Golf Digest's 4,200 Best Places to Play

2nd Edition

Fodor's Travel Publications, Inc.
New York • Toronto • London • Sydney • Auckland

The essay "Taking Your Game on the Road,"
by Peter Andrews, adapted from GOLF DIGEST'S *Places to Play* 1991, copyright © 1991, 1996 Golf Digest/Tennis, Inc.

Special Sales
Fodor's Travel Publications are available at special discounts for bulk purchases for sales promotions or premiums. Special editions, including personalized covers, excerpts of existing guides, and corporate imprints, can be created in large quantities for special needs. For more information, contact your local bookseller or write to Special Markets, Fodor's Travel Publications, 201 East 50th Street, New York, NY 10022. Inquiries from Canada should be directed to your local Canadian bookseller or sent to Random House of Canada, Ltd., Marketing Department, 1265 Aerowood Drive, Mississauga, Ontario L4W 1B9. Inquiries from the United Kingdom should be sent to Fodor's Travel Publications, 20 Vauxhall Bridge Road, London SW1V 2SA, England.

PRINTED IN THE
UNITED STATES OF AMERICA
10 9 8 7 6 5 4 3 2 1

Cover photographs by Stephen Szurlej, taken at Coeur d'Alene Resort Golf Course on Lake Coeur d'Alene, Idaho. Spine photo by Stephen Szurlej, taken at Sandpiper Golf Course, Goleta, California.

Contents

Welcome to Golf Digest's Best Places to Play

GOLF DIGEST'S listing of Places to Play, begun in 1963 and significantly enlarged with 10,000 subscribers' evaluations and comments in 1994, has with this edition become even more comprehensive. Based on the responses of some 23,000 subscribers, it covers more than 4,000 courses.

The ballots of subscribers were analyzed by a tabulation survey service and fed into databases. More than 20 GOLF DIGEST editors and coordinators, following carefully established criteria, then reviewed subscriber evaluations, chose representative comments, checked facts, and edited for style.

Subscribers were asked to judge each course on the quality of the golf experience and the value of the course in relation to others in the area. The Star Ratings, judging the golfing experience, and the Super and Great Value seals as well as the new Frugal Picks are therefore determined from ballots from dedicated players, who paid their green fees, scrutinized the greens, and relaxed in the clubhouses. All-new ratings appear in this edition, based on evaluations of courses played since 1993.

The Star Ratings (*see the key,* How to Use This Guide, *on p. 16*) differ from GOLF DIGEST's course rankings, which are numerical listings of each state's and the nation's top courses. The latter are based solely upon an evaluation of the architectural merits of each course by a GOLF DIGEST panel of experts. There are some highly ranked courses that, as total golf experiences, don't quite measure up in the eyes of subscribers.

The Super and Great Values are based on the average Value Rating for a course. To rate as either, a course had to be at least 3½ stars and average at least 4.0 on the 5.0 Value scale. The top 40 point-getters are Super Values, the very best courses for the money. The next 125 courses are Great Values. New for this edition are the Frugal Golfer Picks, courses that don't rate particularly high as a golfing experience but are still extremely affordable.

Only in this guide's Subscriber Comments will you learn where the wacky new holes are, where you can get a great burger, and where you ought to bring along a ball retriever or bug spray.

If you enjoy public and resort golf in America, Mexico, Canada and the Caribbean, you're likely to enjoy this latest edition of GOLF DIGEST's 4,200 BEST PLACES TO PLAY and find it indispensable in your travels.

—THE EDITORS

Taking Your Game on the Road
There's Much More to a Golf Vacation Than Just Packing Your Clubs and Booking the Tee Times

By Peter Andrews

Mark McCumber puts it nicely. "The easiest part of golf for me is inside the ropes," he says. "Once I get there, all I have to do is play. It's all the traveling that makes the tour so difficult."

Now, Mark McCumber is one of the most meticulously organized men on the PGA Tour. If they ever revive "The Odd Couple," McCumber would be just right for the Tony Randall part. Mark takes, perhaps, 50 golf trips a year and still finds them a chore to organize. How then, are you and I going to fare in figuring out our annual golf vacation? Not well, unless we get some help. And that is what I bring you.

At first blush, I might not seem to be the ideal writer for this assignment. I am probably the most disorganized traveler since "Wrong Way" Corrigan. I pack my suitcase in the manner of a schoolyard basketball player throwing up a soft hook shot. All items landing inside the valise get to go on the trip. The rest stay home and I worry about them later.

I have the sense of direction of a hooded falcon. I have lived in roughly the same area 50 miles north of New York City for two decades and I still get lost driving home at least twice a year. I not only lose myself, I lose important documents as a matter of course. I am not prompt, as a traveler should be. My idea of the proper time to appear at an airport departure gate is when the left inboard engine is starting to turn over.

In my defense, I have seen much of the world without ever missing a flight or losing a piece of luggage. Nevertheless, I realize I may not be the lamp unto which you wish to guide your feet. Therefore, I have marshaled my personal panel of nine experts who really know how to plan a golf trip. The panel includes travel agents as well as golfers, professional and amateur. I have played golf with all of them and know them to be persons of probity and nice judgment. In any given year, we log as much flight time going to golf locations as the entire Peruvian Air Force does going wherever it goes.

Know thy destination. The first step in planning a golf vacation is figuring out what you truly want to do, says Pat O'Brien, who until recently ran a travel agency in Chicago that specialized in packaging golf trips. "Are you traveling specifically to play golf or do you want to go some place pleasant and maybe play a round or two once you get there? Once you've decided that, then you can start picking locations," he says. Pinehurst for the serious player and the Bahamas for the casual golfer, O'Brien suggests. Pat also feels it's important to be sure you're suited for the location. "When I get clients who say they want to go to Scotland only when the wind is down and there's no rain, I try to steer them to Palm Springs."

This article assumes you are traveling on your own and not signing up with a golfing tour in which everything is laid out for you. Unless you are very experienced and know exactly where you're going, however, it is probably a good idea to book a complicated trip through a travel agent, especially one that specializes in golf. The agent often puts a flat percent on your bill, but the money is well spent. You can run up a hefty telephone bill arranging for tee times at Troon by yourself.

Even with an agent, it's not a bad idea to do some forward scouting before you depart. Jack Hogan, the president of Wood & Hogan, a furniture company based in New York, runs an annual golf outing for eight players. He always calls ahead and talks to the starter, not just for tee times, but to check on the quality of play. He especially tries to avoid courses that are holding competitions or whose greens are being aerated. "It's no treat," Hogan says, "to travel a long way and find yourself in the middle of an outing or on greens you can't putt."

Be sure to check with the locals on weather conditions. One year, Hogan's group didn't and some of them wound up playing in Virginia in early April wearing short pants and developing frost on their ankles.

Hogan suggests you keep your vacation on a proper scale, and not schedule more than you can handle. You are not likely to play Crans-sur-Sierre in Valais, Switzerland, and scale the Matterhorn on the same trip. "We used to be more adventurous," Hogan says. "We went to southern Florida, where there are lots of good courses, but everything was a half-hour's drive from every place else. It doesn't sound like much, but when you're trying to get eight players together every day, it gets to be a pain. Now we go to places like the Broadmoor in Colorado, where they have three courses on the same site."

It's well known that booking in advance saves on airfares, but Hogan has found another way to cut down on the transportation costs. "Always spend Saturday night at your destination," Hogan says. If you purchase a ticket 21 days in advance and stay over a Saturday night, you can save up to 75 percent.

Write down your priorities. Mark McCumber is very big on making lists of everything he needs to do and bring before he takes off. It may sound picky, but more than one American golf professional has missed a chance to play in the British Open because he arrived at the airport without his passport.

Most of the panel agree that getting confirmed tee times is vital. "Absolutely," says James FitzGerald, president of GOLF DIGEST. "You can always arrange for dinner reservations later, but get your tee times in advance."

Ed McNulty, a former sales executive with the International Paper Company, agrees. "Beware the guys who tell you to

'Come on down, we'll fit you in.' They're the same people at restaurants who tell you your table is going to be ready in 20 minutes."

Don Barnes, an education specialist from Naples, Florida, disagrees. Don, who is in his late seventies, has taken his 5-handicap around the globe and almost never bothers with confirmed tee times. Don says he and his wife, Sis, once spent six weeks in Scotland at an Edinburgh hotel and played 43 different courses without a tee time. "If one course was too busy to let us on," he says, "there was one 20 minutes away that would." Of course, this deserves a caveat. Barnes's advice may be good for October in Scotland, but you better have advance starting times if you want to play in Phoenix in March.

Bag it up right. When it comes to packing a suitcase for a golf trip, stand aside and let McCumber show you how: "My wife, Paddy, has got me so I can pack for a 10-day golf rotation in one bag including 10 golf shirts, eight pairs of slacks, two sweaters (make sure the sweaters can go with a lot of different outfits), four dress shirts, ties, socks, and underwear. I wear a jacket and one pair of shoes and pack another pair. The trick is to fold everything carefully and make sure the suitcase is fully packed. That way, they stay in place and don't get wrinkled."

Once arrived, McCumber keeps his clothes folded on the spare bed in the hotel room. When he's ready to leave, he puts the clean stuff in the suitcase first, lays in a plastic dry-cleaning bag and then adds his refolded used clothes. The minute he gets back, everything is ready to go to the cleaners.

It's in the bag. McCumber says one of the first things he learned on the PGA Tour was "don't skimp on your luggage. The cheap stuff breaks up in six months." Mark prefers suitcases in heavy tweed fabrics that don't show the dirt. Besides his suitcase and golf bag, Mark always travels with a briefcase equipped with a shoulder strap. That way, he never carries more than two bags with his hands. "Don't carry any bags at all, if you can help it," Mark cautions. "Pulling a muscle in an airport is no way to start a golf trip."

Everyone on the panel agrees the proper packing and transporting of your golf bag is essential. You can always pick up a new visor when you arrive, but a busted 7-iron is tough to replace. Ed McNulty wraps his irons with a towel to keep them from banging up against each other in flight. Jerry Tarde, the editor of GOLF DIGEST, suggests that putting a 46-inch piece of PVC plastic tube inside your bag is a good idea. If your canvas bag cover gets bounced around, there is a good chance your driver will be spared.

McCumber says many golfers make the mistake of not fastening the golf bag's top cover, thinking the carrying case is enough to protect their clubs. It isn't. Mark always packs a pair of shoes wrapped in a towel on the top of the bag and another at the bottom to help balance the weight.

"Never pack spiked shoes in the main pouch," McCumber warns. "If the bag gets dropped or stepped on and the spikes are facing the wrong way, they can pierce the bag and wreck the shafts of your clubs."

Most of the panel suggest taking a Sunday bag, especially when traveling overseas. "European caddies won't carry a big American bag," says FitzGerald. Tarde, however, warns that most carrying cases are not designed for these smaller golf bags, which tend to slosh around inside. Jerry solved that problem by getting married, and now he finds that two Sunday bags fit nicely in a single carrying case.

Making sure it gets there. However you pack your bag, you have to get it there. McNulty takes particular care at the curbside check-in facilities at airports. "Don't just give your bag to the man," Ed says. "Talk to him—tell him your bag is more important than you are." Everyone agrees that a generous tip is in order. The going rate is at least a dollar a bag these days.

Although golf trips are put on plastic, few panel members had any strong thoughts on which credit card to use. In general, they stick with whatever card they are happiest with at the moment. FitzGerald, however, pointed out that some cards now pick up the tab for the collision coverage offered by car-rental companies, which can be a nice fringe benefit. Find out in advance, because it could save you $10 a day or more. Most of the panel take the additional coverage when traveling on their own. "It's expensive for what they offer," O'Brien says, "but your peace of mind is worth something."

Bill Seaman, a sports consultant from Savannah, Georgia, who travels extensively, doesn't see much difference between car rental companies in America, but he says when traveling overseas, you can get some good bargains by arranging to rent cars from local agencies before departing.

What to bring. Any last-minute items to throw into the bag? Seaman, a Southern gentleman of the old school, reminds you to bring your own bourbon if you are leaving the United States.

Mike Roseto of the Wide World of Golf travel agency in Carmel City, California, has an odd thought on something not to bring. Don't bring extra sweaters to Scotland or Ireland because you're almost certainly going to buy one when you get there.

Most of the panel simply ignore the perils of jet lag. But drinking lots of water at regular intervals during the flight forestalls dehydration, which is the most debilitating part of jet lag. Gary Player, who claims to have logged more travel time than Neil Armstrong, once told a colleague of mine that he abstains from drinking alcoholic beverages on board. The alcohol, he says, causes further dehydration. Player also recommends that after an overnight flight, you should do whatever it takes to stay awake the entire next day. For him that means drinking coffee, taking cold showers, and staying active. Then you'll get a good night's sleep and the following morning be adjusted to your new time zone. When McNulty gets on the plane, he sets his watch to the time at his destination and starts thinking in those terms. The panelists do not dose themselves with Lomotil and the rest of the pharmacy of long-distance travel. Seaman brings along a few restoratives on the grounds that, "if I bring them, I never need them, but if I don't, I always do."

Once you're at your destination, a golf trip is much like any other except you have this unwieldy bag to deal with. It is still the most important item in your supply train and ceaseless vigilance is required. "Don't give your clubs to anyone unless you know exactly where he's going," says FitzGerald, "and then get his name." McCumber takes that concept one step further. "The clubs stay with me," he says.

At the course, McNulty likes to check out the golf shop. "I'll buy a hat or some sunscreen and talk to the pro and look over the stock," Ed says. "If they carry XXL sizes, I figure they know their business."

When to book tee times. Slow play is the serpent in the Eden of resort golf, and most of the panel try to avoid it where they can. Tarde suggests that at a busy resort, you try for the earliest tee time possible. "If you play Pebble Beach by 8 in the morning, you can play a round in a little over three hours," says Tarde. "If you don't get off until noon, you'll be out there for more than five." It must be understood that Tarde likes to play golf at about the pace used by the Royal Canadian Mounted Police in lashing a dog-sled team across the tundra with a supply of serum for a sick child. A lot of golfers paying $195 for a round at Pebble Beach want to savor the view as long as they can. Tarde's point is a good one, however. The earlier you start, the faster you will be able to play. McNulty is another speedy player, but years of convention golf have taught him patience. He carries a deck of cards in his bag and is always ready for a few hands of gin rummy or a rubber of bridge.

All agree that caution is called for when playing a new course. Don't try to cut doglegs when you don't know what's out there. As McNulty says, "Don't try to beat the course. Just understand it."

If you are not a trained arborist, trees tend to look like trees, and it's a good idea to stay out of them.

Men in waiting. A word on caddies. Mike Roseto says many of his clients have unrealistic ideas of what a caddie can do for them. They have read all about mythical Scottish caddies who know every blade of grass on the course by its own name. These are mythical stories because they are largely about mythical people.

Good caddies, like good plumbers, are in short supply, and most of them are already booked. Expect your caddie to tell you the distance to the green, maybe, and help you read putts, maybe. If you get any more than that, adopt him.

Tipping at a resort is handled the way you handle it at any place you've not been to before. Ask.

When in Waco . . . . On a more spiritual level, don't forget the whole point of traveling is to experience something new. As Pat O'Brien says, "Go with the local culture." Enjoy what is offered and don't try to insist on your own tastes.

Don't go to Waco, Texas, to dine on *tripes à la mode de Caen* when you can get terrific tamale pie, and don't order a martini at Ballybunion when a pink gin is all a civilized person could ask for.

I like to pick up games with people wherever I go. That's where I can hear the local scandal and find out about the good restaurants. If you make a match with the natives, however, I suggest you keep the bets small. There are variations of golf being played out there that would take a USGA blue blazer and fry it to seersucker. In parts of the South, they play something called "Walking the Doggie," which means if your ball lands behind a tree, you just take your club and bump that little doggie along until it's out some place nice. If everybody does it, I guess it's not cheating, but for a conservative player from the Northeast, it takes a little getting used to. We use our feet when no one's looking.

There's nothing wrong with being hustled out of a reasonable amount of money, by the way. McNulty, Hogan and I once played at Waterville in Ireland with a meat packer from Donegal who went through our pockets for about £8. In return, we got pleasant fellowship, several rude anecdotes and an Irish wind lesson in how to hit a 5-iron that never gets higher than your shoulders. Cheap at twice the price.

I have a good, if boring, tip for those of you leaving the United States. Don't try to play games with the local currency by exchanging money with individuals who offer you a better deal than the official exchange rate. You might pick up the odd bargain, but, before you try, ask yourself two questions. How good are you at spotting a counterfeit dinar? And do you want to spend even a small part of your golf vacation sitting in a room under a lamp talking to a couple of guys in big overcoats?

Parting shots. There are lots of ways to take the sheen off a vacation trip, and playing golf badly is the silliest of them all. Some travelers, however, manage to do just that. Mike Roseto has seen many a golfer, who has spent thousands of dollars to go to some distant and alluring location, slouch off the course full of despair because of a bad round. Try to remember that a high score is no more important at Grand Cypress in Florida than it is at Grand Forks in North Dakota.

I hope you have learned some useful things in this treatise on how to organize a golf trip, and I would ask you now to indulge me in a thought that, perhaps, betrays my own vagaries in such matters. Don't crush your trip with so much organization you squeeze the life out of it. There is more to traveling than arriving and departing on schedule. Crosstown buses do that all the time. Save some time for the unexpected. Let yourself get lost. You'll be found in time and you might discover something wonderful you hadn't known was there.

★★★★★
The Five-Star Courses

Blackwolf Run (River), Kohler, Wis.
The Homestead Resort (Cascades), Hot Springs, Va.
Cog Hill Golf Club (No. 4), Lemont, Ill.
Pebble Beach Golf Links, Pebble Beach, Calif.
Pinehurst No. 2, Pinehurst, N.C.
Pinon Hills Golf Course, Farmington, N.M.
Spyglass Hill Golf Course, Pebble Beach, Calif.
Troon North Golf Club, Scottsdale, Ariz.

The Super Values

 Indicates one of just 40 courses whose combined "Golf Experience" and "Value" scores earned it our highest honor as a Super Value.

Bavarian Hills Golf Course, St. Mary's, Pa.
Bethpage State Park Golf Courses (Black Course), Farmingdale, N.Y.
Binder Park Golf Course, Battle Creek, Mich.
Boiling Springs Golf Club, Woodward, Okla.
Brighton Dale Golf Club (White Birch Course), Kansasville, Wis.
Brown County Golf Course, Oneida, Wis.
Buffalo Dunes Golf Club, Garden City, Kan.
Buffalo (Wyo.) Golf Club
Cambrian Ridge Golf Club, Greenville, Ala.
Cascades Golf Course, Jackson, Mich.
Cheraw (S.C.) State Park Golf Club
Desert Hills Golf Course, Yuma, Ariz.
Gibson Bay Golf Course, Richmond, Ky.
Gold Mountain Golf Course, Bremerton, Wash.
Grand National Golf Club (Lake Course), Opelika, Ala.
Grand National Golf Club (Links Course), Opelika, Ala.
Grand National Golf Club (Short Course), Opelika, Ala.
Green Valley Golf Course, Sioux City, Iowa
Hampshire Golf Club, Dowagiac, Mich.
Heritage Bluffs Golf Club, Channahon, Ill.
Kananaskis Country Golf Club (Mt. Kidd Course), Alberta
Kananaskis Country Golf Club (Mt. Lorette Course), Alberta
L.E. Kaufman Golf Club, Wyoming, Mich.
Lassing Pointe Golf Club, Union, Ky.
The Ledges Golf Club, Roscoe, Ill
Lick Creek Golf Club, Pekin, Ill.
Montauk (N.Y.) Downs State Park
Nemadji Golf Course (East/West), Superior, Wis.
Painted Dunes Desert Golf Club, El Paso
Papago Golf Course, Phoenix
Park Hills Golf Club (West Course), Freeport, Ill.
Pinon Hills Golf Course, Farmington, N.M.
Rock Hollow Golf Club, Peru, Ind.
Ruby View Golf Course, Elko, Nev.
Southern Hills Golf Course, Hot Springs, S.D.
Stoughton Acres Golf Club, Butler, Pa.
Valley View Golf Course, Layton, Utah
Wailua Golf Course, Lihue, Kauai, Hawaii
Walkingstick Golf Course, Pueblo, Colo.
Washatch State Park Golf Club, Midway, Utah

The Great Values

 Indicates one of 125 courses whose combined "Golf Experience" and "Value" scores earned it an honor as a Great Value.

Battlement Mesa Golf Club, Parachute, Colo.
Bethpage State Park Golf Courses, (Red Course), Farmingdale, N.Y.
Birch Creek Golf Club, Smithfield, Utah
Bountiful (Utah) City Golf Course
Bretwood Golf Course, Keene, N.H.
Bryan Park & Golf Club (Champion Course), Brown Summit, N.C.
Bryan Park & Golf Club (Players Course), Brown Summit, N.C.
Bunker Hills Golf Course, Coon Rapids, Minn.
Cacapon Resort State Park, Berkeley Springs, W.Va.
Cape Breton Highlands Golf Links, Nova Scotia
Castlegar Golf Club, British Columbia
Cedar Creek Golf Course, San Antonio, Tex.
Champion Lakes Golf Course, Bolivar, Pa.
The Championship Golf Course at the University of New Mexico, Albuquerque
Chicopee (Mass.) Golf Club
Chicopee Woods Golf Course, Gainesville, Ga.
Chochiti Lake (N.M.) Golf Course
Crown Isle Golf Club, British Columbia
Draper Valley Golf Club, Draper, Va.
Eagle Lake Golf Club, Farmington, Mo.
Edgewood Golf Course, Fargo, N.D.
Fairfield Glade (Tenn.) Resort (Heatherhurst Course).
Fairview Mountain Golf Club, British Columbia
Fall Creek Falls State Park Golf Course, Akeville, Tenn.
Fall River Valley Golf & Country Club, Fall River Mills, Calif.
Fields Ferry Golf Club, Calhoun, Ga.
Flanders Valley Golf Course (Red/Gold Course), Flanders, N.J.
Flanders Valley Golf Course (White/Blue Course), Flanders, N.J.
Foxfire Golf Club, Vidala, Ga.
Gaylord (Mich.) Country Club
Georgia Veterans Golf Course, Cordele, Ga.
Golden Golf & Country Club, British Columbia
Golf Club of Jacksonville (Fla.)
Grandote Golf & Country Club, La Veta, Colo.
Green Lakes State Park Golf Club, Fayetteville, N.Y.
Hangman Valley Golf Course, Spokane, Wash.
Hawthorne Ridge Golf Club, Aledo, Ill.
Henry Horton State Park Golf Course, Chapel Hill, Tenn.
Heritage Hills Golf Course, McCook, Neb.
Hickory Knob Resort Golf Course, McCormick, S.C.
Highland Oaks Golf Club, Dothan, Ala.
Highlands Golf Course, Lincoln, Neb.
Hobble Creek Golf Club, Springville, Utah
The Homestead (The Cascades Course), Hot Springs, Va.
Huron Breeze Golf & Country Club, Au Gres, Mich.
Indian Canyon Golf Course, Spokane, Wash.
J.E. Good Park Golf Club, Akron, Ohio
Jester Park Golf Course, Granger, Iowa
John H. Cain Golf Club, Newport, N.H.
Kearney Hill Golf Links, Lexington, Ky.
Keith Hills Golf Club, Buies Creek, N.C.
Lake Arrowhead Golf Course, Nekoosa, Wis.
Lake Shore Golf Club, Taylorsville, Ill.
Lakewood Shore Resort (Gales Course), Oscoda, Mich.
The Links at Crowbush Cove, Prince Edward Island
Linville (N.C.) Golf Course
Little Traverse Bay Golf Club, Harbor Springs, Mich.
Locust Hill Golf Course, Charles Town, W.Va.

Logan River Golf Course, Logan, Utah
Los Caballeros Golf Club, Wikenburg, Ariz.
Makalei Hawaii Country Club, Kailua-Kona, Hawaii
Mallard Cove Golf Course, Lake Charles, La.
Mariana Butte Golf Course, Loveland, Colo.
Matheson Greens Golf Course, Northport, Mich.
Meadowbrook Golf Course, Rapid City, S.D.
Meadowood Golf Course, Liberty Lake, Wash.
Milham Park Municipal Golf Club, Kalamazoo, Mich.
Mississippi State University Golf Course, Starkville, Miss.
Mistwood Golf Course, Lake Ann, Mich.
Moab (Utah) Golf Club
Mohican Hills Golf Club, Jeromesville, Ohio
Mount Pleasant Golf Club, Baltimore
Naga-Waukee Golf Course, Pewaukee, Wis.
New Richmond (Wis.) Golf Club
Newport News (Va.) Golf Club at Deer Run
NorthWood Golf Club, Rhinelander, Wis.
Oak Hollow Golf Course, High Point, N.C.
Oak Valley Golf Club, Beaumont, Calif.
Orchard Valley Golf Club, Aurora, Ill.
Orgill Park Golf Course, Millington, Tenn.
Osprey Cove Golf Club, St. Marys, Ga.
Oxmoor Valley Golf Club (Short Course), Birmingham, Ala.
Paradise Canyon Golf & Country Club, Alberta
Paragon Golf & Country Club, Nova Scotia
Pebble Creek Country Club, Becker, Minn.
Pinecrest Municipal Golf Course, Idaho Falls, Idaho
Pinecroft Golf Club, Beulah, Mich.
Poppy Hills Golf Course, Pebble Beach, Calif.
Port Royal Golf Course, Bermuda
Prairie Vista Golf Course, Bloomington, Ill.
Pueblo del Sol Golf Course, Sierra Vista, Ariz.
Quail Ridge Golf Course, Winfield, Kan.
River Greens Golf Course, West Lafayette, Ohio
Riverside Golf Course, Janesville, Wis.
Riverton (Wyo.) Country Club
Rolling Meadows Golf Course, Milford, Kan.
San Sabo (Tex.) Municipal Golf Course
Sandridge Golf Club (Dunes Course), Vero Beach, Fla.
Sandridge Golf Club (Lakes Course), Vero Beach, Fla.
Saratoga Spa Golf Course, Saratoga Springs, N.Y.
Sheaffer Memorial Golf Club, Fort Madison, Iowa
Shenandoah Valley Golf Club, Front Royal, Va.
Silver Lakes Golf Course, Glencoe, Ala.
Soaring Eagles Golf Club, Horseheads, N.Y.
Souris Valley Golf Club, Minot, N.D.
Sparta (Wis.) Municipal Golf Club
Spencer (Iowa) Golf & Country Club
St. Lucie West Country Club, Port St. Lucie, Fla.
Sunbrook Golf Club, St. George, Utah
Surf Golf Club, North Myrtle Beach, S.C.
Swan Lake Golf Club, Plymouth, Ind.
Tarry Brae Golf Club, South Fallsburg, N.Y.
Timberton Golf Club, Hattiesburg, Miss.
Tokatee Golf Club, Blue River, Ore.
Torry Pines Golf Course (South Course), LaJolla, Calif.
Trickle Creek Golf Resort, British Columbia
Turtleback Golf & Country Club, Rice Lake, Wis.
Two Rivers Golf Club, Dakota Dunes, S.D.
Wallace Adams Golf Course, McRea, Ga.
Waterville (Me.) Country Club
The Wellman Club, Johnsonville, S.C.
Wildflower at Fair Hills, Detroit Lakes, Minn.
Willinger's Golf Club, Northfield, Minn.
Willow Run Golf Course, Sioux Falls, S.D.
World Woods Golf Club (Pine Barrens), Brooksville, Fla.

The Frugal Golfer's Favorites

Courses with a value rating of 4.0 but less than 3½ stars. Courses are listed alphabetically by state.

Elephant Rocks G.C., Williams, Ariz.
Bennett Valley G.C., Santa Rosa, Calif.
Coronado G.C., Coronado, Calif.
Pacific Grove Mun. G.C., Pacific Grove, Calif.
Fort Morgan G.C., Ft. Morgan Colo.
Deerfield Lakes G.C., Callahan, Fla.
Meadowbrook G.C., Gainesville, Fla.
Twisted Oaks G.C., Beverly Hills, Fla.
Hard Labor Creek State Park G.C., Rutledge, Ga.
Waiehu Mun. G.C., Maui, Hawaii
West Lock, Ewa Beach, Hawaii
Blackfoot G.C. Mun., Blackfoot, Idaho
Bon Vivant C.C., Bourbonnais, Ill.
Bonnie Brook G.C., Waukegan, Ill.
Prairie View G.C., Byron, Ill.
Westview G.C., Quincy, Ill.
Wabach Valley G.C., Geneva, Ind.
Muscatine Mun. G.C., Muscatine, Iowa
Squaw Creek G.C., Marion, Iowa
Les Vieux Chene G.C., Youngsville, La.
Va Jo Wa G.C., Island Falls, Me.
Pine Ridge G.C., Lutherville, Md.
Bay County G.C., Essexville, Mich.
Ella Sharp Park G.C., Jackson, Mich.
Grand View G.C., New Era, Mich.
Kensington Metro Park G.C., Milford, Mich.
Little Crow G.C., Spicer, Minn.
Barker Brook G.C., Oriskany, N.Y.
Bethpage State Park G.C. (Blue Cse.), Farmingdale, N.Y.
Bethpage State Park G.C. (Green Cse.), Farmingdale, N.Y.
Mallard Head G.C., Mooresville, N.C.
Beaver Creek Meadows G.C., Lisbon, Ohio
Forest Hills G.C., Elyria, Ohio
Maple Ridge G.C., Austinberg, Ohio
Sunset Hills G.C., Guymon, Okla.
Meadow Lakes G.C., Prineville, Ore.
Lake Marion G.C., Santee, S.C.
Dyersburg Mun. G.C., Dyersburg, Tenn.
Montgomery Bell State Park G.C., Burns, Tenn.
Andrews County G.C., Andrews, Tex.
Bay Forest G.C., La Porte, Tex.
Chambers Country G.C., Anahuac, Tex.
Delaware Springs G.C., Burnet, Tex.
Devine G.C., Devine, Tex.
Lady Bird Johnson G.C., Fredericksburg, Tex.
Nocona Hills G.C., Nacona, Tex.
Rio Colorado G.C., Bay City, Tex.
Riverside G.C., Victoria, Tex.
Newport News G.C. (Deer Run Cse.), Newport News, Va.
Wolf Creek G.C., Bastian, Va.
Lake Padden G.C., Bellingham, Wash.
Mint Valley G.C., Longview, Wash.
Grandview G.C., Beaver, W.Va.
Greenhills C.C., Ravenswood, W.Va.
Peninsula State Park G.C., Fish Creek, Wis.
Petrifying Springs G.C., Kenosha, Wis.
Reid G. Cse., Appleton, Wis.
Barrhead G.C., Barrhead, Alta.
Ponoka Community G.C., Ponoka, Alta.
Renfrew G.C., Renfrew, Ont.
Mill River Prov. Park G.C., O'Leary, P.E.I.
Cooke G. Cse., Prince Albert, Sask.

How to Use This Guide

The 4,200 golf courses in the USA, Canada, Mexico, and the Caribbean that follow are divided into two parts, East and West, which in turn are arranged alphabetically by state, province, or island. Entries can be read as follows:

Sample Entry

ANYWHERE GOLF RESORT
★★★ANYWHERE GOLF COURSE
PU—100 Anywhere Drive, Centerville (408)000-3213
25 miles south of Somewhere. **Holes:** 18. **Par:** 72/72.
Yards: 6,115/5,692. **Course rating:** 69.8/71.8. **Slope:** 124/120.
Opened: 1965. **Pace of Play rating:** 4:30. **Green fee:** $15/22.
Credit cards: MC, V, AMEX, DISC. **Reduced fees:** Weekdays, Low Season,
  Twilight, Seniors, Juniors.
Caddies: Yes. **Golf carts:** $10 for 18 holes.
Discount golf packages: Yes. **Season:** Year-round. **High:** May–Sept.
On-site lodging: No. **Rental Clubs:** Yes.
Walking policy: Unrestricted walking. **Range:** Yes (grass).
To obtain tee times: Call Wednesday morning for Saturday; Thursday
  morning for Sunday. Call day before for other days.
Subscriber comments: Wonderful course . . . Great conditions . . . Many
  sidehill lies . . . Beginners will love this course . . . Beautiful scenic views of
  the ocean.

Explanation

ANYWHERE GOLF RESORT: The name of the resort (will only appear
  when the facility has more than one course).
★★★—A rating of the golf experience by GOLF DIGEST subscribers. See ratings chart below.
ANYWHERE GOLF COURSE: The name of the course.
PU: Public, daily fee or municipal. **R:** Resort. **SP:** Semi-private.
100 Anywhere Drive, Centerville: Course location.
(408)000-3213: Golf shop phone number.
25 miles south of Somewhere: Distance from nearest major town (as
  determined by a representative from the course).
Holes: The number of holes available for play.
Par: For 18-hole courses the figures shown represent the pars from the
  back/front tees. For 27-hole layouts (three nine-hole courses) the 18-hole
  combinations from the back tees are shown.
Yards: Yardage listed from the back and front tees (18 holes) or from the back
  tees only (27 holes).
Course rating: U.S. Golf Association course rating from both back and front
  (18 holes) or from back tees only (27 holes).
Slope: U.S. Golf Association Slope rating from both back and front
  (18 holes) or from back tees only (27 holes).
Opened: The year the course first opened.
Pace of Play rating: This rating was provided by the course and, in most
  instances, it represents the estimated time to play the course instead of
  the U.S. Golf Association Pace of Play rating, which establishes a specific
  amount of time to play each hole.
Green fee: Fees listed represent the lowest and highest fee for an 18-hole
  round of golf. All fees are subject to change.
Credit cards: MC—MasterCard, V—Visa, AMEX—American Express,
  DISC—Discover or "None" if credit cards are not accepted.
Reduced fees: Times or situations when discount fees are available; call
  ahead for details.
Caddies: If caddies are available at the course.
Golf carts: Either included in green fee or the per person fee for 18 holes. If

a course does not offer a "single" cart rate, the rate is shown for a "full" cart; call ahead for details.

Discount golf packages: If the facility offers package deals at a savings over daily play fees.

Season: Months the facility is open for play.

High: The busy season, when rates are typically higher.

On-site lodging: If lodging is available on the property.

Rental clubs: If rental clubs are available on the property.

Walking policy: Unrestricted walking—walking is allowed at any time without restriction; Walking at certain times—carts or caddies may be mandatory during busy times; or Mandatory carts—carts are always required.

Range: If a practice range is available. Unless noted as "(grass)," the range uses mats for tees.

To obtain tee times: The policy established by the course to secure a playing time.

Subscriber comments: A representative sample of comments made by GOLF DIGEST subscribers in response to a January 1995 survey. These comments apply to conditions, playability and general impressions of the course during the 1994 calendar year and may not be indicative of current conditions or changes made by course management.

NA: Information not made available.

Ratings

★ Basic golf.

★★ Good, not great, but not a rip-off either.

★★★ Very good. Tell a friend it's worth getting off the highway to play.

★★★★ Outstanding. Plan your next vacation around it.

★★★★★ Golf at its absolute best. Pay any price at least once in your life.

½ The equivalent of one-half star.

★ Course not yet rated by GOLF DIGEST subscribers.

Part I

The East

ALABAMA

★★ ALPINE BAY GOLF AND COUNTRY CLUB
R—9855 Renfore Rd., Alpine (205)268-2920, (800)925-0827.
40 miles northwest of Birmingham. **Holes:** 18. **Par:** 72/72.
Yards: 6,518/5,518. **Course rating:** 70.9/69.8. **Slope:** 129/120.
Opened: 1972. **Pace of Play rating:** 4:00. **Green fee:** $12/20.
Credit cards: All major. **Reduced fees:** Weekdays, Resort guests,
Twilight.
Caddies: No. **Golf carts:** $10 for 18 holes.
Discount golf packages: Yes. **Season:** Year-round. **High:** May-Sept.
On-site lodging: Yes. **Rental clubs:** Yes.
Walking policy: Walking at certain times. **Range:** Yes (grass).
To obtain tee times: Call anytime.
Subscriber comments: Good Robert Trent Jones design, but needs better
course maintenance, especially greens . . . Trent Jones marks everywhere
. . . Tree lined . . . Rolling hills . . . Must stay in play . . . Not bad, not
great . . . Upkeep could be improved . . . If traps were repaired, could be
one of the best around . . . Hospitable people . . . Very nice and
accommodating . . . Hard to find.

★★★½ AUBURN LINKS
PU—826 Shell-Toomer Pkwy., Auburn (334)887-5151.
4 miles northwest of Auburn-Opelika. **Holes:** 18. **Par:** 72/72.
Yards: 7,145/5,320. **Course rating:** 72.5/68.5. **Slope:** 129/118.
Opened: 1991. **Pace of Play rating:** N/A. **Green fee:** $28/30.
Credit cards: MC, V. **Reduced fees:** Low season, Resort guests, Seniors,
Juniors.
Caddies: No. **Golf carts:** N/A.
Discount golf packages: Yes. **Season:** Year-round. **High:** June-Oct.
On-site lodging: No. **Rental clubs:** Yes.
Walking policy: Unrestricted walking. **Range:** Yes (grass).
To obtain tee times: One week prior notice.
Subscriber comments: Great tight course . . . A sleeper. Fun to play . . .
Pleasant . . . Tough but fair . . . Lots of sand . . . Shotmaker's course . . .
One of the best in the Southeast . . . Just a step below Grand National . . .
Pretty course, no parallel fairways . . . Fairways and forest, no rough . . .
Better hit it straight . . . Great greens . . . Bent-grass greens . . . Lightning
greens . . . Nos. 1 and 10 are poor holes, rest of course is very nice . . .
Beautiful beginning and finishing holes . . . A well-cared-for course . . .
Enjoyed the layout sheets for each hole.

★★★ AZALEA CITY GOLF CLUB
PU—1000 Gaillard Dr., Mobile (334)342-4221.
10 miles west of Mobile. **Holes:** 18. **Par:** 36/36.
Yards: 6,765/6,491. **Course rating:** 70.9/69.8. **Slope:** 124/121.
Opened: 1957. **Pace of Play rating:** 4:12. **Green fee:** $10/15.
Credit cards: MC, V, AMEX. **Reduced fees:** Twilight.
Caddies: No. **Golf carts:** N/A.
Discount golf packages: No. **Season:** Jan.-Dec. **High:** March-Oct.
On-site lodging: No. **Rental clubs:** Yes.
Walking policy: Unrestricted walking. **Range:** Yes (grass).
To obtain tee times: Call pro shop up to 14 days in advance for weekday
tee times and the Wednesday prior to the weekend call at 8 a.m.
Subscriber comments: Busiest course in Mobile . . . Lots of
improvements recently . . . Constantly being improved . . . Should win
"Most Improved" award . . . Irrigation has helped . . . Greens and fairways
rank with best in area . . . Pro shop leaves something to be desired.

★½ BAY OAKS GOLF CLUB
PU—P.O. Box 651, Bayou La Batre (334)824-2429.
10 miles south of Mobile. **Holes:** 18. **Par:** 72/72.
Yards: 6,208/5,422. **Course rating:** N/A. **Slope:** 124/122.
Opened: N/A. **Pace of Play rating:** N/A. **Green fee:** N/A.
Credit cards: MC, V. **Reduced fees:** Weekdays.
Caddies: No. **Golf carts:** $10 for 18 holes.

Discount golf packages: No. **Season:** Year-round. **High:** Nov.-March.
On-site lodging: No. **Rental clubs:** No.
Walking policy: N/A. **Range:** Yes (grass).
Subscriber comments: Forgiving course, but fairways need work . . .
Good potential, needs help . . . Must play at least once to see the 14th . . . A
600-yard par-5 dogleg around a lake.

BENT BROOK GOLF COURSE
★★★½ **WINDMILL/BROOK/GRAVEYARD**
PU—7900 Dickey Springs Rd., Bessemer (205)424-2368.
10 miles south of Birmingham. **Holes:** 27. **Par:** 71/71/70.
Yards: 6,934/7,053/6,847. **Course rating:** 71.8/71.7/71.1. **Slope:**
119/121/121.
Opened: 1988. **Pace of Play rating:** N/A. **Green fee:** $27.
Credit cards: All major. **Reduced fees:** Weekdays.
Caddies: No. **Golf carts:** $10 for 18 holes.
Discount golf packages: No. **Season:** Year-round.
On-site lodging: No. **Rental clubs:** Yes.
Walking policy: Walking at certain times. **Range:** Yes (grass).
To obtain tee times: Call three days in advance.
Subscriber comments: First-class daily-fee course . . . Fairly new, fun
course . . . Good track . . . Better than average . . . Great public facility . . .
Good variety of holes . . . Not much trouble . . . Best public course in
Southeast . . . Grip it and rip it, wide open . . . Few trees . . . Wide open
now, but wait . . . Always good condition . . . Fairways are excellent . . .
Standing water . . . A swamp when wet . . . Super greens . . . Brook and
Windmill 9s much better than Graveyard . . . Long from tips . . . Cartpath-
only rule makes course too long . . . Need to improve cart rules . . . Not
allowed to walk until after dinner . . . Don't allow pull carts . . . Course
gets better as it matures . . . Wonderful any time of the year.

★ CAHABA VALLEY GOLF AND COUNTRY CLUB
SP—Rte. 2, Trussville (205)655-2095.
Call club for further information.
Subscriber comments: Many different looks . . . First 9 fun, second 9 ho-
hum . . . New ownership making fair track into very good experience . . .
Revamping the course . . . Added three new holes in last three years, made
some fine changes . . . When course changes are complete, will be one of
the finer courses in area.

CAMBRIAN RIDGE GOLF CLUB
★★★★½ **CANYON/LOBLOLLY/SHERLING**
PU—101 Sunbelt Pkwy., Greenville (334)382-9787.
40 miles south of Montgomery. **Holes:** 27. **Par:** 72/71/71.
Yards: 7,424/7,297/7,232. **Course rating:** 75.4/74.6/73.9. **Slope:**
142/140/133.
Opened: 1993. **Pace of Play rating:** 4:00. **Green fee:** $20/27.
Credit cards: All major. **Reduced fees:** Weekdays, Twilight, Seniors,
Juniors.
Caddies: No. **Golf carts** $13 for 18 holes.
Discount golf packages: Yes. **Season:** Year-round.
On-site lodging: No. **Rental clubs:** Yes.
Walking policy: Unrestricted walking. **Range:** Yes (grass).
Complex also includes Short Course, a 9-hole par-3 layout.
Ranked 3rd in Alabama by Golf Digest.
Subscriber comments: Super fun . . . Outstanding! . . . Great course,
treated great! . . . What a hidden treasure . . . A championship course at
public-course rates . . . Challenging but fair . . . Best public course in
Alabama . . . Best of the Robert Trent Jones Trail . . . Beautiful setting . . .
Thought I was in Carolina . . . Very scenic . . . Rolling, large elevated
greens . . . Severe greens . . . Important to drive reasonably long and
accurate . . . Fairway bunkers come into play a lot . . . No flat lies . . . The
most difficult and scenic course I've ever played . . . Canyon and Sherling
are outstanding . . . Sherling a fantastic nine . . . Canyon tough for average

SUPER VALUE

golfer . . . Canyon's par 3s the longest, toughest I've seen . . . Not crowded
. . . Finest overall facility on the planet . . . The greatest thing ever done for
public golf. Everything is first class. No money was spared. Even the rough
was sodded! . . . Too tough for average player . . . No forgiveness . . .
Bring lots of balls . . . Zero to 10 handicap needed to survive . . . Excellent
and courteous staff . . . One 9-hole course short of perfect.

★★ CITRONELLE MUNICIPAL GOLF COURSE

PU—Lakeview Dr., Citronelle (334)866-7881.
Call club for further information.
Subscriber comments: City course . . . Good basic layout . . . Wide open
front nine, back very tight with numerous doglegs . . . Conditions could be
better, layout more interesting . . . Newly rebuilt greens . . . Good course
for high handicapper . . . Usually not crowded.

★½ COLONIAL GOLF CLUB

PU—102 Leesburg St., Huntsville (205)828-0431.
Call club for further information.
Subscriber comments: Flat course, wide open . . . Great greens, vastly
improved last year . . . Best greens around, bent-grass . . . Beautiful greens
but tees, fairways and rough lacking . . . Too much play hurts sparse
Bermuda on fairways . . . No putting green or driving range . . . Can play
all day, walking, on one green fee.

COTTON CREEK CLUB
★★★½ EAST/NORTH/WEST

SP—3840 Cotton Creek Blvd., Gulf Shores (334)968-7766.
40 miles east of Mobile. **Holes:** 27. **Par:** 72/72/72.
Yards: 7,028/6,971/6,975. **Course rating:** 73.9/73.0/73.2. **Slope:**
132/127/131.
Opened: 1987. **Pace of Play rating:** 4:00. **Green fee:** $36/48.
Credit cards: MC, V. **Reduced fees:** Weekdays, Low season.
Caddies: No. **Golf carts:** Included in Green Fee.
Discount golf packages: Yes. **Season:** Year-round. **High:** March-Oct.
On-site lodging: Yes. **Rental clubs:** Yes.
Walking policy: Mandatory cart. **Range:** Yes (grass).
To obtain tee times: Call pro shop up to six months in advance.
Subscriber comments: Arnold Palmer design . . . East/North/West all
great middle-handicap nines . . . Well worth the money . . . Wide open,
well bunkered, fairly flat . . . Some challenging holes . . . Great fairways
. . . Subtle greens . . . Nice, but tricked up holes . . . Some blind shots but
interesting playability . . . New West easy, others are killers . . . North and
East courses are better . . . New nine needs time to mature . . . Without
wind, a relatively easy course; in wind, a monster . . . Great service . . .
Geniuses at growing grass . . . Best layout, best maintained, best run on the
Gulf Coast . . . A place you look forward to playing.

★★½ CULLMAN MUNICIPAL GOLF CLUB

PU—2321 County Rd. 490, Hanceville (205)739-2386.
500 miles north of Birmingham. **Holes:** 18. **Par:** 72/72.
Yards: 6,351/4,577. **Course rating:** 69.8/67.7. **Slope:** 120/115.
Opened: 1950. **Pace of Play rating:** 4:15. **Green fee:** $12.
Credit cards: None. **Reduced fees:** Twilight.
Caddies: No. **Golf carts:** $8 for 18 holes.
Discount golf packages: No. **Season:** Year-round. **High:** May-Aug.
On-site lodging: No. **Rental clubs:** No.
Walking policy: Unrestricted walking. **Range:** Yes (grass).
To obtain tee times: Reservations taken for weekends and holidays only.
Call after 8 a.m. on Wednesday.
Subscriber comments: Great old country course . . . Surprising
conditions for rural course . . . Fun course to play . . . Made a lot of
improvements . . . Continue to do course improvements . . . Improving
daily . . . Excellent new clubhouse . . . Good Bermuda greens . . . Some
holes awkward . . . Best green fee in Birmingham area.

★★ CYPRESS LAKES GOLF AND COUNTRY CLUB
R—1311 E. 6th St., Muscle Shoals (205)386-7783.
50 miles west of Huntsville. **Holes:** 18. **Par:** 70/70.
Yards: 6,309/5,008. **Course rating:** 69.6/67.7. **Slope:** 120/120.
Opened: 1991. **Pace of Play rating:** 4:00. **Green fee:** $12/15.
Credit cards: MC, V. **Reduced fees:** Weekdays, Juniors.
Caddies: No. **Golf carts:** $8 for 18 holes.
Discount golf packages: No. **Season:** Year-round. **High:** March-Oct.
On-site lodging: No. **Rental clubs:** Yes.
Walking policy: Walking at certain times. **Range:** Yes (grass).
To obtain tee times: Call pro shop.
Formerly known as The Oaks Golf Club.
Subscriber comments: Short course, target golf required . . . Good sand,
good amount of water, bent greens . . . A lot of hidden landing areas . . .
Short even from the blues . . . Three or four good holes, otherwise too
short . . . OK for a quick round.

★★★ DEER RUN GOLF COURSE
PU—1175 County Rd. 100, Mouton (205)974-7384.
Call club for further information.
Subscriber comments: Best-kept secret in northern Alabama . . . Good
staff, good greens, good layout . . . Way out, but an excellent, fun course
. . . Beautiful. Away from noise. Quiet . . . Just opened second nine . . .
New holes have grown in nicely . . . Excellent landscaping . . . Excellent
greens . . . Bent-grass greens, always in good condition . . . Very fast
greens . . . Cannot figure out greens. No. 5 is impossible . . . Awesome
uphill par 3 . . . People friendly . . . Walking always allowed . . . If you
walk this one, you will sleep good that night.

★ DON A. HAWKINS GOLF COURSE
PU—8920 Robuck Rd., Birmingham (205)836-7318.
Call club for further information.
Subscriber comments: Municipal course . . . Older, well designed . . .
Excellent potential . . . Needs money . . . Better turf planned for 1995.

★★★ EAGLE POINT GOLF CLUB
PU—4500 Eagle Point Dr., Birmingham (205)991-9070.
Holes: 18. **Par:** 71/70.
Yards: 6,470/4,691. **Course rating:** 70.2/61.9. **Slope:** 127/108.
Opened: 1990. **Pace of Play rating:** N/A. **Green fee:** $19/28.
Credit cards: All major. **Reduced fees:** Seniors.
Caddies: No. **Golf carts:** $9 for 18 holes.
Discount golf packages: No. **Season:** Year-round. **High:** April-Sept.
On-site lodging: No. **Rental clubs:** Yes.
Walking policy: Unrestricted walking. **Range:** Yes (grass).
To obtain tee times: Call up to five days in advance.
Subscriber comments: Excellent location . . . Great mountain scenery
. . . A beautiful setting for golf . . . Has many scenic holes, always in
excellent condition . . . Fun but tough . . . Short and tight, but delightful
. . . Picturesque, but very tight . . . 18 holes where 14 should be . . . First
four holes run parallel to each other . . . Hockey helmet required on first
four holes . . . Short, good for older golfers . . . Tough undulating bent-
grass greens . . . Playable, but a challenge . . . Play it from the tips . . .
Only drawback you can't get off cartpaths . . . This course has really come
a long way . . . Best public course in the area.

★½ FRANK HOUSE MUNICIPAL GOLF CLUB
PU—801 Golf Course Rd., Bessemer (205)424-9540.
15 miles north of Birmingham. **Holes:** 18. **Par:** 72/75.
Yards: 6,320/5,034. **Course rating:** 69.0/63.3. **Slope:** 119/107.
Opened: 1972. **Pace of Play rating:** 4:00. **Green fee:** $14/15.
Credit cards: MC, V, DISC. **Reduced fees:** Weekdays, Low season,
Resort guests, Twilight, Seniors.
Caddies: No. **Golf carts:** $16 for 18 holes.

Discount golf packages: No. **Season:** Year-round. **High:** May-Aug.
On-site lodging: No. **Rental clubs:** Yes.
Walking policy: Walking at certain times. **Range:** No.
To obtain tee times: First come first serve.
Subscriber comments: Fun course, kind of easy. . . Plays kind of slow, yet enjoyable . . . Hilly, very short, lots of pine trees . . . Good for a quickie . . . Needs some work . . . It's hard to keep a good stand of grass on the hills . . . Good people . . . Friendly . . . Best burgers in the area.

GLENLAKES COUNTRY CLUB
★★½ DUNES COURSE
SP—9530 Clubhouse Dr., Foley (334)943-8000, (800)796-4853.
70 miles southeast of Mobile. **Holes:** 18. **Par:** 72/72.
Yards: 6,680/5,019. **Course rating:** 69.1/70.5. **Slope:** 126/120.
Opened: 1987. **Pace of Play rating:** 4:00. **Green fee:** $23/37.
Credit cards: MC, V. **Reduced fees:** Low season, Resort guests, Twilight, Juniors.
Caddies: No. **Golf carts:** Included in Green Fee.
Discount golf packages: Yes. **Season:** Year-round. **High:** Jan.-March.
On-site lodging: No. **Rental clubs:** Yes.
Walking policy: Walking at certain times. **Range:** Yes (grass).
To obtain tee times: Call seven days in advance.
Also has 9-hole Lakes Course.
Subscriber comments: Now 27 holes, interesting but different nines . . . Jekyll and Hyde courses . . . Drastic change from Lakes to Dunes . . . Lakes, less than average . . . Blah . . . Dunes excellent . . . Very good Scottish links . . . New nine improves the Dunes . . . Dunes may be best in lower Alabama . . . Too difficult for 15-handicapper . . . Don't like blind shots, trick doglegs . . . Lacks much, but improving.

★★★½ GOOSE POND COLONY GOLF COURSE
R—417 Ed Hembree Dr., Scottsboro (205)574-5353, (800)268-2884.
40 miles west of Huntsville. **Holes:** 18. **Par:** 72/72.
Yards: 6,860/5,370. **Course rating:** 71.7/70.0. **Slope:** 125/115.
Opened: 1968. **Pace of Play rating:** 4:00. **Green fee:** $14/21.
Credit cards: MC, V, DISC. **Reduced fees:** Weekdays, Resort guests, Seniors, Juniors.
Caddies: No. **Golf carts:** $9 for 18 holes.
Discount golf packages: Yes. **Season:** Year-round. **High:** April-Aug.
On-site lodging: Yes. **Rental clubs:** Yes.
Walking policy: Walking at certain times. **Range:** Yes (grass).
To obtain tee times: Call Monday for weekend three days in advance.
Subscriber comments: Hidden jewel of north Alabama . . . George Cobb design with lots of water. Very scenic . . . Great atmosphere . . . The setting is extraordinary . . . Beautiful course by a lake . . . Prettiest course in northern Alabama . . . Not very well known but very nice. Wonderful greens . . . The secret is out, tends to be crowded . . . Great variation in holes . . . A fun place to play, lots of scoring options . . . Water everywhere . . . A different feel on almost every hole . . . Good test of all shots . . . Competition-quality course, lush fairways, well-kept greens . . . Excellent test. Pick your tee honestly . . . Strong from the tips . . . Prompt tee times . . . Best course in north Alabama . . . Watch out for low-flying geese.

GRAND NATIONAL GOLF CLUB
PU—3000 Sunbelt Pkwy., Opelika (334)749-9042, (800)949-4444.
55 miles east of Montgomery.
Opened: 1992. **Pace of Play rating:** 4:30. **Green fee:** $20/32.
Credit cards: All major.
Caddies: No. **Golf carts:** $13 for 18 holes.
Discount golf packages: Yes. **Season:** Year-round. **High:** March-Oct.
On-site lodging: No. **Rental clubs:** Yes.
Walking policy: Unrestricted walking. **Range:** Yes (grass).
To obtain tee times: Call golf shop.

ALABAMA

★★★★½ LAKE COURSE

Holes: 18. **Par:** 72/72.
Yards: 7,089/4,910. **Course rating:** 74.9/67.4. **Slope:** 138/123.
Reduced fees: Weekdays, Low season, Twilight, Juniors.
Ranked 5th in Alabama by Golf Digest.
Subscriber comments: All the challenge you want . . . Part of the Trent Jones Trail, not laid out for handicaps above 16 . . . Great variety, very scenic . . . Incredible layout, excellent condition . . . Great setting for golf. Memorable course . . . A round to remember on the most beautiful course I've ever seen . . . Azaleas and dogwoods resemble Augusta National, not Grand National . . . Most fun of the Trail courses . . . In 10 years, this course will be five stars . . . It's tough but enjoyable . . . Water, water, water . . . Hit it straight or hit it often . . . Extremely difficult, amplifies mistakes . . . Fairway bunkers, ouch! . . . Island green is tough . . . Greens big but severely slanted . . . Big hitters/good putters course . . . Easier of two long courses . . . Staff was great . . . No problems with 36 holes a day . . . Tough to walk . . . The best bent greens anywhere . . . Best course in Alabama, bar none . . . Probably No. 1 in the country.

★★★★½ LINKS COURSE
Holes: 18. **Par:** 72/72.
Yards: 7,311/4,843. **Course rating:** 74.9/66.8. **Slope:** 141/125.
Reduced fees: Weekdays, Low season, Twilight.
Selected as runner-up for Best New Public Course of 1993 by Golf Digest. Ranked 7th in Alabama by Golf Digest.
Subscriber comments: Fantastic layout . . . Super challenge . . . A beautiful track, absolutely first class . . . Scenic with lakes and pines . . . Golf at its best. A stunning variety of scenery. Isolated . . . Serious target golf, tough to figure yardages . . . Demanding approach shots . . . Interesting holes, tough par 3s . . . Bent greens are an absolute joy . . . Tough greens, better be on same level as flag, or three putt . . . Tougher than the Lake Course, but a must play . . . Bring your best game . . . If you're an 80s golfer, get ready for a 100 . . . Hackers should come here only to use the excellent practice facilities . . . Needs a few years to mature. When it does, it will be as nice as Lake . . . My vote for best of Trent Jones Trail . . . Worth the drive from anywhere . . . Great treatment . . . Young staff, smiling and helpful . . . Best group of par 4's I've ever played . . . Best finishing hole in the state . . . Best course in Alabama .

★★★★½ SHORT COURSE
Holes: 18. **Par:** 54/54.
Yards: 3,328/1,863. **Course rating:** N/A. **Slope:** N/A.
Reduced fees: Weekdays, Low season, Twilight, Juniors.
Subscriber comments: A par-3 course with length and quality. Lots of fun . . . The best par-3 course in captivity. I recommend it highly . . . Great two-hour trip around a golf course . . . Excellent target practice . . . Great variety of lengths due to many tee boxes . . . You can use all of your clubs . . . Everyone should play this course . . . My wife and mother love it . . . Inexpensive if you play it after your regular round . . . Grand National should be on everyone's "Must Play" list . . . All three are great tests of golf . . . Haven't played many that are better.

★★ GULF SHORES GOLF CLUB
PU—520 Clubhouse Dr., Gulf Shores (334)968-7366.
20 miles west of Pensacola, FL. **Holes:** 18. **Par:** 72/72.
Yards: 6,570/5,522. **Course rating:** 72.1/72.0. **Slope:** 122/121.
Opened: 1964. **Pace of Play rating:** N/A. **Green fee:** $32/37.
Credit cards: MC, V. **Reduced fees:** Juniors.
Caddies: No. **Golf carts:** Included in Green Fee.
Discount golf packages: No. **Season:** Year-round. **High:** Jan.–Aug.
On-site lodging: No. **Rental clubs:** Yes.
Walking policy: Mandatory cart. **Range:** Yes (grass).
To obtain tee times: Call pro shop two days in advance.

Subscriber comments: Nice old layout, small greens . . . Older, mature layout. Not too fancy . . . Pleasant play . . . Nice layout for a flat site . . . Open, forgiving, good for the vacationing golfer . . . Seems to be always under construction . . . Improvements being made will make it much better . . . .Course improved since last year.

★★★ GULF STATE PARK GOLF COURSE
PU—20115 State Hwy. 135, Gulf Shores (334)948-4653.
50 miles west of Mobile. Holes: 18. **Par:** 72/72.
Yards: 6,563/5,310. **Course rating:** 72.5/70.4. **Slope:** N/A.
Opened: 1974. **Pace of Play rating:** 4:00. **Green fee:** $19.
Credit cards: MC, V, AMEX. **Reduced fees:** Resort guests, Seniors.
Caddies: No. **Golf carts:** $11 for 18 holes.
Discount golf packages: Yes. **Season:** Year-round. **High:** Feb.-April/June-Aug.
On-site lodging: Yes. **Rental clubs:** Yes.
Walking policy: Unrestricted walking. **Range:** Yes (grass).
To obtain tee times: Call day in advance for weekdays, for weekends, call from Wednesday on.
Subscriber comments: Most impressive for a state park course . . . Top notch . . . Beautiful surroundings . . . Wide fairways and big greens. I love it! . . . Good short course, makes you feel good about the game . . . Good course for old folks . . . Just a fun course . . . Holes have character . . . Crowded but pace maintained . . . Best course marshals I've ever seen . . . Make your reservations early . . . Too much traffic . . . Could be magnificent, needs professional grooming . . . Alligators and monkey squirrels galore . . . Great hamburgers . . . Best course in the area for average golfer . . . The best course on our Gulf Shores vacation.

HAMPTON COVE GOLF CLUB
PU—450 Old Hwy. 431 S., Owens Cross Roads (205)551-1818, (800)949-4444.
5 miles southeast of Huntsville.
Credit cards: All major.
Caddies: No. **Golf carts:** $12 for 18 holes.
Discount golf packages: Yes. **Season:** Year-round. **High:** July-Sept.
On-site lodging: No. **Rental clubs:** Yes.
Walking policy: Unrestricted walking. **Range:** Yes (grass).
To obtain tee times: Tee time required. Call golf shop or 800 number.
★★★½ HIGHLANDS COURSE
Holes: 18. **Par:** 72/72.
Yards: 7,262/4,766. **Course rating:** 74.1/66.0. **Slope:** 134/118.
Opened: 1992. **Pace of Play rating:** N/A. **Green fee:** $20/27.
Reduced fees: Weekdays, Twilight, Juniors.
Subscriber comments: Typical excellent quality of Robert Trent Jones Golf Trail in Alabama . . . Beautiful grounds . . . Outstanding . . . Exquisite . . . Ultimate golf . . . Holes with character . . . Very challenging . . . Gorgeous, difficult course because demand is on accuracy on every shot . . . When in good shape, a true test . . . Much more forgiving than River Course . . . Multi-tiered greens are punitive . . . May be too tough for bogey golfer to enjoy . . . Too many elevated greens, too many bunkers . . . Takes light years to play . . . Average player should choose tee to play, then play the one in front of that . . . Definitely better the second time around . . . Best conditioned course in this area . . . Best public course in north Alabama, bar none.
★★★ RIVER COURSE
Holes: 18. **Par:** 72/72.
Yards: 7,507/5,283. **Course rating:** 75.6/67.0. **Slope:** 135/118.
Opened: 1993. **Pace of Play rating:** N/A. **Green fee:** $20/27.
Reduced fees: Weekdays, Twilight, Juniors.
Subscriber comments: Sprawling layout . . . Links style with few trees . . . Not called River Course for nothing . . . Water everywhere. Tee shots determine your score . . . Best for low handicap, no sand bunkers, lot of water, raised greens . . . Firm, elevated Bermuda greens. Tough to hold in

summer . . . Most holes below flood plain, thus very soggy . . . Not as good as Highland . . . A weak link in the Trent Jones Trail . . . Too many funky holes to be a great course . . . No sand bunkers . . . Built in a swamp . . . Holes lack framing . . . Not easy to find your way around . . . You can walk it.

SHORT COURSE★
Holes: 18. **Par:** 54/54.
Yards: 3,140/1,829. **Course rating:** N/A. **Slope:** N/A.
Opened: N/A. **Pace of Play rating:** N/A. **Green fee:** $13.
Reduced fees: Weekdays, Low season, Twilight, Juniors.

★½HARRY PRITCHETT GOLF COURSE
PU—University of Alabama, Tuscaloosa (205)348-7041.
Call club for further information.
Subscriber comments: OK golf course . . . Some weak holes . . . Very hilly on the front nine . . . Nothing for University of Alabama to brag about . . . Course has improved in the last three years. They have great practice facilities. Driving range, chipping greens and putting green are all kept up nicely . . . Improvements have helped a lot . . . Really becoming better.

HIGHLAND OAKS GOLF CLUB
★★★★ HIGHLANDS/MARSHWOOD/MAGNOLIA

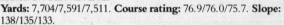

PU—704 Royal Pkwy, Dothan (334)712-2820, (800)949-4444.
Holes: 27. **Par:** 72/72/72.
Yards: 7,704/7,591/7,511. **Course rating:** 76.9/76.0/75.7. **Slope:** 138/135/133.
Opened: 1993. **Pace of Play rating:** N/A. **Green fee:** $20/27.
Credit cards: All major. **Reduced fees:** Weekdays, Low season, Twilight, Juniors.
Caddies: No. **Golf carts:** N/A.
Discount golf packages: Yes. **Season:** Year-round. **High:** March-Oct.
On-site lodging: No. **Rental clubs:** Yes.
Walking policy: Unrestricted walking. **Range:** Yes (grass).
To obtain tee times: Call seven days in advance.
Complex also includes Short Course, a 9-hole par-3 layout.
Highlands/Magnolia 9s ranked 6th in Alabama by Golf Digest.
Subscriber comments: Part of the Robert Trent Jones Trail, the greatest thing ever done for public golf! . . . Gorgeous course, most traditional of the Trail courses . . . Good track with some great holes . . . Excellent test . . . Outstanding fairways. Outstanding greens . . . One of the best anywhere. Large, smooth, big-breaking greens . . . Long, superfast greens, challenging par 5s. Can't believe it's so new . . . All three championship nines are superb . . . Most difficult of all courses on the Trail . . . No fun, too hard . . . Swallow ego and move up a tee box . . . Staff very courteous . . . Second best course I have ever played.

★½ HUNTSVILLE MUNICIPAL GOLF COURSE
PU—2151 Airport Rd., Huntsville (205)883-3647.
Call club for further information.
Subscriber comments: Wide-open course . . . Coming back after tornado cleared trees out four years ago . . . Great because it's wide open. Great for a beginning golfer . . . Very short . . . Not too challenging . . . Cute, but except for 7-iron and putter, not much else is needed . . . Interesting greens . . . Bent greens . . . Convenient location . . . Nice clubhouse . . . Usually busy.

★★½ INDIAN PINES GOLF CLUB
PU—900 Country Club Lane, Auburn (334)821-0880.
Call club for further information.
Subscriber comments: Average public course . . . Decent course . . . Needs maintenance but fun to play . . . Good ego-building course . . . Wide fairways . . . Great greens for public course . . . Gets a lot of play by college students, still in pretty good shape.

★★½ ISLE DAUPHINE GOLF CLUB
PU—100 Orleans Dr., P.O. Box 39, Dauphin Island (334)861-2433.
30 miles south of Mobile. **Holes:** 18. **Par:** 72/72.
Yards: 6,620/5,619. **Course rating:** N/A. **Slope:** 123/122.
Opened: N/A. **Pace of Play rating:** N/A. **Green fee:** N/A.
Credit cards: MC, V. **Reduced fees:** Weekdays.
Caddies: No. **Golf carts:** N/A.
Discount golf packages: No. **Season:** Year-round. **High:** Feb.-May.
On-site lodging: No. **Rental clubs:** No.
Walking policy: N/A. **Range:** No.
Subscriber comments: Beautiful spot along the Gulf . . . Tough, tight
seaside course . . . Atmosphere is great . . . Beautiful views of Gulf. Very
challenging but playable. Wind can change the course dramatically . . . If
only they'd build a few more holes in the dunes . . . Could be beautiful,
needs work . . . Below average conditions . . . Poor fairways . . . Very
sandy . . . Too sandy and unkempt . . . Fun course. Shame it's not in better
condition.

★ JETPORT GOLF COURSE
PU—125 Earl St., Huntsville (205)772-9872.
Call club for further information.
Subscriber comments: A practice course. Wide open. Noisy airport . . .
Very flat, not a lot of character . . . No imagination . . . Redesign has
improved course . . . Could be a nice course but it's never in the best of
shape . . . Greens are usually hard . . . Like granite . . . If you want to get in
trouble, bring your own trees and sand.

★★ JOE WHEELER STATE PARK GOLF CLUB
R—Rte. 4, Box 369A, Rogersville (205)247-9308.
20 miles east of Florence. **Holes:** 18. **Par:** 72/72.
Yards: 7,251/6,055. **Course rating:** 73.1/67.7. **Slope:** 120/109.
Opened: 1974. **Pace of Play rating:** 4:30. **Green fee:** $15.
Credit cards: MC, V, AMEX. **Reduced fees:** Resort guests, Seniors.
Caddies: No. **Golf carts:** $18 for 18 holes.
Discount golf packages: Yes. **Season:** Year-round.
On-site lodging: Yes. **Rental clubs:** Yes.
Walking policy: Unrestricted walking. **Range:** Yes (grass).
To obtain tee times: March to October tee times required for weekends
and holidays taken Monday before play.
Subscriber comments: Nice long-ball course . . . Long, tough . . . Has
scenic holes . . . Lots of hills . . . Elevation changes . . . Elevated greens
. . . Too many blind shots to greens . . . Blind shots ate my lunch . . .
When course is in shape, it is excellent . . . Needs work done on it. Opened
20 years ago and still has rocks, bare spots . . . With some work, could be a
fine course.

★★★½ LAGOON PARK GOLF COURSE
PU—2855 Lagoon Park Dr., Montgomery (334)271-7000.
Holes: 18. **Par:** 72/72.
Yards: 6,773/5,342. **Course rating:** 71.1/69.6. **Slope:** 124/113.
Opened: 1978. **Pace of Play rating:** 4:50. **Green fee:** $14/18.
Credit cards: MC, V, DISC. **Reduced fees:** Weekdays, Low season.
Caddies: No. **Golf carts:** $9 for 18 holes.
Discount golf packages: Yes. **Season:** Year-round. **High:** April-Oct.
On-site lodging: No. **Rental clubs:** Yes.
Walking policy: Unrestricted walking. **Range:** Yes (grass).
To obtain tee times: Call Thursday a.m. for weekend tee times. No
reserved times during week.
Ranked in Second 25 of America's 75 Best Public Golf Courses by Golf
Digest.
Subscriber comments: Perhaps the best-kept secret in Alabama . . . Good
track, must drive well, large greens . . . A real challenge. Doglegs left and
right . . . Must keep drives between trees to score . . . A wonderful course
. . . Tough but fun. You can run a ball up to most greens . . . Had a ball

playing this course . . . Great course but usually damp year around . . .
Don't play after a rain . . . Fair conditioning due to high volume of play . . .
Bermuda greens and fairways, both over-seeded in winter . . . Excellent
course to walk . . . Best public course in south Alabama . . . Best municipal
course I have played.

★★★½ LAKE GUNTERSVILLE GOLF CLUB

PU—7966 Alabama Hwy. 227, Guntersville (205)582-0379.
40 miles south of Huntsville. **Holes:** 18. **Par:** 72/72.
Yards: 6,785/5,776. **Course rating:** 71.2/70.3. **Slope:** 128/124.
Opened: 1974. **Pace of Play rating:** 4:00. **Green fee:** $14.
Credit cards: MC, V, AMEX. **Reduced fees:** Seniors.
Caddies: No. **Golf carts:** $9 for 18 holes.
Discount golf packages: Yes. **Season:** Year-round. **High:** July-Aug.
On-site lodging: Yes. **Rental clubs:** Yes.
Walking policy: Unrestricted walking. **Range:** Yes (grass).
To obtain tee times: Call Wednesday prior to weekend. Tee times for
weekends only.
Subscriber comments: Good state park course . . . A good getaway . . .
Perfect setting . . . Beautiful views . . . Pretty course . . . Variety of holes
. . . Well kept . . . Good greens . . . Tricky greens . . . Greens held balls
nicely this year . . . Wildlife, especially deer, abundant . . . Some funny
holes but fun to play . . . Very hilly and a real challenge . . . Pull out the
driver and leave it out! . . . On the side of a mountain . . . Too many blind
shots . . . Staff very good, service very good . . . No sandwich shop . . .
One of the best state park courses in the Southeast . . . Go in the fall when
the leaves change.

★★★ LAKEPOINT RESORT GOLF COURSE

R—Hwy. 431, Eufaula (334)687-6677, (800)544-5253.
50 miles north of Columbus, GA. **Holes:** 18. **Par:** 72/72.
Yards: 6,752/5,363. **Course rating:** 73.6/69.2. **Slope:** 123.
Opened: 1971. **Pace of Play rating:** N/A. **Green fee:** $13.
Credit cards: MC, V, AMEX. **Reduced fees:** Seniors.
Caddies: No. **Golf carts:** $9 for 18 holes.
Discount golf packages: Yes. **Season:** Year-round. **High:** March-June.
On-site lodging: Yes. **Rental clubs:** Yes.
Walking policy: Unrestricted walking. **Range:** Yes.
To obtain tee times: Call for weekend tee times only.
Subscriber comments: OK for state park course . . . An average, pleasant
course. You enjoy playing it, but are in no hurry to go back . . . Front and
back nines are very different . . . Interesting back nine . . . Plenty of water
. . . Front nine boring . . . State needs to spend money on upkeep . . . Play
is fairly fast after long lines off the first tee . . . Staff is excellent . . . Friendly
. . . Nice people . . . Need to relocate the geese to Canada.

★★½ THE LINKSMAN GOLF CLUB

PU—3700 St. Andrews Dr., Mobile (334)661-0018.
Holes: 18. **Par:** 72/72.
Yards: 6,275/5,416. **Course rating:** 70.1/71.0. **Slope:** 123/121.
Opened: 1987. **Pace of Play rating:** 4:50. **Green fee:** $12.
Credit cards: All major. **Reduced fees:** Weekdays, Resort guests,
Twilight, Seniors, Juniors.
Caddies: No. **Golf carts:** $10 for 18 holes.
Discount golf packages: Yes. **Season:** Year-round. **High:** March-June.
On-site lodging: No. **Rental clubs:** Yes.
Walking policy: Unrestricted walking. **Range:** Yes (grass).
To obtain tee times: Call pro shop.
Subscriber comments: Interesting . . . Water comes into play on almost
all the holes . . . Water on 14 holes . . . Bring lots of golf balls and lots of
patience . . . Confusing layout . . . Too many trick holes . . . Condition
has vastly improved . . . Most improved golf course in Mobile and still
getting better . . . Very courteous staff . . . Tough, tight, water, fun.

MAGNOLIA GROVE GOLF CLUB

PU—7000 Lamplighter Dr., Semmes (334)645-0075, (800)949-4444.
22 miles west of Mobile.
Credit cards: All major. **Reduced fees:** Weekdays, Low season, Twilight, Seniors, Juniors.
Caddies: No. **Golf carts:** $14 for 18 holes.
Discount golf packages: Yes. **Season:** Year-round. **High:** Feb.–April.
On-site lodging: No. **Rental clubs:** Yes.
Walking policy: Unrestricted walking. **Range:** Yes (grass).
To obtain tee times: Call pro shop

★★★★ CROSSINGS COURSE

Holes: 18. **Par:** 72/72.
Yards: 7,150/5,184. **Course rating:** 74.6/N/A. **Slope:** 134/N/A.
Opened: 1992. **Pace of Play rating:** 4:25. **Green fee:** $21/28.
Subscriber comments: World class Trent Jones . . . My favorite on the Robert Trent Jones Trail . . . Most fun of the Jones Trail . . . True Trent Jones designs, great diversity within the same natural layout . . . Sets up great from tees . . . Tests courage . . . Typical Trent Jones, greens Augusta fast . . . Fastest greens I have ever seen . . . Greens putt truer than any I've ever played . . . Good practice areas . . . Lots of sand, changes of elevation, a real test even from the regular tees . . . High handicappers may be disappointed these courses are so tough . . . I was tired after playing this tough course . . . Best course in the area . . . Magnificent course. Great people.

★★★★ FALLS COURSE

Holes: 18. **Par:** 72/72.
Yards: 7,240/5,253. **Course rating:** 75.1/N/A. **Slope:** 137/N/A.
Opened: 1992. **Pace of Play rating:** 4:25. **Green fee:** $21/28.
Ranked 4th in Alabama by Golf Digest.
Subscriber comments: Worth every cent . . . Championship quality . . . Beautiful challenging layout . . . Excellent condition. Good practice areas. Very interesting. All holes different . . . Extremely difficult from back tees . . . Almost too difficult . . . All you can handle from the regular tees . . . Rolling fairways require precise drives. Long par 4s. Large undulating greens . . . Best course at the facility . . . Same as Crossings, a little less difficult . . . Some like it better than Crossings, not me . . . Many forced carries . . . Punishment describes it best . . . Greens are unfair. Some pins impossible . . . Top notch personnel . . . I found both Magnolia Grove courses most playable . . . Excellent rain shelters.

SHORT COURSE★

Holes: 18. **Par:** 54/54.
Opened: 1992. **Green fee:** $13.
Call club for further information.

MARRIOTT'S LAKEWOOD GOLF CLUB

R—Marriott's Grand Hotel, Scenic Hwy. 98, Point Clear (334)990-6312.
30 miles southwest of Mobile.
Opened: 1947. **Pace of Play rating:** 4:00. **Green fee:** $65.
Credit cards: All major. **Reduced fees:** Juniors.
Caddies: No. **Golf carts:** Included in Green Fee.
Discount golf packages: Yes. **Season:** Year-round.
On-site lodging: Yes. **Rental clubs:** Yes.
Walking policy: Mandatory cart. **Range:** Yes (grass).
To obtain tee times: Call pro shop.

★★★ AZALEA COURSE

Holes: 18. **Par:** 72.
Yards: 6,770/5,307. **Course rating:** 72.5/71.3. **Slope:** 128/118.
Subscriber comments: Classic southern course . . . Nice atmosphere, good layout . . . Fair to all . . . Beautiful massive live oak trees . . . Simply magnificent . . . Real southern charm . . . Great for business clients . . . Nice course, nothing outstanding . . . Easier to play since Hurricane Camille . . . New holes superior to old ones . . . Condition of course varies . . . Needs greens rebuilt . . . Very good clubhouse facilities . . . Staff was superb . . . Very hospitable.

★★★ DOGWOOD COURSE
Holes: 18. **Par:** 71/72.
Yards: 6,676/5,532. **Course rating:** 72.1/72.6. **Slope:** 124/122.
Subscriber comments: Very beautiful . . . Lovely setting . . . A pleasant play . . . Good course for all types of shots . . . Narrow fairways . . . Tree lined . . . Balls easily found . . . Good fast greens . . . Toughest back nine in south Alabama . . . Super staff . . . Wonderful service . . . Good hot dogs.

★½ MCFARLAND PARK GOLF COURSE
PU—James M. Spain Dr., City of Florence, Florence (205)760-6428.
120 miles northwest of Birmingham. **Holes:** 18. **Par:** 72/72.
Yards: 6,660/5,741. **Course rating:** 71.9/72.9. **Slope:** N/A.
Opened: 1972. **Pace of Play rating:** N/A. **Green fee:** $6/11.
Credit cards: MC, V. **Reduced fees:** Low season, Seniors, Juniors.
Caddies: No. **Golf carts:** $16 for 18 holes.
Discount golf packages: No. **Season:** Year-round. **High:** May-Oct.
On-site lodging: No. **Rental clubs:** Yes.
Walking policy: N/A. **Range:** Yes (grass).
To obtain tee times: Call Tuesday before upcoming weekend.
Subscriber comments: Tricky course with mounded greens . . . Elevated postage-stamp greens . . . Too many blind shots to the greens . . . Better carry lots of balls. Very narrow, water on every hole . . . Has potential but always wet . . . Lost a lot of trees in freeze last winter . . . Fairways and greens could use a different grass . . . Best tee boxes in Alabama.

★★★ MOUNTAIN VIEW GOLF CLUB
PU—3200 Mtn. View Dr., Graysville (205)674-8362.
Call club for further information.
Subscriber comments: Not long but very hilly . . . Up and down layout . . . Not a championship test, but who cares? . . . A bit short, but enough variety to test your whole bag . . . Very short but interesting . . . Very fun to play . . . Great track for an average golfer . . . Chance for 80 shooters to shoot in 70s . . . Just opened a second nine . . . Pretty views . . . The name fits it perfectly.

★★ OAK MOUNTAIN STATE PARK GOLF COURSE
PU—Findley Dr., Pelham (205)620-2522.
15 miles south of Birmingham. **Holes:** 18. **Par:** 72/72.
Yards: 6,748/5,540. **Course rating:** 71.5/N/A. **Slope:** 127/124.
Opened: 1974. **Pace of Play rating:** 4:30. **Green fee:** $12/18.
Credit cards: MC, V, AMEX. **Reduced fees:** Seniors.
Caddies: No. **Golf carts:** $18 for 18 holes.
Discount golf packages: Yes. **Season:** Year-round. **High:** May-Sept.
On-site lodging: Yes. **Rental clubs:** No.
Walking policy: Unrestricted walking. **Range:** Yes (grass).
To obtain tee times: Call Mondays for upcoming Saturday, Tuesday for Sunday, Wednesday for Monday, etc.
Subscriber comments: Really a pretty course . . . Beautiful layout and location . . . Good aesthetics. Great walking . . . Fun to play . . . Reachable par 5s, fun par 3s, mediocre par 4s . . . Nice design, trouble with year-round care . . . Great design that has been let go . . . Good layout, poor greens . . . Could be a great track . . . Overplayed . . . Makes money for the state. They do not return the favor . . . Heavy traffic . . . Play is too slow . . . State should shovel money at this potential gold mine.

★★½ OLYMPIA SPA GOLF RESORT
SP—Hwy. 231 South, Dothan (334)677-3326.
Holes: 18. **Par:** 72/72.
Yards: 7,242/5,470. **Course rating:** 74.5/71.1. **Slope:** 123/113.
Opened: 1968. **Pace of Play rating:** 4:00. **Green fee:** $12/18.
Credit cards: All major. **Reduced fees:** Twilight.
Caddies: No. **Golf carts:** $10 for 18 holes.
Discount golf packages: Yes. **Season:** Year-round. **High:** March-June.
On-site lodging: Yes. **Rental clubs:** Yes.

Walking policy: Walking at certain times. **Range:** Yes (grass).
To obtain tee times: Call pro shop.
Subscriber comments: A long and demanding course . . . Not too tight, but a good test. Conditioning marginal . . . Huge greens, tough from back tees . . . One of Alabama's hardest from the back tees . . . Toughest holes are 9 and 18 . . . Improved 100 percent in the last two years . . . Staff goes out of its way to be helpful.

OXMOOR VALLEY GOLF CLUB
PU—100 Sunbelt Pkwy., Birmingham (205)942-1177, (800)949-4444.
Credit cards: All major. **Reduced fees:** Weekdays, Low season, Twilight, Seniors, Juniors.
Caddies: No. **Golf carts:** N/A.
Discount golf packages: Yes. **Season:** Year-round. **High:** April-Nov.
On-site lodging: No. **Rental clubs:** Yes.
Walking policy: Unrestricted walking. **Range:** Yes (grass).
To obtain tee times: Call up to seven days in advance. May reserve tee times up to 45 days in advance for an additional $2.

★★★½ RIDGE COURSE
Holes: 18. **Par:** 72/72.
Yards: 7,053/4,869. **Course rating:** 73.5/68.6. **Slope:** 140/130.
Opened: 1992. **Pace of Play rating:** 4:15. **Green fee:** $20/27.
Subscriber comments: Incredible design . . . Spectacular design . . . Magnificent . . . Breathtaking holes throughout . . . Another Robert Trent Jones Golf Trail beauty . . . Target golf, greens very severe . . . Tiered greens are too tough for average duffer. Automatic three putts . . . Too much! . . . Single-digit player course . . . Keeps coming at you . . . Bad golfers, stay away! . . . Get ready to do some hiking . . . More of a cart course . . . Gorgeous scenery, interesting holes, what a pleasure . . . In great shape. Personnel better than my private club . . . Gotta check out these Oxmoor courses.

★★★½ SHORT COURSE
Holes: 18. **Par:** 54/54.
Yards: 3,154/1,990.
Opened: 1992. **Pace of Play rating:** 2:30. **Green fee:** $13.
Subscriber comments: This is a par-3 course, but if played from the tips it is a great course . . . Unbelievable challenge for par 3 . . . Beautiful . . . Magnificent elevation changes . . . Excellent condition . . . Not a rinky dink par 3, a true test. Take every club . . . Fun course that works your game . . . Vary tee box from hole to hole for most enjoyment . . . Great for 12 plus handicaps . . . Best par 3 I've played . . . Best par-3 course in the South.

GREAT VALUE

★★★½ VALLEY COURSE
Holes: 18. **Par:** 72/72.
Yards: 7,240/4,866. **Course rating:** 73.9/65.4. **Slope:** 135/118.
Opened: 1992. **Pace of Play rating:** 4:15. **Green fee:** $20/27.
Subscriber comments: Same old great Robert Trent Jones . . . Good course, very fast greens, no beginners . . . Too tough . . . Killer from the tips . . . If you're playing badly, these courses will make you hate life . . . "Valley" is misleading . . . Exciting elevation changes . . . Target fairways . . . Favors long iron off tees . . . Huge greens . . . Greens are hard . . . Needs at least one flat green . . . Not as scenic as Ridge Course . . . Less tough than Ridge . . . Much better than Ridge except for 18th hole . . . 18th is tough . . . More manageable than Ridge, but keep concentration or it can jump on you, too . . . Indistinguishable holes . . . Service very good . . . Facilities are first rate.

★★★ POINT MALLARD GOLF COURSE
PU—1800 Point Mallard Dr., Decatur (205)351-7776.
20 miles east of Huntsville. **Holes:** 18. **Par:** 72/73.
Yards: 7,113/5,437. **Course rating:** 73.7/N/A. **Slope:** 125/N/A.
Opened: 1970. **Pace of Play rating:** N/A. **Green fee:** $10/15.
Credit cards: MC, V. **Reduced fees:** Weekdays, Low season, Seniors, Juniors.

Caddies: No. **Golf carts:** $16 for 18 holes.
Discount golf packages: Yes. **Season:** Year-round. **High:** April–Sept.
On-site lodging: No. **Rental clubs:** Yes.
Walking policy: Unrestricted walking. **Range:** No.
To obtain tee times: Call Wednesday for Saturday tee times.
Subscriber comments: Long and flat . . . Bring your big sticks . . .
Respectable length, interesting layout . . . Scenic, some good water holes
. . . Not a great deal of trouble . . . Large Bermuda greens . . . Massive
greens, postage-stamp fairways . . . Need a practice area . . . Best shape it
has ever been in. Under new management, very nice people.

★★ QUAIL CREEK GOLF COURSE
PU—19341 Quail Creek Dr., Fairhope (334)990-0240.
20 miles east of Mobile. **Holes:** 18. **Par:** 72/72.
Yards: 6,426/5,305. **Course rating:** 70.1/69.6. **Slope:** 112/114.
Opened: 1988. **Pace of Play rating:** N/A. **Green fee:** $16.
Credit cards: MC, V. **Reduced fees:** Twilight.
Caddies: No. **Golf carts:** $10 for 18 holes.
Discount golf packages: No. **Season:** Year-round. **High:** Jan.–April.
On-site lodging: No. **Rental clubs:** Yes.
Walking policy: Unrestricted walking. **Range:** Yes (grass).
To obtain tee times: May call three days in advance.
Subscriber comments: Very nice, well-maintained public course . . .
Tight, lots of out-of-bounds . . . Wedged into too little space . . . Greens
inconsistent. . . Some poorly designed holes, fairways sloping to lake . . .
Interesting course with varied holes.

★★★★ ROCK CREEK GOLF CLUB
SP—140 Clubhouse Dr., Fairhope (334)928-4223.
10 miles east of Mobile. **Holes:** 18. **Par:** 72/72.
Yards: 6,920/5,135. **Course rating:** 72.2/68.4. **Slope:** 129/117.
Opened: 1993. **Pace of Play rating:** 4:15. **Green fee:** $37/42.
Credit cards: MC, V, AMEX. **Reduced fees:** Twilight.
Caddies: No. **Golf carts:** Included in Green Fee.
Discount golf packages: Yes. **Season:** Year-round. **High:** Spring/Fall.
On-site lodging: No. **Rental clubs:** Yes.
Walking policy: Mandatory cart. **Range:** Yes (grass).
To obtain tee times: Call golf shop for tee time.
Subscriber comments: Nice hilly, woodsy layout . . . Sporty new course
. . . Challenging, but not a back breaker . . . Not penal to average-handicap
golfer, but only good shots let me score . . . Medium difficulty . . . Not
long but makes you think . . . Lots of bunkers, big greens . . . Could write
a page. Most playable course I've ever played . . . Course empty midweek
. . . Still maturing . . . Best new course in south Alabama . . . Good rental
clubs.

SILVER LAKES GOLF COURSE
★★★½ MINDBREAKER/HEARTBREAKER/BACKBREAKER
PU—1 Sunbelt Pkwy., Glencoe (205)892-3268.
15 miles north of Anniston. **Holes:** 27. **Par:** 72/72/72.
Yards: 7,407/7,674/7,425. **Course rating:** N/A. **Slope:** N/A.
Opened: 1993. **Pace of Play rating:** N/A. **Green fee:** $20/27.
Credit cards: All major. **Reduced fees:** Weekdays, Low season, Twilight,
Seniors, Juniors.
Caddies: No. **Golf carts:** $12 for 18 holes.
Discount golf packages: Yes. **Season:** Year-round. **High:** April-Oct.
On-site lodging: No. **Rental clubs:** Yes.
Walking policy: Unrestricted walking. **Range:** Yes (grass).
To obtain tee times: Call golf shop 7 a.m. till dark.
Complex also includes Short Course, a 9-hole par-3 layout.
Subscriber comments: Truly outstanding . . . A real jewel . . . Great
price! Good scenery . . . Very best Trent Jones Trail course . . . Playing
here regularly will make you better . . . Perfect greens . . . Sometimes

unfair . . . Can be a monster . . . Can play up to 7,800 yards! . . . Fairway bunkers everywhere. Ridiculous . . . Toughest on the Trail. Aptly named. Makes being brought to your knees seem enjoyable . . . Country club atmosphere . . . Best treatment you can get. They go to extra effort to please . . . Par-3 course superb.

★★★½ STILL WATERS RESORT

R—1000 Still Waters Dr., Dadeville (205)825-7021, (800)687-3732.
55 miles northeast of Montgomery. **Holes:** 18. **Par:** 72/72.
Yards: 6,407/5,287. **Course rating:** 69.9/71.5. **Slope:** 124/125.
Opened: 1972. **Pace of Play rating:** . **Green fee:** $17/21.
Credit cards: All major. **Reduced fees:** Weekdays, Low season, Juniors.
Caddies: No. **Golf carts:** $11 for 18 holes.
Discount golf packages: Yes. **Season:** Year-round. **High:** March-Oct.
On-site lodging: Yes. **Rental clubs:** Yes.
Walking policy: Unrestricted walking. **Range:** Yes (grass).
To obtain tee times: Call pro shop.
Subscriber comments: Neat course . . . Traditional layout . . . A real treat, beautiful place to play . . . Cut through hills of Lake Martin . . . Great view of lake . . . Shotmaker's course . . . Short but tight . . . Up and down hills . . . Lots of doglegs . . . A pretty course, fun to play . . . Good golf, good buy.

★½ STONEY MOUNTAIN GOLF CLUB

PU—500 Georgia Mtn. Rd., Guntersville (205)582-2598.
Holes: 18. **Par:** 72/72.
Yards: 5,931/4,711. **Course rating:** 67.6/66.2. **Slope:** 118/117.
Opened: N/A. **Pace of Play rating:** N/A. **Green fee:** $15/20.
Credit cards: ,V. **Reduced fees:** Weekdays, Seniors.
Caddies: No. **Golf carts:** N/A.
Discount golf packages: No. **Season:** Year-round. **High:** April-Dec.
On-site lodging: No. **Rental clubs:** Yes.
Walking policy: Walking at certain times. **Range:** No.
To obtain tee times: Call pro shop.
Subscriber comments: Nice course for weekend family outing . . . Wide open and short . . . Straightaway holes. No test . . . Best place to go if you want to play all day.

★★½ TERRAPIN HILLS GOLF ESTATES

PU—Rte. 7, Box 675, Ft. Payne (205)845-4624.
45 miles of Chattanooga, TN. **Holes:** 18. **Par:** 71/71.
Yards: 6,696/5,278. **Course rating:** N/A. **Slope:** 118/N/A.
Opened: N/A. **Pace of Play rating:** N/A. **Green fee:** N/A.
Credit cards: MC, V. **Reduced fees:** Weekdays.
Caddies: No. **Golf carts:** $18 for 18 holes.
Discount golf packages: No. **Season:** Year-round. **High:** April-May/Aug.-Oct.
On-site lodging: No. **Rental clubs:** No.
Walking policy: N/A. **Range:** Yes (grass).
Subscriber comments: Fair course . . . Short but pretty . . . Very playable . . . Good mix of difficulty and forgiveness . . . Unique holes . . . Some tee shots resemble those fantasy holes . . . Nice course, nothing great . . . Too wide open . . . Bet you can't play it only once.

TIMBER RIDGE GOLF CLUB★

SP—101 Ironaton Rd., Talladega (205)362-0346.
40 miles southeast of Birmingham. **Holes:** 18. **Par:** 71/71.
Yards: 6,700/5,346. **Course rating:** 70.0/66.0. **Slope:** 126/122.
Opened: 1988. **Pace of Play rating:** 4:15. **Green fee:** $7/14.
Credit cards: None. **Reduced fees:** Weekdays, Juniors.
Caddies: No. **Golf carts:** $14 for 18 holes.

Discount golf packages: No. **Season:** Year-round. **High:** June–Aug.
On-site lodging: No. **Rental clubs:** Yes.
Walking policy: Unrestricted walking. **Range:** Yes (grass).
To obtain tee times: Call two days in advance.

TIMBERCREEK GOLF CLUB
★★★★ **DOGWOOD/MAGNOLIA/PINES**
PU—9650 TimberCreek Blvd., Daphne (334)621-9900.
10 miles east of Mobile. **Holes:** 27. **Par:** 72/72/72.
Yards: 7,062/6,928/7,090. **Course rating:** 73.8/72.9/74.3. **Slope:**
144/137/143.
Opened: 1993. **Pace of Play rating:** N/A. **Green fee:** $23/28.
Credit cards: MC, V, AMEX. **Reduced fees:** Weekdays, Resort guests,
Twilight.
Caddies: No. **Golf carts:** $12 for 18 holes.
Discount golf packages: Yes. **Season:** Year-round.
On-site lodging: No. **Rental clubs:** Yes.
Walking policy: Walking at certain times. **Range:** Yes (grass).
To obtain tee times: Call pro shop.
Subscriber comments: Great 27 holes . . . Gently rolling Earl Stone
design, very pretty . . . Same architect as Rock Creek . . . Variety of hole
types . . . Plenty of tee options . . . Always fun. Good layout, great
management . . . Very enjoyable, forgiving fairways . . . Conditions better
than expected at a new course . . . Outstanding facility . . . Clubhouse well
designed . . . Best practice facility in state (except for Shoal Creek) . . .
Most enjoyable, not a monster . . . Similar to Magnolia Grove but more
generous . . . Easy access off I-10 . . . A "Must Play" in Mobile.

THE WOODLANDS COURSE AT CRAFT FARMS*
PU—19995 Oak Rd. West, Gulf Shores (334)968-4133, (800)327-2657.
30 miles west of Pensacola, FL. **Holes:** 18. **Par:** 72/72.
Yards: 6,484/5,145. **Course rating:** 70.8/N/A. **Slope:** 123/N/A.
Opened: 1994. **Pace of Play rating:** N/A. **Green fee:** $28/40.
Credit cards: MC, V, AMEX. **Reduced fees:** Low season.
Caddies: No. **Golf carts:** Included in Green Fee.
Discount golf packages: Yes. **Season:** Year-round. **High:** April–Aug.
On-site lodging: No. **Rental clubs:** Yes.
Walking policy: Walking at certain times. **Range:** Yes (grass).
To obtain tee times: Call up to six months in advance.

Notes

★ ALLING MEMORIAL GOLF COURSE
PU—35 Eastern St., New Haven (203)787-8014.
Call club for further information.
Subscriber comments: Fairly flat, improving conditions, good for
average golfers . . . Senior membership makes great value . . . Layout is
good, suits all different levels of players . . . Beginner to intermediate, true
public course.

★ BANNER RESORT & COUNTRY CLUB
PU—10 Banner Rd., Moodus (203)873-9075.
18 miles southeast of Hartford. **Holes:** 18. **Par:** 72/74.
Yards: 6,015/5,776. **Course rating:** 68.9/N/A. **Slope:** 118/N/A.
Opened: 1958. **Pace of Play rating:** 4:30. **Green fee:** $13/22.
Credit cards: None. **Reduced fees:** Weekdays, Low season, Seniors.
Caddies: No. **Golf carts:** $20 for 18 holes.
Discount golf packages: No. **Season:** April-first snow. **High:** June-Aug.
On-site lodging: No. **Rental clubs:** Yes.
Walking policy: Unrestricted walking. **Range:** Yes (grass).
To obtain tee times: Call seven days in advance.
Subscriber comments: Nothing exceptional but good golf . . . Well laid
out. Must position shots . . . Fairly long and flat, fairways could use work
. . . Boring, flat fairways . . . Some holes too close together.

★★½ BEL COMPO GOLF CLUB
PU—65 Nod Rd., Avon (203)678-1679.
10 miles northwest of Hartford. **Holes:** 18. **Par:** 72/72.
Yards: 7,028/5,452. **Course rating:** 73.4/71.6. **Slope:** 131/112.
Opened: 1974. **Pace of Play rating:** 4:30. **Green fee:** $21/25.
Credit cards: None. **Reduced fees:** Seniors.
Caddies: No. **Golf carts:** $24 for 18 holes.
Discount golf packages: No. **Season:** April-Nov. **High:** May-Sept.
On-site lodging: No. **Rental clubs:** Yes.
Walking policy: Unrestricted walking. **Range:** Yes (grass).
To obtain tee times: Call 8 a.m. on Thursday for upcoming weekend.
Subscriber comments: Wide fairways, fifth and 18th holes are unique and
challenging . . . Could be played by all calibers of players. Conditions very
good . . . Some easy holes, some tough ones. Interesting course; will use all
your clubs . . . Easy to walk . . . Flat, long, slower greens, excellent test,
good tees . . . Homey snack bar and grill . . . Front wooded and
challenging, back wide open.

★★★ BLACKLEDGE COUNTRY CLUB
ANDERSON/GILEAD/LINKS
PU—180 West St., Hebron (203)228-0250.
15 miles east of Hartford. **Holes:** 27. **Par:** 72/72/72.
Yards: 6,853/6,823/6,880. **Course rating:** 72.3/N/A/N/A.
Slope: 123/N/A/N/A.
Opened: 1964. **Pace of Play rating:** N/A. **Green fee:** $22/24.
Credit cards: None. **Reduced fees:** Weekdays, Low season, Twilight,
Seniors, Juniors.
Caddies: No. **Golf carts:** N/A.
Discount golf packages: Yes. **Season:** March-Dec. **High:** June-Aug.
On-site lodging: No. **Rental clubs:** No.
Walking policy: Unrestricted walking. **Range:** No.
To obtain tee times: Call one week in advance.
Subscriber comments: Interesting design, beautifully landscaped . . .
Great course, always in good condition tee to green, fun . . . Well run,
always great shape, not too busy, play when in area . . . Solid course, not
overly challenging or memorable, but in good shape. Below average
challenge . . . Good test. Nice condition, nice staff, good for all golfers . . .
Long walk to pro shop and first tee from parking lot . . . Terrific setting,
well-run pro shop, some picturesque holes . . . Nice forgiving layout, new
nine needs to mature, good condition, some wonderful holes.

★½ BRUCE MEMORIAL GOLF COURSE
SP—1300 King St., Greenwich (203)531-7261.
20 miles northeast of New York City. **Holes:** 18. **Par:** 71/73.
Yards: 6,512/5,710. **Course rating:** 71.1/72.0. **Slope:** 124/115.
Opened: 1963. **Pace of Play rating:** 4:30. **Green fee:** $11/12.
Credit cards: None. **Reduced fees:** Weekdays, Seniors, Juniors.
Caddies: No. **Golf carts:** $21 for 18 holes.
Discount golf packages: No. **Season:** April-Nov. **High:** June-Aug.
On-site lodging: No. **Rental clubs:** Yes.
Walking policy: Unrestricted walking. **Range:** Yes.
To obtain tee times: No reserved tee times for weekdays. For weekends
there is a lottery system held on Wednesday nights, or you can call on
Friday after 11 a.m.
Subscriber comments: Service was excellent . . . The head pro is the
nicest guy ever . . . Golf course needs a lot of work . . . Great layout . . .
Greens sub-par but improving, scenic . . . Interesting, well-designed
course.

★★ CANDLEWOOD VALLEY COUNTRY CLUB
PU—401 Danbury Rd., New Milford (203)354-9359.
60 miles northwest of New York City. **Holes:** 18. **Par:** 72/72.
Yards: 6,295/5,403. **Course rating:** 70.3/70.9. **Slope:** 120/126.
Opened: 1961. **Pace of Play rating:** 4:30. **Green fee:** $22/27.
Credit cards: MC, V. **Reduced fees:** Weekdays, Twilight, Seniors.
Caddies: No. **Golf carts:** $11 for 18 holes.
Discount golf packages: No. **Season:** March-Dec. **High:** May-Sept.
On-site lodging: No. **Rental clubs:** No.
Walking policy: Unrestricted walking. **Range:** Yes.
To obtain tee times: Call only Thursday morning at 7:30 a.m. and you
must have at least a threesome.
Subscriber comments: The front nine and back nine are night and day. I
like night . . . Can be slow and requires local knowledge . . . A good
course to brush up your game . . . Back nine tight . . . Fairly flat and easy
walking . . . Greens always very accommodating and in good shape . . .
Flat, not many trees. Don't have to be a long hitter . . . Easy front nine,
very tough back nine, staff is a real pleasure . . . Can't beat it, rebuilt holes
good.

★★★ CEDAR KNOB GOLF CLUB
PU—Billings Rd., Somers (203)749-3550.
11 miles southeast of Springfield, MA. **Holes:** 18. **Par:** 72/74.
Yards: 6,734/5,784. **Course rating:** 72.3/73.8. **Slope:** 119/126.
Opened: 1963. **Pace of Play rating:** 4:30. **Green fee:** $18/20.
Credit cards: None. **Reduced fees:** Weekdays, Low season, Seniors,
Juniors.
Caddies: No. **Golf carts:** $20 for 18 holes.
Discount golf packages: No. **Season:** Year-round. **High:** April-Sept.
On-site lodging: No. **Rental clubs:** Yes.
Walking policy: Unrestricted walking. **Range:** No.
To obtain tee times: Call seven days in advance.
Subscriber comments: Tight fairways, hilly, lots of pines, favors straight
hitters, sloped greens . . . Lovely, rolling, wooded course, big greens, very
long for women . . . Heavy play, large greens, drains well after rain, good
shape, use all clubs . . . Tough par 5s . . . Front nine short, back nine is
long and tight . . . Worth playing anytime . . . Course in excellent shape.
Staff great.

★★★½ CRESTBROOK PARK GOLF COURSE
PU—834 Northfield Rd., Watertown (203)945-5249.
5 miles north of Waterbury. **Holes:** 18. **Par:** 71/75.
Yards: 6,376/5,718. **Course rating:** 73.2/73.8. **Slope:** 132/128.
Opened: 1970. **Pace of Play rating:** 4:30. **Green fee:** $12/22.
Credit cards: None. **Reduced fees:** Weekdays, Seniors, Juniors.
Caddies: No. **Golf carts:** $21 for 18 holes.
Discount golf packages: No. **Season:** April-Dec. **High:** June-Aug.

On-site lodging: No. **Rental clubs:** Yes.
Walking policy: Unrestricted walking. **Range:** Yes (grass).
To obtain tee times: Call two days in advance; phone weekends and holidays only.
Subscriber comments: Toughest greens in Ct. . . . Enjoy front nine, back eats you up . . . Challenging, tough front nine. Great fairways. Large greens . . . Two very different nines . . . Good test for better player. Reasonable pace of play, friendly staff, great condition . . . Very challenging, fun course to play . . . Greens fast but roll true and excellent shape . . . Well-kept tight course, better be straight off the tee . . . Well-maintained muny but difficult with few flat fairways . . . This is a thinking player's course.

D. FAIRCHILD WHEELER GOLF COURSE
PU—2390 Easton Tpke., Fairfield (203)372-6265.
Credit cards: None. **Reduced fees:** N/A.
Caddies: No. **Golf carts:** $20 for 18 holes.
Discount golf packages: No. **Season:** Year-round. **High:** May-Aug.
On-site lodging: No. **Rental clubs:** Yes.
Walking policy: Unrestricted walking. **Range:** No.
To obtain tee times: First come, first serve.
★ BLACK COURSE
Holes: 18. **Par:** 71/73.
Yards: 6,402/5,764. **Course rating:** 70.0/71.9. **Slope:** 124/114.
Opened: 1931. **Pace of Play rating:** 4:30. **Green fee:** $16/20.
Subscriber comments: Black better than Red; the place to play when other courses are full . . . Not kept up, but very accessible . . . Good interesting layout . . . Good variety of holes . . . Wide open fairways, must be long hitter . . . Much more enjoyable since they added 100, 150 and 200 yard markers in fairways.
★ RED COURSE
Holes: 18. **Par:** 72/79.
Yards: 6,775/6,382. **Course rating:** 71.0/78.0. **Slope:** 124/122.
Opened: 1931. **Pace of Play rating:** 4:30. **Green fee:** $16/20.
Subscriber comments: Open year round. Bad condition . . . Four severely hilly holes . . . Fairways hard with little grass . . . Ground is rock hard . . . Good layout lost on poor condition of fairways. Greens usually better than the Black Course.

★½ E.GAYNOR BRENNAN MUNICIPAL GOLF COURSE
PU—451 Stillwater Rd., Stamford (203)324-4185.
Call club for further information.
Subscriber comments: Friendly staff, fairways of several holes are not properly separated and shots can be dangerous . . . Wide-open course, not difficult, not long . . . Big hitter's delight but small greens demand accurate iron shots . . . Tight, dangerous parallel holes on front nine.

★½ EAST HARTFORD GOLF COURSE
PU—130 Long Hill St., East Hartford (203)528-5082.
3 miles east of Hartford. **Holes:** 18. **Par:** 71/72.
Yards: 6,076/5,072. **Course rating:** 68.6/68.1. **Slope:** 114/112.
Opened: 1930. **Pace of Play rating:** 4:30. **Green fee:** $21/23.
Credit cards: None. **Reduced fees:** Seniors, Juniors.
Caddies: No. **Golf carts:** N/A.
Discount golf packages: No. **Season:** April-Dec. **High:** May-Aug.
On-site lodging: No. **Rental clubs:** No.
Walking policy: Unrestricted walking. **Range:** No.
To obtain tee times: Call or come in one week in advance for weekends and holidays.
Subscriber comments: Plain-Jane . . . Basic open municipal course, fair conditions all season . . . Flat, short course . . . The holes are right on top of each other . . . Great shape most of the time . . . Nice public course, not too difficult.

★★½ELMRIDGE GOLF COURSE
RED/BLUE/WHITE

PU—Elmridge Rd., Pawcatuck (203)599-2248.
14 miles east of New London. **Holes:** 27. **Par:** 71/72/71.
Yards: 6,402/6,639/6,449. **Course rating:** N/A. **Slope:** N/A.
Opened: 1968. **Pace of Play rating:** N/A. **Green fee:** $26/29.
Credit cards: MC, V, AMEX. **Reduced fees:** Low season, Twilight.
Caddies: No. **Golf carts:** $11 for 18 holes.
Discount golf packages: Yes. **Season:** March-Dec. **High:** May-Sept.
On-site lodging: No. **Rental clubs:** Yes.
Walking policy: Unrestricted walking. **Range:** Yes (grass).
To obtain tee times: Call Friday for following Monday through Friday.
Call Monday for following weekend and holiday.
Subscriber comments: Front nine straight, open fairways, good for short
basic hitter, back nine quite challenging, golfers need to place their shots
accurately . . . Great mix of holes . . . Beautiful greens. Great personnel
. . . Good beginner course. Not much water. Played with a 70-year old
who kicked my butt . . . Pleasant course, 15 minutes from Foxwoods
Casino, great day . . . Enjoyable to play, course very well kept . . . Wide
open . . . Let it rip.

★★GOODWIN PARK GOLF COURSE

PU—25 Stonington St., Hartford (203)525-3601.
Call club for further information.
Subscriber comments: Much improved course with fun elevated tees, can
be crowded . . . Nice layout . . . Good for your ego . . . Above average
muny with blend of easy and tough holes . . . Great course for seniors . . .
Wide open . . . Forgiving.

★★½GRASSY HILL COUNTRY CLUB

PU—441 Clark Lane, Orange (203)795-1422.
8 miles west of New Haven. **Holes:** 18. **Par:** 70/71.
Yards: 6,118/5,209. **Course rating:** 70.5/71.1. **Slope:** 122/118.
Opened: 1930. **Pace of Play rating:** 4:00–4:30. **Green fee:** $21/38.
Credit cards: MC, V. **Reduced fees:** Weekdays, Seniors.
Caddies: No. **Golf carts:** Included in weekend/holiday green fees; $12 for
18 holes on weekdays.
Discount golf packages: No. **Season:** April.-Nov. **High:** April.-Oct.
On-site lodging: No. **Rental clubs:** Yes.
Walking policy: Walking at certain times. **Range:** Yes.
To obtain tee times: Call in Thursday after 7 a.m. for weekend & holiday
times.
Subscriber comments: Small greens, tough putting challenge . . .
Working hard to improve . . . Open fairways, but some challenging.
Conditions improving . . . Good for medium and high handicappers . . .
Enjoyable, good mix of holes . . . Great local course . . . Long par 5 on
front is a killer . . . Very hilly, 18th hole impossible . . . Great condition.

★★★H. SMITH RICHARDSON GOLF COURSE

PU—2425 Morehouse Hwy., Fairfield (203)255-6094.
Holes: 18. **Par:** 72/72.
Yards: 6,700/5,764. **Course rating:** 71.0/72.8. **Slope:** 127/129.
Opened: 1972. **Pace of Play rating:** 4:30. **Green fee:** $22/27.
Credit cards: None. **Reduced fees:** Weekdays, Twilight, Seniors, Juniors.
Caddies: No. **Golf carts:** $10 for 18 holes.
Discount golf packages: Yes. **Season:** April-Feb. **High:** May-Oct.
On-site lodging: No. **Rental clubs:** Yes.
Walking policy: Unrestricted walking. **Range:** Yes (grass).
To obtain tee times: First come, first serve.
Subscriber comments: One of the best in Fairfield county, love the
finishing hole . . . Very hard to get tee times, impossible on weekends . . .
Good for all levels of players . . . Interesting layout . . . More scenic back

nine . . . Municipal course, well maintained. Gets heavy play and pace of play can be slow . . . Good conditioned course, very interesting, tough greens . . . Nicely groomed . . . Good restaurant . . . Great layout and variety, archaic racking system makes it difficult to get tee times . . . Always in great shape.

★★½ HUNTER GOLF CLUB

PU—685 Westfield Rd., Meriden (203)634-3366.
12 miles south of Hartford. **Holes:** 18. **Par:** 71/72.
Yards: 6,604/5,569. **Course rating:** 71.9/72.7. **Slope:** 124/131.
Opened: N/A. **Pace of Play rating:** 4:20. **Green fee:** $16/22.
Credit cards: MC, V, AMEX. **Reduced fees:** Weekdays, Seniors, Juniors.
Caddies: No. **Golf carts:** $20 for 18 holes.
Discount golf packages: No. **Season:** March-Dec. **High:** June-Aug.
On-site lodging: No. **Rental clubs:** Yes.
Walking policy: Unrestricted walking. **Range:** Yes (grass).
To obtain tee times: Lottery draw system, must come in. Can call for remaining times after lottery times have been given.
Subscriber comments: Room for big drives . . . Very nice scenic layout, especially inward half of both nines . . . Municipal course with heavy play . . . A good challenge that's kept in good shape . . . Always seems 20 degrees colder there than anywhere else in the state . . . Hilly, plays longer against the wind. Accuracy helps for better scoring . . . Blind approach shots . . . Very enjoyable.

★½ KENEY GOLF COURSE

PU—280 Tower Ave, Hartford (203)525-3656.
Holes: 18. **Par:** 70/70.
Yards: 5,969/5,005. **Course rating:** 68.2/67.2. **Slope:** 118/107.
Opened: 1927. **Pace of Play rating:** 4:15. **Green fee:** $11/18.
Credit cards: MC, V. **Reduced fees:** Weekdays, Low season, Twilight, Seniors, Junior
Caddies: No. **Golf carts:** $19 for 18 holes.
Discount golf packages: No. **Season:** April-Nov. **High:** May-Sept.
On-site lodging: No. **Rental clubs:** Yes.
Walking policy: Unrestricted walking. **Range:** No.
To obtain tee times: Call seven days in advance.
Subscriber comments: Course has great potential . . . Lots of target golf. Preshot planning required . . . Old course, old facilities make you feel classic . . . Seems like a lot of regulars and a good secret to pass along . . . Great old Devereux Emmet design . . . Lots of hills and valleys, decent par 5s . . . Great course, accuracy counts, picturesque, elevated tees.

★★½ LAUREL VIEW COUNTRY CLUB

PU—310 W. Shepard Ave., Hamden (203)288-1819.
Call club for further information.
Subscriber comments: Excellent test of golf, back nine much tighter than front . . . Suited for all types of players . . . Very interesting, have to know course to score well . . . Fairways are a bit narrow; big greens . . . Great back nine, very hilly . . . Excellent shape for amount of usage; fun course . . . Put driver in trunk after No. 9 . . . Shot location very important . . . Good value, interesting layout.

★★½ LONGSHORE CLUB PARK

SP—260 Compo Rd. South, Westport (203)222-7535.
13 miles west of Bridgeport. **Holes:** 18. **Par:** 69/73.
Yards: 5,845/5,227. **Course rating:** 69.3/69.9. **Slope:** 115/113.
Opened: 1925. **Pace of Play rating:** N/A. **Green fee:** $11/13.
Credit cards: None. **Reduced fees:** Weekdays, Seniors, Juniors.
Caddies: No. **Golf carts:** $22 for 18 holes.
Discount golf packages: No. **Season:** N/A.
On-site lodging: No. **Rental clubs:** No.
Walking policy: N/A. **Range:** Yes.

To obtain tee times: Guests must be accompanied by a resident.
Subscriber comments: Short course; small, hard, fast greens can be tricky
. . . Beautiful setting in good condition, tough in the wind . . . Course
harder than it looks . . . The front nine not very interesting . . . Pleasant,
good short-game test . . . Old links type . . . The staff goes out of their
way; good walking course.

LYMAN ORCHARDS GOLF CLUB
SP—Rt. 157, Middlefield (203)349-8055.
20 miles south of Hartford.
Credit cards: MC, V. **Reduced fees:** Weekdays, Twilight, Seniors,
Juniors.
Caddies: No.
Discount golf packages: No. **Season:** March-Nov. **High:** May-Oct.
On-site lodging: No. **Rental clubs:** Yes.
Range: Yes (grass).
To obtain tee times: Call the automated tele-tee system 24 hours a day up
to seven days in advance.
★★½ GARY PLAYER COURSE
Holes: 18. **Par:** 71/71.
Yards: 6,660/4,667. **Course rating:** 73.0/67.8. **Slope:** 135/116.
Opened: 1994. **Pace of Play rating:** 4:30. **Green fee:** $31/38.
Golf carts: Included in Green Fee.
Walking policy: Mandatory cart.
Subscriber comments: Gotta play it twice to appreciate it . . . Fascinating
layout; through the hills, great views . . . Wow! When this course grows
up, watch out, must ride (which I usually hate, but you need to here) . . .
Great vistas . . . Shotmaker's course and good compliment to Jones Course,
which is longer and more open . . . Many tee areas . . . New course, needs
maturing. Potential to be a great course . . . Very interesting. Blind shots,
hills, ravines . . . Have to think on tee shots . . . Very challenging golf
course, makes you try harder . . . Feels like you're on TV . . . Most
beautiful golf course I've ever played . . . Very friendly staff, great value
. . . Not for high handicappers . . . Spectacular views; must think on
course, every shot a challenge . . . Course hasn't firmed up yet, but it's an
awesome experience. Some of the most unusual golf holes in Connecticut.
A must play for any serious golfer.
★★★ ROBERT TRENT JONES COURSE
Holes: 18. **Par:** 72/72.
Yards: 7,011/5,812. **Course rating:** 73.5/73.5. **Slope:** 129/122.
Opened: 1969. **Pace of Play rating:** 4:30. **Green fee:** $31/38.
Golf carts: $11 for 18 holes.
Walking policy: Unrestricted walking.
   Formerly known as Lyman Meadow Golf Club.
Subscriber comments: Excellent Robert Trent Jones course with a wide
variety of holes . . . Outstanding layout, good condition . . . Enjoyable to
walk, very playable for mid-level golfer . . . Great course; not very hard,
lots of fun . . . Too wide open for my taste. Staff is five stars though . . .
Good fast greens . . . Helpful staff, very good pro shop . . . Lots of water
and woods, greens hard to read . . . Tough water holes . . . I always play
this course late afternoon after the pros qualify for the Canon GHO. The
course is always in great shape and is very true . . . Greens are quick with a
lot of break.

★★½ MILLBROOK GOLF COURSE
PU—147 Pigeon Hill Rd., Windsor (203)688-2575.
10 miles north of Hartford. **Holes:** 18. **Par:** 71/73.
Yards: 6,258/5,715. **Course rating:** 71.0/71.0. **Slope:** 125/124.
Opened: N/A. **Pace of Play rating:** . **Green fee:** $20/23.
Credit cards: None. **Reduced fees:** N/A.
Caddies: No. **Golf carts:** $11 for 18 holes.
Discount golf packages: Yes. **Season:** April-Nov. **High:** May-Oct.
On-site lodging: No. **Rental clubs:** Yes.
Walking policy: Unrestricted walking. **Range:** No.

To obtain tee times: Call pro shop.
Subscriber comments: Hilly, scenic, very nice staff, plays fast for hilly course . . . Tight in spots, not too long, very well kept . . . The ninth and 18th holes have severe hills. I mean straight up. . . . Excellent greens and fairways : . . A real gem and they care . . . A challenge to score, everyone friendly . . . Layout outstanding. Shotmaker's course . . . Well groomed course, not real difficult, excellent pace . . . Fun course. Tee it up and swing hard!

★★½ NORWICH GOLF COURSE
PU—685 New London Tpke., Norwich (203)889-6973.
Holes: 18. **Par:** 71/71.
Yards: 6,183/5,104. **Course rating:** 69.6/70.2. **Slope:** 123/118.
Opened: 1910. **Pace of Play rating:** 4:15. **Green fee:** $19/27.
Credit cards: None. **Reduced fees:** Twilight.
Caddies: No. **Golf carts:** $10 for 18 holes.
Discount golf packages: No. **Season:** April-Dec. **High:** May-Aug.
On-site lodging: Yes. **Rental clubs:** Yes.
Walking policy: Unrestricted walking. **Range:** Yes.
To obtain tee times: Call same day beginning at 7 a.m. Weekends call Wednesday for Saturday times and Thursday for Sunday times.
Subscriber comments: Short but interesting Ross design . . . Home course, had problems with greens. Tough course; use every club in bag . . . Enjoyed the layout; a tough walk on a hot day . . . Lots of hills . . . From tee to green fantastic . . . Challenge every time out. Nice par 5s . . . Very busy . . . Good contrast on both nines.

★★ OAK HILLS GOLF CLUB
PU—165 Fillow St., Norwalk (203)853-8400.
Call club for further information.
Subscriber comments: Tight parkland course interrupted by several long, wide-open holes . . . Will use all your clubs, nice shape . . . Plays well at all levels . . . Short blind holes . . . Traditional public course . . . Used to be better . . . Good mix of shots required, not overwhelming, crowded on weekends . . . All we need is a clubhouse . . . Tight front nine, open back nine; greens not consistent.

★★½ ORANGE HILLS COUNTRY CLUB
PU—389 Racebrook Rd., Orange (203)795-4161.
7 miles southwest of New Haven. **Holes:** 18. **Par:** 71/74.
Yards: 6,389/5,729. **Course rating:** 71.2/71.5. **Slope:** 114/120.
Opened: 1940. **Pace of Play rating:** 4:30–5:00. **Green fee:** $20/28.
Credit cards: MC, V. **Reduced fees:** No.
Caddies: No. **Golf carts:** $25 for 18 holes.
Discount golf packages: No. **Season:** March-Nov. **High:** May-Oct.
On-site lodging: No. **Rental clubs:** No.
Walking policy: Unrestricted walking. **Range:** No.
To obtain tee times: Call Wednesday 6 p.m. for weekends.
Subscriber comments: Course condition excellent for public course . . . A nice all-around course with some nice water holes . . . Front open, back tight; a lot of work made a good course even prettier . . . Fairways always green; unique holes . . . 16th hole needs an escalator . . . Hilly, many doglegs, well manicured . . . Improving every year, excellent greens, nice staff.

★★★ PEQUABUCK GOLF CLUB
SP—School St., Pequabuck (203)583-7307.
12 miles north of Waterbury. **Holes:** 18. **Par:** 69/72.
Yards: 6,015/5,388. **Course rating:** 69.1/71.0. **Slope:** 122/117.
Opened: 1902. **Pace of Play rating:** 4:15. **Green fee:** $31/31.
Credit cards: None. **Reduced fees:** N/A.
Caddies: No. **Golf carts:** $13 for 18 holes.
Discount golf packages: No. **Season:** April-Dec. **High:** May-Sept.
On-site lodging: No. **Rental clubs:** No.

Walking policy: Unrestricted walking. **Range:** Yes (grass).
To obtain tee times: None taken. Course open to public before 2 p.m. on weekdays and after 2 p.m. on weekends and holidays.
Subscriber comments: Narrow fairways require shot placement, excellent greens, very well kept . . . Great greens, rolling layout . . . Keeps getting better every year . . . Short but demanding course. Variety of shots to play. Excellent condition . . . A fun course, easy holes and very tough holes, a good golfing day.

★★★½ PINE VALLEY COUNTRY CLUB

PU—300 Welch Rd., Southington (203)628-0879.
15 miles west of Hartford. **Holes:** 18. **Par:** 71/73.
Yards: 6,325/5,443. **Course rating:** 70.6/72.0. **Slope:** 122/122.
Opened: 1960. **Pace of Play rating:** N/A. **Green fee:** $20/25.
Credit cards: None. **Reduced fees:** N/A.
Caddies: No. **Golf carts:** N/A.
Discount golf packages: No. **Season:** March-Dec. **High:** June-Aug.
On-site lodging: No. **Rental clubs:** Yes.
Walking policy: Unrestricted walking. **Range:** Yes (grass).
To obtain tee times: Call Wednesday 6 p.m. for Saturday or Sunday. For weekdays call seven days in advance. Must have a foursome to obtain tee time.
Subscriber comments: Nice course, lots of trees . . . The fairways on the front nine are very close . . . Excellent variety in holes, everyone can play here and have fun . . . Great course, you get to use every club in the bag . . . Course in super shape, staff gets an A+ . . . Pretty, lots of par 4s average guy can play well . . . Tree lined, rolling fairways . . . Very good conditions . . . Premium on accuracy, tough on high handicappers . . . Always an enjoyable round.

★★★½ PORTLAND GOLF COURSE

SP—169 Bartlett St., Portland (203)342-6107.
20 miles south of Hartford. **Holes:** 18. **Par:** 71/71.
Yards: 6,213/5,039. **Course rating:** 70.8/68.6. **Slope:** 124/118.
Opened: 1974. **Pace of Play rating:** 4:30. **Green fee:** $21/25.
Credit cards: None. **Reduced fees:** Weekdays, Seniors, Juniors.
Caddies: No. **Golf carts:** $10 for 18 holes.
Discount golf packages: Yes. **Season:** March-Dec. **High:** May-Oct.
On-site lodging: No. **Rental clubs:** Yes.
Walking policy: Unrestricted walking. **Range:** Yes (grass).
To obtain tee times: Call Monday a.m. for weekend.
Subscriber comments: Local knowledge helpful, some tricky shots . . . One of Connecticut's best . . . Short, well maintained, tough greens . . . Very good condition; for all players; helpful personnel . . . Demanding yet forgiving, beautiful greens . . . Too short for most guys, good for ladies and seniors; interesting . . . Narrow fairways, tough doglegs . . . Always a nice golf day . . . Beautiful course, extremely hilly, presents a good challenge . . . Beautiful in the fall. Keep it straight . . . Over the creek and thru the woods. Bring your retriever.

★½ RACEWAY GOLF CLUB

SP—E. Thompson Rd., Thompson (203)521-3156.
Call club for further information.
Subscriber comments: A course with potential if better maintained; great lunch . . . Short but a lot of fun, can score well . . . Have made some improvements . . . All types of players would enjoy, very friendly, wide open fairways, good pace of play.

★★★★ RICHTER PARK GOLF CLUB

PU—100 Aunt Hack Rd., Danbury (203)792-2552.
60 miles northeast of New York City. **Holes:** 18. **Par:** 72/72.
Yards: 6,740/5,627. **Course rating:** 73.0/72.8. **Slope:** 130/122.
Opened: 1971. **Pace of Play rating:** 4:30. **Green fee:** $27/44.
Credit cards: MC, V. **Reduced fees:** Twilight, Seniors, Juniors.

Caddies: No. **Golf carts:** N/A.
Discount golf packages: No. **Season:** April-Nov. **High:** June-Aug.
On-site lodging: No. **Rental clubs:** Yes.
Walking policy: Unrestricted walking. **Range:** No.
To obtain tee times: Nonresidents call Thursday 9 a.m. for weekend.
Ranked in First 25 of America's 75 Best Public Golf Courses by Golf
Digest.
Subscriber comments: Excellent course but very difficult to get tee times
. . . Best suited for low, mid handicap . . . Not for the beginner . . .
Always a pleasure to play . . . Very tough. Doglegs require exacting shots.
Par 3s over water are treacherous. Beautiful, rustic. A fall classic. Above
average . . . Best publicly-owned course I've played . . . Fabulous design
. . . Challenging course, one of best in Northeast . . . Must play to
appreciate . . . I loved the setting . . . Fine layout with hills and water . . .
Terrific public course, tough to get to play, each hole is different . . . Very
difficult for out-of-towner to get tee time . . . 16 water holes . . . Scenic
course, challenging course, worth the trip . . . Even when they had four
temporary greens in 1994, it was still a great course to play . . . Loved it.

★★★ RIDGEFIELD GOLF COURSE
PU—545 Ridgebury Rd., Ridgefield (203)748-7008.
1 mile east of Danbury. **Holes:** 18. **Par:** 70/71.
Yards: 6,380/5,295. **Course rating:** 70.0/70.7. **Slope:** 122/120.
Opened: 1974. **Pace of Play rating:** N/A. **Green fee:** $8/27.
Credit cards: None. **Reduced fees:** Twilight, Seniors, Juniors.
Caddies: No. **Golf carts:** $22 for 18 holes.
Discount golf packages: No. **Season:** April-Dec. **High:** June-Aug.
On-site lodging: No. **Rental clubs:** Yes.
Walking policy: Unrestricted walking. **Range:** Yes (grass).
To obtain tee times: Lottery for reservations Thursday a.m. Telephone
after 9 a.m. Thursday.
Subscriber comments: Pretty course, good front, better back . . . Good
condition, well maintained . . . Enjoyable and challenging . . . Course is
challenging to average golfer . . . Jekyll and Hyde: front nine is short and
wide, back nine is long and tight . . . Great super improves conditions
every year . . . Nice layout with good conditions all seasons . . . A
challenge because it demands accuracy and the greens are fast under all
conditions . . . Excellent course for walking.

★★★ ROCKLEDGE COUNTRY CLUB
PU—289 S. Main St., West Hartford (203)521-3156.
Holes: 18. **Par:** 72/74.
Yards: 6,307/5,608. **Course rating:** 71.3/71.5. **Slope:** 121/118.
Opened: 1949. **Pace of Play rating:** 4:20. **Green fee:** $14/25.
Credit cards: None. **Reduced fees:** Seniors.
Caddies: No. **Golf carts:** $18 for 18 holes.
Discount golf packages: No. **Season:** April-Dec. **High:** June-July.
On-site lodging: No. **Rental clubs:** Yes.
Walking policy: Unrestricted walking. **Range:** Yes.
To obtain tee times: Three days in advance.
Subscriber comments: Well-maintained public course, some blind shots
. . . Course has a couple of short par 5s but fun to play . . . Good layout.
Good shape. Good staff . . . Course for shorter hitters . . . Nice layout,
always good condition, nice practice range, some pretty holes, staff
excellent . . . Beautiful, well-groomed town managed track . . . Easy
course, easy to walk, easy to play, good early in year.

★★★ SHENNECOSSETT MUNICIPAL GOLF COURSE
PU—93 Plant St., Groton (203)445-0262.
2 miles east of New London. **Holes:** 18. **Par:** 72/76.
Yards: 6,491/5,796. **Course rating:** 71.1/73.2. **Slope:** 122/121.
Opened: N/A. **Pace of Play rating:** N/A. **Green fee:** $22/26.
Credit cards: None. **Reduced fees:** No.
Caddies: No. **Golf carts:** N/A.

Discount golf packages: No. **Season:** Year-round. **High:** July-Aug.
On-site lodging: No. **Rental clubs:** No.
Walking policy: Unrestricted walking. **Range:** No.
To obtain tee times: Call Tuesday for Saturday time and Wednesday for Sunday time.
Subscriber comments: Wow! Ross gem . . . Suited to good iron players . . . If you like links style, this course is for you . . . Favors big hitters, tough greens, it can humble you . . . Very different; tee shots over roads; approach shots over railroad tracks . . . Views of Long Island Sound . . . Excellent food . . . Good for average player, wide open . . . Nice oceanside course.

★★★ SIMSBURY FARMS GOLF CLUB
PU—100 Old Farms Rd., West Simsbury (203)658-6246.
15 miles northwest of Hartford. **Holes:** 18. **Par:** 72/72.
Yards: 6,421/5,439. **Course rating:** 71.1/70.1. **Slope:** 124/117.
Opened: 1972. **Pace of Play rating:** 4:00. **Green fee:** $21/25.
Credit cards: None. **Reduced fees:** No.
Caddies: No. **Golf carts:** $22 for 18 holes.
Discount golf packages: No. **Season:** April-Nov. **High:** May-Sept.
On-site lodging: No. **Rental clubs:** Yes.
Walking policy: Unrestricted walking. **Range:** Yes.
To obtain tee times: Call two days in advance at 10 a.m.
Subscriber comments: Beautiful course made tough by seemingly endless uphill approach shots . . . A good test of golf; demanding course . . . Interesting and challenging . . . Hilly, well maintained . . . Very natural, rolling course thru old apple orchard, very long for women . . . Course layout very enjoyable . . . Favors middle to low handicaps . . . True municipal course, family golf place . . . Nice layout, good variety, excellent conditions when other courses were in poor shape . . . Nice little gem in the hills.

★½ SOUTHINGTON COUNTRY CLUB
SP—Savage St., Southington (203)628-7032.
Call club for further information.
Subscriber comments: Easy, good for anyone, slow greens . . . Nice people, some challenging holes . . . Short course, very hilly on front, flat on back, usually good condition . . . You can score on this course . . . Front nine open, back nine tight . . . RIP IT.

★★★ STANLEY GOLF CLUB
BLUE/RED/WHITE
PU—245 Hartford Rd., New Britain (203)827-8144.
10 miles southeast of Hartford. **Holes:** 27. **Par:** 72/71.
Yards: 6,453/6,311/6,138. **Course rating:** 70.5/72.0. **Slope:** 120/122.
Opened: 1930. **Pace of Play rating:** 4:30. **Green fee:** $19/23.
Credit cards: None. **Reduced fees:** Weekdays.
Caddies: No. **Golf carts:** $21 for 18 holes.
Discount golf packages: No. **Season:** April-Dec. **High:** June-Sept.
On-site lodging: No. **Rental clubs:** Yes.
Walking policy: Unrestricted walking. **Range:** No.
To obtain tee times: Call seven days in advance.
Subscriber comments: Blue and White nines are best kept secrets in area . . . Good layout and condition . . . Always in excellent condition. Watch out for foxes stealing golf balls . . . Super public course, always good condition; please don't tell . . . Wide open, but O.B. markers . . . Played it for first time, I enjoyed nearly every hole. Fun! . . . 27 holes of the nicest golf anywhere . . . Greens hold well.

★★★ STERLING FARMS GOLF CLUB
PU—1349 Newfield Ave., Stamford (203)329-7888.
Holes: 18. **Par:** 72/73.
Yards: 6,410/5,600. **Course rating:** 71.7/72.6. **Slope:** 127/121.
Opened: 1969. **Pace of Play rating:** 4:30. **Green fee:** $12/33.

Credit cards: None. **Reduced fees:** Weekdays, Low season, Twilight, Seniors, Junior
Caddies: No. **Golf carts:** $20 for 18 holes.
Discount golf packages: No. **Season:** Year-round. **High:** July-Aug.
On-site lodging: No. **Rental clubs:** Yes.
Walking policy: Unrestricted walking. **Range:** Yes.
To obtain tee times: Call three days in advance.
Subscriber comments: Play it every week. Never boring . . . Always improving. Great greenkeeper . . . Well marshaled, spartan facilities, courteous staff, very good condition . . . Well kept and well managed, a beautiful course . . . Good layout, challenging hole design . . . Interesting variety of holes . . . Great par 4s from the blue tees, too short from whites . . . Tricky course, good use of limited space . . . One of the best public courses I have ever played . . . The fairways and teeing areas are as well maintained as any private country club . . . Rangers make sure you move along on the course . . . Fun course to play . . . Great view from second hole.

★★★½ TALLWOOD COUNTRY CLUB

PU—91 North St., Rt. 85, Hebron (203)646-3437.
15 miles southeast of Hartford. **Holes:** 18. **Par:** 72/72.
Yards: 6,366/5,430. **Course rating:** 70.2/70.8. **Slope:** 119/114.
Opened: 1970. **Pace of Play rating:** 4:30. **Green fee:** $18/22.
Credit cards: None. **Reduced fees:** Low season, Twilight, Seniors, Juniors.
Caddies: No. **Golf carts:** $10 for 18 holes.
Discount golf packages: Yes. **Season:** March-Dec. **High:** May-Sept.
On-site lodging: No. **Rental clubs:** Yes.
Walking policy: Unrestricted walking. **Range:** Yes (grass).
To obtain tee times: Call one week in advance for weekday and Monday a.m. for upcoming weekend.
Subscriber comments: A course for any player. Not extremely long, it has lots of trees and water. Staff excellent, very friendly . . . Scenic course, nice layout, large greens, in trouble if not in fairway . . . New England at its best; woods, water and hills . . . 11 water holes, beautiful fairways . . . Pretty course in fall . . . Good challenge at all levels . . . Perfect greens. Great staff . . . Challenging but fair layout . . . Player should be long and straight. Very well-designed course.

★★½ TASHUA KNOLLS GOLF COURSE

PU—40 Tashua Knolls Lane, Trumbull (203)261-5989.
7 miles north of Bridgeport. **Holes:** 18. **Par:** 72/72.
Yards: 6,502/5,454. **Course rating:** 71.5/72.0. **Slope:** 125/118.
Opened: 1976. **Pace of Play rating:** 4:45. **Green fee:** $20/24.
Credit cards: None. **Reduced fees:** Seniors, Juniors.
Caddies: No. **Golf carts:** $20 for 18 holes.
Discount golf packages: No. **Season:** March-Dec. **High:** May-Sept.
On-site lodging: No. **Rental clubs:** Yes.
Walking policy: Unrestricted walking. **Range:** Yes (grass).
To obtain tee times: Call ahead.
Subscriber comments: Can't beat it in the fall with the church steeple poking out from beyond the first hole . . . Very pretty setting . . . Best course in western Connecticut, not easy to get tee time, seniors play every morning, slow play, worth the wait . . . Good all-around course . . . Surcharge for reserving time in advance . . . Very picturesque back nine . . . If you like doglegs, you'll love this course . . . Very wide open in parts . . . Good challenge for all levels . . . Good condition, variety of holes.

★★★ TIMBERLIN GOLF CLUB

PU—Ken Bates Dr., Kensington (203)828-3228.
18 miles south of Hartford. **Holes:** 18. **Par:** 72/72.
Yards: 6,733/5,477. **Course rating:** 71.9/70.5. **Slope:** 127/109.
Opened: 1970. **Pace of Play rating:** N/A. **Green fee:** $12/24.
Credit cards: None. **Reduced fees:** Seniors, Juniors.

Caddies: No. **Golf carts:** N/A.
Discount golf packages: No. **Season:** April-Nov. **High:** June-Sept.
On-site lodging: No. **Rental clubs:** Yes.
Walking policy: Unrestricted walking. **Range:** Yes (grass).
To obtain tee times: Call two days in advance at 7 a.m.
Subscriber comments: Wide open; let out the driver . . . Beautiful course, very well maintained . . . Excellent course for average player, friendly atmosphere . . . Busy muny . . . Gentle hills, favors long hitters, average golfers . . . One of the better munys . . . Good golf and good food . . . Challenging layout, good condition and interesting . . . Scenery beautiful, especially in fall . . . Requires distance & accuracy . . . Course always in good shape . . . Has character.

TUNXIS PLANTATION COUNTRY CLUB
PU—87 Town Farm Rd., Farmington (203)677-1367.
10 miles south of Hartford.
Credit cards: MC, V, AMEX. **Reduced fees:** Seniors, Juniors.
Caddies: No. **Golf carts:** $24 for 18 holes.
Discount golf packages: No. **Season:** April-Nov. **High:** May-Aug.
On-site lodging: No. **Rental clubs:** Yes.
Walking policy: Unrestricted walking. **Range:** Yes (grass).
To obtain tee times: Call Tuesday prior to weekend at 7:30 a.m.
★★★ **RED/GREEN COURSE**
Holes: 18. **Par:** 72/72.
Yards: 6,647/5,378. **Course rating:** 71.5/71.5. **Slope:** 125/116.
Opened: 1962. **Pace of Play rating:** N/A. **Green fee:** $22/25.
Subscriber comments: Average player will find course a pleasure, good condition, fine treatment by staff . . . Good shape, fun layout; if your tee time is 9:00, you tee off at 9:00 . . . Well maintained and wide open . . . Well-run operation . . . Flat course; easy to walk . . . Always in decent shape and forgiving . . . Good value, not a killer, but an enjoyable place to play. Good greens . . . Some beautiful water holes . . . Well worth the ride. Good service and helpful staff . . . Tunxis is always nice, you can always get on . . . Site of many corporate outings . . . Great golf course, challenges even the best golfer.
★★½ **WHITE COURSE**
Holes: 18. **Par:** 72/72.
Yards: 6,638/5,744. **Course rating:** 72.2/71.5. **Slope:** 129/125.
Opened: 1962. **Pace of Play rating:** N/A. **Green fee:** $22/25.
Subscriber comments: Easy course to walk . . . Good combination of difficult and easier holes . . . Flat, some water, great par 3s . . . Not too long, wide open, well maintained, little sand, water holes, high handicapper can break 100 . . . Confidence-building course, great shape, great service . . . Excellent course for all types of players . . . Conditions are good at all times of the season.

TWIN HILLS COUNTRY CLUB★
PU—Rte. 31, Coventry (203)742-9705.
10 miles east of Hartford. **Holes:** 18. **Par:** 71/71.
Yards: 6,257/5,249. **Course rating:** 68.7/69.5. **Slope:** 118/116.
Opened: 1971. **Pace of Play rating:** 4:30. **Green fee:** $21/23.
Credit cards: None. **Reduced fees:** Seniors.
Caddies: No. **Golf carts:** $20 for 18 holes.
Discount golf packages: No. **Season:** Year-round. **High:** May-Aug.
On-site lodging: No. **Rental clubs:** Yes.
Walking policy: Unrestricted walking. **Range:** No.
To obtain tee times: None taken.

★½ **WESTERN HILLS GOLF CLUB**
PU—Park Rd., Waterbury (203)755-6828.
60 miles east of New York. **Holes:** 18. **Par:** 72/72.
Yards: 6,427/5,393. **Course rating:** 69.6/69.6. **Slope:** 125/122.
Opened: 1961. **Pace of Play rating:** 5:00-5:30. **Green fee:** $11/18.
Credit cards: None. **Reduced fees:** Weekdays, Low season, Seniors,

Juniors.
Caddies: No. **Golf carts:** $9 for 18 holes.
Discount golf packages: No. **Season:** April-Dec. **High:** April-Aug.
On-site lodging: No. **Rental clubs:** Yes.
Walking policy: Unrestricted walking. **Range:** No.
To obtain tee times: Call Thursday for Saturday; Friday for Sunday;
Times start at 7:00 a.m.
Subscriber comments: Great layout but not well maintained . . . Suited
for all types . . . Greens and fairways rock hard, impossible to hold . . . Not
in the best shape but still a fun course to play . . . This course gets a lot of
play, so play it early in the golfing season.

★★½ WHITNEY FARMS GOLF COURSE

PU—175 Shelton Rd., Monroe (203)268-0707.
20 miles north of Bridgeport. **Holes:** 18. **Par:** 72/73.
Yards: 6,628/5,832. **Course rating:** 72.4/72.9. **Slope:** 130/124.
Opened: 1981. **Pace of Play rating:** 4:15. **Green fee:** $32/37.
Credit cards: MC, V, AMEX. **Reduced fees:** Weekdays.
Caddies: No. **Golf carts:** Included in Green Fee.
Discount golf packages: No. **Season:** March-Dec. **High:** June-Aug.
On-site lodging: No. **Rental clubs:** Yes.
Walking policy: Mandatory cart. **Range:** Yes.
To obtain tee times: Call 7 days in advance for weekday; Wednesday
before 8:00 a.m. for weekends. Outing reservations up to one year in
advance.
Subscriber comments: Layout is rural (between houses) challenging for
average golfer . . . Tough, in great condition, tricky greens, good staff . . .
Rock hard, small greens, well maintained . . . Great layout and condition
. . . Some scenic holes . . . Out of bounds border both sides of nearly every
hole . . . Treat outsiders as members . . . Good deal, good test. I'll go back
. . . A sleeper . . . Tight narrow fairways. Plenty of water.

★★★½ WILLIMANTIC COUNTRY CLUB

SP—184 Club Rd., Windham (203)456-1971.
Call club for further information.
Subscriber comments: The course is narrow in many places. The
fairways are plush. The greens are in superb condition . . . The staff is
courteous and helpful . . . Wonderful place to play . . . Tough par 3s, fun to
play . . . Great condition, good layout . . . Challenging greens . . . Top
notch quality, moderately challenging . . . Fun course.

Notes

★½ DEL CASTLE GOLF COURSE

PU—801 McKennans Church Rd., Wilmington (302)995-1990.
Holes: 18. **Par:** 72/72.
Yards: 6,628/5,396. **Course rating:** 70.4/70.9. **Slope:** 116/116.
Opened: 1971. **Pace of Play rating:** 4:00. **Green fee:** $15/19.
Credit cards: None. **Reduced fees:** Weekdays, Low season, Twilight,
Seniors, Juniors.
Caddies: No. **Golf carts:** N/A.
Discount golf packages: No. **Season:** Year-round. **High:** April-Nov.
On-site lodging: No. **Rental clubs:** Yes.
Walking policy: Unrestricted walking. **Range:** Yes (grass).
To obtain tee times:
Come in Monday for following weekend.
Subscriber comments: Quintessential public course . . . Not tricky . . .
Wide open . . . Wide fairways . . . Huge greens . . . Grip it and rip it . . .
Forgiving . . . Slicer's heaven . . . Very crowded . . . Needs additional
parking . . . Needs more water hazards . . . More challenging than appears
. . . Getting better every year.

★½ ED "PORKY" OLIVER GOLF COURSE

PU—800 N. DuPont Rd., Wilmington (302)571-9041.
25 miles south of Philadelphia. **Holes:** 18. **Par:** 69/71.
Yards: 6,115/5,692. **Course rating:** 69.8/71.8. **Slope:** 118/121.
Opened: N/A. **Pace of Play rating:** 4:30. **Green fee:** $15/22.
Credit cards: All major. **Reduced fees:** Weekdays, Low season, Twilight,
Seniors, Juniors.
Caddies: No. **Golf carts:** N/A.
Discount golf packages: No. **Season:** Year-round. **High:** May-Sept.
On-site lodging: No. **Rental clubs:** Yes.
Walking policy: Unrestricted walking. **Range:** Yes (grass).
To obtain tee times: Must be in tee time reservation system.
Subscriber comments: Basic golf . . . Acceptable conditions . . . Shorter
course, easily walked, pretty open . . . Lots of O.B. for right-handed
hookers . . . A couple of good par 4s . . . Unchallenging . . . Very bland
. . . Flat, parallel holes . . . City streets visible . . . Overcrowded . . .
Hackers galore . . . Players don't repair ball marks . . . Have to chase geese
off some holes . . . Love the opening hole.

★★½ RON JAWORSKI'S GARRISONS LAKE GOLF CLUB

PU—101 Fairways Circle East, Smyrna (302)653-6349.
9 miles north of Dover. **Holes:** 18. **Par:** 72/72.
Yards: 7,028/5,460. **Course rating:** 73.1/71.6. **Slope:** 127/126.
Opened: 1963. **Pace of Play rating:** 4:30. **Green fee:** $15/30.
Credit cards: MC, V. **Reduced fees:** Low season, Twilight, Seniors.
Caddies: No. **Golf carts:** $10 for 18 holes.
Discount golf packages: Yes. **Season:** Year-round. **High:** June-Aug.
On-site lodging: No. **Rental clubs:** Yes.
Walking policy: Walking at certain times. **Range:** Yes (grass).
To obtain tee times: Call seven days in advance.
Subscriber comments: Long and tight . . . Solid tree-lined holes require
length and accuracy . . . Tough but fair . . . Over 7,000 yards . . . A very
long day from the back . . . From back tees, makes you respect the pros . . .
Practice your 3-iron! . . . Made for those who fade . . . Easily walked . . .
A challenging bore . . . Huge greens . . . Nice grass range . . . Friendly
course attendants and management . . . Thoroughly enjoyable . . . Best
course in Delaware.

DELAWARE

★★★ **THREE LITTLE BAKERS COUNTRY CLUB**
SP—3542 Foxcroft Dr., Wilmington (302)737-1877.
Holes: 18. **Par:** 71/72.
Yards: 6,609/5,209. **Course rating:** 71.8/70.3. **Slope:** 129/117.
Opened: 1973. **Pace of Play rating:** 4:30. **Green fee:** $21/25.
Credit cards: All major. **Reduced fees:** Weekdays, Low season, Twilight,
Seniors, Juniors.
Caddies: No. **Golf carts:** $11 for 18 holes.
Discount golf packages: No. **Season:** Year-round. **High:** April-Oct.
On-site lodging: Yes. **Rental clubs:** No.
Walking policy: Walking at certain times. **Range:** No.
To obtain tee times: Call Thursday a.m. for following weekend.
Subscriber comments: Great layout . . . Beautiful layout . . . Hilly,
wooded, tight, tough . . . Back nine very tough . . . Several hellishly
difficult holes . . . Some shotmaker holes . . . A place that stretches your
character . . . Topography makes it appealing and challenging . . . Rolling
hills . . . Streams . . . Lots of sidehill lies . . . Greens excellent . . . Offers a
real putting challenge . . . Great par 3s . . . Well groomed . . . Golf
between condominiums . . . Very spread out . . . Some distance from
greens to next tees . . . 16 good holes. No. 1 is a par 3 and No. 10 is a blind
tee shot . . . Wilmington's best . . . Best public course in Delaware . . .
TLB is the most creative layout in the tri-state area.

Notes

DISTRICT OF COLUMBIA

★ **EAST POTOMAC PARK GOLF COURSE**
PU—Ohio Dr., Washington (202)554-7660.
Credit cards: MC, V. **Reduced fees:** Weekdays, Seniors.
Caddies: No. **Golf carts:** $18 for 18 holes.
Discount golf packages: No. **Season:** Year-round. **High:** May-Sept.
On-site lodging: No. **Rental clubs:** Yes.
Walking policy: Unrestricted walking. **Range:** Yes.
To obtain tee times: First come, first served.
Complex also includes nine-hole, par-31 Red Course and nine-hole, par-34
White Course.
★ **BLUE COURSE**
Holes: 18. **Par:** 72/72.
Yards: 6,303/5,761. **Course rating:** 68.5/N/A. **Slope:** 109/N/A.
Opened: 1920. **Pace of Play rating:** 4:30. **Green fee:** $11/17.
Subscriber comments: Where else can you fade the ball off the
Washington Monument? . . . Great view of Washington, D.C. skyline . . .
Great for that nine holes after work . . . Short, but you feel great when you
add up the score . . . Not pristine by any means. Down-to-earth golf . . .
Always crowded . . . Keep your spikes in the car, bring a hardhat . . .
Uninspiring layout . . . Flat . . . No character . . . By a noisy airport . . .
Nice double-decker driving range . . . Wonderful atmosphere of equality.
Everyone's equal on the first tee. No tee times. Just show up with bag and
balls . . . There's always action available . . . They are remodeling . . .
Should be better in '95.

★½ **LANGSTON GOLF COURSE**
PU—2600 Benning Rd. N.E., Washington (202)397-8638.
33 miles northeast of Baltimore. **Holes:** 18. **Par:** 72/N/A.
Yards: 6,340/N/A. **Course rating:** 69.6/N/A. **Slope:** 112/N/A.
Opened: 1939. **Pace of Play rating:** 4:30. **Green fee:** $11/17.
Credit cards: None. **Reduced fees:** Weekdays.
Caddies: No. **Golf carts:** $19 for 18 holes.
Discount golf packages: Yes. **Season:** Year-round. **High:** March-Oct.
On-site lodging: No. **Rental clubs:** Yes.
Walking policy: Unrestricted walking. **Range:** Yes (grass).
To obtain tee times: First come, first served.
Subscriber comments: Best of the three D.C. city courses . . . Best
greens in the area . . . Crew does well with limited funds . . . Added a
sprinkler system . . . Needs a new clubhouse . . . Bunkers need real sand,
fairways need fewer weeds.

★½ **ROCK CREEK PARK GOLF COURSE**
PU—16th & Rittenhouse N.W., Washington (202)882-7332.
Holes: 18. **Par:** 65/65.
Yards: 4,715/N/A. **Course rating:** 62.5/65.5. **Slope:** 112/102.
Opened: 1923. **Pace of Play rating:** N/A. **Green fee:** $11/17.
Credit cards: MC, V. **Reduced fees:** Weekdays, Seniors.
Caddies: No. **Golf carts:** $18 for 18 holes.
Discount golf packages: No. **Season:** Year-round. **High:** June-Aug.
On-site lodging: No. **Rental clubs:** Yes.
Walking policy: Unrestricted walking. **Range:** Yes.
To obtain tee times: First come, first served.
Subscriber comments: Short, fun, inexpensive . . . Very, very short . . .
Very tight . . . Very hilly . . . Poor condition . . . A couple of silly holes
. . . No par 5s, but very tight . . . Leave your driver at home . . . This is the
place to improve your short game . . . Good as a warm-up for your
vacation south.

ADMIRAL LEHIGH GOLF AND RESORT
NORTH COURSE★

R—225 E. Joel Blvd., Lehigh (813)369-2121x2367.
13 miles east of Fort Myers. **Holes:** 18. **Par:** 70/70.
Yards: 5,987/4,849. **Course rating:** 70.0/69.5. **Slope:** 119/121.
Opened: 1965. **Pace of Play rating:** 4:00. **Green fee:** $12/27.
Credit cards: All major. **Reduced fees:** Low season, Resort guests,
Twilight.
Caddies: No. **Golf carts:** $16 for 18 holes.
Discount golf packages: Yes. **Season:** Year-round. **High:** Dec.-April.
On-site lodging: Yes. **Rental clubs:** Yes.
Walking policy: Walking at certain times. **Range:** Yes.
To obtain tee times: Call 24 hours in advance.

AMELIA ISLAND PLANTATION

R—3000 1st Coast Hwy., Amelia Island (904)277-5907, (800)874-6878.
35 miles northeast of Jacksonville.
Credit cards: MC, V, DISC. **Reduced fees:** Low season, Resort guests,
Twilight, Juniors.
Caddies: No. **Golf carts:** Included in Green Fee.
Discount golf packages: Yes. **Season:** Year-round. **High:** April-May.
On-site lodging: Yes. **Rental clubs:** Yes.
Walking policy: Mandatory cart. **Range:** Yes (grass).
To obtain tee times: May be made at the same time reservations are made
at Amelia Island Plantation.

AMELIA LINKS
★★★ OAKMARSH/OYSTERBAY/OCEANSIDE

Holes: 27. **Par:** 72/71/71.
Yards: 6,502/6,026/6,140. **Course rating:** 70.7/68.6/69.3.
Slope: 127/117/120.
Opened: 1972. **Pace of Play rating:** 4:00. **Green fee:** $65/85.
Subscriber comments: Hard but fair . . . Premium on iron play and short
game . . . Very scenic . . . Target course . . . A thinking person's layout
. . . Staff service was excellent . . . Good variety of holes.

★★★½ LONG POINT GOLF CLUB

Holes: 18. **Par:** 72/72.
Yards: 6,775/4,927. **Course rating:** 72.9/69.1. **Slope:** 129/121.
Opened: 1987. **Pace of Play rating:** N/A. **Green fee:** $80/100.
Ranked 51st in America's 75 Best Resort Courses by Golf Digest.
Subscriber comments: Great ocean-front course . . . Play moves quickly
. . . Ocean holes challenging in the wind . . . Very scenic . . . Great course
for women . . . Gorgeous and difficult . . . Very good resort course,
challenging . . . Excellent staff.

★★ APOLLO BEACH GOLF AND SEA CLUB

PU—801 Golf & Sea Blvd., Apollo Beach (813)645-6212.
15 miles south of Tampa. **Holes:** 18. **Par:** 72/72.
Yards: 7,040/4,831. **Course rating:** 73.9/69.1. **Slope:** 130/115.
Opened: 1972. **Pace of Play rating:** N/A. **Green fee:** $35.
Credit cards: All major. **Reduced fees:** Low season, Twilight, Seniors,
Juniors.
Caddies: No. **Golf carts:** Included in Green Fee.
Discount golf packages: Yes. **Season:** Year-round. **High:** Nov.-March.
On-site lodging: No. **Rental clubs:** Yes.
Walking policy: Mandatory cart. **Range:** Yes (grass).
To obtain tee times: Call.
Subscriber comments: Tight fairways and lots of water . . . Long,
straight hitter's course, lots of danger . . . Staff very cooperative . . . Too
many homes.

ARNOLD PALMER'S BAY HILL CLUB AND LODGE
★★★★½ CHALLENGER/CHAMPION

R—9000 Bay Hill Blvd., Orlando (407)876-2429x630.
15 miles southwest of Orlando. **Holes:** 18. **Par:** 72/N/A.
Yards: 7,114/5192. **Course rating:** 74.6/70.3. **Slope:** 141/120.

Opened: 1961. **Pace of Play rating:** 4:10. **Green fee:** $150.
Credit cards: MC, V, AMEX. **Reduced fees:** Resort guests, Juniors.
Caddies: Yes, required when walking. **Golf carts:** $15 for 18 holes.
Discount golf packages: No. **Season:** Year-round. **High:** Jan.–April.
On-site lodging: Yes. **Rental clubs:** Yes.
Walking policy: Unrestricted walking. **Range:** Yes (grass).
To obtain tee times: Tee times made through Lodge reservation.
Also has 9-hole, par-36 Charger Course.
Ranked 89th in America's 100 Greatest Golf Courses by Golf Digest.
Ranked 17th in America's 75 Best Resort Courses by Golf Digest. Ranked
6th in Florida by Golf Digest.
Subscriber comments: Classic golf . . . Staff excellent . . . A very good
course, but not that much better than others costing less . . . Long, longer,
longest, but fun . . . Extremely difficult course . . . Challenging to play,
many bunkers. Large homes . . . Nice to play where pros play . . .
Understated in difficulty and more impressive with each successive round
. . . Tournament-quality golf . . . Very playable . . . Too long for average
player.

★½ **ARROWHEAD GOLF COURSE**
PU—8201 S.W. 24th St., Davie (305)475-8200.
5 miles west of Fort Lauderdale. **Holes:** 18. **Par:** 70/70.
Yards: 6,311/4,838. **Course rating:** 70.8/68.7. **Slope:** 115/109.
Opened: 1976. **Pace of Play rating:** N/A. **Green fee:** $15/40.
Credit cards: MC, V, AMEX. **Reduced fees:** Weekdays, Low season,
Twilight.
Caddies: No. **Golf carts:** Included in Green Fee.
Discount golf packages: Yes. **Season:** Year-round. **High:** Jan.–March.
On-site lodging: No. **Rental clubs:** Yes.
Walking policy: Mandatory cart. **Range:** Yes.
To obtain tee times: Call one week in advance.
Subscriber comments: Course for beginners to average. Well treated by
staff . . . Short . . . Needs sprucing up . . . Semi-tight.

★★★ **ATLANTIS COUNTRY CLUB**
R—190 Atlantis Blvd., Atlantis (407)968-1300.
7 miles south of West Palm Beach. **Holes:** 18. **Par:** 72/72.
Yards: 6,510/5,258. **Course rating:** 71.2/70.9. **Slope:** 126/123.
Opened: 1972. **Pace of Play rating:** 4:00. **Green fee:** $20/50.
Credit cards: MC, V. **Reduced fees:** Weekdays, Low season, Resort
guests.
Caddies: No. **Golf carts:** $15 for 18 holes.
Discount golf packages: Yes. **Season:** Year-round. **High:** Oct.–March.
On-site lodging: Yes. **Rental clubs:** Yes.
Walking policy: Mandatory cart. **Range:** Yes (grass).
To obtain tee times: Non-resort guests call 24 hours in advance. Members
and guests call three days in advance.
Subscriber comments: Well maintained . . . For the straight hitter;
drivers not necessary . . . Tight course . . . Suited for scratch to 20-
handicapper.

★½ **BABE ZAHARIAS GOLF COURSE**
PU—11412 Forest Hills Dr., Tampa (813)932-8932.
Holes: 18. **Par:** 70/71.
Yards: 6,163/5,236. **Course rating:** 68.9/68.9. **Slope:** 121/118.
Opened: 1974. **Pace of Play rating:** 4:00. **Green fee:** $12/25.
Credit cards: MC, V, DISC. **Reduced fees:** Weekdays, Low season,
Twilight, Seniors, Juniors.
Caddies: No. **Golf carts:** Included in Green Fee.
Discount golf packages: No. **Season:** Year-round. **High:** Dec.–May.
On-site lodging: No. **Rental clubs:** Yes.
Walking policy: Unrestricted walking. **Range:** No.
To obtain tee times: Call seven days in advance.
Subscriber comments: City course, fair condition . . . Open. Short

course. Great for new golfers . . . Typical muny, never great shape . . . Only the name is outstanding . . . Average municipal golf course, but a very good $ value.

★★½ BARDMOOR NORTH GOLF CLUB
PU—7919 Bardmoor Blvd., Largo (813)397-0483.
15 miles west of Tampa. **Holes:** 18. **Par:** 72/72.
Yards: 6,960/5,569. **Course rating:** 72.4/71.8. **Slope:** 126/118.
Opened: 1970. **Pace of Play rating:** N/A. **Green fee:** $26/60.
Credit cards: MC, V, AMEX. **Reduced fees:** Weekdays, Low season, Twilight, Juniors.
Caddies: Yes. **Golf carts:** Included in Green Fee.
Discount golf packages: Yes. **Season:** Year-round. **High:** Dec.-April.
On-site lodging: No. **Rental clubs:** Yes.
Walking policy: Mandatory cart. **Range:** Yes (grass).
To obtain tee times: Call four days in advance.
Subscriber comments: In continual redesign . . . Best suited for above-average golfer . . . Playing with caddies was a great time . . . Good, long golf course . . . Former PGA/LPGA Tour's Mixed Team site.

★★½ BAYMEADOWS GOLF CLUB
SP—7981 Baymeadows Circle West, Jacksonville (904)731-5701.
Holes: 18. **Par:** 72/72.
Yards: 7,002/5,309. **Course rating:** 73.7/72.2. **Slope:** 130/130.
Opened: 1969. **Pace of Play rating:** 4:00. **Green fee:** $24/32.
Credit cards: MC, V, AMEX. **Reduced fees:** Twilight.
Caddies: No. **Golf carts:** Included in Green Fee.
Discount golf packages: No. **Season:** Year-round. **High:** Year-round.
On-site lodging: Yes. **Rental clubs:** Yes.

Walking policy: Mandatory cart. **Range:** Yes (grass).
To obtain tee times: Call one week in advance.
Subscriber comments: Older, very fair, open . . . Good layout within residential areas . . . Tight course . . . Good for all clubs . . . Suited for right-to-left player . . . Staff always got me in as a single.

★½ BAYSHORE GOLF COURSE
PU—2301 Alton Rd., Miami Beach (305)532-3350.
Holes: 18. **Par:** 72/73.
Yards: 6,903/5,538. **Course rating:** 73.0/71.6. **Slope:** 127/120.
Opened: N/A. **Pace of Play rating:** 4:00. **Green fee:** $22/45.
Credit cards: MC, V. **Reduced fees:** Weekdays, Low season, Twilight, Juniors.
Caddies: No. **Golf carts:** Included in Green Fee.
Discount golf packages: Yes. **Season:** Year-round. **High:** Dec.-March.
On-site lodging: No. **Rental clubs:** Yes.
Walking policy: Mandatory cart. **Range:** Yes.
To obtain tee times: Call seven days in advance.
Subscriber comments: Scenic . . . Old-time flavor.

★★★★ BAYTREE NATIONAL GOLF LINKS
SP—8207 National Dr., Melbourne (407)259-9060.
50 miles southeast of Orlando. **Holes:** 18. **Par:** 72/72.
Yards: 7,043/4,803. **Course rating:** 73.7/67.5. **Slope:** 129/109.
Opened: 1994. **Pace of Play rating:** N/A. **Green fee:** $35/70.
Credit cards: MC, V, AMEX. **Reduced fees:** Low season, Resort guests, Twilight, Juniors.
Caddies: No. **Golf carts:** Included in Green Fee.
Discount golf packages: Yes. **Season:** Year-round. **High:** Jan.-March.
On-site lodging: No. **Rental clubs:** Yes.
Walking policy: Mandatory cart. **Range:** Yes (grass).
To obtain tee times:
Call six days in advance.
Subscriber comments: Gary Player design with five different tee markers on every hole, playable for every handicap level . . . Definitely a

shotmaker's track . . . Superb design . . . Drains exceptionally well! . . .
Fun to play . . . Best public course in Florida.

★★½ BELLA VISTA GOLF AND YACHT CLUB
SP—P.O. Box 66, Hwy 48, Howey In The Lills (904)324-3233, (800)955-7001.
25 miles west of Orlando. **Holes:** 18. **Par:** 71/71.
Yards: 6,321/5,386. **Course rating:** 68.4/71.9. **Slope:** 119/123.
Opened: 1990. **Pace of Play rating:** 4:00. **Green fee:** $16/38.
Credit cards: MC, V, AMEX. **Reduced fees:** Weekdays, Low season,
Resort guests, Twilight, Seniors, Juniors.
Caddies: No. **Golf carts:** Included in Green Fee.
Discount golf packages: Yes. **Season:** Year-round. **High:** Sept.-April.
On-site lodging: Yes. **Rental clubs:** Yes.
Walking policy: Mandatory cart. **Range:** Yes (grass).
To obtain tee times: Call 48 hours in advance.
Subscriber comments: Not enough land "fore" 18 holes . . . Watch for
snakes . . . Good staff and service . . . Wear a hard hat and stay alert . . .
Fun course to play.

★★ BELLEVIEW MIDO COUNTRY CLUB
R—1501 Indian Rocks Rd., Belleair (813)581-5498.
20 miles west of Tampa. **Holes:** 18. **Par:** 72/74.
Yards: 6,655/5,703. **Course rating:** 70.7/72.1. **Slope:** 118/119.
Opened: 1926. **Pace of Play rating:** 4:00-4:30. **Green fee:** $25/60.
Credit cards: All major. **Reduced fees:** Low season, Resort guests.
Caddies: No. **Golf carts:** N/A.
Discount golf packages: Yes. **Season:** Year-round. **High:** Jan.-April.
On-site lodging: No. **Rental clubs:** Yes.
Walking policy: Walking at certain times. **Range:** Yes (grass).
To obtain tee times: Hotel guests may make tee times at time of
reservation. Non-guests call three days in advance.
Subscriber comments: Easy to score . . . Nice clubhouse . . . A couple of
great holes . . . Fast play . . . Average layout.

★★½ THE BILTMORE GOLF COURSE
PU—1210 Anastasia Ave., Coral Gables (305)460-5364.
3 miles from Miami. **Holes:** 18. **Par:** 71/74.
Yards: 6,642/5,237. **Course rating:** 71.5/70.1. **Slope:** 119/115.
Opened: 1925. **Pace of Play rating:** 3:55. **Green fee:** $39.
Credit cards: MC, V, AMEX. **Reduced fees:** Low season, Twilight,
Juniors.
Caddies: No. **Golf carts:** N/A.
Discount golf packages: No. **Season:** Year-round. **High:** Nov.-April.
On-site lodging: Yes. **Rental clubs:** Yes.
Walking policy: Walking at certain times. **Range:** Yes (grass).
To obtain tee times: Call 24 hours in advance from a touch-tone
telephone. Same day reservation, call starter at (305)460-5365.
Subscriber comments: Great old Donald Ross course . . . Old reliable
Miami course . . . Very popular with college crowd . . . Great public
course . . . Greens variable.

★★★ BINKS FOREST GOLF COURSE
SP—400 Binks Forest Dr., Wellington (407)795-0595.
Holes: 18. **Par:** 72/72.
Yards: 7,065/5,599. **Course rating:** 75.0/71.9. **Slope:** 138/127.
Opened: 1990. **Pace of Play rating:** N/A. **Green fee:** $27/65.
Credit cards: MC, V, AMEX. **Reduced fees:** Weekdays, Low season,
Resort guests, Twilight.
Caddies: No. **Golf carts:** Included in Green Fee.
Discount golf packages: Yes. **Season:** Year-round. **High:** Nov.-April.
On-site lodging: No. **Rental clubs:** Yes.
Walking policy: Mandatory cart. **Range:** Yes (grass).
To obtain tee times: Call one week in advance with credit card.

Subscriber comments: Challenging but fair . . . Narrow and long . . .
Lots of water . . . Great track but often not in good condition . . . Like a
northern course, tree-lined and secluded . . . New owners are improving
course conditions . . . Not overcrowded.

★★★½ BLOOMINGDALE GOLFER'S CLUB

SP—1802 Nature's Way Blvd., Valrico (813)685-4105.
15 miles southeast of Tampa. **Holes:** 18. **Par:** 72/73.
Yards: 7,165/5,506. **Course rating:** 74.4/71.6. **Slope:** 137/129.
Opened: 1983. **Pace of Play rating:** 4:00. **Green fee:** $27/43.
Credit cards: MC, V, AMEX. **Reduced fees:** Weekdays, Low season,
Twilight, Juniors.
Caddies: No. **Golf carts:** $12 for 18 holes.
Discount golf packages: Yes. **Season:** Year-round. **High:** Dec.-April.
On-site lodging: No. **Rental clubs:** Yes.
Walking policy: Mandatory cart. **Range:** Yes (grass).
To obtain tee times: Call up to seven days in advance.
Subscriber comments: Rub shoulders with tour players on range . . .
Good fast greens . . . Accuracy is key here, very little rough for stray shots
. . . Course plays longer than yardage indicates because of soft fairways . . .
Player's course . . . Friendly staff.

BLUEWATER BAY RESORT

R—1950 Bluewater Blvd., Niceville (904)897-3241.
60 miles east of Pensacola.
Opened: 1981. **Pace of Play rating:** 4:00. **Green fee:** $25/33.
Credit cards: All major. **Reduced fees:** Low season, Resort guests.
Caddies: No. **Golf carts:** $12 for 18 holes.
Discount golf packages: Yes. **Season:** Year-round. **High:** Feb.-May
On-site lodging: Yes. **Rental clubs:** Yes.
Walking policy: Walking at certain times. **Range:** Yes (grass).
To obtain tee times: Call anytime.

★★★½ MAGNOLIA/MARSH

Holes: 18. **Par:** 72/72.
Yards: 6,669/5,048. **Course rating:** 72.2/68.4. **Slope:** 131/117.
Subscriber comments: Beautiful layout . . . Pace of play good . . . Staff
was great.

★★★ BAY/LAKE

Holes: 18. **Par:** 72/72.
Yards: 6,803/5,415. **Course rating:** 73.0/70.6. **Slope:** 140/124.
Subscriber comments: Top-flight staff . . . Attractive course with many
trees. Wind off bay . . . Great for the shotmaker . . . Very enjoyable.

BOBBY JONES GOLF COMPLEX

PU—1000 Azinger Way, Sarasota (813)955-8097, (800)955-3529.
Opened: 1927. **Pace of Play rating:** N/A. **Green fee:** $9/18.
Credit cards: MC, V. **Reduced fees:** Low season, Twilight, Juniors.
Caddies: No. **Golf carts:** $10 for 18 holes.
Discount golf packages: No. **Season:** Year-round. **High:** Dec.-April.
On-site lodging: No. **Rental clubs:** Yes.
Walking policy: Walking at certain times. **Range:** Yes.
To obtain tee times: Call automated system from touch-tone phone.
Also has 9-hole, par-30 Colonel Gillespie Course.

★½ AMERICAN COURSE

Holes: 18. **Par:** 71/71.
Yards: 6,009/4,453. **Course rating:** 68.4/65.1. **Slope:** 117/107.
Subscriber comments: Short, lots of irons off tee . . . Good city course;
short and tight back nine.

★½ BRITISH COURSE

Holes: 18. **Par:** 72/72.
Yards: 6,468/5,695. **Course rating:** 70.0/71.8. **Slope:** 111/115.
Subscriber comments: For older player . . . Nice public course . . .
Longer than American Course, but wide open . . . Nice layout.

FLORIDA

BOCA RATON RESORT AND CLUB
R—(407)395-3000x3076.
22 miles south of Palm Beach.
Opened: N/A. **Pace of Play rating:** N/A. **Green fee:** N/A.
Credit cards: All major. **Reduced fees:** Low season, Twilight.
Caddies: No. **Golf carts:** $19 for 18 holes.
Discount golf packages: Yes. **Season:** Year-round. **High:** Oct.-May.
On-site lodging: Yes. **Rental clubs:** No.
Walking policy: N/A. **Range:** Yes (grass).
To obtain tee times: Call club.
COUNTRY CLUB COURSE★
7751 Boca Club Blvd., Boca Raton.
Holes: 18. **Par:** 72/72.
Yards: 6,564/5,565. **Course rating:** N/A. **Slope:** 126/124.
Subscriber comments: Greens and fairways impeccable . . . Nothing
special about layout . . . Course in very good condition.
★★½ RESORT COURSE
501 E. Camino Real, Boca Raton.
Holes: 18. **Par:** 71/71.
Yards: 6,682/5,518. **Course rating:** N/A. **Slope:** 122/124.
Subscriber comments: Condo construction will reduce attractiveness . . .
Redesign planned in '96.

★½ BONIFAY COUNTRY CLUB
SP—State Rd. 177A, Bonifay (904)547-4653.
40 miles north of Panama City. **Holes:** 18. **Par:** 72/72.
Yards: 6,850/5,405. **Course rating:** 73.1/N/A. **Slope:** N/A.
Opened: 1963. **Pace of Play rating:** 4:00. **Green fee:** $17.
Credit cards: MC, V, DISC. **Reduced fees:** Low season, Resort guests,
Twilight, Juniors.
Caddies: No. **Golf carts:** Included in Green Fee.
Discount golf packages: Yes. **Season:** Year-round. **High:** Jan.-April.
On-site lodging: No. **Rental clubs:** Yes.
Walking policy: Walking at certain times. **Range:** Yes (grass).
To obtain tee times: Call up to 24 hours in advance.
Subscriber comments: A very nice little course . . . Staff is fantastic and
beverage cart is major asset.

BOYNTON BEACH MUNICIPAL GOLF COURSE
★★½ RED/WHITE/BLUE
PU—8020 Jog Rd., Boynton Beach (407)969-2201.
10 miles south of West Palm Beach. **Holes:** 27. **Par:** 71/66/65.
Yards: 6,316/5,290/5,062. **Course rating:** 70.1/65.0/63.9.
Slope: 129/N/A/N/A.
Opened: 1984. **Pace of Play rating:** 4:15. **Green fee:** $10/22.
Credit cards: None. **Reduced fees:** Low season, Juniors.
Caddies: No. **Golf carts:** $11 for 18 holes.
Discount golf packages: No. **Season:** Year-round. **High:** Dec.-March.
On-site lodging: No. **Rental clubs:** Yes.
Walking policy: Walking at certain times. **Range:** Yes (grass).
To obtain tee times: Call one day in advance for weekdays and two days
in advance for weekends and holidays.
Subscriber comments: Pro-shop staff of quality . . . Typical muny . . .
Challenging . . . Interesting layouts.

★★ THE BREAKERS CLUB
R—1 South County Rd., Palm Beach (407)659-8407.
2 miles east of West Palm Beach. **Holes:** 18. **Par:** 70/72.
Yards: 6,017/5,582. **Course rating:** 69.3/72.6. **Slope:** 121/122.
Opened: 1897. **Pace of Play rating:** 4:00. **Green fee:** $75.
Credit cards: All major. **Reduced fees:** Resort guests, Twilight, Juniors.
Caddies: Yes. **Golf carts:** Included in Green Fee.
Discount golf packages: Yes. **Season:** Year-round. **High:** Dec.-April.
On-site lodging: Yes. **Rental clubs:** Yes.

Walking policy: Walking at certain times. **Range:** Yes (grass).
To obtain tee times: Tee times obtained as far in advance as needed.
Subscriber comments: Very tight, heavily treed, well maintained, staff excellent . . . Short course, nice finishing hole into ocean wind . . . Target golf. Not long, need accuracy.

★★★½ BREAKERS WEST COUNTRY CLUB
SP—1550 Flagler Pkwy., West Palm Beach (407)653-6320.
10 miles west of West Palm Beach. **Holes:** 18. **Par:** 71/71.
Yards: 6,905/5,385. **Course rating:** 73.9/71.1. **Slope:** 135/123.
Opened: 1969. **Pace of Play rating:** 4:15. **Green fee:** $60/90.
Credit cards: MC, V, AMEX. **Reduced fees:** No.
Caddies: No. **Golf carts:** Included in Green Fee.

Discount golf packages: Yes. **Season:** Year-round. **High:** Nov.-April.
On-site lodging: No. **Rental clubs:** Yes.
Walking policy: Mandatory cart. **Range:** Yes.
To obtain tee times: Must be staying at Breakers Hotel to play here or come as a guest of a member.
Subscriber comments: Excellent layout . . . Good staff . . . Back nine redone, not as good as front . . . Ranger keeps people moving.

★★★ CALUSA LAKES GOLF COURSE
PU—1995 Calusa Lakes Blvd., Nokomis (813)484-8995.
5 miles of Sarasota. **Holes:** 18. **Par:** 72/72.
Yards: 6,760/5,197. **Course rating:** N/A. **Slope:** 124/118.
Opened: N/A. **Pace of Play rating:** N/A. **Green fee:** N/A.
Credit cards: MC, V. **Reduced fees:** Low season, Twilight.
Caddies: No. **Golf carts:** Included in Green Fee.
Discount golf packages: No. **Season:** Year-round. **High:** Jan.-April.
On-site lodging: No. **Rental clubs:** No.
Walking policy: N/A. **Range:** Yes (grass).
Subscriber comments: Restaurant staff is great, plus food is outstanding . . . Nice layout for a home development . . . Fair, but challenging and lots of water holes.

★★ CAPE CORAL GOLF AND TENNIS RESORT
R—4003 Palm Tree Blvd., Cape Coral (813)542-7879, (800)848-1475.
20 miles northeast of Fort Myers. **Holes:** 18. **Par:** 72/72.
Yards: 6,649/5,464. **Course rating:** 71.6/71.2. **Slope:** 122/119.
Opened: 1963. **Pace of Play rating:** 4:00. **Green fee:** $18/50.
Credit cards: All major. **Reduced fees:** Low season, Resort guests, Twilight, Juniors.
Caddies: No. **Golf carts:** Included in Green Fee.
Discount golf packages: Yes. **Season:** Year-round. **High:** Jan.-March.
On-site lodging: Yes. **Rental clubs:** Yes.
Walking policy: Mandatory cart. **Range:** Yes (grass).
To obtain tee times: Call three days in advance after 4 p.m.
Subscriber comments: Flat but good, lots of water . . . Didn't see a ranger . . . Small greens . . . Nicely conditioned.

★½ CAPRI ISLES GOLF CLUB
SP—849 Capri Isles Blvd., Venice (813)485-3371.
60 miles south of Tampa. **Holes:** 18. **Par:** 72/72.
Yards: 6,472/5,480. **Course rating:** 70.0/69.8. **Slope:** 123/113.
Opened: 1972. **Pace of Play rating:** 4:00-4:30. **Green fee:** $23/40.
Credit cards: MC, V. **Reduced fees:** Low season, Twilight.
Caddies: No. **Golf carts:** Included in Green Fee.
Discount golf packages: No. **Season:** Year-round. **High:** Jan.-April.
On-site lodging: No. **Rental clubs:** Yes.
Walking policy: Walking back nine only. **Range:** Yes (grass).
To obtain tee times: Call up to three days ahead.
Subscriber comments: Course recently upgraded . . . Staff friendly.

FLORIDA

★★½ CHAMPIONS CLUB AT JULINGTON CREEK
SP—1111 Durbin Creek Blvd., Jacksonville (904)287-4653.
15 miles south of Jacksonville. **Holes:** 18. **Par:** 72/72.
Yards: 6,872/4,994. **Course rating:** 72.8/68.6. **Slope:** 126/114.
Opened: 1992. **Pace of Play rating:** 4:00. **Green fee:** $29/36.
Credit cards: MC, V. **Reduced fees:** Weekdays, Twilight, Seniors,
Juniors.
Caddies: No. **Golf carts:** Included in Green Fee.
Discount golf packages: No. **Season:** Year-round. **High:** March-
May/Oct.-Dec.
On-site lodging: No. **Rental clubs:** Yes.
Walking policy: Mandatory cart. **Range:** Yes (grass).
To obtain tee times: Call golf shop two days in advance for outside guest
play.
Subscriber comments: Good course . . . Nice people . . . Back nine needs
time . . . Soggy ground in summer, greens very good . . . Treelined . . .
Well designed for all levels.

★★★ THE CHAMPIONS CLUB AT SUMMERFIELD
PU—3400 SE Summerfield Way, Stuart (407)283-1500.
25 miles north of West Palm Beach. **Holes:** 18. **Par:** 72/72.
Yards: 6,809/5,014. **Course rating:** 72.8/69.4. **Slope:** 131/116.
Opened: 1994. **Pace of Play rating:** 4:15. **Green fee:** $20/54.
Credit cards: MC, V. **Reduced fees:** Low season, Twilight, Juniors.
Caddies: No. **Golf carts:** Included in Green Fee.
Discount golf packages: Yes. **Season:** Year-round. **High:** Nov.-April.
On-site lodging: No. **Rental clubs:** Yes.
Walking policy: Mandatory cart. **Range:** Yes (grass).
To obtain tee times: Call seven days in advance during the summer and
four days in advance during the winter.
Subscriber comments: New course, but fun to play . . . Good conditions
especially for new course, friendly people . . . Very fair Fazio design. Well-
organized staff.

★★★½ CIMARRONE GOLF AND COUNTRY CLUB
SP—2690 Cimarrone Blvd., Jacksonville (904)287-2000.
Holes: 18. **Par:** 72/72.
Yards: 6,891/4,707. **Course rating:** N/A. **Slope:** 128/119.
Opened: N/A. **Pace of Play rating:** N/A. **Green fee:** N/A.
Credit cards: MC, V, AMEX. **Reduced fees:** Weekdays, Twilight.
Caddies: No. **Golf carts:** Included in Green Fee.
Discount golf packages: No. **Season:** Year-round. **High:** April-
May/Sept.-Oct.
On-site lodging: No. **Rental clubs:** No.
Walking policy: N/A. **Range:** Yes (grass).
Subscriber comments: Challenging yet enjoyable . . . Water on every
hole . . . Lots of lateral water hazards, good greens . . . Excellent condition
all seasons . . . Relatively new . . . Pace of play good . . . Best
public/semiprivate course around.

CITRUS HILLS GOLF AND COUNTRY CLUB
SP—509 E. Hartford St., Hernando (904)746-4425.
90 miles of Tampa.
Opened: N/A. **Pace of Play rating:** N/A. **Green fee:** N/A.
Credit cards: MC, V. **Reduced fees:** Low season, Twilight.
Caddies: No. **Golf carts:** Included in Green Fee.
Discount golf packages: Yes. **Season:** Year-round. **High:** Dec.-April.
On-site lodging: Yes. **Rental clubs:** No.
Walking policy: N/A. **Range:** Yes (grass).
To obtain tee times: Call club.
★★½ MEADOWS COURSE
Holes: 18. **Par:** 70/70.
Yards: 5,885/4,585. **Course rating:** N/A. **Slope:** 115/112.
Subscriber comments: Wide open . . . Flat, minimal trees . . . Good staff
. . . Need more marshals.

★★★OAKS COURSE
Holes: 18. **Par:** 70/70.
Yards: 6,323/4,647. **Course rating:** N/A. **Slope:** 120/114.
Subscriber comments: Long par 3s . . . Testing both aspects of long and short game . . . Tight fairways . . . No weak holes, playable for the bogey golfer. a good day out . . . Good staff.

CLERBROOK RESORT★
R—20005 US Hwy. No.27, Clermont (904)394-6165.
20 miles west of Orlando. **Holes:** 18. **Par:** 67/67.
Yards: 5,154/4,140. **Course rating:** 65.0/64.0. **Slope:** 110/106.
Opened: 1984. **Pace of Play rating:** 3:15. **Green fee:** $12/20.
Credit cards: MC, V, DISC. **Reduced fees:** Low season, Juniors.
Caddies: No. **Golf carts:** $14 for 18 holes.
Discount golf packages: No. **Season:** Year-round. **High:** Nov.-March.
On-site lodging: Yes. **Rental clubs:** Yes.
Walking policy: Walking at certain times. **Range:** Yes (grass).
To obtain tee times: Call up to five days in advance.

★★★★THE CLUB AT HIDDEN CREEK
SP—3070 PGA Blvd., Navarre (904)939-4604.
20 miles east of Pensacola. **Holes:** 18. **Par:** 72/72.
Yards: 6,862/5,213. **Course rating:** 73.2/70.1. **Slope:** 139/124.
Opened: 1988. **Pace of Play rating:** 3:30-4:00. **Green fee:** $25/50.
Credit cards: All major. **Reduced fees:** Weekdays, Low season, Twilight, Juniors.
Caddies: No. **Golf carts:** Included in Green Fee.
Discount golf packages: Yes. **Season:** Year-round. **High:** Jan.-April.
On-site lodging: No. **Rental clubs:** Yes.
Walking policy: Mandatory cart. **Range:** Yes (grass).
To obtain tee times: Call up to seven days in advance.
Subscriber comments: Great all-around course . . . Good service, very good amenities (dining, pro shop, etc.) . . . Very deceptive, very little water, but well placed . . . Fine course, well maintained . . . Shotmaker's heaven.

★★★THE CLUB AT OAK FORD
MYRTLE/PALMS/LIVE OAK
PU—1522 Palm View Rd., Sarasota (813)371-3680.
60 miles from Tampa. **Holes:** 27. **Par:** N/A.
Yards: N/A. **Course rating:** N/A. **Slope:** N/A.
Opened: N/A. **Pace of Play rating:** N/A. **Green fee:** N/A.
Credit cards: MC, V. **Reduced fees:** Low season.
Caddies: No. **Golf carts:** Included in Green Fee.
Discount golf packages: No. **Season:** Year-round. **High:** Jan.-April.

On-site lodging: No. **Rental clubs:** No.
Walking policy: N/A. **Range:** Yes (grass).
Subscriber comments: Not crowded, scenic . . . Delightful links course, enjoyable . . . Challenging. A real wildlife preserve . . . Enjoyable, wild setting . . . Very narrow at points, slicer's nightmare . . . Worth the drive out of the way . . . Offers several specials month to month. Rangers keep good pace.

COCOA BEACH GOLF COURSE
★★★RIVER/DOLPHIN/LAKES
PU—5000 Tom Warriner Blvd., Cocoa Beach (407)868-3351.
40 miles east of Orlando. **Holes:** 27. **Par:** 71/71/72.
Yards: 6,363/6,393/6,714. **Course rating:** 69.9/70.1/71.7.
Slope: 116/115/119.
Opened: 1992. **Pace of Play rating:** 3:30-4:00. **Green fee:** $17/27.
Credit cards: MC, V. **Reduced fees:** Weekdays, Low season, Twilight, Juniors.
Caddies: No. **Golf carts:** $8 for 18 holes.

Discount golf packages: No. **Season:** Year-round. **High:** Dec.-April.
On-site lodging: No. **Rental clubs:** Yes.
Walking policy: Walking at certain times. **Range:** Yes (grass).
To obtain tee times: Call four days in advance after 4 p.m.
Subscriber comments: Best muny course in area . . . Wide open with lots of water . . . Always windy.

COLONY WEST COUNTRY CLUB
★★★½ CHAMPIONSHIP COURSE
PU—6800 NW 88th Ave., Tamarac (305)726-8430.
10 miles west of Fort Lauderdale. **Holes:** 18. **Par:** 71/71.
Yards: 7,271/5,422. **Course rating:** 75.8/71.6. **Slope:** 138/127.
Opened: 1970. **Pace of Play rating:** 3:30-4:00. **Green fee:** $35/70.
Credit cards: MC, V, AMEX. **Reduced fees:** Weekdays, Low season, Twilight.
Caddies: No. **Golf carts:** Included in Green Fee.
Discount golf packages: Yes. **Season:** Year-round. **High:** Dec.-April.
On-site lodging: No. **Rental clubs:** Yes.
Walking policy: Mandatory cart. **Range:** No.
To obtain tee times: Call pro shop.
Also 18-hole, par-65 Glades Course .
Ranked in Second 25 of America's 75 Best Public Golf Courses by Golf Digest.
Subscriber comments: Tough for average players yet fun to play . . .
Long and sometimes tight, good condition . . . Outstanding course design.

★★ CONTINENTAL COUNTRY CLUB
SP—50 Continental Blvd., Wildwood (904)748-3293.
Call club for further information.
Subscriber comments: Very courteous in clubhouse . . . Accepting of public . . . Many trees.

★ CONTINENTAL GOLF CLUB AT CORAL SPRINGS
SP—9001 W. Sample Rd., Coral Springs (305)752-2140.
20 miles north of Fort Lauderdale. **Holes:** 18. **Par:** 69/70.
Yards: 5,659/4,874. **Course rating:** 67.3/64.9. **Slope:** 120/114.
Opened: 1965. **Pace of Play rating:** 4:30. **Green fee:** $12/26.
Credit cards: MC, V, AMEX. **Reduced fees:** Low season.
Caddies: No. **Golf carts:** Included in Green Fee.
Discount golf packages: No. **Season:** Year-round. **High:** Nov.-April.
On-site lodging: No. **Rental clubs:** Yes.
Walking policy: Mandatory cart. **Range:** No.
To obtain tee times: Call two days in advance.
Subscriber comments: Older course . . . Average . . . Course is in much better shape than a year or two ago.

★★½ CORAL OAKS GOLF COURSE
PU—1800 N. W. 28th Ave., Cape Coral (813)283-4100.
12 miles southwest of Fort Myers. **Holes:** 18. **Par:** 72/72.
Yards: 6,623/4,803. **Course rating:** 71.7/68.9. **Slope:** 123/117.
Opened: 1988. **Pace of Play rating:** 4:00. **Green fee:** $21/25.
Credit cards: MC, V, DISC. **Reduced fees:** No.
Caddies: No. **Golf carts:** Included in Green Fee.
Discount golf packages: Yes. **Season:** Year-round. **High:** Dec.-April.
On-site lodging: No. **Rental clubs:** Yes.
Walking policy: Walking at certain times. **Range:** Yes (grass).
To obtain tee times: Call two days in advance.
Subscriber comments: Any player can enjoy from right tees . . .
Conditions totally inconsistent . . . Great layout.

★★★ THE COUNTRY CLUB AT JACARANDA WEST
SP—601 Jacaranda Blvd., Venice (813)493-2664.
20 miles south of Sarasota. **Holes:** 18. **Par:** 72/72.
Yards: 6,602/5,321. **Course rating:** 71.9/70.7. **Slope:** 126/120.

Opened: 1974. **Pace of Play rating:** 4:00. **Green fee:** $23/36.
Credit cards: MC, V. **Reduced fees:** Low season, Twilight, Juniors.
Caddies: No. **Golf carts:** Included in Green Fee.
Discount golf packages: No. **Season:** Year-round. **High:** Jan.-April.
On-site lodging: No. **Rental clubs:** Yes.
Walking policy: Mandatory cart. **Range:** Yes (grass).
To obtain tee times: Call two days in advance.
Subscriber comments: Very nice local course, lots of sand . . . Short with much sand and water, good greens . . . Nice . . . Good condition . . . Long with lots of water . . . Treated well . . . Nice, mature course.

★★★½ THE COUNTRY CLUB AT SILVER SPRINGS SHORES
SP—565 Silver Rd., Ocala (904)687-2828.
56 miles northwest of Orlando. **Holes:** 18. **Par:** 72/72.
Yards: 6,857/5,188. **Course rating:** 73.7/70.2. **Slope:** 131/120.
Opened: 1969. **Pace of Play rating:** N/A. **Green fee:** $16/32.
Credit cards: All major. **Reduced fees:** Low season, Twilight.
Caddies: No. **Golf carts:** Included in Green Fee.
Discount golf packages: Yes. **Season:** Year-round. **High:** Dec.-April.
On-site lodging: No. **Rental clubs:** Yes.
Walking policy: Mandatory cart. **Range:** Yes (grass).
To obtain tee times: Call up to seven days in advance.
Subscriber comments: Great greens, U.S. Open qualifying site . . . Best greens I played in '94, very challenging . . . Good shape, fair design, great price . . . Greens bring you to your knees . . . Excellent test, great value, best bang for your buck . . . Excellent greens year-round.

★★★ COUNTRY CLUB OF MOUNT DORA
SP—1900 Country Club Blvd., Mount Dora (904)735-2263.
15 miles northwest of Orlando. **Holes:** 18. **Par:** 72/72.
Yards: 6,612/4,689. **Course rating:** 71.5/67.8. **Slope:** 121/118.
Opened: 1991. **Pace of Play rating:** N/A. **Green fee:** $28/40.
Credit cards: MC, V. **Reduced fees:** Weekdays, Low season, Resort guests, Twilight, Juniors.
Caddies: No. **Golf carts:** Included in Green Fee.
Discount golf packages: Yes. **Season:** Year-round. **High:** Jan.-March.
On-site lodging: No. **Rental clubs:** Yes.
Walking policy: Mandatory cart. **Range:** Yes (grass).
To obtain tee times: Call three days in advance.
Subscriber comments: Good combination of water and sand, nice layout, well maintained, worth the drive . . . Good food and very friendly . . . Beautiful setting . . . Play with someone familiar with course, have to use your head . . . Challenging but not brutal.

THE COURSE AT WESTLAND★
SP—Westland Golf Dr., Jacksonville (904)778-4653.
Holes: 18. **Par:** 71/71.
Yards: 6,347/5,380. **Course rating:** 70.3/71.2. **Slope:** 121/118.
Opened: 1974. **Pace of Play rating:** 4:00. **Green fee:** $23/30.
Credit cards: MC, V, AMEX. **Reduced fees:** Weekdays, Twilight, Juniors.
Caddies: No. **Golf carts:** Included in Green Fee.
Discount golf packages: No. **Season:** Year-round.
On-site lodging: No. **Rental clubs:** Yes.
Walking policy: Mandatory cart. **Range:** Yes (grass).
To obtain tee times: Call up to one week in advance.

CRYSTAL LAKE COUNTRY CLUB
PU—3800 Crystal Lake Dr., Pompano Beach (305)942-1900.
5 miles south of Fort Lauderdale.
Pace of Play rating: 4:30. **Green fee:** $28/48.
Credit cards: MC, V, AMEX. **Reduced fees:** Low season, Twilight.
Caddies: No. **Golf carts:** Included in Green Fee.
Discount golf packages: No. **Season:** Year-round. **High:** Nov.-April.

On-site lodging: No. **Rental clubs:** Yes.
Walking policy: Mandatory cart. **Range:** Yes.
To obtain tee times: Call two days in advance.

★★½ TAM O'SHANTER NORTH COURSE
Holes: 18. **Par:** 70/72.
Yards: 6,390/5,205. **Course rating:** 71.0/70.0. **Slope:** 121/118.
Opened: 1967.
Subscriber comments: Very narrow fairways . . . This is a hidden gem always in great shape . . . Courteous staff.

★★½ SOUTH COURSE
Holes: 18. **Par:** 72/72.
Yards: 6,610/5,458. **Course rating:** 71.7/71.5. **Slope:** 120/121.
Opened: 1963.
Subscriber comments: Average course.

★★½ CYPRESS CREEK COUNTRY CLUB
PU—9400 North Military Trail, Boynton Beach (407)727-4202.
10 miles south of West Palm Beach. **Holes:** 18. **Par:** 72/72.
Yards: 6,808/5,530. **Course rating:** 72.0/71.0. **Slope:** 112/109.
Opened: 1964. **Pace of Play rating:** 4:00. **Green fee:** $20/45.
Credit cards: MC, V. **Reduced fees:** Weekdays, Low season.
Caddies: No. **Golf carts:** Included in Green Fee.
Discount golf packages: Yes. **Season:** Year-round. **High:** Nov.-April.
On-site lodging: No. **Rental clubs:** Yes.
Walking policy: Mandatory cart. **Range:** Yes (grass).
To obtain tee times: Call 24 hours in advance at 7 a.m.
Subscriber comments: Good shape . . . Tight fairways . . . Heavy use.

★★★½ CYPRESS KNOLL GOLF CLUB
SP—53 East Hampton Blvd., Palm Coast (904)437-5807, (800)874-2101.
30 miles north of Daytona Beach. **Holes:** 18. **Par:** 72/72.
Yards: 6,591/5,386. **Course rating:** 71.6/69.3. **Slope:** 130/117.
Opened: 1990. **Pace of Play rating:** N/A. **Green fee:** $39/48.
Credit cards: MC, V. **Reduced fees:** Low season, Resort guests, Twilight, Juniors.
Caddies: No. **Golf carts:** Included in Green Fee.
Discount golf packages: Yes. **Season:** Year-round. **High:** Jan.-April.
On-site lodging: No. **Rental clubs:** Yes.
Walking policy: Mandatory cart. **Range:** Yes (grass).
To obtain tee times: Call up to five days in advance.
Subscriber comments: Tight layout, take a lot of balls . . . Many short holes, but must make good shots . . . Very challenging, lots of water and marshes.

DAYTONA BEACH GOLF COURSE
PU—600 Wilder Blvd., Daytona Beach (904)258-3119.
Pace of Play rating: 4:30. **Green fee:** $10/12.
Credit cards: MC, V. **Reduced fees:** Weekdays, Low season, Twilight.
Caddies: No. **Golf carts:** $7 for 18 holes.
Discount golf packages: No. **Season:** Year-round. **High:** Nov.-May.
On-site lodging: No. **Rental clubs:** No.
Walking policy: Unrestricted walking. **Range:** Yes.
To obtain tee times: Call three days in advance.

★½ NORTH COURSE
Holes: 18. **Par:** 72/72.
Yards: 6,567/5,247. **Course rating:** 71.0/69.1. **Slope:** 111/111.
Opened: 1965.
Subscriber comments: Great visual intimidation . . . Too many opposing fairways with no separation.

★½ SOUTH COURSE
Holes: 18. **Par:** 71/71.
Yards: 6,229/5,346. **Course rating:** 69.7/69.6. **Slope:** 106/106.
Opened: 1921.
Subscriber comments: A great layout for a public course.

★★★DEBARY GOLF AND COUNTRY CLUB

SP—300 Plantation Dr., DeBary (407)668-2061.
15 miles northeast of Orlando. **Holes:** 18. **Par:** 72/72.
Yards: 6,776/5,060. **Course rating:** 72.3/68.8. **Slope:** 128/122.
Opened: 1990. **Pace of Play rating:** 4:12. **Green fee:** $25/38.
Credit cards: MC, V. **Reduced fees:** Low season, Juniors.
Caddies: No. **Golf carts:** Included in Green Fee.
Discount golf packages: Yes. **Season:** Year-round. **High:** Feb.-April.
On-site lodging: No. **Rental clubs:** Yes.
Walking policy: Mandatory cart. **Range:** Yes (grass).
To obtain tee times: Call three days in advance.
Subscriber comments: Holes have a lot of character . . . Rolling hills in Florida? You bet . . . Unique finishing holes.

★½DEEP CREEK GOLF CLUB

SP—1260 San Cristobal Ave., Port Charlotte (813)625-6911.
25 miles north of Fort Myers. **Holes:** 18. **Par:** 70/70.
Yards: 6,005/4,860. **Course rating:** 67.5/68.0. **Slope:** 112/110.
Opened: 1985. **Pace of Play rating:** 4:00. **Green fee:** $16/24.
Credit cards: MC, V. **Reduced fees:** Weekdays, Low season, Twilight, Seniors, Juniors.
Caddies: No. **Golf carts:** $10 for 18 holes.
Discount golf packages: No. **Season:** Year-round. **High:** Dec.-April.
On-site lodging: No. **Rental clubs:** Yes.
Walking policy: Walking at certain times. **Range:** Yes (grass).
To obtain tee times: Call up to 48 hours in advance.
Subscriber comments: For straight hitters . . . Challenging . . . A lot of water . . . Short, fun course.

★★★½DEER CREEK GOLF CLUB

SP—2801 Country Club Blvd., Deerfield Beach (305)421-5550.
6 miles north of Fort Lauderdale. **Holes:** 18. **Par:** 72/72.
Yards: 7,038/5,319. **Course rating:** 74.8/71.6. **Slope:** 133/120.
Opened: 1971. **Pace of Play rating:** N/A. **Green fee:** $35/100.
Credit cards: MC, V, AMEX. **Reduced fees:** Weekdays, Low season, Resort guests, Juniors.
Caddies: No. **Golf carts:** Included in Green Fee.
Discount golf packages: Yes. **Season:** Year-round. **High:** Dec.-April.
On-site lodging: No. **Rental clubs:** Yes.
Walking policy: Mandatory cart. **Range:** Yes (grass).
To obtain tee times: Call 72 hours in advance.
Subscriber comments: Many layup shots required . . . Made $2 million in changes. Still not yet mature.

DEER ISLAND GOLFERS' CLUB★

SP—17450 Deer Island Rd 1, Tavares (904)343-7550.
30 miles southeast of Orlando. **Holes:** 18. **Par:** 72/72.
Yards: 6,676/5,298. **Course rating:** 71.7/71.0. **Slope:** 121/118.
Opened: 1994. **Pace of Play rating:** 4:15. **Green fee:** $25/35.
Credit cards: MC, V. **Reduced fees:** Weekdays, Twilight, Seniors.
Caddies: No. **Golf carts:** Included in Green Fee.
Discount golf packages: Yes. **Season:** Year-round. **High:**Oct.-March.
On-site lodging: No. **Rental clubs:** Yes.
Walking policy: Mandatory cart. **Range:** Yes (grass).
To obtain tee times: Call seven days in advance.

★★½DEERFIELD LAKES GOLF COURSE

PU—Lem Turner Rd., Callahan (904)879-1210.
8 miles northwest of Jacksonville. **Holes:** 18. **Par:** 72/74.
Yards: 6,700/5,266. **Course rating:** 70.2/69.0. **Slope:** 114/102.
Opened: N/A. **Pace of Play rating:** 4:00. **Green fee:** $16/25.
Credit cards: MC, V. **Reduced fees:** Weekdays.
Caddies: No. **Golf carts:** Included in Green Fee.
Discount golf packages: No. **Season:** Year-round. **High:** May-Sept.
On-site lodging: No. **Rental clubs:** Yes.

FRUGAL PICK

Walking policy: Walking at certain times. **Range:** Yes (grass).
To obtain tee times: Call for weekend tee times.
Subscriber comments: New management made lots of improvements
. . . Nice little course.

★★★ DELRAY BEACH GOLF CLUB
PU—2200 Highland Ave., Delray Beach (407)243-7380.
18 miles south of West Palm Beach. **Holes:** 18. **Par:** 72/72.
Yards: 6,907/5,189. **Course rating:** 73.0/69.8. **Slope:** 126/117.
Opened: 1923. **Pace of Play rating:** N/A. **Green fee:** $16/37.
Credit cards: MC, V. **Reduced fees:** Low season, Juniors.
Caddies: No. **Golf carts:** Included in Green Fee.
Discount golf packages: No. **Season:** Year-round. **High:** Dec.-March.
On-site lodging: No. **Rental clubs:** Yes.
Walking policy: Walking at certain times. **Range:** Yes (grass).
To obtain tee times: Call two days in advance at 6:30 a.m.
Subscriber comments: Good layout . . . Flat course, no trouble . . . Old
Donald Ross course, refurbished recently.

★★★ DELTONA HILLS GOLF AND COUNTRY CLUB
SP—1120 Elkcam Blvd., Deltona (904)789-4911.
28 miles west of Orlando. **Holes:** 18. **Par:** 72/73.
Yards: 6,892/5,668. **Course rating:** 72.7/72.5. **Slope:** 125/125.
Opened: 1962. **Pace of Play rating:** 4:00. **Green fee:** $21/40.
Credit cards: MC, V. **Reduced fees:** Weekdays, Low season, Resort
guests, Twilight, Juniors.
Caddies: No. **Golf carts:** Included in Green Fee.
Discount golf packages: No. **Season:** Year-round. **High:** Jan.-April.
On-site lodging: No. **Rental clubs:** Yes.
Walking policy: Walking at certain times. **Range:** Yes (grass).
To obtain tee times: Call two days in advance.
Subscriber comments: A mountain course in central Florida . . . Nice
doglegs, good for all golfers . . . Love the sidehill lies . . . New England-
type course . . . Great layout.

DIAMONDBACK GOLF CLUB★
SP—6501 S.R. 544 East, Haines City (813)421-0437.
Holes: 18. **Par:** 72/72.
Yards: 6,805/5,061. **Course rating:** 73.3/70.3. **Slope:** 138/122.
Opened: 1995. **Pace of Play rating:** 4:00. **Green fee:** $42/52.
Credit cards: All major. **Reduced fees:** Weekdays, Twilight, Juniors.
Caddies: No. **Golf carts:** Included in Green Fee.
Discount golf packages: Yes. **Season:** Year-round. **High:** Oct.-March.
On-site lodging: No. **Rental clubs:** Yes.
Walking policy: Mandatory cart. **Range:** Yes (grass).
To obtain tee times: Call seven days in advance.

DIPLOMAT COUNTRY CLUB★
PU—501 Diplomat Pkwy., Hallandale (305)457-2080.
15 miles south of Fort Lauderdale. **Holes:** 18. **Par:** 72/72.
Yards: 6,700/5,400. **Course rating:** 70.6/69.3. **Slope:** 115/110.
Opened: 1957. **Pace of Play rating:** N/A. **Green fee:** $12/38.
Credit cards: MC, V, DISC. **Reduced fees:** Low season.
Caddies: No. **Golf carts:** Included in Green Fee.
Discount golf packages: No. **Season:** Year-round. **High:** Dec.-March.
On-site lodging: No. **Rental clubs:** Yes.
Walking policy: Mandatory cart. **Range:** Yes (grass).
To obtain tee times: Call.
Subscriber comments: Very old course . . . Lots of seniors.

★★ DODGER PINES COUNTRY CLUB
SP—4600 26th St., Vero Beach (407)569-4400.
60 miles north of West Palm Beach. **Holes:** 18. **Par:** 73/74.
Yards: 6,692/5,776. **Course rating:** 71.2/72.3. **Slope:** 122/124.

Opened: 1971. **Pace of Play rating:** N/A. **Green fee:** $14/40.
Credit cards: MC, V, AMEX. **Reduced fees:** Weekdays, Low season, Twilight.
Caddies: No. **Golf carts:** $12 for 18 holes.
Discount golf packages: No. **Season:** Year-round. **High:** Jan.-April.
On-site lodging: No. **Rental clubs:** Yes.
Walking policy: Walking at certain times. **Range:** Yes (grass).
To obtain tee times: Call two days in advance.
Subscriber comments: A very unusual par-6 hole! . . . Front nine goofy with canal in middle of fairway.

★★DON SHULA'S GOLF CLUB
PU—7601 Miami Lakes Dr., Miami Lakes (305)821-1150x3306.
Holes: 18. **Par:** 72/72.
Yards: 7,055/5,639. **Course rating:** 73.0/70.5. **Slope:** 124/120.
Opened: 1963. **Pace of Play rating:** 3:30-4:00. **Green fee:** $32/52.
Credit cards: All major. **Reduced fees:** Weekdays, Low season, Resort guests, Twilight.
Caddies: No. **Golf carts:** $18 for 18 holes.
Discount golf packages: Yes. **Season:** Year-round. **High:** Jan.-April.
On-site lodging: Yes. **Rental clubs:** Yes.
Walking policy: Walking at certain times. **Range:** Yes (grass).
To obtain tee times: Call.
Subscriber comments: Good for all types of players . . . Varied layout, never gets boring.

DORAL GOLF RESORT AND SPA
R—4400 N.W. 87th Ave., Miami (305)592-2000 x 2105, (800)713-6725.
Opened: 1961. **Pace of Play rating:** 4:15.
Credit cards: All major. **Reduced fees:** Low season, Resort guests, Twilight.
Caddies: Yes. **Golf carts:** Included in Green Fee.
Discount golf packages: Yes. **Season:** Year-round. **High:** Oct.-April.
On-site lodging: Yes. **Rental clubs:** Yes.
Walking policy: Walking at certain times. **Range:** Yes (grass).
To obtain tee times: Resort guests may make tee times at time of reservation. Non-guests call one day in advance.

★★★★BLUE COURSE
Holes: 18. **Par:** 72/72.
Yards: 6,939/5,786. **Course rating:** 73.2/73.0. **Slope:** 127/124.
Green fee: $50/150.
Ranked 42nd in America's 75 Best Resort Courses by Golf Digest. Ranked 10th in Florida by Golf Digest.
Subscriber comments: A challenge . . . Beautiful! . . . Solid golf holes from 1 to 18 . . . For average to good players only . . . A classic; caddies in season a nice option . . . Reputation better than reality . . . Raymond Floyd's company coming in to restore and upgrade this long time Tour classic . . . Tough to score when the winds blow, and they always seem to blow hard here.

★★★½GOLD COURSE
Holes: 18. **Par:** 70/70.
Yards: 6,361/5,422. **Course rating:** 70.6/71.4. **Slope:** 127/123.
Green fee: $50/125.
Subscriber comments: As much fun as Blue . . . Need good long game . . . Need to think.

★★RED COURSE
Holes: 18. **Par:** 71/71.
Yards: 6,210/5,254. **Course rating:** 69.9/70.6. **Slope:** 118/118.
Green fee: $50/125.
Subscriber comments: Fun course to play . . . Big letdown after Blue and Gold . . . Fair, watch the water.

★★★WHITE COURSE
Holes: 18. **Par:** 72/72.
Yards: 6,208/5,286. **Course rating:** 69.7/70.1. **Slope:** 117/116.
Green fee: $50/125.
Subscriber comments: Short, water, tight fairways, good course.

DORAL PARK GOLF AND COUNTRY CLUB
★★★½ **SILVER COURSE**
SP—5001 NW 104th Ave., Miami (305)594-0954.
Holes: 18. **Par:** 71/71.
Yards: 6,614/4,661. **Course rating:** 72.0/66.6. **Slope:** 129/113.
Opened: 1984. **Pace of Play rating:** 4:00. **Green fee:** $53/63.
Credit cards: MC, V, AMEX. **Reduced fees:** Weekdays, Low season, Resort guests.
Caddies: No. **Golf carts:** Included in Green Fee.
Discount golf packages: No. **Season:** Year-round. **High:** Jan.-April.
On-site lodging: No. **Rental clubs:** Yes.
Walking policy: Mandatory cart. **Range:** Yes.
To obtain tee times: Call two days in advance.
Subscriber comments: Long, tight track . . . Tough course, keep it out of the rough . . . Many carries over water.

★ DOUG FORD'S LACUNA GOLF CLUB
SP—6400 Grand Lacuna Blvd., Lake Worth (407)433-3006.
5 miles southwest of West Palm Beach. **Holes:** 18. **Par:** 71/71.
Yards: 6,700/5,119. **Course rating:** N/A. **Slope:** 121/111.
Opened: N/A. **Pace of Play rating:** N/A. **Green fee:** N/A.
Credit cards: MC, V. **Reduced fees:** Low season.
Caddies: No. **Golf carts:** N/A.
Discount golf packages: No. **Season:** Year-round. **High:** Nov.-May.
On-site lodging: No. **Rental clubs:** No.
Walking policy: N/A. **Range:** Yes (grass).
Subscriber comments: Excellent layout for left-to-right player (like me) . . . Would be very good if properly kept up . . . Secluded, beautifully kept tree-lined fairways, lots of water.

★★½ DUNEDIN COUNTRY CLUB
SP—1050 Palm Blvd., Dunedin (813)733-7836.
20 miles northwest of Tampa. **Holes:** 18. **Par:** 72/73.
Yards: 6,565/5,726. **Course rating:** 70.3/73.1. **Slope:** 115/121.
Opened: 1928. **Pace of Play rating:** 4:30. **Green fee:** $33/41.
Credit cards: None. **Reduced fees:** Low season, Twilight.
Caddies: No. **Golf carts:** Included in Green Fee.
Discount golf packages: No. **Season:** Year-round. **High:** Dec.-April.
On-site lodging: No. **Rental clubs:** Yes.
Walking policy: Walking at certain times. **Range:** Yes (grass).
To obtain tee times: Call two days in advance.
Subscriber comments: First four holes are torture . . . Old Donald Ross course with brand-new greens, awesome! . . . Good test for long hitters.

★★★★ EAGLE HARBOR GOLF CLUB
SP—2217 Eagle Harbor Pkwy., Orange Park (904)269-9300.
10 miles south of Jacksonville. **Holes:** 18. **Par:** 72/72.
Yards: 6,840/4,980. **Course rating:** 72.6/68.2. **Slope:** 133/121.
Opened: 1993. **Pace of Play rating:** N/A. **Green fee:** $32/40.
Credit cards: MC, V. **Reduced fees:** Weekdays, Twilight, Juniors.
Caddies: No. **Golf carts:** Included in Green Fee.
Discount golf packages: Yes. **Season:** Year-round. **High:** April-June.
On-site lodging: No. **Rental clubs:** Yes.
Walking policy: Walking at certain times. **Range:** Yes (grass).
To obtain tee times: Call two days in advance.
Subscriber comments: New course, excellent condition, good for all types of players . . . Real test of golf, play it before community is built up . . . Left nature in place . . . Needs some maturing, but good layout . . . Wide fairways, large greens.

THE EAGLES GOLF CLUB
★★★ **FOREST/LAKES/OAKS**
SP—16101 Nine Eagles Dr., Odessa (813)920-6681.
10 miles west of Tampa. **Holes:** 27. **Par:** 72/72/72.

Yards: 7,134/7,194/7,068. **Course rating:** 70.3/70.3/70.3. **Slope:** 130/130/130.
Opened: 1973. **Pace of Play rating:** 4:00. **Green fee:** $32/45.
Credit cards: MC, V. **Reduced fees:** Weekdays, Low season, Twilight.
Caddies: No. **Golf carts:** Included in Green Fee.
Discount golf packages: No. **Season:** Year-round. **High:** Jan.–April.
On-site lodging: No. **Rental clubs:** Yes.
Walking policy: Walking at certain times. **Range:** Yes (grass).
To obtain tee times: Call up to four days in advance.
Subscriber comments: Truly enjoyable 27 holes . . . Can't wait for final nine to be completed . . . Top notch, affordable, accuracy important . . . Good course especially Oaks, Forest . . . Drains very slowly . . . Tough but fair, staff very nice . . . Forest most interesting.

★★★½ EASTWOOD GOLF CLUB
PU—13950 Golfway Blvd., Orlando (407)281-4653.
Holes: 18. **Par:** 72/72.
Yards: 7,176/5,393. **Course rating:** 73.9/70.5. **Slope:** 124/117.
Opened: 1989. **Pace of Play rating:** 4:15. **Green fee:** $20/48.
Credit cards: MC, V. **Reduced fees:** Weekdays, Low season, Resort guests, Twilight, Juniors.
Caddies: No. **Golf carts:** Included in Green Fee.
Discount golf packages: Yes. **Season:** Year-round. **High:** Jan.–April.
On-site lodging: No. **Rental clubs:** Yes.
Walking policy: Mandatory cart. **Range:** Yes (grass).
To obtain tee times: Call seven days in advance.
Subscriber comments: Best greens in Orlando . . . Challenging, but fair and superbly maintained . . . Excellent, long layout, very challenging, but you can bail out from bad shots . . . Used every club in the bag.

★★★½ EASTWOOD GOLF COURSE
PU—4600 Bruce Herd Lane, Fort Myers (813)275-4848.
Holes: 18. **Par:** 72/72.
Yards: 6,772/5,116. **Course rating:** 73.3/68.9. **Slope:** 130/120.
Opened: 1977. **Pace of Play rating:** N/A. **Green fee:** $28/47.
Credit cards: MC, V. **Reduced fees:** Weekdays, Low season, Twilight.
Caddies: No. **Golf carts:** Included in Green Fee.
Discount golf packages: No. **Season:** Year-round. **High:** Dec.–March.
On-site lodging: No. **Rental clubs:** Yes.
Walking policy: Walking at certain times. **Range:** Yes (grass).
To obtain tee times: Call one day in advance at 8 a.m.
Ranked in Second 25 of America's 75 Best Public Golf Courses by Golf Digest.
Subscriber comments: Very narrow fairways . . . Course is long and not suited for walkers or beginners . . . For a public course much nicer than many private courses.

★★★ EKANA GOLF CLUB
SP—2100 Ekana Dr., Oviedo (407)366-1211.
10 miles northeast of Orlando. **Holes:** 18. **Par:** 72/72.
Yards: 6,683/5,544. **Course rating:** 72.0/72.1. **Slope:** 130/128.
Opened: 1989. **Pace of Play rating:** N/A. **Green fee:** $22/49.
Credit cards: MC, V. **Reduced fees:** Weekdays, Low season, Twilight.
Caddies: No. **Golf carts:** Included in Green Fee.
Discount golf packages: Yes. **Season:** Year-round. **High:** Jan.–April.
On-site lodging: No. **Rental clubs:** Yes.
Walking policy: Mandatory cart. **Range:** Yes (grass).
To obtain tee times: Call four days in advance.
Subscriber comments: Has some holes you have to be a pro to birdie . . . Serious drainage problems in rainy season . . . Long distances between tees and greens . . . Nice challenge with a variety of holes.

★★★★ EMERALD BAY GOLF COURSE
SP—40001 Emerald Coast Pkwy., Destin (904)837-5197.
15 miles east of Fort Walton Beach. **Holes:** 18. **Par:** 72/72.

Yards: 6,802/5,184. **Course rating:** 73.1/70.1. **Slope:** 135/122.
Opened: 1991. **Pace of Play rating:** 4:00. **Green fee:** $40/75.
Credit cards: MC, V, AMEX. **Reduced fees:** Weekdays, Low season, Resort guests, Juniors.
Caddies: No. **Golf carts:** Included in Green Fee.
Discount golf packages: No. **Season:** Year-round. **High:** March-Nov.
On-site lodging: No. **Rental clubs:** Yes.
Walking policy: Mandatory cart. **Range:** Yes (grass).
To obtain tee times: Call two weeks in advance.
Subscriber comments: Beautiful but flat layout, few trees . . . Large, open course where wind comes into play . . . Staff made you feel welcome . . . Difficult but fair.

★★★★½ EMERALD DUNES GOLF CLUB

PU—2100 Emerald Dunes Dr., West Palm Beach (407)684-4653x1.
Holes: 18. **Par:** 72/72.
Yards: 7,006/4,676. **Course rating:** 73.8/67.1. **Slope:** 133/115.
Opened: 1990. **Pace of Play rating:** 4:15. **Green fee:** $65/125.
Credit cards: All major. **Reduced fees:** Low season, Twilight, Juniors.
Caddies: No. **Golf carts:** Included in Green Fee.
Discount golf packages: No. **Season:** Year-round. **High:** Nov.-April.
On-site lodging: No. **Rental clubs:** Yes.
Walking policy: Mandatory cart. **Range:** Yes (grass).
To obtain tee times: Call and secure with credit card.

Ranked 28th in Florida by Golf Digest.
Subscriber comments: Always interesting . . . Prettiest course I ever played in Florida . . . Timer on cart insures fast play . . . Excellent Fazio course, well maintained . . . Plush, plush, pricey, pricey . . . Awesome golf course . . . Super test of golf . . . Very good-looking course, great design.

★★★ FAIRWINDS GOLF COURSE

PU—4400 Fairwinds Dr., Fort Pierce (407)466-4653, (800)894-1781.
40 miles north of West Palm Beach. **Holes:** 18. **Par:** 72/72.
Yards: 6,783/5,392. **Course rating:** 71.1/68.5. **Slope:** 119/112.
Opened: 1991. **Pace of Play rating:** 4:12. **Green fee:** $20/32.
Credit cards: MC, V. **Reduced fees:** Low season, Juniors.
Caddies: No. **Golf carts:** Included in Green Fee.
Discount golf packages: No. **Season:** Year-round. **High:** Jan.-April.
On-site lodging: No. **Rental clubs:** Yes.
Walking policy: Walking at certain times. **Range:** Yes (grass).
To obtain tee times: Call 48 hours in advance.
Subscriber comments: Great test from the tips. Fun from the front . . . Inclined to be wet. Drainage not up to snuff . . . Very forgiving. Wide fairways.

★★★½ FALCON'S FIRE GOLF CLUB

PU—3200 Seralago Blvd., Kissimmee (407)239-5445.
6 miles south of Orlando. **Holes:** 18. **Par:** 72/72.
Yards: 6,901/5,417. **Course rating:** 72.5/70.4. **Slope:** 125/118.
Opened: 1993. **Pace of Play rating:** 4:00. **Green fee:** $45/74.
Credit cards: MC, V, AMEX. **Reduced fees:** Low season, Twilight, Juniors.
Caddies: No. **Golf carts:** Included in Green Fee.
Discount golf packages: No. **Season:** Year-round. **High:** Jan.-April.
On-site lodging: No. **Rental clubs:** Yes.
Walking policy: Mandatory cart. **Range:** Yes (grass).
To obtain tee times: Call seven days in advance. Groups may call up to six months in advance.
Subscriber comments: Very interesting course, back nine great . . . Four holes wrap around lake . . . Very playable, first class, all the amenities . . . Friendliest staff in central Florida . . . Tourist trap, twice the price for half the golf . . . Great practice facility . . . Stays dry even in rain.

FERNANDINA BEACH MUNICIPAL GOLF COURSE
★★½ NORTH/WEST/SOUTH

PU—2800 Bill Melton Rd., Fernandina Beach (904)277-7370.
35 miles northeast of Jacksonville. **Holes:** 27. **Par:** 72/71/73.
Yards: 6,803/6,412/7,027. **Course rating:** 71.5/69.7/72.6.
Slope: 118/121/123.
Opened: 1954. **Pace of Play rating:** N/A. **Green fee:** $14/17.
Credit cards: None. **Reduced fees:** Weekdays, Juniors.
Caddies: No. **Golf carts:** $9 for 18 holes.
Discount golf packages: No. **Season:** Year-round. **High:** Year-round.
On-site lodging: No. **Rental clubs:** Yes.
Walking policy: Walking at certain times. **Range:** Yes (grass).
To obtain tee times: Call three days in advance.
Subscriber comments: Long, tree-lined . . . Great course for beginner, no
rushing . . . Three nines very different . . . West, long; South, tight . . .
Plenty of forest, live oaks, pines and palms. Good staff and service. Well
worn . . . Not maintained as well as desired . . . Excellent greens. Suited
for good putters.

FONTAINEBLEAU GOLF COURSE
PU—9603 Fontainebleau Blvd., Miami (305)221-5181.
Pace of Play rating: 4:10. **Green fee:** $20/32.
Credit cards: MC, V, AMEX. **Reduced fees:** Weekdays, Low season,
Resort guests, Twilight.
Caddies: No. **Golf carts:** Included in Green Fee.
Discount golf packages: Yes. **Season:** Year-round. **High:** Nov.-April.
On-site lodging: No. **Rental clubs:** Yes.
Walking policy: Mandatory cart. **Range:** Yes.
To obtain tee times: Call up to two weeks in advance.
★½ EAST COURSE
Holes: 18. **Par:** 72/72.
Yards: 7,035/5,586. **Course rating:** 73.3/71.5. **Slope:** 122/119.
Opened: 1969.
★½ WEST COURSE
Holes: 18. **Par:** 72/72.
Yards: 6,944/5,565. **Course rating:** 72.5/71.0. **Slope:** 120/118.
Opened: 1976.

FOREST LAKE GOLF CLUB OF OCOEE★
PU—10521 Clarcona-Ocoee Rd., Ocoee (407)654-4653.
14 miles west of Orlando. **Holes:** 18. **Par:** 72/72.

Yards: 7,083/5,103. **Course rating:** 73.6/69.2. **Slope:** 127/113.
Opened: 1994. **Pace of Play rating:** 4:00. **Green fee:** $23/40.
Credit cards: MC, V. **Reduced fees:** Weekdays, Low season, Twilight,
Juniors.
Caddies: No. **Golf carts:** Included in Green Fee.
Discount golf packages: Yes. **Season:** Year-round.
On-site lodging: No. **Rental clubs:** Yes.
Walking policy: Mandatory cart. **Range:** Yes (grass).
To obtain tee times: Call five days in advance.

★★ FOREST LAKES COUNTRY CLUB
PU—2401 Beneva Rd., Sarasota (813)924-1221.
Call club for further information.
Subscriber comments: Great old course. Homes very close . . . Narrow,
small greens, fairly short . . . Short and wide open, fire away . . . From
good to better after new management.

★★½ FORT MYERS COUNTRY CLUB
PU—3591 McGregor Blvd., Fort Myers (813)936-2457.
120 miles south of Tampa. **Holes:** 18. **Par:** 71/71.
Yards: 6,414/5,135. **Course rating:** N/A. **Slope:** 118/117.
Opened: N/A. **Pace of Play rating:** N/A. **Green fee:** N/A.
Credit cards: N/A. **Reduced fees:** Weekdays, Low season, Twilight.
Caddies: No. **Golf carts:** N/A.

Discount golf packages: No. **Season:** Year-round. **High:** Dec.-April.
On-site lodging: No. **Rental clubs:** No.
Walking policy: N/A. **Range:** Yes (grass).
Subscriber comments: Great old Donald Ross course . . . Recent renovation only made it better . . . Small greens make it a test, older players predominantly . . . Flat but challenging . . . Boring golf, everything is driver, short iron . . . You can walk! . . . Lots of sand at greens . . . A stream runs through when you least expect it.

FORT WALTON BEACH MUNICIPAL GOLF COURSE
PU—(904)862-3922. 50 miles east of Pensacola.
Pace of Play rating: 4:00-4:30. **Green fee:** $15.
Credit cards: None. **Reduced fees:** Twilight.
Caddies: No. **Golf carts:** N/A.
Season: Year-round. **High:** Feb.-Aug.
On-site lodging: No. **Rental clubs:** Yes.
Walking policy: Unrestricted walking. **Range:** Yes (grass).
To obtain tee times: Outside 400-mile radius, may call up to two months in advance.

★★½ OAKS COURSE
1909 Lewis Turner Blvd., Fort Walton Beach.
Holes: 18. **Par:** 72/72.
Yards: 6,409/5,366. **Course rating:** 70.2/67.8. **Slope:** 119/107.
Opened: 1993. **Discount golf packages:** Yes.
Subscriber comments: Player friendly, good place for confidence building . . . Very flat, too easy . . . Front side very tight. Back side very fair . . . Lots of trees, never backed up, always tee times available . . . Easy to walk, fairly crowded year-round.

★★½ PINES COURSE
699 Country Club Dr., Fort Walton Beach.
Holes: 18. **Par:** 72/72.
Yards: 6,802/5,320. **Course rating:** 69.9/69.1. **Slope:** 110/107.
Opened: 1961. **Discount golf packages:** No.
Subscriber comments: Short and tight . . . Very flat . . . Harder of two municipal courses, no trees, wide-open fairways. Fun . . . Rolling terrain in areas. Fun but not a terrific challenge . . . Easy to walk, fairly crowded year-round.

★★★½ FOX HOLLOW GOLF CLUB
PU—10050 Robert Trent Jones Pkwy., New Port Richey (813)376-6333, (800)943-1902.
25 miles northwest of Tampa. **Holes:** 18. **Par:** 71/71.
Yards: 7,138/4,454. **Course rating:** 74.3/65.7. **Slope:** 137/112.
Opened: 1994. **Pace of Play rating:** 4:15. **Green fee:** $32/53.
Credit cards: All major. **Reduced fees:** Weekdays, Low season, Juniors.
Caddies: No. **Golf carts:** Included in Green Fee.
Discount golf packages: Yes. **Season:** Year-round. **High:** Jan.-March.
On-site lodging: No. **Rental clubs:** Yes.
Walking policy: Unrestricted walking. **Range:** Yes (grass).
To obtain tee times: Call up to four days in advance. Groups of eight or more may call up to one year in advance.
Subscriber comments: Nice new layout with six sets of tees to alter course length . . . Well designed, maintained . . . Long, subject to wind from many directions . . . Brutal from backs . . . Fantastic course . . . Beautiful and challenging. You would expect to pay more . . . Difficult.

FOXFIRE GOLF CLUB
★ PINE/PALM/OAK
SP—7200 Proctor Rd., Sarasota (813)921-7757.
50 miles north of Tampa. **Holes:** 27. **Par:** 72/72/72.
Yards: 6,213/6,280/6,101. **Course rating:** 69.8/70.0/69.8. **Slope:** N/A.
Opened: 1975. **Pace of Play rating:** N/A. **Green fee:** $16/45.
Credit cards: MC, V. **Reduced fees:** Low season, Twilight, Juniors.
Caddies: No. **Golf carts:** Included in Green Fee.
Discount golf packages: No. **Season:** Year-round. **High:** Jan.-March.

On-site lodging: No. **Rental clubs:** Yes.
Walking policy: Unrestricted walking. **Range:** Yes (grass).
To obtain tee times: Call anytime three days in advance.
Subscriber comments: Nice layout, some rough areas . . . Poor
maintenance destroys a good layout . . . Naturally preserved, three fine
nine-hole courses . . . Uninspiring course in mediocre condition.

★ FOXWOOD COUNTRY CLUB
SP—4927 Antioch Rd., Crestview (904)682-2012.
40 miles east of Pensacola. **Holes:** 18. **Par:** 72/72.
Yards: 6,210/5,070. **Course rating:** 71.0/69.5. **Slope:** 113/113.
Opened: 1962. **Pace of Play rating:** 3:45. **Green fee:** $8/11.
Credit cards: MC, V. **Reduced fees:** Weekdays, Low season, Twilight.
Caddies: Yes. **Golf carts:** N/A.
Discount golf packages: No. **Season:** Year-round. **High:** Jan.-March.
On-site lodging: No. **Rental clubs:** Yes.
Walking policy: Walking at certain times. **Range:** Yes (grass).
To obtain tee times: Call anytime seven days in advance.
Subscriber comments: Excellent course for all golfers . . . Staff good,
condition of course fair; very short . . . This is the little engine that is trying
. . . Course looks old and outdated.

GADSDEN GOLF AND COUNTRY CLUB★
SP—Solomon Dairy Rd., Quincy (904)627-9631.
20 miles northwest of Tallahassee. **Holes:** 18. **Par:** 72/72.
Yards: 6,642/5,398. **Course rating:** 71.2/70.3. **Slope:** 121/117.
Opened: 1968. **Pace of Play rating:** 4:00. **Green fee:** $13/17.
Credit cards: MC, V. **Reduced fees:** Weekdays.
Caddies: No. **Golf carts:** $11 for 18 holes.
Discount golf packages: No. **Season:** Year-round.
On-site lodging: No. **Rental clubs:** Yes.
Walking policy: Unrestricted walking. **Range:** Yes (grass).
To obtain tee times: Call.

★★★½ GATEWAY GOLF AND COUNTRY CLUB
SP—11360 Championship Dr., Fort Myers (813)561-1010.
Holes: 18. **Par:** 72/72.
Yards: 6,974/5,323. **Course rating:** 73.7/70.6. **Slope:** 130/120.
Opened: 1989. **Pace of Play rating:** 4:33. **Green fee:** $60/90.
Credit cards: MC, V, AMEX. **Reduced fees:** Low season, Twilight.
Caddies: No. **Golf carts:** Included in Green Fee.
Discount golf packages: No. **Season:** Year-round. **High:** Jan.-March.
On-site lodging: No. **Rental clubs:** Yes.
Walking policy: Mandatory cart. **Range:** Yes (grass).
To obtain tee times: Call two days in advance.
Subscriber comments: Tough Fazio design . . . Very nice open links . . .
Lot of fairway bunkers . . . Newer course, open, demanding, wonderful
greens! . . . When mature, will be one of the best . . . Wide fairways . . .
Southwest Florida Seniors hold many tournaments here.

★★ GATOR TRACE GOLF AND COUNTRY CLUB
SP—4302 Gator Trace Drive, Fort Pierce (407)468-4653.
Call club for further information.
Subscriber comments: Many hazards . . . Interesting course with lots of
water . . . Short course, good for seniors . . . Course has to be played with
5-irons through condos, yuk! . . . Tough course, there are only two straight
holes on it.

★½ GOLDEN GATE COUNTRY CLUB
R—4100 Golden Gate Pkwy., Naples (813)455-9498, (800)277-0017.
Holes: 18. **Par:** 72/72.
Yards: 6,570/5,374. **Course rating:** 70.8/70.3. **Slope:** 125/123.
Opened: 1964. **Pace of Play rating:** N/A. **Green fee:** $14/35.
Credit cards: All major. **Reduced fees:** Low season, Resort guests,
Twilight, Juniors.

Caddies: No. **Golf carts:** $15 for 18 holes.
Discount golf packages: Yes. **Season:** Year-round. **High:** Nov.–April.
On-site lodging: Yes. **Rental clubs:** Yes.
Walking policy: Walking at certain times. **Range:** Yes (grass).
To obtain tee times: Public call 48 hours in advance. Hotel guests, at time of reservation.

Subscriber comments: Pretty open, nice shape.

★★★½ GOLDEN OCALA GOLF COURSE
PU—7300 U.S. Hwy. 27 N.W., Ocala (904)622-0198, (800)251-7674.
85 miles north of Orlando. **Holes:** 18. **Par:** 72/72.
Yards: 6,735/5,595. **Course rating:** 72.2/72.2. **Slope:** 132/124.
Opened: 1986. **Pace of Play rating:** 4:30. **Green fee:** $48.
Credit cards: MC, V. **Reduced fees:** Low season, Twilight.
Caddies: No. **Golf carts:** Included in Green Fee.
Discount golf packages: Yes. **Season:** Year-round. **High:** Nov.–April.
On-site lodging: No. **Rental clubs:** Yes.
Walking policy: Mandatory cart. **Range:** Yes (grass).
To obtain tee times: Call one week in advance.
Ranked in Third 25 of America's 75 Best Public Courses by Golf Digest.
Subscriber comments: Replica holes let you play Amen Corner here . . .
Great fun . . . Good idea but no amenities at all! . . . Great fun playing holes
that have historic value . . . Known for replica holes but the others are
superb as well . . . Beautiful layout and poor condition . . . For the $,
closest to St. Andrews I will get . . . Replica holes of Augusta, Troon,
St. Andrews, etc. . . . Replica holes next best thing to being there . . . A
masterpiece that has gone way downhill.

★★★ THE GOLF CLUB AT CYPRESS CREEK
SP—880 Cypress Village Blvd., Ruskin (813)634-8888.
20 miles south of Tampa. **Holes:** 18. **Par:** 72/72.
Yards: 6,839/N/A. **Course rating:** 74.0/66.6. **Slope:** 133/114.
Opened: 1988. **Pace of Play rating:** 4:20. **Green fee:** $20/34.
Credit cards: MC, V. **Reduced fees:** Weekdays, Low season, Resort
guests, Twilight, Seniors.
Caddies: No. **Golf carts:** Included in Green Fee.
Discount golf packages: Yes. **Season:** Year-round. **High:** Feb.–April.
On-site lodging: No. **Rental clubs:** Yes.
Walking policy: Mandatory cart. **Range:** Yes (grass).
To obtain tee times: Call one week in advance.
Also 18-hole executive Upper Creek Course.
Subscriber comments: Tight driving with undulating greens . . . Tough
course, very scenic.

★★★½ THE GOLF CLUB AT CYPRESS HEAD
PU—6231 Palm Vista St., Port Orange (904)756-5449.
5 miles south of Daytona Beach. **Holes:** 18. **Par:** 72/72.
Yards: 6,814/4,909. **Course rating:** 72.4/68.3. **Slope:** 133/116.
Opened: 1992. **Pace of Play rating:** 4:15. **Green fee:** $30/36.
Credit cards: MC, V. **Reduced fees:** Resort guests, Twilight, Juniors.
Caddies: No. **Golf carts:** Included in Green Fee.
Discount golf packages: Yes. **Season:** Year-round. **High:** Feb.–April.
On-site lodging: No. **Rental clubs:** Yes.
Walking policy: Walking at certain times. **Range:** Yes (grass).
To obtain tee times: Call up to three days in advance.
Subscriber comments: Well groomed, good pace . . . Great value for a
muny, beautiful natural scrub areas retained . . . More people should know
about this place . . . Open and windy; good staff and service . . . Best
around for all handicappers . . . Good for long-ball hitters.

★★★½ THE GOLF CLUB AT MARCO
R—3433 Marriott Club Dr., Naples (813)793-6060.
Holes: 18. **Par:** 72/72.
Yards: 6,898/5,416. **Course rating:** 73.4/70.9. **Slope:** 137/122.

Opened: 1991. **Pace of Play rating:** 4:30. **Green fee:** $35/90.
Credit cards: All major. **Reduced fees:** Juniors.
Caddies: No. **Golf carts:** $12 for 18 holes.
Discount golf packages: Yes. **Season:** Year-round. **High:** Jan.-April.
On-site lodging: Yes. **Rental clubs:** Yes.
Walking policy: Mandatory cart. **Range:** Yes (grass).
To obtain tee times: Call 48 hours in advance. Marriott Resort guests may
call 30 days in advance.
Subscriber comments: Nice, tight course . . . Mosquitos! . . . Good
layout but don't play in summer (bugs and wet) . . . Several spectacular
holes . . . Good for seniors.

THE GOLF CLUB OF AMELIA ISLAND★
R—4700 Amelia Island Pkwy., Amelia Island (904)277-8015.
30 miles north of Jacksonville. **Holes:** 18. **Par:** 72/72.
Yards: 6,681/5,039. **Course rating:** 71.7/70.6. **Slope:** 127/122.
Opened: 1987. **Pace of Play rating:** 4:15. **Green fee:** $80.
Credit cards: MC, V, AMEX. **Reduced fees:** Low season, Resort guests,
Twilight, Seniors, Juniors.
Caddies: No. **Golf carts:** Included in Green Fee.
Discount golf packages: Yes. **Season:** Year-round. **High:** May-Sept.
On-site lodging: Yes. **Rental clubs:** Yes.

Walking policy: Mandatory cart. **Range:** Yes (grass).
To obtain tee times: Call.
Subscriber comments: Excellent condition, natural beauty . . . Fun, but
pricey but it's the Ritz's course . . . Friendly staff and fast greens . . . Ritz
Carlton accommodations exceptional . . . Very scenic. Well maintained.
Uncrowded.

★★★½ GOLF CLUB OF JACKSONVILLE
PU—10440 Tournament Lane, Jacksonville (904)779-0800.
Holes: 18. **Par:** 71/71.
Yards: 6,620/5,021. **Course rating:** 70.7/68.0. **Slope:** 120/115.
Opened: 1989. **Pace of Play rating:** N/A. **Green fee:** $21/35.
Credit cards: MC, V, AMEX. **Reduced fees:** Weekdays, Twilight,
Seniors, Juniors.
Caddies: No. **Golf carts:** Included in Green Fee.
Discount golf packages: No. **Season:** Year-round. **High:** March-June.
On-site lodging: No. **Rental clubs:** Yes.
Walking policy: Walking at certain times. **Range:** Yes (grass).
To obtain tee times: Call three days in advance. For Saturday tee times,
call Wednesday.
Subscriber comments: If course had another set of tees between white and
back, it would be golf heaven . . . Tight, lots of water, good test, well cared
for . . . Tough to walk . . . Planes fly over several times per round . . .
Obviously managed by PGA Tour. Very organized . . . Best public course
in Jacksonville . . . Wonderful to walk . . . Excellent design by Weed,
McCumber for all levels. Lots of water and marsh.

(GREAT VALUE)

GOLF CLUB OF MIAMI
PU—6801 Miami Gardens Dr., Miami (305)829-4700.
Opened: 1962. **Pace of Play rating:** 4:00. **Green fee:** $20/65.
Credit cards: All major. **Reduced fees:** Low season, Twilight.
Caddies: No. **Golf carts:** Included in Green Fee.
Discount golf packages: Yes. **Season:** Year-round. **High:** Feb.-Nov.
On-site lodging: No. **Rental clubs:** Yes.
Walking policy: Mandatory cart. **Range:** Yes (grass).
To obtain tee times: Call three days in advance.
★★★ EAST COURSE
Holes: 18. **Par:** 70/70.
Yards: 6,553/5,025. **Course rating:** 70.3/68.8. **Slope:** 124/117.
Subscriber comments: Short in length, but not in challenge . . . Great
greens . . . Ugly buildings everywhere . . . Good shape all year . . . Bikini-
wax greens.

★★★½ WEST COURSE
Holes: 18. **Par:** 72/72.
Yards: 7,017/5,298. **Course rating:** 73.5/70.1. **Slope:** 130/123.
Subscriber comments: Very long and challenging . . . Better than East layout . . . Good shape for muny all year . . . The West Course, a championship test and kept at PGA Tour standards . . . Very difficult, for low handicapper . . . Tough course.

★★½ GOLF HAMMOCK COUNTRY CLUB
SP—2222 Golf Hammock Dr., Sebring (813)382-2151.
90 miles south of Orlando. **Holes:** 18. **Par:** 72/72.
Yards: 6,431/5,352. **Course rating:** 71.0/70.2. **Slope:** 127/118.
Opened: 1976. **Pace of Play rating:** N/A. **Green fee:** $28/35.
Credit cards: MC, V. **Reduced fees:** Low season, Resort guests, Twilight, Juniors.
Caddies: No. **Golf carts:** Included in Green Fee.
Discount golf packages: No. **Season:** Year-round. **High:** Oct.-April.
On-site lodging: No. **Rental clubs:** Yes.
Walking policy: Mandatory cart. **Range:** Yes (grass).
To obtain tee times: Call up to 48 hours in advance.
Subscriber comments: A Sebring favorite, Ron Garl design . . . Trees come into play every hole! . . . Boring . . . Fair all the way.

GRAND CYPRESS RESORT
R—One North Jacaranda, Orlando (407)239-1904, (800)835-7377.
Credit cards: All major. **Reduced fees:** Low season, Twilight, Juniors.
Caddies: Yes, with 48 hour notice. **Golf carts:** Included in Green Fee.
Discount golf packages: Yes. **Season:** Year-round. **High:** Oct.-May.
On-site lodging: Yes. **Rental clubs:** Yes.
Range: Yes (grass).
To obtain tee times: To call starter you must be a guest at the Villas of Grand Cypress or the Hyatt Regency Grand Cypress. You can only book one tee time in advance.

★★★★ NEW COURSE
Holes: 18. **Par:** 72/72.
Yards: 6,773/5,314. **Course rating:** 72.1/69.8. **Slope:** 126/117.
Opened: 1988. **Pace of Play rating:** 4:15. **Green fee:** $80/179.
Walking policy: Unrestricted walking.

Ranked 47th in America's 75 Best Resort Courses by Golf Digest. Ranked 25th in Florida by Golf Digest.
Subscriber comments: If there are courses in heaven, they must be these . . . Tough when the wind blows . . . This is the course to play at Grand Cypress . . . Wide-open design. Great for those who spray the ball . . . Scottish feel, a lot of fun to play . . . Wonderful replica of Old Course at St. Andrews . . . Only thing missing was flock of sheep! . . . Too many double greens.

★★★★ NORTH/SOUTH/EAST
Holes: 27. **Par:** 72/72/72.
Yards: 6,993/6,906/6,955. **Course rating:** 73.9/74.4/73.9.
Slope: 130/132/130.
Opened: 1984. **Pace of Play rating:** 4:15. **Green fee:** $80/175.
Walking policy: Mandatory cart.
North and South 9s ranked 55th in America's 75 Best Resort Courses by Golf Digest. Co-selection as Best New Resort Course of 1984 by Golf Digest. North and South Nines ranked 26th in Florida by Golf Digest.
Subscriber comments: Golfing Nirvana . . . First class from beginning to end, very tough in the wind, you will use all your clubs . . . Tough from tips; looked easy from front . . . Gorgeous but punishing . . . Three fairly different nines. South Nine most difficult . . . Hidden water.

GRAND PALMS GOLF AND COUNTRY CLUB RESORT
★★ GRAND/ROYAL/SABAL
R—110 Grand Palms Dr., Pembrooke Pines (305)437-3334, (800)327-9246.
15 miles south of Fort Lauderdale. **Holes:** 27. **Par:** 72/73/71.

Yards: 6,757/6,736/6,653. **Course rating:** 71.6/71.9/71.5.
Slope: 127/128/124.
Opened: 1987. **Pace of Play rating:** 4:20. **Green fee:** $22/55.
Credit cards: All major. **Reduced fees:** Weekdays, Low season, Resort guests, Twilight.
Caddies: No. **Golf carts:** Included in Green Fee.
Discount golf packages: Yes. **Season:** Year-round. **High:** Dec.-April.
On-site lodging: Yes. **Rental clubs:** Yes.
Walking policy: Mandatory cart. **Range:** Yes (grass).
To obtain tee times: Call three days in advance.
Subscriber comments: Knowing how to read the grain on the greens a must . . . Crowned fairways, too much out-of-bounds . . . Gimmicked course . . . Greens fastest in South Florida, very narrow . . . Newer course . . . Narrow, lots of water.

GRENELEFE GOLF AND TENNIS RESORT
SP—3200 State Rd. 546, Haines City (813)422-7511, (800)237-9549.
25 miles south of Disney World.
Pace of Play rating: N/A. **Green fee:** $32/110.
Credit cards: MC, V, AMEX. **Reduced fees:** Weekdays, Low season, Resort guests, Twilight.
Caddies: No. **Golf carts:** Included in Green Fee.
Discount golf packages: Yes. **Season:** Year-round. **High:** Jan.-April.
On-site lodging: Yes. **Rental clubs:** Yes.
Walking policy: Walking at certain times. **Range:** Yes (grass).
To obtain tee times: Package guests may book starting times one year in advance on the Champions package and 90 days in advance on Classic package.

★★★½ SOUTH COURSE
Holes: 18. **Par:** 71/71.
Yards: 6,869/5,174. **Course rating:** 72.6/69.5. **Slope:** 124/115.
Opened: 1983.
Subscriber comments: South is more open but not easy to score on . . . Most fun of the courses . . . Golf factory . . . Challenging, but not too difficult . . . Fair test of golf . . . Lots of water holes . . . Best for mid-to-short hitters.

★★★★ EAST COURSE
Holes: 18. **Par:** 72/72.
Yards: 6,802/5,114. **Course rating:** 72.5/69.2. **Slope:** 123/114.
Opened: 1978.
Subscriber comments: Good for all types of players . . . Tight, hit it straight . . . Narrow fairways and lots of trees. Trouble when off fairway . . . Good for long hitters.

★★★★ WEST COURSE
Holes: 18. **Par:** 72/72.
Yards: 7,325/5,398. **Course rating:** 75.0/70.9. **Slope:** 130/118.
Opened: 1971.
Ranked 70th in America's 75 Best Resort Courses by Golf Digest. Ranked 30th in Florida by Golf Digest.
Subscriber comments: Don't play West Course from tips unless you're John Daly . . . Great ball-striker's course, always fun to play . . . Tough, narrow fairways . . . Treelined, penalties severe for not being in fairway . . . Most challenging of the three courses . . . Too long for me. Bring out the long irons . . . Fine test of golf . . . Long course for women . . . Great test even for pros, long and tough.

★★★ HABITAT GOLF COURSE
PU—3591 Fairgreen St., Valkaria (407)952-6312.
16 miles south of Melbourne. **Holes:** 18. **Par:** 72/72.
Yards: 6,836/4,969. **Course rating:** 72.9/68.2. **Slope:** 129/115.
Opened: 1991. **Pace of Play rating:** 4:30. **Green fee:** $13/23.
Credit cards: MC, V. **Reduced fees:** Weekdays, Low season, Resort guests, Juniors.
Caddies: No. **Golf carts:** $9 for 18 holes.

Discount golf packages: Yes. **Season:** Year-round. **High:** Dec.-March.
On-site lodging: No. **Rental clubs:** Yes.
Walking policy: Unrestricted walking. **Range:** Yes (grass).
To obtain tee times: Call up to three days in advance.
Subscriber comments: Great character, interesting to play . . . Courteous staff . . . The scenery was stunning. Suits low handicapper . . . Lots of carries on tee shots and approach shots . . . Rolling fairways.

★★★½ HAILE PLANTATION GOLF AND COUNTRY CLUB
PU—9905 SW 44th Ave., Gainesville.
Call club for further information.
Subscriber comments: New Gary Player design . . . Coming of age . . . Mounds around greens . . . Not for the big hitter . . . Take your camera with you . . . Short, cute layout, severe landscaping killed it . . . Mounds and gorgeous greens . . . The layout is fun and very challenging for all calibers of players.

★★★ HALIFAX PLANTATION GOLF CLUB
SP—4000 Old Dixie Hwy., Ormond Beach (904)676-9600.
20 miles north of Daytona Beach. **Holes:** 18. **Par:** 72/72.
Yards: 7,128/4,971. **Course rating:** 73.9/67.6. **Slope:** 129/113.
Opened: 1993. **Pace of Play rating:** 4:00. **Green fee:** $14/22.
Credit cards: MC, V, AMEX. **Reduced fees:** Weekdays, Low season, Resort guests, Twilight.
Caddies: No. **Golf carts:** N/A.
Discount golf packages: Yes. **Season:** Year-round. **High:** Nov.-April.
On-site lodging: No. **Rental clubs:** Yes.
Walking policy: Walking at certain times. **Range:** Yes (grass).
To obtain tee times: Call two days in advance.
Subscriber comments: Nice, large greens . . . Many lookalike holes . . . Friendly staff . . . Wide open . . . Not a parallel fairway.

★★ HARDER HALL COUNTRY CLUB
PU—3600 Golfview Dr., Sebring (813)382-0500.
80 miles south of Orlando. **Holes:** 18. **Par:** 72/72.
Yards: 6,300/5,003. **Course rating:** 70.0/68.5. **Slope:** 116/114.
Opened: 1956. **Pace of Play rating:** 4:00. **Green fee:** $13/30.
Credit cards: MC, V. **Reduced fees:** Low season.
Caddies: No. **Golf carts:** Included in Green Fee.
Discount golf packages: No. **Season:** Year-round. **High:** Jan.-April.
On-site lodging: No. **Rental clubs:** Yes.
Walking policy:: Mandatory cart. **Range:** Yes (grass).
To obtain tee times: Call 48 hours in advance in season.
Subscriber comments: Everything good, most enjoyable . . . Nice old course that needs work . . . Enjoyed seeing the monkey squirrels.

HERITAGE LINKS COUNTRY CLUB AT TURKEY CREEK★
SP—11400 Turkey Creek Blvd., Alachua (904)462-4655.
5 miles northwest of Gainesville. **Holes:** 18. **Par:** 72/72.
Yards: 6,570/5,580. **Course rating:** 71.2/71.8. **Slope:** 121/121.
Opened: 1977. **Pace of Play rating:** 4:00-4:30. **Green fee:** $19/28.
Credit cards: All major. **Reduced fees:** Weekdays, Low season, Resort guests, Seniors.
Caddies: No. **Golf carts:** Included in Green Fee.
Discount golf packages: No. **Season:** Year-round. **High:** Nov.-March.
On-site lodging: Yes. **Rental clubs:** No.
Walking policy: Walking at certain times. **Range:** Yes (grass).
To obtain tee times: Call up to three days in advance for non-members.

★★ HILAMAN PARK MUNICIPAL GOLF COURSE
PU—2737 Blairstone Rd., Tallahassee (904)891-3935.
Holes: 18. **Par:** 72/72.
Yards: 6,364/5,365. **Course rating:** 70.1/70.8. **Slope:** 121/116.
Opened: 1972. **Pace of Play rating:** 4:00. **Green fee:** $11/15.

Credit cards: MC, V. **Reduced fees:** Weekdays, Twilight, Seniors, Juniors.
Caddies: No. **Golf carts:** $9 for 18 holes.
Discount golf packages: No. **Season:** Year-round. **High:** March-June.
On-site lodging: No. **Rental clubs:** Yes.
Walking policy: Walking at certain times. **Range:** Yes (grass).
To obtain tee times: Call one week in advance.
Subscriber comments: Good municipal layout . . . Some elevation changes . . . Very hilly, lots of doglegs . . . Great challenging course . . . Good shotmaker's course.

★★★½ HOMBRE GOLF CLUB

SP—120 Coyote Pass, Panama City Beach (904)234-3673.
100 miles west of Pensacola. **Holes:** 18. **Par:** 72/74.
Yards: 6,820/4,793. **Course rating:** 73.4/67.2. **Slope:** 136/118.
Opened: 1990. **Pace of Play rating:** 4:30. **Green fee:** $60.
Credit cards: MC, V. **Reduced fees:** Low season, Resort guests, Twilight, Juniors.
Caddies: No. **Golf carts:** Included in Green Fee.
Discount golf packages: Yes. **Season:** Year-round. **High:** March-April/June-July.
On-site lodging: No. **Rental clubs:** Yes.
Walking policy: Mandatory cart. **Range:** Yes (grass).
To obtain tee times: Call up to seven days in advance. Golf package tee times up to six months in advance.
Subscriber comments: Don't slice on any hole . . . Lots of water, a good challenge . . . Good public course . . . Tough layout but fair . . . Subtle, not as tough as advertised.

★★★½ HUNTER'S CREEK GOLF COURSE

PU—14401 Sports Club Way, Orlando (407)240-4653.
Holes: 18. **Par:** 72/72.
Yards: 7,432/5,755. **Course rating:** 75.2/72.5. **Slope:** 127/120.
Opened: 1986. **Pace of Play rating:** 4:00. **Green fee:** $31/57.
Credit cards: MC, V. **Reduced fees:** Weekdays, Low season, Twilight.
Caddies: No. **Golf carts:** Included in Green Fee.
Discount golf packages: No. **Season:** Year-round. **High:** Jan.-March.
On-site lodging: No. **Rental clubs:** Yes.
Walking policy: Mandatory cart. **Range:** Yes (grass).
To obtain tee times: Call three days in advance.
Ranked in Second 25 of America's 75 Best Public Golf Courses by Golf Digest.
Subscriber comments: Long, flat, wide open . . . Brush up on drive and long irons first . . . Long course for low handicappers . . . World-class public golf.

★★★ HUNTINGTON HILLS GOLF AND COUNTRY CLUB

SP—2626 Duff Rd., Lakeland (813)859-3689.
33 miles east of Tampa. **Holes:** 18. **Par:** 72/72.
Yards: 6,631/5,011. **Course rating:** 72.5/68.7. **Slope:** 122/115.
Opened: 1992. **Pace of Play rating:** 4:00. **Green fee:** $25/35.
Credit cards: All major. **Reduced fees:** Weekdays, Low season, Twilight.
Caddies: No. **Golf carts:** Included in Green Fee.
Discount golf packages: Yes. **Season:** Year-round. **High:** Dec.-March.
On-site lodging: No. **Rental clubs:** Yes.
Walking policy: Mandatory cart. **Range:** Yes (grass).
To obtain tee times: Call three days in advance.
Subscriber comments: Great design; all levels . . . Everyone treated well . . . Open fairways, little trouble . . . Fairly new course.

★★½ HYDE PARK GOLF CLUB

PU—6439 Hyde Grove Ave., Jacksonville (904)786-5410.
Call club for further information.
Subscriber comments: Donald Ross, fun to play . . . Old courses like this

are fairly challenging . . . Great old course, no hazards marked . . . Dangerous. Too much play, too close . . . Hogan's "11" on par-3 sixth . . . Small greens . . . Fun to play, challenging but fair.

★★½ IMPERIAL LAKES GOLF CLUB

SP—6807 Buffalo Rd., Palmetto (813)747-4653.
25 miles north of Tampa. **Holes:** 18. **Par:** 72/72.
Yards: 6,658/5,270. **Course rating:** 71.5/69.7. **Slope:** 123/117.
Opened: 1987. **Pace of Play rating:** 4:00. **Green fee:** $17/33.
Credit cards: MC, V. **Reduced fees:** Weekdays, Low season, Twilight, Juniors.
Caddies: No. **Golf carts:** Included in Green Fee.
Discount golf packages: No. **Season:** Year-round. **High:** Nov.-April.
On-site lodging: No. **Rental clubs:** Yes.
Walking policy: Walking at certain times. **Range:** Yes (grass).
To obtain tee times: Call or come in two days in advance.
Subscriber comments: Nice variety of holes . . . If you can't hit straight, don't come here . . . Good average course on all counts . . . Flat course, few trees. Wide fairways.

INDIAN BAYOU GOLF AND COUNTRY CLUB
★★★ SEMINOLE/CHOCTAW/CREEK

SP—1 Country Club Drive East, Destin (904)837-6191.
30 miles west of Pensacola. **Holes:** 27. **Par:** 72/72/72.
Yards: 6,958/6,892/7,016. **Course rating:** 73.3/73.1/73.7.
Slope: 126/129/128.
Opened: 1978. **Pace of Play rating:** 4:15. **Green fee:** $37/44.
Credit cards: MC, V, AMEX. **Reduced fees:** No.
Caddies: No. **Golf carts:** N/A.
Discount golf packages: No. **Season:** Year-round. **High:** Feb.-Aug.
On-site lodging: No. **Rental clubs:** Yes.
Walking policy: Walking at certain times. **Range:** Yes (grass).
To obtain tee times: Call up to one month in advance.
Subscriber comments: Big greens . . . Need to play for ball position . . . Great variety created for flat land.

★½ INDIAN CREEK GOLF CLUB

PU—1800 Central Blvd., Jupiter (407)747-6262.
Holes: 18. **Par:** 70/71.
Yards: 6,205/5,150. **Course rating:** 69.9/69.5. **Slope:** 117/118.
Opened: 1982. **Pace of Play rating:** 3:30-4:00. **Green fee:** $26/45.
Credit cards: MC, V. **Reduced fees:** Weekdays, Low season, Twilight.
Caddies: No. **Golf carts:** Included in Green Fee.
Discount golf packages: No. **Season:** Year-round. **High:** Jan.-April.
On-site lodging: No. **Rental clubs:** Yes.
Walking policy: Mandatory cart. **Range:** Yes (grass).
To obtain tee times: Call up to four days in advance.
Subscriber comments: Nice course, friendly service . . . Easier course for high handicappers . . . Easy front nine (four par 3s), back nine tougher.

★★★ INDIGO LAKES GOLF CLUB

SP—312 Indigo Dr., Daytona Beach (904)254-3607.
Holes: 18. **Par:** 72/72.
Yards: 7,168/5,159. **Course rating:** 73.5/69.1. **Slope:** 128/123.
Opened: 1977. **Pace of Play rating:** N/A. **Green fee:** $30/55.
Credit cards: MC, V, AMEX. **Reduced fees:** Weekdays, Low season, Twilight.
Caddies: No. **Golf carts:** Included in Green Fee.
Discount golf packages: Yes. **Season:** Year-round. **High:** Jan.-May.
On-site lodging: Yes. **Rental clubs:** Yes.
Walking policy: Mandatory cart. **Range:** Yes (grass).
To obtain tee times: Call up to three days in advance.
Subscriber comments: Remodeled Lloyd Clifton course . . . Good layout, lots of trees, just good golf . . . Every green well bunkered . . .

Good course, next to race tracks, major highways . . . Deep rough, lots of water . . . Most southerly Florida course with Georgia ambience . . . For all levels.

INNISBROOK HILTON RESORT

R—36750 Hwy. 19 North, Palm Harbor (813)942-2000.
25 miles northwest of Tampa.
Credit cards: All major. **Reduced fees:** Low season, Resort guests, Juniors.
Caddies: No. **Golf carts:** Included in Green Fee.
Discount golf packages: Yes. **Season:** Year-round. **High:** Nov.-April.
On-site lodging: Yes. **Rental clubs:** Yes.
Walking policy: Mandatory cart. **Range:** Yes (grass).
To obtain tee times: Call.
Site of Golf Digest Schools.
★★★★½ **COPPERHEAD COURSE**
Holes: 18. **Par:** 71/71.
Yards: 7,087/5,506. **Course rating:** 74.4/72.0. **Slope:** 140/128.
Opened: 1972. **Pace of Play rating:** 4:30. **Green fee:** $75/120.
Ranked 22nd in America's 75 Best Resort Courses by Golf Digest. Ranked 21st in Florida by Golf Digest.
Subscriber comments: Site of JC Penney Mixed Team Classic . . . Beautiful, challenging . . . Great service . . . Plush . . . Great layout . . . Reminds one of the best of Pinehurst.
★★★★ **ISLAND COURSE**
Holes: 18. **Par:** 72/72.
Yards: 6,999/5,795. **Course rating:** 73.2/74.1. **Slope:** 133/130.
Opened: 1970. **Pace of Play rating:** 4:30. **Green fee:** $60/105.
Ranked 71st in America's 75 Best Resort Courses by Golf Digest.
Subscriber comments: More fun to play than its more famous neighbor, Copperhead . . . Beautiful course . . . Better be creative on shots.
★★★★ **SANDPIPER COURSE-PALMETTO/PALMS/PINES**
Holes: 27. **Par:** 70/70/70.
Yards: 5,969/6,200/6,245. **Course rating:** 68.7/69.8/69.8.
Slope: 122/125/119.
Opened: 1971. **Pace of Play rating:** 4:30. **Green fee:** $50/95.
Subscriber comments: Scenic beauty . . . Great course for not-so-big-hitters . . . Good professional care all around.

★½ INTERNATIONAL GOLF CLUB

R—6351 International Golf Club Rd., Orlando (407)239-6909.
Holes: 18. **Par:** 72/72.
Yards: 6,776/5,077. **Course rating:** 71.7/68.5. **Slope:** 117/109.
Opened: 1986. **Pace of Play rating:** 4:00. **Green fee:** $65.
Credit cards: MC, V. **Reduced fees:** Weekdays, Low season, Resort guests, Twilight, Seniors.
Caddies: No. **Golf carts:** Included in Green Fee.
Discount golf packages: No. **Season:** Year-round. **High:** Jan.-April.
On-site lodging: No. **Rental clubs:** Yes.
Walking policy: Mandatory cart. **Range:** Yes (grass).
To obtain tee times: Call one day in advance.
Subscriber comments: Short, tight course, takes driver out of game . . . Dogleg heaven.

IRONWOOD GOLF COURSE★

PU—2100 N.E. 39th Ave., Gainesville (904)334-2120.
Holes: 18. **Par:** 72/72.
Yards: 6,465/5,234. **Course rating:** 71.3/70.2. **Slope:** 122/117.
Opened: 1964. **Pace of Play rating:** 4:30-5:00. **Green fee:** $10/13.
Credit cards: MC, V, DISC. **Reduced fees:** Weekdays, Low season, Twilight, Seniors, Juniors.
Caddies: No. **Golf carts:** $7 for 18 holes.
Discount golf packages: No. **Season:** Year-round. **High:** Oct.-May.
On-site lodging: No. **Rental clubs:** Yes.
Walking policy: Unrestricted walking. **Range:** Yes (grass).
To obtain tee times: Call two days in advance.

JACARANDA GOLF CLUB

PU—9200 West Broward Blvd., Plantation (305)472-5836.

12 miles west of Fort Lauderdale.

Opened: N/A. **Pace of Play rating:** N/A. **Green fee:** N/A.

Credit cards: MC, V, AMEX. **Reduced fees:** Weekdays, Low season, Twilight.

Caddies: No. **Golf carts:** Included in Green Fee.

Discount golf packages: Yes. **Season:** Year-round. **High:** Nov.-May.

On-site lodging: No. **Rental clubs:** No.

Walking policy: . **Range:** Yes (grass).

★★★ EAST COURSE

Holes: 18. **Par:** 72/72.

Yards: 7,170/5,668. **Course rating:** N/A. **Slope:** 130/121.

Subscriber comments: Nice course but can't remember any holes . . . Challenging . . . Another great, flat Florida course.

★★★ WEST COURSE

Holes: 18. **Par:** 72/72.

Yards: 6,729/5,314. **Course rating:** N/A. **Slope:** 135/129.

Subscriber comments: Nice course but little overrated . . . No change from last year . . . Not as challenging as East but still a test.

★★ JACKSONVILLE BEACH GOLF CLUB

PU—605 South Penman Rd., Jacksonville (904)249-8600.

10 miles east of Jacksonville. **Holes:** 18. **Par:** 72/72.

Yards: 6,510/5,245. **Course rating:** 70.5/69.2. **Slope:** 119/114.

Opened: 1959. **Pace of Play rating:** 4:70. **Green fee:** $15/17.

Credit cards: MC, V. **Reduced fees:** Weekdays, Low season, Twilight, Juniors.

Caddies: No. **Golf carts:** N/A.

Discount golf packages: No. **Season:** Year-round. **High:** Spring and Fall.

On-site lodging: No. **Rental clubs:** Yes.

Walking policy: Walking at certain times. **Range:** Yes (grass).

To obtain tee times: Call Monday at 7 a.m. for next seven days only.

Subscriber comments: Golf course is a challenge; the wind is always changing the degree of difficulty . . . Big, open field; can stray and be in play.

★½ KEY WEST RESORT GOLF COURSE

PU—6450 East College Rd., Key West (305)294-5232.

Holes: 18. **Par:** 70/70.

Yards: 6,526/5,183. **Course rating:** 71.2/70.1. **Slope:** 124/118.

Opened: N/A. **Pace of Play rating:** N/A. **Green fee:** $42/53.

Credit cards: MC, V, AMEX. **Reduced fees:** Low season, Twilight, Juniors.

Caddies: No. **Golf carts:** N/A.

Discount golf packages: Yes. **Season:** Year-round. **High:** Nov.-April.

On-site lodging: No. **Rental clubs:** Yes.

Walking policy: Walking at certain times. **Range:** Yes.

To obtain tee times: Call up to 14 days in advance.

Subscriber comments: Nice alternative from sightseeing . . . Key West is the only course open to the public in the Florida Keys. This par-70 Rees Jones layout is watery and tight. Raised greens are in fine condition year-round and give an impression of elevation. From the blue tees with a little wind, long enough for anyone.

KILLEARN COUNTRY CLUB AND INN

★★★½ SOUTH/EAST/NORTH

R—100 Tyron Circle, Tallahassee (904)893-2144, (800)476-4101.

Holes: 27. **Par:** 72/72/72.

Yards: 7,025/6,760/6,899. **Course rating:** 73.9/73.1/73.3.

Slope: 133/131/132.

Opened: N/A. **Pace of Play rating:** 4:00. **Green fee:** $30/35.

Credit cards: MC, V, AMEX, DISC. **Reduced fees:** Weekdays, Twilight, Juniors.

Caddies: No. **Golf carts:** N/A.
Discount golf packages: Yes. **Season:** Year-round. **High:** March-Aug.
On-site lodging: Yes. **Rental clubs:** Yes.
Walking policy: Walking at certain times. **Range:** Yes (grass).
To obtain tee times: Call one week in advance.
Subscriber comments: South and East have hard, long par 4s from blues . . . One of the best I played this year.

★★½ KISSIMMEE BAY COUNTRY CLUB

SP—2801 Kissimmee Bay Blvd., Kissimmee (407)348-4653.
10 miles south of Orlando. **Holes:** 18. **Par:** 71/71.
Yards: 6,846/5,171. **Course rating:** 70.1/71.0. **Slope:** 119/109.
Opened: 1990. **Pace of Play rating:** 4:00. **Green fee:** $35/60.
Credit cards: MC, V, DISC. **Reduced fees:** Weekdays, Low season, Twilight.
Caddies: No. **Golf carts:** Included in Green Fee.
Discount golf packages: Yes. **Season:** Year-round. **High:** Jan.-April.
On-site lodging: No. **Rental clubs:** Yes.
Walking policy: Mandatory cart. **Range:** Yes (grass).
To obtain tee times: Call seven days in advance.
Subscriber comments: A few interesting holes; most are easy . . . Nice people.

★★ KISSIMMEE GOLF CLUB

SP—3103 Florida Coach Dr., Kissimmee (407)847-2816.
15 miles south of Orlando. **Holes:** 18. **Par:** 72/72.
Yards: 6,537/5,083. **Course rating:** 71.4/68.6. **Slope:** 119/109.
Opened: 1970. **Pace of Play rating:** 3:48. **Green fee:** $30/45.
Credit cards: MC, V. **Reduced fees:** Low season, Resort guests, Twilight.
Caddies: No. **Golf carts:** Included in Green Fee..
Discount golf packages: Yes. **Season:** Year-round. **High:** Dec.-April.
On-site lodging: No. **Rental clubs:** Yes.
Walking policy: Walking at certain times. **Range:** Yes (grass).
To obtain tee times: Call up to four days in advance.
Subscriber comments: Has improved recently, nice clubhouse, good staff and range.

★★ LAKE WORTH GOLF CLUB

PU—1-7th Ave. North, Lake Worth (407)582-9713.
7 miles south of Palm Beach. **Holes:** 18. **Par:** 70/70.
Yards: 6,113/5,413. **Course rating:** 68.6/69.6. **Slope:** 116/113.
Opened: N/A. **Pace of Play rating:** N/A. **Green fee:** $10/23.
Credit cards: None. **Reduced fees:** Weekdays, Twilight, Juniors.
Caddies: No. **Golf carts:** N/A.
Discount golf packages: Yes. **Season:** Year-round. **High:** Jan.-March.
On-site lodging: No. **Rental clubs:** Yes.
Walking policy: Unrestricted walking. **Range:** No.
To obtain tee times: Call one day in advance.
Subscriber comments: Nice layout overlooking the Intracoastal . . . Rather short, easy to play.

★★½ LANSBROOK GOLF CLUB

SP—2500 Village Center Dr., Palm Harbor (813)784-7333.
20 miles west of Tampa. **Holes:** 18. **Par:** 72/72.
Yards: 6,719/5,264. **Course rating:** 71.6/69.3. **Slope:** 126/119.
Opened: 1975. **Pace of Play rating:** N/A. **Green fee:** $30/45.
Credit cards: MC, V. **Reduced fees:** Weekdays, Low season, Twilight.
Caddies: No. **Golf carts:** Included in Green Fee.
Discount golf packages: No. **Season:** Year-round. **High:** Dec.-April.
On-site lodging: No. **Rental clubs:** Yes.
Walking policy: Mandatory cart. **Range:** Yes (grass).
To obtain tee times: Call four days in advance.
Subscriber comments: Fair test for straight hitter . . . Front nine good, back nine boring.

★★★★ LELY FLAMINGO ISLAND CLUB

PU—8004 Lely Resort Blvd., Naples (813)793-2223, (800)388-4653.
30 miles south of Fort Myers. **Holes:** 18. **Par:** 72/72.
Yards: 7,171/5,377. **Course rating:** 73.9/70.6. **Slope:** 135/126.
Opened: 1990. **Pace of Play rating:** 4:15–4:30. **Green fee:** $25/90.
Credit cards: All major. **Reduced fees:** Low season, Twilight.
Caddies: No. **Golf carts:** Included in Green Fee.
Discount golf packages: No. **Season:** Year-round. **High:** Nov.-April.
On-site lodging: No. **Rental clubs:** Yes.
Walking policy: Mandatory cart. **Range:** Yes (grass).
To obtain tee times: Call up to three days in advance, Mastercard or Visa,
November through April.
Subscriber comments: A lot of dead areas, you can golf and shop at mall
on one hole . . . Traps well placed . . . Wide open but challenging . . . Fun
to play . . . Great Trent Jones course.

LEMON BAY GOLF CLUB★

SP—9600 Eagle Preserve Dr., Englewood (813)697-3729.
28 miles south of Sarasota. **Holes:** 18. **Par:** 71/71.
Yards: 6,176/4,992. **Course rating:** 69.2/67.8. **Slope:** 119/114.
Opened: 1982. **Pace of Play rating:** 4:17. **Green fee:** $19/44.
Credit cards: MC, V. **Reduced fees:** Low season.
Caddies: No. **Golf carts:** Included in Green Fee.
Discount golf packages: No. **Season:** Year-round. **High:** Jan.-April.
On-site lodging: No. **Rental clubs:** Yes.
Walking policy: Walking at certain times. **Range:** Yes (grass).
To obtain tee times: Call two days in advance.

★★★★ LINKS AT KEY BISCAYNE

PU—6700 Crandon Blvd., Key Biscayne (305)361-9129.
Holes: 18. **Par:** 72/72.
Yards: 7,070/5,662. **Course rating:** 75.2/73.1. **Slope:** 139/129.
Opened: 1972. **Pace of Play rating:** 4:30. **Green fee:** $45/75.
Credit cards: MC, V, AMEX. **Reduced fees:** Weekdays, Low season,
Twilight.
Caddies: No. **Golf carts:** Included in Green Fee.
Discount golf packages: No. **Season:** Year-round. **High:** Dec.-May.
On-site lodging: No. **Rental clubs:** Yes.
Walking policy: Walking at certain times. **Range:** Yes (grass).
To obtain tee times: Call up to 24 hours in advance.
Ranked in Second 25 of America's 75 Best Public Golf Courses by Golf
Digest.
Subscriber comments: Best to play just after senior event . . . Suits a long
hitter . . . Great views, challenging waterfront course. Better since the
makeover . . . Take lots of balls . . . Tough on a windy day.

★★★½ THE LINKS AT POLO TRACE

SP—13397 Hagen Ranch Rd., Delray Beach (407)495-5300.
30 miles north of Miami. **Holes:** 18. **Par:** 72/72.
Yards: 7,096/5,314. **Course rating:** 73.4/71.0. **Slope:** 134/124.
Opened: 1989. **Pace of Play rating:** N/A. **Green fee:** $25/80.
Credit cards: All major. **Reduced fees:** Weekdays, Low season, Twilight,
Juniors.
Caddies: No. **Golf carts:** Included in Green Fee.
Discount golf packages: Yes. **Season:** Year-round. **High:** Dec.-April.
On-site lodging: No. **Rental clubs:** Yes.
Walking policy: Mandatory cart. **Range:** Yes (grass).
To obtain tee times: Call pro shop.
Subscriber comments: A little pricey but very good track . . . Great links
course, very scenic . . . Not a course for high handicappers . . . Room to
roam. Fun for all players . . . Best Broward course around . . . About the
hardest course in South Florida . . . Great condition, treacherous wind . . .
Generous fairways . . . Great greens, nice pace of play . . . Excellent design,
like old Scotland.

★★½ THE LINKS OF LAKE BERNADETTE
SP—5430 Links Lane, Zephyrhills (813)788-4653.
20 miles north of Tampa. **Holes:** 18. **Par:** 71/71.
Yards: 6,392/5,031. **Course rating:** 70.0/68.0. **Slope:** 117/118.
Opened: 1985. **Pace of Play rating:** N/A. **Green fee:** $20/30.
Credit cards: MC, V. **Reduced fees:** Weekdays, Low season, Twilight.
Caddies: No. **Golf carts:** Included in Green Fee.
Discount golf packages: No. **Season:** Year-round. **High:** Jan.-April.
On-site lodging: No. **Rental clubs:** Yes.
Walking policy: Mandatory cart. **Range:** No.
To obtain tee times: Call three days in advance.
Subscriber comments: Well-kept secret. Nice, little course . . . Always a good deal. Fun course. Outstanding fast greens, great bargain in summer . . . Staff concerned that we enjoyed outing.

★★½ LOCHMOOR COUNTRY CLUB
SP—3911 Orange Grove Blvd., North Fort Myers (813)995-0501.
Holes: 18. **Par:** 72/72.
Yards: 7,908/5,152. **Course rating:** 73.1/69.1. **Slope:** 128/116.
Opened: 1972. **Pace of Play rating:** 4:15-4:30. **Green fee:** $25/45.
Credit cards: MC, V. **Reduced fees:** Low season, Twilight.
Caddies: No. **Golf carts:** Included in Green Fee.
Discount golf packages: No. **Season:** Year-round. **High:** Jan.-April.
On-site lodging: No. **Rental clubs:** Yes.
Walking policy: Walking at certain times. **Range:** Yes (grass).
To obtain tee times: Call 48 hours in advance.
Subscriber comments: Best layout around . . . A lot of boring holes . . . Big hitter's delight . . . Nice layout.

LONGBOAT KEY CLUB
★★★ HARBOURSIDE COURSE - RED/WHITE/BLUE
R—1600 Harbourside Dr., Longboat Key (813)383-9571.
3 miles northwest of Sarasota. **Holes:** 27.
Call club for further information.
Subscriber comments: Good bay vistas . . . Many good holes, lots of water, breezy . . . Almost all greens on high mounds.
★★★½ ISLANDSIDE COURSE
R—361 Gulf of Mexico Dr., Longboat Key (813)383-0781.
3 miles northwest of Sarasota. **Holes:** 18. **Par:** 72/72.
Yards: 6,792/5,198. **Course rating:** N/A. **Slope:** 138/121.
Opened: N/A. **Pace of Play rating:** N/A. **Green fee:** N/A.
Credit cards: MC, V, AMEX. **Reduced fees:** Low season.
Caddies: No. **Golf carts:** Included in Green Fee.
Discount golf packages: Yes. **Season:** Year-round. **High:** Dec.-May.
On-site lodging: Yes. **Rental clubs:** No.
Walking policy: N/A. **Range:** Yes (grass).
Subscriber comments: Unfair penalties (hidden trouble), great target golf . . . Beautiful course, much water, not a high-handicapper's course . . . Almost all greens on high mounds.

LOST LAKE GOLF CLUB★
SP—8310 S.E. Fazio Dr., Hobe Sound (407)220-6666.
25 miles north of West Palm Beach. **Holes:** 18. **Par:** 72/72.
Yards: 6,850/5,106. **Course rating:** 73.4/69.5. **Slope:** 135/123.
Opened: 1992. **Pace of Play rating:** 4:00-4:15. **Green fee:** $20/45.
Credit cards: MC, V. **Reduced fees:** Low season.
Caddies: No. **Golf carts:** Included in Green Fee.
Discount golf packages: No. **Season:** Year-round. **High:** Jan.-April.
On-site lodging: No. **Rental clubs:** Yes.
Walking policy: Mandatory cart. **Range:** Yes (grass).
To obtain tee times: Call one day in advance.

LPGA INTERNATIONAL★
PU—300 Champions Dr., Daytona Beach (904)274-3880.
40 miles east of Orlando. **Holes:** 18. **Par:** 72/72.

Yards: 7,088/5,131. **Course rating:** 74.0/68.9. **Slope:** 134/122.
Opened: 1994. **Pace of Play rating:** 4:24. **Green fee:** $25/60.
Credit cards: MC, V, AMEX. **Reduced fees:** Low season, Twilight.
Caddies: No. **Golf carts:** Included in Green Fee.
Discount golf packages: Yes. **Season:** Year-round. **High:** Nov.-Dec.
On-site lodging: No. **Rental clubs:** Yes.
Walking policy: Mandatory cart. **Range:** Yes (grass).
To obtain tee times: Call seven days in advance.

★★ MAGNOLIA VALLEY COUNTRY CLUB

SP—7223 Massachusetts Ave., New Port Richey (813)847-2342.
Call club for further information.
Subscriber comments: Challenging and interesting greens . . . Fairly long
but mostly wide open. Long hitters can score well.

★½ MANATEE COUNTY GOLF CLUB

PU—5290 66th St. W., Bradenton (813)794-2835.
Call club for further information.
Subscriber comments: Flat but challenging . . . Great potential.

★★★ MANGROVE BAY GOLF COURSE

PU—875 62nd Ave. NE, St. Petersburg (813)893-7800.
Holes: 18. **Par:** 72/72.
Yards: 6,779/5,204. **Course rating:** 71.5/68.5. **Slope:** 120/112.
Opened: 1978. **Pace of Play rating:** N/A. **Green fee:** $16/19.
Credit cards: MC, V, DISC. **Reduced fees:** Low season, Twilight.
Caddies: No. **Golf carts:** N/A.
Discount golf packages: No. **Season:** Year-round. **High:** Nov.-
Feb./April-May.
On-site lodging: No. **Rental clubs:** Yes.
Walking policy: Unrestricted walking. **Range:** Yes (grass).
To obtain tee times: Call seven days in advance.
Subscriber comments: Only course I can find that will let me walk! . . .
Flat with some water . . . Tee times mean little . . . Often have to plan on
five-hour round . . . Really nice course for the price . . . Very good senior
course. Greens are on the fast side and true.

MARCO SHORES COUNTRY CLUB

PU—1450 Mainsail Dr., Naples (813)394-2581.
Holes: 18. **Par:** 72/72.
Yards: 6,879/5,634. **Course rating:** 73.0/72.3. **Slope:** 125/121.
Opened: 1974. **Pace of Play rating:** N/A. **Green fee:** $22/60.
Credit cards: MC, V. **Reduced fees:** Low season, Twilight, Juniors.
Caddies: No. **Golf carts:** Included in Green Fee.
Discount golf packages: No. **Season:** Year-round. **High:** Jan.-April.
On-site lodging: No. **Rental clubs:** Yes.
Walking policy: Mandatory cart. **Range:** Yes (grass).
To obtain tee times: Call or in person four days in advance.
Subscriber comments: A fun course . . . Interesting and playable for
everyone . . . Reduced fees for kids, good deal.

★★★★ MARCUS POINTE GOLF CLUB

PU—2500 Oak Pointe Dr., Pensacola (904)484-9770, (800)362-7287.
Holes: 18. **Par:** 72/72.
Yards: 6,737/5,252. **Course rating:** 72.3/69.6. **Slope:** 129/119.
Opened: 1990. **Pace of Play rating:** N/A. **Green fee:** $20/30.
Credit cards: MC, V. **Reduced fees:** Weekdays, Low season, Twilight,
Juniors.
Caddies: No. **Golf carts:** $13 for 18 holes.
Discount golf packages: Yes. **Season:** Year-round. **High:** Feb.-May.
On-site lodging: No. **Rental clubs:** Yes.
Walking policy: Walking at certain times. **Range:** Yes (grass).
To obtain tee times: Call up to three days in advance.
Subscriber comments: Has character, well defined, excellent fairway
targets . . . Just a very nice layout . . . Challenge from blues . . .
Picturesque course . . . Finest course in Florida Panhandle.

MARRIOTT AT SAWGRASS RESORT
★★★★ MARSH LANDING GOLF CLUB
SP—1000 TPC Blvd., Ponte Vedra Beach (904)273-3720.
15 miles east of Jacksonville. **Holes:** 18. **Par:** 72/72.
Yards: 6,841/6,001. **Course rating:** N/A. **Slope:** 131/120.
Opened: N/A. **Pace of Play rating:** N/A. **Green fee:** N/A.
Credit cards: All major. **Reduced fees:** Low season.
Caddies: No. **Golf carts:** N/A.
Discount golf packages: Yes. **Season:** Year-round. **High:** March-May.
On-site lodging: Yes. **Rental clubs:** No.
Walking policy: N/A. **Range:** Yes (grass).
Subscriber comments: A golfer's golf course . . . A course you never get tired of, tough greens . . . Rates up with TPC courses, one of best-kept secrets, just outstanding . . . Great if you like marshes and wide-open fairways . . . Not for beginners . . . Hard course in windy conditions . . . Superlative setting.

★★★ OAK BRIDGE GOLF CLUB
R—254 Alta Mar Dr., Ponte Vedra Beach (904)285-0204.
12 miles east of Jacksonville. **Holes:** 18. **Par:** 70/70.
Yards: 6,383/4,869. **Course rating:** 70.3/67.8. **Slope:** 126/116.
Opened: 1972. **Pace of Play rating:** 4:00. **Green fee:** $25.
Credit cards: MC, V. **Reduced fees:** No.
Caddies: No. **Golf carts:** $15 for 18 holes.
Discount golf packages: Yes. **Season:** Year-round. **High:** Feb.-May.
On-site lodging: No. **Rental clubs:** Yes.
Walking policy: Walking at certain times. **Range:** Yes (grass).
To obtain tee times: May book tee times through travel agents when making resort reservations.
Subscriber comments: Out-of-bounds and tight layout on many holes, fast greens . . . Excellent par 5s and par 3s . . . Short, tight course; lots of water . . . Interesting layout, always a challenge!

MARRIOTT'S BAY POINT RESORT
★★★ CLUB MEADOWS COURSE
SP—100 Delwood Beach Rd., Panama City Beach (904)235-6937.
90 miles east of Pensacola. **Holes:** 18. **Par:** 72/72.
Yards: 6,913/4,999. **Course rating:** 73.3/68.0. **Slope:** 126/118.
Opened: 1975. **Pace of Play rating:** 3:00-4:00. **Green fee:** $70.
Credit cards: MC, V, AMEX. **Reduced fees:** Low season, Resort guests, Juniors.
Caddies: No. **Golf carts:** Included in Green Fee.
Discount golf packages: No. **Season:** Year-round. **High:** Feb.-June.
On-site lodging: Yes. **Rental clubs:** Yes.
Walking policy: Mandatory cart. **Range:** Yes (grass).
To obtain tee times: Call computerized tee times (904)235-6909.
Subscriber comments: Great member's course . . . Pleasant course to play, no pushover . . . Every par 4 seems to be the same.

★★★½ THE LAGOON LEGEND
PU—4110 Marriott Dr., Panama City Beach (909)234-3307.
90 miles east of Pensacola. **Holes:** 18. **Par:** 72/72.
Yards: 6,885/4,942. **Course rating:** 75.3/69.8. **Slope:** 152/127.
Opened: 1986. **Pace of Play rating:** 4:30. **Green fee:** $70.
Credit cards: MC, V, AMEX. **Reduced fees:** Low season, Resort guests, Twilight, Juniors.
Caddies: No. **Golf carts:** Included in Green Fee.
Discount golf packages: No. **Season:** Year-round. **High:** June-Oct.
On-site lodging: Yes. **Rental clubs:** Yes.
Walking policy: Mandatory cart. **Range:** No.
To obtain tee times: Call computerized tee times (904)235-6909.
Ranked 43rd in America's 75 Best Resort Courses by Golf Digest.
Subscriber comments: Tough test for any golfer . . . 18th hole a doozy . . . Super golf course, too tough for average player . . . Harder than Pine Valley and Congressional combined . . . Water, water, water . . . From back tees ridiculous, unfair . . . Very challenging, bring lots of balls . . . Very difficult. Too hard . . . Got to try it! . . . Great course for shotmakers. Add some wind to the water and you'll use every club.

★★½ MARRIOTT'S ORLANDO WORLD CENTER

R—8701 World Center Dr., Orlando (407)238-8660.
Holes: 18. **Par:** 71/71.
Yards: 6,307/4,988. **Course rating:** 69.8/68.5. **Slope:** 121/115.
Opened: 1986. **Pace of Play rating:** 4:15. **Green fee:** $60/115.
Credit cards: All major. **Reduced fees:** Resort guests, Twilight, Juniors.
Caddies: No. **Golf carts:** Included in Green Fee.
Discount golf packages: Yes. **Season:** Year-round. **High:** Jan.–April.

On-site lodging: Yes. **Rental clubs:** Yes.
Walking policy: Mandatory cart. **Range:** Yes (grass).
To obtain tee times: Call up to one week in advance. Hotel guests may
make tee times up to 90 days in advance.
Subscriber comments: Driver not necessary . . . Tight fairways, a lot of
water . . . Good place for tourists while family is at Disney . . . Tougher
than it looks . . . Deceptively easy to get in trouble. Bring straight shots
. . . Some really long holes for women . . . Need to know course to play
well.

MARTIN COUNTY GOLF AND COUNTRY CLUB

PU—2000 S.E. Saint Lucie Blvd., Stuart (407)287-3747.
40 miles north of West Palm Beach.
Opened: 1925. **Pace of Play rating:** 4:15. **Green fee:** $10/22.
Credit cards: None. **Reduced fees:** Low season, Juniors.
Caddies: No. **Golf carts:** N/A.
Discount golf packages: No. **Season:** Year-round. **High:** Dec.–April.
On-site lodging: No. **Rental clubs:** Yes. **Range:** Yes (grass).
To obtain tee times: Call five days in advance. Must call pro shop for PIN
number.

★★½ BLUE/GOLD COURSE

Holes: 18. **Par:** 72/72.
Yards: 5,900/5,236. **Course rating:** 67.5/69.1. **Slope:** 120/120.
Walking policy: Mandatory cart.
Subscriber comments: Short but interesting . . . This course lacks
definition. It is hard to tell where the fairways end and the greens start . . .
Challenging course. Very narrow. Lots of hazards.

★★½ RED/WHITE COURSE

Holes: 18. **Par:** 72/73.
Yards: 6,200/5,400. **Course rating:** 69.1/70.4. **Slope:** 116/120.
Walking policy: Walking at certain times.
Subscriber comments: Walking is great. Love it . . . Second most played
course in the USA. Torrey Pines in San Diego, Calif., is most played . . .
Too crowded, too many walkers.

★★★½ MATANZAS WOODS GOLF CLUB

SP—398 Lakeview Dr., Palm Coast (904)446-6360, (800)874-2101.
30 miles north of Daytona Beach. **Holes:** 18. **Par:** 72/72.
Yards: 6,985/5,336. **Course rating:** 73.3/71.2. **Slope:** 132/126.
Opened: 1985. **Pace of Play rating:** N/A. **Green fee:** $39/48.
Credit cards: MC, V. **Reduced fees:** Low season, Resort guests,
Twilight, Juniors.
Caddies: No. **Golf carts:** Included in Green Fee.
Discount golf packages: Yes. **Season:** Year-round. **High:** Jan.–April.
On-site lodging: No. **Rental clubs:** Yes.
Walking policy: Mandatory cart. **Range:** Yes (grass).
To obtain tee times: Call up to five days in advance.
Subscriber comments: Challenge, some wicked shots . . . Great Arnold
Palmer design . . . Target golf, good layout . . . Lots of water . . . Solid
test of golf . . . Best by far of Palm Coast group . . . In a survey by N.E.
Florida golf writers, holes 13, 14, 15 were listed as northeast Florida's Amen
Corner.

★½ MAYFAIR COUNTRY CLUB

SP—3536 Country Club Rd., Sanford (407)322-2531.
15 miles north of Orlando. **Holes:** 18. **Par:** 72/72.
Yards: 6,375/5,223. **Course rating:** N/A. **Slope:** 119/115.

Opened: N/A. **Pace of Play rating:** N/A. **Green fee:** N/A.
Credit cards: MC, V, DISC. **Reduced fees:** Weekdays, Low season.
Caddies: No. **Golf carts:** N/A.
Discount golf packages: Yes. **Season:** Year-round. **High:** Dec.–April.
On-site lodging: No. **Rental clubs:** No.
Walking policy: N/A. **Range:** Yes (grass).
Subscriber comments: Good beginner's course . . . Nice course but too many distractions, mainly highway traffic.

★★½ MEADOWBROOK GOLF CLUB

SP—10401 N.W. 37th Place, Gainesville (904)332-0577.
60 miles southwest of Jacksonville. **Holes:** 18. **Par:** 72/72.
Yards: 6,289/4,720. **Course rating:** 69.9/66.7. **Slope:** 119/117.
Opened: 1987. **Pace of Play rating:** N/A. **Green fee:** $7/14.
Credit cards: MC, V, DISC. **Reduced fees:** Weekdays, Twilight.
Caddies: No. **Golf carts:** N/A.
Discount golf packages: No. **Season:** Year-round. **High:** Jan.–April.
On-site lodging: No. **Rental clubs:** Yes.
Walking policy: Walking at certain times. **Range:** Yes (grass).
To obtain tee times: Call 24 hours in advance.
Subscriber comments: Tight and sporty . . . Holes too close together . . . When dry, extremely fast greens, difficult pin positions . . . Challenging to all calibers of play.

(FRUGAL PICK)

★ MELREESE GOLF COURSE

PU—1802 N.W. 37th Ave., Miami (305)633-4583.
Holes: 18. **Par:** 70/72.
Yards: 6,784/5,684. **Course rating:** 72.0/72.0. **Slope:** 118/113.
Opened: 1962. **Pace of Play rating:** 4:00. **Green fee:** $14.
Credit cards: MC, V. **Reduced fees:** Weekdays, Low season, Twilight, Juniors.
Caddies: No. **Golf carts:** $10 for 18 holes.
Discount golf packages: No. **Season:** Year-round. **High:** Jan.–April.
On-site lodging: No. **Rental clubs:** Yes.
Walking policy: Walking at certain times. **Range:** Yes (grass).
To obtain tee times: Call 24 hours in advance.
Subscriber comments: A mere shell of its former self . . . Still feeling effects of Hurricane Andrew . . . Nice view of Miami's expressways.

★★★½ METROWEST COUNTRY CLUB

SP—2100 S. Hiawasse Rd., Orlando (407)299-1099.
Holes: 18. **Par:** 72/72.
Yards: 7,051/5,325. **Course rating:** 73.1/69.6. **Slope:** 126/117.
Opened: 1987. **Pace of Play rating:** 4:00. **Green fee:** $42/65.
Credit cards: MC, V, AMEX. **Reduced fees:** Low season, Twilight, Juniors.
Caddies: No. **Golf carts:** Included in Green Fee.
Discount golf packages: Yes. **Season:** Year-round. **High:** Jan.–May.
On-site lodging: No. **Rental clubs:** Yes.
Walking policy: Mandatory cart. **Range:** Yes (grass).
To obtain tee times: Call up to seven days in advance.
Subscriber comments: Brutally long . . . Close to airport . . . Rip it, wide-open course, playable for all . . . No one hole is like the other . . . Hilly . . . R.T. Jones design that is fun and challenging.

★★ MIAMI SHORES COUNTRY CLUB

SP—10000 Biscayne Blvd., Miami Shores (305)795-2366.
15 miles north of Miami. **Holes:** 18. **Par:** 71/72.
Yards: 6,400/5,400. **Course rating:** 70.6/71.3. **Slope:** 121/126.
Opened: 1938. **Pace of Play rating:** 4:00. **Green fee:** $30/50.
Credit cards: MC, V, AMEX. **Reduced fees:** Weekdays, Low season, Twilight.
Caddies: No. **Golf carts:** Included in Green Fee.
Discount golf packages: No. **Season:** Year-round. **High:** Dec.–April.
On-site lodging: No. **Rental clubs:** Yes.

Walking policy: Mandatory cart. **Range:** No.
To obtain tee times: Call up to three days in advance.
Subscriber comments: Very helpful staff. Recent renovation of several holes.

★★½ MILL COVE GOLF CLUB
PU—1700 Monument Rd., Jacksonville (904)646-4653.
Holes: 18. **Par:** 71/71.
Yards: 6,671/4,719. **Course rating:** 71.7/66.3. **Slope:** 129/112.
Opened: 1990. **Pace of Play rating:** N/A. **Green fee:** $13/22.
Credit cards: MC, V, AMEX. **Reduced fees:** Weekdays, Low season, Twilight, Seniors, Juniors.
Caddies: No. **Golf carts:** $13 for 18 holes.
Discount golf packages: No. **Season:** Year-round. **High:** Year-round.
On-site lodging: No. **Rental clubs:** Yes.
Walking policy: Walking at certain times. **Range:** Yes (grass).
To obtain tee times: Call three days in advance.
Subscriber comments: Nice Arnold Palmer design . . . Fun course with some challenges . . . Hills, water, and woods . . . Adjacent to airport, noise sometimes bothersome . . . Good golf course for average player, average condition year-round.

MISSION INN GOLF AND TENNIS RESORT
SP—10400 County Rd. 48, Howey-in-the-Hills (904)324-3885.
30 miles northwest of Orlando.
Credit cards: All major. **Reduced fees:** Weekdays, Low season, Twilight, Seniors, Juniors.
Caddies: No. **Golf carts:** Included in Green Fee.
Discount golf packages: Yes. **Season:** Year-round. **High:** Feb.-April.
On-site lodging: Yes. **Rental clubs:** Yes.
Walking policy: Mandatory cart. **Range:** Yes (grass).
To obtain tee times: Call.

★★★½ EL CAMPEON COURSE
Holes: 18. **Par:** 72/73.
Yards: 6,852/4,709. **Course rating:** 73.5/68.0. **Slope:** 134/122.
Opened: 1926. **Pace of Play rating:** 4:30. **Green fee:** $38/75.
Subscriber comments: Beautiful, tight and challenging; locals can get deals . . . Nice hideaway, nothing close . . . Memorable holes, top notch, good food and service . . . Challenging old course with elevation changes unusual in Florida . . . "Old Florida" style . . . Very hilly and long . . . Hilly for Florida, long par 4s, great test for good players.

★★★ LAS COLINAS COURSE
Holes: 18. **Par:** 72/71.
Yards: 6,867/4,500. **Course rating:** 72.7/65.2. **Slope:** 128/109.
Opened: 1992. **Pace of Play rating:** 4:30. **Green fee:** $38/65.
Subscriber comments: Brand-new course, narrow and difficult. Nice though . . . Good, new Florida course; good greens, good condition . . . Good new course. Wide open . . . Golf course is maturing nicely.

★★★ THE MOORS GOLF CLUB
PU—3220 Avalon Blvd., Milton (904)995-4653, (800)727-1010.
6 miles northeast of Pensacola. **Holes:** 18. **Par:** 71/71.
Yards: 6,956/5,340. **Course rating:** 73.3/70.3. **Slope:** 126/117.
Opened: 1993. **Pace of Play rating:** 4:25. **Green fee:** $20/26.
Credit cards: All major. **Reduced fees:** Weekdays, Resort guests, Juniors.
Caddies: No. **Golf carts:** $12 for 18 holes.
Discount golf packages: No. **Season:** Year-round. **High:** April-May/Sept.-Oct.
On-site lodging: No. **Rental clubs:** Yes.
Walking policy: Walking at certain times. **Range:** Yes (grass).
To obtain tee times: Call three days in advance.
Subscriber comments: New course, improves every year, beautiful facilities, staff is outstanding . . . Fun course to play . . . Course tends to be wet on the edges, will improve with age.

★★½ NAPLES BEACH HOTEL AND GOLF CLUB
SP—851 Gulf Shore Blvd. North, Naples (813)261-2222, (800)237-7600.
Holes: 18. **Par:** 72/72.
Yards: 6,500/5,300. **Course rating:** 71.2/70.1. **Slope:** 122/115.
Opened: 1930. **Pace of Play rating:** N/A. **Green fee:** $39/90.
Credit cards: All major. **Reduced fees:** Resort guests.
Caddies: No. **Golf carts:** Included in Green Fee.
Discount golf packages: Yes. **Season:** Year-round. **High:** Jan.-April.
On-site lodging: Yes. **Rental clubs:** Yes.
Walking policy: Mandatory cart. **Range:** Yes (grass).
To obtain tee times: Hotel guests 90 days in advance, non-guests call
three days in advance.
Subscriber comments: Don't go to sleep on course, it will bite . . . A
great golf getaway; challenging course and a hotel on the beach . . . Super
hotel course, people treat you fine . . . In good shape, there is a lot of play
on it, just keep the ball in play, the staff and service were good . . . Pleasant
staff, friendly track, good condition, great location.

NORMANDY SHORES GOLF COURSE★
PU—2401 Biarritz Dr., Miami Beach (305)868-6502.
Holes: 18. **Par:** 71/73.
Yards: 6,402/5,527. **Course rating:** 70.5/71.0. **Slope:** 120/119.
Opened: 1938. **Pace of Play rating:** 4:00. **Green fee:** $18/135.
Credit cards: MC, V. **Reduced fees:** Weekdays, Low season, Twilight.
Caddies: No. **Golf carts:** Included in Green Fee.
Discount golf packages: Yes. **Season:** Year-round. **High:** Nov.-April.
On-site lodging: No. **Rental clubs:** Yes.
Walking policy: Walking at certain times. **Range:** Yes (grass).
To obtain tee times: Call one week in advance.

NORTH PALM BEACH COUNTRY CLUB★
PU—951 U.S. Hwy. 1, North Palm Beach (407)626-4344.
5 miles north of West Palm Beach. **Holes:** 18. **Par:** 72/72.
Yards: 6,275/5,055. **Course rating:** 70.0/69.0. **Slope:** 117/115.
Opened: 1963. **Pace of Play rating:** 4:30. **Green fee:** $20/50.
Credit cards: MC, V. **Reduced fees:** Low season, Juniors.
Caddies: No. **Golf carts:** Included in Green Fee.
Discount golf packages: No. **Season:** Year-round. **High:** Nov.-May.
On-site lodging: No. **Rental clubs:** Yes.
Walking policy: Mandatory cart. **Range:** Yes (grass).
To obtain tee times: Call one day in advance at 8 a.m.

★★½ NORTHDALE GOLF CLUB
SP—4417 Northdale Blvd., Tampa (813)962-0428.
Holes: 18. **Par:** 72/72.
Yards: 6,791/5,397. **Course rating:** 72.1/71.0. **Slope:** 119/113.
Opened: 1978. **Pace of Play rating:** N/A. **Green fee:** $35.
Credit cards: MC, V. **Reduced fees:** Twilight.
Caddies: No. **Golf carts:** Included in Green Fee.
Discount golf packages: No. **Season:** Year-round. **High:** Dec.-April.
On-site lodging: No. **Rental clubs:** Yes.
Walking policy: Mandatory cart. **Range:** No.
To obtain tee times: Call up to three days in advance.

Subscriber comments: Short course, good for high handicapper . . .
Usually crowded causing somewhat slow play . . . Nice layout, very slow
pace of play . . . Good variety of holes, shots, for average player.

★★★ OAK HILLS GOLF CLUB
PU—10059 Northcliff Blvd., Spring Hill (904)683-6830.
37 miles northwest of Tampa. **Holes:** 18. **Par:** 72/72.
Yards: 6,774/5,468. **Course rating:** 72.2/71.1. **Slope:** 123/119.
Opened: 1982. **Pace of Play rating:** 4:10. **Green fee:** $18/27.
Credit cards: All major. **Reduced fees:** Weekdays, Low season, Twilight,
Seniors, Juniors.

Caddies: No. **Golf carts:** Included in Green Fee.
Discount golf packages: Yes. **Season:** Year-round. **High:** Dec.-March.
On-site lodging: No. **Rental clubs:** Yes.
Walking policy: Walking at certain times. **Range:** Yes (grass).
To obtain tee times: Call.
Subscriber comments: Back nine is a great challenge . . . Pretty course, kept in good shape . . . My favorite bargain course. Great hills and elevations. Pretty setting. Friendly people . . . No trouble, good for 100-scorer.

★★★½OLDE HICKORY GOLF AND COUNTRY CLUB

SP—14670 Olde Hickory Blvd., Fort Myers (813)768-3335.
Call club for further information.
Subscriber comments: Well-kept course, tough for any player, a lot of water, good staff . . . Tight layout, but a good pace of play . . . Has best deal in town during summer . . . Great condition for being new.

★★½ORANGE LAKE COUNTRY CLUB

R—8505 W. Irlo Bronson Mem. Hwy., Kissimmee (407)239-1050.
15 miles west of Orlando. **Holes:** 27. **Par:** 72/72/72.
Yards: 6,531/6,670/6,571. **Course rating:** 72.6/72.6/72.3.
Slope: 132/131/131.
Opened: 1982. **Pace of Play rating:** 4:00. **Green fee:** $30/65.
Credit cards: MC, V, AMEX. **Reduced fees:** Weekdays, Low season, Resort guests, Twilight, Juniors.
Caddies: No. **Golf carts:** Included in Green Fee.
Discount golf packages: Yes. **Season:** Year-round. **High:** Jan.-April.
On-site lodging: Yes. **Rental clubs:** Yes.
Walking policy: Mandatory cart. **Range:** Yes (grass).
To obtain tee times: Call.
Subscriber comments: Medium course, service good, pace good . . . 27 holes, each nine different, good test, greens suffer in summer . . . Beautiful but not cheap. Lots of trouble . . . Have to stay in fairway . . . Very challenging, fast greens.

★½ORIOLE GOLF AND TENNIS CLUB OF MARGATE

PU—8000 W. Margate Blvd., Margate (305)972-8140.
5 miles north of Fort Lauderdale. **Holes:** 18. **Par:** 72/72.
Yards: 6,418/4872. **Course rating:** 70.9/67.7. **Slope:** 120/112.
Opened: 1972. **Pace of Play rating:** N/A. **Green fee:** $12/32.
Credit cards: MC, V. **Reduced fees:** Low season, Twilight.
Caddies: No. **Golf carts:** Included in Green Fee.
Discount golf packages: No. **Season:** Year-round. **High:** Jan.-April.
On-site lodging: No. **Rental clubs:** Yes.
Walking policy: Mandatory cart. **Range:** Yes (grass).
To obtain tee times: Call two days in advance.
Subscriber comments: Easy, short course but very well maintained, excellent staff . . . Place to go to beat the ball around . . . Open course, a little short but kept nice . . . Excellent bargain, get what you paid for . . . Above average course priced within reason.

★★½OXBOW GOLF CLUB

SP—1 Oxbow Dr., La Belle (813)675-4411.
Call club for further information.
Subscriber comments: Excellent off-season value. Course sneaks up on you. Great weekend getaway . . . Fun layout, good condition, not crowded . . . Open course, moves well, good staff . . . Old Florida. Large oak trees. Friendly people . . . Nice challenge. Great golf packages. Good food, and "lots-a-room at the inn" . . . Great place to disappear . . . Good course. Price is right.

★★★½PALISADES GOLF CLUB

SP—16510 Palisades Blvd., Clermont (904)394-0085.
20 miles west of Orlando. **Holes:** 18. **Par:** 72/72.

Yards: 6,988/5,528. **Course rating:** 73.8/72.1. **Slope:** 127/122.
Opened: 1991. **Pace of Play rating:** 4:90. **Green fee:** $30/55.
Credit cards: MC, V. **Reduced fees:** Weekdays, Low season, Resort guests, Twilight, Seniors, Juniors.
Caddies: No. **Golf carts:** Included in Green Fee.

Discount golf packages: Yes. **Season:** Year-round. **High:** Jan.-April.
On-site lodging: No. **Rental clubs:** Yes.
Walking policy: Mandatory cart. **Range:** Yes (grass).
To obtain tee times: Call up to 30 days in advance. Deposit required.
Subscriber comments: Fun, quiet course. Tough, from back tees . . . Good layout, reasonably priced . . . Courteous staff. New management putting $ into course . . . Beautiful elevations, double hazards require pinpoint shotmaking . . . Easy to find out-of-bounds. Tough test for high handicapper . . . A nice surprise, uncrowded and quiet . . . Remote but worth the drive . . . Hilly and challenging, but fair.

PALM AIRE SPA RESORT AND COUNTRY CLUB
R—2601 Palm Aire Dr. North, Pompano Beach (305)974-7699.
10 miles north of Ft. Lauderdale.
Pace of Play rating: 4:30. **Green fee:** $20/42.
Credit cards: MC, V, AMEX. **Reduced fees:** No.
Caddies: No. **Golf carts:** $15 for 18 holes.
Discount golf packages: Yes. **Season:** Year-round. **High:** May-Sept.
On-site lodging: Yes. **Rental clubs:** Yes.
Walking policy: Mandatory cart. **Range:** Yes (grass).
To obtain tee times: Members can submit cards five to seven days in advance.
Also has 18-hole, par-3 Sabals Course.
★★ **THE PALMS COURSE**
Holes: 18. **Par:** 72/72.
Yards: 6,932/5,434. **Course rating:** 73.7/70.9. **Slope:** 128/120.
Opened: 1962.
Subscriber comments: Lots of water, very pretty course with lots of birds but not many birdies . . . OK place to play on weekdays, average condition.
★½ **THE PINES COURSE**
Holes: 18. **Par:** 72/72.
Yards: 6,610/5,232. **Course rating:** 71.3/69.4. **Slope:** 122/115.
Opened: 1969.

PALM AIRE SPA RESORT AND COUNTRY CLUB
R—3701 Oaks Clubhouse Dr., Pompano Beach (305)978-1737.
Pace of Play rating: 4:30. **Green fee:** $20/42.
Credit cards: MC, V, AMEX. **Reduced fees:** No.
Caddies: No. **Golf carts:** $15 for 18 holes.
Discount golf packages: Yes. **Season:** Year-round. **High:** May-Sept.
On-site lodging: Yes. **Rental clubs:** Yes.
Walking policy: Mandatory cart. **Range:** Yes (grass).
To obtain tee times: Members can submit card five to seven days in advance.
THE OAKS★
Holes: 18. **Par:** 72/72.
Yards: 6,747/5,402. **Course rating:** 72.2/70.4. **Slope:** 122/114.
Opened: 1973.
THE CYPRESS★
Holes: 18. **Par:** 72/72.
Yards: 6,868/5,447. **Course rating:** 73.3/70.8. **Slope:** 128/118.
Opened: 1979.

★★ **PALM BEACH GARDENS MUNICIPAL GOLF COURSE**
PU—11401 Northlake Blvd., Palm Beach Gardens (407)775-2556.
8 miles north of West Palm Beach. **Holes:** 18. **Par:** 72/72.
Yards: 6,375/4,663. **Course rating:** 71.1/66.5. **Slope:** 125/110.
Opened: 1991. **Pace of Play rating:** 4:15. **Green fee:** $8/27.

Credit cards: MC, V. **Reduced fees:** Weekdays, Low season, Twilight, Seniors, Juniors.
Caddies: No. **Golf carts:** N/A.
Discount golf packages: Yes. **Season:** Year-round. **High:** Dec.-April.
On-site lodging: No. **Rental clubs:** Yes.
Walking policy: Walking at certain times. **Range:** Yes (grass).
To obtain tee times: Call up to three days in advance.
Subscriber comments: Tough, tough, tough . . . Lots of water, narrow fairways . . . Very, very wet after heavy rain. Bring lots of balls . . . Tight and scenic; you either love it or hate it . . . Beautiful course. Great layout. A former wildlife refuge. Nice staff.

PALM BEACH POLO AND COUNTRY CLUB
R—11830 Polo Club Rd., West Palm Beach (407)798-7401.
Pace of Play rating: 4:30. **Green fee:** $75/100.
Credit cards: MC, V, AMEX.
Caddies: No. **Golf carts:** $14 for 18 holes.
Discount golf packages: Yes. **Season:** Year-round. **High:** Dec.-April.
On-site lodging: Yes. **Rental clubs:** Yes.
Walking policy: Mandatory cart. **Range:** Yes (grass).
To obtain tee times: Must be a registered resort guest, guest of a member or member of another private country club arranged through their golf pro. Also the 9-hole, par-36 Olde Course.

★★★½ CYPRESS COURSE
Holes: 18. **Par:** 72/72.
Yards: 7,116/5,172. **Course rating:** 74.4/69.8. **Slope:** 138/121.
Opened: 1977. **Reduced fees:** Resort guests, Twilight.
Subscriber comments: First-class course, condition, staff . . . Great fun for better golfers . . . Last three holes will leave you reeling.

★★★★ DUNES COURSE
Holes: 18. **Par:** 72/72.
Yards: 7,050/5,516. **Course rating:** 73.6/71.4. **Slope:** 132/122.
Opened: 1984. **Reduced fees:** Twilight.
Ranked 57th in America's 75 Best Resort Courses by Golf Digest.
Subscriber comments: Wonderful . . . Good course, well maintained . . . Superior resort course . . . Excellent layout. Excellent condition . . . Good people. Good track.

★★½ PALM HARBOR GOLF CLUB
SP—Palm Harbor Pkwy., Palm Coast (904)445-0845, (800)874-2101.
30 miles north of Daytona Beach. **Holes:** 18. **Par:** 72/72.
Yards: 6,572/5,346. **Course rating:** 71.8/71.2. **Slope:** 127/128.
Opened: 1973. **Pace of Play rating:** N/A. **Green fee:** $39/48.
Credit cards: MC, V. **Reduced fees:** Low season, Resort guests, Twilight, Juniors.
Caddies: No. **Golf carts:** Included in Green Fee.
Discount golf packages: Yes. **Season:** Year-round. **High:** Jan.-May.
On-site lodging: No. **Rental clubs:** Yes.
Walking policy: Mandatory cart. **Range:** Yes (grass).
To obtain tee times: Call up to five days in advance.
Subscriber comments: Tricky but fun course, good staff, good condition . . . Good for high handicapper, short but tight . . . Good course to walk . . . Tough public course. Water everywhere. Narrow fairways.

★½ PALM RIVER COUNTRY CLUB
SP—Palm River Blvd., Naples (813)597-6082.
6 miles from Naples. **Holes:** 18. **Par:** 72/72.
Yards: 6,718/5,830. **Course rating:** N/A. **Slope:** 120/121.
Opened: N/A. **Pace of Play rating:** N/A. **Green fee:** N/A.
Credit cards: MC, V. **Reduced fees:** Low season, Twilight.
Caddies: No. **Golf carts:** N/A.
Discount golf packages: No. **Season:** Year-round. **High:** Jan.-March.
On-site lodging: No. **Rental clubs:** No.
Walking policy: N/A. **Range:** No.

Subscriber comments: Good for average golfer, always improving . . .
Long, open; nice program for kids in summer.

★★ PALMETTO GOLF COURSE
PU—9300 S.W. 152nd, Miami (305)238-2922.
Holes: 18. **Par:** 70/73.
Yards: 6,713/5,725. **Course rating:** 72.7/73.4. **Slope:** 128/125.
Opened: 1959. **Pace of Play rating:** 4:00. **Green fee:** $12/25.
Credit cards: MC, V, AMEX. **Reduced fees:** Weekdays, Low season,
Twilight, Juniors.
Caddies: No. **Golf carts:** $13 for 18 holes.
Discount golf packages: Yes. **Season:** Year-round. **High:** Jan.–March.
On-site lodging: No. **Rental clubs:** Yes.
Walking policy: Unrestricted walking. **Range:** Yes.
To obtain tee times: Call automatic system service seven days in advance.
Subscriber comments: Good muny, well run, wide open . . . Hurt by
Hurricane Andrew, replanted hundreds of palm trees . . . Very playable.
Done a great job since Andrew . . . Crowded but always in great shape.

PELICAN BAY COUNTRY CLUB
★★★ SOUTH COURSE
PU—550 Sea Duck Dr., Daytona Beach (904)788-6496.
40 miles northeast of Orlando. **Holes:** 18. **Par:** 72/72.
Yards: 6,630/5,278. **Course rating:** N/A. **Slope:** 123/126.
Opened: N/A. **Pace of Play rating:** N/A. **Green fee:** N/A.
Credit cards: MC, V. **Reduced fees:** Weekdays, Low season, Twilight.
Caddies: No. **Golf carts:** Included in Green Fee.
Discount golf packages: Yes. **Season:** Year-round. **High:** Dec.–April.
On-site lodging: No. **Rental clubs:** No.
Walking policy: . **Range:** No.
Subscriber comments: Sporty layout. Great snack bar . . . Short, fun to
play, nice design . . . Island green is a challenge . . . Service excellent and
pace of play generally OK. We play all year and conditions are excellent.
Except after heavy rains such as Gordan this past year . . . Plenty of water.
Long hitters need not apply.

PELICAN'S NEST GOLF CLUB
★★★★ HURRICANE/GATOR/SEMINOLE/PANTHER
PU—4450 Pelican's Nest Dr., Bonita Springs (813)947-4600,
(800)952-6378.
15 miles south of Fort Myers. **Holes:** 36. **Par:** 72/72.
Yards: 7,016/5,201. **Course rating:** 74.8/69.2. **Slope:** 140/122.
Opened: 1985. **Pace of Play rating:** N/A. **Green fee:** $38/115.
Credit cards: MC, V, AMEX. **Reduced fees:** Low season, Twilight,
Juniors.
Caddies: No. **Golf carts:** Included in Green Fee.
Discount golf packages: No. **Season:** Year-round. **High:** Jan.–March.
On-site lodging: No. **Rental clubs:** Yes.
Walking policy: Mandatory cart. **Range:** Yes (grass).
To obtain tee times: Call 48 hours in advance.
Subscriber comments: Always in A-1 shape . . . The nest is the best! . . .
Tough course but as good as it gets . . . Great layout, very pleasant staff,
always top condition . . . The finest all-round in the area, challenging, staff
great, a beautiful course . . . Only the accurate need apply . . .

★★★ PERDIDO BAY GOLF CLUB
R—One Doug Ford Dr., Pensacola (904)492-1223.
Holes: 18. **Par:** 72/72.
Yards: 7,154/5,478. **Course rating:** 73.6/71.4. **Slope:** 125/121.
Opened: 1963. **Pace of Play rating:** 4:10. **Green fee:** $32/45.
Credit cards: MC, V. **Reduced fees:** Resort guests, Twilight, Juniors.
Caddies: No. **Golf carts:** Included in Green Fee.
Discount golf packages: Yes. **Season:** Year-round. **High:** Jan.–April.
On-site lodging: Yes. **Rental clubs:** Yes.

Walking policy: Mandatory cart. **Range:** Yes (grass).
To obtain tee times: Call. Credit card required if more than seven days in advance.
Subscriber comments: One of the best when in good shape, former PGA Tour site; good, longtime staff . . . Nice resort course, pleasant to play.

PGA NATIONAL RESORT AND SPA
R—1000 Ave. of the Champions, Palm Beach Gardens (407)627-1800, (800)633-9150.
15 miles north of West Palm Beach.
Credit cards: MC, V, AMEX. **Reduced fees:** Low season.
Caddies: No. **Golf carts:** $18 for 18 holes.
Discount golf packages: Yes. **Season:** Year-round. **High:** Jan.-April.
On-site lodging: Yes. **Rental clubs:** Yes.
Walking policy: Mandatory cart. **Range:** Yes (grass).
To obtain tee times: Registered resort guests may call up to one year in advance.

★★★★ CHAMPION COURSE
Holes: 18. **Par:** 72/72.
Yards: 7,022/5,377. **Course rating:** 74.7/71.1. **Slope:** 142/123.
Opened: 1981. **Pace of Play rating:** 4:30. **Green fee:** $125.
Ranked 72nd in America's 75 Best Resort Courses by Golf Digest.
Subscriber comments: Overrated Nicklaus course, designed for pros . . . You feel like a Tour player here . . . Too expensive but worth it once . . . The toughest course in central Florida . . . Must be lottery winner, even out of season . . . Tough for beginners, beautiful facility . . . Very good course, service good, conditioning good . . . A great tournament course in excellent condition . . . Great course, facility . . . Professional in all aspects.

★★★½ ESTATE COURSE
Holes: 18. **Par:** 72/72.
Yards: 6,784/4,903. **Course rating:** 73.4/68.4. **Slope:** 131/118.
Opened: 1984. **Pace of Play rating:** 4:30. **Green fee:** $85.
Subscriber comments: Great shape for early fall, four-hour rounds, course fun, played behind Donald Trump . . . Off-season, best value in area . . . A real sleeper and well-maintained . . . Good greens, fairly short, easiest of resort to score on . . . Enjoyable and fun . . . Watch out for first hole.

★★★ GENERAL COURSE
Holes: 18. **Par:** 72/72.
Yards: 6,768/5,324. **Course rating:** 73.0/71.0. **Slope:** 130/122.
Opened: 1984. **Pace of Play rating:** 4:30. **Green fee:** $85.
Subscriber comments: Good layout, well-maintained, pleasant staff, reasonable price . . . Water, water, water; every hole a challenge.

★★★½ HAIG COURSE
Holes: 18. **Par:** 72/72.
Yards: 6,806/5,645. **Course rating:** 73.0/72.5. **Slope:** 130/121.
Opened: 1980. **Pace of Play rating:** 4:30. **Green fee:** $85.
Subscriber comments: Tough course for average golfer, yet fun to play, nice staff . . . New greens make this course one of Fazio's best . . . Relatively easy . . . Hard course . . . Not too long, I liked it.

★★★ SQUIRE COURSE
Holes: 18. **Par:** 72/72.
Yards: 6,478/4,982. **Course rating:** 71.3/69.8. **Slope:** 127/123.
Opened: 1981. **Pace of Play rating:** 4:30. **Green fee:** $85.
Subscriber comments: Position course, shorter than others . . . Just redone, good layout, good condition.

★★½ PINE LAKES COUNTRY CLUB
SP—400 Pine Lakes Pkwy., Palm Coast (904)445-0852, (800)874-2101.
30 miles north of Daytona Beach. **Holes:** 18. **Par:** 72/72.
Yards: 7,074/5,166. **Course rating:** 73.5/71.4. **Slope:** 126/124.
Opened: 1980. **Pace of Play rating:** N/A. **Green fee:** $39/48.
Credit cards: MC, V. **Reduced fees:** Low season, Resort guests, Twilight, Juniors.

Caddies: No. **Golf carts:** Included in Green Fee.
Discount golf packages: Yes. **Season:** Year-round. **High:** Jan.-April.
On-site lodging: No. **Rental clubs:** Yes.
Walking policy: Mandatory cart. **Range:** Yes (grass).
To obtain tee times: Call up to five days in advance.
Subscriber comments: Good, solid, straightforward course.

PLANT CITY GOLF CLUB★

SP—3102 Coronet Rd., Plant City (813)752-1524.
20 miles east of Tampa. **Holes:** 18. **Par:** 72/72.
Yards: 6,479/4,929. **Course rating:** 70.4/67.3. **Slope:** 118/109.
Opened: 1932. **Pace of Play rating:** 4:00. **Green fee:** $18/25.
Credit cards: MC, V, DISC. **Reduced fees:** Weekdays, Low season,
Twilight, Juniors.
Caddies: No. **Golf carts:** Included in Green Fee.
Discount golf packages: No. **Season:** Year-round. **High:** Nov.-April.
On-site lodging: No. **Rental clubs:** Yes.
Walking policy: Walking at certain times. **Range:** Yes (grass).
To obtain tee times: Call two days in advance.

PLANTATION GOLF AND COUNTRY CLUB

SP—500 Rockley Blvd., Venice (813)493-2000.
15 miles south of Sarasota.
Pace of Play rating: N/A. **Green fee:** $31/52.
Credit cards: MC, V, DISC. **Reduced fees:** Low season, Resort guests.
Caddies: No. **Golf carts:** $11 for 18 holes.
Discount golf packages: No. **Season:** Year-round. **High:** Oct.-April.
On-site lodging: Yes. **Rental clubs:** Yes.
Walking policy: Walking at certain times. **Range:** Yes (grass).
To obtain tee times: Public may call two days in advance. Resort guests,
three days in advance.

★★★ BOBCAT COURSE

Holes: 18. **Par:** 72/72.
Yards: 6,840/5,023. **Course rating:** 73.0/70.6. **Slope:** 130/121.
Opened: 1981.
Subscriber comments: Great layout, good maintenance, good greens . . .
Rolling terrain, pot bunkers a real challenge . . . Good test, improved
layout.

★★★ PANTHER COURSE

Holes: 18. **Par:** 72/72.
Yards: 6,311/4,751. **Course rating:** 70.7/68.0. **Slope:** 124/117.
Opened: 1985.
Subscriber comments: Target course, tough par 3s . . . Nicer of the two
courses . . . Links course, rolling hills, tiered greens, accuracy needed . . .
Very nice layout in good condition . . .

PLANTATION INN AND GOLF RESORT
★★ CHAMPIONSHIP COURSE

R—9301 West Fort Island Trail, Crystal River (904)795-7211, (800)632-
6262.
80 miles north of Orlando. **Holes:** 18. **Par:** 72/72.
Yards: 6,502/5,395. **Course rating:** 71.6/71.1. **Slope:** 126/117.
Opened: 1956. **Pace of Play rating:** 4:15. **Green fee:** $15/32.
Credit cards: MC, V, AMEX. **Reduced fees:** Weekdays, Low season,
Resort guests, Twilight, Juniors.
Caddies: No. **Golf carts:** Included in Green Fee.
Discount golf packages: Yes. **Season:** Year-round. **High:** Feb.-April.
On-site lodging: Yes. **Rental clubs:** Yes.
Walking policy: Walking at certain times. **Range:** Yes (grass).
To obtain tee times: Call two days in advance.
Subscriber comments: Floods very easily . . . Average layout, often very
wet . . . Dead flat with parallel holes . . . Average layout, average player.

★★½ POINCIANA GOLF AND RACQUET RESORT
R—500 E. Cypress Pkwy., Kissimmee (407)933-5300, (800)331-7743.
14 miles south of Orlando. **Holes:** 18. **Par:** 72/72.
Yards: 6,700/4,938. **Course rating:** 72.2/68.4. **Slope:** 125/118.
Opened: 1973. **Pace of Play rating:** 4:15. **Green fee:** $20/40.
Credit cards: MC, V, AMEX. **Reduced fees:** Low season, Resort guests,
Twilight, Juniors.
Caddies: No. **Golf carts:** Included in Green Fee.
Discount golf packages: Yes. **Season:** Year-round. **High:** Jan.-April.
On-site lodging: Yes. **Rental clubs:** Yes.
Walking policy: Mandatory cart. **Range:** Yes (grass).
To obtain tee times: Call seven days in advance.
Subscriber comments: Played it once and fell in love . . . Interesting
course, good food . . . Real nice, good service, on-course snack bar unique
. . . Treated good by staff. Pace of play good . . . Good course to play and
have fun.

POMPANO BEACH GOLF COURSE
PU—1101 N. Federal Hwy., Pompano Beach (305)781-0426.
7 miles north of Ft. Lauderdale.
Opened: 1954. **Pace of Play rating:** N/A. **Green fee:** $20/36.
Credit cards: None. **Reduced fees:** Low season, Twilight, Juniors.
Caddies: No. **Golf carts:** N/A.
Discount golf packages: No. **Season:** Year-round. **High:** Jan.-April.
On-site lodging: No. **Rental clubs:** Yes.
Walking policy: Unrestricted walking. **Range:** Yes (grass).
To obtain tee times: First come, first served.
★★ PALMS COURSE
Holes: 18. **Par:** 71/72.
Yards: 6,356/5,426. **Course rating:** 69.4/70.2. **Slope:** 113/114.
Subscriber comments: Heavy play . . . Long, open . . . Wonderful staff.
★★½ PINES COURSE
Holes: 18. **Par:** 72/74.
Yards: 6,886/5,980. **Course rating:** 72.2/73.4. **Slope:** 123/117.
Subscriber comments: Nice municipal course . . . Long and challenging
. . . Good test . . . City-owned.

★★½ PONCE DE LEON GOLF AND CONFERENCE RESORT
R—4000 U.S. Hwy. 1 North, St. Augustine (904)829-5314, (800)228-2821.
25 miles south of Jacksonville. **Holes:** 18. **Par:** 72/72.
Yards: 6,823/5,308. **Course rating:** 72.9/70.7. **Slope:** 131/125.
Opened: 1916. **Pace of Play rating:** 4:00. **Green fee:** $39/47.
Credit cards: MC, V, AMEX. **Reduced fees:** Low season, Resort guests,
Twilight.
Caddies: No. **Golf carts:** $16 for 18 holes.
Discount golf packages: Yes. **Season:** Year-round. **High:** Feb.-
May/Oct.-Nov.
On-site lodging: Yes. **Rental clubs:** Yes.
Walking policy: Mandatory cart. **Range:** Yes (grass).
To obtain tee times: Book tee times with hotel reservations up to one year
in advance. Others call five days in advance; with priority card, two days in
advance.
Subscriber comments: Donald Ross course, fair condition . . . Can't beat
Donald Ross . . . My wife's favorite . . . Nice diversity on both sides . . .
Great layout but very tough when the wind is up . . . Too much play,
Donald Ross would cringe . . . Good service, course fair for all, good pace
. . . Super pace of play, ranger keeps you moving.

PONTE VEDRA INN AND CLUB
R—200 Ponte Vedra Blvd., Ponte Vedra Beach (904)285-1111,
(800)234-7842.
20 miles southeast of Jacksonville.
Opened: 1928. **Pace of Play rating:** 4:00. **Green fee:** $58/67.
Credit cards: All major. **Reduced fees:** Low season.
Caddies: No. **Golf carts:** N/A.

Discount golf packages: Yes. **Season:** Year-round. **High:** March-May.
On-site lodging: Yes. **Rental clubs:** Yes.
Walking policy: Walking at certain times. **Range:** Yes (grass).
To obtain tee times: May call as soon as Inn reservation is made.

★★★ LAGOON COURSE

Holes: 18. **Par:** 70/70.
Yards: 5,574/4,641. **Course rating:** 66.2/66.9. **Slope:** 110/113.
Subscriber comments: Tougher than reputation. Lots of water. No better
staff or service than P.V. Inn . . . Short course but a skill test. Must be
accurate . . . Too short, but interesting.

★★★ OCEAN COURSE

Holes: 18. **Par:** 72/72.
Yards: 6,573/5,237. **Course rating:** 71.3/69.6. **Slope:** 120/119.
Subscriber comments: A welcome change for Florida golfers with hills,
ravines, beautiful and very reasonable . . . A great old seaside course. First
island green . . . Condition very good. Facilities very good to excellent . . .
Fun old course, bring your wind ball . . . Old southern resort atmosphere.

★★★ RAINTREE GOLF COURSE

R—1600 S. Hiatus Rd., Pembroke Pines (305)432-4400, (800)346-5332.
8 miles southwest of Ft. Lauderdale. **Holes:** 18. **Par:** 72/72.
Yards: 6,461/5,382. **Course rating:** 70.8/70.2. **Slope:** 126/122.
Opened: 1985. **Pace of Play rating:** 4:00. **Green fee:** $27/55.
Credit cards: All major. **Reduced fees:** Weekdays, Low season, Resort
guests, Twilight, Seniors, Juniors.
Caddies: No. **Golf carts:** Included in Green Fee.
Discount golf packages: Yes. **Season:** Year-round. **High:** Nov.-April.
On-site lodging: Yes. **Rental clubs:** Yes.
Walking policy: Mandatory cart. **Range:** Yes.
To obtain tee times: Call three days in advance.
Subscriber comments: Birdie opportunities; water on every hole . . .
Unique, three par3s, 4s, 5s on each side . . . Love the 6-6-6 layout . . . Nice
layout. Good golf. Good service.

★★★½ RAVINES GOLF AND COUNTRY CLUB

SP—2932 Ravines Rd., Middleburg (904)282-7888.
3 miles southwest of Jacksonville. **Holes:** 18. **Par:** 72/70.
Yards: 6,733/4,817. **Course rating:** 72.4/67.4. **Slope:** 133/120.
Opened: 1979. **Pace of Play rating:** 4:30. **Green fee:** $25/50.
Credit cards: All major. **Reduced fees:** No.
Caddies: No. **Golf carts:** Included in Green Fee.
Discount golf packages: No. **Season:** Year-round. **High:** March-May.
On-site lodging: Yes. **Rental clubs:** Yes.
Walking policy: Mandatory cart. **Range:** Yes (grass).
To obtain tee times: Call seven days in advance.
Subscriber comments: Beautiful mountain course set up for above-
average player . . . You'll never get tired of playing this one . . . It's highly-
rated for good reason . . . Overrated, poor condition . . . Ravines it has . . .
Mountains in Florida? See for yourself . . . Landscape makes this fun and
challenging . . . A real adventure to play, requires hitting the ball straight
and clean.

REDLAND GOLF AND COUNTRY CLUB★

PU—24451 S.W. 177th Ave., Homestead (305)247-8503.
20 miles north of Miami. **Holes:** 18. **Par:** 72/72.
Yards: 6,613/5,639. **Course rating:** 72.6/73.0. **Slope:** 123/123.
Opened: 1946. **Pace of Play rating:** 4:00. **Green fee:** $22/40.
Credit cards: MC, V. **Reduced fees:** Low season.
Caddies: No. **Golf carts:** Included in Green Fee.
Discount golf packages: No. **Season:** Year-round. **High:** Nov.-April.
On-site lodging: No. **Rental clubs:** Yes.
Walking policy: Mandatory cart. **Range:** Yes (grass).
To obtain tee times: Call one week in advance.

★★★ RIDGEWOOD LAKES GOLF CLUB

SP—200 Eagle Ridge Dr., Davenport (813)424-8688.
10 miles southwest of Orlando. **Holes:** 18. **Par:** 72/72.
Yards: 7,016/5,217. **Course rating:** 73.7/69.9. **Slope:** 129/116.
Opened: 1993. **Pace of Play rating:** N/A. **Green fee:** $15/45.
Credit cards: MC, V. **Reduced fees:** Weekdays, Low season, Twilight.
Caddies: No. **Golf carts:** Included in Green Fee.
Discount golf packages: Yes. **Season:** Year-round. **High:** Nov.-April.
On-site lodging: No. **Rental clubs:** Yes.
Walking policy: Mandatory cart. **Range:** Yes (grass).
To obtain tee times: Call up to seven days in advance.
Subscriber comments: Good course, watch for hidden water . . . Best
new course in area, good test for all handicaps . . . More water than I can
handle . . . Nice course built on old lake bottom . . . Professional staff
throughout course.

★★★ RIVER BEND GOLF CLUB

SP—730 Airport Rd., Ormond Beach (904)673-6000, (800)334-8841.
3 miles north of Daytona Beach. **Holes:** 18. **Par:** 72/72.
Yards: 6,821/5,112. **Course rating:** 72.3/69.6. **Slope:** 126/120.
Opened: 1990. **Pace of Play rating:** 4:15. **Green fee:** $27/38.
Credit cards: MC, V, AMEX. **Reduced fees:** Weekdays, Low season,
Twilight, Juniors.
Caddies: No. **Golf carts:** Included in Green Fee.
Discount golf packages: Yes. **Season:** Year-round. **High:** Jan.-April.
On-site lodging: No. **Rental clubs:** Yes.
Walking policy: Mandatory cart. **Range:** Yes (grass).
To obtain tee times: Call up to four days in advance.
Subscriber comments: Course set up for average player, pace OK, staff
OK . . . Narrow fairways a good challenge . . . Hard course to walk,
distance from green to next tee . . . Good place to play your round, short
but narrow . . . Has a 600-yard par 5.

★★★½ THE RIVER CLUB

PU—6600 River Club Blvd., Bradenton (813)751-4211.
45 miles south of Tampa. **Holes:** 18. **Par:** 72/72.
Yards: 7,004/5,252. **Course rating:** N/A. **Slope:** 133/122.
Opened: N/A. **Pace of Play rating:** N/A. **Green fee:** N/A.
Credit cards: MC, V. **Reduced fees:** Low season, Twilight.
Caddies: No. **Golf carts:** N/A.
Discount golf packages: Yes. **Season:** Year-round. **High:** Jan.-April.
On-site lodging: No. **Rental clubs:** No.
Walking policy: . **Range:** Yes (grass).
Subscriber comments: Beautiful course. Rangers keep play moving
nicely . . . Best golf in Manatee County . . . Easy tee times, great fees,
excellent course, good facilities, good wildlife, be accurate, must play . . . A
tough challenge for the weekend golfer.

★★★½ RIVER HILLS COUNTRY CLUB

SP—3943 New River Hills Pkwy., Valrico (813)653-3323.
20 miles west of Tampa. **Holes:** 18. **Par:** 72/72.
Yards: 7,004/5,236. **Course rating:** 74.0/70.4. **Slope:** 132/124.
Opened: 1989. **Pace of Play rating:** 4:00. **Green fee:** $21/40.
Credit cards: MC, V. **Reduced fees:** Low season, Twilight.
Caddies: No. **Golf carts:** $15 for 18 holes.
Discount golf packages: Yes. **Season:** Year-round. **High:** Jan.-April.
On-site lodging: No. **Rental clubs:** Yes.
Walking policy: Mandatory cart. **Range:** Yes (grass).
To obtain tee times: Call 48 hours in advance.
Subscriber comments: Challenging course, nice facilities, professional
staff . . . One of the best in Tampa Bay . . . Nice course, well managed.

★½ RIVER RUN GOLF LINKS

PU—1801 27th St. East, Bradenton (813)747-6331.
30 miles south of St. Petersburg. **Holes:** 18. **Par:** 70/70.

Yards: 5,900/4,811. **Course rating:** 67.9/66.5. **Slope:** 115/110.
Opened: 1987. **Pace of Play rating:** 4:30. **Green fee:** $8/16.
Credit cards: None. **Reduced fees:** Weekdays, Low season, Twilight.
Caddies: No. **Golf carts:** $9 for 18 holes.
Discount golf packages: No. **Season:** Year-round. **High:** Jan.-April.
On-site lodging: No. **Rental clubs:** Yes.
Walking policy: Unrestricted walking. **Range:** No.
To obtain tee times: Call 48 hours in advance.
Subscriber comments: Very short course. Some tight fairways. Fair condition . . . This short but quite well-groomed course is great fun, staff very nice . . . Player friendly . . . City course. OK for shorter hitters.

★★★★ RIVERWOOD GOLF CLUB

SP—4100 Riverwood Dr., Port Charlotte (813)764-6661.
45 miles south of Sarasota. **Holes:** 18. **Par:** 72/72.
Yards: 6,938/4,695. **Course rating:** 73.2/67.1. **Slope:** 131/111.
Opened: 1993. **Pace of Play rating:** 4:20. **Green fee:** $35/65.
Credit cards: MC, V. **Reduced fees:** Low season, Resort guests, Twilight.
Caddies: No. **Golf carts:** Included in Green Fee.
Discount golf packages: Yes. **Season:** Year-round. **High:** Dec.-April.
On-site lodging: Yes. **Rental clubs:** Yes.
Walking policy: Mandatory cart. **Range:** Yes (grass).
To obtain tee times: Call two days in advance.
Subscriber comments: Good shape for new course . . . Great practice facilities . . . Makes you very welcome . . . Only course played in '94 that really had fair women's tee boxes . . . Best in the area. Beautifully manicured. Accuracy a must. Great friendly staff.

RIVIERA COUNTRY CLUB★

SP—500 Calle Grande, Ormond Beach (904)677-2464.
4 miles north of Daytona Beach. **Holes:** 18. **Par:** 71/72.
Yards: 6,302/5,207. **Course rating:** 68.0/69.9. **Slope:** 113/122.
Opened: 1935. **Pace of Play rating:** 4:00. **Green fee:** $18/28.
Credit cards: MC, V. **Reduced fees:** Low season, Resort guests, Twilight.
Caddies: No. **Golf carts:** Included in Green Fee.
Discount golf packages: Yes. **Season:** Year-round. **High:** Jan.-March.
On-site lodging: No. **Rental clubs:** Yes.
Walking policy: Mandatory cart. **Range:** Yes (grass).
To obtain tee times: First come, first served. Call ahead to insure course availability.

★½ ROCKY POINT GOLF COURSE

PU—4151 Dana Shores Dr., Tampa (813)884-5141.
Holes: 18. **Par:** 71/71.
Yards: 6,398/4,910. **Course rating:** 71.1/65.7. **Slope:** 122/111.
Opened: 1983. **Pace of Play rating:** 4:25. **Green fee:** $20/25.
Credit cards: MC, V. **Reduced fees:** Low season.
Caddies: No. **Golf carts:** Included in Green Fee.
Discount golf packages: No. **Season:** Year-round. **High:** Year-round.
On-site lodging: No. **Rental clubs:** Yes.
Walking policy: Unrestricted walking. **Range:** No.
To obtain tee times: Call Thursday a.m. for the following week.
Subscriber comments: Fair shape, a good deal if I want to work on my swing . . . Average but affordable . . . There is no escape from water hazards . . . Best of city-owned courses . . . Always crowded, causing slow play.

★★ ROGERS PARK GOLF COURSE

PU—7910 N. 30th St., Tampa (813)234-1911.
Holes: 18. **Par:** 72/72.
Yards: 6,500/5,900. **Course rating:** 71.0/67.0. **Slope:** 120/114.
Opened: 1950. **Pace of Play rating:** 4:15. **Green fee:** $20/25.

Credit cards: MC, V. **Reduced fees:** Weekdays, Low season, Twilight, Seniors, Juniors.
Caddies: No. **Golf carts:** $18 for 18 holes.
Discount golf packages: No. **Season:** Year-round. **High:** Jan.-April.
On-site lodging: No. **Rental clubs:** Yes.
Walking policy: Unrestricted walking. **Range:** Yes (grass).
To obtain tee times: Call one week in advance.
Subscriber comments: Needs work, could be outstanding . . . Fair condition. Staff very nice and polite . . . Can almost always get on without a tee time . . . Good public course.

★½ ROLLING GREEN GOLF CLUB

SP—4501 N. Tuttle Ave., Sarasota (813)355-7621.
Holes: 18. **Par:** 72/72.
Yards: 6,495/5,387. **Course rating:** 70.3/70.5. **Slope:** 113/113.
Opened: 1968. **Pace of Play rating:** 4:00. **Green fee:** $10/20.
Credit cards: MC, V. **Reduced fees:** Low season, Seniors.
Caddies: No. **Golf carts:** $11 for 18 holes.
Discount golf packages: No. **Season:** Year-round. **High:** Nov.-April.
On-site lodging: No. **Rental clubs:** Yes.
Walking policy: Mandatory cart. **Range:** Yes (grass).
To obtain tee times: Call two days in advance.
Subscriber comments: Great course for amount of play, good for all talent, great staff . . . Wide open. Fairways and little rough make it easy to score well.

★★½ ROLLING HILLS HOTEL AND GOLF RESORT

R—3501 West Rolling Hills Circle, Fort Lauderdale (305)475-3010.
Holes: 18. **Par:** 72/72.
Yards: 6,905/5,630. **Course rating:** 72.7/71.7. **Slope:** 124/121.
Opened: 1953. **Pace of Play rating:** 4:30. **Green fee:** $20/50.
Credit cards: All major. **Reduced fees:** Weekdays, Low season, Resort guests, Twilight.
Caddies: No. **Golf carts:** Included in Green Fee.
Discount golf packages: Yes. **Season:** Year-round. **High:** Jan.-April.
On-site lodging: Yes. **Rental clubs:** Yes.
Walking policy: Mandatory cart. **Range:** Yes (grass).
To obtain tee times: Call three days in advance.
Subscriber comments: One of most playable courses in Miami/Ft. Lauderdale area during the rainy season due to a somewhat higher elevation . . . Great oak trees add beauty and difficulty . . . I bet Bill Murray didn't break 90 . . . Overrated from the movie "Caddy Shack" but good . . . Northern type course in south Florida.

★★★ ROSEDALE GOLF AND COUNTRY CLUB

SP—5100 87th St. East, Bradenton (813)756-0004.
30 miles south of Tampa. **Holes:** 18. **Par:** 72/72.
Yards: 6,779/5,169. **Course rating:** 72.6/69.7. **Slope:** 130/120.
Opened: 1993. **Pace of Play rating:** N/A. **Green fee:** $29/48.
Credit cards: MC, V. **Reduced fees:** Low season, Resort guests, Twilight.
Caddies: No. **Golf carts:** Included in Green Fee.
Discount golf packages: Yes. **Season:** Year-round. **High:** Oct.-May.
On-site lodging: No. **Rental clubs:** Yes.
Walking policy: Walking at certain times. **Range:** Yes (grass).
To obtain tee times: Call up to two days in advance.
Subscriber comments: Very nice, newer course demands accuracy . . . Tight . . . Accuracy, not length, a must . . . Hit straight or walk in the pines. Can't be overpowered . . . Tricky layout with some hard greens, patience and all shots needed. Course is tight between homes, not a relaxing course . . . Very tight and borders on unfair . . . Tight with great finishing holes.

★½ ROSEMONT GOLF AND COUNTRY CLUB

SP—4224 Clubhouse Rd., Orlando (407)298-1230.
Call club for further information.

★★½ ROYAL OAK GOLF CLUB

SP—2150 Country Club Dr., Titusville (407)268-1550, (800)884-2150.
35 miles east of Orlando. **Holes:** 18. **Par:** 71/72.
Yards: 6,709/5,471. **Course rating:** 72.3/71.5. **Slope:** 126/128.
Opened: 1964. **Pace of Play rating:** 3:45. **Green fee:** $16/39.
Credit cards: MC, V, AMEX, Diners Club. **Reduced fees:** Weekdays,
Low season, Resort guests, Twilight, Seniors, Juniors.
Caddies: No. **Golf carts:** Included in Green Fee.
Discount golf packages: Yes. **Season:** Year-round. **High:** Jan.-March.
On-site lodging: Yes. **Rental clubs:** Yes.
Walking policy: Walking at certain times. **Range:** Yes (grass).
To obtain tee times: Call one week in advance.
Subscriber comments: Plays well for older Florida course . . . Heavy
play.

SABAL POINT COUNTRY CLUB★

SP—2662 Sabal Club Way, Longwood (407)869-4622.
5 miles north of Orlando. **Holes:** 18. **Par:** 72/72.
Yards: 6,603/5,278. **Course rating:** 71.6/70.0. **Slope:** 129/119.
Opened: 1981. **Pace of Play rating:** 4:15. **Green fee:** $25/55.
Credit cards: MC, V, AMEX. **Reduced fees:** Weekdays, Low season,
Twilight, Juniors.
Caddies: No. **Golf carts:** Included in Green Fee.
Discount golf packages: No. **Season:** Year-round. **High:** Jan.-April.
On-site lodging: No. **Rental clubs:** Yes.
Walking policy: Mandatory cart. **Range:** Yes (grass).
To obtain tee times: Call two days in advance.

SADDLEBROOK RESORT

R—5700 Saddlebrook Way, Wesley Chapel (813)973-1111, (800)729-8383.
30 miles north of Tampa.
Opened: 1983. **Pace of Play rating:** N/A.
Credit cards: All major. **Reduced fees:** Low season, Resort guests.
Caddies: No. **Golf carts:** Included in Green Fee.
Discount golf packages: Yes. **Season:** Year-round. **High:** Nov.-April.
On-site lodging: Yes. **Rental clubs:** Yes.
Walking policy: Mandatory cart. **Range:** Yes (grass).
To obtain tee times: Call 48 hours in advance. Resort guests may reserve
tee times 60 days in advance.

★★★ PALMER COURSE

Holes: 18. **Par:** 71/71.
Yards: 6,469/5,212. **Course rating:** 71.0/70.2. **Slope:** 126/121.
Green fee: $35/95.
Subscriber comments: Trees, trees and more trees, very scenic . . . Hard
shotmaker's course. Great service. Tough rough . . . Great value in
summer, a little forgiving.

★★★½ SADDLEBROOK COURSE

Holes: 18. **Par:** 70/70.
Yards: 6,603/5,183. **Course rating:** 72.0/70.8. **Slope:** 124/124.
Subscriber comments: Tough course with lots of water, excellent staff
. . . Good people, good facilities . . . Super value during summer months,
18th hole one of top finishing holes anywhere . . . Use every club in the
bag.

★★★½ ST. JOHNS COUNTY GOLF CLUB

PU—4900 Cypress Links Blvd., Eckton (904)825-4900.
30 miles south of Jacksonville. **Holes:** 18. **Par:** 72/72.
Yards: 6,926/5,173. **Course rating:** 72.9/68.8. **Slope:** 130/117.
Opened: 1983. **Pace of Play rating:** N/A. **Green fee:** $15.
Credit cards: MC, V. **Reduced fees:** Twilight.
Caddies: No. **Golf carts:** $9 for 18 holes.
Discount golf packages: No. **Season:** Year-round. **High:** Jan.-April.
On-site lodging: No. **Rental clubs:** Yes.
Walking policy: Walking at certain times. **Range:** Yes (grass).
To obtain tee times: Call up to seven days in advance.

Subscriber comments: Great conditions, getting better with age and care, great staff . . . Course is a good challenge for any class of player. Huge, sloped greens and long tees. Challenging water carry. Take off as much as you dare!

★★★★ ST. LUCIE WEST COUNTRY CLUB

SP—951 SW Country Club Dr., Port St. Lucie (407)340-1911.
45 miles north of West Palm Beach. **Holes:** 18. **Par:** 72/72.
Yards: 6,801/5,054. **Course rating:** 72.7/69.8. **Slope:** 130/121
Opened: 1987. **Pace of Play rating:** 4:10. **Green fee:** $25/50.
Credit cards: All major. **Reduced fees:** Low season, Twilight, Juniors.
Caddies: No. **Golf carts:** Included in Green Fee.
Discount golf packages: No. **Season:** Year-round. **High:** Jan.-March.
On-site lodging: No. **Rental clubs:** Yes.
Walking policy: Mandatory cart. **Range:** Yes (grass).
To obtain tee times: Call 48 hours in advance.

Subscriber comments: Great layout, excellent service, good course anytime . . . Course always in top shape and challenging. Staff pleasant.

SANDESTIN BEACH HILTON GOLF AND TENNIS RESORT

R—9300 Hwy. 98 West, Destin (904)267-8155 (Baytowne), (904)267-6500 (Sandestin).
20 miles east of Fort Walton Beach.
Credit cards: All major. **Caddies:** No.
Discount golf packages: Yes.
Season: Year-round. **High:** March-April/Sept.-Oct.
On-site lodging: Yes. **Rental clubs:** Yes.
To obtain tee times: Call three days in advance.

★★★½ BAYTOWNE GOLF COURSE-TROON/DUNES/HARBOR

Holes: 27. **Par:** 72/72/72.
Yards: 7,185/6,890/6,891. **Course rating:** 74.6/73.4/73.9.
Slope: 128/127/127.
Opened: 1985. **Pace of Play rating:** 4:30. **Green fee:** $55/85.
Reduced fees: Low season, Resort guests, Twilight.
Golf carts: N/A.
Walking policy: Walking at certain times. **Range:** Yes.
Subscriber comments: Beautiful layout, tricky, well kept . . . Lots of mounds in fairways; greens good, hard to read . . . Scenery great. Staff very helpful . . . Superb maintenance, most effective and friendly marshals.

BURNT PINES GOLF COURSE*

Holes: 18. **Par:** 72/72.
Yards: 7,046/5,950. **Course rating:** 74.1/68.7. **Slope:** 135/124.
Opened: 1994. **Pace of Play rating:** 3:15. **Green fee:** $60/75.
Reduced fees: Resort guests.
Golf carts: $15 for 18 holes.
Walking policy: Unrestricted walking. **Range:** Yes (grass).

★★★½ THE LINKS COURSE

Holes: 18. **Par:** 72/72.
Yards: 6,710/4,969. **Course rating:** 72.8/69.2. **Slope:** 124/115.
Opened: 1977. **Pace of Play rating:** 4:30. **Green fee:** $55/85.
Reduced fees: Low season, Resort guests, Twilight.
Golf carts: $15 for 18 holes.
Walking policy: Walking at certain times. **Range:** Yes.
Subscriber comments: Can be real hard if the wind blows, great bay view . . . Friendly staff. Course excellent condition year round . . . Wonderful weekend there . . . Great food . . . Narrow and a lot of water, challenging course . . . Very nice resort course . . . Flat.

★★½ SANDPIPER GOLF AND COUNTRY CLUB

SP—6001 Sandpipers Dr., Lakeland (813)859-5461.
30 miles northeast of Tampa. **Holes:** 18. **Par:** 70/70.
Yards: 6,442/5,024. **Course rating:** 70.4/67.7. **Slope:** 120/109.
Opened: 1986. **Pace of Play rating:** 4:00. **Green fee:** $29/32.
Credit cards: MC, V. **Reduced fees:** Weekdays, Low season, Twilight.

Caddies: No. **Golf carts:** Included in Green Fee.
Discount golf packages: Yes. **Season:** Year-round. **High:** Jan.–March.
On-site lodging: No. **Rental clubs:** Yes.
Walking policy: Mandatory cart. **Range:** No.
To obtain tee times: Call a minimum of two days in advance and a maximum of four days.
Subscriber comments: Short course. Low handicapper can really score . . . Links course.

SANDRIDGE GOLF CLUB
PU—5300 73rd St., Vero Beach (407)770-5000.
70 miles north of West Palm Beach.
Pace of Play rating: 4:00. **Green fee:** $12/32.
Credit cards: MC, V, DISC. **Reduced fees:** Weekdays, Low season, Twilight, Juniors.
Caddies: No. **Golf carts:** Included in Green Fee.
Discount golf packages: Yes. **Season:** Year-round. **High:** Jan.–March.
On-site lodging: No. **Rental clubs:** Yes.
Walking policy: Walking at certain times. **Range:** Yes (grass).
To obtain tee times: Automated tee time system through telephone.

★★★½ **DUNES COURSE**
Holes: 18. **Par:** 72/72.
Yards: 6,900/4,922. **Course rating:** 72.2/68.8. **Slope:** 123/109.
Opened: 1986.

Subscriber comments: Makes a transplanted Yankee think he's home . . . Good staff, good layout, good condition . . . Ranger polite but firm, which kept pace of play good . . . One of the nicest, best-kept courses around Vero Beach area.

★★★★ **LAKES COURSE**
Holes: 18. **Par:** 72/72.
Yards: 6,200/4,625. **Course rating:** 69.3/66.6. **Slope:** 120/109.
Opened: 1992.
Subscriber comments: This course requires strategy as well as distance to shoot a reasonable score . . . Even better than the Dunes Course . . . Short and narrow layout with lots of water . . . Very well treated, played within 4½ hours . . . Staff extremely courteous and cheerful.

★★ SANTA ROSA GOLF AND BEACH CLUB
SP—334 Golf Club Dr., Santa Rosa Beach (904)267-2229.
15 miles east of Destin. **Holes:** 18. **Par:** 72/72.
Yards: 6,474/4,988. **Course rating:** 71.8/68.8. **Slope:** 128/115.
Opened: 1969. **Pace of Play rating:** 4:30. **Green fee:** $28/36.
Credit cards: MC, V, AMEX. **Reduced fees:** Low season, Twilight, Juniors.
Caddies: No. **Golf carts:** $13 for 18 holes.
Discount golf packages: No. **Season:** Year-round. **High:** April-Sept.
On-site lodging: No. **Rental clubs:** Yes.
Walking policy: Walking at certain times. **Range:** Yes (grass).
To obtain tee times: Call three days in advance.

★★ SARASOTA GOLF CLUB
SP—7280 N. Leewynn Dr., Sarasota (813)371-2431.
Holes: 18. **Par:** 72/72.
Yards: 7,066/5,004. **Course rating:** 73.0/67.4. **Slope:** 120/106.
Opened: 1950. **Pace of Play rating:** 4:00-4:15. **Green fee:** $22/33.
Credit cards: MC, V. **Reduced fees:** Low season, Resort guests, Twilight, Seniors, Juniors.
Caddies: No. **Golf carts:** Included in Green Fee.
Discount golf packages: Yes. **Season:** Year-round. **High:** Jan.-April.
On-site lodging: No. **Rental clubs:** Yes.
Walking policy: Walking at certain times. **Range:** Yes (grass).
To obtain tee times: Call three days in advance.
Subscriber comments: Relatively open course with four sets of tee boxes . . . Fun place to play. Very friendly . . . Plays long. Not dazzling but decent . . . Flat, easy layout . . . Wide open, reasonable, good for moral.

★½ SAVANNAHS AT SYKES CREEK GOLF CLUB
PU—3915 Savannahs Tr., Merritt Island (407)455-1375.
Call club for further information.
Subscriber comments: Not long but lots of water. Small greens. Straight hitter can score well.

★★ SCENIC HILLS COUNTRY CLUB
PU—8891 Burning Tree Rd., Pensacola (904)476-0611.
Holes: 18. **Par:** 71/71.
Yards: 6,689/5,187. **Course rating:** N/A. **Slope:** 135/116.
Opened: N/A. **Pace of Play rating:** N/A. **Green fee:** N/A.
Credit cards: MC, V, AMEX. **Reduced fees:** Weekdays, Low season, Resort guests, Twilight.
Caddies: No. **Golf carts:** Included in Green Fee.
Discount golf packages: Yes. **Season:** Year-round. **High:** Feb.–April.
On-site lodging: No. **Rental clubs:** No.
Walking policy: N/A. **Range:** Yes.
Subscriber comments: Improved since Jerry Pate renovated it last . . . Hilly and tough doglegs.

★★½ SCHALAMAR CREEK GOLF AND COUNTRY CLUB
SP—4500 US Hwy 92E, Lakeland (813)666-1623.
30 miles east of Tampa. **Holes:** 18. **Par:** 72/72.
Yards: 6,399/4,363. **Course rating:** 70.9/64.8. **Slope:** 124/106.
Opened: 1987. **Pace of Play rating:** 4:00. **Green fee:** $8/21.
Credit cards: MC, V. **Reduced fees:** Weekdays, Low season, Twilight.
Caddies: No. **Golf carts:** $16 for 18 holes.
Discount golf packages: No. **Season:** Year-round. **High:** Jan.–April.
On-site lodging: No. **Rental clubs:** Yes.
Walking policy: Walking at certain times. **Range:** Yes (grass).
To obtain tee times: Call two days in advance.
Subscriber comments: Fun course . . . Fair condition. Easy course.

★★★ SEASCAPE RESORT
R—100 Seascape Dr., Destin (904)654-7888, (800)874-9106.
45 miles east of Pensacola. **Holes:** 18. **Par:** 71/71.
Yards: 6,488/5,029. **Course rating:** 71.5/70.3. **Slope:** 120/113.
Opened: 1969. **Pace of Play rating:** N/A. **Green fee:** $35/54.
Credit cards: MC, V, AMEX. **Reduced fees:** Low season, Resort guests, Juniors.
Caddies: No. **Golf carts:** Included in Green Fee.
Discount golf packages: Yes. **Season:** Year-round. **High:** March-Oct.
On-site lodging: Yes. **Rental clubs:** Yes.
Walking policy: Walking at certain times. **Range:** Yes (grass).
To obtain tee times: Call up to two days in advance.

Subscriber comments: Tricky layout . . . Nice staff even though it's a resort, they make locals feel good . . . A nice resort course . . . Getting better with upgraded course construction.

★★ SEBASTIAN MUNICIPAL GOLF COURSE
PU—101 E. Airport Dr., Sebastian (407)589-6801.
75 miles northwest of Orlando. **Holes:** 18. **Par:** 72/72.
Yards: 6,717/4,579. **Course rating:** 71.0/64.6. **Slope:** 112/101.
Opened: 1981. **Pace of Play rating:** N/A. **Green fee:** $17/28.
Credit cards: MC, V. **Reduced fees:** Low season, Twilight, Juniors.
Caddies: No. **Golf carts:** Included in Green Fee.
Discount golf packages: No. **Season:** Year-round. **High:** Dec.-April.
On-site lodging: No. **Rental clubs:** Yes.
Walking policy: Walking at certain times. **Range:** Yes (grass).
To obtain tee times: Call (407)589-6800.
Subscriber comments: Long but very open . . . Good shape for a muny.

★★ SEMINOLE GOLF CLUB

PU—2550 Pottsdamer St., Tallahassee (904)644-2582.
Holes: 18. **Par:** 72/72.
Yards: 7,033/5,930. **Course rating:** 73.4/73.0. **Slope:** 121/111.
Opened: N/A. **Pace of Play rating:** 3:45. **Green fee:** $11/16.
Credit cards: MC, V, DISC. **Reduced fees:** Weekdays, Resort guests, Twilight, Juniors.
Caddies: No. **Golf carts:** $9 for 18 holes.
Discount golf packages: No. **Season:** Year-round.
On-site lodging: No. **Rental clubs:** Yes.
Walking policy: Walking at certain times. **Range:** Yes.
To obtain tee times: Call on Monday for weekend tee times only.
Subscriber comments: Good average course . . . Not bad for a public course.

★★★½ SEVEN HILLS GOLFERS CLUB

SP—10599 Fairchild Rd., Spring Hill (904)688-8888.
35 miles north of Tampa. **Holes:** 18. **Par:** 72/72.
Yards: 6,715/4,902. **Course rating:** 70.5/66.5. **Slope:** 126/109.
Opened: 1989. **Pace of Play rating:** 4:00. **Green fee:** $29.
Credit cards: None. **Reduced fees:** Weekdays, Low season, Twilight.
Caddies: No. **Golf carts:** Included in Green Fee.
Discount golf packages: No. **Season:** Year-round. **High:** Dec.-April.
On-site lodging: No. **Rental clubs:** Yes.
Walking policy: Mandatory cart. **Range:** Yes (grass).
To obtain tee times: Call up to one week in advance.
Subscriber comments: Very challenging. I could play there every day and did . . . Great course, great condition, staff runs tight ship . . . Lots, lots of water . . . Treated very well. Good pace of play.

★★★½ SEVEN SPRINGS GOLF AND COUNTRY CLUB CHAMPIONSHIP COURSE

SP—3535 Trophy Blvd., New Port Richey (813)376-0035.
12 miles northwest of Tampa. **Holes:** 18. **Par:** 72/72.
Yards: 6,566/5,250. **Course rating:** N/A. **Slope:** 123/112.
Opened: N/A. **Pace of Play rating:** N/A. **Green fee:** N/A.
Credit cards: MC, V. **Reduced fees:** Low season, Twilight.
Caddies: No. **Golf carts:** Included in Green Fee.
Discount golf packages: No. **Season:** Year-round. **High:** Jan.-April.
On-site lodging: No. **Rental clubs:** No.
Walking policy: N/A. **Range:** Yes (grass).
Subscriber comments: Hard to beat for quality and reasonable price . . . Great to play in summer. Good service. Rangers do a great job . . . Nice, tight course. Must hit fairways. Greens excellent.

★★★ SEVILLE GOLF AND COUNTRY CLUB

PU—18200 Seville Clubhouse Dr., Weeki Wachee (904)596-7888, (800)232-1363.
70 miles north of Tampa. **Holes:** 18. **Par:** 72/72.
Yards: 7,140/5,236. **Course rating:** 74.9/70.8. **Slope:** 138/126.
Opened: 1988. **Pace of Play rating:** N/A. **Green fee:** $10/25.
Credit cards: MC, V, DISC. **Reduced fees:** Weekdays, Low season, Twilight.
Caddies: No. **Golf carts:** Included in Green Fee.
Discount golf packages: No. **Season:** Year-round. **High:** Jan.-April.
On-site lodging: No. **Rental clubs:** Yes.
Walking policy: Mandatory cart. **Range:** Yes (grass).
To obtain tee times: Call.
Subscriber comments: Hills and sand and long; championship caliber . . . Physically demanding, true golfing test . . . Make sure to bring your sand wedge . . . Has bomb-crater bunkers . . . Course plays long, but fair . . . Plays longer than it looks . . . Tough course, staff OK. Good layout . . . People sometimes get lost in waste bunkers.

FLORIDA

★★½ SHALIMAR POINTE GOLF AND COUNTRY CLUB
SP—302 Country Club Rd., Shalimar (904)651-1416, (800)964-2833.
45 miles east of Pensacola. **Holes:** 18. **Par:** 72/72.
Yards: 6,765/5,427. **Course rating:** 72.9/70.7. **Slope:** 125/115.
Opened: 1968. **Pace of Play rating:** 4:15. **Green fee:** $25/44.
Credit cards: MC, V, AMEX. **Reduced fees:** Weekdays, Low season,
Resort guests, Twilight.
Caddies: No. **Golf carts:** Included in Green Fee.
Discount golf packages: Yes. **Season:** Year-round. **High:** Jan.-April.
On-site lodging: No. **Rental clubs:** Yes.
Walking policy: Mandatory cart. **Range:** Yes (grass).
To obtain tee times: Call up to five days in advance.
Subscriber comments: Some scenic holes on bay . . . Easy to get a tee
time on a very well-kept course . . . Better each year . . . Nice resort
course.

★★★ SHERMAN HILLS GOLF CLUB
PU—31200 Eagle Falls Dr., Brooksville (904)544-0990.
45 miles north of Tampa. **Holes:** 18. **Par:** 72/72.
Yards: 6,778/4,959. **Course rating:** 72.1/68.2. **Slope:** 118/110.
Opened: 1993. **Pace of Play rating:** N/A. **Green fee:** $15/30.
Credit cards: MC, V. **Reduced fees:** Weekdays, Low season, Twilight.
Caddies: No. **Golf carts:** Included in Green Fee.
Discount golf packages: Yes. **Season:** Year-round. **High:** Oct.-April.
On-site lodging: No. **Rental clubs:** Yes.
Walking policy: Mandatory cart. **Range:** Yes (grass).
To obtain tee times: Call up to one week in advance.
Subscriber comments: Good golf, great price, out-of-the-way location
. . . Front nine, very traditional; back nine, let it ride . . . Front nine,
woody; back, no trees . . . Nice for a new course . . . Nice driving range.

★½ SHOAL RIVER COUNTRY CLUB
SP—1100 Shoal River Dr., Crestview (904)689-1010.
25 miles north of Fort Walton Beach. **Holes:** 18. **Par:** 72/72.
Yards: 6,782/5,183. **Course rating:** 73.5/70.3. **Slope:** 136/124.
Opened: 1986. **Pace of Play rating:** N/A. **Green fee:** $18.
Credit cards: MC, V, AMEX. **Reduced fees:** Weekdays, Low season,
Twilight, Juniors.
Caddies: No. **Golf carts:** $15 for 18 holes.
Discount golf packages: Yes. **Season:** Year-round. **High:** Feb.-March.
On-site lodging: No. **Rental clubs:** Yes.
Walking policy: Walking at certain times. **Range:** Yes (grass).
To obtain tee times: Call up to three days in advance.
Subscriber comments: Some pasture-like fairways. Could be great with
some work . . . A crooked hitter's nightmare.

SIGNAL HILL GOLF AND COUNTRY CLUB★
PU—9615 N. Thomas Drive, Panama City Beach (904)234-5051.
10 miles west of Panama City. **Holes:** 18. **Par:** 71/71.
Yards: 5,617/4,790. **Course rating:** 63.6/63.0. **Slope:** 101/103.
Opened: N/A. **Pace of Play rating:** N/A. **Green fee:** $12/15.
Credit cards: MC, V, DISC. **Reduced fees:** Low season.
Caddies: No. **Golf carts:** N/A.
Discount golf packages: No. **Season:** Year-round. **High:** April-Sept.
On-site lodging: No. **Rental clubs:** Yes.
Walking policy: Unrestricted walking. **Range:** No.
To obtain tee times: Call or come in up to seven days in advance.

SILVER OAKS GOLF AND COUNTRY CLUB★
SP—36841 Clubhouse Drive, Zephyrhills (813)788-1225, (800)853-4653.
20 miles northeast of Tampa. **Holes:** 18. **Par:** 72/72.
Yards: 6,632/5,147. **Course rating:** 71.1/68.8. **Slope:** 120/109.
Opened: 1988. **Pace of Play rating:** 4:15. **Green fee:** $16/35.
Credit cards: MC, V. **Reduced fees:** Weekdays, Low season, Resort
guests, Twilight, Seniors, Juniors.

Caddies: No. **Golf carts:** Included in Green Fee.
Discount golf packages: Yes. **Season:** Year-round. **High:** Dec.-May.
On-site lodging: No. **Rental clubs:** Yes.
Walking policy: Mandatory cart. Walking for members only.
Range: Yes (grass).
To obtain tee times: Call, fax or come in person to make tee time.

★½ SOUTH COURSE AT MIRROR LAKES

R—670 Milwaukee Ave, Lehigh (813)369-1322.
12 miles east of Ft. Myers. **Holes:** 18. **Par:** 73/73.
Yards: 7,058/5,697. **Course rating:** 74.0/72.9. **Slope:** 123/125.
Opened: 1973. **Pace of Play rating:** 4:00. **Green fee:** $12/27.
Credit cards: All major. **Reduced fees:** Low season, Resort guests,
Twilight.

Caddies: No. **Golf carts:** $16 for 18 holes.
Discount golf packages: Yes. **Season:** Year-round. **High:** Dec.-April.
On-site lodging: No. **Rental clubs:** Yes.
Walking policy: Walking at certain times. **Range:** Yes (grass).
To obtain tee times: Call 24 hours in advance.
Subscriber comments: What a layout, used every club in my bag . . .
Great course . . . Short, easy . . . Good for average golfer.

★★★★ SOUTHERN DUNES GOLF AND COUNTRY CLUB

PU—2888 Southern Dunes Blvd., Haines City (813)421-4653,
(800)632-6400.
20 miles southwest of Orlando. **Holes:** 18. **Par:** 72/72.
Yards: 7,200/5,200. **Course rating:** 74.7/72.4. **Slope:** 135/126.
Opened: 1993. **Pace of Play rating:** 4:00. **Green fee:** $27/47.
Credit cards: MC, V. **Reduced fees:** Weekdays, Low season, Juniors.
Caddies: No. **Golf carts:** Included in Green Fee.
Discount golf packages: Yes. **Season:** Year-round. **High:** Oct.-April.
On-site lodging: No. **Rental clubs:** Yes.
Walking policy: Mandatory cart. **Range:** Yes (grass).
To obtain tee times: Call three days in advance.
Subscriber comments: Immaculate . . . Unique course, lots of choices on
shots . . . One of the best new courses in central Florida . . . A desert course
in Florida? Feels like I'm in Arizona . . . This course will be awesome at
maturity . . . A true, natural links course built on real sandhills . . .
Lightning greens . . . Amazingly good condition for new course . . . New
links-type course, sits high for good view, challenge . . . Players will enjoy,
moved well.

★½ SPRING HILL GOLF CLUB

SP—12079 Coronado Dr., Spring Hill (904)683-2261.
35 miles north of Tampa. **Holes:** 18. **Par:** 72/73.
Yards: 6,917/5,588. **Course rating:** 73.0/71.8. **Slope:** 133/127.
Opened: 1975. **Pace of Play rating:** 4:00. **Green fee:** $27.
Credit cards: None. **Reduced fees:** Weekdays, Low season, Twilight.
Caddies: No. **Golf carts:** Included in Green Fee.
Discount golf packages: No. **Season:** Year-round. **High:** Dec.-March.
On-site lodging: No. **Rental clubs:** Yes.
Walking policy: Walking at certain times. **Range:** Yes (grass).
To obtain tee times: Call up to one week in advance.
Subscriber comments: Course in poor shape, facilities need to be
upgraded.

★★½ SPRING LAKE GOLF AND TENNIS RESORT
OSPREY/HAWK/EAGLE

R—100 Clubhouse Lane, Sebring (813)655-1276, (800)635-7277.
65 miles south of Orlando. **Holes:** 27. **Par:** 71/71/72.
Yards: 6,531/6,398/6,673. **Course rating:** 71.3/70.1/71.8.
Slope: 127/116/125.
Opened: 1977. **Pace of Play rating:** 4:15. **Green fee:** $17/36.
Credit cards: All major. **Reduced fees:** Resort guests, Twilight.
Caddies: No. **Golf carts:** Included in Green Fee.

Discount golf packages: Yes. **Season:** Year-round. **High:** Jan.–March.
On–site lodging: Yes. **Rental clubs:** Yes.
Walking policy: Mandatory cart. **Range:** Yes (grass).
To obtain tee times: Call 48 hours in advance.
Subscriber comments: OK layout, fairly easy . . . Entire staff treated us like Nick Price.

★★½ SPRUCE CREEK COUNTRY CLUB

SP—1900 Country Club Dr., Daytona Beach (904)756-6114.
45 miles northeast of Orlando. **Holes:** 18. **Par:** 72/72.
Yards: 6,751/5,157. **Course rating:** 72.2/70.3. **Slope:** 125/121.
Opened: 1971. **Pace of Play rating:** 4:00. **Green fee:** $20/26.
Credit cards: MC, V. **Reduced fees:** Low season, Resort guests,
Twilight, Juniors.
Caddies: No. **Golf carts:** Included in Green Fee.
Discount golf packages: No. **Season:** Year-round. **High:** Jan.–April.
On–site lodging: No. **Rental clubs:** Yes.
Walking policy: Mandatory cart. **Range:** Yes (grass).
To obtain tee times: Call 48 hours in advance.
Subscriber comments: Course condition improving with new green
superintendent . . . Average course.

STOUFFER VINOY GOLF CLUB★

R—600 Snell Isle Blvd. N.E., St. Petersburg (813)896-8000.
Holes: 18. **Par:** 70/71.
Yards: 6,267/4,818. **Course rating:** 70.0/67.3. **Slope:** 118/111.
Opened: 1992. **Pace of Play rating:** 4:00. **Green fee:** $65.
Credit cards: All major. **Reduced fees:** Twilight.
Caddies: Yes. **Golf carts:** N/A.
Discount golf packages: Yes. **Season:** Year-round. **High:** Jan.–April.
On–site lodging: Yes. **Rental clubs:** Yes.
Walking policy: Walking at certain times. **Range:** Yes (grass).
To obtain tee times: Unlimited time frame for resort guests.

SUGAR MILL COUNTRY CLUB
★★★½ RED/WHITE/BLUE

SP—100 Clubhouse Circle, New Smyrna Beach (904)426-5210.
10 miles south of Daytona Beach. **Holes:** 27. **Par:** 72/72/72.
Yards: 6,766/6,695/6,749. **Course rating:** 72.1/72.4/72.6.
Slope: 125/128/129.
Opened: 1970. **Pace of Play rating:** . **Green fee:** $29/60.
Credit cards: MC, V. **Reduced fees:** Low season.
Caddies: No. **Golf carts:** Included in Green Fee.
Discount golf packages: No. **Season:** Year-round. **High:** Jan.–April.
On–site lodging: No. **Rental clubs:** Yes.
Walking policy: Mandatory cart. **Range:** Yes (grass).
To obtain tee times: Call up to two days in advance.
Subscriber comments: Expensive but worth it. Excellent condition. Will
play often . . . The original two nines are the best in the Daytona Beach area
. . . Could enjoy playing this course every day.

★★★ SUMMERFIELD GOLF CLUB

SP—13050 Summerfield Blvd., Riverview (813)671-3311.
70 miles northeast of Tampa. **Holes:** 18. **Par:** 71/71.
Yards: 6,883/5,139. **Course rating:** 73.0/69.6. **Slope:** 125/114.
Opened: 1986. **Pace of Play rating:** 4:00. **Green fee:** $18/34.
Credit cards: MC, V. **Reduced fees:** Low season, Twilight.
Caddies: No. **Golf carts:** Included in Green Fee.
Discount golf packages: Yes. **Season:** Year-round. **High:** Jan.–April.
On–site lodging: No. **Rental clubs:** Yes.
Walking policy: Mandatory cart. **Range:** Yes (grass).
To obtain tee times: Call.
Subscriber comments: Requires accurate iron play . . . Quasi-links-
course style . . . Links course, well-kept fairways and greens, usually busy
. . . Course always in good shape, lots of mounds, water.

SUNNYBREEZE PALMS GOLF COURSE★

SP—8135 SW Sunnybreeze Rd., Arcadia (813)625-0424.
58 miles southeast of St. Petersburg. **Holes:** 18. **Par:** 71/71.
Yards: 6,007/5,009. **Course rating:** 66.6/67.5. **Slope:** 114/119.
Opened: 1971. **Pace of Play rating:** N/A. **Green fee:** $10/25.
Credit cards: MC, V, DISC. **Reduced fees:** Weekdays, Low season.
Caddies: No. **Golf carts:** N/A.
Discount golf packages: Yes. **Season:** Year-round. **High:** Dec.-April.
On-site lodging: No. **Rental clubs:** Yes.
Walking policy: Unrestricted walking. **Range:** Yes (grass).
To obtain tee times: Call one week in advance.

SUNRISE COUNTRY CLUB★

SP—7400 N.W. 24th Place, Sunrise (305)742-4333.
Holes: 18. **Par:** 72/72.
Yards: 6,624/5,317. **Course rating:** 71.8/69.8. **Slope:** 126/119.
Opened: 1959. **Pace of Play rating:** 4:00. **Green fee:** $25/45.
Credit cards: MC, V, AMEX. **Reduced fees:** Twilight.
Caddies: No. **Golf carts:** Included in Green Fee.
Discount golf packages: No. **Season:** Year-round. **High:** Dec.-April.
On-site lodging: No. **Rental clubs:** Yes.
Walking policy: Mandatory cart. **Range:** Yes (grass).
To obtain tee times: Call seven days in advance.

SUNRISE GOLF CLUB★

SP—5710 Draw Lane, Sarasota (813)924-1402.
7 miles southeast of Sarasota. **Holes:** 18. **Par:** 72/72.
Yards: 6,455/5,271. **Course rating:** 70.6/69.3. **Slope:** 122/117.
Opened: 1970. **Pace of Play rating:** 4:00. **Green fee:** $15/40.
Credit cards: MC, V. **Reduced fees:** Low season, Twilight, Juniors.
Caddies: No. **Golf carts:** Included in Green Fee.
Discount golf packages: Yes. **Season:** Year-round. **High:** Feb.-April.
On-site lodging: No. **Rental clubs:** Yes.
Walking policy: Walking at certain times. **Range:** Yes (grass).
To obtain tee times: Call three days in advance.

★★½ TANGLEWOOD GOLF AND COUNTRY CLUB

PU—5916 Tanglewood Dr., Milton (904)623-6176.
10 miles east of Pensacola. **Holes:** 18. **Par:** 72/72.
Yards: 6,455/5,295. **Course rating:** 70.0/69.9. **Slope:** 115/118.
Opened: 1964. **Pace of Play rating:** 4:00 **Green fee:** $17/20.
Credit cards: MC, V. **Reduced fees:** Low season, Seniors.
Caddies: No. **Golf carts:** $10 for 18 holes.
Discount golf packages: No. **Season:** Year-round. **High:** April-Nov.
On-site lodging: No. **Rental clubs:** Yes.
Walking policy: Unrestricted walking. **Range:** Yes (grass).
To obtain tee times: Call anytime.
Subscriber comments: Requires precise tee shots, short course . . . Nice
course with pleasant employees. Enjoyable golfing experience.

★★½ TARPON WOODS GOLF AND COUNTRY CLUB

SP—1100 Tarpon Woods Blvd., Palm Harbor (813)784-2273.
20 miles west of Tampa. **Holes:** 18. **Par:** 72/72.
Yards: 6,466/5,205. **Course rating:** 71.2/69.5. **Slope:** 128/115.
Opened: 1975. **Pace of Play rating:** 3:30. **Green fee:** $32/46.
Credit cards: MC, V, AMEX. **Reduced fees:** Weekdays, Low season,
Twilight.
Caddies: No. **Golf carts:** Included in Green Fee.
Discount golf packages: Yes. **Season:** Year-round. **High:** Jan.-May.
On-site lodging: No. **Rental clubs:** Yes.
Walking policy: Walking at certain times. **Range:** Yes (grass).
To obtain tee times: Call in advance.
Subscriber comments: Nice wooded course . . . Good layout, fair
condition, could be excellent with work.

★★★ TATUM RIDGE GOLF LINKS

SP—421 North Tatum Rd., Sarasota (813)378-4211.
Holes: 18. **Par:** 72/72.
Yards: 6,757/5,149. **Course rating:** 71.9/68.9. **Slope:** 124/114.
Opened: 1989. **Pace of Play rating:** N/A. **Green fee:** $18/35.
Credit cards: MC, V. **Reduced fees:** Low season, Seniors.
Caddies: No. **Golf carts:** Included in Green Fee.
Discount golf packages: No. **Season:** Year-round. **High:** Nov.-May.
On-site lodging: No. **Rental clubs:** Yes.
Walking policy: Mandatory cart. **Range:** Yes (grass).
To obtain tee times: Call three days in advance.
Subscriber comments: Links-style course . . . Very good attention to grounds and people . . . Great links course, always in top shape, staff excellent . . . Better than average public course . . . Good facilities. Scottish-style links course . . . Very nice public course with links look. Strong finish.

TIGER POINT GOLF AND COUNTRY CLUB

SP—1255 Country Club Rd., Gulf Breeze (904)932-1333.
15 miles southeast of Pensacola.
Credit cards: MC, V, AMEX. **Reduced fees:** Weekdays, Low season, Twilight.
Caddies: No. **Golf carts:** Included in Green Fee.
Discount golf packages: Yes. **Season:** Year-round. **High:** Feb.-April/Oct.-Nov.
On-site lodging: No. **Rental clubs:** Yes. **Range:** Yes (grass).
To obtain tee times: Call up to seven days in advance between 8 a.m. and 4 p.m.

★★★½ EAST COURSE

Holes: 18. **Par:** 72/72.
Yards: 7,033/5,217. **Course rating:** 73.8/70.2. **Slope:** 132/125.
Opened: 1979. **Pace of Play rating:** N/A. **Green fee:** $37/48.
Walking policy: Mandatory cart.
Subscriber comments: Course has character, lots of wind from Gulf, semi-tough . . . Water, water everywhere, but does have "outs."

★★½ WEST COURSE

Holes: 18. **Par:** 71/72.
Yards: 6,715/5,314. **Course rating:** 72.2/70.2. **Slope:** 119/121.
Opened: 1965. **Pace of Play rating:** N/A. **Green fee:** $33/38.
Walking policy: Walking at certain times.
Subscriber comments: Great course for medium-handicapper . . . Have never played course when it was not very wet.

★★★½ TIMACUAN GOLF AND COUNTRY CLUB

SP—550 Timacuan Blvd., Lake Mary (407)321-0010.
15 miles northeast of Orlando. **Holes:** 18. **Par:** 72/72.
Yards: 7,019/5,401. **Course rating:** 73.5/72.1. **Slope:** 137/123.
Opened: 1987. **Pace of Play rating:** N/A. **Green fee:** $29/85.
Credit cards: MC, V, AMEX. **Reduced fees:** Weekdays, Low season, Resort guests, Twilight, Juniors.
Caddies: No. **Golf carts:** Included in Green Fee.
Discount golf packages: Yes. **Season:** Year-round. **High:** Jan.-April.
On-site lodging: No. **Rental clubs:** Yes.
Walking policy: Mandatory cart. **Range:** Yes (grass).
To obtain tee times: Call three days in advance.
Subscriber comments: Good facility, well-run . . . One of my favorites . . . Excellent Ron Garl design. Natural feeling.

★½ TOMOKA OAKS GOLF AND COUNTRY CLUB

SP—20 Tomoka Oaks Blvd., Ormond Beach (904)677-7117.
Call club for further information.
Subscriber comments: Just a nice old course . . . Great chance to use all clubs. Trees add challenge . . . Well drained. Well maintained, considering volume.

TOURNAMENT PLAYERS CLUB AT SAWGRASS

R—110 TPC Blvd., Ponte Vedra Beach (904)273-3235.

15 miles southeast of Jacksonville.

Credit cards: MC, V, AMEX, Resort Charge. **Reduced fees:** Low season, Juniors.

Caddies: No. **Golf carts:** N/A.

Discount golf packages: No. **Season:** Year-round. **High:** March-May.

On-site lodging: Yes. **Rental clubs:** Yes.

Walking policy: Unrestricted walking, players must bring a caddie or use motorized pullcart. **Range:** Yes (grass).

To obtain tee times: Guests of Marriott call golf reservations at (800)457-4653.

★★★★½ STADIUM COURSE

Holes: 18. **Par:** 72/72.

Yards: 6,857/5,034. **Course rating:** 74.0/64.7. **Slope:** 135/123.

Opened: 1980. **Pace of Play rating:** 4:02. **Green fee:** $85/135.

Ranked 40th in America's 100 Greatest Golf Courses by Golf Digest. Ranked 7th in America's 75 Best Resort Courses by Golf Digest. Ranked 2nd in Florida by Golf Digest.

Subscriber comments: Got to do it, if only once . . . Once a year affordable . . . Super layout, challenging for best . . . Awesome, must play, toughest course in Florida . . . One of the very best in the world . . . Either hit it straight or bring plenty of golf balls . . . Expensive but you have to play it . . . I died and went to heaven . . . Play it once and get it out of your system . . . Hard, hard, hard. Not as hard when first opened but hard . . . Golf in heaven should be like this . . . A walk amongst the gods! . . . A national shrine on the way . . . 18 great holes, Dye framed each hole nicely . . . Overrated, 17th hole island is what everyone plays for.

★★★★ VALLEY COURSE

Holes: 18. **Par:** 72/72.

Yards: 6,864/5,126. **Course rating:** 72.6/63.8. **Slope:** 129/117.

Opened: 1987. **Pace of Play rating:** 4:02. **Green fee:** $65/90.

Subscriber comments: Almost as great as Stadium . . . More forgiving than its sister course . . . More enjoyable than Stadium. Super challenge . . . Terrific layout and conditioning, could play it every week . . . Easier to get tee time vs. Stadium.

TOURNAMENT PLAYERS CLUB OF TAMPA BAY★

SP—5100 Terrain de Golf Dr., Lutz (813)949-0091.

15 miles northwest of Tampa. **Holes:** 18. **Par:** 71/71.

Yards: 6,898/5,036. **Course rating:** 73.4/69.1. **Slope:** 130/119.

Opened: 1991. **Pace of Play rating:** 4:20. **Green fee:** $42/75.

Credit cards: MC, V, AMEX. **Reduced fees:** Weekdays, Low season, Twilight, Juniors.

Caddies: No. **Golf carts:** Included in Green Fee.

Discount golf packages: No. **Season:** Year-round. **High:** Jan.-April.

On-site lodging: No. **Rental clubs:** Yes.

Walking policy: Mandatory cart. **Range:** Yes (grass).

To obtain tee times: Call seven days in advance.

TURNBERRY ISLE RESORT AND CLUB

R—19999 W. Country Club Dr., Aventura (305)933-6929, (800)327-7208.

10 miles south of Ft. Lauderdale.

Opened: 1971. **Pace of Play rating:** N/A. **Green fee:** $35/75.

Credit cards: MC, V, AMEX. **Reduced fees:** Low season.

Caddies: No. **Golf carts:** $16 for 18 holes.

Discount golf packages: Yes. **Season:** Year-round. **High:** Nov.-April.

On-site lodging: Yes. **Rental clubs:** Yes.

Walking policy: Mandatory cart. **Range:** Yes (grass).

To obtain tee times: Reserve tee times when making hotel reservations.

★★½ NORTH COURSE

Holes: 18. **Par:** 70/70.

Yards: 6,348/4,991. **Course rating:** 70.3/67.9. **Slope:** 127/107.

Subscriber comments: Enjoyable . . . Front nine is prettiest of the complex.

★★★½ SOUTH COURSE
Holes: 18. **Par:** 72/72.
Yards: 7,003/5,581. **Course rating:** 73.7/71.3. **Slope:** 136/116.
Subscriber comments: Much better than North . . . Good resort golf, meticulous condition.

★★ TURTLE CREEK GOLF CLUB
PU—1278 Admiralty Blvd., Rockledge (407)632-2520.

35 miles east of Orlando. **Holes:** 18. **Par:** 72/72.
Yards: 6,709/4,880. **Course rating:** 70.1/68.8. **Slope:** 129/113.
Opened: 1970. **Pace of Play rating:** 4:15. **Green fee:** $20/43.
Credit cards: MC, V, AMEX. **Reduced fees:** Weekdays, Low season, Twilight, Juniors.
Caddies: No. **Golf carts:** Included in Green Fee.
Discount golf packages: Yes. **Season:** Year-round. **High:** Jan.–April.
On-site lodging: No. **Rental clubs:** Yes.
Walking policy: Mandatory cart. **Range:** Yes (grass).
To obtain tee times: Call up to seven days in advance.
Subscriber comments: Nice course. Lots of water. Easy front nine, tough back nine.

★★★ TWISTED OAKS GOLF CLUB
PU—4545 Forest Ridge Blvd., Beverly Hills (904)746-6257.
Call club for further information.
Subscriber comments: Long, wide open. Fast, true greens. Staff friendly . . . Looks easy but isn't . . . Poor man's Black Diamond.

(FRUGAL PICK)

★★½ UNIVERSITY OF SOUTH FLORIDA GOLF COURSE
PU—13120 46th St., Tampa (813)974-2071.

Holes: 18. **Par:** 72/72.
Yards: 6,942/5,393. **Course rating:** 73.1/69.8. **Slope:** 131/115.
Opened: 1967. **Pace of Play rating:** 4:15. **Green fee:** $10/18.
Credit cards: MC, V. **Reduced fees:** Weekdays, Low season, Twilight, Seniors, Juniors.
Caddies: No. **Golf carts:** N/A.
Discount golf packages: No. **Season:** Year-round. **High:** Nov.–April.
On-site lodging: No. **Rental clubs:** Yes.
Walking policy: Unrestricted walking. **Range:** No.
To obtain tee times: Call.
Subscriber comments: Nice, challenging course for price . . . Greatly improved over past years . . . Fairly long but in good shape.

★★★★ UNIVERSITY PARK COUNTRY CLUB
SP—7671 Park Blvd., University Park (813)359-9999.
45 miles south of Tampa. **Holes:** 18. **Par:** 72/72.
Yards: 6,951/5,511. **Course rating:** 73.4/71.3. **Slope:** 132/120.
Opened: 1991. **Pace of Play rating:** 4:15. **Green fee:** $50/85.
Credit cards: MC, V, DISC. **Reduced fees:** Weekdays, Low season, Twilight.
Caddies: No. **Golf carts:** Included in Green Fee.
Discount golf packages: No. **Season:** Year-round. **High:** Nov.–April.
On-site lodging: No. **Rental clubs:** Yes.
Walking policy: Walking at certain times. **Range:** No.
To obtain tee times: Call two days in advance.
Subscriber comments: Excellent course, beautifully maintained, great staff . . . Probably the best public course in this area . . . Wow! A must play worth the cost, award-winning course, run first class, one of the best in town . . . Class act! . . . Great course and condition, friendly, pricey.

★★★½ VIERA EAST GOLF CLUB
PU—2300 Clubhouse Dr., Viera (407)639-6500.
5 miles north of Melbourne. **Holes:** 18. **Par:** 72/72.
Yards: 6,720/5,428. **Course rating:** N/A. **Slope:** N/A.
Opened: 1994. **Pace of Play rating:** 4:00. **Green fee:** $20/25.
Credit cards: MC, V, AMEX. **Reduced fees:** Low season, Resort guests, Juniors.

Caddies: No. **Golf carts:** N/A.

Discount golf packages: No. **Season:** Year-round. **High:** Dec.-April.

On-site lodging: No. **Rental clubs:** Yes.

Walking policy: Walking at certain times. **Range:** Yes (grass).

To obtain tee times: Call 48 hours in advance starting at 7 a.m.

Subscriber comments: Good, honest, fair layout, fairly priced . . . For a new course, excellent maintenance and playability . . . A lot tougher than their rating . . . Tough course with railroad-bunkered greens.

★★★ WALDEN LAKES GOLF AND COUNTRY CLUB

SP—2001 Club House Drive, Plant City (813)754-8575.

Call club for further information.

Subscriber comments: Non-demanding. Good course for 90-scorers and above . . . A test for 15-handicapper, better golfers may appreciate more challenge . . . The staff is very helpful and friendly. Has one of the better driving ranges I've used.

WALT DISNEY WORLD RESORT

Credit cards: MC, V, AMEX, The Disney Card. **Reduced fees:** Low season, Resort guests, Twilight.

Caddies: No. **Golf carts:** Included in Green Fee.

Discount golf packages: Yes. **Season:** Year-round. **High:** Jan.-April.

On-site lodging: Yes. **Rental clubs:** Yes.

Range: Yes (grass).

To obtain tee times: Resort guests with confirmed reservation may call 30 days in advance. Non-guests call four days in advance.

★★★★ EAGLE PINES GOLF COURSE

R—3451 Golf View Dr., Lake Buena Vista (407)824-2675.

20 miles southwest of Orlando Airport. **Holes:** 18. **Par:** 72/72.

Yards: 6,772/4,838. **Course rating:** 72.3/68.0. **Slope:** 131/111.

Opened: 1992. **Pace of Play rating:** 4:00. **Green fee:** $85/115.

Walking policy: Mandatory cart.

Subscriber comments: A nice getaway while at Disney . . . Difficult, enjoyable, excellent . . . Playable Pete Dye course, maybe too much so . . . Expensive but a great golf experience, immaculate . . . Disney is always first class; condition of course, staff attitude and pace of play is terrific. A must-play course.

★★★½ LAKE BUENA VISTA GOLF COURSE

R—One Club Lake Dr., Lake Buena Vista (407)828-3741.

20 miles southwest of Orlando Airport. **Holes:** 18. **Par:** 72/73.

Yards: 6,819/5,194. **Course rating:** 72.7/69.4. **Slope:** 128/120.

Opened: 1972. **Pace of Play rating:** 4:00. **Green fee:** $85/95.

Walking policy: Walking at certain times.

Subscriber comments: Enjoyable to play, well kept, courteous staff . . . Great course, resort prices . . . Good, solid, fun resort course. Send the hackers and beginners here from the other Disney courses . . . Underrated compared to new Disney courses.

★★★★ MAGNOLIA GOLF COURSE

R—1950 W. Magnolia Palm Dr., Lake Buena Vista (407)824-2288.

25 miles southwest of Orlando Airport. **Holes:** 18. **Par:** 72/72.

Yards: 7,190/5,232. **Course rating:** 73.9/70.5. **Slope:** 133/123.

Opened: 1971. **Pace of Play rating:** 4:30. **Green fee:** $85/95.

Walking policy: Mandatory cart.

Subscriber comments: Long hitters fair better . . . Very long course but like all Disney courses, great . . . Excellent conditon, greens great . . . Terrific course, a little expensive . . . Very long, No.6 bunker looks like Mickey, a fun round . . . Good test of golf, Disney maintained, "nuf said."

★★★★½ OSPREY RIDGE GOLF COURSE

R—3451 Golf View Dr., Lake Buena Vista (407)824-2675.

20 miles southwest of Orlando Airport. **Holes:** 18. **Par:** 72/72.

Yards: 7,101/5,402. **Course rating:** 73.9/70.5. **Slope:** 135/122.

Opened: 1992. **Pace of Play rating:** 4:30. **Green fee:** $85/115.

Walking policy: Mandatory cart.

Ranked 27th in Florida by Golf Digest.

Subscriber comments: Best at Disney, in a few years will be a great course . . . Lots of sand, use long irons to stay out of trouble . . . A must at Disney, great conditioning, challenging layout, Disney staff are No.1 . . . Take a camera . . . My favorite . . . Best Fazio I've played . . . The best of Disney . . . Good Fazio design. Hard from the back. Fair from the front . . . Last five holes can kill a good round . . . Wow.

★★★★ PALM GOLF COURSE
R—1950 W. Magnolia Dr., Lake Buena Vista (407)824-2288.
25 miles southwest of Orlando Airport. **Holes:** 18. **Par:** 72/72.
Yards: 6,957/5,311. **Course rating:** 73.0/70.4. **Slope:** 133/124.
Opened: 1971. **Pace of Play rating:** 4:00. **Green fee:** $85/95.
Walking policy: Mandatory cart.
Ranked 61st in America's 75 Best Resort Courses by Golf Digest.
Subscriber comments: No.2 of Disney's five, challenging from tips, bring extra sleeves . . . Good solid track . . . Plush! Great holes, no "Mickey Mouse" course! . . . Would be hard to go wrong at Disney . . . Favorite Disney course, tough even from white markers.

★★★ WATERFORD GOLF CLUB
PU—1454 Gleneagles Dr., Venice (813)484-6621.
15 miles from Sarasota. **Holes:** 18. **Par:** 72/72.
Yards: 6,601/5,242. **Course rating:** N/A. **Slope:** 124/116.
Opened: N/A. **Pace of Play rating:** N/A. **Green fee:** N/A.
Credit cards: MC, V. **Reduced fees:** Low season.
Caddies: No. **Golf carts:** N/A.
Discount golf packages: No. **Season:** Year-round. **High:** Jan.-April.
On-site lodging: No. **Rental clubs:** No.
Walking policy: N/A. **Range:** Yes (grass).
Subscriber comments: Excellent middle-value course . . . Nice course, good upkeep, good staff . . . Course has a variety of holes and now in good condition . . . Nice course and nice folks.

WEDGEWOOD GOLF AND COUNTRY CLUB★
SP—401 Carpenter's Way, Lakeland (813)858-4451.
25 miles west of Tampa. **Holes:** 18. **Par:** 70/70.
Yards: 6,402/4,885. **Course rating:** 69.1/68.1. **Slope:** 115/113.
Opened: 1984. **Pace of Play rating:** N/A. **Green fee:** $16/25.
Credit cards: MC, V. **Reduced fees:** Weekdays, Low season, Twilight.

Caddies: No. **Golf carts:** Included in Green Fee.
Discount golf packages: No. **Season:** Year-round. **High:** Nov.-May.
On-site lodging: No. **Rental clubs:** No.
Walking policy: Mandatory cart. **Range:** Yes (grass).
To obtain tee times: Call three days in advance.

★★★ WEKIVA GOLF CLUB
PU—200 Hunt Club Blvd., Longwood (407)862-5113.
Call club for information.
Comments: Hidden jewel of area. Narrow in spots . . . Best-kept secret in central Florida, course is always in great shape, low price, one of best pro shops in the area . . . Fun local course.

★★★ WEST PALM BEACH MUNICIPAL COUNTRY CLUB
PU—7001 Parker Ave., West Palm Beach (407)582-2019.
Holes: 18. **Par:** 72/72.
Yards: 6,789/5,884. **Course rating:** 72.8/73.3. **Slope:** 124/126.
Opened: 1947. **Pace of Play rating:** 4:00. **Green fee:** $13/30.
Credit cards: MC, V, DISC. **Reduced fees:** Low season, Twilight, Juniors.
Caddies: No. **Golf carts:** $10 for 18 holes.
Discount golf packages: No. **Season:** Year-round. **High:** Dec.-April.
On-site lodging: No. **Rental clubs:** Yes.
Walking policy: Walking at certain times. **Range:** Yes (grass).
To obtain tee times: Lottery system. One person per foursome enters names evening before day of play at 7 p.m. As slips are drawn golfer gets

choice of available times. Other: call starter after lottery or day of play to secure a time. Saturday and Sunday double crossover lottery. Wednesday evening for Saturday and Thursday for Sunday at 7:30 p:m.
Ranked in Second 25 of America's 75 Best Public Golf Courses by Golf Digest.
Subscriber comments: Excellent course, no water . . . Dick Wilson course, gets heavy play . . . Tough to get tee times due to popularity . . . Best bet in south Florida. I love this place . . . West Palm Beach's pride and joy. Usually in great shape. No water, some sand . . . Great old public course.

★★★½ WESTCHASE GOLF CLUB
PU—10307 Radcliffe Dr., Tampa (813)854-2331
Holes: 18. **Par:** 72/72.
Yards: 6,710/5,205. **Course rating:** 71.8/69.1. **Slope:** 130/121.
Opened: 1992. **Pace of Play rating:** N/A. **Green fee:** $35/45.
Credit cards: All major. **Reduced fees:** Weekdays, Low season, Twilight, Juniors.
Caddies: No. **Golf carts:** Included in Green Fee.
Discount golf packages: No. **Season:** Year-round. **High:** Jan.-April.
On-site lodging: No. **Rental clubs:** Yes.
Walking policy: Mandatory cart. **Range:** Yes (grass).
To obtain tee times: Call up to three days in advance.
Subscriber comments: Always a pleasure to play . . . Very challenging and always in good shape . . . In great shape for young course, staff nice . . . A guaranteed tough day for wild hitters. Lot of water, marsh, sawgrass.

★★★ WESTCHESTER GOLF AND COUNTRY CLUB
SP—12250 Westchester Club Drive, Boynton Beach (407)734-6300.
12 miles south of West Palm Beach. **Holes:** 18. **Par:** 72/72.
Yards: 6,760/4,886. **Course rating:** 72.0/67.5. **Slope:** 128/111.
Opened: 1988. **Pace of Play rating:** 4:30. **Green fee:** $28/55.
Credit cards: MC, V, AMEX. **Reduced fees:** Weekdays, Low season, Resort guests.
Caddies: No. **Golf carts:** Included in Green Fee.
Discount golf packages: Yes. **Season:** Year-round. **High:** Nov.-April.
On-site lodging: No. **Rental clubs:** Yes.
Walking policy: Mandatory cart. **Range:** Yes (grass).
To obtain tee times: Call two days in advance.
Subscriber comments: This golf mecca has it all for practice and play . . . Well run but takes forever to play 18 . . . Good challenge, superbly maintained, friendly staff, country club atmosphere, but still laid back.

★★★½ WINDSOR PARKE GOLF CLUB
PU—4747 Hodges Blvd., Jacksonville (904)223-4653.
Holes: 18. **Par:** 72/72.
Yards: 6,740/5,206. **Course rating:** 71.9/69.4. **Slope:** 133/123.
Opened: 1991. **Pace of Play rating:** N/A. **Green fee:** $42/48.
Credit cards: All major. **Reduced fees:** Weekdays, Twilight, Seniors, Juniors.
Caddies: Yes. **Golf carts:** Included in Green Fee.
Discount golf packages: Yes. **Season:** Year-round. **High:** March-May.
On-site lodging: No. **Rental clubs:** Yes.

Walking policy: Walking at certain times. **Range:** Yes.
To obtain tee times: Call five days in advance.
Subscriber comments: A bit more expensive but worth it . . . Great course for the amount of play . . . Nice pro shop, friendly, mostly open fairways . . . Best public course in town . . . For all levels. Flat with mounds. Well maintained. Good staff. Pace of play moderate. Wide fairways. Some water. Very challenging.

★★★½ WINSTON TRAILS GOLF CLUB
PU—6101 Winston Trails Blvd., Lake Worth (407)439-3700.
15 miles south of West Palm Beach. **Holes:** 18. **Par:** 72/72.
Yards: 6,835/5,405. **Course rating:** 72.8/71.1. **Slope:** 123/117.
Opened: 1993. **Pace of Play rating:** N/A. **Green fee:** $30/65.
Credit cards: MC, V, AMEX. **Reduced fees:** Weekdays, Low season,
Twilight.
Caddies: No. **Golf carts:** Included in Green Fee.
Discount golf packages: Yes. **Season:** Year-round. **High:** March-Nov.
On-site lodging: No. **Rental clubs:** Yes.
Walking policy: Mandatory cart. **Range:** Yes (grass).
To obtain tee times: Call two days in advance.
Subscriber comments: Enjoyable to play, knowledgable staff . . . New
course, good open fairways for us duffers . . . Good shape, all-round nice
course . . . Wide open with great big greens and fast . . . Excellent greens
for a young course.

WORLD WOODS GOLF CLUB
R—17590 Ponce De Leon Blvd., Brooksville (904)796-5500.
60 miles north of Tampa.
Opened: 1993. **Pace of Play rating:** 4:20. **Green fee:** $50/75.
Credit cards: MC, V. **Reduced fees:** Weekdays, Low season.
Caddies: No. **Golf carts:** Included in Green Fee.
Discount golf packages: Yes. **Season:** Year-round. **High:** Jan.-April.
On-site lodging: No. **Rental clubs:** Yes.
Walking policy: Mandatory cart. **Range:** Yes (grass).
To obtain tee times: Call up to 30 days in advance with credit card.

GREAT VALUE

★★★★½ PINE BARRENS COURSE
Holes: 18. **Par:** 71/71.
Yards: 6,902/5,301. **Course rating:** 73.7/70.9. **Slope:** 140/132.
Selected as Best New Resort Course of 1994 by Golf Digest. Ranked 8th in
Florida by Golf Digest.
Subscriber comments: Outstanding, awesome, superb shape. If you are
in central Florida, you can't afford not to play . . . You have to play it to
believe it . . . Fazio has created "Pine Valley of the South" . . . A great 36-
hole day . . . I want to be buried here, I love this place . . . Pleeease don't
tell everyone about this place . . . As good as golf gets . . . Finest golf
facility I've ever seen. Well worth the cost. Serious golfer will like it best.
Incredibly maintained. Excellent practice facility. Service was outstanding.
No homes around, it is dedicated to golf.

★★★★½ ROLLING OAKS COURSE
Holes: 18. **Par:** 72/72.
Yards: 6,985/5,245. **Course rating:** 73.5/70.7. **Slope:** 136/128.
Ranked 19th in Florida by Golf Digest.
Subscriber comments: Almost as good as Pine Barrens . . . Outstanding
design, great greens . . . No bad golf holes here, fast-tracking greens, lots of
sand, very good course, top notch practice facility . . . Just plain fun,
especially after Pine Barrens . . . Would look at home in Northeast . . .
Staff is very friendly and anxious to please . . . Most beautiful fairways in
Florida . . . More playable than Pine Barrens, better greens.

★★½ ZELLWOOD STATION COUNTRY CLUB
SP—2126 Spillman Drive, Zellwood (407)886-3303.
20 miles north of Orlando. **Holes:** 18. **Par:** 72/74.
Yards: 6,400/5,377. **Course rating:** 70.5/71.1. **Slope:** 122/122.
Opened: 1977. **Pace of Play rating:** 4:00. **Green fee:** $22/30.
Credit cards: None. **Reduced fees:** Low season, Twilight.
Caddies: No. **Golf carts:** Included in Green Fee.
Discount golf packages: No. **Season:** Year-round. **High:** Nov.-April.
On-site lodging: No. **Rental clubs:** Yes.
Walking policy: Mandatory cart. **Range:** Yes.
To obtain tee times: Call 48 hours in advance.
Subscriber comments: Nice course for high handicapper . . . Excellent
conditions, four of the easiest and four of the hardest holes in central Florida
. . . Good deal, love the hills . . . Long holes. Fast greens.

★½ BACON PARK GOLF COURSE
CYPRESS/MAGNOLIA/LIVE OAK
PU—Shorty Cooper Dr., Savannah (912)354-2625.
Holes: 27. **Par:** 72/72/72.
Yards: 6,573/6,679/6,740. **Course rating:** 69.9/70.5/70.7.
Slope: 118/119/120.
Opened: 1927. **Pace of Play rating:** 3:54. **Green fee:** $12/14.
Credit cards: MC, V. **Reduced fees:** Weekdays, Low season, Twilight, Seniors, Juniors.
Caddies: No. **Golf carts:** N/A.
Discount golf packages: No. **Season:** Year-round. **High:** June-Aug.
On-site lodging: No. **Rental clubs:** Yes.
Walking policy: Walking at certain times. **Range:** Yes (grass).
To obtain tee times: Call up to 30 days in advance.
Subscriber comments: A good course for beginners . . . Public course, played a lot, good weekday stop : . . Could be very good except for poor drainage.

★★★ BARRINGTON HALL GOLF CLUB
SP—7100 Zebulon Rd., Macon (912)757-8358.
65 miles south of Atlanta. **Holes:** 18. **Par:** 72/72.
Yards: 7,062/5,012. **Course rating:** 73.8/69.3. **Slope:** 138/118.
Opened: 1992. **Pace of Play rating:** 4:20. **Green fee:** $19/29.
Credit cards: MC, V. **Reduced fees:** Weekdays.
Caddies: No. **Golf carts:** $10 for 18 holes.
Discount golf packages: Yes. **Season:** Year-round. **High:** April-May.
On-site lodging: No. **Rental clubs:** Yes.
Walking policy: Walking at certain times. **Range:** Yes (grass).
To obtain tee times: Call pro shop.
Subscriber comments: A narrow fairway-type layout, it really is not for a high handicapper . . . Beautiful course, tight fairways and lots of woods . . . Excellent new course, will age into a great one . . . A fun, challenging place.

BEAVER KREEK GOLF CLUB★
SP—Rte. 4, Box 167, Hwy. 221 N., Douglas (912)384-8230.
60 miles northeast of Valdosta. **Holes:** 18. **Par:** 72/72.
Yards: 6,543/5,424. **Course rating:** 71.1/N/A. **Slope:** 119/N/A.
Opened: 1988. **Pace of Play rating:** 3:30. **Green fee:** $24.
Credit cards: MC, V. **Reduced fees:** No.
Caddies: No. **Golf carts:** $16 for 18 holes.
Discount golf packages: Yes. **Season:** Year-round. **High:** April-Oct.
On-site lodging: No. **Rental clubs:** Yes.
Walking policy: Walking at certain times. **Range:** Yes (grass).
To obtain tee times: Call pro shop.

★★½ BELLE MEADE COUNTRY CLUB
PU—2660 Twin Pine Rd., N.W., Thomson (706)595-4511.
35 miles west of Augusta. **Holes:** 18. **Par:** 72/73.
Yards: 6,212/5,362. **Course rating:** 69.9/68.6. **Slope:** 120/113.
Opened: 1968. **Pace of Play rating:** N/A. **Green fee:** $18/26.
Credit cards: MC, V. **Reduced fees:** Weekdays, Seniors.
Caddies: No. **Golf carts:** N/A.
Discount golf packages: No. **Season:** Year-round. **High:** May-Aug.
On-site lodging: No. **Rental clubs:** Yes.
Walking policy: Walking at certain times. **Range:** Yes (grass).
To obtain tee times: Call pro shop.
Subscriber comments: Short, tough, small greens . . . Very enjoyable, suited for all types of players. Excellent condition all year . . . Front nine is open and flat, back nine is very hilly and wooded . . . Friendly staff, unhurried atmosphere, good condition, small-town flavor.

GEORGIA

BLACK CREEK GOLF CLUB★
SP—Bill Futch Rd., Ellabell (912)858-4653.
30 miles east of Savannah. **Holes:** 18. **Par:** 72/72.
Yards: 6,287/4,551. **Course rating:** 70.4/66.0. **Slope:** 130/109.
Opened: 1994. **Pace of Play rating:** 4:30. **Green fee:** $23/27.
Credit cards: MC, V. **Reduced fees:** Seniors, Juniors.
Caddies: No. **Golf carts:** $8 for 18 holes.
Discount golf packages: Yes. **Season:** Year-round. **High:** April-Sept.
On-site lodging: No. **Rental clubs:** Yes.
Walking policy: Unrestricted walking. **Range:** Yes (grass).
To obtain tee times: Call seven days in advance.

★ BOBBY JONES GOLF CLUB
PU—384 Woodward Way, Atlanta (404)355-1009.
Holes: 18. **Par:** 71/71.
Yards: 6,155/4,661. **Course rating:** 69.0/67.6. **Slope:** 119/114.
Opened: 1932. **Pace of Play rating:** 3:30-4:00. **Green fee:** $19/33.
Credit cards: MC, V. **Reduced fees:** Weekdays, Twilight, Seniors,
Juniors.
Caddies: No. **Golf carts:** $10 for 18 holes.
Discount golf packages: No. **Season:** Year-round. **High:** May-Sept.
On-site lodging: No. **Rental clubs:** Yes.
Walking policy: Mandatory cart. **Range:** No.
To obtain tee times: Call pro shop.
Subscriber comments: Course suited for beginners . . . Where everyone
goes for their first golf outing. Lots of hills, always great fun though . . .
OK for old municipal course, but hilly . . . Very crowded and slow, not a
bad little public course . . . Fairways and greens are kept in good condition,
more of a weekend-golfer course . . . Short course, crowded, fair
conditions.

★★★★ THE BOULDERS COURSE AT LAKE ACWORTH
PU—4200 Nance Rd., Acworth (404)917-5151.
20 miles north of Atlanta. **Holes:** 18. **Par:** 71/71.
Yards: 6,759/5,400. **Course rating:** 73.1/71.5. **Slope:** 140/129.
Opened: 1993. **Pace of Play rating:** 4:15. **Green fee:** $34/45.
Credit cards: MC, V. **Reduced fees:** Weekdays, Low season, Twilight,
Seniors, Juniors.
Caddies: No. **Golf carts:** $10 for 18 holes.
Discount golf packages: No. **Season:** Year-round. **High:** March-Oct.
On-site lodging: No. **Rental clubs:** Yes.
Walking policy: Walking at certain times. **Range:** Yes (grass).
To obtain tee times: Call four days in advance at 7:30 a.m.
Ranked 10th in Georgia by Golf Digest.
Subscriber comments: Excellent design and layout . . . Don't play from
back tees; too hard for a public course; beautiful layout . . . Best public
course I've played, tough yet fun . . . This is a difficult course, average
golfer wouldn't enjoy . . . Toughest, best laid out public course . . .
Picturesque layout. Can play long. Designed for straight hitters . . . Best
public course in Georgia. Immaculate condition, no bad holes . . . Very
demanding, very attractive . . . Don't bother playing this course if you
don't have your game face on! . . . Beautiful scenery. Back nine is brutal. A
little pricey . . . Fun course, great views of lake . . . Great par 3s, incredible
views . . . New, great conditions, tough for beginners, service good . . .
Great course, very difficult, a lot of water.

★★ BRICKYARD PLANTATION GOLF CLUB
DUTCHESS/WATERS/MOUNDS
PU—US 280E, Americus (912)874-1234.
Call club for further information.
Subscriber comments: Fun course to play . . . Looks as if it was a farm at
one time . . . Neat place, different, down-home style . . . Good course for
high handicapper. Short with small greens . . . A bit rough in fairway
condition . . . The par 5 on water will get you.

★★ BROWNS MILL GOLF COURSE

PU—480 Cleveland Ave., Atlanta (404)366-3573.
Holes: 18. **Par:** 72/72.
Yards: 6,539/5,545. **Course rating:** 71.0/71.4. **Slope:** 123/118.
Opened: 1969. **Pace of Play rating:** 4:15. **Green fee:** $19/22.
Credit cards: MC, V. **Reduced fees:** Weekdays, Twilight, Seniors, Juniors.
Caddies: No. **Golf carts:** $11 for 18 holes.
Discount golf packages: No. **Season:** Year-round. **High:** March-Oct.
On-site lodging: No. **Rental clubs:** Yes.
Walking policy: Unrestricted walking. **Range:** Yes (grass).
To obtain tee times: Call pro shop.
Subscriber comments: Fine municipal layout in good condition, but greens are slow and grainy . . . Very well kept. Slow on weekends. Attentive staff . . . Best of Atlanta city courses, decent track, inconsistent greens . . . Not too many hazards, but nicely laid out with some water holes. The staff is great.

BULL CREEK GOLF COURSE

PU—7333 Lynch Rd., Columbus (706)561-1614.
10 miles east of Columbus.
Opened: 1972. **Pace of Play rating:** 4:00. **Green fee:** $13/15.
Credit cards: MC, V. **Reduced fees:** Weekdays, Seniors, Juniors.
Caddies: No. **Golf carts:** $9 for 18 holes.
Discount golf packages: Yes. **Season:** Year-round. **High:** April-Aug.
On-site lodging: No. **Rental clubs:** Yes.
Walking policy: Unrestricted walking. **Range:** Yes (grass).
To obtain tee times: Call pro shop.

★★★ EAST COURSE

Holes: 18. **Par:** 72/74.
Yards: 6,705/5,430. **Course rating:** 71.2/69.8. **Slope:** 124/114.
Subscriber comments: Acceptable-to-good course, not hard to play . . . Not for beginners . . . Great golf on both courses . . . Course is tight, requires accuracy . . . Great public layout. Clubhouse, service OK . . . Solid course, well thought-out, holes have personality.

★★★ WEST COURSE

Holes: 18. **Par:** 72/74.
Yards: 6,921/5,385. **Course rating:** 72.5/69.9. **Slope:** 130/121.
Ranked in First 25 of America's 75 Best Public Golf Courses by Golf Digest.
Subscriber comments: Considering number of rounds played, course in excellent condition . . . Course is tight, requires accuracy, courteous staff . . . Very good public courses . . . Very interesting, many doglegs . . . Need to spend some money to bring up to standard . . . Hilly but fun . . . Great public course, lots of challenges.

CALLAWAY GARDENS RESORT

R—U.S. Hwy. 27, Pine Mtn. (706)663-2281 (800)282-8181
27 miles north of Columbus.
Credit cards: All major. **Reduced fees:** Low season, Twilight.
Caddies: No. **Golf carts:** Included in Green Fee.
Discount golf packages: Yes. **Season:** Year-round. **High:** Feb.-March/June-Aug.
On-site lodging: Yes. **Rental clubs:** Yes.
Walking policy: Walking at certain times. **Range:** Yes (grass).
To obtain tee times: Resort guests can make tee times when room reservations are guaranteed. Nonguests call 800 number 48 hours in advance or pro shop day of play.
Also 9-hole Sky View Course.

★★★ GARDENS VIEW COURSE

Holes: 18. **Par:** 72/72.
Yards: 6,392/5,848. **Course rating:** 70.7/72.7. **Slope:** 121/123.
Opened: 1964. **Pace of Play rating:** 4:30-5:00. **Green fee:** $55/65.
Subscriber comments: Wide open, well kept . . . Good family vacation

spot . . . Beautiful, but greens are sometimes too slow . . . Fee to enter park should be included in green fee . . . All three courses are good layouts, different . . . Stop and grab a handful of berries to eat on the course.

★★★ LAKE VIEW COURSE

Holes: 18. **Par:** 70/71.
Yards: 6,006/5,452. **Course rating:** 69.4/70.3. **Slope:** 115/122.
Opened: 1964. **Pace of Play rating:** 4:30–5:00. **Green fee:** $55/65.
Subscriber comments: Wide open, good design, pleasure to play, picturesque . . . Best of three joyful courses . . . Beautiful . . . Friendly to higher handicap . . . Something for everyone, service excellent, play tends to be slow . . . Should not charge to enter park . . . Lovely little course in great condition.

★★★★ MOUNTAIN VIEW COURSE

Holes: 18. **Par:** 72/74.
Yards: 7,057/5,848. **Course rating:** 74.1/73.2. **Slope:** 138/122.
Opened: 1968. **Pace of Play rating:** 4:15. **Green fee:** $40/80.
Ranked 56th in America's 75 Best Resort Courses by Golf Digest. Ranked 16th in Georgia by Golf Digest.
Subscriber comments: Long, but great, home of Buick Southern Open . . . A brute requiring distance, accuracy, shotmaking skills . . . Tough course, narrow fairways, very well maintained . . . Long, tough, absolutely beautiful condition, can't walk . . . Excellent condition, friendly staff, pressure to play well is tremendous after spending so much money . . . Must keep ball in fairway, pros make it look easy . . . Tees fair for all classes of golfers. I think they price it a little high . . . Course is superb, well worth the price . . . Long and brutal but fun and beautiful.

★★½ CENNTENNIAL GOLF CLUB

PU—522 Woodstock Rd., Acworth (404)975-1000.
15 miles south of Atlanta. **Holes:** 18. **Par:** 72/72.
Yards: 6,850/5,095. **Course rating:** 73.1/69.5. **Slope:** 134/122.
Opened: 1990. **Pace of Play rating:** 4:00. **Green fee:** $35/45.
Credit cards: All major. **Reduced fees:** Twilight, Seniors, Juniors.
Caddies: No. **Golf carts:** Included in Green Fee.
Discount golf packages: No. **Season:** Year-round. **High:** June-Oct.
On-site lodging: No. **Rental clubs:** Yes.
Walking policy: Unrestricted walking. **Range:** Yes (grass).
To obtain tee times: Call seven days in advance.
Subscriber comments: Nice track, difficult putting course, worth it . . . Requires good club selection. Some blind greens . . . Target golf from start to finish . . . Hilly mountain course, nice clubhouse . . . Too many layups off the tee.

★★★ THE CHAMPIONS CLUB OF ATLANTA

SP—15135 Hopewell Rd., Alpharetta (404)343-9700.
20 miles north of Atlanta. **Holes:** 18. **Par:** 72/72.
Yards: 6,725/4,470. **Course rating:** 72.9/65.2. **Slope:** 131/108.
Opened: 1991. **Pace of Play rating:** 4:15. **Green fee:** $42/59.
Credit cards: MC, V. **Reduced fees:** Twilight.
Caddies: No. **Golf carts:** Included in Green Fee.
Discount golf packages: No. **Season:** Year-round. **High:** March-Dec.
On-site lodging: No. **Rental clubs:** Yes.
Walking policy: Mandatory cart. **Range:** Yes (grass).
To obtain tee times: Call up to three days in advance.
Subscriber comments: Medium-width fairways, slightly more expensive than other courses in area . . . Staff friendly, course is rough around the edges . . . Plays better from back tees . . . Still maturing, nice facilities, friendly staff . . . Challenging, need to play from back tees . . . Fun but short, good for mid-high handicap . . . Short course, gives high handicapper confidence . . . Rolling hills, good fairways and greens.

★★★½ CHATEAU ELAN GOLF CLUB
R—6060 Golf Club Dr., Braselton (404)271-6050, (800)233-9463.
45 miles northeast of Atlanta. **Holes:** 18. **Par:** 71/71.
Yards: 7,030/5,092. **Course rating:** 73.5/70.8. **Slope:** 136/124.
Opened: 1989. **Pace of Play rating:** 4:30. **Green fee:** $55/60.
Credit cards: MC, V, AMEX. **Reduced fees:** No.
Caddies: No. **Golf carts:** Included in Green Fee.
Discount golf packages: Yes. **Season:** Year-round. **High:** April/Oct.
On-site lodging: Yes. **Rental clubs:** Yes.
Walking policy: Mandatory cart. **Range:** Yes (grass).
To obtain tee times: Call up to seven days in advance. Weekend tee times
guaranteed with credit card.
Site of Golf Digest Schools. Also has 9-hole walking course.
Subscriber comments: Good layout in good shape with good amenities
and good staff, but high priced . . . Helpful staff, challenging course, great
practice areas . . . Very good range and par-3 course . . . Excellent facility,
outstanding track, helps to be long . . . Wonderful greens and generous
fairways . . . Enjoyable mountain course. Super clubhouse service.
Excellent condition . . . Best practice range I've found.

★★★ CHATTAHOOCHEE GOLF CLUB
PU—301 Tommy Aaron Dr., Gainesville (404)532-0066.
50 miles north of Atlanta. **Holes:** 18. **Par:** 72/72.
Yards: 6,700/5,000. **Course rating:** 72.1/64.5. **Slope:** 125/110.
Opened: 1955. **Pace of Play rating:** 4:00. **Green fee:** $14/29.
Credit cards: MC, V, AMEX. **Reduced fees:** Twilight, Seniors, Juniors.
Caddies: No. **Golf carts:** $10 for 18 holes.
Discount golf packages: No. **Season:** Year-round. **High:** April-Sept.
On-site lodging: No. **Rental clubs:** Yes.
Walking policy: Walking at certain times. **Range:** Yes (grass).
To obtain tee times: Call three days in advance.
Subscriber comments: Traditional layout, excellent value and condition,
mature . . . Nine doglegs left, great greens, fairly short . . . Slicer's
nightmare, lots of lefthand doglegs . . . Very nice course, beautiful greens
. . . Good, solid, public course, decent design with a lot of trees.

★★★½ CHICOPEE WOODS GOLF COURSE
PU—2515 Atlanta Hwy., Gainesville (404)534-7322.
30 miles northeast of Atlanta. **Holes:** 18. **Par:** 72/72.
Yards: 7,040/5,001. **Course rating:** 74.0/69.0. **Slope:** 135/117.
Opened: 1991. **Pace of Play rating:** 4:00-4:30. **Green fee:** $27.
Credit cards: MC, V, AMEX. **Reduced fees:** Twilight.
Caddies: No. **Golf carts:** $8 for 18 holes.
Discount golf packages: No. **Season:** Year-round. **High:** April-Sept.
On-site lodging: No. **Rental clubs:** Yes.
Walking policy: Unrestricted walking. **Range:** Yes (grass).
To obtain tee times: Call three days in advance at 9 a.m.
Subscriber comments: Hilly, challenging, well bunkered, contoured
greens . . . Play this course from the back and it will humble you . . . Hilly
. . . Great little layout. A test from the tips. Love hole No. 6! . . . Too
many blind second shots . . . Great course, fair and fun, hilly enough to
warrant a cart . . . Good test of shotmaking.

(GREAT VALUE)

★½ CITY CLUB MARIETTA
PU—510 Powder Spring St., Marietta (404)528-0799.
15 miles north of Atlanta. **Holes:** 18. **Par:** 71/71.
Yards: 5,721/4,715. **Course rating:** 67.3/67.5. **Slope:** 118/115.
Opened: 1991. **Pace of Play rating:** 4:20. **Green fee:** $32/40.
Credit cards: MC, V, AMEX. **Reduced fees:** Weekdays, Seniors,
Juniors.
Caddies: No. **Golf carts:** Included in Green Fee.
Discount golf packages: Yes. **Season:** Year-round. **High:** April-Aug.
On-site lodging: No. **Rental clubs:** Yes.
Walking policy: Unrestricted walking. **Range:** Yes (grass).

To obtain tee times: Call seven days in advance.

Subscriber comments: Plays a lot harder than yardage, narrow fairways . . . Small, short, little challenge, but good shape . . . Short but very interesting. Slow pace at times. Beautiful scenery all year . . . If you like to hit the driver on every hole, don't play here.

★★★½ EAGLE WATCH GOLF CLUB

SP—3055 Eagle Watch Dr., Woodstock (404)591-1000.
25 miles north of Atlanta. **Holes:** 18. **Par:** 72/72.
Yards: 6,900/5,243. **Course rating:** 72.6/68.9. **Slope:** 136/126.
Opened: 1989. **Pace of Play rating:** 4:30. **Green fee:** $40/65.
Credit cards: MC, V, AMEX. **Reduced fees:** Weekdays, Low season, Resort guests, Twilight, Seniors, Juniors.
Caddies: No. **Golf carts:** Included in Green Fee.
Discount golf packages: No. **Season:** Year-round. **High:** June-Aug.
On-site lodging: No. **Rental clubs:** Yes.
Walking policy: Mandatory cart. **Range:** Yes (grass).
To obtain tee times: Call three days in advance.
Subscriber comments: One of the best courses in Georgia, great layout and condition . . . Very hilly and tight . . . Tough for average golfers from blues, all uneven lies . . . Solid Palmer design . . . Best in area but will be private soon . . . Excellent course, fun to play, very few level lies . . . Greens very difficult, challenging.

★★★½ FIELDS FERRY GOLF CLUB

PU—581 Fields Ferry Dr., Calhoun (706)625-5666.
50 miles north of Atlanta. **Holes:** 18. **Par:** 72/72.
Yards: 6,824/5,355. **Course rating:** 71.8/70.5. **Slope:** 123/120.
Opened: 1992. **Pace of Play rating:** 4:10. **Green fee:** $13/25.

Credit cards: MC, V. **Reduced fees:** Weekdays, Twilight, Seniors, Juniors.
Caddies: No. **Golf carts:** $8 for 18 holes.
Discount golf packages: No. **Season:** Year-round. **High:** April-Oct.
On-site lodging: No. **Rental clubs:** Yes.
Walking policy: Unrestricted walking. **Range:** Yes (grass).
To obtain tee times: Call three days in advance.
Subscriber comments: Tremendous three finishing holes . . . Young course that is already a pleasant outing . . . Condition greatly improved . . . New and very good course. Country setting . . . Links style, most wide open, lots of play, good service . . . Great layout, 50 miles from metropolitan area, easy tee times . . . Wide open, needs trees but was in good condition . . . Interesting layout, good variety of holes.

★★½ THE FIELDS GOLF CLUB

SP—257 South Smith Rd., LaGrange (706)845-7425.
30 miles north of Columbus. **Holes:** 18. **Par:** 72/72.
Yards: 6,650/5,000. **Course rating:** 71.4/67.4. **Slope:** 128/113.
Opened: 1990. **Pace of Play rating:** 4:00. **Green fee:** $11/19.
Credit cards: MC, V. **Reduced fees:** Weekdays, Low season, Twilight, Seniors.
Caddies: No. **Golf carts:** $9 for 18 holes.
Discount golf packages: Yes. **Season:** Year-round. **High:** March-Oct.
On-site lodging: No. **Rental clubs:** Yes.
Walking policy: Walking at certain times. **Range:** Yes (grass).
To obtain tee times: Call Monday a.m. prior to weekend.
Subscriber comments: Good course, will be better in a couple of years . . . Smart layout, not overly difficult . . . New course good for tournaments. Playable at all levels . . . Wide open, plenty of blind shots . . . Nice course, better for mid to upper handicapper.

★★★ FOREST HILLS GOLF CLUB

PU—1500 Comfort Rd., Augusta (706)733-0001.
Holes: 18. **Par:** 72/72.
Yards: 6,780/4,875. **Course rating:** 72.8/69.8. **Slope:** 124/117.

Opened: 1926. **Pace of Play rating:** 4:00. **Green fee:** $15/22.
Credit cards: MC, V. **Reduced fees:** Juniors.
Caddies: No. **Golf carts:** $10 for 18 holes.
Discount golf packages: No. **Season:** Year-round. **High:** March–Nov.
On-site lodging: No. **Rental clubs:** Yes.
Walking policy: Unrestricted walking. **Range:** Yes (grass).
To obtain tee times: Call up to one week in advance.
Subscriber comments: Very busy course, tee time highly recommended
. . . Old course renewed, excellent . . . Easy to walk. Good condition for a
municipal . . . Wonderful Donald Ross layout, needs better maintenance
. . . Nice old course.

FORSYTH COUNTRY CLUB★

PU—400 Country Club Dr., Forsyth (912)994-5328.
20 miles north of Macon. **Holes:** 18. **Par:** 72/72.
Yards: 6,051/4,521. **Course rating:** 68.1/65.4. **Slope:** 112/107.
Opened: 1936. **Pace of Play rating:** N/A. **Green fee:** $10/12.
Credit cards: None. **Reduced fees:** No.
Caddies: No. **Golf carts:** $20 for 18 holes.
Discount golf packages: No. **Season:** Year-round.
On-site lodging: No. **Rental clubs:** Yes.
Walking policy: Walking at certain times. **Range:** Yes (grass).
To obtain tee times: First come, first served.

★★★ FOXFIRE GOLF CLUB

SP—1916 Foxfire Dr., Vidalia (912)538-8670.
75 miles west of Savannah. **Holes:** 18. **Par:** 72/71.
Yards: 6,118/4,757. **Course rating:** 69.3/67.5. **Slope:** 125/116.
Opened: 1992. **Pace of Play rating:** 4:30. **Green fee:** $21/25.
Credit cards: MC, V. **Reduced fees:** Weekdays, Seniors, Juniors.
Caddies: No. **Golf carts:** Included in Green Fee.
Discount golf packages: Yes. **Season:** Year-round. **High:** March–Sept.
On-site lodging: No. **Rental clubs:** Yes.
Walking policy: Walking at certain times. **Range:** Yes (grass).
To obtain tee times: Call one day in advance.
Subscriber comments: Great new course, needs work in rough but very
good . . . 13 holes have water on them . . . Best secret in Georgia. Fun to
play. Has everything . . . New course on its way.

★★ FRANCIS LAKE GOLF COURSE

PU—5366 Golf Dr., Lake Park (912)559-7961.
12 miles north of Valdosta. **Holes:** 18. **Par:** 72/72.
Yards: 6,458/5,709. **Course rating:** 71.4/70.1. **Slope:** 124/117.
Opened: 1973. **Pace of Play rating:** N/A. **Green fee:** $18/22.
Credit cards: MC, V. **Reduced fees:** Weekdays, Resort guests, Twilight,
Juniors.
Caddies: No. **Golf carts:** Included in Green Fee.
Discount golf packages: Yes. **Season:** Year-round. **High:** May–Aug.
On-site lodging: No. **Rental clubs:** Yes.
Walking policy: Walking at certain times. **Range:** No.
To obtain tee times: Call in advance.
Subscriber comments: Course will play for most any handicap, but needs
to be better maintained . . . Good course. Very friendly staff. Short.

GEORGIA NATIONAL GOLF CLUB★

PU—1715 Lake Dow Rd., McDonough. (404)914-9994
30 miles south of Atlanta. **Holes:** 18. **Par:** 71/71.
Yards: 6,874/5,741. **Course rating:** 73.3/73.0. **Slope:** 132/130.
Opened: 1994. **Pace of Play rating:** 4:00–4:30. **Green fee:** $35/45.
Credit cards: All Major. **Reduced fees:** Seniors, Juniors.
Caddies: No. **Golf carts:** Included in Green Fee.

Discount golf packages: No. **Season:** Year-round. **High:** April–Sept.
On-site lodging: No. **Rental clubs:** Yes.
Walking policy: Walking at certain times. **Range:** Yes (grass).
To obtain tee times: Call five days in advance.

★★★½ GEORGIA VETERANS STATE PARK GOLF COURSE

PU—2315 Hwy. 280 West, Cordele (912)276-2377.
45 miles south of Macon. **Holes:** 18. **Par:** 72/72.
Yards: 7,088/5,171. **Course rating:** 72.1/73.5. **Slope:** 130/124.
Opened: 1990. **Pace of Play rating:** 3:59. **Green fee:** $15/20.
Credit cards: MC, V. **Reduced fees:** Weekdays, Twilight, Seniors, Juniors.
Caddies: No. **Golf carts:** $14 for 18 holes.
Discount golf packages: Yes. **Season:** Year-round. **High:** April–Sept.
On-site lodging: Yes. **Rental clubs:** Yes.
Walking policy: Unrestricted walking. **Range:** Yes (grass).
To obtain tee times: Tee times accepted daily.
Subscriber comments: Long, long, long from tips . . . Very well designed, suitable for any golfer . . . Beautiful course, fun to play . . . Very good, especially for state park . . . Friendliest staff I've ever encountered . . . Par 72. Straight hitters . . . One of two oustanding Georgia owned/operated golf courses. Great layout. Playable. Tough from back tees . . . Great for weekend golfer . . . Challenging but fun. Neat to see alligators on course.

(GREAT VALUE)

★★½ GOSHEN PLANTATION COUNTRY CLUB

SP—1601 Goshen Clubhouse Dr., Augusta (706)793-1168.
Holes: 18. **Par:** 72/72.
Yards: 6,902/5,688. **Course rating:** 72.6/70.9. **Slope:** 130/125.
Opened: 1970. **Pace of Play rating:** 3:50. **Green fee:** $22/28.
Credit cards: MC, V. **Reduced fees:** Weekdays, Low season, Twilight, Seniors, Juniors.
Caddies: No. **Golf carts:** Included in Green Fee.
Discount golf packages: No. **Season:** Year-round. **High:** March–Oct.
On-site lodging: No. **Rental clubs:** Yes.
Walking policy: Walking at certain times. **Range:** Yes (grass).
To obtain tee times: Call two days in advance. Members, seven days in advance.
Subscriber comments: Tough little course, but in good shape . . . Good except after heavy rains. You may as well walk . . . Still rough with new construction.

HAMILTON MILL GOLF CLUB★

PU—1995 Hamilton Mill Pkwy., Dacula (404)945-4653.
10 miles west of Buford. **Holes:** 18. **Par:** 72/72.
Yards: 6,810/4,744. **Course rating:** N/A. **Slope:** N/A.
Opened: 1995. **Pace of Play rating:** 4:15. **Green fee:** $42/50.
Credit cards: MC, V, AMEX. **Reduced fees:** No.
Caddies: No. **Golf carts:** Included in Green Fee.
Discount golf packages: No. **Season:** Year-round. **High:** May–Sept.
On-site lodging: No. **Rental clubs:** Yes.
Walking policy: Mandatory cart. **Range:** Yes (grass).
To obtain tee times: Call seven days in advance.

★★★½ HAMPTON CLUB

SP—100 Tabbystone, St. Simons Island (912)634-0255.
70 miles south of Jacksonville, FL. **Holes:** 18. **Par:** 72/72.
Yards: 6,400/5,233. **Course rating:** 71.4/71.0. **Slope:** 130/123.
Opened: 1989. **Pace of Play rating:** 4:00. **Green fee:** $60.
Credit cards: MC, V, AMEX. **Reduced fees:** Resort guests, Juniors.
Caddies: No. **Golf carts:** $15 for 18 holes.
Discount golf packages: Yes. **Season:** Year-round. **High:** March–April.
On-site lodging: No. **Rental clubs:** Yes.
Walking policy: Mandatory cart. **Range:** Yes (grass).

To obtain tee times: Call 48 hours in advance.
Subscriber comments: Picturesque course, marsh holes good, numerous doglegs . . . Very challenging, accurate shotmaking required . . . Lots of bugs . . . Friendly staff, stunningly beautiful, must shape the tee shots . . . Accuracy required, very scenic, environmentally sensitive . . . The marsh holes are great fun . . . Scenery outstanding, course in great shape . . . Nice staff, one ill-tempered alligator.

HARBOR CLUB★

SP—One Club Dr., Greensboro (706)453–4414, (800)505–4653.
70 miles east of Atlanta. **Holes:** 18. **Par:** 72/72.
Yards: 6,988/5,207. **Course rating:** 73.7/70.2. **Slope:** 135/123.
Opened: 1991. **Pace of Play rating:** N/A. **Green fee:** $32/62.
Credit cards: MC, V, AMEX. **Reduced fees:** Weekdays, Low season, Resort guests, Seniors, Juniors.
Caddies: No. **Golf carts:** N/A.
Discount golf packages: Yes. **Season:** Year-round. **High:** March-Oct.
On-site lodging: Yes. **Rental clubs:** Yes.
Walking policy: Walking at certain times. **Range:** Yes (grass).
To obtain tee times: Call one week in advance.
Ranked 12th in Georgia by Golf Digest.

★★½ HARD LABOR CREEK STATE PARK GOLF COURSE

PU—Knox Chapel Rd., Rutledge (706)557-3006.
45 miles east of Atlanta. **Holes:** 18. **Par:** 72/75.
Yards: 6,437/4,854. **Course rating:** 71.5/68.6. **Slope:** 129/123.
Opened: 1967. **Pace of Play rating:** 4:30. **Green fee:** $17.

Credit cards: MC, V. **Reduced fees:** Twilight, Seniors, Juniors.
Caddies: No. **Golf carts:** N/A.
Discount golf packages: Yes. **Season:** Year-round. **High:** April-Oct.
On-site lodging: Yes. **Rental clubs:** Yes.
Walking policy: Unrestricted walking. **Range:** Yes (grass).
To obtain tee times: Call up to two weeks in advance.
Subscriber comments: Vastly underrated. Wonderful, peaceful setting, fine layout . . . Great natural layout always in need of care . . . Tight, tight course. Hilly, good little course for all levels . . . My favorite course, rolling hills, diverse scenery and layout. Streams and waterfalls line the fairways; greens in poor shape, though . . . A gem worth finding; heavily wooded, deer add to scenery, great par 3s.

HENDERSON GOLF CLUB★

PU—1 Al Henderson Dr., Savannah (912)920–4653.
Holes: 18. **Par:** 71/71.
Yards: 6,650/4,788. **Course rating:** N/A. **Slope:** N/A.
Opened: 1995. **Pace of Play rating:** 4:00. **Green fee:** $26/33.
Credit cards: MC, V, AMEX. **Reduced fees:** Weekdays, Twilight, Seniors, Juniors.
Caddies: No. **Golf carts:** Included in Green Fee.
Discount golf packages: No. **Season:** Year-round. **High:** May-Sept.
On-site lodging: No. **Rental clubs:** Yes.
Walking policy: Walking at certain times. **Range:** Yes (grass).
To obtain tee times: Call 14 days in advance.

★★½ HIGHLAND GOLF CLUB

PU—2271 Flat Shoals Rd., Conyers (404)483-4235.
Call club for further information.
Subscriber comments: Wide-open course, well maintained . . . Resort-style layout, wide open, few bunkers, good value, a fun course . . . Fun to play, not too difficult, several good holes . . . Recent improvements make big difference . . . Excellent public course, well maintained, good bent-grass greens . . . Enjoyable, playable, well maintained, a test from the back tees.

★★ INNSBRUCK RESORT AND GOLF CLUB

R—Bahn Innsbruck, Helen (706)878-2100, (800)642-2709.
65 miles northeast of Atlanta. **Holes:** 18. **Par:** 72/72.
Yards: 6,748/5,174. **Course rating:** 72.4/N/A. **Slope:** 136/118.
Opened: 1987. **Pace of Play rating:** N/A. **Green fee:** $30/40.
Credit cards: MC, V, AMEX. **Reduced fees:** Low season, Resort guests,
Twilight, Seniors, Juniors.
Caddies: No. **Golf carts:** Included in Green Fee.
Discount golf packages: Yes. **Season:** Year-round. **High:** April-Oct.
On-site lodging: Yes. **Rental clubs:** Yes.
Walking policy: Mandatory cart. **Range:** Yes (grass).
To obtain tee times: Resort guests may call any time.
Subscriber comments: Scenic mountain golf . . . Very well laid out in the
north Georgia mountains; requires a lot of skill to play but it is a lot of fun
. . . Very scenic, lots of wildlife . . . Always a deer or wild turkey to see
. . . Mountainous, needs work in places, unusual layout . . . Typical
mountain course. Spectacular views with very few level lies.

★½ INTERNATIONAL CITY MUNICIPAL GOLF COURSE

PU—100 Sandy Run Lane, Warner Robins (912)922-3892.
15 miles south of Macon. **Holes:** 18. **Par:** 70/70.
Yards: 5,900/4,900. **Course rating:** 66.4/64.4. **Slope:** 112/106.
Opened: 1957. **Pace of Play rating:** 3:43. **Green fee:** $5/14.
Credit cards: None. **Reduced fees:** Weekdays, Seniors, Juniors.
Caddies: No. **Golf carts:** $7 for 18 holes.
Discount golf packages: No. **Season:** Year-round. **High:** June-Aug.
On-site lodging: No. **Rental clubs:** Yes.
Walking policy: Unrestricted walking. **Range:** Yes (grass).
To obtain tee times: Reservations accepted for holidays and weekends
only. Must have three or four players in group.
Subscriber comments: Short course, nice staff, average greens . . .
Excellent course for beginners/walkers . . . Acceptable, needs work and
TLC . . . Great little short course, getting in better shape every year.

JEKYLL ISLAND GOLF RESORT

R—322 Captain Wylly Rd., Jekyll Island (912)635-2368.
70 miles north of Jacksonville, FL.
Green fee: $26. **Credit cards:** MC, V, DISC. **Reduced fees:** Twilight.
Caddies: No. **Golf carts:** $12 for 18 holes.
Discount golf packages: Yes. **Season:** Year-round. **High:** Feb.–April
On-site lodging: No. **Rental clubs:** Yes.
Walking policy: Walking at certain times. **Range:** Yes (grass).
To obtain tee times: May call anytime up to one year in advance.
Also has 9-hole Oceanside Course.

★★★ INDIAN MOUND COURSE

Holes: 18. **Par:** 72/72.
Yards: 6,596/5,345. **Course rating:** 71.1/N/A. **Slope:** 127/122.
Opened: 1975. **Pace of Play rating:** 4:00.
Subscriber comments: The best in Georgia for the money . . . Good
scenery. Well manicured. Friendly staff . . . Very good resort course, fun
for all levels . . . Great course for average golfer, pretty layouts . . . Good
all-around course, staff OK . . . Very courteous staff, good condition year-
round.

★★★ OLEANDER COURSE

Holes: 18. **Par:** 72/72.
Yards: 6,679/5,654. **Course rating:** 72.0/72.6. **Slope:** 128/124.
Opened: 1964. **Pace of Play rating:** 4:00.
Subscriber comments: Wide fairways, lets you spray a little; beware of
heat . . . Great layout, good condition, well run . . . Enjoyed very much.
Wide fairways, good greens. Greatly improved from past years . . . Lets
you play every club in your bag . . . Best on island. Tons of wildlife.
Relaxing atmosphere . . . Longer course but fair.

★★★ PINE LAKES COURSE

Holes: 18. **Par:** 72/72.

Yards: 6,802/5,742. **Course rating:** 71.9/71.9. **Slope:** 130/124.
Opened: 1968. **Pace of Play rating:** 4:00.
Subscriber comments: Flat, but challenging . . . Great scenery. Well
manicured. Good greens . . . Nothing great but OK on all counts . . .
Good public course, nice pro shop and people . . . Tight fairways, our
favorite Jekyll Island course.

★★★½ JONES CREEK GOLF CLUB
PU—4101 Hammond's Ferry Rd., Evans (706)860-4228.
5 miles west of Augusta. **Holes:** 18. **Par:** 72/72.
Yards: 7,008/5,430. **Course rating:** 73.8/72.4. **Slope:** 137/130.
Opened: 1986. **Pace of Play rating:** 4:00. **Green fee:** $21/31.
Credit cards: MC, V, AMEX. **Reduced fees:** Seniors, Juniors.
Caddies: No. **Golf carts:** $11 for 18 holes.
Discount golf packages: No. **Season:** Year-round. **High:** April-Aug.
On-site lodging: No. **Rental clubs:** Yes.
Walking policy: Walking at certain times. **Range:** Yes (grass).
To obtain tee times: Call on Friday for following week and weekend.
Ranked in Third 25 of America's 75 Best Public Golf Courses by Golf
Digest.
Subscriber comments: Great views, great fun, could play it every day . . .
Great Old South course . . . One of the best public courses I've played on,
nice test . . . Fast greens. Tight fairways. Very professional . . . Very fine
course, not easy, but a good test . . . Too many houses . . . Enjoyable
course, staff great.

★½ LAKE ARROWHEAD COUNTRY CLUB
SP—L.A. Station 20, Waleska (404)479-5505.
55 miles northwest of Atlanta. **Holes:** 18. **Par:** 72/71.
Yards: 6,400/4,468. **Course rating:** 71.2/66.3. **Slope:** 135/117.
Opened: 1975. **Pace of Play rating:** N/A. **Green fee:** $31/39.
Credit cards: All major. **Reduced fees:** Weekdays, Resort guests, Juniors.
Caddies: No. **Golf carts:** Included in Green Fee.
Discount golf packages: Yes. **Season:** Year-round. **High:** May-Aug.
On-site lodging: Yes. **Rental clubs:** Yes.
Walking policy: Mandatory cart. **Range:** Yes (grass).
To obtain tee times: Resort guests may reserve tee times at time of
reservation; all others call two days in advance.
Subscriber comments: Tops in potential, terrible maintenance . . . With a
little care could be outstanding, mountain beauty at its best . . . A diamond
in the rough, if they would just polish it . . . Fun, great, mountainous
design, but rough conditions, especially greens.

★★★½ LAKE LANIER ISLANDS HILTON RESORT
R—7000 Holiday Rd., Lake Lanier (404)945-8787, (800)768-5253.
35 miles northeast of Atlanta. **Holes:** 18. **Par:** 72/72.
Yards: 6,341/4,935. **Course rating:** 70.1/68.3. **Slope:** 124/117.
Opened: 1989. **Pace of Play rating:** N/A. **Green fee:** $39/48.
Credit cards: All major. **Reduced fees:** Weekdays, Low season, Twilight.
Caddies: No. **Golf carts:** Included in Green Fee.
Discount golf packages: Yes. **Season:** Year-round. **High:** April-Sept.
On-site lodging: Yes. **Rental clubs:** Yes.
Walking policy: Mandatory cart. **Range:** Yes (grass).
To obtain tee times: Call one week in advance.
Subscriber comments: Great course, service, facilities . . . Tough course,
very scenic overlooking lake . . . Water, water everywhere, and the balls
did sink . . . Great staff, target golf, short but tough, use every club . . .
Beautiful and enjoyable . . . Excellent course, sometimes crowded . . .
Short course but challenging from gold tees . . . Beautiful lake vistas, great
on a warm sunny day.

★★½ LAKESIDE COUNTRY CLUB
PU—3600 Old Fairburn Rd., Atlanta (404)344-3629.
Holes: 18. **Par:** 71/71.
Yards: 6,522/5,279. **Course rating:** 71.4/70.7. **Slope:** 127/121.
Opened: 1962. **Pace of Play rating:** 4:00. **Green fee:** $27/32.
Credit cards: MC, V. **Reduced fees:** Weekdays, Low season, Twilight, Seniors.
Caddies: No. **Golf carts:** Included in Green Fee.
Discount golf packages: Yes. **Season:** Year-round. **High:** March-May.
On-site lodging: No. **Rental clubs:** Yes.
Walking policy: Mandatory cart. **Range:** Yes (grass).
To obtain tee times: Call two weeks in advance.
Subscriber comments: Good layout, poor drainage on many holes . . .
Friendly professional staff, a must play . . . Average player should score
well . . . A good layout, excellent staff . . . An old George Cobb design,
good test.

LAKEVIEW GOLF CLUB★
SP—College Ave. Extension, Blackshear (912)449-4411.
100 miles northeast of Savannah. **Holes:** 18. **Par:** 72/72.
Yards: 6,505/4,928. **Course rating:** 69.7/69.5. **Slope:** 113/113.
Opened: 1971. **Pace of Play rating:** 4:00. **Green fee:** $15.
Credit cards: None. **Reduced fees:** No.
Caddies: No. **Golf carts:** $8 for 18 holes.
Discount golf packages: No. **Season:** Year-round. **High:** July-Sept.
On-site lodging: No. **Rental clubs:** Yes.
Walking policy: Unrestricted walking. **Range:** Yes (grass).
To obtain tee times: First come, first served.

LANDINGS GOLF CLUB
★★★ TRESTLE/BLUFF/CREEK
SP—309 Statham's Way, Warner Robins (912)923-5222.
15 miles southeast of Macon. **Holes:** 27. **Par:** 72/72/72.
Yards: 6,998/6,671/6,819. **Course rating:** 73.1/71.9/72.6.
Slope: 133/130/131.
Opened: 1987. **Pace of Play rating:** 4:00. **Green fee:** $16/23.
Credit cards: MC, V. **Reduced fees:** No.
Caddies: No. **Golf carts:** $9 for 18 holes.
Discount golf packages: Yes. **Season:** Year-round. **High:** March-Dec.
On-site lodging: No. **Rental clubs:** Yes.
Walking policy: Unrestricted walking. **Range:** Yes (grass).
To obtain tee times: Nonmembers call two days in advance.
Subscriber comments: Three nine-holers through a high rent-district . . .
Very enjoyable. Twenty-seven challenging holes of golf . . . A terrific
course for the better player . . . Every hole has character . . . Creek nine too
short, tricked up; Bluff nine great.

★★★½ LANE CREEK GOLF CLUB
PU—2360 Cole Springs Rd., Bishop (706)769-6699, (800)842-6699.
8 miles south of Athens. **Holes:** 18. **Par:** 72/72.
Yards: 6,725/5,195. **Course rating:** 72.6/68.4. **Slope:** 134/115.
Opened: 1992. **Pace of Play rating:** 4:15. **Green fee:** $27/35.
Credit cards: MC, V. **Reduced fees:** Weekdays, Twilight, Seniors, Juniors.
Caddies: No. **Golf carts:** Included in Green Fee.
Discount golf packages: No. **Season:** Year-round. **High:** Year-round.
On-site lodging: No. **Rental clubs:** Yes.
Walking policy: Walking at certain times. **Range:** Yes (grass).
To obtain tee times: Call up to seven days in advance.
Subscriber comments: Better now than before, staff nice, steady pace . . .
Outstanding, getting better with age . . . A diamond in the rough; must
play . . . Fabulous layout, requires thoughtful shot selection . . . Have fallen
in love with this golf course. Will drive 60 minutes just to play it.

GEORGIA

★★THE LINKS GOLF CLUB
PU—340 Hewell Rd., Jonesboro (706)461-5100.
Call club for further information.
Subscriber comments: Very nice municipal course . . . Nice big bunkers, lots of water . . . Great course. Fun for both high and low handicapper . . . A mixed bag: some fun holes and some very questionable ones . . . Rolling links land with a few blind shots, friendly staff.

MAPLE CREEK GOLF COURSE★
PU—1735 Cashtown Rd., Bremen (404)537-4172.
40 miles west of Atlanta. **Holes:** 18. **Par:** 70/70.
Yards: 5,404/4,454. **Course rating:** 65.6/65.3. **Slope:** 114/112.
Opened: 1993. **Pace of Play rating:** 3:12. **Green fee:** $10/17.
Credit cards: None. **Reduced fees:** Weekdays, Low season, Twilight, Seniors.
Caddies: No. **Golf carts:** $8 for 18 holes.
Discount golf packages: No. **Season:** Year-round. **High:** March-Oct.
On-site lodging: No. **Rental clubs:** Yes.
Walking policy: Unrestricted walking. **Range:** No.

★★★MAPLE RIDGE GOLF CLUB
PU—4700 Maple Ridge Trail, Columbus (706)569-0966.
Holes: 18. **Par:** 71/71.
Yards: 6,652/5,030. **Course rating:** 72.2/68.9. **Slope:** 132/127.
Opened: 1993. **Pace of Play rating:** 3:45. **Green fee:** $15/20.
Credit cards: MC, V, AMEX. **Reduced fees:** Weekdays, Low season, Twilight, Seniors, Juniors.
Caddies: No. **Golf carts:** N/A.
Discount golf packages: No. **Season:** Year-round. **High:** April-July.
On-site lodging: No. **Rental clubs:** Yes.
Walking policy: Unrestricted walking. **Range:** Yes (grass).
To obtain tee times: Call or appear in person one week in advance.
Subscriber comments: New course, needs to season . . . Fast play, friendly staff . . . Good facilities. Good course. Holes laid out nicely . . . Beautiful setting, quite challenging greens . . . New course, just needs maturity, very good clubhouse . . . Believe the ridge part, hit them straight.

★★★METROPOLITAN GOLF CLUB
SP—300 Fairington Pkwy., Lithonia (404)981-7696.
10 miles southeast of Atlanta. **Holes:** 18. **Par:** 72/72.
Yards: 6,030/5,966. **Course rating:** 74.2/74.8. **Slope:** 138/131.
Opened: 1967. **Pace of Play rating:** 4:05. **Green fee:** $32/43.
Credit cards: MC, V, AMEX. **Reduced fees:** Weekdays, Twilight.
Caddies: No. **Golf carts:** Included in Green Fee.
Discount golf packages: No. **Season:** Year-round. **High:** April-Sept.
On-site lodging: No. **Rental clubs:** Yes.
Walking policy: Walking at certain times. **Range:** Yes (grass).
To obtain tee times: Call five days in advance.
Subscriber comments: R.T. Jones layout, hilly; wooded, no weak holes, tough from blues . . . Great greens, good high-handicap course . . . Challenging but not spectacular . . . Everything an average golfer could ask for . . . All handicaps can enjoy. Course flat. Not a lot of scenery . . . It has tight fairways, hazards and big doglegs, plus lightning-fast greens. You must bring a lot of your shots, ie. draws . . . Trent Jones classic design, usually in good shape.

★★MYSTERY VALLEY GOLF COURSE
PU—6094 Shadowrock Dr., Lithonia (404)469-6913.
20 miles east of Atlanta. **Holes:** 18. **Par:** 72/75.
Yards: 6,705/5,928. **Course rating:** 71.5/67.9. **Slope:** 124/115.
Opened: 1965. **Pace of Play rating:** N/A. **Green fee:** $13/20.
Credit cards: None. **Reduced fees:** Weekdays, Seniors, Juniors.
Caddies: No. **Golf carts:** $10 for 18 holes.
Discount golf packages: No. **Season:** Year-round. **High:** March-Sept.

On-site lodging: No. **Rental clubs:** Yes.
Walking policy: Unrestricted walking. **Range:** Yes (grass).
To obtain tee times: Call one day in advance for weekdays and one week in advance for weekends.
Subscriber comments: Great public course, slow play due to traffic . . . Excellent public course but too much catering to the good ol' boys . . . Not always in best of condition. Usually crowded . . . Challenging public course, courteous staff, poor condition . . . Wide and long with some hills and water. They often have problems with greens conditions . . . The course is hilly with wide fairways for the average player. As popularity increased over the years, treatment and service declined.

★★★½ NOB NORTH GOLF COURSE
PU—298 Nob North Dr., Cohutta (706)694-8505.
15 miles south of Chattanooga, TN. **Holes:** 18. **Par:** 72/72.
Yards: 6,573/5,448. **Course rating:** 71.7/71.7. **Slope:** 128/126.
Opened: 1978. **Pace of Play rating:** N/A. **Green fee:** $19.
Credit cards: MC, V. **Reduced fees:** Seniors, Juniors.
Caddies: No. **Golf carts:** N/A.
Discount golf packages: No. **Season:** Year-round. **High:** March-Nov.
On-site lodging: No. **Rental clubs:** Yes.
Walking policy: Unrestricted walking. **Range:** Yes (grass).
To obtain tee times: Call five days in advance.
Subscriber comments: Best-kept secret in Georgia: great greens, good layout, friendly staff, year-round play . . . Outstanding, fair for bogey golfers to score on . . . Par 5s somewhat different: long, double doglegs, uphill . . . One of the best public courses I have played . . . Good test of golf, nice scenery, fun golf . . . Long, tight, great greens, staff and service good, slow play on days of high play.

★★ NORTH FULTON GOLF COURSE
PU—216 West Wieuca Rd., Atlanta (404)255-0723.
Holes: 18. **Par:** 71/71.
Yards: 6,570/5,120. **Course rating:** 71.8/69.5. **Slope:** 126/118.
Opened: 1935. **Pace of Play rating:** N/A. **Green fee:** $14/16.
Credit cards: MC, V. **Reduced fees:** Weekdays, Low season, Twilight, Seniors, Juniors.
Caddies: No. **Golf carts:** N/A.
Discount golf packages: Yes. **Season:** Year-round. **High:** July.
On-site lodging: No. **Rental clubs:** Yes.
Walking policy: Unrestricted walking. **Range:** No.
To obtain tee times: Call up to four days in advance.
Subscriber comments: When maintained, it's a good course . . . Very crowded. So-so fairways. Greens OK . . . Heavy use . . . Outstandingly designed old municipal . . . Back nine has a great layout. Overcrowding is a big problem, though . . . Best municipal course in Atlanta, overcrowded . . . Wonderful design, not manicured; spotty greens.

★★★½ OAK GROVE ISLAND GOLF CLUB
SP—100 Clipper Bay, Brunswick (912)262-9575.
70 miles south of Savannah. **Holes:** 18. **Par:** 72/72.
Yards: 6,910/4,855. **Course rating:** 73.2/67.6. **Slope:** 132/116.
Opened: 1993. **Pace of Play rating:** 4:14. **Green fee:** $11/16.
Credit cards: MC, V, AMEX. **Reduced fees:** Weekdays, Resort guests, Twilight, Seniors, Juniors.
Caddies: No. **Golf carts:** N/A.
Discount golf packages: No. **Season:** Year-round. **High:** April-Sept.
On-site lodging: No. **Rental clubs:** Yes.
Walking policy: Walking at certain times. **Range:** Yes (grass).
To obtain tee times: Call seven days in advance.
Subscriber comments: Beautiful course. Needs time to mature, only one to two years old . . . Good layout, will be great in another year . . . Will become widely known and heavily played; loved it . . . Still maturing, nice layout, world-class mosquitoes . . . New, not fully developed, getting better as it grows . . . Nice staff.

★★★ THE OAKS GOLF COURSE

PU—11240 Brown Bridge Rd., Covington (404)221-0200.
30 miles east of Atlanta. **Holes:** 18. **Par:** 70/70.
Yards: 6,420/4,600. **Course rating:** 69.5/64.5. **Slope:** 118/107.
Opened: 1990. **Pace of Play rating:** 3:50. **Green fee:** $24/38.
Credit cards: All major. **Reduced fees:** Weekdays, Low season, Resort
guests, Twilight, Seniors, Juniors.
Caddies: No. **Golf carts:** Included in Green Fee.
Discount golf packages: Yes. **Season:** Year-round. **High:** April-Sept.
On-site lodging: No. **Rental clubs:** Yes.
Walking policy: Walking at certain times. **Range:** Yes (grass).
To obtain tee times: Call for weekends only.
Subscriber comments: Short but fun to play all year, excellent condition
. . . Hacker's heaven . . . Walk-up, no tee times. Nice short course . . .
Good seniors' course, good service, great shape . . . Nice course, well taken
care of, not too long . . . Several blind tee shots . . . Hilly with wide
fairways for the average players.

★★★ OLDE ATLANTA GOLF CLUB

SP—5750 Olde Atlanta Pkwy., Suwanee (404)497-0097.
15 miles northeast of Atlanta. **Holes:** 18. **Par:** 71/71.
Yards: 6,800/5,147. **Course rating:** 73.1/69.3. **Slope:** 132/120.
Opened: 1993. **Pace of Play rating:** 4:20. **Green fee:** $38/45.
Credit cards: MC, V, AMEX. **Reduced fees:** Twilight, Seniors.
Caddies: No. **Golf carts:** Included in Green Fee.
Discount golf packages: No. **Season:** Year-round. **High:** April-Sept.
On-site lodging: No. **Rental clubs:** Yes.
Walking policy: Walking at certain times. **Range:** Yes (grass).
To obtain tee times: Call one week in advance.
Subscriber comments: Nice Arthur Hills layouts . . . Scenic, beautiful
layout, amphitheater greens, mounding hides greens . . . Good design and
test of golf, needs maturity . . . Developer sacrificed course design for golf
lots . . . Needs more time to grow up, good layout, clubhouse nice . . .
New course, but already in very good shape, makes you hit all clubs . . .
Good course in upscale neighborhood, several interesting holes.

★★★½ ORCHARD HILLS GOLF CLUB

PU—600 E. Hwy. 16, Newnan (404)251-5683.
33 miles southwest of Atlanta. **Holes:** 18. **Par:** 72/72.
Yards: 7,100/5,304. **Course rating:** 73.7/69.5. **Slope:** 132/116.
Opened: 1990. **Pace of Play rating:** 4:30. **Green fee:** $34/39.
Credit cards: All major. **Reduced fees:** Weekdays, Low season, Twilight,
Seniors, Juniors.
Caddies: No. **Golf carts:** $20 for 18 holes.
Discount golf packages: Yes. **Season:** Year-round. **High:** April-May.
On-site lodging: No. **Rental clubs:** Yes.
Walking policy: Walking at certain times. **Range:** Yes (grass).
To obtain tee times: Call seven days in advance.
Subscriber comments: Beautiful course. Can be enjoyed by players of all
levels . . . Links style, often windy; excellent, fast greens, mounding . . .
Good links layout, excellent staff, very happy to see you . . . Hard
fairways, no deep bunkers, PGA card discount, good range . . . Linkish, no
trees on one nine. Hell in the wind . . . Seaside golf without the ocean . . .
Open course layout, excellent shape, best service . . . Best greens of any
course I've played . . . Better than average. Friendly, understanding staff
. . . A surprise. Looks easier than it is. Mostly very open . . . Tough on a
windy winter day! . . . Great condition. Outstanding greens. Wide open,
only challenging from tips . . . Great shape, good course for seniors.

★★★★½ OSPREY COVE GOLF CLUB

SP—123 Osprey Dr., St. Marys (912)882-5575, (800)352-5575.
35 miles north of Jacksonville, FL. **Holes:** 18. **Par:** 72/72.
Yards: 6,791/5,263. **Course rating:** 73.0/71.1. **Slope:** 130/120.
Opened: 1990. **Pace of Play rating:** 4:00. **Green fee:** $30/35.

Credit cards: MC, V, AMEX. **Reduced fees:** Juniors.
Caddies: No. **Golf carts:** $12 for 18 holes.
Discount golf packages: Yes. **Season:** Year-round. **High:** Feb-July.
On-site lodging: No. **Rental clubs:** Yes.
Walking policy: Walking at certain times. **Range:** Yes (grass).
To obtain tee times: Call up to one week in advance.
Ranked 14th in Georgia by Golf Digest.
Subscriber comments: Beautiful, McCumber's best design so far . . . All-around best we've played. Super staff, classiest we've been to . . . So impressed I purchased property there . . . Mark McCumber did a great job . . . Great golf, great views . . . Some outstanding holes, some long rides from green to tee . . . A resort couse, beautiful and remote . . . Bag boy remembered my wife and me from three months before. Course a real challenge but still fun . . . Lots of sand and water, nice staff, good pace . . . Outstanding views, very playable, great staff, quick rounds . . . A gem, must play if you're within 100 miles . . . Scenery and condition top notch, quality pro shop and staff . . . Watch out for the gators; outstanding course . . . Do again. Unique, marsh views, well maintained, double green.

PINE BLUFF GOLF AND COUNTRY CLUB*

PU—Hwy. 341 S., Eastman (912)374-0991.
50 miles north of Macon. **Holes:** 18. **Par:** 72/72.
Yards: 6,499/5,065. **Course rating:** 70.6/69.1. **Slope:** 125/119.
Opened: 1994. **Pace of Play rating:** 4:00. **Green fee:** $16/18.
Credit cards: MC, V. **Reduced fees:** Twilight, Seniors, Juniors.
Caddies: No. **Golf carts:** Included in Green Fee.
Discount golf packages: Yes. **Season:** Year-round. **High:** March-May.
On-site lodging: No. **Rental clubs:** Yes.
Walking policy: Walking at certain times. **Range:** Yes (grass).
To obtain tee times: Call seven days in advance.

★★★½ PORT ARMOR GOLF AND COUNTRY CLUB

R—One Port Armor Pkwy., Greensboro (706)453-4564, (800)804-7678.
50 miles east of Atlanta. **Holes:** 18. **Par:** 72/72.
Yards: 6,926/5,177. **Course rating:** 74.0/72.8. **Slope:** 140/131.
Opened: 1986. **Pace of Play rating:** N/A. **Green fee:** $35.
Credit cards: MC, V, AMEX. **Reduced fees:** Low season, Resort guests.
Caddies: No. **Golf carts:** $12 for 18 holes.
Discount golf packages: Yes. **Season:** Year-round. **High:** April-Oct.
On-site lodging: Yes. **Rental clubs:** Yes.
Walking policy: Walking at certain times. **Range:** Yes (grass).
To obtain tee times: Call pro shop.
Ranked 19th in Georgia by Golf Digest.
Subscriber comments: Great layout, making good improvements, friendly staff . . . Too many tricked-up holes (i.e., blind shots) . . . Several holes on lake, very scenic . . . Real placement course. Course has had major problems in past years. New owners making improvements . . . Some blind shots to elevated greens . . . Neat course, good shape, nice staff, some weird holes . . . Very interesting, tests every shot you have . . . Great routing of holes, but inconsistent conditioning.

REYNOLD'S PLANTATION

R—130 Wood Crest Dr. N.E., Eatonton (706)485-0235.
70 miles north of Macon.
Credit cards: MC, V, AMEX. **Caddies:** No.
Discount golf packages: Yes. **Season:** Year-round.
On-site lodging: Yes. **Rental clubs:** Yes.
Walking policy: Walking at certain times. **Range:** Yes (grass).
To obtain tee times: Call three days in advance.
★★★★½ GREAT WATERS COURSE
Holes: 18. **Par:** 72/72.
Yards: 7,058/5,057. **Course rating:** 73.8/69.2. **Slope:** 135/114.
Opened: 1992. **Pace of Play rating:** 4:20. **Green fee:** $75/95.
Reduced fees: Weekdays, Resort guests.

Golf carts: $16 for 18 holes. **High:** April–Oct.

Selected as runner-up for Best New Resort Course of 1993 by Golf Digest. Ranked 5th in Georgia by Golf Digest.

Subscriber comments: Fantastic layout, breathtaking, playable for all levels . . . Very challenging; superb condition, courteous staff, beautiful! . . . Outstanding Nicklaus course on lake, excellent condition . . . After Augusta National, best course in Georgia, at a bargain price . . . Excellent condition, newer course, good variety of holes . . . Best Nicklaus course I've played, fair to 80-90 shooters . . . A great test for low-handicap players . . . Second nine has magnificent lake holes, difficult in wind . . . Nicklaus finally did course real people can play . . . Great course, long hitters have smaller landing areas . . . Must play! My favorite course. Course always in excellent condition. No waiting. Fast pace. Staff is accommodating to no end. Scenery is exceptional. All levels of players can enjoy . . . Nicklaus is a genius; scenic, long but fair. I wish I could play here every day . . . A playable Nicklaus course, gorgeous holes along lake.

★★★★ PLANTATION COURSE

Holes: 18. **Par:** 71/72.

Yards: 6,656/5,162. **Course rating:** 71.2/69.1. **Slope:** 125/117.

Opened: 1987. **Pace of Play rating:** 4:00. **Green fee:** $50.

Reduced fees: Resort guests.

Golf carts: $13 for 18 holes. **High:** April–Aug.

Ranked 18th in Georgia by Golf Digest.

Subscriber comments: Well-conditioned course that all levels can enjoy . . . Great condition, very scenic, good staff, very friendly, good pro shop selection . . . Magnificent views, tough but fair, super condition, world class . . . Only has 14 sand bunkers, but well placed . . . Lush, great shape, fun and fair, very nice . . . Fairest course ever played; favorite course.

★★★ RIVER'S EDGE GOLF COURSE

SP—40 Southern Golf Court, Fayetteville (404)460-1098.

19 miles south of Atlanta. **Holes:** 18. **Par:** 71/71.

Yards: 6,810/5,641. **Course rating:** 72.9/69.9. **Slope:** 135/121.

Opened: 1990. **Pace of Play rating:** 3:44. **Green fee:** $30/40.

Credit cards: MC, V. **Reduced fees:** Weekdays, Twilight, Seniors, Juniors.

Caddies: No. **Golf carts:** Included in Green Fee.

Discount golf packages: Yes. **Season:** Year-round. **High:** March-Oct.

On-site lodging: No. **Rental clubs:** Yes.

Walking policy: Mandatory cart. **Range:** Yes (grass).

To obtain tee times: Call three days in advance.

Formerly known as Champions Club at Rivers Edge.

Subscriber comments: Nice course, heavily wooded . . . Good for short, accurate hitters . . . Narrow fairways, shotmakers' course . . . Layout is outstanding. Staff is nice . . . Best value in Atlanta, outstanding condition, nice variety of holes . . . When course is in shape it is a great one.

★★★ RIVERPINES GOLF CLUB

PU—4775 Old Alabama Rd., Alpharetta (404)442-5960.

20 miles northeast of Atlanta. **Holes:** 18. **Par:** 70/70.

Yards: 6,511/4,279. **Course rating:** 71.3/64.7. **Slope:** 126/107.

Opened: 1993. **Pace of Play rating:** 4:00. **Green fee:** $45.

Credit cards: MC, V, AMEX. **Reduced fees:** Juniors.

Caddies: No. **Golf carts:** Included in Green Fee.

Discount golf packages: Yes. **Season:** Year-round. **High:** April-Sept.

On-site lodging: No. **Rental clubs:** Yes.

Walking policy: Walking at certain times. **Range:** Yes (grass).

To obtain tee times: Call on Mondays only.

Subscriber comments: Four or five goofy holes keep it from being very good . . . Short, only two par 5s . . . Good practice facilities, course well kept . . . Best range in Atlanta . . . Short course but well worth the money; excellent practice facilities . . . Good public course; fair course for all types of players . . . Requires good course management.

★★★½ ROYAL LAKES GOLF AND COUNTRY CLUB
SP—4700 Royal Lakes Dr., Flowery Branch (404)535-8800.
35 miles northeast of Atlanta. **Holes:** 18. **Par:** 72/72.
Yards: 6,871/5,325. **Course rating:** 72.0/70.4. **Slope:** 131/125.
Opened: 1989. **Pace of Play rating:** N/A. **Green fee:** $37/44.
Credit cards: MC, V, AMEX. **Reduced fees:** Weekdays, Twilight,
Juniors.
Caddies: No. **Golf carts:** Included in Green Fee.
Discount golf packages: No. **Season:** Year-round. **High:** March-Sept.
On-site lodging: No. **Rental clubs:** Yes.
Walking policy: Walking at certain times. **Range:** Yes (grass).
To obtain tee times: Tee times required. Call four days in advance.
Subscriber comments: Excellent layout, fun to play but difficult . . . Fast
greens, a lot of water hazards, sand, great course . . . Fast undulating greens
. . . Good course, but tough the first time out . . . Atlanta area sleeper,
slick, difficult and true greens . . . Fun, mountain layout, good conditions
. . . Lots of water, but a great, fun course . . . Excellent test for sidehill
game . . . Always in excellent condition year-round, has beauty and
challenge.

★★ ROYAL OAKS GOLF CLUB
SP—256 Summit Ridge Dr., Cartersville (404)382-3999.
40 miles south of Atlanta. **Holes:** 18. **Par:** 71/75.
Yards: 6,309/4,890. **Course rating:** 70.0/71.0. **Slope:** 124/121.
Opened: 1978. **Pace of Play rating:** 4:00. **Green fee:** $27/32.
Credit cards: MC, V. **Reduced fees:** Weekdays, Low season, Twilight,
Seniors, Juniors.
Caddies: No. **Golf carts:** $10 for 18 holes.
Discount golf packages: Yes. **Season:** Year-round. **High:** April-Oct.
On-site lodging: No. **Rental clubs:** Yes.
Walking policy: Walking at certain times. **Range:** Yes (grass).
To obtain tee times: Call seven days in advance.
Subscriber comments: Course knowledge needed to play well; lots of
blind shots . . . Good, tight rolling fairways require semi-precise
shotmaking; no flat areas, which is great, this gives you a real feeling for
being away from everyone else and all alone . . . Hilly course, tight layout
. . . Fun mountain track, usually in good condition . . . Tight and hilly
course for us high handicaps.

ST. MARLO GOLF CLUB★
PU—7755 St. Marlo Country Club Pkwy., Duluth (404)495-7725
25 miles south of Atlanta. **Holes:** 18. **Par:** 72/72.
Yards: 6,900/5,300. **Course rating:** 73.6/70.3. **Slope:** 137/121.
Opened: 1995. **Pace of Play rating:** 4:00. **Green fee:** $55/65.
Credit cards: MC, V, DISC. **Reduced fees:** Weekdays, Juniors.
Caddies: No. **Golf carts:** $12 for 18 holes.
Discount golf packages: No. **Season:** Year-round. **High:** April-Oct.
On-site lodging: No. **Rental clubs:** Yes.
Walking policy: Unrestricted walking. **Range:** Yes (grass).
To obtain tee times: Call four days in advance.

★★★½ ST. SIMONS ISLAND CLUB
PU—100 Kings Way, St. Simons Island (912)638-5130.
4 miles east of Brunswick. **Holes:** 18. **Par:** 72/72.
Yards: 6,490/5,361. **Course rating:** 71.8/70.0. **Slope:** 133/124.
Opened: 1974. **Pace of Play rating:** 4:15. **Green fee:** $45.
Credit cards: MC, V, AMEX. **Reduced fees:** Low season, Resort guests,
Twilight, Juniors.
Caddies: Yes. **Golf carts:** $15 for 18 holes.
Discount golf packages: No. **Season:** Year-round. **High:** March-April.
On-site lodging: No. **Rental clubs:** Yes.
Walking policy: Walking at certain times. **Range:** Yes (grass).
To obtain tee times: Call.
Site of Golf Digest Schools.

Subscriber comments: It's a much better course than Sea Island across the street, which gets all the publicity. Play is fast, greens are big and fast . . . Traditional design with lots of water, good staff and shop . . . Resort golf, good course for seniors . . . Excellent course in good condition, helpful staff . . . Short and somewhat tight, but a really good course . . . My favorite Sea Island course, all aspects are A-1 . . . Good test; tight; fun to play . . . Course is underrated and underplayed. I loved it.

SCONTI GOLF CLUB
★★★ CHOCTAW/CHEROKEE/CREEK
R—Sconti Golf Club, Big Canoe (706)268-3323.
50 miles north of Atlanta. **Holes:** 27. **Par:** 72/72/72.
Yards: 6,371/6,276/6,247. **Course rating:** 71.0/70.2/70.4.
Slope: 136/132/134.
Opened: 1972. **Pace of Play rating:** N/A. **Green fee:** $30/55.
Credit cards: All major. **Reduced fees:** Weekdays, Low season.
Caddies: No. **Golf carts:** Included in Green Fee.
Discount golf packages: No. **Season:** Year-round. **High:** April-Oct.
On-site lodging: Yes. **Rental clubs:** Yes.
Walking policy: Mandatory cart. **Range:** Yes (grass).
To obtain tee times: Call 48 hours in advance.
Subscriber comments: Extremely nice mountain course, not too difficult . . . Great course . . . Beautiful in fall . . . Narrow track, great shape . . . Short but challenging.

★★★ SHERATON SAVANNAH RESORT & COUNTRY CLUB
R—612 Wilmington Island Rd., Savannah (912)897-1612.
Holes: 18. **Par:** 72/72.
Yards: 6,876/5,328. **Course rating:** 73.5/70.6. **Slope:** 137/128.
Opened: 1927. **Pace of Play rating:** . **Green fee:** $30/48.
Credit cards: MC, V, AMEX. **Reduced fees:** Weekdays, Low season, Resort guests, Twilight, Seniors, Juniors.
Caddies: Yes. **Golf carts:** Included in Green Fee.
Discount golf packages: Yes. **Season:** Year-round. **High:** June-Sept.
On-site lodging: No, hotel is closed. **Rental clubs:** Yes.
Walking policy: Walking at certain times. **Range:** Yes (grass).
To obtain tee times: Call up to 10 months in advance.
Subscriber comments: This could be a super course with better upkeep . . . Donald Ross design, no frills, just good golf . . . Really nice old golf course . . . Great layout for all handicaps, OK staff, neglected jewel . . . Course could be a jewel with needed money.

SEA ISLAND GOLF CLUB
R—100 Retreat Ave., St. Simons Island (912)638-5118, (800)732-4752.
50 miles north of Jacksonville, FL.
Opened: 1927. **Pace of Play rating:** 4:00. **Green fee:** $75/90.
Credit cards: MC, V, Sea Island Card. **Reduced fees:** Low season, Resort guests, Twilight, Juniors.
Caddies: Yes. **Golf carts:** $15 for 18 holes.
Discount golf packages: Yes. **Season:** Year-round.
On-site lodging: Yes. **Rental clubs:** Yes.
Walking policy: Walking at certain times. **Range:** Yes (grass).
To obtain tee times: Call.
Site of Golf Digest Schools.
★★★½ RETREAT/MARSHSIDE
Holes: 18. **Par:** 72/72.
Yards: 6,518/5,056. **Course rating:** 71.2/69.5. **Slope:** 130/111.
Subscriber comments: Great old course, excellent practice facilities . . . Walking with caddies available, very good golf cart fleet, greens tend to be slower than necessary, huge practice range . . . Pretty course, well taken care of, easy if you keep it in play . . . Resort golf at its best, first class . . . All nines are great. Super condition. Excellent service.

GEORGIA

★★★★ SEASIDE/PLANTATION
Holes: 18. **Par:** 72/72.
Yards: 6,900/5,178. **Course rating:** 73.2/69.1. **Slope:** 134/115.
Ranked 62nd in America's 75 Best Resort Courses by Golf Digest. Ranked 7th in Georgia by Golf Digest.
Subscriber comments: Great range, can get windy, not many crowds, best 18 at Sea Island . . . Seaside nine my favorite; excellent conditioning, pro shop is the best, caddies, great . . . Greens tend to be slower than necessary . . . Course in good condition, staff very good . . . All rounds played here were great . . . Very lovely course, best suited for low-to medium-handicap player.

SEA PALMS RESORT
★★½ TALL PINES/GREAT OAKS/SEA PALMS
R—5445 Frederica Rd., St. Simons Island (912)638-9041, (800)841-6268.
65 miles north of Jacksonville, FL. **Holes:** 27. **Par:** 72/72/72.
Yards: 6,658/6,350/6,198. **Course rating:** 71.3/71.1/69.7.
Slope: 128/126/124.
Opened: 1966. **Pace of Play rating:** N/A. **Green fee:** $35/40.
Credit cards: MC, V, AMEX. **Reduced fees:** Weekdays, Low season, Resort guests, Twilight, Juniors.
Caddies: No. **Golf carts:** $14 for 18 holes.
Discount golf packages: Yes. **Season:** Year-round. **High:** Feb.-May.
On-site lodging: Yes. **Rental clubs:** Yes.
Walking policy: Mandatory cart. **Range:** Yes (grass).
To obtain tee times: Call seven days in advance. Hotel guest may call one month in advance.
Subscriber comments: Excellent resort-type course, tall pines, great oaks, sea palms . . . Course is fun but the maintenance has run down in the last few years . . . Nice setting, difficult finishing hole, pesky sand gnats . . . Condition fair. Outstanding layout.

★★★ SKY VALLEY GOLF CLUB
R—One Sky Valley, Sky Valley (706)746-5303, (800)437-2416.
100 miles south of Atlanta. **Holes:** 18. **Par:** 72/72.
Yards: 6,452/5,017. **Course rating:** 71.7/69.0. **Slope:** 128/118.
Opened: 1971. **Pace of Play rating:** N/A. **Green fee:** $25/40.
Credit cards: All major. **Reduced fees:** Low season, Resort guests, Twilight.
Caddies: No. **Golf carts:** Included in Green Fee.
Discount golf packages: No. **Season:** Year-round. **High:** April-Oct.
On-site lodging: Yes. **Rental clubs:** Yes.
Walking policy: Walking at certain times. **Range:** Yes (grass).
To obtain tee times: Call up to one month in advance.
Subscriber comments: Great greens, great scenery, a true gem . . . Bent greens and fairways, beautiful views, much improved . . . Great mountain course, small greens . . . Beautiful mountain course, and well maintained, which was a surprise . . . Very good and challenging.

★★★½ SOUTHBRIDGE GOLF CLUB
SP—415 Southbridge Blvd., Savannah (912)651-5455.
Holes: 18. **Par:** 72/72.
Yards: 6,990/5,181. **Course rating:** 73.4/69.2. **Slope:** 136/118.
Opened: 1988. **Pace of Play rating:** 4:00. **Green fee:** $30/36.
Credit cards: All major. **Reduced fees:** Weekdays, Low season, Seniors.
Caddies: No. **Golf carts:** Included in Green Fee.
Discount golf packages: No. **Season:** Year-round. **High:** April-May.
On-site lodging: No. **Rental clubs:** Yes.
Walking policy: Mandatory cart. **Range:** Yes (grass).
To obtain tee times: Call two weeks in advance.
Subscriber comments: A championship course, great challenging greens, beautiful . . . Good practice area, some holes stay wet well after rain,

friendly staff . . . Played a lot, stays in fair shape all year . . . Back nine in wilds (saw wild pigs on No.10), good golf . . . Challenging at all times . . . Excellent course, nice driving range . . . A young Rees Jones course that could be great with time and better maintenance.

★★★½ SOUTHERNESS GOLF CLUB

SP—4871 Flat Bridge Rd., Stockbridge (404)808-6000.
20 miles east of Atlanta. **Holes:** 18. **Par:** 72/72.
Yards: 6,766/4,956. **Course rating:** 72.2/69.0. **Slope:** 127/119.
Opened: 1991. **Pace of Play rating:** 4:30. **Green fee:** $25/47.
Credit cards: MC, V, AMEX. **Reduced fees:** Twilight.
Caddies: No. **Golf carts:** Included in Green Fee.
Discount golf packages: No. **Season:** Year-round. **High:** April-Sept.
On-site lodging: No. **Rental clubs:** Yes.
Walking policy: Walking at certain times. **Range:** Yes (grass).
To obtain tee times: Call five days in advance.
Subscriber comments: A real test of golf, one of the best in the South . . . Very tough three finishing holes, good practice area, personable staff . . . Tight side-by-side fairways. In winter, greens need work . . . Great greens, fun for all the players . . . Greens have come back since '93, good layout . . . Fun course to play, good track, several beautiful holes . . . Good test of your golfing skills . . . One of the better public courses, food great . . . Links course, accommodating staff.

STONEBRIDGE GOLF CLUB★

PU—685 Stonebridge Dr., Rome (404)498-5715.
Holes: 18. **Par:** 72/72.
Yards: 6,816/5,130. **Course rating:** 72.6/64.6. **Slope:** 123/109.
Opened: 1994. **Pace of Play rating:** 4:00. **Green fee:** $31/37.
Credit cards: MC, V, AMEX. **Reduced fees:** Twilight, Seniors, Juniors.
Caddies: No. **Golf carts:** Included in Green Fee.
Discount golf packages: Yes. **Season:** Year-round. **High:** March-Sept.
On-site lodging: No. **Rental clubs:** Yes.
Walking policy: Unrestricted walking. **Range:** Yes (grass).
To obtain tee times: Call seven days in advance.

STONE MOUNTAIN PARK GOLF COURSE

R—P.O. Box 778, Stone Mtn. (404)498-5715.
12 miles east of Atlanta.
Pace of Play rating: 4:15. **Green fee:** $38.
Credit cards: All major. **Reduced fees:** No.
Caddies: No. **Golf carts:** Included in Green Fee.
Discount golf packages: Yes. **Season:** Year-round. **High:** April-Oct.
On-site lodging: Yes. **Rental clubs:** Yes.
Walking policy: Mandatory cart. **Range:** Yes (grass).
To obtain tee times: Call Tuesday for following weekend and holidays starting at 9 a.m. For weekdays call one week in advance.
Stonemont/Woodmont ranked in Third 25 of America's 75 Best Public Golf Courses by Golf Digest.

★★★ LAKEMONT/WOODMONT

Holes: 18. **Par:** 72/72.
Yards: 6,595/5,231. **Course rating:** 71.6/69.4. **Slope:** 130/120.
Opened: 1987.
Subscriber comments: Nice layout, scenic . . . Front nine is short. Back nine is great R. T. Jones design . . . Great out-of-town course when in shape, good staff . . . Good test. Demanding but fair . . . Grand views, well maintained for public course . . . Very tight, but all handicaps can enjoy. Pace can be very slow . . . Excellent layout, narrow landings, must be able to keep it in play . . . Lakemont is too target oriented, Woodmont remains solid nine . . . Excellent state course with some demanding holes . . . Some very scenic holes, with Stone Mountain as backdrop; park entrance fee should be reimbursed.

GEORGIA

★★★ STONEMONT COURSE
Holes: 18. **Par:** 72/72.
Yards: 6,683/5,020. **Course rating:** 72.6/69.1. **Slope:** 133/121.
Opened: 1971.
Subscriber comments: Beautiful view of scenic Stone Mountain . . .
Slow play on weekends, hardest opening hole par 4 in state . . . Long and
tough . . . Beautiful course, unbelievable views on some holes . . . Great
scenery, good for mountain goats . . . Excellent facilities. Pretty good
course . . . Should have left the original 18 intact.

★★★ STOUFFER PINEISLE RESORT
R—9000 Holiday Rd., Lake Lanier Islands (404)945-8922, (800)468-3571.
45 miles northeast of Atlanta. **Holes:** 18. **Par:** 72/72.
Yards: 6,527/5,297. **Course rating:** 71.6/70.6. **Slope:** 132/127.
Opened: 1973. **Pace of Play rating:** 4:30. **Green fee:** $54/59.
Credit cards: All major. **Reduced fees:** No.
Caddies: No. **Golf carts:** Included in Green Fee.
Discount golf packages: Yes. **Season:** Year-round. **High:** April-Oct.
On-site lodging: Yes. **Rental clubs:** Yes.
Walking policy: Walking at certain times. **Range:** Yes (grass).
To obtain tee times: Hotel guests may make tee times with confirmed
reservation of room. Seven days in advance for all others.
Subscriber comments: Gary Player design . . . Great course for middle to
low handicappers . . . Best part of course starts on the lake . . . Tough and
narrow, too much up and down . . . Very difficult up/down/sidehill
course, beautiful layout . . . Layout and scenery exceptional . . . Resort
course. Challenging but not overwhelming. Good corporate fun course . . .
Gorgeous course and scenery, keep it on the fairways . . . Great golf but not
worth the high price.

★½ SUGAR HILL GOLF CLUB
PU—6094 Suwanee Dam Rd., Sugar Hill (404)271-0519.
35 miles northeast of Atlanta. **Holes:** 18. **Par:** 72/72.
Yards: 6,423/4,207. **Course rating:** 70.7/65.3. **Slope:** 127/112.
Opened: 1992. **Pace of Play rating:** 4:00-4:30. **Green fee:** $30/40.
Credit cards: MC, V. **Reduced fees:** Low season, Twilight, Seniors,
Juniors.
Caddies: No. **Golf carts:** Included in Green Fee.
Discount golf packages: Yes. **Season:** Year-round. **High:** April-Oct.
On-site lodging: No. **Rental clubs:** Yes.
Walking policy: Walking at certain times. **Range:** Yes (grass).
To obtain tee times: Tee times taken 48 hours in advance.
Subscriber comments: Good new course with good potential . . . Very
hilly; do not walk this course . . . Country setting, nice people . . .
Mountain course . . . Quite a few blind tee shots, nine to be exact. The
course does not allow too much room for error . . . Fair variety and
difficulty, fairways and greens fair, staff OK.

TOWNE LAKE HILLS GOLF CLUB★
PU—1003 Towne Lake Hills East, Woodstock (404)592-9969.
25 miles north of Atlanta. **Holes:** 18. **Par:** 72/72.
Yards: 6,757/4,984. **Course rating:** 72.3/69.0. **Slope:** 133/116.
Opened: 1994. **Pace of Play rating:** 4:30. **Green fee:** $39/49.
Credit cards: MC, V. **Reduced fees:** Low season, Twilight.
Caddies: No. **Golf carts:** Included in Green Fee.
Discount golf packages: Yes. **Season:** Year-round. **High:** May-Oct.
On-site lodging: No. **Rental clubs:** Yes.
Walking policy: Unrestricted walking. **Range:** Yes (grass).
To obtain tee times: Call four days in advance.

★★★½ UNIVERSITY OF GEORGIA GOLF CLUB
PU—2600 Riverbend Rd., Athens (706)369-5739, (800)936-4833.
60 miles east of Atlanta. **Holes:** 18. **Par:** 72/73.
Yards: 6,890/5,713. **Course rating:** 73.4/74.0. **Slope:** 133/128.

Opened: 1968. **Pace of Play rating:** 4:08. **Green fee:** $10/20.
Credit cards: MC, V. **Reduced fees:** Weekdays, Twilight.
Caddies: No. **Golf carts:** $9 for 18 holes.
Discount golf packages: No. **Season:** Year-round. **High:** March-June.
On-site lodging: Yes. **Rental clubs:** Yes.
Walking policy: Unrestricted walking. **Range:** Yes (grass).
To obtain tee times: Call one day in advance for weekdays and Thursday after 1 p.m. for weekend.
Subscriber comments: Excellent course for all types of players . . . Wooded, traditional layout . . . Bring the long straight sticks . . . Very good test for better players, needs work . . . Great track for college course; wide open . . . Long course, but enjoyable; nice par 3s . . . Too much play, excellent design, marginal conditioning . . . One of best in state when in shape.

★★★½ **WALLACE ADAMS GOLF COURSE**

PU—Hwy. 441 N., McRae (912)868-6651.
75 miles southeast of Macon. **Holes:** 18. **Par:** 72/72.
Yards: 6,625/5,001. **Course rating:** 70.8/69.1. **Slope:** 128/120.
Opened: 1965. **Pace of Play rating:** 4:00. **Green fee:** $15/20.
Credit cards: MC, V. **Reduced fees:** Resort guests, Seniors.
Caddies: Yes. **Golf carts:** N/A.
Discount golf packages: Yes. **Season:** Year-round. **High:** Spring/Fall.
On-site lodging: Yes. **Rental clubs:** Yes.
Walking policy: Unrestricted walking. **Range:** Yes (grass).
To obtain tee times: First come, first served.
Subscriber comments: Another tremendous state park course. Always excellent condition . . . Well laid out, great variety of holes, staff was great . . . The service and pace of play are fine and the course is always in the best of shape . . . Best-kept secret in the state. Outstanding test of golf skills . . . An excellent place to play: no lines and 3½-hour rounds are normal . . . Fun layout, get to use all clubs, all-day green fee great . . . By far the best-maintained state park course I have seen.

WHITE COLUMNS GOLF CLUB★
PU—300 White Columns Dr., Alpharetta (404)343-9025.
25 miles north of Atlanta. **Holes:** 18. **Par:** 72/72.
Yards: 7,053/6,015. **Course rating:** 73.6/69.0. **Slope:** 137/116.
Opened: 1994. **Pace of Play rating:** 4:15. **Green fee:** $70/80.
Credit cards: MC, V, AMEX. **Reduced fees:** Weekdays.
Caddies: No. **Golf carts:** Included in Green Fee.
Discount golf packages: No. **Season:** Year-round. **High:** March-Oct.
On-site lodging: No. **Rental clubs:** Yes.
Walking policy: Unrestricted walking. **Range:** Yes (grass).
To obtain tee times: Call pro shop.

★★★½ **WHITEWATER CREEK COUNTRY CLUB**
SP—1904 Redwine Rd., Fayetteville (404)461-6545.
30 miles south of Atlanta. **Holes:** 18. **Par:** 72/72.
Yards: 6,739/4,909. **Course rating:** 72.3/68.2. **Slope:** 133/123.
Opened: 1988. **Pace of Play rating:** 4:00. **Green fee:** $32/42.
Credit cards: MC, V, AMEX. **Reduced fees:** Weekdays, Low season, Twilight, Seniors, Juniors.
Caddies: No. **Golf carts:** Included in Green Fee.
Discount golf packages: Yes. **Season:** Year-round. **High:** March-Oct.
On-site lodging: No. **Rental clubs:** Yes.
Walking policy: Mandatory cart. **Range:** Yes (grass).
To obtain tee times: Call three days in advance.
Subscriber comments: My favorite course in Atlanta . . . Excellent condition, can use all clubs in bag, well-kept secret . . . Little-known Georgia jewel . . . Palmer course. Challenging . . . Speedy bent greens, fun round from proper tees.

★½ WILLOWPEG CREEK GOLF COURSE

SP—1 Clubhouse Dr., Rincon (912)826-2092.
Call club for further information.
Subscriber comments: Excellent staff, great layouts, rough as heck . . .
Fun, difficult, slow, fairways poor but growing . . . As a senior who does
not hit real long, it is a joy to play a course that is not long but is still a
challenge.

★★★½ WINDSTONE GOLF CLUB

SP—9230 Windstone Dr., Ringgold (615)894-1231.
6 miles south of Chattanooga. **Holes:** 18. **Par:** 72/72.
Yards: 6,626/4,956. **Course rating:** 71.1/66.8. **Slope:** 119/108.
Opened: 1990. **Pace of Play rating:** N/A. **Green fee:** $16/21.
Credit cards: All major. **Reduced fees:** Low season, Seniors.
Caddies: No. **Golf carts:** $11 for 18 holes.
Discount golf packages: No. **Season:** Year-round. **High:** April-Oct.
On-site lodging: No. **Rental clubs:** Yes.
Walking policy: Unrestricted walking. **Range:** Yes (grass).
To obtain tee times: Call two days in advance.
Subscriber comments: Good layout, uses all shots . . . Tough layout,
narrow, good scramble course . . . Very friendly and challenging course,
great . . . Good elevation and well laid out . . . Great back nine, will use
every club.

Notes

INDIANA

★★★½ AUTUMN RIDGE GOLF CLUB
SP—11420 Old Auburn Rd., Fort Wayne (219)637-8727.
Holes: 18. **Par:** 72/72.
Yards: 7,103/5,273. **Course rating:** 73.9/70.1. **Slope:** 134/122.
Opened: 1993. **Pace of Play rating:** 4:15. **Green fee:** $22/28.
Credit cards: MC, V. **Reduced fees:** Low season, Twilight, Seniors.
Caddies: No. **Golf carts:** $11 for 18 holes.
Discount golf packages: No. **Season:** March-Dec. **High:** May-Sept.
On-site lodging: No. **Rental clubs:** Yes.
Walking policy: Walking at certain times. **Range:** Yes (grass).
To obtain tee times: Call five days in advance.
Subscriber comments: The course targets true golfers, golf cart is highly
recommended, course is in excellent shape all year round when open,
service is quality . . . Best available to public in this area . . . Great new
course . . . Still developing . . . Spread out but nice . . . Too much water
and too many holes running parallel to major roads . . . Water used to trick
up some . . . Best play for an accurate hitter . . . Great practice area . . .
Stay away if you don't like water, 16 ponds on 18 holes . . . Best public
course in the area.

★★★★ BEAR SLIDE GOLF CLUB
SP—6770 E. 231st St., Cicero (317)984-3837, (800)252-8337.
20 miles north of Indianapolis. **Holes:** 18. **Par:** 71/71.
Yards: 7,041/4,831. **Course rating:** 74.6/69.5. **Slope:** 136/117.
Opened: 1993. **Pace of Play rating:** N/A. **Green fee:** $50.
Credit cards: MC, V. **Reduced fees:** No.
Caddies: Yes. **Golf carts:** $12 for 18 holes.
Discount golf packages: No. **Season:** March-Dec. **High:** May-Oct.
On-site lodging: No. **Rental clubs:** Yes.
Walking policy: Unrestricted walking. **Range:** Yes (grass).
To obtain tee times: Call one week in advance.
Subscriber comments: You'll use every club, thinking golf course . . .
Excellent practice facilities . . . Super challenging from back tees, unique
design . . . Combo of weather and water . . . Great course design, as it
matures will be one of best in Midwest . . . Interesting combination of
target/power golf . . . Long and demanding . . . Two different nines, one
traditional, other Scottish . . . Gives you a false sense of distance . . .
Variety in hole layouts . . . Two distinctly unique nines, two gimmicky
holes on back nine . . . Open front side, wooded backside . . . Could give
the pros fits . . . Still needs some finishing touches . . . Mixed bag of holes,
very hard, very easy, some tricked up holes . . . Best course in Indiana.

★★½ BLACK SQUIRREL GOLF CLUB
PU—Hwy. 119 S., Goshen (219)533-1828.
19 miles southeast of South Bend. **Holes:** 18. **Par:** 72/72.
Yards: 6,483/5,018. **Course rating:** 69.8/67.8. **Slope:** 115/110.
Opened: 1989. **Pace of Play rating:** 4:10. **Green fee:** $14/18.
Credit cards: MC, V. **Reduced fees:** Weekdays, Low season.
Caddies: No. **Golf carts:** $10 for 18 holes.
Discount golf packages: No. **Season:** March-Nov. **High:** June-Aug.
On-site lodging: No. **Rental clubs:** Yes.
Walking policy: Unrestricted walking. **Range:** No.
To obtain tee times: Call up to seven days in advance.
Formerly known as Larimer Greens.
Subscriber comments: A game fixer course . . . Bent fairways and greens
great shape . . . Too far between some holes . . . Will become a good
course with time. Current management has significantly improved course
. . . Greens are hard, fast, but still a fun course . . . Need cart, excessive
green to tee distance . . . Challenging, but a little costly.

★★★★ BLACKTHORN GOLF CLUB
PU—6100 Nimtz Pkwy., South Bend (219)232-4653.
Holes: 18. **Par:** 72/72.
Yards: 7,105/5,036. **Course rating:** 75.2/71.0. **Slope:** 135/120.

Opened: 1994. **Pace of Play rating:** 4:30. **Green fee:** $28/45.
Credit cards: MC, V, AMEX. **Reduced fees:** Weekdays, Twilight, Juniors.
Caddies: No. **Golf carts:** $11 for 18 holes.
Discount golf packages: No. **Season:** April-Nov. **High:** May-Sept.
On-site lodging: No. **Rental clubs:** Yes.
Walking policy: Unrestricted walking. **Range:** Yes (grass).
To obtain tee times: Call up to seven days in advance.
Also has a 19th practice hole.
Subscriber comments: Stunning golf course. Total golf experience . . .
City course that feels private, beautiful scenic holes, very challenging . . .
Will be one of best in Midwest . . . Has warm up hole . . . First two holes
disappointing, thereafter the most challenging, rewarding and fun course
I've ever played . . . Best course in northern Indiana . . . Too many tiers
. . . Probably best top 5 city course in country . . . I like the idea . . . They
want you to ride but walk it . . . Is going to be the best course in Indiana
. . . 260-yard practice hole (par 4) . . . Excellent use of existing woodlands
and landscape. Impossible to say enough about Blackthorn . . . I dare you
not to love playing this course. With the phenomenal use of existing
landscape and woods, you'd think it had been here for 40 years, not just
opening in 1994, as it did.

★★★★½ BRICKYARD CROSSING GOLF CLUB

R—4400 W. 16th St., Indianapolis (317)484-6572.
Holes: 18. **Par:** 72/72.
Yards: 6,994/5,038. **Course rating:** 74.5/68.3. **Slope:** 137/116.
Opened: 1993. **Pace of Play rating:** 4:30. **Green fee:** $60.
Credit cards: MC, V, AMEX. **Reduced fees:** .
Caddies: No. **Golf carts:** Included in Green Fee.
Discount golf packages: No. **Season:** April-Oct. **High:** May-Aug.
On-site lodging: Yes. **Rental clubs:** Yes.
Walking policy:: Mandatory cart. **Range:** Yes (grass).
To obtain tee times: Call 30 days in advance.
Selected as runner-up for Best New Resort Course of 1994 by Golf Digest.
Ranked 3rd in Indiana by Golf Digest.
Subscriber comments: Fantastic track . . . Classic Pete Dye, last 4 holes
killer . . . A great experience. Enormous greens and lush fairways . . . In
outstanding condition for first year . . . Dye's handprints abound, fair to all
levels and handicaps . . . Multiple tees allow you to bite off what you want
. . . Very challenging, but good pace of play . . . Greens are brutally tough,
fairways are wide . . . Used track area well . . . Awesome golf course.
Pricey but worth it . . . True championship golf, fastest greens in Indy . . .
Track makes for neat atmosphere . . . Contrived at times in layout, neat
inside race track . . . Best greens in midwest, best new design in Midwest
. . . Just perfection, easy to drive, but wait till you get on greens . . . A bit
expensive but worth it at least once a year . . . Four holes inside 500
Speedway . . . Perfect! If you can get a tee time . . . Same old locker room
. . . What quality golf is all about, forgiving yet challenging . . . Never a
flat putt . . . The best and hardest public course in Indiana . . . Challenge to
all . . . Dye-abolical greens, undulations bordering on unfair . . . Slow play
but not course or staff fault . . . Good, fun course . . . Beats the old
Speedway course.

BROADMOOR COUNTRY CLUB★

PU—4300 W 81st St., Merrillville (219)769-5444.
Call course for additional information.

★★ BROOKSHIRE GOLF CLUB

SP—12120 Brookshire Pkwy., Carmel (317)846-7431.
15 miles north of Indianapolis. **Holes:** 18. **Par:** 72/75.
Yards: 6,651/5,635. **Course rating:** 71.8/74.4. **Slope:** 123/129.
Opened: 1971. **Pace of Play rating:** 4:00. **Green fee:** $28/38.
Credit cards: MC, V, AMEX. **Reduced fees:** Weekdays, Twilight, Juniors.

Caddies: No. **Golf carts:** Included in Green Fee.
Discount golf packages: No. **Season:** Year-round. **High:** May-Oct.
On-site lodging: No. **Rental clubs:** Yes.
Walking policy: Mandatory cart. **Range:** Yes (grass).
To obtain tee times: Call up to three days in advance.
Subscriber comments: Tight course with interesting holes . . . Short and
tight . . . Creek runs thru, more difficult than appears . . . Spring, summer,
fall have really improved with new supt . . . Perfect in spring and fall . . .
Too dry in summer. Suited for all handicaps . . . Looks old, fair test of golf
. . . Must be able to hit straight . . . New sand helps, greens still hard . . .
Very clean course for early November.

★★★½ BROOKWOOD GOLF CLUB
PU—10304 Bluffton Rd., Fort Wayne (219)747-3136.
Holes: 18. **Par:** 72/73.
Yards: 6,700/6,250. **Course rating:** 70.3/67.9. **Slope:** 123/111.
Opened: 1925. **Pace of Play rating:** 4:15. **Green fee:** $ 15.
Credit cards: MC, V, DISC. **Reduced fees:** N/A
Caddies: No. **Golf carts:** $18 for 18 holes.
Discount golf packages: No. **Season:** March-Dec. **High:** April-Sept.
On-site lodging: No. **Rental clubs:** Yes.
Walking policy: Unrestricted walking. **Range:** Yes (grass).
To obtain tee times: Call ahead.
Subscriber comments: Very fine traditional old course . . . Best public
course here and best buy . . . A good course even though the F-16s from
nearby Air National Guard are distracting at times . . . Air traffic noise can
be disturbing . . . Best public course in Fort Wayne . . . Older style course.
Changing to bent fairways . . . Pleasant fun track . . . Well maintained . . .
Lots of sand, long par 4s . . . The course always looks great and is
wonderfully challenging. You definitely get your money's worth . . . Look
out for low-flying airplanes . . . A nice surprise . . . Best public course in
northern Indiana.

CHRISTMAS LAKE GOLF CLUB★
PU—1 Country Club Dr., Santa Claus (812)544-2271, (800)927-2971.
45 miles east of Evansville. **Holes:** 18. **Par:** 72/72.
Yards: 7,191/5,135. **Course rating:** 74.4/69.2. **Slope:** 134/117.
Opened: 1968. **Pace of Play rating:** N/A. **Green fee:** $20/35.
Credit cards: MC, V. **Reduced fees:** Weekdays, Low season, Twilight.
Caddies: No. **Golf carts:** Included in Green Fee.
Discount golf packages: Yes. **Season:** Feb-Dec. **High:** May-Oct.
On-site lodging: No. **Rental clubs:** Yes.
Walking policy: Walking at certain times. **Range:** Yes (grass).
To obtain tee times: Call seven days in advance.

COFFIN GOLF CLUB★
PU—2401 Cold Springs Rd., Indianapolis (317)327-7845.
Holes: 18. **Par:** 72/72.
Yards: 6,709/5,135. **Course rating:** N/A. **Slope:** N/A.
Opened: N/A. **Pace of Play rating:** 4:00. **Green fee:** $18/20.
Credit cards: MC, V. **Reduced fees:** Twilight, Seniors, Juniors.
Caddies: No. **Golf carts:** $13 for 18 holes.
Discount golf packages: No. **Season:** March-Dec. **High:** N/A.
On-site lodging: No. **Rental clubs:** Yes.
Walking policy: Unrestricted walking. **Range:** No.
To obtain tee times: Call up to one week in advance.
Completely renovated course and clubhouse opened July 1995.
Subscriber comments: The course was closed in late 1993 for a complete
makeover . . . Will re-open in 1995, should be great . . . Renovated course
will be among top five in state.

★½ COOL LAKE GOLF CLUB

SP—520 E. 750 N., Lebanon (317)325-9271.

35 miles northwest of Indianapolis. **Holes:** 18. **Par:** 70/72.

Yards: 6,000/4,827. **Course rating:** 66.0/71.0. **Slope:** 100/102.

Opened: 1968. **Pace of Play rating:** 4:00. **Green fee:** $14/18.

Credit cards: MC, V. **Reduced fees:** N/A

Caddies: No. **Golf carts:** $10 for 18 holes.

Discount golf packages: No. **Season:** March-Dec. **High:** May-Sept.

On-site lodging: No. **Rental clubs:** No.

Walking policy: Walking at certain times. **Range:** Yes (grass).

To obtain tee times: Call anytime in advance.

Subscriber comments: Nice little course . . . Front short, back long and narrow fairways . . . Front nine new irrigation enhances overall course quality.

★★★★ COVERED BRIDGE GOLF CLUB

SP—12510 Covered Bridge Rd., Sellersburg (812)246-8880.

10 miles north of Louisville, KY. **Holes:** 18. **Par:** 72/72.

Yards: 6,832/5,943. **Course rating:** 73.0/74.7. **Slope:** 128/126.

Opened: 1994. **Pace of Play rating:** 4:15. **Green fee:** $43/48.

Credit cards: MC, V, AMEX. **Reduced fees:** Weekdays, Low season.

Caddies: No. **Golf carts:** Included in Green Fee.

Discount golf packages: No. **Season:** Year-round. **High:** April-Oct.

On-site lodging: No. **Rental clubs:** Yes.

Walking policy: Mandatory cart. **Range:** Yes (grass).

To obtain tee times: General public call four days in advance. Must guarantee tee time with a credit card.

Ranked 7th in Indiana by Golf Digest.

Subscriber comments: Zoeller design in lovely hills, will improve with age . . . Great turf . . . Well run . . . Could not be better at this time . . . Rough too thick, outstanding clubhouse . . . Beautiful layout, zoysia, drains slowly . . . No negatives here, great view of course from clubhouse . . . Beautiful layout, spectacular ninth and 18th shared green . . . Best, fairest greens around . . . The most playable course in Midwest.

CRESSMOOR COUNTRY CLUB★

PU—601 N. Wisconsin St., Hobart (219)942-9300.

Call course for additional information.

★★★ CURTIS CREEK COUNTRY CLUB

SP—Rte. 3, Rensselaer (219)866-7729.

Call course for additional information.

Subscriber comments: Short course, old oaks line 2/3rds of the course . . . Good surroundings . . . Excellent greens . . . Short but sweet . . . Back nine makes the course.

★★½ DYKEMAN PARK GOLF COURSE

PU—Eberts Rd., Logansport (219)753-0222.

Holes: 18. **Par:** 70/73.

Yards: 6,185/5,347. **Course rating:** 69.4/69.8. **Slope:** 118/102.

Opened: N/A. **Pace of Play rating:** 4:30. **Green fee:** $12.

Credit cards: None. **Reduced fees:** Twilight, Seniors, Juniors.

Caddies: No. **Golf carts:** $8 for 18 holes.

Discount golf packages: Yes. **Season:** March-Dec. **High:** April-Aug.

On-site lodging: No. **Rental clubs:** Yes.

Walking policy: Unrestricted walking. **Range:** Yes.

To obtain tee times: Two days in advance.

Subscriber comments: A good city course located in the country, no houses or buildings to look at . . . Great greens, slow play and very busy . . . Work the ball . . . Best greens around, quick, hard . . . Best municipal course in the state. Very informal.

INDIANA

★★½ EAGLE CREEK GOLF CLUB
PU—8802 W. 56th St., Indianapolis (317)297-3366.
Holes: 18. **Par:** 72/72.
Yards: 7,159/5,800. **Course rating:** 74.6/68.2. **Slope:** 139/116.
Opened: 1974. **Pace of Play rating:** 5:00. **Green fee:** $18/20.
Credit cards: MC, V. **Reduced fees:** Weekdays, Low season, Twilight,
Seniors, Juniors.
Caddies: No. **Golf carts:** $12 for 18 holes.
Discount golf packages: No. **Season:** Feb.-Dec. **High:** June-Aug.
On-site lodging: No. **Rental clubs:** Yes.
Walking policy: Unrestricted walking. **Range:** Yes (grass).
To obtain tee times: Call one week in advance for weekdays and call
Monday for the following weekend.
Also has 9-hole par-36 West course.
Ranked in Third 25 of America's 75 Best Public Golf Courses by Golf
Digest.
Subscriber comments: Early Pete Dye. Best shape I've seen for years . . .
New sand in bunkers . . . Could be best in state if they spend money . . .
Deep, deep, deep rough . . . Beautiful scenery, hilly and treelined . . .
Finally beginning to equal its reputation again . . . Fantastic layout . . .
Course was in tour caliber shape by mid-summer . . . Very long and
demanding from back tees. Tough for high handicap . . . Deserves
reputation as one of top munys in America . . . No two holes the same,
great character on all 3s, 5s . . . Potential top five courses in state . . . Really
improved, great shape, some holes tight, most long . . . Very scenic, very
tight. Must plan every shot . . . Choppy layout with many blind shots . . .
Good test for precise shotmaking. Back in shape after many repairs . . .
Little leafy in fall . . . Take camera . . . Long, sand, hilly; need good tee ball
placement . . . Finally in great shape! . . . Improved 200% in last year . . .
A tour caliber course for city course fees.

★★★ ELBEL PARK GOLF COURSE
PU—26595 Auten Rd., South Bend (219)271-9180.
Holes: 18. **Par:** 72/73.
Yards: 6,700/5,750. **Course rating:** 70.7/71.4. **Slope:** 113/114.
Opened: 1963. **Pace of Play rating:** 4:00. **Green fee:** $15/17.
Credit cards: None. **Reduced fees:** Weekdays, Low season, Twilight,
Seniors, Juniors.
Caddies: No. **Golf carts:** $10 for 18 holes.
Discount golf packages: No. **Season:** March-Dec. **High:** June-Aug.
On-site lodging: No. **Rental clubs:** Yes.
Walking policy: Unrestricted walking. **Range:** Yes (grass).
To obtain tee times: Weekend tee times only. Call on Monday after 6
p.m. for upcoming weekend.
Subscriber comments: Very good muny course . . . Beautiful wetlands
scenery . . . Lots of swamps and doglegs, plush fairways . . . Very scenic
. . . Good, well maintained golf course, great value . . . Could be best
public course in state . . . Too good for daily fee muny . . . Good shape.
Slow greens. Challenging . . . Holes on front being redesigned . . . Best
golf value for 10s of miles.

★★★ ERSKINE PARK GOLF CLUB
PU—4200 Miami St., South Bend (219)291-3216.
Holes: 18. **Par:** 70/76.
Yards: 6,100/5,882. **Course rating:** 69.0/69.1. **Slope:** 121/121.
Opened: 1925. **Pace of Play rating:** 4:30. **Green fee:** $ 10/17.
Credit cards: MC, V. **Reduced fees:** Twilight, Seniors, Juniors.
Caddies: No. **Golf carts:** $10 for 18 holes.
Discount golf packages: Yes. **Season:** March-Nov. **High:** April-Sept.
On-site lodging: No. **Rental clubs:** Yes.
Walking policy: Unrestricted walking. **Range:** No.
To obtain tee times: Call seven days in advance.
Subscriber comments: Hilly, old style, excellent maintenance, short, fun
. . . Not what 17 used to be . . . Ladies tees too long, requires very straight

tee shots, toughest back nine in the area . . . Mature with good greens, great value . . . Very good holes on back nine . . . Outstanding par 3s . . . Tee boxes too close to adjacent greens . . . Heavily used and some difficulty getting times . . . Always very green. Parallel fairways . . . Killer par 3s determine your score. You'd never know this is a public course.

ETNA ACRES GOLF COURSE*
SP—9803 W. 600 S., Andrews (219)468-2906.
16 miles north of Marion. **Holes:** 18. **Par:** 72/72.
Yards: 6,096/5,142. **Course rating:** 68.6/68.9. **Slope:** 109/108.
Opened: 1960. **Pace of Play rating:** 4:00. **Green fee:** $10/12.
Credit cards: None. **Reduced fees:** Weekdays, Low season, Seniors, Juniors.
Caddies: No. **Golf carts:** $8 for 18 holes.
Discount golf packages: Yes. **Season:** March-Nov. **High:** June-Aug.
On-site lodging: No. **Rental clubs:** Yes.
Walking policy: Unrestricted walking. **Range:** Yes (grass).
To obtain tee times: Call pro shop.
Subscriber comments: Rural course, hard cores only . . . New back nine is still rough, demanding layout but needs cosmetic improvements . . . In a few years, will be very nice.

★½ FAIRVIEW GOLF COURSE
PU—7102 S. Calhoun St., Fort Wayne (219)745-7093.
Holes: 18. **Par:** 72/72.
Yards: 6,620/5,125. **Course rating:** 70.8/71.1. **Slope:** 119/108.
Opened: 1927. **Pace of Play rating:** . **Green fee:** $10.
Credit cards: MC, V. **Reduced fees:** No.
Caddies: No. **Golf carts:** $17 for 18 holes.
Discount golf packages: No. **Season:** March-Oct. **High:** May-Sept.
On-site lodging: No. **Rental clubs:** Yes.
Walking policy: Unrestricted walking. **Range:** Yes (grass).
To obtain tee times: Weekend tee times only. Call Tuesday prior to weekend.
Subscriber comments: Front and back nine like two separate courses . . . The least expensive in Fort Wayne . . . Very reasonable rates, course improving . . . Front nine skip it, play back nine twice . . . Short old nine is Donald Ross design . . . Front nine long. Back nine hilly and more trouble . . . Good course for the beginner . . . Best I have seen this course in years . . . They switched the nines in '94 . . . Need better traps.

★½ FENDRICH GOLF COURSE
PU—1900 Diamond Ave., Evansville (812)435-6070.
Holes: 18. **Par:** 70/70.
Yards: 5,791/5,232. **Course rating:** 67.1/69.2. **Slope:** 106/109.
Opened: 1945. **Pace of Play rating:** 4:30. **Green fee:** $10.
Credit cards: None. **Reduced fees:** .
Caddies: No. **Golf carts:** $18 for 18 holes.
Discount golf packages: No. **Season:** Year-round. **High:** April-Sept.
On-site lodging: No. **Rental clubs:** Yes.
Walking policy: Unrestricted walking. **Range:** Yes (grass).
To obtain tee times: Call seven days in advance.
Subscriber comments: Not long, but a few challenging holes . . . Recent Bermuda fairways hold up better . . . Short course . . . Not too challenging. Overused and often slow . . . Greens are too slow and thick . . . It's making a turnaround.

★★½ FOREST PARK GOLF COURSE
PU—P.O. Box 42, Brazil (812)442-5681.
15 miles northeast of Terre Haute. **Holes:** 18. **Par:** 71/73.
Yards: 6,012/5,647. **Course rating:** 68.0/69.8. **Slope:** 110/112.
Opened: 1935. **Pace of Play rating:** 4:00. **Green fee:** $11/13.
Credit cards: None. **Reduced fees:** Low season, Twilight.
Caddies: No. **Golf carts:** $9 for 18 holes.

Discount golf packages: No. **Season:** Year-round. **High:** March-Nov.
On-site lodging: No. **Rental clubs:** No.
Walking policy: Unrestricted walking. **Range:** No.
To obtain tee times: Tee times are not taken in advance.
Subscriber comments: Nice small town muny . . . Get rid of out-of-bounds between Nos. 6 and 7 . . . Short course but fun, greens incredibly quick, short par 4s and 5s. Fun, inexpensive, good for any level player . . . Small town, good course; plays tougher than I thought . . . Flat with little hazards . . . Very casual atmosphere.

FOREST PARK GOLF COURSE★

PU—1155 Sheffield Dr., Valparaiso (219)462-5144.
60 miles east of South Bend. **Holes:** 18. **Par:** 70/72.
Yards: 5,731/5,339. **Course rating:** 67.4/70.7. **Slope:** 114/111.
Opened: 1973. **Pace of Play rating:** 4:30. **Green fee:** $13/18.
Credit cards: None. **Reduced fees:** Twilight, Juniors.
Caddies: No. **Golf carts:** $18 for 18 holes.
Discount golf packages: No. **Season:** April-Dec. **High:** June-Sept.
On-site lodging: No. **Rental clubs:** Yes.
Walking policy: Unrestricted walking. **Range:** No.
To obtain tee times: Call after 8 a.m. Wednesday prior to weekend.
Subscriber comments: A quick change from front to back . . . Front is flat and back everything elevated, great shape . . . 12th hole is gimmicky, unfair on second shot . . . Worth price of play if you like sightseeing while playing. This place is beautiful.

★★★ FOX PRAIRIE GOLF CLUB

PU—8465 E. 196th St., Noblesville (317)776-6357.
15 miles north of Indianapolis. **Holes:** 18. **Par:** 72/75.
Yards: 6,946/5,533. **Course rating:** 72.6/71.4. **Slope:** 118/114.
Opened: 1970. **Pace of Play rating:** 4:30. **Green fee:** $17/22.
Credit cards: MC, V. **Reduced fees:** Weekdays, Twilight.
Caddies: No. **Golf carts:** $11 for 18 holes.
Discount golf packages: Yes. **Season:** March-Nov. **High:** June-Aug.
On-site lodging: No. **Rental clubs:** Yes.
Walking policy: Unrestricted walking. **Range:** Yes (grass).
To obtain tee times: Call pro shop.
Subscriber comments: Very good public course, being upgraded with new traps and sand . . . Bring your driver. Toughest consecutive three holes (Nos. 10 - 12) around . . . Great casual course . . . Requires every club in bag . . . Toughest back nine in area, large greens . . . Some fun holes . . . Several good, challenging holes . . . Nice staff, will fit you in, huge greens, bring your short game, always in good shape . . . Great greens, front nine and back nine very different . . . One of the best municipal courses around.

FRENCH LICK SPRINGS RESORT

R—Hwy. 56, French Lick (812)936-9300, (800)457-4042.
60 miles northwest of Louisville, KY.
Credit cards: All major. **Reduced fees:** Low season, Resort guests, Twilight.
Caddies: No. **Golf carts:** $12 for 18 holes.
Discount golf packages: Yes. **Season:** March-Nov. **High:** May-Oct.
On-site lodging: Yes. **Rental clubs:** Yes.
Walking policy: Mandatory cart. **Range:** No.
To obtain tee times: Call pro shop. Preference given to hotel guests.

★★★½ HILL COURSE

Holes: 18. **Par:** 70/71.
Yards: 6,650/5,927. **Course rating:** 71.6/70.3. **Slope:** 119/116.
Opened: 1920. **Pace of Play rating:** 4:30. **Green fee:** $35.
Subscriber comments: One of the best courses in southwest Indiana . . . An old course with great tradition . . . Great course, history surrounds golf course; would play everyday . . . Big greens, severe greens, great greens . . . Great old course when maintained . . . Great design, you can feel the tradition, tight layout, very enjoyable . . . Very deep valleys . . . Very

rolling, good layout, good mix of length, make good approaches, better be able to putt, still playable for all . . . The staff was great and we did not have to wait long to tee up, pace of play was very fast . . . Very tough greens, but fun for players of all abilities . . . Greens make this course . . . Tough greens . . . Old Donald Ross course being restored, but slowly . . . Must hit it on the correct side of the green . . . Tough, fast greens . . . This course has never been better . . . Staff very good . . . Good for low to mid-handicap golfers . . . Really tough; slopes . . . Nice resort course package . . . Hoosier hospitality.

★½ VALLEY COURSE

Holes: 18. **Par:** 70/71.
Yards: 6,001/5,627. **Course rating:** 67.6/66.0. **Slope:** 110/106.
Opened: 1905. **Pace of Play rating:** 4:00. **Green fee:** $18.
Walking policy: Walking at certain times. **Range:** Yes (grass).
Subscriber comments: Flat, short, wet, well kept, helpful staff, less than four hours . . . Easy walk . . . May be a good course for beginners, stick to Hill course . . . Old course, needs facelift . . . Acceptable at best . . . Challenge, plays to hotel guest . . . Put some money into this and it would be little jewel in the valley.

★★★ GENEVA HILLS GOLF CLUB

PU—R.R. No. 3, Clinton (317)832-8384.
15 miles north of Terre Haute. **Holes:** 18. **Par:** 72/72.
Yards: 6,768/4,785. **Course rating:** 70.2/67.3. **Slope:** 118/115.
Opened: 1970. **Pace of Play rating:** N/A. **Green fee:** $14/17.
Credit cards: MC, V. **Reduced fees:** Weekdays, Low season, Twilight, Seniors, Juniors.
Caddies: No. **Golf carts:** $10 for 18 holes.
Discount golf packages: No. **Season:** Year-round. **High:** April-Oct.
On-site lodging: No. **Rental clubs:** Yes.
Walking policy: Unrestricted walking. **Range:** Yes (grass).
To obtain tee times: Call up to five days in advance.
Subscriber comments: Very playable . . . Good layout, always improving, no sand . . . Back nine greens very undulating . . . Greens fine, rest of course shaggy . . . Back nine greens devilish to putt . . . Lots of driving area . . . Hole Nos. 12, 13, 14 the Amen Corner of Indiana . . . A fun course to play.

★★★½ GOLF CLUB OF INDIANA

PU—I 65 at Zionsville Exit 130, Lebanon (317)769-6388.
16 miles northwest of Indianapolis. **Holes:** 18. **Par:** 72/72.
Yards: 7,084/5,498. **Course rating:** 73.2/72.7. **Slope:** 140/122.
Opened: 1974. **Pace of Play rating:** 4:30. **Green fee:** $30/35.
Credit cards: MC, V. **Reduced fees:** Low season, Twilight.
Caddies: No. **Golf carts:** $5 for 18 holes.
Discount golf packages: No. **Season:** Feb-Dec. **High:** May-Sept.
On-site lodging: No. **Rental clubs:** Yes.
Walking policy: Unrestricted walking. **Range:** Yes (grass).
To obtain tee times: Call pro shop.
Ranked in Third 25 of America's 75 Best Public Golf Courses by Golf Digest.
Subscriber comments: Challenging layout without gimmicks . . . Great layout, good challenge for all levels of golfers . . . Well manicured, bunkers and greens and water make up for lack of trees . . . Huge greens, lots of sand . . . Tough No. 5 par 4, lots of sand, large tiered greens . . . Largest greens ever played . . . Good golf, but expensive, great practice facilities . . . Tee early for nice round . . . Many holes look like each other . . . Bring your sand wedge . . . Will be fair and challenging for all levels of players if tee selection matches ability . . . Always fun, sometimes slow . . . Always looking to improve course.

★★★ GRAND OAK GOLF CLUB

SP—370 Grand Oak Dr., West Harrison (812)637-3943.
25 miles west of Cincinnati, OH. **Holes:** 18. **Par:** 71/71.

Yards: 6,363/4,842. **Course rating:** 70.5/69.9. **Slope:** 125/127.
Opened: 1989. **Pace of Play rating:** 4:05. **Green fee:** $18/22.
Credit cards: MC, V. **Reduced fees:** Low season, Seniors, Juniors.
Caddies: No. **Golf carts:** $10 for 18 holes.
Discount golf packages: No. **Season:** Feb-Dec. **High:** April-Oct.
On-site lodging: No. **Rental clubs:** Yes.
Walking policy: Unrestricted walking. **Range:** Yes (grass).
To obtain tee times: Call up to seven days in advance.
Subscriber comments: Dramatic hilly layout . . . Beautiful target . . .
Can't walk, very hilly, very often unfair, some very scenic holes . . . Tight
and tough to walk, but still enjoyable . . . Target golf extraordinaire,
excellent test, reasonable rates, greens good . . . Virtually unwalkable . . .
Quiet, isolated holes . . . Great hidden treasure . . . You can use every club
in your bag . . . You have to be a mountain climber to enjoy course . . .
Spectacular in fall season . . . Thinker's course. A few odd holes though . . .
Good design but definitely a shotmaker's course. Hilly and woodsy and
potential trouble everywhere . . . Excellent sets of par 3 holes . . . 10 yards
off fairway wilderness . . . Tough course, blind shots, very scenic, friendly
. . . Just 20 minutes west of Cincinnati. Best kept secret in town.

★★★ GREEN ACRES GOLF CLUB
PU—1300 Green Acres Dr., Kokomo (317)883-5771.
Holes: 18. **Par:** 72/76.
Yards: 6,782/5,653. **Course rating:** 72.8/72.7. **Slope:** 128/122.
Opened: 1968. **Pace of Play rating:** 4:30. **Green fee:** $10/17.
Credit cards: MC, V. **Reduced fees:** Low season, Seniors, Juniors.
Caddies: No. **Golf carts:** $10 for 18 holes.
Discount golf packages: No. **Season:** March-Dec. **High:** May-Oct.
On-site lodging: No. **Rental clubs:** Yes.
Walking policy: Unrestricted walking. **Range:** Yes (grass).
To obtain tee times: Call up to seven days in advance.
Subscriber comments: Well designed, with woods, good challenge,
unusual, No. 8 has two greens, men 558 over water; women's 426 on this
side of creek, nice! . . . Good layout, play condition improving with new
management . . . Some position shots, some wide open, a little bit of
everything . . . Great layout, not always well maintained, drainage
problems . . . Tight on new nine . . . Some very long par 5s . . . A lot of
doglegs . . . Too tight. Cussed entire round. Lost more golf balls than ever
. . . Best kept secret in central Indiana.

★★½ GREENFIELD COUNTRY CLUB
SP—145 S. Morristown Pike, Greenfield (317)462-2706.
15 miles east of Indianapolis. **Holes:** 18. **Par:** 72/73.
Yards: 6,773/5,501. **Course rating:** 71.2/73.5. **Slope:** 119/120.
Opened: 1927. **Pace of Play rating:** 4:15. **Green fee:** $16/21.
Credit cards: MC, V. **Reduced fees:** Weekdays.
Caddies: No. **Golf carts:** $11 for 18 holes.
Discount golf packages: No. **Season:** March-Nov. **High:** May-Sept.
On-site lodging: No. **Rental clubs:** No.
Walking policy: Unrestricted walking. **Range:** Yes (grass).
To obtain tee times: Call one week in advance.
Subscriber comments: Super small town club . . . Pleasant to play . . .
Nothing outstanding but would play again . . . Becoming a very good
course, improvements each year help . . . Pleasant surprise, great greens,
accommodating pro shop . . . Pretty good old course.

★★★½ HANGING TREE GOLF CLUB
SP—2302 W. 161st St., Westfield (317)896-2474.
20 miles north of Indianapolis. **Holes:** 18. **Par:** 71/71.
Yards: 6,519/5,151. **Course rating:** 72.6/70.6. **Slope:** 130/122.
Opened: 1990. **Pace of Play rating:** 4:15-4:30. **Green fee:** $39/46.
Credit cards: MC, V, DISC. **Reduced fees:** Weekdays, Low season,
Twilight.
Caddies: No. **Golf carts:** Included in Green Fee.

Discount golf packages: No. **Season:** Year-round. **High:** April-Nov.
On-site lodging: No. **Rental clubs:** Yes.
Walking policy: Mandatory cart. **Range:** Yes (grass).
To obtain tee times: Call anytime. As far in advance as needed.
Subscriber comments: Pleasant rolling layout with dramatic bunkers . . .
Pain in the butt creek (16 of 18 holes), pace of play excellent . . . Good
greens, well trapped . . . Too many hidden hazards . . . Wind always a
factor . . . Myrtle Beach type fairways, very professional layout . . . One
tough but fun course to play, loads of sand, water . . . Bent-grass fairways
. . . Somewhat tricked up . . . Couple of great holes . . .Compact layout
. . . Bent-grass fairways are beautiful; first four holes back and forth, then
good golf . . . Courteous staff . . . Excellent condition, any golfer can play
here. Staff is incredibly nice. High class facility . . . Neat setting with old
farmhouse for clubhouse . . . Country club quality and service for the
general public . . . I hate that damn creek that runs thru it.

★½ HART GOLF COURSE
PU—2500 E 550 N., Marion (317)662-8236.
Call club for further information.
Subscriber comments: Course mostly flat, lacks character, new
construction should help . . . Major changes in '94 and '95, watered
fairways and new tees. Will be an excellent layout and long . . . Good
course for average handicap . . . Best greens in Indiana.

★★ HELFRICH GOLF COURSE
PU—1550 Mesker Park Dr., Evansville (812)435-6075.
Holes: 18. **Par:** 71/74.
Yards: 6,306/5,506. **Course rating:** 69.8/71.4. **Slope:** 124/117.
Opened: 1923. **Pace of Play rating:** 4:00-4:20. **Green fee:** $10.
Credit cards: , V, DISC. **Reduced fees:** .
Caddies: No. **Golf carts:** $9 for 18 holes.
Discount golf packages: No. **Season:** Year-round. **High:** April-Oct.
On-site lodging: No. **Rental clubs:** Yes.
Walking policy: Unrestricted walking. **Range:** No.
To obtain tee times: Call one week in advance.
Subscriber comments: Hilly, not long, a few tough holes . . . Hills, sand,
water, you can play this course well, you play anywhere . . . Two bad
holes, double out-of-bounds on No. 12 . . . Most greens have enough slope
to keep you honest . . . Great challenging greens . . . Must use every club in
bag . . . Too many blind shots.

★★★ HIDDEN CREEK GOLF CLUB
PU—4975 Utica Sellersburg Rd., Sellersburg (812)246-2556.
4 miles north of Louisville, KY. **Holes:** 18. **Par:** 71/71.
Yards: 6,756/5,245. **Course rating:** 73.0/70.6. **Slope:** 133/123.
Opened: 1992. **Pace of Play rating:** 4:20. **Green fee:** $15/17.
Credit cards: MC, V, AMEX. **Reduced fees:** Low season, Twilight.
Caddies: No. **Golf carts:** $10 for 18 holes.
Discount golf packages: Yes. **Season:** Year-round. **High:** March-Oct.
On-site lodging: No. **Rental clubs:** Yes.
Walking policy: Unrestricted walking. **Range:** Yes (grass).
To obtain tee times: Nonmembers may call four days in advance for
weekday tee times and weekend times after 11 a.m. Call day before for
weekend tee times before 11 a.m.
Subscriber comments: Great little course . . . Hilly, lots of water . . .
Open and treelined fairways . . . Fairways close together, always ducking
. . . Bent fairways, greens . . . Course could have used 30 more acres . . .
16th hole still roadblock . . . Tough, tight back nine; pack extra balls . . .
Runs out of room in back . . . Has always been a pleasure to play.

★★★ HONEYWELL GOLF COURSE
PU—3360 W. Division Rd., Wabash (219)563-8663.
45 miles southwest of Fort Wayne. **Holes:** 18. **Par:** 72/72.
Yards: 6,550/5,650. **Course rating:** 69.4/70.4. **Slope:** 120/124.

Opened: 1980. **Pace of Play rating:** 4:15. **Green fee:** $16/20.
Credit cards: MC, V. **Reduced fees:** Weekdays, Low season.
Caddies: No. **Golf carts:** $10 for 18 holes.
Discount golf packages: No. **Season:** March-Nov. **High:** June-Sept.
On-site lodging: No. **Rental clubs:** Yes.
Walking policy: Unrestricted walking. **Range:** Yes (grass).
To obtain tee times: Call in advance.
Subscriber comments: Nice little rural course . . . Super back nine . . .
Fast greens, doing some renovations . . . Pleasant staff . . . Old style front,
Hills back, nine very good consistent greens . . . Once I stayed away, now I
cannot get away . . . Disappointed that they are building homes around it
. . . Demanding with focus on accuracy, great greens . . . Best kept secret
in Indiana.

★★★½ HULMAN LINKS GOLF COURSE
PU—990 N. Chamberlain St., Terre Haute (812)877-2096.
Holes: 18. **Par:** 72/72.
Yards: 7,225/5,775. **Course rating:** 74.9/73.4. **Slope:** 144/134.
Opened: 1978. **Pace of Play rating:** . **Green fee:** $19/22.
Credit cards: MC, V. **Reduced fees:** Low season.
Caddies: No. **Golf carts:** $11 for 18 holes.
Discount golf packages: No. **Season:** March-Dec. **High:** May-Sept.
On-site lodging: No. **Rental clubs:** Yes.
Walking policy: Unrestricted walking. **Range:** Yes (grass).
To obtain tee times: Call anytime for weekday play. Call Wednesday for
following weekend.
Ranked in Third 25 of America's 75 Best Public Golf Courses by Golf
Digest.
Subscriber comments: Worth the drive, great traditional layout, drive it
straight and long . . . Great layout could be kept up better . . . Best suited
for accurate driving, tight fairways . . . New fairways have helped make
this one of state's best . . . Hardest course from tips I've ever played . . .
Has some unfair holes . . . Play it from the gold tees and hang on . . .
Tight, No. 11 is unfair, great finishing hole, fun . . . Excellent, new
fairways . . . Greens big and smooth, nice to walk, course tough on
beginners, 11th hole almost impossible . . . Many holes require course
management . . . Best municipal course in Indiana.

★★★ INDIANA UNIVERSITY GOLF CLUB
PU—State Rd. 46 Bypass, Bloomington (812)855-7543.
45 miles south of Indianapolis. **Holes:** 18. **Par:** 71/72.
Yards: 6,891/5,661. **Course rating:** 72.4/73.1. **Slope:** 129/123.
Opened: 1959. **Pace of Play rating:** 4:00. **Green fee:** $16/17.
Credit cards: None. **Reduced fees:** .
Caddies: No. **Golf carts:** $10 for 18 holes.
Discount golf packages: Yes. **Season:** March-Dec. **High:** April-Oct.
On-site lodging: No. **Rental clubs:** Yes.
Walking policy: Walking at certain times. **Range:** Yes (grass).
To obtain tee times: Call one week in advance.
Also has 9-hole par-3 course.
Subscriber comments: Very pretty, very tight, located at center of
university . . . Rolling and bordered with trees . . . Well managed, well
kept, generous fairways, beautiful rolling hills . . . Tight, too many trees on
front nine, back nine wide open . . . Hilly for Indiana . . . Courteous staff.
Course has character. Good value . . . Lovely, wooded course, Slicers stay
away . . . Keep the ball below the hole . . . A beautiful fall course . . . Great
layout, condition varies, long and hilly . . . No fairway sand . . . Very
hilly, all par 3s over 200 yds, play in spring or fall, dries out in summer.

IRONHORSE GOLF CLUB★
PU—20 Cedar Island, Logansport (219)722-1110.
Holes: 18. **Par:** 71/72.
Yards: 6,100/5,400. **Course rating:** 67.8/64.8. **Slope:** 109/103.
Opened: . **Pace of Play rating:** N/A. **Green fee:** $ 9/11.

Credit cards: MC, V. **Reduced fees:** .
Caddies: No. **Golf carts:** $10 for 18 holes.
Discount golf packages: No. **Season:** March-Dec. **High:** May-Sept.
On-site lodging: No. **Rental clubs:** Yes.
Walking policy: Walking at certain times. **Range:** Yes (grass).
To obtain tee times: Call pro shop.
Formerly known as Logansport Golf Club.
Subscriber comments: Play fast . . . Short course. Lots of water. Pretty
flat.

★★½ IRONWOOD GOLF CLUB
PU—10955 Fall Rd., Fishers (317)842-0551.
Call club for further information.
Subscriber comments: Old sunbelt course. Very nice updates . . .
Recently renovated . . . Some rough edges . . . New bent grass . . . Good
potential.

★★½ JASPER MUNICIPAL GOLF COURSE
PU—17th and Jackson, Jasper (812)482-4600.
Call club for further information.
Subscriber comments: Unusual public course . . . First nine not much
challenge, back nine very tough . . . Very scenic front nine, excellent
condition . . . Front open, back tight, municipal, very friendly staff . . .
Newer back nine is outstanding! . . . Suited for accuracy. Don't have to hit
long.

★★★½ JUDAY CREEK GOLF COURSE
PU—14770 Lindy Dr., Granger (219)277-4653.
5 miles east of South Bend. **Holes:** 18. **Par:** 72/72.
Yards: 6,940/5,000. **Course rating:** 73.3/67.1. **Slope:** 133/116.
Opened: 1989. **Pace of Play rating:** 4:00-4:30. **Green fee:** $19/24.
Credit cards: MC, V, AMEX. **Reduced fees:** Twilight, Seniors, Juniors.
Caddies: No. **Golf carts:** $10 for 18 holes.
Discount golf packages: No. **Season:** March-Oct. **High:** June-Aug.
On-site lodging: No. **Rental clubs:** Yes.
Walking policy: Walking at certain times. **Range:** Yes (grass).
To obtain tee times: Call anytime.
Subscriber comments: Florida type . . . OK for housing development
course . . . I just happened upon this jewel . . . Great bent-grass greens and
fairways . . . No trees only water . . . Fun to play, great condition for
young course . . . Will be quite a challenge when trees mature . . . Bent-
grass fairways not common here . . . Repetitive design . . . Good use of
odd shape property . . . Plenty of water comes into play . . . Flat but
winding . . . Tough in wind . . . Good treatment by staff . . . Superb par
5s. Excellent course architecture . . . Young, plenty of water, challenging
. . . One of Indiana's best.

★★½ LAFAYETTE MUNICIPAL GOLF CLUB
PU—800 Golf View Dr., Lafayette (317)742-4505.
Call club for further information.
Subscriber comments: Elevated greens on flat course . . . Raised greens
that putt fast and true . . . Very good condition for a municipal course . . .
Elevated greens make it tough to judge pin . . . Plays more difficult than it
looks . . . Flat course, elevated greens, good value for $ . . . Fraternal
atmosphere prevails.

★ LAKE HILLS GOLF CLUB
FRONT/MIDDLE/BACK
PU—10001 W. 85th Ave., St. John (219)365-8601.
30 miles southeast of Chicago. **Holes:** 27. **Par:** 71/71/70.
Yards: 5,947/5,889/6,194. **Course rating:** 67.5/67.5/69.0. **Slope:**
120/120/120.
Opened: 1925. **Pace of Play rating:** N/A. **Green fee:** $13/27.

Credit cards: All major. **Reduced fees:** Weekdays, Low season, Twilight, Seniors, Juniors.
Caddies: No. **Golf carts:** $8 for 18 holes.
Discount golf packages: Yes. **Season:** March-Nov. **High:** June-Sept.
On-site lodging: No. **Rental clubs:** Yes.
Walking policy: Unrestricted walking. **Range:** No.
To obtain tee times: Call either number listed or (312)878-2727.
Subscriber comments: Tricky fast greens and great terrain . . . Small greens, no hazards, hilly and bad slope . . . Fairways need better care, some greens have problems . . . Postage stamp size greens that won't hold darts . . . Very hilly, take a cart; lots of variety; conditions vary.

★★ LAKE JAMES GOLF CLUB
PU—1445 W. 275 N., Angola (219)833-3967.
Call club for further information.
Subscriber comments: Best kept secret in northeast Indiana . . . Several holes have great views . . . Has great potential, needs sprucing up, needs better clubhouse . . . Hilly and one of the toughest courses in this area . . . Challenging hills for Indiana, needs water in summer . . . Playable, for experienced players, good treatment by staff, good pace . . . Be in shape or cart it, old trees, great layout . . . Best finishing hole in Indiana.

LAUREL LAKES GOLF COURSE★
PU—2460 E. State Rd. 26 E., Hartford City (317)348-4876.
Call club for further information.
Subscriber comments: Good course, good pace, seldom too crowded, back nine very difficult, front average . . . Some challenging holes, a fun course . . . Builds confidence.

★★★½ THE LEGENDS OF INDIANA GOLF COURSE
PU—Hurricane Rd., Franklin (317)736-8186.
12 miles south of Indianapolis. **Holes:** 18. **Par:** 72/72.
Yards: 7,044/5,244. **Course rating:** 74.0/71.1. **Slope:** 132/121.
Opened: 1991. **Pace of Play rating:** 4:20. **Green fee:** $25/29.
Credit cards: MC, V. **Reduced fees:** Twilight.
Caddies: No. **Golf carts:** $10 for 18 holes.
Discount golf packages: Yes. **Season:** March-Dec. **High:** May-Oct.
On-site lodging: No. **Rental clubs:** Yes.
Walking policy: Walking at certain times. **Range:** Yes (grass).
To obtain tee times: Call seven days in advance.
Ranked 6th in Indiana by Golf Digest.
Subscriber comments: Championship layout, Jim Fazio design . . . Needs more trees to guard fairways, but very nice . . . Greens are great, otherwise generic golf . . . Lots of sand, good greens for fast roll . . . Lacks some character, should get better with age, best range anywhere . . . Unique and challenging enough for any golfer . . . Mounding good fun . . . Well kept, challenging but conquerable . . . Some holes crowded . . . Keeps getting better with age . . . Not a natural layout but good fun . . . Tougher than it appears. Play long and always windy . . . Good variety of holes and breaks up flat terrain . . . Best conditioned in Indiana . . . Fun to play, can get windy out in the cornfields . . . Few trees and lots of bunkers . . . Cornfield to golf course . . . Beautiful job.

★★½ LIBERTY COUNTRY CLUB
SP—1391 N. U.S. 27, Liberty (317)458-5664.
35 miles north of Cincinnati, OH. **Holes:** 18. **Par:** 70/71.
Yards: 6,203/4,544. **Course rating:** 70.5/69.3. **Slope:** 120/115.
Opened: 1927. **Pace of Play rating:** 4:00. **Green fee:** $16.
Credit cards: None. **Reduced fees:** Twilight.
Caddies: No. **Golf carts:** $9 for 18 holes.
Discount golf packages: No. **Season:** Year-round. **High:** June-Aug.

On-site lodging: No. **Rental clubs:** No.
Walking policy: Unrestricted walking. **Range:** Yes (grass).
To obtain tee times: Call three days in advance.
Subscriber comments: Well maintained, courteous staff . . . Challenging holes . . . Best suited for a draw, fast play.

★★★ THE LINKS GOLF CLUB
PU—11425 N. Shelby 700 W., New Palestine (317)861-4466.
15 miles southeast of Indianapolis. **Holes:** 18. **Par:** 72/72.
Yards: 7,054/5,018. **Course rating:** 73.3/68.4. **Slope:** 122/100.
Opened: 1972. **Pace of Play rating:** 4:00. **Green fee:** $19/32.
Credit cards: MC, V. **Reduced fees:** Weekdays, Low season, Twilight.
Caddies: No. **Golf carts:** $5 for 18 holes.
Discount golf packages: No. **Season:** Year-round. **High:** May-Sept.
On-site lodging: No. **Rental clubs:** Yes.
Walking policy: Walking at certain times. **Range:** Yes (grass).
To obtain tee times: Call one week in advance.
Subscriber comments: A hidden jewel . . . Best links course around . . . Off the beaten path but worth the effort . . . Somewhat isolated . . . Mostly flat, but has some good holes . . . Huge greens, lacks character . . . Flat but trouble is available in creeks and ponds . . . Worth seeing . . . Great practice area, exchange gravel for sand . . . Good layout, good staff, good value.

THE LINKS GOLF COURSE★
SP—IN 60, Mitchell (812)849-4653.
Call club for further information.

★½ MAPLEWOOD GOLF CLUB
SP—4261 E. County Rd. 700 S., Muncie (317)284-8007.
Holes: 18. **Par:** 72/76.
Yards: 6,013/5,759. **Course rating:** 68.5/68.5. **Slope:** 115/115.
Opened: 1961. **Pace of Play rating:** . **Green fee:** $10/12.
Credit cards: MC, V. **Reduced fees:** Weekdays, Low season.
Caddies: No. **Golf carts:** $9 for 18 holes.
Discount golf packages: No. **Season:** April-Oct. **High:** July-Sept.
On-site lodging: No. **Rental clubs:** Yes.
Walking policy: Unrestricted walking. **Range:** Yes (grass).
To obtain tee times: Call after Tuesday for weekend play.
Subscriber comments: A fun course . . . Short easy course, slow play, OK staff, beginner to average play . . . Not enough land for a golf course . . . Down and back . . . Hard greens, needs work . . . Many course improvements, owner very congenial . . . No watered fairways, wide open . . . Very friendly people.

★★½ MAXWELTON GOLF CLUB
SP—5721 E. Elkhart County Line Rd., Syracuse (219)457-3504.
45 miles southeast of South Bend. **Holes:** 18. **Par:** 72/72.
Yards: 6,490/5,992. **Course rating:** 70.1/73.4. **Slope:** 124/128.
Opened: 1930. **Pace of Play rating:** 4:00. **Green fee:** $17/19.
Credit cards: All major. **Reduced fees:** No.
Caddies: No. **Golf carts:** $10 for 18 holes.
Discount golf packages: No. **Season:** March-Nov. **High:** May-Sept.
On-site lodging: No. **Rental clubs:** Yes.
Walking policy: Unrestricted walking. **Range:** Yes.
To obtain tee times: Call anytime.
Subscriber comments: Seasoned course . . . Pleasantly surprised . . . Crowded, takes a beating . . . Super lake resort course . . . Super friendly staff . . . Reachable par 4s . . . A fun course to play. Very few straight putts . . . Best it has ever been.

★★ MICHIGAN CITY MUNICIPAL GOLF COURSE
PU—400 E. Michigan Blvd., Michigan City (219)873-1516.
55 miles southeast of Chicago. **Holes:** 18. **Par:** 72/74.
Yards: 6,169/5,363. **Course rating:** 67.6/68.6. **Slope:** 113/113.
Opened: 1930. **Pace of Play rating:** 4:00. **Green fee:** $12.50/16.50.
Credit cards: None. **Reduced fees:** Weekdays, Low season, Twilight, Seniors, Juniors.
Caddies: No. **Golf carts:** $9 for 18 holes.
Discount golf packages: No. **Season:** April-Nov. **High:** June-Aug.
On-site lodging: No. **Rental clubs:** Yes.
Walking policy: Unrestricted walking. **Range:** No.
To obtain tee times: Call one week in advance.
Subscriber comments: Typical city course, easy but interesting, not long in distance, anyone can play it . . . Not too challenging, pretty much open . . . Excellent for scrambles.

OAK GROVE COUNTRY CLUB★
PU—State Rd. 55 S., Oxford (317)385-2713.
15 miles northwest of Lafayette. **Holes:** 18. **Par:** 71/73.
Yards: 6,050/5,410. **Course rating:** 69.2/68.4. **Slope:** 113/113.
Opened: 1928. **Pace of Play rating:** 4:00. **Green fee:** $9/13.
Credit cards: None. **Reduced fees:** Weekdays, Low season, Juniors.
Caddies: No. **Golf carts:** $8 for 18 holes.
Discount golf packages: No. **Season:** Year-round. **High:** June-Aug.
On-site lodging: No. **Rental clubs:** Yes.
Walking policy: Unrestricted walking. **Range:** No.
To obtain tee times: Call pro shop.
Subscriber comments: Established course, good condition but short . . . Good variety, gets better every year.

OAK KNOLL GOLF COURSE★
PU—11200 Whitcomb St., Crown Point (219)663-3349.
Call club for further information.

★★★ OTIS PARK GOLF CLUB
PU—607 Tunnelton Rd., Bedford (812)279-9092.
75 miles north of Indianapolis. **Holes:** 18. **Par:** 72/72.
Yards: 6,308/5,184. **Course rating:** 70.0/69.3. **Slope:** 128/122.
Opened: 1920. **Pace of Play rating:** 4:30. **Green fee:** $ 13/16.
Credit cards: None. **Reduced fees:** No.
Caddies: No. **Golf carts:** $16 for 18 holes.
Discount golf packages: No. **Season:** March-Dec. **High:** May-Oct.
On-site lodging: No. **Rental clubs:** Yes.
Walking policy: Unrestricted walking. **Range:** Yes (grass).
To obtain tee times: Call anytime.
Subscriber comments: Great old course . . . Hilly, hidden greens . . . Lots of hills, rolling greens . . . Love the backdrop (stone fence), rolling terrain a pleasure . . . Excellent value, course could be great with better conditioning . . . Par 5 17th hole features tee on cliff overlooking fairway; Nos. 14 and 15 known as "Death Valley" . . . Some unique holes . . . Not one level lie . . . Will make you a player . . . Course takes advantage of geography for some dramatic holes . . . Best municipal course in state of Indiana.

★★★★ OTTER CREEK GOLF CLUB
PU—11522 E. 50 N., Columbus (812)579-5227.
35 miles south of Indianapolis. **Holes:** 18. **Par:** 72/72.
Yards: 7,258/5,690. **Course rating:** 74.2/72.1. **Slope:** 137/116.
Opened: 1964. **Pace of Play rating:** 4:10. **Green fee:** $40/68.
Credit cards: All major. **Reduced fees:** Weekdays, Low season.
Caddies: No. **Golf carts:** Included in Green Fee.
Discount golf packages: Yes. **Season:** March-Nov. **High:** May-Sept.
On-site lodging: No. **Rental clubs:** Yes.
Walking policy: Unrestricted walking. **Range:** Yes (grass).

To obtain tee times: Call as far in advance as needed. Credit card necessary to hold reservation.

Ranked in First 25 of America's 75 Best Public Golf Courses by Golf Digest. Ranked 5th in Indiana by Golf Digest.

Subscriber comments: Good Trent Jones course . . . Still the jewel of southern Indiana . . . New nine holes look great . . . The ultimate championship course . . . One of the best in state . . . A great test of the game, always great condition . . . Nice facilities . . . Has everything, water, trees, and sand . . . U.S. Open type layout . . . Excellent layout requires accurate iron play, fast undulating greens . . . As good as courses that are rated as "once in a lifetime experience" . . . Best public course in Indiana, beautifully manicured, no tricks, all day fares great value in early summer . . . Well bunkered, many holes surrounded by sand . . . No-nonsense great golf . . . Fountains in ponds spoil natural appearance . . . You know you've played real golf . . . I am a member and I live in Ohio, that is how good it really is! . . . Long off tee. Excellent pace of play. Use every club in bag . . . Great layout, traditional type course, not tricked up . . . Most overrated course in Indiana . . . Great gem in out of the way place . . . Too expensive but Monday and Tuesday daily fee rate an excellent value . . . Should host a major . . . Hospitality best in Indiana.

★★½ PALMIRA GOLF AND COUNTRY CLUB

SP—12111 W. 109th St., St. John (219)365-4331.

40 miles southeast of Chicago. **Holes:** 18. **Par:** 71/73.

Yards: 6,421/5,863. **Course rating:** 70.9/74.2. **Slope:** 118/117.

Opened: 1972. **Pace of Play rating:** . **Green fee:** $15/20.

Credit cards: MC, V. **Reduced fees:** Weekdays, Low season, Twilight, Seniors, Juniors.

Caddies: No. **Golf carts:** $22 for 18 holes.

Discount golf packages: No. **Season:** Year-round. **High:** May-Sept.

On-site lodging: No. **Rental clubs:** Yes.

Walking policy: Unrestricted walking. **Range:** Yes (grass).

To obtain tee times: Call pro shop.

Subscriber comments: Good average course . . . Must be long off tee and straight, long par 4s like the pros play, large greens and fast. If you hate three putts don't play this course. Still have a 710-yard par 5, cut to 580 for short hitters, course kept up nice, staff friendly, too many golf outings . . . 17th is one tough par 5 . . . Greens are small circles and rectangles, no definition . . . Will improve with age . . . Some outstanding holes. Trying to improve course.

PEBBLE BROOK GOLF AND COUNTRY CLUB

PU—3110 Westfield Rd., Noblesville (317)896-5596.

30 miles north of Indianapolis. **Green fee:** $23/27.

Credit cards: MC, V. **Reduced fees:** Weekdays.

Caddies: No. **Golf carts:** $11 for 18 holes.

Discount golf packages: No. **Season:** March-Dec. **High:** May-Sept.

On-site lodging: No. **Rental clubs:** Yes.

Walking policy: Walking at certain times. **Range:** Yes (grass).

To obtain tee times: Call on Tuesday for upcoming weekend and on Sunday for following weekday.

★★½ SOUTH COURSE

Holes: 18. **Par:** 72/72.

Yards: 6,557/5,261. **Course rating:** 70.5/71.9. **Slope:** 121/115.

Opened: 1974. **Pace of Play rating:** 4:00-4:30.

Subscriber comments: Wide open, kept in good shape but lacks bunkers and water to tighten it up . . . Not a lot of trouble . . . Back nine more fun . . . Tough par 3s but easy to score on this course . . . Pretty to look at . . . Easier of two.

★★½ NORTH COURSE

Holes: 18. **Par:** 70/70.
Yards: 6,392/5,806. **Course rating:** 70.5/74.1. **Slope:** 118/115.
Opened: 1989. **Pace of Play rating:** 4:00–4:30.
Subscriber comments: Better course than the South Course, more character in layout . . . Too many holes alike . . . Challenging course, small greens . . . Way too many back and forth holes . . . Very tight fairways, shotmaker's dream . . . Tough finishing hole . . . I like the North Course's bent grass fairways . . . Will be better when trees are added . . . One of best courses in area.

★★★½ PHEASANT VALLEY GOLF CLUB

SP—3838 W. 141st Ave., Crown Point (219)663-5000.
30 miles southeast of Chicago. **Holes:** 18. **Par:** 72/73.
Yards: 6,869/6,166. **Course rating:** 72.3/72.6. **Slope:** 126/N/A.
Opened: 1967. **Pace of Play rating:** 4:30. **Green fee:** $15/25.
Credit cards: MC, V. **Reduced fees:** Weekdays, Low season, Twilight, Seniors, Juniors.
Caddies: No. **Golf carts:** $20 for 18 holes.
Discount golf packages: No. **Season:** April-Dec. **High:** May-Oct.
On-site lodging: No. **Rental clubs:** Yes.
Walking policy: Unrestricted walking. **Range:** No.
To obtain tee times: Call a week ahead.
Subscriber comments: The course is great . . . Great shape, nice greens, all fairways difficult, better than average, requires all clubs . . . Only for straight hitters, trees everywhere . . . Long, tough, hilly . . . Northwest Indiana's best public course . . . One 90 degree dogleg. Best set of par 3s around . . . Diamond in the rough . . . Unfair, sloped fairways . . . Staff and fees make it well worth it.

PLYMOUTH ROCK GOLF COURSE*

PU—12641 7B Rd., Plymouth (219)936-4405.
25 miles south of South Bend. **Holes:** 18. **Par:** 72/74.
Yards: 6,716/5,391. **Course rating:** 66.1/68.2. **Slope:** 104/108.
Opened: 1960. **Pace of Play rating:** 4:00. **Green fee:** $ 6/12.
Credit cards: None. **Reduced fees:** Weekdays, Low season, Twilight, Seniors, Juniors.
Caddies: No. **Golf carts:** $10 for 18 holes.
Discount golf packages: No. **Season:** Year-round. **High:** May-Sept.
On-site lodging: No. **Rental clubs:** Yes.
Walking policy: Unrestricted walking. **Range:** Yes (grass).
To obtain tee times: Call in advance in summer.

★★½ THE POINTE GOLF AND TENNIS RESORT

R—2250 E. Pointe Rd., Bloomington (812)824–4040, (800)860-8604.
Holes: 18. **Par:** 71/71.
Yards: 6,604/5,186. **Course rating:** 73.0/71.2. **Slope:** 140/126.
Opened: 1973. **Pace of Play rating:** 4:30. **Green fee:** $26/40.
Credit cards: All major. **Reduced fees:** Weekdays, Low season, Twilight.
Caddies: No. **Golf carts:** Included in Green Fee.
Discount golf packages: Yes. **Season:** Year-round. **High:** May-Sept.
On-site lodging: Yes. **Rental clubs:** Yes.
Walking policy: Mandatory cart. **Range:** Yes (grass).
To obtain tee times: Call anytime in advance.
Subscriber comments: Pleasant atmosphere, beautiful location . . . Hilly and long, well kept, big greens, pleasure to play . . . Was expecting more . . . Lots of sand . . . Overplayed, need a second 18 . . . All uphill . . . Very nice staff. Play fast . . . Lots of uphill, downhill, sidehill lies. A fun course . . . Fairly long with big greens and lot of sand . . . Greens are very fast and hard to putt if above hole . . . Back nine lacks character . . . Out-of-bounds on nearly every hole . . . Friendly atmosphere.

PURDUE UNIVERSITY GOLF COURSE
PU—1202 Cherry Lane, West Lafayette (317)494-3139.
60 miles northwest of Indianapolis. & **Green fee:** $ 8/10.
Credit cards: All major. **Reduced fees:** Weekdays, Low season, Twilight, Seniors, Juniors.
Caddies: No. **Golf carts:** $11 for 18 holes.
Discount golf packages: No. **Season:** March-Nov. **High:** May-Oct.
On-site lodging: Yes. **Rental clubs:** Yes.
Walking policy: Unrestricted walking. **Range:** Yes (grass).
To obtain tee times: Call on Monday for that week or upcoming weekend.

★½ NORTH COURSE
Holes: 18. **Par:** 72/72.
Yards: 6,852/5,961. **Course rating:** 72.4/N/A. **Slope:** 116/N/A.
Pace of Play rating: 4:15.
Subscriber comments: Wide, short, and in average shape . . . All level play . . . Flat, open relatively long . . . All par 3s, 190 or more . . . Long, every hole seems to be a 470-yd, par 4 . . . Longer, but flatter than Purdue South . . . Not as good as Purdue South . . . Lots of play from students.

★★★ SOUTH COURSE
Holes: 18. **Par:** 71/72.
Yards: 6,428/5,382. **Course rating:** 70.5/N/A. **Slope:** 122/N/A.
Opened: 1934. **Pace of Play rating:** 4:15. **Green fee:** 10/13.
Subscriber comments: Cheap golf on a memorable design, hilly with lots of trees . . . Great hilly layout with many blind spots. Great staff . . . Better than North Course . . . Position course . . . Several fun holes, far from lush, but okay . . . OK for a college course . . . Lots of hills and valleys . . . Fun course, little bit of everything, variety, contoured . . . Usually in great shape but Purdue parks cars on No. 2 fairway during home football games. Go Boilermakers!

★ RABER GOLF COURSE
BLUE/WHITE/RED
PU—19396 St. Rd. No.120, Bristol (219)848-4020.
Call club for further information.
Subscriber comments: No bunkers, no water, but good inexpensive place to practice . . . Playable . . . No rough and marginal fairways . . . Easy to get on and moves fast.

★½ REA PARK GOLF COURSE
PU—3500 So. 7th St., Terre Haute (812)232-0709.
Holes: 18. **Par:** 72/72.
Yards: 6,482/5,353. **Course rating:** 70.2/71.7. **Slope:** 110/110.
Pace of Play rating: N/A. **Green fee:** $ 10/12.
Credit cards: MC, V. **Reduced fees:** Low season, Juniors.
Caddies: No. **Golf carts:** $10 for 18 holes.
Discount golf packages: No. **Season:** March-Dec. **High:** May-Aug.
On-site lodging: No. **Rental clubs:** Yes.
Walking policy: Unrestricted walking. **Range:** Yes.
To obtain tee times: Call Wednesday for upcoming weekend.
Subscriber comments: Flat, very little trouble, staff very friendly, pace is quick . . . Ho-hummer, flat, open, holes all the same . . . Wide open course, no water, small greens . . . Needs fairways redone, greens need work.

★★ RIVERBEND GOLF COURSE
PU—7207 St. Joe Rd., Fort Wayne (219)485-2732.
Holes: 18. **Par:** 72/72.
Yards: 6,702/5,633. **Course rating:** 72.5/72.5. **Slope:** 127/124.
Opened: 1974. **Pace of Play rating:** . **Green fee:** $14/20.
Credit cards: MC, V. **Reduced fees:** Weekdays, Low season, Twilight, Seniors, Juniors.
Caddies: No. **Golf carts:** $9 for 18 holes.
Discount golf packages: No. **Season:** March-Oct. **High:** May-Sept.

On-site lodging: No. **Rental clubs:** Yes.
Walking policy: Unrestricted walking. **Range:** No.
To obtain tee times: Call pro shop.
Subscriber comments: Sporty track . . . Strong finishing holes . . . Nice course, challenging layout . . . Many birdie opportunities . . . Front nine has water everywhere, back nine more open . . . Course has potential to be one of the best in the area but mediocre maintenance practices and lack of improvements hold it back . . . Greens very undulating and sloped . . . A neat course. Interesting, crowded holes.

★½ RIVERSIDE GOLF COURSE
PU—3502 White River Pkwy., Indianapolis (317)327-7300.
Holes: 18. **Par:** 70/71.
Yards: 6,156/5,385. **Course rating:** 67.9/69.7. **Slope:** 100/100.
Opened: 1935. **Pace of Play rating:** 3:45. **Green fee:** $ 8/11.
Credit cards: MC, V, DISC. **Reduced fees:** Twilight, Seniors, Juniors.
Caddies: No. **Golf carts:** $11 for 18 holes.
Discount golf packages: No. **Season:** Year-round. **High:** May-Aug.
On-site lodging: No. **Rental clubs:** Yes.
Walking policy: Unrestricted walking. **Range:** No.
To obtain tee times: Call seven days in advance. Call Monday at 7 a.m. for upcoming weekend.
Subscriber comments: Parkland course without much trouble . . . Needs tee boxes for juniors, womens and seniors . . . Decent public course with several good holes . . . Good starting course, wide open, few trouble spots . . . Old city course. Needs work . . . Ego builder but needs bunkers.

★★★★ ROCK HOLLOW GOLF CLUB
PU—County Rd. 250 W., Peru (317)473-6100.
15 miles north of Kokomo. **Holes:** 18. **Par:** 72/72.
Yards: 6,944/4,967. **Course rating:** 74.0/64.8. **Slope:** 132/112.
Opened: 1994. **Pace of Play rating:** 4:30. **Green fee:** $20/25.
Credit cards: MC, V. **Reduced fees:** .
Caddies: No. **Golf carts:** $10 for 18 holes.
Discount golf packages: No. **Season:** March-Oct. **High:** June-Sept.
On-site lodging: No. **Rental clubs:** Yes.
Walking policy: Unrestricted walking. **Range:** Yes (grass).
To obtain tee times: Call up to two weeks in advance.
Subscriber comments: Wow! Future No. 1 course in state. Very tough course. Well-designed, secluded fairways . . . Outstanding . . . Great design, a feast . . . New course looks like an old course, very fair to all . . . Accuracy needed . . . This is going to be a great course . . . Indiana's new hidden gem.

(SUPER VALUE)

★★★ ROYAL HYLANDS GOLF CLUB
PU—7629 S. Greensboro Pike, Knightstown (317)345-2123.
23 miles east of Indianapolis. **Holes:** 18. **Par:** 71/71.
Yards: 6,452/4,590. **Course rating:** 71.9/68.8. **Slope:** 130/122.
Opened: 1982. **Pace of Play rating:** 4:15. **Green fee:** $18/22.
Credit cards: MC, V. **Reduced fees:** Weekdays, Low season, Juniors.
Caddies: No. **Golf carts:** $11 for 18 holes.
Discount golf packages: Yes. **Season:** March-Dec. **High:** May-Aug.
On-site lodging: No. **Rental clubs:** Yes.
Walking policy: Unrestricted walking. **Range:** Yes (grass).
To obtain tee times: Call pro shop.
Subscriber comments: Scottish feel and look . . . No. 10 is a neat hole . . . Lots of heather . . . Heather? Must mean don't mow the rough, but a fun course . . . Cheap trip to Scotland, with heather . . . If you haven't mastered your putter, beware . . . Pot bunkers . . . With continued

improvements Royal Hylands is becoming one of the nicest in our area . . . Tough first hole. Staff is the best anywhere . . . Best course in area . . . Tough from back tees . . . Fast undulating greens . . . Best greens in state . . . Good mix of holes . . . Hidden gem that's got everybody talking.

★★½ SADDLEBROOK GOLF CLUB
5516 Arabian Rd., Indianapolis (317)290-0539.
Call club for further information.
Subscriber comments: Old course, trees in the right places . . . Challenging but short . . . Hit them straight . . . Great staff, short course, tight, wind makes you use all your clubs . . . Lots of water, back nine very narrow . . . Houses are too close to the course . . . Short but fun target golf . . . New nine needs maturing . . . Some holes seem to be afterthoughts . . . Front nine young but good layout, back nine good, mature layout . . . New nine built around houses, too close at times . . . A pleasure to play.

★★★ SALT CREEK GOLF CLUB
PU—Hwy. 46 E. and Salt Creek Rd., Nashville (812)988-7888.
45 miles south of Indianapolis. **Holes:** 18. **Par:** 72/72.
Yards: 6,407/5,001. **Course rating:** 71.2/68.8. **Slope:** 132/122.
Opened: 1992. **Pace of Play rating:** N/A. **Green fee:** $33.
Credit cards: MC, V, DISC. **Reduced fees:** No.
Caddies: No. **Golf carts:** $12 for 18 holes.
Discount golf packages: Yes. **Season:** March-Nov. **High:** May-Aug.
On-site lodging: No. **Rental clubs:** Yes.
Walking policy: Walking at certain times. **Range:** Yes (grass).
To obtain tee times: Call pro shop.
Subscriber comments: Beautiful layout, fun to play . . . Tight rolling course, different . . . Bring extra sleeve of balls . . . Short but tight, some great holes . . . Tricked up; hole No. 6, 476 yard par 4 with creek that forces lay up on tee shot? . . . Front nine in low area . . . Beautifully landscaped course, cut in the hills and trees . . . Gorgeous setting . . . Good layout, treelined, but too short . . . Neat, unique layout . . . New and a lot of potential . . . Attractive wooded holes . . . Faders paradise . . . Slow, bring a lot of balls. Picturesque . . . Back nine is beautiful . . . Back nine worth the trip . . . Going to be super.

SANDY PINES GOLF COURSE★
SP—U.S. 231 and County Rd. 1100 N., De Motte (219)987-3611.
60 miles south of Chicago. **Holes:** 18. **Par:** 72/72.
Yards: 6,500/4,935. **Course rating:** 71.0/71.4. **Slope:** 120/N/A.
Opened: 1974. **Pace of Play rating:** 4:20. **Green fee:** $14/17.
Credit cards: None. **Reduced fees:** Low season, Twilight, Seniors, Juniors.
Caddies: No. **Golf carts:** $9 for 18 holes.
Discount golf packages: No. **Season:** April-Nov. **High:** June-Aug.
On-site lodging: No. **Rental clubs:** No.
Walking policy: Unrestricted walking. **Range:** No.
To obtain tee times: Call one week in advance.

★½ SARAH SHANK GOLF COURSE
PU—2901 South Keystone, Indianapolis (317)784-0631.
Holes: 18. **Par:** 72/72.
Yards: 6,491/5,352. **Course rating:** 68.9/70.8. **Slope:** 106/115.
Opened: 1940. **Pace of Play rating:** 4:00. **Green fee:** $12/13.
Credit cards: MC, V. **Reduced fees:** Weekdays, Low season, Twilight, Seniors, Juniors.
Caddies: No. **Golf carts:** $20 for 18 holes.
Discount golf packages: No. **Season:** Year-round. **High:** March-Sept.
On-site lodging: No. **Rental clubs:** Yes.
Walking policy: Unrestricted walking. **Range:** No.

To obtain tee times: Call seven days in advance.
Subscriber comments: Typical city course . . . Weak greens but fun . . .
Holes too close together . . . A fun course, long holes open . . . Not bad for
an overplayed muny . . . Mature, but not difficult . . . Long front nine,
very dry fairways in summer, price is fair . . . Economical, OK municipal
course.

★★½ SCHERWOOD GOLF COURSE
PU—600 E. Joliet St., Schererville (219)865-2554.
25 miles south of Chicago. **Holes:** 18. **Par:** 72/72.
Yards: 6,710/5,053. **Course rating:** 72.0/67.3. **Slope:** 127/108.
Opened: 1967. **Pace of Play rating:** 4:30. **Green fee:** $16/21.
Credit cards: MC, V, AMEX. **Reduced fees:** Weekdays, Low season.
Caddies: No. **Golf carts:** $10 for 18 holes.
Discount golf packages: Yes. **Season:** April-Dec. **High:** May-Sept.
On-site lodging: No. **Rental clubs:** Yes.
Walking policy: Unrestricted walking. **Range:** Yes (grass).
To obtain tee times: Call in anytime.
Also has 18-hole executive course.
Subscriber comments: Huge greens, nice fairways, wide open . . . Too
many hidden creeks. Not always in good shape. Big play every day. Greens
not consistent . . . They do a very good job considering the amount of play
. . . Poor maintained greens and traps . . . A nice walk in the park.

★★½ SHADY HILLS GOLF COURSE
PU—1520 W. Chapel Pike, Marion (317)668-8256.
50 miles north of Indianapolis. **Holes:** 18. **Par:** 71/72.
Yards: 6,513/5,595. **Course rating:** 71.6/71.6. **Slope:** 123/110.
Opened: 1957. **Pace of Play rating:** N/A. **Green fee:** $12/15.
Credit cards: MC, V. **Reduced fees:** Seniors, Juniors.
Caddies: No. **Golf carts:** $10 for 18 holes.
Discount golf packages: No. **Season:** March-Nov. **High:** June-Aug.
On-site lodging: Yes. **Rental clubs:** Yes.
Walking policy: Unrestricted walking. **Range:** Yes (grass).
To obtain tee times: Call anytime.
Subscriber comments: Worthwhile, enjoyable, busy but it keeps moving
. . . Some greens are ridiculous and unfair, poor tee boxes . . . Average . . .
A lot of variety, good course for short hitter . . . Several challenging holes,
usually crowded . . . Overlooked by many.

★★ SMOCK GOLF COURSE
PU—3910 S. County Line Rd. E., Indianapolis (317)888-0036.
Holes: 18. **Par:** 72/72.
Yards: 7,055/6,230. **Course rating:** 73.7/75.7. **Slope:** 125/127.
Opened: 1976. **Pace of Play rating:** N/A. **Green fee:** $12/13.
Credit cards: MC, V. **Reduced fees:** Twilight, Seniors, Juniors.
Caddies: No. **Golf carts:** $11 for 18 holes.
Discount golf packages: No. **Season:** Year-round. **High:** May-Sept.
On-site lodging: No. **Rental clubs:** Yes.
Walking policy: Unrestricted walking. **Range:** Yes (grass).
To obtain tee times: Call pro shop up to seven days in advance.
Subscriber comments: Interesting long public course . . . Pro is a class act
. . . Good length and bunkers . . . Tougher than it looks . . . Staff
knowledgable . . . Fine layout. Use all clubs in bag . . . Layout condition
varies, very long but open . . . Windy at all times . . . Great shape, tough
par 5s . . . Greatly improved since the city has leased it to private
management.

★½ SOUTH GROVE GOLF COURSE
PU—1800 W. 18th St., Indianapolis (317)327-7350.
Holes: 18. **Par:** 70/74.
Yards: 6,259/5,126. **Course rating:** 69.3/74.5. **Slope:** 108/108.
Opened: 1902. **Pace of Play rating:** 4:00. **Green fee:** $ 8/11.
Credit cards: MC, V, DISC. **Reduced fees:** Twilight, Seniors, Juniors.

Caddies: No. **Golf carts:** $11 for 18 holes.
Discount golf packages: No. **Season:** Year-round. **High:** May-Aug.
On-site lodging: No. **Rental clubs:** Yes.
Walking policy: Unrestricted walking. **Range:** No.
To obtain tee times: Call seven days in advance. Monday at 7 a.m. for upcoming weekend.
Subscriber comments: Typical city course, lots of trees . . . Watered fairways improvement . . . Well maintained year round . . . Needs more bunkers . . . Don't go behind greens or else . . . Best greens in any public course . . . Best municipal course in the city of Indy . . . Tight fairways and small greens . . . Simple, old style, inner city, golf like grandpa played in town.

★★ SOUTH SHORE GOLF CLUB
PU—10601 State Rd. 13, Syracuse (219)457-5711.
Call club for further information.
Subscriber comments: A place to play at the lakes . . . Great greens, good front nine, boring back, OK golf . . . Flat but plays fast . . . Another good lake resort track, All players treated well. Average pace of play . . . Poor practice area . . . Nice trees, mature . . . OK course for lake area.

★★★½ SULTAN'S RUN GOLF COURSE
PU—1490 N. Meridian Rd., Jasper (812)482-1009.
60 miles west of Louisville, KY. **Holes:** 18. **Par:** 72/72.
Yards: 7,060/5,343. **Course rating:** 72.8/68.1. **Slope:** 132/120.
Opened: 1992. **Pace of Play rating:** N/A. **Green fee:** $32/36.
Credit cards: MC, V. **Reduced fees:** Weekdays, Low season, Twilight, Juniors.
Caddies: No. **Golf carts:** Included in Green Fee.
Discount golf packages: Yes. **Season:** Year-round. **High:** April-Oct.
On-site lodging: No. **Rental clubs:** Yes.
Walking policy: Unrestricted walking. **Range:** Yes (grass).
To obtain tee times: Call seven days in advance.
Subscriber comments: A great massive course . . . A beautiful course; great experience . . . Greens need air . . . Great 18th hole . . . A killer, scenic layout . . . When mature, Otter Creek will have to make room at the top . . . Four sets tees, play where you belong . . . Struggling with grass . . . Perhaps most difficult in state . . . Terrific par 3s . . . Nice course . . . Scenic, challenging and worth the trip to Jasper . . . Other than the length of drives to get over a lake or ravine (18th hole particularly) most any golfer would enjoy . . . Nothing like it in southern Indiana. The waterfall behind No. 18 takes your breath away. Each hole is named after a racehorse. Neat idea . . . Challenging layout . . . Best course and value in southern Indiana . . . Super place, great people . . . Yardage markers on front and back of tee boxes to middle of landing areas . . . Spectacular setting, too new to judge condition . . . Quality throughout, no two holes the same. The views are all breathtaking. 18th is classiest finishing hole in Indiana. Go across the street and learn to ride at a world-class horse facility . . . One of the best courses within a 75-mile radius.

★½ SUMMERTREE GOLF CLUB
PU—2323 E. 101st St., Crown Point (219)663-0800.
35 miles southeast of Chicago. **Holes:** 18. **Par:** 71/72.
Yards: 6,586/5,654. **Course rating:** 71.9/72.3. **Slope:** 124/117.
Opened: 1975. **Pace of Play rating:** 4:00. **Green fee:** $ 15/21.
Credit cards: MC, V. **Reduced fees:** Low season, Seniors.
Caddies: No. **Golf carts:** $21 for 18 holes.
Discount golf packages: No. **Season:** Year-round. **High:** April-Oct.
On-site lodging: No. **Rental clubs:** Yes.
Walking policy: Unrestriacted walking. **Range:** Yes (grass).

To obtain tee times: Call one week in advance.
Subscriber comments: Fun course . . . Best condition in northwest Indiana. Clean as houndstooth . . . A good run for the buck . . . Fairways beautiful, sandtraps rough, greens slow, bumpy . . . Rough varies from none to knee deep . . . Potential to be great course if kept in better condition.

SWAN LAKE GOLF CLUB

PU—5203 Plymouth LaPorte Trail, Plymouth (219)936-9798.
30 miles southwest of South Bend. **Green fee:** $10/14.
Credit cards: MC, V. **Reduced fees:** Weekdays, Twilight, Seniors.
Caddies: No. **Golf carts:** $11 for 18 holes.
Discount golf packages: No. **Season:** March-Oct. **High:** April-June.
On-site lodging: Yes. **Rental clubs:** Yes.
Walking policy: Unrestricted walking. **Range:** Yes (grass).
To obtain tee times: Call pro shop.

GREAT VALUE

★★★½ EAST COURSE

Holes: 18. **Par:** 72/72.
Yards: 6,345/5,289. **Course rating:** 69.9/69.4. **Slope:** 120/109.
Opened: 1967. **Pace of Play rating:** 4:15.
Subscriber comments: Good variety on two courses . . . Was better before they turned 18 into 36 . . . Treelined holes . . . No bunkers, no water, but good inexpensive place to practice . . . East is much better than West . . . Better hit it straight, tough greens to chip and putt, fun course . . . East Course: tough, fair; West Course: longer but easier . . . 36 holes of golfing joy.

WEST COURSE★

Holes: 18. **Par:** 72/72.
Yards: 6,507/5,545. **Course rating:** 70.5/71.7. **Slope:** 117/106.
Opened: 1967. **Pace of Play rating:** 4:15.

TAMEKA WOODS GOLF CLUB★

PU—State Rd. 135 and County Rd. 450W, Trafalgar (317)878-4331.
24 miles south of Indianpolis. **Holes:** 18. **Par:** 72/72.
Yards: 6,526/5,341. **Course rating:** 69.1/68.3. **Slope:** 106/105.
Opened: 1991. **Pace of Play rating:** N/A. **Green fee:** $14/16.
Credit cards: , V. **Reduced fees:** Weekdays, Twilight.
Caddies: No. **Golf carts:** $10 for 18 holes.
Discount golf packages: No. **Season:** Year-round. **High:** June-Aug.
On-site lodging: No. **Rental clubs:** Yes.
Walking policy: Unrestricted walking. **Range:** No.
To obtain tee times: Call one week in advance.

★★★ TIMBER RIDGE GOLF CLUB

PU—12507 County Rd. 44, Millersburg (219)642-3252.
Call club for further information.
Subscriber comments: Several good holes; very playable . . . Varied design . . . Two different style nines . . . Interesting island green . . . Bluegrass fairways, nice greens . . . Flat and pretty wide open . . . Best secret in northern Indiana . . . New course; needs age . . . Last three on back will break your heart.

★★ TIPTON MUNICIPAL GOLF COURSE

PU—Golf Course Rd., Tipton (317)675-6627.
Call club for further information.
Subscriber comments: Nines are different as night and day . . . Front is flat, too close, back is a better challenge . . . Very country, small clubhouse, friendly pro, well laid out . . . Awesome practice facilities; greens are superior . . . Plain course, length of backside offers a challenge . . . Fairways not great . . . Extremely long when wind blowing, good shape . . . Likeable, friendly, simple.

★½ TRI COUNTY GOLF CLUB
PU—8170 N. CR 400 W., Middletown (317)533–4107.
Call club for further information.
Subscriber comments: Cheap public golf . . . Greens are like mohair sweater, fairways like a brick . . . Fun course for beginner . . . Mostly flat . . . Wide open long course, 600+ yard par 5, can hit ball anywhere without too much trouble, good pace, good staff . . . No definition.

★ TRI-WAY GOLF CLUB
PU—12939-4A Rd., Plymouth (219)936-9517.
16 miles south of South Bend. **Holes:** 18. **Par:** 71/71.
Yards: 6,175/5,386. **Course rating:** 69.9/68.6. **Slope:** 110/110.
Opened: 1966. **Pace of Play rating:** N/A. **Green fee:** $ 8/10.
Credit cards: None. **Reduced fees:** Weekdays, Low season.
Caddies: No. **Golf carts:** $15 for 18 holes.
Discount golf packages: Yes. **Season:** April-Oct. **High:** June-Aug.
On-site lodging: No. **Rental clubs:** Yes.
Walking policy: Unrestricted walking. **Range:** No.
To obtain tee times: Call pro shop.
Subscriber comments: Decent course, needs work . . . Yardage grossly overstated . . . Conditions could be better, great week-day specials . . . A lot of variety, nice greens good for short hitter, a little slow . . . Good for novices.

★★½ TURKEY CREEK COUNTRY CLUB
SP—6400 Harrison St., Merrillville (219)980-5170.
Call club for further information.
Subscriber comments: Nice course . . . Uses terrain well, sloped greens challenging . . . Offers a chance to use a wide variety of clubs . . . Rolling hills and narrow fairways . . . Improving public course, crowded on weekends . . . Lots of water holes . . . Creek crosses fairway 10 times . . . Greens very slow . . . Seniors' hangout.

★★ TURKEY RUN GOLF COURSE
PU—R.R. 1, Waveland (317)435-2048.
Call club for further information.
Subscriber comments: Beautiful, challenging hilly course in densely wooded region . . . Very playable . . . No tricks, thoughtful layout . . . Most holes unique and memorable . . . Some grassy problems . . . Greens putt like Astroturf . . . Beautiful surroundings.

★★½ VALLE VISTA GOLF CLUB
PU—755 E. Main St., Greenwood (317)888-5313.
10 miles south of Indianapolis. **Holes:** 18. **Par:** 70/74.
Yards: 6,306/5,680. **Course rating:** 70.0/73.1. **Slope:** 117/113.
Opened: 1971. **Pace of Play rating:** 4:20. **Green fee:** $19/25.
Credit cards: All major. **Reduced fees:** Weekdays, Low season.
Caddies: No. **Golf carts:** $10 for 18 holes.
Discount golf packages: Yes. **Season:** Year-round. **High:** May-Sept.
On-site lodging: No. **Rental clubs:** Yes.
Walking policy: Unrestricted walking. **Range:** No.
To obtain tee times: Call one week in advance.
Subscriber comments: Spread around a suburban housing area . . . Very tight, leave driver in bag . . . Too many holes the same look and feel . . . Well taken care of, houses too close to course, O.B. every hole . . . Not overly great or difficult . . . Kind of back and forth . . . All tees and greens elevated . . . Not a course to spray your tee shots, several tough greens . . . Walking encouraged.

★★★ VALLEY VIEW GOLF CLUB
PU—3748 Lawrence Banet Rd., Floyd Knobs (812)923-7291.
5 miles west of Louisville. **Holes:** 18. **Par:** 71/76.
Yards: 6,523/5,488. **Course rating:** 71.0/71.0. **Slope:** 125/122.
Opened: 1962. **Pace of Play rating:** 4:00. **Green fee:** $10/18.

Credit cards: MC, V. **Reduced fees:** Weekdays, Twilight, Seniors.
Caddies: No. **Golf carts:** $10 for 18 holes.
Discount golf packages: No. **Season:** Year-round. **High:** April-Sept.
On-site lodging: No. **Rental clubs:** Yes.
Walking policy: Unrestricted walking. **Range:** No.
To obtain tee times: Call one to two days in advance.
Subscriber comments: Joy to play . . . Very fair to hard . . . You must keep carts on path, then go 90 degrees to your ball, bad! . . . Open . . . Quick greens. Long . . . Best fairways in southern Indiana . . . 18th fairway is a little weird . . . Low places, does not handle rain well . . . Greens have improved . . . Wonderfully kept for a public course.

★★★ VALLEY VIEW GOLF COURSE

SP—6950 W. County Rd. 850 N., Middletown (317)354-2698.
7 miles east of Anderson. **Holes:** 18. **Par:** 72/72.
Yards: 6,421/5,281. **Course rating:** 70.3/69.9. **Slope:** 114/109.
Opened: 1964. **Pace of Play rating:** 4:00. **Green fee:** $13/16.
Credit cards: None. **Reduced fees:** Seniors.
Caddies: No. **Golf carts:** $10 for 18 holes.
Discount golf packages: No. **Season:** March-Nov. **High:** May-Sept.
On-site lodging: No. **Rental clubs:** No.
Walking policy: Unrestricted walking. **Range:** No.
To obtain tee times: Call for weekends and holidays only.
Subscriber comments: Who said there are no hills in east central Indiana? . . . Every hole is different (elevated tees, elevated greens) . . . Take a cart, some water, very enjoyable . . . Very slick greens . . . Small, very fast greens make up for short holes . . . Could be very tough with more sand.

★★★ WABASH VALLEY GOLF CLUB

PU—207 North Dr., Geneva (219)368-7388.
32 miles south of Fort Wayne. **Holes:** 18. **Par:** 71/71.
Yards: 6,375/5,018. **Course rating:** 70.5/69.8. **Slope:** 117/106.
Opened: 1963. **Pace of Play rating:** N/A. **Green fee:** $13/15.
Credit cards: MC, V. **Reduced fees:** No.
Caddies: No. **Golf carts:** $9 for 18 holes.
Discount golf packages: No. **Season:** March-Nov. **High:** June-Aug.
On-site lodging: No. **Rental clubs:** Yes.
Walking policy: Unrestricted walking. **Range:** Yes (grass).
To obtain tee times: Call one week in advance.
Subscriber comments: Beautiful, challenging, exceptional . . . Very inexpensive, new holes are good, local knowledge is a plus . . . Good golf with good prices . . . Not terribly long, but tight and interesting holes . . . New holes simply outstanding, carved from swamps, woods . . . Front nine through marsh . . . Another new course, didn't build tees big enough . . . Beautiful course cut through woods and wetlands, a hidden treasure . . . Hardest public course in area.

(FRUGAL PICK)

★★★ WALNUT CREEK GOLF COURSE

PU—7453 E. 400 S., Marion (317)998-7651.
25 miles south of Fort Wayne. **Holes:** 18. **Par:** 72/72.
Yards: 6,880/5,154. **Course rating:** 72.1/68.5. **Slope:** 121/109.
Opened: 1970. **Pace of Play rating:** 4:00. **Green fee:** $12/16.
Credit cards: MC, V. **Reduced fees:** No.
Caddies: No. **Golf carts:** $10 for 18 holes.
Discount golf packages: Yes. **Season:** April-Dec. **High:** June-Aug.
On-site lodging: No. **Rental clubs:** Yes.
Walking policy: Unrestricted walking. **Range:** No.
To obtain tee times: Call at least one day in advance.
Subscriber comments: One of the nicest public courses around . . . Disappointing conditions . . . Great country course . . . Interesting . . .

Great mix of shots required, well run . . . Many good holes with a couple that don't match rest of golf course . . . Best kept secret in Indiana . . . Excellent course. No alcohol or coolers. Beautiful foliage in autumn. Not a flat putt on the course . . . Very playable course, nice surprise, fast play encountered . . . Friendliest staff north of Ohio River.

★★ WICKER MEMORIAL PARK GOLF COURSE

PU—Indianapolis Blvd. and Ridge Rd., Highland (219)838-9809.
1 mile north of Hammond. **Holes:** 18. **Par:** 72/73.
Yards: 6,515/5,301. **Course rating:** 70.8/69.3. **Slope:** 106/107.
Opened: 1927. **Pace of Play rating:** N/A. **Green fee:** $12/16.
Credit cards: None. **Reduced fees:** Weekdays, Low season, Twilight, Seniors, Juniors.
Caddies: No. **Golf carts:** $11 for 18 holes.
Discount golf packages: Yes. **Season:** Year-round. **High:** May-Sept.
On-site lodging: No. **Rental clubs:** Yes.
Walking policy: Unrestricted walking. **Range:** Yes (grass).
To obtain tee times: Call in advance.
Subscriber comments: Tremendous piece of property . . . Fantastic greens for town course, gets too much play, good layout . . . Wooded, several long 4s . . . Keep the ball out of the trees and course is a piece of cake. Fast greens . . . Course looks easy but its not; hard to get on weekends . . . Calvin Coolidge dedicated this course . . . Long towering oaks . . . Old course, 1920's with large cottonwoods.

★½ WILLIAM SAHM GOLF COURSE

PU—6800 E. 91st. St., Indianapolis (317)842-5076.
Holes: 18. **Par:** 70/70.
Yards: 6,384/5,459. **Course rating:** 69.2/69.2. **Slope:** 105/104.
Opened: 1963. **Pace of Play rating:** 4:30. **Green fee:** $ 13/14.
Credit cards: MC, V. **Reduced fees:** Twilight, Seniors, Juniors.
Caddies: No. **Golf carts:** $10 for 18 holes.
Discount golf packages: No. **Season:** Year-round. **High:** April-Oct.
On-site lodging: No. **Rental clubs:** Yes.
Walking policy: Unrestricted walking. **Range:** Yes (grass).
To obtain tee times: Call seven days in advance.
Subscriber comments: Early season tune-up couarse . . . Very flat, no sand . . . No real problem with hazards . . . No sand, little water . . . Wide open with no water . . . One of Pete Dye's earlier courses, although he probably won't admit it.

★★★ WINCHESTER GOLF CLUB

PU—Simpson Dr., Winchester (317)584-5151.
20 miles east of Muncie. **Holes:** 18. **Par:** 72/74.
Yards: 6,540/5,023. **Course rating:** 70.4/67.6. **Slope:** 115/106.
Opened: 1973. **Pace of Play rating:** 4:00. **Green fee:** $12/16.
Credit cards: None. **Reduced fees:** Weekdays, Low season.
Caddies: No. **Golf carts:** $11 for 18 holes.
Discount golf packages: No. **Season:** Year-round. **High:** April-Oct.
On-site lodging: No. **Rental clubs:** Yes.
Walking policy: Unrestricted walking. **Range:** Yes (grass).
To obtain tee times: Call up to two weeks in advance.
Subscriber comments: Small town gem . . . New back nine needs to mature . . . Best consistency of greens around . . . Some tough holes, need improvements . . . Great pro, glad to see you.

★½ WOODED VIEW GOLF CLUB

PU—2404 Greentree N., Clarksville (812)283-9274.
5 miles north of Louisville, KY. **Holes:** 18. **Par:** 71/73.
Yards: 6,385/5,059. **Course rating:** 70.4/69.6. **Slope:** 125/110.
Opened: 1978. **Pace of Play rating:** N/A. **Green fee:** $ 5/15.
Credit cards: None. **Reduced fees:** Weekdays, Low season, Seniors, Juniors.
Caddies: No. **Golf carts:** $8 for 18 holes.

Discount golf packages: No. **Season:** Year-round. **High:** March-Oct.
On-site lodging: No. **Rental clubs:** Yes.
Walking policy: Unrestricted walking. **Range:** Yes (grass).
To obtain tee times: Call three days in advance.
Subscriber comments: Must be a straight hitter on this aptly named course . . . Wonderfully kept for a public course.

★★★ **ZOLLNER GOLF COURSE AT TRI-STATE UNIVERSITY**
PU—300 W. Park St., Angola (219)665-4269.
30 miles north of Fort Wayne. **Holes:** 18. **Par:** 72/73.
Yards: 6,628/5,259. **Course rating:** 71.1/69.4. **Slope:** 124/117.
Opened: 1971. **Pace of Play rating:** 4:00. **Green fee:** $15/18.
Credit cards: MC, V. **Reduced fees:** Weekdays, Low season, Twilight, Seniors, Juniors.
Caddies: No. **Golf carts:** $11 for 18 holes.
Discount golf packages: Yes. **Season:** March-Dec. **High:** May-Sept.
On-site lodging: No. **Rental clubs:** Yes.
Walking policy: Unrestricted walking. **Range:** Yes (grass).
To obtain tee times: Call one week in advance.
Subscriber comments: Great older course . . . Big greens perfect . . . Rolling, challenging course, good variety of holes . . . Don't keep up as well as it could be . . . Great course for university, some tight holes make the course interesting . . . Hilly and very long, lots of blind shots, po well maintained . . . Short par 5s . . . Scenic, well kept, best feature not a single residence around . . . Lots of big hills . . . Probably past its prime but at $25 no complaints . . . Challenging. Fun to play. Fast greens but true. Excellent pace . . . Well designed . . . Every hole different . . . Too bad the university can't put more $ back into the course . . . Quaintness, fine challenge, oak trees, always memorable.

Notes

KENTUCKY

★★★ BARREN RIVER STATE PARK GOLF COURSE
PU—1149 State Park Rd., Lucas (502)646-4653.
30 miles southeast of Bowling Green. **Holes:** 18. **Par:** 72/72.
Yards: 6,440/4,919. **Course rating:** 69.1/66.6. **Slope:** 118/106.
Opened: 1957. **Pace of Play rating:** 4:20. **Green fee:** $16.
Credit cards: All major. **Reduced fees:** Twilight.
Caddies: No. **Golf carts:** $9 for 18 holes.
Discount golf packages: Yes. **Season:** Year-round. **High:** April-Sept.
On-site lodging: Yes. **Rental clubs:** Yes.
Walking policy: Unrestricted walking. **Range:** Yes.
To obtain tee times: Call anytime.
Subscriber comments: Hills, hills and more hills; beautiful . . . Front nine
excellent for beginners. Beautiful setting . . . Back 9 challenging. Beautiful
view of lake. See deer on course . . . Challenging par 5s . . . Very scenic in
spring and fall; lots of wildlife . . . Medium tough . . . Back nine new but
fun to play . . . Nice layout. Scenic. Courteous staff . . . Tight but fair; one
of the best Kentucky state park courses.

★ BOB-O-LINK GOLF COURSE
PU—1014 Mary Elizabeth, Lawrenceburg (502)839-4029, (800)963-2626.
35 miles west of Lexington. **Holes:** 18. **Par:** 71/71.
Yards: 6,430/4,889. **Course rating:** 69.7/67.5. **Slope:** 109/105.
Opened: 1968. **Pace of Play rating:** 4:00. **Green fee:** $12/15.
Credit cards: MC, V. **Reduced fees:** Weekdays, Low season, Seniors,
Juniors.
Caddies: No. **Golf carts:** $9 for 18 holes.
Discount golf packages: No. **Season:** Year-round. **High:** April-Oct.
On-site lodging: No. **Rental clubs:** Yes.
Walking policy: Walking at certain times. **Range:** Yes (grass).
To obtain tee times: Call.
Subscriber comments: Typical small-town course. Novices can gain
confidence here . . . Fairways rough . . . Plain, good greens . . . Not
exciting, not very well manicured . . . Treated fine by staff . . . Suited for
the bump-and-run player . . . Lots of potential, poor maintenance . . . No-
frills course.

★★½ BOONE LINKS
PU—19 Clubhouse Dr., Florence (606)371-7550.
10 miles south of Cincinnati. **Holes:** 27. **Par:** 70/72/70.
Yards: 5,950/6,634/6,110. **Course rating:** 68.4/72.1/69.2.
Slope: 118/128/122.
Opened: 1980. **Pace of Play rating:** N/A. **Green fee:** $17/18.
Credit cards: MC, V. **Reduced fees:** Seniors, Juniors.
Caddies: No. **Golf carts:** $10 for 18 holes.
Discount golf packages: No. **Season:** Feb.-Dec. **High:** May-Aug.
On-site lodging: No. **Rental clubs:** Yes.
Walking policy: Unrestricted walking. **Range:** No.
To obtain tee times: Call one week in advance for weekdays at 7:30 a.m.
Subscriber comments: Nice public course . . . Nicely conditioned. A few
odd holes. Numerous great holes . . . Championship layout from the back
. . . Fine test from back tees, underrated . . . Course in good shape . . . One
of the 9s plays like a par 3 . . . "Short Nine" perfect for kids . . . Ridgeview
9 very scenic . . . Short, small greens . . . Second best muny in northern
Kentucky.

★★½ BOOTS RANDOLPH GOLF COURSE
PU—Hwy. 68 W., Cadiz (502)924-9076.
80 miles northeast of Nashville. **Holes:** 18. **Par:** 72/73.
Yards: 6,751/5,191. **Course rating:** 72.7/70.2. **Slope:** 131/121.
Opened: 1973. **Pace of Play rating:** 4:30. **Green fee:** $16.
Credit cards: All major. **Reduced fees:** Twilight.
Caddies: No. **Golf carts:** $18 for 18 holes.
Discount golf packages: No. **Season:** Year-round. **High:** May-Oct.
On-site lodging: No. **Rental clubs:** Yes.

Walking policy: Unrestricted walking. **Range:** Yes (grass).
To obtain tee times: Up to one year in advance.
Subscriber comments: Beautiful scenery, very nice course . . . Scenery great, nice staff . . . Stay in the fairway, rough is "rough" . . . Beautiful wooded course, generous fairways, greens lumpy, bumpy . . . Course gets a great deal of play . . . Fair state park course . . . Fun course to play . . . Not as nice as used to be . . . Front nine and back nine are very different . . . Flat but challenging . . . Front nine better than back. Inconsistent conditioning . . . Picturesque . . . Backside boring . . . Best of the state park system courses.

★½ BRIGHT LEAF GOLF RESORT
R—200 Adam, 1742 Danville Rd., Harrodsburg (606)734-4231.
29 miles southwest of Lexington. **Holes:** 18. **Par:** 72/77.
Yards: 6,500/5,400. **Course rating:** 69.8/66.1. **Slope:** 118/109.
Opened: 1966. **Pace of Play rating:** 4:30. **Green fee:** $15/17.
Credit cards: MC, V. **Reduced fees:** Weekdays, Low season, Twilight.
Caddies: No. **Golf carts:** $20 for 18 holes.
Discount golf packages: No. **Season:** March-Oct. **High:** March-Oct.
On-site lodging: Yes. **Rental clubs:** Yes.
Walking policy: Unrestricted walking. **Range:** No.
To obtain tee times: Call one week in advance.
Subscriber comments: Ma and Pa small resort, Nine holes and 18 holes plus nine lighted . . . Crowded on weekends . . . OK but greens way too slow . . . Greens and fairways not well delineated. Several difficult water holes makes course interesting . . . Very easy, anybody can shoot in 70s. Long slow greens . . . Serious golfers don't make the trip. Group fun . . . Fun course . . . Good family place.

★½ CABIN BROOK GOLF CLUB
PU—2260 Lexington Rd., Versailles (606)873-8404.
7 miles west of Lexington. **Holes:** 18. **Par:** 72/72.
Yards: 7,017/5,233. **Course rating:** 72.4/68.3. **Slope:** 117/108.
Opened: 1965. **Pace of Play rating:** 4:00. **Green fee:** $10/12.
Credit cards: None. **Reduced fees:** No.
Caddies: No. **Golf carts:** N/A.
Discount golf packages: No. **Season:** Year-round. **High:** May-Sept.
On-site lodging: No. **Rental clubs:** Yes.
Walking policy: Walking at certain times. **Range:** Yes (grass).
To obtain tee times: Call one week in advance.
Subscriber comments: Good average public course . . . Fairways like bowling lanes . . . Good course, but rough, needs maintenance . . . Good course for a small budget . . . Aesthetically not outstanding . . . Greens always seemed to be sanded or irrigated . . . Very straight . . . Good ego-boosting course. Few obstacles . . . Wide open fairways, some water . . . Not fancy. Good beginner course.

★★ CHARLIE VETTINER GOLF COURSE
PU—10207 Mary Dell Lane, Jeffersontown (502)267-9958.
25 miles southeast of Louisville. **Holes:** 18. **Par:** 72/72.
Yards: 6,914/5,388. **Course rating:** 72.3/70.0. **Slope:** 123/116.
Opened: 1967. **Pace of Play rating:** 4:30. **Green fee:** $7.
Credit cards: None. **Reduced fees:** Twilight, Seniors.
Caddies: No. **Golf carts:** $9 for 18 holes.
Discount golf packages: No. **Season:** Year-round. **High:** April-Sept.
On-site lodging: No. **Rental clubs:** Yes.
Walking policy: Unrestricted walking. **Range:** No.
To obtain tee times: Call two days in advance.
Subscriber comments: The addition of a back nine has made this an outstanding muny . . . Two totally different personalities from front to back . . . Long, very tough public course . . . Needs a ranger on weekends . . . Course could use more care . . . Challenging back nine . . . Nice layout, but never good condition, especially tee areas.

★½ CONNEMARA GOLF LINKS

PU—2327 Lexington Rd., Nicholasville (606)885-4331.
7 miles south of Lexington. **Holes:** 18. **Par:** 71/71.
Yards: 6,533/4,956. **Course rating:** 71.1/69.5. **Slope:** 115/111.
Opened: 1992. **Pace of Play rating:** 4:30. **Green fee:** $12/17.
Credit cards: All major. **Reduced fees:** Weekdays, Low season, Twilight, Seniors, Juniors.
Caddies: No. **Golf carts:** $9 for 18 holes.
Discount golf packages: No. **Season:** Year-round. **High:** April-Sept.
On-site lodging: No. **Rental clubs:** Yes.
Walking policy: Walking at certain times. **Range:** Yes (grass).
To obtain tee times: Call five days in advance. Tee times will be accepted further in advance for long-distance travelers.
Subscriber comments: New course, on the right track . . . Fairly new course, rough around the edges . . . Uphill, downhill, straight design, no charm . . . Relatively new but maturing, most holes well designed . . . Several unique "signature" type holes . . . Interesting layout through old horse farm . . . Fun, very tough, long course, use all your clubs . . . Front nine great, back nine rough . . . 16th a very pretty par 3 . . . Looks pretty from road. That's it . . . Strange layout. Great service and staff. Good family course.

★★★½ CROOKED CREEK GOLF CLUB

SP—781 Crooked Creek Dr., London (606)877-1993.
76 miles south of Lexington. **Holes:** 18. **Par:** 72/72.
Yards: 7,007/5,087. **Course rating:** 73.4/71.3. **Slope:** 134/122.
Opened: 1993. **Pace of Play rating:** 4:15. **Green fee:** $23/28.
Credit cards: MC, V. **Reduced fees:** Weekdays, Low season, Twilight, Juniors.
Caddies: No. **Golf carts:** $10 for 18 holes.
Discount golf packages: No. **Season:** Year-round. **High:** March-Oct.
On-site lodging: No. **Rental clubs:** Yes.
Walking policy: Unrestricted walking. **Range:** Yes (grass).
To obtain tee times: Call 24 hours in advance.
Subscriber comments: Still young, great layout . . . Excellent design with dramatic, scenic layout . . . Best staff in state . . . Good new course, nice variety of holes . . . Will be one of Kentucky's best public . . . Excellent design, very challenging. Rough eats balls for lunch. Some extreme changes in elevation. Very picturesque, nice fairways. Watch out for snakes . . . New Bermuda grass came in great . . . Overall very enjoyable day . . . Only needs maturing to be a great layout . . . Keep the ball in play, think. Good course for chippers . . . You choose the tee box to make it tough . . . From the tips it is a trial . . . Worth the drive from Lexington . . . Must hit fairways or you're doomed . . . Best public-access course in the state.

★★★ DOE VALLEY GOLF CLUB

SP—1 Doe Valley Pkwy, Brandenburg (502)422-3397.
30 miles southwest of Louisville. **Holes:** 18. **Par:** 71/72.
Yards: 6,471/5,519. **Course rating:** 69.8/70.3. **Slope:** 119/118.
Opened: 1972. **Pace of Play rating:** 4:15. **Green fee:** $13/32.
Credit cards: MC, V, AMEX. **Reduced fees:** Twilight, Seniors.
Caddies: No. **Golf carts:** $12 for 18 holes.
Discount golf packages: Yes. **Season:** Year-round. **High:** April-Sept.
On-site lodging: No. **Rental clubs:** Yes.
Walking policy: Walking at certain times. **Range:** No.
To obtain tee times: Call seven days in advance.
Subscriber comments: Located outside of Fort Knox . . . Beautiful surroundings. All placement . . . Beautiful, hilly, trees . . . Challenging layout, course conditions improving . . . Bring one dozen balls. Lots of heavy woods. Fun course . . . Saw four deer . . . Nice course for wildlife and golfers.

EAGLE TRACE GOLF COURSE★

SP—1000 Ramey Ridge Rd., Morehead (606)783-9973.
60 miles west of Lexington. **Holes:** 18. **Par:** 72/72.
Yards: 6,902/5,247. **Course rating:** N/A. **Slope:** N/A.
Opened: 1995. **Pace of Play rating:** 4:00. **Green fee:** $18.
Credit cards: MC, V. **Reduced fees:** No.
Caddies: No. **Golf carts:** $9 for 18 holes.
Discount golf packages: No. **Season:** Year-round. **High:** April-Sept.
On-site lodging: No. **Rental clubs:** No.
Walking policy: Unrestricted walking. **Range:** Yes (grass).
To obtain tee times: Call eight days in advance.

★★½ EAGLE'S NEST COUNTRY CLUB

SP—Hwy. 39 N., Somerset (606)679-7754.
70 miles south of Lexington. **Holes:** 18. **Par:** 71/72.
Yards: 6,404/5,010. **Course rating:** 69.8/67.9. **Slope:** 117/109.
Opened: 1979. **Pace of Play rating:** N/A. **Green fee:** $21.
Credit cards: MC, V. **Reduced fees:** No.
Caddies: No. **Golf carts:** $9 for 18 holes.
Discount golf packages: No. **Season:** Feb.-Dec. **High:** May-Oct.
On-site lodging: No. **Rental clubs:** Yes.
Walking policy: Unrestricted walking. **Range:** Yes (grass).
To obtain tee times: Call in advance. If you live within the county, you
must be a member of the course to play.
Subscriber comments: Challenging, good, tough holes . . . Contrasting
nines . . . Nos. 1 and 10 are difficult par 4s across a gully . . . Nice looking
course, very hilly . . . Laid out very well for terrain it's in . . . Hard back
nine . . . Condition of course varies.

★★★ FRANCES E. MILLER GOLF COURSE

PU—Rte. 6, Box 347 A, Murray (502)762-2238.
50 miles northwest of Paducah. **Holes:** 18. **Par:** 71/71.
Yards: 6,592/5,058. **Course rating:** 71.6/68.9. **Slope:** 125/117.
Opened: 1983. **Pace of Play rating:** 4:00-4:30. **Green fee:** $14.
Credit cards: MC, V. **Reduced fees:** Twilight, Seniors, Juniors.
Caddies: No. **Golf carts:** $8 for 18 holes.
Discount golf packages: No. **Season:** Year-round. **High:** May-Aug.
On-site lodging: No. **Rental clubs:** Yes.
Walking policy: Walking at certain times. **Range:** Yes (grass).
To obtain tee times: Call.
Subscriber comments: One of the best courses in western Kentucky . . .
Excellent fairways and greens; hilly front side, good practice facilities . . .
Mature course . . . Play moves well . . . Very good for learning hazard play
. . . Leave driver in bag except on No. 8 . . . Maintained by Murray State
University . . . In great condition, friendly service . . . Very hilly.
Challenging to keep ball in play. Play is fairly quick . . . Slow greens, too
many blind shots . . . Try it, you'll like it.

★½ GENERAL BURNSIDE STATE PARK GOLF COURSE

PU—P.O. Box 488, Burnside (606)561-4104.
71 miles south of Lexington. **Holes:** 18. **Par:** 71/71.
Yards: 5,905/5,905. **Course rating:** 67.5/71.6. **Slope:** N/A.
Opened: 1958. **Pace of Play rating:** 4:00. **Green fee:** $14.
Credit cards: All major. **Reduced fees:** Twilight, Seniors.
Caddies: No. **Golf carts:** $9 for 18 holes.
Discount golf packages: No. **Season:** Year-round. **High:** April-Sept.
On-site lodging: No. **Rental clubs:** Yes.
Walking policy: Unrestricted walking. **Range:** No.
Subscriber comments: State park, lots of play, needs maintenance . . .
Short par 4s . . . Birdies are plentiful . . . Neglected by state . . . Nice
course, beautiful walk, play can be slow . . . Fun course.

★★★½ GIBSON BAY GOLF COURSE
PU—2000 Gibson Bay Dr., Richmond (606)623-0225.
20 miles south of Lexington. **Holes:** 18. **Par:** 72/72.
Yards: 7,113/5,069. **Course rating:** 74.1/69.1. **Slope:** 128/115.
Opened: 1993. **Pace of Play rating:** 4:30. **Green fee:** $10/14.
Credit cards: MC, V. **Reduced fees:** Weekdays, Twilight, Seniors,
Juniors.
Caddies: No. **Golf carts:** $9 for 18 holes.
Discount golf packages: No. **Season:** Year-round.
On-site lodging: No. **Rental clubs:** Yes.
Walking policy: Unrestricted walking. **Range:** Yes (grass).
To obtain tee times: Call one week in advnace.
Subscriber comments: Challenging and scenic layout in the foothills of
Richmond . . . Tough to walk, lots of hills . . . Fairways were perfect . . .
Outstanding hospitality . . . New, very hilly layout in superb condition . . .
All the potential in the world . . . Plenty of fairway to stay in . . . Good use
of natural terrain . . . Challenging, variety of shots required, top notch . . .
Michael Hurdzan design . . . Real golf enjoyment . . . A little more work
on the rough and it is off the chart . . . Nice job of fitting course to contours
. . . Challenging yet fair, great staff . . . Most par 5s reachable . . . Superb
five sets of tees. All bent grass . . . One of the best public courses in the state
. . . Great layout; however, almost impossible to walk . . . Long and tough
on windy day . . . Best public course in central Kentucky.

★★ HARTLAND MUNICIPAL GOLF COURSE
PU—1031 Wilkinson Trace, Bowling Green (502)843-5559, (800)786-7263.
Holes: 18. **Par:** 71/72.
Yards: 6,512/5,044. **Course rating:** 69.9/68.3. **Slope:** 119/113.
Opened: 1989. **Pace of Play rating:** . **Green fee:** $11.
Credit cards: MC, V, AMEX. **Reduced fees:** Weekdays, Low season,
Twilight, Seniors, Juniors.
Caddies: No. **Golf carts:** $9 for 18 holes.
Discount golf packages: No. **Season:** Year-round. **High:** July-Aug.
On-site lodging: No. **Rental clubs:** Yes.
Walking policy: Walking at certain times. **Range:** No.
To obtain tee times: Call seven days in advance.
Subscriber comments: New, will get better and safer as trees grow. An
easy course . . . Not much trouble, fairways and roughs not well groomed
. . . Water hazards won't hold water . . . Improving with time . . . 18 holes
squeezed into space for 12 holes . . . I thought dry lake beds were only in
the California desert . . . Flat and windy, can play long, excellent greens and
Bermuda fairways . . . Doglegs too easy . . . Condition improving.

★★ IROQUOIS GOLF COURSE
PU—1501 Rundill Rd., Louisville (502)363-9520.
Holes: 18. **Par:** 71/73.
Yards: 6,138/5,004. **Course rating:** 67.3/70.2. **Slope:** 106/112.
Opened: 1947. **Pace of Play rating:** 4:00. **Green fee:** $8/9.
Credit cards: None. **Reduced fees:** Twilight, Seniors, Juniors.
Caddies: No. **Golf carts:** $9 for 18 holes.
Discount golf packages: No. **Season:** Year-round. **High:** April-Nov.
On-site lodging: No. **Rental clubs:** Yes.
Walking policy: Unrestricted walking. **Range:** No.
To obtain tee times: Call two days in advance.
Subscriber comments: Nice hilly course and different stance after every
shot . . . Front nine is tree-lined, back nine is wide open . . . Slow play on
weekends but course condition worth the wait . . . Bermuda fairways make
this a great course . . . Very good public course . . . Tight front nine . . .
Good mixture of holes . . . Tight, walkable . . . Best-kept public course in
Louisville.

★★ JUNIPER HILLS GOLF COURSE
PU—800 Louisville Rd., Frankfort (502)875-8559.
Holes: 18. **Par:** 70/74.
Yards: 6,200/5,904. **Course rating:** 68.7/67.7. **Slope:** 111/106.
Opened: 1956. **Pace of Play rating:** 3:45. **Green fee:** $10.
Credit cards: None. **Reduced fees:** Twilight.
Caddies: No. **Golf carts:** $10 for 18 holes.
Discount golf packages: No. **Season:** Year-round. **High:** April-Oct.
On-site lodging: No. **Rental clubs:** Yes.
Walking policy: Unrestricted walking. **Range:** No.
To obtain tee times: Call seven days in advance.
Subscriber comments: Hilly course with super greens . . . Short, hilly, plain . . . Wooded. Some water . . . Good course for high handicapper . . . Fun course to play . . . Course gets lots of play . . . Tree lines can cause problems . . . Has improved over last year.

★★★★ KEARNEY HILL GOLF LINKS
PU—3403 Kearney Rd., Lexington (606)253-1981.
Holes: 18. **Par:** 72/72.
Yards: 6,987/5,362. **Course rating:** 73.5/70.1. **Slope:** 128/118.
Opened: 1989. **Pace of Play rating:** N/A. **Green fee:** $20.
Credit cards: MC, V. **Reduced fees:** Twilight, Seniors, Juniors.
Caddies: No. **Golf carts:** N/A.
Discount golf packages: No. **Season:** Year-round. **High:** April-Oct.
On-site lodging: No. **Rental clubs:** Yes.
Walking policy: Unrestricted walking. **Range:** Yes (grass).
To obtain tee times: Call up to seven days in advance for threesomes or foursomes.
Ranked 10th in Kentucky by Golf Digest.
Subscriber comments: Great links-style layout, nice muny . . . A cut above . . . Pete Dye and son layout, site of Senior Tour event. Excellent condition . . . Immaculate, not a weed anywhere . . . Nicest condition you'll find. White tees are plenty . . . Wide open fairways, wind major factor . . . Great finishing hole . . . Lots of sidehill lies, deep bunkers, heavy rough . . . What a thrill . . . A true challenge for every caliber of player . . . Love it, wish I could play it every day. Lots of sand and grass bunkers . . . Needs trees . . . Open and windy . . . Difficult fast greens. Good variety and excellent staff . . . Challenging but fun, usually in good shape . . . Easy fairways but large, very different Pete Dye greens . . . Great course. Scottish feel . . . Slow playing with carts on path . . . Soft, nice fairways, great clubhouse, great water shots, best public course in Kentucky.

★★★ KENTUCKY DAM VILLAGE STATE RESORT PARK GOLF COURSE
R—Hwy. 641, Gilbertsville (502)362-8658.
20 miles east of Paducah. **Holes:** 18. **Par:** 72/72.
Yards: 6,704/5,094. **Course rating:** 73.0/70.0. **Slope:** 135/124.
Opened: 1952. **Pace of Play rating:** 4:30-5:00. **Green fee:** $16.
Credit cards: All major. **Reduced fees:** Twilight.
Caddies: No. **Golf carts:** N/A.
Discount golf packages: Yes. **Season:** Year-round. **High:** March-Oct.
On-site lodging: Yes. **Rental clubs:** Yes.
Walking policy: Unrestricted walking. **Range:** Yes (grass).
To obtain tee times: Call pro shop.
Subscriber comments: State park course, mature, tree-lined fairways, difficult uphill par 5 finishing hole . . . Tough course, very natural, attractive, needs maintenance . . . Heavy play, course is demanding . . . New greens are undulating and quick . . . One of the best public courses in the state . . . Flat to rolling hills . . . Average difficulty. Good course. Getting a lot of play . . . . Plush Bermuda fairways, good greens, lots of trees . . . New greens too severe . . . Great recreation area, fishing, outdoors.

★½ LA GRANGE WOODS COUNTRY CLUB

SP—2820 S. Hwy. 53, La Grange (502)222-7927.
25 miles north of Louisville. **Holes:** 18. **Par:** 71/71.
Yards: 6,104/4,577. **Course rating:** 68.9/65.8. **Slope:** 115/106.
Opened: 1970. **Pace of Play rating:** 4:30. **Green fee:** $12/16.
Credit cards: MC, V. **Reduced fees:** Weekdays, Seniors.
Caddies: No. **Golf carts:** N/A.
Discount golf packages: Yes. **Season:** Year-round. **High:** March-Oct.
On-site lodging: No. **Rental clubs:** Yes.
Walking policy: Walking at certain times. **Range:** Yes.
To obtain tee times: Call seven days in advance.
Subscriber comments: Increased to 18, has potential if maintenance
improves . . . Nice local course. Scenic wooded holes. A few weak holes
. . . Not on my list to play again . . . Short, fun; With new fairways
maturing, it will improve . . . Quite easy . . . Friendly service.

★★ LAKESIDE GOLF CLUB

PU—3725 Richmond Rd., Lexington (606)263-5315.
Call club for further information.
Subscriber comments: Very popular city course, not well groomed but a
bargain . . . Always busy, lots of kids, fairways quite narrow, good practice
areas . . . Overplayed, long course that's fun to play . . . Heavy play has
worn this course down . . . Good public course, needs improvements to be
great . . . Not a very challenging course . . . No. 9 more than 600 yards,
use every club here . . . Could be the best course in America for $10.

★★★★ LASSING POINTE GOLF CLUB

PU—2266 Double Eagle Dr., Union (606)384-2266.
12 miles south of Cincinnati. **Holes:** 18. **Par:** 71/71.
Yards: 6,724/5,153. **Course rating:** 72.2/69.5. **Slope:** 132/122.
Opened: 1994. **Pace of Play rating:** N/A. **Green fee:** $17/18.
Credit cards: MC, V. **Reduced fees:** Seniors, Juniors.
Caddies: No. **Golf carts:** $10 for 18 holes.
Discount golf packages: No. **Season:** April-Oct. **High:** May-Aug.
On-site lodging: No. **Rental clubs:** Yes.
Walking policy: Unrestricted walking. **Range:** Yes (grass).
To obtain tee times: Call one week in advance for weekdays.
Ranked 6th in Kentucky by Golf Digest.
Subscriber comments: Wonderful course for first year, great service . . .
Fine new course. Few weak holes, target golf . . . In excellent condition . . .
Great staff, big greens and tees . . . Some real interesting holes . . . Anyone
can play here . . . Tough, challenging, nice greens . . . Tremendous new
course, a joy to play . . . Four-hour round, very courteous staff, excellent
condition . . . Best course in northern Kentucky, public or private.

SUPER VALUE

★★½ LINCOLN HOMESTEAD STATE PARK GOLF COURSE

PU—5079 Lincoln Park Rd., Springfield (606)336-7461.
50 miles northwest of Louisville. **Holes:** 18. **Par:** 71/73.
Yards: 6,359/5,472. **Course rating:** 70.0/71.0. **Slope:** 119/118.
Opened: 1938. **Pace of Play rating:** 3:00. **Green fee:** $16.
Credit cards: All major. **Reduced fees:** Weekdays, Low season, Twilight.
Caddies: No. **Golf carts:** $9 for 18 holes.
Discount golf packages: Yes. **Season:** Year-round. **High:** April-Oct.
On-site lodging: No. **Rental clubs:** Yes.
Walking policy: Walking at certain times. **Range:** No.
To obtain tee times: Call or come in person.
Subscriber comments: Rolling hills, creek, nice greens . . . Hard to
locate, so sparsely played. Three-hour round very possible, narrow
fairways quite hilly . . . Front side harder than back nine . . . Overall not
bad . . . Country course but lots of blind shots . . . Challenging state park
course . . . Several elevated tees. Beautiful views . . . Good course for older
players . . . Scenic . . . Well-hidden gem in middle of Kentucky, one of
best-maintained state courses.

★★ LONG RUN GOLF CLUB

PU—1605 Flatrock Rd., Anchorage (502)245-0702.
Call club for further information.
Subscriber comments: Pretty easy public course . . . Front nine lulls you, back nine goes for the jugular . . . Fun course, nice for average golfer . . . Has some very good holes . . . Back nine several years old . . . One of the hardest back nines I have ever played.

★★★ MARRIOTT'S GRIFFIN GATE RESORT GOLF CLUB

R—1720 Newtown Pike, Lexington (606)254-4101.
Holes: 18. **Par:** 72/72.
Yards: 6,801/4,979. **Course rating:** 73.3/69.3. **Slope:** 132/119.
Opened: 1981. **Pace of Play rating:** 4:00-4:30. **Green fee:** $28/55.
Credit cards: All major. **Reduced fees:** Weekdays, Low season, Twilight.
Caddies: No. **Golf carts:** Included in Green Fee.
Discount golf packages: Yes. **Season:** Year-round. **High:** April-Oct.
On-site lodging: Yes. **Rental clubs:** Yes.
Walking policy: Mandatory cart. **Range:** No.
To obtain tee times: Hotel guests may make reservations up to 60 days in advance. Outside guests up to three days in advance.
Subscriber comments: Over the rolling hills of Kentucky . . . Housing has ruined its looks . . . Good test, well maintained . . . Typical resort course, wide open, designed to move players along . . . Nice facilities, slow play, average greens . . . Challenging . . . Lots of tricks . . . Too many townhouses near fairways . . . Excellent fast greens, challenging sand and water designs, fairways like walking on carpet . . . Holes are very tightly bunched . . . Have to shape the ball, draw shot a lot . . . One of the top 10 in state; staff great . . . Southern hospitality at its finest . . . Quality from start to finish.

MAYWOOD GOLF COURSE★

PU—130 Maywood Ave., Bardstown (502)348-6600.
34 miles south of Louisville. **Holes:** 18. **Par:** 72/72.
Yards: 6,965/4,711. **Course rating:** 72.2/66.5. **Slope:** 121/107.
Opened: 1995. **Pace of Play rating:** 4:00. **Green fee:** $16/18.
Credit cards: MC, V, AMEX. **Reduced fees:** Twilight.
Caddies: No. **Golf carts:** $10 for 18 holes.
Discount golf packages: Yes. **Season:** Year-round. **High:** March-Nov.
On-site lodging: No. **Rental clubs:** Yes.
Walking policy: Unrestricted walking. **Range:** Yes (grass).
To obtain tee times: Call two weeks in advance.

★★½ MY OLD KENTUCKY HOME STATE PARK GOLF CLUB

PU—Hwy. 49, Bardstown (502)349-6542.
30 miles northeast of Louisville. **Holes:** 18. **Par:** 70/71.
Yards: 6,065/5,239. **Course rating:** 69.5/70.2. **Slope:** 119/118.
Opened: 1938. **Pace of Play rating:** 4:30. **Green fee:** $16.
Credit cards: All major. **Reduced fees:** Weekdays.
Caddies: No. **Golf carts:** $9 for 18 holes.
Discount golf packages: No. **Season:** Year-round. **High:** Year-round.
On-site lodging: No. **Rental clubs:** Yes.
Walking policy: Unrestricted walking. **Range:** Yes (grass).
To obtain tee times: Call in prior Tuesday.
Subscriber comments: Old nine contrasts with new nine on state park course . . . Front nine old, plain; back nine new, great . . . Greens like postage stamps . . . New back nine very challenging . . . Nice walking course; pleasant layout, not too long . . . New nine holes very good, reminds me of South Carolina or Georgia . . . Pretty easy public course; the back is better . . . Best back short nine in state, great for older players . . . The bells ringing "My Old Kentucky Home" is special.

★★★ NEVEL MEADE GOLF COURSE
PU—3123 Nevel Meade Dr., Prospect (502)228-9522.
10 miles north of Louisville. **Holes:** 18. **Par:** 72/72.
Yards: 6,956/5,616. **Course rating:** 72.2/70.4. **Slope:** 122/117.
Opened: 1991. **Pace of Play rating:** 4:30. **Green fee:** $15/21.
Credit cards: MC, V. **Reduced fees:** Low season, Twilight, Seniors, Juniors.
Caddies: No. **Golf carts:** $9 for 18 holes.
Discount golf packages: No. **Season:** Year-round. **High:** March–Oct.
On-site lodging: No. **Rental clubs:** Yes.
Walking policy: Unrestricted walking. **Range:** Yes (grass).
To obtain tee times: Call four days in advance for weekdays and Wednesday morning for weekend tee times.
Subscriber comments: Modeled after old Scottish links . . . Interesting links type . . . Very tough . . . Enjoyable, plays a good 300 yards longer . . . Long, full of bunkers . . . Need a road map first time around . . . Good track, no trees . . . I played on a very windy day, not fun . . . Must stay on fairway . . . Totally unlike any course I've played in Kentucky . . . Hard course but very good for average or better player . . . Enough sand to cover St. Louis . . . Very popular. Well kept . . . Great practice green . . . A real treasure for Louisville.

OLD BRIDGE GOLF CLUB★
SP—1 Old Bridge Rd., Danville (606)236-6051, (800)783-7153.
20 miles southwest of Lexington. **Holes:** 18. **Par:** 72/72.
Yards: 6,400/4,600. **Course rating:** 68.0/64.9. **Slope:** 117/104.
Opened: 1990. **Pace of Play rating:** 4:00. **Green fee:** $10/14.
Credit cards: MC, V. **Reduced fees:** Low season.
Caddies: No. **Golf carts:** N/A.
Discount golf packages: Yes. **Season:** Year-round.
On-site lodging: No. **Rental clubs:** Yes.
Walking policy: Unrestricted walking. **Range:** Yes (grass).
To obtain tee times: Call in advance anytime.

★½ PARK MAMMOTH GOLF CLUB
SP—Hwy. U.S. 31W., Park City (502)749-4101.
19 miles east of Bowling Green. **Holes:** 18. **Par:** 70/74.
Yards: 6,073/5,299. **Course rating:** 68.0/72.0. **Slope:** 114/107.
Opened: 1962. **Pace of Play rating:** 4:00. **Green fee:** $10.
Credit cards: MC, V, AMEX. **Reduced fees:** No.
Caddies: No. **Golf carts:** $8 for 18 holes.
Discount golf packages: Yes. **Season:** Year-round. **High:** April–June.
On-site lodging: No. **Rental clubs:** No.
Walking policy: Unrestricted walking. **Range:** No.
To obtain tee times: Call 48 hours in advance.
Subscriber comments: Average course . . . Fairly easy course, wide open . . . In rough shape . . . Great view . . . Great duffer specials . . . Needs cartpaths . . . Has improved . . . Great for beginners.

★★ PAXTON PARK GOLF CLUB
PU—841 Berger Rd., Paducah (502)444-9514.
Call club for further information.
Subscriber comments: Good layout. Tough par 3s . . . Staff extra nice and helpful . . . Holes are too close together . . . Gets a lot of beginner and senior play . . . Not bad; small greens make it challenging . . . Muny with a lot of potential, they're finally spending some money . . . Excellent Bermuda greens . . . One of the lowest green fees in western Kentucky.

★★½ PINE VALLEY COUNTRY CLUB & RESORT
R—805 Pine Valley Dr., Elizabethtown (502)737-8300, (800)844-1904.
35 miles south of Louisville. **Holes:** 18. **Par:** 72/73.
Yards: 6,613/5,357. **Course rating:** 71:3/69.6. **Slope:** 119/114.
Opened: 1968. **Pace of Play rating:** 4:15. **Green fee:** $12/17.
Credit cards: MC, V. **Reduced fees:** Weekdays, Low season, Resort

guests, Twilight, Seniors, Juniors.
Caddies: No. **Golf carts:** $9 for 18 holes.
Discount golf packages: Yes. **Season:** Year-round. **High:** April-Oct.
On-site lodging: Yes. **Rental clubs:** Yes.
Walking policy: Walking at certain times. **Range:** Yes (grass).
To obtain tee times: Call 800 number.
Subscriber comments: A challenge, pretty . . . Near Fort Knox. Nice
scenic layout with a lot of trees . . . Should be better by now . . . Needs
more upkeep . . . Cartpaths are a long way from the fairways . . . Fun track
. . . Had been neglected, getting turned around . . . Know your shot
distance . . . Sentimental favorite.

★★★½ PLAYERS CLUB OF LEXINGTON
SP—4850 Leestown Rd., Lexington (606)255-1011.
Call club for further information.
Subscriber comments: Excellent new course, lots of water, great! . . . A
really fun layout. Good clubhouse . . . New layout, numerous lakes come
into play . . . Great par 3s . . . Excellent bent greens and fairways . . .
Rolling Kentucky course . . . Challenging layout, greens and fairways very
good, no waiting . . . Back side has plenty of water . . . Great club, fun,
wind a factor . . . First few fairways almost duplicate each other . . . All
angles of golf presented here . . . An authentic signature island hole is
treacherous . . . Not a monotonous back and forth course . . . Fun to play
for all abilities . . . Great staff . . . Food and drink very congenial, course
personnel friendly . . . Very imaginative course requiring imaginative shot
selection . . . Best public course in Kentucky. Thinking man's course . . .
Not for the faint-hearted . . . Island green No. 8 is awesome . . . Best new
course in Lexington area.

QUAIL CHASE GOLF CLUB
★★★½ SOUTH/WEST/EAST
PU—7000 Cooper Chapel Rd., Louisville (502)239-2110.
Holes: 27. **Par:** 72/72/72.
Yards: 6,728/6,715/6,493. **Course rating:** 71.7/72.0/70.5.
Slope: 127/133/124.
Opened: 1988. **Pace of Play rating:** 4:45. **Green fee:** $14/17.
Credit cards: MC, V, AMEX. **Reduced fees:** Weekdays, Low season,
Twilight, Seniors, Juniors.
Caddies: No. **Golf carts:** N/A.
Discount golf packages: Yes. **Season:** Year-round. **High:** June-Aug.
On-site lodging: No. **Rental clubs:** Yes.
Walking policy: Unrestricted walking. **Range:** Yes (grass).
To obtain tee times: Call two days in advance. Out-of-town players may
call up to one year in advance.
Subscriber comments: The place to play in Jefferson County . . . All
three nines are well designed . . . Excellent public course, has lots of play
. . . Great condition . . . East toughest . . . 27 holes of great golf in
Louisville . . . Very fair public course in good condition . . . East Course is
wonderful . . . Challenging . . . Fairways looked like greens . . . Three of
the finest and well-groomed nines . . . Probably the best public course in
the area.

★★½ SENECA GOLF COURSE
PU—2300 Seneca Park Rd., Louisville (502)458-9298.
Holes: 18. **Par:** 72/73.
Yards: 7,034/5,469. **Course rating:** 73.7/71.5. **Slope:** 130/122.
Opened: 1935. **Pace of Play rating:** 4:00. **Green fee:** $8/9.
Credit cards: None. **Reduced fees:** Weekdays, Twilight, Seniors, Juniors.
Caddies: No. **Golf carts:** $18 for 18 holes.
Discount golf packages: No. **Season:** Year-round. **High:** April-Sept.
On-site lodging: No. **Rental clubs:** Yes.
Walking policy: Unrestricted walking. **Range:** Yes (grass).
To obtain tee times: Call seven days in advance.

Subscriber comments: Most challenging public course in area . . . Above average muny . . . Best public course in below six hours . . . Hilly with so-so conditions . . . Still the best public course in Louisville . . . Gary Player won his first U.S. tour event here . . . Greens leave a lot to be desired; don't walk . . . Most popular course in town, so expect slow play.

★★½ SHAWNEE GOLF COURSE
PU—460 Northwestern Pkwy., Louisville (502)776-9389.
Holes: 18. **Par:** 70/70.
Yards: 6,072/5,476. **Course rating:** 65.1/68.5. **Slope:** 100/105.
Opened: 1933. **Pace of Play rating:** 4:00. **Green fee:** $8.
Credit cards: None. **Reduced fees:** Twilight.
Caddies: No. **Golf carts:** N/A.
Discount golf packages: No. **Season:** Year-round. **High:** May-Oct.
On-site lodging: No. **Rental clubs:** Yes.
Walking policy: Unrestricted walking. **Range:** Yes (grass).
To obtain tee times: Call two days in advance.
Subscriber comments: Flat and wide . . . Flat and open, few obstacles, beautiful view of Ohio River . . . Nice scenery on the river . . . Good confidence builder . . . Fun to play . . . If your game is down, you can watch the Ohio River traffic.

★½ SOUTHWIND GOLF COURSE
SP—2480 New Boonesboro Rd., Winchester (606)744-0375.
15 miles east of Lexington. **Holes:** 18. **Par:** 71/71.
Yards: 6,265/4,700. **Course rating:** 67.1/70.0. **Slope:** 113/102.
Opened: 1992. **Pace of Play rating:** 4:00. **Green fee:** $11/13.
Credit cards: None. **Reduced fees:** Weekdays, Low season, Twilight, Seniors.
Caddies: No. **Golf carts:** $8 for 18 holes.
Discount golf packages: Yes. **Season:** Feb.-Dec. **High:** May-Sept.
On-site lodging: No. **Rental clubs:** Yes.
Walking policy: Walking at certain times. **Range:** Yes (grass).
To obtain tee times: Call for weekend tee times only.
Subscriber comments: New course, needs work, way too many blind shots . . . Too cramped . . . Too little grass . . . Has potential to be great with right maintenance . . . New and getting better . . . You can lose your ball in the fairway . . . Not real long; rolling hills . . . Hope I live to see this course develop.

★★ TANGLEWOOD GOLF COURSE
PU—245 Tanglewood Dr., Taylorsville (502)477-2468.
25 miles southeast of Louisville. **Holes:** 18. **Par:** 72/72.
Yards: 6,626/5,275. **Course rating:** 70.2/68.8. **Slope:** 121/115.
Opened: 1984. **Pace of Play rating:** N/A. **Green fee:** $10/15.
Credit cards: MC, V. **Reduced fees:** Weekdays, Low season, Resort guests, Twilight, Seniors, Juniors.
Caddies: No. **Golf carts:** $9 for 18 holes.
Discount golf packages: Yes. **Season:** Year-round. **High:** May-Sept.
On-site lodging: Yes. **Rental clubs:** Yes.
Walking policy: Unrestricted walking. **Range:** Yes (grass).
To obtain tee times: Call three days in advance.
Subscriber comments: Big secret, good course, hard to play . . . Does not get its due . . . Very few flat fairways . . . Driver placement a must . . . Weirdest layout I've ever played; no level shots . . . 3½-hour rounds most weekdays . . . Getting better, challenging . . . Improving conditions, fairways a little close to each other . . . Fun to play after you get to know it . . . Hilly, good shape, little water, greens small . . . Hard to find; a nice course but sometimes "the mower breaks" . . . Nice, challenging, moves well, not crowded.

★½ TATES CREEK GOLF COURSE
PU—1400 Gainesway Dr., Lexington (606)272-3428.
Holes: 18. **Par:** 72/73.
Yards: 6,240/5,260. **Course rating:** 69.5/69.3. **Slope:** 120/117.
Opened: 1950. **Pace of Play rating:** 4:00. **Green fee:** $10.
Credit cards: MC, V. **Reduced fees:** Twilight, Seniors, Juniors.
Caddies: No. **Golf carts:** $14 for 18 holes.
Discount golf packages: No. **Season:** Year-round. **High:** April-Oct.
On-site lodging: No. **Rental clubs:** Yes.
Walking policy: Unrestricted walking. **Range:** No.
To obtain tee times: Call seven days in advance.
Subscriber comments: Typical city course . . . Mature city course . . .
Use imagination for yardage . . . Limited access, makes it very tight! Stay
awake, beginners can hit you . . . Friendly staff, back nine best . . . Run of
the mill . . . Stay out of the trees . . . Good public course to walk . . . Older
course. Good for nine after work . . . I like this golf course; very fun.

THE GOLF COURSES AT KENTON COUNTY
PU—3908 Richardson Rd., Independence (606)371-3200.
15 miles south of Cincinnati.
Credit cards: MC, V. **Caddies:** No.
Discount golf packages: No. **Season:** April-Oct. **High:** May-Aug.
On-site lodging: No. **Rental clubs:** Yes. **Range:** Yes (grass).
To obtain tee times: Call or come in 10 days in advance for weekends and
seven days in advance for weekdays.

★★★½ FOX RUN COURSE
Holes: 18. **Par:** 72/72.
Yards: 7,055/4,707. **Course rating:** 74.8/68.1. **Slope:** 143/123.
Opened: 1992. **Pace of Play rating:** 4:40. **Green fee:** $33.
Reduced fees: No. **Golf carts:** Included in Green Fee.
Walking policy: Mandatory cart.
Subscriber comments: Typical Arthur Hills . . . Don't plan on running
ball onto these greens, all carry . . . Proves a good course can be built
anywhere . . . One of the best public courses . . . N0. 18 is too difficult . . .
Overpampered. Six great holes, six so-so holes, six unfair holes . . . Well-
kept fairways and greens . . . Great shape, only one bad hole: No.18 . . .
Beautiful course, interesting layout, fun to play.

★★ THE PIONEER COURSE
Holes: 18. **Par:** 70/71.
Yards: 6,059/5,336. **Course rating:** 67.9/69.5. **Slope:** 114/115.
Opened: 1968. **Pace of Play rating:** 4:15. **Green fee:** $8/15.
Reduced fees: Weekdays, Seniors, Juniors. **Golf carts:** $11 for 18 holes.
Walking policy: Unrestricted walking.
Subscriber comments: Pretty and well maintained . . . Adequate . . .
Hackers' paradise, wide open, friendly staff . . . Front is short, back is
longer and steeper . . . Short course makes good walk . . . A course anyone
can play, anytime.

★★★ THE WILLOWS COURSE
Holes: 18. **Par:** 72/72.
Yards: 6,791/5,669. **Course rating:** 72.5/74.0. **Slope:** 130/129.
Opened: 1976. **Pace of Play rating:** 4:30. **Green fee:** $14/17.
Reduced fees: Seniors, Juniors. **Golf carts:** $10 for 18 holes.
Walking policy: Unrestricted walking.
Subscriber comments: The mid-level course at Kenton. Almost too hilly
to walk in the summer heat . . . Fairly tough, interesting, good greens,
good staff . . . Fast greens, second shot almost always on hillside . . . High
quality golf . . . Better than Fox Run.

★★½ WEISSINGER HILLS GOLF COURSE
PU—2240 Mt. Eden Rd., Shelbyville (502)633-7332.
15 miles east of Louisville. **Holes:** 18. **Par:** 72/73.
Yards: 6,534/5,165. **Course rating:** 70.8/69.0. **Slope:** 118/112.
Opened: N/A. **Pace of Play rating:** N/A. **Green fee:** $12/17.
Credit cards: MC, V. **Reduced fees:** Weekdays, Low season, Twilight,

Juniors.
Caddies: No. **Golf carts:** $9 for 18 holes.
Discount golf packages: Yes. **Season:** Year-round. **High:** April-Sept.
On-site lodging: No. **Rental clubs:** Yes.
Walking policy: Walking at certain times. **Range:** Yes (grass).
To obtain tee times: Call seven days in advance.
Subscriber comments: Rural setting . . . Layout on old dairy farm, unique clubhouse, nice layout, par 5s reachable in two . . . Need to make two par 5s into par 4s . . . Best greens I've played in Kentucky . . . Excellent greens . . . Good across the board . . . Unfortunately, this course has not matured . . . Short par 5s . . . Fun course. Not too hard . . . Very average in all respects . . . Improving all the time . . . Neat looking clubhouse, "old mule barn" . . . Walkable, a comfortable course, nice staff . . . Great place to avoid long weekend rounds.

★★★ **WESTERN HILLS GOLF COURSE**
PU—2160 Russellville Rd., Hopkinsville (502)885-6023.
60 miles north of Nashville. **Holes:** 18. **Par:** 72/72.
Yards: 6,907/3,921. **Course rating:** 73.8/64.0. **Slope:** 134/109.
Opened: 1985. **Pace of Play rating:** 4:00. **Green fee:** $11/13.
Credit cards: MC, V. **Reduced fees:** Weekdays, Seniors, Juniors.
Caddies: No. **Golf carts:** N/A.
Discount golf packages: No. **Season:** Year-round. **High:** May-Sept.
On-site lodging: No. **Rental clubs:** No.
Walking policy: Walking at certain times. **Range:** Yes (grass).
To obtain tee times: Call up to seven days in advance.
Subscriber comments: A good test for every level of golf . . . Played from the championship tees, it's the longest public course in Kentucky . . . Ladies tee boxes are suited for the typical ladies game . . . Greens are always in fabulous condition . . . Well maintained, spacious fairways, large greens . . . Very challenging. Lots of water hazards. Very well kept. Long course . . . Can be PGA Tour long . . . Holes for all types of players, long or short hitters . . . Good golf for public course. Good greens . . . Diamond in the rough. Great layout for one and all . . . Best course layout for women in the U.S.

★★½ **WOODSON BEND RESORT**
R—14 Woodson Bend, Bronston (606)561-5316.
60 miles south of Lexington. **Holes:** 18. **Par:** 72/75.
Yards: 6,189/5,155. **Course rating:** 69.2/72.0. **Slope:** 117/113.
Opened: 1973. **Pace of Play rating:** 4:30. **Green fee:** $18/23.
Credit cards: MC, V. **Reduced fees:** Low season, Juniors.
Caddies: No. **Golf carts:** Included in Green Fee.
Discount golf packages: Yes. **Season:** Feb.-Dec. **High:** May-Sept.
On-site lodging: Yes. **Rental clubs:** Yes.
Walking policy: Mandatory cart. **Range:** Yes (grass).
To obtain tee times: Call one week in advance.
Subscriber comments: Short resort course . . . Back nine exceptionally scenic . . . Fairways were a bit ragged . . . Very narrow fairways on back . . . Common to see deer romping in the fairways.

MAINE

★★★ AROOSTOOK VALLEY COUNTRY CLUB
SP—Russell Rd., Fort Fairfield (207)476-8083.
15 miles northeast of Presque Isle. **Holes:** 18. **Par:** 72/72.
Yards: 6,304/5,393. **Course rating:** 71.5/71.5. **Slope:** 117/108.
Opened: 1929. **Pace of Play rating:** 4:00. **Green fee:** $22/22.
Credit cards: MC, V. **Reduced fees:** Low season.
Caddies: No. **Golf carts:** $20 for 18 holes.
Discount golf packages: No. **Season:** May-Oct. **High:** July-Aug.
On-site lodging: No. **Rental clubs:** Yes.
Walking policy: Unrestricted walking. **Range:** Yes (grass).
To obtain tee times: Call two days in advance.
Subscriber comments: Course and clubhouse in Canada. Pro shop in
USA . . . Very scenic . . . Great layout . . . Requires player to place the ball
correctly or the next shot can be very difficult . . . Great views . . . You can
knock the ball out of the country.

★★½ BANGOR MUNICIPAL GOLF COURSE
PU—278 Webster Ave., Bangor (207)941-0232.
Holes: 18. **Par:** 71/71.
Yards: 6,345/5,173. **Course rating:** 67.9/69.1. **Slope:** 112/111.
Opened: 1964. **Pace of Play rating:** 4:00. **Green fee:** $16/17.
Credit cards: None. **Reduced fees:** Weekdays, Twilight.
Caddies: No. **Golf carts:** N/A.
Discount golf packages: No. **Season:** April-Nov. **High:** June-Aug.
On-site lodging: No. **Rental clubs:** Yes.
Walking policy: Unrestricted walking. **Range:** Yes (grass).
To obtain tee times: Call up to one week in advance on the nine-hole
course. No tee times taken on the 18-hole course.
Subscriber comments: Good track . . . Wide open, super-large greens
great for higher handicappers . . . Course conditions good . . . Excellent
municipal course, difficult from back tees, otherwise you can score . . .
Could be a really great course . . . Short, develops wedge game . . . Ego
builder, looks tough, plays easy . . . Always enjoy this course, not great but
good.

★½ BAR HARBOR GOLF CLUB
SP—Rt. 3 Trenton (207)667-7505.
Call club for further information.
Subscriber comments: Great location and layout . . . Needs a lot of work
. . . Interesting and pretty . . . Does not look that tough, but is real difficult
. . . Long and narrow, good greens . . . Tricky holes . . . Tremendous
potential on this ocean-side layout . . . Great scenery, but the course is
poorly maintained.

★★ BETHEL INN AND COUNTRY CLUB
R—Broad St., Bethel (207)824-6276, (800)654-0125.
70 miles northwest of Portland. **Holes:** 18. **Par:** 72/72.
Yards: 6,663/5,280. **Course rating:** 72.3/71.4. **Slope:** 133/129.
Opened: 1915. **Pace of Play rating:** 4:00. **Green fee:** $26/33.
Credit cards: All major. **Reduced fees:** Weekdays, Low season, Resort
guests, Twilight.
Caddies: No. **Golf carts:** $24 for 18 holes.
Discount golf packages: Yes. **Season:** May-Oct. **High:** July-Aug.
On-site lodging: Yes. **Rental clubs:** Yes.
Walking policy: Unrestricted walking. **Range:** Yes (grass).
To obtain tee times: 48 hours in advance.
Subscriber comments: Good course for everyone's game, you will use all
clubs . . . The new holes are beautiful . . . Tough par 3s, new holes are the
best . . . Fun vacation course. If you stay in condo on course, beware of golf
balls . . . Beautiful views, some outstanding holes . . . Old and new nines
completely different . . . Staff friendly . . . Course redesigned, needs
maturing . . . Great blend of old with new . . . Has really developed well.

★★★ BIDDEFORD SACO GOLF CLUB
SP—101 Old Orchard Rd., Saco (207)282-5883.
13 miles south of Portland. **Holes:** 18. **Par:** 71/72.
Yards: 6,192/5,053. **Course rating:** 69.6/69.2. **Slope:** 123/110.
Opened: 1921. **Pace of Play rating:** 4:30. **Green fee:** $25/25.
Credit cards: MC, V. **Reduced fees:** Twilight.
Caddies: No. **Golf carts:** $20 for 18 holes.
Discount golf packages: No. **Season:** April-Nov. **High:** June-Aug.
On-site lodging: No. **Rental clubs:** Yes.
Walking policy: Unrestricted walking. **Range:** Yes (grass).
To obtain tee times: Call three days in advance.
Subscriber comments: Front nine Donald Ross, back nine newer, more
modern . . . Good course for average golfers . . . Excellent course and
facility . . . Front nine is wide open and nondescript, back nine is tight.
Reminds me of playing in South Carolina . . . Two tests of golf with
different green sizes and layouts . . . Staff real nice . . . Back nine requires a
shotmaker . . . A fun experience, well worth it, staff excellent.

★★★ BRUNSWICK GOLF CLUB
PU—River Rd., Brunswick. (207)725-8224.
Call club for further information.
Subscriber comments: Delightful, pleasant and interesting . . . Very
good condition with some good golf holes . . . Large, open clubhouse and
exterior deck overlooking challenging No. 9 green . . . Well groomed . . .
Back nine a lovely piece of Wayne Stiles work . . . All players can enjoy it
. . . Three water holes . . . A real sleeper . . . Course is well kept. I will
return! . . . Course is tight with lots of pines . . . Easy walking, favors
longer hitter . . . Staff is very helpful and attentive to your needs.

★★½ CAPE ARUNDEL GOLF CLUB
SP—Old River Rd., Kennebunkport. (207)967-3494.
20 miles south of Portland. **Holes:** 18. **Par:** 69/70.
Yards: 5,869/5,134. **Course rating:** 67.0/68.6. **Slope:** 117/106.
Opened: 1901. **Pace of Play rating:** 4:00. **Green fee:** $30/30.
Credit cards: None. **Reduced fees:** No.
Caddies: Yes. **Golf carts:** $20 for 18 holes.
Discount golf packages: No. **Season:** April-Oct. **High:** July-Sept.
On-site lodging: No. **Rental clubs:** Yes.
Walking policy: Unrestricted walking. **Range:** No.
To obtain tee times: Call one day in advance.
Subscriber comments: A gem . . . Scottish links style, small greens, very
difficult . . . Very picturesque; cliffs and rocks . . . Very hospitable . . .
Good for all golfers . . . Scenic course with some good holes . . . Pot
bunkers . . . Can be delayed by fog . . . Pretty layout, good condition . . .
"Hello, George Bush" . . . Old New England fun.

★★ DUTCH ELM GOLF CLUB
PU—R.R. No.4 Brimstone Rd., Arundel (207)282-9850.
20 miles south of Portland. **Holes:** 18. **Par:** 72/73.
Yards: 6,230/5,384. **Course rating:** 68.8/70.1. **Slope:** 119/115.
Opened: 1965. **Pace of Play rating:** 4:00. **Green fee:** $20/25.
Credit cards: MC, V. **Reduced fees:** Weekdays, Low season, Resort
guests, Twilight, Seniors.
Caddies: No. **Golf carts:** $0 for 18 holes.
Discount golf packages: Yes. **Season:** April-Nov. **High:** July-Aug.
On-site lodging: No. **Rental clubs:** Yes.
Walking policy: Unrestricted walking. **Range:** Yes (grass).
To obtain tee times: Call.
Subscriber comments: Consecutive par 3s twice, three consecutive par 5s!
. . . Easy course, some holes boring but some on back nine are challenging
. . . Three par 5s in a row, unusual . . . Staff very courteous.

MAINE

★★ FAIRLAWN GOLF & COUNTRY CLUB

SP—R.R. 4, Auburn (207)998-4277.
Call club for further information.
Subscriber comments: Open, always have a shot . . . Long wide open, big greens, flat . . . Enjoyable course for all levels of play . . . Lots of fun par 4s . . . A real pretty course in fall.

★★½ GORHAM GOLF CLUB

SP—134 McClellan Rd., Gorham (207)839-3490.
Call club for further information.
Subscriber comments: Tremendous layout; rolling hills, trees . . . Could be a real gem but suffers from poor conditioning . . . Very fair and challenging, rewarded for good shots, punished for the bad ones . . . Great finishing holes . . . Small greens . . . Good for average player . . . Outstanding treatment by staff.

★★★½ KEBO VALLEY GOLF COURSE

PU—Eagle Lake Rd., Bar Harbor (207)288-3000.
42 miles southeast of Bangor. **Holes:** 18. **Par:** 70/72.
Yards: 6,112/5,440. **Course rating:** 69.0/68.0. **Slope:** 129/125.
Opened: 1888. **Pace of Play rating:** 4:00–4:30. **Green fee:** $20/34.
Credit cards: MC, V. **Reduced fees:** Low season.
Caddies: No. **Golf carts:** $14 for 18 holes.
Discount golf packages: No. **Season:** April-Nov. **High:** July-Aug.
On-site lodging: No. **Rental clubs:** Yes.
Walking policy: Unrestricted walking. **Range:** No.
To obtain tee times: Call two days in advance.
Subscriber comments: Laid out in 1888, a challenge then and now . . . Links-type course, greens roll true, spectacular scenery . . . Great old traditional course . . . Hilly, some tough holes . . . Very well kept . . . Nice layout . . . Great experience . . . One of the best in Maine . . . I liked the clubhouse and staff . . . Well designed amidst northeast beauty . . . Very demanding . . . Look forward to playing here every year . . . Every hole is uniquely challenging . . . Wonderful coastline scenery . . . Beautiful fall foliage.

★★★ KENNEBEC HEIGHTS GOLF CLUB

PU—Green Meadow Dr., Farmingdale (207)623-9831.
Call club for further information.
Subscriber comments: New back nine three years old; demands you stay in play on beautiful fairway that is soft and well groomed . . . Very scenic, woodsy with good mix of par 3s, 4s, and 5s . . . Front easy and open . . . Exciting new back nine . . . Two different nines, requires adjustment, back nine super . . . Challenging course.

★½ MINGO SPRINGS GOLF COURSE

SP—Proctor Rd. & Rte. 4, Rangeley (207)864-5021.
120 miles north of Portland. **Holes:** 18. **Par:** 70/70.
Yards: 5,923/5,334. **Course rating:** 66.3/67.4. **Slope:** 109/110.
Opened: 1925. **Pace of Play rating:** . **Green fee:** $23/23.
Credit cards: None. **Reduced fees:** .
Caddies: No. **Golf carts:** N/A.
Discount golf packages: No. **Season:** May-Oct. **High:** July-Sept.
On-site lodging: No. **Rental clubs:** Yes.
Walking policy: Unrestricted walking. **Range:** Yes (grass).
To obtain tee times: No tee times taken.
Subscriber comments: Real family course . . . Staff made us feel very welcome . . . Front nine, accurate short shots a must . . . Very natural feel, wind and elements make course more difficult than appears . . . Views of mountains . . . Gorgeous greens, not huge, yet not tiny, making for a lot of bump-and-run shots . . . Beautiful views of Rangeley Lake.

★★★ NATANIS GOLF CLUB
PU—Webber Pond Rd., Vassalboro (207)622-3561.
Call club for further information.
Subscriber comments: Outstanding course; three nine-hole layouts with good conditions . . . The new nine is a "5" . . . Well operated . . . New holes are nicer than original 18 holes . . . Good solid public layout . . . Perfect late fall course, fabulous greens . . . 27 holes, all different . . . Pleasant and relaxing place to play.

★★★ PENOBSCOT VALLEY COUNTRY CLUB
SP—366 Main St., Orono (207)866-2423.
5 miles south of Bangor. **Holes:** 18. **Par:** 72/74.
Yards: 6,450/5,856. **Course rating:** 70.3/73.2. **Slope:** 123/126.
Opened: 1923. **Pace of Play rating:** 4:00. **Green fee:** $45/45.
Credit cards: MC, V. **Reduced fees:** .
Caddies: No. **Golf carts:** $26 for 18 holes.
Discount golf packages: No. **Season:** April-Oct. **High:** June-Aug.
On-site lodging: No. **Rental clubs:** Yes.
Walking policy: Unrestricted walking. **Range:** Yes (grass).
To obtain tee times: Call seven days in advance.
Subscriber comments: Donald Ross with lush greens . . . Service very good . . . Wide open, conditions good all year . . . Open, small, sloped greens are the soul of the course . . . Local knowledge course . . . Great treatment, good shape . . . It doesn't get any better than this . . . The course has majestic scenery and is well manicured . . . A player's club, fast tiny greens, require good irons.

★★ POLAND SPRING COUNTRY CLUB
R—Rte. 26, Poland Spring (207)998-6002.
20 miles northwest of Portland. **Holes:** 18. **Par:** 71/74.
Yards: 6,200/5,393. **Course rating:** 68.2/71.6. **Slope:** 119/117.
Opened: 1896. **Pace of Play rating:** 4:00. **Green fee:** $18.
Credit cards: All major. **Reduced fees:** Resort guests.
Caddies: Yes. **Golf carts:** $18 for 18 holes.
Discount golf packages: Yes. **Season:** May-Nov. **High:** June-Sept.
On-site lodging: Yes. **Rental clubs:** Yes.
Walking policy: Unrestricted walking. **Range:** Yes (grass).
To obtain tee times: Call up to one year in advance.
Subscriber comments: Not too demanding. Wide open, few obstacles . . . Nice views from some tees . . . Very scenic . . . Staff good, great views, challenging greens . . . Beautiful country setting . . . A birdie and bogey course . . . Variety of holes . . . Hilly, requires golf cart.

★½ PRESQUE ISLE COUNTRY CLUB
SP—35 Parkhurst Siding Rd., Presque Isle (207)764-0430.
Holes: 18. **Par:** 72/73.
Yards: 6,794/5,708. **Course rating:** 71.0/72.4. **Slope:** 118/119.
Opened: 1958. **Pace of Play rating:** N/A. **Green fee:** $18.
Credit cards: None. **Reduced fees:** Low season.
Caddies: No. **Golf carts:** $18 for 18 holes.
Discount golf packages: Yes. **Season:** May-Oct. **High:** June-Aug.
On-site lodging: No. **Rental clubs:** Yes.
Walking policy: Unrestricted walking. **Range:** Yes (grass).
Subscriber comments: Enjoyed it . . . Staff helpful and courteous.

★½ PROSPECT HILL GOLF COURSE
SP—694 S. Main St., Auburn (207)782-9220.
5 miles east of Lewiston. **Holes:** 18. **Par:** 71/73.
Yards: 5,846/5,227. **Course rating:** 66.9/68.7. **Slope:** 111/119.
Opened: 1957. **Pace of Play rating:** 4:00. **Green fee:** $15.
Credit cards: MC, V. **Reduced fees:** Twilight.
Caddies: No. **Golf carts:** $18 for 18 holes.
Discount golf packages: Yes. **Season:** April-Nov. **High:** April-Nov.
On-site lodging: No. **Rental clubs:** No.

Walking policy: Unrestricted walking. **Range:** No.
To obtain tee times: First come, first served.
Subscriber comments: Short but very challenging, very pleasant . . . Fun for high handicap golfer . . . The two nines play very differently . . . Some interesting holes . . . Two different nines, one old and one new . . . Friendly staff.

★★½ RIVERSIDE MUNICIPAL GOLF COURSE

PU—1158 Riverside St., Portland (207)797-3524.
Holes: 18. **Par:** 72/72.
Yards: 6,450/5,640. **Course rating:** 69.5/70.7. **Slope:** 115/112.
Opened: 1935. **Pace of Play rating:** 4:30. **Green fee:** $15/18.
Credit cards: MC, V. **Reduced fees:** Seniors, Juniors.
Caddies: No. **Golf carts:** $18 for 18 holes.
Discount golf packages: No. **Season:** April-Nov. **High:** July-Aug.
On-site lodging: No. **Rental clubs:** Yes.
Walking policy: Unrestricted walking. **Range:** Yes (grass).
To obtain tee times: Call Wednesday prior to weekend of play.
Subscriber comments: A good public course, site of Maine Open . . . Wide open, long, easy . . . Interesting and challenging . . . Front nine short and easy, back is difficult . . . Excellent municipal course, busy on weekends . . . Have rangers to speed play . . . Some lovely holes, especially par 3s . . . Only a couple of tough holes . . . Excellent design and very challenging shotmaker's course.

★★½ ROCKLAND GOLF CLUB

SP—606 Old County Rd., Rockland (207)594-9322.
45 miles east of Augusta. **Holes:** 18. **Par:** 70/73.
Yards: 6,121/5,583. **Course rating:** 68.6/71.8. **Slope:** 114/119.
Opened: 1932. **Pace of Play rating:** 4:00. **Green fee:** $20/25.
Credit cards: MC, V. **Reduced fees:** Twilight.
Caddies: No. **Golf carts:** $10 for 18 holes.
Discount golf packages: No. **Season:** April-Oct. **High:** June-Sept.
On-site lodging: No. **Rental clubs:** Yes.
Walking policy: Unrestricted walking. **Range:** No.
To obtain tee times: Call two days in advance.
Subscriber comments: Requires ball placement on several holes . . . Great course, good condition . . . Beautiful ocean scenery . . . Open course with good greens . . . Ninth, 10th and 11th are all par 3s . . . Basic golf, slicer's delight . . . Beautiful, well taken care of course . . . Best greens in Maine . . . Great scenery, great price.

★★★½ SABLE OAKS GOLF CLUB

PU—505 Country Club Dr., South Portland (207)775-6257.
Holes: 18. **Par:** 70/72.
Yards: 6,359/4,786. **Course rating:** 71.8/0. **Slope:** 138/121.
Opened: 1989. **Pace of Play rating:** 4:30. **Green fee:** $23/29.
Credit cards: MC, V. **Reduced fees:** Twilight.
Caddies: No. **Golf carts:** $22 for 18 holes.
Discount golf packages: No. **Season:** April-Dec. **High:** April-Sept.
On-site lodging: No. **Rental clubs:** Yes.
Walking policy: Unrestricted walking. **Range:** No.
Subscriber comments: Long; well-groomed fairways . . . Large clubhouse with well-stocked pro shop and staff to attend your needs . . . Course is demanding of good shotmaking off the tee and second shot to greens that are fast . . . Long walk without cart . . . Nice setting in town . . . Great course, one of the best on the list . . . Long and narrow but fair, best for control players . . . Beautiful condition . . . Great shape, good challenge, enjoyable to play . . . Tight, tough, target golf . . . High handicapper will struggle . . . Some tough carries, but interesting and in

good condition . . . Rolling hills; good condition; greens excellent . . .
Difficult doglegs and par 5s, some long 4s . . . Rock ledges are beautiful
. . . Requires careful course management . . . Good players only, bring all
your clubs . . . Great condition but too many blind shots . . . You need to
think.

★★★½ SAMOSET RESORT GOLF CLUB

R—220 Warrenton St., Rockport (207)594-1431, (800)341-1650.
80 miles northeast of Portland. **Holes:** 18. **Par:** 70/71.
Yards: 6,417/5,360. **Course rating:** 69.3/69.1. **Slope:** 125/117.
Opened: 1978. **Pace of Play rating:** 4:00–4:30. **Green fee:** $35/60.
Credit cards: All major. **Reduced fees:** Low season, Resort guests.
Caddies: No. **Golf carts:** $14 for 18 holes.
Discount golf packages: Yes. **Season:** April-Nov. **High:** June-Sept.
On-site lodging: Yes. **Rental clubs:** Yes.
Walking policy: Walking at certain times. **Range:** Yes (grass).
To obtain tee times: Call well in advance.
Ranked 26th in America's 75 Best Resort Courses by Golf Digest. Ranked
2nd in Maine by Golf Digest.
Subscriber comments: Excellent resort course in a beautiful location . . .
Maine's best, great condition, once a year treat . . . Great greens, great
views, carts on paths only . . . Relatively flat, walkable, terrific views of
ocean . . . New holes open, should be more challenging . . . Could be the
Pebble Beach of the East . . . Great staff . . . Very good condition . . . Very
difficult with wind off Atlantic . . . A class operation . . . Picturesque . . . A
real gem right on the ocean, some great holes . . . Some very difficult holes,
ocean winds tricky . . . If you come to Maine, you must play here.

★★★★ SUGARLOAF GOLF CLUB

R—RR No.1, P.O. Box 5000, Carrabassett Valley (207)237-2000x6806,
(800)843-5623.
100 miles north of Portland. **Holes:** 18. **Par:** 72/72.
Yards: 6,451/5,376. **Course rating:** 70.8/73.7. **Slope:** 137/136.
Opened: 1986. **Pace of Play rating:** 4:30. **Green fee:** $54.
Credit cards: MC, V, AMEX. **Reduced fees:** Low season, Resort guests,
Twilight, Juniors.
Caddies: No. **Golf carts:** $14 for 18 holes.
Discount golf packages: Yes. **Season:** May-Oct. **High:** Aug-Sept.
On-site lodging: Yes. **Rental clubs:** Yes.
Walking policy: Unrestricted walking. **Range:** Yes (grass).
To obtain tee times: Call anytime two weeks in advance.
Ranked 63rd in America's 75 Best Resort Courses by Golf Digest. Ranked
1st in Maine by Golf Digest.
Subscriber comments: Absolutely the best, pro quality . . . Must be
accurate . . . Conditions great all year, service terrific . . . Unparalleled
scenery . . . Beautiful mountain course, very challenging R. T. Jones Jr.
course with some outstanding holes . . . Need more rough between
fairways and woods . . . Beautiful setting with tight white birch-lined
fairways . . . What a track . . . Wonderful elevations . . . Incredible scenery
. . . Great course which plays longer than it seems . . . Everything you ever
wanted . . . Most beautiful in autumn . . . The back nine is breathtaking
. . . Astounding mountain course. Double doglegs. Unforgettable . . .
Very short season, a bit out-of-the-way but worth it . . . Beautiful birches,
rivers.

★★½ VA JO WA GOLF COURSE

R—142A Walker Rd., Island Falls (207)463-2128.
85 miles northeast of Bangor. **Holes:** 18. **Par:** 72/72.
Yards: 6,223/5,065. **Course rating:** 70.4/69.6. **Slope:** 121/115.
Opened: 1964. **Pace of Play rating:** 3:30–4:00. **Green fee:** $20/20.
Credit cards: MC, V, DISC. **Reduced fees:** Resort guests, Twilight.
Caddies: No. **Golf carts:** N/A

(FRUGAL PICK)

Discount golf packages: Yes. **Season:** May-Oct. **High:** July-Sept.
On-site lodging: Yes. **Rental clubs:** Yes.
Walking policy: Unrestricted walking. **Range:** Yes (grass).
To obtain tee times: Call 24 hours in advance.
Subscriber comments: Very scenic . . . Hard to find.

★★★ VAL HALLA GOLF COURSE

PU—1 Val Halla Rd., Cumberland (207)829-2225.
10 miles north of Portland. **Holes:** 18. **Par:** 72/72.
Yards: 6,574/5,437. **Course rating:** 71.1/70.4. **Slope:** 126/116.
Opened: 1965. **Pace of Play rating:** 4:00. **Green fee:** $17/22.
Credit cards: MC, V. **Reduced fees:** Weekdays, Seniors, Juniors.
Caddies: No. **Golf carts:** N/A.
Discount golf packages: Yes. **Season:** April-Oct. **High:** June-Sept.
On-site lodging: No. **Rental clubs:** Yes.
Walking policy: Unrestricted walking. **Range:** Yes.
To obtain tee times: Call one week in advance.
Subscriber comments: Shot my career round there, must be great . . .
Won't kill high handicapper, but good challenge for better golfers . . . Nice
staff, course is long and well cared for . . . Wide open, some tough par 4s
. . . A few blind holes, must ring a bell . . . Friendly staff; interesting golf,
not overly difficult . . . Up and coming.

★★★★ WATERVILLE COUNTRY CLUB

SP—Country Club Rd., Oakland (207)465-9861.
8 miles west of Waterville. **Holes:** 18. **Par:** 70/73.
Yards: 6,412/5,466. **Course rating:** 69.6/71.4. **Slope:** 124/121.
Opened: 1916. **Pace of Play rating:** 4:00. **Green fee:** $38.
Credit cards: None. **Reduced fees:** No.
Caddies: No. **Golf carts:** $20 for 18 holes.
Discount golf packages: No. **Season:** April-Nov. **High:** May-Sept.
On-site lodging: No. **Rental clubs:** No.
Walking policy: Unrestricted walking. **Range:** Yes (grass).
To obtain tee times: Call five days in advance.
Subscriber comments: Championship layout, nice condition . . . Good
overall challenge with tight layout . . . The very best . . . Maintenance is
great and staff is great . . . Course conditions were outstanding, even
during drought . . . Challenging yet very playable . . . Value is
unbelievable, compares with best private courses in the state . . . Well-
marked with impeccable greens . . . Nice layout, in good shape. Look
forward to playing again.

GREAT VALUE

★★ WILLOWDALE GOLF CLUB

PU—52 Willowdale Rd., Scarborough (207)883-9351.
9 miles south of Portland. **Holes:** 18. **Par:** 70/70.
Yards: 5,980/5,344. **Course rating:** 68.7/73.7. **Slope:** 110/112.
Opened: 1924. **Pace of Play rating:** 4:30. **Green fee:** $20.
Credit cards: MC, V. **Reduced fees:** Twilight.
Caddies: No. **Golf carts:** $10 for 18 holes.
Discount golf packages: No. **Season:** April-Oct. **High:** July-Aug.
On-site lodging: No. **Rental clubs:** Yes.
Walking policy: Unrestricted walking. **Range:** No.
To obtain tee times: Call Wednesday for following weekend.
Subscriber comments: Very enjoyable, very nice people, heavy play in
summer . . . Back nine much better layout than front nine . . . Easy
walking . . . Well conditioned . . . Buggy, abuts a marsh . . . Flat and
straight, few challenges . . . Wide open, good greens . . . Course being
improved.

★★½ THE BAY CLUB

R—9122 Libertytown Rd., Berlin (800)229-2582, (800)229-2582.
7 miles east of Ocean City. **Holes:** 18. **Par:** 72/72.
Yards: 6,958/5,609. **Course rating:** 73.1/71.3. **Slope:** 126/118.
Opened: 1989. **Pace of Play rating:** 5:00. **Green fee:** $20/45.
Credit cards: MC, V, AMEX. **Reduced fees:** Weekdays, Low season,
Resort guests, Twilight.
Caddies: No. **Golf carts:** Included in Green Fee.
Discount golf packages: Yes. **Season:** Year-round. **High:** April–Oct.
On-site lodging: No. **Rental clubs:** Yes.
Walking policy: Mandatory cart. **Range:** Yes (grass).
To obtain tee times: Call up to one year in advance.
Subscriber comments: Difficult and tight, many risk/reward decisions,
14th too long for island green . . . Nos. 9 and 18 great par 5s . . . Good
ocean resort course . . . Lots of woods and water . . . Nice layout. great for
average golfer, several challenging holes . . . Good people, fair greens, good
water holes, excellent finishing hole . . . Flat and generally uninteresting
. . . Flat property, greens small, slow . . . Challenging par 3s, good variety
of holes.

BAY HILLS GOLF CLUB★

SP—545 Bay Hills Dr., Arnold (410)974-0669.
30 miles south of Baltimore. **Holes:** 18. **Par:** 70/70.
Yards: 6,423/5,029. **Course rating:** 70.8/69.2. **Slope:** 118/121.
Opened: 1969. **Pace of Play rating:** 4:15. **Green fee:** $26/32.
Credit cards: None. **Reduced fees:** Twilight.
Caddies: No. **Golf carts:** Included in Green Fee.
Discount golf packages: No. **Season:** Year-round. **High:** April–Oct.
On-site lodging: No. **Rental clubs:** Yes.
Walking policy: Mandatory cart. **Range:** No.
To obtain tee times: Call up to three days in advance.

★★★ THE BEACH CLUB GOLF LINKS

SP—9715 Deer Park Rd., Berlin (410)641-4653, (800)435-9223.
7 miles west of Ocean City. **Holes:** 18. **Par:** 72/72.
Yards: 7,020/5,167. **Course rating:** 73.0/69.0. **Slope:** 128/117.
Opened: 1991. **Pace of Play rating:** N/A. **Green fee:** $25/45.
Credit cards: All major. **Reduced fees:** Low season, Twilight.
Caddies: No. **Golf carts:** Included in Green Fee.
Discount golf packages: Yes. **Season:** Year-round. **High:** April–Oct.
On-site lodging: No. **Rental clubs:** Yes.
Walking policy: Mandatory cart. **Range:** Yes (grass).
To obtain tee times: Call anytime. Confirm with credit card.
Subscriber comments: Some good holes, very narrow, must be straight
. . . Middle of road, not too difficult . . . Pleasant experiences, will continue
to play again and again . . . Pretty course. Congenial staff . . . Great greens.
Course is coming into its own . . . Not too easy/not too difficult . . . A
beautiful course in its infancy, potential gem on the shore . . . Good use of
woods and water. Demands a variety of shots . . . Nice layout, long rounds
in summer.

★★½ BEAVER CREEK COUNTRY CLUB

SP—9535 Mapleville Rd., Hagerstown (301)733-5152.
60 miles west of Baltimore. **Holes:** 18. **Par:** 72/73.
Yards: 6,878/5,636. **Course rating:** 71.6/71.4. **Slope:** 120/124.
Opened: 1956. **Pace of Play rating:** 4:00. **Green fee:** $9/21.
Credit cards: None. **Reduced fees:** Weekdays, Low season, Twilight,
Seniors, Juniors.
Caddies: No. **Golf carts:** $10 for 18 holes.
Discount golf packages: No. **Season:** Jan–Dec. **High:** May–Oct.
On-site lodging: No. **Rental clubs:** Yes.
Walking policy: Walking at certain times. **Range:** Yes (grass).
To obtain tee times: Call one week in advance.

Subscriber comments: Tough from back tees, lots of trees . . . Mature course opened in 50's, has some tight holes, excellent greens . . . Up-and-down course, good layout . . . Nice course, good value . . . New pro fall '94, service has dramatically improved.

★★★½ BLACK ROCK GOLF COURSE
PU—20025 Mt. Aetna Rd., Hagerstown (301)791-3040.
70 miles west of Baltimore. **Holes:** 18. **Par:** 72/74.
Yards: 6,646/5,179. **Course rating:** 70.7/64.7. **Slope:** 124/112.
Opened: 1989. **Pace of Play rating:** 4:15. **Green fee:** $11/20.
Credit cards: MC, V. **Reduced fees:** Twilight, Seniors, Juniors.
Caddies: No. **Golf carts:** $10 for 18 holes.
Discount golf packages: Yes. **Season:** Year-round. **High:** May-Sept.
On-site lodging: No. **Rental clubs:** Yes.
Walking policy: Unrestricted walking. **Range:** Yes (grass).
To obtain tee times: Call seven days in advance for weekday tee times. Call Monday prior to weekend at 7:30 a.m.
Subscriber comments: Pretty good layout, good condition, friendly people . . . Great course, nice facilities and personnel, maintained well, a bear to walk . . . Mountain course with picture postcard views. I would love to play it again . . . Best kept secret in Maryland . . . President Clinton shot 80 . . . Relatively new public course. Short but interesting . . . Staff is excellent, great short course, excellent holes . . . Good elevation changes, good views, tricky 13th green.

★½ BRANTWOOD GOLF CLUB
PU—1190 Augustine Herman Hwy., Elkton (410)398-8849.
Call club for further information.
Subscriber comments: Flat course, not very challenging . . . Continues to improve, still needs work . . . Fairly flat but challenging . . . Course condition fair. Staff courteous, very knowledgeable . . . Short and fun. Doesn't try to be what it's not.

★★★ BRETON BAY GOLF AND COUNTRY CLUB
SP—Rte. 3, P.O. Box 25K, Leonardtown (301)475-2300.
Holes: 18. **Par:** 72/73.
Yards: 6,933/5,457. **Course rating:** 73.0/70.0. **Slope:** 126/117.
Opened: 1974. **Pace of Play rating:** 4:00. **Green fee:** $20.
Credit cards: None. **Reduced fees:** Juniors.
Caddies: No. **Golf carts:** $32 for 18 holes.
Discount golf packages: No. **Season:** March-Dec. **High:** May-Aug.
On-site lodging: No. **Rental clubs:** Yes.
Walking policy: Unrestricted walking. **Range:** Yes (grass).
To obtain tee times: Call after Thursday for the weekends.
Subscriber comments: Varied, open to tight, rural, excellent value . . . Beautiful view of Potomac River, two different nines, unique . . . Fun course. Each hole gives you a different look . . . Nice pool . . . No. 1 very scenic.

CAMBRIDGE COUNTRY CLUB★
SP—Horns Point Rd., Cambridge (410)228-4808.
40 miles north of Salisbury. **Holes:** 18. **Par:** 72/73.
Yards: 6,387/5,416. **Course rating:** 69.3/71.0. **Slope:** 113/118.
Opened: 1925. **Pace of Play rating:** 4:00. **Green fee:** $35.
Credit cards: MC, V. **Reduced fees:** Resort guests.
Caddies: No. **Golf carts:** N/A.
Discount golf packages: Yes. **Season:** Year-round. **High:** May-Oct.
On-site lodging: No. **Rental clubs:** Yes.
Walking policy: Unrestricted walking. **Range:** Yes (grass).
To obtain tee times: Only members and guests of members can play on the weekends. No tee time required for weekdays.

★★ CLUSTERED SPIRES GOLF COURSE

PU—8415 Gas House Pike, Frederick (301)694-6249.
45 miles west of Baltimore. **Holes:** 18. **Par:** 72/72.
Yards: 6,769/5,230. **Course rating:** 70.5/70.0. **Slope:** 115/124.
Opened: 1991. **Pace of Play rating:** N/A. **Green fee:** $14/22.
Credit cards: MC, V. **Reduced fees:** Weekdays, Twilight, Seniors, Juniors.
Caddies: No. **Golf carts:** $9 for 18 holes.
Discount golf packages: No. **Season:** Year-round. **High:** April-Oct.
On-site lodging: No. **Rental clubs:** Yes.
Walking policy: Unrestricted walking. **Range:** Yes (grass).
To obtain tee times: Call up to five days in advance.
Subscriber comments: Good for all levels of golfers, big fairways . . .
Fun course, cordial staff . . . Good for a relatively new course . . . Fun,
open layout from whites, much more challenging from blue tees. Still
young, should improve as it ages . . . Needs time to acquire personality . . .
Nice people, nice track.

★★½ DIAMOND RIDGE GOLF COURSE

PU—2309 Ridge Rd., Woodlawn (410)944-6607.
10 miles west of Baltimore. **Holes:** 18. **Par:** 70/72.
Yards: 6,550/5,833. **Course rating:** 71.0/73.2. **Slope:** 120/123.
Opened: 1968. **Pace of Play rating:** 4:30. **Green fee:** $15/17.
Credit cards: None. **Reduced fees:** Twilight, Seniors, Juniors.
Caddies: No. **Golf carts:** $18 for 18 holes.
Discount golf packages: No. **Season:** Year-round. **High:** April-Oct.
On-site lodging: No. **Rental clubs:** Yes.
Walking policy: Unrestricted walking. **Range:** Yes (grass).
To obtain tee times: Call anytime.
Subscriber comments: Hilly course, tough on windy days . . . Rolling
hills and woods, very nice challenge . . . Rolling muny. Easy walk. Dry in
summer . . . Well kept with some terrific par 4s . . . Very nice course, good
price, very crowded . . . Straightforward layout, little water.

★★★½ EAGLE'S LANDING GOLF CLUB

PU—12367 Eagle's Nest Rd., Berlin (410)213-7277.
3 miles south of Ocean City. **Holes:** 18. **Par:** 72/72.
Yards: 7,003/4,896. **Course rating:** 74.3/69.3. **Slope:** 126/115.
Opened: 1991. **Pace of Play rating:** 4:00. **Green fee:** $16/23.
Credit cards: MC, V, AMEX. **Reduced fees:** Weekdays, Low season, Twilight.
Caddies: No. **Golf carts:** $12 for 18 holes.
Discount golf packages: Yes. **Season:** Year-round. **High:** April-Oct.
On-site lodging: No. **Rental clubs:** Yes.
Walking policy: N/A. **Range:** No.
To obtain tee times: Call within 90 days.
Subscriber comments: Overplayed but good challenge . . . Beautiful
layout, Bermuda fairways, requires precise shots off tee . . . Ball-eating
course . . . 17th and 18th are awesome . . . Phenomenal course . . . Very
interesting layout . . . Gorgeous views, condition varies, walking allowed!
. . . On a scale of 1-5, it's an 8! . . . No weak holes, pace of play very good,
beautiful sights . . . Excellent new course, maturing gracefully . . . Best in
Ocean City . . . Target golf in preserved wetlands . . . Pars on Nos. 17 and
18 are great scores . . . My favorite beach course . . . Better than Pinehurst
. . . Beautiful view of the bay.

★½ EISENHOWER GOLF COURSE

PU—1576 General Hwy., Crownsville (410)222-7922.
27 miles south of Baltimore. **Holes:** 18. **Par:** 71/71.
Yards: 6,693/4,853. **Course rating:** 71.3/66.9. **Slope:** 122/96.
Opened: 1970. **Pace of Play rating:** 4:30. **Green fee:** $15.
Credit cards: None. **Reduced fees:** Twilight, Seniors, Juniors.
Caddies: No. **Golf carts:** $22 for 18 holes.
Discount golf packages: No. **Season:** Year-round. **High:** May-Oct.

On-site lodging: No. **Rental clubs:** Yes.
Walking policy: Unrestricted walking. **Range:** Yes.
To obtain tee times: Call seven days in advance.
Subscriber comments: An average muny course . . . Great layout, never know what the condition will be . . . Pretty ragged . . . Shotmaker's course, very demanding . . . Course is a nice layout and could be beautiful . . . Requires very good iron play . . . Some water. Fun course.

★★★ ENTERPRISE GOLF COURSE
PU—2802 Enterprise Rd., Mitchellville (301)249-2040.
2 miles east of Washington D.C. **Holes:** 18. **Par:** 72/72.
Yards: 6,586/5,157. **Course rating:** 71.7/69.6. **Slope:** 128/114.
Opened: 1976. **Pace of Play rating:** 4:30. **Green fee:** $11/22.
Credit cards: MC, V. **Reduced fees:** Weekdays, Low season, Twilight, Seniors, Juniors.
Caddies: No. **Golf carts:** $21 for 18 holes.
Discount golf packages: No. **Season:** Year-round. **High:** March-Oct.
On-site lodging: No. **Rental clubs:** Yes.
Walking policy: Walking at certain times. **Range:** Yes.
To obtain tee times: First come, first served.
Subscriber comments: Joy to play, always in top shape, easy to walk . . . My favorite Maryland public course, always in great condition . . . Good mix of holes . . . Too many blind shots . . . Good pro shop and cafe, great course . . . Very busy, sometimes tough to get a tee time . . . Good layout, offering a variety of shots.

★½ FALLS ROAD GOLF CLUB
PU—10800 Falls Rd., Potomac (301)299-5156.
20 miles southeast of Washington, D.C. **Holes:** 18. **Par:** 71/75.
Yards: 6,257/5,476. **Course rating:** 67.7/59.3. **Slope:** 120/111.
Opened: 1955. **Pace of Play rating:** 4:30. **Green fee:** $15/24.
Credit cards: None. **Reduced fees:** Seniors, Juniors.
Caddies: No. **Golf carts:** $20 for 18 holes.
Discount golf packages: No. **Season:** Year-round. **High:** April-Nov.
On-site lodging: No. **Rental clubs:** Yes.
Walking policy: Unrestricted walking. **Range:** Yes.
To obtain tee times: Call one week in advance for weekends only.
Subscriber comments: A good beginner's course . . . Pleasant course. Back nine is best . . . Great course for husband and wife . . . Pleasant old public course . . . Back nine has more imagination.

★½ FOREST PARK GOLF CLUB
PU—2900 Hillsdale Rd., Baltimore (410)448-4653.
Holes: 18. **Par:** 71/71.
Yards: 6,127/4,824. **Course rating:** 68.2/66.0. **Slope:** 116/100.
Opened: N/A. **Pace of Play rating:** N/A. **Green fee:** $10.
Credit cards: None. **Reduced fees:** Weekdays, Twilight, Seniors, Juniors.
Caddies: No. **Golf carts:** N/A.
Discount golf packages: No. **Season:** Year-round. **High:** April-Oct.
On-site lodging: No. **Rental clubs:** Yes.
Walking policy: Unrestricted walking. **Range:** No.
To obtain tee times: Call pro shop.
Subscriber comments: Made a hole-in-one on No. 13 . . . Good old course for everyone . . . Wide fairways, no water or gimmicky holes . . . Very good course, challenging and fun all year . . . Best deal for the money . . . Urban golf . . . Short with postage-stamp greens . . . Best kept secret in Baltimore.

★★½ GLENN DALE COUNTRY CLUB
SP—11501 Old Prospect Hill Rd., Glenn Dale (301)464-0904.
15 miles northeast of Washington, D.C. **Holes:** 18. **Par:** 70/70.
Yards: 6,282/4,809. **Course rating:** 70.0/67.2. **Slope:** 115/107.
Opened: 1955. **Pace of Play rating:** 4:00. **Green fee:** $22/27.
Credit cards: MC, V. **Reduced fees:** Low season, Twilight, Seniors, Juniors.

Caddies: No. **Golf carts:** $20 for 18 holes.
Discount golf packages: No. **Season:** Year-round. **High:** April–Oct.
On-site lodging: No. **Rental clubs:** Yes.
Walking policy: Walking at certain times. **Range:** Yes.
To obtain tee times: Call one day in advance.
Subscriber comments: Relatively short, emphasis on chipping and putting, very challenging . . . Lots of doglegs . . . Good county course, looks like a private club all year . . . Water, woods, well kept, heavy play . . . Some good holes, greens good.

★★★½ THE GOLF CLUB AT WISP

R—Marsh Hill Rd., McHenry (301)387-4911.
90 miles southeast of Pittsburgh, Pa. **Holes:** 18. **Par:** 72/72.
Yards: 7,122/5,542. **Course rating:** 73.0/72.0. **Slope:** 137/128.
Opened: 1973. **Pace of Play rating:** 4:15. **Green fee:** $40/48.
Credit cards: All major. **Reduced fees:** Low season, Resort guests, Twilight.
Caddies: No. **Golf carts:** Included in Green Fee.
Discount golf packages: Yes. **Season:** April–Oct. **High:** July–Sept.
On-site lodging: Yes. **Rental clubs:** Yes.
Walking policy: Walking at certain times. **Range:** Yes.
To obtain tee times: Call.
Subscriber comments: Alpine golf . . . Very challenging, narrow fairways . . . Fun all the way . . . Beautiful side on the mountain course, great views . . . Wonderful view, people very accomodating . . . Fast greens, mountain course by ski slope.

★★★ HARBOURTOWNE GOLF RESORT & COUNTRY CLUB

R—Rt. 33 at Martingham Dr., St. Michaels (410)745-5183, (800)446-9066.
75 miles southeast of Washington, D.C. **Holes:** 18. **Par:** 70/71.
Yards: 6,320/5,036. **Course rating:** 69.5/68.5. **Slope:** 120/113.
Opened: 1971. **Pace of Play rating:** 4:00–4:30. **Green fee:** $38.
Credit cards: All major. **Reduced fees:** Low season, Resort guests.
Caddies: No. **Golf carts:** $12 for 18 holes.
Discount golf packages: Yes. **Season:** Year-round. **High:** April–Oct.
On-site lodging: Yes. **Rental clubs:** Yes.
Walking policy: Mandatory cart. **Range:** Yes (grass).
To obtain tee times: Call.
Subscriber comments: Good Pete Dye course, good condition, tight, fun . . . Good mixture of open and wooded, tight fairways . . . Ho-hum front nine, back nine prettier and more challenging . . . Hole Nos. 10 through 15 difficult . . . Very good course, beautiful scenery.

★★★★ HOG NECK GOLF COURSE

PU—10142 Old Cordova Rd., Easton (410)822-6079.
50 miles east of Baltimore. **Holes:** 18. **Par:** 72/72.
Yards: 7,000/5,500. **Course rating:** 73.8/71.1. **Slope:** 125/118.
Opened: 1976. **Pace of Play rating:** 4:20. **Green fee:** $28.
Credit cards: MC, V. **Reduced fees:** Twilight, Juniors.
Caddies: No. **Golf carts:** $11 for 18 holes.
Discount golf packages: No. **Season:** Feb–Dec. **High:** April–Oct.
On-site lodging: No. **Rental clubs:** Yes.
Walking policy: Unrestricted walking. **Range:** Yes.
To obtain tee times: Call on Saturday for upcoming week.
Ranked in First 25 of America's 75 Best Public Golf Courses by Golf Digest. Ranked 10th in Maryland by Golf Digest.
Also has a nine-hole executive course.
Subscriber comments: Requires every shot in bag, beautiful course, tons of fun to play . . . Excellent course, great contrast between front and back nines . . . Long and narrow on back, open with sand and water on front . . . Front side is like an ocean course, back side in the woods . . . Every hole a sight to behold . . . Distance is measured in meters not yards . . . Challenging layout, good staff but no 19th hole . . . World-class public course . . . Great course, great layout. Get rid of metric system, though . . . Good test for all abilities. No clubhouse a drawback.

★½ LAYTONSVILLE GOLF COURSE

PU—7130 Dorsey Rd., Laytonsville (301)948-5288.
18 miles north of Washington D.C. **Holes:** 18. **Par:** 70/73.
Yards: 6,311/5,439. **Course rating:** 69.8/71.4. **Slope:** 117/113.
Opened: 1973. **Pace of Play rating:** N/A. **Green fee:** $18/23.
Credit cards: None. **Reduced fees:** Seniors, Juniors.
Caddies: No. **Golf carts:** N/A.
Discount golf packages: No. **Season:** Year-round. **High:** April-Sept.
On-site lodging: No. **Rental clubs:** Yes.
Walking policy: Unrestricted walking. **Range:** Yes (grass).
To obtain tee times: Call on Monday at 7 a.m. for weekends and holidays
only.
Subscriber comments: Good test from back tees, large greens, good
condition, fun . . . Short course, not much trouble . . . Not always in good
shape . . . A fun course, not crowded and not difficult, seniors love it.

★½ MAPLE RUN GOLF CLUB

PU—13610-A Moser Rd., Thurmont (301)271-7870.
15 miles north of Frederick. **Holes:** 18. **Par:** 72/72.
Yards: 6,553/4,822. **Course rating:** N/A. **Slope:** N/A.
Opened: 1992. **Pace of Play rating:** 4:15. **Green fee:** $15/19.
Credit cards: MC, V. **Reduced fees:** Weekdays, Low season, Twilight,
Seniors.
Caddies: No. **Golf carts:** $9 for 18 holes.
Discount golf packages: Yes. **Season:** Year-round. **High:** April-Oct.
On-site lodging: No. **Rental clubs:** Yes.
Walking policy: Unrestricted walking. **Range:** Yes.
To obtain tee times: Call pro shop.
Subscriber comments: Great new course, diverse . . . Nice front nine, the
back is different . . . Gimmicky course . . . Narrow 90-degree doglegs . . .
Strange back nine.

★½ MARLBOROUGH COUNTRY CLUB

SP—4750 John Rodgers Blvd., Upper Marlboro (301)952-1350.
20 miles east of Washington, D.C. **Holes:** 18. **Par:** 71/71.
Yards: 6,119/5,130. **Course rating:** 69.5/69.5. **Slope:** 127/120.
Opened: 1974. **Pace of Play rating:** 4:15. **Green fee:** $22/27.
Credit cards: MC, V, AMEX. **Reduced fees:** Weekdays, Low season,
Twilight.
Caddies: No. **Golf carts:** $11 for 18 holes.
Discount golf packages: Yes. **Season:** Year-round. **High:** April-Oct.
On-site lodging: No. **Rental clubs:** Yes.
Walking policy: Walking at certain times. **Range:** Yes.
To obtain tee times: Call one week in advance.
Subscriber comments: Very tight, lack of space . . . Greens need
improvement . . . Short but interesting and challenging . . . Doglegs and
some elevated greens, woods and water come into play on a majority of the
holes.

★★★½ MOUNT PLEASANT GOLF CLUB

PU—6001 Hillen Rd., Baltimore (410)254-5100.
Holes: 18. **Par:** 71/73.
Yards: 6,757/5,489. **Course rating:** 72.0/71.0. **Slope:** 121/120.
Opened: 1933. **Pace of Play rating:** N/A. **Green fee:** $11/12.

Credit cards: None. **Reduced fees:** Weekdays, Twilight, Seniors, Juniors.
Caddies: No. **Golf carts:** $9 for 18 holes.
Discount golf packages: No. **Season:** Year-round. **High:** June-Aug.
On-site lodging: No. **Rental clubs:** Yes.
Walking policy: Unrestricted walking. **Range:** No.
To obtain tee times: Lottery times for weekends. Two weeks in advance
for weekdays.
Subscriber comments: Home of the old Eastern Open . . . Best
Baltimore city course . . . Course and staff are great . . . Very difficult, not
a course to build confidence . . . Open fairways, large greens, few facilities,

enjoyable round . . . Inner-city beauty, well kept, course with character . . . Good course, low cost, very busy . . . Practice those long irons! . . . Can't imagine better golf in the middle of a city . . . Classic old design, great bargain but crowded and a bit shabby overall.

★★ NASSAWANGO COUNTRY CLUB

SP—3940 Nassawango Rd., Snow Hill (410)632-3144.
18 miles southeast of Salisbury. **Holes:** 18. **Par:** 72/73.
Yards: 6,644/5,760. **Course rating:** 70.2/72.1. **Slope:** 125/125.
Opened: 1970. **Pace of Play rating:** 4:00–4:15. **Green fee:** $21.
Credit cards: None. **Reduced fees:** Low season.
Caddies: No. **Golf carts:** $11 for 18 holes.
Discount golf packages: Yes. **Season:** Year-round. **High:** May-Oct.
On-site lodging: No. **Rental clubs:** Yes.
Walking policy: Mandatory cart. **Range:** No.
To obtain tee times: Call.
Subscriber comments: Nice course, wooded . . . Tight course with fast greens . . . Great value . . . Good honest golf . . . Long and narrow . . . OK golf, too few really good holes.

★★ NEEDWOOD GOLF COURSE

PU—6724 Needwood Rd., Derwood (301)948-1075.
22 miles south of Washington, D.C. **Holes:** 18. **Par:** 70/72.
Yards: 6,254/5,112. **Course rating:** 69.1/69.2. **Slope:** 113/105.
Opened: 1969. **Pace of Play rating:** N/A. **Green fee:** $18/23.
Credit cards: MC, V. **Reduced fees:** Seniors, Juniors.
Caddies: No. **Golf carts:** $22 for 18 holes.
Discount golf packages: No. **Season:** Year-round. **High:** May-Sept.
On-site lodging: No. **Rental clubs:** Yes.
Walking policy: Unrestricted walking. **Range:** Yes.
To obtain tee times: Weekday, first come, first served; weekend, reservations optional.
Also have a nine-hole, par-29 executive course.
Subscriber comments: Lake hole No. 18 is a test . . . Some good holes, remodeled clubhouse is nice . . . A forgiving course with tough finish . . . Hard to walk, very hilly . . . Short, fun course . . . Kept in fair condition, service and pace are good.

★★½ NORTHWEST PARK GOLF COURSE

PU—15701 Layhill Rd., Wheaton (301)598-6100.
15 miles south of Washington, D.C. **Holes:** 18. **Par:** 72/74.
Yards: 7,185/6,325. **Course rating:** 74.0/74.5. **Slope:** 122/126.
Opened: 1964. **Pace of Play rating:** 4:30. **Green fee:** $18/19.
Credit cards: None. **Reduced fees:** Seniors, Juniors.
Caddies: No. **Golf carts:** $11 for 18 holes.
Discount golf packages: No. **Season:** Year-round. **High:** June-Aug.
On-site lodging: No. **Rental clubs:** Yes.
Walking policy: Unrestricted walking. **Range:** Yes.
To obtain tee times: Call up to six days in advance for weekdays, Monday a.m. for upcoming weekend.
Also has a par-34, nine-hole course.
Subscriber comments: Wide open course, you can let it fly safely. Also has a nine-hole executive course . . . Long and wide open, just blast away . . . Very, very long, don't walk if faint of heart . . . Long, very open, needs work, good test for all levels of play . . . With a little attention this could be a very good course . . . Great price, course consistently in good shape . . . John Daly would love it, 7,200 yards wide open.

★★½ NUTTERS CROSSING GOLF CLUB

SP—30287 S. Hampton Bridge Rd., Salisbury (410)860-4653.
Holes: 18. **Par:** 70/70.
Yards: 6,033/4,800. **Course rating:** 67.1/66.5. **Slope:** 115/110.
Opened: 1991. **Pace of Play rating:** 4:00. **Green fee:** $30.
Credit cards: MC, V. **Reduced fees:** Twilight.
Caddies: No. **Golf carts:** Included in Green Fee.

Discount golf packages: No. **Season:** Year-round. **High:** April-Oct.
On-site lodging: No. **Rental clubs:** Yes.
Walking policy: Unrestricted walking. **Range:** Yes (grass).
To obtain tee times: Call anytime during the week.
Subscriber comments: Hard to find any trouble, higher handicappers win the bets . . . Very enjoyable layout, well-groomed, excellent, young staff . . . Short but strategic course . . . Good beginner's course, very busy, nice amenities . . . Short course, ladies will love it . . . Very playable. Good marshals keep it moving.

OCEAN CITY GOLF AND YACHT CLUB
R—11401 Country Club Dr., Berlin (410)641-1779, (800)442-3570.
150 miles east of Washington, D.C.
Pace of Play rating: N/A. **Green fee:** $13/29.
Credit cards: MC, V. **Reduced fees:** Weekdays, Low season.
Caddies: No. **Golf carts:** $11 for 18 holes.
Discount golf packages: Yes. **Season:** Year-round. **High:** April-Oct.
On-site lodging: No. **Rental clubs:** Yes.
Walking policy: Walking at certain times. **Range:** Yes (grass).
To obtain tee times: Call. Credit card needed to guarantee tee time.

★★½ BAYSIDE COURSE
Holes: 18. **Par:** 72/72.
Yards: 6,526/5,396. **Course rating:** 71.7/71.3. **Slope:** 121/119.
Opened: N/A.
Subscriber comments: Flat course, easy to play, enjoyable . . . Interesting water holes . . . Lots of woods and marsh, requires careful shots not length . . . Beautiful bay views . . . Nice scenery, tough if windy . . . Small greens, narrow fairways . . . Take bug repellent in summer . . . Many memorable holes through woods and marsh . . . These two courses are surprisingly different from each other. Both offer fun and challenge . . . Nicer 18 of the two.

★★½ SEASIDE COURSE
Holes: 18. **Par:** 73/75.
Yards: 6,520/5,848. **Course rating:** 70.9/73.1. **Slope:** 115/119.
Opened: 1959.
Subscriber comments: Flat, wide open . . . Good old courses . . . Easier than Bayside Course . . . Gorgeous, great course and management . . . Easy course . . . Playable but not exciting . . . Mature course. Steady not thrilling.

★½ PATUXENT GREENS COUNTRY CLUB
SP—14415 Greenview Dr., Laurel (301)776-5533.
15 miles north of Washington, D.C. **Holes:** 18. **Par:** 71/71.
Yards: 6,482/5,456. **Course rating:** 71.0/71.8. **Slope:** 126/119.
Opened: 1970. **Pace of Play rating:** 4:30. **Green fee:** $20/44.
Credit cards: MC, V, AMEX. **Reduced fees:** Weekdays, Low season, Twilight.
Caddies: No. **Golf carts:** Included in Green Fee.
Discount golf packages: No. **Season:** Year-round. **High:** March-Oct.
On-site lodging: No. **Rental clubs:** Yes.
Walking policy: Walking at certain times. **Range:** No.
To obtain tee times: Call five days in advance.
Subscriber comments: Course is in wetlands, always soggy . . . Not in the best condition, no range facilities . . . Lots of water make it tough for high handicappers . . . Leave your woods at home, tight, lots of water . . . Not a bad layout . . . Flat layout. Water in play on 16 holes. Good course to walk . . . This could be an outstanding course if the fairways drained better. Service was excellent. Challenging back nine . . . Short course with tight doglegs. Better suited for mid- to high-handicappers.

★★★ PINE RIDGE GOLF COURSE
PU—2101 Dulaney Valley Rd., Lutherville (410)252-1408.
15 miles north of Baltimore. **Holes:** 18. **Par:** 72/72.
Yards: 6,820/5,732. **Course rating:** 72.0/72.0. **Slope:** 122/120.
Opened: 1958. **Pace of Play rating:** N/A. **Green fee:** $11/12.

Credit cards: MC, V. **Reduced fees:** Weekdays, Twilight, Seniors, Juniors.
Caddies: No. **Golf carts:** N/A.
Discount golf packages: No. **Season:** Year-round. **High:** June-Aug.
On-site lodging: No. **Rental clubs:** Yes.
Walking policy: Walking at certain times. **Range:** Yes.
To obtain tee times: Reserve tee times up to two weeks in advance. Weekday tee times cost $2 in person, $5 over the phone with a credit card. Weekend a.m. tee times are sold in a lottery, weekend p.m. times are $5.
Subscriber comments: Great layout among pine trees, greens average, easy par 5s . . . Made for the left-to-right player . . . Former LPGA Tour site, they are working hard to bring it back . . . Great layout, suffers from overplay . . . Set among woods, water and wildlife, the course offers a pleasant experience . . . Wonderful, scenic, challenging, hard to get on . . . Nice layout around reservoir . . . Great layout with lots of variety. Beautiful when dogwoods are in bloom . . . No. 8 is one of hardest in area . . . Greens need work . . . Could be better groomed . . . Most scenic course in Baltimore, very crowded.

★★ POOLESVILLE GOLF COURSE
PU—16601 W. Willard Rd., Poolesville (301)428-8143.
25 miles northwest of Washington, D.C. **Holes:** 18. **Par:** 71/73.
Yards: 6,757/5,599. **Course rating:** 72.3/71.4. **Slope:** 123/118.
Opened: 1959. **Pace of Play rating:** 4:30-5:00. **Green fee:** $13/26.
Credit cards: None. **Reduced fees:** Seniors, Juniors.
Caddies: No. **Golf carts:** N/A.
Discount golf packages: No. **Season:** Year-round. **High:** June.
On-site lodging: No. **Rental clubs:** Yes.
Walking policy: Unrestricted walking. **Range:** Yes (grass).
To obtain tee times: Call or come in one week in advance for weekends and holidays.
Subscriber comments: Challenging, long, good par 4s; quiet, in the middle of nowhere . . . Long with several water holes, some conditioning needed . . . Interesting layout . . . Very long second hole, 605 yards . . . I never score well here . . . Straightforward course, playable but not very interesting . . . Fun, relatively easy, not usually crowded . . . True public course . . . Favorite Maryland course, long, fair; on weekdays not much traffic.

QUEENSTOWN HARBOR GOLF LINKS
PU—310 Links Lane, Queenstown (410)827-6611, (800)827-5257.
45 miles southeast of Baltimore.
Opened: 1991. **Pace of Play rating:** 4:00-4:30. **Green fee:** $47/55.
Credit cards: MC, V. **Reduced fees:** Weekdays, Twilight.
Caddies: No. **Golf carts:** Included in Green Fee.
Discount golf packages: No. **Season:** Year-round. **High:** April-Oct.
On-site lodging: No. **Rental clubs:** Yes.
Walking policy: Unrestricted walking. **Range:** Yes (grass).
To obtain tee times: Call one week in advance after 12 p.m.
★★★½ LAKES COURSE
Holes: 18. **Par:** 71/71.
Yards: 6,537/4,576. **Course rating:** 71.0/66.6. **Slope:** 124/111.
Subscriber comments: Wonderful scenic course, excellent conditions . . . Great condition . . . Country club condition, not for high handicapper . . . Always in her big sister's shadow . . . Not as good as River Course, but still tough . . . Par-5 18th is a bear . . . The best for pure enjoyment of the game . . . Not as challenging as River Course but still worth the money . . . Must be accurate . . . Can humble you quickly!
★★★★ RIVER COURSE
Holes: 18. **Par:** 72/72.
Yards: 7,110/5,026. **Course rating:** 74.2/69.0. **Slope:** 138/123.
Ranked 6th in Maryland by Golf Digest.
Subscriber comments: Beautiful setting, many good holes . . . Tough par 4s, scenic views of the water . . . Fun to play but too demanding for high

handicapper . . . Bent fairways and greens in outstanding shape . . . Always in great shape . . . Looks great and plays tough . . . Hit it straight or bring lots of balls. I loved it! . . . Nice facilities and range . . . Spectacular golf, not for the faint of heart nor weak of wallet . . . Beautiful scenery . . . Better than any course in Myrtle Beach . . . Beautiful scenery, too many forced carries . . . Back nine is four strokes harder than front nine.

★★★ REDGATE MUNICIPAL GOLF COURSE

PU—14500 Avery Rd., Rockville (301)309-3055.
8 miles north of Washington, D.C. **Holes:** 18. **Par:** 71/71.
Yards: 6,432/5,271. **Course rating:** 71.7/70.2. **Slope:** 131/121.
Opened: 1974. **Pace of Play rating:** 4:00-4:30. **Green fee:** $18/20.
Credit cards: None. **Reduced fees:** Seniors, Juniors.
Caddies: No. **Golf carts:** $11 for 18 holes.
Discount golf packages: No. **Season:** Year-round. **High:** April-Nov.
On-site lodging: No. **Rental clubs:** Yes.
Walking policy: Unrestricted walking. **Range:** Yes (grass).
To obtain tee times: Tee times for weekends only. Call Monday 7:30 a.m. for upcoming weekend.
Subscriber comments: Very hilly course, you get a workout by walking it, very fast greens . . . Tough public course, especially last three holes . . . Best greens in area for public course, very, very fast . . . No. 16 par 5 is hardest hole in D.C. area . . . Mountain goat course . . . Very hilly, excellent for walkers . . . Small in length but great in play, narrow fairways, lots of hills and good greens.

★★★ RIVER RUN GOLF CLUB

PU—11433 Beauchamp Rd., Berlin (410)641-7200, (800)733-7786.
110 miles southeast of Washington, D.C. **Holes:** 18. **Par:** 71/71.
Yards: 6,705/5,002. **Course rating:** 70.4/73.1. **Slope:** 128/117.
Opened: 1991. **Pace of Play rating:** N/A. **Green fee:** $8/36.
Credit cards: All major. **Reduced fees:** Weekdays, Low season, Resort guest, Twilight.
Caddies: No. **Golf carts:** $12 for 18 holes.
Discount golf packages: Yes. **Season:** Year-round. **High:** April-Oct.
On-site lodging: Yes. **Rental clubs:** Yes.
Walking policy: Walking at certain times. **Range:** Yes (grass).
To obtain tee times: Call.
Subscriber comments: Course is new, interesting . . . Great layout, many great holes . . . Tough and tight. Must stay in fairway. Fun round . . . First nine is links-style, second forested . . . Needs work, nice layout, easy course . . . Great Gary Player design, greens need water, very hard . . . Super course with holes that beg you to gamble, especially par 5s . . . Nice test of golf, new course, needs to grow in.

★★½ ROCKY POINT GOLF CLUB

PU—1935 Back River Neck Rd., Essex (410)391-2906.
9 miles east of Baltimore. **Holes:** 18. **Par:** 72/74.
Yards: 6,785/5,150. **Course rating:** 72.3/73.1. **Slope:** 122/121.
Opened: 1967. **Pace of Play rating:** 4:30. **Green fee:** $15/17.
Credit cards: MC, V. **Reduced fees:** Weekdays, Twilight, Seniors, Juniors.
Caddies: No. **Golf carts:** $18 for 18 holes.
Discount golf packages: No. **Season:** Year-round. **High:** April-Sept.
On-site lodging: No. **Rental clubs:** Yes.
Walking policy: Unrestricted walking. **Range:** Yes (grass).
To obtain tee times: Call six days in advance or in person seven days in advance.
Subscriber comments: Wide open, kind of flat . . . 11th looks out over water, watch out for winds . . . For as much play as it gets, course in remarkably good shape . . . Scenery of the bay is excellent . . . Lots of diversity, beautiful scenery, a real treat . . . The only time the course is in bad shape is when we get no rain . . . Nice public facility, good layout, good value . . . A few really good holes.

MARYLAND

★★★★ SWAN POINT GOLF CLUB
SP—11550 Swan Point Blvd., Issue (301)259-0047, (800)706-3488.
50 miles southeast of Washington, D.C. **Holes:** 18. **Par:** 72/72.
Yards: 6,761/5,009. **Course rating:** 72.5/69.3. **Slope:** 126/116.
Opened: 1985. **Pace of Play rating:** 4:30. **Green fee:** $37/60.
Credit cards: MC, V. **Reduced fees:** Weekdays, Low season, Twilight,
Seniors, Juniors.
Caddies: No. **Golf carts:** Included in Green Fee.
Discount golf packages: Yes. **Season:** March-Dec. **High:** June-Sept.
On-site lodging: No. **Rental clubs:** Yes.
Walking policy: Walking at certain times. **Range:** Yes (grass).
To obtain tee times: Call one week in advance with credit card.
Subscriber comments: Tight fairways, good variety, grass range included
with green fee . . . Fairly long, tough water holes, excellent condition . . .
Marshes and pine trees, thought I was in Myrtle Beach . . . Rewards
accuracy over distance, lots of water . . . It's a bit of a hike from D.C. but
after playing it, return trip is inevitable . . . Prettiest course in Maryland, it's
a must . . . Myrtle Beach quality in Maryland . . . Mixture woods and
wetlands . . . Some breathtaking holes . . . Two of the nastiest par 3s back-
to-back on back nine . . . Lots of interesting holes.

TROTTERS GLEN GOLF COURSE★
PU—16501 Batchellors Forest Rd., Olney (301)570-4951.
15 miles northeast of Washington, D.C. **Holes:** 18. **Par:** 72/72.
Yards: 6,220/4,983. **Course rating:** 69.3/68.2. **Slope:** 113/111.
Opened: 1993. **Pace of Play rating:** 4:15. **Green fee:** $18/23.
Credit cards: All major. **Reduced fees:** Weekdays, Low season.
Caddies: No. **Golf carts:** $22 for 18 holes.
Discount golf packages: No. **Season:** Year-round. **High:** June-Aug.
On-site lodging: Yes. **Rental clubs:** Yes.
Walking policy: Unrestricted walking. **Range:** Yes (grass).
To obtain tee times: Call Monday 8 a.m. for that week and weekend.

TURF VALLEY HOTEL AND COUNTRY CLUB
R—2700 Turf Valley Rd., Ellicott City (410)465-1504, (800)666-8873.
20 miles west of Baltimore.
Opened: 1959. **Pace of Play rating:** 4:00. **Green fee:** $30/50.
Credit cards: All major. **Reduced fees:** Weekdays, Low season, Resort
guests, Twilight.
Caddies: No. **Golf carts:** $11 for 18 holes.
Discount golf packages: Yes. **Season:** Year-round. **High:** April-Oct.
On-site lodging: Yes. **Rental clubs:** Yes.
Walking policy: Walking at certain times. **Range:** Yes (grass).
To obtain tee times: In person, seven days in advance. By phone, six days
in advance.

★★½ NORTH COURSE
Holes: 18. **Par:** 71/71.
Yards: 6,633/5,600. **Course rating:** 69.5/71.8. **Slope:** 117/124.
Subscriber comments: New holes are gorgeous, placement course, not
long . . . Still new, great beauty, challenging . . . Very enjoyable course to
play, friendly . . . Spotty conditions.

★★½ EAST COURSE
Holes: 18. **Par:** 71/71.
Yards: 6,592/5,564. **Course rating:** 72.0/71.6. **Slope:** 128/131.
Subscriber comments: Narrow, not particularly long, good shape . . .
Great variety, some holes tight . . . Good competitive course, staff
professional . . . A pure course . . . Interesting course. Short but tight . . .
Tight, trees, lots of blind shots. Take lots of balls.

★★ SOUTH COURSE
Holes: 18. **Par:** 70/72.
Yards: 6,323/5,572. **Course rating:** 69.2/72.8. **Slope:** 113/126.
Opened: 1963. **Pace of Play rating:** 4:00.
Subscriber comments: Easiest of three courses at Turf Valley, pretty, not
long . . . Nice resort course . . . Golf factory . . . Wide open, easy play, not
too interesting . . . Big greens, wonderful staff, good course, lots of trees
. . . Area is picturesque, course is interesting . . . Best course at this resort
. . . Some well-designed holes.

★★½ TWIN SHIELDS GOLF CLUB

PU—2425 Roarty Rd., Dunkirk (410)257-7800.

15 miles east of Washington, D.C. **Holes:** 18. **Par:** 70/70.
Yards: 6,321/5,305. **Course rating:** 68.2/67.0. **Slope:** 118/113.
Opened: 1969. **Pace of Play rating:** 4:00. **Green fee:** $25/30.
Credit cards: None. **Reduced fees:** Twilight, Seniors, Juniors.
Caddies: No. **Golf carts:** $25 for 18 holes.
Discount golf packages: No. **Season:** Year-round. **High:** April-Oct.
On-site lodging: No. **Rental clubs:** No.
Walking policy: Walking at certain times. **Range:** Yes (grass).
To obtain tee times: Call three days in advance.
Subscriber comments: Workingman's golf course . . . Neat par 3s . . .
Several challenging holes, good value . . . Varied terrain. Hills and trees . . .
When the rough is long and thick you need to be very strong. I'm not . . .
Your average short public golf course, conditions can be good one month,
bad the next, very nice staff . . . Some scenic holes . . . Fast, true greens,
excellent fairways.

★★½ UNIVERSITY OF MARYLAND GOLF COURSE

SP—University Blvd., College Park (301)403-4299.

5 miles east of Washington, D.C. **Holes:** 18. **Par:** 71/72.
Yards: 6,654/5,563. **Course rating:** 71.7/71.1. **Slope:** 120/117.
Opened: 1956. **Pace of Play rating:** 4:00. **Green fee:** $22/26.
Credit cards: None. **Reduced fees:** Weekdays, Low season, Twilight,
Seniors, Juniors.
Caddies: No. **Golf carts:** $10 for 18 holes.
Discount golf packages: No. **Season:** Year-round. **High:** April-Oct.
On-site lodging: No. **Rental clubs:** No.
Walking policy: Walking at certain times. **Range:** Yes (grass).
To obtain tee times: Call six days in advance.
Subscriber comments: Very pretty, fastest greens in D.C. area . . . Nos.
1, 2, 5, 6, and 7 are some of the toughest par 4s around . . . Good course,
plays long, narrow fairways . . . Some interesting and fun holes . . .
Working on improving all the time . . . Good value for alumni, good holes
. . . Course is rapidly improving with new water system.

★★★ WAKEFIELD VALLEY GOLF & CONFERENCE CENTER

SP—1000 Fenby Farm Rd., Westminster (410)876-6662.

30 miles north of Baltimore. **Holes:** 27. **Par:** 72/72/72.
Yards: 6,933/7,038/6,823. **Course rating:** 74.4/74.1/73.6.
Slope: 139/138/139.
Opened: 1978. **Pace of Play rating:** 4:30. **Green fee:** $29/36.
Credit cards: MC, V. **Reduced fees:** Low season, Twilight, Seniors,
Juniors.
Caddies: No. **Golf carts:** Included in Green Fee.
Discount golf packages: No. **Season:** March-Dec. **High:** June-Sept.
On-site lodging: Yes. **Rental clubs:** Yes.
Walking policy: Walking at certain times. **Range:** Yes (grass).
To obtain tee times: Call or come in.
Subscriber comments: Tour-level greens . . . 27 pretty holes, well
maintained, sneaky, long, very tough greens . . . Beautiful clubhouse and
layout . . . Green/White combo, tough enough but fair . . . Marvelous par
5s . . . Fairly wide open from tee, will allow for slice . . . White nine the
easiest . . . Practice facility is great. Greens are very tricky . . . Always fun
to play, good condition, friendly staff.

★★½ WHITE PLAINS REGIONAL PARK GOLF CLUB

PU—St. Charles Pkwy., White Plains (301)843-2947.

Call club for further information.
Subscriber comments: Good layout, not for beginners . . . Tight course,
a lot of trees . . . Tree-lined course can be challenging. Greens usually
decent . . . Nice holes, different holes, good staff, great hot dogs . . . Keep
ball in play or else.

★★ **WICOMICO SHORES MUNICIPAL GOLF COURSE**
PU—Rte. 234, 20621 Aviation Yacht & CC Rd., Chaptico (301)934-8191.
45 miles southeast of Washington, D.C. **Holes:** 18. **Par:** 72/72.
Yards: 6,482/5,460. **Course rating:** 70.7/68.3. **Slope:** 120/120.
Opened: 1962. **Pace of Play rating:** 4:30. **Green fee:** $15/19.
Credit cards: None. **Reduced fees:** Weekdays, Twilight, Seniors, Juniors.
Caddies: No. **Golf carts:** $12 for 18 holes.
Discount golf packages: Yes. **Season:** Year-round. **High:** May-Sept.
On-site lodging: No. **Rental clubs:** Yes.
Walking policy: Unrestricted walking. **Range:** Yes (grass).
To obtain tee times: Call Monday for upcoming weekend or holiday.
Subscriber comments: Great finishing hole . . . Good scenery, good for
average player . . . Need chair lift to come up to 18th hole! Most fun to play
. . . Slowly getting better . . . Nice layout. Fun course . . . Will be really
good once improvements are done . . . Some holes long and open, others
tight and tree-lined.

Notes

★★★ ATLANTIC COUNTRY CLUB

PU—450 Little Sandy Pond Rd., Plymouth (508)888-6644.
50 miles south of Boston. **Holes:** 18. **Par:** 72/72.
Yards: 6,728/4,918. **Course rating:** 71.5/67.4. **Slope:** 130/113.
Opened: 1994. **Pace of Play rating:** 4:30. **Green fee:** $25/28.
Credit cards: MC, V. **Reduced fees:** Weekdays, Twilight.
Caddies: No. **Golf carts:** $12 for 18 holes.
Discount golf packages: No. **Season:** March-Dec. **High:** June-Aug.
On-site lodging: No. **Rental clubs:** Yes.
Walking policy: Unrestricted walking. **Range:** Yes (grass).
To obtain tee times: Call two days in advance.
Subscriber comments: New course . . . Challenging . . . Looks great . . .
A must . . . Has great potential . . . Excellent practice facilities . . . Very
good for all level golfers, nice layout . . . Fairways best in Massachusetts.

★★★ BALLYMEADE COUNTRY CLUB

SP—125 Falmouth Woods Rd., N. Falmouth (508)540-4005.
58 miles south of Boston. **Holes:** 18. **Par:** 72/70.
Yards: 6,928/4,722. **Course rating:** 72.3/66.3. **Slope:** 137/112.
Opened: 1988. **Pace of Play rating:** N/A. **Green fee:** $40/65.
Credit cards: All major. **Reduced fees:** Weekdays, Low season, Twilight,
Seniors.
Caddies: No. **Golf carts:** Included in Green Fee.
Discount golf packages: No. **Season:** Year-round. **High:** June-Aug.
On-site lodging: No. **Rental clubs:** Yes.
Walking policy: Mandatory cart. **Range:** Yes (grass).
To obtain tee times: Call seven days in advance.
Subscriber comments: Unusual Cape course . . . Great course for all
levels . . . Great views . . . You can hit it straight and still be in trouble . . .
Excellent facility and staff . . . Great course, not for the timid . . . Played as
outing guest, course too tough for me . . . Always memorable, course you
love to hate . . . Tees in better shape than some greens on other courses in
the area . . . Lots of hills, rolling fairways, suited for the low-handicap
player, difficult course, picturesque, excellent service . . . Requires good
course management . . . Played off season, must be great in season . . . Just
too tough for a group of 16 to 24 handicappers. Blind shots, long carries
over water, severe greens made play very slow. Many balls off fairway
were lost . . . Recent improvements to the course . . . Target golf at its
ultimate . . . Change tees and it's a different course . . . Excellent service,
staff terrific, must be long and accurate to score well . . . Long and hilly.
Hard to walk . . . Very pretty and beautiful views from elevated tees.

★★ BASS RIVER GOLF COURSE

PU—Highbank Rd., South Yarmouth (508)398-9079.
70 miles south of Boston. **Holes:** 18. **Par:** 72/72.
Yards: 6,129/5,343. **Course rating:** 79.3/69.3. **Slope:** 122/111.
Opened: 1902. **Pace of Play rating:** N/A. **Green fee:** $10/28.
Credit cards: MC, V. **Reduced fees:** Low season, Twilight.
Caddies: No. **Golf carts:** $21 for 18 holes.
Discount golf packages: No. **Season:** Year-round. **High:** May-Sept.
On-site lodging: No. **Rental clubs:** Yes.
Walking policy: Unrestricted walking. **Range:** No.
To obtain tee times: Call four days in advance.
Subscriber comments: Quaint Cape course, loaded with charm . . .
Excellent greens and fairways, course is made for anyone . . . Good "pick-
me-up" course . . . Wind off river can make it tough . . . Plenty of
character and variety . . . Nice course. Great par 3 over water . . . Blind
shots and wind make it tough . . . Two different nines keep it interesting.

★★ BAY POINTE COUNTRY CLUB

SP—Onset Ave., Onset (508)759-8802.
Call club for further information.
Subscriber comments: Typical short Cape course . . . Good blend of

hard and easy holes, very hilly, land short of green on No. 10 . . . Short but tricky, greens were especially tough . . . Good par 3s, nice staff . . . Too many par 3 holes of the same yardage . . . Lots of improvements . . . A better course than most people realize.

★★★ BAYBERRY HILLS GOLF COURSE
PU—West Yarmouth Rd., West Yarmouth (508)394-5597.
75 miles south of Boston. **Holes:** 18. **Par:** 72/72.
Yards: 7,172/5,275. **Course rating:** 73.5/69.2. **Slope:** 132/111.
Opened: 1987. **Pace of Play rating:** N/A. **Green fee:** $10/28.
Credit cards: MC, V. **Reduced fees:** Low season, Twilight.
Caddies: No. **Golf carts:** $21 for 18 holes.
Discount golf packages: No. **Season:** N/A. **High:** May-Oct.
On-site lodging: No. **Rental clubs:** Yes.
Walking policy: Unrestricted walking. **Range:** Yes (grass).
To obtain tee times: Call four days in advance.
Subscriber comments: Was a good secret on the Cape . . . Challenge increases dramatically in the wind . . . Layout allows you to feel you have the course all to yourself even on a busy day . . . Gold tees great test . . . Driver's paradise . . . A real pleasure . . . Very well run muny . . . Large, true greens a big plus . . . Great course, 18th hole is cool . . . Fun to play, distance between greens and tees long . . . Fair test, could be the sleeper of Cape courses.

★★ BLISSFUL MEADOWS GOLF CLUB
SP—801 Chockalog Rd., Uxbridge (508)278-6133.
20 miles south of Worcester. **Holes:** 18. **Par:** 72/72.
Yards: 6,656/5,072. **Course rating:** N/A. **Slope:** N/A.
Opened: 1992. **Pace of Play rating:** N/A. **Green fee:** $18/22.
Credit cards: MC, V, AMEX. **Reduced fees:** Low season, Twilight, Seniors.
Caddies: No. **Golf carts:** $10 for 18 holes.
Discount golf packages: No. **Season:** April-Nov. **High:** May-Oct.
On-site lodging: No. **Rental clubs:** No.
Walking policy: Unrestricted walking. **Range:** Yes (grass).
To obtain tee times: Call up to two days in advance.
Subscriber comments: New course, has great potential, very interesting . . . Undulating greens, need accurate approach shots and good reads . . . Very tight . . . Leave the driver in the bag . . . Great layout, must work the ball, small rocks in fairway just under surface scratch clubs when taking divot . . . Nice turf practice area . . . Great staff.

★★ BRADFORD COUNTRY CLUB
PU—201 Chadwick Rd., Bradford (508)372-8587.
25 miles north of Boston. **Holes:** 18. **Par:** 70/70.
Yards: 6,511/4,939. **Course rating:** 72.8/67.8. **Slope:** 141/129.
Opened: 1990. **Pace of Play rating:** 4:30. **Green fee:** $18/29.
Credit cards: MC, V, AMEX. **Reduced fees:** Weekdays, Low season, Twilight, Seniors, Juniors.
Caddies: No. **Golf carts:** $10 for 18 holes.
Discount golf packages: Yes. **Season:** April-Dec. **High:** May-Sept.
On-site lodging: No. **Rental clubs:** Yes.
Walking policy: Unrestricted walking. **Range:** No.
To obtain tee times: Call up to five days in advance.
Subscriber comments: Very good condition all season, forces you to manage your game, back nine very difficult, need cart . . . Two very different nines . . . You need a Sherpa along on the back nine, very steep . . . Tough course. Not for beginners . . . Target golf . . . Good greens, back nine cruel . . . Many carries over swamps, steep hills, blind shots . . . Very demanding course . . . Requires your best control game. Tough to walk . . . Accuracy a key. No.12 should be a par 10 . . . 12th hole is a BEAR.

MASSACHUSETTS

★½ BROOKMEADOW COUNTRY CLUB
PU—100 Everendon Rd., Canton (617)828-4444.
20 miles southwest of Boston. **Holes:** 18. **Par:** 72/72.
Yards: 6,660/5,690. **Course rating:** 71.6/71.2. **Slope:** 123/114.
Opened: 1968. **Pace of Play rating:** N/A. **Green fee:** N/A.
Credit cards: MC, V, DISC. **Reduced fees:** Low season, Twilight,
Seniors, Juniors.
Caddies: No. **Golf carts:** N/A.
Discount golf packages: No. **Season:** Year-round. **High:** April-Oct.
On-site lodging: No. **Rental clubs:** Yes.
Walking policy: Unrestricted walking. **Range:** Yes (grass).
To obtain tee times: For weekdays call one day in advance. For weekends
call five days in advance.
Subscriber comments: Flat course . . . Easy walk, not difficult to score,
fun . . . Can hit driver here . . . Few bunkers . . . Good beginner's course
. . . Back nine more challenging than front . . . Flat layout, but tight
fairways . . . Long par 3s . . . Simple layout, good for a leisurely day,
conditioning spotty.

★★★ CAPE COD COUNTRY CLUB
PU—Theater Rd., Hatchville (508)563-9842.
50 miles south of Boston. **Holes:** 18. **Par:** 71/72.
Yards: 6,404/5,348. **Course rating:** 71.0/70.6. **Slope:** 122/119.
Opened: 1929. **Pace of Play rating:** N/A. **Green fee:** $20/30.
Credit cards: MC, V. **Reduced fees:** Weekdays, Low season, Twilight,
Juniors.
Caddies: No. **Golf carts:** $22 for 18 holes.
Discount golf packages: Yes. **Season:** Year-round. **High:** March-Oct.
On-site lodging: No. **Rental clubs:** Yes.
Walking policy: Unrestricted walking. **Range:** No.
To obtain tee times: Call Friday for following Friday, Saturday or
Sunday. One week in advance for weekdays.
Subscriber comments: Classic layout . . . Good variety, several tough
approaches to uphill greens . . . Good course with Cape flavor . . .
Challenging from the start; hills, hills, hills . . . Too hot to walk in the
summer, but this is a "must stop" on our monthly trips to the Cape . . .
Wide open. Easy to scramble . . . Elevated greens, well kept . . . Fun Cape
course. Greens challenging. Lots of hills. Must be straight. Hit a lot of irons
. . . Pro shop and restaurant staff were superb . . . Old Cape Cod course,
well run, good challenge for average golfer. Very busy in summer . . . Staff
very helpful getting you out, even when busy . . . Good greens, hilly . . .
Not bad for an old course.

★★★½ CAPTAINS GOLF COURSE
PU—1000 Freeman's Way, Brewster (508)896-5100.
100 miles southeast of Boston. **Holes:** 18. **Par:** 72/72.
Yards: 6,794/5,388. **Course rating:** 72.7/70.5. **Slope:** 130/117.
Opened: 1985. **Pace of Play rating:** 4:14. **Green fee:** $20/35.
Credit cards: None. **Reduced fees:** Low season, Twilight.
Caddies: No. **Golf carts:** N/A.
Discount golf packages: No. **Season:** March-Dec. **High:** May-Oct.
On-site lodging: No. **Rental clubs:** Yes.
Walking policy: Unrestricted walking. **Range:** Yes (grass).
To obtain tee times: Call two days prior at 6 p.m. on automated system
or prepaid by calling throughout the year with payment by check at least
two weeks prior to play date.
Ranked in First 25 of America's 75 Best Public Golf Courses by Golf
Digest. Selected Best New Public Course of 1985 by Golf Digest.
Subscriber comments: Great course, great condition, nice people . . . Not
much trouble off the tee. A great driving day gives a great score . . . Terrific
Cape Cod layout . . . Scores harder than it looks . . . The most peaceful yet
stimulating course . . . Superb condition . . . Tough to get tee times . . .
Real pleasure . . . Small greens, need to be accurate . . . Back nine a real
challenge. Good mix of holes . . . Great layout, greens are the best

anywhere, go for the pin . . . On par with any private course, and you can walk it . . . Well-maintained, tight tree-lined course . . . Chance to see all your clubs . . . Good design, good for all handicaps . . . Sand traps like sifted sand . . . If there is a golf course in heaven, this is it . . . This is Cape Cod golf at its best.

★★★½ CHICOPEE GOLF CLUB

PU—1290 Burnett Rd., Chicopee (413)592-4156.
Call club for further information.
Subscriber comments: Course conditions excellent, staff helpful and friendly . . . Hilly, some blind shots, not too difficult . . . Heavily favors a draw from back tees; good mixture of tight, semi-tight and open holes . . . Scenic, large greens, very good test of golf . . . Fairways and greens in great shape . . . Best public course for a 1960's price . . . Easy to walk, white tees and ladies tees make it fun but testing . . . Next to airport, you can almost see the pilots eyes . . . Great for any golfer, hilly, narrow fairways . . . Many long holes, very large greens, a lot of three-putts . . . Par on No. 5 would make your year . . . The greens are hard during the summer . . . Diverse, variety of holes all level players can score on . . . Please remove this course from the list; sometimes a good thing should be kept quiet.

★★ COLONIAL COUNTRY CLUB

PU—1 Audubon Rd., Wakefield (617)245-9300.
12 miles north of Boston. **Holes:** 18. **Par:** 70/72.
Yards: 6,565/5,280. **Course rating:** 72.8/69.5. **Slope:** 130/109.
Opened: 1929. **Pace of Play rating:** 4:05. **Green fee:** $39/49.
Credit cards: All major. **Reduced fees:** Low season, Twilight, Seniors, Juniors.
Caddies: No. **Golf carts:** Included in Green Fee.
Discount golf packages: Yes. **Season:** April-Dec. **High:** May-Oct.
On-site lodging: Yes. **Rental clubs:** Yes.
Walking policy: Mandatory cart. **Range:** Yes (grass).
To obtain tee times: Hotel guests 21 days in advance. Public, seven days in advance.
Subscriber comments: Good golf experience . . . This is where we head when our club closes . . . Good public course for mid- to high-handicappers . . . Wide variety of holes, very diverse course . . . Elevations on course make it interesting . . . Not too tough, slow greens . . . Decent course, nothing spectacular.

★★★½ CRANBERRY VALLEY GOLF COURSE

PU—183 Oak St., Harwich (508)430-7560.
85 miles south of Boston. **Holes:** 18. **Par:** 72/72.
Yards: 6,745/5,518. **Course rating:** 71.9/71.3. **Slope:** 129/115.
Opened: 1974. **Pace of Play rating:** 4:08. **Green fee:** $30/35.
Credit cards: None. **Reduced fees:** Weekdays, Low Season, Twilight.
Caddies: No. **Golf carts:** $20 for 18 holes.
Discount golf packages: No. **Season:** Year-round. **High:** March-Nov.
On-site lodging: No. **Rental clubs:** Yes.
Walking policy: Unrestricted walking. **Range:** Yes (grass).
To obtain tee times: Pre-payment by check or cash starting March 1st or two days in advance, with no pre-payment, starting at 8 a.m.
Subscriber comments: Great Cape Cod layout by Cornish . . . Tremendous layout, you can gamble off every tee . . . 18th hole is marvelous . . . Well run with a polite, accommodating staff; particularly helpful with rainchecks . . . Very good, a little of everything, makes you think . . . Great traps . . . Another tough one to get on, but worth the wait . . . Tree lined but generous fairway widths . . . Watch out for the woods . . . Well-trapped . . . Tough, long par 3s, quick to close in wet weather . . . No.10 is a real tough nut . . . Outstanding vistas . . . Requires good mid-long iron play . . . Great track, best finishing hole on the Cape . . . Emphasis on accuracy over distance . . . Plays longer than card suggests . . . One word, outstanding . . . Some quirky holes, especially 18, a double dogleg to the right . . . Best public course on Cape, gets tons of play.

★★★★ CRUMPIN-FOX CLUB

SP—Parmenter Rd., Bernardston (413)648-9101.
30 miles north of Springfield. **Holes:** 18. **Par:** 72/72.
Yards: 7,007/5,432. **Course rating:** 73.8/71.5. **Slope:** 141/131.
Opened: 1978. **Pace of Play rating:** N/A. **Green fee:** $55.
Credit cards: All major. **Reduced fees:** Resort guests, Juniors.
Caddies: Yes. **Golf carts:** $12 for 18 holes.
Discount golf packages: Yes. **Season:** April-Nov. **High:** June-Oct.
On-site lodging: Yes. **Rental clubs:** Yes.
Walking policy: Unrestricted walking. **Range:** Yes (grass).
To obtain tee times: Two days in advance for public. Members or golf
and dinner packages may book as far in advance as desired.
Ranked 9th in Massachusetts by Golf Digest.
Subscriber comments: A great golf experience . . . Tight, hilly course,
good condition all season, friendly staff . . . Every hole has its own
character . . . Doesn't get much better . . . Local knowledge very helpful
. . . Amenities are great, course picturesque . . . Worth the long drive to the
middle of nowhere . . . The new nine, now mature, and the dinner package
make this one of the best places to play anywhere! . . . Take a caddy and
enjoy the experience . . . Could probably hold the U.S. Open here . . . Top
notch in all areas. A course like the pros play . . . Hills, tough greens,
doglegs, beautiful . . . Great track, a diamond in the rough, can't wait to
play it again . . . A tough but fair test. Beautiful. Staff friendly . . . Better
players will enjoy it the most. Caddies, what a treat! . . . The cat's meow! . . .
Great par 5s around water . . . True challenge, tough but fair, demands all
clubs, great scenery . . . One of the state's most picturesque . . . Best
bunker conditions around . . . Great golf course in rustic surroundings.

★★½ CRYSTAL SPRINGS GOLF CLUB

PU—940 North Broadway, Haverhill (508)374-9621.
Call club for further information.
Subscriber comments: Old time golf . . . Fairways and greens well
maintained . . . Tight front nine. Well-bunkered greens . . . Service and
staff excellent . . . Open front, wooded back side . . . Front nine more
difficult than back nine . . . Very friendly atmosphere.

★½ D.W. FIELD GOLF CLUB

PU—331 Oak St., Brockton (508)580-7855.
Holes: 18. **Par:** 70/70.
Yards: 5,972/5,415. **Course rating:** 68.4/70.1. **Slope:** 127/111.
Opened: 1926. **Pace of Play rating:** 4:30. **Green fee:** $17/21.
Credit cards: None. **Reduced fees:** Low season, Twilight, Juniors.
Caddies: No. **Golf carts:** $22 for 18 holes.
Discount golf packages: No. **Season:** Year-round. **High:** June-Aug.
On-site lodging: No. **Rental clubs:** Yes.
Walking policy: Unrestricted walking. **Range:** No.
To obtain tee times: First come, first serve.
Subscriber comments: Short but interesting municipal course . . . Wide
open, great confidence builder . . . No gimmicks . . . No water . . . Good
public course with some interesting holes . . . Great course to learn the
game on.

★★★ DENNIS HIGHLANDS GOLF COURSE

PU—825 Old Bass River Rd., Dennis (508)385-8698.
80 miles south of Boston. **Holes:** 18. **Par:** 71/71.
Yards: 6,464/4,927. **Course rating:** 70.4/67.4. **Slope:** 118/112.
Opened: 1984. **Pace of Play rating:** 3:47. **Green fee:** $20/30.
Credit cards: MC, V. **Reduced fees:** Low season, Twilight.
Caddies: No. **Golf carts:** $21 for 18 holes.
Discount golf packages: No. **Season:** Year-round. **High:** April-Nov.
On-site lodging: No. **Rental clubs:** Yes.
Walking policy: Unrestricted walking. **Range:** Yes (grass).

To obtain tee times: Call four days in advance or guarantee with pre-payment (no refunds) anytime in advance.

Subscriber comments: Course name is good description of the feel of this layout . . . Tough in wind, fun . . . Can be tough with crowned fairways . . . Challenging undulating greens . . . Well kept, hills up and down . . . Fine public course, varied and challenging for the amateur . . . Well laid out, greens make this course . . . Enjoyable, easy to recover from errant shots . . . The average player loves this course . . . A must if on the Cape . . . Great big greens, not tight, but need to be accurate, tough when wind blows . . . Front nine hilly, back flatter . . . Greens are great to putt.

★★★ DENNIS PINES GOLF COURSE

PU—Golf Course Rd., East Dennis (508)385-8698.
80 miles south of Boston. **Holes:** 18. **Par:** 72/73.
Yards: 7,029/5,798. **Course rating:** 71.9/73.2. **Slope:** 127/128.
Opened: 1964. **Pace of Play rating:** 4:04. **Green fee:** $20/30.
Credit cards: MC, V. **Reduced fees:** Low season, Twilight.
Caddies: No. **Golf carts:** $21 for 18 holes.
Discount golf packages: No. **Season:** Year-round. **High:** April-Nov.
On-site lodging: No. **Rental clubs:** Yes.
Walking policy: Unrestricted walking. **Range:** Yes.
To obtain tee times: Call four days in advance or guarantee with pre-payment (no refund) anytime in advance.
Subscriber comments: Old course, difficult landing areas for many drives, challenging . . . Must hit it straight . . . Not much room for error, can be blocked out in fairway . . . Very good track, need to execute shots . . . Long and tight, good challenge for low handicapper . . . Nice course on the Cape . . . Another must stop on our monthly trips to the Cape . . . Friendly staff. Great pro shop. Well kept. Our favorite course . . . Narrow design, many doglegs, small greens . . . Must think your way around course . . . Use all your clubs; all types of hill lies . . . A jewel, a painting should be done of holes 10 and 11 . . . One of the best kept secrets on the Cape.

★★★ FAR CORNER GOLF CLUB

PU—Main St. & Barker Rd., West Boxford (508)352-8300.
Call club for further information.
Subscriber comments: If you want to test your game, this is the place, can play tough . . . Hard to get to, but year in and year out, consistent . . . Great variety in shots, beautiful trip through wooded back . . . Nice design, tough course from tips . . . Nice, playable, just long enough, need llama . . . Course suited for all abilities, a thinking player's course . . . Tremendous scenery on the back nine . . . Long course. Wide fairways but challenging . . . Well maintained. Fun to play, nice setting . . . Greens that are four-puttable . . . Some great holes . . . Big greens, tough par 3s; par 5s reachable . . . Well-groomed public course with some class.

★★★★ FARM NECK GOLF CLUB

SP—Farm Neck Way, Oak Bluffs (508)693-3057.
90 miles south of Boston. **Holes:** 18. **Par:** 72/72.
Yards: 6,709/5,022. **Course rating:** 71.8/68.9. **Slope:** 130/109.
Opened: 1969. **Pace of Play rating:** 4:15. **Green fee:** $33/66.
Credit cards: MC, V, AMEX. **Reduced fees:** Low season.
Caddies: No. **Golf carts:** $22 for 18 holes.
Discount golf packages: No. **Season:** April-Dec. **High:** July-Aug.
On-site lodging: No. **Rental clubs:** Yes.
Walking policy: Walking at certain times. **Range:** Yes (grass).
To obtain tee times: Call two days in advance.
Subscriber comments: Beautiful, many scenic holes . . . Bring your camera . . . Several visually stunning holes . . . Great condition . . . Great layout, superb greens . . . Fantastic course, just hard to get to . . . Absolutely wonderful. The best in New England . . . Stunning ocean

views. Good service . . . Lots of interesting holes, meant to be played in the wind . . . Superb scenery and layout not to be missed . . . Incredible . . . Hidden gem . . . Thank God there's no bridge to Martha's Vineyard . . . Challenging . . . Great condition, good service . . . If it's good enough for Bill Clinton it's good enough for me.

★½ FRANCONIA GOLF COURSE

PU—619 Dwight Rd., Springfield (413)734-9334.
Call club for further information.
Subscriber comments: Just a good muny . . . A fair course for a fair price for a fair player . . . Reworked over the years; city-owned, gets a good amount of play . . . Tricky on the back nine; greens in fairly good shape for the amount of play course receives . . . A few holes have drainage problems . . . Very busy year round . . . Suited for every level of player, not difficult, but fun to play. Pace of play is fast mid-week, slow on weekends . . . Staff very helpful.

★★★ GANNON MUNICIPAL GOLF COURSE

PU—Great Woods Rd., Lynn (617)592-8238.
Call club for further information.
Subscriber comments: Target golf, blind greens . . . Good condition . . . The course is best suited for any type of golfer; walking the front side is tough . . . Scenic views, need every club in your bag . . . Great holes and great shape for amount of play . . . Hilly, cart recommended, beautiful grass, best muny around.

★★★ GARDNER MUNICIPAL GOLF COURSE

PU—152 Eaton St., Gardner (508)632-9703.
20 miles north of Worcester. **Holes:** 18. **Par:** 71/75.
Yards: 6,106/5,653. **Course rating:** 68.9/72.2. **Slope:** 124/123.
Opened: 1936. **Pace of Play rating:** 3:33. **Green fee:** $15/25.
Credit cards: None. **Reduced fees:** Weekdays, Twilight.
Caddies: No. **Golf carts:** $11 for 18 holes.
Discount golf packages: No. **Season:** April-First snow. **High:** June-Sept.
On-site lodging: No. **Rental clubs:** Yes.
Walking policy: Unrestricted walking. **Range:** Yes (grass).
To obtain tee times: Call two days in advance. Thursday for Saturday and Friday for Sunday.
Subscriber comments: Front nine very easy, back nine quite a challenge . . . Back nine difficult to walk, slows pace of play to a crawl . . . Front nine open, back hilly and tight; excellent greens . . . Very playable for the average golfer, but still a challenge for the low-handicap player; staff is professional and friendly.

★★★ GEORGE WRIGHT GOLF COURSE

PU—420 West St., Hyde Park (617)364-8997.
5 miles south of Boston. **Holes:** 18. **Par:** 70/70.
Yards: 6,400/5,500. **Course rating:** 69.5/70.3. **Slope:** 126/115.
Opened: . **Pace of Play rating:** 4:30. **Green fee:** $18/21.
Credit cards: MC, V. **Reduced fees:** Seniors, Juniors.
Caddies: No. **Golf carts:** $22 for 18 holes.
Discount golf packages: Yes. **Season:** Year-round. **High:** June-Aug.
On-site lodging: No. **Rental clubs:** Yes.
Walking policy: Unrestricted walking. **Range:** No.
To obtain tee times: Call on Thursday for upcoming weekend.
Subscriber comments: Forgotten Ross gem . . . Play and accept conditions . . . Great layout in urban setting . . . Tight, very difficult to walk, hilly . . . Potentially best in area, has character . . . Interesting contours . . . Great price, and it's in Boston! . . . Very challenging; a lot of blind shots . . . Golfers know this is best public course in Massachusetts . . . A jewel in the city . . . Great greens, as good as any private . . . A gem hidden in the city . . . Play well here and you play well anywhere . . . God built this course, Donald Ross tweaked it.

★★ GREEN HARBOR GOLF CLUB

PU—624 Webster St., Marshfield (617)834-7303.
30 miles south of Boston. **Holes:** 18. **Par:** 71/71.
Yards: 6,211/5,355. **Course rating:** 69.1/69.3. **Slope:** 115/109.
Opened: 1971. **Pace of Play rating:** 4:00. **Green fee:** $24/25.
Credit cards: None. **Reduced fees:** Twilight.
Caddies: No. **Golf carts:** N/A.
Discount golf packages: No. **Season:** March-Dec.
On-site lodging: No. **Rental clubs:** Yes.
Walking policy: Unrestricted walking. **Range:** No.
To obtain tee times: Two days prior at 6 a.m. for 18 holes; day of play at 6 a.m. for 9 holes.
Subscriber comments: Reasonable challenge . . . Nice views . . . Good course to build confidence, very flat, good for any handicap . . . Nice course, wide open . . . When wind kicks up it's five shots harder . . . A beginner's paradise . . . No carts, easy walk . . . A few real challenging holes . . . A good bargain for the buck.

★★ HEATHER HILL COUNTRY CLUB

PU—149 W. Bacon St., Plainville (508)695-0309.
Call club for further information.
Subscriber comments: 18-hole layout good . . . First hole on nine-hole course is a par 3 . . . Staff always makes you feel welcome . . . Recent expansion makes course very accessible . . . Course improving . . . Shot placement critical on some holes . . . A fun course, wide open, let out the shaft . . . If your rent the carts you must use them on the path with 90 degree rule . . . Quite hilly, some fairways narrow, blind tee shots, remainder rather tough. Nine-hole layout fairly open . . . Small greens make course tough even though it's short.

★★★½ HICKORY RIDGE COUNTRY CLUB

SP—191 West Pomeroy Lane, Amherst (413)253-9320.
Holes: 18. **Par:** 72/72.
Yards: 6,794/5,340. **Course rating:** 72.5/70.3. **Slope:** 129/114.
Opened: 1970. **Pace of Play rating:** 4:30. **Green fee:** $32/43.
Credit cards: MC, V, AMEX. **Reduced fees:** Weekdays, Juniors.
Caddies: No. **Golf carts:** $25 for 18 holes.
Discount golf packages: No. **Season:** April-Nov. **High:** May-Sept.
On-site lodging: No. **Rental clubs:** Yes.
Walking policy: Unrestricted walking. **Range:** Yes (grass).
To obtain tee times: Outside play: 24 hours in advance.
Subscriber comments: Playing Hickory Ridge is a pleasure . . . 18th hole is signature hole: 440+ to elevated green . . . Holds interest exceedingly well; options, options . . . Very fair from ladies tees . . . Extremely accommodating staff, try hard to fit singles in . . . Large greens, pretty flat and open, good for mid-handicap player . . . Average, golfer friendly . . . Great conditions, good test of your ability . . . Great finishing hole . . . Beautiful, well kept. Scenic . . . Nice staff . . . Always in great shape, just an enjoyable course to play . . . A long course from back tees with a variety of shots required.

★★ HIGHLAND GOLF LINKS

PU—Highland Light Rd. P.O. Box 162, North Truro (508)487-9201.
45 miles north of Hyannis. **Holes:** 18. **Par:** 70/74.
Yards: 5,299/4,782. **Course rating:** 65.0/67.4. **Slope:** 103/107.
Opened: 1892. **Pace of Play rating:** 3:35. **Green fee:** $25.
Credit cards: None. **Reduced fees:** Low season.
Caddies: No. **Golf carts:** $21 for 18 holes.
Discount golf packages: Yes. **Season:** April-Nov. **High:** June-Sept.
On-site lodging: No. **Rental clubs:** Yes.
Walking policy: Unrestricted walking. **Range:** No.
To obtain tee times: Call 48 hrs. in advance.
Subscriber comments: Hilly links course, staff very accommodating and friendly . . . Dates to 1892, oldest on Cape Cod; panoramic, feels like

Scotland . . . Fantastic ocean views . . . A touch of Scotland in New England . . . Fun and not too difficult, unless windy . . . The way golf was meant to be played . . . Majestic views . . . True links golf, quite a challenge . . . One would swear they were in England . . . It is over 100 years old and right on the ocean; even has a lighthouse, one of my favorites.

★★½ HYANNIS GOLF CLUB AT IYANOUGH HILLS

SP—Rte. 132, Hyannis (508)362-2606.
3 miles north of Hyannis. **Holes:** 18. **Par:** 71/72.
Yards: 6,514/5,149. **Course rating:** 70.2/69.0. **Slope:** 121/125.
Opened: N/A. **Pace of Play rating:** N/A. **Green fee:** $25/35.
Credit cards: All major. **Reduced fees:** Weekdays, Low season, Twilight, Seniors.
Caddies: No. **Golf carts:** $12 for 18 holes.
Discount golf packages: Yes. **Season:** Year-round. **High:** June-Sept.
On-site lodging: No. **Rental clubs:** Yes.
Walking policy: Walking at certain times. **Range:** Yes.
To obtain tee times: Call pro shop.
Subscriber comments: Old standby on the Cape . . . This course has come a long way, great greens, friendly staff . . . Has some interesting holes . . . Nice driving range, very busy in summer . . . Hilly course with wide fairways, greens are good . . . Nice course, would play again . . . Not a level lie on the course . . . A real sleeper . . . Interesting, challenging, doing a lot to improve conditions.

★★★ JUNIPER HILL GOLF COURSE

PU—202 Brigham St., Northboro (508)393-2444.
Call club for further information.
Subscriber comments: Tough to decide which 18 you should play . . . Riverside, wide fairways, small greens, great condition, great staff . . . Like Riverside Course better than Lakeside Course, not as narrow . . . Both courses tough, bring your best game . . . New Lakeside Course is beautiful . . . Lakeside Course for everyone, holes have character, views great . . . Two courses, one open, one tight, lots of play . . . Lakeside Course, shotmaker's layout, lots of trouble . . . Riverside Course had great greens all season . . . Lakeside Course better! . . . Riverside Course top notch, well laid out . . . Old course for average player, new course more of a challenge . . . Variety of holes, requires all the clubs . . . Riverside is one of the best courses around . . . Riverside has several blind tee shots.

★★½ LAKEVILLE COUNTRY CLUB

PU—44 Clear Pond Rd, Lakeville (508)947-6630.
50 miles south of Boston. **Holes:** 18. **Par:** 72/72.
Yards: 6,274/5,297. **Course rating:** 70.1/68.5. **Slope:** 123/118.
Opened: 1970. **Pace of Play rating:** N/A. **Green fee:** $20/25.
Credit cards: MC, V, DISC. **Reduced fees:** No.
Caddies: No. **Golf carts:** $20 for 18 holes.
Discount golf packages: No. **Season:** Year-round. **High:** May-Sept.
On-site lodging: No. **Rental clubs:** No.
Walking policy: Unrestricted walking. **Range:** No.
To obtain tee times: Tee times can be made one week ahead with a major credit card. Foursomes only on weekends and holidays during the morning.
Subscriber comments: A short hitter's mecca . . . Long front nine, too many par 3s on back nine . . . 16th hole: try to land a golf ball on a postage stamp . . . Beautiful finishing holes with two par 3s over water . . . Great par 4s, quick play, suited nicely for the short hitter; 16th is the best . . . Short, a lot of water holes, good test for short and medium irons . . . Nice friendly staff. Great greens, course always in good condition . . . Some fun par 5s . . . Two of the three finishing holes par 3s . . . Challenging course with plenty of water hazards; can be rewarding . . . Fairways run side by side, dangerous . . . Short but still fun, didn't need the woods at all . . . Ego builder, all greens reachable in regulation . . . Must hit ball straight. Big slow greens. Can score well here.

★★★ LARRY GANNON GOLF CLUB
PU—42 Great Woods Rd., Lynn (617)592-8238.
Call club for further information.
Subscriber comments: Great seaside test . . . Great test in wind, devilish greens . . . Good views.

★★★½ MAPLEGATE COUNTRY CLUB
PU—160 Maple St., Bellingham (508)966-4040.
25 miles southwest of Boston. **Holes:** 18. **Par:** 72/72.
Yards: 6,815/4,852. **Course rating:** 74.2/70.2. **Slope:** 133/124.
Opened: 1990. **Pace of Play rating:** 4:10. **Green fee:** $19/37.
Credit cards: MC, V. **Reduced fees:** Weekdays, Low season, Twilight, Juniors.
Caddies: No. **Golf carts:** $49 for 18 holes.
Discount golf packages: No. **Season:** April-Dec. **High:** May-Sept.
On-site lodging: No. **Rental clubs:** Yes.
Walking policy: Walking at certain times. **Range:** Yes (grass).
To obtain tee times: Call six days in advance for foursomes; previous day after 4 p.m. for all others.
Subscriber comments: Pretty, wooded new course . . . Interesting . . . Fairly tight, medium-sized greens, fair conditions . . . Par 3 eighth is a classic; waterfall and swans . . . Excellent layout, an all-around pleasant golf experience . . . When it matures, it will be magnificent . . . Great forest golf, many doglegs, many carries over swamp . . . Calm front nine, back shorter, tighter, more imagination . . . Excellent new course, tight fairways, but decent landing areas. A real comer . . . This is what fun golf is all about. Leave the woods in the bag . . . Premium on accuracy off the tee . . . Makes you think . . . Excellent condition peak season, staff very nice . . . Superb design. Good layout. Needs time to be noticed.

★½ MERRIMACK GOLF CLUB
PU—210 Howe St., Methuen (508)685-9717.
Call club for further information.
Subscriber comments: Wet in spring, honest layout, blue-collar . . . Drainage poor, needs care . . . You get what you pay for . . . Too swampy . . . Course has great potential.

★★★ NEW ENGLAND COUNTRY CLUB
PU—180 Paine St., Bellingham (508)883-2300.
35 miles south of Boston. **Holes:** 18. **Par:** 71/71.
Yards: 6,378/4,908. **Course rating:** 71.1/68.7. **Slope:** 129/121.
Opened: 1990. **Pace of Play rating:** 4:50. **Green fee:** $25/40.
Credit cards: MC, V. **Reduced fees:** Weekdays, Low season, Twilight.
Caddies: No. **Golf carts:** Included in Green Fee.
Discount golf packages: Yes. **Season:** April-Nov. **High:** June-Sept.
On-site lodging: No. **Rental clubs:** No.
Walking policy: Walking at certain times. **Range:** Yes (grass).
To obtain tee times: Call pro shop no more than five days in advance.
Subscriber comments: Spectacular and scenic . . . Some superior holes, some unique holes . . . Has a lot of promise . . . Difficult course, several hidden hazards; bring extra balls . . . Significant forced carries . . . Tight, target golf, friendly staff, enjoyable . . . Accurate approach shots a must; good test . . . Good service, course excellent, not for the beginner . . . Could be special . . . Wonderful variety of challenging holes . . . Tough course, especially on high handicappers . . . Many long walks to next hole . . . Love the course, you have to think . . . Keep your driver in the bag . . . More ups and downs than a rollercoaster . . . All that golf should be . . . You can't beat it.

NEW SEABURY COUNTRY CLUB
R—P.O. Box 549, New Seabury (508)477-9110.
70 miles south of Boston.
Opened: 1964. **Pace of Play rating:** 4:30. **Green fee:** $30/60.
Credit cards: MC, V, AMEX. **Reduced fees:** Low season, Twilight.

Caddies: No. **Golf carts:** $15 for 18 holes.
Discount golf packages: Yes. **Season:** Year-round. **High:** July–Aug.
On-site lodging: Yes. **Rental clubs:** Yes.
Walking policy: Walking at certain times. **Range:** Yes.
To obtain tee times: Guests of the resort may make tee times one day in advance.

★★★★ BLUE COURSE
Holes: 18. **Par:** 72/72.
Yards: 7,200/5,764. **Course rating:** 75.3/73.8. **Slope:** 130/128.
Ranked 69th in America's 75 Best Resort Courses by Golf Digest. Ranked 5th in Massachusetts by Golf Digest.
Subscriber comments: Beautiful oceanside course, good conditions, always windy . . . Constant breeze, are you really a golfer? . . . All you want from back tees . . . Front nine seaside, back nine condo-side . . . Great golf course. Oh, the wind . . . Worth every penny, beautiful seaside views . . . This is a beautiful place and we truly love to get beaten into the ground by it. A most delightful lesson in humility . . . A championship test, great ocean holes, huge greens . . . Beauty on Nantucket Sound. Good views of Martha's Vineyard. Great shape . . . Front nine is spectacular, back nine is challenging . . . Like playing two different courses . . . Could play every day and never get bored . . . Always a delight to play . . . One of the best on Cape Cod . . . Tough as a Nor'easter, beautiful as a wildlife sanctuary . . . Great scenery, all-around great course running along ocean.

★★★ GREEN COURSE
Holes: 18. **Par:** 70/68.
Yards: 5,939/5,105. **Course rating:** 67.0/66.3. **Slope:** 117/110.
Subscriber comments: Greens are unbelievably tough, be prepared . . . Was like playing on a private course . . . Pretty little course in great shape . . . Nice course for social golf, for relaxing; excellent condition . . . Shorter course, not designed for low handicappers in a competitive mood.

★ NORWOOD COUNTRY CLUB
PU—400 Providence Hwy., Norwood (617)769-5880.
20 miles south of Boston. **Holes:** 18. **Par:** 71/71.
Yards: 6,009/4,997. **Course rating:** 67.1/68.7. **Slope:** 112/108.
Opened: 1975. **Pace of Play rating:** 4:30. **Green fee:** $16/20.
Credit cards: None. **Reduced fees:** Weekdays, Twilight, Seniors, Juniors.
Caddies: No. **Golf carts:** $11 for 18 holes.
Discount golf packages: No. **Season:** Year-round. **High:** June–Sept.
On-site lodging: Yes. **Rental clubs:** Yes.
Walking policy: Unrestricted walking. **Range:** Yes.
To obtain tee times: Call one week in advance for weekends and holidays only.
Subscriber comments: All short straight holes, can be boring . . . Very short, good course for beginners or seniors . . . Straight, short, flat, wide, will make you feel like a pro . . . Very flat with lots of lateral hazards . . . Good for walking, not tough, not in great shape, but enjoyable . . . Almost every hole looks the same; flat, tree-lined.

★★★½ OAK RIDGE GOLF CLUB
PU—850 S. Westfield St., Feeding Hills (413)789-7307.
10 miles northwest of Springfield. **Holes:** 18. **Par:** 70/70.
Yards: 6,819/5,307. **Course rating:** 71.2/70.0. **Slope:** 124/N/A.
Opened: 1974. **Pace of Play rating:** N/A. **Green fee:** $20/25.
Credit cards: None. **Reduced fees:** Weekdays, Seniors, Juniors.
Caddies: No. **Golf carts:** $12 for 18 holes.
Discount golf packages: No. **Season:** March–Dec. **High:** June–Sept.
On-site lodging: No. **Rental clubs:** Yes.
Walking policy: N/A. **Range:** No.
To obtain tee times: Call one week in advance for weekday and Wednesdays for weekend play.
Subscriber comments: Great shotmaking course . . . Fun and friendly. Easy to walk . . . Well-groomed layout; tees allow it to play to a variety of skill levels . . . Too many tournaments and outings . . . Always in pristine

condition, has the feel of a private club . . . Excellent rolling layout; need all clubs . . . Covered bridge! . . . Outstanding in every way . . . Good course for intermediate to good golfer . . . A bit short from the whites but a good test from the blue tees . . . Lots of flowers everywhere. Good staff and clubhouse . . . Need to have your putter working . . . Beautiful, aesthetically pleasing course, very challenging with four sets of tees . . . Every hole has character . . . Large flat greens, very good par 3s.

★★★½ OCEAN EDGE GOLF CLUB

R—832 Villages Dr., Brewster (508)896-5911.
90 miles south of Boston. **Holes:** 18. **Par:** 72/72.
Yards: 6,665/5,098. **Course rating:** 71.9/73.2. **Slope:** 129/129.
Opened: 1986. **Pace of Play rating:** 4:30. **Green fee:** $26/46.
Credit cards: MC, V, AMEX. **Reduced fees:** Weekdays, Low season, Resort guests, Juniors.
Caddies: No. **Golf carts:** $13 for 18 holes.
Discount golf packages: Yes. **Season:** March-Dec. **High:** June-Sept.
On-site lodging: Yes. **Rental clubs:** Yes.
Walking policy: Walking at certain times. **Range:** Yes (grass).
To obtain tee times: Hotel guests may make tee times at time of room reservation.
Subscriber comments: Friendly staff, great conditions, fun to play . . . Need a good eye for distance off the tees. Take a yardage book . . . Treated like royalty . . . Tight course, little room for error . . . Outstanding shape, excellent staff, super layout . . . Ocean Edge, outstanding . . . Unique, challenging course for all levels . . . Test of your game . . . Not long, but wind can play havoc with your game . . . Simply the best on the Cape . . . Except for a couple of holes, a real gem . . . Those pot bunkers will kill you . . . Beautiful course, but too hard for me on the day I played . . . Unbeatable par 5s . . . No "ocean" on this Ocean Edge course . . . Fine, natural course with no gimmicks, a true test . . . Interesting course with some very challenging holes, always in excellent condition.

★★★½ OLDE BARNSTABLE FAIRGROUNDS GOLF COURSE

PU—Rte. 149, Marstons Mills (508)420-1141.
55 miles south of Boston. **Holes:** 18. **Par:** 71/71.
Yards: 6,503/5,162. **Course rating:** 70.7/69.2. **Slope:** 123/118.
Opened: 1992. **Pace of Play rating:** 4:30. **Green fee:** $20/35.
Credit cards: MC, V. **Reduced fees:** Weekdays, Twilight.
Caddies: No. **Golf carts:** $21 for 18 holes.
Discount golf packages: No. **Season:** Year-round. **High:** April-Nov.
On-site lodging: No. **Rental clubs:** Yes.
Walking policy: Unrestricted walking. **Range:** Yes.
To obtain tee times: Call 48 hours in advance at 10 a.m. Prepaid reservations by mail with no restrictions.
Subscriber comments: Excellent layout, very enjoyable . . . Excellent greens . . . No.18 is a picture hole . . . Lots of fun, greens fast and hilly . . . Excellent course, all greens heavily protected, fast with lots of break . . . Needs time to mature; challenging shot selection . . . This course keeps getting better . . . True country-club feeling. Course is a delight to play, enjoyed every hole . . . Super course, enjoyable to play, nice undulations in fairways and on greens . . . Must wait on 10th as small planes fly overhead . . . Wish I played it again . . . Par 3s super . . . More variety than many Cape Cod courses.

★★★ PEMBROKE COUNTRY CLUB

SP—West Elm St., Pembroke (617)826-3983.
Call club for further information.
Subscriber comments: Hit straight or you're in for a long day . . . Tough par fours . . . Nice track, usually in good shape . . . Great lounge, nice layout, easy walking . . . One of the best in the area, lots of challenging

holes . . . Bring the big sticks; fairways suck the ball right, slicers beware!
. . . Long and narrow, fast greens, plenty of water . . . Course is a lot
harder than ratings indicate; must use every club in bag . . . Tough course
that doesn't get much respect . . . One of the nicest on the shore.

★½ PONKAPOAG GOLF CLUB

PU—2167 Washington St., Canton (617)828-5828.
10 miles south of Boston.
Call club for further information.
Subscriber comments: With a little more work this will be a great public
course . . . A few good challenging holes . . . All levels of play can enjoy
this course and walk away with change in your pocket . . . Great potential,
many improvements and more to come . . . Old gem on comeback trail,
lots of character, not what it used to be . . . Superb layout and improving
conditions . . . Blue-collar golf at its best . . . Great course for beginners
. . . The basic beauty of a Donald Ross course exists.

★★★½ POQUOY BROOK GOLF CLUB

PU—20 Leonard St., Lakeville (508)947-5261.
Call club for further information.
Subscriber comments: Good early Cornish design . . . They don't come
better than this . . . Very pleasant staff . . . Nice rolling hills with beautiful
views . . . Great condition, nice practice facilities . . . Treated well, play
was moving along, good course for all handicaps, better for long and
straight hitters, tough greens . . . Good test of golf, big greens . . . Some
good risk and reward holes . . . Attractive course, kept up to top level,
challenging but can finish without giving up on game . . . Love the 18th
. . . Always a pleasant experience . . . No complaints on entire round,
would play anytime . . . A great public track . . . Scenery is absolutely
gorgeous, this course is for all levels of players . . . Superb golfing
experience . . . Best maintained public course, played last fall, no leaves!
. . . Us oldsters need a cart . . . Tree lined, fairly tight fairways . . . The
greens are always in perfect shape . . . Staff keeps play moving along . . .
Good walking course . . . Low and high handicaps can enjoy a round here.

★★½ QUASHNET VALLEY COUNTRY CLUB

SP—309 Old Barnstable Rd., Mashpee (508)477-4412.
55 miles south of Boston. **Holes:** 18. **Par:** 72/72.
Yards: 6,602/5,094. **Course rating:** 71.7/70.3. **Slope:** 132/119.
Opened: 1974. **Pace of Play rating:** 4:00–4:30. **Green fee:** $18/36.
Credit cards: MC, V. **Reduced fees:** Low season, Twilight.
Caddies: No. **Golf carts:** $11 for 18 holes.
Discount golf packages: No. **Season:** Year-round. **High:** April-Oct.
On-site lodging: No. **Rental clubs:** Yes.
Walking policy: Walking at certain times. **Range:** Yes (grass).
To obtain tee times: Call one week in advance.
Subscriber comments: Unique . . . The cranberry bogs swallow errant
balls . . . Must be accurate with every shot . . . Great layout, the front and
back are distinctively different . . . Pretty but cannot use woods on several
tees because of driving through the fairway . . . Staff makes you feel
welcome . . . Tough course, narrow fairways with lots of interesting holes
and fast greens . . . Course in good shape. Tough challenge unless your
shots are accurate . . . Stunning scenery . . . Tight front nine, eats golf balls.
Hit it straight and score . . . Demanding tee shots . . . Not for beginners,
lots of hazards . . . Very difficult design through cranberry bogs, finishing
holes killers . . . Most par 4s reachable in two, no bad holes, a fun course
. . . You either like it or hate it.

REHOBOTH COUNTRY CLUB★

PU—155 Perryville Rd., Rehoboth (508)252-6259.
15 miles east of Providence. **Holes:** 18. **Par:** 72/75.
Yards: 6,950/5,450. **Course rating:** 72.5/70.4. **Slope:** 125/115.
Opened: 1966. **Pace of Play rating:** 3:50. **Green fee:** $17/22.
Credit cards: None. **Reduced fees:** Twilight, Seniors, Juniors.

Caddies: No. **Golf carts:** $10 for 18 holes.
Discount golf packages: No. **Season:** Year-round. **High:** May-Sept.
On-site lodging: No. **Rental clubs:** No.
Walking policy: Unrestricted walking. **Range:** No.
To obtain tee times: Tee times taken three days in advance for weekends only.

★½ RIDDER GOLF CLUB
PU—300 Oak St., Rte. 14, Whitman (617)447-6614.
20 miles south of Boston. **Holes:** 18. **Par:** 70/70.
Yards: 5,847/5,400. **Course rating:** 67.6/67.6. **Slope:** 109/109.
Opened: 1961. **Pace of Play rating:** 4:00. **Green fee:** $15/24.
Credit cards: None. **Reduced fees:** Low season, Juniors.
Caddies: No. **Golf carts:** $21 for 18 holes.
Discount golf packages: No. **Season:** March-Dec. **High:** May-Sept.
On-site lodging: No. **Rental clubs:** Yes.
Walking policy: Unrestricted walking. **Range:** Yes (grass).
To obtain tee times: Call up to 48 hours in advance.
Subscriber comments: Another short hitter's dream . . . Surprisingly tough back nine . . . Short, greens good, no such thing as an easy course . . . A regular guy's (and lady's) course, very forgiving . . . A confidence builder . . . Fairways open; greens break a lot . . . Great for beginners and seniors . . . Usually a well-maintained course . . . Owners are very loyal to customers . . . Faders find trouble . . . The place to play if you have only one golf ball.

★★ ROUND HILL COUNTRY CLUB
SP—Round Hill Rd., E. Sandwich (508)888-3384.
50 miles south of Boston. **Holes:** 18. **Par:** 71/70.
Yards: 6,300/4,800. **Course rating:** 71.4/68.1. **Slope:** 124/115.
Opened: 1972. **Pace of Play rating:** 4:30. **Green fee:** $40.
Credit cards: MC, V. **Reduced fees:** Weekdays, Low season, Twilight, Juniors.
Caddies: No. **Golf carts:** Included in Green Fee.
Discount golf packages: No. **Season:** Year-round. **High:** May-Oct.
On-site lodging: No. **Rental clubs:** Yes.
Walking policy: Walking at certain times. **Range:** Yes (grass).
To obtain tee times: Call seven days in advance.
Subscriber comments: Tough hilly course, usually windy, service was great . . . Mountain goats love this place . . . Never a wait, take a cart . . . Let me see the PGA Tour here! . . . Endurance test, most shots are blind . . . Nice course, but don't walk it on a hot day . . . Saddleback fairways . . . Well treated by staff . . . Has its up and downs. Lots of fun.

★★½ SADDLE HILL COUNTRY CLUB
PU—204 Saddle Hill Rd., Hopkinton (508)435-4630.
Call club for further information.
Subscriber comments: Very playable course . . . Tough course to walk, conditions varies . . . Well marked distances, real challenge from blues . . . Lots of hills, doglegs, woods, no water . . . Requires every club in your bag . . . Nothing fancy . . . Greens very consistent, a true test . . . A great course for the common man, we need more of these.

★★ SAGAMORE SPRINGS GOLF CLUB
PU—1287 Main St., Lynnfield (617)334-6969.
15 miles north of Boston. **Holes:** 18. **Par:** 70/70.
Yards: 5,936/4,784. **Course rating:** 68.6/66.5. **Slope:** 119/112.
Opened: 1929. **Pace of Play rating:** N/A. **Green fee:** $26/30.
Credit cards: MC, V, DISC. **Reduced fees:** Low season, Seniors.
Caddies: No. **Golf carts:** $11 for 18 holes.
Discount golf packages: No. **Season:** March-Dec. **High:** June-Sept.
On-site lodging: No. **Rental clubs:** Yes.
Walking policy: Unrestricted walking. **Range:** Yes.

To obtain tee times: Call four days in advance between 9 a.m. and 5 p.m.
Subscriber comments: Average player will have an average challenge . . .
Seeing Elvis easier than getting tee time . . . Short but very enjoyable,
tough par 3s, good staff . . . Outstanding course for all levels, beautiful in
the fall . . . Long par 3s and reachable par 5s . . . Good drainage makes it a
springtime winner . . . Easy course to shoot a low score . . . Very well
maintained, no trick shots required.

★★½ SANDY BURR COUNTRY CLUB
PU—103 Cochituate Rd., Wayland (508)358-7211.
Call club for further information.
Subscriber comments: This course has character . . . Reachable par 5s
. . . Holes very close to each other, "Fore" . . . Wide open, forgiving . . .
Good, old New England course, historic clubhouse . . . Slow on weekends
. . . Challenging layout, pretty in fall . . . Donald Ross design, easy par 5s,
great par 3s . . . Nice fairways, easy play, kept in good condition.

★★★ SHAKER HILLS GOLF CLUB
PU—Shaker Rd., Harvard (508)772-2227.
35 miles northwest of Boston. **Holes:** 18. **Par:** 71/71.
Yards: 6,850/5,001. **Course rating:** 72.3/67.9. **Slope:** 135/116.
Opened: 1991. **Pace of Play rating:** 4:20. **Green fee:** $45/50.
Credit cards: MC, V. **Reduced fees:** Twilight.
Caddies: Yes. **Golf carts:** Included in Green Fee.
Discount golf packages: No. **Season:** April-Nov. **High:** June-Sept.
On-site lodging: No. **Rental clubs:** Yes.
Walking policy: Walking at certain times. **Range:** Yes (grass).
To obtain tee times: Call automated 24-hour tee time reservations.
Selected as runner-up for Best New Public Course of 1992.
Subscriber comments: Super layout, very interesting . . . A class above
all others, worth playing a few times . . . Excellent layout with great holes,
super staff, greens inconsistent . . . Excellent, except for the greens . . .
Carts only on paths, should use 90 degree rule, fairways immaculate,
though . . . Very tough, challenging, requires cart, very hilly . . . Wow!
Tough track . . . Very nice course . . . Lots of rangers on the course, keep it
moving . . . Thinking man's layout, one of Brian Silva's best . . . Good
course, but too tough for average golfer, too tight in spots . . . Too many
holes with O.B. on right . . . Great elevated tees, not for beginners . . .
Nice variations from hole to hole . . . Everyone is courteous and helpful;
great clubhouse; course has something for all levels . . . Four fantastic par
3s.

★★★½ SOUTH SHORE COUNTRY CLUB
SP—274 South St., Hingham (617)749-8479.
Call club for further information.
Subscriber comments: Challenging course, lots of uphill and sidehill lies
. . . Hard to get up and down . . . Very hilly, greens excellent, especially
early fall; fasten seatbelt on downhills . . . Staff friendly . . . Ball position is
important, greens break a lot . . . Tough course to walk . . . Tremendous,
fun test of golf for mid-handicapper. Elevated greens and tees . . . 15th
through 18th holes are fantastic finishing holes . . . Good layout, tough
approaches to greens.

STOW ACRES COUNTRY CLUB
PU—58 Randall Rd., Stow (508)568-1100.
25 miles west of Boston.
Credit cards: None. **Reduced fees:** Weekdays, Low season, Twilight,
Seniors, Juniors.
Caddies: No. **Golf carts:** $24 for 18 holes.
Discount golf packages: No. **Season:** March-Dec. **High:** April-Nov.
On-site lodging: No. **Rental clubs:** Yes.
Walking policy: Unrestricted walking. **Range:** Yes.
To obtain tee times: Call five days in advance.

★★★ NORTH COURSE
Holes: 18. **Par:** 72/72.
Yards: 6,950/6,011. **Course rating:** 72.8/70.6. **Slope:** 130/120.
Opened: 1965. **Pace of Play rating:** 4:10. **Green fee:** $30/37.
Subscriber comments: Course is wonderful . . . Straightforward, good layout, good variety . . . As good as they come in public courses . . . Good intermediate course . . . Great public golf, well run, good test, must play every year . . . Good walking course, can hit all your clubs . . . Good test of skill and patience . . . Improvements are outstanding: bunker renovations, conversion to bent grass, many amenities . . . Beautiful course in the country, difficult and long . . . Six hour round common, people play like they are trying to qualify for the Open . . . Cream of the crop for public golf courses. Shot values excellent. Must drive the golf ball . . . Ninth hole impossible . . . Would be great if not for endless dogleg lefts . . . Good mix of holes, nine shots tougher than South course . . . Play can be slow . . . Great 9th hole . . . Country club conditions; must play if in the area . . . Very ambitious for ladies . . . Long wait some days, plays slow but usually worth it . . . A solid golf course where you earn a good score.

★★★ SOUTH COURSE
Holes: 18. **Par:** 72/72.
Yards: 6,520/5,642. **Course rating:** 71.8/69.7. **Slope:** 120/116.
Opened: 1955. **Pace of Play rating:** 4:08. **Green fee:** $28/37.
Subscriber comments: A very underrated shotmaker's course . . . The wind is a big factor on this layout; fun course . . . Not as tough as North. Back nine is beautiful in the fall. Play is sometimes slow . . . Hilly, heck of a challenge . . . Excellent condition, best grass changeover . . . Left to rights and rights to lefts. Excellent test . . . Manageable for all levels, with excellent par 5s . . . Easier and more enjoyable of the two courses . . . True treasure of a course, need to think course management on every hole, greens are true and fast, course is lush with lots of water and tight fairways; a great experience.

★★ SWANSEA COUNTRY CLUB
PU—299 Market St., Swansea (508)379-9886.
10 miles east of Providence, RI. **Holes:** 18. **Par:** 72/72.
Yards: 6,809/5,103. **Course rating:** 72.6/69.3. **Slope:** 129/111.
Opened: 1963. **Pace of Play rating:** N/A. **Green fee:** $20/25.
Credit cards: None. **Reduced fees:** Weekdays, Low season, Twilight, Seniors, Juniors.
Caddies: No. **Golf carts:** N/A.
Discount golf packages: No. **Season:** Year-round. **High:** May-Sept.
On-site lodging: No. **Rental clubs:** Yes.
Walking policy: Unrestricted walking. **Range:** Yes (grass).
To obtain tee times: Call five days in advance.
Subscriber comments: Cornish design . . . Long, tough course with narrow fairways, a lot of trees . . . Nice layout, challenging to every level of golfer . . . Nice course, able to use all clubs . . . Needs tender loving care . . . A challenge from the tips, owner making steady improvements on a great layout . . . Best greens in the area, need to be straight and long to score well.

★★★★ TACONIC GOLF CLUB
SP—Meacham St., Williamstown (413)458-3997.
35 miles east of Albany, NY. **Holes:** 18. **Par:** 71/N.A.
Yards: 6,614/N/A. **Course rating:** 70.5/N/A. **Slope:** 127/111.
Opened: 1896. **Pace of Play rating:** 4:00. **Green fee:** $80.
Credit cards: MC, V. **Reduced fees:** N/A.
Caddies: No. **Golf carts:** Included in Green Fee.
Discount golf packages: No. **Season:** April-Nov.
On-site lodging: No. **Rental clubs:** Yes.
Walking policy: Mandatory cart. **Range:** Yes (grass).
To obtain tee times: Call up to one week in advance.
Subscriber comments: Great example of New England mountain golf; not too long, but difficult from back tees . . . Beautiful views, crowded in

peak season, staff excellent . . . One of the best tracks anywhere . . .
Excellent staff and conditions, scenic views, great layout . . . I've never
played Augusta; these greens must be comparable . . . A great golf course.
Trees planted after built . . . Course should be in the Ivy League: it's tough
to get into and even harder to get out of . . . Every hole is excellent . . .
Challenge to low or high handicaps . . . Can't have a more beautiful setting.
Greens are deadly, fast, and severe . . . One of best kept secrets in golf, will
host 1996 U.S. Senior Amateur; play it in the fall . . . A favorite, right in
the Berkshire Mountains, great layout.

★★★½ TARA FERNCROFT COUNTRY CLUB

R—50 Ferncroft Rd., Danver (508)777-5614.
Holes: 18. **Par:** 72/73.
Yards: 6,601/5,543. **Course rating:** 73.2/71.4. **Slope:** 131/118.
Opened: 1970. **Pace of Play rating:** 4:15. **Green fee:** $75.
Credit cards: All major. **Reduced fees:** No.
Caddies: No. **Golf carts:** Included in Green Fee.
Discount golf packages: Yes. **Season:** April-Dec. **High:** May-Oct.
On-site lodging: Yes. **Rental clubs:** Yes.
Walking policy: Mandatory cart. **Range:** Yes (grass).
To obtain tee times: Hotel guests 2 days prior to play.
Subscriber comments: Split-personality nines combine for good test . . .
Superb! . . . Always a delight, good condition . . . Can't take carts off path
. . . Tourist's heaven. Good layout. Everything you need for golf . . .
Outstanding Robert Trent Jones layout . . . Lots of water on front nine . . .
Play it if you want to see a real golf course . . . Very nice course. Well
maintained. Great service . . . LPGA used to play here, great golf . . .
Fairways are always in great shape . . . Top notch all around.

★★★ TRULL BROOK GOLF COURSE

PU—170 River Rd., Tewksbury (508)851-6731.
28 miles northwest of Boston. **Holes:** 18. **Par:** 72/72.
Yards: 6,350/5,385. **Course rating:** 68.4/70.2. **Slope:** 118/118.
Opened: 1963. **Pace of Play rating:** 4:12. **Green fee:** $30/32.
Credit cards: MC, V. **Reduced fees:** Weekdays, Low season, Twilight,
Seniors, Juniors.
Caddies: No. **Golf carts:** $11 for 18 holes.
Discount golf packages: No. **Season:** March-Nov. **High:** June-Aug.
On-site lodging: No. **Rental clubs:** Yes.
Walking policy: Unrestricted walking. **Range:** No.
To obtain tee times: Call up to seven days in advance.
Subscriber comments: Always in good shape, can be crowded, lots of
hills, attack par 5s . . . Fun course, room for error, very busy . . . Fairly
tight, huge greens . . . Don't walk; many deceptive tee shots . . . A gem,
well maintained, challenging course . . . Too short for real test, too hilly for
comfortable walk . . . Interesting Cornish course, good mix of holes . . .
Varied terrain that's fun to play . . . Makes you think . . . Awesome
scenery in fall . . . A little too formal, but very pretty and interesting . . .
Good maintenance despite heavy play . . . Too many blind approach shots
. . . A beautiful, well manicured, and very scenic golf course. I find it to be
a demanding course . . . Pretty holes, not real tough, but super greens.

★★★½ WACHUSETT COUNTRY CLUB

SP—187 Prospect St., West Boylston (508)835-4453.
7 miles north of Worcester. **Holes:** 18. **Par:** 72/N/A.
Yards: 6,608/6,216. **Course rating:** 71.7/N/A. **Slope:** 124/N/A.
Opened: 1928. **Pace of Play rating:** 4:15. **Green fee:** $25/28.
Credit cards: MC, V. **Reduced fees:** Weekdays, Low season, Twilight.
Caddies: No. **Golf carts:** $12 for 18 holes.
Discount golf packages: No. **Season:** April-Nov. **High:** May-Oct.
On-site lodging: No. **Rental clubs:** Yes.
Walking policy: Unrestricted walking. **Range:** Yes (grass).
To obtain tee times: Call.
Subscriber comments: Excellent, challenging course for intermediate

players. Courteous staff, course remains in good shape all season . . . Good test of golf, bring your driver . . . Old layout, plays well, very enjoyable . . . Gorgeous . . . Nice layout, private conditions . . . Nice views, top condition even after tough New England winters . . . Interesting mountain course . . . Great course you never tire of . . . Very open, tends to be windy, small greens . . . Suits all players. Staff O.K. Pace O.K. Fine shape . . . Spectacular views on several holes . . . True Donald Ross, good par 4s . . . Great risk and reward on par 5s.

★★★½ WAHCONAH COUNTRY CLUB

SP—15 Orchard Rd., Dalton (413)684-1333.
4 miles north of Pittsfield. **Holes:** 18. **Par:** 71/73.
Yards: 6,541/5,597. **Course rating:** 71.4/71.2. **Slope:** 122/113.
Opened: 1930. **Pace of Play rating:** 4:15. **Green fee:** $40/50.
Credit cards: MC, V. **Reduced fees:** N/A.
Caddies: No. **Golf carts:** $22 for 18 holes.
Discount golf packages: No. **Season:** April-Nov. **High:** April-Nov.
On-site lodging: No. **Rental clubs:** No.
Walking policy: Unrestricted walking. **Range:** Yes (grass).
To obtain tee times: Call eight days in advance.
Subscriber comments: Scenic location . . . Difficult, tricky greens to putt . . . Challenging back nine . . . Great improvements in course conditioning . . . Each nine very different; well conditioned . . . Fun for everyone.

★★★ WAUBEEKA GOLF LINKS

PU—137 New Ashford Rd., S. Williamstown (413)458-8355.
12 miles north of Pittsfield. **Holes:** 18. **Par:** 72/72.
Yards: 6,296/5,086. **Course rating:** 70.9/71.2. **Slope:** 127/111.
Opened: 1966. **Pace of Play rating:** 3:52. **Green fee:** $17/22.
Credit cards: MC, V, AMEX. **Reduced fees:** Low season, Juniors.
Caddies: No. **Golf carts:** N/A.
Discount golf packages: No. **Season:** April-Nov. **High:** July-Aug.
On-site lodging: No. **Rental clubs:** Yes.
Walking policy: Unrestricted walking. **Range:** Yes (grass).
To obtain tee times: Call in advance.
Subscriber comments: Beautiful setting, need to know the course . . . Nice mix of holes . . . Play in the fall, views are wonderful . . . Great course for all . . . Challenging holes. Good service. Very accessible . . . Cooperative and courteous staff . . . Many bunkers and hazards . . . Beautiful views and wildlife.

★★½ WESTMINSTER COUNTRY CLUB

SP—51 Ellis Rd., Westminster (508)874-5938.
22 miles north of Worcester. **Holes:** 18. **Par:** 71/71.
Yards: 6,491/5,453. **Course rating:** 70.9/70.0. **Slope:** 133/115.
Opened: 1957. **Pace of Play rating:** 4:00. **Green fee:** $20/25.
Credit cards: MC, V, AMEX. **Reduced fees:** Twilight.
Caddies: No. **Golf carts:** $20 for 18 holes.
Discount golf packages: No. **Season:** April-Nov. **High:** May-Sept.
On-site lodging: No. **Rental clubs:** Yes.
Walking policy: Unrestricted walking. **Range:** No.
To obtain tee times: Call one day in advance for weekdays and on Friday for weekend times.
Subscriber comments: Wonderful restaurant, great course . . . Good price. Good staff. Good for mid-handicaps . . . Tough back nine . . . Great greens. The scenery is outstanding. Play it! . . . Fine course conditions.

★★½ WESTOVER GOLF COURSE

PU—South St., Granby (413)547-8610.
10 miles northeast of Springfield. **Holes:** 18. **Par:** 72/72.
Yards: 7,025/5,980. **Course rating:** 73.9/72.0. **Slope:** 131/118.
Opened: 1957. **Pace of Play rating:** 4:30. **Green fee:** $13/15.
Credit cards: None. **Reduced fees:** Twilight, Seniors, Juniors.
Caddies: No. **Golf carts:** $11.

MASSACHUSETTS

Discount golf packages: No. **Season:** April-Dec. **High:** June-Sept.
On-site lodging: No. **Rental clubs:** Yes.
Walking policy: Unrestricted walking. **Range:** Yes (grass).
To obtain tee times: Call or come in 48 hours in advance.
Subscriber comments: Excellent layout. Long, favors a fader, quality of the greens keep it from being excellent test of golf . . . Has seen better days, but is an enjoyable course to play . . . Could be terrific course, but designed for slicer . . . Next to runway of Westover, almost daily huge planes land . . . Tight layout, blind shots . . . Very long course, adjacent to air base; at times very loud . . . Easy to walk . . . Watch out for aircraft . . . Be long or be gone . . . Make up with your driver the night before . . . Looooong.

Notes

BROADWATER RESORT

Green fee: $40. **Credit cards:** All major. **Reduced fees:** Low season, Resort guests, Twilight.
Caddies: No. **Golf carts:** Included in Green Fee.
Discount golf packages: Yes. **Season:** Year-round. **High:** Feb.–May.
On-site lodging: Yes. **Rental clubs:** Yes.
Walking policy: Mandatory cart.
To obtain tee times: Call pro shop.

★★ SEA COURSE

R—2000 Beach Dr., Gulfport (601)385–4085, (800)647–3964.
Holes: 18. **Par:** 71/73.
Yards: 6,214/5,403. **Course rating:** 70.0/72.0. **Slope:** 118/113.
Opened: 1908. **Pace of Play rating:** 4:00. **Range:** No.
Subscriber comments: Chance to play a course little changed this century . . . Small greens, good staff . . . Needs some repair work . . . Old-style course in average condition . . . Some tight holes, some challenging . . . Nothing spectacular but fun, harmless . . . No. 4 most beautiful hole in Mississippi.

★★ SUN COURSE

R—2000 Beauvoir, Biloxie (601)385–4081, (800)647–3964.
3 miles east of Gulfport. **Holes:** 18. **Par:** 72/72.
Yards: 7,168/5,485. **Course rating:** 72.0/72.0. **Slope:** 126/120.
Opened: 1968. **Pace of Play rating:** 4:00. **Range:** Yes (grass).
Subscriber comments: Must hit long ball . . . Long but fair, super staff . . . Long. Small greens. Practice area. Fun to play . . . Wide open, long, just enough sand and water . . . Down from past conditions . . . Very nice but crowded in summer.

DIAMONDHEAD COUNTRY CLUB

R—7600 Country Club Circle, Diamondhead (601)255–3910, (800)346–8741.
20 miles west of Gulfport.
Pace of Play rating: N/A. **Green fee:** $26/38.
Credit cards: All major. **Reduced fees:** Low season, Resort guests, Juniors.
Caddies: No. **Golf carts:** $12 for 18 holes.
Discount golf packages: Yes. **Season:** Year-round. **High:** Feb.–May.
On-site lodging: Yes. **Rental clubs:** Yes.
Walking policy: Walking at certain times. **Range:** Yes (grass).
To obtain tee times: Advance tee times only available through golf packages. Call (800)221-2423 and/or (800)345-7915 for package information. Packages also available through hotels and motels along the coast.

★★★½ CARDINAL COURSE

Holes: 18. **Par:** 72/72.
Yards: 6,831/5,065. **Course rating:** 72.7/68.9. **Slope:** 132/117.
Opened: 1972.
Subscriber comments: Beautiful; well maintained . . . Beautiful scenery. Some drainage problems . . . Staff friendly and accommodating . . . For all golfers.

★★★ PINE COURSE

Holes: 18. **Par:** 72/72.
Yards: 6,817/5,313. **Course rating:** 73.6/71.1. **Slope:** 133/118.
Opened: 1977.
Subscriber comments: Been redone. A lovely course. Nice facilities . . . Good community course . . . Nice layout, some short holes, nice staff.

EAGLE RIDGE GOLF COURSE★

PU—Hwy. 18 S., Raymond (601)857–5993.
10 miles southwest of Jackson. **Holes:** 18. **Par:** 72/72.
Yards: 6,500/5,135. **Course rating:** 70.5/N/A. **Slope:** 113/N/A.
Opened: 1955. **Pace of Play rating:** 4:00. **Green fee:** $9/12.
Credit cards: MC, V. **Reduced fees:** Weekdays, Seniors.

Caddies: No. **Golf carts:** $16 for 18 holes.
Discount golf packages: No. **Season:** Year-round. **High:** March-Aug.
On-site lodging: No. **Rental clubs:** Yes.
Walking policy: Unrestricted walking. **Range:** Yes (grass).
To obtain tee times: Call Thursday for upcoming weekend.

★½ EDGEWATER BAY GOLF COURSE
R—2674 Pass Rd., Biloxi (601)388-9670.
Call club for further information.
Subscriber comments: Nice layout . . . Fairways need help. Picturesque
back nine . . . Not enough fairway grass, plenty of dead spots . . . Average
track, fairways skinned . . . Good for a practice round.

★½ GRAND OAKS RESORT
R—Corner of Lyles Dr. and Hwy. 7, Oxford (601)236-3008,
(800)541-3881. 60 miles south of Memphis. **Holes:** 18. **Par:** 70/70.
Yards: 5,956/5,012. **Course rating:** N/A. **Slope:** N/A.
Opened: 1994. **Pace of Play rating:** 4:30. **Green fee:** $15/32.
Credit cards: All major. **Reduced fees:** Weekdays, Low season, Twilight,
Seniors, Juniors.
Caddies: No. **Golf carts:** Included in Green Fee.
Discount golf packages: Yes. **Season:** Year-round. **High:** March-Oct.
On-site lodging: No. **Rental clubs:** Yes.
Walking policy: Walking at certain times. **Range:** Yes (grass).
To obtain tee times: Call pro shop.
Subscriber comments: Too new to rate . . . Extremely tight; lost a lot of
golf balls . . . Opened too early . . . .Needs maturity . . . Short and tight
. . . Very short, very good greens.

★½ HOLIDAY GOLF CLUB
SP—11300 Goodman Rd., Olive Branch (901)525-2402.
2 miles south of Memphis. **Holes:** 18. **Par:** 72/72.
Yards: 6,498/5,114. **Course rating:** 70.8/N/A. **Slope:** 116/N/A.
Opened: 1975. **Pace of Play rating:** 4:00. **Green fee:** $15/19.
Credit cards: MC, V. **Reduced fees:** Resort guests, Seniors, Juniors.
Caddies: No. **Golf carts:** N/A.
Discount golf packages: Yes. **Season:** Year-round. **High:** May-Sept.
On-site lodging: Yes. **Rental clubs:** Yes.
Walking policy: Walking at certain times. **Range:** Yes (grass).
To obtain tee times: Call five days in advance.
Subscriber comments: Good public course . . . Too crowded . . .
Relatively easy layout . . . Good service . . . Plain Jane course, nothing
special, well-stocked pro shop . . . Good for average player . . . Very nice
course, walkable . . . Fun course, heavily played . . . No.1 pro shop in area
. . . Fairways could be better . . . Nothing to celebrate, short holes
interesting . . . All Bermuda course . . . Entices you to go for it a few
times.

★★★½ KIRKWOOD NATIONAL GOLF CLUB
SP—P.O. Box 747, Holly Springs (601)252-4888.
40 miles southeast of Memphis. **Holes:** 18. **Par:** 72/72.
Yards: 7,129/4,898. **Course rating:** N/A. **Slope:** N/A.
Opened: 1994. **Pace of Play rating:** 4:30. **Green fee:** $25/42.
Credit cards: MC, V. **Reduced fees:** Weekdays, Low season, Seniors,
Juniors.
Caddies: No. **Golf carts:** Included in Green Fee.
Discount golf packages: Yes. **Season:** Year-round. **High:** June-Aug.
On-site lodging: No. **Rental clubs:** No.
Walking policy: Unrestricted walking. **Range:** Yes (grass).
To obtain tee times: Call seven days in advance.
Subscriber comments: Marvelous new course! Must play if in area . . .
New course needs to mature, good design . . . Excellent layout, best course

in Memphis area . . . Great variety of holes, nothing tricky or tricked up
. . . Inexpensive for its quality . . . Great track, tough on high handicapper
. . . Very challenging . . . Still needs attention to some areas . . . Course is
well groomed . . . Super layout, super service, well worth the wait . . .
Unbelievable course; in time will be the best in Mississippi.

★★★ MISSISSIPPI NATIONAL GOLF CLUB
PU—900 Hickory Hill Dr., Gautier (601)497-2372, (800)477-4044.
15 miles east of Biloxi. **Holes:** 18. **Par:** 72/72.
Yards: 7,003/5,229. **Course rating:** 73.1/69.6. **Slope:** 128/113.
Opened: 1965. **Pace of Play rating:** 4:00. **Green fee:** $15/30.
Credit cards: MC, V. **Reduced fees:** Weekdays, Low season, Resort
guests.
Caddies: No. **Golf carts:** $10 for 18 holes.
Discount golf packages: Yes. **Season:** Year-round. **High:** Feb.-April.
On-site lodging: Yes. **Rental clubs:** Yes.
Walking policy: Walking at certain times. **Range:** Yes (grass).
To obtain tee times: Call seven days in advance.
Formerly known as Hickory Hill.
Subscriber comments: Old course that can play tough . . . Good layout
for all players . . . Beautiful course, very enjoyable to play . . . Testing par
3s . . . Flat. Fun to play. Evidence of great course at one time . . . Changes
expected to improve overall . . . Wide fairways, long course . . . Enjoyable
layout, can be a little long . . . Best course in immediate area.

★★★ MISSISSIPPI STATE UNIVERSITY GOLF COURSE
PU—1520 Old Hwy. 82E, Starkville (601)325-3028.
120 miles northeast of Jackson. **Holes:** 18. **Par:** 72/72.
Yards: 6,926/5,443. **Course rating:** 73.5/71.8. **Slope:** 130/121.
Opened: 1989. **Pace of Play rating:** 4:00. **Green fee:** $10/15.
Credit cards: All major. **Reduced fees:** Weekdays, Juniors.

Caddies: No. **Golf carts:** $8 for 18 holes.
Discount golf packages: No. **Season:** Year-round. **High:** March-Sept.
On-site lodging: No. **Rental clubs:** Yes.
Walking policy: Unrestricted walking. **Range:** Yes (grass).
To obtain tee times: Call Wednesday for following week.
Subscriber comments: Terrific golf facility for as much play as it gets . . .
Best college course in South . . . Great college course, challenging but fair
. . . Bermuda greens, good in warm months, bumpy in winter . . . Fast
greens. Nice fairways . . . Good condition. Excellent fairways. A little
slow. Good staff . . . Great bargain . . . Whew! 600-plus-yard finishing
hole is tough in the heat . . . Fun walkable layout . . . A doozie from the
tips . . . Go Bulldogs! A very nice golf course.

★★ NATCHEZ TRACE GOLF CLUB
SP—Beech Springs Rd., Saltillo (601)869-2166.
Holes: 18. **Par:** 72/72.
Yards: 6,841/4,791. **Course rating:** 72.3/69.3. **Slope:** 116/108.
Opened: 1964. **Pace of Play rating:** 4:00. **Green fee:** $15/24.
Credit cards: None. **Reduced fees:** Weekdays.
Caddies: No. **Golf carts:** $18 for 18 holes.
Discount golf packages: No. **Season:** Year-round. **High:** June-Aug.
On-site lodging: No. **Rental clubs:** No.
Walking policy: Unrestricted walking. **Range:** Yes (grass).
To obtain tee times: First come, first served.
Subscriber comments: Lots of water and narrow fairways, hills . . . Good
test for mid to low handicappers . . . A lot of sharp doglegs . . . Average
course, nothing special, not always in good shape . . . Unmemorable . . .
Uneven lies . . . Makes you play every club in your bag . . . With a little
money and work could be good.

★★★ OLE MISS GOLF CLUB
PU—Rte. 3 College Hill Rd., Oxford (601)234-4816.
70 miles south of Memphis, TN. **Holes:** 18. **Par:** 72/72.
Yards: 6,682/5,276. **Course rating:** 72.8/70.9. **Slope:** 129/120.
Opened: 1965. **Pace of Play rating:** 4:30. **Green fee:** $10/14.
Credit cards: MC, V. **Reduced fees:** No.
Caddies: No. **Golf carts:** $18 for 18 holes.
Discount golf packages: No. **Season:** Year-round. **High:** May-Aug.
On-site lodging: No. **Rental clubs:** Yes.
Walking policy: Unrestricted walking. **Range:** Yes (grass).
To obtain tee times: Call in advance.
Subscriber comments: Severe test . . . Few fairway bunkers . . . Requires
you to use all clubs in your bag . . . A magnificent setting for golf . . . Poor
sand traps . . . A premium is placed on tee shots . . . Toughest 18 holes in
Mississippi.

★★½ PASS CHRISTIAN ISLES GOLF CLUB
SP—150 Country Club Dr., Pass Christian (601)452-3830.
16 miles west of Gulfport. **Holes:** 18. **Par:** 72/72.
Yards: 6,438/5,428. **Course rating:** 69.7/71.6. **Slope:** 124/120.
Opened: 1951. **Pace of Play rating:** 3:30. **Green fee:** $24.
Credit cards: MC, V, AMEX. **Reduced fees:** .
Caddies: No. **Golf carts:** $12 for 18 holes.
Discount golf packages: Yes. **Season:** Year-round. **High:** Feb.-April.
On-site lodging: No. **Rental clubs:** Yes.
Walking policy: Walking at certain times. **Range:** No.
To obtain tee times: Call in advance.
Subscriber comments: Nice layout . . . Good condition . . . Nothing
special . . . Good for medium-handicap player . . . Pleasant help . . . Just
enough water and sand traps, short, easy to play.

★½ PINE ISLAND GOLF CLUB
SP—2021 Beachview Dr., Ocean Springs (601)875-1674.
4 miles east of Biloxi. **Holes:** 18. **Par:** 71/71.
Yards: 6,369/4,915. **Course rating:** 70.9/67.8. **Slope:** 129/109.
Opened: 1973. **Pace of Play rating:** 4:00. **Green fee:** $14/25.
Credit cards: MC, V. **Reduced fees:** Weekdays, Low season, Resort
guests, Twilight.
Caddies: No. **Golf carts:** $12 for 18 holes.
Discount golf packages: Yes. **Season:** Year-round. **High:** Feb.-April.
On-site lodging: No. **Rental clubs:** Yes.
Walking policy: Walking at certain times. **Range:** Yes (grass).
To obtain tee times: Call pro shop.
Subscriber comments: Tight course, lots of trees, small greens, very
challenging . . . Narrow with hazards, not well kept . . . Tight fairways,
off the fairways get in lots of trouble . . . Short, tight, not much fun . . .
Bring bug spray . . . Nice scenery.

★★★ PLANTATION GOLF COURSE
SP—9425 Plantation Rd., Olive Branch (601)895-3530.
10 miles south of Memphis, TN. **Holes:** 18. **Par:** 72/72.
Yards: 6,773/5,055. **Course rating:** 72.0/64.4. **Slope:** 122/109.
Opened: 1990. **Pace of Play rating:** 4:15. **Green fee:** $19/23.
Credit cards: MC, V. **Reduced fees:** Weekdays, Low season, Twilight,
Seniors, Juniors.
Caddies: No. **Golf carts:** N/A.
Discount golf packages: No. **Season:** Year-round. **High:** March-Sept.
On-site lodging: No. **Rental clubs:** Yes.
Walking policy: Walking at certain times. **Range:** Yes (grass).
To obtain tee times: Call five days in advance.
Subscriber comments: Jewel of a muny in Memphis area . . . Great
zoysia fairways and bent grass greens . . . Average amateur will like it . . .
Some holes are crowded together . . . Good layout. Not too much trouble.
Best suited for mid handicappers . . . Best finishing hole in area, friendly

staff . . . Another nice course . . . Front is short target golf, back is long,
wide open . . . Some holes forced . . . Do not play when hot . . . Bent
grass suffers from heat, fairways best in area . . . Scenic classy layout . . .
The staff is extremely helpful with outings . . . Places a premium on
shotmaking ability . . . Very challenging layout . . . No. 18 very scenic
approach.

★★ ST. ANDREWS COUNTRY CLUB
SP—2 Golfing Green Dr., Ocean Springs (601)875-7730.
40 miles west of Mobile. **Holes:** 18. **Par:** 72/72.
Yards: 6,460/4,960. **Course rating:** 69.7/67.8. **Slope:** 119/111.
Opened: 1968. **Pace of Play rating:** 4:00. **Green fee:** $12/25.
Credit cards: MC, V. **Reduced fees:** No.
Caddies: No. **Golf carts:** $11 for 18 holes.
Discount golf packages: Yes. **Season:** Year-round. **High:** Feb.-March.
On-site lodging: Yes. **Rental clubs:** No.
Walking policy: Walking at certain times. **Range:** Yes (grass).
To obtain tee times: Call pro shop.
Subscriber comments: Total renovation underway . . . Had a good
round going until alligator showed up.

SONNY GUY MUNICIPAL GOLF COURSE★
PU—3200 Woodrow Wilson Dr., Jackson (601)960-1905.
Holes: 18. **Par:** 72/72.
Yards: 6,935/5,217. **Course rating:** 71.9/69.0. **Slope:** 117/104.
Opened: 1949. **Pace of Play rating:** 4:00. **Green fee:** $6/8.
Credit cards: MC, V. **Reduced fees:** Weekdays, Twilight, Seniors,
Juniors.
Caddies: No. **Golf carts:** $14 for 18 holes.
Discount golf packages: Yes. **Season:** Year-round. **High:** March-July.
On-site lodging: No. **Rental clubs:** Yes.
Walking policy: Unrestricted walking. **Range:** No.
To obtain tee times: Call one day in advance.

SOUTHWIND COUNTRY CLUB★
SP—15312 Dismuke Dr., Biloxi (601)392-0400.
50 miles west of Mobile. **Holes:** 18. **Par:** 72/72.
Yards: 6,202/5,577. **Course rating:** 65.0/66.0. **Slope:** 113/113.
Opened: 1992. **Pace of Play rating:** 4:00. **Green fee:** $22.
Credit cards: MC, V. **Reduced fees:** No.
Caddies: No. **Golf carts:** $10 for 18 holes.
Discount golf packages: Yes. **Season:** Year-round. **High:** Feb.-April.
On-site lodging: No. **Rental clubs:** Yes.
Walking policy: Unrestricted walking. **Range:** No.
To obtain tee times: Call two days in advance.

★★ SUNKIST COUNTRY CLUB
R—2381 Sunkist Country Club Rd., Biloxi (601)388-3961.
Holes: 18. **Par:** 72/72.
Yards: 6,000/5,300. **Course rating:** 69.0/71.0. **Slope:** 117/121.
Opened: 1954. **Pace of Play rating:** 4:08. **Green fee:** $20/37.
Credit cards: MC, V, DISC. **Reduced fees:** Weekdays, Low season,
Twilight.
Caddies: No. **Golf carts:** Included in Green Fee.
Discount golf packages: No. **Season:** Year-round. **High:** Feb.-April.
On-site lodging: No. **Rental clubs:** No.
Walking policy: Mandatory cart. **Range:** Yes (grass).
To obtain tee times: Call as far in advance as necessary.
Subscriber comments: Nice for average golfer . . . Challenging
undulating greens . . . Fair maintenance, good staff . . . Tough course to
walk . . . Sand and water, nice staff . . . Too many out-of-bounds . . .
Near to great shape . . . Hometown folks.

★★★★ TIMBERTON GOLF CLUB

PU—22 Clubhouse Dr., Hattiesburg (601)584-4653.
90 miles north of New Orleans. **Holes:** 18. **Par:** 72/72.
Yards: 7,028/5,439. **Course rating:** 73.1/71.4. **Slope:** 131/128.
Opened: 1991. **Pace of Play rating:** 4:00. **Green fee:** $25/35.
Credit cards: MC, V. **Reduced fees:** No.
Caddies: No. **Golf carts:** Included in Green Fee.
Discount golf packages: Yes. **Season:** Year-round. **High:** March-April.
On-site lodging: No. **Rental clubs:** Yes.
Walking policy: Mandatory cart. **Range:** Yes (grass).
To obtain tee times: Call up to 60 days in advance. Credit card required.
Ranked 4th in Mississippi by Golf Digest.
Subscriber comments: Top notch in all respects . . . Great layout, large
greens, excellent fairways . . . Very good, enjoyable, struggle and enjoy the
course beauty . . . Great tifdwarf Bermuda greens . . . First class . . . Most
congenial staff I've ever dealt with . . . Layout is somewhat vanilla . . .
Longer than card. Tough course but fair. 18th is hard but wonderful . . .
Best layout in Mississippi. Good greens. A hidden gem . . . In fantastic
shape . . . Always in excellent shape, plays well to all . . . Hope you can
slice the ball . . . Best service ever received; course is heaven . . .
Outstanding golf . . . Some outstanding holes . . . Superb conditioning and
a staff that cares . . . Great course, staff and pace of play; best secret in
Mississippi.

★★ TRAMARK GOLF COURSE

PU—P.O. Box 6631, Gulfport (601)863-7808.
65 miles east of New Orleans. **Holes:** 18. **Par:** 72/72.
Yards: 6,350/5,800. **Course rating:** 68.5/69.5. **Slope:** 116/109.
Opened: 1967. **Pace of Play rating:** 3:45. **Green fee:** $12.
Credit cards: MC, V. **Reduced fees:** Juniors.
Caddies: No. **Golf carts:** $16 for 18 holes.
Discount golf packages: Yes. **Season:** Year-round. **High:** Feb.-April.
On-site lodging: No. **Rental clubs:** Yes.
Walking policy: Unrestricted walking. **Range:** Yes (grass).
To obtain tee times: Call anytime.
Subscriber comments: $12 ego booster . . . Short, no trouble, for
beginners . . . Lots of retirees . . . Have to wait on many holes . . . Not
much . . . Friendly staff, condition needs improvement, generous layout.

★ USM'S VAN HOOK GOLF COURSE

PU—One Golf Course Rd., Hattiesburg (601)264-1872.
60 miles north of Biloxi. **Holes:** 18. **Par:** 72/73.
Yards: 6,660/5,226. **Course rating:** 69.0/70.0. **Slope:** N/A.
Opened: 1957. **Pace of Play rating:** 3:50. **Green fee:** $7/13.
Credit cards: MC, V. **Reduced fees:** Weekdays, Low season, Twilight,
Seniors, Juniors.
Caddies: No. **Golf carts:** N/A.
Discount golf packages: Yes. **Season:** Year-round. **High:** May-June.
On-site lodging: No. **Rental clubs:** Yes.
Walking policy: Unrestricted walking. **Range:** Yes (grass).
To obtain tee times: Call 24 hours in advance.
Subscriber comments: Few hazards; good for high handicappers and
beginners . . . Rarely in top shape . . . Mediocre at best . . . Nice little
course . . . You get what you pay for . . . One bunker on the course . . .
Just needs some money for upkeep.

★★★ WEDGEWOOD GOLF COURSE

SP—5206 Tournament Dr., Olive Branch (901)521-8275.
5 miles south of Memphis. **Holes:** 18. **Par:** 72/72.
Yards: 6,863/5,627. **Course rating:** 72.8/69.1. **Slope:** 127/118.
Opened: 1990. **Pace of Play rating:** 4:06. **Green fee:** $23.
Credit cards: MC, V. **Reduced fees:** Weekdays, Low season, Resort
guests, Twilight, Seniors, Juniors.
Caddies: No. **Golf carts:** $10 for 18 holes.

Discount golf packages: Yes. **Season:** Year-round. **High:** May–Sept.
On-site lodging: Yes. **Rental clubs:** Yes.
Walking policy: Walking at certain times. **Range:** Yes (grass).
To obtain tee times: Call seven days in advance.
Subscriber comments: A fun course for players of all levels . . . Don't like 20 foot-deep ditches and kudzu vines close to fairways . . . Excellent bentgrass greens. You'd better be straight . . . Lots of kudzu . . . Tight and demanding. Love it . . . Good course, great finishing holes . . . Too many ditches . . . Fun, challenging, beginners beware: out-of-bounds, water, trees . . . A few questionable holes . . . Needs cleaning up around edges . . . Long and tough . . . Needs some esthetics, dull looking . . . Best greens in Mid-South . . . Back side is the better of the nines . . . Toughest greens to read and putt in this area.

★★★½ **WINDANCE COUNTRY CLUB**
SP—19385 Champion Circle, Gulfport (601)832-4871.
60 miles east of New Orleans. **Holes:** 18. **Par:** 72/72.
Yards: 6,678/5,179. **Course rating:** 72.1/70.1. **Slope:** 129/120.
Opened: 1986. **Pace of Play rating:** 4:15. **Green fee:** $60.
Credit cards: MC, V, AMEX. **Reduced fees:** No.
Caddies: No. **Golf carts:** Included in Green Fee.
Discount golf packages: Yes. **Season:** Year-round. **High:** Feb.–April.
On-site lodging: No. **Rental clubs:** Yes.
Walking policy: Mandatory cart. **Range:** Yes (grass).
To obtain tee times: All tee times are held with a credit card, and cancellation policy is 24 hours prior to tee time. Packages available through most hotels in the area.
Subscriber comments: Beautiful fairways that roll through forest and subdivision . . . Worth every penny . . . Course designed for long straight hitter . . . Scenic and tough but fun to play . . . They should change the front nine to the back nine. Better closing hole at nine . . . Lots of trouble for errant shots . . . Pleasant staff . . . Fun. Recommended . . . Excellent maintenance, good staff, excellent pace . . . Demanding from the get go . . . Good layout, great shape . . . Good coast course, smooth play, keep it in play . . . Love the layout, super staff . . . Pay attention to yardage markers . . . Best course on Mississippi Gulf Coast, hit it straight here.

Notes

★★½ AMHERST COUNTRY CLUB

PU—76 Ponemah Rd., Amherst (603)673-9908.
10 miles west of Nashua. **Holes:** 18. **Par:** 72/74.
Yards: 6,520/5,532. **Course rating:** 71.0/74.2. **Slope:** 123/129.
Opened: 1965. **Pace of Play rating:** 4:12. **Green fee:** $22/29.
Credit cards: MC, V. **Reduced fees:** Weekdays, Seniors.
Caddies: No. **Golf carts:** $12 for 18 holes.
Discount golf packages: No. **Season:** March-Dec. **High:** May-Oct.
On-site lodging: No. **Rental clubs:** Yes.
Walking policy: Unrestricted walking. **Range:** No.
To obtain tee times: Call three days in advance.
Subscriber comments: Easy course, friendly staff, four-hour round is
normal . . . Good mix of holes, fun risk/reward, tough contoured greens
. . . The course is made for a target golf player. Sand traps everywhere . . .
The staff was outstanding. With their new tee times system, play is great
. . . The course is always in great shape throughout the year . . . Hit it
straight and score . . . Fast greens, tree-lined fairways . . . Well marshaled,
greens and fairways excellent.

THE BALSAMS GRAND RESORT HOTEL
★★★½ PANORAMA GOLF CLUB

R—Rte. 26, Dixville Notch (603)255-4961.
110 miles northwest of Portland, Maine. **Holes:** 18. **Par:** 72/72.
Yards: 6,804/5,069. **Course rating:** 73.9/69.9. **Slope:** 136/124.
Opened: 1912. **Pace of Play rating:** 4:02. **Green fee:** $40.
Credit cards: All major. **Reduced fees:** Resort guests.
Caddies: No. **Golf carts:** $13 for 18 holes.
Discount golf packages: Yes. **Season:** May-Oct. **High:** July-Aug.
On-site lodging: Yes. **Rental clubs:** Yes.
Walking policy: Unrestricted walking. **Range:** Yes (grass).
To obtain tee times: Hotel guests call up to seven days in advance all
others up to three days.
Subscriber comments: Play it! Just go play it . . . Superb course, on top
of mountain, fall view spectacular . . . Outstanding course . . . Nice resort
course, management excellent . . . Incredible location and clubhouse . . .
Nice old course in good shape . . . Course is tough, lots of hills . . . The
most beautiful golf course I've ever played . . . Wow! Long, beautiful and
fun . . . Great staff.

★★½ BEAVER MEADOW GOLF CLUB

PU—1 Beaver Meadow Dr., Concord (603)228-8954.
Holes: 18. **Par:** 72/72.
Yards: 6,356/5,519. **Course rating:** 70.0/71.8. **Slope:** 121/123.
Opened: 1896. **Pace of Play rating:** N/A. **Green fee:** $15/25.
Credit cards: None. **Reduced fees:** Weekdays, Low season, Twilight,
Seniors, Juniors.
Caddies: No. **Golf carts:** N/A.
Discount golf packages: No. **Season:** April-Nov. **High:** May-Sept.
On-site lodging: No. **Rental clubs:** Yes.
Walking policy: Unrestricted walking. **Range:** Yes.
To obtain tee times: Call two days in advance.
Subscriber comments: Two very different nines. The front is flat, more
deceptive. The back is longer, more obvious challenges . . . Tougher than it
looks . . . Back long and hard . . . Tight fairways . . . Oldest golf course in
the state of New Hampshire . . . Pretty layout, easy to walk.

★½ BETHLEHEM COUNTRY CLUB

PU—Main St., Rte. 302, Bethlehem (603)869-5745.
Holes: 18. **Par:** 70/70.
Yards: 5,826/5,314. **Course rating:** 67.7/71.8. **Slope:** 113/121.
Opened: 1898. **Pace of Play rating:** N/A. **Green fee:** $18/22.
Credit cards: MC, V. **Reduced fees:** Weekdays, Resort guests, Twilight,
Seniors, Juniors.
Caddies: No. **Golf carts:** N/A.

Discount golf packages: Yes. **Season:** May-Oct. **High:** July-Aug.
On-site lodging: No. **Rental clubs:** Yes.
Walking policy: Unrestricted walking. **Range:** No.
To obtain tee times: Call.
Subscriber comments: Large boulders in fairways come into play often
. . . Nice mountain course, continues to improve . . . Nice layout, some
real neat holes . . . New pro and course superintendent are making this into
one of the most pleasant of golf experiences . . . Very friendly . . . Excellent
club repair facility.

★★★★ BRETWOOD GOLF COURSE

PU—East Surry Rd., Keene (603)352-7626.
Holes: 18. **Par:** 72/72.
Yards: 6,974/5,140. **Course rating:** 73.9/70.1. **Slope:** 134/120.
Opened: 1968. **Pace of Play rating:** 4:30. **Green fee:** $22/28.
Credit cards: None. **Reduced fees:** Twilight.
Caddies: No. **Golf carts:** $10 for 18 holes.
Discount golf packages: No. **Season:** April-Nov. **High:** June-Oct.
On-site lodging: No. **Rental clubs:** Yes.
Walking policy: Unrestricted walking. **Range:** Yes (grass).
To obtain tee times: Call Wednesday for upcoming weekend.
Ranked 8th in New Hampshire by Golf Digest.
Previously 27-hole course. Added a new nine to create two 18-hole courses.
The new course opened in 1995.
Subscriber comments: Great test of golf, beautiful scenery, four sets of
tees . . . Fun course yet tough . . . Great milkshakes at the clubhouse . . .
Open, fun course, lots of water . . . Good test from back tees . . . Easy
course for experts and novices . . . Fun, creative, wide open . . . Course
always in good shape . . . Gorgeous in the fall . . . Outstanding holes . . .
New 18 very scenic. Love it . . . Tough and very long, big greens, very
demanding . . . Course has an island-green hole.

★★★ CAMPBELL'S SCOTTISH HIGHLANDS GOLF COURSE

PU—79 Brady Ave., Salem (603)894-4653.
30 miles north of Boston. **Holes:** 18. **Par:** 71/71.
Yards: 6,249/5,056. **Course rating:** 69.5/68.4. **Slope:** 120/114.
Opened: 1994. **Pace of Play rating:** N/A. **Green fee:** $22/26.
Credit cards: MC, V. **Reduced fees:** Weekdays, Twilight, Seniors.
Caddies: No. **Golf carts:** $9 for 18 holes.
Discount golf packages: No. **Season:** April-Nov. **High:** July-Aug.
On-site lodging: No. **Rental clubs:** Yes.
Walking policy: Unrestricted walking. **Range:** No.
To obtain tee times: Call three days in advance.
Subscriber comments: Nice new course, short but sweet . . . Beautiful
greens, great staff . . . New course, great potential . . . Not long but very
interesting holes for the average golfer . . . May not be a challenge for better
golfers . . . Welcome newcomer that can only get better . . . Superb
facilities for handicapped golfers . . . Hidden secret . . . Hard to believe it's
only a year old . . . Short but tricky, great condition . . . Big fast greens,
lots of breaks.

★★ CANDIA WOODS GOLF LINKS

PU—313 South Rd., Candia (603)483-2307.
10 miles east of Manchester. **Holes:** 18. **Par:** 71/73.
Yards: 6,558/5,582. **Course rating:** 70.9/72.2. **Slope:** 121/130.
Opened: 1964. **Pace of Play rating:** N/A. **Green fee:** $21/28.
Credit cards: MC, V. **Reduced fees:** Weekdays, Low season, Twilight,
Juniors.
Caddies: No. **Golf carts:** $11 for 18 holes.
Discount golf packages: No. **Season:** March-Dec. **High:** June.
On-site lodging: No. **Rental clubs:** No.
Walking policy: Unrestricted walking. **Range:** Yes (grass).
To obtain tee times: Call five days in advance.
Subscriber comments: Good wide-open course for average player . . .

Somewhat rough but nice layout . . . Trying very hard to be upscale . . . Best chocolate-chip cookies . . . Nice course, nice people . . . Relatively flat but challenging . . . Long par 4s, great views, all greens run toward Rte. 101.

★★★★ CONCORD COUNTRY CLUB
SP—Country Club Lane, Concord (603)228-8936.
Call club for further information.
Subscriber comments: Truly awesome greens, lightning fast . . . Very challenging back nine. Tight, tough driving holes . . . A total pleasure . . . Some wonderful holes . . . Good pro shop . . . Need all your clubs . . . Better suited for better players.

★★★ COUNTRY CLUB OF NEW HAMPSHIRE
PU—Kearsarge Valley Rd., North Sutton (603)927-4246.
30 miles south of Concord. **Holes:** 18. **Par:** 72/72.
Yards: 6,727/5,446. **Course rating:** 71.6/71.7. **Slope:** 125/127.
Opened: 1957. **Pace of Play rating:** N/A. **Green fee:** $20/30.
Credit cards: MC, V, DISC. **Reduced fees:** Weekdays, Twilight.
Caddies: No. **Golf carts:** $11 for 18 holes.
Discount golf packages: Yes. **Season:** April-Nov. **High:** July-Sept.
On-site lodging: Yes. **Rental clubs:** Yes.
Walking policy: Unrestricted walking. **Range:** Yes (grass).
To obtain tee times: Call up to seven days in advance. Motel guests and outings can book anytime.
Ranked 10th in New Hampshire by Golf Digest.
Subscriber comments: Hilly, difficult from back tees . . . Well designed, challenging with great variety . . . Wilderness setting with tight fairways, requires accurate tee shots . . . Personnel very cordial . . . Well conditioned . . . Use cart . . . Every hole is different, big greens, scenic . . . This is what golf is all about . . . Picturesque . . . Great greens . . . Front flat but interesting back . . . A pleasure, must think on several holes . . . Always in great shape . . . I go out of my way to play it every year.

★½ DERRYFIELD COUNTRY CLUB
PU—625 Mammoth Rd., Manchester (603)669-0235.
Holes: 18. **Par:** 70/74.
Yards: 6,100/5,535. **Course rating:** 68.7/71.0. **Slope:** 113/125.
Opened: 1932. **Pace of Play rating:** . **Green fee:** $24/24.
Credit cards: None. **Reduced fees:** N/A.
Caddies: Yes. **Golf carts:** N/A.
Discount golf packages: No. **Season:** April-Dec. **High:** June-Sept.
On-site lodging: No. **Rental clubs:** No.
Walking policy: Unrestricted walking. **Range:** No.
To obtain tee times: Call on Thursday for upcoming weekend and holiday.
Subscriber comments: An up and down course. Golf cart a must, especially on hot days . . . Challenging old front nine. So-so new back nine . . . Very nice . . . Suited for all players.

★★★ EASTMAN GOLF LINKS
PU—Clubhouse Lane, Grantham (603)863-4500.
43 miles northwest of Concord. **Holes:** 18. **Par:** 71/73.
Yards: 6,731/5,369. **Course rating:** 73.5/71.9. **Slope:** 137/128.
Opened: 1973. **Pace of Play rating:** N/A. **Green fee:** $35/35.
Credit cards: MC, V. **Reduced fees:** N/A.
Caddies: No. **Golf carts:** $16 for 18 holes.
Discount golf packages: No. **Season:** May-Nov. **High:** July-Sept.
On-site lodging: No. **Rental clubs:** No.
Walking policy: Walking at certain times. **Range:** Yes.
To obtain tee times: Call two days in advance.
Ranked 9th in New Hampshire by Golf Digest.
Subscriber comments: Long, tight and hilly . . . Have played it since it

opened and it continues to impress me with demands for shotmaking . . .
Terrific course, beautiful setting . . . Lots of blind shots, need to play three
or four rounds to score well . . . Rewarding challenge for an average player
. . . Excellent greens . . . Typical northern New England views . . . Tough
to walk.

GREEN MEADOW GOLF CLUB
PU—59 Steele Rd., Hudson (603)889-1555.
11 miles south of Manchester.
Green fee: $20/26.
Credit cards: MC, V. **Reduced fees:** Weekdays, Low season, Twilight,
Seniors, Juniors.
Caddies: Yes. **Golf carts:** N/A.
Discount golf packages: No. **Season:** March-Dec. **High:** April-Aug.
On-site lodging: No. **Rental clubs:** Yes.
Walking policy: Unrestricted walking. **Range:** Yes (grass).
To obtain tee times: N/A.
★½NORTH COURSE
Holes: 18. **Par:** 72/72.
Yards: 6,495/5,102. **Course rating:** 67.6/68.3. **Slope:** 109/113.
Opened: 1959. **Pace of Play rating:** N/A.
One week in advance in person or call on Monday for upcoming weekend.
Subscriber comments: Golf for the masses, needs more attention to
maintenance . . . Friendly staff, great practice facilities . . . Average tracks,
good for beginners . . . Two courses both good for golf ego . . . Course
gets a lot of play . . . Decent place . . . Wide open fairways, good greens,
fairly easy.
SOUTH COURSE★
Holes: 18. **Par:** 72/72.
Yards: 6,598/5,173. **Course rating:** 70.0/71.2. **Slope:** 114/120.
Opened: 1959. **Pace of Play rating:** N/A.

★★★HANOVER COUNTRY CLUB
PU—Rope Ferry Rd., Hanover (603)646-2000.
10 miles south of Lebanon. **Holes:** 18. **Par:** 69/73.
Yards: 5,876/5,468. **Course rating:** 68.7/72.7. **Slope:** 118/127.
Opened: 1899. **Pace of Play rating:** 4:00. **Green fee:** $30.
Credit cards: MC, V. **Reduced fees:** Twilight.
Caddies: No. **Golf carts:** $14 for 18 holes.
Discount golf packages: Yes. **Season:** April-Nov. **High:** June-Sept.
On-site lodging: No. **Rental clubs:** Yes.
Walking policy: Unrestricted walking. **Range:** No.
To obtain tee times: Call seven days in advance.
Subscriber comments: Tricky old layout, bring at least three wedges . . .
Greenkeeper does an excellent job . . . Good course. Extremely hilly, in
good shape . . . Not for novices . . . Nice layout, very hilly old course,
good condition . . . Tough to walk 18 holes unless you're in good shape.
My wife was ready to call a cab after 15 . . . Target golf, challenging.

★★½JACK O'LANTERN RESORT
R—Rte. 3, Box A, Woodstock (603)745-3636.
60 miles north of Manchester. **Holes:** 18. **Par:** 70/70.
Yards: 5,829/4,725. **Course rating:** 67.5/67.5. **Slope:** 113/113.
Opened: 1947. **Pace of Play rating:** 4:30. **Green fee:** $26/32.
Credit cards: All major. **Reduced fees:** Weekdays, Resort guests,
Twilight.
Caddies: No. **Golf carts:** $12 for 18 holes.
Discount golf packages: Yes. **Season:** May-Oct.
On-site lodging: Yes. **Rental clubs:** Yes.
Walking policy: Walking at certain times. **Range:** No.
To obtain tee times: Call 24 hours in advance.
Subscriber comments: Very friendly . . . Small greens, good condition

. . . Fairways, like the greens, perfect in every way . . . Beautiful views . . .
Challenging for all handicaps . . . One of the best . . . Lots of doglegs, nice
to work on mid-iron game . . . Enjoyable course and challenging . . .
Trees, little creatures, and breathtaking scenery.

★★★½ JOHN H. CAIN GOLF CLUB

SP—Unity Rd., Newport (603)863-7787.
35 miles west of Concord. **Holes:** 18. **Par:** 71/71.
Yards: 6,415/4,738. **Course rating:** 71.4/63.8. **Slope:** 133/112.
Opened: 1920. **Pace of Play rating:** 4:00. **Green fee:** $20/25.
Credit cards: MC, V. **Reduced fees:** Weekdays, Low season, Twilight,
Seniors, Juniors.
Caddies: No. **Golf carts:** $11 for 18 holes.
Discount golf packages: Yes. **Season:** April-Nov. **High:** July-Sept.
On-site lodging: No. **Rental clubs:** Yes.
Walking policy: Unrestricted walking. **Range:** Yes (grass).
To obtain tee times: Call seven days in advance.
Subscriber comments: Course one of the finest, fairways excellent, staff
courteous . . . For hacker through serious amateur . . . Wide variety;
mountain, flats, and river bottom . . . Would be my favorite if it were
closer to home . . . Awesome, lots of water . . . Challenging from back
tees, good condition.

★★★½ KEENE COUNTRY CLUB

SP—755 West Hill Rd., Keene (603)352-9722.
60 miles east of Manchester. **Holes:** 18. **Par:** 72/75.
Yards: 6,200/5,900. **Course rating:** 69.0/72.2. **Slope:** 121/130.
Opened: 1900. **Pace of Play rating:** 4:00. **Green fee:** $40.
Credit cards: MC, V. **Reduced fees:** N/A.
Caddies: No. **Golf carts:** $30 for 18 holes.
Discount golf packages: Yes. **Season:** April-Nov. **High:** May-Sept.
On-site lodging: No. **Rental clubs:** Yes.
Walking policy: Unrestricted walking. **Range:** Yes (grass).
To obtain tee times: Call ahead.
Subscriber comments: A difficult course that is easy to play . . . Great
scenery, nice people everywhere . . . Nice old course, very tricky . . . Very
tough for short course . . . Members only until 1 p.m. on weekends . . .
Premium on direction, not distance . . . Old course, requires shotmaking
. . . Good test of skills.

★★★ LACONIA COUNTRY CLUB

SP—607 Elm St., Laconia (603)524-1273.
24 miles north of Concord. **Holes:** 18. **Par:** 72/72.
Yards: 6,483/5,552. **Course rating:** 71.7/72.1. **Slope:** 128/125.
Opened: 1926. **Pace of Play rating:** 3:47. **Green fee:** $60.
Credit cards: MC, V. **Reduced fees:** Low season, Resort guests, Juniors.
Caddies: Yes. **Golf carts:** Included in Green Fee.
Discount golf packages: No. **Season:** April-Nov. **High:** June-Sept.
On-site lodging: No. **Rental clubs:** Yes.
Walking policy: Mandatory cart. **Range:** Yes (grass).
To obtain tee times: Call Thursday for upcoming weekend.
Subscriber comments: Best suited for long, accurate hitters . . . Greens
good, fairways excellent . . . Staff treated us well . . . Play was at times
slow . . . Greens are smooth and fast. Tougher course than it looks . . .
Condition excellent. Layout nice. All levels of play . . . Everyone should
play this course . . . Well manicured, scenic, challenging . . . Thinker's
course.

★½ MAPLEWOOD COUNTRY CLUB

PU—Rte. 302, Bethlehem (603)869-3335.
80 miles north of Concord. **Holes:** 18. **Par:** 72/72.
Yards: 6,100/5,200. **Course rating:** 67.5/68.4. **Slope:** 113/114.
Opened: 1907. **Pace of Play rating:** 4:00. **Green fee:** $18/20.
Credit cards: MC, V. **Reduced fees:** Weekdays, Low season, Twilight.

Caddies: No. **Golf carts:** $11 for 18 holes.
Discount golf packages: Yes. **Season:** May-Oct. **High:** May-Sept.
On-site lodging: No. **Rental clubs:** Yes.
Walking policy: Unrestricted walking. **Range:** Yes (grass).
To obtain tee times: Call anytime.
Subscriber comments: Nice views, greens were a little on rough side but still playable . . . Staff is very nice . . . Beautiful scenery and a great challenge . . . Love that par 6 . . . Nice course, but maintenance not always good.

★★½ MOUNT WASHINGTON GOLF COURSE

R—Rte. 302, Bretton Woods (603)278-1000.
90 miles north of Concord. **Holes:** 18. **Par:** 71/71.
Yards: 6,638/5,336. **Course rating:** 70.1/70.1. **Slope:** 123/118.
Opened: 1915. **Pace of Play rating:** 4:00. **Green fee:** $20/30.
Credit cards: All major. **Reduced fees:** Resort guests.
Caddies: No. **Golf carts:** $20 for 18 holes.
Discount golf packages: Yes. **Season:** May-Oct. **High:** July-Sept.
On-site lodging: Yes. **Rental clubs:** Yes.
Walking policy: Unrestricted walking. **Range:** No.
To obtain tee times: Call anytime in advance.
Subscriber comments: The clear view and air make golfing great . . . Absolutely beautiful scenery . . . Course in fair shape, good layout . . . Nice rolling greens . . . Fun course to play, links style . . . Scenery was great . . . All can find this challenging.

★★★ NORTH CONWAY COUNTRY CLUB

SP—Norcross Circle, North Conway (603)356-9391.
Holes: 18. **Par:** 71/71.
Yards: 6,659/5,530. **Course rating:** 71.9/71.4. **Slope:** 126/120.
Opened: 1895. **Pace of Play rating:** 4:00. **Green fee:** $28/35.
Credit cards: MC, V. **Reduced fees:** Low season, Twilight, Seniors, Juniors.
Caddies: No. **Golf carts:** $22 for 18 holes.
Discount golf packages: No. **Season:** May-Oct. **High:** June-Oct.
On-site lodging: No. **Rental clubs:** Yes.
Walking policy: Unrestricted walking. **Range:** Yes (grass).
To obtain tee times: Call three days in advance.
Ranked 7th in New Hampshire by Golf Digest.
Subscriber comments: Excellent condition . . . Very picturesque, snuggled in mountains . . . Has a train 20 yards behind first tee. Hope you have concentration . . . Course plays all of stated yardage . . . Very scenic course with mountains . . . Very interesting and demanding holes . . . Mostly flat with wide fairways. Very enjoyable to play . . . Good course, nice people.

★★★½ OVERLOOK COUNTRY CLUB

PU—5 Overlook Dr., Hollis (603)465-2909.
60 miles north of Boston. **Holes:** 18. **Par:** 71/72.
Yards: 6,290/5,230. **Course rating:** 69.7/70.4. **Slope:** 130/126.
Opened: 1989. **Pace of Play rating:** 4:30. **Green fee:** $26/32.
Credit cards: MC, V. **Reduced fees:** Weekdays, Twilight.
Caddies: No. **Golf carts:** $20 for 18 holes.
Discount golf packages: No. **Season:** April-Dec. **High:** June-Aug.
On-site lodging: No. **Rental clubs:** Yes.
Walking policy: Unrestricted walking. **Range:** No.
To obtain tee times: Call one week in advance.
Subscriber comments: Short, tight, lot of water, good condition, nice staff . . . Course knowledge important . . . Short course, good layout, nothing but enjoyment . . . Interesting course for all levels . . . Great test, lot of doglegs . . . Well-run course and good test of accuracy . . . Requires all types of shots . . . Very playable public course . . . Good variety of holes . . . Starter very helpful, pace of play a little slow . . . Fine course, nice layout, quite playable . . . Pleasant course with varying terrain and holes.

NEW HAMPSHIRE

★★★ PASSACONAWAY COUNTRY CLUB
PU—12 Midway Ave., Litchfield (603)424-4653.
5 miles south of Manchester. **Holes:** 18. **Par:** 71/72.
Yards: 6,855/5,369. **Course rating:** 72.2/70.3. **Slope:** 126/118.
Opened: 1989. **Pace of Play rating:** 4:30. **Green fee:** $20/30.
Credit cards: MC, V. **Reduced fees:** Weekdays, Low season, Twilight,
Seniors, Juniors.
Caddies: No. **Golf carts:** N/A.
Discount golf packages: No. **Season:** April-Dec. **High:** May-Sept.
On-site lodging: No. **Rental clubs:** Yes.
Walking policy: Unrestricted walking. **Range:** Yes (grass).
To obtain tee times: Call seven days in advance for weekdays and five
days in advance for weekends.
Subscriber comments: Some long holes on front nine, shorter but
bunkered on back . . . Wind can make this real tough, nice greens . . .
Mounding between fairways makes complaints of no trees absolutely
ludicrous . . . Anyone who knows golf will fall in love here . . . Ladie's tees
very fair . . . Some pretty holes, some holes too close together. Be careful
. . . Beautiful use of length, terrain and greens design . . . Little to no shade
. . . Good course for big hitters . . . Long and open links-style course,
meticulously maintained . . . Best-kept secret in New Hampshire . . . Can
be easily hit by sliced tee shots in parallel fairways . . . Measures long from
tips but quite forgiving, enjoyable.

★★½ PEASE GOLF COURSE
PU—2 Country Club Rd., Portsmouth (603)433-1331.
Holes: 18. **Par:** 70/70.
Yards: 6,228/5,291. **Course rating:** 70.8/69.9. **Slope:** 128/120.
Opened: N/A. **Pace of Play rating:** 4:00. **Green fee:** $26.
Credit cards: MC, V. **Reduced fees:** N/A.
Caddies: No. **Golf carts:** $20 for 18 holes.
Discount golf packages: No. **Season:** April-Nov. **High:** June-Aug.
On-site lodging: No. **Rental clubs:** Yes.
Walking policy: Unrestricted walking. **Range:** Yes (grass).
To obtain tee times: Call three days in advance.
Subscriber comments: Short course, but enjoyable to play . . .
Improvements in progress . . . Average challenge for average golfer . . .
Good novice course . . . Scenic, tough in the wind . . . Flat and narrow . . .
Several challenging holes . . . Nice shape. Not very pretty, slow . . . Great
yardage markers . . . Easy and short but accuracy needed . . . Excellent
greens . . . My favorite in the area.

★★ PLAUSAWA VALLEY COUNTRY CLUB
SP—42 Whittemore Rd., Pembroke (603)224-6267.
Holes: 18. **Par:** 72/73.
Yards: 6,545/5,391. **Course rating:** 72.6/71.5. **Slope:** 131/128.
Opened: 1963. **Pace of Play rating:** 5:00. **Green fee:** $24/27.
Credit cards: MC, V. **Reduced fees:** Weekdays, Low season, Resort
guests, Twilight, Seniors, Juniors.
Caddies: No. **Golf carts:** $24 for 18 holes.
Discount golf packages: Yes. **Season:** April-Nov. **High:** July-Aug.
On-site lodging: No. **Rental clubs:** Yes.
Walking policy: Unrestricted walking. **Range:** Yes (grass).
To obtain tee times: Call seven days in advance.
Subscriber comments: Easy frontside, very difficult back . . . A great
place for beginners . . . Front is open, back nine through forest . . . Old and
new nines of completely different character . . . Picturesque in the fall . . .
Solid golf . . . Staff was knowledgeable. Service was good . . . Very fair,
pretty good condition . . . Would rather play back nine twice.

★★★★ PORTSMOUTH COUNTRY CLUB
SP—1 Country Club Lane, Greenland (603)436-9719.
3 miles west of Portsmouth. **Holes:** 18. **Par:** 72/78.
Yards: 7,050/6,202. **Course rating:** 74.1/77.1. **Slope:** 127/135.

Opened: 1957. **Pace of Play rating:** N/A. **Green fee:** $40.
Credit cards: MC, V, DISC. **Reduced fees:** Twilight.
Caddies: No. **Golf carts:** $20 for 18 holes.
Discount golf packages: No. **Season:** April-Nov. **High:** June-Sept.
On-site lodging: No. **Rental clubs:** Yes.
Walking policy: Unrestricted walking. **Range:** Yes (grass).
To obtain tee times: Call one day in advance.
Ranked 4th in New Hampshire by Golf Digest.
Subscriber comments: Nice shotmaker's course . . . Driver's paradise, fast greens, could play every day . . . This is a Robert Trent Jones gem . . . Poor man's Ocean Course, real tough when windy . . . Very enjoyable for all handicaps . . . A wind-swept delight on shores of Great Bay . . . Great layout. Scenic view along the water . . . Long, wide and flat.

★★½ ROCHESTER COUNTRY CLUB
SP—Church St., Gonic (603)332-9892.
2 miles of Rochester. **Holes:** 18. **Par:** 72/73.
Yards: 6,596/5,414. **Course rating:** 72.7/70.4. **Slope:** 125/123.
Opened: 1916. **Pace of Play rating:** 4:15-4:30. **Green fee:** $37/42.
Credit cards: MC, V. **Reduced fees:** N/A.
Caddies: No. **Golf carts:** Included in Green Fee.
Discount golf packages: No. **Season:** April-Nov. **High:** June-Aug.
On-site lodging: No. **Rental clubs:** Yes.
Walking policy: Mandatory cart. **Range:** No.
To obtain tee times: First come, first serve. Weekdays must play before 3 p.m. Weekends can't play before 2 p.m.
Subscriber comments: Well-manicured course . . . Polite and helpful staff . . . Fun course, hilly . . . Always great conditions . . . Few flat lies, open front and tree lined back . . . Excellent layout.

★★ SAGAMORE-HAMPTON GOLF CLUB
PU—101 North Rd., North Hampton (603)964-5341.
50 miles north of Boston. **Holes:** 18. **Par:** 71/71.
Yards: 6,489/5,822. **Course rating:** 70.5/67.1. **Slope:** 101/101.
Opened: 1963. **Pace of Play rating:** N/A. **Green fee:** $23.
Credit cards: None. **Reduced fees:** Low season.
Caddies: No. **Golf carts:** N/A.
Discount golf packages: No. **Season:** April-Dec. **High:** May-Sept.
On-site lodging: No. **Rental clubs:** Yes.
Walking policy: Unrestricted walking. **Range:** No.
To obtain tee times: Call seven days in advance for weekends and holidays and two days in advance for weekdays.
Subscriber comments: Great condition, easy walker . . . Takes you from wide open to wooded fairways, a fun round . . . Ego booster. Best suited for high handicappers . . . Short course. Wide open. Grip and rip . . . Fun course to play . . . Average golfer has minimal challenge . . . Wide open front nine with severly sloped greens, tougher back nine . . . Easy, good course to help you out of a slump.

★★★★ SHATTUCK GOLF COURSE
PU—28 Dublin Rd., Jaffrey (603)532-4300.
20 miles east of Keene. **Holes:** 18. **Par:** 71/71.
Yards: 6,701/4,632. **Course rating:** 74.1/73.1. **Slope:** 145/139.
Opened: 1991. **Pace of Play rating:** 4:30-5:00. **Green fee:** $35/35.
Credit cards: MC, V. **Reduced fees:** Weekdays, Low season, Twilight.
Caddies: No. **Golf carts:** $12 for 18 holes.
Discount golf packages: Yes. **Season:** May-Oct. **High:** June-Sept.
On-site lodging: No. **Rental clubs:** No.
Walking policy: Unrestricted walking. **Range:** Yes (grass).
To obtain tee times: Call 30 days in advance for weekdays. For weekends call the Tuesday prior to upcoming weekend starting at 7 a.m.
Ranked 1st in New Hampshire by Golf Digest.
Subscriber comments: Very difficult . . . Excellent target course . . . Hit it straight or bring lots of ammo. Leave woods in the bag . . . Very friendly

pro shop . . . Scary from the back tees . . . Enjoy the scenery and forget about scoring . . . Difficult for high handicapper . . . Bring your whole game, or don't bother. Plan on losing at least a sleeve! . . . A tiger of a course, bring your "A" game . . . Gets better each time you play it. The ultimate test . . . Play the blues and bring a dozen balls . . . Try to break 100. Good luck . . . PGA Tour should try this place from the tips . . . Each hole separate and demanding . . . Favorite course. Jaw dropped on almost every hole . . . Must be played if you live in New England . . . Great golf course, may be the most demanding course in the region . . . Every golfer should have the experience . . . Not good for a hacker. An unforgettable round. We lost 30 balls . . . The golf course from Hell. Beautiful setting and fun once a year . . . Challenging thinking-man's course . . . Spectacular views, long carries over water . . . Tight, hilly, lots of trees, very tough course to play, challenging . . . Golf for masochists . . . Target golf, small greens, forced carries.

★★★★ SKY MEADOW COUNTRY CLUB
SP—6 Mtn. Laurels Dr., Nashua (603)888-3000.
30 miles north of Boston. **Holes:** 18. **Par:** 72/72.
Yards: 6,590/5,127. **Course rating:** 73.3/71.2. **Slope:** 133/131.
Opened: 1986. **Pace of Play rating:** 4:15. **Green fee:** $53/80.
Credit cards: MC, V, AMEX. **Reduced fees:** N/A.
Caddies: No. **Golf carts:** Included in Green Fee.
Discount golf packages: No. **Season:** April-Nov. **High:** June-Sept.
On-site lodging: No. **Rental clubs:** Yes.
Walking policy: Mandatory cart. **Range:** Yes.
To obtain tee times: Guests may make reservations two days in advance.
Ranked 5th in New Hampshire by Golf Digest.
Subscriber comments: Great layout and conditions . . . Lovely scenery, good test of golf . . . What a view! . . . Nice facilities, friendly . . . Once-a-year kind of place . . . Course knowledge important . . . Great clubhouse and staff, course always in great condition, big greens . . . One of the more breathtaking par 5s anywhere. Need to think your way around the course . . . Demanding, narrow scenic track with strategic layout . . . What a pearl . . . Astonishing views . . . Extremely fast greens . . . Public course with private service.

★★★ SOUHEGAN WOODS GOLF CLUB
PU—65 Thorton Ferry Rd., Amherst (603)673-0200.
Call club for further information.
Subscriber comments: Excellent layout, challenging although very flat . . . So many sand traps each player should carry a rake . . . Fun place to play, well run . . . Nice condition, good practice area, spacious putting area . . . Friendly clubhouse . . . Look for coupon special . . . Tight, long par 4s. Use 3-wood, leave driver at home . . . Lots of woods and heavily trapped . . . Better bring your sand wedge . . . Easy to walk . . . Suited for all players, staff excellent . . . Bunkers, bunkers, everywhere.

★★½ WAUKEWAN GOLF CLUB
PU—P.O. Box 403, Meredith (603)279-6661.
50 miles south of Manchester. **Holes:** 18. **Par:** 71/73.
Yards: 5,735/5,010. **Course rating:** 67.1/68.7. **Slope:** 120/112.
Opened: 1961. **Pace of Play rating:** N/A. **Green fee:** $20/25.
Credit cards: MC, V. **Reduced fees:** Low season.
Caddies: No. **Golf carts:** $20 for 18 holes.
Discount golf packages: No. **Season:** May-Oct. **High:** June-Sept.
On-site lodging: No. **Rental clubs:** Yes.
Walking policy: Unrestricted walking. **Range:** Yes (grass).
To obtain tee times: Call up to 48 hours in advance.
Subscriber comments: Piece of heaven . . . First tee mountain view . . . Hilly but all levels can achieve satisfaction at this wonderful course . . .

Plenty of water. Tough course for a slicer . . . Fun course, not terribly difficult . . . Short, fun layout . . . Nice people, loyal membership . . . Out of the way, but worth playing . . . Don't be fooled by short holes . . . Fall foliage is great . . . Uncrowded and relaxing.

★ WAUMBEK GOLF CLUB

PU—Rte. 2, Jefferson (603)586-7777.
Holes: 18. **Par:** 71/71.
Yards: 5,874/4,772. **Course rating:** N/A. **Slope:** 107/107.
Call club for further information.
Subscriber comments: Fun . . . Gem in the rough . . . Excellent views, fair golf.

★★★½ WENTWORTH-BY-THE-SEA COUNTRY CLUB

SP—Wentworth Rd., Portsmouth (603)433-5010.
60 miles south of Boston. **Holes:** 18. **Par:** 70/70.
Yards: 6,162/5,097. **Course rating:** 67.8/70.5. **Slope:** 123/119.
Opened: 1897. **Pace of Play rating:** 4:00. **Green fee:** $50/75.
Credit cards: All major. **Reduced fees:** Weekdays, Low season.
Caddies: Yes. **Golf carts:** $14 for 18 holes.
Discount golf packages: No. **Season:** April-Nov. **High:** May-Sept.
On-site lodging: No. **Rental clubs:** Yes.
Walking policy: Unrestricted walking. **Range:** No.
To obtain tee times: Call three days in advance.
Subscriber comments: Scenic . . . Tight with water . . . For players of all handicaps . . . Staff and service excellent, condition of course very good . . . Different challenge on every hole . . . Short seaside course . . . Chance to score . . . Beautiful views . . . Must be accurate, don't need length . . . Well maintained course . . . Great dining . . . A lot of blind shots and tricky greens . . . Always fun to play . . . Scenic, old course along ocean inlet . . . A wonderful course that requires all your skill . . . Tough seaside test, especially when the wind blows.

★★½ WHITE MOUNTAIN COUNTRY CLUB

PU—Ashland Rd., Ashland (603)536-2227.
300 miles north of Concord. **Holes:** 18. **Par:** 71/73.
Yards: 6,408/5,410. **Course rating:** 70.4/70.2. **Slope:** 125/118.
Opened: 1974. **Pace of Play rating:** N/A. **Green fee:** $12/27.
Credit cards: MC, V. **Reduced fees:** Weekdays, Low season, Twilight.
Caddies: No. **Golf carts:** $11 for 18 holes.
Discount golf packages: No. **Season:** May-Oct. **High:** July-Sept.
On-site lodging: Yes. **Rental clubs:** Yes.
Walking policy: Unrestricted walking. **Range:** Yes (grass).
To obtain tee times: Call up to seven days in advance.
Subscriber comments: Wide open, let it rip, very friendly . . . Great playing course . . . Beautiful scenery, well-maintained course, great dining . . . Fun course good weekend getaway . . . Love the par-5 fifth . . . A solid test of golf from back tees but not tricky or overly punishing . . . Great little course. Greens are terrific . . . A fun course, watch out for low flying hanggliders . . . Forgiving course, not hilly in spite of name.

WINDHAM GOLF AND COUNTRY CLUB*

PU—Londonderry Rd., Windham (603)434-2093.
12 miles south of Manchester. **Holes:** 18. **Par:** 72/72.
Yards: 6,442/5,127. **Course rating:** 71.3/69.0. **Slope:** 136/132.
Opened: 1995. **Pace of Play rating:** 4:00-4:30. **Green fee:** $25/30.
Credit cards: MC, V. **Reduced fees:** No.
Caddies: No. **Golf carts:** $11 for 18 holes.
Discount golf packages: No. **Season:** Year-round. **High:** May-Oct.
On-site lodging: No. **Rental clubs:** Yes.
Walking policy: Unrestricted walking. **Range:** Yes (grass).
To obtain tee times: Call Thursday at 8:30 a.m. for the weekend.

★½ APPLE MOUNTAIN GOLF CLUB

PU—Rd 2, Box 24, Belvidere (908)453-3023.
40 miles west of New York City. **Holes:** 18. **Par:** 72/72.
Yards: 6,593/5,214. **Course rating:** 71.8/69.8. **Slope:** 121/123.
Opened: 1973. **Pace of Play rating:** 4:15. **Green fee:** $17/38.
Credit cards: MC, V. **Reduced fees:** Weekdays, Low season, Twilight, Seniors, Juniors.
Caddies: No. **Golf carts:** N/A.
Discount golf packages: Yes. **Season:** Year-round. **High:** June-Aug.
On-site lodging: No. **Rental clubs:** Yes.
Walking policy: Walking at certain times. **Range:** No.
To obtain tee times: Call.
Subscriber comments: Great view from No. 7 tee . . . Confusing layout, many side-by-side fairways with danger from errant shots . . . Course has improved 199% in last year . . . Challenging, hilly course . . . Great lunch, great view of Delaware Valley . . . Need hard hats . . . Extremely hilly. Tough greens. Always an unusual angle to fairway. Few bunkers . . . Walking this course tires you quickly . . . Long downhill par 3s make club selection interesting.

★★ ASH BROOK GOLF COURSE

PU—1210 Raritan Rd., Scotch Plains (908)668-8503.
15 miles southwest of Newark **Holes:** 18. **Par:** 72/72.
Yards: 6,916/6,373. **Course rating:** N/A. **Slope:** 115/121.
Opened: 1955. **Pace of Play rating:** N/A. **Green fee:** $23/27.
Credit cards: N/A. **Reduced fees:** Weekdays.
Caddies: No. **Golf carts:** $22 for 18 holes.
Discount golf packages: No. **Season:** Year-round. **High:** March-Oct.
On-site lodging: No. **Rental clubs:** No.
Walking policy: N/A. **Range:** No.
Subscriber comments: Feels like the longest public course in New Jersey . . . Challenging course. Heavy play . . . Terrain mixed . . . The course has a natural look surrounded by woods . . . Municipal course, long waiting, most people courteous . . . Stacks up golfers like the planes at O'Hare . . . Long, nice layout.

★★ AVALON COUNTRY CLUB

SP—1510 Rte. 9 N., Cape May Court House (609)465-4653, (800)643-4766.
30 miles south of Atlantic City. **Holes:** 18. **Par:** 71/72.
Yards: 6,325/4,924. **Course rating:** 70.3/70.7. **Slope:** 122/122.
Opened: 1971. **Pace of Play rating:** 4:00. **Green fee:** $20/55.
Credit cards: MC, V, AMEX. **Reduced fees:** Weekdays, Low season, Twilight, Juniors.
Caddies: No. **Golf carts:** Included in Green Fee.
Discount golf packages: Yes. **Season:** Year-round. **High:** May-Sept.
On-site lodging: No. **Rental clubs:** Yes.
Walking policy: Walking at certain times. **Range:** Yes.
To obtain tee times: Call two weeks in advance.
Subscriber comments: Course is wide open and fairly easy . . . Great shore golf course, difficult, scenic and fun, back nine is fantastic . . . Staff super . . . Fall and winter rates are bargains . . . Pace of play too slow . . . Packed in summer . . . Bring bug spray for No. 16 . . . Staff very helpful . . . Heavily played.

★★★ BEAVER BROOK COUNTRY CLUB

SP—Rte. No. 31 South, Country Club Rd., Clinton (908)735-4022, (800)433-8567.
45 miles west of New York City. **Holes:** 18. **Par:** 72/72.
Yards: 6,546/5,283. **Course rating:** 71.6/70.4. **Slope:** 122/112.
Opened: 1964. **Pace of Play rating:** 4:00. **Green fee:** $30/46.
Credit cards: MC, V, AMEX. **Reduced fees:** Twilight.
Caddies: No. **Golf carts:** $28 for 18 holes.
Discount golf packages: No. **Season:** March-Dec. **High:** June-Aug.
On-site lodging: No. **Rental clubs:** Yes.

Walking policy: Walking at certain times. **Range:** Yes (grass).
To obtain tee times: Call one week in advance.
Subscriber comments: Very scenic . . . Hilly course with great setting in valley . . . Outstanding greens . . . Some blind shots and sidehill lies, but really nice course . . . Fairly wide-open front nine . . . Interesting and well-maintained hilly course . . . Fast greens. Good condition . . . Not for beginners . . . Extremely hard for average golfer . . . Excellent mountain layout . . . Interesting layout, courteous staff.

★½ BECKETT GOLF CLUB
PU—RD No. 2, P.O. Box 76A, Swedesboro (609)467-4700.
Call club for further information.
Subscriber comments: Good for average golfer, services adequate . . .
Too many doglegs, blind shots . . . Condition fair . . . Easy to walk . . .
Mediocre . . . Nice little course . . . 27 holes, no par 4s over 400 yards.

★★½ BEY LEA GOLF CLUB
PU—1536 North Bay Ave., Toms River (908)349-0566.
Call club for further information.
Subscriber comments: Some challenging holes across water . . . Excellent back nine . . . Good for walking, fairly open . . . Always in good condition . . . Overcrowded but decent condition . . . Great New Jersey golf . . .
Wide open, yet challenging . . . Huge greens.

★★★★ BLUE HERON PINES GOLF CLUB
PU—550 W. Country Club Dr., Galloway (609)965-4653.
18 miles south of Atlantic City. **Holes:** 18. **Par:** 72/72.
Yards: 6,777/5,053. **Course rating:** 73.0/68.4. **Slope:** 136/116.
Opened: 1993. **Pace of Play rating:** 4:15. **Green fee:** $50/86.
Credit cards: All major. **Reduced fees:** Weekdays, Low season, Twilight.
Caddies: No. **Golf carts:** Included in Green Fee.
Discount golf packages: No. **Season:** Year-round. **High:** May-Oct.
On-site lodging: No. **Rental clubs:** Yes.
Walking policy: Unrestricted walking. **Range:** Yes (grass).
To obtain tee times: Call up to five days in advance.
Subscriber comments: Great new layout, good conditions, interesting holes . . . Not for high handicapper . . . A real gem, very playable . . .
Variety of tees, great for everyone . . . Outstanding layout facilites and service. Bring your "A" game . . . Like walking on carpet . . . Great golf will get better with age . . . Pace is good, staff is courteous, course is in good condition . . . Beautiful course, similar to courses in Myrtle Beach . . . They keep traffic moving . . . Exceptional pro shop and facilities . . . A great golf experience, Pine Valley-look on several holes.

★★★½ BOWLING GREEN GOLF CLUB
SP—Schoolhouse Rd., Milton (201)697-8688.
50 miles northwest of New York City. **Holes:** 18. **Par:** 72/72.
Yards: 6,689/4,966. **Course rating:** 72.9/69.4. **Slope:** 131/122.
Opened: 1966. **Pace of Play rating:** 4:15. **Green fee:** $26/43.
Credit cards: MC, V, AMEX. **Reduced fees:** Weekdays, Twilight.
Caddies: No. **Golf carts:** $15 for 18 holes.
Discount golf packages: No. **Season:** March-Dec. **High:** April-Sept.
On-site lodging: No. **Rental clubs:** No.
Walking policy: Unrestricted walking. **Range:** Yes.
To obtain tee times: Call two days in advance after 7 a.m.
Subscriber comments: Must hit them straight . . . Nestled amongst tall pines . . . Front nine very tight . . . Fourth hole gimicky due to condos . . .
Great grill room . . . Too many trees . . . Very tough but enjoyable course . . . Challenging, well-maintained course . . . Most players will use all clubs in bag . . . Great course in the mountains, layout is terrific . . . 18th hole is long and hard . . . Very fast greens . . . Beautiful scenery.

★★ BRIGANTINE GOLF LINKS
PU—Roosevelt Blvd. and North Shore, Brigantine (609)266-1388.
2 miles north of Atlantic City. **Holes:** 18. **Par:** 72/72.

Yards: 6,520/6,233. **Course rating:** N/A. **Slope:** 123/120.
Opened: N/A. **Pace of Play rating:** N/A. **Green fee:** N/A.
Credit cards: MC, V. **Reduced fees:** Low season, Resort guests, Twilight.
Caddies: Yes. **Golf carts:** N/A.
Discount golf packages: Yes. **Season:** Year-round. **High:** May-Sept.
On-site lodging: No. **Rental clubs:** No.
Walking policy: N/A. **Range:** No.
To obtain tee times: Call five days in advance.
Subscriber comments: Fun course, but too many houses in play . . .
Difficult course when ocean breezes pick up . . . Easy and fun, pleasant
layout . . . No liquor license . . . Good value and challenging "tight" layout
. . . Cooperative staff . . . Too many houses close to fairways . . . Water
and marsh hazards common . . . Excellent greens . . . Bugs a problem . . .
Lots of water, nice staff, great layout.

★★★½ **BUENA VISTA COUNTRY CLUB**
PU—Box 307, Rte. 40 & Country Club Lane, Buena (609)697-3733.
30 miles southeast of Philadelphia. **Holes:** 18. **Par:** 72/72.
Yards: 6,869/5,651. **Course rating:** 73.5/72.2. **Slope:** 131/128.
Opened: 1957. **Pace of Play rating:** N/A. **Green fee:** $24/27.
Credit cards: None. **Reduced fees:** Weekdays, Low season, Twilight.
Caddies: No. **Golf carts:** $10 for 18 holes.
Discount golf packages: No. **Season:** Year-round. **High:** May-Oct.
On-site lodging: No. **Rental clubs:** Yes.
Walking policy: Walking at certain times. **Range:** Yes (grass).
To obtain tee times: Call six days in advance.
Subscriber comments: Fun to play, well-kept secret . . . Pinehurst in
New Jersey, best public-access course in state . . . Suited to above average
golfer . . . Staff courteous . . . Conditions above average . . . Gets a lot of
play throughout the year, but well kept and challenging . . . Good greens,
bad mosquitoes . . . Tough long par 3s . . . Excellent pines course . . .
Don't miss the 10th hole . . . Tight and long, definitely target golf . . .
Tight fairways and lots of sand, fast hard greens, good test of skills.

★★★ **CAPE MAY NATIONAL GOLF CLUB**
SP—Rte. 9, Cape May (609)884-1563.
35 miles south of Atlantic City. **Holes:** 18. **Par:** 71/71.
Yards: 6,857/4,696. **Course rating:** 72.9/68.8. **Slope:** 136/115.
Opened: 1991. **Pace of Play rating:** 4:15. **Green fee:** $35/65.
Credit cards: MC, V. **Reduced fees:** Weekdays, Low season, Twilight, Juniors.
Caddies: No. **Golf carts:** Included in Green Fee.
Discount golf packages: Yes. **Season:** Year-round. **High:** May-Oct.
On-site lodging: No. **Rental clubs:** Yes.
Walking policy: Walking at certain times. **Range:** Yes (grass).
To obtain tee times: Call seven days in advance.
Subscriber comments: Great layout, marshals make you play fast . . .
Good quality golf in New Jersey's southernmost tip . . . Nice people
running the course . . . Narrow and wooded . . . Great day of golf . . .
Beautiful links-type scenery . . . Interesting layout, great finishing hole . . .
Still improving as it grows . . . Excellent condition for young course . . .
Difficult for the average golfer, lots of water . . . Links-type course . . .
Great course . . . Can't believe you're in New Jersey.

★★ **CEDAR CREEK GOLF COURSE**
PU—Tilton Blvd., Bayville (908)269-4460.
50 miles north of Altantic City. **Holes:** 18. **Par:** 72/72.
Yards: 6,325/5,173. **Course rating:** 71.2/72.5. **Slope:** 115/116.
Opened: 1981. **Pace of Play rating:** 4:30. **Green fee:** $8/22.
Credit cards: None. **Reduced fees:** Weekdays, Twilight, Seniors, Juniors.
Caddies: No. **Golf carts:** $23 for 18 holes.
Discount golf packages: No. **Season:** Year-round. **High:** May-Sept.
On-site lodging: No. **Rental clubs:** Yes.

Walking policy: Unrestricted walking. **Range:** No.
To obtain tee times: No tee times.
Subscriber comments: Back nine hilly with water, more challenging . . .
Good for all levels . . . Many seniors play . . . Needs work, could be great,
nice layout . . . No. 1 handicap hole 234–yard par 3 on a hill.

★★½ CENTERTON GOLF CLUB
PU—Rte. No.540-Almond Rd., Elmer (609)358-2220.
10 miles west of Vineland. **Holes:** 18. **Par:** 71/71.
Yards: 6,725/5,525. **Course rating:** 69.2/71.5. **Slope:** 120/120.
Opened: 1962. **Pace of Play rating:** N/A. **Green fee:** $10/16.
Credit cards: MC, V. **Reduced fees:** Weekdays, Low season, Twilight.
Caddies: No. **Golf carts:** $26 for 18 holes.
Discount golf packages: Yes. **Season:** Year-round. **High:** May-Aug.
On-site lodging: No. **Rental clubs:** Yes.
Walking policy: Walking at certain times. **Range:** Yes (grass).
To obtain tee times: Call six days in advance.
Subscriber comments: Staff very friendly, holes offer enough variety to
keep a round interesting . . . Wide fairways, big greens, peaceful setting,
rural, good separation of holes . . . Harder than it looks . . . Decent test,
not long . . . Good basic track in fine condition . . . Nice course, good
condition, confidence builder . . . Suitable for all levels of play.

★½ COHANZICK COUNTRY CLUB
SP—Bridgeton-Fairton Rd., Fairton (609)455-2127.
Call club for further information.
Subscriber comments: Friendly and supportive staff . . . A bit short,
some nice par 3s, swampy, near river, lots of bugs . . . Scenic course, short
but challenging . . . Short course, lots of doglegs, very small greens, good
par 3s.

★★ CRANBURY GOLF CLUB
SP—49 Southfield Rd., Cranbury (609)799-0341.
6 miles east of Princeton. **Holes:** 18. **Par:** 71/72.
Yards: 6,312/5,545. **Course rating:** 70.0/72.0. **Slope:** 117/118.
Opened: N/A. **Pace of Play rating:** N/A. **Green fee:** $22/30.
Credit cards: MC, V, AMEX. **Reduced fees:** Weekdays, Low season,
Twilight, Juniors.
Caddies: No. **Golf carts:** $13 for 18 holes.
Discount golf packages: No. **Season:** Year-round. **High:** May-Sept.
On-site lodging: No. **Rental clubs:** Yes.
Walking policy: Walking at certain times. **Range:** Yes (grass).
To obtain tee times: Call one week in advance.
Subscriber comments: Two very tough par 3s. Nice use of sand traps on
most holes . . . Short, fairly tight . . . Decent design with acceptable
conditions for a lot of play . . . Flat but many challenging holes . . . Good
course to walk . . . Friendly staff, many improvements underway . . . Fun
course, small greens, big bunkers.

★★½ CREAM RIDGE GOLF CLUB
SP—181 Rte. 539, Cream Ridge (609)259-2849.
20 miles northwest of Trent. **Holes:** 18. **Par:** 71/71.
Yards: 6,630/5,101. **Course rating:** 72.3/72.3. **Slope:** 119/119.
Opened: 1958. **Pace of Play rating:** 4:30. **Green fee:** $14/25.
Credit cards: ,V. **Reduced fees:** Weekdays, Low season, Twilight,
Seniors, Juniors.
Caddies: No. **Golf carts:** $25 for 18 holes.
Discount golf packages: No. **Season:** Year-round. **High:** May-Sept.
On-site lodging: No. **Rental clubs:** No.
Walking policy: Walking at certain times. **Range:** Yes (grass).
To obtain tee times: Call one week in advance for weekends.
Subscriber comments: Few good holes, sporty layout . . . Challenging
for high handicapper, deceiving greens . . . Challenging layout, great

variety of holes, No. 18 eats your lunch . . . Water on 10 holes, but not very long, fair test of golf . . . Fun course, playable, scenic, some surprises . . . Out in the country, farms, rolling hills, water, worth the drive . . . A few excellent holes . . . Nice people, low-key atmosphere.

★★★½ CRYSTAL SPRINGS GOLF CLUB

SP—123 Crystal Springs Rd., Hamburg (201)827-1444.
56 miles northwest of New York City. **Holes:** 18. **Par:** 72/72.
Yards: 6,857/5,131. **Course rating:** 73.3/70.5. **Slope:** 132/123.
Opened: 1991. **Pace of Play rating:** . **Green fee:** $33/61.
Credit cards: MC, V, AMEX. **Reduced fees:** Weekdays, Twilight.
Caddies: No. **Golf carts:** Included in Green Fee.
Discount golf packages: No. **Season:** April-Nov. **High:** May-Sept.
On-site lodging: No. **Rental clubs:** Yes.
Walking policy: Mandatory cart. **Range:** Yes (grass).
To obtain tee times: Call seven days in advance.
Subscriber comments: Difficult for the average player, condition good, great design . . . Can't take cart off path . . . Strange bounces due to mounds in fairways . . . Very pretty course, par-3 10th outstanding . . . Tremendously scenic . . . Toughest course in New Jersey . . . Very tough, shotmaker's course, have your best game ready . . . Hilly and tight and long . . . Quarry holes are memorable . . . Tee shot on No. 10 is best of all time . . . Poor choice for high handicappers . . . Best suited for low handicap, course is too tricked up . . . Good maintenance, links-style rough is severe.

★★½ DARLINGTON GOLF COURSE

PU—2777 Campgaw Rd., Mahwah (201)818-0777.
Call club for further information.
Subscriber comments: Excellent layout but fairways too narrow . . . Layout average, well kept for use . . . Lots of trees, large greens . . . Despite heavy usage, Grounds crews do a great job . . . Too many geese! . . . Very challenging for country course . . . Slow pace of play, excellent condition.

★ EAST ORANGE GOLF COURSE

SP—440 Parsonage Hill Rd., Short Hills (201)379-7190.
10 miles west of Newark. **Holes:** 18. **Par:** 72/73.
Yards: 6,120/5,640. **Course rating:** 67.6/69.8. **Slope:** 100/105.
Opened: 1920. **Pace of Play rating:** N/A. **Green fee:** $25/30.
Credit cards: None. **Reduced fees:** Weekdays, Twilight, Juniors.
Caddies: No. **Golf carts:** $20 for 18 holes.
Discount golf packages: No. **Season:** April-Dec. **High:** May-Sept.
On-site lodging: No. **Rental clubs:** No.
Walking policy: Unrestricted walking. **Range:** No.
To obtain tee times: First come, first serve after 11 a.m. weekends only.
Subscriber comments: A practice course only . . . Pace good, staff good . . . Four tough finishing holes, needs more upkeep . . . Some nice holes . . . Flat and uneventful layout . . . Improving but long way to go.

★½ EMERSON GOLF CLUB

PU—99 Palisade Ave., Emerson (201)261-1100.
15 miles northeast of New York City. **Holes:** 18. **Par:** 71/71.
Yards: 6,702/5,625. **Course rating:** 71.1/70.8. **Slope:** 118/117.
Opened: 1963. **Pace of Play rating:** 4:30. **Green fee:** $30/45.
Credit cards: MC, V, AMEX. **Reduced fees:** Weekdays, Low season, Twilight, Juniors.
Caddies: No. **Golf carts:** $15 for 18 holes.
Discount golf packages: No. **Season:** April-Jan. **High:** May-Aug.
On-site lodging: No. **Rental clubs:** Yes.
Walking policy: Walking at certain times. **Range:** Yes (grass).
To obtain tee times: Call up to five days in advance.
Subscriber comments: Long, flat, dull . . . Not much trouble, wide open . . . Flat course . . . Nothing fancy, just good golf . . . Greens are excellent

. . . Course in general requires a little better upkeep . . . Too flat and not in best shape . . . Front nine long and flat, back nine more wooded and enjoyable . . . Nice speed policy.

FARMSTEAD GOLF AND COUNTRY CLUB
★★★ CLUBVIEW/LAKEVIEW/VALLEYVIEW
PU—88 Lawrence Rd., Lafayette (201)383-1666.
50 miles west of New York City. **Holes:** 27. **Par:** 71/69/68.
Yards: 6,680/6,221/6,161. **Course rating:** 71.3/69.3/68.9.
Slope: 118/117/116.
Opened: N/A. **Pace of Play rating:** N/A. **Green fee:** $20/34.
Credit cards: MC, V, AMEX. **Reduced fees:** Twilight, Seniors.
Caddies: No. **Golf carts:** N/A.
Discount golf packages: No. **Season:** April-Nov. **High:** May-Oct.
On-site lodging: No. **Rental clubs:** Yes.
Walking policy: Mandatory cart. **Range:** No.
To obtain tee times: Call one week in advance. For weekends call after 10 a.m.
Subscriber comments: Clubview and Lakeview are solid nines . . . Fun course, excellent condition, picturesque . . . Nice restaurant, pro shop, no range and poor putting green, always great condition . . . Worth ride from metro area . . . Scenery great, staff helpful . . . Great three-nines course, varied holes . . . Lack of a practice range facility keeps Farmstead from being a top notch course . . . A bit too much water . . . Each nine has its own personality . . . Valleyview Nine needs work . . . Very good bar.

FLANDERS VALLEY GOLF COURSE
PU—Pleasant Hill Rd., Flanders (201)584-5382.
50 miles west of New York City.
Opened: 1963. **Pace of Play rating:** 4:20. **Green fee:** $11/53.
Credit cards: None. **Reduced fees:** Weekdays, Twilight, Seniors.
Caddies: No. **Golf carts:** $25 for 18 holes.
Discount golf packages: No. **Season:** April-Nov. **High:** May-Aug.
On-site lodging: No. **Rental clubs:** Yes.
Walking policy: Unrestricted walking. **Range:** No.
To obtain tee times: Call.
★★★½ RED/GOLD
Holes: 18. **Par:** 72/73.
Yards: 6,770/5,540. **Course rating:** 72.6/72.0. **Slope:** 126/121.

Subscriber comments: Maintained like a private course . . . Outstanding course maintenance . . . Best buy in New Jersey . . . Front side level, back side hilly with beautiful views . . . Back nine hilly, No. 13 a killer . . . Hard to walk, too much space between tee boxes . . . Very scenic and hilly, fair test of golf . . . Superb course, very hard to get tee times, long wait.
★★★★ WHITE/BLUE
Holes: 18. **Par:** 72/72.
Yards: 6,765/5,534. **Course rating:** 72.7/72.6. **Slope:** 126/122.
Subscriber comments: Outstanding course, great condition . . . Great course, requires straight drives and good putting . . . Well conditioned, true greens, a bit more difficult than Red/Gold . . . Classic 18 but too difficult to get a starting time . . . One of the best public courses in New Jersey, groomed to perfection . . . Blue/White truly like a private club . . . Great course, compares to many fine private courses . . . Long par 4s make it difficult, drive it straight . . . Truly championship caliber.

★★½ FRANCIS A. BYRNE GOLF CLUB
PU—1100 Pleasant Valley Way, West Orange (201)736-2306.
Holes: 18. **Par:** 70/72.
Yards: 6,653/5,384. **Course rating:** 70.2/73.0. **Slope:** 128/125.
Opened: 1920. **Pace of Play rating:** 5:00. **Green fee:** $20/24.
Credit cards: None. **Reduced fees:** Seniors, Juniors.
Caddies: No. **Golf carts:** $22 for 18 holes.
Discount golf packages: No. **Season:** April-Dec. **High:** June-Aug.
On-site lodging: No. **Rental clubs:** No.

Walking policy: Walking at certain times. **Range:** No.
To obtain tee times: First come, first served.
Subscriber comments: Good public course, very busy, long waits . . .
Challenging layout . . . Very hilly, lots of sidehill lies . . . Very tough
public course, few level shots . . . Good views . . . Hilly . . . Scenic.

★ FREEWAY GOLF COURSE
PU—1858 Sicklerville Rd., Sicklerville (609)227-1115.
16 miles east of Philadelphia. **Holes:** 18. **Par:** 72/72.
Yards: 6,536/5,395. **Course rating:** 73.6/73.4. **Slope:** 111/115.
Opened: 1968. **Pace of Play rating:** 4:30. **Green fee:** $10/18.
Credit cards:, V. **Reduced fees:** Weekdays, Low season, Twilight,
Seniors, Juniors.
Caddies: No. **Golf carts:** Included in Green Fee.
Discount golf packages: No. **Deason:** Year-round. **High:** April-June.
On-site lodging: No. **Rental clubs:** Yes.
Walking policy: Walking at certain times. **Range:** Yes (grass).
To obtain tee times: Call or come in.
Subscriber comments: Two different nines; front long, open; back short,
tight . . . Needs work . . . Good beginner course . . . Courteous staff . . .
First hole, 624 yards . . . Average course with long holes.

★½ GALLOPING HILL GOLF COURSE
PU—P.O. Box 898, Union (908)686-1556.
Holes: 18. **Par:** 73/76.
Yards: 6,690/5,514. **Course rating:** 71.3/N/A. **Slope:** 122/N/A.
Opened: 1920. **Pace of Play rating:** 4:00. **Green fee:** $23/27.
Credit cards: None. **Reduced fees:** Weekdays, Twilight, Seniors, Juniors.
Caddies: No. **Golf carts:** $22 for 18 holes.
Discount golf packages: No. **Season:** Year-round. **High:** April-Oct.
On-site lodging: No. **Rental clubs:** Yes.
Walking policy: Unrestricted walking. **Range:** No.
To obtain tee times: First come, first served.
Also has a nine-hole course.
Subscriber comments: Great layout makes up for poor condition . . .
Challenging, fun layout . . . Hilly course, but collects a lot of water after
rain . . . Tough to walk . . . Long course, very hilly, OK shape, drainage
problems, hacker's dream, fairways and greens need work, nice scenery.

★ GAMBLER RIDGE GOLF CLUB
PU—P.O. Box 109, Cream Ridge (609)758-3588.
Call club for further information.
Subscriber comments: Fair shape, uninspiring layout . . . Wide open and
short, suited for high handicappers . . . Wide open, great value, good pace,
easy course . . . Good practice course . . . Too easy, makes me look good
. . . Course needs to mature.

★★ GOLDEN PHEASANT GOLF CLUB
SP—141 Country Club Dr. & Eayrestown Rd., Medford (609)267-4276.
20 miles east of Philadelphia. **Holes:** 18. **Par:** 72/72.
Yards: 6,273/5,105. **Course rating:** 68.1/68.4. **Slope:** 119/114.
Opened: 1963. **Pace of Play rating:** 4:30. **Green fee:** $12/25.
Credit cards: MC, V. **Reduced fees:** Weekdays, Twilight, Seniors.
Caddies: No. **Golf carts:** $11 for 18 holes.
Discount golf packages: No. **Season:** Year-round. **High:** April-Oct.
On-site lodging: No. **Rental clubs:** Yes.
Walking policy: Walking at certain times. **Range:** Yes (grass).
To obtain tee times: Call Monday before weekend and holiday.
Subscriber comments: Average tree-lined course tight and short . . .
Holes too close together . . . Front nine OK, back nine excellent . . .
Couple of blind and dangerous holes . . . Unique layout, a little tight in
places, crowded at times . . . A lot of challenging holes . . . Interesting, not
difficult, enjoyable . . . Parallel holes are dangerous.

GREAT GORGE COUNTRY CLUB
★★★½ LAKE/QUARRY/RAIL
PU—Rte. 517, McAfee (201)827-5757.
50 miles northwest of New York. **Holes:** 27. **Par:** 71/71/72.
Yards: 6,819/6,826/6,921. **Course rating:** 73.3/72.7/73.4.
Slope: 131/126/128.
Opened: 1971. **Pace of Play rating:** N/A. **Green fee:** $49/72.
Credit cards: MC, V, AMEX, JCB. **Reduced fees:** Weekdays, Low
season, Resort guests, Twilight, Seniors.
Caddies: No. **Golf carts:** Included in Green Fee.
Discount golf packages: Yes. **Season:** March-Nov. **High:** May-Oct.
On-site lodging: Yes. **Rental clubs:** Yes.
Walking policy: Mandatory cart. **Range:** Yes (grass).
To obtain tee times: Call up to 30 days in advance.
Subscriber comments: Super layout and conditioning on all three courses,
suits all levels of play . . . Good variety of holes . . . Challenging, well kept;
Rail and Quarry, the best nines . . . Good test for better player . . . Hilly
terrain, good greens, scenic layout . . . Great quarry holes . . . Challenging,
fair, want to play again . . . Lake aptly named . . . All three courses up and
down hills . . . Quarry/Lake interesting layout . . . OK for most golfers,
well run, excellent greens.

★★★ GREATE BAY RESORT AND COUNTRY CLUB
R—901 Mays Landing Rd., Somers Point (609)927-0066.
8 miles south of Atlantic City. **Holes:** 18. **Par:** 71/71.
Yards: 6,750/5,495. **Course rating:** N/A. **Slope:** 130/126.
Opened: N/A. **Pace of Play rating:** N/A. **Green fee:** N/A.
Credit cards: MC, V, AMEX. **Reduced fees:** Low season, Resort guests,
Twilight.
Caddies: No. **Golf carts:** Included in Green Fee.
Discount golf packages: Yes. **Season:** Year-round. **High:** May-Sept.
On-site lodging: Yes. **Rental clubs:** No.
Walking policy: N/A. **Range:** Yes (grass).
Subscriber comments: Small greens, lots of wind, The LPGA Tour goes
here for a reason . . . Lives up to reputation . . . Service and amenities
terrific . . . Best hot dogs at the 10th hole . . . Nice course, varied holes . . .
Somewhat short . . . Course OK, well organized and very convenient at
shore . . . White tees short, LPGA should play from blues . . . Great
traditional layout.

★★ GREEN KNOLL GOLF COURSE
PU—587 Garretson Rd., Bridgewater (908)722-1301.
30 miles west of New York City. **Holes:** 18. **Par:** 71/72.
Yards: 6,443/5,349. **Course rating:** 70.9/73.0. **Slope:** 117/121.
Opened: 1960. **Pace of Play rating:** 3:52. **Green fee:** $20/35.
Credit cards: MC, V. **Reduced fees:** Seniors, Juniors.
Caddies: No. **Golf carts:** $22 for 18 holes.
Discount golf packages: No. **Season:** March-Nov. **High:** May-Sept.
On-site lodging: No. **Rental clubs:** Yes.
Walking policy: Unrestricted walking. **Range:** No.
To obtain tee times: Call for 24-hour access for a per reservation fee.
Also has a nine-hole pitch and putt course.
Subscriber comments: Three or four very good holes No. 8, No. 15, No.
18 . . . As a novice, Green Knoll does not have many trees to get in your
way, however there are various water hazards to conquer . . . Open and
hilly. Only a couple of challenging holes . . . Flat with a few hills . . . Good
for average golfer . . . Open course, few hazards . . . Nice view of course
from clubhouse.

★★ HANOVER COUNTRY CLUB
SP—Larrison Rd., Wrightstown (609)758-8301.
Call club for further information.
Subscriber comments: Difficult par 4s, very difficult finishing hole . . .
Fairly straight and open, decent shape . . . Long, flat and open . . . Open

course, room for mistakes . . . Nice greens . . . 18th hole 625-yards with water at 150-yard marker.

★ HENDRICKS FIELD GOLF COURSE

PU—Franklin Ave., Belleville (201)751-0178.
Call club for further information.
Subscriber comments: Well-kept public course, crowded, slow play . . .
Tight layout . . . Pace fair, staff good . . . Good neighborhood course . . .
Not for the serious golfer . . . Average public course . . . Tees in poor
shape . . . Back nine short.

★ HIDDEN HILLS GOLF CLUB

PU—1 Schooley's Mt. Rd., Rte. 24, Hackettstown (908)852-5694.
Call club for further information.
Subscriber comments: Good layout, could be great . . . Poor condition,
nice layout, polite people, trying to fix it . . . Short, tricky, sloppy back
nine . . . Getting better, trying harder . . . Needs a little work.

★★½ HIGH MOUNTAIN GOLF CLUB

SP—845 Ewing Ave., Franklin Lakes (201)891-4653.
15 miles west of New York. **Holes:** 18. **Par:** 71/71.
Yards: 6,347/5,426. **Course rating:** 69.5/70.0. **Slope:** 118/117.
Opened: 1967. **Pace of Play rating:** 4:00–4:30. **Green fee:** $27/34.
Credit cards: None. **Reduced fees:** Weekdays, Twilight.
Caddies: No. **Golf carts:** Included in Green Fee.
Discount golf packages: No. **Season:** April-Nov. **High:** May-Oct.
On-site lodging: No. **Rental clubs:** Yes.
Walking policy: Walking at certain times. **Range:** Yes (grass).
To obtain tee times: Call Monday of the week of play.
Subscriber comments: Condition improved over last three years . . .
Convenient to NYC . . . Very easy, can be boring, needs work . . . Back
nine better than front . . . Some hilly spots, but not too tough for medium
handicappers . . . Scenic, some holes have severe elevation change.

★★★ HIGH POINT COUNTRY CLUB

SP—P.O. Box 1154, Montague (201)293-3282.
Call club for further information.
Subscriber comments: Tough layout, too much OB, courteous staff,
friendly . . . A real sleeper, better have a good long game . . . Good
challenge, doglegs left and right . . . Remote . . . Beautiful starting hole,
appears easier than it plays . . . Have to play several times to enjoy course.
Many doglegs . . . Need every club in the bag . . . Beautiful setting.

★★½ HOLLY HILLS GOLF CLUB

PU—374 Freisburg Rd., Alloway (609)455-5115.
25 miles east of Wilmington, Del. **Holes:** 18. **Par:** 72/72.
Yards: 6,376/5,056. **Course rating:** 70.8/68.0. **Slope:** 120/114.
Opened: 1970. **Pace of Play rating:** N/A. **Green fee:** $20/35.
Credit cards: MC, V, AMEX. **Reduced fees:** Weekdays, Low season,
Twilight, Juniors.
Caddies: No. **Golf carts:** $12 for 18 holes.
Discount golf packages: Yes. **Season:** Year-round. **High:** April-Oct.
On-site lodging: No. **Rental clubs:** No.
Walking policy: Walking at certain times. **Range:** Yes (grass).
To obtain tee times: Call one week in advance for weekend tee times
only.
Subscriber comments: Excellent layout, variety of hole designs make it
exciting . . . Interesting layout, unusual terrain for N.J. . . . Hilly, very
scenic . . . Nice elevation changes, fast greens, too short, enjoyable . . .
Tough back nine, remote, lots of hills for south Jersey, tough to walk . . .
Too tough to walk all those hills! . . . Secluded.

★★★½ HOMINY HILL GOLF COURSE

PU—92 Mercer Rd., Colts Neck (908)462-9222.
50 miles north of Philadelphia. **Holes:** 18. **Par:** 72/72.

Yards: 7,056/5,794. **Course rating:** 74.4/73.9. **Slope:** 132/128.
Opened: 1964. **Pace of Play rating:** N/A. **Green fee:** $17/34.
Credit cards: None. **Reduced fees:** Weekdays, Twilight, Seniors, Juniors.
Caddies: No. **Golf carts:** $28 for 18 holes.
Discount golf packages: No. **Season:** March-Dec. **High:** May-Oct.
On-site lodging: No. **Rental clubs:** Yes.
Walking policy: Unrestricted walking. **Range:** Yes (grass).
To obtain tee times: Call seven days in advance.
Ranked in First 25 of America's 75 Best Public Golf Courses by Golf
Digest.
Subscriber comments: Excellent layout, very challenging par 3s . . . A
Robert Trent Jones masterpiece . . . Simply the best, truly a championship
layout . . . Had problems with greens . . . Great course . . . Getting back to
Top 25 condition . . . Tough to get on . . . Must have long drives . . .
Robert Trent Jones at his best . . . Sand is everywhere . . . Lots of sand and
real rough . . . Extremely difficult from back tees, OK for everyone from
regular tees, but not for beginners.

★★★★ HOWELL PARK GOLF COURSE
PU—Yellow Brook and Preventorium Rd., Farmingdale (908)938-4771.
40 miles north of Philadelphia. **Holes:** 18. **Par:** 72/72.
Yards: 6,885/5,693. **Course rating:** 73.0/72.5. **Slope:** 128/125.
Opened: 1972. **Pace of Play rating:** N/A. **Green fee:** $20/49.
Credit cards: None. **Reduced fees:** Weekdays, Twilight.
Caddies: No. **Golf carts:** N/A.
Discount golf packages: No. **Season:** March-Dec. **High:** April-Oct.
On-site lodging: No. **Rental clubs:** No.
Walking policy: Unrestricted walking. **Range:** No.
To obtain tee times: Call seven days in advance.
Ranked in Second 25 of America's 75 Best Public Golf Courses by Golf
Digest.
Subscriber comments: Outstanding course, not for beginners . . . Top-
of-the-line course, tough to get tee times . . . Course always in good
condition, well-run and maintained county course . . . Excellently
maintained . . . Hard to get on . . . Fairways are like greens, hate to take
divot . . . Slow play but great course . . . Great fairways, fast greens. Good
practice facility.

★★½ JUMPING BROOK GOLF AND COUNTRY CLUB
SP—210 Jumping Brook Rd., Neptune (908)922-6140.
50 miles south of New York City. **Holes:** 180. **Par:** 72/72.
Yards: 6,591/5,316. **Course rating:** 71.4/71.2. **Slope:** 122/118.
Opened: 1925. **Pace of Play rating:** N/A. **Green fee:** $28/35.
Credit cards: MC, V, AMEX. **Reduced fees:** Weekdays, Twilight,
Seniors, Juniors.
Caddies: No. **Golf carts:** $15 for 18 holes.
Discount golf packages: No. **Season:** Year-round. **High:** May-Sept.
On-site lodging: No. **Rental clubs:** Yes.
Walking policy: Walking at certain times. **Range:** Yes (grass).
To obtain tee times: Call three days in advance or Wednesday for the
upcoming weekend.
Subscriber comments: Hilly, long, must be innovative in shotmaking
. . . Greens are fast, fast, fast . . . Very long, old course which could be
great if upgraded . . . Getting better every year . . . A gem of a course,
greens are excellent and fast, front nine the hardest . . . Nice staff, tight
fairways, sloping greens, most improved course in '94 . . . Can see all 18
holes from clubhouse.

KNOLL COUNTRY CLUB
PU—1001 Parsippany Blvd., Parsippany (201)263-7115.
Call club for further information.
★½ EAST COURSE
Subscriber comments: Doesn't have the amenities but a good test, fun
. . . Course good for beginner . . . Course too tight, can be hazardous

when crowded . . . Nice layout . . . Very accommodating . . . Not bad for a public course.

★★★ WEST COURSE

Subscriber comments: Single players made to feel welcome . . . Some very long and challenging par 4s . . . Difficult greens . . . Beautiful clubhouse, nice layout . . . Good test for good player . . . Tree-lined fairways . . . Old-style layout, deep bunkers.

★½ LAKEWOOD COUNTRY CLUB

PU—145 Country Club Dr., Lakewood (908)364-8899.
40 miles south of New York City. **Holes:** 18. **Par:** 72/74.
Yards: 6,200/5,800. **Course rating:** 71.0/70.7. **Slope:** 117/116.
Opened: 1902. **Pace of Play rating:** 4:00-4:30. **Green fee:** $14/22.
Credit cards: None. **Reduced fees:** Weekdays, Twilight.
Caddies: No. **Golf carts:** $11 for 18 holes.
Discount golf packages: No. **Season:** Year-round. **High:** June-Aug.
On-site lodging: No. **Rental clubs:** Yes.
Walking policy: Unrestricted walking. **Range:** Yes.
To obtain tee times: Call one day in advance.
Subscriber comments: An architectural museum piece, fun course should be preserved with conditioning upgrade . . . Fairly short, small greens . . . Improvements under way should help . . . Usually easy to get tee time . . . Good course for mid- to high-handicappers . . . Tough course needs work . . . Tiny greens . . . 90-year old course, rolling greens, good course for average golfer.

MARRIOTT'S SEAVIEW RESORT

R—401 South New York Rd., Absecon (609)748-7680.
8 miles northwest of Atlantic City.
Green fee: $35/80.
Credit cards: All major. **Reduced fees:** Low season, Twilight.
Caddies: No. **Golf carts:** Included in Green Fee.
Discount golf packages: Yes. **Season:** Year-round.
On-site lodging: Yes. **Rental clubs:** Yes.
Walking policy: Mandatory cart. **Range:** Yes (grass).
To obtain tee times: Hotel guests call 30 days in advance. Others call three days in advance Monday-Thursday. One day in advance for Friday-Sunday.

★★★ BAY COURSE

Holes: 18. **Par:** 71/72.
Yards: 6,263/5,586. **Course rating:** 69.0/70.7. **Slope:** 113/115.
Opened: 1915. **Pace of Play rating:** 4:15.
Subscriber comments: Fun to play, scenic, wide open . . . Nice Donald Ross design, Snead's first PGA Championship '42 . . . Old, mature course, nice day of golf . . . Wind, small greens make up for lack of length . . . Bug problem in summer . . . Nice atmosphere. Good tune-up for Pines . . . Wonderfully maintained Donald Ross course, tough when wind blows . . . Outstanding old-time historic resort setting . . . Short, not very challenging.

★★★½ PINES COURSE

Holes: 18. **Par:** 71/75.
Yards: 6,885/5,837. **Course rating:** 73.0/73.2. **Slope:** 132/128.
Opened: 1931. **Pace of Play rating:** 4:30.
Subscriber comments: Tough course, tight fairways, heavily bunkered . . . Narrow and well-bunkered fairways, off-line shots end up in pine trees . . . Tight and demanding, bring your "A" game . . . Beautiful course, very well kept . . . Outstanding hole design . . . Great clubhouse . . . Outstanding course when not overbooked . . . Need every club in bag . . . Tight, tough, not for beginners.

★½ MAYS LANDING COUNTRY CLUB

PU—1855 Cates Rd., McKee City (609)641-4411.
13 miles west of Atlantic City. **Holes:** 18. **Par:** 72/71.
Yards: 6,662/5,432. **Course rating:** 71.1/70.3. **Slope:** 116/114.
Opened: 1962. **Pace of Play rating:** 4:00. **Green fee:** $15/27.

Credit cards: MC, V. **Reduced fees:** Weekdays, Low season, Twilight.
Caddies: No. **Golf carts:** $13 for 18 holes.
Discount golf packages: No. **Season:** Year-round. **High:** April–Oct.
On-site lodging: No. **Rental clubs:** Yes.
Walking policy: Walking at certain times. **Range:** Yes (grass).
To obtain tee times: Call up to seven days in advance.
Subscriber comments: Championship layout, needs a little TLC . . . A
good course you can play in a reasonable time frame . . . Some nice holes
. . . Course needs work . . . Nice layout, polite staff . . . An interesting flat
course.

MEADOWS GOLF CLUB★

SP—79 Two Bridges Rd., Lincoln Park (201)696-7212.
22 miles west of New York City. **Holes:** 18. **Par:** 68/68.
Yards: 6,100/4,600. **Course rating:** 67.6/64.7. **Slope:** 110/99.
Opened: N/A. **Pace of Play rating:** N/A. **Green fee:** $17/30.
Credit cards: None. **Reduced fees:** Weekdays, Twilight, Seniors.
Caddies: No. **Golf carts:** $26 for 18 holes.
Discount golf packages: No. **Season:** Year-round.
On-site lodging: No. **Rental clubs:** Yes.
Walking policy: Walking at certain times. **Range:** No.
To obtain tee times: Call for weekend tee times only.

★★½ MERCER OAKS GOLF CLUB

PU—c/o County Parks Commissioner, Trenton (609)936-9603.
Call club for further information.
Subscriber comments: Great layout, maturing quickly . . . Should be
very good in a few years . . . Very long course . . . Wide open . . . New,
developing course with character, will be excellent . . . Challenging links-
type course . . . Layout is fantastic . . . Ninth hole tough but only 380-
yards . . . I loved it, my wife didn't.

★★ MIRY RUN COUNTRY CLUB

PU—106 B. Sharon Rd., Robbinsville (609)259-1010.
Call club for further information.
Formerly known as Skyview C.C.
Subscriber comments: Open course, needs more definition . . . A few
good holes . . . Pretty course, a few tough holes, needs some work . . . Flat
but fun course . . . Potential is high . . . Good course for long hitter.

★★½ MOUNTAIN VIEW GOLF COURSE

PU—Bear Tavern Rd., West Trenton (609)882-4093.
Call club for further information.
Subscriber comments: Front is open, back has more character . . .
Challenging and hilly, small greens, length, and hills make this course a real
test . . . Always crowded, plays very long . . . Hole Nos. 12, 13, and 14 are
magnificent when played from blue tees.

★★ OCEAN ACRES COUNTRY CLUB

SP—925 Buccaneer Lane, Manahawkin (609)597-9393.
12 miles west of Long Beach Island. **Holes:** 18. **Par:** 72/72.
Yards: 6,548/5,412. **Course rating:** 70.5/70.7. **Slope:** 120/118.
Opened: 1967. **Pace of Play rating:** N/A. **Green fee:** $15/22.
Credit cards: MC, V, AMEX. **Reduced fees:** Low season, Twilight.
Caddies: No. **Golf carts:** $20 for 18 holes.
Discount golf packages: No. **Season:** Year-round. **High:** June–Aug.
On-site lodging: No. **Rental clubs:** Yes.
Walking policy: Walking at certain times. **Range:** No.
To obtain tee times: Call five days in advance for weekends and holidays
only.
Subscriber comments: Great island par 3 . . . Accuracy is a must . . .
Good back nine, front too open, tough to get on . . . Too crowded, tourist
haven . . . Flat, open on front, back tight and better challenge . . . Pleasant
course . . . Beautiful back nine.

★★★ OCEAN COUNTY GOLF COURSE AT ATLANTIS
PU—Country Club Blvd., Tuckerton (609)296-2444.
30 miles north of Atlantic City. **Holes:** 18. **Par:** 72/72.
Yards: 6,845/5,579. **Course rating:** 73.6/71.8. **Slope:** 134/124.
Opened: 1961. **Pace of Play rating:** 4:30. **Green fee:** $10/28.
Credit cards: None. **Reduced fees:** Twilight, Seniors, Juniors.
Caddies: No. **Golf carts:** $22 for 18 holes.
Discount golf packages: No. **Season:** Year-round. **High:** Aug.
On-site lodging: No. **Rental clubs:** Yes.
Walking policy: Walking at certain times. **Range:** Yes.
To obtain tee times: Call eight days in advance at 6 p.m. I.D. card
required.
Subscriber comments: Difficult and tight, stay out of the woods! . . .
Very good all-round course . . . Nice old fashioned course . . . Tough
course, must be straight . . . A gem . . . Great facility and course . . .
Mosquitoes are awful in summer . . . Great place to play.

★★ OLD ORCHARD COUNTRY CLUB
SP—54 Monmouth Rd., Eatontown (908)542-7666.
40 miles south of New York City. **Holes:** 18. **Par:** 72/72.
Yards: 6,588/5,575. **Course rating:** 70.5/70.8. **Slope:** 116/115.
Opened: 1929. **Pace of Play rating:** N/A. **Green fee:** $13/27.
Credit cards: MC, V. **Reduced fees:** Weekdays, Low season, Twilight,
Seniors.
Caddies: No. **Golf carts:** $28 for 18 holes.
Discount golf packages: No. **Season:** Year-round. **High:** May-Sept.
On-site lodging: No. **Rental clubs:** Yes.
Walking policy: Unrestricted walking. **Range:** Yes.
To obtain tee times: Call for current month.
Subscriber comments: Several interesting holes . . . Seventh hole is island
green, can make or break your day/round . . . Easy front, challenge on
back . . . Pleasant course, not special . . . Short fun course, well kept, small
greens . . . Interesting layout, condition needs improvement.

★½ OVERPECK GOLF COURSE
PU—E Cedar Lane, Teaneck (201)837-9666.
Call club for further information.
Subscriber comments: Too many geese . . . OK for county course,
terrible drainage . . . Flat, lots of water . . . Heavily played . . . Good
amount of water, wide open . . . Well laid out, nice greens . . . Lots of
water, basically flat . . . Water does not drain well.

★★ PARAMUS GOLF CLUB
PU—314 Paramus Rd., Paramus (201)440-6079.
15 miles west of New York City. **Holes:** 18. **Par:** 71/70.
Yards: 6,212/5,241. **Course rating:** 69.1/72.0. **Slope:** 118/117.
Opened: 1976. **Pace of Play rating:** 4:30. **Green fee:** $22/28.
Credit cards: None. **Reduced fees:** Weekdays, Seniors.
Caddies: No. **Golf carts:** $23 for 18 holes.
Discount golf packages: No. **Season:** Year-round. **High:** April-Nov.
On-site lodging: No. **Rental clubs:** Yes.
Walking policy: Unrestricted walking. **Range:** No.
To obtain tee times: No tee times.
Subscriber comments: Getting a tee time is problematic . . . Short and
open, not too much trouble . . . Friendly . . . Very flat, not very difficult
. . . A great old course . . . Good par 3s . . . A lot of doglegs . . . Municipal
course, flat and easy . . . Too crowded.

★½ PASCACK BROOK GOLF AND COUNTRY CLUB
SP—15 Rivervale Rd., River Vale (201)664-5886.
Call club for further information.
Subscriber comments: First tee you shoot over water . . . Most holes
extremely tight, poor drainage . . . Great course for 25 to 30 handicappers,
pace of play a little slow though . . . OK for most golfers, very small greens
. . . Not bad at all, some par 4s that can be eagled.

PASSAIC COUNTY GOLF COURSE
PU—209 Totowa Rd., Wayne (201)881-4921.
Call club for further information.

★½**BLUE COURSE**
Subscriber comments: Easy, wide open course for average player . . .
Not bad for public course, gets a lot of play . . . Varied, interesting holes,
both very crowded most of the time.

★½**RED COURSE**
Subscriber comments: Better layout than Blue Course . . . Lots of
potential . . . Conditions could be better.

★★★**PENNSAUKEN COUNTRY CLUB**
PU—3800 Haddonfield Rd., Pennsauken (609)662-4961.
Call club for further information.
Subscriber comments: Good course for all levels . . . Nice golf course,
some tight holes, good test . . . Challenging track, great greens, hard to get
out, overplayed . . . Good clubhouse and restaurant . . . Easy to score on, a
good confidence builder . . . Best public course in greater Philadelphia area
. . . Course was in very good condition, nice layout, little on short side . . .
Good balance of difficult and easy holes.

★★½**PINE BROOK GOLF CLUB**
PU—1 Covered Bridge Blvd., Englishtown (908)536-7272.
Call club for further information.
Subscriber comments: Executive course for all levels, excellent condition
. . . Tough par 61! . . . Good course for beginners and to work on your
irons . . . Great for senior citizens like myself . . . Nice staff, well-kept for
small course, good track to practice iron game.

★½**PINELANDS GOLF CLUB**
PU—887 S. Mays Landing Rd., Winslow (609)561-8900.
25 miles northwest of Altantic City. **Holes:** 18. **Par:** 71/71.
Yards: 6,224/5,375. **Course rating:** 69.7/70.4. **Slope:** 114/119.
Opened: 1963. **Pace of Play rating:** 4:30. **Green fee:** $12/23.
Credit cards: MC, V. **Reduced fees:** Weekdays, Low season, Twilight.
Caddies: No. **Golf carts:** $11 for 18 holes.
Discount golf packages: No. **Season:** Year-round. **High:** May-Nov.
On-site lodging: No. **Rental clubs:** Yes.
Walking policy: Walking at certain times. **Range:** Yes (grass).
To obtain tee times: Call five days in advance for minimum of three
players.
Subscriber comments: Narrow, bad fairways, good greens . . . Great
layout, some blind holes, polite staff . . . Blue-collar golf, nice layout,
decent challenge . . . Great, tight layout, but turf maintenance is bad . . .
Seems to be improving each year, nice track.

★½**PRINCETON GOLF CLUB**
PU—Wheeler Way, Princeton (609)452-9382.
Call club for further information.
Subscriber comments: Pleasant little, accessible, surprise course . . . Short
but tight course, accuracy a must . . . Don't play here after heavy rain,
otherwise excellent . . . Course very playable for us old duffers . . . Too
short . . . Great course to learn iron play . . . Tight but flat.

★★½**QUAIL BROOK GOLF COURSE**
PU—625 New Brunswick Rd., Somerset (908)560-9528.
30 miles west of New York City. **Holes:** 18. **Par:** 71/72.
Yards: 6,591/5,385. **Course rating:** 70.8/69.9. **Slope:** 119/115.
Opened: 1982. **Pace of Play rating:** 3:52. **Green fee:** $20/35.
Credit cards: MC, V. **Reduced fees:** Seniors, Juniors.
Caddies: No. **Golf carts:** $22 for 18 holes.
Discount golf packages: No. **Season:** Year-round. **High:** May-Sept.
On-site lodging: No. **Rental clubs:** Yes.
Walking policy: Unrestricted walking. **Range:** No.
To obtain tee times: 24-hour access for tee time for a per reservation fee.

Subscriber comments: Nice front nine, back nine has poor layout for walking . . . Short shotmaker's course . . . Good course, but long walk between holes on back nine . . . Great public course, short, but challenging . . . Challenges all levels . . . Pace of play is slow but acceptable for a public course in New Jersey . . . Make sure you're in shape for the hilly back nine.

RAMBLEWOOD COUNTRY CLUB
★★½ **RED/WHITE/BLUE**

PU—200 Country Club Pkwy., Mt. Laurel (609)235-2118.
8 miles east of Philadelphia. **Holes:** 27. **Par:** 72/72/72.
Yards: 6,883/6,624/6,723. **Course rating:** 72.9/71.1/72.1.
Slope: 130/129/130.
Opened: 1962. **Pace of Play rating:** N/A. **Green fee:** $40/48.
Credit cards: MC, V. **Reduced fees:** Weekdays, Low season, Twilight, Seniors.
Caddies: No. **Golf carts:** N/A.
Discount golf packages: Yes. **Season:** Year-round. **High:** April-Oct.
On-site lodging: No. **Rental clubs:** Yes.
Walking policy: Walking at certain times. **Range:** No.
To obtain tee times: Call seven days in advance.
Subscriber comments: If you hit it long, you'll love it; short hitters, stay away . . . Convenient location, three nines, very nicely maintained, good facilities except for lack of driving range, flat greens . . . Easy courses, very pretty, well laid out . . . Good condition in summer, poor in wet season, pretty good layout . . . Course is fairly flat, not much of challenge, suited for beginner to average player . . . Well kept, straightforward . . . Open, fun layout . . . Fair condition.

★★★ RANCOCAS GOLF CLUB

PU—Clubhouse Dr., Willingboro (609)877-5344.
10 miles north of Philadelphia. **Holes:** 18. **Par:** 71/72.
Yards: 6,634/5,284. **Course rating:** 73.0/73.0. **Slope:** 130/127.
Opened: 1968. **Pace of Play rating:** 4:15. **Green fee:** $19/32.
Credit cards: MC, V. **Reduced fees:** Weekdays, Low season, Twilight, Seniors, Juniors.
Caddies: No. **Golf carts:** Included in Green Fee.
Discount golf packages: Yes. **Season:** Year-round. **High:** April-Nov.
On-site lodging: No. **Rental clubs:** Yes.
Walking policy: Walking at certain times. **Range:** Yes.
To obtain tee times: Call up to seven days in advance.
Subscriber comments: R.T. Jones course with odd mixture of easy and picturesque holes . . . 13th hole, downhill, uphill, double-dogleg par 5 . . . A shotmaker's course . . . Front nine open, many traps, back tight . . . Great design by R.T. Jones . . . Front nine open, back nine tree-lined . . . Good condition, fast greens, back nine very tight.

★★★ RIVER VALE COUNTRY CLUB

PU—660 Rivervale Rd., River Vale (201)391-2300.
30 miles north of New York City. **Holes:** 18. **Par:** 72/74.
Yards: 6,470/5,293. **Course rating:** 70.1/68.6. **Slope:** 116/107.
Opened: 1928. **Pace of Play rating:** 4:30. **Green fee:** $58/82.
Credit cards: MC, V, AMEX. **Reduced fees:** Low season, Twilight.
Caddies: No. **Golf carts:** Included in Green Fee.
Discount golf packages: Yes. **Season:** March-Nov. **High:** June-Sept.
On-site lodging: No. **Rental clubs:** Yes.
Walking policy: Mandatory cart. **Range:** Yes.
To obtain tee times: Call in advance.
Subscriber comments: Short, open, hilly, good maintenance, very strict . . . Good test. Some interesting holes . . . Well kept and challenging but not worth the money . . . Interesting layout . . . Sporty course . . . Well maintained, efficiently run, varied terrain.

★ ROCKLEIGH GOLF COURSE

PU—15 Paris Ave., Rockleigh (201)768-6353.
Call club for further information.
Subscriber comments: Good for beginner . . . County course, not in
exceptionally good condition . . . Potential to be excellent course, shame
. . . No. 7 on Red, 445-yard par 4 uphill, is toughest hole in North
America.

★★½ RON JAWORSKI'S EAGLES' NEST COUNTRY CLUB

SP—Woodbury-Glassboro Rd., Sewell (609)468-3542.
12 miles south of Camden. **Holes:** 18. **Par:** 71/71.
Yards: 6,376/5,210. **Course rating:** 71.3/71.2. **Slope:** 130/125.
Opened: N/A. **Pace of Play rating:** N/A. **Green fee:** $18/25.
Credit cards: MC, V, AMEX. **Reduced fees:** Weekdays, Low season,
Twilight, Seniors.
Caddies: No. **Golf carts:** $10 for 18 holes.
Discount golf packages: No. **Season:** Year-round. **High:** April-Oct.
On-site lodging: No. **Rental clubs:** No.
Walking policy: Walking at certain times. **Range:** No.
To obtain tee times: Call anytime.
Subscriber comments: Nice clubhouse, condition of greens above
average, nice topography . . . Nine easy holes, nine tough holes . . . Back
nine hilly, hilly . . . Front nine open, back nine tight . . . Owner football
star Ron Jaworski friendly . . . Out of the way but worth the trip . . . Holes
seven through 15 very interesting . . . Suits all types of players . . . Features
the dangerous combination of high handicappers and parallel fairways . . .
Very good test on back nine . . . Nos. 7 and 15 awesome par 5s.

★★½ RUTGERS GOLF CLUB

PU—777 Hoes Lane, Piscataway (908)932-2631.
Call club for further information.
Subscriber comments: One of the nicest courses I've played . . . Beautiful
wide-open course, great use of water and sand . . . Some holes are too
short, drive and pitch . . . Easy course, good for beginners . . . Can play
short, two good finishing holes . . . Best-kept secret, nice layout, no
restaurant and bar . . . Nice walking course for seniors . . . Flat course . . .
University course, relatively easy, moderate to heavy play . . . Scenic
through campus . . . Challenging . . . Nice but plain.

★★★ SHARK RIVER GOLF COURSE

PU—320 Old Corlies Ave., Neptune (908)922-4141.
50 miles of Newark. **Holes:** 18. **Par:** 71/71.
Yards: 6,176/5,532. **Course rating:** N/A. **Slope:** 112/116.
Call club for further information.
Subscriber comments: Awkward layout, but in good condition . . . Hard
not to like this quirky course with a mix of very easy and very difficult holes
. . . Great layout, some short holes even from the blue tees, but don't be
fooled, you will use every club in the bag . . . Nice shape, a little short . . .
Good for ego . . . Well-kept clubhouse . . . Short course, small greens, but
fun to play . . . Enjoyable to play, some holes too short, some too long . . .
Best 3s around, good iron play.

★★ SPOOKY BROOK GOLF COURSE

PU—Elizabeth Ave., Somerset (908)873-2242.
30 miles west of New York City. **Holes:** 18. **Par:** 71/72.
Yards: 6,612/5,376. **Course rating:** 70.5/73.5. **Slope:** 113/120.
Opened: 1970. **Pace of Play rating:** 3:47. **Green fee:** $20/35.
Credit cards: MC, V. **Reduced fees:** Seniors, Juniors.
Caddies: No. **Golf carts:** $22 for 18 holes.
Discount golf packages: No. **Season:** Year-round. **High:** May-Sept.
On-site lodging: No. **Rental clubs:** Yes.
Walking policy: Unrestricted walking. **Range:** Yes (grass).
To obtain tee times: 24-hour access number for a per reservation fee.

Subscriber comments: Wide open, let it rip . . . Some real nice holes on the back, Nos. 13, 14, 15, 17 . . . Larger greens, enjoyable all golfers . . . A likeable course, kept well, flat and open . . . Favors beginners. Good-size greens . . . Long but very plain . . . Nice to walk. Back nine more challenging.

★★½SPRING MEADOW GOLF COURSE
PU—4181 Atlantic Ave., Farmingdale (908)449-0806.
40 miles east of Trenton. **Holes:** 18. **Par:** 72/76.
Yards: 5,953/5,310. **Course rating:** 68.1/69.7. **Slope:** 113/114.

Opened: 1920. **Pace of Play rating:** 4:30. **Green fee:** $13/16.
Credit cards: None. **Reduced fees:** Weekdays, Twilight, Seniors.
Caddies: No. **Golf carts:** $20 for 18 holes.
Discount golf packages: No. **Season:** Year-round. **High:** April-Oct.
On-site lodging: No. **Rental clubs:** Yes.
Walking policy: Unrestricted walking. **Range:** Yes (grass).
To obtain tee times: First come, first served.
Subscriber comments: Unusual mix of holes . . . Price is right for this fun and gimmicky course . . . Small knock-around course, only course in N.J. owned by the state . . . Interesting short course . . . Has some very unusual holes, good value . . . Deceivingly difficult, short layout . . . No. 10 par-4 426 all uphill, is a killer ; my first hole-in-one on No. 9.

★★★½SUNSET VALLEY GOLF COURSE
PU—47 West Sunset Rd., Pompton Plains (201)835-1515.
13 miles north of Newark. **Holes:** 18. **Par:** 70/70.
Yards: 6,483/5,274. **Course rating:** 71.7/70.8. **Slope:** 129/123.
Opened: 1974. **Pace of Play rating:** 4:30. **Green fee:** $11/32.
Credit cards: None. **Reduced fees:** Twilight, Seniors.
Caddies: No. **Golf carts:** $32 for 18 holes.
Discount golf packages: No. **Season:** April-Dec. **High:** May-Sept.
On-site lodging: No. **Rental clubs:** Yes.
Walking policy: Unrestricted walking. **Range:** No.
To obtain tee times: Automated tee time or come in person.
Subscriber comments: Course has a lot of character, fast greens, beautiful valley scenery . . . Very fast greens, everything breaks down the mountains . . . Big fast greens. Stay below the holes . . . 16th hole a killer . . . Three of the best finishing holes in N.J. . . . Fast, hilly greens, can four-putt . . . Toughest greens north of Augusta! Bikini wax is an understatement . . . Good course, great back nine.

TAMARACK GOLF COURSE
★½RED/WHITE/BLUE/GOLD
PU—97 Hardenburg Lane, East Brunswick (908)821-8881.
6 miles east of New Brunswick. **Holes:** 36. **Par:** 72/72.
Yards: 7,025/5,810. **Course rating:** 73.3/72.5. **Slope:** 118/113.
Opened: 1970. **Pace of Play rating:** 4:00. **Green fee:** $6/50.
Credit cards: None. **Reduced fees:** Seniors, Juniors.
Caddies: No. **Golf carts:** $22 for 18 holes.
Discount golf packages: No. **Season:** Year-round. **High:** March-Oct.
On-site lodging: No. **Rental clubs:** Yes.
Walking policy: Unrestricted walking. **Range:** Yes.
To obtain tee times: First come, first served.
Subscriber comments: Flat, lots of doglegs, river and lakes in play . . . Tough course. Greens so-so . . . The Red and White nines are championship design, but conditioning is poor . . . Great potential, needs lots of work . . . Interesting and challenging, variety with four nines, condition needs some improvement.

★VALLEYBROOK GOLF COURSE
PU—1 Golf View, Blackwood (609)227-3171.
10 miles southeast of Camden. **Holes:** 18. **Par:** 72/72.
Yards: 6,123/5,319. **Course rating:** 70.6/69.1. **Slope:** 125/120.
Opened: 1990. **Pace of Play rating:** 4:00. **Green fee:** $12/16.
Credit cards: None. **Reduced fees:** Weekdays, Twilight.

Caddies: No. **Golf carts:** N/A.
Discount golf packages: Yes. **Season:** Year-round. **High:** April-Oct.
On-site lodging: No. **Rental clubs:** Yes.
Walking policy: Unrestricted walking. **Range:** Yes (grass).
To obtain tee times: Call seven days in advance.
Subscriber comments: Short, tricked-up back nine . . . Needs some
work, good for beginners . . . This is what $16 golf is all about . . . Old-
style challenging holes . . . Redesign in the '80's . . . Terrible layout. I like
their driving range . . . Course needs a lot of work.

★½ WARRENBROOK GOLF COURSE
PU—500 Warrenville Rd., Warren (908)754-8402.
30 miles west of New York City. **Holes:** 18. **Par:** 71/70.
Yards: 6,372/5,095. **Course rating:** 71.1/69.8. **Slope:** 127/121.
Opened: 1978. **Pace of Play rating:** 3:47. **Green fee:** $20/35.
Credit cards: MC, V. **Reduced fees:** Seniors, Juniors.
Caddies: No. **Golf carts:** $22 for 18 holes.
Discount golf packages: No. **Season:** April-Nov. **High:** May-Sept.
On-site lodging: No. **Rental clubs:** Yes.
Walking policy: Unrestricted walking. **Range:** No.
To obtain tee times: 24-hour access number for a per reservation fee.
Subscriber comments: Tight, small, tricky greens, not for high
handicappers . . . Great layout, fun course, good value . . . Has a lot of
potential . . . Very tight fairways, lots of woods, driver stays in the bag . . .
Hilly, some blind shots . . . A billy goat course, but fun . . . A beautiful and
challenging course that has narrow tree-lined fairways and is an excellent
test for the low handicapper. Unfortunately it is falling into disrepair.

★½ WEDGEWOOD COUNTRY CLUB
PU—200 Hurffville Rd., Turnersville (609)227-5522.
Call club for further information.
Subscriber comments: Good layout, difficult, condition has suffered . . .
Up and down, hilly, tight fairways . . . Don't like driving across two roads
. . . Love the back . . . Could be a gem . . . What a layout, No. 13 the
devil's creation of a par 4 . . . OK. Love the 13th hole . . . Great potential
but poorly taken care of.

★★ WESTWOOD GOLF CLUB
PU—850 Kings Hwy., Woodbury (609)845-2000.
Call club for further information.
Subscriber comments: Medium difficult, has improved last two years
. . . Family run with love and it shows. Ken and Janet are great hosts,
lovely daughter Jennifer makes best chili outside of Texas . . . Nice, short
course . . . Gimmicky course . . . Easy to walk, nothing fancy . . . Ever
improving . . . Front nine very forgiving, back nine gets a little tighter . . .
Needs more time to ripen.

★★½ WILLOW BROOK COUNTRY CLUB
SP—4310 Bridgeboro Rd., Moorestown (609)461-0131.
10 miles southeast of Cherry Hills. **Holes:** 18. **Par:** 72/72.
Yards: 6,457/5,028. **Course rating:** 71.2/68.3. **Slope:** 125/110.
Opened: 1967. **Pace of Play rating:** 4:30. **Green fee:** $19/28.
Credit cards: MC, V, DISC. **Reduced fees:** Weekdays, Low season,
Twilight, Seniors.
Caddies: No. **Golf carts:** $10 for 18 holes.
Discount golf packages: No. **Season:** Year-round. **High:** May-Sept.
On-site lodging: No. **Rental clubs:** Yes.
Walking policy: Walking at certain times. **Range:** Yes (grass).
To obtain tee times: Call Monday to Friday for weekend tee time and call
anytime for weekday.
Subscriber comments: Very well maintained, good practice facilities . . .
Mandatory cart policy on weekends and peak daily times is stupid . . .
Great 18th hole. Decent public course . . . Pleasant setting, nice location
. . . Challenging back nine, 18th terrific hole . . . Good course with a creek
running through it.

★★★ WOODLAKE GOLF AND COUNTRY CLUB

SP—25 New Hampshire Ave., Lakewood (908)367-4500.
45 miles south of Newark. **Holes:** 18. **Par:** 72/74.
Yards: 6,766/5,557. **Course rating:** 72.5/72.2. **Slope:** 126/120.
Opened: 1972. **Pace of Play rating:** 3:30-4:30. **Green fee:** $29/50.
Credit cards: MC, V. **Reduced fees:** Weekdays, Low season, Twilight.
Caddies: No. **Golf carts:** Included in Green Fee.
Discount golf packages: Yes. **Season:** Year-round. **High:** May-Aug.
On-site lodging: No. **Rental clubs:** Yes.
Walking policy: Mandatory cart. **Range:** Yes (grass).
To obtain tee times: Nonmembers call two days in advance.
Subscriber comments: Sometimes floods, otherwise very good to top-notch . . . Good, tight layout with a lot of water . . . Excellent layout, usually wet with long grass on fairways. If in better shape I would rate it a lot higher . . . Excellent layout, but too much housing . . . Great course from back tees . . . Loved it, lots of water, long, tight, tough greens, great pin placements . . . Beautiful track, challenging course, must keep ball in play, tight fairways on some holes.

Notes

NEW YORK

★★½ ADIRONDACK GOLF & COUNTRY CLUB
PU—88 Golf Rd., Peru (518)643-8403, (800)346-1761.
70 miles south of Montreal. **Holes:** 18. **Par:** 72/72.
Yards: 6,851/5,069. **Course rating:** 71.9/67.9. **Slope:** 123/115.
Opened: 1990. **Pace of Play rating:** 5:00. **Green fee:** $15/28.
Credit cards: MC, V, DISC. **Reduced fees:** Weekdays, Low season,
Twilight, Seniors, Juniors.
Caddies: No. **Golf carts:** N/A.
Discount golf packages: No. **Season:** March-Dec. **High:** July-Aug.
On-site lodging: No. **Rental clubs:** Yes.
Walking policy: Unrestricted walking. **Range:** Yes (grass).
To obtain tee times: Call Wednesday for upcoming Saturday, Sunday and
Monday. Call Sunday for Tuesday through Friday.
Subscriber comments: Best suited for low to middle handicappers.
Woods line both sides of fairways on most holes. Very nice layout and
scenic . . . Staff quite friendly . . . Definitely not for your beginner . . .
Very tight fairways.

★½ AFTON GOLF CLUB
PU—Afton Lake Rd., Afton (607)639-2454.
Call club for further information.
Subscriber comments: Short, easy . . . Best for higher handicappers . . .
Nice little course, fairly easy, well maintained, fun to play . . . People very
nice . . . Very friendly and accommodating staff . . . A very good course
for beginners and intermediate players . . . Fun place to get away from the
pressure.

★★ ALBAN HILLS COUNTRY CLUB
PU—129 Alban Hills Dr., Johnstown (518)762-3717.
40 miles west of Albany. **Holes:** 18. **Par:** 70/70.
Yards: 5,819/5,015. **Course rating:** 66.3/67.6. **Slope:** 103/105.
Opened: 1980. **Pace of Play rating:** 4:30. **Green fee:** $8/14.
Credit cards: None. **Reduced fees:** Weekdays, Low season, Twilight,
Seniors, Juniors.
Caddies: No. **Golf carts:** $18 for 18 holes.
Discount golf packages: No. **Season:** April-Nov. **High:** June-Aug.
On-site lodging: No. **Rental clubs:** Yes.
Walking policy: Unrestricted walking. **Range:** No.
To obtain tee times: Call seven days in advance.
Subscriber comments: Wide open, undulating large greens . . . Too few
bunkers . . . Needs more water hazards . . . Becomes a test after first four
holes . . . Service and staff is five stars.

★½ AMHERST AUDUBON GOLF COURSE
PU—500 Maple Rd., Williamsville (716)631-7139.
Call club for further information.
Subscriber comments: Course is best suited for average player . . .
Fairway and greens good . . . New clubhouse . . . Only three par 5s . . .
Too many down and back long par 4s. Easy course layout . . . Wide open.

★★★ AMSTERDAM MUNICIPAL GOLF COURSE
PU—Upper Van Dyke Ave., Amsterdam (518)842-4265.
15 miles northwest of Schenectady. **Holes:** 18. **Par:** 71/74.
Yards: 6,370/5,352. **Course rating:** 70.2/70.2. **Slope:** 120/110.
Opened: 1938. **Pace of Play rating:** 4:30. **Green fee:** $16/ 18.
Credit cards: None. **Reduced fees:** Seniors.
Caddies: No. **Golf carts:** $20 for 18 holes.
Discount golf packages: No. **Season:** April-Nov. **High:** July-Aug.
On-site lodging: No. **Rental clubs:** Yes.
Walking policy: Unrestricted walking. **Range:** Yes (grass).
To obtain tee times: Call two days in advance for weekends only.

Subscriber comments: Need riding cart, hills make course challenging . . . Tough test for municipal . . . Two best finishing par 4s . . . One of RT Jones' first courses . . . Hilly, small greens, good exercise, blind holes . . . Wide open fairways . . . Interesting variety of holes.

★★★ ARROWHEAD GOLF COURSE

PU—7185 East Taft Rd., East Syracuse (315)656-7563.
Holes: 18. **Par:** 72/ 73.
Yards: 6,700/5,156. **Course rating:** 70.9/68.5. **Slope:** 113/109.
Opened: 1968. **Pace of Play rating:** 4:30. **Green fee:** $15.
Credit cards: None. **Reduced fees:** Seniors, Juniors.
Caddies: No. **Golf carts:** $16 for 18 holes.
Discount golf packages: No. **Season:** April-Nov. **High:** May-Sept.
On-site lodging: No. **Rental clubs:** Yes.
Walking policy: Unrestricted walking. **Range:** No.
To obtain tee times: First come, first served.
Subscriber comments: Great par 5s . . . Well maintained, always improving . . . Course was in excellent shape all season . . . Staff and management always helpful . . . The course is flat throughout which makes for easy walking . . . The layout seems like it was designed for safety . . . No problem with errant balls from other fairways . . . The greens which are always in good shape favor the straight ball hitter . . . Big difference from the tips . . . Water on 15 holes.

★★ AUBURN GOLF & COUNTRY CLUB

PU—RD 6, East Lake Rd., Auburn (315)253-3152.
Call club for further information.
Subscriber comments: Great for high-handicap player . . . Food was excellent . . . It seems like it is all par 4s . . . Greens excellent . . . Grand old layout, investing to bring it back . . . With a little work, golf course would be good.

★★★ BALLSTON SPA COUNTRY CLUB

SP—Rte. 67, Ballston Spa (518)885-7935.
20 miles north of Albany. **Holes:** 18. **Par:** 71/74.
Yards: 6,215/5,757. **Course rating:** 69.3/69.4. **Slope:** 124/122.
Opened: 1926. **Pace of Play rating:** 4:00. **Green fee:** $40.
Credit cards: None. **Reduced fees:** N/A.
Caddies: No. **Golf carts:** Included in Green Fee.
Discount golf packages: No. **Season:** April-Nov. **High:** June-Sept.
On-site lodging: No. **Rental clubs:** Yes.
Walking policy: Mandatory cart. **Range:** Yes (grass).
To obtain tee times: Call one week in advance.
Subscriber comments: Very playable . . . Many hidden brooks . . . Very pretty . . . Tough greens . . . You better be below the hole . . . Short narrow layout, demands accuracy more than distance . . . Great attitude towards guests . . . Clean as a whistle . . . Only straight hitters need apply . . . Water on 10 holes.

★★½ BARKER BROOK GOLF COURSE

PU—Rogers Rd., Oriskany Falls (315)821-9992.
Call club for further information.
Subscriber comments: My personal favorite . . . Greens are the course's biggest asset . . . Groomed the best, front nine goes from open to very tight . . . Staff very nice . . . Food good . . . Good test for middle/high handicappers . . . Course management absolutely super.

★½ BATAVIA COUNTRY CLUB

SP—7909 Batavia-Byron Rd., Batavia (716)343-7600.
Call club for further information.
Subscriber comments: Nice course for beginners, not much trouble . . . 4th hole is very interesting . . . Friendly staff . . . Not a bad layout, fairly wide open, good pace, condition O.K.

NEW YORK

★★½ BATTLE ISLAND GOLF COURSE
PU—Rte. 48, Battle Island State Park, Fulton (315)592-3361.
21 miles north of Syracuse. **Holes:** 18. **Par:** 72/72.
Yards: 5,973/5,561. **Course rating:** 67.9/68.7. **Slope:** 109/N/A.
Opened: N/A. **Pace of Play rating:** 4:30-5:00. **Green fee:** $13/16.
Credit cards: None. **Reduced fees:** Seniors, Juniors.
Caddies: No. **Golf carts:** $18 for 18 holes.
Discount golf packages: No. **Season:** April-Nov. **High:** Aug.-Sept.
On-site lodging: No. **Rental clubs:** Yes.
Walking policy: Unrestricted walking. **Range:** No.
To obtain tee times: First come, first served.
Subscriber comments: Hard to believe it is not a private course . . . Hills
and trouble everywhere ; short, small greens . . . Wide open course ; heavy
play . . . Shooting gallery when busy . . . Very scenic, fine variety of holes
. . . Fun course for all players.

★★ BEAVER ISLAND STATE PARK GOLF CLUB
PU—Beaver Island State Park, Grand Island (716)773-4668.
8 miles north of Buffalo. **Holes:** 18. **Par:** 72/72.
Yards: 6,595/6,201. **Course rating:** N/A. **Slope:** N/A.
Opened: N/A. **Pace of Play rating:** 4:10. **Green fee:** $14/17.
Credit cards: None. **Reduced fees:** Weekdays, Seniors, Juniors.
Caddies: No. **Golf carts:** $18 for 18 holes.
Discount golf packages: No. **Season:** April-Nov. **High:** July-Aug.
On-site lodging: No. **Rental clubs:** No.
Walking policy: Unrestricted walking. **Range:** No.
To obtain tee times
Call Thursday for upcoming weekend.
Subscriber comments: Front nine long and windy . . . Back nine tight
. . . In great shape . . . Lush fairways . . . Relatively wide open, stray shots
not penalized . . . Lots of water, but flat . . . The staff keeps you moving at
a comfortable pace . . . Good walking course . . . Great test for average and
lower handicaps.

BEEKMAN GOLF CLUB
★½ TACONIC/HIGHLAND/VALLEY
SP—11 Country Club Rd., Hopewell Junction (914)226-7700.
36 miles north of White Plains. **Holes:** 27. **Par:** 71/70/71.
Yards: 6,387/6,213/6,300. **Course rating:** 71.8/71.2/71.6.
Slope: 126/124/124.
Opened: 1963. **Pace of Play rating:** 3:50. **Green fee:** $16/23.
Credit cards: MC, V. **Reduced fees:** Weekdays, Low season, Twilight,
Seniors.
Caddies: No. **Golf carts:** Included in Green Fee.
Discount golf packages: Yes. **Season:** April-Nov. **High:** July-Aug.
On-site lodging: No. **Rental clubs:** Yes.
Walking policy: Walking at certain times. **Range:** Yes (grass).
To obtain tee times: Call.
Subscriber comments: Hilly secluded layout . . . Good golf deal . . .
Three nines all well laid out . . . Enjoyable for all handicaps . . . Pace of
play fair . . . Carts, golf, lunch for a nominal fee during the week.

★★ BERGEN POINT COUNTRY CLUB
PU—69 Bergen Ave., West Babylon (516)661-8282.
30 miles east of New York City. **Holes:** 18. **Par:** 71/71.
Yards: 6,637/5,707. **Course rating:** 71.4/71.8. **Slope:** 120/122.
Opened: 1972. **Pace of Play rating:** 4:30. **Green fee:** $17/20.
Credit cards: None. **Reduced fees:** Weekdays, Low season, Twilight,
Seniors, Juniors.
Caddies: No. **Golf carts:** $12 for 18 holes.
Discount golf packages: Yes. **Season:** March-Dec. **High:** June-Oct.
On-site lodging: No. **Rental clubs:** Yes.
Walking policy: Unrestricted walking. **Range:** Yes.
To obtain tee times: Call same day.

Subscriber comments: Making effort to improve layout and quality . . . Next to a sewage treatment plant . . . It is a county course recently turned over to a private concern to run and they are doing wonders . . . The drawback now is it has become a popular place to play . . . Mammoth improvements have made it a sensational course . . . Glad I came back! Links type, strong winds make course difficult .

BETHPAGE STATE PARK GOLF COURSES
PU—Farmingdale (516)293-8899.
18 miles east of New York City.
Pace of Play rating: 5:00-5:30. **Green fee:** $14/18.
Credit cards: None. **Reduced fees:** Weekdays, Low season, Twilight, Seniors.
Caddies: No. **Golf carts:** $24 for 18 holes.
Discount golf packages: Yes. **Season:** Year-round. **High:** May-Sept.
On-site lodging: No. **Rental clubs:** Yes.
Walking policy: Unrestricted walking. **Range:** Yes.
To obtain tee times: Call one week in advance for reservations.

★★★★ BLACK COURSE

Holes: 18. **Par:** 71/71.
Yards: 7,065/6,556. **Course rating:** 75.4/78.9. **Slope:** 144/146.
Opened: 1935.
Ranked in Second 25 of America's Best Public Golf Courses by Golf Digest. Ranked 11th in New York by Golf Digest.
Subscriber comments: Unbelievable course, would love to see the pros play from the back tees . . . Tillinghast's best tee to green, if only everyone else would go away . . . One of the best "tests" of golfing aptitude anywhere . . . Tough course, hilly . . . You use every club . . . Challenging layout but playable . . . Serious pace of play problem . . . A thinking man's course . . . Great course for low handicappers . . . Go and be humbled . . . Only for accomplished players . . . Tough, tougher, toughest, must be strong and scratch player . . . Fairways unreachable for average golfer . . . Bring your "A" game and comfortable shoes . . . A visual treat . . . You must love to climb hills . . . A death march on a hot day . . . Great pro shop . . . Still a phenomenal public test . . . A true test, need every shot in the book . . . Can't find ball inches off the fairway . . . There is a sign at the first hole stating "for low handicaps only" . . . Take my advice, this sign is right . . . Slow play because of lots of difficulty . . . Lots of bogies.

★★★ BLUE COURSE
Holes: 18. **Par:** 72/72.
Yards: 6,684/6,213. **Course rating:** 72.2/75.5. **Slope:** 126/130.
Opened: 1930.
Subscriber comments: Fair for all handicaps . . . A step below the Black, but a fine test of golf . . . Tough front nine . . . Back nine makes it fair ; in good shape . . . Heavy woods, small greens . . . Steep hills and plenty of them . . . Deceptively difficult driving holes . . . Par 4s are long but straight . . . Every bit as exciting as the Black . . . Good course but not worth the ridiculous wait . . . Lots and lots of doglegs . . . Good and consistant greens . . . Short hitters at major disadvantage . . . Very good condition for the number of rounds that are played.

★★★ GREEN COURSE
Holes: 18. **Par:** 71/71.
Yards: 6,267/5,903. **Course rating:** 69.8/73.3. **Slope:** 121/125.
Opened: 1930.
Subscriber comments: Fun course . . . You'll always say "I should have scored better" . . . Course to play if you can not get on the Black . . . More interesting than its fabled sister course . . . The sleeper of the five . . . Not too long, tricky undulating greens, tests short game and putting . . . Old time course with treacherous greens . . . I love this course . . . Slow play . . . Fairly easy test . . . Not too long, but requires all the clubs in your bag . . . Lots of fun . . . Beautiful walk . . . Like a miniature Black, more forgiving but hilly . . . Most interesting greens of entire complex.

★★★ RED COURSE
Holes: 18. **Par:** 70/70.
Yards: 6,756/6,198. **Course rating:** 73.0/76.0. **Slope:** 127/131.
Opened: 1930.
Subscriber comments: Toughest first hole in the world . . . 460-yard par 4 uphill . . . Worth the wait . . . Picturesque, challenging, my favorite . . . Too many doglegs make it tough for mid to high handicappers . . . Easier than Black or Blue . . . Best overall variety at Bethpage . . . The "Black" course for twenty handicappers . . . Not as famous as Black, but just as good . . . Requires all types of shots.

★★½ YELLOW COURSE
Holes: 18. **Par:** 71/71.
Yards: 6,316/5,680. **Course rating:** 70.1/67.2. **Slope:** 121/115.
Opened: 1930.
Subscriber comments: Fun course, easy to play . . . Four or five tough holes . . . Subject to slow play, beginners course . . . Wide open, fairly flat . . . Yellow course is the easiest but still a challenge . . . Good pro shop . . . Good 19th hole . . . Good test for irons . . . Great course for short hitters . . . Good course to learn to play . . . Wife loved it.

★★★ BLUE HILL GOLF CLUB
SP—285 Blue Hill Rd., Pearl River (914)735-2094.
20 miles north of New York. **Holes:** 18. **Par:** 72/72.
Yards: 6,471/5,651. **Course rating:** 70.6/70.6. **Slope:** 116/117.
Opened: 1924. **Pace of Play rating:** 4:15. **Green fee:** $27/33.
Credit cards: None. **Reduced fees:** Weekdays, Twilight.
Caddies: No. **Golf carts:** $26 for 18 holes.
Discount golf packages: No. **Season:** March-Dec. **High:** June-Sept.
On-site lodging: Yes. **Rental clubs:** No.
Walking policy: Unrestricted walking. **Range:** Yes.
To obtain tee times: Call one day in advance.
Subscriber comments: Short, wide open, great for beginners . . . Fast and true greens . . . Tricky par 3s . . . Watch the wind . . . Always in good shape . . . 10th hole is special . . . Club selection impossible in wind . . . Like teeing off a mountain . . . Fairways are always perfect . . . Many holes on front nine similar . . . Play to fade . . . Back more varied . . . Looking forward to new nine holes . . . Open and relatively easy . . . Good for beginners . . . Wide fairways . . . A confidence builder.

BLUE STONE GOLF COURSE*
PU—1 Grant St., Oxford (607)843-8352.
Call club for further information.
Subscriber comments: Extremely steep greens . . . Very steep fairways . . . Ball placement and cart a must.

★★★ BLUFF POINT GOLF & COUNTRY CLUB
SP—75 Bluff Point Dr., Plattsburgh (518)563-3420, (800)438-0985.
60 miles south of Montreal. **Holes:** 18. **Par:** 72/74.
Yards: 6,309/5,295. **Course rating:** 70.6/71.0. **Slope:** 122/121.
Opened: 1890. **Pace of Play rating:** 4:00. **Green fee:** $24/29.
Credit cards: MC, V. **Reduced fees:** Low season, Twilight.
Caddies: No. **Golf carts:** $11 for 18 holes.
Discount golf packages: Yes. **Season:** April-Nov. **High:** June-Sept.
On-site lodging: No. **Rental clubs:** Yes.
Walking policy: Unrestricted walking. **Range:** Yes (grass).
To obtain tee times: Guests may call five days in advance.
Subscriber comments: Well suited for low to middle handicappers . . . One of the oldest courses in the Adirondacks! . . . Much better shape than in the past . . . On Lake Champlain . . . Great view, great mountains . . . Great staff.

★½ BRAEMAR COUNTRY CLUB

SP—4704 Ridge Rd. West, Spencerport (716)352-1535.
Call club for further information.
Subscriber comments: Very small greens, accurate iron play a must . . .
Good test of long and mid irons . . . Long and challenging fours and fives
. . . Tight golf course . . . O.B. and water, could be better with proper
maintainance.

★½ BRANTINGHAM GOLF CLUB

PU—P.O. Box 151, Brantingham (315)348-8218.
55 miles north of Utica. **Holes:** 18. **Par:** 71/74.
Yards: 5,268/4,886. **Course rating:** 64.5/N/A. **Slope:** 97/N/A.
Opened: N/A. **Pace of Play rating:** 4:30. **Green fee:** $12.
Credit cards: None. **Reduced fees:** Twilight.
Caddies: No. **Golf carts:** $16 for 18 holes.
Discount golf packages: No. **Season:** April-Oct. **High:** July-Aug.
On-site lodging: No. **Rental clubs:** Yes.
Walking policy: Unrestricted walking. **Range:** No.
To obtain tee times: First come, first served.
Subscriber comments: Fun course, owners make you feel welcome . . .
Flat course . . . Front nine excellent, back nine needs work.

★½ BRENTWOOD COUNTRY CLUB

PU—100 Pennsylvania Ave., Brentwood (516)436-6060.
45 miles east of New York City. **Holes:** 18. **Par:** 72/72.
Yards: 6,173/5,835. **Course rating:** N/A. **Slope:** 121/118.
Opened: 1920. **Pace of Play rating:** 4:00. **Green fee:** $16/26.
Credit cards: None. **Reduced fees:** Weekdays, Low season, Twilight,
Seniors, Juniors.
Caddies: No. **Golf carts:** $23 for 18 holes.
Discount golf packages: No. **Season:** March-Dec. **High:** May-July.
On-site lodging: No. **Rental clubs:** Yes.
Walking policy: Unrestricted walking. **Range:** No.
To obtain tee times: Call three days in advance for weekends only for a $2
fee per person.
Subscriber comments: Very short and flat . . . Good for seniors and
walkers . . . Service was very good . . . Play sometimes real slow . . .
Conditions usually good . . . Needs water hazards and deeper rough . . .
Excellent par 4 holes.

★½ BRIGHTON PARK GOLF COURSE

PU—Brompton Rd., Town of Tonawanda (716)695-2580.
5 miles north of Buffalo. **Holes:** 18. **Par:** 72/73.
Yards: 6,535/5,852. **Course rating:** 70.7/73.5. **Slope:** 108/109.
Opened: 1963. **Pace of Play rating:** 4:15. **Green fee:** $15/18.
Credit cards: N/A. **Reduced fees:** Weekdays, Low season, Twilight,
Seniors.
Caddies: No. **Golf carts:** $16 for 18 holes.
Discount golf packages: No. **Season:** April-Nov. **High:** June-Aug.
On-site lodging: No. **Rental clubs:** No.
Walking policy: Unrestricted walking. **Range:** Yes.
To obtain tee times: Call seven days in advance.
Subscriber comments: Good beginner's course . . . Excellent greens,
fairways are in bad shape . . . Flat, long course, service and staff very good
. . . Too easy and very flat . . . No challenge.

★★★½ BRISTOL HARBOUR GOLF CLUB

R—5500 Seneca Point Rd, Canandaigua (716)396-2460, (800)288-8248.
40 miles south of Rochester. **Holes:** 18. **Par:** 72/72.
Yards: 6,700/5,500. **Course rating:** 72.6/73.0. **Slope:** 126/126.
Opened: 1972. **Pace of Play rating:** 4:30. **Green fee:** $25/45.
Credit cards: MC, V. **Reduced fees:** Weekdays, Low season, Resort
guests, Twilight, Seniors, Juniors.
Caddies: No. **Golf carts:** Included in Green Fee.

Discount golf packages: Yes. **Season:** April-Nov. **High:** June-Sept. **On-site lodging:** Yes. **Rental clubs:** Yes. **Walking policy:** Mandatory cart. **Range:** Yes (grass). **To obtain tee times:** General public can call up to seven days in advance. **Subscriber comments:** Very challenging ; rangers keep it moving great . . . A "must play" in the Finger Lakes ; tight back nine . . . Great layout, some of the best greens I've played . . . Unbelievable view of lake and hills . . . Great course, fine staff ; ultimate in golf . . . Excellent mountain course, good resort accommodations . . . Accuracy a must . . . Super greens and staff . . . A must play . . . Great views of Canandaigua Lake . . . No. 14 second shot has 100-foot drop to green . . . Don't miss this one . . . Great views, make a day of it . . . Have to learn the "grain" of the greens.

★★½ BROCKPORT COUNTRY CLUB
SP—3739 County Line Rd, Brockport (716)638-6486.
Call club for further information.
Subscriber comments: Good course for high handicap players . . . Friendly people . . . Small greens, same blind shots, holds your interest well . . . Lots of O.B. right . . . Variety of length on par 4s . . . Challenging, but fair, front and back like playing two totally different courses.

★★½ BYRNCLIFF GOLF CLUB
R—Rte. 20A, Varysburg (716)535-7300.
35 miles southeast of Buffalo. **Holes:** 18. **Par:** 72/73.
Yards: 6,783/5,545. **Course rating:** 73.1/75.1. **Slope:** 115/119.
Opened: 1965. **Pace of Play rating:** 4:30. **Green fee:** $18.
Credit cards: All major. **Reduced fees:** Low season, Resort guests, Twilight, Seniors.
Caddies: No. **Golf carts:** $20 for 18 holes.
Discount golf packages: Yes. **Season:** April-Nov. **High:** June-Aug.
On-site lodging: Yes. **Rental clubs:** Yes.
Walking policy: Unrestricted walking. **Range:** Yes.
To obtain tee times: Call on phone to reserve tee time.
Subscriber comments: Hilly with very fast greens . . . Need to play a few times to learn placement . . . A fun course with interesting scenery . . . Have to be a mountain goat . . . Very challenging course, lots of trouble holes . . . Good test, well groomed greens . . . Nice place to spend weekend.

★★ CAMILLUS COUNTRY CLUB
SP—5690 Bennetts Corners Rd, Camillus (315)672-3770.
8 miles west of Syracuse. **Holes:** 18. **Par:** 73/73.
Yards: 6,368/5,573. **Course rating:** 70.1/71.4. **Slope:** 115/110.
Opened: 1962. **Pace of Play rating:** 4:15. **Green fee:** $15/18.
Credit cards: MC, V. **Reduced fees:** Weekdays, Low season, Seniors, Juniors.
Caddies: No. **Golf carts:** $9 for 18 holes.
Discount golf packages: Yes. **Season:** April-Nov. **High:** June-Aug.
On-site lodging: No. **Rental clubs:** Yes.
Walking policy: Unrestricted walking. **Range:** Yes (grass).
To obtain tee times: Call up to three days in advance.
Subscriber comments: A lot of blind shots to greens . . . Hills, hills, hills . . . Bring your mountain climbing gear . . . Staff is nice. Wide fairways, big greens . . . Need good legs . . . Great condition all seasons . . . Must play position shots . . . Country setting and very quiet . . . Will test your skills from a number of different lies.

★½ CANAJOHARIE COUNTRY CLUB
SP—Box 57 or Rte. 163, Canajoharie (518)673-8183.
37 miles southeast of Utica. **Holes:** 18. **Par:** 70/71.
Yards: 5,744/4,833. **Course rating:** 66.4/65.7. **Slope:** 109/105.
Opened: 1940. **Pace of Play rating:** 4:00. **Green fee:** $12/16.
Credit cards: MC, V. **Reduced fees:** Juniors.
Caddies: No. **Golf carts:** $19 for 18 holes.

Discount golf packages: No. **Season:** April-Oct. **High:** June-Aug.
On-site lodging: No. **Rental clubs:** Yes.
Walking policy: Unrestricted walking. **Range:** Yes (grass).
To obtain tee times: Call pro shop for weekend starting times.
Subscriber comments: Great fun, even in the rain . . . Great burgers . . .
Exceptionally friendly people . . . New, very short front nine . . . Hilly,
wide open back nine located in small valley.

★★½ CANASAWACTA CC

SP—Country Club Rd., Norwich (607)336-2685.
37 miles northeast of Binghamton. **Holes:** 18. **Par:** 70/71.
Yards: 6,271/5,166. **Course rating:** 69.9/68.8. **Slope:** 120/114.
Opened: 1920. **Pace of Play rating:** 4:00. **Green fee:** $18/22.
Credit cards: None. **Reduced fees:** Low season, Twilight, Juniors.
Caddies: No. **Golf carts:** $10 for 18 holes.
Discount golf packages: No. **Season:** April-Oct. **High:** June-Aug.
On-site lodging: No. **Rental clubs:** Yes.
Walking policy: Unrestricted walking. **Range:** No.
To obtain tee times: Call pro shop no more than three days in advance.
Subscriber comments: Good staff and service . . . Well maintained . . .
Very hilly, be in good shape if you walk it . . . Interesting layout, a little
short, some elevated tees are nice . . . Too many blind holes . . . Fun
course, long par 4s.

CARDINAL HILLS GOLF COURSE★

PU—Conewango Rd., Randolph (716)358-5409.
Call club for further information.
Subscriber comments: Employees are really helpful and accommodating
. . . Bring a hammer to drive tees into ground . . . Postage stamp size
greens, tees need improvement . . . If unfamiliar could be easily confused as
to location of next tee.

★ CASOLWOOD GOLF COURSE

PU—New Boston Rd., Canastota (315)697-9164.
Call club for further information.
Subscriber comments: Hospitable staff . . . Very short course . . . Very
easy to put ball in another fairway . . . Greens very small, pace of play
moderate.

CEDAR VIEW GOLF COURSE★

PU—Rte. 37C, Rooseveltown (315)764-9104.
Call club for further information.
Subscriber comments: Nice . . . Relatively open fairways . . . Large
greens.

★★★ CENTERPOINTE COUNTRY CLUB

SP—1940 Brickyard Rd, Canandaigua (716)924-5346.
25 miles southeast of Rochester. **Holes:** 18. **Par:** 71/71.
Yards: 6,717/5,213. **Course rating:** 70.7/68.3. **Slope:** 116/107.
Opened: 1963. **Pace of Play rating:** 4:15. **Green fee:** $15/22.
Credit cards: MC, V. **Reduced fees:** Weekdays, Low season, Twilight,
Seniors.
Caddies: No. **Golf carts:** $20 for 18 holes.
Discount golf packages: Yes. **Season:** April-Nov. **High:** June-Aug.
On-site lodging: No. **Rental clubs:** Yes.
Walking policy: Unrestricted walking. **Range:** Yes (grass).
To obtain tee times: Call Thursday after 7 a.m. for weekends (Friday-
Sunday). First come, first serve on weekdays.
Subscriber comments: Solid, always in top shape . . . Nice course, some
architectural changes would be nice . . . For all level players, very flat,
relatively matured trees, used to be wide open . . . Challenging and in good
condition . . . Tough back nine . . . Excellent service from golf pro's staff.

★½ CENTRAL VALLEY GOLF CLUB
PU—210 Smith Clove Rd, Central Valley (914)928-6924.
50 miles north of New York City. **Holes:** 18. **Par:** 70/73.
Yards: 5,644/5,317. **Course rating:** 67.7/70.9. **Slope:** 116/120.
Opened: 1922. **Pace of Play rating:** 4:00-4:30. **Green fee:** $21/31.
Credit cards: MC, V, AMEX. **Reduced fees:** Weekdays, Low season,
Twilight, Seniors, Juniors.
Caddies: No. **Golf carts:** $12 for 18 holes.
Discount golf packages: No. **Season:** April-Nov. **High:** May-Aug.
On-site lodging: No. **Rental clubs:** Yes.
Walking policy: Unrestricted walking. **Range:** No.
  To obtain tee times: Call pro shop up to seven days in advance.
Subscriber comments: Short tight course, good for most players, good
condition . . . Mountain golf, take a cart . . . Good course for the first time
. . . Challenging approach shots . . . Tough greens to hold.

CHAUTAUQUA GOLF CLUB
R—Rte. 394, Chautauqua (716)357-6211.
70 miles south of Buffalo.
Green fee: $15/28.
Credit cards: MC, V. **Reduced fees:** Weekdays, Low season, Twilight.
Caddies: No. **Golf carts:** $10 for 18 holes.
Discount golf packages: Yes. **Season:** April-Nov. **High:** June-Aug.
On-site lodging: No. **Rental clubs:** Yes.
Walking policy: Unrestricted walking. **Range:** Yes (grass).
To obtain tee times: Call pro shop one week in advance. Large groups
will be able to arrange tee times further in advance.

★★★ THE HILL COURSE
Holes: 18. **Par:** 72/72.
Yards: 6,412/5,076. **Course rating:** 72.1/72.7. **Slope:** 118/110.
Opened: 1994. **Pace of Play rating:** 4:30.
Subscriber comments: Watch out for those greens . . . Beautiful views,
beautiful challenge . . . Great staff . . . Open ; favors long hitter . . . Greens
slow . . . Great pace of play . . . Well kept . . . Nice walk . . . Challenge
for all levels . . . Very scenic.

★★★ THE LAKE COURSE
Holes: 18. **Par:** 72/74.
Yards: 6,462/5,423. **Course rating:** 71.1/71.7. **Slope:** 115/108.
Opened: 1913. **Pace of Play rating:** 4:00.
Subscriber comments: Wonderful resort course . . . Very playable for all
abilities . . . Short but tricky . . . Greens tough . . . Well maintained, very
enjoyable to play service and pace of play was very good . . . Would return
again.

CHEMUNG GOLF COURSE*
PU—County Rd. 60, Waverly (607)565-2323.
12 miles east of Elmira. **Holes:** 18. **Par:** 69/69.
Yards: 6,000/5,525. **Course rating:** 66.3/66.0. **Slope:** N/A.
Opened: 1962. **Pace of Play rating:** 4:00. **Green fee:** $10/12.
Credit cards: None. **Reduced fees:** Weekdays, Low season, Twilight,
Seniors.
Caddies: No. **Golf carts:** $18 for 18 holes.
Discount golf packages: Yes. **Season:** Year-round. **High:** May-Sept.
On-site lodging: No. **Rental clubs:** No.
Walking policy: Unrestricted walking. **Range:** No.
To obtain tee times: First come, first served.
Subscriber comments: Fun little course at good price.

★★½ CHENANGO VALLEY GOLF COURSE
PU—153 State Park Rd, Chenango Forks (607)648-9804.
Call club for further information.
Subscriber comments: Requires accurate shots . . . Playable for all levels

. . . Tough course ; lots of blind tee and fairway shots . . . Difficult, wooded, narrow fairways . . . Greens could be better . . . In New York State Forest . . . Excellent golf in the woods . . . Use all clubs in bag . . . Good mix of holes.

★★½ CHESTNUT HILL COUNTRY CLUB

PU—1330 Broadway, Darien Center (716)547-9699.
Call club for further information.
Subscriber comments: Always have a good time . . . Well kept . . . Great crews . . . Great conditions all year . . . Good facilities . . . Good pace, continually upgrading . . . Good fairways with semi-soft greens . . . Front nine more interesting . . . Few sand traps . . . Super people . . . Course in great shape . . . Greens excellent . . . Nice greens and new large tees . . . Low handicap a plus . . . Very fast and hilly greens, a lot of blind shots into the greens.

★½ CHILI COUNTRY CLUB

SP—760 Scottsville - Chili Rd., Scottsville (716)889-9325.
10 miles south of Rochester. **Holes:** 18. **Par:** 72/72.
Yards: 6,628/5,498. **Course rating:** 71.7/70.4. **Slope:** 117/110.
Opened: 1959. **Pace of Play rating:** 4:30. **Green fee:** $14/16.
Credit cards: MC, V. **Reduced fees:** Weekdays, Low season, Twilight, Seniors, Juniors.
Caddies: No. **Golf carts:** $18 for 18 holes.
Discount golf packages: No. **Season:** Year-round. **High:** July-Aug.
On-site lodging: No. **Rental clubs:** Yes.
Walking policy: Unrestricted walking. **Range:** Yes (grass).
To obtain tee times: Call pro shop.
Subscriber comments: Flat and wide open, good for high handicappers . . . Pro shop has best prices anywhere . . . Good spring and fall golf . . . Dust bowl during the summer . . . This is the place to buy clubs . . . Course needs lots of work . . . Good for most players.

★½ CLEARVIEW GOLF CLUB

PU—202-12 Willets Point Blvd., Bayside (718)229-2570.
Call club for further information.
Subscriber comments: Flat and forgiving, best conditions for off season for a muny . . . Layout has potential . . . So very New York! . . . Most incredible view of the Throg's Neck Bridge! . . . Flat and wide open . . . Pace too slow . . . Boring yet enjoyable experience . . . Very crowded course.

CONCORD RESORT HOTEL

R—Kiamesha Lake (914)794-4000, (800)431-3850.
90 miles northwest of New York.
Credit cards: All major. **Reduced fees:** Weekdays, Resort guests, Twilight.
Golf carts: Included in Green Fee.
Discount golf packages: Yes. **Season:** April-Nov. **High:** June-Aug.
On-site lodging: Yes. **Rental clubs:** Yes. **Range:** Yes (grass).
To obtain tee times: Will take times all year with credit card number. 72 hour cancellation policy.

★★★ INTERNATIONAL GOLF COURSE

Holes: 18. **Par:** 71/71.
Yards: 5,968/5,564. **Course rating:** 71.8/73.6. **Slope:** 124/125.
Opened: 1950. **Pace of Play rating:** 4:00. **Green fee:** $40/55.
Caddies: No. **Walking policy:** Unrestricted walking.
Subscriber comments: Terrific golf course, my favorite, very fast greens . . . Good conditions, friendly staff . . . Fun course . . . Super staff and service with a smile . . . Always a good alternative to the Monster.

★★★½ THE MONSTER GOLF COURSE

Holes: 18. **Par:** 72/72.
Yards: 7,471/6,548. **Course rating:** 76.4/78.5. **Slope:** 142/144.
Opened: 1963. **Pace of Play rating:** 5:00. **Green fee:** $60/90.

Caddies: Yes. **Walking policy:** Mandatory cart.
Ranked 45th in America's 75 Best Resort Courses by Golf Digest.
Subscriber comments: Long . . . Very hard for the handicap of 15 or
more . . . Great condition . . . Much too difficult for me, interesting layout
. . . Truly a monster, you never tire of it . . . Best esthetics and best test of
golf in area . . . It is not called the Monster for nothing . . . Fantastic views
and great people . . . Carts must be kept on paved paths . . . Cart paths add
to slow play . . . Fun, hilly, big greens, bunkers, wide fairways, good test.

★★★½ CONKLIN PLAYERS CLUB

PU—1520 Conklin Rd., Conklin (607)775-3042.
70 miles south of Syracuse. **Holes:** 18. **Par:** 72/72.
Yards: 6,772/4,699. **Course rating:** 72.5/67.8. **Slope:** 127/116.
Opened: 1991. **Pace of Play rating:** 4:30. **Green fee:** $18/25.
Credit cards: MC, V. **Reduced fees:** Weekdays, Low season, Seniors.
Caddies: No. **Golf carts:** $10 for 18 holes.
Discount golf packages: No. **Season:** April-Nov. **High:** May-Oct.
On-site lodging: No. **Rental clubs:** Yes.
Walking policy: Walking at certain times. **Range:** Yes (grass).
To obtain tee times: Call pro shop.
Subscriber comments: Scoreable for all levels . . . Great course, very
scenic, must play once . . . Very interesting holes . . . Fairways are excellent
. . . Tough for high handicaps . . . Most people need cart . . . Outstanding
architecture, this course is beautiful, no two holes alike . . . Well
maintained, good variety of holes . . . Tough to walk back nine . . . Every
par 5 offers a challenging gamble . . . Bent fairways and greens, island
green, very pleasant staff . . . Best par 3s anywhere . . . Demands
intelligent golf. Tremendous views on the 15th, 16th, 17th, and 18th.

★★½ COPAKE COUNTRY CLUB

PU—Lake Copake, Craryville (518)325-4338.
Call club for further information.
Subscriber comments: Some nice interesting holes . . . Nice side stop
while in area . . . Your score will surprise you . . . Tricky greens and small,
too!

★★★ CRAB MEADOW GOLF CLUB

PU—Waterside Ave., Northport (516)757-8800.
32 miles east of New York City. **Holes:** 18. **Par:** 72/72.
Yards: 6,575/5,807. **Course rating:** 70.2/72.6. **Slope:** 116/116.
Opened: 1960. **Pace of Play rating:** 4:30. **Green fee:** $30.
Credit cards: None. **Reduced fees:** Twilight, Seniors, Juniors.
Caddies: No. **Golf carts:** $24 for 18 holes.
Discount golf packages: No. **Season:** March-Dec. **High:** April-Sept.
On-site lodging: No. **Rental clubs:** Yes.
Walking policy: Unrestricted walking. **Range:** Yes.
To obtain tee times: Call (516)757-2300 one week in advance.
Subscriber comments: Good pace, great for walking . . . Nice diversity
. . . Good for average golfer . . . Terrific course . . . Beautiful views . . .
Good condition all the time . . . Pleasantly surprised . . . Nice overall golf
experience . . . A very playable layout, interesting . . . Score early, it gets
harder later . . . Always tee off on time ; greens and traps perfect.

★★★ CRAIG WOOD GOLF COURSE

PU—Cascade Rd., Rt. 73, Lake Placid (518)523-9811, (800)421-9811.
135 miles south of Albany. **Holes:** 18. **Par:** 72/72.
Yards: 6,554/5,500. **Course rating:** 70.6/70.2. **Slope:** 114/118.
Opened: 1920. **Pace of Play rating:** 4:15. **Green fee:** $17.
Credit cards: MC, V. **Reduced fees:** Resort guests, Twilight.
Caddies: No. **Golf carts:** $12 for 18 holes.
Discount golf packages: Yes. **Season:** May-Oct. **High:** July-Aug.
On-site lodging: No. **Rental clubs:** Yes.
Walking policy: Unrestricted walking. **Range:** Yes (grass).
To obtain tee times: Call pro shop.

Subscriber comments: Well suited for high handicapper ; wide fairways . . . Beautiful views ; great shape . . . Fun course . . . Open but hilly . . . Good pace of play, better than average . . . Challenge from the back tees, requires good drives to score well . . . Can be crowded . . . Open links first nine, wooded second nine . . . Great course . . . Had a fox follow us for four holes . . . Beautiful during fall foliage.

★½ CRONIN'S GOLF RESORT

PU—Golf Course Rd., Warrensburg (518)623-9336.
Call club for further information.
Subscriber comments: Made to feel at home . . . Difficult and tricky back nine . . . Course conditions improving every year . . . Very friendly family operation . . . Second and third holes along river.

★★½ DANDE FARMS COUNTRY CLUB

-6883 Cedar Str., Akron (716)542-2027.
Call club for further information.
Subscriber comments: Out of farm country . . . Peaceful . . . No sand traps . . . Walkable . . . Wide open, few hazards, well kept . . . I hope the secret doesn't get around . . . Good combination of easy and hard holes . . . Not a long course, but interesting . . . Good greens . . . Not real exciting, but a nice course . . . Well-kept . . . Very slow at times.

DEERFIELD COUNTRY CLUB
★★★½ (NORTH/SOUTH)

SP—100 Craig Hill Dr., Brockport (716)392-8080.
20 miles west of Rochester. **Holes:** 18. **Par:** 72/72.
Yards: 7,083/5,623. **Course rating:** 73.9/72.4. **Slope:** 138/123.
Opened: 1963. **Pace of Play rating:** 4:30. **Green fee:** $12/21.
Credit cards: MC, V. **Reduced fees:** Low season, Seniors, Juniors.
Caddies: No. **Golf carts:** $10 for 18 holes.
Discount golf packages: No. **Season:** April-Dec. **High:** June-Aug.
On-site lodging: No. **Rental clubs:** Yes.
Walking policy: Unrestricted walking. **Range:** Yes (grass).
To obtain tee times: Call pro shop one week in advance.
Also has 9-hole East course.
Subscriber comments: Long par 4s . . . Large greens, big breaks . . . Use every club in your bag, a test of self . . . Helps to be a big hitter on some par 4s . . . Nos. 11 and 16 very difficult par fours . . . North is toughest nine . . . Easy to get a tee time . . . Long, tight, great greens, toughest in area . . . Very challenging.

★★★ DEERWOOD GOLF COURSE

PU—1818 Sweeney St., North Tonawanda (716)695-8525.
12 miles north of Buffalo. **Holes:** 18. **Par:** 72/73.
Yards: 6,948/6,150. **Course rating:** 73.0/75.0. **Slope:** 117/123.
Opened: 1975. **Pace of Play rating:** 4:30. **Green fee:** $17/20.
Credit cards: None. **Reduced fees:** Weekdays, Twilight.
Caddies: No. **Golf carts:** $9 for 18 holes.
Discount golf packages: No. **Season:** April-Dec. **High:** June-Aug.
On-site lodging: No. **Rental clubs:** No.
Walking policy: Unrestricted walking. **Range:** Yes (grass).
To obtain tee times: First come first served. Three golfers with tickets may hold a spot for a threesome or foursome. Twosomes and singles will be matched up to make threesomes or foursomes.
Subscriber comments: Great public course, get there early . . . Challenging from back tees . . . Pace varies . . . Relatively long, but wide fairways . . . Flat, but long, very well groomed for public course . . . Par 5 on 12th (565) and par 3 on 13th (207) great holes and you've had a great day! . . . Nice course and good service . . . Not enough yardage markers . . . Water comes into play on some holes.

★★ DOMENICO'S GOLF COURSE
PU—13 Church Rd., Whitesboro (315)736-9812.
4 miles west of Utica. **Holes:** 18. **Par:** 72/75.
Yards: 6,715/5,458. **Course rating:** 70.5/71.5. **Slope:** 118/N/A.
Opened: 1982. **Pace of Play rating:** 4:10. **Green fee:** $12/14.
Credit cards: None. **Reduced fees:** Weekdays, Twilight.
Caddies: No. **Golf carts:** $10 for 18 holes.
Discount golf packages: No. **Season:** March-Nov. **High:** May-Aug.
On-site lodging: No. **Rental clubs:** Yes.
Walking policy: Unrestricted walking. **Range:** No.
To obtain tee times: Call pro shop.
Subscriber comments: Nothing fancy . . . Staff is nice . . . Fairways side by side . . . Back nine is better . . . Course improving each year.

★ DOUGLASTON GOLF CLUB
PU—63-20 Marathon Pkwy., Douglaston (718)224-6566.
Call club for further information.
Subscriber comments: In fair condition, interesting blind shots, not regulation, too many par 3s . . . Hilly, many blind shots, great for irons . . . Back nine is pitch and putt . . . Some very good holes . . . Great views of Manhattan . . . A place to hit balls . . . Short . . . Seven par 3's . . . Good for high handicapper . . . This course seemed to deteriorate over the year . . . Conditions could be better.

★½ DRUMLINS WEST GOLF CLUB
PU—800 Nottingham Rd., Syracuse (315)446-5580.
5 miles east of Syracuse. **Holes:** 18. **Par:** 70/70.
Yards: 6,030/4,790. **Course rating:** 68.2/71.0. **Slope:** N/A.
Opened: 1935. **Pace of Play rating:** N/A. **Green fee:** $14.
Credit cards: MC, V, DISC. **Reduced fees:** Seniors, Juniors.
Caddies: No. **Golf carts:** $22 for 18 holes.
Discount golf packages: Yes. **Season:** April-Nov. **High:** May-Aug.
On-site lodging: No. **Rental clubs:** Yes.
Walking policy: Unrestricted walking. **Range:** Yes (grass).
To obtain tee times: Call pro shop.
Subscriber comments: Good layout in poor condition . . . Greens OK . . . Fairways and rough indistinguishable . . . Needs attention . . . Very scenic, challenging . . . Take a cart . . . Lots of yardage on back nine . . . Front nine through woods . . . Back nine a shooting gallery.

★★ DUNWOODIE GOLF CLUB
PU—Wasylenko Lane, Yonkers (914)968-2771.
Holes: 18. **Par:** 70/72.
Yards: 5,815/4,511. **Course rating:** 68.3/67.8. **Slope:** 117/117.
Opened: N/A. **Pace of Play rating:** 4:00. **Green fee:** $37/42.
Credit cards: MC, V, AMEX. **Reduced fees:** Twilight, Seniors, Juniors.
Caddies: No. **Golf carts:** $22 for 18 holes.
Discount golf packages: No. **Season:** April-Dec. **High:** April-Nov.
On-site lodging: No. **Rental clubs:** Yes.
Walking policy: Unrestricted walking. **Range:** Yes (grass).
To obtain tee times: Call (914)593-4653.
Subscriber comments: In excellent shape condsidering all the play . . . Computerized tee time reservation system working well . . . You need to be a mountain goat . . . Way too short, four par 3s on back nine . . . Bring your hiking boots . . . Hilly layout . . . Must be straight to score . . . Fairways and greens in superb condition . . . Staff courteous, pace of play very good . . . Greens always good . . . Front tight, accuracy a premium . . . Back open . . . Many blind fairway shots.

★★★ DURAND EASTMAN GOLF COURSE
PU—1200 Kings Hwy. North, Rochester (716)342-9810.
Holes: 18. **Par:** 70/72.
Yards: 6,089/5,727. **Course rating:** 68.8/71.7. **Slope:** 112/113.
Opened: 1935. **Pace of Play rating:** 4:30. **Green fee:** $12/13.

Credit cards: None. **Reduced fees:** Weekdays, Low season, Seniors, Juniors.
Caddies: No. **Golf carts:** $16 for 18 holes.
Discount golf packages: Yes. **Season:** April-Nov. **High:** June-Aug.
On-site lodging: No. **Rental clubs:** Yes.
Walking policy: Unrestricted walking. **Range:** Yes (grass).
To obtain tee times: None taken.
Subscriber comments: Great layout by Lake Ontario . . . Very hilly, recommend cart . . . Tough terrain . . . "Postage stamp" greens, great shape for extensive public play . . . What a course . . . Don't miss it in the fall . . . Only bright spot in a visit to the in-laws upstate . . . Beautiful course, slow play hurts . . . Must hit good shots . . . Staff very good.

★★★ DUTCH HOLLOW COUNTRY CLUB
SP—Benson Rd, Owasco (315)784-5052.
19 miles southwest of Syracuse. **Holes:** 18. **Par:** 71/72.
Yards: 6,460/5,045. **Course rating:** 70.3/70.3. **Slope:** 120/113.
Opened: 1968. **Pace of Play rating:** 4:00-4:30. **Green fee:** $15/18.
Credit cards: MC, V. **Reduced fees:** Weekdays, Low season, Twilight, Seniors, Juniors.
Caddies: No. **Golf carts:** $10 for 18 holes.
Discount golf packages: Yes. **Season:** April-Nov. **High:** May-Sept.
On-site lodging: No. **Rental clubs:** Yes.
Walking policy: Unrestricted walking. **Range:** Yes (grass).
To obtain tee times: Call pro shop.
Subscriber comments: Water, water everywhere . . . Interesting course . . . Well-designed . . . Facilities average . . . Food excellent . . . Treated well . . . Great scramble course . . . Water on most of the holes on front nine . . . You will need your driver here . . . Great test of golf, tests your whole game . . . Great greens . . . Tricky short course, several gambling holes . . . Lots of right and left doglegs with small greens . . . Water on a number of holes as a stream snakes its way through the course.

★½ DYKER BEACH GOLF COURSE
PU—86th St. and 7th Ave., Brooklyn (718)836-9722.
Holes: 18. **Par:** 71/72.
Yards: 6,548/5,696. **Course rating:** 68.8/N/A. **Slope:** 113/N/A.
Opened: 1928. **Pace of Play rating:** 4:30-5:00. **Green fee:** $15/17.
Credit cards: MC, V. **Reduced fees:** Weekdays, Twilight, Seniors, Juniors.
Caddies: No. **Golf carts:** $23 for 18 holes.
Discount golf packages: No. **Season:** Year-round. **High:** May-Oct.
On-site lodging: No. **Rental clubs:** Yes.
Walking policy: Unrestricted walking. **Range:** No.
To obtain tee times: Call Tee time number up to eleven days in advance.
Subscriber comments: Not challenging enough for low handicapper . . . Pace of play slow . . . Conditions vary . . . Staff friendly, easy course, good confidence builder . . . Have to pay for parking . . . Terrible condition at beginning of season . . . Shows great improvement . . . Short but challenging for five to 20 handicap . . . Course for all players . . . Fast greens . . . Long waits and very long rounds . . . Tree-lined fairways. Hilly elevated greens . . . A little bit of rustic heaven in middle of the city . . . Undulating fairways, tricky greens, trees, no water . . . Nice challenge . . . Decent condition, wide open.

★★½ EAGLE CREST GOLF COURSE
PU—1004 Ballston Lake Rd., Ballston Lake (518)877-7082.
Call club for further information.
Subscriber comments: Friendly place to play . . . Improvements being made, some unfair holes and greens . . . Usually open before the others, but very muddy in spring . . . Forgiving fairways ; challenging greens ; great driving range . . . Improved a lot but still has more potential . . . Owners are making the effort to improve . . . Nice course for all levels, short,

excellent shape . . . Back nine is longer and more difficult . . . Easily accessible on weekdays . . . Crowded on weekends . . . Bring the family ; nice staff ; working hard to upgrade . . . A course to watch . . . Getting better each year . . . Rolling greens, elephants buried here.

★★½ EAGLE VALE GOLF COURSE

PU—4344 Nine Mile Point Rd., Fairport (716)377-5200.
15 miles southeast of Rochester. **Holes:** 18. **Par:** 70/72.
Yards: 6,524/5,787. **Course rating:** 70.9/72.8. **Slope:** 123/120.
Opened: 1987. **Pace of Play rating:** 4:25. **Green fee:** $25/32.
Credit cards: MC, V, AMEX. **Reduced fees:** Weekdays, Low season, Seniors, Juniors.
Caddies: No. **Golf carts:** Included in Green Fee.
Discount golf packages: Yes. **Season:** April-Dec. **High:** June-Aug.
On-site lodging: No. **Rental clubs:** Yes.
Walking policy: Walking at certain times. **Range:** Yes.
To obtain tee times: Call 24 hrs. in advance for weekdays and 72 hrs. in advance for weekends and holidays.
Subscriber comments: Nice greens, interesting holes, good pace . . . A pleasant, relaxing course with subtle difficulties . . . Course plays well at all levels . . . Outstanding pro shop, nice mix of holes, play back tees . . . Continues to improve . . . Super pro shop, good practice area . . . Tough greens and tough back nine when windy . . . Holes run close together . . . Be alert for stray shots.

EISENHOWER PARK GOLF

PU—Eisenhower Park, East Meadow (516)542-0015.
20 miles east of New York City.
Pace of Play rating: 4:30. **Green fee:** $7/28.
Credit cards: None. **Reduced fees:** Weekdays, Low season, Seniors.
Caddies: No. **Golf carts:** $22 for 18 holes.
Discount golf packages: No. **Season:** Year-round. **High:** May-Oct.
On-site lodging: No. **Rental clubs:** Yes.
Walking policy: Unrestricted walking. **Range:** Yes.
To obtain tee times: Walk in.

★½ BLUE COURSE

Holes: 18. **Par:** 72/72.
Yards: 6,026/5,800. **Course rating:** 68.7/74.1. **Slope:** 112/122.
Opened: 1947.
Subscriber comments: Solid, well maintained course . . . In good condition, holes all look alike . . . Staff friendly . . . Wide open fairways . . . Generic golf, but decent layout . . . Greens always kept in great shape . . . New greenkeeper has improved course tremendously . . . Relatively flat . . . Few gentle doglegs, elevated greens, well groomed year round . . . Easy with all par fives reachable . . . Ego booster . . . Good walker's course . . . Every green elevated and surrounded by traps . . . Simple layout, very good beginner's course . . . Plain Jane.

★★½ RED COURSE

Holes: 18. **Par:** 72/72.
Yards: 6,756/5,449. **Course rating:** 71.5/69.8. **Slope:** 119/115.
Opened: 1914.
Subscriber comments: Solid course, big sand traps, interesting layout . . . Flat, longest of three courses . . . Long waits for tee times and long rounds . . . By far the better public course there . . . Wide open, forgiving, pleasant . . . It is a nice layout for an average golfer . . . Flat, but well trapped . . . Oh, what a public course! . . . Simple layout, very good beginner's course . . . Wife and I loved it . . . Great condition: greens and fairways . . . Overall in good shape.

★½ WHITE COURSE

Holes: 18. **Par:** 72/72.
Yards: 6,269/5,920. **Course rating:** 69.5/71.4. **Slope:** 115/117.
Opened: 1947.
Subscriber comments: The most boring course ever! . . . Vanilla generic

golf, all holes are straight . . . Pool table golf, but in good condition . . .
Flat fairways, never in trouble, nice greens . . . No diversity in layout . . .
Lots of sand, good bunker practice . . . Greens in great shape all year . . .
Very good beginner's course . . . Greens well protected by deep traps.

★★ ELM TREE GOLF COURSE
PU—283 St. Rte. No.13, Cortland (607)753-1341.
30 miles south of Syracuse. **Holes:** 18. **Par:** 70/74.
Yards: 6,251/5,520. **Course rating:** 66.4/66.3. **Slope:** 100/ 99.
Opened: 1966. **Pace of Play rating:** 4:00. **Green fee:** $9/13.
Credit cards: MC, V. **Reduced fees:** Weekdays, Low season, Resort
guests, Twilight, Seniors, Juniors.
Caddies: No. **Golf carts:** $18 for 18 holes.
Discount golf packages: Yes. **Season:** April-Nov. **High:** June-Aug.
On-site lodging: No. **Rental clubs:** No.
Walking policy: Unrestricted walking. **Range:** Yes (grass).
To obtain tee times: Call one day in advance.
Subscriber comments: Good hilly layout . . . Has really improved in last
five years . . . Fun course to play . . . Easy course makes you feel like a pro
. . . Chock full of subtle nuances, never tire of the course.

★★ ELMA MEADOWS GOLF CLUB
PU—1711 Girdle Rd., Elma (716)652-2022.
Call club for further information.
Subscriber comments: Sometimes very crowded but a great course . . .
Staff good . . . Accuracy a must . . . Very crowded, must go in the early
a.m. . . . Fairly long and wide open . . . Can't get into lots of trouble . . .
They keep this course in very good playing condition for the amount of
play they get.

★½ ELY PARK MUNICIPAL GOLF COURSE
-13905 Mt. Prospect, Binghamton (607)772-7231.
Call club for further information.
Subscriber comments: Hilly course, few bunkers ; friendly . . . Steep
hills, good for any handicap . . . Lots of beginners play here . . . Used most
clubs . . . Great staff . . . Suited for everyone.

★★★½ EN-JOIE GOLF CLUB
PU—722 West Main St., Endicott (607)785-1661.
9 miles west of Binghamton, N.Y. **Holes:** 18. **Par:** 72/74.
Yards: 7,016/5,205. **Course rating:** 73.0/69.8. **Slope:** 125/118.
Opened: 1927. **Pace of Play rating:** 4:00. **Green fee:** $18/20.
Credit cards: MC, V. **Reduced fees:** Weekdays, Low season, Seniors,
Juniors.
Caddies: No. **Golf carts:** $10 for 18 holes.
Discount golf packages: No. **Season:** March-Dec. **High:** May-Sept.
On-site lodging: No. **Rental clubs:** Yes.
Walking policy: Unrestricted walking. **Range:** Yes (grass).
To obtain tee times: Weekdays first come, first served. Tee times for
weekends only.
Subscriber comments: Lot of trees, narrow fairways . . . Got it all . . .
Scenery, serious golf playability, conditioning, ambiance, PGA Tour stop
. . . Always seems to be working on course . . . Always a pleasure, very
friendly people . . . Very walkable and picturesque . . . En-Joie was a thrill
to play . . . Narrow tree-lined fairways . . . Site of B.C. Open . . . Good
staff, cordial . . . Course closed week before B.C. Open . . . Flat, good
walking course, water in play.

★★★ ENDWELL GREENS GOLF CLUB
PU—3675 Sally Piper Rd., Endwell (607)785-4653.
5 miles west of Binghamton. **Holes:** 18. **Par:** 72/76.
Yards: 7,053/5,382. **Course rating:** 73.6/70.6. **Slope:** 121/117.
Opened: 1968. **Pace of Play rating:** 4:00. **Green fee:** $16/18.
Credit cards: MC, V, DISC, Marketing Exchange. **Reduced fees:**

Weekdays, Low season, Seniors.
Caddies: No. **Golf carts:** $11 for 18 holes.
Discount golf packages: No. **Season:** April-Nov. **High:** May-Aug.
On-site lodging: No. **Rental clubs:** Yes.
Walking policy: Unrestricted walking. **Range:** Yes (grass).
To obtain tee times: Public play call two days in advance. Also take advance times for outings. Members can book tee times up to a week in advance.
Subscriber comments: Very hilly, seldom a level lie, congenial staff . . . Well groomed, very few flat lies, tough walk . . . Not for beginners . . . Greens are treacherous when fast . . . Always kept in good condition . . . Greens always in good shape, fun place to play.

FILLMORE GOLF CLUB★
PU—Tollgate Rd., Locke (315)497-3145.
Call club for further information.

★ FORD HILL COUNTRY CLUB
RED/WHITE/BLUE/ORANGE
PU—Rte. 26, Ford Hill Rd., Whitney Point (607)692-8938.
Call club for further information.
Subscriber comments: Can play almost anytime with no problems . . . Staff and management go out of their way to make you feel welcome.

FOREST PARK GOLF COURSE★
PU—Forest Park Dr., Woodhaven (718)296-0999.
Holes: 18. **Par:** 67/67.
Yards: 5,820/5,431. **Course rating:** 67.5/69.5. **Slope:** 111/116.
Opened: 1901. **Pace of Play rating:** 4:50. **Green fee:** $7/17.
Credit cards: MC, V. **Reduced fees:** Weekdays, Low season, Twilight, Seniors, Juniors.
Caddies: No. **Golf carts:** $23 for 18 holes.
Discount golf packages: No. **Season:** Year-round. **High:** April-Sept.
On-site lodging: No. **Rental clubs:** Yes.
Walking policy: Unrestricted walking. **Range:** No.
To obtain tee times: Call in advance up to seven days.

★★★½ FOXFIRE GOLF CLUB
PU—One Village Blvd., Baldwinsville (315)638-2930.
9 miles northwest of Syracuse. **Holes:** 18. **Par:** 72/72.
Yards: 6,887/5,405. **Course rating:** 72.8/71.5. **Slope:** 127/115.
Opened: 1974. **Pace of Play rating:** 4:00-4:30. **Green fee:** $18/20.
Credit cards: MC, V. **Reduced fees:** Seniors, Juniors.
Caddies: No. **Golf carts:** $10 for 18 holes.
Discount golf packages: Yes. **Season:** March-Nov. **High:** June-Aug.
On-site lodging: No. **Rental clubs:** Yes.
Walking policy: Walking at certain times. **Range:** Yes (grass).
To obtain tee times: Call pro shop five days in advance.
Subscriber comments: Long, fast green, lots of O.B. . . . Great staff ; good course, always good shape . . . Long and tough, a good test . . . Good design, nice greens, good sand, active rangers . . . Long par 5s, condominiums a little close for a stray shot . . . Great challenging course, use all your clubs . . . One of central New York's best conditioned courses . . . Narrow, tree-lined, plenty of bunkers and some water.

★★★ GARRISON GOLF CLUB
SP—RT 9, Garrison (914)424-3605.
50 miles north of New York City. **Holes:** 18. **Par:** 72/70.
Yards: 6,470/5,041. **Course rating:** 71.3/69.3. **Slope:** 130/122.
Opened: 1962. **Pace of Play rating:** N/A. **Green fee:** $20/55.
Credit cards: MC, V. **Reduced fees:** Weekdays, Twilight, Seniors.
Caddies: No. **Golf carts:** $15 for 18 holes.
Discount golf packages: No. **Season:** April-Nov. **High:** June-Aug.
On-site lodging: No. **Rental clubs:** Yes.

Walking policy: Walking at certain times. **Range:** Yes (grass).
To obtain tee times: Call up to one week in advance.
Subscriber comments: Would rival any great private course layout . . .
Very difficult greens and grain . . . Outstanding views . . . Course in great
shape . . . Front and back like two different courses . . . Accuracy and
length rewarded . . . Very friendly and helpful staff . . . Hilly, it would help
to have one leg shorter than the other or be related to a mountain goat . . .
Well maintained for amount of play it receives . . . Truly a gem and it is not
even hidden . . . Great scenic views: West Point and Hudson River . . .
Frustrating for high handicapper but great design.

GENESEE VALLEY GOLF COURSE
PU—1000 East River Rd., Rochester (716)424-2920.
Pace of Play rating: 4:30-5:00. **Green fee:** $12/13.
Credit cards: None. **Reduced fees:** Low season, Twilight, Seniors,
Juniors.
Caddies: No. **Golf carts:** $9 for 18 holes.
Discount golf packages: Yes. **Season:** April-Nov. **High:** June-July.
On-site lodging: No. **Rental clubs:** Yes.
Walking policy: Unrestricted walking. **Range:** No.
To obtain tee times: First come, first served.

★½ NEW COURSE
Holes: 18. **Par:** 67/69.
Yards: 5,270./5,270 **Course rating:** N/A/67.7. **Slope:** 93.0/100.
Opened: 1927.
Subscriber comments: Fairly flat . . . Great for beginners . . . Overly
simple with few, if any challenges, course shows its age . . . Greens are
small and challenging . . . No hazards, very open . . . Too short, good for
new golfers and kids . . . Fairly open, shorter than Old Course, not hard.

★ OLD COURSE
Holes: 18. **Par:** 71/77.
Yards: 6,374-6,007. **Course rating:** 69.3/73.2. **Slope:** 104/102.
Opened: 1900.
Subscriber comments: Old course: long, very tough par 3s.

★★★½ GLEN OAK GOLF COURSE
R—711 Smith Rd., East Amherst (716)688-5454.
Holes: 18. **Par:** 72/72.
Yards: 6,730/5,561. **Course rating:** 72.4/71.9. **Slope:** 129/118.
Opened: 1969. **Pace of Play rating:** 4:00. **Green fee:** $22/40.
Credit cards: MC, V. **Reduced fees:** Weekdays, Low season, Twilight,
Seniors.
Caddies: No. **Golf carts:** Included in Green Fee.
Discount golf packages: No. **Season:** April-Nov. **High:** June-Aug.
On-site lodging: No. **Rental clubs:** Yes.
Walking policy: Mandatory cart. **Range:** Yes (grass).
To obtain tee times: Call three days in advance. Pre-booking available for
groups or outings.
Subscriber comments: Use all your clubs . . . Great finishing hole . . .
Incredibly challenging, every hole different . . . Must be nifty with a
wedge! . . . Need all the shots and lots of balls . . . Fine layout, good
condition except for traps . . . Lots of water . . . Excellent driving range
and putting green . . . Challenging for all levels . . . With proper care, it
could be a championship course . . . Well kept course, great use of water.

GOLDEN OAK GOLF CLUB★
PU—Rte. 79 South, Windsor (607)655-3217.
15 miles east of Binghamton. **Holes:** 18. **Par:** 69/69.
Yards: 5,500/4,500. **Course rating:** 67.0/65.0. **Slope:** 117/115.
Opened: 1972. **Pace of Play rating:** 4:00-4:30. **Green fee:** $10/13.
Credit cards: MC, V. **Reduced fees:** Weekdays.
Caddies: No. **Golf carts:** $9 for 18 holes.

Discount golf packages: Yes. **Season:** April-Nov. **High:** June-Aug.
On-site lodging: No. **Rental clubs:** Yes.
Walking policy: Unrestricted walking. **Range:** No.
To obtain tee times: Call 48 hours in advance.

★★★½ GREEN LAKES STATE PARK GOLF CLUB

PU—7900 Green Lakes Rd., Fayetteville (315)637-0258.
7miles south of Syracuse. **Holes:** 18. **Par:** 71/74.
Yards: 6,212/5,481. **Course rating:** 68.4/70.6. **Slope:** 113/120.
Opened: 1936. **Pace of Play rating:** 4:00. **Green fee:** $14/17.
Credit cards: None. **Reduced fees:** No.
Caddies: No. **Golf carts:** $20 for 18 holes.
Discount golf packages: No. **Season:** April-Nov. **High:** May-Sept.
On-site lodging: No. **Rental clubs:** Yes.
Walking policy: Unrestricted walking. **Range:** No.
To obtain tee times: Call two days in advance.
Subscriber comments: Has 18 challenging holes, good test for low and
high handicappers . . . Friendly and courteous staff . . . Course gets a lot of
play, so pace of play can be slow at times . . . Plush fairways . . . Great
clubhouse . . . So good that it is too busy . . . Beautiful course . . . Scenic
. . . Tough putting on undulating greens . . . Staff is extremely nice . . .
Good design. Prepare for extreme lies and tough putting . . . Not a walker's
course . . . One of Trent Jones' first . . . Great view from clubhouse . . .
Back side through the woods with some tight fairways . . . Breathtakingly
beautiful . . . It clears you mind and tests your ability.

★★★★½ GROSSINGER RESORT
LAKE/VALLEY/VISTA

R—26 Rte. 52 East, Liberty (914)292-9000.
98 miles northwest of New York. **Holes:** 27. **Par:** 72/72/72.
Yards: 6,839/6,750/6,625. **Course rating:** 72.9/72.5/72.1.
Slope: 134/133/132.
Opened: 1965. **Pace of Play rating:** N/A. **Green fee:** $38/69.
Credit cards: MC, V, AMEX. **Reduced fees:** Weekdays, Low season,
Resort guests, Twilight.
Caddies: No. **Golf carts:** Included in Green Fee.
Discount golf packages: Yes. **Season:** April-Nov. **High:** June-Sept.
On-site lodging: Yes. **Rental clubs:** Yes.
Walking policy: Mandatory cart. **Range:** Yes (grass).
To obtain tee times: Call up to two weeks in advance.
Subscriber comments: Great layout makes you play all shots . . . Nice
layout, three nines, scenic . . . Excellent condition . . . Fast greens . . .
Getting expensive, but one of my favorites . . . Some holes have no level
lies . . . Immaculate condition, great vistas . . . Sssssh! Best kept secret in
New York, great mountain course . . . Too expensive to play regularly, but
worth it for a special round . . . Great condition, outstanding views, helpful
staff . . . Big greens, makes you think all the time . . . A great golf course,
not for beginners . . . Really no place of quality to eat but you can golf till
you drop . . . Lunch included with green fees . . . Spectacular back nine . . .
Fast play and greens are like lightning. Its the best! . . . Conditioned to
perfection.

★ GROVER CLEVELAND GOLF COURSE

PU—3781 Main St., Amherst (716)836-7398.
3 miles north of Buffalo. **Holes:** 18. **Par:** 69/N/A.
Yards: 5,584/N/A. **Course rating:** 67.5/N/A. **Slope:** 101/N/A.
Opened: 1912. **Pace of Play rating:** 4:00. **Green fee:** $9/10.
Credit cards: None. **Reduced fees:** Weekdays, Seniors, Juniors.
Caddies: No. **Golf carts:** N/A.
Discount golf packages: No. **Season:** Feb.-Nov. **High:** June-Aug.
On-site lodging: No. **Rental clubs:** No.
Walking policy: Unrestricted walking. **Range:** Yes.
To obtain tee times: First come first serve.

Subscriber comments: One of the oldest courses around . . . Flat, open course . . . Fair condition . . . Home of 1912 U.S. Open (originally Country Club of Buffalo) . . . Good for B and C players, too easy for A's . . . Short, wide open, good for beginners.

★★½ HANAH COUNTRY CLUB

R—Rte. 30, Margaretville (914)586-4849, (800)752-6494.
42 miles west of Kingston. **Holes:** 18. **Par:** 72/72.
Yards: 7,033/5,294. **Course rating:** 73.5/69.7. **Slope:** 133/123.
Opened: 1992. **Pace of Play rating:** 5:00. **Green fee:** $33/50.
Credit cards: MC, V. **Reduced fees:** Weekdays, Low season, Resort guests, Twilight, Seniors.
Caddies: No. **Golf carts:** $11 for 18 holes.
Discount golf packages: Yes. **Season:** April-Oct. **High:** June-July.
On-site lodging: Yes. **Rental clubs:** Yes.
Walking policy: Mandatory cart. **Range:** Yes (grass).
To obtain tee times: You must call and make a tee time.
Subscriber comments: Unusual layout, beautiful scenery . . . Great layout, good challenge from blues . . . Last three holes make or break you if you're in contention . . . Staff courteous . . . Pace average . . . Better bring a lot of balls when you play this course . . . Pleasant staff, need a road map to find first tee . . . Leisurely round . . . Lots of water in play, need to be straight not long . . . Huge practice facilities . . . Too many blind shots . . . Pace very fast . . . Very tight fairways . . . Punished for missing fairways . . . Balls lost in brambles . . . The perfect golf vacation. If you want a stress-free round, come to Hanah.

HARBOUR POINTE COUNTRY CLUB★

PU—Rte. 18 & 98, Waterport (716)798-3010.
Call club for further information.
Subscriber comments: Very short, needs work . . . Good for beginners . . . This site has tremendous potential.

★★½ HAUPPAUGE COUNTRY CLUB

SP—Veterans Memorial Hwy., Hauppauge (516)724-7500.
30 miles east of New York City. **Holes:** 18. **Par:** 72/74.
Yards: 6,525/5,925. **Course rating:** 71.0/75.5. **Slope:** 122/131.
Opened: 1960. **Pace of Play rating:** N/A. **Green fee:** $35.
Credit cards: None. **Reduced fees:** Weekdays, Low season, Twilight, Seniors, Juniors.
Caddies: No. **Golf carts:** $15 for 18 holes.
Discount golf packages: No. **Season:** March-Dec. **High:** May-Oct.
On-site lodging: No. **Rental clubs:** Yes.
Walking policy: Walking at certain times. **Range:** Yes.
To obtain tee times: First come, first served.
Subscriber comments: Challenging fairways, great use of water . . . Wide open for good beginners . . . Nice greens for public course . . . Very little trouble . . . Great facility . . . Very fast play . . . Greens good . . . Great starting hole . . . Lots of water on back nine . . . Always in good shape. Good course for the intermediate player.

★★★½ HILAND GOLF CLUB

SP—67 Haviland Rd., Queensbury (518)761-4653.
45 miles north of Albany. **Holes:** 18. **Par:** 72/72.
Yards: 6,632/5,677. **Course rating:** 73.0/72.9. **Slope:** 135/123.
Opened: 1988. **Pace of Play rating:** 3:30-4:00. **Green fee:** $25.
Credit cards: MC, V, AMEX. **Reduced fees:** Weekdays, Low season, Twilight.
Caddies: No. **Golf carts:** $13 for 18 holes.
Discount golf packages: No. **Season:** April-Nov. **High:** June-Sept.
On-site lodging: No. **Rental clubs:** Yes.
Walking policy: Unrestricted walking. **Range:** Yes (grass).
To obtain tee times: Call. Tee times required.
Subscriber comments: New course that should mature beautifully . . .

Has good length and playability . . . Course needs trees . . . Good tournament course . . . Has holes requiring distance as well as some that require common sense . . . Staff good, pace average . . . Wide open . . . Good shape, can get windy . . . Very enjoyable . . . Very nice public course, playable, yet challenging . . . Good condition . . . Only the greens keep this from being a "5" . . . Lots of water, fairly new course, conditions good . . . Somewhat flat, reminded me of a Florida course . . . Beautiful course in great shape . . . A "must" when in New York . . . Loved it, great greens: big and soft . . . Need to be well above average golfer to score well . . . Site of Michelob New York State Open . . . Great condition, very good layout, "must play" if visiting Lake George.

★½ HILLENDALE GOLF COURSE

PU—218 Applegate Rd., Ithaca (607)273-2363, (800)286-2838.
50 miles south of Syracuse. **Holes:** 18. **Par:** 71/73.
Yards: 6,002/5,705. **Course rating:** 68.8/69.3. **Slope:** 115/116.
Opened: 1912. **Pace of Play rating:** 4:30. **Green fee:** $12/13.
Credit cards: MC, V. **Reduced fees:** Weekdays, Low season, Twilight, Seniors, Juniors.
Caddies: No. **Golf carts:** $16 for 18 holes.
Discount golf packages: Yes. **Season:** April-Oct. **High:** June-Aug.
On-site lodging: No. **Rental clubs:** Yes.
Walking policy: Unrestricted walking. **Range:** Yes (grass).
To obtain tee times: No tee times taken.
Subscriber comments: Nice pro shop . . . Good course . . . Service well suited for average player . . . Hacker's Heaven . . . Front nine is very short . . . Back is interesting.

★★½ HOLIDAY VALLEY RESORT

R—Rte. 219, Ellicottville (716)699-2346.
48 miles south of Buffalo. **Holes:** 18. **Par:** 72/73.
Yards: 6,555/5,381. **Course rating:** 71.3/74.0. **Slope:** 125/115.
Opened: 1961. **Pace of Play rating:** 4:20. **Green fee:** $15/25.
Credit cards: All major. **Reduced fees:** Low season, Twilight.
Caddies: No. **Golf carts:** $10 for 18 holes.
Discount golf packages: Yes. **Season:** April-Oct. **High:** June-Sept.
On-site lodging: Yes. **Rental clubs:** Yes.
Walking policy: Unrestricted walking. **Range:** Yes (grass).
To obtain tee times: Call three days in advance.
Subscriber comments: Back nine almost like a large putt-putt course . . . Pack mules needed for the back nine . . . Very accommodating staff . . . No. 11 hole should be used for summer skiing . . . Very scenic . . . Good test, hilly . . . Front open but tricky . . . Back is tight . . . Good condition and pace . . . If you spray your shots, I'll find your balls next week. Clubhouse and facilities are the very best.

HYDE PARK GOLF COURSE

PU—4300 Porter Rd., Niagara Falls (716)297-2067.
20 miles northwest of Buffalo.
Opened: 1920. **Pace of Play rating:** 4:00. **Green fee:** $13/17.
Credit cards: None. **Reduced fees:** Seniors, Juniors.
Caddies: No. **Golf carts:** N/A.
Discount golf packages: No. **Season:** April-Nov. **High:** June-Sept.
On-site lodging: No. **Rental clubs:** Yes.
Walking policy: Unrestricted walking. **Range:** Yes (grass).
To obtain tee times: First come, first served.

★½ NORTH COURSE

Holes: 18. **Par:** 70/70.
Yards: 6,400/5,700. **Course rating:** 70.0/72.0. **Slope:** 110/110.
Subscriber comments: Used to be excellent . . . Excellent potential . . . High traffic . . . Very open and spacious . . . Great for a beginner.

★ RED/WHITE COURSE
Holes: 18. **Par:** 71/71.
Yards: 6,850/6,500. **Course rating:** N/A. **Slope:** N/A.
Subscriber comments: White nine: plenty of water . . . A very solid nine
. . . Needs sand in traps . . . Beginner's course.

IBM MID HUDSON VALLEY GOLF COURSE★
SP—575 South Rd., Poughkeepsie (914)433-2222.
70 miles north of New York City. **Holes:** 18. **Par:** 72/72.
Yards: 6,691/4,868. **Course rating:** 72.4/67.9. **Slope:** 130/117.
Opened: 1944. **Pace of Play rating:** 4:30. **Green fee:** $30/35.
Credit cards: All major. **Reduced fees:** Weekdays, Twilight, Juniors.
Caddies: No. **Golf carts:** $22 for 18 holes.
Discount golf packages: No. **Season:** March-Dec. **High:** March-Dec.
On-site lodging: No. **Rental clubs:** Yes.
Walking policy: Walking at certain times. **Range:** Yes.
To obtain tee times: Call one day in advance at 7:45 a.m. for weekdays.
Call Sunday at 2:00 p.m. for following weekend.

★★ INDIAN ISLAND COUNTRY CLUB
PU—Riverside Dr., Riverhead (516)727-7776.
70 miles east of New York City. **Holes:** 18. **Par:** 72/72.
Yards: 6,353/5,524. **Course rating:** 71.0/72.8. **Slope:** 124/126.
Opened: 1972. **Pace of Play rating:** 4:30. **Green fee:** $15/19.
Credit cards: None. **Reduced fees:** Low season, Twilight, Seniors,
Juniors.
Caddies: No. **Golf carts:** $12 for 18 holes.
Discount golf packages: Yes. **Season:** March-Dec. **High:** May-Sept.
On-site lodging: No. **Rental clubs:** Yes.
Walking policy: Unrestricted walking. **Range:** Yes.
To obtain tee times: Available only to Suffolk County green key card
holders.
Subscriber comments: Nice course for young or old . . . Tricky, nice
views . . . Very fair and very playable . . . Terrific conditions, especially
greens . . . No need for fairway woods . . . Interesting from back tees only
. . . Easy play, lots of enjoyment, no tour types . . . Front nine a bear when
wind blows . . . Average layout . . . Conditions could be better . . . Short
but tough due to wind off bay.

★★★ ISLAND'S END GOLF & COUNTRY CLUB
SP—Rt. 25, Greenport (516)477-0777.
Call club for further information.
Subscriber comments: Flat and open, great greens . . . Sweetheart of a
layout . . . Great view of Long Island Sound . . . Difficult to get tee-off
time . . . Cost higher than most but worth it . . . Easy to walk . . . Very
reasonable length and nicely run . . . 16th is Pebble Beach of Long Island
. . . Great for average golfer . . . Fine staff, pace great . . . Nicely kept, a
pleasant round of golf . . . Wide open with wind.

★★ JAMES BAIRD STATE PARK GOLF CLUB
PU—122C Freedom Plains Rd., Pleasant Valley (914)473-1052.
5 miles east of Poughkeepsie. **Holes:** 18. **Par:** 71/74.
Yards: 6,616/5,541. **Course rating:** 71.3/75.2. **Slope:** 124/131.
Opened: N/A. **Pace of Play rating:** 4:30. **Green fee:** $14/17.
Credit cards: None. **Reduced fees:** Low season, Twilight, Seniors,
Juniors.
Caddies: No. **Golf carts:** $20 for 18 holes.
Discount golf packages: No. **Season:** April-Nov. **High:** May-Aug.
On-site lodging: No. **Rental clubs:** Yes.
Walking policy: Unrestricted walking. **Range:** Yes.
To obtain tee times: Call two days in advance.
Subscriber comments: Fairly flat and open . . . Tough greens . . . Not
very long course . . . Good service . . . More difficult than it looks . . . The
par 5 13th hole one of the hardest I've ever played . . . Front nine wide open

. . . Easy to walk . . . Staff very polite . . . Course in very good condition
. . . Course for all handicappers . . . Excellent food at rest . . . Classic Trent
Jones design . . . Tiny greens in good condition. Subtle rolls in fairway
make for an interesting round. Beautiful in autumn . . . 13th is toughest par
5 in area . . . Great scenery and service.

★ KISSENA PARK GOLF COURSE
PU—164-15 Booth Memorial Ave., Flushing (718)939-4594.
Holes: 18. **Par:** 64/64.
Yards: 4,727/4,425. **Course rating:** 61.8/65.6. **Slope:** 101/106.
Opened: 1937. **Pace of Play rating:** 3:15. **Green fee:** $16/18.
Credit cards: None. **Reduced fees:** Weekdays, Twilight, Seniors, Juniors.
Caddies: No. **Golf carts:** N/A.
Discount golf packages: No. **Season:** Year-round.
On-site lodging: No. **Rental clubs:** Yes.
Walking policy: Unrestricted walking. **Range:** No.
To obtain tee times: Call seven days in advance.
Subscriber comments: Short, but interesting, tricky greens . . . Practice
your pitching . . . Needs lots of improvement in tee areas and fairways . . .
Good practice course with five good par 3s ; other 3s are short . . . Leave
woods at home . . . Short course . . . Very unforgiving . . . A short 18-
hole course, challenging for a novice and surprisingly hilly for Queens . . .
Watch out for the pheasants that roam the course.

★★★ KUTSHER'S COUNTRY CLUB
R—Kutsher Rd., Monticello (914)794-6000.
80 miles north of New York City. **Holes:** 18. **Par:** 71/71.
Yards: 7,001/5,676. **Course rating:** 73.5/72.3. **Slope:** 123/119.
Opened: 1962. **Pace of Play rating:** 4:30. **Green fee:** $39.
Credit cards: None. **Reduced fees:** Resort guests, Twilight.
Caddies: No. **Golf carts:** Included in Green Fee.
Discount golf packages: Yes. **Season:** April-Nov. **High:** July-Aug.
On-site lodging: Yes. **Rental clubs:** Yes.
Walking policy: Mandatory cart. **Range:** Yes (grass).
To obtain tee times: Call one week in advance. Hotel guests may call one
month in advance.
Subscriber comments: Nice little hideaway course, tougher than it
appears . . . Good but not special . . . Nice test and tight . . . Large greens
. . . Deep greenside bunkers . . . Lots of trees . . . Natural setting . . . Fair
to all levels . . . Nice facility . . . Played three days there, poured every day
and course still very playable . . . Good demanding course, slick greens . . .
Fun, long, hilly, big greens, best in August.

★★½ LA TOURETTE GOLF CLUB
PU—1001 Richmond Hill Rd., Staten Island (718)351-1889.
Holes: 18. **Par:** 72/72.
Yards: 6,692/5,493. **Course rating:** 70.7/70.9. **Slope:** 119/115.
Opened: 1930. **Pace of Play rating:** 4:30-5:00. **Green fee:** $20/22.
Credit cards: MC, V. **Reduced fees:** Twilight, Seniors, Juniors.
Caddies: No. **Golf carts:** $24 for 18 holes.
Discount golf packages: No. **Season:** Year-round. **High:** May-Sept.
On-site lodging: No. **Rental clubs:** Yes.
Walking policy: Unrestricted walking. **Range:** No.
To obtain tee times: Call one week in advance.
Subscriber comments: Long and open fairways, midsized greens . . .
Favorite city course, very wide . . . Forgiving fairways . . . Extremely slow
play . . . Long and challenging, tees and greens could be better . . .
Deceptive, long for average player, some excellent holes . . . Very good
course for beginners . . . Course in good shape during summer . . . Good
for walking . . . A good mix of holes to challenge mid to high handicappers
. . . Good staff.

LAKE PLACID RESORT
R—Mirror Lake Dr., Lake Placid (518)523-4460, (800)577-4653.
20 miles west of Plattsburgh.
Opened: 1895. **Pace of Play rating:** 4:00. **Green fee:** $60.
Credit cards: MC, V, AMEX. **Reduced fees:** Low season, Resort guests,
Twilight, Juniors.
Caddies: No. **Golf carts:** $24 for 18 holes.
Discount golf packages: Yes. **Season:** May-Oct. **High:** July-Aug.
On-site lodging: Yes. **Rental clubs:** Yes.
Walking policy: Unrestricted walking. **Range:** Yes (grass).
To obtain tee times: Call or come in person.
Also has 9-hole executive course.
★★ **LOWER COURSE**
Holes: 18. **Par:** 70/74.
Yards: 6,235/5,658. **Course rating:** 69.0/73.0. **Slope:** 115/113.
Subscriber comments: Play it! Long and tricky . . . Short par 3s . . .
Scotland without the air fare . . . Memorable golf . . . Staff good, service
good . . . Very flat, open . . . Great mountain-links course, long but not
difficult.
★★ **UPPER COURSE**
Holes: 18. **Par:** 70/75.
Yards: 5,852/5,463. **Course rating:** 69.0/72.0. **Slope:** 115/0.
Subscriber comments: Great mountain scenery . . . Better test than
Lower . . . Fun course . . . Good course for average player . . . Hilly, lots
of sidehill lies . . . Couple of blind shots to greens.

★★★ **LAKE SHORE COUNTRY CLUB**
SP—1165 Greenleaf Rd., Rochester (716)663-0300.
Holes: 18. **Par:** 70/73.
Yards: 6,343/5,561. **Course rating:** 67.2/72.0. **Slope:** 116/117.
Opened: 1932. **Pace of Play rating:** 4:30. **Green fee:** $21.
Credit cards: MC, V, DISC. **Reduced fees:** No.
Caddies: No. **Golf carts:** $21 for 18 holes.
Discount golf packages: No. **Season:** April-Nov. **High:** June-Aug.
On-site lodging: No. **Rental clubs:** No.
Walking policy: Unrestricted walking. **Range:** Yes (grass).
To obtain tee times: Call same day for weekdays. Call Thursday for
upcoming weekend.
Subscriber comments: Very traditional, lake breeze, good pace, easy to
score . . . Pretty open but you need every club in your bag . . . Nice layout,
friendly staff, well-kept . . . Very playable, small greens, great practice area
. . . A real challenge from blue tees, small greens . . . Lots of O.B.

★½ **LE ROY COUNTRY CLUB**
SP—7759 East Main Rd., Le Roy (716)768-7330.
20 miles east of Rochester. **Holes:** 18. **Par:** 71/74.
Yards: 6,382/5,752. **Course rating:** 69.6/71.0. **Slope:** 115/117.
Opened: 1930. **Pace of Play rating:** 4:30. **Green fee:** $13/16.
Credit cards: MC, V. **Reduced fees:** Weekdays, Low season, Twilight,
Seniors, Juniors.
Caddies: Yes. **Golf carts:** $21for 18 holes.
Discount golf packages: Yes. **Season:** April-Oct. **High:** June-Aug.
On-site lodging: No. **Rental clubs:** Yes.
Walking policy: Unrestricted walking. **Range:** Yes (grass).
To obtain tee times: Call.
Subscriber comments: Good beginning course . . . Heavily played and
abused . . . Solid course . . . Nothing fancy . . . Lightning greens, great
shape. Length good, staff OK, not much trouble.

★★★★ **LEATHERSTOCKING GOLF COURSE**
R—Nelson Ave., Cooperstown (607)547-5275.
50 miles southwest of Albany. **Holes:** 18. **Par:** 72/72.
Yards: 6,324/5,254. **Course rating:** 71.0/69.2. **Slope:** 124/116.
Opened: 1909. **Pace of Play rating:** 4:30-4:45. **Green fee:** $45/55.

Credit cards: MC, V, AMEX. **Reduced fees:** Weekdays, Resort guests.
Caddies: No. **Golf carts:** $15 for 18 holes.
Discount golf packages: Yes. **Season:** April-Oct. **High:** June-Sept.
On-site lodging: Yes. **Rental clubs:** Yes.
Walking policy: Walking at certain times. **Range:** No.
To obtain tee times: Call six days in advance.
Subscriber comments: Excellent challenge from the blues . . . Last three
holes are the best you'll find . . . Not to be missed, package includes
Baseball Hall of Fame . . . Breathtaking views, excellent playing conditions
. . . Very interesting and challenging . . . Excellent staff . . . The par 5 18th
is 3000 miles east of and $200.00 less than Pebble Beach . . . Everyone must
play here at least once . . . Hall of Fame course . . . Love to play here . . .
Challenging well trapped, great greens, pretty . . . 18th tee shot can be very
tough over water.

★★½ LIMA GOLF & COUNTRY CLUB
PU—2681 Plank Rd., Lima (716)624-1490.
20 miles south of Rochester. **Holes:** 18. **Par:** 72/74.
Yards: 6,338/5,624. **Course rating:** 69.2/74.0. **Slope:** 115/117.
Opened: 1963. **Pace of Play rating:** 4:00-4:30. **Green fee:** $12/17.
Credit cards: MC, V. **Reduced fees:** Weekdays, Low season, Seniors.
Caddies: No. **Golf carts:** $9 for 18 holes.
Discount golf packages: No. **Season:** April-Oct. **High:** June-Sept.
On-site lodging: No. **Rental clubs:** Yes.
Walking policy: Unrestricted walking. **Range:** Yes (grass).
To obtain tee times: Call pro shop up to one week in advance.
Subscriber comments: Very fast but true greens . . . The greens are
among the best but the layout is weak . . . Greens spectacular . . . Pace is
slow on weekends . . . Course in good shape, staff very courteous, always
improving course . . . Fairly long, but easy driving course, great greens . . .
Long and straight, good food, friendly staff.

THE LINKS AT HIAWATHA LANDING★
PU—2350 Marshland Rd., Apalachin (607)687-6952.
10 miles east of Binghamton. **Holes:** 18. **Par:** 72/72.
Yards: 7,067/5,101. **Course rating:** 73.5/68.4. **Slope:** 131/113.
Opened: 1994. **Pace of Play rating:** 4:15. **Green fee:** $25/40.
Credit cards: All major. **Reduced fees:** Weekdays, Low season, Twilight.
Caddies: No. **Golf carts:** Included in Green Fee.
Discount golf packages: Yes. **Season:** April-Nov. **High:** June-Sept.
On-site lodging: No. **Rental clubs:** Yes.
Walking policy: Unrestricted walking. **Range:** Yes (grass).
To obtain tee times: Call one week in advance.

★★ LIVERPOOL GOLF & COUNTRY CLUB
PU—7209 Morgan Rd., Liverpool (315)457-7170.
5 miles north of Syracuse. **Holes:** 18. **Par:** 71/69.
Yards: 6,412/5,487. **Course rating:** 70.7/69.3. **Slope:** 114/113.
Opened: 1943. **Pace of Play rating:** 4:00. **Green fee:** $15/17.
Credit cards: None. **Reduced fees:** Weekdays, Low season, Twilight,
Seniors, Juniors.
Caddies: No. **Golf carts:** $15 for 18 holes.
Discount golf packages: No. **Season:** Year-round. **High:** April-Nov.
On-site lodging: No. **Rental clubs:** Yes.
Walking policy: Unrestricted walking. **Range:** No.
To obtain tee times: Call.
Subscriber comments: Friendly atmosphere, a few holes would give a pro
a challenge . . . Island par 3 puts as much terror into a golfer as 17th at
Sawgrass . . . Well managed . . . Generally easy to walk . . . Good public
course, flat but interesting . . . Strong course from tips . . . Great people
. . . Moderately difficult from back tees. Fairly easy from front.

MALONE GOLF CLUB

SP—Country Club Rd., Malone (518)483-2926.
70 miles south of Montreal.
Pace of Play rating: 4:30. **Green fee:** $26.
Credit cards: MC, V, AMEX. **Reduced fees:** Twilight.
Caddies: No. **Golf carts:** $22 for 18 holes.
Discount golf packages: Yes. **Season:** April-Oct. **High:** June-Aug.
On-site lodging: No. **Rental clubs:** Yes.
Walking policy: Unrestricted walking. **Range:** No.
To obtain tee times: Call one week in advance.

★★★½ EAST COURSE

Holes: 18. **Par:** 72/73.
Yards: 6,545/5,224. **Course rating:** 71.9/40.1. **Slope:** 127/115.
Opened: 1939.
Subscriber comments: Staff shared their brownies . . . Challenging, the
greens difficult to read . . . Challenging course in good condition . . .
Original course opened by Babe Ruth . . . Hilly, long with difficult par 3s
. . . Always in top shape.

★★★ WEST COURSE

Holes: 18. **Par:** 71/71.
Yards: 6,592/5,272. **Course rating:** 71.3/70.0. **Slope:** 126/119.
Opened: 1987.
Subscriber comments: Challenging, set in Adirondack Mountains . . .
Elevations, stay in fairway or else . . . New course, already in excellent
shape . . . Staff very friendly and helpful.

★½ MAPLEMOOR GOLF COURSE

PU—1128 North St., White Plains (914)946-1830.
20 miles north of New York City. **Holes:** 18. **Par:** 71/74.
Yards: 6,226/5,812. **Course rating:** 68.8/71.9. **Slope:** 110/119.
Opened: 1923. **Pace of Play rating:** 5:00. **Green fee:** $15/40.
Credit cards: MC, V. **Reduced fees:** Twilight, Seniors, Juniors.
Caddies: No. **Golf carts:** $22 for 18 holes.
Discount golf packages: No. **Season:** April-Dec. **High:** May-Aug.
On-site lodging: No. **Rental clubs:** Yes.
Walking policy: Unrestricted walking. **Range:** No.
Subscriber comments: Not challenging to low handicappers . . . Staff
courteous, pace of play a little slow . . . Great staff . . . Course has character
. . . Could be better maintained but pleasant round and scenic holes . . .
Boring, slow, all holes are straight . . . Played course only once, had a good
time . . . Very forgiving, wide open.

★ MARINE PARK GOLF CLUB

PU—2880 Flatbush Ave., Brooklyn (718)338-7113.
Holes: 18. **Par:** 72/72.
Yards: 6,866/5,323. **Course rating:** 70.5/N/A. **Slope:** 118/N/A.
Opened: 1964. **Pace of Play rating:** 4:30-5:00. **Green fee:** $8/18.
Credit cards: MC, V. **Reduced fees:** Weekdays, Low season, Twilight,
Seniors, Juniors.
Caddies: No. **Golf carts:** $23 for 18 holes.
Discount golf packages: No. **Season:** Year-round. **High:** May-Aug.
On-site lodging: No. **Rental clubs:** Yes.
Walking policy: Unrestricted walking. **Range:** No.
To obtain tee times: Call seven days in advance.
Subscriber comments: Greens good . . . Very forgiving . . . Have to pay
for parking . . . Fairway open but in poor shape . . . Fairly tough course
due to wind . . . Much too crowded in summer . . . Great layout for
beginners . . . No water, few trees . . . So-so conditions. The length makes
up for it.

★★★ MARK TWAIN GOLF CLUB

PU—Corning Rd., Elmira (607)737-5770.
50 miles east of Binghamton. **Holes:** 18. **Par:** 72/76.
Yards: 6,829/5,571. **Course rating:** 73.6/72.3. **Slope:** 123/121.

Opened: N/A. **Pace of Play rating:** 4:30. **Green fee:** $13/15.
Credit cards: None. **Reduced fees:** Weekdays, Twilight, Seniors, Juniors.
Caddies: No. **Golf carts:** $11 for 18 holes.
Discount golf packages: No. **Season:** April-Oct. **High:** June-Aug.
On-site lodging: No. **Rental clubs:** Yes.
Walking policy: Unrestricted walking. **Range:** Yes (grass).
To obtain tee times: Call.
Subscriber comments: Big fast greens, wide fairways . . . Tough layout, open enough for all golfers . . . Original Donald Ross . . . Tricky greens . . . Gorgeous scenery and layout . . . A value at twice the price . . . Blind shots to all par 3s . . . Great front nine . . . Boring back nine.

★★ MARRIOTT'S GOLF CLUB AT WIND WATCH

R—1717 Vanderbuilt Motor Pkwy., Hauppauge (516)232-9850.
30 miles east of New York City. **Holes:** 18. **Par:** 71/71.
Yards: 6,425/5,135. **Course rating:** 71.2/68.6. **Slope:** 133/118.
Opened: 1990. **Pace of Play rating:** 4:15. **Green fee:** $39/69.
Credit cards: All major. **Reduced fees:** Low season, Resort guests, Twilight, Juniors.
Caddies: No. **Golf carts:** Included in Green Fee.
Discount golf packages: No. **Season:** Year-round. **High:** April-Oct.
On-site lodging: Yes. **Rental clubs:** Yes.
Walking policy: Mandatory cart. **Range:** Yes (grass).
To obtain tee times: Hotel guests may call one week in advance. Nonguests call three days in advance.
Subscriber comments: Good layout, bad shape . . . Not worth the price . . . Very challenging . . . Very attentive staff . . . Conditions could be better . . . Course condition does not warrant high price . . . A South Carolina resort-style clone . . . Plays shorter than card distances . . . Staff treats you very well . . . The white tees make it a very fair course . . . Acceptable layout.

MASSENA COUNTRY CLUB

PU—Rte. 131, Massena (315)769-2293.
160 miles north of Syracuse. **Holes:** 18. **Par:** 71/75.
Yards: 6,602/5,361. **Course rating:** 70.1/70.0. **Slope:** 110/111.
Opened: 1958. **Pace of Play rating:** 4:00. **Green fee:** $22.
Credit cards: MC, V. **Reduced fees:** Low season, Twilight.
Caddies: Yes. **Golf carts:** $20 for 18 holes.
Discount golf packages: No. **Season:** May-Oct. **High:** June-Aug.
On-site lodging: No. **Rental clubs:** Yes.
Walking policy: Unrestricted walking. **Range:** Yes (grass).
To obtain tee times: Two day advance.
Subscriber comments: Beautiful setting on the St. Lawrence River . . . Great view . . . Always cool in summer heat.

★★½ McCANN MEMORIAL GOLF CLUB

PU—155 Wilbur Blvd., Poughkeepsie (914)471-3917.
65 miles north of New York City. **Holes:** 18. **Par:** 72/72.
Yards: 6,524/5,354. **Course rating:** 72.0/71.4. **Slope:** 128/123.
Opened: 1972. **Pace of Play rating:** 4:30. **Green fee:** $25/28.
Credit cards: None. **Reduced fees:** Seniors, Juniors.
Caddies: No. **Golf carts:** $22 for 18 holes.
Discount golf packages: No. **Season:** March-Dec. **High:** April-Oct.
On-site lodging: No. **Rental clubs:** Yes.
Walking policy: Unrestricted walking. **Range:** Yes (grass).
To obtain tee times: Call.
Subscriber comments: Good for all handicaps, very friendly, pace better than most . . . Excellent facilities, great course layout . . . A lot of back and forth holes . . . Everybody hitting out of wrong fairways, always need to duck . . . Pro-shop folks are first class . . . Very large greens and well kept fairways . . . Good course, too easy . . . Designed for high handicaps . . . Very narrow fairways . . . Wear hard hat on front nine! . . . Service is good.

★★ MIDDLE ISLAND COUNTRY CLUB
DOGWOOD/OAKTREE/SPRUCE
PU—Yapank Rd., Middle Island (516)924-5100.
75 miles east of New York City. **Holes:** 27. **Par:** 72/72/72.
Yards: 6,934/7,027/7,015. **Course rating:** 73.4/73.4/73.4.
Slope: 128/128/128.
Opened: 1964. **Pace of Play rating:** N/A. **Green fee:** $22.
Credit cards: None. **Reduced fees:** No.
Caddies: No. **Golf carts:** $14 for 18 holes.
Discount golf packages: No. **Season:** Year-round. **High:** April-Oct.
On-site lodging: No. **Rental clubs:** Yes.
Walking policy: Walking at certain times. **Range:** No.
To obtain tee times: Call one week in advance.
Subscriber comments: Needs better care on the fairways and greens . . .
Great length from tips . . . Three different nines, good for average golfer
. . . Tight, challenging course . . . Conditions have gone downhill . . . No.
9 on the Oak Course is about the tightest par 5 I've seen, O.B. on the right,
trees left . . . Narrow, not long but must stay in fairway . . . Staff
exceptionally courteous . . . Rough is extremely difficult . . . Nice test of
golf . . . Interesting layout . . . Can be challenging for the intermediate
player.

★★½ MOHANSIC GOLF CLUB
PU—Baldwin Rd., Yorktown Heights (914)962-4049.
37 miles north of New York City. **Holes:** 18. **Par:** 70/75.
Yards: 6,500/5,594. **Course rating:** 69.9/75.2. **Slope:** 120/127.
Opened: 1925. **Pace of Play rating:** 4:30. **Green fee:** $35/40.
Credit cards: None. **Reduced fees:** Weekdays, Twilight, Seniors, Juniors.
Caddies: No. **Golf carts:** $21 for 18 holes.
Discount golf packages: No. **Season:** April-Dec. **High:** June-Aug.
On-site lodging: No. **Rental clubs:** Yes.
Walking policy: Unrestricted walking. **Range:** Yes.
To obtain tee times: Call computerized tee times (914)962-4065
Subscriber comments: Very good course, well maintained . . . Always
windy, if you can't play in the wind, don't show up . . . Challenging test,
scenic and quiet . . . Well cared for . . . Good layout, variety of holes . . .
Could be fantastic with some tender loving care . . . Too many hills for
older folks . . . Wide open course with some long par 4s.

★★★★ MONTAUK DOWNS STATE PARK GOLF COURSE
PU—South Fairview Ave., Montauk (516)668-1100.
110 miles east of New York City. **Holes:** 18. **Par:** 72/72.
Yards: 6,762/5,797. **Course rating:** 73.3/75.9. **Slope:** 133/135.
Opened: 1968. **Pace of Play rating:** 4:30. **Green fee:** $20/25.
Credit cards: None. **Reduced fees:** Twilight, Seniors.
Caddies: No. **Golf carts:** $12 for 18 holes.
Discount golf packages: No. **Season:** April-Dec. **High:** July-Sept.
On-site lodging: No. **Rental clubs:** Yes.
Walking policy: Unrestricted walking. **Range:** Yes.
To obtain tee times: Call seven to nine days in advance.

Ranked in Second 25 of America's 75 Best Public Golf Courses by Golf
Digest.
Subscriber comments: Legendary course . . . Worth the hassle to get
there . . . Staff friendly and helpful . . . Great conditions . . . If the wind is
blowing, hang onto your scorecard . . . Underrated, great course . . . Too
bad it's at the end of the earth . . . Good all-around course, not for the
beginner . . . It is a beautiful place to play and enjoy the scenery . . . I love
this course . . . For a state course, conditions are like a private club . . .
Hard to get a tee time . . . A jewel on the tip of the Island . . . U.S. Open
rough and British Open wind . . . Trent Jones at his best . . . Could play
forever . . . Never tire of it . . . Poor man's Shinnecock . . . Outrageously

wonderful . . . Please don't tell anyone about this place . . . Can play up to 12,000 yards on windy day . . . Great layout . . . Forces you to hit all types of shots and all clubs . . . This course has class . . . The best on the Island . . . Well kept and friendly atmosphere.

★ MOSHOLU GOLF COURSE AND DRIVING RANGE
PU—3700 Jerome Ave., Bronx (718)655-9164.
Call club for further information.
Subscriber comments: Crowded, good course to learn to play on.

★★★ NEVELE COUNTRY CLUB
R—Rte. 209, Ellenville , (800)647-6000.
90 miles north of New York. **Holes:** 18. **Par:** 70/70.
Yards: 6,600/4,600. **Course rating:** 71.9/71.1. **Slope:** 128/126.
Opened: N/A. **Pace of Play rating:** 4:00-5:00. **Green fee:** $25/35.
Credit cards: MC, V, AMEX. **Reduced fees:** Weekdays, Resort guests, Twilight.
Caddies: No. **Golf carts:** N/A.
Discount golf packages: Yes. **Season:** April-Dec. **High:** May-Sept.
On-site lodging: Yes. **Rental clubs:** Yes.
Walking policy: Unrestricted walking. **Range:** Yes (grass).
To obtain tee times: Hotel guests call three weeks in advance. Non guests call two weeks in advance.
Subscriber comments: Short but tight . . . Excellent design . . . Very well maintained, a joy to play . . . Good layout . . . Conditions above average . . . Staff excellent . . . Best in the fall . . . Excellent greens . . . Beautiful water holes . . . Really tough from blues . . . A tight challenging course accuracy is a necessity.

★★½ THE NEW COURSE AT ALBANY
PU—65 O'Neil Rd., Albany (518)489-3526.
Holes: 18. **Par:** 71/71.
Yards: 6,300/4,990. **Course rating:** 69.4/72.0. **Slope:** 117/113.
Opened: 1991. **Pace of Play rating:** N/A. **Green fee:** $10/18.
Credit cards: None. **Reduced fees:** Twilight.
Caddies: No. **Golf carts:** $9 for 18 holes.
Discount golf packages: No. **Season:** April-Nov. **High:** June-Aug.
On-site lodging: No. **Rental clubs:** Yes.
Walking policy: Unrestricted walking. **Range:** Yes (grass).
To obtain tee times: Call 24 hours in advance.
Subscriber comments: Course is for any type of player . . . Not a flat lie on the course . . . Excellent practice facilities . . . Much improved . . . Very hilly but wide open, greens are fast and hard . . . Tiring to walk, especially back nine.

★½ NIAGARA COUNTY GOLF COURSE
PU—314 Davison Rd., Lockport (716)434-6669.
Call club for further information.
Subscriber comments: Nice course . . . Flat wide open course . . . Elevated greens . . . Well suited for average player . . . Few bunkers, little water, but usually in good shape . . . Driver-wedge all day.

★½ OLD HICKORY GOLF CLUB
SP—6653 Big Tree Rd., Livonia (716)346-2450.
20 miles south of Rochester. **Holes:** 18. **Par:** 72/72.
Yards: 6,650/5,450. **Course rating:** 70.2/70.7. **Slope:** 109/111.
Opened: 1990. **Pace of Play rating:** 4:00. **Green fee:** $13/14.
Credit cards: None. **Reduced fees:** Low season, Seniors, Juniors.
Caddies: No. **Golf carts:** N/A.
Discount golf packages: No. **Season:** April-Oct. **High:** May-Sept.
On-site lodging: No. **Rental clubs:** Yes.

Walking policy: Unrestricted walking. **Range:** Yes (grass).
To obtain tee times: Call one week in advance.
Subscriber comments: Will be a great course when the trees grow . . .
Well kept . . . Plays long due to wind . . . Very open, easy to score, easy to
get on, great pro.

★★★ OYSTER BAY TOWN GOLF COURSE

PU—Southwood Rd., Woodbury (516)364-3977.
35 miles east of New York. **Holes:** 18. **Par:** 70/70.
Yards: 6,351/5,109. **Course rating:** 71.5/70.4. **Slope:** 131/126.
Opened: 1989. **Pace of Play rating:** 4:45. **Green fee:** $40/50.
Credit cards: None. **Reduced fees:** Weekdays, Low season, Twilight,
Seniors, Juniors.
Caddies: No. **Golf carts:** N/A.
Discount golf packages: No. **Season:** Year-round. **High:** April-Oct.
On-site lodging: No. **Rental clubs:** Yes.
Walking policy: Unrestricted walking. **Range:** Yes.
To obtain tee times: First come, first serve.
Subscriber comments: Very tight and challenging layout . . . Last five
holes are awesome . . . Beautiful course, looks like it was made for a pro
tour, very rough . . . I'd rate it high, but then it would get even more
crowded . . . Not for beginners . . . Really shoehorned into the site . . .
Last three holes significantly tougher than first fifteen . . . Warning: remove
driver from bag . . . Great test from back tees . . . Large greens ; always
windy . . . Last three holes present a very difficult test for any golfer.

★★★½ PEEK'N PEAK RESORT

R—1405 Olde Rd., Clymer (716)355-4141.
20 miles southeast of Erie, PA. **Holes:** 18. **Par:** 72/72.
Yards: 6,260/4,820. **Course rating:** 69.0/69.5. **Slope:** 115/112.
Opened: 1974. **Pace of Play rating:** 4:30-5:00. **Green fee:** $19/27.
Credit cards: All major. **Reduced fees:** Weekdays, Low season, Seniors.
Caddies: No. **Golf carts:** $10 for 18 holes.
Discount golf packages: Yes. **Season:** April-Nov. **High:** June-Sept.
On-site lodging: Yes. **Rental clubs:** Yes.
Walking policy: Unrestricted walking. **Range:** Yes (grass).
To obtain tee times: Call pro shop.
Also has 9-hole, par-36 course called Upper Golf Club.
Subscriber comments: Nice course for couples on a weekend getaway
. . . One of the most enjoyable courses I've ever played in addition to being
very challenging . . . It is very well kept with each hole having a
breathtaking view . . . Suited for low and middle handicappers . . . Good
food, great staff.

PELHAM-SPLIT ROCK GOLF COURSE

PU—870 Shore Rd., Bronx (718)885-1258.
Opened: 1932. **Pace of Play rating:** 4:00-4:15. **Green fee:** $15/17.
Credit cards: MC, V. **Reduced fees:** Weekdays, Twilight, Seniors,
Juniors.
Caddies: No. **Golf carts:** $12 for 18 holes.
Discount golf packages: No. **Season:** Year-round. **High:** May-Sept.
On-site lodging: No. **Rental clubs:** Yes.
Walking policy: Unrestricted walking. **Range:** Yes.
To obtain tee times: Call up to 12 days in advance for weekends and up to
seven days in advance for weekdays. Credit card is needed to hold
reservation for weekend.

★½ PELHAM COURSE

Holes: 18. **Par:** 71/71.
Yards: 6,991/5,634. **Course rating:** 69.6/N/A. **Slope:** 114/115.
Subscriber comments: Open but interesting layout . . . Never know you
were in New York City . . . A little dull but forgiving . . . Wide open,
good warm-up course . . . Condition getting much better, some fine holes
. . . Easy par 5s.

★½ SPLIT ROCK

Holes: 18. **Par:** 71/71.
Yards: 6,714/5,509. **Course rating:** 71.9/71.7. **Slope:** 125/122.
Subscriber comments: Super layout . . . Very challenging . . . With better conditioning would rival the best . . . Not great, not bad, just acceptable . . . Must be straight off the tee, narrow fairways . . . Nice layout, good for beginners.

★½ PHILIP J. ROTELLA GOLF COURSE

PU—Thiells and Mt. Ivy Rds., Thiells (914)354-1616.
20 miles north of New York City. **Holes:** 18. **Par:** 72/72.
Yards: 6,502/4,856. **Course rating:** 71.4/71.7. **Slope:** 126/123.
Opened: 1985. **Pace of Play rating:** N/A. **Green fee:** $22/30.
Credit cards: None. **Reduced fees:** Twilight, Seniors.
Caddies: No. **Golf carts:** $22 for 18 holes.
Discount golf packages: Yes. **Season:** March-Dec. **High:** May-July.
On-site lodging: No. **Rental clubs:** Yes.
Walking policy: Walking at certain times. **Range:** Yes (grass).
To obtain tee times: Call pro shop.
Subscriber comments: Six par 3s, six par 4s, and six par 5s . . . Tough course . . . Lots of water . . . Tees too close to adjacent greens . . . Needs to be maintained better. Poor ladies' tees . . . Courteous staff . . . Lots of trees, fair fairways, fun course.

★★★ PINE HILLS COUNTRY CLUB

SP—162 Wading River Rd., Manorville (516)878-4343.
Call club for further information.
Subscriber comments: Great condition . . . Well kept, easier than it looks, good greens. Just a nice place to play . . . Good pace, good treatment, open favors long hitters . . . Challenging, but not bad for high handicappers . . . Back nine has a lot of character . . . Good fairways, first nine flat, black nine very hilly, wide fairways . . . Private course conditions, friendly personnel, tricky greens . . . Best maintained course on Long Island . . . Good for beginning to above average golfers . . . Fun course! What else can I say?

★★½ PUTNAM COUNTRY CLUB

SP—Hill St., Mahopac (914)628-4200.
50 miles north of New York City. **Holes:** 18. **Par:** 71/73.
Yards: 6,774/5,799. **Course rating:** 72.1/73.7. **Slope:** 131/132.
Opened: . **Pace of Play rating:** . **Green fee:** $16/ 24.
Credit cards: MC, V. **Reduced fees:** Weekdays, Twilight, Seniors, Juniors.
Caddies: No. **Golf carts:** $12 for 18 holes.
Discount golf packages: No. **Season:** April-Nov. **High:** June-Sept.
On-site lodging: No. **Rental clubs:** Yes.
Walking policy: Walking at certain times. **Range:** No.
To obtain tee times: Call one week in advance.
Subscriber comments: Very long uphill par 4 ninth hole . . . Good fairways, in good condition for a course that welcomes non-members . . . Many holes identical . . . Good service and pace . . . Challenging greens . . . Some great par 4s . . . Too many tee boxes right next to greens.

★★★★ RADISSON GREENS GOLF CLUB

SP—8055 Potter Rd., Baldwinsville (315)638-0092.
15 miles northwest of Syracuse. **Holes:** 18. **Par:** 72/73.
Yards: 7,010/5,543. **Course rating:** 73.3/70.0. **Slope:** 128/124.
Opened: 1977. **Pace of Play rating:** 4:15. **Green fee:** $19/22.
Credit cards: None. **Reduced fees:** Seniors.
Caddies: No. **Golf carts:** $22 for 18 holes.
Discount golf packages: No. **Season:** April-Nov. **High:** May-Sept.
On-site lodging: No. **Rental clubs:** No.
Walking policy: Walking at certain times. **Range:** Yes (grass).
To obtain tee times: Call Monday for upcoming weekend.

Subscriber comments: Scenic, challenging at times, exceptionally maintained . . . Lovely, great staff and condition . . . Tree lined, keep it in play . . . Most holes are straight back and forth, flat, tight . . . Difficult course not for high handicapper . . . A lot of water ; a lot of condos . . . For most players . . . Good service . . . From back tees, very difficult . . . Long wooded, well trapped fairways and greens . . . Subtly contoured greens . . . Four outstanding water holes . . . A real sleeper . . . Course always in good shape . . . Hard to get on . . . Beautiful course . . . pleasure to play.

★★★½ RIVER OAKS GOLF CLUB
SP—201 Whitehaven Rd., Grand Island (716)773-3336.
10 miles south of Buffalo. **Holes:** 18. **Par:** 72/72.
Yards: 7,389/5,747. **Course rating:** 75.5/72.0. **Slope:** 131/118.
Opened: 1971. **Pace of Play rating:** 4:10. **Green fee:** $12/36.
Credit cards: MC, V, AMEX. **Reduced fees:** Low season, Resort guests.
Caddies: No. **Golf carts:** $11 for 18 holes.
Discount golf packages: Yes. **Season:** April-Nov. **High:** June-Sept.
On-site lodging: Yes. **Rental clubs:** Yes.
Walking policy: Mandatory cart. **Range:** Yes (grass).
To obtain tee times: Call two days in advance.
Subscriber comments: Good layout, long, half links, half tree-lined . . . Could be hard for average golfer . . . Pace and staff good . . . Nos. 4 through 6 are meadow golf . . . Excellent condition, highly challenging, excellent clubhouse . . . Narrow fairways, tough greens . . . Hope it never goes private . . . Great test of golf, super course.

★★★ ROCK HILL COUNTRY CLUB
PU—105 Clancy Rd., Manorville (516)878-2250.
60 miles east of New York City. **Holes:** 18. **Par:** 71/72.
Yards: 7,050/5,390. **Course rating:** 73.7/71.4. **Slope:** 128/121.
Opened: 1965. **Pace of Play rating:** 4:30. **Green fee:** $23/27.
Credit cards: None. **Reduced fees:** Weekdays, Low season, Twilight, Seniors, Juniors.
Caddies: No. **Golf carts:** $28 for 18 holes.
Discount golf packages: No. **Season:** Year-round. **High:** May-Sept.
On-site lodging: No. **Rental clubs:** No.
Walking policy: Walking at certain times. **Range:** Yes (grass).
To obtain tee times: Call seven days in advance.
Subscriber comments: Most fairways are wide open, the back nine is especially forgiving of an errant tee ball . . . If you like wind, it's always in your face in May and August . . . Course is very demanding for lower handicapped players . . . Tough, hilly and sharp doglegs . . . Front nine target golf, Back nine let shaft out . . . Tough greens to read . . . Conditions are better than in past . . . Great finishing holes . . . Course needed work last time I played it . . . Tough walk, but nice condition . . . Perfect course . . . Played during a monsoon.

ROCKLAND LAKE STATE PARK GOLF CLUB
★★★ NORTH CSE
–Rt. 9W, P.O. Box 217, Bear Mtn. (914)268-6250.
Call club for further information.
Subscriber comments: Must know layout to score . . . Great layout but always a long round . . . Good layout not too challenging but fun to play . . . Worth two hour trip from Long Island . . . Easier to win lotto than get tee time . . . Ideal walking, well maintained, good for twelve plus handicaps . . . A beautiful golf course, a challenge for all levels, good pace.

★★½ ROME COUNTRY CLUB
SP—5342 Rte. 69, Rome (315)336-6464.
Holes: 18. **Par:** 72/75.
Yards: 6,775/5,505. **Course rating:** 71.8/70.4. **Slope:** 125/N/A.
Opened: 1929. **Pace of Play rating:** 4:00. **Green fee:** $16/20.
Credit cards: MC, V. **Reduced fees:** Weekdays.
Caddies: No. **Golf carts:** $20 for 18 holes.

Discount golf packages: Yes. **Season:** Year-round. **High:** May-Aug.
On-site lodging: No. **Rental clubs:** Yes.
Walking policy: Unrestricted walking. **Range:** Yes (grass).
To obtain tee times: Call.
Subscriber comments: Can be wet . . . Front has two par 3s in a row . . .
Back nine has potential . . . Lots of hills and small greens . . . Hidden
trouble . . . Ditches not well marked . . . Poor balance . . . Four par 5s in
five holes (Nos. 7, 9, 10, and 11) . . . True test of shotmaking.

ROTHLAND GOLF COURSE
★★½ **RED/GOLD/WHITE**
PU—12089 Clarence Center Rd., Akron (716)542-4325.
15 miles east of Buffalo. **Holes:** 27. **Par:** 72/72/72.
Yards: 6,486/6,216/6,044. **Course rating:** 70.5/69.5/69.0.
Slope: 113/108/105.
Opened: 1980. **Pace of Play rating:** 4:00-4:30. **Green fee:** $15/18.
Credit cards: None. **Reduced fees:** Weekdays, Low season, Twilight,
Seniors.
Caddies: No. **Golf carts:** $10 for 18 holes.
Discount golf packages: No. **Season:** April-Nov. **High:** June-Sept.
On-site lodging: No. **Rental clubs:** Yes.
Walking policy: Unrestricted walking. **Range:** Yes (grass).
To obtain tee times: Call seven days in advance.
Subscriber comments: Gold Course the tightest with many trees . . . Just
a good course and nice place to play . . . Most greens crowned, tough to
hold . . . OK for a pick up game . . . Red Course long and wide open . . .
White Course, third hole has tree in middle of fairway! . . . Gold is best test
. . . Suitable for all golfers . . . Well groomed, nice people.

★★★★ THE SAGAMORE GOLF CLUB
R—110 Sagamore Rd., Bolton Landing (518)644-9400.
60 miles north of Albany. **Holes:** 18. **Par:** 70/71.
Yards: 6,890/5,261. **Course rating:** 72.9/73.0. **Slope:** 130/122.
Opened: 1928. **Pace of Play rating:** 4:00. **Green fee:** $70.
Credit cards: All major. **Reduced fees:** N/A.
Caddies: No. **Golf carts:** Included in Green Fee.
Discount golf packages: Yes. **Season:** April-Nov. **High:** May-Oct.
On-site lodging: Yes. **Rental clubs:** Yes.
Walking policy: Mandatory cart. **Range:** Yes (grass).
To obtain tee times: You can make tee times when you book your
reservations with the resort.
Subscriber comments: Good, hard course, you'll like it . . . Brings you to
your knees . . . Wow! Good layout, should be easy, but can jump up and
bite you . . . Tough, don't play if your handicap is above 10 . . .
Spectacular, what condition . . . A steal . . . Superb . . . We'll be back . . .
Ideal for all player levels . . . Great course . . . A lot of character . . . Must
make shots . . . Classic untouched Ross, this is a must play . . . Elevated
greens on every hole, narrow tree-lined fairways . . . Extremely pleasant
staff . . . Can't afford it everyday, but worth the price . . . Heavily wooded,
hilly back nine is extremely tight . . . Very scenic views of Lake George and
Adirondacks.

ST. LAWRENCE UNIVERSITY GOLF COURSE★
PU—Rte. 11, Canton (315)386-4600.
68 miles south of Ottawa, Canada. **Holes:** 18. **Par:** 72/73.
Yards: 6,694/5,430. **Course rating:** 72.1/73.1. **Slope:** 122/120.
Opened: 1930. **Pace of Play rating:** 4:00. **Green fee:** $13/20.
Credit cards: MC, V. **Reduced fees:** Weekdays, Low season, Resort
guests, Twilight, Juniors.
Caddies: No. **Golf carts:** $22 for 18 holes.
Discount golf packages: Yes. **Season:** April-Oct. **High:** June-Aug.
On-site lodging: Yes. **Rental clubs:** Yes.
Walking policy: Unrestricted walking. **Range:** Yes (grass).
To obtain tee times: Call two days in advance.

★½ SALMON CREEK COUNTRY CLUB

SP—355 Washington St., Spencerport (716)352-4300.
Call club for further information.
Subscriber comments: Lots of doglegs, long course, but friendly . . .
Upkeep and condition of course marginal . . . Interesting layout . . . Some
blind shots . . . Fun to play, tough greens to putt.

★★★½ SARATOGA SPA GOLF COURSE

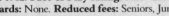

PU—Saratoga Spa State Park, Saratoga Springs (518)584-2006.
24 miles north of Albany. **Holes:** 18. **Par:** 72/72.
Yards: 7,149/5,649. **Course rating:** 73.7/72.5. **Slope:** 130/122.
Opened: 1962. **Pace of Play rating:** N/A. **Green fee:** $12/ 14.
Credit cards: None. **Reduced fees:** Seniors, Juniors.
Caddies: No. **Golf carts:** N/A.
Discount golf packages: No. **Season:** April-Nov. **High:** June-Aug.
On-site lodging: Yes. **Rental clubs:** Yes.
Walking policy: Unrestricted walking. **Range:** Yes (grass).
To obtain tee times: First come, first seraved for weekdays. Tee times
Saturday and Sunday only.
Also has 9-hole, par-29 course.
Subscriber comments: Fairways lined with tall pines . . . A great place to
play hooky from work . . . Great course and conditions, lots of rangers,
long waits on weekends . . . Great course crippled by slow play . . . Too
busy in racing season . . . The best . . . Can't beat the locale (keep this a
secret) . . . Avoid in August (near racetrack) . . . Bring sand wedge . . .
Saratoga Spa practically across the road from the Saratoga Racetrack . . .
Lots of pressure holes . . . Requires good approaches . . . Course well kept
. . . Fun to play . . . Clubhouse and services very good.

★★ SAXON WOODS GOLF COURSE

PU—315 Mamaroneck Ave., Scarsdale (914)725-3814.
5 miles north of White Plains. **Holes:** 18. **Par:** 71/73.
Yards: 6,397/5,617. **Course rating:** 70.2/71.2. **Slope:** 119/120.
Opened: 1931. **Pace of Play rating:** 5:00. **Green fee:** $12/40.
Credit cards: None. **Reduced fees:** Weekdays, Twilight, Seniors, Juniors.
Caddies: No. **Golf carts:** $20 for 18 holes.
Discount golf packages: No. **Season:** April-Dec. **High:** June-Aug.
On-site lodging: No. **Rental clubs:** Yes.
Walking policy: Unrestricted walking. **Range:** No.
To obtain tee times: Call.
Subscriber comments: A strong layout and potentially fine course,
however, too much play and brutally slow, tees need work . . . Condition
is mediocre . . . Routine public course, not much trouble . . . Course good
for skins game . . . If you can score here, you can score anywhere . . .
Course layout is very good . . . Borders on excellent.

★★ SCHENECTADY GOLF COURSE

PU—400 Oregon Ave., Schenectady (518)382-5155.
18 miles east of Albany. **Holes:** 18. **Par:** 72/72.
Yards: 6,570/5,275. **Course rating:** 71.1/68.1. **Slope:** 123/115.
Opened: 1935. **Pace of Play rating:** 4:30. **Green fee:** $14/16.
Credit cards: None. **Reduced fees:** Seniors, Juniors.
Caddies: No. **Golf carts:** $19 for 18 holes.
Discount golf packages: No. **Season:** April-Nov. **High:** May-Aug.
On-site lodging: No. **Rental clubs:** Yes.
Walking policy: Unrestricted walking. **Range:** Yes (grass).
To obtain tee times: Call 48 hours in advance.
Subscriber comments: Nice municipal course with large greens . . .
Good layout ; staff working on it . . . Good roll off the tee, plays short for
long hitters . . . Spread my ashes on the 17th tee . . . Good course for
walking . . . Good muny course . . . Lots of play . . . Takes water well all
seasons.

★★★ SEGALLA COUNTRY CLUB

PU—P.O. Box C, Amenia (914)373-9200.
25 miles west of Poughkeepsie, N.Y. **Holes:** 18. **Par:** 72/72.
Yards: 6,617/5,601. **Course rating:** 72.0/72.3. **Slope:** 133/129.
Opened: 1992. **Pace of Play rating:** 4:30. **Green fee:** $21/27.
Credit cards: MC, V, AMEX. **Reduced fees:** Low season, Twilight,
Seniors, Juniors.
Caddies: No. **Golf carts:** N/A.
Discount golf packages: No. **Season:** April-Nov. **High:** May-Sept.
On-site lodging: No. **Rental clubs:** Yes.
Walking policy: Walking at certain times. **Range:** Yes.
To obtain tee times: Call six days in advance starting at 6:30 a.m.
Subscriber comments: Excellent new course wide open but tough,
difficult greens . . . Good for all handicaps . . . Young, but very promising
. . . Wide open . . . Treatment is first rate . . . Sometimes narrow, suited
for low handicappers . . . Good 19th hole . . . Back nine has gorgeous view
in the fall, fun course for all players . . . Needs to mature . . . My wife liked
it better than I did . . . Stay out of the rough . . . First class all the way . . .
Young, outstanding course . . . Service, space, conditions top notch for all
. . . Very polite but firmly move you along the course to keep the play
moving . . . Needs some more trees . . . Interesting course . . . Greens need
to settle . . . A couple of beautiful water holes . . . Front nine open, back
more challenging . . . Many holes play left to right, need to be good
shotmaker . . . Challenging holes with blind approaches . . . The clubhouse
and restaurant are excellent . . . Please don't let this course die before
puberty . . . Accuracy, not distance, a must.

★★★★ SEVEN OAKS GOLF CLUB

SP—East Lake and Payne Streets, Hamilton (315)824-1432.
41 miles of Syracuse. **Holes:** 18. **Par:** 72/72.
Yards: 6,915/5,849. **Course rating:** N/A. **Slope:** 128/125.
Opened: N/A. **Pace of Play rating:** N/A. **Green fee:** N/A.
Credit cards: MC, V. **Reduced fees:** Resort guests.
Caddies: Yes. **Golf carts:** N/A.
Discount golf packages: Yes. **Season:** April-Oct. **High:** June-Aug.
On-site lodging: No. **Rental clubs:** No.
Walking policy: N/A. **Range:** Yes (grass).
Subscriber comments: Wonderful challenge, beautiful course and campus
. . . Great course, big greens, tough winds, must position ball off tees . . .
Dynamite course, friendly staff, good value, premium on direction . . . A
test for above-average golfer . . . Tremendous layout ; scenic . . . Excellent
golf facility, challenging layout and good service in pro shop . . . Rough
sometimes too difficult, even for strong players . . . Be careful of hidden
water . . . Better for long hitters . . . The Colgate University "course" is a
"graduate" examination of your game . . . Bring your "A" swing. Great,
wonderful, long holes, very challenging.

★★½ SHADOW LAKE GOLF & RAQUET CLUB

PU—1850 Five Mile Line Rd., Penfield (716)385-2010.
10 miles southeast of Rochester. **Holes:** 18. **Par:** 71/72.
Yards: 6,164/5,498. **Course rating:** 68.5/70.5. **Slope:** 111/112.
Opened: 1977. **Pace of Play rating:** 4:00. **Green fee:** $10/22.
Credit cards: MC, V, AMEX. **Reduced fees:** Weekdays, Low season,
Twilight, Seniors.
Caddies: No. **Golf carts:** $11 for 18 holes.
Discount golf packages: No. **Season:** Marchch-Dec. **High:** June-Aug.
On-site lodging: No. **Rental clubs:** Yes.
Walking policy: Walking at certain times. **Range:** No.
To obtain tee times: Call one week in advance.
Also has 9-hole, par-31 executive course.
Subscriber comments: Lots of trees and water, I can't break 80 . . .

Excellent maintainance . . . Excellent clubhouse and staff . . . Flowers everywhere . . . Close to nature . . . High handicaps will score well here . . . Short course gets a ton of play . . . Bring your driver, wedge, and putter, that's all you need . . . Greens need work . . . Most players will enjoy . . . Very good staff . . . Service excellent.

★★★ SHADOW PINES GOLF CLUB
PU—600 Whalen Rd., Penfield (716)385-8550.
10 miles southeast of Rochester. **Holes:** 18. **Par:** 72/72.
Yards: 6,763/5,292. **Course rating:** 72.1/73.1. **Slope:** 121/124.
Opened: 1985. **Pace of Play rating:** 4:30-5:00. **Green fee:** $15/22.
Credit cards: MC, V, AMEX. **Reduced fees:** Weekdays, Low season, Twilight, Seniors.
Caddies: No. **Golf carts:** $11 for 18 holes.
Discount golf packages: No. **Season:** April-Oct. **High:** June-Aug.
On-site lodging: No. **Rental clubs:** Yes.
Walking policy: Mandatory cart. **Range:** Yes (grass).
To obtain tee times: Call one week in advance for locals. For out-of-town or large groups call one year in advance.
Subscriber comments: More trees than water, cute doglegs, tough fast contoured greens . . . Excellent clubhouse and staff . . . Front nine wide open, back nine tight and hilly . . . Rolling terrain . . . Good variety . . . A must for the golf lover to play . . . Tough . . . Easy to post a good score here . . . Staff friendly and helpful.

★★★ SHERIDAN PARK GOLF CLUB
PU—Center Park Dr., Town of Tonawanda (716)875-1811.
3 miles north of Buffalo. **Holes:** 18. **Par:** 71/74.
Yards: 6,534/5,656. **Course rating:** 71.5/74.0. **Slope:** 116/116.
Opened: 1933. **Pace of Play rating:** 4:15. **Green fee:** $15/18.
Credit cards: None. **Reduced fees:** Weekdays, Twilight.
Caddies: No. **Golf carts:** $16 for 18 holes.
Discount golf packages: No. **Season:** April-Nov. **High:** June-Aug.
On-site lodging: No. **Rental clubs:** No.
Walking policy: Unrestricted walking. **Range:** No.
To obtain tee times: Call (716)873-1100 seven days in advance.
Subscriber comments: Nice layout, good pace . . . Toughest area course, if you can score here, you can score anywhere . . . Lots of water and narrow fairways . . . Excellent layout, good skills test . . . Challenging back nine . . . For better handicapper . . . You will use all clubs.

★½ SILVER LAKE GOLF COURSE
PU—915 Victory Blvd., Staten Island (718)447-5686.
Holes: 18. **Par:** 69/69.
Yards: 6,050/5,202. **Course rating:** 67.7/71.2. **Slope:** 110/119.
Opened: 1931. **Pace of Play rating:** N/A. **Green fee:** $15/17.
Credit cards: MC, V. **Reduced fees:** Weekdays, Low season, Twilight, Seniors, Juniors.
Caddies: No. **Golf carts:** $23 for 18 holes.
Discount golf packages: Yes. **Season:** Year-round. **High:** May-Sept.
On-site lodging: No. **Rental clubs:** Yes.
Walking policy: Unrestricted walking. **Range:** Yes.
To obtain tee times: Call.
Subscriber comments: Very pretty, narrow . . . Leave the driver in the bag . . . A real shooting gallery . . . Welcome to Dodge City . . . Service is good but the pace of play is slow because of high usage . . . It is narrow and hilly . . . Short but tight fairways . . . Nice scenery . . . Very hilly, tough walking course . . . Forget your driver and brush up on your irons.

★½ SIX-S GOLF COURSE
WEST COURSE
PU—Transit Bridge Rd., Belfast (716)365-2201.
65 miles southeast of Buffalo. **Holes:** 18. **Par:** 72/72.
Yards: 6,210/4826. **Course rating:** 69.5/69.7. **Slope:** 120/115.

Opened: 1965. **Pace of Play rating:** 4:00. **Green fee:** $11/12.
Credit cards: MC, V, AMEX. **Reduced fees:** Weekdays, Twilight,
Seniors, Juniors.
Caddies: No. **Golf carts:** $8 for 18 holes.
Discount golf packages: No. **Season:** March-Nov. **High:** July-Aug.
On-site lodging: No. **Rental clubs:** No.
Walking policy: Unrestricted walking. **Range:** Yes.
To obtain tee times: First come, first served. Tee times required only for
tournaments.
New 18-hole, par-72 East course opened June 1995.
Subscriber comments: Staff very helpful . . . Incredibly busy . . . Well
maintained, long par 5s, great use of hills.

★★★ SMITHTOWN LANDING GOLF CLUB

PU—495 Landing Ave., Smithtown (516)360-7618.
35 miles east of New York. **Holes:** 18. **Par:** 72/72.
Yards: 6,114/5,263. **Course rating:** 70.9/69.8. **Slope:** 125/122.
Opened: 1961. **Pace of Play rating:** 5:00. **Green fee:** $15/23.
Credit cards: None. **Reduced fees:** Weekdays, Low season.
Caddies: No. **Golf carts:** $12 for 18 holes.
Discount golf packages: No. **Season:** Year-round. **High:** May-Sept.
On-site lodging: No. **Rental clubs:** No.
Walking policy: Unrestricted walking. **Range:** Yes.
To obtain tee times: Tee times taken weekends and holidays for residents
only.
Also has a 9-hole, par-3 course.
Subscriber comments: Huge greens, putter's delight . . . Great ninth hole
. . . Need every club in bag . . . Good condition . . . Best land use of
beautiful terrain . . . Long and hilly, fun finishing hole . . . Nice greens . . .
Well maintained greens could be better . . . Good service and staff . . . Well
protected greens, no water, challenging but enjoyable to all golfers . . .
Easy course . . . No distinguished holes . . . Conditions are fair . . .
Premium on shotmaking . . . Small greens and very scenic . . . Not very
long, but fun . . . Friendly people, but much too crowded.

★★★½ SOARING EAGLES GOLF CLUB

PU—201 Middle Rd., Horseheads (607)796-9350.
10 miles north of Elmira. **Holes:** 18. **Par:** 72/72.
Yards: 6,625/4,930. **Course rating:** 71.6/67.5. **Slope:** 117/108.
Opened: 1940. **Pace of Play rating:** 4:00-4:30. **Green fee:** $7/19.
Credit cards: None. **Reduced fees:** Twilight, Seniors, Juniors.
Caddies: No. **Golf carts:** $20 for 18 holes.
Discount golf packages: No. **Season:** April-Nov. **High:** June-Sept.
On-site lodging: No. **Rental clubs:** Yes.
Walking policy: Unrestricted walking. **Range:** Yes (grass).
To obtain tee times: Call one week in advance.
Subscriber comments: Right price, not over-crowded . . . Usually in
good shape . . . Easy to walk . . . Friendly pro shop . . . Most notable
feature is the large undulating greens . . . Favors long hitter, tough greens,
top-notch shape . . . Best course in area . . . Use every club in bag . . .
Very demanding par 3s.

★★★½ SPOOK ROCK GOLF COURSE

PU—233 Spook Rock Rd., Suffern (914)357-3085.
30 miles northwest of New York City. **Holes:** 18. **Par:** 72/72.
Yards: 6,894/4,953. **Course rating:** 73.3/70.9. **Slope:** 129/118.
Opened: 1970. **Pace of Play rating:** 4:30. **Green fee:** $30/40.
Credit cards: None. **Reduced fees:** Twilight.
Caddies: No. **Golf carts:** $24 for 18 holes.
Discount golf packages: No. **Season:** April-Nov. **High:** May-Sept.
On-site lodging: No. **Rental clubs:** Yes.
Walking policy: Unrestricted walking. **Range:** Yes.
To obtain tee times: Call Sunday after 6 p.m. for weekdays and Thursday
after 7 a.m. for weekend play.

Ranked in First 25 of America's 75 Best Public Golf Courses by Golf Digest.

Subscriber comments: Will be even better when reconstruction complete . . . Course is difficult for women, I am a 27 handicap and really have a hard time . . . . Fair service and pace . . . Good layout, but disappointed in ongoing construction . . . Good for beginners to mid-level players . . . Excellent golf course, but virtually impossible to get starting time . . . Championship layout with challenging holes . . . Mangagement should be congratulated on its maintenance program . . . Dynamite.

★½ SPRAIN LAKE GOLF CLUB
PU—290 Grassy Sprain Rd., Yonkers (914)779-9827.
Holes: 18. **Par:** 70/71.
Yards: 6,010/5,500. **Course rating:** 68.6/70.2. **Slope:** 114/115.
Opened: N/A. **Pace of Play rating:** 4:30. **Green fee:** $35/45.
Credit cards: None. **Reduced fees:** Weekdays, Twilight, Seniors, Juniors.
Caddies: No. **Golf carts:** $23 for 18 holes.
Discount golf packages: No. **Season:** April-Dec. **High:** June-Aug.
On-site lodging: No. **Rental clubs:** Yes.
Walking policy: Unrestricted walking. **Range:** No.
To obtain tee times: Call.
Subscriber comments: Geese problem (surrounds reservoir) getting better now that they have a dog to chase them away . . . Nice course, some very good holes . . . Greens bigger than infield at Yankee Stadium! . . . OK to play when everyplace else is booked up.

★★★ SPRING LAKE GOLF CLUB
PU—30 E. Bartlett Rd., Middle Island (516)924-5115.
45 miles east of New York City. **Holes:** 18. **Par:** 72/72.
Yards: 7,048/5,732. **Course rating:** 73.2/70.0. **Slope:** 128/120.
Opened: 1967. **Pace of Play rating:** 4:15. **Green fee:** $23/25.
Credit cards: None. **Reduced fees:** Weekdays, Twilight.
Caddies: No. **Golf carts:** $13 for 18 holes.
Discount golf packages: No. **Season:** Year-round. **High:** April-Oct.
On-site lodging: No. **Rental clubs:** Yes.
Walking policy: Walking at certain times. **Range:** Yes (grass).
To obtain tee times: Call.
Subscriber comments: Beautiful course, plays longer than card shows . . . Nice mix of holes, greens are fast . . . If you can draw ball you will score . . . Beautiful superbly kept grounds . . . Always mint condition . . . Long rough, long rounds . . . Enjoyable walking . . . Not a beginner's course . . . One of the best kept courses around . . . Long and difficult from back tees.

★★½ STONY FORD GOLF CLUB
PU—550 Rte. 416, Montgomery (914)457-1532.
70 miles north of New York City. **Holes:** 18. **Par:** 72/72.
Yards: 6,550/4,856. **Course rating:** 72.4/72.4. **Slope:** 128/128.
Opened: 1968. **Pace of Play rating:** N/A. **Green fee:** $10/28.
Credit cards: None. **Reduced fees:** Weekdays, Low season, Twilight, Seniors.
Caddies: No. **Golf carts:** $10 for 18 holes.
Discount golf packages: No. **Season:** April-Nov. **High:** May-Sept.
On-site lodging: No. **Rental clubs:** Yes.
Walking policy: Unrestricted walking. **Range:** Yes (grass).
To obtain tee times: Call five days in advance for weekdays or in person one week in advance. Call Wednesday for upcoming weekend after 12 noon or one week in advance if you come in person.
Subscriber comments: Very forgiving, not real difficult . . . Plenty of water and sand . . . Staff is great and so are the facilities . . . A level lie is hard to find . . . Not a course for beginners . . . The views from different elevations are beautiful . . . Better than average municipal course . . . Needs upgraded maintenance.

★★ SUNKEN MEADOW STATE PARK GOLF CLUB
BLUE/RED/GREEN
PU—Sunken Meadow State Park, Kings Park (516)269-3838.
40 miles east of New York City. **Holes:** 27. **Par:** 71/72/71.
Yards: 6,100/6,165/6,185. **Course rating:** 73.2/73.6/73.2.
Slope: 120/120/119.
Opened: 1964. **Pace of Play rating:** 5:00. **Green fee:** $9/11.
Credit cards: None. **Reduced fees:** Seniors.
Caddies: No. **Golf carts:** Not available.
Discount golf packages: No. **Season:** April-Nov. **High:** April-Sept.
On-site lodging: No. **Rental clubs:** Yes.
Walking policy: Unrestricted walking. **Range:** Yes (grass).
To obtain tee times: First come, first served.
Subscriber comments: On the easy side but a good value . . . Generally
very slow play, Blue Course most challenging . . . Can only sign up for
nine, must wait to sign again . . . Impossible to get in 18 holes . . . Strictly
nine holes . . . For beginners this course and value are exceptional . . . Good
for quick nine . . . Municipal nightmare . . . Three excellent well kept nines
. . . Everybody and their non-golfing buddies plays there . . . Excellent
condition for a heavily trafficked public course.

★★★ SWAN LAKE GOLF CLUB
PU—373 River Rd., Manorville (516)369-1818.
10 miles west of Riverhead. **Holes:** 18. **Par:** 72/72.
Yards: 7,011/5,245. **Course rating:** 72.5/69.0. **Slope:** 121/112.
Opened: 1979. **Pace of Play rating:** 4:30. **Green fee:** $25/27.
Credit cards: None. **Reduced fees:** Twilight.
Caddies: No. **Golf carts:** $26 for 18 holes.
Discount golf packages: No. **Season:** Year-round. **High:** April-Oct.
On-site lodging: No. **Rental clubs:** Yes.
Walking policy: Walking at certain times. **Range:** No.
To obtain tee times: Call up to one week in advance.
Subscriber comments: Pin placements on extra-large greens make club
selection difficult . . . Very little rough . . . Very forgiving course . . .
Country club setting . . . Always in great condition . . . Greens are too big!
. . . Great staff, good test, I wish I lived closer . . . Your "greens in
regulation" average should go up here . . . Well maintained but needs some
rough . . . Good "rest" stops . . . Lots of water but relatively wide open
. . . Challenging when the wind is up, but you can really score on still days
. . . Huge greens . . . Beautiful fairways . . . Wide open and always well
maintained year round . . . The home of the four-putt green! . . . No such
thing as rough . . . The par-3 16th hole is spectacular . . . Very playable for
high or low handicapper . . . Ornamental water . . . Easy and fun layout.

★ SYCAMORE GREENS GOLF COURSE
PU—Pangburn Rd., Duanesburg (518)355-6145.
Call club for further information.
Subscriber comments: OK for once-a-week golfer . . . Needs a lot of
work.

★★★½ TARRY BRAE GOLF CLUB
PU—Pleasant Valley Rd., So. Fallsburg (914)434-2620.
10 miles northeast of Monticello. **Holes:** 18. **Par:** 72/72.
Yards: 6,888/6,270. **Course rating:** 73.1/72.1. **Slope:** 128/123.
Opened: 1962. **Pace of Play rating:** 4:00. **Green fee:** $18/25.
Credit cards: None. **Reduced fees:** Weekdays, Low season, Twilight.
Caddies: No. **Golf carts:** $12 for 18 holes.
Discount golf packages: No. **Season:** April-Nov. **High:** June-Sept.
On-site lodging: No. **Rental clubs:** Yes.
Walking policy: Walking at certain times. **Range:** Yes (grass).
To obtain tee times: Call the Wednesday piro to weekend.
Subscriber comments: Good mountain golf, too tough to walk on warm

GREAT VALUE

day . . . Well worth discovering . . . Love the course, clubhouse a bit small, beautiful holes . . . Very hilly, must keep ball on fairway, rough is deep . . . One of my favorites. The kind of course you never tire of . . . Take a cart if you're not in shape . . . Great muny in the Catskills.

★★★ TENNANAH LAKE GOLF & TENNIS CLUB

R—P.O. Box 487 - Hankins Rd., Roscoe (607)498-5502.
60 miles north of Middletown. **Holes:** 18. **Par:** 72/74.
Yards: 6,769/5,797. **Course rating:** 71.2/72.5. **Slope:** 121/115.
Opened: 1904. **Pace of Play rating:** 4:00–4:30. **Green fee:** $20/26.
Credit cards: MC, V, AMEX. **Reduced fees:** Weekdays, Resort guests, Twilight, Seniors, Juniors.
Caddies: No. **Golf carts:** $26 for 18 holes.
Discount golf packages: Yes. **Season:** May-Oct. **High:** June-Aug.
On-site lodging: Yes. **Rental clubs:** Yes.
Walking policy: Walking at certain times. **Range:** No.
To obtain tee times: Open book policy: Call starting May 1st for time anytime through the season.
Subscriber comments: Hilly, very small greens, very scenic . . . Eight or nine breathtaking holes, the rest are plain and too long . . . Walk on, no wait, great pace, well maintained, excellent golf at all levels of play.

★★★ TERRY HILLS GOLF COURSE

PU—5122 Clinton St. Rd., Batavia (716)343-0860, (800)825-8633.
30 miles east of Buffalo. **Holes:** 18. **Par:** 72/72.
Yards: 6,072/5,107. **Course rating:** 68.7/68.0. **Slope:** 108/102.
Opened: 1930. **Pace of Play rating:** 4:25. **Green fee:** $15/19.
Credit cards: MC, V. **Reduced fees:** Low season, Twilight, Seniors.
Caddies: No. **Golf carts:** $10 for 18 holes.
Discount golf packages: Yes. **Season:** March-Nov. **High:** June-Aug.
On-site lodging: No. **Rental clubs:** Yes.
Walking policy: Walking at certain times. **Range:** Yes (grass).
To obtain tee times: Call up to one week in advance.
Subscriber comments: Finesse course, few holes require long drives . . . Hilly, some water, tight fairways . . . Front nine long par 5s and small greens on back . . . Great confidence building course . . . Lots of variety in hole length and design . . . Chance to create a lot of shots . . . A nice challenge especially for women golfers . . . Challenges you with everything . . . Back nine has nice water holes . . . True greens hold shots . . . Breaks are true . . . Friendly, pleasant, efficient staff . . . Over use of trees . . . Course in nice condition all year . . . Enjoyable for average and higher handicapped players.

★★★½ THENDARA GOLF CLUB

SP—Rte. 28, Thendara (315)369-3136.
55 miles north of Utica. **Holes:** 18. **Par:** 72/73.
Yards: 6,435/5,757. **Course rating:** 70.2/72.8. **Slope:** 124/121.
Opened: 1921. **Pace of Play rating:** 4:00. **Green fee:** $20.
Credit cards: None. **Reduced fees:** Twilight.
Caddies: No. **Golf carts:** N/A.
Discount golf packages: No. **Season:** May-Oct. **High:** July-Sept.
On-site lodging: No. **Rental clubs:** Yes.
Walking policy: Walking at certain times. **Range:** Yes (grass).
To obtain tee times: Members call one week in advance. Non-members may call one day in advance. Certain tee times are reserved for members on weekends.
Subscriber comments: A little jewel on the mountains . . . Great course, short but tough, hilly and wooded, great greens, huge horrible flies . . . Tight back nine, follows along river, beautiful in fall . . . Very unusual holes, a test for better golfers . . . Beware of bears! Donald Ross did original back nine, a lot of fun in a peaceful setting . . . Gorgeous anytime of year, bring your spikes: it's a climb . . . Front and back like two different courses . . . Ninth green is impossible.

★★★ THOMAS CARVEL COUNTRY CLUB

PU—Ferris Rd, Pine Plains (518)398-7101.

30 miles northeast of Paughkeepsie. **Holes:** 18. **Par:** 73/75.
Yards: 7,025/5,066. **Course rating:** 73.5/69.0. **Slope:** 127/115.
Opened: 1962. **Pace of Play rating:** 4:30. **Green fee:** $32/37.
Credit cards: MC, V. **Reduced fees:** Weekdays, Low season, Twilight,
Seniors.
Caddies: No. **Golf carts:** Included in Green Fee.
Discount golf packages: Yes. **Season:** April-Nov. **High:** May-Sept.
On-site lodging: No. **Rental clubs:** Yes.
Walking policy: Mandatory cart. **Range:** Yes (grass).
To obtain tee times: Call up to seven days in advance.
Subscriber comments: Excellent greens, worth the speeding ticket . . .
Good conditions all season, friendly staff, fast pace . . . Great 19th hole . . .
Needs a "Fudgie the Whale" shaped green . . . Very hilly, excellent service,
but a great challenge for better golfers . . . Really improved, greens real
slick . . . Course in good shape . . . Greens fast even in rain . . . You start
off in a valley and all the rest of the holes are up in the hills . . . Great fall
course . . . Impossible to walk . . . Worth an hour and a half drive to get
there . . . Not for short hitters . . . Challenging for all levels of play,
murder the first time.

★★ THOUSAND ISLANDS GOLF CLUB

R—County Rd. No.100 Wellesley Island East, Wellesley Island (315)482-
9454.

35 miles north of Watertown. **Holes:** 18. **Par:** 72/74.
Yards: 6,302/5,240. **Course rating:** 69.2/68.5. **Slope:** 118/114.
Opened: 1894. **Pace of Play rating:** 4:00. **Green fee:** $22/24.
Credit cards: MC, V, AMEX. **Reduced fees:** Weekdays, Low season,
Resort guests, Twilight, Juniors.
Caddies: No. **Golf carts:** $22 for 18 holes.
Discount golf packages: Yes. **Season:** April-Nov. **High:** June-Sept.
On-site lodging: Yes. **Rental clubs:** Yes.
Walking policy: Walking at certain times. **Range:** Yes (grass).
To obtain tee times: Call. No restrictions.
Subscriber comments: Old course, short, nice setting on river . . .
Course needs work . . . Great food and staff courteous . . . Just a fun resort
course . . . Great signature holes.

TIMBER POINT GOLF COURSE
★½ RED/WHITE/BLUE

PU—Great River Rd., Great River (516)581-2401.

50 miles east of New York City. **Holes:** 27. **Par:** 72/72/72.
Yards: 6,642/6,525/6,441. **Course rating:** 72.9/71.9/70.6.
Slope: 121/116/116.
Opened: 1927. **Pace of Play rating:** 5:00. **Green fee:** $19/31.
Credit cards: None. **Reduced fees:** Weekdays, Low season, Twilight,
Seniors, Juniors.
Caddies: No. **Golf carts:** $24 for 18 holes.
Discount golf packages: No. **Season:** Year-round. **High:** June-Aug.
On-site lodging: No. **Rental clubs:** Yes.
Walking policy: Unrestricted walking. **Range:** Yes.
To obtain tee times: Residents with green key card may call seven days in
advance.
Subscriber comments: White is an after-thought ; the Red nine is great ;
Blue has some nice holes . . . Beautiful holes along Great South Bay . . . A
links-style course, I liked it better when it was 18 holes . . . Good layout,
gets a lot of play but still decent condition . . . Drainage problem on bayside holes . . . On a windy day, which is frequent, it presents a real
challenge . . . A good course to learn to play in the wind . . . Skip the
White nine . . . Must be accurate . . . Some good holes, the original 18 was
great . . . Family of osprey watch your shots.

★★★ TOWN OF WALLKILL GOLF CLUB
PU—40 Sands Rd., Middletown (914)361-1022.
55 miles northwest of New York City. **Holes:** 18. **Par:** 72/72.
Yards: 6,437/5,171. **Course rating:** N/A. **Slope:** 128/122.
Opened: N/A. **Pace of Play rating:** 4:30. **Green fee:** $22/31.
Credit cards: None. **Reduced fees:** Weekdays, Twilight, Seniors.
Caddies: No. **Golf carts:** $12 for 18 holes.
Discount golf packages: No. **Season:** April-Nov. **High:** June-Aug.
On-site lodging: No. **Rental clubs:** Yes.
Walking policy: Unrestricted walking. **Range:** Yes (grass).
To obtain tee times: Call Saturdays for following week.
Subscriber comments: Short, but fun . . . Tightly lined fairways, target-type golf . . . The facilities are great and so is the staff . . . It is a great English-style course . . . A lot of doglegs, play from the tips . . . Blind tee shots everywhere . . . Irons off many tees . . . Best new muny area . . . Young greens won't hold approach shots . . . Blind tee shots on four holes . . . Beautiful and tough, well maintained.

★★★½ TRI COUNTY COUNTRY CLUB
SP—Rt. 39, Forestville (716)965-9723.
50 miles south of Buffalo. **Holes:** 18. **Par:** 71/72.
Yards: 6,639/5,574. **Course rating:** 70.9/71.0. **Slope:** 118/113.
Opened: 1924. **Pace of Play rating:** 4:10. **Green fee:** $20/22.
Credit cards: MC, V. **Reduced fees:** Weekdays.
Caddies: No. **Golf carts:** $22 for 18 holes.
Discount golf packages: Yes. **Season:** April-Oct. **High:** July-Aug.
On-site lodging: No. **Rental clubs:** No.
Walking policy: Unrestricted walking. **Range:** Yes (grass).
To obtain tee times: Call pro shop.
Subscriber comments: Tricky greens . . . Two different front nines . . . Front short and tight . . . Back long and wide open, few traps . . . You need to hit the ball straight and long . . . Very walkable, polite staff, remote location.

★★½ VALLEY VIEW GOLF CLUB
PU—620 Memorial Pkwy., Utica (315)732-8755.
Holes: 18. **Par:** 71/73.
Yards: 6,583/5,942. **Course rating:** 69.2/72.6. **Slope:** 118/116.
Opened: 1936. **Pace of Play rating:** 4:30. **Green fee:** $11/14.
Credit cards: None. **Reduced fees:** Twilight.
Caddies: No. **Golf carts:** $10 for 18 holes.
Discount golf packages: No. **Season:** April-Nov. **High:** April-Aug.
On-site lodging: No. **Rental clubs:** Yes.
Walking policy: Unrestricted walking. **Range:** No.
To obtain tee times: First come, first served.
Subscriber comments: Wide open . . . A little hilly . . . Very busy city course with excellent design . . . Conditions hurt by use . . . Average player's course.

★½ VAN CORTLANDT GOLF CLUB
PU—Van Cortlandt Park S. and Bailey Ave., Bronx (718)543-4595.
5 miles north of New York. **Holes:** 18. **Par:** 70/70.
Yards: 6,122/5,421. **Course rating:** 68.9/73.0. **Slope:** 112/120.
Opened: 1895. **Pace of Play rating:** 4:00. **Green fee:** $19/21.
Credit cards: MC, V. **Reduced fees:** Twilight, Seniors, Juniors.
Caddies: No. **Golf carts:** $23 for 18 holes.
Discount golf packages: Yes. **Season:** March-Dec. **High:** April-Oct.
On-site lodging: No. **Rental clubs:** Yes.
Walking policy: Unrestricted walking. **Range:** No.
To obtain tee times: Call 10 days in advance. Prepay with credit card.
Subscriber comments: One of the oldest public courses in America . . . Lots of walking between holes . . . 18 beautiful holes, the last four of which are steep hills in contrast to rolling terrain of the first 14 . . . Play is fast,

rarely crowded, only disadvantage is that the first hole is a half-mile from the clubhouse! . . . Only choice for city dwellers without friends at Winged Foot . . . Take a cart, green to tee can be ten minute walk . . . Great access via subway from Columbia University.

★★½ VICTOR HILLS GOLF CLUB
PU—1460 Brace Rd., Victor (716)924-3480.
Call club for further information.
Subscriber comments: Thirty-six holes (plus a 9 hole executive course) to choose from, always fun to play . . . Don't let "farmer's field" looks fool you, there is good golf to be played here . . . North Course very hilly . . . Thirty-six holes of very interesting and challenging terrain . . . Greens and fairways in very good shape for a public course . . . Blind second shot on many holes . . . Four nines give a lot of variety . . . Beginner golfers everywhere.

★★★½ VILLA ROMA COUNTRY CLUB
SP—Villa Roma Rd., Callicoon (914)887-5097, (800)727-8455.
100 miles north of New York City. **Holes:** 18. **Par:** 71/72.
Yards: 6,231/4,791. **Course rating:** 70.6/68.3. **Slope:** 125/117.
Opened: 1987. **Pace of Play rating:** 4:00. **Green fee:** $35/48.
Credit cards: All major. **Reduced fees:** Weekdays, Resort guests, Twilight, Seniors.
Caddies: No. **Golf carts:** Included in Green Fee.
Discount golf packages: Yes. **Season:** April-Nov. **High:** May-Sept.
On-site lodging: Yes. **Rental clubs:** Yes.
Walking policy: Mandatory cart. **Range:** Yes (grass).
To obtain tee times: Call pro shop.
Subscriber comments: Beautiful views well worth finding . . . Hilly, scenic, plush, big greens, well maintained . . . Everything does run to the valley . . . Out of the way but worth trip . . . Half the course seems links-like, half seems like target golf, like two different designs . . . The course isn't very long but you must think about good placement of shots for best angles to very hard-to-read greens . . . This course is suited for all types of players, from resort beginners to professionals . . . The staff here is exceptional . . . Hard to get on if you're not staying at the resort . . . Beautiful mountain layout . . . Greens almost unfair . . . Shotmaker's course . . . Challenging layout . . . Good greens.

★★★ WATERTOWN GOLF CLUB
SP—Watertown (315)782-4040.
70 miles south of Syracuse. **Holes:** 18. **Par:** 72/73.
Yards: 6,309/5,492. **Course rating:** 69.4/67.9. **Slope:** 113/114.
Opened: 1926. **Pace of Play rating:** 4:00. **Green fee:** $20.
Credit cards: None. **Reduced fees:** Twilight.
Caddies: No. **Golf carts:** $9 for 18 holes.
Discount golf packages: Yes. **Season:** April-Oct. **High:** June-Aug.
On-site lodging: No. **Rental clubs:** Yes.
Walking policy: Unrestricted walking. **Range:** Yes (grass).
To obtain tee times: Call Wednesday for upcoming weekend and call Friday for next Tuesday and Wednesday.
Subscriber comments: Outstanding condition . . . A shotmaker's course . . . Staff friendly and accommodating.

★★★★ WAYNE HILLS COUNTRY CLUB
SP—2250 Gannett Rd., Lyons (315)946-6944.
30 miles east of Rochester. **Holes:** 18. **Par:** 72/73.
Yards: 6,854/5,556. **Course rating:** 72.8/72.0. **Slope:** 125/116.
Opened: 1959. **Pace of Play rating:** 4:00. **Green fee:** $33.
Credit cards: None. **Reduced fees:** .
Caddies: No. **Golf carts:** $11 for 18 holes.
Discount golf packages: No. **Season:** April-Nov. **High:** May-Sept.
On-site lodging: No. **Rental clubs:** No.
Walking policy: Mandatory cart. **Range:** Yes (grass).

To obtain tee times: Call three days in advance after 3 p.m.
Subscriber comments: Tree-lined fairways, great greens, very tough course, always well kept . . . From back tees a real golfing challenge . . . Course speaks for itself . . . A diamond in the rough, worth the money, don't miss . . . A real sleeper, great layout, good condition . . . Suitable for all levels of golfer.

WEBSTER GOLF CLUB
PU—440 Salt Rd., Webster (716)265-1920.
Call club for further information.

★★★ EAST COURSE
Subscriber comments: Some long holes, good use of limited space . . . From the back it is a pretty good challenge . . . Wide open, short, fun course, beginner's heaven . . . Good layout and distance for all levels . . . Fantastic shape year-round.

★½ WEST COURSE
Subscriber comments: Watch out for wild shots from adjoining holes . . . Nice older layout, mature trees . . . Good for novice, no sand . . . Nice fairly easy course to start your season with . . . Relatively flat, easy to walk . . . Preferred by average golfers and seniors.

★★½ WEST SAYVILLE GOLF CLUB
PU—Montauk Hwy., West Sayville (516)567-1704.
45 miles east of New York. **Holes:** 18. **Par:** 72/72.
Yards: 6,715/5,387. **Course rating:** 72.5/71.2. **Slope:** 124/119.
Opened: 1968. **Pace of Play rating:** N/A. **Green fee:** $18/ 18.
Credit cards: DISC. **Reduced fees:** Weekdays, Low season, Twilight, Seniors, Juniors.
Caddies: No. **Golf carts:** $12 for 18 holes.
Discount golf packages: No. **Season:** Year-round. **High:** May-Sept.
On-site lodging: No. **Rental clubs:** Yes.
Walking policy: Unrestricted walking. **Range:** Yes (grass).
To obtain tee times: Must be resident of Suffolk and purchase green key reservations card.
Subscriber comments: Great pro staff . . . True test even for scratch golfers . . . Layout makes golf a contact sport . . . Take "fore" seriously . . . Flat with tricky hazards . . . Can hit green from just about any fairway . . . Great, even in the rain.

★★★ WESTPORT COUNTRY CLUB
PU—Liberty St., Westport (518)962-4470.
Call club for further information.
Subscriber comments: Good course for high handicappers, wide fairways, however wind is a factor on most days . . . A wonderful old course. Good original back nine . . . Needs trees on front . . . Great scenery in a nice town with friendly people.

★★★ WHITEFACE INN RESORT GOLF CLUB
R—P.O. Box 231, Lake Placid (518)523-2551.
150 miles north of Albany. **Holes:** 18. **Par:** 72/74.
Yards: 6,490/5,635. **Course rating:** 70.6/73.9. **Slope:** 123/113.
Opened: 1900. **Pace of Play rating:** 4:00. **Green fee:** $20/29.
Credit cards: All major. **Reduced fees:** Weekdays, Low season, Resort guests, Twilight, Juniors.
Caddies: No. **Golf carts:** $24 for 18 holes.
Discount golf packages: Yes. **Season:** May-Oct. **High:** July-Aug.
On-site lodging: Yes. **Rental clubs:** Yes.
Walking policy: Unrestricted walking. **Range:** Yes (grass).
To obtain tee times: Call any time.
Subscriber comments: Beautiful views, good mountain golf . . . Narrow . . . Fairways narrow, walk single file . . . Incredible views, courteous staff . . . Suitable for most all golfers . . . Numerous doglegs with very challenging greens.

★★½ WILD WOOD COUNTRY CLUB

SP—1201 West Rush Rd., Rush (716)334-5860.
25 miles south of Rochester. **Holes:** 18. **Par:** 71/72.
Yards: 6,431/5,368. **Course rating:** 70.2/70.1. **Slope:** 120/116.
Opened: 1968. **Pace of Play rating:** 4:30. **Green fee:** $18/20.
Credit cards: MC, V. **Reduced fees:** Low season, Seniors.
Caddies: No. **Golf carts:** $20 for 18 holes.
Discount golf packages: Yes. **Season:** April-Oct. **High:** July-Aug.
On-site lodging: No. **Rental clubs:** Yes.
Walking policy: Unrestricted walking. **Range:** Yes (grass).
To obtain tee times: Call pro shop.
Subscriber comments: Scenic layout, water on nine holes, very tight, lots
of trees . . . Wet in spring . . . Improving yearly. Terrific back nine . . .
Target golf in a great setting . . . Staff friendly, service good.

★★★ WILLOWBROOK COUNTRY CLUB

PU—4200 Lake Ave., Lockport (716)434-0111.
25 miles north of Buffalo. **Holes:** 18. **Par:** 71/71.
Yards: 6,018/5,713. **Course rating:** 68.9/67.7. **Slope:** 112/112.
Opened: 1956. **Pace of Play rating:** 4:00. **Green fee:** $13/18.
Credit cards: MC, V. **Reduced fees:** Weekdays, Low season, Twilight,
Seniors.
Caddies: No. **Golf carts:** $9 for 18 holes.
Discount golf packages: Yes. **Season:** April-Nov. **High:** June-Aug.
On-site lodging: No. **Rental clubs:** Yes.
Walking policy: Unrestricted walking. **Range:** Yes (grass).
To obtain tee times: Call one week in advance.
Subscriber comments: Front nine too easy, back nine ridiculously hard
. . . Short but challenging . . . Pace sometimes slow . . . Maintenance
works constantly to improve the course . . . Short, somewhat hilly, fast
greens, fairways cut very short, well conditioned . . . Fun to play all year
. . . Sharp doglegs . . . Club selection important . . . These greens will have
you talking to yourself.

★★★½ WINDHAM COUNTRY CLUB

PU—South St., Windham (518)734-9910.
Call club for further information.
Subscriber comments: Nicely maintained with beautiful scenery . . .
Looks easy, be careful . . . Good variety . . . Greens best in area.

★★ WINGED PHEASANT GOLF LINKS

SP—1433 Sand Hill Rd., Shortsville (716)289-8846.
20 miles southeast of Rochester. **Holes:** 18. **Par:** 70/72.
Yards: 6,400/5,835. **Course rating:** 69.0/72.0. **Slope:** 118/119.
Opened: 1963. **Pace of Play rating:** 4:30. **Green fee:** $18/20.
Credit cards: MC, V, AMEX. **Reduced fees:** Weekdays, Low season,
Resort guests, Twilight, Seniors, Juniors.
Caddies: Yes. **Golf carts:** $20 for 18 holes.
Discount golf packages: No. **Season:** March-Nov. **High:** June-Aug.
On-site lodging: No. **Rental clubs:** Yes.
Walking policy: Walking at certain times. **Range:** Yes (grass).
To obtain tee times: Call seven days in advance.
Subscriber comments: Small greens, very well kept, friendly staff, a few
rough spots . . . Good short, beginner's course . . . Tough par 3s on back
. . . Sneaky tough, nice greens with subtle breaks . . . Plenty of challenge
for all levels . . . Diamond in the rough.

★★★★ BALD HEAD ISLAND CLUB

R—P.O. Box 3070, Bald Head Island (910)457-7310, (800)234-1666.
30 miles south of Wilmington. Holes: 18. **Par:** 72/72.
Yards: 6,855/4,810. **Course rating:** 74.2/69.5. **Slope:** 143/121.
Opened: 1975. **Pace of Play rating:** 4:00. **Green fee:** $36/45.
Credit cards: MC, V, AMEX. **Reduced fees:** Low season, Resort guests, Juniors.
Caddies: No. **Golf carts:** $12 for 18 holes.
Discount golf packages: Yes. **Season:** Year-round. **High:** March-Nov.
On-site lodging: Yes. **Rental clubs:** Yes.
Walking policy: Unrestricted walking. **Range:** Yes (grass).
To obtain tee times: Call pro shop seven days in advance.
Subscriber comments: Beautiful, wonderful track . . . Boat ride to island is great . . . Very picturesque and lots of bird wildlife . . . Beautifully conditioned course . . . All golfers can enjoy this one . . . Very pleasant staff, fees are typical of resort course . . . Superb atmosphere, service. Watch out for gators . . . George Cobb design, a departure from the ordinary. Watch out for mosquitos . . . Super test, great location, will test you as a wind player . . . Fun and fair . . . Last three holes very challenging . . . Well groomed, most holes lined with trouble, accuracy needed . . . Best kept secret in North Carolina.

★★½ BEACON RIDGE GOLF AND COUNTRY CLUB

R—6000 Longleaf Dr., West End (910)673-2950, (800)416-5204.
65 miles northwest of Greensboro. Holes: 18. **Par:** 36/36.
Yards: 3,128/2,349. **Course rating:** 70.7/67.1. **Slope:** 125/115.
Opened: 1988. **Pace of Play rating:** 4:00. **Green fee:** $20/36.
Credit cards: MC, V. **Reduced fees:** Weekdays, Low season, Resort guests, Twilight, Seniors, Juniors.
Caddies: No. **Golf carts:** $16 for 18 holes.
Discount golf packages: Yes. **Season:** Year-round. **High:** Spring/Fall.
On-site lodging: Yes. **Rental clubs:** Yes.
Walking policy: Walking at certain times. **Range:** Yes (grass).
To obtain tee times: Call anytime.
Subscriber comments: Fair course, not too hard . . . Needs improved cart paths, too dusty . . . Nice holes . . . Pretty, rolling course, challenging, good condition . . . Beautiful pines . . . This course is for straight line hitters . . . Three tough finishing holes . . . Spotty, not always in condition . . . Fun course to play.

★★½ BEAU RIVAGE PLANTATION COUNTRY CLUB

SP—6230 Carolina Beach Rd., Wilmington (910)392-9022, (800)628-7080.
Holes: 18. **Par:** 72/72.
Yards: 6,709/4,612. **Course rating:** 72.5/69.0. **Slope:** 136/114.
Opened: 1986. **Pace of Play rating:** 4:30-5:00. **Green fee:** $30/49.
Credit cards: All major. **Reduced fees:** Low season, Resort guests, Twilight, Seniors.
Caddies: No. **Golf carts:** Included in Green Fee.
Discount golf packages: Yes. **Season:** Year-round. **High:** March-Sept.
On-site lodging: Yes. **Rental clubs:** Yes.
Walking policy: Mandatory cart. **Range:** Yes (grass).
To obtain tee times: Call pro shop between 7 a.m. and 7 p.m.
Subscriber comments: Hilly course for the coast . . . Have to play more than once to enjoy . . . Local knowledge mandatory . . . Too many blind shots . . . Long distance between holes . . . Can get lost going from 9th green to 10th tee . . . Fun and fair . . . This is a good course but doesn't really test the better players' shotmaking . . . Some holes tricked up but generally challenging . . . My favorite beach course . . . Short but fun . . . Fine service, never a crowd . . . Great challenge, relaxed atmosphere.

★ BEL AIRE GOLF CLUB

PU—1517 Pleasant Ridge Rd., Greensboro (910)668-2413.
Call club for further information.
Subscriber comments: Great beginners golf course . . . Uninteresting

front nine . . . Good twilight rates . . . Hilly, open with close parallel fairways . . . Airport is your next door neighbor . . . Domed greens tough to hold . . . Wide open, par 5s are all reachable . . . Heavily played due to location, usually only in fair condition . . . Front nine hackers' delight . . . Wide open . . . Back nine is a fair challenge.

BELVEDERE PLANTATION GOLF AND COUNTRY CLUB★

SP—2368 Country Club Dr., Hampstead (910)270-2703.
15 miles north of Wilmington. **Holes:** 18. **Par:** 71/72.
Yards: 6,401/4,992. **Course rating:** 71.2/68.5. **Slope:** 128/113.
Opened: 1970. **Pace of Play rating:** 4:15. **Green fee:** $ 20/40.
Credit cards: MC, V. **Reduced fees:** Low season, Resort guests.
Caddies: No. **Golf carts:** Included in Green Fee.
Discount golf packages: Yes. **Season:** Year-round. **High:** March-May.
On-site lodging: Yes. **Rental clubs:** Yes.
Walking policy: Mandatory cart. **Range:** Yes (grass).
To obtain tee times: Call one week in advance.

★★ BLACK MOUNTAIN GOLF COURSE

PU—106 Montreat Rd., Black Mtn. (704)669-2710.
15 miles north of Asheville. **Holes:** 18. **Par:** 71/71.
Yards: 6,181/5,780.
Call club for further information.
Subscriber comments: Mountain course . . . Average course, nothing spectacular . . . Fun, different type of course, has par 6 . . . Interesting par 6, tight in places . . . One unique hole, a 747-yard par 6 . . . Remarkable . . . Real fun, staff helpful . . . Scenic, tight mountain course.

★½ BLAIR PARK GOLF CLUB

PU—1901 S. Main St., High Point (910)883-3497.
18 miles west of Greensboro. **Holes:** 18. **Par:** 72/72.
Yards: 6,449/5,171. **Course rating:** 69.4/67.3. **Slope:** 111/107.
Opened: 1936. **Pace of Play rating:** 4:30. **Green fee:** $10/12.
Credit cards: None. **Reduced fees:** Twilight, Seniors, Juniors.
Caddies: No. **Golf carts:** $9 for 18 holes.
Discount golf packages: No. **Season:** Year-round. **High:** June-Aug.
On-site lodging: No. **Rental clubs:** Yes.
Walking policy: Walking at certain times. **Range:** No.
To obtain tee times: Call one week in advance.
Subscriber comments: Hacker's paradise . . . Short, has several interesting holes . . . Not memorable . . . Muny course . . . Power lines through course . . . Few bunkers . . . Borders very good . . . Front nine is low and stays wet . . . Challenging par 3s . . . Not accommodating to women . . . Easy course.

★★ BOGUE BANKS COUNTRY CLUB

SP—152 Oak Leaf Dr. Rte. 3, Pine Knoll Shores (919)726-1034.
Call club for further information.
Subscriber comments: Short, exciting, gorgeous scenery, hidden gem . . . Lots of water, no sand traps . . . Oceanside course . . . Very tight course . . . Not long course, but no room for error . . . Short but very enjoyable layout, it has a links feel to it . . . Nice little seaside course . . . Short course, player who hits straight can score well . . . Play lots of irons on tee shots . . . Beautiful view.

★★★ BOONE GOLF CLUB

PU—Fairway Dr., Boone (704)264-8760.
90 miles west of Winston Salem. **Holes:** 18. **Par:** 71/75.
Yards: 6,401/5,172. **Course rating:** 70.1/69.1. **Slope:** 120/113.
Opened: 1958. **Pace of Play rating:** 4:00. **Green fee:** $25/35.
Credit cards: MC, V. **Reduced fees:** Weekdays, Low season, Twilight.
Caddies: No. **Golf carts:** $10 for 18 holes.
Discount golf packages: Yes. **Season:** April-Nov. **High:** June-Aug.
On-site lodging: No. **Rental clubs:** Yes.

Walking policy: Walking at certain times. **Range:** No.
To obtain tee times: Call one week in advance.
Subscriber comments: Superb Ellis Maples design . . . Nothing fancy here . . . Relatively flat for mountain course . . . A lot of fun, well kept, nice staff . . . Nice views . . . Very nice layout, wide open for the most part . . . Short and easy to score . . . Beautiful setting . . . Pleasure just to be there . . . Interesting and challenging . . . Medium length . . . Slick undulating greens . . . Large greens . . . Front nine flat for mountains, nice fall retreat . . . Great public course, not as hilly as you might expect . . . Where my golf addiction began.

★★½ BRANDYWINE BAY GOLF AND COUNTRY CLUB

SP—Hwy. 70 W., Rte. 2, Morehead City (919)247-2541.
Holes: 18. **Par:** 71/71.
Yards: 6,609/5,191. **Course rating:** 72.2/68.5. **Slope:** 119/119.
Opened: 1980. **Pace of Play rating:** 4:30. **Green fee:** $10/20.
Credit cards: None. **Reduced fees:** Low season, Twilight.
Caddies: No. **Golf carts:** $15 for 18 holes.
Discount golf packages: Yes. **Season:** Year-round. **High:** March-Oct.
On-site lodging: No. **Rental clubs:** No.
Walking policy: Walking at certain times. **Range:** Yes (grass).
To obtain tee times: Call anytime.
Subscriber comments: A tight, fun golf course . . . Good design with some beautiful holes . . . Extremely tight course . . . Miss it and you're O.B. . . . Not recommended after rain . . . Deceiving water on course . . . Challenging all year . . . 18 holes fit into a small area . . . Too much hardpan sand . . . Holds lots of water in fairways . . . Best course in the area by far.

★★ BRICK LANDING PLANTATION

R—1900 Goose Creek Rd., Ocean Isle Beach (910)754-5545, (800)438-3006.
15 miles north of N. Myrtle Beach, SC. **Holes:** 18. **Par:** 72/71.
Yards: 6,752/4,707. **Course rating:** 72.1/67.0. **Slope:** 141/116.
Opened: 1988. **Pace of Play rating:** 4:20. **Green fee:** $31/61.
Credit cards: MC, V. **Reduced fees:** Twilight, Juniors.
Caddies: No. **Golf carts:** Included in Green Fee.
Discount golf packages: Yes. **Season:** Year-round. **High:** March-April/Oct.
On-site lodging: Yes. **Rental clubs:** Yes.
Walking policy: Mandatory cart. **Range:** Yes (grass).
To obtain tee times: Call pro shop.
Subscriber comments: A true target golf course . . . Bring a dozen golf balls . . . If you like target golf, this is a must. Plenty of water hazards, must be aware of hazards and place shots accordingly . . . Good for any handicap, course management necessary . . . Beautiful, sporty, unusual . . . Par 3s too short . . . One par 3 is under 100 yards, very congested . . . First four holes an adventure, after that good solid holes . . . Shotmaker's delight, water on 16 holes; wore out my four wood off tee . . . Must play from back tees . . . Very enjoyable golf, but I like to hit my driver more . . . Tight holes on marshland holes . . . Too punishing for slightly offline shots . . . I bet you will never play all 18 with one ball!

★★½ BRIERWOOD GOLF CLUB

SP—Hwy. 179, Shallotte (910)754-4660.
25 miles southwest of Wilmington. **Holes:** 18. **Par:** 72/72.
Yards: 6,607/4,812. **Course rating:** 71.0/67.0. **Slope:** 129/114.
Opened: 1966. **Pace of Play rating:** 4:25. **Green fee:** $15/38.
Credit cards: MC, V. **Reduced fees:** Weekdays, Low season, Twilight, Seniors.
Caddies: No. **Golf carts:** Included in Green Fee.
Discount golf packages: Yes. **Season:** Year-round. **High:** April-Oct.
On-site lodging: No. **Rental clubs:** Yes.
Walking policy: Walking at certain times. **Range:** No.
To obtain tee times: Call pro shop.

Subscriber comments: Lots of water, slicers nightmare . . . Bad tees . . . Short course . . . Ideal for seniors and women . . . No practice area . . . Just wasn't impressed with the layout . . . Attentive staff, real enjoyable golf . . . Staff very loose . . . Small, hard Bermuda greens . . . Far better than one would expect.

★★★ BRUNSWICK PLANTATION GOLF LINKS
R—Hwy. 17 N., Calabash (910)287-7888, (800)848-0290.
25 miles north of Myrtle Beach, SC. **Holes:** 18. **Par:** 72/72.
Yards: 6,779/5,210. **Course rating:** 72.7/70.4. **Slope:** 131/115.
Opened: 1992. **Pace of Play rating:** 4:30. **Green fee:** $25/45.
Credit cards: MC, V. **Reduced fees:** No.
Caddies: No. **Golf carts:** Included in Green Fee.
Discount golf packages: Yes. **Season:** Year-round. **High:** March-April/Oct.
On-site lodging: Yes. **Rental clubs:** Yes.
Walking policy: Mandatory cart. **Range:** Yes (grass).
To obtain tee times: Obtain tee times through Myrtle Beach packages or call direct.
Subscriber comments: Beautiful Willard Byrd layout, a sleeper, must play . . . Super greens . . . Lovely laid-out holes, not too tough . . . Friendly staff, enjoyable round . . . Suited for any player . . . Beautiful but difficult undulating greens, medium length course . . . Good greens, generous landing areas . . . Lots of fairway bunkers, better be down the middle . . . Little O.B. . . . Challenge for all handicaps . . . Great, quick greens . . . No two holes the same . . . Interesting blend of holes . . . A little more forgiving test than the marsh–type courses.

★★½ BRUSHY MOUNTAIN GOLF CLUB
PU—P.O. Box 457, Taylorsville (704)632-4804.
Call club for further information.
Subscriber comments: Good public course, play there often . . . Was playable . . . Needs better care of traps . . . Short but challenging, average maintainance . . . Slick rolling greens in summer . . . One of the nicest courses in the area . . . Wonderful country course, you'll use every club.

BRYAN PARK AND GOLF CLUB
PU—6275 Bryan Park Rd., Brown Summit (910)375-2200.
10 miles northeast of Greensboro. **Green fee:** $15/30.
Credit cards: MC, V, AMEX. **Reduced fees:** Low season, Twilight, Seniors, Juniors.
Caddies: No. **Golf carts:** $10 for 18 holes.
Discount golf packages: Yes. **Season:** Year-round. **High:** April-Sept.
On-site lodging: No. **Rental clubs:** Yes.
Walking policy: Walking at certain times. **Range:** Yes (grass).
To obtain tee times: Call up to one month in advance for weekdays. Call Wednesday at 8 a.m. for weekend and holidays.

★★★★ CHAMPIONS COURSE
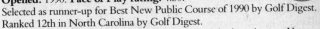

Holes: 18. **Par:** 72/72.
Yards: 7,135/5,395. **Course rating:** 74.0/72.0. **Slope:** 130/123.
Opened: 1990. **Pace of Play rating:** 4:30.
Selected as runner-up for Best New Public Course of 1990 by Golf Digest. Ranked 12th in North Carolina by Golf Digest.
Subscriber comments: One of the better layouts in America . . . Very playable and fun for all golfers and a challenge. One of the better courses anywhere . . . Municipal golf course that is well maintained and continuing to improve . . . Broad-shouldered test . . . Condition poor . . . Very long and challenging . . . Great track, great value, beautiful scenery . . . Back tees make it a monster . . . Great layout . . . Feel welcome, very challenging for us weekend players . . . Great layout; you will hit every shot in your bag . . . Beautiful Rees Jones layout . . . One of the very best municipal courses . . . Don't walk, further from greens to tee than tee to green . . . Tough backside with lake in play on five holes . . . Want to play Tour? Try and break par here . . . What public golf can be . . . Good

psychological builder . . . Scoring chances are often available . . . GGO needs to move here . . . Tough to beat, beauty, price, playability, staff . . . Great layout, tough for high handicap players . . . Real golf, with real greens and real fairways and real rough . . . Among the best in North Carolina . . . Always excellent and it's a muny!

★★★½ PLAYERS COURSE

Holes: 18. **Par:** 72/72.
Yards: 7,076/5,260. **Course rating:** 73.0/70.5. **Slope:** 128/120.
Opened: 1974. **Pace of Play rating:** 4:30.

Subscriber comments: Beautiful George Cobb layout . . . A good course. Very enjoyable for 18 handicap or better, bit of a struggle for others . . . Hilly . . . Some good lake views . . . Not as long as Champions but requires more shotmaking . . . One of the best groups of par 3s I've ever seen . . . Play blue tees . . . Solid classic design . . . State-of-the-art practice facility planned.

★½ BUNCOMBE COUNTY MUNICIPAL GOLF CLUB

PU—226 Fairway Dr., Asheville (704)298-1867.
Call club for further information.
Subscriber comments: Public Donald Ross layout . . . Up and down, up and down the hills . . . Easy front . . . Hard back . . . Flat, wide open front nine, good for short hitters . . . Overplayed muny . . . Good public layout suffers from not enough capital infusion.

★★ CAPE GOLF AND RACQUET CLUB

SP—535 The Cape Blvd., Wilmington (910)799-3110.
Holes: 18. **Par:** 72/72.
Yards: 6,790/4,948. **Course rating:** 73.1/69.3. **Slope:** 133/118.
Opened: 1985. **Pace of Play rating:** 4:30. **Green fee:** $18/40.
Credit cards: MC, V, DISC. **Reduced fees:** Weekdays, Low season, Twilight, Seniors.
Caddies: No. **Golf carts:** Included in Green Fee.
Discount golf packages: Yes. **Season:** Year-round. **High:** April.
On-site lodging: Yes. **Rental clubs:** Yes.
Walking policy: Mandatory cart. **Range:** Yes (grass).
To obtain tee times: Call one day in advance.
Subscriber comments: Resort quality golf at city park prices if maintained . . . Good layout needs work . . . Water on backside . . . Nice mix of holes . . . Enjoyable course, but not always in good shape . . . Condition varies between beautiful to okay . . . Worth the trip, good layout, fair price . . . Watch for gators.

★★★ CAROLINA LAKES GOLF CLUB

PU—Rte. 6, Box 7, Sanford (919)499-5421, (800)942-8633.
18 miles north of Fayetteville. **Holes:** 18. **Par:** 70/70.
Yards: 6,397/5,010. **Course rating:** 70.7/67.0. **Slope:** 117/110.
Opened: 1981. **Pace of Play rating:** 4:00. **Green fee:** $10/15.
Credit cards: MC, V. **Reduced fees:** Weekdays, Low season, Resort guests, Twilight, Seniors, Juniors.
Caddies: No. **Golf carts:** $10 for 18 holes.
Discount golf packages: Yes. **Season:** Year-round. **High:** March-May.
On-site lodging: No. **Rental clubs:** Yes.
Walking policy: Unrestricted walking. **Range:** Yes (grass).
To obtain tee times: Call up to one week in advance.
Subscriber comments: Excellent course at any time of the year and a great staff . . . Short but interesting, excellent course for older people . . . Good layout . . . Difficult greens to read . . . Solid course . . . Friendly atmosphere and good to play . . . Hilly and challenging . . . Interesting, fair test . . . Beautiful country layout and nice place to relax and enjoy beauty . . . Tricky greens . . . Short course, good for beginners.

★★CAROLINA PINES GOLF AND COUNTRY CLUB

SP—390 Carolina Pines Blvd., New Bern (919)444-1000.
Holes: 18. **Par:** 72/72.
Yards: 6,250/5,900. **Course rating:** N/A. **Slope:** 115/111.
Call club for further information.
Subscriber comments: Improving facility . . . Greens not up to standards
of course layout . . . Short course but interesting . . . Fun to play for all . . .
Staff friendly . . . Play in winter, not many on course . . . Too many 90-
degree holes . . . Tight course, a lot of out of bounds . . . Not outstanding,
but a beautiful signature hole.

★★½CAROLINA SHORES GOLF AND COUNTRY CLUB

PU—99 Carolina Shores Dr., Calabash (910)579-2181.
7 miles north of Myrtle Beach. **Holes:** 18. **Par:** 72/72.
Yards: 6,783/6,231. **Course rating:** N/A. **Slope:** 128/122.
Call club for further information.
Subscriber comments: Good Tom Jackson design . . . More sand than
the Sahara . . . Tough first hole . . . Too many sand traps . . . Favorite
course in Myrtle area for fun . . . 98 sand traps . . . I've only played this one
once but I enjoyed it . . . No surprises . . . Hit it straight . . . Will wear out
sand wedge . . . Sand, sand everywhere . . . If you like traps, this is the
place . . . Good tournament course.

★★½CHARLOTTE GOLF LINKS

PU—11500 Providence Rd., Charlotte (704)846-7990.
Holes: 18. **Par:** 71/72.
Yards: 6,700/5,279. **Course rating:** 71.5/70.3. **Slope:** 121/117.
Opened: 1993. **Pace of Play rating:** 4:20. **Green fee:** $19/25.
Credit cards: MC, V, AMEX. **Reduced fees:** Low season, Twilight,
Seniors, Juniors.
Caddies: No. **Golf carts:** $12 for 18 holes.
Discount golf packages: Yes. **Season:** Year-round. **High:** April-Nov.
On-site lodging: No. **Rental clubs:** Yes.
Walking policy: Walking at certain times. **Range:** Yes (grass).
To obtain tee times: Call one week in advance.
Subscriber comments: Exceptional links-style layout . . . Shotmaker's
course . . . Relatively new, will get better with age . . . Interesting links-
style golf . . . Opened too soon . . . Miss the fairway and in for a long day
. . . Accuracy a premium . . . Some sand and water . . . Course is harder
than it looks . . . Large and small greens, rolling fairways . . . Lots of go-
for-broke holes . . . Neat and hard par 3s . . . Very playable.

CHATUGE SHORES GOLF COURSE★

PU—Rt. 2, P.O. Box 145-E, Hayesville (704)389-8940.
110 miles west of Asheville. **Holes:** 18. **Par:** 72/36.
Yards: 6,687/4,950. **Course rating:** 71.3/68.3. **Slope:** 123/120.
Opened: 1971. **Pace of Play rating:** 4:00-4:30. **Green fee:** $18.
Credit cards: MC, V. **Reduced fees:** No.
Caddies: No. **Golf carts:** $6 for 18 holes.
Discount golf packages: No. **Season:** Year-round. **High:** June-Aug.
On-site lodging: No. **Rental clubs:** Yes.
Walking policy: Unrestricted walking. **Range:** Yes.
To obtain tee times: Call up to three days in advance.

CHEROKEE HILLS GOLF AND COUNTRY CLUB★

R—Harshaw Rd., Murphy (704)837-5853, (800)334-3905.
90 miles north of Altanta. **Holes:** 18. **Par:** 72/72.
Yards: 6,724/5,172. **Course rating:** 70.0/68.0. **Slope:** 113/117.
Opened: 1969. **Pace of Play rating:** 4:00. **Green fee:** $15.
Credit cards: MC, V, AMEX. **Reduced fees:** Resort guests, Juniors.
Caddies: No. **Golf carts:** $10 for 18 holes.
Discount golf packages: Yes. **Season:** Year-round. **High:** May-Nov.
On-site lodging: Yes. **Rental clubs:** Yes.

Walking policy: Walking at certain times. **Range:** Yes (grass).
To obtain tee times: Call 48 hours in advance. Tee times can also be made at the same time as reservation of golf package.

★½ CHEVIOT HILLS GOLF CLUB
SP—7301 Capital Blvd., Raleigh (919)876–9920.
Call club for further information.
Subscriber comments: Challenging golf with minimal gimmicks . . .
Basic layout . . . Not exciting . . . Some fun holes . . . Usually good greens
. . . No beer allowed . . . Heavily used . . . Condition fluctuates during the
year . . . Played course for the first time recently and will return . . . Great
walker's course . . . Good length for public course, iffy shape at times . . .
Rolling Hills would be a better name.

★★★ CLEGHORN PLANTATION GOLF AND COUNTRY CLUB
PU—200 Golf Circle, Rutherfordton (704)286–9117.
70 miles west of Charlotte. **Holes:** 18. **Par:** 72/73.
Yards: 6,903/4,751. **Course rating:** 74.6/68.1. **Slope:** 134/111.
Opened: 1969. **Pace of Play rating:** 4:30. **Green fee:** $22/30.
Credit cards: MC, V. **Reduced fees:** Weekdays.
Caddies: No. **Golf carts:** Included in Green Fee.
Discount golf packages: Yes. **Season:** Year-round. **High:** April–Sept.
On-site lodging: No. **Rental clubs:** Yes.
Walking policy: Mandatory cart. **Range:** Yes (grass).
To obtain tee times: Call in advance.
Subscriber comments: Great layout by George Cobb, hard! Really good
mountain course . . . Will give your cart a workout . . . Loads of fun . . .
Large greens with some severe undulations . . . Placement of shots required
for good score . . . Excellent greens . . . Hardest golf course known to man
(Bad shots get worse) . . . Played for the first time this year and was
impressed. Nice layout, pretty quiet during the week, Bermuda rough is
too tough . . . Too many hills. Too little fairway and small greens. You
have to play every club in bag, rewards good shots, very good, tough golf,
great staff, kills you with lies in rough . . . Hidden secret in foothills of
mountains . . . Sand in bunkers is like quicksand . . . We lost one member
of our foursome in one of the bunkers . . . Great golf setting . . . Need your
long and strong game here . . . Best in area.

★★★ THE CLUB AT LONGLEAF
SP—2001 Midland Rd., Southern Pines (910)692–6100, (800)889–5323.
60 miles south of Raleigh. **Holes:** 18. **Par:** 71/71.
Yards: 6,600/4,719. **Course rating:** 69.7/65.7. **Slope:** 117/108.
Opened: 1988. **Pace of Play rating:** 4:00. **Green fee:** $25/53.
Credit cards: MC, V. **Reduced fees:** Low season, Resort guests, Twilight, Juniors.
Caddies: No. **Golf carts:** Included in Green Fee.
Discount golf packages: Yes. **Season:** Year-round. **High:** March–May/Oct.
On-site lodging: Yes. **Rental clubs:** Yes.
Walking policy: Walking at certain times. **Range:** Yes (grass).
To obtain tee times: Call the above 800 number.
Subscriber comments: Dan Maples design . . . Two distinct nines . . .
Front wide-open; back, woods and hills . . . One of the better values in
Pinehurst area . . . Some holes play through the old horse track . . . Fine
layout, great for all . . . Front nine and back nine have different styles . . .
Varied routes to the hole makes challenge for low and high handicappers
. . . Staff cordial and welcome to visitor, course was in excellent shape, well
kept, artistic . . . Just a nice place to play . . . Would recommend to anyone!
Sporty course for average golfer . . . First nine open, second nine treed . . .
One of Dan Maples' best.

COUNTRY CLUB OF WHISPERING PINES

SP—2 Clubhouse Blvd., Whispering Pines (910)949-2311.
55 miles southwest of Raleigh. **Green fee:** $40.
Credit cards: MC, V, AMEX. **Reduced fees:** Low season, Resort guests, Juniors.
Caddies: No. **Golf carts:** $15 for 18 holes.
Discount golf packages: Yes. **Season:** Year-round. **High:** March–Oct.
On-site lodging: Yes. **Rental clubs:** Yes.
Walking policy: Mandatory cart. **Range:** Yes (grass).
To obtain tee times: Call two days in advance.

★★★ EAST COURSE

Holes: 18. **Par:** 72/72.
Yards: 7,138/5,542. **Course rating:** 73.9/72.0. **Slope:** 125/123.
Opened: 1959. **Pace of Play rating:** 4:00.
Subscriber comments: Fun course with good use of natural surroundings
. . . Great facilities, we were treated like members of the club . . . Good test
for middle handicappers . . . Difficult but fair course . . . Challenge but
okay for high handicap . . . Relaxed and friendly . . . Pretty course, good
food.

★★★ WEST COURSE

Holes: 18. **Par:** 71/71.
Yards: 6,363/5,135. **Course rating:** 70.3/69.8. **Slope:** 128/121.
Opened: 1959. **Pace of Play rating:** 4:00.
Subscriber comments: Shorter, tighter . . . Pretty scenery . . . Par 5s can
be killers . . . Good course for average player . . . Excellent fairways, good
greens . . . Lots of trees, narrow fairways, fun course . . . Old established
course.

★ CRYSTAL SPRINGS GOLF CLUB

SP—P.O. Box 9, Pineville (704)588-2640.
Call club for further information.
Subscriber comments: Woodsy setting . . . All uphill . . . Has potential
. . . Favors fade . . . Local knowledge a must . . . Hilly course that's hard to
maintain . . . Nice folks . . . Needs some upkeep.

★★½ CYPRESS LAKES GOLF COURSE

PU—Rt. 1, Cypress Lakes Rd., Hope Mills (910)483-0359.
10 miles north of Fayetteville. **Holes:** 18. **Par:** 72/74.
Yards: 7,240/5,685. **Course rating:** 74.2/72.1. **Slope:** 126/116.
Opened: 1968. **Pace of Play rating:** 4:00. **Green fee:** $13/15.
Credit cards: MC, V. **Reduced fees:** Weekdays.
Caddies: No. **Golf carts:** N/A.
Discount golf packages: Yes. **Season:** Year-round. **High:** Spring/Fall.
On-site lodging: No. **Rental clubs:** Yes.
Walking policy: Unrestricted walking. **Range:** Yes (grass).
To obtain tee times: Call anytime.
Subscriber comments: Almost every fairway a separate hole with skillful
use of terrain . . . Water on most holes . . . Long with great greens and sand
traps . . . A joy to play . . . Terrific in wet winters, Like Pinehurst . . .
Home of the Floyds, is great for its value and playability . . . The layout
area is 7,240 from the back, you'd better hit the ball long and be able to
work it both ways . . . Fun course to play all year round.

★★★½ DEERCROFT GOLF AND COUNTRY CLUB

SP—3000 Deercroft Dr., Wagram (910)369-3107.
19 miles south of Pinehurst. **Holes:** 18. **Par:** 72/72.
Yards: 6,745/5,443. **Course rating:** 72.6/67.0. **Slope:** 125/113.
Opened: 1984. **Pace of Play rating:** 4:30. **Green fee:** $40/60.
Credit cards: MC, V. **Reduced fees:** Weekdays, Low season, Twilight,
Seniors, Juniors.
Caddies: No. **Golf carts:** Included in Green Fee.
Discount golf packages: Yes. **Season:** Year-round. **High:** Spring/Fall.
On-site lodging: No. **Rental clubs:** Yes.
Walking policy: Mandatory cart. **Range:** Yes (grass).

To obtain tee times: Call pro shop. Tee times also available through most hotels in the area.

Subscriber comments: A hidden gem in the Pinehurst area . . . Great land and layout . . . Interesting. Scenic, challenging, well maintained . . . Sleeper, worth playing . . . Good layout, seldom crowded, usually in good shape . . . Good, good, good, good, great layout. Excellent shot values . . . Fun course for all levels of players . . . Good variation of shots required . . . One of the best courses in the area . . . Very friendly staff . . . Stay in fairway . . . Tough rough . . . Best-kept secret in Sandhills, every hole unique.

★★★½ DEVIL'S RIDGE GOLF CLUB

SP—5107 Linksland Dr., Holly Springs (919)557-6100.
10 miles southwest of Raleigh. **Holes:** 18. **Par:** 72/72.
Yards: 7,002/5,244. **Course rating:** 73.7/69.8. **Slope:** 138/121.
Opened: 1991. **Pace of Play rating:** 4:15. **Green fee:** $20/28.
Credit cards: MC, V. **Reduced fees:** Weekdays, Low season, Twilight, Seniors, Juniors.
Caddies: No. **Golf carts:** $12 for 18 holes.
Discount golf packages: Yes. **Season:** Year-round. **High:** June-Aug.
On-site lodging: No. **Rental clubs:** Yes.
Walking policy: Walking at certain times. **Range:** Yes (grass).
To obtain tee times: Call one week in advance.
Subscriber comments: Earned its name . . . Would like to play it now that I know the layout . . . Gorgeous, needs all shots here . . . Seldom a level lie . . . Unbelievable . . . Not a weak hole on the course . . . Condition of greens a little inconsistent . . . Residential construction beginning to impinge . . . Shotmaker's course . . . Gently rolling terrain, narrow, very challenging, par 72 old-style course that calls for every club in your bag . . . Fair layout, emphasis on all tee shots . . . Very penal . . . Spotty greens holding back better rating . . . Long distances between greens and tees . . . Conditioning sometimes suspect . . . Excellent from blues and fun from whites . . . Very tough, very hilly . . . One of the most challenging in the area . . . Interesting variety, love the large greens . . . Play it everytime I'm in Raleigh area . . . A joy to play . . . Very courteous staff, great cheeseburgers . . . Great finishing holes . . . Always interesting, plays fair for all levels, different each time out.

★★ DUCK WOODS COUNTRY CLUB

SP—50 Dogwood Trail, Kitty Hawk (919)261-2609.
70 miles south of Norfolk, VA. **Holes:** 18. **Par:** 72/73.
Yards: 6,650/5,407. **Course rating:** 71.3/70.7. **Slope:** 132/127.
Opened: 1968. **Pace of Play rating:** 4:15. **Green fee:** $32/42.
Credit cards: None. **Reduced fees:** No.
Caddies: No. **Golf carts:** $10 for 18 holes.
Discount golf packages: No. **Season:** Year-round. **High:** May-Sept.
On-site lodging: No. **Rental clubs:** Yes.
Walking policy: Mandatory cart. **Range:** Yes (grass).
To obtain tee times: Call two days in advance.
Subscriber comments: Any hole can jump up and bite you . . . Water on 14 holes . . . Not an easy place to build a good quality course . . . If you have a slice or a push, stay away from this one . . . Water nearly all holes.

★★★½ DUKE UNIVERSITY GOLF CLUB

R—Rte. 751 and Science Dr., Durham (919)681-2288.
Holes: 18. **Par:** 72/73.
Yards: 7,045/5,505. **Course rating:** 73.9/71.2. **Slope:** 137/124.
Opened: 1957. **Pace of Play rating:** 4:15. **Green fee:** $30/45.
Credit cards: MC, V. **Reduced fees:** Weekdays, Low season, Resort guests, Twilight, Seniors, Juniors.
Caddies: No. **Golf carts:** $15 for 18 holes.
Discount golf packages: Yes. **Season:** Year-round. **High:** March-Sept.
On-site lodging: Yes. **Rental clubs:** Yes.
Walking policy: Unrestricted walking. **Range:** Yes (grass).

To obtain tee times: Call up to seven days in advance.

Ranked 11th in North Carolina by Golf Digest.

Subscriber comments: Terrific since remodeling in 1994 . . . Redesigned and has improved looks, still very challenging . . . Great for strong, young folks . . . Few level areas. Wonderful, challenging course, very helpful staff . . . Bermuda fairways throughout . . . They got better with recent conditioning . . . Rees Jones nicely re-made this into a great course . . . Very good after redesign . . . Tough carries and greens . . . Better keep it in fairways . . . Great future . . . Great course for a university great university also . . . Remodeled and improved.

EAGLE CREST GOLF COURSE*

PU—4400 Auburn Church Rd., Garner (919)772-6104.

5 miles south of Raleigh. **Holes:** 18. **Par:** 71/71.

Yards: 6,514/4,875. **Course rating:** N/A. **Slope:** N/A.

Opened: 1968. **Pace of Play rating:** 4:00. **Green fee:** $12/19.

Credit cards: MC, V. **Reduced fees:** Weekdays, Twilight, Seniors, Juniors.

Caddies: No. **Golf carts:** $9 for 18 holes.

Discount golf packages: No. **Season:** Year-round. **High:** April-Sept.

On-site lodging: No. **Rental clubs:** Yes.

Walking policy: Unrestricted walking. **Range:** Yes (grass).

To obtain tee times: Call one week in advance.

★★½ ECHO FARMS GOLF AND COUNTRY CLUB

SP—4114 Echo Farms Blvd., Wilmington (910)791-9318.

Holes: 18. **Par:** 72/72.

Yards: 7,014/5,142. **Course rating:** 74.2/70.7. **Slope:** 132/121.

Opened: 1974. **Pace of Play rating:** 4:00. **Green fee:** $20/35.

Credit cards: All major. **Reduced fees:** Low season, Resort guests.

Caddies: No. **Golf carts:** Included in Green Fee.

Discount golf packages: Yes. **Season:** Year-round. **High:** April-Oct.

On-site lodging: No. **Rental clubs:** Yes.

Walking policy: Mandatory cart. **Range:** Yes (grass).

To obtain tee times: Call ahead.

Subscriber comments: Coastal course . . . Good all around course . . . A course that you want to go back and play again . . . Plain Jane for beach area . . . Bring long irons . . . Too long for average golfer from back tees . . . Lovely wooded course . . . Bent greens . . . Nothing special . . . Straightforward . . . No surprises . . . No, it just is not exciting golf . . . Length and price make this standard layout worthwhile.

★★★½ THE EMERALD GOLF CLUB

SP—5000 Clubhouse Dr., New Bern (919)633-4440.

18. **Par:** 72/72.

Yards: 6,924/5,287. **Course rating:** 74.0/71.3. **Slope:** 125/119.

Opened: 1988. **Pace of Play rating:** 4:00-4:20. **Green fee:** $20/42.

Credit cards: MC, V. **Reduced fees:** No.

Caddies: No. **Golf carts:** Included in Green Fee.

Discount golf packages: Yes. **Season:** Year-round. **High:** March-May/Oct.

On-site lodging: No. **Rental clubs:** Yes.

Walking policy: Mandatory cart. **Range:** Yes (grass).

To obtain tee times: Call two days in advance.

Subscriber comments: Always in tip-top condition . . . Tight course, good for shotmaking, a lot of iron play, beautiful layout . . . Carts on paths only . . . Fine layout with fine views and different look on every hole . . . Greens well-positioned . . . If we had been allowed to walk, it would have been a wonderful day, but carts manditory and cart paths only ruin everything . . . Best in area . . . Very well-maintained, challenging but playable . . . Super course from back tees . . . Great finishing hours . . . Toughest 18th hole ever, water all the way down on the right . . . Really nice course for the average player all year . . . Worth the drive to play . . . Best-kept secret, I hope, in eastern North Carolina.

★★★½ **ETOWAH VALLEY COUNTRY CLUB**
SOUTH/WEST/NORTH
R—450 Brickyard Rd., Etowah (704)891-7141, (800)451-8174.
18 miles southeast of Asheville. **Holes:** 27. **Par:** 72/73/73.
Yards: 7,108/7,005/6,911. **Course rating:** 73.3/73.1/72.4. **Slope:**
125/125/125.
Opened: 1967. **Pace of Play rating:** 4:30. **Green fee:** $20/25.
Credit cards: MC, V, DISC. **Reduced fees:** Low season.
Caddies: No. **Golf carts:** $14 for 18 holes.
Discount golf packages: Yes. **Season:** Year-round. **High:** April-Oct.
On-site lodging: Yes. **Rental clubs:** Yes.
Walking policy: Walking at certain times. **Range:** Yes (grass).
To obtain tee times: Call two days in advance.
Subscriber comments: All three nines are good challenges. Different . . .
A long course, but fair to all golfers . . . Just a great place to stay . . . Most
enjoyable resort, fine course to play . . . Overrated . . . Nice mountain
course . . . Great resort . . . Relaxing and quiet . . . S/W nines are best . . .
Long tough par 4s . . . Beautiful layout and staff friendly . . . Lawn
bowling . . . Clubhouse/restaurant beautiful . . . From back tees the PGA
Tour would not embarass the course record . . . Course beautiful . . .
Personnel friendly and helpful . . . Lodging nice . . . Food was good . . .
Greens very good . . . Fairway well kept . . . Rough was rough . . .
Variety, always well maintained . . . Great staff . . . Nice variety of golf
holes, North nine is best of the three . . . 27 holes tough but fair . . .
Various terrain adds challenge . . . Ego and body exhausted!

FAIRFIELD HARBOUR COUNTRY CLUB
SP—1100 Pelican Dr., New Bern (919)514-0050.
100 miles southeast of Raleigh. **Green fee:** $24.
Credit cards: All major. **Reduced fees:** Low season, Twilight.
Caddies: No. **Golf carts:** $10 for 18 holes.
Discount golf packages: Yes. **Season:** Year-round. **High:** Spring/Fall.
On-site lodging: Yes. **Rental clubs:** Yes.
Walking policy: Walking at certain times. **Range:** Yes (grass).
To obtain tee times: Call in advance.
★★ **HARBOUR POINTE COURSE**
Holes: 18. **Par:** 72/72.
Yards: 6,650/5,100. **Course rating:** 71.8/68.6. **Slope:** 125/111.
Opened: 1989. **Pace of Play rating:** 4:30
Subscriber comments: Flat coastal course, interesting and playable . . .
Need to know it to play it well . . . Touristy . . . Too much water, sand,
swamp. Too remote . . . This could be a superb course . . . Challenging
. . . Don't be fooled by the dirt road and clubhouse in a trailer; diverse,
imaginative layout that rewards shotmaking.
SHORELINE COURSE★
Holes: 18. **Par:** 72/72.
Yards: 6,802/5,200. **Course rating:** 72.1/70.0. **Slope:** 128/118.
Opened: 1972. **Pace of Play rating:** 4:30.

FAIRFIELD MOUNTAINS
R—201 Blvd. of the Mountains, Lake Lure (704)625-2888.
50 miles east of Asheville. **Credit cards:** All major. **Reduced fees:** Low
season.
Caddies: No. **Golf carts:** Included in Green Fee.
Discount golf packages: Yes. **Season:** Year-round. **High:** April-Oct.
On-site lodging: Yes. **Rental clubs:** Yes.
Range: No.
To obtain tee times: Call pro shop one month in advance.
Formerly known as Colony Lake Lure.
★★★ **APPLE VALLEY GOLF CLUB**
Holes: 18. **Par:** 72/72.
Yards: 6,726/4,661. **Course rating:** 72.6/66.3. **Slope:** 138/114.
Opened: 1986. **Pace of Play rating:** 4:30. **Green fee:** $39.
Walking policy: Mandatory cart.

Subscriber comments: Interesting mountain course . . . Great views . . . Great shape . . . great views . . . Best of the two . . . No. 18 is a bear . . . Quality course, well maintained, friendly staff . . . Solid from whites, long and strong from blues . . . Plays to all levels . . . Great front side, narrow, tough . . . A fun course . . . Well maintained, good test of golf . . . Good variety of golf holes . . . Staff good, pace good, service good, tough course . . . Difficulty caused by rough . . . Scenery is wonderful, must play accurate tee shots, excellent family resort.

★★½ BALD MOUNTAIN GOLF CLUB

Holes: 18. **Par:** 72/72.
Yards: 6,575/4,808. **Course rating:** 70.9/66.9. **Slope:** 125/112.
Opened: 1974. **Pace of Play rating:** 4:30. **Green fee:** $27.
Golf carts: $12 for 18 holes.
Walking policy: Walking at certain times.
Subscriber comments: Wonderful scenery. Beautiful setting . . . Back side much more interesting than front . . . Enjoyable with beautiful scenery . . . Ideal for short players . . . Plays to all skill levels . . . Practice range up to 200 yards only . . . Interesting mountain course . . . Shotmaker's special.

★★ FINLEY GOLF CLUB

PU—Finley Golf Club Rd., Chapel Hill (919)962-2349.
5 miles south of Durham. **Holes:** 18. **Par:** 72/73.
Yards: 6,580/5,277. **Course rating:** 71.3/69.7. **Slope:** 127/118.
Opened: 1949. **Pace of Play rating:** 4:30. **Green fee:** $8/22.
Credit cards: MC, V. **Reduced fees:** Weekdays, Twilight, Seniors, Juniors.
Caddies: No. **Golf carts:** $10 for 18 holes.
Discount golf packages: No. **Season:** Year-round. **High:** April-Oct.
On-site lodging: No. **Rental clubs:** Yes.
Walking policy: Unrestricted walking. **Range:** Yes (grass).
To obtain tee times: Call Monday prior to weekend or University holiday . . . Call no earlier than two days in advance for weekdays.
Subscriber comments: Nice layout for university course, average condition . . . Always enjoy Finley, but condition could improve . . . Honest, traditional design . . . Marginal layout . . . Walkable . . . Rewards long hitter . . . Quite crowded during school term . . . Great old design . . . Davis loves it. Probably ate this course alive at University of North Carolina.

★½ FOX SQUIRREL COUNTRY CLUB

SP—591 S. Shore Dr., Boiling Spring Lake (910)845-2625.
25 miles north of Wilmington. **Holes:** 18. **Par:** 72/72.
Yards: 6,762/5,349. **Course rating:** 72.5/70.7. **Slope:** 125/117.
Opened: 1962. **Pace of Play rating:** 4:00. **Green fee:** $15/20.
Credit cards: MC, V. **Reduced fees:** No.
Caddies: No. **Golf carts:** $12 for 18 holes.
Discount golf packages: Yes. **Season:** Year-round. **High:** June-Sept.
On-site lodging: No. **Rental clubs:** Yes.
Walking policy: Unrestricted walking. **Range:** No.
To obtain tee times: Call 24 hours in advance.
Subscriber comments: Average course, pleasant in pro shop . . . Hard course, slope should be higher . . . Always in good shape . . . Fun to walk this course . . . Nice vacation course . . . Too many doglegs . . . There is a difference between challenging and needing to be lucky . . . Nice vacation course.

FOXFIRE RESORT AND COUNTRY CLUB

R—9 Foxfire Blvd., Jackson Springs (910)295-4563.
60 miles north of Raleigh. **Green fee:** $35/64.
Credit cards: All major. **Reduced fees:** Low season, Resort guests, Juniors.
Caddies: No. **Golf carts:** Included in Green Fee.
Discount golf packages: Yes. **Season:** Year-round. **High:** March-June/Sept.

On-site lodging: Yes. **Rental clubs:** Yes.
Walking policy: Mandatory cart. **Range:** Yes (grass).
To obtain tee times: Call anytime.

★★½ EAST COURSE
Holes: 18. **Par:** 72/72.
Yards: 6,851/5,256. **Course rating:** 73.5/70.5. **Slope:** 131/119.
Opened: 1968. **Pace of Play rating:** 4:30.
Subscriber comments: Pretty open, lots of doglegs . . . Fun course, good food . . . The ultimate example of average . . . One my favorite courses . . . Good staff . . . Cart paths a mess . . . Course needs sprucing up . . . Suited to long hitters . . . Pretty open, lots of doglegs . . . Treated women golfers very nice . . . A super location to focus on golf . . . Tees allow for many challenges . . . Good course, nice retreat, plan to stay on-site . . . Would be very good if improved conditions . . . Better than the West Course.

★★★ WEST COURSE
Holes: 18. **Par:** 72/72.
Yards: 6,742/5,273. **Course rating:** 72.4/70.3. **Slope:** 129/115.
Opened: 1968. **Pace of Play rating:** 4:30.
Subscriber comments: Good design and balance . . . Has excellent potential . . . Very good layout . . . Challenging to anyone . . . Nice interesting layout . . . A slower pace than East . . . It does not seem to be kept up as well . . . Would be very good with some improved conditions . . . Hilly course . . . Needs some length . . . Okay if in Pinehurst, but not a draw in itself.

★★½ FRENCH BROAD GOLF CENTER
PU—5 French Broad Ave., Fletcher (704)687-8545.
Call club for further information.
Subscriber comments: New course, needs to mature, above average staff, greens fast but fair . . . In excellent condition now after being set back by severe flooding in April 1994 . . . Had to reseed the fairways and some greens . . . Good design . . . Superb dining facilities . . . Good layout, great practice area . . . Several challenging holes with water coming into play, slick greens, course does not drain well in wet weather . . . A challenge from blue or gold tees . . . Water on 14 holes . . . Best greens in area . . . Great potential if floods don't ruin it . . . Greens slick as bikini wax, McCord would like it . . . Very nice.

★★ GASTONIA MUNICIPAL GOLF CLUB
PU—530 Niblick Dr., Gastonia (704)866-6945.
Call club for further information.
Subscriber comments: Epitome of the Old South . . . Tight, lots of ditches . . . Fairways tend to be moderately hard with some bare spots . . . Course is very open and essentially without bunkers . . . Give it a try.

★★★½ GATES FOUR COUNTRY CLUB
SP—6775 Irongate Dr., Fayetteville (910)425-2176.
Holes: 18. **Par:** 72/72.
Yards: 6,865/5,368. **Course rating:** 73.4/70.5. **Slope:** 122/115.
Opened: 1971. **Pace of Play rating:** 4:00. **Green fee:** $15/23.
Credit cards: MC, V. **Reduced fees:** Weekdays, Low season, Resort guests.
Caddies: No. **Golf carts:** $9 for 18 holes.
Discount golf packages: Yes. **Season:** Year-round. **High:** Spring/Fall.
On-site lodging: No. **Rental clubs:** Yes.
Walking policy: Walking at certain times. **Range:** Yes (grass).
To obtain tee times: Call one week in advance.
Subscriber comments: Tough golf course from the back tees, new greens . . . Nice course with very good greens . . . Very narrow fairways . . . Deep rough, tough, course . . . Many different style holes . . . Have to hit it straight . . . Pro shop personnel very cordial.

★★★ THE GAUNTLET AT ST. JAMES PLANTATION

SP—Hwy. 211, Southport (910)253-3008, (800)247-4806.
28 miles south of Wilmington. **Holes:** 18. **Par:** 72/72.
Yards: 7,022/5,048. **Course rating:** 75.0/69.7. **Slope:** 142/119.
Opened: 1990. **Pace of Play rating:** 4:30. **Green fee:** $40/60.
Credit cards: MC, V, AMEX. **Reduced fees:** Low season, Twilight,
Seniors.
Caddies: Yes. **Golf carts:** Included in Green Fee.
Discount golf packages: Yes. **Season:** Year-round. **High:** March-May.
On-site lodging: No. **Rental clubs:** Yes.
Walking policy: Mandatory cart. **Range:** Yes (grass).
To obtain tee times: Call pro shop.
Subscriber comments: Whoever said golf was relaxing never played here
. . . Tricked up . . . Great operation . . . Course built in marsh . . . Very
good character . . . High slope. If you don't crush it, don't play it . . . Back
tee butt-kicker . . . Typical P.B. Dye course . . . Where's the earth mover?
. . . Only one bad hole . . . Take plenty of extra balls. Challenging Dye
course . . . Tough Bermuda greens . . . Tougher than the slope rating . . .
Finishing holes memorable . . . Monster from tips . . . So unique you will
not mind the difficult or tricky holes . . . Good menu and restaurant . . .
Marsh everywhere . . . Quality customer service . . . Superintendent has
done fantastic job . . . Some blind tee shots can get you in trouble on your
first visit . . . Staff gives good directions . . . Bring woods for par-4
approaches . . . Toughest course in Brunswick County . . . 75.0 rating is
no joke.

★★★ GLEN CANNON COUNTRY CLUB

SP—Wilson Rd., Brevard (704)884-9160.
25 miles south of Asheville. **Holes:** 18. **Par:** 72/72.
Yards: 6,548/5,172. **Course rating:** 71.7/69.1. **Slope:** 124/117.
Opened: 1967. **Pace of Play rating:** 4:15. **Green fee:** $20/50.
Credit cards: MC, V. **Reduced fees:** Low season, Twilight.
Caddies: No. **Golf carts:** Included in Green Fee.
Discount golf packages: No. **Season:** Year-round. **High:** April-Oct.
On-site lodging: No. **Rental clubs:** Yes.
Walking policy: Mandatory cart. **Range:** Yes (grass).
To obtain tee times: Call one day in advance.
Subscriber comments: One of the nicest courses in the mountains . . .
Excellent . . . Used all clubs, bunkers well maintained . . . Scenic and fun to
play . . . No. 2 with waterfall is beautiful . . . Couple of small greens . . .
good staff, friendly members . . . Well kept, nicely laid out . . . Play every
day after work . . . Fun course for all players . . . Pretty, not difficult, but
tricky . . . Good mix of holes . . . gorgeous trick greens . . . Some holes
could be on postcards; a par 3 with waterfall background.

★ GREAT SMOKIES RESORT GOLF CLUB

R—One Hilton Dr., Asheville (704)253-5874, (800)733-3211.
Holes: 18. **Par:** 70/70.
Yards: 5,900/4,600. **Course rating:** 69.5/67.0. **Slope:** 118/113.
Opened: 1974. **Pace of Play rating:** 4:00. **Green fee:** $17/30.
Credit cards: All major. **Reduced fees:** Weekdays, Low season, Resort
guests, Twilight.
Caddies: No. **Golf carts:** $13 for 18 holes.
Discount golf packages: Yes. **Season:** Year-round. **High:** April-Oct.
On-site lodging: Yes. **Rental clubs:** Yes.
Walking policy: Walking at certain times. **Range:** No.
To obtain tee times: Hotel guests may call one year in advance; outside
play two days in advance.
Subscriber comments: Better be in shape to play this course . . . Leave
the driver home . . . Tight fairways with doglegs . . . Bring plenty of balls
. . . Roller coaster course, up and down . . . Tight fairways, mountain
course . . . Barely golf, short hilly course in fair condition . . . Plush, slow
greens only good point . . . Too many blind shots . . . Poor fairway
maintainance, but interesting mountain course.

★★½ THE GROVE PARK INN RESORT
R—290 Macon Ave., Asheville (704)252-2711, (800)438-5800.
Holes: 18. **Par:** 71/71.
Yards: 6,520/4,687. **Course rating:** 71.7/68.6. **Slope:** 125/111.
Opened: 1894. **Pace of Play rating:** 4:30. **Green fee:** $20/44.
Credit cards: All major. **Reduced fees:** Low season, Twilight.
Caddies: No. **Golf carts:** N/A.
Discount golf packages: Yes. **Season:** Year-round. **High:** April-Nov.
On-site lodging: Yes. **Rental clubs:** Yes.
Walking policy: Walking at certain times. **Range:** No.
To obtain tee times: Call anytime.
Subscriber comments: Old, short, narrow, fun . . . Terrain is incredible
. . . Mountain course in good condition . . . Bunkers need sand . . . A lot
of fun, basically alone on the course . . . A fun course in a camp-out area
. . . Mountain greens tough to read . . . Played it in fall during indian
summer, simply beautiful! Gorgeous setting for a golf course . . . Not what
it used to be . . . Lots of class and tradition! Enough said . . . Golf course is
average but the scenery and hotel make this a must experience.

★★ HAWKSNEST GOLF AND SKI RESORT
PU—1800 Skyland Dr., Seven Devils (704)963-6561.
70 miles west of Winston-Salem. **Holes:** 18. **Par:** 72/72.
Yards: 6,244/4,799. **Course rating:** N/A. **Slope:** 113/110.
Opened: N/A. **Pace of Play rating:** N/A. **Green fee:** N/A.
Credit cards: MC, V, DISC. **Reduced fees:** Weekdays, Low season,
Twilight.
Caddies: No. **Golf carts:** Included in Green Fee.
Discount golf packages: Yes. **Season:** Year-round. **High:** July-Aug.
On-site lodging: No. **Rental clubs:** No.
Walking policy: N/A. **Range:** No.
Subscriber comments: Very enjoyable . . . A few strange holes . . . Hard
to club, many interesting holes . . . Nice mountain course . . . Narrow,
steep, windy . . . If you're in the fairway, you're in good shape . . . One of
my favorites . . . Nice scenery . . . Easy to get on and not crowded. Great
mountain views . . . At over 4,000 feet an excellent ego builder.

★★ HIGH HAMPTON INN AND COUNTRY CLUB
R—Hwy. 107 S., Box 338, Cashiers (704)743-2450, (800)334-2551.
65 miles south of Asheville. **Holes:** 18. **Par:** 71.
Yards: 6,012. **Course rating:** 68.5. **Slope:** 120.
Opened: 1923. **Pace of Play rating:** 4:30. **Green fee:** $17/34.
Credit cards: MC, V, AMEX. **Reduced fees:** Low season, Resort guests,
Twilight.
Caddies: No. **Golf carts:** $11 for 18 holes.
Discount golf packages: Yes. **Season:** April-Nov. **High:** June-Aug.
On-site lodging: Yes. **Rental clubs:** Yes.
Walking policy: Unrestricted walking. **Range:** Yes (grass).
To obtain tee times: Call pro shop.
Subscriber comments: Great views, short and simple . . . No sand, I
mean not a single sand trap . . . Beautiful scenery . . . Hard to judge
distances because of elevation changes . . . Beautiful scenery, fairways
average . . . Not as challenging as other courses in western North Carolina
. . . Drivable par 4s . . . Short hitter can have fun . . . Good but nothing
special . . . Wonderful, old accommodations, course adequate . . .
Magnificent scenery.

★★★½ HIGHLAND CREEK GOLF CLUB
PU—7001 Highland Creek Pkwy., Charlotte (704)875-9000.
Holes: 18. **Par:** 72/72.
Yards: 7,008/5,005. **Course rating:** 73.3/70.1. **Slope:** 133/128.
Opened: 1993. **Pace of Play rating:** 4:30. **Green fee:** $40/46.
Credit cards: MC, V, AMEX. **Reduced fees:** Weekdays.
Caddies: No. **Golf carts:** Included in Green Fee.
Discount golf packages: No. **Season:** Year-round. **High:** April-Sept.

On-site lodging: No. **Rental clubs:** Yes.
Walking policy: Mandatory cart. **Range:** Yes (grass).
To obtain tee times: Call three days in advance.
Subscriber comments: Best kept secret in Carolinas! Nice new public course, will be great when it matures . . . Very challenging course particularly its par 5s . . . Use all your clubs . . . Has everything you want in a golf course . . . Beautiful layout . . . Good variety in holes . . . Great finishing hole . . . In good enough condition to warrant the fees . . . No. 18 is unforgettable . . . Tough, but fun holes . . . Wonderful layout . . . Pleasure to play, need all the shots . . . Layout long but fair . . . Best public course in Charlotte area by far.

HILLCREST GOLF CLUB★
CEDAR SIDE/HILL SIDE/LAKE SIDE
PU—2450 S. Stratford Rd., Winston-Salem (910)765-5269.
Holes: 27. **Par:** 72/72/72.
Yards: 5,839/5,869/5,848. **Course rating:** 66.5/66.5/66.5. **Slope:** 104/104/104.
Opened: 1931. **Pace of Play rating:** 4:00. **Green fee:** $12/16.
Credit cards: MC, V. **Reduced fees:** Twilight, Juniors.
Caddies: No. **Golf carts:** $10 for 18 holes.
Discount golf packages: No. **Season:** Year-round. **High:** March–Sept.
On-site lodging: No. **Rental clubs:** No.
Walking policy: Unrestricted walking. **Range:** No.
To obtain tee times: Call Friday 8 a.m. for upcoming weekend.

★★★ HOLLY FOREST COUNTRY CLUB
R—4000 Hwy. 64 West, Sapphire (704)743-1174.
60 miles south of Asheville. **Holes:** 18. **Par:** 70/70.
Yards: 6,147/5,690. **Course rating:** N/A. **Slope:** 119/118.
Opened: N/A. **Pace of Play rating:** N/A. **Green fee:** N/A.
Credit cards: MC, V. **Reduced fees:** Low season.
Caddies: No. **Golf carts:** Included in Green Fee.
Discount golf packages: Yes. **Season:** Year-round. **High:** May–Sept.
On-site lodging: Yes. **Rental clubs:** No.
Walking policy: N/A. **Range:** Yes (grass).
Subscriber comments: Unique mountain course . . . Tough greens, beautiful mountain scenery . . . No. 13 beautiful and tough . . . Bunkers need maintainance . . . Good course for any type player, well maintained, staff friendly, helpful . . . Fun, several great holes . . . Tight, must be accurate . . . Short, but interesting . . . How many mulligans do I get? . . . Tight, short, test . . . Beautiful layout, variety of holes for all skill levels . . . Watch out for No. 4 . . . Beautiful views.

★★★½ HOUND EARS CLUB
SP—P.O. Box 188, Blowing Rock (704)963-5831.
90 miles west of Asheville. **Holes:** 18. **Par:** 72/73.
Yards: 6,165/4,959. **Course rating:** 69.4/66.8. **Slope:** 122/110.
Opened: 1963. **Pace of Play rating:** 4:00. **Green fee:** $35/75.
Credit cards: MC, V, AMEX. **Reduced fees:** No.
Caddies: No. **Golf carts:** $12 for 18 holes.
Discount golf packages: Yes. **Season:** April–Nov. **High:** June–Sept.
On-site lodging: Yes. **Rental clubs:** Yes.
Walking policy: Walking at certain times. **Range:** Yes (grass).
To obtain tee times: Call two days in advance.
Subscriber comments: Favorite mountain course . . . The balls fly farther up here . . . Beautiful, very playable . . . Mountain course, great fairways . . . Short but fun, too . . . Short, beautiful scenery, excellent condition . . . Great . . . Play every opportunity . . . Class act.

★★½ HYLAND HILLS GOLF CLUB
PU—4100 U.S. No.1 N., Southern Pines (910)692-3752.
5 miles east of Pinehurst. **Holes:** 18. **Par:** 72/72.
Yards: 6,726/4,677. **Course rating:** 70.4/66.8. **Slope:** 124/109.

Opened: 1974. **Pace of Play rating:** 4:00. **Green fee:** $18/35.
Credit cards: MC, V. **Reduced fees:** No.
Caddies: No. **Golf carts:** $16 for 18 holes.
Discount golf packages: Yes. **Season:** Year-round. **High:** March-May/Oct.
On-site lodging: Yes. **Rental clubs:** Yes.
Walking policy: Walking at certain times. **Range:** Yes (grass).
To obtain tee times: Call in advance.
Subscriber comments: Not a traditional Pinehurst course . . . Good resort, has improved . . . Mixture of difficult and easy holes . . . Long carries over water on two holes . . . Great course, nice people, a hoot . . . Always have afternoon specials . . . Good course for average player . . . Price a little below average for Sandhills . . . Can use every club in your bag . . . Challenging for average player . . . Best buy in Pinehurst . . . What a turnaround . . . Four finishing holes allow for aggressiveness . . . Pinehurst golf on the economy plan.

INDIAN VALLEY GOLF COURSE*
PU—1005 Indian Valley Dr., Burlington (910)584-7871.
20 miles east of Greensboro. **Holes:** 18. **Par:** 70/70.
Yards: 6,610/5,606. **Course rating:** 71.3/68.4. **Slope:** 115/113.
Opened: 1967. **Pace of Play rating:** 4:15. **Green fee:** $9/14.
Credit cards: MC, V. **Reduced fees:** Weekdays, Low season, Resort guests, Twilight, Seniors, Juniors.
Caddies: No. **Golf carts:** $9 for 18 holes.
Discount golf packages: Yes. **Season:** Year-round. **High:** April-Oct.
On-site lodging: No. **Rental clubs:** No.
Walking policy: Unrestricted walking. **Range:** Yes (grass).
To obtain tee times: Call Monday for weekend tee times at 8 a.m.

★★★ JAMESTOWN PARK GOLF CLUB
PU—7014 E. Fork Rd., Jamestown (910)454-4912.
3 miles east of Greensboro. **Holes:** 18. **Par:** 72/72.
Yards: 6,665/5,298. **Course rating:** 72.6/70.7. **Slope:** 126/118.
Opened: 1972. **Pace of Play rating:** 4:00-4:30. **Green fee:** $14/16.
Credit cards: None. **Reduced fees:** Weekdays, Seniors, Juniors.
Caddies: No. **Golf carts:** $8 for 18 holes.
Discount golf packages: No. **Season:** Year-round. **High:** May-Sept.
On-site lodging: No. **Rental clubs:** Yes.
Walking policy: Walking at certain times. **Range:** Yes (grass).
To obtain tee times: Call one week in advance for weekdays. Call Thursday prior to weekend of play.
Subscriber comments: Very good municipal golf course . . . Better conditioning would lift the course a level . . . Lots of placement shots . . . Some challenging holes . . . Good, but could be great with better maintainance . . . Great test, risk/reward, opportunities abound . . . Greens deceptively difficult . . . Course is long but fairly wide open . . . Great hot dogs, good pro shop.

★★★½ JEFFERSON LANDING CLUB
PU—Box 110, Jefferson (910)246-5555.
80 miles northwest of Winston Salem. **Holes:** 18. **Par:** 72/72.
Yards: 7,111/4,960. **Course rating:** N/A. **Slope:** 121/103.
Opened: N/A. **Pace of Play rating:** N/A. **Green fee:** N/A.
Credit cards: All major. **Reduced fees:** Weekdays, Low season, Resort guests, Twilight.
Caddies: No. **Golf carts:** Included in Green Fee.
Discount golf packages: Yes. **Season:** March-Nov. **High:** June-Sept.
On-site lodging: Yes. **Rental clubs:** N/A.
Walking policy: N/A. **Range:** Yes (grass).
Subscriber comments: Flat layout in mountains . . . Good mountain course . . . Good layout, very scenic, challenging holes . . . Everything was fine. Good but not great, great greens, unusually flat . . . Tough to get to, but outstanding; beautiful greens . . . Top notch operation . . . Too open

. . . Don't expect much scenery for a mountain course . . . Great mountain views from several tees . . . Interesting holes, lots of water . . . Wide fairways, pretty course . . . Good variety of holes . . . Strong course, carts stay on paths, then 90-degree cart rule in effect . . . Pretty location . . . One of the better mountain courses.

★★★★ KEITH HILLS COUNTRY CLUB

SP—Country Club Dr., Buies Creek (910)893-5051, (800)334-4111.
30 miles south of Raleigh. **Holes:** 18. **Par:** 72/72.
Yards: 6,660/5,225. **Course rating:** 71.6/69.6. **Slope:** 129/120.
Opened: 1975. **Pace of Play rating:** 4:15. **Green fee:** $17/24.
Credit cards: MC, V. **Reduced fees:** Juniors.
Caddies: No. **Golf carts:** N/A
Discount golf packages: Yes. **Season:** Year-round. **High:** March-June.
On-site lodging: No. **Rental clubs:** Yes.
Walking policy: Walking at certain times. **Range:** Yes (grass).
To obtain tee times: Call pro shop.
Subscriber comments: Another shotmaker's course . . . Outstanding quality for public course . . . Always in great shape, a real test for anyone . . . Not easy, but playable for most average players . . . The golfer must make all the shots to score . . . Stays in great shape all year . . . Enjoyable course, does not get all the recognition it deserves . . . Get the "orange-ade" . . . Love the view . . . Bermuda fairways as good as anywhere, great staff . . . One of the best ever! Terrific Ellis Maple design . . . Beautiful and well-kept . . . Hilly, a lot of doglegs, rarely crowded . . . Very few weak holes . . . Too many "don't do this and don't that" signs . . . Probably most underrated in North Carolina . . . Possibly the best golf deal in North Carolina. I'd take an out-of-state guest here . . . Long, well designed . . . Excellent, beautiful setting . . . Augusta-like . . . Best orange-ade and lemon-ade . . . I love this course . . . The best university course I've ever played . . . Extra good for a college course . . . Best-kept secret in North Carolina . . . Best snack bar, fine staff . . . Big time course in small town . . . One of North Carolina's hidden treasures.

★★★½ LANE TREE GOLF COURSE

SP—2317 Salem Church Rd., Goldsboro (919)734-1245.
43 miles southeast of Raleigh. **Holes:** 18. **Par:** 71/71.
Yards: 6,963/5,168. **Course rating:** 72.4/68.9. **Slope:** 131/120.
Opened: 1992. **Pace of Play rating:** 4:00. **Green fee:** $10/20.
Credit cards: MC, V. **Reduced fees:** Weekdays, Low season, Resort guests.
Caddies: No. **Golf carts:** $10 for 18 holes.
Discount golf packages: No. **Season:** Year-round. **High:** April-Sept.
On-site lodging: No. **Rental clubs:** No.
Walking policy: Walking at certain times. **Range:** Yes (grass).
To obtain tee times: Call three days in advance.
Subscriber comments: Enjoyable golf . . . Very fair . . . Front side plays completely differently than back . . . A nice new course, wide open, good, fast bent-grass greens, can be tricky on a windy day . . . A good challenge . . . Fairways close together . . . A fader's course . . . 18th young, needs to mature, very tough . . . Back tees are punishing, regular tees are fair . . . Not yet mature . . . Very large greens . . . The best greens in the area, makes you use all the shots.

★★★½ LEGACY GOLF LINKS

PU—U.S. Hwy. 15-501 S., Aberdeen (910)944-8825, (800)344-8825.
2 miles south of Pinehurst. **Holes:** 18. **Par:** 72/72.
Yards: 6,989/4,948. **Course rating:** 73.2/68.3. **Slope:** 132/120.
Opened: 1991. **Pace of Play rating:** 4:15. **Green fee:** $36/75.
Credit cards: MC, V, AMEX. **Reduced fees:** Low season, Resort guests, Juniors.
Caddies: No. **Golf carts:** Included in Green Fee.
Discount golf packages: Yes. **Season:** Year-round. **High:** Spring/Fall.
On-site lodging: No. **Rental clubs:** Yes.

Walking policy: Mandatory cart. **Range:** Yes (grass).
To obtain tee times: Call in advance.
Subscriber comments: A superb layout by Jack Nicklaus Jr. . . . Good test from all tee boxes . . . Nice course, good character, a treat to play, can be played by all handicaps . . . Staff is good, know their jobs well . . . Pace is usually very good, enjoyable . . . User friendly . . . Tough course even from white tees . . . Don't miss this one . . . Easy to get good tee times . . . Good variety . . . Jack Jr.'s best. Great design . . . Course short, but very compettitve . . . Very playable . . . A real jewel . . . Great variety . . . Very nice people . . . Very good course . . . Can run ball onto greens . . . Each hole is an experience . . . One of the best in North Carolina or South Carolina . . . Impossible gem . . . Best/toughest finishing hole in North Carolina . . . Lots of fun, great staff, model for public golf . . . Starter goes over cart rules and course, every club should do this . . . Very nice design, last three holes a super finish . . . Every hole different, interesting to play.

LINCOLN COUNTRY CLUB★

SP—2108 Country Club Rd., Lincolnton (704)735-1382.
20 miles northwest of Charlotte. **Holes:** 18. **Par:** 72/72.
Yards: 6,467/5,011. **Course rating:** 70.4/69.0. **Slope:** 125/118.
Opened: 1991. **Pace of Play rating:** 4:20. **Green fee:** $22/28.
Credit cards: MC, V. **Reduced fees:** Weekdays, Seniors, Juniors.
Caddies: No. **Golf carts:** Included in Green Fee.
Discount golf packages: No. **Season:** Year-round. **High:** April-Oct.
On-site lodging: No. **Rental clubs:** No.
Walking policy: Unrestricted walking. **Range:** Yes (grass).
To obtain tee times: Call three days in advance.

★★★★ LINVILLE GOLF COURSE

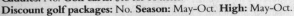

R—Linville Ave., Linville (704)733-4363.
60 miles northeast of Asheville. **Holes:** 18. **Par:** 72/72.
Yards: 6,780/5,086. **Course rating:** 72.7/69.3. **Slope:** 135/119.
Opened: 1924. **Pace of Play rating:** 4:15-4:30. **Green fee:** $35.
Credit cards: None. **Reduced fees:** No.
Caddies: No. **Golf carts:** $13 for 18 holes.
Discount golf packages: No. **Season:** May-Oct. **High:** May-Oct.
On-site lodging: Yes. **Rental clubs:** Yes.
Walking policy: Mandatory cart. **Range:** Yes (grass).
To obtain tee times: Must be a guest at Eseeola Lodge.
Ranked 16th in North Carolina by Gof Digest.
Subscriber comments: It doesn't get any better . . . Donald Ross at his best . . . Wonderful ambience . . . Beautiful mountain scenery, friendly staff . . . Fantastic layout. My all time favorite public course . . . Use all your clubs . . . Wonderful course . . . Best of Donald Ross . . . Stay at the lodge. A wonderful experience . . . Still one of the best . . . Next to the Cascades Course at the Homestead, this is a mountain masterpiece . . . Breathtaking, tight, bit out of way but worth it . . . One of the best Donald Ross courses I've played . . . Great views of Grandfather Mountain . . . Fastest greens on earth . . . Trout in all the streams . . . Best mountain resort in the state.

★★★½ LION'S PAW GOLF LINKS

R—351 Ocean Ridge Pkwy., Sunset Beach (910)287-1717, (800)233-1801.
9 miles north of North Myrtle Beach, SC. **Holes:** 18. **Par:** 72/72.
Yards: 7,003/5,363. **Course rating:** 74.6/69.1. **Slope:** 138/118.
Opened: 1991. **Pace of Play rating:** 4:30. **Green fee:** $35/75.
Credit cards: All major. **Reduced fees:** Weekdays, Low season, Resort guests, Twilight, Juniors.
Caddies: No. **Golf carts:** $15 for 18 holes.
Discount golf packages: Yes. **Season:** Year-round. **High:** Spring/Fall.
On-site lodging: No. **Rental clubs:** Yes.
Walking policy: Mandatory cart. **Range:** Yes (grass).
To obtain tee times: Golf packages or call pro shop.
Additional 9 holes added to Panther's Run Course due to open Sept. '95.

Subscriber comments: Wild driver's dream, pretty . . . A poke to get to landing areas from tees . . . Hit all the clubs in the bag . . . Bugs will carry you off in spring . . . Toughest set of par 3s . . . Fun to play . . . Greens smooth as a baby's bottom . . . Add one club on par 3s . . . My favorite on our annual golf trip to beach . . . Each are nicely done . . . Good contrast between nines . . . Look forward to the new 36 . . . New "Panther Run" very, very nice . . . Good course for good golfer . . . Nice course; if you get the chance, play it . . . Look out for the paw hole . . . Best course for the money in Brunswick Country coast.

★½ LOCHMERE GOLF CLUB

SP—2511 Kildare Farm Rd., Cary (919)851-0611.
5 miles west of Raleigh. **Holes:** 18. **Par:** 72/74.
Yards: 6,867/5,052. **Course rating:** 71.8/68.1. **Slope:** 124/113.
Opened: 1986. **Pace of Play rating:** 4:15. **Green fee:** $18/28.
Credit cards: MC, V. **Reduced fees:** Weekdays, Twilight, Seniors, Juniors.
Caddies: No. **Golf carts:** $12 for 18 holes.
Discount golf packages: No. **Season:** Year-round. **High:** N/A.
On-site lodging: No. **Rental clubs:** Yes.
Walking policy: Walking at certain times. **Range:** Yes (grass).
To obtain tee times: Call one week in advance.
Subscriber comments: OK course, built in a valley, usually stays wet . . . Don't go if it has rained in the last month . . . Player-friendly appearance, but can get sloppy . . . Needs some course work . . . Tight, but easy to walk.

★★★ LOCKWOOD GOLF LINKS

SP—19 Clubhouse Dr. S.W., Supply (910)842-5666, (800)443-7891.
40 miles north of Myrtle Beach, SC. **Holes:** 18. **Par:** 72/72.
Yards: 6,836/5,524. **Course rating:** 73.5/70.0. **Slope:** 135/121.
Opened: 1988. **Pace of Play rating:** N/A. **Green fee:** $25/62.
Credit cards: MC, V. **Reduced fees:** Low season, Resort guests, Juniors.
Caddies: No. **Golf carts:** Included in Green Fee.
Discount golf packages: Yes. **Season:** Year-round. **High:** Spring/Fall.
On-site lodging: Yes. **Rental clubs:** Yes.
Walking policy: Mandatory cart. **Range:** Yes (grass).
To obtain tee times: Call up to one year in advance between 7 a.m. and 5 p.m.
Subscriber comments: Tight. Tough from the blue tees . . . Beautiful course . . . Off the beaten path . . . Nice tight course . . . Need to be straight off tee . . . Great views of marsh . . . Little off the main roads . . . Good beach course, good layout . . . Some layup holes off tee . . . This course can be enjoyed by true golfers of any skill level.

★★★ MAGGIE VALLEY RESORT GOLF CLUB

R—340 Country Club Rd., Maggie Valley (704)926-6013.
40 miles west of Asheville. **Holes:** 18. **Par:** 72/73.
Yards: 6,336/5,195. **Course rating:** 69.8/69.4. **Slope:** 121/117.
Opened: 1963. **Pace of Play rating:** 4:30. **Green fee:** $15/33.
Credit cards: All major. **Reduced fees:** Weekdays, Low season, Twilight, Juniors.
Caddies: No. **Golf carts:** $15 for 18 holes.
Discount golf packages: Yes. **Season:** Year-round. **High:** March-Nov.
On-site lodging: Yes. **Rental clubs:** Yes.
Walking policy: Walking at certain times. **Range:** Yes (grass).
To obtain tee times: Call one day in advance.
Subscriber comments: Beautiful layout, front nine in the valley . . . Great layout . . . Front and back vastly different . . . Tough back nine, hilly . . . Course design uses mountains very well . . . Great food . . . Nothing special, some nice holes . . . Just a good place for a golfing holiday . . . Appeals to all level of players . . . Easy front nine more difficult back . . .

Great staff . . . Accommodations are old but clean . . . Fun to play with friends . . . Staff was very helpful and friendly . . . Nice greens, mostly flat and open . . . Some awesome, unfair greens . . . Sadistic pin placements on back make you hold your breath . . . I love it!

★½ MAGNOLIA COUNTRY CLUB

SP—171 Magnolia Lane, Magnolia (910)289-2126.
40 miles south of Wilmington. **Holes:** 18. **Par:** 71/71.
Yards: 6,400/4,600. **Course rating:** 69.8/68.3. **Slope:** 116/109.
Opened: 1974. **Pace of Play rating:** 3:30. **Green fee:** $7/13.
Credit cards: None. **Reduced fees:** Weekdays, Resort guests, Twilight, Seniors, Juniors.
Caddies: No. **Golf carts:** $8 for 18 holes.
Discount golf packages: No. **Season:** Year-round. **High:** June-Aug.
On-site lodging: No. **Rental clubs:** Yes.
Walking policy: Unrestricted walking. **Range:** No.
To obtain tee times: Call for weekend tee times only.
Subscriber comments: Good course for iron play . . . You get what you pay for . . . The course is flat; greens very small, but simple . . . Easy, flat country course, kinda backwoodsy . . . Fun to play, fine staff . . . Wonderful, a stranger has never left this course.

★★★ MALLARD HEAD COUNTRY CLUB

SP—P.O. Box 480, Mooresville (704)664-7031.
Call club for further information.
Subscriber comments: Pleasant surprise for the cost . . . Tough but fair test of golf, Great greens, Keep it a secret . . . Need to improve the intangibles . . . Too much O.B. . . . Lots of friendly dogs! Good layout, could be in better shape . . . Very good, little known course . . . Still has Hugo damage . . . Best deal around Charlotte.

★★★½ MARSH HARBOUR GOLF LINKS

PU—Hwy. 179, Calabash (910)579-3161, (800)377-2315.
15 miles north of Myrtle Beach, SC. **Holes:** 18. **Par:** 71/71.
Yards: 6,690/4,795. **Course rating:** 72.4/67.7. **Slope:** 134/115.
Opened: 1980. **Pace of Play rating:** 4:30. **Green fee:** $30/75.
Credit cards: MC, V, AMEX. **Reduced fees:** Low season, Resort guests.
Caddies: No. **Golf carts:** $17 for 18 holes.
Discount golf packages: Yes. **Season:** Year-round. **High:** March-April/Oct.
On-site lodging: No. **Rental clubs:** Yes.
Walking policy: Mandatory cart. **Range:** Yes (grass).
To obtain tee times: Call up to nine months in advance. Deposit required during high season.
Ranked in Second 25 of America's 75 Best Public Golf Courses by Golf Digest.
Subscriber comments: A unique pleasure and challenge . . . Beautiful . . . Target golf . . . Beautiful holes on intracoastal waterway . . . Favorite place to play . . . Great use of natural coast . . . Best yardage books . . . Woody and tough . . . Good for players who keep ball in play . . . Great test from back tees . . . Marsh in play a lot . . . Not in top shape . . . Neat scenery . . . Good greens . . . Great fishing holes, scenic . . . The best course in the area . . . Shotmaker's course . . . Two great finishing holes . . . Good golf course except I hate the 17th hole . . . Better than her Oyster sister . . . Par-5 17th is fantastic . . . I made par! Target course, last two holes beautiful . . . 17th green at sunset is the best in the world.

★★★½ MID PINES GOLF CLUB

R—1010 Midland Rd., Southern Pines (910)692-9362, (800)323-2114.
70 miles south of Raleigh. **Holes:** 18. **Par:** 72/75.
Yards: 6,515/5,592. **Course rating:** 71.4/72.3. **Slope:** 127/128.
Opened: 1921. **Pace of Play rating:** 4:30. **Green fee:** $30/60.
Credit cards: MC, V, AMEX. **Reduced fees:** Low season, Resort guests, Twilight.

Caddies: No. **Golf carts:** $18 for 18 holes.
Discount golf packages: Yes. **Season:** Year-round.
On-site lodging: Yes. **Rental clubs:** Yes.
Walking policy: Mandatory cart. **Range:** Yes (grass).
To obtain tee times: Call in advance.
Subscriber comments: Classical Donald Ross . . . Excellent course, beautifully designed . . . Challenging. A + + + . . . Tight/short, fun course, great hotel. Great, great, great, great. Slick greens . . . Great old course to play . . . Tight fairways, fast greens . . . Good use of water and sand . . . Some tight drives, no schlocky holes . . . Always a pleasure to play . . . Pure Donald Ross . . . A Pinehurst bargain . . . Bermuda rough is tough . . . Getting better after sold to Pine Needles . . . Very enjoyable Ross course . . . Tight fairways, need to be long and straight of the tee . . . Great fader's course . . . A Ross classic with plateau greens . . . This course proves you don't need to be 7,000 yards plus to be considered a great course . . . Beautiful, scenic, course cut out of woods, can feel the history . . . Golf takes top priority now, and it shows . . . Aged like a great bottle of wine.

★★ MONROE COUNTRY CLUB
PU—Hwy. 601-S., Monroe (704)282-4661.
20 miles southeast of Charlotte. **Holes:** 18. **Par:** 72/73.
Yards: 6,759/4,964. **Course rating:** 71.8/68.6. **Slope:** 118/117.
Opened: 1936. **Pace of Play rating:** 4:00-4:30. **Green fee:** $12/17.
Credit cards: None. **Reduced fees:** Weekdays.
Caddies: No. **Golf carts:** $9 for 18 holes.
Discount golf packages: No. **Season:** Year-round. **High:** May-Aug.
On-site lodging: No. **Rental clubs:** Yes.
Walking policy: Unrestricted walking. **Range:** Yes (grass).
To obtain tee times: Weekend tee times only. Call Thursday prior to the weekend.
Subscriber comments: Two different nines . . . Front nine beautiful; back nine fair . . . Nine holes by Donald Ross (best nine) . . . Front Tom Jackson design . . . Back Donald Ross . . . Short course, some tight holes, good pace . . . Good course for a short hitter like me . . . Worth a look.

MOORESVILLE GOLF COURSE★
PU—W. Wilson Rd., Mooresville (704)663-2539.
25 miles north of Charlotte. **Holes:** 18. **Par:** 72/72.
Yards: 6,528/4,976. **Course rating:** 72.5/68.6. **Slope:** 124/115.
Opened: 1963. **Pace of Play rating:** 4:00-5:00. **Green fee:** $9/12.
Credit cards: MC, V. **Reduced fees:** Seniors, Juniors.
Caddies: No. **Golf carts:** $10 for 18 holes.
Discount golf packages: No. **Season:** Year-round. **High:** April-Nov.
On-site lodging: No. **Rental clubs:** Yes.
Walking policy: Walking at certain times. **Range:** Yes (grass).
To obtain tee times: Call 24 hours in advance for weekdays and one week in advance for weekends and holidays.

★½ MOREHEAD CITY COUNTRY CLUB
SP—Country Club Rd., Morehead City (919)726-4917.
Call club for further information.
Subscriber comments: Very good golf for a small town country club . . . Two par 5s together . . . Nice people . . . Grip it/rip it course, short and forgiving, the average player will play well here . . . Poor tee boxes . . . Not very scenic . . . Simple design . . . Small, flat greens are the downfall here . . . Average course, easy recovery from bad shots.

★★★½ MOUNT MITCHELL GOLF CLUB
PU—7590 Hwy. 80 S., Burnsville (704)675-5454.
55 miles northeast of Asheville. **Holes:** 18. **Par:** 72/72.
Yards: 6,475/5,455. **Course rating:** 70.0/69.5. **Slope:** 121/117.
Opened: 1975. **Pace of Play rating:** 4:00. **Green fee:** $30/45.
Credit cards: MC, V. **Reduced fees:** Weekdays, Low season, Resort guests.

Caddies: No. **Golf carts:** Included in Green Fee.
Discount golf packages: Yes. **Season:** April-Nov. **High:** May-Oct.
On-site lodging: Yes. **Rental clubs:** Yes.
Walking policy: Walking at certain times. **Range:** No.
To obtain tee times: Call two weeks in advance. You must guarantee
with credit card during times of heavy play.
Subscriber comments: Delightful mountain golf with steep hills . . . Gem
in the mountains . . . Enjoyable and memorable . . . Lovely, challenging
course . . . Finest public course around, but no range . . . Scenery and
course excellent . . . Marvelous fairways and greens . . . Must play. Course
running at base of mountain . . . Back nine is unbelievable . . . Beautiful
and tough . . . Real treat to play . . . Played early spring through early fall,
course always outstanding . . . Breathtaking beauty . . . The best mountain
course in North Carolina.

★★½ MOUNTAIN AIRE GOLF CLUB
PU—1104 Golf Course Rd., West Jefferson (910)877-4716.
80 miles west of Winston-Salem. **Holes:** 18. **Par:** 71/71.
Yards: 6,107/4,143. **Course rating:** 71.0/66.0. **Slope:** 113/113.
Opened: 1950. **Pace of Play rating:** 4:00. **Green fee:** $12/17.
Credit cards: MC, V. **Reduced fees:** Weekdays, Low season, Twilight,
Juniors.
Caddies: No. **Golf carts:** $9 for 18 holes.
Discount golf packages: Yes. **Season:** March-Nov. **High:** June-Aug.
On-site lodging: Yes. **Rental clubs:** Yes.
Walking policy: Unrestricted walking. **Range:** Yes (grass).
To obtain tee times: Call pro shop.
Subscriber comments: Needs growth . . . Best kept secret . . . Beautiful
course, most fun ever . . . Great people . . . Back nine in good shape . . .
Fair value . . . Best mountain course for the money.

★★★½ MOUNTAIN GLEN GOLF CLUB
SP—Newland (704)733-5804.
Call club for further information.
Subscriber comments: George Cobb track . . . Very nice mountain
course . . . Course is better each time you play . . . Nice mountain course
and nice people . . . You use every club in your bag . . . Beautiful mountain
course . . . Fast greens . . . Great views . . . Enjoyable . . . Good shape and
fun . . . Short, nice mountain setting.

★★★ NAGS HEAD GOLF LINKS
R—5615 S. Seachase Dr., Nags Head (919)441-8073, (800)851-9404.
75 miles south of Virginia Beach, VA. **Holes:** 18. **Par:** 71/71.
Yards: 6,200/5,800. **Course rating:** 68.8/66.9. **Slope:** 130/126.
Opened: 1987. **Pace of Play rating:** 4:30. **Green fee:** $25/75.
Credit cards: MC, V. **Reduced fees:** Weekdays, Low season, Resort
guests, Twilight, Seniors, Juniors.
Caddies: No. **Golf carts:** Included in Green Fee.
Discount golf packages: Yes. **Season:** Year-round. **High:** June-Aug.
On-site lodging: Yes. **Rental clubs:** Yes.
Walking policy: Mandatory cart. **Range:** Yes (grass).
To obtain tee times: Call pro shop up to one year in advance.
Subscriber comments: A hidden gem, don't tell anyone . . . Too narrow
. . . The wind is mean . . . Don't hit it straight, stay home . . . Almost
unplayable into wind . . . Beautiful holes on backside . . . Fun, short, tight,
beautiful views of the sound, driver rarely needed and usually bad idea . . .
Staff very friendly and courteous . . . A new course everyday, depending
on wind . . . Links style among dunes . . . Best suited for straight shooter
. . . Severe penalties if out of fairway . . . Leave your driver in the trunk
. . . Gorgeous views along the sound . . . Very well maintained . . . I love
putting on fast greens that will hold a 3-iron. Brace yourself for the wind
. . . Very polite staff . . . Short, tight, learn to play the wind . . . Try to
finish your round at sunset.

★★★½ THE NEUSE GOLF CLUB

SP—918 Birkdale Dr., Clayton (919)550-0550.
15 miles east of Raleigh. **Holes:** 18. **Par:** 72/72.
Yards: 7,010/5,478. **Course rating:** 73.5/72.2. **Slope:** 136/126.
Opened: 1993. **Pace of Play rating:** 4:30. **Green fee:** $18/24.
Credit cards: MC, V. **Reduced fees:** Weekdays, Low season, Twilight,
Seniors, Juniors.
Caddies: No. **Golf carts:** $12 for 18 holes.
Discount golf packages: No. **Season:** Year-round. **High:** April-Oct.
On-site lodging: No. **Rental clubs:** Yes.
Walking policy: Walking at certain times. **Range:** Yes (grass).
To obtain tee times: Call pro shop.
Subscriber comments: Devil's Ridge with more elevation changes . . .
New course, good character, best suited for mid and low handicappers . . .
Best use of natural landscape east of Pebble Beach . . . Course is very good
. . . A little more difficult than your usual course . . . Overall, it is very fun
to play, rolling hills make it scenic . . . Great layout . . . Good staff . . . For
better players . . . Wonderful new course . . . Good new course . . . A little
immature . . . Interesting holes; needs to be rated on challenge, not yardage
. . . Great layout using all natural resources including rocks, streams . . .
Just needs time . . . Great holes along the Neuse River . . . One of the best
around, sensational vistas . . . Well designed . . . Tough, must be accurate
on every shot . . . From 12th on, unforgettable . . . Watch for ricocheting
balls on No. 14 . . . Great signature hole . . . Four great finishing holes . . .
Hoorah! Allows walking . . . Surprising how hilly this was . . . Dramatic
use of rocks and boulders, fun to play and challenging . . . Up-and-down
terrain . . . Super greens.

★★★★ NORTH SHORE COUNTRY CLUB

SP—101 N. Shore Dr., Sneads Ferry (910)327-2410, (800)828-5035.
25 miles north of Wilmington. **Holes:** 18. **Par:** 72/72.
Yards: 6,866/5,039. **Course rating:** 72.8/68.7. **Slope:** 134/122.
Opened: 1988. **Pace of Play rating:** 4:30. **Green fee:** $24/45.
Credit cards: MC, V. **Reduced fees:** Weekdays, Low season, Twilight,
Juniors.
Caddies: No. **Golf carts:** Included in Green Fee.
Discount golf packages: Yes. **Season:** Year-round. **High:** March-Nov.
On-site lodging: No. **Rental clubs:** Yes.
Walking policy: Mandatory cart. **Range:** Yes (grass).
To obtain tee times: Call up to one year in advance.
Subscriber comments: Plush, nice, good, lush . . . Fun, fair, 36 holes in
one day possible . . . Great bar . . . Wide open, but demanding due to lots
of wind . . . Don't miss this one . . . Gorgeous, wooded and clean, bent
greens, great staff, excellent . . . Outstanding greens, good test for all
golfers . . . A hidden jewel, large greens . . . Excellent shape . . . Test for
good players . . . Superb course . . . Very playable. You will play this
course more than once . . . A little out-of-the-way . . . Keeps your
attention . . . Every hole is different, scenic, blues are challenging . . .
Beautiful even in winter . . . Big, big, big, fast, slick, sweet, true greens
. . . Management very nice to walk-ons . . . Best course on the coast of
North Carolina.

★★★½ OAK HOLLOW GOLF COURSE

PU—1400 Oakview Rd., High Point (910)883-3260.
8 miles east of Greensboro. **Holes:** 18. **Par:** 72/72.
Yards: 6,483/4,796. **Course rating:** 71.6/67.4. **Slope:** 124/114.
Opened: 1972. **Pace of Play rating:** 4:30. **Green fee:** $12/15.
Credit cards: None. **Reduced fees:** Seniors, Juniors.
Caddies: No. **Golf carts:** $9 for 18 holes.
Discount golf packages: No. **Season:** Year-round. **High:** April-Aug.
On-site lodging: No. **Rental clubs:** Yes.
Walking policy: Unrestricted walking. **Range:** Yes (grass).
To obtain tee times: Call 48 hours in advance for weekdays. Call
Thursday for upcoming weekend.

Ranked in Third 25 of America's 75 Best Public Golf Courses by Golf Digest.

Subscriber comments: Early Pete Dye layout . . . Puts premium on chipping and putting. Can not beat value . . . Lots of water, interesting layout . . . Fun to play . . . Tough but fair . . . Best to play the first time with someone who knows the course layout . . . Not memorable . . . Windy, beside a lake . . . Very good muny, winds around large lake . . . Tough putting during boat races . . . Tough front nine . . . Staff very courteous . . . Slick, undulating greens . . . Shotmaker's course with some length . . . Great layout, challenge everywhere . . . Two nines are completely different . . . Unbeatable value for Pete Dye.

★★½ OAK ISLAND GOLF AND COUNTRY CLUB

PU—928 Caswell Beach Rd., Caswell Beach (910)278-5275.
23 miles south of Wilmington. **Holes:** 18. **Par:** 72/72.
Yards: 6,608/5,437. **Course rating:** N/A. **Slope:** 128/121.
Opened: N/A. **Pace of Play rating:** N/A. **Green fee:** N/A.
Credit cards: MC, V. **Reduced fees:** Weekdays, Low season.
Caddies: No. **Golf carts:** N/A.
Discount golf packages: Yes. **Season:** Year-round. **High:** June-Oct.
On-site lodging: No. **Rental clubs:** No.
Walking policy: N/A. **Range:** Yes (grass).
Subscriber comments: Fine old Cobb course . . . Good layout . . . Can be windy . . . Made improvements, better greens . . . A fun course to play, has some very tough holes . . . Ocean breeze usually makes finishing holes tough . . . Nice old beach course, people nice . . . Some fine holes . . . Course is best it has been in five years.

★½ OAKWOOD HILLS GOLF CLUB

R—U.S. Hwy. No. 1 S., Pinebluff (910)281-3169.
12 miles south of Pinehurst. **Holes:** 18. **Par:** 72/70.
Yards: 6,583/4,677. **Course rating:** 71.8/66.0. **Slope:** 127/103.
Opened: 1972. **Pace of Play rating:** 4:00. **Green fee:** $15.
Credit cards: MC, V. **Reduced fees:** Weekdays, Low season, Resort guests, Twilight.
Caddies: No. **Golf carts:** $20 for 18 holes.
Discount golf packages: Yes. **Season:** Year-round. **High:** Spring/Fall.
On-site lodging: Yes. **Rental clubs:** Yes.
Walking policy: Walking at certain times. **Range:** Yes (grass).
To obtain tee times: Call pro shop up to five months in advance.
Subscriber comments: Course has great potential . . . Staff excellent . . . Staff better than course . . . Eroded cartpaths . . . They were putting in new sprinkler system when we played.

★★ OCEAN ISLE BEACH GOLF COURSE

PU—6000 Pro Shop Dr., S.W., Ocean Isle Beach (910)579-2610.
30 miles of Myrtle Beach. **Holes:** 18. **Par:** 72/72.
Yards: 6,626/5,075. **Course rating:** N/A. **Slope:** 126/116.
Opened: N/A. **Pace of Play rating:** N/A. **Green fee:** N/A.
Credit cards: MC, V. **Reduced fees:** Twilight.
Caddies: No. **Golf carts:** N/A.
Discount golf packages: Yes. **Season:** Year-round. **High:** March/May-Sept./Nov.
On-site lodging: No. **Rental clubs:** No.
Walking policy: . **Range:** Yes (grass).
Subscriber comments: Pretty good little track, fun to walk . . . Wide open . . . Fun course . . . Very appreciative of your business . . . Hilly beach course . . . This course is always well taken care of, but it is just golf, nothing special . . . One of the best, always fun to play . . . A nice warm-up for the big boys in Myrtle Beach.

★★★ OLDE BEAU GOLF CLUB

SP—Hwy. 21, Roaring Gap (910)363-3044.
Call club for further information.

Subscriber comments: Trickery at its best . . . Some rather wacky holes . . . Worth the drive for the scenery, especially in the fall . . . Tight driving; if not in the fairway you're dead . . . 17th hole is like falling off a mountain . . . Target golf uphill . . . A challenging course, but it has a few easy holes . . . Absolutely gorgeous, breathtaking . . . Mountain course with fabulous views . . . Staff treatment was outstanding . . . Wonderful scenic views, but the course has some quirky holes . . . Beautiful views, great staff, makes bad round enjoyable, worth the price . . . Bring climbing boots . . . A great course, take a camera . . . Autumn is simply breathtaking . . . I'd play it again just for the unbelievable scenery.

★★★ OLDE POINT COUNTRY CLUB

SP—Country Club Dr. and Hwy. 17 N., Hampstead (910)270-2403.
18 miles north of Wilmington. **Holes:** 18. **Par:** 72/72.
Yards: 6,913/5,133. **Course rating:** 72.5/69.0. **Slope:** 136/115.
Opened: 1974. **Pace of Play rating:** 4:00–4:30 **Green fee:** $25/45.
Credit cards: MC, V, AMEX. **Reduced fees:** Weekdays, Low season.
Caddies: No. **Golf carts:** Included in Green Fee.
Discount golf packages: Yes. **Season:** Year-round. **High:** March–May.
On-site lodging: Yes. **Rental clubs:** Yes.
Walking policy: Mandatory cart. **Range:** Yes (grass).
To obtain tee times: Call pro shop in advance.
Subscriber comments: Course is a sleeper, very hilly design . . .
Beautifully wooded course, bent greens . . . Above average public course, fair condition . . . Interesting track . . . Nice course . . . No. 11 a memorable par 5 . . . Tight fairways and doglegs . . . Best in Pender County . . . Best hot dogs anywhere.

★★★½ OYSTER BAY GOLF LINKS

PU—Hwy. 179, Sunset Beach (910)579-7391, (800)377-2315.
18 miles north of Myrtle Beach, SC. **Holes:** 18. **Par:** 71/71.
Yards: 6,785/4,825. **Course rating:** 74.1/67.7. **Slope:** 137/117.
Opened: 1983. **Pace of Play rating:** N/A. **Green fee:** $30/75.
Credit cards: MC, V, AMEX. **Reduced fees:** Low season, Resort guests.
Caddies: No. **Golf carts:** $17 for 18 holes.
Discount golf packages: Yes. **Season:** Year-round. **High:** March–April/Oct.
On-site lodging: No. **Rental clubs:** Yes.
Walking policy: Mandatory cart. **Range:** Yes (grass).
To obtain tee times: Call up to nine months in advance. Deposit required during high season. Reservations
available for all six Legends Group courses and Legends Resorts.
Ranked in Second 25 of America's 75 Best Public Golf Courses by Golf Digest. Selected Best New Resort Course of 1983 by Golf Digest.
Subscriber comments: A scenic beauty . . . Lots of water . . . Wonderful layout, super shape . . . Beautiful scenery . . . Beauty and a beast . . . Postcard holes almost "too cute" . . . Wish I lived closer . . . One of my coastal favorites . . . One of the most enjoyable . . . One of the prettiest golf courses anywhere on the coast . . . I've never played a Maples course that was not special . . . When it is ready for play it is gorgeous . . . What a course! Play it every time I go to Myrtle Beach.

★½ PAWTUCKET GOLF CLUB

SP—One Pawtucket Rd., Charlotte (704)394-5909.
Call club for further information.
Subscriber comments: Fair course with some trick holes . . . Couple of very short par 3s, otherwise competitive course . . . Poorly planned, can't be improved . . . Some interesting holes . . . Rough course, all bent-grass greens . . . Sparse . . . Fair condition . . . Standard of public golf in Charlotte.

THE PEARL GOLF LINKS

PU—1300 Pearl Blvd. S.W., Sunset Beach (910)579-8132.
10 miles north of Myrtle Beach, S.C. **Green fee:** $31/69.

Credit cards: All major. **Reduced fees:** Twilight, Juniors.
Caddies: No. **Golf carts:** Included in Green Fee.
Discount golf packages: No. **Season:** Year-round. **High:** Spring/Fall.
On-site lodging: No. **Rental clubs:** Yes.
Walking policy: Mandatory cart. **Range:** Yes (grass).
To obtain tee times: Call pro shop.

★★★½ **EAST COURSE**
Holes: 18. **Par:** 72/72.
Yards: 6,749/5,125. **Course rating:** 73.1/73.9. **Slope:** 135/129.
Opened: 1987. **Pace of Play rating:** 4:30-5:00
Subscriber comments: Outstanding, a real gem . . . Pretty layout . . .
Good bent grass greens . . . Choose your tees well here, it can eat your
lunch . . . Always in good condition but always a long, long, long round of
golf. . . Bring your "A" game or sit in the bar and drink "Bullfrogs" . . .
Bring your whole game in summer . . . Three feet off greens and your ball
is only half visible . . . Excellent condition . . . A treat to play again and
again.

★★★½ **WEST COURSE**
Holes: 18. **Par:** 72/72.
Yards: 7,000/5,188. **Course rating:** 73.2/73.4. **Slope:** 132/127.
Opened: 1987. **Pace of Play rating:** 4:30-5:00.

Subscriber comments: Outstanding Dan Maples design . . . Great coastal
layout, many waste areas . . . Nice course, very fair . . . Good links-type
layout . . . Favorite place in Myrtle Beach . . . Treat juniors as humans . . .
Pebble Beach of the East Coast! These two courses are identical as far as
rating them goes . . . Great tracks . . . Beautiful scenery . . . Five par 5s,
five par 3s, fun . . . Great finishing holes . . . Multitudes of trouble: marsh,
oyster shells, lovegrass, sand and water.

PINE GROVE GOLF CLUB★
PU—1108 Costner Rd., Shelby (704)487-0455.
45 miles west of Charlotte. **Holes:** 18. **Par:** 70/70.
Yards: 6,238/4,774. **Course rating:** 67.9/63.5. **Slope:** 110/100.
Opened: 1960 **Pace of Play rating:** 4:00. **Green fee:** $12/22.
Credit cards: MC, V. **Reduced fees:** Weekdays, Seniors.
Caddies: No. **Golf carts:** Included in Green Fee.
Discount golf packages: No. **Season:** Year-round. **High:** June-Aug.
On-site lodging: No. **Rental clubs:** No.
Walking policy: Walking at certain times. **Range:** No.
To obtain tee times: Call for weekends and holidays.

PINE KNOLLS GOLF COURSE★
PU—1100 Quail Hollow Rd., Kernersville (910)993-8300.
9 miles east of Winston Salem. **Holes:** 18. **Par:** 72/72.
Yards: 6,287/4,480. **Course rating:** 70.0/65.0. **Slope:** 121/92.
Opened: 1969. **Pace of Play rating:** 4:00. **Green fee:** $13/16.
Credit cards: MC, V. **Reduced fees:** Seniors, Juniors.
Caddies: No. **Golf carts:** $10 for 18 holes.
Discount golf packages: No. **Season:** Year-round. **High:** May-Oct.
On-site lodging: No. **Rental clubs:** Yes.
Walking policy: Walking at certain times. **Range:** Yes (grass).
To obtain tee times: Call or come in Thursday for upcoming weekend.

★★★★ **PINE NEEDLES GOLF CLUB**
R—1005 Midland Rd., Southern Pines (910)692-8611, (800)747-7272.
70 miles south of Raleigh. **Holes:** 18. **Par:** 71/71.
Yards: 6,708/5,039. **Course rating:** 72.2/68.4. **Slope:** 131/118.
Opened: 1927. **Pace of Play rating:** 4:10. **Green fee:** $65.
Credit cards: MC, V, AMEX. **Reduced fees:** Low season, Resort guests.
Caddies: No. **Golf carts:** $18 for 18 holes.
Discount golf packages: Yes. **Season:** Year-round. **High:** Spring/Fall.
On-site lodging: Yes. **Rental clubs:** Yes.
Walking policy: Walking at certain times. **Range:** Yes (grass).
To obtain tee times: Call pro shop once a room reservation is made.

Outside play is taken on a space-available basis up to 30 days in advance.
Subscriber comments: Old Donald Ross magic . . . Super layout/tough finishing hole . . . Great course for all golfers . . . Peggy Kirk Bell great . . . Recent improvements help a great deal . . . Excellent facilities and a fair test for any golfer . . . Mrs. Bell and her staff have done an incredible job with this gem of a course . . . Fast turtle-back greens . . . Getting ready for Women's Open . . . Even better than Mid Pines . . . Top quality . . . My first visit was everything I had hoped for . . . Similar to Pinehurst No. 2 in value of shotmaking . . . Playable at every level . . . Nice training facility . . . Best practice facility in area . . . In top two or three in Pinehurst area.

★½ PINE TREE GOLF CLUB
PU—1680 Pine Tree Lane, Kernersville (910)993-5598.
18 miles west of Greensboro. **Holes:** 18. **Par:** 71/71.
Yards: 6,604/4,897. **Course rating:** 71.0/67.0. **Slope:** 113/110.
Opened: 1970. **Pace of Play rating:** 4:00. **Green fee:** $14/18.
Credit cards: MC, V. **Reduced fees:** Seniors.
Caddies: No. **Golf carts:** $10 for 18 holes.
Discount golf packages: No. **Season:** Year-round. **High:** April-Oct.
On-site lodging: No. **Rental clubs:** Yes.
Walking policy: Walking at certain times. **Range:** Yes (grass).
To obtain tee times: Call up to 10 days in advance.
Subscriber comments: Terrific layout . . . Poor conditioning . . . Course could be upgraded . . . Large greens, good for ego . . . Fairly open . . . Not too crowded . . . Getting much better with new owners . . . Easy to get tee times . . . Wide open course . . . Just enough challenge . . . A pleasant game.

★★★★½ PINEHURST PLANTATION GOLF CLUB
SP—Midland Rd., Pinehurst (910)695-3193, (800)633-2685.
50 miles south of Raleigh. **Holes:** 18. **Par:** 72/72.
Yards: 7,135/5,046. **Course rating:** 74.5/68.8. **Slope:** 140/125.
Opened: 1993. **Pace of Play rating:** 3:55. **Green fee:** $53/110.
Credit cards: MC, V, AMEX. **Reduced fees:** No.
Caddies: No. **Golf carts:** Included in Green Fee.
Discount golf packages: No. **Season:** Year-round. **High:** April-May/Oct.
On-site lodging: No. **Rental clubs:** Yes.
Walking policy: Mandatory cart. **Range:** Yes (grass).
To obtain tee times: Have head pro set up a tee time or call golf shop out of season.
Ranked 20th in North Carlina by Golf Digest.
Subscriber comments: Super course, super use of lands, great greens, great challenge . . . Arnold Palmer layout . . . Great greens, great course . . . Excellent service . . . Great test of golf . . . Best course in Pinehurst besides No. 2 . . . Very fast greens . . . Super course, super use of lands . . . great greens . . . Great challenge.

PINEHURST RESORT AND COUNTRY CLUB
R—Carolina Vista St., Pinehurst (910)295-8141, (800)795-4653.
70 miles southwest of Raleigh.
Credit cards: All major. **Reduced fees:** Low season, Twilight.
Caddies: Yes. **Golf carts:** $19 for 18 holes.
Discount golf packages: Yes. **Season:** Year-round. **High:** Spring/Fall.
On-site lodging: Yes. **Rental clubs:** Yes.
Walking policy: Unrestricted walking. **Range:** Yes (grass).
To obtain tee times: Call 1-800-ITS-GOLF.
★★★ PINEHURST NO. 1
Holes: 18. **Par:** 70/73.
Yards: 5,780/5,329. **Course rating:** 67.4/70.1. **Slope:** 114/117.
Opened: 1899. **Pace of Play rating:** N/A. **Green fee:** $38/70.
Subscriber comments: Typically Pinehurst . . . Best sporty, short course for all golfers . . . Ladies will love it . . . Scenic, great greens . . . Good traditional type course . . . Fine seniors course, not too long . . . Kept clean

and neat . . . Hospitality good, staff treats you like family . . . Testy but short . . . Maddening Ross greens . . . Wonderful golf, enjoyable, makes you feel like you are a good player . . . Nice course, not too demanding.

★★★★★ **PINEHURST NO. 2**

Holes: 18. **Par:** 72/74.

Yards: 7,020/5,966. **Course rating:** 74.1/74.2. **Slope:** 131/135.

Opened: 1901. **Pace of Play rating:** N/A. **Green fee:** $113/145.

Ranked 9th in America's 100 Greatest Golf Courses by Golf Digest. Ranked 2nd in America's 75 Best Resort Courses by Golf Digest. Ranked 1st in North Carolina by Golf Digest.

Subscriber comments: This course needs no introduction . . . Memorable, but too expensive . . . My favorite for playability on all levels . . . The best!!! Must take a caddy to enjoy . . . Great atmosphere, intimidating greens . . . Superb! Would play everyday of the week . . . Take caddie and really see this course . . . This is what golf is all about . . . Wish I could afford to play daily . . . Deceptive looking course . . . Much more difficult than it appears . . . Fine accommodations . . . Not difficult for high handicappers, but a real test for low handicappers . . . Long, hard second shots with woods and long irons . . . Enjoy the walk through history, an honor to play it . . . The only course where I don't care what I shoot . . . The perfect golf experience . . . I had chills going up my spine coming up 18 . . . The best ever . . . Classic that will always challenge . . . Change nothing! The pinnacle, better than Pebble Beach . . . The best of Ross . . . Pinehurst No. 2 akin to religious experience. World–class resort, best clubhouse in America. The masterpiece, what else to say? Tougher to score than it looks . . . An 80 feels like a 70 . . . A premier course, expensive but worth it . . . The best, plain and simple.

★★★ **PINEHURST NO. 3**

Holes: 18. **Par:** 70/72.

Yards: 5,593/5,198. **Course rating:** 67.2/71.1. **Slope:** 112/114.

Opened: 1907. **Pace of Play rating:** N/A **Green fee:** $38/70.

Subscriber comments: Short but tricky . . . Tough greens . . . Most difficult to hit . . . Tough to putt . . . Greens even more challenging than No. 2 . . . Enjoyable.

★★★½ **PINEHURST NO. 4**

Holes: 18. **Par:** 72/73.

Yards: 6,919/5,696. **Course rating:** 73.3/71.8. **Slope:** 126/119.

Opened: 1912. **Pace of Play rating:** N/A. **Green fee:** $38/70.

Subscriber comments: Not No. 2, more fun for average golfer . . . Spectacular, third best of the seven . . . Last three holes toughest in Pinehurst . . . Fast, firm greens . . . Hidden jewel . . . Fun, classic, fair course . . . In best shape of Pinehurst courses . . . Lots of variety, a must play course . . . Best after No. 2.

★★★ **PINEHURST NO. 5**

Holes: 18. **Par:** 72/73.

Yards: 6,827/5,658. **Course rating:** 73.4/74.7. **Slope:** 130/131.

Opened: 1961. **Pace of Play rating:** N/A. **Green fee:** $38/70.

Subscriber comments: A different course for Pinehurst . . . Tough layout, challenging, well placed shots . . . More challenging than No. 1 or No. 3 . . . Lots of O.B.s . . . Hardly an easy par on course . . . Not the same as 20 years ago . . . Toughest course at Pinehurst . . . Too many O.B. with condos and houses . . . It's Pinehurst, enough said.

★★★½ **PINEHURST NO. 6**

Holes: 18. **Par:** 72/72.

Yards: 7,157/5,430. **Course rating:** 75.6/71.2. **Slope:** 139/125.

Opened: 1979. **Pace of Play rating:** N/A. **Green fee:** $38/70.

Credit cards: All major. **Reduced fees:** Low season, Twilight.

Caddies: No.

Subscriber comments: Another gem at Pinehurst . . . Sweet course . . . Easy layout, fun and fair . . . Too many condos and such . . . My second favorite scenic, watery challenge . . . Interesting . . . Not the best Pinehurst can offer . . . Love to play it, great design, beautiful surroundings . . . From the tips, one of the most difficult courses you can find anywhere . . . Good addition to group . . . Fine staff. Tough, tough, tough! A hidden Tom

Fazio gem . . . Must include on your Pinehurst agenda . . . Good variety when playing Pinehurst . . . Lives in the shadow of No. 2.

★★★★ **PINEHURST NO. 7**

Holes: 18. **Par:** 72/72.
Yards: 7,114/4,924. **Course rating:** 75.6/69.7. **Slope:** 145/124.
Opened: 1986. **Pace of Play rating:** N/A. **Green fee:** $83/115.
Caddies: No.

Ranked 23rd in America's 75 Best Resort Courses by Golf Digest. Ranked 15th in North Carolina by Golf Digest.

Subscriber comments: Not to be overlooked among their wonderful collection . . . Tough, but beautiful . . . Tough greens . . . The only thing better is No. 2 . . . More forgiving than No. 2 around greens . . . There is just too much to like about Pinehurst . . . Hard greens, you've got to keep your head on straight to play it . . . Just outstanding. Very difficult . . . Maybe the best of the seven, tough but fair . . . Tough to enjoy an 85 being a four handicapper but I did on No. 7! Best of the Pinehurst seven . . . Wow! Too hard for us . . . A true gem, love it . . . All OK . . . Courteous and helpful staff . . . Tough, very hilly . . . Contoured greens, awesome! Terrific Rees Jones test, fair, hard, interesting . . . You will not score well the first time you play . . . Rees Jones rose to the challenge of Donald Ross.

★★★ **THE PIT GOLF LINKS**

PU—Hwy. 5, Pinehurst (910)944-1600, (800)574-4653
35 miles west of Fayetteville. **Holes:** 18. **Par:** 72/72.
Yards: 6,600/4,759. **Course rating:** 72.3/68.4. **Slope:** 139/121.
Opened: 1985. **Pace of Play rating:** N/A. **Green fee:** $25/64.
Credit cards: MC, V. **Reduced fees:** Low season, Twilight, Juniors.
Caddies: No. **Golf carts:** $17 for 18 holes.
Discount golf packages: Yes. **Season:** Year-round. **High:** March/May-Oct.
On-site lodging: No. **Rental clubs:** Yes.
Walking policy: Unrestricted walking. **Range:** Yes (grass).
To obtain tee times: Call 800-574-4653.

Ranked in Second 25 of America's 75 Best Public Golf Courses by Golf Digest.

Subscriber comments: Unique layout, loads of fun . . . Great layout . . . Like full-length miniature golf . . . Course very unique, truly a test, particularly from the tips . . . Very unusual, very enjoyable . . . Has no room for errant shots . . . You love it or you hate it . . . Lots of elevations . . . Watch the greens . . . Miss a fairway and you're dead . . . Tough layout for novices . . . You'll lose every ball in your bag if you're off line . . . Too tricked up . . . Lots of character . . . A must play! Great terrain . . . Accuracy a must . . . Would have to play several times . . . Tight! A thinking golfer's course, shot placement critical . . . Funkier than Snoop Doggy Dog . . . A real club-snapper . . . Target course, lots of water and trouble . . . You want to come back and beat the course.

★★★½ **PORTERS NECK COUNTRY CLUB**

SP—1202 Porters Neck Rd., Wilmington (910)686-1177.
3 miles north of Raleigh. **Holes:** 18. **Par:** 72/72.
Yards: 7,209/5,268. **Course rating:** 74.4/70.1. **Slope:** 130/115.
Opened: 1991. **Pace of Play rating:** 4:00. **Green fee:** $30/60.
Credit cards: MC, V, AMEX. **Reduced fees:** Weekdays, Low season, Resort guests, Twilight.
Caddies: No. **Golf carts:** Included in Green Fee.
Discount golf packages: Yes. **Season:** Year-round. **High:** Feb.-May
On-site lodging: No. **Rental clubs:** Yes.
Walking policy: Mandatory cart. **Range:** Yes (grass).
To obtain tee times: Call pro shop in advance.

Ranked 13th in North Carolina by Golf Digest.

Subscriber comments: Fazio treasure . . . Costly but must play at least once . . . Beautiful surroundings . . . Fascinating Fazio . . . Fun course, just right for average players . . . Giant sand traps . . . Pretty area . . . Tight course in nice condition . . . Several risk/reward holes . . . Beach golf with its beach . . . New Tom Fazio layout is fun to play, wide fairways, challenging approaches and tough greens . . . Tournament caliber when dry . . . Bring on the pros.

★★ QUAIL RIDGE GOLF COURSE
SP—5634 Quail Ridge Dr., Sanford (919)776-6623, (800)344-6276.
30 miles south of Raleigh. **Holes:** 18. **Par:** 72/73.
Yards: 6,875/5,280. **Course rating:** 73.2/70.8. **Slope:** 125/117.
Opened: 1965. **Pace of Play rating:** 3:30-4:00. **Green fee:** $25/35.
Credit cards: MC, V. **Reduced fees:** Weekdays, Low season, Twilight, Seniors, Juniors.
Caddies: No. **Golf carts:** Included in Green Fee.
Discount golf packages: Yes. **Season:** Year-round. **High:** Spring/Fall.
On-site lodging: Yes. **Rental clubs:** Yes.
Walking policy: Walking at certain times. **Range:** Yes (grass).
To obtain tee times: Call pro shop.
Subscriber comments: Beautiful setting, playable, friendly . . . Very good course for the average player, wonderful people in charge . . . Challenging and playable . . . Hilly layout, some very good holes . . . Fair condition . . . Conditions improving . . . Nice course, deep bunkers . . . Need every shot in your bag . . . Somewhat hilly, large sand traps . . . Good design, desperately needs better maintainance . . . Down-to-earth staff.

★ QUAKER MEADOWS GOLF CLUB
PU—826 N. Green St., Morganton (704)437-2677.
Call club for further information.
Subscriber comments: Playable, needs better maintainance . . . Good public course, very busy, many brainless approach shots . . . For the weekend golfer.

QUAKER NECK COUNTRY CLUB★
SP—299 Country Club Rd., Trenton (919)224-5736.
10 miles south of New Bern. **Holes:** 18. **Par:** 72/73.
Yards: 6,405/5,080. **Course rating:** 68.0/69.0. **Slope:** 108/106.
Opened: 1976. **Pace of Play rating:** 4:00. **Green fee:** $10/15.
Credit cards: MC, V. **Reduced fees:** Weekdays.
Caddies: No. **Golf carts:** $10 for 18 holes.
Discount golf packages: No. **Season:** Year-round. **High:** June-Aug.
On-site lodging: No. **Rental clubs:** Yes.
Walking policy: Unrestricted walking. **Range:** Yes (grass).
To obtain tee times: Call pro shop.

★★★ QUARRY HILLS COUNTRY CLUB
SP—George Bason Rd., Graham (910)578-2602.
Call club for further information.
Subscriber comments: Underrated test, better have your "A" game ready . . . Very tough short course, tough par 3s . . . Long hitter's course, tricky greens . . . Good finishing holes.

★★½ REEDY CREEK GOLF CLUB
PU—585 Reedy Creek Rd., Four Oaks (919)934-7502, (800)331-2572.
20 miles south of Raleigh. **Holes:** 18. **Par:** 72/72.
Yards: 6,401/5,115. **Course rating:** 70.5/68.5. **Slope:** 117/115.
Opened: 1988. **Pace of Play rating:** 4:15. **Green fee:** $12/20.
Credit cards: MC, V. **Reduced fees:** Weekdays, Resort guests, Twilight, Seniors, Juniors.
Caddies: No. **Golf carts:** $9 for 18 holes.
Discount golf packages: Yes. **Season:** Year-round. **High:** April-Sept.
On-site lodging: No. **Rental clubs:** Yes.
Walking policy: Walking at certain times. **Range:** Yes (grass).
To obtain tee times: Call pro shop at least one week in advance for your choice on weekends.

Subscriber comments: Unique farmland turned golf course . . . Worth drive from Raleigh . . . Fun course . . . Has some character, too. Sandy but enjoyable . . . A hidden jewel . . . Another well-kept secret . . . Course, slow Bermuda greens . . . Some really tough holes . . . No. 13 is a killer . . . Noisy . . . Fun course, wide open . . . Very friendly staff . . . short but interesting, good course for seniors . . . Excellent par 3s . . . Let driver fly . . . Can be deceptively hard.

★★★½ REEMS CREEK GOLF CLUB
SP—Pink Fox Cove Rd., Weaverville (704)645-4393, (800)762-8379.
12 miles north of Asheville. **Holes:** 18. **Par:** 72/72.
Yards: 6,477/4,605. **Course rating:** 71.6/66.9. **Slope:** 133/114.
Opened: 1989. **Pace of Play rating:** 4:30. **Green fee:** $37/40.
Credit cards: MC, V. **Reduced fees:** Weekdays, Low season, Resort guests.
Caddies: No. **Golf carts:** Included in Green Fee.
Discount golf packages: Yes. **Season:** Year-round. **High:** March-Oct.
On-site lodging: No. **Rental clubs:** Yes.
Walking policy: Mandatory cart. **Range:** Yes (grass).
To obtain tee times: Call two weeks in advance. Groups larger than 24 players call six months in advance.
Subscriber comments: Last two years Reems Creek has been in immaculate condition . . . Great staff wanted you to be there . . . Good mountain course . . . Challenging course, good staff, take starter's advice . . . Beautiful scenery . . . Best conditioned course in North Carolina . . . Nice mountain layout, great views . . . Staff very organized and very helpful . . . Rolling terrain . . . Short but tough . . . Scenery great, people great and practice area beautiful . . . Very slick greens . . . No cursing allowed on No. 14 . . . Excellent course, would definitely go back . . . Too much walking from cart . . . Rough was unplayable . . . Carts remain on paths . . . Relatively short, good elevation changes, several blind shots . . . Great mountain course.

★½ REYNOLDS PARK GOLF CLUB
PU—2391 Reynolds Park Rd., Winston-Salem (910)650-7660.
2 miles south of Winston-Salem. **Holes:** 18. **Par:** 71/72.
Yards: 6,350/5,538. **Course rating:** 70.0/70.0. **Slope:** 118/118.
Opened: 1939. **Pace of Play rating:** 4:15. **Green fee:** $14/16.
Credit cards: MC, V. **Reduced fees:** Weekdays, Low season, Twilight, Seniors, Juniors.
Caddies: No. **Golf carts:** Included in Green Fee.
Discount golf packages: No. **Season:** Year-round. **High:** April-Sept.
On-site lodging: No. **Rental clubs:** Yes.
Walking policy: Walking at certain times. **Range:** Yes (grass).
To obtain tee times: Call seven days in advance.
Subscriber comments: What you expect of a North Carolina muny . . . Needs scenic additions: Lakes, color scrubs, flowers . . . Number of good and bad holes . . . Has improved over the last couple of years . . . New watering system installed three years ago . . . Improvements made . . . The traditional city public golf course . . . Different, shotmaker's course . . . Good public course for Wake Forest students.

★★★ RIVER BEND GOLF CLUB
PU—3005 Longwood Dr., Shelby (704)482-4286.
45 miles west of Charlotte. **Holes:** 18. **Par:** 72/72.
Yards: 6,610/4,920. **Course rating:** 71.0/66.0. **Slope:** 130/102.
Opened: 1965. **Pace of Play rating:** 4:00. **Green fee:** $14/18.
Credit cards: MC, V. **Reduced fees:** Seniors, Juniors.
Caddies: No. **Golf carts:** $11 for 18 holes.
Discount golf packages: Yes. **Season:** Year-round. **High:** May-Oct.
On-site lodging: No. **Rental clubs:** Yes.
Walking policy: Walking at certain times. **Range:** Yes (grass).
To obtain tee times: Call pro shop one day to one week in advance.
Subscriber comments: Comfortable surroundings . . . Excellent for mid-

to-high handicaps . . . Fairly simple; it is kept in excellent condition all year round . . . Not too challenging, but fair service and good pace . . . Too many out-of-bounds stakes . . . Best kept secret in the state.

★★★ ROCK BARN CLUB OF GOLF

SP—3791 Golf Dr., Conover (704)459-9279.
60 miles southeast of Charlotte. **Holes:** 18. **Par:** 72/72.
Yards: 6,778/4,812. **Course rating:** 72.2/67.7. **Slope:** 132/117.
Opened: 1969. **Pace of Play rating:** 4:10. **Green fee:** $31/36.
Credit cards: MC, V. **Reduced fees:** Weekdays, Seniors.
Caddies: No. **Golf carts:** $11 for 18 holes.
Discount golf packages: No. **Season:** Year-round. **High:** April-Oct.
On-site lodging: No. **Rental clubs:** Yes.
Walking policy: Unrestricted walking. **Range:** Yes (grass).
To obtain tee times: Call three days in advance.
Subscriber comments: A treat for all golfers . . . A hidden jewel, a real must . . . Not super tough, great for outings . . . Always a pleasure to play . . . Great greens, too many O.B. stakes . . . Worth the drive . . . Good course for women to beat men on . . . Championship caliber, well maintained . . . Player's course, long, good condition . . . Very good condition, fun to play, good grill room . . . Don't miss this one if you're in the area.

★★★ SANDPIPER BAY GOLF AND COUNTRY CLUB

PU—800 Sandpiper Bay Dr., Sunset Beach (910)579-9120, (800)356-5827.
25 miles north of Myrtle Beach, SC. **Holes:** 18. **Par:** 71/71.
Yards: 6,503/4,869. **Course rating:** 71.6/68.3. **Slope:** 119/113.
Opened: 1987. **Pace of Play rating:** 4:30. **Green fee:** $14/46.
Credit cards: MC, DISC. **Reduced fees:** Weekdays, Low season.
Caddies: No. **Golf carts:** $16 for 18 holes.
Discount golf packages: Yes. **Season:** Year-round. **High:** Spring/Fall.
On-site lodging: No. **Rental clubs:** Yes.
Walking policy: Mandatory cart. **Range:** Yes (grass).
To obtain tee times: Call pro shop.
Subscriber comments: Real pleasure to play, wide fairways, minimum rough . . . Nice wide fairways . . . Short and fun, five par 3s and five par 5s . . . Enjoyable for every level of golfer . . . Fair layout, doesn't beat you up . . . Nice course on very hot day . . . Well-maintained Maples layout . . . Beautiful greens and not too severe . . . Good course for women . . . Terriffic bent greens. Immaculate conditions in stiffling mid-summer heat . . . Anyone can play this course . . . Even the flora and fauna were friendly.

★½ SANDY RIDGE GOLF COURSE

PU—2025 Sandy Ridge Rd., Colfax (910)668-0408.
5 miles west of Greensboro. **Holes:** 18. **Par:** 72/72.
Yards: 6,025/5,600. **Course rating:** N/A. **Slope:** N/A.
Opened: 1970. **Pace of Play rating:** 4:00. **Green fee:** $12/15.
Credit cards: None. **Reduced fees:** Seniors.
Caddies: No. **Golf carts:** $8 for 18 holes.
Discount golf packages: No. **Season:** Year-round. **High:** June-Sept.
On-site lodging: No. **Rental clubs:** No.
Walking policy: Walking at certain times. **Range:** No.
To obtain tee times: Call Monday before weekend wanting to play.
Subscriber comments: Nice little layout, not very challenging . . . No sand traps, not real long . . . Easy course . . . Staff has worked to improve this layout and it shows.

★½ SCOTHURST COUNTRY CLUB

SP—Hwy. 20 E. Box 88, Lumber Bridge (910)843-5357.
20 miles south of Fayetteville. **Holes:** 18. **Par:** 72/72.
Yards: 7,000/5,150. **Course rating:** 72.9/70.0. **Slope:** 118/111.
Opened: 1965. **Pace of Play rating:** 4:00. **Green fee:** $25.
Credit cards: None. **Reduced fees:** Weekdays, Low season.

Caddies: No. **Golf carts:** Included in Green Fee.
Discount golf packages: Yes. **Season:** Year-round. **High:** March-Sept.
On-site lodging: No. **Rental clubs:** No.
Walking policy: Walking at certain times. **Range:** No.
To obtain tee times: Call pro shop.
Subscriber comments: Course could be a much tougher test with a little work . . . This one is up and down; sometimes in great shape, others bad.

★★½ SEA SCAPE GOLF COURSE

R—300 Eckner St., Kitty Hawk (919)261-2158.
70 miles south of Norfolk, VA. **Holes:** 18. **Par:** 72/73.
Yards: 6,409/5,536. **Course rating:** 70.4/70.9. **Slope:** 120/115.
Opened: 1968. **Pace of Play rating:** 4:45. **Green fee:** $35/60.
Credit cards: MC, V. **Reduced fees:** Low season, Resort guests,
Twilight, Juniors.
Caddies: No. **Golf carts:** Included in Green Fee.
Discount golf packages: No. **Season:** Year-round. **High:** May-Oct.
On-site lodging: No. **Rental clubs:** Yes.
Walking policy: Mandatory cart. **Range:** Yes (grass).
To obtain tee times: Call anytime between 7 a.m. and 7 p.m.
Reservations can be made up to one year in advance.
Subscriber comments: Different terrain on front and back make it interesting . . . Wind sneaks up on you here . . . Can be tough to score well . . . Heavy play, very challenging . . . Best suited for straight shooters . . . Severe penalties if out of the fairway.

SEA TRAIL PLANTATION AND GOLF LINKS

R—211 Clubhouse Rd., Sunset Beach (910)287-1122, (800)546-5748.
20 miles north of Myrtle Beach, SC. **Credit cards:** All major. **Reduced fees:** Resort guests, Juniors.
Caddies: No. **Golf carts:** $16 for 18 holes.
Discount golf packages: Yes. **Season:** Year-round. **High:** March-April/Oct.
On-site lodging: Yes. **Rental clubs:** Yes.
Walking policy: Mandatory cart. **Range:** Yes (grass).
To obtain tee times: Call anytime.

★★★½ WILLARD BYRD COURSE

Holes: 18. **Par:** 72/72.
Yards: 6,750/4,697. **Course rating:** 72.1/69.1. **Slope:** 128/121.
Opened: 1990. **Pace of Play rating:** 4:30 **Green fee:** $15/48.
Subscriber comments: A must Myrtle Beach area resort . . . Could play everyday. Best course at Sea Trails . . . Scenic . . . Good resort courses . . . Very nice but I like other Sea Trail courses better . . . Very demanding on some holes . . . Play is enjoyable and challenging . . . A challenging course but fair for average golfer . . . Good Byrd layout, only a hair below Jones . . . Fun, nice people, have great time . . . Best three golf courses to play from Wilmington to Myrtle Beach . . . Love to play there . . . Very well maintained course, good for all levels . . . Wonderful greens . . . Pleasant day of golf on an attractive course . . . Narrow fairways . . . Water on many holes . . . Good, but enjoyed sister courses more . . . Good housing . . . Good course for better golfer . . . Good variety of holes . . . Excellent opportunity to play three different courses at one site.

★★★½ DAN MAPLES COURSE

Holes: 18. **Par:** 72/72.
Yards: 6,751/5,090. **Course rating:** 71.7/68.5. **Slope:** 121/108.
Opened: 1985. **Pace of Play rating:** 4:30. **Green fee:** $ 15/48.
Subscriber comments: Three courses at one site . . . Scenic, great layout, good challenge, fast . . . Condos too close, too much O.B. . . . Very fair, excellent layouts usually in fine condition . . . Clubhouse very good . . . Short and tight . . . Several new greens . . . Conditions are always good . . . Treated great at each course . . . Probably least severe of three courses . . . Fun course . . . Will not get bored . . . Short but great design . . . Caters to tourists . . . Staff friendly . . . A Sandhills layout at the beach . . . More terrific par 5s . . . Opportunity for three different, enjoyable golf courses.

★★★½ REES JONES COURSE
Holes: 18. **Par:** 72/72.
Yards: 6,761/4,912. **Course rating:** 72.4/68.5. **Slope:** 132/115.
Opened: 1989. **Pace of Play rating:** 4:30. **Green fee:** $20/58.
Subscriber comments: A "must play" . . . The best of the Sea Trail courses . . . Great course, slick greens . . . But other two are good, too . . . Real championship course in great shape, good staff . . . Will play each time I am in North Carolina . . . Very long but enjoyable . . . Has every type of golf hole imaginable . . . Superior greens . . . Ladies can compete with men . . . Most fun I've had in a while . . . Great variety of holes . . . First visit and not my last . . . Great greens! No. 9 needs better marking, water is in play . . . Extremely accommodating, handled last-minute addition to group tee time with a smile . . . Must play thinking man's golf.

★★★½ SEVEN LAKES COUNTRY CLUB
SP—Seven Lakes Dr., West End (910)673-1092.
10 miles west of Pinehurst. **Holes:** 18. **Par:** 72/73.
Yards: 6,927/5,192. **Course rating:** 74.4/70.6. **Slope:** 133/123.
Opened: 1976. **Pace of Play rating:** N/A. **Green fee:** $30/45.
Credit cards: None. **Reduced fees:** Low season, Juniors.
Caddies: No. **Golf carts:** $14 for 18 holes.
Discount golf packages: Yes. **Season:** Year-round. **High:** Spring/Fall.
On-site lodging: Yes. **Rental clubs:** Yes.
Walking policy: Mandatory cart. **Range:** Yes (grass).
To obtain tee times: Call pro shop.
Subscriber comments: Friendly environment . . . Best kept secret in Pinehurst area . . . Beautiful condition . . . Well maintained . . . Won't kill you unless you play from the back . . . Great test of golf . . . Great condition and staff . . . A real gem . . . Was in perfect shape in late fall . . . Interesting holes. Good test . . . Bring balls . . . Peter Tufts design . . . Challenging, every hole unique . . . Beautiful stern test . . . You could play this course often and enjoy it.

SHAMROCK GOLF CLUB★
PU—1722 Shamrock Dr., Burlington (910)226-7045, (800)849-0995.
35 miles east of Greensboro. **Holes:** 18. **Par:** 72/72.
Yards: 6,416/5,017. **Course rating:** 69.0/67.5. **Slope:** 113/113.
Opened: 1952. **Pace of Play rating:** 3:55. **Green fee:** $12/15.
Credit cards: MC, V. **Reduced fees:** Weekdays, Low season, Twilight, Seniors, Juniors.
Caddies: No. **Golf carts:** Included in Green Fee.
Discount golf packages: Yes. **Season:** Year-round. **High:** March-Oct.
On-site lodging: No. **Rental clubs:** Yes.
Walking policy: Walking at certain times. **Range:** Yes (grass).
To obtain tee times: Call up to one month in advance.

★★½ SILVER CREEK GOLF CLUB
PU—Star Rte., Swansboro (919)393-8058.
25 miles north of Jacksonville. **Holes:** 18. **Par:** 72/72.
Yards: 6,526/5,412. **Course rating:** 71.6/68.1. **Slope:** 117/110.
Opened: 1986. **Pace of Play rating:** 4:30. **Green fee:** $20/40.
Credit cards: MC, V. **Reduced fees:** Low season, Resort guests, Seniors.
Caddies: No. **Golf carts:** Included in Green Fee.
Discount golf packages: Yes. **Season:** Year-round. **High:** May-Oct.
On-site lodging: No. **Rental clubs:** Yes.
Walking policy: Walking at certain times. **Range:** Yes (grass).
To obtain tee times: Call in advance.
Subscriber comments: Long, windy course . . . Tough course when the wind blows . . . Wide open . . . Conditions have deteriorated in recent years . . . Will be better as trees mature . . . Good potential . . . A little flat and featureless, but developing . . . A lot of water to carry . . . Elevated greens are tough. Can always somehow seem to work in another foursome.

★★ SOURWOOD GOLF COURSE

PU—8055 Pleasanthill Church Rd., Snow Camp (910)376-8166.
Call club for further information.
Subscriber comments: Nice layout, shotmaker's course, friendly staff.
Fun course . . . New course constantly improving . . . Needs to mature
. . . Fun, short, course but very enjoyable. summer . . . Old farmland . . .
Excellent greens . . . Best greens within 50 miles.

★★★ SOUTHERN PINES GOLF CLUB

SP—280 Country Club Dr., Southern Pines (910)692-6551.
50 miles northwest of Raleigh. **Holes:** 18. **Par:** 71/74.
Yards: 6,500/5,400. **Course rating:** 70.3/70.9. **Slope:** 124/118.
Opened: 1912. **Pace of Play rating:** 4:00. **Green fee:** $37/54.
Credit cards: MC, V, AMEX. **Reduced fees:** Weekdays, Low season,
Resort guests, Twilight, Seniors.
Caddies: No. **Golf carts:** $15 for 18 holes.
Discount golf packages: Yes. **Season:** Year-round. **High:** March–Oct.
On-site lodging: No. **Rental clubs:** Yes.
Walking policy: Mandatory cart. **Range:** Yes (grass).
To obtain tee times: Call anytime.
Also has extra 9 holes.
Subscriber comments: Classic Donald Ross . . . In good condition . . .
Friendly staff, good scenery . . . Fun, short course . . . Hard, but fair . . .
Surprisingly difficult . . . Not long but tricky . . . Good staff . . .
Conditions have varied from good to bad, but this year they were the best
ever . . . Donald Ross design, a pleasure to play . . . Greens are typical
Ross. Fun to play, fairly short.

★★★ SPRINGDALE COUNTRY CLUB

SP—Rte. 2, Box 271, Canton (704)235-8451.
15 miles west of Asheville. **Holes:** 18. **Par:** 72/72.
Yards: 6,812/5,421. **Course rating:** N/A. **Slope:** 126/113.
Opened: N/A. **Pace of Play rating:** N/A. **Green fee:** N/A.
Credit cards: MC, V. **Reduced fees:** Twilight.
Caddies: No. **Golf carts:** N/A.
Discount golf packages: Yes. **Season:** Year-round. **High:** April–May.
On-site lodging: Yes. **Rental clubs:** No.
Walking policy: N/A. **Range:** No.
Subscriber comments: Out-of-the-way course in Mountain Valley . . .
Nice course, fantastic scenery, great mountain golf . . . Wide-open course,
back nine has a lot of blind approach shots . . . Mountain course with
private feel . . . Have played every year for the last nine years . . . Very
enjoyable . . . Might give high handicappers fits . . . Easy par 5s . . . Killer
par 4s . . . Nice views but no mixed drinks!

★★½ STAR HILL GOLF AND COUNTRY CLUB
SANDS/PINES/LAKES

SP—202 Clubhouse Dr., Cape Carteret (919)393-8111.
25 miles west of Jacksonville. **Holes:** 27. **Par:** 72/71/71.
Yards: 6,301/6,448/6,361. **Course rating:** 70.5/70.2/70.9. **Slope:**
115/113/118.
Opened: 1967. **Pace of Play rating:** 4:00. **Green fee:** $15/35.
Credit cards: MC, V. **Reduced fees:** Low season, Resort guests,
Twilight.
Caddies: No. **Golf carts:** $11 for 18 holes.
Discount golf packages: Yes. **Season:** Year-round. **High:** June–Aug.
On-site lodging: No. **Rental clubs:** Yes.
Walking policy: Walking at certain times. **Range:** Yes (grass).
To obtain tee times: Call to reserve time for any month of current year.
Subscriber comments: Variety of 27 holes . . . Most improved. I keep
going back, enjoyable . . . A fun course . . . Has a Pinehurst feel to it . . .
Fine sand in the rough . . . All nines good . . . Enjoyable layout for average
golfer, accommodating staff . . . Good condition . . . Best-kept course in
our area, always a joy to visit.

★★★ STONEY CREEK GOLF CLUB

PU—911 Golf House Rd. E., Stoney Creek (910)449-5688.
12 miles east of Greensboro. **Holes:** 18. **Par:** 72/72.
Yards: 7,063/4,737. **Course rating:** 74.1/69.8. **Slope:** 144/123.
Opened: 1992. **Pace of Play rating:** N/A. **Green fee:** $18/22.
Credit cards: MC, V, AMEX. **Reduced fees:** Weekdays, Low season,
Twilight, Seniors, Juniors.
Caddies: No. **Golf carts:** $12 for 18 holes.
Discount golf packages: Yes. **Season:** Year-round. **High:** Spring/Fall.
On-site lodging: No. **Rental clubs:** Yes.
Walking policy: Walking at certain times. **Range:** Yes (grass).
To obtain tee times: Call seven days in advance.
Subscriber comments: Newer course but already established . . . All
greens are slanted at an angle . . . Watch out for first hole . . . Always a
challenge . . . Very difficult for high handicapper. Great layout, don't miss
. . . Hardest golf course, but love it . . . Greens hard . . . Accuracy is
critical . . . Many blind shots, local knowledge needed . . . A bit tricked up
. . . Must keep ball in play to score . . . First hole is a bear . . . Best yardage
marked course ever played . . . Best staff in area . . . Must be at top of your
game to play the back tees with the slope of 144 . . . Shotmaker's course,
super-fast greens . . . Killer hole No. 1, fun after that. Not an easy track
. . . One of the great new courses in the area.

★★★★ TALAMORE RESORT

PU—1595 Midland Rd., Southern Pines (910)692-5884.
2 miles east of Pinehurst. **Holes:** 18. **Par:** 71/72.
Yards: 7,020/4,945. **Course rating:** 72.9/69.0. **Slope:** 142/125.
Opened: 1992. **Pace of Play rating:** 4:20. **Green fee:** $40/75.
Credit cards: MC, V. **Reduced fees:** Low season, Twilight.
Caddies: Yes. **Golf carts:** Included in Green Fee.
Discount golf packages: Yes. **Season:** Year-round. **High:** Spring/Fall.
On-site lodging: No. **Rental clubs:** Yes.
Walking policy: Mandatory cart. **Range:** Yes (grass).
To obtain tee times: Call pro shop.
Ranked 18th in North Carolina by Golf Digest.
Subscriber comments: A majestic Sandhills creation . . . Magnificent
course . . . Wonderful variety of holes . . . A true test of golf . . . The hills
and layout memorable . . . Best course in North Carolina . . . Superb Rees
Jones design . . . Llama caddies! . . . Rees Jones masterpiece . . . Difficult
but enjoyable . . . One of the area's best courses . . . Pretty, great greens
. . . Love Rees Jones, play everyday . . . Many sand traps . . . Beautiful
course with lots of elevation changes . . . A challenge from all tees . . .
Excellent layout, four tees so anybody can play . . . Lots of traps . . . A
"must play" on my Pinehurst list . . . Excellent course, doglegs, water,
sand . . . Llamas were out of town.

TANGLEWOOD PARK GOLF COURSES

PU—Hwy. 158 W., Clemmons (910)766-5082. *778-6300*
8 miles west of Winston-Salem. **Green fee:** $16/50.
Credit cards: None. **Reduced fees:** Weekdays, Low season, Resort
guests, Twilight, Seniors, Juniors.
Caddies: No. **Golf carts:** $14 for 18 holes.
Discount golf packages: Yes. **Season:** Year-round. **High:** Spring/Fall.
On-site lodging: Yes. **Rental clubs:** Yes.
Walking policy: Walking at certain times. **Range:** Yes (grass).
To obtain tee times: Call seven days in advance. Lodge guests may make
tee times when booking reservations.

★★★★ CHAMPIONSHIP COURSE

Holes: 18. **Par:** 72/74.
Yards: 7,022/5,119. **Course rating:** 74.5/70.9. **Slope:** 140/130.
Opened: 1957. **Pace of Play rating:** 4:15.
Ranked in First 25 of America's 75 Best Public Golf Courses by Golf
Digest. Ranked 10th in North Carolina by Golf Digest.
Subscriber comments: Championship layout, great to play where the big

boys play . . .

True championship test . . . Excellent layout, challenging for both scratch and duffer . . . Struggle for weaker . . . The seniors ought to play the back tees! . . . You get your money's worth . . . Unfair traps . . . Fairways are like carpet . . . Sand traps will keep me honest . . . Championship clubhouse . . . Possibly my favorite course . . . The best public course I have played, must hit it long . . . Well done . . . Excellent facility . . . Bring your shovel . . . Brought me to my knees . . . Beautiful park, beautiful course . . . No grandstands for me? Super layout, always in excellent shape . . . Bring your camel . . . One of the finest public courses in the country.

★★★½ REYNOLDS COURSE

Holes: 18. **Par:** 72/72.
Yards: 6,469/5,432. **Course rating:** 71.0/70.2. **Slope:** 125/120.
Opened: 1959. **Pace of Play rating:** 4:15.
Subscriber comments: Great public course, well kept, tight layout . . . Best suited for player that can hit high approach shots . . . Best course for the money . . . Few holes really require a driver, lots of woods, tougher course than Championship to keep ball in play . . . Looks easy but tough . . . Better suited for shorter hitters than championship course . . . Not as long as championship course but still very challenging . . . No place for a slicer . . . Bring your beachwear, sand everywhere . . . Few flags visible from the tee . . . Good test from back tees . . . Looks easy, but looks are deceiving . . . Excellent course for the money . . . Dollar for dollar, play the Reynolds course.

THE LODGE GOLF COURSE★

PU—Rte. 3, Hwy. 74 E., Lauringburg (910)277-0311.
50 miles south of Fayetteville. **Holes:** 18. **Par:** 72/72.
Yards: 6,570/4,830. **Course rating:** 69.4/65.5. **Slope:** 112/102.
Opened: 1982. **Pace of Play rating:** 4:10. **Green fee:** $17/21.
Credit cards: None. **Reduced fees:** Twilight, Seniors.
Caddies: No. **Golf carts:** Included in Green Fee.
Discount golf packages: Yes. **Season:** Year-round. **High:** April-Sept.
On-site lodging: No. **Rental clubs:** Yes.
Walking policy: Unrestricted walking. **Range:** Yes (grass).
To obtain tee times: First come, first served.
Formerly known as Ine's Lodge Country Club.

THE SOUND GOLF LINKS★

SP—101 Clubhouse Dr., Hertford (919)426-5555, (800)535-0704.
80 miles southwest of Norfolk, VA. **Holes:** 18. **Par:** 72/72.
Yards: 6,500/4,665. **Course rating:** 70.1/66.3. **Slope:** 125/113.
Opened: 1990. **Pace of Play rating:** 4:30. **Green fee:** $30.
Credit cards: MC, V. **Reduced fees:** Weekdays, Juniors.
Caddies: No. **Golf carts:** Included in Green Fee.
Discount golf packages: No. **Season:** Year-round. **High:** April-Sept.
On-site lodging: No. **Rental clubs:** No.
Walking policy: Mandatory cart. **Range:** Yes (grass).
To obtain tee times: Call four months in advance.
Subscriber comments: Strong scenic course . . . Location too remote . . . Facilities attractive . . . I would recommend it to any serious golfer . . . Too narrow for mid to high handicappers . . . Challenging . . . Difficult for senior players . . . Using every club in the bag . . . Dan Maple's pearl on the Albermarle.

TWIN OAKS GOLF COURSE★

PU—3250 Twin Oaks Dr., Statesville (704)872-3979.
50 miles north of Charlotte. **Holes:** 18. **Par:** 72/72.
Yards: 6,368/4,632. **Course rating:** 69.2/70.2. **Slope:** 112/114.
Opened: 1960. **Pace of Play rating:** 4:00. **Green fee:** $12/22.
Credit cards: MC, V, AMEX. **Reduced fees:** Weekdays, Low season.
Caddies: No. **Golf carts:** $22 for 18 holes.

Discount golf packages: No. **Season:** Year-round. **High:** April-Aug.
On-site lodging: No. **Rental clubs:** Yes.
Walking policy: Walking at certain times. **Range:** Yes (grass).
To obtain tee times: Call anytime.

WAKE FOREST COUNTRY CLUB★
SP—13239 Capital Blvd., Wake Forest (919)556-3416.
9 miles north of Raleigh. **Holes:** 18. **Par:** 72/72.
Yards: 6,952/5,124. **Course rating:** 74.4/70.0. **Slope:** 135/122.
Opened: 1961. **Pace of Play rating:** 4:00. **Green fee:** $16/21.
Credit cards: MC, V. **Reduced fees:** Twilight, Seniors, Juniors.
Caddies: No. **Golf carts:** $12 for 18 holes.
Discount golf packages: No. **Season:** Year-round. **High:** April-June.
On-site lodging: No. **Rental clubs:** Yes.
Walking policy: Walking at certain times. **Range:** Yes (grass).
To obtain tee times: Weekday tee times are available seven days in
advance. Weekend times are available on Thursday at noon. A credit card is
required for weekend tee times.

WALNUT WOOD GOLF COURSE★
PU—3172 Alamance Church Rd., Julian (910)697-8140.
25 miles east of Greensboro. **Holes:** 18. **Par:** 73/73.
Yards: 6,390/5,334. **Course rating:** 69.1/69.7. **Slope:** 113/111.
Opened: 1978. **Pace of Play rating:** 4:00. **Green fee:** $18/21.
Credit cards: MC, V. **Reduced fees:** Seniors.
Caddies: No. **Golf carts:** Included in Green Fee.
Discount golf packages: No. **Season:** Year-round. **High:** May-Sept.
On-site lodging: No. **Rental clubs:** Yes.
Walking policy: Walking at certain times. **Range:** Yes.
To obtain tee times: First come, first served.

★★½ WAYNESVILLE COUNTRY CLUB INN
R—Ninevah Rd., Waynesville (704)452-4617.
25 miles east of Asheville. **Holes:** 27. **Par:** 70/70/70.
Yards: 5,798/5,803/5,943. **Course rating:** 66.4/66.4/66.8. **Slope:**
103/105/104.
Opened: 1926. **Pace of Play rating:** 4:08. **Green fee:** $13/26.
Credit cards: MC, V. **Reduced fees:** Low season, Resort guests,
Twilight, Juniors.
Caddies: No. **Golf carts:** $13 for 18 holes.
Discount golf packages: Yes. **Season:** Year-round. **High:** March-Oct.
On-site lodging: Yes. **Rental clubs:** Yes.
Walking policy: Walking at certain times. **Range:** No.
To obtain tee times: Call one day in advance. Guests at the hotel may
make tee times at time of reservation.
Subscriber comments: Beautiful 27 holes . . . Newest nine the toughest
. . . Little character . . . Mostly wide fairways . . . Short beautiful course in
good condition . . . All you need is a 1-iron . . . Great for senior golfers . . .
Very congenial service people . . . Free drop for hitting cars? Pretty scenery
. . . Nice layouts . . . Fun to play . . . Challenging, hilly course, well-
maintained.

★½ WENDELL COUNTRY CLUB
SP—180 Jake May Dr., Wendell (919)365-7337.
Call club for further information.
Subscriber comments: Fun country course, friendly staff makes you
comfortable . . . good experience . . . Each hole has a distinct character . . .
Hard, fast greens all year . . . Need to water fairways . . . Nice open
course, very personal staff.

★½ WESTPORT GOLF COURSE
PU—7494 Golf Course Dr. S., Denver (704)483-5604.
25 miles north of Charlotte. **Holes:** 18. **Par:** 72/72.
Yards: 6,805/5,600. **Course rating:** 72.3/69.5. **Slope:** 123/118.

Opened: 1968. **Pace of Play rating:** 4:30. **Green fee:** $11/20.
Credit cards: None. **Reduced fees:** Weekdays, Twilight, Seniors.
Caddies: No. **Golf carts:** $11 for 18 holes.
Discount golf packages: No. **Season:** Year-round. **High:** April-Oct.
On-site lodging: No. **Rental clubs:** Yes.
Walking policy: Walking at certain times. **Range:** Yes (grass).
To obtain tee times: Call one week in advance.
Subscriber comments: Terrific around the edges . . . Decent condition,
year round . . . Very playable . . . Tough test of golf . . . You'll wear out
your long irons . . . Right to left course . . . A few forced carries . . .
Average day's golf.

★★½ WHISPERING WOODS GOLF CLUB

SP—26 Sandpiper Dr., Whispering Pines (910)949-4653, (800)224-5061.
6 miles northeast of Pinehurst. **Holes:** 18. **Par:** 70/70.
Yards: 6,334/4,924. **Course rating:** 70.5/68.7. **Slope:** 122/122.
Opened: 1975. **Pace of Play rating:** 4:30. **Green fee:** $25/50.
Credit cards: All major. **Reduced fees:** Low season, Twilight, Seniors,
Juniors.
Caddies: No. **Golf carts:** $15 for 18 holes.
Discount golf packages: Yes. **Season:** Year-round. **High:** Spring/Fall.
On-site lodging: No. **Rental clubs:** Yes.
Walking policy: Mandatory cart. **Range:** No.
To obtain tee times: Call up to one year in advance up to day of play.
Credit card required for out of town reservation.
Subscriber comments: Doglegs, water, sand, tight . . . Five par 3s . . .
Very good layout . . . Fun course, nice people . . . Excellent senior course
. . . Some areas need work . . . Backside is a great test . . . Reasonable . . .
Better condition than in the past . . . Staff wants you to come back.

★★★ WOODBRIDGE GOLF LINKS

PU—1007 New Camp Creek Church Rd., Kings Mtn. (704)482-0353.
30 miles west of Charlotte. **Holes:** 18. **Par:** 72/74.
Yards: 6,743/5,151. **Course rating:** 71.9/69.3. **Slope:** 131/116.
Opened: 1976. **Pace of Play rating:** 4:30. **Green fee:** $25/32.
Credit cards: MC, V. **Reduced fees:** No.
Caddies: No. **Golf carts:** Included in Green Fee.
Discount golf packages: No. **Season:** Year-round. **High:** April-Oct.
On-site lodging: No. **Rental clubs:** Yes.
Walking policy: Walking at certain times. **Range:** Yes (grass).
To obtain tee times: Call up to one week in advance.
Subscriber comments: A superb course design, will make you use all
your clubs . . . Very good course, allows you to play all the clubs . . .
Requires good course management . . . Course conditions are outstanding
in every way, except the traps . . . Great southern hospitality great . . .
Challenging holes . . . One of the better public courses around . . . Usually
in outstanding condition . . . Second best in the area . . . Bridges on back
nine are nice to walk . . . In the top five public courses around Charlotte
. . . Very playable, but challenging . . . You are missing a great course.

WOODLAKE COUNTRY CLUB
★★★½ LAKE SHORE/CYPRESS CREEK

R—150 Woodlake Blvd., Vass (910)245-4686, (800)334-1126.
60 miles south of Raleigh. **Holes:** 18. **Par:** 72/72.
Yards: 7,012/5,255. **Course rating:** 73.4/71.4. **Slope:** 134/128.
Opened: 1973. **Pace of Play rating:** 4:30. **Green fee:** $30/70.
Credit cards: MC, V. **Reduced fees:** Weekdays, Low season, Resort
guests, Twilight.
Caddies: No. **Golf carts:** Included in Green Fee.
Discount golf packages: Yes. **Season:** Year-round. **High:** March-May.
On-site lodging: Yes. **Rental clubs:** No.
Walking policy: Mandatory cart. **Range:** Yes (grass).
To obtain tee times: Call up to one year in advance.
Also has 9-hole par-36 Cranes Cove Course.

Subscriber comments: Plenty of water, bring all your clubs for this one
. . . Tough from tips, bring an extra dozen . . . Eighteen-hole course very
enjoyable . . . Nice old course in great shape . . . Very nice resort . . . Plan
to go early and play all 27 holes . . . Great Captain's Choice course . . .
Good fun and good lunch . . . If you are off target, bring plenty of balls . . .
Solid, challenging course with great variety of conditions and scenery . . .
Last three holes will wear you out . . . Great service . . . Lots of water . . .
Should play once before keeping score. Very good for all golfers . . . Often
overlooked by the Pinehurst crowd.

Notes

★½ AIRPORT GOLF COURSE

PU—900 N. Hamilton Rd., Columbus (614)645-3127.

Holes: 18. **Par:** 70/72.

Yards: 6,383/5,504. **Course rating:** 68.1/N/A. **Slope:** 107/N/A.

Opened: 1965. **Pace of Play rating:** 4:30. **Green fee:** $12/14.

Credit cards: MC, V. **Reduced fees:** Low season, Twilight, Seniors, Juniors.

Caddies: No. **Golf carts:** $19 for 18 holes.

Discount golf packages: No. **Season:** Year-round. **High:** May-Sept.

On-site lodging: No. **Rental clubs:** Yes.

Walking policy: Unrestricted walking. **Range:** No.

To obtain tee times: Call Sunday after 6 p.m. for the following weekend.

Subscriber comments: Short course, small greens, jets and airplanes fly very low over the course . . . Short from the whites but an ample track. Water and pine trees . . . For a city- owned course well maintained . . . Lots of play, good variety of shots and holes . . . Courteous staff. Maintenance could be better. Good value.

★★★½ APPLE VALLEY GOLF CLUB

PU—433 Clubhouse Dr., Howard (614)397-7664, (800)359-7664.

6 miles east of Mt. Vernon. **Holes:** 18. **Par:** 72/75.

Yards: 6,946/6,116. **Course rating:** 72.4/74.9. **Slope:** 116/120.

Opened: 1971. **Pace of Play rating:** 4:00. **Green fee:** $14/18.

Credit cards: MC, V. **Reduced fees:** Seniors.

Caddies: No. **Golf carts:** $10 for 18 holes.

Discount golf packages: No. **Season:** March-Oct. **High:** June-Aug.

On-site lodging: No. **Rental clubs:** No.

Walking policy: Walking at certain times. **Range:** Yes (grass).

To obtain tee times: Call as far in advance as possible.

Subscriber comments: Long course, huge greens use every club in bag, nice track . . . Love this course, only problem is everyone does, hard to get on . . . Course always in good shape and very friendly staff . . . Excellent getaway weekend course . . . Good challenge, from back tees . . . Scenic, well kept, long par 4s on back, great price . . . Great condition, long for average players, great value.

★★ ATWOOD RESORT GOLF COURSE

R—2650 Lodge Rd., Dellroy (216)735-2211, (800)362-6406.

25 miles southeast of Canton. **Holes:** 18. **Par:** 70/70.

Yards: 6,152/4,188. **Course rating:** 65.7/62.0. **Slope:** 102/91.

Opened: 1951. **Pace of Play rating:** 4:00. **Green fee:** $10/18.

Credit cards: All major. **Reduced fees:** Weekdays, Low season, Resort guests, Seniors, Juniors.

Caddies: No. **Golf carts:** $10 for 18 holes.

Discount golf packages: Yes. **Season:** Year-round. **High:** June-Sept.

On-site lodging: Yes. **Rental clubs:** Yes.

Walking policy: Unrestricted walking. **Range:** Yes.

To obtain tee times: Call pro shop.

Also has lighted 9-hole par-3 course.

Subscriber comments: Beautiful scenery, fine greens . . . Short, hilly, but challenging to par it . . . Nice course. Fast greens. Nice scenery . . . Five star hotel on course . . . Sand, lakes and big greens . . . Good resort course, par 3s are great.

★★★★ AVALON LAKES GOLF COURSE

R—One American Way, Warren (216)856-8898.

40 miles southeast of Cleveland. **Holes:** 18. **Par:** 71/71.

Yards: 6,868/5,324. **Course rating:** 73.4/70.9. **Slope:** 128/116.

Opened: 1968. **Pace of Play rating:** 4:30. **Green fee:** $ 43.

Credit cards: MC, V, AMEX. **Reduced fees:** Weekdays, Low season, Twilight.

Caddies: No. **Golf carts:** Included in Green Fee.

Discount golf packages: No. **Season:** April-Oct. **High:** June-Aug.

On-site lodging: Yes. **Rental clubs:** Yes.

Walking policy: Mandatory cart. **Range:** Yes (grass).
To obtain tee times: Call pro shop.
Subscriber comments: Great test, greens are mysterious . . . Early Pete Dye course, usually in good condition . . . Another gem. Great fairways and greens. A well-bunkered beauty . . . Great shape . . . Better for long ball hitter, service fine, cart required, cost fair . . . Mostly flat, but very challenging, nice staff . . . Can get crowded but a wonderful challenge . . . LPGA tour stop.

★ AVON FIELD GOLF COURSE

PU—4081 Reading Rd., Cincinnati (513)281-0322.
Holes: 18. **Par:** 66/66.
Yards: 5,186/4,618. **Course rating:** 63.9/63.5. **Slope:** 99/98.
Opened: 1914. **Pace of Play rating:** N/A. **Green fee:** $11/14.
Credit cards: MC, V. **Reduced fees:** Low season, Seniors, Juniors.
Caddies: No. **Golf carts:** $10 for 18 holes.
Discount golf packages: Yes. **Season:** Year-round. **High:** May-Aug.
On-site lodging: No. **Rental clubs:** Yes.
Walking policy: Unrestricted walking. **Range:** Yes (grass).
To obtain tee times: Call pro shop 24 hours in advance or use XETA Tee Time service.
Subscriber comments: No par 5s, bring your short game . . . Short and easy, especially back nine, with driveable par 4s. Conditions vastly improved . . . Good course for iron use, well maintained and priced . . . Good course for a novice/beginner . . . A good walking course.

★½ BARBERTON BROOKSIDE COUNTRY CLUB

SP—3727 Golf Course Dr., Barberton (216)825-4539.
Call club for further information.
Subscriber comments: Much improved with new watering systems . . . Back nine long . . . Very open layout, few holes required much beyond club selection . . . Getting better.

★★★ BEAVER CREEK MEADOWS GOLF COURSE

PU—12774 St. Rte. 7, Lisbon (216)385-3020.
30 miles south of Youngstown. **Holes:** 18. **Par:** 71/72.
Yards: 6,500/5,500. **Course rating:** 68.7/68.5. **Slope:** N/A.
Opened: 1984. **Pace of Play rating:** 4:30. **Green fee:** $11/14.
Credit cards: None. **Reduced fees:** Weekdays, Low season.
Caddies: No. **Golf carts:** $16 for 18 holes.
Discount golf packages: No. **Season:** March-Dec. **High:** June-Aug.
On-site lodging: No. **Rental clubs:** Yes.
Walking policy: Unrestricted walking. **Range:** Yes (grass).
To obtain tee times: Call pro shop.
Subscriber comments: Short, kept in good shape . . . Plenty of water for the automatic water system, the course has five lakes, this is probably the best course in the area . . . Continuing improvement each year.

★ BEDFORD TRAILS GOLF COURSE

PU—713 Bedford Rd., Lowellville (216)536-2234.
1 miles east of Youngstown. **Holes:** 18. **Par:** 70/70.
Yards: 6,160/5,170. **Course rating:** N/A. **Slope:** N/A.
Opened: 1962. **Pace of Play rating:** 4:30. **Green fee:** $10/14.
Credit cards: MC, V. **Reduced fees:** Weekdays, Low season, Seniors, Juniors.
Caddies: No. **Golf carts:** $8 for 18 holes.
Discount golf packages: No. **Season:** Year-round. **High:** May-Sept.
On-site lodging: No. **Rental clubs:** No.
Walking policy: Unrestricted walking. **Range:** Yes (grass).
To obtain tee times: Call pro shop.
Subscriber comments: Back nine needs maturing, tight and wooded . . . Challenging. Quick pace. Back nine narrow and difficult.

★★★ BELLEFONTAINE COUNTRY CLUB

SP—665 Rd. 190 W., Bellefontaine (513)592-4653.
Call club for further information.
Subscriber comments: Good pace . . . Great course, friendly staff, great value . . . New nine needs a few years.

★★★½ BENT TREE GOLF CLUB

PU—350 Bent Tree Rd., Sunbury (614)965-5140.
20 miles north of Columbus. **Holes:** 18. **Par:** 72/72.
Yards: 6,805/5,280. **Course rating:** 72.1/69.2. **Slope:** 122/113.
Opened: 1988. **Pace of Play rating:** 4:15. **Green fee:** $40/50.
Credit cards: MC, V, DISC. **Reduced fees:** Low season, Twilight, Seniors.
Caddies: No. **Golf carts:** Included in Green Fee.
Discount golf packages: Yes. **Season:** March-Dec. **High:** May-Oct.
On-site lodging: No. **Rental clubs:** Yes.
Walking policy: Walking at certain times. **Range:** Yes (grass).
To obtain tee times: Call up to one week in advance, make reservations with credit card number.
Subscriber comments: Overpriced but perfect golf . . . Courteous staff, treated well, course in great condition . . . Sand, sand, sand . . . Short back nine, takes driver out of bag . . . Great condition, great service, private-club feel, too open, but traps keep it interesting . . . Course rewards accuracy. Wind can be a factor.

★★½ BIG MET GOLF CLUB

PU—4811 Valley Pkwy., Fairview Park (216)331-1070.
2 miles west of Cleveland. **Holes:** 18. **Par:** 72/74.
Yards: 6,125/5,870. **Course rating:** 68.0/72.0. **Slope:** 108/113.
Opened: 1926. **Pace of Play rating:** 4:42. **Green fee:** $11/15.
Credit cards: MC, V. **Reduced fees:** Low season, Seniors, Juniors.
Caddies: No. **Golf carts:** $18 for 18 holes.
Discount golf packages: Yes. **Season:** March-Dec. **High:** May-Aug.
On-site lodging: No. **Rental clubs:** No.
Walking policy: Unrestricted walking. **Range:** No.
To obtain tee times: Call five days in advance.
Subscriber comments: Nice layout, great condition considering very heavy play, needs sand bunkers . . . Lots of play, good shape, mature trees, not difficult . . . Good condition for so much play, very convenient for quick nine . . . Excellent condition for amount of play . . . Not real challenging, but great condition, excellent for a quick round after work . . . It's a flat course.

★★★ BLACKHAWK GOLF CLUB

PU—8830 Dustin Rd., Galena (614)965-1042.
20 miles northeast of Columbus. **Holes:** 18. **Par:** 71/71.
Yards: 6,550/4,726. **Course rating:** 70.6/66.0. **Slope:** 115/106.
Opened: 1964. **Pace of Play rating:** 4:30. **Green fee:** $18/19.
Credit cards: MC, V, DISC. **Reduced fees:** Low season, Twilight, Seniors.
Caddies: No. **Golf carts:** $10 for 18 holes.
Discount golf packages: No. **Season:** March-Dec. **High:** May-Oct.
On-site lodging: No. **Rental clubs:** Yes.
Walking policy: Unrestricted walking. **Range:** Yes (grass).
To obtain tee times: Call seven days in advance for Friday, Saturday and Sunday.
Subscriber comments: Challenging, well maintained . . . Accuracy counts, good condition all year, tough to get tee time . . . Gets progressively difficult at the finishing holes . . . . A number of challenging holes, green speed erratic . . . Narrow and trees.

BLACKLICK WOODS GOLF COURSE
★★★ **GOLD COURSE**

PU—7309 E. Livingston Ave., Reynoldsburg (614)861-3193.
5 miles east of Columbus. **Holes:** 18. **Par:** 72/75.
Yards: 7,069/5,633. **Course rating:** 72.2/70.9. **Slope:** 120/116.
Opened: 1965. **Pace of Play rating:** 4:00. **Green fee:** $13.
Credit cards: None. **Reduced fees:** Weekdays, Low season, Twilight.
Caddies: No. **Golf carts:** $17 for 18 holes.
Discount golf packages: No. **Season:** Year-round. **High:** May-Aug.
On-site lodging: No. **Rental clubs:** Yes.
Walking policy: Unrestricted walking. **Range:** Yes (grass).
To obtain tee times: Call five days in advance.
Also has 18-hole executive Green Course.
Subscriber comments: Good course; well run; very busy though . . .
Long course, kept up very well, best city course . . . Closing May '95 and
will reopen in May '96; Executive course is open . . . Longer from whites
than many from blues, but fair . . . Being reworked . . . Polite personnel
. . . Some fun holes with elevated tees . . . Can't beat the deal . . . Not a flat
green on the course . . . One of my favorites, and a city course to boot . . .
Best value in Ohio.

★★★½ BLUE ASH GOLF COURSE

PU—4040 Cooper Rd., Cincinnati (513)745-8577.
15 miles north of Cincinnati. **Holes:** 18. **Par:** 72/72.
Yards: 6,643/5,125. **Course rating:** 72.6/70.3. **Slope:** 127/124.
Opened: 1979. **Pace of Play rating:** 4:20. **Green fee:** $ 18.
Credit cards: None. **Reduced fees:** Low season, Seniors, Juniors.
Caddies: No. **Golf carts:** $19 for 18 holes.
Discount golf packages: No. **Season:** Year-round. **High:** May-Sept.
On-site lodging: No. **Rental clubs:** Yes.
Walking policy: Unrestricted walking. **Range:** No.
To obtain tee times: Non residents call five days in advance.
Ranked in Third 25 of America's 75 Best Public Golf Courses by
Golf Digest.
Subscriber comments: Long, tight hilly, great shape even in summer . . .
You've got to hit it long from the back tees . . . Great course, well
maintained, slow due to difficulty . . . Great course but they close out
nonresidents . . . Excellent course, difficult, some poorly designed holes
. . . Enjoyable for all levels, pin placements can make extremely challenging
. . . Well maintained, difficult to get tee time . . . Large undulating greens
make the course . . . Excellent layout, great challenge, too busy . . .
Difficult to get on. Nice course to play . . . Excellent condition,
immaculate. Condo golf on back nine . . . Hard walking. Extremely hilly
course. In good shape . . . Seven greens are blind shots . . . Long,
challenging, well maintained. Difficult starting holes . . . Difficult course,
play is slow, suited for good to excellent players.

★½ BLUFFTON GOLF CLUB

PU—8575 N. Dixie Hwy., Bluffton (419)358-6230.
15 miles north of Lima. **Holes:** 18. **Par:** 72/72.
Yards: 6,633/5,822. **Course rating:** 69.2/69.8. **Slope:** 103/95.
Opened: 1941. **Pace of Play rating:** 4:00. **Green fee:** $ 12.
Credit cards: None. **Reduced fees:** Weekdays, Low season, Seniors,
Juniors.
Caddies: No. **Golf carts:** $8 for 18 holes.
Discount golf packages: No. **Season:** March-Nov. **High:** June-Aug.
On-site lodging: No. **Rental clubs:** Yes.
Walking policy: Unrestricted walking. **Range:** Yes (grass).
To obtain tee times: Call one week in advance.
Subscriber comments: Good grass. Maintenance needs upgrading. Good
service.

★½ BOB-O-LINK GOLF COURSE
RED/WHITE/BLUE
PU—4141 Center Rd., Avon (216)934–6217.
20 miles west of Cleveland. **Holes:** 27. **Par:** 71/71/72.
Yards: 6,263/6,052/6,383. **Course rating:** 66.6/66.6/68.4. **Slope:** 108/115/115.
Opened: 1969. **Pace of Play rating:** 4:00. **Green fee:** $12/14.
Credit cards: None. **Reduced fees:** Weekdays, Seniors, Juniors.
Caddies: No. **Golf carts:** $16 for 18 holes.
Discount golf packages: No. **Season:** Year-round. **High:** May-Sept.
On-site lodging: No. **Rental clubs:** Yes.
Walking policy: Unrestricted walking. **Range:** Yes (grass).
To obtain tee times: Call one week in advance.
Subscriber comments: Blue course is the best, Red second, White third
. . . Needs to come into '90's with maintenance . . . Great lake views . . .
Great place to play by yourself when working on your game. Hardly ever
crowded. Great for beginners . . . A good late year course, very few tree
leaves.

★½ BOLTON FIELD GOLF COURSE
PU—6005 Alkire Rd., Galloway (614)645-3050.
81 miles southwest of Columbus. **Holes:** 18. **Par:** 72/72.
Yards: 7,034/5,204. **Course rating:** 71.0/N/A. **Slope:** 115/N/A.
Opened: 1971. **Pace of Play rating:** 4:00-4:30. **Green fee:** $12/14.
Credit cards: MC, V. **Reduced fees:** Weekdays, Low season, Twilight,
Seniors, Juniors.
Caddies: No. **Golf carts:** $9 for 18 holes.
Discount golf packages: Yes. **Season:** Year-round. **High:** May-Sept.
On-site lodging: No. **Rental clubs:** Yes.
Walking policy: Unrestricted walking. **Range:** Yes (grass).
To obtain tee times: Call Sunday night prior to weekend. For weekdays,
call one week in advance.
Subscriber comments: Reasonable challenge, solid golf, could be
maintained better . . . Large greens and some short par 4s and long par 3s.
Not a lot of trouble but good challenge . . . Long but open, good scoring
course . . . A better city course. Nothing fancy, but it can reach up and grab
you.

★½ BOSTON HILLS COUNTRY CLUB
PU—105/124 E. Hines Hill Rd., Boston Heights (216)656-2438.
30 miles south of Cleveland. **Holes:** 18. **Par:** 71/71.
Yards: 6,117/4,987. **Course rating:** 68.2/67.4. **Slope:** 110/105.
Opened: 1923. **Pace of Play rating:** 4:00 **Green fee:** $16/20.
Credit cards: None. **Reduced fees:** Weekdays, Low season, Seniors,
Juniors.
Caddies: No. **Golf carts:** $19 for 18 holes.
Discount golf packages: No. **Season:** Year-round. **High:** June-Aug.
On-site lodging: Yes. **Rental clubs:** Yes.
Walking policy: Unrestricted walking. **Range:** Yes (grass).
To obtain tee times: Call one week in advance.
Subscriber comments: Short, easy . . . Nice new sheltered driving range.
Good outing facility . . . Short course, dime-size greens . . . Needs better
maintenance. Excellent practice facility.

★★ BRANDYWINE COUNTRY CLUB
PU—555 Akron Peninsula Rd., Peninsula (216)657-2525.
3 miles southwest of Akron. **Holes:** 18. **Par:** 72/75.
Yards: 7,100/5,625. **Course rating:** 70.2/70.5. **Slope:** 113/113.
Opened: 1962. **Pace of Play rating:** 4:00. **Green fee:** $ 22.
Credit cards: None. **Reduced fees:** Weekdays, Twilight, Seniors.
Caddies: No. **Golf carts:** $20 for 18 holes.
Discount golf packages: Yes. **Season:** Year-round. **High:** May-Sept.
On-site lodging: No. **Rental clubs:** Yes.

Walking policy: Unrestricted walking. **Range:** No.
To obtain tee times: Call one week in advance.
Subscriber comments: Jekyll and Hyde front nine vs. back nine . . . Front side open, back side hilly, tight . . . Front open and treelined, back hilly and narrow, pace on back nine can be very slow . . . For good players. Good staff. Pace OK . . . Front side builds confidence; back side destroys it . . . Back nine is bizarre.

★½ BRIARDALE GREENS GOLF COURSE
PU—24131 Briardale Ave., Euclid (216)289-8574.
8 miles east of Cleveland. **Holes:** 18. **Par:** 70/70.
Yards: 6,127/4,977. **Course rating:** 69.1/70.5. **Slope:** 116/118.
Opened: N/A. **Pace of Play rating:** 4:00. **Green fee:** $14/15.
Credit cards: MC, V. **Reduced fees:** Weekdays, Low season, Twilight, Seniors, Juniors.
Caddies: No. **Golf carts:** $8 for 18 holes.
Discount golf packages: Yes. **Season:** March–Nov. **High:** May–Sept.
On-site lodging: No. **Rental clubs:** Yes.
Walking policy: Unrestricted walking. **Range:** Yes (grass).
To obtain tee times: Call one week in advance.
Subscriber comments: A classic muny. Fast greens, very popular . . . A fairly flat course with a few water hazards and sand traps . . . Good links-style course. Excellent value during winter.

★★½ BRIARWOOD GOLF COURSE–
BEN/GLENS/LOCHS
PU—2737 Edgerton Rd., Broadview Heights (216)237-5271.
22 miles south of Cleveland. **Holes:** 27. **Par:** 71/72/71.
Yards: 6,405/6,985/6,500. **Course rating:** 70.1/72.8/70.8. **Slope:** 117/125/117.
Opened: 1965. **Pace of Play rating:** 4:00. **Green fee:** $18/22.
Credit cards: None. **Reduced fees:** Weekdays, Low season, Twilight, Seniors, Juniors.
Caddies: No. **Golf carts:** $10 for 18 holes.
Discount golf packages: No. **Season:** April–Dec. **High:** May–Sept.
On-site lodging: No. **Rental clubs:** Yes.
Walking policy: Unrestricted walking. **Range:** Yes (grass).
To obtain tee times: Call Saturday a.m. for following weekend.
Subscriber comments: Three nines add variety, tough to get tee time . . . Sporty course, twists, turns and canyons, needs more sand . . . Challenging layout with hills and doglegs. Not too long or short.

★★½ BUCKEYE HILLS GOLF COURSE
PU—13204 Miami Trace Rd., Greenfield (513)981-4136.
Call club for further information.
Subscriber comments: County course attracting city attention, above average greens . . . Very good challenge . . . Surprising. Greens fast. Scenic. Good shape.

★★ BUNKER HILL GOLF COURSE
PU—3060 Pearl R., Medina (216)722-4174.
20 miles south of Cleveland. **Holes:** 18. **Par:** 70/72.
Yards: 6,044/5,481. **Course rating:** 67.1/68.9. **Slope:** 107/110.
Opened: 1927. **Pace of Play rating:** 4:00. **Green fee:** $17/19.
Credit cards: MC, V. **Reduced fees:** Weekdays, Low season, Seniors, Juniors.
Caddies: No. **Golf carts:** $17 for 18 holes.
Discount golf packages: No. **Season:** March–Nov. **High:** May–Aug.
On-site lodging: No. **Rental clubs:** Yes.
Walking policy: Walking at certain times. **Range:** No.

To obtain tee times: Call on weekends and holidays.
Subscriber comments: Small greens, must manage play, well conditioned course . . . Good condition, decent pace of play, hilly . . . The accent is on "hill". Many blind holes . . . Short course, but enough hazards to test you . . . Rolling, interesting course, conditions good considering amount of play.

★★ CALIFORNIA GOLF COURSE

PU—5920 Kellogg Ave., Cincinnati (513)231-4734.
Holes: 18. **Par:** 70/71.
Yards: 6,216/5,626. **Course rating:** 70.0/71.4. **Slope:** 116/113.
Opened: 1936. **Pace of Play rating:** 4:00. **Green fee:** $16/17.
Credit cards: None. **Reduced fees:** Low season, Seniors, Juniors.
Caddies: No. **Golf carts:** $19 for 18 holes.
Discount golf packages: No. **Season:** Year-round. **High:** April–Sept.
On-site lodging: No. **Rental clubs:** Yes.
Walking policy: Unrestricted walking. **Range:** No.
To obtain tee times: Call one day in advance.
Subscriber comments: Long walk around city reservoir, well maintained . . . Short, tricky, shot making required . . . Hills, water, woods, blind shots . . . Good conditions with scenic views . . . Great staff. Nines are very different . . . Older-style course, for mid-high handicap.

★★½ CARROLL MEADOWS GOLF COURSE

PU—1130 Meadowbrook, Carrollton (216)627-2663.
Call club for further information.
Subscriber comments: Greens excellent, fairly new course, needs more trees and maturing . . . Links type, good greens, inexpensive . . . Service and pace of play are very good . . . Reasonable rates . . . Tight course, fairways close to each other.

★★★ CASSEL HILLS GOLF CLUB

PU—201 South Cassel Rd., Vandalia (513)890-1300.
Call club for further information.
Subscriber comments: Back nine extremely hilly and tough, front rebuilt '94, very good . . . Way too many blind shots on this course. Scenic . . . Improving condition offers variety, playable condition . . . Changed front nine, made it safer. Well groomed and challenging . . . Back nine probably toughest and prettiest in area.

CHAMPION LINKS GOLF CLUB★

PU—4891 Clovercrest Dr., N.W., Warren (216)847-0383.
Call club for further information.

★★★½ CHAMPIONS GOLF COURSE

PU—3900 Westerville Rd., Columbus (614)645-7111.
Holes: 18. **Par:** 70/72.
Yards: 6,555/5,427. **Course rating:** 71.2/71.2. **Slope:** 127/127.
Opened: 1952. **Pace of Play rating:** 4:30. **Green fee:** $25/27.
Credit cards: MC, V. **Reduced fees:** Weekdays, Low season, Twilight, Seniors, Juniors.
Caddies: No. **Golf carts:** $9 for 18 holes.
Discount golf packages: Yes. **Season:** Year-round. **High:** May–Oct.
On-site lodging: No. **Rental clubs:** Yes.
Walking policy: Walking at certain times. **Range:** Yes (grass).
To obtain tee times: Call seven days in advance.
Subscriber comments: Nice old track, city needs to spend some money to restore beauty . . . Course layout superb, upkeep leaves a lot to be desired . . . Tight course, some tough holes . . . Wonderful layout, tees too small for public play.

★★½ CHAPEL HILLS GOLF COURSE
PU—3381 Austinburg Rd., Ashtabula (216)997-3791, (800)354-9608.
45 miles east of Cleveland. **Holes:** 18. **Par:** 72/72.
Yards: 5,971/4,507. **Course rating:** 68.6/65.7. **Slope:** 112/104.
Opened: 1957. **Pace of Play rating:** 4:00. **Green fee:** $11/15.
Credit cards: MC, V. **Reduced fees:** Weekdays, Seniors, Juniors.
Caddies: No. **Golf carts:** $8 for 18 holes.
Discount golf packages: No. **Season:** April-Nov. **High:** June-Sept.
On-site lodging: No. **Rental clubs:** Yes.
Walking policy: Unrestricted walking. **Range:** Yes (grass).
To obtain tee times: Call pro shop.
Subscriber comments: Well conditioned, maintained, some challenging
holes . . . Easy to play, but a lot of doglegs.

★★★ CHARDON LAKES GOLF CLUB
PU—470 South St., Chardon (216)285-4653.
35 miles southeast of Cleveland. **Holes:** 18. **Par:** 71/73.
Yards: 6,789/5,077. **Course rating:** 73.1/66.6. **Slope:** 135/111.
Opened: 1931. **Pace of Play rating:** 4:30. **Green fee:** $18/23.
Credit cards: All major. **Reduced fees:** Low season, Seniors, Juniors.
Caddies: No. **Golf carts:** $10 for 18 holes.
Discount golf packages: No. **Season:** April-Nov. **High:** June-Sept.
On-site lodging: Yes. **Rental clubs:** Yes.
Walking policy: Unrestricted walking. **Range:** Yes (grass).
To obtain tee times: Call two weeks in advance for weekdays. Call after 8
a.m. Monday for upcoming weekend and holiday.
Subscriber comments: Excellent conditions year-round, very fast greens
. . . Good length. Keep approach shots below the holes . . . Long, tough
putting . . . Tough established course. Hard to get on . . . Tough course
demands accuracy everywhere.

★½ CHEROKEE HILLS GOLF CLUB
PU—5740 Center Rd., Valley City (216)225-6122.
31 miles nortwest of Akron. **Holes:** 18. **Par:** 70/70.
Yards: 6,210/5,480. **Course rating:** 69.8/N/A. **Slope:** 120/N/A.
Opened: 1981. **Pace of Play rating:** 4:30. **Green fee:** $10/18.
Credit cards: MC, V. **Reduced fees:** Weekdays, Low season, Seniors,
Juniors.
Caddies: No. **Golf carts:** $25 for 18 holes.
Discount golf packages: Yes. **Season:** Year-round. **High:** April-Oct.
On-site lodging: No. **Rental clubs:** Yes.
Walking policy: Unrestricted walking. **Range:** No.
To obtain tee times: Call in advance.
Subscriber comments: Getting better now with watered fairways . . .
Overall condition fair, postage stamp greens, heavy league play.

★★½ CHEROKEE HILLS GOLF COURSE
SP—4622 County Rd., 49 N., Bellefontaine (513)599-3221.
45 miles north of Columbus. **Holes:** 18. **Par:** 71/74.
Yards: 6,448/5,327. **Course rating:** 70.8/70.3. **Slope:** 115/108.
Opened: 1970. **Pace of Play rating:** 4:30. **Green fee:** $13/16.
Credit cards: MC, V. **Reduced fees:** Weekdays, Low season, Juniors.
Caddies: No. **Golf carts:** $9 for 18 holes.
Discount golf packages: Yes. **Season:** March-Dec. **High:** May-Sept.
On-site lodging: No. **Rental clubs:** Yes.
Walking policy: Unrestricted walking. **Range:** No.
To obtain tee times: Call one week in advance.
Subscriber comments: Reasonable costs, good overall condition, average
golf challenge . . . Wide variety from open to tight, nice family run
atmosphere . . . Way too crowded. Pace not enforced . . . No holdups,
staff kept players moving.

OHIO

★★★ CHIPPEWA GOLF CLUB
PU—12147 Shank Rd., Doylestown (216)658-6126, (800)321-1701.
5 miles south of Akron. **Holes:** 18. **Par:** 71/72.
Yards: 6,273/4,877. **Course rating:** 69.1/67.0. **Slope:** 109/103.
Opened: 1962. **Pace of Play rating:** N/A. **Green fee:** $11/18.
Credit cards: All major. **Reduced fees:** Weekdays, Low season, Seniors, Juniors.
Caddies: No. **Golf carts:** $19 for 18 holes.
Discount golf packages: No. **Season:** Year-round. **High:** April-Oct.
On-site lodging: No. **Rental clubs:** Yes.
Walking policy: Unrestricted walking. **Range:** Yes (grass).
To obtain tee times: Call pro shop.
Subscriber comments: Good challenge. lots of variety in holes . . . First nine too short, great back nine, great conditions . . . Power lines distracting . . . Nos. 14, 15, and 16: "the Devil's Triangle", a great test of golf . . . This course is kept in beautiful shape. Staff is true to the tee times . . . Well maintained year round, fast and hilly greens.

CLIFFSIDE GOLF COURSE★
SP—100 Cliffside Dr., Gallipolis (614)446-4653.
30 miles northeast of Huntington, WV. **Holes:** 18. **Par:** 72/72.
Yards: 6,598/5,268. **Course rating:** 70.5/66.8. **Slope:** 115/109.
Opened: 1988. **Pace of Play rating:** 4:00. **Green fee:** $11/14.
Credit cards: MC, V. **Reduced fees:** Low season.
Caddies: No. **Golf carts:** $10 for 18 holes.
Discount golf packages: No. **Season:** Year-round. **High:** April-Oct.
On-site lodging: No. **Rental clubs:** Yes.
Walking policy: Unrestricted walking. **Range:** No.
To obtain tee times: Call one week in advance.
Subscriber comments: Challenging course with spacious fairways . . . Good course, all abilities, well maintained even in hot summer . . . Tricky doglegs . . . Always in good shape but expect 5 + hour round.

★★★ COLONIAL HILLS GOLF CLUB
PU—10985 Harding Hwy., Lafayette (419)649-3350.
Call club for further information.
Subscriber comments: This is a gem, and unlikely location for what's sure to be one of the 10 best new public courses . . . Excellent condition, staff very good . . . Accuracy very important . . . Long walks between tees.

★★★★ COOKS CREEK GOLF CLUB
PU—16405 U.S. Hwy. 23 S., Ashville (614)983-3636.
Call club for further information.
Subscriber comments: Long course, mounded greens . . . Tree-lined fairways . . . You can surely practice your fairway woods and long irons. Very long par 4s.

★★½ COPELAND HILLS GOLF COURSE
PU—41703 Metz Rd., Columbiana (216)482-3221.
Call club for further information.
Subscriber comments: Fastest greens around, very windy, sand on many holes . . . Wide open spaces, wind makes it longer and harder than it appears . . . Young course, nice layout, will get better with age.

★★★ COUNTRY ACRES GOLF CLUB
SP—17374 St. Rte. 694, Ottawa (419)532-3434.
20 miles north of Lima. **Holes:** 18. **Par:** 72/72.
Yards: 6,464/4,961. **Course rating:** 69.9/67.9. **Slope:** 126/113.
Opened: 1978. **Pace of Play rating:** 4:15. **Green fee:** $13/15.
Credit cards: MC, V. **Reduced fees:** Seniors, Juniors.
Caddies: No. **Golf carts:** $10 for 18 holes.
Discount golf packages: Yes. **Season:** March-Dec. **High:** June-Sept.

On-site lodging: No. **Rental clubs:** Yes.
Walking policy: Unrestricted walking. **Range:** Yes (grass).
To obtain tee times: Call one week in advance.
Subscriber comments: Course layout good. Fairways hard, greens soft
. . . Reasonable rates, not too long . . . Condition average at best.

★½ COUNTRYSIDE GOLF COURSE

PU—1421 Struthers Coit Rd., Lowellville (216)755-0016.
5 miles south of Youngstown. **Holes:** 18. **Par:** 71/71.
Yards: 6,461/5,399. **Course rating:** 70.5/70.1. **Slope:** N/A.
Opened: N/A. **Pace of Play rating:** 4:00. **Green fee:** $14/16.
Credit cards: MC, V. **Reduced fees:** Weekdays, Low season, Seniors,
Juniors.
Caddies: No. **Golf carts:** $8 for 18 holes.
Discount golf packages: No. **Season:** March-Nov. **High:** May-Aug.
On-site lodging: No. **Rental clubs:** No.
Walking policy: Unrestricted walking. **Range:** No.
To obtain tee times: Call pro shop.
Subscriber comments: Very tight but beautiful, hazards everywhere,
don't use a driver . . . Hilly, lots of trees, scenic course . . .
Accommodating, challenging course, attentive staff.

★★★ CROOKED TREE GOLF CLUB

SP—3595 Mason Montgomery Rd., Mason (513)398-3933.
Call club for further information.
Subscriber comments: Walkable, must use all your clubs, tight in spots,
plenty water holes . . . Great variety of holes. Big tees . . . Good layout.
Needs a little more maturation . . . Grueling par 3s . . . Very tight. Gobbles
golf balls.

★★½ DARBY CREEK GOLF COURSE

PU—19300 Orchard Rd., Marysville (513)349-7491, (800)343-2729.
18 miles northwest of Columbus. **Holes:** 18. **Par:** 72/72.
Yards: 7,054/5,245. **Course rating:** 72.7/68.1. **Slope:** 124/114.
Opened: 1993. **Pace of Play rating:** 4:00-4:30. **Green fee:** $18/24.
Credit cards: MC, V. **Reduced fees:** Weekdays, Twilight, Seniors.
Caddies: No. **Golf carts:** $10 for 18 holes.
Discount golf packages: Yes. **Season:** Year-round. **High:** May-Oct.
On-site lodging: No. **Rental clubs:** Yes.
Walking policy: Walking at certain times. **Range:** Yes (grass).
To obtain tee times: Call 60 days in advance.
Subscriber comments: Front open, links style; back cut out of woods . . .
New course, will get better, good value . . . Good shot values, each hole
challenging, some holes too close . . . Too young to be on that price scale
but lots of potential . . . Front nine needs a few years to mature, tight back
nine . . . Hated the front 9 but it's growing on me, love the back 9, two
completely different tracks.

★★½ DEER CREEK STATE PARK GOLF COURSE

R—20635 Waterloo Rd., Mt. Sterling (614)869-3088.
45 miles southwest of Columbus. **Holes:** 18. **Par:** 72/72.
Yards: 7,134/5,611. **Course rating:** 73.7/71.7. **Slope:** 113/113.
Opened: 1982. **Pace of Play rating:** 4:30. **Green fee:** $15/18.
Credit cards: MC, V. **Reduced fees:** Weekdays, Low season, Resort
guests, Twilight, Seniors, Juniors.
Caddies: No. **Golf carts:** $10 for 18 holes.
Discount golf packages: Yes. **Season:** Year-round. **High:** May-Sept.
On-site lodging: Yes. **Rental clubs:** Yes.
Walking policy: Unrestricted walking. **Range:** Yes (grass).
To obtain tee times: If staying at a facility in the park, call anytime for tee
times. If coming just for the day, call Monday morning of the week you
want to play.

Subscriber comments: A state park course, very long . . . Fun course, fairly long, but wide open, lot of sand, but few trees . . . Flat wide open fairways, rolling greens, lots of bunkers . . . Will be very good course when trees mature . . . User friendly, good treatment, fine place, fine condition . . . Played in fall, wide open, good fairways, lovely course, easy to walk . . . Take the family, rent a cabin, stay a day or two.

★½ DEER LAKE GOLF CLUB
PU—6300 Lake Rd. W., Geneva (216)466–8450.
Call club for further information.
Subscriber comments: Good greens, a good place to work on your game . . . Difficult greens, some surprise hazards . . . Flat, plain layout, very accommodating family operation.

★★½ DEER TRACK GOLF CLUB
PU—9488 Leavitt Rd., Elyria (216)986–5881.
30 miles west of Cleveland. **Holes:** 18. **Par:** 71/71.
Yards: 6,410/5,191. **Course rating:** 70.3/68.7. **Slope:** 104/115.
Opened: 1989. **Pace of Play rating:** 4:10. **Green fee:** $14/15.
Credit cards: MC, V. **Reduced fees:** Low season, Seniors.
Caddies: No. **Golf carts:** $17 for 18 holes.
Discount golf packages: No. **Season:** Year-round. **High:** April-Oct.
On-site lodging: No. **Rental clubs:** No.
Walking policy: Unrestricted walking. **Range:** Yes (grass).
To obtain tee times: Call pro shop.
Subscriber comments: Mounds, trees, and/or water, stay in fairway . . . Tight, short, always crowded, friendly, water on back nine . . . Friendly staff, good layout, not crowded.

★★★ DETWILER GOLF COURSE
PU—4001 N. Summit St., Toledo (419)726–9353.
Call club for further information.
Subscriber comments: Flat course that plays longer than yardage; forgiving from the tee but to score need good middle-iron game . . . It's a tricky Arthur Hills design . . . For amount of play, course was in good condition . . . Well maintained good test for average golfer . . . Nice fairways, large greens, sprayers course, excellent range . . . Great natural setting, adjacent to Lake Erie, great wildlife.

★★ DORLON PARK GOLF COURSE
PU—18000 Station Rd., Columbia Station (216)236–8234.
22 miles southwest of Cleveland. **Holes:** 18. **Par:** 72/74.
Yards: 7,154/5,691. **Course rating:** 74.0/67.4. **Slope:** 131/118.
Opened: 1970. **Pace of Play rating:** 4:00. **Green fee:** $18.
Credit cards: None. **Reduced fees:** Seniors.
Caddies: No. **Golf carts:** $16 for 18 holes.
Discount golf packages: No. **Season:** April-Nov. **High:** May-Sept.
On-site lodging: No. **Rental clubs:** Yes.
Walking policy: Unrestricted walking. **Range:** Yes (grass).
To obtain tee times: Call 8 a.m. to 2 p.m. Monday thru Friday.
Subscriber comments: Tough course, hard fast greens in summer . . . Long course. Good for big hitters, some hidden obstacles can be a nuisance. Keep it in fairway, pace OK . . . A flat course with a variety of wooded and more open holes.

★★★★ EAGLE STICKS GOLF COURSE
PU—2655 Maysville Pike, Zanesville (614)454–4900, (800)782–4493.
60 miles east of Columbus. **Holes:** 18. **Par:** 70/70.
Yards: 6,412/4,137. **Course rating:** 70.1/63.7. **Slope:** 120/96.
Opened: 1990. **Pace of Play rating:** 4:30. **Green fee:** $26/36.
Credit cards: MC, V, AMEX. **Reduced fees:** Weekdays, Low season, Twilight, Seniors, Juniors.
Caddies: No. **Golf carts:** $10 for 18 holes.

Discount golf packages: Yes. **Season:** April-Dec. **High:** June-Aug.
On-site lodging: No. **Rental clubs:** Yes.
Walking policy: Unrestricted walking. **Range:** Yes (grass).
To obtain tee times: Call pro shop up to one year in advance.
Ranked 19th in Ohio by Golf Digest.
Subscriber comments: Challenging layout from back tees . . . .
Wonderful, short but pin placements put a premium on iron play . . . Great
course, red tees short for women, recommend they play white . . . All
golfers should play here at least once . . . Very demanding course and was
in excellent shape . . . Beautiful, tough, rough, more expensive but worth it
. . . Take a cart. Bet you can't walk all 18. Great mix of holes . . . Distances
are very deceptive . . . Bent-grass fairways . . . Sand everywhere . . .
Excellent layout, greens and fairways, you use all 14 clubs, shotmaker's
course.

★½ EAGLES NEST GOLF COURSE

PU—1540 St. Rte. No. 28, Loveland (513)722-1241.
15 miles east of Cincinnati. **Holes:** 18. **Par:** 71/71.
Yards: 6,145/4,868. **Course rating:** 69.7/66.9. **Slope:** 120/108.
Opened: N/A. **Pace of Play rating:** 4:00. **Green fee:** $12/14.
Credit cards: MC, V, DISC. **Reduced fees:** Low season, Twilight,
Seniors, Juniors.
Caddies: No. **Golf carts:** $9 for 18 holes.
Discount golf packages: No. **Season:** Year-round. **High:** April-Sept.
On-site lodging: No. **Rental clubs:** Yes.
Walking policy: Unrestricted walking. **Range:** Yes (grass).
To obtain tee times: Call seven days in advance.
Subscriber comments: On flat terrain with woods and water . . . Tight,
must be accurate . . . Flat, no challenge . . . Easy, flat, wide open course,
not too many places to get into trouble . . . New ownership, improving
course yearly.

★★ THE ELMS COUNTRY CLUB

PU—1608 Manchester Rd., S.W., North Lawrence (216)833-2668,
(800)600-3567.
45 miles south of Cleveland. **Holes:** 27. **Par:** 72/71/73.
Yards: 6,545/6,054/6,633. **Course rating:** 69.9/67.7/70.1. **Slope:**
110/104/108.
Opened: 1932. **Pace of Play rating:** 4:00. **Green fee:** $15/16.
Credit cards: MC, V. **Reduced fees:** Weekdays, Low season, Twilight,
Seniors, Juniors.
Caddies: No. **Golf carts:** $25 for 18 holes.
Discount golf packages: Yes. **Season:** Feb-Dec. **High:** May-Sept.
On-site lodging: No. **Rental clubs:** Yes.
Walking policy: Unrestricted walking. **Range:** Yes (grass).
To obtain tee times: Call pro shop.
Subscriber comments: Older course, fairly wide open . . . Nice layout
but poor drainage, great greens . . . Straightforward course.

EMERALD WOODS GOLF CLUB
★ AUDREY'S/HEATHER STONE

PU—12501 N. Boone Rd., Columbia Station (216)236-8940.
Call club for further information.
Subscriber comments: Variety in layout, plays fast . . . Fairway and
rough blend together . . . Not maintained well . . . Good course for errant
tee shots, room for error.

★ ST. ANDREWS/PINE VALLEY

Call club for further information.
Subscriber comments: Mostly wide open . . . Good course for average
golfer . . . Terrific layout, worth playing at least once . . . Pine Valley nine
is short, tight, challenging, makes you think.

★★½ ERIE SHORES GOLF COURSE
PU—7298 Lake Rd., E., North Madison (216)428-3164.
Call club for further information.
Subscriber comments: Course in good shape, used to be too easy, but
they toughened it up . . . Very scenic, long enjoyable walk, staff friendly,
pace good.

★½ ESTATE CLUB GOLF COURSE
PU—3871 Tschopp Rd., Lancaster (614)654-4444, (800)833-8463.
4 miles north of Columbus. **Holes:** 18. **Par:** 71/72.
Yards: 6,405/5,680. **Course rating:** 69.9/N/A. **Slope:** 115/113.
Opened: 1967. **Pace of Play rating:** 4:00. **Green fee:** $12/15.
Credit cards: MC, V. **Reduced fees:** Weekdays, Twilight, Seniors,
Juniors.
Caddies: No. **Golf carts:** $18 for 18 holes.
Discount golf packages: Yes. **Season:** Year-round. **High:** June-Sept.
On-site lodging: No. **Rental clubs:** Yes.
Walking policy: Unrestricted walking. **Range:** Yes (grass).
To obtain tee times: Call one week in advance.
Subscriber comments: Lot of water in tight fairways . . . For a course so
heavily played, it was in excellent condition when I played it . . . Good
walking course.

★★½ FAIRFIELD GOLF CLUB
PU—2200 John Gray Rd., Fairfield (513)867-5385.
2 miles north of Cincinnati. **Holes:** 18. **Par:** 70/70.
Yards: 6,250/4,900. **Course rating:** 69.5/68.8. **Slope:** 123/113.
Opened: 1968. **Pace of Play rating:** 4:00. **Green fee:** $17.
Credit cards: None. **Reduced fees:** Seniors, Juniors.
Caddies: No. **Golf carts:** $20 for 18 holes.
Discount golf packages: No. **Season:** March-Dec. **High:** June-Aug.
On-site lodging: No. **Rental clubs:** Yes.
Walking policy: Walking at certain times. **Range:** No.
To obtain tee times: Call nine days in advance.
Subscriber comments: Fun course, some tough holes, good conditions
. . . A rolling course with plenty of doglegs . . . Great condition for public
course . . . Lovely course, short but tight . . . Conditions can vary from
month to month.

★★½ FAIRWAY PINES GOLF COURSE
PU—1777 Blaise-Nemeth Rd., Painesville (216)357-7800.
Call club for further information.
Subscriber comments: Flat course, moderately challenging . . . Easy
layout, nice to play . . . Nice mix of wide and narrow fairways . . . Newer
course getting better each year, great pro shop . . . More difficult than it
appears, layout hole design tougher than expected. Plays generally fast, new
course, needs some work.

★ FALLEN TIMBERS FAIRWAYS GOLF CLUB
SP—7711 Stitt Rd., Waterville (419)878-4653.
12 miles south of Toledo. **Holes:** 18. **Par:** 71/71.
Yards: 6,026/4,969. **Course rating:** 69.4/70.4. **Slope:** 109/111.
Opened: 1992. **Pace of Play rating:** 4:15. **Green fee:** $14/17.
Credit cards: MC, V. **Reduced fees:** Weekdays, Low season, Twilight,
Seniors, Juniors.
Caddies: No. **Golf carts:** $9 for 18 holes.
Discount golf packages: No. **Season:** April-Oct. **High:** June-Aug.
On-site lodging: No. **Rental clubs:** Yes.
Walking policy: Unrestricted walking. **Range:** Yes (grass).
To obtain tee times: Call seven days in advance.
Subscriber comments: New course, has potential . . . No trees, too open.
No diversity in holes . . . New course, greens are good, fairways and rough
need time.

★★½ **FLAGSTONE GOLF CLUB**
PU—13683 St. Rt. 38, Marysville (513)642-1816, (800)742-0899.
15 miles west of Columbus. **Holes:** 18. **Par:** 72/72.
Yards: 6,323/5,111. **Course rating:** 69.6/68.9. **Slope:** 115/113.
Opened: 1925. **Pace of Play rating:** 4:30. **Green fee:** $14/19.
Credit cards: MC, V. **Reduced fees:** Weekdays, Low season, Twilight,
Seniors.
Caddies: No. **Golf carts:** $9 for 18 holes.
Discount golf packages: No. **Season:** Year-round. **High:** May-Sept.
On-site lodging: No. **Rental clubs:** Yes.
Walking policy: Unrestricted walking. **Range:** No.
To obtain tee times: Call up to one week in advance.
Subscriber comments: Gets a lot of play . . . Good pace . . . Interesting
holes, reachable in regulation by average golfer.

★★½ **FOREST HILLS GOLF CENTER**
PU—41971 Oberlin Rd., Elyria (216)323-2632.
Call club for further information.
Subscriber comments: Maintenance gets better every year . . . Accuracy
helps, stay out of trees . . . Inexpensive and well maintained. Pace flows
well . . . Greens are always good.

(FRUGAL PICK)

★ **FOREST OAKS GOLF COURSE**
PU—U.S. Rte. No. 422 and St. Rte. No. 305, Southington (216)898-2852.
Call club for further information.
Subscriber comments: Few challenging holes, hard ground
conditions, price fair . . . Fair test of golf, reasonable rates.

★★★★ **FOWLER'S MILL GOLF CLUB**
BLUE/WHITE/RED
PU—13095 Rockhaven Rd., Chesterland (216)729-7569.
35 miles east of Cleveland. **Holes:** 27. **Par:** 72/72/72.
Yards: 7,002/6,385/6,595. **Course rating:** 74.7/70.7/72.1. **Slope:**
136/125/128.
Opened: 1972. **Pace of Play rating:** 4:30. **Green fee:** $19/39.
Credit cards: MC, V. **Reduced fees:** Weekdays, Low season, Twilight,
Seniors, Juniors.
Caddies: No. **Golf carts:** $3 for 18 holes.
Discount golf packages: No. **Season:** March-Oct. **High:** June-Aug.
On-site lodging: No. **Rental clubs:** Yes.
Walking policy: Unrestricted walking. **Range:** Yes (grass).
To obtain tee times: Call up to one month in advance.
Subscriber comments: Split fairways make it great, a must to play . . .
Pete Dye course well maintained . . . Great layout, very challenging, best
$22 I have ever spent . . . Great design; slick greens; somewhat short
yardage . . . They have weekday special after 3 p.m., Blue and White
layouts worth it, Red shorter . . . Tough course. Greens usually always fast
. . . Good layout with tough holes. Excellent condition . . . Pete Dye
makes you use every club in your bag. Tee times a must . . . Great course,
plays slow, White and Blue nine excellent, Red good, slow play caused by
using each nine as a starting point . . . Interesting layout with creeks
splitting two fairways . . . Worth a stop here.

★★★ **FOX DEN GOLF CLUB**
PU—2770 Call Rd., Stow (216)673-3443.
8 miles north of Akron. **Holes:** 18. **Par:** 72/72.
Yards: 6,468/5,431. **Course rating:** 70.4/69.0. **Slope:** 115/114.
Opened: 1966. **Pace of Play rating:** 4:00. **Green fee:** $13/23.
Credit cards: MC, V. **Reduced fees:** Weekdays, Low season, Seniors,
Juniors.
Caddies: No. **Golf carts:** $18 for 18 holes.
Discount golf packages: No. **Season:** March-Nov. **High:** May-Sept.
On-site lodging: No. **Rental clubs:** No.
Walking policy: Unrestricted walking. **Range:** Yes (grass).

To obtain tee times: Call ahead anytime.

Subscriber comments: Short course, but interesting and fun, well kept
. . . Short but country club conditions . . . Challenging, sporty, scenic, well
groomed, adventuresome . . . Challenging prettiest course, not too tough.
Great shape year round . . . A lot of course design being updated to bring
the challenge up, plantings are hard to beat, some beautiful views . . .
Challenging but not intimidating . . . Well groomed, challenging for all
levels, gets better every year.

FOXFIRE GOLF CLUB
PU—10799 St. Rte. 104, Lockbourne (614)224-3694.
15 miles south of Columbus. **Green fee:** $18.
Credit cards: MC, V. **Reduced fees:** Low season.
Caddies: No. **Golf carts:** $10 for 18 holes.
Discount golf packages: No. **Season:** Year-round. **High:** June-Sept.
On-site lodging: No. **Rental clubs:** Yes.
Walking policy: Unrestricted walking. **Range:** Yes (grass).
To obtain tee times: Tee times taken two weeks in advance for weekends
and holidays only; weekdays are first come, first play.

THE PLAYERS CLUB AT FOXFIRE★
Holes: 18. **Par:** 72/72.
Yards: 7,077/5,255. **Course rating:** 74.2/70.3. **Slope:** 132/121.
Opened: 1993. **Pace of Play rating:** 4:15.

★★★½ THE FOXFIRE COURSE
Holes: 18. **Par:** 72/72.
Yards: 6,891/5,175. **Course rating:** 71.1/69.1. **Slope:** 118/112.
Opened: 1974. **Pace of Play rating:** 4:30.

Subscriber comments: Foxfire good course, long, difficult. Players Club,
tight in spots, not for average player, great shape . . . Good shape, tough
from back tees . . . Well maintained, fun course, hard to get tee time . . .
Some greens too small for shots required to them . . . Back nine fairways
extremely tight . . . Very challenging . . . A bit higher price than city
courses. Worth the extra money you pay . . . With the addition of "The
Players Club" this is a good deal . . . Players Club is outstanding,
challenging; plush fairways; greens hold and nice size . . . Tough par 5s . . .
Let's keep this a secret.

★★½ GENEVA ON THE LAKE GOLF CLUB
PU—Golf Ave., Geneva On The Lake (216)466-8797.
Call club for further information.

Subscriber comments: Woody and rolling, long . . . Play can be slow,
greens usually excellent . . . Good test of all shots . . . Hilly . . . Lots of
trees, short . . . Well laid out, shotmaking course . . . Basic golf course, no
frills.

★ GLENEAGLES GOLF CLUB
PU—2615 Glenwood Dr., Twinsburg (216)425-3334.
Call club for further information.

Subscriber comments: Course still a bit raw, challenging . . . Layout
great . . . Looks open from road, very tight, super course . . . New course,
excellent design, needs two more years of growth . . . Outside of fairways
very, very rough . . . Fairways still need work . . . Some holes are
challenging but others are over-hazarded endeavors of championship
trickery. Trickery and high rough made the course over-priced experience
. . . Layout is nice but still too young.

★★★ GLENVIEW GOLF COURSE
PU—10965 Springfield Pike, Cincinnati (513)771-1747.
Holes: 18. **Par:** 72/72.
Yards: 6,965/5,091. **Course rating:** 72.3/69.9. **Slope:** 132/110.
Opened: 1974. **Pace of Play rating:** N/A. **Green fee:** $20.
Credit cards: None. **Reduced fees:** Low season, Seniors, Juniors.
Caddies: No. **Golf carts:** $20 for 18 holes.
Discount golf packages: No. **Season:** Year-round. **High:** May-Sept.

On-site lodging: No. **Rental clubs:** Yes.
Walking policy: Unrestricted walking. **Range:** Yes (grass).
To obtain tee times: Automated tee time service allows subscribers to call seven days in advance. Nonsubscribers call one day in advance. Out of town players call pro shop.
Subscriber comments: Mid-handicap, new back nine very challenging . . . Trees abundant . . . Two totally different nines, great price, need cart on back nine . . . Pricey, new nine is tough, course is much tougher from back tees, all-year golf . . . Good use of terrain, difficult to walk . . . Overplayed, needs better upkeep . . . New nine opened in excellent condition and looks like it's been there for years . . . Difficult. Staff good. You want to return.

★★½ GRANDVIEW GOLF CLUB
PU—13404 Old State Rd., Middlefield (216)834-1824.
Call club for further information.
Subscriber comments: The name says it all, "Grandview" . . . Unusual course. Very steep hills . . . Very tough greens, sloped . . . Interesting doglegs and lakes.

★★★½ GRANVILLE GOLF CLUB
PU—555 Newark Rd., Granville (614)587-4653.
30 miles east of Columbus. **Holes:** 18. **Par:** 71/72.
Yards: 6,612/5,413. **Course rating:** 71.3/70.6. **Slope:** 126/121.
Opened: 1935. **Pace of Play rating:** 4:30. **Green fee:** $22/27.
Credit cards: MC, V, DISC. **Reduced fees:** No.
Caddies: Yes. **Golf carts:** $11 for 18 holes.
Discount golf packages: No. **Season:** Year-round. **High:** April-Nov.
On-site lodging: Yes. **Rental clubs:** Yes.
Walking policy: Walking at certain times. **Range:** Yes (grass).
To obtain tee times: Call seven days in advance.
Subscriber comments: Very scenic in small college town, easy . . . Great Donald Ross course; four new holes added on back nine don't fit with the rest of the course . . . Watered fairways, beautiful track . . . Short, but requires accuracy . . . Redesign of back did not hurt . . . This is Donald Ross. Breathtaking view from 18th tee. Worth every penny . . . Rolling. Several elevated greens . . . Must hit center of greens, always a pleasure . . . Very challenging but fair . . . Unexpectedly interesting. Unique . . . All the free balls you can hit on the range. I like it . . . Donald Ross design at an affordable price.

★½ GREAT TRAIL GOLF COURSE
PU—E. Line Rd., Minerva (216)868-6770.
Call club for further information.
Subscriber comments: Very hilly, definitely need cart . . . Great breakfast with golf package . . . Small greens . . . Fun course in a scenic setting.

★½ GREEN CREST GOLF COURSE
PU—7813 Bethany Rte. 1, Middletown (513)777-2090.
Call club for further information.
Subscriber comments: Slow play, carts on path cause most of delay . . . Short and too compact . . . Well-kept, a little short but interesting, flat and walkable . . . Good mix of long and short holes . . . Tougher than it looks. Long par 4s. In good shape . . . Flat with water on four holes. As trees grow it will get harder.

★★★ GREEN HILLS GOLF CLUB
PU—1959 S. Main St., Clyde (419)547-7947.
Call club for further information.
Subscriber comments: Short but very sweet, well maintained . . . Nice people, good greens, nice track . . . Flat countryside.

OHIO

★½ GREEN VALLEY GOLF CLUB

SP—2673 Pleasant Valley Rd., N.E., New Philadelphia (216)364-2812.
Holes: 18. **Par:** 72/73.
Yards: 6,500/5,200. **Course rating:** 71.5/69.5. **Slope:** 117/113.
Opened: 1961. **Pace of Play rating:** 4:00. **Green fee:** $11.
Credit cards: None. **Reduced fees:** Weekdays, Low season, Twilight.
Caddies: No. **Golf carts:** $15 for 18 holes.
Discount golf packages: Yes. **Season:** March-Nov. **High:** May-Aug.
On-site lodging: No. **Rental clubs:** Yes.
Walking policy: Unrestricted walking. **Range:** Yes (grass).
To obtain tee times: Call one day in advance.
Subscriber comments: Very hilly, good variety . . . New watering
system has helped . . . Nice scenic course, greens are nice, fairways are
terribly narrow, control players will score well.

★★★★ HAWKS NEST GOLF CLUB

PU—2800 E. Pleasant Home Rd., Creston (216)435-4611.
20 miles south of Akron. **Holes:** 18. **Par:** 72/72.
Yards: 6,670/4,767. **Course rating:** 71.5/67.9. **Slope:** 124/110.
Opened: 1993. **Pace of Play rating:** 4:09. **Green fee:** $18/20.
Credit cards: MC, V. **Reduced fees:** Seniors.
Caddies: No. **Golf carts:** $10 for 18 holes.
Discount golf packages: Yes. **Season:** April-Dec. **High:** May-Oct.
On-site lodging: No. **Rental clubs:** Yes.
Walking policy: Unrestricted walking. **Range:** Yes (grass).
To obtain tee times: Call pro shop.
Subscriber comments: New course layout on old farm; needs to mature
. . . Good challenge . . . Some tees, fairways too parallel for comfort . . .
Lot of sand traps, nice greens . . . Every hole a different look, great
condition . . . Lots of teeing areas, great practice area, great course, still
young . . . Must hit straight. Tough from back tees . . . Offers opportunity
for using every club . . . Not easy but fair . . . Course layout and condition
excellent. Price high, but worth it . . . They keep play moving along . . .
Need a short game . . . Hard to believe it's only two years old, great shape
. . . Great surprise . . . 12 links holes, six traditional . . . Waited extra year
to open all 18 holes and worth the wait, greens lush . . . Young course,
several dynamite holes, awesome potential.

★★★½ HAWTHORNE HILLS GOLF CLUB

SP—1000 Fetter Rd., Lima (419)221-1891.
Call club for further information.
Subscriber comments: Keep in fairways, big trouble in woods . . . Lots
of variety . . . Short course . . . You will use every club in the bag . . . The
price is right and sand on every hole . . . Good bent-grass fairways . . .
Some holes are forgiving. Some will eat you alive . . . Staff is excellent,
pace of play a little slow.

★★★½ HEATHERWOODE GOLF CLUB

PU—88 Heatherwoode Blvd., Springboro (513)748-3222.
15 miles south of Dayton. **Holes:** 18. **Par:** 71/71.
Yards: 6,730/5,069. **Course rating:** 72.9/70.3. **Slope:** 142/129.
Opened: 1991. **Pace of Play rating:** 4:30. **Green fee:** $27/29.
Credit cards: MC, V, AMEX. **Reduced fees:** Seniors, Juniors.
Caddies: No. **Golf carts:** $11 for 18 holes.
Discount golf packages: No. **Season:** March-Dec. **High:** June-Aug.
On-site lodging: No. **Rental clubs:** Yes.
Walking policy: Walking at certain times. **Range:** Yes (grass).
To obtain tee times: Call one week in advance.
Subscriber comments: Water-haters nightmare . . . Target golf . . . A
very nice course but a little expensive for the area . . . Carts mandatory
during prime time and must stay on paths using 90 degree rule to fairways
. . . Fun course, hidden targets, risk and reward driver play . . . Many blind

shots, hilly . . . Don't bring a slice . . . Course always in top condition, lots of water on front nine that require shot accuracy . . . Super practice facilities . . . They lowered their price this year . . . Has a great variety of holes . . . Excellent layout, site of Nike Tournament . . . Many different challenges, must use many types of shots. Fast greens . . . Couple tricked up holes.

★★★½ HEMLOCK SPRINGS GOLF CLUB

PU—4654 Cold Springs Rd., Geneva (216)466-4044, (800)436-5625.
40 miles east of Cleveland. **Holes:** 18. **Par:** 72/72.
Yards: 6,812/5,453. **Course rating:** 72.8/73.8. **Slope:** 123/115.
Opened: 1961. **Pace of Play rating:** 4:30. **Green fee:** $15/19.
Credit cards: None. **Reduced fees:** Weekdays, Low season, Twilight, Seniors, Juniors.
Caddies: No. **Golf carts:** $10 for 18 holes.
Discount golf packages: Yes. **Season:** April-Nov. **High:** June-Aug.
On-site lodging: No. **Rental clubs:** Yes.
Walking policy: Unrestricted walking. **Range:** Yes (grass).
To obtain tee times: Call at anytime for any date.
Subscriber comments: Well maintained, design variety, wooded . . . You need to be long and straight, large greens . . . Long, challenging, well-maintained, can be humbling . . . Hilly and interesting . . . Extremely playable for all levels; excellent conditions all season, friendly staff, great value.

★★ HIAWATHA GOLF COURSE

PU—901 Beech St., Mt. Vernon (614)393-2886.
40 miles northeast of Columbus. **Holes:** 18. **Par:** 72/74.
Yards: 6,721/5,100. **Course rating:** 71.5/68.5. **Slope:** N/A.
Opened: 1962. **Pace of Play rating:** 4:30. **Green fee:** $11/13.
Credit cards: None. **Reduced fees:** Weekdays, Low season, Twilight, Seniors, Juniors.
Caddies: No. **Golf carts:** $9 for 18 holes.
Discount golf packages: Yes. **Season:** March-Nov. **High:** July-Aug.
On-site lodging: No. **Rental clubs:** No.
Walking policy: Unrestricted walking. **Range:** No.
To obtain tee times: Call pro shop.
Subscriber comments: Tough course, lot of hazards . . . Old course, you can rip it here . . . Water comes into play on 12 holes. Relatively flat.

★½ HICKORY FLAT GREENS GOLF CLUB

PU—54188 Lafayette Township Rd. 155, West Lafayette (614)545-7796.
25 miles southwest of New Philadelphia. **Holes:** 18. **Par:** 72/72.
Yards: 6,600,5,124. **Course rating:** 70.4/68.3. **Slope:** 109/105.
Opened: 1970. **Pace of Play rating:** 4:30. **Green fee:** $ 13.
Credit cards: None. **Reduced fees:** Low season, Twilight, Seniors, Juniors.
Caddies: No. **Golf carts:** $20 for 18 holes.
Discount golf packages: Yes. **Season:** Year-round. **High:** May-Sept.
On-site lodging: No. **Rental clubs:** Yes
Walking policy: Unrestricted walking. **Range:** Yes (grass).
To obtain tee times: Call anytime.
Subscriber comments: Wide open with a few tough holes . . . Lots of water . . . Pace slow at times . . . Good unadvertised specials if you ask.

★★½ HICKORY GROVE GOLF CLUB

PU—6302 State Rte. 294, Harpster (614)496-2631, (800)833-6619.
15 miles north of Marion. **Holes:** 18. **Par:** 72/76.
Yards: 6,874/5,376. **Course rating:** 71.0/69.1. **Slope:** 108/105.
Opened: 1963. **Pace of Play rating:** 4:00. **Green fee:** $10/12.
Credit cards: MC, V, DISC. **Reduced fees:** Weekdays, Twilight.
Caddies: No. **Golf carts:** $17 for 18 holes.
Discount golf packages: Yes. **Season:** March-Nov. **High:** June-Aug.

On-site lodging: No. **Rental clubs:** Yes.
Walking policy: Unrestricted walking. **Range:** Yes (grass).
To obtain tee times: Call pro shop.
Subscriber comments: Has gold tees for seniors, a nice feature . . . OK layout, just fun to play . . . Long, flat, not exciting, easy to play.

★½ HICKORY NUT GOLF CLUB

PU—23601 Royalton Rd., Columbia Township. (216)236-8008.
1 mile west of Strongsville. **Holes:** 18. **Par:** 71/73.
Yards: 6,424. **Course rating:** 69.5. **Slope:** 124.
Opened: 1968. **Pace of Play rating:** 4:00. **Green fee:** $15/17.
Credit cards: None. **Reduced fees:** Seniors.
Caddies: No. **Golf carts:** $18 for 18 holes.
Discount golf packages: No. **Season:** April-Oct. **High:** April-Oct.
On-site lodging: No. **Rental clubs:** Yes.
Walking policy: Unrestricted walking. **Range:** No.
To obtain tee times: First come, first served.
Subscriber comments: Average facility. Average price.

★★½ HICKORY WOODS GOLF COURSE

PU—1240 Hickory Woods Dr., Loveland (513)575-3900.
15 miles north of Cincinnati. **Holes:** 18. **Par:** 70/71.
Yards: 6,105/5,115. **Course rating:** 70.1/69.4. **Slope:** 119/113.
Opened: 1983. **Pace of Play rating:** 4:10. **Green fee:** $17/27.
Credit cards: MC, V. **Reduced fees:** Low season, Seniors, Juniors.
Caddies: No. **Golf carts:** $10 for 18 holes.
Discount golf packages: No. **Season:** Year-round. **High:** April-Aug.
On-site lodging: No. **Rental clubs:** Yes.
Walking policy: Unrestricted walking. **Range:** No.
To obtain tee times: Call six days in advance.
Subscriber comments: Very hilly back nine, accuracy a premium . . . Layout in woods . . . Tight but playable, use all your clubs . . . Going from the front to back is like playing another course . . . Short, tight course with a premium of being in the fairway . . . Front nine wide open and back nine treelined and tight . . . Rustic course but tough to walk . . . Good condition for heavy use . . . Short, but good. Position course, good condition . . . A short course but, the back nine has trouble everywhere with thick woods and steep hills.

★ HIDDEN HILLS GOLF CLUB

SP—4886 County Rd. 16, Woodville (419)849-3693.
Call club for further information.
Subscriber comments: Inexpensive. Get what you pay for . . . A few really pretty holes.

★ HIDDEN LAKE GOLF COURSE

PU—5370 E. State Rd. 571, Tipp City (513)667-8880.
12 miles south of Dayton. **Holes:** 18. **Par:** 72/72.
Yards: 6,562/5,357. **Course rating:** 70.5/69.3. **Slope:** 114/111.
Opened: 1988. **Pace of Play rating:** 4:00. **Green fee:** $ 9/18.
Credit cards: All major. **Reduced fees:** Low season, Seniors, Juniors.
Caddies: No. **Golf carts:** $9 for 18 holes.
Discount golf packages: No. **Season:** Year-round. **High:** March-Nov.
On-site lodging: No. **Rental clubs:** Yes.
Walking policy: Unrestricted walking. **Range:** Yes.
To obtain tee times: Call one week in advance.
Subscriber comments: Three island greens . . . Very difficult to walk . . . Too far green to tee making it a must to take cart . . . Tee ball very important . . . Tough sloping greens . . . Condition fair . . . Greens above average . . . Postage stamp greens.

★½ HIGHLAND PARK GOLF CLUB
PU—3550 Green Rd., Cleveland (216)348-7273.
Call club for further information.
Subscriber comments: Long straight course, some challenging par 4s . . .
Acceptable and good rate.

★★½ HILLCREST GOLF CLUB
PU—800 W. Bigelow, Findlay (419)423-7211.
Call club for further information.
Subscriber comments: These greens hold, shoot for the pin, only one
trap, not too difficult . . . Tight starting holes, open thereafter . . .
Expensive to play for quality . . . Good course for anyone . . . Variety of
shots needed.

★★★ HILLIARD LAKES GOLF CLUB
PU—31665 Hilliard Rd., Westlake (216)871-9578.
15 miles east of Cleveland. **Holes:** 18. **Par:** 72/75.
Yards: 6,680/5,636. **Course rating:** 70.0/74.0. **Slope:** 124/118.
Opened: 1968. **Pace of Play rating:** N/A. **Green fee:** $18.
Credit cards: None. **Reduced fees:** Weekdays, Seniors, Juniors.
Caddies: No. **Golf carts:** $24 for 18 holes.
Discount golf packages: No. **Season:** March-Nov. **High:** May-Sept.
On-site lodging: No. **Rental clubs:** No.
Walking policy: Unrestricted walking. **Range:** Yes (grass).
To obtain tee times: First come, first served.
Subscriber comments: On the short side, back nine very tight, just a fun
place to play . . . Too short, but scenic & relaxing . . . Lots of water . . .
Tight fairways, easier greens . . . Lots of tall trees . . . Flat as a pancake,
somewhat easy if you can hit it straight.

★★★ HINCKLEY HILLS GOLF COURSE
PU—300 State Rd., Hinckley (216)278-4861.
17 miles south of Cleveland. **Holes:** 18. **Par:** 73/72.
Yards: 6,704/5,478. **Course rating:** 73.6/70.1. **Slope:** N/A.
Opened: 1964. **Pace of Play rating:** 3:51. **Green fee:** $22.
Credit cards: MC, V. **Reduced fees:** No.
Caddies: No. **Golf carts:** $22 for 18 holes.
Discount golf packages: Yes. **Season:** April-Nov. **High:** May-Sept.
On-site lodging: No. **Rental clubs:** Yes.
Walking policy: Walking at certain times. **Range:** No.
To obtain tee times: Call pro shop.
Subscriber comments: Great layout, but needs water . . . Very hilly,
some blind spots . . . A little pricey but wonderful layout, spectacular view
. . . Hilly beautiful scenery, some tough, some easy holes . . . Great course
for big hitters . . . Name decribes course, very hilly . . . Large, undulating
greens . . . Not enough variety . . . Wind always a factor.

★½ HOLLY HILLS GOLF CLUB
PU—4699 N. State Hwy. 42, Waynesville (513)897-4921.
Call club for further information.
Subscriber comments: Plays tougher than it looks (wide open) . . . Front
open, back tight . . . Well-maintained greens . . . Picturesque valley, wide
fairways . . . Back nine has more character . . . Two courses, inside and
outside. The outside course has beautiful scenery.

★★½ HOMESTEAD GOLF COURSE
PU—5327 Worley Rd., Tipp City (513)698-4876.
Call club for further information.
Subscriber comments: Super fast greens for a public course . . . Ponds,
woods . . . Doglegs abound . . . Best course value anywhere . . . Well-kept
. . . Always mowed, short course . . . Very undulating greens . . . Course
good for all levels of golfer.

★½ HOMESTEAD SPRINGS GOLF COURSE
PU—5888 London – Lancaster Rds., Groveport (614)836-5872.
Call club for further information.
Subscriber comments: Greens are interesting and challenging . . . Good condition for amount of play. A fun layout . . . Very accomodating staff . . . Back nine a true challenge.

★★★ HUBBARD GOLF COURSE
PU—6233 W. Liberty St. S.E., Hubbard (216)534-9026.
Call club for further information.
Subscriber comments: Always in great condition, club selection makes it a challenge . . . Short, small greens put emphasis on wedge play . . . Short small greens, pleasant staff . . . Some drivable par 4s . . . Good test . . . Not too long . . . Rewards good chipping.

★★★½ HUESTON WOODS STATE PARK GOLF RESORT
R—6962 Brown Rd., Oxford (513)523-8081, (800)282-7275.
25 miles north of Cincinnati. **Holes:** 18. **Par:** 72/72.
Yards: 7,005/5,176. **Course rating:** 73.1/68.9. **Slope:** 132/N/A.
Opened: 1968. **Pace of Play rating:** 4:45-5:00. **Green fee:** $15/20.
Credit cards: MC, V. **Reduced fees:** Weekdays, Twilight, Seniors.
Caddies: No. **Golf carts:** $31 for 18 holes.
Discount golf packages: No. **Season:** April-Oct. **High:** June-Sept.
On-site lodging: Yes. **Rental clubs:** Yes.
Walking policy: Walking at certain times. **Range:** Yes (grass).
To obtain tee times: Call one week in advance for weekdays. Call 7:30 a.m. Tuesday for upcoming weekend. Hotel guests may make tee times at any time with reservation number.
Subscriber comments: Woods, woods, woods. Long course, bring extra balls . . . Beautiful setting in early fall . . . Great par 3s . . . Course was in good shape, price is right . . . Very challenging. Long, hilly and tight . . . treelined fairways . . . Trees everywhere and fast greens . . . Many blind shots . . . Bring fade tee shot . . . Excellent course, sometimes crowded . . . Target golf. Lots of big trees, slow play . . . Water hole a whopper. Easy to walk . . . Dogleg heaven, greens fair . . . Long doglegs left and right . . . Miami University's home track, last three holes are evil! . . . Great course for a state park, leave your hook and slice at home . . . Another treasure in a state park.

★★★★ INDIAN SPRINGS GOLF CLUB
PU—11111 State Rte. 161, Mechanicsburg (513)834-2111, (800)752-7846.
23 miles west of Columbus. **Holes:** 18. **Par:** 72/72.
Yards: 7,123/5,733. **Course rating:** 73.8/72.6. **Slope:** 126/122.
Opened: 1990. **Pace of Play rating:** 4:30. **Green fee:** $28.
Credit cards: MC, V, DISC. **Reduced fees:** Weekdays, Low season, Twilight.
Caddies: No. **Golf carts:** $10 for 18 holes.
Discount golf packages: No. **Season:** March-Oct. **High:** June-Aug.
On-site lodging: No. **Rental clubs:** Yes.
Walking policy: Unrestricted walking. **Range:** Yes (grass).
To obtain tee times: Call one week in advance.
Subscriber comments: Short grass roughs keep play moving . . . Back nine more difficult . . . Very tough . . . Always windy . . . Look forward to beating this course, well laid out . . . Great practice green . . . Rolling fairways, elevation changes, tiered greens, challenging . . . Great course but priced too high . . . Excellent design, best for your dollar . . . Very long, tight fairways . . . Fast contoured greens . . . Don't pass this up . . . Can play it conservative or take chances . . . Two distinct nines, back nine very tight and long . . . Multiple tee boxes . . . Must be accurate or you are in jail . . . Pace was medium to fast . . . Played in summer, lush fairways, tight, wooded, punishing rough, well kept . . . Some killer par 5s . . . Too long with too many tricky greens . . . Great layout, location is remote.

IRISH HILLS GOLF COURSE★
PU—7020 Newark Rd., Mt. Vernon (614)397-6252.
40 miles south of Mansfield. **Holes:** 18. **Par:** 71/75.
Yards: 6,503/5,890. **Course rating:** 70.2/N/A. **Slope:** N/A.
Opened: N/A. **Pace of Play rating:** 4:00-4:30. **Green fee:** $10/12.
Credit cards: None. **Reduced fees:** No.
Caddies: No. **Golf carts:** $8 for 18 holes.
Discount golf packages: No. **Season:** March-Nov. **High:** June-Aug.
On-site lodging: No. **Rental clubs:** No.
Walking policy: Unrestricted walking. **Range:** No.
To obtain tee times: Call pro shop.
Subscriber comments: Recently built back nine needs time . . . Good shape, tight course.

★★★ IRONWOOD GOLF CLUB
SP—1015 W. Leggett, Wauseon (419)335-0587.
30 miles west of Toledo. **Holes:** 18. **Par:** 72/74.
Yards: 6,965/5,306. **Course rating:** 72.2/69.2. **Slope:** 112/106.
Opened: 1971. **Pace of Play rating:** 4:00. **Green fee:** $ 9/16.
Credit cards: None. **Reduced fees:** Weekdays.
Caddies: No. **Golf carts:** $9 for 18 holes.
Discount golf packages: No. **Season:** March-Nov. **High:** June-Aug.
On-site lodging: No. **Rental clubs:** Yes.
Walking policy: Unrestricted walking. **Range:** Yes (grass).
To obtain tee times: Call seven days in advance.
Subscriber comments: Long, wide open course; good for all games . . . Open, breezy course, country hospitality . . . Long course, big greens, no trouble . . . Pace is OK . . . Course is maturing, will get better and better . . . Good course and fun for occasional rounds . . . Inexpensive, but country club conditions.

★★★ IRONWOOD GOLF COURSE
SP—445 State Rd., Hinckley (216)278-7171.
Call club for further information.
Subscriber comments: Hilly course; challenging par 3s; semi-private status makes tough to get weekend times . . . Excellent rolling terrain, good variety of holes . . . Good course makeup, need to use all clubs in bag . . . Always seems windy there . . . No traps . . . Holy smokes, what a view . . . Short but challenging . . . Very hilly, fast, sloping green.

★★★½ J.E. GOOD PARK GOLF CLUB
PU—530 Nome Ave., Akron (216)864-0020.
Holes: 18. **Par:** 71/71.
Yards: 6,663/4,926. **Course rating:** 72.0/69.1. **Slope:** 123/115.
Opened: 1926. **Pace of Play rating:** 3:50. **Green fee:** $16/18.
Credit cards: None. **Reduced fees:** Low season, Seniors, Juniors.
Caddies: No. **Golf carts:** $9 for 18 holes.
Discount golf packages: No. **Season:** March-Dec. **High:** May-Oct.
On-site lodging: No. **Rental clubs:** No.
Walking policy: Unrestricted walking. **Range:** Yes.
To obtain tee times: Call one week in advance.

Subscriber comments: Maintained very well . . . Fast greens, long and skinny . . . Densely wooded; well manicured considering much play; tough challenge for good amateurs . . . Best value in the county . . . Tough track . . . Not long, but tight, got to hit it straight . . . No tee times during the week . . . Tough par 3s . . . Good greens, well trapped . . . Playable for the high handicapper, but challenging for the low handicapper . . . Use all your clubs . . . Beautiful old course, plays longer than you think . . . Layout has stood the test of time . . . Many doglegs . . . Need accuracy off tee . . . Could be a private course. Unbelievable for a city course . . . Huge trees . . . Challenging, super conditioning for the amount of play it gets . . . Easy to walk.

★½ JAMAICA RUN GOLF CLUB
PU—8781 Jamaica Rd., Germantown (513)866-4333.
15 miles southeast of Dayton. **Holes:** 18. **Par:** 72/72.
Yards: 6,587/5,092. **Course rating:** 71.0/69.2. **Slope:** 121/115.
Opened: 1989. **Pace of Play rating:** 4:15. **Green fee:** $15/17.
Credit cards: MC, V. **Reduced fees:** Low season, Seniors, Juniors.
Caddies: No. **Golf carts:** $10 for 18 holes.
Discount golf packages: No. **Season:** Year-round. **High:** April–Sept.
On-site lodging: No. **Rental clubs:** Yes.
Walking policy: Unrestricted walking. **Range:** Yes (grass).
To obtain tee times: Call seven days in advance.
Subscriber comments: Some interesting holes . . . Needs trees . . . A few
unique holes. Still maturing . . . Overplayed by inconsiderate hackers.
Greens full of ball marks. Divots never fixed. Sand always needs raking . . .
A meandering creek adds character to many holes.

★★½ JAYCEE GOLF COURSE
SP—12100 Pleasant Valley Rd., Chillicothe (614)775-7659.
Subscriber comments: A forgiving course . . . Very big difference front
to back, rather ordinary but fun . . . Back nine wide open, several water
holes . . . Tricky greens.

★★½ JAYCEE PUBLIC GOLF COURSE
PU—2710 Jackson Rd., Zanesville (614)452-1860.
Holes: 18. **Par:** 71/76.
Yards: 6,660/6,200. **Course rating:** 67.8/72.3. **Slope:** N/A.
Opened: 1949. **Pace of Play rating:** 4:00. **Green fee:** $10/12.
Credit cards: None. **Reduced fees:** Twilight, Seniors, Juniors.
Caddies: No. **Golf carts:** $10 for 18 holes.
Discount golf packages: No. **Season:** Year-round. **High:** May–Sept.
On-site lodging: No. **Rental clubs:** Yes.
Walking policy: Unrestricted walking. **Range:** No.
To obtain tee times: Call one week in advance for weekends only.
Subscriber comments: Condition improving . . . No tee times required
during the week, wide open course . . . Blind shots . . . Best around for
money versus challenge versus maintenance versus views.

★★ KINGS MILL GOLF COURSE
SP—2500 Berringer Rd., Waldo (614)726-2626.
35 miles north of Columbus. **Holes:** 18. **Par:** 70/74.
Yards: 6,099/5,318. **Course rating:** 68.1/68.8. **Slope:** 106/109.
Opened: 1966. **Pace of Play rating:** 4:00. **Green fee:** $14/15.
Credit cards: MC, V, AMEX. **Reduced fees:** Low season, Juniors.
Caddies: No. **Golf carts:** $16 for 18 holes.
Discount golf packages: Yes. **Season:** March–Dec. **High:** May–Oct.
On-site lodging: No. **Rental clubs:** Yes.
Walking policy: Unrestricted walking. **Range:** No.
To obtain tee times: Call seven days in advance or longer with a credit
card.
Subscriber comments: Short course, easy but fun for a change . . . It's
not overly crowded . . . Terrain varies . . . Staff went out of their way to
help . . . Course has character at the right price . . . Good value, looks easy
but couple of tight spots.

★½ KINGSWOOD GOLF COURSE
PU—4188 Irwin Simpson Rd., Mason (513)398-5252.
Call club for further information.
Subscriber comments: Short, pretty easy, questionable maintenance . . .
Short and easy . . . Long, condition marginal, at least a couple weird holes
. . . Short and good shape . . . Front nine is more difficult, some interesting
holes . . . Front nine is competitive, back nine is short.

KITTY HAWK GOLF CLUB

PU—3383 Chuck Wagner Lane, Dayton (513)237-5424.
Green fee: $15.
Credit cards: None. **Reduced fees:** Low season, Seniors, Juniors.
Caddies: No. **Golf carts:** $18 for 18 holes.
Discount golf packages: No. **Season:** Year-round. **High:** April-Oct.
On-site lodging: No. **Rental clubs:** Yes.
Walking policy: Unrestricted walking. **Range:** Yes (grass).
To obtain tee times: Call Tuesday at noon for upcoming weekend.
Also has 18-hole par-3 course called Kitty Course.

★½ EAGLE COURSE

Holes: 18. **Par:** 72/75.
Yards: 7,115/5,887. **Course rating:** 72.8/74.3. **Slope:** 120/123.
Opened: 1962. **Pace of Play rating:** 4:15.
Subscriber comments: Water on too many holes . . . Sturdy course, big fairways, big greens accommodate a lot of traffic . . . Water everywhere, bring extra golf balls, small greens . . . City improving course, gets lots of play . . . Scenic course, generally conditioned . . . Large sand bunkers.

HAWK COURSE★

Holes: 18. **Par:** 72/73.
Yards: 6,766/5,638. **Course rating:** 71.1/73.3. **Slope:** 118/121.
Opened: 1962. **Pace of Play rating:** 4:15.

LAKESIDE GREENS GOLF COURSE★

PU—2404 S.E. River Rd., Lake Milton (216)547-2797.
Call club for further information.
Subscriber comments: Fair condition, back is short but tight.

★★ LARCH TREE GOLF COURSE

PU—2765 N. Snyder Rd., Trotwood (513)854-1951.
6 miles northwest of Dayton. **Holes:** 18. **Par:** 72/74.
Yards: 6,982/5,912. **Course rating:** 71.5/72.7. **Slope:** 107/107.
Opened: 1965. **Pace of Play rating:** 4:00. **Green fee:** $ 15/19.
Credit cards: None. **Reduced fees:** Low season, Juniors.
Caddies: No. **Golf carts:** $10 for 18 holes.
Discount golf packages: No. **Season:** Year-round. **High:** May-Aug.
On-site lodging: No. **Rental clubs:** Yes.
Walking policy: Unrestricted walking. **Range:** Yes (grass).
To obtain tee times: Call seven days in advance.
Subscriber comments: Nice greens but plain everywhere else . . . Treelined . . . Plain and simple . . . The greens are in excellent shape throughout the season, but the fairways become stressed and hard during the summer heat period. The staff is very courteous. Pace of play is average . . . Rough is a challenge.

★★ LICKING SPRINGS TROUT AND GOLF CLUB

PU—2250 Horns Hill Rd., Newark (614)366-2770.
35 miles east of Columbus. **Holes:** 18. **Par:** 72/72.
Yards: 6,400/5,035. **Course rating:** 70.0/68.7. **Slope:** 116/107.
Opened: 1960. **Pace of Play rating:** 4:30. **Green fee:** $13/14.
Credit cards: MC, V. **Reduced fees:** Low season, Seniors.
Caddies: No. **Golf carts:** $9 for 18 holes.
Discount golf packages: No. **Season:** Year-round. **High:** May-Sept.
On-site lodging: No. **Rental clubs:** Yes.
Walking policy: Unrestricted walking. **Range:** No.
To obtain tee times: Call. Tee times required for weekends.
Subscriber comments: Very hilly, most lies are either uphill or downhill. Greens elevated . . . Hidden creeks, lots of trees, prepare to scramble . . . Challenging course for faders . . . Blind shots, hard to walk . . . Blind shot heaven . . . Back nine very hard and very well maintained . . .

OHIO

★★½ LOCUST HILLS GOLF CLUB
PU—5575 North River Rd., Springfield (513)265-5152.
Call club for further information.
Subscriber comments: Enjoyable layout for the price . . . Fairly tight, easy, very good pace of play . . . Short hitters course, some interesting putting . . . Well maintained family owned course has come a long way in the last eight-10 years. Fairways vast, greens great, not difficult . . . Fun and challenging . . . Take your own golf cart when you go.

★½ LOST NATION GOLF COURSE
PU—38890 Hodgson Rd., Willoughby (216)953-4280.
25 miles east of Cleveland. **Holes:** 18. **Par:** 72/73.
Yards: 6,400/5,700. **Course rating:** 69.4/70.9. **Slope:** 113/112.
Opened: 1928. **Pace of Play rating:** 4:30. **Green fee:** $13/17.
Credit cards: None. **Reduced fees:** Weekdays, Low season, Seniors, Juniors.
Caddies: No. **Golf carts:** $9 for 18 holes.
Discount golf packages: Yes. **Season:** Year-round. **High:** May-Oct.
On-site lodging: No. **Rental clubs:** No.
Walking policy: Unrestricted walking. **Range:** Yes (grass).
To obtain tee times: Call one week in advance.
Subscriber comments: No frills golf at its finest . . . Old track needs work, too much play . . . City of Willoughby is making a good effort . . . Interesting, good walk, pace varies.

★ LOYAL OAK GOLF COURSE
FIRST/SECOND
PU—2909 S. Cleve-Mass Rd., Norton (216)825-2904.
10 miles west of Akron. **Holes:** 18. **Par:** 70/73.
Yards: 6,390. **Course rating:** 68.8/N/A. **Slope:** 115/N/A.
Opened: 1931. **Pace of Play rating:** 4:00. **Green fee:** $13/17.
Credit cards: None. **Reduced fees:** Seniors, Juniors.
Caddies: No. **Golf carts:** $17 for 18 holes.
Discount golf packages: No. **Season:** March-Nov. **High:** May-Sept.
On-site lodging: No. **Rental clubs:** Yes.
Walking policy: Unrestricted walking. **Range:** No.
To obtain tee times: Call anytime.
Also has 9-hole Third Course.
Subscriber comments: Wide, open, flat course . . . Maintenance only average . . . Setting good. Fair price . . . Short, small greens, staff very friendly.

★½ LYONS DEN GOLF
PU—Rte. 93 at 21, Canal Fulton (216)854-9910, (800)801-6007.
14 miles south of Akron. **Holes:** 18. **Par:** 69/69.
Yards: 5,774/5,228. **Course rating:** 65.0/N/A. **Slope:** 97/102.
Opened: 1962. **Pace of Play rating:** 4:00. **Green fee:** $ 8/16.
Credit cards: MC, V. **Reduced fees:** Weekdays, Low season, Seniors, Juniors.
Caddies: No. **Golf carts:** $16 for 18 holes.
Discount golf packages: No. **Season:** Year-round. **High:** May-Sept.
On-site lodging: No. **Rental clubs:** Yes.
Walking policy: Unrestricted walking. **Range:** Yes (grass).
To obtain tee times: Call pro shop.
Subscriber comments: Good course for egos, short par 4s, short par 3s . . . Nice course for high hadicap to score well . . . Very scenic . . . Conditioning improving.

★ MAHONING COUNTRY CLUB
PU—700 E Liberty St., Girard (216)545-2517,
Call club for further information.
Subscriber comments: Rolling terrain and several picturesque holes . . . Front nine short and wide open, back nine longer and narrower . . . Improvements have been made.

★★★½ MANAKIKI GOLF CLUB
PU—35501 Eddy Rd., Willoughby (216)942-2500.
18 miles east of Cleveland. **Holes:** 18. **Par:** 72/72.
Yards: 6,302/5,739. **Course rating:** 71.4/72.8. **Slope:** 128/121.
Opened: 1929. **Pace of Play rating:** 4:30. **Green fee:** $ 19.
Credit cards: MC, V. **Reduced fees:** Low season, Seniors, Juniors.
Caddies: No. **Golf carts:** $10 for 18 holes.
Discount golf packages: No. **Season:** March–Dec. **High:** May–Sept.
On-site lodging: No. **Rental clubs:** Yes.
Walking policy: Unrestricted walking. **Range:** No.
To obtain tee times: Call five days in advance beginning at noon.
Subscriber comments: Tough back nine must drive ball straight . . .
Wide landing areas . . . Beautiful Donald Ross layout, restoration
improving course . . . Most holes require big carry . . . Crowded but a
challenging course . . . Nicely groomed . . . Long par 4s and narrow
fairways . . . Fair shape, too many elevated greens for me . . . Not easy,
lots of hills . . . Crowded at peak times . . . Must be a shotmaker.

★★½ MAPLE RIDGE GOLF COURSE
PU—Rte. 45, Austinburg (216)969-1368, (800)922-1368.
50 miles east of Cleveland. **Holes:** 18. **Par:** 70/70.
Yards: 6,001/5,400. **Course rating:** 68.5/69.0. **Slope:** 118/118.
Opened: 1960. **Pace of Play rating:** N/A. **Green fee:** $12/14.
Credit cards: None. **Reduced fees:** Seniors, Juniors.
Caddies: No. **Golf carts:** $16 for 18 holes.
Discount golf packages: No. **Season:** March–Nov. **High:** June–Aug.
On-site lodging: No. **Rental clubs:** Yes.
Walking policy: Unrestricted walking. **Range:** No.
To obtain tee times: Call two weeks in advance.
Subscriber comments: Not too long, forgiving, friendly . . . Short,
wooded course . . . Excellent shape, good value . . . Challenging and fun
. . . Straight hitter's course.

(FRUGAL PICK)

★★½ MAPLECREST GOLF COURSE
PU—219 Tallmadge Rd., Kent (216)673-2722.
3 miles west of Akron. **Holes:** 18. **Par:** 71/72.
Yards: 6,412/5,285. **Course rating:** 69.2/67.8. **Slope:** 108/113.
Opened: 1926. **Pace of Play rating:** 4:00. **Green fee:** $15/22.
Credit cards: None. **Reduced fees:** Weekdays, Seniors.
Caddies: No. **Golf carts:** $18 for 18 holes.
Discount golf packages: No. **Season:** March–Oct. **High:** May–Aug.
On-site lodging: No. **Rental clubs:** No.
Walking policy: Unrestricted walking. **Range:** Yes (grass).
To obtain tee times: Call after Sunday for upcoming weekend.
Subscriber comments: Toughest par 3s around . . . Fun course in nice
shape all year . . . Elevated greens on par 3s . . . Good pace of play on busy
days . . . Always in great shape.

★★★★ MAUMEE BAY STATE PARK GOLF COURSE
PU—1750 Park Rd. No. 2, Oregon (419)836-9009.
12 miles east of Toledo. **Holes:** 18. **Par:** 72/72.
Yards: 6,941/5,221. **Course rating:** 73.3/70.5. **Slope:** 129/118.
Opened: 1990. **Pace of Play rating:** 4:30. **Green fee:** $20/25.
Credit cards: All major. **Reduced fees:** Weekdays, Low season, Twilight,
Seniors.
Caddies: No. **Golf carts:** $12 for 18 holes.
Discount golf packages: Yes. **Season:** April–Oct. **High:** May–Aug.
On-site lodging: Yes. **Rental clubs:** Yes.
Walking policy: Walking at certain times. **Range:** Yes (grass).
To obtain tee times: Call one week in advance for weekdays. Call on
Wednesday at 8 a.m. for upcoming weekend and holidays.

Subscriber comments: Must hit straight . . . Links style, lots of wind from the lake . . . Very few trees but challenging bunkers . . . Expensive but interesting links-style layout, watch out for wind . . . The final four are a bear . . . Great potential . . . No trees but lots of wind, playable by anyone.

MAYFAIR COUNTRY CLUB
SP—2229 Raber Rd., Uniontown (216)699-2209.
Call club for further information.

★½ EAST COURSE
Subscriber comments: Well maintained, very short . . . Needs more maintenance . . . Short holes and flat, nice for beginners to mid-handicappers. Few traps and water.

★★★ WEST COURSE
Call club for further information.
Subscriber comments: Good greens to hit and hold, not a long course, must have good short game . . . Gets a lot of play, well groomed course, challenging . . . Lot of sand, long from back tees, fair value weekdays . . . Varied holes, moderate lengths . . . Front nine open, back tight . . . Good bargain year-round, heavy play . . . Big greens, well maintained . . . Fairly open, reasonable shape.

★½ MIAMI SHORES GOLF COURSE
PU—Rutherford Dr., Troy (513)335-4457.
15 miles north of Dayton. **Holes:** 18. **Par:** 72/73.
Yards: 6,200/5,417. **Course rating:** 67.6/68.5. **Slope:** 97/101.
Opened: 1949. **Pace of Play rating:** 4:00. **Green fee:** $11.
Credit cards: None. **Reduced fees:** No.
Caddies: No. **Golf carts:** $9 for 18 holes.
Discount golf packages: No. **Season:** March-Dec. **High:** June-Aug.
On-site lodging: No. **Rental clubs:** Yes.
Walking policy: Unrestricted walking. **Range:** No.
To obtain tee times: Call one week in advance.
Subscriber comments: Short, wide open . . . Easy walking . . . Variety of holes, deep rough . . . Fairly easy course, but conditions good and great value.

★★★ MIAMI WHITEWATER FOREST GOLF COURSE
PU—8801 Mt. Hope Rd., Harrison (513)367-4627.
18 miles west of Cincinnati. **Holes:** 18. **Par:** 72/72.
Yards: 6,780/5,093. **Course rating:** 71.9/68.8. **Slope:** 120/104.
Opened: 1959. **Pace of Play rating:** 4:25. **Green fee:** $16.
Credit cards: None. **Reduced fees:** Seniors, Juniors.
Caddies: No. **Golf carts:** $11 for 18 holes.
Discount golf packages: No. **Season:** March-Dec. **High:** June-Aug.
On-site lodging: No. **Rental clubs:** Yes.
Walking policy: Unrestricted walking. **Range:** Yes.
To obtain tee times: Call five days in advance starting at 6 p.m.
Subscriber comments: Wide fairways suited for long but not so accurate drives, large greens make accurate long putts a necessity . . . Beautiful setting, well kept, back nine difficult to walk . . . Very open, scenic lakes, deer, woods, birds . . . Beautiful course, often see deer on course . . . Excellent value and well maintained . . . Great layout . . . Elevation changes . . . Rough and mounds cut too high, interesting front nine, back boring, great condition, all year . . . Management always terrific.

★★½ MILL CREEK GOLF CLUB
SP—7259 Penn Rd., Ostrander (614)666-7711, (800)695-5175.
10 miles north of Columbus. **Holes:** 18. **Par:** 72/72.
Yards: 6,300/5,100. **Course rating:** 69.0/70.0. **Slope:** 111/111.
Opened: 1973. **Pace of Play rating:** 4:30. **Green fee:** $14/18.
Credit cards: MC, V, DISC. **Reduced fees:** Weekdays, Low season, Seniors, Juniors.
Caddies: No. **Golf carts:** $8 for 18 holes.

Discount golf packages: Yes. **Season:** March-Dec. **High:** June-Sept.
On-site lodging: No. **Rental clubs:** No.
Walking policy: Unrestricted walking. **Range:** Yes (grass).
To obtain tee times: Call up to two weeks in advance, guarantee with credit card.
Subscriber comments: Easy holes, not much water . . . True concern for making golfers enjoy the course . . . Short course, can be test . . . Often overlooked but good track . . . Not real long, but good value, some tricky holes.

MILL CREEK PARK GOLF COURSE

PU—W. Golf Dr., Boardman (216)758-7926.
7 miles southwest of Youngstown. **Green fee:** $14/19.
Credit cards: MC, V. **Reduced fees:** Low season, Seniors, Juniors.
Caddies: No. **Golf carts:** $19 for 18 holes.
Discount golf packages: No. **Season:** April-Nov. **High:** June-Sept.
On-site lodging: No. **Rental clubs:** No.
Walking policy: Unrestricted walking. **Range:** No.
To obtain tee times: Call or come in Wednesday 6 a.m. for upcoming weekend.
Also have an 18-hole par-3 course.

★★★ NORTH COURSE

Holes: 18. **Par:** 70/74.
Yards: 6,412/5,889. **Course rating:** 71.9/74.4. **Slope:** 124/117.
Opened: 1928. **Pace of Play rating:** 3:46.
Subscriber comments: Natural beauty, complete test of golf . . . Always well maintained, tight fairways . . . Great treelined tight course, small greens . . . Tight, well bunkered . . . Has it all. Water, sand, trees, elevated greens . . . Usually overcrowded . . . Cut out of a park, treelined beautiful course that is deadly if you spray the ball.

★★★½ SOUTH COURSE

Holes: 18. **Par:** 70/75.
Yards: 6,511/6,102. **Course rating:** 71.8/74.9. **Slope:** 129/118.
Opened: 1937. **Pace of Play rating:** 3:44.
Subscriber comments: Challenging, good condition . . . Usually in good shape considering amount of play . . . Tight fairways, a placement course . . . Well maintained and reasonable . . . Truly a test of golf . . . Precise test of skills . . . Excellent par 3s. Postage-stamp holes.

★½ MINERVA LAKE GOLF CLUB

PU—2955 Minerva Lake Rd., Columbus (614)882-9988.
10 miles north of Columbus. **Holes:** 18. **Par:** 69.
Yards: 5,513. **Course rating:** 67.8. **Slope:** 103.
Opened: 1931. **Pace of Play rating:** 4:15. **Green fee:** $12/15.
Credit cards: MC, V, DISC. **Reduced fees:** Weekdays, Low season, Twilight, Seniors.
Caddies: No. **Golf carts:** $17 for 18 holes.
Discount golf packages: No. **Season:** March-Dec. **High:** May-July.
On-site lodging: No. **Rental clubs:** Yes.
Walking policy: Unrestricted walking. **Range:** No.
To obtain tee times: Call one week in advance for weekends and holidays until 11 a.m.
Subscriber comments: Very courteous, average pace, fair condition . . . Short but interesting, some tough holes . . . Small, but fun and not a pushover . . . Best tune-up course around . . . Forgiving . . . Very nice quaint course, short, usually well-kept . . . Short, but can cause trouble.

★★★½ MOHICAN HILLS GOLF CLUB

PU—25 Ashland County Rd. 1950, Jeromesville (419)368-3303.
10 miles east of Wooster. **Holes:** 18. **Par:** 72/72.
Yards: 6,536/4,976. **Course rating:** 71.1/67.9. **Slope:** 122/112.
Opened: 1972. **Pace of Play rating:** 4:10. **Green fee:** $14/16.
Credit cards: None. **Reduced fees:** Weekdays.
Caddies: No. **Golf carts:** $8 for 18 holes.

Discount golf packages: No. **Season:** April-Dec. **High:** June-Aug.
On-site lodging: No. **Rental clubs:** Yes.
Walking policy: Unrestricted walking. **Range:** Yes (grass).
To obtain tee times: Call one week in advance.
Subscriber comments: Great layout, condition and staff a well kept secret
. . . First nine holes might put you to sleep, better wake up from nine on
. . . Must hit long, big greens . . . undulating greens, challenging . . . Great
view, fairways and greens well maintained . . . One of the best kept courses
in the area . . . Different layout, creek cuts through several holes . . . Golf
in fall, fast greens, green fees worth the ride.

★★ NEUMANN GOLF COURSE
WHITE/BLUE/RED
PU—7215 Bridgetown Rd., Cincinnati (513)574–1320.
Holes: 27. **Par:** 71/70/71.
Yards: 6,218/6,115/5,989. **Course rating:** 69.0/68.5/68.4. **Slope:** 109/109/111.
Opened: 1965. **Pace of Play rating:** 4:30. **Green fee:** $ 15.
Credit cards: None. **Reduced fees:** Low season, Seniors, Juniors.
Caddies: No. **Golf carts:** $10 for 18 holes.
Discount golf packages: No. **Season:** Year-round. **High:** March-Nov.
On-site lodging: No. **Rental clubs:** Yes.
Walking policy: Unrestricted walking. **Range:** Yes.
To obtain tee times: Call 24 hours in advance.
Subscriber comments: Most improved course in the area condition-wise
. . . Red, not too hard; White, challenging; Blue tough . . . Easy to walk
. . . OK but hilly, good for city owned course . . . Fun to play . . . Long
waits to start.

NORTHMOOR GOLF CLUB★
SP—8330 State Rte. 703 E., Celina (419)394–4896.
40 miles southeast of Lima. **Holes:** 18. **Par:** 70/70.
Yards: 5,802/5,086. **Course rating:** 66.8/68.0. **Slope:** 102/102.
Opened: 1923. **Pace of Play rating:** 4:00. **Green fee:** $12/14.
Credit cards: MC, V. **Reduced fees:** Low season.
Caddies: No. **Golf carts:** $8 for 18 holes.
Discount golf packages: No. **Season:** Year-round. **High:** April-Oct.
On-site lodging: No. **Rental clubs:** Yes.
Walking policy: Unrestricted walking. **Range:** Yes (grass).
To obtain tee times: Tee times available two weeks before date and
mandatory on weekends and holidays only.

OAK KNOLLS GOLF CLUB
PU—6700 State Rte. 43, Kent (216)673-6713.
10 miles northeast of Akron. **Green fee:** $15/21.
Credit cards: None. **Reduced fees:** Weekdays, Low season, Seniors, Juniors.
Caddies: No. **Golf carts:** $9 for 18 holes.
Discount golf packages: No. **Season:** March-Nov. **High:** May-Sept.
On-site lodging: No. **Rental clubs:** No.
Walking policy: Unrestricted walking. **Range:** Yes (grass).
To obtain tee times: Call anytime.
★★ EAST COURSE
Holes: 18. **Par:** 71/72.
Yards: 6,483/5,279. **Course rating:** 70.5/69.7. **Slope:** 111/107.
Opened: 1963. **Pace of Play rating:** 4:00.
Subscriber comments: Open fairways. Good shape year-round . . .
Open, greens all flat no break . . . Course well designed, only fair condition
. . . Small greens.
★★½ WEST COURSE
Holes: 18. **Par:** 72/72.
Yards: 6,373/5,681. **Course rating:** 69.0/71.3. **Slope:** 112/112.

Opened: 1970. **Pace of Play rating:** 4:00. **Season:** April-Sept.
Subscriber comments: Fun course when windy . . . This course will test all aspects of your game . . . Big driving range for practice . . . Long hilly blind shots . . . Good greens . . . Open fairways . . . Wide open but high rough.

★★★½ ORCHARD HILLS GOLF AND COUNTRY CLUB

SP—11414 Caves Rd., Chesterland (216)729-1963.
20 miles east of Cleveland. **Holes:** 18. **Par:** 72/72.
Yards: 6,409/5,651. **Course rating:** 71.1/72.6. **Slope:** 126/122.
Opened: 1962. **Pace of Play rating:** 4:30. **Green fee:** $15/20.
Credit cards: MC, V. **Reduced fees:** No.
Caddies: No. **Golf carts:** $20 for 18 holes.
Discount golf packages: No. **Season:** April-Nov. **High:** May-Sept.
On-site lodging: No. **Rental clubs:** Yes.
Walking policy: Unrestricted walking. **Range:** No.
To obtain tee times: Tee times for members only.
Subscriber comments: Accuracy key, superb condition, unknown gem . . . Prettiest course in area, best maintained, some say unfair but it is tough . . . Plays through apple orchard . . . Hilly, beautiful greens are very difficult . . . A very tough test; strong finishing holes . . . Good challenge and variety among holes.

★★★ OTTAWA PARK GOLF COURSE

PU—1 Walden Pond, Toledo (419)472-2059.
Call club for further information.
Subscriber comments: Layout deceptive, wind constantly changing factor . . . Short track that makes you think from the tee, several shorter par 4s; to score well need accurate short-iron game . . . Tight course . . . Treelined; very small extra-fast greens . . . Short and sweet . . . Beautiful old trees, short but tight . . . Even though the course is fairly short, its rolling hills make it difficult . . . Always excellent shape; at $15.75 to walk 18 during the week, it doesn't get any better.

★★½ OXBOW GOLF AND COUNTRY CLUB

PU—County Rd. 85, Belpre (614)423-6771, (800)423-0443.
120 miles south of Columbus. **Par:** 71/72.
Yards: 6,558/4,858. **Course rating:** 70.9/68.8. **Slope:** 117/109.
Opened: 1974. **Pace of Play rating:** 4:00. **Green fee:** $13/15.
Credit cards: MC, V, DISC. **Reduced fees:** Seniors, Juniors.
Caddies: No. **Golf carts:** $10 for 18 holes.
Discount golf packages: Yes. **Season:** Year-round. **High:** May-July.
On-site lodging: No. **Rental clubs:** Yes.
Walking policy: Unrestricted walking. **Range:** Yes (grass).
To obtain tee times: Call pro shop.
Subscriber comments: Good, variety of shots needed . . . Good value for green fees, fun course . . . Too severe . . . Lots of sidehill and downhill shots . . . Greens are true, good pace of play . . . Excellent par 3s.

★★★ PEBBLE CREEK GOLF CLUB

PU—4300 Algire Rd., Lexington (419)884-3434.
8 miles south of Mansfield. **Holes:** 18. **Par:** 72/72.
Yards: 6,554/5,195. **Course rating:** 70.8/69.1. **Slope:** 117/113.
Opened: 1971. **Pace of Play rating:** 4:50. **Green fee:** $15/18.
Credit cards: MC, V. **Reduced fees:** Weekdays, Seniors, Juniors.
Caddies: No. **Golf carts:** $10 for 18 holes.
Discount golf packages: No. **Season:** March-Oct. **High:** March-Oct.
On-site lodging: No. **Rental clubs:** Yes.
Walking policy: Unrestricted walking. **Range:** Yes (grass).
To obtain tee times: Call within two weeks of date requested for groups of 20 or less. Groups over 20 can call up to one year in advance for tee times.

Subscriber comments: Expensive, needs some work, but a really nice course . . . A little tight but beautiful layout . . . Hilly, blind holes everywhere . . . Stern test from tips. Glass greens.

★ PHEASANT RUN GOLF COURSE
PU—711 Pheasant Run Dr., La Grange (216)355-5035.
Call club for further information.
Subscriber comments: Flat course with some tight holes . . . Narrow fairways . . . Flat, short, needs help.

★½ PINE BROOK GOLF COURSE
PU—11043 N. Durkee Rd., Grafton (216)748-2939.
22 miles west of Cleveland. **Holes:** 18. **Par:** 70/70.
Yards: 6,062/5,225. **Course rating:** 66.8/68.9. **Slope:** 110/109.
Opened: 1959. **Pace of Play rating:** 3:30-3:58. **Green fee:** $14/16.
Credit cards: MC, V. **Reduced fees:** Weekdays, Seniors, Juniors.
Caddies: No. **Golf carts:** $18 for 18 holes.
Discount golf packages: Yes. **Season:** Year-round. **High:** June-Aug.
On-site lodging: No. **Rental clubs:** Yes.
Walking policy: Unrestricted walking. **Range:** Yes (grass).
To obtain tee times: Call anytime.
Subscriber comments: Very good greens to putt, suited to all types, some holes weak . . . Short open course . . . Some good holes mixed in with some ho-hum holes, good staff . . . Not especially long, but a few holes are challenging.

★★½ PINE HILL GOLF CLUB
SP—4382 Kauffman Rd., Carroll (614)837-3911.
Call club for further information.
Subscriber comments: Long, hilly, tough greens . . . Scenic hills with blind shots, good treatment, good pace . . . Flat course with some hills, good for better players . . . Always in great shape. Nice combo of easy and tough holes . . . Great golf value.

★★★★ PINE HILLS GOLF CLUB
PU—433 W. 130th St., Hinckley (216)225-4477.
15 miles south of Cleveland. **Holes:** 18. **Par:** 72/73.
Yards: 6,482/5,685. **Course rating:** 71.2/74.3. **Slope:** 124/126.
Opened: 1957. **Pace of Play rating:** 4:00. **Green fee:** $22.
Credit cards: MC, V. **Reduced fees:** No.
Caddies: No. **Golf carts:** $9 for 18 holes.
Discount golf packages: No. **Season:** April-Nov. **High:** April-Nov.
On-site lodging: No. **Rental clubs:** Yes.
Walking policy: Unrestricted walking. **Range:** No.
To obtain tee times: Call pro shop.
Subscriber comments: Narrow fairways . . . Hit the landing zones or forget it . . . Great course, a little pricey but well worth money . . . Overpriced in relationship to comparable courses . . . Good test of golf skills, not for the occasional golfer . . . Very hilly. Cart is a must . . . No range is a negative . . . Good combo of short/long holes . . . Hard to get a starting time . . . Short, great par 3s . . . If you enjoy nature through woods, this is it . . . Thinking golfer's layout, keep it straight.

★½ PINE RIDGE COUNTRY CLUB
PU—30601 Ridge Rd., Wickliffe (216)943-0293, (800)254-7275.
15 miles northeast of Cleveland. **Holes:** 18. **Par:** 71/75.
Yards: 6,137/5,672. **Course rating:** 69.6/73.0. **Slope:** 118/122.
Opened: 1924. **Pace of Play rating:** 4:30. **Green fee:** $13/17.
Credit cards: MC, V. **Reduced fees:** Weekdays, Low season, Twilight, Seniors.
Caddies: Yes. **Golf carts:** $12 for 18 holes.
Discount golf packages: Yes. **Season:** Year-round. **High:** April-Oct.
On-site lodging: No. **Rental clubs:** Yes.
Walking policy: Mandatory cart. **Range:** Yes.

To obtain tee times: Call 7:00 a.m. Thursday for upcoming weekend. Call one week in advance for weekdays.

Subscriber comments: Many blind holes . . . Sporty, not real tight . . . Increased play since going public, needs better conditioning . . . Short but interesting. Tricky greens, A-1 shape.

★★ PINE VALLEY GOLF CLUB

PU—469 Reimer Rd., Wadsworth (216)335-3375.
1 mile east of Wadsworth. **Holes:** 18. **Par:** 72/74.
Yards: 6,097/5,268. **Course rating:** 68.5/67.9. **Slope:** 109/107.
Opened: 1962. **Pace of Play rating:** 4:00. **Green fee:** $13/17.
Credit cards: None. **Reduced fees:** Weekdays, Seniors, Juniors.
Caddies: No. **Golf carts:** $18 for 18 holes.
Discount golf packages: No. **Season:** March-Nov. **High:** May-Oct.
On-site lodging: No. **Rental clubs:** No.
Walking policy: Unrestricted walking. **Range:** No.
To obtain tee times: Call pro shop for starting times.
Subscriber comments: Super-wide fairways . . . Nice old course, family owned and very friendly . . . Well maintained short course . . . Long course with a lot of ups and downs . . . Average player can succeed. Greens usually slow.

★★★½ PIPESTONE GOLF CLUB

PU—4344 Benner Rd., Miamisburg (513)866-4653.
8 miles south of Dayton. **Holes:** 18. **Par:** 72/72.
Yards: 6,939/5,207. **Course rating:** 72.1/69.2. **Slope:** 137/121.
Opened: 1992. **Pace of Play rating:** N/A. **Green fee:** $23/29.
Credit cards: MC, V. **Reduced fees:** Twilight.
Caddies: No. **Golf carts:** $10 for 18 holes.
Discount golf packages: No. **Season:** March-Dec. **High:** June-Aug.
On-site lodging: No. **Rental clubs:** Yes.
Walking policy: Unrestricted walking. **Range:** Yes (grass).
To obtain tee times: Call pro shop seven days in advance.
Subscriber comments: Fair, undulating fairways . . . Great layout and greens, great value and managed the right way . . . Too many parallel fairways. Needs time to mature . . . Newer course, with time it could become great . . . A little tight with sloping fairways . . . Some holes do not reward you for a good shot . . . Placement off tee essential . . . Excellent greens, good variety in holes, course will toughen up as it matures . . . Hilly, flat, doglegs, can give you trouble.

★★ PLEASANT HILL GOLF CLUB

PU—6487 Hankins Rd., Middletown (513)539-7220.
20 miles north of Cincinnati. **Holes:** 18. **Par:** 71/71.
Yards: 6,586/4,723. **Course rating:** 70.2/65.6. **Slope:** 111/101.
Opened: 1969. **Pace of Play rating:** 4:00. **Green fee:** $13/16.
Credit cards: MC, V. **Reduced fees:** Weekdays, Low season, Seniors, Juniors.
Caddies: No. **Golf carts:** $10 for 18 holes.
Discount golf packages: No. **Season:** Year-round. **High:** June-July.
On-site lodging: No. **Rental clubs:** Yes.
Walking policy: Unrestricted walking. **Range:** Yes (grass).
To obtain tee times: Call Monday for weekend; call anytime for weekday.
Subscriber comments: Flat, parallel fairways, slow play . . . Short and straight, interesting water holes . . . Fairly flat, good variety of holes, always windy . . . Needs some improvements in shot values.

★½ PLEASANT HILL GOLF COURSE
BACK/FRONT/MIDDLE

PU—12316 Old State Rd., Chardon (216)286-9961.
Call club for further information.
Subscriber comments: Very hilly, heavily wooded, interesting layout . . . Fun to play, conditions usually suspect.

★★★ PLEASANT VALLEY COUNTRY CLUB

SP—3830 Hamilton Rd., Medina (216)725-5770.
Call club for further information.
Subscriber comments: Front nine fairly open, back nine needs accuracy
. . . Heavy play but in great shape in August . . . Tough course for better
golfers . . . Great variety of holes . . . Long from tips with 3- and 4-irons
on second shots to par 4s. Usually plays fairly fast . . . Good challenge,
water, hills.

★½ WOOLDRIDGE GOLF AND SWIM CLUB

PU—1313 S. Main St., Mansfield (419)756-1026.
Call club for further information.
Formerly known as Possum Run Golf Club.
Subscriber comments: Nice course, hilly, small greens . . . Very hilly,
has cart lift for walkers . . . Made great improvements in past two years,
still has a way to go.

★★ POWDERHORN GOLF COURSE

PU—3991 Bates Rd., Madison (216)428-5951, (800)863-3742.
40 miles northeast of Cleveland. **Holes:** 18. **Par:** 70/70.
Yards: 6,004/4,881. **Course rating:** 68.5/67.6. **Slope:** 117/113.
Opened: 1981. **Pace of Play rating:** 4:30. **Green fee:** $ 9/15.
Credit cards: MC, V. **Reduced fees:** Weekdays, Low season, Twilight,
Seniors, Juniors.
Caddies: No. **Golf carts:** $8 for 18 holes.
Discount golf packages: Yes. **Season:** Year-round. **High:** April-Oct.
On-site lodging: No. **Rental clubs:** Yes.
Walking policy: Unrestricted walking. **Range:** No.
To obtain tee times: Call one week ahead.
Subscriber comments: Very wooded . . . Gotta hit long and straight, nice
greens, not a walking course . . . Too long between tees, tough holes, hilly.

PRAIRIE VIEW GOLF COURSE*

PU—Rte. 1, Waynesfield (419)568-7888.
12 miles east of Wapakoneta. **Holes:** 18. **Par:** 72/72.
Yards: 6,348/5,575. **Course rating:** N/A. **Slope:** N/A.
Opened: 1991. **Pace of Play rating:** 4:00. **Green fee:** $12.
Credit cards: None. **Reduced fees:** No.
Caddies: No. **Golf carts:** $17 for 18 holes.
Discount golf packages: No. **Season:** March-Nov. **High:** May-Sept.
On-site lodging: No. **Rental clubs:** Yes.
Walking policy: Unrestricted walking. **Range:** Yes (grass).
To obtain tee times: Call 24 hours in advance.
Subscriber comments: A very young course developing more character
each year . . . Good service, price right.

★★★½ PUNDERSON STATE PARK GOLF COURSE

PU—11755 Kingman Rd., Newbury (216)564-5465.
Call club for further information.
Subscriber comments: Very challenging, strong layout, have to think
your way . . . Long, demanding from back tees, good greens, suits better
players . . . Well maintained for a state park course . . . Outstanding
course, fall colors spectacular . . . Lots of play . . . Doglegs and sand traps.

★★★★ QUAIL HOLLOW RESORT

R—11080 Concord Hambden Rd., Concord (216)352-6201, (800)792-0258.
30 miles east of Cleveland. **Holes:** 18. **Par:** 72/72.
Yards: 6,712/4,389. **Course rating:** 72.2/65.7. **Slope:** 130/107.
Opened: 1972. **Pace of Play rating:** 4:11. **Green fee:** $65/90.
Credit cards: All major. **Reduced fees:** Weekdays, Low season, Twilight,
Juniors.
Caddies: No. **Golf carts:** Included in Green Fee.
Discount golf packages: Yes. **Season:** April-Nov. **High:** June-Aug.
On-site lodging: Yes. **Rental clubs:** Yes.

Walking policy: Walking at certain times. **Range:** Yes (grass).
To obtain tee times: Call when making room reservations.
Subscriber comments: Great variety, elevations, woods, doglegs . . .
Very fast greens . . . Hard to get on . . . Little pricey . . . Very fast greens,
slow play on weekends . . . Can't afford to spray and better be able to putt
. . . Nike Tour site. Challenging.

★★½ RACCOON HILL GOLF COURSE
PU—485 Judson Rd., Kent (216)673-2111.
10 miles southeast of Akron. **Holes:** 18. **Par:** 71/71.
Yards: 6,068/4,650. **Course rating:** 69.2/67.0. **Slope:** 115/106.
Opened: N/A **Pace of Play rating:** 4:30. **Green fee:** $12/22.
Credit cards: None. **Reduced fees:** Weekdays, Low season, Twilight,
Seniors.
Caddies: No. **Golf carts:** $9 for 18 holes.
Discount golf packages: No. **Season:** March-Nov. **High:** May-Sept.
On-site lodging: No. **Rental clubs:** No.
Walking policy: Unrestricted walking. **Range:** No.
To obtain tee times: Call pro shop.
Subscriber comments: Back nine plays like links course . . . Great greens,
current owner has improved course . . . Open . . . Flat . . . A number of
high risk/high reward holes . . . Great to walk.

★★½ RACCOON INTERNATIONAL GOLF CLUB
PU—3275 Worthington Rd. S.W., Granville (614)587-0921.
25 miles east of Columbus. **Holes:** 18. **Par:** 72/72.
Yards: 6,586/6,094. **Course rating:** N/A. **Slope:** 125/116.
Opened: N/A. **Pace of Play rating:** N/A. **Green fee:** N/A.
Credit cards: MC, V. **Reduced fees:** Weekdays, Low season.
Caddies: No. **Golf carts:** N/A.
Discount golf packages: No. **Season:** Year-round. **High:** March-Oct.
On-site lodging: No. **Rental clubs:** No.
Walking policy: N/A. **Range:** Yes.
Subscriber comments: Front nine is very tight . . . Moderately long, little
trouble . . . Still awaiting promised improvement . . . Holes have been
remodeled . . . Nice tight holes require accuracy on driving . . . Course had
recent renovations . . . Making improvements to course, should be really
nice soon.

★★★ RAINTREE COUNTRY CLUB
SP—4350 Mayfair Rd., Uniontown (216)699-3232, (800)371-0017.
5 miles south of Akron. **Holes:** 18. **Par:** 72/72.
Yards: 6,811/5,030. **Course rating:** 73.0/68.5. **Slope:** 127/114.
Opened: 1992. **Pace of Play rating:** 4:30-5:00. **Green fee:** $16/26.
Credit cards: MC, V. **Reduced fees:** Weekdays, Low season, Twilight,
Seniors, Juniors.
Caddies: No. **Golf carts:** $10 for 18 holes.
Discount golf packages: Yes. **Season:** Year-round. **High:** April-Oct.
On-site lodging: No. **Rental clubs:** Yes.
Walking policy: Walking at certain times. **Range:** Yes (grass).
To obtain tee times: Call or in person all season. May reconfirm one year
in advance.
Subscriber comments: Young track, very demanding from blues . . .
Much of the course out in the open. Lacks perspective . . . Fairways too
close together . . . Very scenic, tough but not unrealistic . . . Lots of traps
. . . Almost like playing three courses, wooded, links, water . . . New
course, greens usually inconsistent and spiked up, eventually will become a
great course . . . Excellent greens . . . Should get better when greens
mature.

★★ RAYMOND MEMORIAL GOLF CLUB
PU—3860 Trabue Rd., Columbus (614)274-1895.
Call club for further information.
Subscriber comments: Tough to putt, very reasonable, sometimes slow

. . . City has a diamond in the rough . . . Flat, good for all, staff OK, gets very heavy play, pace sometimes slow . . . Good value, inconsistent condition . . . Some hard doglegs . . . Long but open . . . Fine layout, gets a lot of play.

★½ REEVES GOLF COURSE

PU—4747 Playfield Lane, Cincinnati (513)321-1433.
Holes: 18. **Par:** 70/74.
Yards: 6,200/5,630. **Course rating:** 68.4/70.2. **Slope:** 109/102.
Opened: 1965. **Pace of Play rating:** 4:00. **Green fee:** $15.
Credit cards: None. **Reduced fees:** Low season, Seniors, Juniors.
Caddies: No. **Golf carts:** $10 for 18 holes.
Discount golf packages: No. **Season:** Year-round. **High:** May-Sept.
On-site lodging: No. **Rental clubs:** Yes.
Walking policy: Unrestricted walking. **Range:** Yes (grass).
To obtain tee times: Xeta computer system or call 24 hours in advance. Also has a 9-hole par-3 course.
Subscriber comments: Easy to walk . . . Course is flat and wide open, no trouble, great greens and fairways . . . Wide open, flat course, next to small airport . . . Walking course . . . Flat and uninspiring.

REID PARK MEMORIAL GOLF COURSE

PU—1325 Bird Rd., Springfield (513)324-7725.
43 miles west of Columbus. **Green fee:** $16.
Credit cards: None. **Reduced fees:** Twilight.
Caddies: No. **Golf carts:** $20 for 18 holes.
Discount golf packages: No. **Season:** Year-round. **High:** May-Oct.
On-site lodging: No. **Rental clubs:** No.
Walking policy: Unrestricted walking. **Range:** No.
To obtain tee times: Call eight days in advance.

★★★ NORTH COURSE

Holes: 18. **Par:** 72/72.
Yards: 6,760/5,035. **Course rating:** 72.5/69.2. **Slope:** 130/118.
Opened: 1967. **Pace of Play rating:** 4:15.
Subscriber comments: Great course design, hilly, wooded . . . Fun course to play, not long but scenic . . . Tight course . . . Good condition . . . Fair, large greens . . . You'll use every club in your bag . . . Hilly, but fair, rates good.

★★ SOUTH COURSE

Holes: 18. **Par:** 72/72.
Yards: 6,500/4,895. **Course rating:** 69.0/66.5. **Slope:** 110/102.
Opened: 1967. **Pace of Play rating:** 4:15.
Subscriber comments: Long course requires shotmaking . . . Easy, wide open, no bunkers, two lakes . . . Can be hard. Well maintained . . . Short, no traps . . . Course gets lots of play.

★★ RICKENBACKER GOLF CLUB

SP—5600 Airbase Rd., Groveport (614)491-5000.
10 miles south of Columbus. **Holes:** 18. **Par:** 72/72.
Yards: 7,003/5,476. **Course rating:** 72.6/71.2. **Slope:** 117/117.
Opened: 1959. **Pace of Play rating:** 4:15. **Green fee:** $10/17.
Credit cards: MC, V. **Reduced fees:** Weekdays, Low season, Twilight, Seniors, Juniors.
Caddies: No. **Golf carts:** $9 for 18 holes.
Discount golf packages: Yes. **Season:** Year-round. **High:** June-Aug.
On-site lodging: No. **Rental clubs:** Yes.
Walking policy: Unrestricted walking. **Range:** Yes (grass).
To obtain tee times: Call pro shop five days in advance.
Formerly known as Steeplechase Country Club.
Subscriber comments: Long course, interesting . . . Needs work, long from blues . . . Good test of golf, variety of types of holes . . . Fast greens . . . New management seems determined to do well.

★★½ RIDGE TOP GOLF COURSE

PU—7441 Tower Rd., Medina (216)725-5500.
20 miles south of Cleveland. **Holes:** 18. **Par:** 71/71.
Yards: 6,211/4,968. **Course rating:** 70.0/67.9. **Slope:** 109/106.
Opened: 1970. **Pace of Play rating:** 3:45. **Green fee:** $14/18.
Credit cards: MC, V. **Reduced fees:** Weekdays, Low season, Seniors, Juniors.
Caddies: No. **Golf carts:** $17 for 18 holes.
Discount golf packages: No. **Season:** March-Nov. **High:** June-Aug.
On-site lodging: No. **Rental clubs:** No.
Walking policy: Unrestricted walking. **Range:** No.
To obtain tee times: Call pro shop.
Subscriber comments: Great course, excellent condition, friendly atmosphere . . . Fast undulating greens for a public course . . . Very popular course, well maintained . . . Has some interesting holes, you have to think . . . Good value.

★ RIVER BEND GOLF COURSE

PU—5567 Upper River Rd., Miamisburg (513)859-8121.
5 miles south of Dayton. **Holes:** 18. **Par:** 72/75.
Yards: 7,000/5,980. **Course rating:** 70.8/N/A. **Slope:** 112/N/A.
Opened: 1963. **Pace of Play rating:** 4:00. **Green fee:** $13/16.
Credit cards: None. **Reduced fees:** Low season, Seniors, Juniors.
Caddies: No. **Golf carts:** $9 for 18 holes.
Discount golf packages: No. **Season:** Year-round. **High:** June-Aug.
On-site lodging: No. **Rental clubs:** Yes.
Walking policy: Unrestricted walking. **Range:** No.
To obtain tee times: Call seven days in advance.
Subscriber comments: Plain, simple and wide open, a very good value . . . Making a comeback since new irrigation system installed . . . Flat and very little trouble . . . Easy to walk . . . Good practice/warm-up course.

★★★★ RIVER GREENS GOLF COURSE

PU—22749 State Rte. 751, West Lafayette (614)545-7817.
25 miles southwest of New Philadelphia. **Holes:** 18 **Par:** 72/73.
Yards: 6,588/5,409. **Course rating:** 70.9/70.2. **Slope:** 114/113.
Opened: 1967. **Pace of Play rating:** 4:30. **Green fee:** $ 16.
Credit cards: MC, V. **Reduced fees:** No.
Caddies: No. **Golf carts:** $10 for 18 holes.
Discount golf packages: Yes. **Season:** March-Dec. **High:** March-Sept.
On-site lodging: No. **Rental clubs:** Yes.
Walking policy: Unrestricted walking. **Range:** Yes (grass).
To obtain tee times: Call one week in advance.
Also has 9-hole par-36 Pine Course.
Subscriber comments: Must keep ball in fairway. Trees and high rough . . . Very good fairways and greens . . . Stay out of pines . . . Good course to walk . . . Prices higher than other area course, but worth it . . . Always great condition . . . Green speed and conditions outstanding . . . Good prices . . . Beautiful but tight . . . Good conditions always . . . Another top course, you want to go back again.

★★★ RIVERBY HILLS GOLF COURSE

PU—16571 West River Rd., Bowling Green (419)878-5941.
Call club for further information.
Subscriber comments: Long course with flat, open front nine versus hilly, narrow back nine. Helps to be accurate off tee to set up middle to long irons, usually in good condition all season . . . Can be tough in the wind . . . Great course, challenging but not too hard always in top notch shape . . . Average layout, some strange holes.

★½ ROCKY FORK GOLF AND TENNIS CENTER

PU—9965 State Rte. 124, Hillsboro (513)393-9004.

Call club for further information.

Subscriber comments: Nicely maintained, never crowded, friendly, a few hokey holes . . . Back nine hilly, wooded and tight . . . Play moves along good.

★★★½ ROYAL AMERICAN LINKS GOLF CLUB

SP—3300 Miller Paul Rd., Galena (614)965-1215.

17 miles north of Columbus. **Holes:** 18. **Par:** 72/72.

Yards: 6,809/5,171. **Course rating:** 72.7/70.1. **Slope:** 126/111.

Opened: 1992. **Pace of Play rating:** 4:30. **Green fees:** $20/35.

Credit cards: MC, V, DISC. **Reduced fees:** Weekdays, Low season, Twilight, Seniors, Juniors.

Caddies: No. **Golf carts:** $10 for 18 holes.

Discount golf packages: No. **Season:** March-Dec. **High:** June-Sept.

On-site lodging: No. **Rental clubs:** Yes.

Walking policy: Unrestricted walking. **Range:** Yes (grass).

To obtain tee times: Call one week in advance.

Subscriber comments: Tough test, bring a lot of balls, better players only . . . Tough in the wind . . . Tough and interesting, pricey . . . Lots of water, mounds and many good holes. Hit it straight . . . High green fees, but worth playing, never crowded . . . Fairways too narrow, sneaky water.

★ RUNNING FOX GOLF COURSE
RED/WHITE/BLUE

PU—310 Sunset, Chillicothe (614)775-9955.

42 miles south of Columbus. **Holes:** 27. **Par:** 72/72/72.

Yards: 6,538/6,568/6,432. **Course rating:** 70.5/70.5/70.5. **Slope:** 113/113/113.

Opened: 1974. **Pace of Play rating:** 4:00. **Green fee:** $10/12.

Credit cards: MC, V. **Reduced fees:** Seniors, Juniors.

Caddies: No. **Golf carts:** $19 for 18 holes.

Discount golf packages: Yes. **Season:** Year-round. **High:** June-July.

On-site lodging: No. **Rental clubs:** Yes.

Walking policy: Unrestricted walking. **Range:** Yes (grass).

To obtain tee times: Call anytime.

Subscriber comments: Basic golf except river holes which are beautiful . . . Price meets my pocketbook.

★½ SAFARI GOLF CLUB

PU—P.O. Box 400, Powell (614)645-3444.

Call club for further information.

Subscriber comments: Holes too close together . . . Not always in good condition, they have shortened holes . . . Course has been upgraded with new tee boxes and irrigation system . . . Not great, but improved. Anyone can play it.

★★★ SALEM HILLS GOLF AND COUNTRY CLUB

SP—12688 Salem-Warren Rd., Salem (216)337-8033.

15 miles south of Youngstown. **Holes:** 18. **Par:** 72/72.

Yards: 7,146/5,597. **Course rating:** 74.3/69.7. **Slope:** 126/114.

Opened: 1966. **Pace of Play rating:** 5:00. **Green fee:** $16/18.

Credit cards: MC, V. **Reduced fees:** Weekdays, Seniors, Juniors.

Caddies: No. **Golf carts:** $9 for 18 holes.

Discount golf packages: Yes. **Season:** April-Nov. **High:** June-Aug.

On-site lodging: No. **Rental clubs:** No.

Walking policy: Unrestricted walking. **Range:** Yes (grass).

To obtain tee times: Call pro shop.

Subscriber comments: Long course, wide fairways, greens tough to hit . . . Straight drives a must . . . Very challenging, getting better each year . . . Long and lean. Well manicured . . . Challenging for all golfers.

★★★ SALT FORK STATE PARK GOLF COURSE
PU—14755 Cadiz Rd., Lore City (614)432-7185, (800)282-7275.
6 miles east of Cambridge. **Holes:** 18. **Par:** 71/71.
Yards: 6,056/5,241. **Course rating:** 68.3/69.7. **Slope:** 110/113.
Opened: 1972. **Pace of Play rating:** 4:00–4:30. **Green fee:** $13.
Credit cards: MC, V. **Reduced fees:** Low season, Resort guests, Seniors.
Caddies: No. **Golf carts:** $12 for 18 holes.
Discount golf packages: Yes. **Season:** Year-round. **High:** May–Oct.
On-site lodging: Yes. **Rental clubs:** Yes.
Walking policy: Unrestricted walking. **Range:** Yes (grass).
To obtain tee times: Call pro shop as far in advance as you like.
Subscriber comments: Not a walking course, very hilly, very pretty . . .
Beautiful course, target course, large undulating greens . . . Short but very
challenging . . . Staying on path slows play . . . Good challenging course.
Only complaint, must keep carts on paths, should have 90 degree rule . . .
Tight fairways . . . Good mountain layout; use your head . . . Must be
straight.

★★★½ SAWMILL CREEK GOLF AND RACQUET CLUB
R—2401 Cleveland Rd. W., Huron (419)433-3789.
65 miles west of Cleveland. **Holes:** 18. **Par:** 71/74.
Yards: 6,813/5,416. **Course rating:** 72.3/70.6. **Slope:** 128/120.
Opened: 1973. **Pace of Play rating:** 4:30. **Green fee:** $43.
Credit cards: MC, V, AMEX. **Reduced fees:** Low season.
Caddies: No. **Golf carts:** $24 for 18 holes.
Discount golf packages: Yes. **Season:** April–Oct. **High:** June–Sept.
On-site lodging: Yes. **Rental clubs:** Yes.
Walking policy: Unrestricted walking. **Range:** No.
To obtain tee times: Call pro shop; out of season call Sawmill Creek
Resort at 1-800-SAWMILL.
Subscriber comments: Short and tight, usually windy . . . Plush, long,
challenging resort course, expensive . . . Tough in wind, good track . . .
Huge greens, can hit every one and still three-putt each . . . Lake Erie wind
adds to challenge, well manicured.

★★★★½ SHAKER RUN GOLF COURSE
PU—4361 Greentree Rd., Lebanon (513)727-0007.
18 miles north of Cincinnati. **Holes:** 18. **Par:** 72/72.
Yards: 6,965/5,075. **Course rating:** 75.4/68.8. **Slope:** 141/121.
Opened: 1979. **Pace of Play rating:** 4:30. **Green fee:** $49/58.
Credit cards: MC, V, AMEX. **Reduced fees:** Low season, Twilight,
Seniors, Juniors.
Caddies: No. **Golf carts:** Included in Green Fee.
Discount golf packages: No. **Season:** March–Dec. **High:** May–Oct.
On-site lodging: No. **Rental clubs:** Yes.
Walking policy: Walking at certain times. **Range:** Yes (grass).
To obtain tee times: Call pro shop seven days in advance.
Ranked 20th in Ohio by Golf Digest.
Subscriber comments: Excellent course, very tough especially finishing
hole on both nines, somewhat overpriced. Need length and accuracy . . .
My favorite course but a little pricey, enjoy everything but price . . . Great
layout and tight fairways, a real challenge . . . Tight, lightning fast greens, I
wish I could play it every day . . . You just won't believe this place. Glad it
went public . . . Often crowded . . . Scenic, bring camera . . . Good golfers
can bite off all they can chew . . . Excellent target golf course . . .
Expensive but best course in the area . . . Very demanding from the back
tees.

★½ SHAMROCK GOLF CLUB
PU—4436 Powell Rd., Powell (614)792-6630.
12 miles south of Columbus. **Holes:** 18. **Par:** 71/71.
Yards: 6,300/5,400. **Course rating:** 67.5/68.0. **Slope:** 115/110.
Opened: 1988. **Pace of Play rating:** 4:15. **Green fee:** $14/19.
Credit cards: MC, V, DISC. **Reduced fees:** Low season, Twilight,

Seniors, Juniors.
Caddies: No. **Golf carts:** $11 for 18 holes.
Discount golf packages: No. **Season:** Year-round. **High:** May-Oct.
On-site lodging: No. **Rental clubs:** Yes.
Walking policy: Walking at certain times. **Range:** Yes (grass).
To obtain tee times: Call seven days in advance.
Subscriber comments: Parallel fairways, no trees, wear a hard hat . . .
Warning: This is a hard hat area . . . Narrow, crowded course, fairways,
greens, very nice.

★★★½ SHARON WOODS GOLF COURSE
PU—11355 Swing Rd., Cincinnati (513)769-4325.
15 miles north of Cincinnati. **Holes:** 18. **Par:** 70/70.
Yards: 6,652/5,288. **Course rating:** 72.3/69.7. **Slope:** 127/114.
Opened: 1938. **Pace of Play rating:** 4:30. **Green fee:** $16/17.
Credit cards: None. **Reduced fees:** Seniors, Juniors.
Caddies: No. **Golf carts:** $11 for 18 holes.
Discount golf packages: No. **Season:** March-Dec. **High:** April-Sept.
On-site lodging: No. **Rental clubs:** Yes.
Walking policy: Unrestricted walking. **Range:** No.
To obtain tee times: Call pro shop five days in advance by telephone only
starting at 6 p.m. (i.e. call Monday for Saturday.)
Subscriber comments: Tight, tough long par 4s . . . Difficult to walk,
best of the country courses . . . Front nine is very long. Good test. Back is
shorter but tighter, lots of hills. Always crowded. Nice . . . Not a fair
course layout, tough and very difficult to walk . . . Tougher than it looks
from any tee . . . An old course recently reworked. A challenge . . . Tough
par 3s . . . Nice course other than slow rounds and hard greens . . . Old
style, natural terrain.

★★½ SHAWNEE HILLS GOLF COURSE
PU—18753 Egbert Rd., Bedford (216)232-7184.
10 miles southeast of Cleveland. **Holes:** 18. **Par:** 71/73.
Yards: 6,160/6,029. **Course rating:** 68.7/72.5. **Slope:** 112/116.
Opened: 1957. **Pace of Play rating:** 3:50. **Green fee:** $11/15.
Credit cards: MC, V. **Reduced fees:** Low season, Seniors, Juniors.
Caddies: No. **Golf carts:** $18 for 18 holes.
Discount golf packages: Yes. **Season:** March-Dec. **High:** May-Sept.
On-site lodging: No. **Rental clubs:** Yes.
Walking policy: Unrestricted walking. **Range:** Yes.
To obtain tee times: Call pro shop five days in advance.
Subscriber comments: Too crowded, easy and short . . . Beautiful, tree
filled 18-hole layout, only three sandtraps, greens excellent . . . New holes
add a good deal of challenge; leave the driver at home . . . Average person
can afford green fees, need to work on playing conditions.

★★ SHAWNEE LOOKOUT GOLF CLUB
PU—2030 Lawrencburg, North Bend (513)941-0120.
Call club for further information.
Subscriber comments: Very hilly, hard to walk . . . Cart a must, difficult
to walk. Does not get a crowd . . . Reasonable, excellent greens . . . Target
golf.

★★★ SHAWNEE STATE PARK GOLF COURSE
PU—P.O. Box 148, Friendship (614)858-6681.
Call club for further information.
Subscriber comments: Deserted during week, excellent golf layout . . .
State owned, good test of skill . . . Subtle doglegs invite "guts" shots . . .
Great for golf vacation.

★★★ SHELBY OAKS GOLF CLUB
SOUTH/WEST/NORTH
PU—9900 Sidney Freyburg Rd., Sidney (513)492-2883.
31 mile south of Lima. **Holes:** 27. **Par:** 72/72/72.

Yards: 6,651/6.650/6,561. **Course rating:** 71.2/60.9/70.5. **Slope:** 115/115/115.
Opened: 1964. **Pace of Play rating:** 4:30. **Green fee:** $ 15/17.
Credit cards: MC, V. **Reduced fees:** Twilight.
Caddies: No. **Golf carts:** $9 for 18 holes.
Discount golf packages: No. **Season:** March-Nov. **High:** May-Oct.
On-site lodging: No. **Rental clubs:** Yes.
Walking policy: Unrestricted walking. **Range:** Yes.
To obtain tee times: Call one week in advance.
Subscriber comments: A few hilly holes, lots of trees on old course . . .
Not too tough, not too easy, just right for average golfer . . . Tight from
blues . . . Well maintained.

★★½ SKYLAND GOLF CLUB
PU—2085 Center Rd., Hinckley (216)225-5698.
Call club for further information.
Subscriber comments: Small greens . . . Well maintained . . . Fairways
and greens well kept . . . Tough tight course, good view.

★★★ SKYLAND PINES GOLF CLUB
SP—3550 Columbus Rd. N.E., Canton (216)454-5131.
5 miles east of Canton. **Holes:** 18. **Par:** 72/72.
Yards: 6,467/5,279. **Course rating:** 69.6/69.6. **Slope:** 113/113.
Opened: N/A. **Pace of Play rating:** 4:15. **Green fee:** $14/20.
Credit cards: MC, V, DISC. **Reduced fees:** Low season.
Caddies: No. **Golf carts:** $9 for 18 holes.
Discount golf packages: No. **Season:** Feb.-Dec. **High:** April-Nov.
On-site lodging: No. **Rental clubs:** Yes.
Walking policy: Walking at certain times. **Range:** Yes (grass).
To obtain tee times: Call pro shop in advance.
Subscriber comments: Very good greens, hold water like a sponge . . .
Not a long course, but has lots of trees, greens real fast . . . Lightning
greens, short, good layout . . . Playable old course . . . The course is
somewhat long and fair condition. Pace of play was good four hours.

SLEEPY HOLLOW GOLF COURSE★
PU—6029 E. State Rte. 101, Clyde (419)547-0770.
50 miles east of Toledo. **Holes:** 18. **Par:** 71/72.
Yards: 6,371/5,204. **Course rating:** 69.3/68.4. **Slope:** 113/110.
Opened: 1961. **Pace of Play rating:** 4:15. **Green fee:** $13/15.
Credit cards: MC, V, DISC. **Reduced fees:** Weekdays, Low season,
Twilight, Seniors, Juniors.
Caddies: No. **Golf carts:** $18 for 18 holes.
Discount golf packages: No. **Season:** April-Nov. **High:** June-Aug.
On-site lodging: No. **Rental clubs:** Yes.
Walking policy: Unrestricted walking. **Range:** Yes (grass).
To obtain tee times: Call up to six days in advance.

★★★½ SLEEPY HOLLOW GOLF COURSE
PU—9445 Brecksville Rd., Brecksville (216)526-4285.
15 miles south of Cleveland. **Holes:** 18. **Par:** 71/73.
Yards: 6,630/5,715. **Course rating:** 71.9/73.5. **Slope:** 124/128.
Opened: . **Pace of Play rating:** 4:00. **Green fee:** $19.
Credit cards: MC, V. **Reduced fees:** Weekdays, Low season, Seniors,
Juniors.
Caddies: No. **Golf carts:** $10 for 18 holes.
Discount golf packages: No. **Season:** March-Dec. **High:** May-Sept.
On-site lodging: No. **Rental clubs:** Yes.
Walking policy: Unrestricted walking. **Range:** Yes.
To obtain tee times: Call pro shop at noon five days in advance.
Subscriber comments: Good condition, hit tee ball straight or you're dead
. . . Mature course, don't be above hole, top amateurs love it, lots of play
. . . Always in good shape, but must ride . . . Tight with difficult greens
. . . Fairways and greens can be excellent or poor depending on the amount

of play and weather . . . Lots of ravines and very difficult. Tricky greens
. . . Wow, incredible greens . . . Very crowded at peak times, public golf at
its best . . . Humbling. Very tough but incredibly awesome, excellent value
. . . Premier course, almost too popular.

SNOW HILL COUNTRY CLUB★
SP—11093 State Rte. 73, New Vienna (513)987-2922.
Call club for further information.
Subscriber comments: Not very challenging on the front nine. Good
greens . . . Looks easy, not much trouble.

★★½ ST. ALBANS GOLF CLUB
PU—3833 Northridge Rd. N.W., Alexandria (614)924-8885.
25 miles east of Columbus. **Holes:** 18. **Par:** 71/71.
Yards: 6,717/5,498. **Course rating:** 71.6/71.1. **Slope:** 112/112.
Opened: 1988. **Pace of Play rating:** 4:20. **Green fee:** $11/13.
Credit cards: None. **Reduced fees:** Low season, Seniors.
Caddies: No. **Golf carts:** $23 for 18 holes.
Discount golf packages: No. **Season:** March-Dec. **High:** May-Aug.
On-site lodging: No. **Rental clubs:** No.
Walking policy: Unrestricted walking. **Range:** No.
To obtain tee times: Call pro shop.
Subscriber comments: Wide open, wind makes it a good test of golf . . .
Family run, well maintained ego boost . . . Flat . . . Staff good, pace good,
plays short, well taken care of year- round . . . Decent daily fee course,
offers rolling terrain, very reasonable fee.

★★★½ SUGAR BUSH GOLF COURSE
PU—11186 N. St., State Rte. 88, Garrettsville (216)527-4202.
Call club for further information.
Subscriber comments: A real sleeper, long and tight . . . Quick greens
. . . Good layout, needs better maintenance . . . Tough course, busy but
accommodating . . . Front nine tougher than back . . . Premium on driving
. . . Shotmaker's course.

★½ SUGAR CREEK GOLF COURSE
SP—950 Elmore E. Rd., Elmore (419)862-2551.
20 miles south of Toledo. **Holes:** 18. **Par:** 71/71.
Yards: 6,331/5,092. **Course rating:** 66.5/64.4. **Slope:** 102/98.
Opened: 1963. **Pace of Play rating:** 4:00. **Green fee:** $12/14.
Credit cards: MC, V. **Reduced fees:** Weekdays, Low season, Twilight,
Seniors, Juniors.
Caddies: No. **Golf carts:** $18 for 18 holes.
Discount golf packages: Yes. **Season:** March-Dec. **High:** June-Sept.
On-site lodging: No. **Rental clubs:** Yes.
Walking policy: Walking at certain times. **Range:** Yes (grass).
To obtain tee times: Call anytime.
Subscriber comments: Short, good for beginner, good variety of holes.

★★½ SUGAR ISLE GOLF COUNTRY
PU—2469 Dayt-Lakeview Rd., New Carlisle (513)845-8699.
1 mile north of Dayton. **Holes:** 18. **Par:** 72/72.
Yards: 6,743/5,651. **Course rating:** 70.2/71.1. **Slope:** 107/110.
Opened: 1974. **Pace of Play rating:** 4:30. **Green fee:** $13/16.
Credit cards: MC, V. **Reduced fees:** Weekdays, Seniors.
Caddies: No. **Golf carts:** $10 for 18 holes.
Discount golf packages: No. **Season:** Year-round. **High:** June-Sept.
On-site lodging: No. **Rental clubs:** Yes.
Walking policy: Unrestricted walking. **Range:** Yes (grass).
To obtain tee times: Call one week from date wanted, unless group of 20
or more with deposit down.
Subscriber comments: Great fun, need better facilities, good golf . . .
Good variety of holes . . . Usually in good shape in summer . . . Two-
tiered greens.

★½ SUGARCREEK GOLF COURSE
PU—Winklepleck Rd., Sugarcreek (216)852-9989.
8 miles west of New Philadelphia. **Holes:** 18. **Par:** 72/72.
Yards: 6,200. **Course rating:** 67.4/64.6. **Slope:** 107/100.
Opened: 1929. **Pace of Play rating:** N/A. **Green fee:** N/A.
Credit cards: None. **Reduced fees:** Weekdays, Seniors, Juniors.
Caddies: No. **Golf carts:** $10 for 18 holes.
Discount golf packages: No. **Season:** Year-round. **High:** N/A.
On-site lodging: No. **Rental clubs:** Yes.
Walking policy: Unrestricted walking. **Range:** No.
To obtain tee times: Call pro shop.
Subscriber comments: Maintenance OK . . . Front nine, small greens;
back is wide open and tough . . . Scenic Amish country.

★★ SUNNYHILL GOLF CLUB
PU—3734 Sunnybrook Rd., Kent (216)673-1785.
5 miles east of Akron. **Holes:** 18. **Par:** 71/72.
Yards: 6,289/5,083. **Course rating:** 68.4/68.4. **Slope:** 110/107.
Opened: 1921. **Pace of Play rating:** 4:00. **Green fee:** $10/19.
Credit cards: MC, V, DISC. **Reduced fees:** Weekdays, Low season,
Seniors, Juniors.
Caddies: No. **Golf carts:** Included in Green Fee.
Discount golf packages: No. **Season:** March-Jan. **High:** May-Aug.
On-site lodging: No. **Rental clubs:** No.
Walking policy: Unrestricted walking. **Range:** Yes (grass).
To obtain tee times: Call ahead.
Also has 9-hole par-34 Middle Course.
Subscriber comments: A lot of blind shots and water . . . Wide open.

★★ SWEETBRIAR GOLF AND PRO SHOP
FIRST/SECOND/THIRD
PU—750 Jaycox Rd., Avon Lake (216)933-9001.
20 miles west of Cleveland. **Holes:** 27. **Par:** 72/72/70.
Yards: 6,491/6,292/6,075. **Course rating:** 68.7/67.5/66.3. **Slope:**
106/104/100.
Opened: 1966. **Pace of Play rating:** 4:15. **Green fee:** $14/17.
Credit cards: MC, V. **Reduced fees:** Low season, Twilight, Seniors,
Juniors.
Caddies: No. **Golf carts:** $17 for 18 holes.
Discount golf packages: No. **Season:** Year-round. **High:** May-Oct.
On-site lodging: No. **Rental clubs:** Yes.
Walking policy: Unrestricted walking. **Range:** Yes.
To obtain tee times: Call on Wednesday morning for upcoming
weekend. No tee times for weekdays.
Subscriber comments: Flat, no sand, much water . . . Easy course, nice
pro shop and range, a lot of play here . . . Keep play moving well for large
numbers . . . Accuracy important . . . Mature trees, good shape.

★★ SYCAMORE HILLS GOLF CLUB
SP—3728 W. Hayes Ave., Fremont (419)332-5716.
35 miles southeast of Toledo. **Holes:** 18. **Par:** 70/72.
Yards: 6,221/5,076. **Course rating:** 67.3/66.3. **Slope:** 110/107.
Opened: 1964. **Pace of Play rating:** 4:15. **Green fee:** $12/15.
Credit cards: MC, V. **Reduced fees:** Weekdays, Low season, Seniors,
Juniors.
Caddies: No. **Golf carts:** $17 for 18 holes.
Discount golf packages: No. **Season:** March-Dec. **High:** April-Sept.
On-site lodging: No. **Rental clubs:** Yes.
Walking policy: Unrestricted walking. **Range:** Yes (grass).
To obtain tee times: Call in advance for weekends and holidays.
Subscriber comments: Winds off the lake can make course play 10 strokes
harder . . . Excellent greens . . . Challenging, well kept . . . Good value.

★★½ TABLE ROCK GOLF CLUB

PU—3005 Wilson Rd., Centerburg (614)625-6859, (800)688-6859.
20 miles north of Columbus. **Holes:** 18. **Par:** 72/72.
Yards: 6,694/5,565. **Course rating:** 70.7/71.3. **Slope:** 113/N/A.
Opened: 1973. **Pace of Play rating:** 4:30. **Green fee:** $15/18.
Credit cards: All major. **Reduced fees:** Weekdays, Low season, Twilight, Seniors.
Caddies: No. **Golf carts:** $10 for 18 holes.
Discount golf packages: No. **Season:** Year-round. **High:** May-Sept.
On-site lodging: No. **Rental clubs:** Yes.
Walking policy: . **Range:** Yes (grass).
To obtain tee times: Call two weeks in advance.
Subscriber comments: Layout a little too flat but decent course with some length . . . Short but difficult, back nine has lots of trees . . . Good variety of holes, well kept . . . Front and back nines are like two separate courses; front is open; back is tight.

TAM O'SHANTER GOLF COURSE

PU—5055 Hills and Dales Rd. N.W., Canton (216)478-6501, (800)462-9964.
50 miles south of Cleveland.
Green fee: $22
Credit cards: MC, V. **Reduced fees:** Weekdays, Low season, Resort guests, Seniors, Juniors.
Caddies: No. **Golf carts:** $8 for 18 holes.
Discount golf packages: Yes. **Season:** March-Dec. **High:** April-Oct.
On-site lodging: No. **Rental clubs:** No.
Walking policy: Unrestricted walking. **Range:** Yes.
To obtain tee times: Call up to one year in advance with credit card to guarantee.

★★★½ DALES COURSE

Holes: 18. **Par:** 70/75.
Yards: 6,569/5,384. **Course rating:** 70.4/69.7. **Slope:** 110/109.
Opened: 1928. **Pace of Play rating:** 4:30.
Subscriber comments: Beautiful, rolling hills, consistent terrain . . . Pace of play maintained . . . A shot in the rough is truly a penalty . . . Nice layout, site of Ohio Open . . . Well-maintained good test, deceptively long, greens true but slow, nice pace of play . . . Old style course . . . Always in great condition, too busy.

★★★ HILLS COURSE

Holes: 18. **Par:** 70/75.
Yards: 6,385/5,076. **Course rating:** 69.1/67.4. **Slope:** 104/102.
Opened: 1928. **Pace of Play rating:** 4:30.
Subscriber comments: Lot of shotmaking . . . Fair layout for any golfer . . . Hilly but walkable . . . Best from tips . . . Good pace and excellent condition.

TAMARAC GOLF CLUB★

PU—500 Stevick Rd., Lima (419)331-2951.
Holes: 18. **Par:** 72/72.
Yards: 6,109/5,029. **Course rating:** 69.8/67.9. **Slope:** N/A.
Opened: 1950. **Pace of Play rating:** 4:00. **Green fee:** $12/15.
Credit cards: MC, V. **Reduced fees:** Twilight, Seniors.
Caddies: No. **Golf carts:** $15 for 18 holes..
Discount golf packages: Yes. **Season:** March-Dec. **High:** April-Sept.
On-site lodging: No. **Rental clubs:** Yes.
Walking policy: Unrestricted walking. **Range:** Yes (grass).
To obtain tee times: Call anytime.
Also has 9-hole par-3 course.

★★ TAMER WIN GOLF AND COUNTRY CLUB

PU—2940 Niles Cortland Rd. N.E., Cortland (216)637-2881.
20 miles north of Youngstown. **Holes:** 18. **Par:** 71/74.
Yards: 6,275/5,623. **Course rating:** 68.8/68.8. **Slope:** 112/112.

Opened: 1961. **Pace of Play rating:** 4:00. **Green fee:** $15/17.
Credit cards: MC, V. **Reduced fees:** Low season, Seniors, Juniors.
Caddies: No. **Golf carts:** $8 for 18 holes.
Discount golf packages: No. **Season:** April-Nov. **High:** May-Sept.
On-site lodging: No. **Rental clubs:** No.
Walking policy: Unrestricted walking. **Range:** No.
To obtain tee times: Call for weekends and holidays.
Subscriber comments: Short front, long back, wooded . . . Back nine too narrow but fun . . . Good condition.

★½ TANGLEWOOD GOLF CLUB
PU—1086 Cheshire Rd., Delaware (614)548-6715.
Call club for further information.
Subscriber comments: No rough . . . A great course for walking, kept in remarkably good condition . . . Flat and open but fun.

★★½ TANNENHAUF GOLF CLUB
PU—11411 McCallum Ave., Alliance (216)823-4402, (800)533-5140.
10 miles east of Canton. **Holes:** 18. **Par:** 72/72.
Yards: 6,666/5,455. **Course rating:** 72.0/70.8. **Slope:** 111/109.
Opened: 1959. **Pace of Play rating:** 4:00. **Green fee:** $18/19.
Credit cards: MC, V. **Reduced fees:** Weekdays, Low season, Seniors, Juniors.
Caddies: No. **Golf carts:** $17 for 18 holes.
Discount golf packages: Yes. **Season:** April-Oct. **High:** June-Aug.
On-site lodging: No. **Rental clubs:** Yes.
Walking policy: Unrestricted walking. **Range:** Yes (grass).
To obtain tee times: Call pro shop.
Subscriber comments: Good course from the blues; tight, small greens . . . Open course with deep narrow greens . . . Kept in nice shape, greens tricky . . . Well maintained since water installed . . . Long and challenging.

THE GOLF CENTER AT KINGS ISLAND
R—6042 Fairway Dr., Mason (513)398-7700.
25 miles north of Cincinnati. **Green fee:** $30/48.
Credit cards: All major. **Reduced fees:** Weekdays, Low season, Twilight.
Caddies: No. **Golf carts:** $12 for 18 holes.
Discount golf packages: No. **Season:** March-Dec. **High:** May-Sept.
On-site lodging: No. **Rental clubs:** Yes.
Walking policy: Walking at certain times. **Range:** Yes (grass).
To obtain tee times: Call up to seven days in advance.
Formerly known as The Jack Nicklaus Sports Center.
★★★½ THE GRIZZLY COURSE
Holes: 18. **Par:** 71/72.
Yards: 6,731/5,256. **Course rating:** 72.6/68.5. **Slope:** 131/115.
Opened: 1971. **Pace of Play rating:** 4:30.
Subscriber comments: Great course, good shape . . . Well maintained, tough greens . . . Nice course, expensive for our area but probably worth it . . . Excellent driving range . . . Hard to get tee times . . . Like a garden. Has everything . . . Well cared for, fairways are extra soft.
★★½ THE BRUIN COURSE
Holes: 18. **Par:** 61.
Yards: 3,428/3,428. **Course rating:** N/A. **Slope:** N/A.
Subscriber comments: A shorter course kept in excellent condition but pricey . . . Little long for beginning players. Greens were in excellent shape.

THE GOLF CLUB AT YANKEE TRACE*
PU—10000 Yankee Rd., Centerville (513)438-4653.
15 miles north of Dayton. **Holes:** 18. **Par:** 72/72.
Yards: 7,139/5,204. **Course rating:** 75.5/70.5. **Slope:** 140/124.
Opened: 1995. **Pace of Play rating:** 4:00. **Green fee:** $33/44.
Credit cards: MC, V, DISC. **Reduced fees:** Twilight, Seniors, Juniors.
Caddies: No. **Golf carts:** $11 for 18 holes.

Discount golf packages: Yes. **Season:** Year-round. **High:** March-Oct.
On-site lodging: No. **Rental clubs:** Yes.
Walking policy: Unrestricted walking. **Range:** Yes (grass).
To obtain tee times: Call seven days in advance.

★★★★ THE VINEYARD GOLF COURSE
PU—600 Nordyke Rd., Cincinnati (513)474-3007.
Holes: 18. **Par:** 71/71.
Yards: 6,789/4,747. **Course rating:** 73.0/65.7. **Slope:** 129/113.
Opened: 1987. **Pace of Play rating:** 4:20. **Green fee:** $ 22.
Credit cards: None. **Reduced fees:** Seniors, Juniors.
Caddies: No. **Golf carts:** $10 for 18 holes.
Discount golf packages: Yes. **Season:** March-Nov. **High:** May-Sept.
On-site lodging: No. **Rental clubs:** Yes.
Walking policy: Unrestricted walking. **Range:** No.
To obtain tee times: Call five days in advance of play at 6 p.m.
Subscriber comments: Course short but tight, very well kept. Interesting tiered greens, good putting a necessity to score well . . . Fast play, great pro and staff, if this were a private club I'd sell the wife and farm to be a member . . . Plays long, well kept, trees and lakes . . . Very professionally run public course, tough course . . . Short but well manicured . . . New bent grass fairways for '95 . . . Outstanding staff, good conditions and pace of play . . . Proper club selection a must . . . Treat us like country club members . . . Back nine has more character, staff is excellent.

THE WOODS GOLF CLUB★
PU—12083 U.S. 127 S., Van Wert (419)238-0441.
40 miles east of Ft. Wayne. **Holes:** 18. **Par:** 72/72.
Yards: 6,775/5,025. **Course rating:** 70.4/70.4. **Slope:** 118/116.
Opened: 1962. **Pace of Play rating:** 4:30. **Green fee:** $12/13.
Credit cards: MC, V. **Reduced fees:** No.
Caddies: No. **Golf carts:** $9 for 18 holes.
Discount golf packages: No. **Season:** March-Dec. **High:** May-Sept.
On-site lodging: No. **Rental clubs:** Yes.
Walking policy: Unrestricted walking. **Range:** Yes (grass).
To obtain tee times: Call starting the Monday prior to upcoming weekend.

★½ THORN APPLE COUNTRY CLUB
SP—1051 Alton Darby Creek Rd., Columbus-Galloway (614)878-7703.
Holes: 18. **Par:** 72/74.
Yards: 7,037/5,901. **Course rating:** 72.6/71.7. **Slope:** 116/115.
Opened: 1966. **Pace of Play rating:** 4:30. **Green fee:** $15/16.
Credit cards: MC, V. **Reduced fees:** Twilight.
Caddies: No. **Golf carts:** $18 for 18 holes.
Discount golf packages: No. **Season:** Year-round. **High:** April-Oct.
On-site lodging: No. **Rental clubs:** Yes.
Walking policy: Unrestricted walking. **Range:** No.
To obtain tee times: Call one week in advance for weekends and holidays.
Subscriber comments: Challenging course showing considerable wear from lots of play and not enough grooming . . . Long and windy . . . Looks short, plays long.

★★½ THUNDER HILL GOLF CLUB
PU—7050 Griswold Rd., South Madison (216)298-3474.
35 miles east of Cleveland. **Holes:** 18. **Par:** 72/72.
Yards: 7,223/5,524. **Course rating:** 78.0/N/A. **Slope:** 151/127.
Opened: 1976. **Pace of Play rating:** 4:30-5:00. **Green fee:** $25/30.
Credit cards: MC, V. **Reduced fees:** Low season, Seniors, Juniors.
Caddies: No. **Golf carts:** Included in Green Fee.
Discount golf packages: Yes **Season:** April-Dec. **High:** May-Sept.
On-site lodging: No. **Rental clubs:** No.
Walking policy: Mandatory cart. **Range:** No.
To obtain tee times: Call anytime.

Subscriber comments: Water, water, everywhere. Only a few holes don't have water, must be very accurate . . . Woody, narrow . . . Long and straight . . . Bring lots of balls . . . Built from old fish hatchery, 90 lakes within the course, challenging but fun . . . Humbling experience off longer tees . . . Extra long, must be in fairway . . . Excellent chipping and putting skills needed . . . A bear but fun.

THUNDERBIRD HILLS GOLF CLUB
PU—1316 Mudbrook Rd., Huron (419)433-4552.
40 miles west of Cleveland. **Green fee:** $18.
Credit cards: MC, V, DISC. **Reduced fees:** Weekdays, Low season, Seniors.
Caddies: No. **Golf carts:** $18 for 18 holes.
Discount golf packages: No. **Season:** Year-round. **High:** April-Nov.
On-site lodging: No. **Rental clubs:** Yes.
Walking policy: Unrestricted walking. **Range:** No.
To obtain tee times: Call pro shop.
★★★ **NORTH COURSE**
Holes: 18. **Par:** 72/74.
Yards: 6,464/5,993. **Course rating:** 70.3/74.0. **Slope:** 109/121.
Opened: 1960. **Pace of Play rating:** 4:00.
Subscriber comments: Well maintained year-round . . . Excellent conditions, run by people who appreciate the golfer . . . Rolling hills, challenging small greens . . . No bunkers . . . Gets better each year; great pro shop, well run.
SOUTH COURSE★
Holes: 18. **Par:** 72/72.
Yards: 6,587/5,385. **Course rating:** N/A. **Slope:** N/A.
Opened: 1995. **Pace of Play rating:** 4:30. **Green fee:** $ 20.
Golf carts: $20 for 18 holes.
Walking policy: Walking at certain times.

★★½ **TURKEYFOOT LAKE GOLF LINKS**
FIRST/SECOND/THIRD
PU—294 W. Turkeyfoot Lake Rd., Akron (216)644-5971.
Holes: 27. **Par:** 36/35/35.
Yards: 6,168/5,122/5,452. **Course rating:** 70.0/65.0/66.8. **Slope:** 116.
Opened: 1925. **Pace of Play rating:** 4:00. **Green fee:** $15/20.
Credit cards: None. **Reduced fees:** Weekdays, Low season, Seniors, Juniors.
Caddies: No. **Golf carts:** $20 for 18 holes.
Discount golf packages: No. **Season:** Year-round. **High:** May-Sept.
On-site lodging: No. **Rental clubs:** No.
Walking policy: Unrestricted walking. **Range:** No.
To obtain tee times: Call for weekend tee times.
Subscriber comments: Great condition, variety of holes, polite staff . . . Short, great greens and drainage . . . Third nine very short, first and second nines good test from blues . . . Best conditioned and maintained in area, lots of play, open most of year . . . Good pace of play.

★★★ **TURNBERRY GOLF COURSE**
PU—1145 Clubhouse Rd., Pickerington (614)645-2582.
12 miles east of Columbus. **Holes:** 18. **Par:** 72/73.
Yards: 6,636/5,440. **Course rating:** 71.1/68.8. **Slope:** 114/110.
Opened: 1991. **Pace of Play rating:** 4:00. **Green fee:** $16/22.
Credit cards: MC, V. **Reduced fees:** Weekdays, Low season, Twilight, Seniors, Juniors.
Caddies: No. **Golf carts:** $9 for 18 holes.
Discount golf packages: Yes. **Season:** Year-round. **High:** April-Oct.
On-site lodging: No. **Rental clubs:** Yes.
Walking policy: Walking at certain times. **Range:** Yes (grass).
To obtain tee times: Call seven days in advance.
Subscriber comments: Excellent links course, requires all 14 clubs in bag

. . . Green fees well worth the price, course much improved . . . Get tee times . . . Very tough in windy conditions . . . You can get on with almost no notice . . . Elevated greens, open and rough . . . Not very difficult, but still challenging, a nice change of pace.

★½ TWIN LAKES GOLF COURSE
PU—2220 Marion Ave. Rd., Mansfield (419)529-3777.
Call club for further information.
Subscriber comments: Fun to play . . . Wood and wedge . . . Short, older course.

★½ TWIN RUN GOLF COURSE
PU—2505 Eaton Rd., Hamilton (513)868-5833.
15 miles northwest of Cincinnati. **Holes:** 18. **Par:** 72/74.
Yards: 6,551/5,391. **Course rating:** 70.8/69.9. **Slope:** 123/112.
Opened: 1963. **Pace of Play rating:** 4:15. **Green fee:** $ 9/14.
Credit cards: None. **Reduced fees:** Low season, Seniors, Juniors.
Caddies: No. **Golf carts:** $18 for 18 holes.
Discount golf packages: No. **Season:** March-Nov. **High:** May-Sept.
On-site lodging: No. **Rental clubs:** Yes.
Walking policy: Unrestricted walking. **Range:** Yes (grass).
To obtain tee times: E
Call seven days in advance.
Subscriber comments: Older course. Very hilly . . . Well-kept. Gets lots of play, short course . . . Looking better all the time.

★★ VALLEY VIEW GOLF CLUB
VALLEY/RIVER/LAKES
PU—1212 Cuyahoga St., Akron (216)928-9034.
Holes: 27. **Par:** 72/72/72.
Yards: 6,293/6,183/6,168. **Course rating:** 68.7/68.2/68.2. **Slope:** 111/111/109.
Opened: 1956. **Pace of Play rating:** 4:45. **Green fee:** $14/16.
Credit cards: None. **Reduced fees:** Weekdays, Seniors.
Caddies: No. **Golf carts:** $9 for 18 holes.
Discount golf packages: No. **Season:** March-Nov. **High:** May-Sept.
On-site lodging: No. **Rental clubs:** No.
Walking policy: Unrestricted walking. **Range:** No.
To obtain tee times: Call seven days in advance.
Subscriber comments: Challenging course over steep hills . . . Has lot of play . . . Has some great holes if you like risky tee shots . . . Good use of water on second and third nines. Decent year-round condition . . . Not too easy, not too hard, asks for a variety of shots.

★★★½ VALLEYWOOD GOLF CLUB
SP—13502 Airport Hwy., Swanton (419)826-3991.
15 miles west of Toledo. **Holes:** 18. **Par:** 71/73.
Yards: 6,364/5,588. **Course rating:** 68.4/71.6. **Slope:** 115/121.
Opened: 1929. **Pace of Play rating:** 4:00. **Green fee:** $19/22.
Credit cards: None. **Reduced fees:** Seniors.
Caddies: No. **Golf carts:** $10 for 18 holes.
Discount golf packages: No. **Season:** Feb-Dec. **High:** .
On-site lodging: No. **Rental clubs:** Yes.
Walking policy: Unrestricted walking. **Range:** No.
To obtain tee times: Call seven days in advance.
Subscriber comments: Enjoyable course, but plays slow. Need to be good with short irons to score well . . . Lush fairways . . . Short and premium on accuracy . . . Old style course with elevated greens, great conditions all times of year . . . Well maintained . . . Excellent greens.

WEATHERWAX GOLF COURSE
PU—5401 Mosiman Rd., Middletown (513)425-7886.
35 miles north of Cincinnati. **Green fee:** $14/16.
Credit cards: None. **Reduced fees:** Seniors, Juniors.

Caddies: No. **Golf carts:** $10 for 18 holes.
Discount golf packages: No. **Season:** Year-round. **High:** April-Nov.
On-site lodging: No. **Rental clubs:** Yes.
Walking policy: Unrestricted walking. **Range:** Yes (grass).
To obtain tee times: Call or come in one week in advance for weekends and holidays.

★★★ VALLEYVIEW/HIGHLANDS
Holes: 18. **Par:** 72/72.
Yards: 6,756/5,253. **Course rating:** 72.0/69.8. **Slope:** 120/114.
Opened: 1972. **Pace of Play rating:** 4:30.
Subscriber comments: Tight, hilly, tough, easy to get on . . . Prices under most area courses . . . Good city course, hard to get on . . . Best 36 holes for the money . . . Must hit good long irons, slick greens . . . Long off tee. Use every club in bag . . . Always in good shape . . . Weatherwax provides the best bargain in southwestern Ohio.

★★★ WOODSIDE/MEADOWS
Holes: 18. **Par:** 72/72.
Yards: 7,174/5,669. **Course rating:** 73.4/71.5. **Slope:** 116/112.
Opened: 1972. **Pace of Play rating:** 4:30.
Subscriber comments: Long course, straight drives needed, birdie holes scarce, play all year . . . Long and tight at times, always in good shape . . . Long from the tips . . . Great value . . . Hard to get tee times . . . Good test for long hitters . . . Always in good shape, fairly open course.

★½ WESTERN RESERVE GOLF AND COUNTRY CLUB
SP—1543 Fixler Rd., Sharon Center (216)239-2839.
Call club for further information.
Subscriber comments: Very fast greens . . . Narrow, 3-wood important.

★ WESTERN ROW GOLF COURSE
PU—7392 Mason-Montgomery Rd., Mason (513)398-8886.
10 miles north of Cincinnati. **Holes:** 18. **Par:** 72/72.
Yards: 6,746/5,701. **Course rating:** 71.4/71.2. **Slope:** 121/120.
Opened: 1963. **Pace of Play rating:** 4:30. **Green fee:** $13/16.
Credit cards: MC, V, DISC.&RReduced fees: Weekdays, Low season, Twilight, Seniors, Juniors.
Caddies: No. **Golf carts:** $18 or 18 holes.
Discount golf packages: No. **Season:** Year-round. **High:** April-Oct.
On-site lodging: No. **Rental clubs:** Yes.
Walking policy: Unrestricted walking. **Range:** No.
To obtain tee times: First come, first served.
Subscriber comments: Course is wide open. Need to improve fairways . . . A flat, open course with little trouble, good for those learning the game, longer than many, priced reasonably . . . Flat, few trees, greens very undulated.

★★½ WHETSTONE GOLF AND SWIM CLUB
PU—5211 Marion Mt. Gilead Rd., Caledonia (614)383-4343, (800)272-3215.
6 miles northeast of Marion. **Holes:** 18. **Par:** 72/72.
Yards: 6,674/5,023. **Course rating:** 71.7/73.6. **Slope:** 120/111.
Opened: 1971. **Pace of Play rating:** 4:10. **Green fee:** $12/15.
Credit cards: MC, V, AMEX. **Reduced fees:** Weekdays, Seniors.
Caddies: No. **Golf carts:** $21 for 18 holes.
Discount golf packages: No. **Season:** April-Oct. **High:** April-Oct.
On-site lodging: No. **Rental clubs:** No.
Walking policy: Unrestricted walking. **Range:** Yes (grass).
To obtain tee times: Call seven days in advance.
Subscriber comments: Nice, some tight holes, some wide, no sand, well kept . . . Good value, nice greens. Mostly open.

★½ WILLOW CREEK GOLF CLUB
PU—15905 Darrow Rd., Vermilion (216)967-4101.
40 miles west of Cleveland. **Holes:** 18. **Par:** 72/76.
Yards: 6,356/5,419. **Course rating:** 68.0/68.0. **Slope:** 108/111.
Opened: 1948. **Pace of Play rating:** 4:30. **Green fee:** $13/15.
Credit cards: MC, V. **Reduced fees:** Weekdays, Low season, Seniors.
Caddies: No. **Golf carts:** $8 for 18 holes.
Discount golf packages: Yes. **Season:** March-Dec. **High:** April-Sept.
On-site lodging: No. **Rental clubs:** Yes.
Walking policy: Unrestricted walking. **Range:** Yes (grass).
To obtain tee times: Call one week in advance for upcoming weekend.
Subscriber comments: Made many improvements . . . Narrow fairways,
lots of trees.

★★ WILLOW RUN GOLF COURSE
PU—State Rtes. 310 and 161, Pataskala (614)927-1932.
Call club for further information.
Subscriber comments: Course in very good condition . . . Must be
managed well to score . . . Short course, creek meanders throughout . . .
Fairly easy, good condition, sometimes play is slow.

★★★★ WINDMILL LAKES GOLF CLUB
PU—6544 State Rte. 14, Ravenna (216)297-0440.
30 miles southeast of Cleveland. **Holes:** 18. **Par:** 70/70.
Yards: 6,936/5,368. **Course rating:** 73.8/70.4. **Slope:** 128/115.
Opened: 1971. **Pace of Play rating:** 4:15. **Green fee:** $16/28.
Credit cards: MC, V. **Reduced fees:** Low season, Twilight, Seniors,
Juniors.
Caddies: No. **Golf carts:** $9 for 18 holes.
Discount golf packages: No. **Season:** March-Nov. **High:** May-Sept.
On-site lodging: No. **Rental clubs:** Yes.
Walking policy: Unrestricted walking. **Range:** Yes (grass).
To obtain tee times: Call 48 hours in advance. If requesting tee times
longer than 48 hours in advance, a credit card is needed.
Subscriber comments: Undulating, quick greens; well-stocked pro shop
. . . Good layout, good condition year-round, expensive rates . . . Great
pro shop, great staff, No.1 reason why Kent State is becoming a golf power
. . . Relatively flat . . . Plays long, must carry shots to green . . . Long
course from back tees, difficult par 3s. Good challenge . . . L-o-n-g . . .
Tough test but fair . . . Fun course, crosses river on several holes . . .
Rangers keep things moving . . . Outstanding layout, well maintained and
fun. Great clubhouse . . . Higher priced but condition was excellent . . .
Very nice course, makes you want to come back . . . Excellent course with
a great pro shop . . . Not an easy hole to be found. Best staff ever seen.

★★½ WINTON WOODS GOLF CLUB
THE MILL COURSE
PU—1515 W. Sharon Rd., Cincinnati (513)825-3770.
Holes: 18. **Par:** 72/72.
Yards: 6,376/4,554. **Course rating:** 70.0/66.6. **Slope:** 120/108.
Opened: 1941. **Pace of Play rating:** 4:14. **Green fee:** $16.
Credit cards: None. **Reduced fees:** Seniors, Juniors.
Caddies: No. **Golf carts:** $10 for 18 holes.
Discount golf packages: Yes. **Season:** March-Dec. **High:** May-Sept.
On-site lodging: No. **Rental clubs:** Yes.
Walking policy: Unrestricted walking. **Range:** Yes (grass).
To obtain tee times: Tee times taken only by phone five days in advance.
Subscriber comments: Redone in 1993, much improved . . . New course
design has improved course . . . Excellent large greens . . . Large complete
new complex but needs to age . . . Remodeled course that needs more time
to heal . . . Tough layout through trees . . . Course renovation has paid off
. . . Excellent practice facility . . . Great value. Reacaently rebuilt. Will get
better.

★★★ WOODLAND GOLF CLUB

PU—4900 Swisher Rd., Cable (513)653-8875.
36 miles southeast of Columbus. **Holes:** 18. **Par:** 71/71.
Yards: 6,407/4,965. **Course rating:** 70.1/67.7. **Slope:** 116/110.
Opened: 1972. **Pace of Play rating:** 4:30. **Green fee:** $17/20.
Credit cards: MC, V, DISC. **Reduced fees:** Weekdays, Low season,
Twilight, Seniors, Juniors.
Caddies: No. **Golf carts:** $10 for 18 holes.
Discount golf packages: No. **Season:** Year-round. **High:** March-Sept.
On-site lodging: No. **Rental clubs:** Yes.
Walking policy: Unrestricted walking. **Range:** Yes (grass).
To obtain tee times: Call anytime ahead.
Subscriber comments: Blind shots all day long . . . Lots of trouble if you
don't find the fairways . . . Strategy, not power course . . . Used every club
in bag.

★½ WYANDOT GOLF COURSE

SP—3032 Columbus Rd., Centerburg (614)625-5370, (800)986-4653.
20 miles north of Columbus. **Holes:** 18. **Par:** 72/72.
Yards: 6,422/5,486. **Course rating:** 68.4/70.3. **Slope:** 113/115.
Opened: 1978. **Pace of Play rating:** 4:00. **Green fee:** $11/14.
Credit cards: MC, V. **Reduced fees:** Weekdays, Low season, Seniors.
Caddies: No. **Golf carts:** $9 for 18 holes.
Discount golf packages: No. **Season:** Year-round. **High:** April-Oct.
On-site lodging: No. **Rental clubs:** Yes.
Walking policy: Unrestricted walking. **Range:** No.
To obtain tee times: Call pro shop.
Subscriber comments: Tee times always available; great course for
practice . . . Short . . . Inexpensive; pace relatively good.

★★★★ YANKEE RUN GOLF COURSE

PU—7610 Warren Sharon Rd., Brookfield (216)448-8096, (800)446-5346.
60 miles northwest of Pittsburgh, PA. **Holes:** 18. **Par:** 70/73.
Yards: 6,501/5,140. **Course rating:** 70.7/69.0. **Slope:** 119/109.
Opened: 1931. **Pace of Play rating:** 4:30 **Green fee:** $20/23.
Credit cards: MC, V. **Reduced fees:** Weekdays, Low season, Seniors,
Juniors.
Caddies: No. **Golf carts:** Included in Green Fee.
Discount golf packages: Yes. **Season:** March-Nov. **High:** May-Sept.
On-site lodging: No. **Rental clubs:** Yes.
Walking policy: Unrestricted walking. **Range:** No.
To obtain tee times: Tee times taken Oct. 1st for next season.
Subscriber comments: Courteous staff, acceptable pace . . . Big, fast
greens, worth price . . . Medium length . . . Rolling terrain . . . Beautiful
scenery. Elevated greens and some hidden holes . . . Family run course,
excellent shape, good pace of play on weekends, nice atmosphere.

★★★ ZOAR VILLAGE GOLF CLUB

PU—P.O. Box 647, Zoar (216)874-4653.
6 miles south of Dover. **Holes:** 18. **Par:** 72/72.
Yards: 6,535/5,235. **Course rating:** 70.7/69.7. **Slope:** 117/115.
Opened: 1975. **Pace of Play rating:** 4:15. **Green fee:** $18.
Credit cards: None. **Reduced fees:** Weekdays, Seniors.
Caddies: No. **Golf carts:** $18 for 18 holes.
Discount golf packages: Yes. **Season:** March-Dec. **High:** July-Aug.
On-site lodging: No. **Rental clubs:** Yes.
Walking policy: Walking at certain times. **Range:** Yes (grass).
To obtain tee times: Call up to 10 months in advance.
Subscriber comments: Not real tight but has large greens with plenty of
humps in them, must hit short irons accurately to get close to the pin . . .
Flat course but good conditions . . . Everyone loves to play this course,
must stay out of bunkers . . . Secluded, very well kept . . . Plays longer
than it is.

PENNSYLVANIA

★★ ALLENTOWN MUNICIPAL GOLF COURSE
PU—3400 Tilghman St., Allentown (610)395-9926.
65 miles south of Philadelphia. **Holes:** 18. **Par:** 73/73.
Yards: 7,085/5,635. **Course rating:** 72.0/71.3. **Slope:** 127/123.
Opened: 1955. **Pace of Play rating:** 4:30. **Green fee:** $12/16.
Credit cards: None. **Reduced fees:** Low season, Twilight, Seniors,
Juniors.
Caddies: No. **Golf carts:** $20 for 18 holes.
Discount golf packages: No. **Season:** Year-round. **High:** May–Sept.
On-site lodging: No. **Rental clubs:** Yes.
Walking policy: Unrestricted walking. **Range:** Yes.
To obtain tee times: In person 7 days in advance.
Subscriber comments: Good condition for municipal . . . Services
adequate . . . Interesting layout . . . Winding creek makes driving tough for
average hitters . . . Decent municipal course . . . Heavy play . . . Need to
hit the ball long to truly enjoy . . . Long and open . . . Dry in summer . . .
Easy to walk . . . Need more par 3s . . . Big hitter kind of course . . . Old
parkland course with good 4s . . . Your typical muny . . . Well groomed
but predictable . . . Super value . . . some very tough holes . . . Great walk
or drive . . . Need watering system, otherwise nice course . . . a mature
course . . . Long . . . Mostly tree trouble . . . Fun and very economical.

★ ARNOLD'S GOLF CLUB
PU—RD No.2, Nescopeck (717)752-7022.
Call club for further information.
Subscriber comments: Excellent layout for beginners . . . Very easy
course with no traps and very short par 4s . . . Short, open . . . A
confidence builder . . . Very tight in some places.

ARROWHEAD GOLF COURSE
★★½ RED/WHITE
PU—1539 Weavertown Rd., Douglassville (610)582-4258.
9 miles east of Reading. **Holes:** 18. **Par:** 71/71.
Yards: 6,002/6,002. **Course rating:** 68.9/73.4. **Slope:** 116/124.
Opened: 1954. **Pace of Play rating:** 4:30–5:00. **Green fee:** $14/17.
Credit cards: None. **Reduced fees:** Weekdays, Low season, Twilight.
Caddies: No. **Golf carts:** $17 for 18 holes.
Discount golf packages: Yes. **Season:** Year-round.
On-site lodging: No. **Rental clubs:** Yes.
Walking policy: Unrestricted walking. **Range:** Yes (grass).
To obtain tee times: Call pro shop or come in.
Also has nine-hole, par-35 Blue course.
Subscriber comments: Great greens . . . Tough finishing four . . . Used
to be great course until added golf cart alarm when you leave cart path . . .
Easy walk . . . Very reasonable . . . nice rural layout . . . 254-yard par 3,
longest I've ever seen . . . In middle of nowhere . . . Plain Jane, but nice
. . . Close to private club conditions . . . Some unique holes . . . Large
greens . . . No rough . . . Walking permitted . . . Good mix of open and
tight holes . . . Course in good condition . . . Hills and trees . . . Suited for
average to good player . . . Easy walking . . . Tree-lined with water.

★½ AUBREYS GOLF CLUB
PU—Mercer Rd., Butler (412)287-4832.
Call club for further information.
Subscriber comments: Back nine a real test of golf . . . Tough course but
nice . . . Back nine is very hard and hilly . . . Front nine very open, almost
mundane . . . Back nine very tight . . . Almost unfair.

★★★½ BAVARIAN HILLS GOLF COURSE
PU—Mulligan Rd., St. Mary's (814)834-3602.
135 miles north of Pittsburgh. **Holes:** 18. **Par:** 71/73.
Yards: 6,290/4,845. **Course rating:** N/A. **Slope:** N/A.
Opened: 1990. **Pace of Play rating:** 4:30. **Green fee:** $17.
Credit cards: None. **Reduced fees:** Twilight, Juniors.

Caddies: No. **Golf carts:** $17 for 18 holes.
Discount golf packages: No. **Season:** April–Nov. **High:** June–Aug.
On-site lodging: No. **Rental clubs:** Yes.
Walking policy: Unrestricted walking. **Range:** Yes.
To obtain tee times: Call Monday for upcoming weekend.
Subscriber comments: Great new course . . . Variety of lies . . .
Awesome scenery . . . Exceptional design . . . Good variety of holes . . .
Very hilly . . . Course still developing . . . Two to three years from being
very good.

★★½ BEDFORD SPRINGS GOLF COURSE

PU—Rd. No.6, Bedford (814)623-8999.
Call club for further information.
Subscriber comments: Donald Ross . . . You can still tell what it must
have been like . . . Excellent course and hilly . . . Makes you think . . .
You'll hit almost every club in the bag . . . Good design for the most part
. . . Old favorite . . . Good Donald Ross layout . . . Course needs work
. . . Great layout . . . Great potential . . . Stay out of the rough . . . Still a
fine course . . . Improving historical old layout.

★★½ BETHLEHEM MUNICIPAL GOLF CLUB

PU—400 Illicks Mills Rd., Bethlehem (610)691-9393.
Holes: 18. **Par:** 71/71.
Yards: 6,830/5,119. **Course rating:** 70.6/ 69.1. **Slope:** 112/N.A.
Opened: 1956. **Pace of Play rating:** 4:30. **Green fee:** $10/20.
Credit cards: None. **Reduced fees:** Weekdays, Twilight, Seniors, Juniors.
Caddies: No. **Golf carts:** $10 for 18 holes.
Discount golf packages: No. **Season:** Year-round. **High:** March–Oct.
On-site lodging: No. **Rental clubs:** Yes.
Walking policy: Unrestricted walking. **Range:** Yes (grass).
To obtain tee times: Residents sign up Thursday, others sign up Friday
for $1.00 fee.
Also has a nine-hole executive course.
Subscriber comments: Fine municipal course . . . Greens hard . . .
Fairways hard all year . . . Good layout . . . Good finishing hole . . . Long-
ball hitter's course . . . No water hazards . . . Fairly straight . . . Easy walk
. . . Long, wide open . . . Fairly open . . . Limited trouble . . . No water
. . . Staff accommodating.

BLACK HAWK GOLF COURSE

PU—644 Blackhawk Rd., Beaver Falls (412)843-2542.
Call club for further information.
★★ FIRST COURSE
Subscriber comments: Course in decent shape . . . Too many short par 4s
. . . Gets a lot play during season . . . Unremarkable holes . . . Originally
18 holes, now 36 holes . . . Quality lost out . . . One of the few flat courses
in Pennsylvania.
★★ SECOND COURSE
Subscriber comments: Nice shape . . . Kind of plain . . . Nothing
outstanding . . . Small greens . . . Fun to play . . . Busy place . . . Need to
be half mountain goat . . . Excellent bar . . . Better layout of the two at
Black Hawk.

★★½ BLACKWOOD GOLF COURSE

PU—410 Red Corner Rd., Douglassville (610)385-6922.
12 miles east of Reading. **Holes:** 18. **Par:** 70/70.
Yards: 6,403/4,826. **Course rating:** 68.6/62.0. **Slope:** 115/ 95.
Opened: 1970. **Pace of Play rating:** 4:00-4:30. **Green fee:** $10/17.
Credit cards: None. **Reduced fees:** Weekdays, Low season, Twilight,
Seniors.
Caddies: No. **Golf carts:** N/A.
Discount golf packages: No. **Season:** Year-round. **High:** May-Sept.
On-site lodging: No. **Rental clubs:** Yes.
Walking policy: Unrestricted walking. **Range:** Yes (grass).

To obtain tee times: Call Monday two weeks in advance.
Subscriber comments: Good variety of holes . . . A little tight . . .
Comprehensive facility . . . Gets better every year . . . Inexpensive . . .
Courteous staff . . . Very plain layout . . . Fairly open and not too difficult
. . . Average course . . . Wide open . . . Not a lot of hazards . . . Parallel
fairways can be dangerous . . . Forgiving, fun and cheap . . . Too many
holes similar . . . Nos. 5, 6, 7, and 8 are crammed together.

★★ BLUE MOUNTAIN VIEW GOLF COURSE

PU—Blue Mt. Dr., RD 1, Box 106, Fredericksburg (717)865-4401.
23 miles east of Harrisburg. **Holes:** 18. **Par:** 71/73.
Yards: 6,010/4,520. **Course rating:** 68.2/64.9. **Slope:** 110/101.
Opened: 1963. **Pace of Play rating:** 4:00. **Green fee:** $16/18.
Credit cards: None. **Reduced fees:** Weekdays, Low season, Seniors,
Juniors.
Caddies: No. **Golf carts:** $20 for 18 holes.
Discount golf packages: No. **Season:** Year-round. **High:** April–Sept.
On-site lodging: No. **Rental clubs:** No.
Walking policy: Unrestricted walking. **Range:** Yes.
To obtain tee times: Call pro shop.
Subscriber comments: Rustic but well worth the low fees . . . Short and
hilly . . . Outstanding views . . . Very nice course . . . A few interesting
holes but nothing to excite one . . . Short but challenging.

★ BON AIR GOLF CLUB

PU—McCormick Rd., Corapolis (412)262-2992.
10 miles west of Pittsburgh. **Holes:** 18. **Par:** 71/73.
Yards: 5,821/4,809. **Course rating:** 68.5/69.5. **Slope:** 117/120.
Opened: 1932. **Pace of Play rating:** 3:30-4:00. **Green fee:** $16/18.
Credit cards: None. **Reduced fees:** Weekdays, Low season, Seniors.
Caddies: No. **Golf carts:** $12 for 18 holes.
Discount golf packages: Yes. **Season:** Year-round. **High:** April–Sept.
On-site lodging: No. **Rental clubs:** Yes.
Walking policy: Walking at certain times. **Range:** No.
To obtain tee times: Call 24 hours in advance.
Subscriber comments: Excellent conditions . . . Short course more for
high handicapper . . . Hilly . . . Blind shots . . . Near airport, noisy . . .
Not in very good shape . . . Half of the holes are acceptable . . . Greens
were in excellent shape but course is short . . . Great public course greens
. . . Good location from Pittsburgh and airport.

BRIARWOOD GOLF CLUB

PU—4775 W. Market St., York (717)792-9776, (800)432-1555.
Pace of Play rating: 4:30-5:00. **Green fee:** $16/ 22.
Credit cards: MC, V, MAC/Cirrus. **Reduced fees:** Weekdays, Low
season, Resort guests, Twilight, Seniors.
Caddies: No. **Golf carts:** $10 for 18 holes.
Discount golf packages: Yes. **Season:** Year-round. **High:** March–Oct.
On-site lodging: No. **Rental clubs:** Yes.
Walking policy: Unrestricted walking. **Range:** Yes (grass).
To obtain tee times: Call. No restrictions as to advanced bookings.
★★ EAST COURSE
Holes: 18. **Par:** 72/72.
Yards: 6,550/5,120. **Course rating:** 69.7/67.8. **Slope:** 116/112.
Opened: 1955.
Subscriber comments: Your basic public course . . . Nothing special but
OK . . . Flat, uneventful, beginner will enjoy . . . Fairly wide open . . .
Made good use of what hills they have . . . Spray hitter's heaven . . . Nice
greens for a public course.
★★½ WEST COURSE
Holes: 18. **Par:** 70/70.
Yards: 6,300/4,820. **Course rating:** 69.7/67.3. **Slope:** 119/112.
Opened: 1990.
Subscriber comments: Still needs to grow in . . . Short course . . . Not a

lot of trouble . . . Better and more challenging than East Course . . . Too many short par 4s . . . Great potential . . . Stop on ladies' Futures Tour . . . Short course . . . Par 70 . . . Nice layout.

BUCK HILL GOLF CLUB
★★★ WHITE/BLUE/RED
SP—Golf Dr., Buck Hill Falls (717)595-7730.
50 miles north of Allentown. **Holes:** 27. **Par:** 72/70/70.
Yards: 6,450/6,150/6,300. **Course rating:** 71.0/69.8/70.4.
Slope: 126/120/122.
Opened: 1901. **Pace of Play rating:** 4:00. **Green fee:** $30/45.
Credit cards: MC, V. **Reduced fees:** Twilight.
Caddies: No. **Golf carts:** $14 for 18 holes.
Discount golf packages: No. **Season:** April-Nov. **High:** June-Sept.
On-site lodging: No. **Rental clubs:** Yes.
Walking policy: Mandatory cart. **Range:** Yes (grass).
To obtain tee times: Call one week in advance. Groups of 12 or more may call farther in advance.
Subscriber comments: Tougher than hell . . . More trees than all of Canada . . . A bear . . . Fine mountain layout . . . White/Blue are best nines . . . Very peaceful round . . . Few adjacent fairways . . . Beautiful and lush . . . Great design . . . Fabulous course . . . Donald Ross gem . . . Good mix of holes.

★★★½ BUCKNELL GOLF CLUB
SP—Rte. No.1, Lewisburg (717)523-8193.
60 miles north of Harrisburg. **Holes:** 18. **Par:** 70/71.
Yards: 6,268/5,387. **Course rating:** 70.3/71.2. **Slope:** 128/122.
Opened: 1930. **Pace of Play rating:** 4:00. **Green fee:** $21/26.
Credit cards: All major. **Reduced fees:** N/A.
Caddies: No. **Golf carts:** $12 for 18 holes.
Discount golf packages: No. **Season:** March-Nov. **High:** June-Aug.
On-site lodging: No. **Rental clubs:** Yes.
Walking policy: Unrestricted walking. **Range:** Yes (grass).
To obtain tee times: Call one week in advance.
Subscriber comments: Beautiful shotmaker's course . . . Great condition . . . Not long, but difficult . . . Great course . . . Nice old style . . . Tree-lined fairways . . . Plays tougher than it looks . . . Walking course . . . Good test . . . Becoming my favorite.

★★★ BUTLER'S GOLF COURSE
PU—800 Rock Run Rd., Elizabeth (412)751-9121.
15 miles south of Pittsburgh. **Holes:** 27. **Par:** 72/N/A.
Yards: 6,616/N/A. **Course rating:** 70.3/N/A. **Slope:** 115/N/A.
Opened: 1928. **Pace of Play rating:** 4:15. **Green fee:** $17/24.
Credit cards: All major. **Reduced fees:** Weekdays, Low season, Twilight, Seniors, Juniors.
Caddies: No. **Golf carts:** $10 for 18 holes.
Discount golf packages: No. **Season:** Year-round. **High:** April-Oct.
On-site lodging: Yes. **Rental clubs:** Yes.
Walking policy: Walking at certain times. **Range:** Yes (grass).
To obtain tee times: Call one week in advance for weekday. Call Tuesday 10 a.m. for upcoming weekend play.
Subscriber comments: Good condition . . . Nice service . . . Nice public layout . . . Worth taking time to play . . . Heavy play on weekends . . . Need some length on some holes . . . Wide open . . . Suited for all players . . . Three very tough finishing holes . . . Flowers around tee boxes are a nice touch . . . Outstanding restaurant.

CARROLL VALLEY GOLF RESORT
Pace of Play rating: 4:30.
Credit cards: MC, V, DISC.
Caddies: No. **Golf carts:** $12 for 18 holes.
Discount golf packages: Yes. **Rental clubs:** Yes.
To obtain tee times: Tee times are available every Friday for the following

Monday through Sunday. Golf packages and group outings may make tee times at any time.

★★★ MOUNTAIN VIEW COURSE
PU—Bullfrog Rd., Fairfield (717)642-5848.
8 miles west of Harrisburg. **Holes:** 18. **Par:** 71/70.
Yards: 6,343/5,024. **Course rating:** 70.2/68.2. **Slope:** 122/113.
Opened: 1979. **Green fee:** $18/22.
Reduced fees: Weekdays, Low season, Resort guests.
Season: March-Nov. **High:** April-Oct.
On-site lodging: No.
Walking policy: Unrestricted walking. **Range:** Yes (grass).
Subscriber comments: Love the first hole . . . Driveable par 4s . . . Front nine open, back nine tight . . . Nothing tricky . . . Fun to play . . . Can walk course easily . . . Good greens . . . Great layout . . . Scenery is great . . . Variety of good holes . . . Lots of fun . . . Rolling hills . . . Great . . . One good nine, one ordinary.

★★★½ CARROLL VALLEY COURSE
R—121 Sanders Rd., Fairfield (717)642-8252, (800)548-8504.
10 miles west of Harrisburg. **Holes:** 18. **Par:** 71/72.
Yards: 6,633/5,005. **Course rating:** 71.2/67.6. **Slope:** 120/114.
Opened: 1965. **Green fee:** $21/25.
Reduced fees: Low season, Resort guests.
Season: Year-round. **High:** April-Oct.
On-site lodging: Yes.
Walking policy: Walking at certain times. **Range:** No.
Subscriber comments: Solid course . . . Good for all levels . . . Scenic . . . Ski and golf on the same day . . . Beautiful view of Blue Ridge mountains . . . Set in the beautiful rolling hills of Pennsylvania . . . This one a real treat . . . Varying types of holes . . . Challenging . . . Some water to overcome . . . Hilly and challenging . . . Tough par 3s . . . Good condition . . . value . . . Some interesting holes . . . Won't kill you . . . President Clinton shot 88 here . . . Very long . . . Long par 3s . . . Good par 5s.

★★½ CASTLE HILLS GOLF COURSE
PU—110 W. Oakwood Way, New Castle (412)652-8122.
50 miles north of Pittsburgh. **Holes:** 18. **Par:** 72/73.
Yards: 6,415/5,784. **Course rating:** 69.7/73.3. **Slope:** 118/113.
Opened: 1930. **Pace of Play rating:** 4:30. **Green fee:** $14/16.
Credit cards: None. **Reduced fees:** Low season, Seniors, Juniors.
Caddies: No. **Golf carts:** $9 for 18 holes.
Discount golf packages: No. **Season:** March-Dec. **High:** May-Sept.
On-site lodging: No. **Rental clubs:** No.
Walking policy: Unrestricted walking. **Range:** Yes (grass).
To obtain tee times: Call.
Subscriber comments: Beautiful old course . . . Easy to walk . . . Hilly . . . Excellent greens . . . Short, tight course . . . Course mostly flat and easy to walk.

★★ CEDAR RIDGE GOLF COURSE
PU—1225 Barlow Two Taverns Rd., Gettysburg (717)359-4480.
43 miles north of Harrisburg. **Holes:** 18. **Par:** 72/N/A.
Yards: 6,132/ 5,546. **Course rating:** 69.5/ 69.3. **Slope:** 114/114.
Opened: 1987. **Pace of Play rating:** 4:30. **Green fee:** $10/14.
Credit cards: None. **Reduced fees:** Low season, Twilight.
Caddies: No. **Golf carts:** $9 for 18 holes.
Discount golf packages: No. **Season:** Year-round. **High:** April-Nov.
On-site lodging: No. **Rental clubs:** Yes.
Walking policy: Unrestricted walking. **Range:** No.
To obtain tee times: Call.
Subscriber comments: Some very unusual holes can catch you . . . Improving, but still a long way to go . . . Nos. 10 and 11 are interesting holes . . . Great for a new player . . . Front nine open . . . . Flat course . . . Very few hazards.

CEDARBROOK GOLF COURSE

PU—R.D. No.3, Belle Vernon (412)929-8300.
25 miles southwest of Pittsburgh.
Opened: N/A. **Pace of Play rating:** 4:30.
Credit cards: MC, V, DISC. **Reduced fees:** Low season, Seniors, Juniors.
Caddies: No. **Golf carts:** $10 for 18 holes.
Discount golf packages: No. **Season:** Year-round. **High:** April-Sept.
On-site lodging: No. **Rental clubs:** Yes. **Range:** Yes (grass).
To obtain tee times: Call seven days in advance of day of play.

★★★ GOLD COURSE

Holes: 18. **Par:** 72/72.
Yards: 6,701/5,211. **Course rating:** 71.6/68.6. **Slope:** 135/123.
Green fee: $17/24. **Walking policy:** Walking at certain times.
Subscriber comments: A challenging, well-maintained course . . . A few
great holes . . . Real nice . . . Good test of golf . . . Put the back nines
together and you'll have a great course . . . Beautiful views . . . Longer than
Red Course . . . Challenging.

★★ RED COURSE

Holes: 18. **Par:** 71/71.
Yards: 6,100/4,600. **Course rating:** 67.2/64.6. **Slope:** 118/107.
Green fee: $15/21. **Walking policy:** Unrestricted walking.
Subscriber comments: Much easier than the Gold Course . . . Front nine
is too short, back nine too open, barren . . . Everything is squeezed too
tight together . . . Red Course too short . . . Beautiful views, country club
fairways . . . Managable distances . . . Front nine short and too easy, back
nine makes up for front nine's flaws.

★★ CENTER SQUARE GOLF CLUB

SP—Rte. 73 & Whitehall Rd., Center Square (610)584-5700.
20 miles west of Philadelphia. **Holes:** 18. **Par:** 71/73.
Yards: 6,296/5,598. **Course rating:** 69.3/70.6. **Slope:** 119/114.
Opened: 1963. **Pace of Play rating:** 4:15. **Green fee:** $17/24.
Credit cards: MC, V. **Reduced fees:** Low season, Twilight, Seniors.
Caddies: No. **Golf carts:** $35 for 18 holes.
Discount golf packages: No. **Season:** Year-round. **High:** April-Oct.
On-site lodging: No. **Rental clubs:** Yes.
Walking policy: Walking at certain times. **Range:** Yes (grass).
To obtain tee times: Call eight days in advance for weekdays. Call
Wednesday a.m. for upcoming weekend.
Subscriber comments: Interesting course . . . Improving with
renovations . . . Beautiful layout . . . Good layout for a short course . . .
One of the better public courses in southeast Pennsylvania. Hosted 1980
Women's Public Links Championship . . . Relatively open . . . Front flat,
back hilly . . . Wide open . . . Hard greens . . . Good for average golfer . . .
Easy course . . . Mid- handicap golfer will find it challenging . . .
Challenging course but too wide open . . . All holes unique . . . They keep
all the woods cleared out so you can find your ball.

★★★★ CENTER VALLEY CLUB

PU—3300 Center Valley Pky., Center Valley (610)791-5580.
3 miles south of Allentown. **Holes:** 18. **Par:** 72/72.
Yards: 6,904/4,932. **Course rating:** 74.1/70.6. **Slope:** 135/123.
Opened: 1991. **Pace of Play rating:** 4:30. **Green fee:** $31/38.
Credit cards: MC, V. **Reduced fees:** Twilight.
Caddies: No. **Golf carts:** $13 for 18 holes.
Discount golf packages: No. **Season:** Year-round. **High:** May-Oct.
On-site lodging: No. **Rental clubs:** Yes.
Walking policy: Walking at certain times. **Range:** Yes (grass).
To obtain tee times: Call up to seven days in advance with credit card.
Subscriber comments: Excellent private course quality . . . This is the
best course in tri-state area . . . Discourage walkers . . . 45-60 min. drive
from civilization . . . World class golf . . . Worth the premium price . . .
Course offered a real putting challenge . . . A good short game paid
dividends here . . . Some holes on back are unfair . . . Starkly contrasting

nines . . . Championship layout . . . A monster from the tips . . . Fantastic layout . . . No. 18 is great finish . . . Links nine excellent, back nine too penal . . . Many good holes but I don't care for the mounds . . . Difficult course . . . Good amenities . . . Good condition . . . Front nine, Scottish links; back nine, tight.

★★★★ CHAMPION LAKES GOLF COURSE

PU—RD 1, Box 285, Bolivar (412)238-5440.
50 miles east of Pittsburgh. **Holes:** 18. **Par:** 71/74.
Yards: 6,608/5,556. **Course rating:** 69.0/72.1. **Slope:** 128/127.
Opened: 1968. **Pace of Play rating:** 4:00. **Green fee:** $20/25.
Credit cards: None. **Reduced fees:** Weekdays, Low season.

Caddies: No. **Golf carts:** $10 for 18 holes.
Discount golf packages: No. **Season:** April-Dec. **High:** May-Sept.
On-site lodging: Yes. **Rental clubs:** Yes.
Walking policy: Unrestricted walking. **Range:** Yes (grass).
To obtain tee times: Call.
Subscriber comments: True championship . . . Test of golf . . . Tight, tight, tight, accuracy No.1 . . . Scenic, fun, challenging . . . Tough, tight track with pleasant pro and personnel . . . Would go play anytime . . . Watch out for soft, heavy bunker sand! . . . Difficult layout . . . Cheap for course of this quality . . . Narrow and treacherous, but delightfully challenging . . . Owned by former Pirate, Dick Groat . . . Best value in western Pennsylvania . . . Remote but worth it . . . Fix tee boxes and this course is five stars.

★½ CHEROKEE GOLF COURSE

PU—217 Elysburg Rd., Danville (717)275-2005.
50 miles north of Harrisburg. **Holes:** 18. **Par:** 72/72.
Yards: 6,037/4,524. **Course rating:** N/A. **Slope:** N/A.
Opened: 1973. **Pace of Play rating:** 4:00. **Green fee:** $14/17.
Credit cards: MC, V, DISC. **Reduced fees:** Weekdays.
Caddies: No. **Golf carts:** $9 for 18 holes.
Discount golf packages: No. **Season:** Year-round. **High:** May-Aug.
On-site lodging: No. **Rental clubs:** Yes.
Walking policy: Unrestricted walking. **Range:** No.
To obtain tee times: Call pro shop anytime.
Subscriber comments: Flat, no sand . . . Plenty of water . . . Greens are upside-down saucers . . . Very tough greens, all sloped and hard to hold . . . Small short course . . . Great for beginners, no sand traps . . . Nice walking course . . . Good variety of holes.

★★★½ CHESTNUT RIDGE GOLF CLUB

PU—RD No.1, Blairsville (412)459-7188.
35 miles east of Pittsburgh. **Holes:** 18. **Par:** 72/72.
Yards: 6,321/5,130. **Course rating:** 70.7/70.2. **Slope:** 129/119.
Opened: 1964. **Pace of Play rating:** 4:00-4:30. **Green fee:** $23.
Credit cards: MC, V, AMEX. **Reduced fees:** Weekdays.
Caddies: No. **Golf carts:** $10 for 18 holes.
Discount golf packages: Yes. **Season:** April-Nov. **High:** May-Sept.
On-site lodging: No. **Rental clubs:** No.
Walking policy: Unrestricted walking. **Range:** Yes (grass).
To obtain tee times: Call seven days in advance.
Subscriber comments: Beautiful restaurant and clubhouse . . . Excellent views of the Laurel mountains . . . Improving every year . . . Has improved in last two year . . . Beautiful surroundings and nice atmosphere . . . Good greens and lush fairways . . . Good '60s-style layout.

★½ COBB'S CREEK GOLF COURSE

PU—72 Landsdowne Ave., Philadelphia (215)877-8707.
Holes: 18. **Par:** 71/71.
Yards: 6,660/6,130. **Course rating:** 68.6/68.1. **Slope:** 117/114.
Opened: 1916. **Pace of Play rating:** 4:00-4:30. **Green fee:** $22/26.
Credit cards: All major. **Reduced fees:** Weekdays, Twilight, Seniors, Juniors.

Caddies: No. **Golf carts:** $26 for 18 holes.
Discount golf packages: No. **Season:** Year-round. **High:** April-Oct.
On-site lodging: No. **Rental clubs:** Yes.
Walking policy: Unrestricted walking. **Range:** Yes (grass).
To obtain tee times: Call one week in advance.
Also has 18-hole Karakung Golf Course.
Subscriber comments: One of the best layouts in the city but it's overplayed and in poor shape . . . Very good city course . . . Very challenging . . . Site of 1955 PGA Daily News Open . . . Short front . . . long back . . . Designed by same architect as Merion . . . Pace was medium for the type of play but good for a Saturday away from wife, kids, and work . . . A golf factory . . . Spent two weeks there one day . . . Hugh Wilson design . . . One of the best public links in the area . . . Weird par 3s.

★★½ COLONIAL GOLF CLUB

PU—Duck Hollow Rd., Uniontown (412)439-3150.
Call club for further information.
Subscriber comments: Enjoyable front nine . . . Jungle-like back . . . Constant improvements being made . . . Good course to play in fall when leaves change in mountains . . . good layout . . . All kinds of holes.

★★ CONLEY'S RESORT INN

R—740 Pittsburgh Rd., Butler (412)586-7711, (800)344-7303.
30 miles north of Pittsburgh. **Holes:** 18. **Par:** 72/72.
Yards: 6,200/5,625. **Course rating:** 69.0/69.0. **Slope:** 110/110.
Opened: 1963. **Pace of Play rating:** 4:00. **Green fee:** $17/25.
Credit cards: All major. **Reduced fees:** Weekdays, Low season, Resort guests, Twilight, Seniors.
Caddies: No. **Golf carts:** $10 for 18 holes.
Discount golf packages: Yes. **Season:** Year-round. **High:** April-Oct.
On-site lodging: Yes. **Rental clubs:** Yes.
Walking policy: Walking at certain times. **Range:** No.
To obtain tee times: Call up to one year in advance.
Subscriber comments: Toughest finishing hole . . . Too narrow greens . . . Not bad for a quick round of golf . . . A blah golf course . . . Dull layout.

★★½ COOL CREEK COUNTRY CLUB

PU—Cool Creek Rd., Wrightsville (717)252-3691, (800)942-2444.
10 miles west of Lancaster. **Holes:** 18. **Par:** 71/70.
Yards: 6,521/5,703. **Course rating:** 71.1/72.6. **Slope:** 118/118.
Opened: 1948. **Pace of Play rating:** 4:00. **Green fee:** $17/25.
Credit cards: MC, V. **Reduced fees:** Weekdays, Low season, Resort guests, Twilight, Seniors, Juniors.
Caddies: No. **Golf carts:** $12 for 18 holes.
Discount golf packages: Yes. **Season:** Year-round. **High:** April-Oct.
On-site lodging: No. **Rental clubs:** Yes.
Walking policy: Walking at certain times. **Range:** Yes.
To obtain tee times: Call. Credit cards are required to reserve tee times during high season on weekends.
Subscriber comments: Nice old course . . . Great fairways and greens . . . Above average . . . Nice layout, hilly . . . Nice course, well run . . . Improving with age . . . Mature course in great shape . . . Good value . . . Variety of holes . . . Interesting course . . . Great shape . . . Front nine boring, back nine good . . . Nice layout for position player . . . Can play tough.

★★ COREY CREEK GOLF CLUB

SP—U.S. Rte. No.6 East, Mansfield (717)662-3520.
35 miles southwest of Elmira, NY. **Holes:** 18. **Par:** 72/72.
Yards: 6,571/4,920. **Course rating:** 71.1/66.0. **Slope:** 120/110.
Opened: 1927. **Pace of Play rating:** 4:12. **Green fee:** $12/20.
Credit cards: MC, V. **Reduced fees:** Weekdays, Low season, Twilight.
Caddies: No. **Golf carts:** $12 for 18 holes.
Discount golf packages: Yes. **Season:** April-Nov. **High:** May-Oct.

On-site lodging: No. **Rental clubs:** Yes.
Walking policy: Walking at certain times. **Range:** No.
To obtain tee times: Call anytime in advance.
Subscriber comments: Great staff and scenery . . . Pretty layout . . .
Difficult greens . . . Blind holes . . . New clubhouse and restaurant . . .
Staff friendly . . . Course is fair.

★★★★ COUNTRY CLUB AT WOODLOCH SPRINGS
R—Woodloch Dr., Hawley (717)685-2100.
50 miles east of Scranton. **Holes:** 18. **Par:** 72/72.
Yards: 6,579/4,973. **Course rating:** 72.3/71.6. **Slope:** 143/130.
Opened: 1992. **Pace of Play rating:** 4:45. **Green fee:** $46/56.
Credit cards: MC, V, AMEX. **Reduced fees:** Weekdays.
Caddies: No. **Golf carts:** Included in Green Fee.
Discount golf packages: No. **Season:** May-Oct. **High:** June-Aug.
On-site lodging: Yes. **Rental clubs:** Yes.
Walking policy: Walking at certain times. **Range:** Yes (grass).
To obtain tee times: Call one week in advance.
You must own property or be staying at one of the townhouses to play the
course.
Subscriber comments: Lightning greens . . . Enjoyable course . . .
Challenging target golf . . . Tough course from back tees . . . Beautifully
maintained . . . Fantastic layout and views . . . Truly worthy of its ranking
as one of the best new resort courses . . . Best course in Pennsylvania . . .
Tremendous . . . Target golf on a mountain setting . . . A lot of thinking
. . . New mountain course . . . Some long carries . . . Nice layout.

CROSS CREEK RESORT
★★ NORTH COURSE
PU—P.O. Box 432, Titusville (814)827-9611.
25 miles of Erie. **Holes:** 18. **Par:** 70/70.
Yards: 6,495/5,285. **Course rating:** N/A. **Slope:** 112/108.
Opened: N/A. **Pace of Play rating:** N/A. **Green fee:** N/A.
Credit cards: MC, V, DISC. **Reduced fees:** Weekdays, Low season.
Caddies: No. **Golf carts:** N/A.
Discount golf packages: Yes. **Season:** April-Oct. **High:** June-Aug.
On-site lodging: Yes. **Rental clubs:** No.
Walking policy: N/A. **Range:** Yes.
Subscriber comments: Very good shape . . . Fairways watered . . . Good
test of golf . . . Pleasant, well organized . . . Outstanding food . . . .
Facilities OK . . . Food good . . . Some very nice holes.

CULBERTSON HILLS GOLF RESORT★
R—Rte. 6N West, Edinboro (814)734-3114.
15 miles south of Eric. **Holes:** 18. **Par:** 72/73.
Yards: 6,763/5,815. **Course rating:** 71.7/72.9. **Slope:** 126/114.
Opened: 1931. **Pace of Play rating:** 4:30. **Green fee:** $15/22.
Credit cards: MC, V. **Reduced fees:** Weekdays, Low season, Resort
guests, Twilight, Seniors, Juniors.
Caddies: No. **Golf carts:** $10 for 18 holes.
Discount golf packages: Yes. **Season:** April-Nov. **High:** June-Aug.
On-site lodging: Yes. **Rental clubs:** Yes.
Walking policy: Walking at certain times. **Range:** No.
To obtain tee times: Call.

★★½ CUMBERLAND GOLF CLUB
PU—2395 Ritner Hwy., Carlisle (717)249-5538.
Call club for further information.
Subscriber comments: Old course . . . Heavily played . . . Good
condition for all the traffic . . . Clubhouse needs work . . . A fair test
overall . . . Wide open and watered fairways . . . Nos. 17 and 18 are not for
average players . . . Great older course . . . Much improved due to course
watering . . . Long par 3s are a real test! No. 17 tough par four . . . Staff
friendly . . . Best course in the area for the price.

★★½ DONEGAL HIGHLANDS GOLF CLUB

PU—RD No.1, Donegal (412)423-7888.
35 miles west of Pittsburgh. **Holes:** 18. **Par:** 72/72.
Yards: 6,130/4,520. **Course rating:** 69.6/65.7. **Slope:** 121/113.
Opened: 1991. **Pace of Play rating:** 4:30. **Green fee:** $17/23.
Credit cards: MC, V. **Reduced fees:** Weekdays, Low season, Seniors, Juniors.
Caddies: No. **Golf carts:** $20 for 18 holes.
Discount golf packages: Yes. **Season:** March-Nov. **High:** June-Aug.
On-site lodging: No. **Rental clubs:** Yes.
Walking policy: Unrestricted walking. **Range:** Yes (grass).
To obtain tee times: Call seven days in advance.
Subscriber comments: Improving with age . . . Great new course just off Pennsylvania Turnpike. . . . A must play . . . You have to think at this course . . . Very enjoyable . . . Good new course . . . Wide open front, tight back . . . Beautiful views, nature at its best . . . Great variety (trees, moguls, sand, water) . . . Reminds me of Scottish Highlands . . . Terrific greens . . . Very easy, short.

★★★ DOWNRIVER GOLF CLUB

PU—RD No.2, P.O. Box 628, Everett (814)652-5193.
40 miles south of Altoona. **Holes:** 18. **Par:** 72/73.
Yards: 6,855/5,513. **Course rating:** 70.5/71.6. **Slope:** 115/118.
Opened: 1967. **Pace of Play rating:** 4:30. **Green fee:** $13/15.
Credit cards: All major. **Reduced fees:** Weekdays, Twilight, Juniors.
Caddies: No. **Golf carts:** $10 for 18 holes.
Discount golf packages: Yes. **Season:** April-Nov. **High:** June-Sept.
On-site lodging: No. **Rental clubs:** No.
Walking policy: Unrestricted walking. **Range:** Yes (grass).
To obtain tee times: Call up to one week in advance.
Subscriber comments: Excellent course at a fair price . . . Would recommend to anyone . . . Local people don't realize the gem they have . . . Good walking . . . Wide open . . . Fun . . . Good course, a true test . . . Flat, wide open . . . Average flat course . . . Course is fairly flat and open but plays long for the senior player from the white tees . . . Very well taken care of.

★★★ DOWNING GOLF COURSE

PU—Troupe Rd., Harborcreek (814)899-5827.
6 miles east of Erie. **Holes:** 18. **Par:** 72/74.
Yards: 7,175/6,259. **Course rating:** 73.0/74.4. **Slope:** 114/115.
Opened: 1962. **Pace of Play rating:** 4:45. **Green fee:** $12/15.
Credit cards: None. **Reduced fees:** Low season, Twilight.
Caddies: No. **Golf carts:** $15 for 18 holes.
Discount golf packages: No. **Season:** Year-round. **High:** March-Nov.
On-site lodging: No. **Rental clubs:** No.
Walking policy: Unrestricted walking. **Range:** Yes (grass).
To obtain tee times: For Saturday call on Wednesday; call anytime for other days.
Subscriber comments: Quite long for the average golfer . . . Excellent shape in 1994 . . . Long, flat, not crowded . . . Long, tough layout . . . Winds a factor . . . Long, flat, not too interesting . . . It is a long public course but hard ground and no rough make it play much shorter.

★ DOWNINGTON COUNTRY CLUB

PU—P.O. Box 408, Rte. 30, Downington (215)269-2000.
25 miles of Philadelphia. **Holes:** 18. **Par:** 72/72.
Yards: 6,585/5,665. **Course rating:** N/A. **Slope:** 120/115.
Opened: N/A. **Pace of Play rating:** N/A. **Green fee:** N/A.
Credit cards: MC, V, AMEX. **Reduced fees:** Weekdays, Low season, Twilight.
Caddies: No. **Golf carts:** N/A.
Discount golf packages: Yes. **Season:** Year-round. **High:** May-Sept.
On-site lodging: No. **Rental clubs:** No.

Walking policy: N/A. **Range:** Yes.
Subscriber comments: Nice old, tree-lined course . . . Fazio course . . .
Fair condition at best . . . Great layout but has been let go . . . Greens need
work . . . Great potential. Poor conditions on a nice track . . . Could be
great . . . Great potential . . . Poor course maintenance . . . Probably was a
very good course years ago . . . A real shame . . . Once wonderful Fazio
design ruined by poor maintenance.

★★★★ EAGLE LODGE COUNTRY CLUB

R—Ridge Pike & Manor Roads, Lafayette Hill (610)825-9198.
10 miles west of Philadelphia. **Holes:** 18. **Par:** 71/71.
Yards: 6,759/5,260. **Course rating:** 72.8/70.4. **Slope:** 130/123.
Opened: 1983. **Pace of Play rating:** 4:00-5:00. **Green fee:** $80/90.
Credit cards: MC, V, AMEX. **Reduced fees:** Low season.
Caddies: No. **Golf carts:** Included in Green Fee.
Discount golf packages: Yes. **Season:** Year-round. **High:** April-Oct.
On-site lodging: Yes. **Rental clubs:** Yes.
Walking policy: Mandatory cart. **Range:** Yes (grass).
To obtain tee times: Call with credit card to hold reservation.
Subscriber comments: Very good course . . . Tough greens . . . Some
long par 3s . . . Hard course . . . Long but fun to play . . . Rees Jones
layout is fun and tough . . . Very challenging course . . . Very fast play . . .
Good staff . . . Incredible greens . . . Great course . . . Very hilly . . . Long
par 3s . . . I love this course . . . Facilities great . . . From back tees the pros
would enjoy it . . . Hills, hills, hills, no level lies . . . A corporate
playground . . . Excellent staff . . . Great pace . . . A gem . . . Some of the
purest greens around.

★★★ EDGEWOOD IN THE PINES GOLF COURSE

PU—Edgewood Rd., Drums (717)788-1101.
25 miles south of Wilkes-Barre. **Holes:** 18. **Par:** 72/72.
Yards: 6,721/5,184. **Course rating:** 71.9/69.9. **Slope:** N/A.
Opened: 1980. **Pace of Play rating:** 4:20. **Green fee:** $15/17.
Credit cards: None. **Reduced fees:** Weekdays, Low season, Twilight.
Caddies: No. **Golf carts:** $12 for 18 holes.
Discount golf packages: No. **Season:** April-Nov. **High:** May-Aug.
On-site lodging: No. **Rental clubs:** Yes.
Walking policy: Walking at certain times. **Range:** No.
To obtain tee times: Call one week in advance.
Subscriber comments: Good risk/reward holes . . . Good mix of holes
. . . Course always in great condition . . . Always treated well . . . Great
place to play . . . Course will show you how good you really are . . . Long,
narrow fairways . . . Plenty of water . . . Staff nice . . . Play is slow . . .
Very good golf course . . . Personnel are the best . . . Picturesque . . .
Monotonous . . . Holes too close together . . . Fairly flat mountain course
. . . Beautiful scenery . . . Good use of water . . . Lots of traps . . .
Enjoyable course.

★★★½ EMPORIUM COUNTRY CLUB

SP—Cameron Rd., Star Rte., Emporium (814)486-7715.
50 miles east of Bradford. **Holes:** 18. **Par:** 72/72.
Yards: 6,032/5,233. **Course rating:** 68.5/69.0. **Slope:** 118/115.
Opened: N/A. **Pace of Play rating:** 4:10. **Green fee:** $16/18.
Credit cards: None. **Reduced fees:** Weekdays, Twilight, Juniors.
Caddies: No. **Golf carts:** $9 for 18 holes.
Discount golf packages: Yes. **Season:** March-Nov. **High:** April-Sept.
On-site lodging: No. **Rental clubs:** Yes.
Walking policy: Walking at certain times. **Range:** Yes (grass).
To obtain tee times: Call. Tee times usually not necessary during the
week.
Subscriber comments: On side of a mountain . . . Very tough course . . .
Hilly but interesting . . . Breathtaking in fall . . . Tight front nine . . . Open
back . . . Very enjoyable . . . Tight back nine . . . Good greens . . . Lots of
sidehill lies.

★★ ERIE GOLF CLUB
PU—6050 Old Zuck Rd., Erie (814)866-0641.
Holes: 18. **Par:** 69/ 72.
Yards: 5,682/ 4,977. **Course rating:** 67.2/68.2. **Slope:** 111/ 109.
Opened: 1920. **Pace of Play rating:** 4:00. **Green fee:** $11/14.
Credit cards: None. **Reduced fees:** Twilight.
Caddies: No. **Golf carts:** $15 for 18 holes.
Discount golf packages: No. **Season:** March-Nov. **High:** April-Oct.
On-site lodging: No. **Rental clubs:** Yes.
Walking policy: Unrestricted walking. **Range:** No.
To obtain tee times: Call Wednesday for Saturday.
Subscriber comments: Very hilly with tough downhill, uphill, and
sidehill lies . . . Very hilly . . . Short . . . Good condition . . . Too many
hills . . . When it is dry the ball really rolls.

★ EXETER GOLF CLUB
PU—811 Shelbourne Rd., Reading (610)779-1211.
Holes: 18. **Par:** 70/70.
Yards: 6,085/5,300. **Course rating:** 69.0/67.0. **Slope:** N/A.
Opened: 1957. **Pace of Play rating:** 4:00-4:30. **Green fee:** $12/18.
Credit cards: MC, V. **Reduced fees:** Weekdays, Twilight, Seniors.
Caddies: No. **Golf carts:** $10 for 18 holes.
Discount golf packages: No. **Season:** Year-round. **High:** April-Nov.
On-site lodging: No. **Rental clubs:** Yes.
Walking policy: Unrestricted walking. **Range:** No.
To obtain tee times: Call anytime, no restrictions.
Subscriber comments: Still needs lots of work . . . Average public course
in every way . . . The course has improved over the years . . . The staff is
great . . . Major improvements recently in design and quality . . . Fairly
easy course . . . Nice for a quick round.

★★★ FAIRVIEW GOLF COURSE
PU—Rt. 72, Quentin (717)273-3411.
5 miles south of Lebanon. **Holes:** 18. **Par:** 71/73.
Yards: 6,227/5,221. **Course rating:** 69.2/72.9. **Slope:** 106/115.
Opened: 1959. **Pace of Play rating:** 4:15. **Green fee:** $10/20.
Credit cards: MC, V. **Reduced fees:** Weekdays, Low season, Twilight,
Seniors, Juniors.
Caddies: No. **Golf carts:** $11 for 18 holes.
Discount golf packages: No. **Season:** Year-round. **High:** May-Sept.
On-site lodging: No. **Rental clubs:** Yes.
Walking policy: Unrestricted walking. **Range:** Yes.
To obtain tee times: Call up to two weeks in advance.
Subscriber comments: Relatively short . . . Fun . . . Demands accuracy
. . . Hidden gem . . . No frills, just great golf . . . Average public course
. . . Well maintained . . . Nice par 3s . . . Not long . . . Course short . . .
Condition good . . . Service good . . . Both nines end with par 3s . . .
Some very good holes, most routine . . . Couple of blind holes . . .
Beautiful course . . . Everyone should enjoy this course . . . Old, mature
course is pretty wide open.

★½ FERNWOOD RESORT AND COUNTRY CLUB
R—Rte. 209, Bushkill (717)588-9500.
42 miles southeast of Scranton. **Holes:** 18. **Par:** 72/72.
Yards: 6,100/4,800. **Course rating:** 68.8/ 63.3. **Slope:** 125/115.
Opened: 1972. **Pace of Play rating:** 4:00. **Green fee:** $40/50.
Credit cards: MC, V, AMEX. **Reduced fees:** Low season, Resort guests,
Twilight.
Caddies: No. **Golf carts:** Included in Green Fee.
Discount golf packages: Yes. **Season:** April-Nov. **High:** July-Sept.
On-site lodging: Yes. **Rental clubs:** Yes.
Walking policy: Mandatory cart. **Range:** Yes (grass).
To obtain tee times: Call anytime.
Subscriber comments: Resort-type course . . . Blind holes . . . Hilly . . .

Mountain course . . . Too narrow and hilly . . . Green very fast (many three putts) . . . Nothing special to set it apart from others . . . Some ridiculous holes . . . Making some well-needed repairs on course . . . Some difficult holes . . . Homes close to fairways.

★★½ FIVE PONDS GOLF CLUB

PU—1225 West St. Rd., Warminster (215)956-9727.
14 miles north of Philadelphia. **Holes:** 18. **Par:** 71/71.
Yards: 6,760/5,430. **Course rating:** 71.0/70.1. **Slope:** 121/117.
Opened: N/A. **Pace of Play rating:** 4:30. **Green fee:** $19/23.
Credit cards: MC, V, MAC. **Reduced fees:** Weekdays, Low season, Twilight, Seniors.
Caddies: No. **Golf carts:** $12 for 18 holes.
Discount golf packages: No. **Season:** Year-round. **High:** April-Sept.
On-site lodging: No. **Rental clubs:** Yes.
Walking policy: Walking at certain times. **Range:** Yes (grass).
To obtain tee times: Call one week in advance.
Subscriber comments: Fairways too close to each other . . . Not trees but ponds come into play . . . Easy front nine . . . Good par 3s . . . Greens great . . . Too many parallel holes . . . Good back nine especially . . . Long par 4s . . . Plenty of water . . . Difficult course . . . Not long, but lots of water . . . Best public course in southeast Pennsylvania . . . Beautiful scenery . . . . Average layout . . . Good design . . . Interesting holes . . . A bit crowded between 4:00 - 8:00 P.M. . . . Excellent course . . . Holes too close together . . . Crowded in season . . . Nice little course.

★★½ FLATBUSH GOLF COURSE

PU—940 Littlestown Rd., Littlestown (717)359-7125.
40 miles south of Harrisburg. **Holes:** 18. **Par:** 71/71.
Yards: 6,717/5,401. **Course rating:** 72.4/72.2. **Slope:** 122/120.
Opened: 1989. **Pace of Play rating:** 4:30. **Green fee:** $13/17.
Credit cards: None. **Reduced fees:** Low season, Twilight.
Caddies: No. **Golf carts:** $9 for 18 holes.
Discount golf packages: No. **Season:** Year-round. **High:** May-Sept.
On-site lodging: No. **Rental clubs:** Yes.
Walking policy: Unrestricted walking. **Range:** Yes (grass).
To obtain tee times: Call seven to 10 days in advance, especially for weekends.
Subscriber comments: Nice layout . . . Wide open . . . Good layout . . . Easy to walk . . . Staff good . . . Always improving layout . . . Boring . . . Very flat course . . . Front flat and open back . . . Hilly and long . . . Ordinary, not too challenging.

★★★ FLYING HILLS GOLF COURSE

PU—10 Village Center Dr., Reading (610)775-4063.
Holes: 18. **Par:** 70/70.
Yards: 6,023/5,176. **Course rating:** 68.2/68.8. **Slope:** 118/118.
Opened: 1971. **Pace of Play rating:** 4:30. **Green fee:** $14/17.
Credit cards: None. **Reduced fees:** Weekdays, Low season.
Caddies: No. **Golf carts:** $10 for 18 holes.
Discount golf packages: No. **Season:** Year-round. **High:** March-Sept.
On-site lodging: No. **Rental clubs:** Yes.
Walking policy: Unrestricted walking. **Range:** No.
To obtain tee times: Call pro shop.
Subscriber comments: Short course but great holes . . . Beautiful area . . . Great layout . . . Shotmaker's course . . . Beautiful . . . Not too long but extremely tight . . . Tight and hilly . . . Must be accurate . . . Good value . . . Can walk . . . Must be able to play uphill, downhill, sidehill lies. Nice to get away from condos and traffic . . . A very good back nine . . . A little too narrow around the condos on the front nine . . . Make sure your homeowner's is paid . . . Great shape, challenging . . . Good restaurant . . . Short, but very narrow . . . Play with irons and you'll score well . . . Not crowded . . . A well-hidden gem . . . Great value . . . Worth drive from Philadelphia . . . Pleasant people . . . Beautiful condition . . . Great layout, interesting . . . Keep it a secret.

★½ FOUR SEASONS GOLF CLUB

PU—750 Slocum Ave., Exeter (717)655-8869.

6 miles north of Wilkes-Barre. **Holes:** 18. **Par:** 70/70.

Yards: 5,748/4,306. **Course rating:** N/A. **Slope:** N/A.

Opened: 1960. **Pace of Play rating:** N/A. **Green fee:** $11/13.

Credit cards: None. **Reduced fees:** Weekdays, Twilight.

Caddies: No. **Golf carts:** $9 for 18 holes.

Discount golf packages: No. **Season:** Year-round. **High:** May-Sept.

On-site lodging: No. **Rental clubs:** Yes.

Walking policy: Unrestricted walking. **Range:** Yes.

To obtain tee times: Call Monday for upcoming weekend or holiday.

Subscriber comments: Course open year-round . . . Winter play is great . . . Best suited for beginners . . . Fun layout, good condition year round . . . Every hole the same . . . Flat course . . . Little trouble . . . Wide open . . . Short and ratty . . . Some tough par 3s . . . Nothing special here . . . Below average for area . . . Holes squeezed together.

★★½ FOX HOLLOW GOLF CLUB

PU—2020 Trumbauersville Rd., Quakertown (215)538-1920.

Holes: 18. **Par:** 71/71.

Yards: 6,595/5,411. **Course rating:** 70.2/67.0. **Slope:** 117/106.

Opened: 1957. **Pace of Play rating:** 4:30. **Green fee:** $16/22.

Credit cards: MC, V. **Reduced fees:** Weekdays, Low season, Twilight, Seniors, Juniors.

Caddies: No. **Golf carts:** $10 for 18 holes.

Discount golf packages: No. **Season:** Year-round. **High:** May-Sept.

On-site lodging: No. **Rental clubs:** Yes.

Walking policy: Walking at certain times. **Range:** Yes (grass).

To obtain tee times: Call anytime in advance.

Subscriber comments: Challenge . . . Fun golf . . . Nice price . . . This course is getting better and better . . . Suited for middle handicappers . . . Course is not difficult . . . Very different . . . Loved it first time we played . . . Well-kept course doesn't play long . . . Best public course around Philadelphia area . . . Continuing to improve . . . Courteous staff . . . Large, well-manicured undulating greens . . . Not long but a real pleasure to play . . . Nice variety of holes . . . OK but needs work.

★★½ FOX RUN GOLF COURSE

PU—RD No.2 River Rd., Beaver Falls (412)847-3568.

30 miles northwest of Pittsburgh. **Holes:** 18. **Par:** 70/72.

Yards: 6,488/5,337. **Course rating:** 69.6/72.2. **Slope:** 113/117.

Opened: 1962. **Pace of Play rating:** 4:30. **Green fee:** $14/16.

Credit cards: None. **Reduced fees:** Low season, Seniors.

Caddies: No. **Golf carts:** N/A.

Discount golf packages: No. **Season:** Year-round. **High:** May-Sept.

On-site lodging: No. **Rental clubs:** No.

Walking policy: Unrestricted walking. **Range:** Yes (grass).

To obtain tee times: Call.

Subscriber comments: West Pennsylvania's most improved course . . . Suited for all levels . . . Making improvements . . . Spending money . . . Dry, hard greens . . . Two of the prettiest par 3s I've seen . . . Must rank as the most improved public course in the area . . . Most improved course in the area . . . Great teaching staff . . . Four really good par 3s . . . All water in play . . . Great staff and clubhouse.

★★★½ FOXCHASE GOLF CLUB

PU—300 Stevens Rd., Stevens (717)336-3673.

40 miles northeast of Philadelphia. **Holes:** 18. **Par:** 72/72.

Yards: 6,689/4,690. **Course rating:** 72.7/66.9. **Slope:** 124/116.

Opened: 1991. **Pace of Play rating:** N/A. **Green fee:** $15/35.

Credit cards: MC, V. **Reduced fees:** Weekdays, Low season, Twilight, Seniors, Juniors.

Caddies: No. **Golf carts:** Included in Green Fee.

Discount golf packages: No. **Season:** Year-round. **High:** May-Oct.

On-site lodging: No. **Rental clubs:** Yes.
Walking policy: Walking at certain times. **Range:** Yes (grass).
To obtain tee times: Call pro shop eight days prior to day of play or use credit card to obtain tee times prior to eight days.
Subscriber comments: One of the best layouts from back tees in the area . . . Maturing into one of the best values in east Pennsylvania . . . Eighth and 14th holes worth price of admission . . . Short par 5s . . . Great greens . . . Short . . . No. 14 a bear . . . Very clean clubhouse and pro shop . . . Built on farmland . . . Needs to mature . . . On short side . . . Great clubhouse and driving range . . . New course . . . Will come of age in three to five years . . . First-class driving range . . . Great clubhouse . . . Nice layout . . . Young course . . . Well kept . . . Will be terrific when it matures . . . Links style . . . Windy . . . Beautifully conditioned course . . . A bit short even from the blues.

★★★ GALEN HALL COUNTRY CLUB
PU—Galen Hall Rd., Wernersville (610)678-9535.
Call club for further information.
Subscriber comments: Tough par 3s . . . Super-sloped . . . Fast greens . . . Excellent service and bar and restaurant . . . Hilly, open course . . . Scenic . . . Great conditions . . . You better be a good putter . . . Several gimmicky holes . . . 15th is par-3 moat hole . . . New irrigation big improvement . . . Beautiful scenery . . . Two holes play over public roads . . . OK layout . . . Faster than ice greens . . . Ever seen greens break uphill? Try the second hole! . . . Mandatory carts . . . Very fast greens . . . Scenic . . . Some unusual holes . . . Uncrowded weekdays . . . Impossible greens . . . Fun course . . . Putts break uphill . . . Very hilly . . . Small greens . . . Great 19th hole restaurant . . . Very nice . . . Food is excellent . . . Mountain style . . . Tough and small greens . . . Short course . . . Fun for a day.

★★ GENERAL WASHINGTON GOLF COURSE
PU—2750 Egypt Rd., Audubon (610)666-7602.
4 miles west of Philadelphia. **Holes:** 18. **Par:** 70/72.
Yards: 6,300/5,300. **Course rating:** 67.5/67.4. **Slope:** N/A.
Opened: 1945. **Pace of Play rating:** 4:30. **Green fee:** $16/20.
Credit cards: None. **Reduced fees:** Low season, Twilight, Seniors, Juniors.
Caddies: No. **Golf carts:** $22 for 18 holes.
Discount golf packages: Yes. **Season:** Year-round. **High:** April-Oct.
On-site lodging: No. **Rental clubs:** Yes.
Walking policy: Unrestricted walking. **Range:** No.
To obtain tee times: 7 days in advance.
Subscriber comments: Doglegs abound . . . A lot of short doglegs, par 4s . . . Must be able to hit straight and long to score . . . Multi-tier greens . . . Course condition is always excellent . . . Greens need work . . . Used to be in horrible shape but better now . . . Lots of doglegs . . . Poor condition, but good design . . . Easy to walk . . . Doesn't drain well . . . Great potential yet to be realized . . . Very good layout.

★★ GLEN BROOK COUNTRY CLUB
PU—Glenbrook Rd., Stroudsburg (717)421-3680.
75 miles west of New York. **Holes:** 18. **Par:** 72/72.
Yards: 6,536/5,234. **Course rating:** 71.4/69.4. **Slope:** 123/117.
Opened: 1924. **Pace of Play rating:** N/A. **Green fee:** $33/37.
Credit cards: N/A. **Reduced fees:** Weekdays, Low season, Resort guests, Twilight, Seniors.
Caddies: No. **Golf carts:** Included in Green Fee.
Discount golf packages: Yes. **Season:** April-Nov. **High:** May-Oct.
On-site lodging: Yes. **Rental clubs:** Yes.
Walking policy: Walking at certain times. **Range:** No.
To obtain tee times: Call pro shop.
Subscriber comments: Up-and-down holes . . . Acceptable layout . . . Some hokey holes . . . Longish rambling layout . . . Plenty of challenge . . . Need to play smart . . . Wet a lot of time . . . Great to walk in the

afternoon and evening . . . Tough par 3s . . . Old course . . . Small greens . . . Nice course . . . Long . . . Hilly . . . Difficult for double-digit handicappers . . . Average course . . . Good layout.

★★ GRANDVIEW GOLF CLUB

PU—2779 Carlisle Rd., York (717)764-2674, (800)942-2444.
4 miles north of York. **Holes:** 18. **Par:** 72/73.
Yards: 6,639/5,578. **Course rating:** 70.5/71.1. **Slope:** 119/120.
Opened: 1924. **Pace of Play rating:** 4:00-4:30. **Green fee:** $15/20.
Credit cards: MC, V. **Reduced fees:** Weekdays, Low season, Resort guests, Twilight, Seniors, Juniors.
Caddies: No. **Golf carts:** $10 for 18 holes.
Discount golf packages: Yes. **Season:** Year-round. **High:** April-Oct.
On-site lodging: No. **Rental clubs:** Yes.
Walking policy: Unrestricted walking. **Range:** No.
To obtain tee times: Call pro shop at 800 number.
Subscriber comments: Very challenging and easy holes . . . Dangerous parallel fairways . . . Old mature course . . . Very long for average player . . . Lots of uphill and downhill shots . . . Old course . . . Good fun course . . . Service good . . . Superb little course . . . Well groomed . . . Oldest public course in this area (and can test your skill) . . . Shows its age . . . Some interesting holes.

★★ GREEN ACRES GOLF CLUB

PU—RD No.4, Rte. 408, Titusville (814)827-3589.
Call club for further information.
Subscriber comments: Great little course . . . Some water, some trees . . . Very fast greens . . . Easy and short . . . Average . . . Ego builder . . . Short and open course . . . Too open . . . No character . . . Nice course . . . Slow greens . . . Not too interesting, reasonable.

★½ GREEN MEADOWS GOLF COURSE

PU—2451 N Brickyard Rd., North East (814)725-5009.
Call club for further information.
Subscriber comments: Very flat with many very small elevated greens . . . Short . . . Fun to play . . . Mounded greens on first nine . . . Easy, but fun . . . Back nine new . . . Needs time.

GREEN MEADOWS GOLF COURSE*

PU—R.D. 2, Box 224 Rt 19, Volant (412)530-7330.
45 miles north of Pittsburgh. **Holes:** 18. **Par:** 72/72.
Yards: 6,196/5,220. **Course rating:** 68.4/N/A. **Slope:** 108/N/A.
Opened: 1964. **Pace of Play rating:** 4:00. **Green fee:** $9/16.
Credit cards: MC, V. **Reduced fees:** Weekdays, Low season, Seniors, Juniors.
Caddies: No. **Golf carts:** $9 for 18 holes.
Discount golf packages: Yes. **Season:** March-Dec. **High:** April-Sept.
On-site lodging: No. **Rental clubs:** Yes.
Walking policy: Unrestricted walking. **Range:** Yes (grass).
To obtain tee times: Call pro shop anytime.
Subscriber comments: Nice course . . . Very plain . . . Becoming one of the best . . . Wide open . . . Nice greens . . . Easy to score . . . Back nine more interesting . . . Too many blind holes . . . Wide fairways . . . Still good for novice or big hitter . . . Well groomed . . . Wide fairways . . . Good greens . . . Too many flowers . . . Great par 3s . . . Usually not crowded . . . Built on farmland.

★½ GREEN POND COUNTRY CLUB

PU—3604 Farmersville Rd., Bethlehem (610)691-9453.
Holes: 18. **Par:** 71/74.
Yards: 6,521/5,541. **Course rating:** 69.4/69.7. **Slope:** 126/112.
Opened: N/A. **Pace of Play rating:** 4:00. **Green fee:** $16/20.
Credit cards: None. **Reduced fees:** Weekdays, Twilight, Seniors, Juniors.
Caddies: No. **Golf carts:** $10 for 18 holes.

Discount golf packages: No. **Season:** Year-round. **High:** April–Nov.
On-site lodging: No. **Rental clubs:** Yes.
Walking policy: Unrestricted walking. **Range:** Yes (grass).
To obtain tee times: Tee times only on weekends, call the Monday before.
Subscriber comments: Short but tight . . . Easy to walk . . . Small, hard greens . . . Seasoned course . . . Short . . . Good senior citizen's course . . . Needs better maintenance . . . Hard to hold greens . . . Crowded . . . Narrow . . . Short course excellent for mid-range handicappers who have a decent game . . . Will cut four to six strokes off your handicap if you can drive over 200 yards.

★★★½ GREENCASTLE GREENS GOLF CLUB
PU—2000 Castlegreen Dr., Greencastle (717)597-1188.
75 miles northwest of Baltimore. **Holes:** 18. **Par:** 72/74.
Yards: 6,908/5,315. **Course rating:** 72.6/70.3. **Slope:** 129/124.
Opened: 1991. **Pace of Play rating:** 5:00. **Green fee:** $11/21.
Credit cards: MC, V. **Reduced fees:** Weekdays, Low season, Twilight, Seniors, Juniors.
Caddies: No. **Golf carts:** $11 for 18 holes.
Discount golf packages: Yes. **Season:** Year-round. **High:** April–Oct.
On-site lodging: No. **Rental clubs:** Yes.
Walking policy: Walking at certain times. **Range:** Yes (grass).
To obtain tee times: Call up to 2 weeks in advance.
Subscriber comments: Nice course and clubhouse . . . Long distances from green to next tee . . . One of the best . . . Fun to play . . . My favorite course . . . Many outstanding holes . . . Hard to walk . . . Too far between greens and tees . . . Good par 3s . . . Lots of hills . . . Fronted by water . . . Great scenery . . . Waterfall third hole . . . Will be top course when mature . . . Few blind shots . . . Challenge . . . A fun course . . . Scenic . . . Memorable holes with waterfalls, ponds . . . New course . . . Great layout . . . Bring extra balls first time around.

DEEP VALLEY GOLF COURSE★
PU—169 Hartmann Rd., Harmony (412)452-8021.
25 miles south of Pittsburgh. **Holes:** 18. **Par:** 72/N/A.
Yards: 6,310/N/A. **Course rating:** N/A. **Slope:** N/A.
Opened: 1958. **Pace of Play rating:** 4:30. **Green fee:** $11/15.
Credit cards: None. **Reduced fees:** Low season, Seniors.
Caddies: No. **Golf carts:** $10 for 18 holes.
Discount golf packages: No. **Season:** Year-round. **High:** March–Oct.
On-site lodging: No. **Rental clubs:** Yes.
Walking policy: Unrestricted walking. **Range:** No.
To obtain tee times: First come, first served.

★★★ HAWK VALLEY GOLF CLUB
PU—1319 Crestview Dr., Denver (717)445-5445, (800)522-4295.
25 miles east of Lancaster. **Holes:** 18. **Par:** 72/72.
Yards: 6,628/5,661. **Course rating:** 70.3/70.2. **Slope:** 132/119.
Opened: 1971. **Pace of Play rating:** 4:30. **Green fee:** $17/20.
Credit cards: MC, V, AMEX. **Reduced fees:** Juniors.
Caddies: No. **Golf carts:** $13 for 18 holes.
Discount golf packages: Yes. **Season:** Year-round. **High:** April–Nov.
On-site lodging: No. **Rental clubs:** Yes.
Walking policy: Walking at certain times. **Range:** No.
To obtain tee times: Weekday call eight days in advance; weekend and holidays call anytime in advance.
Subscriber comments: Subtle greens . . . Nice test of iron game . . . Nice layout . . . Very fair greens . . . Nice clubhouse . . . Great course . . . A real sleeper . . . I hope people don't find it . . . Pretty tough course but fun to play . . . Average course . . . Many holes look similar . . . Good shape . . . Very good staff . . . Course rangers actually move play . . . Some good holes . . . Tough in windy conditions . . . Good pro shop and large undulating greens . . . Good test, challenging but not a killer . . . Very

good somewhat flat type golf course . . . A good challenge . . . Supersonic putting surfaces . . . Good layout . . . Some very tricky putting greens . . . Very slick greens . . . Layout OK . . . Green contours drive you crazy!

★★★½ HERITAGE HILLS GOLF RESORT

R—2700 Mt. Rose Ave., York (717)755-4653, (800)942-2444.
25 miles south of Harrisburg. **Holes:** 18. **Par:** 71/71.
Yards: 6,330/5,075. **Course rating:** 70.6/69.5. **Slope:** 120/116.
Opened: 1989. **Pace of Play rating:** 5:00. **Green fee:** $26.
Credit cards: All major. **Reduced fees:** Low season, Twilight, Seniors.
Caddies: No. **Golf carts:** $12 for 18 holes.
Discount golf packages: No. **Season:** Year-round. **High:** April-Sept.
On-site lodging: No. **Rental clubs:** Yes.
Walking policy: Walking at certain times. **Range:** Yes.
To obtain tee times: Call pro shop.
Subscriber comments: Nice clubhouse, pro shop . . . Good test from blue tees . . . Fairways too close to each other . . . Large greens . . . Nice variety of holes . . . Long par 4s . . . Tough but fun to play . . . Good shape . . . Some holes too close . . . Friendly staff . . . Good facilities . . . Rolling hills . . . The tough holes have an out for the squeamish . . . Great finishing hole . . . Relatively new course . . . Interesting up-and-down holes over a quarry . . . Slow play but worth playing . . . Great layout . . . Tough putting greens . . . Needs maturity . . . Beautiful course . . . Lots of water.

HERSHEY COUNTRY CLUB

R—1000 E. Derry Rd., Hershey (717)533-2464, (800)900-4653.
12 miles east of Harrisburg.
Reduced fees: Weekdays, Twilight.
Caddies: No. **Golf carts:** Included in Green Fee.
Discount golf packages: Yes. **Season:** Year-round. **High:** May-Oct.
On-site lodging: Yes. **Rental clubs:** Yes.
Walking policy: Mandatory cart. **Range:** Yes (grass).
To obtain tee times: Call 60 days in advance without fee.

★★★½ EAST COURSE

Holes: 18. **Par:** 71/71.
Yards: 7,061/5,645. **Course rating:** 73.6/71.6. **Slope:** 128/127.
Opened: 1970. **Pace of Play rating:** N/A. **Green fee:** $64/69.
Credit cards: MC, V, AMEX.
Subscriber comments: Not comparable to West Course. Long, tough, uninteresting . . . Too many holes similar to each other . . . Wide-open course, but still challenging due to length and elevated greens . . . Monster from the blue tees . . . Well designed in most respects but not enough variety . . . Long . . . Excellent course . . . Great condition . . . Good design . . . Best set of par 5s on east coast. Gracious, beautiful in old tradition . . . Well done in all respects . . . Underrated compared to West . . . Has some great holes . . . Longer, more open than West Course.

★★★★ WEST COURSE

Holes: 18. **Par:** 73/76.
Yards: 6,860/5,908. **Course rating:** 73.1/74.7. **Slope:** 131/127.
Opened: 1930. **Pace of Play rating:** N/A. **Green fee:** $84/89.
Credit cards: MC, V.
Subscriber comments: First class course . . . Immaculate condition . . . Great layout . . . Don't miss this one . . . Beautiful course . . . Typical resort course . . . Carts required . . . Greens relatively slow . . . Championship-type course . . . Excellent condition . . . Beautiful old style . . . Hilly course . . . Awesome layout . . . Fast greens . . . Mature trees . . . Worth every penny . . . Ambiance is outstanding . . . Smell the chocolate . . . Golfer's delight . . . Most enjoyable course and chocolate smell . . . If factory is working, no better smelling course . . . Great old course . . . Site of Lady Keystone Open . . . Superb layout . . . Fifth hole par 3, magnificent view of Milton Hershey mansion . . . One of best courses in Pennsylvania . . . Play it every chance I can . . . Historic . . . Hosted PGA and LPGA tournaments . . . Well maintained . . . Very challenging.

★★★½ HERSHEY PARKVIEW GOLF COURSE

PU—600 West Derry Rd., Hershey (717)534-3450, (800)900-4653.
12 miles east of Harrisburg. **Holes:** 18. **Par:** 70/71.
Yards: 6,103/4,817. **Course rating:** 69.8/69.6. **Slope:** 121/107.
Opened: 1927. **Pace of Play rating:** N/A. **Green fee:** $35/43.
Credit cards: MC, V, AMEX. **Reduced fees:** Weekdays, Twilight.
Caddies: No. **Golf carts:** N/A.
Discount golf packages: Yes. **Season:** Year-round. **High:** May-Oct.
On-site lodging: Yes. **Rental clubs:** Yes.
Walking policy: Walking at certain times. **Range:** Yes.
To obtain tee times: Call seven days in advance without fee; eight-60 days
in advance subject to $3.00 per player reservation fee.
Subscriber comments: Tight . . . Older course . . . Best in spring and
early fall . . . Fun course . . . Different holes, elevations . . . Use of creek is
great . . . Unique layout . . . Fun course . . . Fast greens . . . Scenic . . .
Shotmaker's course . . . Interesting but very short . . . Small greens . . .
Tight fairways . . . Not nearly the course it was ten years ago . . . Great
public course . . . Challenging . . . Well kept . . . No par 5s with length
. . . Beautiful layout . . . Worth trip and money . . . A tribute to Mr.
Hershey . . . Shot placement very critical . . . Short, old layout . . . Fun but
a good test . . . Wonderful shotmaker's course . . . A very good, old
course.

★★ HICKORY HEIGHTS GOLF CLUB

PU—116 Hickory Heights Dr., Bridgeville (412)257-0300.
12 miles south of Pittsburgh. **Holes:** 18. **Par:** 72/72.
Yards: 6,504/5,057. **Course rating:** 71.8/69.9. **Slope:** 132/126.
Opened: 1992. **Pace of Play rating:** 4:30. **Green fee:** $22/38.
Credit cards: MC, V. **Reduced fees:** Weekdays, Low season, Twilight,
Seniors, Juniors.
Caddies: No. **Golf carts:** N/A.
Discount golf packages: No. **Season:** Year-round. **High:** April-Oct.
On-site lodging: No. **Rental clubs:** Yes.
Walking policy: Walking at certain times. **Range:** Yes (grass).
To obtain tee times: Call five days in advance.
Subscriber comments: Some interesting holes . . . Very hilly . . . Some
good holes . . . Some silly holes . . . Fairly new, especially second nine . . .

Doing their best with difficult steep terrain . . . Nice layout . . . Four hard
par 3s . . . Greens are true but it's like playing in the Alps . . . Good practice
range . . . Lots of hills . . . Very challenging par 3s . . . Michael Hurdzan
did a wonderful job . . . Some very funky, unfair par 3s . . . Interesting and
challenging layout despite short length . . . A super fun course . . . Back
nine is real tight . . . Front has one goofy-golf par 3.

★★★ HICKORY VALLEY GOLF CLUB

PU—1921 Ludwig Rd., Gilbertsville (610)754-9862.
Call club for further information.
Subscriber comments: Very good layout . . . Fun to mix nines . . . Blue
and Red longer and tighter than White . . . Excellent all year . . . Beautiful
course and scenery . . . Most challenging . . . Well run . . . crowded . . .
Three separate nines . . . White is poor . . . Three nines nice . . . Well-run
operation . . . Fourth nine on the way . . . Play on weekdays when walking
is allowed . . . Beautiful 27 holes . . . Flat terrain . . . Excellent condition
. . . Course is beautiful in the fall . . . Great scenic holes.

★★★ GOLF CLUB AT HIDDEN VALLEY

R—One Craighead Dr., Hidden Valley (814)443-6454, (800)946-5348.
60 miles southeast of Pittsburgh. **Holes:** 18. **Par:** 72/72.
Yards: 6,579/5,097. **Course rating:** 73.5/69.2. **Slope:** 142/129.
Opened: 1987. **Pace of Play rating:** 4:30. **Green fee:** $31/41.
Credit cards: All major. **Reduced fees:** Weekdays, Low season, Resort
guests, Twilight.
Caddies: No. **Golf carts:** $16 for 18 holes.
Discount golf packages: Yes. **Season:** April-Nov. **High:** June-Aug.

On-site lodging: Yes. **Rental clubs:** Yes.
Walking policy: Walking at certain times. **Range:** Yes (grass).
To obtain tee times: Call 800 number. Weekday tee times taken two weeks in advance.
Subscriber comments: Nice scenery . . . Good layout . . . Had fun . . . Beautiful setting . . . Country club golf at muny prices . . . Very hilly . . . Four great holes in woods . . . A few scenic mountain course holes . . . Very scenic and tight . . . Not long . . . Accuracy a must . . . Nice start . . . Some short par 4s but a very good course . . . Outstanding, best in area . . . Scenery outstanding . . . Tough course with narrow, guarded fairways . . . This is not the course for you if you can't hit the ball straight . . . Kept in excellent condition . . . Staff was good . . . Pace of play is moderate.

★★★½ HONEY RUN GOLF AND COUNTRY CLUB
SP—3131 South Salem Church Rd., York (717)792-9771, (800)475-4657.
Holes: 18. **Par:** 72/72.
Yards: 6,797/5,948. **Course rating:** 72.4/74.0. **Slope:** 123/125.
Opened: 1971. **Pace of Play rating:** 4:00 - 4:30. **Green fee:** $20/29.
Credit cards: MC, V. **Reduced fees:** Weekdays, Low season, Resort guests, Twilight, Seniors, Juniors.
Caddies: No. **Golf carts:** $9 for 18 holes.
Discount golf packages: Yes. **Season:** Year-round. **High:** May-Aug.
On-site lodging: No. **Rental clubs:** Yes.
Walking policy: Walking at certain times. **Range:** Yes (grass).
To obtain tee times: Call pro shop as far in advance as needed.
Subscriber comments: Great test of golf from back tees . . . Super greens . . . Tricky holes . . . A real challenge . . . Worth 60 minute drive from Baltimore . . . Long, long par 3s . . . Fun but long . . . Good design . . . Very challenging . . . Excellent greens . . . Lots of doglegs . . . Poor finishing hole . . . Has decent practice area . . . Poor clubhouse facilities . . . Championship course . . . Very, very good . . . Hosted Nike Tour in '93 . . . Fun course . . . Front nine straight open . . . Back nine, trees and doglegs . . . Interesting par 5s.

★ HORSHAM VALLEY GOLF CLUB
PU—500 Babylon Rd., Ambler (215)646-4707.
15 miles northwest of Philadelphia. **Holes:** 18. **Par:** 66/66.
Yards: 5,019/4,307. **Course rating:** 61.7/61.7. **Slope:** 101/101.
Opened: 1957. **Pace of Play rating:** 4:00. **Green fee:** $18/24.
Credit cards: All major. **Reduced fees:** Weekdays, Low season, Twilight, Seniors, Juniors.
Caddies: No. **Golf carts:** $24 for 18 holes.
Discount golf packages: Yes. **Season:** Year-round. **High:** April-Oct.
On-site lodging: No. **Rental clubs:** Yes.
Walking policy: Unrestricted walking. **Range:** Yes (grass).
To obtain tee times: Weekdays one day in advance; weekends one week in advance.
Subscriber comments: Course is way too short . . . Too many par 3s . . . Short . . . Many par 4s drivable . . . This is a short course . . . Good place to practice your irons . . . Par is generous by two to three strokes . . . Short course . . . Needs work . . . Very friendly atmosphere . . . Short course . . . Enjoyed the company and the fresh air.

★★★½ IRON MASTERS COUNTRY CLUB
SP—RD No.1, Roaring Spring (814)224-2915.
15 miles south of Altoona. **Holes:** 18. **Par:** 72/75.
Yards: 6,644/5,683. **Course rating:** 72.2/73.6. **Slope:** 130/119.
Opened: 1962. **Pace of Play rating:** 4:30. **Green fee:** $25.
Credit cards: MC, V. **Reduced fees:** Weekdays.
Caddies: No. **Golf carts:** $11 for 18 holes.
Discount golf packages: Yes. **Season:** April-Dec. **High:** June-Aug.
On-site lodging: No. **Rental clubs:** Yes.
Walking policy: Unrestricted walking. **Range:** Yes.
To obtain tee times: Call two weeks in advance.
Subscriber comments: Attractive rolling course . . . Excellent condition

. . . Pleasant staff . . . Short, but tricky . . . Keep it straight . . . Greens were good . . . Excellent mountain course . . . Very fair . . . Scenic . . . Treelined . . . Hilly, suitable for all levels . . . Requires a lot of different shots . . . Very hilly with doglegs right and left.

★½ JOHN F. BYRNE GOLF COURSE

PU—9500 Leon St., Philadelphia (215)632-8666.
Holes: 18. **Par:** 67/67.
Yards: 5,200/4,662. **Course rating:** 65.0/61.4. **Slope:** 107/*98.
Opened: N/A. **Pace of Play rating:** 4:30. **Green fee:** $17/20.
Credit cards: All major. **Reduced fees:** Weekdays, Low season, Twilight, Seniors.
Caddies: No. **Golf carts:** $25 for 18 holes.
Discount golf packages: Yes. **Season:** Year-round. **High:** May-Oct.
On-site lodging: No. **Rental clubs:** Yes.
Walking policy: Unrestricted walking. **Range:** No.
To obtain tee times: Call seven days in advance.
Subscriber comments: A worn-out track . . . Lots of water . . . A good test . . . Heavy traffic . . . Fairways too close together . . . Extreme hills on nine and 18 . . . Very nice course . . . Always well kept . . . Short course . . . Small greens.

★★ KIMBERTON GOLF CLUB

PU—Rte. 23, Kimberton (215)933-8836.
Call club for further information.
Subscriber comments: Fairly open for average golfer . . . Nice staff . . . Tough par 3s . . . Longish par 4s for average golfer . . . Fairly open . . . Back nine hillier . . . Few good holes . . . Flat plain course . . . OK shape . . . G. Fazio design . . . Very forgiving . . . Nothing unusual . . . Always an interesting round here . . . Third hole my overall favorite . . . Flat with few traps . . . Most holes flat and straightforward . . . Third hole over lake the best in area . . . Good value . . . Tough greens . . . Nice course . . . Challenging.

★★ LENAPE HEIGHTS GOLF COURSE

PU—950 Golf Course Rd., Ford City (412)763-2201.
40 miles northeast of Pittsburgh. **Holes:** 18. **Par:** 71/71.
Yards: 6,145/4,869. **Course rating:** 69.0/67.4. **Slope:** 120/114.
Opened: 1967. **Pace of Play rating:** 4:00. **Green fee:** $12/15.
Credit cards: MC, V. **Reduced fees:** Weekdays.
Caddies: No. **Golf carts:** $9 for 18 holes.
Discount golf packages: No. **Season:** March-Nov. **High:** April-Sept.
On-site lodging: No. **Rental clubs:** Yes.
Walking policy: Unrestricted walking. **Range:** No.
To obtain tee times: Call Tuesday for upcoming weekend.
Subscriber comments: Course needs some work . . . Good staff . . . Course interesting . . . Good surroundings . . . Two nines look like two different designers . . . Back nine more challenging . . . Hilly course with some interesting holes.

LIMEKILN GOLF CLUB
★★ RED/WHITE/BLUE

PU—1176 Limekiln Pike, Ambler (215)643-0643.
10 miles north of Philadelphia. **Holes:** 27. **Par:** 70/70/70.
Yards: 6,213/6,415/6,176. **Course rating:** 67.8/68.7/N/A.
Slope: 114/114/N/A.
Opened: 1966. **Pace of Play rating:** 4:00–4:30. **Green fee:** $21/26.
Credit cards: None. **Reduced fees:** Twilight, Seniors.
Caddies: No. **Golf carts:** $12 for 18 holes.
Discount golf packages: No. **Season:** Year-round. **High:** May-July.
On-site lodging: No. **Rental clubs:** Yes.
Walking policy: Walking at certain times. **Range:** Yes (grass).
To obtain tee times: Call Monday for upcoming weekend.
Subscriber comments: Good course . . . Three nines help speed play . . . Three nines all different . . . Excellent shape . . . Poor shape and too busy

. . . Nice water holes . . . Flat, uninteresting layout . . . Too short . . . Lots of driver-wedge par 4s . . . Blue No. 7 tough. Red nine too short . . . Blue and White are nice and fair test . . . Good public layout, overplayed however.

★★½ LINDEN HALL GOLF CLUB
R—R.D. No.1, Dawson (412)529-2366.
37 miles south of Pittsburgh. **Holes:** 18. **Par:** 72/77.
Yards: 6,675/5,900. **Course rating:** 71.2/N/A. **Slope:** N/A.
Opened: N/A. **Pace of Play rating:** 4:00-4:30. **Green fee:** $15/22.
Credit cards: All major. **Reduced fees:** Weekdays, Low season, Resort guests, Seniors, Juniors.
Caddies: No. **Golf carts:** $20 for 18 holes.
Discount golf packages: Yes. **Season:** Year-round. **High:** March-Nov.
On-site lodging: Yes. **Rental clubs:** Yes.
Walking policy: Unrestricted walking. **Range:** No.
To obtain tee times: Call pro shop.
Subscriber comments: Great walker's course . . . Good length . . . Always a favorite place to play . . . Great no. 18 . . . Challenging for all levels of players . . . Nice mountain resort . . . A true test for all levels of play . . . Excellent scenery especially in the fall . . . Need bug spray in summer . . . Good design . . . Best local value . . . Non-golf amenities are slipping . . . Layout OK but not excellent . . . Some tough holes.

★½ LOCH NAIRN GOLF CLUB
PU—RR No.1, McCue Rd., Avondale (215)268-2234.
Call club for further information.
Subscriber comments: Good restaurant in clubhouse . . . Good potential . . . A best-kept secret untill now . . . Great water holes . . . Friendly staff . . . Uncrowded . . . Few amenities . . . Short, attractive, and challenging . . . Two very different nines, lots of fun . . . Long distance between holes . . . Elevated greens drain to sides, tough to hold . . . Nice course if you like water . . . Nice layout . . . Needs work . . . Beautiful farmhouse . . . Narrow . . . Fun . . . Hard . . . Great challenge . . . First five holes very good . . . Fast greens underrated . . . Some good holes on back . . . Tough walk . . . A mix of interesting and dull holes . . . Tough on high handicappers . . . Lots of water . . . Nice layout . . . Country golf . . . Suited for all levels of play . . . Challenging holes.

★★★ LOCUST VALLEY GOLF CLUB
PU—5525 Locust Valley Rd., Coopersburg (610)282-4711.
45 miles north of Philadelphia. **Holes:** 18. **Par:** 72/74.
Yards: 6,451/5,444. **Course rating:** 71.0/71.3. **Slope:** 132/121.
Opened: 1954. **Pace of Play rating:** 4:00. **Green fee:** $18/24.
Credit cards: MC, V. **Reduced fees:** Low season, Twilight, Seniors.
Caddies: No. **Golf carts:** $11 for 18 holes.
Discount golf packages: No. **Season:** March-Dec. **High:** May-Sept.
On-site lodging: No. **Rental clubs:** Yes.
Walking policy: Walking at certain times. **Range:** No.
To obtain tee times: Call one week in advance.
Subscriber comments: Old-time feel . . . Country setting . . . Great course . . . Try it . . . Great view of mountains . . . Short, tight, tough course . . . Greens are very small . . . Very tight, not for beginners . . . Tight, challenging course with great views . . . Good, challenging shotmaker's course . . . Bring the long sticks . . . Very tight . . . Good golf test . . . Picturesque . . . Used all my clubs . . . Small greens . . . Fairways need work . . . Tough in wind . . . Outstanding 18th hole . . . A tree-lined slicer's nightmare . . . Challenging course . . . Strict dress code . . . Former country club . . . Great old course . . . Good variety of holes . . . Used to be private club and has seen better days.

★★★ LOST CREEK GOLF CLUB
PU—Rte. No. 35, Oakland Mills (717)463-2450.
Call club for further information.
Subscriber comments: Great course for the price . . . Country

atmosphere . . . Beautiful scenery . . . Nice people . . . Walking permitted
. . . Beautiful setting . . . Mountains nearby . . . Amish in horse and
buggies travel surrounding roads . . . A hidden gem . . . Great scenery in
fall . . . Excellent large greens and fine finishing holes.

★★ MACOBY RUN GOLF COURSE

PU—5275 McLeans Station Rd., Green Lane (215)541-0161.
20 miles southeast of Allentown. **Holes:** 18. **Par:** 72/N/A.
Yards: 6,319/N/A. **Course rating:** 69.5/N/A. **Slope:** 118/N/A.
Opened: 1991. **Pace of Play rating:** N/A. **Green fee:** $11/16.
Credit cards: None. **Reduced fees:** Low season, Twilight, Seniors,
Juniors.
Caddies: No. **Golf carts:** $9 for 18 holes.
Discount golf packages: No. **Season:** Year-round. **High:** May-Sept.
On-site lodging: No. **Rental clubs:** Yes.
Walking policy: Unrestricted walking. **Range:** Yes (grass).
To obtain tee times: Call seven days in advance.
Subscriber comments: Wide open and difficult . . . Long course lots of
fun to play . . . Tough walking front nine . . . Course is a nicely designed
on rolling farmland in hill area . . . Testy little tract . . . Something for all
levels . . . No bunkers . . . Simple layout . . . Great bar . . . Some trick
holes . . . Getting better every year . . . Treat everyone great . . . Family
owned . . . Wide but cannot spray shots . . . Very interesting . . . Will be
excellent when mature . . . New course but coming along . . . Hilly,
several great holes . . . Back nine needs maturing . . . Best food for miles
around! . . . Exceptional family-run restaurant.

★★★ MAJESTIC RIDGE GOLF CLUB

PU—2437 Adin Lane, Chambersburg (717)267-3444.
Call club for further information.
Subscriber comments: Great scenery . . . Lots of hills and blind shots . . .
One of the best new courses in area . . . Much improved . . . First year I
hated it but I'm fast falling in love . . . Lots of hills . . . Streams . . .
Doglegs . . . Place drives with irons . . . Very hilly . . . Blind shots . . .
Maturing nicely . . . Some great holes of golf . . . Too many holes to lay up
from tees.

★½ MANADA GOLF CLUB

PU—R.D. No.1, Box 5250, Grantville (717)469-2400.
15 miles north of Harrisburg. **Holes:** 18. **Par:** 72/72.
Yards: 6,705/5,276. **Course rating:** 70.7/68.8. **Slope:** 117/111.
Opened: 1963. **Pace of Play rating:** 4:00-5:00. **Green fee:** $14/18.
Credit cards: MC, V. **Reduced fees:** Weekdays, Low season, Twilight,
Seniors, Juniors.
Caddies: No. **Golf carts:** $11 for 18 holes.
Discount golf packages: No. **Season:** Year-round. **High:** April-Sept.
On-site lodging: No. **Rental clubs:** Yes.
Walking policy: Unrestricted walking. **Range:** Yes.
To obtain tee times: Weekends phone early.
Subscriber comments: Wide open . . . Let 'em fly public course . . .
Nothing outstanding . . . Needs water . . . Nice course . . . Greens were
hard and fast . . . In good shape during rain . . . Golf course dry during
peak season . . . You get what you pay for here . . . Wide-open course . . .
Public course condition.

★★ MANOR GOLF CLUB

PU—Brian Rd., Sinking Spring (215)678-9597.
Call club for further information.
Subscriber comments: Short . . . Very visually appealing . . . Fast
rounds . . . Short but nice . . . Scenic . . . Very nice atmosphere . . . Too
hilly for me . . . Fairly easy course . . . Front nine wide open, back nine
tree-lined . . . Tight course . . . Hilly . . . Woods . . . Need to be accurate
. . . Many blind shots . . . Short . . . Blind second shots . . . Very hilly.

★½ MANOR VALLEY GOLF CLUB

PU—2095 Denmark Manor Rd., Export (412)744-4242.
28 miles east of Pittsburgh. **Holes:** 18. **Par:** 72/79.
Yards: 6,327/6,327. **Course rating:** 69.9/71.7. **Slope:** N/A.
Opened: 1963. **Pace of Play rating:** 4:00. **Green fee:** $13/14.
Credit cards: None. **Reduced fees:** Seniors.
Caddies: No. **Golf carts:** $9 for 18 holes.
Discount golf packages: No. **Season:** March-Dec. **High:** April-Oct.
On-site lodging: No. **Rental clubs:** Yes.
Walking policy: Unrestricted walking. **Range:** Yes.
To obtain tee times: Call anytime.
Subscriber comments: Quiet . . . Easy place to get swing right . . . Fair
. . . Not many hazards . . . Great for seniors . . . Beautiful scenery . . .
Crowned greens hard to hold . . . Greens and course hard as a rock in
summer . . . Greens small . . . Almost all elevated . . . Too firm.

★½ MAYAPPLE GOLF LINKS

PU—1 Mayapple Dr., Carlisle (717)258-4088.
15 miles south of Harrisburg. **Holes:** 18. **Par:** 71/72.
Yards: 6,541/5,595. **Course rating:** 71.3/69.6. **Slope:** 116/114.
Opened: 1992. **Pace of Play rating:** 4:00. **Green fee:** $12/19.
Credit cards: MC, V, AMEX. **Reduced fees:** Weekdays, Low season,
Resort guests, Twilight, Seniors.
Caddies: No. **Golf carts:** $30 for 18 holes.
Discount golf packages: No. **Season:** Year-round. **High:** May-Sept.
On-site lodging: No. **Rental clubs:** No.
Walking policy: Unrestricted walking. **Range:** Yes (grass).
To obtain tee times: Call up to one week in advance.
Subscriber comments: Some interesting holes . . . Wide open . . . New
course . . . Must mature . . . Has one great par 5 . . . No trees . . . Wide
open . . . Not very challenging . . . Tough course first time out . . . Greens
small and hard to hit . . . Good short game is essential . . . Some very short
holes . . . Interesting design and features. Will improve with age . . . Two
or three good holes . . . About as British as an English muffin.

★★★ MAYFIELD GOLF CLUB

PU—I-80 Exit 9N Pa. Rte. 68, Clarion (814)226-8888.
90 miles north of Pittsburgh. **Holes:** 18. **Par:** 72/72.
Yards: 6,990/5,439. **Course rating:** 73.0/71.0. **Slope:** 117/118.
Opened: 1974. **Pace of Play rating:** 4:00. **Green fee:** $12/22.
Credit cards: None. **Reduced fees:** Weekdays.
Caddies: No. **Golf carts:** $10 for 18 holes.
Discount golf packages: Yes. **Season:** April-Oct. **High:** June-Aug.
On-site lodging: Yes. **Rental clubs:** No.
Walking policy: Walking at certain times. **Range:** Yes (grass).
To obtain tee times: Call.
Subscriber comments: Greens considerably sloped . . . Don't get above
hole . . . Challenging greens, otherwise forgiving . . . Very nice course . . .
Back nine a challenge . . . Good for all levels of play . . . Front wide open,
some tight spots on back nine.

★★½ MEADOWINK GOLF CLUB

PU—4076 Bulltown Rd., Murrysville (412)327-8243.
20 miles east of Pittsburgh. **Holes:** 18. **Par:** 72/72.
Yards: 6,139/5,103. **Course rating:** 68.2/66.9. **Slope:** 125/118.
Opened: 1970. **Pace of Play rating:** 4:00-4:30. **Green fee:** $15/18.
Credit cards: MC, V. **Reduced fees:** Weekdays, Low season, Seniors.
Caddies: No. **Golf carts:** $9 for 18 holes.
Discount golf packages: Yes. **Season:** Year-round. **High:** April-Sept.
On-site lodging: No. **Rental clubs:** Yes.
Walking policy: Unrestricted walking. **Range:** No.
To obtain tee times: Call one week in advance. One year in advance for
group outings over 16 people.
Subscriber comments: Confidence builder! Short . . . Beautiful course
. . . Not for the faint of heart . . . Demanding . . . Take extra balls for the

back nine . . . No. 11 is the best par 3 in the area . . . Short holes . . . Some target golf . . . Tight holes . . . Nice layout . . . Good service . . . Too many blind holes . . . Enjoyable, well-maintained course.

★½ MERCER PUBLIC GOLF COURSE
PU—Rte. No.58 and Golf Rd., Mercer (412)662-9951.
60 miles north of Pittsburgh. **Holes:** 18. **Par:** 72/72.
Yards: 6,194/5,366. **Course rating:** 70.4/69.9. **Slope:** 111/111.
Opened: 1959. **Pace of Play rating:** 4:30. **Green fee:** $12/15.
Credit cards: None. **Reduced fees:** Low season, Seniors.
Caddies: No. **Golf carts:** $9 for 18 holes.
Discount golf packages: No. **Season:** Year-round. **High:** May-Sept.
On-site lodging: No. **Rental clubs:** Yes.
Walking policy: Walking at certain times. **Range:** Yes (grass).
To obtain tee times: Call pro shop.
Subscriber comments: Short, well maintained . . . Picturesque . . . Tight but short . . . Nice public course . . . Good 19th hole.

★ MIDDLETOWN COUNTRY CLUB
PU—420 North Bellevue Ave., Langhorne (215)757-6953.
14 miles north of Philadelphia. **Holes:** 18. **Par:** 68/ 68.
Yards: 5,812/ 5,572. **Course rating:** N/A. **Slope:** N/A.
Opened: N/A. **Pace of Play rating:** 4:00-4:30. **Green fee:** $14/20.
Credit cards: All major. **Reduced fees:** Weekdays, Low season, Twilight, Seniors, Juniors.
Caddies: No. **Golf carts:** $12 for 18 holes.
Discount golf packages: Yes. **Season:** Year-round. **High:** May-Oct.
On-site lodging: No. **Rental clubs:** Yes.
Walking policy: Unrestricted walking. **Range:** No.
To obtain tee times: Call.
Subscriber comments: Poor condition . . . Short . . . Challenging course for all handicaps . . . Too short . . . Some real weak holes . . . Very strange layout . . . 82-yard par 3 downhill and 285-yard par 4 . . . Open but hilly . . . Some par 4s should be 3s.

★★★ MILL RACE GOLF COURSE
R—RR No.2, Benton (717)925-2040.
35 miles southeast of Wilke-Barre. **Holes:** 18. **Par:** 70/71.
Yards: 6,096/4,791. **Course rating:** 68.6/68.3. **Slope:** 126/122.
Opened: 1970. **Pace of Play rating:** 4:20. **Green fee:** $14/18.
Credit cards: MC, V. **Reduced fees:** Weekdays, Seniors, Juniors.
Caddies: No. **Golf carts:** $10 for 18 holes.
Discount golf packages: No. **Season:** March-Nov. **High:** May-Aug.
On-site lodging: No. **Rental clubs:** Yes.
Walking policy: Walking at certain times. **Range:** Yes (grass).
To obtain tee times: Call one week in advance.
Subscriber comments: Water comes into play . . . Plenty of water . . . Nice scenic course at base of mountain . . . Flat . . . Beautiful scenery . . . A real challenge from the blues . . . Some holes are quality . . . Water, water, water, like a Florida course.

★★ MOCCASIN RUN GOLF COURSE
PU—P.O. Box 172A, Schoff Rd., Atglen (610)593-7341.
40 miles west of Philadelphia. **Holes:** 18. **Par:** 72/72.
Yards: 6,336/5,275. **Course rating:** 69.0/67.7. **Slope:** 113/113.
Opened: 1988. **Pace of Play rating:** 4:30. **Green fee:** $15/20.
Credit cards: None. **Reduced fees:** Weekdays, Low season, Twilight, Seniors, Juniors.
Caddies: No. **Golf carts:** $10 for 18 holes.
Discount golf packages: Yes. **Season:** Year-round. **High:** April-Oct.
On-site lodging: No. **Rental clubs:** Yes.
Walking policy: Unrestricted walking. **Range:** Yes (grass).
To obtain tee times: Call one week in advance.
Subscriber comments: Many wedge shots to greens . . . Give it five years

to mature . . . Great finishing hole . . . Great greens . . . Very good . . . Wide open, you can hit it anywhere . . . Wonderful course . . . Very friendly staff . . . Great scenery . . . Good back nine . . . Very good condition . . . Very open . . . Nice holes on back nine . . . First few holes can be dangerous . . . Fairly new . . . Nice layout.

★★★ MOHAWK TRAILS GOLF COURSE
PU—RD No.7, Box 243, New Castle (412)667-8570.
50 miles north of Pittsburgh. **Holes:** 18. **Par:** 72/N/A.
Yards: 6,324/N/A. **Course rating:** 70.3/N/A. **Slope:** 108/N/A.
Opened: 1965. **Pace of Play rating:** 4:30. **Green fee:** $13/14.
Credit cards: None. **Reduced fees:** Weekdays, Low season, Seniors.
Caddies: No. **Golf carts:** $8 for 18 holes.
Discount golf packages: No. **Season:** March-Dec. **High:** May-Sept.
On-site lodging: No. **Rental clubs:** Yes.
Walking policy: Unrestricted walking. **Range:** No.
To obtain tee times: Call on Wednesday for upcoming weekend. Weekday tee times for 12 or more.
Subscriber comments: Nice layout . . . Tends to burn out in summer . . . Well-groomed short course . . . Good staff . . . Great price . . . Heavy play, can be slow . . . Priced right, wide open.

★★★ MONROE VALLEY GOLF CLUB
PU—RD No.1, Jonestown (717)865-2375.
Call club for further information.
Subscriber comments: Wide open . . . Wind a big factor . . . Long course . . . Course favors long hitters . . . Nice views . . . Solid par 3s . . . Nestled between rows of mountains . . . Breathtaking views . . . Very fun course . . . Very good layout with several scenic mountain holes . . . Heavy play but maintenance OK . . . Usually well kept . . . Some challenging holes . . . Well kept with tough back nine.

★★★ MOUNT AIRY LODGE GOLF COURSE
R—42 Woodland Rd., Mount Pocono (717)839-8811x7088, (800)441-4410.
30 miles east of Scranton. **Holes:** 18. **Par:** 72/73.
Yards: 7,123/5,771. **Course rating:** 74.3/73.3. **Slope:** 138/122.
Opened: 1980. **Pace of Play rating:** 4:30. **Green fee:** $40/50.
Credit cards: All major. **Reduced fees:** Weekdays, Resort guests, Twilight.
Caddies: No. **Golf carts:** $16 for 18 holes.
Discount golf packages: Yes. **Season:** April-Nov. **High:** May-Sept.
On-site lodging: Yes. **Rental clubs:** Yes.
Walking policy: Mandatory cart. **Range:** Yes.
To obtain tee times: Call any time of year, but at least two weeks in advance.
Subscriber comments: Conditons, staff, amenities very fine . . . Great views and layout . . . Very good condition . . . Too many blind shots . . . Best scenery in northeast Pennsylvania. Good course for average golfer . . . Relatively open, rough is kept short . . . Slow on weeekends . . . Resort golf . . . Overrated . . . For the price, fun if you have a lot of time . . . A great course, long and challenging . . . Scenic beauty . . . Outstanding scenery . . . Was once a great course, needs maintenance . . . Tight, hilly.

★★ MOUNT ODIN PARK GOLF CLUB
PU—Mt. Odin Park Dr., Greensburg (412)834-2640.
30 miles east of Pittsburgh. **Holes:** 18. **Par:** 70/72.
Yards: 5,395/4,733. **Course rating:** 65.0/68.0. **Slope:** 108/104.
Opened: 1935. **Pace of Play rating:** 3:30-4:00. **Green fee:** $13/15.
Credit cards: None. **Reduced fees:** N/A.
Caddies: No. **Golf carts:** $8 for 18 holes.
Discount golf packages: Yes. **Season:** Year-round. **High:** April-Sept.
On-site lodging: No. **Rental clubs:** Yes.
Walking policy: Unrestricted walking. **Range:** Yes (grass).

To obtain tee times: Come in person weekend prior or call on Monday for upcoming weekend.
Subscriber comments: Very hilly . . . Course is nice . . . Needs work . . . Too short . . . Very hilly . . . Well kept . . . Fun course . . . Extremely tight . . . . Beautiful views, best value . . . Manageable distances . . . Short . . . Too many blind shots.

★★★½ MOUNTAIN LAUREL GOLF CLUB

R—Rte. 534 & I80, White Haven (717)443-7424, (800)458-5921.
80 miles northeast of Philadelphia. **Holes:** 18. **Par:** 72/72.
Yards: 6,798/5,631. **Course rating:** 72.3/71.9. **Slope:** 113/113.
Opened: 1969. **Pace of Play rating:** 4:30. **Green fee:** $40/50.
Credit cards: All major. **Reduced fees:** Low season, Resort guests, Twilight, Seniors.
Caddies: No. **Golf carts:** Included in Green Fee.
Discount golf packages: Yes. **Season:** April-Nov. **High:** June-Aug.
On-site lodging: Yes. **Rental clubs:** Yes.
Walking policy: Walking at certain times. **Range:** Yes (grass).
To obtain tee times: Tee times are required with a credit card to guarantee.
Subscriber comments: Good resort-type golf course . . . Pretty surroundings . . . One of the best in area . . . Price reflects Pocono region . . . Good resort course . . . Nice scenery . . . Interesting short holes . . . A nice layout for all players . . . Nicest course in the Poconos . . . Great layout . . . Bear from the tips . . . Back nine traffic . . . Starts out slow . . . Awesome after first three holes.

MOUNTAIN MANOR INN AND GOLF CLUB

SP—Creek Rd., Marshall's Creek (717)223-1290.
100 miles north of Philadelphia.
Opened: 1945. **Pace of Play rating:** 4:30. **Green fee:** $14/24.
Credit cards: None. **Reduced fees:** Weekdays, Low season, Resort guests, Twilight.
Caddies: No. **Golf carts:** $25 for 18 holes.
Discount golf packages: Yes. **Season:** April-Oct. **High:** April-Oct.
On-site lodging: Yes. **Rental clubs:** Yes.
Walking policy: Unrestricted walking. **Range:** Yes (grass).
To obtain tee times: No tee times.
Also has 18-hole par-3 course
★★½ BLUE/YELLOW
Holes: 18. **Par:** 71/71.
Yards: 6,233/5,079. **Course rating:** 68.5/68.5. **Slope:** 115/115.
Subscriber comments: Blue and Yellow are very spacious . . . Silver and Orange can rattle anyone . . . Good for walking at any age . . . Fun to play . . . Flat, boring . . . Hard in summer . . . Greens hard and very small . . . Great par 4s . . . Fun resort course . . . Maintained well . . . Crowded in season . . . Flat, nice walk . . . Wide open . . . Bland.
★★½ ORANGE/SILVER
Holes: 18. **Par:** 73/73.
Yards: 6,426/5,146. **Course rating:** 71.0/ 71.5. **Slope:** 132/ 124.
Subscriber comments: Fun and challenging . . . A lot of uphill, downhill lies . . . Tough mountain course . . . Lots of hilly lies . . . Good condition . . . Several unusual holes . . . Hilly . . . Long . . . Silver course brings you to your knees in first three holes . . . Can you imagine a real par 6? . . . Resort course with par 6! Take a guide or caddie . . . Orange is nicest of the two . . . Unusual course . . . Excellent condition . . . Hilly.

★★ MOUNTAIN VALLEY GOLF COURSE

PU—Burma Rd., Mahanoy City (717)467-2242.
Call club for further information.
Subscriber comments: Great possibilities . . . Hilly course cut into mountains . . . Love it! Condition could improve but excellent layout . . . Difficult walk.

★ MULBERRY HILL GOLF CLUB

PU—RD No.6, Box 2057, Mt. Pleasant (412)547-1909.
17 miles southeast of Pittsburgh. **Holes:** 18. **Par:** 72/71.
Yards: 6,147/4,655. **Course rating:** 68.4/72.0. **Slope:** 122/121.
Opened: 1983. **Pace of Play rating:** 4:00. **Green fee:** $14/14.
Credit cards: MC, V. **Reduced fees:** Weekdays, Low season, Seniors,
Juniors.
Caddies: No. **Golf carts:** $10 for 18 holes.
Discount golf packages: No. **Season:** Year-round. **High:** April-Oct.
On-site lodging: No. **Rental clubs:** Yes.
Walking policy: Walking at certain times. **Range:** No.
To obtain tee times: Call 7 a.m. - 9 a.m., first come first served.
Subscriber comments: Poorly-designed course . . . Poorly maintained
. . . Too many blind holes . . . Good service . . . Nice clubhouse . . . Hilly
with blind shots . . . Too much in such a small area . . . Nice scenery . . .
Pretty course.

★ MURRYSVILLE GOLF CLUB

PU—3804 Sardis Rd., Murrysville (412)327-0726.
20 miles east of Pittsburgh. **Holes:** 18. **Par:** 70/74.
Yards: 5,575/5,250. **Course rating:** 64.4/67.2. **Slope:** 99/107.
Opened: 1938. **Pace of Play rating:** 4:00. **Green fee:** $14/16.
Credit cards: None. **Reduced fees:** Seniors.
Caddies: No. **Golf carts:** $9 for 18 holes.
Discount golf packages: No. **Season:** April-Nov. **High:** June-Aug.
On-site lodging: No. **Rental clubs:** Yes.
Walking policy: Unrestricted walking. **Range:** No.
Subscriber comments: Fair . . . Not much trouble . . . No sand . . . No
water hazards . . . OK as practice course . . . Nothing fancy . . . Wide
open, easy course.

NEMACOLIN WOODLANDS RESORT

R—Rte. 40E., Farmington (412)329-6111, (800)422-2736.
50 miles southeast of Pittsburgh.
Credit cards: MC, V, AMEX.
Caddies: No. **Golf carts:** Included in Green Fee.
Discount golf packages: Yes. **Season:** April-Nov. **High:** May-Oct.
On-site lodging: Yes. **Rental clubs:** Yes.
Walking policy: Mandatory cart. **Range:** Yes (grass).
To obtain tee times: Resort guests call 45 days in advance. Daily fee may
call seven days in advance.

MYSTIC ROCK GOLF CLUB★

Holes: 18. **Par:** 72/72.
Yards: 7,196/4,991. **Course rating:** 73.7/69.9. **Slope:** 161/124.
Opened: 1995. **Pace of Play rating:** 4:30. **Green fee:** $79/90.
Reduced fees: Low season.

★★★½ THE LINKS GOLF CLUB

Holes: 18. **Par:** 71/71.
Yards: 6,814/4,825. **Course rating:** 73.0/68.1. **Slope:** 131/115.
Opened: 1976. **Pace of Play rating:** 4:20. **Green fee:** $55/62.
Reduced fees: Weekdays, Low season, Twilight.
Subscriber comments: In top shape always . . . A fun layout . . .
Challenging . . . Shortish course . . . Fun to play . . . Well groomed . . . A
lot of steep ups and downs . . . Blind greens make first couple of rounds
difficult . . . My wife and I play here about 40 times a year . . . It is located
on a mountain top, hence it is very scenic, but not many hills . . . Beautiful
mountain course, some long, tough holes . . . Nice design . . . Resort is
fabulous . . . Course always in great shape . . . Think you've got the course
down until you reach Nos. 16, 17, and 18 . . . Great mountain resort . . .
Enjoyable resort atmosphere.

★★ NORTH FORK GOLF AND TENNIS CLUB

SP—RD No.4, Box 218, Johnstown (814)288-2822.
65 miles west of Pittsburgh. **Holes:** 18. **Par:** 72/72.

Yards: 6,470/5,762. **Course rating:** 71.1/72.0. **Slope:** 124/114.
Opened: 1934. **Pace of Play rating:** 3:30. **Green fee:** $16/18.
Credit cards: MC, V, AMEX. **Reduced fees:** Seniors, Juniors.
Caddies: No. **Golf carts:** $9 for 18 holes.
Discount golf packages: No. **Season:** April-Oct. **High:** June-Aug.
On-site lodging: No. **Rental clubs:** No.
Walking policy: Unrestricted walking. **Range:** No.
To obtain tee times: Call up to seven days in advance. Open to the public Monday, Wednesday and Friday after 2 p.m.
Subscriber comments: Challenging layout . . . What an improvement . . . Nothing exceptional . . . Variety of holes . . . Good greens . . . Just an average course . . . Fine course.

★★★ NORTH HILLS GOLF CLUB

PU—1450 N. Center St., Corry (814)664-4477.
24 miles southeast of Erie. **Holes:** 18. **Par:** 71/72.
Yards: 6,800/5,146. **Course rating:** 71.0/71.4. **Slope:** 115/119.
Opened: 1967. **Pace of Play rating:** 4:00. **Green fee:** $11/17.
Credit cards: None. **Reduced fees:** Weekdays, Low season, Twilight.
Caddies: No. **Golf carts:** $10 for 18 holes.
Discount golf packages: No. **Season:** April-Oct. **High:** July-Aug.
On-site lodging: No. **Rental clubs:** Yes.
Walking policy: Unrestricted walking. **Range:** No.
To obtain tee times: First come, first served.
Subscriber comments: Nice old, mature course . . . Challenging . . . Four great finishing holes . . . This is a very nice public course . . . Well managed.

★★½ NORTH PARK GOLF COURSE

PU—Kummer Rd., Allison Park (412)935-1967.
Call club for further information.
Subscriber comments: Short and hilly . . . Great value for a well-maintained county course . . . Short, gimmicky holes . . . Tough from back tees . . . Excellent county-owned course, tournament caliber . . . Good muny but playable . . . Good shape for amount of play . . . Wide open, good place to learn the game . . . Very good par 3s.

★★½ NORTHAMPTON VALLEY COUNTRY CLUB

SP—Rte. 332, Richboro (215)355-2234.
15 miles northeast of Philadelphia. **Holes:** 18. **Par:** 71/76.
Yards: 6,377/5,586. **Course rating:** 69.2/70.0. **Slope:** 123/118.
Opened: 1964. **Pace of Play rating:** 4:30. **Green fee:** $15/27.
Credit cards: MC, V, AMEX. **Reduced fees:** Weekdays, Twilight, Seniors.
Caddies: No. **Golf carts:** $13 for 18 holes.
Discount golf packages: No. **Season:** Year-round. **High:** April-Oct.
On-site lodging: No. **Rental clubs:** Yes.
Walking policy: Walking at certain times. **Range:** No.
To obtain tee times: Call one week in advance for weekends only.
Subscriber comments: Flat, not very inventive . . . Boring layout . . . Lots of similar holes . . . Nice greens . . . Tight course but straight . . . Good condition . . . Nice course . . . Big greens . . . Course was in good condition . . . Played slow . . . 18th hole best very short par 4 I've ever seen . . . Radar-equipped putter a must.

★★ OAKBROOK GOLF COURSE

PU—RD No.1, Box 102, Stoystown (814)629-5892.
60 miles east of Pittsburgh. **Holes:** 18. **Par:** 71/73.
Yards: 5,935/5,530. **Course rating:** 67.4/70.4. **Slope:** 109/113.
Opened: 1955. **Pace of Play rating:** 4:30. **Green fee:** $14/16.
Credit cards: None. **Reduced fees:** N/A.
Caddies: No. **Golf carts:** N/A.
Discount golf packages: No. **Season:** April-Nov. **High:** June-Aug.
On-site lodging: No. **Rental clubs:** Yes.

Walking policy: Unrestricted walking. **Range:** Yes (grass).
To obtain tee times: Ball back system.
Subscriber comments: Basic public course . . . Condition vary . . . Fun
to play . . . Front nine is better than back nine . . . Short . . . Good scoring
course . . . Nice views . . . Very friendly staff.

★★ OVERLOOK GOLF COURSE
PU—2040 Lititz Pike, Lancaster (717)569-9551.
60 miles west of Philadelphia. **Holes:** 18. **Par:** 70/71.
Yards: 6,100/4,962. **Course rating:** 69.2/68.4. **Slope:** 110/113.
Opened: 1930. **Pace of Play rating:** 4:30. **Green fee:** $14/21.
Credit cards: MC, V. **Reduced fees:** Low season, Seniors.
Caddies: No. **Golf carts:** $11 for 18 holes.
Discount golf packages: No. **Season:** Year-round. **High:** May-Aug.
On-site lodging: No. **Rental clubs:** Yes.
Walking policy: Unrestricted walking. **Range:** No.
To obtain tee times: Call one week in advance for weekends only.
Subscriber comments: Wide open . . . Fairly easy course . . . Getting
better all the time . . . Too many parallel fairways close together . . . Fairly
flat and easy . . . Good course . . . Back and forth, not very challenging . . .
Unusual design, par 4s either very long or very short . . . I played over 100
rounds here in 1994 . . . A hidden gem and getting better . . . Great staff
. . . Beautiful setting for golf course . . . Boring . . . Straightaway holes
. . . Crowded . . . Difficult to get into trouble . . . Few memorable holes.

★★★ PARK GOLF COURSE
PU—RD 4, Conneaut Lake (814)382-9974.
Call club for further information.
Subscriber comments: Very short . . . Nice level golf course . . . Not
long . . . Interesting layout . . . Confidence booster . . . Easy to score . . .
All-around great course . . . Atmosphere, value fun . . . Beautiful greens
. . . Watch out for creeks.

★★½ PARK HILLS COUNTRY CLUB
PU—Highland Ave., Altoona (814)944-2631.
Call club for further information.
Subscriber comments: Nothing special . . . Some holes are weird . . .
Course stays soft after heavy rains . . . Driver-sand wedge course . . . Great
course . . . Good challenge . . . Short course.

★★★ PAXON HOLLOW COUNTRY CLUB
SP—850 Paxon Hollow Rd., Media (215)353-0220.
Call club for further information.
Subscriber comments: Fantastic greens . . . Great shotmaking necessary
. . . Course is challenging and in great shape . . . Plenty of woods . . .
Short but challenging . . . Below average clubhouse . . . Good condition
. . . Very hilly . . . Short . . . Good tune-up course . . . Excellent condition
. . . Beautiful course, scenery . . . Short but difficult and tight . . . Good
old golf course . . . Short but fun . . . 18th is absolute bear . . . Tough to
walk . . . Hilly . . . Short . . . Tight course . . . Excellent greens . . . Fun to
play No. 17, a par 3 downhill 110 yards. . . . Beautiful vistas . . . Short but
sweet . . . Fun to play.

★★★½ PENN NATIONAL GOLF CLUB
SP—3720 Clubhouse Dr., Fayetteville (717)352-3000, (800)221-7366.
39 miles northeast of Harrisburg. **Holes:** 18. **Par:** 72/72.
Yards: 6,919/5,331. **Course rating:** 73.2/70.1. **Slope:** 129/116.
Opened: 1968. **Pace of Play rating:** 4:00-5:00. **Green fee:** $18/27.
Credit cards: MC, V. **Reduced fees:** Low season, Twilight, Seniors,
Juniors.
Caddies: No. **Golf carts:** $13 for 18 holes.
Discount golf packages: Yes. **Season:** Year-round. **High:** May-Oct.
On-site lodging: Yes. **Rental clubs:** Yes.
Walking policy: Walking at certain times. **Range:** Yes (grass).
To obtain tee times: Call.

Subscriber comments: Beautiful layout in mountains . . . Tough driving course . . . Friendly staff . . . Easy walking . . . Beautiful course . . . Challenging layout . . . Minimal clubhouse . . . Very mature well-maintained course, fairways and greens excellent . . . Views beautiful, well worth the trip . . . Best-kept secret in the northeast . . . Great layout . . . Mature trees . . . Some tight holes . . . Good par 3s . . . A challenging, fun-to-play course . . . Very modest clubhouse . . . Friendly staff . . . Afternoon rates are great for a course of high caliber . . . Definitely a "must play" . . . Cordial service . . . Great shape . . . Staff and service good . . . Open course . . . Good for anyone . . . Good shape.

PENNSYLVANIA STATE UNIVERSITY GOLF COURSE
PU—1523 West College Ave., State College (814)865-4653.
90 miles southeast of Harrisburg.
Pace of Play rating: 4:00-4:30.
Credit cards: MC, V, DISC. **Reduced fees:** Twilight.
Caddies: No. **Golf carts:** $10 for 18 holes.
Discount golf packages: Yes. **Season:** March-Nov. **High:** June-Sept.
On-site lodging: Yes. **Rental clubs:** Yes.
Walking policy: Walking at certain times. **Range:** Yes.
To obtain tee times: Call up to one week in advance.
★★★½ **BLUE COURSE**
Holes: 18. **Par:** 72/72.
Yards: 6,525/5,128. **Course rating:** 72.0/69.8. **Slope:** 128/118.
Opened: 1970. **Green fee:** $23.
Subscriber comments: Better of two courses . . . Recently revised . . . Interesting . . . Challenging course . . . Great layout . . . Well kept . . . Just beautiful . . . Average golfer will not break 85 . . . New holes are great . . . New back nine is great . . . Excellent course . . . Tough to get on . . . New back nine needs to mature . . . New holes couple years away . . . Fairly flat . . . As a Penn State grad, I can't believe they killed "Old Blue" with the new design.
★★½ **WHITE COURSE**
Holes: 18. **Par:** 70/70.
Yards: 6,008/5,212. **Course rating:** 68.2/69.4. **Slope:** 115/116.
Opened: 1994. **Green fee:** $18.
Subscriber comments: Anything at Penn State is outstanding, Go Lions! . . . Not as good as Blue Course . . . Flat, open course . . . Long walks between greens and tees (which isn't bad) . . . Good variety of par 3s . . . Course has great potential . . . Needs attention . . . Not nearly as good as Blue Course . . . Still a good value . . . Enjoyable to play over and over . . . Good golf on an OK layout . . . Easy . . . Wide open . . . A few nice holes, but very long walk . . . Historic . . . Short but challenging.

★½ **PERRY GOLF COURSE**
PU—220 Zion's Church Rd., Shoemakersville (610)562-3510.
Call club for further information.
Subscriber comments: Wide open field . . . Front nine poor, Back nine great . . . Muddy in spring . . . Nothing tough . . . No hazards . . . The course is OK . . . Staff is great . . . For beginners to average player . . . Good pace . . . Wide open . . . Postage stamp greens . . . Walking permitted . . . Wide open short course . . . Good place to learn to play.

★★½ **PICKERING VALLEY GOLF CLUB**
PU—South White Horse Rd., Phoenixville (610)933-2223.
20 miles west of Philadelphia. **Holes:** 18. **Par:** 72/72.
Yards: 6,530/5,235. **Course rating:** 70.3/64.5. **Slope:** 122/111.
Opened: 1985. **Pace of Play rating:** 4:30-5:00. **Green fee:** $18/22.
Credit cards: None. **Reduced fees:** Weekdays, Twilight, Seniors.
Caddies: No. **Golf carts:** Included in Green Fee.
Discount golf packages: Yes. **Season:** Year-round. **High:** April-Oct.
On-site lodging: No. **Rental clubs:** Yes.
Walking policy: Walking at certain times. **Range:** Yes (grass).
To obtain tee times: Call seven days in advance on weekends.

Subscriber comments: An average course . . . Wide open . . . Pace good . . . Nice layout . . . Good for all levels . . . Staff and service OK . . . Slow at times . . . Friendly staff . . . Hilly . . . Variety of holes . . . Pretty in fall . . . OK public course . . . Very scenic . . . Ups and downs . . . Nice greens . . . Very hilly . . . Back nine is tighter . . . Slow play . . . Excellent service . . . Closest course to corporate corridor, very heavy play . . . Tough greens . . . Three-putt heaven . . . Difficult to walk especially back . . . Great design . . . Huge greens . . . Watch for four putts . . . 18th hole great . . . . Back nine is delightful and tight . . . Very challenging, tough par 3s . . . Great terrain . . . Nice staff.

★★★½ PINE ACRES COUNTRY CLUB
SP—1401 W. Warren Rd., Bradford (814)362-2005.
80 miles south of Buffalo, N.Y. **Holes:** 18. **Par:** 72/72.
Yards: 6,700/5,600. **Course rating:** 70.3/72.3. **Slope:** 120/120.
Opened: 1965. **Pace of Play rating:** 4:00. **Green fee:** $16/22.
Credit cards: MC, V. **Reduced fees:** Weekdays, Low season, Seniors, Juniors.
Caddies: No. **Golf carts:** $9 for 18 holes.
Discount golf packages: No. **Season:** April-Oct. **High:** June-Aug.
On-site lodging: No. **Rental clubs:** Yes.
Walking policy: Unrestricted walking. **Range:** Yes (grass).
To obtain tee times: Call one week in advance for weekends and holidays only.
Subscriber comments: Very well maintained . . . Variety of shots and lies challenging . . . Best course in area . . . Very scenic . . . Creeks and mountains.

★★½ PINE CREST GOLF CLUB
PU—101 Country Club Dr., Lansdale (215)855-6112.
Call club for further information.
Subscriber comments: Long distance from some greens to next tee makes walking almost impossible . . . Some good holes . . . Nice course but too overdeveloped with townhouses . . . Short course from back tees but very enjoyable . . . Well groomed . . . Very short course . . . Only two par 5s but always in good shape . . . Sporty layout . . . Nice greens . . . No range a minus . . . Nice restaurant.

★★★ PINE GROVE GOLF COURSE
PU—401 Diamond Rd., Grove City (412)458-9942.
Call club for further information.
Subscriber comments: Average-length flat course . . . Great layout . . . Nice setting . . . Easy to walk . . . Treated well . . . Price good and run well . . . Great position golf . . . Water on five holes . . . Friendly owners . . . Short and tight . . . Great layout . . . Decent price . . . Easy to walk and fun to play.

PINE HILL GOLF COURSE*
PU—263 Leech Rd., Greenville (412)588-8053.
Call club for further information.

★ PINE HILLS GOLF COURSE
PU—140 S. Keyser Ave, Taylor (717)562-0138.
Call club for further information.
Subscriber comments: Located inside city limits . . . Lots of play because of location . . . Fair condition . . . Always busy . . . Young course . . . Excellent condition . . . Very reasonable rates . . . Needs a lot of work . . . Short and straight . . . No trouble . . . Confidence builder . . . Good place for youngsters to learn the game . . . Boring design but dries from rain quickly.

★★½ PITTSBURGH NORTH GOLF CLUB
PU—3800 Bakerstown Rd., Bakerstown (412)443-3800.
16 miles north of Pittsburgh. **Holes:** 18. **Par:** 72/73.
Yards: 7,021/5,075. **Course rating:** 68.8/68.3. **Slope:** 128/114.

Opened: 1950. **Pace of Play rating:** 4:30. **Green fee:** $15/20.
Credit cards: None. **Reduced fees:** Low season, Seniors, Juniors.
Caddies: No. **Golf carts:** $18 for 18 holes.
Discount golf packages: No. **Season:** Year-round. **High:** June-Aug.
On-site lodging: No. **Rental clubs:** Yes.
Walking policy: Walking at certain times. **Range:** Yes.
To obtain tee times: Call 7 days in advance.
Subscriber comments: All agree it's a good course . . . Hilly but a good test . . . Ball is always above or below your feet . . . Conditions great even in summer heat.

★★ PLEASANT VALLEY GOLF CLUB

PU—R.D. No.4, Box 4164, Stewartstown (717)993-2184.
22 miles north of Towson, Md. **Holes:** 18. **Par:** 72/74.
Yards: 6,540/5,250. **Course rating:** 69.4/70.5. **Slope:** 119/117.
Opened: 1964. **Pace of Play rating:** 4:15. **Green fee:** $12/15.
Credit cards: MC, V. **Reduced fees:** Weekdays, Low season, Twilight, Seniors, Junior

Caddies: No. **Golf carts:** $10 for 18 holes.
Discount golf packages: Yes. **Season:** Year-round. **High:** March-Oct.
On-site lodging: No. **Rental clubs:** Yes.
Walking policy: Unrestricted walking. **Range:** No.
To obtain tee times: Call. Credit card needed to hold reservation.
Subscriber comments: Tough crowned, fast greens . . . Plenty of value packages for money conscious golfer . . . Wide-open farm course with hard greens . . . Excellent . . . Weekday deal including breakfast, lunch, and 18 holes . . . Gets boring since most of it is back-and-forth over former farmland . . . Long par 4s . . . Very nice course with great scenery . . . Most of course is fairly open . . . Straightforward . . . Fun for everyone . . . Busy . . . Super view . . . Some very interesting holes . . . Fair value but nothing exciting . . . Decent . . . Hard getting tee time.

PLEASANT VALLEY GOLF COURSE★

PU—R.R. No.1, Box 58, Vintondale (814)446-6244.
10 miles north of Johnstown. **Holes:** 18. **Par:** 71/72.
Yards: 6,498/5,361. **Course rating:** 69.8/70.3. **Slope:** 124/115.
Opened: 1966. **Pace of Play rating:** 4:00. **Green fee:** $13/15.
Credit cards: MC, V, DISC. **Reduced fees:** Weekdays, Low season, Juniors.
Caddies: No. **Golf carts:** $11 for 18 holes.
Discount golf packages: Yes. **Season:** March-Dec. **High:** May-Oct.
On-site lodging: No. **Rental clubs:** Yes.
Walking policy: Walking at certain times. **Range:** Yes (grass).
To obtain tee times: Call pro shop.
Subscriber comments: A nice day of golf for the money . . . Open . . . Good course for beginner . . . Could be a good layout . . . Greens need work.

POCONO MANOR INN AND GOLF CLUB

PU—P.O. Box 7, Pocono Manor (717)839-7111.
20 miles of Scranton.
Opened: N/A. **Pace of Play rating:** N/A. **Green fee:** N/A.
Credit cards: MC, V, AMEX. **Reduced fees:** Weekdays, Resort guests, Twilight.
Caddies: No. **Golf carts:** $28 for 18 holes.
Discount golf packages: Yes. **Season:** April-Nov. **High:** May-Oct.
On-site lodging: Yes. **Rental clubs:** No.
Walking policy: N/A. **Range:** Yes (grass).

★★ EAST COURSE

Holes: 18. **Par:** 72/72.
Yards: 6,480/6,113. **Course rating:** N/A. **Slope:** N/A.
Subscriber comments: Quaint mountain layout . . . Lot of blind shots . . . Many interesting holes . . . Poor condition . . . Needs TLC . . . Majestic old mountain course . . . Uninspired layout . . . Course could use some redesign . . . Small greens . . . Fairways tend to get dry in the

summer . . . Sporty mountain course . . . Fun to play . . . Good condition
. . . A lot of fun holes . . . Too short.

★½ WEST COURSE
Holes: 18. **Par:** 72/72.
Yards: 6,857/5,706. **Course rating:** N/A. **Slope:** N/A.
Subscriber comments: Uninteresting holes . . . Poor condition . . . Less
fun than East Course . . . West is easier . . . Long holes . . . Wide open . . .
Boring . . . Nice layout . . . Excellent staff . . . Fairly challenging and open
. . . Greens are small and hard . . . You need to play a nice, soft lob shot on
every hole.

★★ QUAIL VALLEY GOLF CLUB
SP—901 Teeter Rd., Littletown (717)359-8453.
45 miles northeast of Baltimore. **Holes:** 18. **Par:** 72/72.
Yards: 7,042/5,218. **Course rating:** 72.9/69.5. **Slope:** 123/113.
Opened: 1993. **Pace of Play rating:** 4:30–5:00. **Green fee:** $15/20.
Credit cards: MC, V. **Reduced fees:** Weekdays, Low season, Twilight,
Seniors.
Caddies: No. **Golf carts:** $10 for 18 holes.
Discount golf packages: No. **Season:** Year-round. **High:** March-Oct.
On-site lodging: No. **Rental clubs:** No.
Walking policy: Unrestricted walking. **Range:** Yes (grass).
To obtain tee times: Call one week in advance.
Subscriber comments: Will be tough when mature . . . Very good for
new course . . . Interesting . . . Best new course in central Pennsylvania
. . . 175-yard par-3 island hole . . . Fairly new course . . . Nice mix of open
and wooded . . . Will be nice in a few years . . . Plays long . . . All skill
levels can enjoy . . . A new two-year old course with lots of promise . . .
Pretty course . . . Potential is there to be a good course . . . Killer par 5 on
back.

★★★½ QUICKSILVER GOLF CLUB
PU—2000 Quicksilver Rd., Midway (412)796-1811.
18 miles west of Pittsburgh. **Holes:** 18. **Par:** 72/74.
Yards: 7,120/ 5,067. **Course rating:** 75.7/68.6. **Slope:** 145/115.
Opened: 1990. **Pace of Play rating:** 4:10. **Green fee:** $60.
Credit cards: All major. **Reduced fees:** Low season, Twilight, Seniors,
Juniors.
Caddies: No. **Golf carts:** $0 for 18 holes.
Discount golf packages: No. **Season:** March-Dec. **High:** May-Oct.
On-site lodging: No. **Rental clubs:** Yes.
Walking policy: Walking at certain times. **Range:** Yes (grass).
To obtain tee times: Call or come in five days in advance.
Subscriber comments: Top notch . . . Tough but fair . . . Fast greens . . .
Lacks scenery . . . A true test for all levels . . . World-class clubhouse . . .
Young course with lightning fast greens . . . Offers a true test for all . . .
Would play here every weekend if I wouldn't go broke before the golf
season was half over . . . Some great holes on back . . . Too many blind
shots . . . Long course . . . Watch out for wind . . . Tough course . . .
First-class facilities . . . Hosts Senior Tour event.

★★ RICH MAIDEN GOLF COURSE
PU—R.D. No.2, Box 2099, Fleetwood (610)926-1606.
10 miles south of Reading. **Holes:** 18. **Par:** 69/70.
Yards: 5,635/5,145. **Course rating:** 63.7/65.1. **Slope:** 97/ 99.
Opened: 1932. **Pace of Play rating:** N/A. **Green fee:** $13/19.
Credit cards: None. **Reduced fees:** Low season, Twilight, Seniors.
Caddies: No. **Golf carts:** $19 for 18 holes.
Discount golf packages: Yes. **Season:** Year-round. **High:** April-Sept.
On-site lodging: No. **Rental clubs:** Yes.
Walking policy: Unrestricted walking. **Range:** No.
To obtain tee times: Call or come in.
Subscriber comments: Lots of par 3s . . . In great shape . . . Wide open
. . . Not difficult . . . Nice course for all levels . . . Too crowded . . . Many
elevated greens . . . . Open . . . . Fun . . . Country setting . . . Ego builder

short course . . . Small, elevated greens . . . Fairly short . . . Nice layout
. . . . Very short track . . . Plain . . . Five or six nice holes . . . Very short
. . . Rarely need woods . . . A lot of short par 3s . . . Easy layout.

★★★½ RIVERSIDE GOLF COURSE

PU—RD No.2, Box 281, Cambridge Springs (814)398-4537.
18 miles of Erie. **Holes:** 18. **Par:** 70/70.
Yards: 6,113/5,232. **Course rating:** N/A. **Slope:** 116/117.
Opened: N/A. **Pace of Play rating:** N/A. **Green fee:** N/A.
Credit cards: MC, V. **Reduced fees:** Weekdays, Low season, Twilight.
Caddies: No. **Golf carts:** N/A.
Discount golf packages: Yes. **Season:** March-Oct. **High:** June-Sept.
On-site lodging: No. **Rental clubs:** No.
Walking policy: N/A. **Range:** Yes (grass).
Subscriber comments: Tough par 3s . . . Challenging . . . Usually good
shape . . . Long par 4s . . . Challenging par 3s . . . Beautifully groomed
. . . Tough championship layout . . . True test of golf . . . Excellent
fairways, bunkers . . . Good service . . . Pretty course . . . Fair course . . .
Flat, easy to walk . . . Many improvements made over the last four to five
years.

★★½ ROLLING GREEN GOLF CLUB

PU—228 King Richard Dr., McMurray (412)222-9671.
Call club for further information.
Subscriber comments: Excellent greens . . . Need better traps and more
traps . . . Average public course . . . Simple layout . . . Good course just to
swing the clubs . . . Great course to take your kids . . . Likeable course.

★½ ROLLING HILLS GOLF COURSE

PU—RD No.1, Rte. 208, Pulaski (412)964-8201.
10 miles east of Youngstown. **Holes:** 18. **Par:** 71/76.
Yards: 6,000/5,552. **Course rating:** N/A. **Slope:** N/A.
Opened: 1967. **Pace of Play rating:** 4:30. **Green fee:** $12/13.
Credit cards: MC, V. **Reduced fees:** Weekdays, Low season, Seniors.
Caddies: No. **Golf carts:** $8 for 18 holes.
Discount golf packages: No. **Season:** Year-round. **High:** June-Aug.
On-site lodging: No. **Rental clubs:** Yes.
Walking policy: Unrestricted walking. **Range:** No.
To obtain tee times: Call in advance. Required on weekends.
Subscriber comments: Matches its name . . . Can be easy . . . No. 7 is
fun . . . One of my favorites . . . . Average place to play . . . Nice place for
price . . . Small greens . . . Back nine on a mountain.

★★★★ ROYAL OAKS GOLF COURSE

PU—3350 West Oak St., Lebanon (717)274-2212.
15 miles east of Hershey. **Holes:** 18. **Par:** 71/71.
Yards: 6,542/4,687. **Course rating:** 71.3/66.6. **Slope:** 118/108.
Opened: 1992. **Pace of Play rating:** 4:00-4:30. **Green fee:** $16/29.
Credit cards: MC, V, DISC. **Reduced fees:** Weekdays, Low season,
Seniors, Juniors.
Caddies: No. **Golf carts:** $10 for 18 holes.
Discount golf packages: No. **Season:** Year-round. **High:** April-Nov.
On-site lodging: No. **Rental clubs:** No.
Walking policy: Unrestricted walking. **Range:** Yes (grass).
To obtain tee times: Available one week in advance unless credit card
number or deposit is taken. Tee times required seven days a week.
Subscriber comments: Myrtle Beach in Pennsylvania . . . Excellent value
. . . Gorgeous fairways . . . Newer design . . . Mounds . . . Tough layout
. . . Some heroic holes add to the fun . . . Super value . . . Great layout . . .
Beautiful course . . . Lush and wide open . . . Challenging links course . . .
Doesn't get any better than this . . . Tough but very playable if you use
your head . . . Excellent use of the terrain . . . Best-kept secret in eastern
Pennsylvania . . . First hole breathtaking . . . Inviting course . . . Beautiful
course . . . True golfing challenge . . . Still needs to mature a little.

★★★ SAXON GOLF COURSE

PU—839 Ekastown Rd., Sarver (412)353-2130.
Call club for further information.
Subscriber comments: Flat course . . . Good length . . . Very hard, fast greens . . . Flattest course in area . . . Wooded . . . Enjoyable back nine . . . Two different nines . . . Small greens on front . . . Bigger greens on back . . . Fun course . . . Easy to walk.

★★★ SCRANTON MUNICIPAL GOLF COURSE

PU—RD 4, Lake Ariel (717)689-2686.
Call club for further information.
Subscriber comments: Needs work on layout . . . Made great improvements to clubhouse . . . Wide open . . . Excellent greens . . . Great value . . . A good public course . . . Don't be above the pin on the fourth green . . . Excellent condition but rather easy . . . Short and fairly straight.

★½ SEVEN SPRINGS COUNTRY CLUB

PU—357 Pineview Dr., Elizabeth (412)384-7730.
Call club for further information.
Subscriber comments: Good scenery on mountain top . . . Course is short but well maintained . . . Fair . . . Not much trouble . . . Hilly, short course . . . Great duffer course . . . Hilly and barren . . . Short par 5s (almost par 4s) . . . Lots of sidehill lies.

★★★½ SEVEN SPRINGS MOUNTAIN RESORT GOLF COURSE

R—RD No.1, Champion (814)352-7777.
60 miles southeast of Pittsburgh. **Holes:** 18. **Par:** 71/72.
Yards: 6,360/4,934. **Course rating:** 70.6/68.3. **Slope:** 116/111.
Opened: 1969. **Pace of Play rating:** 4:30-5:00. **Green fee:** $55/60.
Credit cards: MC, V, DISC. **Reduced fees:** Weekdays, Low season, Resort guests, Twilight.
Caddies: No. **Golf carts:** Included in Green Fee.
Discount golf packages: Yes. **Season:** April-Oct. **High:** July-Aug.
On-site lodging: Yes. **Rental clubs:** Yes.
Walking policy: Walking at certain times. **Range:** Yes (grass).
To obtain tee times: Call 48 hours in advance unless a guest at the resort then tee times can be made same time as reservation.
Subscriber comments: Great course . . . Good holes . . . Treatment good . . . Best in western Pennsylvania . . . . Manicured . . . Scenic . . . Tough . . . Panoramic views . . . Very tough finishing holes . . . Excellent course on top of mountain . . . True resort golf . . . Beautiful surroundings . . . Next to ski slopes . . . Back nine very long for ladies . . . Greens like putting on porcelain . . . Some poor holes . . . Long par 4s . . . Overall good layout . . . Some so-so holes . . . Scenic.

★½ SHADOW BROOK GOLF COURSE

PU—Rd 6, Tunkhannock (717)836-5417.
Call club for further information.
Subscriber comments: Interesting front nine . . . Good ice cream . . . Very hilly second nine . . . Stays open 10 months . . . Always busy . . . Good for get-away . . . Front nine open, back nine extremely hilly . . . Fair to marginal golf course . . . Tiny greens . . . Hilly on back . . . Middle of the road . . . Front is nicely laid out, back nine on a hill and gimmicky.

SHAWNEE INN AND GOLF RESORT
★★½ BLUE/RED/WHITE

R—River Rd., Shawnee-on-Delaware (717)421-1500x1425, (800)742-9633.
90 miles west of New York City. **Holes:** 27. **Par:** 72/72/72.
Yards: 6,589/6,665/6,800. **Course rating:** 72.4/72.8/72.2.
Slope: 131/129/132.
Opened: 1904. **Pace of Play rating:** N/A. **Green fee:** $32/65.
Credit cards: All major. **Reduced fees:** Weekdays, Low season, Resort guests, Twilight.
Caddies: No. **Golf carts:** Included in Green Fee.
Discount golf packages: Yes. **Season:** April-Nov. **High:** May-Aug.
On-site lodging: Yes. **Rental clubs:** Yes.

Walking policy: Mandatory cart. **Range:** Yes.
To obtain tee times: Confirm tee times with credit card. Cancellation policy is 24 hours.
Subscriber comments: Couple tough water holes . . . Good resort course . . . Fun to play . . . Challenging yet rewarding . . . Interesting and fun . . . Three interesting nines . . . Good staff . . . Too many bugs in summer . . . Nice hole over Delaware river . . . Great course on the Delaware . . . The rough is killer . . . Challenging 27 holes . . . Fast, undulating greens . . . Beautiful in fall . . . Nice views of mountains . . . Could be very, very good . . . Good course, very scenic on river.

★ SILVER SPRINGS GOLF COURSE

PU—136 Sample Bridge Rd., Mechanicsburg (717)766-0462.
10 miles of Harrisburg. **Holes:** 18. **Par:** 70/70.
Yards: 6,000/5,500. **Course rating:** N/A. **Slope:** 114/109.
Opened: N/A. **Pace of Play rating:** N/A. **Green fee:** N/A.
Credit cards: MC, V. **Reduced fees:** Weekdays, Low season, Twilight.
Caddies: No. **Golf carts:** N/A.
Discount golf packages: No. **Season:** Year-round. **High:** March-Nov.
On-site lodging: No. **Rental clubs:** No.
Walking policy: N/A. **Range:** Yes.
Subscriber comments: A straight hitter's course . . . Not long but interesting . . . Fun . . . Very short course . . . Four par 3s on the back . . . Too wet in spring . . . Very reasonable . . . Easy course . . . Course too small . . . Not very challenging . . . Holes are crammed together . . . Almost an executive course.

★★★ SINKING VALLEY COUNTRY CLUB

PU—Cape Cod Rd., Altoona (814)684-0662.
Call club for further information.
Subscriber comments: Great beginner's course . . . Small course and greens . . . Lots of play . . . Good ego builder . . . Glorified chip 'n' putt course . . . Good course for seniors and beginners . . . Very friendly staff . . . Short but improving lately . . . Very friendly.

★ SKYLINE GOLF COURSE

PU—Rte. 247, R.D. No.1, Carbondale (717)282-5993.
15 miles of Scranton. **Holes:** 18. **Par:** 66/66.
Yards: 4,719/3,866. **Course rating:** N/A. **Slope:** N/A.
Opened: 1959. **Pace of Play rating:** N/A. **Green fee:** N/A.
Credit cards: N/A. **Reduced fees:** N/A.
Caddies: No. **Golf carts:** N/A.
Discount golf packages: No. **Season:** April-Nov. **High:** June-Aug.
On-site lodging: No. **Rental clubs:** Yes.
Walking policy: Unrestricted walking. **Range:** No.
Subscriber comments: If you can find it, play it! . . . Generous driving areas . . . Fast . . . Very sloped greens . . . Enjoyed lush grass and scenery . . . Beautiful scenery . . . Excellent greens . . . Friendly atmosphere . . . Great value . . . Very, very beautiful view.

★★½ SKYTOP LODGE GOLF CLUB

R—Skytop (717)595-8910.
35 miles east of Scranton. **Holes:** 18. **Par:** 71/ 75.
Yards: 6,256/5,683. **Course rating:** 70.2/ 72.8. **Slope:** 121/122.
Opened: 1928. **Pace of Play rating:** N/A. **Green fee:** $35/50.
Credit cards: MC, V, AMEX,. **Reduced fees:** Resort guests.
Caddies: No. **Golf carts:** $15 for 18 holes.
Discount golf packages: Yes. **Season:** April-Oct. **High:** June-Sept.
On-site lodging: Yes. **Rental clubs:** Yes.
Walking policy: Walking at certain times. **Range:** No.
To obtain tee times: Required on weekends and holidays. Call pro shop.
Subscriber comments: Quiet course . . . Great facility . . . Scenic views . . . Good shape . . . Interesting course . . . Fun resort course . . . A little short for big hitters . . . Gorgeous setting . . . Maintenance greatly improved.

★★★½ SOUTH HILLS COUNTRY CLUB

SP—Brownsville Rd. & Clairton Rd., Pittsburgh (412)884–5111.
Call club for further information.
Subscriber comments: Challenging course . . . Well kept . . . Great
greens . . . Too slick and rolling for me . . . Lots of deer around . . . Hilly
with woods and some water . . . Nice course . . . Good old course . . . .
Short course with excellent greens.

★★★ SOUTH HILLS GOLF CLUB

PU—925 Westminster Ave., Hanover (717)637-7500.
40 miles north of Baltimore. **Holes:** 18. **Par:** 71/71.
Yards: 6,575/5,749. **Course rating:** 71.0/72.0. **Slope:** 121/119.
Opened: 1959. **Pace of Play rating:** 4:30. **Green fee:** $10/19.
Credit cards: None. **Reduced fees:** Weekdays, Low season, Twilight,
Seniors, Juniors.
Caddies: No. **Golf carts:** $10 for 18 holes.
Discount golf packages: No. **Season:** Year-round. **High:** May-Oct.
On-site lodging: No. **Rental clubs:** Yes.
Walking policy: Walking at certain times. **Range:** Yes (grass).
To obtain tee times: Call pro shop.
New nine holes opened spring of 1995.
Subscriber comments: Fast and tricky greens . . . Nice layout . . . Not
long but challenging . . . Not a flat spot on the course . . . Good shape . . .
Fun layout . . . Friendly . . . Wonderful experience . . . Rolling hills . . .
Huge undulating greens . . . Interesting holes . . . OK facilities . . . A fun
course with old-style design features . . . One of the best courses in central
Pennsylvania . . . Great shape and plays fast . . . Great course . . . Tends to
dry out in hot weather . . . Great farmland setting . . . Short but interesting
. . . Huge greens . . . Easy to get on but watch those three-putts.

★★ SOUTH PARK GOLF COURSE

PU—East Park Dr., Library (412)835-3545.
Call club for further information.
Subscriber comments: Amazing shape for the heavy play . . . Always
friendly . . . Cheap . . . Hilly . . . Lot of uneven lies . . . Very challenging
. . . Some tough par 4s . . . Greens good . . . County park . . . Could be
great and upscale . . . Where I lost my virginity, golfwise . . . Never a flat
lie . . . One of the hilliest in area . . . Decent back nine . . . Layout average
. . . Greens real slow.

★½ SPORTSMANS GOLF CLUB

SP—3800 Linglestown Rd., Harrisburg (717)545-0023.
Call club for further information.
Subscriber comments: Good layout . . . Much improved in 1994 . . .
Long par 3s and 5s . . . Narrow greens . . . Acceptable conditions and
course layout . . . Could be good . . . Needs work . . . Tough tree-lined
course . . . Many good improvements being made . . . Getting better all the
time . . . Greens very good . . . Some challenging holes . . . Wide open . . .
Not a very interesting course . . . Receives a lot of play because of its
location . . . Course maintenance has improved recently . . . Tees and
greens close.

SPRINGDALE GOLF CLUB★

PU—R.D. No.3, Box 40C, Uniontown (412)439-4400.
50 miles south of Pittsburgh. **Holes:** 18. **Par:** 70/71.
Yards: 6,100/5,350. **Course rating:** 67.5/68.5. **Slope:** 115/115.
Opened: . **Pace of Play rating:** 4:00. **Green fee:** $12/13.
Credit cards: None. **Reduced fees:** Weekdays, Low season, Seniors.
Caddies: No. **Golf carts:** $18 for 18 holes.
Discount golf packages: No. **Season:** . **High:** June-Aug.
On-site lodging: No. **Rental clubs:** Yes.
Walking policy: Unrestricted walking. **Range:** No.
To obtain tee times: First come, first served.
Subscriber comments: Small greens . . . Worn out . . . Very small greens
. . . Great to walk . . . Beginners . . . Wide open with very small hard
greens . . . Good beginner's course . . . Needs bunkers.

★½ STANDING STONE GOLF CLUB

PU— Rte. 26 North, Huntingdon (814)643-2422.
25 miles south of State College. **Holes:** 18. **Par:** 70/70.
Yards: 6,593/5,528. **Course rating:** 71.4/71.1. **Slope:** 120/120.
Opened: 1973 **Pace of Play rating:** 4:08. **Green fee:** $20/25.
Credit cards: None. **Reduced fees:** Twilight.
Caddies: No. **Golf carts:** Included in Green Fee.
Discount golf packages: No. **Season:** March-Nov. **High:** March-Sept.
On-site lodging: No. **Rental clubs:** Yes.
Walking policy: Mandatory cart. **Range:** Yes (grass).
To obtain tee times: Call seven days in advance.
Subscriber comments: Geoffrey Cornish design . . . Needs better
maintenance . . . Good 19th hole . . . Good course to play . . . Maturing
trees . . . Fun course . . . Not a tournament course . . . Hit it long and
straight . . . Good design . . . Slow greens.

★★★½ STATE COLLEGE ELKS COUNTRY CLUB

SP—Rte. 322 Box 8, Boalsburg (814)466-6451.
5 miles east of State College. **Holes:** 18. **Par:** 71/72.
Yards: 6,358/5,125. **Course rating:** 70.9/70.2. **Slope:** 123/119.
Opened: 1964. **Pace of Play rating:** 4:00. **Green fee:** $28.
Credit cards: None. **Reduced fees:** N/A.
Caddies: No. **Golf carts:** $28 for 18 holes.
Discount golf packages: No. **Season:** April-Nov. **High:** May-Sept.
On-site lodging: No. **Rental clubs:** Yes.
Walking policy: Unrestricted walking. **Range:** Yes (grass).
To obtain tee times: Call one week in advance.
Formerly known as Elks Lodge and Country Club.
Subscriber comments: Interesting . . . Some very tough holes . . . Long,
imposing, hilly course . . . Very challenging holes . . . Friendly staff and
excellent restaurant . . . Challenging course . . . Water on five holes . . .
Hilly with lots of sidehill lies . . . Good value . . . Fairly open . . . Par 3s
and 4s are solid, 5s weak.

★★★½ STONE HEDGE COUNTRY CLUB

PU—R.D. No.4, Tunkhannock (717)836-5108.
22 miles west of Scranton. **Holes:** 18. **Par:** 71/71.
Yards: 6,506/4,992. **Course rating:** 71.9/69.7. **Slope:** 124/122.
Opened: 1991. **Pace of Play rating:** 4:00. **Green fee:** $18/25.
Credit cards: None. **Reduced fees:** Weekdays, Low season, Twilight,
Seniors.
Caddies: No. **Golf carts:** $8 for 18 holes.
Discount golf packages: No. **Season:** April-Dec. **High:** May-Sept.
On-site lodging: No. **Rental clubs:** No.
Walking policy: Mandatory cart. **Range:** Yes (grass).
To obtain tee times: Call three days in advance or earlier if out of town.
Subscriber comments: Beautiful course, everyone should play it . . .
Tight but fair . . . Wow! Still young but challenging to all levels . . .
Putting their money into the course instead of clubhouse . . . Great value
. . . Should be on PGA Tour . . . Excellent . . . Scenic . . . New course on
rise . . . Great layout . . . Good course, no clubhouse . . . Rolling parkland,
open combination . . . Nice layout . . . Difficult second hole . . . Could
play this course everyday . . . This is the course that dares you to want to
go back to do better . . . Very, very tough . . . Mountain course . . .
Beautiful . . . A hidden gem . . . Great scenery . . . Use all the clubs in your
bag . . . Very good greens . . . No amenities . . . Beautiful course . . . Top
notch . . . A sleeper.

★★★ STOUGHTON ACRES GOLF CLUB

SUPER VALUE

PU—904 Sunset Dr., Butler (412)285-3633.
Call club for further information.
Subscriber comments: Fast greens . . . Scenic . . . Courteous staff . . .
Treat you as guests . . . Course has some nice holes . . . Management treats
you great . . . Fun little course . . . Low prices . . . Quality holes . . . Great
value . . . Tough to get on . . . Incredible value . . . Well maintained with
heavy play . . . Fair test . . . Well kept . . . Pretty scenic back nine . . .

Family owned . . . Very fair but tricky back nine . . . Best public course
. . . Employees treat you like a king . . . No smoking or drinking.

★★★½ SUGARLOAF GOLF CLUB
PU—R.D. No.2, Sugarloaf (717)384-4097.
6 miles west of Hazleton. **Holes:** 18. **Par:** 72/72.
Yards: 6,845/5,620. **Course rating:** 73.0/72.8. **Slope:** 122/120.
Opened: 1967. **Pace of Play rating:** 4:00-4:30. **Green fee:** $15.
Credit cards: MC, V, MAC. **Reduced fees:** Twilight.
Caddies: No. **Golf carts:** $22 for 18 holes.
Discount golf packages: No. **Season:** March-Nov. **High:** July-Aug.
On-site lodging: No. **Rental clubs:** Yes.
Walking policy: Walking at certain times. **Range:** Yes (grass).
To obtain tee times: Call.
Subscriber comments: Back nine outstanding . . . Tough to walk . . .
Great shape . . . Interesting holes . . . Friendly staff . . . Average but fun to
play . . . Open . . . Very good hard par 3s . . . Long carries of 200 yards
over water . . . Just love the layout . . . Great course . . . Slow play . . .
Good staff . . . Wide open . . . Very scenic . . . Long, challenging . . .
Awesome scenery . . . Good layout! . . . Great greens . . . Back nine better
than front . . . Nice mountain course . . . Good shape . . . Friendly.

★★½ SUNSET GOLF COURSE
PU—783 S. Geyer's Church Rd., Middletown (717)944-5415.
Call club for further information.
Subscriber comments: Interesting short course . . . Nice public course
. . . Average in all aspects . . . Monster hill from 18th to clubhouse . . .
Nice course . . . Good for beginner . . . Nice layout with views . . .
Affordable . . . Not crowded . . . Has variety . . . Short . . . Great fun . . .
A 737 every minute, right on flight path to HIA airport . . . Don't let view
of Three Mile Island scare you . . . 10th hole drop is stunning . . . Some
nice holes . . . Open course . . . Some outstanding views.

SYLVAN HEIGHTS GOLF COURSE★
PU—Rte. 65, Ellwood - New Castle Rd., New Castle (412)658-8021.
50 miles south of Pittsburgh. **Holes:** 18. **Par:** 71/ 71.
Yards: 6,081/ 5,781. **Course rating:** N/A. **Slope:** N/A.
Opened: N/A. **Pace of Play rating:** 4:15. **Green fee:** $9.
Credit cards: None. **Reduced fees:** Seniors.
Caddies: No. **Golf carts:** $15 for 18 holes.
Discount golf packages: No. **Season:** Year-round. **High:** April-Oct.
On-site lodging: No. **Rental clubs:** No.
Walking policy: Unrestricted walking. **Range:** No.
To obtain tee times: Call anytime.
Subscriber comments: Excellent layout . . . Needs more attention on
mowing but nice for city course . . . Needs watering system to handle
heavy play . . . Good greens . . . Decent course for the money.

★★★½ TAM O'SHANTER GOLF CLUB
PU—I-80 And Rte. 18 North, Hermitage (412)981-3552.
40 miles northwest of Pittsburgh. **Holes:** 18. **Par:** 72/76.
Yards: 6,537/5,385. **Course rating:** 69.4/70.2. **Slope:** 121/113.
Opened: 1931. **Pace of Play rating:** 4:00. **Green fee:** $17/19.
Credit cards: MC, V, DISC. **Reduced fees:** Weekdays, Low season,
Resort guests, Seniors, Juniors.
Caddies: Yes. **Golf carts:** $9 for 18 holes.
Discount golf packages: Yes. **Season:** March-Nov. **High:** June-Sept.
On-site lodging: Yes. **Rental clubs:** Yes.
Walking policy: Unrestricted walking. **Range:** Yes (grass).
To obtain tee times: Call pro shop, times available daily.
Subscriber comments: Could play this every day . . . Treated great . . .
Everyone should spend time here . . . Some unusual holes across ravines
. . . Beautiful views, great layout . . . Well groomed . . . Pretty course . . .
Great people . . . Nice course but very crowded . . . Tough to get on . . .
Beautiful layout, good location . . . Mature course.

★★★ TAMIMENT RESORT AND CONFERENCE CENTER

R—Bushkill Falls Rd., Tamiment (717)588-6652, (800)233-8105.
75 miles west of New York. Holes: 18. **Par:** 72/72.
Yards: 6,858/5,598. **Course rating:** 72.7/71.9. **Slope:** 130/124.
Opened: 1951. **Pace of Play rating:** 4:15. **Green fee:** $22/30.
Credit cards: All major. **Reduced fees:** Weekdays, Low season, Resort
guests, Twilight, Juniors.
Caddies: No. **Golf carts:** $15 for 18 holes.
Discount golf packages: Yes. **Season:** April-Nov. **High:** May-Sept.
On-site lodging: Yes. **Rental clubs:** Yes.
Walking policy: Walking at certain times. **Range:** No.
To obtain tee times: Hotel guests at time room reservations are made.
Nonguests may call up to one month in advance.
Subscriber comments: Great layout . . . Large greens . . . A challenge
. . . Great Robert Trent Jones layout . . . Poor condition . . . Good old
course . . . A few scenic mountain course holes . . . Awesome . . . Long
. . . Fast greens . . . Up-and-down hills . . . Long tough par 4s . . . Very
long mountain course . . . Difficult par 3s . . . Very hilly . . . Good design
. . . Long, narrow and hilly . . . A true "placement" course with exciting
par 3s . . . Lots of fun and worth it.

★½ TANGLEWOOD MANOR GOLF CLUB

PU—Scotland Rd., Quarryville (717)786-2220.
Call club for further information.
Subscriber comments: Well kept . . . Making improvements . . . Short
course . . . It will get better with age . . . Average public course . . .
Beautiful layout . . . Think and plan your approach shots . . . Nice layout
. . . Back nine tight, challenging . . . Reasonable rates . . . Tough par 3s.

★★★★ TOFTREES RESORT

R—1 Country Club Lane, State College (814)238-7600, (800)452-3602.
90 miles northwest of Harrisburgh. Holes: 18. **Par:** 72/72.
Yards: 7,018/5,555. **Course rating:** 74.3/71.8. **Slope:** 134/126.
Opened: 1968. **Pace of Play rating:** 4:30-5:00. **Green fee:** $31/45.
Credit cards: All major. **Reduced fees:** Weekdays, Low season, Twilight,
Juniors.
Caddies: No. **Golf carts:** Included in Green Fee.
Discount golf packages: Yes. **Season:** April-Nov. **High:** June-Sept.
On-site lodging: Yes. **Rental clubs:** Yes.
Walking policy: Walking at certain times. **Range:** Yes (grass).
To obtain tee times: Public, 30 days in advance; Resort guests, 60 days in
advance.
Subscriber comments: Great golf course . . . Well designed in wooded
setting . . . First-class in every way . . . Always fun to play . . . Beautiful,
beautiful . . . Nice staff . . . Everything thought out . . . Great golf course
. . . Breathtaking views . . . Every hole is challenging . . . No let up . . .
Outstanding course . . . Monster when wet . . . Wow! State college beauty
with outstanding condition . . . Every hole is different . . . Almost every
hole bordered by forest . . . Spectacular . . . Holes one through five the best
. . . Fairways like greens . . . Spectacular 9th from back tees . . . Excellent
experience . . . Challenging for all levels of players . . . Big layout . . . Well
maintained . . . No bad holes.

★★★★ TOM'S RUN GOLF COURSE

PU—R.D. 1, Box 578, Blairsville (412)459-7188.
35 miles east of Pittsburgh. Holes: 18. **Par:** 72/72.
Yards: 6,705/5,363. **Course rating:** 72.9/71.2. **Slope:** 134/126.
Opened: 1993. **Pace of Play rating:** 4:30. **Green fee:** $40.
Credit cards: MC, V, AMEX. **Reduced fees:** Weekdays.
Caddies: No. **Golf carts:** $10 for 18 holes.
Discount golf packages: Yes. **Season:** April-Nov. **High:** April-Nov.
On-site lodging: No. **Rental clubs:** No.
Walking policy: Unrestricted walking. **Range:** Yes (grass).
To obtain tee times: Call 7 days in advance.
Subscriber comments: First four holes very interesting . . . Two
distinctively different nines . . . Third and fourth are beautiful and

challenging holes . . . Has 90 sand traps . . . Keep rake handy . . . Needs to mature . . . Has promise . . . Terrific new course . . . Superb condition . . . Nice clubhouse . . . Tom's Run is a new course but is developing a solid reputation . . . Scenic and picturesque . . . Wonderful views . . . A few average holes keep it from being outstanding.

★★½ TOWANDA COUNTRY CLUB

SP—RR 06, Box 6180, Towanda (717)265-6939.
100 miles north of Harrisburg. **Holes:** 18. **Par:** 71/76.
Yards: 6,100/5,600. **Course rating:** 68.0/67.0. **Slope:** 119/102.
Opened: 1927. **Pace of Play rating:** 4:00. **Green fee:** $14/17.
Credit cards: MC, V. **Reduced fees:** Seniors, Juniors.
Caddies: No. **Golf carts:** $20 for 18 holes.
Discount golf packages: Yes. **Season:** April-Dec. **High:** May-Sept.
On-site lodging: No. **Rental clubs:** Yes.
Walking policy: Mandatory cart. **Range:** No.
To obtain tee times: Call pro shop.
Subscriber comments: Hilly layout but short and challenging . . . Fun, short course . . . Hilly . . . Hilly . . . Very few level lies . . . Excellent greens . . . Beautiful scenery . . . Greens break toward river . . . Short but sassy . . . Short par 4s . . . Small fast greens.

TREASURE LAKE GOLF CLUB
★★★★ GOLD COURSE

PU—687 Treasure Lake, Dubois (814)375-1807.
Call club for further information.
Subscriber comments: Tunnel golf . . . Not suited for meek . . . Championship track . . . Staff outstanding . . . A gem in the forest . . . Hope nobody else finds out about it . . . Narrow, tree-lined fairways, not for the slicer . . . Very tight in places . . . Too tough . . . No room for error . . . Picturesque settings.

★★ TURBOT HILLS GOLF COURSE

PU—RR No.2, Milton (717)742-9852.
Call club for further information.
Subscriber comments: Too many blind approach shots . . . An old small-town course . . . Challenging . . . Improvements make the course better each year . . . Strange layout, hilly . . . It's OK . . . Fun and fair . . . Very hilly . . . Tiny greens . . . Course lacked personality.

★½ TWIN PONDS GOLF COURSE

PU—654 Gilbertsville Rd., Gilbertsville (215)369-1901.
Call club for further information.
Subscriber comments: Short, fun course . . . Great place to hold an outing . . . Lots of short par 4s . . . Always a brisk round . . . Nice course for average golfer . . . Homey atmosphere . . . Nice staff . . . Short but interesting . . . Best played with no woods in the bag . . . Hilly, easy courses . . . Nothing fancy . . . Easy.

★½ TWINING VALLEY GOLF CLUB

PU—1400 Twining Rd., Dresher (215)659-9917.
Call club for further information.
Subscriber comments: Course is not very difficult . . . Clubhouse is the best part . . . Course not so good . . . Long in the tooth . . . Well worn . . . Great staff . . . Good course . . . Easy six holes . . . Great six holes . . . Bizarre six holes . . . Small greens . . . Busy . . . Nice course.

★★★★ TYOGA COUNTRY CLUB

SP—RD No.6, Wellsboro (717)724-1653.
Call club for further information.
Subscriber comments: Beautiful views . . . Even deer on the course . . . Outstanding scenery . . . Excellent layout . . . Exceptional mountain scenery . . . I'm moving there so I can play this course more often . . . Unusual up-and-down course . . . Very good golf package . . . Scenic . . . Beautiful setting . . . Challenging tight course . . . Golf packages are unbelievable value . . . Gorgeous mountain course . . . Coupled with

Corry Creek, this makes for a fantastic weekend . . . Front side hilly and tree-lined, back more open . . . Very fair.

★★★ UPPER PERK GOLF COURSE

PU—Rte. 663 & Ott Rd., Pennsburg (215)679-5594.
50 miles northeast of Philadelphia. **Holes:** 18. **Par:** 71/71.
Yards: 6,381/5,249. **Course rating:** 70.0/69.6. **Slope:** 117/113.
Opened: 1977. **Pace of Play rating:** 4:00. **Green fee:** $16/20.
Credit cards: None. **Reduced fees:** Weekdays, Low season, Twilight, Seniors, Juniors.
Caddies: No. **Golf carts:** $20 for 18 holes.
Discount golf packages: No. **Season:** March–Dec. **High:** May–Sept.
On-site lodging: No. **Rental clubs:** No.
Walking policy: Unrestricted walking. **Range:** No.
To obtain tee times: Call up to two weeks in advance.
Subscriber comments: Always in great shape for amount of play it gets . . . Very nice course . . . Can be slow . . . Great condition . . . Great course . . . Large greens . . . Groomed well . . . Trees maturing . . . Course becoming tougher . . . Nice open course . . . Lots of play . . . Gets better with age . . . Well-kept course . . . Flat . . . Well maintained . . . Varied . . . Challenging . . . Busy . . . Interesting course . . . Need a variety of shots . . . Frequent "risk or safe" shot choices.

★ VALLEY FORGE GOLF CLUB

PU—401 North Gulf Rd., King Of Prussia (610)337-1776.
25 miles west of Philadelphia. **Holes:** 18. **Par:** 71/71.
Yards: 6,200/5,668. **Course rating:** 68.9/71.1. **Slope:** N/A.
Opened: 1929. **Pace of Play rating:** 4:00. **Green fee:** $18/23.
Credit cards: None. **Reduced fees:** N/A.
Caddies: No. **Golf carts:** $26 for 18 holes.
Discount golf packages: No. **Season:** March–Nov. **High:** June–July.
On-site lodging: No. **Rental clubs:** Yes.
Walking policy: Unrestricted walking. **Range:** No.
To obtain tee times: Call seven days in advance.
Subscriber comments: Good beginner's course . . . Good value . . . Extremely hilly . . . Not a walkable course for most people . . . If you walk you will crawl back to the clubhouse . . . Old style . . . Small greens . . . Wide open . . . Lots of play . . . Nothing special . . . Good, open starter course . . . Par 3s on back nine excellent . . . Acceptable . . . Being so close to Philly, it's always crowded.

★½ VALLEY GREEN GOLF AND COUNTRY CLUB

PU—RD No.2, Box 449F, Greensburg (412)837-6366.
40 miles southeast of Pittsburgh. **Holes:** 18. **Par:** 72/72.
Yards: 6,345/5,450. **Course rating:** 67.5/67.5. **Slope:** 104/104.
Opened: 1965. **Pace of Play rating:** 4:50. **Green fee:** $15/16.
Credit cards: None. **Reduced fees:** Seniors.
Caddies: No. **Golf carts:** $18 for 18 holes.
Discount golf packages: No. **Season:** Year-round. **High:** April–Sept.
On-site lodging: No. **Rental clubs:** Yes.
Walking policy: Unrestricted walking. **Range:** No.
To obtain tee times: Call pro shop.
Subscriber comments: Beat-up, poor fairways . . . Practice course . . . Potential if maintained . . . Nice layout . . . Maintenance poor . . . Layout is great . . . Greens fair . . . Long course . . . Good course for a quick nine after work.

★★ VALLEY GREEN GOLF COURSE

PU—1227 Valley Green Rd., Etters (717)938-4200.
15 miles south of Harrisburg. **Holes:** 18. **Par:** 71/71.
Yards: 6,000/5,500. **Course rating:** 67.0/67.0. **Slope:** 110/109.
Opened: 1964. **Pace of Play rating:** 4:00. **Green fee:** $11/18.
Credit cards: MC, V. **Reduced fees:** Weekdays, Low season, Twilight, Seniors, Juniors.
Caddies: No. **Golf carts:** $10 for 18 holes.

Discount golf packages: No. **Season:** March–Nov. **High:** April–Oct.
On-site lodging: No. **Rental clubs:** Yes.
Walking policy: Unrestricted walking. **Range:** No.
To obtain tee times: Call pro shop one week in advance.
Subscriber comments: Short course, hilly, hard to hold greens . . . Well-kept course but not too many par 4s under 300 yds . . . Clubhouse is not much . . . Nice short course . . . Good neighborhood course . . . Great twilight deal . . . Easy front, tough back nine.

★½ VENANGO TRAIL GOLF COURSE

SP—970 Freeport Rd., Mars (412)776-4400.
18 miles north of Pittsburgh. **Holes:** 18. **Par:** 72/72.
Yards: 6,200/5,518. **Course rating:** 69.9/74.0. **Slope:** 120/117.
Opened: 1954. **Pace of Play rating:** 4:00. **Green fee:** $11/20.
Credit cards: All major. **Reduced fees:** Weekdays, Low season, Seniors, Juniors.
Caddies: No. **Golf carts:** $10 for 18 holes.
Discount golf packages: Yes. **Season:** Year-round. **High:** April-Oct.
On-site lodging: No. **Rental clubs:** No.
Walking policy: Walking at certain times. **Range:** No.
To obtain tee times: Call 48 hours in advance.
Subscriber comments: Great restaurant . . . Very hilly . . . Good greens . . . Up and down hills all day . . . Short, very tight course . . . Another hilly course with some tough holes . . . Hilly with small, hard greens.

VENANGO VALLEY INN AND GC★

R—Rte.19, Venango (814)398-4330.
Call club for further information.
Subscriber comments: Little maintenance . . . Good layout but poorly maintained . . . OK for just hitting balls.

★★½ WATER GAP COUNTRY CLUB

SP—P.O. Box 188, Mtn. Rd., Delaware Water Gap (717)476-0200.
70 miles of New York City. **Holes:** 18. **Par:** 72/72.
Yards: 6,186/5,175. **Course rating:** N/A. **Slope:** 125/114.
Opened: N/A. **Pace of Play rating:** N/A. **Green fee:** N/A.
Credit cards: All major. **Reduced fees:** Weekdays.
Caddies: No. **Golf carts:** N/A.
Discount golf packages: Yes. **Season:** March-Nov. **High:** July-Sept.
On-site lodging: Yes. **Rental clubs:** No.
Walking policy: N/A. **Range:** No.
Subscriber comments: Several interesting holes . . . Short course but very tricky . . . Good greens . . . Old, challenging, scenic . . . Fun to play . . . Impossible hills . . . Great views . . . Fun holes . . . Open . . . Tough to walk . . . Very dry in summer . . . Beautiful scenery in the fall . . . Walter Hagen played there . . . Very nice . . . Old course . . . Hilly lies . . . Sloped fairways . . . Fun course.

★★½ WEDGEWOOD GOLF CLUB

PU—4875 Limeport Pike, Coopersburg (610)797-4551.
4 miles south of Allentown. **Holes:** 18. **Par:** 71/72.
Yards: 6,162/5,622. **Course rating:** 68.8/65.8. **Slope:** 122/108.
Opened: 1963. **Pace of Play rating:** 4:30. **Green fee:** $16/30.
Credit cards: MC, V. **Reduced fees:** Weekdays, Low season, Twilight, Seniors.
Caddies: No. **Golf carts:** Included in Green Fee.
Discount golf packages: No. **Season:** Year-round. **High:** April-Sept.
On-site lodging: No. **Rental clubs:** Yes.
Walking policy: Walking at certain times. **Range:** Yes (grass).
To obtain tee times: Call pro shop.
Subscriber comments: Good average public course . . . Short but some tough holes . . . Short course but excellent condition . . . Fun, easy course to play . . . Short course . . . . Well maintained . . . Beautiful surroundings . . . Nice . . . Well maintained . . . Interesting course . . . Very good for

the average player . . . Flat with lots of water and sand . . . Some demanding holes . . . Wide open . . . Better suited for beginners.

WHITE DEER PARK AND GOLF COURSE
PU—R.R. No.1, P.O. Box 183, Montgomery (717)547-2186.
8 miles north of Williamsport.
Opened: 1965. **Pace of Play rating:** 4:00-4:30. **Green fee:** $14/18.
Credit cards: MC, V, DISC. **Reduced fees:** Weekdays, Low season, Seniors, Juniors.
Caddies: No. **Golf carts:** $11 for 18 holes.
Discount golf packages: No. **Season:** Year-round. **High:** May-Sept.
On-site lodging: No. **Rental clubs:** Yes.
Walking policy: Unrestricted walking. **Range:** Yes (grass).
To obtain tee times: Call Monday after 6 p.m. for upcoming weekend. For weekdays call three days in advance.
Also has a nine-hole, par-3 course.

★★★ CHALLENGE COURSE
Holes: 18. **Par:** 72/72.
Yards: 6,605/4,742. **Course rating:** 71.6/ 68.4. **Slope:** 133/125.
Subscriber comments: Course still maturing . . . Will be one of the finest . . . Great layout . . . Nice layout . . . Newer course . . . Very pretty course . . . Fairly short . . . Challenging . . . Scenic . . . Don't try walking . . . Spectacular views but course needs maturing.

★★ VINTAGE COURSE
Holes: 18. **Par:** 72/72.
Yards: 6,405/4,843. **Course rating:** 69.7/ 68.5. **Slope:** 122/120.
Subscriber comments: Plain vanilla course . . . No special toppings . . . Fun course . . . Good condition . . . Good challenge . . . Older, less challenging . . . Very good value . . . Open, some challenging holes . . . Getting better . . . Fun to play . . . Interesting layout.

★★★ WHITE TAIL GOLF CLUB
PU—2679 Klein Rd., Bath (610)837-9626.
7 miles north of Allentown. **Holes:** 18. **Par:** 72/72.
Yards: 6,432/5,228. **Course rating:** 70.1/N/A. **Slope:** 113/N/A.
Opened: 1993. **Pace of Play rating:** 4:30. **Green fee:** $18/25.
Credit cards: None. **Reduced fees:** Weekdays, Twilight, Seniors, Juniors.
Caddies: No. **Golf carts:** $10 for 18 holes.
Discount golf packages: Yes. **Season:** April-Dec. **High:** May-Sept.
On-site lodging: No. **Rental clubs:** Yes.
Walking policy: Walking at certain times. **Range:** Yes (grass).
To obtain tee times: Call seven days in advance, seven days a week.
Subscriber comments: Would not want to walk the front nine on hot, humid day . . . Relatively new but grown in nicely . . . Interesting mix of holes . . . Super, ultra-fast greens and very imaginative design . . . Tough, fast greens . . . A number of very good holes . . . Young course . . . Should mature to be even better . . . New course needs time . . . Fastest greens in Lehigh Valley . . . Fun to play . . . New front nine not as good as back nine . . . Several short holes . . . Hilly . . . Wind can be a big factor . . . New course . . . Will be a dandy.

★★★ WILKES-BARRE GOLF CLUB
PU—1001 Fairway Dr., Wilkes-Barre (717)472-3590.
25 miles south of Scranton. **Holes:** 18. **Par:** 72/74.
Yards: 6,912/5,690. **Course rating:** 72.8/73.2. **Slope:** 125/115.
Opened: 1968. **Pace of Play rating:** 4:30. **Green fee:** $20/20.
Credit cards: MC, V, AMEX. **Reduced fees:** Weekdays, Low season, Twilight, Seniors, Juniors.
Caddies: No. **Golf carts:** $11 for 18 holes.
Discount golf packages: Yes. **Season:** April-Nov. **High:** June-Aug.
On-site lodging: No. **Rental clubs:** Yes.
Walking policy: Walking at certain times. **Range:** Yes (grass).
To obtain tee times: Call one week in advance.
Subscriber comments: A very good course . . . Kept in good repair . . .

Good mix of holes . . . Greens need some work . . . Nice mountain top layout . . . A real nice course to play, it has it all . . . Great course . . . Best in area . . . Championship layout . . . Very busy . . . Fantastic greens . . . Consistent . . . Not the typical muny . . . Lots of woods . . . Nice shape all year round . . . Very scenic . . . Treelined . . . Worth playing . . . Long . . . Played in mid-summer . . . Course in excellent condition . . . For a municipal public course, very reasonable . . . Challenging.

★★½ WILLOW HOLLOW GOLF COURSE
PU—RD No.1, Box 1366, Prison Rd., Leesport (610)373-1505.
6 miles north of Reading. **Holes:** 18. **Par:** 70/70.
Yards: 5,810/4,435. **Course rating:** 67.1/N/A. **Slope:** 105/ 90.
Opened: 1959. **Pace of Play rating:** 4:00. **Green fee:** $9/18.
Credit cards: None. **Reduced fees:** Weekdays, Twilight, Seniors, Juniors.
Caddies: No. **Golf carts:** $10 for 18 holes.
Discount golf packages: No. **Season:** Year-round. **High:** May-Sept.
On-site lodging: No. **Rental clubs:** Yes.
Walking policy: Walking at certain times. **Range:** No.
To obtain tee times: Call up to one month in advance for weekends. For weekdays call up to two weeks in advance.
Subscriber comments: Variety of holes . . . Pleasant golf experience . . . Short . . . Public . . . Open course . . . Always in great shape . . . Has some super holes: Nos. 7, 9 and 11. Lots of par 3s . . . Back nine has good holes . . . Very short, but fun to play . . . Fun to play . . . Front and back nines are different worlds.

★★ WOODLAND HILLS COUNTRY CLUB
SP—Lower Saucon Rd., Hellertown (215)838-7192.
Call club for further information.
Subscriber comments: Course upkeep has improved . . . Tough greens . . . Last three holes good . . . Nice layout . . . Could improve range . . . Condition varies week to week from good to fair . . . A decent 18 . . . Superb course . . . Well maintained.

★★★★ WYNCOTE GOLF CLUB
SP—50 Wyncote Dr., Oxford (610)932-8900.
55 miles southwest of Philadelphia. **Holes:** 18. **Par:** 72/72.
Yards: 7,012/5,454. **Course rating:** 73.8/71.6. **Slope:** 128/126.
Opened: 1993. **Pace of Play rating:** 4:00-4:30. **Green fee:** $30/57.
Credit cards: All major. **Reduced fees:** Weekdays, Twilight, Seniors, Juniors.
Caddies: Yes. **Golf carts:** $12 for 18 holes.
Discount golf packages: No. **Season:** March-Dec. **High:** May-Oct.
On-site lodging: No. **Rental clubs:** Yes.
Walking policy: Walking at certain times. **Range:** Yes (grass).
To obtain tee times: Call one week in advance. Credit card must be used to reserve weekend tee times.
Ranked 13th in Pennsylvania by Golf Digest.
Subscriber comments: Gorgeous . . . Tough . . . Very challenging . . . One of the hottest I've played . . . Fairways like walking on a rug . . . Great holes . . . Friendly staff . . . Open and windy with wetland areas . . . Very unusual links course . . . Slope should be 150 . . . Links-style course in the country . . . Great links-style course and helpful staff . . . Beautiful fairways and greens . . . A bit of Scotland or Ireland . . . Very windy . . . Try playing in a 40-mph wind . . . Just like Scotland . . . Unique layout . . . No trees . . . Many areas of brush . . . Very tough from tips . . . Bring enough balls . . . New club . . . Expensive but fun . . . Ashamed to take divot in fairway . . . Great shape . . . Like country club . . . You'll use every club.

★★ COUNTRY VIEW GOLF CLUB

PU—Colwell Rd., RR No.4, Harrisville (401)568-7157.
15 miles north of Providence. **Holes:** 18. **Par:** 70/70.
Yards: 6,067/4,755. **Course rating:** 69.2/67.0. **Slope:** 119/105.
Opened: 1965. **Pace of Play rating:** 3:50. **Green fee:** $15/23.
Credit cards: None. **Reduced fees:** Weekdays, Low season, Twilight,
Seniors.
Caddies: No. **Golf carts:** $22 for 18 holes.
Discount golf packages: No. **Season:** March-Nov. **High:** June-Sept.
On-site lodging: No. **Rental clubs:** Yes.
Walking policy: Unrestricted walking. **Range:** Yes.
To obtain tee times: Call up to seven days in advance for weekdays. For
weekends call Monday.
Subscriber comments: Nice country track . . . Staff pleasant . . . So far
out your boss can't find you . . . Good challenge even for beginner . . .
Never broken 80? Here's the place . . . Fun layout, good views . . .
Crowned greens, must plan approach shots short . . . Clubhouse personnel
and starter very cordial . . . Small greens . . . Conditions are good . . . Fun
to play, can swing away . . . Easy back nine.

★★ CRANSTON COUNTRY CLUB

PU—69 Burlingame Rd., Cranston (401)826-1683.
7 miles south of Providence. **Holes:** 18. **Par:** 71/72.
Yards: 6,750/5,499. **Course rating:** 72.4/N/A. **Slope:** 124/N/A.
Opened: 1970. **Pace of Play rating:** 4:30. **Green fee:** $20/27.
Credit cards: None. **Reduced fees:** Twilight, Seniors.
Caddies: No. **Golf carts:** $10 for 18 holes.
Discount golf packages: No. **Season:** March-Dec. **High:** May-Sept.
On-site lodging: No. **Rental clubs:** Yes.
Walking policy: Unrestricted walking. **Range:** No.
To obtain tee times: Call Tuesday for upcoming weekend. For weekdays
call three days in advance.
Subscriber comments: Nothing spectacular, about average . . . Could be
a much better course with some work . . . Has lots of potential . . . Some
interesting holes on back nine . . . From the blues, a real challenge.

★★★½ EXETER COUNTRY CLUB

PU—320 Ten Rod Rd., Exeter (401)295-1178.
15 miles of Warwick. **Holes:** 18. **Par:** 72/72.
Yards: 6,919/5,733. **Course rating:** N/A. **Slope:** 123/115.
Opened: N/A. **Pace of Play rating:** N/A. **Green fee:** N/A.
Credit cards: MC, V. **Reduced fees:** Low season, Twilight.
Caddies: No. **Golf carts:** N/A.
Discount golf packages: No. **Season:** March-Nov. **High:** June-Sept.
On-site lodging: Yes. **Rental clubs:** No.
Walking policy: N/A. **Range:** Yes (grass).
Subscriber comments: Interesting design . . . Fairways well kept, shots
need to be precise . . . Back nine more difficult than front . . . Great course
for all levels of golfers . . . Well maintained, wide open fairways without
much trouble . . . Among the best in the area, I just can't score there. Oh
well . . . Absolutely the most fun of any course we play . . . One of the best
in Rhode Island. Superbly groomed and excellent test of golf . . .
Championship layout . . . Unique layout, back nine completely surrounds
the front nine . . . For all handicaps . . . Nice scenery ; worth a trip . . .
Layout has nice variety . . . Long par 3s.

★★½ FOSTER COUNTRY CLUB

SP—67 Johnson Rd., Foster (401)397-7750.
32 miles west of Providence. **Holes:** 18. **Par:** 72/74.
Yards: 6,200/5,500. **Course rating:** 69.5/70.0. **Slope:** 114/112.
Opened: 1964. **Pace of Play rating:** 4:30-5:00. **Green fee:** $18/20.
Credit cards: MC, V. **Reduced fees:** N/A.
Caddies: No. **Golf carts:** $18 for 18 holes.
Discount golf packages: Yes. **Season:** April-Nov. **High:** May-Aug.

On–site lodging: No. **Rental clubs:** Yes.
Walking policy: Walking at certain times. **Range:** No.
To obtain tee times: Call three days in advance.
Subscriber comments: Numerous blind shots and sharp doglegs . . . It
helps if you know the course layout . . . Challenging, three doglegs . . .
Accuracy needed on back nine ; bad finish with two par 3s . . . Fun course,
good staff . . . Front side open, back nine a hilly hike in the woods . . .
Good value; good restaurant ; several tough holes . . . Something for all
handicaps . . . Good food . . . Very good for any level golfer.

★★½ GREEN VALLEY COUNTRY CLUB

SP—371 Union St., Portsmouth (401)849-2162.
5 miles south of Newport. **Holes:** 18. **Par:** 71/71.
Yards: 6,830/5,459. **Course rating:** 72.0/69.5. **Slope:** 126/120.
Opened: 1957. **Pace of Play rating:** N/A. **Green fee:** $24/29.
Credit cards: MC, V. **Reduced fees:** Weekdays, Twilight.
Caddies: No. **Golf carts:** $20 for 18 holes.
Discount golf packages: No. **Season:** March–Dec. **High:** May–Sept.
On–site lodging: No. **Rental clubs:** Yes.
Walking policy: Unrestricted walking. **Range:** Yes (grass).
To obtain tee times: Call three days in advance.
Subscriber comments: A pretty fun course to play, greens good . . .
Remarkably beautiful and challenging . . . Excellent . . . Very crowded
course . . . Well maintained . . . Some nice views . . . Long course, can be
very windy.

★★½ LAUREL LANE GOLF COURSE

SP—309 Laurel Lane, West Kingston (401)783-3844.
25 miles south of Providence. **Holes:** 18. **Par:** 71/70.
Yards: 5,806/5,381. **Course rating:** 68.1/70.8. **Slope:** 113/115.
Opened: 1961. **Pace of Play rating:** 4:00. **Green fee:** $15/18.
Credit cards: None. **Reduced fees:** Twilight.
Caddies: No. **Golf carts:** N/A.
Discount golf packages: No. **Season:** March–Dec. **High:** June–Sept.
On–site lodging: No. **Rental clubs:** No.
Walking policy: Unrestricted walking. **Range:** No.
To obtain tee times: First come first serve.
Subscriber comments: Nothing distinctive, but a good course . . . Fun
course, plays shorter than card . . . Short but some tough holes, especially
the back nine . . . A good course to learn the game . . . Nice course ; nice
people . . . Wide open front nine. Narrow back . . . Well maintained, two
different nines: front is flat, back is hilly.

★ MELODY HILL GOLF COURSE

PU—Off Saw Mill Rd., Harmony (401)949-9851.
Call club for further information.
Subscriber comments: Fun course . . . Doglegs, fairways tough, greens
hard . . . Beautiful layout, in poor shape . . . Could be nicer, but still a
good value.

★★★ MONTAUP COUNTRY CLUB

SP—500 Anthony Rd., Portsmouth (401)683-9882.
Call club for further information.
Subscriber comments: Beautiful layout, very good condition . . . The
true look of a links course . . . Treated well . . . Nice layout . . . Good for
long-ball hitters . . . Nice course, lots of trees and water . . . Unusually
windy. Fairly tight course . . . Very picturesque . . . Good golf holes. Very
good condition . . . Toughest first three holes I've ever seen . . . Great back
nine. Stay below the hole! . . . Good all–around experience . . . Always in
good shape; good for all golfers . . . A real test of skills.

★★★½ NORTH KINGSTOWN MUNICIPAL GOLF COURSE

PU—1 Callahan Rd., North Kingstown (401)294-4051.
15 miles south of Providence. **Holes:** 18. **Par:** 70/70.
Yards: 6,161/5,227. **Course rating:** 69.7/69.5. **Slope:** 119/115.
Opened: 1943. **Pace of Play rating:** 4:30. **Green fee:** $13/23.
Credit cards: None. **Reduced fees:** Weekdays, Low season, Twilight.
Caddies: No. **Golf carts:** $20 for 18 holes.
Discount golf packages: No. **Season:** April-Nov. **High:** May-Oct.
On-site lodging: No. **Rental clubs:** Yes.
Walking policy: Unrestricted walking. **Range:** Yes (grass).
To obtain tee times: Call one day in advance beginning at 8 a.m. during regular season.
Subscriber comments: Good test for all levels . . . Old course, old facility, good value . . . Varied layout . . . Well constructed in traditional fashion . . . Back nine near ocean, very windy . . . A real gem, well maintained . . . Nice conditions, seaside links course . . . Enjoyable course . . . Some long holes . . . Abuts Quonset Air Base. Likely to see some Navy planes . . . Has the feel of the bar in "Top Gun" . . . Great course. Very popular . . . Everyone scores well . . . Old Navy course, well maintained, good bargain.

★★★½ RICHMOND COUNTRY CLUB

PU—74 Sandy Pond Rd., Richmond (401)364-9200.
30 miles south of Providence. **Holes:** 18. **Par:** 71/71.
Yards: 6,826/4,974. **Course rating:** 72.1/N/A. **Slope:** 121/N/A.
Opened: 1993. **Pace of Play rating:** 4:00. **Green fee:** $24/29.
Credit cards: None. **Reduced fees:** Weekdays, Twilight.
Caddies: No. **Golf carts:** $20 for 18 holes.
Discount golf packages: No. **Season:** April-Nov. **High:** June-Sept.
On-site lodging: No. **Rental clubs:** Yes.
Walking policy: Unrestricted walking. **Range:** No.
To obtain tee times: Call one day in advance beginning at 7 a.m.
Subscriber comments: A shotmaker's course, narrow fairways lined by 100-foot pines . . . Very well maintained, great staff . . . Blue and gold markers make it very challenging . . . Great course, staff very good, service good . . . Great walking course, feels like North Carolina . . . Wonderful clubhouse . . . Course for everyone . . . Short but tight, very beautiful setting . . . A joy to play . . . Must play. Sculpted course, bent grass tee to green, any golfer will enjoy . . . Tight fairways . . . Wonderful facility . . . Greens perfectly groomed. Fairways like carpet . . . Golf heaven . . . Hidden gem, leave driver home . . . Must play from back tees for any challenge . . . Myrtle Beach feel in the backwoods of Rhode Island . . . Made me feel like I was in Florida; lots of bunkers and pinewoods on each hole.

★★★ TRIGGS MEMORIAL GOLF COURSE

PU—1533 Chalkstone Ave., Providence (401)521-8460.
Holes: 18. **Par:** 72/73.
Yards: 6,596/5,598. **Course rating:** 71.9/N/A. **Slope:** 126/N/A.
Opened: 1933. **Pace of Play rating:** 4:00. **Green fee:** $21/25.
Credit cards: None. **Reduced fees:** Low season, Seniors.
Caddies: No. **Golf carts:** $23 for 18 holes.
Discount golf packages: No. **Season:** Year-round. **High:** June-Aug.
On-site lodging: No. **Rental clubs:** Yes.
Walking policy: Unrestricted walking. **Range:** No.
To obtain tee times: Call.
Subscriber comments: Links-type course, very long . . . Need to keep ball in play to score . . . Conditions improving yearly on this Donald Ross gem . . . Very difficult opening three holes . . . Fairways and greens nice . . . A long and challenging course . . . Good test for all golfers . . . Great layout. Long. Conditions vary greatly off fairways.

★★½ **WINNAPAUG COUNTRY CLUB**
SP—184 Shore Rd., Westerly (401)596-1237.
30 miles south of Providence. **Holes:** 18. **Par:** 72/72.
Yards: 6,337/5,113. **Course rating:** 68.9/69.0. **Slope:** 113/110.
Opened: 1922. **Pace of Play rating:** 4:00. **Green fee:** $22/28.
Credit cards: MC, V, AMEX. **Reduced fees:** Twilight.
Caddies: No. **Golf carts:** $11 for 18 holes.
Discount golf packages: Yes. **Season:** Year-round. **High:** June-Sept.
On-site lodging: Yes. **Rental clubs:** Yes.
Walking policy: Unrestricted walking. **Range:** Yes (grass).
To obtain tee times: Call seven days in advance
Subscriber comments: Some holes have nice views of the Block Island
Sound . . . Nice course to play when on a summer vacation . . . All levels
of play can enjoy this seaside course . . . Tight, short fairways, very
demanding greens, heavy play, fun course . . . Surf and Turf . . . Ross
design . . . Tight course, lots of O.B. . . . Good food . . . One of my
favorite layouts. Great variety with four unique par 3s.

Notes

★★★ ARCADIAN SHORES GOLF CLUB

PU—701 Hilton Rd., Myrtle Beach (803)449-5217, (800)249-9228.
Holes: 18. **Par:** 72/72.
Yards: 6,938/5,229. **Course rating:** 73.2/69.9. **Slope:** 136/117.
Opened: 1974. **Pace of Play rating:** 4:30. **Green fee:** $39/78.
Credit cards: MC, V, AMEX. **Reduced fees:** Low season, Resort guests.
Caddies: No. **Golf carts:** Included in Green Fee.
Discount golf packages: Yes. **Season:** Year-round. **High:** March-May/Oct.
On-site lodging: Yes. **Rental clubs:** Yes.
Walking policy: Mandatory cart. **Range:** Yes (grass).
To obtain tee times: Call up to one year in advance or book a golf package through the golf department at the Myrtle Beach Hilton.
Subscriber comments: Long, tough, but very nice . . . Nice straight forward golf course . . . New greens for '95 . . . Much better after recent greens change . . . Great layout, greens hard as a brick . . . Green recently rebuilt . . . Not Myrtle's best . . . Good practice area . . . Old but very nice . . . Interesting design and enjoyable to play . . . Beautiful course . . . Great old South Carolina course . . . Dogleg right, dogleg left, long and short, got it all.

★★★½ ARROWHEAD GOLF CLUB

PU—1201 Burcal Rd., Myrtle Beach (803)236-3243.
Holes: 18. **Par:** 72/72.
Yards: 6,666/4,812. **Course rating:** 71.1/N/A. **Slope:** 130/N/A.
Opened: 1994. **Pace of Play rating:** 4:00. **Green fee:** $31/79.
Credit cards: MC, V. **Reduced fees:** No.
Caddies: No. **Golf carts:** Included in Green Fee.
Discount golf packages: Yes. **Season:** Year-round. **High:** Spring/Fall.
On-site lodging: No. **Rental clubs:** Yes.
Walking policy: Mandatory cart. **Range:** Yes (grass).
To obtain tee times: Book through accommodations host or call pro shop.
Additional 9 holes to open September '95.
Subscriber comments: New course. Excellent layout . . . Too much water for average player . . . Very very nice for a new course . . . Easy if you keep ball dry . . . Bermuda greens, Distances deceiving . . . Water on almost every hole . . . Will be super when in matures . . . Gimmicks include trees between fairways to middle of greens . . . Few people know about it yet . . . Best in Myrtle . . . Nicest and hardest course ever played.

★★ AZALEA SANDS GOLF CLUB

PU—2100 Hwy. 17 S., North Myrtle Beach (803)272-6191, (800)252-2312.
Holes: 18. **Par:** 72/72.
Yards: 6,902/5,172. **Course rating:** 72.5/70.2. **Slope:** 123/119.
Opened: 1972. **Pace of Play rating:** 4:30-5:00. **Green fee:** $20/49.
Credit cards: MC, V. **Reduced fees:** Low season, Resort guests, Twilight.
Caddies: No. **Golf carts:** Included in Green Fee.
Discount golf packages: Yes. **Season:** Year-round. **High:** Spring/Fall.
On-site lodging: No. **Rental clubs:** Yes.
Walking policy: Walking at certain times. **Range:** No.
To obtain tee times: Call pro shop.
Subscriber comments: Centrally located, well maintained, always a pleasure to play . . . Fine greens, open at times . . . Best suited for the straight hitter . . . Name says it all, "Sand everywhere" . . . Good standard kind of course . . . Too little course . . . Pro shop, people very accommodating . . . Good starting course for vacations.

BAY TREE GOLF PLANTATION

PU—P.O. Box 240, North Myrtle Beach (803)249-1487, (800)845-6191.
Green fee: $17/40.
Credit cards: MC, V. **Reduced fees:** Low season.
Caddies: No. **Golf carts:** $15 for 18 holes.

Discount golf packages: Yes. **Season:** Year-round. **High:** March-April.
On-site lodging: Yes. **Rental clubs:** Yes.
Walking policy: Walking at certain times. **Range:** Yes.
To obtain tee times: Call anytime.

★★½ GOLD COURSE
Holes: 18. **Par:** 72/72.
Yards: 6,942/5,264. **Course rating:** 72.0/69.7. **Slope:** 135/117.
Opened: 1971. **Pace of Play rating:** 4:00.
Subscriber comments: Interesting layout, especially last three holes . . .
Course showed effects of heavy play, but conditions good . . . Only one of
Bay Tree courses above average . . . Course can be tough but flat . . . A
great place to pretend you're on the PGA Tour . . . From the back tees,
windy day, it's almost unplayable . . . Check greens in summer . . .
Challenging course, best experience of three Bay Tree courses

★★½ GREEN COURSE
Holes: 18. **Par:** 72/72.
Yards: 7,044/5,362. **Course rating:** 72.5/69.0. **Slope:** 135/118.
Opened: 1971. **Pace of Play rating:** 4:00.
Subscriber comments: Position golf is at a premium . . . Great course for
big hitters to let it rip, great practice facilities . . . Conditions uneven,
heavily played course, good wet weather course, drains well . . . Fun to
play . . . Best out of three . . . Lots of water, bunkers, good service . . .
The toughest of the Bay Tree layouts.

★★ SILVER COURSE
Holes: 18. **Par:** 72/72.
Yards: 6,871/5,417. **Course rating:** 70.5/69.0. **Slope:** 131/116.
Opened: 1971. **Pace of Play rating:** 4:00.
Subscriber comments: Most enjoyable for beach course . . . Simple
greens were like trampolines in spring . . . A real "meat grinder" . . . Very
average course . . . Plain course, nothing spectacular.

★★★ BEACHWOOD GOLF CLUB
PU—1520 Hwy. 17 S., North Myrtle Beach (803)272-6168.
Call club for further information.
Subscriber comments: Good tourist course . . . Some great holes . . .
Great cheeseburger . . . Staff did good job with a lot of traffic . . . User-
friendly warm up course . . . Traditional style for Myrtle Beach area . . .
Short course . . . Good senior and ego course . . . Straight forward course
. . . Wide fairways . . . Generous openings to most greens . . . Resort
course makes you feel good.

BERKELEY COUNTRY CLUB★
SP—Old Hwy. 52, Moncks Corner (803)761-4880.
20 miles south of Charleston. **Holes:** 18. **Par:** 72/72.
Yards: 6,696/5,100. **Course rating:** 71.2/67.9. **Slope:** 114/106.
Opened: 1959. **Pace of Play rating:** N/A. **Green fee:** $14/18.
Credit cards: MC, V, DISC. **Reduced fees:** Low season, Seniors.
Caddies: No. **Golf carts:** $9 for 18 holes.
Discount golf packages: No. **Season:** Year-round. **High:** April-Aug.
On-site lodging: No. **Rental clubs:** Yes.
Walking policy: Walking at certain times. **Range:** Yes (grass).
To obtain tee times: Call three days in advance.

★★★½ BLACKMOOR GOLF CLUB
R—6100 Longwood Rd., Hwy. 707, Murrells Inlet (803)650-5555.
12 miles south of Myrtle Beach. **Holes:** 18. **Par:** 72/72.
Yards: 6,614/4,807. **Course rating:** 71.1/67.9. **Slope:** 126/115.
Opened: 1990. **Pace of Play rating:** 4:30-5:00. **Green fee:** $22/60.
Credit cards: MC, V. **Reduced fees:** Low season, Resort guests, Juniors.
Caddies: No. **Golf carts:** $16 for 18 holes.
Discount golf packages: Yes. **Season:** Year-round. **High:** April-Oct.
On-site lodging: No. **Rental clubs:** Yes.
Walking policy: Mandatory cart. **Range:** Yes (grass).
To obtain tee times: Call pro shop.

Subscriber comments: Way to go, Gary Player . . . Worth the ride . . . Wonderful course . . . Staff very helpful . . . Great golf, tight course . . . Several holes too narrow . . . Lush, tight but not too much . . . Gives options . . . Enjoyable, fun course . . . Very playable . . . A great fun course . . . Interesting but not too hard . . . You never wonder how far it is to the green . . . Varied types of holes, blind doglegs . . . Need good iron play . . . Lot of wildlife . . . Very wet and marshy . . . Best hamburgers . . . Beautiful scenery . . . Best kept secret in Myrtle Beach . . . Found over 12 balls.

★½ **BONNIE BRAE GOLF COURSE**
SP—1316 Fork Shoals Rd., Greenville (803)277-4178.
Call club for further information.
Subscriber comments: Old course, but OK . . . Favors fade . . . Good fair course, tough opening hole . . . Good cart paths . . . Developing into a good course . . . Fun course that's improving conditions every year.

★★ **BOSCOBEL COUNTRY CLUB**
SP—Hwy. 76, Pendleton (803)646-3991.
Call club for further information.
Subscriber comments: Old-style course that plays to straight hitter. Greens will test your putter . . . Golfer has to use all his talents . . . Interesting layout; some good holes . . . Small fast greens, average condition, lots of undulations on greens . . . Nice bent greens, hilly . . . Greens are very difficult, many breaks and fast.

★★½ **BUCK CREEK GOLF PLANTATION**
MEADOW/CYPRESS/TUPELO
PU—701 Bucks Trail, Hwy. 9, Longs (803)249-5996, (800)344-0982.
6 miles west of Myrtle Beach. **Holes:** 27. **Par:** 72/72/72.
Yards: 6,751/6,865/6,726. **Course rating:** 71.1/72.4/71.6. **Slope:** 126/132/128.
Opened: 1990. **Pace of Play rating:** 4:00. **Green fee:** $22/66.
Credit cards: MC, V. **Reduced fees:** Low season, Twilight, Juniors.
Caddies: No. **Golf carts:** $16 for 18 holes.
Discount golf packages: Yes. **Season:** Year-round. **High:** Spring/Fall.
On-site lodging: No. **Rental clubs:** Yes.
Walking policy: Mandatory cart. **Range:** Yes (grass).
To obtain tee times: Call pro shop.
Subscriber comments: Many different challenges . . . A well-kept secret . . . Low lying course . . . Choose hard, medium, or easy. Just enough sand and water . . . Very tight, lots of trouble . . . Must be accurate to score . . . Must be accurate with tee shot . . . Tough course . . . One tough nine, two very good nines . . . Very playable, you can use all your clubs . . . Not too exciting . . . It's hard to beat this place . . . Good layout, can be windy, tough greens . . . Cypress is the only good one . . . Best course with abundant wildlife.

BURNING RIDGE GOLF CLUB
R—Hwy. 501 W., Conway (803)247-0538.
5 miles northwest of Myrtle Beach. **Green fee:** $56.
Credit cards: MC, V, DISC. **Reduced fees:** Weekdays, Low season, Twilight.
Caddies: No. **Golf carts:** Included in Green Fee.
Discount golf packages: Yes. **Season:** Year-round. **High:** Feb.-Oct.
On-site lodging: No. **Rental clubs:** Yes.
Walking policy: Mandatory cart. **Range:** Yes (grass).
To obtain tee times: Call two days in advance.
★★½ **EAST COURSE**
Holes: 18. **Par:** 72/72.
Yards: 6,780/4,524. **Course rating:** 72.8/65.4. **Slope:** 128/111.
Opened: 1985. **Pace of Play rating:** 4:00.
Subscriber comments: Commercial vacation-type course . . . Good course, treatment very good . . . Nice, good setup . . . Good layout, good

variety . . . Easy, average and difficult holes . . . Excellent practice area . . . Interesting layout, average golfer can enjoy . . . Great par 3s. Good sand traps . . . Tight with a good amount of water . . . Every hole is tight. Hit it in the fairway. Not long.

★★½ WEST COURSE
Holes: 18. **Par:** 72/72.
Yards: 6,714/4,831. **Course rating:** 71.8/67.2. **Slope:** 122/118.
Opened: 1980. **Pace of Play rating:** 4:00.
Subscriber comments: Interesting layout, several water holes . . . Hard course, almost unfairly bunkered . . . Average golf for South Carolina . . . Lots of well-placed water . . . Well-kept secret.

★★★★½ CALEDONIA GOLF AND FISH CLUB
PU—369 Caledonia Dr., Pawleys Island (803)237-3675.
15 miles south of Myrtle Beach. **Holes:** 18. **Par:** 70/70.
Yards: 6,503/4,968. **Course rating:** 70.8/68.2. **Slope:** 130/113.
Opened: 1994. **Pace of Play rating:** 4:00. **Green fee:** $95.
Credit cards: All major. **Reduced fees:** No.
Caddies: No. **Golf carts:** Included in Green Fee.
Discount golf packages: Yes. **Season:** Year-round. **High:** Spring/Fall.
On-site lodging: No. **Rental clubs:** Yes.
Walking policy: Mandatory cart. **Range:** No.
To obtain tee times: Call pro shop or have hotel golf director book tee times.
Ranked 12th in South Carolina by Golf Digest.
Subscriber comments: Enjoyable new course . . . A lot of sand with some grass thrown in . . . Beautiful, enjoyable, must play . . . Very special layout, similar to Augusta National in beauty . . . Excellent golf course, 18th hole will be a classic . . . New course . . . Fun to play . . . Not too long . . . Great course, bring your best game to score well . . . What golf is all about . . . Great course, a must play for the oak tree-lined drive . . . Target golf . . . A great gem in Myrtle Beach, will be one of the best . . . Great old oak trees. Play every club . . . Outstanding hole designs . . . Great experience. Staff was excellent . . . Great design, tees for everyone, beautiful golf course . . . This is a fun course to play . . . Creative layout requiring good shotmaking . . . Wonderful plantation setting, excellent, courteous staff, several long par 4s . . . Enjoyable to play, great to look at, best public golf at Myrtle Beach.

★★ CALHOUN COUNTRY CLUB
SP—Rte. 3 Country Club Rd., St. Matthews (803)823-2465.
30 miles south of Columbia. **Holes:** 18. **Par:** 71/71.
Yards: 6,339/4,812. **Course rating:** 70.9/66.4. **Slope:** 119/110.
Opened: 1957. **Pace of Play rating:** 4:00. **Green fee:** $10/25.
Credit cards: MC, V. **Reduced fees:** Weekdays, Twilight, Seniors, Juniors.
Caddies: No. **Golf carts:** Included in Green Fee.
Discount golf packages: No. **Season:** Year-round. **High:** March–April.
On-site lodging: No. **Rental clubs:** No.
Walking policy: Walking at certain times. **Range:** Yes (grass).
To obtain tee times: Call pro shop.
Subscriber comments: Nice layout . . . Well maintained, tight and challenging . . . Fair condition . . . Good designs . . . Great treatment.

★★★★ CALLAWASSIE ISLAND CLUB
PALMETTO/DOGWOOD/MAGNOLIA
SP—P.O. Drawer 2297, Beaufort (803)521-1533, (800)221-8431.
15 miles north of Hilton Head Island. **Holes:** 27. **Par:** 72/72/72.
Yards: 6,936/6,956/7,070. **Course rating:** 73.2/73.9/74.8. **Slope:** 130/132/138.
Opened: 1985. **Pace of Play rating:** 4:00. **Green fee:** $52/73.
Credit cards: MC, V, AMEX. **Reduced fees:** N/A.
Caddies: No. **Golf carts:** Included in Green Fee.
Discount golf packages: No. **Season:** Year-round. **High:** Spring/Fall.

On-site lodging: No. **Rental clubs:** Yes.
Walking policy: Mandatory cart. **Range:** Yes (grass).
To obtain tee times: Call pro shop.
Subscriber comments: One of Fazio's finest . . . Three solid nines . . .
Bring your sand wedge . . . Exceptional course, just want to keep on
playing . . . Outstanding Fazio course . . . For all levels of players . . .
Beautiful layout . . . First-class practice . . . As good a course as you can
find . . . Enjoyable, want to play again . . . Hidden gem . . . Callawassie,
great layout in the middle of nowhere . . . Worth the detour.

★★½ **CAROLINA SPRINGS COUNTRY CLUB**
WILLOWS/PINES/CEDAR
SP—1680 Scuffletown Rd., Fountain Inn (803)862-3551.
8 miles south of Greenville. **Holes:** 27. **Par:** 72/72/72.
Yards: 6,676/6,815/6,643. **Course rating:** 71.7/72.1/71.2. **Slope:**
125/121/121.
Opened: 1968. **Pace of Play rating:** 4:30. **Green fee:** $17/25.
Credit cards: MC, V. **Reduced fees:** Weekdays, Low season, Twilight,
Seniors, Juniors.
Caddies: No. **Golf carts:** $11 for 18 holes.
Discount golf packages: Yes. **Season:** Year-round. **High:** April-Sept.
On-site lodging: No. **Rental clubs:** Yes.
Walking policy: Unrestricted walking. **Range:** Yes (grass).
To obtain tee times: Call up to five days in advance.
Subscriber comments: Good solid public course . . . Wide open for the
most part . . . Bent greens, common Bermuda fairways . . . Best nines are
Willows and Pines . . . Fine 27-hole layout . . . Good for average player
. . . Three very different nines . . . Willows and Pines favor draw . . . All
the nines are imaginative . . . Great greens . . . Rangers keep players
moving . . . Five sets of tees, three nines, great place to learn.

★★½ **CAT ISLAND GOLF CLUB**
SP—8 Waveland Ave., Beaufort (803)524-0300, (800)221-9582.
40 miles north of Savannah, GA. **Holes:** 18. **Par:** 71/71.
Yards: 6,518/4,933. **Course rating:** 71.0/67.4. **Slope:** 127/116.
Opened: 1985. **Pace of Play rating:** 3:30. **Green fee:** $35.
Credit cards: MC, V. **Reduced fees:** Resort guests, Twilight, Juniors.
Caddies: No. **Golf carts:** Included in Green Fee.
Discount golf packages: Yes. **Season:** Year-round. **High:** Year-round.
On-site lodging: No. **Rental clubs:** Yes.
Walking policy: Mandatory cart. **Range:** Yes (grass).
To obtain tee times: Call up to 30 days in advance.
Subscriber comments: Picturesque . . . Water and marsh views, wildlife
. . . Fun course . . . Low country scenery . . . Beautiful par 3s . . . Best-
kept secret on the islands . . . Nice low country holes . . . Worth leaving
Hilton Head Island to play . . . Could be very good with better
conditioning.

★★★★ **CEDAR CREEK GOLF CLUB**
SP—2475 Club Dr., Aiken (803)648-4206.
25 miles west of Augusta, GA. **Holes:** 18. **Par:** 72/72.
Yards: 7,206/5,231. **Course rating:** 73.3/69.1. **Slope:** 125/115.
Opened: 1991. **Pace of Play rating:** 4:00. **Green fee:** $25/35.
Credit cards: MC, V, AMEX. **Reduced fees:** Resort guests, Seniors.
Caddies: No. **Golf carts:** Included in Green Fee.
Discount golf packages: Yes. **Season:** Year-round. **High:** April-Sept..
On-site lodging: No. **Rental clubs:** Yes.
Walking policy: Walking at certain times. **Range:** Yes (grass).
To obtain tee times: Call seven days in advance.
Subscriber comments: Fine Arthur Hills course . . . Excellent course . . .
New course, maturing fast, well worth a visit . . . This fun layout is sneaky
difficult . . . Very tough . . . Very challenging, gets better every year . . .
Hard to find . . . Deep bunkers . . . Bermuda roughs . . . Elevated greens.
Waste bunkers in fairways . . . Best-kept secret in Augusta/Aiken area,

TPC level course . . . Cedar Creek is a hidden jewel! Arthur Hill did a superb job. Very testing, yet enjoyable and beautiful . . . Holes wind through undeveloped woods, excellent conditions, abundant wildlife . . . A secret worth keeping.

★★½ CHARLESTON MUNICIPAL GOLF COURSE

PU—2110 Maybank Hwy., Charleston (803)795-6517.
Holes: 18. **Par:** 72/72.
Yards: 6,411/5,202. **Course rating:** 70.2/69.2. **Slope:** 112/114.
Opened: 1927. **Pace of Play rating:** 4:00. **Green fee:** $9/11.
Credit cards: None. **Reduced fees:** Twilight, Seniors, Juniors.
Caddies: No. **Golf carts:** $10 for 18 holes.
Discount golf packages: No. **Season:** Year-round. **High:** Spring/Fall.
On-site lodging: No. **Rental clubs:** Yes.
Walking policy: Unrestricted walking. **Range:** Yes (grass).
To obtain tee times: Call or come in one week in advance for threesomes and foursomes.
Subscriber comments: One of only a handful of truly public courses in the state . . . Good layout . . . Small greens . . . Good course for average player . . . For a muny course in great shape.

★★★ CHARLESTON NATIONAL COUNTRY CLUB

SP—1360 National Dr., Mt. Pleasant (803)884-7799.
10 miles east of Charleston. **Holes:** 18. **Par:** 72/72.
Yards: 6,928/5,103. **Course rating:** 73.5/70.8. **Slope:** 137/126.
Opened: 1991. **Pace of Play rating:** 4:15. **Green fee:** $25/50.
Credit cards: MC, V, DISC. **Reduced fees:** Weekdays, Low season, Twilight.
Caddies: Yes. **Golf carts:** Included in Green Fee.
Discount golf packages: Yes. **Season:** Year-round. **High:** Spring/Fall.
On-site lodging: No. **Rental clubs:** Yes.
Walking policy: Walking at certain times. **Range:** Yes (grass).
To obtain tee times: Call pro shop.
Subscriber comments: Best target golf in Charleston . . . Scenic . . . Even enjoy delay time . . . Too many forced carries . . . Most scenic course in area, new clubhouse is first-class . . . Very mean if wind gets up . . . Very good before Hurricane Hugo, lost so many trees . . . Very unforgiving . . . Lots of carries over marsh . . . Demanding . . . Staff friendly and accommodating. Varied layout . . . Beautiful marsh course. Bring lots of balls . . . Scenic marshes. Challenging but fair test of golf . . . Plays quick . . . Best kept secret in U.S. . . . Beautiful!

★★★½ CHERAW STATE PARK GOLF COURSE

PU—Rte. 2, Box 888, Cheraw (803)537-2215.
40 miles north of Florence. **Holes:** 18. **Par:** 72/72.
Yards: 6,900/5,408. **Course rating:** N/A. **Slope:** 130/120.
Opened: N/A. **Pace of Play rating:** N/A. **Green fee:** N/A.
Credit cards: MC, V. **Reduced fees:** Weekdays, Twilight.
Caddies: No. **Golf carts:** N/A.
Discount golf packages: Yes. **Season:** Year-round. **High:** March-June.
On-site lodging: Yes. **Rental clubs:** No.
Walking policy: N/A. **Range:** Yes (grass).
Subscriber comments: A diamond in the rough . . . Sandhill area of South Carolina makes for challenging play . . . Best-kept secret around . . . Golf course is for everyone, outstanding in every way. I drive 83 miles to play . . . Bent greens, well maintained . . . Very short, very tight, accurate iron play a must . . . Very good course, but couldn't walk even if allowed . . . Course is well-laid out, fun to play . . . State is doing great job in using park lands . . . Outstanding Sandhills layout . . . Unknown diamond . . . Great to play on the way to Myrtle Beach . . . Best kept secret in South Carolina . . . Nice layout, good condition, very pleasant . . . Great people work there . . . Probably the best state-owned course in the South. Absolutely gorgeous.

★★½ **CHESTER GOLF CLUB**
PU—Dawson Dr., Chester (803)581-5733.
Call club for further information.
Subscriber comments: Nothing outstanding . . . Good solid public
course . . . 40 miles from Charlotte or Columbia and worth the drive . . .
Good bent greens . . . Never real crowded . . . Best-kept secret in the
Piedmont.

★½ **CHICKASAW POINT COUNTRY CLUB**
SP—500 Hogan Dr., Westminster (803)972-9623.
Call club for further information.
Subscriber comments: Design allows good golf for all handicaps . . . Not
a pretty course . . . Not user-friendly . . . Course layout is great, needs
ground work . . . Has good potential to improve.

THE CLUB AT SEABROOK ISLAND
R—1002 Landfall Way, Seabrook Island (803)768-1000.
20 miles south of Charleston. & **Green fee:** $50/75.
Credit cards: All major. **Reduced fees:** No.
Caddies: No. **Golf carts:** Included in Green Fee.
Discount golf packages: Yes. **Season:** Year-round. **High:** Feb-Aug.
On-site lodging: Yes. **Rental clubs:** Yes.
Walking policy: Mandatory cart. **Range:** Yes (grass).
To obtain tee times: Have to be at resort three days ahead of time.
★★★ **CROOKED OAKS COURSE**
D**Holes:** 18. **Par:** 72/72.
Yards: 6,832/5,250. **Course rating:** 73.2/70.1. **Slope:** 126/119.
Opened: 1982. **Pace of Play rating:** 4:00.
Subscriber comments: Postcard low country golf course . . . Fun to play,
look out for trees . . . Poor facilities . . . Very playable and enjoyable for the
higher handicapper . . . Pricey but not crowded. Good place to take your
wife . . . Excellent resort course.
★★★½ **OCEAN WINDS COURSE**
Holes: 18. **Par:** 72/72.
Yards: 6,805/5,524. **Course rating:** 73.5/73.1. **Slope:** 130/127.
Opened: 1976. **Pace of Play rating:** 4:00.
Subscriber comments: Excellent resort course . . . Excellent greens . . .
Nice variety. Couple of weak holes . . . Best course in Charleston for the
money.

★★★ **COBB'S GLEN COUNTRY CLUB**
SP—2201 Cobb's Way, Anderson (803)226-7688, (800)624-7688.
28 miles south of Greenville. **Holes:** 18. **Par:** 72/72.
Yards: 7,002/5,312. **Course rating:** 72.3/72.0. **Slope:** 129/121.
Opened: 1975. **Pace of Play rating:** 4:00. **Green fee:** $20/25.
Credit cards: MC, V, AMEX. **Reduced fees:** Weekdays, Seniors,
Juniors.
Caddies: No. **Golf carts:** $10 for 18 holes.
Discount golf packages: Yes. **Season:** Year-round. **High:** April-Oct.
On-site lodging: No. **Rental clubs:** Yes.
Walking policy: Walking at certain times. **Range:** Yes (grass).
To obtain tee times: Call 48 hours in advance.
Subscriber comments: George Cobb design . . . Challenging course,
usually in top condition . . . Generous fairways . . . Demands full variety of
shots . . . Good layout . . . Very large greens . . . Big, soft greens that putt
fast . . . Traps in poor condition . . . Good for relaxing layout, good rolling
greens . . . Large, sloping, fast greens, very fair course . . . One of upstate
South Carolina's best.

COLDSTREAM COUNTRY CLUB★
SP—Hwy. 60, Irmo (803)781-0114.
14 miles northwest of Columbia. **Holes:** 18. **Par:** 71/71.
Yards: 6,155/5,097. **Course rating:** 70.1/68.7. **Slope:** 122/N/A
Opened: 1974. **Pace of Play rating:** 4:00. **Green fee:** $22/28.

Credit cards: MC, V. **Reduced fees:** Weekdays, Low season, Resort guests, Twilight, Seniors, Juniors.
Caddies: No. **Golf carts:** Included in Green Fee.
Discount golf packages: No. **Season:** Year-round. **High:** April-Oct.
On-site lodging: No. **Rental clubs:** Yes.
Walking policy: Mandatory cart. **Range:** No.
To obtain tee times: Call 48 hours in advance. Members have priority tee times on weekends.

★★★ COLONIAL CHARTERS GOLF CLUB
PU—301 Charter Dr., Longs (803)249-8809.
3 miles north of North Myrtle Beach. **Holes:** 18. **Par:** 72/72.
Yards: 6,901/6,372. **Course rating:** N/A. **Slope:** 127/120.
Opened: N/A. **Pace of Play rating:** N/A. **Green fee:** N/A.
Credit cards: All major. **Reduced fees:** Low season, Twilight.
Caddies: No. **Golf carts:** $14 for 18 holes.
Discount golf packages: Yes. **Season:** Year-round. **High:** Spring/Fall.
On-site lodging: Yes. **Rental clubs:** No.
Walking policy: N/A. **Range:** Yes (grass).
Subscriber comments: Very good course . . . Great sights on the eighth
. . . Challenging course . . . Disappointed with playing conditions . . .
More enjoyable each time I play it . . . Some interesting holes . . . A cart is
a must, from one hole to the next is a drive through the pines, . . . Seldom
see another fairway, safest course I know . . . One of my favorites . . . Lots
of fun . . . Excellent Bermuda greens . . . A few tricky holes . . . Will be
nice residential course.

COOPER'S CREEK GOLF CLUB★
SP—700 Wagener Hwy. No.113, Pelion (803)894-3666, (800)828-8463.
25 miles west of Columbia. **Holes:** 18. **Par:** 72/73.
Yards: 6,582/4,565. **Course rating:** 70.8/63.6. **Slope:** 120/99.
Opened: 1973. **Pace of Play rating:** 4:00. **Green fee:** $7/17.
Credit cards: MC, V. **Reduced fees:** Weekdays, Low season, Resort
guests, Twilight, Seniors, Juniors.
Caddies: No. **Golf carts:** $15 for 18 holes.
Discount golf packages: Yes. **Season:** Year-round. **High:** April-Oct.
On-site lodging: No. **Rental clubs:** Yes.
Walking policy: Unrestricted walking. **Range:** Yes (grass).
To obtain tee times: Call up to three days in advance.

COOSAW CREEK COUNTRY CLUB★
PU—4210 Club Course Dr., North Charleston (803)767-9000.
Holes: 18. **Par:** 71/71.
Yards: 6,593/5,064. **Course rating:** 71.3/64.4. **Slope:** 129/115.
Opened: 1993. **Pace of Play rating:** 4:00. **Green fee:** $26/32.
Credit cards: MC, V, AMEX. **Reduced fees:** Weekdays, Low season.
Caddies: No. **Golf carts:** $12 for 18 holes.
Discount golf packages: Yes. **Season:** Year-round. **High:** Spring/Fall.
On-site lodging: No. **Rental clubs:** Yes.
Walking policy: Walking at certain times. **Range:** Yes (grass).
To obtain tee times: Call up to seven days in advance.

★★½ COUNTRY CLUB OF BEAUFORT
SP—8 Barnwell Dr., Beaufort (803)522-1605, (800)869-1617.
45 miles north of Savannah, GA. **Holes:** 18. **Par:** 72/72.
Yards: 6,506/4,880. **Course rating:** 71.2/67.8. **Slope:** 118/120.
Opened: 1973. **Pace of Play rating:** 4:00. **Green fee:** $24.
Credit cards: MC, V, AMEX. **Reduced fees:** Twilight.
Caddies: No. **Golf carts:** $12 for 18 holes.
Discount golf packages: Yes. **Season:** Year-round. **High:** Spring/Fall.
On-site lodging: No. **Rental clubs:** Yes.
Walking policy: Unrestricted walking. **Range:** Yes (grass).
To obtain tee times: Call up to seven days in advance.
Subscriber comments: Coastal beauty with classic character . . . One of

my all time favorites . . . Rather wild around the edges . . . Water on 13 holes . . . Good entertainment at good price . . . Treated well . . . Fun to play . . . Largest alligators in the state!

★★★½ COUNTRY CLUB OF HILTON HEAD

SP—70 Skull Creek Dr., Hilton Head Island (803)681-4653.
35 miles northeast of Savannah, GA. **Holes:** 18. **Par:** 72/72.
Yards: 6,919/5,373. **Course rating:** 73.6/71.3. **Slope:** 132/123.
Opened: 1987. **Pace of Play rating:** 4:20. **Green fee:** $44/73.
Credit cards: All major. **Reduced fees:** Low season, Twilight.
Caddies: No. **Golf carts:** Included in Green Fee.
Discount golf packages: No. **Season:** Year-round. **High:** Spring/Fall
On-site lodging: No. **Rental clubs:** Yes.
Walking policy: Mandatory cart. **Range:** Yes (grass).
To obtain tee times: Call up to three months in advance.
Subscriber comments: Solid Rees Jones . . . Clubhouse exceptional . . . Some good holes . . . Very much like northern country club . . . A favorite of mine, woods kept clear of underbrush, lets you play back out . . . Pleasant . . . Long course, well groomed . . . Good test, good layout . . . Super course . . . Well laid out . . . First-class . . . Put on your Hilton Head list.

★★★ CRICKENTREE COUNTRY CLUB

SP—1084 Langford Rd., Blythewood (803)754-8600.
Call club for further information.
Subscriber comments: Nice layout . . . Tough course. Lot of character . . . Good greens, must be accurate . . . One of few bent-grass courses in area . . . When the greens are right, this is heaven . . . Beautiful tree-lined layout . . . Excellent challenging course. I hope to play it again soon . . . Beautiful, interesting to play . . . Tight and challenging . . . Time will make it a gem.

★★★½ CROWFIELD GOLF AND COUNTRY CLUB

SP—300 Hamlet Circle, Goose Creek (803)764-4618.
20 miles west of Charleston. **Holes:** 18. **Par:** 72/72.
Yards: 7,003/5,682. **Course rating:** 73.7/67.3. **Slope:** 134/N/A.
Opened: 1990. **Pace of Play rating:** 4:00-4:30. **Green fee:** $22/33.
Credit cards: All major. **Reduced fees:** Weekdays, Low season, Twilight.
Caddies: No. **Golf carts:** $13 for 18 holes.
Discount golf packages: Yes. **Season:** Year-round. **High:** Spring.
On-site lodging: No. **Rental clubs:** Yes.
Walking policy: Walking at certain times. **Range:** Yes (grass).
To obtain tee times: Call one week in advance.
Subscriber comments: Awesome track . . . This is a very challenging course that requires accuracy off the tee . . . Miss the fairway and you can just about guarantee a bogey at best . . . Many pinpoint shots, lots of fun to play, well laid out . . . Hardest course I ever played . . . Recent changes to course make it very playable . . . Nice layout, plenty of water, good pace. Tough, mounded fairways . . . Keep this a secret . . . Take your opponent there if you hit it straight and he does not . . . Gimmicky . . . Very hard par 3s . . . Super, modern design . . . Big rolling greens . . . Undiscovered gem . . . Very unforgiving, all holes isolated from others . . . The most underrated course in the low country of South Carolina . . . If you're not patient, don't play here . . . Very good course, lots of moguls, water, marsh. I loved it.

DEER TRACK GOLF RESORT

R—460 Platt Blvd., Surfside Beach (803)650-2146, (800)548-9186.
8 miles south of Myrtle Beach. **Green fee:** $8/38.
Credit cards: MC, V. **Reduced fees:** Weekdays, Low season, Resort guests, Twilight, Juniors.
Caddies: No. **Golf carts:** $16 for 18 holes.
Discount golf packages: Yes. **Season:** Year-round. **High:** Spring/Fall.
On-site lodging: Yes. **Rental clubs:** Yes.

Walking policy: Walking at certain times. **Range:** Yes (grass).
To obtain tee times: Call pro shop.

★★ NORTH COURSE
Holes: 18. **Par:** 72/72.
Yards: 7,203/5,353. **Course rating:** 73.5/69.6. **Slope:** 121/119.
Opened: 1974. **Pace of Play rating:** N/A.
Subscriber comments: Gets lots of play, not always in good shape . . .
Enjoyable for all levels . . . Too many blind shots for my taste . . . Too
many hidden hazards . . . Tight fairways . . . Nothing special . . . Excellent
greens . . . For long hitters, wide fairways . . . Very nice layout, an
enjoyable play . . . Some holes lined with condos both sides, so hit it
straight . . . Good pro shop.

★★ SOUTH COURSE
Holes: 18. **Par:** 71/71.
Yards: 6,916/5,226. **Course rating:** 72.9/70.6. **Slope:** 119/120.
Opened: 1974. **Pace of Play rating:** N/A.
Subscriber comments: Fun courses . . . Water on both sides of fairways
so bring lots of balls . . . Very nice layout . . . Typical resort course . . .
Fair.

★★★½ THE DUNES WEST GOLF CLUB
SP—3535 Wando Plantation Way, Mt. Pleasant (803)856-9000, (800)591-
5809.
10 miles east of Charleston. **Holes:** 18. **Par:** 72/72.
Yards: 6,871/5,278. **Course rating:** 73.4/69.2. **Slope:** 131/118.
Opened: 1991. **Pace of Play rating:** 4:15. **Green fee:** $30/60.
Credit cards: MC, V, AMEX. **Reduced fees:** Weekdays, Low season,
Juniors.
Caddies: Yes. **Golf carts:** Included in Green Fee.
Discount golf packages: Yes. **Season:** Year-round. **High:** March-
May/Oct.
On-site lodging: No. **Rental clubs:** Yes.
Walking policy: Walking at certain times. **Range:** Yes (grass).
To obtain tee times: Call. A credit card must be used if you are reserving
more than two weeks in advance.
Subscriber comments: Outstanding golf course, fair, fun and scenic . . .
Nice public course, but almost unfair at places into wind . . . Huge greens
and fairways . . . Fair layout for all types of golfers . . . Tough with lots of
sand . . . Great golf course with some very scenic marsh views . . . Hard
when the wind blows, need to play more than once to know where to aim
. . . Great traditional beach course, spectacular views . . . Wide fairways,
large greens, fun for any handicapper . . . Fun, beautiful course . . . Overall
better than Wild Dunes . . . Enjoyed the experience every time. Course is
really maturing . . . Good layout, No. 18 is great finishing hole . . . Very
nice course . . . Good greens . . . Open enough for sprayers . . . Best
course for the money in the Charleston area.

★★★ EAGLE NEST GOLF CLUB
R—Hwy. 17 N., North Myrtle Beach (803)249-1449, (800)543-3113.
Holes: 18. **Par:** 72/72.
Yards: 6,901/5,105. **Course rating:** 73.0/69.8. **Slope:** 120/116.
Opened: 1971. **Pace of Play rating:** 4:30. **Green fee:** $12/39.
Credit cards: MC, V, AMEX. **Reduced fees:** Resort guests, Twilight.
Caddies: No. **Golf carts:** $15 for 18 holes.
Discount golf packages: Yes. **Season:** Year-round. **High:** March-
April/Oct.
On-site lodging: No. **Rental clubs:** Yes.
Walking policy: Walking at certain times. **Range:** Yes (grass).
To obtain tee times: Call up to one year in advance.
Subscriber comments: A surprising find . . . A northern-type course in
the south . . . Tough little course . . . Beautiful course with fun and
challenging holes . . . Good finishing holes, especially 17 . . . Overplayed
. . . Equally balanced between straight and doglegs holes . . . 16, 17, and
18th holes magnificent . . . Three tough finishing holes . . . Enjoyable

course . . . Picturesque layout, well kept, by the water . . . Much improved condition, challenging finish . . . The last three holes hardest I've ever played in a row . . . Great finishing holes, 16, 17, 18 . . . Great for all players . . . Win a lot or lose a lot of money on the last three holes.

★★½ EASTPORT GOLF CLUB
PU—Hwy. 17, North Myrtle Beach (803)249-3997, (800)334-9035.
Holes: 18. **Par:** 70/70.
Yards: 6,047/4,560. **Course rating:** 66.2/65.7. **Slope:** 116/114.
Opened: 1988. **Pace of Play rating:** 4:00-4:30. **Green fee:** $6/27.
Credit cards: MC, V. **Reduced fees:** Weekdays.
Caddies: No. **Golf carts:** $15 for 18 holes.
Discount golf packages: No. **Season:** Year-round. **High:** March-May.
On-site lodging: No. **Rental clubs:** Yes.
Walking policy: Mandatory cart. **Range:** No.
To obtain tee times: Call 48 hours in advance.
Subscriber comments: Reachable, readable, rewarding, tell all seniors a must in Myrtle Beach . . . Good seniors course . . . Short, tight course but lots of fun . . . Very narrow, no overlap between fairways . . . Easy to score well . . . Too short . . . Tricky, interesting though short . . . Lots of sand . . . Short, tight and interesting, No. 18 too tough . . . Enjoyed it so much I played it twice.

★★½ EDISTO BEACH GOLF CLUB
R—24 Fairway Dr., Edisto Island (803)869-1111.
45 miles south of Charleston. **Holes:** 18. **Par:** 71/72.
Yards: 6,212/5,306. **Course rating:** 69.5/70.3. **Slope:** 118/120.
Opened: 1973. **Pace of Play rating:** 4:00. **Green fee:** $42.
Credit cards: MC, V. **Reduced fees:** Weekdays, Low season, Resort guests, Juniors.
Caddies: No. **Golf carts:** Included in Green Fee.
Discount golf packages: Yes. **Season:** Year-round. **High:** April-Oct.
On-site lodging: Yes. **Rental clubs:** Yes.
Walking policy: Walking at certain times. **Range:** No.
To obtain tee times: Call pro shop.
Formerly known as Country Club at Edisto.
Subscriber comments: Lots of water . . . Tight course . . . Lots of water and sand. Good layout . . . May have tried to force some of the design into too small an area . . . Very small greens . . . Lot of doglegs, short tee shots, placement course . . . If one wants a natural, low key setting, this is one of the best . . . Pretty course. Tight on some holes . . . Too far away from everywhere . . . Much water . . . Don't need driver . . . Very fine course, brings you back.

★½ FALCON'S LAIR GOLF COURSE
SP—1308 Falcon's Dr., Walhalla (803)638-0000.
40 miles northwest of Greenville. **Holes:** 18. **Par:** 72/74.
Yards: 6,955/5,238. **Course rating:** 72.1/70.6. **Slope:** 124/123.
Opened: 1991. **Pace of Play rating:** 4:30. **Green fee:** $22/26.
Credit cards: MC, V. **Reduced fees:** Weekdays, Low season, Twilight, Seniors, Juniors.
Caddies: No. **Golf carts:** $10 for 18 holes.
Discount golf packages: Yes. **Season:** Year-round. **High:** March-Oct.
On-site lodging: No. **Rental clubs:** Yes.
Walking policy: Walking at certain times. **Range:** Yes (grass).
To obtain tee times: First come, first served.
Subscriber comments: Many interesting holes . . . Layout is difficult . . . A few holes need redesign . . . Will improve . . . Some suspect holes. Narrow mountain course . . . A lot of potential.

★★½ FORT MILL GOLF CLUB
SP—101 Country Club Dr., Fort Mill (803)547-2044.
15 miles south of Charlotte, NC. **Holes:** 18. **Par:** 72/72.
Yards: 6,865/5,448. **Course rating:** 72.5/70.0. **Slope:** 123/123.

Opened: 1948. **Pace of Play rating:** 4:15. **Green fee:** $20.
Credit cards: None. **Reduced fees:** No.
Caddies: No. **Golf carts:** $32 for 18 holes.
Discount golf packages: No. **Season:** Year-round. **High:** April-Sept.
On-site lodging: No. **Rental clubs:** No.
Walking policy: Mandatory cart. **Range:** No.
To obtain tee times: Call on Wednesday for upcoming weekend.
Weekdays call one or two days in advance.
Subscriber comments: OK public course . . . Lot of play but well
conditioned . . . Coming into maturity . . . Tough greens to putt . . . One
of the better public layouts in upstate South Carolina.

★★★ FOX CREEK GOLF CLUB

SP—Hwy. 15 S., Lydia (803)332-0613.

20 miles west of Florence. **Holes:** 18. **Par:** 72/72.
Yards: 6,903/5,271. **Course rating:** 72.3/67.9. **Slope:** 123/106.
Opened: 1988. **Pace of Play rating:** 4:30. **Green fee:** $13/18.
Credit cards: MC, V. **Reduced fees:** Weekdays, Resort guests, Seniors,
Juniors.
Caddies: No. **Golf carts:** $10 for 18 holes.
Discount golf packages: Yes. **Season:** Year-round. **High:** Feb-
May/Sept.-Nov.
On-site lodging: No. **Rental clubs:** Yes.
Walking policy: Walking at certain times. **Range:** Yes (grass).
Subscriber comments: Fun, challenging course . . . Big greens . . . Open
. . . High handicapper's delight . . . Very pleasant experience all three times
. . . Requires shot selection on some holes . . . If you can find it, play it.

FOXBORO GOLF CLUB★

R—1438 Wash Davis Rd., Summerton (803)478-7000, (800)468-7061.
75 miles southeast of Charleston. **Holes:** 18. **Par:** 72/72.
Yards: 6,889/5,386. **Course rating:** 71.1/68.4. **Slope:** 117/114.
Opened: 1988. **Pace of Play rating:** 4:30. **Green fee:** $15/29.
Credit cards: MC, V. **Reduced fees:** Low season.
Caddies: No. **Golf carts:** Included in Green Fee.
Discount golf packages: Yes. **Season:** Year-round. **High:** Spring/Fall.
On-site lodging: No. **Rental clubs:** Yes.
Walking policy: Mandatory cart. **Range:** No.
To obtain tee times: Call pro shop.

★★★ GATOR HOLE GOLF COURSE

PU—700 Hwy. 17., North Myrtle Beach (803)249-3543, (800)447-2668.
Holes: 18. **Par:** 70/70.
Yards: 6,000/4,685. **Course rating:** 69.8/65.9. **Slope:** 116/112.
Opened: 1980. **Pace of Play rating:** 4:00. **Green fee:** $32/56.
Credit cards: MC, V. **Reduced fees:** Twilight, Juniors.
Caddies: No. **Golf carts:** Included in Green Fee.
Discount golf packages: No. **Season:** Year-round. **High:** March-May.
On-site lodging: No. **Rental clubs:** Yes.
Walking policy: Mandatory cart. **Range:** Yes (grass).
To obtain tee times: Call 13 months in advance.
Subscriber comments: No gators here, but holes will bite ya . . . Will
make you think or you are dead . . . Short but tough, has six par 3s . . .
Absolute fun . . . Unusual beach course . . . Lots of water, bunkers, good
service . . . Nonpunishing opening hole . . . Best kept secret on Myrtle
Beach . . . Love it.

★★½ THE GAUNTLET AT LAUREL VALLEY

PU—253 Chinquapin Rd., Tigerville (803)895-6758, (800)531-0098.
15 miles north of Greenville. **Holes:** 18. **Par:** 72/72.
Yards: 6,713/4,545. **Course rating:** 72.1/69.7. **Slope:** 135/119.
Opened: 1993. **Pace of Play rating:** 4:30. **Green fee:** $25/40.
Credit cards: MC, V, AMEX. **Reduced fees:** Weekdays, Low season,
Twilight, Seniors, Juniors.

Caddies: No. **Golf carts:** Included in Green Fee.
Discount golf packages: No. **Season:** Year-round. **High:** March–Oct.
On-site lodging: No. **Rental clubs:** Yes.
Walking policy: Walking at certain times. **Range:** Yes (grass).
To obtain tee times: Call up to five days in advance.
Subscriber comments: New . . . Wonderfully scenic . . . Gorgeous
mountain views . . . Remote . . . Great prospects, good layout . . . Needs
maturing, lots of blind shots . . . Great views . . . Too many tricky holes
. . . Easy front nine, tough back nine . . . Opened too early . . . Wife broke
100 first time . . . A fairly tough course, will get better with age . . .
Fantastic scenery . . . Difficult to hit elevated greens . . . Fun course . . .
Tougher than at first look.

★ GEORGE MILER GOLF COURSE
PU—400 Country Club Blvd., Summerville (803)873-2210.
Call club for further information.
Subscriber comments: Tight fairways, good old course . . . Crowded
. . . Poorly maintained . . . Needs work, cart paths are terrible.

★★½ GOLDEN HILLS GOLF AND COUNTRY CLUB
SP—100 Scotland Dr., Lexington (803)957-3355.
Call club for further information.
Subscriber comments: Narrow course, challenging : . . Off fairway is
probably lost ball . . . Some nice holes . . . Terrible rough, prepare to spend
time looking for balls . . . Pretty course that has not yet matured . . .
Getting better.

★★★★½ HARBOUR TOWN GOLF LINKS
R—11 Lighthouse Lane, Hilton Head Island (803)363-4485, (800)955-8337.
30 miles northeast of Savannah, GA. **Holes:** 18. **Par:** 71/71.
Yards: 6,916/5,019. **Course rating:** 74.0/69.0. **Slope:** 136/117.
Opened: 1969. **Pace of Play rating:** 4:00-4:30. **Green fee:** $78/142.
Credit cards: All major. **Reduced fees:** Low season, Resort guests,
Twilight, Juniors.
Caddies: Yes. **Golf carts:** $18 for 18 holes.
Discount golf packages: Yes. **Season:** Year-round. **High:** Spring/Fall.
On-site lodging: Yes. **Rental clubs:** Yes.
Walking policy: Walking at certain times. **Range:** Yes (grass).
To obtain tee times: Call and hold tee time with credit card.
Ranked 57th in America's 100 Greatest Golf Courses by Golf Digest.
Ranked 9th in America's 75 Best Resort Courses by Golf Digest. Ranked
2nd in South Carolina by Golf Digest.
Subscriber comments: Easier and more enjoyable to play than seems on
TV . . . A barrel of fun worth the price . . . Beautiful, thoughtful and
challenging layout, staff very courteous . . . Deserving of Top 100 rating
. . . Expected better maintenance . . . Out of bounds on almost every hole
. . . Conditions greatly improved . . . A beautiful ambiance . . . Good test
. . . Too much play . . . Par 3s are scenic . . . Solid layout . . . Upkeep up
and down seasonally . . . Staff professional and friendly, condition of
course improved over prior years . . . Wall-to-wall golfers . . . Tight
fairways and small greens . . . Great layout. Small greens . . . Holes 17 and
18 fantastic . . . This course is always in good shape . . . Prestigious . . .
Spike marks destroy greens . . . Could play here every day forever . . .
Where else can you hit a drive in the middle of the fairway and still be
behind a tree? . . . Great test of ability . . . Not a bad hole . . . Best course
in the south.

★★★★ HEATHER GLEN GOLF LINKS
RED/WHITE/BLUE
R—Hwy. 17 N., Little River (803)249-9000, (800)868-4536.
15 miles south of Myrtle Beach. **Holes:** 27. **Par:** 72/72/72.
Yards: 6,769/6,808/6,771. **Course rating:** 72.4/72.4/72.4. **Slope:**
130/130/127.
Opened: 1987. **Pace of Play rating:** 4:30. **Green fee:** $ 30/81.

Credit cards: MC, V, AMEX. **Reduced fees:** No.
Caddies: No. **Golf carts:** Included in Green Fee.
Discount golf packages: No. **Season:** Year-round. **High:** March–May/Oct.
On-site lodging: No. **Rental clubs:** Yes.
Walking policy: Mandatory cart. **Range:** Yes (grass).
To obtain tee times: Call anytime.
Ranked in Second 25 of America's 75 Best Public Golf Courses by Golf Digest. Selected Best New Public Course of 1987 by Golf Digest.
Subscriber comments: Nice change of pace from other Myrtle Beach courses . . . A true delight . . . Unique course . . . Could play this course over and over . . . Good practice facilities . . . Very friendly . . . All three nines are great, real good shape . . . Very tough course . . . Even with heavy play, well kept . . . This course is a hidden treasure . . . Best course I played all year . . . A thorough pleasure to play . . . Top shelf . . . Neat terrain . . . Good solid layouts . . . Precision shotmaking . . . Great par 5 finishing hole . . . A really great place one of my best golf experiences . . . Each hole has a different character.

★★★★ HERITAGE CLUB
PU—Hwy. 17 S., Pawleys Island (803)237-3424, (800)377-2315.
20 miles south of Myrtle Beach. **Holes:** 18. **Par:** 71/71.
Yards: 7,100/5,325. **Course rating:** 74.2/71.0. **Slope:** 137/125.
Opened: 1986. **Pace of Play rating:** 4:30. **Green fee:** $ 36/85.
Credit cards: MC, V, AMEX. **Reduced fees:** Low season, Resort guests.
Caddies: No. **Golf carts:** $17 for 18 holes.
Discount golf packages: Yes. **Season:** Year-round. **High:** March/April/Oct.
On-site lodging: No. **Rental clubs:** Yes.
Walking policy: Mandatory cart. **Range:** Yes (grass).
To obtain tee times: Call up to nine months in advance. Deposit required during high season.
Ranked in Second 25 of America's 75 Best Public Golf Courses by Golf Digest.
Subscriber comments: Beautiful plantation setting. Undulating greens . . . Excellent golf in peaceful setting . . . First class! Something for everyone . . . Beauty on all sides . . . Moss-draped oaks, tough holes, a challenge . . . An undiscovered jewel, so don't tell anyone . . . Gorgeous clubhouse . . . Beautiful layout . . . Old plantation . . . Most scenic course in area . . . Difficult, but the scenery makes up for it . . . A few difficult forced carries . . . Some memorable holes . . . South at its best . . . One fine course, fairways always seem soft, lots of trouble, need to play course once before scoring well.

★★½ HERON POINT GOLF CLUB
PU—6980 Blue Heron Blvd., Myrtle Beach (803)650-6664.
60 miles north of Charleston. **Holes:** 18. **Par:** 72/72.
Yards: 6,477/4,734. **Course rating:** 71.0/69.2. **Slope:** 120/121.
Opened: 1988. **Pace of Play rating:** 4:00. **Green fee:** $35.
Credit cards: MC, V. **Reduced fees:** Weekdays, Low season, Resort guests, Twilight, Seniors, Juniors.
Caddies: No. **Golf carts:** Included in Green Fee.
Discount golf packages: Yes. **Season:** Year-round. **High:** Spring/Fall.
On-site lodging: No. **Rental clubs:** Yes.
Walking policy: Mandatory cart. **Range:** Yes (grass).
To obtain tee times: Call one week in advance.
Subscriber comments: Target golf . . . Narrow fairways . . . Tight fairways . . . Fast greens, water, nice course . . . Hard to find . . . 18th hole is a classic . . . A lot of trees and too many houses . . . Friendly alligators.

★★★½ HICKORY KNOB GOLF CLUB
R—off Hwy. 378, McCormick (803)391-2450, (800)491-1764.
38 miles north of Augusta. **Holes:** 18. **Par:** 72/72.
Yards: 6,560/4,905. **Course rating:** 72.1/67.3. **Slope:** 119/120.

Opened: 1982. **Pace of Play rating:** 4:30. **Green fee:** $12/16.
Credit cards: MC, V. **Reduced fees:** Twilight, Seniors.
Caddies: No. **Golf carts:** $10 for 18 holes.
Discount golf packages: Yes. **Season:** Year-round. **High:** April–Oct.
On-site lodging: Yes. **Rental clubs:** Yes.
Walking policy: Unrestricted walking. **Range:** Yes (grass).
To obtain tee times: Call pro shop.
Subscriber comments: A real lakeside beauty . . . Excellent for a state
park . . . As pretty as Augusta . . . Beautiful setting . . . Challenging layout
with good practice range and a boat dock . . . More yardages and
description needed for first time players . . . Slow greens, nothing
remarkable . . . Good view of lake . . . Narrow, tough, requires good
shotmaking . . . Lots of water . . . For your money it's the best in the south
. . . Poor man's Augusta National . . . State park golf . . . Converted
greens from bent back to Bermuda about two years ago. Was probably a
logical choice by management . . . Not long, but plays long. Absolutely
demands accuracy.

★★ HILLCREST GOLF CLUB
PU—1099 Old St. Matthews Rd., Orangeburg (803)533-6030.
35 miles southeast of Columbia. **Holes:** 18. **Par:** 72/72.
Yards: 6,722/5,208. **Course rating:** 70.5/67.8. **Slope:** 119/107.
Opened: 1972. **Pace of Play rating:** 4:30. **Green fee:** $12/14.
Credit cards: MC, V. **Reduced fees:** Low season.
Caddies: No. **Golf carts:** $8 for 18 holes.
Discount golf packages: Yes. **Season:** Year-round. **High:** March–May.
On-site lodging: No. **Rental clubs:** Yes.
Walking policy: Unrestricted walking. **Range:** Yes (grass).
To obtain tee times: Call pro shop.
Subscriber comments: Very tight. Very hilly. Think on every shot . . .
Good muny, not long . . . Not very challenging . . . Good public course,
easy layout . . . Not crowded.

★★★½ HILTON HEAD NATIONAL GOLF CLUB
PU—P.O. Box 23227, Hilton Head Island (803)842-5900.
30 miles northeast of Savannah, GA. **Holes:** 18. **Par:** 72/72.
Yards: 6,779/5,589. **Course rating:** N/A. **Slope:** 124/115.
Opened: 1989. **Pace of Play rating:** N/A. **Green fee:** N/A.
Credit cards: MC, V, AMEX. **Reduced fees:** Weekdays, Low season,
Resort guests, Twilight.
Caddies: No. **Golf carts:** $15 for 18 holes.
Discount golf packages: Yes. **Season:** Year-round. **High:** Spring/Fall.
On-site lodging: No. **Rental clubs:** No.
Walking policy: N/A. **Range:** Yes (grass).
Subscriber comments: Not too long, not too easy . . . Some tricked up
holes . . . Tight with many right to left turns . . . Down home staff . . . A
gem . . . Very enjoyable, hazards can be avoided . . . Keep ball in fairway
. . . Watch the gnats . . . A decent course at a decent price . . . Not a lot of
trouble . . . Rolling fairways. Beware of gators in the marsh . . . A pleasure
to play. Great variety in holes.

HUNTER'S CREEK PLANTATION GOLF CLUB★
SP—702 Hunter's Creek Blvd., Greenwood (803)223-9286.
47miles south of Greenville. **Holes:** 18. **Par:** 72/72.
Yards: 6,999/4,954. **Course rating:** 73.6/67.5. **Slope:** 133/119.
Opened: 1994. **Pace of Play rating:** 4:00. **Green fee:** $26/35.
Credit cards: MC, V. **Reduced fees:** Weekdays, Low season, Juniors.
Caddies: No. **Golf carts:** Included in Green Fee.
Discount golf packages: No. **Season:** Year-round. **High:** April–June.
On-site lodging: No. **Rental clubs:** Yes.
Walking policy: Unrestricted walking. **Range:** Yes (grass).
To obtain tee times: Call seven days in advance.

★★ INDIAN WELLS GOLF CLUB

PU—100 Woodlake Dr., Garden City (803)651-1505, (800)833-6337.
10 miles south of Myrtle Beach. **Holes:** 18. **Par:** 72/72.
Yards: 6,624/4,872. **Course rating:** 71.9/68.2. **Slope:** 125/118.
Opened: 1984. **Pace of Play rating:** 4:00–4:30. **Green fee:** $5/40.
Credit cards: MC, V, DISC. **Reduced fees:** Low season, Resort guests, Twilight, Juniors.
Caddies: No. **Golf carts:** $16 for 18 holes.
Discount golf packages: Yes. **Season:** Year-round. **High:** Spring/Fall.
On-site lodging: No. **Rental clubs:** Yes.
Walking policy: Walking at certain times. **Range:** Yes (grass).
To obtain tee times: Call up to one year in advance.
Subscriber comments: Good beach course . . . Lots of water . . . Easy to play . . . Fun course, good layout, bring extra balls, nice staff . . . Nice layout. Good fairways . . . Nice short course . . . Favors left to right player . . . Must fly the ball over lots of water.

★★½ INDIGO CREEK GOLF CLUB

PU—P.O. Box 15437, Surfside Beach (803)650-0381, (800)833-6337.
10 miles south of Myrtle Beach. **Holes:** 18. **Par:** 72/72.
Yards: 6,750/4,921. **Course rating:** 72.2/69.2. **Slope:** 128/120.
Opened: 1990. **Pace of Play rating:** 4:00. **Green fee:** $26/60.
Credit cards: MC, V, DISC. **Reduced fees:** Low season, Twilight.
Caddies: No. **Golf carts:** Included in Green Fee.
Discount golf packages: No. **Season:** Year-round. **High:** Spring/Fall.
On-site lodging: No. **Rental clubs:** Yes.
Walking policy: Mandatory cart. **Range:** Yes (grass).
To obtain tee times: Call 800 number two days in advance.
Subscriber comments: Solid layout, very playable . . . Good layout . . . Nothing outstanding . . . Not long, but tight . . . Easy to play . . . Very open course. No major problems . . . Lots of water and O.B., not always visible from tee . . . Enjoyable course, challenging, nice staff . . . Decent layout . . . Enjoyable course, typical Myrtle Beach vacation.

★★★½ INDIGO RUN GOLF CLUB

SP—72 Colonial Dr., Hilton Head Island (803)689-2200.
42 miles northeast of Savannah, GA. **Holes:** 18. **Par:** 72/72.
Yards: 7,014/4,974. **Course rating:** 73.7/69.3. **Slope:** 132/120.
Opened: 1992. **Pace of Play rating:** 4:15. **Green fee:** $30/53.
Credit cards: MC, V, AMEX, Diners Club. **Reduced fees:** Low season, Resort guests, Twilight, Juniors.
Caddies: No. **Golf carts:** $17 for 18 holes.
Discount golf packages: Yes. **Season:** Year-round. **High:** March–May/Oct.
On-site lodging: No. **Rental clubs:** Yes.
Walking policy: Mandatory cart. **Range:** Yes (grass).
To obtain tee times: Call pro shop between 6:30 a.m. - 6:30 p.m.
Subscriber comments: Tight course through pine forest, fair but tough, still maturing . . . Friendly, fair course . . . Great layout for women . . . Easy to play . . . Tight fairways . . . Must be accurate . . . Beautiful layout . . . Fair forward tees . . . Fun course, rewards good shots . . . Bring balls, will need . . . Staff very nice . . . Maybe the most reasonable price on Hilton Head.

★★ ISLAND GREEN GOLF CLUB
DOGWOOD/HOLLY/TALL OAKS

PU—455 Sunehanna Dr., Unit STE-1, Myrtle Beach (803)650-2186.
Call club for further information.
Subscriber comments: Short tight course, leave woods at home . . . Hard to find . . . Course was tight, good layout . . . Fairways too close to condos . . . Felt at home the moment I arrived, outstanding staff . . . Three short but challenging nines . . . Can't be afraid of water.

★★½ ISLAND WEST GOLF CLUB

R—U.S. Hwy. 278, Bluffton (803)689-6660.
25 miles northeast of Savannah, GA. **Holes:** 18. **Par:** 72/72.
Yards: 6,803/4,938. **Course rating:** 72.1/66.5. **Slope:** 129/116.
Opened: 1991. **Pace of Play rating:** 4:00-4:30. **Green fee:** $23/44.
Credit cards: MC, V, AMEX. **Reduced fees:** Low season, Resort guests,
Twilight, Juniors.
Caddies: No. **Golf carts:** $18 for 18 holes.
Discount golf packages: Yes. **Season:** Year-round. **High:** March-
April/Oct.
On-site lodging: No. **Rental clubs:** Yes.
Walking policy: Walking at certain times. **Range:** Yes (grass).
To obtain tee times: Call up to one year in advance. Reservations for eight
or more players require credit card.
Subscriber comments: Nice course with a lot of forced carries . . .
Average but pleasant to play . . . Needs time to improve . . . Hit it straight
or you are done . . . No holes that stick in your mind . . . Requires accurate
iron play . . . An early Fuzzy design, hope the next is a little better . . .
Course hadn't matured but nice layout . . . Needs more definition for first
time player . . . Fine club facilities.

KIAWAH ISLAND RESORT

R—Kiawah Beach Dr., Kiawah Island (803)768-2121, (800)845-2471.
21 miles south of Charleston.
Credit cards: All major. **Reduced fees:** Low season, Resort guests,
Twilight, Juniors.
Caddies: No. **Golf carts:** $18 for 18 holes.
Discount golf packages: Yes. **Season:** Year-round. **High:** Spring/Fall.
On-site lodging: Yes. **Rental clubs:** Yes.
Walking policy: Walking at certain times. **Range:** Yes (grass).
To obtain tee times: May call five days in advance with credit card to hold
tee times.

★★½ MARSH POINT COURSE

Holes: 18. **Par:** 71/71.
Yards: 6,472/4,944. **Course rating:** 71.8/69.5. **Slope:** 126/122.
Opened: 1976. **Pace of Play rating:** 4:00. **Green fee:** $40/75.
Subscriber comments: Pleasant golf experience . . . Slated for major
upgrade . . . Short but water provides a challenge . . . Beautiful view . . .
Lots of water . . . Keep it play . . . Acceptable but not great . . . Lots of
gators . . . Beautiful island course, for everyone . . . Target golf . . .
Thinking man's (or woman's) course.

★★★★ OSPREY POINT COURSE

R—Governors Dr., Kiawah Island
Holes: 18. **Par:** 72/72.
Yards: 6,678/5,122. **Course rating:** 71.8/69.6. **Slope:** 124/120.
Opened: 1988. **Pace of Play rating:** 4:00. **Green fee:** $50/90.
Ranked 54th in America's 75 Best Resort Courses by Golf Digest.
Subscriber comments: Prettiest of the Kiawah courses . . . The staff are
very attentive and greet everyone with a smile . . . Beautiful . . . Everyone
will enjoy . . . A very playable course for all handicaps . . . Not as
challenging as Ocean or Turtle . . . Good finishing holes . . . Good layout,
challenging water, marsh holes . . . Terrific from Fazio . . . Multiple
risk/reward choices . . . Great short course for seniors . . . Beautiful, fair, a
must! . . . Windy . . . Looks tough, plays easy . . . Low handicappers
should play blues . . . Lots of gators . . . Great course, close to the Ocean
Course, very friendly place . . . Challenging, but more than fair . . . Why
can't more places include range balls like this? . . . Good compliment to
other Kiawah courses.

★★★★½ THE OCEAN COURSE

R—1000 Ocean Course Dr., Kiawah Island (803)768-7272.
Holes: 18. **Par:** 72/72.
Yards: 7,371/5,327. **Course rating:** 76.9/72.9. **Slope:** 149/133.
Opened: 1991. **Pace of Play rating:** 4:30. **Green fee:** $80/115.
Credit cards: MC, V, AMEX. **Reduced fees:** N/A.

Golf carts: Included in Green Fee.
Discount golf packages: Yes. **Season:** Year-round. **High:** March–May.
Walking policy: Unrestricted walking. **Range:** Yes (grass).
To obtain tee times: Call sixty days in advance.
Ranked 3rd in America's 75 Best Resort Courses by Golf Digest. Selected as Best New Resort Course of 1991 by Golf Digest. Ranked 6th in South Carolina by Golf Digest.
Subscriber comments: The ultimate golfing experience . . . Most difficult course in the states . . . Must play once . . . Scenery unbelievable . . . Unique American links course . . . In the same league as Pinehurst and Pebble Beach . . . Very tough . . . Too damn hard . . . Very difficult, I've never gotten more satisfaction out of a par on a hole . . . If it's not on the fairway or green, it's lost . . . Brutal wind . . . Only course played that should be rated over 80.0 . . . Staggering . . . Tough course, awesome ocean holes, one of the best in country . . . A completely unique golf experience . . . Sympathize with Langer, no gimmes over six inches . . . Wish I could afford to play weekly . . . Need to play on a calm day . . . The challenge and scenery are exceptional . . . So hard it is almost work to play . . . Target golf and you better know where to hit it . . . A special treat and test for any golfer . . . No.1 on the island . . . A humbling course . . . I've played Pine Valley and Oakmont and Kiawah is tougher! . . . Weather and wind can make or break you . . . Even the pros grumble . . . Awesome views . . . Brutal Dye classic . . . Made for match play . . . This will be the course of the future.

★★★★ TURTLE POINT COURSE
R—Turtle Point Lane, Kiawah Island (803)768-2121.
Holes: 18. **Par:** 72/72.
Yards: 6,915/5,285. **Course rating:** 73.5/69.8. **Slope:** 132/122.
Opened: 1981. **Pace of Play rating:** 4:00. **Green fee:** $50/90.
Ranked 44th in America's 75 Best Resort Courses by Golf Digest.
Subscriber comments: A Nicklaus seaside beauty . . . Fun watching gators . . . A lot of fun to play . . . Lots of water . . . Best all around at Kiawah . . The three oceanside holes are nicest . . . Development detracts from ocean holes . . . Distracted by bikini on ocean holes . . . Beautiful course . . . Fun to play . . . Scoreable . . . Course for all handicaps . . . Brutal when windy . . . Ocean holes are good and most of other holes are better than average resort course . . . Fader's course . . . Good design and test of ability. Pretty surroundings . . . Nice Nicklaus layout . . . Saw a nine-foot alligator.

★ KINGS GRANT COUNTRY CLUB
SP—222 Fairington Dr., Summerville (803)873-7110.
20 miles east of Charleston. **Holes:** 18. **Par:** 72/72.
Yards: 6,712/5,025. **Course rating:** 70.5/68.5. **Slope:** 115/115.
Opened: 1971. **Pace of Play rating:** 4:00. **Green fee:** $11/16.
Credit cards: MC, V. **Reduced fees:** Weekdays, Low season, Resort guests.
Caddies: No. **Golf carts:** $11 for 18 holes.
Discount golf packages: Yes. **Season:** Year-round. **High:** April–June.
On-site lodging: No. **Rental clubs:** Yes.
Walking policy: Unrestricted walking. **Range:** Yes (grass).
To obtain tee times: Call pro shop.
Subscriber comments: Good course in dry times, well laid out . . . This isn't a long course but there is trouble all around . . . Has good potential . . . Needs TLC . . . Never try to play after a moderate rain . . . Wildlife and Ashley River makes for worthwhile play.

★★★ LAKE MARION GOLF CLUB
PU—P.O. Box 160, Santee (803)854-2554, (800)344-6534.
50 miles south of Columbia. **Holes:** 18. **Par:** 72/72.
Yards: 6,670/5,254. **Course rating:** 71.6/69.8. **Slope:** 117/112.
Opened: 1974. **Pace of Play rating:** 4:00. **Green fee:** $25/40.
Credit cards: MC, V. **Reduced fees:** Juniors.
Caddies: No. **Golf carts:** Included in Green Fee.

FRUGAL PICK

Discount golf packages: Yes. **Season:** Year-round. **High:** March–May.
On-site lodging: No. **Rental clubs:** Yes.
Walking policy: Mandatory cart. **Range:** Yes (grass).
To obtain tee times: Call pro shop.
Subscriber comments: Good modest course . . . Good all-around course to play . . . The course was well laid out, great for the golfer who plays once or twice a week . . . Forgiving on some holes but harder on others . . . Serves mid-handicapper very well . . . Friendly, courteous, and interested in people . . . Old traditional course . . . Off-season, course in very good condition . . . Enjoyable . . . Really a fun course . . . Overplayed . . . Good design, great value . . . A well-maintained muny course, not crowded, price is right . . . The whole town is glad you're there and shows it.

★★½ LAKEWOOD LINKS
SP—3600 Greenview Pkwy., Sumter (803)481-5700.
Call club for further information.
Subscriber comments: Short but good . . . Not too impressive . . . Water on 10 holes . . . Tight course . . . Fun course . . . Short, but has some interesting holes . . . Target golf, nice course but some trick holes.

LEGEND OAKS PLANTATION GOLF CLUB★
PU—118 Legend Oaks Way, Summerville (803)821-4077.
19 miles north of Charleston. **Holes:** 18. **Par:** 72/72.
Yards: 6,974/4,954. **Course rating:** 72.3/69.4. **Slope:** 124/116.
Opened: 1994. **Pace of Play rating:** 4:00. **Green fee:** $38.
Credit cards: MC, V. **Reduced fees:** Low season, Twilight.
Caddies: No. **Golf carts:** $12 for 18 holes.
Discount golf packages: Yes. **Season:** Year-round. **High:** March–Nov.
On-site lodging: No. **Rental clubs:** Yes.
Walking policy: Unrestricted walking. **Range:** No.
To obtain tee times: Call seven days in advance.

LEGENDS RESORTS
R—Hwy. 501, Myrtle Beach (803)236-9318, (800)377-2315.
Green fee: $30/75.
Credit cards: MC, V, AMEX. **Reduced fees:** Low season, Resort guests.
Caddies: No. **Golf carts:** $17 for 18 holes.
Discount golf packages: Yes. **Season:** Year-round. **High:** March–April/Oct.
On-site lodging: Yes. **Rental clubs:** Yes.
Walking policy: Mandatory cart. **Range:** Yes (grass).
To obtain tee times: Call up to nine months in advance.

★★★½ HEATHLAND AT THE LEGENDS
Holes: 18. **Par:** 71/71.
Yards: 6,785/5,115. **Course rating:** 74.5/71.0. **Slope:** 127/121.
Opened: 1990. **Pace of Play rating:** 4:30-5:00.
Subscriber comments: Scotland without the airfare . . . As close to Scotland as you can get . . . Dynamic shotmaker's course, stayed extra day to play again . . . Extremely well conditioned, a little too wide open . . . Best golf facility on east coast . . . Awesome clubhouse . . . Fantastic golf . . . This course is superb . . . The staff was excellent . . . Must play in wind . . . Courses are tough but fun to play . . . Wide open links style . . . Unbelievable greens . . . Wind very much a factor . . . Bad shots can be played . . . Great facility . . . Not tricked up . . . You have to play this course at least once . . . Leave the driver in the bag . . . Heathland best of three . . . If you like Links Golf you'll love these three. Low handicappers, go back to the tees. Terrific practice area . . . Call me anytime.

★★★½ MOORLAND AT THE LEGENDS
Holes: 18. **Par:** 72/72.
Yards: 6,799/4,905. **Course rating:** 76.8/72.8. **Slope:** 140/127.
Opened: 1990. **Pace of Play rating:** 4:30-5:00.
Subscriber comments: Typical tough P.B. Dye . . . Very tough. Great challenge . . . Very different holes . . . Gets a bad rap, really . . . Dye went overboard . . . Great golf, period . . . Not typical Myrtle Beach track . . .

Supposed to be a bear, but actually very playable . . . Do or die golf, I love it . . . Humbled . . . Unique layout some great holes, few from a moonscape . . . Designed for somebody who hits very long . . . Best facility in Myrtle Beach area.

★★★½ PARKLAND AT THE LEGENDS

Holes: 18. **Par:** 72/72.
Yards: 7,170/5,570. **Course rating:** 74.3/72.9. **Slope:** 131/127.
Opened: 1992. **Pace of Play rating:** 4:30-5:00.
&Subscriber comments: Augusta without azaleas . . . Nice change of place . . . Only one dumb hole . . . Not quite as good as Heathland but nice . . . Wide open, tough sand traps . . . More work than fun . . . Well designed . . . No wimpy par 4s here . . . 7,000 yard layouts are appreciated . . . Don't be weak here . . . Superb practice facilities . . . A pleasure to play . . . Excellent course, best for low handicap golfer . . . Extremely tough, bring plenty of balls . . . Interesting park style course . . . Good holes in natural settings . . . Tough, but fair. Better be on top of your game to play well . . . Largest greens I've seen . . . Traditional layout . . . What a clubhouse . . . Easier layout than Heathland and much prettier.

★★½ THE LINKS AT CYPRESS BAY

PU—P.O. Box 680, Little River (803)249-1025, (800)833-6337.
25 miles south of Myrtle Beach. **Holes:** 18. **Par:** 72/72.
Yards: 6,502/5,004. **Course rating:** 70.0/69.0. **Slope:** 118/113.
Opened: 1970. **Pace of Play rating:** 4:30. **Green fee:** $31/54.
Credit cards: MC, V, DISC. **Reduced fees:** Low season, Resort guests, Twilight, Juniors.
Caddies: No. **Golf carts:** $16 for 18 holes.
Discount golf packages: Yes. **Season:** Year-round. **High:** March-June/Sept.
On-site lodging: Yes. **Rental clubs:** Yes.
Walking policy: Walking at certain times. **Range:** No.
To obtain tee times: Call 24 hours in advance.
Subscriber comments: Pleasant surprise . . . Narrow fairways . . . Not too tough, great par 3s, fun . . . Greens in great shape, interesting layout . . . Some tough holes . . . Short course, not too challenging, good condition, fun to play . . . Lots of sand and water . . . Not too long or too tight . . . Very playable.

★★½ THE LINKS AT STONO FERRY

PU—5365 Forest Oaks Dr., Hollywood (803)763-1817.
12 miles south of Charleston. **Holes:** 18. **Par:** 72/72.
Yards: 6,606/4,928. **Course rating:** 68.3/69.2. **Slope:** 115/119.
Opened: 1989. **Pace of Play rating:** 4:00. **Green fee:** $12/30.
Credit cards: MC, V. **Reduced fees:** Weekdays, Low season, Twilight, Seniors.
Caddies: No. **Golf carts:** Included in Green Fee.
Discount golf packages: Yes. **Season:** Year-round. **High:** March-May/Oct.
On-site lodging: No. **Rental clubs:** Yes.
Walking policy: Walking at certain times. **Range:** Yes (grass).
To obtain tee times: Call pro shop up to one week in advance.
Subscriber comments: Beautiful course, challenging and fun, some long carries over salt marsh . . . 10 miles from nowhere . . . Very tough on right to left hitters but nice track . . . Easy, but scenic . . . Off the beaten path, good shape . . . Good course . . . Lovely inland waterway layout . . . Beautiful island course, for everyone . . . Treelined fairways require accuracy . . . Course was very fair . . . Best golf in low country.

★★★½ LINKS O'TRYON

SP—11250 New Cut Rd., Campobello (803)468-4961.
Call club for further information.
Subscriber comments: A pleasure to play . . . Good course but off the beaten track . . . No. 13 a great hole . . . Must enjoy putting slick greens . . . Played at bad time of year and still had a good time . . . Best greens

around . . . Good mix of blind holes and challenging holes . . . Diverse holes . . . No trees . . . Pro shop staff tops, you can see efforts to continue improvements . . . Fun, fun, fun . . . Challenged everytime you tee it up . . . Tough but fun . . . Wide open fairways, greens very firm . . . Love to play . . . Best public course in the area.

★★½ LINRICK GOLF COURSE
PU—356 Campground Rd., Columbia (803)754-6331.
7 miles north of Columbia. **Holes:** 18. **Par:** 73/73.
Yards: 6,919/5,243. **Course rating:** 72.8/69.4. **Slope:** 125/N/A.
Opened: 1972. **Pace of Play rating:** 4:30. **Green fee:** $10/12.
Credit cards: None. **Reduced fees:** Seniors, Juniors.
Caddies: No. **Golf carts:** $8 for 18 holes.
Discount golf packages: No. **Season:** Year-round. **High:** March-Sept.
On-site lodging: No. **Rental clubs:** Yes.
Walking policy: Unrestricted walking. **Range:** Yes (grass).
To obtain tee times: Tuesday through Friday available Monday morning after 9 a.m.; Saturday through Monday
available on Thursday morning after 9 a.m. Daily times available open to close of business.
Subscriber comments: Very tough hilly layout . . . Muny course with low senior rates, lots of blind tee shots, variable conditioning . . . Long par 4s, short par 3s . . . Several great tests of ability . . . Most holes are wide open . . . Play is fairly quick.

★★★ LITCHFIELD COUNTRY CLUB
R—Hwy. 17, Pawleys Island (803)237-3411, (800)922-6348.
20 miles south of Myrtle Beach. **Holes:** 18. **Par:** 72/72.
Yards: 6,752/5,264. **Course rating:** 72.6/70.8. **Slope:** 130/119.
Opened: 1966. **Pace of Play rating:** 3:36. **Green fee:** $30/60.
Credit cards: All major. **Reduced fees:** Low season, Juniors.
Caddies: No. **Golf carts:** Included in Green Fee.
Discount golf packages: Yes. **Season:** Year-round. **High:** Spring/Fall.
On-site lodging: Yes. **Rental clubs:** Yes.
Walking policy: Mandatory cart. **Range:** Yes (grass).
To obtain tee times: Call anytime.
Subscriber comments: Classic southern country club . . . Good old-type layout . . . Very fair . . . Not as hard as some . . . Good layout . . . Lots of water . . . Front side flat, back side leave driver in the car . . . Good par 3s . . . Playable by all levels . . . Good for seniors. Be accurate . . . Fairways were soft . . . More difficult than it looks . . . Old course but still very enjoyable.

★★★★ THE LONG BAY CLUB
R—Hwy. 9, Longs (803)399-2222, (800)344-5590.
15 miles west of North Myrtle Beach. **Holes:** 18. **Par:** 72/72.
Yards: 7,021/5,598. **Course rating:** 74.3/72.1. **Slope:** 137/127.
Opened: 1988. **Pace of Play rating:** 4:30. **Green fee:** $27/75.
Credit cards: All major. **Reduced fees:** Low season, Resort guests.
Caddies: No. **Golf carts:** $16 for 18 holes.
Discount golf packages: Yes. **Season:** Year-round. **High:** March-April/Oct.
On-site lodging: No. **Rental clubs:** Yes.
Walking policy: Mandatory cart. **Range:** Yes (grass).
To obtain tee times: Contact your hotel golf director or call tee time central up to one year in advance.
Ranked 19th in South Carolina by Golf Digest.
Subscriber comments: Typical small, tricky Nicklaus . . . The course you love to hate . . . Conditions only so-so . . . Fantastic potential . . . Would like to see what pros would shoot here, very challenging, enjoyed it . . . Tough course in good shape . . . This one is exciting, very tough from all tees . . . Would like to play it again . . . A lot of sand . . . Long as you want . . . Mounds everywhere . . . Large greens . . . I'd like to see Jack play it from the back tees! . . . Always fun to putt . . . Shotmaker's course for

good golfers . . . Break the piggy bank, it's worth it . . . Just what you'd expect . . . Visually something to remember . . . Bring the long irons . . . Hit the driver well and it's fun, hit the driver bad and it's a killer . . . Difficult, beautiful . . . Creative golf course . . . I'd play it again . . . Big Jack could shoot par but not anyone else.

★★½ MIDLAND VALLEY GOLF CLUB

SP—Hwy. 1, Aiken (803)663-7332.
Call club for further information.
Subscriber comments: Good layout, mature, changes in elevation . . . All par 3s the same length . . . Basic golf . . . Beautiful course in residential area . . . Ellis Maples design . . . Extremely fast Bermuda greens . . . Greens putt like countertops . . . Rolling hills . . . Open fairways . . . Nice greens . . . Some long, tough holes . . . Finally got greens right.

MYRTLE BEACH NATIONAL GOLF CLUB

R—4900 National Dr., Myrtle Beach (803)448-2308, (800)344-5590.
5 miles west of Myrtle Beach. **Green fee:** $10/45.
Credit cards: All major. **Reduced fees:** Low season, Resort guests.
Caddies: No. **Golf carts:** $16 for 18 holes.
Discount golf packages: Yes. **Season:** Year-round. **High:** March-April/Oct.
On-site lodging: No. **Rental clubs:** Yes.
Walking policy: Mandatory cart. **Range:** Yes (grass).
To obtain tee times: Contact your hotel golf director or call tee time central up to one year in advance.

★★★ NORTH COURSE

Holes: 18. **Par:** 72/72.
Yards: 6,759/5,047. **Course rating:** 72.9/68.0. **Slope:** 125/113.
Opened: 1974. **Pace of Play rating:** 4:30.
Subscriber comments: Very enjoyable course to play . . . Feels like you're alone on course . . . Great water holes . . . Plain vanilla . . . Good layout but poor greens . . . All par 3s are short . . . Calls for accurate tee shots . . . Great par 3 island green . . . Courteous people and well run.

★★★ SOUTHCREEK COURSE

Holes: 18. **Par:** 72/72.
Yards: 6,416/4,723. **Course rating:** 70.5/66.5. **Slope:** 123/109.
Opened: 1973. **Pace of Play rating:** 4:30.
Walking policy: Walking at certain times.
To obtain tee times: Contact your hotel golf director or call tee time central up to one year in advance.
Subscriber comments: Short and lots of trees, fun to play, busy . . . More interesting . . . Nice course . . . Must be very accurate with approach shot . . . A fun course to play . . . Bent-grass greens were a little thin in October . . . Staff can handle the mass of golfers well each day . . . We play the course on every trip to the beach . . . You can count on it being in great shape.

★★★ WEST COURSE

Holes: 18. **Par:** 72/72.
Yards: 6,866/5,307. **Course rating:** 73.0/69.0. **Slope:** 119/109.
Opened: 1974. **Pace of Play rating:** 4:30.
Subscriber comments: Good for most levels . . . Fun to play . . . Busy, busy, busy . . . Nice course . . . Must be very straight . . . Tough but fair . . . Fast greens . . . Good course and staff . . . Courteous people and well run . . . Best in Myrtle Beach for women.

★★½ MYRTLE WEST GOLF CLUB

PU—Hwy. 9 W., North Myrtle Beach (803)249-1478, (800)842-8390.
11 miles northeast of Myrtle Beach. **Holes:** 18. **Par:** 72/72.
Yards: 6,787/4,859. **Course rating:** 72.7/67.9. **Slope:** 132/113.
Opened: 1989. **Pace of Play rating:** 4:30. **Green fee:** $25/55.
Credit cards: MC, V, AMEX. **Reduced fees:** Low season.
Caddies: No. **Golf carts:** Included in Green Fee.
Discount golf packages: Yes. **Season:** Year-round. **High:** Spring/Fall.

On-site lodging: No. **Rental clubs:** No.
Walking policy: Mandatory cart. **Range:** Yes (grass).
To obtain tee times: Call up to nine months in advance. With golf card or coupon book, 48 hours in advance.
Subscriber comments: A well-run course . . . Lots of sand . . . Average difficulty . . . Interesting course . . . Good greens . . . Nice facilities, well maintained, level with moguls, long drive from Myrtle Beach . . . Nice course . . . Must use strategy. Short . . . People were real nice . . . Best-kept secret in the beach area.

MYRTLEWOOD GOLF CLUB

SP—Hwy. 17 at 48th Ave. N., Myrtle Beach (803)449-5134, (800)283-3633.
Credit cards: All major. **Reduced fees:** Low season, Resort guests, Juniors.
Caddies: No. **Golf carts:** $15 for 18 holes.
Discount golf packages: Yes. **Season:** Year-round. **High:** Spring/Fall.
On-site lodging: No. **Rental clubs:** Yes.
Walking policy: Mandatory cart. **Range:** Yes (grass).
To obtain tee times: Phone pro shop or 800 number to reserve a time. Deposit or credit card number required in high season to secure tee time or contact hotel golf director to make arrangements for you.

★★★½ PALMETTO COURSE

Holes: 18. **Par:** 72/72.
Yards: 6,957/5,305. **Course rating:** 72.7/70.1. **Slope:** 121/117.
Opened: 1973. **Pace of Play rating:** 4:10. **Green fee:** $10/43.
Subscriber comments: Two very fine courses, generally in fine condition . . . Fairest, good shape, really fun course . . . Long an open, well-maintained course . . . Very good course . . . Good fairways, nice greens . . . No gimmicks, two great finishing holes . . . Straightforward golf.

★★★½ PINEHILLS COURSE

Holes: 18. **Par:** 72/72.
Yards: 6,640/4,906. **Course rating:** 72.0/67.4. **Slope:** 125/113.
Opened: 1993. **Pace of Play rating:** 4:10. **Green fee:** $15/47.
Subscriber comments: New Arthur Hills layout, tricky, lots of water, good condition . . . Great since being rebuilt . . . Very enjoyable . . . Lots of shots over water . . . May be best in Myrtle Beach . . . Redesign has really enhanced course, now tough for average golfer . . . Not as nice as the Palmetto course . . . Excellent bent greens, not long but demanding . . . Not another course like this in Myrtle Beach.

★★★ NORTHWOODS GOLF CLUB

PU—201 Powell Rd., Columbia (803)786-9242.
4 miles south of Columbia. **Holes:** 18. **Par:** 72/72.
Yards: 6,800/5,000. **Course rating:** 71.9/67.8. **Slope:** 122/116.
Opened: 1990. **Pace of Play rating:** 4:15. **Green fee:** $19/28.
Credit cards: MC, V, AMEX. **Reduced fees:** Weekdays, Low season, Twilight, Seniors, Juniors.
Caddies: No. **Golf carts:** $11 for 18 holes.
Discount golf packages: Yes. **Season:** Year-round. **High:** May-Oct.
On-site lodging: No. **Rental clubs:** Yes.
Walking policy: Unrestricted walking. **Range:** Yes (grass).
To obtain tee times: Call seven days in advance. Out of state players may call a month in advance.
Subscriber comments: Excellent P.B. Dye layout . . . Nice course, will be better as it matures . . . Course a little tricky . . . Loved the speed of greens . . . Greens slope away from approach . . . Best greens you can putt . . . Much improved since its inception . . . Great staff . . . Some challenging holes . . . Great shape anytime I've played . . . Too many gimmick holes . . . Nice course on small amount of land . . . Best conditioned course in Columbia.

★★½ OAK HILLS GOLF CLUB

PU—7629 Fairfield Rd., Columbia (803)735-9830.
Holes: 18. **Par:** 72/72.

Yards: 6,894/4,574. **Course rating:** N/A. **Slope:** 122/110.
Opened: N/A. **Pace of Play rating:** N/A. **Green fee:** N/A.
Credit cards: MC, V. **Reduced fees:** Weekdays, Low season, Twilight, Seniors, Juniors.
Caddies: No. **Golf carts:** N/A.
Discount golf packages: Yes. **Season:** Year-round. **High:** April-Aug.
On-site lodging: No. **Rental clubs:** No.
Walking policy: N/A. **Range:** Yes (grass).
Subscriber comments: Fairly new course, lots of work going on, getting better . . . Too many rocks, too few clubs . . . Course has potential, needs grooming . . . Ruined a wedge on the fairway (rock) . . . Several challenging holes . . . Great layout, rolling hills and greens . . . A lot of target golf.

★★★ OAK POINT GOLF COURSE
PU—4255 Bohicket Rd., Johns Island (803)768-7431.
20 miles south of Charleston. **Holes:** 18. **Par:** 72/72.
Yards: 6,759/4,671. **Course rating:** 71.2/69.8. **Slope:** 132/121.
Opened: 1989. **Pace of Play rating:** 4:00. **Green fee:** $30/49.
Credit cards: MC, V. **Reduced fees:** Weekdays, Low season, Twilight, Juniors.
Caddies: No. **Golf carts:** Included in Green Fee.
Discount golf packages: Yes. **Season:** Year-round. **High:** April-Oct.
On-site lodging: No. **Rental clubs:** Yes.
Walking policy: Walking at certain times. **Range:** Yes (grass).
To obtain tee times: Call anytime.
Subscriber comments: A pretty decent course . . . Has come a long way in last year, potential to be one of the best in area . . . Quite nice . . . Abundant wildlife . . . No clubhouse . . . Good but needs maturing . . . . Fun from all tees . . . Like the course, much improved in last few years . . . Playable, fun . . . Blind shots end up in unseen hazards, which is unfair when many players are first time tourists . . . Wind can play havoc on exposed holes . . . Why play Kiawah? Just as good for half the cost.

OAKDALE COUNTRY CLUB★
SP—3700 W. Lake Dr., Florence (803)662-0368.
Holes: 18. **Par:** 72/73.
Yards: 6,300/5,000. **Course rating:** 70.0/67.1. **Slope:** 117/109.
Opened: 1964. **Pace of Play rating:** 4:00. **Green fee:** $12/17.
Credit cards: V. **Reduced fees:** No.
Caddies: No. **Golf carts:** $8 for 18 holes.
Discount golf packages: No. **Season:** Year-round. **High:** March.
On-site lodging: No. **Rental clubs:** Yes.
Walking policy: Walking at certain times. **Range:** Yes (grass).
To obtain tee times: Call pro shop.

OCEAN POINT GOLF LINKS★
R—250 Ocean Point Dr., Fripp Island (803)838-2309, (800)845-4100.
20 miles southeast of Beaufort. **Holes:** 18. **Par:** 72/72.
Yards: 6,590/4,951. **Course rating:** 72.2/69.5. **Slope:** 129/113.
Opened: 1964. **Pace of Play rating:** 4:10. **Green fee:** $34/41.
Credit cards: All major. **Reduced fees:** Weekdays, Low season, Resort guests, Juniors.
Caddies: No. **Golf carts:** $16 for 18 holes.
Discount golf packages: Yes. **Season:** Year-round. **High:** Spring/Fall.
On-site lodging: Yes. **Rental clubs:** Yes.
Walking policy: Walking at certain times. **Range:** Yes (grass).
To obtain tee times: Call pro shop or make reservation through resort.

★★★ OLD SOUTH GOLF LINKS
PU—50 Buckingham Plantation Dr., Bluffton (803)785-5353, (800)257-8997.
1 miles west of Hilton Head Island. **Holes:** 18. **Par:** 72/71.
Yards: 6,772/4,776. **Course rating:** 72.4/69.6. **Slope:** 129/123.

Opened: 1991. **Pace of Play rating:** 4:20. **Green fee:** $35/70.
Credit cards: MC, V, AMEX. **Reduced fees:** Low season, Resort guests,
Twilight, Juniors.
Caddies: No. **Golf carts:** Included in Green Fee.
Discount golf packages: Yes. **Season:** Year-round. **High:** March/April-
Oct.
On-site lodging: No. **Rental clubs:** Yes.
Walking policy: Walking at certain times. **Range:** Yes (grass).
To obtain tee times: Call up to 60 days in advance.
Subscriber comments: Well designed, variety, scenic . . . Very playable
for average golfer . . . Interesting, over marshes . . . Par 3s are tough . . .
Two trick holes . . . Short but takes great shots . . . Plays to all skill levels
. . . Fair test of golf . . . Some tough carries . . . Plays in front of marshes
. . . Well designed, variety, scenic . . . Best-kept secret on Hilton Head.

★★★½ OYSTER REEF GOLF CLUB
SP—155 High Bluff Rd., Hilton Head Island (803)681-7717.
35 miles northeast of Savannah, GA. **Holes:** 18. **Par:** 72/72.
Yards: 7,027/5,288. **Course rating:** 73.7/69.8. **Slope:** 131/118.
Opened: 1982. **Pace of Play rating:** 4:00. **Green fee:** $48/79.
Credit cards: All major. **Reduced fees:** Low season, Resort guests,
Juniors.
Caddies: No. **Golf carts:** Included in Green Fee.
Discount golf packages: Yes. **Season:** Year-round. **High:** Spring/Fall.
On-site lodging: No. **Rental clubs:** Yes.
Walking policy: Mandatory cart. **Range:** Yes (grass).
To obtain tee times: Call up to 90 days in advance.
Subscriber comments: Interesting, good condition, fun to play . . . Good
tight course, nice layout . . . Good Rees Jones layout has improved . . .
Every hole pretty . . . A very good course, no tricks, be careful on a windy
day . . . Can play very long . . . One of the most playable courses on the
island . . . Interesting, good conditions, fun to play.

PALMETTO DUNES RESORT
R—P.O. Box 5849, Hilton Head Island (803)785-1140, (800)827-3006.
50 miles northeast of Savannah, GA.
Credit cards: MC, V, AMEX. **Reduced fees:** Resort guests.
Caddies: No. **Golf carts:** Included in Green Fee.
Discount golf packages: Yes. **Season:** Year-round. **High:** March/Oct.
On-site lodging: Yes. **Rental clubs:** Yes.
Walking policy: Mandatory cart. **Range:** Yes (grass).
To obtain tee times: Call 24 hours in advance.
★★★½ ARTHUR HILLS COURSE
Holes: 18. **Par:** 72/72.
Yards: 6,651/4,999. **Course rating:** 71.4/68.5. **Slope:** 127/118.
Opened: 1986. **Pace of Play rating:** 4:15. **Green fee:** $55/80.
Subscriber comments: Nice change from the Jones and Fazio courses . . .
Plenty of trouble, but a great test . . . Has some funny holes . . . Best of
Palmetto Dunes' courses . . . 12 and 17 border on sadism . . . Have to play
more than once to appreciate . . . No. 17 requires strategy and nerve . . .
Big disappointment . . . Not gimmicked up . . . Love them Arthur Hills
Courses.
★★★ GEORGE FAZIO COURSE
(803)785-1130.
Holes: 18. **Par:** 70/70.
Yards: 6,875/5,273. **Course rating:** 74.2/69.2. **Slope:** 132/117.
Opened: 1974. **Pace of Play rating:** 4:15. **Green fee:** $50/70.
Walking policy: Walking at certain times.
Subscriber comments: One of the toughest..Excellent in every way . . .
Hard course with a lot of sand . . . Revised in last year . . . Lots of water
. . . As tough as resort courses get . . . Tough par fours, I used every club
in the bag . . . Good variety . . . Awesome layout . . . Winding waterways
and gators make for a great afternoon . . . Tough! Tough! Small greens . . .
Great channel views . . . Great views, watch for gators . . . Tough for even

the best players . . . One of Hilton Head's best.

★★★ROBERT TRENT JONES COURSE
(803)785-1136.
Holes: 18. **Par:** 72/72.
Yards: 6,710/5,425. **Course rating:** 72.2/70.7. **Slope:** 123/117.
Opened: 1969. **Pace of Play rating:** 4:00. **Green fee:** $55/73.
Walking policy: Mandatory cart.
To obtain tee times: Resort guests call 60 days in advance. Outside guests call 30 days in advance.
Subscriber comments: Most forgiving course at this resort . . . Nine holes with wind and nine holes against the wind . . . Staff pleasant . . . Some holes on back nine too similar . . . Fairly unimaginative . . . Very scenic and very playable for all players . . . Solid track, no tricks, some treats . . . 10th hole plays to beach . . . Unusual layout.

PALMETTO HALL PLANTATION
R—108 Fort Howell Dr., Hilton Head Island (803)689-4100, (800)827-3006. 30 miles northeast of Savannah, GA. **Green fee:** $55/75.
Credit cards: MC, V, AMEX. **Reduced fees:** Resort guests, Juniors.
Caddies: No. **Golf carts:** Included in Green Fee.
Discount golf packages: Yes. **Season:** Year-round. **High:** Spring/Fall.
On-site lodging: No. **Rental clubs:** Yes.
Walking policy: Mandatory cart. **Range:** Yes (grass).
To obtain tee times: Call pro shop.

★★★★ARTHUR HILLS COURSE
Holes: 18. **Par:** 72/72.
Yards: 6,918/4,956. **Course rating:** 72.2/68.6. **Slope:** 132/119.
Opened: 1991. **Pace of Play rating:** 4:00–4:30.
Subscriber comments: Arthur Hills at his best . . . Suited for mid-to-low handicap . . . Beautiful, challenging . . . Fine golf course, good test . . . Fun to play, a challenge, don't miss an opportunity to play . . . A jewel, visit to Hilton Head must include this one . . . Too many holes resemble each other. Great 18th hole . . . Great use of natural hazards . . . Nine and 18 hard? President Clinton doesn't have enough mulligans to par these holes . . . Varied . . . Great course, better finishing hole than Harbour Town . . . Excellent condition, blend of woods, water, fast greens . . . Best kept secret on Hilton Head Island.

★★½ROBERT CUPP COURSE
Holes: 18. **Par:** 72/72.
Yards: 7,079/5,220. **Course rating:** 74.8/71.1. **Slope:** 141/126.
Opened: 1993. **Pace of Play rating:** 4:00–4:30.
Subscriber comments: A real non-traditional treat . . . Play the Hills Course . . . Different geometric layout, breaks the monotony . . . Too many right angles . . . Geometric shapes are all hype . . . Unusual, but fun . . . Wild golf course . . . Unique geometric design . . . Unique and challenging layout; forget the geometric designs, it's a good course . . . Reminiscent of high school geometry class . . . Fun in a sadistic sort of way . . . Computer designed, sharp angles . . . Different but fun to play . . . Silly mounding, not natural . . . Better after you have played it a couple of times . . . I didn't know the Egyptians had colonized South Carolina.

PARKLAND GOLF CLUB★
SP—295 E. Deadfall Rd., Greenwood (803)229-5086. 40 miles south of Greenville. **Holes:** 18. **Par:** 72/72.
Yards: 6,520/5,130. **Course rating:** 70.8/68.3. **Slope:** 124/115.
Opened: 1985. **Pace of Play rating:** 3:45. **Green fee:** $14/18.
Credit cards: MC, V. **Reduced fees:** Weekdays, Seniors, Juniors.
Caddies: No. **Golf carts:** $10 for 18 holes.
Discount golf packages: Yes. **Season:** Year-round. **High:** March-Nov.
On-site lodging: No. **Rental clubs:** No.
Walking policy: Unrestricted walking. **Range:** Yes (grass).
To obtain tee times: Call for weekends and holidays.

★★ PATRIOTS POINT LINKS
PU—100 Clubhouse Dr., Mt. Pleasant (803)881-0042.
2 miles north of Charleston. **Holes:** 18. **Par:** 72/72.
Yards: 6,838/5,562. **Course rating:** 72.1/71.0. **Slope:** 118/115.
Opened: 1981. **Pace of Play rating:** 4:00. **Green fee:** $18/25.
Credit cards: MC, V, AMEX. **Reduced fees:** Weekdays, Low season, Twilight.
Caddies: No. **Golf carts:** $11 for 18 holes.
Discount golf packages: Yes. **Season:** Year-round. **High:** Spring/Fall.
On-site lodging: No. **Rental clubs:** Yes.
Walking policy: Walking at certain times. **Range:** Yes (grass).
To obtain tee times: Call anytime one week in advance.
Subscriber comments: Easy start, hard finish . . . Duck . . . Beautiful location . . . Basic ocean course . . . Too busy . . . Good layout, tought at times . . . Flat course with lots of water, staff very nice, good facilities, fun to play . . . Good for hot Charleston summers . . . Harbor winds help . . . Scenic Charleston harbor . . . Wide open on Charleston harbor.

★★★½ PAWLEY'S PLANTATION GOLF CLUB
SP—Hwy. 17, Pawley's Island (803)237-1736.
Call club for further information.
Ranked 18th in South Carolina by Golf Digest.
Subscriber comments: Good Nicklaus layout, good mixture of holes . . . Water, water, everywhere . . . Bring extra balls . . . Absolutely beautiful, wonderful design, very challenging . . . Narrow and long . . . Have to see it to believe it . . . Excellent beach course . . . Long and tough . . . Too hard, not everybody can play like Jack . . . You pay for your mistakes . . . Lots of sand . . . Pretty tight fairways . . . Typical Nicklaus. Not set up for average 15 handicaps. 67-yard par 3 is ridiculous . . . Wonderfully hard, a joy to play, very beautiful, view of ocean and marshes and wildlife. Very friendly staff . . . Nicklaus has done better . . . Tough to score on hard layout . . . Tough in the wind . . . What a track.

★★★ PERSIMMON HILL GOLF CLUB
PU—Rte. 3, Saluda (803)275-3522.
35 miles east of Augusta, GA. **Holes:** 18. **Par:** 72/73.
Yards: 6,925/5,449. **Course rating:** 72.3/71.1. **Slope:** 122/121.
Opened: 1962. **Pace of Play rating:** 4:00. **Green fee:** $10/18.
Credit cards: MC, V, AMEX. **Reduced fees:** Weekdays, Low season, Twilight.
Caddies: No. **Golf carts:** $12 for 18 holes.
Discount golf packages: Yes. **Season:** Year-round. **High:** March-May.
On-site lodging: No. **Rental clubs:** Yes.
Walking policy: Walking at certain times. **Range:** Yes (grass).
To obtain tee times: Call one week in advance.
Subscriber comments: Great golf in the middle of nowhere . . . Remember, no mulligans . . . Good course for the better than average golfer . . . Worth the trip from at least 60-70 miles . . . Good course improvements since 1993, please continue . . . Love the layout . . . Great golf surroundings . . . Great old course . . . Fun course, tight . . . Need all clubs and shots. Great water holes . . . Easy if you can get over the water . . . Nice layout, all players, staff fine, service fine . . . A worthwhile drive . . . Great par 5s over water . . . Showing its age . . . Big, big greens . . . Brisk pace of play even on weekends.

★★★ PINE FOREST COUNTRY CLUB
SP—1000 Congressional Blvd., Summerville (803)851-1193.
20 miles west of Charleston. **Holes:** 18. **Par:** 72/72.
Yards: 6,905/5,007. **Course rating:** 73.0/67.7. **Slope:** 127/120.
Opened: 1992. **Pace of Play rating:** 4:30. **Green fee:** $25/40.
Credit cards: MC, V. **Reduced fees:** Weekdays, Low season, Twilight, Juniors.
Caddies: No. **Golf carts:** Included in Green Fee.
Discount golf packages: Yes. **Season:** Year-round. **High:** May-Sept.

On-site lodging: No. **Rental clubs:** Yes.
Walking policy: Unrestricted walking. **Range:** Yes (grass).
To obtain tee times: Call pro shop.
Subscriber comments: Beautiful course . . . Seldom a wait at tee boxes
. . . Great course, very challenging, lots of water . . . Water on right of 16
holes . . . Tough if you miss the mounded greens . . . Too many bad
bounces, left to right player won't like . . . Bad news if you have a slice or a
hook . . . Challenging . . . Water everywhere . . . Very demanding . . .
Best-kept secret in Charleston area.

★★★ PINE LAKES INTERNATIONAL COUNTRY CLUB

SP—5603 Woodside Ave., Myrtle Beach (803)449-6459, (800)446-6817.
Holes: 18. **Par:** 71/71.
Yards: 6,609/5,376. **Course rating:** 71.5/71.6. **Slope:** 125/122.
Opened: 1927. **Pace of Play rating:** 4:30. **Green fee:** $45/95.
Credit cards: MC, V, AMEX. **Reduced fees:** Resort guests.
Caddies: No. **Golf carts:** $20 for 18 holes.
Discount golf packages: Yes. **Season:** Year-round. **High:** March-April.
On-site lodging: No. **Rental clubs:** Yes.
Walking policy: Mandatory cart. **Range:** Yes (grass).
To obtain tee times: Call up to a year in advance. Must have deposit.
Subscriber comments: A "don't miss" for Myrtle Beach . . . Tradition,
classic, must play . . . Great ambiance . . . Great old course, difficult,
warmly received . . . One of the best courses in Myrtle Beach . . . Front
nine doesn't have character of back nine . . . Watch that drink on No. 4 tee
. . . Where you are treated like royalty . . . My favorite at the beach.
Service and grace beyond your dreams . . . Overrated "Grandaddy" of
Myrtle Beach . . . Old fashioned, traditional garden variety design . . . The
most fair and most challenging course I've played anywhere . . . Fair to all
levels of golfers . . . Myrtle Beach experience not complete without
playing.

★★★ PINE RIDGE COUNTRY CLUB

SP—425 Pine Ridge Rd., Edgefield (803)637-3570.
Call club for further information.
Subscriber comments: Super fun layout always in good shape . . . Well-
maintained course for average player . . . Small town golf at its best, worth
a visit . . . If you can find it, you get your money's worth . . . Long par 3s
make this course challenging . . . Very good course in the middle of
nowhere . . . Just a good, solid no frills layout . . . Has excellent Bermuda
greens in summertime.

★½ PINELAND PLANTATION GOLF CLUB

PU—Rte. 1, Box 54-C, Mayesville (803)659-4359.
15 miles northeast of Sumter. **Holes:** 18. **Par:** 72/72.
Yards: 7,084/5,307. **Course rating:** N/A. **Slope:** 122/119.
Opened: N/A. **Pace of Play rating:** N/A. **Green fee:** N/A.
Credit cards: MC, V. **Reduced fees:** Weekdays, Low season, Twilight.
Caddies: No. **Golf carts:** $N/A for 18 holes.
Discount golf packages: Yes. **Season:** Year-round. **High:** March-May.
On-site lodging: No. **Rental clubs:** No.
Walking policy: N/A. **Range:** Yes (grass).
Subscriber comments: Excellent test, shabby conditions . . . Watch for
fire ants . . . Fairways are like my backyard . . . Say they are going to
upgrade.

★★ PINETUCK GOLF CLUB

SP—2578 Tuckaway Rd., Rock Hill (803)327-1141.
20 miles south of Charlotte. NC. **Holes:** 18. **Par:** 71/74.
Yards: 6,567/4,870. **Course rating:** 71.7/68.2. **Slope:** 127/111.
Opened: 1971. **Pace of Play rating:** 4:30. **Green fee:** $15/20.
Credit cards: MC, V. **Reduced fees:** Weekdays, Twilight, Seniors.
Caddies: No. **Golf carts:** $11 for 18 holes.
Discount golf packages: Yes. **Season:** Year-round. **High:** March-Oct.

On-site lodging: No. **Rental clubs:** No.
Walking policy: Walking at certain times. **Range:** Yes (grass).
To obtain tee times: Call anytime for weekends and holidays.
Subscriber comments: Wide open and forgiving . . . Very hard surface
. . . Vastly improved over the years . . . Friendly staff . . . Good challenge,
improved condition with new management . . . Best improved in the area.

★★½ POCALLA SPRINGS COUNTRY CLUB

SP—1700 Hwy. 15 S., Sumter (803)481-8322.
Holes: 18. **Par:** 71/71.
Yards: 6,350/5,500. **Course rating:** 68.0/65.0. **Slope:** 115/111.
Opened: 1920. **Pace of Play rating:** 4:00. **Green fee:** $7/10.
Credit cards: MC, V. **Reduced fees:** Weekdays, Low season, Resort
guests, Twilight, Seniors, Juniors.
Caddies: No. **Golf carts:** Included in Green Fee.
Discount golf packages: Yes. **Season:** Year-round. **High:** April-Sept.
On-site lodging: No. **Rental clubs:** Yes.
Walking policy: Unrestricted walking. **Range:** Yes (grass).
To obtain tee times: Call pro shop.
Subscriber comments: Very short . . . Flat, not much variety . . . You
need to fade and draw ball.

PORT ROYAL GOLF CLUB

R—10A Grasslawn Ave., Hilton Head Island (803)686-8801, (800)234-6318.
Credit cards: MC, V, AMEX. **Reduced fees:** Low season, Resort guests,
Twilight, Juniors.
Caddies: No. **Golf carts:** Included in Green Fee.
Discount golf packages: Yes. **Season:** Year-round. **High:** March-
May/Sept..
On-site lodging: No. **Rental clubs:** Yes.
Walking policy: Mandatory cart. **Range:** Yes (grass).
To obtain tee times: Call 800 number for reservation office.

★★½ BARONY COURSE

Holes: 18. **Par:** 72/72.
Yards: 6,530/5,253. **Course rating:** 71.2/70.1. **Slope:** 124/115.
Opened: 1968. **Pace of Play rating:** 4:00. **Green fee:** $49/80.
Subscriber comments: Enjoyable, must play on fairway to score well . . .
Average course, average conditions . . . Wide open . . . Fun to play . . .
Small greens, target course . . . Good resort course, very open . . . Not
very challenging . . . Watch out for the alligators!

★★½ PLANTER'S ROW COURSE

Holes: 18. **Par:** 72/72.
Yards: 6,520/5,126. **Course rating:** 72.1/68.9. **Slope:** 128/116.
Opened: 1983. **Pace of Play rating:** 4:00. **Green fee:** $49/80.
Subscriber comments: Narrow, tough course . . . Some good holes, a
Williard Byrd redo . . . Tight . . . Parallel fairways with much woods
between . . . Greens needed a shave . . . Fair test . . . Bland and generous
. . . Extremely tight, but not long . . . Tight but not unfair.

★★★ ROBBER'S ROW COURSE

Holes: 18. **Par:** 72/72.
Yards: 6,642/5,000. **Course rating:** 72.6/70.4. **Slope:** 134/114.
Opened: 1968. **Pace of Play rating:** 4:30. **Green fee:** $54/80.
Subscriber comments: Excellent Pete Dye redesign . . . More open than
Planter's Row . . . Very tight, demanding layout . . . Excellent redesign,
tough par 3s from blue tees . . . True test of target golf . . . Wind, water,
bunkers . . . One of my favorites, narrow, tough, good greens, beautiful
location even on a wet day . . . Great coastal course . . . Much, much better
since Pete fixed it up.

★★½ POSSUM TROT GOLF CLUB

R—Possum Trot Rd., North Myrtle Beach (803)272-5341, (800)626-8768.
Holes: 18. **Par:** 72/72.
Yards: 6,966/5,160. **Course rating:** 73.0/69.6. **Slope:** 118/111.
Opened: 1968. **Pace of Play rating:** 4:00. **Green fee:** $32/57.

Credit cards: All major. **Reduced fees:** Weekdays, Twilight.
Caddies: No. **Golf carts:** Included in Green Fee.
Discount golf packages: Yes. **Season:** Year-round. **High:** March-April/Sept..
On-site lodging: No. **Rental clubs:** Yes.
Walking policy: Walking at certain times. **Range:** Yes (grass).
To obtain tee times: Call anytime.
Subscriber comments: Comfortable as an old shoe . . . What a golf course should be . . . Pleasant staff . . . Good variation from hole to hole . . . Always fun to play . . . Swampy . . . A favorite of locals in Myrtle Beach . . . Friendly staff, superb practice facility . . . Needs more upkeep . . . Great for second round of day . . . Friendly and courteous and lot of fun. We'll be back . . . Cheap beach golf . . . Good old course, enjoyable time, an old friend . . . When you've lost all your new golf balls during your golf vacation to the beach, borrow one and go to Possum Trot. It will renew your spirit and give you a false sense of confidence.

REGENT PARK GOLF CLUB★
PU—6000 Regent Pkwy., Fort Mill (803)547-1300.
16 miles south of Charlotte. **Holes:** 18. **Par:** 72/72.
Yards: 6,861/5,258. **Course rating:** N/A. **Slope:** N/A.
Opened: 1994. **Pace of Play rating:** 4:20. **Green fee:** $32/36.
Credit cards: All major. **Reduced fees:** No.
Caddies: No. **Golf carts:** Included in Green Fee.
Discount golf packages: No. **Season:** Year-round. **High:** April-Oct.
On-site lodging: Yes. **Rental clubs:** Yes.
Walking policy: Mandatory cart. **Range:** Yes (grass).
To obtain tee times: Call three days in advance.

★★★½ THE RIVER CLUB
R—Hwy. 17 S., Pawleys Island (803)237-8755, (800)344-5590.
12 miles south of Myrtle Beach. **Holes:** 18. **Par:** 72/72.
Yards: 6,677/5,084. **Course rating:** 72.2/67.7. **Slope:** 125/120.
Opened: 1986. **Pace of Play rating:** 4:40. **Green fee:** $20/52.
Credit cards: All major. **Reduced fees:** Low season, Resort guests.
Caddies: No. **Golf carts:** $16 for 18 holes.
Discount golf packages: Yes. **Season:** Year-round. **High:** March-April/Oct.
On-site lodging: Yes. **Rental clubs:** Yes.
Walking policy: Walking at certain times. **Range:** No.
To obtain tee times: Contact your hotel golf director or call up to one year in advance.
Subscriber comments: Beautiful low country layout . . . Double digit handicaps beware, slope should be higher than listed . . . Challenging second shots . . . Fair track, be careful of the yardages . . . Lots of water . . . A real challenge, beautiful . . . Nicely laid out, interesting . . . Beautiful shape . . . Good course but severely crowded . . . Loved it every time, great staff, great par 3s and hard, short par 4s . . . Well kept, visually impressive, plays longer than rating . . . Plays tough in summer with heavy Bermuda rough . . . Par-5 18th reachable in two by average golfer if he is courageous . . . Lots of water that is not in play . . . One of the better courses in Pawleys area.

★★★½ RIVER FALLS PLANTATION
PU—100 Player Blvd., Duncan (803)433-9192.
10 miles north of Greenville. **Holes:** 18. **Par:** 72/72.
Yards: 6,734/4,928. **Course rating:** 72.1/68.2. **Slope:** 127/125.
Opened: 1990. **Pace of Play rating:** 4:00-4:30. **Green fee:** $31/39.
Credit cards: MC, V. **Reduced fees:** Low season, Resort guests, Seniors, Juniors.
Caddies: No. **Golf carts:** Included in Green Fee.
Discount golf packages: Yes. **Season:** Year-round. **High:** April-Aug.
On-site lodging: No. **Rental clubs:** Yes.
Walking policy: Walking at certain times. **Range:** Yes (grass).

To obtain tee times: Call pro shop.
Subscriber comments: Difficult Gary Player course . . . Challenging, unusual, fun . . . A few gimmicky holes . . . Holes require precise shot placements . . . Good use of hilly terrain and sharp slopes. Several fun shots from high tees to targets far below . . . Excellent course . . . Some holes are hard to play without course knowledge . . . Getting better with age . . . Too many blind tee shots . . . Good layout . . . High rough everywhere . . . Variety of shots required . . . Some unusual holes, some weak holes . . . Tight and challenging . . . Unparalleled variety of holes . . . Interesting . . . Shotmaker's course . . . Beautiful course, beautiful layout . . . Most scenic course I ever played. Must see this layout.

★★★ RIVER HILLS GOLF AND COUNTRY CLUB
PU—3670 Cedar Creek Run, Little River (803)399-2100, (800)264-3810.
10 miles north of Myrtle Beach. **Holes:** 18. **Par:** 72/72.
Yards: 6,829/4,861. **Course rating:** 73.0/68.0. **Slope:** 133/120.
Opened: 1989. **Pace of Play rating:** 4:30. **Green fee:** $14/44.
Credit cards: All major. **Reduced fees:** Twilight.
Caddies: No. **Golf carts:** $16 for 18 holes.
Discount golf packages: Yes. **Season:** Year-round. **High:** April-Oct.
On-site lodging: No. **Rental clubs:** Yes.
Walking policy: Mandatory cart. **Range:** Yes (grass).
To obtain tee times: Call up to one year in advance.
Subscriber comments: You won't believe it untill you play it. A real challenge . . . Bring lots of balls, the back side will kill you . . . Diverse collection of fairways . . . One poor hole . . . Best back nine I've played at Myrtle Beach . . . Lots of water and interesting holes . . . A true test but enjoyable . . . Lots of water . . . Best-kept secret in South Carolina . . . Hilly for Myrtle Beach but in great shape . . . Friendly people, bring an extra sleeve of balls for No. 17 . . . Fun course, good for all playing levels, not very busy for Myrtle.

★★½ RIVER OAKS GOLF PLANTATION
OTTER/BEAR/FOX
R—831 River Oaks Dr., Myrtle Beach (803)236-2222.
Holes: 27. **Par:** 72/72/72.
Yards: 6,877/6,778/6,791. **Course rating:** 72.5/72.0/71.7. **Slope:** 125/126/125.
Opened: 1987. **Pace of Play rating:** 4:30. **Green fee:** $25/46.
Credit cards: MC, V. **Reduced fees:** Low season, Resort guests, Twilight, Juniors.
Caddies: No. **Golf carts:** Included in Green Fee.
Discount golf packages: Yes. **Season:** Year-round. **High:** March-April.
On-site lodging: No. **Rental clubs:** Yes.
Walking policy: Mandatory cart. **Range:** Yes (grass).
To obtain tee times: Any local hotel can arrange tee times or call pro shop.
Subscriber comments: Three nines all challenging . . . Three different fun nines, always a value . . . Well-kept course, short and narrow . . . Very pretty . . . Don't leave fairway . . . Housing development is taking away all neighboring trees, eroding beauty, serenity . . . Tough but fair.

★★ ROBBERS ROOST GOLF COURSE
PU—Hwy. 17 N., North Myrtle Beach (803)249-1471, (800)352-2384.
Holes: 18. **Par:** 70/72.
Yards: 7,148/5,387. **Course rating:** 74.4/70.2. **Slope:** 137/116.
Opened: 1968. **Pace of Play rating:** 4:30. **Green fee:** $29/56.
Credit cards: MC, V, AMEX. **Reduced fees:** Low season, Twilight.
Caddies: No. **Golf carts:** Included in Green Fee.
Discount golf packages: No. **Season:** Year-round. **High:** March-April.
On-site lodging: No. **Rental clubs:** Yes.
Walking policy: Mandatory cart. **Range:** Yes (grass).
To obtain tee times: Call up to one year in advance.
Subscriber comments: Majestic old course, pretty lakes, and moss draped

trees . . . Pleasant surprise, good greens . . . 16th great par 5 . . . Best-kept secret . . . Some fine holes . . . One of the finest back nines at Myrtle Beach . . . Appreciate the old style golf in North Myrtle Beach.

★★ ROLLING HILLS GOLF CLUB
PU—1790 Hwy. 501, Galavants Ferry (803)358-4653, (800)633-2380. 25 miles west of Myrtle Beach. **Holes:** 18. **Par:** 72/72. **Yards:** 6,749/5,141. **Course rating:** 71.4/86.3. **Slope:** 120/109. **Opened:** 1988. **Pace of Play rating:** 3:50. **Green fee:** $10/20. **Credit cards:** MC, V. **Reduced fees:** Weekdays, Low season, Resort guests, Twilight, Seniors, Juniors. **Caddies:** No. **Golf carts:** $15 for 18 holes. **Discount golf packages:** Yes. **Season:** Year-round. **High:** Spring/Fall. **On-site lodging:** No. **Rental clubs:** Yes. **Walking policy:** Walking at certain times. **Range:** Yes (grass). **To obtain tee times:** Call 800 number. **Subscriber comments:** For those on a budget . . . New facilities . . . Fair course, sort of long, wide open . . . Fairly open layout, some real good holes on the front . . . Always wet . . . Fair for average golfer . . . Relaxing rounds.

★★★ ROSE HILL COUNTRY CLUB
EAST/SOUTH/WEST
SP—One Clubhouse Dr., Bluffton (803)757-2160. Call club for further information. **Subscriber comments:** Best rates in the Hilton Head area, fit for low-medium handicappers . . . Could use some work on unflattening the course . . . Ho-hum . . . West is by far the best nine . . . This course is suited for all players . . . Never a crowd . . . Beautiful traditional layout . . . Pleasant to play . . . This course seems to get better every year.

★★ SALUDA VALLEY COUNTRY CLUB
SP—598 Beaver Dam Rd., Williamston (803)847-7102. 20 miles south of Greenville. **Holes:** 18. **Par:** 72/72. **Yards:** 6,430/5,126. **Course rating:** 70.8/69.4. **Slope:** 119/114. **Opened:** 1964. **Pace of Play rating:** 4:30. **Green fee:** $10/15. **Credit cards:** None. **Reduced fees:** Weekdays. **Caddies:** No. **Golf carts:** $8 for 18 holes. **Discount golf packages:** No. **Season:** Year-round. **High:** April-Sept. **On-site lodging:** No. **Rental clubs:** No. **Walking policy:** Unrestricted walking. **Range:** Yes (grass). **To obtain tee times:** Call three days in advance. **Subscriber comments:** Course not too hard, favors higher handicaps . . . Short course, good greens, wide open, few trees . . . Getting better since installing irrigation system.

★★½ SANTEE NATIONAL GOLF CLUB
R—Hwy. 6 W., Santee (803)854-3531, (800)448-0152. 60 miles north of Charleston. **Holes:** 18. **Par:** 72/72. **Yards:** 6,858/4,748. **Course rating:** 72.1/68.2. **Slope:** 120/116. **Opened:** 1989. **Pace of Play rating:** 4:00. **Green fee:** $25/36. **Credit cards:** All major. **Reduced fees:** Resort guests, Seniors, Juniors. **Caddies:** No. **Golf carts:** Included in Green Fee. **Discount golf packages:** Yes. **Season:** Year-round. **High:** March-April/Oct. **On-site lodging:** No. **Rental clubs:** Yes. **Walking policy:** Mandatory cart. **Range:** Yes (grass). **To obtain tee times:** Call 800 number. **Subscriber comments:** A surprise in the middle of nowhere . . . Fairways generally open . . . Greens small and fast . . . Not crowded . . . Enjoyed round . . . The whole town is glad you're there and show it . . . Easy playing . . . Good staff . . . Small town atmosphere . . . Old fashioned . . .

Very good country course . . . Staff treats you like family . . . Good potential . . . A good deal for the bargain hunter . . . Nice and easy, I shot better than my age here . . . Good layout . . . My wife's favorite . . . Nondescript front nine, outstanding back nine . . . Good one!

★★ SEA GULL GOLF CLUB

PU—P.O. Box 2607, Pawleys Island (803)448-5931.
20 miles north of Myrtle Beach. **Holes:** 18. **Par:** 72/72.
Yards: 6,910/5,250. **Course rating:** N/A. **Slope:** 128/115.
Opened: N/A. **Pace of Play rating:** N/A. **Green fee:** N/A.
Credit cards: MC, V. **Reduced fees:** Low season.
Caddies: No. **Golf carts:** N/A.
Discount golf packages: No. **Season:** Year-round. **High:** Spring/Fall.
On-site lodging: Yes. **Rental clubs:** No.
Walking policy: N/A. **Range:** No.
Subscriber comments: Improving each month . . . Old timer . . . Appears overplayed . . . Nice of them to give you a bag of ice to keep your beer in . . . Few memorable holes, but a fair test . . . Maintenance has improved . . . Playable and the owners try to keep it up . . . One of our most improved courses.

SEA PINES SPORTS AND CONFERENCE CENTER

R—100 N. Sea Pines Dr., Hilton Head Island (803)842-1894, (800)955-8337.
30 miles northeast of Savannah, GA. **Green fee:** $70/77.
Credit cards: All major. **Reduced fees:** Low season, Resort guests, Twilight, Juniors.
Caddies: No. **Golf carts:** Included in Green Fee.
Discount golf packages: Yes. **Season:** Year-round. **High:** Spring/Fall.
On-site lodging: Yes. **Rental clubs:** Yes.
Walking policy: Walking at certain times. **Range:** Yes (grass).
To obtain tee times: Call 800 number.

★★★ OCEAN COURSE

Holes: 18. **Par:** 72/72.
Yards: 6,614/5,284. **Course rating:** 71.0/69.7. **Slope:** 125/111.
Opened: 1960. **Pace of Play rating:** 4:30.
Redesigned by Mark McCumber. Course to reopen in September 1995.
Subscriber comments: Anxiously awaiting the opening of a redesigned course . . . Fun to play . . . Nice surrounding . . . Fun course, friendly staff . . . Beauty and golf all in one, love the par 5s . . . Beautiful . . . More enjoyable than Harbour Town . . . Great par 3 facing the ocean . . . Super play. Great layout. Nice holes . . . Tough final four holes . . . Can't wait to see the redone course.

★★½ SEA MARSH COURSE

Holes: 18. **Par:** 72/72.
Yards: 6,515/5,054. **Course rating:** 70.0/69.8. **Slope:** 120/123.
Opened: 1960. **Pace of Play rating:** 4:30.
Subscriber comments: Staff is always friendly, course is a fair, well-designed resort course . . . Fun to play . . . Redone three years ago . . . Great finishing hole . . . Nice but not as neatly manicured as the Ocean Course . . . Challenging second shots. Tight fairways . . . Very nice course. Good condition . . . Long and challenging . . . Good across the board.

★★½ SHADOWMOSS PLANTATION GOLF CLUB

SP—20 Dunvegan Dr., Charleston (803)556-8251, (800)338-4971.
Holes: 18. **Par:** 72/72.
Yards: 6,700/5,200. **Course rating:** 72.4/70.2. **Slope:** 123/120.
Opened: 1971. **Pace of Play rating:** 4:00. **Green fee:** $8/20.
Credit cards: MC, V, AMEX. **Reduced fees:** Weekdays, Low season, Resort guests, Twilight, Seniors, Juniors.
Caddies: No. **Golf carts:** $12 for 18 holes.
Discount golf packages: Yes. **Season:** Year-round. **High:** March-May.
On-site lodging: No. **Rental clubs:** Yes.

Walking policy: Walking at certain times. **Range:** Yes (grass).
To obtain tee times: Call. Tee times taken six months in advance.
Subscriber comments: Average layout surrounded by homes . . . Best golf value in Charleston . . . Ditches everywhere . . . Nice course . . . Some tight fairways, water and wooded areas built around a housing development . . . Fun to play . . . Nice people, accomodating . . . Good course for average player . . . Well-maintained course, wide fairways . . . Needs more yardage markers.

★★★ SHIPYARD GOLF CLUB
GALLEON/BRIGANTINE/CLIPPER
R—P.O. Drawer 7229, Hilton Head Island (803)686–8802.
Call club for further information.
Subscriber comments: A wonderful layout . . . Nice course, poor drainage on some holes . . . Great course, great facilities lots of water . . . Very average . . . Usually too wet . . . Great pro shop . . . Lots of water. Narrow. Shotmaker's course . . . Nice greens. Plush fairways, always fun . . . Great resort course . . . Good layout with wide fairways . . . Enjoyed each course . . . Good vacation stop.

★★½ SPRING LAKE COUNTRY CLUB
SP—1375 Spring Lake Rd., York (803)684–4898.
20 miles south of Charlotte, NC. **Holes:** 18. **Par:** 72/72.
Yards: 6,748/4,975. **Course rating:** 72.8/67.3. **Slope:** 126/108.
Opened: 1960. **Pace of Play rating:** 4:00. **Green fee:** $15/21.
Credit cards: MC, V. **Reduced fees:** Weekdays, Juniors.
Caddies: No. **Golf carts:** $11 for 18 holes.
Discount golf packages: No. **Season:** Year-round. **High:** May-Oct.
On-site lodging: No. **Rental clubs:** Yes.
Walking policy: Walking at certain times. **Range:** Yes (grass).
To obtain tee times: Call for Fridays, weekends and holidays.
Subscriber comments: Very nice course . . . Good for average golfer . . . Very challenging from back tees . . . Very fast greens . . . Played during renovations, rating could improve . . . Very family oriented.

★★★ STONEY POINT GOLF CLUB
SP—709 Swing About Rd., Greenwood (803)942–0900.
35 miles south of Greenville. **Holes:** 18. **Par:** 72/72.
Yards: 6,760/5,060. **Course rating:** 72.1/70.3. **Slope:** 125/120.
Opened: 1990. **Pace of Play rating:** 4:00. **Green fee:** $14/19.
Credit cards: MC, V. **Reduced fees:** Twilight, Seniors, Juniors.
Caddies: No. **Golf carts:** $11 for 18 holes.
Discount golf packages: No. **Season:** Year-round. **High:** Spring/Fall.
On-site lodging: No. **Rental clubs:** Yes.
Walking policy: Walking at certain times. **Range:** Yes (grass).
To obtain tee times: Call seven days in advance.
Subscriber comments: Nice course, beautiful setting . . . Fun to play, fairly open . . . Good shape, some difficult holes for seniors . . . Very firm course to play . . . Never crowded . . . Narrow fairways, water . . . Just don't overdevelop with houses.

★★ SUMMERSETT GOLF CLUB
SP—111 Pilot Rd., Greenville (803)834–4781.
Holes: 18. **Par:** 72/72.
Yards: 6,025/4,910. **Course rating:** 68.3/67.6. **Slope:** 114/119.
Opened: 1938. **Pace of Play rating:** 4:00. **Green fee:** $11/16.
Credit cards: MC, V. **Reduced fees:** Seniors.
Caddies: No. **Golf carts:** $10 for 18 holes.
Discount golf packages: Yes. **Season:** Year-round. **High:** April-Aug.
On-site lodging: No. **Rental clubs:** Yes.
Walking policy: Walking at certain times. **Range:** No.
To obtain tee times: Call one week in advance.
Subscriber comments: Short but a challenge . . . Another older course

. . . Beautiful mountain course . . . Nice walk . . . Don't have to be long hitter . . . Tight fairways and small greens . . . Hilly, but watch the grain on the greens . . . Some fairways need attention . . . No driver required. Remember your short game.

★★★★ SURF GOLF AND BEACH CLUB

SP—1701 Springland Lane, North Myrtle Beach (803)249-1524, (800)765-7873.
60 miles south of Wilmington. **Holes:** 18. **Par:** 72/72.
Yards: 6,842/5,178. **Course rating:** 72.6/68.2. **Slope:** 126/111.
Opened: 1960. **Pace of Play rating:** 4:00. **Green fee:** $13/57.
Credit cards: MC, V. **Reduced fees:** Low season.
Caddies: No. **Golf carts:** $14 for 18 holes.
Discount golf packages: Yes. **Season:** Year-round. **High:** Spring/Fall.
On-site lodging: No. **Rental clubs:** Yes.
Walking policy: Mandatory cart. **Range:** Yes (grass).
To obtain tee times: Contact pro shop directly or have hotel make tee times.
Subscriber comments: Lots of class, plantation-type setting . . . Great people . . . If I could be a member here I'd be happy . . . Wonderful layout and condition . . . Great finishing holes . . . Old course . . . No tricks, just a great track . . . Recently redesigned by John LaFoy . . . Good test, fun . . . Loved this course. Several dogleg rights . . . Wide open, but a test . . . Very good design fair well kept, good food . . . Traditional course, not tricked up, nice layout . . . Clean classic old time course. No.1 at Myrtle . . . One of the playable courses at North Myrtle Beach . . . Course renovations successful . . . One of the finest traditional courses.

★★★★½ TIDEWATER GOLF CLUB

PU—4901 Little River Neck Rd., North Myrtle Beach (803)249-3829, (800)446-5363.
Holes: 18. **Par:** 72/72.
Yards: 7,150/4,665. **Course rating:** 73.7/67.5. **Slope:** 134/127.
Opened: 1990. **Pace of Play rating:** 4:30-5:00. **Green fee:** $40/77.
Credit cards: MC, V, AMEX. **Reduced fees:** Juniors.
Caddies: No. **Golf carts:** $16 for 18 holes.
Discount golf packages: No. **Season:** Year-round. **High:** Year-round.
On-site lodging: Yes. **Rental clubs:** Yes.
Walking policy: Mandatory cart. **Range:** Yes (grass).
To obtain tee times: Call pro shop, send deposit, time is then reconfirmed.
Selected as Best New Public Course of 1990 by Golf Digest. Ranked 9th in South Carolina by Golf Digest.
Subscriber comments: Beautiful to look at, consistently interesting to play . . . Very high fees for Myrtle Beach. Most unusual course in area . . . Difficult for women . . . Not too long, great scenery, unusual par 3s . . . Beautiful, tranquil, challenging, great staff . . . Tough course for average player . . . True test of golf skills . . . Beautiful . . . Not much of a clubhouse . . . Free ball mark repair tool nice touch . . . Best conditioned traditional layout ever . . . Some dramatic holes . . . Challenges all phases of golf game . . . Impossible to walk due to distance between greens and tees . . . Second best at Myrtle Beach . . . One of the toughest and most fun . . . Some great holes . . . Top quality course, I wish I could afford to play here everyday . . . The best at the beach . . . A real test from blues . . . Many choke shots . . . Fantastic views . . . What a course, scenery, great condition, spectacular . . . Gorgeous marsh views . . . Expensive but I loved every minute and every hole . . . Some spectacular holes . . . Tremendous challenge but fair . . . No two holes alike.

★★★½ TIMBERLAKE PLANTATION GOLF CLUB

SP—1700-A Amicks Ferry Rd., Chapin (803)345-9909.
30 miles north of Columbia. **Holes:** 18. **Par:** 72/72.
Yards: 6,703/5,111. **Course rating:** 73.2/69.8. **Slope:** 132/118.
Opened: N/A. **Pace of Play rating:** N/A. **Green fee:** $16/22.

Credit cards: MC, V, AMEX. **Reduced fees:** Weekdays, Low season, Resort guests, Twilight, Seniors, Juniors.
Caddies: No. **Golf carts:** $10 for 18 holes.
Discount golf packages: Yes. **Season:** Year-round. **High:** April-May/Aug-Nov.
On-site lodging: Yes. **Rental clubs:** Yes.
Walking policy: Unrestricted walking. **Range:** Yes (grass).
To obtain tee times: Call one week in advance.
Subscriber comments: Very good Byrd design on lake . . . Beautiful, challenging layout, par 5 18th hole on Lake Murray as scenic as any hole anywhere . . . Don't miss the boat ride to get there . . . Super nice course, a lot of variety, great closing hole . . . Good design . . . Scenic but condition varies . . . Awesome . . . Nice, tough, good variety hole to hole . . . Use all the clubs . . . Absolutely loved it . . . No. 18 one of the most scenic holes in the south.

★★★½ VERDAE GREENS GOLF CLUB
R—650 Verdae Blvd., Greenville (803)676-1500.
Holes: 18. **Par:** 72/72.
Yards: 6,773/5,012. **Course rating:** 71.9/68.1. **Slope:** 126/116.
Opened: 1989. **Pace of Play rating:** 4:00. **Green fee:** $27/44.
Credit cards: MC, V, AMEX. **Reduced fees:** Low season, Resort guests, Seniors, Juniors.
Caddies: No. **Golf carts:** Included in Green Fee.
Discount golf packages: Yes. **Season:** Year-round. **High:** March-Nov.
On-site lodging: Yes. **Rental clubs:** Yes.
Walking policy: Walking at certain times. **Range:** Yes (grass).
To obtain tee times: Call seven days in advance.
Subscriber comments: Beautiful, hilly, and fun to play . . . Mountain-type course, scenic and playable for average golfer . . . Interesting layout . . . Best course in area, need precision shotmaking to score . . . Greens always very firm . . . Long holes for average golfer . . . Good test of ability . . . An excellent track, challenging, need all shots . . . The biggest surprise, great layout . . . Quickest greens I've putted . . . Will be an outstanding course when it matures . . . Well designed and well maintained . . . Service of a country club . . . Changes in greens have helped . . . Nike Tour stops here.

★½ VILLAGE GREEN GOLF CLUB
PU—Hwy. 176, Gramling (803)472-2411.
Call club for further information.
Subscriber comments: Good practice course . . . Wear your best tank top . . . Starting to fix this course up, still needs work . . . Nice course, double dogleg 18th . . . Making improvements . . . Challenging, almost too hard for a high handicapper.

★★½ WATERWAY HILLS GOLF CLUB
OAKS/LAKES/RAVINES
R—Hwy. 17N, Restaurant Row, Myrtle Beach (803)449-6488, (800)344-5590.
Holes: 27. **Par:** 72/72/72.
Yards: 6,461/6,339/6,470. **Course rating:** 71.0/70.6/70.8. **Slope:** 120/122/121.
Opened: 1975. **Pace of Play rating:** 4:15. **Green fee:** $10/45.
Credit cards: All major. **Reduced fees:** Low season, Resort guests.
Caddies: No. **Golf carts:** $16 for 18 holes.
Discount golf packages: Yes. **Season:** Year-round. **High:** March-April/Oct.
On-site lodging: No. **Rental clubs:** Yes.
Walking policy: Walking at certain times. **Range:** Yes (grass).
To obtain tee times: Call your hotel golf director of call "Tee Time Central" at (800)344-5590 up to one year in advance.
Subscriber comments: One of the best staffs; even got a rain check! . . . Blind holes with water not noted on scorecard . . . Nice ride over water to

clubhouse . . . Great shape, tight fairways . . . Sand and water on every hole . . . It's too aggravating getting on and off the golf course . . . The tram is too slow . . . Interesting, well maintained, has character . . . Don't fall for cable car ride to clubhouse . . . How many clubs have accidentally fallen off gondola?

★★ WEDGEFIELD PLANTATION COUNTRY CLUB

SP—100 Manor Dr., Georgetown (803)546-8587.
20 miles south of Myrtle Beach. **Holes:** 18. **Par:** 72/73.
Yards: 6,705/5,249. **Course rating:** 72.2/69.9. **Slope:** 123/119.
Opened: 1974. **Pace of Play rating:** 4:30. **Green fee:** $35/55.
Credit cards: MC, V. **Reduced fees:** Low season, Twilight.
Caddies: No. **Golf carts:** Included in Green Fee.
Discount golf packages: Yes. **Season:** Year-round. **High:** Spring/Fall.
On-site lodging: Yes. **Rental clubs:** Yes.
Walking policy: Walking at certain times. **Range:** Yes (grass).
To obtain tee times: Call pro shop.
Subscriber comments: Good old course in good shape . . . Good track from back tees, back nine exceptional . . . Wet in spring and winter . . . Good layout, wet at times . . . Doesn't get the play it deserves on Myrtle Beach packages.

★★★ THE WELLMAN CLUB

SP—328 Country Club Dr., Johnsonville (803)386-2521, (800)258-2935.
42 miles west of Myrtle Beach. **Holes:** 18. **Par:** 72/72.
Yards: 7,018/5,281. **Course rating:** 73.9/69.5. **Slope:** 129/105.
Opened: 1966. **Pace of Play rating:** 4:00. **Green fee:** $16/28.
Credit cards: MC, V. **Reduced fees:** Weekdays, Low season, Resort guests, Juniors.
Caddies: No. **Golf carts:** $12 for 18 holes.
Discount golf packages: Yes. **Season:** Year-round. **High:** Feb-May.
On-site lodging: Yes. **Rental clubs:** Yes.
Walking policy: Walking at certain times. **Range:** Yes (grass).
To obtain tee times: Call at least 48 hours in advance.
Subscriber comments: A real gem . . . Nice place to play golf . . . A little off the beaten path, but worth the drive . . . Good layout, not well known . . . Never crowded, nice folks . . . Excellent greens and fairways and never crowded . . . Excellent course . . . Good test of golf . . . Best-kept secret around . . . I'd play this course everyday if I could . . . Out of the mainstream but an excellent layout . . . One of South Carolina's best-kept secrets.

GREAT VALUE

WHITE PINES GOLF CLUB★

PU—614 Mary Lane, Camden (803)432-7442.
20 miles northeast of Columbia. **Holes:** 18. **Par:** 72/N/A.
Yards: 6,800/4,806. **Course rating:** 71.3/66.9. **Slope:** 125/112.
Opened: 1989. **Pace of Play rating:** 4:00. **Green fee:** $15.
Credit cards: None. **Reduced fees:** Weekdays, Low season, Resort guests, Twilight, Seniors, Juniors.
Caddies: No. **Golf carts:** Included in Green Fee.
Discount golf packages: Yes. **Season:** Year-round. **High:** April-Oct.
On-site lodging: No. **Rental clubs:** Yes.
Walking policy: Mandatory cart. **Range:** No.
To obtain tee times: First come, first served.
Subscriber comments: Gem hidden in horse country . . . Do it . . . Can lose balls, but a nice course . . . Needs work.

WILD DUNES RESORT

R—5881 Palmetto Dr., Isle of Palms (803)886-2301, (800)845-8880.
12 miles southwest of Charleston. **Credit cards:** All major. **Reduced fees:** Weekdays, Low season, Resort guests.
Caddies: No. **Golf carts:** Included in Green Fee.
Discount golf packages: Yes. **Season:** Year-round. **High:** Spring/Fall.
On-site lodging: Yes. **Rental clubs:** Yes.

Walking policy: Mandatory cart. **Range:** No.
To obtain tee times: Call pro shop.

★★★½ HARBOR COURSE
Holes: 18. **Par:** 70/70.
Yards: 6,446/4,774. **Course rating:** 70.9/68.1. **Slope:** 124/117.
Opened: 1986. **Pace of Play rating:** 4:00–4:30. **Green fee:** $29/75.
Subscriber comments: Tougher than Links, not as pretty though . . .
Solid and enjoyable . . . Target golf at its best . . . Well-kept course but
short and narrow . . . Lots of water, I spent more time admiring the homes
than the course . . . Could play this every day for the rest of my life . . .
Short, tight, no need for woods . . . Tough par 3s . . . Have to play more
than once to appreciate . . . Coastal winds make club selection tricky . . .
Six par 3s . . . Long rides between holes . . . Cheaper than Links but not as
good a track . . . Wonderful layout. Nos. 17 and 18 tough, tough, tough
. . . Lots of marsh and water . . . Target golf with wind translates to tough.

★★★★½ LINKS COURSE
R—5757 Palm Blvd., Isle of Palms (803)886-2180, (800)845-8880.
Holes: 18. **Par:** 72/72.
Yards: 6,722/4,849. **Course rating:** 72.7/69.1. **Slope:** 131/121.
Opened: 1980. **Pace of Play rating:** 4:12. **Green fee:** $39/110.
Walking policy: Unrestricted walking. **Range:** Yes (grass).
Ranked 91st in America's 100 Greatest Golf Courses by Golf Digest.
Ranked 13th in America's 75 Best Resort Courses by Golf Digest. Ranked
5th in South Carolina by Golf Digest.
Subscriber comments: Expensive, but a real classic . . . Better than the
average ocean course . . . True links golf test . . . Far too crowded on
weekend, Harbor Course a better bet . . . Tremendous challenge . . . Great
golf, beautiful course, wonderful resort area . . . One fine layout, very hard
in wind, scenic . . . This resort defines class . . . Tough design, but fair,
good layout, elevated tees and greens . . . I though I was at Pebble . . . This
course is beautiful . . . Could play this everyday for the rest of my life . . .
Strong, scenic, everyone should play it once . . . As good as it gets . . .
Extremely difficult if the wind is blowing . . . Best public course in the
southeast even after Hugo . . . My No. 1 favorite . . . Still one of the best
around . . . Can't get enough of the course . . . Love the 17th and 18th by
the ocean . . . Treated like a king . . . First time I ever had to hit 5-iron on a
short par 3. Windy but beautiful . . . A target golf course with a lot of water
. . . If wind is blowing order pizza in the condo . . . Does not get much
better than this, three great finishing holes . . . Worth the price, back nine is
as good as any around. Famous course, not the same after Hurricane Hugo
but still great.

WILD WING PLANTATION
R—1000 Wild Wing Blvd., Conway (803)347-9464, (800)736-9464.
7 miles north of Myrtle Beach. **Credit cards:** All major. **Reduced fees:**
Weekdays, Low season, Resort guests.
Caddies: No. **Golf carts:** $16 for 18 holes.
Discount golf packages: Yes. **Season:** Year-round. **High:** April/Oct.
On-site lodging: No. **Rental clubs:** Yes.
Walking policy: Mandatory cart. **Range:** Yes (grass).
To obtain tee times: Call tee time operations by phone or in person.
Times must be guaranteed with a credit card or pre-paid. If booking on a
golf package, the hotel will be responsible for the tee time.

★★★★ AVOCET COURSE
Holes: 18. **Par:** 72/72.
Yards: 7,127/5,298. **Course rating:** 74.2/70.4. **Slope:** 128/118.
Opened: 1993. **Pace of Play rating:** 4:00–4:30. **Green fee:** $28/83.
Ranked 17th in South Carolina by Golf Digest.
Subscriber comments: A little manufactured but great, good variety of
holes . . . Friendly staff that warned me of green fee when I made tee time
. . . There are now four courses, all of them super . . . Great condition . . .
Tough layout, very difficult greens . . . One of the best courses I ever
played . . . Best complex at beach . . . No place else close . . . Great range,
great putting range . . . Favorite course in Myrtle Beach. Many teeing

options . . . Good solid course . . . One of the best I ever played . . . Good players course . . . High handicappers, stay home . . . Larry Nelson's sure-fire winner . . . Fantastic, imaginative . . . Nothing natural in the landscape . . . Fantastic complex. Good variety of holes. Enjoyable for all handicaps . . . Unusual but interesting . . . Straight, no doglegs, no tricks, but long par 4s, always excellent condition . . . Take some humility pills.

FALCON COURSE★
Holes: 18. **Par:** 72/72.
Yards: 7,082/5,190. **Course rating:** N/A. **Slope:** N/A.
Opened: 1994. **Pace of Play rating:** 4:00-4:30. **Green fee:** $28/83.
Walking policy: Walking at certain times.

★★★½ HUMMINGBIRD COURSE
Holes: 18. **Par:** 72/72.
Yards: 6,853/5,168. **Course rating:** 73.0/69.5. **Slope:** 131/123.
Opened: 1992. **Pace of Play rating:** 4:00-4:30. **Green fee:** $17/70.
Subscriber comments: Very challenging, you have to make the right club selection . . . Shotmaker's course . . . Great but tough, too difficult in 35 m.p.h winds . . . Great range, great putting green . . . Well-conditioned fairways and greens, good condition, tough in wind . . . Very good condition . . . Another wide-open course . . . Well kept . . . Super greens . . . Lots of hazards, good condition . . . Very enjoyable for all levels of golfers . . . Unfair pin placement detracts from playability . . . Marsh is in the perfect spots . . . Great restaurant and clubhouse, beautifully manicured courses, very helpful staff . . . Fun, lots of trouble, several 200 yard carries required from regular tees . . . Loved it.

★★★★ WOOD STORK COURSE
Holes: 18. **Par:** 72/72.
Yards: 7,044/5,409. **Course rating:** 73.6/70.7. **Slope:** 126/121.
Opened: 1991. **Pace of Play rating:** 4:00-4:30. **Green fee:** $17/70.
Subscriber comments: Wonderful basic course . . . Beautiful . . . My favorite at Myrtle Beach . . . Great course, many nice touches . . . All four of Wild Wings' courses different and a great day of golf . . . Long course for seniors, very fast greens . . . Smooth bent-grass greens . . . Traditional American course, anybody can play . . . Best of the four courses for the average player . . . Excellent condition, staff offers superb treatment . . . Wonderful golfing experience . . . Lots of trees, very tight . . . Friendly staff and starters, nice tour through wetland area. Lots of birds . . . Course was interesting to play, staff friendly & helpful . . . Do they sell stock?

★★★½ WILLBROOK PLANTATION GOLF CLUB
R—Hwy. 17, Pawleys Island (803)237-4900.
22 miles south of Myrtle Beach. **Holes:** 18. **Par:** 72/72.
Yards: 6,704/4,963. **Course rating:** 71.8/67.9. **Slope:** 125/118.
Opened: 1988. **Pace of Play rating:** 4:20. **Green fee:** $36/74.
Credit cards: MC, V, AMEX. **Reduced fees:** Resort guests.
Caddies: No. **Golf carts:** Included in Green Fee.
Discount golf packages: Yes. **Season:** Year-round. **High:** March-April.
On-site lodging: Yes. **Rental clubs:** Yes.
Walking policy: Walking at certain times. **Range:** Yes (grass).
To obtain tee times: Call pro shop.
Subscriber comments: Very nice course, a Dan Maples classic, not well known, great people . . . Outstanding Bermuda greens . . . First two holes are hardest . . . Beautiful landscapes, interesting history . . . Very, very good for all players . . . Charming setting, wetlands, good greens narrow fairways . . . Beautiful. A must play. Played three times . . . Great track . . . Some good holes . . . Historic setting . . . Secluded, excellent layout, fun course . . . Fine course tests your skills . . . One of the very best in Myrtle Beach.

★★★★ THE WITCH
R—1900 Hwy. 544, Conway (803)448-1300.
8 miles north of Myrtle Beach. **Holes:** 18. **Par:** 71/71.
Yards: 6,702/4,812. **Course rating:** 71.2/69.0. **Slope:** 133/109.
Opened: 1989. **Pace of Play rating:** N/A. **Green fee:** $39/84.

Credit cards: MC, V. **Reduced fees:** Twilight.
Caddies: No. **Golf carts:** Included in Green Fee.
Discount golf packages: Yes. **Season:** Year-round. **High:** Feb-May/Sept.-Nov.
On-site lodging: No. **Rental clubs:** Yes.
Walking policy: Mandatory cart. **Range:** Yes (grass).
To obtain tee times: Call pro shop. Deposit required during peak season.
Subscriber comments: One of a kind! Isolated and beautiful . . . Challenging and enjoyable, Maples' best . . . Interesting course set in the woods . . . Better be able to putt . . . Five star course and staff . . . Have plenty of insect spray . . . Routed through beautiful woodlands . . . Many great golf holes . . . Excellent service, lost a lot of balls, if you're out of the fairway you are out of luck . . . Beautiful, need to see to believe . . . Test your ability . . . Nature preserve setting, good Maples' design . . . One of three toughest courses I ever played . . . Absolutely gorgeous . . . Beautiful wetlands. Excellent golf variety . . . Totally different 9s . . . Tough course, with long carries over marsh . . . Great clubhouse . . . Watch out for s-s-snakes . . . Terrific from tips.

Notes

★ AUDUBON PARK GOLF COURSE

PU—4160 Park Ave., Memphis (901)683-6941.
Call club for further information.

Subscriber comments: Good for quick round after work in the summer
. . . Average muny course, needs improvement around greens . . . Typical
muny course, now being improved . . . Fairly short, recommended for
seniors, fun for high handicappers . . . City course, not well kept . . . Wide
open, new improvements will make for extra nice muny course.

★½ BANEBERRY GOLF AND RESORT

PU—704 Harrison Ferry Rd., Baneberry (615)674-2500, (800)951-4653.
35 miles east of Knoxville. **Holes:** 18. **Par:** 71/72.
Yards: 6,694/4,829. **Course rating:** 72.6/68.5. **Slope:** 125/117.
Opened: 1972. **Pace of Play rating:** 4:25. **Green fee:** $11/14.
Credit cards: All major. **Reduced fees:** No.
Caddies: No. **Golf carts:** $10 for 18 holes.
Discount golf packages: Yes. **Season:** Year-round. **High:** April-
May/Oct.
On-site lodging: Yes. **Rental clubs:** Yes.
Walking policy: Unrestricted walking. **Range:** Yes (grass).
To obtain tee times: Call pro shop.
Subscriber comments: Good family fun . . . A good course for the
average player . . . Course in average condition . . . Making
improvements.

★★½ BENT CREEK GOLF RESORT

R—3919 E. Parkway, Gatlinburg (615)436-3947, (800)251-9336.
40 miles east of Knoxville. **Holes:** 18. **Par:** 72/73.
Yards: 6,182/5,111. **Course rating:** 70.3/69.2. **Slope:** 127/117.
Opened: 1972. **Pace of Play rating:** 4:00. **Green fee:** $15/30.
Credit cards: MC, V. **Reduced fees:** Low season, Resort guests,
Twilight.
Caddies: No. **Golf carts:** $13 for 18 holes.
Discount golf packages: Yes. **Season:** Year-round. **High:** March-Nov.
On-site lodging: Yes. **Rental clubs:** Yes.
Walking policy: Walking at certain times. **Range:** Yes (grass).
To obtain tee times: Tee times may be made up to a year in advance and
must be guaranteed with a major credit card.
Subscriber comments: Gary Player made the most of what he had to
work with . . . Good mountain course . . . Only the front nine can be
considered good . . . Great views, back nine needs improving . . . Front
nine traditional, back nine circus . . . Very challenging for 10–plus
handicapper, good mix of golf, absolutely gorgeous front . . . Wear snake
boots for copperheads in summer! . . . Mountain creek comes into play
often. Beautiful setting . . . Flat front, lots of water; mountain back, target
golf, best from blue tees . . . Great scenery and helpful staff, but expect
slow play.

★★★½ BIG CREEK GOLF CLUB

SP—6195 Woodstock-Cuba Rd., Millington (901)353-1654.
12 miles north of Memphis. **Holes:** 18. **Par:** 72/72.
Yards: 7,052/5,086. **Course rating:** 72.8/69.6. **Slope:** 121/111.
Opened: 1977. **Pace of Play rating:** 4:30. **Green fee:** $14/21.
Credit cards: MC, V. **Reduced fees:** Weekdays, Low season, Twilight,
Seniors, Juniors.
Caddies: No. **Golf carts:** $10 for 18 holes.
Discount golf packages: No. **Season:** Year-round. **High:** April-Sept.
On-site lodging: No. **Rental clubs:** Yes.
Walking policy: Unrestricted walking. **Range:** Yes (grass).
To obtain tee times: Public may call four days in advance; out-of-town
people and season-pass holders may call seven days in advance.
Subscriber comments: Bent-grass greens, front flat, back hilly . . . Vastly
improved in last one to two years, good test . . . Good course, can be long,
great greens . . . Greens in good shape. Front nine lacks character . . . Long

course. Good layout . . . Above average course, well maintained . . . Good condition but not very interesting, a challenging, relatively flat course . . . Can hit the ball wildly and still be in play. Parallel fairways . . . Challenging for high and medium handicapper . . . Front nine flat and dull, back nine hilly with doglegs . . . Course becoming better under new ownership.

★★ BRAINERD GOLF COURSE
PU—5203 Old Mission Rd., Chattanooga (615)855-2692.
Holes: 18. **Par:** 72/72.
Yards: 6,468/5,403. **Course rating:** 69.8/69.9. **Slope:** 119/118.
Opened: 1926. **Pace of Play rating:** 4:00. **Green fee:** $13/16.
Credit cards: MC, V. **Reduced fees:** Weekdays, Seniors, Juniors.
Caddies: No. **Golf carts:** $9 for 18 holes.
Discount golf packages: No. **Season:** Year-round. **High:** April-Sept.
On-site lodging: No. **Rental clubs:** No.
Walking policy: Walking at certain times. **Range:** No.
To obtain tee times: Call two days in advance.
Subscriber comments: Short but challenging . . . Good course for players starting out . . . Improvements are helping . . . Plenty of trees, older course . . . Ross design . . . Fairways and greens excellent condition . . . Easy to walk.

★★★½ BRIARWOOD GOLF COURSE
PU—P.O. Box 288, Crab Orchard (615)484-5285.
45 miles west of Knoxville. **Holes:** 18. **Par:** 72/72.
Yards: 6,689/5,021. **Course rating:** 74.2/70.9. **Slope:** 132/123.
Opened: 1988. **Pace of Play rating:** N/A. **Green fee:** $25/36.
Credit cards: All major. **Reduced fees:** Weekdays, Low season.
Caddies: No. **Golf carts:** Included in Green Fee.
Discount golf packages: Yes. **Season:** Year-round. **High:** April-Oct.
On-site lodging: Yes. **Rental clubs:** Yes.
Walking policy: Mandatory cart. **Range:** Yes (grass).
To obtain tee times: Call weekdays at 8 a.m. and weekends at 7 a.m.
Subscriber comments: Breathtaking scenery; some of the most beautiful holes in area . . . Course stays in average shape, mountain course . . . The most impressive mountain scenery I have ever seen . . . With a little more money and maturity could be great. Scenic . . . Mountain golf, hidden creeks, tight fairways . . . This is one layout you won't forget, take a lot of balls . . . Absolutely beautiful, long and tough . . . Many picturesque holes, can be tough . . . Remote area, difficult course, no place for duffers . . . Well-kept secret . . . Spectacular location on Cumberland Plateau . . . Best-kept secret in Tennessee . . . A top-of-the-mountain course with stunning views for about 100 miles to all points of the compass. Wooded hillsides and valleys make all par 4s and 5s a tradeoff between distance off the tee and accuracy . . . Scenic and beautiful, excellent condition . . . Tough, need to be long hitter . . . Outstanding variety of holes. Natural beauty . . . Breathtaking. Impeccably maintained, a real test . . . Beautiful vistas, bring your long irons, great track.

★★½ BROWN ACRES GOLF COURSE
PU—406 Brown Rd., Chattanooga (615)855-2680.
Call club for further information.
Subscriber comments: Well maintained, some interesting holes, close to city . . . Challenging course. All types of players. Good staff . . . A very good muny course . . . Wide open, very little trouble . . . Would be better except for I-75 through the course . . . Good and improving.

★½ BUFFALO VALLEY GOLF COURSE
PU—90 Country Club Dr., Unicoi (615)928-1022.
3 miles southeast of Johnson City. **Holes:** 18. **Par:** 71/72.
Yards: 6,624/4,968. **Course rating:** 71.7/69.6. **Slope:** 119/111.
Opened: N/A. **Pace of Play rating:** 4:00. **Green fee:** $15/17.
Credit cards: MC, V. **Reduced fees:** Weekdays.
Caddies: No. **Golf carts:** $27 for 18 holes.

Discount golf packages: Yes. **Season:** Year-round. **High:** April-Sept.
On-site lodging: Yes. **Rental clubs:** Yes.
Walking policy: Unrestricted walking. **Range:** Yes (grass).
To obtain tee times: Call 48 hours in advance.
Subscriber comments: Course has improved over past few years . . .
Very beautiful course. Challenging . . . Course has great potential, needs
work . . . Slowly becoming a good course.

CAMELOT GOLF COURSE★
PU—Hwy. No. 94, Rogersville (615)272-7499.
Call club for further information.
Subscriber comments: Beautiful scenery. Wide open course, not real
memorable . . . Needs a lot of work.

★ CARROLL LAKE GOLF CLUB
SP—1305 Carroll Lake Rd., McKenzie (901)352-5998.
45 miles north of Jackson. **Holes:** 18. **Par:** 71/71.
Yards: 5,517/4,868. **Course rating:** 68.0/68.0. **Slope:** N/A.
Opened: 1961. **Pace of Play rating:** 4:30. **Green fee:** $14.
Credit cards: MC, V. **Reduced fees:** Weekdays, Low season, Seniors,
Juniors.
Caddies: No. **Golf carts:** $9 for 18 holes.
Discount golf packages: No. **Season:** Year-round. **High:** April-Nov.
On-site lodging: No. **Rental clubs:** Yes.
Walking policy: Unrestricted walking. **Range:** No.
To obtain tee times: Call pro shop.
Subscriber comments: Would be excellent course if they had funds to fix
it; very rough . . . Old course, needs work.

★★ COUNTRY HILLS GOLF COURSE
PU—1501 Saundersville Rd., Hendersonville (615)824-1100.
10 miles north of Nashville. **Holes:** 18. **Par:** 70/70.
Yards: 6,100/4,800. **Course rating:** 71.2/67.8. **Slope:** 119/114.
Opened: 1990. **Pace of Play rating:** 4:30. **Green fee:** $13/20.
Credit cards: MC, V, AMEX. **Reduced fees:** Weekdays, Low season,
Twilight, Seniors, Juniors.
Caddies: No. **Golf carts:** $10 for 18 holes.
Discount golf packages: Yes. **Season:** Year-round. **High:** March-Oct.
On-site lodging: No. **Rental clubs:** Yes.
Walking policy: Unrestricted walking. **Range:** Yes (grass).
To obtain tee times: Call seven days in advance.
Subscriber comments: A few poorly designed holes spoil course . . .
Hilly with two very unfair holes, otherwise good service, speed good . . . A
beautiful, well-maintained course, challenging hills, lakes, favors a golfer
who hits a draw . . . Reasonable course except for a couple of "goofy" golf
holes . . . Wooded, hilly course. Straight hitter . . . Strange, tough layout,
blind shots, steep hills . . . Scenic with excellent elevation changes . . .
Mountain goat would love the hills . . . Challenging course, narrow
fairways, good shape, fun to play.

★★½ CREEK'S BEND GOLF CLUB
PU—5900 Hixson Pike, Hixson (615)842-5911.
Call club for further information.
Subscriber comments: Scenery outstanding; not for high handicap . . .
Forgiving fairways, great bent-rass greens . . . Very nice, very good
condition . . . Fair course. A little short . . . Fair course, stays flooded a lot.

THE CROSSINGS GOLF CLUB★
SP—2585 Hwy. 81 N., Jonesborough (615)348-8844.
7 miles west of Johnson City. **Holes:** 18. **Par:** 72/72.
Yards: 6,366/5,072. **Course rating:** 70.0/68.2. **Slope:** 118/112.
Opened: 1994. **Pace of Play rating:** 4:30. **Green fee:** $25.
Credit cards: None. **Reduced fees:** No.
Caddies: No. **Golf carts:** $8 for 18 holes.

Discount golf packages: No. **Season:** Year-round. **High:** March-Oct.
On-site lodging: No. **Rental clubs:** Yes.
Walking policy: Unrestricted walking. **Range:** Yes (grass).
To obtain tee times: Call five days in advance.

★½ DAVY CROCKETT GOLF COURSE
PU—4380 Rangeline, Memphis (901)358-3375.
Holes: 18. **Par:** 72/72.
Yards: 6,200/5,900.
Call club for further information.
Subscriber comments: Tightly wooded, good test for any golfer. Tight
and challenging, one of the city's best . . . Short, hilly, testy . . . With
continued care and improvements this will be a very good municipal
course.

DEER CREEK GOLF CLUB*
SP—1055 Deer Creek Dr., Crossville (615)456-0178.
60 miles west of Knoxville. **Holes:** 18. **Par:** 72/72.
Yards: 6,251/4,917. **Course rating:** 69.6/67.2. **Slope:** 122/114.
Opened: 1989. **Pace of Play rating:** 4:15. **Green fee:** $15/20.
Credit cards: MC, V. **Reduced fees:** Twilight, Juniors.
Caddies: No. **Golf carts:** $10 for 18 holes.
Discount golf packages: Yes. **Season:** Year-round. **High:** April-Oct.
On-site lodging: No. **Rental clubs:** Yes.
Walking policy: Walking at certain times. **Range:** Yes (grass).
To obtain tee times: Call one week in advance.

★★½ DYERSBURG MUNICIPAL GOLF COURSE
PU—Golf Course Rd., Dyersburg (901)286-7620.
Call club for further information.
Subscriber comments: Excellent condition for a muny, unbeatable for
eight bucks . . . Good for average golfer . . . All Bermuda-grass course
good for summer play only.

FRUGAL PICK

★★★ EASTLAND GREEN GOLF COURSE
PU—550 Club House Lane, Clarksville (615)358-9051.
Holes: 18. **Par:** 72/72.
Yards: 6,437/4,790. **Course rating:** 71.5/68.4. **Slope:** 123/116.
Opened: 1990. **Pace of Play rating:** 4:00. **Green fee:** $12/17.
Credit cards: MC, V. **Reduced fees:** Weekdays, Twilight, Seniors,
Juniors.
Caddies: No. **Golf carts:** $16 for 18 holes.
Discount golf packages: No. **Season:** Year-round. **High:** July-Aug.
On-site lodging: No. **Rental clubs:** Yes.
Walking policy: Unrestricted walking. **Range:** Yes (grass).
To obtain tee times: Call five days in advance.
Subscriber comments: Nice facilities and fairways, rough is tall grass,
well laid out, water on one hole . . . Good layout, challenging holes, sporty
. . . Short course very challenging, well kept, courteous staff . . . Very nice
course, fun to play. Always treated well . . . Fairways offer many surprises
such as hidden bunkers and water hazards.

★★★½ EGWANI FARMS GOLF COURSE
PU—3920 Singleton Station Rd., Rockford (615)970-7132.
8 miles south of Knoxville. **Holes:** 18. **Par:** 72/72.
Yards: 6,708/4,680. **Course rating:** 71.9/66.1. **Slope:** 126/113.
Opened: 1991. **Pace of Play rating:** 4:00. **Green fee:** $40/50.
Credit cards: MC, V. **Reduced fees:** Juniors.
Caddies: No. **Golf carts:** Included in Green Fee.
Discount golf packages: No. **Season:** Year-round. **High:** April-Oct.
On-site lodging: No. **Rental clubs:** Yes.
Walking policy: Mandatory cart. **Range:** Yes (grass).
To obtain tee times: Call one week in advance.
Subscriber comments: A good course, run by nice women . . . Good

greens, not much of a layout . . . Very nice course. Well groomed. Helpful staff . . . Beautiful course and greens, friendliest and best staff around, including Sandy the dog . . . Quiet, peaceful setting, but a little pricey . . . Front is flat and bland. Back is hilly and very scenic . . . Layout maturing and has recovered nicely from big flood . . . Excellent condition . . . Staff treats you like you own the place . . . Youthful, expect rapid improvement.

★★ ELIZABETHTON MUNICIPAL GOLF CLUB

PU—Golf Club Rd., Elizabethton (615)542-8051.
9 miles east of Johnson City. **Holes:** 18. **Par:** 72/72.
Yards: 6,339/4,335. **Course rating:** 71.2/67.7. **Slope:** 129/118.
Opened: 1934. **Pace of Play rating:** 4:30. **Green fee:** $17/30.
Credit cards: MC, V. **Reduced fees:** No.
Caddies: No. **Golf carts:** Included in Green Fee.
Discount golf packages: No. **Season:** Year-round. **High:** April-Sept.
On-site lodging: No. **Rental clubs:** Yes.
Walking policy: Walking at certain times. **Range:** Yes (grass).
To obtain tee times: Call one week in advance.
Subscriber comments: Very difficult 6,300-yard course . . . Recently rebuilt, well done . . . New design challenging . . . City owned . . . Great scenery.

★★★½ FALL CREEK FALLS STATE PARK GOLF COURSE

PU—Rte. 3, Pikeville (615)881-5706.
70 miles north of Chattanooga. **Holes:** 18. **Par:** 72/72.
Yards: 6,669/6,051. **Course rating:** 71.6/74.8. **Slope:** 127/126.
Opened: 1972. **Pace of Play rating:** 4:30. **Green fee:** $16.

Credit cards: MC, V, AMEX. **Reduced fees:** Seniors, Juniors.
Caddies: No. **Golf carts:** $9 for 18 holes.
Discount golf packages: No. **Season:** Year-round. **High:** May-Oct.
On-site lodging: Yes. **Rental clubs:** Yes.
Walking policy: Unrestricted walking. **Range:** Yes (grass).
To obtain tee times: Call at least two weeks in advance.
Ranked in Third 25 of America's 75 Best Public Golf Courses by Golf Digest.
Subscriber comments: Beautiful scenery. In state park. An hour from everywhere . . . Secluded, quiet, not crowded . . . For any golfer; excellent condition . . . State park gem . . . Great location, Joe Lee course . . . Great course winding through the woods, deer everywhere . . . Lots of sand, hills, woods . . . Can be narrow . . . Tight, tree-lined fairways. Beautiful setting . . . Pretty state park golf course, lots of sand . . . No water, lots of sand. Beautiful mountain setting . . . Best greens in the state. Doglegs for days . . . Any level, staff good, service good, good course, good getaway . . . Excellent staff.

★★ FORREST CROSSING GOLF COURSE

PU—750 Riverview Dr., Franklin (615)794-9400.
15 miles south of Nashville. **Holes:** 18. **Par:** 72/72.
Yards: 6,968/5,011. **Course rating:** 73.6/69.1. **Slope:** 125/114.
Opened: 1988. **Pace of Play rating:** 4:15. **Green fee:** $5/22.
Credit cards: MC, V. **Reduced fees:** Weekdays, Low season, Twilight.
Caddies: No. **Golf carts:** $12 for 18 holes.
Discount golf packages: No. **Season:** Year-round. **High:** April-Sept.
On-site lodging: No. **Rental clubs:** Yes.
Walking policy: Walking at certain times. **Range:** Yes (grass).
To obtain tee times: Call seven days in advance.
Subscriber comments: Nice layout. Shows wear throughout summer . . . Layout so-so. Not in good shape in 1994 . . . Excellent layout, very good greens. Fairways sparse due to winterkill . . . Course rough in spring due to flooding, but course overall hard to play. Pins and greens placed to make it challenging . . . Good course, you keep ball straight or it's wet . . . Course doesn't drain well, lost fairways all of '94.

★½ FOX MEADOWS GOLF COURSE
PU—3064 Clarke Rd., Memphis (901)362-0232.
Holes: 18. **Par:** 71/72.
Yards: 6,545/5,095. **Course rating:** 69.9/66.7. **Slope:** 108/102.
Opened: 1960. **Pace of Play rating:** 4:00. **Green fee:** $11/12.
Credit cards: None. **Reduced fees:** Seniors, Juniors.
Caddies: No. **Golf carts:** $16 for 18 holes.
Discount golf packages: No. **Season:** Year-round. **High:** May-Sept.
On-site lodging: No. **Rental clubs:** Yes.
Walking policy: Unrestricted walking. **Range:** No.
To obtain tee times: Call anytime.
Subscriber comments: Bermuda greens, wide open, long, average golfer
. . . Wide-open muny, no great challenge, nice fairways and greens . . .
Good public course, walkable . . . Slightly better than average muny course
. . . Not a destination, but you can work on your swing.

★★½ GATLINBURG GOLF COURSE
PU—520 Dollywood Lane, Pigeon Forge (615)453-3912.
34 miles west of Knoxville. **Holes:** 18. **Par:** 71/72.
Yards: 6,281/4,718. **Course rating:** 72.3/68.9. **Slope:** 125/117.
Opened: 1955. **Pace of Play rating:** 4:15. **Green fee:** $25.
Credit cards: MC, V. **Reduced fees:** Twilight, Juniors.
Caddies: No. **Golf carts:** $14 for 18 holes.
Discount golf packages: Yes. **Season:** Year-round. **High:** May-Oct.
On-site lodging: No. **Rental clubs:** Yes.
Walking policy: Walking at certain times. **Range:** No.
To obtain tee times: Call one week in advance.
Subscriber comments: Holy phobia, Batman, severe elevation . . .
Accurate tee shots needed; too many sloping fairways . . . Hills, hills, and
more hills . . . Front nine open, back nine hilly and scenic . . . Front side
enjoyable. Back side too much mountain golf . . . Short but challenging
mountain course . . . Fair course, great views.

★★★★ GRAYSBURG HILLS GOLF COURSE
KNOBS/FODDERSTACK/CHIMNEYTOP
PU—910 Graysburg Hills Rd., Chuckey (615)234-8061.
12 miles northeast of Greenville. **Holes:** 27. **Par:** 72/72/72.
Yards: 6,834/6,875/6,743. **Course rating:** 72.8/73.0/72.2.
Slope: 128/134/133.
Opened: 1978. **Pace of Play rating:** N/A. **Green fee:** $20/25.
Credit cards: MC, V, AMEX. **Reduced fees:** No.
Caddies: No. **Golf carts:** $10 for 18 holes.
Discount golf packages: Yes. **Season:** Year-round. **High:** April-Oct.
On-site lodging: No. **Rental clubs:** Yes.
Walking policy: Unrestricted walking. **Range:** Yes (grass).
To obtain tee times: Call up to one year in advance.
Subscriber comments: One of the nicest public courses I have played . . .
Rees Jones course, good challenge from white tees, tough from blues,
terrific personnel, courteous, friendly, great condition year-round . . .
Course is always in good shape . . . Three great nines in the middle of
nowhere . . . A hidden jewel . . . Good test, good people, well maintained
. . . Good test for bogey player . . . Great family owners, friendly, kind and
helpful. Course is always well groomed and beautiful.

★★½ HARPETH HILLS GOLF COURSE
PU—2424 Old Hickory Blvd., Nashville (615)862-8493.
Holes: 18. **Par:** 72/72.
Yards: 6,900/5,200. **Course rating:** 73.1/71.2. **Slope:** 126/124.
Opened: 1968. **Pace of Play rating:** 4:30. **Green fee:** $14.
Credit cards: None. **Reduced fees:** No.
Caddies: No. **Golf carts:** $16 for 18 holes.
Discount golf packages: No. **Season:** Year-round. **High:** May-Sept.
On-site lodging: No. **Rental clubs:** Yes.
Walking policy: Unrestricted walking. **Range:** Yes (grass).

To obtain tee times: Call seven days in advance.
Subscriber comments: Challenging city course, for mid to low handicap. Muny course, usually crowded . . . Best public course in Nashville. Best greens . . . Good layout for metro course, sometimes slow . . . Good layout, got to keep it in fairway to score . . . Challenging, good condition for city course.

★★★★ HEATHERHURST GOLF CLUB
PINE/CREEK/MOUNTAIN

R—P.O. Box 2000, Fairfield Glade (615)484-3799.
6 miles west of Crossfield. **Holes:** 27. **Par:** 72/72/72.
Yards: 6,650/6,700/6,800. **Course rating:** 69.4/69.2/70.2.
Slope: 120/119/123.
Opened: 1988. **Pace of Play rating:** 4:00. **Green fee:** $16/35.
Credit cards: All major. **Reduced fees:** No.
Caddies: No. **Golf carts:** $10 for 18 holes.
Discount golf packages: Yes. **Season:** Year-round. **High:** April-Oct.
On-site lodging: Yes. **Rental clubs:** Yes.
Walking policy: Walking at certain times. **Range:** Yes (grass).
To obtain tee times: Call five days in advance.
Subscriber comments: Short but fun course, well maintained . . . Breathtaking scenery . . . Excellent short course, very playable . . . Three nice courses, good for husband/wife outing . . . Scenery is great, fun courses to play, course designed with all types of golfers in mind . . . Wooded, wildlife, deer, turkeys, fox, fun . . . Course in good condition, friendly people . . . Excellent course, some really great holes, beautiful.

★★★½ HENRY HORTON STATE PARK GOLF COURSE

PU—4358 Nashville Hwy., Chapel Hill (615)364-2319.
30 miles south of Nashville. **Holes:** 18. **Par:** 72/73.
Yards: 7,060/5,625. **Course rating:** 74.3/72.1. **Slope:** 128/117.
Opened: 1963. **Pace of Play rating:** 5:00. **Green fee:** $16.
Credit cards: MC, V, AMEX. **Reduced fees:** Seniors, Juniors.
Caddies: No. **Golf carts:** $18 for 18 holes.
Discount golf packages: No. **Season:** Year-round. **High:** May-June.
On-site lodging: Yes. **Rental clubs:** Yes.
Walking policy: Unrestricted walking. **Range:** Yes (grass).
To obtain tee times: Call Tuesday for upcoming weekend.
Subscriber comments: Course is long, greens are enormous . . . Nothing luxurious, just great golf . . . Great state park course, try a park restaurant buffet . . . Wide open, but long. A few very challenging holes, always in great shape . . . One of the better state park courses; large bent greens . . . Long and demanding hills and trees . . . Great state park course, large greens, fairly long, good condition . . . It's not for short hitters.

★★★½ HERMITAGE GOLF COURSE

PU—3939 Old Hickory Blvd., Old Hickory (615)847-4001.
10 miles east of Nashville. **Holes:** 18. **Par:** 72/72.
Yards: 6,775/5,475. **Course rating:** 71.9/70.8. **Slope:** 122/120.
Opened: 1986. **Pace of Play rating:** 4:00-4:30. **Green fee:** $19/24.
Credit cards: All major. **Reduced fees:** Twilight.
Caddies: No. **Golf carts:** $10 for 18 holes.
Discount golf packages: No. **Season:** Year-round. **High:** April-Oct.
On-site lodging: No. **Rental clubs:** Yes.
Walking policy: Walking at certain times. **Range:** Yes (grass).
To obtain tee times: Call five days in advance. May make tee times up to one year in advance with credit card.
Subscriber comments: Well-conditioned, scenic, open course that plays tight . . . Good layout, fair course . . . Staff excellent, very good condition, challenging . . . One of the best in Nashville . . . Wonderful layout, beautiful scenery, great staff . . . Very good course, very well maintained . . . A beautiful layout, an outstanding test of skill . . . LPGA Sara Lee stop, course condition suffers in summer after the tournament . . . Flat, semi-long course, suited for good iron and putter player . . . Sometimes

crowded, very scenic course, friendly staff . . . So many golf outings, hard to get tee times . . . Great. Use all clubs; moderate to low challenge, fairways and greens in good condition in summer . . . Good layout for the average amateur.

★ HUNTERS POINT GOLF CLUB

PU—1500 Hunters Point Pike, Lebanon (615)444-7521.
25 miles east of Nashville. **Holes:** 18. **Par:** 72/73.
Yards: 6,573/5,600. **Course rating:** 69.6/71.5. **Slope:** 108/111.
Opened: 1966. **Pace of Play rating:** 4:00-4:30. **Green fee:** $8/12.
Credit cards: MC, V. **Reduced fees:** Weekdays, Low season, Seniors, Juniors.
Caddies: No. **Golf carts:** $9 for 18 holes.
Discount golf packages: Yes. **Season:** Year-round. **High:** May-Oct.
On-site lodging: No. **Rental clubs:** Yes.
Walking policy: Unrestricted walking. **Range:** Yes (grass).
To obtain tee times: First come, first served.
Subscriber comments: Very rough . . . Course good for average golfer . . . Course not maintained very well. Friendly people in the pro shop . . . Improving.

★★ INDIAN HILLS GOLF CLUB

PU—405 Calumet Trace, Murfreesboro (615)898-0152.
25 miles southeast of Nashville. **Holes:** 18. **Par:** 71/71.
Yards: 6,495/5,686. **Course rating:** 72.8/70.3. **Slope:** 125/118.
Opened: 1988. **Pace of Play rating:** 4:15-4:30. **Green fee:** $10/21.
Credit cards: MC, V. **Reduced fees:** Weekdays, Low season, Twilight, Seniors, Juniors.
Caddies: No. **Golf carts:** $9 for 18 holes.
Discount golf packages: Yes. **Season:** Year-round. **High:** April-Oct.
On-site lodging: No. **Rental clubs:** Yes.
Walking policy: Walking at certain times. **Range:** Yes (grass).
To obtain tee times: Call three days in advance.
Subscriber comments: Scenic and interesting . . . Course is short, but very tight, good for accurate iron player . . . Needs TLC . . . Not a good layout for walking. Challenging but fair . . . Needs grooming but getting better . . . Nice course. Building too many houses near golf course . . . Fun course, pretty layout.

★½ IRONWOOD GOLF COURSE

PU—3801 Ironwood Rd., Cookeville (615)528-2331.
80 miles west of Nashville. **Holes:** 18. **Par:** 72/72.
Yards: 6,311/5,023. **Course rating:** 70.7/68.5. **Slope:** 123/112.
Opened: 1971. **Pace of Play rating:** 3:30-4:00. **Green fee:** $11.
Credit cards: MC, V, DISC. **Reduced fees:** Weekdays, Low season, Seniors, Juniors.
Caddies: No. **Golf carts:** $9 for 18 holes.
Discount golf packages: No. **Season:** Year-round. **High:** April-Sept.
On-site lodging: No. **Rental clubs:** Yes.
Walking policy: Unrestricted walking. **Range:** Yes (grass).
To obtain tee times: First come, first served.
Subscriber comments: Nice course for average golfers . . . Neglected layout that has a pasture feeling to it . . . Could be a good course with proper care . . . Course improving under new owner.

★½ KNOXVILLE GOLF COURSE

PU—3925 Schaad Rd., Knoxville (615)691-7143.
Holes: 18. **Par:** 72/72.
Yards: 6,528/5,325. **Course rating:** 71.5/69.7. **Slope:** 119/110.
Opened: 1984. **Pace of Play rating:** N/A. **Green fee:** $10/14.
Credit cards: MC, V. **Reduced fees:** Weekdays, Twilight, Seniors, Juniors.
Caddies: No. **Golf carts:** $10 for 18 holes.
Discount golf packages: No. **Season:** Year-round. **High:** April-Nov.

On-site lodging: No. **Rental clubs:** Yes.
Walking policy: Unrestricted walking. **Range:** No.
To obtain tee times: Call one week in advance.
Subscriber comments: Your average muny, friendly folks, fun golf . . . Workingman's course . . . Fairways need work . . . Nice course for a muny . . . Challenging, playable, walkable.

★★½ LAMBERT ACRES GOLF CLUB
RED/WHITE/ORANGE
SP—3428 Tuckaleechee Park, Maryville (615)982-9838.
18 miles south of Knoxville. **Holes:** 27. **Par:** 72/72/72.
Yards: 6,480/6,282/6,292. **Course rating:** 70.8/70.1/69.6.
Slope: 118/121/119.
Opened: 1965. **Pace of Play rating:** 4:30. **Green fee:** $15.
Credit cards: None. **Reduced fees:** No.
Caddies: No. **Golf carts:** $8 for 18 holes.
Discount golf packages: No. **Season:** Year-round. **High:** May-Oct.
On-site lodging: No. **Rental clubs:** Yes.
Walking policy: Unrestricted walking. **Range:** No.
To obtain tee times: First come, first served.
Subscriber comments: Wide open, 27 fair amateur holes . . . OK course, beautiful scenery . . . Beautiful mountain course . . . Fine condition for heavily played public course . . . Best suited for high handicap . . . Good layout, enjoyable and challenging, walkable.

LEGENDS CLUB OF TENNESSEE
SP—1500 Legends Club Lane, Franklin (615)790-1300.
15 miles south of Nashville.
Opened: 1992. **Pace of Play rating:** 4:00-4:15. **Green fee:** $49/65.
Credit cards: All major. **Reduced fees:** Weekdays.
Caddies: No. **Golf carts:** Included in Green Fee.
Discount golf packages: Yes. **Season:** Year-round. **High:** April-Oct.
On-site lodging: No. **Rental clubs:** Yes.
Walking policy: Mandatory cart. **Range:** Yes (grass).
To obtain tee times: Call up to 30 days in advance.
★★★★ NORTH COURSE
Holes: 18. **Par:** 72/72.
Yards: 7,190/5,333. **Course rating:** 75.0/70.9. **Slope:** 132/119.
Subscriber comments: The best greens in Tennessee, with a lot of sand, zoysia fairways . . . Very solid course; fun, excellent condition . . . Hard course; long, longer and longest, very scenic . . . Service great, beautiful fairways, lots of sand, fast greens . . . Long but fun to play. Very open . . . Great for all types of golfers . . . Kite/Cupp masterpiece, bravo . . . Great staff, good layout, well-marked . . . Great layout for all players.
★★★★ SOUTH COURSE
Holes: 18. **Par:** 71/71.
Yards: 7,113/5,290. **Course rating:** 74.7/71.4. **Slope:** 129/121.
Subscriber comments: Excellent example of modern golf architecture, beautiful layout . . . Semi-links style, much mounding, great course conditions . . . Good golf, treated well . . . Very testing course, average to good golfer . . . North Course tighter, both have zoysia fairways and fast bent greens . . . Drive it long, putt it true, else you'll be blue . . . Greens, fairways are in excellent shape year-round. Little wait for tee times and play moves well . . . Tom Kite/Bob Cupp design . . . Outstanding layout and course, super greens, staff very courteous and professional.

★½ LONG HOLLOW GOLF COURSE
PU—1080 Long Hollow Pike, Gallatin (615)451-3120.
Call club for further information.
Subscriber comments: For amount of use, kept relatively well; wide-open course . . . Needs manicure . . . Good for weekend players. Short but fun . . . Easy, but could be hard if you don't like water.

★★★ MARRIOTT'S GOLF CLUB AT SHILOH FALLS
SP—P.O. Box 11, Pickwick Dam (901)689-5050.
100 miles east of Memphis. **Holes:** 18. **Par:** 72/72.
Yards: 6,713/5,156. **Course rating:** 73.1/71.3. **Slope:** 136/128.
Opened: 1993. **Pace of Play rating:** N/A. **Green fee:** $34/44.
Credit cards: All major. **Reduced fees:** Weekdays, Low season, Resort guests, Juniors.
Caddies: No. **Golf carts:** Included in Green Fee.
Discount golf packages: Yes. **Season:** Year-round. **High:** April-Oct.
On-site lodging: Yes. **Rental clubs:** Yes.
Walking policy: Walking at certain times. **Range:** Yes (grass).
To obtain tee times: Call up to seven days in advance.
Subscriber comments: A little time and it will be tops . . . New course; beautiful design . . . Need all the shots, all holes are solid and straightforward . . . Tough Jerry Pate/Fred Couples layout, iron shots are a must . . . Beautiful new course. Signature hole not completed . . . Diamond in the rough . . . Nice hilly course close to Tennessee River. Cut out of woods . . . Bent-grass greens and a few blind second shots . . . Someday this will be an exceptional course, especially when it finally has full 18 holes open.

★½ MCCABE FIELD GOLF COURSE
MIDDLE/NORTH/SOUTH
PU—46th Ave & Murphy Rd., Nashville (615)862-8491.
Holes: 27. **Par:** 70/71/71.
Yards: 6,023/6,481/6,522. **Course rating:** 68.6/69.6/69.7.
Slope: 110/112/111.
Opened: 1939. **Pace of Play rating:** 4:00. **Green fee:** $14.
Credit cards: None. **Reduced fees:** Seniors, Juniors.
Caddies: No. **Golf carts:** $16 for 18 holes.
Discount golf packages: No. **Season:** Year-round. **High:** April-Sept.
On-site lodging: No. **Rental clubs:** Yes.
Walking policy: Unrestricted walking. **Range:** No.
To obtain tee times: Call seven days in advance.
Subscriber comments: Worn out; heavy play . . . Down and back; some interesting holes . . . Weather took its toll in '94. Promising outlook '95 . . . Easy, open.

★★ MOCCASIN BEND GOLF CLUB
PU—381 Moccasin Bend Rd., Chattanooga (615)267-3585.
Holes: 18. **Par:** 72/72.
Yards: 6,469/5,290. **Course rating:** 69.6/69.0. **Slope:** 111/109.
Opened: 1966. **Pace of Play rating:** 4:00. **Green fee:** $11/15.
Credit cards: MC, V. **Reduced fees:** Seniors, Juniors.
Caddies: No. **Golf carts:** $9 for 18 holes.
Discount golf packages: Yes. **Season:** Year-round. **High:** April-Oct.
On-site lodging: No. **Rental clubs:** Yes.
Walking policy: Walking at certain times. **Range:** Yes (grass).
To obtain tee times: Call for weekends and holidays.
Subscriber comments: Easy walking, fairly short and compact . . . Good place to learn to play and build confidence . . . Wide open and flat. Gets too much play. Good staff . . . The staff is very nice. Lost fairways last spring but improving.

★★★ MONTGOMERY BELL STATE PARK GOLF COURSE
PU—800 Hotel Ave., Burns (615)797-2578.
35 miles west of Nashville. **Holes:** 18. **Par:** 71/72.
Yards: 6,091/4,961. **Course rating:** 69.3/68.8. **Slope:** 121/116.
Opened: 1970. **Pace of Play rating:** 4:30. **Green fee:** $16.
Credit cards: MC, V, AMEX. **Reduced fees:** Seniors, Juniors.
Caddies: No. **Golf carts:** $16 for 18 holes.
Discount golf packages: Yes. **Season:** Year-round. **High:** April-Nov.
On-site lodging: No. **Rental clubs:** No.
Walking policy: Unrestricted walking. **Range:** Yes (grass).

To obtain tee times: Call six days in advance.
Subscriber comments: Fader's dream, short . . . Hi[...]
player . . . Beautiful setting, deer a regular in the gallery[...]
private . . . Great layout for intermediate to advanced playe[...]
condition all year long, lots of woods . . . Very scenic; hit driv[...]
slow greens; deer everywhere . . . State course, wooded, short [...]
park course in good shape. Fun and challenging.

★★★ NASHBORO VILLAGE GOLF COURSE

PU—2250 Murfreesboro Rd., Nashville (615)367-2311.
Holes: 18. **Par:** 72/75.
Yards: 6,887/5,485. **Course rating:** 73.5/72.3. **Slope:** 134/121.
Opened: 1974. **Pace of Play rating:** 4:30. **Green fee:** $18/22.
Credit cards: MC, V, AMEX. **Reduced fees:** Weekdays, Low season,
Resort guests, Twilight, Juniors.
Caddies: No. **Golf carts:** $11 for 18 holes.
Discount golf packages: Yes. **Season:** Year-round. **High:** April-Sept.
On-site lodging: No. **Rental clubs:** Yes.
Walking policy: Walking at certain times. **Range:** Yes (grass).
To obtain tee times: Weekend tee times may be made beginning the
Tuesday prior to the weekend. Weekday tee times may be made up to two
weeks in advance.
Subscriber comments: Challenging layout with good mix of holes . . .
Nice elevation changes, tough course . . . Long course from back, good
greens in mid summer . . . Great course, tight fairways, greens very good.
Some slow play . . . Fun to play. Tough but fair . . . Lots of variety.

★★★½ ORGILL PARK GOLF COURSE

PU—9080 Bethuel Rd., Millington (901)872-3610.
10 miles north of Memphis. **Holes:** 18. **Par:** 70/71.
Yards: 6,284/4,574. **Course rating:** 66.8/68.3. **Slope:** 109/108.
Opened: 1972. **Pace of Play rating:** 3:30-5:00. **Green fee:** $13/14.
Credit cards: All major. **Reduced fees:** Weekdays, Seniors, Juniors.
Caddies: No. **Golf carts:** N/A.
Discount golf packages: No. **Season:** Year-round. **High:** April-Sept.
On-site lodging: No. **Rental clubs:** Yes.
Walking policy: Unrestricted walking. **Range:** Yes (grass).
To obtain tee times: Call one day in advance for weekdays and two days
in advance for weekends.
Subscriber comments: Best public course in Shelby County . . .
Memphis area's best course; good layout, well maintained . . . Probably has
best fairways in Memphis . . . Very interesting course. Hilly . . . Anyone
can play, course is always nice . . . Better personal attention and courtesies
than home. If they had bunkers, it would be a championship course . . .
Best muny in area . . . Open, some water, no sand . . . Excellent fairways
and summer greens.

GREAT VALUE

★★★ PARIS LANDING GOLF CLUB

PU—Rte. 1, P.O. Box 77, Buchanan (901)644-1332.
Call club for further information
Subscriber comments: State park, beautiful scenery, tight course but fair
. . . Carved out of forest, by lake, awesome . . . Outstanding because of
natural beauty; wildlife everywhere . . . Heavy play, great test of skill . . .
Very demanding, not for beginners . . . Bermuda-grass fairways. Bent
greens . . . Beautiful views of the lake . . . Hilly and gorgeous. Eagles (real
ones) nest around there . . . Good course for all capabililties. Nicest and
most scenic Tennessee state park. No. 4 has vista worth beholding.

★★★ PICKWICK LANDING STATE PARK GOLF COURSE

PU—Hwy. No. 57, Pickwick Dam (901)689-3149.
Call club for further information.
Subscriber comments: Tight and hilly; very playable greens; for mid-low

g hills, good fun golf course . . .
nt greens. Nice Bermuda
many straight holes, but good

–9434.

66.7. **Slope:** 114/116.
. **Green fee:** $9/11.
fees: Seniors, Juniors.

Discount golf packages: No. **Season:** Year-round. **High:** April-Aug.
On-site lodging: No. **Rental clubs:** Yes.
Walking policy: Unrestricted walking. **Range:** Yes (grass).
To obtain tee times: First come, first served.
Subscriber comments: Interesting old design; for any golfer . . .
Inexpensive, nice old muny. Greens always good.

★★★ QUAIL RIDGE GOLF COURSE
PU—4055 Altruria Rd., Bartlett (901)386-6951.
5 miles north of Memphis. **Holes:** 18. **Par:** 71/70.
Yards: 6,600/5,206. **Course rating:** 71.8/N/A. **Slope:** 128/N/A.
Opened: 1994. **Pace of Play rating:** 4:15-4:30. **Green fee:** $20/23.
Credit cards: MC, V, DISC. **Reduced fees:** Weekdays, Seniors, Juniors.
Caddies: No. **Golf carts:** $10 for 18 holes.
Discount golf packages: No. **Season:** Year-round. **High:** April-Oct.
On-site lodging: No. **Rental clubs:** No.
Walking policy: Walking at certain times. **Range:** Yes (grass).
To obtain tee times: Call five days in advance.
Subscriber comments: New course, will be one of the best in town in
another year or two. The best greens in Memphis . . . Very challenging,
but fair layout . . . New course. Tight . . . Short, tight fun course, some
great holes . . . Very good new course, nice staff, diverse . . . New
superintendent, great layout, needs seasoning, moderate to low challenge;
high handicapper will find it difficult.

★★ THE QUARRY GOLF CLUB
PU—1001 Reads Lake Rd., Chattanooga (615)875-8888.
Call club for further information.
Subscriber comments: Nice layout, tough holes in the quarry . . . With a
lot of work could be a landmark.

★★★★ RIVER ISLANDS GOLF CLUB
PU—9610 Kodak Rd., Kodak (615)933-0100, (800)347-4837.
15 miles east of Knoxville. **Holes:** 18. **Par:** 72/72.
Yards: 7,001/4,973. **Course rating:** 75.4/69.4. **Slope:** 133/118.
Opened: 1990. **Pace of Play rating:** 4:00. **Green fee:** $29/45.
Credit cards: MC, V, AMEX. **Reduced fees:** Weekdays, Low season,
Twilight.
Caddies: No. **Golf carts:** Included in Green Fee.
Discount golf packages: Yes. **Season:** Year-round. **High:** April-Oct.
On-site lodging: No. **Rental clubs:** No.
Walking policy: Mandatory cart. **Range:** Yes (grass).
To obtain tee times: Call pro shop.
Subscriber comments: Best course in east Tennessee . . . Zoysia fairways,
many different types of holes, must play . . . Great Arthur Hills layout,
many trees, difficult water holes, greens and fairways in good shape . . .
Challenging, shotmaker's tune up your short game . . . Pretty, scenic,
interesting and unusual layout. Hard to get to . . . Excellent greens,
challenge for any level from varied tees . . . A gorgeous course, may be

finest in Tennessee . . . Best course I've ever played . . . Very long from back tees. Must cross river three times . . . Golf course a "10" although not that great a piece of land to work with. Some forced carries over water, but not long ones . . . Beautiful scenery. Plays around river . . . Not for beginners . . . This is Tennessee and golf at their best.

★★★½ ROAN VALLEY GOLF ESTATES

SP—Hwy. 421 S., Mountain City (615)727-7931.
15 miles north of Boone, NC. **Holes:** 18. **Par:** 72/72.
Yards: 6,736/4,370. **Course rating:** 71.8/68.9. **Slope:** 120/107.
Opened: 1982. **Pace of Play rating:** 4:15. **Green fee:** $29/37.
Credit cards: MC, V. **Reduced fees:** Weekdays, Low season, Juniors.
Caddies: No. **Golf carts:** Included in Green Fee.
Discount golf packages: No. **Season:** April–Nov. **High:** May–Oct.
On-site lodging: Yes. **Rental clubs:** Yes.
Walking policy: Walking at certain times. **Range:** No.
To obtain tee times: Call anytime.
Subscriber comments: Course is good for all, staff treats you like family . . . Beautiful mountain scenery . . . Nice mountain course. Fun to play . . . Staff always glad to see you . . . Beautiful golf course. Long distance from green to tee . . . Breathtakingly beautiful in the fall . . . Very memorable, autumn leaves beautiful, very fun to play.

★★★ SPRINGHOUSE GOLF CLUB

R—18 Springhouse Lane, Nashville (615)871-7759.
Holes: 18. **Par:** 72/72.
Yards: 7,007/5,126. **Course rating:** 74.0/70.2. **Slope:** 133/118.
Opened: 1990. **Pace of Play rating:** 4:00–4:30. **Green fee:** $45.
Credit cards: All major. **Reduced fees:** Seniors.
Caddies: No. **Golf carts:** Included in Green Fee.
Discount golf packages: No. **Season:** Year-round. **High:** April–Oct.
On-site lodging: Yes. **Rental clubs:** Yes.
Walking policy: Mandatory cart. **Range:** Yes (grass).
To obtain tee times: Tee times are required and are taken up to seven days in advance.
Ranked 10th in Tennessee by Golf Digest.
Subscriber comments: Gimmicky moguls are a nuisance, but still a fun course . . . Average course, but upkeep exceptional . . . Bikini-waxed greens, lots of mounds, service good . . . Too little land, course feels cramped, Senior PGA Tour stop . . . Polite service, beautifully manicured . . . Pure target golf. Forced carries . . . Excellent scenery, good greens . . . Great staff. Boring course. Good conditioning. Long, narrow, too many mounds, fast greens . . . Overrated, mounding looks artificial and is . . . Very nice course, challenging but fair.

★★★ STONEBRIDGE GOLF COURSE

PU—3049 Davies Plantation Rd., Memphis (901)382-1886.
Holes: 18. **Par:** 71/71.
Yards: 6,788/5,012. **Course rating:** 73.3/66.8. **Slope:** 133/113.
Opened: 1972. **Pace of Play rating:** 4:30. **Green fee:** $21.
Credit cards: MC, V, AMEX. **Reduced fees:** Weekdays, Low season.
Caddies: No. **Golf carts:** $10 for 18 holes.
Discount golf packages: No. **Season:** Year-round. **High:** April–Sept.
On-site lodging: No. **Rental clubs:** Yes.
Walking policy: Walking at certain times. **Range:** Yes (grass).
To obtain tee times: Call five days in advance.
Subscriber comments: Too many houses; otherwise very good challenge . . . Lost greens in summer of '93, but recovered nicely . . . Not a good course for beginners . . . Excellent course. Too crowded on weekends . . . Good golf year-round, challenging course, fine staff . . . O.B. and/or water on every hole. Bent greens . . . Nice layout counteracted by old bent that can't handle Memphis heat . . . Good course, long, always eats my lunch . . . Tighter course with O.B. and trees.

★★★★ STONEHENGE GOLF CLUB
R—100 Fairfield Blvd., Fairfield Glade (615)484-3731, (800)624-8755.
60 miles west of Knoxville. **Holes:** 18. **Par:** 72/72.
Yards: 6,549/5,000. **Course rating:** 71.5/70.2. **Slope:** 131/124.
Opened: 1984. **Pace of Play rating:** 4:30. **Green fee:** $35/50.
Credit cards: MC, V, AMEX. **Reduced fees:** Low season, Resort guests, Twilight, Juniors.
Caddies: No. **Golf carts:** Included in Green Fee.
Discount golf packages: Yes. **Season:** Year-round. **High:** April-Oct.
On-site lodging: Yes. **Rental clubs:** Yes.
Walking policy: Mandatory cart. **Range:** Yes (grass).
To obtain tee times: Written, 30 days in advance to Central Tee Times, P.O. Box 2000, Fairfield Glade, TN 38558. Call five days in advance.
Ranked 14th in America's 75 Best Resort Courses by Golf Digest.
Selected Best New Resort Course of 1985 by Golf Digest.
Subscriber comments: Soft fairways; do not play if wet; beautiful in fall . . . As good as anywhere; superb, challenging layout in gorgeous setting . . . 100 percent bent-grass course, beautiful layout . . . Requires accuracy off the tees and then good long irons, plenty of sand but most greens accept run-up shot . . . Great course and scenic, fairways always soggy . . . Excellent condition, all bent grass, little roll . . . Very challenging. A must if in the area! . . . Tough for the high handicapper, beautiful course . . . No.15 is as good a par 5 as any . . . Great back nine, fairways always seem to be wet . . . Best golf course I have ever played.

★★ SWAN LAKE COUNTRY CLUB
PU—581 Dunbar Cave Rd., Clarksville (615)648-0479.
Call for further information.
Subscriber comments: Older city park course, small greens . . . Nice layout with some really long par 4s; lake has ducks, no swans . . . Good course for average player, condition questionable . . . Front nine flat and open. Back side hilly with tight fairways. Suited for all types of play.

★★ T.O. FULLER GOLF COURSE
PU—1400 Pavillion Dr., Memphis (901)543-7771.
Holes: 18. **Par:** 72/73.
Yards: 6,000/5,656. **Course rating:** 71.0/72.0. **Slope:** 117/110.
Opened: 1956. **Pace of Play rating:** 4:00. **Green fee:** $8/12.
Credit cards: MC, V, AMEX. **Reduced fees:** Weekdays, Low season, Seniors.
Caddies: No. **Golf carts:** $18 for 18 holes.
Discount golf packages: No. **Season:** Year-round. **High:** May-Dec.
On-site lodging: No. **Rental clubs:** Yes.
Walking policy: Unrestricted walking. **Range:** No.
To obtain tee times: Call five days in advance.
Subscriber comments: Good municipal course, out of the way . . . Very hilly . . . Long and rough . . . Memphis' best-kept secret, challenging . . . Too many hills, good people . . . Course is not kept up as well as most, but has several very interesting holes . . . Could be better maintained.

★★½ TED RHODES GOLF COURSE
PU—1901 Ed Temple Blvd., Nashville (615)862-8463.
Holes: 18. **Par:** 72/72.
Yards: 6,660/5,732. **Course rating:** 71.8/68.3. **Slope:** 120/115.
Opened: 1954. **Pace of Play rating:** No. **Green fee:** $14.
Credit cards: None. **Reduced fees:** Seniors, Juniors.
Caddies: No. **Golf carts:** $14 for 18 holes.
Discount golf packages: No. **Season:** Year-round. **High:** May-Sept.
On-site lodging: No. **Rental clubs:** Yes.
Walking policy: Unrestricted walking. **Range:** Yes (grass).
To obtain tee times: Call one week in advance.
Subscriber comments: Lots and lots of water . . . New nine needs couple of years . . . Wide open, lots of water . . . Finally 18 holes, will mature . . . Interesting for public course.

★★★ THREE RIDGES GOLF COURSE

PU—6101 Wise Springs Rd., Knoxville (615)687-4797.
Holes: 18. **Par:** 72/72.
Yards: 6,825/5,225. **Course rating:** 73.2/70.7. **Slope:** 128/121.
Opened: 1991. **Pace of Play rating:** 4:30. **Green fee:** $8/19.
Credit cards: All major. **Reduced fees:** Weekdays, Twilight, Seniors, Juniors.
Caddies: No. **Golf carts:** $10 for 18 holes.
Discount golf packages: No. **Season:** Year-round. **High:** April-Oct.
On-site lodging: No. **Rental clubs:** Yes.
Walking policy: Unrestricted walking. **Range:** Yes (grass).
To obtain tee times: Call seven days in advance.
Subscriber comments: Very nice, well-conditioned layout, new Nike Tour stop . . . Love the layout; needs money reinvested in course conditioning . . . Challenging course, uses every club in bag . . . Very good course, bent greens and Bermuda fairways . . . Shotmaker's course; fast, true greens . . . Improves every year . . . Tough track, you'll need lots of shots . . . Good people selling good golf.

★★½ THUNDER HOLLOW GOLF CLUB

R—815 Tennessee Ave., Crossville (615)456-4060.
60 miles west of Knoxville. **Holes:** 18. **Par:** 72/72.
Yards: 6,411/4,844. **Course rating:** 71.9/70.0. **Slope:** 124/121.
Opened: 1983. **Pace of Play rating:** 4:30. **Green fee:** $24.
Credit cards: None. **Reduced fees:** No.
Caddies: No. **Golf carts:** Included in Green Fee.
Discount golf packages: Yes. **Season:** Year-round. **High:** April-Sept.
On-site lodging: Yes. **Rental clubs:** Yes.
Walking policy: Walking at certain times. **Range:** Yes (grass).
To obtain tee times: Call.
Subscriber comments: Any player will enjoy; challenging hazards . . . Watch out for deep ravines everywhere . . . Up-and-coming course . . . 16 great holes, two Mickey Mouse holes, mostly secluded in woods.

★★ TWO RIVERS GOLF COURSE

PU—3140 McGavock Pike, Nashville (615)889-2675.
Holes: 18. **Par:** 72/72.
Yards: 6,595/5,336. **Course rating:** 71.5/70.4. **Slope:** 120/116.
Opened: 1971. **Pace of Play rating:** 4:00. **Green fee:** $14.
Credit cards: None. **Reduced fees:** No.
Caddies: No. **Golf carts:** N/A.
Discount golf packages: No. **Season:** Year-round. **High:** April-Sept.
On-site lodging: No. **Rental clubs:** Yes.
Walking policy: Unrestricted walking. **Range:** No.
To obtain tee times: Call up to seven days in advance, seven days a week.
Subscriber comments: Open course, small greens, good for all levels . . . Good all-around muny course . . . Nice course. Better than average conditions . . . Easy, very crowded, not bad for city-owned course.

★★ WARRIOR'S PATH STATE PARK GOLF COURSE

PU—P.O. Box 5026, Kingsport (615)323-4990.
90 miles east of Knoxville. **Holes:** 18. **Par:** 72/72.
Yards: 6,581/5,328. **Course rating:** 71.2/72.4. **Slope:** 115/117.
Opened: 1972. **Pace of Play rating:** 4:30. **Green fee:** $14/16.
Credit cards: MC, V. **Reduced fees:** Weekdays, Low season, Seniors, Juniors.
Caddies: No. **Golf carts:** $9 for 18 holes.
Discount golf packages: Yes. **Season:** Year-round. **High:** July-Aug.
On-site lodging: No. **Rental clubs:** Yes.
Walking policy: Unrestricted walking. **Range:** Yes (grass).
To obtain tee times: Call anytime beginning in January. Tee times needed for Saturday, Sunday, Monday and holidays.
Subscriber comments: Very hilly state course . . . New water system has improved course 100 percent . . . High-handicap golf but nice layout.

TENNESSEE

★★★½ WILLOW CREEK GOLF CLUB

PU—12003 Kingston Pike, Knoxville (615)675-0100.
12 miles west of Knoxville. **Holes:** 18. **Par:** 72/74.
Yards: 7,266/5,557. **Course rating:** 73.5/71.9. **Slope:** 130/119.
Opened: 1988. **Pace of Play rating:** N/A. **Green fee:** $20/28.
Credit cards: MC, V, AMEX. **Reduced fees:** Low season, Juniors.
Caddies: No. **Golf carts:** $12 for 18 holes.
Discount golf packages: No. **Season:** Year-round. **High:** April-Oct.
On-site lodging: No. **Rental clubs:** Yes.
Walking policy: Walking at certain times. **Range:** Yes (grass).
To obtain tee times: Call one week in advance.
Subscriber comments: Former Nike Tour stop, always well conditioned
. . . Good test of golf, good practice area . . . Well done, good walking, can
be a real challenge . . . Challenging, great layout on par 5s. Excellent
greens, be ready for a five-hour round on weekends . . . Long, difficult;
good driver, short game needed . . . Bermuda fairways, bent-grass greens
and zoysia fringes. Holes have character . . . Control is important. Huge
bent greens . . . Challenging and playable for all players.

★★½ WINDTREE GOLF COURSE

PU—810 Nonaville Rd., Mt. Juliet (615)754-4653.
15 miles east of Nashville. **Holes:** 18. **Par:** 72/72.
Yards: 6,557/5,126. **Course rating:** 71.1/69.6. **Slope:** 124/117.
Opened: 1991. **Pace of Play rating:** 4:00-4:15. **Green fee:** $19/23.
Credit cards: MC, V, AMEX. **Reduced fees:** Twilight.
Caddies: No. **Golf carts:** N/A.
Discount golf packages: No. **Season:** Year-round. **High:** April-Sept.
On-site lodging: No. **Rental clubs:** Yes.
Walking policy: Walking at certain times. **Range:** Yes (grass).
To obtain tee times: Call Mondays for upcoming weekend.
Subscriber comments: New, has potential . . . Front nine flat, back hilly,
like playing two different courses . . . Hilly, but open, not difficult, but
enjoyable to play . . . Back nine too hilly to walk . . . Would be great if not
for "cartpath - 90 degree rule", nice elevation . . . Not far from being great.
Good changes in elevations . . . New, needs more mature trees, will be
outstanding in years . . . Try it, you'll like it.

Notes

ALBURG COUNTRY CLUB★

SP—Rte. 129, South Alburg (802)796-3586.
40 miles north of Burlington. **Holes:** 18. **Par:** 72/75.
Yards: 6,388/5,621. **Course rating:** 69.4/70.8. **Slope:** 110/106.
Opened: 1967. **Pace of Play rating:** 4:00. **Green fee:** $12/20.
Credit cards: None. **Reduced fees:** Weekdays, Low season, Twilight, Juniors.
Caddies: No. **Golf carts:** $20 for 18 holes.
Discount golf packages: Yes. **Season:** May-Oct. **High:** July-Aug.
On-site lodging: No. **Rental clubs:** Yes.
Walking policy: Unrestricted walking. **Range:** Yes (grass).
To obtain tee times: Call on Wednesday for upcoming weekend.

★★½ BASIN HARBOR GOLF CLUB

R—Basin Harbor Rd., Vergennes (802)475-2309.
30 miles south of Burlington. **Holes:** 18. **Par:** 72/72.
Yards: 6,513/5,745. **Course rating:** 71.5/74.8. **Slope:** 122/125.
Opened: 1927. **Pace of Play rating:** 4:30. **Green fee:** $25/35.
Credit cards: MC, V. **Reduced fees:** Weekdays, Low season, Resort guests, Twilight, Juniors.
Caddies: No. **Golf carts:** $24 for 18 holes.
Discount golf packages: Yes. **Season:** May-Oct. **High:** July-Aug.
On-site lodging: Yes. **Rental clubs:** Yes.
Walking policy: Walking at certain times. **Range:** Yes (grass).
To obtain tee times: Public may call two days prior to tee time. Resort guests can make tee times any time before their stay.
Subscriber comments: Long course . . . Has small air field . . . Flat layout . . . Beautiful lake views, nice condition . . . Nice older course, greens in good shape . . . Flat, easy to walk . . . Great par 3s on back nine . . . Not what you'd expect in Vermont . . . A family course . . . Meticulously maintained, smallish greens, a couple of tough par 3s.

CHAMPLAIN COUNTRY CLUB★

SP—Box 856, St. Albans (802)527-1187.
3 miles north of St. Albans. **Holes:** 18. **Par:** 70/70.
Yards: 6,145/5,217. **Course rating:** 69.6/69.4. **Slope:** 120/106.
Opened: 1915. **Pace of Play rating:** 4:00. **Green fee:** $21/24.
Credit cards: MC, V, DISC. **Reduced fees:** Weekdays, Twilight, Juniors.
Caddies: No. **Golf carts:** $22 for 18 holes.
Discount golf packages: No. **Season:** April-Oct. **High:** July-Aug.
On-site lodging: No. **Rental clubs:** Yes.
Walking policy: Unrestricted walking. **Range:** No.
To obtain tee times: June 1 through October 1 call three days in advance for weekends and holidays.
Subscriber comments: Suited for all . . . Great management . . . Excellent conditions . . . Fun course, wide open.

★★★ COUNTRY CLUB OF BARRE

PU—Plainfield Rd., Barre (802)476-7658.
Holes: 18. **Par:** 71/71.
Yards: 6,191/5,515. **Course rating:** 70.2/72.0. **Slope:** 123/116.
Opened: 1924. **Pace of Play rating:** 4:00. **Green fee:** $30.
Credit cards: MC, V. **Reduced fees:** N/A.
Caddies: No. **Golf carts:** $14 for 18 holes.
Discount golf packages: No. **Season:** April-Oct. **High:** June-Aug.
On-site lodging: No. **Rental clubs:** No.
Walking policy: Unrestricted walking. **Range:** Yes (grass).
To obtain tee times: Tee times may be made seven days in advance.
Subscriber comments: Short and hilly . . . One of most scenic in New England . . . Conditions improving with new greenkeeper . . . Lots of fun and challenge . . . No bad holes, tight fairways . . . Need to drive the ball well to score . . . Really interesting ups and downs . . . Great views.

★★★ CROWN POINT COUNTRY CLUB

SP—Weathersfield Center Rd., Springfield (802)885-1010.
100 miles north of Hartford, Ct. **Holes:** 18. **Par:** 72/72.
Yards: 6,572/5,542. **Course rating:** 72.0/71.3. **Slope:** 123/117.
Opened: 1953. **Pace of Play rating:** 4:12. **Green fee:** $27/34.
Credit cards: MC, V. **Reduced fees:** Weekdays, Twilight, Juniors.
Caddies: No. **Golf carts:** $27 for 18 holes.
Discount golf packages: No. **Season:** April-Oct. **High:** May-Sept.
On-site lodging: No. **Rental clubs:** Yes.
Walking policy: Unrestricted walking. **Range:** Yes (grass).
To obtain tee times: Call up to three days in advance.
Subscriber comments: Fall nice to play . . . Just fun to play . . . Beautiful
location, rolling hills and mountain backdrop . . . Nice folks . . . Wide
fairways, lots of sidehill lies . . . Real gem . . . Friendly staff . . .
Picturesque course . . . One of Vermont's best courses and values.

★ ESSEX COUNTRY CLUB

PU—332 Old Stage Rd., Essex Junction (802)879-3232.
10 miles northeast of Burlington. **Holes:** 18. **Par:** 72/72.
Yards: 6,500/5,700. **Course rating:** 70.4/69.0. **Slope:** 117/112.
Opened: . **Pace of Play rating:** 4:00. **Green fee:** $18.
Credit cards: MC, V. **Reduced fees:** Twilight.
Caddies: No. **Golf carts:** $20 for 18 holes.
Discount golf packages: No. **Season:** April-Nov. **High:** April-Oct.
On-site lodging: No. **Rental clubs:** Yes.
Walking policy: Unrestricted walking. **Range:** No.
To obtain tee times: Call pro shop.
Subscriber comments: Very narrow greens and fairways . . . Tight, no
sand . . . Uncrowded so far . . . Think before you hit . . . A test.

★★★½ GLENEAGLES GOLF COURSE

R—Historic Rte. 7-A, Manchester Village (802)362-3223.
70 miles southeast of Albany. **Holes:** 18. **Par:** 71/71.
Yards: 6,423/5,082. **Course rating:** 71.3/65.2. **Slope:** 129/117.
Opened: 1926. **Pace of Play rating:** 4:30. **Green fee:** $70/80.
Credit cards: All major. **Reduced fees:** Twilight.
Caddies: No. **Golf carts:** $18 for 18 holes.
Discount golf packages: Yes. **Season:** May-Oct.
On-site lodging: Yes. **Rental clubs:** Yes.
Walking policy: Walking at certain times. **Range:** No.
To obtain tee times: Call two days in advance.
Ranked 3rd in Vermont by Golf Digest.
Subscriber comments: Exceptional scenery . . . Forgiving fairways . . .
Excellent re-design, pleasant to play for golfers of all abilities . . .
Beautifully manicured and wide open . . . Beautiful setting between two
mountain ridges . . . Very difficult for high handicappers, but fun . . .
Classic Vermont! Tough, classy, well manicured.

★★★ HAYSTACK GOLF CLUB

SP—Mann Rd., Wilmington (802)464-8301.
100 miles north of Hartford, Ct. **Holes:** 18. **Par:** 72/74.
Yards: 6,549/5,471. **Course rating:** 71.5/71.3. **Slope:** 125/120.
Opened: 1972. **Pace of Play rating:** 4:50. **Green fee:** $39/45.
Credit cards: All major. **Reduced fees:** Weekdays, Low season, Resort
guests, Juniors.
Caddies: No. **Golf carts:** $14 for 18 holes.
Discount golf packages: Yes. **Season:** May-Nov. **High:** July-Aug.
On-site lodging: No. **Rental clubs:** Yes.
Walking policy: Walking at certain times. **Range:** Yes (grass).
To obtain tee times: Call in advance.
Subscriber comments: What a beautiful course, well kept and challenging
. . . Great views . . . Plays long . . . Very narrow course . . . Wonderful
layout . . . Back nine has some great holes . . . Awesome back nine, wild
11th and 14th . . . Very hilly . . . Some unforgettable holes.

★★★ KILLINGTON GOLF COURSE

R—Killington Rd., Killington (802)422-6700.
16 miles east of Rutland. **Holes:** 18. **Par:** 72/72.
Yards: 6,326/5,108. **Course rating:** 70.6/71.2. **Slope:** 126/123.
Opened: 1984. **Pace of Play rating:** 4:30. **Green fee:** $36.
Credit cards: All major. **Reduced fees:** Twilight, Juniors.
Caddies: No. **Golf carts:** $13 for 18 holes.
Discount golf packages: Yes. **Season:** May-Oct.
On-site lodging: Yes. **Rental clubs:** Yes.
Walking policy: Unrestricted walking. **Range:** Yes.
To obtain tee times: Call up to 5 days in advance or if booking a golf
package, when hotel reservations are made.
Subscriber comments: Greatly improved . . . Nice mountain course, fall
is beautiful . . . Thoroughly entertaining, a fun, hilly layout with nice vistas
. . . Strange golf; 100 ft. and 200 ft. drops . . . Mountain course
conditioning . . . Always in good condition . . . Short, tough course . . .
Soft, fast greens . . . Better be able to hit them straight . . . Mountainside
golf at its best.

★★ KWINIASKA GOLF CLUB

SP—Spear St., Shelburne (802)985-3672.
7 miles south of Burlington. **Holes:** 18. **Par:** 72/72.
Yards: 7,067/5,670. **Course rating:** 72.5/72.6. **Slope:** 128/119.
Opened: 1964. **Pace of Play rating:** 4:30. **Green fee:** $22.
Credit cards: MC, V. **Reduced fees:** Twilight.
Caddies: No. **Golf carts:** $20 for 18 holes.
Discount golf packages: No. **Season:** April-Nov. **High:** June-Aug.
On-site lodging: No. **Rental clubs:** Yes.
Walking policy: Unrestricted walking. **Range:** Yes (grass).
To obtain tee times: Call one day in advance.
Subscriber comments: New greenkeeper has course shaping up. Should
be excellent in a few years . . . If you're in the area, don't miss it . . . Tough
on windy days . . . Great shape when there is plenty of rain . . . Has
improved over the years . . . A good challenge . . . Flat front nine, very
hilly back nine . . . Friendly staff . . . Long hitter's course . . . Fun . . .
Long course, you get to use all your clubs.

MONTAGUE GOLF CLUB★

SP—2 Golf Lane, Randolph (802)728-3806.
20 miles south of Montepelier. **Holes:** 18. **Par:** 70/71.
Yards: 5,910/5,064. **Course rating:** 68.6/68.7. **Slope:** 120/111.
Opened: 1925. **Pace of Play rating:** 4:30. **Green fee:** $18/24.
Credit cards: MC, V. **Reduced fees:** Weekdays, Low season, Twilight.
Caddies: No. **Golf carts:** $10 for 18 holes.
Discount golf packages: Yes. **Season:** April-Oct. **High:** June-Aug.
On-site lodging: No. **Rental clubs:** Yes.
Walking policy: Unrestricted walking. **Range:** No.
To obtain tee times: Call two days in advance.
Subscriber comments: Expanded to 18 three years ago . . . Good country
course . . . Friendly . . . Good shape . . . Many narrow fairways.

★★★½ MOUNT SNOW GOLF CLUB

R—Country Club Rd., West Dover (802)464-5642, (800)451-4211.
70 miles east of Albany, N.Y. **Holes:** 18. **Par:** 72/74.
Yards: 6,894/5,839. **Course rating:** 72.4/72.5. **Slope:** 130/118.
Opened: 1964. **Pace of Play rating:** 4:30. **Green fee:** $45.
Credit cards: MC, V, AMEX. **Reduced fees:** Low season, Resort guests,
Twilight, Juniors.
Caddies: No. **Golf carts:** $14 for 18 holes.
Discount golf packages: Yes. **Season:** May-Oct. **High:** July-Aug.
On-site lodging: Yes. **Rental clubs:** Yes.
Walking policy: Unrestricted walking. **Range:** Yes (grass).
To obtain tee times: Call pro shop.
Subscriber comments: Lovely course, magnificent setting . . . Tough for

seniors . . . Our foursome liked it . . . Very hilly, with blind second shots
. . . If you play in the autumn months bring extra balls, leaves everywhere
. . . Long course, very hilly with beautiful scenery . . . Nothing more
scenic . . . Great back nine, tough greens . . . My annual golf school
pilgrimage . . . Good course, gets lots of play . . . None more pretty in fall
. . . Beautiful, but watch out for golf school sessions . . . This is an
outstanding value . . . The golf course is great, a beautiful layout.

★★½ MT. ANTHONY GOLF & TENNIS CENTER
PU—943 Bank St., Bennington (802)447-7079.
Call club for further information.
Subscriber comments: Super fast small greens . . . Mountain course . . .
Scenery outstanding . . . Never a flat lie, very hilly . . . Good condition . . .
Friendly staff . . . No snack facilities . . . Real hilly . . . Fun course.

★★½ NEWPORT COUNTRY CLUB
SP—Pine Hill Rd., Newport (802)334-2391.
80 miles from Burlington. **Holes:** 18. **Par:** 72/72.
Yards: 6,117/5,312. **Course rating:** N/A. **Slope:** 120/111.
Opened: N/A. **Pace of Play rating:** N/A. **Green fee:** N/A.
Credit cards: MC, V. **Reduced fees:** Twilight.
Caddies: No. **Golf carts:** N/A.
Discount golf packages: No. **Season:** April-Oct. **High:** July-Aug.
On-site lodging: No. **Rental clubs:** No.
Walking policy: . **Range:** Yes (grass).
Subscriber comments: Very friendly, pro helpful . . . Suited for all
players . . . Scenic . . . Course relatively easy . . . Very nice, good views of
the lake . . . Some blind tee shots.

★★ ORLEANS COUNTRY CLUB
SP—Rte. 58, Orleans (802)754-2333.
Call club for further information.
Subscriber comments: Wilderness setting, very scenic . . . Great
clubhouse and people . . . Good food . . . Good challenging course where
you can score well . . . Great restaurant . . . Short but subtle, enjoyable and
well conditioned . . . Good course for average player.

★★★ PROCTOR—PITTSFORD COUNTRY CLUB
PU—Corn Hill Rd., Pittsford (802)483-9379.
3 miles north of Rutland. **Holes:** 18. **Par:** 70/72.
Yards: 6,052/5,446. **Course rating:** 69.4/66.1. **Slope:** 121/115.
Opened: . **Pace of Play rating:** 4:15. **Green fee:** $25.
Credit cards: MC, V. **Reduced fees:** Twilight, Juniors.
Caddies: No. **Golf carts:** $11 for 18 holes.
Discount golf packages: No. **Season:** April-Nov. **High:** July-Aug.
On-site lodging: No. **Rental clubs:** Yes.
Walking policy: Unrestricted walking. **Range:** Yes (grass).
To obtain tee times: Tee times required on weekends and holidays. Call
Thursday for Saturday time; call Friday for Sunday time.
Subscriber comments: Beautiful course, not crowded . . . Hidden gem,
out of the way . . . Typical beautiful views, would go back . . . Friendly
. . . Fun course. Lots of challenge for all levels . . . A little short but very
pleasant . . . Beautiful in foliage season.

★★½ RALPH MYHRE COUNTRY CLUB
SP—Rte. 1, Middlebury (802)388-3711.
Call club for further information.
Subscriber comments: Front and back are two different courses . . . Fun
to play . . . Picturesque college town . . . All-around good course,
interesting layout . . . Kept in very good condition . . . Seldom seems
crowded . . . Nice views from various spots around the course . . . A
course the average golfer can play and feel good with his score . . .
Challenges better golfers . . . One of my favorites.

★★½ ROCKY RIDGE GOLF CLUB

SP—68 Ledge Rd., Burlington (802)482-2191.
12 miles south of Burlington. **Holes:** 18. **Par:** 72/72.
Yards: 6,000/5,230. **Course rating:** 69.1/68.7. **Slope:** 124/110.
Opened: 1963. **Pace of Play rating:** 4:00. **Green fee:** $19.
Credit cards: None. **Reduced fees:** Twilight.
Caddies: No. **Golf carts:** $20 for 18 holes.
Discount golf packages: No. **Season:** April-Nov. **High:** July-Aug.
On-site lodging: No. **Rental clubs:** Yes.
Walking policy: Unrestricted walking. **Range:** Yes (grass).
To obtain tee times: Call early Thursday morning for upcoming weekend.
Subscriber comments: Very interesting, 15th hole has over 100 ft. vertical drop . . . Very short, very narrow fairways . . . Great scenery . . . Designed for the average player . . . Well maintained . . . Definitely get a cart . . . Lots of woods . . . Nice people . . . Has some unique holes.

★★★★ RUTLAND COUNTRY CLUB

SP—North Grove St., Rutland (802)773-3254.
Holes: 18. **Par:** 70/71.
Yards: 6,100/5,446. **Course rating:** 69.7/71.6. **Slope:** 125/125.
Opened: 1901. **Pace of Play rating:** 4:00. **Green fee:** $50.
Credit cards: MC, V. **Reduced fees:** No.
Caddies: No. **Golf carts:** $27 for 18 holes.
Discount golf packages: No. **Season:** April-Oct. **High:** June-Aug.
On-site lodging: No. **Rental clubs:** Yes.
Walking policy: Mandatory cart. **Range:** Yes.
To obtain tee times: Call one day in advance.
Walking permitted for members only.
Ranked 4th in Vermont by Golf Digest.
Subscriber comments: My home course, what can I say? Visitors always rave about the excellent conditon of the course . . . Tough greens . . . One of my favorites . . . Excellent, fast greens . . . Simple layout . . . Well kept . . . Incredible par 3 on front nine . . . Beautiful setting, mountains come into play . . . Never plays the same . . . Excellent greens, beautiful scenery . . . Not an easy course even though it's short.

★★½ STOWE GOLF COURSE

R—Cape Cod Rd., Stowe (802)253-4893.
37 miles east of Burlington. **Holes:** 18. **Par:** 72/72.
Yards: 6,206/5,346. **Course rating:** 70.4/66.5. **Slope:** 122/115.
Opened: 1950. **Pace of Play rating:** 4:30. **Green fee:** $45.
Credit cards: All major. **Reduced fees:** Twilight.
Caddies: Yes. **Golf carts:** $15 for 18 holes.
Discount golf packages: No. **Season:** May-Oct. **High:** July-Sept.
On-site lodging: No. **Rental clubs:** Yes.
Walking policy: Unrestricted walking. **Range:** Yes (grass).
To obtain tee times: Call anytime. Credit card is required for weekends and holidays to hold tee time.
Subscriber comments: Beautiful rolling hills . . . One of the most beautiful courses I have ever played . . . . Manicured greens and tees are in a dramatic mountain setting. Spectacular downhill par 3s add spice to the challenge . . . Highly recommended for all . . . Picturesque mountain course with easy greens to putt . . . Semi-mountainous, fun and challenging . . . Tough to walk . . . Good greens . . . Busy in summer.

STRATTON MOUNTAIN RESORT
★★★½ LAKE/MOUNTAIN/FOREST

R—RR 1 Box 145, Stratton Mtn. (802)297-4114, (800)787-2886.
40 miles south of Rutland. **Holes:** 27. **Par:** 72/72/72.
Yards: 6,526/6,478/6,602. **Course rating:** 71.2/71.2/72.0. **Slope:** 125/126/125.
Opened: 1965. **Pace of Play rating:** 4:20. **Green fee:** $46/64.
Credit cards: All major. **Reduced fees:** Weekdays, Low season, Resort

guests, Juniors.
Caddies: No. **Golf carts:** $14 for 18 holes.
Discount golf packages: Yes. **Season:** May-Oct. **High:** July-Aug.
On-site lodging: Yes. **Rental clubs:** Yes.
Walking policy: Walking at certain times. **Range:** Yes (grass).
To obtain tee times: Call one week in advance.
Subscriber comments: Must be accurate . . . Gorgeous views . . .
Excellent staff . . . Great golf for all . . . Fun. Always play all three nines,
friendly place . . . All three nines different, fun and challenging . . . Great
mountain golf . . . New superintendent has it in best shape ever . . . LPGA
knows a good thing . . . Some good, tough holes . . . Good resort course,
well maintained . . . Beautiful setting . . . Each nine has distinct character
. . . Friendly, helpful staff . . . Fair test of golf.

★★★½ SUGARBUSH GOLF COURSE

R—Golf Course Rd., Warren (802)583-2722, (800)537-8427.
45 miles south of Burlington. **Holes:** 18. **Par:** 72/72.
Yards: 6,524/5,187. **Course rating:** 71.7/70.4. **Slope:** 128/119.
Opened: 1962. **Pace of Play rating:** 4:30. **Green fee:** $38/49.
Credit cards: All major. **Reduced fees:** Weekdays, Low season, Resort
guests, Twilight, Juniors.
Caddies: No. **Golf carts:** $15 for 18 holes.
Discount golf packages: Yes. **Season:** May-Oct. **High:** July-Oct.
On-site lodging: Yes. **Rental clubs:** Yes.
Walking policy: Walking at certain times. **Range:** Yes (grass).
To obtain tee times: Public may call 24 hrs. in advance ; preferred tee
times can be arranged through golf packages.
Subscriber comments: Need to use course management, beautiful greens
. . . Tough mountain course, very hilly, rolling greens . . . Great mountain
scenery . . . Few flat lies ; this will test your handicap . . . Friendly staff . . .
Big greens . . . What views! . . . Dramatic changes in elevation from tee to
green . . . Staff is pleasant and very helpful . . . Must be able to work the
ball both ways . . . New England golf . . . Set snuggly in the mountains,
great locale, challenging and fun . . . Great Robert Trent Jones course in the
Green Mountains . . . Fair condition and superb ambience.

★½ WEST BOLTON GOLF CLUB

PU—RD 1 Box 305, West Bolton Rd., Jericho (802)434-4321.
23 miles south of Burlington. **Holes:** 18. **Par:** 70/71.
Yards: 5,880/5,094. **Course rating:** 66.3/65.7. **Slope:** 109/103.
Opened: 1983. **Pace of Play rating:** 4:00. **Green fee:** $15/17.
Credit cards: MC, V. **Reduced fees:** Twilight, Seniors, Juniors.
Caddies: No. **Golf carts:** $18 for 18 holes.
Discount golf packages: No. **Season:** May-Oct. **High:** June-Aug.
On-site lodging: No. **Rental clubs:** Yes.
Walking policy: Unrestricted walking. **Range:** No.
To obtain tee times: Call one week prior.
Subscriber comments: Scenic . . . Short, with tiny greens . . . Cart
country . . . Good for the average golfer.

WILLISTON GOLF CLUB★

PU—P.O. Box 541, Williston (802)878-3747.
7 miles east of Burlington. **Holes:** 18. **Par:** 69/72.
Yards: 5,685/4,753. **Course rating:** 68.0/64.1. **Slope:** 118/106.
Opened: 1926. **Pace of Play rating:** 4:20. **Green fee:** $18.
Credit cards: None. **Reduced fees:** Twilight.
Caddies: No. **Golf carts:** $20 for 18 holes.
Discount golf packages: No. **Season:** May-Nov. **High:** July-Aug.
On-site lodging: No. **Rental clubs:** Yes.
Walking policy: Unrestricted walking. **Range:** No.
To obtain tee times: Call 7:00 a.m. or after on Thursday before weekend;
weekdays come in and register name.

★★★½ **WOODSTOCK COUNTRY CLUB**
R—Fourteen The Green, Woodstock (802)457-6674.
140 miles north of Boston. **Holes:** 18. **Par:** 69/71.
Yards: 6,001/4,924. **Course rating:** 69.0/67.0. **Slope:** 121/113.
Opened: 1895. **Pace of Play rating:** 3:30-4:00. **Green fee:** $55/55.
Credit cards: MC, V, AMEX. **Reduced fees:** Weekdays, Low season,
Resort guests, Twilight.
Caddies: No. **Golf carts:** $15 for 18 holes.
Discount golf packages: Yes. **Season:** May-Nov. **High:** July-Aug.
On-site lodging: Yes. **Rental clubs:** Yes.
Walking policy: Unrestricted walking. **Range:** Yes (grass).
To obtain tee times: Call the same day of play.
Subscriber comments: Water everywhere, bring plenty of balls . . . Well
maintained . . . Very short, tight, excellent condition . . . Simple design,
fun to play . . . Exact placement required, stream in play on 13 holes . . .
Fun Robert Trent Jones course . . . Not a difficult course . . . Magnificent
course tucked in a little valley behind the Woodstock Inn . . . Conditions
were superb . . . Walk to really appreciate the character.

Notes

VIRGINIA

★★½ ALGONKIAN REGIONAL PARK GOLF COURSE
PU—47001 Fairway Dr., Sterling (703)450-4655.
20 miles west of Washington, D.C. **Holes:** 18. **Par:** 72/72.
Yards: 7,015/5,795. **Course rating:** 73.5/74.0. **Slope:** 125/113.
Opened: 1972. **Pace of Play rating:** 4:30. **Green fee:** $18/22.
Credit cards: MC, V. **Reduced fees:** Weekdays, Resort guests, Seniors,
Juniors.
Caddies: No. **Golf carts:** $21 for 18 holes.
Discount golf packages: No. **Season:** Year-round. **High:** May-Dec.
On-site lodging: Yes. **Rental clubs:** Yes.
Walking policy: Unrestricted walking. **Range:** Yes.
To obtain tee times: Call or come into shop Tuesdays at 11 a.m. for
following Friday, Saturday, Sunday and any upcoming holiday.
Subscriber comments: Solid public course, nice back nine . . . Too long
for average golfer, no variety in shots . . . You'll wear out a 3-wood . . .
Slightly bland design but fair and fun . . . Long par 4s . . . Flat and great to
walk . . . Long, lots of trees . . . A day of long irons . . . Great cookies in
the snack bar . . . Long, beautiful, well maintained . . . Lots of challenging,
long par 4s . . . Above average muny-type course, great value for D.C.
area.

★★ BELMONT GOLF COURSE
PU—1600 Hilliard Rd., Richmond (804)266-4929.
10 miles north of Richmond. **Holes:** 18. **Par:** 71/73.
Yards: 6,350/5,418. **Course rating:** 70.6/72.6. **Slope:** 126/130.
Opened: 1903. **Pace of Play rating:** 4:00. **Green fee:** $17/20.
Credit cards: None. **Reduced fees:** Seniors, Juniors.
Caddies: No. **Golf carts:** $10 for 18 holes.
Discount golf packages: No. **Season:** Year-round. **High:** April-Oct.
On-site lodging: No. **Rental clubs:** Yes.
Walking policy: Unrestricted walking. **Range:** No.
To obtain tee times: May call seven days in advance and Monday
morning for the upcoming weekend.
Subscriber comments: A very good, fun Donald Ross . . . Good course
to walk . . . Boring back and forth back nine . . . Tough first hole . . .
Tillinghast redone by D. Ross, rehabilitated to excellent condition . . . OK
course, not very challenging.

★ BIDE-A-WEE GOLF CLUB
PU—1 Bide-A-Wee Lane, Portsmouth (804)393-5269.
5 miles east of Norfolk. **Holes:** 18. **Par:** 72/74.
Yards: 7,069/5,518. **Course rating:** 72.2/66.4. **Slope:** 121/113.
Opened: 1955. **Pace of Play rating:** 4:15. **Green fee:** $8/9.
Credit cards: None. **Reduced fees:** Weekdays, Juniors.
Caddies: No. **Golf carts:** $14 for 18 holes.
Discount golf packages: No. **Season:** Year-round. **High:** April-Sept.
On-site lodging: No. **Rental clubs:** Yes.
Walking policy: Unrestricted walking. **Range:** Yes (grass).
To obtain tee times: Call 24 hours in advance.
Subscriber comments: Lots of play all year . . . Getting better . . . Service
OK . . . Was good muny course when privately run.

★★★ BIRDWOOD GOLF COURSE
SP—Rte. 250 West, Charlottesville (804)293-4653.
1 mile west of Charlottesville. **Holes:** 18. **Par:** 72/72.
Yards: 6,820/5,041. **Course rating:** 72.8/65.2. **Slope:** 132/116.
Opened: 1984. **Pace of Play rating:** 3:44. **Green fee:** $12/50.
Credit cards: MC, V. **Reduced fees:** Weekdays, Low season, Resort
guests, Twilight, Seniors, Juniors.
Caddies: No. **Golf carts:** $11 for 18 holes.
Discount golf packages: Yes. **Season:** Year-round. **High:** April-Oct.
On-site lodging: Yes. **Rental clubs:** Yes.
Walking policy: Unrestricted walking. **Range:** Yes (grass).
To obtain tee times: Tee times are available 24 hours in advance.
Subscriber comments: Fast greens, too many blind shots . . . Tough to

walk! Best part of the course are the greens . . . Long distance between some holes . . . Great back nine, very scenic . . . Good challenge. Hilly, average length . . . Open front, wooded back, beautiful setting, maturing nicely.

★★ BIRKDALE GOLF AND COUNTRY CLUB

SP—8511 Royal Birkdale Dr., Chesterfield (804)739-8800.
15 miles southwest of Richmond. **Holes:** 18. **Par:** 71/71.
Yards: 6,544/4,459. **Course rating:** 71.1/N/A. **Slope:** 122/N/A.
Opened: 1990. **Pace of Play rating:** 4:15. **Green fee:** $32/38.
Credit cards: MC, V, AMEX. **Reduced fees:** Weekdays, Low season, Resort guests, Twilight, Seniors, Juniors.
Caddies: No. **Golf carts:** Included in Green Fee.

Discount golf packages: Yes. **Season:** Year-round. **High:** May–Oct.
On-site lodging: No. **Rental clubs:** Yes.
Walking policy: Mandatory cart. **Range:** Yes (grass).
To obtain tee times: Call one week in advance.
Subscriber comments: No. 11 ridiculous with tree in middle of fairway . . . Nice layout, not too tough, good greens, must be played from tips . . . Beautiful course, beautiful snack bar . . . Premium on tee shots . . . Not Dan Maples' best work but fun to play . . . Nos. 9 and 18 outstanding . . . Fun to play but lacks maturity.

★½ BOW CREEK MUNICIPAL GOLF COURSE

PU—3425 Clubhouse Rd., Virginia Beach (804)431-3763.
10 miles west of Norfolk. **Holes:** 18. **Par:** 70/70.
Yards: 5,917/5,181. **Course rating:** 70.4/68.4. **Slope:** 114/104.
Opened: 1960. **Pace of Play rating:** 4:30. **Green fee:** $17.
Credit cards: DISC. **Reduced fees:** Low season, Twilight, Seniors, Juniors.
Caddies: No. **Golf carts:** $16 for 18 holes.
Discount golf packages: No. **Season:** Year-round. **High:** April–Sept.
On-site lodging: Yes. **Rental clubs:** Yes.
Walking policy: Unrestricted walking. **Range:** Yes (grass).
To obtain tee times: Call by 8 a.m. on Friday for weekend tee times. Through the week it's first come, first served.
Subscriber comments: Fair layout, easy to walk . . . Smaller course. Good for ego . . . Short and nothing special. Nice little muny . . . Too close to houses.

★★★½ BRISTOW MANOR GOLF CLUB

PU—11507 Valley View Dr., Bristow (703)368-3558.
25 miles southwest of Washington, D.C. **Holes:** 18. **Par:** 72/74.
Yards: 7,102/5,527. **Course rating:** 72.9/73.4. **Slope:** 129/128.
Opened: 1993. **Pace of Play rating:** 4:00. **Green fee:** $22/29.
Credit cards: MC, V, AMEX. **Reduced fees:** Weekdays, Low season, Twilight, Seniors, Juniors.
Caddies: No. **Golf carts:** $12 for 18 holes.
Discount golf packages: No. **Season:** Year-round. **High:** March–Nov.
On-site lodging: No. **Rental clubs:** Yes.
Walking policy: Walking at certain times. **Range:** Yes (grass).
To obtain tee times: Call as far in advance as desired.
Subscriber comments: New course, with age will become excellent . . . Links-style course . . . Very open and windy . . . Lots of marsh requires carries, lots of trouble . . . Tough links-style layout. Exceedingly deep rough slows play since errant shots are hard to find . . . Hit it straight or reload . . . Bring a lot of balls . . . Beauty. This is it. Bought a house unit . . . Wish it was private so I could join . . . Good par 3s, mediocre par 5s . . . You will play it better the second time after you figure it out . . . Best upscale course in northern Virginia . . . Practice range second to none . . . Front nine terrific, back has some gimmick holes.

VIRGINIA

★ THE BROOKWOODS GOLF CLUB
PU—7325 Club Dr., Quinton (804)932-3737, (800)932-3737.
12 miles east of Richmond. **Holes:** 18. **Par:** 72/72.
Yards: 6,557/4,897. **Course rating:** 71.2/69.5. **Slope:** 123/119.
Opened: 1974. **Pace of Play rating:** 4:30. **Green fee:** $14/17.
Credit cards: MC, V. **Reduced fees:** Twilight, Seniors, Juniors.
Caddies: No. **Golf carts:** $10 for 18 holes.
Discount golf packages: Yes. **Season:** Year-round. **High:** April-Oct.
On-site lodging: No. **Rental clubs:** Yes.
Walking policy: Walking at certain times. **Range:** Yes (grass).
To obtain tee times: Call anytime prior to day of play.
Subscriber comments: Hilly, lots of doglegs, great variety, wooded,
scruffy around edges . . . OK for hackers like me . . . Needs work, nice
layout . . . Excellent design, needs maintenance . . . Every hole looks the
same.

★★★ BRYCE RESORT GOLF COURSE
R—P.O. Box 3, Basye (703)856-2124.
100 miles southwest of Washington, D.C. **Holes:** 18. **Par:** 71/71.
Yards: 6,261/5,240. **Course rating:** 68.8/70.1. **Slope:** 122/120.
Opened: 1968. **Pace of Play rating:** 4:30. **Green fee:** $10/26.
Credit cards: MC, V, AMEX. **Reduced fees:** Weekdays, Low season,
Resort guests, Twilight.
Caddies: No. **Golf carts:** $13 for 18 holes.
Discount golf packages: Yes. **Season:** March-Dec. **High:** May-Aug.
On-site lodging: Yes. **Rental clubs:** Yes.
Walking policy: Mandatory cart. **Range:** Yes (grass).
To obtain tee times: Up to three days in advance for nonmembers.
Subscriber comments: Nice scenery in mountains, not too tough . . .
Beautiful, short course . . . Uninspiring . . . Course rather flat . . . My
favorite place to go every fall for foliage and views . . . Go in the winter and
ski . . . Wide creek comes into play . . . Challenging holes but fun to play.

★½ CARPER'S VALLEY GOLF CLUB
PU—1400 Millwood Pike, Winchester (703)662-4319.
65 miles northwest of Washington, D.C. **Holes:** 18. **Par:** 70/71.
Yards: 6,135/5,100. **Course rating:** 69.1/70.7. **Slope:** 118/119.
Opened: 1962. **Pace of Play rating:** 4:00. **Green fee:** $10/20.
Credit cards: MC, V. **Reduced fees:** Weekdays, Low season, Twilight.
Caddies: No. **Golf carts:** Included in Green Fee.
Discount golf packages: No. **Season:** Year-round. **High:** April-Oct.
On-site lodging: No. **Rental clubs:** Yes.
Walking policy: Walking at certain times. **Range:** Yes (grass).
To obtain tee times: Call or come in up to five days in advance.
Subscriber comments: Basically open, straightforward course . . .
Fairways bare, greens hard . . . The wind seems to blow all the time . . .
Open holes and wooded holes. This year some hole changes. Fun to play.
Good greens . . . Good local course. Burns out in the summertime . . .
Hilly, some interesting holes.

★★★ CAVERNS COUNTRY CLUB
R—Airport Rd., Luray (703)743-7111.
80 miles west of Washington, D.C. **Holes:** 18. **Par:** 72/72.
Yards: 6,499/5,499. **Course rating:** 71.2/72.4. **Slope:** 117/120.
Opened: 1976. **Pace of Play rating:** 4:30-5:00. **Green fee:** $18/24.
Credit cards: MC, V, DISC. **Reduced fees:** N/A.
Caddies: No. **Golf carts:** $9 for 18 holes.
Discount golf packages: Yes. **Season:** Year-round. **High:** April-
June/Sept.-Oct.
On-site lodging: No. **Rental clubs:** No.
Walking policy: Unrestricted walking. **Range:** No.
To obtain tee times: Reserve tee time when booking golf package.
Subscriber comments: Great scenes of mountains . . . Beautiful mountain
course next to historic Luray Caverns . . . Great mountain course for all

skill levels. Scenic. Better each year . . . Tough track, keep 'em straight . . . Great mountain views, quiet, peaceful golf.

CEDAR HILLS COUNTRY CLUB*
SP—RR No.1 Box 598, Jonesville (703)346-1535.
85 miles north of Knoxville, Tenn. **Holes:** 18. **Par:** 71/71.
Yards: 6,466/5,057. **Course rating:** 69.3/65.2. **Slope:** 111/101.
Opened: 1967. **Pace of Play rating:** 4:00. **Green fee:** $10/15.
Credit cards: None. **Reduced fees:** Weekdays, Juniors.
Caddies: No. **Golf carts:** $8 for 18 holes.
Discount golf packages: No. **Season:** Year-round. **High:** April-Oct.
On-site lodging: No. **Rental clubs:** Yes.
Walking policy: Unrestricted walking. **Range:** Yes (grass).
To obtain tee times: Call anytime.
Subscriber comments: Staff courteous and helpful . . . Greens are great, probably comparable to resort greens . . . Excellent . . . A lot of very tight fairways and little or no bunkers, only downside to course . . . An excellent value for golfing dollar.

★★★ CHESTNUT CREEK GOLF CLUB
SP—360 Chestnut Creek Dr., Hardy (703)721-4214.
Call club for further information.
Subscriber comments: Outstanding mountain course, nice layout . . . Excellent young course, will only get better . . . Front very tight and young, back is nice . . . Very hilly. Some gimmicky holes . . . A few trick holes, but generally an excellent course . . . Almost every hole unique.

THE COLONIAL GOLF COURSE*
PU—8285 Diascund Rd., James City County (804)566-1600.
17 miles north of Newport News. **Holes:** 18. **Par:** 72/72.
Yards: 6,809/4,568. **Course rating:** 73.1/66.3. **Slope:** 132/109.
Opened: 1995. **Pace of Play rating:** 4:00. **Green fee:** $60.
Credit cards: MC, V. **Reduced fees:** Weekdays, Twilight, Seniors, Juniors.
Caddies: No. **Golf carts:** Included in Green Fee.
Discount golf packages: No. **Season:** Year-round. **High:** April-Oct.
On-site lodging: No. **Rental clubs:** Yes.
Walking policy: Unrestricted walking. **Range:** Yes (grass).
To obtain tee times: Call anytime.

★★★ THE CROSSINGS GOLF CLUB
PU—800 Virginia Center Pkwy., Glen Allen (804)261-0000.
9 miles north of Richmond. **Holes:** 18. **Par:** 72/72.
Yards: 6,619/5,625. **Course rating:** 70.7/73.2. **Slope:** 126/128.
Opened: 1979. **Pace of Play rating:** 4:20. **Green fee:** $27/45.
Credit cards: MC, V. **Reduced fees:** Weekdays, Low season, Seniors, Juniors.
Caddies: No. **Golf carts:** Included in Green Fee.
Discount golf packages: No. **Season:** Year-round. **High:** March-Nov.
On-site lodging: No. **Rental clubs:** Yes.
Walking policy: Walking at certain times. **Range:** Yes (grass).
To obtain tee times: Call seven days in advance.
Subscriber comments: Great course when it's in good shape, good atmosphere . . . Excellent public course, reasonable, challenging . . . Very good public course, good for high handicappers, great chili dogs . . . Pleasant, flat layout, for all levels, friendly . . . First-rate course, cozy shop and snack bar . . . Tough course, demands accurate shotmaking. Good challenge for all skill levels . . . Well set up for women and seniors . . . Difficult course on a beautiful layout . . . Demanding second shots to par 4s . . . Tough layout but so much fun you want to replay everything . . . Some interesting, diverse holes . . . Great Joe Lee design, best condition summer and fall.

★★★½ DRAPER VALLEY GOLF CLUB

PU—Rte. 1, Box 104, Draper (703)980-4653.
60 miles south of Roanoke. **Holes:** 18. **Par:** 72/72.
Yards: 7,046/4,793. **Course rating:** 73.3/65.6. **Slope:** 125/113.
Opened: 1992. **Pace of Play rating:** 4:30. **Green fee:** $16/21.
Credit cards: MC, V. **Reduced fees:** Weekdays, Low season.
Caddies: No. **Golf carts:** $9 for 18 holes.
Discount golf packages: Yes. **Season:** Year-round. **High:** March-Nov.
On-site lodging: No. **Rental clubs:** Yes.
Walking policy: Walking at certain times. **Range:** Yes (grass).
To obtain tee times: Call seven days in advance.
Subscriber comments: Great young course, can't wait to come back in 15
years and see how all the trees have grown in . . . Best public course in
Virginia, excellent everything . . . Very long course, new, will get better
with age . . . Has some awesome holes . . . Long, long uphill par 3s . . .
Excruciatingly tough greens.

FORD'S COLONY COUNTRY CLUB

R—240 Ford's Colony Dr., Williamsburg (804)258-4130.
40 miles west of Richmond.
Pace of Play rating: 4:30. **Green fee:** $40/90.
Credit cards: MC, V, AMEX. **Reduced fees:** Weekdays, Low season,
Resort guests, Twilight.
Caddies: No. **Golf carts:** Included in Green Fee.
Discount golf packages: Yes. **Season:** Year-round. **High:** April-Oct.
On-site lodging: Yes. **Rental clubs:** Yes.
Walking policy: Mandatory cart. **Range:** Yes (grass).
To obtain tee times: Call seven days in advance.

★★★★ BLUE/GOLD COURSE

Holes: 18. **Par:** 71/71.
Yards: 6,769/5,424. **Course rating:** 72.3/N/A. **Slope:** 124/109.
Opened: 1987.
Subscriber comments: Wonderful challenge . . . A golfer's dream . . .
Great test of golf for all players, great Dan Maples design . . . Excellent
greens, tough doglegs . . . Upscale with country club atmosphere . . .
Blue/Gold better than Red/White . . . I would recommend to any person
. . . Great course, good test, staff and food service excellent . . . Great
condition . . . A must if visiting Williamsburg.

★★★½ RED/WHITE COURSE

Holes: 18. **Par:** 72/72.
Yards: 6,755/5,614. **Course rating:** 72.3/73.2. **Slope:** 126/132.
Opened: 1985.
Subscriber comments: Lots of woods and water but still fairly easy to
play . . . Absolutely impeccable . . . Great layout, always good condition
. . . Plan your vacation around it . . . Courses remind me of Pinehurst . . .
Nice blend of hills and lakes . . . Ranked second to Blue/Gold but don't
believe it.

★★½ GLENWOOD GOLF CLUB

PU—3100 Creighton Rd., Richmond (804)226-1793.
Holes: 18. **Par:** 71/75.
Yards: 6,464/5,197. **Course rating:** 70.0/72.1. **Slope:** 114/120.
Opened: 1927. **Pace of Play rating:** 4:06. **Green fee:** $13/20.
Credit cards: None. **Reduced fees:** Weekdays, Twilight, Seniors, Juniors.
Caddies: No. **Golf carts:** $10 for 18 holes.
Discount golf packages: No. **Season:** Year-round. **High:** May-Oct.
On-site lodging: No. **Rental clubs:** Yes.
Walking policy: Unrestricted walking. **Range:** No.
To obtain tee times: Call one week in advance.
Subscriber comments: Decent course . . . Well maintained, open year
round, great staff, home course, wide-open . . . Good public course, super
value . . . Best-kept course in the area. Hard to get on . . . Excellent
condition. Friendly staff. Very forgiving course . . . Year-round in great
shape.

GOLDEN HORSESHOE GOLF CLUB

R—401 South England St., Williamsburg (804)220-7696, (800)447-8679.
45 miles east of Richmond.
Pace of Play rating: 4:30. **Green fee:** $85/100.
Credit cards: MC, V, AMEX. **Reduced fees:** Low season, Resort guests, Twilight.
Caddies: Yes. **Golf carts:** Included in Green Fee.
Discount golf packages: No. **Season:** Year-round. **High:** April–Oct.
On-site lodging: Yes. **Rental clubs:** Yes.
Walking policy: Unrestricted walking. **Range:** Yes (grass).
To obtain tee times: Reserve tee times when making hotel reservations otherwise call one week prior to play.

★★★★½ GOLD COURSE

Holes: 18. **Par:** 71/71.
Yards: 6,700/5,159. **Course rating:** 73.1/66.2. **Slope:** 137/120.
Opened: 1963.
Ranked 30th in America's 75 Best Resort Courses by Golf Digest. Ranked 4th in Virginia by Golf Digest. Site of Golf Digest Schools.
Also nine-hole executive course.
Subscriber comments: Classic R.T. Jones Sr. . . . Only the single digit handicap survives, a "must play" for all . . . Best par 3s I ever played, excellent shape all year, difficult . . . The best of the best, excellent layout, greens, personnel . . . Four of the finest par 3s I've ever played . . . A jewel to be played and replayed . . . Two great courses, expensive but worth every cent . . . Appreciate it more each time I play it . . . Could not be better in any respect . . . Pretty. Challenging. Historic . . . A real golf mecca, play when flowers are in bloom . . . Wonderful layout, immaculate condition . . . Best group of par 3s on one course in U.S . . . Great par 3s. Bring lots of money . . . Great course, very beautiful, last five holes tough . . . If within two hours of the course, call the wife and say you need an extra day off to play this great course.

★★★★ GREEN COURSE

Holes: 18. **Par:** 72/72.
Yards: 7,120/5,348. **Course rating:** 73.4/69.3. **Slope:** 134/109.
Opened: 1992.
Subscriber comments: Not quite in same league as Gold Course . . . Great, challenging, very well maintained . . . I like it every bit as much as its older sister . . . Great companion to Gold, more open . . . Top notch course and good pace and scenic woodlands abound, superb treatment by cooperative staff . . . Much improved as it matures, good service, great condition, easier than Gold but definitely a challenge . . . Interesting mounding along fairways . . . Different from Gold but great in its own right . . . Much fairer than Gold Course . . . Excellent Rees Jones, beautiful setting and clubhouse . . . Take another day and play this one too. Great course.•

★½ GOOSE CREEK GOLF CLUB

SP—43001 Golf Club Rd., Leesburg (703)729-2500.
35 miles west of Washington, D.C. **Holes:** 18. **Par:** 72/72.
Yards: 6,400/5,235. **Course rating:** 70.3/71.3. **Slope:** 121/120.
Opened: 1952. **Pace of Play rating:** 4:00. **Green fee:** $20/39.
Credit cards: MC, V, AMEX. **Reduced fees:** Weekdays, Low season, Twilight, Seniors, Juniors.
Caddies: No. **Golf carts:** N/A.
Discount golf packages: No. **Season:** Year-round. **High:** April–Sept.
On-site lodging: No. **Rental clubs:** Yes.
Walking policy: Walking at certain times. **Range:** No.
To obtain tee times: Call Wednesday 9 a.m. for weekend tee times.
Subscriber comments: Course is improving, but long way to go . . . Poorly-kept golf course . . . Very hilly requires well-placed drive on most holes . . . Not bad. Some greens very tricky . . . For a quick practice round it's OK . . . Interesting course, often tight . . . Reachable par 5s . . . Dangerous blind shots, firm, tiny greens . . . Small greens, holes are too close to each other . . . Typical public links. No frills.

GORDEN TRENT GOLF COURSE★
PU—Rd. No. 632, Stuart (703)694-3805.
Call club for further information.
Subscriber comments: Good for beginners and quite short, very uncrowded with nice setting . . . OK for local play.

★½ GREEN'S FOLLY GOLF COURSE
PU—Sinai Rd., South Boston (804)572-4998.
Call club for further information.
Subscriber comments: Par 3s are chip shots . . . Huge 667-yard par 5 . . . Good layout for average player . . . Average condition . . . Challenging course.

★★ THE GREENS OF FREDERICKSBURG
PU—2801 Plank Rd., Fredericksburg (703)786-8385.
Holes: 18. **Par:** 72/72.
Yards: 6,921/5,486. **Course rating:** 72.9/72.1. **Slope:** 135/124.
Opened: 1971. **Pace of Play rating:** 4:30. **Green fee:** $27/34.
Credit cards: MC, V. **Reduced fees:** Weekdays, Low season, Resort guests, Twilight.
Caddies: No. **Golf carts:** Included in Green Fee.
Discount golf packages: Yes. **Season:** Year-round. **High:** March-June/Nov.
On-site lodging: Yes. **Rental clubs:** Yes.
Walking policy: Mandatory cart. **Range:** Yes (grass).
To obtain tee times: Call seven days in advance.
Formerly known as Shannon Green.
Subscriber comments: Long hitter's course. Wide fairways . . . Long and open but not easy . . . Nice rolling layout, good for all handicappers . . . Excellent layout (very long) but in uneven condition . . . Good for low- to mid-handicapper . . . Commercial development infringing onto course.

THE HAMPTONS GOLF COURSE
★★★ WOODS/LAKES/LINKS
PU—320 Butler Farm Rd., Hampton (804)766-9148.
Holes: 27. **Par:** 71/71/70.
Yards: 6,401/6,283/5,940. **Course rating:** 69.9/69.4/67.8.
Slope: 110/110/106.
Opened: 1989. **Pace of Play rating:** 4:30. **Green fee:** $14/17.
Credit cards: MC, V, AMEX. **Reduced fees:** Weekdays, Low season, Seniors, Juniors.
Caddies: No. **Golf carts:** $9 for 18 holes.
Discount golf packages: No. **Season:** Year-round. **High:** March-Sept.
On-site lodging: No. **Rental clubs:** Yes.
Walking policy: Walking at certain times. **Range:** Yes (grass).
To obtain tee times: Call 48 hours in advance for weekends only.
Subscriber comments: Noise of naval jet planes taking off over course was too much . . . Affordable, beautiful scenery golf course in great condition . . . Short course, John Daly would use 7-iron through sand wedge . . . Three very distinct nines, nice clubhouse, friendly staff . . . Each nine is a change . . . Woods and Lakes best . . . Shotmaker's course, good for tuning up.

★★★ HANGING ROCK GOLF CLUB
PU—1500 Red Lane, Salem (703)389-7275, (800)277-7497.
9 miles west of Roanoke. **Holes:** 18. **Par:** 73/72.
Yards: 6,828/4,463. **Course rating:** 72.3/62.6. **Slope:** 125/106.
Opened: 1991. **Pace of Play rating:** 4:47. **Green fee:** $19/23.
Credit cards: MC, V. **Reduced fees:** Weekdays, Low season, Resort guests, Twilight, Seniors, Juniors.
Caddies: No. **Golf carts:** $12 for 18 holes.
Discount golf packages: Yes. **Season:** Year-round. **High:** April-Oct.
On-site lodging: No. **Rental clubs:** Yes.
Walking policy: Walking at certain times. **Range:** Yes (grass).

To obtain tee times: Call one day in advance for weekday. Call Wednesday at 9 a.m. for upcoming weekend and holiday.

Subscriber comments: Beautiful scenery. Placement course in mountains . . . Needs to mature, fun golf with lovely topography . . . Need all your clubs, can be tough when windy . . . Very nice and well-kept course, interesting and difficult holes . . . Unusual layout, course is still maturing . . . Challenging first hole . . . New course but good.

★★★½ HELL'S POINT GOLF COURSE

PU—2700 Atwoodtown Rd., Virginia Beach (804)721-3400.

15 miles east of Norfolk. **Holes:** 18. **Par:** 72/72.
Yards: 6,966/5,003. **Course rating:** 73.3/71.2. **Slope:** 130/116.
Opened: 1982. **Pace of Play rating:** 4:18. **Green fee:** $25/47.
Credit cards: MC, V. **Reduced fees:** Weekdays, Low season, Resort guests, Twilight.
Caddies: No. **Golf carts:** Included in Green Fee.
Discount golf packages: Yes. **Season:** Year-round. **High:** May-Aug.
On-site lodging: No. **Rental clubs:** No.
Walking policy: Unrestricted walking. **Range:** Yes (grass).
To obtain tee times: Call one week in advance or book through hotel golf package up to one year in advance.

Subscriber comments: Scenic, tough, great shape, good pro shop . . . Rees Jones design, most enjoyable round of the year . . . Need a cart to play, long distance between holes . . . Best course in Virginia Beach area . . . Long difficult course, positioning important . . . Very difficult, always good condition, worth the money . . . Great sandwiches . . . Great design, no two holes the same.

★★½ HERNDON CENTENNIAL GOLF CLUB

PU—909 Ferndale Ave., Herndon (703)471-5769.

20 miles northwest of Washington, D.C. **Holes:** 18. **Par:** 71/71.
Yards: 6,445/5,025. **Course rating:** 68.7/69.0. **Slope:** 116/121.
Opened: 1979. **Pace of Play rating:** 4:30. **Green fee:** $25.
Credit cards: None. **Reduced fees:** Weekdays, Seniors, Juniors.
Caddies: No. **Golf carts:** $24 for 18 holes.
Discount golf packages: No. **Season:** Year-round. **High:** May-Sept.
On-site lodging: No. **Rental clubs:** Yes.
Walking policy: Unrestricted walking. **Range:** Yes (grass).
To obtain tee times: Call 24 hours in advance.

Subscriber comments: Short, open, relatively easy . . . Short but sweet par 4s are easily reached . . . Excellent golf course, good muny . . . Short but challenging, nice to walk . . . Short but exceptionally well groomed . . . Very forgiving. A 25-handicap should break 90 here . . . Nice muny. Good for ego . . . Short from the white tees. Must play from the blues . . . Confidence booster, little trouble, reachable par 5s . . . Wide variety of holes, excellent condition . . . Long hitters will not use many medium to long clubs.

★★★ HIDDEN CREEK GOLF CLUB

SP—11599 North Shore Dr., Reston (703)437-4222.
Call club for further information.

Subscriber comments: A tough, long course . . . Much improved course, challenge for all . . . Good solid layout . . . Great, tough par 4s on front nine.

★½ HOLLOWS GOLF COURSE

SP—14408 Cherry Hill Rd., Montpelier (804)798-2949.

10 miles northwest of Richmond. **Holes:** 18. **Par:** 72/72.
Yards: 6,505/5,020. **Course rating:** 70.7/68.1. **Slope:** 118/108.
Opened: 1984. **Pace of Play rating:** 4:00. **Green fee:** $14/20.
Credit cards: None. **Reduced fees:** Weekdays, Low season, Twilight, Seniors, Junior
Caddies: No. **Golf carts:** $10 for 18 holes.
Discount golf packages: No. **Season:** Year-round. **High:** April-Oct.
On-site lodging: No. **Rental clubs:** Yes.

Walking policy: Unrestricted walking. **Range:** Yes (grass).
To obtain tee times: Call seven days in advance.
Subscriber comments: Very bland, Nos. 17 and 18 are the best holes . . .
Fun course, 17th hole great challenge . . . Relatively open course with water
coming into play on last two holes only . . . Very short, too open, good
seniors' course . . . Terrain is flat and very open . . . Nice little course, good
condition.

HOLSTON HILLS GOLF CLUB★
SP—Country Club Rd., Marion (703)783-7484.
Call club for further information.
Subscriber comments: Super course . . . Excellent greens . . .
Uncrowded.

THE HOMESTEAD RESORT
R—P.O. Box 2000, Hot Springs (703)839-7994.
150 miles west of Richmond.
Credit cards: All major. **Reduced fees:** Low season, Resort guests,
Twilight, Juniors.
Caddies: Yes. **Golf carts:** $18 for 18 holes.
Discount golf packages: Yes. **Season:** April-Oct. **High:** April-Oct.
On-site lodging: Yes. **Rental clubs:** Yes.
Walking policy: Walking at certain times. **Range:** Yes (grass).
To obtain tee times: Call.

★★★★★ CASCADES COURSE
Holes: 18. **Par:** 70/71.
Yards: 6,566/5,448. **Course rating:** 72.9/72.9. **Slope:** 136/137.
Opened: 1923. **Pace of Play rating:** 4:25. **Green fee:** $60/90.
Ranked 39th in America's 100 Greatest Golf Courses by Golf Digest.
Ranked 12th in America's 75 Best Resort Courses by Golf Digest. Ranked
1st in Virginia by Golf Digest.
Subscriber comments: Lightning fast greens, like putting on a billiard
table . . . Heaven, no matter how you play. The staff and course define the
best in golf . . . Memorable in every aspect . . . Mecca, best mountain
course in U.S. . . . My all-time favorite . . . World class experience,
great layout, conditions and staff . . . The original Scots would be proud
. . . Unbelievable golf course. Unbelievable challenge, would play every
day forever. Staff super . . . Expensive but worth it, really felt pampered
. . . Very challenging, but fair to women and shorter hitters.

★★★½ HOMESTEAD COURSE
(703)839-7740.
Holes: 18. **Par:** 71/72.
Yards: 6,200/5,150. **Course rating:** 70.1/70.0. **Slope:** 121/117.
Opened: 1892. **Pace of Play rating:** 4:25. **Green fee:** $40/65.
Subscriber comments: Very historic setting for golf but course is not as
good as Cascades . . . Fun course, short . . . Fun course to play . . . Easier
to score than Cascades . . . Pretty setting overlooking hotel . . . Great old
course, great condition, need all clubs . . . Same as The Greenbrier but
more sedate . . . Short but fun, old world charm.

★★★½ LOWER CASCADES COURSE
(703)839-7995.
Holes: 18. **Par:** 72/70.
Yards: 6,619/4,726. **Course rating:** 72.2/65.5. **Slope:** 127/116.
Opened: 1962. **Pace of Play rating:** 4:25. **Green fee:** $65.
Subscriber comments: Easier than Cascades by several strokes . . .
Gorgeous golf course . . . Always score well here, love to play it . . . More
forgiving than Cascades . . . Good but not up to the other Homestead
courses.

★★★ HONEY BEE GOLF CLUB
SP—5016 S. Independence Blvd., Virginia Beach (804)471-2768.
Holes: 18. **Par:** 70/70.
Yards: 6,075/4,929. **Course rating:** 69.6/67.0. **Slope:** 123/104.
Opened: 1986. **Pace of Play rating:** 4:22. **Green fee:** $23/40.
Credit cards: MC, V. **Reduced fees:** Weekdays, Low season, Twilight,
Seniors, Juniors.

Caddies: No. **Golf carts:** Included in Green Fee.
Discount golf packages: Yes. **Season:** Year-round. **High:** March–Oct.
On-site lodging: No. **Rental clubs:** Yes.
Walking policy: Walking at certain times. **Range:** Yes (grass).
To obtain tee times: Call Wednesday for upcoming weekend. Otherwise call one week in advance.
Subscriber comments: Nice layout except for too many houses along fairway . . . Short course, but beware of last four holes from back tees, long and hard . . . Last three holes are excellent, rest of course is uneventful . . . Short but demanding . . . Short and uneventful . . . Nice green and fairways. A few holes are close to homes . . . Fun par 3s, nice pro shop and restaurant, very good practice area . . . Too much distance between greens and next tee . . . Relatively flat, challenging for average player.

★★½ IVY HILL GOLF CLUB
PU—Rte. 2, Forest (804)525-2680.
Call club for further information.
Subscriber comments: Hilly, shortish, very open, scenic, good greens, some tough holes . . . OK but needs improvement . . . A well-kept, challenging course . . . Extremely hilly, large and fast greens . . . Good hilly test, can beat you up.

★ JORDAN POINT GOLF CLUB
PU—Jordan Point Rd., Hopewell (804)458-0141.
Call club for further information.
Subscriber comments: Early holes flat, later up and down . . . Nice workingman's course . . . Not in great shape, challenging back nine . . . Impossible to walk back nine . . . Starting with No. 8, there are some tough holes.

★½ KEMPSVILLE GREENS GOLF CLUB
PU—4840 Princess Anne Rd., Virginia Beach (804)474-8441.
Holes: 18. **Par:** 70/70.
Yards: 5,849/4,538. **Course rating:** 67.8/63.8. **Slope:** 114/94.
Opened: N/A. **Pace of Play rating:** N/A. **Green fee:** $10/18.
Credit cards: None. **Reduced fees:** Resort guests, Seniors, Juniors.
Caddies: No. **Golf carts:** $8 for 18 holes.
Discount golf packages: Yes. **Season:** Year-round. **High:** June–Aug.
On-site lodging: No. **Rental clubs:** Yes.
Walking policy: Unrestricted walking. **Range:** Yes (grass).
To obtain tee times: Call Friday after 8 a.m. for upcoming weekend and holiday. Open play during the week.
Subscriber comments: Some good holes but not many . . . Tight course . . . Houses line course . . . No. 11 is greatest hole I ever played . . . Tough back nine, lots of water . . . Too many houses and condos.

★★★½ KILN CREEK GOLF AND COUNTRY CLUB
SP—1003 Brick Kiln Blvd., Newport News (804)988-3220.
30 miles west of Norfolk. **Holes:** 18. **Par:** 72/72.
Yards: 6,889/5,313. **Course rating:** 73.4/69.5. **Slope:** 130/119.
Opened: 1989. **Pace of Play rating:** 4:00. **Green fee:** $35/50.
Credit cards: MC, V, AMEX. **Reduced fees:** Weekdays, Low season.
Caddies: No. **Golf carts:** Included in Green Fee.
Discount golf packages: No. **Season:** Year-round. **High:** April–Oct.
On-site lodging: Yes. **Rental clubs:** Yes.
Walking policy: Mandatory cart. **Range:** Yes (grass).
To obtain tee times: Call one week in advance.
Subscriber comments: Great course, this one will kick the big boys' butts! . . . The back nine is harder, and Nos. 16, 17, 18 are great finishing holes . . . One of four or five best in state of Virginia, wonderful layout . . . Good public course, noisy next to interstate and airport . . . Tough but fun.

KINGSMILL RESORT

R—1010 Kingsmill Rd., Williamsburg (804)253-3906, (800)832-5665.
50 miles east of Richmond.
Pace of Play rating: 4:15. **Green fee:** $45/110.
Credit cards: All major. **Reduced fees:** Low season, Resort guests,
Twilight.
Caddies: No. **Golf carts:** Included in Green Fee.
Discount golf packages: Yes. **Season:** Year-round. **High:** April–Oct.
On-site lodging: Yes. **Rental clubs:** Yes.
Walking policy: Mandatory cart. **Range:** Yes (grass).
To obtain tee times: Resort guests may make tee times at time of room
reservation. Others may call 24 hours in advance.

★★★½ PLANTATION COURSE

Holes: 18. **Par:** 72/72.
Yards: 6,605/4,880. **Course rating:** 72.1/69.2. **Slope:** 126/122.
Opened: 1986.
Subscriber comments: Especially good for mid-range players . . . Good
golf but not impressive . . . Fun and demanding, good condition year
round, great par 5s . . . Excellent course, nothing fancy . . . Good golf . . .
More playable for average golfer than River . . . Well maintained and
probably better than River Course . . . Quality courses, great pro shop and
staff . . . Good course to play in afternoon after River Course . . . River
Course much better . . . Great course, but overshadowed by River Course.

★★★★ RIVER COURSE

Holes: 18. **Par:** 71/71.
Yards: 6,797/4,606. **Course rating:** 73.3/67.4. **Slope:** 137/109.
Opened: 1975.
Ranked 7th in Virginia by Golf Digest.
Subscriber comments: Good test for better players but will not destroy
others . . . Incredible setting, a bit slow and not a great place to slice . . .
Locals' chance to play where the pros are . . . Excellent course, last four
holes memorable . . . Course is too cute for words . . . Classic Pete Dye,
difficult, scenic and fun . . . Demanding layout, fast greens, well maintained
. . . Site of PGA Tout's Anheuser Busch. Good but expensive . . . Fun to
play on Tour course. Not as difficult as expected . . . Favorite Virginia
course, expensive but well worth it . . . Some long carries from back tees,
incredible 18th green . . . One of Dye's masterpieces . . . Good design,
target golf, condos too close to course.

WOODS COURSE★

Holes: 18. **Par:** 72/72.
Yards: 6,784/5,140. **Course rating:** 72.7/68.7. **Slope:** 125/120.
Opened: 1994.

★★★ LAKE MONTICELLO GOLF CLUB

PU—51 Bunker Blvd., Palmyra (804)589-3075.
Call club for further information.
Subscriber comments: Long from blue tees, hilly, tight, challenging . . .
Scenic. Every hole isolated. Bring balls . . . Trees and water make
placement golf at its best. On most tees leave your woods in the bag . . .
Course will come of age in '95.

★½ LAKE WRIGHT GOLF COURSE

SP—6280 North Hamden Blvd., Norfolk (804)461-2246.
Holes: 18. **Par:** 70/70.
Yards: 6,174/5,297. **Course rating:** 68.8/68.2. **Slope:** 116/105.
Opened: 1969. **Pace of Play rating:** 4:00. **Green fee:** $16/18.
Credit cards: MC, V. **Reduced fees:** Weekdays, Low season, Seniors.
Caddies: No. **Golf carts:** $18 for 18 holes.
Discount golf packages: No. **Season:** Year-round. **High:** April–Nov.
On-site lodging: Yes. **Rental clubs:** Yes.
Walking policy: Walking at certain times. **Range:** Yes (grass).
To obtain tee times: Call one day in advance for weekends only.
Subscriber comments: Wide open all the way . . . Holes too close
together . . . Good for family golf . . . Short, wide open, no scenery . . .

Borders international airport . . . No. 5 is the only real golf hole, one of the toughest holes around . . . Greatly improved . . . Too close to interstate highway (distracting) . . . Nice public course, staff very friendly and helpful . . . Could be better than it is.

LAKEVIEW GOLF COURSE
★★★½ LAKE/PEAK/SPRING
SP—Rte. 11, Harrisonburg (703)434–8937.
Holes: 27. **Par:** 72/72/72.
Yards: 6,517/6,640/6,303. **Course rating:** 71.0/71.3/70.9.
Slope: 119/121/120.
Opened: 1962. **Pace of Play rating:** 3:44. **Green fee:** $18/18.
Credit cards: None. **Reduced fees:** Twilight.
Caddies: No. **Golf carts:** $10 for 18 holes.
Discount golf packages: No. **Season:** Year-round. **High:** April-Oct.
On-site lodging: No. **Rental clubs:** Yes.
Walking policy: Unrestricted walking. **Range:** Yes.
To obtain tee times: Call up to seven days in advance.
Subscriber comments: Fun, scenic, well kept, friendly, must return . . . Course is challenging but open enough that play moves along. Very good value . . . Mountain course, average greens, well-manicured . . . Tough nines, can't walk the mountain nine, nice . . . 27 holes, one nine wide open, one nine tree-lined fairways, one nine water and trees, great view of mountain ranges . . . Very creative use of available land . . . Spring and Lake top quality . . . Each nine holes is different . . . Wonderful course and views.

★★★½ LANSDOWNE GOLF CLUB
R—44050 Woodridge Pkwy., Lansdowne (703)729–4071, (800)541–4801.
35 miles west of Washington, D.C. **Holes:** 18. **Par:** 72/72.
Yards: 7,057/5,213. **Course rating:** 73.3/75.0. **Slope:** 126/134.
Opened: 1991. **Pace of Play rating:** 4:30. **Green fee:** $80/90.
Credit cards: MC, V, AMEX. **Reduced fees:** Low season, Resort guests, Juniors.
Caddies: No. **Golf carts:** Included in Green Fee.
Discount golf packages: Yes. **Season:** Year-round. **High:** April-Nov.
On-site lodging: Yes. **Rental clubs:** Yes.
Walking policy: Mandatory cart. **Range:** Yes (grass).
To obtain tee times: Call 48 hours in advance.
Subscriber comments: Back nine is unforgettable . . . Robert Trent Jones Jr. at his best . . . Lots of elevation on back nine, very challenging, picturesque, well maintained . . . Why I play this game . . . Pricey, but a real treat . . . Robert Trent Jones Jr. layout with all the trimmings . . . Some excellent par 3s . . . Great use of terrain . . . Worth every cent . . . Beautiful course. Front nine is OK, back nine more than makes up for it . . . Awesome finishing holes . . . The tees were better than many courses' greens.

LEE PARK GOLF COURSE★
PU—3108 Homestead Dr., Petersburg (804)733-5667.
25 miles north of Richmond. **Holes:** 18. **Par:** 70/70.
Yards: 6,037/4,946. **Course rating:** 68.0/62.2. **Slope:** 108/96.
Opened: 1945. **Pace of Play rating:** 4:00. **Green fee:** $20/25.
Credit cards: None. **Reduced fees:** Weekdays, Twilight, Seniors, Juniors.
Caddies: No. **Golf carts:** Included in Green Fee.
Discount golf packages: No. **Season:** Year-round. **High:** June-Aug.
On-site lodging: No. **Rental clubs:** Yes.
Walking policy: Unrestricted walking. **Range:** Yes (grass).
To obtain tee times: None taken.

★★★ LEE'S HILL GOLFERS' CLUB
PU—10200 Old Dominion Pkwy., Fredericksburg (703)891-0111, (800)930-3636.
50 miles north of Richmond. **Holes:** 18. **Par:** 72/72.
Yards: 6,805/5,064. **Course rating:** 72.4/69.2. **Slope:** 128/115.

Opened: 1993. **Pace of Play rating:** 4:15. **Green fee:** $13/33.
Credit cards: MC, V. **Reduced fees:** Weekdays, Low season, Twilight,
Seniors, Juniors.
Caddies: No. **Golf carts:** $12 for 18 holes.
Discount golf packages: Yes. **Season:** Year-round. **High:** April-Oct.
On-site lodging: No. **Rental clubs:** Yes.
Walking policy: Mandatory cart. **Range:** Yes (grass).
To obtain tee times: Call on day in advance.
Subscriber comments: New course, still rough on some edges but great
potential . . . Woods and water, straight tee shots a must, big, rolling, fast
greens . . . Civil War setting interesting . . . Will be outstanding with
maturity, rough needs work, full of rocks . . . Novel tee markers . . .
Private club atmosphere . . . Young, very tight and beautiful, how I like it!
. . . Very good new course but has rocky spots in fairways and spotty
rough . . . Course gets sloppy after rain . . . Great staff, good layout, great
twilight value, friendly to ladies . . . Historical signs throughout course.

★★ LEESBURG WESTPARK HOTEL GOLF CLUB
R—59 Clubhouse Dr. S.W., Leesburg (703)777-1910.
Call club for further information.
Subscriber comments: Several long walks between green and tee . . .
Nice little course, small greens . . . Short but challenging . . . Nice walk in
the park . . . Course is good for all level of golfers . . . Holes side by side.
Balls flying everywhere . . . Very interesting layout . . . Excellent greens,
nice course.

★★ MASSANUTTEN GOLF CLUB
R—P.O. Box 1227, Harrisonburg (703)289-9441.
Call club for further information.
Subscriber comments: Cardiac hill, very hard on seniors . . . Ski resort
course . . . Most holes slope from left to right . . . Beautiful mountain
course . . . Tight and beautiful, especially in the fall with the trees changing
color . . . Everything rolls downhill . . . Very tough course, narrow
fairways, very good greens . . . Severe sidehill fairways . . . Very scenic,
tricky mountain golf . . . Tough mountainside course.

★½ MEADOWCREEK GOLF COURSE
PU—1400 Pen Park Rd., Charlottesville (804)977-0615.
Holes: 18. **Par:** 71/71.
Yards: 6,030/4,628. **Course rating:** 68.5/62.0. **Slope:** 118/105.
Opened: 1973. **Pace of Play rating:** 3:52. **Green fee:** $20.
Credit cards: MC, V. **Reduced fees:** Twilight, Seniors, Juniors.
Caddies: No. **Golf carts:** $10 for 18 holes.
Discount golf packages: No. **Season:** Year-round. **High:** April-Sept.
On-site lodging: No. **Rental clubs:** Yes.
Walking policy: Unrestricted walking. **Range:** Yes (grass).
To obtain tee times: Call 48 hours in advance.
Subscriber comments: Hilly, very interesting, scenic, friendly, well kept,
some unique holes . . . Good condition and maintenance, affordable golf,
helpful, good staff . . . Too many blind shots . . . Nice logo . . . 15 good
holes.

★★★ MEADOWS FARMS GOLF COURSE
PU—4300 Flat Run Rd., Locust Grove (703)854-9890.
14 miles west of Fredericksburg. **Holes:** 18. **Par:** 72/72.
Yards: 7,005/4,541. **Course rating:** 73.2/65.2. **Slope:** 129/110.
Opened: 1993. **Pace of Play rating:** 4:40. **Green fee:** $24/34.
Credit cards: MC, V. **Reduced fees:** Low season, Twilight, Seniors.
Caddies: No. **Golf carts:** Included in Green Fee.
Discount golf packages: No. **Season:** Year-round. **High:** April-Sept.
On-site lodging: No. **Rental clubs:** Yes.
Walking policy: Walking at certain times. **Range:** Yes (grass).
To obtain tee times: Call at least one week in advance.
Subscriber comments: Lots of interesting holes . . . Good landscaping,
because owner operates a nursery . . . 841-yard par 6 . . . Has 19 holes . . .

Warm-up hole . . . First hole is practice, good idea . . . For those of us who will never get to play Pebble Beach, an overall great golfing experience . . . Too many gimmicks . . . Nice warm-up hole to begin round . . . Practice hole and par 6 just great . . . Island green like Sawgrass . . . Beautiful course kept in outstanding condition . . . Greens may be too tough for high handicapper . . . Too bad I don't live closer . . . Unique idea, practice hole to start . . . Interesting, but needs maturity.

★★½ MILL QUARTER PLANTATION GOLF COURSE

SP—1525 Mill Quarter Dr., Powhatan (804)598-4221.
22 miles west of Richmond. **Holes:** 18. **Par:** 72/72.
Yards: 6,970/5,280. **Course rating:** 73.2/N/A. **Slope:** 127/109.
Opened: 1973. **Pace of Play rating:** 4:00. **Green fee:** $8/25.
Credit cards: None. **Reduced fees:** Weekdays, Low season, Resort guests, Twilight, Seniors, Juniors.
Caddies: No. **Golf carts:** N/A.
Discount golf packages: Yes. **Season:** Year-round. **High:** April-Sept.
On-site lodging: No. **Rental clubs:** Yes.
Walking policy: Unrestricted walking. **Range:** Yes (grass).
To obtain tee times: Call one week in advance.
Subscriber comments: Course is a good challenge and fun to play . . . Average length, not difficult, good condition . . . Par-5 barn hole is a real standout . . . An oasis, good golf in middle of nowhere . . . Great fun, difficult, friendly, beautiful, something for all . . . Laid back, friendly atmosphere, fun course, it tests you but it doesn't kill you.

NEWPORT NEWS GOLF CLUB AT DEER RUN

PU—13564 Jefferson Ave., Newport News (804)886-7925.
30 miles west of Norfolk.
Opened: 1966. **Pace of Play rating:** 4:00. **Green fee:** $12/13.
Credit cards: MC, V. **Reduced fees:** Weekdays, Low season, Seniors, Juniors.
Caddies: No. **Golf carts:** $15 for 18 holes.
Discount golf packages: No. **Season:** Year-round. **High:** April-Nov.
On-site lodging: No. **Rental clubs:** Yes.
Walking policy: Walking at certain times. **Range:** Yes (grass).
To obtain tee times: Call seven days in advance for weekdays. Call Thursday beginning at 7 a.m. for weekends and holidays.

★★★ CARDINAL COURSE

Holes: 18. **Par:** 72/72.
Yards: 6,624/5,603. **Course rating:** 70.9/65.7. **Slope:** 118/98.
Subscriber comments: Nice course, new clubhouse gives country club atmosphere . . . Get there early and see the deer . . . Excellent shape year-round . . . Helpful and courteous staff, good maintenance . . . Excellent facilities . . . Hard to believe these two courses are operated by the city.

★★★ DEER RUN COURSE

Holes: 18. **Par:** 72/72.
Yards: 7,081/6,332. **Course rating:** 73.7/70.0. **Slope:** 133/113.
Opened: 1966. **Pace of Play rating:** 4:00.
Subscriber comments: Terrific, lots of wildlife, especially deer by the herd . . . Outstanding municipal course . . . Staff know their job and how to treat golfers in distress . . . Generous fairways . . . Challenging, long par 4s a struggle for the high handicapper, great value . . . Beautiful public course.

★ OCEAN VIEW GOLF COURSE

PU—9610 Norfolk Ave., Norfolk (804)480-2094.
Holes: 18. **Par:** 70/70.
Yards: 6,200/5,642. **Course rating:** 69.5/69.0. **Slope:** 117/116.
Opened: 1929. **Pace of Play rating:** 4:30. **Green fee:** $15.
Credit cards: MC, V. **Reduced fees:** Weekdays, Low season, Twilight, Seniors, Juniors.
Caddies: No. **Golf carts:** Included in Green Fee.
Discount golf packages: Yes. **Season:** Year-round. **High:** April-Oct.
On-site lodging: No. **Rental clubs:** Yes.

Walking policy: Walking at certain times. **Range:** No.
To obtain tee times: Call one week in advance.
Subscriber comments: Inexpensive, friendly staff . . . Affordable, lots of play . . . Municipal course . . . Old course, fairly short, good for beginners . . . Nice staff, tolerant with hackers . . . Typical muny. Needs work.

★★★½ OLDE MILL GOLF COURSE
R—Rte. 1, Box 84, Laurel Fork (703)398-2211.
80 miles southwest of Roanoke. **Holes:** 18. **Par:** 72/72.
Yards: 6,833/4,876. **Course rating:** 72.7/70.4. **Slope:** 127/134.
Opened: 1973. **Pace of Play rating:** 4:30. **Green fee:** $23/28.
Credit cards: MC, V. **Reduced fees:** Weekdays, Low season, Resort guests, Twilight.
Caddies: No. **Golf carts:** $12 for 18 holes.
Discount golf packages: Yes. **Season:** Year-round. **High:** April-Oct.
On-site lodging: Yes. **Rental clubs:** Yes.
Walking policy: Walking at certain times. **Range:** Yes (grass).
To obtain tee times: Call between 8 a.m. and 6 p.m. anytime.
Subscriber comments: Great getaway for men to be boys . . . A great mountain course . . . Excellent course, wonderful course . . . Very nice mountain golf, tough course . . . Interesting layout, well maintained, clear mountain air . . . Excellent holes, beautiful view and setting . . . Beautiful views, lots of water . . . Challenging with water on 13 of 18 holes . . . Splendid . . . Out of the way.

★ OLE MONTEREY GOLF CLUB
PU—1112 Tinker Creek Lane, Roanoke (703)563-0400.
Holes: 18. **Par:** 71/71.
Yards: 6,712/6,287. **Course rating:** N/A. **Slope:** 116/112.
Opened: N/A. **Pace of Play rating:** N/A. **Green fee:** N/A.
Credit cards: N/A. **Reduced fees:** Weekdays.
Caddies: No. **Golf carts:** N/A.
Discount golf packages: No. **Season:** Year-round. **High:** April-Oct.
On-site lodging: No. **Rental clubs:** No.
Walking policy: N/A. **Range:** No.
Subscriber comments: Good starter course . . . A mature course open and forgiving, on the upswing, it is being maintained better than in recent years . . . Needs lots of work, could be very good . . . Layout outstanding, but not developed.

★★½ PENDERBROOK GOLF CLUB
SP—3700 Golf Trail Lane, Fairfax (703)385-3700.
Holes: 18. **Par:** 71/72.
Yards: 6,152/5,042. **Course rating:** 71.2/69.1. **Slope:** 130/121.
Opened: 1980. **Pace of Play rating:** 4:30. **Green fee:** $27/35.
Credit cards: MC, V. **Reduced fees:** Weekdays, Low season, Seniors, Juniors.
Caddies: No. **Golf carts:** $13 for 18 holes.
Discount golf packages: No. **Season:** Year-round. **High:** March-Oct.
On-site lodging: No. **Rental clubs:** Yes.
Walking policy: Unrestricted walking. **Range:** No.
To obtain tee times: Call three days in advance starting at 8 a.m.
Subscriber comments: Tight, tough for occasional golfer . . . Better hit it straight, second shot into No. 12 toughest on planet . . . Some very tough water holes . . . Hilly and tight with some water . . . OK layout with new housing . . . Tight, hilly, houses too close to some fairways . . . Very demanding for seniors . . . No. 12 rates special mention, good tee shot leaves 179-yard carry over water . . . Friendly staff. Good mix of holes and water, woods, quality public golf . . . Leave driver at home . . . Location great. Easy access to D.C. Metro area . . . Long distances between some holes on back nine.

★★★ POHICK BAY REGIONAL GOLF COURSE

PU—10301 Gunston Rd., Lorton (703)339-8585.
15 miles of Washington, D.C. **Holes:** 18. **Par:** 72/72.
Yards: 6,405/5,897. **Course rating:** N/A. **Slope:** 131/126.
Opened: N/A. **Pace of Play rating:** N/A. **Green fee:** N/A.
Credit cards: MC, V. **Reduced fees:** Weekdays, Low season.
Caddies: No. **Golf carts:** N/A.
Discount golf packages: No. **Season:** Year-round. **High:** April-Nov.
On-site lodging: No. **Rental clubs:** No.
Walking policy: N/A. **Range:** Yes.
Subscriber comments: Very hilly course, tough to walk . . . Killer terrain
. . . Very tight, several greens need resloping, way too severe . . . Very nice
layout, wooded and hilly, a good challenge, not long but very tight . . .
Tough par 3s . . . Tricky. Greens sloped severely and hilly. Fun . . . Good
course for the mountain climbers . . . Bring your irons if you hook or slice
. . . Good design, has character. Well maintained . . . Toughest short
course you will ever play, target golf . . . Tight, great greens . . . Tough,
tree-lined, crowned fairways.

★★½ RED WING LAKE GOLF COURSE

PU—1080 Prosperity Rd., Virginia Beach (804)437-4845.
Holes: 18. **Par:** 72/72.
Yards: 7,080/5,285. **Course rating:** 73.7/68.1. **Slope:** 125/102.
Opened: 1971. **Pace of Play rating:** 4:30. **Green fee:** $20.
Credit cards: None. **Reduced fees:** Seniors, Juniors.
Caddies: No. **Golf carts:** $16 for 18 holes.
Discount golf packages: Yes. **Season:** Year-round. **High:** April-Oct.
On-site lodging: No. **Rental clubs:** Yes.
Walking policy: Unrestricted walking. **Range:** Yes (grass).
To obtain tee times: Call 24 hours in advance.
Subscriber comments: Wide-open, long, some real good holes . . .
Intermediate level golfers find a challenge, long and wide, heavily played,
slow on weekends, marginal restaurant, OK pro shop, outstanding
volunteer marshals, friendly pros . . . Good course, lots of water . . . Wide
open course, poor drainage on some holes . . . Nos. 9 and 18 reach out and
bite you . . . Good layout, maintenance is improving . . . Heavy play ruins
nice layout . . . High handicappers get breaks with wide open fairways . . .
Excellent par 5s on Nos. 9 and 18.

★★★ RESTON NATIONAL GOLF COURSE

PU—11875 Sunrise Valley Dr., Reston (703)620-9333.
25 miles west of Washington, D.C. **Holes:** 18. **Par:** 71/72.
Yards: 6,871/5,936. **Course rating:** 72.9/74.3. **Slope:** 126/132.
Opened: 1967. **Pace of Play rating:** 4:30. **Green fee:** $24/37.
Credit cards: MC, V, AMEX. **Reduced fees:** Weekdays, Low season,
Twilight, Seniors, Juniors.
Caddies: Yes. **Golf carts:** $13 for 18 holes.
Discount golf packages: Yes. **Season:** Year-round. **High:** April-Oct.
On-site lodging: Yes. **Rental clubs:** Yes.
Walking policy: Unrestricted walking. **Range:** Yes.
To obtain tee times: Call Monday at 8 a.m. for weekdays. Call
Wednesday at 8 a.m. for upcoming weekend.
Subscriber comments: Challenging, great condition, fast greens, good
par 4s . . . Beautiful course in great setting . . . Good golf for better than
average golfer . . . Overcrowded because it's best in area . . .
Improvements in conditioning would help rating . . . Great for any level.
Always in good condition . . . Classic layout without gimmicks, good, true
golf challenge . . . Quality, traditional layout . . . A shotmaker's dream,
every hole a delightful surprise.

★★½ RINGGOLD GOLF CLUB

PU—Rte. No.1 Box 1960, Ringgold (804)822-8728.
5 miles east of Danville. **Holes:** 18. **Par:** 72/72.
Yards: 6,588/4,816. **Course rating:** 72.3/64.2. **Slope:** 124/107.
Opened: 1976. **Pace of Play rating:** 4:30. **Green fee:** $16/18.

Credit cards: MC, V. **Reduced fees:** Weekdays, Low season, Seniors.
Caddies: No. **Golf carts:** $8 for 18 holes.
Discount golf packages: No. **Season:** Year-round. **High:** April-Sept.
On-site lodging: No. **Rental clubs:** Yes.
Walking policy: Unrestricted walking. **Range:** Yes.
To obtain tee times: Call after Wednesday for threesomes and foursomes. Less than three on Blue only.
Also has nine-hole, par-35 Blue Course.
Subscriber comments: Good public course . . . Well-designed course for every type player but fairways need more grass.

★★★ RIVER'S BEND GOLF AND COUNTRY CLUB

SP—11700 Hogans Alley, Chester (804)530-1000.
10 miles south of Richmond. **Holes:** 18. **Par:** 71/71.
Yards: 6,671/4,932. **Course rating:** 71.9/67.8. **Slope:** 132/117.
Opened: 1990. **Pace of Play rating:** 4:15. **Green fee:** $14/29.
Credit cards: MC, V. **Reduced fees:** Weekdays, Twilight, Seniors, Juniors.
Caddies: No. **Golf carts:** $12 for 18 holes.
Discount golf packages: No. **Season:** Year-round. **High:** April-Sept.
On-site lodging: No. **Rental clubs:** Yes.
Walking policy: Walking at certain times. **Range:** Yes (grass).
To obtain tee times: Call one week in advance.
Subscriber comments: Up and down, many blind shots . . . Fantastic, two of best par 4s, Nos. 2 and 18, ever played . . . Tee it up from the back on 18 . . . Has some very unique holes . . . Bobby Wadkins' home course . . . Lots of woods and water, so bring many balls . . . Fairly new, along the James River, great scenery, check out No. 17, 100 yards straight uphill . . . Excellent vistas on finishing holes . . . Some borderline goofy holes . . . Great tee box on No. 18, view of James River . . . Don't play it on windy day if keeping score.

★★★ ROYAL VIRGINIA GOLF CLUB

PU—3181 Dukes Rd., Hadensville (804)457-2041.
31 miles southeast of Charlottesville. **Holes:** 18. **Par:** 72/N/A.
Yards: 7,106/N/A. **Course rating:** 73.4/N/A. **Slope:** 131/N/A.
Opened: 1993. **Pace of Play rating:** 4:30. **Green fee:** $15/24.
Credit cards: MC, V. **Reduced fees:** Weekdays, Low season, Twilight, Seniors.
Caddies: No. **Golf carts:** $12 for 18 holes.
Discount golf packages: No. **Season:** Year-round. **High:** Dec.-Feb.
On-site lodging: No. **Rental clubs:** No.
Walking policy: Walking at certain times. **Range:** No.
To obtain tee times: Call seven days in advance.
Subscriber comments: Long and tight, good pace of play, made for tight hitters . . . Long course, challenging, quick greens . . . Too long for average golfer, wide-open, needs maturing . . . Best public course value, a good secret, publicity will ruin it . . . Great new public course, difficult, nice layout . . . New course cut out of woods, very nice once it matures.

★★★ SHENANDOAH CROSSING RESORT AND COUNTRY CLUB

R—Rt. 2, Box 416, Gordonsville (703)832-9543, (800)467-0592.
30 miles west of Charlottesville. **Holes:** 18. **Par:** 72/72.
Yards: 6,192/4,713. **Course rating:** 69.8/66.5. **Slope:** 119/111.
Opened: 1991. **Pace of Play rating:** 4:19. **Green fee:** $28/38.
Credit cards: All major. **Reduced fees:** Weekdays, Low season, Twilight, Seniors, Juniors.
Caddies: No. **Golf carts:** Included in Green Fee.
Discount golf packages: Yes. **Season:** Year-round. **High:** May-Sept.
On-site lodging: Yes. **Rental clubs:** Yes.
Walking policy: Walking at certain times. **Range:** Yes (grass).
To obtain tee times: Call 5 days in advance.
Subscriber comments: Little-known, nice greens, short interesting

hideaway . . . Nice resort course, worth staying over for the night . . . Not very long but accuracy is extremely important. Beautiful course, rolling greens . . . New course but a joy to play . . . No water holes . . . My favorite course, great condition, follows natural terrain . . . Way off the beaten track but worth the ride . . . Hidden gem! . . . Enjoyable woods course . . . Short and fun, each hole well defined, quiet and peaceful golf.

★★★½ SHENANDOAH VALLEY GOLF CLUB

SP—Rte. 2 Box 1240, Front Royal (703)636-4653.
15 miles south of Winchester. **Holes:** 27. **Par:** 71/71/72.
Yards: 6,121/6,330/6,399. **Course rating:** 69.0/70.2/70.0.
Slope: 115/117/116.
Opened: 1960. **Pace of Play rating:** 4:30. **Green fee:** $12/45.
Credit cards: All major. **Reduced fees:** Weekdays, Low season, Twilight.
Caddies: No. **Golf carts:** Included in Green Fee.
Discount golf packages: Yes. **Season:** Year-round. **High:** March-Oct.
On-site lodging: Yes. **Rental clubs:** Yes.
Walking policy: Unrestrictd walking. **Range:** Yes (grass).
To obtain tee times: Weekly tee sheets come out Monday morning.
Subscriber comments: If you want to play golf all day long, go here . . . Very scenic in fall . . . Blue Nine is most challenging, Blue Nos. 3, 4, and 5 is the "devil's triangle." You can't escape with three pars . . . 27 beautiful holes . . . Short but challenging, usually in good shape . . . Relatively short layout, isn't too difficult, perfect for the golfer who's at the office too much . . . 27 holes of fun . . . Red Nine is the easiest . . . Excellent 27 holes. Always immaculate. Great staff. No bad surprises . . . Very, very pretty views . . . Three lovely nines, short, always treated well . . . Left with a good feeling . . . A favorite, must play in spring or fall . . . Well worth the drive from D.C., gorgeous location.

THE SHENVALEE
★★½ CREEK/MILLER/OLDE

R—P.O. Box 930, New Market (703)740-9930.
95 miles west of Washington, D.C. **Holes:** 27. **Par:** 71/71/71.
Yards: 6,595/6,297/6,358. **Course rating:** 71.1/70.1/70.1.
Slope: 120/119/117.
Opened: 1924. **Pace of Play rating:** 4:00. **Green fee:** $18/20.
Credit cards: MC, V. **Reduced fees:** Low season, Resort guests, Twilight.
Caddies: No. **Golf carts:** $10 for 18 holes.
Discount golf packages: Yes. **Season:** Year-round. **High:** April-Oct.
On-site lodging: Yes. **Rental clubs:** Yes.
Walking policy: Walking at certain times. **Range:** Yes (grass).
To obtain tee times: Call pro shop.
Subscriber comments: Great view of mountains . . . Great view on No. 12 . . . Sporty layout. Very scenic. New nine added. New holes blend in well . . . Old 18 holes very short, new nine holes better designed . . . Great for women, short, friendly staff . . . Short course, good for ego . . . Interesting old course, low key, reasonable, good food.

SKYLAND LAKES GOLF COURSE★

PU—Rte. 1, Fancy Gap (703)728-4923.
Call club for further information.
Subscriber comments: Course is tight but fun to play . . . Improved . . . Short, easier track, uncrowded usually.

★★★ SLEEPY HOLE GOLF COURSE

PU—4700 Sleepy Hole Rd., Suffolk (804)538-4100.
12 miles southwest of Norfolk. **Holes:** 18. **Par:** 71/72.
Yards: 6,695/5,121. **Course rating:** 71.7/64.8. **Slope:** 122/108.
Opened: 1972. **Pace of Play rating:** 2:00. **Green fee:** $9/16.
Credit cards: None. **Reduced fees:** Weekdays, Seniors, Juniors.
Caddies: No. **Golf carts:** $11 for 18 holes.
Discount golf packages: No. **Season:** Year-round. **High:** April-Oct.

On-site lodging: No. **Rental clubs:** Yes.
Walking policy: Walking at certain times. **Range:** Yes (grass).
To obtain tee times: 24 hours in advance for mid-week times. 9 a.m.
Thursday for weekend and holiday times.
Subscriber comments: Front nine tight, back nine open . . . Short,
expensive . . . Good, fun course . . . This was and could be again, a very
beautiful place to golf . . . A great course . . . Good layout with good
variety, conditions need upgrading . . . Best bang for the buck, good
condition . . . Former LPGA Tour stop needs TLC to really shine . . . 18th
hole incredible approach shot . . . 18th hole is a gem . . . Great value,
couple of super holes, and you can walk.

★★½ SOUTH WALES GOLF COURSE

PU—18363 Golf Lane, Jeffersonton (703)451-1344.
30 miles north of Fredericksburg. **Holes:** 18. **Par:** 71/73.
Yards: 7,077/5,020. **Course rating:** 73.2/68.5. **Slope:** 123/104.
Opened: 1960. **Pace of Play rating:** 4:30. **Green fee:** $15/20.
Credit cards: MC, V, DISC. **Reduced fees:** Weekdays, Low season,
Twilight, Seniors.
Caddies: No. **Golf carts:** $22 for 18 holes.
Discount golf packages: No. **Season:** Year-round. **High:** April-Oct.
On-site lodging: No. **Rental clubs:** Yes.
Walking policy: Unrestricted walking. **Range:** Yes.
To obtain tee times: Call on Wednesday for upcoming weekend.
Subscriber comments: Good course, could be better kept. Good staff.
Good speed of play . . . Long par 5s, interesting layout, elevations, relaxing
atmosphere . . . Nice course needs work . . . Slowly getting better . . . Not
a single bad hole. Long and difficult . . . Good old layout showing neglect
. . . Great layout.

★★½ STONELEIGH GOLF CLUB

SP—35271 Prestwick Court, Round Hill (703)589-1402.
40 miles west of Washington, D.C. **Holes:** 18. **Par:** 72/71.
Yards: 6,903/5,014. **Course rating:** 73.4/69.8. **Slope:** 132/119.
Opened: 1992. **Pace of Play rating:** 4:30. **Green fee:** $45/55.
Credit cards: MC, V. **Reduced fees:** N/A.
Caddies: No. **Golf carts:** Included in Green Fee.
Discount golf packages: Yes. **Season:** Year-round. **High:** April-Oct.
On-site lodging: No. **Rental clubs:** Yes.
Walking policy: Walking at certain times. **Range:** Yes (grass).
To obtain tee times: Call golf shop.
Subscriber comments: Some silly holes, but an otherwise solid design
. . . Great course, great views, friendly staff, excellent facility . . . Enjoyed
the view from No. 2 green . . . Needs maturing but good layout . . . Hilly,
rugged, imaginative, Scottish layout, unique . . . Feels like Ireland. View
from No. 2 is heaven . . . Amusement park front nine. Too many unfair
holes . . . Fun course, some wild holes, need go play a few times . . . Good
mountain layout. Need to play it more than once. Very scenic . . . Course
too hilly, not fully grown in.

★★ STUMPY LAKE GOLF CLUB

PU—4797 E. Indian River Rd., Virginia Beach (804)467-6119.
Holes: 18. **Par:** 72/72.
Yards: 6,800/5,200. **Course rating:** 72.2/67.1. **Slope:** 119/97.
Opened: 1957. **Pace of Play rating:** 4:00. **Green fee:** $17.
Credit cards: All major. **Reduced fees:** Weekdays, Low season, Twilight,
Seniors, Juniors.
Caddies: No. **Golf carts:** $9 for 18 holes.
Discount golf packages: No. **Season:** Year-round. **High:** April-Oct.
On-site lodging: No. **Rental clubs:** Yes.
Walking policy: Walking at certain times. **Range:** Yes (grass).
To obtain tee times: First come, first serve.
Subscriber comments: Holds your interest, average condition . . . A few
water holes . . . Course is really improving, greens are much better . . .
Righties better know how to draw the ball, doglegs right-to-left galore . . .

Nice layout in the woods, beware of snakes and mosquitos . . . Wonderful Robert Trent Jones design . . . Fair test, public course facilities and maintenance.

★★★ SUFFOLK GOLF COURSE
PU—1227 Holland Rd., Suffolk (804)539-6298.
20 miles west of Suffolk. **Holes:** 18. **Par:** 72/72.
Yards: 6,340/5,561. **Course rating:** 70.3/71.1. **Slope:** 121/112.
Opened: 1950. **Pace of Play rating:** 4:00. **Green fee:** $11/12.
Credit cards: None. **Reduced fees:** Seniors, Juniors.
Caddies: No. **Golf carts:** $7 for 18 holes.
Discount golf packages: No. **Season:** Year-round. **High:** May-Sept.
On-site lodging: No. **Rental clubs:** Yes.
Walking policy: Walking at certain times. **Range:** Yes.
To obtain tee times: Weekdays, a week in advance. Weekends, 8 a.m. Wednesday.
Subscriber comments: Out-of-the-way public course in fine shape . . . Beautiful natural layout . . . Good course, great price . . . Has some tough holes, a challenge . . . Very strange back nine . . . Nice track, excellent value, interesting.

★ SUMMIT GOLF CLUB
PU—140 Country Club Dr., Cross Junction (703)888-4188.
Call club for further information.
Subscriber comments: Potential for good hilly course . . . Needs lot of work . . . Front nine hard, back nine fair . . . Out-of-the-way mountain course . . . Mountainous, tight, OK pace, needs better upkeep.

★★★ SYCAMORE CREEK GOLF COURSE
PU—1991 Manakin Rd., Manakin Sabot (804)784-3544.
15 miles east of Richmond. **Holes:** 18. **Par:** 70/70.
Yards: 6,256/5,149. **Course rating:** 69.7/64.6. **Slope:** 124/114.
Opened: 1992. **Pace of Play rating:** 4:00. **Green fee:** $29/36.
Credit cards: MC, V. **Reduced fees:** Weekdays, Low season, Twilight, Seniors, Juniors.
Caddies: No. **Golf carts:** Included in Green Fee.
Discount golf packages: No. **Season:** Year-round. **High:** April-Oct.
On-site lodging: No. **Rental clubs:** Yes.
Walking policy: Mandatory cart. **Range:** Yes (grass).
To obtain tee times: Call three days in advance. Wednesdays for weekends and holidays.
Subscriber comments: U.S. Open-like rough . . . Don't play the whites . . . Back nine makes the course . . . Very challenging new course will only get better . . . Beautiful greens. Very tight. Tough second hole . . . Very short and easy. A duck shoot for a good golfer but fun nonetheless. Green all year. Good staff . . . Excellent use of terrains. Well-planned layout. A bit short . . . Will be nice when it matures.

★★★★ THE TIDES INN
GOLDEN EAGLE GOLF COURSE
R—Golden Eagle Dr., Irvington (804)438-5501, (800)843-3746.
70 miles east of Richmond. **Holes:** 18. **Par:** 72/72.
Yards: 6,963/5,384. **Course rating:** 73.0/69.9. **Slope:** 130/121.
Opened: 1976. **Pace of Play rating:** 4:15-4:30 **Green fee:** $38/65.
Credit cards: MC, V, AMEX. **Reduced fees:** Weekdays, Low season, Resort guests.
Caddies: No. **Golf carts:** $15 for 18 holes.
Discount golf packages: Yes. **Season:** March-Dec. **High:** April-Oct.
On-site lodging: No. **Rental clubs:** Yes.
Walking policy: Unrestricted walking. **Range:** Yes (grass).
To obtain tee times: Please call pro shop. Hotel guests may reserve tee times as far in advance as they wish.
Subscriber comments: Great course and condition, first class fun . . . Long, tight and wet. Nos. 9 and 18 require long carry over water . . . A jewel to be played and replayed . . . I played 36 holes in one day, both rounds less than 3¼ hours! . . . The best way to play these two courses is

the Tartan in a.m. and Golden Eagle in p.m. That way you can start the day off in a good mood . . . Golden Eagle plays longer than card says. Neither is easy . . . Some really tough holes. Long carries over water . . . Beautiful layout and good test.

★★★½ TIDES LODGE RESORT AND COUNTRY CLUB
THE TARTAN COURSE

R—1 St. Andrews Lane, Irvington (804)438-6200, (800)248-4337.
65 miles east of Richmond. **Holes:** 18. **Par:** 72/72.
Yards: 6,586/5,121. **Course rating:** 71.5/69.2. **Slope:** 124/116.
Opened: 1959. **Pace of Play rating:** 3:30. **Green fee:** $25/53.
Credit cards: MC, V, AMEX. **Reduced fees:** Weekdays, Low season, Resort guests, Twilight.
Caddies: Yes. **Golf carts:** $15 for 18 holes.
Discount golf packages: Yes. **Season:** March-Dec. **High:** May-Oct.
On-site lodging: Yes. **Rental clubs:** Yes.
Walking policy: Unrestricted walking. **Range:** Yes (grass).
To obtain tee times: Call at least one week in advance to get desired time.
Subscriber comments: Less elegant than Golden Eagle but just as enjoyable . . . Fun, old Virginia atmosphere at this resort . . . Classic course, well-designed . . . Good course, well-maintained, leave your driver in your bag . . . Staff helpful, course in good shape in spring, good for beginners and up . . . Nice breather after Golden Eagle.

★★ TWIN LAKES GOLF COURSE

PU—6100 Clifton Rd., Clifton (703)631-9099.
20 miles west of Washington, D.C. **Holes:** 18. **Par:** 73/73.
Yards: 7,010/5,935. **Course rating:** 73.0/72.6. **Slope:** 121/118.
Opened: 1967. **Pace of Play rating:** 4:05. **Green fee:** $19/23.
Credit cards: MC, V. **Reduced fees:** Weekdays, Seniors, Juniors.
Caddies: No. **Golf carts:** $20 for 18 holes.
Discount golf packages: No. **Season:** Year-round. **High:** May-Sept.
On-site lodging: No. **Rental clubs:** Yes.
Walking policy: Unrestricted walking. **Range:** No.
To obtain tee times: Call (703)758-1800 for advance times, pro shop number for day of play/walk-on times (if available). Tee time strongly recommended.
Subscriber comments: Joe Sixpack and his three buddies are always in front of you . . . One of best municipal course I've played . . . Good confidence builder, wide-open . . . Wildlife galore, wide-open course, good for bad golfers . . . Well maintained considering the amount of play . . . Some challenging holes . . . Let 'er rip, open, long, my kind of course . . . Good water holes, little above average public course . . . Very nice public golf course, nice layout . . . Good, well-maintained county course. Very limited snack bar.

VIRGINIA OAKS GOLF AND COUNTRY CLUB★

PU—8101 Virginia Oaks Dr., Gainsville (703)551-2103.
25 miles west of Washington DC. **Holes:** 18. **Par:** 72/72.
Yards: 6,925/4,852. **Course rating:** 73.3/N/A. **Slope:** 133/N/A.
Opened: 1995. **Pace of Play rating:** 4:00. **Green fee:** $28/46.
Credit cards: MC, V, AMEX. **Reduced fees:** Twilight.
Caddies: No. **Golf carts:** $11 for 18 holes.
Discount golf packages: Yes. **Season:** Year-round. **High:** April-Oct.
On-site lodging: No. **Rental clubs:** Yes.
Walking policy: Walking at certain times. **Range:** Yes (grass).
To obtain tee times: Call seven days in advance.

WINTERGREEN RESORT

R—P.O. Box 706, Wintergreen (804)325-8240, (800)325-2200.
43 miles west of Charlottesville.
Green fee: $45/65.
Credit cards: MC, V, AMEX. **Reduced fees:** Weekdays, Low season, Resort guests.
Caddies: No. **Golf carts:** $16 for 18 holes.
Discount golf packages: Yes. **Season:** April-Nov. **High:** May-Oct.

On-site lodging: Yes. **Rental clubs:** Yes.
Walking policy: Mandatory cart. **Range:** Yes (grass).
To obtain tee times: Call pro shop up to 90 days in advance.

★★★★ DEVIL'S KNOB GOLF CLUB

Holes: 18. **Par:** 70/70.
Yards: 6,576/5,101. **Course rating:** 72.4/68.6. **Slope:** 126/118.
Opened: 1977. **Pace of Play rating:** 4:15.
Subscriber comments: Shotmaker's course. Extremely well suited for short accurate golfer, great views, wonderful staff . . . Fascinating when fog is on fairways . . . Nice layout in Blue Ridge Mountains, great tee sights . . . Beautiful setting, narrow mountain course . . . Great vistas in mountain setting . . . The funnest course around. Newton would be proud . . . Views of Shenandoah Valley from Devil's Knob must be seen . . . Wonderful mountain course, leave driver in trunk . . . Mountaintop course. Severe elevation changes . . . Devil's Knob shorter but more interesting . . . Narrow fairways, challenging, enjoyable.

★★★★ STONEY CREEK AT WINTERGREEN

Holes: 18. **Par:** 72/72.
Yards: 7,003/5,500. **Course rating:** 74.0/71.0. **Slope:** 132/125.
Opened: 1988. **Pace of Play rating:** 4:30.
Ranked 34th in America's 75 Best Resort Courses by Golf Digest. Selected as runner-up for Best New Resort Course of 1989 by Golf Digest. Ranked 6th in Virginia by Golf Digest.
Subscriber comments: Can ski and golf at same resort in same day! . . . Golf outstanding, a must play place in Virginia . . . Super course at foot of beautiful mountains . . . Great course. Long from back tees. Good service. Super summertime course. Good food . . . Best manicured golf course north of Augusta . . . Outstanding golf course, spectacular holes . . . Great compliment to Devil's Knob. Play 'em both . . . Rees Jones at his best, beautiful mountains.

★★★ WOLF CREEK GOLF & COUNTRY CLUB

SP—Rte. 1 Box 421, Bastian (703)688-4610.
120 miles west of Roanoke. **Holes:** 18. **Par:** 71/71.
Yards: 6,215/4,788. **Course rating:** 68.7/71.0. **Slope:** 107/128.
Opened: 1982. **Pace of Play rating:** 4:00. **Green fee:** $13/18.
Credit cards: None. **Reduced fees:** Weekdays, Low season, Resort guests, Twilight, Seniors, Juniors.
Caddies: No. **Golf carts:** $10 for 18 holes.
Discount golf packages: Yes. **Season:** Year-round. **High:** April-Oct.
On-site lodging: No. **Rental clubs:** Yes.
Walking policy: Walking at certain times. **Range:** No.
To obtain tee times: Call one week in advance for weekends; two days in advance for weekdays.
Subscriber comments: Good courses, good value . . . Beautiful scenery. Hilly, tough greens . . . Great course in the middle of nowhere . . . A short, sporty, challenging, scenic course with a good number of birdie holes for the above average golfer. Yet accuracy is a must off the tee. Plenty of hills, water and sand traps in a country atmosphere . . . Who'd have thought that one damn creek could cross six holes?

(FRUGAL PICK)

★★ WOODLANDS GOLF COURSE

PU—9 Woodland Rd., Hampton (804)727-1195.
Holes: 18. **Par:** 69/69.
Yards: 5,482/4,399. **Course rating:** 64.6/64.8. **Slope:** 99/100.
Opened: 1927. **Pace of Play rating:** 4:00. **Green fee:** $10/14.
Credit cards: MC, V. **Reduced fees:** Seniors, Juniors.
Caddies: No. **Golf carts:** $14 for 18 holes.
Discount golf packages: No. **Season:** Year-round. **High:** April-Sept.
On-site lodging: No. **Rental clubs:** Yes.
Walking policy: Unrestricted walking. **Range:** No.
To obtain tee times: Call pro shop 2½ days at noon, in advance of the day of play.
Subscriber comments: Lots of water for such a short course . . . Excellent for senior players, well-kept course . . . Terrific, unknown gem . . . Small quaint course . . . a good walking course.

★½ BEL MEADOW COUNTRY CLUB

SP—Rte. 1 Box 450, Mt. Clare (304)623-3701.
5 miles south of Clarksburg. **Holes:** 18. **Par:** 72/72.
Yards: 6,938/5,517. **Course rating:** 73.0/71.5. **Slope:** 126/122.
Opened: 1965. **Pace of Play rating:** 4:30. **Green fee:** N/A.
Credit cards: MC, V, DISC. **Reduced fees:** Weekdays, Low season,
Twilight, Seniors.
Caddies: No. **Golf carts:** $10 for 18 holes.
Discount golf packages: No. **Season:** Year-round. **High:** May-Aug.
On-site lodging: No. **Rental clubs:** Yes.
Walking policy: Unrestricted walking. **Range:** Yes (grass).
To obtain tee times: Call one week in advance during season (April-Oct.)
weekends only.
Subscriber comments: Very good layout. Has been in poor condition,
but improving last two years . . . Has potential to be a very good course
. . . Robert Trent Jones layout, strong holes, poor shape.

★½ BIG BEND GOLF CLUB

PU—Riverview Dr., Tornado (304)341-8023.
Call club for further information.
Subscriber comments: Layout is basic with room for errant shots,
playable by all . . . Fairways could be in better shape . . . Better course for
us moderate players . . . Nice layout.

★★★½ CACAPON STATE PARK RESORT GOLF COURSE

R—Rte. 1, Box 304, Berkeley Springs (304)258-1022, (800)225-5982
25 miles north of Winchester, Va. **Holes:** 18. **Par:** 72/72.
Yards: 6,940/5,510. **Course rating:** 72.4/72.1. **Slope:** 121/116.
Opened: 1974. **Pace of Play rating:** 4:30. **Green fee:** $19/22.
Credit cards: MC, V, AMEX. **Reduced fees:** Low season, Seniors.
Caddies: No. **Golf carts:** $19 for 18 holes.
Discount golf packages: Yes. **Season:** Year-round. **High:** April-Oct.
On-site lodging: Yes. **Rental clubs:** Yes.
Walking policy: Unrestricted walking. **Range:** Yes (grass).
To obtain tee times: Resort guests with lodging deposit ; all others one
week in advance.
Subscriber comments: Beautiful mountain setting, excellent greens . . . A
beautiful course in the fall . . . Deer sometimes hold up play . . . Mountain
masterpiece . . . Play in October when leaves are on fire . . . Easy front
nine. Hilly and more difficult back nine . . . Well maintained, much wildlife
seen . . . Bring bug spray . . . Excellent Robert Trent Jones course, located
in a state park, very severe.

(GREAT VALUE)

★★★ CANAAN VALLEY STATE PARK RESORT GOLF COURSE

R—Rte. 1, Box 330, Davis (304)866-4121x2632, (800)622-4121.
Holes: 18. **Par:** 72/72.
Yards: 6,982/5,820. **Course rating:** 73.4/71.8. **Slope:** 125/115.
Opened: 1968. **Pace of Play rating:** 4:30. **Green fee:** $24.
Credit cards: All major. **Reduced fees:** Seniors.
Caddies: No. **Golf carts:** $27 for 18 holes.
Discount golf packages: Yes. **Season:** April-Nov. **High:** June-Aug.
On-site lodging: Yes. **Rental clubs:** Yes.
Walking policy: Unrestricted walking. **Range:** Yes (grass).
To obtain tee times: Lodge guest can and should make tee times when
they make room reservations.
Subscriber comments: Value, aesthetics, condition, pace, people all
excellent . . . Beautiful park. Impossible to lose a ball . . . Bring a sweater
. . . Very open but very long all the way back from blues . . . Outstanding
state park course . . . Good conditions and great greens.

★★½ ESQUIRE COUNTRY CLUB

SP—Esquire Dr., Barboursville (304)736-1476.
Call club for further information.
Subscriber comments: A well-kept secret, "barn" clubhouse is very nice

. . . Houses crowd most fairways, otherwise high marks . . . Good layout.
Back tighter than front . . . Good from hole No. 14 on, others so-so . . .
Very long course, course is very well laid out.

★★★★ GLADE SPRINGS RESORT

R—3000 Lake Dr., Daniels (304)763-2050, (800)634-5233.
8 miles south of Beckley. **Holes:** 18. **Par:** 72/72.
Yards: 6,941/4,884. **Course rating:** 73.5/67.6. **Slope:** 135/118.
Opened: 1973. **Pace of Play rating:** 4:15. **Green fee:** $40/50.
Credit cards: MC, V, AMEX. **Reduced fees:** Weekdays, Low season,
Resort guests, Twilight, Juniors.
Caddies: No. **Golf carts:** Included in Green Fee.
Discount golf packages: Yes. **Season:** Year-round. **High:** May-Oct.
On-site lodging: Yes. **Rental clubs:** Yes.
Walking policy: Unrestricted walking. **Range:** Yes (grass).
To obtain tee times: Resort guests may make tee times with confirmed
room reservation. Public should call seven days in advance.
Ranked 5th in West Virginia by Golf Digest.
Subscriber comments: Excellent course, tough when windy . . . Good
golf, good getaway . . . Was very impressed all around . . . Beautiful and
tough, come ready to play . . . Wide open course, very long and tough
from back tees . . . Challenging, scenic, final three holes are great . . . Good
condition, improved greatly in last three years.

GOLF CLUB OF WEST VIRGINIA★

PU—Box 199, Rte. 1, Waverly (304)464-4420.
10 miles northeast of Parkersburg. **Holes:** 18. **Par:** 70/71.
Yards: 6,018/5,011. **Course rating:** 68.9/67.9. **Slope:** 116/109.
Opened: 1950. **Pace of Play rating:** 4:00. **Green fee:** $20/25.
Credit cards: MC, V, DISC. **Reduced fees:** Juniors.
Caddies: No. **Golf carts:** N/A.
Discount golf packages: Yes. **Season:** Year-round. **High:** April-Sept.
On-site lodging: No. **Rental clubs:** Yes.
Walking policy: Unrestricted walking. **Range:** No.
To obtain tee times: Call anytime.
Subscriber comments: Heavy play. Easy scoring course . . . Excellent
staff.

★★★ GRANDVIEW COUNTRY CLUB

(FRUGAL PICK)

SP—440 Scottridge Dr., Beaver (304)763-2520.
Call club for further information.
Subscriber comments: Nice course, some scenic holes . . . Wide open,
greens are humpbacked . . . Exceptional mountain views . . . Well designed
and very good scenery . . . A real bargain, good layout and conditions.

THE GREENBRIER

R—White Sulphur Spr. (304)536-7851, (800)624-6070.
250 miles southhwest of Washington, D.C.
Green fee: $42/85.
Credit cards: MC, V, AMEX. **Reduced fees:** Low season.
Caddies: Yes. **Golf carts:** $34 for 18 holes.
Discount golf packages: Yes. **Season:** March-Nov. **High:** April-Oct.
On-site lodging: Yes. **Rental clubs:** Yes.
Walking policy: Mandatory cart. **Range:** Yes (grass).
To obtain tee times: Call two weeks in advance. Reservations requested.

★★★★½ GREENBRIER COURSE

Holes: 18. **Par:** 72/72.
Yards: 6,681/5,280. **Course rating:** 73.7/71.5. **Slope:** 136/123.
Opened: 1925. **Pace of Play rating:** 4:30.
Ranked 33rd in America's 75 Best Resort Courses by Golf Digest. Ranked
1st in West Virginia by Golf Digest.
Subscriber comments: A super place, the course and people capture you
. . . Absolutely wonderful layout . . . Tough course, great condition and
views, No. 6 tough . . . Seniors won't score well but who cares, it's
beautiful. Outstanding in all respects . . . Old World grand treatment . . .
Ryder Cup and Solheim Cup, need I say more? . . . Great Nicklaus course.

★★★½ LAKESIDE COURSE
Holes: 18. **Par:** 70/70.
Yards: 6,336/5,175. **Course rating:** 70.4/69.9. **Slope:** 121/115.
Opened: 1963. **Pace of Play rating:** 4:00.
Subscriber comments: An enjoyable outing, in good shape, super first hole . . . Tougher course than it looks . . . Interesting layout, outstanding maintenance . . . Fine course, enjoyable and interesting . . . Easy course, ideal for slicers.

★★★★ OLD WHITE COURSE
Holes: 18. **Par:** 70/70.
Yards: 6,640/5,658. **Course rating:** 72.7/73.7. **Slope:** 128/126.
Opened: 1913. **Pace of Play rating:** 4:00.
Ranked 3rd in West Virginia by Golf Digest.
Subscriber comments: Definitely a "must play" if you like a traditional design, well-suited for all levels of play . . . Most holes relatively easy from tee to green, but the greens are as tough as any I've played . . . Stay below hole on greens! . . . Plush, outstanding course maintenance . . . Staff makes you feel like Sam Snead . . . A traditional course that's fun to play . . . Old C.B. Macdonald design . . . A great traditional course, outstanding conditions.

GREENBRIER VALLEY COUNTRY CLUB★
SP—Rte. 219 North, Lewisburg (304)645-3660.
Call club for further information.

★★★ GREENHILLS COUNTRY CLUB
SP—Rte. 56, Ravenswood (304)273-3396.

FRUGAL PICK

38 miles north of Charleston. **Holes:** 18. **Par:** 72/74.
Yards: 6,056/5,018. **Course rating:** 68.6/69.0. **Slope:** 119/108.
Opened: 1960. **Pace of Play rating:** 4:00. **Green fee:** $11/16.
Credit cards: MC, V, DISC. **Reduced fees:** Weekdays, Low season, Resort guests.
Caddies: No. **Golf carts:** $9 for 18 holes.
Discount golf packages: Yes. **Season:** Year-round. **High:** April-Oct.
On-site lodging: Yes. **Rental clubs:** No.
Walking policy: Unrestricted walking. **Range:** Yes (grass).
To obtain tee times: Call.
Subscriber comments: Public course with exceptional greens and fairways . . . Very good condition . . . Lots of variety . . . A lot of elevated greens, blind shots, back nine hilly . . . Fast greens, lots of sand.

★★★★ HAWTHORNE VALLEY GOLF COURSE
R—10 Snowshoe Dr., Snowshoe (304)572-1000.
20 miles north of Marlinton. **Holes:** 18. **Par:** 72/72.
Yards: 7,045/4,363. **Course rating:** 72.1/64.3. **Slope:** 130/103.
Opened: 1994. **Pace of Play rating:** 5:00. **Green fee:** $43/58.
Credit cards: MC, V, AMEX. **Reduced fees:** Weekdays, Low season, Resort guests.
Caddies: No. **Golf carts:** Included in Green Fee.
Discount golf packages: Yes. **Season:** May-Nov. **High:** July-Sept.
On-site lodging: Yes. **Rental clubs:** Yes.
Walking policy: Mandatory cart. **Range:** Yes (grass).
To obtain tee times: Call.
Ranked 2nd in West Virginia by Golf Digest.
Subscriber comments: Maybe the nicest I've ever played. Cut from mountainside . . . Excellent new course, scenery second to none, great course, great employees . . . Very hilly, take plenty of balls . . . A Gary Player masterpiece, would be trouble for high handicapper . . . Greens hard, must hit it straight or you will never find ball . . . Thank you, Gary Player!

★½ HIGHLAND SPRINGS GOLF COURSE
PU—1600 Washington Pike, Wellsburg (304)737-2201.
Call club for further information.
Subscriber comments: Super staff, nice challenging course . . . Very

forgiving for average golfers with several tests for the good golfer . . . Five holes in Pennsylvania, 13 holes in West Virginia . . . Poor conditions, no great holes . . . Wide open, grip it and rip it.

LAKEVIEW RESORT & CONFERENCE CENTER

R—Rte. 6 Box 88A, Morgantown (304)594-2011, (800)624-8300.
60 miles south of Pittsburgh.
Pace of Play rating: 4:30. **Green fee:** $20/35.
Credit cards: All major. **Reduced fees:** Weekdays, Low season, Resort guests, Juniors.
Caddies: No. **Golf carts:** $14 for 18 holes.
Discount golf packages: Yes. **Season:** Year-round. **High:** June-Sept.
On-site lodging: Yes. **Rental clubs:** Yes.
Walking policy: Mandatory cart. **Range:** Yes (grass).
To obtain tee times: Hotel guests may call up to 14 days in advance. Call 10 days in advance if not staying at the hotel.

★★★½ LAKEVIEW COURSE

Holes: 18. **Par:** 72/72.
Yards: 6,800/5,432. **Course rating:** 72.8/71.8. **Slope:** 130/118.
Opened: 1953.
Ranked 4th in West Virginia by Golf Digest.
Subscriber comments: Woods and beautiful views, always great shape . . . Very challenging, excellent staff, first-class resort . . . The view of Cheat Lake is spectacular . . . Next to Greenbrier, West Virginia's best course. Incredible wooded layout . . . Good test . . . Super tough . . . Extremely, challenging, well manicured, No. 18 is a real gem . . . Jack may have made it in two on 18 but you won't.

★★½ MOUNTAINVIEW COURSE

Holes: 18. **Par:** 72/72.
Yards: 6,447/5,242. **Course rating:** 70.7/69.4. **Slope:** 119/122.
Opened: 1984.
Subscriber comments: Good sister to Lakeview . . . Challenging and fun . . . Short but hilly . . . Nos. 9 and 18 very hilly . . . Hilly, blind holes, fast greens . . . Very tight, lots of O.B., hilly, shotmaker's course, leave driver in bag.

★★½ LAVELETTE GOLF CLUB

PU—Lynn Oak Dr., Lavalette (304)525-7405.
5 miles south of Huntington. **Holes:** 18. **Par:** 71/71.
Yards: 6,262/5,257. **Course rating:** 69.5/72.6. **Slope:** 118/120.
Opened: 1991. **Pace of Play rating:** 4:30. **Green fee:** $12/15.
Credit cards: MC, V, DISC. **Reduced fees:** N/A.
Caddies: No. **Golf carts:** $9 for 18 holes.
Discount golf packages: No. **Season:** Year-round. **High:** May-Sept.
On-site lodging: No. **Rental clubs:** Yes.
Walking policy: Unrestricted walking. **Range:** Yes (grass).
To obtain tee times: Call one week in advance.
Subscriber comments: Young course . . . Nice 700-yard, par-6 hole . . . Fair but tough . . . Different layout with a mix of flat and hilly terrain . . . Every golfer should play once . . . Different from anything you ever played . . . Nice clubhouse and staff, pretty scenery, little gimmicky with par 6 and a double green . . . Needs some time to mature.

LEWISBURG ELKS COUNTRY CLUB★

PU—Rte. 219 N., Lewisburg (304)645-3660.
70 miles south of Roanoke. **Holes:** 18. **Par:** 70/70.
Yards: 5,609/4,373. **Course rating:** 65.0/65.5. **Slope:** 108/110.
Opened: 1940. **Pace of Play rating:** 4:00. **Green fee:** $14/17.
Credit cards: MC, V. **Reduced fees:** Weekdays, Low season.
Caddies: No. **Golf carts:** $9 for 18 holes.
Discount golf packages: Yes. **Season:** Year-round. **High:** April-Nov.
On-site lodging: No. **Rental clubs:** Yes.
Walking policy: Unrestricted walking. **Range:** No.
To obtain tee times: Call.
Subscriber comments: Short but challenging course . . . Great staff . . . Needs some maintenance.

★★★½ LOCUST HILL GOLF COURSE

SP—1 St. Andrews Dr., Charles Town (304)728-7300.
60 miles west of Washington, D.C. **Holes:** 18. **Par:** 72/72.
Yards: 7,005/5,112. **Course rating:** 73.5/72.0. **Slope:** 128/120.
Opened: 1991. **Pace of Play rating:** 4:00–4:30. **Green fee:** $16/22.
Credit cards: MC, V. **Reduced fees:** Weekdays, Low season, Twilight.
Caddies: No. **Golf carts:** $10 for 18 holes.
Discount golf packages: Yes. **Season:** Year-round. **High:** May–Oct.
On-site lodging: No. **Rental clubs:** Yes.
Walking policy: Walking at certain times. **Range:** Yes (grass).
To obtain tee times: Call Wednesday after 11 a.m. for weekend tee times.
Weekday times can be made seven days in advance.
Subscriber comments: Great layout, needs clubhouse . . . Great country
setting . . . Pleasant surprise . . . Lots of water and great finishing hole . . .
Down-to-earth fun golf course, you never get tired out playing this course
. . . Good course, good value . . . Good condition and staff . . . A real gem,
fine condition and a challenging layout . . . Hidden jewel . . . Super practice
area . . . Easy front, challenging back . . . Long from the tips.

MEADOW PONDS GOLF COURSE★

PU—Rte. 7 West, Cassville (304)328-5570.
60 miles south of Pittsburgh. **Holes:** 18. **Par:** 69/69.
Yards: 5,328/5,026. **Course rating:** 64.9/63.9. **Slope:** 102/100.
Opened: 1963. **Pace of Play rating:** N/A. **Green fee:** $10/12.
Credit cards: All major. **Reduced fees:** Weekdays.
Caddies: No. **Golf carts:** N/A.
Discount golf packages: No. **Season:** Year-round.
On-site lodging: No. **Rental clubs:** Yes.
Walking policy: Unrestricted walking. **Range:** Yes (grass).
To obtain tee times: Call Mondays.
Subscriber comments: Hilly in spots. Some gullies to shoot over, many
sidehill holes with greens on top of ridges . . . Very hilly, short course . . .
Very short, three clubs and putter course, poor shape.

OGLEBAY PARK

PU—Oglebay Park, Rte. 88N., Wheeling (304)243-4050, (800)624-6988.
55 miles south of Pittsburgh.
Opened: 1971. **Pace of Play rating:** 4:00–4:30. **Green fee:** $31/36.
Credit cards: All major. **Reduced fees:** Weekdays, Resort guests.
Caddies: Yes. **Golf carts:** $12 for 18 holes.
Discount golf packages: Yes. **Season:** March–Nov. **High:** May–Aug.
On-site lodging: Yes. **Rental clubs:** Yes.
Walking policy: Unrestricted walking. **Range:** No.
To obtain tee times: Call up to 60 days in advance. Guest at resort may
call up to one year with reservation.

★½ CRISPIN COURSE

Holes: 18. **Par:** 71/71.
Yards: 5,670/5,100. **Course rating:** 66.6/68.4. **Slope:** 103/108.
Subscriber comments: A good hilly test for all levels . . . Friendly, fun to
play, something for all . . . Not for the serious golfer.

★★★½ SPEIDEL COURSE

Holes: 18. **Par:** 71/71.
Yards: 7,000/5,515. **Course rating:** 72.7/72.0. **Slope:** 126/120.
Subscriber comments: A tough course in design and play, a great
challenge . . . Lush and long, very hilly . . . Public golf at its best, many
difficult par 4s . . . Excellent course from back tees, lots of hills . . . Former
LPGA Tour course . . . Beautiful mountain course, don't walk it! . . .
Course beats you to death.

★★★ PIPESTEM GOLF CLUB

PU—Pipestem State Park, Pipestem (304)466-1800.
Holes: 18. **Par:** 72/72.
Yards: 6,884/5,623. **Course rating:** 73.1/71.3. **Slope:** 129/117.
Opened: 1970. **Pace of Play rating:** 4:00–4:30 **Green fee:** $17/22.
Credit cards: MC, V, AMEX. **Reduced fees:** Weekdays, Low season,
Seniors.

Caddies: No. **Golf carts:** $10 for 18 holes.
Discount golf packages: Yes. **Season:** Year-round. **High:** May-Sept.
On-site lodging: Yes. **Rental clubs:** Yes.
Walking policy: Unrestricted walking. **Range:** Yes (grass).
To obtain tee times: Guests may make tee times at time of room
reservation otherwise call one week in advance.
Also has nine-hole, par-3 course
Subscriber comments: Excellent course in beautiful location . . .
Excellent driving range . . . Good layout, but little room for error off the
tee on a few holes . . . First-class par-3 course also . . . One of West
Virginia's beauties . . . All golfers will enjoy the beautiful scenery and
wildlife.

RIVERSIDE GOLF CLUB★
PU—Rte. 1, Mason (304)773-5354, (800)261-3031.
60 miles northwest of Charleston. **Holes:** 18. **Par:** 70/72.
Yards: 6,198/4,842. **Course rating:** 69.2/72.0. **Slope:** 118/117.
Opened: 1975. **Pace of Play rating:** 4:30. **Green fee:** $12/14.
Credit cards: MC, V. **Reduced fees:** Weekdays.
Caddies: No. **Golf carts:** $8 for 18 holes.
Discount golf packages: No. **Season:** Year-round. **High:** April-Sept.
On-site lodging: No. **Rental clubs:** Yes.
Walking policy: Unrestricted walking. **Range:** No.
To obtain tee times: Call.
Subscriber comments: Deceiving in degree of difficulty . . . Flat but you
must play smart on doglegs . . . Nice layout.

★★ SANDY BRAE GOLF COURSE
PU—19 Osborne Mills Rd., Clendenin (304)965-7700.
Holes: 18. **Par:** 69/74.
Yards: 5,648/5,312. **Course rating:** N/A. **Slope:** N/A.
Opened: 1965. **Pace of Play rating:** 5:00. **Green fee:** $11/14.
Credit cards: MC, V. **Reduced fees:** Weekdays, Low season, Twilight,
Seniors.
Caddies: No. **Golf carts:** $8 for 18 holes.
Discount golf packages: No. **Season:** Year-round. **High:** April-Oct.
On-site lodging: No. **Rental clubs:** Yes.
Walking policy: Unrestricted walking. **Range:** No.
To obtain tee times: Call seven days in advance.
Subscriber comments: Much improved, good greens, well maintained
. . . Lots of elevated tee shots . . . Good scenery . . . Hilly, lot of fun.

★★½ SCARLET OAKS COUNTRY CLUB
SP—1 Dairy Rd., Poca (304)755-8079.
15 miles northwest of Charleston. **Holes:** 18. **Par:** 72/72.
Yards: 6,700/5,036. **Course rating:** 72.3/69.3. **Slope:** 129/109.
Opened: 1980. **Pace of Play rating:** 4:30. **Green fee:** $27/30.
Credit cards: MC, V, AMEX. **Reduced fees:** No.
Caddies: No. **Golf carts:** Included in Green Fee.
Discount golf packages: No. **Season:** March-Dec. **High:** June-July.
On-site lodging: No. **Rental clubs:** Yes.
Walking policy: Mandatory cart. **Range:** Yes (grass).
To obtain tee times: Call seven days in advance.
Subscriber comments: Layout is fair at best . . . Good layout, but some
holes have too narrow a landing area to use driver . . . Better suited to
accurate hitter . . . Tight with some tough finishing holes.

★ SLEEPY HOLLOW GOLF & COUNTRY CLUB
SP—Golf Course Rd., Charles Town (304)725-5210.
Holes: 18. **Par:** 72/72.
Yards: 6,600/5,766. **Course rating:** 70.0/72.3. **Slope:** 112/104.
Opened: 1962. **Pace of Play rating:** 4:00. **Green fee:** $10/17.
Credit cards: None. **Reduced fees:** Weekdays, Low season, Twilight,
Seniors.
Caddies: No. **Golf carts:** $10 for 18 holes.

Discount golf packages: No. **Season:** Year-round. **High:** May-Aug.
On-site lodging: No. **Rental clubs:** Yes.
Walking policy: Unrestricted walking. **Range:** Yes (grass).
To obtain tee times: Call anytime.

Subscriber comments: Just someplace to play . . . Aptly named, sleepy
and laid back . . . Course maintenance needs improvement . . . Fair for all,
excellent finishing hole.

SOUTH HILLS GOLF CLUB★
PU—1253 Gihon Rd., Parkersburg (304)422-8381.
70 miles north of Charleston. **Holes:** 18. **Par:** 71/71.
Yards: 6,467/4,842. **Course rating:** 71.2/70.3. **Slope:** 129/115.
Opened: 1953. **Pace of Play rating:** 4:15. **Green fee:** $13/15.
Credit cards: MC, V, DISC. **Reduced fees:** Low season, Seniors.
Caddies: No. **Golf carts:** $9 for 18 holes.
Discount golf packages: Yes. **Season:** Year-round. **High:** May-Sept.
On-site lodging: No. **Rental clubs:** Yes.
Walking policy: Unrestricted walking. **Range:** Yes (grass).
To obtain tee times: Call.
Formerly known as Willow Brook Golf Course.

STONEBRIDGE GOLF CLUB★
SP—Burke St. Ext., Rte. 5, Martinsburg (304)263-4653, (800)225-5982.
60 miles west of Washington, D.C. **Holes:** 18. **Par:** 71/72.
Yards: 6,161/4,996. **Course rating:** 69.7/67.9. **Slope:** 119/108.
Opened: 1922. **Pace of Play rating:** 3:30-4:00. **Green fee:** $10/22.
Credit cards: MC, V. **Reduced fees:** Weekdays, Low season, Resort
guests, Twilight.
Caddies: No. **Golf carts:** $10 for 18 holes.
Discount golf packages: Yes. **Season:** March-Dec. **High:** May-Sept.
On-site lodging: No. **Rental clubs:** Yes.
Walking policy: Walking at certain times. **Range:** Yes (grass).
To obtain tee times: Call one week in advance.

★★½ SUGARWOOD GOLF AND COUNTRY CLUB
PU—Sugarwood Rd., Lavalette (304)523-6500.
Call club for further information.
Subscriber comments: Has an alcohol-free clubhouse . . . Layout is basic
with a couple of interesting holes on back nine . . . Playable by all . . . New
holes on front nine, good back side . . . Lots of par 3s, and lots of water.

★★ TWIN FALLS STATE PARK GOLF COURSE
PU—P.O. Box 1023, Mullens (304)294-4044, (800)225-5982.
28 miles southwest of Beckley. **Holes:** 18. **Par:** 71/71.
Yards: 6,382/5,202. **Course rating:** 70.1/69.5. **Slope:** 122/112.
Opened: 1968. **Pace of Play rating:** 4:00. **Green fee:** $19/23.
Credit cards: MC, V, AMEX. **Reduced fees:** Weekdays, Low season,
Seniors.
Caddies: No. **Golf carts:** N/A.
Discount golf packages: Yes. **Season:** Year-round. **High:** June-Oct.
On-site lodging: Yes. **Rental clubs:** Yes.
Walking policy: Unrestricted walking. **Range:** No.
To obtain tee times: Call.
Subscriber comments: Back nine tight. Potentially dangerous . . . Tight
fairways, shotmaker's course . . . Too many gimmicky holes.

★★★ TYGART LAKE COUNTRY CLUB
SP—Rte.1 Knottsville Rd., Grafton (304)265-3100.
Call club for further information.
Subscriber comments: Good for average player . . . Tough par 3s . . .
Good for all handicaps . . . Fun, use all clubs in bag.

VALLEY VIEW GOLF COURSE★
PU—Rte. No.220, Moorefield (304)538-6564.
Call club for further information.
Subscriber comments: Easy, "let her rip" course . . . Nice little course in the country . . . Really fun course, nice people, condition very good.

★★★½ WOODRIDGE PLANTATION GC
PU—301 Woodridge Dr., Mineral Wells (304)489-1800.
Call club for further information.
Subscriber comments: A young course with character . . . Will be a fantastic place to play . . . Good layout but needs to mature . . . Short, greens excellent.

THE WOODS RESORT
★★★ MOUNTAIN VIEW GOLF COURSE
R—Mtn. Lake Rd., Hedgesville (304)754-7222.
90 miles west of Washington D.C. **Holes:** 18. **Par:** 72/71.
Yards: 6,608/4,900. **Course rating:** 72.2/68.5. **Slope:** 121/107.
Opened: 1989. **Pace of Play rating:** 4:15. **Green fee:** $20/25.
Credit cards: MC, V, AMEX. **Reduced fees:** Weekdays, Low season, Twilight, Seniors, Juniors.
Caddies: No. **Golf carts:** $11 for 18 holes.
Discount golf packages: Yes. **Season:** Year-round. **High:** April-Sept.
On-site lodging: Yes. **Rental clubs:** Yes.
Walking policy: Walking at certain times. **Range:** Yes (grass).
To obtain tee times: Call five days in advance.
Also had nine-hole Stony Lick Course
Subscriber comments: Great mix of holes . . . A nice course to play 27 holes . . . 27 holes and newest nine not very good yet . . . Fascinating layout, great use of mountain terrain . . . Great view, front nine great . . . Love it, got my first hole-in-one on old No. 12 . . . Makes me want to buy a retirement home and I'm only 35 . . . Has character . . . Well maintained . . . In a beautiful setting . . . Fun layout, great par 3s . . . Challenging 27 holes . . . Peaceful resort course in a nice setting.

Notes

★½ BELMONT GOLF & COUNTRY CLUB

R—P.O. Box WK 251, Warwick (809)236-6400.

5 miles west of Hamilton. **Holes:** 18. **Par:** 70/72.

Yards: 5,800/4,900. **Course rating:** 68.6/67.7. **Slope:** 128/116.

Opened: 1928. **Pace of Play rating:** 4:00. **Green fee:** $75.

Credit cards: MC, V, AMEX. **Reduced fees:** Twilight, Juniors.

Caddies: No. **Golf carts:** Included in Green Fee.

Discount golf packages: No. **Season:** Year-round. **High:** Oct.-May.

On-site lodging: Yes. **Rental clubs:** Yes.

Walking policy: Walking at certain times. **Range:** No.

To obtain tee times: Call 48 hours in advance. Hotel guests may call two months in advance.

Subscriber comments: Tight course, enjoyed their greens . . . Beautiful views; lots of blind shots . . . Like stepping back in time, neat old course.

★★★½ CASTLE HARBOUR GOLF CLUB

R—6 Paynters Rd., Hamilton Parish (809)293-2040.

Holes: 18. **Par:** 71/71.

Yards: 6,440/4,995. **Course rating:** 71.3/69.2. **Slope:** 128/116.

Opened: 1930. **Pace of Play rating:** 4:30. **Green fee:** $$57/90.

Credit cards: MC, V, AMEX, Bermuda. **Reduced fees:** Low season, Twilight, Juniors.

Caddies: No. **Golf carts:** $20 for 18 holes.

Discount golf packages: Yes. **Season:** Year-round. **High:** April-June/ Sept.-Nov.

On-site lodging: Yes. **Rental clubs:** Yes.

Walking policy: Mandatory cart. **Range:** No.

To obtain tee times: Call 48 hours in advance or when booking golf package.

Subscriber comments: Lots of blind shots . . . Very hilly . . . Great views, interesting holes, best value resort course . . . Fun course, not too long . . . Good resort value. Staff was super and very friendly . . . Very good course. When the wind blows it becomes tough . . . Breathtaking first tee, well groomed . . . Nice layout, beautiful views, a treat to play.

★★★★ PORT ROYAL GOLF COURSE

PU—Middle Rd., Southampton (809)234-0972.

Holes: 18. **Par:** 71/72.

Yards: 6,565/5,571. **Course rating:** 72.0/72.5. **Slope:** 134/127.

Opened: 1970. **Pace of Play rating:** 4:30-5:00. **Green fee:** $50.

Credit cards: MC, V, AMEX. **Reduced fees:** Twilight, Seniors, Juniors.

Caddies: No. **Golf carts:** $28 for 18 holes.

Discount golf packages: Yes. **Season:** Year-round. **High:** April-Dec.

On-site lodging: No. **Rental clubs:** Yes.

Walking policy: Walking at certain times. **Range:** Yes.

To obtain tee times: Call (809)295-6500 up to four days in advance.

Subscriber comments: View from par 3 signature hole was outstanding . . . Very scenic course, a real challenge . . . Tough but fun . . . Great layout, long course, especially on a windy day . . . Outstanding Trent Jones course; 16th hole beautiful . . . Don't miss this course . . . Play it for the scenery . . . With the views, it doesn't matter how you play . . . Great service and condition . . . Best course on the island . . . One of my favorites; bring every club and your camera . . . Quality shot values, good condition, a pleasure.

THE BAHAMAS

ABACO

TREASURE CAY GOLF CLUB★
R—(800)327-1584.
Holes: 18. **Par:** 72/73.
Yards: 6,985/5,690. **Course rating:** N/A. **Slope:** N/A.
Opened: 1965. **Pace of Play rating:** N/A. . **Green fee:** $40.
Credit cards: MC, V, AMEX. **Reduced fees:** Resort guests.
Caddies: No. **Golf carts:** $25 for 18 holes.
Discount golf packages: Yes. **Season:** Year-round. **High:** Nov.–April.
On-site lodging: Yes. **Rental clubs:** Yes.
Walking policy: Walking at certain times. **Range:** Yes.
To obtain tee times: None.

GRAND BAHAMA ISLAND

BAHAMAS PRINCESS RESORT AND CASINO
R—P.O. Box F 207, Freeport (809)352-6721.
Opened: 1964. **Pace of Play rating:** 4:00. **Green fee:** $49/63.
Credit cards: All major. **Reduced fees:** Resort guests, Juniors.
Caddies: No. **Golf carts:** Included in Green Fee.
Discount golf packages: Yes. **Season:** Year-round. **High:** Nov.–April.
On-site lodging: Yes. **Rental clubs:** Yes.
Walking policy: Mandatory cart. **Range:** Yes (grass).
To obtain tee times: Call. Tee times required November through April.
★★½ **EMERALD COURSE**
Holes: 18. **Par:** 72/75.
Yards: 6,679/5,722. **Course rating:** 72.3/73.1. **Slope:** 121/121.
Subscriber comments: Bring lots of balls as shots outside of fairway are
unretrievable due to jungle . . . Good condition, treated well . . .
Wonderful, excellent greens, fairways.
★★½ **RUBY COURSE**
Holes: 18. **Par:** 72/74.
Yards: 6,750/5,622. **Course rating:** 72.4/72.4. **Slope:** 122/120.
Subscriber comments: Good condition . . . Good pace . . . Average test.

LUCAYA GOLF AND COUNTRY CLUB★
R—P.O. Box F42500, Freeport (809)373-1066.
Holes: 18. **Par:** 72/75.
Yards: 6,824/5,978. **Course rating:** 72.1/74.5. **Slope:** 128/129.
Opened: 1962. **Pace of Play rating:** 4:00. **Green fee:** $75.
Credit cards: MC, V, AMEX. **Reduced fees:** Low season, Resort guests,
Juniors.
Caddies: No. **Golf carts:** Included in Green Fee.
Discount golf packages: Yes. **Season:** Year-round. **High:** Oct.–March.
On-site lodging: No. **Rental clubs:** Yes.
Walking policy: Mandatory cart. **Range:** Yes (grass).
To obtain tee times: Call one day in advance.
Subscriber comments: Great place to play . . . Beautiful, quiet . . .
Excellent staff . . . Don't miss the fairway!

NEW PROVIDENCE

CABLE BEACH GOLF CLUB★
R—West Bay St., Nassau (809)327-6000, (800)432-0221.
Holes: 18. **Par:** 72/72.
Yards: 7,040/6,114. **Course rating:** 72.0/72.0.
Opened: 1929. **Pace of Play rating:** N/A. **Green fee:** $55/60.
Credit cards: MC, V, AMEX. **Reduced fees:** Low season, Resort guests,
Twilight, Seniors, Juniors.
Caddies: No. **Golf carts:** $45 for 18 holes.

Discount golf packages: Yes. **Season:** Year-round. **High:** Dec.-April.
On-site lodging: Yes. **Rental clubs:** Yes.
Walking policy: Walking at certain times. **Range:** Yes (grass).
To obtain tee times: Call club.

PARADISE ISLAND GOLF★
SP—P.O. Box N-4777, Nassau (809)363-3925.
Holes: 18. **Par:** 72/72.
Yards: 6,770/5,871. **Course rating:** 71.6/67.0. **Slope:** 114/105.
Opened: 1961. **Pace of Play rating:** 4:30. **Green fee:** $86/135.
Credit cards: MC, V, AMEX. **Reduced fees:** Low season, Resort guests.
Caddies: No. **Golf carts:** Included in Green Fee.
Discount golf packages: Yes. **Season:** Year-round. **High:** Nov-April.
On-site lodging: No. **Rental clubs:** Yes.
Walking policy: Mandatory cart. **Range:** Yes.
To obtain tee times: Call two days in advance.
Subscriber comments: Some fun holes . . . Well constructed. Magnificent scenery . . . Good test.

SOUTH OCEAN GOLF AND BEACH RESORT★
R—South Ocean Dr., Nassau (809)362-4391x23.
Holes: 18. **Par:** 72/72.
Yards: 6,707/5,908. **Course rating:** 72.5/75.0. **Slope:** 128/130.
Opened: N/A. **Pace of Play rating:** N/A. **Green fee:** $45/45.
Credit cards: All major. **Reduced fees:** Low season, Resort guests, Juniors.
Caddies: No. **Golf carts:** $25 for 18 holes.
Discount golf packages: Yes. **Season:** Year-round.
On-site lodging: Yes. **Rental clubs:** Yes.
Walking policy: Mandatory cart. **Range:** Yes (grass).
To obtain tee times: Call 24 hours in advance.

BARBADOS

SANDY LANE GOLF CLUB★
R—Sandy Lane, St. James (809)432-1311.
Holes: 18. **Par:** 72/72.
Yards: 6,553/5,520. **Course rating:** 70.2/70.8. **Slope:** 122/120.
Opened: 1961. **Pace of Play rating:** 4:00. **Green fee:** $55/85.
Credit cards: MC, V, AMEX. **Reduced fees:** Low season, Resort guests, Twilight.
Caddies: Yes. **Golf carts:** N/A.
Discount golf packages: No. **Season:** Year-round. **High:** Dec.-April.
On-site lodging: Yes. **Rental clubs:** Yes.
Walking policy: Unrestricted walking. **Range:** Yes (grass).
To obtain tee times: Call 48 hours in advance. Resort guests may book tee times at time of room reservation.
Subscriber comments: Four and a half hours to play . . . Hard course . . . Good staff.

DOMINICAN REPUBLIC

CASA DE CAMPO RESORT AND COUNTRY CLUB
R—La Romana (809)523-3333x3158.
45 miles northwest of Santo Domingo.
Credit cards: MC, V, AMEX. **Reduced fees:** Juniors.
Caddies: Yes. **Golf carts:** Included in Green Fee.
Discount golf packages: Yes. **Season:** Year-round. **High:** Dec.-April.
On-site lodging: Yes. **Rental clubs:** Yes.
Walking policy: Walking at certain times. **Range:** Yes (grass).
To obtain tee times: Fax Golf Office 809-523-8800.
★★★★ **TEETH OF THE DOG**
Holes: 18. **Par:** 72/72.
Yards: 6,888/5,571. **Course rating:** 74.1/72.9. **Slope:** 140/130.
Opened: 1970. **Pace of Play rating:** N/A. **Green fee:** $100.
Subscriber comments: Best course I've played worldwide . . . Super course, beautiful views . . . Great caddies . . . Incredible golf course,

beautiful scenery . . . Could play here all day, every day . . . Better than Pebble Beach . . . More fun than St. Andrews . . . Stunning vistas, ocean breeze makes club selection important.

★★★½ THE LINKS COURSE
Holes: 18. **Par:** 71/71.
Yards: 6,461/4,521. **Course rating:** 70.0/65.7. **Slope:** 124/113.
Opened: 1976. **Pace of Play rating:** N/A. **Green fee:** $70.
Subscriber comments: A reasonably good test for all levels of play . . . Almost as good as Teeth of the Dog . . . Great shape and tremendous caddies . . . Excellent condition.

★½ RADISSON PUERTO PLATA GOLF RESORT
R—Playa Dorado Dr., Puerto Plata (809)586-5360.
Call club for further information.
Subscriber comments: Good resort course, tee times easy to get . . . Caddies a must . . . Tough short Bermuda grasses, putts all straight.

JAMAICA

CAYMANAS GOLF COURSE★
SP— St. Catherine (809)968-3003.
10 miles east of Kingston. **Holes:** 18. **Par:** 72/72.
Yards: 6,570/6,130. **Course rating:** 71.0/70.0. **Slope:** 70/72.
Opened: 1958 **Pace of Play rating:** N/A. **Green fee:** N/A.
Credit cards: MC, V, AMEX. **Reduced fees:** Juniors.
Caddies: Yes. **Golf carts:** $12 for 18 holes.
Discount golf packages: No. **Season:** Year-round.
On-site lodging: No. **Rental clubs:** Yes.
Walking policy: Unrestricted walking. **Range:** Yes (grass).
To obtain tee times: No tee time required.

★★½ HALF MOON GOLF CLUB
R—Rose Hall, Montego Bay (809)953-2560, (809)626-0592.
7 miles west of Montego Bay. **Holes:** 18. **Par:** 72/72.
Yards: 7,119/5,148. **Course rating:** 73.7/68.9. **Slope:** 127/115.
Opened: 1961. **Pace of Play rating:** 3:56. **Green fee:** $50/85.
Credit cards: MC, V, AMEX. **Reduced fees:** Low season, Resort guests.
Caddies: Yes. **Golf carts:** $25 for 18 holes.
Discount golf packages: Yes. **Season:** Year-round.
On-site lodging: Yes. **Rental clubs:** Yes.
Walking policy: Unrestricted walking. **Range:** Yes (grass).
To obtain tee times: Call or come in. Caddies are mandatory.
Subscriber comments: Very pleasant experience . . . Beautiful, A+ . . . Excellent greens . . . All players can play it.

★½ IRONSHORE GOLF AND COUNTRY CLUB
R—P.O. Box 531, Montego Bay No.2, St. James (809)953-2800.
Holes: 18. **Par:** 72/73.
Yards: 6,600/5,400. **Course rating:** 72.0/73.0. **Slope:** N/A.
Opened: 1971. **Pace of Play rating:** N/A. **Green fee:** $34/45.
Credit cards: MC, V, AMEX. **Reduced fees:** Low season, Resort guests, Juniors.
Caddies: Yes. **Golf carts:** $29 for 18 holes.
Discount golf packages: Yes. **Season:** Year-round. **High:** Dec.-April.
On-site lodging: No. **Rental clubs:** Yes.
Walking policy: Unrestricted walking. **Range:** Yes (grass).
To obtain tee times: Call.
Subscriber comments: Greens are fairly true, fairways can be barren . . . Enjoyable.

★ SANDALS GOLF AND COUNTRY CLUB
SP—Upton, Ocho Rios (809)975-0119, (800)726-3257.
Holes: 18. **Par:** 71/72.
Yards: 6,424/5,080. **Course rating:** N/A. **Slope:** N/A.
Opened: 1954. **Pace of Play rating:** N/A. **Green fee:** $50.
Credit cards: MC, V, AMEX. **Reduced fees:** Resort guests.
Caddies: Yes, mandatory at $10. **Golf carts:** N/A.

Discount golf packages: Yes. **Season:** Year-round. **High:** Dec.-March.
On-site lodging: No. **Rental clubs:** Yes.
Walking policy: Unrestricted walking. **Range:** No.
To obtain tee times: Call one week in advance.
Subscriber comments: Could be great some day . . . Caddies were great.

★★ SUPER CLUBS GOLF CLUB AT RUNAWAY BAY

R—Runaway Bay P.O. Box 58, St. Ann (809)973-2561.
15 miles west of Ocho Rios. **Holes:** 18. **Par:** 72/72.
Yards: 6,871/5,389. **Course rating:** 72.4/70.3. **Slope:** 124/117.
Opened: 1960. **Pace of Play rating:** 4:30. **Green fee:** $50.
Credit cards: MC, V, AMEX. **Reduced fees:** Low season, Resort guests.
Caddies: Yes. **Golf carts:** $25 for 18 holes.
Discount golf packages: Yes. **Season:** Year-round. **High:** Jan.-Feb.
On-site lodging: Yes. **Rental clubs:** Yes.
Walking policy: Unrestricted walking. **Range:** Yes (grass).
To obtain tee times: First come, first served.
Subscriber comments: Caddies are knowledgeable about the game and
course staff friendly . . . Suitable to all levels of play . . . Nice view of
ocean.

★★★ TRYALL GOLF TENNIS AND BEACH RESORT

PU—Sandy Bay Main Rd., Hanover (809)956-5681.
15 miles of Montego Bay. **Holes:** 18. **Par:** 71/73.
Yards: 6,920/5,669. **Course rating:** 72.5/72.5. **Slope:** 133/122.
Opened: 1959. **Pace of Play rating:** 4:00. **Green fee:** $40/60.
Credit cards: MC, V, AMEX, Diners Club. **Reduced fees:** No.
Caddies: Yes. **Golf carts:** $27 for 18 holes.
Discount golf packages: Yes. **Season:** Year-round. **High:** Dec.-April.
On-site lodging: Yes. **Rental clubs:** Yes.
Walking policy: Unrestricted walking. **Range:** Yes.
To obtain tee times: Call 24 hours in advance.
Subscriber comments: Interesting holes . . . Great fun . . . Tough greens
for even a good putter . . . Diverse layout . . . Ocean holes are challenging.

★★★½ WYNDHAM ROSE HALL RESORT

R— Montego Bay (809)953-2650x89.
10 miles northeast of Montego Bay. **Holes:** 18. **Par:** 72/73.
Yards: 6,991/5,309. **Course rating:** 71.8/73.5. **Slope:** 130/118.
Opened: 1973. **Pace of Play rating:** 3:58. **Green fee:** $40/50.
Credit cards: MC, V, AMEX. **Reduced fees:** Low season, Resort guests.
Caddies: Yes. **Golf carts:** $33 for 18 holes.
Discount golf packages: Yes. **Season:** Year-round. **High:** Nov.-May.
On-site lodging: Yes. **Rental clubs:** Yes.
Walking policy: Mandatory cart. **Range:** Yes (grass).
To obtain tee times: Must contact golf shop (ext. 89). Tee times may be
made in advance of stay.
Subscriber comments: Back nine very scenic . . . A pleasure, the staff and
course were very enjoyable . . . Love the mountainside, good caddies.

NEVIS

FOUR SEASONS RESORT NEVIS★

R—Pinney's Beach, (809)469-1111.
Holes: 18. **Par:** 71/71.
Yards: 6,766/5,153. **Course rating:** 71.7/69.3. **Slope:** 125/117.
Opened: 1991. **Pace of Play rating:** 4:00. **Green fee:** $81/110.
Credit cards: All major. **Reduced fees:** Juniors.
Caddies: No. **Golf carts:** Included in Green Fee.
Discount golf packages: Yes. **Season:** Year-round. **High:** Dec.-April.
On-site lodging: Yes. **Rental clubs:** Yes.
Walking policy: Mandatory cart. **Range:** Yes (grass).
To obtain tee times: Call in advance once you have resort reservations or
make them daily.
Subscriber comments: Sensational golf course in paradise. Uncrowded.

BAHIA BEACH PLANTATION★

PU—Rt. 187 Km. 4.2, Rio Grande (809)256-5600.
16 miles east of San Juan. **Holes:** 18. **Par:** 72/72.
Yards: 6,695/5,648. **Course rating:** 71.5/72.5. **Slope:** 124/124.
Opened: 1991. **Pace of Play rating:** 4:00. **Green fee:** $40/50.
Credit cards: MC, V, AMEX. **Reduced fees:** Weekdays, Low season,
Twilight, Seniors, Juniors.
Caddies: No. **Golf carts:** Included in Green Fee.
Discount golf packages: No. **Season:** Year-round. **High:** Nov.-April.
On-site lodging: No. **Rental clubs:** Yes.
Walking policy: Mandatory cart. **Range:** Yes (grass).
To obtain tee times: Call one week in advance.

BERWIND COUNTRY CLUB★

SP—Route 187 KM 4.7, Rio Grande (809)876-3056.
15 miles east of San Juan. **Holes:** 18. **Par:** 72/72.
Yards: 7,011/5,772. **Course rating:** 72.6/72.1. **Slope:** 127/123.
Opened: 1962. **Pace of Play rating:** N/A. **Green fee:** $35/45.
Credit cards: MC, V, AMEX. **Reduced fees:** Juniors.
Caddies: No. **Golf carts:** Included in Green Fee.
Discount golf packages: No. **Season:** Year-round. **High:** Oct.-April.
On-site lodging: No. **Rental clubs:** Yes.
Walking policy: Mandatory cart. **Range:** Yes (grass).
To obtain tee times: Open to non-members only on Monday, Tuesday,
Thursday and Fridays before 11:00 a.m.

★½ THE GOLF CLUB AT EL CONQUISTADOR

R—Road 987, K.M. 3.4, Las Croabas (809)863-8899.
31 miles east of San Juan. **Holes:** 18. **Par:** 72/72.
Yards: 6,662/5,131. **Course rating:** 70.6/67.2. **Slope:** 122/113.
Opened: N/A. **Pace of Play rating:** 4:00. **Green fee:** $95.
Credit cards: All major. **Reduced fees:** Juniors.
Caddies: No. **Golf carts:** Included in Green Fee.
Discount golf packages: Yes. **Season:** Year-round. **High:** Dec.-March.
On-site lodging: Yes. **Rental clubs:** Yes.
Walking policy: Mandatory cart. **Range:** Yes (grass).
To obtain tee times: Call.
Subscriber comments: Very hilly . . . Beautiful scenery . . . Quite a
challenge.

HYATT DORADO BEACH RESORT

R—Carr. 693, Dorado (809)796-8961.
22 miles west of San Juan.
Opened: 1958. **Pace of Play rating:** 4:30. **Green fee:** $75.
Credit cards: All major. **Reduced fees:** Resort guests, Twilight, Juniors.
Caddies: No. **Golf carts:** $40 for 18 holes.
Discount golf packages: Yes. **Season:** Year-round. **High:** Dec.-March.
On-site lodging: Yes. **Rental clubs:** Yes.
Walking policy: Mandatory cart. **Range:** Yes (grass).
To obtain tee times: Hotel guest call in advance. Nonguests call same day.
★★★½ EAST COURSE
Holes: 18. **Par:** 72/74.
Yards: 6,985/5,883. **Course rating:** 72.8/72.6. **Slope:** 127/124.
Subscriber comments: A good course from back tees. Good ocean holes
. . . Was in Puerto Rico on business and had the most wonderful time on
the best course I ever played . . . The views on this course are outstanding.
★★★★ WEST COURSE
Holes: 18. **Par:** 72/74.
Yards: 6,913/5,883. **Course rating:** 72.6/73.1. **Slope:** 127/125.
Subscriber comments: Nice blend of difficulty and enjoyability . . . Good
golf, great resort . . . Good challenge.

HYATT REGENCY CERROMAR BEACH

R—Rt. 693, Dorado (809)796-8915.
26 miles west of San Juan.
Opened: 1971. **Pace of Play rating:** 4:30. **Green fee:** $30/100.
Credit cards: All major. **Reduced fees:** Weekdays, Low season, Resort guests, Twilight, Juniors.
Caddies: No. **Golf carts:** $20 for 18 holes.
Discount golf packages: Yes. **Season:** Year-round. **High:** Dec.-March.
On-site lodging: Yes. **Rental clubs:** Yes.
Walking policy: Mandatory cart. **Range:** Yes (grass).
To obtain tee times: Hotel guests call anytime during their stay. Nonguests call day of play.

★★★½ NORTH COURSE

Holes: 18. **Par:** 72/72.
Yards: 6,843/5,547. **Course rating:** 72.2/71.1. **Slope:** 125/121.
Subscriber comments: Good layout, tough from back tees . . . Rich, lush, windy, R.T. Jones in truth . . . Very well maintained, friendly staff, interesting scenery.

★★★ SOUTH COURSE

Holes: 18. **Par:** 72/72.
Yards: 7,047/5,486. **Course rating:** 73.1/70.8. **Slope:** 127/120.
Subscriber comments: OK golf, good resort . . . Fun course.

★★★ PALMAS DEL MAR RESORT

R—Route 3, KM 86.4, Humacao (809)852-6000, (809)725-6270.
35 miles south of San Juan. **Holes:** 18. **Par:** 72/72.
Yards: 6,803/5,432. **Course rating:** 72.8/71.5. **Slope:** 127/122.
Opened: 1974. **Pace of Play rating:** 4:30. **Green fee:** $44/70.
Credit cards: All major. **Reduced fees:** Weekdays, Low season, Resort guests, Twilight.
Caddies: No. **Golf carts:** Included in Green Fee.
Discount golf packages: Yes. **Season:** Year-round. **High:** Dec.-March.
On-site lodging: Yes. **Rental clubs:** Yes.
Walking policy: Mandatory cart. **Range:** Yes (grass).
To obtain tee times: Resort guest on golf package upon confirmation. Guests without golf package call three days in advance. All others call same day.
Subscriber comments: Front and back two different courses . . . Course suited to all levels . . . Tight front nine but short back nine.

ST. KITTS

ROYAL ST. KITTS GOLF CLUB ✶

PU—P.O. Box 315, Frigate Bay (809)465-8339.
2 miles north of Basseterre. **Holes:** 18. **Par:** 72/72.
Yards: 6,918/5,349. **Course rating:** 73.0/69.0. **Slope:** 125/N/A.
Opened: 1976. **Pace of Play rating:** N/A. **Green fee:** $31/35.
Credit cards: All major. **Reduced fees:** Resort guests, Seniors, Juniors.
Caddies: No. **Golf carts:** $40 for 18 holes.
Discount golf packages: Yes. **Season:** Year-round. **High:** Dec.-May.
On-site lodging: No. **Rental clubs:** Yes.
Walking policy: Mandatory cart. **Range:** Yes (grass).
To obtain tee times: Call.

ST. MAARTEN

MULLET BAY GOLF CLUB ✴
R—P.O. Box 309, Phillipsburg 011-5995-52801, (800)468-5538.
10 miles from Phillipsburg. **Holes:** 18. **Par:** 70/71.
Yards: 6,300/5,700. **Course rating:** 69.0/68.0. **Slope:** 115/111.
Opened: 1971. **Pace of Play rating:** 4:00. **Green fee:** $65/125.
Credit cards: MC, V, AMEX. **Reduced fees:** Resort guests.
Caddies: No. **Golf carts:** Included in Green Fee.
Discount golf packages: Yes. **Season:** Year-round. **High:** Nov.-May.
On-site lodging: Yes. **Rental clubs:** Yes.
Walking policy: Mandatory cart. **Range:** Yes (grass).
To obtain tee times: Call golf professional.
Subscriber comments: Lots of water but fun . . . Although the fairways
are not in very good condition, I enjoy this course as much as any I've
played . . . The scenery is outstanding.

TURKS & CAICOS ISLAND

PROVO GOLF CLUB ✴
R—Grace Bay Rd., Providenciales (809)946-5991.
Holes: 18. **Par:** 72/72.
Yards: 6,217/4,979. **Course rating:** 71.2/68.5. **Slope:** 124/116.
Opened: 1992. **Pace of Play rating:** 4:00. **Green fee:** $50/80.
Credit cards: MC, V, AMEX. **Reduced fees:** Low season, Resort guests,
Juniors.
Caddies: No. **Golf carts:** Included in Green Fee.
Discount golf packages: Yes. **Season:** Year-round. **High:** Dec.-April.
On-site lodging: Yes. **Rental clubs:** Yes.
Walking policy: Mandatory cart. **Range:** Yes (grass).
To obtain tee times: Call.

THE VIRGIN ISLANDS

ST. CROIX

BUCCANEER HOTEL GOLF COURSE★
R—P.O. Box 218, (809)773-2100.
3 miles of Christiansted. **Holes:** 18. **Par:** 71/71.
Yards: 6,117/4,490. **Slope:** 116/108.
Opened: N/A. **Pace of Play rating:** N/A. **Green fee:** N/A.
Credit cards: All major. **Reduced fees:** Low season, Resort guests.
Caddies: No. **Golf carts:** N/A.
Discount golf packages: Yes. **Season:** Year-round. **High:** Dec.-April.
On-site lodging: Yes. **Rental clubs:** No.
Walking policy: N/A. **Range:** No.
Subscriber comments: Particularly enjoyable for the average golfer, not a
championship course, but sufficiently challenging for most . . . Excellent
snack bar.

CARAMBOLA GOLF CLUB★
SP—72 Estate River, Kingshill (809)778-5638.
Holes: 18. **Par:** 72/73.
Yards: 6,843/5,424. **Course rating:** 72.7/71.0. **Slope:** 131/123.
Opened: 1966. **Pace of Play rating:** N/A. **Green fee:** $35/55.
Credit cards: MC, V, AMEX. **Reduced fees:** Low season, Resort guests,
Twilight.
Caddies: No. **Golf carts:** Included in Green Fee.
Discount golf packages: No. **Season:** Year-round. **High:** Dec.-April.
On-site lodging: Yes. **Rental clubs:** Yes.
Walking policy: Mandatory cart. **Range:** Yes (grass).
To obtain tee times: Resort guests by mail or phone up to 30 days in
advance. Nonguests call 24 hours in advance.
Subscriber comments: One of the best courses I have ever played . . . A
real treat for a vacation course.

★★ **MAHOGANY RUN GOLF COURSE**
PU—No.1 Mahogany Run Rd. N., (809)775-5000, (800)253-7103.
Holes: 18. **Par:** 70/70.
Yards: 6,022/4,873. **Course rating:** 70.1/72.6. **Slope:** 123/111.
Opened: 1980. **Pace of Play rating:** N/A. **Green fee:** $50/70.
Credit cards: All major. **Reduced fees:** Low season, Twilight.
Caddies: No. **Golf carts:** $15 for 18 holes.
Discount golf packages: Yes. **Season:** Year-round. **High:** Dec.-April.
On-site lodging: Yes. **Rental clubs:** Yes.
Walking policy: Mandatory cart. **Range:** Yes (grass).
To obtain tee times: Call 48 hours in advance; if you have a golf package call 72 hours prior to play.

Notes

NEW BRUNSWICK

FREDERICTON GOLF COURSE★
SP—P.O. Box 504, Fredericton (506)458-1003.
Call club for further information.
Subscriber comments: Need accurate shots but fun to play, will return
. . . Relatively short and hilly . . . Best greens around . . . Good challenge
for intermediate players . . . Good facilities and staff.

GOWAN BRAE GOLF & COUNTRY CLUB★
SP—Youghall Rd., Bathurst (506)546-2707.
Holes: 18. **Par:** 72/74.
Yards: 6,577/5,979. **Course rating:** 71.3/73.0. **Slope:** 129/125.
Opened: 1958. **Pace of Play rating:** 4:30. **Green fee:** $32.
Credit cards: MC, V. **Reduced fees:** No.
Caddies: No. **Golf carts:** $24 for 18 holes.
Discount golf packages: No. **Season:** May-Nov. **High:** July-Aug.
On-site lodging: No. **Rental clubs:** Yes.
Walking policy: Unrestricted walking. **Range:** Yes (grass).
To obtain tee times: Call two days in advance.
Subscriber comments: Outstanding seaside course. Serious back nine.
Scenic . . . One of New Brunswick's best . . . Book ahead . . . Challenging
for all levels, good conditions . . . Great setting. Variety.

★★ MONCTON GOLF CLUB
SP—P.O. Box 7070, Riverview (506)387-3855.
Call club for further information.
Subscriber comments: Mature . . . Relatively short and well groomed
. . . Tough par 3s. Has held many national tournaments . . . Good value in
a nice setting . . . Nice amenities.

PINE NEEDLES GOLF & COUNTRY CLUB
RIVER/ORCHARD/PINE★
PU—RR No.1, P.O. Box 1, Shediac (506)532-4634.
20 miles east of Moncton. **Holes:** 27. **Par:** 72/71/73.
Yards: 6,091/5,919/6,430. **Course rating:** 67.6/66.2/69.7.
Slope: 112/106/119.
Opened: N/A. **Pace of Play rating:** 5:00. **Green fee:** $24.
Credit cards: MC, V. **Reduced fees:** Twilight.
Caddies: No. **Golf carts:** $24 for 18 holes.
Discount golf packages: No. **Season:** May-Oct. **High:** July-Aug.
On-site lodging: No. **Rental clubs:** Yes.
Walking policy: Unrestricted walking. **Range:** No.
To obtain tee times: Call two days in advance for weekends and holidays.
Subscriber comments: New River nine quite tough, not for everyone . . .
Reasonably well maintained. Best suited to experienced players . . . The
River nine, it's the most scenic and challenging of the three.

★★½ THE ALGONQUIN RESORT
SEASIDE COURSE
R—150 Reed Ave., St. Andrews (506)529-3062.
60 miles southwest of Saint John. **Holes:** 18. **Par:** 72/73.
Yards: 6,474/5,949. **Course rating:** 69.3/73.0. **Slope:** 114/N/A.
Opened: 1894. **Pace of Play rating:** N/A. **Green fee:** $25/36.
Credit cards: All major. **Reduced fees:** Weekdays, Low season, Twilight.
Caddies: No. **Golf carts:** $28 for 18 holes.
Discount golf packages: Yes. **Season:** April-Oct. **High:** July-Aug.
On-site lodging: Yes. **Rental clubs:** Yes.
Walking policy: Unrestricted walking. **Range:** Yes (grass).

To obtain tee times: Call anytime throughout season. During off season, tee times can be obtained when booking accommodation.
Also has 9-hole, par-31 executive course called Woodland.
Subscriber comments: Nice old course, great view, good condition. Watch out for the wind . . . Donald Ross design and very scenic . . . Fun to play, but lacks conditioning; play spring and fall.

NEWFOUNDLAND

BLOMIDON GOLF & COUNTRY CLUB★
SP—Wess Valley Rd., Corner Brook (709)634-5550.
Holes: 18. **Par:** 69/72.
Yards: 5,500/5,400. **Course rating:** 67.0/70.0. **Slope:** 116/121.
Opened: 1952. **Pace of Play rating:** 4:00. **Green fee:** $25.
Credit cards: MC, V. **Reduced fees:** N/A.
Caddies: No. **Golf carts:** $22 for 18 holes.
Discount golf packages: No. **Season:** May-Oct. **High:** June-Aug.
On-site lodging: No. **Rental clubs:** Yes.
Walking policy: Unrestricted walking. **Range:** No.
To obtain tee times: Call or come in up to three days in advance.
Subscriber comments: Many blind shots . . . Short par 4s; remainder of course challenging . . . Short course . . . Hard, fast greens . . . Short season, but very accommodating . . . Very hilly.

★★★½ TWIN RIVERS GOLF COURSE
R—General Delivery, Port Blandford (709)543-2626.
140 miles west of St. John's. **Holes:** 18. **Par:** 71/71.
Yards: 6,546/5,433. **Course rating:** 71.9/72.5. **Slope:** 128/129.
Opened: 1984. **Pace of Play rating:** 5:00. **Green fee:** $27/34.
Credit cards: All major. **Reduced fees:** Weekdays, Low season, Resort guests, Twilight, Juniors.
Caddies: Yes. **Golf carts:** $13 for 18 holes.
Discount golf packages: Yes. **Season:** May-Oct. **High:** July-Sept.
On-site lodging: Yes. **Rental clubs:** Yes.
Walking policy: Unrestricted walking. **Range:** Yes (grass).
To obtain tee times: Call anytime during the season. Reserve tee times with credit card.
Subscriber comments: Ocean views, generous fairways, difficult greens, beautiful scenery . . . Best suited for low-ball players, staff is excellent, service and pace of play very good . . . A must to play. Something for everyone . . . Great walk with nature.

NOVA SCOTIA

★★★ ABERCROMBIE GOLF CLUB
SP—P.O. Box 516, New Glasgow (902)752-6249.
Holes: 18. **Par:** 72.
Yards: 6,300. **Course rating:** 71.0. **Slope:** 124.
Opened: 1967. **Pace of Play rating:** 4:30. **Green fee:** $30.
Credit cards: V. **Reduced fees:** Weekdays, Twilight.
Caddies: No. **Golf carts:** $13 for 18 holes.
Discount golf packages: No. **Season:** May-Sept. **High:** July-Aug.
On-site lodging: No. **Rental clubs:** Yes.
Walking policy: Unrestricted walking. **Range:** Yes (grass).
To obtain tee times: Call one day in advance.
Subscriber comments: Long and demanding but fair . . . Challenging . . . New irrigation system installed for 1995 . . . Excellent condition. Suited for low and medium handicappers . . . Difficult for high handicappers or beginners . . . Well worth the price.

★★½ AMHERST GOLF CLUB
SP—P.O. Box 26, Amherst (902)667-8730.
Call club for further information.
Subscriber comments: Fun to play. Good for lefties . . . Friendly atmosphere, worth every cent . . . Room to move the ball . . . Seldom busy . . . Never a problem to get on . . . Geographic location allows for great fairway conditions . . . Good course for all players.

★★★½ ASHBURN GOLF CLUB

SP—P.O. Box 22038, Halifax (902)861-4013.
Call club for information.
Subscriber comments: Long and fast greens. Sidehill lies. Good shot values . . . Excellent condition. Left-hander's nightmare . . . Wonderful test of golf . . . Tough layout . . . Greens difficult for the average player . . . A real challenge for low-handicap players and pros . . . Course well-suited for the long-ball hitters . . . Beautifully manicured, a real challenge.

BRIGHTWOOD GOLF & COUNTRY CLUB★

SP—227 School St., Dartmouth (902)469-7879.
Call club for further information.
Subscriber comments: Short course but must keep ball in play; good all-around course . . . Nice clubhouse, used year-round . . . Hilly and difficult . . . Lots of blind shots and tough lies . . . Very confusing layout.

★★★★ CAPE BRETON HIGHLANDS GOLF LINKS

PU—Cape Breton Highlands Nt'l Pk., Ingonish Beach (902)285-2600.
70 miles south of Sydney. **Holes:** 18. **Par:** 72/76.
Yards: 6,596/5,664. **Course rating:** 73.9/73.3. **Slope:** 139/131.
Opened: 1942. **Pace of Play rating:** N/A. **Green fee:** $25.
Credit cards: MC, V. **Reduced fees:** Twilight, Juniors.
Caddies: Yes. **Golf carts:** None.
Discount golf packages: Yes. **Season:** May-Oct. **High:** July-Aug.
On-site lodging: Yes. **Rental clubs:** Yes.
Walking policy: Unrestricted walking. **Range:** No.
To obtain tee times: Call 24 hours in advance; exceptions made for lodge guests.
Subscriber comments: Excellent views, being renovated, long walks . . . A lot of walking on the side of mountain. Scenery outstanding . . . Wide open fairways which are also long . . . Ideal for long drivers . . . Variety of holes and layout makes for a challenging game . . . Great layout, best in Nova Scotia . . . Fabulous views, ocean and hills . . . Beautiful autumn course . . . Miles from anywhere but worth it . . . Return to another era . . . Best-kept secret in golf . . . Hospitality plus!

★★½ DUNDEE RESORT GOLF COURSE

R—R.R. 32, West Bay (902)345-0420, (800)565-1774.
155 miles east of Halifax. **Holes:** 18. **Par:** 72/72.
Yards: 6,475/5,236. **Course rating:** 71.9/71.9. **Slope:** 135/131.
Opened: 1977. **Pace of Play rating:** 4:30. **Green fee:** $24/32.
Credit cards: All major. **Reduced fees:** Weekdays, Resort guests, Twilight.
Caddies: No. **Golf carts:** $28 for 18 holes.
Discount golf packages: Yes. **Season:** May-Oct. **High:** June-Sept.
On-site lodging: Yes. **Rental clubs:** Yes.
Walking policy: Unrestricted walking. **Range:** No.
To obtain tee times: Call 24 hours in advance.
Subscriber comments: Hilly but playable, great view of Lake Bras D'or . . . Challenging course as fairways are narrow, with majority of holes played uphill or on a slope . . . Breathtaking scenery of lake; very classy resort; hills make every shot an adventure for even the most skilled player . . . The course is best suited for the golfer who has an imagination and has the ability to control it.

★★★ KEN-WO COUNTRY CLUB

SP—P.O. Box 465, Wolfville (902)681-5388.
60 miles east of Halifax. **Holes:** 18. **Par:** 70/73.
Yards: 6,308/5,915. **Course rating:** 69.2/73.5. **Slope:** 118/118.
Opened: 1921. **Pace of Play rating:** 4:00. **Green fee:** $30.
Credit cards: MC, V. **Reduced fees:** Twilight.
Caddies: No. **Golf carts:** $22 for 18 holes.
Discount golf packages: No. **Season:** April-Nov. **High:** June-Aug.
On-site lodging: No. **Rental clubs:** Yes.
Walking policy: Unrestricted walking. **Range:** Yes (grass).
To obtain tee times: Call two days in advance.

Subscriber comments: Great course, nice pro shop and clubhouse . . . Good golf test . . . Very crowded, but staff very helpful . . . Every hole different . . . Fairways at times overlap which can be confusing to first-time player . . . Wide fairways with minimal rough make it ideal for players with hooks and slices . . . Excellent facilities. Layout tight . . . Beautiful, mature course.

LINGAN COUNTRY CLUB★
SP—P.O. Box 1641, Sydney (902)562-1112.
Call club for further information.
Subscriber comments: Will test your game . . . Open course, suits any golfer.

★★★PARAGON GOLF & COUNTRY CLUB
SP—368 Brookside Dr., Kingston (902)765-2554.
100 miles northwest of Halifax. **Holes:** 18. **Par:** 72/72.
Yards: 6,245/5,580. **Course rating:** 69.5/72.1. **Slope:** 123/123.
Opened: 1964. **Pace of Play rating:** 4:15. **Green fee:** $27/29.
Credit cards: V. **Reduced fees:** No.
Caddies: No. **Golf carts:** $20 for 18 holes.
Discount golf packages: No. **Season:** April-Oct. **High:** May-Aug.
On-site lodging: No. **Rental clubs:** Yes.
Walking policy: Unrestricted walking. **Range:** No.
To obtain tee times: Nonmembers call one day in advance.
Subscriber comments: Good variety of holes, interesting and scenic . . . Some greens are small . . . Open and flat course, suits any golfer . . . Well-groomed. Busy on weekends . . . Course improves every year, offers challenges.

★★★½THE PINES RESORT HOTEL GOLF COURSE
R—P.O. Box 70, Digby (902)245-4104.
150 miles southwest of Halifax. **Holes:** 18. **Par:** 71/76.
Yards: 6,204/5,865. **Course rating:** 70.0/73.0. **Slope:** 121/129.
Opened: 1932. **Pace of Play rating:** 4:15. **Green fee:** $28.
Credit cards: All major. **Reduced fees:** N/A.
Caddies: No. **Golf carts:** $24 for 18 holes.
Discount golf packages: Yes. **Season:** May-Oct. **High:** July-Sept.
On-site lodging: Yes. **Rental clubs:** Yes.
Walking policy: Unrestricted walking. **Range:** No.
To obtain tee times: Call. No restrictions.
Subscriber comments: Fine older course, usually well kept . . . Very quiet and in great shape . . . Good for average golfer . . . Beautiful course and mostly wide open. Nice mix of holes . . . Exceptional resort course . . . Bring your "A" game . . . Good staff, pleasant pace, usually in good shape.

★★½THE TRURO GOLF CLUB
SP—Golf St., Truro (902)893-4650.
50 miles west of Halifax. **Holes:** 18. **Par:** 71/72.
Yards: 6,500/5,636. **Course rating:** 70.9/72.4. **Slope:** 123/125.
Opened: 1903. **Pace of Play rating:** 3:50. **Green fee:** $30.
Credit cards: MC, V. **Reduced fees:** Twilight.
Caddies: No. **Golf carts:** $22 for 18 holes.
Discount golf packages: No. **Season:** April-Nov. **High:** May-Sept.
On-site lodging: No. **Rental clubs:** Yes.
Walking policy: Unrestricted walking. **Range:** Yes (grass).
To obtain tee times: Call 24 hours in advance.
Subscriber comments: Flat, easy to walk, good service, pace of play very good . . . Nice layout, very fair, good greens . . . Good challenge, flat, friendly . . . Well groomed, a hidden gem . . . Course suited to short hitter.

★★★★ ANGUS GLEN GOLF CLUB

PU—4495 Major Mackenzie E., Markham (905)887-5157.
25 miles north of Toronto.
Holes: 18. **Par:** 72/72. **Yards:** 7,300/5,721. **Course rating:** N/A. **Slope:** N/A.
Opened: 1994. **Pace of Play rating:** 4:40. **Green fee:** $65/90.
Credit cards: MC, V, AMEX. **Reduced fees:** Low season.
Caddies: No. **Golf carts:** Included in Green Fee.
Discount golf packages: No. **Season:** April-Nov. **High:** May-Oct.
On-site lodging: No. **Rental clubs:** Yes.
Walking policy: Mandatory cart. **Range:** Yes (grass).
To obtain tee times: Call one month in advance.
Subscriber comments: New course opened to public in May; outstanding layout . . . Excellent shape. Exciting and tough . . . Will be a great test when it matures . . . Great design by Doug Carrick.

★★½ BAY OF QUINTE COUNTRY CLUB

SP—R.R. No. 2 Trent Rd., Belleville (613)968-7063.
115 miles east of Toronto.
Holes: 18. **Par:** 72/73. **Yards:** 6,840/5,701. **Course rating:** 72.4/71.4. **Slope:** 125/113.
Opened: 1921. **Pace of Play rating:** 4:00. **Green fee:** $33/38.
Credit cards: MC, V. **Reduced fees:** Low season, Twilight, Juniors.
Caddies: No. **Golf carts:** $30 for 18 holes.
Discount golf packages: No. **Season:** April-Nov. **High:** May-Sept.
On-site lodging: No. **Rental clubs:** Yes.
Walking policy: Unrestricted walking. **Range:** Yes (grass).
To obtain tee times: Call five days in advance for weekday and Thursday noon for weekends and Monday holidays.
Subscriber comments: Flat layout . . . A long walk, must cross train tracks twice . . . Picturesque . . . Demanding, well-conditioned site of 1996 Ontario Amateur . . . Length, trees and rough make up for lack of topographical variation.

★½ BEECHWOOD GOLF AND COUNTRY CLUB

SP—4680 Thorold Townline Rd., Niagara Falls (905)680-4653.
Holes: 18. **Par:** 72/72. **Yards:** 6,700/5,400. **Course rating:** 71.0/70.5. **Slope:** N/A.
Opened: 1960. **Pace of Play rating:** 4:15-4:30. **Green fee:** $25/28.
Credit cards: MC, V. **Reduced fees:** Weekdays, Low season.
Caddies: No. **Golf carts:** $25 for 18 holes.
Discount golf packages: Yes. **Season:** April-Nov. **High:** April-Sept.
On-site lodging: No. **Rental clubs:** No.
Walking policy: Unrestricted walking. **Range:** Yes (grass).
To obtain tee times: Local nonmembers call or come in up to four days in advance. Visitors may reserve in advance without restrictions.
Subscriber comments: Excellent service, large greens, a few tough holes . . . Very busy course, slow play, both offset by friendly capable staff . . . A lot of fun to play, some severe climbs, green fee less than average, good condition . . . Tight fairways, require straight shots . . . Flat, simple course, retirees' course, improving maintenance.

★★★½ BLUE SPRINGS GOLF CLUB

SP—170 York St., Acton (519)853-4434.
Call club for further information.
Subscriber comments: Best course in the area, esthetically pleasing, different tee boxes from different angles make course suitable to all, ponds and streams used well, lots of variation, half the price of comparable courses . . . Too long and hilly to walk . . . Spectacular scenery, elevated tees, greens, lots of water and long . . . Challenging, well-bunkered, beautiful countryside, tree-lined, home of Canadian PGA . . . Good layout but impossible to walk. Conditioning should be improved . . . Good women's tees . . . Good condition, very tough. Good pace . . . Tough track, greens too severe, some very good holes, average condition . . . Beautiful scenery in fall . . . It's a blaze of color in the fall.

★★★ BROCKVILLE COUNTRY CLUB

SP—P.O. Box 42, Brockville (613)342-2468.
Call club for further information.
Subscriber comments: Narrow fairways, lots of rough, challenging . . .
Mixture of trees, open and trapped holes. Suitable for all handicaps . . .
Good design using natural terrain . . . An interesting old course in a nice
setting.

★★½ BROOKLEA GOLF AND COUNTRY CLUB
NORTH/SOUTH

SP—751 Young St., Midland (705)526-7532.
90 miles north of Toronto.
Holes: 18. **Par:** 72/72. **Yards:** 6,625/5,540. **Course rating:** 61.2/71.4.
Slope: 126/126.
Opened: 1959. **Pace of Play rating:** 4:00-5:00. **Green fee:** $30/34.
Credit cards: MC, V, AMEX. **Reduced fees:** Weekdays, Resort guests,
Twilight.
Caddies: No. **Golf carts:** $13 for 18 holes.
Discount golf packages: Yes. **Season:** Year-round. **High:** June-Sept.
On-site lodging: No. **Rental clubs:** Yes.
Walking policy: Unrestricted walking. **Range:** Yes (grass).
To obtain tee times: Call up to 48 hours in advance.
Also has 9-hole executive West Course.
Subscriber comments: Back nine older, longer, tree-lined, tough, staff
excellent, golf package perfect, front nine new and well designed . . . Short
but not dull, quite well groomed . . . Varied layout, offering combination
of mature tree-lined holes with linksland type holes.

★★½ CALABOGIE HIGHLANDS RESORT AND GOLF CLUB

PU—Barryville Rd., Calabogie (613)752-2171.
55 miles southwest of Ottawa.
Holes: 18. **Par:** 72/72. **Yards:** 6,735/5,632. **Course rating:** 71.4/72.0.
Slope: 126/N.A.
Opened: 1983. **Pace of Play rating:** 4:25. **Green fee:** $22/25.
Credit cards: MC, V, Interac. **Reduced fees:** Weekdays, Low season,
Resort guests, Twilight, Juniors.
Caddies: No. **Golf carts:** $13 for 18 holes.
Discount golf packages: Yes. **Season:** April-Nov. **High:** June-Aug.
On-site lodging: Yes. **Rental clubs:** Yes.
Walking policy: Unrestricted walking. **Range:** Yes (grass).
To obtain tee times: Call seven days in advance.
Subscriber comments: Fast true greens, fantastic view. Friendly staff. Fall
is best . . . Lots of hills, but course is always green. Never dry . . . Hilly
cottage country, beautiful vistas, a course for all levels . . . Small greens,
good shape, lots of character.

★★½ CALEDON COUNTRY CLUB

PU—2121 Old Baseline Rd., R.R. No. 1, Inglewood (905)838-0121.
Call club for further information.
Subscriber comments: Very tight, tree-lined, fun course . . . Short,
interesting course, good value. Busy but playable in 4 hrs . . . Nestled in
beautiful Caledon Hills. Very scenic in fall . . . Tough, hilly layout, needs
all the shots.

★★ CARDINAL GOLF CLUB
EAST/WEST

PU—2740 Hwy. 9, R.R. No. 1, Kettleby (905)841-2195.
20 miles north of Toronto.
Holes: 36. **Par:** 72/72. **Yards:** 6,450/6,500 **Course rating:** 71.5/72.0.
Slope: N/A.
Opened: 1989. **Pace of Play rating:** 4:00. **Green fee:** $18/35.
Credit cards: MC, V, AMEX. **Reduced fees:** Weekdays, Low season,
Twilight, Seniors, Juniors.
Caddies: No. **Golf carts:** $13 for 18 holes.
Discount golf packages: No. **Season:** April-Nov. **High:** June-Aug.
On-site lodging: No. **Rental clubs:** Yes.

Walking policy: Unrestricted walking. **Range:** Yes (grass).
To obtain tee times: Call up to seven days in advance.
Also has 18-hole par-58 short course.
Subscriber comments: Good value for the money . . . Interesting holes
with numerous water hazards and challenging green placements, enjoyable
course for the better club player . . . Lots of improvement being made . . .
Course in good shape, but very flat and wide open . . . Will be better when
trees mature.

★★★ CARLISLE GOLF AND COUNTRY CLUB
PU—523 Carlisle Rd., Carlisle (905)689-8820, (800)661-4343.
10 miles north of Burlington.
Holes: 18. **Par:** 72/72. **Yards:** 6,557/5,232. **Course rating:** 70.6/72.9.
Slope: 119/105.
Opened: 1991. **Pace of Play rating:** 4:30. **Green fee:** $35/40.
Credit cards: MC, V, AMEX. **Reduced fees:** Weekdays, Low season,
Seniors, Juniors.
Caddies: No. **Golf carts:** $15 for 18 holes.
Discount golf packages: Yes. **Season:** April-Nov. **High:** June-Aug.
On-site lodging: No. **Rental clubs:** Yes.
Walking policy: Unrestricted walking. **Range:** No.
To obtain tee times: Call up to one week in advance.
Subscriber comments: Absolutely the best value, new clubhouse in '95,
great course, narrow, just enough bunkers . . . Course is in great shape . . .
Well groomed, need helmet for stray shots from adjoining holes . . . Need
to use every club in the bag . . . Outstanding in every category from the
staff to the course . . . Beautiful layout and a good challenge from the back
tees.

★★★ CHESTNUT HILL GOLF AND COUNTRY CLUB
SP—13300 Leslie St., Richmond Hill (416)213-7456.
20 miles north of Toronto.
Holes: 18. **Par:** 72/73. **Yards:** 7,087/5,492. **Course rating:** 74.5/70.5.
Slope: N/A.
Opened: 1994. **Pace of Play rating:** 4:00. **Green fee:** $60/75.
Credit cards: MC, V, AMEX. **Reduced fees:** Weekdays, Juniors.
Caddies: Yes. **Golf carts:** $20 for 18 holes.
Discount golf packages: No. **Season:** April-Oct. **High:** June-Aug.
On-site lodging: No. **Rental clubs:** Yes.
Walking policy: Unrestricted walking. **Range:** Yes (grass).
To obtain tee times: Call three days in advance.
Subscriber comments: Suited for all levels of players because of open
fairways . . . Newly developed . . . Needs maturity . . . Great track, will
mature into outstanding course . . . Avoid playing at dusk or the
mosquitoes will devour you . . . New course, nice layout, green fees
somewhat prohibitive.

★★★ CHIPPEWA GOLF AND COUNTRY CLUB
SP—Hwy. 21 N., Southampton (519)797-3684.
23 miles west of Owen Sound.
Holes: 18. **Par:** 72/72. **Yards:** 6,420/5,392. **Course rating:** 69.5/70.0.
Slope: 116/109.
Opened: 1964. **Pace of Play rating:** 4:00. **Green fee:** $20/25.
Credit cards: MC, V. **Reduced fees:** Low season, Twilight.
Caddies: No. **Golf carts:** $24 for 18 holes.
Discount golf packages: Yes. **Season:** April-Nov. **High:** May-Sept.
On-site lodging: No. **Rental clubs:** Yes.
Walking policy: Unrestricted walking. **Range:** Yes (grass).
To obtain tee times: Call Sunday for the upcoming week.
Subscriber comments: Easy to walk. Good condition . . . Interesting
design, simply a joy to play . . . Good condition for country course, slow
play, nice facilities.

★★½ DEER RUN GOLF CLUB
PU—Bloomfield Rd., R.R. No. 3, Blenheim (519)676-1566.
11 miles south of Chothom.

Holes: 18. **Par:** 72/72. **Yards:** 6,386/5,303. **Course rating:** 70.4/65.0.
Slope: N/A.
Opened: 1993. **Pace of Play rating:** 4:00. **Green fee:** $12/18.
Credit cards: MC, V, AMEX. **Reduced fees:** Weekdays, Low season, Twilight.
Caddies: No. **Golf carts:** $12 for 18 holes.
Discount golf packages: Yes. **Season:** April-Nov. **High:** June-July.
On-site lodging: No. **Rental clubs:** Yes.
Walking policy: Unrestricted walking. **Range:** Yes (grass).
To obtain tee times: Call pro shop.
Subscriber comments: New course, large greens, tough target golf, small fairways. Has big potential . . . New, accuracy needed, better as it ages.

DEERHURST RESORT
R—R.R. No. 4, Huntsville (705)789-2381.
120 miles north of Toronto.
Credit cards: MC, V, AMEX. **Reduced fees:** Weekdays, Low season, Twilight.
Caddies: No. **Golf carts:** Included in Green Fee.
Discount golf packages: Yes. **Season:** May-Oct. **High:** June-Aug.
On-site lodging: Yes. **Rental clubs:** Yes.
Range: Yes (grass).
To obtain tee times: Call seven days in advance.

★★★★½ DEERHURST HIGHLANDS GOLF COURSE
Holes: 18. **Par:** 72/73. **Yards:** 7,011/5,393. **Course rating:** 74.5/71.2.
Slope: 140/125.
Opened: 1990. **Pace of Play rating:** 4:00. **Green fee:** $79/84.
Walking policy: Mandatory cart.
Subscriber comments: All types of golf wrapped into 18 holes . . . Great challenge; rough is jungle, bring lots of ammo . . . Best resort test in Ontario . . . Very scenic . . . Exceptional setting with fabulous layout . . . Lots of trees. Demanding length . . . The course makes excellent use of the natural terrain for both scenic and functional purposes. Of particular note are the unique greens and wide separations between holes . . . Splendid combination of wilderness and links type holes, brutal from back tees . . . Imaginative, scenic, demanding design cut out of woods terrain; some long forced carries . . . Masterpiece without destroying nature.

★★½ DEERHURST LAKESIDE GOLF COURSE
Holes: 18. **Par:** 65/65. **Yards:** 4,500/3,800. **Course rating:** 62.4/63.0.
Slope: 101/104.
Opened: 1972. **Pace of Play rating:** 4:00. **Green fee:** $20/30.
Reduced fees: Low season, Resort guests, Juniors.
Walking policy: Walking at certain times.
Subscriber comments: Short but never dull . . . Front nine scenic and good test, back nine weak . . . A pleasant resort track . . . Shorter course. Good fun. Great staff. Enough challenge . . . Above average executive track, a pleasant walk, fast greens.

DELHI GOLF AND COUNTRY CLUB★
SP—905 James St., Delhi (519)582-1621.
40 miles southeast of London.
Holes: 18. **Par:** 71/72. **Yards:** 6,400/5,200. **Course rating:** 71.3/69.4.
Slope: 114/103.
Opened: 1960. **Pace of Play rating:** 4:00. **Green fee:** $21/24.
Credit cards: MC, V, AMEX. **Reduced fees:** Weekdays, Twilight, Seniors, Juniors.
Caddies: No. **Golf carts:** $24 for 18 holes.
Discount golf packages: Yes. **Season:** March-Dec. **High:** June-Aug.
On-site lodging: No. **Rental clubs:** Yes.
Walking policy: Unrestricted walking. **Range:** Yes (grass).
To obtain tee times: Call pro shop.
Subscriber comments: Mixture of new and old nines results in inconsistent greens.

★½ DON VALLEY GOLF COURSE
PU—4200 Young St., Toronto (416)392-2465.
Holes: 18. **Par:** 71/71. **Yards:** 6,300/6,150. **Course rating:** N/A. **Slope:** N/A.
Opened: N/A. **Pace of Play rating:** N/A. **Green fee:** N/A.
Credit cards: MC, V, AMEX. **Reduced fees:** Twilight.
Caddies: Yes. **Golf carts:** N/A.
Discount golf packages: No. **Season:** April-Nov. **High:** July-Aug.
On-site lodging: No. **Rental clubs:** No.
Walking policy: N/A. **Range:** Yes (grass).
Subscriber comments: Currently being renovated. Back nine open this season . . . Good tough muny track . . . Testing layout. Good value but too crowded . . . Water on some holes. Narrow par 5s . . . Great muny course, long waiting period rewarded.

★★ DOON VALLEY GOLF CLUB
PU—500 Doon Valley Dr., Kitchener (519)741-2711.
Call club for further information.
Subscriber comments: Good variety of holes, heavy play keeps it from showing its best . . . Great course, tough to score, delight to play . . . Well maintained, not very challenging, some very short, open par 4s . . . Excellent for an average and new player. They are improving yearly.

★★★★ EAGLE CREEK GOLF CLUB
SP—109 Royal Troon Lane, Dunrobin (613)832-0728.
18 miles west of Ottawa.
Holes: 18. **Par:** 72/72. **Yards:** 7,067/5,413. **Course rating:** 74.3/71.5.
Slope: N/A.
Opened: 1991. **Pace of Play rating:** 4:00. **Green fee:** $48.
Credit cards: MC, V, AMEX. **Reduced fees:** Low season, Juniors.
Caddies: No. **Golf carts:** $12 for 18 holes.
Discount golf packages: No. **Season:** April-Nov. **High:** June-Aug.
On-site lodging: No. **Rental clubs:** Yes.
Walking policy: Unrestricted walking. **Range:** Yes (grass).
To obtain tee times: Call three days in advance. Out of town reservations anytime with full payment.
Subscriber comments: Narrow, great variety, up and down to greens . . . Excellent Venturi design in marshland/wooded setting. Will challenge any player. The golf is so good you don't worry about lack of a proper clubhouse . . . Excellent layout . . . Best suited for medium to high handicaps, good variety of holes . . . Course remains the same, fun to play for any level, big greens, tight, long . . . Challenging, fair target golf course, drainage excellent.

★★ FANSHAWE GOLF CLUB
SP—R.R. No. 5, London (519)455-2770.
Call club for further information.
Subscriber comments: Mature course. Open fairways. Blue/White nines nice combination . . . Gentle parkland setting . . . Makes you think out loud . . . This course run by local parks department. At times in very poor condition, due to constant use.

FIRE FIGHTERS GORMLEY GREEN GOLF CLUB
PU—P.O. Box 278, Gormley (905)888-1219.
12 miles north of Toronto. **Green fee:** $24/38.
Credit cards: V, AMEX. **Reduced fees:** Weekdays, Low season, Twilight, Seniors.
Caddies: No. **Golf carts:** $9 for 18 holes.
Discount golf packages: No. **Season:** April-Nov. **High:** June-Sept.
On-site lodging: No. **Rental clubs:** Yes.
Walking policy: Unrestricted walking. **Range:** Yes (grass).
To obtain tee times: Call pro shop.
★½ CIRCLE COURSE
Holes: 18. **Par:** 70/70. **Yards:** 6,618/5,658. **Course rating:** 72.0/N/A.

Slope: 115/N.A.
Opened: N/A. **Pace of Play rating:** N/A.
Subscriber comments: A simple course for beginners or advanced golfers . . . Gently rolling links-style course . . . Course in nice shape, value is good, facilities only adequate.

★★½ CREEK COURSE
Holes: 18. **Par:** 72/72. **Yards:** 6,948/5,958. **Course rating:** 73.1/N.A.
Slope: 128/N.A.
Opened: N/A. **Pace of Play rating:** 4:15.
Subscriber comments: Interesting elevations include tree-lined and links design. Pace is slow at peak times . . . Very challenging, interesting layout. Tight . . . Very windy, always.

★ FIRE FIGHTERS ROLLING HILLS GOLF CLUB
BLUE/RED COURSE
PU—P.O. Box 519, Gormley (905)888-1955.
12 miles north of Toronto.
Holes: 36. **Par:** 72/70. **Yards:** 6,428/5,210 **Course rating:** 68.5/61.3.
Slope: 112/95.
Opened: N/A. **Pace of Play rating:** 4:30. **Green fee:** $16/32.
Credit cards: MC, V, AMEX. **Reduced fees:** Weekdays, Low season, Twilight, Seniors.
Caddies: No. **Golf carts:** $18 for 18 holes.
Discount golf packages: No. **Season:** April-Nov. **High:** June-Sept.
On-site lodging: No. **Rental clubs:** Yes.
Walking policy: Unrestricted walking. **Range:** No.
To obtain tee times: Call pro shop.
Also has 18-hole par-62 Gold Course.
Subscriber comments: Adequate, good for tournaments, easy to walk . . . Open, and ego building course. Good value for mid-high handicappers . . . Basic layout, but price is right.

★★½ FLAMBOROUGH HILLS GOLF CLUB
SP—P.O. Box 9, Copetown (905)627-1743.
Call club for further information.
Subscriber comments: New nine offers good variety, excellent value for money . . . 27 holes, scenic, lots of water . . . New nine gives nice 27-hole mix . . . Good course for the average player in very good condition . . . Fast greens. Good putting required.

★★★★ FOREST CITY NATIONAL GOLF CLUB
PU—R.R. 6, London (519)451-0994.
Call club for further information.
Subscriber comments: Superb layout, 1/2 parkland, 1/2 links, excellent condition, fair test for all levels . . . Numerous tees give different look every time you play, course well designed for all types of players . . . Excellent conditions, hard greens and very fast . . . Good variety of holes, length and difficulty.

★★★★ GLEN ABBEY GOLF CLUB
PU—1333 Dorval Dr., Oakville (905)844-1811.
20 miles west of Toronto.
Holes: 18. **Par:** 73/74. **Yards:** 7,112/5,520. **Course rating:** 77.0/73.5.
Slope: 128/N.A.
Opened: 1977. **Pace of Play rating:** 4:30. **Green fee:** $75/125.
Credit cards: MC, V, AMEX. **Reduced fees:** Low season.
Caddies: No. **Golf carts:** Included in Green Fee.
Discount golf packages: No. **Season:** April-Oct. **High:** May-Oct.
On-site lodging: No. **Rental clubs:** Yes.
Walking policy: Unrestricted walking. **Range:** Yes (grass).
To obtain tee times: Begin accepting tee times March 1st for the upcoming season. Booking must be prepaid with credit card. No changes or cancellations will be accepted.
Subscriber comments: The valley holes are superb, long difficult, great condition, best for low handicaps . . . Nice to play course pros play, expensive . . . Not as difficult as expected, make your own mistakes here

. . . Overpriced, though you are treated well . . . All holes challenging, even flat front nine . . . Home of the Canadian Open . . . Beautiful, thinker's course . . . Always a pleasure, I like the way Nicklaus lets me enjoy the game from the middle tees . . . Superb, well groomed and challenging, worth every penny . . . Water on nine holes, provides great golf, at a price . . . Everyone should pay the price just once . . . Excellent conditions all season . . . Outstanding, great risk/reward holes, beautiful setting, premium experience.

★★★ HAWK RIDGE GOLF CLUB
PU—P.O. Box 874, Orilla (705)329-4653.
Call club for further information.
Subscriber comments: Three nine hole layouts, each different and challenging . . . Links-style, great shape, superior value . . . Front is open, very long; back is tight, in forest. Fast large greens . . . Good variety of holes.

★★★ HOCKLEY VALLEY RESORT
R—R.R. No. 1, Orangeville (519)942-0754.
30 miles northwest of Toronto.
Holes: 18. **Par:** 70/70. **Yards:** 6,391/4,646. **Course rating:** 71.0/71.0.
Slope: N/A.
Opened: 1989. **Pace of Play rating:** 4:30. **Green fee:** $46/59.
Credit cards: All major. **Reduced fees:** Low season, Resort guests, Twilight.
Caddies: No. **Golf carts:** Included in Green Fee.
Discount golf packages: Yes. **Season:** April-Nov. **High:** June-Aug.
On-site lodging: Yes. **Rental clubs:** Yes.
Walking policy: Mandatory cart. **Range:** Yes (grass).
To obtain tee times: Hotel guests can book anytime. All others call four days in advance.
Subscriber comments: Target golf, beautiful scenery, not a walking course . . . Rolling and hilly links course . . . Terrific par 3s with large elevation changes . . . Carts are mandatory for good reason, great layout, great scenery . . . Grass bunkers vs. sand is a nice touch; par 3s are wicked . . . Fair for short hitter and women . . . Picturesque. A lot of fun . . . All 18 holes are difficult and interesting . . . Best kept secret in Ontario, very good, very tough with wind.

★ HORNBY TOWER GOLF CLUB
PU—Hornby Rd., Hornby (905)878-3421.
Call club for further information.
Subscriber comments: Basic layout . . . Slicers delight . . . Long course, very flat, average fun area . . . Few traps and water . . . Open, few hazards, little rough, fast, not very challenging.

★★★½ HORSESHOE VALLEY RESORT
VALLEY COURSE
R—R.R. No. 1, Barrie (705)835-2790.
60 miles north of Toronto.
Holes: 18. **Par:** 72/72. **Yards:** 6,167/5,232. **Course rating:** 71.0/67.0.
Slope: 131/122.
Opened: 1974. **Pace of Play rating:** 4:15. **Green fee:** $34.
Credit cards: MC, V, AMEX, Diners Club. **Reduced fees:** Resort guests, Twilight.
Caddies: No. **Golf carts:** $26 for 18 holes.
Discount golf packages: No. **Season:** April-Oct. **High:** June-Aug.
On-site lodging: Yes. **Rental clubs:** Yes.
Walking policy: Unrestricted walking. **Range:** Yes (grass).
To obtain tee times: Resort guests may make tee times at time of reservation. Others, call one week in advance.
Also 9-hole par-36 Highlands Course.
Subscriber comments: Fantastic layout, narrow, tree-lined fairways, many elevated greens . . . Avoid early summer play, fall is gorgeous . . . Short but tight, a long walk, but scenic . . . Great resort course, scenic with some beautiful vistas, good value . . . Tight fairways, fast greens. Tough par 3s . . . Lots of variety. Well maintained . . . Great in fall with leaf colors.

★½ INDIAN CREEK GOLF AND COUNTRY CLUB

SP—120 Indian Creek Rd. W., Chatham (519)354-7666.
Holes: 18. **Par:** 71/73. **Yards:** 6,200/5,471. **Course rating:** 68.6/71.4.
Slope: 113/119.
Opened: 1956. **Pace of Play rating:** 4:00. **Green fee:** $15/18.
Credit cards: MC, V. **Reduced fees:** Low season, Twilight, Seniors, Juniors.
Caddies: No. **Golf carts:** $22 for 18 holes.
Discount golf packages: Yes. **Season:** March-Dec. **High:** May-Oct.
On-site lodging: No. **Rental clubs:** Yes.
Walking policy: Unrestricted walking. **Range:** Yes (grass).
To obtain tee times: Call up to one week in advance.
Subscriber comments: Lots of trees, best greens in area . . . Short, flat course, very good for beginners, busy.

★★★½ KANATA LAKES GOLF AND COUNTRY CLUB

SP—7000 Campeau Dr., Kanata (613)592-1631.
10 miles west of Ottawa.
Holes: 18. **Par:** 70/70. **Yards:** 6,730/5,328. **Course rating:** 73.0/70.0.
Slope: N/A.
Opened: 1991. **Pace of Play rating:** 4:00. **Green fee:** $42/46.
Credit cards: MC, V. **Reduced fees:** No.
Caddies: No. **Golf carts:** $15 for 18 holes.
Discount golf packages: No. **Season:** April-Oct. **High:** July-Aug.
On-site lodging: No. **Rental clubs:** Yes.
Walking policy: Unrestricted walking. **Range:** Yes.
To obtain tee times: Call two days in advance after 8 a.m.
Subscriber comments: Good maintenance . . . Small greens, narrow fairways, meanders through residential subdivision . . . Immaculate shape, well contoured course. Accuracy off the tee.

★★★ KINGSVILLE GOLF CLUB
RED/WHITE/GOLD

SP—Hwy. 18 W., Kingsville (519)733-6585.
25 miles south of Detroit.
Holes: 27. **Par:** 72/72/72. **Yards:** 6,297/6,305/6,518. **Course rating:** 70.6/71.1/72.1. **Slope:** N/A.
Opened: 1925. **Pace of Play rating:** 4:30. **Green fee:** $ 33.
Credit cards: MC, V. **Reduced fees:** Low season, Twilight, Juniors.
Caddies: No. **Golf carts:** $13 for 18 holes.
Discount golf packages: No. **Season:** March-Nov. **High:** June-Aug.
On-site lodging: No. **Rental clubs:** No.
Walking policy: Unrestricted walking. **Range:** Yes (grass).
To obtain tee times: Call two days in advance.
Subscriber comments: Can play here year round. Three nines, a good test . . . Easy walking. Mature fairways of oak and maple . . . Gold most challenging, beautiful new clubhouse.

★★ THE LINKS OF ROCKWAY GLEN

SP—3290 9th St. South, St. Catharines .
Call club for further information.
Subscriber comments: Setting is in old vineyard, grass has not taken well . . . Potentially great, needs to mature . . . New course needs maturing, still very good layout, challenging . . . Good layout, every hole different, rough needs work, good value.

LIONHEAD GOLF AND COUNTRY CLUB

PU—8525 Mississauga Rd., Brampton (905)455-4900.
10 miles west of Toronto. **Credit cards:** MC, V, AMEX. **Reduced fees:** Low season.
Caddies: No. **Golf carts:** Included in Green Fee.
Discount golf packages: No. **Season:** April-Nov. **High:** May-Oct.
On-site lodging: No. **Rental clubs:** Yes.
Walking policy: Mandatory cart. **Range:** Yes (grass).
To obtain tee times: Book with credit card one to 60 days in advance.

★★★★ LEGENDS COURSE

Holes: 18. **Par:** 72/72. **Yards:** 7,198/5,730. **Course rating:** 77.0/74.0.
Slope: 151/137.
Opened: 1991. **Pace of Play rating:** 4:30. **Green fee:** $75/125.
Subscriber comments: Expensive but outstanding, difficult but fair . . .
Course maintenance and customer treatment are on the private course level
. . . Very demanding, can pull the feet out from under you at anytime . . .
Beautiful holes, in great shape all season. A little tough with long carries on
some holes . . . The only time in my life I wanted to be John Daly . . .
Course is tough but fair. Staff treats you like royalty . . . Challenging,
difficult greens . . . Overrated. Disappointed after all the hype. Too
expensive but friendly.

★★★★ MASTERS COURSE

Holes: 18. **Par:** 72/72. **Yards:** 7,035/5,553. **Course rating:** 75.0/72.5.
Slope: 146/131.
Opened: 1991. **Pace of Play rating:** 4:30. **Green fee:** $75/110.
Subscriber comments: Long carries needed . . . Not as tough as Legends
by a long shot but still great fun . . . For low handicap players (because of
narrow fairways and difficult approach shots) . . . Choose the right tees or it
won't be fun . . . Beautiful in fall, fast greens . . . Good service . . . The
meek shall not score here, fabulously maintained, but too expensive . . .
Second best public course in Ontario, worth every dollar . . . Better than
Legends, more character.

★★★½ LOCH MARCH GOLF AND COUNTRY CLUB

PU—1755 Old Carp Rd., Kanata (613)839-5885.
28 miles west of Ottawa.
Holes: 18. **Par:** 72/72. **Yards:** 6,750/4,878. **Course rating:** 72.0/72.0.
Slope: 129/113.
Opened: 1987. **Pace of Play rating:** 4:30. **Green fee:** $40.
Credit cards: MC, V, AMEX, Interact. **Reduced fees:** No.
Caddies: No. **Golf carts:** $22 for 18 holes.
Discount golf packages: Yes. **Season:** May-Nov. **High:** June-Aug.
On-site lodging: No. **Rental clubs:** Yes.
Walking policy: Unrestricted walking. **Range:** No.
To obtain tee times: Call two days in advance.
Subscriber comments: Very challenging, yet every level of player can
enjoy . . . Every hole offers choices, beautiful facility . . . Tight,
challenging, walk only if in good shape yourself . . . Challenging course,
good opening holes, greens are tricky . . . Public course with country club
service.

LOMBARD GLEN GOLF CLUB★

SP—R.R. No. 1, Lombardy (613)283-5318.
Call club for further information.
Subscriber comments: Maturing nicely . . . Newly redesigned 18 holes,
nine with water . . . Very playable, good value for money.

★ MANDERLEY ON THE GREEN

SP—R.R. No. 3, North Gower (613)489-2066.
6 miles south of Ottawa.
Holes: 18. **Par:** 71/71. **Yards:** 6,414/5,668. **Course rating:** 70.0/72.0.
Slope: N/A.
Opened: 1964. **Pace of Play rating:** 4:30. **Green fee:** $15/32.
Credit cards: MC, V, AMEX. **Reduced fees:** Weekdays, Low season,
Twilight.
Caddies: No. **Golf carts:** $14 for 18 holes.
Discount golf packages: Yes. **Season:** April-Oct. **High:** June-Sept.
On-site lodging: No. **Rental clubs:** Yes.
Walking policy: Unrestricted walking. **Range:** Yes (grass).
To obtain tee times: Call 48 hours in advance.
Subscriber comments: Picturesque, well kept . . . Very dry, reasonable
rates, very good layout . . . Public course, good in spring, afterwards traffic
takes its toll.

★★½ MAPLES OF BALLANTRAE LODGE AND GOLF CLUB

R—R.R. No. 4, Stouffville (905)640-6077.

30 miles northeast of Toronto.

Holes: 18. **Par:** 72/73. **Yards:** 6,600/5,250. **Course rating:** 70.0/69.5.
Slope: 126/N/A.

Opened: 1982. **Pace of Play rating:** 4:30. **Green fee:** $25/30.

Credit cards: MC, V, AMEX. **Reduced fees:** Weekdays, Low season,
Twilight, Seniors, Juniors.

Caddies: No. **Golf carts:** $13 for 18 holes.

Discount golf packages: Yes. **Season:** April-Nov. **High:** June-Aug.

On-site lodging: Yes. **Rental clubs:** Yes.

Walking policy: Unrestricted walking. **Range:** Yes (grass).

To obtain tee times: Call one day in advance for weekdays. Call
Thursday at 8 a.m. for weekend and holiday.

Subscriber comments: Short but interesting, good women's course . . .
Very demanding, tough greens . . . Course is good but long to walk, very
good facilities . . . Easy walking . . . Water in play on 11 holes.

★★★ MARKHAM GREEN GOLF AND COUNTRY CLUB

SP—8028 9th Line, Markham (905)294-6156.

5 miles northeast of Toronto.

Holes: 18. **Par:** 71/72. **Yards:** 6,538/5,292. **Course rating:** 71.1/71.0.
Slope: 127/113.

Opened: 1954. **Pace of Play rating:** 4:30. **Green fee:** $40/45.

Credit cards: MC, V, AMEX. **Reduced fees:** Low season, Twilight,
Juniors.

Caddies: No. **Golf carts:** $15 for 18 holes.

Discount golf packages: No. **Season:** April-Nov. **High:** May-Sept.

On-site lodging: No. **Rental clubs:** Yes.

Walking policy: Unrestricted walking. **Range:** Yes (grass).

To obtain tee times: Call up to five days in advance.

Subscriber comments: Very good private course, gone semi-private, not
overly tough but nice.

★★ MILL RUN GOLF AND COUNTRY CLUB

SP—RO No. 1, Uxbridge (905)852-6212.

Call club for further information.

Subscriber comments: Good mix of open, wide holes and tight marshy
ones . . . Front nine so-so, back nine target golf . . . Needs to mature a bit
more.

★★★★ MONTERRA GOLF COURSE

R—R.R. No. 3, Collingwood (705)445-0231x407.

100 miles north of Toronto.

Holes: 18. **Par:** 72/72. **Yards:** 6,581/5,139. **Course rating:** 71.8/69.5.
Slope: 129/N/A.

Opened: 1989. **Pace of Play rating:** 4:30. **Green fee:** $22/42.

Credit cards: MC, V, AMEX. **Reduced fees:** Low season, Resort guests,
Twilight.

Caddies: No. **Golf carts:** $15 for 18 holes.

Discount golf packages: Yes. **Season:** May-Nov. **High:** May-Oct.

On-site lodging: Yes. **Rental clubs:** Yes.

Walking policy: Unrestricted walking. **Range:** Yes (grass).

To obtain tee times: Resort guest, when confirming reservation. General
public call three days in advance.

Subscriber comments: Links-style fairways, many bunkers . . . Course
well marked, rewards accuracy and not distance . . . Staff, pace and
condition were very good, not a walker's course . . . Shotmakers course
. . . Need all clubs. Plays long when windy . . . Beautiful setting . . .
Tough golf course, great weekend getaway . . . Very challenging from all
tees. A thinking man's course.

★★★ NOBLETON LAKES GOLF CLUB

PU—125 Nobleton Lakes Dr., Nobleton (905)859-4070.

20 miles north of Toronto.

Holes: 18. **Par:** 72/72. **Yards:** 7,089/5,819. **Course rating:** 75.3/72.8.

Slope: 145/N/A.
Opened: 1975. **Pace of Play rating:** 5:00. **Green fee:** $52/59.
Credit cards: MC, V, AMEX. **Reduced fees:** Low season, Twilight.
Caddies: No. **Golf carts:** Included in Green Fee.
Discount golf packages: No. **Season:** April-Nov. **High:** May-Oct.
On-site lodging: No. **Rental clubs:** Yes.
Walking policy: Mandatory cart. **Range:** Yes (grass).
To obtain tee times: Call three days in advance.
Subscriber comments: Front nine tight with extreme elevation, back opens up, always a challenge . . . Fairly difficult, design has too many blind tee shots . . . Easy access but 5½ hour rounds, very busy. Nice layout, average condition . . . Strong layout, rough will penalize you, very well kept . . . Not for the faint of heart.

★★ NORTH RIDGE MUNICIPAL GOLF COURSE
PU—320 Balmoral Dr., Branford (519)753-6112.
Call club for further information.
Subscriber comments: Not overly interesting or difficult but kept in good condition . . . Back nine less challenging than front . . . Straight up, straight down, no challenge.

★★½ THE OAKS OF ST. GEORGE GOLF CLUB
SP—269 German School Rd., Paris (519)448-3673.
2 miles north of Brantford.
Holes: 18. **Par:** 72/72. **Yards:** 6,328/5,628. **Course rating:** 71.1/67.9.
Slope: 123/115.
Opened: 1992. **Pace of Play rating:** 4:15. **Green fee:** $25/30.
Credit cards: MC, V. **Reduced fees:** Twilight, Seniors.
Caddies: No. **Golf carts:** $26 for 18 holes.
Discount golf packages: Yes. **Season:** May-Oct. **High:** June-Sept.
On-site lodging: No. **Rental clubs:** Yes.
Walking policy: Unrestricted walking. **Range:** Yes (grass).
To obtain tee times: Call pro shop.
Subscriber comments: Needs a cart, walking could be tiring, lots of hills and valleys . . . Course is challenging and picturesque . . . A four-year-old David Moote design, challenging course, demands extreme accuracy off the tee.

★★★★ OSPREY VALLEY HEATHLANDS GOLF COURSE
PU—R.R. No. 2, Alton (416)454-4653.
20 miles northwest of Toronto.
Holes: 18. **Par:** 71/71. **Yards:** 6,810/5,248. **Course rating:** N/A. **Slope:** N/A.
Opened: N/A. **Pace of Play rating:** N/A. **Green fee:** $ N/A.
Credit cards: MC, V, AMEX. **Reduced fees:** Weekdays, Resort guests, Twilight.
Caddies: Yes. **Golf carts:** N/A.
Discount golf packages: Yes. **Season:** April-Dec. **High:** May-Sept.
On-site lodging: No. **Rental clubs:** No.
Walking policy: N/A. **Range:** No.
Subscriber comments: Great links-style course, very demanding, tight fairways, rolling greens . . . Doug Carrick great design, cheap, thought I played in Scotland, even has a railroad going past . . . Blind shots make first time difficult . . . Just needs a clubhouse to complete a great golf experience . . . High mounding gives Scottish effect and isolated holes; good values despite very basic facilities.

PAKENHAM HIGHLANDS GOLF CLUB★
PU—Hwy. 15 at McWatty Rd., Pakenham (613)624-5550.
25 miles west of Ottawa.
Holes: 18. **Par:** 72/72. **Yards:** 6,561/5,360. **Course rating:** 71.0/72.0.
Slope: N/A.
Opened: 1994. **Pace of Play rating:** 4:15. **Green fee:** $24/27.
Credit cards: MC, V, Interac. **Reduced fees:** Weekdays, Twilight.
Caddies: No. **Golf carts:** $22 for 18 holes.
Discount golf packages: Yes. **Season:** April-Oct. **High:** June-Aug.

On-site lodging: No. **Rental clubs:** Yes.
Walking policy: Unrestricted walking. **Range:** Yes (grass).
To obtain tee times: Call five days in advance.

★★★½ PENINSULA LAKES GOLF CLUB
PU—569 Hwy. 20 W., Fenwick (905)892-8844.
Call club for further information
Subscriber comments: Built in an old quarry so sand plentiful, but tends to have a lot of sidehill slope, short but difficult, need a cart, especially for older golfers, always in excellent condition . . . Greens lightning fast . . . Four lakes come into play. Just delightful . . . Scenic course. Many challenges over and around water, great golf . . . New holes on back nine a real challenge. Tough course to walk . . . Spectacular views. Will only get better with age.

★★★ PHEASANT RUN GOLF CLUB
SOUTHRN UPLAND/MIDLANDS/HIGHLANDS
PU—18033 Con. 5 R.R. No. 1, Sharon (416)898-3917.
Call club for further information.
Subscriber comments: The hilltop holes are extremely scenic . . . Hilly forested course. All 27 holes exciting . . . Some holes are just plain unfair, great scenery though . . . Narrow fairways takes driver out of bag for mid-handicappers.

★★½ PINE KNOT GOLF AND COUNTRY CLUB
SP—5421 Hamilton Rd., Dorchester (519)268-3352.
7 miles east of London.
Holes: 18. **Par:** 71/71. **Yards:** 6,500/5,003. **Course rating:** 70.0/69.0.
Slope: N/A.
Opened: 1992. **Pace of Play rating:** 3:45. **Green fee:** $26/32.
Credit cards: MC, V, AMEX. **Reduced fees:** Low season.
Caddies: No. **Golf carts:** $25 for 18 holes.
Discount golf packages: Yes. **Season:** April-Nov. **High:** June-Aug.
On-site lodging: No. **Rental clubs:** Yes.
Walking policy: Unrestricted walking. **Range:** Yes (grass).
To obtain tee times: Call up to seven days in advance.
Subscriber comments: Have your shoes laced, first four holes very challenging. If you survive you can have a good round, lots of water, one or two gimmicky holes. Definitely play blues . . . Fairly open but enough water for a test . . . Pleasant dining too . . . Needs work, is very rough and young. They try very hard.

PINES OF GEORGINA GOLF CLUB★
SP—P.O. Box 44, Hwy. 48, Pefferlaw (705)437-1669.
50 miles northeast of Toronto.
Holes: 18. **Par:** 70/70. **Yards:** 6,012/5,457. **Course rating:** 67.8/65.7.
Slope: 112/107.
Opened: 1992. **Pace of Play rating:** 4:00. **Green fee:** $15/20.
Credit cards: MC, V. **Reduced fees:** Weekdays, Low season, Twilight.
Caddies: No. **Golf carts:** $9 for 18 holes.
Discount golf packages: Yes. **Season:** April-Nov. **High:** June-Aug.
On-site lodging: No. **Rental clubs:** Yes.
Walking policy: Unrestricted walking. **Range:** Yes (grass).
To obtain tee times: Call one week in advance.

★★ PINESTONE RESORT AND CONFERENCE CENTER
SP—P.O. Box 809, Haliburton (705)457-3444.
120 miles northeast of Toronto.
Holes: 18. **Par:** 71/73. **Yards:** 6,023/5,533. **Course rating:** 69.0/70.0.
Slope: N/A.
Opened: 1976. **Pace of Play rating:** 4:00-4:15 **Green fee:** $30/35.
Credit cards: MC, V, AMEX. **Reduced fees:** Weekdays, Low season, Resort guests.
Caddies: No. **Golf carts:** $25 for 18 holes.
Discount golf packages: Yes. **Season:** May-Oct. **High:** July-Sept.
On-site lodging: Yes. **Rental clubs:** Yes.

Walking policy: Unrestricted walking. **Range:** Yes (grass).
To obtain tee times: Call 6 a.m. to 6 p.m. daily.
Subscriber comments: Lovely resort course, short in yardage, but must be accurate . . . Highland course, tight, not always good condition . . . Needs work on greens, natural beauty . . . Short but tricky and very narrow . . . Good range of difficulty of holes. Fair to average golfer.

★★★ RENFREW GOLF CLUB
SP—P.O. Box 276, Renfrew (613)432-7729.
Call club for further information.
Subscriber comments: Old Scottish-type course. Demanding but fair . . . Hilly course, trees but little water, good test for all handicaps . . . Challenging, long for women, pretty in the fall.

★★★ RICHMOND HILL GOLF CLUB
PU—8755 Bathurst St., Richmond Hill (905)889-4653.
5 miles north of Toronto.
Holes: 18. **Par:** 70/70. **Yards:** 6,004/4,935. **Course rating:** 67.8/64.0.
Slope: 120/N/A.
Opened: 1992. **Pace of Play rating:** 4:00-4:30. **Green fee:** $18/45.
Credit cards: MC, V. **Reduced fees:** Weekdays, Low season, Twilight, Seniors.
Caddies: No. **Golf carts:** $29 for 18 holes.
Discount golf packages: Yes. **Season:** April-Nov. **High:** June-Aug.
On-site lodging: No. **Rental clubs:** Yes.
Walking policy: Unstricated walking. **Range:** Yes.
To obtain tee times: Call one day in advance with credit card. Purchase a green fee package for four day advance booking.
Subscriber comments: Short but well laid out . . . Just proves that length is not a premium . . . A good relatively short course with a forgiving front nine and a narrow, tough back nine . . . Well-trapped, small greens.

★½ RICHVIEW GOLF AND COUNTRY CLUB
SP—2406 Bronty Rd., Oakville (905)827-1211.
Call club for further information.
Subscriber comments: Good layout, shape has deteriorated in last couple of years . . . Very variable course conditions but open Year-round. if no snow on the ground.

RIVENDELL GOLF CLUB★
PU—R.R. No. 1, Verona (613)374-3404.
18 miles north of Kingston.
Holes: 18. **Par:** 71/71. **Yards:** 6,070/5,127. **Course rating:** 67.0/69.0.
Slope: N/A.
Opened: 1980. **Pace of Play rating:** 4:00. **Green fee:** $17/21.
Credit cards: MC, V. **Reduced fees:** Low season, Resort guests, Twilight.
Caddies: No. **Golf carts:** $10 for 18 holes.
Discount golf packages: No. **Season:** May-Oct. **High:** June-Sept.
On-site lodging: No. **Rental clubs:** Yes.
Walking policy: Unrestricted walking. **Range:** No.
To obtain tee times: Call pro shop.
Subscriber comments: Put in back nine a few years ago, could be very good course with some money and work.

★★ RIVER ROAD GOLF COURSE
PU—2115 River Rd., London (519)452-1822.
Call club for further information.
Subscriber comments: Short and straight, leave driver at home. If lost balls are your measure of a course, this is definitely over par . . . New course will improve with age, a testing layout.

★★½ ROSELAND GOLF AND CURLING CLUB
PU—455 Kennedy Dr., West, Windsor (519)969-3810.
Holes: 18. **Par:** 72/74. **Yards:** 6,588/5,914. **Course rating:** 70.6/73.1.
Slope: 119/123.

Opened: 1928. **Pace of Play rating:** 5:00. **Green fee:** $19/25.
Credit cards: MC, V. **Reduced fees:** Weekdays, Low season, Twilight,
Seniors.
Caddies: No. **Golf carts:** $13 for 18 holes.
Discount golf packages: No. **Season:** April-Oct. **High:** June-Aug.
On-site lodging: No. **Rental clubs:** Yes.
Walking policy: Unrestricted walking. **Range:** No.
To obtain tee times: Call Wednesday 9 a.m. for Saturday and Thursday 9
a.m. for Sunday and Monday holidays.
Subscriber comments: Very tight, elevated greens . . . Good value for a
Donald Ross course, very busy, too busy.

★★★½ ROYAL WOODBINE GOLF CLUB
SP—195 Galaxy Blvd., Etobicoke (416)674-4653.
Call club for further information.
Subscriber comments: Extremely narrow, target golf, metro location,
slow . . . Favors right to left player, too close to Toronto International
Airport . . . A good test and always in great shape . . . Good layout, water
and tough greens, low-mid handicap, staff good. Pace of Play fair.
Condition good spring-summer . . . Excellent creek on almost every hole.
But a treat to play. Super condition, new clubhouse, watch out for low-
flying planes.

★★★½ SILVER LAKES GOLF AND COUNTRY CLUB
SP—21114 Yonge Str., R.R. No. 1, Newmarket (905)836-8070.
20 miles north of Toronto.
Holes: 18. **Par:** 72/74. **Yards:** 6,910/5,210. **Course rating:** 74.5/73.5.
Slope: 135/N/A.
Opened: 1994. **Pace of Play rating:** 4:30. **Green fee:** $42/52.
Credit cards: MC, V, AMEX. **Reduced fees:** Weekdays, Low season,
Twilight, Seniors, Juniors.
Caddies: No. **Golf carts:** $12 for 18 holes.
Discount golf packages: No. **Season:** April-Nov. **High:** June-Aug.
On-site lodging: No. **Rental clubs:** Yes.
Walking policy: Unrestricted walking. **Range:** Yes (grass).
To obtain tee times: Call one week in advance.
Subscriber comments: A sleeper of a course, must be straight and smart,
great practice range . . . Extremely tight tree-lined course, fairways still
new, demanding test of golf . . . Established, mature trees; doesn't play like
new course.

★★★½ ST. ANDREWS VALLEY GOLF CLUB
PU—368 St. John Sideroad E., Aurora (905)727-7888.
20 miles north of Toronto.
Holes: 18. **Par:** 72/72. **Yards:** 7,304/5,536. **Course rating:** 77.4/68.5.
Slope: N/A.
Opened: 1993. **Pace of Play rating:** 4:30. **Green fee:** $38/58.
Credit cards: MC, V, AMEX. **Reduced fees:** Weekdays, Twilight.
Caddies: No. **Golf carts:** $14 for 18 holes.
Discount golf packages: Yes. **Season:** April-Nov. **High:** June-Aug.
On-site lodging: No. **Rental clubs:** Yes.
Walking policy: Unrestricted walking. **Range:** Yes (grass).
To obtain tee times: Call up to two weeks in advance.
Subscriber comments: Plush, challenging course, target type . . . A must
play, plays anywhere from 6,000–7,000 yds, very well maintained . . . New
young greens, good variety of holes . . . Very challenging links style with
trees and water . . . Huge greens. Six sets of tees. A monster from the back
but playable and fun from the whites . . . 10 minute tee off-times, good
speed of play . . . Long, tough well-trapped, fast undulating greens, bring
"A" game.

★★½ ST. CLAIR PARKWAY GOLF COURSE
PU—Moore Rd. 6, Mooretown (519)867-2810.
12 miles south of Sarnia.
Holes: 18. **Par:** 71/72. **Yards:** 6,720/5,731. **Course rating:** 70.5/71.0.
Slope: 118/122.

Opened: 1971. **Pace of Play rating:** 4:15. **Green fee:** $24.
Credit cards: MC, V. **Reduced fees:** Low season, Twilight.
Caddies: No. **Golf carts:** $27 for 18 holes.
Discount golf packages: No. **Season:** April-Nov. **High:** July-Aug.
On-site lodging: No. **Rental clubs:** Yes.
Walking policy: Unrestricted walking. **Range:** No.
To obtain tee times: Call up to seven days in advance.
Subscriber comments: Nice layout, treated well by staff, challenging . . .
Rolling, narrow, fairways with large greens . . . Long, good shape, not
busy, many risk/reward holes.

SUMMERHEIGHTS GOLF LINKS★
SOUTH/NORTH/WEST

PU—R.R. No. 2, South Branch Rd., Cornwall (613)938-8009.
70 miles south of Ottawa.
Holes: 27. **Par:** 72/72/72. **Yards:** 6,391/6,591/6,450. **Course rating:**
70.0/71.0/70.0. **Slope:** 121/123/123.
Opened: 1962. **Pace of Play rating:** 4:30. **Green fee:** $21/25.
Credit cards: MC, V. **Reduced fees:** Low season, Twilight.
Caddies: No. **Golf carts:** $25 for 18 holes.
Discount golf packages: No. **Season:** May-Oct. **High:** June-Aug.
On-site lodging: No. **Rental clubs:** Yes.
Walking policy: Unrestricted walking. **Range:** Yes (grass).
To obtain tee times: Call two days in advance.

★★ SUTTON CREEK GOLF AND COUNTRY CLUB

SP—R.R. No. 2, Walker and Guesto, Essex (519)726-6900.
Call club for further information.
Subscriber comments: Very inexpensive, front inland style with water in
play a lot, back nine, rolling links, nice conditioning, well laid out . . . Lots
of water, flat, good shape, nice staff, not that interesting.

★★ THAMES VALLEY GOLF COURSE

PU—850 Sunnyhill Ave., London (519)471-5750.
Call club for further information.
Subscriber comments: Scenic, mature layout, good conditions Year-
round. considering heavy traffic . . . A very challenging and tight old
course, very busy at times . . . Tough course. Good pace. Can enjoy it
better if you are a good straight hitter.

★★★ THUNDERBIRD GOLF AND COUNTRY CLUB

SP—995 Myrtle Rd., W., Ashburn (905)686-1121.
18 miles northeast of Toronto.
Holes: 18. **Par:** 72/72. **Yards:** 6,819/5,828. **Course rating:** 72.9/71.0.
Slope: 127/N/A.
Opened: 1959. **Pace of Play rating:** 4:30. **Green fee:** $20/40.
Credit cards: MC, V, AMEX. **Reduced fees:** Weekdays, Low season,
Twilight, Seniors, Juniors.
Caddies: No. **Golf carts:** $13 for 18 holes.
Discount golf packages: Yes. **Season:** April-Nov. **High:** June-Aug.
On-site lodging: No. **Rental clubs:** Yes.
Walking policy: Unrestricted walking. **Range:** Yes (grass).
To obtain tee times: Call seven days in advance. Credit card needed to
hold weekend tee time.
Subscriber comments: Slow, has character, rough in spots . . . Requires
good course management . . . Most holes are long for average golfer. Can
be fast greens . . . Excellent test, need all your clubs.

★★★ UPPER CANADA GOLF COURSE

SP—R.R. No. 1, Morrisburg (613)543-2003.
50 miles south of Montreal.
Holes: 18. **Par:** 72/73. **Yards:** 7,100/5,800. **Course rating:** 73.7/70.1.
Slope: N/A.
Opened: 1969. **Pace of Play rating:** 4:30. **Green fee:** $27/31.
Credit cards: MC, V. **Reduced fees:** Low season, Twilight, Juniors.
Caddies: No. **Golf carts:** $28 for 18 holes.

Discount golf packages: Yes. Season: April-Nov. High: June-Aug.
On-site lodging: No. Rental clubs: Yes.
Walking policy: Unrestricted walking. Range: Yes (grass).
To obtain tee times: Call three days in advance.
Subscriber comments: Long, challenging course, lots of geese, terrific value . . . Along St. Lawrence seaway . . . Canadian geese make walking an adventure on back nine . . . Great course at reasonable rates . . . Fairways with large greens and pleasing shapes.

★★★½ WHIRLPOOL GOLF COURSE
PU—Niagara Pkwy., Niagara Falls (905)356-1140.
25 miles north of Buffalo.
Holes: 18. Par: 72/71. Yards: 6,994/5,929. Course rating: 73.5/73.0.
Slope: 130/124.
Opened: 1951. Pace of Play rating: 4:30-5:00. Green fee: $30/32.
Credit cards: MC, V, AMEX. Reduced fees: Low season, Twilight.
Caddies: No. Golf carts: $28 for 18 holes.
Discount golf packages: Yes. Season: March-Nov. High: June-Sept.
On-site lodging: No. Rental clubs: Yes.
Walking policy: Unrestricted walking. Range: No.
To obtain tee times: Call as far in advance as you want. Must reserve with credit card.
Subscriber comments: Lovely course to play in mid-summer with the mist from the falls . . . Suitable for all levels of expertise . . . Stunning surroundings and scenery, course is long but it's O.K. to spray it here . . . Classic Stanley Thompson design along the Niagara Gorge . . . Run by the Niagara Parks Commission and maintained beautifully but slow. In spite of that it should not be missed . . . Nice course, but helicopters seem to buzz course every five minutes.

★½ WILLO-DELL GOLF CLUB
PU—P.O. Box 234, Niagara Falls (905)295-8181.
Call club for further information.
Subscriber comments: Great course, slow to play . . . Great value, well maintained . . . Expensive green fees for a very average course . . . Good layout, good shape, nice clubhouse atmosphere.

PRINCE EDWARD ISLAND

★★★½ BRUDENELL RIVER PROVINCIAL GOLF COURSE
PU—P.O. Box 1189, Roseneath (902)652-2342.
30 miles east of Charlottetown. Holes: 18. Par: 72/69.
Yards: 6,037/5,082. Course rating: 70.2/70.5. Slope: 131/129.
Opened: 1969. Pace of Play rating: 4:15. Green fee: $28/34.
Credit cards: MC, V, AMEX. Reduced fees: Low season, Resort guests, Twilight, Seniors, Juniors.
Caddies: Yes (advance notice required). Golf carts: $25 for 18 holes.
Discount golf packages: Yes. Season: May-Nov. High: June-Sept.
On-site lodging: Yes. Rental clubs: Yes.
Walking policy: Unrestricted walking. Range: Yes (grass).
To obtain tee times: Call in advance.
Subscriber comments: Owned, operated, maintained by the Province; well above average . . . In good condition all the time; long, underplayed; nice people . . . Great layout, fantastic value . . . Intimate woodland course, especially back nine . . . Good accommodations and great amenities . . . Beautiful, tight course, suits any player . . . Generous fairways, strategic bunkering, fast greens, well maintained . . . Best suited for longer hitters . . . Service excellent.

★★★ GREEN GABLES GOLF COURSE
PU—Rte. No.6, Cavendish (902)963-2488.
25 miles northwest of Charlottetown. Holes: 18. Par: 72/74.
Yards: 6,500/5,790. Course rating: 70.5/73.0. Slope: 120/122.
Opened: 1939. Pace of Play rating: 4:30. Green fee: $24/28.

Credit cards: MC, V. **Reduced fees:** Weekdays, Low season, Twilight.
Caddies: No. **Golf carts:** $24 for 18 holes.
Discount golf packages: No. **Season:** May-Oct. **High:** July-Aug.
On-site lodging: No. **Rental clubs:** Yes.
Walking policy: Unrestricted walking. **Range:** Yes (grass).
To obtain tee times: Call.
Subscriber comments: Okay condition, beautiful scenery, great pro, play is slow depending on time of day . . . Wooded, solitude, beauty, natural . . . Nice old course, good seaside holes . . . Great staff . . . Lots of woods and variety . . . Play early or late in season . . . Extremely busy in the heart of the tourist season . . . Very long, hilly course, small greens, very challenging.

★★★★½ THE LINKS AT CROWBUSH COVE

PU—P.O. Box 204, Morell (902)961-31000, (800)377-8337.
20 miles east of Charlottetown. **Holes:** 18. **Par:** 72/72.
Yards: 6,936/5,490. **Course rating:** 75.0/68.0. **Slope:** 134/114.
Opened: 1993. **Pace of Play rating:** 4:15. **Green fee:** $35/45.
Credit cards: MC, V. **Reduced fees:** Low season, Resort guests, Twilight, Seniors.
Caddies: No. **Golf carts:** $15 for 18 holes.
Discount golf packages: Yes. **Season:** May-Oct. **High:** July-Aug.
On-site lodging: No. **Rental clubs:** Yes.
Walking policy: Unrestricted walking. **Range:** Yes (grass).
To obtain tee times: Call ten days in advance with credit card number.
Selected as Best New Canadian Public Course of 1994 by Golf Digest.
Subscriber comments: An excellent course with scenery you cannot find anywhere else in the world . . . Excellent new course, long and difficult, good services, great scenery . . . Nothing short of spectacular! . . . Best links I've ever played . . . Too tough for me, but I still enjoy it, great condition . . . This course is out of this world . . . Excellent golf, lots of doglegs, small and large greens, tight and generous fairways, difficult greens, beautifully manicured, white-sand bunkers, excellent service . . . Best suited for high-ball, right-to-left players . . . Could play every day for the rest of my life . . . Best links course on the island . . . Every hole memorable . . . Staff great. The view from 11th tee is the reason I play golf . . . Can only get better with age.

★★★ MILL RIVER GOLF COURSE

R—P.O. Box 13, O'Leary (902)859-2238, (800)367-8337.
35 miles southeast of Summerside. **Holes:** 18. **Par:** 72/72.
Yards: 6,827/5,983. **Course rating:** 75.0/70.5. **Slope:** 132/127.
Opened: 1971. **Pace of Play rating:** 4:24. **Green fee:** $22/28.
Credit cards: MC, V. **Reduced fees:** Low season, Twilight, Seniors.
Caddies: No. **Golf carts:** $24 for 18 holes.
Discount golf packages: Yes. **Season:** May-Oct. **High:** June-Sept.
On-site lodging: Yes. **Rental clubs:** Yes.
Walking policy: Unrestricted walking. **Range:** Yes (grass).
To obtain tee times: Call up to ten days in advance.
Subscriber comments: Tricky course, good condition, well run, beautiful layout . . . Excellent value . . . Fun to play . . . Good for beginners and amateurs . . . Long, hilly course, tight fairways, water holes abound, great golf, tough to score when wind is high . . . Excellent service, pace is good . . . An out-of-the-way orphan . . . Best value on the island.

★½ RUSTICO RESORT GOLF & COUNTRY CLUB

R—RR No.3, South Rustico (902)963-2357, (800)465-3734.
12 miles north of Charlottetown. **Holes:** 18. **Par:** 72/72.
Yards: 6,675/5,550. **Course rating:** N/A. **Slope:** N/A.
Opened: 1980. **Pace of Play rating:** 3:30. **Green fee:** $15/22.
Credit cards: MC, V. **Reduced fees:** Weekdays, Low season, Resort guests, Twilight, Seniors, Juniors.
Caddies: No. **Golf carts:** $22 for 18 holes.
Discount golf packages: Yes. **Season:** April-Oct. **High:** July-Aug.
On-site lodging: Yes. **Rental clubs:** Yes.
Walking policy: Unrestricted walking. **Range:** Yes (grass).

To obtain tee times: Call.
Subscriber comments: Small greens, open fairways . . . Nice, short, sporty course . . . Not very interesting. Suited for occasional golfers . . . Two or three excellent holes, crowded.

★★ STANHOPE GOLF & COUNTRY CLUB
PU—York RR No.1, Stanhope (902)672-2842.
15 miles north of Charlottetown. **Holes:** 18. **Par:** 72/74.
Yards: 6,439/5,785. **Course rating:** 71.0/72.0. **Slope:** 118/N/A.
Opened: 1970. **Pace of Play rating:** 4:00-4:30. **Green fee:** $20/27.
Credit cards: V. **Reduced fees:** Weekdays, Low season, Resort guests.
Caddies: Yes. **Golf carts:** $23 for 18 holes.
Discount golf packages: Yes. **Season:** May-Oct. **High:** July-Aug.
On-site lodging: No. **Rental clubs:** Yes.
Walking policy: Unrestricted walking. **Range:** Yes (grass).
To obtain tee times: Call anytime.
Subscriber comments: Very scenic . . . Blue-collar course . . . Mix of links and woodland styles . . . Relaxed atmosphere . . . Hard course with a strong on-shore wind . . . Challenging greens, not crowded . . . Water, water, water.

★½ SUMMERSIDE GOLF CLUB
PU—120 Water St., Summerside (902)436-2505.
30 miles of Charlottetown. **Holes:** 18. **Par:** 72/72.
Yards: 6,428/6,106. **Course rating:** N/A. **Slope:** 123/121.
Opened: N/A. **Pace of Play rating:** N/A. **Green fee:** N/A.
Credit cards: MC, V, AMEX. **Reduced fees:** Low season, Twilight.
Caddies: No. **Golf carts:** N/A.
Discount golf packages: Yes. **Season:** May-Oct. **High:** July-Aug.
On-site lodging: No. **Rental clubs:** No.
Walking policy: N/A. **Range:** Yes (grass).
Subscriber comments: Some interesting holes . . . Nice, quiet local course, good condition . . . An old course, but well kept . . . Easy walk.

QUEBEC

BAIE MISSISQUOI GOLF CLUB★
PU—321 Ave. Venise West, Venise-en-Quebec (514)244-5932.
40 miles south of Montreal. **Holes:** 18. **Par:** 72/73.
Yards: 6,357/5,664. **Course rating:** 71.0/73.0. **Slope:** N/A.
Opened: 1962. **Pace of Play rating:** 4:15. **Green fee:** $14/28.
Credit cards: MC, V. **Reduced fees:** Weekdays, Low season, Twilight, Juniors.
Caddies: No. **Golf carts:** $23 for 18 holes.
Discount golf packages: No. **Season:** April-Oct. **High:** June-Aug.
On-site lodging: Yes. **Rental clubs:** Yes.
Walking policy: Unrestricted walking. **Range:** Yes (grass).
To obtain tee times: Call three days in advance.

DORVAL GOLF CLUB★
PU—2000 Aveneu Revechon, Dorval (514)631-6624.
Call club for further information.

GOLF LE MIRAGE
SP—3737 Chemin Martin, Terrebonne
15 miles northeast of Montreal.
Opened: 1993. **Pace of Play rating:** 4:30. **Green fee:** $35/45.
Credit cards: MC, V, AMEX, A.T.M., Enroute, Diners. **Reduced fees:** Weekdays.
Caddies: Yes. **Golf carts:** $24 for 18 holes.
Discount golf packages: Yes. **Season:** May-Nov. **High:** July-Aug.
On-site lodging: No. **Rental clubs:** Yes.
Walking policy: Unrestricted walking. **Range:** Yes (grass).
To obtain tee times: Call up to five days in advance for weekdays and two days in advance for weekends.

ARIZONA COURSE★
(514)477-4854.
Holes: 18. **Par:** 71/72.
Yards: 6,210/5,217. **Course rating:** 70.5/70.8. **Slope:** 129/131.
CAROLINA COURSE★
(514)477-4254.
Holes: 18. **Par:** 71/71.
Yards: 6,708/5,701. **Course rating:** 71.5/71.9. **Slope:** 125/123.

GRAY ROCKS GOLF CLUB★
SP—525 Rue Principale, Mont Tremblant (819)425-2771, (800)567-6744.
78 miles west of Montreal. **Holes:** 18. **Par:** 72/72.
Yards: 6,320/5,750. **Course rating:** 69.4/68.7. **Slope:** 119/118.
Opened: 1927. **Pace of Play rating:** 4:30. **Green fee:** $30/40.
Credit cards: MC, V, AMEX. **Reduced fees:** Weekdays, Low season,
Resort guests, Twilight.
Caddies: Yes. **Golf carts:** $32 for 18 holes.
Discount golf packages: Yes. **Season:** May-Oct. **High:** July-Aug.
On-site lodging: Yes. **Rental clubs:** Yes.
Walking policy: Unrestricted walking. **Range:** Yes (grass).
To obtain tee times: Call one week in advance for weekdays and 48 hours
in advance for weekends.
Subscriber comments: Good all-around course . . . Service, pace very
good . . . Scenic and challenging . . . In the mountains . . . Lake views,
good condition, great atmosphere.

LE CHATEAU MONTEBELLO★
SP—392 Rue Notre Dame, Montebello (819)423-4653.
60 miles east of Ottawa. **Holes:** 18. **Par:** 70/72.
Yards: 6,235/4,998. **Course rating:** 70.0/72.0. **Slope:** N/A.
Opened: 1929. **Pace of Play rating:** 4:30. **Green fee:** $54.
Credit cards: All major. **Reduced fees:** Weekdays, Low season, Twilight.
Caddies: No. **Golf carts:** Included in Green Fee.
Discount golf packages: Yes. **Season:** May-Oct. **High:** June-Sept.
On-site lodging: Yes. **Rental clubs:** Yes.
Walking policy: Mandatory cart. **Range:** Yes (grass).
To obtain tee times: Call seven days in advance.

LE CLUB DE GOLF CARLING LAKE★
R—Rte. 327 North, Pine Hill (514)476-1212.
601 miles north of Montreal. **Holes:** 18. **Par:** 72/72.
Yards: 6,691/5,352. **Course rating:** 72.0/71.0. **Slope:** 126/N/A.
Opened: 1961. **Pace of Play rating:** 4:30. **Green fee:** $37/40.
Credit cards: MC, V, AMEX. **Reduced fees:** Weekdays, Low season,
Twilight.
Caddies: No. **Golf carts:** $21 for 18 holes.
Discount golf packages: No. **Season:** May-Oct. **High:** June-Sept.
On-site lodging: Yes. **Rental clubs:** Yes.
Walking policy: Mandatory cart. **Range:** Yes.
To obtain tee times: Call and give credit card number for confirmation.
Subscriber comments: Gorgeous setting. Accommodations excellent . . .
Fun, beautiful, difficult, great course . . . Real challenge, hilly but has flat
sections . . . Best value around, staff and club A+.

LE GOLF CHANTECLER★
PU—Box 165, Ste. Adele (514)229-3742.
30 miles north of Montreal. **Holes:** 18. **Par:** 70/70.
Yards: 6,280/6,110. **Course rating:** N/A. **Slope:** N/A.
Opened: N/A. **Pace of Play rating:** N/A. **Green fee:** N/A.
Credit cards: MC, AMEX. **Reduced fees:** Weekdays, Low season.
Caddies: No. **Golf carts:** Included in Green Fee.
Discount golf packages: Yes. **Season:** May-Oct. **High:** June-Sept.
On-site lodging: Yes. **Rental clubs:** No.
Walking policy: N/A. **Range:** No.

MANOIR RICHELIEU★
R—181 Ave., Richelieu, Point-au-Pic (418)665-3703.
90 miles of Quebec. **Holes:** 18. **Par:** 70/70.
Yards: 6,255/5,980.
Call club for further information.

MONTREAL MUNICIPAL GOLF COURSE★
PU—7501 Francois Perrawet, Office 100, Montreal (514)872-1143.
Call club for further information.

OWL'S HEAD★
R—181 Chemin Owl's Head, Mansonville (514)292-3666.
75 miles east of Montreal. **Holes:** 18. **Par:** 72/72.
Yards: 6,705/5,295. **Course rating:** 72.0/69.0. **Slope:** N/A.
Opened: 1992. **Pace of Play rating:** 4:30. **Green fee:** $30/36.
Credit cards: MC, V. **Reduced fees:** Weekdays, Low season, Twilight.
Caddies: No. **Golf carts:** $13 for 18 holes.
Discount golf packages: Yes. **Season:** May-Oct. **High:** June-Aug.
On-site lodging: Yes. **Rental clubs:** Yes.
Walking policy: Unrestricted walking. **Range:** Yes.
To obtain tee times: Hotel guests can reserve anytime. General public can
reserve up to five days in advance.
Subscriber comments: Probably the best course within the area (40
minutes from Newport, Vt.) . . . Still young, maturing quickly into true
championship layout.

Notes

Part II

The West

★★½ ANCHORAGE GOLF COURSE

PU—3651 O'Malley Rd., Anchorage (907)522-3363.
Holes: 18. **Par:** 72/72.
Yards: 6,616/4,848. **Course rating:** 72.1/68.2. **Slope:** 130/119.
Opened: 1987. **Pace of Play rating:** N/A. **Green fee:** $25/37.
Credit cards: MC, V, DISC. **Reduced fees:** Resort guests, Seniors, Juniors.
Caddies: No. **Golf carts:** $10 for 18 holes.
Discount golf packages: No. **Season:** May-Oct. **High:** June-Aug.
On-site lodging: No. **Rental clubs:** Yes.
Walking policy: Walking at certain times. **Range:** Yes (grass).
To obtain tee times: Residents call five days in advance, nonresidents three days in advance.
Ranked 2nd in Alaska by Golf Digest.
Subscriber comments: Interesting layout . . . Scenic views of Mt. McKinley . . . Long, tight and hilly, a real challenge . . . Very tight, need to hit a straight ball . . . Condition is OK . . . Gets better each year . . . Fine clubhouse . . . Peak-hour rounds are slow . . . Probably the best course in Anchorage . . . Will be the best in Alaska.

★★½ EAGLEGLEN GOLF COURSE

PU—23-100 Elmendorf A.F.B., Anchorage (907)552-3821.
Holes: 18. **Par:** 72/72.
Yards: 6,689/5,457. **Course rating:** 71.6/70.4. **Slope:** 128/123.
Opened: 1973. **Pace of Play rating:** 4:00-5:00. **Green fee:** $9/28.
Credit cards: MC, V. **Reduced fees:** Low season, Twilight, Seniors.
Caddies: No. **Golf carts:** N/A.
Discount golf packages: No. **Season:** May-Oct. **High:** June-Aug.
On-site lodging: No. **Rental clubs:** Yes.
Walking policy: Unrestricted walking. **Range:** Yes.
To obtain tee times: Either call reservation system or show-up.
Ranked 1st in Alaska by Golf Digest.
Subscriber comments: Interesting Robert Trent Jones layout . . . Well laid out, uses water very well . . . Avoidable water . . . Many high risk, high reward holes . . . Three par 5s in the first five holes . . . Back nine has lots of character with creek crossings . . . Air Force course . . . Military has preferential tee times . . . Greens pretty good . . . Greens come around earlier here . . . Lots of fun, nothing too hard . . . Best in Alaska . . . Very scenic . . . Excellent photo opportunities.

★½ KENAI GOLF CLUB

PU—1420 Lawton Dr., Kenai (907)283-7500.
Call club for further information.
Subscriber comments: Good front nine, unimaginative back nine . . . Accessible, very reasonable . . . Course condition, especially greens, varies depending upon previous winter snow cover.

★★ MOOSE RUN GOLF COURSE

PU—P.O. Box 5130, Ft. Richardson (907)428-0056.
Holes: 18. **Par:** 72/72.
Yards: 6,499/5,382. **Course rating:** N/A. **Slope:** 119/120.
Opened: N/A. **Pace of Play rating:** N/A. **Green fee:** N/A.
Credit cards: MC, V. **Reduced fees:** Twilight.
Caddies: No. **Golf carts:** N/A.
Discount golf packages: No. **Season:** May-Oct. **High:** July-Aug.
On-site lodging: No. **Rental clubs:** No.
Walking policy: Unrestricted walking. **Range:** Yes.
Ranked 3rd in Alaska by Golf Digest.
Subscriber comments: Military course . . . Like two separate courses . . . Mostly wide open front nine, up and down back nine . . . Be sure to ring the bell for following players . . . Great scenery, including moose . . . Needs more upkeep and maintenance . . . Poor greens detract from good course . . . Friendliest course in the area . . . Nice folks . . . Can play 16 hours on a summer day . . . Play two rounds, same fee good all day . . . As the name suggests, watch out for moose.

ALASKA

NORTH STAR GOLF COURSE*

SP—330 Golf Club Dr., Fairbanks (907)457-4653.
Holes: 18. **Par:** 72/72.
Yards: 6,852/5,995. **Course rating:** N/A. **Slope:** N/A.
Opened: 1993. **Pace of Play rating:** 4:40. **Green fee:** $20/24.
Credit cards: MC, V. **Reduced fees:** Weekdays, Resort guests, Juniors.
Caddies: No. **Golf carts:** $10 for 18 holes.
Discount golf packages: No. **Season:** May-Oct. **High:** June-Sept.
On-site lodging: No. **Rental clubs:** Yes.
Walking policy: Walking at certain times. **Range:** Yes (grass).
To obtain tee times: Call 24 hours in advance. Members up to seven days in advance.
Subscriber comments: Northernmost course in U.S. . . . They have foxes on course . . . Play becomes delayed for moose and sandhill cranes, but I consider animal sightings to be a bonus.

★½ PALMER GOLF COURSE

PU—1000 Lepak Ave., Palmer (907)745-4653.
42 miles north of Anchorage. **Holes:** 18. **Par:** 72/73.
Yards: 7,125/5,895. **Course rating:** 74.5/74.6. **Slope:** 132/127.
Opened: 1990. **Pace of Play rating:** 4:25. **Green fee:** $20/22.
Credit cards: MC, V. **Reduced fees:** Seniors, Juniors.
Caddies: No. **Golf carts:** $18 for 18 holes.
Discount golf packages: Yes. **Season:** May-Sept. **High:** May-July.
On-site lodging: No. **Rental clubs:** Yes.
Walking policy: Unrestricted walking. **Range:** Yes (grass).
To obtain tee times: Call pro shop.
Subscriber comments: First to open in spring . . . Beautiful farmland and glacier surroundings . . . Best buy for 18 holes of great scenery . . . The most grand scenery in the world . . . Great views of Matanuska River and Chugach Mountains . . . Links style . . . Long but wide open. Swing away . . . Difficult when wind blows off glacier.

★★★ SETTLERS BAY GOLF CLUB

PU—Mile 8 Knik Rd., Wasilla (907)376-5466.
Call club for further information.
Subscriber comments: Great little nine holes . . . Wonderful . . . Best deal in Alaska . . . Beautiful course, good staff, plays fast . . . Short, but don't go to sleep . . . Best shape of any in Alaska . . . Best grass in state . . . Gets in good shape early . . . Second nine in progress . . . Wait until second nine is in.

Notes

★★ **AHWATUKEE COUNTRY CLUB**
SP—12432 S. 48th St., Phoenix (602)893-1161.
Holes: 18. **Par:** 72/72.
Yards: 6,713/5,506. **Course rating:** 71.5/70.3. **Slope:** 124/118.
Opened: 1971. **Pace of Play rating:** N/A. **Green fee:** N/A.
Credit cards: MC, V. **Reduced fees:** Weekdays, Low season, Twilight.
Caddies: No. **Golf carts:** $12 for 18 holes.
Discount golf packages: No. **Season:** Year-round. **High:** Jan.-March.
On-site lodging: No. **Rental clubs:** Yes.
Walking policy: Mandatory cart. **Range:** Yes (grass).
To obtain tee times: Call golf shop up to seven days in advance.
Subscriber comments: Mature, classic layout . . . Retirement style . . .
Tight condo course . . . 3 iron/3 wood course . . . Nice variety of holes . . .
A lot of traffic noise . . . Undergoing upgrades . . . Best shape in quite a
while.

ANTELOPE HILLS GOLF COURSE
PU—1 Perkins Dr., Prescott (602)776-7888.
90 miles north of Phoenix.
Pace of Play rating: N/A. **Green fee:** $22/32.
Credit cards: MC, V. **Reduced fees:** Low season, Twilight, Juniors.
Caddies: No. **Golf carts:** N/A.
Discount golf packages: Yes. **Season:** Year-round. **High:** April-Oct.
On-site lodging: No. **Rental clubs:** Yes.
Walking policy: Unrestricted walking. **Range:** Yes (grass).
To obtain tee times: Call three days in advance.
★★★ **NORTH COURSE**
Holes: 18. **Par:** 72/74.
Yards: 6,778/6,097. **Course rating:** 71.4/74.3. **Slope:** 131/126.
Opened: 1956.
Subscriber comments: Inexpensive traditional golf experience . . . Very
nice older-style course . . . Well established . . . Some long par 4s, lots of
trees . . . Mature trees . . . Narrow fairways . . . Tough greens, you had
better be good at putting . . . Not memorable . . . Great escape in the
summer . . . Good mountain getaway . . . A cool break from a desert
summer.
★★½ **SOUTH COURSE**
Holes: 18. **Par:** 72/72.
Yards: 7,014/5,560. **Course rating:** 71.3/71.0. **Slope:** 124/113.
Opened: 1992.
Subscriber comments: New course with few trees . . . Sprayer's delight
. . . Well laid out, interesting, playable . . . Some interesting holes . . .
Some short holes, good finishing holes. . . . The 18th can ruin a scorecard
. . . Not mature yet . . . Needs more growth time . . . North course gets
the ink, but the South is a player's course . . . Not much trouble . . . Not as
challenging as the North . . . Less character than North . . . Nondescript
. . . Killer course in the wind . . . Worth the drive.

★★½ **ARIZONA GOLF RESORT**
R—425 South Power Rd., Mesa (602)832-1661.
25 miles from Phoenix. **Holes:** 18. **Par:** 71/71.
Yards: 6,574/6,195. **Course rating:** N/A. **Slope:** 123/117.
Opened: N/A. **Pace of Play rating:** N/A. **Green fee:** N/A.
Credit cards: All major. **Reduced fees:** Weekdays, Low season, Resort
guests, Twilight.
Caddies: No. **Golf carts:** Included in Green Fee.
Discount golf packages: Yes. **Season:** Year-round. **High:** Jan.-March.
On-site lodging: Yes. **Rental clubs:** No.
Walking policy: N/A. **Range:** Yes (grass).
Subscriber comments: Oldtimer course . . . Nice resort course . . .
Traditional . . . Lots of trees . . . Lots of sand . . . Some water . . . Sporty
greens . . . Tight fairways . . . Winds between homes on both sides . . .
Fun, but not the most exciting . . . Not visually attractive . . . Not a
destination course . . . Improvements have been made . . . Good staff.

ARIZONA

ARIZONA BILTMORE COUNTRY CLUB
SP—24th St. and Missouri, Phoenix (602)955-9655.
Pace of Play rating: 4:50. **Green fee:** $38/95.
Credit cards: MC, V, AMEX. **Reduced fees:** Low season.
Caddies: No. **Golf carts:** Included in Green Fee.
Discount golf packages: Yes. **Season:** Year-round. **High:** Jan.-May.
On-site lodging: Yes. **Rental clubs:** Yes.
Walking policy: Mandatory cart. **Range:** Yes (grass).
To obtain tee times: May call five days in advance.
★★★ ADOBE COURSE
Holes: 18. **Par:** 72/73.
Yards: 6,800/6,101. **Course rating:** 71.5/74.3. **Slope:** 121/123.
Opened: 1928.

Subscriber comments: Older course . . . Bill Bell layout, akin to Riviera, many similar holes . . . Old time park course . . . Trees like midwest courses . . . Midwest in the desert . . . A little flat . . . Flat and uninteresting . . . Plain vanilla . . . Not much scenery . . . Surrounding homes more interesting than course . . . Super nice shape . . . Always in top condition . . . Just a comfortable course . . . Staff makes it an enjoyable day . . . They do treat you like a million bucks.
★★★ LINKS COURSE
Holes: 18. **Par:** 71/71.
Yards: 6,300/4,747. **Course rating:** 69.3/68.0. **Slope:** 122/107.
Opened: 1978.
Subscriber comments: Fun course . . . Imaginative, with taste and class . . . Hilly, shorter and sportier than Adobe . . . Bill Johnston design . . . Uses terrain well . . . Winds through mountain foothills, great views . . . All trouble is easily seen . . . All Bermuda grass . . . Not too demanding . . . Not outstanding . . . Nothing spectacular . . . Great hotel, average golf course . . . Mediocre practice facilities . . . Courteous staff . . . Service good . . . Flowers a plus.

★★★ ARROWHEAD RANCH COUNTRY CLUB
SP—19888 N. 73rd Ave., Glendale (602)561-9600.
Call club for further information.
Subscriber comments: Great Palmer course design . . . Challenging . . . Need all the shots . . . User friendly . . . Quite forgiving, very playable and yet fun . . . Good layout, a little windy . . . Water on nine holes. . . Thought I was at the beach . . . Great 18th . . . Not allowed to carry bag or use pull cart.

★★ ARTHUR PACK DESERT GOLF CLUB
PU—9101 North Thornydale Rd., Tucson (602)744-3322.
Holes: 18. **Par:** 72/72.
Yards: 6,900/5,100. **Course rating:** 71.6/67.6. **Slope:** 118/108.
Opened: 1975. **Pace of Play rating:** 4:00. **Green fee:** $12/20.
Credit cards: MC, V. **Reduced fees:** Low season, Seniors, Juniors.
Caddies: No. **Golf carts:** $16 for 18 holes.
Discount golf packages: No. **Season:** Year-round. **High:** Nov.-May.
On-site lodging: No. **Rental clubs:** Yes.
Walking policy: Unrestricted walking. **Range:** Yes (grass).
To obtain tee times: May call up to seven days in advance.
Subscriber comments: Very nice design . . . One of Tucson's many good courses . . . The fairest desest course in Tuscon . . . Lots of desert, accurate shots a must . . . Just fair in all areas . . . Great new improvements . . . Very short from the whites . . . Bring water, there's nothing to drink on the course . . . Ancient golf carts . . . Greens above average, sand traps in poor condition . . . Condition of greens is always excellent.

THE BOULDERS CLUB
R—34631 North Tom Darlington Dr., Carefree (602)488-9028.
Pace of Play rating: N/A. **Green fee:** N/A.
33 miles north of Phoenix.
Credit cards: All maior. **Reduced fees:** Low season.

Caddies: No. **Golf carts:** Included in Green Fee.
Discount golf packages: Yes. **Season:** Year-round. **High:** Feb.–May.
On-site lodging: Yes. **Rental clubs:** No.
Walking policy: N/A. **Range:** Yes (grass).
NORTH COURSE
★★★★ **Holes:** 18. **Par:** 72/72.
Yards: 6,731/4,893. **Course rating:** N/A. **Slope:** 135/113.
Opened: 1984.
Ranked 52nd in America's 75 Best Resort Courses by Golf Digest. Ranked 12th in Arizona by Golf Digest.
Subscriber comments: Great experience . . . Always a pleasure . . . Sheer beauty . . . Desert golf at its best . . . Target golf for the short and straight average hitter . . . Local knowledge very important . . . Beautifully designed and maintained . . . Expensive, but the avid golfer should play it at any price . . . The best desert course . . . Too much desert . . . Great, great condition, greater treatment . . . Service personnel are super.

★★★★½ **SOUTH COURSE**
Holes: 18. **Par:** 71/71.
Yards: 6,589/4,715. **Course rating:** N/A. **Slope:** 137/107.
Opened: N/A.
Ranked 15th in Arizona by Golf Digest.
Subscriber comments: Gorgeous . . . Lovely setting. Interesting layout . . . Great greens . . . Love it! . . . Views out of sight. Green fees are, too . . . Worth every penny at least once . . . Tough course, No. 17 in particular . . . Near perfect condition . . . We loved both Boulders . . . Maybe it's just the scenery. Nah, it's great golf . . . Service is outstanding. I will return.

★★★½ **CANOA HILLS GOLF COURSE**

SP—300 W. Calle Urbano, Green Valley (602)648-1880.
25 miles south of Tucson. **Holes:** 18. **Par:** 72/72.
Yards: 6,610/2,533. **Course rating:** 70.8/68.5. **Slope:** 126/116.
Opened: 1984. **Pace of Play rating:** N/A. **Green fee:** $21/52.
Credit cards: MC, V. **Reduced fees:** Low season, Twilight, Juniors.
Caddies: No. **Golf carts:** Included in Green Fee.
Discount golf packages: No. **Season:** Year-round. **High:** Jan.–April.
On-site lodging: No. **Rental clubs:** Yes.
Walking policy: Mandatory cart. **Range:** Yes (grass).
To obtain tee times: Call two days in advance.
Subscriber comments: Mature south Arizona course . . . Desert target golf . . . Tight fairways, Mesquite trees . . . Every hole a new adventure . . . Starts out ordinary, builds to quality finishing holes . . . Demands great control on tees . . . Lots of desert to catch errant shots . . . Testing holes for iron play . . . Tremendous greens . . . Bent-grass greens . . . Lightning fast . . . High handicappers should avoid . . . Good staff and restaurant . . . Carts must stay on path . . . Slows play . . . Impeccable groundskeeping, never a bad lie . . . Best overall course condition in southern Arizona . . . Best condition of any Arizona course . . . Best-kept secret in the state.

★★ **CASA GRANDE MUNICIPAL GOLF COURSE**
PU—2121 N. Thornton Rd., Casa Grande (602)836-9216.
Call club for further information.
Subscriber comments: Wide open . . . Flat . . . Friendly . . . Unimaginative . . . Maintenance was marginal . . . Sometimes hard to find next tee.

CAVE CREEK GOLF CLUB
PU—15202 N. 19th Ave., Phoenix (602)866-8076.
Holes: 18. **Par:** 72/72.
Yards: 6,876/5,614. **Course rating:** 71.1/70.0. **Slope:** 122/112.
Opened: 1994. **Pace of Play rating:** 4:30. **Green fee:** $17/25.
Credit cards: None. **Reduced fees:** Low season, Twilight, Seniors, Juniors.
Caddies: No. **Golf carts:** $15 for 18 holes.

Discount golf packages: No. **Season:** Year-round. **High:** Nov.-April.
On-site lodging: No. **Rental clubs:** Yes.
Walking policy: Unrestricted walking. **Range:** Yes (grass).
To obtain tee times: Call two days in advance.
Subscriber comments: Long, busy course . . . So-so front nine, challenging back nine . . . Challenging but not unreasonable . . . Muny built on a landfull and looks it . . . Thin fairways . . . Could be a great track with more maintenance . . . Greens in nice shape . . . Undulating greens . . . Some greens are very tough . . . For a muny, it always seems to find a way to be challenging.

CLUB TERRAVITA★
SP—34034 North 69th Way, Scottsdale (602)488-1333.
Holes: 18. **Par:** 72/72.
Yards: 7,186/5,367. **Course rating:** 74.4/70.3. **Slope:** 139/127.
Opened: 1994. **Pace of Play rating:** 4:20. **Green fee:** $115.
Credit cards: MC, V, AMEX. **Reduced fees:** No.
Caddies: No. **Golf carts:** $14 for 18 holes.
Discount golf packages: No. **Season:** Year-round. **High:** Nov.-May.
On-site lodging: No. **Rental clubs:** Yes.
Walking policy: Mandatory cart. **Range:** Yes.
To obtain tee times: Nonmembers can call 24 hours in advance.

★★★ CLUB WEST GOLF CLUB
PU—16400 S. 14th Ave., Phoenix (602)460-4400.
Holes: 18. **Par:** 72/72.
Yards: 7,057/4,985. **Course rating:** 73.1/63.5. **Slope:** 129/104.
Opened: 1993. **Pace of Play rating:** 4:00. **Green fee:** $35/79.
Credit cards: All major. **Reduced fees:** Low season, Twilight.
Caddies: No. **Golf carts:** Included in Green Fee.
Discount golf packages: No. **Season:** Year-round. **High:** Jan.-April.
On-site lodging: No. **Rental clubs:** Yes.
Walking policy: Mandatory cart. **Range:** Yes (grass).
To obtain tee times: Call seven days in advance with credit card number.
Subscriber comments: User-friendly desert-style course . . . Great links . . . Service second to none. Great clubhouse . . . Ho-hum . . . Too many short holes . . . Easy for the better golfer . . . Course has not developed yet . . . Nos. 3 and 7 are great golf holes . . . No. 17 has two greens. Make your choice! Awesome hole.

CONCHO VALLEY COUNTRY CLUB★
SP—HC-30, Box 900, Concho (602)337-4644.
28 miles northeast of Show Low. **Holes:** 18. **Par:** 72/72.
Yards: 6,656/5,559. **Course rating:** 69.1/70.0. **Slope:** 119/128.
Opened: 1975. **Pace of Play rating:** 3:30. **Green fee:** $12/20.
Credit cards: None. **Reduced fees:** Low season, Resort guests, Twilight, Seniors, Juniors.
Caddies: No. **Golf carts:** $10 for 18 holes.
Discount golf packages: Yes. **Season:** Year-round. **High:** May-Sept.
On-site lodging: Yes. **Rental clubs:** Yes.
Walking policy: Unrestricted walking. **Range:** Yes (grass).
To obtain tee times: Call seven days in advance.

★★★ COYOTE LAKES GOLF CLUB
PU—18800 N. Coyote Lakes Pkwy., Surprise (602)566-2323.
8 miles northwest of Phoenix. **Holes:** 18. **Par:** 71/71.
Yards: 6,159/4,708. **Course rating:** 68.9/68.0. **Slope:** 114/107.
Opened: 1993. **Pace of Play rating:** N/A. **Green fee:** $20/40.
Credit cards: MC, V. **Reduced fees:** Weekdays, Low season, Twilight, Juniors.
Caddies: No. **Golf carts:** Included in Green Fee.
Discount golf packages: No. **Season:** Year-round. **High:** Jan.-April.
On-site lodging: No. **Rental clubs:** Yes.

Walking policy: Mandatory cart. **Range:** Yes (grass).
To obtain tee times: Call seven days in advance.
Subscriber comments: New, short target course . . . Fun layout . . . Fun to play . . . Worthwhile . . . Interesting use of land . . . In a desert wash . . . Unusual layout, very uneven fairways . . . Not a level placement on the course . . . Beautiful course for straight drivers . . . Position golf . . . Rewards accuracy, not power . . . Tricky holes . . . Every hole different, great fun for the money . . . Narrow. Tough. Great greens . . . Dare to reach No. 6 in two? Beware the rock wall . . . Young course, will be outstanding in about 10 years . . . A sleeper . . . Not fully developed but lots of fun . . . Fun, but short . . . Needs conditioning and a better practice range . . . On the verge of being too expensive . . . One of the most pleasurable courses I've ever played.

DAVE WHITE MUNICIPAL GOLF COURSE*
PU—2121 N. Thornton Rd., Casa Grande (602)836-9216.
Holes: 18. **Par:** 72/72.
Yards: 6,316/5,038. **Course rating:** 68.8/66.5. **Slope:** 115/100.
Opened: 1978. **Pace of Play rating:** 4:00. **Green fee:** $15.
Credit cards: MC, V. **Reduced fees:** Weekdays, Low season, Twilight, Seniors, Juniors.
Caddies: No. **Golf carts:** $8 for 18 holes.
Discount golf packages: No. **Season:** Year-round. **High:** Nov.-March.
On-site lodging: No. **Rental clubs:** Yes.
Walking policy: Unrestricted walking. **Range:** Yes (grass).
To obtain tee times: Call three days in advance.
Subscriber comments: Small-town friendly . . . Worth the drive when tee times are all but impossible in Phoenix . . . Front nine needs remodeling to match the great new back nine.

★★½ DESERT HILLS GOLF COURSE
PU—1245 Desert Hills Dr., Yuma (520)344-4653.
175 miles west of Phoenix. **Holes:** 18. **Par:** 72/74.
Yards: 6,800/5,726. **Course rating:** 71.1/72.4. **Slope:** 117/122.
Opened: 1973. **Pace of Play rating:** 4:00-4:30. **Green fee:** $8/16.
Credit cards: None. **Reduced fees:** Low season, Juniors.
Caddies: No. **Golf carts:** $9 for 18 holes.
Discount golf packages: No. **Season:** Year-round. **High:** Dec.-April.
On-site lodging: No. **Rental clubs:** Yes.
Walking policy: Unrestricted walking. **Range:** Yes (grass).
To obtain tee times: Call computerized reservation up to 48 hours in advance. You need a nine-digit number to make reservations (such as a social security number).
subscriber comments: A municipal course, but you wouldn't know it . . . A gem in an out-of-the-way place . . . A good test of golf, but wide open in most areas so pace of play is good . . . Long and challenging . . . Good for long ball hitters . . . Best municipal course I've seen.

★★ DOBSON RANCH GOLF CLUB
PU—2155 S. Dobson Rd., Mesa (602)644-2270.
15 miles east of Phoenix. **Holes:** 18. **Par:** 72/72.
Yards: 6,593/5,598. **Course rating:** 71.0/71.3. **Slope:** 117/116.
Opened: 1973. **Pace of Play rating:** N/A. **Green fee:** $13/21.
Credit cards: MC, V, AMEX. **Reduced fees:** Low season, Twilight, Juniors.
Caddies: No. **Golf carts:** N/A.
Discount golf packages: No. **Season:** Year-round. **High:** Nov.-April.
On-site lodging: No. **Rental clubs:** Yes.
Walking policy: Unrestricted walking. **Range:** Yes (grass).
To obtain tee times: Call four days in advance.
Subscriber comments: Standard course . . . Straightforward golf . . . No frills . . . Huge greens . . . Easy layout, some interesting holes . . . Well-kept . . . Very crowded . . . Slow, slow and more slow . . . Slowest pace of play in the valley . . . Should overseed fairways in the winter . . . Very playable for most golfers.

ARIZONA

★★★ EAGLE'S NEST COUNTRY CLUB AT PEBBLE CREEK
SP—3639 Clubhouse Dr., Goodyear (602)935-6750, (800)795-4663.
15 miles west of Phoenix. **Holes:** 18. **Par:** 72/72.
Yards: 6,860/5,030. **Course rating:** 72.6/68.0. **Slope:** 127/111.
Opened: 1991. **Pace of Play rating:** N/A. **Green fee:** $20/45.
Credit cards: MC, V. **Reduced fees:** Low season, Twilight.
Caddies: No. **Golf carts:** $8 for 18 holes.
Discount golf packages: No. **Season:** Year-round. **High:** Jan.-March.
On-site lodging: No. **Rental clubs:** Yes.
Walking policy: Unrestricted walking. **Range:** Yes (grass).
To obtain tee times: Call two days in advance.
Subscriber comments: New . . . Links layout . . . Level ground molded
into rolling course . . . Wide fairways, lightly played . . . Cart-paths-only
policy the only negative . . . Carts-on-path policy slows play to a crawl . . .
Friendly staff.

★★½ ELDEN HILLS GOLF CLUB
PU—2380 N. Oakmont Dr., Flagstaff (602)527-7999.
Holes: 18. **Par:** 73/73.
Yards: 6,029/5,280. **Course rating:** 66.6/70.5. **Slope:** 115/120.
Opened: 1960. **Pace of Play rating:** N/A. **Green fee:** $25.
Credit cards: MC, V, AMEX. **Reduced fees:** Weekdays, Low season,
Twilight, Juniors.
Caddies: No. **Golf carts:** $13 for 18 holes.
Discount golf packages: No. **Season:** March-Nov. **High:** May-Sept.
On-site lodging: No. **Rental clubs:** Yes.
Walking policy: Unrestricted walking. **Range:** Yes (grass).
To obtain tee times: May call up to three days in advance.
Subscriber comments: "Hills" is well named . . . Hilly mountain course
. . . Very difficult in places. Don't walk . . . Lots of trees . . . Pretty short
. . . Shorter in high altitude . . . Rough around the edges . . . Sand traps
need more sand, fairways need more water . . . Worth the drive from
Phoenix in the summer.

★★★ GOLF CLUB AT EL DORADO LAKES
PU—1800 West Guadalupe, Gilbert (602)926-3589, (800)468-7918.
10 miles east of Phoenix. **Holes:** 18. **Par:** 72/72.
Yards: 6,716/4,992. **Course rating:** 72.2/68.8. **Slope:** 132/120.
Opened: 1993. **Pace of Play rating:** N/A. **Green fee:** $30/75.
Credit cards: MC, V, AMEX. **Reduced fees:** Weekdays, Low season,
Resort guests, Twilight.
Caddies: No. **Golf carts:** Included in Green Fee.
Discount golf packages: Yes. **Season:** Year-round. **High:** Jan.-April.
On-site lodging: No. **Rental clubs:** Yes.
Walking policy: Mandatory cart. **Range:** Yes (grass).
To obtain tee times: Call seven days in advance.
Subscriber comments: Young, up-and-coming daily fee. We need more
like this . . . Great fairways and greens . . . Small, elevated greens . . .
Elephant buried in every green . . . Plan your shots . . . Sneaky easy . . . A
little confusing at times . . . Asking too much for a course not yet mature
. . . Is going to be popular.

★★★ ELEPHANT ROCKS GOLF CLUB
PU—2200 Country Club Rd., Williams (602)635-4935.
30 miles west of Flagstaff. **Holes:** 9. **Par:** 70/72.
Yards: 5,937/5,309. **Course rating:** 67.6/67.3. **Slope:** 123/126.
Opened: 1990. **Pace of Play rating:** N/A. **Green fee:** $16/18.
Credit cards: MC, V, DISC. **Reduced fees:** Weekdays, Juniors.
Caddies: No. **Golf carts:** $16 for 18 holes.
Discount golf packages: No. **Season:** April-Oct. **High:** May-Sept.
On-site lodging: No. **Rental clubs:** Yes.
Walking policy: Unrestricted walking. **Range:** Yes (grass).
To obtain tee times: Call one week in advance.
Subscriber comments: Wonderful nine-hole layout . . . Fairly new . . .
Cute layout . . . Located at about 6700 feet elevation, among the pines . . .

FRUGAL PICK

Winds through the forest . . . Narrow fairways mean you have to hit the ball pretty straight . . . Not a long course, but No. 8 is a killer. A very long hole and straight uphill . . . Very quiet. No trouble getting on . . . Outstanding value for a nine-hole course . . . Play a second nine holes from longer tees . . . Best nine-hole course in Arizona . . . Most picturesque course in Arizona.

★★½ ELOY-TOHONO MUNICIPAL GOLF COURSE

PU—1-10 and Toltect Rd., Eloy (602)466-7734.

47 miles southeast of Tucson. **Holes:** 18. **Par:** 72/72.

Yards: 7,100/5,363. **Course rating:** 72.3/69.8. **Slope:** 117/112.

Opened: 1992. **Pace of Play rating:** 4:30. **Green fee:** $24.

Credit cards: MC, V. **Reduced fees:** Low season, Juniors.

Caddies: No. **Golf carts** $7 for 18 holes.

Discount golf packages: Yes. **Season:** Year-round. **High:** Oct.-April.

On-site lodging: No. **Rental clubs:** Yes.

Walking policy: Unrestricted walking. **Range:** Yes (grass).

To obtain tee times: Call seven days in advance.

Subscriber comments: New desert course . . . Great layout but in the middle of nowhere . . . Delightful and devious design . . . Wild yet fun . . . Innovative greens . . . No. 2 is the longest hole in Arizona . . . Promising course . . . Needs to age a little . . . Will be very playable . . . Give it five more years . . . Will be great when it grows up.

★★★ EMERALD CANYON GOLF COURSE

PU—72 Emerald Canyon Dr., Parker (602)667-3366.

150 miles east of Phoenix. **Holes:** 18. **Par:** 72/71.

Yards: 6,657/4,754. **Course rating:** 71.5/66.2. **Slope:** 131/119.

Opened: 1989. **Pace of Play rating:** N/A. **Green fee:** $16/28.

Credit cards: MC, V. **Reduced fees:** Weekdays, Low season, Twilight, Juniors.

Caddies: No. **Golf carts:** Included in Green Fee.

Discount golf packages: Yes. **Season:** Year-round. **High:** Nov.-March.

On-site lodging: No. **Rental clubs:** Yes.

Walking policy: Mandatory cart. **Range:** Yes (grass).

To obtain tee times: Call up to one week in advance.

Subscriber comments: An unexpected pleasure . . . Fantastic, unusual layout. Different kind of golf . . . Every hole different . . . Canyon fairways . . . Set in between stony cliffs and bluffs. Narrow fairways and hidden greens challenge you . . . It's a nightmare the first time around . . . Large greens with character and complexity, lots of ups and downs . . . Stunning surroundings . . . A jewel in the desert . . . Rocky, not fair in places . . . Don't play in the heat . . . Not walkable . . . Best bargain in Arizona . . . Bring lots of ammo!

★★ ENCANTO PARK GOLF COURSE

PU—2705 N. 15th Ave., Phoenix (602)253-3963.

Holes: 18. **Par:** 70/72.

Yards: 6,386/5,731. **Course rating:** 69.0/70.5. **Slope:** 111/111.

Opened: 1937. **Pace of Play rating:** 4:30. **Green fee:** $11/26.

Credit cards: MC, V. **Reduced fees:** Low season, Twilight, Seniors, Juniors.

Caddies: No. **Golf cart:** $18 for 18 holes.

Discount golf packages: No. **Season:** Year-round. **High:** Feb.-April.

On-site lodging: No. **Rental clubs:** Yes.

Walking policy: Unrestricted walking. **Range:** Yes (grass).

Complex also includes a 9 hole par 3 course.

To obtain tee times: Call two days in advance.

Subscriber comments: Nice old-fashioned course . . . Flat with few traps . . . In good condition year-round . . . Plain and simple but fun . . . Not much of a challenge . . . OK golf for the economy-minded . . . Love the green fee . . . Old, established, flat, easy, cheap, fun.

★★ ESTRELLA MOUNTAIN GOLF COURSE

PU—Golf Course Dr., Goodyear (602)932-3714.
15 miles west of Phoenix. **Holes:** 18. **Par:** 71/73.
Yards: 6,767/5,383. **Course rating:** 71.2/71.2. **Slope:** 121/116.
Opened: 1962. **Pace of Play rating:** 4:00. **Green fee:** $10/22.
Credit cards: MC, V. **Reduced fees:** Low season, Twilight, Seniors, Juniors.
Caddies: No. **Golf carts:** N/A.
Discount golf packages: No. **Season:** Year-round. **High:** Dec.-April.
On-site lodging: No. **Rental clubs:** Yes.
Walking policy: Unrestricted walking. **Range:** Yes (grass).
To obtain tee times: Call seven days in advance.
Subscriber comments: A casual play . . . Not a bad place to play for a public course . . . Interesting holes . . . Not crowded . . . Fairly easy for seniors . . . Upgraded in recent years . . . Maybe worth the trip out there, maybe not.

★★★ THE 500 CLUB

PU—4707 W. Pinnacle Peak Rd., Glendale (602)492-9500.
20 miles northwest of Phoenix. **Holes:** 18. **Par:** 72/73.
Yards: 6,543/5,557. **Course rating:** 69.8/69.8. **Slope:** 116/112.
Opened: 1989. **Pace of Play rating:** 4:30. **Green fee:** $20/45.
Credit cards: MC, V, AMEX. **Reduced fees:** Weekdays, Juniors.
Caddies: No. **Golf carts:** $10 for 18 holes.
Discount golf packages: No. **Season:** Year-round. **High:** Nov.-April.
On-site lodging: No. **Rental clubs:** Yes.
Walking policy: Unrestricted walking. **Range:** Yes (grass).
To obtain tee times: Call up to three days in advance.

Subscriber comments: Another up-and-comer . . . Great desert course . . . Very pleasant, particularly for the average player . . . Picturesque as any, this course lulls you with its deceptive distances . . . Very fair and playable . . . Improving as it matures . . . Smoothest greens anywhere . . . Great except last four holes . . . Last three holes need to be redesigned . . . Not for wild people . . . Don't miss fairways, you'll wreck your clubs . . . A plus is a chance to meet Indy 500 winner Tom Sneva . . . Tom Sneva tends bar here!

★★★ THE FOOTHILLS GOLF CLUB

PU—2201 E. Clubhouse Dr., Phoenix (602)460-4653.
Holes: 18. **Par:** 72/72.
Yards: 6,958/5,438. **Course rating:** 72.3/70.1. **Slope:** 122/114.
Opened: 1987. **Pace of Play rating:** 4:15. **Green fee:** $25/85.
Credit cards: MC, V, AMEX. **Reduced fees:** Weekdays, Low season, Twilight, Juniors.
Caddies: No. **Golf carts:** Included in Green Fee.
Discount golf packages: No. **Season:** Year-round. **High:** Jan.-March.
On-site lodging: No. **Rental clubs:** Yes.
Walking policy: Mandatory cart. **Range:** Yes (grass).
To obtain tee times: Call up to seven days in advance.
Subscriber comments: Nice desert golf . . . Nice scenery . . . Nice track . . . Nice course, making a comeback . . . The greens are back in great shape. Finally! . . . Course has gotten better. Great shape.

★★★½ FOOTHILLS CLUB WEST

PU—16400 South 14th Ave., Phoenix (602)460-4400.
Call club for further information.
Subscriber comments: Nice start for a new course . . . One of the finest new public courses in a while . . . Fabulous . . . A sleeper . . . Excellent shape, excellent layout, excellent view . . . Great challenge . . . No pushover . . . Great par 3s, large elevation changes . . . Everybody can play it . . . A spread-out course . . . Pretty holes on back nine . . . Too many hazards and obstructions. Blind shots are ridiculous . . . Greens are still too hard . . . One of my favorites in the Valley . . . My favorite course in Arizona.

★★★ FOUNTAIN HILLS GOLF CLUB

SP—10440 Indian Wells Dr., Fountain Hills (602)837-1173.
14 miles east of Scottsdale. **Holes:** 18. **Par:** 71/71.
Yards: 6,087/5,035. **Course rating:** 68.9/68.9. **Slope:** 119/112.
Opened: 1971. **Pace of Play rating:** N/A. **Green fee:** $30/70.
Credit cards: All major. **Reduced fees:** Low season, Twilight, Juniors.
Caddies: No. **Golf carts:** N/A.
Discount golf packages: No. **Season:** Year-round. **High:** Jan.-April.
On-site lodging: No. **Rental clubs:** Yes.
Walking policy: Walking at certain times. **Range:** Yes (grass).
To obtain tee times: Call up to three days in advance.
Subscriber comments: A very pretty and panoramic course . . .
Gorgeous area . . . Tourists' delight . . . Beautiful mountain views from
most tees . . . Great scenery . . . A course to ponder your shots . . . A
stimulating variety of challenges . . . Very different for a desert course . . .
Lots of hills, some blind shots, but fair. A good workout . . . Short, but oh
so sweet! . . . Would be better if it was longer . . . Many sporty holes, but
too many tricks . . . Too many blind shots . . . No. 18 is a strange hole . . .
18th is unfair and a bad design. Cement traps . . . Only one fountain at
Fountain Hills, but it has all the hills.

★★ FRANCISCO GRANDE RESORT AND GOLF CLUB

R—26000 Gila Bend Hwy., Casa Grande (602)426-9205, (800)237-4238.
45 miles south of Phoenix. **Holes:** 18. **Par:** 72/72.
Yards: 7,594/5,554. **Course rating:** 74.9/69.9. **Slope:** 126/112.
Opened: 1961. **Pace of Play rating:** 4:00. **Green fee:** $20/60.
Credit cards: MC, V, AMEX, Diners Club. **Reduced fees:** Low season,
Juniors.
Caddies: No. **Golf carts:** Included in Green Fee.
Discount golf packages: Yes. **Season:** Year-round. **High:** Nov.-April.
On-site lodging: Yes. **Rental clubs:** Yes.
Walking policy: Mandatory cart. **Range:** Yes (grass).
To obtain tee times: Call up to five days in advance.
Subscriber comments: Very good. Very long . . . Extremely long . . .
Longest Arizona course from the tips . . . A real challenge . . . Try this one
from the "Willie Mays" tees . . . Always great fairways . . . Greens not too
challenging . . . Living on its reputation. Not much of a resort . . . Bush
league . . . Friendly staff . . . Very accommodating.

★★½ FRED ENKE GOLF COURSE

PU—8251 E. Erwington Rd., Tucson (602)296-8607.
Holes: 18. **Par:** 72/72.
Yards: 6,807/4,700. **Course rating:** 73.3/68.8. **Slope:** 137/111.
Opened: 1982. **Pace of Play rating:** 4:30. **Green fee:** $20.
Credit cards: MC, V. **Reduced fees:** Low season, Twilight, Seniors,
Juniors.
Caddies: No. **Golf carts:** $14 for 18 holes.
Discount golf packages: No. **Season:** Year-round. **High:** Dec.-April.
On-site lodging: No. **Rental clubs:** Yes.
Walking policy: Unrestricted walking. **Range:** Yes (grass).
To obtain tee times: Call one week in advance.
Subscriber comments: A desert pearl in public golf . . . Well laid-out . . .
Innovative and demanding . . . Good desert experience . . . Lots of desert
. . . Desert golf with coyotes . . . Stay out of the desert . . . Spot golf . . . If
you're off, kiss it goodbye . . . A hard muny . . . Many blind holes . . .
Local knowledge helps . . . Difficult to keep ball in play . . . Leave your
driver home . . . All you can handle from blue tees . . . Too many blind tee
shots for a public course . . . Very penal if you miss a fairway . . . Not
enough turf . . . Usually not in best of shape . . . Fairways need work . . .
Tees, greens need attention . . . Hard course to follow. Poorly marked . . .
Toughest public layout in Tucson . . . Best public course in Tucson . . .
Tucson's best-kept secret.

GAINEY RANCH GOLF CLUB
★★★½ **DUNES/LAKES/ARROYO**
R—7600 Gainey Club Dr., Scottsdale (602)483-2582.
Holes: 27. **Par:** 72/72/72.
Yards: 6,800/6,614/6,662. **Course rating:** 71.9/71.1/70.7.
Slope: 128/126/124.
Opened: 1984. **Pace of Play rating:** N/A. **Green fee:** $70/105.
Credit cards: Must charge to hotel room. **Reduced fees:** Low season.
Caddies: No. **Golf carts:** Included in Green Fee.
Discount golf packages: Yes. **Season:** Year-round. **High:** Jan.–April.
On-site lodging: Yes. **Rental clubs:** Yes.
Walking policy: Mandatory cart. **Range:** Yes (grass).
To obtain tee times: Hotel guests make tee times with hotel golf coordinator.
Subscriber comments: Nice layout, tough from the blues . . . Each nine is different . . . Every hole is different . . . A real resort, just fun to play sometimes . . . Arroyo/Lakes is the worthwhile 18 . . . Too crowded. In the early days it was a pleasure . . . One of the best in the Phoenix Valley.

★★★½ **GOLD CANYON GOLF CLUB**
R—6100 S. Kings Ranch Rd., Apache Junction (602)982-9449, (800)624-6445.
35 miles southeast of Phoenix. **Holes:** 18. **Par:** 71/72.
Yards: 6,398/4,876. **Course rating:** 69.8/67.5. **Slope:** 135/112.
Opened: 1982. **Pace of Play rating:** 4:30. **Green fee:** $32/99.
Credit cards: All major. **Reduced fees:** Weekdays, Low season, Resort guests, Twilight.
Caddies: No. **Golf carts:** Included in Green Fee.
Discount golf packages: Yes. **Season:** Year-round. **High:** Jan.–March.
On-site lodging: Yes. **Rental clubs:** Yes.
Walking policy: Mandatory cart. **Range:** Yes (grass).
To obtain tee times: Call and reserve up to 60 days in advance with a credit card, three days without a credit card.
Subscriber comments: Beautiful location . . . The view is worth the price . . . Out of this world . . . Tough course . . . Some tight desert shots. Some open fairways. Much wildlife . . . Starts slow, nails you, ends slow . . . Reputation based on back nine . . . Front nine not impressive . . . Back nine fantastic in mountain area . . . Breathtaking setting in the Superstition Mountains . . . Wild back nine . . . Watch for cougars . . . Back nine is second to none . . . Should be played by all golfers at least once . . . Some holes almost impossible . . . Very unforgiving . . . Penalties for even small errors . . . Best back nine in the Valley . . . Don't tell anyone about this little bit of heaven.

GRAYHAWK GOLF CLUB
PU—19600 N. Pima Rd., Scottsdale (602)502-1800
Credit cards: MC, V, AMEX. **Reduced fees:** Low season.
Caddies: No. **Golf carts:** Included in Green Fee.
Discount golf packages: No. **Season:** Year-round. **High:** Oct.–May
On-site lodging: No. **Rental clubs:** Yes.
Walking policy: Unrestricted walking. **Range:** Yes (grass).
To obtain tee times: Call up to 30 days in advance.
TALON COURSE★
Holes: 18. **Par:** 72/72.
Yards: 7,001/5,143. **Course rating:** 74.3/70.0 **Slope:** 141/121.
Opened: 1994. **Pace of Play rating:** 4:20. **Green fee:** $75/155
RAPTOR COURSE★
Holes: 18. **Par:** 71.
Yards: 7,025. **Course rating:** N/A. **Slope:** N/A.
Opened: 1995. **Pace of Play rating:** 4:20. **Green fee:** $95/175

★★★ HAPPY TRAILS GOLF RESORT
SP—17200 W. Bell Rd., Surprise (602)584-6000.
20 miles northwest of Phoenix. **Holes:** 18. **Par:** 72/72.
Yards: 6,646/5,146. **Course rating:** 72.1/68.7. **Slope:** 124/113.
Opened: 1983. **Pace of Play rating:** 4:15. **Green fee:** $15/40.
Credit cards: MC, V, DISC. **Reduced fees:** Weekdays, Low season,
Resort guests, Twilight, Juniors.
Caddies: No. **Golf carts:** Included in Green Fee.
Discount golf packages: No. **Season:** Year-round. **High:** Nov.-April.
On-site lodging: No. **Rental clubs:** Yes.
Walking policy: Mandatory cart. **Range:** Yes (grass).
To obtain tee times: Call three days in advance during season. Call seven
days in advance during summer.
Subscriber comments: A surprisingly good course . . . Links type . . .
Mixture of good holes, some testy ones . . . Six easy holes, then look out!
. . . Excellent greens . . . Lickety-split bent-grass greens . . . Best greens in
Phoenix . . . Best golfing value in the Valley of the Sun . . . Let's keep it a
secret.

★★ HAVEN GOLF CLUB
PU—110 North Abrego, Green Valley (602)625-4281.
Call club for further information.
Subscriber comments: Traditional fun course . . . Flat, short . . . Fast
play the norm . . . Very average layout . . . Very nondescript . . . Wide
open, so just turn and burn . . . Hackers Haven. Slice your heart out . . .
An honest track at an incredibly low price . . . Best value in Green Valley
year round.

★★★½ HILLCREST GOLF CLUB
PU—20002 Star Ridge Rd., Sun City West (602)584-1500.
10 miles from Phoenix. **Holes:** 18. **Par:** 72/72.
Yards: 6,960/5,880. **Course rating:** N/A. **Slope:** 127/119.
Opened: N/A. **Pace of Play rating:** N/A. **Green fee:** N/A.
Credit cards: MC, V, AMEX. **Reduced fees:** Weekdays, Low season,
Resort guests, Twilight.
Caddies: No. **Golf carts:** Included in Green Fee.
Discount golf packages: No. **Season:** Year-round. **High:** Nov.-May.
On-site lodging: Yes. **Rental clubs:** No.
Walking policy: . **Range:** Yes (grass).
Subscriber comments: Super golf course . . . Attractive, well-managed,
fun to play . . . Pretty course, palm trees, white sand bunkers, forgiving
fairways . . . A 'generous fairways' course . . . Golf on a grand scale . . .
Wide open . . . Bring your driver . . . Let 'er rip! . . . Course can make
golfer look good . . . No big surprises for first time player . . . Still plays in
four hours . . . Huge tricky greens . . . Great practice facilities . . . They've
got a good thing and they know it . . . Pro shop personnel pleasant and
helpful . . . One of the best staffs in Phoenix area . . . Best value in
Phoenix.

★★★ KARSTEN GOLF COURSE AT ASU
PU—1125 East Rio Salado Parkway, Tempe (602)921-8070.
5 miles southeast of Phoenix. **Holes:** 18. **Par:** 72/72.
Yards: 7,057/4,765. **Course rating:** 74.3/63.4. **Slope:** 133/110.
Opened: 1989. **Pace of Play rating:** 4:50. **Green fee:** $30/84.
Credit cards: MC, V, AMEX. **Reduced fees:** Weekdays, Low season,
Juniors.
Caddies: No. **Golf carts:** Included in Green Fee.
Discount golf packages: No. **Season:** Year-round. **High:** Jan.-April.
On-site lodging: No. **Rental clubs:** Yes.
Walking policy: Mandatory cart. **Range:** Yes (grass).
To obtain tee times: Call golf shop up to five days in advance.
Subscriber comments: Desert course in the city . . . University course
. . . Good Pete Dye course on very few acres . . . Pete Dye at his best . . .
Did a great job considering the original setting . . . Very puttable greens

. . . Mounds throughout . . . Lunar golf . . . Like golfing on the moon . . . Use every club in your bag and get every lie imaginable . . . Fun and exhilarating . . . Good test of golf if played from appropriate tees . . . When in Arizona, play this course . . . Need to know the course . . . Lots of blind shots to greens; lots of downhill, uphill, sidehill lies . . . Pete Dye at his worst . . . Too many moguls. Pete should learn other design techniques . . . Too many mounds in the fairways . . . Good shots are unrewarded . . . Hate the Pete Dye mounds . . . Dye is tough on the average player . . . If you hook or slice, look out . . A nightmare for the high handicapper . . . Good course to teach students to hate the game . . . Good course, lousy scenery . . . Too many power lines . . . Power lines are ugly . . . Service is first class . . . ASU staff is charming . . . Staff is full of sugar and spice.

★★ KEN MCDONALD GOLF CLUB

PU—800 Divot Dr. - A, Tempe (602)350-5256.

4 miles southeast of Phoenix. **Holes:** 18. **Par:** 72/73.
Yards: 6,743/5,872. **Course rating:** 70.8/70.8. **Slope:** 115/112.
Opened: 1974. **Pace of Play rating:** 4:00–4:25. **Green fee:** $17.
Credit cards: MC, V. **Reduced fees:** Twilight.
Caddies: Yes. **Golf carts:** $8 for 18 holes.
Discount golf packages: No. **Season:** Year-round. **High:** Nov.-April.
On-site lodging: No. **Rental clubs:** Yes.
Walking policy: Unrestricted walking. **Range:** Yes (grass).
To obtain tee times: Call up to two days in advance.
Subscriber comments: Good muny course . . . Pleasant round . . . Best condition in 12 years . . . Winter overseeding a big plus . . . Not very interesting . . . Typical muny, overcrowded, overplayed . . . Best local course for the price.

LA PALOMA COUNTRY CLUB
★★★½ RIDGE/CANYON/HILL

R—3660 E. Sunrise Dr., Tucson (602)299-1500, (800)222-1249.
Holes: 27. **Par:** 72/72/72.
Yards: 7,088/7,017/6,997. **Course rating:** 75.2/74.2/74.8.
Slope: 152/150/151.
Opened: 1984. **Pace of Play rating:** N/A. **Green fee:** $65/105.
Credit cards: All major. **Reduced fees:** Low season, Resort guests.
Caddies: No. **Golf carts:** Included in Green Fee.
Discount golf packages: Yes. **Season:** Year-round. **High:** Jan.-May.
On-site lodging: Yes. **Rental clubs:** Yes.
Walking policy: Mandatory cart. **Range:** Yes (grass).
To obtain tee times: Resort guests up to 60 days in advance.
Ridge and Canyon nines ranked 59th in America's 75 Best Resort Courses by Golf Digest. Ridge and Canyon nines ranked 13th in Arizona by Golf Digest.
Subscriber comments: Tough Nicklaus target desert course . . . Very difficult . . . Not for the fainthearted . . . Beautiful golf holes, need every shot to score well . . . Tough layout in the foothills . . . Intimidating . . . Even the easy holes can bite . . . On a good day, you can almost see the landing areas from the back tees . . . Only course with fairway caddies . . . Great variety with three nines . . . Immaculate but unexciting . . . Too much target golf . . . Too difficult for the average golfer . . . Better without the annoying mounds . . . Unfair. Good shots are penalized and poor shots are rewarded . . . Worn-out range balls . . . Best course I've played in long time . . . One of the best 27-hole layouts in Arizona . . . Great all-round resort experience . . . Worth staying . . . Great service . . . Treated well.

LAS SENDAS GOLF CLUB★

PU—7555 East Eagle Crest Dr., Mesa (602)396-4000.
Holes: 18. **Par:** 71/71.
Yards: 6,836/5,100. **Course rating:** 73.8/69.9. **Slope:** 149/126.
Opened: 1995. **Pace of Play rating:** 4:15. **Green fee:** $45/98.
Credit cards: All major. **Reduced fees:** Low season.
Caddies: No. **Golf carts:** Included in Green Fee.

Discount golf packages: No. **Season:** Year-round. **High:** Jan.–April.
On-site lodging: No. **Rental clubs:** Yes.
Walking policy: Walking at certain times. **Range:** Yes (grass).
To obtain tee times: Call seven days in advance.

★★★½ **THE LEGEND GOLF RESORT AT ARROWHEAD**
PU—21027 North 67th Ave., Glendale (602)561-1902, (800)468-7918.
15 miles northwest of Phoenix. **Holes:** 18. **Par:** 72/72.
Yards: 7,005/5,233. **Course rating:** 73.0/71.2. **Slope:** 129/119.
Opened: 1989. **Pace of Play rating:** N/A. **Green fee:** $25/85.
Credit cards: MC, V, AMEX. **Reduced fees:** Weekdays, Low season,
Twilight.
Caddies: No. **Golf carts:** Included in Green Fee.
Discount golf packages: No. **Season:** Year-round. **High:** Jan.–April.
On-site lodging: No. **Rental clubs:** Yes.
Walking policy: Mandatory cart. **Range:** Yes (grass).
To obtain tee times: Call seven days in advance.
Subscriber comments: Tough-as-nails Arnold Palmer track . . .
Underrated and underplayed, many great holes . . . Better than Arrowhead
but gets less press . . . Well-designed . . . Challenges all skills . . . Premium
on placement . . . Uneven lies on most holes . . . Demanding approach
shots . . . With four tee selections, it sets up nicely for all levels . . . Love
this Palmer layout . . . I'd play it everyday if possible . . . Killer greens . . .
Tough to read and putt . . . No level putts . . . Long way between Nos. 9
and 10 . . . Okay, but not great . . . Traps are poor . . . Spartan services
. . . Needs a real clubhouse . . . Needs a pro shop . . . Needs a ranger . . .
One of Palmer's best . . . The best Palmer course in Arizona . . . The best
course in Glendale.

LONDON BRIDGE GOLF CLUB
PU—2400 Clubhouse Dr., Lake Havasu City (602)855-2719.
180 miles southeast of Phoenix.
Pace of Play rating: 4:00. **Credit cards:** MC, V.
Caddies: No. **Golf carts:** Included in Green Fee.
Discount golf packages: Yes. **Season:** Year-round. **High:** Jan.–April.
On-site lodging: No. **Rental clubs:** Yes.
Walking policy: Mandatory cart. **Range:** Yes (grass).
To obtain tee times: Call.
★★★ **LONDON BRIDGE COURSE**
Holes: 18. **Par:** 71/72.
Yards: 6,618/5,756. **Course rating:** 70.4/73.5. **Slope:** 122/133.
Opened: 1969. **Green fee:** $35/50.
Reduced fees: Low season, Twilight, Seniors, Juniors.
Subscriber comments: Not a bad little course . . . Not great, but best in
the area . . . Bunkers need work . . . Summer afternoons are hot-hot-hot
. . . "Pop and drop" course. The times I went a nine took no more than 90
minutes . . . Two completely different courses make for great two-day
tournaments.
★★ **STONEBRIDGE COURSE**
Holes: 18. **Par:** 71/71.
Yards: 6,166/5,045. **Course rating:** 68.8/68.6. **Slope:** 114/118.
Opened: 1979. **Green fee:** $30/35.
Reduced fees: Weekdays, Low season, Resort guests, Twilight, Seniors.
Subscriber comments: A lot of fun to play . . . Good test . . .
Deceptively long . . . Hilly course . . . Challenging for all games . . . Two
street crossings.

★★★★ **LOS CABALLEROS GOLF CLUB**
R—1551 S. Vulture Mine Rd., Wickenburg (602)684-2704.
50 miles northwest of Phoenix. **Holes:** 18. **Par:** 72/72.
Yards: 6,962/5,690. **Course rating:** 73.4/73.8. **Slope:** 136/128.
Opened: 1979. **Pace of Play rating:** 4:00. **Green fee:** $50/90.
Credit cards: MC, V. **Reduced fees:** Low season, Resort guests.
Caddies: No. **Golf carts:** Included in Green Fee.

Discount golf packages: Yes. **Season:** Year-round. **High:** Feb.-April.
On-site lodging: Yes. **Rental clubs:** Yes.
Walking policy: Mandatory cart. **Range:** Yes (grass).
To obtain tee times: Call two days in advance.
Ranked 16th in Arizona by Golf Digest.
Subscriber comments: An ultimate desert course . . . Spectacular desert
scenery . . . What a desert course should look like. No glitz . . . Excellent
all the way around . . . Great views, wonderful greens . . . Sneaks up on
you . . . Bring all your game . . . 16, 17 and 18, what a finish! . . . This
course can eat your lunch very quickly, but I love it . . . Only desert course
I ever liked . . . Deer, quail sightings common . . . Great resort . . .
Courteous, very uncrowded . . . Fantastic facilities . . . Can't be beat for the
money . . . Always enjoy playing here . . . Best greens in Arizona . . .
Best-kept secret in Arizona.

MARRIOTT'S CAMELBACK GOLF CLUB
R—7847 N. Mockingbird Lane, Scottsdale (602)948-6770, (800)242-2635.
Opened: 1974. **Pace of Play rating:** N/A. **Green fee:** $30/90.
Credit cards: All major. **Reduced fees:** Weekdays, Low season, Resort
guests, Twilight.
Caddies: No. **Golf carts:** Included in Green Fee.
Discount golf packages: Yes. **Season:** Year-round. **High:** Jan.-April.
On-site lodging: Yes. **Rental clubs:** Yes.
Walking policy: Mandatory cart. **Range:** Yes (grass).
To obtain tee times: Call up to seven days in advance. If you are a
member or Marriott guest, call up to 30 days in advance.

★★INDIAN BEND COURSE
Holes: 18. **Par:** 72/72.
Yards: 7,014/5,917. **Course rating:** 71.9/72.0. **Slope:** 117/118.
Subscriber comments: Average course for the average golfer . . . Simple,
unimpressive resort course . . . Plays straight out and back along a wash
. . . Not too many interesting features . . . Arroyos and wind . . . Wide
fairways to let out the driver . . . Nice but ordinary . . . Not a lot of
variation . . . Uneventful . . . Not as pretty as the sister course . . . Good
practice facility . . . Excellent clubhouse . . . Attentive staff . . . I played as a
walk-on single, was treated wonderfully by the staff.

★★½PADRE COURSE
Holes: 18. **Par:** 71/73.
Yards: 6,559/5,626. **Course rating:** 70.3/71.1. **Slope:** 117/117.
Subscriber comments: More traditional than Indian Bend . . . Flat with
trees . . . Many trees . . . Pretty course . . . Very busy . . . Uninspiring . . .
Unimaginative . . . Very nicely groomed . . . Easier in the winter when
rough is dormant . . . Super practice facilities . . . Superb service . . . Super
slow play . . . Best pro shop in the Valley.

★★MARYVALE GOLF COURSE
PU—5902 W. Indian School Rd., Phoenix (602)846-4022.
Holes: 18. **Par:** 72/72.
Yards: 6,539/5,656. **Course rating:** 69.8/70.2. **Slope:** 115/113.
Opened: 1961. **Pace of Play rating:** 4:00. **Green fee:** $6/26.
Credit cards: None. **Reduced fees:** Weekdays, Low season, Twilight,
Seniors, Juniors.
Caddies: No. **Golf carts:** N/A.
Discount golf packages: No. **Season:** Year-round. **High:** Nov.-April.
On-site lodging: No. **Rental clubs:** Yes.
Walking policy: Unrestricted walking. **Range:** Yes (grass).
To obtain tee times: Call two days in advance. Three tee times per hour
are reserved for walk-on play.
Subscriber comments: City course . . . Easy and convenient . . . Kind of
flat . . . Short par 4s . . . Driver, wedge . . . Short par 5s . . . Nice Midwest
feel . . . Lots of trees . . . Bring an ax . . . Typical muny condition . . .
Sometimes scruffy . . . Greens are good, the rest isn't . . . Needs new golf
carts badly . . . Fun to walk.

McCORMICK RANCH GOLF CLUB
R—7505 E. McCormick Parkway, Scottsdale (602)948-0260.
Opened: 1972. **Pace of Play rating:** 4:30. **Green fee:** $34/85.
Credit cards: MC, V. **Reduced fees:** Weekdays, Low season, Resort guests, Twilight.
Caddies: No. **Golf carts:** Included in Green Fee.
Discount golf packages: Yes. **Season:** Year-round. **High:** Jan.-June.
On-site lodging: Yes. **Rental clubs:** Yes.
Walking policy: Mandatory cart. **Range:** Yes (grass).
To obtain tee times: Call two days in advance. You may call one week in advance when staying at one of 10 Scottsdale hotels.

★★★ PALM COURSE
Holes: 18. **Par:** 72/72.
Yards: 7,032/5,210. **Course rating:** 73.7/70.2. **Slope:** 133/120.
Subscriber comments: Venerable layout . . . Newly redone . . . New greens . . . Water and sand getting tougher . . . Does have some good holes . . . Interesting mix of holes . . . Not crowded . . . Always a pleasant visit . . . Biggest disappointment in Arizona . . . Fun golf course if you have lots of time . . . Staff trained to a "T".

★★★ PINE COURSE
Holes: 18. **Par:** 72/72.
Yards: 7,013/5,367. **Course rating:** 73.2/71.0. **Slope:** 133/120.
Subscriber comments: Pleasurable . . . Long, tough layout, makes you use your head . . . Beautiful and harmonious in its diversity . . . Sometimes rough is too long, but still is a terrific course . . . Good transition to Bermuda greens . . . Nice, but not very exciting . . . Friendly staff . . . Excellent service.

MT. GRAHAM MUNICIPAL GOLF COURSE★
PU—Golf Course Rd., Safford (602)348-3140.
120 miles east of Tucson. **Holes:** 18. **Par:** 72/73.
Yards: 6,354/5,691. **Course rating:** 69.5/70.6. **Slope:** 116/117.
Opened: N/A. **Pace of Play rating:** 4:00. **Green fee:** $13.
Credit cards: None. **Reduced fees:** Twilight, Juniors.
Caddies: No. **Golf carts:** $14 for 18 holes.
Discount golf packages: No. **Season:** Year-round.
On-site lodging: No. **Rental clubs:** Yes.
Walking policy: Unrestricted walking. **Range:** Yes (grass).
Subscriber comments: A fairly easy course from tee to green . . . Lots of water . . . Very tricky, hard to hold and very fast . . . Good muny for the money.

★★★½ OAKCREEK COUNTRY CLUB
SP—690 Bell Rock Blvd., Sedona (602)284-1660.
Holes: 18. **Par:** 72/72.
Yards: 6,854/5,555. **Course rating:** 71.0/71.6. **Slope:** 129/130.
Opened: 1967. **Pace of Play rating:** 4:30. **Green fee:** $50.
Credit cards: MC, V. **Reduced fees:** Twilight, Juniors.
Caddies: No. **Golf carts:** Included in Green Fee.
Discount golf packages: No. **Season:** Year-round. **High:** June-Oct.
On-site lodging: No. **Rental clubs:** Yes.
Walking policy: Walking at certain times. **Range:** Yes (grass).
To obtain tee times: Call six days in advance.
Subscriber comments: Magnificent views of red rocks . . . Unsurpassed beauty . . . Scenery next to none . . . The most spectacular views in the state . . . Hard to concentrate on your game . . . Rolling hills . . . Well-maintained . . . Some tricky holes . . . Leave your driver in the bag as much as possible . . . Good finishing hole . . . A must in Arizona . . . If you have the chance, play it at least once.

OCOTILLO GOLF CLUB
★★★★ BLUE/WHITE/GOLD
PU—3751 S. Clubhouse Dr., Chandler (602)220-9000.

15 miles southeast of Phoenix. **Holes:** 27. **Par:** 71/72/71.
Yards: 6,533/6,729/6,612. **Course rating:** 70.8/71.3/71.4.
Slope: 128/131/128.
Opened: 1986. **Pace of Play rating:** 4:15. **Green fee:** $32/80.
Credit cards: MC, V, AMEX. **Reduced fees:** Low season, Twilight.
Caddies: No. **Golf carts:** Included in Green Fee.
Discount golf packages: No. **Season:** Year-round. **High:** Jan.–April.
On-site lodging: No. **Rental clubs:** Yes.
Walking policy: Mandatory cart. **Range:** Yes (grass).
To obtain tee times: Call two days in advance in season and one week in advance off season.
Subscriber comments: Exciting if you like water . . . The wettest 27 holes in Arizona . . . Surprising to find this much water in the desert . . . A Florida course in the desert . . . Short-hitting shotmaker's dream . . . Really pretty . . . Everything top notch . . . Water everywhere but not a threat . . . Fun golf except for water on first five holes . . . Well, you get the idea . . . Not fun for everyday play . . . Only course I've played that looked exactly as pictured . . . So much water it has its own weather system . . . One of most beautiful courses I've ever seen, but too much water . . . Awesome shape . . . Best-maintained course in Arizona . . . A must play! . . . Best-kept secret in the Valley . . . Best-kept secret in the West.

★★½ ORANGE TREE GOLF CLUB
R—10601 N. 56th St., Scottsdale (602)948-3730, (800)228-0386.
Holes: 18. **Par:** 72/72.
Yards: 6,762/5,632. **Course rating:** 71.3/71.8. **Slope:** 122/116.
Opened: 1957. **Pace of Play rating:** 4:15. **Green fee:** $29/98.
Credit cards: MC, V, AMEX, Diners Club. **Reduced fees:** No.
Caddies: No. **Golf carts:** Included in Green Fee.
Discount golf packages: Yes. **Season:** Year-round. **High:** Jan.–March.
On-site lodging: No. **Rental clubs:** Yes.
Walking policy: Mandatory cart. **Range:** Yes (grass).
To obtain tee times: Call seven days in advance.
Subscriber comments: Good metropolitan course . . . An old course that has maintained its beauty and style . . . Reminiscent of Midwestern courses with mature trees . . . Kind of flat but still interesting . . . Generous fairways but long. Fun for big-ball hitters . . . Some small greens . . . Great finishing hole . . . Not too thrilling . . . All holes look the same . . . Needs a little polish . . . Mature with trees, flat, fast greens, good staff . . . Second-best staff in Arizona.

★ PAINTED MOUNTAIN GOLF CLUB
PU—6210 E. McKellips Rd., Mesa (602)832-0156.
Call club for further information.
Formerly known as Camelot Golf Club.
Subscriber comments: Easy layout . . . Good for the beginner . . . Course has really improved in last couple of years . . . Good improvements. Will go up a notch or two in the next couple of years . . . No holes worth remembering . . . Very nice people, willing to talk to you about problems.

★★★½ PALM VALLEY GOLF CLUB
SP—2211 N. Litchfield Rd., Goodyear (602)935-2500.
15 miles west of Phoenix. **Holes:** 18. **Par:** 72/72.
Yards: 7,015/5,300. **Course rating:** 72.8/68.7. **Slope:** 130/109.
Opened: 1993. **Pace of Play rating:** No. **Green fee:** $19/55.
Credit cards: MC, V. **Reduced fees:** Weekdays, Low season, Twilight, Juniors.
Caddies: No. **Golf carts:** $12 for 18 holes.
Discount golf packages: No. **Season:** Year-round. **High:** Jan.–March.
On-site lodging: No. **Rental clubs:** Yes.
Walking policy: Unrestricted walking. **Range:** Yes (grass).
To obtain tee times: Call up to four days in advance

Subscriber comments: New course . . . Desert type . . . Semi-difficult
. . . Real nice layout, plays right-to-left and left-to-right . . . A good
players course . . . Very wide fairways for long ball hitters . . . Ninth is the
toughest hole in Arizona . . . No outstanding characteristics . . . Not
enough natural hazards . . . Needs trees for shade . . . Too spread out to
walk . . . Will only get better with age . . . Will be a winner with time . . .
Friendly clubhouse staff.

★★★½ PAPAGO GOLF COURSE

PU—5595 E. Moreland St., Phoenix (602)275-8428.
Holes: 18. **Par:** 72/72.
Yards: 7,068/5,781. **Course rating:** 73.3/72.4. **Slope:** 132/119.
Opened: 1963. **Pace of Play rating:** 4:30-5:00. **Green fee:** $17/26.
Credit cards: None. **Reduced fees:** Low season, Twilight, Seniors,
Juniors.
Caddies: No. **Golf carts:** $10 for 18 holes.
Discount golf packages: No. **Season:** Year-round. **High:** Jan.-May.

On-site lodging: No. **Rental clubs:** Yes.
Walking policy: Unrestricted walking. **Range:** Yes (grass).
To obtain tee times: Call two days in advance beginning at 6:30 a.m.
Subscriber comments: Great track . . . Top caliber . . . A fine old mature
course . . . An oasis in the desert . . . A premier muny. Every bit as good as
Torrey Pines . . . A lot of trees, have to stay in the fairways . . . You won't
believe you're playing a municipal, considering how many balls you'll end
up losing . . . Public golf as it should be . . . Only problem is getting on in
the winter because of its popularity . . . Close to the airport, a great round
on a flight delay . . . Just try to get on! . . . Best municipal in Phoenix . . .
Best public links in Arizona . . . Best muny anywhere . . . One of best in
the West . . . If you didn't bring your game, you won't find it here.

(SUPER VALUE)

★½ PAVILION LAKES GOLF CLUB

PU—8870 E. Indian Bend Rd., Scottsdale (602)948-3370.
Holes: 18. **Par:** 71/69.
Yards: 6,499/5,057. **Course rating:** 70.1/68.0. **Slope:** 120/110.
Opened: 1992. **Pace of Play rating:** 4:00. **Green fee:** $9/48.
Credit cards: MC, V. **Reduced fees:** Low season, Twilight, Juniors.
Caddies: No. **Golf carts:** N/A.
Discount golf packages: No. **Season:** Year-round. **High:** Jan.-April.
On-site lodging: No. **Rental clubs:** Yes.
Walking policy: Walking at certain times. **Range:** Yes (grass).
To obtain tee times: Call up to seven days in advance.
   Formerly known as Pima Golf Resort.
Subscriber comments: Recently renovated . . . Sparse but fun . . . In
good shape except for the greens . . . It's green and flat . . . Fun for a cheap
date . . . Used to be a lot tougher . . . Working on improving . . .
Improves every time we play . . . Course has shade trees.

★ PAYSON GOLF COURSE

PU—1504 West Country Club Dr., Payson (602)474-2273.
85 miles northeast of Phoenix. **Holes:** 18. **Par:** 71/71.
Yards: 5,854/5,094. **Course rating:** 66.9/66.7. **Slope:** 114/113.
Opened: 1976. **Pace of Play rating:** N/A. **Green fee:** $20/28.
Credit cards: None. **Reduced fees:** Weekdays, Low season, Juniors.
Caddies: No. **Golf carts:** $10 for 18 holes.
Discount golf packages: No. **Season:** Year-round. **High:** April-Oct.
On-site lodging: No. **Rental clubs:** Yes.
Walking policy: Unrestricted walking. **Range:** Yes (grass).
To obtain tee times: Call up to one week in advance.
Subscriber comments: Out in the country . . . Layout in foothills and
meadows . . . Some dull holes, some unique ones . . . Strange back nine
. . . Back nine holes too bunched together . . . Hidden doglegs, in-course
out of bounds . . . Never have I laughed at a course as much as this one . . .
Only game in town.

ARIZONA

★★★½ **THE PHOENICIAN GOLF CLUB**
R—6000 East Camelback Rd., Scottsdale (602)423-2449, (800)888-8234.
Holes: 18. **Par:** 71/71.
Yards: 6,487/5,058. **Course rating:** 71.2/68.2. **Slope:** 134/122.
Opened: 1988. **Pace of Play rating:** 4:30. **Green fee:** $70/125.
Credit cards: All major. **Reduced fees:** Low season, Resort guests.
Caddies: No. **Golf carts:** Included in Green Fee.
Discount golf packages: Yes. **Season:** Year-round. **High:** Oct.-May.
On-site lodging: Yes. **Rental clubs:** Yes.
Walking policy: Mandatory cart. **Range:** Yes (grass).
Subscriber comments: Perfect, gorgeous, well-kept, challenging . . .
Beautiful setting. Front nine lush and green, back nine a desert layout with
elevation changes . . . Breathtaking views and holes . . . Plush place . . .
Expensive, but you get the royal treatment . . . If you can afford it, this is
fun. Take your time . . . Where is The Phoenician we had before? . . . Carts
not allowed off paths. Paths are hidden from fairways . . . Excellent food
and rooms . . . Outstanding in all aspects . . . One of the best in the area.

POHLCAT MOUNTAIN VIEW GOLF CLUB
PU—5740 W. Baseline Rd., Laveen (602)237-4567.
10 miles southwest of Phoenix.
Credit cards: MC, V, AMEX. **Reduced fees:** Weekdays, Low season,
Twilight, Seniors, Juniors.
Caddies: No. **Golf carts:** $10 for 18 holes.
Discount golf packages: No. **Season:** Year-round. **High:** Dec.-March.
On-site lodging: No. **Rental clubs:** Yes.
Walking policy: Unrestricted walking. **Range:** Yes (grass).
To obtain tee times: Call seven days in advance.
★½ **EAST COURSE**
Holes: 18. **Par:** 72/74.
Yards: 6,875/5,945. **Course rating:** 71.7/72.3. **Slope:** 119/114.
Opened: 1994. **Pace of Play rating:** N/A. **Green fee:** $10/30.
Subscriber comments: Very young course . . . I liked it. Nice fairways
and greens . . . Very open. Erratic hitters' paradise . . . A few years of tree
growth will help . . . Not impressed in the least . . . Better make some
greens changes if they want to survive . . . Hard to find in Phoenix.
★½ **WEST COURSE**
Holes: 18. **Par:** 71/71.
Yards: 6,646/5,770. **Course rating:** 70.9/71.6. **Slope:** 121/116.
Opened: 1993. **Pace of Play rating:** N/A. **Green fee:** $20/30.
Subscriber comments: Simple layout . . . Set up for fast play. No hazards
. . . Too new to have good conditions . . . Promises to be fun in a few years
. . . Courses side by side, not very inspiring . . . Hackers everywhere. Wear
a hard hat . . . Little imagination on holes . . . Even when it matures, it will
put you to sleep . . . Clubhouse a treat . . . Excellent practice facility.

★★★½ **THE POINTE GOLF CLUB ON LOOKOUT MOUNTAIN**
R—11111 N. 7th St., Phoenix (602)866-6356.
Holes: 18. **Par:** 72/72.
Yards: 6,617/4,552. **Course rating:** 71.7/65.3. **Slope:** 131/113.
Opened: 1989. **Pace of Play rating:** 4:30. **Green fee:** $50/130.
Credit cards: All major. **Reduced fees:** Weekdays, Low season, Resort
guests, Twilight.
Caddies: No. **Golf carts:** Included in Green Fee.
Discount golf packages: No. **Season:** Year-round. **High:** Nov.-May.
On-site lodging: Yes. **Rental clubs:** Yes.
Walking policy: Mandatory cart. **Range:** Yes (grass).
To obtain tee times: Resort guests call 30 days in advance.
Subscriber comments: Scenic, adventurous course . . . If you want target
mountain golf, this is it . . . A ball placement course . . . Good for control
hitters . . . Lots of topography . . . Very difficult terrain . . . Good solid
test . . . Great views . . . Fun course, offers a lot of diversity in hole design
. . . Great course, too short . . . Ever-encroaching houses spoiling the
setting . . . No substance . . . Target golf at its worst . . . You never know

how much club to use off tee to target fairway . . . Not well-positioned clubhouse. First hole is 1/4 mile away . . . Staff is outstanding, service is excellent. They extend every courtesy you would expect.

★★½ THE POINTE GOLF CLUB ON SOUTH MOUNTAIN

R—777 S. Pointe Parkway, Phoenix (602)431-6480, (800)876-4682.
Holes: 18. **Par:** 70/70.
Yards: 6,003/4,550. **Course rating:** 68.1/66.2. **Slope:** 117/107.
Opened: 1988. **Pace of Play rating:** 4:00–4.30. **Green fee:** $32/85.
Credit cards: All major. **Reduced fees:** Low season, Twilight.
Caddies: No. **Golf carts:** Included in Green Fee.
Discount golf packages: Yes. **Season:** Year-round. **High:** Jan.-April.
On-site lodging: Yes. **Rental clubs:** Yes.
Walking policy: Mandatory cart. **Range:** No.
To obtain tee times: Call golf shop seven days in advance. For resort guests, call 30 days in advance.
Subscriber comments: Half desert, half regular . . . Normal front, desert back nine . . . Short, target-type course . . . Playable target course . . . Front nine really interesting. Back nine okay . . . . . . Disappointing. Did not like the difference between front and back nines . . . Back nine very quirky . . . Back nine too tricky, blind shots and small greens . . . Not enough length . . . Can't use driver enough . . . Some holes impossible to play . . . Great mountain/desert course . . . Always enjoyed it . . . I've got find way to retire and work there.

★★★ PRESCOTT COUNTRY CLUB

SP—1030 Prescott C.C. Blvd., Dewey (602)772-8984.
Call club for further information.
Subscriber comments: Well laid-out . . . A little of everything. Tests all your shots . . . Good driving course . . . Hilly, very windy . . . Par 3s all seemed monotonous . . . 18th hole ends with an exceedingly steep return to clubhouse . . . Not that well-known . . . A great escape . . . Good treatment . . . Make you feel welcome.

★★★½ PUEBLO DEL SOL GOLF COURSE

PU—2770 St. Andrews Dr., Sierra Vista (602)378-6444.
70 miles southeast of Tucson. **Holes:** 18. **Par:** 72/74.
Yards: 6,880/5,818. **Course rating:** 72.0/72.3. **Slope:** 125/126.
Opened: 1975. **Pace of Play rating:** 4:15. **Green fee:** $11/25.
Credit cards: MC, V, DISC. **Reduced fees:** Low season, Twilight, Juniors.
Caddies: No. **Golf carts:** N/A.
Discount golf packages: No. **Season:** Year-round. **High:** Feb.-March/June-Oct.
On-site lodging: No. **Rental clubs:** Yes.
Walking policy: Unrestricted walking. **Range:** Yes (grass).
To obtain tee times: Call one day in advance for weekdays. Call starting Wednesdays for weekends.
Subscriber comments: Year in and year out, some of the best putting surfaces you'll ever see . . . The fastest greens in town . . . Fastest and truest greens I've ever played . . . Fast, fast, fast . . . Fastest greens in the state . . . Best greens in southern Arizona . . . Best bent-grass greens in Arizona . . . Year round, the best greens on the planet, period . . . Gary McCord would love these greens. Slick as all get-out.

★★½ PUEBLO EL MIRAGE COUNTRY CLUB

SP—11201 N. El Mirage Rd., El Mirage (602)583-0425.
10 miles west of Phoenix. **Holes:** 18. **Par:** 72/72.
Yards: 6,521/5,563. **Course rating:** 70.0/71.0. **Slope:** 119/117.
Opened: 1985. **Pace of Play rating:** N/A. **Green fee:** $12/38.
Credit cards: MC, V. **Reduced fees:** Weekdays, Low season, Twilight, Juniors.
Caddies: No. **Golf carts:** Included in Green Fee.
Discount golf packages: Yes. **Season:** Year-round. **High:** Nov.-March.
On-site lodging: Yes. **Rental clubs:** Yes.

Walking policy: Walking at certain times. **Range:** Yes (grass).
To obtain tee times: Call golf shop three days in advance.
Subscriber comments: Retirement community . . . Nice small course . . .
Layout interesting . . . No frills . . . Fairways not very forgiving, bordered
by desert . . . Short on course upkeep . . . Needs closer mowing . . .
Potential as best-kept secret in West Valley.

★★ RANCHO MANANA GOLF COURSE

SP—5734 E. Rancho Manana Blvd., Cave Creek (602)488-0398.
20 miles north of Phoenix. **Holes:** 18. **Par:** 72/73.
Yards: 6,378/5,910. **Course rating:** N/A/68.8. **Slope:** 127/114.
Opened: 1988. **Pace of Play rating:** N/A. **Green fee:** $20/75.
Credit cards: All majors. **Reduced fees:** Weekdays, Low season,
Twilight.
Caddies: No. **Golf carts:** Included in Green Fee.
Discount golf packages: Yes. **Season:** Year-round. **High:** Jan.-April.
On-site lodging: No. **Rental clubs:** Yes.
Walking policy: Mandatory cart. **Range:** Yes (grass).
To obtain tee times: Call up to seven days in advance.
Subscriber comments: Short, tight target course in foothills. Great views.
Fun to play . . . Potential to be an awesome layout . . . Very interesting,
not always kept up . . . I see coyotes, quail, hawks every time out . . .
Worst example of desert golf . . . Not a cheap thrill, a thrill that is cheap.

RANDOLPH PARK GOLF COURSE

PU—600 S. Alvernon, Tucson (602)325-2811.
Credit cards: MC, V, DISC. **Reduced fees:** Low season, Twilight,
Seniors, Juniors.
Caddies: No. **Golf carts:** $14 for 18 holes.
Discount golf packages: No. **Season:** Year-round. **High:** Oct.-May.
On-site lodging: No. **Rental clubs:** Yes.
Walking policy: Unrestricted walking. **Range:** Yes (grass).

★★★ NORTH COURSE

Holes: 18. **Par:** 72/73.
Yards: 6,902/5,972. **Course rating:** 72.5/73.7. **Slope:** 128/124.
Opened: 1925. **Pace of Play rating:** 4:30. **Green fee:** $15/22.
Subscriber comments: Nice course in the middle of Tucson . . . Old-
style layout . . . High-quality muny . . . Good test . . . Lots of traffic, plays
long . . . Greens roll very true, average 10 on the Stimpmeter year round
. . . Good enough for the pros . . . Tour stop you can play for under $20
. . . Far too easy for LPGA-caliber play . . . Best muny in the area . . . One
of the best public course in America . . . Best true public course in country
. . . When they figure it out, it should be nice.

★★ SOUTH COURSE

Holes: 18. **Par:** 70/72.
Yards: 6,229/5,568. **Course rating:** 68.1/69.6. **Slope:** 101/108.
Opened: 1964. **Pace of Play rating:** 4:00. **Green fee:** 13/20.
Subscriber comments: Pretty old municipal course . . . A short fill-in
course. Good ego builder . . . Undergoing major renovations in 1995 that
will drastically alter it . . . Not close to North Course, but beginning to
redesign . . . Proposed redesign looks interesting.

★★★½ RED MOUNTAIN RANCH COUNTRY CLUB

SP—6425 E. Teton, Mesa (602)985-0285.
15 miles east of Phoenix. **Holes:** 18. **Par:** 72/72.
Yards: 6,797/4,982. **Course rating:** 73.8/69.4. **Slope:** 134/120.
Opened: 1987. **Pace of Play rating:** 4:15. **Green fee:** $29/125.
Credit cards: MC, V, AMEX, Diners Club. **Reduced fees:** Weekdays,
Low season, Twilight.
Caddies: No. **Golf carts:** Included in Green Fee.
Discount golf packages: No. **Season:** Year-round. **High:** Jan.-April.
On-site lodging: No. **Rental clubs:** Yes.
Walking policy: Mandatory cart. **Range:** Yes (grass).
To obtain tee times: Call three days prior at 7:30 a.m. with credit card.

Subscriber comments: Another great Pete Dye design . . . If you like Pete Dye, you'll love this course . . . Beautiful . . . Major task from the tips . . . Must keep ball in the fairway . . . Too tight for driver . . . Lots of blind shots . . . Fair, but mistakes cost you big-time . . . Lob wedge a must . . . Love those railroad ties! . . . Desert transition areas, water hazards make it a tough course to bogey . . . Very gimmicky . . . A Pete Dye torture chamber . . . Thanks, Pete Dye . . . Best greens in Phoenix in the summer.

★★★½ RIO RICO RESORT & CC
R—1069 Camino Caralampi, Rio Rico (602)281-8567.
Call club for further information.
Subscriber comments: Great location . . . No rush, great scenery . . . Fine Trent Jones Sr. course . . . Fun. Interesting holes . . . Front and back very different . . . One nine tough, other easier . . . Back nine one of the best in Arizona . . . Demandingly long . . . Lots of sand . . . A little hard for us oldtimers . . . Could play here all the time . . . Better know how to play . . . Don't tell anyone! Trent Jones' best-kept secret . . . Sign warns high handicappers to stay off the blue tees. Great idea!

★★★½ SAN IGNACIO GOLF CLUB
PU—4201 S. Camino Del Sol, Green Valley (602)648-3468.
25 miles south of Tucson. **Holes:** 18. **Par:** 71/72.
Yards: 6,704/5,200. **Course rating:** 71.4/68.7. **Slope:** 129/116.
Opened: 1989. **Pace of Play rating:** N/A. **Green fee:** $22/58.
Credit cards: MC, V. **Reduced fees:** Low season.
Caddies: No. **Golf carts:** $11 for 18 holes.
Discount golf packages: No. **Season:** Year-round. **High:** Jan.-April.
On-site lodging: No. **Rental clubs:** Yes.
Walking policy: Mandatory cart. **Range:** Yes (grass).
To obtain tee times: Call four days in advance.
Subscriber comments: One of southern Arizona's premier desert courses . . . Quality course . . . A jewel . . . Picture-postcard vistas . . . A layout you'll never forget . . . Sneaky tough . . . Tees for all players . . . Soft, lush greens . . . Best greens we played on all year . . . Good planning necessary for each shot . . . Some interesting decisions to be made on each hole . . . You have to think! . . . Now I know why everyone talks about Arthur Hills . . . Unfair in several places. Tee shot landing areas not compatible with lengths of holes . . . Desert blind shots . . . Too many lay-ups off tees . . . They destroyed this beauty when houses replaced surrounding desert . . . Best in southern Arizona . . . Will be one of Arizona's best when it matures.

★★★ SAN MARCOS GOLF & COUNTRY CLUB
SP—100 N. Dakota St., Chandler (602)963-3358.
15 miles north of Phoenix. **Holes:** 18. **Par:** 72/73.
Yards: 6,501/5,386. **Course rating:** 70.0/69.4. **Slope:** 117/112.
Opened: 1923. **Pace of Play rating:** 4:00. **Green fee:** $30/75.
Credit cards: All major. **Reduced fees:** Weekdays, Low season, Twilight.
Caddies: No. **Golf carts:** Included in Green Fee.
Discount golf packages: Yes. **Season:** Year-round. **High:** Jan.-April.
On-site lodging: Yes. **Rental clubs:** Yes.
Walking policy: Mandatory cart. **Range:** Yes (grass).
To obtain tee times: Call seven days in advance.
Subscriber comments: One of the oldest courses in Arizona . . . You can feel the history . . . Old course design is always a joy . . . One of a few in Arizona where the fairways are lined by trees . . . Lots of tree shade . . . Went to seed for years, coming back nicely . . . Beautifully kept fairways and greens . . . Never a bad lie . . . Small, firm greens allow pitch-and-run . . . Very forgiving . . . Staff is extremely friendly . . . Can't say enough about it.

SANTA RITA GOLF CLUB★
PU—16461 Houghton Rd., Tucson (602)762-5620.
Holes: 18. **Par:** 71/72.
Yards: 6,406/5,539. **Course rating:** 70.9/69.7. **Slope:** 117/117.
Opened: 1976. **Pace of Play rating:** 4:05. **Green fee:** $15/25.

Credit cards: All major. **Reduced fees:** Weekdays, Low season, Twilight, Seniors, Juniors.
Caddies: No. **Golf carts:** $8 for 18 holes.
Discount golf packages: Yes. **Season:** Year-round. **High:** Jan.–April.
On-site lodging: No. **Rental clubs:** Yes.
Walking policy: Unrestricted walking. **Range:** Yes (grass).
To obtain tee times: Call up to seven days in advance.

SCOTTSDALE COUNTRY CLUB
★★½NORTH/SOUTH/EAST
SP—7702 E. Shea Blvd., Scottsdale (602)948-6000.
Holes: 27. **Par:** 70/71/71.
Yards: 6,085/6,335/6,292. **Course rating:** 68.8/69.6/69.7.
Slope: 118/118/119.

Opened: 1954. **Pace of Play rating:** 4:15. **Green fee:** $25/85.
Credit cards: MC, V, AMEX. **Reduced fees:** Weekdays, Low season, Twilight.
Caddies: No. **Golf carts:** Included in Green Fee.
Discount golf packages: No. **Season:** Year-round. **High:** Jan.–April.
On-site lodging: No. **Rental clubs:** Yes.
Walking policy: Mandatory cart. **Range:** No.
To obtain tee times: Public, two days in advance.
Subscriber comments: Great little 27-hole facility . . . Short but demands accuracy from the back tees . . . Very small greens . . . Play the North and South layout, which has adjacent fairways and trees . . . Lots of shade . . . East is the best nine . . . East nine is fantastic . . . Not much scenery . . . Not memorable . . . Has seen its day . . . No driving range . . . Not always well-kept, but it's always fun.

★★★★SEDONA GOLF RESORT
PU—7260 Hwy. 179, Sedona (602)284-9355.
100 miles north of Phoenix. **Holes:** 18. **Par:** 71/71.
Yards: 6,642/5,030. **Course rating:** 70.3/67.0. **Slope:** 129/109.
Opened: 1988. **Pace of Play rating:** N/A. **Green fee:** $50/60.
Credit cards: MC, V, AMEX. **Reduced fees:** Weekdays, Low season, Twilight.
Caddies: No. **Golf carts:** N/A.
Discount golf packages: Yes. **Season:** Year-round. **High:** March-Nov.
On-site lodging: No. **Rental clubs:** Yes.
Walking policy: Unrestricted walking. **Range:** Yes (grass).
To obtain tee times: Call up to 14 days in advance with credit card.
Ranked 10th in Arizona by Golf Digest.
Subscriber comments: Magnificent . . . One of the most beautiful mountain courses on earth . . . Stunning views of Sedona Valley . . . Scenic with framing red rocks . . . Fabulous views . . . Wonderful place to play. Top marks in everything . . . Superb design . . . Good use of land . . . Isolated fairways . . . Lots of character . . . Striking views . . . Best scenery this side of Pebble Beach . . . Bring your camera . . . Can't think of a more beautiful place to play golf . . . Hard to stay focused . . . Hard to pay attention to golf with unique red rock setting . . . Scenery overwhelms even a great score . . . Simply the most picturesque location anywhere . . . Best greens anywhere . . . Challenging greens. No such thing as a straight putt . . . Always in top condition, but bunkers need to be upgraded . . . Course also overwatered . . . Most beautiful course in Arizona . . . Worth the drive 90 miles north from Phoenix . . . The scenery alone is worth it . . . Best course in Arizona, without a doubt . . . Heaven above, cooler than Phoenix.

SHADOW MOUNTAIN GOLF CLUB★
SP—1105 Irene St., Pearce (602)826-3412.
70 miles east of Tucson. **Holes:** 18. **Par:** 36/36.
Yards: 6,632/5,980. **Course rating:** 71.8/72.3. **Slope:** 127/125.
Opened: N/A. **Pace of Play rating:** 4:00. **Green fee:** $10/15.
Credit cards: MC, V. **Reduced fees:** Low season, Juniors.
Caddies: No. **Golf carts:** $9 for 18 holes.

Discount golf packages: No. **Season:** Year-round. **High:** Jan.-May.
On-site lodging: No. **Rental clubs:** Yes.
Walking policy: Unrestricted walking. **Range:** Yes (grass).
To obtain tee times: Call one day in advance.
Subscriber comments: Small subtle greens . . . Lots of O.B. . . . Uncrowded and unhurried. You can take your time.

SHERATON EL CONQUISTADOR COUNTRY CLUB

R—10555 North La Canada, Tucson (602)544-1800.
Opened: 1984. **Pace of Play rating:** 4:30. **Green fee:** $40/105.
Credit cards: All major. **Reduced fees:** Low season, Resort guests.
Caddies: No. **Golf carts:** Included in Green Fee.
Discount golf packages: Yes. **Season:** Year-round. **High:** Feb.-April.
On-site lodging: Yes. **Rental clubs:** Yes.
Walking policy: Mandatory cart. **Range:** Yes (grass).

★★★ SUNRISE COURSE

Holes: 18. **Par:** 72/72.
Yards: 6,819/5,255. **Course rating:** 71.7/69.4. **Slope:** 123/116.
Subscriber comments: Very honest course . . . Nice greens, bunkers, fairways . . . Some spectacular holes . . . Requires very accurate shots. Not much room for error . . . More difficult than its rating . . . Challenging par 3s . . . One really unfair par 3 spoils it for me . . . Better of the two courses . . . Could be improved with a little imagination . . . Rough is very rocky . . . Totally well managed . . . Always in good shape . . . But miles away from the hotel.

★★★ SUNSET COURSE

Holes: 18. **Par:** 72/72.
Yards: 6,763/5,323. **Course rating:** 71.2/69.5. **Slope:** 123/114.
Subscriber comments: Desert course . . . A challenging course, demands good distance off the tee . . . Elevated greens with protective bunkers . . . Elevated greens make approach shots difficult . . . Blind shots . . . Underrated, too low of a slope rating . . . Much tougher than Sunrise . . . Lots of construction of homes . . . Biggest challenge was avoiding construction workers . . . Wait a year to play this one . . . "BBH" (Beautiful Before Housing) . . . Too far from the hotel . . . A great resort . . . Outstanding service. They extend every courtesy you would expect.

★★★½ SILVER CREEK GOLF CLUB

PU—2051 Silver Lake Blvd., White Mtn. Lake (602)537-2744.
10 miles south of Show Low. **Holes:** 18. **Par:** 71/71.
Yards: 6,813/5,193. **Course rating:** 71.5/68.0. **Slope:** 131/120.
Opened: 1985. **Pace of Play rating:** 4:30. **Green fee:** $17/35.
Credit cards: MC, V, DISC. **Reduced fees:** Weekdays, Low season, Twilight, Seniors, Juniors.
Caddies: No. **Golf carts:** $11 for 18 holes.
Discount golf packages: Yes. **Season:** Year-round. **High:** June-Sept.
On-site lodging: Yes. **Rental clubs:** Yes.
Walking policy: Unrestricted walking. **Range:** No.
To obtain tee times: Call three days in advance.
Subscriber comments: High desert layout . . . Off the beaten track . . . A great hideway in the Arizona mountains . . . Great course, never busy . . . Regular tees manageable. Back tees very tough . . . Don't miss fairways into desert . . . Always manicured 100% . . . Excellent treatment by staff . . . Do not miss this one . . . Best unknown course in Arizona.

★½ SILVERBELL GOLF COURSE

PU—3600 N. Silverbell, Tucson (602)743-7284.
Holes: 18. **Par:** 72/73.
Yards: 6,824/5,800. **Course rating:** 71.2/71.5. **Slope:** 123/118.
Opened: 1978. **Pace of Play rating:** 4:10. **Green fee:** $18.
Credit cards: None. **Reduced fees:** Low season, Twilight, Seniors, Juniors.
Caddies: No. **Golf carts:** N/A.
Discount golf packages: No. **Season:** Year-round. **High:** Oct.-April.
On-site lodging: No. **Rental clubs:** Yes.

Walking policy: Unrestricted walking. **Range:** Yes (grass).
To obtain tee times: Call.
Subscriber comments: Easy, flat metro course . . . Always windy . . .
Could be a good one . . . Currently getting new irrigation . . . Upgrades
will improve course . . . Very busy with snowbird tourists.

★★★★ STARR PASS GOLF CLUB
SP—3645 W. Starr Pass Blvd., Tucson (602)670-0400.
Holes: 18. **Par:** 71/71.
Yards: 6,910/5,071. **Course rating:** 74.6/70.7. **Slope:** 139/121.
Opened: 1986. **Pace of Play rating:** 4:15. **Green fee:** $48/95.
Credit cards: MC, V, AMEX. **Reduced fees:** Low season, Resort guests,
Twilight.
Caddies: No. **Golf carts:** Included in Green Fee.
Discount golf packages: Yes. **Season:** Year-round. **High:** Jan.-May.
On-site lodging: Yes. **Rental clubs:** Yes.
Walking policy: Mandatory cart. **Range:** Yes (grass).
To obtain tee times: Call up to 30 days in advance.
Ranked 18th in Arizona by Golf Digest.
Subscriber comments: True desert golf . . . Target golf at its best . . .
Former TPC, tough . . . Accuracy a must . . . Always terrific . . . One of
the most enjoyable in the area . . . Very hilly . . . Very scenic . . . Tricked
up, but a great setting . . . Fun, but us hackers shouldn't keep score . . .
Too many blind shots and too many uneven stances in the fairways . . .
Gimmicky, but still fun to play . . . Large tricky greens . . . Best greens in
southern Arizona . . . Best greens I've ever seen in August . . . One of the
most picturesque and challenging layouts, being ruined by housing
construction throughout. A real shame . . . Toughest course in the state . . .
Best course for the money in Tucson . . . Great staff with a course to match
. . . Best pro shop in Tucson. You will buy something.

★★★ STONECREEK, THE GOLF CLUB
SP—4435 E. Paradise Village Parkway South, Paradise Valley (602)953-
9111.
1 miles southwest of Phoenix. **Holes:** 18. **Par:** 71/71.
Yards: 6,839/5,098. **Course rating:** 72.6/68.4. **Slope:** 134/118.
Opened: 1989. **Pace of Play rating:** 4:30. **Green fee:** $20/94.
Credit cards: All major. **Reduced fees:** Weekdays, Low season, Juniors.
Caddies: No. **Golf carts:** Included in Green Fee.
Discount golf packages: Yes. **Season:** Year-round. **High:** Jan.-April.
On-site lodging: No. **Rental clubs:** Yes.
Walking policy: Mandatory cart. **Range:** Yes (grass).
To obtain tee times: Call three days in advance or up to a year through a
local hotel.
Subscriber comments: Position golf . . . Stay on the fairways or else . . .
All the challenge you want on a links-type course . . . Many interesting
holes . . . Deceptively difficult. Possible double on every hole . . . Great
shape for the amount of play . . . Good, not memorable . . . Bent greens
take a beating . . . Suffer in summer . . . Lose that stupid meandering creek
that winds mindlessly throughout the course . . . Best-run course in north
Phoenix . . . Good driving range and clubhouse. Great restaurant . . .
Outstanding management . . . Everyone is very professional . . . Service is
one of the best.

★★★½ SUN CITY VISTOSO GOLF CLUB
SP—1495 E. Rancho Vistoso Blvd., Tucson (602)825-3110.
Holes: 18. **Par:** 72/72.
Yards: 6,723/5,109. **Course rating:** 71.8/68.3. **Slope:** 137/114.
Opened: 1987. **Pace of Play rating:** 4:20. **Green fee:** $35.
Credit cards: MC, V. **Reduced fees:** No.
Caddies: No. **Golf carts:** $13 for 18 holes.
Discount golf packages: No. **Season:** Year-round. **High:** Nov.-April.
On-site lodging: No. **Rental clubs:** Yes.
Walking policy: Mandatory cart. **Range:** Yes (grass).
To obtain tee times: Call one week in advance.

Subscriber comments: Tough! . . . Challenging . . . Not at all boring
. . . Must hit a straight ball . . . Just as difficult as Tucson National . . .
Spectacular mountain and desert scenery . . . Still one of the best if you can
get on.

★★★½SUPERSTITION SPRINGS GOLF CLUB
R—6542 E. Baseline Rd., Mesa (602)985-5622, (800)468-7918.
20 miles east of Phoenix. **Holes:** 18. **Par:** 72/72.
Yards: 7,005/5,328. **Course rating:** 74.1/70.9. **Slope:** 135/120.
Opened: 1986. **Pace of Play rating:** N/A. **Green fee:** $24/95.
Credit cards: MC, V, AMEX. **Reduced fees:** Weekdays, Low season,
Twilight.
Caddies: No. **Golf carts:** Included in Green Fee.
Discount golf packages: Yes. **Season:** Year-round. **High:** Oct.-April.
On-site lodging: No. **Rental clubs:** Yes.
Walking policy: Mandatory cart. **Range:** Yes (grass).
To obtain tee times: Accepted up to seven days in advance. Tee time
accepted eight to 60 days in advance for surcharge fee of $7.
Subscriber comments: Wonderful . . . Spectacular design . . . Unique
holes . . . Lots of interesting holes, many with water features . . . Rolling
fairways with grass bunkers . . . Demanding second shots . . . Watch out
for sand! . . . Some really tough holes . . . Nine and 18 are awesome . . .
Best holes in the state . . . Best course in the East Valley . . . Would prefer
walking it . . . A must if you come to Phoenix . . . Wish I could play it
more . . . Head pro makes you feel like it's your course . . . Great
restaurant . . . Super lunch.

★★★TATUM RANCH GOLF CLUB
PU—29888 N. Tatum Ranch Dr., Cave Creek (602)585-2399, (800)468-
7918.
25 miles north of Phoenix. **Holes:** 18. **Par:** 72/72.
Yards: 6,870/5,609. **Course rating:** 73.4/71.5. **Slope:** 128/116.
Opened: 1987. **Pace of Play rating:** . **Green fee:** $30/95.
Credit cards: MC, V, AMEX. **Reduced fees:** Weekdays, Low season,
Twilight, Juniors.
Caddies: No. **Golf carts:** Included in Green Fee.
Discount golf packages: No. **Season:** Year-round. **High:** Nov.-April.
On-site lodging: No. **Rental clubs:** Yes.
Walking policy: Mandatory cart. **Range:** Yes (grass).
To obtain tee times: Call seven days in advance for no charge. Call up to
60 days in advance with a surcharge.
Subscriber comments: How well do you play from desert lies? . . .
Superb introduction to desert golf . . . Less severe desert-style course . . .
Mark a spot where you want to be. There's a lot of desert waiting for
company . . . Keep straight like a straight arrow . . . A lot of course
compared to some nearby competition . . . No monster. Lots of pars out
there . . . Lots of blind holes. Need to know where you're going . . .
Somewhat removed from the mainstream . . . Tucked away from the city.
You'll hear nothing but yourself having fun . . . Everything about it is great
. . . Great hot dogs at the turn.

★★★½TONTO VERDE GOLF CLUB
SP—18402 El Circulo Dr., Rio Verde (602)471-2710.
20 miles northeast of Scottsdale. **Holes:** 18. **Par:** 72/72.
Yards: 6,736/5,376. **Course rating:** 71.1/70.8. **Slope:** 132/124.
Opened: 1994. **Pace of Play rating:** N/A. **Green fee:** $35/90.
Credit cards: MC, V. **Reduced fees:** Low season.
Caddies: No. **Golf carts:** Included in Green Fee.
Discount golf packages: No. **Season:** Year-round. **High:** Dec.-April.
On-site lodging: Yes. **Rental clubs:** Yes.
Walking policy: Walking at certain times. **Range:** Yes (grass).
To obtain tee times: Tee time must be made no sooner than four days in
advance. Saturday tee time may be booked on Wednesday.
Ranked 14th in Arizona by Golf Digest.

Subscriber comments: Terrific new course . . . Graham-Panks course . . . Superb layout . . . One of the most scenic of new courses. Lots of desert running through fairways . . . Lots of cacti . . . Beautiful country . . . Awesome views . . . Solid golf . . . Better get off of the tee straight . . . Top condition for new course . . . Very lush . . . Strange bunker placements . . . Homes under construction and truck noise distracting . . . Too far from town . . . Well worth the drive . . . A public equivalent of Troon. More user-friendly, but not easy . . . Great greens . . . Needs some time, will be super.

TOURNAMENT PLAYERS CLUB OF SCOTTSDALE

R—17020 North Hayden Rd., Scottsdale (602)585-3939.
Credit cards: MC, V, AMEX.
Caddies: No. **Golf carts:** N/A.
Discount golf packages: No. **Season:** Year-round. **High:** Oct.-April.
On-site lodging: Yes. **Rental clubs:** Yes.
Walking policy: Unrestricted walking. **Range:** Yes (grass).
To obtain tee times: Call up to seven days in advance.

★★½ DESERT COURSE

Holes: 18. **Par:** 71/71.
Yards: 6,552/4,715. **Course rating:** 71.4/66.3. **Slope:** 112/109.
Opened: 1987. **Pace of Play rating:** N/A. **Green fee:** $11/18.
Reduced fees: Low season, Twilight, Seniors, Juniors.
Subscriber comments: Companion course to TPC Phoenix Open course . . . Sporty . . . Short but well laid out. Fits terrain . . . Pro condition fairways and greens . . . Easy enough to score on from the whites, very playable from all tees . . . Spraying is okay . . . Unfortunately getting too popular . . . Good course, just too short . . . Not overseeded in winter . . . There are much better desert courses in town . . . Pass on this one and play the Stadium . . . Has better greens than the Stadium Course . . . Greens are great to putt . . . Very good practice facility . . . Best deal in the area . . . Best bargain in the U.S.A.

★★★½ STADIUM COURSE

Holes: 18. **Par:** 71/71.
Yards: 6,992/5,567. **Course rating:** 73.9/71.6. **Slope:** 131/122.
Opened: 1986. **Pace of Play rating:** N/A. **Green fee:** $34/97.
Reduced fees: Low season, Twilight.
Ranked in Second 25 of America's 75 Best Public Golf Courses by Golf Digest. Ranked 17th in Arizona by Golf Digest.
Subscriber comments: Magnificent . . . Incredible for a public course . . . Home of the Phoenix Open . . . Those pros sure are lucky . . . Fun, challenging, playable . . . Tough in the wind . . . Nice to play where the pros play . . . Now appreciate what pros can do . . . Fast greens, fast fairways . . . Some greens unique . . . Finally the greens are in good shape . . . Great course, everything in prime condition . . . Truly a championship layout . . . Not as scenic as other Arizona courses . . . Looks better on TV than in person . . . Overrated as a tour stop that I can play . . . Disappointed in layout. Expected more . . . Nice, but there are better courses in area . . . Staff was great . . . They treat you like a high roller . . . Excellent operation. You'll come away happy . . . Best TPC course along with Sawgrass.

★½ TRINI ALVAREZ EL RIO MUNICIPAL GOLF COURSE

PU—1400 West Speedway Blvd., Tucson (520)623-6783.
Holes: 18. **Par:** 70/73.
Yards: 6,418/5,624. **Course rating:** 69.6/72.2. **Slope:** 110/115.
Opened: 1929. **Pace of Play rating:** 4:00. **Green fee:** $10/20.
Credit cards: MC, V. **Reduced fees:** Weekdays, Low season, Twilight, Seniors, Juniors.
Caddies: No. **Golf carts:** $7 for 18 holes.
Discount golf packages: Yes. **Season:** Year-round. **High:** Oct.-March.
On-site lodging: No. **Rental clubs:** Yes.
Walking policy: Unrestricted walking. **Range:** Yes (grass).
To obtain tee times: Call central reservation system for all municipal courses.

Subscriber comments: One of Tucson's oldest . . . Short, flat, small greens . . . Wide-open . . . Windy . . . Small, tight greens make scoring difficult . . . Small, hard greens spoil it . . . Could be in much better shape.

★★★★★ **TROON NORTH GOLF CLUB**
SP—10320 E. Dynamite Blvd., Scottsdale (602)585-5300.
Holes: 18. **Par:** 72/72.
Yards: 7,008/5,050. **Course rating:** 73.1/69.0. **Slope:** 146/116.
Opened: 1990. **Pace of Play rating:** 4:30. **Green fee:** $75/135.
Credit cards: MC, V, AMEX. **Reduced fees:** Low season, Juniors.
Caddies: No. **Golf carts:** Included in Green Fee.
Discount golf packages: No. **Season:** Year-round. **High:** Nov.-May.
On-site lodging: No. **Rental clubs:** Yes.
Walking policy: Unrestricted walking. **Range:** Yes (grass).
To obtain tee times: Call five days in advance of play.
Ranked 90th in America's 100 Greatest Golf Courses by Golf Digest.
Ranked 4th in Arizona by Golf Digest. Site of Golf Digest Schools.
Subscriber comments: The Augusta of Arizona . . . The Pebble Beach of the desert . . . Fantastic Weiskopf/Morrish design . . . Every hole a desert scene of unbelievable beauty . . . Fantastic views from tee to green . . . This is real target golf at it's best . . . Will challenge the best golfers . . . Top billing and getting better . . . No detail left out . . . Truly outstanding . . . Best fairway to green course I've ever played . . . So smooth, could putt from tee to green . . . One of the all time great courses . . . Second best behind Pebble Beach . . . Best course east of Pebble, west of Pine Valley . . . Magnificent greens . . . The greatest greens anywhere. None better at any place . . . Impeccable! . . . Bring a dozen balls if you slice . . . Bring a camera, leave your clubs at home . . . You've heard it all: Expensive, but a must at least once . . . Too bad I need to remortgage my house to play . . . Spend the money . . . Pay extra and play in winter . . . You pay your green fees, but then won' t get nickeled and dimed to death . . . Free range balls! . . . Beautiful now, but won't be when fully developed. Many homes on small lots . . . New clubhouse finalizes the experience . . . Employees were extremely helpful . . . The best of the desert courses . . . The ultimate desert golf experience . . . A piece of art . . . Well deserving of an outstanding rating.

★★½ **TUBAC GOLF RESORT**
R—1 Otera Rd., Tubac (602)398-2211.
Call club for further information.
Subscriber comments: Small, secluded resort . . . Lovely location . . . Great place to get away . . . Nice tourist course, easy to play . . . Each nine has a different look . . . The back nine is absolutely gorgeous . . . Play over the river and bird watch. Golf is secondary . . . My wife loved it while I fought it . . . Condition improved much over last year . . . Charming staff and site.

TUCSON NATIONAL RESORT AND CONFERENCE CENTER
★★★½ **ORANGE/GOLD/GREEN**
R—2727 West Club Dr., Tucson (602)575-7540, (800)528-4856.
Holes: 27. **Par:** 73/73/72.
Yards: 7,108/6,860/6,692. **Course rating:** 74.8/74.7/74.6.
Slope: 136/135/134.
Opened: 1962. **Pace of Play rating:** 4:20. **Green fee:** $50/125.
Credit cards: All major. **Reduced fees:** Resort guests.
Caddies: No. **Golf carts:** Included in Green Fee.
Discount golf packages: No. **Season:** Year-round. **High:** Oct.-May.
On-site lodging: Yes. **Rental clubs:** Yes.
Walking policy: Mandatory cart. **Range:** Yes (grass).
To obtain tee times: Call two days in advance. Resort guests call 30 days in advance.
Subscriber comments: Truly a diamond in the desert . . . Has it all . . . Conventional design . . . Nice to get back to a traditional course . . . A joy to play . . . Gets better with age . . . PGA Tour course . . . Great greens

. . . Avoid the Green nine, it does not measure up . . . Green nine is an afterthought . . . Some holes unfairly tightened . . . Love it, but it is hard . . . I'm going back to this one . . . One of the best courses out there . . . One of Tucson's best . . . All the makings of one of the best in the western U.S. . . . Super pro shop and dining . . . Exceptional service.

VENTANA CANYON GOLF AND RACQUET CLUB
R—6200 N. Clubhouse Lane, Tucson (602)577-4061, (800)828-5701.
Green fee: $65/135.
Credit cards: MC, V, AMEX. **Reduced fees:** Low season, Resort guests.
Caddies: No. **Golf carts:** Included in Green Fee.
Discount golf packages: No. **Season:** Year-round. **High:** Oct.-May.
On-site lodging: Yes. **Rental clubs:** Yes.
Walking policy: Mandatory cart. **Range:** Yes (grass).
To obtain tee times: Call seven days in advance.

★★★½ CANYON COURSE
Holes: 18. **Par:** 72/72.
Yards: 6,819/4,919. **Course rating:** 72.7/68.3. **Slope:** 141/114.
Opened: 1987. **Pace of Play rating:** 4:45.
Ranked 19th in Arizona by Golf Digest.
Comments: The essence of desert golf . . . Tough target golf on a beautiful desert course . . . Be able to steer it . . . Tremendous course . . . Tom Fazio at his best . . . Fine resort course, average player has fun . . . Should be for tour players . . . Beautiful scenery . . . Hotel and waterfall backdrops on 18 are stunning . . . If you didn't play golf, you would still enjoy the scenery and wildlife . . . Two or three shots easier than the Mountain . . . As tough as the Mountain Course . . . Better than the Mountain Course . . . They should overseed. I don't like brown greens in winter . . . Miles of twisting cart paths, a long way from green to tee . . . Seems like the Sierra Club would want to know about the poor cactus shots . . . Arizona's most scenic . . . Resort is one of the best in Tucson.

★★★½ MOUNTAIN COURSE
Holes: 18. **Par:** 72/72.
Yards: 6,926/4,789. **Course rating:** 74.2/68.3. **Slope:** 146/117.
Opened: 1984. **Pace of Play rating:** 4:20.
Ranked 28th in America's 75 Best Resort Courses by Golf Digest. Ranked 11th in Arizona by Golf Digest.
Subscriber comments: Underrated Tom Fazio course . . . Excellent course, but tight . . . May be the finest desert layout . . . Target golf at its best . . . Nature at its best . . . Interesting par 3s . . . Par 3 3rd hole is awesome! . . . 3rd hole is in a class by itself . . . A great course, testy for all . . . More difficult and more spectacular than the Canyon . . . Not for beginners . . . So hard, both courses were virtually unplayable . . . Great fairways, poor greens . . . Greens inconsistent . . . Perfect location for golf-only vacation . . . Bring a fat wallet and a shag bag full of balls . . . As good as it gets . . . Best course in Tucson . . . These two are a dynamic golf experience.

★★½ THE VISTAS CLUB
PU—18823 N. Country Club Pkwy., Peoria (602)566-1633.
Call club for further information.
Subscriber comments: Not long, a fun course . . . Rolling fairways . . . Nice variety . . . Reasonable . . . Greens as soft as a parking lot . . . Good atmosphere . . . Senior-friendly.

★★★½ WESTBROOK VILLAGE GOLF CLUB
SP—19260 N. Westbrook Pkwy., Peoria (602)933-0174.
Call club for further information.
Subscriber comments: Nice course . . . Nice staff . . . Good test . . . Short but well laid-out . . . Flat but nice variety . . . Not too hard . . . Wide open fairways . . . 17th is a great par 3 . . . Great scenery . . . Good atmosphere . . . Not the best sand . . . Fun and diverse.

★★ **WESTERN SKIES GOLF CLUB**
PU—1245 E. Warner Rd., Gilbert (602)545-8542.
Call club for further information.
subscriber comments: Young course . . . Not overpowering . . . Flat as a
cotton field . . . Fairways hard and fast . . . Very little trouble . . . Good
course for a scatter ball . . . More new courses should be built like this . . .
Long par 3s . . . Kinda boring . . . I loved bouncing balls off passing freight
trains on the practice range . . . Super staff. They are the best in Arizona
. . . A former secret . . . Lots of potential.

THE WIGWAM GOLF AND COUNTRY CLUB
R—451 N. Litchfield Rd., Litchfield Park (602)272-4653, (800)909-4224.
20 miles west of Phoenix.
Pace of Play rating: N/A. **Green fee:** $27/95.
Credit cards: All major. **Reduced fees:** Low season, Resort guests.
Caddies: Yes. **Golf carts:** Included in Green Fee.
Discount golf packages: Yes. **Season:** Year-round. **High:** Jan.-May.
On-site lodging: Yes. **Rental clubs:** Yes.
Walking policy: Mandatory cart. **Range:** Yes (grass).
To obtain tee times: Five day advance reservation. Hotel guests can book
up to six months in advance.
★★★ **BLUE COURSE**
Holes: 18. **Par:** 70/70.
Yards: 6,130/5,235. **Course rating:** 67.9/69.8. **Slope:** 115/112.
Opened: 1961.
Subscriber comments: Best of the three . . . Classic Robert Trent Jones
. . . Traditional, flat with trees . . . Short but tricky . . . Beautiful par 3s
. . . Easy course. Great for the poor golfer . . . Uninteresting . . . ZZZ. I
prefer something more visually appealing . . . Never seems to be mowed
properly . . . During summer heat, no drinking water on course . . . Played
in summer in three hours . . . Excellent place to stay and play . . .
Courteous staff . . . Bring $$$s . . . Total operation well-run.
★★★½ **GOLD COURSE**
Holes: 18. **Par:** 72/72.
Yards: 7,021/5,737. **Course rating:** 73.6/72.2. **Slope:** 129/120.
Opened: 1964.
Ranked 9th in Arizona by Golf Digest.
Subscriber comments: Best of the three . . . Grande Dame of desert
courses . . . Old Arizona . . . Venerable Robert Trent Jones Sr. layout . . .
Plays like Midwest course . . . Good challenge from the back tees . . . Flat
but with difficult elevated greens . . . Plays even longer and tougher due to
elevation of greens . . . Greens hard to hold . . . A lot of sand traps . . .
Some impossible-to-reach-in-two par 5s . . . Great risk/reward layout . . .
You must manage this course . . . A great break from target golf . . . Long
hitter's special . . . Wigwam's "monster" . . . A classic test of anyone's
game . . . Best played as part of hotel package . . . Vastly overrated . . .
Not terribly interesting . . . You must play it . . . Condition improved this
past year.
★★★ **RED COURSE**
Holes: 18. **Par:** 72/72.
Yards: 6,867/5,821. **Course rating:** 71.8/71.9. **Slope:** 118/115.
Opened: 1974.
Subscriber comments: Best of the three . . . Old fashioned . . .
Pleasurable, less challenging, more relief than Gold Course . . . Beats the
Gold Course hands down . . . Three tough closing holes . . . Front nine
OK, back nine too easy . . . Being a resort, play is very heavy . . . Excellent
facilities . . . Ideal course . . . The best-kept secret of the three Wigwam
courses.

★★½ BEN GEREN REGIONAL PARK GOLF COURSE
PU—7200 S. Zero, Fort Smith (501)646-5301.
Holes: 18. **Par:** 72/73.
Yards: 6,782/5,023. **Course rating:** 71.7/67.7. **Slope:** 120/109.
Opened: 1972. **Pace of Play rating:** 4:30. **Green fee:** $11/13.
Credit cards: None. **Reduced fees:** Weekdays, Twilight, Seniors, Juniors.
Caddies: No. **Golf carts:** $20 for 18 holes.
Discount golf packages: No. **Season:** Year-round. **High:** April-Oct.
On-site lodging: No. **Rental clubs:** Yes.
Walking policy: Unrestricted walking. **Range:** Yes (grass).
To obtain tee times: One day in advance.
Subscriber comments: Better than average . . . Good though not
spectacular . . . Generally flat with water . . . Wide open . . . Well kept . . .
Excellent Bermuda fairways . . . Beautiful bent-grass greens . . . Very slick
. . . Greens as good as any in the area . . . Greens best in the state for a
public course . . . Inadequate snack bar . . . Tremendous number of players
'til dark during most of the season . . . Busy and rushed . . . Friendly
service.

BURNS PARK GOLF COURSE
PU—30 River Rd., North Little Rock (501)758-5800.
Credit cards: None. **Reduced fees:** Twilight, Seniors, Juniors.
Caddies: No. **Golf carts:** $17 for 18 holes.
Discount golf packages: No. **Season:** Year-round. **High:** N/A.
On-site lodging: No. **Rental clubs:** Yes.
Walking policy: Unrestricted walking. **Range:** Yes (grass).
To obtain tee time:
Call one week in advance.

★½ CHAMPIONSHIP COURSE
Holes: 18. **Par:** 71/71.
Yards: 6,354/5,189. **Course rating:** 69.5/67.8. **Slope:** 106/97.
Opened: 1964. **Pace of Play rating:** N/A. **Green fee:** $ 8/10.
Subscriber comments: Typical central Arkansas muny . . . Something
for everyone . . . Flat front nine, back nine tight . . . Hilly and curvy . . .
Few bunkers . . . Drab design . . . Worn out . . . Doesn't drain well . . .
Very clayish . . . Sometimes mud is a problem . . . Very hard and dry in
summer . . . Cheap, but maddening when ground is hard . . . Great view
of Arkansas River . . . Now 36 holes . . . Should help weekend crowds . . .
Sixsomes allowed.

TOURNAMENT COURSE*
Holes: 18. **Par:** 70/70.
Yards: 5,688/4,512. **Course rating:** N/A. **Slope:** N/A.
Opened: 1994. **Pace of Play rating:** N/A. **Green fee:** $ 8/10.
Subscriber comments: Old short nine with new back nine, recently
opened . . . Will ease the crowds.

★★★½ CHEROKEE VILLAGE
SOUTH COURSE
R—Laguna Dr., Cherokee Village (501)257-2555.
145 miles north of Little Rock. **Holes:** 18. **Par:** 72/72.
Yards: 7,058/5,270. **Course rating:** 73.5/70.4. **Slope:** 128/116.
Opened: 1972. **Pace of Play rating:** 4:00. **Green fee:** $10/20.
Credit cards: MC, V. **Reduced fees:** No.
Caddies: No. **Golf carts:** $N/A for 18 holes.
Discount golf packages: No. **Season:** Year-round. **High:** May-Sept.
On-site lodging: No. **Rental clubs:** Yes.
Walking policy: Unrestricted walking. **Range:** Yes (grass).
To obtain tee times: First come, first served.
Complex also includes private North Course.
Subscriber comments: A hidden diamond in Arkansas . . . Beautiful
mountain course . . . Great design . . . Greatly improved in last three years
. . . Bent greens and Bermuda fairways . . . Greens are very good . . . A

long challenge with sand and hills . . . Gas carts a must with the hills . . .
Need every club . . . No water hazards . . . Nice scenery, quick play . . .
Well kept, secluded . . . Not crowded at all . . . Terrific staff . . . Friendly
atmosphere . . . I felt at home . . . 1995 should be its best year yet.

THE CREEKS PUBLIC LINKS★

PU—P.O. Box 190, Cave Springs (501)248-1000.
10 miles north of Fayetteville. **Holes:** 18. **Par:** 71.
Yards: 6,009/5,367. **Course rating:** 67.5/64.2. **Slope:** 111/104.
Opened: 1990. **Pace of Play rating:** NA. **Green fee:** $7/15.
Credit cards: MC, V, AMEX. **Reduced fees:** Weekdays, Seniors,
Juniors.
Caddies: No. **Golf carts:** $8 for 18 holes.
Discount golf packages: Yes. **Season:** Year-round. **High:** April-July.
On-site lodging: No. **Rental clubs:** Yes.
Walking policy: Unrestricted walking. **Range:** Yes (grass).
To obtain tee times: Call anytime in advance.

★★½DAWN HILL GOLF CLUB

R—R.R. No. 1 Dawn Hill Rd., Siloam Springs (501)524-4838, (800)423-
3786.
35 miles northwest of Fayetteville. **Holes:** 18. **Par:** 72/73.
Yards: 6,852/5,330. **Course rating:** 71.3/69.1. **Slope:** 114/110.
Opened: 1966. **Pace of Play rating:** 4:00. **Green fee:** $10/20.
Credit cards: All major. **Reduced fees:** Twilight.
Caddies: No. **Golf carts:** $N/A for 18 holes.
Discount golf packages: Yes. **Season:** Year-round. **High:** May-Oct.
On-site lodging: Yes. **Rental clubs:** Yes.
Walking policy: Walking at certain times. **Range:** Yes (grass).
To obtain tee times: Call anytime in advance.
Subscriber comments: Long and wide, set in a valley . . . Good routing
. . . Good layout, too much play . . . Not very crowded, no tee times
needed . . . If greens were better, it would be great . . . Open. Few hazards
. . . Course not the best of fun . . . More like a muny than a resort . . .
Very courteous staff . . . Pleasant people.

★★½DEGRAY STATE PARK GOLF COURSE

PU—Rte. 3, Box 490, Bismarck (501)865-2807, (800)737-8355.
25 miles south of Hot Springs. **Holes:** 18. **Par:** 72/72.
Yards: 6,930/5,731. **Course rating:** 60.7/67.0. **Slope:** 134/123.
Opened: 1976. **Pace of Play rating:** 4:00. **Green fee:** $10/11.
Credit cards: All major. **Reduced fees:** Seniors.
Caddies: No. **Golf carts:** $16 for 18 holes.
Discount golf packages: Yes. **Season:** Year-round. **High:** April-Sept.
On-site lodging: No. **Rental clubs:** Yes.
Walking policy: Unrestricted walking. **Range:** Yes (grass).
To obtain tee times: Call anytime.
Subscriber comments: Nice state park course . . . A different course, and
wild . . . Entertaining . . . Beautiful scenery . . . Front nine open, back
tighter . . . Back nine was too hard for high handicaps . . . Bring your
driver. You can use it on 15 holes . . . Really hilly . . . Carts are a good idea
. . . Not overrun with golfers . . . Excellent pace of play year round . . .
Pace continually monitored . . . Not great, could be better . . . Needs better
upkeep . . . Fairways in 1994 were much better, as were the greens . . .
Helpful staff . . . Comfortable lodging.

★½DIAMOND HILLS GOLF COURSE

SP—Rte. 7 N. Diamond Blvd., Diamond City (501)422-7613
Call club for further information.
Subscriber comments: Neat layout, hard to find . . . Nice mountain
setting . . . Greens were good but fairways were poor . . . All grass cut at
the same height.

★★½ HINDMAN PARK GOLF COURSE

PU—60 Brookview Dr., Little Rock (501)565-6450.
Holes: 18. **Par:** 72/72.
Yards: 6,393/4,349. **Course rating:** 68.9/N/A. **Slope:** 109/N/A.
Opened: N/A. **Pace of Play rating:** N/A. **Green fee:** $ 8/10.
Credit cards: None. **Reduced fees:** Low season, Twilight, Seniors, Juniors.
Caddies: No. **Golf carts:** $17 for 18 holes.
Discount golf packages: No. **Season:** Year-round. **High:** May-Aug.
On-site lodging: No. **Rental clubs:** Yes.
Walking policy: Unrestricted walking. **Range:** Yes (grass).
To obtain tee times: Tee time reservations may be made one week in advance of playing date. Saturday, Sunday, Monday and Tuesday: Tee time reservation must be made in person at the golf course.
Wednesday, Thursday and Friday: Tee time reservations may be made in person or by telephoning the golf pro shop.
Complex includes 18-hole par-65 War Memorial Golf Course.
Subscriber comments: Decent muny, could be great . . . Demanding course. Doglegs, creeks, water . . . Streams but no sand . . . No bunkers . . . Very tight . . . Treelined . . . Hilly, must keep ball in the air . . . Very nice layout. Have upgraded it some . . . Conditioning has been improved. Was in excellent shape in 1994 . . . Most enjoyable in the area . . . Best of the three Little Rock courses.

HOT SPRINGS COUNTRY CLUB

R—2100 Malvern Ave., Hot Springs (501)624-2661.
60 miles west of Little Rock.
Credit cards: MC, V, AMEX. **Reduced fees:** Weekdays, Resort guests.
Caddies: No. **Golf carts:** Included in Green Fee.
Discount golf packages: Yes. **Season:** Year-round. **High:** March-Oct.
On-site lodging: No. **Rental clubs:** Yes.
Walking policy: Mandatory cart. **Range:** Yes (grass).
To obtain tee times: Call two days in advance.
Complex also includes 9-hole par-33 Pineview Course.

★★★ ARLINGTON COURSE

Holes: 18. **Par:** 72/74.
Yards: 6,646/6,206. **Course rating:** 72.0/75.6. **Slope:** 127/137.
Opened: 1932. **Pace of Play rating:** 4:30. **Green fee:** $65/75.
Subscriber comments: Great old course . . . Challenging . . . Excellent . . . Beautiful . . . Very enjoyable . . . Forgiving for high handicaps . . . Nice traditional layout . . . PGA type course . . . Lots of hills . . . I remember the hills . . . Just rebuilt . . . Redesigned greens and water hazards by Ben Crenshaw's company . . . Two courses in one. Front nine control, back nine length . . . Good country club atmosphere . . . Great service . . . Staff treated us well.

★★½ MAJESTIC COURSE

Holes: 18. **Par:** 72/72.
Yards: 6,715/5,541. **Course rating:** 72.7/70.9. **Slope:** 131/121.
Opened: 1908. **Pace of Play rating:** 4:30. **Green fee:** $50/55.
Subscriber comments: Classic . . . Steeped in tradition . . . Originally designed by Willie Park Jr . . . Short course, not nearly as hard as Arlington . . . Very beautiful . . . Compacted together, holes almost on top of each other . . . Tight with blind shots. Stay on Arlington . . . Could be a good track if they would put in some money and effort . . . Pipeline being laid throughout . . . Bent greens recently installed have attracted increased play . . . Wonderful clubhouse . . . Excellent accommodations.

★★½ LONGHILLS GOLF CLUB

SP—327 Hwy. 5 N., Benton (501)794-9907.
9 miles southwest of Little Rock. **Holes:** 18. **Par:** 72/73.
Yards: 6,539/5,350. **Course rating:** 69.9/69.5. **Slope:** 110/110.
Opened: 1955. **Pace of Play rating:** 3:55. **Green fee:** $ 9/13.
Credit cards: MC, V. **Reduced fees:** Juniors.
Caddies: No. **Golf carts:** $8 for 18 holes.

Discount golf packages: No. **Season:** Year-round. **High:** April-Sept.
On-site lodging: No. **Rental clubs:** Yes.
Walking policy: Unrestricted walking. **Range:** Yes (grass).
To obtain tee times: Call anytime for weekdays. For weekends and
holidays call Wednesday beginning at 8 a.m.
Subscriber comments: Very nice public track, but very crowded . . . Lots
of variety here . . . Both tight tree-lined holes on front and open holes on
back . . . Many doglegs and narrow fairways . . . Good test especially if the
wind blows . . . $20 gets cart, golf, bucket of balls, Coke and candy . . .
Very enjoyable. Only three bad holes . . . Heat hurts the bent greens in
summer . . . Great staff that takes golf seriously . . . Treated super . . . Best
public course in the area . . . The most improved . . . One of Arkansas
nicest public courses.

★★★★ MOUNTAIN RANCH GOLF CLUB
R—820 Lost Creek Pkwy., Fairfield Bay (501)884-3400.
84 miles north of Little Rock. **Holes:** 18. **Par:** 72/72.
Yards: 6,780/5,134. **Course rating:** 71.8/69.8. **Slope:** 129/121.
Opened: 1983. **Pace of Play rating:** 4:30. **Green fee:** $28.
Credit cards: MC, V. **Reduced fees:** Weekdays, Low season, Resort
guests, Twilight, Juniors.
Caddies: No. **Golf carts:** $10 for 18 holes.
Discount golf packages: Yes. **Season:** Year-round. **High:** May-Oct.
On-site lodging: Yes. **Rental clubs:** Yes.
Walking policy: Walking at certain times. **Range:** Yes (grass).
To obtain tee times: Call up to two weeks in advance.
Subscriber comments: Excellent resort course hidden in the hills of
Arkansas . . . Hard to find . . . Picture book setting . . . Beautiful Ozark
mountain vistas . . . Superb . . . Majestic . . . Naturally beautiful . . . Hilly,
undulating fairways . . . Carts are a good idea . . . Very tight . . .
Unforgiving . . . You better hit the fairway or you've got a lost ball . . .
With all of the sand and water hazards, you really have to be on your toes
. . . Tournament quality . . . With all the trimmings . . . Always in good
shape . . . Women's tees were realistically placed . . . Pace was slow, but
surroundings worth the wait . . . Hilly with blind drives and approaches.
Need a map! . . . Well-stocked pro shop. Staff is warm, friendly, helpful
. . . Good vacation spot. Just super . . . Definitely one of best in state.

★★★ PRAIRIE CREEK COUNTRY CLUB
SP—Hwy. 12 E., Rogers (501)925-2414.
100 miles east of Tulsa, OK. **Holes:** 18. **Par:** 72/77.
Yards: 6,707/5,921. **Course rating:** 73.4/76.3. **Slope:** 130/127.
Opened: 1968. **Pace of Play rating:** 4:30. **Green fee:** $12/13.
Credit cards: None. **Reduced fees:** Weekdays, Resort guests, Twilight.
Caddies: No. **Golf carts:** $8 for 18 holes.
Discount golf packages: Yes. **Season:** Year-round. **High:** April-Sept.
On-site lodging: No. **Rental clubs:** Yes.
Walking policy: Unrestricted walking. **Range:** Yes (grass).
To obtain tee times: First come, first served.
Subscriber comments: Very surprising . . . Beautiful setting . . . Front
nine on top of a hill . . . On ridge tops . . . Back nine down in a valley . . .
Almost two different courses . . . One of toughest tests around . . . Only
for golfers who enjoy a difficult course . . . In fall, color from hardwood
trees is great . . . Too tough for normal mortals . . . If you can't keep it
straight, forget it . . . Don't look for lost balls . . . Well maintained family
operation . . . Best kept secret in Arkansas.

★★★ QUAPAW GOLF LINKS
PU—110 St. Hwy. 391 N., North Little Rock (501)945-0945.
Holes: 18. **Par:** 72/72.
Yards: 6,972/5,118. **Course rating:** 72.4/70.3. **Slope:** 119/120.
Opened: 1993. **Pace of Play rating:** 4:30. **Green fee:** $12/20.
Credit cards: MC, V. **Reduced fees:** Weekdays, Low season, Twilight,
Seniors, Juniors.

Caddies: No. **Golf carts:** $16 for 18 holes.
Discount golf packages: Yes. **Season:** Year-round. **High:** March-Oct.
On-site lodging: No. **Rental clubs:** Yes.
Walking policy: Unrestricted walking. **Range:** Yes (grass).
To obtain tee times: Call five days in advance.
Subscriber comments: Fresh new course . . . Rough European–style layout . . . Very unique for Arkansas . . . Completely different . . . Wide open . . . Links type . . . Real fun . . . A driving challenge . . . Impossible rough . . . Lots of water . . . Man–made dunes . . . Sand and grass bunkers . . . Several good holes . . . No. 10 is quite challenging . . . Very flat . . . No targets . . . Not a single tree on the course . . . Frustrating losing balls in the tall grass . . . Attempt at Brittish style course comes off well. A little rough around the edges . . . Best course in Little Rock area for straight hitters . . . Best bent grass greens in the area . . . Best greens in Arkansas.

★½ REBSAMEN PARK GOLF COURSE
PU—Rebsamen Park Rd., Little Rock (501)666-7965.
Call club for further information.
Complex includes a 9-hole par-33 course.
Subscriber comments: Old Little Rock muny . . . Strictly a short, open, public course . . . Flat . . . Right on the banks of Arkansas River . . . Very forgiving of wayward shots . . . Can hit driver on every par 4 and 5 . . . Not as challenging as Burns Park . . . No challenge, but a good place to work on your swing . . . Short nine, great for super seniors.

★★½ THE RED APPLE INN AND COUNTRY CLUB
R—325 Club Rd., Heber Springs (501)362-3131, (800)255-8900.
65 miles south of Little Rock. **Holes:** 18. **Par:** 71/71.
Yards: 6,402/5,137. **Course rating:** 70.0/69.0. **Slope:** 121/110.
Opened: 1984. **Pace of Play rating:** N/A. **Green fee:** $25.
Credit cards: All major. **Reduced fees:** No.
Caddies: No. **Golf carts:** $17 for 18 holes.
Discount golf packages: No. **Season:** Year-round. **High:** April-Nov.
On-site lodging: Yes. **Rental clubs:** Yes.
Walking policy: Walking at certain times. **Range:** Yes (grass).
To obtain tee times: Call 24 hours in advance.
Subscriber comments: Scenic . . . Well laid out . . . Hilly . . . Steep . . . Treelined . . . Tight in places . . . No. 2 is a great hole . . . Great course if you leave out two holes . . . Poor hard Bermuda greens keep this from being an excellent course . . . Greens not in very good shape anytime . . . Greens do not hold as well as they should . . . Great scenery during the year.

SOUTH HAVEN GOLF CLUB★
PU—Rte. 10, Box 201, Texarkana (501)774-5771.
Holes: 18. **Par:** 71/71.
Yards: 6,227/4,951. **Course rating:** 69.3/69.8. **Slope:** 123/117.
Opened: 1931. **Pace of Play rating:** 3:30-4:00. **Green fee:** $10/12.
Credit cards: None. **Reduced fees:** Seniors, Juniors.
Caddies: No. **Golf carts:** $16 for 18 holes.
Discount golf packages: No. **Season:** Year-round. **High:** April-Sept.
On-site lodging: No. **Rental clubs:** Yes.
Walking policy: Unrestricted walking. **Range:** Yes (grass).
To obtain tee times: Call for weekdays only.

TWIN LAKES GOLF CLUB★
SP—Rte. 4, Box 110-A, Mountain Home (501)425-2028.
120 miles southeast of Springfield, MO. **Holes:** 18. **Par:** 70/70.
Yards: 5,910/5,018. **Course rating:** 67.2/69.1. **Slope:** 110/106.
Opened: 1959. **Pace of Play rating:** 3:47. **Green fee:** $18.
Credit cards: None. **Reduced fees:** Low season.
Caddies: No. **Golf carts:** Included in Green Fee.

Discount golf packages: Yes. **Season:** Year-round. **High:** N/A.
On-site lodging: No. **Rental clubs:** Yes.
Walking policy: Unrestricted walking. **Range:** No.
To obtain tee times: First come, first served.

★½ VACHE GRASSE COUNTRY CLUB
SP—Country Club Rd., Greenwood (501)996-4191.
15 miles west of Ft. Smith. **Holes:** 18. **Par:** 72/72.
Yards: 6,502/4,966. **Course rating:** 70.5/67.4. **Slope:** 114/113.
Opened: 1968. **Pace of Play rating:** N/A. **Green fee:** $ 8/12.
Credit cards: None. **Reduced fees:** No.
Caddies: No. **Golf carts:** $14 for 18 holes.
Discount golf packages: No. **Season:** Year-round. **High:** May-Sept.
On-site lodging: No. **Rental clubs:** No.
Walking policy: Unrestricted walking. **Range:** Yes (grass).
To obtain tee times: Tee times taken only in the summer by calling one day in advance.
Subscriber comments: Strange layout . . . Built on rocky terrain . . . Lacks fairway grass . . . Even in the fairways your good lies will be on rock . . . Easy to damage irons . . . Don't use your good clubs . . . Has the makings for a good course but very little work has been done.

Notes

★★½ ADOBE CREEK GOLF CLUB

PU—1901 Frates Rd., Petaluma (707)765-3000.

25 miles north of San Francisco. **Holes:** 18. **Par:** 72/72.

Yards: 6,825/5,027. **Course rating:** 73.8/69.4. **Slope:** 131/120.

Opened: 1990. **Pace of Play rating:** 4:15. **Green fee:** $10/55.

Credit cards: MC, V. **Reduced fees:** Weekdays, Twilight, Seniors, Juniors.

Caddies: No. **Golf carts:** $10 for 18 holes.

Discount golf packages: No. **Season:** Year-round. **High:** May-Oct.

On-site lodging: No. **Rental clubs:** Yes.

Walking policy: Unrestricted walking. **Range:** Yes (grass).

To obtain tee times: Call one week in advance.

Subscriber comments: Very fair Robert Trent Jones Jr. design . . . Very windy in spring . . . Too many buried Volkswagens . . . Rough was so high, miss a fairway, lose a ball . . . Still a young course, no trees to speak of . . . Great shape for a new course . . . Fairly ordinary, but Nos. 2 and 16 are tough . . . Links-style course . . . Too many mounds . . . Not many trees . . . Lots of grassy mounds . . . Tough greens, interesting layout . . . Fun to play, considering it's a flat site . . . Good irons course . . . Extremely accommodating to women . . . Uninspired track, too many houses . . . Getting better.

★½ ALHAMBRA MUNICIPAL GOLF COURSE

PU—630 S. Almansor St., Alhambra (818)570-5059.

10 miles east of Los Angeles. **Holes:** 18. **Par:** 70/71.

Yards: 5,300/4,876. **Course rating:** 64.5/67.3. **Slope:** 107/105.

Opened: 1982. **Pace of Play rating:** 4:30-5:00. **Green fee:** $12/17.

Credit cards: MC, V. **Reduced fees:** Twilight, Seniors, Juniors.

Caddies: No. **Golf carts:** $19 for 18 holes.

Discount golf packages: No. **Season:** Year-round. **High:** N/A .

On-site lodging: No. **Rental clubs:** Yes.

Walking policy: Unrestricted walking. **Range:** Yes.

To obtain tee times: Call seven days in advance at 5:30 a.m.

Subscriber comments: Good muny course. Some challenging holes . . . Fairly open, easy to walk . . . Short but interesting course . . . A hackers' convention, slow . . . Several interesting holes with some water . . . Short with excellent greens . . . Too many "new" players, don't know etiquette, don't repair ball and spike marks . . . Average front, good back. Friendly staff. Good shape for amount of play.

★★★ THE ALISAL RANCH GOLF COURSE

R—1054 Alisal Rd., Solvang (805)688-4215.

40 miles north of Santa Barbara. **Holes:** 18. **Par:** 72/73.

Yards: 6,396/5,709. **Course rating:** 70.7/73.5. **Slope:** 121/127.

Opened: 1955. **Pace of Play rating:** 4:15. **Green fee:** $50.

Credit cards: All major. **Reduced fees:** No.

Caddies: No. **Golf carts:** $24 for 18 holes.

Discount golf packages: Yes. **Season:** Year-round. **High:** May-Oct.

On-site lodging: Yes. **Rental clubs:** Yes.

Walking policy: Unrestricted walking. **Range:** Yes (grass).

To obtain tee times: Weekdays, seven days in advance. Weekend, Thursday prior to weekend.

Subscriber comments: One of the most beautiful courses around . . . No. 1 handicap hole truly tough! . . . Beautiful setting, short but challenging, watch for deer . . . Small greens, well bunkered . . . A bit short; ninth hole from blue tees may be best par 3 in southern California . . . Short with narrow fairways . . . Beautiful setting, very serene, good shape . . . Several greens are being rebuilt, course will be very good when work is done . . . Delightful, pleasant surroundings . . . Well maintained, fine old course . . . Go in February, you will get June sunshine.

★★★ ALTA SIERRA GOLF AND COUNTRY CLUB

SP—11897 Tammy Way, Grass Valley (916)273-2010.

50 miles northeast of Sacramento. **Holes:** 18. **Par:** 72/72.

Yards: 6,537/5,984. **Course rating:** 71.2/74.6. **Slope:** 128/128.

Opened: 1964. **Pace of Play rating:** N/A. **Green fee:** $35/40.
Credit cards: MC, V. **Reduced fees:** Weekdays, Juniors.
Caddies: No. **Golf carts:** $10 for 18 holes.
Discount golf packages: No. **Season:** Year-round. **High:** April-June.
On-site lodging: Yes. **Rental clubs:** Yes.
Walking policy: Unrestricted walking. **Range:** Yes (grass).
To obtain tee times: Call on first of the month to book for upcoming month.
Subscriber comments: Great Foothill course . . . O.B. on every hole, bring your straight game! . . . Trees and deer make for a relaxing round . . . Hills, water and pine trees, nice layout . . . Challenging mountain course . . . Nice variety . . . Rattlesnakes and rough, narrow fairways . . . Tight and tough . . . Hilly, tight; for short, straight hitters . . . Always a good challenge . . . Country atmosphere . . . This course has improved over the last two years . . . Enjoyable change during summer heat.

★★½ ANAHEIM HILLS GOLF COURSE
PU—6501 Nohl Ranch Rd., Anaheim (714)748-8900.
25 miles south of Los Angeles. **Holes:** 18. **Par:** 71/72.
Yards: 6,218/5,356. **Course rating:** 70.0/70.0. **Slope:** 119/115.
Opened: 1972. **Pace of Play rating:** N/A. **Green fee:** $16/22.
Credit cards: None. **Reduced fees:** Twilight, Seniors.
Caddies: No. **Golf carts:** N/A.
Discount golf packages: No. **Season:** Year-round.
On-site lodging: No. **Rental clubs:** Yes.
Walking policy: Unrestricted walking. **Range:** Yes.
To obtain tee times: Call one week in advance.
Subscriber comments: Unique hilly course . . . To play the course you have to be a mountain goat, every lie is uphill, sidehill or downhill . . . Simple little course. Little imagination . . . Great public layout. Good condition . . . A couple of bizarre holes . . . Too hilly for me . . . Each hole offers a different challenge . . . Unique design, takes advantage of the terrain, short but tight, well maintained . . . Hilly, beautiful vistas, good golf round . . . Best city-owned course in California.

★★½ ANCIL HOFFMAN GOLF COURSE
PU—6700 Tarshes Dr., Carmichael (916)482-5660.
12 miles southwest of Sacramento. **Holes:** 18. **Par:** 72/73.
Yards: 6,794/5,954. **Course rating:** 72.5/73.4. **Slope:** 123/123.
Opened: 1965. **Pace of Play rating:** 4:00-4:30. **Green fee:** $16/23.
Credit cards: None. **Reduced fees:** Weekdays, Twilight, Seniors, Juniors.
Caddies: No. **Golf carts:** $19 for 18 holes.
Discount golf packages: Yes. **Season:** Year-round. **High:** N/A.
On-site lodging: No. **Rental clubs:** Yes.
Walking policy: Unrestricted walking. **Range:** Yes (grass).
To obtain tee times: Call one week in advance. Call Monday morning for the following Saturday, Sunday and Monday.
Ranked in Third 25 of America's 75 Best Public Golf Courses by Golf Digest.
Subscriber comments: Beautiful setting next to river . . . Course always under repair . . . Beautiful layout . . . Living on past ratings . . . Tough muny course, lots of trees . . . Excellent test, friendly place . . . Greens and fairways have declined greatly . . . Course looks tired . . . Very difficult No. 16 . . . Loses points for condition . . . Accuracy a must . . . Nice muny, well tended . . . Trees! Don't miss the fairway in the fall . . . Well kept, good staff, challenging course, beautiful . . . Maintenance is not as good as it use to be.

★★★ APTOS SEASCAPE GOLF COURSE
PU—610 Clubhouse Dr., Aptos (408)688-3213.
20 miles northeast of San Jose. **Holes:** 18. **Par:** 72/72.
Yards: 6,116/5,576. **Course rating:** 69.8/72.6. **Slope:** 126/127.
Opened: 1926. **Pace of Play rating:** 4:30. **Green fee:** $16/55.
Credit cards: MC, V, AMEX. **Reduced fees:** Weekdays, Low season, Resort guests, Twilight, Seniors, Juniors.

Caddies: Yes. **Golf carts:** $26 for 18 holes.
Discount golf packages: No. **Season:** Year-round. **High:** June-Oct.
On-site lodging: No. **Rental clubs:** Yes.
Walking policy: Unrestricted walking. **Range:** Yes.
To obtain tee times: Call one week in advance for weekdays. Three week advance reservation for an additional $3 per player.
Subscriber comments: Gem of a little course . . . Beautiful ambiance, well groomed, excellent food . . . Near the ocean, elevated tees to narrow fairways . . . Great vegetation . . . First hole is the world's easiest . . . The central coast's best-kept secret . . . Well maintained and enjoyable . . . Beautiful setting, a little short, par 5s reachable with irons . . . Been around awhile, still in good shape . . . Fun course. Not great conditions . . . Lots of trees to make it interesting . . . Ocean breezes . . . Best public course in the area . . . One of the best "unknown courses" . . . Superb wooded course . . . Course wet much of the time, doesn't drain well . . . Well bunkered . . . Great scenery, a little slow . . . Driving range is irons only . . . But there is no "seascape."

★★★★ AVIARA GOLF CLUB
R—7447 Batiquitos Dr., Carlsbad (619)929-0077.
30 miles north of San Diego. **Holes:** 18. **Par:** 72/72.
Yards: 7,007/5,007. **Course rating:** 74.9/69.1. **Slope:** 141/119.
Opened: 1991. **Pace of Play rating:** 4:30. **Green fee:** $95/115.
Credit cards: MC, V, AMEX, Diners Club, JCB. **Reduced fees:**
Weekdays, Twilight.
Caddies: No. **Golf carts:** Included in Green Fee.
Discount golf packages: No. **Season:** Year-round. **High:** April-Aug.
On-site lodging: No. **Rental clubs:** Yes.
Walking policy: Mandatory cart. **Range:** Yes (grass).
To obtain tee times: Available six days in advance.
Ranked 26th in California by Golf Digest.
Subscriber comments: Arnold Palmer track . . . 18th hole in top five of state . . . Service was the best I've ever had on a golf course . . . The most beautiful par 3s I've ever played . . . Immaculate! . . . Greens too severe for resort course . . . Course is gorgeous . . . Options from each tee . . . Tough, Should have to be single digit handicap to play . . . Probably one of Southern California's best courses . . . Fantastic daily fee . . . Augusta look alike in Southern California . . . One of the best of the new . . . A "don't miss" course . . . Five tee boxes allow for lots of variety, beautiful with brutal finishing hole . . . A gem, Arnie and Ed Seay's best . . . Callaway and Cobra factories five miles away . . . Gigantic greens . . . Best course in San Diego area . . . Beautiful, hilly, well conditioned . . . Great course, but greens are gigantic! . . . Wish the landscape architect would do my backyard.

★★★ AVILA BEACH RESORT GOLF COURSE
PU—P.O. Box 2140, Avila Beach (805)595-2307.
8 miles south of San Luis Obispo. **Holes:** 18. **Par:** 71/71.
Yards: 6,443/5,116. **Course rating:** 70.9/69.9. **Slope:** 122/126.
Opened: 1969. **Pace of Play rating:** 4:30. **Green fee:** $23/30.
Credit cards: MC, V. **Reduced fees:** Twilight, Seniors, Juniors.
Caddies: No. **Golf carts:** $11 for 18 holes.
Discount golf packages: Yes. **Season:** Year-round. **High:** April-Nov.
On-site lodging: No. **Rental clubs:** Yes.
Walking policy: Walking at certain times. **Range:** Yes (grass).
To obtain tee times: One week in advance.
Subscriber comments: What a nifty layout: doglegs, elevation changes, coastal California jewel . . . Lots of river crossings . . . Kikuyu grass taking over . . . Front nine rolling hills, back nine all over water . . . A few gimmicky holes . . . Overlooks ocean . . . Some hills, water, generally good to excellent condition . . . Two distinct nines . . . Narrow and requires course knowledge to play well . . . Outstanding 10th hole . . . Interesting layout, great setting . . . Front nine very tough, back nine great . . . Best in the area.

CALIFORNIA

★AZUSA GREENS GOLF COURSE
PU—919 W. Sierra Madre Blvd., Azusa (818)969-1727.
Call club for further information.
Subscriber comments: Good but short . . . Not being adequately
maintained . . . Reworking golf course . . . Flat, no water, lots of hardpan
. . . Plain, dusty . . . Esthetically unappealing, narrow fairways . . . Must
love golf in a rock pile . . . Fairways are grass-sand mix . . . Dry fairways,
not well maintained . . . Not bad for a public course.

★½BALBOA PARK GOLF CLUB
PU—2600 Golf Course Dr., San Diego (619)239-1632.
Call club for further information.
Subscriber comments: Easy course, short, not a lot of trouble . . . A
fairly short but fair test of golf . . . Undergoing never-ending renovation
. . . Flat layout, good views of marina and bridge . . . Well maintained for a
heavy traffic public course . . . Interesting short course . . . Should be better
after renovations.

BARTLEY W. CAVANAUGH GOLF COURSE★
PU—8301 Freeport Blvd., Sacramento (916)433-6307.
Holes: 18. **Par:** 71/712.
Yards: 6,265/4,723. **Course rating:** N/A. **Slope:** N/A.
Opened: 1995. **Pace of Play rating:** 4:30. **Green fee:** $15/20.
Credit cards: No. **Reduced fees:** Weekdays, Twilight, Seniors, Juniors.
Caddies: No. **Golf carts:** $10 for 18 holes.
Discount golf packages: No. **Season:** Year-round. **High:** May–Sept.
On-site lodging: No. **Rental clubs:** Yes.
Walking policy: Mandatory cart. **Range:** No.
To obtain tee times: Call seven days in advance.

★★★BEAU PRE GOLF CLUB
SP—1777 Norton Rd., McKinleyville (707)839-2342, (800)931-6690.
10 miles north of Eureka. **Holes:** 18. **Par:** 71/72.
Yards: 5,910/4,976. **Course rating:** 68.1/67.6. **Slope:** 116/116.
Opened: 1967. **Pace of Play rating:** 3:30–4:00. **Green fee:** $15/20.
Credit cards: MC, V. **Reduced fees:** Weekdays, Twilight, Juniors.
Caddies: No. **Golf carts:** $15 for 18 holes.
Discount golf packages: Yes. **Season:** Year-round. **High:** May–Sept.
On-site lodging: No. **Rental clubs:** Yes.
Walking policy: Unrestricted walking. **Range:** Yes (grass).
To obtain tee times: Call pro shop.
Subscriber comments: A gem in the North, all-around great . . . Lots of
water and woods . . . Short and flat, nice . . . Long rough . . . Challenging
course . . . Interesting variety of holes, hillside holes are attractive . . .
Unusual layout . . . Nice little course . . . Located in paradise!

★★½BENNETT VALLEY GOLF COURSE
PU—3330 Yulupa Ave., Santa Rosa (707)528-3673.
50 miles north of San Francisco. **Holes:** 18. **Par:** 72/75.
Yards: 6,600/5,958. **Course rating:** 70.6/72.5. **Slope:** 112/123.
Opened: 1969. **Pace of Play rating:** N/A **Green fee:** $8/18.
Credit cards: None. **Reduced fees:** Weekdays, Twilight, Seniors, Juniors.
Caddies: No. **Golf carts:** $18 for 18 holes.
Discount golf packages: No. **Season:** Year-round. **High:** May–Sept.
On-site lodging: No. **Rental clubs:** Yes.
Walking policy: Unrestricted walking. **Range:** Yes (grass).
To obtain tee times: Call one week in advance.
Subscriber comments: Shorter course with best greens of any public
course . . . Flat, a few really good holes . . . Nice setting, fun for average
golfers . . . Suffered some decline . . . Some well-made holes in good
condition . . . Simple but fun . . . Very tough driving holes, great 19th hole
. . . Typical muny, not memorable . . . A rare species in northern
California . . . Course in great shape considering how many rounds are
played . . . Great greens! . . . Best muny in California.

(FRUGAL PICK)

★★ BIDWELL PARK GOLF COURSE

PU—Wildwood Ave., Chico (916)891-8417.
90 miles south of Sacramento. **Holes:** 18. **Par:** 70/71.
Yards: 6,157/5,855. **Course rating:** 68.6/73.1. **Slope:** 115/123.
Opened: 1930. **Pace of Play rating:** 4:30. **Green fee:** $14/18.
Credit cards: None. **Reduced fees:** Twilight, Seniors, Juniors.
Caddies: No. **Golf carts:** $18 for 18 holes.
Discount golf packages: No. **Season:** Year-round. **High:** June-July.
On-site lodging: No. **Rental clubs:** Yes.
Walking policy: Unrestricted walking. **Range:** No.
To obtain tee times: Call two days in advance.
Subscriber comments: Beautiful canyon setting . . . Fun course, new
holes under construction . . . Same hole over and over . . . Parallel fairways
are dangerous . . . Very good layout, lots of trees . . . Heavy play, good
condition . . . Laid out to challenge the intermediate to advanced golfer . . .
Getting better every year . . . Average public course . . . Nice setting and
deer on course . . . Very tired looking . . . Under renovation, will make
this an outstanding course.

★½ BING MALONEY GOLF COURSE

PU—6801 Freeport Blvd., Sacramento (916)428-9401.
40 miles east of Stockton. **Holes:** 18. **Par:** 72/73.
Yards: 6,281/5,972. **Course rating:** 69.7/72.6. **Slope:** 109/119.
Opened: 1952. **Pace of Play rating:** 4:30. **Green fee:** $14/16.
Credit cards: None. **Reduced fees:** Twilight, Seniors, Juniors.
Caddies: No. **Golf carts:** $19 for 18 holes.
Discount golf packages: No. **Season:** Year-round. **High:** March-May.
On-site lodging: No. **Rental clubs:** Yes.
Walking policy: Unrestricted walking. **Range:** Yes.
To obtain tee times: Call one week in advance.
Subscriber comments: High-traffic course . . . Good public course with
lots of play . . . Flat course, flat greens, old style of play . . . Flat, straight
and wide fairways, tree-lined, terrible greens . . . Good course to build
confidence because of wide-open fairways . . . A lot of traffic, but course
wears well . . . Some hard holes but most are easy . . . Good Sunday
course, some good holes, fun to play any time of year.

★★★ BLACK LAKE GOLF CLUB

R—1490 Golf Course Lane, Nipomo (805)343-1214, (800)423-0981.
10 miles south of Santa Maria. **Holes:** 18. **Par:** 72/72.
Yards: 6,412/5,614. **Course rating:** 70.3/71.8. **Slope:** 120/122.
Opened: 1964. **Pace of Play rating:** 4:50-5:00. **Green fee:** $40/55.
Credit cards: MC, V, AMEX. **Reduced fees:** Weekdays, Low season,
Resort guests, Twilight, Seniors, Juniors.
Caddies: No. **Golf carts:** $24 for 18 holes.
Discount golf packages: Yes. **Season:** Year-round. **High:** May-Sept.
On-site lodging: Yes. **Rental clubs:** Yes.
Walking policy: Walking at certain times. **Range:** Yes (grass).
To obtain tee times: Resort guests tee times are set when reservation is
made. Nonguests call seven days in advance.
Subscriber comments: A plush, beautiful, challenging course . . . Short
shotmaker's course; excellent turf maintenance . . . Every hole is different
. . . Beautiful setting . . . Mature, very playable . . . One of the best
manicured . . . Nice coastal course . . . A long round of golf . . . Back nine
very scenic, water on front nine . . . Well-maintained resort course . . . A
fair test, not too difficult if you can handle hilly lies . . . Worst rap:
mandatory carts until 3 p.m. . . . Fair course, rolling hills, pretty area . . .
The weather can change without notice . . . Just a beautiful course; one of
my favorites.

★ BLUE SKIES COUNTRY CLUB

PU—55100 Martinez Trail, Yucca Valley (619)365-4111.
Call club for further information.
Subscriber comments: Flat, lots of trees . . . Staff is very accommodating
. . . Needs better watering system . . . Out in the middle of nowhere.

BLYTHE GOLF CLUB★
PU—4708 Wells Rd., Blythe (619)922-7272.
4 miles north of Blythe. **Holes:** 18. **Par:** 72/73.
Yards: 6,567/5,684. **Course rating:** 70.7/70.6. **Slope:** 109/110.
Opened: 1968. **Pace of Play rating:** 4:00–4:30. **Green fee:** $5.
Credit cards: None. **Reduced fees:** No.
Caddies: No. **Golf carts:** $7 for 18 holes.
Discount golf packages: No. **Season:** Year-round. **High:** Dec.–April.
On-site lodging: No. **Rental clubs:** Yes.
Walking policy: Unrestricted walking. **Range:** Yes (grass).
To obtain tee times: Taken January through April one day in advance
starting at 7 a.m.
Subscriber comments: Want a surprise in the desert? Try it . . . Short
course, good for the ego . . . Interesting and challenging, enjoyed playing
. . . No waiting to tee off during Christmas break . . . A real gem!

★★★½ BODEGA HARBOUR GOLF LINKS
R—21301 Heron Dr., Bodega Bay (707)875-3538.
20 miles west of Santa Rosa. **Holes:** 18. **Par:** 70/71.
Yards: 6,260/4,749. **Course rating:** 71.9/67.7. **Slope:** 130/120.
Opened: 1976. **Pace of Play rating:** 4:30. **Green fee:** $25/70.
Credit cards: MC, V. **Reduced fees:** Weekdays, Low season, Resort
guests, Twilight.
Caddies: Yes. **Golf carts:** $15 for 18 holes.
Discount golf packages: Yes. **Season:** Year-round. **High:** April-Oct.
On-site lodging: Yes. **Rental clubs:** Yes.
Walking policy: Walking at certain times. **Range:** No.
To obtain tee times: Call up to 60 days in advance.
Subscriber comments: Fantastic seaside links . . . Tough, especially when
fog is in . . . Views to kill for when not foggy . . . Last three holes are very
challenging . . . Two different nines, big swings in weather . . . Make sure
the wind ain't blowin'! . . . Front side is the nine from hell! . . . Great views
of Pacific Ocean . . . Spectacular views and layout, very challenging . . .
Straight drive too often ends in a bunker . . . Classiest staff in northern
California . . . 18th impossible from back tees . . . Ocean view each hole
. . . Three fun finishing holes . . . Play in a.m. before wind howls; a beast
from the tips . . . When weather is good this course cannot be beat . . . Not
a long course, but excellent layout and tough greens . . . No driving range,
tiny putting green . . . New front nine is different (pot bunkers) . . . Great
views! No.16 is a hoot! . . . Winds through subdivision . . . On a clear day,
no better experience . . . Could be best in northern California . . . Unique
layout, every hole different . . . Almost always foggy . . . Poor man's
Pebble Beach . . . Took excellent nine hole course, made contrived 18 . . .
Best three finishing holes you can find . . . A challenge and a workout, if
you have the guts to walk . . . Front nine has a lot of sidehill lies and tricky
greens . . . A cakewalk on a rare calm day.

★★ BOUNDARY OAKS COUNTRY CLUB
PU—3800 Valley Vista Rd., Walnut Creek (510)934-6212.
Call club for further information.
Subscriber comments: Good combination of hills, valleys . . . Very
crowded, but greens are good, interesting . . . A good walk, play is slow
. . . They have lengthened the course . . . Great layout, course usually in
lousy shape . . . Beware of rattlesnakes in the rough . . . Great design,
conditions getting better . . . Long course with tricky greens . . . A couple
of interesting holes make it playable . . . Surprisingly good test, good
practice range . . . Miserable tees and very poor greens! . . . Making a come
back, crowded . . . Very good municipal course . . . Long from the tips
. . . Most improved layout in northern California.

BROOKSIDE GOLF CLUB
PU—1133 N. Rosemont Ave., Pasadena (818)796-8151.
Pace of Play rating: N/A. **Green fee:** $14/30.
Credit cards: MC, V. **Reduced fees:** Weekdays, Twilight, Seniors,
Juniors.

Caddies: No. **Golf carts:** $10 for 18 holes.
Discount golf packages: No. **Season:** Year-round. **High:** April–Oct.
On-site lodging: No. **Rental clubs:** Yes.
Walking policy: Walking at certain times. **Range:** Yes (grass).
To obtain tee times: Call seven days ahead for weekdays. Call Mondays after 9:30 a.m. for Saturday tee times and call Tuesdays after 9:30 for Sunday times.

★★½ C.W. KOINER COURSE
Holes: 18. **Par:** 72/75.
Yards: 7,037/6,104. **Course rating:** 74.5/74.7. **Slope:** 134/128.
Opened: 1928.
Subscriber comments: Very enjoyable round by the Rose Bowl! . . . Crowded, very slow . . . Long but generous fairways; greens are bumpy . . . Very good course, long, good condition most of year . . . Clean, fun to play . . . . Excellent, long course. Has it all. Three par 4's over 440. Well kept . . . Among the top 10 public facilities in southern California . . . Getting better and better . . . Flat course, boon for long hitters . . . Condition not always good due to Rose Bowl parking.

★★½ E.O. NAY COURSE
Holes: 18. **Par:** 70/71.
Yards: 6,046/5,377. **Course rating:** 68.4/70.5. **Slope:** 115/117.
Opened: 1948.
Subscriber comments: Always in good playable condition . . . Short course, needs a lot of work and regular maintenance . . . Staff is good, pace of play can be slow in mid-morning . . . Good track for weekend golfer . . . Avoid during football season, when course is parking lot for preschool . . . Short but tough holes . . . Lengthening made it a better course; small greens are difficult.

★★ CAMARILLO SPRINGS GOLF COURSE
PU—791 Camarillo Springs Rd., Camarillo (805)484-1075.
54 miles north of Los Angeles. **Holes:** 18. **Par:** 72/72.
Yards: 6,375/5,297. **Course rating:** 70.2/70.2. **Slope:** 115/116.
Opened: 1972. **Pace of Play rating:** 4:00. **Green fee:** $22/60.
Credit cards: MC, V. **Reduced fees:** Weekdays, Resort guests, Twilight, Seniors, Juniors.
Caddies: No. **Golf carts:** Included in Green Fee.
Discount golf packages: Yes. **Season:** Year-round. **High:** May–Aug.
On-site lodging: No. **Rental clubs:** Yes.
Walking policy: Mandatory cart. **Range:** Yes.
To obtain tee times: Call seven days in advance.
Subscriber comments: Good layout, great greens . . . Good condition for a busy course . . . Course is too wet, does not drain properly . . . Good greens, poor fairways and tees . . . Nothing to write home about! . . . Unbelievably crowded . . . On-board computers fun . . . Good muny track, can be very slow . . . Fun public course . . . Carts have electronic yardage meter, you'll always pick the right club . . . Well-suited for the straight hitter.

★★★ CANYON LAKES COUNTRY CLUB
PU—640 Bollinger Canyon Way, San Ramon (510)735-6511.
30 miles east of San Francisco. **Holes:** 18. **Par:** 71/71.
Yards: 6,731/5,234. **Course rating:** 70.9/69.9. **Slope:** 124/121.
Opened: 1987. **Pace of Play rating:** 4:30. **Green fee:** $55/70.
Credit cards: MC, V. **Reduced fees:** No.
Caddies: No. **Golf carts:** Included in Green Fee.
Discount golf packages: No. **Season:** Year-round. **High:** Feb.-Oct.
On-site lodging: No. **Rental clubs:** Yes.
Walking policy: Mandatory cart. **Range:** No.
To obtain tee times: Call seven days in advance.
Subscriber comments: Nice track, good condition . . . Nice. Nos. 17 and 18 are windy nightmares . . . Very playable . . . Beautifully maintained . . . Beautiful views . . . First time around, make sure to check yardage . . . Excellently maintained. Great shot values. Lots of upscale homes to hit . . . A few gimmicky holes . . . Tough when windy. Good layout. Among top five public courses in the Bay Area.

★★★ CANYON OAKS GOLF CLUB

SP—999 Yosemite Dr., Chico (916)343-2582.

85 miles north of Sacramento. **Holes:** 18. **Par:** 72/72.
Yards: 6,804/5,030. **Course rating:** 72.7/70.4. **Slope:** 133/127.
Opened: N/A. **Pace of Play rating:** N/A. **Green fee:** $15/28.
Credit cards: MC, V. **Reduced fees:** Twilight, Seniors, Juniors.
Caddies: No. **Golf carts:** N/A.
Discount golf packages: No. **Season:** Year-round. **High:** N/A.
On-site lodging: No. **Rental clubs:** Yes.
Walking policy: Unrestricted walking. **Range:** No.
To obtain tee times: One week in advance.
Subscriber comments: Carved through a beautiful canyon . . . You just
can't grip it and rip it on this course . . . Do you like rattlesnakes? . . .
Excellent greens, sloping fairways, much trouble . . . Too hard for higher
handicaps . . . Golf and views are outstanding . . . Lots of fun, good layout
. . . Very challenging for a reasonably new course . . . Will be a very
challenging course when it finally settles.

★½ CANYON SOUTH GOLF COURSE

PU—1097 Murray Canyon Dr., Palm Springs (619)327-2019.

100 miles east of Los Angeles. **Holes:** 18. **Par:** 71/71.
Yards: 6,536/5,685. **Course rating:** 69.8/72.0. **Slope:** 119/117.
Opened: 1963. **Pace of Play rating:** 4:00. **Green fee:** $25/60.
Credit cards: MC, V, AMEX. **Reduced fees:** Weekdays, Low season,
Twilight.
Caddies: No. **Golf carts:** Included in Green Fee.
Discount golf packages: No. **Season:** Nov.–Sept. **High:** Jan.–March
On-site lodging: No. **Rental clubs:** Yes.
Walking policy: Mandatory cart. **Range:** Yes (grass).
To obtain tee times: We take tee times up to one week in advance.
Subscriber comments: Nice course. Nothing special . . . Needs more
water, greens are good . . . Getting very run–down . . . Beautiful scenery
. . . Enjoyable . . . Flat, good for high handicappers . . . Flat, featureless
. . . Flat but interesting . . . Plays long. Flat, very heavy play . . . Not a
very interesting track . . . Good course design, older established plantings.

★★★ CARLTON OAKS COUNTRY CLUB

R—9200 Inwood Dr., Santee (619)448-8500.

20 miles northeast of San Diego. **Holes:** 18. **Par:** 72/72.
Yards: 7,088/4,548. **Course rating:** 75.7/62.1. **Slope:** 144/114.
Opened: 1960. **Pace of Play rating:** 4:30. **Green fee:** $55/65.
Credit cards: MC, V, AMEX. **Reduced fees:** Resort guests, Twilight.
Caddies: No. **Golf carts:** Included in Green Fee.
Discount golf packages: Yes. **Season:** Year-round. **High:** N/A.
On-site lodging: Yes. **Rental clubs:** Yes.
Walking policy: Walking at certain times. **Range:** Yes (grass).
To obtain tee times: Call up to seven days in advance.
Subscriber comments: Huge course, a real challenge from the tips, great
layout . . . Great layout, some poor turf conditions . . . Bring your class
"A" game . . . Can't drive carts on the blue-grass fairways . . . Tough but
fair, small greens, narrow fairways . . . Ted Robinson excellence, a great
challenge . . . Demands accuracy . . . Best around, not for the timid . . .
Fairways are the best . . . Outstanding in all aspects . . . Take all your clubs
and be long off tee . . . 90 percent of the cart paths on the left side. If you
slice, you walk twice as far . . . Super job of remodeling a couple years ago
. . . Toughest golf course in southern California.

★★ CARMEL HIGHLAND DOUBLETREE GOLF AND TENNIS RESORT

R—14455 Penasquitos Dr., San Diego (619)672-9100, (800)622-9223.
Holes: 18. **Par:** 72/72.
Yards: 6,428/5,361. **Course rating:** 70.7/71.9. **Slope:** 123/125.
Opened: 1967. **Pace of Play rating:** 4:30. **Green fee:** $32/52.
Credit cards: MC, V, AMEX. **Reduced fees:** Weekdays, Low season,
Resort guests, Twilight, Seniors, Juniors.

Caddies: No. **Golf carts:** Included in Green Fee.
Discount golf packages: Yes. **Season:** Year-round. **High:** Jan.-April.
On-site lodging: Yes. **Rental clubs:** Yes.
Walking policy: Walking at certain times. **Range:** Yes.
To obtain tee times: Call seven days in advance. Golf packages 30 days in advance.
Subscriber comments: Fun resort course, nice place to stay, sometimes slow . . . Very disjointed throughout . . . Good for high handicappers. Average layout . . . Greens a little lumpy . . . Resort course, lacks something . . . Great for working on your downhill, sidehill shots . . . Nothing memorable about this layout . . . Looks easy but it's not . . . Rolling hills . . . Fast greens all break toward freeway.

★★★ CARMEL MOUNTAIN RANCH COUNTRY CLUB

PU—14050 Carmel Ridge Rd., San Diego (619)487-9224.
Holes: 18. **Par:** 72/72.
Yards: 6,728/5,372. **Course rating:** 71.9/71.0. **Slope:** 131/122.
Opened: 1986. **Pace of Play rating:** 4:20. **Green fee:** $30/60.
Credit cards: MC, V, AMEX. **Reduced fees:** Twilight, Seniors, Juniors.
Caddies: No. **Golf carts:** Included in Green Fee.
Discount golf packages: No. **Season:** Year-round. **High:** N/A.
On-site lodging: No. **Rental clubs:** Yes.
Walking policy: Mandatory cart. **Range:** Yes (grass).
To obtain tee times: Call up to seven days in advance.
Subscriber comments: Exceptionally good course, greens tough to read, nice fairways . . . Each hole is in a different neighborhood . . . Condo golf . . . Too many sidehill lies, too many silly holes . . . Layout grows on you . . . Houses too close to greens and tees . . . Rambling. Much too far from green to tee . . . Some holes not playable for a short hitter . . . Hardest greens ever . . . Lots of uphill/downhill holes . . . Great before homes were built, now the beauty is missing . . . Demanding, long course, long carries over barrancas required on some holes, fun to play . . . Best greens in San Diego County.

CARMEL VALLEY RANCH GOLF CLUB★

R—1 Old Ranch Rd., Carmel (408)626-2510, (800)422-7635.
Holes: 18. **Par:** 70/70.
Yards: 6,515/5,088. **Course rating:** 70.1/69.6. **Slope:** 124/135.
Opened: 1981. **Pace of Play rating:** 4:15. **Green fee:** $115/125.
Credit cards: All major. **Reduced fees:** Resort guests, Juniors.
Caddies: No. **Golf carts:** Included in Green Fee.
Discount golf packages: Yes. **Season:** Year-round. **High:** July-Oct.
On-site lodging: Yes. **Rental clubs:** Yes.
Walking policy: Mandatory cart. **Range:** Yes (grass).
To obtain tee times: Resort guests anytime with resort reservation. Public, call pro shop.

★★ CASTLE CREEK COUNTRY CLUB

SP—8797 Circle R Dr., Escondido (619)749-2422, (800)619-2465.
40 miles north of San Diego. **Holes:** 18. **Par:** 72/72.
Yards: 6,396/4,800. **Course rating:** 70.8/67.4. **Slope:** 124/108.
Opened: 1956. **Pace of Play rating:** 4:00-4:15. **Green fee:** $22/32.
Credit cards: MC, V, AMEX. **Reduced fees:** Weekdays, Twilight.
Caddies: No. **Golf carts:** $10 for 18 holes.
Discount golf packages: Yes. **Season:** Year-round. **High:** Jan.-April.
On-site lodging: Yes. **Rental clubs:** Yes.
Walking policy: Unrestricted walking. **Range:** No.
To obtain tee times: Call seven days in advance.
Subscriber comments: Nice quiet country setting, good variety of holes, lots of trees, so a banana ball won't be any fun . . . Lumpy greens . . . Discount golfers' haven . . . Fun, small woodsy course . . . Long irons and chipping are key . . . Nothing special . . . Fun to play, but watch for O.B. . . . Very playable and pleasant . . . Work on course in 1994 has improved conditions greatly . . . Length satisfying from blues only . . . Wide-open with forced water carries; best public course in area . . . Course in best shape ever.

★★★½ CASTLE OAKS GOLF CLUB
PU—1000 Castle Oaks Dr., Ione (209)274-0167.
30 miles southeast of Sacramento. **Holes:** 18. **Par:** 71/71.
Yards: 6,739/4,953. **Course rating:** 72.3/67.3. **Slope:** 129/114.
Opened: 1994. **Pace of Play rating:** N/A. **Green fee:** $16/32.
Credit cards: MC, V. **Reduced fees:** Weekdays, Twilight, Seniors,
Juniors.
Caddies: No. **Golf carts:** $10 for 18 holes.
Discount golf packages: No. **Season:** Year-round. **High:** Spring/Fall.
On-site lodging: No. **Rental clubs:** Yes.
Walking policy: Walking at certain times. **Range:** Yes (grass).
To obtain tee times: Call one week in advance.
Subscriber comments: Hot new course . . . Best-kept secret in northern
California . . . Lots of water hazards . . . Every hole could be a signature
hole! . . . Great new course doesn't play "new" . . . Two super finishing
holes . . . Right down to the marshals, the staff is the best anywhere . . .
Last hole has a double fairway, great hole . . . Hidden secret . . . With five
sets of tees, something for everyone . . . Has outstanding potential . . .
Fantastic three finishing holes . . . Thinking man's course . . . Outstanding
course, very well kept . . . Many swampy areas, need to keep ball on
fairway . . . Don't miss this one . . . Need accurate drives, lots of water . . .
Best new course around Sacramento in quite a while . . . Fairly flat, some
distances between greens and tees . . . Best public golf course in northern
California.

★★½ CHALK MOUNTAIN GOLF CLUB
PU—10000 El Bordo Ave., Atascadero (805)466-8848.
Call club for further information.
Subscriber comments: A quirky municipal course . . . Unsuited hilly
terrain needed more grading during construction . . . Hilly, well-kept
course . . . Offers challenges for golfers of all abilities . . . Good shape for
muny . . . With roaming deer to distract you! . . . Two differently-styled
nines . . . Twists and turns through oak trees . . . A little short, but great
fun . . . Lots of lay-ups . . . Lots of trees . . . Nice target track . . .
Conditions inconsistent . . . Fantastic layout for a muny, could use some
TLC . . . Rough was dirt, high weeds and/or rocks . . . Hilly course
challenges you to hit landing areas . . . Tougher than it looks.

THE CHARDONNAY GOLF CLUB
SP—2555 Jameson Canyon Rd. Hwy. 12, Napa (707)257-8950.
45 miles north of San Francisco.
Credit cards: MC, V, AMEX, JCB.
Caddies: No. **Golf carts:** Included in Green Fee.
On-site lodging: No. **Rental clubs:** Yes. **Range:** Yes (grass).
To obtain tee times: Call up to two weeks in advance.
THE CLUB SHAKESPEARE★
Holes: 18. **Par:** 72/72.
Yards: 7,001/5,448. **Course rating:** 74.5/70.9. **Slope:** 137/125.
Opened: 1992. **Pace of Play rating:** 4:00. **Green fee:** $60/100.
Reduced fees: Weekdays, Low season, Twilight, Seniors, Juniors.
Discount golf packages: No. **Season:** Year-round. **High:** April-Oct.
Walking policy: Walking at certain times.
★★★ THE VINEYARDS COURSE
Holes: 18. **Par:** 71/71.
Yards: 6,811/5,200. **Course rating:** 73.7/70.1. **Slope:** 133/126.
Opened: 1987. **Pace of Play rating:** 4:00-4:30. **Green fee:** $40/75.
Reduced fees: Weekdays, Low season, Twilight, Seniors.
Discount golf packages: Yes.
Walking policy: Mandatory cart.
Subscriber comments: A fun course in a beautiful setting . . . Beautiful
when grape vines have color . . . Poor maintenance around green and tees
. . . Golf in producing vineyards, beautiful layout . . . Fair test of golf,
pure, no gimmicks . . . Wind can be overpowering (any p.m.) . . . Could
be in better shape; good design . . . Wind and very poor conditions of
fairway takes the fun out . . . Links layout; varied abilities can play . . .

Very tough, small greens . . . Nice vineyards experience. Not dramatic . . . A challenge; very memorable, outstanding layout . . . Fairways a little crude, still growing . . . Best suited for straight hitters . . . Will be a great course someday.

★★ CHERRY ISLAND GOLF COURSE

PU—2360 Elverta Rd., Elverta (916)991-7293.
10 miles north of Sacramento. **Holes:** 18. **Par:** 72/72.
Yards: 6,562/5,163. **Course rating:** 71.1/70.0. **Slope:** 124/117
Opened: 1990. **Pace of Play rating:** 4:30. **Green fee:** $16/23
Credit cards: None. **Reduced fees:** Low season, Twilight, Seniors, Juniors.
Caddies: No. **Golf carts:** $9 for 18 holes.
Discount golf packages: No. **Season:** Year-round. **High:** April-Nov.
On site lodging: No. **Rental clubs:** Yes.
Walking policy: Unrestricted walking. **Range:** Yes (grass).
To obtain tee times: Call one week in advance starting at 6:30 a.m. Call on Monday for weekend tee times.
Subscriber comments: Very difficult precision shot course . . . Lay-up par 4s? 3-iron drive on par 5? If you are a player looking for a challenge, skip it . . . Great layout, rammed into too few acres . . . Too much in-course O.B. . . . A real challenge, you have to think about club selection on all holes . . . Four poorly designed golf holes . . . Can't see the fairways from the trees . . . Finesse course gives you a workout . . . Some holes puzzling and difficult . . . First hole you have to hit 6- or 7-iron off tee on par 4 . . . First hole is a bad design, holds up play . . . Constant noise of planes overhead is distracting . . . Good condition for public course . . . Getting better with age. Good county course . . . A few unfair holes, players either love it or hate it . . . Some holes traditional, some target golf, some water . . . Some good holes, but mostly a waste of good location . . . Tricky layout, but a good change of pace . . . Local knowledge helpful.

★½ CHESTER WASHINGTON GOLF COURSE

PU—1930 W. 120th St., Los Angeles (213)779-2803.
20 miles of Los Angeles. **Holes:** 18. **Par:** 70/70.
Yards: 6,348/5,646. **Course rating:** N/A. **Slope:** 107/115.
Opened: N/A. **Pace of Play rating:** N/A. **Green fee:** N/A.
Credit cards: N/A. **Reduced fees:** Weekdays.
Caddies: No. **Golf carts:** N/A.
Discount golf packages: No. **Season:** Year-round. **High:** June-Aug.
On-site lodging: No. **Rental clubs:** No.
Walking policy: N/A. **Range:** Yes.
Subscriber comments: A surprise, well maintained . . . Course has improved . . . Should improve after renovations completed . . . Dry fairways but great layout . . . Old course, wide fairways, easy to play but slow on weekends . . . Old-style layout . . . Tee times will soon be golden! This is a comer!

CHINA LAKE GOLF CLUB★

SP—411 Midway, China Lake (619)939-2990.
Call club for further information.
Subscriber comments: Military course . . . Challenging layout, high desert air is a factor . . . Desert course, hot and dry, great layout, tough rough . . . No. 5 will eat your lunch.

CHUCK CORICA GOLF COMPLEX

PU—No. 1 Clubhouse Memorial Rd., Alameda (510)522-4321.
5 miles west of Oakland.
Pace of Play rating: 4:30. **Green fee:** $14/25.
Credit cards: MC, V. **Reduced fees:** Weekdays, Twilight, Seniors, Juniors.
Caddies: No. **Golf carts:** $9 for 18 holes.
Discount golf packages: No. **Season:** Year-round. **High:** May-Oct.
On-site lodging: No. **Rental clubs:** Yes.
Walking policy: Unrestricted walking. **Range:** Yes (grass).

To obtain tee times: Call seven days in advance.

★★½ EARL FRY COURSE
Holes: 18. **Par:** 71/72.
Yards: 6,141/5,560. **Course rating:** 69.2/71.0. **Slope:** 119/114.
Opened: 1927.
Subscriber comments: Great practice facilities, relatively easy course . . .
Good condition, very high use . . . Plays a little short, greens could use a
little improvement . . . Basic muny . . . Watch out for goose droppings . . .
Good greens, short, an ego builder . . . Always lush and green, muny
course that feels like a country club . . . When the wind blows this is a
challenging course.

★★ JACK CLARK SOUTH COURSE
Holes: 18. **Par:** 71/71.
Yards: 6,559/5,473. **Course rating:** 70.8/70.0. **Slope:** 119/110.
Opened: N/A.
Subscriber comments: Nice, green, sleepy course . . . Well-maintained
muny, South Course underrated, great for high handicappers . . . Great
greens, otherwise it's not much to talk about . . . Flat, open . . . North
Course requires more position play. South a bit longer but not as well
conditioned . . . Better test than North but very scruffy in summer . . .
Plain Jane golf . . . Longer with less water than the North Course . . . I
didn't know cheap golf was this good.

★★ CHULA VISTA MUNICIPAL GOLF COURSE
PU—4475 Bonita Rd., Bonita (619)479-4141, (800)833-8463.
10 miles south of San Diego. **Holes:** 18. **Par:** 73/74.
Yards: 6,759/5,776. **Course rating:** 72.3/72.7. **Slope:** 128/124.
Opened: N/A. **Pace of Play rating:** 4:30. **Green fee:** $18/24.
Credit cards: MC, V. **Reduced fees:** Weekdays, Twilight, Seniors,
Juniors.
Caddies: No. **Golf carts:** $10 for 18 holes.
Discount golf packages: No. **Season:** Year-round. **High:** July-Sept.
On-site lodging: No. **Rental clubs:** Yes.
Walking policy: Unrestricted walking. **Range:** Yes (grass).
To obtain tee times: Call five days in advance. Call eight to 30 days in
advance for $1 surcharge.
Subscriber comments: Requires accuracy and control, narrow fairways
. . . Flat, long and straight . . . Fun to walk . . . Tight in areas, wide open
in others . . . Good greens all year . . . Needs a lot of everything for
improvement . . . Difficult water hazards if you slice . . . Often floods
following heavy rains . . . New greens OK, others need work.

★½ CITY OF SAN MATEO GOLF COURSE
PU—1700 Coyote Point Dr., San Mateo (415)347-1461.
18 miles south of San Francisco. **Holes:** 18. **Par:** 70/72.
Yards: 5,853/5,451. **Course rating:** 67.0/69.8. **Slope:** 104/115.
Opened: 1933. **Pace of Play rating:** N/A. **Green fee:** $19/23.
Credit Cards: None. **Reduced fees:** Weekdays, Twilight, Juniors.
Caddies: No. **Golf carts:** $9 for 18 holes.
Discount golf packages: No. **Season:** Year-round. **High:** N/A.
On-site lodging: No. **Rental clubs:** Yes.
Walking policy: Unrestricted walking. **Range:** No.
To obtain tee times: Call seven days in advance.
Subscriber comments:
High traffic muny that is acceptable . . . Flat, straight course . . . Short, fun
course, pretty open with afternoon wind . . . Overcrowded, run down . . .
Flat, but the back nine has some nice holes . . . Signs of improvement in
clubhouse and course.

COPPER RIVER COUNTRY CLUB★
SP—11500 N. Friant Rd., Fresno (209)434-5200.
Holes: 18. **Par:** 72/72.
Yards: 7,029/5,5,374. **Course rating:** 73.6/70.5. **Slope:** 130/120.
Opened: 1995. **Pace of Play rating:** 4:30. **Green fee:** $35/40.
Credit cards: MC, V. **Reduced fees:** Weekdays, Twilight, Juniors.

Caddies: No. **Golf carts:** $20 for 18 holes.
Discount golf packages: No. **Season:** Year-round. **High:** March-Sept.
On-site lodging: No. **Rental clubs:** Yes.
Walking policy: Unrestricted walking. **Range:** Yes (grass).
To obtain tee times: Call two days in advance.

★★★ CORONADO GOLF COURSE

PU—2000 Visalia Row, Coronado (619)435-3121.
2 miles south of San Diego. **Holes:** 18. **Par:** 72/72.
Yards: 6,633/5,784. **Course rating:** 71.8/73.7. **Slope:** 124/126.
Opened: 1957. **Pace of Play rating:** 4:30. **Green fee:** $20.
Credit cards: MC, V. **Reduced fees:** Twilight, Juniors.
Caddies: No. **Golf carts:** $10 for 18 holes.

Discount golf packages: No. **Season:** Year-round. **High:** All.
On-site lodging: No. **Rental clubs:** Yes.
Walking policy: Walking at certain times. **Range:** Yes.
To obtain tee times: Call two days in advance at 7 a.m. Fourteen days in advance you may buy a time for 11 a.m. or later for $30. Fee must be paid at least three days in advance.
Subscriber comments: Landfill on harbor, absolutely flat . . . Fun track; good greens, super bay surroundings . . . Wonderful course, fun, kept in good condition . . . Blessed with great location, but what a disappointment . . . Flat, long, good challenge . . . Simple course, but outstanding views of San Diego Bay . . . Always in good condition, suited for everyone . . . Best golf deal in the San Diego area . . . Basic, but tough with the wind . . . Great scenery . . . Course could be in better shape . . . Easy, flat but fun . . . The best muny in San Diego, great finishing holes . . . Hard to get a morning tee time, but worth playing anytime.

COSTA MESA COUNTRY CLUB
PU—1701 Golf Course Dr., Costa Mesa (714)540-7500.
25 miles south of Los Angeles.
Opened: N/A. **Pace of Play rating:** 5:00. **Green fee:** $17/22.
Credit cards: None. **Reduced fees:** Twilight, Seniors, Juniors.
Caddies: No. **Golf carts:** $20 for 18 holes.
Discount golf packages: No. **Season:** Year-round. **High:** Year-round.
On-site lodging: No. **Rental clubs:** Yes.
Walking policy: Unrestricted walking. **Range:** Yes (grass).
To obtain tee times: Call one week in advance or Monday for Saturday, Sunday, Monday times.

★½ LOS LAGOS COURSE
Holes: 18. **Par:** 72/72.
Yards: 6,542/5,925. **Course rating:** 70.7/73.3. **Slope:** 116/118.
Subscriber comments: Well-designed old-style course . . . Unfortunately poor condition, unimaginative layout . . . Slow, bumpy greens . . . Fairway and green conditions always marginal . . . In fair shape for a public course. Easy to play . . . Can't chip, ground too hard . . . Good municipal course. Walkable. Needs better care . . . Gets lots of play . . . Lucky to find grass on some fairways . . . Somewhat interesting for a short course, good bunkers by greens . . . Course always has challenging pin placements.

★½ MESA LINDA COURSE
Holes: 18. **Par:** 70/70.
Yards: 5,486/4,591. **Course rating:** 66.0/65.6. **Slope:** 104/103.
Subscriber comments: Executive-type course, easy . . . Short course . . . Nice course, needs TLC, slow play . . . Average to poor muny. Poor condition . . . Small greens. Tight fairways . . . Very crowded, flat, fair condition . . . Great program for kids . . . Biggest bargain in Orange County . . . Too crowded, poor greens . . . Several short par 4s detract from overall challenge . . . Improving, but a long way to go.

★½ CREEKSIDE GOLF COURSE
PU—701 Lincoln Ave., Modesto (209)571-5123.
25 miles south of Stockton. **Holes:** 18. **Par:** 72/72.
Yards: 6,610/5,496. **Course rating:** 70.3/69.5. **Slope:** 115/108.

Opened: 1992. **Pace of Play rating:** 4:10. **Green fee:** $9/18.
Credit cards: None. **Reduced fees:** Weekdays, Twilight, Seniors, Juniors.
Caddies: No. **Golf carts:** $18 for 18 holes.
Discount golf packages: No. **Season:** Year-round. **High:** May-Sept.
On-site lodging: No. **Rental clubs:** Yes.
Walking policy: Unrestricted walking. **Range:** Yes (grass).
To obtain tee times: Call one week in advance for weekdays. Call
Monday for upcoming weekend beginning at 6:30 a.m.
Subscriber comments: Short fairways, extra-large greens . . . Young
course, needs maturing . . . Easy, open course . . . Tough putting greens,
hard fairways . . . Good practice facilities . . . When foliage grows it will
rate an easy four stars . . . Wide open, drives roll forever . . . Foxes, egrets,
ducks, critters abound . . . Front nine more challenging and tight than back
nine . . . Hardly a good lie. No trees . . . Grass in fairways needed more
time to settle in, but once all the trees grow, it will become a tough course
. . . Crowned fairways at times too severe . . . Will be tough when the trees
grow.

★½ CRYSTAL SPRINGS GOLF CLUB
SP—6650 Golf Course Dr., Burlingame (415)342-0603.
200 miles south of San Francisco. **Holes:** 18. **Par:** 72/72.
Yards: 6,683/5,920. **Course rating:** 72.1/74.0. **Slope:** 125/130.
Opened: 1920. **Pace of Play rating:** 4:00. **Green fee:** $40/50.
Credit cards: MC, V. **Reduced fees:** Weekdays, Twilight.
Caddies: No. **Golf carts:** N/A.
Discount golf packages: No. **Season:** Year-round. **High:** March-Oct.
On-site lodging: No. **Rental clubs:** Yes.
Walking policy: Walking at certain times. **Range:** Yes.
To obtain tee times: Call one week in advance for weekdays. For
weekends, call Monday before.
Subscriber comments: Tough old course . . . Excellent scenic location,
tough slopes . . . Skip the front nine, play back twice . . . Difficult driving,
shot-shaping fairways . . . Course condition varies from poor to acceptable
. . . Many unfair landing areas. Penalizes too many good shots . . . Good
layout, usually windy . . . Aerobic golf, up-down-up-down . . . Marginal
condition always . . . Great greens . . . Not a flat spot on it.

★★★ CYPRESS GOLF CLUB
PU—4921 Katella Ave., Los Alamitos (714)527-1800.
22 miles south of Los Angeles. **Holes:** 18. **Par:** 71/71.
Yards: 6,510/4,569. **Course rating:** 72.6/66.5. **Slope:** 140/117.
Opened: 1992. **Pace of Play rating:** N/A. **Green fee:** $45/95.
Credit cards: All major. **Reduced fees:** Weekdays, Twilight, Seniors.
Caddies: No. **Golf carts:** Included in Green Fee.
Discount golf packages: Yes. **Season:** Year-round. **High:** April-Oct.
On-site lodging: No. **Rental clubs:** Yes.
Walking policy: Unrestricted walking. **Range:** Yes (grass).
To obtain tee times: Call up to seven days in advance.
Subscriber comments: Too many mounds . . . Very, very narrow . . .
Claustrophobic course to play . . . Water on 14 holes . . . Very nice layout
in a tight space . . . Best greens in Orange County . . . Too much course in
too small a space. Tough for all golfers . . . Well done . . . One of the most
interesting courses I've ever played. A real challenge, lots of fun, a first-class
golf experience . . . Bermuda fairways, bent greens . . . Target golf. Lots of
water. A miniature PGA West (Stadium) . . . All fairways packed together
. . . Excellent course with potential . . . Fun layout. Too many moguls . . .
Good track, fun and challenging, plays longer than the yardage . . . Like
playing in Candyland . . . Stay out of the monkey grass . . . Not enough
land for 18 holes . . . Too cramped, no elbow room.

★★ DAD MILLER GOLF COURSE
PU—430 N. Gilbert St., Anaheim (714)774-8055.
Call club for further information.
Subscriber comments: Fair municipal course. Walkable. Needs better care
. . . Ordinary, non-descript . . . Good place for a warm-up round . . .

Wide open . . . The last two holes are the longest . . . Greens are in poor shape, dead spots . . . Pace of play slow when busy. Too many short par 4s . . . Wide open and flat, good beginners course . . . Divotmaster paradise, wear a helmet and duck! The 4th of July without the explosions.

★★½ DEBELL GOLF CLUB
PU—1500 Walnut Ave., Burbank (818)845-0022.
Holes: 18. **Par:** 71/73.
Yards: 5,610/5,412. **Course rating:** 67.4/70.8. **Slope:** 108/118.
Opened: 1958. **Pace of Play rating:** 5:00. **Green fee:** $15/19.
Credit cards: None. **Reduced fees:** Weekdays, Low season, Twilight, Seniors, Juniors.
Caddies: No. **Golf carts:** $18 for 18 holes.
Discount golf packages: No. **Season:** Year-round. **High:** Year-round.
On-site lodging: No. **Rental clubs:** Yes.
Walking policy: Unrestricted walking. **Range:** Yes.
To obtain tee times: Call pro shop.
Subscriber comments: A hidden gem carved out of the Verdugo Mountains . . . Too many trick hazards: arroyos, ditches, etc. . . . Tight; interesting course . . . If you score well at Debell you should score very well on spacious courses . . . Nice scenic course, well maintained . . . Weeds aplenty . . . Short and fun, thinking man's golf . . . Lots of uphill fairways . . . Hilly, target-type course . . . Mountainside course . . . Tough putting . . . Great views of Los Angeles on a clear day . . . Spectacular views of San Fernando Valley and the Los Angeles Basin . . . Back nine very short (executive length), front side more challenging.

★★★ DELAVEAGA GOLF CLUB
PU—401 Upper Park Rd., Santa Cruz (408)423-7214.
25 miles south of San Jose. **Holes:** 18. **Par:** 72/72.
Yards: 6,010/5,331. **Course rating:** 70.4/70.6. **Slope:** 133/125.
Opened: 1970. **Pace of Play rating:** 4:18. **Green fee:** $24/32.
Credit cards: None. **Reduced fees:** Weekdays, Twilight.
Caddies: No. **Golf carts:** N/A.
Discount golf packages: No. **Season:** Year-round. **High:** N/A.
On-site lodging: No. **Rental clubs:** Yes.
Walking policy: Unrestricted walking. **Range:** Yes.
To obtain tee times: Call one week in advance.
Subscriber comments: Beautiful, challenging, hidden in the Santa Cruz hills . . . Wooded and tight, accuracy a must . . . Many players I know refuse to play it because it's too tough . . . Ball rolls off the fairways . . . Can't wait till I can play this one again . . . Killer terrain, one foot off fairway, lost ball . . . Hardest municipal course in U.S.A. . . . Requires an arsenal of shots . . . Giant trees. Gorgeous layout . . . Extremely tight.

Must think off tee. Great views . . . Too many sloping fairways with rolls into elephantine rough . . . Hit it straight; if not you're in the canyons . . . Can be muddy . . . Fairways lean towards trouble . . . Outstanding little sister to Pasatiempo. Everyone's favorite.

★★★★ DESERT DUNES GOLF CLUB
PU—19300 Palm Dr., Desert Hot Springs (619)251-5367, (800)766-2767.
5 miles north of Palm Springs. **Holes:** 18. **Par:** 72/72.
Yards: 6,876/5,359. **Course rating:** 73.8/70.7. **Slope:** 142/122.
Opened: 1989. **Pace of Play rating:** N/A. **Green fee:** $30/100.
Credit cards: MC, V, AMEX. **Reduced fees:** Weekdays, Low season, Resort guests, Twilight, Seniors, Juniors.
Caddies: No. **Golf carts:** Included in Green Fee.
Discount golf packages: Yes. **Season:** Year-round. **High:** Jan.–May.
On-site lodging: No. **Rental clubs:** Yes.
Walking policy: Unrestricted walking. **Range:** Yes (grass).
To obtain tee times: Call seven days in advance.
Ranked in Second 25 of America's 75 Best Public Golf Courses by Golf Digest.
Subscriber comments: Spectacular links design, nothing like it in Palm Desert . . . Sometimes not in good shape, but a fun track . . . Lose the wind

. . . Super design . . . No condos on course, beautiful scenery . . . Nice change of pace in Dye-dominated desert . . . Best-kept secret in Palm Desert . . . Howling winds . . . Very windy . . . Great desert challenge . . . A real dunes course . . . Best-kept secret in Palm Springs area except when windy . . . Trent Jones Jr. course must be played with a light wind . . . The best! . . . The wind blows and blows, will try even the best golfers' patience and wind game . . . Course is in a wind tunnel . . . Long links style, very challenging terrain . . . Best course in the desert, I could play here everyday . . . A tough course with many hazards. Usually high scores for high handicappers . . . No homes or condos. Desert golf at its best.

★★★½ DESERT FALLS COUNTRY CLUB
SP—1111 Desert Falls Pkwy., Palm Desert (619)341-4020.
Holes: 18. **Par:** 72/72.
Yards: 7,017/5,313. **Course rating:** 75.0/71.7. **Slope:** 145/124.
Opened: 1984. **Pace of Play rating:** 4:00–4:15. **Green fee:** $30/130.
Credit cards: MC, V. **Reduced fees:** Low season, Twilight.
Caddies: No. **Golf carts:** Included in Green Fee.
Discount golf packages: No. **Season:** Year-round. **High:** Nov.-April.
On-site lodging: Yes. **Rental clubs:** Yes.
Walking policy: Mandatory cart. **Range:** Yes (grass).
To obtain tee times: Call three days in advance with credit card.
Subscriber comments: Another jewel in the desert . . . Great desert course, excellent shape . . . Varied design, all holes different, no cookie cutter here . . . Best course in Palm Springs area. Not as tricked up as so many others . . . Nice links layout, very playable . . . Unusual golf holes . . . Local knowledge necessary to score well the first time . . . Tough for the average golfer . . . Challenging, very pretty . . . Long par 4s . . . Standing on the tees, you can't tell where to aim . . . What time, I'll be there.

DESERT PRINCESS COUNTRY CLUB AND RESORT
★★★ LA VISTA/EL CIELO/LOS LAGOS
R—28-555 Landau Blvd., Cathedral City (619)322-2280, (800)637-0577.
2 miles southeast of Palm Springs. **Holes:** 27. **Par:** 72/72/72.
Yards: 6,764/6,587/6,667. **Course rating:** 72.5/71.2/71.8.
Slope: 126/121/123.
Opened: 1984. **Pace of Play rating:** 4:30. **Green fee:** $45/95.
Credit cards: MC, V, AMEX. **Reduced fees:** Weekdays, Low season, Resort guests, Twilight.
Caddies: No. **Golf carts:** Included in Green Fee.
Discount golf packages: Yes. **Season:** Year-round. **High:** Nov.-May.
On-site lodging: Yes. **Rental clubs:** Yes.
Walking policy: Mandatory cart. **Range:** Yes (grass).
To obtain tee times: Resort guests call up to 30 days in advance.
Subscriber comments: Three interesting nines . . . Windy and flat, uninspiring . . . The original 18 holes are great . . . Not really tough . . . Very good course design, turf always in very good condition . . . Lots of water . . . Takes seven minutes to get from clubhouse to the first tee. El Cielo is the best nine.

★★ DIABLO CREEK GOLF COURSE
PU—4050 Port Chicago Hwy., Concord (510)686-6262.
50 miles northeast of San Francisco. **Holes:** 18. **Par:** 71/72.
Yards: 6,866/5,872. **Course rating:** 72.2/72.5. **Slope:** 122/119.
Opened: 1962. **Pace of Play rating:** 4:30. **Green fee:** $17/19.
Credit cards: MC, V. **Reduced fees:** Weekdays, Twilight, Seniors, Juniors.
Caddies: No. **Golf carts:** $10 for 18 holes.
Discount golf packages: Yes. **Season:** Year-round. **High:** N/A.
On-site lodging: No. **Rental clubs:** Yes.
Walking policy: Unrestricted walking. **Range:** Yes.
To obtain tee times: Call Mondays at noon to get available tee times.
Subscriber comments: Good greens, a good public course . . . Slow play a major drawback . . . Flat as a pancake, little challenge . . . Needs work,

but moving in right direction . . . Solid course for the average golfer . . .
Long, traditional . . . Some fair holes, good design . . . Greens are in good
shape, very flat course . . . Heavy play but good condition . . . Flat, a little
boring . . . 660-yard par-5 third hole is a hoot.

★½ DIAMOND BAR GOLF CLUB

PU—22751 E. Golden Springs Dr., Diamond Bar (909)861-8282.
25 miles east of Los Angeles. **Holes:** 18. **Par:** 72/73.
Yards: 6,810/6,009. **Course rating:** 72.8/73.9. **Slope:** 125/122.
Opened: 1964. **Pace of Play rating:** 4:00-5:00. **Green fee:** $12/21.
Credit cards: All major. **Reduced fees:** Weekdays, Twilight, Seniors,
Juniors.
Caddies: No. **Golf carts:** $10 for 18 holes.
Discount golf packages: No. **Season:** Year-round. **High:** N/A.
On-site lodging: No. **Rental clubs:** Yes.
Walking policy: Unrestricted walking. **Range:** Yes.
To obtain tee times: Call or come in one week in advance.
Subscriber comments: Nice course, good greens . . . In poor condition;
has potential . . . Shaggy, inconsistent fairways . . . Interesting layout.
Good challenge . . . Worn-out fairways . . . Always a portion of course in
bad shape, mostly the greens . . . Seems every hole is next to the freeway.
You lose your voice at the end of day due to shouting . . . Excellent layout
if someone could keep it in playable condition year-round.

★★½ DIAMOND OAKS GOLF CLUB

PU—349 Diamond Oaks Rd., Roseville (916)783-4947.
15 miles east of Sacramento. **Holes:** 18. **Par:** 72/73.
Yards: 6,283/5,608. **Course rating:** 69.5/70.5. **Slope:** 115/112.
Opened: 1963. **Pace of Play rating:** N/A. **Green fee:** $14/17.
Credit cards: MC, V. **Reduced fees:** Weekdays, Twilight, Seniors,
Juniors.
Caddies: No. **Golf carts:** $8 for 18 holes.
Discount golf packages: No. **Season:** Year-round. **High:** April-Oct.
On-site lodging: No. **Rental clubs:** Yes.
Walking policy: Walking at certain times. **Range:** Yes.
To obtain tee times: Call one week in advance for weekday. Call Monday
for upcoming weekend.
Subscriber comments: Good old course. Big established oak trees come
into play often . . . Very busy . . . A nice friendly municipal course . . .
Needs more parking . . . Short course, green condition depends on time of
year . . . Very much improved over past three years . . . Easy course, wide
open . . . Fun course, not too difficult, good condition . . . Tougher than
yardage suggests . . . Very playable, good scoring opportunities.

★★★ DRY CREEK RANCH GOLF COURSE

PU—809 Crystal Way, Galt (209)745-4653.
20 miles south of Sacramento. **Holes:** 18. **Par:** 72/74.
Yards: 6,773/5,952. **Course rating:** 72.7/73.9. **Slope:** 129/128.
Opened: 1962. **Pace of Play rating:** 4:30. **Green fee:** $16/26.
Credit cards: MC, V. **Reduced fees:** Weekdays, Low season, Twilight.
Caddies: No. **Golf carts:** $18 for 18 holes.
Discount golf packages: No. **Season:** Year-round. **High:** April-July.
On-site lodging: No. **Rental clubs:** Yes.
Walking policy: Unrestricted walking. **Range:** Yes (grass).
To obtain tee times: Call two weeks in advance.
Subscriber comments: Great old design . . . Toughest course year-round
in northern California, need to draw ball . . . Good tournament course . . .
Mature, well-bunkered greens . . . Favors non-slicers, demands driving
accuracy . . . Good valley course . . . Tough, fair, quality course . . .
Always seems to sandwich in too many people . . . The mother of slow
play was born here . . . Fog can be serious in winter . . . Rough too long
. . . Killer first, 18th holes . . . Very friendly, mellow round . . . No. 18
should be par 5 . . . Great greens! Very fast and perfect . . . Best public
course in Sacramento area . . . Demands accurate irons to small greens . . .
One of the best northern California public courses.

★★ DRYDEN PARK GOLF COURSE

PU—920 Sunset Ave., Modesto (209)577-5359.
Holes: 18. **Par:** 72/74.
Yards: 6,574/6,048. **Course rating:** 69.8/72.5. **Slope:** 119/115.
Opened: 1953. **Pace of Play rating:** 4:15. **Green fee:** $14/16.
Credit cards: None. **Reduced fees:** Weekdays, Twilight, Seniors, Juniors.
Caddies: No. **Golf carts:** $18 for 18 holes.
Discount golf packages: No. **Season:** Year-round. **High:** May-Sept.

On-site lodging: No. **Rental clubs:** Yes.
Walking policy: Unrestricted walking. **Range:** Yes (grass).
To obtain tee times: Call one week in advance for weekdays and the
Monday before for weekends beginning at 6:30 a.m.
Subscriber comments: Solid, old-fashioned muny . . . Wide fairways,
small greens, very playable, fun . . . Average muny course . . . Typical
muny course, large trees . . . Mature course; old, small greens need TLC
. . . Can get some bad lies in fairways, greens bumpy . . . No. 1 handicap
hole: "don't let them cut down the oak" . . . Good summer course, flat . . .
Conditions improving but a dull course to play . . . Needs creative
updating . . . Cheap, simple layout, friendly staff.

★★★ EAGLE CREST GOLF CLUB

PU—1656 Cloverdale Rd., Escondido (619)737-9762.
20 miles northeast of San Diego. **Holes:** 18. **Par:** 72/72.
Yards: 6,417/4,941. **Course rating:** 71.6/69.9. **Slope:** 136/123.
Opened: 1993. **Pace of Play rating:** N/A. **Green fee:** $30/55.
Credit cards: All major. **Reduced fees:** Twilight, Seniors, Juniors.
Caddies: No. **Golf carts:** Included in Green Fee.
Discount golf packages: No. **Season:** Year-round. **High:** Jan.-April.
On-site lodging: No. **Rental clubs:** Yes.
Walking policy: Walking at certain times. **Range:** Yes (grass).
To obtain tee times: Call seven days in advance.
Subscriber comments: An undiscovered jewel! . . . Facilities consist of a
trailer . . . Tough course, pick your targets carefully . . . Great new course
. . . First few holes very demanding . . . Bring a couple of extra balls . . .
Enjoyable course, short on amenities . . . Very tough layout, great scenic
course . . . Ecological areas can make it a tough front nine . . . Play it before
they build the houses . . . Use a lot of sticks . . . Short, tight and interesting
. . . Wide variety of holes . . . Poor placement of O.B. stakes make it tight
. . . Narrow fairways, O.B. very unforgiving . . . Good test of golf,
impressive concern given to environment . . . Best-kept secret in San Diego
county.

★★★ EASTLAKE COUNTRY CLUB

PU—2375 Clubhouse Dr., Chula Vista (619)482-5757.
20 miles southeast of San Diego. **Holes:** 18. **Par:** 72/72.
Yards: 6,606/5,118. **Course rating:** 70.7/68.8. **Slope:** 116/114.
Opened: 1991. **Pace of Play rating:** 4:00. **Green fee:** $30/46.
Credit cards: MC, V. **Reduced fees:** Weekdays, Seniors, Juniors.
Caddies: No. **Golf carts:** $12 for 18 holes.
Discount golf packages: No. **Season:** Year-round. **High:** Jan.-June.
On-site lodging: No. **Rental clubs:** Yes.
Walking policy: Unrestricted walking. **Range:** Yes (grass).
To obtain tee times: Call after 3 p.m. five days in advance.
Subscriber comments: Typical Ted Robinson, several par 4s drivable
from the blues . . . Young course, will get tougher with age . . . A good
practice course . . . Excellent conditioning, user-friendly course . . . Lots of
sand . . . Beautifully landscaped, a joy to play . . . Not a difficult course,
but a very enjoyable experience . . . User-friendly . . . Greens are a pleasure
to putt . . . A well-kept secret . . . Nice, forgiving course . . . Fairly new,
turf not established . . . The greens make the course, power hitters and
finesse players can enjoy . . . I fell asleep. Haven't I played this hole already?
. . . Cool, computerized yardage markers in carts.

★★½ EL DORADO PARK GOLF CLUB

PU—2400 Studebaker Rd., Long Beach (310)430-5411.

Call club for further information.

Subscriber comments: A beautiful, scenic place to play . . . Often crowded and slow . . . Hard to get on, widely played . . . Established course . . . Every hole has personality . . . Short, unexciting . . . Flat course with lots of trees; it will sneak up on you . . . Not a typical muny, challenging layout . . . Toughest of the three public courses in Long Beach . . . Fine municipal course. Hit it straight or you pay the price . . . Very mature, tree-lined fairways; small, elevated greens . . . Best of Long Beach trio.

EL PRADO GOLF COURSES

PU—6555 Pine Ave., Chino (909)597-1751.

30 miles east of Los Angeles.

Opened: 1976. **Pace of Play rating:** N/A. **Green fee:** $13/21.

Credit cards: None. **Reduced fees:** Weekdays, Low season, Twilight, Seniors, Juniors.

Caddies: No. **Golf carts:** $11 for 18 holes.

Discount golf packages: No. **Season:** Year-round. **High:** Year-round.

On-site lodging: No. **Rental clubs:** No.

Walking policy: Unrestricted walking. **Range:** Yes (grass).

To obtain tee times: For weekdays call one week in advance. Call Monday for upcoming weekend.

★★ BUTTERFIELD STAGE COURSE

Holes: 18. **Par:** 72/73.

Yards: 6,508/5,503. **Course rating:** 69.7/70.2. **Slope:** 108/118.

Subscriber comments: Out in the country, has character . . . Dairy farms nearby . . . Not long, great greens and interesting layouts . . . Cattle nearby . . . Surroundings add flavor . . . Greens usually best in area . . . Can be lots of insects and cow odors . . . Nice simple course . . . Dairy farms abound add ambiance . . . A little conditioning would really help . . . Wide-open course with forced water carries . . . Needs work on fairways . . . Has unrealized potential.

★★½ CHINO CREEK COURSE

Holes: 18. **Par:** 72/73.

Yards: 6,671/5,596. **Course rating:** 71.0/70.8. **Slope:** 114/115.

Subscriber comments: Tougher of the two 18s, great greens, tough finishing hole . . . Hard finishing holes, good walking course . . . Can hit it anywhere and still score . . . Tough back nine with Chino Creek running through it . . . Course rough is "rough" . . . In dairy country so the smell is strong . . . Wide open, but has trouble . . . Level. Easy to play. Good, fun course . . . Good greens, better of the two layouts . . . You better like cows! Excellent greens, good challenge . . . Greens always good, confidence builder.

★★ EL RANCHO VERDE COUNTRY CLUB

PU—Country Club Dr., Rialto (909)875-5346.

5 miles from San Bernardino. **Holes:** 18. **Par:** 72/72.

Yards: 6,800/5,589. **Course rating:** N/A. **Slope:** 124/118.

Opened: N/A. **Pace of Play rating:** N/A. **Green fee:** N/A.

Credit cards: MC, V. **Reduced fees:** Weekdays, Low season, Twilight.

Caddies: No. **Golf carts:** N/A.

Discount golf packages: No. **Season:** Year-round. **High:** Year-round.

On-site lodging: No. **Rental clubs:** No.

Walking policy: N/A. **Range:** Yes (grass).

Subscriber comments: Little-known great golf . . . Very nice layout, could be outstanding if course was better maintained . . . Very hard-packed rough. Lack of water . . . Best-kept secret around the area. I've played private country clubs with worse greens . . . Not bad, needs some TLC . . . Good course to practice on . . . Wide-open course for the most part, no water hazards, pretty much flat . . . Wide fairways . . . Uninteresting layout . . . Forced water carries, slow greens, the best public course in the area.

★★★ EL RIVINO COUNTRY CLUB

PU—5530 El Rivino Rd., P.O. Box 3369, Riverside (909)684-8905.
3 miles from San Bernardino. **Holes:** 18. **Par:** 73/73.
Yards: 6,466/5,863. **Course rating:** N/A. **Slope:** 111/113.
Opened: N/A. **Pace of Play rating:** N/A **Green fee:** N/A.
Credit cards: MC, V. **Reduced fees:** Weekdays, Twilight.
Caddies: No. **Golf carts:** N/A.
Discount golf packages: No. **Season:** Year-round. **High:** Year-round.
On-site lodging: No. **Rental clubs:** No.
Walking policy: N/A . **Range:** No.
Subscriber comments: Best-kept course in Riverside County . . . No
brown spots, just beautiful green grass everywhere . . . Beautiful layout,
like a private club . . . Very reasonable, good variety of holes . . . Easy
course, you can score well here . . . Unusual par 6 . . . One of the most
improved tracks in southern California . . . Well maintained. Parallel
fairways a problem . . . Best-kept public course around . . . Only par 6 I've
ever played . . . Fun golf wide open . . . Water on five holes . . . Avoid
windy days . . . Easy, very open, great greens . . . No snack shop . . .
Vending machines.

★★★ ELKINS RANCH GOLF CLUB

PU—1386 Chambersburg Rd., Fillmore (805)524-1440.
20 miles west of Valencia. **Holes:** 18. **Par:** 71/73.
Yards: 6,302/5,650. **Course rating:** 69.9/72.6. **Slope:** 117/122.
Opened: 1959. **Pace of Play rating:** 4:30. **Green fee:** $22/27.
Credit cards: None. **Reduced fees:** Weekdays, Twilight, Seniors, Juniors.
Caddies: No. **Golf carts:** $11 for 18 holes.
Discount golf packages: No. **Season:** Year-round. **High:** April-Oct.
On-site lodging: No. **Rental clubs:** Yes.
Walking policy: Unrestricted walking. **Range:** Yes (grass).
To obtain tee times: Call up to 10 days in advance.
Subscriber comments: Nice location between orange groves and
mountains . . . Just another golf course . . . Really a nice course out in
nowhere . . . Back nine lots of fun . . . Tree varieties abound . . . Nice
elevated tees . . . Good variety of holes, topography . . . 17th hole the best
. . . Beautiful course and views . . . Snack shop has the best burgers on
earth . . . Tricky greens, somewhat tough and weird layout . . . Tight
course. Mature . . . Easy but interesting . . . This course could be
outstanding . . . Could be a great course.

★★★★ FALL RIVER VALLEY GOLF AND COUNTRY CLUB

PU—42889 State Hwy., 299 E., Fall River Mills (916)336-5555.
70 miles northeast of Redding. **Holes:** 18. **Par:** 72/72.
Yards: 7,365/6,200. **Course rating:** 74.1/74.6. **Slope:** 129/127.
Opened: 1978. **Pace of Play rating:** N/A. **Green fee:** $9/22.
Credit cards: None. **Reduced fees:** Weekdays, Twilight, Seniors, Juniors.
Caddies: No. **Golf carts:** N/A.
Discount golf packages: No. **Season:** March-Nov. **High:** May-Sept.
On-site lodging: No. **Rental clubs:** Yes.
Walking policy: Unrestricted walking. **Range:** Yes (grass).
To obtain tee times: Call two weeks in advance.

GREAT VALUE

Subscriber comments: What a gem of a course . . . Best-kept secret in
northern California . . . Beautiful mountain course . . . Hate to mention
this course, because it won't be the best-kept secret for a California course
. . . Staff is pleasant and friendly . . . Long, can be brutal if not an accurate
shooter . . . Every hole is a separate challenge, great greens . . . Wonderful
greens . . . Hidden gem of northern California . . . Wide open and
spectacular . . . Out in the boonies . . . Beautiful scenery; superb course . . .
The eighth wonder of the world, well maintained . . . Wow! The ambiance!
What a relaxing experience and view . . . A great test, long . . . Little
known value in the mountains . . . Third hole is an exceptional 666-yard
par 5 . . . Golf in the morning and fly fish in the afternoon.

CALIFORNIA

★★ FALLBROOK GOLF CLUB
PU—2757 Gird Rd., Fallbrook (619)728-8334.
40 miles north of San Diego. **Holes:** 18. **Par:** 72/72.
Yards: 6,223/5,597. **Course rating:** 69.8/71.4. **Slope:** 117/119.
Opened: 1961. **Pace of Play rating:** N/A. **Green fee:** $9/28.
Credit cards: MC, V, DISC. **Reduced fees:** Weekdays, Twilight, Juniors.
Caddies: No. **Golf carts:** $18 for 18 holes.
Discount golf packages: No. **Season:** Year-round. **High:** Year-round.
On-site lodging: No. **Rental clubs:** Yes.
Walking policy: Unrestricted walking. **Range:** Yes (grass).
To obtain tee times: Call up to 10 days in advance.
Subscriber comments: Tight golf course, a good test of shotmaking . . .
Muny condition . . . Great setting for a 16 hole course, nine and 18 an
afterthought . . . Older course with two distinct nines . . . Older course,
worth a try . . . Back nine really tight, nice setting . . . Back nine looks like
a park . . . Good layout . . . Some hills, a creek, many trees . . . Fun course
for medium and high handicapper, maintenance so-so . . . Everything
about average . . . Off the beaten path, fun, moderate difficulty . . . Funky
old course . . . Back nine especially beautiful because of very large mature
trees . . . Don't play back nine in the fall . . . Oak leaves are too much.

★★ FIG GARDEN GOLF CLUB
SP—7700 N. Van Ness Blvd., Fresno (209)439-2928.
Holes: 18. **Par:** 72/72.
Yards: 6,621/5,605. **Course rating:** 70.6/71.9. **Slope:** 113/120.
Opened: 1958. **Pace of Play rating:** 4:15. **Green fee:** $29.
Credit cards: All major. **Reduced fees:** Weekdays, Twilight, Juniors.
Caddies: No. **Golf carts:** $24 for 18 holes.
Discount golf packages: No. **Season:** Year-round. **High:** Year-round.
On-site lodging: No. **Rental clubs:** Yes.
Walking policy: Unrestricted walking. **Range:** Yes.
To obtain tee times: Call pro shop.
Subscriber comments: Good ol' course, some interesting holes . . . Tight
course with lots of big trees . . . Staff was very good . . . Flat, but lots of
trees . . . Short, but must hit target . . . Flat course, poor greens . . . Greens
need work and get heavy play . . . Rather easy. Any golfer can have some
fun . . . They can't seem to get a grip on their greens . . . Acceptable
condition for amount of play.

FORT ORD GOLF COURSE
PU—1 McClure Way, Fort Ord (408)899-2351.
8 miles south of Pebble Beach. **Green fee:** $15/50.
Credit cards: MC, V. **Reduced fees:** Twilight.
Caddies: No. **Golf carts:** $10 for 18 holes.
Discount golf packages: No. **Season:** Year-round. **High:** March-Nov.
On-site lodging: No. **Rental clubs:** Yes.
Walking policy: Unrestricted walking. **Range:** Yes (grass).
To obtain tee times: Call two weeks in advance.
★★★½ BAYONET COURSE
Holes: 18. **Par:** 72/72.
Yards: 6,982/5,680. **Course rating:** 74.0/73.7. **Slope:** 132/134.
Opened: 1954. **Pace of Play rating:** N/A.
Subscriber comments: Best-kept secret on the Monterey Peninsula . . . In
transition from military ownership . . . U.S. Open caliber . . . One of the
most challenging in Monterey . . . Will wear you down; almost no sand,
but none is needed . . . Best-kept secret in California . . . What happens
when the Army leaves? . . . This course can eat you alive . . . Toughest I
have ever seen . . . Trees on this course make Poppy Hills look like a desert
. . . Demands accurate shots, must be straight or in the trees . . . Putting an
adventure . . . The pros should play here in the AT&T, great layout . . .
Best public course in area . . . Hardest track on the peninsula . . . Probably
the toughest golf course in Monterey, tough, hard to read greens . . . Poor
man's Spyglass . . . Bring longest shots in your bag . . . Not what it used to
be . . . Three-foot putts break three feet . . . Mediocre grooming but great

layout . . . Long, demanding, no hidden tricks . . . Interesting holes laid out in an old forest . . . Great ocean views . . . Mostly wooded, narrow . . . A big-hitters course. Par 4s are long! . . . Did I mention trees? . . . Amenities were spartan . . . Trees have overgrown into fairways, too tight . . . Tough, long, tight, "Bayonet" is the correct name for this course.

★★★ BLACKHORSE COURSE

Holes: 18. **Par:** 72/72.
Yards: 6,396/5,613. **Course rating:** 69.8/72.5. **Slope:** 120/129.
Opened: 1974. **Pace of Play rating:** N/A.
Subscriber comments: Not many know it's open to the public . . . Shorter than Bayonet but just as good . . . Play this before you play Bayonet . . . Tight, tough, poor maintenance . . . Putt-putt course alongside of Bayonet . . . Lots of plants and somewhat hilly . . . Beautiful course, good greens . . . Mediocre grooming. No really memorable holes . . . Very challenging if you wander off of fairways. Low, low limbs on trees . . . Tough, straight shooters only, shorter but still difficult to score . . . Somebody was playing a trick in design . . . Easier of two courses but also hilly. Some long walks between greens. You must be in shape to carry your bag.

★★★½ FOUNTAINGROVE RESORT AND COUNTRY CLUB

SP—1525 Fountaingrove Pkwy., Santa Rosa (707)579-4653.
50 miles north of San Francisco. **Holes:** 18. **Par:** 72/72.
Yards: 6,797/5,644. **Course rating:** 72.8/72.1. **Slope:** 132/128.
Opened: 1985. **Pace of Play rating:** 4:30. **Green fee:** $45/70.
Credit cards: MC, V, AMEX. **Reduced fees:** Weekdays, Twilight.
Caddies: No. **Golf carts:** Included in Green Fee.
Discount golf packages: Yes. **Season:** Year-round. **High:** May-Oct.
On-site lodging: No. **Rental clubs:** Yes.
Walking policy: Mandatory cart. **Range:** Yes.
To obtain tee times: Call up to seven days in advance.
Subscriber comments: Good Ted Robinson design . . . Wow! Love No. 17 over water . . . Windiest day of the year, still great golf . . . Prettiest course north of Pebble Beach! . . . Needs markers for blind shots . . . Outstanding in all aspects . . . Some very exciting holes . . . Very hilly, many uphill shots with little roll . . . Many blind shots will test you first time out . . . Good conditions, a few marginal holes, a few great holes . . . A fine maturing track . . . Good course for the low handicapper . . . Variety of holes requires strategic driving, calculated risk . . . Mandatory carts on paths only, too tiring up and down walking path to ball . . . One of the best in Sonoma county . . . Beautiful old oak trees . . . For mature adults only . . . Great layout, resort treatment . . . Heard great things, but with the exception of a couple holes, overall average . . . O.B. abounds . . . Tight O.B. due to condos not fair . . . Worthwhile to go out of your way to play . . . One of the top five in northern California.

★★½ FRANKLIN CANYON GOLF COURSE

PU—Hwy. 4, Rodeo (510)799-6191.
22 miles east of San Francisco. **Holes:** 18. **Par:** 72/72.
Yards: 6,776/5,516. **Course rating:** 70.9/71.2. **Slope:** 118/123.
Opened: 1968. **Pace of Play rating:** N/A. **Green fee:** $21/32.
Credit cards: MC, V. **Reduced fees:** Weekdays, Low season, Twilight, Seniors, Juniors.
Caddies: No. **Golf carts:** $11 for 18 holes.
Discount golf packages: No. **Season:** Year-round. **High:** N/A.
On-site lodging: No. **Rental clubs:** Yes.
Walking policy: Unrestricted walking. **Range:** Yes.
To obtain tee times: Tee times made for two or more up to seven days in advance.
Subscriber comments: Windy course in secluded canyon . . . Tough and long, course maintenance needs improving . . . It is a great course, but the tees need a lot of work . . . Frankly dry and high . . . Five par 5s, good layout . . . Always a good challenge . . . Nice scenery . . . Well maintained. Playable course . . . Very diverse layout and good greens . . . A few nice blind holes . . . Good muny course . . . Great greens for so much play, nice condition for public course . . . A fine course hampered by consistent slow

play . . . Best public course in area . . . Mostly flat, wide fairways . . . Good par 3s and par 5s . . . Basic golf . . . If the wind blows this gem will be all you can handle.

★★½ FRESNO WEST GOLF AND COUNTRY CLUB

PU—23986 W. Whitesbridge Rd., Kerman (209)846-8655.
23 miles west of Fresno. **Holes:** 18. **Par:** 72/73.

Yards: 6,959/6,000. **Course rating:** 72.6/74.1. **Slope:** 118/118.
Opened: 1966. **Pace of Play rating:** 4:00-4:15. **Green fee:** $13/16.
Credit cards: MC, V. **Reduced fees:** Weekdays, Low season, Twilight, Seniors, Juniors.
Caddies: No. **Golf carts:** $20 for 18 holes.
Discount golf packages: No. **Season:** Year-round. **High:** N/A.
On-site lodging: No. **Rental clubs:** Yes.
Walking policy: Unrestricted walking. **Range:** Yes (grass).
To obtain tee times: Call one week in advance.
Subscriber comments: A player needs distance for this course nestled in the fruitful San Joaquin Valley . . . Windy conditions make this a monster, love it . . . Long course, very open, tough in frequent wind . . . Good conditions, no surprises . . . Wind a factor . . . The view is not suited for postcard material . . . Greens are tough because of grain and wind . . . Good layout for a muny. A real test from the tips . . . Flat, long, lots of water, great greens . . . Flat, some water hazards . . . A little out of the way.

★★½ FURNACE CREEK GOLF COURSE

R—P.O. Box 187, Death Valley (619)786-2301.
140 miles north of Las Vegas. **Holes:** 18. **Par:** 70/71.
Yards: 6,093/5,238. **Course rating:** 67.7/69.2. **Slope:** 103/111.
Opened: 1937. **Pace of Play rating:** N/A. **Green fee:** $36.
Credit cards: All major. **Reduced fees:** Low season, Resort guests, Twilight.
Caddies: No. **Golf carts:** $10 for 18 holes.
Discount golf packages: Yes. **Season:** Year-round. **High:** Oct.-May.
On-site lodging: Yes. **Rental clubs:** Yes.
Walking policy: Unrestricted walking. **Range:** Yes (grass).
To obtain tee times: Call anytime.
Subscriber comments: Below sea level . . . Ball doesn't carry . . . Very poor shape! . . . Short, subpar course . . . Needs all-round work but still has excellent potential . . . Beautiful course for winter . . . "Get a sunburn" getaway . . . Flat track, wide open, good for beginners . . . Easy course, great place . . . Poor design, OK for where it is . . . Golf at the bottom of the U.S.!

GOLF RESORT AT INDIAN WELLS

R—44-500 Indian Wells Lane, Indian Wells (619)346-4653.
19 miles east of Palm Springs.
Opened: 1986. **Pace of Play rating:** N/A. **Green fee:** $40/105.
Credit cards: MC, V, AMEX. **Reduced fees:** Weekdays, Low season, Resort guests, Twilight.
Caddies: No. **Golf carts:** Included in Green Fee.
Discount golf packages: Yes. **Season:** Year-round. **High:** Jan.-May.
On-site lodging: Yes. **Rental clubs:** Yes.
Walking policy: Mandatory cart. **Range:** Yes (grass).
To obtain tee times: Stay at one of four participating hotels or call three days in advance.

★★★ EAST COURSE

Holes: 18. **Par:** 72/72.
Yards: 6,157/5,408. **Course rating:** 70.3/70.0. **Slope:** 116/111.
Subscriber comments: Alternate desert course . . . The mountains are so close you can touch them . . . Kind of a golf factory, busy . . . Kept well for a desert course, nice scenery . . . Yawn! Uninspiring resort course . . . Nothing special. Great hotel . . . Great resort course, good condition . . . Wide-open easy course, pretty . . . Tough but playable . . . Beautiful finishing hole! . . . Course in excellent condition year-round but serious

overcrowding and slow play at times, unfortunately . . . Nice layout, wide open, not too intimidating for women . . . Plays harder than rating . . . Best practice facility.

★★★ WEST COURSE
Holes: 18. **Par:** 72/72.
Yards: 6,500/5,408. **Course rating:** 70.3/70.0. **Slope:** 116/111.
Subscriber comments: Good desert course . . . Many elevation changes . . . The course is maintained beautifully year-round . . . My favorite desert course in Vacationland . . . Fun course, good greens, nothing special . . . Country club treatment . . . Nice resort layout. Requires some shotmaking . . . Fine clubhouses, fun greens . . . Very nice for all players . . . Possibly one of the lushest courses in area . . . Marshals try to keep the pace moving, but it is a resort . . . Good resort golf next to two great hotels . . . Very plush, almost boring . . . Not a weed in sight.

★★★½ GRAEAGLE MEADOWS GOLF COURSE
R—Hwy. 89, Graeagle (916)836-2323.
58 miles north of Reno, NV. **Holes:** 18. **Par:** 72/72.
Yards: 6,680/5,640. **Course rating:** 70.7/71.3. **Slope:** 118/118.
Opened: 1967. **Pace of Play rating:** N/A. **Green fee:** $30.
Credit cards: MC, V. **Reduced fees:** Twilight.
Caddies: No. **Golf carts:** N/A.

Discount golf packages: Yes. **Season:** April-Nov. **High:** July-Aug.
On-site lodging: Yes. **Rental clubs:** Yes.
Walking policy: Unrestricted walking. **Range:** Yes (grass).
To obtain tee times: Call after February 1st for times during season.
Subscriber comments: A great mountain course in the Sierras . . . Beautiful setting, tranquil . . . Laid out in a meadow along the Feather River, elevated tees, beautiful course . . . Some interesting holes . . . Breathtaking vistas, good long course . . . Relaxed, worth the drive . . . Hidden gem in the Sierras . . . Greens not always at their best . . . Blends well with nature . . . Another sleeper, there are no easy holes, condition is good for a mountain course . . . Scenic Sierra course, well thought-out, calm . . . They treat us well . . . Wonderful scenery. Hospitable community. Great trout fishing. Go! . . . Hidden treasure in California golf . . . Great climate, superb course, all holes are challenging . . . Relaxed atmosphere . . . Flat, a nice resort course . . . Good variety, average holes, scenic.

GREEN RIVER GOLF COURSE
PU—5215 Green River Rd., Corona (909)737-7393.
25 miles south of San Bernardino.
Opened: 1965. **Pace of Play rating:** 4:30. **Green fee:** $20/25.
Credit cards: MC, V, DISC.
Caddies: No. **Golf carts:** $11 for 18 holes.
Discount golf packages: No. **Season:** Year-round. **High:** N/A.
On-site lodging: No. **Rental clubs:** Yes.
Walking policy: Unrestricted walking. **Range:** Yes (grass).
To obtain tee times: Call seven days in advance for weekday tee times. Call Monday for upcoming Friday to Sunday.

★★ ORANGE COURSE
Holes: 18. **Par:** 71/72.
Yards: 6,416/5,744. **Course rating:** 70.4/75.7. **Slope:** 119/125.
Reduced fees: Juniors.
Subscriber comments: Great old-style layout . . . Only drawback is very slow play . . . Play early before wind and smog . . . Open, but with mature trees . . . Home of the fivesome . . . Needs work on course . . . OK for a weekend player . . . Greens sometimes in poor shape . . . Long and challenging. Average condition . . . Flat, tight fairways and small greens . . . Will never go there again . . . Nothing much, in between freeway 91 and railroad . . . Too many trees . . . Should have put their money into the course and not the million-dollar clubhouse . . . Very mature with lots of trees, tough when windy . . . Many unique holes . . . Tougher of the two.

★★½ RIVERSIDE COURSE
Holes: 18. **Par:** 71/71.
Yards: 6,275/5,467. **Course rating:** 69.2/73.9. **Slope:** 117/121.
Reduced fees: Twilight, Juniors.
Subscriber comments: Getting better all the time . . . Great finishing hole
. . . Very crowded all the time . . . Go for the pin, because you can't putt
these greens . . . Home of the six-hour round . . . Mountains and horses
viewed on back nine . . . Enjoyable course. Heavily wooded. Straight and
short pays premium . . . Greens maintenance needs attention, very bumpy
and a lot of dry spots . . . Heavily played muny course . . . Great clubhouse
. . . Fun, every hole asks for something different . . . Lots of trees, small
greens, slow play due to poor condition . . . Has charm, can be difficult
even though it's short.

★★ GREEN TREE GOLF CLUB
PU—999 Leisure Town Rd., Vacaville (707)448-1420.
30 miles west of Sacramento. **Holes:** 18. **Par:** 71/71.
Yards: 6,017/5,318. **Course rating:** 68.2/69.5. **Slope:** 114/117.
Opened: 1962. **Pace of Play rating:** 4:30. **Green fee:** $10/18.
Credit cards: MC, V. **Reduced fees:** Twilight, Seniors, Juniors.
Caddies: No. **Golf carts:** $10 for 18 holes.
Discount golf packages: No. **Season:** Year-round. **High:** March-Nov.
On-site lodging: No. **Rental clubs:** Yes.
Walking policy: Unrestricted walking. **Range:** Yes.
To obtain tee times: Call up to seven days in advance.
Also has 9-hole executive course.
Subscriber comments: Greens are as good as at country clubs . . . Flat
course, well kept . . . Could provide more drinking water . . .
Unremarkable, simple design . . . Best greens in area . . . Rough areas
poorly maintained all year . . . Has really improved over last five years,
greens are in great shape, but fairways are often patchy . . . Walkable . . .
Flat, open course, average greens . . . Best all-round course in area; some
challenging, interesting holes.

GRIFFITH PARK
PU—4730 Crystal Springs Dr., Los Angeles (213)664-2255.
Pace of Play rating: 4:50. **Green fee:** $10/21.
Credit cards: None. **Reduced fees:** Weekdays, Twilight, Seniors, Juniors.
Caddies: No. **Golf carts:** $10 for 18 holes.
Discount golf packages: No. **Season:** Year-round. **High:** March-Sept.
On-site lodging: No. **Rental clubs:** Yes.
Walking policy: Unrestricted walking. **Range:** Yes.
To obtain tee times: Must have a city of L.A. reservation card to make tee
times over the phone. To obtain a card, pick up an application at any city
course, fill out, pay fee, receive card. You can always come to
the course and put your name on the waiting list with the starter.

★★ HARDING COURSE
Holes: 18. **Par:** 72/73.
Yards: 6,536/6,028. **Course rating:** 70.4/72.5. **Slope:** 112/118.
Opened: 1924.
Subscriber comments: Old, tall trees, small greens . . . Gets heavy play,
greens poor, beautiful setting, poor maintenance . . . Too many flies and
people, long waits . . . Great old layout, but the greens are too slow . . .
Saved by interesting routings . . . Two of the best L.A. muny courses . . .
Don't play in summer because of bugs . . . Slow play but well worth the
wait . . . One of the best munys in L.A. . . . Pleasant course, some
challenging holes . . . Lousy condition, boring course . . . Tediously slow
and crowded . . . Fairways never in great shape. Mature course . . . Great
track, beautiful . . . Probably the busiest course in southern California.

★★½ WILSON COURSE
Holes: 18. **Par:** 72/73.
Yards: 6,942/6,330. **Course rating:** 72.7/74.6. **Slope:** 115/119.
Opened: 1923.
Subscriber comments: The better of the two park courses . . . Good old-
style golf . . . Good old-fashioned course, good for long hitters . . . Could

be so good . . . An old classic but very slow . . . Long and challenging, great tournament course . . . Scenic metro course . . . Mature, picturesque course, but greens are inconsistent, bumpy . . . Good public course . . . Heavy play, flat but interesting . . . Usually poor course conditions throughout the year . . . Good, traditional golf.

HAGGIN OAKS GOLF COURSE

PU—3645 Fulton Ave., Sacramento (916)481-4507.
Pace of Play rating: 4:45. **Green fee:** $14/16.
Credit cards: MC, V, DISC. **Reduced fees:** Weekdays, Twilight, Seniors, Juniors.
Caddies: No. **Golf carts:** $10 for 18 holes.
Discount golf packages: No. **Season:** Year-round. **High:** April-Sept.
On-site lodging: No. **Rental clubs:** Yes.
Walking policy: Unrestricted walking. **Range:** Yes.
To obtain tee times: Call one week in advance for weekdays and call Tuesday after 9:30 a.m. for weekends and holidays.

★½ NORTH COURSE

Holes: 18. **Par:** 72/72.
Yards: 6,631/5,853. **Course rating:** 71.4/71.7. **Slope:** 115/111.
Opened: N/A.
Subscriber comments: Greens boring . . . Bunkering nonexistent . . . Distance comes in handy, but poor shots add up quickly . . . Always my second choice . . . Flat, boring, straight holes . . . Very forgiving course . . . Best in area for quick nine or fun-filled 18 . . . Greens need a lot of help . . . Nice oak trees, maintenance is only fair . . . Bring a six pack to join the crowd . . . You can hit it anywhere . . . Great starter course . . . Needs better upkeep, but fun.

★★ SOUTH COURSE

Holes: 18. **Par:** 72/72.
Yards: 6,602/5,732. **Course rating:** 70.6/71.4. **Slope:** 113/113.
Opened: 1932.
Subscriber comments: Alister Mackenzie design, low cost, poor shape . . . The other two nines are better than this one . . . Great old design, 1930s-style course . . . Another course that fails to reach its true potential . . . Through old oaks . . . Full-grown trees but nothing outstanding . . . Flat and long, not much of a challenge . . . Interesting holes, but greens are inconsistent . . . Needs a little tenderness . . . The whole city plays here . . . They spiff it up for big tournaments but let it go in between . . . Great character, lots of trees and doglegs . . . Once upon a time, this was a great course.

★★★½ HALF MOON BAY GOLF LINKS

R—2000 Fairway Dr., Half Moon Bay (415)726-4438.
20 miles south of San Francisco. **Holes:** 18. **Par:** 72/72.
Yards: 7,131/5,769. **Course rating:** 74.5/73.3. **Slope:** 136/125.
Opened: 1973. **Pace of Play rating:** 5:00. **Green fee:** $77/97.
Credit cards: MC, V. **Reduced fees:** Weekdays, Resort guests, Twilight.
Caddies: No. **Golf carts:** Included in Green Fee.
Discount golf packages: Yes. **Season:** Year-round. **High:** N/A.
On-site lodging: Yes. **Rental clubs:** Yes.
Walking policy: Mandatory cart. **Range:** No.
To obtain tee times: Call one week in advance.
Subscriber comments: Poor man's Pebble Beach . . . Fairways always groomed like carpet . . . The 18th fronts the ocean . . . With the wind at your back, try to drive the barranca . . . Awesome finishing hole . . . No driving range . . . Lots of fog in early morning . . . The premier public course in San Francisco Bay area . . . Front nine not as scenic as back nine . . . Challenging layout, beautiful coastal setting . . . Scenic, hard in wind, too many condos . . . Wonderful 18th hole, good test . . . Beautiful and challenging . . . Three great finishing holes . . . Most of the course is condo golf, last two holes on ocean . . . Tougher than Pebble from blues . . . Ordinary except for the 18th . . . Strong, honest course . . . Four tough finishing holes . . . 18th tee is breathtaking . . . Still looking for one good

hole . . . Tough in the sea breeze . . . Overrated. Holes Nos. 1-17 boring
. . . Great course. Use all your clubs. See if you hit fewer houses than your
handicap . . . Very scenic, target golf off tee . . . Very nice course, well
maintained . . . View at 16, 17 and 18 is "Wow" . . . One of the best in the
west, Joe DiMaggio plays it.

HANSEN DAM GOLF COURSE★
PU—10400 Glen Oaks Blvd., Pacoima (818)896-0050.
15 miles north of Los Angeles. **Holes:** 18. **Par:** 72/75.
Yards: 6,715/6,090. **Course rating:** 69.9/73.5. **Slope:** 112/119.
Opened: 1977. **Pace of Play rating:** 4:30. **Green fee:** $15/20.
Credit cards: None. **Reduced fees:** Weekdays, Twilight, Seniors, Juniors.
Caddies: No. **Golf carts:** $15 for 18 holes.
Discount golf packages: No. **Season:** Year-round. **High:** N/A.
On-site lodging: No. **Rental clubs:** Yes.
Walking policy: Unrestricted walking. **Range:** Yes.
To obtain tee times: Advance reservations require an L.A. city reservation
card. Daily, first-come, first-served.

★★ HARDING PARK GOLF CLUB
PU—Harding Park Rd. and Skyline Blvd., San Francisco (415)664-4690.
Holes: 18. **Par:** 72/73.
Yards: 6,743/6,205. **Course rating:** 72.1/74.1 **Slope:** 124/120.
Opened: 1925. **Pace of Play rating:** 4:30. **Green fee:** $24/29.
Credit cards: None. **Reduced fees:** Weekdays, Twilight, Seniors, Juniors.
Caddies: No. **Golf carts:** $22 for 18 holes.
Discount golf packages: No. **Season:** Year-round. **High:** April-Nov.
On-site lodging: No. **Rental clubs:** Yes.
Walking policy: Unrestricted. **Range:** Yes.
Subscriber comments: A San Francisco classic but needs upgrading . . .
Bumpy greens . . . Good layout, good condition considering amount of
play . . . Agonizingly long time to get through 18 holes . . . A real gem,
poorly maintained . . . Poor man's Olympic Club . . . Desperately needs
help . . . Fairways a bit choppy . . . Next to shooting range . . . Too bad
such a good course is so rundown . . . Why can't the city of San Francisco
maintain its golf courses? The best holes face the Olympic Club. Is that a
coincidence? . . . Great layout, challenging, could be fabulous if it had some
grass on the fairways . . . Typhoon, hurricane or snow, they never close
. . . I never played here when it was not raining . . . Very good municipal
course for the regular golfer . . . Greens need work . . . Sad to see
prestigious course in bad shape.

★★★½ HESPERIA GOLF AND COUNTRY CLUB
SP—17970 Bangor Ave., Hesperia (619)244-9301.
15 miles north of San Bernardino. **Holes:** 18. **Par:** 72/72.
Yards: 6,996/6,136. **Course rating:** 74.6/73.9. **Slope:** 133/124.
Opened: 1955. **Pace of Play rating:** 3:30-4:00. **Green fee:** $15/20.
Credit cards: MC, V. **Reduced fees:** Juniors.
Caddies: No. **Golf carts:** $20 for 18 holes.
Discount golf packages: Yes. **Season:** Year-round. **High:** Spring/Fall.
On-site lodging: No. **Rental clubs:** Yes.
Walking policy: Unrestricted walking. **Range:** Yes.
To obtain tee times: Call two weeks ahead, if possible.
Subscriber comments: Desert secret, a treat to play . . . Nice course,
tough . . . Best-kept secret in southern California, greens are perfect . . .
Best course in Victor Valley . . . One of the best public courses in southern
California, great challenge . . . Great golf in the middle of nowhere . . .
Fast! Very much worth the drive from L.A. . . . Best in high desert . . .
Excellent layout and greens. Weather can be tough on the course . . .
Narrow, challenging . . . The secret is out.

★★★½ HORSE THIEF COUNTRY CLUB
R—28930 Horse Thief Dr., Stallion Spring, Tehachapi (805)822-5581.
50 miles east of Bakersfield. **Holes:** 18. **Par:** 72/72.

Yards: 6,678/5,677. **Course rating:** 72.1/72.1. **Slope:** 124/124.
Opened: 1972. **Pace of Play rating:** 4:50. **Green fee:** $30.
Credit cards: All major. **Reduced fees:** Weekdays, Twilight, Seniors, Juniors.
Caddies: No. **Golf carts:** N/A.
Discount golf packages: Yes. **Season:** Year-round. **High:** May-Sept.

On-site lodging: Yes. **Rental clubs:** Yes.
Walking policy: Unrestricted walking. **Range:** Yes.
To obtain tee times: Resort guests may make tee times up to one year in advance at time of room reservation. Nonguests call up to ten days in advance.
Subscriber comments: Wild layout . . . Need straight shots . . . Lots of rocks and elevation . . . Big rocks in the middle of fairways . . . Just plain fun . . . Interesting and fun to play, maintenance is fair, deer often roam the course . . . Beautiful track . . . Lush . . . Altitude makes me John Daly . . . Fantastic . . . Lots of tough putts . . . Isolated, beautiful setting . . . Oak trees . . . Great golf course in great shape. Has every shot in the book . . . Best-kept secret in southern California, don't tell anyone.

★★★½ HUNTER RANCH GOLF COURSE
PU—4041 Hwy. 46 E., Paso Robles (805)237-7444.
25 miles north of San Luis Obispo. **Holes:** 18. **Par:** 72/72.
Yards: 6,741/5,639. **Course rating:** 72.2/71.1. **Slope:** 128/125.
Opened: 1994. **Pace of Play rating:** 4:00. **Green fee:** $25/35.
Credit cards: MC, V. **Reduced fees:** Juniors.
Caddies: No. **Golf carts:** $22 for 18 holes.
Discount golf packages: No. **Season:** Year-round. **High:** May-Oct.
On-site lodging: No. **Rental clubs:** Yes.
Walking policy: Unrestricted walking. **Range:** Yes (grass).
To obtain tee times: Call one week in advance.
Subscriber comments: Outstanding! . . . What a course! . . . Stay on the fairway . . . Beautiful views over rolling hills, yet easy to walk . . . Hidden gem of central California . . . Nice mix of long, open and tight holes, great greens . . . Very mature for a new course . . . Well laid-out, interesting, and beautiful oaks . . . Great hilly new course, makes you want to play again soon . . . Beautiful setting, foothills with oaks and views of vineyards . . . What a deal! . . . Picturesque. Interesting. Friendly staff . . . Too many blind shots. Back nine confusing . . . Absolutely beautiful setting . . . Fabulous . . . Lots of blind shots . . . Big league track . . . Excellent putting greens . . . Need to play it more than once to get used to it . . . Great! Will get even better when it grows up.

★★ IMPERIAL GOLF CLUB
PU—2200 E. Imperial Hwy., Brea (714)529-3923.
Call club for further information.
Subscriber comments: Great course, great views . . . Forgiving . . . Long course. Not easy. Best for long ball hitter . . . Always in good playable condition . . . All-time easiest golf course, makes you feel like Arnold Palmer . . . Very average course, not much feel . . . Always some construction . . . Fairways could be improved . . . Wide open, watch for nesting hawks on No. 1.

★★½ INDIAN HILLS GOLF COURSE
PU—5700 Clubhouse Dr., Riverside (909)360-2090.
Holes: 18. **Par:** 70/72.
Yards: 6,104/5,562. **Course rating:** 70.0/70.7. **Slope:** 126/118.
Opened: 1964. **Pace of Play rating:** 4:30. **Green fee:** $16/35.
Credit cards: MC, V. **Reduced fees:** Weekdays, Low season, Twilight, Seniors, Juniors.
Caddies: No. **Golf carts:** N/A.
Discount golf packages: Yes. **Season:** Year-round. **High:** Nov.-June.
On-site lodging: No. **Rental clubs:** Yes.
Walking policy: Unrestricted walking. **Range:** Yes.
To obtain tee times: Call pro shop.

Subscriber comments: Interesting, hilly layout . . . Maintenance OK . . . Great layout, tough par 3s . . . Very hilly but a great challenge . . . Need to improve maintenance of course . . . More hilly than flat . . . Reasonably well maintained for public course . . . Tight, small greens, potential to be great . . . Back nine in the hills, great views . . . Lots of elevation changes and narrow fairways, requires planning . . . A very good course, my favorite, great variety of shots . . . Range is a cage with mats . . . Short and choppy layout . . . 16th hole tees off 90-foot cliff . . . Should buy some new golf carts.

★★ INDIAN PALMS COUNTRY CLUB

PU—4863 Old Monroe Rd., Indio (619)347-2326.
Call club for further information.
Subscriber comments: Old course with three nines, good condition . . . 27 holes, mature course, narrow fairways . . . Lots of desert wildlife . . . Course in poor condition . . . Fairways too narrow. Houses too close . . . Challenge for controlled shots . . . Great finishing holes . . . Tight course, good challenge, no bunkers, some water . . . Great layout for couples, course quality being updated . . . Needs some sand traps! . . . Basic golf, no frills.

★½ INDIAN SPRINGS COUNTRY CLUB

PU—46-080 Jefferson St., La Quinta (619)775-3360.
6 miles south of Palm Desert. **Holes:** 18. **Par:** 71/72.
Yards: 6,369/5,717. **Course rating:** 69.8/72.4. **Slope:** 112/117.
Opened: 1960. **Pace of Play rating:** 4:15. **Green fee:** $15/40.
Credit cards: MC, V, DISC. **Reduced fees:** No.
Caddies: No. **Golf carts:** N/A.
Discount golf packages: Yes. **Season:** Year-round. **High:** Nov.-May.
On-site lodging: No. **Rental clubs:** Yes.
Walking policy: Unrestricted walking. **Range:** Yes (grass).
To obtain tee times: Call up to seven days in advance.
Subscriber comments: Old design, very basic, fair condition . . . Good for beginners . . . Vastly improved, very respectable.

★★½ INDIAN VALLEY GOLF CLUB

PU—3035 Novato Blvd., Novato (415)897-1118.
22 miles north of San Francisco. **Holes:** 18. **Par:** 72/72.
Yards: 6,253/5,238. **Course rating:** 69.2/70.9. **Slope:** 119/128.
Opened: 1958. **Pace of Play rating:** 4:00. **Green fee:** $12/35.
Credit cards: MC, V, AMEX. **Reduced fees:** Weekdays, Twilight, Seniors, Juniors.
Caddies: No. **Golf carts:** $20 for 18 holes.
Discount golf packages: No. **Season:** Year-round. **High:** May-Sept.
On-site lodging: No. **Rental clubs:** Yes.
Walking policy: Walking at certain times. **Range:** Yes.
To obtain tee times: Call one week in advance.
Subscriber comments: Beautiful hilly setting . . . Fun course, up and down hills . . . Nice old course, well maintained . . . Very hilly, creates interesting tee shots, always enjoyable . . . Good layout, can make a high handicapper feel good . . . Having a cart helps . . . Very playable in wet weather, good drainage . . . Every hole is different; had problems with greens but that is solved now . . . Many elevated tees make for good aerial views . . . Great layout, greens need to be rebuilt . . . Really good all-around.

INDUSTRY HILLS SHERATON RESORT AND CONFERENCE CENTER

R—One Industry Hills Pkwy., City of Industry (818)810-4653.
25 miles east of Los Angeles.
Pace of Play rating: 4:30. **Green fee:** $42/57.
Credit cards: All major.
Caddies: No. **Golf carts:** Included in Green Fee.
Discount golf packages: Yes. **Season:** Year-round. **High:** April-July.
On-site lodging: Yes. **Rental clubs:** Yes.

Walking policy: Mandatory cart. **Range:** Yes.
To obtain tee times: Call three days in advance.

★★★½ EISENHOWER COURSE

Holes: 18. **Par:** 72/73.
Yards: 7,181/5,589. **Course rating:** 76.6/73.1. **Slope:** 149/135.
Opened: 1979.
Reduced fees: Weekdays, Low season, Twilight, Seniors, Juniors.
Subscriber comments: What a monster . . . Nice view on ride between ninth and 10th holes . . . A little more forgiving than the Babe . . . You will play every club you have! Just a great tough course . . . Have to play at least twice . . . One of the best in L.A. . . . Very narrow with treacherous rough . . . Better than Zaharias course, longer but not as punishing . . . Too tough for average golfer . . . Dare the pros to beat Ike . . . Incredible, breathtaking views for a public course . . . Very hilly. Blind shots, you need a spotter or lots of balls . . . Tricked up, unfair . . . Best course in southern California, excellent condition, large greens, scenic . . . The more you play the more you'll like this course . . . Long, narrow, major elevation changes, can be intimidating . . . Can be smoggy . . . Very tough, a little gaudy but maintained well . . . Break par on this course and you are ready for PGA Tour . . . Truly impossible layout, but very fun at the same time . . . Built on a landfill . . . Lightning-quick greens, many undulations . . . Tough as nails . . . All work is on the greens. 10-foot flags . . . Not fun for high handicappers, far and away hardest course in southern California . . . From the tips, no course in the world is harder . . . Usually find more balls in the rough than you started with . . . Whew!

★★★½ BABE DIDRIKSON ZAHARIAS COURSE

Holes: 18. **Par:** 71/71.
Yards: 6,778/5,363. **Course rating:** 74.2/72.4. **Slope:** 144/133.
Opened: 1980.
Reduced fees: Weekdays, Low season, Twilight, Seniors.
Subscriber comments: Ego deflater, punishes good shots . . . Stay in fairways, ball-devouring rough . . . Long and narrow, too smoggy . . . Not as tough as reputation . . . Punishing rough . . . Must be able to keep ball in play or afford lots of balls . . . Good for straight, short hitter . . . Too much course but I love it . . . Much tougher than Ike if playing from black tees . . . Hard, elevated greens, no approach options . . . Tough greens, no easy pin placements . . . Not the most fun course to play . . .

Forget your score and have fun . . . No fairway wider than 20 yards . . . Bring your control game here, greens are hard and fast . . . Like driving down a bowling alley . . . Zaharias course shouldn't have black tees! . . . Tight but well thought out, great condition year round . . . My driveway is wider than the fairways . . . Always in great shape . . . Best shape of any course on planet.

★½ THE ISLAND CLUB

PU—3303 Gateway Rd., Bethel Island (510)684-2654.
25 miles southeast of Stockton. **Holes:** 18. **Par:** 72/74.
Yards: 6,632/5,813. **Course rating:** 70.8/72.2. **Slope:** 118/117.
Opened: 1960. **Pace of Play rating:** 3:45. **Green fee:** $11/22.
Credit cards: MC, V, AMEX. **Reduced fees:** Weekdays, Low season, Twilight, Seniors, Juniors.
Caddies: No. **Golf carts:** N/A.
Discount golf packages: Yes. **Season:** Year-round. **High:** April-Oct.
On-site lodging: No. **Rental clubs:** Yes.
Walking policy: Unrestricted walking. **Range:** Yes (grass).
To obtain tee times: Call up to one week in advance.
Subscriber comments: Friendly place to practice . . . Usually not crowded . . . Nice little muny . . . Lots of water, great par 3s . . . Very good in winter, excellent drainage . . . Don't play on a windy day . . . Attempting to fix up greens and fairways . . . Nice layout for prevailing wind conditions . . . It's there when you need it!

★★ JURUPA HILLS COUNTRY CLUB

PU—6161 Moraga Ave., Riverside (909)685-7214.
Holes: 18. **Par:** 70/71.
Yards: 6,022/5,773. **Course rating:** 68.2/73.4. **Slope:** 112/121.
Opened: 1960. **Pace of Play rating:** N/A. **Green fee:** $16/24.
Credit cards: MC, V. **Reduced fees:** Weekdays, Low season, Twilight,
Seniors, Juniors.
Caddies: No. **Golf carts:** Included in Green Fee.
Discount golf packages: Yes. **Season:** Year-round. **High:** N/A.
On-site lodging: No. **Rental clubs:** Yes.
Walking policy: Walking at certain times. **Range:** Yes (grass).
To obtain tee times: Call club.
Subscriber comments: Course is well laid-out, a challenge, fun . . . A fine
public golf course . . . Some fairways and greens in poor, terrible condition
all year . . . Good greens, short but fun . . . Not much . . . Nice place to
play . . . Fair condition, higher handicaps would enjoy, staff good . . .
Modest layout. Fair condition . . . The greens make this course, they don't
give up birdies . . . Bikini wax on the greens . . . OK design, too many
trees . . . Some very testy holes . . . Fastest greens in the west!

★★ KERN RIVER GOLF COURSE

PU—Rudal Rd., Bakersfield (805)872-5128.
Holes: 18. **Par:** 70/73.
Yards: 6,458/5,971. **Course rating:** 70.5/72.3. **Slope:** 117/116.
Opened: 1920. **Pace of Play rating:** N/A. **Green fee:** $9/12.
Credit cards: MC, V. **Reduced fees:** Weekdays, Twilight, Seniors,
Juniors.
Caddies: No. **Golf carts:** $8 for 18 holes.
Discount golf packages: No. **Season:** Year-round. **High:** N/A.
On-site lodging: No. **Rental clubs:** Yes.
Walking policy: Unrestricted walking. **Range:** Yes (grass).
To obtain tee times: Call Wednesday at 7 a.m. for weekends. Call 24
hours in advance for weekdays.
Subscriber comments: Interesting public layout . . . Good public course
. . . Some tough holes . . . Basic public course, fairly good maintenance
. . . Tough par 3s and long par 4s . . . Suited for all golfers . . . Good
layout, but upkeep could use some work . . . Not a real good test . . .
Mature course, good for beginners and average golfers . . . Plan to stay a
long time . . . Had a great time, lots of trees, better be straight . . . Could
be a much better course with better care.

★★★½ LA CONTENTA GOLF CLUB

SP—1653 Hwy. 26, Valley Springs (209)772-1081, (800)446-5321.
30 miles east of Stockton. **Holes:** 18. **Par:** 71/72.
Yards: 6,425/5,120. **Course rating:** 70.2/70.8. **Slope:** 125/120.
Opened: 1972. **Pace of Play rating:** 4:30. **Green fee:** $20/31.
Credit cards: MC, V. **Reduced fees:** Weekdays, Resort guests, Twilight,
Seniors, Juniors.
Caddies: No. **Golf carts:** $10 for 18 holes.
Discount golf packages: Yes. **Season:** Year-round. **High:** March-Oct.
On-site lodging: Yes. **Rental clubs:** Yes.
Walking policy: Unrestricted walking. **Range:** No.
To obtain tee times: Tee times available 90 days in advance through
Double Eagle automated tee time reservation system.
Subscriber comments: Another out-of-the-way gem . . . Steep hilly
layout . . . Great mountain foothill course, some great golf holes . . . Hilly
resort-style course, several blind holes with challenging elevations . . . Love
the challenging hills, can walk 18 holes but better to use a cart . . . Too
much O.B. . . . If you haven't played it before, the hills, the valleys and the
trees will confound you . . . One major downer: no range, only nets . . .
Well maintained, good basic layout . . . Very challenging and enjoyable,
bring every club! . . . Fun, fun, fun, course not long. Greens are always
good. Par 3s are dynamite . . . Fun course but you need a local guide . . .
Too many blind shots to uphill greens . . . Fun course. Secluded in the
foothills of the Sierras . . . Central valley jewel, a must play despite its
remote location.

LA COSTA RESORT AND SPA
R—2100 Costa Del Mar Rd., Carlsbad (619)438-9111.
30 miles north of San Diego.
Opened: 1964. **Pace of Play rating:** 4:30. **Green fee:** $110/170.
Credit cards: All major. **Reduced fees:** Weekdays, Resort guests, Twilight.
Caddies: Yes. **Discount golf packages:** Yes. **Season:** Year-round.
On-site lodging: Yes. **Rental clubs:** Yes.
Walking policy: Mandatory cart. **Range:** Yes (grass).
To obtain tee times: Call starter at extension 25.

★★★½ NORTH COURSE
Holes: 18. **Par:** 72/73.
Yards: 6,987/5,939. **Course rating:** 74.8/74.0. **Slope:** 137/127.
Golf carts: Included in Green Fee.
Subscriber comments: World-class . . . Great spa . . . Excellent conditions and a true test of golf . . . Spa city with mud baths . . . Too difficult for average golfer . . . Very bland, looks like most other courses . . . Courses are well maintained; best resort I've ever been to . . . Fun to play . . . Should not charge for range balls . . . Excellent championship golf . . . Take caddie, if available . . . Two of the best golf experiences . . . Very overrated . . . Incredible condition for a resort course, spa is world class . . . The best. Doesn't get much better than this . . . Great greens, very fair golf courses . . . A lot of sand . . . Fair and exciting.

★★★½ SOUTH COURSE
Holes: 18. **Par:** 72/74.
Yards: 6,894/5,612. **Course rating:** 74.4/72.1. **Slope:** 138/123.
Golf carts: $20 for 18 holes.
Subscriber comments: Fantastic all the way around . . . Nice views, good greens . . . Some challenging holes . . . Trouble everywhere, good challenge for better players . . . Great resort course, good condition, fun to play . . . Disappointed, poor shape . . . Lovely course . . . One of the few places to get a caddie in southern California . . . Best greens I've ever seen! Wonderfully traditional . . . Carpet-like fairways, but pace of play was toooo slow . . . Very posh, as it should be.

★★½ LA MIRADA GOLF COURSE
PU—15501 E. Alicante Rd., La Mirada (310)943-7123.
20 miles southeast of Los Angeles. **Holes:** 18. **Par:** 70/71.
Yards: 6,044/5,632. **Course rating:** 67.2/71.7. **Slope:** 109/115.
Opened: 1962. **Pace of Play rating:** N/A. **Green fee:** $17/21.
Credit cards: MC, V. **Reduced fees:** Weekdays, Twilight, Seniors, Juniors.
Caddies: No. **Golf carts:** $10 for 18 holes.
Discount golf packages: No. **Season:** Year-round. **High:** N/A.
On-site lodging: No. **Rental clubs:** Yes.
Walking policy: Unrestricted walking. **Range:** Yes (grass).
To obtain tee times: Call seven days in advance.
Subscriber comments: Fine muny course, first-class greenkeeper . . . Hilly, good condition, fast greens . . . Great short course . . . Variation from hole to hole . . . Good for all. Wide open fairways in good shape . . . Good greens, fairways so-so, challenging design makes up for hilly, short length . . . Fun, six par 3s . . . Easy, but pleasant golf experience . . . Good fast greens for county course . . . Short, lots of hills, easy scoring.

★★★★ LA PURISIMA GOLF COURSE
PU—3455 State Hwy. 246, Lompoc (805)735-8395.
40 miles north of Santa Barbara. **Holes:** 18. **Par:** 72/72.
Yards: 7,105/5,762. **Course rating:** 74.9/74.3. **Slope:** 143/131.
Opened: 1986. **Pace of Play rating:** 4:15. **Green fee:** $25/35.
Credit cards: MC, V. **Reduced fees:** Juniors.
Caddies: No. **Golf carts:** $22 for 18 holes.
Discount golf packages: No. **Season:** Year-round. **High:** May-Oct.
On-site lodging: No. **Rental clubs:** Yes.
Walking policy: Unrestricted walking. **Range:** Yes (grass).

To obtain tee times: Call one week in advance.
Subscriber comments: Fantastic test of golf . . . Golf course from hell . . . Afternoon breezes add to challenges, great views, great course, hard but fair . . . A beauty . . . Wind makes it very difficult . . . Don't get out of fairway . . . Please, no hackers . . . Awesome . . . What a challenge . . . Wow! . . . Hidden jewel. One of best values in southern California . . . Very tough, not for the high handicapper . . . Fab! . . . Good layout with immaculate maintenance of turf, elegant mission-style facilities . . . When the wind

blows, it's almost unplayable . . . Graves' best . . . Great course, not a bad hole in sight. Nasty, tough greens. Gorgeous! . . . Great R.M. Graves layout . . . Very penal, devastating wind in afternoon . . . Still not that well known . . . Constant hurricane . . . Before you go to Q school . . . All types of topography. Good condition . . . Many birds fouling the course . . . Wind, windy, windy . . . Pebble Beach, watch out! . . . Outstanding condition year round. Walked off 18th green first time and could recall all 18 holes! Could hold U.S. Open here, it's that tough.

LA QUINTA RESORT AND CLUB
SP—50–200 Vista Bonita, La Quinta (619)564-7686.
15 miles east of Palm Springs.
Credit cards: MC, V, AMEX, Diners Club. **Reduced fees:** Weekdays, Low season, Resort guests, Twilight.
Caddies: No. **Golf carts:** Included in Green Fee.
Discount golf packages: Yes. **Season:** Year-round. **High:** Nov.-April.
On-site lodging: Yes. **Rental clubs:** Yes.
Walking policy: Mandatory cart. **Range:** Yes (grass).
To obtain tee times: Hotel Guests may make tee times up to one year in advance. Nonguests three days in advance. Call 619-564-5729 for all advance tee times.

★★★★ MOUNTAIN COURSE
Holes: 18. **Par:** 72/72.
Yards: 6,758/5,010. **Course rating:** 74.1/68.4. **Slope:** 140/120.
Opened: 1981. **Pace of Play rating:** 4:25. **Green fee:** $60/210.
Subscriber comments: Awesome course, beautiful scenery . . . Beautiful layout, great challenge of golf game . . . Quality Dye . . . Tough but fun . . . I was in golf heaven . . . The best from Pete Dye . . . Spectacular closing holes, great course . . . Difficult course. Crowned hard greens with rough close by make scoring difficult . . . Plays long with sidehill lies and lots of trouble . . . Great layout, you've got to be lucky to play this one . . . Fun to play and relax . . . Wild coyotes and very pretty scenery . . . Top of the line golf experience . . . Classic desert layout, good challenge . . . Very good course, target golf . . . I loved the dramatic tee shots . . . Best course in the desert.

★★★½ DUNES COURSE
Holes: 18. **Par:** 72/72.
Yards: 6,747/5,005. **Course rating:** 73.1/68.0. **Slope:** 137/114.
Opened: 1981. **Pace of Play rating:** 4:15. **Green fee:** $60/140.
Ranked 75th in America's 75 Best Resort Courses by Golf Digest.
Subscriber comments: Good, fair Pete Dye layout . . . Outstanding scenery, demanding, long . . . Not in best shape . . . Almost as good as the Mountain . . . Take your sand wedge . . . Very good condition, scenic, some tough holes, fun to play . . . Start with ordinary topography, even Pete can't help . . . Stay out of those huge bunkers . . . No. 17 is one tough hole . . . Good resort track, plays well for average golfer . . . Wonderful design, better than the Mountain . . . Fun course . . . Great driving holes.

★★★ LAGUNA SECA GOLF CLUB
PU—10520 York Rd., Monterey (408)373-3701.
Holes: 18. **Par:** 71/72.
Yards: 6,125/5,186. **Course rating:** 70.4/70.2. **Slope:** 123/119.
Opened: 1970. **Pace of Play rating:** 4:40. **Green fee:** $55.
Credit cards: MC, V, AMEX. **Reduced fees:** Twilight.
Caddies: No. **Golf carts:** $25 for 18 holes.
Discount golf packages: Yes. **Season:** Year-round. **High:** June-Aug.

On-site lodging: No. **Rental clubs:** Yes.
Walking policy: Unrestricted walking. **Range:** No.
To obtain tee times: Call 30 days in advance for weekdays and seven days in advance for weekends.
Subscriber comments: Hilly, narrow, nice . . . Extremely different nines . . . Beautiful scenery, fine condition, interesting . . . Lush, green course . . . Magnificent views . . . Interesting back nine . . . Good test of shotmaking . . . Better maintenance difficult in wet, foggy location . . . Good facilities, clean and nicely cut course, tough layout, you can't be in rough . . . Beautiful layout with good shot values . . . 15th hole is a great experience every time you play it.

★★ LAKE CHABOT GOLF COURSE
PU—11450 Golf Links Rd., Oakland (510)351-5812.
Call club for further information.
Subscriber comments: Fun, hilly course, back nine the most unique around with great views of San Francisco Bay . . . Best muny course in Bay area . . . Interesting layout . . . Not well-kept . . . Ridiculously steep hills . . . 400-foot drop in elevation . . . Monster finishing hole . . . Last hole is fun . . . Billy goat is course logo . . . High in the hills, severe slopes . . . More ups and downs than a yo-yo . . . Commonly known as "Lake Shabby" . . . Not the best condition . . . Very long and hilly, well-kept, definitely rent a cart . . . You have to play it to believe it, not a great course, but very memorable.

★½ LAKE DON PEDRO GOLF CLUB
PU—Ranchito Hernandez, La Grange (209)852-2242.
Call club for further information.
Subscriber comments: Few level lies . . . Hilly, open course, some good holes, fun course . . . Never lost so many balls in the fairway . . . Good course . . . Not a flat spot except tees . . . Well-designed, open course, unfortunately poorly maintained and conditioned . . . Has maintenance problems during dry season . . . Layout is interesting.

LAKE SHASTINA GOLF RESORT
★★★½ CHAMPIONSHIP COURSE
R—5925 Country Club Dr., Weed (916)938-3205, (800)358-4653.
7 miles north of Weed. **Holes:** 18. **Par:** 72/72.
Yards: 6,969/5,530. **Course rating:** 72.6/N/A. **Slope:** 126/117.
Opened: 1973. **Pace of Play rating:** 4:30. **Green fee:** $22/45.
Credit cards: MC, V, AMEX. **Reduced fees:** Low season, Resort guests, Twilight, Juniors.
Caddies: No. **Golf carts:** $15 for 18 holes.
Discount golf packages: Yes. **Season:** Year-round. **High:** May-Sept.
On-site lodging: Yes. **Rental clubs:** Yes.
Walking policy: Unrestricted walking. **Range:** Yes (grass).
To obtain tee times: Call pro shop one month in advance.
Also has nine-hole Scottish Nine.
Subscriber comments: One of the great courses in northern California . . . Course offers enough of a challenge to make it interesting but is not a mean course . . . Most impressive course, wonderful views, well kept . . . Beautiful setting, fair, challenging . . . Great layout, winds are tough . . . Wide open, no exceptional holes . . . Well designed, must play every club in bag, wind often a factor, can be slow . . . Incredible views of Mt. Shasta . . . Great layout, mountain air adds distance . . . Majestic, beauty . . . Good test, resort atmosphere.

★★★ LAKE TAHOE GOLF COURSE
PU—2500 Emerald Bay Rd. Hwy. 50, South Lake Tahoe (916)577-0788.
60 miles southwest of Reno. **Holes:** 18. **Par:** 71/72.
Yards: 6,685/5,654. **Course rating:** 70.9/70.1. **Slope:** 120/115.
Opened: 1960. **Pace of Play rating:** 4:30. **Green fee:** $31.
Credit cards: MC, V. **Reduced fees:** Low season, Twilight, Juniors.
Caddies: No. **Golf carts:** $13 for 18 holes.

Discount golf packages: Yes. **Season:** May-Oct. **High:** June-Sept.
On-site lodging: No. **Rental clubs:** Yes.
Walking policy: Walking at certain times. **Range:** Yes (grass).
To obtain tee times: Reservations available 60 days in advance with $5 reservation fee.
Subscriber comments: Valley floor course . . . Tough course if you get lazy. Great 16th! . . . 19th hole is like drinking beer in your closet . . . Gorgeous setting, flat and tree-lined fairways make for a good time for all . . . Has some great dogleg holes . . . Average to poor conditions . . . Course primarily flat and straight . . . Thin air, use one club less . . . Front nine fairly open and back nine is tough! . . . Back nine plays over river on most holes . . . Beautiful setting, course doesn't overreach . . . Scenic track, good mountain test . . . Public golf course but feel and treated like country club . . . Well maintained with great greens . . . Good course for all levels. Great views.

★★½ LAKEWOOD COUNTRY CLUB

PU—3101 E. Carson St., Lakewood (310)421-3741.
Holes: 18. **Par:** 72/73.
Yards: 7,045/5,920. **Course rating:** 72.9/74.1. **Slope:** 113/121.
Opened: 1935. **Pace of Play rating:** 5:00. **Green fee:** $17/21.
Credit cards: MC, V. **Reduced fees:** Weekdays, Twilight, Seniors, Juniors.
Caddies: No. **Golf carts:** $19 for 18 holes.
Discount golf packages: No. **Season:** Year-round. **High:** April-Oct.
On-site lodging: No. **Rental clubs:** Yes.
Walking policy: Unrestricted walking. **Range:** Yes.
To obtain tee times: One week in advance by phone or in person.
Subscriber comments: Old, but well-groomed course . . . Solid public course; flat, but good greens . . . Easy to walk and play . . . Is subject to slow play on the weekends . . . Fairways well groomed . . . Fairly challenging . . . An older course, but worth playing . . . Marginal conditioning, some great holes, some very weak . . . A long but fair course. Back tees impossible for high handicappers . . . Course is a bear from the back tees.

★★½ LAS POSITAS GOLF COURSE

PU—917 Clubhouse Dr., Livermore (510)443-3122.
1 miles west of Livermore. **Holes:** 18. **Par:** 72/72.
Yards: 6,725/5,270. **Course rating:** 72.0/70.1. **Slope:** 126/120.
Opened: 1965. **Pace of Play rating:** 4:30. **Green fee:** $24/29.
Credit cards: MC, V. **Reduced fees:** Weekdays, Low season, Twilight, Juniors.
Caddies: No. **Golf carts:** $11 for 18 holes.
Discount golf packages: No. **Season:** Year-round. **High:** April-June.
On-site lodging: No. **Rental clubs:** Yes.
Walking policy: Unrestricted walking. **Range:** Yes (grass).
To obtain tee times: Taken by computer one week in advance beginning at 5 a.m.
Also has nine-hole executive course.
Subscriber comments: Probably everything a muny should be . . . Two very different nines . . . Back nine is really neat . . . Well designed for all level of players . . . Getting better with renovations . . . Mix of good and mediocre holes, conditions only so-so . . . New back nine needs maturing . . . Lots of airplane noise . . . Thoughtful layout . . . Good course. Crowded. Course is showing wear . . . Number of blind shots required . . . Wooded front nine, links-style back nine . . . Nothing to write home about . . . Fair. Play early, it gets windy . . . Greens always so-so . . . Between freeway and airport, very noisy . . . No. 18 a nasty finisher . . . Flat, but wind makes it a test.

LAWRENCE WELK'S DESERT OASIS COUNTRY CLUB
★★½ LAKEVIEW/MOUNTAIN/RESORT

SP—34567 Cathedral Canyon Dr., Cathedral City (619)328-6571.
10 miles southeast of Palm Springs. **Holes:** 27. **Par:** 72/72/72.

Yards: 6,505/6,477/6,366. **Course rating:** 71.6/70.9/70.3.
Slope: 128/119/118.
Opened: 1975. **Pace of Play rating:** 4:30. **Green fee:** $35/85.
Credit cards: All major. **Reduced fees:** Weekdays, Low season, Twilight.
Caddies: No. **Golf carts:** Included in Green Fee.
Discount golf packages: Yes. **Season:** Year-round. **High:** Jan.-April.
On-site lodging: No. **Rental clubs:** Yes.
Walking policy: Mandatory cart. **Range:** Yes (grass).
To obtain tee times: Call up to four days in advance.
Subscriber comments: Very crowded and popular course . . . Lakeview
and Mountain are best . . . Well kept but very short . . . Sort of boring, but
nice . . . Easy, plays fast, it's OK . . . Lots of water. Short . . . Resort nine
is a very mundane layout, course condition only fair . . . Great mountain
views from desert. Good condition . . . Lake and Mountain nines great,
Resort OK . . . A lot of water! . . . Tight at times, watch the water . . .
Considering it's Palm Springs, it should be better . . . Great shape, greens
and fairways better than past years.

★★LEMOORE GOLF COURSE
PU—350 Iona Ave., Lemoore (209)924-9658.
30 miles south of Fresno. **Holes:** 18. **Par:** 72/72.
Yards: 6,431/5,126. **Course rating:** 69.8/67.9. **Slope:** 118/118.
Opened: 1930. **Pace of Play rating:** N/A. **Green fee:** $12/15.
Credit cards: MC, V. **Reduced fees:** No.
Caddies: No. **Golf carts:** N/A .
Discount golf packages: No. **Season:** Year-round. **High:** N/A.
On-site lodging: No. **Rental clubs:** Yes.
Walking policy: Unrestricted walking. **Range:** Yes (grass).
To obtain tee times: Call Thursday for weekend times.
Subscriber comments: Nice course, well kept . . . Fun course, uniquely
different nines, small greens . . . Back side still new, when it grows up will
be good.

★★LINCOLN PARK GOLF COURSE
PU—34th Ave. and Clement St., San Francisco (415)221-9911.
Holes: 18. **Par:** 68/70.
Yards: 5,149/4,984. **Course rating:** 64.4/67.4. **Slope:** 106/108.
Opened: 1916. **Pace of Play rating:** 4:25. **Green fee:** $21/25.
Credit cards: None. **Reduced fees:** Weekdays, Twilight, Juniors.
Caddies: No. **Golf carts:** $20 for 18 holes.
Discount golf packages: No. **Season:** Year-round. **High:** April-Nov.
On-site lodging: No. **Rental clubs:** Yes.
Walking policy: Unrestricted walking. **Range:** No.
To obtain tee times: Call seven days in advance for weekdays; three days
in advance for weekends.
Subscriber comments: A walk in the park, pleasant short course . . . Best
view of Golden Gate there is . . . Golf is so-so . . . 17th hole only reason to
play here . . . Looks like park land converted into golf course . . .
Outstanding views of Golden Gate Bridge . . . 17th by the Golden Gate
. . . Shame such a beautiful layout has deteriorated so badly . . . Bad layout,
views are fantastic . . . Great views, a must for tourists with medium to
high handicaps . . . Little beat up . . . Excellent vistas, challenging short
course . . . 17th is one of the most beautiful holes in the world . . . Greens
like shag carpet . . . Most difficult short course in northern California . . .
Course needs a little work . . . Some of the best views from any course,
anywhere.

★★★★ THE LINKS AT SPANISH BAY
R—2700 17 Mile Dr., Pebble Beach (408)647-7495, (800)654-9300.
2 miles south of Monterey. **Holes:** 18. **Par:** 72/72.
Yards: 6,820/5,309. **Course rating:** 74.6/70.6. **Slope:** 142/129.
Opened: 1987. **Pace of Play rating:** 4:30. **Green fee:** $125/135.
Credit cards: MC, V, AMEX. **Reduced fees:** Resort guests, Twilight.
Caddies: Yes. **Golf carts:** $20 for 18 holes.

Discount golf packages: Yes. **Season:** Year-round. **High:** Sept.-Nov.
On-site lodging: Yes. **Rental clubs:** Yes.
Walking policy: Unrestricted walking. **Range:** No.
To obtain tee times: Resort guest call one year in advance; outside play may reserve maximum of 60 days in advance.
Ranked 24th in America's 75 Best Resort Courses by Golf Digest. Selected as Best New Resort Course of 1988 by Golf Digest. Ranked 12th in California by Golf Digest.
Subscriber comments: True links, surrounded by protected dunes, with wind very challenging . . . Best links course played outside of Scotland . . . Beautiful links course by the ocean . . . Love the scenery . . . Best links course in California . . . Very impressed with their dedication to maintaining the environment . . . Very friendly, but needs driving range . . . Sand dunes are different . . . Not very interesting, not too scenic . . . Putting greens need to be improved . . . True seaside links requiring shotmaking and strategy; very tough finish in the wind . . . Absolutely terrific . . . Authentic . . . Every hole is a memorable challenge . . . A reasonable facsimile of Scottish golf but greatly Americanized . . . Environmentally sensitive areas ruin play . . . Best golfing value of the big three . . . Rivals Pebble . . . Slow, bumpy greens, fun to play in the wind . . . Best secret on 17 Mile Drive, half the price of Pebble, just as much fun . . . Bagpiper plays over dunes at sunset, goosebumps! . . . Unique target golf, beautiful coastal links . . . Better stay on fairway . . . Everyone should play it once, beautiful . . . Seems like architects couldn't make up their mind to make this links or inland . . . Something special in the sand . . . Little bit of a tricked-up course, need to play a lot to enjoy . . . Lots of run shots. Low-ball course . . . Great views. Can be very windy and cold . . . It's a lot of money for ocean views, but I'd go back.

LOS ANGELES ROYAL VISTA GOLF COURSE
★½ **NORTH/SOUTH/EAST**
SP—20055 E. Colima Rd., Walnut (909)595-7441.
22 miles east of Los Angeles. **Holes:** 27. **Par:** 71/71/72.
Yards: 6,381/6,071/6,182. **Course rating:** 69.0/67.6/68.5.
Slope: 115/110/112.
Opened: 1963. **Pace of Play rating:** 4:30. **Green fee:** $17/28.
Credit cards: MC, V. **Reduced fees:** Weekdays, Low season, Resort guests, Twilight, Seniors, Juniors.
Caddies: No. **Golf carts:** Included in Green Fee.
Discount golf packages: Yes. **Season:** Year-round. **High:** April-Sept.
On-site lodging: No. **Rental clubs:** Yes.
Walking policy: Unrestricted walking. **Range:** Yes.
To obtain tee times: Call seven days in advance.
Subscriber comments: Practice course . . . Lots of tough lies . . . Heavy play, worn out . . . Nice layout, poor maintenance . . . Condition marginal . . . OK . . . Making several needed improvements . . . Funky course, poor condition . . . Hilly, unfair lies, always crowded . . . Course under reconstruction.

★★½ LOS ROBLES GOLF CLUB
PU—299 S. Moorpark Rd., Thousand Oaks (805)495-6171.
30 miles north of Los Angeles. **Holes:** 18. **Par:** 70/70.
Yards: 6,274/5,333. **Course rating:** 69.4/70.1. **Slope:** 118/117.
Opened: 1965. **Pace of Play rating:** 5:00. **Green fee:** $14/20.
Credit cards: MC, V. **Reduced fees:** Weekdays, Twilight, Seniors, Juniors.
Caddies: No. **Golf carts:** $16 for 18 holes.
Discount golf packages: Yes. **Season:** Year-round. **High:** N/A.
On-site lodging: No. **Rental clubs:** Yes.
Walking policy: Unrestricted walking. **Range:** Yes.
To obtain tee times: Residents eight days in advance; all others seven days.
Subscriber comments: Pretty course, varied holes . . . Beautiful tree-lined . . . Solid track for muny, greens can be very good . . . Good test of golf,

good condition . . . Good muny course . . . Charming and fun . . . Well maintained and heavily played . . . Great city course, nice scenery . . . Hilly muny course, average condition . . . Very slow play, but good greens and layout . . . Very nice municipal course, poor condition . . . Slow, slow, slow. Bring your lunch . . . Very pretty course, good layout in the hills . . . The slowest play in Los Angeles . . . Best-kept public course in the area.

LOS SERRANOS LAKES GOLF AND COUNTRY CLUB
PU—15656 Yorba Ave., Chino Hills (909)597-1711.
40 miles east of Los Angeles.
Opened: 1925. **Pace of Play rating:** 3:30–4:00.
Credit cards: MC, V, DISC. **Reduced fees:** Weekdays, Twilight, Seniors.
Caddies: No. **Golf carts:** $11 for 18 holes.
Discount golf packages: No. **Season:** Year-round. **High:** March-June.
On-site lodging: No. **Rental clubs:** Yes.
Walking policy: Unrestricted walking. **Range:** Yes (grass).
To obtain tee times: Call pro shop seven days in advance.

★★★ **NORTH COURSE**
Holes: 18. **Par:** 72/74.
Yards: 6,440/5,949. **Course rating:** 70.4/74.5. **Slope:** 120/118.
Green fee: $20/30.
Subscriber comments: Short shotmaker's course, good variety . . . Enjoyable layout, very playable . . . Not as good as the South Course . . . Nice mature course, challenging layout . . . Sister course is much nicer . . . Well maintained. Fun layout . . . Championship from tips, windy in afternoons, much improved . . . Good layout and condition, very hilly . . . Not in class of South Course, but above average . . . Long ball hitters have more fun . . . Shorter than South but makes you think . . . Can be very windy . . . Small greens, generally in good shape, good for iron practice . . . Some good holes, well kept, interesting . . . Lumpy greens . . . One of the best courses in southern California.

★★★½ **SOUTH COURSE**
Holes: 18. **Par:** 74/74.
Yards: 7,036/5,957. **Course rating:** 74.3/73.5. **Slope:** 133/123.
Green fee: $24/30.
Subscriber comments: Good layout and condition, very hilly . . . One of the best and toughest layouts in southern California . . . Good shape for amount of play . . . Par 74, six par 5s, let the big dog eat . . . Classic old-style course . . . Long from blues, but fairly open, mature trees, good elevation changes . . . Back nine is wonderful, front nine is torture . . . Plays similar to Riviera . . . Six par 5s encourage birdies . . . More character than North Course . . . Unbelievably long (par 74!) . . . Never lets up . . . Wonderful, lots of character . . . Worth playing any time of year . . . Beautiful views.

★★½ **LOS VERDES GOLF COURSE**
PU—7000 W. Los Verdes Dr., Rancho Palos Verdes (310)377-0338.
17 miles west of Los Angeles. **Holes:** 18. **Par:** 71/72.
Yards: 6,651/5,738. **Course rating:** 72.4/71.8. **Slope:** 122/118.
Opened: 1964. **Pace of Play rating:** 4:30–5:00. **Green fee:** $17/21.
Credit cards: MC, V. **Reduced fees:** Weekdays, Twilight, Seniors, Juniors.
Caddies: No. **Golf carts:** $10 for 18 holes.
Discount golf packages: No. **Season:** Year-round. **High:** June-Sept.
On-site lodging: No. **Rental clubs:** Yes.
Walking policy: Unrestricted walking. **Range:** Yes.
To obtain tee times: Call one week in advance, 6 a.m. on weekdays and 5 a.m. on weekends.
Subscriber comments: Best-kept secret in southern California . . . Beautiful course, ocean views . . . Best view in Los Angeles area . . . Impossible to get on, people sleep in their cars overnight . . . Course is a little ratty at times, but you can't beat the view . . . More like private club

. . . Very popular . . . Great setting, very thin fairways . . . A great ocean course, very tricky greens . . . Best view of Catalina Island . . . Poor man's Torrey Pines . . . The nearby ocean makes putting a real challenge! . . . Good course when taken care of . . . Very few flat lies . . . Work in progress . . . One of the prettiest courses in California.

★★ MACE MEADOWS GOLF AND COUNTRY CLUB
PU—26570 Fairway Dr., Pioneer (209)295-7020.
Call club for further information.
Subscriber comments: Peaceful meadow, mountain course . . . Nice greens . . . Good mountain course, nice test . . . Opposing holes very close to each other . . . Very rough driving course, must be able to work the ball both ways and hit it straight . . . Wear a flak vest and helmet on back nine . . . Some beautiful picture holes in mountain setting . . . Kind of chopped up . . . Ruined a good nine-hole course by making it 18 . . . Needs more upkeep . . . Somewhat mundane course, but nice setting . . . Beautiful and fun, not too many know about it.

★★ MADERA MUNICIPAL GOLF COURSE
PU—23200 Ave. 17, Madera (209)675-3504.
Call club for further information.
Subscriber comments: Relaxed atmosphere, nice small-town course . . . Greens are large and lightning-quick, three-putts abound . . . Undulating greens are tough . . . Plain and uninteresting . . . Plain vanilla muny . . .

Wide open, good muny, great greens . . . Up-and-coming course for the future . . . Needs maturing, well designed . . . Still in developmental stage, young trees . . . Best greens in San Joaquin Valley.

★★★ MALIBU COUNTRY CLUB
PU—901 Encinal Canyon Rd., Malibu (818)889-6680.
30 miles east of Los Angeles. **Holes:** 18. **Par:** 72/72.
Yards: 6,740/5,627. **Course rating:** 72.3/71.4. **Slope:** 130/120.
Opened: 1976. **Pace of Play rating:** 4:00-4:30. **Green fee:** $48/68.
Credit cards: MC, V, JCB. **Reduced fees:** Seniors.
Caddies: No. **Golf carts:** Included in Green Fee.
Discount golf packages: No. **Season:** Year-round. **High:** N/A.
On-site lodging: No. **Rental clubs:** Yes.
Walking policy: Mandatory cart. **Range:** No.
To obtain tee times: Call pro shop.
Subscriber comments: Only high-end public-access course in Los Angeles county . . . Nice layout but in mediocre condition . . . Never crowded weekdays, pleasant way to get away . . . Sporty layout, no driving range . . . Well conditioned year-round. Fast pace of play . . . Interesting course in the Santa Monica Mountains. Mainly elevation changes . . . Fun layout. Greens break toward the ocean . . . Nice course, inadequately maintained . . . Excellent greens, layout demands a complete game . . . Susceptible to heavy fog, needs a decent driving range . . . Course condition good . . . Mostly elevated greens, use one or two clubs more.

MARRIOTT'S DESERT SPRINGS RESORT AND SPA
R—74-855 Country Club Dr., Palm Desert (619)341-1756.
85 miles east of Los Angeles.
Opened: 1987. **Pace of Play rating:** 4:00-4:30. **Green fee:** $65/130.
Credit cards: All major. **Reduced fees:** Weekdays, Low season, Resort guests, Twilight.
Caddies: No. **Golf carts:** Included in Green Fee.
Discount golf packages: Yes. **Season:** Year-round. **High:** Oct.-May.
On-site lodging: Yes. **Rental clubs:** Yes.
Walking policy: Mandatory cart. **Range:** Yes (grass).
To obtain tee times: Hotel guest can call up to 30 days in advance. Nonguests may call three days in advance.

★★★½ **PALM COURSE**

Holes: 18. **Par:** 72/72.

Yards: 6,761/5,492. **Course rating:** 72.0/70.8. **Slope:** 124/116.

Subscriber comments: Beautiful mature course very lush in the middle of the desert . . . Well designed (Ted Robinson) . . . Not as well maintained as past years . . . Last five holes are excellent . . . First class from start to finish . . . Both Valley, Palm courses are beautiful . . . Tougher than Valley . . . Beautiful course, good use of water . . . Great facilities, best practice area . . . Total experience . . . Both golf courses are excellent resort courses and the hotel is magnificent. Too hot to play in summer months . . . Immaculate and pretty landscaping. Cute . . . Best par 4 in the valley . . . A little bit of everything . . . Palms pretty, but lots of water . . . Well laid-out, great condition . . . Visually pretty, but relatively easy, good resort course . . . Challenging and just beautiful. Few flat lies . . . Over the fence, off the light post, around the swimming pool, down the cart path, into the water.

★★★½ **VALLEY COURSE**

Holes: 18. **Par:** 72/72.

Yards: 6,679/5,330. **Course rating:** 72.1/69.6. **Slope:** 124/110.

Subscriber comments: Easier of the two . . . OK, not as nice as Palm Course . . . Fun course, beautiful sights . . . Tedious, monotonous . . . Not nearly as good as Palm . . . All holes look the same . . . No. 17 is spectacular, lots of water, lush . . . Layout lacks imagination and challenge . . . Perfect shape, better layout with less slopes . . . Challenging but not impossible to score well . . . Great surroundings and playing conditions . . . Beautiful and fun . . . Take a camera.

MARRIOTT'S RANCHO LAS PALMAS RESORT AND COUNTRY CLUB

★★½ **NORTH/SOUTH/WEST**

R—42000 Bob Hope Dr., Rancho Mirage (619)568-0955.

5 miles west of Palm Springs. **Holes:** 27. **Par:** 71/69/70.

Yards: 6,019/5,569/5,550. **Course rating:** 67.2/65.5/65.3.

Slope: 115/106/105.

Opened: 1978. **Pace of Play rating:** N/A. **Green fee:** $50/95.

Credit cards: All major. **Reduced fees:** Weekdays, Low season, Resort guests, Twilight.

Caddies: No. **Golf carts:** N/A.

Discount golf packages: Yes. **Season:** Year-round. **High:** Jan.-April.

On-site lodging: Yes. **Rental clubs:** Yes.

Walking policy: Mandatory cart. **Range:** Yes (grass).

To obtain tee times: Call seven days in advance. Must be guest at hotel.

Subscriber comments: Fun to play and a great environment . . . OK, not great . . . Too many holes up and down through a wash . . . Uninteresting. Built among condos . . . OK course, flat . . . Nice course plays easy! . . . Crowded during season . . . Fun resort course, some water, some narrow holes . . . Short and fun, fair-to-easy, all can play.

MATHER GOLF COURSE★

PU—4013 Eagles Nest Rd., Mather (916)368-0193.

65 miles east of Modesto. **Holes:** 18. **Par:** 72/74.

Yards: 6,721/5,976. **Course rating:** 71.3/72.4. **Slope:** 119/119.

Opened: 1952. **Pace of Play rating:** N/A. **Green fee:** $16/23.

Credit cards: None. **Reduced fees:** Weekdays, Low season, Twilight, Seniors, Juniors.

Caddies: No. **Golf carts:** $18 for 18 holes.

Discount golf packages: No. **Season:** Year-round. **High:** May-Aug.

On-site lodging: No. **Rental clubs:** Yes.

Walking policy: Unrestricted walking. **Range:** Yes (grass).

To obtain tee times: Call one week in advance at 6:30 a.m.

MEADOW LAKE COUNTRY CLUB

★★ **MEADOW LAKE COUNTRY CLUB**

SP—10333 Meadow Glen Way, Escondido (619)749-1620.

30 miles north of San Diego. **Holes:** 18. **Par:** 72/74.

Yards: 6,521/5,758. **Course rating:** 72.5/72.8. **Slope:** 131/123.

Opened: 1965. **Pace of Play rating:** 4:30. **Green fee:** $24/32.

Credit cards: All major. **Reduced fees:** Weekdays, Resort guests, Twilight, Juniors.
Caddies: No. **Golf carts:** $12 for 18 holes.
Discount golf packages: Yes. **Season:** Year-round. **High:** N/A.
On-site lodging: No. **Rental clubs:** Yes.
Walking policy: Walking at certain times. **Range:** Yes (grass).
To obtain tee times: Call pro shop seven days in advance.
Subscriber comments: One of San Diego county's best-kept secrets . . . Good test, very hilly with tilted fairways, fast greens, sharpest doglegs in the county . . . Hilly, tight, difficult for most golfers . . . Accuracy a must, some blind shots, course knowledge needed . . . Chopped up course. Difficult hillsides . . . Don't like playing uphill . . . Short, tight, bring all your clubs, a shotmaker's course . . . Too many blind shots, lots of trees. Marginal maintenance . . . Outstanding views, very quiet course . . . Fun to play, needs more grass.

★★★ MENIFEE LAKES COUNTRY CLUB

SP—29875 Menifee Lakes Dr., Menifee (909)672-3090.
20 miles south of Riverside. **Holes:** 18. **Par:** 72/72.
Yards: 6,472/5,421. **Course rating:** 71.2/71.3. **Slope:** 128/119.
Opened: 1989. **Pace of Play rating:** 3:40. **Green fee:** $20/49.
Credit cards: MC, V. **Reduced fees:** Weekdays, Twilight, Juniors.
Caddies: No. **Golf carts:** Included in Green Fee.
Discount golf packages: No. **Season:** Year-round. **High:** N/A.
On-site lodging: No. **Rental clubs:** Yes.
Walking policy: Mandatory cart. **Range:** Yes (grass).
To obtain tee times: Call starter six days in advance for weekday tee times and the Wednesday before the weekend for weekend tee times.
Also new 9-hole course.
Subscriber comments: A good test of golf with several very unique holes . . . Play early before the wind comes up . . . A gem, great test. Good condition and beautiful scenery . . . Not a tough course but tight in some areas . . . Not much variety. Water on most holes . . . Short, requires good iron play. Good greens . . . Flat, uneventful course . . . Water in play on over half the holes . . . They buried 100 elephants under the greens . . . Pleasant to play, water a major factor, good speed of play . . . Wide open fairways. Lots of water, but it seldom comes into play.

★★★ MESQUITE GOLF AND COUNTRY CLUB

PU—2700 E. Mesquite Ave., Palm Springs (619)323-1502.
120 miles outside of Los Angeles. **Holes:** 18. **Par:** 72/72.
Yards: 6,328/5,244. **Course rating:** N/A. **Slope:** 117/118.
Opened: N/A. **Pace of Play rating:** N/A. **Green fee:** N/A.
Credit cards: MC, V, AMEX. **Reduced fees:** Weekdays, Low season, Twilight.
Caddies: No. **Golf carts:** Included in Green Fee.
Discount golf packages: No. **Season:** Year-round. **High:** Nov.-May.
On-site lodging: No. **Rental clubs:** No.
Walking policy: N/A. **Range:** Yes (grass).
Subscriber comments: Top-notch facility, tricky layout, some water . . . Electronic "caddie" on cart icing on beautiful course . . . Some holes not well laid out . . . Charming quality course . . . Well maintained, good shot values, pleasant experience . . . Turf conditions usually good, tight course layout . . . Not very well-manicured in peak season . . . Narrow parallel fairways, FORE! . . . Unique course, beautiful . . . Nice golf in the heart of Palm Springs.

★★ MICKE GROVE GOLF LINKS

PU—11401 N. Micke Grove Rd., Lodi (209)369-4410.
5 miles north of Stockton. **Holes:** 18. **Par:** 72/72.
Yards: 6,565/5,286. **Course rating:** 71.1/69.7. **Slope:** 118/111.
Opened: 1989. **Pace of Play rating:** 4:30. **Green fee:** $15/22.
Credit cards: MC, V. **Reduced fees:** Weekdays, Twilight, Seniors, Juniors.

Caddies: No. **Golf carts:** $10 for 18 holes.
Discount golf packages: No. **Season:** Year-round. **High:** March-Nov.
On-site lodging: No. **Rental clubs:** Yes.
Walking policy: Unrestricted walking. **Range:** Yes (grass).
To obtain tee times: Call seven days in advance.
Subscriber comments: New course, has a chance to be a good one . . .
Lots of water and sand, great open course . . . Poor design, condition
average, slow . . . Cookie-cutter golf course . . . Challenging greens, fairly
new but growing out . . . Wind is biggest difficulty, no wind equals a good
score . . . Fun course but wind is usually a major factor to deal with . . .
Needs better maintenance . . . New layout. Has potential when mature . . .
A real jewel, a surprise.

★★½ MILE SQUARE GOLF CLUB

PU—10401 Warner Ave., Fountain Valley (714)968-4556.
30 miles north of Los Angeles. **Holes:** 18. **Par:** 72/72.
Yards: 6,629/5,545. **Course rating:** 71.4/70.5. **Slope:** 121/109.
Opened: 1967. **Pace of Play rating:** 4:00–4:30. **Green fee:** $22.
Credit cards: None. **Reduced fees:** Twilight.
Caddies: Yes. **Golf carts:** $21 for 18 holes.
Discount golf packages: No. **Season:** Year-round. **High:** March-Sept.
On-site lodging: No. **Rental clubs:** Yes.
Walking policy: Unrestricted walking. **Range:** Yes.
To obtain tee times: Call one week in advance for weekdays; call Monday
for Saturday and Tuesday for Sunday.
Subscriber comments: The epitome of a public course . . . It's OK, if you
like playing the same par 4 eight times . . . Very well maintained for heavy
play . . . Easy course if you hit it straight . . . Well kept, fair test . . . Trees
grown to improve it . . . Open and wide, gives you back your confidence
. . . Fine public, flat course, excellent condition . . . Flat and wide; big,
well-kept greens . . . Lots of wind and trees.

★★★★ MISSION HILLS NORTH GOLF COURSE

PU—70-705 Ramon Rd., Rancho Mirage (619)770-9496, (800)358-2211.
5 miles east of Palm Springs. **Holes:** 18. **Par:** 72/72.
Yards: 7,062/4,907. **Course rating:** 73.9/68.0. **Slope:** 134/118.
Opened: 1991. **Pace of Play rating:** 4:30. **Green fee:** $55/120.
Credit cards: MC, V, AMEX. **Reduced fees:** Weekdays, Low season,
Resort guests, Twilight.
Caddies: No. **Golf carts:** Included in Green Fee.
Discount golf packages: Yes. **Season:** Year-round. **High:** Oct.-April.
On-site lodging: Yes. **Rental clubs:** Yes.
Walking policy: Mandatory cart. **Range:** Yes (grass).
To obtain tee times: Public may call within seven days. If staying at the
Westin Mission Hills Resort Hotel, you may book tee times upon room
confirmation.
Subscriber comments: Beautiful course, one tough hole after another . . .
No condos, beautiful scenery. Tees to challenge all golfers . . . Great desert
layout . . . Call me anytime, I'll call in sick . . . Best new course in
Coachella Valley . . . Best-manicured course of any I've ever played . . .
Thought I was in golf paradise . . . Many bunkers . . . You'll like this one if
you hate trees . . . Very pretty, playable course. Lots of mounding, fast
greens . . . Very nice layout, good service, well maintained . . . A must
visit . . . Great condition, greens as fast as any, fun . . . Playable for anyone
. . . Gary Player's best, breathtaking . . . Fine layout, not a typical desert
course . . . One of the best desert courses. Each hole is prettier than the
other . . . Smooth, fast greens.

★★★ MISSION LAKES COUNTRY CLUB

SP—8484 Clubhouse Blvd., Desert Hot Springs (619)329-8061.
10 miles north of Palm Springs. **Holes:** 18. **Par:** 71/72.
Yards: 6,737/5,390. **Course rating:** 72.8/71.2. **Slope:** 131/122.
Opened: 1973. **Pace of Play rating:** 4:15. **Green fee:** $30/60.
Credit cards: MC, V. **Reduced fees:** Weekdays, Low season, Resort
guests, Twilight, Juniors.

Caddies: No. **Golf carts:** Included in Green Fee.
Discount golf packages: No. **Season:** Year-round. **High:** Jan.–May.
On-site lodging: Yes. **Rental clubs:** Yes.
Walking policy: Mandatory cart. **Range:** Yes (grass).
To obtain tee times: Call three days ahead.
Subscriber comments: A must play whenever I'm in Palm Springs,
excellent greens . . . Outstanding course . . . Holes 15 through 18 are
toughest four finishing holes in Palm Springs area . . . Will never be
confused with Mission Hills . . . Strange layout . . . Slow play my only
complaint . . . Beautiful conditions and course, great shape and challenge
. . . Interesting muny layout, tough . . . Outstanding in all respects . . .
Hardest finishing four in southern California.

★★★ MONARCH BEACH GOLF LINKS

R—23841 Stonehill Dr., Dana Point (714)240-8247.
60 miles north of San Diego. **Holes:** 18. **Par:** 70/70.
Yards: 6,227/5,046. **Course rating:** 69.2/68.5. **Slope:** 128/120.
Opened: 1984. **Pace of Play rating:** 4:30. **Green fee:** $75/100.
Credit cards: MC, V, AMEX, Diners Club. **Reduced fees:** No.
Caddies: No. **Golf carts:** Included in Green Fee.
Discount golf packages: No. **Season:** Year-round. **High:** Year-round.
On-site lodging: No. **Rental clubs:** No.
Walking policy: Unrestricted walking. **Range:** Yes.
To obtain tee times: Seven days in advance. Also eight to 30 days in
advance with an additional $15 per player pre-book fee. Times are held with
credit card which will be charged if 24 hour cancellation is not given.
Subscriber comments: Some beautiful views . . . Condo golf with two
ocean holes . . . Well-maintained links course, very unique! . . . They must
understand they are not Pebble Beach . . . Greatly improved from three
years ago, great views! . . . Good track that can get better . . . OK course, a
bit rich . . . Breathtaking views . . . Short but challenging, fun to play . . .
Condition of course year-round is poor . . . Pretty course, complete game
required, greens can be spotty . . . Disappointing condition needs
improvement . . . Two ocean holes . . . Some great holes . . . Tricked up
with sand traps . . . Lots of water holes, greatly improved condition.

★★½ MONTEBELLO GOLF CLUB

PU—901 Via San Clemente, Montebello (213)723-2971.
9 miles east of Los Angeles. **Holes:** 18. **Par:** 71/72.
Yards: 6,671/5,979. **Course rating:** 70.4/72.4. **Slope:** 114/117.
Opened: 1928. **Pace of Play rating:** 4:00. **Green fee:** $18/21.
Credit cards: None. **Reduced fees:** No.
Caddies: No. **Golf carts:** $20 for 18 holes.
Discount golf packages: No. **Season:** Year-round. **High:** April–Oct.
On-site lodging: No. **Rental clubs:** No.
Walking policy: Unrestricted walking. **Range:** Yes.
To obtain tee times: Call seven days in advance.
Subscriber comments: Another great Los Angeles muny . . . Nice
course, excellent condition . . . Could do a lot more with what they have
available . . . Always solid . . . Very smoggy in summer . . . Flat . . .
Good, long for the average golfer . . . Course is old and gets lots of play.
Still fun . . . Forgiving wide fairways. Good for slicers and hookers . . .
Nice local course. Nothing spectacular but fun to play.

MORENO VALLEY RANCH GOLF CLUB
★★★½ MOUNTAIN/LAKE/VALLEY

PU—28095 John F. Kennedy Dr., Moreno Valley (909)924-4444.
15 miles east of Riverside. **Holes:** 27. **Par:** 72/72/72.
Yards: 6,684/6,898/6,880. **Course rating:** 73.1/74.1/74.2.
Slope: 139/138/140.
Opened: 1988. **Pace of Play rating:** 4:00–4:30. **Green fee:** $30/53.
Credit cards: All major. **Reduced fees:** Weekdays, Low season, Twilight,
Seniors, Juniors.
Caddies: No. **Golf carts:** Included in Green Fee.

Discount golf packages: Yes. **Season:** Year-round. **High:** Nov.-May.
On-site lodging: No. **Rental clubs:** Yes.
Walking policy: Mandatory cart. **Range:** Yes (grass).
To obtain tee times: Call seven days in advance.
Ranked in Third 25 of America's 75 Best Public Golf Courses by Golf Digest.
Subscriber comments: Best-kept secret. Pete Dye strikes again . . . Mountain course is quite nice, the other two are so-so . . . Each nine is different and fun . . . Mountain and Lake nines the best . . . Always a treat, Mountain nine too tricked up, best combo is Valley/Lake . . . Excellent course, beautiful setting . . . Touched by the master . . . A Pete Dye gem . . . Mountain/Lake best combo, course maintenance has slipped in the last two years . . . Just another target golf course . . . Superb in every way, all year . . . Tight, don't miss the fairway! Nice scenery . . . Good players should play from tips; always has good, fast greens . . . Snows on mountain nine . . . This is one course that makes me think Pete Dye is a nice fellow.

★★★ MORRO BAY GOLF COURSE

PU—State Park Rd., Morro Bay (805)772-4341.
15 miles north of San Luis Obispo. **Holes:** 18. **Par:** 71/72.
Yards: 6,360/5,055. **Course rating:** 70.4/69.5. **Slope:** 118/117.
Opened: 1929. **Pace of Play rating:** 4:15-4:30. **Green fee:** $20/26.
Credit cards: None. **Reduced fees:** Twilight, Seniors, Juniors.
Caddies: No. **Golf carts:** $10 for 18 holes.

Discount golf packages: No. **Season:** Year-round. **High:** April-Aug.
On-site lodging: No. **Rental clubs:** Yes.
Walking policy: Unrestricted walking. **Range:** Yes (grass).
To obtain tee times: Starting times can be made one day in advance for weekdays; weekend times are taken on Saturday for the following weekend. Reservations can be made by phone or in person.
Subscriber comments: The poor man's beach-front course! . . . Practice your putting . . . Quick greens, lots of breakers . . . Great views of Morro Bay . . . Beautiful layout, a few quirky holes . . . Terrific mix of scenery, challenging layout, and good greenkeeping . . . Blue tees actually too much . . . Seaside course, relaxing course for average players . . . Always in good shape and heavily played. Interesting layout and great views . . . One of the best public courses in California . . . In a state park . . . Wouldn't miss it . . . Most enjoyable, great vistas . . . Ocean view from every hole . . . Good for amount of play . . . Pebble Beach views at muny prices . . . Good customer relations . . . Busy but fun, tricky greens but playable . . . Only minor negative was no sand traps . . . Beautiful layout.

★★★½ MT. WOODSON COUNTRY CLUB

SP—16422 N. Woodson Dr., Ramona (619)788-3555.
25 miles northeast of San Diego. **Holes:** 18. **Par:** 70/70.
Yards: 6,180/4,441. **Course rating:** 68.8/64.7. **Slope:** 130/108.
Opened: 1991. **Pace of Play rating:** 4:30. **Green fee:** $28/58.
Credit cards: MC, V, AMEX. **Reduced fees:** Weekdays, Twilight, Juniors.
Caddies: No. **Golf carts:** Included in Green Fee.
Discount golf packages: Yes. **Season:** Year-round. **High:** N/A.
On-site lodging: No. **Rental clubs:** Yes.
Walking policy: Mandatory cart. **Range:** Yes.
To obtain tee times: Call seven days in advance.
Subscriber comments: Amazing little course, awesome holes, going back for more . . . Short, but a test, beautifully landscaped and cared for . . . Disneyland-like holes . . . A great bridge . . . Very narrow and winding fairway . . . Fabulous scenery . . . Short, tight, challenging, beautiful . . . Beautiful architecture . . . Target golf, leave your driver at home . . . Golfer's Disneyland . . . Very hilly and unusual layout, big elevation drops, super greens and upkeep . . . Lots of carry-type shots, but wide open landing areas . . . Very beautiful, well maintained and scenic . . . Best short course in California . . . Remote, but well worth it. Don't let the short yardage fool you, it's a one-of-a-kind course . . . Tightest design ever, great

shape, makes you think! . . . Play each hole with an eye on the vistas, very nice . . . You had better hit it straight or own lots of balls . . . Scenic but hilly . . . Where is the fairway? . . . Fantastic views . . . Beautiful, but much too tough for anyone but low handicapper . . . Cool bag tags . . . San Diego Rocky Mountain golf course.

★★★ MOUNTAIN MEADOWS GOLF CLUB

PU—1875 N. Fairplex Dr., Pomona (909)623-3704.
20 miles east of Los Angeles. **Holes:** 18. **Par:** 72/72.
Yards: 6,509/5,637. **Course rating:** 71.5/71.5. **Slope:** 125/117.
Opened: 1977. **Pace of Play rating:** 4:30-5:00. **Green fee:** $14/21.
Credit cards: MC, V. **Reduced fees:** Weekdays, Low season, Twilight, Seniors, Juniors.
Caddies: No. **Golf carts:** $10 for 18 holes.
Discount golf packages: No. **Season:** Year-round. **High:** May-Aug.
On-site lodging: No. **Rental clubs:** Yes.
Walking policy: Unrestricted walking. **Range:** Yes (grass).
To obtain tee times: Call one week in advance; weekdays at 6 a.m.; weekends and holidays at 5 a.m.
Subscriber comments: Los Angeles' best-kept secret . . . Nice challenging course, hilly . . . Slow play, could be in better condition . . . Excellent maintenance for Los Angeles county course. Fast greens . . . Lots of hills and valleys. Very busy, tough on high handicappers . . . As good a public course as you'll find . . . Interesting muny with changes in elevation . . . Lots of hills . . . Nice layout, good shape . . . Always in good condition, nice layout . . . Some challenging holes on back nine . . . More challenging than you think . . . One of the most interesting layouts in southern California.

MOUNTAIN SHADOWS GOLF COURSE

PU—100 Golf Course Dr., Rohnert Park (707)584-7766.
7 miles south of Santa Rosa.
Pace of Play rating: 4:30.
Credit cards: MC, V. **Reduced fees:** Weekdays, Twilight, Seniors, Juniors.
Caddies: No. **Golf carts:** $12 for 18 holes.
Discount golf packages: No. **Season:** Year-round. **High:** April-Oct.
On-site lodging: No. **Rental clubs:** Yes. **Range:** Yes.
To obtain tee times: One week in advance.

★★ NORTH COURSE

Holes: 18. **Par:** 72/72.
Yards: 7,035/5,503. **Course rating:** 72.1/70.5. **Slope:** N/A.
Opened: 1974. **Green fee:** $16/35.
Walking policy: Walking at certain times.
Subscriber comments: Not long but makes you think, refreshing . . . Big fairways, big greens . . . Well-designed, interesting layout . . . Water in play on many holes . . . Good conditioning, but nothing special . . . Flat course. Scenery only OK . . . OK, not exceptional . . . Locals call it Mountain Shambles . . . Good greens, maintenance average . . . Laughably bad. Where's Dan Jenkins when you need him? . . . Beautiful condition but uninspired design . . . Very soggy in winter, poor drainage . . . Always muddy . . . Fun course but enough water and doglegs to keep it interesting.

★½ SOUTH COURSE

Holes: 18. **Par:** 72/72.
Yards: 6,720/5,805. **Course rating:** 70.1/71.4. **Slope:** 115/122.
Opened: 1963. **Green fee:** $12/30.
Walking policy: Unrestricted walking.
Subscriber comments: Flat, lots of trees, nice . . . Too many ducks and geese on course . . . Tight, small greens . . . Old course, uninteresting, unplayable in winter, no good drainage . . . Mickey Mouse front nine, good back nine . . . Good course for the duffer, open fairways . . . Clay-like mud sticks to clubs . . . Very different nines, wears the traffic well . . . Tough back nine . . . Needs major renovation . . . Good carries required on several holes . . . Not much excitement . . . No design. Holes all the same.

CALIFORNIA

★★½ MOUNTAIN SPRINGS GOLF CLUB

PU—1000 Championship Dr., Sonora (209)532-1000.
45 miles east of Stockton. **Holes:** 18. **Par:** 72/71.
Yards: 6,665/5,195. **Course rating:** 71.9/68.8. **Slope:** 128/112.
Opened: 1990. **Pace of Play rating:** 4:30-5:00. **Green fee:** $10/25.
Credit cards: MC, V. **Reduced fees:** Twilight, Seniors, Juniors.
Caddies: No. **Golf carts:** $10 for 18 holes.
Discount golf packages: Yes. **Season:** Year-round. **High:** April-Sept.
On-site lodging: No. **Rental clubs:** Yes.
Walking policy: Unrestricted walking. **Range:** Yes.
To obtain tee times: Call two weeks in advance.
Subscriber comments: Set in valley, fair shape, few trees, good greens,
good price . . . New course will mature nicely with good care . . . Great
mountain course, slick greens, great scenery . . . Fun, but too many blind
shots . . . Great design, several challenging holes . . . Take a guide first time
around, fairways are blind . . . Must think through every shot, the more
you play the more you enjoy . . . Needs to mature, some bare spots, some
really fun holes . . . Sometimes hard to know where to hit . . . Well kept,
good layout but hilly . . . If you're ever near Yosemite, don't miss this one.

★★½ MOUNTAIN VIEW COUNTRY CLUB

PU—2121 Mountain View Dr., Corona (909)737-9798.
10 miles west of Riverside. **Holes:** 18. **Par:** 72/73.
Yards: 6,433/5,374. **Course rating:** 70.8/71.7. **Slope:** 124/120.
Opened: 1963. **Pace of Play rating:** 4:00. **Green fee:** $27/37.
Credit cards: MC, V. **Reduced fees:** Weekdays, Low season, Resort
guests, Twilight, Seniors, Juniors.
Caddies: No. **Golf carts:** Included in Green Fee.
Discount golf packages: Yes. **Season:** Year-round. **High:** Oct.-June.
On-site lodging: No. **Rental clubs:** Yes.
Walking policy: Walking at certain times. **Range:** Yes (grass).
To obtain tee times: Call two weeks in advance.
Subscriber comments: Some interesting holes, elevation changes . . . Not
well groomed . . . Nice layout, not kept up very well . . . Very narrow
course with O.B. on both sides of 14 holes . . . Needs a little more TLC,
but has improved over the years.

★★½ NAPA MUNICIPAL GOLF CLUB

PU—2295 Streblow Dr., Napa (707)255-4333.
45 miles northwest of San Francisco. **Holes:** 18. **Par:** 72/73.
Yards: 6,730/5,956. **Course rating:** 71.7/76.8. **Slope:** 127/137.
Opened: 1967. **Pace of Play rating:** 4:00. **Green fee:** $14/25.
Credit cards: None. **Reduced fees:** Weekdays, Low season, Twilight,
Seniors, Juniors.
Caddies: No. **Golf carts:** $20 for 18 holes.
Discount golf packages: No. **Season:** Year-round. **High:** April-Nov.
On-site lodging: No. **Rental clubs:** Yes.
Walking policy: Unrestricted walking. **Range:** Yes.
To obtain tee times: Seven days in advance by phone or in person.
Subscriber comments: Uses all clubs in your bag, good layout . . . Nice
layout, but too unkempt for my taste . . . Good test, thin fairways, 14
water holes . . . Needs minor work . . . A real tester . . . Well groomed,
nice golf experience . . . Tough greens, very good muny . . . Tough track,
could use better conditioning . . . A nice municipal track. A little soggy in
winter . . . Could use some wine during rounds.

★★½ NEEDLES MUNICIPAL GOLF COURSE

PU—144 Marina Dr., Needles (619)326-3931.
100 miles south of Las Vegas. **Holes:** 18. **Par:** 70/70.
Yards: 6,550/5,850. **Course rating:** 70.1/71.1. **Slope:** 107/114.
Opened: 1962. **Pace of Play rating:** 4:00. **Green fee:** $15/19.
Credit cards: MC, V. **Reduced fees:** Low season, Seniors, Juniors.
Caddies: No. **Golf carts:** $10 for 18 holes.
Discount golf packages: No. **Season:** Year-round. **High:** Nov.-April.
On-site lodging: No. **Rental clubs:** Yes.

Walking policy: Unrestricted walking. **Range:** Yes (grass).
To obtain tee times: Two days in advance for weekdays; one week in advance for weekends. Call after 6 a.m.
Subscriber comments: On Colorado River, dry desert course, friendly staff, good for beginners, fun course . . . Summer too hot. Dry! Dry! Dry! . . . A bargain if the weather cooperates . . . An excellent public course . . . Not a bad course, considering where you are.

★★★ NORTHSTAR-AT-TAHOE RESORT GOLF COURSE
R—Hwy. 267 and Northstar Dr., Truckee (916)562-2490, (800)466-6784.
40 miles west of Reno, NV. **Holes:** 18. **Par:** 72/72.
Yards: 6,897/5,470. **Course rating:** 72.0/71.2. **Slope:** 137/134.
Opened: 1975. **Pace of Play rating:** N/A. **Green fee:** $45/70.
Credit cards: All major. **Reduced fees:** Low season, Resort guests, Twilight, Seniors, Juniors.
Caddies: No. **Golf carts:** Included in Green Fee.
Discount golf packages: Yes. **Season:** May-Oct. **High:** July-Aug.
On-site lodging: Yes. **Rental clubs:** Yes.
Walking policy: Unrestricted walking. **Range:** Yes.
To obtain tee times: Call 21 days in advance, unless hotel guest.
Subscriber comments: Two diverse nines . . . Easy front nine, tough back . . . Open front nine . . . Long, tough, tree-lined; need distance off the tee to score, even with altitude . . . Gorgeous and challenging, some greens need work . . . Through forested canyon . . . Conditions so-so . . . Back nine better than front . . . Two different nines: one tight in woods, one open meadow . . . Course in fair shape, back nine very challenging . . . Narrow fairways, scenic and fun . . . Two courses in one, Meadow and Woods, beautiful . . . Usually in good shape for a high altitude course . . . Must have a guide the first time around.

★★★★ OAK VALLEY GOLF CLUB
PU—37-600 14th St., Beaumont (909)769-7200.
20 miles east of San Bernadino. **Holes:** 18. **Par:** 72/72.
Yards: 7,003/5,494. **Course rating:** 73.9/71.1. **Slope:** 136/122.
Opened: 1990. **Pace of Play rating:** N/A. **Green fee:** $30/50.
Credit cards: MC, V, AMEX. **Reduced fees:** Weekdays, Twilight.
Caddies: No. **Golf carts:** Included in Green Fee.
Discount golf packages: Yes. **Season:** Year-round. **High:** March-June.
On-site lodging: No. **Rental clubs:** Yes.
Walking policy: Mandatory cart. **Range:** Yes (grass).
To obtain tee times: Call seven days in advance.

Subscriber comments: What a find . . . Beautiful location, especially in winter with snow-capped mountains . . . One of the best-kept secrets in southern California . . . Best course between the desert and the ocean . . . A true "golfer's course" . . . A hidden jewel! Play it before everyone finds out about it . . . Great layout, she bites back, no real clubhouse . . . Back nine is awesome, No. 17 a great hole, can be very windy at times . . . Will be better with permanent clubhouse . . . Palm Springs type course without the cost, don't try it in the wind . . . One of southern California's best . . . Jewel of a course . . . Sleeper. Not busy . . . Quite demanding on a calm day, when the wind blows, watch out! . . . Could play here every day, never crowded . . . Needs maturity, but is capable of being best course in Riverside area . . . The best public course in southern California . . . 12th a classic! . . . Links to rolling hills, fantastic shot values, every hole different . . . Greens consistently fast . . . Worth the drive from Los Angeles . . . Excellent, well-maintained course, scenic . . . Tremendous design, great hole variety.

★★★½ OAKHURST COUNTRY CLUB
SP—1001 Peacock Creek Dr., Clayton (510)672-9737.
2 miles south of Concord. **Holes:** 18. **Par:** 72/72.
Yards: 6,739/5,285. **Course rating:** 73.1/70.3. **Slope:** 132/123.
Opened: 1990. **Pace of Play rating:** N/A. **Green fee:** $50/70.
Credit cards: MC, V, DISC. **Reduced fees:** Twilight, Seniors, Juniors.
Caddies: No. **Golf carts:** Included in Green Fee.

Discount golf packages: No. **Season:** Year-round. **High:** N/A.
On-site lodging: No. **Rental clubs:** Yes.
Walking policy: Mandatory cart. **Range:** Yes (grass).
To obtain tee times: Call three days in advance.
Subscriber comments: A touch of class . . . A real gem, great finishing hole . . . Best new course in area . . . Interesting layout . . . Must play several times to get the feel . . . Bring your best game . . . Perfect maintenance, tough, nice layout . . . A real test, long driving holes, tough par 3s . . . Windy location . . . Thoroughly satisfying golf experience . . . Target golf at its best, bring every iron you own . . . Greens are too hard and fast. Terrific layout . . . Impossible from black tees . . . Well maintained, good shot values . . . Too much walking with carts on path only . . . Young course but a real test already . . . Great golf but do you think they can build any more houses on 18th hole? . . . Fastest greens in northern California; the older it gets, the better . . . Northern California could use more high-end daily fees like this.

OAKMONT GOLF CLUB
★★★ **WEST COURSE**
SP—7025 Oakmont Dr., Santa Rosa (707)539-0415.
55 miles north of Santa Rosa. **Holes:** 18. **Par:** 72/72.
Yards: 6,379/5,573. **Course rating:** 70.5/71.9. **Slope:** 121/128.
Opened: 1963. **Pace of Play rating:** 4:30. **Green fee:** $25/32.
Credit cards: MC, V. **Reduced fees:** Twilight.
Caddies: No. **Golf carts:** $11 for 18 holes.
Discount golf packages: No. **Season:** Year-round. **High:** N/A.
On-site lodging: No. **Rental clubs:** Yes.
Walking policy: Unrestricted walking. **Range:** Yes (grass).
To obtain tee times: Call one week in advance for weekends and holidays and one day ahead during the week.
Also has 18-hole par-63 East Course.
Subscriber comments: Beautiful, manicured fairways among large old oak trees . . . Makes you play a lot of shots, well maintained . . . Ho-hum layout . . . Very playable, not a lot of trouble . . . Good old-style course . . . Nice course . . . Always in wonderful condition. Testy greens . . . Pleasant layout through a retirement community . . . Course plays long due to heavy watering . . . Well kept, walkable . . . Best unknown course in Sonoma County.

★½ OCEANSIDE MUNICIPAL GOLF COURSE
PU—825 Douglas Dr., Oceanside (619)433-1360.
30 miles north of San Diego. **Holes:** 18. **Par:** 72/72.
Yards: 6,450/5,398. **Course rating:** 70.8/71.6. **Slope:** 118/121.
Opened: 1974. **Pace of Play rating:** 4:00-5:00. **Green fee:** $16/21.
Credit cards: MC, V. **Reduced fees:** Weekdays, Twilight, Seniors, Juniors.
Caddies: No. **Golf carts:** $18 for 18 holes.
Discount golf packages: No. **Season:** Year-round. **High:** Year-round.
On-site lodging: No. **Rental clubs:** Yes.
Walking policy: Unrestricted walking. **Range:** Yes (grass).
To obtain tee times: Call eight days in advance.
Subscriber comments: Nice, old, well-done layout . . . Pretty wilderness, I saw seven types of ducks and loved it . . . Harder than rating/slope indicates . . . Gets a lot of play, in good condition for amount of play . . . Poor greens ruin a good layout . . . Muny course but in good shape . . . Nothing special about course; staff very friendly.

★★★★ OJAI VALLEY INN
R—Country Club Rd., Ojai (805)646-2420, (800)422-6524.
60 miles south of Los Angeles. **Holes:** 18. **Par:** 70/71.
Yards: 6,235/5,225. **Course rating:** 70.6/70.2. **Slope:** 123/123.
Opened: 1923. **Pace of Play rating:** 4:30. **Green fee:** $86.
Credit cards: All major. **Reduced fees:** Resort guests, Twilight.
Caddies: No. **Golf carts:** $14 for 18 holes.

Discount golf packages: Yes. **Season:** Year-round. **High:** March–Oct.
On-site lodging: Yes. **Rental clubs:** Yes.
Walking policy: Unrestricted walking. **Range:** Yes (grass).
To obtain tee times: Resort guests may make tee times 90 days in advance. All others three days in advance.
Subscriber comments: Lovely old charming hotel and great course, loved it . . . Back nine worth the price of admission; finish early and turn a second 18 for only the cart cost . . . Good old-style course . . . Nice layout for good iron player . . . Gorgeous and challenging . . . Great setting, relaxing resort course . . . First-class resort . . . Fast, true greens, kept in excellent condition . . . Wonderful old course . . . All around course suitable to all golfers . . . Noisy and numerous maintenance vehicles abound . . . Short but extremely demanding . . . Outstanding service, but not a championship course . . . Beautiful, well kept, every hole a picture . . . Immaculate, picturesque but very short. Easy to score . . . Needs more length . . . A great standard for courses, everything is the best . . . Hidden treasure of the L.A. area . . . Superb little course . . . A true shotmaker's course. No. 6 is the most difficult short par 4 I've played . . . Fun place and area . . . It's the best in all categories! . . . Tough course. Beautiful surroundings. Take an extra sleeve of balls . . . Hardest short course you will ever play, conditions excellent . . . An experience to cherish . . . Very well-conditioned course since it was rebuilt . . . Best-kept secret in California!

★★★ OLD DEL MONTE GOLF COURSE

PU—1300 Sylvan Rd., Monterey (408)373-2436.
Holes: 18. **Par:** 72/74.
Yards: 6,278/5,431. **Course rating:** 70.8/71.1. **Slope:** 122/118.
Opened: 1897. **Pace of Play rating:** 3:50–4:00. **Green fee:** $50.
Credit cards: All major. **Reduced fees:** Resort guests, Twilight, Seniors, Juniors.
Caddies: Yes. **Golf carts:** $15 for 18 holes.
Discount golf packages: No. **Season:** Year-round. **High:** April–Oct.
On-site lodging: Yes. **Rental clubs:** Yes.
Walking policy: Unrestricted walking. **Range:** No.
To obtain tee times: Call up to 60 days in advance.
Subscriber comments: Old, charming and challenging . . . Worth playing the oldest course west of Mississippi . . . Very forgiving, beautiful setting . . . Still a great golf course . . . Easy to walk with beautiful old trees . . . Oldest golf course in California . . . Maturity a plus . . . Best muny ever, Pebble Beach without the ocean . . . Sublime . . . Good warm-up prior to taking on tougher tracks . . . No driving range . . . Sand, sand, sand . . . No water . . . Oldest course west of Mississippi . . . Not much of a match compared to other area courses . . . Old charm with character.

★★½ OLIVAS PARK GOLF COURSE

PU—3750 Olivas Park Dr., Ventura (805)642-4303.
60 miles north of Los Angeles. **Holes:** 18. **Par:** 72/72.
Yards: 6,760/5,501. **Course rating:** 71.3/71.3. **Slope:** 119/117.
Opened: 1964. **Pace of Play rating:** 4:00. **Green fee:** $16/21.
Credit cards: None. **Reduced fees:** Twilight, Juniors.
Caddies: No. **Golf carts:** $20 for 18 holes.
Discount golf packages: No. **Season:** Year-round. **High:** May–Sept.
On-site lodging: No. **Rental clubs:** Yes.
Walking policy: Unrestricted walking. **Range:** Yes (grass).
To obtain tee times: Call seven days in advance.
Subscriber comments: Flat as a pancake, but wind makes it tough . . . Good muny, flat and wide open, usually in good shape . . . More open course than desired . . . Flat but very enjoyable, lots of wind in p.m. . . . Mushroom factory next door noticeable for nine holes . . . Flat muny track. Wide open . . . A flat, windswept course which is extremely fair . . . Great if there is no wind . . . Nothing special . . . Very open, very forgiving . . . Maintenance sometimes poor . . . Improved condition. Staff attentive . . . Good speed of play.

★★★ PACIFIC GROVE MUNICIPAL GOLF LINKS

PU—77 Asilomar Blvd., Pacific Grove (408)648-3175.
17 miles west of Salinas. **Holes:** 18. **Par:** 70/72.
Yards: 5,732/5,305. **Course rating:** 67.5/70.5. **Slope:** 117/114.
Opened: 1932. **Pace of Play rating:** 4:00. **Green fee:** $24/28.
Credit cards: None. **Reduced fees:** Twilight, Juniors.
Caddies: No. **Golf carts:** N/A.
Discount golf packages: No. **Season:** Year-round. **High:** N/A.
On-site lodging: No. **Rental clubs:** Yes.
Walking policy: Unrestricted walking. **Range:** Yes (grass).
To obtain tee times: Call seven days in advance (each day for same day
next week) 6:50 a.m. Monday through Friday, 6:30 a.m. Saturday, Sunday
and holidays.
Subscriber comments: A real gem . . . Good way to experience peninsula
golf . . . Two different nines . . . Best value on peninsula . . . Nice, easy to
get on . . . Back nine links layout with ocean . . . Front tight and tree-lined,
back out by the ocean under lighthouse, very scenic and breathtaking views
. . . Skip the front, play the back twice . . . Not difficult, but enjoyable . . .
Best-kept secret around . . . Best deal in the west . . . Very, very windy in
afternoon, ice plant makes accuracy a must . . . Front nine is warm-up . . .
Postage-stamp greens . . . A sleeper . . . Fun sights, too short . . . Fun
course, lots of deer on it . . . Scottish links feel, great views of Pacific Ocean
. . . Overrated in last survey; five good holes in the dunes, rest is forgettable
. . . Love the ocean dunes . . . Miniature Spyglass.

★★★ PAJARO VALLEY GOLF CLUB

PU—967 Salinas Rd., Watsonville (408)724-3851.
20 miles south of Santa Cruz. **Holes:** 18. **Par:** 72/72.
Yards: 6,234/5,694. **Course rating:** 70.0/72.3. **Slope:** 122/123.
Opened: 1927. **Pace of Play rating:** 3:30-4:00. **Green fee:** $27/55.
Credit cards: MC, V, AMEX. **Reduced fees:** Weekdays, Twilight.
Caddies: No. **Golf carts:** $25 for 18 holes.
Discount golf packages: Yes. **Season:** Year-round. **High:** April-Nov.
On-site lodging: No. **Rental clubs:** Yes.
Walking policy: Unrestricted walking. **Range:** Yes.
To obtain tee times: Call anytime.
Subscriber comments: Forgiving, nice wide fairways, old and established

. . . Ho-hum course, in good condition . . . Doesn't live up to potential,
can be nice . . . Challenging course for the average player, fairways make
each shot hard . . . A hidden gem. Better than courses that cost more . . .
Pretty hill setting . . . Well taken care of . . . Good course for average
player . . Easy but scenic track . . . Never a level lie . . . Play is slow!
Tough finishing holes to walk, might be the toughest public course around
anywhere.

★★★½ PALA MESA RESORT

R—2001 S. Hwy. 395, Fallbrook (619)728-5881, (800)722-4700.
40 miles south of San Diego. **Holes:** 18. **Par:** 72/73.
Yards: 6,528/5,848. **Course rating:** 72.0/74.5. **Slope:** 131/128.
Opened: 1964. **Pace of Play rating:** 4:30. **Green fee:** $35/70.
Credit cards: MC, V, AMEX. **Reduced fees:** Weekdays, Low season,
Resort guests, Twilight, Juniors.
Caddies: No. **Golf carts:** Included in Green Fee.
Discount golf packages: Yes. **Season:** Year-round. **High:** Jan.-May.
On-site lodging: Yes. **Rental clubs:** Yes.
Walking policy: Mandatory cart. **Range:** Yes (grass).
To obtain tee times: Call seven days in advance.
Site of Golf Digest Schools.
Subscriber comments: A real little gem . . . Back nine outstanding . . .
Best and fastest greens in southern California: short layout but the trees help
to penalize the long and crooked, always in great shape . . . Way too much
O.B. . . . Very demanding, but a joy to play . . . Trees galore . . . Two
nines each have their own personality . . . Much variety . . . Slick,

undulating greens . . . Fun course and good conditions . . . Old and super narrow, O.B. everywhere, bring your best game . . . Great greens but not much else to talk about . . . Well maintained, good fast pace of play . . . Narrow and short. Don't bet against seniors on this course.

★★★ PALM DESERT RESORT COUNTRY CLUB

R—77-333 Country Club Dr., Palm Desert (619)345-2791.
Holes: 18. **Par:** 72/72.
Yards: 6,585/5,670. **Course rating:** 70.8/71.8. **Slope:** 117/123.
Opened: 1980. **Pace of Play rating:** 4:00. **Green fee:** $70/85.
Credit cards: MC, V, AMEX. **Reduced fees:** Weekdays, Low season, Twilight.
Caddies: No. **Golf carts:** Included in Green Fee.
Discount golf packages: Yes. **Season:** Nov.-Sept. **High:** Nov.-April.
On-site lodging: Yes. **Rental clubs:** Yes.
Walking policy: Mandatory cart. **Range:** Yes (grass).
To obtain tee times: Call five days in advance.
Subscriber comments: Well kept, lightly used, some easy holes . . . Relatively easy, good for seniors, high handicappers . . . Short . . . Uncrowded, very quiet . . . Good condo course, nice condition, big greens . . . So-so layout, not too tough . . . Course has matured well plays nicely.

★★★½ PALOS VERDES GOLF CLUB

SP—3301 Via Campesina, Palos Verdes Estates (310)375-2759.
20 miles north of Los Angeles. **Holes:** 18. **Par:** 71/70.
Yards: 6,116/5,506. **Course rating:** 70.4/73.3. **Slope:** 131/128.
Opened: 1924. **Pace of Play rating:** 4:30. **Green fee:** $85.
Credit cards: MC, V, AMEX. **Reduced fees:** Juniors.
Caddies: No. **Golf carts:** Included in Green Fee.
Discount golf packages: No. **Season:** Year-round. **High:** June-Aug.
On-site lodging: No. **Rental clubs:** Yes.
Walking policy: Mandatory cart. **Range:** No.
To obtain tee times: Call seven days in advance.
Subscriber comments: Classic 1920's course . . . Spectacular holes, hilly . . . The best-kept secret in southern California . . . Great shape, character . . . Requires good shotmaking through canyons . . . Rather play somewhere else, not a good layout . . . Terrific setting, loved the scenery . . . Hilly with some excellent views if the weather permits. Conditioning is always suspect . . . Great location . . . Short deceiving course, small greens, not many flat lies . . . Great competitive course, need all the clubs in your bag . . . Fine old course in excellent condition . . . My favorite, gotta play.

★★★ PARADISE VALLEY GOLF COURSE

PU—3950 Paradise Valley Dr., Fairfield (707)426-1600.
45 miles northeast of San Francisco. **Holes:** 18. **Par:** 72/72.
Yards: 6,993/5,413. **Course rating:** 74.1/71.1. **Slope:** 135/119.
Opened: 1993. **Pace of Play rating:** 4:30. **Green fee:** $22/31.
Credit cards: MC, V, AMEX. **Reduced fees:** Weekdays, Low season, Resort guests, Twilight.
Caddies: No. **Golf carts:** $11 for 18 holes.
Discount golf packages: Yes. **Season:** Year-round.
On-site lodging: No. **Rental clubs:** Yes.
Walking policy: Unrestricted walking. **Range:** Yes (grass).
To obtain tee times: Call seven days in advance.

Subscriber comments: Excellent course, flat but very interesting . . . Great architecture . . . Huge greens . . . You're in for a treat . . . New, still needs some work . . . Greens are new and hard to putt . . . Combo wide, narrow fairways, a beauty . . . Where's the trees? . . . Very nice, new, upscale muny . . . Suffering growing pains, newness wearing off . . . Tough in the wind . . . Difficult to play . . . Lots of bunkers and water. Need good sand play and ball placement . . . The best all-around public facility, unbelievable clubhouse and sports bar! . . . Can't help to be one of the best in northern Calif. . . . Challenging par 3s . . . Bad design on No.10

. . . Takes advantage of many natural creeks and mature trees, has potential to be a great public golf course . . . Practice your putting . . . No.10 is awesome . . . Can not believe this is city course . . . For an immature course this is fantastic, I can't wait for the course to mature.

★★★★½ PASATIEMPO GOLF CLUB
SP—18 Clubhouse Rd., Santa Cruz (408)459-9155.
Holes: 18. **Par:** 71/72.
Yards: 6,483/5,647. **Course rating:** 72.9/73.6. **Slope:** 138/135.
Opened: 1929. **Pace of Play rating:** 4:15. **Green fee:** $100.
Credit cards: MC, V, AMEX. **Reduced fees:** Weekdays, Twilight.
Caddies: Yes. **Golf carts:** $32 for 18 holes.
Discount golf packages: No. **Season:** Year-round. **High:** June-Sept.
On-site lodging: No. **Rental clubs:** Yes.
Walking policy: Unrestricted walking. **Range:** Yes (grass).
To obtain tee times: Call seven days for weekdays. Call Monday for upcoming weekend at 10 a.m.
Ranked 99th in America's 100 Greatest Golf Courses by Golf Digest. Ranked in First 25 of America's 75 Best Public Golf Courses by Golf Digest. Ranked 10th in California by Golf Digest.
Subscriber comments: Great old course by terrific designer . . . Challenging, needs some grooming . . . Alister Mackenzie, enough said . . . One of the best in northern California . . . Hilly, tree-lined . . . A classic . . . Outstanding, traditional and illustrious . . . Par-3 18th hole . . . Old-time favorite . . . I'll never play Pebble again . . . Demands good iron play . . . Comparable to Pebble Beach . . . Can destroy you . . . Tight in spots . . . Not a flat lie anywhere . . . A must for any golf nut, some of the best holes you'll ever play . . . Back nine will take you to your knees . . . See the Santa Cruz boardwalk from first tee, beautiful . . . A few long holes over canyons. Great and tough . . . An absolute must-play for low handicappers who like to walk . . . When you think you can walk on water, try this one . . . . . . Class. Must play five times before you start to understand it . . . Challenging 15th hole worth the entire round . . . Everyone here knows it's as good as Pebble . . . Could be the best in California . . . Mackenzie and God built this one . . . Top-notch traditional golf, always in great condition . . . The best golf experience I've ever had . . . Each hole different, great golfing experience . . . Wow! This one is great.

★½ PEACOCK GAP GOLF AND COUNTRY CLUB
SP—333 Biscayne Dr., San Rafael (415)453-4940.
12 miles from San Francisco. **Holes:** 18. **Par:** 71/71.
Yards: 6,354/5,629. **Course rating:** N/A. **Slope:** 121/128.
Opened: N/A. **Pace of Play rating:** N/A. **Green fee:** N/A.
Credit cards: MC, V. **Reduced fees:** Twilight.
Caddies: No. **Golf carts:** N/A.
Discount golf packages: Yes. **Season:** Year-round. **High:** March-Oct.
On-site lodging: No. **Rental clubs:** No.
Walking policy: N/A. **Range:** Yes.
Subscriber comments: Course needs better maintenance . . . Windy most of the time, not in good condition . . . Good challenge, nice setting . . . Hard and fast in summer, nice in spring . . . Good condition . . . It's OK . . . Not enough real estate for the money . . . Excellent course worth playing . . . Hilly good views, not well maintained . . . Flat, easy, unimaginative . . . All the holes are the same . . . Layout is dull.

★★★★★ PEBBLE BEACH GOLF LINKS
R—17 Mile Dr., Pebble Beach (408)624-3811, (800)654-9300.
Holes: 18. **Par:** 72/72.
Yards: 6,799/5,197. **Course rating:** 74.4/71.9. **Slope:** 142/130.
Opened: 1919. **Pace of Play rating:** 4:30-5:00. **Green fee:** $175/225.
Credit cards: All major. **Reduced fees:** Twilight.
Caddies: Yes. **Golf carts:** Included in Green Fee.
Discount golf packages: Yes. **Season:** Year-round. **High:** Sept.-Oct.
On-site lodging: Yes. **Rental clubs:** Yes.

Walking policy: Unrestricted walking. **Range:** Yes.
To obtain tee times: Call one day in advance.
Ranked 3rd in America's 100 Greatest Golf Courses by Golf Digest. Ranked 1st in America's 75 Best Resort Courses by Golf Digest. Ranked 1st in California by Golf Digest.
Subscriber comments: A religious experience . . . You'll need a home equity loan to play, but do it! . . . Any way you look at this course, it is one of the great ones . . . Mecca . . . The best course on earth, or anywhere else! . . . Golfer's heaven, but must be a player . . . There's only Pebble . . . Heaven on earth at any price . . . One of the scenic places on the planet . . . Great to be able to walk . . . A course that lives up to and deserves its reputation. Truly memorable . . . Mother Earth's finest piece of golf real estate . . . Awesome . . . You're not a golfer unless you've played it. Must walk to get your money's worth. Six of the finest holes in golf . . . Moslems go to Mecca, golfers go to Pebble Beach . . . Expected something tougher, I guess that's Spyglass . . . Cart paths ruin it . . . Unreal landscape . . . Slow play but who cares? . . . Play is very slow but views are awesome . . . Unmatched setting. Must play once. Reeks of tradition . . . No. 1 in the world . . . What else can be written, how can it get more expensive . . . Lives up to continued accolades . . . Still the dream course . . . A shrine . . . Ghosts walk the course . . . Most enjoyable scenery in history . . . Simply the best!

PELICAN HILL GOLF CLUB

R—22651 Pelican Hill Rd., Newport Coast (714)759-5190.
40 miles north of Los Angeles.
Pace of Play rating: N/A. **Green fee:** $125/145.
Credit cards: MC, V, AMEX, Diners Club, JCB. **Reduced fees:** Resort guests, Twilight.
Caddies: No. **Golf carts:** Included in Green Fee.
Discount golf packages: Yes. **Season:** Year-round. **High:** Year-round.
On-site lodging: No. **Rental clubs:** Yes.
Walking policy: Mandatory cart. **Range:** Yes (grass).
To obtain tee times: Call six days in advance with credit card beginning at 6:30 a.m. Noncancellable reservations may be made 14 days in advance.

★★★★ THE LINKS COURSE

Holes: 18. **Par:** 71/71.
Yards: 6,856/5,800. **Course rating:** 73.6/73.0. **Slope:** 136/125.
Opened: 1993.
Ranked 14th in California by Golf Digest.
Subscriber comments: Too cool . . . Clearly one of the best courses in California . . . Can't find a better view . . . The best in Los Angeles with ocean views, only one thing to complain about, too expensive . . . Bad location for driving range . . . As good as the ocean . . . Beautiful views of ocean from every hole . . . Don't be camera-shy . . . Very tricky, local knowledge helps . . . Resort course with gorgeous views, great greens, helpful computerized cart yardage indicators . . . Wonderful views, excellent condition . . . Wonderful Fazio test, great shape, prepare to five-putt! . . . Great course, but not on par with Pebble . . . Beautiful setting high above Newport Beach, sweeping vistas of ocean beaches . . . It doesn't get much better, fairways like carpets . . . You pay a hefty fee but I feel it is worth it . . . Still new, trees still growing . . . The Pebble Beach of southern California.

★★★★ THE OCEAN COURSE

Holes: 18. **Par:** 70/70.
Yards: 6,634/5,409. **Course rating:** 72.8/72.5. **Slope:** 138/124.
Opened: 1991.
Selected as Best New Resort Course of 1992 by Golf Digest. Ranked 19th in California by Golf Digest.
Subscriber comments: Next to Pebble, probably most scenic in California . . . Worth a try, stay on the fairways . . . Tom Fazio's finest, canyons and ocean plus elevation changes, spectacular in every way . . . Yuppie heaven . . . Breathtaking view of the Pacific . . . Fazio is numero uno . . . Great ocean location . . . Gorgeous . . . Best golf in southern

California . . . A putting challenge, bring an extra sleeve . . . Both courses are golfing delights . . . Better than links course . . . Prettier and tougher than the Links, too pricey for mortals . . . A great use of the environment . . . Best if played on company expense account.

PGA WEST RESORT

R—56-150 PGA Blvd., La Quinta (619)564-7170.
30 miles southeast of Palm Springs.
Pace of Play rating: N/A. **Credit cards:** MC, V, AMEX, Diners Club, JCB.
Reduced fees: Weekdays, Low season, Resort guests, Twilight.
Caddies: No. **Golf carts:** Included in Green Fee.
Discount golf packages: Yes. **Season:** Year-round. **High:** Jan.-April.
On-site lodging: No. **Rental clubs:** Yes.
Walking policy: Mandatory cart. **Range:** Yes(grass).
To obtain tee times: Call.

★★★★ **JACK NICKLAUS RESORT COURSE**
Holes: 18. **Par:** 72/72.
Yards: 7,126/5,043. **Course rating:** 75.5/69.0. **Slope:** 138/116.
Opened: 1987. **Green fee:** $70/180.
Ranked 35th in America's 75 Best Resort Courses by Golf Digest. Ranked 23rd in California by Golf Digest.

Subscriber comments: Most beautiful and fairest Nicklaus course I've played . . . Tough, fair and immaculate, great test of your game . . . Way to many shots required that the average golfer just can't hit . . . Will frustrate the crooked hitter, challenging . . . More enjoyable than Stadium Course . . . Enjoyed the experience . . . A lot of deep bunkers . . . Can't wait to play again! Each hole very distinctive, tough but fair . . . Jack must have had a great deal on sand! . . . A bit rich in season . . . Very long traps . . . Fantastic layout . . . Ninth hole is a classic, shares a double green with the 18th . . . High handicappers steer clear, no wonder I'm a Palmer fan . . . Spectacular, just great golf . . . Too penal, stick with the Stadium Course . . . Best course in the desert.

★★★★ **TPC STADIUM COURSE**
Holes: 18. **Par:** 72/72.
Yards: 7,261/5,087. **Course rating:** 77.3/70.3. **Slope:** 151/124.
Opened: 1986. **Green fee:** $75/210.
Ranked 16th in America's 75 Best Resort Courses by Golf Digest. Ranked 16th in California by Golf Digest.
Subscriber comments: Tough, tough, tough! . . . Amazing design . . . Fair test of golf, just demanding and very unforgiving . . . Killer! . . . Every golfer should try this torture test at least once . . . Too tricked up, Nicklaus course far prettier . . . Incredible from back tees . . . Large mounds premium on driving into fairway . . . No. 1 in California for shotmaking, stay out of bunkers and water . . . Brutally unforgiving . . . Not for the average "Bear" . . . Don't drink and drive here . . . Incredible experience . . . Dye's greatness shows . . . Bring frogman suit . . . Tough! Its not easy to stop the ball on par-3 17th island green . . . Every hole an adventure . . . Watch out for Alcatraz! . . . Bring your lob wedge . . . A head scratcher! Not for the faint of heart . . . Bunkers are bigger than some beaches! . . . This is one of the greatest golf courses on earth, forget about the crybaby whiners who think this course is too hard.

★★★½ PINE MOUNTAIN LAKE COUNTRY CLUB

SP—19228 Pine Mountain Dr., Groveland (209)962-8620.
Call club for further information.
Subscriber comments: Interesting layout. A hidden gem . . . Mountain course in very good condition has everything you like . . . Fun to play . . . Love it. Hard to get to but worth the trip . . . Excellent mountain course in good shape . . . Breathtaking mountain views . . . Can't wait to play it again . . . Good solid course. Condition and service improving! . . . Best little country club in the Sierras.

CALIFORNIA

★★½ PITTSBURG DELTA VIEW GOLF COURSE
PU—2242 Golf Club Rd., Pittsburg (510)439-4040.
40 miles east of San Francisco. **Holes:** 18. **Par:** 72/72.
Yards: 6,359/5,405. **Course rating:** 70.4/70.1. **Slope:** 124/120.
Opened: 1950. **Pace of Play rating:** 4:30. **Green fee:** $11/18.
Credit cards: MC, V. **Reduced fees:** Twilight, Seniors, Juniors.
Caddies: No. **Golf carts:** $18 for 18 holes.
Discount golf packages: No. **Season:** Year-round.
On-site lodging: No. **Rental clubs:** Yes.
Walking policy: Unrestricted walking. **Range:** Yes (grass).
To obtain tee times: Call pro shop one week in advance.
Subscriber comments: Quiet, remote, rural setting . . . Some good holes
. . . Carnival front nine, good to practice your wind game . . . New greens,
back nine will be very good . . . Tough walk . . . Slow play, condition of
course marginal . . . Great remodeling effort.

★★★ PLUMAS LAKE GOLF AND COUNTRY CLUB
SP—1551 Country Club Avenue, Marysville (916)742-3201.
Holes: 18. **Par:** 71/72.
Yards: 6,437/5,759. **Course rating:** 70.5/70.3. **Slope:** 122/126.
Opened: 1926. **Pace of Play rating:** 4:30. **Green fee:** $15/20.
Credit cards: None. **Reduced fees:** Twilight, Seniors, Juniors.
Caddies: No. **Golf carts:** $18 for 18 holes.
Discount golf packages: No. **Season:** Year-round. **High:** April-Oct.
On-site lodging: No. **Rental clubs:** Yes.
Walking policy: Unrestricted walking. **Range:** Yes (grass).
To obtain tee times: Call seven days in advance:
Subscriber comments: Treelined, narrow, many doglegs, very fast greens
. . . Best course in northern Calif. . . . Out of the way, but in great
condition, fun . . . Good staff, decent course layout for average player . . .
Wonderful greens and lots of trees . . . Top-notch course . . . Well
maintained . . . A good small town layout, good treatment by staff . . .
Average but not too exciting . . . Longer than yardage, good shot values
. . . Plays long but fair, great park-land style course . . . Rural location . . .
Best greens in northern California.

★★★½ PLUMAS PINES COUNTRY CLUB
PU—402 Poplar Valley Rd., Blairsden (916)836-1420.
63 miles of Reno, Nev. **Holes:** 18. **Par:** 72/72.
Yards: 6,504/5,106. **Course rating:** N/A. **Slope:** 127/122.
Opened: N/A. **Pace of Play rating:** N/A. **Green fee:** N/A.
Credit cards: MC, V, AMEX. **Reduced fees:** Weekdays, Low season,
Twilight.
Caddies: No. **Golf carts:** N/A.
Discount golf packages: Yes. **Season:** April-Oct. **High:** June-Sept.
On-site lodging: Yes. **Rental clubs:** No.
Walking policy: N/A. **Range:** Yes (grass).
Subscriber comments: Real sleeper . . . Tough layout for inaccurate
hitters . . . Beautiful mountain course . . . Beautiful golf course along
Feather River, narrow in places . . . Back nine interesting, front nothing
special . . . Shotmaker's course . . . Tight fairways, take lots of balls . . .
Houses too intrusive on otherwise good course . . . Beautiful, well
designed, some great holes . . . Good golf experience but speed up the pace!
. . . Pretty landscape, short course . . . Beautiful resort-type course, for all
golfers . . . Water on 11 holes, skinny and short, lots trees . . . Beautiful,
scenic course, some elevated tees . . . Touristy . . . Often overbooked . . .
Pricey . . . Very scenic.

★★★★ POPPY HILLS GOLF COURSE
PU—3200 Lopez Rd., Pebble Beach (408)625-2154.
60 miles south of San Jose. **Holes:** 18. **Par:** 72/72.
Yards: 6,861/5,473. **Course rating:** 74.8/71.2. **Slope:** 143/131.
Opened: 1986. **Pace of Play rating:** 4:30-5:00. **Green fee:** $45/95.
Credit cards: MC, V. **Reduced fees:** Juniors.
Caddies: No. **Golf carts:** N/A.

GREAT VALUE

Discount golf packages: No. **Season:** Year-round. **High:** May-Aug.
On-site lodging: No. **Rental clubs:** Yes.
Walking policy: Unrestricted walking. **Range:** Yes (grass).
To obtain tee times: Call up to 30 days in advance.
Subscriber comments: A real pleasure. First class . . . As tough as they
come . . . Every tee is a picture postcard . . . Good layout, huge greens,
course of tricky holes . . . Best in every aspect for the price . . . Keeps
kicking my butt . . . Wildlife abounds . . . Great woodsy area, fun to walk
. . . Better than Spyglass and less money . . . A golf adventure, Monterey
Peninsula-style, requires good shot decisions . . . Must be able to steer the
ball, first outing there is to learn the course, easier second round, gorgeous
. . . Excellent track . . . Greens are treacherous if not in proper place,
playing golf with deer . . . Superb conditioning, quite playable . . .
Penalizes bad shots heavily but doesn't reward good shots . . . True test of
golf. Better be able to putt . . . No. 1 on my list to never play again . . .
True test of your skill . . . Poppy is getting easier, and more fun . . . Check
out the deer . . . Maturing nicely. Unfairly criticized . . . Poppy is poppy!
. . . Tough par 4s . . . Great to challenge your game. Must stay straight . . .
A seriously flawed first hole . . . Best overall golf in Monterey area . . . See
how you rate with the big boys . . . The Monterey Cathedral . . . Large
tough, greens . . . Bunkers hidden in middle of fairways . . . A jewel. The
input from the pros playing the Crosby/AT&T has made it easier . . . As
tough as Spyglass . . . Cheaper than Pasatiempo . . . A working man's
Pebble Beach! . . . Very good design, but it takes a few times around to
know where to hit it . . . Constant tinkering has turned this course from
good to great!

★★★½ **RAMS HILL COUNTRY CLUB**
SP—1881 Rams Hill Rd., Borrego Springs (619)767-5124.
70 miles from San Diego. **Holes:** 18. **Par:** 72/72.
Yards: 6,866/5,694. **Course rating:** N/A. **Slope:** 133/119.
Opened: N/A. **Pace of Play rating:** N/A. **Green fee:** N/A.
Credit cards: MC, V, AMEX. **Reduced fees:** Low season, Resort guests,
Twilight.
Caddies: No. **Golf carts:** Included in Green Fee.
Discount golf packages: Yes. **Season:** Nov.-Sept. **High:** Nov.-April.
On-site lodging: Yes. **Rental clubs:** No.
Walking policy: N/A. **Range:** Yes (grass).
Subscriber comments: Great layout, deserves more acclaim . . . A great
course, but it's in the middle of nowhere . . . Very tough but fair test of golf
with excellent greens . . . A really surprising golfing challenge . . . Desert
course, good condition, can be windy, great scenery . . . Beautiful desert
course, wonderful experience . . . Serene setting, excellent condition . . .
Turn the water on! . . . Fun course, well designed . . . A really surprising
golfing challenge.

RANCHO BERNARDO INN AND COUNTRY CLUB
★★★ **WEST COURSE**
R—17550 Bernardo Oaks Dr., San Diego (619)675-8470, (800)662-6439.
Holes: 18. **Par:** 72/72.
Yards: 6,458/5,448. **Course rating:** 70.6/71.2. **Slope:** 122/119.
Opened: 1962. **Pace of Play rating:** 4:45. **Green fee:** $58/75.
Credit cards: All major. **Reduced fees:** Weekdays, Resort guests,
Twilight, Juniors.
Caddies: No. **Golf carts:** Included in Green Fee.
Discount golf packages: Yes. **Season:** Year-round. **High:** Dec-May.
On-site lodging: Yes. **Rental clubs:** Yes.
Walking policy: Walking at certain times. **Range:** Yes (grass).
To obtain tee times: Hotel guest call anytime; outside guest, seven days in
advance.
Subscriber comments: A good old course, well suited to terrain,
comfortable to play . . . Too many concrete-lined ditches across fairway
. . . Fairways in fair condition . . . Beautiful resort course, great pro shop
and service . . . Combines beauty, scenery, tough golf, great layout . . .

This course is very challenging and in first-class shape . . . Nothing special, average course . . . Nice course; long, challenging holes . . . Best French restaurant in southern California.

RANCHO CANADA GOLF CLUB
PU—4860 Carmel Valley Rd., Carmel (408)624-0111.
8 miles south of Monterey.
Credit cards: MC, V, AMEX, Diners Club. **Reduced fees:** Twilight.
Caddies: No. **Golf carts:** $13 for 18 holes.
Discount golf packages: Yes. **Season:** Year-round. **High:** April-Oct.
On-site lodging: No. **Rental clubs:** Yes.
Walking policy: Unrestricted walking. **Range:** Yes (grass).
To obtain tee times: For out of town quests, call pro shop any time.
★★★ **EAST COURSE**
Holes: 18. **Par:** 71/72.
Yards: 6,113/5,279. **Course rating:** 70.1/69.5. **Slope:** 124/118.
Opened: 1971. **Pace of Play rating:** 4:00. **Green fee:** $45.
Subscriber comments: Need all shots and clubs you've got . . . A tough course. Windy and fair. Lots of challenging holes . . . Trying to return it to its former glory, still too early to tell . . . Lots of elevation change. Some great holes . . . Need local knowledge! . . . Wide fairways, fairways and greens getting better . . . Great traditional design . . . Best finishing hole in southern California.

★★★ **WEST COURSE**
Holes: 18. **Par:** 72/73.
Yards: 6,338/5,574. **Course rating:** 71.1/71.6. **Slope:** 126/121.
Opened: 1970. **Pace of Play rating:** 4:00. **Green fee:** $65.
Subscriber comments: Great Carmel course zigs over Carmel River, great fishing spots . . . Beautiful, varied, challenging . . . Short, narrow, trees . . . Has some very interesting holes, always well maintained . . . A hidden jewel . . . Nice setting, but some holes seem a trifle unfair . . . East is easier, West is a better course . . . The West is best but the East is almost as good . . . Well kept facility, easier of two, fun to play . . . Short, pretty course, not very interesting . . . A few greens need hard work . . . Good track for the average player. Not too challenging, except for a few holes on the back nine . . . Not Pebble, but a cut above average, good condition.

★★ RANCHO MARIA GOLF CLUB
PU—1950 Casmalia Rd., Santa Maria (805)937-2019.
3 miles southwest of Santa Maria. **Holes:** 18. **Par:** 72/73.
Yards: 6,390/5,504. **Course rating:** 70.2/71.3. **Slope:** 119/123.
Opened: 1965. **Pace of Play rating:** 3:30-4:00. **Green fee:** $15/25.
Credit cards: MC, V. **Reduced fees:** Weekdays, Twilight, Seniors, Juniors.
Caddies: No. **Golf carts:** $9 for 18 holes.
Discount golf packages: No. **Season:** Year-round. **High:** Year-round.
On-site lodging: No. **Rental clubs:** Yes.
Walking policy: Unrestricted walking. **Range:** Yes (grass).
To obtain tee times: Two days in advance for weekdays; seven days in advance for weekends and holidays.
Subscriber comments: A very nice country municipal. Pleasant atmosphere . . . Not long, but accuracy a must . . . Rural setting . . . Fairly challenging, hilly layout, very windy in afternoons . . . Easy course, usually in good condition . . . Beginners would enjoy this course . . . Hilly, fun course with beautiful views . . . Nice, small public course.

RANCHO MURIETA COUNTRY CLUB
SP—7000 Alameda Dr., Rancho Murieta (916)354-3440.
15 miles east of Sacramento.
Green fee: $50/75.
Credit cards: MC, V, AMEX. **Reduced fees:** Low season, Resort guests, Juniors.
Caddies: No. **Golf carts:** Included in Green Fee.

Discount golf packages: No. **Season:** Year-round. **High:** April–Oct.
On-site lodging: Yes. **Rental clubs:** Yes.
Walking policy: Mandatory cart. **Range:** Yes (grass).
To obtain tee times: Call three days in advance.

★★★½ NORTH COURSE

Holes: 18. **Par:** 72/72.
Yards: 6,839/5,608. **Course rating:** 72.8/71.6. **Slope:** 131/136.
Opened: 1971. **Pace of Play rating:** 4:15.
Subscriber comments: One of the hardest to score on . . . Need a variety
of shots . . . You need to play this more than once to appreciate it . . . It
will beat you to death . . . Good par 4s . . . Single digit handicappers are the
happiest here, tough track . . . Can be very physically tiring . . . Think
first, then shoot . . . Good layout, green design too severe . . . Stay below
the hole . . . Very difficult greens . . . Extremely tight fairways: even when
you hit the fairway it may not be level . . . Always beats me up, but I keep
coming back.

★★★½ SOUTH COURSE

Holes: 18. **Par:** 72/72.
Yards: 6,886/5,527. **Course rating:** 72.6/71.6. **Slope:** 127/122.
Opened: 1971. **Pace of Play rating:** 4:15.
Subscriber comments: Course designed for greater shot options than
North . . . Good course, some holes need more character . . . Nos. 9, 10
and 11 may be nicest in northern California . . . Not as nice as North . . . A
little more forgiving than the North Course . . . Tees make it playable for
all levels, O.B. too close three holes . . . Hilly layout gives poor lies,
trouble is easy to get into . . . Great golf course, need all shots, excellent
greens.

★★★½ RANCHO PARK GOLF COURSE

PU—10460 West Pico Blvd., Los Angeles (310)839-4374.
Holes: 18. **Par:** 71/71.
Yards: 6,585/5,928. **Course rating:** N/A. **Slope:** 124/122.
Call club for further information.
Subscriber comments: A great old course . . . Best public course in use
. . . Best public course in Los Angeles, private-type course, a must . . . Well
maintained, hard to get on . . . Plays slow, but always in very good
condition for such a crowded course . . . Amazing shape for amount of play
. . . Seen better days . . . Terrific course, better be straight and have some
length, too . . . Use of alternate greens too frequent . . . Great muny,
conditions inconsistent . . . Absolutely impossible to get on . . . Best public
course in area . . . Fine course with much tradition . . . Played my first
round here in 1958 and we've both slipped.

RANCHO SAN DIEGO GOLF CLUB

PU—3121 Willow Glen Dr., El Cajon (619)442-9891.
20 miles from San Diego.
Call club for further information.

★★½ IVANHOE COURSE

Holes: 18. **Par:** 72/72.
Yards: 7,011/5,624. **Course rating:** N/A. **Slope:** 129/116.
Subscriber comments: Challenging, always has best greens around, great
variety . . . Facilities need updating . . . Older course, long, wide open,
very puttable . . . Easy going course, no gimmicks, fun for all levels of
golfers . . . Fair test of golf, enjoyable to play . . . Boring . . . Very
ordinary . . . Generally in good condition for a public course . . . Best
greens in San Diego Country.

★½ MONTE VISTA COURSE

Holes: 18. **Par:** 71/71.
Yards: 6,110/5,407. **Course rating:** N/A. **Slope:** 108/109.
Subscriber comments: New holes designed to toughen up course . . .
Short, but fairly tight . . . Short course, not too demanding, flat, good for
beginners . . . First hole is a backbreaker . . . Good course, needs more
maintenance. Heavy play . . . New layout messed up a good course . . .
Totally ruined this course with two 630-yard holes . . . Bad layout . . .

Good for walking, prone to flooding . . . Good layout. Good greens . . . Not as nice as sister Ivanhoe . . . Not impressed with the new holes. Greens are great.

★½ RANCHO SAN JOAQUIN GOLF CLUB
PU—1 Sandburg Way, Irvine (714)786-5522.
Call club for further information.
Subscriber comments: Constant improvements . . . Gets windy, otherwise not too tough . . . Good condition for amount of play . . . They are making improvements . . . Boring . . . The greens are too hilly . . . Very slow play, fair condition, average challenge, typical public course . . . Some great memorable holes amid many average holes . . . Course seems to always be under repair . . . Recent changes frame course nicely.

★★★ RANCHO SOLANO GOLF COURSE
PU—3250 Rancho Solano Parkway, Fairfield (707)429-4653.
30 miles west of Sacramento. **Holes:** 18. **Par:** 72/72.
Yards: 6,705/5,206. **Course rating:** 72.6/69.6. **Slope:** 127/117.
Opened: 1991. **Pace of Play rating:** 4:30. **Green fee:** $22/31.
Credit cards: MC, V, AMEX. **Reduced fees:** Weekdays, Twilight, Seniors, Juniors.
Caddies: No. **Golf carts:** N/A.
Discount golf packages: Yes. **Season:** Year-round. **High:** June-Sept.
On-site lodging: No. **Rental clubs:** Yes.
Walking policy: Unrestricted walking. **Range:** Yes (grass).
To obtain tee times: Call one week in advance.
Subscriber comments: Gigantic greens . . . Forgiving fairways, big, tough greens which slow play down . . . A real wind tunnel, need lead shoes . . . Need to be a good putter . . . Very windy, scruffy layout . . . Rolling hills . . . Largest greens you'll ever see . . . Hilly, open, long . . . Huge greens (some could be subdivided for housing) that have sneaky breaks . . . Interesting course but condition deteriorating . . . Always in great shape, challenging layout, fun to play . . . New course, will develop as it matures . . . Four-putt greens everywhere . . . Scary putting . . . Cheers again, city of Fairfield . . . Fairfield should be proud of its two great courses.

★★★ RECREATION PARK GOLF COURSE
PU—5001 Deukmejian Dr., Long Beach (310)494-5000.
15 miles south of Los Angeles. **Holes:** 18. **Par:** 72/74.
Yards: 6,317/5,793. **Course rating:** 69.0/72.6. **Slope:** 112/120.
Opened: 1924. **Pace of Play rating:** 4:30. **Green fee:** $17/21.
Credit cards: MC, V. **Reduced fees:** Weekdays, Twilight, Seniors, Juniors.
Caddies: No. **Golf carts:** $10 for 18 holes.
Discount golf packages: No. **Season:** Year-round.
On-site lodging: No. **Rental clubs:** Yes.
Walking policy: Unrestricted walking. **Range:** Yes.
To obtain tee times: Must have reservation card ($10.00 a year) to obtain tee times up to six days in advance. Without card call one day in advance after 12:30 p.m.
Subscriber comments: A fine older course, very well groomed . . . Very nice old public course . . . Very mature course, excellent test . . . Riviera Country Club in Long Beach, beautiful old-style course . . . Just plain fun! . . . Very old, short but beautiful. Each hole memorable . . . Old country club turned muny . . . Very, very, very crowded, mostly fivesomes . . . Superb public course . . . Good condition always, plays slow, very busy . . . Way overrated, overcrowded for no apparent reason . . . One of the best public courses in the Los Angeles area.

★★★★ REDHAWK GOLF CLUB
SP—45100 Redhawk Parkway, Temecula (909)695-1424, (800)451-4295.
30 miles south of Riverside. **Holes:** 18. **Par:** 72/72.
Yards: 7,139/5,510. **Course rating:** 75.7/72.0. **Slope:** 149/124.

Opened: 1991. **Pace of Play rating:** 4:30. **Green fee:** $46/70.
Credit cards: MC, V, AMEX. **Reduced fees:** Twilight, Juniors.
Caddies: No. **Golf carts:** Included in Green Fee.
Discount golf packages: No. **Season:** Year-round.
On-site lodging: No. **Rental clubs:** Yes.
Walking policy: Mandatory cart. **Range:** Yes (grass).
To obtain tee times: Available five days in advance.
Subscriber comments: One of the most beautifully landscaped courses

. . . Every blade of grass in place . . . New, excellent turf and maintenance
. . . Would not want to play everyday, but fun to play . . . A real test . . .
Incredible! . . . Tremendous track. Great golf experience . . . Strong course
with dramatic holes . . . Too many tricks, it cackles at you for no good
reason . . . Best putting green ever . . . Great holes . . . Great in every area
. . . Worth the trip . . . Great water holes . . . Play from tees of your
ability, this course is beautiful but mean . . . Practice green intimidating,
out of the way, but worth it . . . More like a resort course . . . Prettiest
course in southern California . . . Will be a bear when it grows up . . .
Immaculate, super-fast greens . . . Needs restaurant . . . Worth playing
several times . . . Very challenging, should be a PGA Tour course . . . Big
reputation, some tricked up holes, need lots of local knowledge . . . Very
nice layout, great shape, learn to putt first . . . Best finishing hole . . . Some
great picture holes . . . No. 12 hole the prettiest . . . Very fair, what you see
is what you get . . . Best course I'd never heard of.

★★★½ RESORT AT SQUAW CREEK
R—400 Squaw Creek Rd., Olympic Valley (916)583-6300, (800)327-3353.
45 miles east of Reno, Nevada. **Holes:** 18. **Par:** 71/71.
Yards: 6,931/5,097. **Course rating:** 72.9/68.9. **Slope:** 140/127.
Opened: 1992. **Pace of Play rating:** 4:00-4:30. **Green fee:** $110/120.
Credit cards: MC, V, AMEX. **Reduced fees:** Weekdays, Low season,
Twilight.
Caddies: No. **Golf carts:** Included in Green Fee.
Discount golf packages: Yes. **Season:** May-Oct. **High:** July-Aug.
On-site lodging: Yes. **Rental clubs:** Yes.
Walking policy: Walking at certain times. **Range:** Yes.
To obtain tee times: Call pro shop and give credit card number to hold a
tee time.
Subscriber comments: Challenging design to maintain wetlands . . .
Great links-style golf course, very well maintained . . . Bring at least a
dozen balls, not enjoyable . . . Terrific scenery . . . Target golf; resort golf
it is not . . . A real change . . . Expensive frustration for occasional
vacationing golfers . . . Very scenic and unique layout, difficult but fun . . .
Outstanding, simply outstanding, accuracy a key . . . Beautiful setting,
must keep the ball in play . . . A gimmick course . . . Stunning course, very
challenging . . . Beautiful vistas, some holes almost unfair, you better hit it
straight.

RIDGEMARK GOLF AND COUNTRY CLUB
R—3800 Airline Highway, Hollister (408)637-1010, (800)637-8151.
40 miles southeast of San Jose.
Opened: 1972. **Pace of Play rating:** 4:10. **Green fee:** $40/55.
Credit cards: All major. **Reduced fees:** Twilight.
Caddies: No. **Golf carts:** Included in Green Fee.
Discount golf packages: Yes. **Season:** Year-round. **High:** Year-round.
On-site lodging: Yes. **Rental clubs:** Yes.
Walking policy: Mandatory cart. **Range:** Yes (grass).
To obtain tee times: Call seven days in advance.
★★★ DIABLO COURSE
Holes: 18. **Par:** 72/72.
Yards: 6,603/5,475. **Course rating:** 71.9/72.0. **Slope:** 123/123.
Subscriber comments: Fun layout for most levels, condition almost
always good . . . Fun course, many challenging holes requiring shot
placement . . . Kept challenging for average player . . . OK course, not
great . . . Interesting design, well maintained . . . Fairways too narrow
fairways . . . Shot placement is the key.

★★½ GABILAN COURSE
Holes: 36. **Par:** 72/72.
Yards: 6,781/5,683. **Course rating:** 72.0/72.7. **Slope:** 124/124.
Subscriber comments: Nice layout, a lot of variance in holes . . . Too many houses, fairways widely dispersed . . . Long, hilly . . . Need a cart, 1/4 mile from green to next tee . . . Split course a big mistake . . . Great greens and design . . . Doesn't compare to Diablo . . . Fun track, some great holes.

★★★★ RIO BRAVO COUNTRY CLUB
R—15200 Casa Club Dr., Bakersfield (805)871-4653.
Call club for further information.
Subscriber comments: Superior design, excellent course, memorable . . . Great greens, long and hot . . . Challenging, good layout, must get off the tee . . . Tough . . . Strong course, very enjoyable . . . Good challenge . . . Very well maintained, big tough greens, long, hilly course . . . Must be a solid striker of the ball, good putter on fast greens . . . Very long, no shade, tough.

★★★ RIO HONDO GOLF CLUB
PU—10627 Old River School Rd., Downey (310)927-2329.
15 miles east of Los Angeles. **Holes:** 18. **Par:** 71/71.
Yards: 6,344/5,080. **Course rating:** 70.2/69.4. **Slope:** 119/117.

Opened: 1921. **Pace of Play rating:** N/A. **Green fee:** $25/35.
Credit cards: MC, V. **Reduced fees:** Twilight, Seniors, Juniors.
Caddies: No. **Golf carts:** N/A.
Discount golf packages: No. **Season:** Year-round. **High:** Year-round.
On-site lodging: No. **Rental clubs:** Yes.
Walking policy: Unrestricted walking. **Range:** Yes.
To obtain tee times: Call seven days in advance at 6 a.m.
Subscriber comments: A newly redesigned course . . . Most courses in the area not up to these standards . . . Course closed for a year and remodeled, outstanding . . . Newly refurbished fairways and greens. Fun layout . . . Flat, fun course . . . Nice layout good for high handicappers, a little crowded . . . Greens in poor shape . . . Remake of boring flat course is a boring bumpy course . . . Common cart paths between opposing fairways are an accident in waiting . . . Will be great publinks . . . A heck of a course.

★★★ RIVER COURSE AT THE ALISAL
PU—150 Alisal Rd., Solvang (805)688-6042.
35 miles northwest of Santa Barbara. **Holes:** 18. **Par:** 72/72.
Yards: 6,830/5,815. **Course rating:** 73.1/73.4. **Slope:** 126/127.
Opened: 1992. **Pace of Play rating:** 4:15. **Green fee:** $35/45.
Credit cards: MC, V, AMEX. **Reduced fees:** Weekdays, Resort guests, Seniors, Juniors.
Caddies: No. **Golf carts:** $11 for 18 holes.
Discount golf packages: Yes. **Season:** Year-round. **High:** Jan-March, May, Oct.
On-site lodging: No. **Rental clubs:** Yes.
Walking policy: Unrestricted walking. **Range:** Yes (grass).
To obtain tee times: Call or come in seven days in advance.
Subscriber comments: Nice new course, very open . . . Good condition, but pretty blah course . . . Well conditioned, great place to play all day . . . New and immature course, not very challenging . . . Fine young course, good character, great scenery of Solvang . . . Windy, flat, undistinguished . . . Will improve with mature trees . . . Flat, fun, relaxed play . . . Tough but fair. Good greens . . . Staff at River Course is sincere . . . Outstanding in all parts . . . Too many fairways side by side, learn how to say "fore" . . . Good restaurant . . . What a pleasant surprise from back tees.

★★ RIVER RIDGE GOLF CLUB
PU—2401 W. Vineyard Ave., Oxnard (805)983-4653.
Call club for further information.
Subscriber comments: Forgiving course with some nice challenging holes

. . . Rebuilding (in progress) will help . . . Five shots over water . . . Good greens, hard fairways, occasionally smelly from dump . . . Very challenging when the wind kicks up, which is often . . . A couple of strange holes . . . Long course to walk, especially between tees and greens . . . Going to redo front nine, why stop? . . . Built on top of old landfill, we call it "Rubbish Ridge" . . . Great layout, consistent greens . . . Only problem is smell from mushroom processing plant . . . Back nine tough with lots of water and an island green . . . Good staff, good conditions.

★½ RIVER VIEW GOLF COURSE
PU—1800 W. 22nd St., Santa Ana (714)543-1115.
2 miles south of Santa Ana. **Holes:** 18. **Par:** 71/71.
Yards: 6,450/6,100. **Course rating:** 69.0/66.1. **Slope:** 106/103.
Opened: 1964. **Pace of Play rating:** 4:30. **Green fee:** $10/16.
Credit cards: MC, V. **Reduced fees:** Weekdays, Low season, Resort guests, Twilight, Seniors, Juniors.
Caddies: No. **Golf carts:** $18 for 18 holes.
Discount golf packages: Yes. **Season:** Year-round. **High:** March-Dec.
On-site lodging: No. **Rental clubs:** Yes.
Walking policy: Unrestricted walking. **Range:** Yes (grass).
To obtain tee times: Call within 10 days of desired time.
Subscriber comments: Spend the $ on practice balls . . . Mature layout, needs TLC, could be nice . . . Sand pit . . . Not bad when it's not flooded . . . Short tight, well groomed . . . Needs care and maintenance . . . Average course.

★★ RIVERSIDE GOLF CLUB
PU—9770 Monterey Rd., Coyote (408)463-0622.
8 miles south of San Jose. **Holes:** 18. **Par:** 72/73.
Yards: 6,881/5,942. **Course rating:** 72.2/72.5. **Slope:** 127/118.
Opened: 1957. **Pace of Play rating:** 4:30-5:00. **Green fee:** $23/34.
Credit cards: None. **Reduced fees:** Weekdays, Low season, Twilight, Seniors, Juniors.
Caddies: No. **Golf carts:** N/A.
Discount golf packages: Yes. **Season:** Year-round.
On-site lodging: No. **Rental clubs:** Yes.
Walking policy: Unrestricted walking. **Range:** Yes (grass).
To obtain tee times: Call one week in advance.
Subscriber comments: Fine public course, old-style greens . . . Very long, a test of the hitter . . . Sameness of each hole makes for dull golf . . . Poor man's country club . . . Nice course to play, good condition . . . Hard greens, fun to play for anyone . . . Course condition is poor at times. Needs work . . . Windy late in day . . . Need to improve fairways and rough . . . Not in great shape but wide open for big hitters . . . Long and flat, conditions improving.

★★ RIVERSIDE OF FRESNO GOLF CLUB
PU—7672 N. Josephine, Fresno (209)275-5900.
Holes: 18. **Par:** 72/75.
Yards: 6,621/6,008. **Course rating:** 71.2/73.9. **Slope:** 122/125.
Opened: 1939. **Pace of Play rating:** 4:15. **Green fee:** $8/17.
Credit cards: MC, V. **Reduced fees:** Twilight, Seniors, Juniors.
Caddies: No. **Golf carts:** $9 for 18 holes.
Discount golf packages: No. **Season:** Year-round. **High:** April-Oct.
On-site lodging: No. **Rental clubs:** Yes.
Walking policy: Unrestricted walking. **Range:** Yes (grass).
To obtain tee times: Call seven days in advance starting at 6:00 a.m.
Subscriber comments: Traditional simple layout. Not a wimpy muny . . . Short, tight public course . . . Very good playing course with nice layout . . . Tight course for beginners . . . Two new greens . . . Improvements noticeable . . . Most improved public course in California . . . Interesting track . . . Mix length with making accurate shots. Finally got their greens in great putting shape . . . Could be an outstanding course.

★★★½ THE SCGA MEMBERS' CLUB AT RANCHO CALIFORNIA

PU—38275 Murrieta Hot Springs Rd., Murrieta (909)677-7446, (800)752-9724.

45 miles north of San Diego. **Holes:** 18. **Par:** 72/72.
Yards: 7,059/5,355. **Course rating:** 73.9/70.5. **Slope:** 132/116.
Opened: 1972. **Pace of Play rating:** N/A. **Green fee:** $45/55.
Credit cards: MC, V. **Reduced fees:** Weekdays, Twilight, Juniors.
Caddies: No. **Golf carts:** Included in Green Fee.
Discount golf packages: No. **Season:** Year-round. **High:** Jan-May.
On-site lodging: No. **Rental clubs:** Yes.
Walking policy: Unrestricted walking. **Range:** Yes (grass).
To obtain tee times: Members call 10 days in advance, nonmembers seven days.
Subscriber comments: Rustic, very physical golf links, you could be in Scotland . . . Great setting . . . Who needs Pebble Beach? . . . Do not tell anybody . . . No. 8 is a beautiful golf hole, No. 9 most difficult . . . Very playable, great design. Hard to get to but lots of fun . . . Immaculate condition . . . Very challenging oceanside layout, very windy . . . Beautiful course, too windy . . . Isolated.

★ SALINAS FAIRWAYS GOLF COURSE

PU—45 Skyway Blvd, Salinas (408)758-7300.
Call club for further information.
Subscriber comments: Overplayed, tired course . . . Poor condition, fair layout . . . Very affordable . . . Unkempt paths and fairways. Bare spots and crabgrass . . . Nice track, complete golf experience . . . Not well kept . . . Gets a tremendous amount of play and is rather sparse in some places . . . Greens too long and too soft . . . Only if you want to get some exercise.

★★ SAN BERNARDINO GOLF CLUB

PU—1494 South Waterman, San Bernardino (909)885-2414.
2 miles south of San Bernardino. **Holes:** 18. **Par:** 70/73.
Yards: 5,782/5,226. **Course rating:** 67.4/70.0. **Slope:** 112/112.
Opened: 1967. **Pace of Play rating:** 4:00. **Green fee:** $7/20.
Credit cards: MC, V. **Reduced fees:** Weekdays, Twilight, Seniors, Juniors.
Caddies: No. **Golf carts:** $9 for 18 holes.
Discount golf packages: No. **Season:** Year-round. **High:** April-May/Sept.-Oct.
On-site lodging: No. **Rental clubs:** Yes.
Walking policy: Unrestricted walking. **Range:** Yes.
To obtain tee times: Call up to one week in advance.
Subscriber comments: Wide-open course with forced water carries, slow greens . . . Short but challenging . . . Fun to play, requires course management . . . Better than most public courses, always in good shape . . . Dangerous with parallel fairways and mature hackers . . . Well maintained, lots of lay-up shots . . . Water forces you to use many clubs, good test . . . Short and uninteresting . . . Fairways acceptable, greens good.

★★ SAN CLEMENTE MUNICIPAL GOLF CLUB

PU—150 E. Magdalena, San Clemente (714)492-1997.
60 miles north of San Diego. **Holes:** 18. **Par:** 72/73.
Yards: 6,447/5,722. **Course rating:** 70.2/72.4. **Slope:** 118/117.
Opened: 1929. **Pace of Play rating:** 4:00-5:00. **Green fee:** $17/24.
Credit cards: None. **Reduced fees:** Weekdays, Twilight, Seniors, Juniors.
Caddies: No. **Golf carts:** $18 for 18 holes.
Discount golf packages: No. **Season:** Year-round. **High:** June-Aug.
On-site lodging: No. **Rental clubs:** Yes.
Walking policy: Unrestricted walking. **Range:** Yes.
To obtain tee times: Call seven days in advance. Three open times per hour for walk-ons.

Subscriber comments: A pleasant municipal . . . Best value in the West if they only had greens . . . Good muny, fun to play, trick greens, lots of play . . . Old city course, great layout and condition . . . Not challenging or exciting . . . Watch for "break-to-ocean" putts on the greens . . . Wide fairways makes for a high handicapper's delight . . . Great views of ocean . . . Toughest last four holes in southern California.

★★½ SAN DIMAS CANYON GOLF CLUB

PU—2100 Terrebonne Ave., San Dimas (909)599-2313.
25 miles east of Los Angeles. **Holes:** 18. **Par:** 72/74.
Yards: 6,314/5,571. **Course rating:** 70.2/73.9. **Slope:** 118/123.
Opened: N/A. **Pace of Play rating:** N/A. **Green fee:** $16/34.
Credit cards: MC, V. **Reduced fees:** Weekdays, Twilight, Seniors, Juniors.
Caddies: No. **Golf carts:** N/A.
Discount golf packages: Yes. **Season:** Year-round. **High:** April-Sept.
On-site lodging: No. **Rental clubs:** Yes.
Walking policy: Unrestricted walking. **Range:** Yes.
To obtain tee times: Call seven days in advance starting at 5:30 a.m.
Subscriber comments: Leisurely walk in the country . . . Not too shabby . . . Good golf, too much play, too slow . . . Nice little track, lots of character for a muny . . . Keep it straight to score . . . Nice layout, stunning foothill views . . . Hills, valleys, water . . . Lots of character, great shape . . . Great for any golfer, friendly staff . . . Not difficult but interesting . . . Beautiful mountain views, wild deer roam course in the afternoon.

★★★ SAN GERONIMO GOLF CLUB

SP—5800 Sir Francis Drake Blvd., San Geronimo (415)488-4030.
20 miles northwest of San Francisco. **Holes:** 18. **Par:** 72/72.
Yards: 6,801/5,140. **Course rating:** 73.3/69.9. **Slope:** 130/125.
Opened: 1963. **Pace of Play rating:** 4:30. **Green fee:** $30/55.
Credit cards: MC, V. **Reduced fees:** Weekdays, Twilight, Seniors, Juniors.
Caddies: No. **Golf carts:** N/A.
Discount golf packages: No. **Season:** Year-round. **High:** March-Oct.
On-site lodging: No. **Rental clubs:** Yes.
Walking policy: Unrestricted walking. **Range:** No.
To obtain tee times: Call one week in advance.
Subscriber comments: Great variety in layout. Killer-fast greens . . . Most improved course over past two years . . . A lot of irrigation work done and it shows. Big improvement . . . Never tire of golf here . . . Great shape for a public course . . . Front nine is very straightforward, the back nine offers many challenges . . . Four, five very fun holes, others fairly routine . . . Challenging layout, plays long, tricky greens . . . Nothing memorable . . . Super greens, fairways are only fair . . . True challenge, toughest greens in northern California.

★★ SAN JOSE MUNICIPAL GOLF COURSE

PU—1560 Oakland Rd., San Jose (408)441-4653.
Holes: 18. **Par:** 72/72.
Yards: 6,602/5,594. **Course rating:** 70.1/69.7. **Slope:** 108/112.
Opened: N/A. **Pace of Play rating:** N/A. **Green fee:** $24/32.
Credit cards: None. **Reduced fees:** Weekdays, Twilight, Seniors, Juniors.
Caddies: No. **Golf carts:** N/A.
Discount golf packages: No. **Season:** Year-round.
On-site lodging: No. **Rental clubs:** Yes.
Walking policy: Unrestricted walking. **Range:** Yes.
To obtain tee times: Call or come in one week in advance for weekdays. Call Tuesday before 7 a.m. for weekend, alternating one reservation by phone and one in person.
Subscriber comments: Flat, very few challenges but in good condition . . . Nice for muny, crowded . . . Flat and not much trouble . . . Suited for average player . . . OK in a pinch . . . No penalty for missed drives . . .

Easy course, always surprised at good condition, considering extensive play . . . Flat, flat, flat, flat, etc. . . . Vanilla layout, good greens . . . Best muny in South Bay.

★½ SAN JUAN HILLS COUNTRY CLUB

PU—32120 San Juan Creek Rd., San Juan Capistrano (714)493-1167.
60 miles north of San Diego. **Holes:** 18. **Par:** 71/71.
Yards: 6,295/5,402. **Course rating:** 69.5/71.4. **Slope:** 116/122.
Opened: 1966. **Pace of Play rating:** N/A. **Green fee:** $20/30.
Credit cards: MC, V. **Reduced fees:** Weekdays, Twilight.
Caddies: No. **Golf carts:** $10 for 18 holes.
Discount golf packages: No. **Season:** Year-round. **High:** May-Sept.
On-site lodging: No. **Rental clubs:** Yes.
Walking policy: Walking at certain times. **Range:** No.
To obtain tee times: Call up to 10 days in advance.
Subscriber comments: Needs a lot of work on fairways . . . Lots of hardpan if it's dry . . . Fun layout, new holes add more character . . . Up-and-down hills . . . An enjoyable muny . . . Terrible layout, always in deplorable condition . . . New three holes in the back, almost different course . . . Continuing problems with greens . . . Bumpy greens, even new holes are showing wear . . . The new 13th, 14th and 15th are beautiful . . . Good design, poor maintenance, dead grass . . . Fun layout but poorly maintained.

★★½ SAN LUIS REY DOWNS COUNTRY CLUB

R—31474 Golf Club Dr., Bonsall (619)758-9699.
40 miles of San Diego. **Holes:** 18. **Par:** 72/72.
Yards: 6,750/5,493. **Course rating:** 72.6/71.4. **Slope:** 128/124.
Opened: 1963. **Pace of Play rating:** 4:30. **Green fee:** $25/45.
Credit cards: MC, V, AMEX. **Reduced fees:** Twilight, Juniors.
Caddies: No. **Golf carts:** Included in Green Fee.
Discount golf packages: Yes. **Season:** Year-round. **High:** Jan-May.
On-site lodging: Yes. **Rental clubs:** Yes.
Walking policy: Walking at certain times. **Range:** Yes (grass).
To obtain tee times: Call seven days in advance.
Subscriber comments: A challenging deceptive layout, good condition . . . Best greens in southern California . . . Real pleasure, excellent condition, close to private caliber . . . Good course, holes Nos. 8, 9 and 10 very difficult . . . Many improvements in condition this year . . . Due to many large trees, it plays very hard for its length, tee shots difficult . . . Good challenge, trees, placement important . . . Beautiful, peaceful countryside . . . Some holes border on unfair; must be able to curve ball . . . Good windy course in the afternoon.

★½ SAN RAMON ROYAL VISTA GOLF CLUB

SP—9430 Fircrest Lane, San Ramon (510)828-6100.
15 miles south of Walnut Creek. **Holes:** 18. **Par:** 72/73.
Yards: 6,560/5,770. **Course rating:** 70.9/72.7. **Slope:** 115/119.
Opened: 1960. **Pace of Play rating:** N/A. **Green fee:** $21/31.
Credit cards: MC, V. **Reduced fees:** Twilight, Seniors, Juniors.
Caddies: No. **Golf carts:** N/A.
Discount golf packages: No. **Season:** Year-round. **High:** May-Sept.
On-site lodging: No. **Rental clubs:** Yes.
Walking policy: Unrestricted walking. **Range:** Yes.
To obtain tee times: Call seven days in advance.
Subscriber comments: Straight, narrow fairways, short, good for beginners . . . Mediocre . . . Fairways dry, lots of bare ground . . . Staff could be more friendly . . . Not a great muny . . . Nice course kept well, good for everyday . . . Dry and hard, too many trick holes . . . Good layout, each hole difficult . . . Front and back nines different, mixing tight fairways with links style . . . Long par 3s need better landscape maintenance . . . Between homes and narrow, but fun to play.

★★★½ SAN VICENTE GOLF CLUB

SP—24157 San Vincente Rd., Ramona (619)789-3477.
25 miles northeast of San Diego. **Holes:** 18. **Par:** 72/72.
Yards: 6,610/5,543. **Course rating:** 71.5/72.8. **Slope:** 123/128.
Opened: 1972. **Pace of Play rating:** 4:00-4:30. **Green fee:** $41/51.
Credit cards: MC, V, AMEX. **Reduced fees:** Twilight.
Caddies: No. **Golf carts:** Included in Green Fee.
Discount golf packages: Yes. **Season:** Year-round.
On-site lodging: Yes. **Rental clubs:** No.
Walking policy: Walking at certain times. **Range:** Yes (grass).
To obtain tee times: Call up to five days in advance.
Subscriber comments: Delightful surprise in back country, great layout
and atmosphere . . . Fun and fair . . . Makes your game look good . . . Fun
course, must hit it straight, and keep ball in the fairway . . . A classic . . .
Sporty, picturesque, rolling course, fun to play . . . Good greens, poor
fairways . . . Never get tired playing this course, always a challenge . . .
Great little layout. Always in mint condition, the long drive is worth it . . .
Well kept but overbooked.

★★★★ SANDPIPER GOLF COURSE

PU—7925 Hollister Avenue, Goleta (805)968-1541.
100 miles north of Los Angeles. **Holes:** 18. **Par:** 72/73.
Yards: 7,068/5,725. **Course rating:** 74.5/73.3. **Slope:** 134/125.

Opened: 1972. **Pace of Play rating:** 4:00. **Green fee:** $55/75.
Credit cards: MC, V. **Reduced fees:** Weekdays, Juniors.
Caddies: No. **Golf carts:** $22 for 18 holes.
Discount golf packages: No. **Season:** Year-round. **High:** May-Oct.
On-site lodging: No. **Rental clubs:** Yes.
Walking policy: Unrestricted walking. **Range:** Yes (grass).
To obtain tee times: Call one week in advance.
Ranked in First 25 of America's 75 Best Public Golf Courses.
Subscriber comments: Now there's a great Bell design . . . Long and
pretty setting on cliffs above Pacific . . . Southern California's Pebble Beach
. . . Holes right on Pacific make it a must-play . . . Sea-cliff terrain . . .
Beautiful . . . Breathtaking views, strong holes, good, fast greens . . . Poor
man's Pebble Beach . . . What a view! Better weather than Pebble . . . Back
nine worth the price of admission . . . Pebble Beach for the middle class . . .
Best in Santa Barbara area . . . Pebble Beach South . . . Uses nature well
. . . On cliffs looking over the ocean . . . Has own personality . . . Fun
ocean course, don't let front nine lull you . . . Gorgeous setting. Overall
satisfying golf experience . . . Next to the ocean but doesn't feel like it . . .
Nice layout, windy conditions a bear . . . You pay for the views . . .
Prettiest layout south of Pebble Beach . . . Way too windy! . . .
Magnificent setting along Pacific coast . . . Seaside beauty. Not pretentious
. . . Big three-putt greens . . . Great shape. Try it from the tips, good luck.

★★½ SANTA ANITA GOLF COURSE

PU—405 S. Santa Anita Avenue, Arcadia (818)447-7156.
6 miles southeast of Pasadena. **Holes:** 18. **Par:** 71/74.
Yards: 6,368/5,908. **Course rating:** 70.4/73.1. **Slope:** 122/121.
Opened: 1936. **Pace of Play rating:** N/A. **Green fee:** $17/21.
Credit cards: MC, V. **Reduced fees:** Twilight, Seniors, Juniors.
Caddies: No. **Golf carts:** $20 for 18 holes.
Discount golf packages: No. **Season:** Year-round.
On-site lodging: No. **Rental clubs:** Yes.
Walking policy: Walking at certain times. **Range:** Yes (grass).
To obtain tee times: Call.
Subscriber comments: Great layout, but municipal conditions . . . Fun
course, not many flat lies . . . Built in 30s, went to pot in 80s, is being
brought back. Looks flat but is not . . . Mounds in center of well-
maintained fairways, penalize good drivers . . . Better than average muny
. . . Excellent short walking course, greens are a little too firm . . . Wide-
open public course, heavy play . . . Pleasant surprise, sleeper, well
maintained, good challenge . . . Fine design for public course. Greens can

be iffy . . . Generally good course with no complaints except slow play . . .
Best public golf course in Los Angeles area, continues to improve.

★★ SANTA BARBARA GOLF CLUB
PU—3500 McCaw Ave., Santa Barbara (805)687-7087.
90 miles north of Los Angeles. **Holes:** 18. **Par:** 70/72.
Yards: 6,014/5,541. **Course rating:** 67.6/71.9. **Slope:** 113/121.
Opened: 1958. **Pace of Play rating:** 4:00-4:30. **Green fee:** $18/20.
Credit cards: None. **Reduced fees:** Weekdays, Twilight, Seniors, Juniors.
Caddies: No. **Golf carts:** $10 for 18 holes.
Discount golf packages: No. **Season:** Year-round. **High:** May-Sept.
On-site lodging: No. **Rental clubs:** Yes.
Walking policy: Unrestricted walking. **Range:** Yes.
To obtain tee times: Reservations required. Monday for Saturday,
Sunday and Monday, call seven days in advance.
Subscriber comments: Low-priced muny but interesting enough, decent
shape, reachable par 5s . . . Nos. 10, 11, 12, 13, 14 are a great stretch of
holes . . . Good for a muny course but play can be very slow . . . Very
heavy play and condition shows it . . . Lots of uphill holes, challenging for
high handicappers but not discouraging . . . Your usual muny, crowded
and overplayed . . . Course is for all players. In fair shape . . . Lot of ups
and downs . . . No outstanding holes . . . Very busy yet playable, good old
course.

★½ SANTA CLARA GOLF AND TENNIS CLUB
PU—5155 Stars and Stripes Dr., Santa Clara (408)980-9515.
12 miles west of San Jose. **Holes:** 18. **Par:** 72/72.
Yards: 6,822/5,639. **Course rating:** 73.0/71.5. **Slope:** 126/115.
Opened: 1987. **Pace of Play rating:** N/A. **Green fee:** $17/27.
Credit cards: MC, V, AMEX. **Reduced fees:** Weekdays, Resort guests,
Twilight, Seniors, Juniors.
Caddies: No. **Golf carts:** $10 for 18 holes.
Discount golf packages: No. **Season:** Year-round. **High:** April-Sept.
On-site lodging: Yes. **Rental clubs:** Yes.
Walking policy: Unrestricted walking. **Range:** Yes.
To obtain tee times: General public, seven days in advance. Santa Clara
residents and Westin Hotel guests, eight days in advance.
Subscriber comments: Bay winds are tough . . . Tough angles and
hidden pins . . . Nice layout but poorly maintained . . . Great design,
terrible condition . . . Too many blind shots and not well groomed . . .
Windblown, wide open, no memorable holes . . . Located next to a landfill;
in summer it gets quite smelly . . . Long, challenge for mid- to high-
handicapper . . . Could be a good course except some greens and fairways
need work . . . Condition is bad because of rising gas (old dump area) . . .
Great layout, helps to know how to turn ball both ways, greens need help
. . . Best municipal layout in area.

★★★ SANTA TERESA GOLF CLUB
PU—260 Bernal Rd., San Jose (408)225-2650.
Holes: 18. **Par:** 71/73.
Yards: 6,742/6,032. **Course rating:** 71.1/73.5. **Slope:** 121/125.
Opened: 1963. **Pace of Play rating:** N/A. **Green fee:** $24/34.
Credit cards: MC, V, DISC. **Reduced fees:** Weekdays, Twilight,
Seniors, Juniors.
Caddies: No. **Golf carts:** N/A.
Discount golf packages: No. **Season:** Year-round. **High:** April-Sept.
On-site lodging: No. **Rental clubs:** Yes.
Walking policy: Unrestricted walking. **Range:** Yes.
To obtain tee times: Call up to one week in advance.
Subscriber comments: Darn good course . . . Good condition, good
layout, very slow play . . . Course plays well for heavy play . . . Best
public course in Silicon Valley . . . Boring, good condition S-L-O-W . . .
Nice combo of hills and flat holes, well maintained . . . Great course, the
best in the San Jose area . . . The best-conditioned municipal track around,

tough to score. Schizophrenic muny course. Some ridiculously easy, some very difficult holes . . . Good variety of holes . . . Great practice sand, chipping area . . . Course offers good shot variety, especially back nine . . . Best muny in Santa Clara County.

★★★½ THE SEA RANCH GOLF LINKS
PU—49300 Hwy. 1, The Sea Ranch (707)785-2468.
Call club for further information.
Subscriber comments: Another good muny, young, getting lots of play . . . Best new public course in area . . . The back nine is tough . . . Superb greens . . . Trees will define course . . . Front and back nines completely different in shape and character . . . Gotta love it! . . . young, maturing, challenging layout . . . Very short par 3s . . . Front nine is short with an excess of water and O.B., (much of the latter due to environmental preserves); back nine is very good . . . High volume of play . . . Muny course trying to give country club atmosphere. Why? . . . New, needs more grass.

★★ SELMA VALLEY GOLF COURSE
PU—12389 East Rose Avenue, Selma (209)896-2424.
Call club for further information.
Subscriber comments: Short and sweet . . . Short course, fairly tight but easy . . . Good variation of holes . . . Course needs work . . . Short, good course for seniors . . . Very short but demands accuracy, slow greens . . . Only two long holes . . . Short holes, but fun . . . Good condition. Play it all year.

SEPULVEDA GOLF COURSE
PU—16821 Burbank Blvd., Encino (818)986-4560.
15 miles northwest of Los Angeles.
Opened: 1960. **Pace of Play rating:** N/A. **Green fee:** $16/21.
Credit cards: None. **Reduced fees:** Weekdays, Twilight, Seniors, Juniors.
Caddies: No. **Golf carts:** $11 for 18 holes.
Discount golf packages: No. **Season:** Year-round. **High:** April-Sept.
On-site lodging: No. **Rental clubs:** Yes.
Walking policy: Unrestricted walking. **Range:** Yes.
★½ BALBOA COURSE
Holes: 18. **Par:** 70/72.
Yards: 6,359/5,912. **Course rating:** 68.8/70.9. **Slope:** 107/115.
Subscriber comments: Slow and crowded, layout not bad for public course . . . Not a difficult test . . . Acceptable to average golfer . . . Extremely wide fairways, these courses are very flat with no water . . . Good for practice . . . Wide-open municipal course, dull . . . In good shape most of the year . . . Course suited to accurate irons . . . Greens always seem to be in bad shape . . . Adequate golf.
★½ ENCINO COURSE
Holes: 18. **Par:** 72/75.
Yards: 6,863/6,133. **Course rating:** 70.8/73.4. **Slope:** 112/119.
Subscriber comments: Greens large, wide fairways very forgiving . . . Beautiful par 3s . . . Greens vary in quality too much . . . Municipal course, a lot of play . . . Straightforward layout . . . Nice layout but course conditions are still suffering . . . Pretty and well maintained . . . Better course than Balboa . . . A big, wide-open course, all levels can score here . . . Best conditions in many years.

★★½ SEVEN HILLS GOLF COURSE
PU—1537 S. Lyon St., Hemet (909)925-4815.
Call club for further information.
Subscriber comments: Nice course, fair price, slow play . . . Average municipal course . . . Nice little muny, short, snowbirds take over in winter . . . Moves along well . . . Fun, flat course, trees and some water. Not always in best shape in winter . . . Played course in a rainstorm and still enjoyed it.

★★★ SHANDIN HILLS GOLF CLUB

PU—3380 Little Mountain Dr., San Bernardino (909)886-0669.
Holes: 18. **Par:** 72/72.
Yards: 6,517/5,592. **Course rating:** 70.3/71.6. **Slope:** 120/122.
Opened: 1980. **Pace of Play rating:** 4:00. **Green fee:** $8/25.
Credit cards: MC, V. **Reduced fees:** Weekdays, Twilight, Seniors, Juniors.
Caddies: No. **Golf carts:** $10 for 18 holes.
Discount golf packages: Yes. **Season:** Year-round. **High:** Oct.
On-site lodging: No. **Rental clubs:** Yes.
Walking policy: Unrestricted walking. **Range:** Yes (grass).
To obtain tee times: Call seven days in advance.
Subscriber comments: A hidden gem . . . Only negative is Freeway 215 through middle of course . . . This is one course that just gets better with age . . . Many sand traps around greens . . . Great front nine . . . Always run down a little. Never have everything fixed . . . Good public course, nothing exciting about it . . . Some very interesting holes . . . Fun and challenging hillside lies . . . Don't miss it if you're in the San Bernardino Mountains . . . Good shot values . . . Filled in some sand traps, why? . . . Short but interesting, very busy, worth playing.

★½ SHARP PARK GOLF COURSE

PU—Highway 1, Pacifica (415)355-8546.
15 miles southwest of San Francisco. **Holes:** 18. **Par:** 72/74.
Yards: 6,273/6,095. **Course rating:** 70.0/73.0. **Slope:** 115/120.
Opened: 1929. **Pace of Play rating:** N/A. **Green fee:** $21/25.
Credit cards: None. **Reduced fees:** Weekdays, Twilight, Juniors.
Caddies: No. **Golf carts:** $20 for 18 holes.
Discount golf packages: Yes. **Season:** Year-round. **High:** April-Oct.
On-site lodging: No. **Rental clubs:** Yes.
Walking policy: Unrestricted walking. **Range:** No.
To obtain tee times: Call one week in advance for weekdays and four days in advance for weekends.
Subscriber comments: A good course, damaged by storms . . . Course needs overhaul, but it's an Alister Mackenzie . . . Usually wet to swampy fairways and green . . . Wet a lot, close to ocean . . . Pretty, oceanside course . . . Classic course, poor maintenance . . . Beautiful setting, course has seen better days . . . Nice layout with nice ambiance . . . Bad shape most of the year . . . Great course . . . Muddy fairways are unkempt . . . Doing the best they can . . . This could be a great public course with maintenance . . . Slowest greens in area . . . Three devilish par 3s with the wind blowing.

★★½ SHERWOOD FOREST GOLF CLUB

PU—79 N. Frankwood Avenue, Sanger (209)787-2611.
18 miles east of Fresno. **Holes:** 18. **Par:** 71/72.
Yards: 6,205/5,605. **Course rating:** 67.5/70.8. **Slope:** 110/115.
Opened: 1968. **Pace of Play rating:** N/A. **Green fee:** $14/17.
Credit cards: MC, V. **Reduced fees:** Juniors.
Caddies: No. **Golf carts:** N/A.
Discount golf packages: No. **Season:** Year-round. **High:** April-June.
On-site lodging: No. **Rental clubs:** Yes.
Walking policy: Unrestricted walking. **Range:** Yes (grass).
To obtain tee times: Call up to one week in advance.
Subscriber comments: Scenic, lots of oak trees . . . Scenic, river makes it interesting . . . Short course, good for ego . . . Not the greatest, but there are a few holes to keep your interest . . . Beautiful course, some very tight holes . . . Short, fairly tight, in the middle of nowhere . . . Scenic river bottom, tree-lined . . . Out and away at the base of foothills, plays easy . . . Well-maintained course but very slow to play . . . Has great potential . . . Peaceful course.

★★ SHORELINE GOLF LINKS

PU—2600 N. Shoreline Blvd., Mountain View (415)969-2041.
10 miles north of San Jose. **Holes:** 18. **Par:** 72/72.

Yards: 6,744/5,532. **Course rating:** 72.5/71.7. **Slope:** 125/121.
Opened: 1982. **Pace of Play rating:** 4:15. **Green fee:** $17/42.
Credit cards: MC, V, AMEX. **Reduced fees:** Weekdays, Twilight,
Seniors, Juniors.
Caddies: No. **Golf carts:** $22 for 18 holes.
Discount golf packages: No. **Season:** Year-round. **High:** May-Sept.

On-site lodging: No. **Rental clubs:** Yes.
Walking policy: Unrestricted walking. **Range:** Yes (grass).
To obtain tee times: Call six days in advance. Call Monday for weekend.
Subscriber comments: Robert Trent Jones Jr. course, long and longer in
the wind, tired greens . . . Traps are often wet caked sand . . . Great layout,
ruined by lack of care . . . Par 3s are challenging, every hole offers
something new . . . Coots ruin fairways and greens . . . Has potential, not
in great shape . . . Much improved, coot invasion unfortunate . . .
Interesting layout, if the wind kicks up be prepared to alter your strategy
. . . U.S. Open rough on the links-style course . . . Has great potential . . .
Par 3s ridiculous, especially with wind . . . One of the best muny courses
around.

★½ SIERRA VIEW PUBLIC GOLF COURSE
PU—12608 Avenue 264 At Rd. 124, Visalia (209)732-2078.
Call club for further information.
Subscriber comments: Good beginner's course . . . Needs some work on
fairways and greens . . . A very good public course, some holes a bit short
. . . Not in very good shape.

SILVERADO COUNTRY CLUB AND RESORT
R—1600 Atlas Peak Rd., Napa (707)257-5460, (800)532-0500.
50 miles northeast of San Francisco.
Opened: 1955. **Pace of Play rating:** N/A. **Green fee:** $50/100.
Credit cards: All major. **Reduced fees:** Low season, Resort guests,
Twilight.
Caddies: No. **Golf carts:** Included in Green Fee.
Discount golf packages: Yes. **Season:** Year-round. **High:** March-Nov.
On-site lodging: Yes. **Rental clubs:** Yes.
Walking policy: Mandatory cart. **Range:** Yes (grass).
To obtain tee times: May take tee times as far in advance as hotel
reservations.

★★★½ SOUTH COURSE
Holes: 18. **Par:** 72/72.
Yards: 6,685/5,672. **Course rating:** 72.4/71.8. **Slope:** 129/123.
Subscriber comments: Afternoon in Napa Valley can't be beat . . . Both
courses show a lot of wear . . . Very pleasant, relaxed setting . . . Boring
. . . The best in the West . . . Beautiful setting . . . Great course, well
maintained . . . Even in a cold rain it's worth it . . . Has all you want from
the tips . . . Great course in the wine country . . . Memorable course with
wide landing areas through tree-lined fairways . . . Good challenge for
average golfer . . . Wonderful layout, tough greens, try the tuna sandwich
at snack shop . . . North course is better but South has Transamerica . . .
Scenic Napa Valley gives course character and beauty . . . Lots of water and
wind . . . Some very difficult holes but fair . . . Love those tour courses.

★★★½ NORTH COURSE
Holes: 18. **Par:** 72/72.
Yards: 6,900/5,857. **Course rating:** 73.4/73.1. **Slope:** 131/128.
Subscriber comments: Great course, just beautiful, plays long . . . Lots of
trees, better stay in fairway . . . Not quite as good as the South but great
. . . More interesting than South Course . . . Much better course than
South . . . A little but easier than South Course . . . Beautiful scenery,
deceiving distances, caution to the bogey golfer . . . Tough course, long
when wet . . . Offers challenging holes and views, good service . . .
Challenging resort course, superb condition . . . Great weekend idea, not
tough, but enjoyable . . . Next-best thing to a true golf test.

★★★ SIMI HILLS GOLF CLUB
PU—5031 Alamo, Simi Valley (805)522-0813.
Call club for further information.

Subscriber comments: Good public course but greens are inconsistent at best . . . Great course, always in great condition . . . Pace of play slow on front . . . One of the best public courses in southern California . . . Interesting layout, challenging, good staff . . . Very nice municipal course, excellent condition . . . Greens have been bad in past, but they're trying to improve . . . Good condition. Easy to score well. Slow, very busy . . . Nice muny, tougher than rated . . . Challenging and fun . . . Second-slowest course in Los Angeles.

SINGING HILLS COUNTRY CLUB
R—3007 Dehesa Rd., El Cajon (619)442-3425, (800)457-5568.
17 miles east of San Diego.
Green fee: $29/34.
Credit cards: MC, V, AMEX. **Reduced fees:** Weekdays, Twilight, Juniors.
Caddies: No. **Golf carts:** N/A.
Discount golf packages: Yes. **Season:** Year-round.
On-site lodging: Yes. **Rental clubs:** Yes.
Walking policy: Unrestricted walking. **Range:** Yes (grass).
To obtain tee times: Weekday, seven days prior; weekends, call prior Monday.
Also has 18-hole par-54 Willow Glen Course.

★★★ OAK GLEN COURSE
Holes: 18. **Par:** 72/72.
Yards: 6,597/5,549. **Course rating:** 71.3/71.4. **Slope:** 122/124.
Opened: 1956. **Pace of Play rating:** N/A.
Subscriber comments: Excellent golfing facility . . . Excellent short course, good condition, good weather year-round . . . Fine public course, excellent staff . . . New back nine excellent, greens excellent . . . Great resort, course easy for average player . . . Older course, huge trees . . . Nice location; mature, scenic course, playable . . . I would take someone there . . . Good course for all levels. Play it slow. Good walking course . . . Good competitive course . . . Staff friendly, boring layout . . . Not all it's projected to be . . . Very professional staff . . . Either course is a worthwhile experience.

★★★½ WILLOW GLEN COURSE
Holes: 18. **Par:** 72/72.
Yards: 6,605/5,585. **Course rating:** 72.0/72.8. **Slope:** 124/122.
Opened: 1956. **Pace of Play rating:** N/A.
Subscriber comments: Good layout, nice resort, good practice facility . . . Tougher than it looks. Really tough if windy . . . Always in great shape, staff best I've seen, a must-play . . . Two holes much too short to be par 4s . . . One of kind in country, beautiful . . . Beautiful use of flower plantings . . . Top-of-the-line treatment . . . For a resort course, they always keep the course in good shape . . . Short, but well kept . . . Great course, many tournaments held here . . . Wonderful resort facility.

★½ SKYLINKS GOLF CLUB
PU—4800 E. Wardlow Rd., Long Beach (310)429-0030.
Call club for further information.

Subscriber comments: Tough par 3s, a pleasure to play . . . Very well conditioned for a public course . . . A flat muny course with small greens and tight fairways . . . Course not very well maintained. Slow play . . . Well maintained. True greens . . . Plain and simple . . . Flat, nothing special . . . Of fair interest, not terribly difficult . . . Lots of airplane noise . . . Play under landing planes.

★★ SKYWEST GOLF CLUB
PU—1401 Golf Course Rd., Hayward (510)278-6188.
22 miles southeast of San Francisco. **Holes:** 18. **Par:** 72/73.
Yards: 6,930/6,171. **Course rating:** 72.8/74.3. **Slope:** 121/123.

Opened: 1965. **Pace of Play rating:** 5:00. **Green fee:** $16/20.
Credit cards: MC, V. **Reduced fees:** Seniors, Juniors.
Caddies: No. **Golf carts:** N/A.
Discount golf packages: No. **Season:** Year-round.
On-site lodging: No. **Rental clubs:** Yes.
Walking policy: Unrestricted walking. **Range:** Yes.
To obtain tee times: Call seven days in advance.
Subscriber comments: Standard muny golf . . . Hard to get starting times
. . . Last three holes all into afternoon wind . . . Flat, wide fairways . . .
Long, busy, but well maintained . . . Slowest-playing course around, but
good layout . . . Inconsistent greens . . . A good test but also good for
beginners . . . Some tough grass and bare spots . . . Very long par 4s,
fairway needs work . . . Slow play ruins the day . . . Ball washers and spike
scrapers on each tee. Well placed port-o-potties . . . Your average track.

★★★½ SOBOBA SPRINGS COUNTRY CLUB
SP—1020 Soboba Rd., San Jacinto (909)654-9354.
25 miles west of Palm Springs. **Holes:** 18. **Par:** 73/74.
Yards: 6,829/5,762. **Course rating:** 73.5/73.2. **Slope:** 135/131.
Opened: 1965. **Pace of Play rating:** N/A. **Green fee:** $36/45.
Credit cards: MC, V, AMEX. **Reduced fees:** Twilight, Juniors.
Caddies: No. **Golf carts:** Included in Green Fee.
Discount golf packages: No. **Season:** Year-round. **High:** Oct.-May.
On-site lodging: No. **Rental clubs:** No.
Walking policy: Mandatory cart. **Range:** Yes (grass).
To obtain tee times: Call seven days in advance.
Subscriber comments: A pleasant course in this isolated area . . . Really
nice course, some tough water holes . . . Fine setting in river bed, great
character . . . Great layout, lots of trees, good water holes, unique look for
that area . . . A well-kept secret, hope it stays that way . . . Reasonably well
maintained . . . Too many birds, mudhens, ducks, noisy crows . . . Old
Desmond Muirhead design, well worth the effort to find . . . Great holes
around the lakes, several challenging tee shots . . . Just keep leaves off
fairways . . . Always a great golfing experience.

★★★★ SONOMA GOLF CLUB
PU—17700 Arnold Dr., Sonoma (707)996-0300, (800)956-4653.
45 miles south of San Francisco. **Holes:** 18. **Par:** 72/72.
Yards: 7,069/5,519. **Course rating:** 74.9/71.5. **Slope:** 135/128.
Opened: 1991. **Pace of Play rating:** 4:50. **Green fee:** $45/65.
Credit cards: MC, V. **Reduced fees:** Weekdays, Low season, Twilight.
Caddies: No. **Golf carts:** Included in Green Fee.
Discount golf packages: Yes. **Season:** Year-round. **High:** April-Oct.
On-site lodging: No. **Rental clubs:** Yes.
Walking policy: Unrestricted walking. **Range:** Yes (grass).
To obtain tee times: Two weeks in advance.
Subscriber comments: One classic layout . . . Wonderful old-style
course, well maintained . . . Fairly tough from blues . . . Great course,
great pro shop, great restaurant . . . Super greens . . . All segments of this
club are great, but too expensive . . . Excellent layout, greens recently
rebuilt . . . Updated with new bunkers, greens . . . One of the great courses
in northern California . . . Beautiful traditional layout . . . Interesting holes
. . . Reconditioned a fine old course into a great one . . . Fantastic layout
. . . Wonderful place to play, variety of holes, excellent condition always
. . . Great, not a bad hole on the course . . . Hidden jewel in Napa/Sonoma
region . . . Too many mounds . . . Fast PGA-like greens . . . Greens as
good as the Olympic Club's . . . Not well known . . . Best course in
Sonoma county . . . Country club environment . . . A daily fee that treats
you like a member . . . Worth seeking, one of the best in northern
California.

★★★ SOULE PARK GOLF COURSE
PU—1033 East Ojai Avenue, Ojai (805)646-5633.
16 miles northeast of Ventura. **Holes:** 18. **Par:** 72/72.
Yards: 6,350/5,894. **Course rating:** 69.1/71.0. **Slope:** 107/115.

Opened: 1962. **Pace of Play rating:** N/A. **Green fee:** $18/23.
Credit cards: None. **Reduced fees:** Weekdays, Twilight, Seniors, Juniors.
Caddies: No. **Golf carts:** N/A.
Discount golf packages: No. **Season:** Year-round.
On-site lodging: Yes. **Rental clubs:** Yes.
Walking policy: Unrestricted walking. **Range:** Yes (grass).
To obtain tee times: Call seven days in advance starting at 7 a.m.
Subscriber comments: Best muny around, up there with Ojai Valley . . .
Keep the ball in the air . . . On the short side, driveable par 4s . . . Fairways
are usually average, but some of the best greens around . . . Great setting in
Ojai, a lot of character . . . Great fun, great scenery, as nice as public golf
gets, easy to score . . . Just down the road from Ojai Valley . . . A delight
in every possible way . . . A course you never grow tired of . . . Course not
in as good condition as it should be . . . Tricked up too much . . . Beautiful
course and setting, No. 7 is very tough . . . Needs better fairways with
more grass. Nice layout . . . All types of terrain. Interesting shots. Good for
all players . . . Trees get in the way . . . Rural atmosphere. Beautiful
scenery . . . Best kept secret in Ventura County. A real treat!

★★★ SOUTHRIDGE GOLF CLUB

SP—9413 S. Butte Rd., Sutter (916)755-4653.
8 miles west of Yuba City. **Holes:** 18. **Par:** 72/72.
Yards: 7,047/5,541. **Course rating:** 72.7/71.3. **Slope:** 130/122.
Opened: 1992. **Pace of Play rating:** 4:30. **Green fee:** $22/29.
Credit cards: MC, V, AMEX. **Reduced fees:** Weekdays, Low season,
Twilight, Seniors, Juniors.
Caddies: No. **Golf carts:** $10 for 18 holes.
Discount golf packages: Yes. **Season:** Year-round. **High:** March-
June/Sept.-Nov.
On-site lodging: No. **Rental clubs:** Yes.
Walking policy: Walking at certain times. **Range:** Yes (grass).
To obtain tee times: Seven days in advance.
Subscriber comments: Two courses in one . . . Hope it's not windy . . .
Hilly, do not walk . . . Links front nine, radical hills/hillside on back nine
. . . Front nine full of water, back impossible to walk . . . Not one level tee
box . . . A little ragged but with great potential. Scenic but unwalkable . . .
Beautiful conditions and scenery . . . Long between holes, some unfair
fairways . . . Relatively new so much of the scenery has not fully developed
. . . Back nine in mountains . . . Par-5 16th worth the price of admission
. . . Very fun and different . . . Back nine is very tough . . . No. 16 can ruin
your round, but it will be the hole you talk about.

★★½ SPRING VALLEY GOLF CLUB

PU—3441 E. Calaveras Blvd, Milpitas (408)262-1722.
Call club for further information.
Subscriber comments: Short but excitingly, difficult lies and shot-shaping
fairways . . . Bring your best putter! . . . Scenic and challenging, some
crowding . . . Challenging . . . Must be straight. Three holes over water
. . . Fairly hairy course, but nice walk. Foothill layout with tricky greens
. . . Nice track for a muny, but course needs lots of work . . . Not very
inspiring or challenging . . . A nice little surprise course that has improved
in past year.

★★★★★ SPYGLASS HILL GOLF COURSE

R—Spyglass Hill Rd. and Stevenson Dr., Pebble Beach (408)625-8563,
(800)654-9300.
Holes: 18. **Par:** 72/74.
Yards: 6,859/5,642. **Course rating:** 75.9/73.7. **Slope:** 143/133.
Opened: 1966. **Pace of Play rating:** 5:00. **Green fee:** $150/175.
Credit cards: All major. **Reduced fees:** Resort guests, Twilight.
Caddies: Yes. **Golf carts:** Included in Green Fee.
Discount golf packages: Yes. **Season:** Year-round. **High:** Aug.-Nov.
On-site lodging: No. **Rental clubs:** Yes.
Walking policy: Unrestricted walking. **Range:** Yes (grass).

To obtain tee times: Call reservations up to 18 months in advance if you're staying at resort or 30 days in advance if you are not.

Ranked 34th in America's 100 Greatest Golf Courses by Golf Digest. Ranked 6th in America's 75 Best Resort Courses by Golf Digest. Ranked 7th in California by Golf Digest.

Subscriber comments: The ultimate test of golf . . . Doesn't get its due respect, wonderful . . . As good as Pebble Beach . . . Ocean and forest plus charm . . . Beats me to death but I love it . . . Worth every George Washington . . . Think you're good, try this! . . . Best of the Peninsula, stirs the blood, sea, trees, sand, it has it all . . . Toughest course on the Monterey Peninsula . . . So majestic . . . Lace up your shoes and pray you brought your "A" game . . . Each hole a different challenge . . . First five holes are like Pine Valley . . . The quiet jewel of the Peninsula. More tenacity than Pebble. True golfer's hangout . . . May be toughest and most interesting course in the U.S. . . . Better than Pebble Beach. Great test for low handicappers . . . About the closest I'll ever get to Augusta . . . Awesome, everything you want in a golf course . . . Bring your fairway woods . . . Thrilling course, tantalizing to come back . . . Ambiance worth the money . . . As good as people say . . . Best course on the planet. Soooo difficult . . . One can not play without being impressed, great course . . . Golf heaven, Part II. Wow!!!

STEELE CANYON GOLF CLUB
★★★½ CANYON/RANCH/MEADOW
PU—3199 Stonefield Dr., Jamul (619)441-6900.
20 miles east of San Diego. **Holes:** 27. **Par:** 71/72/71.
Yards: 6,741/7,001/6,672. **Course rating:** 72.7/74.0/72.2.
Slope: 135/137/134.
Opened: 1991. **Pace of Play rating:** 4:00. **Green fee:** $40/50.
Credit cards: MC, V, AMEX. **Reduced fees:** Twilight, Seniors, Juniors.
Caddies: No. **Golf carts:** Included in Green Fee.
Discount golf packages: No. **Season:** Year-round. **High:** Dec.-May.
On-site lodging: No. **Rental clubs:** No.
Walking policy: Mandatory cart. **Range:** Yes (grass).
To obtain tee times: Call seven days in advance.
Subscriber comments: Three different nines, can be long, tight, or just fun . . . Excellent views down the canyon . . . The type of course you only play one time . . . Canyon nine has five holes where green surface is hidden . . . Best 27 holes in town, course needs more maintenance . . . Great fun, and very interesting . . . Requires good driving shots from back . . . Fantastic course. It's a thinking man's course. Not just beautiful, but different every time I play . . . Some good holes but generally nothing extra-special overall . . . One of the most dramatic courses ever . . . Difficult target golf, a little gimmicky . . . Don't play here if you're not straight . . . Canyon is ridiculously tricked-up, but the other two are gems . . . Canyon nine is great layout . . . If this is typical of Gary Player courses, I want to play them all . . . Gary Player design . . . Poorly designed par 5s, otherwise fine layout . . . Hilly, well conditioned new course, no facilities . . . Best layout in San Diego county.

★★ SUMMIT POINTE GOLF CLUB
PU—1500 Country Club Dr., Milpitas (408)262-8813.
Call club for further information.
Subscriber comments: Very hilly . . . Tough greens, hard to score well here . . . Hilly with a lot of uneven lies . . . Great back nine . . . Unforgiving . . . Foothill layout with some water hazards . . . Back nine has eight water holes . . . Beautiful course, great scenery . . . Some fairways angled too steep to hold a good drive, hilly, tough . . . Not a flat lie on the front and the back nine is very narrow . . . Great 16th hole . . . Good challenge for a little money.

★★★½ SUN CITY PALM SPRINGS GOLF CLUB
R—38-180 Del Webb Blvd., Bermuda Dunes (619)772-2200.
10 miles east of Palm Springs. **Holes:** 18. **Par:** 72/72.
Yards: 6,720/5,305. **Course rating:** 73.0/70.3. **Slope:** 131/118.

Opened: 1992. **Pace of Play rating:** 4:15. **Green fee:** $30/68.
Credit cards: MC, V. **Reduced fees:** Weekdays, Low season, Twilight.
Caddies: No. **Golf carts:** Included in Green Fee.
Discount golf packages: No. **Season:** Year-round.
On-site lodging: Yes. **Rental clubs:** Yes.

Walking policy: Mandatory cart. **Range:** Yes (grass).
To obtain tee times: Call three days in advance.
Subscriber comments: Very nice desert, resort course . . . Flat course, not
very impressed, lined by condos . . . Nice layout, good condition all year
. . . Runs between homes . . . A beautifully maintained course,
progressively demanding . . . Thin fairways and greens, fun layout . . .
Excellent golf, very windy at times . . . Greens not lush, but roll very true
. . . Pristine condition, beautiful, challenging . . . Short course but lots of
fun . . . Only the best I've ever played.

★★★ SUN LAKES COUNTRY CLUB

SP—850 South Country Club Dr., Banning (909)845-2135.
20 miles west of Palm Springs. **Holes:** 18. **Par:** 72/72.
Yards: 7,035/5,516. **Course rating:** 74.3/72.7. **Slope:** 132/118.
Opened: 1987. **Pace of Play rating:** N/A. **Green fee:** $57.
Credit cards: MC, V. **Reduced fees:** Twilight, Juniors.
Caddies: No. **Golf carts:** $45 for 18 holes.
Discount golf packages: No. **Season:** Year-round. **High:** April-Oct.
On-site lodging: No. **Rental clubs:** No.
Walking policy: Unrestricted walking. **Range:** Yes (grass).
To obtain tee times: Call up to four days in advance.
Subscriber comments: A championship course, a real test to any golfer,
bunkers and water placed to gather up any errant shot . . . Not very
exciting, but OK shape . . . Fun track through houses . . . 100 bunkers, six
lakes, fine shot values . . . Good wide fairways, well kept . . . Thin air
affects club selection, be forewarned!

★★ SUNNYVALE MUNICIPAL GOLF COURSE

PU—605 Macara Lane, Sunnyvale (408)738-3666.
5 miles north of San Jose. **Holes:** 18. **Par:** 70/71.
Yards: 6,249/5,305. **Course rating:** 69.7/70.2. **Slope:** 119/120.
Opened: 1986. **Pace of Play rating:** N/A. **Green fee:** $14/28.
Credit cards: None. **Reduced fees:** Weekdays, Low season, Twilight.
Caddies: No. **Golf carts:** N/A.
Discount golf packages: No. **Season:** Year-round. **High:** March-Sept.
On-site lodging: No. **Rental clubs:** Yes.
Walking policy: Unrestricted walking. **Range:** No.
To obtain tee times: Call seven days in advance.
Subscriber comments: A good fader's course . . . Easy muny, good for
the ego . . . Well maintained all year. Good character for flat bay-side
course . . . Flat and uninteresting . . . Very well maintained for a muny . . .
Busy, flat muny course, nothing special . . . Looks easy, but deceptive,
troublesome.

SUNOL VALLEY GOLF COURSE

PU—6900 Mission Rd., Sunol.
7 miles south of Hayward.
Opened: 1968. **Pace of Play rating:** 4:30-5:00. **Green fee:** $42/57.
Credit cards: MC, V. **Reduced fees:** Twilight.
Caddies: No. **Golf carts:** Included in Green Fee.
Discount golf packages: No. **Season:** Year-round. **High:** April-Sept.
On-site lodging: No. **Rental clubs:** Yes.
Walking policy: Walking at certain times. **Range:** Yes (grass).
To obtain tee times: Call seven days in advance.
★★ PALM COURSE
(510)862-0414.
Holes: 18. **Par:** 72/74.
Yards: 6,843/5,997. **Course rating:** 72.2/74.4. **Slope:** 118/124.
Subscriber comments: Great in morning, tough late in day . . . Average

course in fair condition . . . Hilly and steep, challenging experience . . . Can get hurricane winds late in the day . . . Watch for flying balls . . . Needs major maintenance . . . Long par 3s . . . Scenic, but very windy in the afternoons . . . Wide-open fairways, like playing in a wind tunnel . . . Rolling hills, good condition for muny-type course . . . Course has no real character . . . Has some great holes . . . Sloping greens make putting hard.

★★ CYPRESS COURSE

(510)862-2404.
Holes: 18. **Par:** 72/72.
Yards: 6,195/5,458. **Course rating:** 69.1/70.1. **Slope:** 115/115.
Subscriber comments: Good course and facilities . . . Not as good as Palm Course . . . Flat and trees, narrow . . . Needs work . . . Not real long, good for faders . . . Good diversity in holes. Very fast greens in summer . . . Scenic, shorter and easier than Palm . . . Good walking course, wide fairways . . . Palm Course a little more difficult. Still a nice layout.

★★ SWENSON PARK GOLF CLUB

PU—6803 Alexandria Place, Stockton (209)937-7360.
Holes: 18. **Par:** 72/74.
Yards: 6,485/6,266. **Course rating:** 70.0/73.8. **Slope:** 110/117.

Opened: 1952. **Pace of Play rating:** 4:30. **Green fee:** $14.
Credit cards: None. **Reduced fees:** Weekdays, Low season, Twilight, Seniors, Juniors.
Caddies: No. **Golf carts:** $18 for 18 holes.
Discount golf packages: Yes. **Season:** Year-round.
On-site lodging: No. **Rental clubs:** Yes.
Walking policy: Unrestricted walking. **Range:** Yes (grass).
To obtain tee times: Call one week in advance.
Also 9-hole par-3 course.
Subscriber comments: Hot Central Valley course in summer . . . Needs improvement, needs to be more interesting . . . Overplayed muny course, slow play . . . Good, old public course, huge trees . . . Tight lies through tall oaks . . . Biggest oak trees ever . . . 300-year-old oak tree . . . So many trees, they are numbered with large signs to help you find your tee shot . . . Par 4s have wide, tree-lined fairways . . . Not particularly long, but your shots must be accurate . . . Best muny in Stockton, well maintained.

★½ SYCAMORE CANYON GOLF CLUB

PU—500 Kenmar Lane, Arvin (805)854-3163.
25 miles southeast of Bakersfield. **Holes:** 18. **Par:** 72/73.
Yards: 7,100/5,744. **Course rating:** 72.8/71.6. **Slope:** 125/120.
Opened: 1989. **Pace of Play rating:** N/A. **Green fee:** $10/13.
Credit cards: MC, V. **Reduced fees:** Weekdays, Twilight, Seniors, Juniors.
Caddies: No. **Golf carts:** $8 for 18 holes.
Discount golf packages: No. **Season:** Year-round. **High:** Feb.-Oct.
On-site lodging: No. **Rental clubs:** Yes.
Walking policy: Unrestricted walking. **Range:** Yes (grass).
To obtain tee times: Call seven days in advance.
Subscriber comments: Length, water, sand, in all the right places . . . Interesting layout, nice greens . . . It's like playing in a rice paddy . . . Long, open, hard ground . . . Could be a great course . . . Well maintained, when the trees grow and come into play, it will make the course more difficult . . . Water where it counts, flat . . . In time, a great course.

★½ TABLE MOUNTAIN GOLF COURSE

PU—2700 Oro Dam Blvd. West, Oroville (916)533-3922.
70 miles north of Sacramento. **Holes:** 18. **Par:** 72/68.
Yards: 6,500/5,000. **Course rating:** 69.8/66.5. **Slope:** 116/104.
Opened: 1956. **Pace of Play rating:** 4:00. **Green fee:** $13/15.
Credit cards: MC, V. **Reduced fees:** Weekdays, Twilight, Seniors, Juniors.
Caddies: No. **Golf carts:** N/A.

Discount golf packages: Yes. **Season:** Year-round. **High:** May–Sept.
On-site lodging: No. **Rental clubs:** Yes.
Walking policy: Unrestricted walking. **Range:** Yes (grass).
To obtain tee times: Call seven days in advance.
Subscriber comments: Easy, flat layout . . . Few real hazards, fast play
the norm . . . Course could be in better condition . . . Water holes make
course tougher . . . Flat valley course. Good greens. Very dry in summer
. . . Best greens in area. Flat, easy and uninteresting.

★★★½ TAHOE DONNER GOLF CLUB
PU—12850 Northwoods Blvd., Truckee (916)587-9440.
40 miles west of Reno, NV. **Holes:** 18. **Par:** 72/72.
Yards: 6,952/6,487. **Course rating:** N/A. **Slope:** 130/127.
Call club for further information.
Subscriber comments: Spyglass of the Sierras. Very tough. Great
condition . . . Tough mountain course . . . Excellent mountain course . . .
Very quiet . . . A gem in the rough . . . Fun to walk this tree-lined course
. . . Beautiful course, difficult greens . . . Course layout in a figure-eight
. . . Super mountain golf . . . Limited season . . . Tight course. Leave the
driver at home! . . . No. 1 sets the tone. Long uphill. Forest left and right
. . . Beautiful high mountain setting. Long hitter's paradise . . . Best hot
dogs . . . A tough layout at 6,500 feet . . . Tight fairways, lots of trees . . .
Mountain golf at its best.

TAHQUITZ CREEK PALM SPRINGS GOLF RESORT
R—1885 Golf Club Dr., Palm Springs (619)328-1956.
3 miles east of Palm Springs.
Pace of Play rating: 4:00.
Credit cards: MC, V, AMEX. **Reduced fees:** Low season, Twilight.
Caddies: No. **Golf carts:** $20 for 18 holes.
Discount golf packages: No. **Season:** Year-round. **High:** Jan–May.
On-site lodging: No. **Rental clubs:** Yes.
Walking policy: Walking at certain times. **Range:** Yes (grass).
To obtain tee times: N/A.
★★ OLD COURSE
Holes: 18. **Par:** 71/73.
Yards: 6,040/5,800. **Course rating:** 69.5/72.6. **Slope:** 107/115.
Opened: 1959. **Green fee:** $18/35.
Call three days in advance.
Subscriber comments: Fun municipal course . . . No sand! No water!
Fast and friendly anytime . . . Flat, poor condition . . . Grass bunkers . . .
Fun course, can be very easy . . . Fun course, excellent condition for a
public course . . . Well kept considering traffic . . . First nine's drama to
second nine's charm.
RESORT COURSE*
(619)328-1005.
Holes: 18. **Par:** 72/72.
Yards: 6,705/5,206. **Course rating:** 71.4/70.0. **Slope:** 120/119.
Opened: 1995. **Green fee:** $75/85.

TEMECULA CREEK INN
★★★½ CREEK/OAKS/STONEHOUSE
R—44501 Rainbow Canyon Rd., Temecula (909)676-2405, (800)962-7335.
50 miles north of San Diego. **Holes:** 27. **Par:** 72/72/72.
Yards: 6,784/6,693/6,605. **Course rating:** 72.6/72.6/71.8.
Slope: 125/130/123.
Opened: 1970. **Pace of Play rating:** 4:30. **Green fee:** $33/49.
Credit cards: All major. **Reduced fees:** Weekdays, Low season, Resort
guests, Twilight, Juniors.
Caddies: No. **Golf carts:** N/A.
Discount golf packages: Yes. **Season:** Year-round.
On-site lodging: Yes. **Rental clubs:** Yes.
Walking policy: Walking at certain times. **Range:** Yes (grass).
To obtain tee times: Call up to seven days in advance.

Subscriber comments: Shotmaker's course, elevation, doglegs . . . Oaks and Stonehouse courses are good . . . Stonehouse nine is gorgeous . . . All three nines exceptional . . . Creek is a so-so nine, but it is enjoyable . . . Striking views on many holes . . . My wife loves it! . . . Scenic, challenging . . . I love this place, the best . . . Nice for the bucks . . . 27 holes for great variety. Fun to play . . . Stonehouse very unique. Creek and Oak traditional, tree-lined . . . Fantastic, well kept . . . Very pleasant place to play . . . Play Oak front nine and you will love Stonehouse back nine . . . Very pleasant, walkable course in good condition . . . Very scenic, hilly and lots of trees . . . Watch for snakes . . . Beautiful mountain views . . . Oak and Stonehouse best challenge, good condition always . . . Best course in Temecula area . . . Keep ball in the fairway on the first three holes . . . Front side doesn't prepare you for back.

★★½ TIERRA DEL SOL GOLF CLUB
PU—10300 N. Loop Dr., California City (619)373-2384.
Call club for further information.
Subscriber comments: Fun course, but wind always a factor . . . Long, hot in summer, dry in winter, fast greens . . . Severely sloped greens, fairways have bare spots . . . Great greens, windy, very sparse . . . Desert course. Windy, never plays the same . . . Condition fair on backside . . . Worth the trouble. Drive to find . . . No scenery. Windy but playable . . . Best greens around, fairways need help . . . An isolated gem in the desert.

★★★½ TIJERAS CREEK GOLF CLUB
PU—29082 Tijeras Creek Rd., Rancho Santa Margarita (714)589-9793.
50 miles south of Los Angeles. **Holes:** 18. **Par:** 72/72.
Yards: 6,601/5,130. **Course rating:** 71.8/70.1. **Slope:** 125/115.
Opened: 1990. **Pace of Play rating:** 4:30-5:00. **Green fee:** $60/80.
Credit cards: MC, V, AMEX. **Reduced fees:** Twilight, Juniors.
Caddies: No. **Golf carts:** Included in Green Fee.
Discount golf packages: No. **Season:** Year-round.
On-site lodging: No. **Rental clubs:** Yes.
Walking policy: Mandatory cart. **Range:** Yes (grass).
To obtain tee times: Call seven days in advance.
Subscriber comments: Very nice Ted Robinson design . . . 17th hole great . . . Super course . . . Front nine does not prepare you for the tough back . . . Outstanding, blazing fast greens . . . Nice layout, but concrete is softer than these greens! . . . Front nine and back nine are Dr. Jekyll and Mr. Hyde . . . Easy front, tough back . . . Nice course, usually in great condition, nice challenge . . . Back nine clearly more interesting . . . Need to get greens in better shape . . . Front nine, piece of cake, back nine nightmare alley . . . Two different nines entirely . . . One of the best back nines . . . Breathtaking back nine requiring accuracy . . . Canyon back nine . . . Front nine is resort golf, back nine is rural . . . Back nine as great as anywhere in U.S. . . . Bring extra balls for the back nine . . . Requires pre-shot planning on many holes . . . Best public course in Orange County.

★★½ TILDEN PARK GOLF COURSE
PU—Grizzley Peak and Shasta Rd., Berkeley (510)848-7373.
10 miles east of San Francisco. **Holes:** 18. **Par:** 70/71.
Yards: 6,300/5,400. **Course rating:** 69.9/69.2. **Slope:** 120/116.
Opened: 1936. **Pace of Play rating:** 4:15. **Green fee:** $18/25.
Credit cards: MC, V. **Reduced fees:** Weekdays, Twilight, Seniors, Juniors.
Caddies: No. **Golf carts:** $22 for 18 holes.
Discount golf packages: No. **Season:** Year-round. **High:** April-Oct.
On-site lodging: No. **Rental clubs:** Yes.
Walking policy: Unrestricted walking. **Range:** No.
To obtain tee times: Call one week in advance.
Subscriber comments: Older public course with much play, lovely setting . . . Hilly course, lots of ups, downs, and sideways . . . Fun course, hidden in Berkeley Hills . . . Helmet required . . . Very rough off fairway . . . Tough opening par 4 . . . Can't be a slicer or hooker, many trees, beautiful scenery . . . Narrow fairways, challenging . . . Requires patience

. . . Best muny in Bay area . . . Fun, short layout ruined by poor maintenance . . . Toughest opening hole around . . . Great scenery, No. 10 tee is on top of a cliff and is spectacular . . . Classic park-land course, excellent par 3s . . . You think you are at the Olympic Club . . . Hilly, tree-lined course. Be in shape to carry your bag . . . Delightful experience . . . A good muny except in wet weather, a real mudder . . . Classic old style, no frills . . . Pristine park location . . . Better maintenance could put it over the top.

★½ TONY LEMA GOLF CLUB

PU—13800 Neptune Dr., San Leandro (510)895-2162.
Call club for further information.
Subscriber comments: Wide open, I mean wide open; windy always . . . Good for novice . . . Bad condition when wet or dry, needs a lot of work . . . A lot of fun . . . Very windy. Some poor course conditions . . . On a clear day you can see San Francisco skyline . . . Great Bay views . . . Good place to play . . . Very good staff, great course for high handicappers, scratch players won't be challenged . . . Too many waterfowl make fairways a mess . . . They keep trying to improve fairways and greens . . . Shoddy practice mats.

TORREY PINES GOLF COURSE

PU—11480 North Torrey Pines Rd., La Jolla (619)452-3226, (800)985-4653.
10 miles north of San Diego.
Opened: 1957. **Pace of Play rating:** N/A. **Green fee:** $75/90.
Credit cards: MC, V, AMEX. **Reduced fees:** No.
Caddies: No. **Golf carts:** Included in Green Fee.
Discount golf packages: Yes. **Season:** Year-round.
On-site lodging: Yes. **Rental clubs:** Yes.
Walking policy: Mandatory cart. **Range:** Yes (grass).
To obtain tee times: You may call four to six weeks in advance.

★★★½ NORTH COURSE

Holes: 18. **Par:** 72/74.
Yards: 6,647/6,118. **Course rating:** 72.1/75.4. **Slope:** 129/134.
Ranked in Third 25 of America's 75 Best Public Golf Courses by Golf Digest.
Subscriber comments: Good all around, not real long, unique golf holes . . . Disappointing . . . Not quite the pure test of golf as its South neighbor but still a super track. A very fair test of golf . . . Always jammed . . . Greens excellent, maintenance improving . . . Very gorgeous setting, a user-friendly course . . . Very scenic holes along ocean . . . Terrific scenery, long par 4s look easy . . . Beautiful, playable but not easy, sixth hole is a spectacular par 3 . . . Beautiful scenery, good course, acceptable condition . . . Almost as good as South Course . . . More playable than South . . . Absolute steal for residents, $100 round for $14 . . . Conditions of course always best in winter and spring, a joy to walk . . . Year-round maintenance not good . . . Not quite as good as South Course, but still better than most.

★★★★ SOUTH COURSE

Holes: 18. **Par:** 72/76.
Yards: 7,055/6,457. **Course rating:** 74.6/77.3. **Slope:** 136/139.
Ranked in Second 25 of America's 75 Best Public Golf Courses by Golf Digest. Ranked 22nd in California by Golf Digest.

Subscriber comments: If you can't afford Pebble Beach, Torrey Pines' South Course is the next best thing . . . If you can get on, play it. Next to Pebble, best seaside course in the west . . . Right on the ocean . . . Greens very true . . . Great for long hitters . . . Last hole is a risk-reward hole . . . This is the greatest muny on earth. A tremendous test of golf. Very fair but very tough. No.12 is my pick for toughest hole I've ever played . . . Needs to be more accessible . . . Keep the ball on the fairway here. The view sometimes takes away from your game . . . Still one of the best all-around munys . . . Especially good after tournament . . . Best public course in San Diego . . . A poor man's Pebble Beach complete with hang gliders . . . Plays long with no roll in fairways . . . Can understand why the tour stops here . . . Enjoyable but no great holes . . . Course condition, especially greens, very unpredictable year round . . . Longer and more difficult than North . . . Slow, slow but what a golf course! . . . Sweeping cliff views are breathtaking . . . Best muny course by far . . . Pros can't score either when wind picks up . . . Overrated . . . Much better course than North Course . . . Best muny south of San Francisco.

★★½ TRACY GOLF AND COUNTRY CLUB
PU—35200 South Chrisman Rd., Tracy (209)835-9463.
Call club for further information.
Subscriber comments: Lots of fun, well maintained . . . Good valley track, excellent small greens . . . Lots of water and strategic trees and bunkers. Tough walk . . . Nos. 9 and 10, not near clubhouse; course straddles freeway . . . Keep the ball low. Windy. A good test for all handicaps . . . Nothing noteworthy . . . Very windy in the afternoon.

★★★½ TUSTIN RANCH GOLF CLUB
PU—12442 Tustin Ranch Rd., Tustin (714)730-1611.
Holes: 18. **Par:** 72/72.
Yards: 6,736/5,204. **Course rating:** 72.9/70.3. **Slope:** 129/118.
Opened: 1989. **Pace of Play rating:** N/A **Green fee:** $65/95.
Credit cards: MC, V, AMEX. **Reduced fees:** Weekdays, Seniors, Juniors.
Caddies: No. **Golf carts:** Included in Green Fee.
Discount golf packages: No. **Season:** Year-round. **High:** June-Oct.
On-site lodging: No. **Rental clubs:** Yes.
Walking policy: Mandatory cart. **Range:** Yes (grass).
To obtain tee times: Call seven days in advance.
Subscriber comments: Fun for all, very pleasant surroundings . . . Great par 3s . . . Lush, resort-style course, lots of water . . . Not as hard as it looks . . . Pedestrian layout . . . Perfect condition, good layout . . . Fees seem to be an attempt to privatize course . . . Interesting contouring landscaping from a flat piece of land . . . Another good Ted Robinson design . . . Price is way out of line with facilities . . . Expensive even by California standards . . . Easy course with tough three-level greens . . . The 18th hole at sundown is murder. You hit it right into the sun . . . Well manicured, fun course . . . Very nice layout with interesting bunkers . . . Target golf layout . . . Too many holes play the same . . . Carts on path is a bit of a negative.

★★★ TWIN OAKS GOLF COURSE
PU—1425 N. Twin Oaks Valley Rd., San Marcos (619)591-4653.
3 miles west of Escondido. **Holes:** 18. **Par:** 72/72.
Yards: 6,535/5,423. **Course rating:** 71.2/71.6. **Slope:** 124/120.
Opened: 1993. **Pace of Play rating:** 4:00. **Green fee:** $25/50.
Credit cards: All major. **Reduced fees:** Weekdays, Twilight, Juniors.
Caddies: No. **Golf carts:** Included in Green Fee.
Discount golf packages: Yes. **Season:** Year-round.
On-site lodging: No. **Rental clubs:** Yes.
Walking policy: Mandatory cart. **Range:** Yes (grass).
To obtain tee times: Call up to seven days in advance.
Subscriber comments: Typical Ted Robinson design . . . Young course, will get better . . . Not much course control . . . Course too new, very plain . . . Landing areas are narrow, fairways slope too severely to some hazards . . . Enjoyable new course, many short par 4s . . . Good condition . . . New course, nice facilities, average conditioning . . . Super greens . . . New interesting holes . . . Best-kept secret in San Diego area.

★★ UPLAND HILLS COUNTRY CLUB
SP—1231 East 16th St., Upland (909)946-4711.
20 miles east of Los Angeles. **Holes:** 18. **Par:** 70/70.
Yards: 5,827/4,813. **Course rating:** 67.1/66.5. **Slope:** 111/106.
Opened: 1983. **Pace of Play rating:** N/A. **Green fee:** $17/27.
Credit cards: All major. **Reduced fees:** No.
Caddies: No. **Golf carts:** $11 for 18 holes.

Discount golf packages: No. **Season:** Year-round.
On-site lodging: No. **Rental clubs:** Yes.
Walking policy: Walking at certain times. **Range:** No.
To obtain tee times: Call seven days in advance.
Subscriber comments: Tough course, O.B., trees, water . . . Greens are in great shape . . . Leave the driver at home . . . Nice course. Excellent greens . . . Best greens anywhere . . . Course laid out east to west, always into wind or downwind . . . Narrow, must hit it straight. Course is simple, greens are like ice . . . Maintenance is very poor . . . Short and uneventful course.

VALLE GRANDE GOLF COURSE*
PU—1119 Watts Dr., Bakersfield (805)832-2259.
Holes: 18. **Par:** 72/72.
Yards: 6,240/5,531. **Course rating:** 69.8/68.9. **Slope:** 116/114.
Opened: 1952. **Pace of Play rating:** 4:00. **Green fee:** $9/12.
Credit cards: None. **Reduced fees:** Twilight, Seniors, Juniors.
Caddies: No. **Golf carts:** $8 for 18 holes.
Discount golf packages: No. **Season:** Year-round.
On-site lodging: No. **Rental clubs:** No.
Walking policy: Unrestricted walking. **Range:** Yes (grass).
To obtain tee times: Call seven days in advance.

★★ VAN BUSKIRK PARK GOLF COURSE
PU—1740 Houston Ave, Stockton (209)937-7357.
Holes: 18. **Par:** 72/74.
Yards: 6,928/5,927. **Course rating:** 72.2/72.2. **Slope:** 118/113.
Opened: 1961. **Pace of Play rating:** 4:30. **Green fee:** $13.
Credit cards: None. **Reduced fees:** Twilight, Seniors, Juniors.
Caddies: No. **Golf carts:** $20 for 18 holes.
Discount golf packages: No. **Season:** Year-round.
On-site lodging: No. **Rental clubs:** Yes.
Walking policy: Unrestricted walking. **Range:** Yes (grass).
To obtain tee times: Call Monday for upcoming weekend.
Subscriber comments: Typical muny layout with fairly wide fairways . . . Long hitter's course . . . Muny course, long, good test . . . Great muny, good conditions . . . Lots of quality improvement this year, greens need work . . . Best public course greens in this area . . . A well-conditioned, long, fast-moving muny, fun to play . . . Potential for being a great muny.

★★½ VICTORVILLE MUNICIPAL GOLF COURSE
SP—14414 Green Tree Blvd., Victorville (619)245-4860.
25 miles north of San Bernardino. **Holes:** 18. **Par:** 72/72.
Yards: 6,640/5,878. **Course rating:** 71.2/72.7. **Slope:** 121/118.
Opened: 1965. **Pace of Play rating:** 4:00. **Green fee:** $17/20.
Credit cards: MC, V. **Reduced fees:** Weekdays, Low season, Resort guests, Twilight, Seniors, Juniors.
Caddies: No. **Golf carts:** $10 for 18 holes.
Discount golf packages: Yes. **Season:** Year-round. **High:** May-Sept.
On-site lodging: Yes. **Rental clubs:** Yes.
Walking policy: Walking at certain times. **Range:** No.
To obtain tee times: Call up to 14 days in advance.
Subscriber comments: City course . . . Very good shape . . . Wide open . . . Windy at times . . . Well maintained, fun course to play . . . Putting at this course will make you crazy . . . Kept in outstanding condition year-round.

★★★ THE VINEYARD AT ESCONDIDO
PU—925 San Pasqual Rd., Escondido (619)735-9545.
15 miles north of San Diego. **Holes:** 18. **Par:** 70/70.
Yards: 6,531/5,073. **Course rating:** 70.3/70.3. **Slope:** 125/117.
Opened: 1993. **Pace of Play rating:** N/A. **Green fee:** $25/40.

Credit cards: MC, V, AMEX. **Reduced fees:** Weekdays, Low season,
Twilight, Seniors, Juniors.
Caddies: No. **Golf carts:** $10 for 18 holes.
Discount golf packages: No. **Season:** Year-round.
On-site lodging: No. **Rental clubs:** Yes.
Walking policy: Walking at certain times. **Range:** Yes.
To obtain tee times: Call seven days in advance.

★★ WASCO VALLEY ROSE GOLF COURSE
PU—301 North Leonard Ave., Wasco (805)758-8301.
19 miles north of Bakersfield. **Holes:** 18. **Par:** 72/72.
Yards: 6,862/5,356. **Course rating:** 72.5/70.5. **Slope:** 121/119.
Opened: 1991. **Pace of Play rating:** 4:10. **Green fee:** $10/12.
Credit cards: MC, V, AMEX. **Reduced fees:** Weekdays, Low season,
Twilight, Seniors, Juniors.
Caddies: No. **Golf carts:** $20 for 18 holes.
Discount golf packages: No. **Season:** Year-round. **High:** April-
June/Oct.
On-site lodging: No. **Rental clubs:** Yes.
Walking policy: Unrestricted walking. **Range:** Yes (grass).
To obtain tee times: Call seven days in advance.
Subscriber comments: Super-fast greens . . . Isolated out in the country
. . . Wonderful, fun, great test . . . Will be more challenging when the trees
grow up . . . Will play tougher when the course gets older . . . Flat course,
lots of doglegs . . . Good for average player . . . Well-maintained public
course in the middle of nowhere . . . Flat, good greens, no trees, hackers
delight . . . Even better if all the water hazards were full.

★★★½ THE WESTIN MISSION HILLS RESORT
R—71-501 Dinah Shore & Bob Hope Dr., Rancho Mirage (619)328-3198,
(800)358-2211.
10 miles east of Palm Springs. **Holes:** 18. **Par:** 70/70.
Yards: 6,987/4,841. **Course rating:** 73.7/67.4. **Slope:** 136/107.
Opened: 1987. **Pace of Play rating:** 4:15. **Green fee:** $55/120.
Credit cards: MC, V, AMEX. **Reduced fees:** Resort guests.
Caddies: No. **Golf carts:** Included in Green Fee.
Discount golf packages: Yes. **Season:** Year-round. **High:** Oct.-April.
On-site lodging: Yes. **Rental clubs:** Yes.
Walking policy: Mandatory cart. **Range:** Yes (grass).
To obtain tee times: Call two days in advance for outside play and three
months in advance for hotel guests.
Subscriber comments: A reasonable Pete Dye course, you'll come back
for more . . . very good resort course, multiple tees, fun for everyone . . .
Easier than North Course, playable for beginner . . . Another Pete Dye
course, if you like his stuff! . . . Resort golf at it's finest . . . Are greens
linoleum or what? . . . Too narrow, hemmed in by condos . . . Difficult if
you stray . . . Plush, pretty, looks intimidating but is very playable . . . A
resort course, too artificial . . . Fun layout, water everywhere . . .
Uninteresting design . . . Nice job, Pete.

WHISPERING PALMS LODGE AND COUNTRY CLUB
★½ EAST/SOUTH/NORTH
SP—5690 Cancha de Golf, Rancho Santa Fe (619)756-2471.
20 miles north of San Diego. **Holes:** 27. **Par:** 71/72/71.
Yards: 6,141/6,443/6,346. **Course rating:** 68.8/70.2/69.7.
Slope: 110/112/112.
Pace of Play rating: 4:00. **Green fee:** $35/45.
Credit cards: MC, V, AMEX. **Reduced fees:** Twilight.
Caddies: No. **Golf carts:** $10 for 18 holes.
Discount golf packages: Yes. **Season:** Year-round.
On-site lodging: Yes. **Rental clubs:** Yes.
Walking policy: Unrestricted walking. **Range:** Yes.
To obtain tee times: Call seven days in advance.

★½ WHITTIER NARROWS GOLF COURSE

PU—8640 E Rush St., Rosemead (818)288-1044.

Call club for further information.

Subscriber comments: Wide open, long but hard fairways made it play shorter . . . Between the model airplane park and the shooting range, too noisy . . . Course is long enough to be challenging . . . Needs better snack shop, restrooms too far away . . . Wide open, good place to work on game.

★★½ WILLOW PARK GOLF CLUB

PU—17007 Redwood Rd., Castro Valley (510)537-8989.

20 miles southeast of Oakland. **Holes:** 18. **Par:** 71/71.

Yards: 6,227/5,193. **Course rating:** 67.4/69.2. **Slope:** 110/117.

Opened: 1967. **Pace of Play rating:** 4:30. **Green fee:** $16/22.

Credit cards: None. **Reduced fees:** No.

Caddies: No. **Golf carts:** N/A.

Discount golf packages: No. **Season:** Year-round.

On-site lodging: No. **Rental clubs:** No.

Walking policy: Unrestricted walking. **Range:** Yes.

To obtain tee times: Call Monday for weekday at 7 a.m. and at 10 a.m. for weekend.

Subscriber comments: Delightful design . . . Fairways like a battlefield . . . Heavy play . . . Canyon course . . . Uninteresting flat course . . . No bathroom facilities on course . . . Deer on course nine out of 10 times . . . Short, tight, scenic fun . . . Wind does not affect play, deer do affect it . . . Very tight, short and picturesque . . . Tight layout, death to slicers . . . Lots of scenery and wildlife . . . Nondescript holes, lacks maintenance . . . Sporty course for straight hitter . . . Short and tight, hazards on most holes . . . Good layout, lots of challenging shots.

★★★½ WINDSOR GOLF CLUB

PU—6555 Skylane Blvd., Windsor (707)838-7888.

6 miles north of Santa Rosa. **Holes:** 18. **Par:** 72/72.

Yards: 6,650/5,116. **Course rating:** 72.3/69.3. **Slope:** 126/125.

Opened: 1989. **Pace of Play rating:** 4:15. **Green fee:** $22/35.

Credit cards: MC, V. **Reduced fees:** Weekdays, Twilight, Seniors, Juniors.

Caddies: No. **Golf carts:** N/A.

Discount golf packages: No. **Season:** Year-round.

On-site lodging: No. **Rental clubs:** Yes.

Walking policy: Unrestricted walking. **Range:** Yes (grass).

To obtain tee times: Call seven days in advance at 6:30 a.m.

Subscriber comments: Well laid-out course . . . A bit gimmicky on some holes, but a well-maintained course . . . Tightest target golf I have ever played . . . Nike Tour plays here . . . Big oak trees . . . Beautiful course but disgraceful greens . . . One of the best in California . . . Most greens in very bad shape; shame, it's a great layout, fun to play . . . Lots of variety to par 3s . . . Good layout needs maturing, especially greens . . . A gem of a golf course . . . Rough can be mean, tough par 3s . . . Best driving range north of Poppy Hills . . . Bring a good sand game . . . Bring plenty of straight shots with you . . . Frequently overlooked great course in a great golfing area . . . Creatively uses the natural terrain and trees . . . Great track for the money.

★½ WOODLEY LAKES GOLF CLUB

PU—6331 Woodley Ave., Van Nuys (818)787-8163.

Call club for further information.

Subscriber comments: Old reliable, but getting a much needed facelift . . . Easy, no great ego builder . . . Dull course, nice greens . . . Greens better than other city courses . . . Very plain public layout . . . Great for duffers scoring between 90 and 100 . . . Long, flat, dull, bunkers not in play . . . Designed for fast play . . . Wide open, good greens, a nice course for beginners . . . Wide fairways, big greens . . . Adequate golf . . . No trees, no trouble, no fun.

★★½ ADOBE CREEK NATIONAL GOLF COURSE

PU—876 18½ Rd., Fruita (303)858-0521.

9 miles west of Grand Junction. **Holes:** 18. **Par:** 72/72.

Yards: 6,997/4,980. **Course rating:** 71.2/55.1. **Slope:** 119/ 97.

Opened: 1992. **Pace of Play rating:** 4:10. **Green fee:** $16/ 22.

Credit cards: None. **Reduced fees:** Weekdays, Low season, Twilight, Seniors, Juniors.

Caddies: No. **Golf carts:** $16 for 18 holes.

Discount golf packages: No. **Season:** May-Dec. **High:** May-Sept.

On-site lodging: No. **Rental clubs:** Yes.

Walking policy: Unrestricted walking. **Range:** Yes (grass).

To obtain tee times: Call two days in advance.

Subscriber comments: New Course, will get better as it matures, nice people, good service . . . Gorgeous views of Colorado . . . Good course layout.

★★ APPLETREE GOLF COURSE

PU—10150 Rolling Ridge Rd., Colorado Springs (719)382-3649, (800)844-6531.

80 miles south of Denver. **Holes:** 18. **Par:** 72/72.

Yards: 6,407/5,003. **Course rating:** 68.6/66.9. **Slope:** 122/113.

Opened: 1972. **Pace of Play rating:** N/A. **Green fee:** $10/ 20.

Credit cards: MC, V. **Reduced fees:** Weekdays, Low season, Seniors, Juniors.

Caddies: No. **Golf carts:** $20 for 18 holes.

Discount golf packages: No. **Season:** Year-round. **High:** May-Sept.

On-site lodging: No. **Rental clubs:** Yes.

Walking policy: Unrestricted walking. **Range:** Yes (grass).

To obtain tee times: Call up to seven days in advance.

Subscriber comments: Friendly people, challenging for medium level player, course needs some work . . . Good family course, mostly flat, some water, very courteous staff . . . Vastly improved with additional bunkers and mounds . . . Beautiful course, reasonable price, worth the trip.

★★ APPLEWOOD GOLF COURSE

PU—14001 W. 32nd Ave., Golden (303)279-3003.

13 miles west of Golden. **Holes:** 18. **Par:** 71/72.

Yards: 6,229/5,374. **Course rating:** 68.2/69.0. **Slope:** 122/118.

Opened: 1954. **Pace of Play rating:** 4:30. **Green fee:** $15/ 21.

Credit cards: MC, V, AMEX. **Reduced fees:** Weekdays, Twilight, Seniors, Juniors.

Caddies: No. **Golf carts:** $10 for 18 holes.

Discount golf packages: Yes. **Season:** Year-round. **High:** April-Oct.

On-site lodging: No. **Rental clubs:** Yes.

Walking policy: Unrestricted walking. **Range:** Yes (grass).

To obtain tee times: Call six days in advance.

Subscriber comments: Dry fairways, very open layout . . . An environmentally friendly course . . . No pesticides used . . . Tee times seven to eight minutes apart . . . Crowded . . . Lack of water! Allow fivesomes, slow . . . OK for environment, marginal for golf.

★★★½ ARROWHEAD GOLF CLUB

PU—10850 W. Sundown Trail, Littleton (303)973-9614.

15 miles south of Denver. **Holes:** 18. **Par:** 70/72.

Yards: 6,682/5,465. **Course rating:** 70.9/70.0. **Slope:** 134/123.

Opened: 1978. **Pace of Play rating:** 4:30-5:00. **Green fee:** $45/80.

Credit cards: MC, V, AMEX. **Reduced fees:** Weekdays, Low season, Twilight, Seniors.

Caddies: No. **Golf carts:** Included in Green Fee.

Discount golf packages: No. **Season:** March-Nov. **High:** June-Sept.

On-site lodging: No. **Rental clubs:** Yes.

Walking policy: Mandatory cart. **Range:** Yes (grass).

To obtain tee times: Call seven days in advance with credit card.

Ranked in Third 25 of America's 75 Best Public Golf Courses by Golf Digest. Ranked 18th in Colorado by Golf Digest.

COLORADO

Subscriber comments: Beautiful scenery, worth the price one time . . . Spectacular red rock formations . . . Most beautiful golf course east of the Rockies, sandstone formations, lakes, deer, eagles . . . Only affordable in off-season and twilight . . . Has never reached its potential . . . Could be great . . . Bring your oxygen because you'll get a Colorado "high" from this course . . . Most scenic course I have ever played . . . God built it, humans planted the grass.

★★ ASPEN GOLF COURSE
PU—408 East Cooper, Aspen (303)925-2145.
Holes: 18. **Par:** 71/72.
Yards: 7,165/5,591. **Course rating:** 72.2/69.9. **Slope:** 125/116.
Opened: 1962. **Pace of Play rating:** 4:15. **Green fee:** $35/55.
Credit cards: MC, V. **Reduced fees:** Low season, Seniors, Juniors.
Caddies: No. **Golf carts:** $13 for 18 holes.
Discount golf packages: No. **Season:** April-Oct. **High:** July-Sept.
On-site lodging: No. **Rental clubs:** Yes.
Walking policy: Unrestricted walking. **Range:** Yes (grass).
To obtain tee times: Call three days in advance.
Subscriber comments: Too flat . . . Nice grass for mountains . . . Multi-tiered greens . . . Every hole a statement . . . Practice putting before playing here . . . Long, but flat and not inspiring . . . Scenery saves it . . . For the laid back, non-serious golfer.

★½ AURORA HILLS GOLF COURSE
PU—50 S. Peoria St., Aurora (303)364-6111.
10 miles east of Denver. **Holes:** 18. **Par:** 72/73.
Yards: 6,735/5,919. **Course rating:** 70.0/71.3. **Slope:** 115/109.
Opened: 1968. **Pace of Play rating:** 4:15. **Green fee:** $13/20.
Credit cards: MC, V. **Reduced fees:** Twilight, Seniors, Juniors.
Caddies: No. **Golf carts:** $9 for 18 holes.
Discount golf packages: No. **Season:** Year-round. **High:** May-Sept.
On-site lodging: No. **Rental clubs:** Yes.
Walking policy: Unrestricted walking. **Range:** Yes (grass).
To obtain tee times: Call pro shop.
Subscriber comments: Very flat, relatively easy, public course . . . Front nine is the better side . . . Back nine flat . . . Wide open . . . Like playing in a big field . . . Wonderful cook in the grill . . . Fairly easy, good warm-up course.

★★★½ BATTLEMENT MESA GOLF CLUB
PU—3930 N. Battlement Pkwy., Parachute (303)285-7274.
42 miles east of Glenwood Springs. **Holes:** 18. **Par:** 72/72.
Yards: 7,309/5,386. **Course rating:** 73.9/69.9. **Slope:** 132/112.
Opened: 1987. **Pace of Play rating:** 4:15. **Green fee:** $18/26.
Credit cards: All major. **Reduced fees:** Weekdays, Low season, Seniors, Juniors.

Caddies: No. **Golf carts:** $12 for 18 holes.
Discount golf packages: Yes. **Season:** March-Nov. **High:** June-Aug.
On-site lodging: Yes. **Rental clubs:** Yes.
Walking policy: Unrestricted walking. **Range:** Yes (grass).
To obtain tee times: Call three days in advance or up to one year with lodging and golf package.
Subscriber comments: A Colorado sleeper . . . Very good course, great weekend packages . . . Challenging, imaginative and scenic course, can be a brute when windy . . . Very scenic, great variety, use all clubs, knowledge helps . . . Wonderful course and accommodations . . . A buy at twice the price . . . Tough . . . Rewards smart golf . . . Excellent greens.

★★★ BEAVER CREEK GOLF CLUB
R—P.O. Box 915, Avon (303)845-5775.
100 west of Denver. **Holes:** 18. **Par:** 70/70.
Yards: 6,752/5,200. **Course rating:** 69.2/70.2. **Slope:** 133/121.
Opened: 1982. **Pace of Play rating:** 4:30. **Green fee:** $100.

Credit cards: All major. **Reduced fees:** Low season, Resort guests.
Caddies: No. **Golf carts:** Included in Green Fee.
Discount golf packages: No. **Season:** May-Oct. **High:** May-June.
On-site lodging: Yes. **Rental clubs:** Yes.
Walking policy: Mandatory cart. **Range:** Yes (grass).
To obtain tee times: Call for information, depends on where you are staying.
Subscriber comments: The view was breathtaking . . . First four and last four holes the best . . . Another great mountain course . . . Great variety of holes, last three are super . . . A little pricey . . . Fun, short, mountain course, some beautiful tree-lined holes.

★★★ BOOMERANG LINKS

PU—7309 West 4th St., Greeley (303)351-8934, (800)266-6371.
40 miles north of Denver. **Holes:** 18. **Par:** 72/72.
Yards: 7,214/5,285. **Course rating:** 72.6/68.5. **Slope:** 131/113.
Opened: 1991. **Pace of Play rating:** 4:00. **Green fee:** $15/18.
Credit cards: MC, V, DISC. **Reduced fees:** Weekdays, Low season, Twilight, Seniors, Juniors.
Caddies: No. **Golf carts:** $18 for 18 holes.
Discount golf packages: No. **Season:** Year-round. **High:** June-Sept.
On-site lodging: No. **Rental clubs:** Yes.
Walking policy: Unrestricted walking. **Range:** Yes (grass).
To obtain tee times: Call Monday for the following seven days.
Subscriber comments: Impossible front nine with OB left water right . . . Straight hitter's course . . . Shotmaking, accuracy a must! . . . Narrow fairways make course a real challenge . . . Fun course, good staff, good weekend rates . . . Still new course, needs to mature a little.

★★★★ BRECKENRIDGE GOLF CLUB

PU—200 Clubhouse Dr., Breckenridge (303)453-9104.
80 miles west of Denver. **Holes:** 18. **Par:** 72/72.
Yards: 7,279/5,066. **Course rating:** 73.1/67.7. **Slope:** 146/118.
Opened: 1985. **Pace of Play rating:** 4:30. **Green fee:** $45/58.
Credit cards: MC, V, AMEX. **Reduced fees:** Low season, Twilight.
Caddies: No. **Golf carts:** $12 for 18 holes.
Discount golf packages: No. **Season:** May-Oct. **High:** July-Sept.
On-site lodging: No. **Rental clubs:** Yes.
Walking policy: Walking at certain times. **Range:** Yes (grass).
To obtain tee times: Call two days in advance.
Ranked 14th in Colorado by Golf Digest.
Subscriber comments: You want to know how good you are, play here . . . Outstanding layout, difficult to get a tee time . . . Always beautiful, a challenge, well run . . . Too hard for most golfers, some greens too small to be fair . . . Hard to concentrate with all the beauty around you . . . A Colorado classic . . . Best mountain track for the money . . . A "must" play . . . Superb Nicklaus course at high altitude.

BROADMOOR GOLF CLUB
★★★★ EAST COURSE

R—1 Pourtales Dr., Colorado Springs (719)577-5790, (800)634-7711.
60 miles south of Denver. **Holes:** 18. **Par:** 72/73.
Yards: 7,091/5,873. **Course rating:** 73.0/74.1. **Slope:** 129/126.
Opened: 1918. **Pace of Play rating:** 4:10. **Green fee:** $83.
Credit cards: All major. **Reduced fees:** No.
Caddies: Yes. **Golf carts:** $15 for 18 holes.
Discount golf packages: Yes. **Season:** Year-round. **High:** April-Oct.
On-site lodging: Yes. **Rental clubs:** Yes.
Walking policy: Mandatory cart or Caddie. **Range:** Yes (grass).
To obtain tee times: Confirm reservations in hotel. Call pro shop.
Ranked 29th in America's 75 Best Resort Courses by Golf Digest. Ranked 10th in Colorado by Golf Digest.
Subscriber comments: Marvelous old golf course, very challenging . . . Ross didn't build bad ones! Women's Open will find a good test on this fine

course . . . Grand old lady . . . Broadmoor spring and fall packages are outstanding values . . . Old line character, but a lot of use . . . Great courses . . . Can get a good deal at right time . . . Great golf in a five star resort . . . A Donald Ross open to the public!

★★★½ SOUTH COURSE

R—1 Pourtales Dr., Colorado Springs (719)577-5790.
60 miles south of Denver. **Holes:** 18. **Par:** 72/72.
Yards: 6,781/4,834. **Course rating:** 72.1/68.4. **Slope:** 135/117.
Opened: 1976. **Pace of Play rating:** 4:10. **Green fee:** $83.
Credit cards: All major. **Reduced fees:** No.
Caddies: Yes. **Golf carts:** $15 for 18 holes.
Discount golf packages: Yes. **Season:** Year-round. **High:** April-Oct.
On-site lodging: Yes. **Rental clubs:** Yes.
Walking policy: Mandatory cart or Caddie. **Range:** Yes (grass).
To obtain tee times: Call golf club.
Ranked 19th in Colorado by Golf Digest.
Subscriber comments: Too much target from tee . . . Real challenge, great food, closes too soon . . . Outstanding place to play golf. Arnold Palmer at his best . . . Have to aim at flags on many drives (Blind shots) . . . Target golf in the mountains, great fun.

★★★★ WEST COURSE

R—1 Pourtales Dr., Colorado Springs (719)577-5790, (800)634-7711.
60 miles south of Denver. **Holes:** 18. **Par:** 72/73.
Yards: 6,937/5,505. **Course rating:** 73.0/71.6. **Slope:** 133/122.
Opened: 1918. **Pace of Play rating:** 4:10. **Green fee:** 83.
Credit cards: All major. **Reduced fees:** No.
Caddies: Yes. **Golf carts:** $15 for 18 holes.
Discount golf packages: Yes. **Season:** Year-round. **High:** April-Oct.
On-site lodging: Yes. **Rental clubs:** Yes.
Walking policy: Mandatory cart or Caddie. **Range:** Yes (grass).
To obtain tee times: Call pro shop.
Ranked 58th in America's 75 Best Resort Courses by Golf Digest. Ranked 16th in Colorado by Golf Digest.
Subscriber comments: Great staff, nice course, new club is something . . . My favorite . . . Good course, tough greens, excellent views . . . Not as good as East, but very good . . . Excellent shop . . . Spectacular course, awesome scenery, serious golf.

★½ CITY PARK GOLF CLUB

PU—2500 York, Denver (303)295-2095
Call club for further information.
Subscriber comments: Muny course, good value for seniors, little difficulty . . . Easy fairways, challenge on greens, nice public course . . . Great views of mountains and city scape . . . Not much trouble, a muny course and shows it . . . Best BBQ in Colorado!

★★★ COAL CREEK GOLF COURSE

PU—275 S. Lark Ave., Louisville (303)666-7888.
4 miles east of Boulder. **Holes:** 18. **Par:** 72/72.
Yards: 6,957/5,168. **Course rating:** 71.1/68.4. **Slope:** 130/114.
Opened: 1990. **Pace of Play rating:** N/A. **Green fee:** $14/23.
Credit cards: MC, V. **Reduced fees:** Weekdays, Low season, Twilight, Seniors, Juniors.
Caddies: No. **Golf carts:** $18 for 18 holes.
Discount golf packages: No. **Season:** Year-round. **High:** April-Sept.
On-site lodging: No. **Rental clubs:** Yes.
Walking policy: Unrestricted walking. **Range:** Yes (grass).
To obtain tee times: Call three days in advance beginning 8 a.m.
Subscriber comments: Good variety of holes . . . Requires using most of the irons and woods in your bag . . . Super friendly for juniors . . . Only course in the area that lets my six-year-old go with me . . . Great layout, creek comes into play on several holes . . . Nice practice area . . . Young course but value is excellent, will get better with age . . . Houses built around course have hurt the beauty of the course.

★★ COLLINDALE GOLF CLUB

PU—1441 E. Horsetooth Rd., Fort Collins (303)221-6651.
60 miles north of Denver. **Holes:** 18. **Par:** 71/73.
Yards: 7,011/5,472. **Course rating:** 71.5/69.9. **Slope:** 126/113.
Opened: 1972. **Pace of Play rating:** 4:00-4:30. **Green fee:** $13/14.
Credit cards: MC, V. **Reduced fees:** Weekdays, Low season, Twilight,
Seniors, Juniors.
Caddies: No. **Golf carts:** $16 for 18 holes.
Discount golf packages: No. **Season:** Year-round. **High:** May-Sept.
On-site lodging: No. **Rental clubs:** Yes.
Walking policy: Unrestricted walking. **Range:** Yes (grass).
To obtain tee times: Call three days in advance.
Subscriber comments: Friendly and knowledgeable staff . . . Excellent
greens, best I've seen on a public course . . . So flat it puts you to sleep . . .
Easy walking . . . Great greens year round . . . Flat, but interesting . . .
Great condition in Colorado climate.

★★½ COPPER MOUNTAIN RESORT
COPPER CREEK GOLF CLUB

R—104 Wheeler Circle, Copper Mountain (303)968-2882.
75 miles west of Denver. **Holes:** 18. **Par:** 70/70.
Yards: 6,094/4,374. **Course rating:** 67.6/63.8. **Slope:** 124/100.
Opened: 1976. **Pace of Play rating:** 4:00. **Green fee:** $55/65.
Credit cards: All major. **Reduced fees:** Low season, Resort guests,
Twilight.
Caddies: No. **Golf carts:** Included in Green Fee.
Discount golf packages: Yes. **Season:** June-Oct. **High:** July-Aug.
On-site lodging: Yes. **Rental clubs:** Yes.
Walking policy: Mandatory cart. **Range:** Yes (grass).
To obtain tee times: Resort guests, sixty days in advance, nonguests call
four days in advance.
Subscriber comments: Beautiful views, after 3:00 package great . . .
Short, but demanding target golf . . . Fun layout . . . Holes go down ski
slopes . . . Very short . . . A couple of great holes.

★★★★ DALTON RANCH GOLF CLUB

SP—589 C.R. 252, Durango (303)247-8774.
Holes: 18. **Par:** 72/72.
Yards: 6,934/5,539. **Course rating:** 72.4/71.7. **Slope:** 135/125.
Opened: 1993. **Pace of Play rating:** 4:15. **Green fee:** $21/31.
Credit cards: MC, V. **Reduced fees:** Low season, Resort guests,
Twilight.
Caddies: No. **Golf carts:** $9 for 18 holes.
Discount golf packages: Yes. **Season:** April-Nov. **High:** June-Sept.
On-site lodging: No. **Rental clubs:** Yes.
Walking policy: Unrestricted walking. **Range:** Yes (grass).
To obtain tee times: Call pro shop.
Subscriber comments: Greens demand lofted approaches, water on
fourteen holes . . . A hidden jewel. Don't miss it. Great service . . . Not
long, but a real test.

★★★ DOS RIOS GOLF CLUB

PU—501 Camino Del Rio, Gunnison (303)641-1482.
Call club for further information.
Subscriber comments: Not very long but oh, so much water . . . Lots of
fun, two totally different nines . . . Challenging course, employees go out
of the way to be nice.

★★★ EAGLE VAIL GOLF CLUB

PU—0431 Eagle Dr., Avon (303)949-5267.
107 miles west of Denver. **Holes:** 18. **Par:** 72/72.
Yards: 6,819/4,856. **Course rating:** 70.9/67.3. **Slope:** 131/114.
Opened: 1975. **Pace of Play rating:** 4:30. **Green fee:** $40/70.
Credit cards: MC, V, AMEX. **Reduced fees:** Low season, Twilight.

Caddies: No. **Golf carts:** Included in Green Fee.
Discount golf packages: No. **Season:** May-Oct. **High:** June-Sept.
On-site lodging: No. **Rental clubs:** Yes.
Walking policy: Mandatory cart. **Range:** Yes (grass).
To obtain tee times: Call two days in advance.
Subscriber comments: Good course but tricky . . . Balls just seem to fly forever . . . Many improvements over the years, interesting holes . . . Great distance due to altitude . . . Beautiful setting . . . Shotmaker's course . . . Best hot dogs at the turn . . . Some goofy holes, even for a mountain resort course.

★★½ EAGLES NEST GOLF CLUB
PU—305 Golden Eagle Rd., Silverthorne (303)468-0681.
67 miles west of Denver. **Holes:** 18. **Par:** 72/72.
Yards: 7,024/5,556. **Course rating:** 72.6/71.9. **Slope:** 141/126.
Opened: 1985. **Pace of Play rating:** 4:30. **Green fee:** $25/70.
Credit cards: MC, V. **Reduced fees:** Weekdays, Low season, Twilight, Juniors.
Caddies: No. **Golf carts:** Included in Green Fee.
Discount golf packages: Yes. **Season:** May-Oct. **High:** July-Sept.
On-site lodging: No. **Rental clubs:** Yes.
Walking policy: Mandatory cart. **Range:** Yes (grass).
To obtain tee times: Call seven days in advance.
Subscriber comments: This course is more like an amusement park . . . Another goofy, gimmicky course, fun but too many blind shots . . . A must at least once . . . Beautiful mountain layout . . . Wildlife . . . Great setting.

★★½ ESTES PARK GOLF COURSE
PU—1080 S. Saint Vrain Ave., Estes Park (303)586-8146.
60 miles west of Denver. **Holes:** 18. **Par:** 71/72.
Yards: 6,326/5,250. **Course rating:** 68.3/68.3. **Slope:** 118/115.
Opened: 1957. **Pace of Play rating:** 3:47. **Green fee:** $20/28.
Credit cards: MC, V. **Reduced fees:** Low season, Twilight.
Caddies: No. **Golf carts:** $10 for 18 holes.
Discount golf packages: Yes. **Season:** April-Oct. **High:** June-Sept.
On-site lodging: No. **Rental clubs:** Yes.
Walking policy: Unrestricted walking. **Range:** Yes (grass).
To obtain tee times: Call seven days in advance.
Subscriber comments: Play through elk herds . . . Redesigned and fun to play, ball goes forever in altitude . . . Mountain course, some blind shots . . . Fun course set in spectacular mountain setting . . . Best buy for mountain course.

★★★ FAIRFIELD PAGOSA GOLF CLUB
PINON/PONDEROSA/MEADOWS
R—One Pines Club Place, Pagosa Springs (303)731-4755.
55 miles east of Durango. **Holes:** 27. **Par:** 71/72/71.
Yards: 6,670/7,221/6,913. **Course rating:** 69.4/72.9/70.9.
Slope: 119/125/123.
Opened: 1973. **Pace of Play rating:** N/A. **Green fee:** $22/28.
Credit cards: All major. **Reduced fees:** Low season, Twilight, Juniors.
Caddies: No. **Golf carts:** $10 for 18 holes.
Discount golf packages: Yes. **Season:** April-Oct. **High:** July-Aug.
On-site lodging: Yes. **Rental clubs:** Yes.
Walking policy: Unrestricted walking. **Range:** Yes (grass).
To obtain tee times: Call one week in advance.
Subscriber comments: Few know about this course . . . Great variety of holes and nines . . . Good greens . . . Lovely view of mountains . . . Scenery is terrific.

★★ FLATIRONS GOLF COURSE
PU—5706 Arapahoe Rd., Boulder (303)442-7851.
15 miles northwest of Denver. **Holes:** 18. **Par:** 70/71.
Yards: 6,765/5,615. **Course rating:** 69.9/71.1. **Slope:** 125/115.

Opened: 1933. **Pace of Play rating:** 4:10. **Green fee:** $14/18.
Credit cards: MC, V. **Reduced fees:** No.
Caddies: No. **Golf carts:** $9 for 18 holes.
Discount golf packages: No. **Season:** Year-round. **High:** March–Sept.
On-site lodging: No. **Rental clubs:** Yes.
Walking policy: Unrestricted walking. **Range:** Yes (grass).
To obtain tee times: Call one day in advance for weekdays at 7 a.m. and
three days in advance for weekends at 7 p.m.
Subscriber comments: The "flat" in the name says it all . . . Old course
. . . Lots of trees . . . Fun course and not overly difficult . . . Plain layout
. . . Inexpensive . . . Flat and open, easy enough . . . Great mountain
views.

★★½ FOOTHILLS GOLF COURSE
PU—3901 S. Carr St., Denver (303)989-3901.
Holes: 18. **Par:** 72/74.
Yards: 6,908/6,028. **Course rating:** 71.1/73.4. **Slope:** 122/118.
Opened: 1971. **Pace of Play rating:** N/A. **Green fee:** $15.
Credit cards: MC, V. **Reduced fees:** No.
Caddies: No. **Golf carts:** $10 for 18 holes.
Discount golf packages: No. **Season:** Year-round. **High:** April–Oct.
On-site lodging: No. **Rental clubs:** Yes.
Walking policy: Unrestricted walking. **Range:** Yes (grass).
To obtain tee times: Nonresidents call two days in advance.
Subscriber comments: Helpful people . . . Great value for the money . . .
What you see is what you get . . . Course finally maturing after 20 years
. . . Potential to be a good course if better maintained . . . New irrigation
system improved course . . . Great practice site.

★★½ FORT MORGAN GOLF COURSE
PU—17586 Colorado Rd., T.5, Fort Morgan (303)867-5990.
70 miles northeast of Denver. **Holes:** 18. **Par:** 73/74.
Yards: 6,470/5,615. **Course rating:** 69.7/70.1. **Slope:** 117/113.
Opened: N/A. **Pace of Play rating:** 3:50. **Green fee:** $12/18.
Credit cards: MC, V. **Reduced fees:** Weekdays.
Caddies: No. **Golf carts:** N/A.
Discount golf packages: No. **Season:** Year-round. **High:** April–Oct.
On-site lodging: No. **Rental clubs:** Yes.
Walking policy: Unrestricted walking. **Range:** Yes (grass).
To obtain tee times: Call seven days in advance for weekdays and three
days in advance for weekends and holidays.
Subscriber comments: Nice course, all levels enjoy this one . . . Good
little country course.

(FRUGAL PICK)

★★★★ FOX HOLLOW AT LAKEWOOD GOLF COURSE
CANYON/MEADOW/LINKS
PU—13410 W. Morrison Rd., Lakewood (303)986-7888.
15 miles west of Denver. **Holes:** 27. **Par:** 71/72/71.
Yards: 6,808/6,888/7,030. **Course rating:** 71.2/71.1/72.3.
Slope: 138/132/134.
Opened: 1993. **Pace of Play rating:** 4:45. **Green fee:** $27.
Credit cards: MC, V. **Reduced fees:** Seniors, Juniors.
Caddies: No. **Golf carts:** $12 for 18 holes.
Discount golf packages: No. **Season:** Year-round. **High:** April–Oct.
On-site lodging: No. **Rental clubs:** Yes.
Walking policy: Unrestricted walking. **Range:** Yes (grass).
To obtain tee times: Call six days in advance for nonresidents after 5 p.m.
Canyon and Meadow nines selected as runner-up for Best New Public
Course of 1994 by Golf Digest. Canyon and Meadow nines ranked 12th in
Colorado by Golf Digest.
Subscriber comments: One of the best public courses in America . . . It's
like a great country club . . . Canyon/Meadow the best . . . Good layout,
will develop into great one . . . Public, but as good as most courses which
boast exclusive rates and resort quality . . . What can I say? Wish they had

54 holes! . . . They treat you like a CC member . . . Looks like a 20-year-old masterpiece in only two years . . . Two nines are great, the third is good . . . Very friendly staff, kind of course I'd like to play daily . . . Spikeless from November to April.

★★★ GRAND LAKE GOLF COURSE
PU—1415 County Rd. 48, Grand Lake (303)627-8008.
100 miles northwest of Denver. **Holes:** 18. **Par:** 72/74.
Yards: 6,542/5,685. **Course rating:** 70.5/70.9. **Slope:** 131/123.
Opened: 1964. **Pace of Play rating:** 4:20. **Green fee:** $40.
Credit cards: MC, V. **Reduced fees:** No.
Caddies: No. **Golf carts:** N/A.
Discount golf packages: No. **Season:** May-Oct. **High:** July-Aug.
On-site lodging: No. **Rental clubs:** Yes.
Walking policy: Unrestricted walking. **Range:** Yes (grass).
To obtain tee times: Call two days in advance for weekdays and Thursday 6:30 a.m. for weekend.
Subscriber comments: Fun mountain course good service . . . Cut into mountains, beautiful surprises . . . Each hole carved out of woods, hit it straight, beautiful setting . . . Leave driver at home, narrow, trees everywhere, beautiful.

★★★★ GRANDOTE GOLF AND COUNTRY CLUB
R—5540 Hwy. 12, La Veta (719)742-3122, (800)762-9513.
45 miles south of Pueblo. **Holes:** 18. **Par:** 72/72.
Yards: 7,085/5,608. **Course rating:** 72.8/70.7. **Slope:** 133/117.
Opened: 1986. **Pace of Play rating:** 4:00. **Green fee:** $30/45.

Credit cards: MC, V. **Reduced fees:** Weekdays, Low season.
Caddies: No. **Golf carts:** $20 for 18 holes.
Discount golf packages: Yes. **Season:** April-Oct. **High:** July-Sept.
On-site lodging: No. **Rental clubs:** Yes.
Walking policy: Unrestricted walking. **Range:** Yes (grass).
To obtain tee times: Call anytime.
Ranked 3rd in Colorado by Golf Digest.
Subscriber comments: Hard to get there, but worth it . . . Great course, all day green fee . . . Probably the best kept secret in Colorado . . . Super staff, beautiful view, nice secret . . . Stay at Great Sand Dunes for food . . . If you hit it in the rough, forget it . . . A hidden jewel in the southern Colorado mountains . . . Outstanding value and uncrowded! Would play there everyday . . . Love this course, great golf packages.

★★★½ GREAT SAND DUNES COUNTRY CLUB
R—5303 Hiwy. 150, Mosca (719)378-2357, (800)284-9213.
30 miles northeast of Alamosa. **Holes:** 18. **Par:** 72/72.
Yards: 7,006/5,327. **Course rating:** 71.2/67.8. **Slope:** 126/118.
Opened: 1990. **Pace of Play rating:** N/A. **Green fee:** $65.
Credit cards: All major. **Reduced fees:** No.
Caddies: No. **Golf carts:** Included in Green Fee.
Discount golf packages: Yes. **Season:** May-Oct. **High:** July-Sept.
On-site lodging: Yes. **Rental clubs:** Yes.
Walking policy: Unrestricted walking. **Range:** Yes (grass).
To obtain tee times: Call pro shop.
Subscriber comments: Too much rough . . . Buffalo and deer abound . . . A beautiful and fair course . . . It is quite long . . . Course is better since they have redesigned it . . . Very courteous staff.

★★★ HIGHLAND HILLS GOLF COURSE
PU—2200 Clubhouse Dr., Greeley (303)330-7327.
50 miles north of Denver. **Holes:** 18. **Par:** 71/75.
Yards: 6,700/6,002. **Course rating:** 71.4/72.8. **Slope:** 128/120.
Opened: 1961. **Pace of Play rating:** 4:00. **Green fee:** $16/20.
Credit cards: MC, V, DISC. **Reduced fees:** Weekdays, Low season, Twilight, Seniors, Juniors.
Caddies: No. **Golf carts:** N/A.

Discount golf packages: Yes. **Season:** Year-round. **High:** May-Oct.
On-site lodging: No. **Rental clubs:** Yes.
Walking policy: Unrestricted walking. **Range:** Yes (grass).
To obtain tee times: Call seven days in advance.
Subscriber comments: May be the best muny track in Colorado . . . Got to hit them straight . . . Very friendly staff . . . Strong muny course, lots of trees, well maintained . . . Tree-lined fairways.

★★½ HILLCREST GOLF CLUB
SP—2300 Rim Dr., Durango (303)247-1499.
Holes: 18. **Par:** 71/71.
Yards: 6,838/5,252. **Course rating:** 71.3/68.1. **Slope:** 127/111.
Opened: 1969. **Pace of Play rating:** 4:00. **Green fee:** $15.
Credit cards: MC, V. **Reduced fees:** Twilight.
Caddies: No. **Golf carts:** $15 for 18 holes.
Discount golf packages: No. **Season:** March-Nov. **High:** June-Aug.
On-site lodging: No. **Rental clubs:** Yes.
Walking policy: Unrestricted walking. **Range:** Yes (grass).
To obtain tee times: Call one week in advance.
Subscriber comments: Well maintained, great value, friendly staff, mountain scenery . . . Hillcrest is a really good public course . . . Beautiful setting, bargain! A real buy from a money standpoint . . . The greens are in remarkable shape for the amount of play.

★★★½ INDIAN PEAKS GOLF CLUB
PU—2300 Indian Peaks Trail, Lafayette (303)666-4706.
10 miles west of Boulder. **Holes:** 18. **Par:** 72/72.
Yards: 7,083/5,468. **Course rating:** 72.5/69.9. **Slope:** 134/116.
Opened: 1993. **Pace of Play rating:** 4:10. **Green fee:** $22/25.
Credit cards: MC, V. **Reduced fees:** Weekdays.
Caddies: No. **Golf carts:** $10 for 18 holes.
Discount golf packages: No. **Season:** Year-round. **High:** May-Sept.
On-site lodging: No. **Rental clubs:** Yes.
Walking policy: Unrestricted walking. **Range:** Yes (grass).
To obtain tee times: Call one day in advance for weekdays. Call Monday for Saturday tee time and Tuesday for a Sunday tee time.
Subscriber comments: A good test from Hale Irwin . . . Great views, tough in spots, thinking man's course . . . Will be outstanding when greens mature . . . Great staff, fun track that won't whip you . . . Well-run course, great shape for its age . . . User-friendly wide fairways . . . Hard to get on but worth it . . . Plays like Hale: steady and tough . . . Beautiful large driving range . . . Irwin carved a beauty . . . Good place to take customers.

★★½ INDIAN TREE GOLF CLUB
PU—7555 Wadsworth Blvd., Arvada (303)423-3450.
10 miles northwest of Denver. **Holes:** 18. **Par:** 70/75.
Yards: 6,742/5,850. **Course rating:** 69.6/71.4. **Slope:** 114/116.
Opened: 1971. **Pace of Play rating:** 4:30. **Green fee:** $18.
Credit cards: MC, V. **Reduced fees:** No.
Caddies: No. **Golf carts:** $18 for 18 holes.
Discount golf packages: No. **Season:** Year-round. **High:** May-Sept.
On-site lodging: No. **Rental clubs:** Yes.
Walking policy: Unrestricted walking. **Range:** Yes (grass).
To obtain tee times: Call 24 hours in advance.
Also has 9-hole par-3 course.
Subscriber comments: Average public course, nothing special, but enjoyed . . . A lot of up and down terrain . . . Being upgraded . . . Very nice staff, always willing to help . . . Great layout, challenging, but not tricky.

★★★★ INVERNESS GOLF COURSE
R—200 Inverness Dr. W., Englewood (303)799-9660.
3 miles south of Denver. **Holes:** 18. **Par:** 70/70.
Yards: 6,948/6,407. **Course rating:** N/A. **Slope:** 136/129.

Opened: 1974. **Pace of Play rating:** N/A. **Green fee:** N/A.
Credit cards: All major. **Reduced fees:** Twilight.
Caddies: No. **Golf carts:** N/A.
Discount golf packages: Yes. **Season:** Year-round. **High:** June-Aug.
On-site lodging: Yes. **Rental clubs:** No.
Walking policy: N/A. **Range:** Yes (grass).
Subscriber comments: Play it from the tips, great holes . . . Well conditioned, great greens, staff works hard to keep pace of play quick . . . One of the best in town, a little pricey, never boring . . . As a hotel guest, the value is very good for this course.

★★ JOHN F. KENNEDY GOLF CLUB

PU—10500 E. Hampden Ave., Aurora (303)755-0105.
6 miles east of Denver. **Holes:** 27. **Par:** 71/71/72.
Yards: 6,868/6,753/7,009. **Course rating:** 71.6/70.9/71.7.
Slope: 131/124/118.
Opened: 1963. **Pace of Play rating:** 4:30. **Green fee:** $14/19.
Credit cards: None. **Reduced fees:** Seniors, Juniors.
Caddies: No. **Golf carts:** $20 for 18 holes.
Discount golf packages: No. **Season:** Year-round. **High:** April-Sept.
On-site lodging: No. **Rental clubs:** Yes.
Walking policy: Unrestricted walking. **Range:** Yes.
To obtain tee times: Must purchase card.
Also has a par 3 course.
Subscriber comments: Excellent muny, with better maintenance would be first rate . . . New nine outstanding by Dick Phelps . . . Long and not much trouble . . . Large greens . . . Wide open.

★★★½ KEYSTONE RANCH GOLF COURSE

R—P.O. Box 38, Keystone (303)468-4250.
75 miles west of Denver. **Holes:** 18. **Par:** 72/72.
Yards: 7,090/5,596. **Course rating:** 71.4/70.7. **Slope:** 130/129.
Opened: 1980. **Pace of Play rating:** 4:30. **Green fee:** $82/92.
Credit cards: All major. **Reduced fees:** Low season, Resort guests, Twilight, Juniors.
Caddies: No. **Golf carts:** Included in Green Fee.
Discount golf packages: Yes. **Season:** May-Oct. **High:** June-Sept.
On-site lodging: Yes. **Rental clubs:** Yes.
Walking policy: Walking at certain times. **Range:** Yes (grass).
To obtain tee times: Call seven days in advance.
Ranked 41st in America's 75 Best Resort Courses by Golf Digest. Ranked 6th in Colorado by Golf Digest.
Subscriber comments: The staff pampers you . . . Great views . . . Good condition for a mountain course . . . Good rates after 5:00 for locals . . . Wonderful layout, superb mountain golf . . . A great experience . . . Overpriced, but worth one time . . . Very diverse . . . Fun track . . . Long tough mountain course . . . Too expensive for course conditions.

★½ LAKE ARBOR GOLF COURSE

PU—8600 Wadsworth Blvd., Arvada (303)423-1643.
15 miles north of Denver. **Holes:** 18. **Par:** 70/69.
Yards: 5,865/4,965. **Course rating:** 66.7/71.1. **Slope:** 108/113.
Opened: 1971. **Pace of Play rating:** 4:00. **Green fee:** $16.
Credit cards: MC, V. **Reduced fees:** No.
Caddies: No. **Golf carts:** $17 for 18 holes.
Discount golf packages: No. **Season:** Year-round. **High:** April-Sept.
On-site lodging: Yes. **Rental clubs:** Yes.
Walking policy: Unrestricted walking. **Range:** Yes.
To obtain tee times: For weekdays call one day in advance. For weekends start Wednesday and major holidays, two days in advance.
Subscriber comments: Short course, some water and sand . . . Too small an area for the course . . . Best greens in Metro Denver . . . Hit 'em straight.

★★½ LAKE VALLEY GOLF CLUB
SP—4400 Lake Valley Dr., Longmont (303)444-2114.
3 miles north of Boulder. **Holes:** 18. **Par:** 70/70.
Yards: 6,725/5,713. **Course rating:** 69.6/71.8. **Slope:** 121/119.
Opened: 1964. **Pace of Play rating:** N/A. **Green fee:** $13/23.
Credit cards: MC, V. **Reduced fees:** Weekdays, Twilight, Seniors, Juniors.
Caddies: No. **Golf carts:** $19 for 18 holes.
Discount golf packages: Yes. **Season:** Year-round. **High:** April-Aug.
On-site lodging: No. **Rental clubs:** Yes.
Walking policy: Unrestricted walking. **Range:** Yes (grass).
To obtain tee times: Call three days in advance.
Subscriber comments: Wide open, year-round course . . . Conditions improving due to new computerized watering system . . . Two for one cart and green fees in fall . . . The wind can really blow out here . . . Excellent front nine.

★★★★ LEGACY RIDGE GOLF COURSE
PU—10801 Legacy Ridge Pkwy., Westminster (303)438-8997x2210.
15 miles northwest of Denver. **Holes:** 18. **Par:** 72/72.
Yards: 7,251/5,383. **Course rating:** 74.0/70.6. **Slope:** 134/122.
Opened: 1994. **Pace of Play rating:** 4:15. **Green fee:** $23/27.
Credit cards: MC, V. **Reduced fees:** Weekdays, Seniors, Juniors.
Caddies: No. **Golf carts:** $18 for 18 holes.
Discount golf packages: No. **Season:** Year-round. **High:** April-Oct.
On-site lodging: No. **Rental clubs:** Yes.
Walking policy: Unrestricted walking. **Range:** Yes (grass).
To obtain tee times: Nonresidents call one day in advance starting at 5 p.m.
Subscriber comments: Must ride, too long to walk . . . Blind shots . . . Nice clubhouse . . . Demands good shot placement . . . This is the future of public golf . . . Interesting holes with variety . . . Long and straight shots needed . . . Wind can be tough . . . Outstanding tough course . . . Arthur Hills has developed the best new Colorado course . . . New course needs maturing . . . Gonna' be a great one . . . Designed to work with existing wildlife . . . Nice clubhouse and great food . . . Mature even though new; score early, it gets tougher . . . Country club feel.

★★½ LONE TREE GOLF CLUB
PU—9808 Sunningdale Blvd., Littleton (303)799-9940.
15 miles south of Denver. **Holes:** 18. **Par:** 72/72.
Yards: 7,012/5,340. **Course rating:** 72.1/70.6. **Slope:** 127/120.
Opened: 1983. **Pace of Play rating:** 4:00. **Green fee:** $30/ 40.
Credit cards: All major. **Reduced fees:** Seniors.
Caddies: No. **Golf carts:** $10 for 18 holes.
Discount golf packages: Yes. **Season:** Year-round. **High:** April-Oct.
On-site lodging: Yes. **Rental clubs:** Yes.
Walking policy: Unrestricted walking. **Range:** Yes (grass).
To obtain tee times: Nonresidents call three days in advance after noon.
Subscriber comments: Cost too much for course condition . . . Nice course . . . Back nine has some very difficult holes . . . Country club now a public course . . . Makes you work for a good score . . . Tough track . . . A true Arnold Palmer, hard and rewarding.

★★★ LOVELAND GOLF CLUB
PU—2115 W. 29th St., Loveland (303)667-5256.
45 miles north of Denver. **Holes:** 18. **Par:** 72/71.
Yards: 6,827/5,498. **Course rating:** 69.9/70.6. **Slope:** 120/117.
Opened: 1959. **Pace of Play rating:** 4:00. **Green fee:** $16/18.
Credit cards: MC, V. **Reduced fees:** Weekdays, Twilight, Juniors.
Caddies: No. **Golf carts:** N/A.
Discount golf packages: Yes. **Season:** Year-round. **High:** May-Sept.
On-site lodging: No. **Rental clubs:** Yes.
Walking policy: Unrestricted walking. **Range:** Yes (grass).
To obtain tee times: Call pro shop.

Subscriber comments: Very nice, great condition year round, well run . . . Good shape for overloaded muny . . . Older course, trees good shape, excellent value . . . Excellent public golf course . . . Great city course.

★★★★ MARIANA BUTTE GOLF COURSE

PU—701 Clubhouse Dr., Loveland (303)667-8308.
45 miles north of Denver. **Holes:** 18. **Par:** 72/72.
Yards: 6,572/5,420. **Course rating:** 70.6/70.2. **Slope:** 130/121.
Opened: 1992. **Pace of Play rating:** 4:15–4:30. **Green fee:** $18/25.
Credit cards: MC, V, AMEX. **Reduced fees:** Weekdays, Low season, Twilight.
Caddies: No. **Golf carts:** $12 for 18 holes.
Discount golf packages: Yes. **Season:** March–Nov. **High:** May–Sept.
On-site lodging: No. **Rental clubs:** Yes.
Walking policy: Unrestricted walking. **Range:** Yes (grass).
To obtain tee times: Call pro shop.
Subscriber comments: Best municipal in state . . . Worth the drive from Denver . . . This is a terrific, little-known course . . . Magnificent views, great layout . . . No. 16 from championship tees is best hole in northern Colorado . . . Beautiful course, can't wait to return. Computerized phone reservation is a nightmare! . . . Another jewel by Dick Phelps . . . May be Colorado's best value . . . Used existing hills and terrain perfectly . . . Good layout but short . . . Will be awesome when it matures.

★★★ MEADOW HILLS GOLF COURSE

PU—3609 S. Dawson St., Aurora (303)690-2500.
6 miles east of Denver. **Holes:** 18. **Par:** 70/72.
Yards: 6,717/5,481. **Course rating:** 70.9/70.5. **Slope:** 133/117.
Opened: 1957. **Pace of Play rating:** 3:57. **Green fee:** $15/24.
Credit cards: MC, V. **Reduced fees:** Weekdays, Twilight, Seniors, Juniors.
Caddies: No. **Golf carts:** $11 for 18 holes.
Discount golf packages: No. **Season:** Year-round. **High:** May–Sept.
On-site lodging: No. **Rental clubs:** Yes.
Walking policy: Unrestricted walking. **Range:** Yes (grass).
To obtain tee times: Nonresidents may call three days in advance.
Subscriber comments: Another nice course where shots have to be accurate . . . Country club now public, tough to get a tee time . . . Great views, good mix of holes . . . Tough but fair . . . Tree lined . . . Must be long and strong . . . Best course for money . . . Very well kept . . . Great values in golf shop, staff helpful.

★½ PARK HILL GOLF CLUB

PU—4141 E. 35th Ave., Denver (303)333-5411.
Holes: 18. **Par:** 71/72.
Yards: 6,585/5,811. **Course rating:** 69.4/73.4. **Slope:** 120/124.
Opened: 1931. **Pace of Play rating:** 3:45. **Green fee:** $19/22.
Credit cards: MC, V. **Reduced fees:** No.
Caddies: No. **Golf carts:** $22 for 18 holes.
Discount golf packages: No. **Season:** Year-round. **High:** May–Aug.
On-site lodging: No. **Rental clubs:** Yes.
Walking policy: Unrestricted walking. **Range:** Yes.
To obtain tee times: Call up to six days in advance.
Subscriber comments: Flat mature public course, play is slow but price is right . . . Great food . . . A Denver tradition, it's always open . . . Greens shoveled off and fairways plowed for winter play . . . Open 365 days of the year . . . Hard to lose a ball.

★½ PATTY JEWETT GOLF CLUB

PU—900 E. Espanola, Colorado Springs (719)578-6826.
Holes: 18. **Par:** 72/75.
Yards: 6,811/5,998. **Course rating:** 71.5/73.0. **Slope:** 124/124.
Opened: 1898. **Pace of Play rating:** 4:00. **Green fee:** $13.
Credit cards: None. **Reduced fees:** No.
Caddies: No. **Golf carts:** $16 for 18 holes.

Discount golf packages: No. **Season:** Year-round. **High:** May-Aug.
On-site lodging: No. **Rental clubs:** Yes.
Walking policy: Unrestricted walking. **Range:** No.
To obtain tee times: Call one week in advance.
Also has 9-hole par-35 course.
Subscriber comments: Very heavy traffic, shows wear, easy to play . . .
Your typical muny, incredibly overcrowded dawn to dusk . . . One of the
oldest courses west of the Mississippi River . . . Anyone can play, very nice
staff, play all year . . . Awesome!

★★★½ PINE CREEK GOLF CLUB
PU—9850 Divot Trail, Colorado Springs (719)594-9999.
Holes: 18. **Par:** 72/72.
Yards: 7,194/5,314. **Course rating:** 72.6/69.0. **Slope:** 139/113.
Opened: 1988. **Pace of Play rating:** 4:30. **Green fee:** $22/26.
Credit cards: MC, V. **Reduced fees:** Weekdays, Low season, Twilight,
Seniors, Juniors.
Caddies: No. **Golf carts:** $20 for 18 holes.
Discount golf packages: No. **Season:** Year-round. **High:** April-Oct.
On-site lodging: No. **Rental clubs:** Yes.
Walking policy: Unrestricted walking. **Range:** Yes (grass).
To obtain tee times: Call up to three days in advance.
Subscriber comments: Fun day, always enjoyable . . . Please keep
location secret . . . Some holes reminiscent of Pine Valley . . . Must be able
to keep it in fairways . . . Narrow, challenging, it takes a round to know
the course . . . Tough course rewards smart players . . . Breathtaking view,
well laid-out course, polite and friendly staff . . . Worth your time.

★★★½ PLUM CREEK GOLF AND COUNTRY CLUB
SP—331 Players Club Dr., Castle Rock (303)688-2611, (800)488-2612.
25 miles south of Denver. **Holes:** 18. **Par:** 72/72.
Yards: 6,700/4,875. **Course rating:** 70.1/68.3. **Slope:** 131/118.
Opened: 1985. **Pace of Play rating:** 4:00. **Green fee:** $65/77.
Credit cards: All major. **Reduced fees:** Weekdays, Low season, Twilight.
Caddies: No. **Golf carts:** Included in Green Fee.
Discount golf packages: No. **Season:** Year-round. **High:** June-Sept.
On-site lodging: No. **Rental clubs:** Yes.
Walking policy: Mandatory cart. **Range:** Yes (grass).
To obtain tee times: Call seven days in advance with credit card only.
Ranked 17th in Colorado by Golf Digest.
Subscriber comments: Must be on top of game. Nos. 16, 17, 18 tough
finish . . . Best public course in state, always A-1 condition . . . Pro shop
and staff great. Excellent use of the land . . . Keep carts on path! . . . Love
this Pete Dye course, best three finishing holes in state . . . Typical Pete
Dye penal colony . . . Former TPC course immaculately kept . . .
Spectacular target golf, spectacular view of Rocky Mtns.

★★★★ POLE CREEK GOLF CLUB
PU—P.O. Box 3348, Winter Park (303)726-8847.
80 miles northwest of Denver. **Holes:** 18. **Par:** 72/72.
Yards: 7,107/5,006. **Course rating:** 73.1/67.9. **Slope:** 135/119.
Opened: 1984. **Pace of Play rating:** 4:15. **Green fee:** $34/60.
Credit cards: MC, V, DISC. **Reduced fees:** Weekdays, Low season,
Twilight, Juniors.
Caddies: No. **Golf carts:** $12 for 18 holes.
Discount golf packages: No. **Season:** May-Oct. **High:** June-Sept.
On-site lodging: No. **Rental clubs:** Yes.
Walking policy: Unrestricted walking. **Range:** Yes (grass).
To obtain tee times: Call up to seven days in advance. More than seven
days requires credit card and $5 per player reservation charge.
Ranked in Third 25 of America's 75 Best Public Golf Courses by Golf
Digest. Selected Best New Public Course of 1984 by Golf Digest.
Subscriber comments: Great value at twilight . . . Impossible to locate on
first try . . . Long ride from Denver . . . A real beauty . . . Worth every

mile of the drive . . . Great condition for 45 day growing season . . . Super mountain course . . . Variety of holes . . . Mountain golf at its best.

★★★½ PTARMIGAN COUNTRY CLUB
SP—5412 Vardon Way, Fort Collins (303)226-6600.
60 miles north of Denver. **Holes:** 18. **Par:** 72/72.
Yards: 7,201/5,327. **Course rating:** 73.0/69.0. **Slope:** 135/116.
Opened: 1988. **Pace of Play rating:** 4:20. **Green fee:** $20/40.
Credit cards: MC, V. **Reduced fees:** Weekdays, Low season, Twilight, Seniors, Juniors.
Caddies: No. **Golf carts:** $20 for 18 holes.
Discount golf packages: No. **Season:** Year-round. **High:** May-Sept.
On-site lodging: No. **Rental clubs:** Yes.
Walking policy: Walking at certain times. **Range:** Yes grass).
To obtain tee times: Call two days in advance.
Subscriber comments: Great greens . . . $15 twilight rate, unbelievable, great all around experience . . . Long, wonderful mountain view . . . Take your sand wedge . . . Excellent Jack Nicklaus designed course with courteous personnel . . . Will beat you up if you play wrong tees.

★★ PUEBLO CITY PARK GOLF CLUB
PU—3900 Thatcher Avenue, Pueblo (719)561-4946.
Call club for further information.
Subscriber comments: Too crowded, too long to play a round . . . Flat terrain, no water and few hazards . . . Good all around course . . . Good for beginning, intermediate and senior palyers . . . Course is used extensively . . . Not my favorite layout.

★★★ PUEBLO WEST GOLF COURSE
PU—251 S. McCulloch Blvd., Pueblo West (719)547-2280.
8 miles west of Pueblo. **Holes:** 18. **Par:** 72/72.
Yards: 7,368/5,688. **Course rating:** 73.3/71.4. **Slope:** 125/117.
Opened: 1972. **Pace of Play rating:** N/A. **Green fee:** $13/16.
Credit cards: MC, V. **Reduced fees:** Weekdays, Seniors, Juniors.
Caddies: No. **Golf carts:** $8 for 18 holes.
Discount golf packages: No. **Season:** Year-round. **High:** April-Sept.
On-site lodging: Yes. **Rental clubs:** Yes.
Walking policy: Unrestricted walking. **Range:** Yes (grass).
To obtain tee times: Call pro shop.
Subscriber comments: Long and tight . . . Can be tough when windy, flat and long . . . No trees, lots of houses. Improved management, excellent, truly friendly pros . . . Gorgeous views.

★★★ RACCOON CREEK GOLF CLUB
PU—7301 W. Bowles Ave., Littleton (303)973-4653.
Call club for further information.
Subscriber comments: Good variety, demands good shots, very tough No. 17 . . . Lots of water . . . Shots must be accurate to stay dry . . . Excellent practice facility . . . Must make your tee shots or bomb . . . Tough, but fun . . . Great public course . . . Very busy . . . Great 19th hole.

★★½ RIFLE CREEK GOLF COURSE
SP—3004 State Hwy. 325, Rifle (303)625-1093.
60 miles east of Grand Junction. **Holes:** 18. **Par:** 72/72.
Yards: 6,241/5,131. **Course rating:** 69.3/68.5. **Slope:** 123/109.
Opened: 1960. **Pace of Play rating:** 4:00. **Green fee:** $10/23.
Credit cards: MC, V. **Reduced fees:** Low season, Twilight, Juniors.
Caddies: No. **Golf carts:** $11 for 18 holes.
Discount golf packages: Yes. **Season:** March-Nov. **High:** June-Sept.
On-site lodging: No. **Rental clubs:** Yes.
Walking policy: Unrestricted walking. **Range:** Yes (grass).
To obtain tee times: Call one week in advance.

Subscriber comments: Unbelievable setting, good golf . . . Back nine is tough . . . Staff excellent . . . New nine a real test of skill, hills, gullies, canyons, must see! . . . Two distinctly different nines.

RIVERDALE GOLF CLUB
★★★★ **DUNES COURSE**
PU—13300 Riverdale Rd., Brighton (303)659-6700.
10 miles north of Denver. **Holes:** 18. **Par:** 72/72.
Yards: 7,030/4,903. **Course rating:** 72.1/67.5. **Slope:** 129/109.
Opened: 1985. **Pace of Play rating:** 4:30. **Green fee:** $26.
Credit cards: MC, V. **Reduced fees:** No.
Caddies: No. **Golf carts:** $20 for 18 holes.
Discount golf packages: No. **Season:** Year-round. **High:** May-Sept.
On-site lodging: No. **Rental clubs:** Yes.
Walking policy: Unrestricted walking. **Range:** Yes (grass).
To obtain tee times: Call two days in advance for weekday. Call Monday at 5:30 p.m. for Saturday and Tuesday at 5:30 p.m. for Sunday.
Ranked in First 25 of America's 75 Best Public Golf Courses by Golf Digest. Ranked 8th in Colorado by Golf Digest.
Subscriber comments: A challenge from Pete Dye . . . Bent fairways and greens . . . Always well maintained . . . Great test of golf, it used to be my favorite . . . Need tee length . . . Pete Dye, unusually good design for public . . . Keep it in the fairway or bring many golf balls . . . The best Colorado has to offer . . . Excellent layout . . . Narrow fairways . . . Rough is treacherous . . . Links style . . . Accurate driving is key . . . Good pacing between foursomes . . . Everything is good about this pace, except surroundings . . . Shotmaker's dream, a test.

★★ **KNOLLS COURSE**
PU—13300 Riverdale Rd., Brighton (303)659-6700.
10 miles north of Denver. **Holes:** 18. **Par:** 71/73.
Yards: 6,756/5,931. **Course rating:** 70.2/72.2. **Slope:** 118/117.
Opened: 1963. **Pace of Play rating:** 4:00. **Green fee:** $14/16.
Credit cards: MC, V. **Reduced fees:** No.
Caddies: No. **Golf carts:** $20 for 18 holes.
Discount golf packages: No. **Season:** Year-round. **High:** May-Sept.
On-site lodging: No. **Rental clubs:** Yes.
Walking policy: Unrestricted walking. **Range:** Yes (grass).
To obtain tee times: Call two days in advance for weekdays. Call Monday at 5:30 p.m. for Saturday and Tuesday at 5:30 p.m. for Sunday.
Subscriber comments: Good solid muny . . . Great greens . . . Nothing special, but lots of water and a very reasonable rate . . . The Dune's plain Jane sister, great greens . . . Canals are murder.

★★★½ **SHERATON STEAMBOAT RESORT AND CONFERENCE CENTER**
SHERATON STEAMBOAT GOLF CLUB
R—2000 Clubhouse Dr., Steamboat Springs (303)879-1391, (800)848-8878.
157 miles northwest of Denver. **Holes:** 18. **Par:** 72/72.
Yards: 6,906/5,647. **Course rating:** 71.7/72.6. **Slope:** 134/127.
Opened: 1974. **Pace of Play rating:** 4:15. **Green fee:** $55/80.
Credit cards: All major. **Reduced fees:** Low season, Resort guests, Twilight, Seniors.
Caddies: No. **Golf carts:** $15 for 18 holes.
Discount golf packages: Yes. **Season:** May-Oct. **High:** June-Aug.
On-site lodging: Yes. **Rental clubs:** Yes.
Walking policy: Mandatory cart. **Range:** Yes (grass).
To obtain tee times: Hotel guests up to one year in advance. Nonguests call 24 hours in advance.

Subscriber comments: Extremely tight, bring lots of ammo . . . I only play when they have specials . . . Tight course, many blind shots . . . Fun . . . Beautiful setting . . . Course condition is improved but needs work . . . Stunning . . . Deer generally play through, but nobody minds . . . Inexpensive with golf package . . . Great mountain golf.

★★★★ SKYLAND MOUNTAIN GOLF RESORT

SP—385 Country Club Dr., Crested Butte (303)349-6131, (800)628-5496.
28 miles north of Gunnison. **Holes:** 18. **Par:** 72/72.
Yards: 7,208/5,702. **Course rating:** 72.6/72.4. **Slope:** 129/123.
Opened: 1983. **Pace of Play rating:** N/A. **Green fee:** $30/ 65.
Credit cards: MC, V, AMEX. **Reduced fees:** Low season, Resort guests,
Twilight.
Caddies: No. **Golf carts:** Included in Green Fee.
Discount golf packages: No. **Season:** May-Oct. **High:** July-Aug.
On-site lodging: Yes. **Rental clubs:** Yes.
Walking policy: Mandatory cart. **Range:** Yes (grass).
To obtain tee times: Call in advance.
Subscriber comments: Beautiful setting, tough R.T. Jones Jr. design . . .
Spectacular scenery . . . Above 9,000 feet . . . Leave banana balls home . . .
Rewards shotmaking skills . . . One of Colorado's best courses.

★★★★ SONNENALP GOLF CLUB

R—1265 Berry Creek Rd., Edwards (303)926-3533.
110 miles west of Denver. **Holes:** 18. **Par:** 71/71.
Yards: 7,059/5,293. **Course rating:** 72.3/70.0. **Slope:** 138/115.
Opened: 1981. **Pace of Play rating:** 4:00. **Green fee:** $75/110.
Credit cards: MC, V. **Reduced fees:** Weekdays, Low season, Resort
guests, Twilight, Juniors.
Caddies: No. **Golf carts:** Included in Green Fee.
Discount golf packages: Yes. **Season:** April-Oct. **High:** June-Sept.
On-site lodging: No. **Rental clubs:** Yes.
Walking policy: Mandatory cart. **Range:** Yes (grass).
To obtain tee times: Nonresort guest call day of play. Resort guests may
reserve tee time upon making reservation.
Formerly known as Singletree Golf Club.
Ranked 53rd in America's 75 Best Resort Courses by Golf Digest. Site of
Golf Digest Schools.
Subscriber comments: Great shape, fast greens . . . Terrific staff . . . Best
course in Vail Valley . . . A great layout . . . Value, off season . . .
Excellent greens and layout . . . Excellent condition and personnel.

★★½ SOUTH SUBURBAN GOLF COURSE

PU—7900 S. Colorado Blvd., Littleton (303)770-5500.
9 miles south of Denver. **Holes:** 18. **Par:** 72/72.
Yards: 6,705/5,579. **Course rating:** 69.6/71.0. **Slope:** 120/117.
Opened: 1973. **Pace of Play rating:** N/A. **Green fee:** $14/ 22.
Credit cards: MC, V, DISC. **Reduced fees:** Seniors.
Caddies: No. **Golf carts:** $18 for 18 holes.
Discount golf packages: No. **Season:** Year-round. **High:** April-Oct.
On-site lodging: No. **Rental clubs:** Yes.
Walking policy: Unrestricted walking. **Range:** Yes (grass).
To obtain tee times: Call five days in advance.
Also has 9-hole par-3 course.
Subscriber comments: Too crowded . . . Short . . . Good public course
. . . New master plan being implemented . . . Since adding new watering
system, a lot nicer, great price . . . Good workout for your legs . . . Hilly,
but wide open . . . Greens too hard, no flat spots, extremely fast.

★★½ SOUTHRIDGE GOLF CLUB

PU—5750 S. Lemay Ave., Fort Collins (303)226-2828.
60 miles north of Denver. **Holes:** 18. **Par:** 71/71.
Yards: 6,363/5,508. **Course rating:** 69.1/69.3. **Slope:** 122/118.
Opened: 1984. **Pace of Play rating:** 4:00. **Green fee:** $14/17.
Credit cards: MC, V. **Reduced fees:** Weekdays, Low season, Twilight,
Seniors, Juniors.
Caddies: No. **Golf carts:** $16 for 18 holes.
Discount golf packages: Yes. **Season:** Year-round. **High:** April-Sept.
On-site lodging: No. **Rental clubs:** Yes.
Walking policy: Unrestricted walking. **Range:** Yes (grass).

To obtain tee times: Call up to three days in advance.
Subscriber comments: Very short, greens are a little rough . . . Tight course, must hit straight shots . . . Narrow but interesting . . . Better played from back tees.

TAMARRON RESORT
★★★★ **THE CLIFFS**
R—P.O. Box 3131, Durango (303)259-2000, (800)678-1000.
Holes: 18. **Par:** 72/72.
Yards: 6,885/5,330. **Course rating:** 73.0/71.9. **Slope:** 144/127.

Opened: 1975. **Pace of Play rating:** 4:30. **Green fee:** $60/95.
Credit cards: All major. **Reduced fees:** Low season, Resort guests, Twilight, Seniors, Juniors.
Caddies: No. **Golf carts:** Included in Green Fee.
Discount golf packages: Yes. **Season:** May-Nov. **High:** June-Sept.
On-site lodging: Yes. **Rental clubs:** Yes.
Walking policy: Mandatory cart. **Range:** Yes (grass).
To obtain tee times: Outside play call one day before. Resort guests call two days in advance.
Ranked 20th in Colorado by Golf Digest.
Subscriber comments: Nice place to visit, course is long, well maintained . . . Exceptional experience . . . Outstanding treatment from resort staff . . . Breathtaking scenery, almost distracting . . . Must be able to keep the ball in play . . . Most beautiful course in Colorado.

★★★½ **THE CLUB AT CORDILLERA**
SP—655 Club House Dr., Edwards. (303)926-5100.
100 miles west of Denver. **Holes:** 18. **Par:** 72/72.
Yards: 7,444/ 5,665. **Course rating:** 74.0/71.5. **Slope:** 145/ 138.
Opened: 1994. **Pace of Play rating:** 4:15. **Green fee:** $135.
Credit cards: MC, V, AMEX. **Reduced fees:** No.
Caddies: Yes. **Golf carts:** Included in Green Fee.
Discount golf packages: No. **Season:** May-Oct. **High:** May-Oct.
On-site lodging: Yes. **Rental clubs:** Yes.
Walking policy: Mandatory cart. **Range:** Yes (grass).
To obtain tee times: Call 24 hours in advance.
Subscriber comments: For low handicap golfers only . . . Bring hiking gear . . . Needs a bit more maturing . . . Great setting . . . Places premium on accuracy . . . Spectacular mountain course.

★★★½ **THE COURSES AT HYLAND HILLS**
HYLAND HILLS GOLD COURSE
PU—9650 N. Sheridan Blvd., Westminster (303)428-6526.
10 miles north of Denver. **Holes:** 18. **Par:** 72/73.
Yards: 7,021/5,654. **Course rating:** 71.9/71.9. **Slope:** 132/120.
Opened: 1964. **Pace of Play rating:** N/A. **Green fee:** $19.
Credit cards: MC, V, AMEX. **Reduced fees:** No.
Caddies: No. **Golf carts:** $17 for 18 holes.
Discount golf packages: No. **Season:** Year-round. **High:** June-Aug.
On-site lodging: No. **Rental clubs:** Yes.
Walking policy: Unrestricted walking. **Range:** Yes(grass).
To obtain tee times: Call at 7 a.m. one day in advance for weekdays; for Saturday call Wednesday at 11 a.m. and for Sunday call on Friday at 11 a.m. Also has 9-hole par-37 Blue Course, 9-hole par-27 South Course and 9-hole North Course.
Ranked in First 25 of America's 75 Best Public Golf Courses by Golf Digest.
Subscriber comments: Long course . . . Lots of water for Colorado . . . Excellent condition . . . Great public facility . . . Nos. 17 and 18 good finishing holes, my favorite course in Colorado . . . Beautiful mature course, hard to get on . . . Plays well to good shot placement . . . One of best public courses in the Denver area . . . Greens take abuse from too much play . . . Tough for nonresidents to get weekend times . . . Terrific

views . . . Best test of public golf in Mountain Time Zone . . . You won't find a better public course for under $20 . . . Well maintained for as much play as it gets.

★★★ THE MEADOWS GOLF CLUB

PU—6937 S. Simms, Littleton (303)972-8831.
15 miles southwest of Denver. **Holes:** 18. **Par:** 72/72.
Yards: 6,995/5,416. **Course rating:** 71.6/71.1. **Slope:** 130/123.
Opened: 1984. **Pace of Play rating:** 4:30. **Green fee:** $16/23.
Credit cards: MC, V. **Reduced fees:** Low season, Seniors, Juniors.
Caddies: No. **Golf carts:** $20 for 18 holes.
Discount golf packages: No. **Season:** Year-round. **High:** May-Sept.
On-site lodging: No. **Rental clubs:** Yes.
Walking policy: Unrestricted walking. **Range:** Yes (grass).
To obtain tee times: Nonresidents may call two days in advance.
Subscriber comments: Ditch bisects course, means straight shots . . .
Good layout for all flat terrain . . . Nice fairways if you hit them . . . Fun
target golf . . . Best shape ever . . . Great value . . . Value priced . . .
Accuracy a must, fun course . . . Just a little work to make a great course.

★★★ THE SNOWMASS CLUB GOLF COURSE

R—P.O. Box G-2, Snowmass Village (303)923-3148, (800)525-6200.
7 miles west of Aspen. **Holes:** 18. **Par:** 71/71.
Yards: 6,894/5,008. **Course rating:** 70.5/67.3. **Slope:** 134/114.
Opened: 1970. **Pace of Play rating:** N/A. **Green fee:** $55/95.
Credit cards: All major. **Reduced fees:** Low season, Resort guests,
Twilight, Juniors.

Caddies: No. **Golf carts:** Included in Green Fee.
Discount golf packages: Yes. **Season:** May-Oct. **High:** June-Sept.
On-site lodging: Yes. **Rental clubs:** Yes.
Walking policy: Mandatory cart. **Range:** Yes (grass).
To obtain tee times: Nonguests call one day in advance. Hotel guests two
weeks in advance.
Subscriber comments: Great views . . . Beautiful setting but a bit pricey
. . . Very demanding because elevation changes, beautiful views of valley,
mountains . . . Great recreation layout . . . A great course in a beautiful
place.

★★ THORNCREEK GOLF CLUB

PU—13555 N. Washington St., Thornton (303)450-7055.
18 miles north of Denver. **Holes:** 18. **Par:** 72/72.
Yards: 7,268/5,547. **Course rating:** 73.7/70.5. **Slope:** 136/120.
Opened: 1992. **Pace of Play rating:** N/A. **Green fee:** $26.
Credit cards: MC, V, AMEX. **Reduced fees:** Twilight, Seniors, Juniors.
Caddies: No. **Golf carts:** $10 for 18 holes.
Discount golf packages: No. **Season:** Year-round. **High:** May-Sept.
On-site lodging: No. **Rental clubs:** Yes.
Walking policy: Unrestricted walking. **Range:** Yes (grass).
To obtain tee times: May call up to two weeks in advance.
Subscriber comments: Good layout . . . Too new, hard greens . . .
Heavy play, will be a good course. Everywhere you look are houses.
Starting times too close . . . Played in June rough shape. Played in
September, much better . . . Excellent late day rates . . . Conditions not
always in top shape . . . Distance tee to green discouraging for walkers . . .
U.S. Open conditions around greens . . . Love the course layout.

TWIN PEAKS GOLF COURSE★

PU—1200 Cornell Dr., Longmont (303)772-1722.
35 miles north of Denver. **Holes:** 18. **Par:** 70/71.
Yards: 6,767/5,354. **Course rating:** 71.3/69.1. **Slope:** 120/110.
Opened: 1977. **Pace of Play rating:** 4:00. **Green fee:** $16.
Credit cards: None. **Reduced fees:** Weekdays, Seniors, Juniors.
Caddies: No. **Golf carts:** $16 for 18 holes.

Discount golf packages: No. **Season:** Year-round. **High:** May-Sept.
On-site lodging: No. **Rental clubs:** Yes.
Walking policy: Unrestricted walking. **Range:** Yes (grass).
To obtain tee times: Call or come in two days in advance.

★★★ VAIL GOLF CLUB
PU—1778 Vail Valley Dr., Vail (303)479-2260.
100 miles west of Denver. **Holes:** 18. **Par:** 77/72.
Yards: 7,100/5,291. **Course rating:** 70.8/69.5. **Slope:** 121/114.
Opened: 1968. **Pace of Play rating:** 4:30. **Green fee:** $45/80.
Credit cards: MC, V. **Reduced fees:** Low season.
Caddies: No. **Golf carts:** Included in Green Fee.
Discount golf packages: No. **Season:** May-Oct. **High:** June-Sept.
On-site lodging: No. **Rental clubs:** Yes.
Walking policy: Walking at certain times. **Range:** Yes (grass).
To obtain tee times: Call 48 hours in advance.
Subscriber comments: Playable, yet challenging . . . Very well run
facility . . . Great staff . . . Decent mountain layout . . . Good condition
. . . Good walkable mountain course . . . Very busy . . . Beautiful scenery
. . . Fun course plays short.

★ VALLEY HI GOLF COURSE
PU—610 S. Chelton Rd., Colorado Springs (719)578-6926.
Holes: 18. **Par:** 71/73.
Yards: 6,806/5,384. **Course rating:** 71.1/68.7. **Slope:** 116/110.
Opened: 1954. **Pace of Play rating:** 4:15. **Green fee:** $13.
Credit cards: MC, V. **Reduced fees:** Seniors, Juniors.
Caddies: No. **Golf carts:** $16 for 18 holes.
Discount golf packages: No. **Season:** Year-round. **High:** June-Aug.
On-site lodging: No. **Rental clubs:** Yes.
Walking policy: Unrestricted walking. **Range:** Yes (grass).
To obtain tee times: Call one week in advance.
Subscriber comments: Not in good shape with rough greens . . .
Generally poor condition . . . Fun to play for the money.

★★★★ WALKING STICK GOLF COURSE
PU—4301 Walking Stick Blvd., Pueblo (719)584-3400.
40 miles south of Colorado Springs. **Holes:** 18. **Par:** 72/72.
Yards: 7,147/5,181. **Course rating:** 72.6/69.0. **Slope:** 130/114.
Opened: 1991. **Pace of Play rating:** 4:50. **Green fee:** $15/17.
Credit cards: MC, V. **Reduced fees:** Weekdays, Twilight.
Caddies: No. **Golf carts:** $16 for 18 holes.
Discount golf packages: No. **Season:** Year-round. **High:** May-Sept.
On-site lodging: No. **Rental clubs:** Yes.
Walking policy: Unrestricted walking. **Range:** Yes (grass).
To obtain tee times: Call on Wednesday for Saturday or Sunday. Call
after Saturday for any day during the week.
Subscriber comments: Rolling fairways make you place your shots . . .
Quite possible the best greens in Colorado . . . A new course but fun to
play . . . No wait . . . Inexpensive, good dunes-style layout . . .
Outstanding scenery . . . Price right . . . Worth four times the price . . . A
must play, enjoyable setting . . . Worth drive from Denver . . . I live in
Alaska, going back to play.

★★ WELLSHIRE GOLF COURSE
PU—3333 S. Colorado Blvd., Denver (303)757-1352.
Holes: 18. **Par:** 71/73.
Yards: 6,608/5,890. **Course rating:** 70.1/69.3. **Slope:** 124/121.
Opened: 1927. **Pace of Play rating:** 4:15. **Green fee:** $14/20.
Credit cards: None. **Reduced fees:** Weekdays, Seniors, Juniors.
Caddies: No. **Golf carts:** $20 for 18 holes.
Discount golf packages: No. **Season:** Year-round. **High:** April-Sept.
On-site lodging: No. **Rental clubs:** Yes.
Walking policy: Unrestricted walking. **Range:** Yes.
To obtain tee times: Purchase reservation card $10 for all five Denver city
courses. Call five days in advance at central number (303) 784-4000.

Subscriber comments: Municipal course, needs more upkeep . . . An old country club turned muny . . . If you're allergic to cottonwoods, beware . . . Good traditional design, not too exciting but challenging . . . Floating balls at driving range . . . Old course making improvements . . . City of Denver operation.

★★½ WEST WOODS GOLF CLUB

PU—6655 Quaker St., Arvada (303)424-3334.
14 miles northwest of Denver. **Holes:** 18. **Par:** 72/72.
Yards: 7,035/5,197. **Course rating:** 72.1/69.5. **Slope:** 135/112.
Opened: 1994. **Pace of Play rating:** 4:15. **Green fee:** $22/26.
Credit cards: MC, V. **Reduced fees:** Juniors.
Caddies: No. **Golf carts:** $9 for 18 holes.
Discount golf packages: No. **Season:** Year-round. **High:** April-Aug.
On-site lodging: No. **Rental clubs:** Yes.
Walking policy: Unrestricted walking. **Range:** Yes (grass).
To obtain tee times: Call one day in advance for weekdays. Call Wednesday at 7 a.m. for both Saturday and Sunday.
Subscriber comments: New course, should be better in a year or two . . . Built between houses, far distances from green to next tee . . . Needs to grow, hilly, good value . . . Conditions could be better . . . Nice layout, not too expensive . . . Lots of water.

★★ WILLIS CASE GOLF COURSE

PU—4999 Vrain St., Denver (303)455-9801.
Holes: 18. **Par:** 72/75.
Yards: 6,364/6,144. **Course rating:** 68.7/72.8. **Slope:** 112/115.
Opened: 1929. **Pace of Play rating:** 4:20. **Green fee:** $14/20.
Credit cards: None. **Reduced fees:** Weekdays.
Caddies: No. **Golf carts:** $20 for 18 holes.
Discount golf packages: No. **Season:** Year-round. **High:** June-Aug.
On-site lodging: No. **Rental clubs:** Yes.
Walking policy: Unrestricted walking. **Range:** No.
To obtain tee times: Annual reservation access card or walk on.
Subscriber comments: Too easy, good staff . . . Mature, piney layout . . . Needs more TLC . . . A nice old-fashioned course, bumpy greens all year . . . View on first tee worth the green fee . . . Nice course for every day golf.

WOODLAND PARK FUJIKI GOLF AND COUNTRY CLUB★

SP—100 Lucky Lady Dr., Woodland Park. (719)687-7587.
18 miles east of Colorado Springs. **Holes:** 18. **Par:** 72/72.
Yards: 6,747/5,276. **Course rating:** 71.5/N/A. **Slope:** 129/N/A.
Opened: 1995. **Pace of Play rating:** 4:00-4:30. **Green fee:** $30/35.
Credit cards: All major. **Reduced fees:** Weekdays, Twilight, Seniors, Juniors.
Caddies: No. **Golf carts:** $20 for 18 holes.
Discount golf packages: No. **Season:** Year-round. **High:** May-Sept.
On-site lodging: No. **Rental clubs:** Yes.
Walking policy: Unrestricted walking. **Range:** Yes (grass).
To obtain tee times: Call three days in advance.

★★ YAMPA VALLEY GOLF CLUB

PU—2194 Hwy., 394, Craig (303)824-3673.
200 miles northwest of Denver. **Holes:** 18. **Par:** 72/72.
Yards: 6,344/5,358. **Course rating:** 68.3/69.6. **Slope:** 123/114.
Opened: 1968. **Pace of Play rating:** 3:55. **Green fee:** $18.
Credit cards: MC, V. **Reduced fees:** Seniors, Juniors.
Caddies: No. **Golf carts:** $8 for 18 holes.
Discount golf packages: No. **Season:** April-Oct. **High:** June-Aug.
On-site lodging: No. **Rental clubs:** Yes.
Walking policy: Unrestricted walking. **Range:** Yes (grass).
To obtain tee times: Call three days in advance.
Subscriber comments: Back nine is worth the out-of-the-way trip . . . Pretty little small town . . . Flat but nice . . . Great staff . . . Great price.

★½ ALA WAI GOLF COURSE

PU—404 Kapahulu Ave., Honolulu (Oahu) (808)732-2012.
Holes: 18. **Par:** 70/70.
Yards: 6,019/5,006. **Course rating:** 67.2/67.2. **Slope:** 116/110.
Opened: 1931. **Pace of Play rating:** N/A. **Green fee:** $4/30.
Credit cards: None. **Reduced fees:** Weekdays, Seniors, Juniors.
Caddies: No. **Golf carts:** $12 for 18 holes.
Discount golf packages: No. **Season:** Year-round. **High:** April-Sept.
On-site lodging: No. **Rental clubs:** Yes.
Walking policy: Unrestricted walking. **Range:** Yes.
To obtain tee times: Call one week in advance at 6:30 a.m.
Subscriber comments: Greens in good shape considering amount of play
. . . Almost impossible to get tee times . . . Lots of roll on fairways . . . Flat
and easy . . . Numerous tourists and beginners makes this course one to
avoid . . . Best year-round muny course on Oahu . . . Very busy course,
pace is good before 10:00 a.m. . . . Typical muny, turn and burn . . . Lot of
water hazards.

★★★★ THE CHALLENGE AT MANELE

R—P.O. Box L, Lanai City (Lanai) (808)565-2222.
Holes: 18. **Par:** 72/72.
Yards: 7,039/5,024. **Course rating:** N/A. **Slope:** N/A.
Opened: 1993. **Pace of Play rating:** N/A. **Green fee:** $100.
Credit cards: MC, V, AMEX. **Reduced fees:** Resort guests.
Caddies: No. **Golf carts:** Included in Green Fee.
Discount golf packages: Yes. **Season:** Year-round. **High:** Nov.-Feb.
On-site lodging: Yes. **Rental clubs:** Yes.
Walking policy: Mandatory cart. **Range:** Yes (grass).
To obtain tee times: Call pro shop.
Ranked 5th in Hawaii by Golf Digest.
Subscriber comments: The Challenge, pick the correct tees! Fantastic
ocean course, not for beginners . . . Even better than the Experience . . .
Spectacular ocean views, more playable than most Nicklaus courses . . .
Best vacation spot on earth, great ocean views . . . Challenging course, not
for high handicappers . . . Let 'er rip but with control, lava one side, ocean
other side . . . Mountain air, beautiful . . . Different for Hawaii . . . Target
course . . . Spectacular ocean views . . . It's no wonder why Microsoft's
Bill Gates got married on the 12th tee . . . Absolutely beautiful! Location
more than the course recommends it . . . Super potential.

★★★½ EWA BEACH INTERNATIONAL GOLF CLUB

SP—91-050 Fort Weaver Rd., Ewa Beach (Oahu) (808)689-8317.
18 miles west of Honolulu. **Holes:** 18. **Par:** 72/72.
Yards: 6,777/4,949. **Course rating:** 71.7/68.2. **Slope:** 126/119.
Opened: 1992. **Pace of Play rating:** N/A. **Green fee:** $60/70.
Credit cards: MC, V. **Reduced fees:** Seniors, Juniors.
Caddies: No. **Golf carts:** Included in Green Fee.
Discount golf packages: No. **Season:** Year-round. **High:** Aug./Winter.
On-site lodging: No. **Rental clubs:** Yes.
Walking policy: Mandatory cart. **Range:** Yes.
To obtain tee times: Call one week in advance.
Subscriber comments: Robin Nelson design . . . Short but great . . .
Best-kept secret on Oahu . . . Between holes, beautifully manicured . . .
Good course but ocean salt kills some fairway grass . . . Great design,
playable . . . Nice layout . . . Bunkers! Bunkers! Bunkers! Mature trees for
a newer course, limited public play . . . Very well maintained.

★★★★ THE EXPERIENCE AT KOELE

R—730 Lanai Ave., Lanai City (Lanai) (808)565-4653.
Holes: 18. **Par:** 72/72.
Yards: 7,014/5,425. **Course rating:** 73.3/66.0. **Slope:** 141/123.
Opened: 1991. **Pace of Play rating:** 4:00. **Green fee:** $150.
Credit cards: . **Reduced fees:** Twilight, Juniors.
Caddies: No. **Golf carts:** Included in Green Fee.
Discount golf packages: Yes. **Season:** Year-round. **High:** Dec.-May.
On-site lodging: Yes. **Rental clubs:** Yes.

Walking policy: Mandatory cart. **Range:** Yes (grass).
To obtain tee times: Call 30 days in advance.
Selected as runner-up for Best New Resort Course of 1992 by Golf Digest.
Ranked 13th in Hawaii by Golf Digest.
Subscriber comments: Awesome views and setting, bring your camera
. . . Great eighth hole with tee several hundred feet above fairway . . .
Good challenge, would love to play again . . . Great contrast between nines
. . . Deer, cool weather for Hawaii . . . Front nine very beautiful . . . Back
nine needs maturing . . . Great 18-hole putting course . . . Bring a jacket,
cool . . . Pretty course, bad shape . . . Bent-grass greens . . . Looks
somewhat like an Augusta National . . . Truly an experience.

★★★½ HAPUNA GOLF COURSE

R—62-100 Kauna'oa Dr., Kamuela (808)880-3000.
34 miles south of Kailua-Kona. **Holes:** 18. **Par:** 72/72.
Yards: 6,875/5,067. **Course rating:** 72.1/63.9. **Slope:** 134/117.
Opened: 1992. **Pace of Play rating:** 4:00-4:30. **Green fee:** $80/130.
Credit cards: MC, V, AMEX, JCB, Carte Blanche. **Reduced fees:** Resort
guests, Juniors.
Caddies: No. **Golf carts:** N/A.
Discount golf packages: Yes. **Season:** Year-round. **High:** Nov.-April.
On-site lodging: Yes. **Rental clubs:** Yes.
Walking policy: Mandatory cart. **Range:** Yes (grass).
To obtain tee times: Guests four days in advance. Off-property guests
two days in advance.
Subscriber comments: Try it, you'll like it . . . Unusual resort course,
bring lots of balls . . . Good target-type layout . . . Excellent for a new
course . . . Fabulous condition . . . Need to be low single digit to putt out
with the same ball as you started with . . . Geat new Palmer course, can be
windy. Wonderful test, bring your 'A' game . . . Rated high environmentally because much of landscape was left untouched . . . 40 mph winds
not unusual . . . Rolling fairways, manicured and clean . . . Very playable,
but a little too tricky.

HAWAII KAI GOLF COURSE
★½ CHAMPIONSHIP COURSE

PU—8902 Kalanianaole Hwy., Honolulu (Oahu) (808)395-2358.
12 miles east of Honolulu. **Holes:** 18. **Par:** 72/72.
Yards: 6,614/5,591. **Course rating:** 71.4/72.7. **Slope:** 127/124.
Opened: 1973. **Pace of Play rating:** 4:00. **Green fee:** $80/90.
Credit cards: MC, V, AMEX, JCB. **Reduced fees:** Weekdays, Twilight.
Caddies: No. **Golf carts:** Included in Green Fee.
Discount golf packages: No. **Season:** Year-round. **High:** Year-round.
On-site lodging: No. **Rental clubs:** Yes.
Walking policy: Mandatory cart. **Range:** Yes (grass).
To obtain tee times: Call or Fax request.
Also has an executive course by R.T. Jones Sr.
Subscriber comments: Good greens, mediocre fairways, good warmup
for vacation . . . Good place to play, enjoyable . . . Some tee areas are too
close to homes . . . Tee off early before tourists arrive . . . Poor
maintenance . . . Sloping greens that makes three-putts very common . . .
Excellent to improve your short game . . . Beautiful course, plays long but
pretty much open . . . Much improved over the years . . . Very slow play.

HAWAII PRINCE GOLF CLUB
★★ A/B/C

R—91-1200 Fort Weaver Rd., Ewa Beach (Oahu) (808)944-4567.
20 miles west of Honolulu. **Holes:** 27. **Par:** 72/72/72.
Yards: 7,117/7,255/7,166. **Course rating:** 74.2/75.0/74.4.
Slope: 131/132/134.
Opened: 1992. **Pace of Play rating:** N/A. **Green fee:** $50/135.
Credit cards: MC, V, AMEX, Diners Club, JCB. **Reduced fees:**
Weekdays, Resort guests, Twilight, Seniors, Juniors.
Caddies: No. **Golf carts:** Included in Green Fee.

Discount golf packages: Yes. **Season:** Year-round. **High:** Dec.-Feb.
On-site lodging: No. **Rental clubs:** Yes.
Walking policy: Mandatory cart. **Range:** Yes (grass).
Subscriber comments: I'll never play again. Pace is a bit slow, four-man cart is bad idea . . . If you like playing in the wind, this is for you . . . Nice fairways, greens need to grow grass more . . . Requires accuracy and distance, lots of water, beautiful . . . Very playable for all levels, nothing spectacular, tourist-oriented . . . Resort layout, lots of water, burning sugar cane close by . . . No character to the course . . . Challenging when windy, otherwise pretty boring.

KAANAPALI GOLF COURSE
R—Kaanapali Resort, Lahaina (Maui) (808)661-3691.
Pace of Play rating: 4:00. **Green fee:** $100/120.
Credit cards: MC, V, AMEX. **Reduced fees:** Low season, Resort guests, Twilight.
Caddies: No. **Golf carts:** Included in Green Fee.
Discount golf packages: Yes. **Season:** Year-round. **High:** Dec.-April.
On-site lodging: Yes. **Range:** Yes (grass).
To obtain tee times: Resort guests call four days in advance. Non guests call two days in advance.

★★★ SOUTH COURSE
Holes: 18. **Par:** 71/71.
Yards: 6,555/5,485. **Course rating:** 70.7/69.8. **Slope:** 127/120.
Opened: 1976. **Rental clubs:** No. **Walking policy:** N/A.
Subscriber comments: It's in Maui . . . What else could you ask for? Nice, open, fast greens . . . Incredible views . . . Absolutely great! Great views to match great golf . . . Very easy if it's not windy . . . Convenient and accessible but ordinary . . . Easy, short resort layout, heavy play . . . Definitely not up to resort-type course . . . Great views, staff and service was excellent . . . Fun course . . . Very basic.

★★★ NORTH COURSE
Holes: 18. **Par:** 71/72.
Yards: 6,994/5,417. **Course rating:** 72.8/71.1. **Slope:** 134/123.
Opened: 1963. **Rental clubs:** Yes. **Walking policy:** Mandatory cart.
Subscriber comments: Excellent resort course, challenging but playable . . . Tough, narrow, long rough, greens fast . . . Typical Robert Trent Jones Sr. . . . Another great course to play, excellent condition . . . Subtle design, tough without Pete Dye-type tricks . . . Worth the money, great views, great holes . . . Very scenic . . . Tough in the wind . . . Bring your long irons and your camera . . . Some really poorly designed holes . . . Super tough greens, rest not too spectacular . . . Excellent course booklets to help golfers.

★★★½ KALUAKOI GOLF COURSE
R—P.O. Box 26, Maunaloa (Molokai) (808)552-2739.
20 miles east of Kaunakakai. **Holes:** 18. **Par:** 72/72.
Yards: 6,564/5,461. **Course rating:** 72.3/71.4. **Slope:** 129/119.
Opened: 1977. **Pace of Play rating:** 3:30-4:00. **Green fee:** $55/75.
Credit cards: All major. **Reduced fees:** Low season, Resort guests.
Caddies: No. **Golf carts:** Included in Green Fee.
Discount golf packages: Yes. **Season:** Year-round. **High:** Dec.-March.
On-site lodging: Yes. **Rental clubs:** Yes.
Walking policy: Mandatory cart. **Range:** Yes (grass).
To obtain tee times: Call one month in advance. Groups of 16 and over one year in advance.
Subscriber comments: Great course, always playable, undiscovered . . . More ocean holes than Pebble Beach . . . Great place to play . . . A favorite . . . Lightning fast greens, very windy, breathtaking ocean scenery . . . One of the best-kept island secrets . . . Only resort course on Molokai . . . Staff service and pace great . . . Scenic.

★★★ KANEOHE KLIPPER GOLF CLUB
SP—Kaneohe Marines Corps Air Station, Kanehoe Bay (Oahu) (808)254-2107.
Call club for further information.

Subscriber comments: Holes 13 through 16 worth the price . . . Need military I. D. or sponsor . . . Course could use more irrigation . . . Scenic along shoreline . . . Saw whales frolicking and surfers . . . Gorgeous layout ocean holes take both your breath and tee shot away . . . Open fairways, fast greens, scenic . . . Course needs some TLC , ocean holes help make the course worth it . . . Excellent for all skills . . . Good layout . . . Three beautiful ocean holes . . . Military course . . . Poor man's Pebble Beach.

KAPALUA GOLF CLUB
R—300 Kapalua Dr., Kapalua (Maui)
8 miles north of Lahaina.
Pace of Play rating: 3:30-4:00.
Credit cards: All major. **Reduced fees:** Resort guests, Twilight, Juniors.
Caddies: Yes. **Golf carts:** Included in Green Fee.
Discount golf packages: Yes. **Season:** Year-round. **High:** Dec.-March.
On-site lodging: Yes. **Rental clubs:** Yes.
Walking policy: Walking at certain times. **Range:** Yes (grass).
To obtain tee times: Resort guests may reserve tee times one week in advance. Non guests call four days in advance.

★★★★ THE BAY COURSE
(808)669-8820.
Holes: 18. **Par:** 72/72.
Yards: 6,600/5,124. **Course rating:** 71.7/69.6. **Slope:** 138/121.
Opened: 1975. **Green fee:** $110.
Ranked 36th in America's 75 Best Resort Courses by Golf Digest. Ranked 15th in Hawaii by Golf Digest.
Subscriber comments: Could never understand why pros played here vs. much tougher Village Course . . . Fun course for the whole family . . . Lots of fun to play. Hilly, very scenic . . . Fantastic island golf, doesn't get better . . . Beautiful course, nice layout and views . . . Most beautiful course I've ever played, a marvelous experience . . . Easiest of the Kapalua Trilogy . . . Resort course, too open, not challenging for better players . . . Beautiful, well-groomed courses . . . Pineapple fields and rainforest nearby . . . Wonderful!

★★★★ THE PLANTATION COURSE
(808)669-8877.
Holes: 18. **Par:** 73/73.
Yards: 7,263/5,627. **Course rating:** 75.2/73.2. **Slope:** 142/129.
Opened: 1991. **Green fee:** $120.
Ranked 4th in America's 75 Best Resort Courses by Golf Digest. Selected as runner-up for Best New Resort Course of 1991 by Golf Digest . . . Ranked 3rd in Hawaii by Golf Digest.
Subscriber comments: Golf at its best, excellent facilities, amazing views . . . Beautiful ocean views but too many blind shots and funny bounces . . . Great course, every hole a challenge . . . Best of the Kapalua courses . . . Worth every penny . . . Play at least once in your life . . . My favorite course, great golf and absolutely gorgeous . . . Toughest course you'll ever love to hate . . . 18th hole a must-play . . . Bring lots of balls . . . Anything out of the fairway is history . . . Great view of two neighbor isles . . . Massive greens . . . Much local knowledge required . . . Outrageous greens (too contoured).

★★★½ THE VILLAGE COURSE
(808)669-8835.
Holes: 18. **Par:** 71/71.
Yards: 6,632/5,134. **Course rating:** 73.3/70.9. **Slope:** 139/122.
Opened: 1980. **Green fee:** $110.
Ranked 31st in America's 75 Best Resort Courses by Golf Digest.
Subscriber comments: Watch the whales from many holes . . . Many elevation changes. Fun . . . Golf heaven . . . Beautiful layout . . . Up into the hills, a shotmaker's course . . . Nos. 5, 6 and 7 are amongst most scenic anywhere . . . No pizzazz . . . Great mountain views . . . Difficult uphill shots into the wind . . . Long and narrow . . . A good test; in very good condition . . . Does the wind ever not blow? Course maintenance not up to par . . . Good variety of holes . . . Tighter fairways compared to Plantation . . . Some holes are downhill . . . Excellent course reference booklets.

KAUAI LAGOONS RESORT

R—Kalapaki Beach, Lihue (Kauai) (808)241-6000.
Opened: 1988. **Pace of Play rating:** N/A.
Credit cards: MC, V, AMEX, Diners Club. **Reduced fees:** Resort guests.
Caddies: No. **Golf carts:** Included in Green Fee.
Discount golf packages: Yes. **Season:** Year-round. **High:** Jan.-March/Aug.
On-site lodging: Yes. **Rental clubs:** Yes.
Walking policy: Mandatory cart. **Range:** Yes (grass).
To obtain tee times: Call within 30 days.

★★★★ KIELE COURSE

Holes: 18. **Par:** 72/72.
Yards: 7,070/5,417. **Course rating:** 73.7/66.5. **Slope:** 137/123.
Green fee: $145.
Ranked 15th in America's 75 Best Resort Courses by Golf Digest. Selected as Best New Resort Course of 1989 by Golf Digest. Ranked 6th in Hawaii by Golf Digest.
Subscriber comments: Picture-perfect condition . . . Unhurt by Iniki, best greens in Hawaii . . . More playable than most Nicklaus courses . . . Most beautiful course in Hawaii, but tough, bring lots of balls if windy . . . Move the airport! Jack Nicklaus' best effort . . . Tremendous views! Memorable . . . Very attractive and well-kept test . . . Some beautiful golf holes . . . Never seen so many traps . . . Outstanding golf course and clubhouse amenities . . . Exciting course, never dull, great for the risk taker . . . Just admire the scenery, take one hole at a time.

★★★½ LAGOONS COURSE

Holes: 18. **Par:** 72/72.
Yards: 6,942/5,607. **Course rating:** 72.8/67.0. **Slope:** 135/116.
Green fee: $100.
Subscriber comments: Outstanding layout . . . Much easier for high handicappers . . . Jack Nicklaus designed, good for high handicapper . . . Not quite up to sister course, but a great round . . . Typical Nicklaus course . . . Lots of sand . . . Beautiful course . . . Not as good as the Kiele Course, but more than acceptable.

★★½ KIAHUNA GOLF CLUB

R—2545 Kiahuna Plantation Dr., Poipu (Kauai) (808)742-9595.
15 miles south of Lihue. **Holes:** 18. **Par:** 70/70.
Yards: 6,353/5,631. **Course rating:** 69.7/71.4. **Slope:** 128/119.
Opened: 1983. **Pace of Play rating:** N/A. **Green fee:** $45.
Credit cards: MC, V, AMEX. **Reduced fees:** Resort guests, Twilight.
Caddies: No. **Golf carts:** Included in Green Fee.
Discount golf packages: No. **Season:** Year-round. **High:** Nov.-March.
On-site lodging: No. **Rental clubs:** Yes.
Walking policy: Mandatory cart. **Range:** Yes (grass).
To obtain tee times: Call one day in advance.
Subscriber comments: A slightly short course, poorly maintained . . . I never skip this fast, fun track . . . Good play . . . No crowds . . . Reasonably short course but interesting . . . Terrific lava views . . . A good layout and course condition . . . Very enjoyable . . . Forgettable . . . Too windy to be acceptable . . . Forgiving . . . Great for long hitters who are normally afraid to use their drivers . . . Course was built on landfill and greens still settling.

★★★ KO OLINA GOLF CLUB

R—92-1220 Aliinui Dr., Kapolei (Oahu) (808)676-5300.
20 miles west of Honolulu. **Holes:** 18. **Par:** 72/72.
Yards: 6,867/5,392. **Course rating:** 72.8/71.3. **Slope:** 137/125.
Opened: 1990. **Pace of Play rating:** 4:30. **Green fee:** $95/145.
Credit cards: All major. **Reduced fees:** Resort guests, Twilight.
Caddies: No. **Golf carts:** Included in Green Fee.
Discount golf packages: Yes. **Season:** Year-round. **High:** Dec.-Feb.
On-site lodging: Yes. **Rental clubs:** Yes.
Walking policy: Walking at certain times. **Range:** Yes (grass).
To obtain tee times: Call seven days in advance.

Ranked 67th in America's 75 Best Resort Courses by Golf Digest.
Subscriber comments: Condition of fairways and greens were perfect . . .
Watch out for the black swans . . . Too much noise from airplanes and cars,
fair but non-memorable course . . . More like good muny course than
resort course . . . Great challenging layout, very tough in afternoon . . .
Everything manmade, nothing natural . . . Must be 16 or better handicap to
play the course . . . Typical Ted Robinson design . . . Great resort . . . Lots
of scenery . . . Fun and challenging . . . Windy, good fairways, very
appealing . . . Bogey golfers forget it. Bring lots of balls!

KONA SURF RESORT AND COUNTRY CLUB

PU—78-7000 Alii Dr., Kailua-Kona (808)322-2595.
Pace of Play rating: 4:00. **Green fee:** $60/100.
Credit cards: MC, V, AMEX. **Reduced fees:** Twilight.
Caddies: No. **Golf carts:** Included in Green Fee.
Discount golf packages: No. **Season:** Year-round. **High:** Jan.-March.
On-site lodging: No. **Rental clubs:** Yes.
Walking policy: Mandatory cart. **Range:** Yes.
To obtain tee times: Resort guests may reserve tee times up to one year in
advance.

★★★ MOUNTAIN COURSE

Holes: 18. **Par:** 72/72.
Yards: 6,471/4,906. **Course rating:** 71.5/69.2. **Slope:** 133/125.
Opened: 1985.
Subscriber comments: Great mountain course with views of the ocean
. . . Excellent challenge . . . Terrific finishing hole . . . Best resort course on
Oahu . . . Has some very tough lies on sides of hills.

★★★½ OCEAN COURSE

Holes: 18. **Par:** 72/73.
Yards: 6,579/5,499. **Course rating:** 71.6/71.9. **Slope:** 129/127.
Opened: 1968.
Subscriber comments: Superb scenery, fast play . . . Beach course,
straightforward . . . Can offer some splendid views . . . Lost much of its
excellence of the past . . . As scenic as many more famous courses . . .
Beautiful course at a leisurely pace . . . Well-kept secret on Big Island, not
windy . . . A fun and easy resort course.

★★★½ KOOLAU GOLF COURSE

PU—45-550 Kionaole, Kaneohe (Oahu) (808)236-4653, (800)556-6528.
13 miles north of Honolulu. **Holes:** 18. **Par:** 72/72.
Yards: 7,310/5,119. **Course rating:** 76.4/72.9. **Slope:** 162/134.
Opened: 1992. **Pace of Play rating:** N/A. **Green fee:** $85/100.
Credit cards: MC, V, AMEX. **Reduced fees:** Weekdays, Low season,
Twilight.
Caddies: No. **Golf carts:** Included in Green Fee.
Discount golf packages: Yes. **Season:** Year-round.
On-site lodging: No. **Rental clubs:** Yes.
Walking policy: Unrestricted walking. **Range:** Yes (grass).
To obtain tee times: Call two months in advance.
Ranked 4th in Hawaii by Golf Digest.
Subscriber comments: Long carries over ravines . . . Great layout, must
stay in fairway, course is difficult to find . . . A real test! Toughest course
rating in U.S. . . . Beautiful shape, a must play! Long, challenging, fun,
beautiful views, funnest course I ever played . . . Excellent fairways and
greens . . . Course for masochists . . . Too hard to be fun . . . By far most
challenging . . . Most scenic in Hawaii . . . Every hole a signature hole . . .
18th a must play! Extreme target golf, the Bataan Death March in a golf cart
. . . Difficult, must play target golf, good scenery, bent-grass greens . . .
Very tough . . . Soft, mushy fairways . . . A must-experience course.

★★★ MAKAHA VALLEY COUNTRY CLUB

PU—84-627 Makaha Valley Rd., Waianae (Oahu) (808)695-7111.
40 miles northwest of Honolulu. **Holes:** 18. **Par:** 71/71.
Yards: 6,369/5,720. **Course rating:** 69.2/72.7. **Slope:** 133/120.
Opened: 1969. **Pace of Play rating:** 4:00. **Green fee:** $35/42.

Credit cards: MC, AMEX. **Reduced fees:** Weekdays, Low season.
Caddies: No. **Golf carts:** Included in Green Fee.
Discount golf packages: No. **Season:** Year-round. **High:** Dec.-March.
On-site lodging: No. **Rental clubs:** Yes.
Walking policy: Mandatory cart. **Range:** Yes (grass).
To obtain tee times: Call for tee time.
Subscriber comments: Nice short course . . . Short but some tricky holes
. . . Nice combination of hazards and layout; out of the way, but a should-
play . . . Short course, lots of hills, somewhat forgiving . . . Wide open,
fast, grainy greens, good course . . . Fantastic condition . . . Good for high
handicapper . . . Nice resort course in the valley . . . Fun and easy, play is
almost always very slow on weekends.

★★★★ **MAKALEI HAWAII COUNTRY CLUB**
PU—72-3890 Hawaii Belt Rd., Kailua-Kona (808)325-6625.
Holes: 18. **Par:** 72/72.
Yards: 7,091/5,242. **Course rating:** 73.5/64.9. **Slope:** 143/125.
Opened: 1992. **Pace of Play rating:** 3:30-4:00. **Green fee:** $110.
Credit cards: MC, V, AMEX, Diners Club, JCB. **Reduced fees:** Resort
guests, Twilight.
Caddies: No. **Golf carts:** Included in Green Fee.
Discount golf packages: Yes. **Season:** Year-round. **High:** Dec.-March.
On-site lodging: No. **Rental clubs:** Yes.
Walking policy: Mandatory cart. **Range:** Yes (grass).
To obtain tee times: Call up to one week in advance.
Subscriber comments: This topsoil over crushed lava chewed and scarred
the soles of my irons . . . Wildlife and setting wonderful . . . Don't forget
your sweater. The best all-around track in Hawaii. Entire course is bent
grass. Front nine climbs to 3,000 plus feet. Vistas are tremendous. Do it!
Removed from all human activity, beautiful surroundings, local birds
singing . . . Target golf with nice views, course on mountain slopes, misty
. . . Still very new . . . Tee-to-green, a must play if on Big Island . . . Best
for straight shooters but very fun, very scenic views . . . Cool climate in
mountains, peaceful with natural forest . . . A treasure of bent grass in
scenic mountains . . . Super all-around.

MAKENA RESORT GOLF COURSE
R—5415 Makena Alanui, Kihei (Maui) (808)879-3344, (800)321-6284.
6 miles south of Kihei.
Opened: 1993. **Pace of Play rating:** 4:15. **Green fee:** $110.
Credit cards: MC, V, AMEX, Diners Club, Carte Blanche. **Reduced
fees:** Resort guests, Twilight, Juniors.
Caddies: No. **Golf carts:** Included in Green Fee.
Discount golf packages: Yes. **Season:** Year-round. **High:** Dec.-
April/Aug./Oct.
On-site lodging: Yes. **Rental clubs:** Yes.
Walking policy: Mandatory cart. **Range:** Yes (grass).
To obtain tee times: Three days in advance for anyone not staying at the
resort. Guests staying at the resort or Maui Prince Hotel are allowed to
make tee times one year in advance.
★★★★ **NORTH COURSE**
Holes: 18. **Par:** 72/72.
Yards: 6,914/5,303. **Course rating:** 72.1/70.9. **Slope:** 139/128.
Ranked 9th in Hawaii by Golf Digest.
Subscriber comments: Beautiful, tough course you never hear about . . .
A must play! Bring camera and your best game . . . Best course on Maui
. . . Very plush and scenic . . . Fabulous, demanding, thinking man's
course . . . Beautiful scenery, difficult to score, narrow and fast greens . . .
Beautiful vistas of the ocean everywhere, good course but fairways wide
open, not challenging . . . Love the two-fairway, one-green hole, well
maintained . . . Words don't do it justice . . . Excellent view of neighboring
islands, Molokini, Kahoolawe and Lanai.

★★★★ SOUTH COURSE

Holes: 18. **Par:** 72/72.
Yards: 7,017/5,529. **Course rating:** 72.6/71.1. **Slope:** 138/130.
Ranked 10th in Hawaii by Golf Digest.
Subscriber comments: Pretty layout, bring your driver . . . Great Robert Trent Jones Jr. design . . . Beautiful views . . . Each hole is gorgeous . . . Indescribably beautiful scenery. Average fairways but lush, tree-lined, good greens . . . Just as pretty as the North Course with more elevation . . . Great views and shot values . . . Breathtaking vistas, a must for vacationers to Maui . . . Challenging, but no wind! Very friendly staff . . . Great course, encountered a wild bear on fourth green . . . Needs a better snack shop.

★★★★½ MAUNA KEA BEACH GOLF COURSE

R—62-100 Mauna Kea Beach Dr., Kamuela (808)880-3480.
34 miles south of Kailua-Kona. **Holes:** 18. **Par:** 72/72.
Yards: 7,114/5,277. **Course rating:** 73.6/65.8. **Slope:** 135/109.
Opened: 1965. **Pace of Play rating:** 4:00-4:30. **Green fee:** $80/130.
Credit cards: MC, V, AMEX, JCB, Carte Blanche. **Reduced fees:** Resort guests, Juniors.
Caddies: No. **Golf carts:** Included in Green Fee.
Discount golf packages: Yes. **Season:** Year-round. **High:** Nov.-April.
On-site lodging: Yes. **Rental clubs:** Yes.
Walking policy: Mandatory cart. **Range:** Yes (grass).
To obtain tee times: Guests four days in advance. Off-property guests two days in advance.
Ranked 70th in America's 100 Greatest Golf Courses by Golf Digest.
Ranked 8th in America's 75 Best Resort Courses by Golf Digest. Ranked 1st in Hawaii by Golf Digest.
Subscriber comments: Best in Hawaii . . . The contrast of green, oceaning lava, spectacular . . . The grandaddy of all Hawaiian resorts. Kudos to the greenkeeper. Best course I've ever played . . . Everything you would want . . . No shortcomings . . . The Pebble Beach of Hawaii . . . A must-play, No. 3 is the Polynesian answer to No. 16 at Cypress Point . . . One great old course . . . From the blue tees all the golf you can handle . . . The third is the most beautiful in the "hole" world . . . I think it's overrated, but the course is sculptural and in immaculate condition . . . Greens have been slowed but are very true . . . Views of ocean on most holes, play once at any price.

MAUNA LANI RESORT

R—P.O. Box 4959, Kohala Coast (808)885-6655.
Credit cards: MC, V, AMEX, Diners Club. **Reduced fees:** Low season, Twilight.
Caddies: No. **Golf carts:** Included in Green Fee.
Discount golf packages: Yes. **Season:** Year-round. **High:** Nov.-April.
On-site lodging: Yes. **Rental clubs:** Yes.
Walking policy: Mandatory cart. **Range:** Yes (grass).
To obtain tee times: Call three days in advance.

★★★★ NORTH COURSE

Holes: 18. **Par:** 72/72.
Yards: 6,993/5,474. **Course rating:** 73.2/71.4. **Slope:** 136/124.
Opened: 1981. **Pace of Play rating:** 4:30. **Green fee:** $100/150.
Subscriber comments: The absolute golf experience . . . 10 stars . . . Lava roughs are tight to fairways . . . Mauna Lani courses are the best in Hawaii for playability . . . If I could only play one course, this is it. Better than the South . . . Another monster on the lava . . . Very nice and beautiful course and scenery . . . Great design, playable . . . A magnificent resort in all aspects, challenging, lovely, my favorite . . . A good and fun course.

★★★★ SOUTH COURSE

Holes: 18. **Par:** 72/72.
Yards: 7,029/5,331. **Course rating:** 73.1/70.3. **Slope:** 133/122.
Opened: N/A. **Pace of Play rating:** N/A. **Green fee:** N/A.
Ranked 11th in Hawaii by Golf Digest.

Subscriber comments: Best holes on the water, bring extra balls due to high winds . . . Hard to concentrate, great views . . . Those lava rocks are too distracting . . . Not as intense as the North, still wonderful . . . Not overly challenging but a beautiful experience . . . The best golf experience . . . Beautiful views and excellent conditions . . . Great greens, accuracy counts . . . Best-looking course in Hawaii . . . Great service, interesting layout . . . Unique, dramatic holes make these must-plays . . . Always a pleasurable experience.

★½ MILILANI GOLF CLUB

SP—95-176 Kuahelani Ave., Mililani (Oahu) (808)623-2222.
12 miles southeast of Honolulu. **Holes:** 18. **Par:** 72/72.
Yards: 6,455/5,985. **Course rating:** 69.3/73.6. **Slope:** 121/127.
Opened: 1967. **Pace of Play rating:** 4:30-5:00. **Green fee:** $83/91.
Credit cards: MC, V, AMEX, Diners Club. **Reduced fees:** Weekdays, Twilight, Seniors.
Caddies: No. **Golf carts:** Included in Green Fee.
Discount golf packages: Yes. **Season:** Year-round. **High:** Jan.-Feb./June.
On-site lodging: No. **Rental clubs:** Yes.
Walking policy: Mandatory cart. **Range:** Yes.
To obtain tee times: Call up to one month in advance.
Subscriber comments: Flat, greens too inconsistent . . . Lots of trees everywhere, keep your ball in the fairway and you're OK . . . OK all-around in summer, kind of dry and hard . . . A flat course, muddy during rainy season, relatively easy . . . Nothing exceptional . . . Easy tourist course, average maintenance . . . Solid course in a residential area . . . Flat, slow play . . . Relatively flat, mature course, cooler location . . . Lots of water holes . . . Fairways very inconsistent throughout the year.

★★½ OLOMANA GOLF LINKS

SP—41-1801 Kalanianaole Hwy., Waimanalo (Oahu) (808)259-7926.
Holes: 18. **Par:** 72/73.
Yards: 6,326/5,456. **Course rating:** 70.3/72.4. **Slope:** 129/128.
Opened: 1967. **Pace of Play rating:** 4:30. **Green fee:** $33/39.
Credit cards: MC, V, AMEX, JCB. **Reduced fees:** Weekdays, Twilight, Seniors.
Caddies: No. **Golf carts:** Included in Green Fee.
Discount golf packages: Yes. **Season:** Year-round. **High:** July-Aug.
On-site lodging: No. **Rental clubs:** Yes.
Walking policy: Walking at certain times. **Range:** Yes.
To obtain tee times: Call one month in advance.
Subscriber comments: Nice local course, good greens . . . Routine layout . . . Gets a lot of play . . . Needs better maintenance . . . A little short but challenging . . . Great views . . . Course needs work . . . Well-kept greens . . . Very nice public course . . . Condition vastly improved . . . Short with water hazards . . . Some tees and fairways are dangerously close . . . A somewhat challenging course . . . Good local course, short but fun, easy.

★★★ PALI MUNICIPAL GOLF COURSE

PU—45-050 Kamehameha Hwy., Kaneohe (Oahu) (808)261-9784.
Holes: 18. **Par:** 72/74.
Yards: 6,500/6,050. **Course rating:** 78.8/70.4. **Slope:** 126/127.
Opened: 1954. **Pace of Play rating:** 4:30. **Green fee:** $8/12.
Credit cards: None. **Reduced fees:** Twilight, Seniors, Juniors.
Caddies: No. **Golf carts:** $12 for 18 holes.
Discount golf packages: No. **Season:** Year-round. **High:** June-Aug.
On-site lodging: No. **Rental clubs:** No.
Walking policy: Unrestricted walking. **Range:** Yes (grass).
To obtain tee times: One week in advance.
Subscriber comments: Lots of hills, long, beautiful views . . . Oldish-style public course . . . Beaten by weather and hackers . . . Best public course on Oahu . . . New clubhouse under construction . . . Fun, tough, interesting . . . Long, hilly course, rough greens, best muny on Oahu . . .

With just a bit more maintenance this muny could take the Hawaiian Open away from Waialae! Above-average municipal course, very busy . . . Some long par 4s, especially the sixth, which is 465 yards.

★★★ PEARL COUNTRY CLUB

SP—98-535 Kaonohi St., Aiea (Oahu) (808)487-3802.
10 miles west of Honolulu. **Holes:** 18. **Par:** 72/72.
Yards: 6,787/5,536. **Course rating:** 72.0/72.1. **Slope:** 135/130.
Opened: 1967. **Pace of Play rating:** N/A. **Green fee:** $47/100.
Credit cards: MC, V, AMEX, Diners Club, JCB. **Reduced fees:**
Twilight.
Caddies: No. **Golf carts:** Included in Green Fee.
Discount golf packages: No. **Season:** Year-round. **High:** Year-round.
On-site lodging: No. **Rental clubs:** Yes.
Walking policy: Mandatory cart. **Range:** Yes.
To obtain tee times: Call in advance.
Subscriber comments: Fun but play is slow . . . Older public course, very nice. Good course considering amount it's played . . . Lots of hills and trees . . . Need to be in fairway . . . Great condition . . . Overlooks Pearl Harbor, scenic, would play again . . . Nice course, hard when windy, very hilly . . . Remember, putts break to ocean. Fair layout, wind sneaks up on you.

★★★½ POIPU BAY RESORT GOLF CLUB

R—2250 Ainako St., Koloa (Kauai) (808)742-8711, (800)858-6300.
16 miles southwest of Lihue. **Holes:** 18. **Par:** 72/72.
Yards: 6,959/5,241. **Course rating:** 73.4/70.9. **Slope:** 132/121.
Opened: 1990. **Pace of Play rating:** 4:15. **Green fee:** $95/125.
Credit cards: MC, V, AMEX, Diners Club, JCB. **Reduced fees:** Resort guests, Twilight, Juniors.
Caddies: No. **Golf carts:** Included in Green Fee.
Discount golf packages: Yes. **Season:** Year-round. **High:** Jan.–May.
On-site lodging: Yes. **Rental clubs:** Yes.
Walking policy: Mandatory cart. **Range:** Yes (grass).
To obtain tee times: Call 48 hours in advance.
Ranked 12th in Hawaii by Golf Digest.
Subscriber comments: Young course but excellent layout and land . . . Back nine seaside holes can be tough . . . Good condition . . . Beautiful course, but very poor greens and gale force winds common . . . Finishing holes are excellent but rest are average . . . Too many bunkers in the middle of the fairways . . . Great Robert Trent Jones Jr. course. Play this one . . . Good solid course, often windy . . . Good layout, ocean views, great links course with beautiful scenery.

PRINCEVILLE RESORT

R—(800)826-4400.
Caddies: No. **Golf carts:** Included in Green Fee.
Discount golf packages: Yes. **Season:** Year-round. **High:** Nov.–March.
On-site lodging: Yes. **Rental clubs:** Yes.
Walking policy: Mandatory cart. **Range:** Yes (grass).
To obtain tee times: Call one month in advance.

★★★★ PRINCEVILLE MAKAI GOLF CLUB
OCEAN/LAKES/WOODS

1 Lei O Papa Rd., Princeville (Kauai) (808)826-3580.
30 miles north of Lihue. **Holes:** 27. **Par:** 72/72/72.
Yards: 6,875/6,886/6,901. **Course rating:** 72.7/72.7/72.3.
Slope: 133/134/129.
Opened: 1973. **Pace of Play rating:** 4:00. **Green fee:** $50/110.
Credit cards: MC, V, AMEX, Diners Club. **Reduced fees:** Low season, Resort guests, Twilight, Juniors.
Ocean and Lakes nines ranked 48th in America's 75 Best Resort Courses by Golf Digest. Ocean and Lakes nines ranked 8th in Hawaii by Golf Digest.
Subscriber comments: Gorgeous, quiet, not overplayed, great staff . . . Top notch courses, Princeville Course very unique . . . Makai Ocean outstanding . . . Fun, windy and very quick pace of play . . . Beautiful, no

pressure . . . Very pleasant to play . . . Scenic, well-kept . . . Good for all golfers . . . Fun and playable . . . I could play the course everyday . . . Good course but not in the same class as the other courses on Kauai . . . A pleasant resort layout . . . No great test, a no brainer.

★★★★½ THE PRINCE GOLF CLUB

5-3900 Kuhio Highway, Princeville (Kauai) (808)826-5000.
30 miles north of Lihue. **Holes:** 18. **Par:** 72/72.
Yards: 7,309/5,338. **Course rating:** 75.6/70.0. **Slope:** 144/127.
Opened: 1991. **Pace of Play rating:** 5:00. **Green fee:** $140.
Credit cards: MC, V, AMEX, Diners Club, JCB. **Reduced fees:** Resort guests, Juniors.
Ranked 72nd in America's 100 Greatest Golf Courses by Golf Digest.
Ranked 5th in America's 75 Best Resort Courses by Golf Digest . . .
Selected Best New Resort Course of 1990 by Golf Digest. Ranked 2nd in Hawaii by Golf Digest.
Subscriber comments: It's No. 1 . . . Another difficult course, spectacular scenery. This is golfer's heaven, way out in front in every way . . . Can I live here? Please! Awesome first hole, then it gets better . . . Spectacular course but too difficult for the average player . . . And God created heaven on the Prince Course! Very interesting with great shotmaking holes . . . My most enjoyable golf experience . . . A must . . . Beautiful . . . Some holes a little awkward . . . Great condition . . . If I had one course to play for the rest of my life, this is it! Several beautiful and unusual holes . . . Best in Hawaii . . . Need a lot of balls . . . Tough, windy, wet . . . Excellent, but overrated . . . Wet in winter . . . Terrific torture in the jungle . . . Great condition as most all Hawaii courses . . . Very difficult, bring extra balls.

★★½ PUKALANI COUNTRY CLUB

PU—360 Pukalani St., Pukalani (Maui) (808)572-1314.
Holes: 18. **Par:** 72/74.
Yards: 6,945/5,574. **Course rating:** 72.8/71.1. **Slope:** 121/118.
Opened: 1981. **Pace of Play rating:** N/A. **Green fee:** $55/62.
Credit cards: MC, V. **Reduced fees:** Low season, Twilight.
Caddies: No. **Golf carts:** Included in Green Fee.
Discount golf packages: No. **Season:** Year-round. **High:** Jan.-March.
On-site lodging: No. **Rental clubs:** Yes.
Walking policy: Mandatory cart. **Range:** Yes (grass).
To obtain tee times: Call anytime.
Subscriber comments: Hilly course, tough and green . . . A hidden gem in upcountry . . . Wide open but not easy . . . Best-kept secret on Maui, spectacular views on course cut into side of volcano . . . Great views of central mall from 900–1000 foot elevation on Haleakala . . . Often dry, lacking irrigation . . . Pleasantly surprised but nothing exceptional, some holes with big inclines . . . Killer views from every tee . . . Magnificent views, but poorly designed and maintained . . . Uninspiring.

★★★½ SANDALWOOD GOLF COURSE

PU—2500 Honoapiilani Hwy., Wailuku (Maui) (808)242-4653.
4 miles south of Wailuku. **Holes:** 18. **Par:** 72/72.
Yards: 6,469/5,162. **Course rating:** 71.2/64.8. **Slope:** 129/118.
Opened: 1991. **Pace of Play rating:** 3:30-4:00. **Green fee:** $65/75.
Credit cards: MC, V, AMEX, Diners Club, JCB. **Reduced fees:** Resort guests.
Caddies: No. **Golf carts:** Included in Green Fee.
Discount golf packages: No. **Season:** Year-round. **High:** Jan.-April.
On-site lodging: No. **Rental clubs:** Yes.
Walking policy: Mandatory cart. **Range:** Yes (grass).
To obtain tee times: Call up to one year in advance.
Subscriber comments: Good layout . . . Bring your bazooka for shots into the wind . . . Excellent design . . . Reachable par 5s . . . Tough par 4s . . . Best new course on Maui, don't miss it . . . Can be challenging with tradewinds . . . Good for all levels . . . Narrow, windy . . . Blind tee shots.

★★ SEAMOUNTAIN GOLF COURSE

R—Off Hwy., Punaluu (808)928-6222.
56 miles south of Hilo. **Holes:** 18. **Par:** 72/72.
Yards: 6,492/5,663. **Course rating:** 72.5/70.9. **Slope:** 135/116.
Opened: 1973. **Pace of Play rating:** 3:00. **Green fee:** $25.
Credit cards: MC, V. **Reduced fees:** Resort guests, Juniors.
Caddies: No. **Golf carts:** Included in Green Fee.
Discount golf packages: Yes. **Season:** Year-round. **High:** Jan.-Feb.
On-site lodging: Yes. **Rental clubs:** Yes.
Walking policy: Mandatory cart. **Range:** Yes (grass).
To obtain tee times: Call in reservations accepted any time.
Subscriber comments: At end of land, great fun after you get there . . .
Beautiful ocean and mountain views, poor maintenance . . . Secluded
location but nice layout . . . Best-kept secret in Hawaii . . . Very remote
area of Big Island . . . No crowds.

★★★½ SHERATON MAKAHA RESORT AND COUNTRY CLUB

R—84-626 Makaha Valley Rd., Waianae (Oahu) (808)695-9544.
40 miles west of Honolulu. **Holes:** 18. **Par:** 72/72.
Yards: 7,091/5,880. **Course rating:** 73.2/73.9. **Slope:** 139/129.
Opened: 1969. **Pace of Play rating:** 4:20. **Green fee:** $80/150.
Credit cards: All major. **Reduced fees:** Weekdays, Low season, Resort
guests, Twilight.
Caddies: No. **Golf carts:** Included in Green Fee.
Discount golf packages: Yes. **Season:** Year-round. **High:** Jan.-March.
On-site lodging: Yes. **Rental clubs:** Yes.
Walking policy: Mandatory cart. **Range:** Yes (grass).
To obtain tee times: Call or fax two weeks in advance.
Subscriber comments: Very challenging, but still a fair course . . . Tight,
great from the tips . . . Long and hard, great holes, a must experience for
good golfers, no fun for bad golfers . . . Very good golf course . . .
Peaceful and quiet . . . Always in excellent playing condition . . .
Challenging, fast greens . . . Very tricky greens . . . Length is important
. . . Seldom busy but an excellent course . . . Worth the drive . . . Some
really nice holes and views.

★★★½ SILVERSWORD GOLF CLUB

PU—1345 Piilani Hwy., Kihei (Maui) (808)874-0777.
12 miles north of Kahului. **Holes:** 18. **Par:** 71/71.
Yards: 6,801/5,265. **Course rating:** 72.0/70.0. **Slope:** 124/118.
Opened: 1987. **Pace of Play rating:** N/A. **Green fee:** $57/69.
Credit cards: MC, V. **Reduced fees:** Low season, Twilight.
Caddies: No. **Golf carts:** Included in Green Fee.
Discount golf packages: No. **Season:** Year-round. **High:** Jan.-March.
On-site lodging: No. **Rental clubs:** Yes.
Walking policy: Mandatory cart. **Range:** Yes (grass).
To obtain tee times: Call up to one month in advance.
Subscriber comments: Wind conditions make course difficult . . . Great
new course, very tight . . . Excellent condition for public course . . . Near
the ocean with views . . . A challenge if they are burning sugar cane. Busy,
playable, wide open . . . Great downhill first hole . . . Just beautiful, like a
public country club . . . Must stay in fairways, high rough . . . Needs to
age, well laid-out.

TURTLE BAY HILTON GOLF AND TENNIS RESORT

R—57-091 Kamehameha Hwy., Kahuku (Oahu) (808)293-8574, (800)445-
8667.
38 miles north of Honolulu.
★★★½ THE LINKS AT KUILIMA
Holes: 18. **Par:** 72/72.
Yards: 7,199/4,851. **Course rating:** 75.0/64.3. **Slope:** 141/121.
Opened: 1992. **Pace of Play rating:** 4:30. **Green fee:** $75/125.
Credit cards: All major. **Reduced fees:** Resort guests.
Caddies: No. **Golf carts:** Included in Green Fee.
Discount golf packages: Yes. **Season:** Year-round. **High:** Dec.-March.
On-site lodging: Yes. **Rental clubs:** Yes.

Walking policy: Mandatory cart. **Range:** Yes (grass).
To obtain tee times: Call or fax the golf shop or hotel two months in advance or up to one year in advance if staying at the Turtle Bay Hilton hotel.

Subscriber comments: It doesn't look hard, but bunkers and water always seem to catch your ball . . . Lush fairways, hard pool-table greens . . . Links style on the far side of Oahu . . . Windy . . . Pretty, European-tyle course . . . Friendly service, challenging design . . . Lots of water and howling tradewinds make for a challenging romp through this swamp . . . Arnold Palmer design . . . Very good course . . . Unique design . . . Half links, half like Sawgrass . . . Tee boxes better than most stateside greens . . . Target golf from the tee.

★★★ TURTLE BAY COUNTRY CLUB
Call club for further information.
Subscriber comments: Nine holes to be played twice . . . Boring . . . No challenge . . . Super course if you don't mind lots of wind . . . Beautiful layout . . . Trouble if you slice . . . Best for the better-than-average golfer . . . Very windy.

★★ VOLCANO GOLF AND COUNTRY CLUB
PU—P.O. Box 46, Volcanoes National Park (808)967-7331.
32 miles south of Hilo. Holes: 18. **Par:** 72/72.
Yards: 6,250/5,449. **Course rating:** N/A. **Slope:** 128/117.
Opened: N/A. **Pace of Play rating:** N/A. **Green fee:** N/A.
Credit cards: MC, V, AMEX,. **Reduced fees:** N/A.
Caddies: No. **Golf carts:** Included in Green Fee.
Discount golf packages: No. **Season:** Year-round. **High:** July-Sept.
On-site lodging: No. **Rental clubs:** No.
Walking policy: . **Range:** Yes (grass).
Subscriber comments: Experience playing golf on an active volcano! A nice cool day in the tropics . . . Stunning . . . Beautiful when weather is nice . . . Cool golfing in a volcano area . . . Good course . . . Greens not up to par.

★★ WAIEHU GOLF COURSE
PU—P.O. Box 507, Wailuku (Maui) (808)244-5934.
Holes: 18. **Par:** 72/71.
Yards: 6,330/5,511. **Course rating:** 69.8/70.6. **Slope:** 111/115.
Opened: N/A. **Pace of Play rating:** 4:00-4:30. **Green fee:** $25/30.
Credit cards: None. **Reduced fees:** No.
Caddies: No. **Golf carts:** $15 for 18 holes.
Discount golf packages: No. **Season:** Year-round. **High:** Nov.-March.
On-site lodging: No. **Rental clubs:** Yes.
Walking policy: Unrestricted walking. **Range:** Yes.
To obtain tee times: Call two days in advance.
Subscriber comments: Good setting . . . Needs turf improvement . . . Loved the ocean views . . . Course is fair . . . Bermuda city . . . Give it a miss . . . Boring course . . . No character . . . Great value and scenery . . . Watch the surf if you slice . . . Great ocean holes and views . . . Muny condition . . . Beautiful views along ocean . . . Heavily trafficked . . . Well-maintained . . . Too hilly . . . A real challenge.

(FRUGAL PICK)

★★★ WAIKELE GOLF CLUB
SP—94-200 Paioa Place, Waipahu (Oahu) (808)676-9000.
15 miles west of Honolulu. Holes: 18. **Par:** 72/72.
Yards: 6,663/5,226. **Course rating:** 71.7/65.6. **Slope:** 126/113.
Opened: 1993. **Pace of Play rating:** 4:00-5:00. **Green fee:** $95.
Credit cards: MC, V, AMEX, JCB. **Reduced fees:** Weekdays, Twilight.
Caddies: No. **Golf carts:** Included in Green Fee.
Discount golf packages: No. **Season:** Year-round. **High:** Jan.-Feb.
On-site lodging: No. **Rental clubs:** No.
Walking policy: Mandatory cart. **Range:** Yes (grass).
To obtain tee times: Call golf shop.
Subscriber comments: Wide fairways make you think you're Calvin Peete . . . Nicest new course . . . Short but hilly . . . Nice layout . . . Worst of cart-path golf . . . Rock hard greens . . . Long par 4s . . . New . . .

Difficult . . . Beautiful . . . Lots of O.B. . . . Requires accuracy off the tees and multi-tiered greens require accuracy on approach shots . . . Great challenge . . . Plays harder than it looks . . . Well-maintained . . . New course . . . Needs to mature . . . Young greens . . . Should improve with time . . . Unique and challenging holes . . . Very enjoyable.

WAIKOLOA BEACH RESORT

23 miles south of Kailua-Kona.
Green fee: $95.
Credit cards: All major. **Reduced fees:** Resort guests, Twilight.
Caddies: No. **Golf carts:** Included in Green Fee.
Discount golf packages: Yes. **Season:** Year-round. **High:** Dec.–March.
On-site lodging: Yes. **Rental clubs:** Yes.
Walking policy: Mandatory cart. **Range:** Yes (grass).
To obtain tee times: Call or fax 30 days in advance with major credit card to guarantee.

★★★ BEACH GOLF COURSE

R—1020 Keana Place, Kamuela (808)885-6060.
Holes: 18. **Par:** 72/72.
Yards: 6,566/5,094. **Course rating:** 71.5/69.4. **Slope:** 133/119.
Opened: 1981. **Pace of Play rating:** 4:30.
Subscriber comments: Fun course, not too tough, near the ocean and the hotel . . . Great shape . . . Can be very windy . . . Great condition . . . Good resort course, fun when not slow . . . Fun resort course.

★★★½ KINGS' GOLF COURSE

R—600 Waikoloa Beach Dr., Kamuela (808)885-4647.
Holes: 18. **Par:** 72/72.
Yards: 7,074/5,459. **Course rating:** 73.9/71.0. **Slope:** 133/121.
Opened: 1990. **Pace of Play rating:** 4:30.
Ranked 25th in America's 75 Best Resort Courses by Golf Digest. Selected as runner-up for Best New Resort Course of 1990 by Golf Digest. Ranked 14th in Hawaii by Golf Digest.
Subscriber comments: Wonderful course . . . Helpful staff . . . Resort golf . . . Fantastic, enough said . . . Wonderful resort course . . . A fun course . . . Very good resort course . . . Fair but tough . . . Best course on the island of Hawaii . . . Requires all clubs . . . Good resort course . . . Long but not challenging . . . Windy but playable . . . Good design.

★★★½ WAIKOLOA VILLAGE GOLF CLUB

R—68-1792 Melia St., Waikoloa (808)883-9621.
18 miles north of Kailua-Kona. **Holes:** 18. **Par:** 72/72.
Yards: 6,791/5,479. **Course rating:** 71.8/72.1. **Slope:** 130/119.
Opened: 1972. **Pace of Play rating:** 3:48. **Green fee:** $50/65.
Credit cards: MC, V, AMEX, JCB. **Reduced fees:** Twilight, Juniors.
Caddies: No. **Golf carts:** Included in Green Fee.
Discount golf packages: Yes. **Season:** Year-round. **High:** Dec.–Feb.
On-site lodging: Yes. **Rental clubs:** Yes.
Walking policy: Walking at certain times. **Range:** Yes (grass).
To obtain tee times: Call three days in advance. Groups of 12 or more call one year in advance. Reservations taken 30 days in advance with a 50 percent prepay.
Subscriber comments: Challenging for the low handicappers . . . Long and open . . . Beautiful scenic course . . . Not overly difficult . . . Courses in great shape . . . Beautiful lava hazards and sand . . . Good staff . . . Fast players . . . Another great resort course . . . Very good but a windy mountain course . . . Fabulous views . . . A great course in great shape . . . Fairly forgiving . . . Wonderful time . . . What a lot of wind!

WAILEA GOLF CLUB

R—120 Kaukahi St., Wailea (Maui) (808)875-5111.
17 miles south of Kahului.
Pace of Play rating: N/A.
Credit cards: All major. **Reduced fees:** Resort guests.
Caddies: No. **Golf carts:** Included in Green Fee.
Discount golf packages: Yes. **Season:** Year-round. **High:** Dec.–April.
On-site lodging: Yes. **Rental clubs:** Yes.

Walking policy: Mandatory cart. **Range:** Yes (grass).
To obtain tee times: Call five days in advance if you are a Wailea resort guest.

★★★½ BLUE COURSE
Holes: 18. **Par:** 72/72.
Yards: 6,758/5,291. **Course rating:** 71.6/72.0. **Slope:** 130/117.
Opened: 1972. **Green fee:** $85.
Ranked 66th in America's 75 Best Resort Courses by Golf Digest.
Subscriber comments: Exceptional in all areas . . . Great design . . . Lots to see especially if whales are in . . . Fun course, lush and well-kept grounds on both courses . . . Good course . . . Easy . . . Not overwhelmingly interesting . . . These courses rival Kapalua as best in Hawaii, particularly with the addition of the third course . . . Well-kept . . . Wide fairways.

★★ EMERALD COURSE
Holes: 18. **Par:** 72/72.
Yards: 6,825/5,454. **Course rating:** N/A. **Slope:** N/A.
Opened: 1994. **Green fee:** $85.
Subscriber comments: Outstanding course . . . All players . . . Highly recommend . . . Course not that hard . . . Fairways wide open . . . Beautiful vistas . . . Short course . . . Beautiful scenery . . . Shared greens.

★★★½ GOLD COURSE
Holes: 18. **Par:** 72/72.
Yards: 7,070/5,317. **Course rating:** 73.0/70.3. **Slope:** 139/121.
Opened: 1994. **Green fee:** $90.
Ranked 7th in Hawaii by Golf Digest.
Subscriber comments: Best of three Wailea courses . . . Better than Blue and old Orange courses . . . Great views . . . Lots of Robert Trent Jones Jr. signature traps, elevated greens . . . New course . . . Needs to mature . . . Has potential . . . Beautiful scenic views . . . Course never lets up, makes you think . . . Very good, no complaints . . . Sand, sand everywhere . . . Nice . . . Well- maintained . . . Too many parallel fairways . . . Traps everywhere . . . Great sunsets if finishing at dusk . . . It's on Maui! . . . Good layout.

★★★½ WAILUA GOLF COURSE
PU—3-5351 Kuhio Hwy., Lihue (Kauai) (808)245-8092.
3 miles south of Lihue. **Holes:** 18. **Par:** 36/36.
Yards: 6,981/5,974. **Course rating:** 73.0/73.1. **Slope:** 136/122.
Opened: 1963. **Pace of Play rating:** N/A. **Green fee:** $18/20.
Credit cards: None. **Reduced fees:** Twilight, Seniors.
Caddies: No. **Golf carts:** $14 for 18 holes.
Discount golf packages: No. **Season:** Year-round. **High:** Jan.-April.
On-site lodging: No. **Rental clubs:** Yes.
Walking policy: Unrestricted walking. **Range:** Yes.
To obtain tee times: Call one week in advance, minimum two players.
Ranked in First 25 of America's 75 Best Public Golf Courses by Golf Digest.
Subscriber comments: Good course, sometimes slow . . . Great beat-up public course . . . Needs better grounds, water, and less play to recover . . . Best public course in Hawaii . . . Great challenge . . . Easy access public course . . . A lot of fun . . . Fun all around, good service, conditions . . . Beautiful course in all respects . . . Still the best muny in Hawaii . . . Very beautiful and demanding . . . USGA Public Links Championships here in '75, '85 and '96 . . . Still good even after losing some trees . . . Nice views . . . Good for all levels.

WAIMEA COUNTRY CLUB★
SP—Mamalohoa Hwy., Kamuela (808)885-8777.
Holes: 18. **Par:** 72/72.
Yards 6,661/5,673. **Course rating:** N/A. **Slope:** N/A.
Opened: 1994. **Pace of Play rating:** 4:00. **Green fee:** $75.
Credit cards: MC, V, AMEX. **Reduced fees:** No.
Caddies: No. **Golf carts:** Included in Green Fee.

Discount golf packages: No. **Season:** Year-round.
On-site lodging: No. **Rental clubs:** Yes.
Walking policy: Unrestricted walking. **Range:** Yes.
To obtain tee times: Call anytime.

★★★ WEST LOCH GOLF COURSE

PU—91-1126 Okupe St., Ewa Beach (808)671-2292.
15 miles west of Honolulu. **Holes:** 18. **Par:** 72/72.
Yards: 6,479/5,296. **Course rating:** 70.3/68.6. **Slope:** 123/117.
Opened: 1990. **Pace of Play rating:** 4:00. **Green fee:** $14/18.
Credit cards: None. **Reduced fees:** Twilight, Seniors, Juniors.
Caddies: No. **Golf carts:** Included in Green Fee.
Discount golf packages: No. **Season:** Year-round. **High:** April-Sept.
On-site lodging: No. **Rental clubs:** Yes.
Walking policy: Mandatory cart. **Range:** Yes (grass).
To obtain tee times: Call one week in advance.
Subscriber comments: Some starters need to be friendlier . . . Best
Honolulu muny course . . . Challenging . . . Short, hazards all around . . .
Accuracy and control . . . Lots of water . . . Fast greens . . . Five-star 19th
hole . . . Presently the flagship muny . . . Almost impossible to get on . . .
Average course with some interesting holes . . . Slow, flat municipal course
. . . Poor man's country club . . . Course not in great shape.

Notes

★★★ AVONDALE GOLF CLUB

SP—10745 Avondale Loop Rd., Hayden Lake (208)772-5963.
35 miles east of Spokane, WA. **Holes:** 18. **Par:** 72/74.
Yards: 6,525/4,719. **Course rating:** 71.1/73.2. **Slope:** 118/123.
Opened: 1968. **Pace of play rating:** 4:00. **Green fee:** $20.
Credit cards: MC, V, DISC. **Reduced fees:** Low season, Twilight,
Juniors.
Caddies: No. **Golf carts:** $21 for 18 holes.
Discount golf packages: No. **Season:** March-Oct. **High:** June-Aug.
On-site lodging: No. **Rental clubs:** Yes.
Walking policy: Walking at certain times. **Range:** Yes (grass).
To obtain tee times: Call pro shop seven days in advance.
Subscriber comments: Tight fairways . . . Lots of trees . . . Some hills
. . . Keep them straight . . . Nice variety . . . Nice setting . . . Better than
average . . . Some easy holes . . . Challenging back nine . . . Play with
someone who knows the course . . . Fast greens, some narrow front to
back . . . Good grass . . . Very friendly.

★★★ BLACKFOOT MUNICIPAL GOLF COURSE

PU—3115 Teeples Dr., Blackfoot (208)785-9960.
19 miles north of Pocatello. **Holes:** 18. **Par:** 71/75.
Yards: 6,899/6,385. **Course rating:** 71.5/75.0. **Slope:** 123/124.
Opened: 1959. **Pace of play rating:** 4:30. **Green fee:** $12.
Credit cards: MC, V. **Reduced fees:** Weekdays, Low season.
Caddies: No. **Golf carts:** $15 for 18 holes.
Discount golf packages: No. **Season:** March-Nov. **High:** May-Oct.
On-site lodging: No. **Rental clubs:** Yes.
Walking policy: Unrestricted walking. **Range:** No.
To obtain tee times: Call two days in advance.
Subscriber comments: Tough old front nine, newer open back nine . . .
Excellent front nine . . . Designed by U.S. Amateur champ George von
Elm . . . Fantastic shot values . . . Long par 4s . . . Wind is the biggest
challenge . . . Country club conditions on a public course, all season . . .
Quick play . . . Lack of crowds and low cost add up to a good course . . .
Staff does beautiful job . . . Would recommend this to all players.

★½ BRYDEN CANYON PUBLIC GOLF CLUB

PU—445 O'Connor Rd., Lewiston (208)746-0863.
100 miles northwest of Spokane, WA. **Holes:** 18. **Par:** 71/71.
Yards: 6,103/5,380. **Course rating:** 67.4/69.9. **Slope:** 106/111.
Opened: 1975. **Pace of play rating:** 4:30-5:00. **Green fee:** $11.
Credit cards: MC, V. **Reduced fees:** No.
Caddies: No. **Golf carts:** $11 for 18 holes.
Discount golf packages: Yes. **Season:** Year-round. **High:** Feb.-Sept.
On-site lodging: No. **Rental clubs:** Yes.
Walking policy: Unrestricted walking. **Range:** Yes (grass).
To obtain tee times: Call up to seven days in advance.
Subscriber comments: Hillside golf . . . Fun to play . . . Wide open . . .
Easy greens . . . A variety of terrain . . . Lots of relief . . . A canyon setting
. . . Very hilly . . . Older players need carts . . . Very friendly staff.

★★ CENTENNIAL GOLF CLUB

PU—Box 52, Centennial Dr., Nampa (208)467-3011.
Call club for further information.
Subscriber comments: Sweet little course . . . A new course . . . An open
course with few trees . . . Short but interesting . . . Well groomed . . .
Some water hazards . . . Large greens . . . Accuracy is not critical . . . Ego
builder . . . Easy to break 90 . . . Will be an interesting course to play when
the trees get more growth . . . Staff is the best in Idaho.

CLEAR LAKE COUNTRY CLUB★

SP—403 Clear Lake Lane, Buhl (208)543-4849.
90 miles east of Boise. **Holes:** 18. **Par:** 72/73.
Yards: 5,905/5,378. **Course rating:** 68.2/69.4. **Slope:** 112/113.

Opened: 1987. **Pace of play rating:** 4:30. **Green fee:** $15/20.
Credit cards: MC, V. **Reduced fees:** Weekdays, Juniors.
Caddies: No. **Golf carts:** N/A.
Discount golf packages: No. **Season:** Year-round. **High:** May-Oct.
On-site lodging: No. **Rental clubs:** Yes.
Walking policy: Unrestricted walking. **Range:** Yes (grass).
To obtain tee times: Call four days in advance.

★★★★½ COEUR D'ALENE RESORT GOLF COURSE
R—900 Floating Green Dr., Coeur d'Alene (208)667-4653, (800)688-5253.
32 miles east of Spokane, WA. **Holes:** 18. **Par:** 71/71.
Yards: 6,309/5,490. **Course rating:** 69.9/70.3. **Slope:** 121/118.
Opened: 1991. **Pace of play rating:** 4:22. **Green fee:** $60/125.
Credit cards: All major. **Reduced fees:** Low season, Resort guests.

Caddies: Yes. **Golf carts:** Included in Green Fee.
Discount golf packages: Yes. **Season:** April-Oct. **High:** June-Sept.
On-site lodging: Yes. **Rental clubs:** Yes.
Walking policy: Walking at certain times. **Range:** Yes (grass).
To obtain tee times: Guests may call up to one year in advance.
Ranked 11th in America's 75 Best Resort Courses by Golf Digest. Ranked
1st in Idaho by Golf Digest.
Subscriber comments: Prepare to be pampered . . . Utopian-like
experience for any golfer . . . A wonderful golf experience . . . Fantastic
beauty . . . Fantastic condition . . . Fantastic staff . . . Fantastic service . . .
Floating carpet green is great . . . Forecaddies are superb . . . Attentive,
fleet-footed caddies . . . Fairways mowed like greens . . . No rough . . .
The most enjoyable day I can recall . . . The highlight of our golfing year
. . . No course in the world has better grounds or amenities . . . The boat
trip is a must . . . Every golfer should treat himself to this one . . . I could
happily stay here forever . . . A little short . . . Much easier course than I
had expected . . . Play it on a windy day if you think it's easy . . . Golf and
Idaho at its finest . . . One of a kind scenery . . . Best golf experience in the
Northwest . . . In 28 years of walking the links, this is the all around best
. . . Nice touches : . . Done with class . . . Don't change a thing.

★★½ EAGLE HILLS GOLF COURSE
PU—605 N. Edgewood Lane, Eagle (208)939-0402.
4 miles northwest of Boise. **Holes:** 18. **Par:** 72/72.
Yards: 6,485/5,305. **Course rating:** 70.5/70.2. **Slope:** 118/114.
Opened: 1968. **Pace of play rating:** 4:00. **Green fee:** $14/19.
Credit cards: MC, V. **Reduced fees:** Weekdays, Low season, Twilight,
Seniors, Juniors.
Caddies: No. **Golf carts:** $9 for 18 holes.
Discount golf packages: Yes. **Season:** Year-round. **High:** March-Oct.
On-site lodging: No. **Rental clubs:** Yes.
Walking policy: Unrestricted walking. **Range:** Yes (grass).
To obtain tee times: Call five days in advance.
Subscriber comments: Two distinctive nines . . . Front typical layout in
housing development . . . Tight. Must be mentally on your game . . .
Cross streets between holes . . . Too many houses . . . Back nine more
open . . . Very good back nine . . . Greens improved from years past.

★★★ ELKHORN COUNTRY CLUB
R—Elkhorn Rd., Sun Valley (208)622-3300.
150 miles east of Boise. **Holes:** 18. **Par:** 72/72.
Yards: 7,101/5,424. **Course rating:** 72.4/69.2. **Slope:** 133/120.
Opened: 1975. **Pace of play rating:** 4:00-4:30. **Green fee:** $75.
Credit cards: All major. **Reduced fees:** Resort guests.
Caddies: No. **Golf carts:** Included in Green Fee.
Discount golf packages: Yes. **Season:** May-Oct. **High:** June-Aug.
On-site lodging: Yes. **Rental clubs:** Yes.
Walking policy: Mandatory cart. **Range:** Yes (grass).
To obtain tee times: Public two days in advance or 30 days in advance
with a credit card.

Ranked 64th in America's 75 Best Resort Courses by Golf Digest. Ranked 3rd in Idaho by Golf Digest.
Subscriber comments: Good course in Sun Valley . . . Great views . . . Wildlife evident . . . Typical Robert Trent Jones Jr. course with massive greens . . . Lots of traps . . . Beautiful. Open and rolling . . . Strange holes but fun . . . Good shape for a mountain course . . . Very difficult from back tees . . . Ball still travels a mile . . . Better shape this year than last year.

HIDDEN LAKES GOLF RESORT★
R—8838 Lower Pack River Rd., Sandpoint (208)263-1642.
86 miles northeast of Spokane, WA. **Holes:** 18. **Par:** 71/71.
Yards: 6,655/5,078. **Course rating:** 71.7/68.9. **Slope:** 128/120.
Opened: 1986. **Pace of play rating:** N/A. **Green fee:** $25/29.
Credit cards: MC, V. **Reduced fees:** Low season, Resort guests, Twilight, Seniors, Juniors.
Caddies: No. **Golf carts:** $11 for 18 holes.
Discount golf packages: Yes. **Season:** April-Oct. **High:** April-Oct.
On-site lodging: No. **Rental clubs:** Yes.
Walking policy: Unrestricted walking. **Range:** Yes (grass).
To obtain tee times: Twelve days in advance for members and seven days in advance for nonmembers.

★★½ HIGHLAND GOLF COURSE
PU—201 Von Elm Rd., Pocatello (208)237-9922.
Holes: 18. **Par:** 72/76.
Yards: 6,512/6,100. **Course rating:** 67.5/73.0. **Slope:** 114/117.
Opened: 1963. **Pace of play rating:** 4:30. **Green fee:** $12/13.
Credit cards: None. **Reduced fees:** Seniors, Juniors.
Caddies: No. **Golf carts:** $16 for 18 holes.
Discount golf packages: No. **Season:** March-Oct. **High:** May-Sept.
On-site lodging: No. **Rental clubs:** Yes.
Walking policy: Unrestricted walking. **Range:** Yes (grass).
To obtain tee times: Call Thursday for upcoming weekend.
Subscriber comments: Good public golf . . . Wide open . . . Lots of hills . . . Take a cart.

★★★ THE HIGHLANDS GOLF AND COUNTRY CLUB
PU—N. 701 Inverness Dr., Post Falls (208)773-3673.
30 miles east of Spokane, WA. **Holes:** 18. **Par:** 72/73.
Yards: 6,369/5,115. **Course rating:** 70.7/69.5. **Slope:** 125/121.
Opened: 1991. **Pace of play rating:** N/A. **Green fee:** $21/23.
Credit cards: All major. **Reduced fees:** Weekdays, Low season, Seniors, Juniors.
Caddies: No. **Golf carts:** $22 for 18 holes.
Discount golf packages: No. **Season:** March-Oct. **High:** June-Aug.
On-site lodging: No. **Rental clubs:** Yes.
Walking policy: Walking at certain times. **Range:** Yes (grass).
To obtain tee times: Call one week in advance.
Subscriber comments: Relatively new . . . One of best newer courses . . . Interesting course . . . Accuracy is the focus . . . Some strong holes . . . Some marginal holes . . . Good practice area . . . OB on both sides of most holes . . . Course needs to season . . . Will be great in a few years . . . Could be a gem . . . Nicest clubhouse in Idaho . . . Nice drive-through food service on the 14th.

★★ MCCALL MUNICIPAL GOLF COURSE
PU—off Fairway Dr., McCall (208)634-7200
Call club for further information.
Subscriber comments: Good high-levation course . . . Short . . . Narrow . . . Lots of pines . . . Small greens . . . No sand traps . . . Beautiful setting but doesn't drain well . . . Great atmosphere . . . Good golf experience.

★★★½ PINECREST MUNICIPAL GOLF COURSE

PU—701 E. Elva St., Idaho Falls (208)529-1485.

Holes: 18. **Par:** 70/77.

Yards: 6,394/6,123. **Course rating:** 69.5/74.0. **Slope:** 116/125.

Opened: 1934. **Pace of play rating:** 4:15. **Green fee:** $10/11.

Credit cards: MC, V. **Reduced fees:** No.

Caddies: No. **Golf carts:** $14 for 18 holes.

Discount golf packages: No. **Season:** March-Nov. **High:** May-Sept.

On-site lodging: No. **Rental clubs:** Yes.

Walking policy: Unrestricted walking. **Range:** No.

To obtain tee times: One day in advance starting at 6:30 a.m.

Subscriber comments: Old established course . . . Built during the
Depression Era . . . Grand old course in the middle of the city . . . Many
large pine trees . . . Smallish greens . . . Nicely groomed . . . Log
clubhouse . . . Was a WPA project . . . Best-feeling clubhouse around . . .
New sprinkler system has returned course to prior status . . . Well worth
playing.

(GREAT VALUE)

★★½ PURPLE SAGE GOLF COURSE

PU—15192 Purple Sage Rd., Caldwell (208)459-2223.

25 miles west of Boise. **Holes:** 18. **Par:** 71/71.

Yards: 6,747/5,343. **Course rating:** 70.7/68.9. **Slope:** 117/111.

Opened: 1963. **Pace of play rating:** 4:00. **Green fee:** $12/14.

Credit cards: None. **Reduced fees:** Weekdays.

Caddies: No. **Golf carts:** $16 for 18 holes.

Discount golf packages: No. **Season:** March-Dec. **High:** May-Aug.

On-site lodging: No. **Rental clubs:** Yes.

Walking policy: Unrestricted walking. **Range:** Yes (grass).

To obtain tee times: Call seven days in advance.

Subscriber comments: One of the better public courses . . . Narrow
fairways . . . Good water . . . Great for iron play . . . Big greens . . .
Rather fast . . . With a lot of break in them . . . Few hazards, too straight
. . . New tee boxes . . . There are shots local knowledge will help . . .
Wind can add variety.

★★★ QUAIL HOLLOW GOLF CLUB

SP—4520 N. 36th St., Boise (208)344-7807.

Holes: 18. **Par:** 70/70.

Yards: 6,444/4,530. **Course rating:** 70.7/68.0. **Slope:** 128/129.

Opened: 1982. **Pace of play rating:** 4:50. **Green fee:** $12/19.

Credit cards: MC, V. **Reduced fees:** Weekdays, Low season, Seniors,
Juniors.

Caddies: No. **Golf carts:** $8 for 18 holes.

Discount golf packages: No. **Season:** Year-round. **High:** March-Oct.

On-site lodging: No. **Rental clubs:** Yes.

Walking policy: Unrestricted walking. **Range:** Yes (grass).

To obtain tee times: Call five days in advance.

Subscriber comments: Target golf at its finest . . . Lots of sidehill, uphill
and downhill lies . . . Fast undulating greens that get faster as summer
progresses . . . Bring your "A" game . . . Some very scenic holes . . .
Young trees, big greens . . . Spectacular, but needs maintenance . . . Lots of
hills . . . Do not walk this course . . . They are trying to make it easier. Big
mistake! . . . Undervalued course . . . Best greens in Boise . . . Best in
Idaho for the money.

★★½ RIVERSIDE GOLF COURSE

PU—3500 S. Bannock Hwy., Pocatello (208)232-9515.

Holes: 18. **Par:** 72/75.

Yards: 6,397/5,710. **Course rating:** 69.7/72.2. **Slope:** 114/119.

Opened: 1963. **Pace of play rating:** 4:30. **Green fee:** $12/13.

Credit cards: None. **Reduced fees:** No.

Caddies: No. **Golf carts:** $16 for 18 holes.

Discount golf packages: No. **Season:** March-Oct. **High:** May-Aug.

On-site lodging: No. **Rental clubs:** Yes.

Walking policy: Unrestricted walking. **Range:** Yes (grass).

To obtain tee times: Call Thursday for upcoming weekend.
Subscriber comments: Good solid golf . . . Varied terrain . . . Older front nine is nice . . . Big old trees . . . Tight and fun . . . Back nine flat, open, unspectacular . . . Great greens.

★★½ SAND CREEK GOLF CLUB
PU—5200 S. 25th E., Idaho Falls (208)529-1115.
Holes: 18. **Par:** 72/73.
Yards: 6,805/5,770. **Course rating:** 70.5/72.2. **Slope:** 115/116.
Opened: 1978. **Pace of play rating:** 4:30. **Green fee:** $11/12.
Credit cards: MC, V. **Reduced fees:** Seniors, Juniors.
Caddies: No. **Golf carts:** $14 for 18 holes.
Discount golf packages: No. **Season:** March-Nov. **High:** June-Aug.
On-site lodging: No. **Rental clubs:** Yes.
Walking policy: Unrestricted walking. **Range:** Yes.
To obtain tee times: Call one day in advance.
Subscriber comments: Flat . . . Open . . . Lots of water . . . Firm greens . . . Very slow play anytime of the week . . . Windy.

SCOTCH PINES GOLF COURSE★
PU—10610 Scotch Pines Rd., Payette (208)642-1829.
58 miles northwest of Boise. **Holes:** 18. **Par:** 72/72.
Yards: 6,454/5,586. **Course rating:** 69.4/71.8. **Slope:** 110/116.
Opened: 1960. **Pace of play rating:** 3:45. **Green fee:** $13.
Credit cards: MC, V. **Reduced fees:** No.
Caddies: No. **Golf carts:** $9 for 18 holes.
Discount golf packages: No. **Season:** Feb-Nov. **High:** May-Aug.
On-site lodging: No. **Rental clubs:** Yes.
Walking policy: Unrestricted walking. **Range:** Yes (grass).
To obtain tee times: Call two days in advance.

★★★ SHADOW VALLEY GOLF CLUB
PU—Rt. 1, Hwy. 55, Boise (208)939-6699.
Call club for further information.
Subscriber comments: Challenging . . . two distinct nines . . . Front nine up and down fairways . . . Back nine traditional, through the trees . . . Great front nine. Fun to play . . . Interesting . . . Greens are real tricky to read and putt . . . Always in good shape . . . Fast golf demanded . . . Marshals used expertly . . . Better keep up pace . . . Friendly staff . . . My favorite course. I like it more than it likes me . . . Very underrated . . . Best public course in Boise . . . Idaho's best kept secret.

★★½ STONERIDGE GOLF CLUB
R—1 Blanchard Rd., Blanchard (208)437-4682.
35 miles northeast of Spokane. **Holes:** 18. **Par:** 72/72.
Yards: 6,522/5,678. **Course rating:** 71.4/72.4. **Slope:** 127/126.
Opened: 1971. **Pace of play rating:** 4:30. **Green fee:** $20.
Credit cards: MC, V. **Reduced fees:** Resort guests, Twilight, Seniors, Juniors.
Caddies: No. **Golf carts:** $22 for 18 holes.
Discount golf packages: Yes. **Season:** April-Oct. **High:** May-Sept.
On-site lodging: Yes. **Rental clubs:** Yes.
Walking policy: Unrestricted walking. **Range:** Yes (grass).
To obtain tee times: Call seven days in advance for weekends and holidays; 48 hours for weekdays.
Subscriber comments: A fun resort course . . . Pretty mountain scenery . . . Sand, water, trees, blind shots . . . A good mix of easy and difficult holes . . . Lighting quick greens . . . Slickest greens that ever held a 1-iron . . . Killer rough . . . Great condition . . . A superb layout . . . 17th hole is a monster . . . Uncrowded . . . Still the best kept secret in north Idaho.

★★★★ SUN VALLEY RESORT GOLF COURSE
R—Sun Valley Rd., Sun Valley (208)622-2251, (800)786-8259.
Holes: 18. **Par:** 72/73.
Yards: 6,565/5,241. **Course rating:** 71.1/70.4. **Slope:** 128/125.
Opened: 1938. **Pace of play rating:** 4:30. **Green fee:** $49/83.

Credit cards: All major. **Reduced fees:** Low season, Resort guests.
Caddies: No. **Golf carts:** Included in Green Fee.
Discount golf packages: Yes. **Season:** April-Oct. **High:** June-Sept.
On-site lodging: Yes. **Rental clubs:** Yes.
Walking policy: Walking at certain times. **Range:** Yes (grass).
To obtain tee times: Hotel guests anytime. Public may call 48 hours in advance. All tee times reserved with credit card.
Ranked 60th in America's 75 Best Resort Courses by Golf Digest. Ranked 2nd in Idaho by Golf Digest. Site of Golf Digest Schools.
Subscriber comments: In the heart of Sun Valley . . . Tremendous course . . . Excellent design . . . Majestic setting . . . Awesome scenery . . . A real treat . . . Narrow . . . Lots of pines . . . Lakes . . . Foxes . . . 15th should be on the list of greatest par 3s! . . . Play the blue tees . . . Ball travels a mile . . . Fun to play . . . Some tight places . . . Course management is a must.

★★½ TWIN LAKES VILLAGE GOLF COURSE

SP—E. 2600 Village Blvd., Rathdrum (208)687-1311.
15 miles north of Coeur d'Alene. **Holes:** 18. **Par:** 71/72.
Yards: 6,178/5,370. **Course rating:** 69.7/71.0. **Slope:** 124/121.
Opened: 1975. **Pace of play rating:** 4:00. **Green fee:** $10/20.
Credit cards: MC, V. **Reduced fees:** Low season, Twilight, Seniors, Juniors.
Caddies: No. **Golf carts:** $22 for 18 holes.
Discount golf packages: No. **Season:** April-Oct. **High:** June-Aug.
On-site lodging: Yes. **Rental clubs:** Yes.
Walking policy: Unrestricted walking. **Range:** Yes (grass).
To obtain tee times: Call one week in advance.
Subscriber comments: Nice out-of-the-way track . . . Sporty . . . Cute . . . Front nine good, back nine too narrow . . . Bring your straight sticks . . . Short, but accuracy off the tee is a must . . . Front nine is good for beginners. Back nine is a bit more difficult . . . Dense woods . . . A surprisingly nice challenge . . . Newer back nine is maturing . . . People are always pleasant.

★★½ UNIVERSITY OF IDAHO GOLF COURSE

PU—1215 Nez Perce, Moscow (208)885-6171.
85 miles south of Spokane. **Holes:** 18. **Par:** 72/72.
Yards: 6,639/5,770. **Course rating:** 72.0/73.0. **Slope:** 130/130.
Opened: 1933. **Pace of play rating:** 4:15. **Green fee:** $11/15.
Credit cards: MC, V, DISC. **Reduced fees:** Weekdays, Twilight, Seniors, Juniors.
Caddies: No. **Golf carts:** $20 for 18 holes.
Discount golf packages: Yes. **Season:** March-Oct. **High:** May-Aug.
On-site lodging: No. **Rental clubs:** Yes.
Walking policy: Unrestricted walking. **Range:** Yes.
To obtain tee times: Call up to one week in advance.
Subscriber comments: Good design for rolling hills . . . Up-and-down fairways . . . Steep, hard, fun . . . Handicap raiser . . . Tough lies . . . Too many sidehill lies even after great shots . . . Nice challenge. Very hilly terrain . . . Hard walking . . . Great course when I'm in the area . . . Underrated by many.

★½ WARM SPRINGS GOLF COURSE

PU—2495 Warm Springs Ave., Boise (208)343-5661.
Holes: 18. **Par:** 72/72.
Yards: 6,719/5,660. **Course rating:** N/A. **Slope:** 113/113.
Opened: N/A. **Pace of play rating:** N/A. **Green fee:** N/A.
Credit cards: All major. **Reduced fees:** Weekdays, Twilight.
Caddies: No. **Golf carts:** N/A.
Discount golf packages: No. **Season:** Year-round. **High:** May-Sept.
On-site lodging: No. **Rental clubs:** No.
Walking policy: N/A. **Range:** Yes.
Subscriber comments: Boise's most often played course . . . Pretty basic public course . . . Just stand back and let it fly . . . Flat and unimaginitive . . . Predictable . . . Nice course for higher handicaps . . . I occasionally get a quick nine after work there because of convenience.

★★★★ ALDEEN GOLF CLUB
PU—1900 Reid Farm Rd., Rockford (815)282-4653.
90 miles west of Chicago. **Holes:** 18. **Par:** 72/77.
Yards: 7,058/5,038. **Course rating:** 73.6/69.1. **Slope:** 126/115.
Opened: 1991. **Pace of Play rating:** 3:30. **Green fee:** $30/36.
Credit cards: MC, V, DISC. **Reduced fees:** Weekdays, Twilight.
Caddies: No. **Golf carts:** $24 for 18 holes.
Discount golf packages: No. **Season:** April-Oct. **High:** June-Aug.
On-site lodging: No. **Rental clubs:** Yes.
Walking policy: Unrestricted walking. **Range:** Yes (grass).
To obtain tee times: Call one week in advance. Credit card needed to
reserve starting times.
Subscriber comments: The pride of the community . . . Tee set up is
great for all levels of play . . . Has an excellent driving range . . . Nice
layout, bent grass, lots of bunkers . . . Great course now maturing, best hit
ball straight . . . Lots of water . . . One island hole, many man-made
mounds . . . Four sets of tees . . . Can't decide if it's a municipal course or a
country club . . . Great public course, would be good course for Senior
PGA Tour.

★★★★ ANNBRIAR GOLF COURSE
PU—1524 Birdie Lane, Waterloo (618)939-4653.
25 miles southeast of St. Louis. **Holes:** 18. **Par:** 72/72.
Yards: 6,841/4,792. **Course rating:** 72.3/66.4. **Slope:** 141/110.
Opened: 1993. **Pace of Play rating:** 4:30. **Green fee:** $42/52.
Credit cards: MC, V. **Reduced fees:** Low season.
Caddies: No. **Golf carts:** Included in Green Fee.
Discount golf packages: No. **Season:** Year-round. **High:** April-Oct.
On-site lodging: No. **Rental clubs:** Yes.
Walking policy: Mandatory cart. **Range:** Yes (grass).
To obtain tee times: Call up to seven days in advance.
Subscriber comments: Back nine like Augusta . . . Enjoyed very much,
favorite course . . . Beautiful scenery . . . Course has tee boxes for every
kind of player, very friendly staff and a quick pace . . . The course has really
matured over the past year . . . Lots of mounds . . . Scenery is exceptional
. . . An awesome course . . . Offering a variety of tee boxes (five), wide
fairways, easily visible greens . . . Very nice food, service, people . . . Only
drawback is the cart paths only rule . . . Private club feel . . . Good layout,
front open, back tight, long carry on some tee shots to reach fairway.

★½ ANTIOCH GOLF CLUB
PU—40150 N. Rte. 59, Antioch (708)395-3004.
60 miles northwest of Chicago. **Holes:** 18. **Par:** 72/72.
Yards: 6,321/5,556. **Course rating:** 68.2/72.4. **Slope:** 114/112.
Opened: 1925. **Pace of Play rating:** 4:15. **Green fee:** $14/22.
Credit cards: MC, V, AMEX. **Reduced fees:** Weekdays, Low season,
Twilight, Seniors, Juniors.
Caddies: No. **Golf carts:** $23 for 18 holes.
Discount golf packages: Yes. **Season:** Year-round. **High:** May-Sept.
On-site lodging: No. **Rental clubs:** Yes.
Walking policy: Unrestricted walking. **Range:** Yes.
To obtain tee times: Call up to seven days in advance (credit card
required).
Subscriber comments: Mixed conditions, better score on easy holes . . .
Vastly improved over last three years . . . Undergoing much course
construction . . . Course is somewhat hilly . . . Good for all levels of play
. . . Challenging greens.

★★½ ARBORETUM GOLF CLUB
PU—401 Half Day Rd., Buffalo Grove (708)913-1112.
45 miles northwest of Chicago. **Holes:** 18. **Par:** 72/72.
Yards: 6,477/5,039. **Course rating:** 71.1/68.7. **Slope:** 132/118.
Opened: 1990. **Pace of Play rating:** 4:15-4:30. **Green fee:** $28/38.
Credit cards: MC, V, DISC. **Reduced fees:** Weekdays, Low season,

Twilight.
Caddies: No. **Golf carts:** N/A.
Discount golf packages: Yes. **Season:** March-Dec. **High:** June-Aug.
On-site lodging: No. **Rental clubs:** Yes.
Walking policy: Walking at certain times. **Range:** No.
To obtain tee times: Call five days in advance for non-residents with credit card.
Subscriber comments: Front nine outstanding, back nine very short . . . Better to be straight . . . If you bring your slice, better bring your snorkel . . . Lots of water on front nine . . . Only drawback, mandatory carts before 2 p.m. on weekends . . . Accuracy is a must, plenty of water, love it! . . . Fun golf, some challenging holes . . . No driving range . . . Bring lots of balls . . . Play with someone who knows the course . . . Underrated, not many people know about it . . . Sand and water everywhere . . . Worth a visit . . . Very tight fairways/landing areas . . . Creek makes some holes tricky on front nine . . . Don't hook the ball, O.B. left everywhere . . . Target golf . . . Extremely sloped fairways.

ARROWHEAD GOLF CLUB
★½ **EAST/WEST/SOUTH**
PU—26 W. 151 Butterfield Rd., Wheaton (708)653-5800.
35 miles west of Chicago. **Holes:** 27. **Par:** 71/70/71.
Yards: 6,107/6,217/6,310. **Course rating:** 69.1/69.1/69.1.
Slope: 114/114/114.
Opened: 1924. **Pace of Play rating:** N/A. **Green fee:** $22/25.
Credit cards: MC, V. **Reduced fees:** Weekdays, Twilight, Seniors, Juniors.
Caddies: No. **Golf carts:** $10 for 18 holes.
Discount golf packages: No. **Season:** April-Dec. **High:** May-Oct.
On-site lodging: No. **Rental clubs:** Yes.
Walking policy: Unrestricted walking. **Range:** Yes.
To obtain tee times: Call up to seven days in advance for weekdays, Monday before for weekends.
Subscriber comments: Not a lot of trouble, good course for the occasional golfer . . . Very average . . . City needs to invest more $$ . . . Short, easy, good test for high handicap . . . Better wear a hard hat . . . Fairways are close . . . Many park district improvements, rebuilt holes are a plus . . . Green speed moderate.

★★★½ BALMORAL WOODS COUNTRY CLUB
PU—2500 Balmoral Woods Dr., Crete (708)672-7448.
40 miles south of Chicago. **Holes:** 18. **Par:** 72/72.
Yards: 6,683/5,282. **Course rating:** 72.6/71.8. **Slope:** 131/117.
Opened: 1976. **Pace of Play rating:** 4:00. **Green fee:** $22/37.
Credit cards: All major. **Reduced fees:** Weekdays, Low season, Twilight, Seniors.
Caddies: No. **Golf carts:** Included in Green Fee.
Discount golf packages: Yes. **Season:** March-Nov. **High:** June-Aug.
On-site lodging: No. **Rental clubs:** Yes.
Walking policy: Mandatory cart. **Range:** Yes (grass).
To obtain tee times: Call one week in advance. Credit card required to reserve weekend tee time.
Subscriber comments: Nice people, good golf, medium handicaps can play well . . . Many local tours and qualifiers held here . . . Good test, some outstanding holes . . . Tree-lined fairways, must be able to work the ball . . . Hills, trees, big greens, tough . . . Ex-private club . . . Very difficult first time . . . One of my favorites, always tough . . . Love it . . . Good variety of holes, fun to play . . . Many elevation changes, tough par 3s . . . Best course in Chicago's south suburbs . . . A long drive from Chicago but special prices Tuesday/Thursday make trip worthwhile . . . Slick greens . . . Hilly with numerous mature oak trees. Very well run . . . Nice layout . . . Roller coaster, fast greens . . . Like a private course . . . Friendly place, great challenge in south suburbs.

★★ BARTLETT HILLS GOLF COURSE
PU—800 W. Oneida, Bartlett (708)837-2741.
25 miles northwest of Chicago. **Holes:** 18. **Par:** 71/71.
Yards: 6,482/5,488. **Course rating:** 71.2/71.8. **Slope:** 124/121.
Opened: 1924. **Pace of Play rating:** 4:00-4:30. **Green fee:** $9/26.
Credit cards: MC, V. **Reduced fees:** Weekdays, Low season, Twilight,
Seniors, Juniors.
Caddies: No. **Golf carts:** $12 for 18 holes.
Discount golf packages: No. **Season:** Year-round. **High:** April-Sept.
On-site lodging: No. **Rental clubs:** Yes.
Walking policy: Unrestricted walking. **Range:** Yes (grass).
To obtain tee times: Call up to seven days in advance.
Subscriber comments: Gets a lot of play . . . Some interesting angled
greens . . . Sentimental favorite . . . Redesign of course has improved it a
lot . . . Course a challenge and fun for all golfers, except someone at
championship level . . . Interesting layout . . . Good combination of easy
and tough holes for all golfers . . . Very good neighborhood course.

★★★ BELK PARK GOLF CLUB
PU—880 Belk Park Rd., Wood River (618)251-3115.
10 miles east of St. Louis, MO. **Holes:** 18. **Par:** 72/73.
Yards: 6,761/5,726. **Course rating:** 71.5/70.8. **Slope:** 121/118.
Opened: 1970. **Pace of Play rating:** 4:30. **Green fee:** $21/25.
Credit cards: MC, V. **Reduced fees:** Low season, Twilight, Juniors.
Caddies: No. **Golf carts:** $35 for 18 holes.
Discount golf packages: No. **Season:** Year-round. **High:** May-Sept.
On-site lodging: No. **Rental clubs:** Yes.
Walking policy: Unrestricted walking. **Range:** Yes (grass).
To obtain tee times: Call one week in advance.
Subscriber comments: Large greens, used every club, 14-15-16 is Amen
Corner . . . Beautiful clubhouse, nice staff . . . Many nice new
improvements . . . Well kept, back nine is fun . . . Forgiving layout,
constant improvements make it better all the time . . . New traps and
clubhouse . . . Open front nine and tight back nine . . . Lots of water and
trees.

★★★ BIG RUN GOLF CLUB
PU—17211 W. 135th St., Lockport (815)838-1057.
35 miles southwest of Chicago. **Holes:** 18. **Par:** 72/74.
Yards: 6,980/6,090. **Course rating:** 73.9/75.4. **Slope:** 139/133.
Opened: 1930. **Pace of Play rating:** N/A. **Green fee:** $22/32.
Credit cards: MC, V. **Reduced fees:** Low season, Twilight, Juniors.
Caddies: No. **Golf carts:** $12 for 18 holes.
Discount golf packages: No. **Season:** April-Nov. **High:** June-Aug.
On-site lodging: No. **Rental clubs:** Yes.
Walking policy: Walking at certain times. **Range:** No.
To obtain tee times: Call seven days in advance at 7 a.m.
Subscriber comments: Long! Your fairway woods better be working . . .
Making many changes for good . . . Very good course, best for those with
handicap 12 or less . . . Many local tours and qualifiers held here . . . New
holes built in last couple years are great . . . Very scenic, beautiful vistas . . .
Pars on Nos. 9 and 18 is my goal in life . . . The driver gods better be good
to you there . . . Fine old course, lots of trees . . . Trees, trees everywhere
. . . Very hilly and difficult, elevated greens . . . Don't like mandatory carts
. . . Classic midwest golf . . . Long par 5s, small greens . . . Length here is
an asset . . . Old but fabulous real golf . . . Like putting on a cliff . . . Rich
tradition . . . Hilly in Illinois? . . . They vastly improved the few holes that
needed it . . . Guaranteed three-putt on 7 and 11 . . . Holes range from
wimps to brutal.

★★★ BLACKBERRY OAKS GOLF COURSE
PU—2245 Kennedy Rd., Bristol (708)553-7170.
40 miles west of Chicago. **Holes:** 18. **Par:** 72/72.
Yards: 6,258/5,230. **Course rating:** 69.8/70.1. **Slope:** 121/119.

Opened: 1993. **Pace of Play rating:** 4:30. **Green fee:** $22/27.
Credit cards: All major. **Reduced fees:** Twilight, Seniors, Juniors.
Caddies: No. **Golf carts:** $24 for 18 holes.
Discount golf packages: No. **Season:** April-Nov. **High:** June-Aug..
On-site lodging: No. **Rental clubs:** Yes.
Walking policy: Unrestricted walking. **Range:** Yes (grass).
To obtain tee times: Call up to one week in advance.
Subscriber comments: Different kind of course for suburban Chicago
. . . Fun place to play, good restaurant . . . Well-kept course with good
variety of design . . . Course will improve with age . . . Yes, yes, an
absolute must . . . Short but water keeps you on your toes . . . New
course, in a couple of years it will be outstanding, people are friendly . . .
Short, but shot positioning is vital . . . Not long, must play tips for
challenge . . . Great finishing hole . . . Country club golf at public prices
. . . Lots of water, especially off the tee.

★★★ BON VIVANT COUNTRY CLUB

PU—Career Center Rd., Bourbonnais (815)935-0403, (800)248-7775.
2 miles north of Kankakee. **Holes:** 18. **Par:** 72/75.
Yards: 7,498/5,979. **Course rating:** 76.2/74.7. **Slope:** 128/123.
Opened: 1980. **Pace of Play rating:** 3:58. **Green fee:** $14/20.
Credit cards: MC, V, AMEX. **Reduced fees:** N/A.
Caddies: No. **Golf carts:** $9 for 18 holes.
Discount golf packages: No. **Season:** April-Nov. **High:** May-Sept.
On-site lodging: No. **Rental clubs:** Yes.
Walking policy: Unrestricted walking. **Range:** Yes (grass).
To obtain tee times: Call seven days in advance.
Subscriber comments: Very long course, a good workout for woods and
wedges . . . Very long but wide open, not much trouble, just stay in the
fairway . . . Water on nine holes, wind makes course tricky . . . Worth the
drive from Chicago . . . Hard ground makes this very long course playable
. . . Always a pleasure to play even when I'm not playing well . . . Airport
runways aren't this long . . . Greens the size of Texas . . . From the tips
think "kill" . . . Can't understand why this course does not have more play.

★★★ BONNIE BROOK GOLF CLUB

PU—2800 N. Lewis Ave., Waukegan (708)360-4730.
25 miles north of Chicago. **Holes:** 18. **Par:** 72/73.
Yards: 6,701/5,559. **Course rating:** 72.4/72.2. **Slope:** 126/124.
Opened: 1927. **Pace of Play rating:** 4:15. **Green fee:** $15/27.
Credit cards: MC, V. **Reduced fees:** Twilight, Seniors.
Caddies: No. **Golf carts:** N/A.
Discount golf packages: No. **Season:** April-Nov. **High:** May-Sept.
On-site lodging: No. **Rental clubs:** Yes.
Walking policy: Unrestricted walking. **Range:** Yes (grass).
To obtain tee times: Weekend tee times only. Call three days in advance.
Subscriber comments: Much improved over years . . . Pretty, former
private country club many years ago . . . Public course well maintained
with several memorable holes . . . Friendly atmosphere throughout, very
well maintained . . . Good course, worth a 45-minute drive . . . Two cuts
of rough, great people, reasonably priced food and drinks . . . Best value in
Lake County . . . Nice contours for Illinois . . . Greens are tough, need
proper club selection . . . Deceptive but fair . . . One of the most fun and
best-conditioned public courses I play.

★½ BONNIE DUNDEE GOLF CLUB

PU—16 N. 871 Rte. 25, Carpentersville (708)426-5511.
25 miles northwest of Chicago. **Holes:** 18. **Par:** 69/75.
Yards: 6,176/6,024. **Course rating:** 68.1/72.5. **Slope:** 113/113.
Opened: 1924. **Pace of Play rating:** 4:00. **Green fee:** $13/23.
Credit cards: MC, V, DISC. **Reduced fees:** Weekdays, Twilight,
Seniors, Juniors.
Caddies: No. **Golf carts:** $12 for 18 holes.
Discount golf packages: No. **Season:** April-Nov. **High:** June-Aug.

On-site lodging: No. **Rental clubs:** Yes.
Walking policy: Unrestricted walking. **Range:** No.
To obtain tee times: Call seven days in advance.
Subscriber comments: Newer course will be good one . . . Wide open course, great for beginners . . . Condition OK . . . Best suited for 15 handicap and higher players . . . Spacious fairways . . . Fairways dry out in summer . . . Short holes, little difficulty . . . Needs work on conditioning.

★½ BUFFALO GROVE GOLF CLUB
PU—48 Raupp Blvd., Buffalo Grove (708)459-5520.
40 miles northwest of Chicago. **Holes:** 18. **Par:** 72/75.
Yards: 6,892/6,003. **Course rating:** 71.5/73.5. **Slope:** 120/122.
Opened: 1965. **Pace of Play rating:** N/A. **Green fee:** $12/24.
Credit cards: MC, V, DISC. **Reduced fees:** Low season, Twilight, Seniors, Juniors.
Caddies: No. **Golf carts:** $24 for 18 holes.
Discount golf packages: Yes. **Season:** Year-round. **High:** May-Oct.
On-site lodging: No. **Rental clubs:** Yes.
Walking policy: Unrestricted walking. **Range:** Yes (grass).
To obtain tee times: Monday through Friday first come first served, for weekends and holidays call the prior Monday.
Subscriber comments: Good muny course, forgiving fairways . . . Condition has improved . . . Flat, some trees and water . . . Good for the weekend golfer, friendly atmosphere . . . Little challenge to good golfers, great for newer players . . . Target golf, short from tips . . . Good par 3s . . . Easy for long drivers . . . Heavy play.

★★½ BUNKER LINKS MUNICIPAL GOLF COURSE
PU—3500 Lincoln Park Dr., Galesburg (309)344-1818.
42 miles northwest of Peoria. **Holes:** 18. **Par:** 71/73.
Yards: 5,934/5,354. **Course rating:** 67.4/69.4. **Slope:** 106/108.
Opened: 1922. **Pace of Play rating:** 3:30. **Green fee:** N/A.
Credit cards: None. **Reduced fees:** Twilight.
Caddies: No. **Golf carts:** $9 for 18 holes.
Discount golf packages: No. **Season:** March-Nov. **High:** April-Sept.
On-site lodging: No. **Rental clubs:** No.
Walking policy: Unrestricted walking. **Range:** Yes (grass).
To obtain tee times: Call up to one week in advance for weekends only.
Subscriber comments: Nice golf course for a public facility, well-kept course . . . Pleasant staff, very average course . . . Very little trouble . . . Swift playing muny. Usually well groomed . . . Greens are very fast . . . Wide open, nice greens . . . Courteous staff, good pace of play.

★★½ BUNN GOLF COURSE
PU—2500 S. 11th, Springfield (217)522-2633.
Holes: 18. **Par:** 72/73.
Yards: 6,104/5,355. **Course rating:** 68.7/68.4. **Slope:** 118/119.
Opened: 1901. **Pace of Play rating:** 4:40. **Green fee:** $9/13.
Credit cards: MC, V. **Reduced fees:** Seniors, Juniors.
Caddies: No. **Golf carts:** $9 for 18 holes.
Discount golf packages: No. **Season:** March-Nov. **High:** June-July.
On-site lodging: No. **Rental clubs:** Yes.
Walking policy: Unrestricted walking. **Range:** No.
To obtain tee times: In person seven days in advance with nominal fee.
Subscriber comments: Reasonably well-kept for amount of play . . . A very good course and can be tough . . . Some tough holes . . . Lots of trees . . . Knowledgeable staff . . . A short course with trees, traps and water requiring well-placed tee shots and careful approaches, ideal for average players.

★★½ THE BURR HILL CLUB
PU—5N748 Burr Rd., St. Charles (708)584-8236.
40 miles west of Chicago. **Holes:** 18. **Par:** 72/72.
Yards: 6,640/5,111. **Course rating:** 72.5/70.9. **Slope:** 128/120.

Opened: 1974. **Pace of Play rating:** N/A. **Green fee:** $18/26.
Credit cards: MC, V. **Reduced fees:** Weekdays, Low season, Twilight.
Caddies: No. **Golf carts:** $12 for 18 holes.
Discount golf packages: No. **Season:** Year-round. **High:** May-Aug.
On-site lodging: No. **Rental clubs:** Yes.
Walking policy: Unrestricted walking. **Range:** Yes (grass).
To obtain tee times: Available seven days in advance.
Subscriber comments: Course is getting better, greens are in good
condition . . . Nice layout, long, a little rough with some spotty fairways
. . . Long, a lot of in-course out of bounds . . . Keeps you on your toes . . .
Limited clubhouse accommodations . . . Some holes require accuracy, not
distance . . . Gotta love it, broke 80 here . . . Doglegs, water carries,
position golf.

CANTIGNY GOLF
★★★★ WOODSIDE/LAKESIDE/HILLSIDE
PU—27 W. 270 Mack Rd., Wheaton (708)668-3323.
40 miles west of Chicago. **Holes:** 27. **Par:** 72/72/72.
Yards: 6,709/6,625/6,760. **Course rating:** 72.4/71.1/72.2.
Slope: 130/126/125.
Opened: 1989. **Pace of Play rating:** 4:20. **Green fee:** $57.
Credit cards: All major. **Reduced fees:** Seniors, Juniors.
Caddies: No. **Golf carts:** $13 for 18 holes.
Discount golf packages: No. **Season:** April-Oct. **High:** June-Aug.
On-site lodging: No. **Rental clubs:** Yes.
Walking policy: Unrestricted walking. **Range:** Yes (grass).
To obtain tee times: Call up to seven days in advance.
Woodside and Lakeside 9s (Premier) ranked in First 25 of America's 75 Best
Public Golf Courses by Golf Digest. Selected as Best New Public Course of
1989 by Golf Digest. Woodside and Lakeside 9s (Premier) ranked 18th in
Illinois by Golf Digest.
Subscriber comments: Best staff and service around . . . Like a private
club in service and condition . . . Nice practice range . . . Nice Dick Tracy
sand trap . . . Lots of shotmaking and strategy . . . My favorite public
course in Chicago area . . . Multiple tees . . . 27 holes of heaven! . . . I like
to play different courses, but if I had to pick one to play every day, this is it
. . . Relatively short, well-conditioned, greens very fast, doglegs, some
water, mature trees, fairly heavy play, not too difficult . . . Wonderful
surroundings, highly manicured . . . Can walk anytime . . . Great practice
facilities . . . The very best anywhere, take your camera . . . Leaf rule vital
in October . . . Great hotdogs . . . Trees, trees, trees! Beauty of a course
. . . Captures your interest the whole round . . . If you only do one course
in Illinois, do Cantigny! . . . Leave your woods in your bag . . . Food very
good . . . Pinehurst in Illinois . . . Wonderful in all respects! . . . You can
walk! . . . With three rotations among the nine hole courses you even get
variety! . . . First timers beware hidden hazards off tees . . . True test for
any handicap.

★★★ CARILLON GOLF CLUB
PU—21200 S. Carillon, Plainfield (815)886-2132.
30 miles south of Chicago. **Holes:** 18. **Par:** 71/71.
Yards: 6,607/5,194. **Course rating:** 71.1/68.4. **Slope:** 121/108.
Opened: 1990. **Pace of Play rating:** 4:30. **Green fee:** $34/44.
Credit cards: MC, V, DISC. **Reduced fees:** Weekdays, Low season,
Twilight, Seniors.
Caddies: No. **Golf carts:** Included in Green Fee.
Discount golf packages: Yes. **Season:** March-Nov. **High:** June-Sept.
On-site lodging: No. **Rental clubs:** No.
Walking policy: Walking at certain times. **Range:** Yes (grass).
To obtain tee times: Call seven days in advance.
Subscriber comments: Soft fairways and greens, lots of open spaces . . .

18th hole is brutal . . . Links course in very good condition . . . Need to be accurate . . . Carts only before 4 p.m. a downer . . . Tough layout from back tee, lots of water . . . Good layout, wind plays havoc on this course . . . Huge surprise . . . Bring your best wind game . . . Some really good holes . . . Very nice course, no trees, but very enjoyable.

CHALET HILLS GOLF CLUB★
PU—945 W. Rawson Bridge Rd., Cary (708)639-0666.
40 miles northwest of Chicago. **Holes:** 18. **Par:** 73/73.
Yards: 6,877/4,934. **Course rating:** 72.8/68.1. **Slope:** 130/114.
Opened: 1956. **Pace of Play rating:** N/A. **Green fee:** $22/31.
Credit cards: MC, V. **Reduced fees:** Weekdays, Twilight, Seniors, Juniors.
Caddies: No. **Golf carts:** $11 for 18 holes.
Discount golf packages: No. **Season:** April-Oct. **High:** May-Sept.
On-site lodging: No. **Rental clubs:** Yes.
Walking policy: Walking at certain times. **Range:** Yes (grass).
To obtain tee times: Call pro shop.

★½ CHEVY CHASE GOLF CLUB
PU—1000 N. Milwaukee Ave., Wheeling (708)537-0082.
30 miles northwest of Chicago. **Holes:** 18. **Par:** 72/72.
Yards: 6,721/5,244. **Course rating:** 71.7/69.3. **Slope:** 127/115.
Opened: 1924. **Pace of Play rating:** 4:01. **Green fee:** $16/24.
Credit cards: MC, V, DISC. **Reduced fees:** Low season, Twilight, Seniors, Juniors.
Caddies: No. **Golf carts:** $12 for 18 holes.
Discount golf packages: No. **Season:** Year-round. **High:** April-Oct.
On-site lodging: No. **Rental clubs:** Yes.
Walking policy: Unrestricted walking. **Range:** No.
To obtain tee times: Call one week in advance.
Subscriber comments: Typical park district overplayed layout . . . Very small greens . . . Very, very flat . . . Not too interesting for better golfers . . . High handicapper's course . . . Old traditional course . . . Course needs work . . . It has been upgraded every year . . . Small pro shop . . . Not overly difficult, challenging and fun . . . Good for middle handicap . . . Old course needs help.

★ CHICK EVANS GOLF COURSE
PU—6145 Golf Rd., Morton Grove (708)965-5353.
Holes: 18. **Par:** 73/71.
Yards: 5,680/5,680. **Course rating:** 67.5/63.0. **Slope:** N/A.
Opened: 1940. **Pace of Play rating:** 4:30. **Green fee:** $16/19.
Credit cards: MC, V. **Reduced fees:** Weekdays, Twilight, Seniors, Juniors.
Caddies: No. **Golf carts:** $20 for 18 holes.
Discount golf packages: No. **Season:** March-Dec. **High:** June-Aug.
On-site lodging: No. **Rental clubs:** Yes.
Walking policy: Unrestricted walking. **Range:** Yes (grass).
To obtain tee times: Call seven days in advance.
Subscriber comments: Overplayed muny . . . Tee off from mats on front nine . . . Good high handicap course, confidence builder . . . Changing tees from mats to grass.. Fair condition . . . No traps, heavily used, staff helpful . . . County course, easy and in bad shape.

CINDER RIDGE GOLF LINKS★
PU—24801 Lakepoint Dr., Wilmington (815)476-4000.
55 miles south of Chicago. **Holes:** 18. **Par:** 72/72.
Yards: 6,803/5,644. **Course rating:** N/A. **Slope:** N/A.
Opened: 1995. **Pace of Play rating:** 4:30. **Green fee:** $30/35.
Credit cards: MC, V. **Reduced fees:** Weekdays, Twilight.
Caddies: No. **Golf carts:** Included in Green Fee.

Discount golf packages: No. **Season:** April-Dec. **High:** May-Sept.
On-site lodging: No. **Rental clubs:** Yes.
Walking policy: Unrestricted walking. **Range:** Yes (grass).
To obtain tee times: Call up to seven days in advance with a credit card.
Yearly times may be purchased with three weeks deposit in advance.

COG HILL GOLF CLUB
PU—12294 Archer Ave., Lemont (708)257-5872.
32 miles southwest of Chicago.
Credit cards: MC, V, DISC. **Reduced fees:** Weekdays, Low season
(except for No. 4), Twilight, Juniors. **Caddies:** Yes.
Discount golf packages: No. **Season:** Year-round. **High:** April-Oct.
On-site lodging: No. **Rental clubs:** Yes.
Walking policy: Unrestricted walking. **Range:** Yes (grass).
★★½ **COURSE No.1**
Holes: 18. **Par:** 71/72.
Yards: 6,329/5,594. **Course rating:** 69.9/71.3. **Slope:** 117/118.
Opened: 1928. **Pace of Play rating:** 3:37. **Green fee:** $8/30.
Golf carts: $26 for 18 holes.
To obtain tee times: Call six days in advance.
Subscriber comments: Cog Hill's No. 1 and 3 are fair and challenging
. . . Easy track, excellent outing course . . . Good test, well manicured,
very busy . . . People and conditions great . . . Easiest of Cog Hill courses,
but pleasant . . . Play can be slow . . . Golfers well treated . . . Neat, fair,
interesting . . . Jemsek Course. What else needs to be said?
★★★½ **COURSE No.2**
Holes: 18. **Par:** 72/72.
Yards: 6,268/5,564. **Course rating:** 69.4/72.3. **Slope:** 120/120.
Opened: 1930. **Pace of Play rating:** 3:34. **Green fee:** $19/35.
Golf carts: $26 for 18 holes.
To obtain tee times: 90 days in advance with pre-payment or six days in
advance without.
Subscriber comments: Great cousin to No.4, pretty course, but short . . .
No two holes alike . . . The course is challenging but slow play deters me
from playing . . . Use all clubs . . . Course is wooded, but not real difficult,
very professional staff . . . Nice golf course, great facilities to practice . . .
An old fashioned classic . . . It's nice, but there's no comparison with No. 4
. . . Great little course, great value . . . Strategic type of course . . . With
four courses, staff seems too busy . . . More enjoyable than No. 4 at half the
price . . . Even a cold rainy day couldn't ruin this course or the personnel
. . . Best hot dogs in all of golf . . . Good ball management course . . . Play
it from the "tips" to really test your game . . . Mini-Dubs Dread . . .
Terrific! Rewards good shot, beats the hell out of a poor shot . . . Very
scenic and must think out shots.
★★½ **COURSE No.3**
Holes: 18. **Par:** 72/71.
Yards: 6,437/5,321. **Course rating:** 70.1/69.9. **Slope:** 117/114.
Opened: 1928. **Pace of Play rating:** 3:49. **Green fee:** $8/30.
Golf carts: $26 for 18 holes.
To obtain tee times: Call six days in advance.
Subscriber comments: Course is wooded, but not real difficult . . . Great
practice facilities, great instructors . . . For the weekend golfer, very good
conditions . . . Excellent outing course . . . Nice for a change, but no No.4
or No.2 . . . Very good course for a beginner or someone not straight . . .
Cog Hill No. 3 keeps your interest . . . Sporty and well groomed . . . Nice
layout, roller-coaster, pool table greens . . . Overall condition is good.
★★★★★ **COURSE No. 4**
Holes: 18. **Par:** 72/72.
Yards: 6,930/5,874. **Course rating:** 75.6/76.7. **Slope:** 142/134.
Opened: 1964. **Pace of Play rating:** 3:57. **Green fee:** $80.
Golf carts: Included in Green Fee.
To obtain tee times: Call up to 90 days in advance with pre-pay on credit
card.
Ranked 59th in America's 100 Greatest Golf Courses by Golf Digest.

Ranked in First 25 of America's 75 Best Public Golf Courses by Golf Digest. Ranked 4th in Illinois by Golf Digest.

Subscriber comments: Ask the pros how they feel about the Western Open! . . . Bring your "A" game . . . Outstanding course, sand makes it tough . . . Pros play and we can, too . . . Amazing golf experience . . . Ultimate test, need every club in bag, best in Midwest . . . Best value in Chicagoland, kept in great condition . . . A real gem of a course. U.S. Open? Yes! . . . A must-play once a year . . . Bring your sand game . . . Typical Jemsek course, perfect . . . Tour course, long, hilly . . . I've played this course every year for 20 years and it gets better every year . . . Everyone should play at least once . . . Natural beauty, and tough as hell . . . Great traditional layout . . . Home of the Western Open, says it all . . . The ultimate test, deserves U.S. Open . . . Keep it in the fairway, you will score . . . Even better with a caddie . . . Top 100 . . . Requires great shotmaking and nerve . . . King of the Midwest . . . Still top two or three in Illinois . . . Enjoy it with a caddy (and avoid raking all those bunkers you'll be in) . . . Great old fashioned course . . . No railroad ties . . . No forced carries, not much water . . . The best 18 holes I've found in the Chicago area . . . Long and challenging, staff is very nice. First class!

COLUMBIA GOLF CLUB★
PU—125 AA Rd., Columbia (618)286-4455.
15 miles north of St. Louis, MO. **Holes:** 18. **Par:** 71/72.
Yards: 6,275/5,000. **Course rating:** 69.4/68.4. **Slope:** N/A.
Opened: 1972. **Pace of Play rating:** 4:30. **Green fee:** $12/21.
Credit cards: None. **Reduced fees:** Weekdays, Low season, Seniors.
Caddies: No. **Golf carts:** $10 for 18 holes.
Discount golf packages: No. **Season:** Year-round. **High:** April-Oct.
On-site lodging: No. **Rental clubs:** No.
Walking policy: Unrestricted walking. **Range:** No.
To obtain tee times: Call pro shop.

CRAB ORCHARD GOLF CLUB★
SP—W. Grand Ave, Carterville (618)985-2321.
100 miles southeast of St. Louis. **Holes:** 18. **Par:** 70/71.
Yards: 6,420/5,058. **Course rating:** 71.0/68.4. **Slope:** 129/108.
Opened: 1959. **Pace of Play rating:** 4:00. **Green fee:** $17.
Credit cards: MC, V, DISC. **Reduced fees:** Seniors.
Caddies: No. **Golf carts:** $9 for 18 holes.
Discount golf packages: No. **Season:** Year-round. **High:** April-Oct.
On-site lodging: No. **Rental clubs:** Yes.
Walking policy: Unrestricted walking. **Range:** Yes (grass).
To obtain tee times: Call. Must have threesome or foursome to reserve tee time.

★★½ DEER CREEK GOLF CLUB
PU—26201 South Western Ave., University Park (708)672-6667.
30 miles south of Chicago. **Holes:** 18. **Par:** 72/72.
Yards: 6,755/5,835. **Course rating:** 72.4/73.2. **Slope:** 124/120.
Opened: 1972. **Pace of Play rating:** 4:15. **Green fee:** $17/23.
Credit cards: All major. **Reduced fees:** Weekdays, Twilight, Seniors, Juniors.
Caddies: No. **Golf carts:** $10 for 18 holes.
Discount golf packages: No. **Season:** Year-round. **High:** May-Sept.
On-site lodging: No. **Rental clubs:** Yes.
Walking policy: Unrestricted walking. **Range:** Yes (grass).
To obtain tee times: Call anytime.
Subscriber comments: Trees need to grow . . . A sleeper . . . Plenty of bunkers and water . . . Good course, used in state Open qualifying tournament . . . Good to hard for average player . . . Can spray ball most of time . . . A find, everything is wonderful, heaven . . . Nice staff . . . Good course for anyone, good people.

ILLINOIS

★★ DEERFIELD PARK GOLF CLUB
PU—1201 Saunders Rd., Riverwoods (708)945-8333.
6 miles west of Highland Park. **Holes:** 18. **Par:** 72/74.
Yards: 6,756/5,635. **Course rating:** 71.8/71.9. **Slope:** 125/121.
Opened: N/A. **Pace of Play rating:** 4:15. **Green fee:** $23/28.
Credit cards: MC, V, DISC. **Reduced fees:** Weekdays, Twilight.
Caddies: No. **Golf carts:** $24 for 18 holes.
Discount golf packages: Yes. **Season:** April-Dec. **High:** June-Sept.
On-site lodging: No. **Rental clubs:** Yes.
Walking policy: Unrestricted walking. **Range:** No.
To obtain tee times: Call 48 hours in advance.
Subscriber comments: Tough, fast greens . . . Very underrated course
. . . Tough park district course, nice greens . . . Try not to hit any cars on
the tollway on back nine . . . Has length . . . Nice public play course . . .
Large greens . . . Nice layout, uses all shots . . . Good course, flat, honest
yardages.

★½ DEERPATH PARK GOLF COURSE
PU—500 W. Deerpath, Lake Forest (708)615-4290.
25 miles north of Chicago. **Holes:** 18. **Par:** 70/72.
Yards: 6,105/5,542. **Course rating:** 68.7/72.1. **Slope:** 124/122.
Opened: 1927. **Pace of Play rating:** 4:00. **Green fee:** $17/25.
Credit cards: MC, V. **Reduced fees:** Seniors, Juniors.
Caddies: No. **Golf carts:** $10 for 18 holes.
Discount golf packages: No. **Season:** April-Dec. **High:** June-Aug.
On-site lodging: No. **Rental clubs:** Yes.
Walking policy: Unrestricted walking. **Range:** Yes (grass).
To obtain tee times: First come first serve on day of play.
Subscriber comments: Course is getting tougher because of tree planting
. . . Great practice facility, very easy to walk . . . Nice, short course . . .
Have made many changes on holes . . . Friendly, shorter course, nice staff,
good condition . . . Good, traditional style, old-time feeling to original
holes . . . Good for intermediate golfer.

★★★ EAGLE CREEK RESORT GOLF COURSE
R—Eagle Creek State Park, Findlay (217)756-3456, (800)876-3245.
35 miles south of Decatur. **Holes:** 18. **Par:** 72/72.
Yards: 6,908/4,978. **Course rating:** 73.5/69.1. **Slope:** 132/115.
Opened: 1989. **Pace of Play rating:** 4:30. **Green fee:** $25/45.
Credit cards: All major. **Reduced fees:** Weekdays, Low season, Resort
guests, Twilight, Juniors.
Caddies: No. **Golf carts:** Included in Green Fee.
Discount golf packages: Yes. **Season:** Year-round. **High:** May-Oct.
On-site lodging: Yes. **Rental clubs:** Yes.
Walking policy: Mandatory cart. **Range:** Yes (grass).
To obtain tee times: Call in advance but must be guaranteed with credit
card.
Subscriber comments: Leave driver in the bag a lot . . . Tight course,
driver barely needed, accuracy a must . . . Resort, good for all players from
the right tees . . . Really tight, lots of dogleg holes, good greens . . . Resort
on large lake . . . Beautiful views, tight, up and down course, not well
known . . . Tough rough . . . Very scenic, deer roaming the course . . .
Must keep ball in fairway . . . Off the beaten track, but worth it.

EAGLE RIDGE INN AND RESORT
R—10 Clubhouse Dr., Galena (815)777-5200, (800)892-2269.
20 miles east of Dubuque, IA.
Pace of Play rating: 4:30. **Green fee:** $77/97.
Credit cards: All major. **Reduced fees:** Low season, Resort guests,
Twilight.
Caddies: No. **Golf carts:** $14 for 18 holes.
Discount golf packages: Yes. **Season:** April-Nov. **High:** May-Oct.
On-site lodging: Yes. **Rental clubs:** Yes.

Walking policy: Walking at certain times. **Range:** Yes (grass).
To obtain tee times: Call one week in advance for nonguests.

★★★★ NORTH COURSE

Holes: 18. **Par:** 72/72.
Yards: 6,836/5,578. **Course rating:** 73.4/72.3. **Slope:** 134/127. **Opened:** 1977.
Ranked 39th in America's 75 Best Resort Courses by Golf Digest.
Subscriber comments: Very challenging course, very scenic . . . Beautiful layout, No. 8 is most scenic hole . . . Terrific golf challenge . . . Magnificent scenery! . . . Always fast, difficult greens . . . Concede all fourth putts . . . Postcard views, top notch staff . . . Best holes are 7, 8, 15 . . . No adjacent fairways, beautiful . . . Wonderful course, very fair, despite hilly terrain, must keep it straight . . . Treats you like a country club member . . . Prepare for long round but you'll enjoy every minute . . . Excellent practice facility . . . Gorgeous wooded course . . . No. 7 and No. 8 are most scenic around.

★★★★ SOUTH COURSE

Holes: 18. **Par:** 72/72.
Yards: 6,762/5,609. **Course rating:** 72.9/72.4. **Slope:** 133/128. **Opened:** 1984.
Ranked 38th in America's 75 Best Resort Courses by Golf Digest. Co-selection as Best New Resort Course of 1984 by Golf Digest. Ranked 19th in Illinois by Golf Digest.
Subscriber comments: Lots of challenges . . . Loved the variety of holes . . . Well-run, resort setting . . . Good layout, not as scenic as North course . . . Beautiful views . . . A resort course, suited for lower handicap players . . . Much harder of the two . . . Hard greens, beautiful layout with wildlife . . . Every hole is new and exciting, play it again and again . . . Beautiful Mississippi Valley scenery . . . Staff very friendly, nice pro shop . . . Length not necessary, accuracy the key . . . 18th hole brutal but great . . . If you can play 10, 15, and 18 in par or better, you are a God . . . Multiple tee and green elevations, scientific design, crowned fairways . . . Enjoyable course.

★★★ EDGEBROOK COUNTRY CLUB

SP—2100 Sudyam Rd., Sandwich (815)786-3058.
35 miles west of Aurora. **Holes:** 18. **Par:** 72/73.
Yards: 6,100/5,134. **Course rating:** 69.1/69.5. **Slope:** 119/114.
Opened: 1968. **Pace of Play rating:** 4:16. **Green fee:** $20/22.
Credit cards: MC, V, DISC. **Reduced fees:** Low season.
Caddies: No. **Golf carts:** $22 for 18 holes.
Discount golf packages: No. **Season:** Year-round. **High:** June-Aug.
On-site lodging: No. **Rental clubs:** Yes.
Walking policy: Unrestricted walking. **Range:** Yes (grass).
To obtain tee times: Call at least five days in advance.
Subscriber comments: Two different nines . . . Challenging, shotmaker's course . . . Interesting front nine; boring back . . . A well-maintained short tight course, fun to play . . . Challenging course, nice bartenderess . . . Front nine tight and wooded, back nine open . . . Challenging holes, familiarity with course required to score well . . . Nice old front nine, back nine needs more trees.

★½ ELLIOTT GOLF COURSE

PU—888 South Lyford Rd., Cherry Valley (815)332-5130.
2 miles east of Rockford. **Holes:** 18. **Par:** 72/76.
Yards: 6,393/6,253. **Course rating:** 69.4/74.1. **Slope:** 107/107.
Opened: 1968. **Pace of Play rating:** 4:30. **Green fee:** $12/21.
Credit cards: MC, V. **Reduced fees:** Twilight.
Caddies: No. **Golf carts:** $20 for 18 holes.
Discount golf packages: No. **Season:** April-Oct. **High:** May-Aug.
On-site lodging: No. **Rental clubs:** Yes.
Walking policy: Unrestricted walking. **Range:** Yes.
To obtain tee times: Call or come in seven days in advance.

Subscriber comments: Newer city course, OK layout . . . Good course
. . . Wide open, will be tough when it grows up . . . Helpful pro, good
driving range . . . Wide open course, has some good par 4s . . . When some
water problems are corrected, course will improve . . . Very long open
course, large greens.

FARIES PARK GOLF COURSE*

PU—1 Faries Park, Decatur (217)422-2211.
Call club for further information.

★★★ FOX BEND GOLF COURSE

PU—Route 34, Oswego (708)554-3939.
6 miles south of Aurora. **Holes:** 18. **Par:** 72/74.
Yards: 6,800/5,600. **Course rating:** 71.4/72.5. **Slope:** 118/120.
Opened: 1967. **Pace of Play rating:** N/A. **Green fee:** $26/29.
Credit cards: MC, V. **Reduced fees:** Weekdays, Low season, Twilight,
Seniors, Juniors.
Caddies: No. **Golf carts:** $17 for 18 holes.
Discount golf packages: No. **Season:** March-Dec. **High:** May-Sept.
On-site lodging: No. **Rental clubs:** Yes.
Walking policy: Unrestricted walking. **Range:** Yes (grass).
To obtain tee times: Call one week in advance.
Subscriber comments: Comfortable layout . . . Good for mid to high-
handicappers . . . Worth the drive . . . Pretty wide open . . . Nice little
course, good for everyday player . . . Fun course . . . Nice country course,
friendly, good greens . . . An enjoyable course to play, always in good
condition . . . Variety of different holes . . . Mostly wide open . . . Adding
watering system . . . Sporty, but not championship quality, good condition
. . . Tough, undulated greens . . . Greens are very quick, undulating and
large.

★★★ FOX CREEK GOLF CLUB

PU—6555 Fox Creek Dr., Edwardsville (618)692-9400, (800)692-9401.
20 miles northeast of St. Louis, MO. **Holes:** 18. **Par:** 72/72.
Yards: 7,027/5,185. **Course rating:** 74.9/72.1. **Slope:** 144/132.
Opened: 1992. **Pace of Play rating:** N/A. **Green fee:** $25/35.
Credit cards: MC, V. **Reduced fees:** Weekdays, Low season, Twilight,
Seniors.
Caddies: No. **Golf carts:** Included in Green Fee.
Discount golf packages: Yes. **Season:** Year-round. **High:** May-Sept.
On-site lodging: No. **Rental clubs:** Yes.
Walking policy: Mandatory cart. **Range:** Yes (grass).
To obtain tee times: Call four days in advance.
Subscriber comments: Unfair for first-timer . . . Blind shots . . . Nice
new golf course . . . For good players . . . Lot of trouble, good condition
for new course and getting better . . . Tough par 3s . . . Nice and long
course, little tough for the average player . . . Newer course, filling in
nicely, very tight, water, a terror from backs . . . One of toughest driving
courses I've seen . . . Very narrow fairways, tons of trouble . . . Seniors
need to play from second of four sets of tees . . . Sneaky hazards and wood-
lined fairways, the course keeps you coming back to prove you are not as
bad as your last score . . . Boo, hiss for carts and paths . . . Tight, need
good long irons.

★★ FOX RUN GOLF LINKS

PU—333 Plum Grove Rd., Elk Grove Village (708)980-4653.
20 miles northwest of Chicago. **Holes:** 18. **Par:** 70/70.
Yards: 6,287/5,288. **Course rating:** 70.5/70.2. **Slope:** 119/116.
Opened: 1984. **Pace of Play rating:** 4:10. **Green fee:** $27.
Credit cards: MC, V, AMEX. **Reduced fees:** Weekdays, Twilight.
Caddies: No. **Golf carts:** $24 for 18 holes.
Discount golf packages: No. **Season:** April-Nov. **High:** June-Aug.
On-site lodging: No. **Rental clubs:** Yes.
Walking policy: Unrestricted walking. **Range:** Yes (grass).

To obtain tee times: Call up to seven days in advance.
Subscriber comments: Improvements made to course are excellent . . .
Big rolling greens, tight water back nine . . . Lots of water, especially on
back nine . . . Plays tough into west wind . . . Water on 11 holes . . . Front
average, back nine well above average . . . Bring extra golf balls . . .
Treacherous back nine, tough as nails.

★★★½ GEORGE W. DUNNE NATIONAL GOLF COURSE

PU—16300 South Central, Oak Forest (708)535-3377.
25 miles southwest of Chicago. **Holes:** 18. **Par:** 72/72.
Yards: 7,170/5,535. **Course rating:** 75.1/71.4. **Slope:** 135/121.
Opened: 1982. **Pace of Play rating:** N/A. **Green fee:** $30/40.
Credit cards: MC, V. **Reduced fees:** Weekdays, Twilight, Seniors,
Juniors.
Caddies: No. **Golf carts:** $0 for 18 holes.
Discount golf packages: No. **Season:** March-Dec. **High:** May-Aug.
On-site lodging: No. **Rental clubs:** Yes.
Walking policy: Unrestricted walking. **Range:** Yes.
To obtain tee times: Call (708)429-6886 seven days in advance, 24 hours a
day.
Ranked in First 25 of America's Best Public Courses by Golf Digest.
Subscriber comments: Quick trip from the Loop . . . Excellent layout,
overplayed, therefore extreme wear and tear . . . Great layout . . . Sand
traps and greens need work . . . Great layout, not as well taken care of as in
past . . . Great course, politicians' playground . . . No. 11 is particularly
tough . . . Lots of sand traps and they need attention . . . Great design, I
love the course, needs more care . . . Good range . . . Poor man's Kemper
Lakes . . . Several deer sightings on course . . . Very good forest preserve
course . . . Poor conditioning devalues a fine course.

★★★ GIBSON WOODS GOLF CLUB

PU—Monmouth Park, Monmouth (309)734-9968.
Holes: 18. **Par:** 71/75.
Yards: 6,362/5,885. **Course rating:** 70.9/73.9. **Slope:** 119/119.
Opened: 1966. **Pace of Play rating:** 4:30. **Green fee:** $11/12.
Credit cards: None. **Reduced fees:** Weekdays, Low season, Twilight.
Caddies: No. **Golf carts:** $18 for 18 holes.
Discount golf packages: No. **Season:** March-Nov. **High:** June-Aug.
On-site lodging: No. **Rental clubs:** Yes.
Walking policy: Unrestricted walking. **Range:** Yes (grass).
To obtain tee times: First come, first serve.
Subscriber comments: Tight course, billions of trees, quick greens, some
killer holes . . . This course rewards a straight/accurate hitter. Little sand,
but lots of trees . . . Very cordial staff, totally accomodating . . . Short
course, but very tight, requires accuracy . . . Nice and challenging
municipal course . . . Must hit straight . . . Always well-groomed with
small greens . . . A real sleeper in the Midwest . . . If you can score here,
you can score anywhere. Use all your clubs, but only if you are straight . . .
State high school champs always from here.

★½ GLENDALE LAKES GOLF COURSE

PU—1550 President St., Glendale Heights (708)260-0018.
30 miles east of Chicago. **Holes:** 18. **Par:** 71/71.
Yards: 6,143/5,390. **Course rating:** 62.1/71.1. **Slope:** 121/124.
Opened: 1987. **Pace of Play rating:** 3:44. **Green fee:** $15/21.
Credit cards: All major. **Reduced fees:** Weekdays, Low season, Twilight,
Seniors, Juniors.
Caddies: No. **Golf carts:** $33 for 18 holes.
Discount golf packages: Yes. **Season:** March-Nov. **High:** June-Aug.
On-site lodging: No. **Rental clubs:** Yes.
Walking policy: Walking at certain times. **Range:** No.
To obtain tee times: Call seven days in advance.
Subscriber comments: Nice short fairways, fast greens and a lot of water
. . . Winds through the condos . . . Should be called Glendale Ocean . . .

Short but some difficult holes, good condition, except geese! . . . Target golf, good course to learn how to manage game . . . Not for duffers . . . Condos line many holes . . . Listen to arguments happening in nearby homes and condos . . . A fun course to play . . . Shorter than marked . . . Not a bad little course.

GLENEAGLES GOLF CLUB

PU—13070 McNulty Rd., Lemont (708)257-5466.
25 miles southwest of Chicago.
Opened: 1924. **Pace of Play rating:** 4:40. **Green fee:** $22/28.
Credit cards: None. **Reduced fees:** Low season, Twilight, Seniors.
Caddies: No. **Golf carts:** N/A.
Discount golf packages: No. **Season:** March-Dec. **High:** June-Aug.
On-site lodging: No. **Rental clubs:** Yes.
Walking policy: Unrestricted walking. **Range:** Yes (grass).
To obtain tee times: Call.

★★ RED COURSE

Holes: 18. **Par:** 70/74.
Yards: 6,090/6,090. **Course rating:** 67.6/71.3. **Slope:** 112/111.
Subscriber comments: Flat open layout . . . Very basic . . . Average course, par 3s best holes . . . Easy to get on . . . Short course with nice fairways and nice people . . . Just golf, short but well groomed . . . Somewhat easy . . . Good for seniors, everything is driver/wedge . . . Small greens . . . The greens need traps . . . Good food.

★★½ WHITE COURSE

Holes: 18. **Par:** 70/75.
Yards: 6,080/6,080. **Course rating:** 68.7/72.3. **Slope:** 116/114.
Subscriber comments: Chicago Open played here in late 50s, but it's better now . . . Similar to Red Course, wide open, small greens . . . Course is very consistent . . . Flat, wooded . . . New additions are exciting . . . OK . . . Pleasant shorter layout . . . Needs better practice facilities . . . Good for the everyday hacker.

★★★ GLENWOODIE COUNTRY CLUB

PU—193rd and State, Glenwood (708)758-1212.
25 miles south of Chicago. **Holes:** 18. **Par:** 72/72.
Yards: 6,715/5,176. **Course rating:** 71.8/68.4. **Slope:** 120/108.
Opened: 1923. **Pace of Play rating:** 3:40. **Green fee:** $8/25.
Credit cards: MC, V, DISC. **Reduced fees:** Weekdays, Low season, Twilight, Seniors, Juniors.
Caddies: No. **Golf carts:** N/A.
Discount golf packages: No. **Season:** Year-round. **High:** April-Sept.
On-site lodging: No. **Rental clubs:** Yes.
Walking policy: Unrestricted walking. **Range:** Yes (grass).
To obtain tee times: Call.
Subscriber comments: The two nines are like night and day . . . Good course for all, two or three very hard holes . . . Huge greens . . . 16th is very tough par 4 . . . Easy front, very, very difficult back . . . Expect a triple at No.16 . . . Plays longer than you think . . . Bar and grill well-priced and good staff is very helpful and friendly . . . Good range . . . No. 16 still breaks backs of many golfers . . . Straight driver a must . . . Good course for average golfer . . . Two or three interesting holes . . . Old course with some very nice holes . . . If you like trees, play this one . . . Tough short course, many beautiful scenic approach shots.

★★½ THE GOLF CLUB AT OAK BROOK HILLS

R—3500 Midwest Rd., Oak Brook (708)850-5530, (800)445-3315.
20 miles west of Chicago. **Holes:** 18. **Par:** 70/69.
Yards: 6,372/5,152. **Course rating:** 70.4/69.2. **Slope:** 122/114.
Opened: 1987. **Pace of Play rating:** N/A. **Green fee:** $57/62.
Credit cards: All major. **Reduced fees:** Weekdays, Low season, Twilight, Seniors.
Caddies: No. **Golf carts:** N/A.
Discount golf packages: Yes. **Season:** March-Nov. **High:** April-Sept.

On-site lodging: Yes. **Rental clubs:** Yes.
Walking policy: Walking at certain times. **Range:** No.
To obtain tee times: Call one week in advance. Hotel guests call three weeks in advance.
Subscriber comments: Some tough par 3s . . . Considering a hotel course, not too bad . . . It will be quite nice once it's in full playing condition . . . Treat you well. Some narrow fairways . . . Gets a lot of play, sporty . . . Short resort course but greens are improving . . . Target course . . . Challenging holes . . . A quality test . . . Plenty of sand and water . . . Good resort course, no range, great pro shop, course tight . . . Strong, challenging par 3s.

★★★ GOLF CLUB OF ILLINOIS

PU—1575 Edgewood Rd., Algonquin (708)658-4400.
35 miles northwest of Chicago. **Holes:** 18. **Par:** 71/71.
Yards: 7,011/4,896. **Course rating:** 74.6/68.6. **Slope:** 133/115.
Opened: 1987. **Pace of Play rating:** N/A. **Green fee:** $33/43.
Credit cards: All major. **Reduced fees:** Weekdays, Low season, Twilight, Seniors, Juniors.
Caddies: No. **Golf carts:** $12 for 18 holes.
Discount golf packages: Yes. **Season:** March-Nov. **High:** May-Sept.
On-site lodging: No. **Rental clubs:** Yes.
Walking policy: Walking at certain times. **Range:** Yes (grass).
To obtain tee times: Call seven days in advance with credit card.
Subscriber comments: Not a tree on it . . . Maybe you should list this course under Iowa since that's what the drive feels like from the Loop . . . Lightning fast greens . . . I like to play it for a change of pace . . . Target golf . . . Good if you like links-type course, good greens . . . Good test for the long hitter . . . No trees . . . Find a windless day and go play . . . Great conditioned greens . . . Gets bad rap from players who can't think or hit straight . . . Why don't people like this track? . . . Don't play this course on a windy day . . . Club selection is No.1 here, tight landing areas . . . Pro shop always wants you back . . . No.15 can break mortal men's egos . . . Windy and long . . . Not for the high handicapper . . . Mounds can be tricky . . . Terribly underrated, good risk/reward, No.11 is gorgeous . . . If you like links style, here you go . . . Playable since cutting back of severe rough . . . Don't go off fairway.

★½ GOLFMOHR GOLF CLUB

PU—16724 Hubbard Rd., East Moline (309)496-2434.
Call club for further information.
Subscriber comments: Fair track, well-designed . . . Last three years have had two to three bad greens, but they have replaced them . . . Good course for average golfer . . . Very sporty, all skill levels can enjoy . . . Nice bar and grill . . . Fairly flat courses, open . . . Sporty little course, pretty flat, relatively easy and fun . . . Nice challenge off tee and approach.

★½ GRAND MARAIS GOLF COURSE

PU—4500 Pocket Rd., Centreville (618)398-9999.
7 miles east of St. Louis, MO. **Holes:** 18. **Par:** 72/72.
Yards: 6,600/5,324. **Course rating:** N/A. **Slope:** N/A.
Opened: 1936. **Pace of Play rating:** N/A. **Green fee:** $14/16.
Credit cards: MC, V. **Reduced fees:** Weekdays, Low season, Seniors, Juniors.
Caddies: Yes. **Golf carts:** $22 for 18 holes.
Discount golf packages: No. **Season:** Year-round. **High:** May-Oct.
On-site lodging: No. **Rental clubs:** Yes.
Walking policy: Unrestricted walking. **Range:** Yes (grass).
To obtain tee times: Call one week in advance.
Subscriber comments: Bright future . . . Better now . . . On the way back to a fine course . . . Older course undergoing facelift, promises to be better in '95 . . . New clubhouse just opened, many changes in the course . . . Good track.

★★½ GREENVIEW COUNTRY CLUB

PU—2801 Putter Lane, Centralia (618)532-7395.
Call club for further information.
Subscriber comments: Home of Tom Wargo . . . Greens small . . . Front
nine easy, back will kill you . . . Usually greeted by the lovely Irene Wargo
. . . Lots of woods on back, open on front . . . Could be very good . . .
Condition comes and goes, just like Tom Wargo.

★★★★ HAWTHORNE RIDGE GOLF CLUB

PU—R.R. 2, Hhwy. 94 S., Aledo (309)582-5641.
Call club for further information.
Subscriber comments: Two entirely different nines, lots of fun holes . . .
Wish it was in my backyard . . . If you can find it, you've found a deal . . .
One of the best courses in our area, not nearly enough credit . . . Improve
greenkeeping and you have outstanding course . . . Good layout with three
to four great holes . . . Not many easy pars . . . Scenic and fun to play . . .
Challenging variety of holes, tricky slopes, elevated greens fun . . . Best
local public course by far . . . Lots of water and sand traps . . . Looks easier
than it is . . . The slope in most of the fairways makes the tee shot the most
crucial . . . I feel very lucky to walk away from any of these holes with a par
. . . Very fun shotmaker's course . . . Friendly staff . . . Great layout in the
middle of nowhere.

★★★★ HERITAGE BLUFFS GOLF CLUB

PU—24355 W. Bluff Rd., Channahon (815)467-7888.
45 miles south of Chicago. **Holes:** 18. **Par:** 72/72.
Yards: 7,106/4,967. **Course rating:** 73.9/68.4. **Slope:** 132/112.
Opened: 1993. **Pace of Play rating:** N/A. **Green fee:** $25/35.
Credit cards: MC, V. **Reduced fees:** Weekdays, Twilight, Seniors,
Juniors.
Caddies: No. **Golf carts:** $11 for 18 holes.
Discount golf packages: No. **Season:** April-Oct. **High:** May-Sept.
On-site lodging: No. **Rental clubs:** Yes.
Walking policy: Unrestricted walking. **Range:** Yes (grass).
To obtain tee times: Call five days in advance with credit card
Subscriber comments: Super course, not discovered yet . . . What a
layout . . . Best new course in the area. Very good layout, tees for every
level of play . . . Tough, good mixture of different holes, fair . . . Great
variety of holes . . . Uphill par-4 No.18 requires two great shots . . . Very
tough, a lot like Cog Hill No.4 . . . Good new course with a test for every
player . . . Play from the correct set of tees . . . Best course in Will County
. . . I think this is going to be in the top Will County golf course quickly
. . . Sleeper of a course for being new, staff was great . . . Great layout
variety, doesn't beat you up . . . For a small town municipal it is out of this
world . . . Layout uses bluffs, wetlands, prairie, woods effectively . . . A
masterpiece, plain and simple . . . Four sets of tees . . . Calls for
shotmaking throughout . . . Please don't let this secret out . . . Wow! Can't
wait till next year . . . Beautiful piece of land, natural course, tough to score
. . . People at clubhouse very helpful . . . Can be a wind tunnel . . . Lots of
hills and ravines . . . Dick Nugent's best design.

★★★ HICKORY POINT GOLF CLUB

PU—RR 11, Weaver Rd., Decatur (217)421-7444.
Holes: 18. **Par:** 72/73.
Yards: 6,855/5,896. **Course rating:** 71.4/N/A. **Slope:** 121/N/A.
Opened: 1970. **Pace of Play rating:** 4:00. **Green fee:** $12/15.
Credit cards: MC, V. **Reduced fees:** Twilight, Seniors, Juniors.
Caddies: No. **Golf carts:** $0 for 18 holes.
Discount golf packages: No. **Season:** March-Nov. **High:** June-Aug.
On-site lodging: No. **Rental clubs:** Yes.
Walking policy: Unrestricted walking. **Range:** Yes (grass).
To obtain tee times: Weekdays, call up to seven days in advance.
Weekend and holidays call the Monday prior to starting at 6:30 a.m.

Subscriber comments: Longish, but rewards good shots . . . In the best shape ever . . . Good practice facilities . . . Good back nine . . . Good test of all around golf . . . Need a long drive . . . Greens big, hard . . . Course is always in excellent shape . . . Will become tougher as trees mature.

HICKORY RIDGE GOLF CENTER★
PU—2727 West Glenn Rd., Carbondale (618)529-4386.
100 miles southeast of St. Louis. **Holes:** 18. **Par:** 72/72.
Yards: 6,863/5,506. **Course rating:** 73.3/71.6. **Slope:** 137/134.
Opened: 1993. **Pace of Play rating:** 4:12. **Green fee:** $15/18.
Credit cards: MC, V. **Reduced fees:** Twilight, Seniors, Juniors.
Caddies: No. **Golf carts:** $9 for 18 holes.
Discount golf packages: Yes. **Season:** Year-round. **High:** April-Sept.
On-site lodging: No. **Rental clubs:** Yes.
Walking policy: Unrestricted walking. **Range:** Yes (grass).
To obtain tee times: Call one week in advance.

★★HIGHLAND PARK COUNTRY CLUB
PU—1201 Park Avenue West, Highland Park (708)433-9015.
20 miles north of Chicago. **Holes:** 18. **Par:** 70/70.
Yards: 6,522/5,353. **Course rating:** 72.1/71.8. **Slope:** 130/122.
Opened: 1966. **Pace of Play rating:** N/A. **Green fee:** $40/51.
Credit cards: MC, V. **Reduced fees:** Weekdays, Low season, Twilight.
Caddies: No. **Golf carts:** $14 for 18 holes.
Discount golf packages: No. **Season:** April-Nov. **High:** May-Sept.
On-site lodging: No. **Rental clubs:** Yes.
Walking policy: Walking at certain times. **Range:** Yes (grass).
To obtain tee times: Call seven days in advance.
Subscriber comments: Excessively narrow driving areas . . . Converted private club, mature, straight ball scores well . . . Staff makes you feel like a member . . . Lots of doglegs . . . Will be better when rebuilding is finished . . . Trees planted 20 to 25 years ago becoming factor . . . Short par 4s on back nine . . . Course plays short, par 70 . . . Tree-lined and tight . . . Fair course to all players . . . Many challenging par 4s.

HIGHLAND PARK GOLF COURSE★
PU—1613 S. Main, Bloomington (309)823-4200.
Holes: 18. **Par:** 70/70.
Yards: 5,725/5,530. **Course rating:** N/A. **Slope:** 115/111.
Opened: N/A. **Pace of Play rating:** N/A. **Green fee:** N/A.
Credit cards: , V. **Reduced fees:** Twilight.
Caddies: No. **Golf carts:** N/A.
Discount golf packages: No. **Season:** Year-round.
On-site lodging: No. **Rental clubs:** No.
Walking policy: N/A. **Range:** No.

★★½HIGHLAND SPRINGS GOLF COURSE
PU—9500 35th. St. West, Rock Island (309)787-5814.
5 miles south of Davenport. **Holes:** 18. **Par:** 72/72.
Yards: 6,884/5,875. **Course rating:** 73.0/69.0. **Slope:** 118/N/A.
Opened: 1968. **Pace of Play rating:** N/A. **Green fee:** $10/12.
Credit cards: None. **Reduced fees:** Weekdays, Twilight, Seniors, Juniors.
Caddies: No. **Golf carts:** N/A.
Discount golf packages: No. **Season:** April-Oct. **High:** June-Aug.
On-site lodging: No. **Rental clubs:** Yes.
Walking policy: Unrestricted walking. **Range:** Yes (grass).
To obtain tee times: Call 24 hours in advance for weekends and holidays only.
Subscriber comments: Long course with rolling terrain . . . Nice layout can play reasonably long, surrounded by farms . . . About average for public course in the area . . . Fair design. Large greens. Maintenance OK . . . Good tough layout. Conditions vary.

★★½ HIGHLAND WOODS GOLF COURSE

PU—2775 N. Ela Rd., Hoffman Estates (708)202-0340.
20 miles west of Chicago. **Holes:** 18. **Par:** 72/72.
Yards: 6,995/5,895. **Course rating:** 72.5/72.0. **Slope:** 129/125.
Opened: 1975. **Pace of Play rating:** 4:00. **Green fee:** $21/25.
Credit cards: MC, V. **Reduced fees:** Weekdays, Twilight.
Caddies: No. **Golf carts:** $20 for 18 holes.
Discount golf packages: No. **Season:** March–Dec. **High:** May–Sept.
On-site lodging: No. **Rental clubs:** No.
Walking policy: Unrestricted walking. **Range:** No.
To obtain tee times: Automated call in system.
Subscriber comments: For county course, good condition . . . Easy to
walk, good layout . . . Wide open but not too easy to score, good forest
preserve course . . . Maintenance not consistent . . . Always a crowd . . .
This could be a good course if money was put into it.

★★½ HILLDALE GOLF CLUB

PU—1625 Ardwick Dr., Hoffman Estates (708)310-1100.
40 miles northwest of Chicago. **Holes:** 18. **Par:** 71/72.
Yards: 6,432/5,409. **Course rating:** 71.3/72.1. **Slope:** 125/121.
Opened: 1971. **Pace of Play rating:** N/A. **Green fee:** $25/33.
Credit cards: All major. **Reduced fees:** Weekdays, Low season, Twilight,
Seniors.
Caddies: No. **Golf carts:** $12 for 18 holes.
Discount golf packages: Yes. **Season:** April–Nov. **High:** June–Aug.
On-site lodging: No. **Rental clubs:** Yes.
Walking policy: Walking at certain times. **Range:** Yes (grass).
To obtain tee times: Call up to seven days in advance.
Subscriber comments: Mandatory carts until 3:00 on weekends a minus
. . . Sets up for left to right player . . . OK, convenient to downtown . . .
Suited for average golfer . . . Tight course, "No driver needed" . . .
Getting better . . . Excellent par 5s . . . Robert Trent Jones design . . .
Good for all levels of players . . . Only course in area where you can eat
sushi after 18th hole . . . Holes 10 to 13 can make or break a round . . .
Good challenge and fun for average Joe . . . Back nine much nicer than
front.

★½ HUGHES CREEK GOLF CLUB

PU—1749 Spring Valley Dr., Elburn (708)365-9200.
30 miles west of Chicago. **Holes:** 18. **Par:** 72/72.
Yards: 6,506/5,561. **Course rating:** 70.9/71.7. **Slope:** 117/115.
Opened: 1993. **Pace of Play rating:** 4:00. **Green fee:** $14/22.
Credit cards: MC, V. **Reduced fees:** Weekdays, Low season, Twilight,
Seniors, Juniors.
Caddies: No. **Golf carts:** $12 for 18 holes.
Discount golf packages: No. **Season:** April–Nov. **High:** June–Aug.
On-site lodging: No. **Rental clubs:** Yes.
Walking policy: Unrestricted walking. **Range:** Yes.
To obtain tee times: Call one week in advance.
Subscriber comments: New course needs time . . . Back nine better than
front . . . Needs maturity . . . New course, grounds need work . . . Some
nice holes . . . Very playable for all levels . . . Course has developed nicely
. . . Needs some good maintenance, but a tough layout.

★★½ ILLINOIS STATE UNIVERSITY GOLF COURSE

PU—West Gregory St., Normal (309)438-8065.
100 miles south of Chicago. **Holes:** 18. **Par:** 71/73.
Yards: 6,533/5,581. **Course rating:** 71.1/71.8. **Slope:** 120/119.
Opened: 1964. **Pace of Play rating:** 3:45. **Green fee:** $11.
Credit cards: MC, V. **Reduced fees:** Twilight, Seniors, Juniors.
Caddies: No. **Golf carts:** $8 for 18 holes.
Discount golf packages: No. **Season:** March–Dec. **High:** May–Aug.
On-site lodging: No. **Rental clubs:** Yes.
Walking policy: Unrestricted walking. **Range:** No.

To obtain tee times: Reservation in person date of play Monday through Friday.

Subscriber comments: Staff is helpful in finding golfers to play with . . . Premium on tee shot . . . Great turkey sandwiches . . . Challenging yet playable . . . Lots of trees, lots of sand, small greens, not too hard for short hitters . . . Can be tight with high rough . . . Pin oaks, maple and scrub pines make this a tough course if you're out of the fairways . . . Difficult from championship tees . . . Over 75 traps . . . Good for university course . . . This is a very nice golf course that will challenge the mid-80s golfer.

INDIAN LAKES RESORT

R—250 West Schick Rd., Bloomingdale (708)529-6466, (800)334-3417.
30 miles west of Chicago.
Opened: 1963. **Pace of Play rating:** 4:00-5:00. **Green fee:** $43/48.
Credit cards: All major. **Reduced fees:** Weekdays, Low season, Twilight.
Caddies: No. **Golf carts:** Included in Green Fee.
Discount golf packages: Yes. **Season:** April-Nov. **High:** June-Sept.
On-site lodging: Yes. **Rental clubs:** Yes.
Walking policy: Walking at certain times. **Range:** No.
To obtain tee times: Call up to four weeks in advance. If more than one tee time needed, credit card must be used.

★½ IROQUOIS COURSE
Holes: 18. **Par:** 72/72.
Yards: 6,923/6,239. **Course rating:** 72.4/N/A. **Slope:** 120/N/A.
Subscriber comments: Fair to all golfers . . . Outing course . . . Maintenance could be improved . . . Average resort course, nothing spectacular . . . Does the job, keeps the game in tune . . . Iroquois sits lower than Sioux and was soggy.

★½ SIOUX COURSE
Holes: 18. **Par:** 72/72.
Yards: 6,803/6,225. **Course rating:** 72.1/N/A. **Slope:** 123/N/A.
Subscriber comments: Good golf outing course . . . Long hitters favored, more sand than Sahara . . . OK design and shape . . . A lot of sand with high-lipped traps. Good for all skill levels . . . Staff did great job getting us to safety when lightning occured during my round . . . Good practice for approach shots . . . Flat, long with many fairway bunkers and few trees, makes wind a big factor . . . Some challenging hilly holes in resort setting.

★★½ INGERSOLL MEMORIAL GOLF CLUB

PU—101 Daisyfield Rd., Rockford (815)987-8834.
70 miles west of Chicago. **Holes:** 18. **Par:** 71/74.
Yards: 5,991/5,140. **Course rating:** 68.2/73.3. **Slope:** 108/108.
Opened: 1922. **Pace of Play rating:** N/A. **Green fee:** $12/21.
Credit cards: MC, V. **Reduced fees:** Twilight.
Caddies: No. **Golf carts:** $20 for 18 holes.
Discount golf packages: No. **Season:** April-Oct. **High:** April-Oct.
On-site lodging: No. **Rental clubs:** Yes.
Walking policy: Unrestricted walking. **Range:** Yes.
Subscriber comments: Old city course, short, great trees line fairways, back nine is very challenging, great No.13 and 14 . . . Open, fast greens . . . Player must be straight . . . Trees everywhere . . . Small greens . . . Treated well . . . Can be a nightmare for those with a bad slice or hook . . . Postage stamp greens.

★½ INWOOD GOLF COURSE

PU—3000 W. Jefferson, Joliet (815)741-7265.
40 miles southwest of Chicago. **Holes:** 18. **Par:** 71/71.
Yards: 6,078/5,559. **Course rating:** 69.4/71.4. **Slope:** 117/121.
Opened: 1931. **Pace of Play rating:** 4:30. **Green fee:** $12/24.
Credit cards: MC, V, DISC. **Reduced fees:** Weekdays, Twilight, Seniors, Juniors.
Caddies: No. **Golf carts:** $18 for 18 holes.
Discount golf packages: Yes. **Season:** April-Oct. **High:** June-Aug.
On-site lodging: No. **Rental clubs:** Yes.

Walking policy: Unrestricted walking. **Range:** Yes (grass).
To obtain tee times: Call 24 hours in advance for weekday and Monday for upcoming weekend.
Subscriber comments: Friendly staff, back nine more fun to play than front nine . . . Good all-around course . . . Great confidence builder . . . Morale booster, don't need driver . . . Part of Joliet Park district.

★★ IRONWOOD GOLF COURSE
PU—1901 N. Towanda Ave., Normal (309)454-9620.
100 miles south of Chicago. **Holes:** 18. **Par:** 72/72.
Yards: 6,960/5,385. **Course rating:** 72.4/69.8. **Slope:** 126/113.
Opened: 1990. **Pace of Play rating:** 4:15. **Green fee:** $11/13.
Credit cards: MC, V. **Reduced fees:** Weekdays, Low season, Twilight, Seniors, Juniors.
Caddies: No. **Golf carts:** N/A.
Discount golf packages: Yes. **Season:** March-Nov. **High:** May-July.
On-site lodging: No. **Rental clubs:** Yes.
Walking policy: Unrestricted walking. **Range:** Yes (grass).
To obtain tee times: Call one week in advance.
Subscriber comments: New course needs time to mature . . . Too flat . . . Young course, wide open, not too difficult . . . Some interesting holes . . . Good condition, but not very interesting . . . Basic but not challenging . . . Well-managed, but holes repetitive . . . Laid out very nicely for the intermediate to advanced golfer. The staff was quite courteous and accommodating.

★★½ KELLOGG GOLF COURSE
PU—7716 N. Radnor Rd., Peoria (309)691-0293.
Holes: 18. **Par:** 72/72.
Yards: 6,735/5,675. **Course rating:** 70.9/71.5. **Slope:** 117/120.
Opened: 1974. **Pace of Play rating:** 4:00. **Green fee:** $10/13.
Credit cards: MC, V. **Reduced fees:** Weekdays, Twilight, Juniors.
Caddies: No. **Golf carts:** $10 for 18 holes.
Discount golf packages: No. **Season:** March-Nov. **High:** June-Aug.
On-site lodging: No. **Rental clubs:** Yes.
Walking policy: Unrestricted walking. **Range:** Yes (grass).
To obtain tee times: One week in advance in person. Phone reservations taken only on day of play.
Also 9-hole executive course.
Subscriber comments: Good variety of holes . . . Very wide, few trees, little water . . . Open fairways, big greens . . . Nice clubhouse, good driving range, good challenge . . . Challenging par 5s . . . Big greens can be slippery; open and windy most times . . . Long narrow fairways.

★★★★ KEMPER LAKES GOLF COURSE
PU—Old McHenry Rd., Long Grove (708)320-3450.
25 miles northwest of Chicago. **Holes:** 18. **Par:** 72/72.
Yards: 7,217/5,638. **Course rating:** 75.7/67.9. **Slope:** 140/125.
Opened: 1979. **Pace of Play rating:** 4:00-4:30. **Green fee:** $100.
Credit cards: MC, V. **Reduced fees:** N/A.
Caddies: No. **Golf carts:** Included in Green Fee.
Discount golf packages: No. **Season:** April-Nov. **High:** June-Aug.
On-site lodging: No. **Rental clubs:** Yes.
Walking policy: Unrestricted walking. **Range:** Yes (grass).
To obtain tee times: Call two weeks in advance.
Ranked in First 25 of America's 75 Best Public Golf Courses by Golf Digest. Ranked 14th in Illinois by Golf Digest.
Subscriber comments: Very challenging, great conditioning . . . Finest public course in Illinois . . . The staff is excellent and very helpful . . . Tremendous challenge, great trees, water . . . Like a private club . . . PGA Championship held here . . . Better be long off tee . . . Easy start, resort-type finish . . . Water and sand everywhere . . . Good as 95% of private

clubs in Chicago area . . . Expensive but it's a magnificent golf experience. Good bass fishing but don't get caught . . . Pricey when compared to Cog Hill and Pine Meadow . . . Very hard from the back tees. Miss a green and you'll bogey . . . Held major . . . Big price tag but worth it . . . One of the best!

★★★½ KLEIN CREEK GOLF CLUB

PU—1 N 333 Pleasant Hill Rd., Winfield (708)690-0101.
18 miles west of Chicago. **Holes:** 18. **Par:** 72/72.
Yards: 6,673/4,509. **Course rating:** 71.9/66.2. **Slope:** 127/110.
Opened: 1994. **Pace of Play rating:** N/A. **Green fee:** $54/64.
Credit cards: MC, V, AMEX. **Reduced fees:** Weekdays.
Caddies: No. **Golf carts:** Included in Green Fee.
Discount golf packages: No. **Season:** April-Nov. **High:** June-Sept.
On-site lodging: No. **Rental clubs:** Yes.
Walking policy: Mandatory cart. **Range:** No.
To obtain tee times: Call up to two weeks in advance with credit card.
Subscriber comments: New course, soon to be on everyone's "have to play" list . . . Don't like 90 degree rule . . . Does not allow walkers any time . . . Very tight and unforgiving . . . Target golf, new course with good risk, reward . . . Repeat play is worth it . . . Hidden jewel, can't believe it's public . . . No.5 and No.10 are two quality short par 4s . . . Water on 11 of 18 holes (not just little creeks) . . . 168 traps, 11 holes of water, wetlands, etc . . . . First three holes will decide your round . . . Great test of skill . . . Run like a private country club . . . They treat you like kings . . . Don't come if you can't hit straight . . . Double jeopardy on most par 4s and 5s . . . No bail out, must be straight.

LACOMA GOLF COURSE

PU—8080 Timmerman Rd., East Dubuque (815)747-3874.
1 miles east of Dubuque.
Opened: 1967. **Pace of Play rating:** 4:00-5:00. **Green fee:** $10/14.
Credit cards: MC, V, DISC. **Reduced fees:** N/A.
Caddies: No. **Golf carts:** $18 for 18 holes.
Discount golf packages: No. **Season:** March-First snow. **High:** May-Sept.
On-site lodging: No. **Rental clubs:** Yes.
Walking policy: Unrestricted walking. **Range:** Yes (grass).
To obtain tee times: Call seven days in advance.
Also has 9-hole par-3 course.

★★ BLUE COURSE

Holes: 18. **Par:** 71/71.
Yards: 6,705/5,784. **Course rating:** 71.5/70.0. **Slope:** 118/117.
Subscriber comments: Friendly staff, good service . . . Blue Course is good, rest are easy for wedge players . . . Some unusual shaped holes . . . The scent of the Mississippi River fills the air . . . Not a long course but fun to play . . . Very hilly . . . Original nine are good.

RED/GOLD COURSE★

Holes: 18. **Par:** 69/69.
Yards: 5,552/4,895. **Course rating:** 63.5/63.8. **Slope:** 105/102.

★★½ LAKE OF THE WOODS GOLF CLUB

PU—405 N. Lake of the Woods Rd., Mahomet (217)586-2183.
8 miles west of Champaign. **Holes:** 18. **Par:** 72/72.
Yards: 6,520/5,187. **Course rating:** 70.8/69.1. **Slope:** 118/112.
Opened: 1954. **Pace of Play rating:** 3:50. **Green fee:** $13/16.
Credit cards: MC, V. **Reduced fees:** Seniors, Juniors.
Caddies: No. **Golf carts:** $8 for 18 holes.
Discount golf packages: No. **Season:** March-Dec. **High:** June-Aug.
On-site lodging: No. **Rental clubs:** Yes.
Walking policy: Unrestricted walking. **Range:** Yes (grass).
To obtain tee times: Call seven days in advance.
Also has 9-hole par-3 course.
Subscriber comments: Lots of sand . . . Usually in good condition . . .

Nice course, must be straight . . . Rolling course with tree-lined fairways
. . . Nice park district course that you want to play more than once . . .
Watering system sure helped . . . Beautiful setting with mature trees galore,
hills and water . . . Well-conditioned and staff courteous . . . Short course,
easy to post a good score . . . Interesting holes.

★★★½ LAKE SHORE GOLF CLUB

SP—316 N. Shumway, Taylorsville (217)824-5521.
Call club for further information.
Subscriber comments: Fun to play all levels of ability . . . Gorgeous
layout around lake, polite staff . . . Not for neophytes . . . Lot of slope on
greens . . . Very mature and beautiful layout, suited for long and accurate
hitter . . . Course is very tight, very challenging . . . Wind from lake
always in play . . . A lovely wooded lake shore setting . . . No two holes
alike . . . Courteous staff . . . Lots of doglegs and need good short game.

LAKEWOOD GOLF CLUB★

PU—7900 Briarwood Rd., Lakewood (815)477-0055.
30 miles northwest of Chicago. **Holes:** 18. **Par:** 72/72.
Yards: 6,891/5,437. **Course rating:** 72.1/70.3. **Slope:** 123/116.
Opened: 1991. **Pace of Play rating:** 4:30. **Green fee:** $32/42.
Credit cards: All major. **Reduced fees:** Weekdays, Low season, Twilight,
Seniors, Juniors.
Caddies: No. **Golf carts:** Included in Green Fee.
Discount golf packages: No. **Season:** March-Nov. **High:** June-Aug.
On-site lodging: No. **Rental clubs:** Yes.
Walking policy: Walking at certain times. **Range:** Yes (grass).
To obtain tee times: Call one week in advance.

★★★½ THE LEDGES GOLF CLUB

PU—7111 McCurry Rd., Roscoe (815)389-0979.
10 miles south of Rockford. **Holes:** 18. **Par:** 72/72.
Yards: 6,740/5,881. **Course rating:** 72.5/74.1. **Slope:** 129/129.
Opened: 1978. **Pace of Play rating:** 4:00-4:30. **Green fee:** $14/24.
Credit cards: None. **Reduced fees:** Weekdays, Low season, Twilight,
Seniors, Juniors.
Caddies: No. **Golf carts:** $10 for 18 holes.
Discount golf packages: No. **Season:** April-Oct. **High:** May-Aug.
On-site lodging: No. **Rental clubs:** Yes.
Walking policy: Unrestricted walking. **Range:** Yes (grass).
Subscriber comments: Fantastic public course, No.2 a monster par 5 . . .
Eight water holes, tight holes on back nine . . . Interesting layout and
difficult . . . Bring your long ball, be happy with bogey on No.2 . . . Age
will make this an Illinois must . . . Much water and great variety of holes
. . . Lots of variation. Some wide open holes, others very tight . . . A good
test for the better golfer . . . Need to be a low handicapper . . . Accuracy is
a must.

★★ LEGACY GOLF CLUB

PU—3500 Cargill Rd., Granite City (618)931-4653.
12 miles southwest of St. Louis, MO. **Holes:** 18. **Par:** 71/71.
Yards: 6,300/5,600. **Course rating:** 70.4/69.4. **Slope:** 114/110.
Opened: 1990. **Pace of Play rating:** N/A. **Green fee:** $14/21.
Credit cards: MC. **Reduced fees:** Weekdays, Low season, Twilight,
Seniors, Juniors.
Caddies: No. **Golf carts:** $5 for 18 holes.
Discount golf packages: Yes. **Season:** Year-round. **High:** April-Oct.
On-site lodging: No. **Rental clubs:** Yes.
Walking policy: Unrestricted walking. **Range:** Yes (grass).
To obtain tee times: Call one week in advance.
Subscriber comments: Very tough on windy day . . . Slow due to course

rules that carts must remain on cart paths. 90 degree rule would speed up play . . . Course is very flat, with no trees . . . Flat and open, great greens . . . New course, but well designed . . . A lot of water, in an industrial area . . . Made for John Daly wannabes . . . Will be a very good course when it matures.

★½ LEO DONOVAN GOLF COURSE

PU—5805 Knoxville Ave., Peoria (309)691-8361.
Holes: 18. **Par:** 72/72.
Yards: 6,735/5,675. **Course rating:** 70.9/71.5. **Slope:** 117/120.
Opened: 1929. **Pace of Play rating:** N/A. **Green fee:** $4/12.
Credit cards: MC, V. **Reduced fees:** Weekdays, Twilight, Juniors.
Caddies: No. **Golf carts:** N/A.
Discount golf packages: No. **Season:** March-Nov. **High:** April-Aug.
On-site lodging: No. **Rental clubs:** Yes.
Walking policy: Unrestricted walking. **Range:** No.
To obtain tee times: In person, up to seven days in adavance. By telephone, day of play.
Subscriber comments: Mature course, lots of play but well cared for . . . Good old course, lots of trees . . . Nice track, takes accuracy . . . Flat, small greens, fun to play . . . Seniors and women love it, treated well always . . . Well kept considering it is not irrigated . . . Short but fun.

★★★½ LICK CREEK GOLF COURSE

PU—2210 North Parkway Dr., Pekin (309)346-0077.
12 miles north of Peoria. **Holes:** 18. **Par:** 72/72.
Yards: 6,909/5,729. **Course rating:** 72.8/72.9. **Slope:** 128/125.
Opened: 1976. **Pace of Play rating:** N/A. **Green fee:** $9/16.
Credit cards: MC, V. **Reduced fees:** Weekdays, Twilight, Seniors, Juniors.
Caddies: No. **Golf carts:** $14 for 18 holes.
Discount golf packages: No. **Season:** April-Nov. **High:** June-Sept.
On-site lodging: No. **Rental clubs:** Yes.
Walking policy: Unrestricted walking. **Range:** Yes (grass).
To obtain tee times: Call one week in advance.

Ranked in Third 25 of America's 75 Best Public Golf Courses by Golf Digest.
Subscriber comments: This one will bring you to your knees! . . . A tight course, good variety of trouble, quick greens . . . Tight course and challenging . . . Good greens . . . Leave driver at home . . . Great test, tough for high handicappers if they play the wrong tees . . . One of life's little challenges . . . If you like sidehill lies all day, this is it . . . Hardest course in area . . . Par 3s and 5s are best . . . Super fast greens, shaved with bikini wax (oops) . . . Doesn't let up . . . Treated very well . . . This is a hacker's nightmare . . . The fairways are mostly rolling hillsides and a level lie is rare . . . May be the "All-time best bang for the buck".

★★½ LINCOLN GREENS GOLF COURSE

PU—700 E. Lake Dr., Springfield (217)786-4000.
90 miles north of St. Louis. **Holes:** 18. **Par:** 72/72.
Yards: 6,582/5,625. **Course rating:** 70.3/70.9. **Slope:** 112/114.
Opened: 1957. **Pace of Play rating:** 4:30. **Green fee:** $7/22.
Credit cards: MC, V. **Reduced fees:** Weekdays, Twilight, Seniors, Juniors.
Caddies: No. **Golf carts:** $9 for 18 holes.
Discount golf packages: Yes. **Season:** March-Dec. **High:** June-Aug.
On-site lodging: No. **Rental clubs:** Yes.
Walking policy: Unrestricted walking. **Range:** Yes (grass).
To obtain tee times: Call up to seven days in advance. $2.00 charge per tee time - no refund unless it rains or cancel 24 hours prior to tee time.

Subscriber comments: Suited to all . . . Narrow fairways, nice greens, scenic water holes on lake . . . Course with a lot of character, very established . . . Doglegs and hills make good play . . . Rather straight with a couple interesting holes . . . Getting good again . . . Demanding shotmaker's course must use all your clubs and imagination on course.

★★★ THE LINKS GOLF COURSE
PU—Nichols Park, Jacksonville (217)479-4663.
30 miles west of Springfield. **Holes:** 18. **Par:** 72/72.
Yards: 6,836/5,310. **Course rating:** 71.4/72.4. **Slope:** 112/114.
Opened: 1979. **Pace of Play rating:** 4:00. **Green fee:** $10/14.
Credit cards: DISC. **Reduced fees:** Weekdays, Low season, Seniors, Juniors.
Caddies: No. **Golf carts:** N/A.
Discount golf packages: No. **Season:** March-Nov. **High:** May-Sept.
On-site lodging: No. **Rental clubs:** Yes.
Walking policy: Unrestricted walking. **Range:** Yes (grass).
To obtain tee times: Call one week in advance.
Also has 9-hole course.
Subscriber comments: OK course . . . Most players don't know how to take care of course . . . Most greens are cratered with ballmarks . . . Not very long but challenging, good staff, and good speed of play . . . Better be a good wind player . . . Links is suited for the long player; staff very courteous . . . Very open, a little rough in spots yet fun . . . Lots of sand . . . The Links is a relatively long course, with rather fast greens that are pretty well kept all through the season, and will be a very challenging course once the trees grow up and become a factor . . . Never had a problem getting on.

★★ MACKTOWN GOLF COURSE
PU—2221 Freeport Rd., Rockton (815)624-9931.
Call club for further information.
Subscriber comments: Short (5800 yards), fun to play, staff is great . . . Nos. 17 and 18 good finishing holes . . . Good for senior players . . . Middle/high handicapper shouldn't miss . . . Short, most holes wide open, a couple of tough greens.

★★★ MARENGO RIDGE GOLF CLUB
PU—9508 Harmony Hill Rd., Marengo (815)923-2332.
35 miles west of Chicago. **Holes:** 18. **Par:** 72/73.
Yards: 6,636/5,659. **Course rating:** 71.4/72.2. **Slope:** 122/120.
Opened: 1965. **Pace of Play rating:** 3:55. **Green fee:** $19/24.
Credit cards: MC, V. **Reduced fees:** Weekdays, Low season, Twilight, Seniors, Juniors.
Caddies: No. **Golf carts:** N/A.
Discount golf packages: Yes. **Season:** March-Dec. **High:** May-Sept.
On-site lodging: No. **Rental clubs:** Yes.
Walking policy: Unrestricted walking. **Range:** Yes (grass).
To obtain tee times: Call seven days in advance.
Subscriber comments: On course out of bounds, difficult shot placements . . . Back nine is tough, front nine well built . . . Enjoyable! Enjoyable! . . . New back nine is a treat, good for all golfers . . . One nine wooded, the other an open links style . . . Staff was very professional, asked us to come back . . . The best course no one has ever heard of . . . Good test . . . Many trees . . . Nice clubhouse . . . Multiple tees make it suitable for all levels . . . New clubhouse, locker rooms and practice area. Looking forward to playing it again . . . Excellent for ladies' day . . . Course you love to play.

★★ MARRIOTT'S LINCOLNSHIRE RESORT
R—Ten Marriott Dr., Lincolnshire (708)634-5935.
30 miles north of Chicago. **Holes:** 18. **Par:** 70/69.
Yards: 6,313/4,892. **Course rating:** 71.1/68.9. **Slope:** 129/117.
Opened: 1975. **Pace of Play rating:** N/A. **Green fee:** $35/53.
Credit cards: All major. **Reduced fees:** Low season, Twilight.

Caddies: No. **Golf carts:** Included in Green Fee.
Discount golf packages: Yes. **Season:** April-Oct. **High:** May-Sept.
On-site lodging: Yes. **Rental clubs:** Yes.
Walking policy: Walking at certain times. **Range:** No.
To obtain tee times: Call up to one week in advance. Resort guests may make reservations when they book their room up to ninety days in advance.
Subscriber comments: Good sporty course for a resort . . . Front nine easy, back nine challenging . . . The two nines are completely different . . . Beautiful grounds, well kept . . . Tight course . . . Short, but tough for average player . . . Good George Fazio design.

THE MEADOWS GOLF CLUB OF BLUE ISLAND★
PU—2802 W. 123rd St., Blue Island (708)385-1994.
Holes: 18. **Par:** 71/71.
Yards: 6,550/4,830. **Course rating:** N/A. **Slope:** N/A.
Opened: 1994. **Pace of Play rating:** 4:15. **Green fee:** $12/11.
Credit cards: MC, V. **Reduced fees:** Weekdays, Low season, Twilight, Seniors, Juniors.
Caddies: No. **Golf carts:** $10 for 18 holes.
Discount golf packages: No. **Season:** March-Dec. **High:** May-Sept.
On-site lodging: No. **Rental clubs:** No.
Walking policy: Unrestricted walking. **Range:** Yes (grass).
To obtain tee times: Call pro shop.
Subscriber comments: We called it a "rock & roll" golf course: hit a fairway rock and watch the ball roll . . . New . . . Opened too soon . . . Needs more work.

★★★½ MIDLANE COUNTRY CLUB
PU—14565 W. Yorkhouse Rd., Wadsworth (708)244-1990.
50 miles north of Chicago. **Holes:** 18. **Par:** 72/73.
Yards: 7,073/5,635. **Course rating:** 74.4/72.7. **Slope:** 132/124.
Opened: 1964. **Pace of Play rating:** N/A. **Green fee:** $35/56.
Credit cards: All major. **Reduced fees:** Weekdays, Low season, Twilight, Seniors.
Caddies: No. **Golf carts:** N/A.
Discount golf packages: No. **Season:** March-Nov. **High:** June-Sept.
On-site lodging: No. **Rental clubs:** Yes.
Walking policy: Walking at certain times. **Range:** Yes (grass).
To obtain tee times: Call seven days in advance.
Subscriber comments: Vastly improved, very well maintained . . . Close to private club caliber . . . 18th hole a beauty . . . Good course, nice amenities, fun day . . . Love the course, staff is wonderful . . . It's a shame I never score well there . . . Too many outings . . . Long and tough, not for the high handicapper . . . Tough in wind . . . Eight water holes, large rolling greens . . . Greens are the best and fastest in state . . . When the wind is up, this course is a bear . . . LET MY PEOPLE WALK! . . . The greens are very large and very fast . . . Reworked course from a couple years back . . . My new favorite club . . . Must hit driver in fairway . . . Very tough from back tees . . . Golf Outing Heaven.

★★★ NAPERBROOK GOLF COURSE
PU—22204 111th St., Plainfield (708)378-4215.
24 miles southwest of Chicago. **Holes:** 18. **Par:** 72/72.
Yards: 6,755/5,381. **Course rating:** 71.2/69.5. **Slope:** 120/112.
Opened: 1990. **Pace of Play rating:** 4:15. **Green fee:** $25.
Credit cards: MC, V. **Reduced fees:** Weekdays, Low season, Twilight, Seniors, Juniors.
Caddies: No. **Golf carts:** $21 for 18 holes.
Discount golf packages: No. **Season:** March-Dec. **High:** June-Aug.
On-site lodging: No. **Rental clubs:** Yes.
Walking policy: Unrestricted walking. **Range:** Yes (grass).
To obtain tee times: Call Monday morning the week of play. Holidays are booked Monday through Monday.
Subscriber comments: Nice layout. Some tough shots. Very good

condition . . . One of my favorites. Accuracy pays a big dividend . . . Will continue to get better as course matures . . . Stay out of the love grass . . . Long rough eats golf balls . . . Tough par 3s, short par 4s . . . Tough when wind is up . . . Semi-links. Excellent driving range . . . A real gem, fun for all levels of players . . . Markers plentiful so you know distance . . . Interesting little course, wind plays havoc . . . Four year-old course, links type kept in perfect condition despite heavy play. Will be perfect when all trees mature . . . Count on the wind being a major factor most of the time.

★★½ NETTLE CREEK GOLF CLUB
PU—5355 Saratoga Rd., Morris (815)941-4300.
Call club for further information.
Subscriber comments: Challenging course, No.2 hole is a real treat . . . Well-bunkered course, needs a couple more years to develop . . . Well off the beaten path . . . A well designed, fun to play layout . . . Lots of construction around the course . . . Brand new course, worth the drive.

★★★ NEWMAN GOLF COURSE
PU—2021 W. Nebraska, Peoria (309)674-1663.
Holes: 18. **Par:** 71/74.
Yards: 6,838/5,933. **Course rating:** 71.8/74.2. **Slope:** 119/120.
Opened: 1934. **Pace of Play rating:** N/A. **Green fee:** $5/13.
Credit cards: MC, V. **Reduced fees:** Weekdays, Twilight, Juniors.
Caddies: No. **Golf carts:** N/A.
Discount golf packages: No. **Season:** March-Nov. **High:** April-Aug.
On-site lodging: No. **Rental clubs:** Yes.
Walking policy: Unrestricted walking. **Range:** No.
To obtain tee times: In person up to seven days. Telephone, day of play.
Subscriber comments: Tough par 71 course, rough can be deep . . . Fair . . . Best public course in 50 miles . . . Mature, watered fairways, back nine will wear you down . . . Good test . . . Nice variety of holes, requires all clubs . . . Toughest Peoria course, if you're not playing well by the last four holes, go home . . . Hardest finishing holes around . . . Some very demanding long par 4s . . . Mature course . . . Conditions improved last three years.

★½ NORDIC HILLS RESORT
PU—Nordic Rd., Itasca (708)773-3510.
20 miles of Chicago. **Holes:** 18. **Par:** 71/71.
Yards: 5,910/5,331. **Course rating:** N/A. **Slope:** 105/113.
Opened: N/A. **Pace of Play rating:** N/A. **Green fee:** N/A.
Credit cards: All major. **Reduced fees:** Weekdays, Low season, Twilight.
Caddies: No. **Golf carts:** Included in Green Fee.
Discount golf packages: No. **Season:** April-Nov. **High:** June-Aug.
On-site lodging: Yes. **Rental clubs:** No.
Walking policy: N/A. **Range:** No.
Subscriber comments: Nice course to hold company outings . . . Fun course with tree-lined fairways . . . Relatively easy for guests . . . Old course. Very short and sporty . . . Fairways too tight, always ducking stray balls . . . Short and compact . . . Can shoot low scores, good for ego . . . Very tough for average golfer.

★★½ OAK BROOK GOLF CLUB
PU—2606 York Rd., Oak Brook (708)990-3032.
30 miles west of Chicago. **Holes:** 18. **Par:** 72/72.
Yards: 6,541/5,341. **Course rating:** 71.2/70.9. **Slope:** 121/120.
Opened: 1980. **Pace of Play rating:** 4:30. **Green fee:** $28/32.
Credit cards: MC, V. **Reduced fees:** Twilight.
Caddies: No. **Golf carts:** $12 for 18 holes.
Discount golf packages: No. **Season:** March-Dec. **High:** April-Sept.
On-site lodging: No. **Rental clubs:** Yes.
Walking policy: Unrestricted walking. **Range:** Yes.
To obtain tee times: Call seven days in advance.
Subscriber comments: Great paced course, some challenging holes . . .

Wooded course . . . A great course for afternoon golf . . . Great range . . . Nice, but a little short . . . Bring every shot in golf . . . Short but fair and tough greens . . . Good park district course with lots of water and too many geese . . . Challenging due to many hazards.

★★★ THE OAK CLUB OF GENOA

PU—11770 Ellwood Greens Rd., Genoa (815)784-5678.
50 miles west of Chicago. **Holes:** 18. **Par:** 72/72.
Yards: 7,032/5,556. **Course rating:** 74.1/72.5. **Slope:** 135/127.
Opened: 1973. **Pace of Play rating:** N/A. **Green fee:** $20.
Credit cards: All major. **Reduced fees:** Weekdays, Low season, Twilight, Seniors.
Caddies: No. **Golf carts:** Included in Green Fee.
Discount golf packages: No. **Season:** March-Dec. **High:** May-Sept.
On-site lodging: No. **Rental clubs:** Yes.
Walking policy: Walking at certain times. **Range:** Yes (grass).
To obtain tee times: Call one week in advance.
Subscriber comments: Great course from the tips for a low handicapper . . . I love this course, it's 40 miles west of Chicago and nobody plays it . . . Fastest greens I've ever putted on . . . A natural beauty . . . Scenic with some water . . . Good test . . . Beautiful, no gimmicks here . . . A great staff, good outing course . . . Great dining room . . . You use all 14 clubs . . . Multiple tee boxes, fast and true greens, need to shape your shots, growing in popularity . . . Good variety of holes.

★★½ OAK MEADOWS GOLF CLUB

PU—900 N. Wood Dale Rd., Addison (708)595-0071.
8 miles northwest of Elmhurst. **Holes:** 18. **Par:** 71/73.
Yards: 6871/5,954. **Course rating:** 72.1/73.8. **Slope:** 126/128.
Opened: 1925. **Pace of Play rating:** N/A. **Green fee:** $27/29.
Credit cards: MC, V. **Reduced fees:** Twilight.
Caddies: No. **Golf carts:** $12 for 18 holes.
Discount golf packages: No. **Season:** March-Nov. **High:** June-Sept.
On-site lodging: No. **Rental clubs:** Yes.
Walking policy: Walking at certain times. **Range:** Yes (grass).
To obtain tee times: Call seven days in advance.
Subscriber comments: Nice parkland course . . . Quality layout, converted private club . . . Needs better conditioning . . . Tight course . . . Lots of mature trees, stay out of the woods . . . Narrow fairways . . . Great 19th hole . . . Some good golf holes . . . Old Elmhurst Country Club, country club setting and course at forest preserve prices . . . Waiting to see what upcoming course changes bring . . . Lots of trees, good length, Hogan won here.

OAK RIDGE GOLF CLUB★

SP—658 E. Rt. 6, La Salle (815)223-7273.
90 miles northeast of Chicago. **Holes:** 18. **Par:** 72/72.
Yards: 6,900/5,825. **Course rating:** 72.6/73.0. **Slope:** 117/117.
Opened: 1994. **Pace of Play rating:** 4:15. **Green fee:** $28/32.
Credit cards: MC, V, DISC. **Reduced fees:** Seniors.
Caddies: No. **Golf carts:** Included in Green Fee.
Discount golf packages: No. **Season:** Year-round. **High:** June-Sept.
On-site lodging: No. **Rental clubs:** Yes.
Walking policy: Mandatory cart. **Range:** Yes (grass).
To obtain tee times: Call anytime.

★★★ ODYSSEY GOLF COURSE

PU—19110 S. Ridgeland, Tinley Park (708)429-7400.
20 miles southwest of Chicago. **Holes:** 18. **Par:** 72/72.
Yards: 7,095/5,554. **Course rating:** 72.6/68.9. **Slope:** 128/112.
Opened: 1992. **Pace of Play rating:** 4:00-4:30. **Green fee:** $15/53.
Credit cards: MC, V. **Reduced fees:** Weekdays, Low season, Twilight.
Caddies: No. **Golf carts:** Included in Green Fee.
Discount golf packages: No. **Season:** April-Nov. **High:** June-Aug.

On-site lodging: No. **Rental clubs:** No.
Walking policy: Walking at certain times. **Range:** Yes (grass).
To obtain tee times: Call up to two weeks in advance.
Subscriber comments: Challenging, but not unfair . . . Undiscovered and new, getting better all the time . . . Every green is elevated, lots of water . . . Wind makes course tough . . . One of the toughest courses around, course is on upswing . . . Watch out for the water . . . A very good staff . . . Well maintained with beautiful views . . . Nice for left-to-right player . . . Better be straight or bring lots of ammo . . . Holes 17 and 18 are beautiful . . . Good for all levels . . . An excellent course . . . Super layout, awesome clubhouse, next to World Music Theatre . . . Good golf holes . . . Difficult par 4s . . . Next to a concert facility . . . Some interesting background sounds . . . Great links-style experience with plenty of sand and water . . . Little known, one of Chicago's best.

★★½ OLD OAK COUNTRY CLUB

PU—14200 South Parker Rd., Lockport (708)301-3344.
19 miles southwest of Chicago. **Holes:** 18. **Par:** 71/72.
Yards: 6,535/5,274. **Course rating:** 70.1/N/A. **Slope:** 124/N/A.
Opened: 1926. **Pace of Play rating:** N/A. **Green fee:** $20/27.
Credit cards: All major. **Reduced fees:** Weekdays, Low season, Twilight, Seniors, Juniors.
Caddies: No. **Golf carts:** N/A.
Discount golf packages: No. **Season:** April-Dec. **High:** June-Sept.
On-site lodging: No. **Rental clubs:** Yes.
Walking policy: Unrestricted walking. **Range:** No.
To obtain tee times: Call.
Subscriber comments: Trying to improve and has some interesting strategic holes . . . Another good old-fashioned golf course . . . A bit short but well cared for . . . Old course with mucho trees. Nice challenge . . . Keep ball in fairway . . . Tough greens slanted back to front, no gimmies . . . High handicappers welcomed . . . Getting better each year. Improvements are appreciated.

★★★ OLD ORCHARD COUNTRY CLUB

PU—700 W. Rand Rd., Mt. Prospect (708)255-2025.
20 miles northwest of Chicago. **Holes:** 18. **Par:** 70/70.
Yards: 6,022/5,719. **Course rating:** N/A. **Slope:** 121/119.
Opened: N/A. **Pace of Play rating:** N/A. **Green fee:** N/A.
Credit cards: MC, V, DISC. **Reduced fees:** Weekdays, Twilight.
Caddies: No. **Golf carts:** Included in Green Fee.
Discount golf packages: No. **Season:** April-Nov. **High:** June-July.
On-site lodging: No. **Rental clubs:** No.
Walking policy: N/A. **Range:** Yes (grass).
Subscriber comments: Good unknown course . . . Great special prices . . . Relatively short but hard to score . . . Playable but tough course . . . A thinker's course, two driveable par 4s for big hitters . . . Short but tight . . . Well maintained and pretty course . . . Tight fairways . . . No.17 from blue tees as tough as they come.

★ ORCHARD HILLS COUNTRY CLUB

PU—38342 N. Green Bay Rd., Waukegan (708)336-5118.
40 miles north of Chicago. **Holes:** 18. **Par:** 71/71.
Yards: 6,366/6,043. **Course rating:** 68.8/68.8. **Slope:** 104/104.
Opened: 1930. **Pace of Play rating:** 4:00. **Green fee:** $23/25.
Credit cards: MC, V, DISC. **Reduced fees:** Weekdays, Low season, Twilight.
Caddies: No. **Golf carts:** $12 for 18 holes.
Discount golf packages: Yes. **Season:** March-Jan. **High:** May-Sept.
On-site lodging: No. **Rental clubs:** Yes.
Walking policy: Unrestricted walking. **Range:** Yes (grass).

To obtain tee times: Call up to one week in advance.

Subscriber comments: Wide open, hackers' paradise . . . Greens are very small and fairly fast . . . Suited for high handicappers, wide open and fairly long . . . Ego builder . . . Improvements being added, relatively easy course.

★★★★ ORCHARD VALLEY GOLF CLUB

PU—2411 W. Illinois Ave., Aurora (708)907-0500.
35 miles west of Chicago. **Holes:** 18. **Par:** 72/72.
Yards: 6,745/5,162. **Course rating:** 72.2/70.1. **Slope:** 132/118.
Opened: 1993. **Pace of Play rating:** N/A. **Green fee:** $33/38.
Credit cards: MC, V, AMEX. **Reduced fees:** Twilight, Seniors, Juniors.
Caddies: No. **Golf carts:** N/A.
Discount golf packages: No. **Season:** April-Oct. **High:** June-Sept.
On-site lodging: No. **Rental clubs:** Yes.
Walking policy: Unrestricted walking. **Range:** Yes (grass).
To obtain tee times: Call seven days in advance. Credit card required to secure tee time. Twenty-four hour cancellation policy.
Subscriber comments: Interesting holes, makes you think . . . Great new course, not many trees, course starts off tough . . . Nice staff, well stocked pro shop . . . Country club feel without the price . . . Some very interesting holes . . . Very tough on a windy day . . . Four superb finishing holes, good use of wetlands . . . Toughest par 3s from tips in northern Illinois . . . Fairways separated by mounds, excellent shape, four-star facilities . . . I really liked this course . . . You have to be a player to score well . . . Kavanaugh design, a true test . . . Outstanding city course, lots of sand and water . . . Very helpful staff . . . The wind just blows and blows and blows . . . Tight course with a bunch of water holes . . . Love it . . . Best secret in Chicago . . . Would love to read Gary McCord's subscriber comments on this course! . . . Course is very interesting for all ranges of golfers. Four sets of tees change the course . . . Transition from first to second holes a real wake-up . . . Not a bad hole in the bunch . . . A true test of golf and great Kavanaugh design . . . Fell in love with this new course, simply outstanding.

★★★½ THE ORCHARDS GOLF CLUB

PU—1499 Golf Course Dr., Belleville (618)233-8921, (800)452-0358.
20 miles southeast of St. Louis. **Holes:** 18. **Par:** 71/71.
Yards: 6,405/5,001. **Course rating:** 69.0/70.1. **Slope:** 121/120.
Opened: 1991. **Pace of Play rating:** N/A. **Green fee:** $16/30.
Credit cards: MC, V. **Reduced fees:** Weekdays, Low season, Twilight, Seniors, Juniors.
Caddies: No. **Golf carts:** $10 for 18 holes.
Discount golf packages: No. **Season:** Year-round. **High:** April-Oct.
On-site lodging: No. **Rental clubs:** Yes.
Walking policy: Walking at certain times. **Range:** Yes (grass).
To obtain tee times: Call up to seven days.
Subscriber comments: Front is open, back is a shotmakers' nine, need to place shots for correct approach . . . Fun to play . . . Beautiful course, nice combination of open and wooded holes . . . Enjoyable and well-conditioned . . . New, plenty of natural hazards . . . Excellent driving range. Very difficult par 3s . . . Championship course built in old apple orchard.

★★½ PALATINE HILLS GOLF COURSE

PU—512 W. Northwest Hwy., Palatine (708)359-4020.
25 miles northwest of Chicago. **Holes:** 18. **Par:** 72/72.
Yards: 6,800/5,975. **Course rating:** 71.6/73.2. **Slope:** 120/119.
Opened: 1965. **Pace of Play rating:** N/A. **Green fee:** $24/29.
Credit cards: MC, V. **Reduced fees:** Weekdays, Low season, Twilight.
Caddies: No. **Golf carts:** $12 for 18 holes.
Discount golf packages: Yes. **Season:** April-Nov. **High:** June-Aug.
On-site lodging: No. **Rental clubs:** Yes.
Walking policy: Unrestricted walking. **Range:** Yes (grass).

To obtain tee times: Call two days in advance for weekdays and one week in advance for weekend tee times.

Subscriber comments: Fast greens . . . Very playable . . . Decent condition and improving . . . Fair course, short, conditions may vary . . . Decent park district track . . . Much improved condition recently . . . Good mixture of holes, some flat, some hilly, some water . . . Well maintained and fair public course.

PALOS COUNTRY CLUB
★½ RED/WHITE/BLUE
PU—13100 Southwest Hwy., Palos Park (708)448-6550.
Call club for further information.

Subscriber comments: Nice layout but needs grooming . . . Built on low land . . . Nice course, will definitely play again . . . The Red and White nines were just rebuilt. New layout is easier than the previous layout . . . Good practice course . . . Needs fairway and tee work.

PARK HILLS GOLF CLUB
PU—3240 W. Stephenson, Freeport (815)235-3611.
100 miles west of Chicago.
Pace of Play rating: 4:00. **Green fee:** $12/15.
Credit cards: MC, V. **Reduced fees:** Weekdays, Juniors.
Caddies: No. **Golf carts:** $9 for 18 holes.
Discount golf packages: No. **Season:** April-Nov. **High:** June-Aug.
On-site lodging: No. **Rental clubs:** Yes.
Walking policy: Unrestricted walking. **Range:** Yes (grass).
To obtain tee times: Call seven days in advance.
EAST COURSE★
Holes: 18. **Par:** 72/73.
Yards: 6,477/5,401. **Course rating:** 69.9/69.8. **Slope:** 116/115.
Opened: 1953.
★★★½ WEST COURSE
Holes: 18. **Par:** 72/73.
Yards: 6,622/5,940. **Course rating:** 71.3/76.2. **Slope:** 121/127.
Opened: 1964.

Subscriber comments: Nice variety of holes, very courteous staff . . . Suited for all handicaps . . . This course has really come into prime in the last ten years . . . Very busy, staff works very hard and keeps play moving . . . Great greens . . . Back nine holes are tree lined, better be straight . . . Back nine very difficult, good greens.

★★ PINE LAKES GOLF CLUB
PU—25130 Schuck Rd., Washington (309)745-9344.
Call club for further information.

Subscriber comments: Some great holes, some not so great . . . Back nine is much better than front nine, No. 10 is too hard, rest of back nine is fun . . . They have made the front nine more difficult . . . Usually good conditions, challenging for the high handicapper.

★★★★ PINE MEADOW GOLF CLUB
PU—1 Pine Meadow Lane, Mundelein (708)566-4653.
30 miles north of Chicago. **Holes:** 18. **Par:** 72/72.
Yards: 7,141/5,412. **Course rating:** 74.4/70.9. **Slope:** 131/121.
Opened: 1985. **Pace of Play rating:** 4:00. **Green fee:** $53.
Credit cards: MC, V, DISC. **Reduced fees:** Twilight, Juniors.
Caddies: Yes. **Golf carts:** $13 for 18 holes.
Discount golf packages: No. **Season:** March-Dec. **High:** April-Nov.
On-site lodging: No. **Rental clubs:** Yes.
Walking policy: Unrestricted walking. **Range:** Yes (grass).
To obtain tee times: Call up to six months in advance. Prepayment of green fee is necessary from May 15th to Oct. 1st.
Ranked in First 25 of America's 75 Best Public Golf Courses by Golf Digest. Selected Best New Public Course of 1986 by Golf Digest. Ranked 16th in Illinois by Golf Digest. Site of Golf Digest Schools.

Subscriber comments: One of the best in the Midwest and gets better each passing year . . . Use all your clubs here. Typical Jemsek course . . . Need to use all clubs and your brain . . . Serious golfers' course, great location . . . World's best practice facilities . . . Top notch layout, can play long, sometimes greens get too much play . . . Best overall course in area . . . Simply beautiful, more room than I thought . . . This course is beautiful and challenging, don't let it jump up and bite you . . . I love the length and toughness . . . Absolutely delightful, unrestricted walking, top quality . . . Great old-fashioned layout . . . Could hold PGA Tour event . . . Driving range outstanding . . . Great warm-up facilities. Great snack bar and grill . . . Tougher than Kemper . . . Caddies available . . . My favorite Chicago area course: best layout, greens, traps, practice area and value . . . Great old tree-lined fairways . . . Incredibly difficult from tips, huge greens . . . Everything is A+. I met the owner on No.9 tee, and he asked for our suggestions . . . Two completely different looking nines . . . I could play this course every day . . . They really push you to finish . . . Best kept secret on the North Shore . . . Walkers' paradise . . . Lots of play but they try harder.

★★★ PINECREST GOLF & COUNTRY CLUB

PU—11220 Algonquin Rd., Huntley (708)669-3111.
50 miles west of Chicago. **Holes:** 18. **Par:** 72/72.
Yards: 6,636/5,061. **Course rating:** 71.4/68.9. **Slope:** 119/112.
Opened: 1972. **Pace of Play rating:** 4:00. **Green fee:** $23/29.
Credit cards: MC, V, DISC. **Reduced fees:** Twilight, Seniors, Juniors.
Caddies: No. **Golf carts:** $12 for 18 holes.
Discount golf packages: No. **Season:** March-Dec. **High:** June-Aug.
On-site lodging: No. **Rental clubs:** Yes.
Walking policy: Walking at certain times. **Range:** Yes (grass).
To obtain tee times: Call one week in advance.
Subscriber comments: In the country, pleasant to play . . . Interesting . . . Very agreeable people . . . Fun course to play, traditional style . . . A sleeper, nice course, uncrowded . . . Very friendly pro shop staff . . . Country club conditions at public fee price . . . Course puts money into upkeep and improvements . . . Pretty wide open, well kept, nice people in pro shop . . . Great practice area . . . A good all-around course . . . Greens are fast and fair, fairways in good shape.

★★★½ PLUM TREE NATIONAL GOLF CLUB

PU—19511 Lembcke Rd., Harvard (815)943-7474, (800)851-3578.
35 miles northeast of Chicago. **Holes:** 18. **Par:** 72/72.
Yards: 6,648/5,954. **Course rating:** 72.9/74.9. **Slope:** 128/132.
Opened: 1969. **Pace of Play rating:** 4:15. **Green fee:** $25/48.
Credit cards: All major. **Reduced fees:** Low season, Twilight, Seniors.
Caddies: No. **Golf carts:** Included in Green Fee.
Discount golf packages: No. **Season:** April-Dec. **High:** June-Aug.
On-site lodging: No. **Rental clubs:** Yes.
Walking policy: Walking at certain-times. **Range:** Yes (grass).
To obtain tee times: Call a week in advance.
Subscriber comments: Challenge for 12 to 20 handicapper . . . Will use all your clubs . . . Lots of good traps . . . Joe Lee design . . . Small, but nice grillroom . . . Beautifully bunkered . . . Nestled in rolling terrain, 75 minutes from Chicago . . . Worth the trip out, fun course to play . . . Good for all skill levels . . . Staff accommodating . . . Hidden jewel in the country . . . Gorgeous country setting . . . Tough, long, well groomed.

★★ POPLAR CREEK COUNTRY CLUB

PU—1400 Poplar Creek Dr., Hoffman Estates (708)884-0219.
30 miles northwest of Chicago. **Holes:** 18. **Par:** 70/70.
Yards: 6,108/5,386. **Course rating:** 69.6/69.9. **Slope:** 124/118.
Opened: 1971. **Pace of Play rating:** N/A. **Green fee:** $12/26.
Credit cards: MC, V. **Reduced fees:** Twilight, Seniors, Juniors.
Caddies: No. **Golf carts:** N/A.
Discount golf packages: No. **Season:** March-Nov. **High:** June-Aug.

On-site lodging: No. **Rental clubs:** Yes.
Walking policy: Walking at certain times. **Range:** Yes (grass).
To obtain tee times: Call seven days in advance.
Subscriber comments: Tight, short layout . . . Built on marshland . . .
Lots of irons off tee . . . Nice practice facility . . . Windy conditions, leave
driver in bag . . . My favorite course in Chicagoland, not that difficult but
fun . . . Short course, you must not spray shots, very good new clubhouse.

PRAIRIE ISLE GOLF CLUB★

SP—2216 Rt. 176, Prairie Grove (815)356-0202.
37 miles east of Rockford. **Holes:** 18. **Par:** 72/73.
Yards: 6,469/5,468. **Course rating:** 70.7/71.3. **Slope:** 123/117.
Opened: 1994. **Pace of Play rating:** 4:15. **Green fee:** $23/44.
Credit cards: All major. **Reduced fees:** Weekdays, Low season, Twilight,
Seniors, Juniors.
Caddies: No. **Golf carts:** $12 for 18 holes.
Discount golf packages: No. **Season:** Year-round. **High:** July-Aug.
On-site lodging: No. **Rental clubs:** Yes.
Walking policy: Walking at certain times. **Range:** No.
To obtain tee times: Call two weeks in advance.

★★★★ PRAIRIE LANDING GOLF COURSE

PU—2325 Longest Dr., West Chicago (708)208-7600.
30 miles west of Chicago. **Holes:** 18. **Par:** 72/72.
Yards: 6,862/4,859. **Course rating:** N/A. **Slope:** N/A.
Opened: 1994. **Pace of Play rating:** N/A. **Green fee:** $70.
Credit cards: All major. **Reduced fees:** Low season, Twilight, Juniors.
Caddies: No. **Golf carts:** Included in Green Fee.
Discount golf packages: No. **Season:** April-Nov. **High:** May-Sept.
On-site lodging: No. **Rental clubs:** Yes.
Walking policy: Unrestricted walking. **Range:** Yes (grass).
To obtain tee times: Call up to seven days in advance.
Subscriber comments: New course, great shape, staff is great . . . Tee
boxes for everyone . . . Tough for high handicappers, destined for greatness
. . . Bring your best putting game . . . Robert Trent Jones, Jr. design . . .
Gets very windy in afternoon . . . Links style . . . Good challenge for all
levels . . . Short, but with a zillion traps . . . Links-style, can land 747 in
some fairways . . . Don't get too attached to your ball

★★★★ PRAIRIE VISTA GOLF COURSE

PU—504 Sale Barn Rd., Bloomington (309)823-4217.
Holes: 18. **Par:** 72/71.
Yards: 6,748/5,224. **Course rating:** 71.8/68.9. **Slope:** 128/114.
Opened: 1991. **Pace of Play rating:** 3:52. **Green fee:** $14/16.
Credit cards: MC, V. **Reduced fees:** Twilight, Seniors, Juniors.
Caddies: Yes. **Golf carts:** $0 for 18 holes.
Discount golf packages: No. **Season:** March-Nov. **High:** May-July.
On-site lodging: No. **Rental clubs:** Yes.
Walking policy: Unrestricted walking. **Range:** Yes (grass).
To obtain tee times: Call up to seven days in advance.

Subscriber comments: Lots of hidden hazards . . . Fun course, need all
the shots. Like to keep it hidden . . . Though a new course, it is surprisingly
mature. Its four tee boxes make it playable to many skill levels . . . Destined
to be a jewel . . . The best public course I have played anywhere . . . Very
nice people for employees . . . Hope to keep this one a secret so play doesn't
pick up . . . Large waste bunkers make this a difficult course if your drives
are off the mark . . . Too bad no beer . . . Beautiful layout and great
shotmaking holes . . . Course grows on you . . . Harder than it looks . . .
Course at the wind's mercy.

★★★ PRAIRIEVIEW GOLF COURSE

PU—7993 N. River Rd., Byron (815)234-4653.
12 miles southwest of Rockford. **Holes:** 18. **Par:** 72/72.
Yards: 6,893/5,658. **Course rating:** 72.3/71.6. **Slope:** 123/117.
Opened: 1992. **Pace of Play rating:** N/A. **Green fee:** $16/20.
Credit cards: MC, V. **Reduced fees:** Weekdays, Twilight, Seniors,
Juniors.
Caddies: No. **Golf carts:** N/A.
Discount golf packages: No. **Season:** April-Oct. **High:** June-Aug.
On-site lodging: No. **Rental clubs:** Yes.
Walking policy: Unrestricted walking. **Range:** Yes (grass).
To obtain tee times: Call up to seven days in advance.
Subscriber comments: Great signature holes No.6 and No.11 . . . Tight
holes, water, well maintained . . . Course only four years old, very well
taken care of . . . Interesting terrain, well-suited for male or female . . .
Formidable layout and tough course . . . Lots of variation . . . Two
different links in one. Some extra easy, others very hard.

★★★½ THE RAIL GOLF CLUB

PU—RR No.5-124 North, Springfield (217)525-0365.
100 miles north of St. Louis. **Holes:** 18. **Par:** 72/72.
Yards: 6,583/5,406. **Course rating:** 71.1/70.6. **Slope:** 120/116.
Opened: 1970. **Pace of Play rating:** 4:15. **Green fee:** $25.
Credit cards: MC, V, AMEX. **Reduced fees:** Seniors, Juniors.
Caddies: No. **Golf carts:** $10 for 18 holes.
Discount golf packages: No. **Season:** March-Dec. **High:** May-Sept.
On-site lodging: No. **Rental clubs:** Yes.
Walking policy: Unrestricted walking. **Range:** Yes (grass).
To obtain tee times: Call five days in advance of the day of play.
Subscriber comments: Open fairways, not a lot of trouble . . . Friendly
staff but not a real tough test for the LPGA . . . Fun and interesting . . .
How do those LPGA ladies do it? Tough course from blue tees . . .
Personnel very polite and helpful . . . An assistant pro at the Rail took a half
hour of his time to help me with my swing . . . Sneaky OB's and greens
tough to read . . . Since I am a senior, it is a pleasure to play here. Very nice
indeed . . . Gets better around tournament LPGA time . . . Wide open,
bring driver . . . Best tasting BBQ pork outside of Texas! . . . Played with
Nancy Lopez . . . Great layout.

★★½ RAILSIDE GOLF CLUB

PU—120 W. 19th St., Gibson City (217)784-5000.
25 miles east of Bloomington. **Holes:** 18. **Par:** 72/72.
Yards: 6,801/5,367. **Course rating:** 71.8/70.2. **Slope:** 122/115.
Opened: 1993. **Pace of Play rating:** N/A. **Green fee:** $8/16.
Credit cards: All major. **Reduced fees:** Twilight, Seniors, Juniors.
Caddies: No. **Golf carts:** $9 for 18 holes.
Discount golf packages: Yes. **Season:** Year-round. **High:** May-Sept..
On-site lodging: No. **Rental clubs:** Yes.
Walking policy: Unrestricted walking. **Range:** Yes (grass).
To obtain tee times: Call up to five days in advance.
Subscriber comments: Always a strong wind . . . Personnel very polite
and helpful, new course in very good shape . . . Great practice area . . .
Challenging golf course with lots of elevated greens . . . Course longer than
others in area . . . Rough is impossible . . . Course often windy . . . An
oasis amongst the corn and beans.

★★½ RANDALL OAKS GOLF CLUB

PU—37 W. 361 Binnie Rd., Dundee (708)428-5661.
35 miles northwest of Chicago. **Holes:** 18. **Par:** 71/71.
Yards: 6,160/5,379. **Course rating:** 67.7/70.3. **Slope:** 113/110.
Opened: 1966. **Pace of Play rating:** 4:00. **Green fee:** $15/26.
Credit cards: MC, V, DISC. **Reduced fees:** Weekdays, Twilight,
Seniors, Juniors.
Caddies: No. **Golf carts:** $12 for 18 holes.

Discount golf packages: No. **Season:** April-Nov. **High:** June-Aug.
On-site lodging: No. **Rental clubs:** Yes.
Walking policy: Unrestricted walking. **Range:** Yes (grass).
To obtain tee times: Call seven days in advance.
Subscriber comments: Comfortable course . . . Great for average golfer, excellent short course with slick greens . . . New clubhouse . . . Few straight putts . . . Many doglegs . . . Short holes but excellent greens, fast, good for our senior group . . . Clubhouse inviting . . . For a shotmaker, placement over distance.

★★★½ REND LAKE GOLF COURSE

PU—1600 Marcum Branch Rd., Benton (618)629-2353.
90 miles southeast of St. Louis. **Holes:** 27. **Par:** 72/72/72.
Yards: 6,861/6,812/6,835. **Course rating:** 72.2/71.8/73.0.
Slope: 130/131/133.
Opened: 1975. **Pace of Play rating:** 4:20. **Green fee:** $20/24.
Credit cards: MC, V. **Reduced fees:** Weekdays, Seniors.
Caddies: No. **Golf carts:** $10 for 18 holes.
Discount golf packages: Yes. **Season:** March-Nov. **High:** May-Oct.
On-site lodging: Yes. **Rental clubs:** Yes.
Walking policy: Walking at certain times. **Range:** Yes (grass).
To obtain tee times: Call pro shop.
Subscriber comments: Nice wide fairways . . . Well taken care of, beautiful course . . . Well worth the drive from anywhere, beautiful, tough, great . . . Well groomed, pretty wide open, large greens . . . Mature trees. New nine holes great . . . Staff terrific . . . I played this course in 1994, my friend and I had a wonderful time . . . Somebody escorted us to the first hole, people stopped and asked if everything was all right . . . Recommend it to all golfers, use almost every club in bag, will go back and play this course again . . . Great pro shop . . . Tough with many different types of hole layouts and very nice service and people.

★★★½ RUFFLED FEATHERS GOLF CLUB

SP—1 Pete Dye Dr., Lemont (708)257-1000.
20 miles west of Chicago. **Holes:** 18. **Par:** 72/72.
Yards: 6,878/5,273. **Course rating:** 73.1/65.7. **Slope:** 134/110.
Opened: 1992. **Pace of Play rating:** 4:30. **Green fee:** $50/85.
Credit cards: MC, V, AMEX. **Reduced fees:** Weekdays, Low season, Twilight.
Caddies: No. **Golf carts:** Included in Green Fee.
Discount golf packages: No. **Season:** March-Nov. **High:** April-Oct.
On-site lodging: No. **Rental clubs:** Yes.
Walking policy: Unrestricted walking. **Range:** Yes (grass).
To obtain tee times: Tee times per foursomes only - seven days in advance. Golf events (12 or more players) call any time.
Subscriber comments: Glad it did not go private . . . Keep it straight! . . . Target golf with forced carries . . . After playing this course with my three handicap I felt like a hacker . . . Great Dye track, artistic holes requiring thoughtful approach, excellent condition . . . Water everywhere . . . Not the Ocean course but very tough . . . Tough target golf, some carries off the tee . . . Nature, water, wildlife refuge . . . A real beauty . . . Not for the faint of heart . . . My favorite Southside track . . . A day to remember. First hole only easy one . . . Several holes seem set up to fool you . . . Good range . . . Very tough golf course but very enjoyable . . . Excellent service from the pro shop staff, extremely long, difficult front nine, followed by a short yet challenging back nine . . . The short par 5s and three short tricky par 4s . . . Great tester, fair but still challenges all areas of game, aesthetically pleasing . . . Best par 3s around.

ST. ANDREWS GOLF AND COUNTRY CLUB

PU—3N441 Rte. 59, West Chicago (708)231-3100x0.
30 miles west of Chicago.
Opened: 1926. **Pace of Play rating:** N/A. **Green fee:** $22/29.
Credit cards: MC, V, DISC. **Reduced fees:** Weekdays, Low season,

Twilight, Juniors.
Caddies: No. **Golf carts:** $26 for 18 holes.
Discount golf packages: No. **Season:** Year-round. **High:** May-Sept.
On-site lodging: No. **Rental clubs:** Yes.
Walking policy: Unrestricted walking. **Range:** Yes (grass).
To obtain tee times: For weekdays call six days before day desired. For the weekend, call the prior Monday before the weekend. During the season player may obtain a guaranteed foursome tee time for $114.00 (weekends before 1 p.m.).

★★½ LAKEWOOD COURSE
Holes: 18. **Par:** 72/72.
Yards: 6,666/5,353. **Course rating:** 71.1/69.4. **Slope:** 121/114.
Subscriber comments: Excellent practice facility . . . Old mature course . . . Driving range excellent . . . Good course in old style . . . Meat and potatoes golf for all types of golfers . . . Jemsek country, mostly for outings . . . Best finishing holes in the area . . . Fun course for all handicaps . . . No.2 green redone . . . Large greens . . . Staff very friendly, encourages fast play . . . Like the fact they stay open in winter . . . Simple design, great for regular play . . . They do a lot of outings and the course is always in good playing condition.

★★½ ST. ANDREWS COURSE
Holes: 18. **Par:** 71/71.
Yards: 6,759/5,138. **Course rating:** 71.2/68.2. **Slope:** 118/110.
Subscriber comments: Lots of long, straight holes . . . Beautiful trees, but not in play . . . Good golf experience regardless of skill level . . . A lot of challenging holes . . . Fun track, score on the front, back is tough . . . Joe Jemsek knows what the public golfer wants . . . Redoing No.2 and No.17 green . . . All of the Jemsek courses are very good, improvements are a constant way of business . . . Good for weekend golfer.

★★★ SANDY HOLLOW GOLF COURSE
PU—2500 Sandy Hollow Rd., Rockford (815)987-8836.
70 miles west of Chicago. **Holes:** 18. **Par:** 71/76.
Yards: 6,228/5,883. **Course rating:** 69.4/72.8. **Slope:** 113/113.
Opened: 1930. **Pace of Play rating:** N/A. **Green fee:** $12/21.
Credit cards: MC, V, DISC. **Reduced fees:** Twilight.
Caddies: No. **Golf carts:** $20 for 18 holes.
Discount golf packages: No. **Season:** April-Oct. **High:** June-Aug.
On-site lodging: No. **Rental clubs:** Yes.
Walking policy: Unrestricted walking. **Range:** No.
To obtain tee times: Call one week in advance.
Subscriber comments: Longer, old, challenging city course, but fun . . . Mature course with trees . . . Must work the ball . . . Lots of sand and trees, narrow fairways . . . Suited for all types of players. This past year course was in best shape of the past seven years . . . For number of rounds, stays in good shape . . . Good mixture of holes . . . Fun to play.

★★★ SCHAUMBURG GOLF CLUB
PU—401 N. Roselle Rd., Schaumburg (708)885-9000.
30 miles west of Chicago. **Holes:** 18. **Par:** 71/71.
Yards: 6,522/4,885. **Course rating:** 70.6/67.2. **Slope:** 117/114.
Opened: 1926. **Pace of Play rating:** 4:00. **Green fee:** $23/26.
Credit cards: MC, V. **Reduced fees:** Weekdays, Twilight, Seniors, Juniors.
Caddies: No. **Golf carts:** $13 for 18 holes.
Discount golf packages: No. **Season:** April-Dec. **High:** June-Aug.
On-site lodging: No. **Rental clubs:** Yes.
Walking policy: Unrestricted walking. **Range:** Yes (grass).
To obtain tee times: Call one week in advance.
Also has a 9-hole par-35 course.
Subscriber comments: All three nines were facelifted . . . Well run park

district course . . . Friendly staff, good for any level player . . . Becoming a favorite . . . Another course that has added bunkers, sand traps . . . Tougher now . . . Nice redesign of a tired course . . . New layout fairways and greens have introduced additional landscaping . . . Smallish greens, with maturity a popular municipal course.

★★½ SETTLER'S HILL GOLF COURSE

PU—919 E. Fabyan Pkwy., Batavia (708)232-1636.
Call club for further information.
Subscriber comments: Wide open . . . Variety of holes, some hard shots . . . This was an environmental project built on an old landfill. An amazing renovation . . . Every par 5 is a challenge . . . Plenty of challenges . . . Good everyday course for all . . . Course in good shape, one of the most scenic and panoramic courses around . . . Who would guess a former garbage dump? The best variety of golf in the suburbs . . . Played only once and surprised me . . . Nice mix of links and parkland . . . You will either love it or hate it.

★★★½ SEVEN BRIDGES GOLF CLUB

PU—One Mulligan Dr., Woodridge (708)964-7777.
25 miles west of Chicago. **Holes:** 18. **Par:** 72/72.
Yards: 7,118/5,277. **Course rating:** 74.4/69.8. **Slope:** 132/118.
Opened: 1991. **Pace of Play rating:** 4:30. **Green fee:** $40/75.
Credit cards: MC, V, AMEX. **Reduced fees:** Low season, Twilight.
Caddies: Yes. **Golf carts:** Included in Green Fee.
Discount golf packages: No. **Season:** April-Nov. **High:** May-Oct.
On-site lodging: No. **Rental clubs:** Yes.
Walking policy: Unrestricted walking. **Range:** Yes (grass).
To obtain tee times: Call seven days in advance.
Subscriber comments: Treated like a professional. Let back nine mature, could host tournament someday . . . Front nine is great, so are teaching pros . . . Staff will spoil you for playing other courses . . . They aim to please . . . Great amenities, super clubhouse . . . Most challenging course in the area . . . Nos.10, 11, 12 too tough for average player; great condition . . . There's less water in the Pacific Ocean. Great food . . . Two completely different nines in character . . . Front nine much better than back . . . A challenge right up until you hit the 19th hole . . . Beautiful clubhouse . . . Jekyll and Hyde front nine versus back nine . . . Best pro shop in west suburbs . . . If you think you are a good golfer, play Seven Bridges. It will humble you very fast . . . Water comes into play on 14 of 18.

★½ SHADY LAWN GOLF COURSE

SP—615 Dixie Hwy., Beecher (708)946-2800.
30 miles south of Chicago. **Holes:** 27. **Par:** 72/72/72.
Yards: 6,340/6,485/6,423. **Course rating:** 68.2/68.3/68.5.
Slope: 112/110/111.
Opened: 1927. **Pace of Play rating:** 4:00. **Green fee:** $12/24.
Credit cards: MC, V. **Reduced fees:** Weekdays, Low season, Twilight, Seniors, Juniors.
Caddies: No. **Golf carts:** $12 for 18 holes.
Discount golf packages: Yes. **Season:** Year-round. **High:** June-Sept.
On-site lodging: No. **Rental clubs:** Yes.
Walking policy: Unrestricted walking. **Range:** No.
To obtain tee times: Call anytime.
Subscriber comments: South nine is the best of the three . . . Wide open, let it rip . . . Course is fine for all levels . . . Good beer . . . Great grillroom with nice prices . . . Hackers everywhere. Get out early during season . . . Mixing up of three nines confusing . . . Ideal for middle to high handicapper, plus a few challenging holes.

SILVER LAKE COUNTRY CLUB
PU—147th St. and 82nd Ave., Orland Park (708)349-6940, (800)525-3465.
22 miles southwest of Chicago.
Pace of Play rating: 4:30. **Green fee:** $25/30.
Credit cards: MC, V, DISC. **Reduced fees:** Weekdays, Low season,
Twilight, Seniors, Juniors.
Caddies: No. **Golf carts:** $12 for 18 holes.
Discount golf packages: No. **Season:** March-Jan. **High:** April-Oct.
On-site lodging: No. **Rental clubs:** Yes.
Walking policy: Unrestricted walking. **Range:** No.
To obtain tee times: Tee time may be made by phone (708-833-8463) up
to 14 days in advance.
Also has a 9-hole par-29 course called Rolling Hills.

★★½ NORTH COURSE
Holes: 18. **Par:** 72/77.
Yards: 6,826/5,659. **Course rating:** 71.9/71.5. **Slope:** 116/116.
Opened: 1927.
Subscriber comments: Nice course but no range . . . Local golf outing
mecca . . . Long par 4s . . . Good for the beginner to intermediate golfer
. . . North from the tips a good challenge, must be a good iron player for
South . . . Very good traditional test of golf . . . Not bad . . . Both nice
courses in the middle of Orland Park . . . Long, flat but wooded, nice
greens, great 19th hole . . . We are a varied group with seniors and younger
players (24 members) and are treated very well . . . Course nice, South is
sporty, six par 3s; North a little longer, more challenging.

★★★ SOUTH COURSE
Holes: 18. **Par:** 70/72.
Yards: 5,948/5,138. **Course rating:** 67.9/69.3. **Slope:** 108/109.
Opened: 1929.
Subscriber comments: Great facility, course is short but a shotmaking
challenge . . . Need all the clubs in the bag . . . Better than North course if
you are on a group outing . . . Next time I'd wear a hard hat. Golf balls
flying and no one apologizes . . . Prettier than North. Another nice course
for high to mid handicappers . . . Short but sporty. Has some well-designed
holes . . . Tough, can't shoot my handicap, good greens . . . Shotmakers'
course, great food, excellent staff.

★★ SPARTAN MEADOWS GOLF CLUB
PU—1969 Spartan, Elgin (708)931-5950.
Holes: 18. **Par:** 72/72.
Yards: 6,853/5,353. **Course rating:** 72.7/70.3. **Slope:** 123/116.
Opened: N/A. **Pace of Play rating:** 4:00. **Green fee:** $19/28.
Credit cards: MC, V, DISC. **Reduced fees:** Weekdays, Low season,
Twilight, Seniors, Juniors.
Caddies: No. **Golf carts:** $24 for 18 holes.
Discount golf packages: Yes. **Season:** April-Nov. **High:** May-Sept.
On-site lodging: No. **Rental clubs:** Yes.
Walking policy: Unrestricted walking. **Range:** No.
To obtain tee times: Call seven days in advance.
Subscriber comments: Redesigned course makes it very challenging . . .
Much improved with new tee boxes, pot bunkers and landscaping . . .
Great job of redesigning course in '94 . . . Course in best shape I've ever
seen it in ten years . . . U.S. Open qualifier in 1995 . . . Very nice
combination of holes, good staff, very playable for all golfers . . . Work in
progress.

★★★★ SPENCER T. OLIN COMMUNITY GOLF COURSE
PU—4701 College Ave., Alton (618)465-3111.
25 miles northeast of St. Louis. **Holes:** 18. **Par:** 72/72.
Yards: 6,941/5,049. **Course rating:** 73.8/68.5. **Slope:** 135/117.
Opened: 1989. **Pace of Play rating:** 4:25. **Green fee:** $27/50.
Credit cards: MC, V, AMEX. **Reduced fees:** Weekdays, Low season,
Resort guests, Twilight, Juniors.
Caddies: No. **Golf carts:** Included in Green Fee.

Discount golf packages: Yes. **Season:** Year-round. **High:** April-Oct.
On-site lodging: No. **Rental clubs:** Yes.
Walking policy: Walking at certain times. **Range:** Yes (grass).
To obtain tee times: Tee times accepted seven days in advance - credit card necessary to confirm and hold time. Foursomes only accepted for weekends and holidays.
Subscriber comments: Need to hit from the tips . . . Long and tough . . . Very professionally and personally run by staff. Great challenge . . . Excellent layout and course set up beautifully for prevailing summer winds. Shooting 74 there didn't hurt any opinion of this course . . . Lots of fun . . . Suited to all . . . Arnold Palmer course, best in St. Louis area . . . Good staff, variety of holes . . . Good fairways, traps, and greens. You better know how to putt . . . No artificial obstacles (railroad ties, etc) . . . Tee boxes for everyone . . . A championship course, very good.

★★½ SPORTSMAN'S COUNTRY CLUB

PU—3535 Dundee Rd., Northbrook (708)291-2350.
2 miles north of Deerfield. **Holes:** 18. **Par:** 70/72.
Yards: 6,354/5,500. **Course rating:** 70.5/71.8. **Slope:** 123/125.
Opened: 1931. **Pace of Play rating:** 4:00. **Green fee:** $28.
Credit cards: MC, V. **Reduced fees:** Low season.
Caddies: No. **Golf carts:** $28 for 18 holes.
Discount golf packages: No. **Season:** March-Nov. **High:** June-Aug.
On-site lodging: No. **Rental clubs:** Yes.
Walking policy: Unrestricted walking. **Range:** Yes.
To obtain tee times: Call three days in advance.
Additional 9-hole course.
Subscriber comments: Mature, picturesque track, looks easy enough, but takes its toll quietly on mid to high-handicapper. Bring your sand wedge . . . New nine layout particularly good . . . New bent fairways, new tree plantings, should be excellent course by year 2000 . . . No. 17 a real gambler . . . Large complex for all levels of play . . . Simple yet still fun . . . Easy to walk, great par 4s . . . Short, even from the blues . . . Short but demanding . . . Good for high handicappers, ego booster . . . A nice public course, well-maintained.

★★★ SPRINGBROOK GOLF COURSE

PU—2220 83rd St., Naperville (708)420-4215.
28 miles southwest of Chicago. **Holes:** 18. **Par:** 72/73.
Yards: 6,896/5,850. **Course rating:** 72.6/72.7. **Slope:** 124/125.
Opened: 1974. **Pace of Play rating:** 4:10. **Green fee:** $19/25.
Credit cards: MC, V. **Reduced fees:** Weekdays, Low season, Twilight, Seniors, Juniors.
Caddies: No. **Golf carts:** $21 for 18 holes.
Discount golf packages: No. **Season:** March-Dec. **High:** .
On-site lodging: No. **Rental clubs:** Yes.
Walking policy: Unrestricted walking. **Range:** Yes (grass).
To obtain tee times: Call on Mondays.
Subscriber comments: Always windy, a good challenge . . . Great course, everything is there in front of you . . . When put in tournament condition, the greens are a real treat . . . Good balance between challenging and easy holes . . . Toughest back nine around . . . Long, long, long. Doesn't trick you. You just have to hit it . . . Course and staff very good . . . Last five holes are killers . . . Tough from the back tees . . . Good place to use all your clubs . . . Last six holes as good a challenge as you will find.

★★★½ STEEPLE CHASE GOLF CLUB

PU—200 N. La Vista Dr., Mundelein (708)949-8900.
35 miles northwest of Chicago. **Holes:** 18. **Par:** 72/72.
Yards: 6,827/4,831. **Course rating:** 73.1/68.1. **Slope:** 129/113.
Opened: 1993. **Pace of Play rating:** 3:53. **Green fee:** $34.
Credit cards: All major. **Reduced fees:** Weekdays, Twilight, Seniors, Juniors.
Caddies: No. **Golf carts:** $11 for 18 holes.

Discount golf packages: No. **Season:** April-Nov. **High:** May-Sept.
On-site lodging: No. **Rental clubs:** Yes.
Walking policy: Walking at certain times. **Range:** No.
To obtain tee times: Call seven days in advance at 6 a.m.; foursomes only, credit card required.
Subscriber comments: New course . . . Good layout, will mature nicely . . . A real sleeper, when mature it will be one of a kind . . . Outstanding terrain . . . Tee shot on No.10, wow! . . . 18th hole is one of the best finishes in Chicago area . . . Beautiful, playable new course, excellent tee arrangements, well-groomed, nice amenities, service . . . Great layout, once greens mature it will be a "10" . . . Gorgeous design on former horse farm, a new look on every hole . . . Pin placements can be almost impossible . . . I can't believe how stupid I was to wait 15 months after this jewel opened to take the 20-minute drive from my home to play there . . . Friendly staff, keep ball below hole, tough par 3s . . . Playable for all levels but severe around the greens . . . Fun and playable for all levels. No bikini wax needed on slick greens . . . Nearly perfect, fun-fun-fun new course . . . Front nine open, back tighter . . . Still a baby but tight and interesting.

★★½ SUNSET VALLEY GOLF CLUB
PU—1390 Sunset Rd., Highland Park (708)432-7140.
20 miles north of Chicago. **Holes:** 18. **Par:** 72/72.
Yards: 6,458/5,465. **Course rating:** 70.5/71.6. **Slope:** 121/119.
Opened: 1922. **Pace of Play rating:** 4:00. **Green fee:** $20/29.
Credit cards: MC, V. **Reduced fees:** Weekdays, Low season, Twilight, Seniors, Juniors.
Caddies: No. **Golf carts:** $12 for 18 holes.
Discount golf packages: No. **Season:** March-Nov. **High:** March-Aug.
On-site lodging: No. **Rental clubs:** Yes.
Walking policy: Unrestricted walking. **Range:** No.
To obtain tee times: Tee times can be reserved for three or four people one week in advance. This can be done over the phone. Times are held with a credit card number.
Subscriber comments: My regular course, flat, well conditioned, small greens . . . Reseeding should make '95 great . . . Great greens, short layout but big trees, nice staff . . . Good for accurate iron player and putter . . . Beautiful public course, great hot dogs . . . My favorite on North Shore of Chicago . . . Original greens look like Sarazen should be on 'em . . . Great contours.

★½ TAMARACK COUNTRY CLUB
PU—800 Tamarack Lane, O'Fallon (618)632-6666.
20 miles east of St. Louis, MO. **Holes:** 18. **Par:** 71/74.
Yards: 6,282/5,120. **Course rating:** 68.2/67.7. **Slope:** 106/104.
Opened: 1965. **Pace of Play rating:** 4:30. **Green fee:** $13/16.
Credit cards: MC, V. **Reduced fees:** N/A.
Caddies: No. **Golf carts:** $9 for 18 holes.
Discount golf packages: No. **Season:** Year-round. **High:** April-Sept.
On-site lodging: No. **Rental clubs:** Yes.
Walking policy: Unrestricted walking. **Range:** Yes (grass).
To obtain tee times: Call seven days in advance.
Subscriber comments: Holes slope to water . . . Solid, some great holes, some boring. Good staff . . . Flat, uneventful, short, tight . . . Good for beginning players, rolling greens . . . Lots of water but fair . . . Sand in traps brought over on the Mayflower. Very grainy and sparse . . . Great ego booster for people who want an easy low score.

★★½ TAMARACK GOLF CLUB
SP—24032 Royal Worlington Dr., Naperville (708)904-4004.
20 miles southwest of Chicago. **Holes:** 18. **Par:** 70/70.
Yards: 6,955/5,016. **Course rating:** 74.2/68.8. **Slope:** 131/114.
Opened: 1989. **Pace of Play rating:** 4:20. **Green fee:** $30/49.
Credit cards: MC, V, AMEX. **Reduced fees:** Weekdays, Low season, Twilight, Seniors.

Caddies: No. **Golf carts:** Included in Green Fee.
Discount golf packages: No. **Season:** March-Nov. **High:** June-Sept.
On-site lodging: No. **Rental clubs:** Yes.
Walking policy: Mandatory cart. **Range:** No.
To obtain tee times: Call seven days in advance; credit card number
needed to reserve tee-time. Foursomes only on weekends.
Subscriber comments: Hard course in wind, good staff, rough is high
. . . Tough as any course from back, lots of water . . . No carts on fairway
makes for long round and a waste of time . . . Wind usually a factor . . .
Water on nearly every hole, bring lots of balls . . . Every hole is water right,
sand left . . . Plan on wind . . . Spaciousness is an illusion, water is
everywhere!

★ THUNDERBIRD COUNTRY CLUB

SP—1010 East Northwest Hwy., Barrington (708)381-6500.
15 miles of Chicago. **Holes:** 18. **Par:** 71/72.
Yards: 6,169/5,155. **Course rating:** 69.6/70.3. **Slope:** 115/117.
Opened: 1958. **Pace of Play rating:** 4:30. **Green fee:** $20/27.
Credit cards: MC, V. **Reduced fees:** Low season, Seniors.
Caddies: No. **Golf carts:** $12 for 18 holes.
Discount golf packages: No. **Season:** Year-round. **High:** May-Sept.
On-site lodging: No. **Rental clubs:** Yes.
Walking policy: Unrestricted walking. **Range:** Yes (grass).
To obtain tee times: Call monday at 8:00 a.m. for times Tuesday thru
Sunday. Call Sunday at 3 p.m. for times on Monday.
Subscriber comments: Not that many bunkers, nice back nine . . . Hard
sand traps, poorly aimed tees . . . Under new ownership, getting better . . .
Staff friendly, course may be understaffed . . . Interesting layout . . . Wide
open, but fun.

★★★ TIMBER TRAILS COUNTRY CLUB

PU—11350 Plainfield Rd., La Grange (708)246-0275.
20 miles west of Chicago. **Holes:** 18. **Par:** 71/73.
Yards: 6,197/5,581. **Course rating:** 68.7/71.1. **Slope:** 113/116.
Opened: 1934. **Pace of Play rating:** 4:00. **Green fee:** $26/33.
Credit cards: MC, V. **Reduced fees:** Low season, Twilight, Seniors.
Caddies: No. **Golf carts:** $13 for 18 holes.
Discount golf packages: No. **Season:** March-Dec. **High:** May-Oct.
On-site lodging: No. **Rental clubs:** Yes.
Walking policy: Unrestricted walking. **Range:** No.
To obtain tee times: Call seven days in advance by phone secured by
credit card; accept reservations for foursomes, threesomes and twosomes.
Subscriber comments: Trees, trees, trees. Need to be straight . . . Lots of
trees, fun holes . . . Lots of fun and still challenging . . . Hilly layout . . .
Hit 'em straight . . . Old, tree-lined course, very beautiful, good test for all
. . . Yardage books available . . . Tons of trees, don't try heroic recoveries
. . . Old style . . . Pleasure to not see railroad ties or island greens . . . Be a
straight hitter . . . Like playing in a park . . . Tight holes, put the driver
away . . . Friendly staff, no range . . . Just a real good golf course . . .
Unbelievable landscaping . . . Mature trees give it an Olympia Fields feel.

UNIVERSITY OF ILLINOIS GOLF CLUB

PU—800 Hartwell Dr., Savoy (217)359-5613.
120 miles south of Chicago.
Credit cards: MC, V, DISC. **Reduced fees:** Low season, Twilight,
Seniors.
Caddies: No. **Golf carts:** $17 for 18 holes.
Discount golf packages: No.
On-site lodging: No. **Rental clubs:** Yes.
Walking policy: Unrestricted walking. **Range:** Yes (grass).
To obtain tee times: Call pro shop seven days in advance.
★½ ORANGE COURSE
Holes: 18. **Par:** 72/76.
Yards: 6,817/5,721. **Course rating:** 72.1/72.2. **Slope:** 120/121.

Opened: 1950. **Pace of Play rating:** 4:00-4:30. **Green fee:** $12/15.
Season: March-Nov. **High:** June-Aug.

Subscriber comments: Good value for university students . . . Great potential, if they ever do something to the greens . . . Slopes on these greens are ridiculous . . . Orange Course challenging . . . Sloped greens . . . Small greens . . . Pretty wide open . . . Course has bad local reputation for condition of greens . . . Good course for walking . . . Course was going through renovation in September . . . Orange Course worth it, but tough for beginners . . . Good layout, maintenance very poor . . . Stay below the hole.

BLUE COURSE★

Holes: 18. **Par:** 73/74.
Yards: 6,579/6,129. **Course rating:** 70.4/74.1. **Slope:** 114/118.
Opened: 1966. **Pace of Play rating:** 4:00-4:30. **Green fee:** $10/13.
Season: Year-round. **High:** June-Aug.
Subscriber comments: Blue Course, fun. Less challenging than Orange.

★★ URBAN HILLS COUNTRY CLUB

PU—23520 Crawford Ave., Richton Park (708)747-0306.
20 miles south of Chicago. **Holes:** 18. **Par:** 71/71.
Yards: 6,650/5,266. **Course rating:** 71.1/69.1. **Slope:** 114/110.
Opened: 1967. **Pace of Play rating:** N/A. **Green fee:** $11/19.
Credit cards: MC, V. **Reduced fees:** Weekdays, Low season, Twilight, Seniors, Juniors.
Caddies: No. **Golf carts:** $10 for 18 holes.
Discount golf packages: No. **Season:** Year-round. **High:** April-Oct.
On-site lodging: No. **Rental clubs:** Yes.
Walking policy: Unrestricted walking. **Range:** No.
To obtain tee times: Call one week in advance.
Subscriber comments: Course can help your handicap . . . Easy course, gets lots of play . . . Easy to walk . . . Flat terrain, not too much of a challenge. Nice greens . . . Challenging for middle to high handicapper . . . Course is so popular, it's crowded in December.

★½ VILLA OLIVIA COUNTRY CLUB

PU—Rt. 20 and Naperville Rd., Bartlett (708)289-1000x740.
34 miles of Chicago. **Holes:** 18. **Par:** 73/73.
Yards: 6,165/5,546. **Course rating:** N/A. **Slope:** 122/122.
Opened: N/A. **Pace of Play rating:** N/A. **Green fee:** N/A.
Credit cards: MC, V, DISC. **Reduced fees:** Weekdays, Twilight.
Caddies: No. **Golf carts:** N/A.
Discount golf packages: No. **Season:** March-Nov. **High:** May-Oct.
On-site lodging: No. **Rental clubs:** No.
Walking policy: N/A. **Range:** Yes (grass).
Subscriber comments: First nine good, second nine not very good . . . Bring all your clubs . . . Slow greens . . . Golf in the summer, ski in the winter . . . Improved since it was redone . . . Five new holes added, new tees add length. Front nine flat, back nine has hills . . . You can throw the ball onto par 3 10th . . . Heavy outing play, staff polite.

★½ VILLAGE GREEN COUNTRY CLUB

PU—2501 N. Midlothian Rd., Mundelein (708)566-7373.
25 miles north of Chicago. **Holes:** 18. **Par:** 70/70.
Yards: 6,235/5,600. **Course rating:** 69.2/69.2. **Slope:** 115/118.
Opened: 1963. **Pace of Play rating:** 4:30. **Green fee:** $17/24.
Credit cards: MC, V. **Reduced fees:** Weekdays, Low season, Twilight, Seniors, Juniors.
Caddies: No. **Golf carts:** $25 for 18 holes.
Discount golf packages: Yes. **Season:** April-Oct. **High:** June-Aug.
On-site lodging: No. **Rental clubs:** Yes.
Walking policy: Walking at certain times. **Range:** No.
To obtain tee times: Call seven days in advance.

Subscriber comments: They never close . . . Nice course . . . Nice course to score . . . So tight it's dangerous . . . Very short course, driveable par 4s . . . Nice course for beginners . . . Some good holes, some bad . . . Fairways close together.

★★ VILLAGE GREENS OF WOODRIDGE

PU—1575 W. 75th St., Woodridge (708)985-3610.
25 miles west of Chicago. **Holes:** 18. **Par:** 72/73.
Yards: 6,650/5,847. **Course rating:** 71.2/72.2. **Slope:** 121/119.
Opened: 1959. **Pace of Play rating:** 4:10. **Green fee:** $26/29.
Credit cards: MC, V. **Reduced fees:** Weekdays, Low season, Twilight, Seniors, Juniors.
Caddies: No. **Golf carts:** $12 for 18 holes.
Discount golf packages: No. **Season:** March-Nov. **High:** May-Sept.
On-site lodging: No. **Rental clubs:** Yes.
Walking policy: Unrestricted walking. **Range:** Yes (grass).
To obtain tee times: Non-residents call five days in advance. Credit card required for weekends and holidays.
Subscriber comments: Friendly staff, new drainage a big plus . . . Renovations in process . . . Back nine holes particularly fun . . . Good course to learn on . . . Back nine is better . . . A number of long/difficult par 3s and 4s. Some good risk/reward par 5s . . . Hosts lots of local tournaments.

★★★½ VILLAGE LINKS OF GLEN ELLYN

PU—485 Winchell Way, Glen Ellyn (708)469-8180.
20 miles west of Chicago. **Holes:** 18. **Par:** 71/73.
Yards: 6,933/5,753. **Course rating:** 73.5/73.3. **Slope:** 130/127.
Opened: 1967. **Pace of Play rating:** 3:59. **Green fee:** $39.
Credit cards: All major. **Reduced fees:** Weekdays, Low season, Seniors, Juniors.
Caddies: Yes. **Golf carts:** $13 for 18 holes.
Discount golf packages: No. **Season:** March-Nov.
On-site lodging: No. **Rental clubs:** Yes.
Walking policy: Unrestricted walking. **Range:** Yes (grass).
To obtain tee times: Call or come in seven days in advance.
Also has a 9-hole par-36 course.
Subscriber comments: Sand, sand, sand . . . Hard to score well . . . A challenge from any tee box . . . True test of golf from back tees . . . Terrific range and practice area . . . Looks easy, but is tricky and difficult . . . Nice family course, good pace, good condition . . . Western Open qualifier course . . . Top of the line golf course . . . One of the best kept secrets in the Chicago area . . . Well laid out. Sporty and fair . . . Fine course, top notch shape, rangers keep goofs off course, a nice golf experience . . . You can walk! . . . Good design, mix of short target and long open holes . . . Not cheap for non-residents . . . Real challenge from blues . . . Great test from tips for good golfer, great practice facility . . . "Have a day on us" is a great concept.

★★★ WEDGEWOOD GOLF COURSE

PU—Rt. 59 and Caton Farm Rd., Joliet (815)741-7270.
40 miles southwest of Chicago. **Holes:** 18. **Par:** 72/72.
Yards: 6,519/5,792. **Course rating:** 72.0/72.4. **Slope:** 119/123.
Opened: 1970. **Pace of Play rating:** N/A. **Green fee:** $12/24.
Credit cards: MC, V, DISC. **Reduced fees:** Weekdays, Twilight, Seniors, Juniors.
Caddies: No. **Golf carts:** $18 for 18 holes.
Discount golf packages: Yes. **Season:** April-Oct. **High:** June-Aug.
On-site lodging: No. **Rental clubs:** Yes.
Walking policy: Unrestricted walking. **Range:** Yes (grass).
To obtain tee times: Call 24 hours in advance for weekday and call Monday for upcoming weekend.

Subscriber comments: Excellent park district course, No.13 as difficult a par 3 as there is . . . Several good holes through woods . . . Great way to spend your afternoon . . . Long and tough from tips . . . As good as park district course can be . . . A real and fair test of golf . . . Solid course for all skill levels . . . No.3 follows a river.

WESTGATE VALLEY COUNTRY CLUB
★½ WEST COURSE
SP—13100 S. Ridgeland Ave., Palos Heights (708)385-1810.
20 miles south of Chicago. **Holes:** 18. **Par:** 71/76.
Yards: 6,399/6,048. **Course rating:** 68.3/70.1. **Slope:** 105/115.
Opened: 1929. **Pace of Play rating:** 4:30-5:00. **Green fee:** $20/26.
Credit cards: None. **Reduced fees:** Low season, Twilight.
Caddies: No. **Golf carts:** $12 for 18 holes.
Discount golf packages: No. **Season:** Year-round. **High:** July-Sept.
On-site lodging: No. **Rental clubs:** Yes.
Walking policy: Unrestricted walking. **Range:** Yes.
To obtain tee times: Call two weeks in advance.
Also has 18-hole par-67 East course.
Subscriber comments: Fair course . . . Greens a challenge . . . Good place to learn, wide open, no sand . . . A flat, easy course in fair shape . . . Hardly any water . . . No challenge . . . For a short course with no sand, tough to score on . . . The greens will get you.

★★★ WESTVIEW GOLF COURSE
PU—S. 36th St., Quincy (217)223-7499.
Holes: 18. **Par:** 71/71.
Yards: 5,841/5,898. **Course rating:** 70.1/70.2. **Slope:** 116/114.
Opened: 1946. **Pace of Play rating:** N/A. **Green fee:** $16/18.
Credit cards: None. **Reduced fees:** Low season, Twilight.
Caddies: No. **Golf carts:** $8 for 18 holes.
Discount golf packages: No. **Season:** Jan-Dec. **High:** May-Aug.
On-site lodging: No. **Rental clubs:** Yes.
Walking policy: Unrestricted walking. **Range:** No.
To obtain tee times: Also has 9-hole par-35 South course.
Tee time to be offered on an alternating reserved and open basis throughout the day. Call or come in six days in advance. More than six days in advance $2 per reservation fee.
Subscriber comments: Suited to all . . . Short, but enjoyable . . . Finally getting its act together . . . Course easy . . . Golf pro is very good with everyone, regardless of handicap.

(FRUGAL PICK)

WHITE PINES GOLF CLUB
PU—500 W. Jefferson St., Bensenville (708)766-0304.
10 miles west of Chicago.
Opened: 1930. **Pace of Play rating:** N/A. **Green fee:** $27/28.
Credit cards: MC, V, DISC. **Reduced fees:** Weekdays, Low season, Twilight.
Caddies: No. **Golf carts:** $24 for 18 holes.
Discount golf packages: No. **Season:** Year-round. **High:** May-Oct.
On-site lodging: No. **Rental clubs:** Yes.
Walking policy: Unrestricted walking. **Range:** Yes (grass).
To obtain tee times: Call one week in advance.
★★ EAST COURSE
Holes: 18. **Par:** 71/74.
Yards: 6,412/5,415. **Course rating:** 71.1/71.4. **Slope:** 126/122.
Subscriber comments: White Pines' East course has some nice holes for everyone but I'm glad this is where outings are scheduled, freeing up the West . . . Best winter practice facility in Illinois . . . Small greens, many trees, lots of water, extremely penal, relatively short . . . Flat, some challenging holes . . . Course management a plus . . . Back nine is great. Three finishing holes are tough . . . Good long iron play a must . . . A good test of golf . . . maintained well.

★★½ **WEST COURSE**
Holes: 18. **Par:** 72/74.
Yards: 6,601/5,998. **Course rating:** 71.5/73.4. **Slope:** 119/121.
Subscriber comments: When trees mature this will be tough . . . Small greens require accuracy . . . From back tees good and long . . . Back nine tough . . . Stay home if you can't hit it straight . . . Water comes into play. Choosing right club is critical.

★★ **WILLOW POND GOLF COURSE**
PU—808 Golf Course Rd., Rantoul (217)893-9000.
15 miles north of Champaign. **Holes:** 18. **Par:** 72/72.
Yards: 6,799/6,550. **Course rating:** 71.8/71.9. **Slope:** 115/114.
Opened: 1956. **Pace of Play rating:** 4:15. **Green fee:** $14/16.
Credit cards: MC, V. **Reduced fees:** Twilight, Seniors, Juniors.
Caddies: No. **Golf carts:** $16 for 18 holes.
Discount golf packages: No. **Season:** March-Nov. **High:** June-Aug.
On-site lodging: No. **Rental clubs:** Yes.
Walking policy: Unrestricated walking. **Range:** Yes (grass).
To obtain tee times: Only weekend reservations taken. Call on Tuesday.
Subscriber comments: Average test of golf . . . Usually not too crowded . . . Easy to walk . . . Mature trees, course not real long . . . Small greens and just enough trouble to keep you honest . . . Old military course, well kept . . . Making improvement, fair test of golf . . . Length makes it challenging . . . At least two to three strokes easier than the other park district courses, however, it is usually in very good shape . . . Fun with enough challenge to hold your interest.

★½ **WILMETTE GOLF COURSE**
PU—3900 Fairway Dr., Wilmette (708)256-9646.
10 miles north of Chicago. **Holes:** 18. **Par:** 70/70.
Yards: 6,093/5,760. **Course rating:** 69.5/73.1. **Slope:** 122/127.
Opened: 1922. **Pace of Play rating:** 4:00. **Green fee:** $26/29.
Credit cards: MC, V, DISC. **Reduced fees:** Weekdays, Twilight, Juniors.
Caddies: No. **Golf carts:** $24 for 18 holes.
Discount golf packages: No. **Season:** April-Nov. **High:** June-Sept.
On-site lodging: No. **Rental clubs:** Yes.
Walking policy: Unrestricted walking. **Range:** Yes (grass).
To obtain tee times: Call one day before at 10 a.m. for weekdays and six days prior to weekend and holidays.
Subscriber comments: Gets lots of play, a little tired . . . Ball runs forever . . . Small, old course, overcrowded but it's my home course . . . Relatively easy, fun course . . . Old standby . . . Very good community course, lots of old oak trees . . . Fun greens . . . Natural beauty . . . The greens putt well, and you don't need a driver in your bag . . . Good for intermediate golfer, pace of play slow, but improving.

★★ **WINNETKA GOLF COURSE**
PU—1300 Oak St., Winnetka (708)501-2050.
5 miles north of Chicago. **Holes:** 18. **Par:** 71/72.
Yards: 6,485/5,857. **Course rating:** 70.9/73.3. **Slope:** 125/124.
Opened: 1917. **Pace of Play rating:** 3:52. **Green fee:** $27/30.
Credit cards: None. **Reduced fees:** Weekdays, Low season, Twilight.
Caddies: No. **Golf carts:** N/A.
Discount golf packages: No. **Season:** April-Dec. **High:** May-Aug.
On-site lodging: No. **Rental clubs:** Yes.
Walking policy: Unrestricted walking. **Range:** Yes.
To obtain tee times: Call one week in advance.
Subscriber comments: Nice new clubhouse . . . Good layout and scenery . . . Course provides variety of shots, get to use all clubs . . . Easy to get to from the Loop . . . Challenging configuration . . . Just fine . . . Course is struggling to revitalize greens which they lost year before . . . Good sporty course . . . Wonderful older course, tight, with creeks weaving throughout . . . Great par 3s . . . Enjoyable, not too hard, not too easy.

★★ WOODBINE GOLF COURSE

PU—14240 W. 151st St., Lockport (708)301-1252.
30 miles southwest of Chicago. **Holes:** 18. **Par:** 70/70.
Yards: 6,020/5,618. **Course rating:** 68.1/71.3. **Slope:** 108/113.
Opened: 1988. **Pace of Play rating:** 4:06. **Green fee:** $23/29.
Credit cards: MC, V, AMEX. **Reduced fees:** Weekdays, Low season,
Twilight, Seniors, Juniors.
Caddies: No. **Golf carts:** $24 for 18 holes.
Discount golf packages: No. **Season:** March-Nov. **High:** May-Sept.
On-site lodging: No. **Rental clubs:** Yes.
Walking policy: Unrestricted walking. **Range:** No.
To obtain tee times: Call seven days in advance.
Subscriber comments: Wide open, good place to take kids . . . Always
windy . . . Easy to get tee time, good pace . . . Particularly good bent grass
fairways . . . No driving range, small, functional clubhouse . . . Water
comes into play . . . A very friendly staff . . . This course has the potential
to become a great course, all it needs is time . . . Nice course that is good
for the ego . . . Decent little new course, great shape and price . . . Course
of the future once trees mature.

★★ WOODRUFF GOLF COURSE

PU—Geiger Rd., Joliet (815)741-7272.
40 miles southwest of Chicago. **Holes:** 18. **Par:** 68/68.
Yards: 5,424/5,059. **Course rating:** 64.9/67.8. **Slope:** 99/105.
Opened: 1921. **Pace of Play rating:** N/A. **Green fee:** $12/24.
Credit cards: MC, V, DISC. **Reduced fees:** Weekdays, Twilight,
Seniors, Juniors.
Caddies: No. **Golf carts:** $18 for 18 holes.
Discount golf packages: Yes. **Season:** April-Oct. **High:** June-Aug.
On-site lodging: No. **Rental clubs:** Yes.
Walking policy: Unrestricted walking. **Range:** No.
To obtain tee times: Call 24 hours in advance for weekdays and call
Monday for upcoming weekend.
Subscriber comments: Beautiful course, no par 5s only drawback . . .
Fun back, side/front old municipal . . . Play smart, not long . . . Fall colors
unmatched, easy to walk . . . Very short, but greens are good . . . Beautiful
old course, lots of water on back nine.

Notes

IOWA

★★½ A.H. BLANK GOLF COURSE

PU—801 County Line Rd., Des Moines (515)285-0864.
Holes: 18. **Par:** 72/72.
Yards: 6,815/5,617. **Course rating:** 72.0/N/A. **Slope:** 119/115.
Opened: 1971. **Pace of Play rating:** 4:30. **Green fee:** $13/15.
Credit cards: MC, V. **Reduced fees:** Low season, Twilight, Seniors, Juniors.
Caddies: No. **Golf carts:** $19 for 18 holes.
Discount golf packages: No. **Season:** March–Oct. **High:** May–Aug.
On-site lodging: No. **Rental clubs:** Yes.
Walking policy: Unrestricted walking. **Range:** Yes (grass).
To obtain tee times: Call seven days in advance.
Subscriber comments: Will improve with watered fairways . . . Course for all players, condition is improving . . . Back nine has more character . . . Nice layout. Tough par 3s . . . Good for average and below player . . . Average public course, staff could be friendlier . . . Good layout, par 5s are birdie potentials.

★★★½ AMANA COLONIES GOLF COURSE

PU—451 27th Ave., Amana (319)622-6222, (800)383-3636.
20 miles north of Cedar Rapids. **Holes:** 18. **Par:** 72/72.
Yards: 6,824/5,228. **Course rating:** 73.3/69.7. **Slope:** 136/115.
Opened: 1989. **Pace of Play rating:** 5:00. **Green fee:** $45/50.
Credit cards: MC, V, AMEX. **Reduced fees:** Weekdays, Low season, Twilight.
Caddies: No. **Golf carts:** Included in Green Fee.
Discount golf packages: No. **Season:** March–Nov. **High:** June–Sept.
On-site lodging: Yes. **Rental clubs:** Yes.
Walking policy: Walking at certain times. **Range:** Yes (grass).
To obtain tee times: Call up to 30 days in advance for Monday through Thursday. Credit card required.
Subscriber comments: Long and tight, accuracy demanded, all wooded with many up/downhill shots, outstanding aesthetics . . . Beautiful scenery, keeping cart off course a big drawback . . . Suited for serious golfing . . . Challenging but fair. Staff very friendly . . . Maintained well . . . Too tough for a hacker like me. Beautiful setting, watch out for wildlife, deer, wild turkey . . . Expect this to be a powerhouse course in the future . . . One of Iowa's finest . . . Hills, hills, hills, never a flat lie . . . Will be better with age . . . Nicest public course I have ever played . . . Jewel in middle of cornfields . . . Cut into large oak forest . . . Like playing in a game preserve . . . I hate the 90 degree rule . . . Good for 3-wood off tee . . . Tight course carved through woods. You feel like the only ones on the course. Nice clubhouse, super staff.

AMERICAN LEGION COUNTRY CLUB★

SP—1800 S. Elm St., Shenandoah (712)246-3308.
60 miles southeast of Omaha, NE. **Holes:** 18. **Par:** 70/72.
Yards: 5,803/5,261. **Course rating:** 66.6/69.1. **Slope:** 102/113.
Opened: 1956. **Pace of Play rating:** N/A. **Green fee:** $12/16.
Credit cards: MC, V. **Reduced fees:** N/A.
Caddies: No. **Golf carts:** $8 for 18 holes.
Discount golf packages: Yes. **Season:** April–Oct. **High:** June–Aug.
On-site lodging: No. **Rental clubs:** Yes.
Walking policy: Unrestricted walking. **Range:** No.
To obtain tee times: Call pro shop.
Subscriber comments: Good for average players . . . Front nine excellent challenge, back nine acceptable . . . Front nine water and hills. Back nine trees and hills. Very challenging course.

★★½ BEAVER RUN GOLF COURSE

PU—11200 N.W. Towner Dr., Grimes (515)986-3221.
10 miles northeast of Des Moines, IA. **Holes:** 18. **Par:** 72/73.
Yards: 6,550/5,383. **Course rating:** 70.6/70.0. **Slope:** 118/112.
Opened: 1991. **Pace of Play rating:** 4:18. **Green fee:** $19.

Credit cards: MC, V, AMEX. **Reduced fees:** Weekdays, Seniors, Juniors.
Caddies: No. **Golf carts:** $10 for 18 holes.
Discount golf packages: No. **Season:** March-Nov. **High:** May-Aug.
On-site lodging: No. **Rental clubs:** Yes.
Walking policy: Walking at certain times. **Range:** Yes (grass).
To obtain tee times: Call or come in seven days in advance.
Subscriber comments: When trees grow up course will have more character . . . Nice bent grass fairways with ample greens . . . Monster in 20 years . . . Holes 12 thru 16 tough . . . Well-placed bunkers and water. Wonderful staff . . . Five short par 4s . . . Plays a little short, but narrow fairways challenge . . . Great fairways, stay in them or you are in a pine tree.

★★★★ BOS LANDEN GOLF CLUB

PU—2411 Bos Landen Dr., Pella (515)628-4625, (800)916-7888.
35 miles southeast of Des Moines. **Holes:** 18. **Par:** 72/72.
Yards: 6,932/5,155. **Course rating:** 73.5/70.9. **Slope:** 133/122.
Opened: 1994. **Pace of Play rating:** 4:30. **Green fee:** $14/30.
Credit cards: MC, V, AMEX. **Reduced fees:** Weekdays, Low season, Twilight, Seniors, Juniors.
Caddies: No. **Golf carts:** $10 for 18 holes.
Discount golf packages: Yes. **Season:** April-Nov. **High:** April-Sept.
On-site lodging: Yes. **Rental clubs:** Yes.
Walking policy: Unrestricted walking. **Range:** Yes (grass).
To obtain tee times: Call seven days in advance.
Subscriber comments: Target golf. Lots of irons off the tee . . . Very demanding. Tough but a great experience! . . . Staff was very polite . . . Thick woods . . . Shotmaker's course . . . Nice elevation changes. Nice scenery . . . Variety of terrain, must hit straight . . . Tight, take extra balls . . . The setting at Bos Landen was superb. Course is suited for competent players, especially from the lengthy black tee markers. We played in fall, making scenery with all of its colorful trees especially brilliant . . . Great new track primarily through woods, good condition for brand new course, welcome addition to central Iowa golf scene.

★★½ BRIGGS WOODS GOLF COURSE

PU—2501 Briggs Woods Trail, Webster City (515)832-9572.
17 miles east of Fort Dodge. **Holes:** 18. **Par:** 72/71.
Yards: 6,502/5,267. **Course rating:** 72.0/70.0. **Slope:** 128/118.
Opened: 1971. **Pace of Play rating:** N/A. **Green fee:** $9/13.
Credit cards: MC, V. **Reduced fees:** Weekdays, Low season, Twilight, Juniors.
Caddies: No. **Golf carts:** $15 for 18 holes.
Discount golf packages: Yes. **Season:** April-Oct. **High:** April-Sept.
On-site lodging: No. **Rental clubs:** Yes.
Walking policy: Unrestricted walking. **Range:** No.
To obtain tee times: Call three days in advance.
Subscriber comments: Interesting back nine . . . Contrasting nines. Easy front, difficult back . . . Holes 13, 14, 15, 16 are four toughest consecutive holes in state . . . The last three holes are really tight . . . Front nine is hilly, back nine water and very narrow fairways . . . Good shape, back nine tight, par 5s short. Treated great, played several times in summer.

★★★ BROOKS GOLF CLUB

PU—P.O. Box 499, Hwy. 71 N., Okoboji (712)332-5011.
Call club for further information.
Subscriber comments: Fast greens, fun to play . . . Lots of improvements have been made . . . Fun to play, easy to score on . . . Fun course. Grip it and rip it . . . Good course for all levels . . . Gently sloped course with undulating greens and very good service.

★½ BUNKER HILL GOLF COURSE
PU—2200 Bunker Hill Rd., Dubuque (319)589-4261.
Holes: 18. **Par:** 69/69.
Yards: 5,316/4,318. **Course rating:** 65.7/64.1. **Slope:** 111/113.
Opened: N/A. **Pace of Play rating:** 4:30. **Green fee:** $10/12.
Credit cards: MC, V, AMEX. **Reduced fees:** Weekdays, Twilight,
Seniors, Juniors.
Caddies: No. **Golf carts:** $9 for 18 holes.
Discount golf packages: No. **Season:** March-Nov. **High:** May-Sept.
On-site lodging: No. **Rental clubs:** Yes.
Walking policy: Unrestricted walking. **Range:** No.
To obtain tee times: Call one week in advance.
Subscriber comments: Beautiful views of hilly Dubuque . . . Short
course, local knowledge is vital . . . A very short course that will humiliate
your ego . . . Best suited for a straight hitter . . . Lots of sidehill lies. Much
improved from four or five years ago . . . Short course, some scenic holes.

★★½ BYRNES PARK GOLF COURSE
PU—1101 Campbell, Waterloo (319)234-9271.
Holes: 18. **Par:** 72/72.
Yards: 6,268/5,325. **Course rating:** 68.2/68.6. **Slope:** 113/102.
Opened: 1908. **Pace of Play rating:** 4:00-4:30. **Green fee:** $10.
Credit cards: None. **Reduced fees:** Seniors, Juniors.
Caddies: No. **Golf carts:** $16 for 18 holes.
Discount golf packages: Yes. **Season:** April-Nov. **High:** May-Aug.
On-site lodging: No. **Rental clubs:** Yes.
Walking policy: Unrestricted walking. **Range:** Yes (grass).
To obtain tee times: Call pro shop.
Subscriber comments: Old muny course, lots of play . . . Short, wide
open, small greens . . . Neat old course . . . Heavy play, lots of kids during
summer months . . . Nice beginner's course . . . Discounts for junior
players and college students . . . Average layout, well maintained, staff
friendly.

★★ DODGE PARK GOLF COMPLEX
PU—4041 W. Broadway, Council Bluffs (712)322-9970.
Call club for further information.
Subscriber comments: Flat . . . Good mature, comfortable course . . .
Lots of trees, easy to score, fun course.

★★ DUCK CREEK GOLF CLUB
PU—Locust and Marlow, Davenport (319)326-7824.
Holes: 18. **Par:** 70/74.
Yards: 5,900/5,500. **Course rating:** 67.9/72.0. **Slope:** 115/120.
Opened: N/A. **Pace of Play rating:** 4:00. **Green fee:** $11.
Credit cards: None. **Reduced fees:** Seniors, Juniors.
Caddies: No. **Golf carts:** $16 for 18 holes.
Discount golf packages: No. **Season:** April-Nov. **High:** April-Sept.
On-site lodging: No. **Rental clubs:** Yes.
Walking policy: Unrestricted walking. **Range:** No.
To obtain tee times: Call one day in advance.
Subscriber comments: Short but fun . . . Would rate four or five if sand
traps added . . . Water system was put in last fall, will make summer play
more fun . . . Everyone can enjoy . . . Just made changes on 14 and 15 that
will help make course better . . . Rolling course . . . Good beginner's
course in decent shape . . . Good course for the beginner to advance, fast
play . . . Great family golf, old course.

★½ EDMUNDSON GOLF COURSE
PU—1608 Edmundson Dr., Oskaloosa (515)673-5120.
60 miles southeast of Des Moines. **Holes:** 18. **Par:** 70/70.
Yards: 6,024/4,701. **Course rating:** 68.3/68.0. **Slope:** 114/N/A.
Opened: N/A. **Pace of Play rating:** 4:18. **Green fee:** $8/9.
Credit cards: None. **Reduced fees:** Seniors, Juniors.

Caddies: No. **Golf carts:** $16 for 18 holes.
Discount golf packages: No. **Season:** April-Oct. **High:** May-July.
On-site lodging: No. **Rental clubs:** Yes.
Walking policy: Unrestricted walking. **Range:** Yes (grass).
To obtain tee times: Call on the Thursday before the weekend.
Subscriber comments: Staff is excellent, greens all very good, a lot of uphill and downhill lies . . . Long, open course . . . Great pro shop . . . Wide open but fun to play . . . Great for beginners and average players.

★★ ELLIS PARK MUNICIPAL GOLF COURSE
PU—1401 Zika Ave. N.W., Cedar Rapids (319)398-5180.
Holes: 18. **Par:** 72/72.
Yards: 6,648/5,210. **Course rating:** 72.0/70.8. **Slope:** 124/111.
Opened: 1920. **Pace of Play rating:** 5:00. **Green fee:** $10/11.
Credit cards: None. **Reduced fees:** Weekdays, Twilight, Seniors, Juniors.
Caddies: No. **Golf carts:** $19 for 18 holes.
Discount golf packages: No. **Season:** April-Nov. **High:** June-Aug.
On-site lodging: No. **Rental clubs:** Yes.
Walking policy: Unrestricted walking. **Range:** No.
To obtain tee times: Call Monday through Saturday 9 a.m. to 3 p.m. up to 10 days in advance.
Subscriber comments: Back nine extremely tight . . . Front nine long and wide open, back nine narrow . . . Tests every part of game . . . Very different nines, greens deceptively slow, a good golf test . . . Staff nice, good service . . . Hills on holes 12 thru 15 will wear out walker . . . Some of the back nine really pinched.

★★½ EMEIS GOLF CLUB
PU—4500 W. Central Park, Davenport (319)326-7825.
Holes: 18. **Par:** 72/74.
Yards: 6,500/5,549. **Course rating:** 71.9/74.0. **Slope:** 120/115.
Opened: 1961. **Pace of Play rating:** 4:30. **Green fee:** $11.
Credit cards: None. **Reduced fees:** Seniors, Juniors.
Caddies: No. **Golf carts:** $8 for 18 holes.
Discount golf packages: No. **Season:** April-Oct. **High:** May-Aug.
On-site lodging: No. **Rental clubs:** Yes.
Walking policy: Walking at certain times. **Range:** No.
To obtain tee times: Call or come in one day in advance. A $2 nonrefundable fee required up to one week in advance.
Subscriber comments: No practice facility . . . Good par 4s, all golfers regardless of handicap should enjoy this course . . . Good standard public course . . . Has many interesting holes . . . Wide open, let it rip . . . Heavy play, excellent under the circumstances.

★★★ EMERALD HILLS GOLF CLUB
SP—808 S. Hwy. 71, Arnolds Park (712)332-5672.
103 miles southeast of Sioux City. **Holes:** 18. **Par:** 72/72.
Yards: 6,600/5,956. **Course rating:** 70.6/N/A. **Slope:** 118/N/A.
Opened: 1972. **Pace of Play rating:** 4:00. **Green fee:** $25/30.
Credit cards: MC, V. **Reduced fees:** Weekdays, Low season, Twilight, Juniors.
Caddies: No. **Golf carts:** $10 for 18 holes.
Discount golf packages: Yes. **Season:** April-Oct. **High:** May-Sept.
On-site lodging: No. **Rental clubs:** Yes.
Walking policy: Unrestricted walking. **Range:** Yes (grass).
To obtain tee times: Call anytime.
Subscriber comments: Long, no trouble, score should be good . . . Slick greens with good undulations . . . This is a nice course, challenging and hilly . . . Course begins 5-4-3-5-4-3 with each hole offering different challenges and rewards . . . Rolling course, sloping greens, good service, fast play . . . Nicest course in Iowa . . . Large, well-maintained greens, fair test for above average golfer.

★★★½ FINKBINE GOLF COURSE

PU—1362 W. Melrose Ave., Iowa City (319)335-9556.
110 miles east of Des Moines. **Holes:** 18. **Par:** 72/72.
Yards: 6,989/5,645. **Course rating:** 72.7/73.1. **Slope:** 130/123.
Opened: 1955. **Pace of Play rating:** 4:30. **Green fee:** $18/22.
Credit cards: MC, V. **Reduced fees:** Twilight.
Caddies: No. **Golf carts:** $20 for 18 holes.
Discount golf packages: No. **Season:** April-Nov. **High:** June-Aug.
On-site lodging: No. **Rental clubs:** Yes.
Walking policy: Unrestricted walking. **Range:** Yes (grass).
To obtain tee times: Call seven days in advance.
Subscriber comments: One of the best courses in Iowa . . . A good
course for low/mid range handicappers . . . One of the nicer older courses
. . . You won't regret playing it . . . College course, well kept . . . Good
food . . . No.13 an awesome challenge . . . Ex-Amana VIP course . . .
Need to think . . . No.13 signature hole similar to No.17 at TPC Sawgrass
. . . Hit 'em long and straight! . . . Clubhouse facilities and dining area are
very good . . . Excellent practice facilities . . . Rough very tough . . .
Lovely and good tournament course.

★★★ GATES PARK GOLF COURSE

PU—820 E. Donald St., Waterloo (319)291-4485.
Holes: 18. **Par:** 72/72.
Yards: 6,833/5,635. **Course rating:** 70.0/69.5. **Slope:** 105/105.
Opened: 1953. **Pace of Play rating:** N/A. **Green fee:** $10.
Credit cards: None. **Reduced fees:** Seniors, Juniors.
Caddies: No. **Golf carts:** $16 for 18 holes.
Discount golf packages: No. **Season:** April-Dec. **High:** June-Aug.
On-site lodging: No. **Rental clubs:** Yes.
Walking policy: Unrestricted walking. **Range:** Yes.
To obtain tee times: Call Tuesday after 8 a.m. for upcoming weekend.
Subscriber comments: Where Ray Floyd won National Jaycees . . . Long
course, good fairways and greens . . . A greater investment in care would
make this beautiful course outstanding . . . Long rough and large oak trees,
fast greens in summer . . . Big, smooth greens, lots of different shots
required . . . Nice old layout.

★★★½ GLYNNS CREEK GOLF COURSE

PU—19251 290th St., Long Grove (319)285-6444.
10 miles north of Davenport. **Holes:** 18. **Par:** 72/72.
Yards: 7,036/5,435. **Course rating:** 73.5/70.4. **Slope:** 131/124.
Opened: 1992. **Pace of Play rating:** 4:00–4:30. **Green fee:** $12/17.
Credit cards: MC, V. **Reduced fees:** Weekdays, Low season, Twilight,
Seniors, Juniors.
Caddies: No. **Golf carts:** $9 for 18 holes.
Discount golf packages: No. **Season:** April-Oct. **High:** June-Aug.
On-site lodging: No. **Rental clubs:** Yes.
Walking policy: Walking at certain times. **Range:** Yes (grass).
To obtain tee times: Call up to 30 days in advance.
Subscriber comments: Pretty, lots of wildlife . . . Great golf experience,
will become famous with time . . . A challenge from any tee box . . . Tight
fairways on front nine . . . Very nice course. Two blind holes . . . Large
greens . . . This is so good, I hate to tell you about it, because too many
people will come if they know about it . . . Requires all the shots . . . One
of the longest courses in Iowa from the back tees. Use the short (white) tees
. . . The course is fun for every golfer, the staff very friendly, excellent
service . . . Lots of blind shots . . . Best course in eastern Iowa . . . Fantastic
new course, great layout . . . Newer course, narrow fairways, nice design
. . . For a new course, conditions very good.

★ GRANDVIEW GOLF COURSE

PU—2401 E. 29th. St., Des Moines (515)262-8414.
Holes: 18. **Par:** 70/71.
Yards: 5,422/5,191. **Course rating:** 65.5/N/A. **Slope:** 106/N/A.

Opened: 1898. **Pace of Play rating:** 3:30–4:00. **Green fee:** $13/15.
Credit cards: MC, V. **Reduced fees:** Twilight, Seniors.
Caddies: No. **Golf carts:** $9 for 18 holes.
Discount golf packages: No. **Season:** April–Nov. **High:** June–Aug.
On-site lodging: No. **Rental clubs:** Yes.
Walking policy: Unrestricted walking. **Range:** No.
To obtain tee times: Call on Sunday for Monday tee time and Monday
for the rest of that week.
Subscriber comments: Very short public course, good for junior and
senior golfers . . . Old municipal course . . . Short but tough to get low
score, fun . . . Short, flat course, good for walkers . . . Must stay in
fairways.

★★★½ **GREEN VALLEY GOLF COURSE**
PU—4300 Donner Ave., Sioux City (712)252-2025.
Call club for further information.
Subscriber comments: Long course, huge greens . . . Continue to add
improvements each year . . . Wide open fairways . . . Good shape for
amount of play year-round, plenty of water and sand.

SUPER VALUE

★★★½ **JESTER PARK GOLF COURSE**
PU—R.R. No.1, Granger (515)999-2903.
10 miles northwest of Des Moines. **Holes:** 18. **Par:** 72/73.
Yards: 6,801/6,062. **Course rating:** 72.7/N/A. **Slope:** 125/N/A.
Opened: 1970. **Pace of Play rating:** 4:15. **Green fee:** $11/14.
Credit cards: MC, V. **Reduced fees:** Low season, Twilight, Seniors,
Juniors.
Caddies: No. **Golf carts:** $18 for 18 holes.
Discount golf packages: No. **Season:** March–Oct. **High:** June–Aug.
On-site lodging: No. **Rental clubs:** Yes.
Walking policy: Unrestricted walking. **Range:** Yes (grass).
To obtain tee times: Call one week in advance.
Also has 9-hole par-3 course.
Subscriber comments: Great course, appeals to wide range of skill levels
. . . Basically flat with good length and challenging decisions . . . Placement
a must or you're in trouble . . . Friendly crew . . . Some really long holes
. . . I will buy membership there in '95 . . . Long course, only one severe
water hole . . . Fair test of golf, not a lot of tricks . . . 1994 saw this course
in it's best condition ever . . . Big greens . . . Need to be good lag putter
. . . Tough on windy day . . . Championship caliber golf . . . Great staff
. . . Extremely well maintained . . . Also has a par 3 course that is fun to
play. Good for working on your irons.

GREAT VALUE

★★★½ **LAKE PANORAMA NATIONAL GOLF COURSE**
R—5019 Clover Ridge Rd., Panora (515)755-2024, (800)766-7013.
45 miles west of Des Moine. **Holes:** 18. **Par:** 72/72.
Yards: 7,015/5,765. **Course rating:** 73.2/73.2. **Slope:** 131/121.
Opened: 1970. **Pace of Play rating:** 4:15. **Green fee:** $30/35.
Credit cards: MC, V, AMEX. **Reduced fees:** Low season.
Caddies: No. **Golf carts:** Included in Green Fee.
Discount golf packages: Yes. **Season:** April–Nov. **High:** June–Aug.
On-site lodging: Yes. **Rental clubs:** Yes.
Walking policy: Mandatory cart. **Range:** Yes (grass).
To obtain tee times: Call seven days in advance. Outings with 40 plus
players may book time up to one year in advance.
Subscriber comments: This is one fine course . . . Great golf course for all
levels . . . 17th breathtaking view, need good control . . . Tough but fair,
wish there were more like it . . . Requires long drives and straight irons . . .
Big time course, professionally run, windy . . . Short hitters must have
good short game . . . One of the top five in Iowa accessible to public . . . I
want to play it again, it's a course you need to play often . . . Scenery
beautiful, with some very challenging holes . . . Makes you use all your
sticks.

LAKESIDE MUNICIPAL GOLF COURSE*
PU—R.R. No. 2, Fort Dodge (515)576-6741.
Holes: 18. **Par:** 72/72.
Yards: 6,436/5,540. **Course rating:** 70.1/69.8. **Slope:** 114/109.
Opened: 1976. **Pace of Play rating:** 4:30. **Green fee:** $10/11.
Credit cards: MC, V. **Reduced fees:** N/A.
Caddies: No. **Golf carts:** $14 for 18 holes.
Discount golf packages: No. **Season:** April-Oct. **High:** June-Aug.
On-site lodging: No. **Rental clubs:** Yes.
Walking policy: Unrestricted walking. **Range:** Yes (grass).
To obtain tee times: Call 48 hours in advance.
Subscriber comments: Nice for a public course . . . Recently installed a
sprinkling system . . . Great scenery . . . Nice staff . . . Good average to
sub-average ability course.

★★★ MUSCATINE MUNICIPAL GOLF COURSE

(FRUGAL PICK)

PU—1820 Hwy. 38 N., Muscatine (319)263-4735.
20 miles east of Davenport. **Holes:** 18. **Par:** 72/72.
Yards: 6,471/5,471. **Course rating:** 69.7/72.5. **Slope:** 117/108.
Opened: 1969. **Pace of Play rating:** 4:00. **Green fee:** $8.
Credit cards: None. **Reduced fees:** Seniors, Juniors.
Caddies: No. **Golf carts:** $8 for 18 holes.
Discount golf packages: No. **Season:** March-Nov. **High:** May-June.
On-site lodging: No. **Rental clubs:** Yes.
Walking policy: Unrestricted walking. **Range:** Yes (grass).
To obtain tee times: Call or come in seven days in advance.
Subscriber comments: Wide open on some holes, but tight on others . . .
Keep it a secret . . . Much better with new clubhouse . . . All levels can
enjoy. Courteous staff . . . A good test on approach shots . . . Friendly
people . . . Improvements in the last few years are helping the course
condition . . . They keep the fairways and greens very good . . . Good
layout and experience.

★★½ OKOBOJI VIEW GOLF COURSE
PU—Hwy. 86, Box 412, Spirit Lake (712)337-3372.
74 miles east of Sioux Falls. **Holes:** 18. **Par:** 70/73.
Yards: 6,051/5,441. **Course rating:** 68.5/70.1. **Slope:** 113/113.
Opened: 1962. **Pace of Play rating:** N/A. **Green fee:** $24/26.
Credit cards: MC, V. **Reduced fees:** Low season, Twilight.
Caddies: No. **Golf carts:** $10 for 18 holes.
Discount golf packages: Yes. **Season:** April-Oct. **High:** June-Aug.
On-site lodging: No. **Rental clubs:** Yes.
Walking policy: Unrestricted walking. **Range:** Yes (grass).
To obtain tee times: Tee times taken one day in advance.
Subscriber comments: Nice layout, a little tight on some holes, has a 19th
hole for playoffs . . . Nice course with trees and water . . . Smallish
clubhouse . . . Lots of water and sand. Best 19th hole, 85-yards uphill . . .
Gently sloped course, undulating greens, good service . . . Trying hard to
improve caliber of golf . . . Pleasant, unhurried time.

★★ OTTER CREEK GOLF CLUB
PU—1410 N.E. 36th, Ankeny (515)965-6464.
5 miles north of Des Moines. **Holes:** 18. **Par:** 71/73.
Yards: 6,473/5,889. **Course rating:** 71.0/73.1. **Slope:** 117/119.
Opened: 1981. **Pace of Play rating:** 4:00. **Green fee:** $16.
Credit cards: MC, V. **Reduced fees:** Weekdays, Twilight.
Caddies: No. **Golf carts:** $19 for 18 holes.
Discount golf packages: No. **Season:** April-Oct. **High:** April-Oct.
On-site lodging: No. **Rental clubs:** Yes.
Walking policy: Unrestricted walking. **Range:** Yes (grass).
To obtain tee times: Call one week in advance.
Subscriber comments: Great value, fun to play, a little too easy, great
staff . . . Gets better every year with maturity . . . Fun course for

something different . . . Staff is superb, course is pretty wide open, consistent greens, needs to mature . . . Windiest course in Iowa . . . The fairways are the best . . . This is a public course? . . . The older the course gets, the harder it will play . . . Getting better as years go by . . . Water on six holes . . . You will learn to play in the wind.

★★½ OTTUMWA MUNICIPAL GOLF COURSE

PU—4101 Angle Rd., Ottumwa (515)683-0646.
90 miles northwest of Des Moines. **Holes:** 18. **Par:** 70/70.
Yards: 6,335/4,954. **Course rating:** 70.4/66.7. **Slope:** 118/102.
Opened: 1931. **Pace of Play rating:** 4:00. **Green fee:** $8/10.
Credit cards: None. **Reduced fees:** N/A.
Caddies: No. **Golf carts:** $8 for 18 holes.
Discount golf packages: No. **Season:** March–Nov. **High:** June-Aug.
On-site lodging: No. **Rental clubs:** Yes.
Walking policy: Unrestricted walking. **Range:** Yes (grass).
To obtain tee times: Call anytime.
Subscriber comments: Well maintained with nice fairways and greens . . . Very playable, smallish but good greens, nice friendly atmosphere . . . Good condition for heavy use . . . Short course, very quick greens, great staff, use all the clubs.

★★½ PALMER HILLS MUNICIPAL GOLF COURSE

PU—2999 Middle Rd., Bettendorf (319)332-8296.
3 miles east of Davenport. **Holes:** 18. **Par:** 71/71.
Yards: 6,535/5,923. **Course rating:** 71.5/74.0. **Slope:** 124/130.
Opened: 1975. **Pace of Play rating:** 4:00. **Green fee:** $12.
Credit cards: MC, V. **Reduced fees:** Weekdays, Twilight, Seniors, Juniors.
Caddies: No. **Golf carts:** $16 for 18 holes.
Discount golf packages: No. **Season:** April-Dec. **High:** April-Sept.
On-site lodging: No. **Rental clubs:** Yes.
Walking policy: Unrestricted walking. **Range:** Yes.
To obtain tee times: Call anytime.
Subscriber comments: Tactical course, needs to be played a second time to appreciate it . . . Redesigned three holes last year, harder to play . . . Much work being done to repair and prevent flood damage . . . Some pros practice here rather than Oakwood CC during Hardee's week! . . . Nice old course, very challenging . . . If you want a test of golf, play this course . . . Accommodating and friendly staff . . . Hilly, long . . . Hitting fairways is a must for a good second shot . . . Lots of hills and streams . . . Course makes you use all clubs.

★★★ PHEASANT RIDGE MUNICIPAL GOLF COURSE

PU—3205 W. 12th St., Cedar Falls (319)273-8647.
5 miles west of Waterloo. **Holes:** 18. **Par:** 72/70.
Yards: 6,730/5,179. **Course rating:** 72.5/68.4. **Slope:** 122/101.
Opened: 1972. **Pace of Play rating:** 4:00. **Green fee:** $10.
Credit cards: None. **Reduced fees:** Low season, Seniors, Juniors.
Caddies: No. **Golf carts:** $20 for 18 holes.
Discount golf packages: No. **Season:** April-Nov. **High:** April-Sept.
On-site lodging: No. **Rental clubs:** Yes.
Walking policy: Unrestricted walking. **Range:** Yes (grass).
To obtain tee times: Call up to one week in advance.
Subscriber comments: Excellent course for all golfers, will challenge all . . . More sand than average muny . . . This course is always windy . . . Perfectly placed fairway bunkers . . . Lightning fast greens . . . Favors big hitter . . . Big sand traps . . . Long, windy, flat, small greens . . . Seniors will enjoy . . . Will be tough when trees grow . . . The wind plays a large role . . . Wide open, rolling course, good service, fast play.

★★★½ PLEASANT VALLEY GOLF CLUB

PU—4390 S.E. Sand Rd., Iowa City (319)337-7209.
100 miles west of Des Moines. **Holes:** 18. **Par:** 72/72.
Yards: 6,472/4,754. **Course rating:** 71.0/N/A. **Slope:** 119/N/A.
Opened: 1987. **Pace of Play rating:** N/A. **Green fee:** $15/18.
Credit cards: All major. **Reduced fees:** Weekdays, Seniors, Juniors.
Caddies: No. **Golf carts:** $9 for 18 holes.
Discount golf packages: No. **Season:** April-Oct. **High:** June-July.
On-site lodging: No. **Rental clubs:** Yes.
Walking policy: Unrestricted walking. **Range:** Yes (grass).
To obtain tee times: Call up to one week in advance.
Subscriber comments: Medium length, lots of sand and water good for
test of golf . . . Long front, narrow back . . . Lots of water and sand . . .
Great layout . . . Large clubhouse . . . Not long, thinking man's course . . .
Water hazards on 12 holes . . . A very picturesque layout . . . Will play
again . . . Course is maturing and getting better every year . . . Hidden
surprise, resort-like layout . . . .Well bunkered and very fair but difficult
when windy . . . Like the name says, "Pleasant" . . . If I lived closer I
would play this course all the time . . . Tees for all abilities.

★★ ST. ANDREWS GOLF CLUB

PU—1866 Blairs Ferry Rd. N.E., Cedar Rapids (319)393-9915.
Call club for further information.
Subscriber comments: 18 holes packed into 14 hole layout . . . Always
open before all others . . . Really different nines . . . Tight, short front nine,
Long, open back nine . . . Excellent greens, tight fairways, not easy to score
unless straight . . . Condensed but interesting.

★★★½ SHEAFFER GOLF COURSE

PU—1760 308th Ave., Fort Madison (319)528-6214.
15 miles southwest of Burlington. **Holes:** 18. **Par:** 72/73.
Yards: 6,303/5,441. **Course rating:** 69.9/69.9. **Slope:** 118/113.
Opened: 1962. **Pace of Play rating:** N/A. **Green fee:** $9/11.
Credit cards: None. **Reduced fees:** Weekdays, Twilight, Seniors, Juniors.
Caddies: No. **Golf carts:** $16 for 18 holes.
Discount golf packages: No. **Season:** March-Nov. **High:** June-Aug.
On-site lodging: No. **Rental clubs:** Yes.
Walking policy: Unrestricted walking. **Range:** Yes (grass).
To obtain tee times: Call anytime. Tee times needed on weekends and
holidays only.
Subscriber comments: Suited to all handicaps due to its large tees.
Varying the tee markers either brings in or eliminates some fairway bunkers
from play . . . Front nine tight, back open . . . Course with variety,
doglegs, holes that are in and out of trees . . . With maturity will be tough
. . . All golfers would enjoy . . . Clubhouse old but adequate . . . Rarely
overcrowded.

(GREAT VALUE)

SHORELINE GOLF COURSE★

PU—210 Locust St., Carter Lake (712)347-5173.
3 miles west of Omaha, NE. **Holes:** 18. **Par:** 72/72.
Yards: 7,000/5,439. **Course rating:** 71.9/66.0. **Slope:** 124/107.
Opened: 1991. **Pace of Play rating:** 4:00. **Green fee:** $13/14.
Credit cards: MC, V. **Reduced fees:** Weekdays, Low season, Seniors,
Juniors.
Caddies: No. **Golf carts:** $16 for 18 holes.
Discount golf packages: Yes. **Season:** Year-round. **High:** April-Oct.
On-site lodging: No. **Rental clubs:** Yes.
Walking policy: Unrestricted walking. **Range:** Yes (grass).
To obtain tee times: Call one week in advance.
Subscriber comments: Low handicap player challenged from blue tees,
average player enjoys white tees. Course is tight and rewards well placed
shots . . . Shoreline has water that comes into play on four holes . . . Tough
course for slicers . . . Lots of trees . . . Premium on straight shots.

★★½ SOUTH HILLS GOLF COURSE

PU—1101 Campbell, Waterloo (319)291-4268.

Holes: 18. **Par:** 72/72.

Yards: 6,698/5,818. **Course rating:** 71.4/N/A. **Slope:** 108/N/A.

Opened: 1972. **Pace of Play rating:** 4:00. **Green fee:** $10.

Credit cards: None. **Reduced fees:** Seniors, Juniors.

Caddies: No. **Golf carts:** $16 for 18 holes.

Discount golf packages: No. **Season:** April-Dec. **High:** June-Aug.

On-site lodging: No. **Rental clubs:** Yes.

Walking policy: Unrestricted walking. **Range:** Yes.

To obtain tee times: Call Tuesday after 8 a.m. for upcoming weekend.

Subscriber comments: Hilly and challenging at all times . . . Greens look subtle but are full of unseen breaks . . . Rolling hills, tree-lined fairways . . . Challenging course, use every club in bag, must play smart . . . Back nine is fantastic . . . Nice staff. Needs more hazards . . . Tough course when windy . . . Good service. Good place for average golfer . . . South Hills is maturing nicely . . . Challenging but not too long . . . More difficult than it looks.

★★★★ SPENCER GOLF AND COUNTRY CLUB

SP—2200 W. 18th St., Spencer (712)262-2028.

100 miles northeast of Sioux City. **Holes:** 18. **Par:** 72/73.

Yards: 6,888/5,760. **Course rating:** 73.0/74.5. **Slope:** 127/124.

Opened: 1966. **Pace of Play rating:** 4:00. **Green fee:** $27.

Credit cards: MC, V. **Reduced fees:** N/A.

Caddies: No. **Golf carts:** $11 for 18 holes.

Discount golf packages: No. **Season:** March-Oct. **High:** June-Sept.

On-site lodging: No. **Rental clubs:** Yes.

Walking policy: Unrestricted walking. **Range:** Yes (grass).

To obtain tee times: Call anytime up to one month in advance.

Subscriber comments: Excellent course, a real challenge . . . Watered rough is tough . . . One of the nicest courses in Iowa . . . Beautiful, beautiful course . . . Staff very friendly . . . Just wish that I could play better . . . Long holes and plenty of bunkers . . . One of top five in state . . . Great course, facilities, maintenance superb, highly recommended . . . One of Iowa's best.

★★½ SQUAW CREEK GOLF COURSE

PU—5101 Golf Course Rd., Marion (319)398-5182.

2 miles of Cedar Rapids. **Holes:** 18. **Par:** 72/72.

Yards: 6,629/5,574. **Course rating:** N/A. **Slope:** 111/109.

Opened: N/A. **Pace of Play rating:** N/A. **Green fee:** N/A.

Credit cards: MC, V. **Reduced fees:** N/A.

Caddies: No. **Golf carts:** N/A.

Discount golf packages: No. **Season:** April-Nov. **High:** June-Sept.

On-site lodging: No. **Rental clubs:** No.

Walking policy: N/A. **Range:** Yes (grass).

Subscriber comments: The best pro shop anywhere. If it is made, they have it in four different shafts and four lofts . . . A well-designed course with recent improvements . . . Have made some improvements . . . Many good golf holes . . . Variety of holes . . . Front nine fairly easy but more difficult on the back. Good mix of tree lined and wide open fairways . . . Needs more sand traps . . . Long, not very hilly.

★★★½ VALLEY OAKS GOLF CLUB

SP—3330 Harts Mill Rd., Clinton (319)242-7221.

40 miles north of Davenport. **Holes:** 18. **Par:** 72/73.

Yards: 6,855/5,325. **Course rating:** 72.5/70.3. **Slope:** 124/121.

Opened: 1965. **Pace of Play rating:** N/A. **Green fee:** $13/16.

Credit cards: MC, V. **Reduced fees:** Weekdays, Juniors.

Caddies: No. **Golf carts:** $9 for 18 holes.

Discount golf packages: No. **Season:** April-Oct. **High:** April-Oct.

On-site lodging: No. **Rental clubs:** Yes.

Walking policy: Unrestricted walking. **Range:** Yes (grass).

To obtain tee times: Call up to seven days in advance.
Subscriber comments: Beautiful setting, nice design . . . Charming, spread out and picturesque . . . Super course . . . Lots of oak trees, better bring your chain saw along, if you don't, hit it straight . . . Great improvement last two years in conditioning . . . For all level players . . . Better than 95 percent of courses in state . . . Lots of trees in strategic places . . . Lots of fun to play . . . Creek runs through the course.

★★★½ VEENKER MEMORIAL GOLF COURSE
PU—Stange Rd., Ames (515)294-6727.
30 miles north of Des Moines. **Holes:** 18. **Par:** 72/73.
Yards: 6,543/5,357. **Course rating:** 71.3/70.6. **Slope:** 124/120.
Opened: 1938. **Pace of Play rating:** 4:00. **Green fee:** $15/17.
Credit cards: MC, V. **Reduced fees:** Weekdays, Juniors.
Caddies: No. **Golf carts:** $18 for 18 holes.
Discount golf packages: No. **Season:** March-Nov. **High:** June-Aug.
On-site lodging: No. **Rental clubs:** Yes.
Walking policy: Unrestricted walking. **Range:** Yes (grass).
To obtain tee times: Call up to one week in advance.
Course owned by Iowa State University.
Subscriber comments: Always a challenge . . . Must think on every shot . . . One of top courses in area . . . Bring a few extra balls and be ready for fun . . . Tight with good variety . . . Course will bring you to your knees . . . Staff nice . . . Old college course, be straight or bring lots of balls . . . Good shotmaker's course . . . Long and tight . . . Big greens, water comes into play . . . Beautiful old course, loved it . . . Miss fairway you're in the woods. Lots of elevation changes . . . The best course in Iowa and maybe in the midwest . . . Greens undulating and lightning fast . . . Not long, but hills, woods, water, sidehill lies, and tight fairways makes this a superb target golf course . . . Heavy traffic during school . . . On the short side, but worth every step.

★★★ WAVELAND GOLF COURSE
PU—4908 University Ave., Des Moines (515)242-2911.
Holes: 18. **Par:** 72/71.
Yards: 6,419/5,295. **Course rating:** 71.4/69.4. **Slope:** 126/116.
Opened: 1894. **Pace of Play rating:** 4:00–4:30. **Green fee:** $14/16.
Credit cards: MC, V. **Reduced fees:** Low season, Twilight, Seniors, Juniors.
Caddies: No. **Golf carts:** $19 for 18 holes.
Discount golf packages: Yes. **Season:** March-Nov. **High:** May-Aug.
On-site lodging: No. **Rental clubs:** Yes.
Walking policy: Unrestricted walking. **Range:** No.
To obtain tee times: Call Sunday for Monday tee times and Monday for the balance of the week.
Subscriber comments: Forested and hilly, shotmaker's course, length not required, medium sized greens . . . Great old hilly course demands lots of shots . . . Granddaddy of public courses . . . Old course that is making a comeback . . . Lots of terrain, mature trees . . . Water system helps . . . Grand old oaks . . . Terrific clubhouse, lots of character . . . Bring mountain shoes as only level lies are on tees and greens . . . Accuracy and length won't ensure views of greens but necessary to score . . . No. 3 real TOUGH! . . . Not made for people who spray their shots . . . Difficult course for older player to walk.

★★ WESTWOOD GOLF CLUB
PU—2807-1st Ave. W., Newton (515)792-3087.
25 miles east of Des Moines. **Holes:** 18. **Par:** 71/71.
Yards: 6,245/5,645. **Course rating:** 68.3/74.5. **Slope:** 116/N/A.
Opened: 1927. **Pace of Play rating:** 4:00. **Green fee:** $12/14.
Credit cards: None. **Reduced fees:** Juniors.
Caddies: No. **Golf carts:** $16 for 18 holes.
Discount golf packages: No. **Season:** April-Oct. **High:** June-Aug.
On-site lodging: No. **Rental clubs:** Yes.

Walking policy: Unrestricted walking. **Range:** Yes (grass).
To obtain tee times: Call one week in advance.
Subscriber comments: Suited for average player . . . Includes water, creeks and doglegs . . . Fair challenge . . . Short but interesting. Front nine hilly with no flat lies and small old greens . . . Back is flat with water, big greens . . . Two distinct nines, very friendly staff . . . Course and facilities improve each year.

WILLOW CREEK GOLF CLUB
★★ RED COURSE
PU—140 Army Post Rd., West Des Moines (515)285-4558.
6 miles southwest of Des Moines. **Holes:** 18. **Par:** 71/74.
Yards: 6,465/5,758. **Course rating:** 70.2/71.4. **Slope:** 116/112.
Opened: 1961. **Pace of Play rating:** 3:55. **Green fee:** $17/18.
Credit cards: MC, V, DISC. **Reduced fees:** N/A.
Caddies: No. **Golf carts:** $19 for 18 holes.
Discount golf packages: No. **Season:** April-Oct. **High:** June-Sept.
On-site lodging: No. **Rental clubs:** Yes.
Walking policy: Unrestricted walking. **Range:** Yes (grass).
To obtain tee times: Call pro shop.
Also has 9-hole par-35 White Course and 9-hole par-33 Blue Course.
Subscriber comments: New nine holes makes it worthwhile . . . New holes have improved the course . . . Nice course to play . . . Accommodating clubhouse . . . Family run, friendly, quite open, fun . . . Large greens with risk/reward layout . . . Great practice range . . . New holes have links feel . . . Difference between old and new greens can throw you off.

Notes

KANSAS

★★★★ ALVAMAR GOLF CLUB
SP—1800 Crossgate Dr., Lawrence (913)842-1907.
25 miles southwest of Kansas City. **Holes:** 18. **Par:** 72/72.
Yards: 7,096/5,489. **Course rating:** 75.0/N/A. **Slope:** 135/N/A.
Opened: 1968. **Pace of Play rating:** 4:30. **Green fee:** $15/30.
Credit cards: MC, V, DISC. **Reduced fees:** Weekdays, Low season,
Resort guests, Twilight, Seniors, Juniors.
Caddies: No. **Golf carts:** $12 for 18 holes.
Discount golf packages: Yes. **Season:** Year-round. **High:** May-Sept.
On-site lodging: No. **Rental clubs:** Yes.
Walking policy: Unrestricted walking. **Range:** Yes (grass).
To obtain tee times: Call seven days in advance.
Ranked in Third 25 of America's 75 Best Public Golf Courses by Golf
Digest.
Subscriber comments: The hidden gem of Kansas . . . A strong layout
with a variety of shots required . . . Tight fairways. Accuracy the key . . .
Some outstanding holes . . . Great par 5s . . . A thinking man's course . . .
Tough from the back tees . . . Great zoysia fairways . . . Ball sits up nicely
on zoysia . . . Best zoysia fairways anywhere . . . Marvelous greens . . .
Huge, slick . . . Best greens in the world . . . Best conditioned fairways and
greens in the Kansas City area . . . Needs better sand traps . . . Crusty sand
. . . Wonderful place to play, like a country club . . . Almost as good as
private course next door . . . Maybe better . . . Usually crowded, well
marshaled . . . Nice staff . . . Put on a tournament with no problems . . .
Best public course in Kansas.

★½ BRAEBURN GOLF CLUB AT WICHITA STATE UNIVERSITY
SP—4201 E. 21st, Wichita (316)685-6601.
Holes: 18. **Par:** 70/71.
Yards: 6,320/5,301. **Course rating:** 71.6/71.4. **Slope:** 129/121.
Opened: N/A. **Pace of Play rating:** 4:00. **Green fee:** $13.
Credit cards: MC, V. **Reduced fees:** Weekdays, Low season, Twilight,
Seniors, Juniors.
Caddies: No. **Golf carts:** $17 for 18 holes.
Discount golf packages: No. **Season:** Year-round. **High:** March-Oct.
On-site lodging: No. **Rental clubs:** Yes.
Walking policy: Unrestricted walking. **Range:** Yes (grass).
To obtain tee times: Call Sunday at 3 p.m. for following week.
Subscriber comments: One of the oldest courses in Kansas . . . Sits on a
college campus . . . Old country club gone public . . . Looking better all
the time . . . Some interesting holes . . . Beautiful tree lined fairways . . .
Lots of big trees . . . Bermuda fairways . . . Very small greens . . . Easy
course . . . Short par 5s . . . New tees and watering system will make it
better.

★★★★ BUFFALO DUNES GOLF CLUB
PU—South Star Rte., Garden City (316)276-1210.
180 miles west of Wichita. **Holes:** 18. **Par:** 72/72.
Yards: 6,767/5,598. **Course rating:** 72.5/72.0. **Slope:** 124/114.
Opened: 1976. **Pace of Play rating:** 4:15. **Green fee:** $10/12.
Credit cards: None. **Reduced fees:** Twilight.
Caddies: No. **Golf carts:** $17 for 18 holes.
Discount golf packages: No. **Season:** Year-round. **High:** April-Oct.
On-site lodging: No. **Rental clubs:** Yes.
Walking policy: Unrestricted walking. **Range:** Yes (grass).
To obtain tee times: Call Mondays at 5 p.m. for following week.
Subscriber comments: A jewel in the middle of nowhere . . . What a
surprise . . . As good as any anywhere . . . By far the most challenging,
best kept, fun-to-play public course I've ever played, without being overly
punishing . . . Wonderful dunes course . . . Tough links in west Kansas . . .
Take all your clubs . . . 40 mph winds common . . . Watch out for the
knee-high rough . . . Staff, from greenkeeper to pro, is very interested in

making your round great. They show pride . . . A real gem . . . The best golf value ever . . . Best kept secret in Kansas . . . One of the best public courses in the country . . . Wish this course were closer . . . Buffalo Dunes has proven to me time after time that there's no place like home.

★½ CAREY PARK GOLF CLUB

PU—P.O. Box 1212, Hutchinson (316)694-2698.
Call club for further information.
Subscriber comments: Flat . . . Mature . . . Big cottonwood trees . . . Heavily used . . . No trouble . . . Good course, bad greens . . . Frustrating greens . . . 17 holes are completely flat . . . All holes look alike . . . Some nice improvements over recent years, but a long way to go.

★½ COLLY CREEK GOLF CLUB

PU—3720 S.W. 45th, Topeka (913)267-7888.
Holes: 18. **Par:** 70/70.
Yards: 6,409/4,656. **Course rating:** 70.6/70.0. **Slope:** 125/124.
Opened: 1990. **Pace of Play rating:** 4:30. **Green fee:** $12/15.
Credit cards: MC, V, DISC. **Reduced fees:** Weekdays, Twilight, Seniors, Juniors.
Caddies: No. **Golf carts:** $N/A for 18 holes.
Discount golf packages: No. **Season:** Year-round. **High:** April-Oct.
On-site lodging: No. **Rental clubs:** Yes.
Walking policy: Unrestricted walking. **Range:** Yes (grass).
To obtain tee times: Call Tuesday for following weekend and holiday.
Subscriber comments: Very short and tight . . . Requires careful club selection . . . Trees and water everywhere . . . Small greens . . . Meandering creek . . . Water on every hole . . . Bring at least two sleeves of balls . . . Amateur design . . . Front nine executive length and gimmicky . . . nine holes in area made for six holes . . . Creeks under greens . . . Almost every hole a 90 degree dogleg . . . Back nine more redeeming . . . Second nine a tougher test . . . Hit it straight or you're dead . . . Leave driver in the bag . . . Back nine especially bad . . . Lost balls, poison ivy . . . I like it because of the year-round driving range.

★★★ CUSTER HILL GOLF CLUB

SP—Normandy Drive, Fort Riley (913)239-5412.
Call club for further information.
Subscriber comments: Military course . . . Long . . . Rolling hills . . . Lots of saucer greens . . . Small, fast, sloping greens . . . If you can find it, you'll love it . . . Robert Trent Jones for about 10 bucks . . . Tough par 3s . . . Suffers from lack of quality maintenance . . . Green and fairway conditions vary week to week . . . Tall grass around bunkers . . . Rough means a lost ball . . . Improved toward the end of the season . . . On its way back.

★★★★ DEER CREEK GOLF CLUB

SP—7000 W. 133st, Overland Park (913)681-3100.
15 miles south of Kansas City. **Holes:** 18. **Par:** 72/72.
Yards: 6,870/5,120. **Course rating:** 74.5/68.5. **Slope:** 137/113.
Opened: 1989. **Pace of Play rating:** N/A. **Green fee:** $39/47.
Credit cards: MC, V, DISC. **Reduced fees:** Weekdays, Low season, Twilight.
Caddies: No. **Golf carts:** $N/A for 18 holes.
Discount golf packages: No. **Season:** Year-round. **High:** March-Nov.
On-site lodging: No. **Rental clubs:** Yes.
Walking policy: Unrestricted walking. **Range:** Yes (grass).
To obtain tee times: Call 24 hours in advance.
Subscriber comments: Class design . . . Robert Trent Jones Jr. design . . . Extremely tight . . . Lots of trouble. Water and woods . . . Creek in play on most holes . . . Must position yourself off the tee blocks . . . Rarely need a driver . . . You'd better be accurate . . . Long iron players will love it . . . Short game a must . . . Private club feel and conditions . . . Great zoysia fairways . . . Very good greens . . . A lot of sand . . . Not nearly as

nice as the homes surrounding it . . . Set in a flood plain . . . Very soggy
. . . Sand traps wash out after heavy rain . . . Beautiful clubhouse . . . Great
course, but three times the price of other public courses . . . Never get tired
of playing here . . . Best public course in the Kansas City area.

★★★ DUB'S DREAD GOLF CLUB

PU—12601 Hollingsworth Rd., Kansas City (913)721-1333.
Holes: 18. **Par:** 72/72.
Yards: 6,987/5,454. **Course rating:** 73.6/70.4. **Slope:** 131/121.
Opened: 1965. **Pace of Play rating:** N/A. **Green fee:** $20/27.
Credit cards: MC, V, AMEX. **Reduced fees:** Twilight, Seniors, Juniors.
Caddies: No. **Golf carts:** $12 for 18 holes.
Discount golf packages: No. **Season:** Year-round. **High:** April–Oct.
On-site lodging: No. **Rental clubs:** Yes.
Walking policy: Unrestricted walking. **Range:** Yes (grass).
To obtain tee times: Call or come in up to three days in advance. Credit
card required for weekend and holidays.
Subscriber comments: Old classic course . . . Former semi-private course
. . . Deceptively difficult . . . Great challenge . . . Long and fairly narrow
. . . Every hole outstanding . . . No two holes alike . . . Challenges your
skill to manuever the ball . . . You must work the ball left to right and right
to left . . . From very back tees, all the golf course anyone needs . . .
Definitely a challenge for short knockers . . . Zoysia tees and fairways . . .
Course upkeep improved each of the last three years . . . Need to clean up
small ponds . . . Biggest problem, no distance markers . . . Staff like a
country club . . . Nice course, but a little remote . . . Worth the drive . . .
Best course in the Kansas City area.

★★½ EMPORIA MUNICIPAL GOLF CLUB

PU—R.R. 4, Emporia (316)342-7666.
Call club for further information.
Subscriber comments: Very nice . . . Pretty wide open . . . Wonderful
soft greens . . . Super layout on back nine . . . Undistinctive, but service
was midwest homey . . . Surprisingly well groomed for a small town
muny . . . No waiting! . . . Gets better with age.

★★★ HERITAGE PARK GOLF COURSE

PU—16445 Lackman Road, Olathe (913)829-4653.
12 miles northeast of Kansas City. **Holes:** 18. **Par:** 71/71.
Yards: 6,876/5,797. **Course rating:** 72.6/72.3. **Slope:** 131/121.
Opened: 1990. **Pace of Play rating:** 4:30. **Green fee:** $18/20.
Credit cards: MC, V. **Reduced fees:** Weekdays, Twilight, Seniors,
Juniors.
Caddies: No. **Golf carts:** $22 for 18 holes.
Discount golf packages: No. **Season:** Year-round. **High:** March–Oct.
On-site lodging: No. **Rental clubs:** Yes.
Walking policy: Unrestricted walking. **Range:** Yes (grass).
To obtain tee times: Call five days in advance.
Subscriber comments: Hidden jewel of the area . . . Great design . . .
Several great holes . . . Wide open and windy . . . Worth playing . . .
Championship quality and condition . . . Some tough par 4s . . . Some
long carries over water . . . Severe penalties for missing fairways and greens
. . . Knee high rough on a couple holes . . . Spent a lot of time looking for
balls . . . Good layout but greens badly designed . . . Strange greens . . .
Tough undulating greens . . . Long walk between greens and tees . . .
Quarter of a mile on some holes . . . Too long to walk comfortably . . .
Too much room between holes . . . Could put par 3s between them . . . A
layout made for cart rentals . . . Toughest muny layout in the Kansas City
area.

★★★ HESSTON MUNICIPAL GOLF PARK

PU—520 Golf Course Dr., Hesston (316)327-2331.
35 miles north of Wichita. **Holes:** 18. **Par:** 71/71.
Yards: 6,526/5,475. **Course rating:** 71.4/66.7. **Slope:** 125/118.

Opened: 1976. **Pace of Play rating:** 4:15. **Green fee:** $9/11.
Credit cards: None. **Reduced fees:** Seniors.
Caddies: No. **Golf carts:** $N/A for 18 holes.
Discount golf packages: No. **Season:** Year-round. **High:** May-Sept.
On-site lodging: No. **Rental clubs:** Yes.
Walking policy: Unrestricted walking. **Range:** Yes (grass).
To obtain tee times: Call pro shop.
Subscriber comments: Great fun to play . . . Wide fairways . . . Elevated greens . . . Lots of doglegs . . . Long par 3s . . . Some water, some bunkers . . . Thick rough . . . Not real long, not real short . . . Great shape . . . Plays fast . . . Very tough in the wind, which is everyday . . . A lot of look alike holes . . . Very dry. Needs water . . . Play before it gets hot in summer . . . One of the best courses around.

★★ HIDDEN LAKES GOLF COURSE

PU—6020 South Greenwich Rd., Derby (316)788-2855.
6 miles southeast of Wichita. **Holes:** 18. **Par:** 72/71.
Yards: 6,523/5,212. **Course rating:** 70.8/72.2. **Slope:** 122/120.
Opened: 1960. **Pace of Play rating:** 4:30. **Green fee:** $12/13.
Credit cards: All major. **Reduced fees:** Weekdays, Twilight, Seniors, Juniors
Caddies: No. **Golf carts:** $9 for 18 holes.
Discount golf packages: No. **Season:** Year-round. **High:** March-Oct.
On-site lodging: No. **Rental clubs:** Yes.
Walking policy: Unrestricted walking. **Range:** Yes (grass).
To obtain tee times: Call seven days in advance.
Subscriber comments: Nothing hidden about the lakes . . . Plenty of water . . . Excellent use of water . . . Lush fairways . . . Quite a few doglegs . . . No. 5 is the toughest par 5 in town. Course got an undeserved bad rap last year . . . New grounds crew. Best shape ever . . . Out of the way but worth finding.

★★½ L.W. CLAPP GOLF COURSE

PU—4611 E. Harry, Wichita (316)688-9341.
Holes: 18. **Par:** 70/70.
Yards: 6,087/4,965. **Course rating:** 70.0/69.7. **Slope:** 120/110.
Opened: N/A. **Pace of Play rating:** N/A. **Green fee:** $12.
Credit cards: None. **Reduced fees:** Weekdays, Twilight, Seniors, Juniors.
Caddies: No. **Golf carts:** $9 for 18 holes.
Discount golf packages: No. **Season:** Year-round. **High:** May-Aug.
On-site lodging: No. **Rental clubs:** Yes.
Walking policy: Unrestricted walking. **Range:** No.
To obtain tee times: Call on Sunday at 3 p.m. for following week.
Subscriber comments: Nice course . . . Real short . . . Small greens . . . No trouble . . . Great shape . . . Requires some shotmaking . . . Must be accurate . . . Too many back-and-forth holes . . . Parallel fairways are too tight . . . Could do a lot with this course . . . Space tee times out more and it would be great . . . Added concrete cart paths. Course not big enough to accommodate them . . . Nothing great, but still fun . . . A good course to help you learn.

★★★ LAKE SHAWNEE GOLF COURSE

PU—4141 S.E. Edge Rd., Topeka (913)267-2295.
Holes: 18. **Par:** 69/69.
Yards: 6,013/5,459. **Course rating:** 68.3/70.8. **Slope:** 107/113.
Opened: 1970. **Pace of Play rating:** N/A. **Green fee:** $9/11.
Credit cards: None. **Reduced fees:** Weekdays, Twilight, Seniors, Juniors.
Caddies: Yes. **Golf carts:** $10 for 18 holes.
Discount golf packages: No. **Season:** Year-round. **High:** May-Sept.
On-site lodging: No. **Rental clubs:** Yes.
Walking policy: Unrestricted walking. **Range:** Yes (grass).
To obtain tee times: Call four days in advance.
Subscriber comments: Affordable fun . . . Very pretty . . . Comfortable . . . Rewards good shots . . . Native oaks make fall a great time to play . . .

Can't beat the views . . . Short but challenging . . . Very challenging par 69 . . . Introduction of zoysia fairways over the last three years was annoying but has proven to be worth it . . . Several blind shots to greens, my favorite in Topeka. Getting better all the time . . . Very pretty and great bargain . . . Long lines on weekends . . . Get a cart, the hills are killers . . . Well run county course.

★★★ MACDONALD GOLF COURSE
PU—840 N. Yale, Wichita (316)688-9391.
Call club for further information.
Subscriber comments: One of Kansas's hidden jewels . . . Old park-style course very handsome. Best public course in the area . . . Improvements are scheduled . . . High quality course but needs better upkeep . . . Will be great after rehab coming soon . . . Good staff and service . . . Very enjoyable, well maintained, good challenge . . . Must drive ball accurate and long . . . Big trees.

★★★ MARIAH HILLS GOLF COURSE
PU—R.R. No. 2, Box 40, Dodge City (316)225-8182.
Holes: 18. **Par:** 71/73.
Yards: 6,868/5,559. **Course rating:** 72.4/71.5. **Slope:** 118/112.
Opened: 1975. **Pace of Play rating:** 4:30. **Green fee:** $7/10.
Credit cards: None. **Reduced fees:** Twilight, Juniors.
Caddies: No. **Golf carts:** $15 for 18 holes.
Discount golf packages: No. **Season:** Year-round. **High:** April–Oct.
On-site lodging: No. **Rental clubs:** Yes.
Walking policy: Unrestricted walking. **Range:** Yes (grass).
To obtain tee times: Call Thursday before weekend.
Subscriber comments: Big, fairly wide open, huge greens, good for big hitter . . . Fair for western Kansas hot summers . . . Lost some trees. When the wind blows, add 8-10 strokes . . . The staff is exceptional. I drive from Great Bend to play there and they remember me.

★★½ OVERLAND PARK GOLF CLUB
SOUTH/NORTH/WEST
PU—12501 Quivira Rd., Overland Park (913)897-3809.
9 miles south of Kansas City. **Holes:** 27. **Par:** 70/70/70.
Yards: 6,446/6,455/6,367. **Course rating:** 69.9/69.7/69.9. **Slope:** 113/119/115.
Opened: 1970. **Pace of Play rating:** 4:30. **Green fee:** $14.
Credit cards: MC, V. **Reduced fees:** Twilight, Seniors, Juniors.
Caddies: No. **Golf carts:** $11 for 18 holes.
Discount golf packages: No. **Season:** Year-round. **High:** April–Sept.
On-site lodging: No. **Rental clubs:** Yes.
Walking policy: Walking at certain times. **Range:** Yes.
To obtain tee times: Call seven days in advance.
Also has 9-hole executive course.
Subscriber comments: Busiest course in metro area . . . Friendly new third nine, West links was good addition . . . Out of season OK, in season marshals push and rush . . . Efficient and friendly staff . . . Maintenance wonderful compared to high value play, play spring, summer, and fall . . . Nice greens, help good, can't smoke inside . . . Conditioning a miracle in view of number of rounds . . . Great for walking . . . Too many fivesomes . . . Hit it wherever you want . . . Third nine requires a cart.

★½ PAINTED HILLS GOLF COURSE
PU—7101 Parallel Pkwy., Kansas City (913)334-1111.
Holes: 18. **Par:** 70/70.
Yards: 5,914/4,698. **Course rating:** 67.7/63.5. **Slope:** 119/107.
Opened: 1927. **Pace of Play rating:** 4:00. **Green fee:** $16/18.
Credit cards: MC, V. **Reduced fees:** Weekdays, Twilight, Seniors, Juniors.
Caddies: No. **Golf carts:** $20 for 18 holes.

Discount golf packages: No. **Season:** Year-round. **High:** April-Sept.
On-site lodging: No. **Rental clubs:** Yes.
Walking policy: Unrestricted walking. **Range:** Yes.
To obtain tee times: Call up to two days in advance.
Formerly known as Victory Hills.
Subscriber comments: Recently re-designed . . . Not a long course but you need to be a straight hitter, tight fairways and medium to small greens . . . Eight new golf holes, 17 new multi- level tee boxes, even new irrigation system . . . New layout will be better . . . New course is hands down the best in Kansas City.

★★ PAWNEE PRAIRIE GOLF COURSE
PU—1931 S. Tyler Rd., Wichita (316)721-7474.
Holes: 18. **Par:** 72/72.
Yards: 7,361/5,928. **Course rating:** 74.8/73.3. **Slope:** 123/119.
Opened: 1970. **Pace of Play rating:** 4:20. **Green fee:** $12.
Credit cards: None. **Reduced fees:** Twilight, Seniors, Juniors.
Caddies: No. **Golf carts:** $17 for 18 holes.
Discount golf packages: No. **Season:** Year-round. **High:** May-Sept.
On-site lodging: No. **Rental clubs:** Yes.
Walking policy: Unrestricted walking. **Range:** Yes (grass).
To obtain tee times: Call seven days in advance starting Sunday 3:30 p.m.
Subscriber comments: Long from the tips with plenty of trouble . . . Long with south wind . . . Course is too wide open, play is very slow . . . Huge greens . . . Good variety in holes, fast greens, terrific shape, driving range and large putting greens . . . Not much grass in fairways . . . Never reached it's potential . . . Staff friendly.

★★★½ QUAIL RIDGE GOLF COURSE
PU—3805 Quail Ridge Dr., Winfield (316)221-5645.
35 miles southeast of Wichita. **Holes:** 18. **Par:** 72/72.
Yards: 6,826/5,328. **Course rating:** 73.0/71.4. **Slope:** 130/130.
Opened: 1992. **Pace of Play rating:** 4:10. **Green fee:** $11/13.
Credit cards: MC, V, DISC. **Reduced fees:** Weekdays, Resort guests, Seniors, Juniors.
Caddies: No. **Golf carts:** $8 for 18 holes.
Discount golf packages: Yes. **Season:** Year-round. **High:** April-Oct.
On-site lodging: Yes. **Rental clubs:** Yes.
Walking policy: Unrestricted walking. **Range:** Yes (grass).
To obtain tee times: Call up to one week in advance for weekdays. Call on Monday starting 8 a.m. for following weekend.
Subscriber comments: Only a few years old but becoming one of the area's best . . . Best course in the area . . . Decent new course . . . Good course, great price, motel on property . . . Wow!! One of the best new courses in the midwest. A must . . . Links course, wide open fairways play good in the heat. Getting better all the time . . . A secret place but not for long, too nice . . . Excellent condition all year, pace good . . . Will be top-10 course in Kansas . . . Best public course in area . . . Super greens and fairways . . . Staff polite and friendly, promotes ready play, four hour rounds normal . . . Excellent summer condition. Not much weekday play . . . Best golfing value in Kansas.

★★★½ ROLLING MEADOWS GOLF COURSE
PU—7550 Old Milford Rd., Milford (913)238-4303.
60 miles west of Topeka. **Holes:** 18. **Par:** 72/72.
Yards: 6,879/5,515. **Course rating:** 74.0/70.7. **Slope:** 134/116.
Opened: 1981. **Pace of Play rating:** N/A. **Green fee:** $9/11.
Credit cards: MC, V. **Reduced fees:** Weekdays, Twilight.
Caddies: No. **Golf carts:** $8 for 18 holes.
Discount golf packages: Yes. **Season:** Year-round. **High:** April-Oct.
On-site lodging: No. **Rental clubs:** Yes.
Walking policy: Unrestricted walking. **Range:** Yes (grass).
To obtain tee times: Call Wednesday a.m. for following weekend.
Subscriber comments: Challenging and a bargain . . . Should play in

spring or fall, too hot in summer . . . One of nicest in area, a secret . . .
This is a sleeper, off the beaten path . . . Excellent course, poor range, small
clubhouse . . . Best value in Kansas . . . Never a crowd . . . This course has
water, trees, wind, distance, you name it . . . Summer dream, lots of
mosquitos . . . Great golf for middle of Kansas . . . Excellent staff willing
help you in any way possible. Never a delay . . . Great variety of holes, tees
for every ability . . . A plum . . . Not crowded, very well manicured,
greens excellent and fast . . . One green fee play all day . . . I can't believe I
waited this long to find it.

★★★½ SALINA MUNICIPAL GOLF CLUB
PU—2500 E. Crawford Street, Salina (913)826-7450.
Call club for further information.
Subscriber comments: Super track . . . Fairways among the best in
Kansas . . . Wide open with no real hazards . . . You must have a good
long game for this course . . . Long par 4s, large flat greens . . . Good
condition year round . . . Lot of holes same but fun . . . Very good
fairways even in summer heat . . . Set in hills and valleys, tough greens,
long . . . Helpful staff, busy . . . If you can't hit ball low forget it . . .
Windy.

★★ SIM PARK GOLF COURSE
PU—2020 W. Murdock, Wichita (316)337-9100.
Holes: 18. **Par:** 71/71.
Yards: 6,330/5,048. **Course rating:** 70.5/67.9. **Slope:** 119/103.
Opened: 1920. **Pace of Play rating:** 4:30. **Green fee:** $12.
Credit cards: None. **Reduced fees:** Twilight.
Caddies: No. **Golf carts:** $16 for 18 holes.
Discount golf packages: No. **Season:** Year-round. **High:** April-Sept.
On-site lodging: No. **Rental clubs:** Yes.
Walking policy: Unrestricted walking. **Range:** No.
To obtain tee times: Call pro shop.
Subscriber comments: Course has no water, few traps, 18-plus handicap
dream . . . Nice layout, easy to walk greens, can suffer from overplay . . .
Pace of play slow, service good . . . Course redone several years ago, a little
short but not too easy . . . 2nd best public course in Wichita . . . Absolutly
no water but still worth it . . . Difficult to obtain tee time on weekend . . .
Short course, not much trouble . . . Greens get rough in summer . . . A fun
course for weekend duffers . . . Shoot your low rounds here.

★★ ST. ANDREW'S GOLF COURSE
PU—11099 W. 135th St., Overland Park (913)897-3804.
10 miles south of Kansas City. **Holes:** 18. **Par:** 70/70.
Yards: 6,205/4,713. **Course rating:** 69.5/67.7. **Slope:** 109/108.
Opened: 1962. **Pace of Play rating:** N/A. **Green fee:** $11/13.
Credit cards: MC, V. **Reduced fees:** Twilight, Seniors, Juniors.
Caddies: No. **Golf carts:** $11 for 18 holes.
Discount golf packages: No. **Season:** Year-round. **High:** June-July.
On-site lodging: No. **Rental clubs:** Yes.
Walking policy: Unrestricted walking. **Range:** Yes(grass).
To obtain tee times: Call three days in advance.
Subscriber comments: Better course since front nine redesigned . . .
Impossible par 4s. Should be 72 par . . . Maintenance wonderful compared
to high volume play . . . Marshals are super and keep the pace moving.
Average times 4½ hours . . . Great for walking, conditioning good, odd
layout on back nine . . . Course always crowded . . . Redone front nine
now more interesting.

★★ STAGG HILL GOLF CLUB
PU—4441 Ft. Riley Blvd., Manhattan (913)539-1041.
130 miles west of Kansas City. **Holes:** 18. **Par:** 72/73.
Yards: 6,697/5,642. **Course rating:** 70.3/72.1. **Slope:** 112/117.
Opened: 1968. **Pace of Play rating:** 4:30. **Green fee:** $14/15.

Credit cards: MC, V, DISC. **Reduced fees:** Low season, Twilight, Juniors.
Caddies: No. **Golf carts:** $18 for 18 holes.
Discount golf packages: No. **Season:** Year-round. **High:** April-Oct.
On-site lodging: No. **Rental clubs:** Yes.
Walking policy: Unrestricted walking. **Range:** Yes.
To obtain tee times:
Members call Wednesday for tee times on Friday, Saturday and Sunday. Nonmembers call Thursday for Friday, Saturday and Sunday.
Subscriber comments: Has come back well since flood of 1993 covered course . . . Trees, doglegs, water, its a ball . . . Semi-tough . . . Better than it was . . . Both nines goes to the right, slicer's dream course . . . Bring your bug spray during spring months . . . Will take years to rebuild from flood.

★★★½ SUNFLOWER HILLS GOLF CLUB

PU—122 Riverview, Bonner Springs (913)721-2727.
15 miles west of Kansas City. **Holes:** 18. **Par:** 72/73.
Yards: 7,001/5,850. **Course rating:** 73.3/72.6. **Slope:** 124/124.
Opened: 1977. **Pace of Play rating:** N/A. **Green fee:** $9/15.
Credit cards: MC, V. **Reduced fees:** Weekdays, Twilight, Seniors, Juniors.
Caddies: No. **Golf carts:** $N/A for 18 holes.
Discount golf packages: No. **Season:** Year-round. **High:** April-Sept.
On-site lodging: No. **Rental clubs:** Yes.
Walking policy: Unrestricted walking. **Range:** Yes (grass).
To obtain tee times: Call four days in advance.
Subscriber comments: Very pretty, greens great, attentive staff . . . Good shop staff . . . Demands every club in the bag . . . Has country club appearance . . . Uses plenty of water, always green . . . Best buy in public golf in KC area . . . Long hilly course with some very challenging holes . . . May be best public course in KC metro area . . . When it's windy, it's wild . . . Very tough from blues, great layout, very good greens, large traps . . . Zoysia fairways need to be filled in . . . Great variety of shots . . . Wonderful, challenging, best public course in KC.

★★★★ TERRADYNE RESORT HOTEL AND COUNTRY CLUB

R—1400 Terradyne, Andover (316)733-5851.
10 miles east of Wichita. **Holes:** 18. **Par:** 71/71.
Yards: 6,704/5,048. **Course rating:** 74.3/70.2. **Slope:** 139/121.
Opened: 1987. **Pace of Play rating:** 4:00. **Green fee:** $25/75.
Credit cards: MC, V, AMEX. **Reduced fees:** Resort guests.
Caddies: Yes. **Golf carts:** $10 for 18 holes.
Discount golf packages: Yes. **Season:** Year-round. **High:** April-Oct.
On-site lodging: Yes. **Rental clubs:** Yes.
Walking policy: Unrestricted walking. **Range:** Yes (grass).
To obtain tee times: Resort guests call one week in advance.
Subscriber comments: Terrific course . . . Unusual seaside look using waist high prairie grass . . . Keeps me on my toes . . . Most demanding courses for shotmaking in Kansas . . . Bring extra balls, rough is outrageous . . . Scottish style that exacts a big penalty for those who don't keep it in the fairway . . . Penalized by deep rough . . . Pace of play fast . . . Very tough, semi- long . . . Target golf. Greens perfect. Fun to play if you are straight . . . Best conditioned course in state . . . Magnificent accomodations! Trouble everywhere . . . Love it and hate it. Better keep ball in fairway.

★½ TOMAHAWK HILLS GOLF CLUB

PU—17501 Midland Dr., Shawnee (913)631-8000.
5 miles south of Kansas City. **Holes:** 18. **Par:** 70/71.
Yards: 6,003/5,643. **Course rating:** 69.1/71.1. **Slope:** 118/117.
Opened: 1916. **Pace of Play rating:** N/A. **Green fee:** $15/17.
Credit cards: MC, V. **Reduced fees:** Weekdays, Twilight, Seniors, Juniors.

Caddies: No. **Golf carts:** $22 for 18 holes.
Discount golf packages: No. **Season:** Year-round. **High:** April-Oct.
On-site lodging: No. **Rental clubs:** Yes.
Walking policy: Unrestricted walking. **Range:** Yes (grass).
To obtain tee times: Call two days in advance.
Subscriber comments: Strange course in hills . . . Has two unique par 3s . . . Fairways and tees good, greens bumpy and rough . . . Most fun par 3s in town are 9th and 18th holes . . . Some course work being done . . . Unique bluff shots . . . A few interesting holes . . . Tough walking . . . Hilly and well kept, very scenic . . . Many blind shots . . . Established 1910, one of the oldest courses in continuous use in Kansas City area . . . Excellent value for money, good for short game . . . The staff is good, but best of all cold beer!

★★ TOPEKA PUBLIC GOLF CLUB
PU—2533 S.W. Urish Rd., Topeka (913)272-0511.
Holes: 18. **Par:** 71/71.
Yards: 6,335/5,468. **Course rating:** 70.0/70.1. **Slope:** 114/114.
Opened: 1954. **Pace of Play rating:** 4:00. **Green fee:** $9/11.
Credit cards: None. **Reduced fees:** Seniors, Juniors.
Caddies: No. **Golf carts:** $10 for 18 holes.
Discount golf packages: Yes. **Season:** Year-round. **High:** May-Sept.
On-site lodging: No. **Rental clubs:** Yes.
Walking policy: Unrestricted walking. **Range:** Yes (grass).
To obtain tee times: Call Tuesday after 7 a.m. for weekends and holidays only.
Subscriber comments: Flat prairie style course, hardly any scenery . . . Long lines on weekends . . . Well maintained, need more staff at clubhouse, busy . . . Fairways get very thin during warm months . . . Like putting on a thick shag rug . . . Pace can be slow but still fun . . . Average fairways and greens . . . You could lose a basket ball . . . Need some sand . . . Has some weird greens . . . Very enjoyable, wide open to roam, poor driving range . . . Par 3, No. 8 very tough . . . Long lines on weekends . . . Typical municipal course, women's tees not much help . . . Nice pace of play.

★★★½ TURKEY CREEK GOLF COURSE
PU—1000 Fox Run, McPherson (316)241-8530.
50 miles north of Wichita. **Holes:** 18. **Par:** 70/69.
Yards: 6,241/4,723. **Course rating:** 71.3/66.7. **Slope:** 125/112.
Opened: 1990. **Pace of Play rating:** N/A. **Green fee:** $10/12.
Credit cards: MC, V. **Reduced fees:** Weekdays.
Caddies: No. **Golf carts:** $16 for 18 holes.
Discount golf packages: No. **Season:** Year-round. **High:** April-Sept.
On-site lodging: No. **Rental clubs:** Yes.
Walking policy: Unrestricted walking. **Range:** Yes (grass).
To obtain tee times: Call one week in advance for weekdays. Weekends and holidays call the Wednesday before.
Subscriber comments: Interesting layout, three or four great holes . . . Nice new course, personable staff . . . Lots of water, fairly short . . . Strong value on shot placement . . . Call ahead if it rains because course is subject to flooding . . . Coming back from floods of 1993. Was once super, and may be again sometime soon . . . Great shape and excellent greens . . . Water everywhere, challenging, tight, must be able to hit long irons for many approach shots . . . World's best cart paths . . . Tee boxes need to be leveled and grass added . . . Short but tough . . . Best kept secret in Kansas! A target golf course with lots of water . . . Short and tough.

★★½ VILLAGE GREENS GOLF COURSE
PU—Box 1, Ozawkie (913)876-2255.
Call club for further information.
Subscriber comments: Golf in the country . . . One of best values in area, crowded early . . . They need to take tee times, at least on weekends . . . Very good course . . . Excellent care and being improved each year . . . Poor man's country club. Family atmosphere . . . Love those par 5s . . .

KANSAS

Paradise in the boonies, few amenities but free coffee . . . Friendly owner working hard on improvements . . . Good course if you don't mind waiting an hour to tee off . . . A place to getaway . . . This guy has done a great job!

★★½ WELLINGTON GOLF CLUB

PU—1500 West Harvey, Wellington (316)326-7904.
28 miles south of Wichita. **Holes:** 18. **Par:** 70/70.
Yards: 6,201/5,384. **Course rating:** 70.5/70.9. **Slope:** 135/113.
Opened: 1919. **Pace of Play rating:** N/A. **Green fee:** $10/12.
Credit cards: MC, V. **Reduced fees:** Weekdays, Twilight.
Caddies: No. **Golf carts:** $14 for 18 holes.
Discount golf packages: No. **Season:** Year-round. **High:** April-Sept.
On-site lodging: No. **Rental clubs:** Yes.
Walking policy: Unrestricted walking. **Range:** Yes(grass).
To obtain tee times: Call up to one week in advance.
Subscriber comments: Good city course . . . Excellent pro and staff friendly and accommodating . . . Flat course . . . Nice bluegrass fairways . . . Greens too fast for hackers . . . Very small greens . . . Short but tough layout, newly installed sprinkler system . . . One of the toughest public tracks, elevated pancake greens, shortgame tester.

★★ WESTERN HILLS GOLF CLUB

SP—8533 S. W. 21st. Street, Topeka (913)478-4000.
Holes: 18. **Par:** 70/70.
Yards: 6,089/4,728. **Course rating:** 69.2/66.1. **Slope:** 121/110.
Opened: 1967. **Pace of Play rating:** 4:00-4:30. **Green fee:** $11/13.
Credit cards: All major. **Reduced fees:** Juniors.
Caddies: No. **Golf carts:** $10 for 18 holes.
Discount golf packages: No. **Season:** Year-round. **High:** April-Sept.
On-site lodging: No. **Rental clubs:** Yes.
Walking policy: Unrestricted walking. **Range:** No.
To obtain tee times: Call Wednesday for weekend tee time.
Subscriber comments: Short'n-sweet, watch out for geese . . . Good par 3s, easy to walk, good public course . . . Was a good semi-private, went public . . . Higher fees offset by faster play . . . Straightforward first nine. Challenging back nine . . . New sprinkler system has helped. Great greens . . . Staff OK, four hour round . . . Excellent facilities . . . Nothing special about this course . . . Could use better groundskeeping . . . Hackers will love this place . . . Several short par 4s, lots of water and sand . . . One of the better courses in Topeka area.

★★★½ WILLOW BEND GOLF CLUB

SP—8001 E. Mulberry, Wichita (316)636-4653.
Call club for further information
Subscriber comments: Tom Weiskopf course . . . Good long course . . . Great character . . . Plays better than it looks . . . Wide open, pace of play slow . . . Great layout, super condition and facility . . . Best course in Wichita, very beautiful landscape . . . Staff very helpful . . . Great service, very few trees come into play . . . Best practice facility in area . . . Tough course in spring and fall when rough is high . . . Driving range and great putting green . . . Shorter holes require deft shotmaking . . . Well equipped pro shop, terrific layout, beautiful condition, sculpture on each hole.

LOUISIANA

BAYOU OAKS GOLF COURSES

PU—1040 Filmore, New Orleans (504)483-9396.
Credit cards: None. **Reduced fees:** Twilight, Seniors, Juniors.
Caddies: No. **Golf carts:** $8 for 18 holes.
Discount golf packages: No. **Season:** Year-round. **High:** April-June/
Sept.-Oct.
On-site lodging: No. **Rental clubs:** Yes.
Walking policy: Unrestricted walking. **Range:** Yes (grass).
To obtain tee times: Call one day in advance for weekends and holidays.
Weekdays, first come, first served.
Also has an 18–hole par-68 Little Course.

★½ LAKESIDE COURSE

Holes: 18. **Par:** 70/70.
Yards: 6,054/5,872. **Course rating:** 68.5/70.5. **Slope:** 110/103.
Opened: 1936. **Pace of Play rating:** 4:00-4:30. **Green fee:** $9/11.
Subscriber comments: Beginners course full of beginners . . . Flat, open,
short, not well maintained . . . Pace of play slow . . . Not much variety,
mostly straight holes . . . Very monotonous . . . No sand in traps . . .
Greens inconsistent. Tee boxes not level . . . Pace of play extremely slow,
needs course marshal to correct . . . Good service, friendly professionals,
outstanding teaching areas and personnel.

★★★ CHAMPIONSHIP COURSE

Holes: 18. **Par:** 72/72.
Yards: 7,061/6,013. **Course rating:** 71.5/73.3. **Slope:** 116/118.
Opened: 1936. **Pace of Play rating:** 4:00-4:30. **Green fee:** $12/17.
Subscriber comments: Best of three municipal courses . . . Good public
course, high traffic, slow . . . Pace of play needs improvements, better
ranger patrols. Needs better yardage marks . . . Slow players should stay
away . . . Staff is very courteous . . . Needs fairway bunkers . . . Beautiful
oak trees . . . The work they are doing is paying off.

★★½ WISNER COURSE

Holes: 18. **Par:** 72/72.
Yards: 6,465/5,707. **Course rating:** 70.5/71.8. **Slope:** 111/116.
Opened: 1936. **Pace of Play rating:** 4:00-4:30. **Green fee:** $9/11.
Subscriber comments: Good course, worth the price . . . Many tree-lined
fairways, second best of three courses . . . Great variety, good bargain, gets
crowded . . . Similar to the championship course but less interesting . . .
Good service, friendly professionals . . . Tougher than championship
course for scoring . . . Trees all shots . . . Great for walking . . . Great staff
. . . Does not drain well, should be avoided in rainy season . . . Hard as a
brick on a swamp.

★★★ BELLE TERRE COUNTRY CLUB

SP—111 Fairway Dr., La Place (504)652-5000.
30 miles west of New Orleans. **Holes:** 18. **Par:** 72/72.
Yards: 6,840/5,510. **Course rating:** 72.2/71.6. **Slope:** 130/113.
Opened: 1977. **Pace of Play rating:** 3:30. **Green fee:** $27/38.
Credit cards: MC, V, AMEX. **Reduced fees:** Weekdays.
Caddies: No. **Golf carts:** Included in Green Fee.
Discount golf packages: No. **Season:** Year-round. **High:** April-Oct.
On-site lodging: No. **Rental clubs:** Yes.
Walking policy: Mandatory cart. **Range:** Yes (grass).
To obtain tee times: Call four days in advance for nonmembers.
Subscriber comments: Good layout through bayou . . . Last three holes
on both nines into wind and tough . . . Beautiful course that can run a little
expensive . . . Excellent layout, shaded greens are not usually in top
condition . . . Swampy when wet . . . Course run down, bare areas, bad
bunkers . . . Beautiful, well-kept, fast greens . . . Good fairways . . . Some
houses too close to the course . . . Very tough the first time . . . Has
declined some in maintenance . . . Very flat and lots of water . . . Very
picturesque . . . Challenging layout and plenty of water and sand. Good
staff and facilities. Only play back tees if you are a good ball striker . . .
Water, water, water . . . A real gem.

★★★★½ BLUFFS ON THOMPSON CREEK GOLF CLUB

R—Hwy. 965 and Freeland Rd., St. Francisville (504)634-5551.
25 miles north of Baton Rouge. **Holes:** 18. **Par:** 72/72.
Yards: 7,143/4,813. **Course rating:** 74.6/69.0. **Slope:** 143/123.
Opened: 1989. **Pace of Play rating:** 4:30. **Green fee:** $28/55.
Credit cards: All major. **Reduced fees:** Weekdays, Low season, Resort
guests, Twilight.
Caddies: No. **Golf carts:** $12 for 18 holes.
Discount golf packages: Yes. **Season:** Year-round. **High:** Spring/Fall.
On-site lodging: Yes. **Rental clubs:** Yes.
Walking policy: Walking at certain times. **Range:** Yes (grass).
To obtain tee times: Call four days in advance for weekdays and
Thursday after noon for weekends.
Ranked 3rd in Louisiana by Golf Digest.
Subscriber comments: Very demanding Arnold Palmer design . . .
Beautiful scenery, great course, real challenge, too expensive . . . Maybe
best in state . . . No. 17 is awesome . . . God created it, Palmer unveiled it.
Hated to leave . . . Outstanding hidden gem. This can't be Louisiana . . .
Must be a creative putter . . . Greens are pro quality. A lot of deceiving
elevation changes. Well marked for yardages . . . Very nice course on hills
which is unusual for south Louisiana . . . Wonderful design . . . Unusual
property . . . Bring your tee ball . . . One of my favorites. A good deal . . .
Finest course in Louisiana . . . Scenery makes even a bad round enjoyable
. . . A bit expensive but worth it . . . The best public course in Louisiana
. . . Perfect setting for a golf course. Tree-lined fairways and large greens
. . . Always well groomed, worth every penny . . . Best layout in Baton
Rouge area.

★ BRECHTEL GOLF COURSE

PU—3700 Behrman Place, New Orleans (504)362-4761.
Holes: 18. **Par:** 70/70.
Yards: 6,065/5,556. **Course rating:** 66.0/N/A. **Slope:** 97/N/A.
Opened: 1965. **Pace of Play rating:** 3:30. **Green fee:** $8.
Credit cards: None. **Reduced fees:** Twilight, Seniors, Juniors.
Caddies: No. **Golf carts:** $6 for 18 holes.
Discount golf packages: No. **Season:** Year-round. **High:** April-Oct.
On-site lodging: No. **Rental clubs:** Yes.
Walking policy: Unrestricted walking. **Range:** Yes.
To obtain tee times: First come, first served.
Subscriber comments: Course very short but fun . . . Cheap and pace of
play is good . . . Good shape, friendly people, helpful . . . Interesting public
course . . . Improve 10th hole and whole course improves . . . Some
character . . . Could use a lot of work, tees, traps, greens so-so . . . Would
not mind cost increase if kept up.

★½ CHENNAULT PARK GOLF COURSE

PU—8475 Millhaven Rd., Monroe (318)329-2454.
Holes: 18. **Par:** 72/72.
Yards: 7,044/5,783. **Course rating:** N/A. **Slope:** 118/109.
Opened: N/A. **Pace of Play rating:** N/A. **Green fee:** N/A.
Credit cards: N/A. **Reduced fees:** N/A.
Caddies: No. **Golf carts:** $N/A for 18 holes.
Discount golf packages: No. **Season:** Year-round. **High:** May-Sept.
On-site lodging: No. **Rental clubs:** No.
Walking policy: N/A. **Range:** Yes (grass).
Subscriber comments: Long muny course with great potential for
improvement . . . Year-round, reasonably priced . . . Many trees and water
hazards . . . Needs traps, better physical management . . . Being renovated
. . . Not a bad layout.

★★★½ EASTOVER COUNTRY CLUB

R—5690 Eastover Rd., New Orleans (504)245-7347.
Call club for further information.
Subscriber comments: Fine Joe Lee course, well laid out . . . Begin to feel

like going in a circle. Half the holes are dogleg left . . . Very good course, friendly staff, best layout in area, good value . . . Nothing to brag about but fun to play . . . Solid course with water, sand . . . Spacious layout . . . Links-type course., very interesting . . . Errant shot will find homes . . . Marvelous grass . . . White tees very fair for short hitter . . . Flat, long, medium-fast greens . . . Course crowded most of time . . . Best course in New Orleans.

★ HOWELL PARK GOLF COURSE
PU—5511 Winbourne Ave., Baton Rouge (504)357-9292.
Holes: 18. **Par:** 70/70.
Yards: 5,779/4,577. **Course rating:** 67.6/N/A. **Slope:** N/A.
Opened: 1956. **Pace of Play rating:** 4:00. **Green fee:** $5.
Credit cards: MC, V. **Reduced fees:** Twilight, Juniors.
Caddies: No. **Golf carts:** $14 for 18 holes.
Discount golf packages: No. **Season:** Year-round. **High:** March-Sept.
On-site lodging: No. **Rental clubs:** Yes.
Walking policy: Unrestricted walking. **Range:** No.
To obtain tee times: Call for weekends only.
Subscriber comments: Very easy course . . . Hard greens won't hold a wedge shot . . . Some holes a mite short. Creek is interesting diversion . . . Cheap round of golf, hardly ever crowded, short course . . . Better grass in my yard . . . Will do in a rush.

★★½ HUNTINGTON PARK GOLF COURSE
PU—8300 Pines Rd., Shreveport (318)673-7765.
Holes: 18. **Par:** 72/74.
Yards: 7,294/6,171. **Course rating:** 73.3/74.7. **Slope:** N/A.
Opened: 1969. **Pace of Play rating:** N/A. **Green fee:** $10/13.
Credit cards: MC, V. **Reduced fees:** Weekdays, Twilight, Seniors, Juniors.
Caddies: No. **Golf carts:** $8 for 18 holes.
Discount golf packages: No. **Season:** Year-round. **High:** May-Sept.
On-site lodging: No. **Rental clubs:** Yes.
Walking policy: Unrestricted walking. **Range:** Yes (grass).
To obtain tee times: Call or come in on Thursday at 7 a.m. for upcoming weekend. Weekdays, first come, first served.
Subscriber comments: Long and hilly course, but from the gold tees very enjoyable for shorter hitters . . . Good practice green . . . Back and forth across a ditch . . . Flat, no sand, some water . . . Pace of play good. Good treatment by staff . . . Greens need work . . . Could be a lot nicer with care.

★★½ LES VIEUX CHENES GOLF CLUB
PU—Rte. 2C, Box 15 GC, Youngsville (318)837-1159.
9 miles south of Lafayette. **Holes:** 18. **Par:** 72/74.
Yards: 6,900/5,600. **Course rating:** 70.1/69.1. **Slope:** 119/113.
Opened: 1977. **Pace of Play rating:** 4:30. **Green fee:** $8.
Credit cards: MC, V, AMEX. **Reduced fees:** Twilight, Seniors, Juniors.
Caddies: No. **Golf carts:** $13 for 18 holes.
Discount golf packages: No. **Season:** Year-round. **High:** June-Sept.
On-site lodging: No. **Rental clubs:** No.
Walking policy: Unrestricted walking. **Range:** Yes (grass).
To obtain tee times: Call two days in advance.

Subscriber comments: Average public course but never in very good shape and play is ridiculously slow at times . . . Good course but very crowded and slow, service is friendly . . . Not much character . . . Can't beat the price. Big, well manicured greens. Very tough finishing hole . . . Tough to get tee times . . . Needs more work on drainage . . . Some holes too close to others, ouch! . . . Good course, good value, good location.

★★★½ MALLARD COVE GOLF COURSE
PU—Chennault Air Base, Lake Charles (318)491-1204.
125 miles west of Baton Rouge. **Holes:** 18. **Par:** 72/72.
Yards: 6,903/5,294. **Course rating:** 72.4/70.1. **Slope:** 125/117.

Opened: 1976. **Pace of Play rating:** 4:00. **Green fee:** $10/13.
Credit cards: None. **Reduced fees:** Weekdays, Twilight, Seniors, Juniors.
Caddies: No. **Golf carts:** $14 for 18 holes.
Discount golf packages: No. **Season:** Year-round. **High:** April-Oct.
On-site lodging: No. **Rental clubs:** Yes.
Walking policy: Unrestricted walking. **Range:** Yes (grass).
To obtain tee times: Call or come in 48 hours in advance.
Subscriber comments: Excellent all around course . . . Extremely long.
Brutally hot in the summer (no shade) . . . Nice fairways . . . Very good
test from championship tees . . . One of the finest public courses . . .
Course looks run down. Could be showplace . . . Great fairways. Hard
greens and poor sand traps . . . Water and sand in play on 15 holes . . .
Course needs marshals . . . Fast pace of play for crowded course . . . Best
suited for long hitters . . . The staff is great and pace of play about 3½
hours. Challenge results from length and Bermuda rough, contoured
greens.

★★★½ OAK HARBOR GOLF CLUB

PU—201 Oak Harbor Blvd., Slidell (504)646-0110.
25 miles east of New Orleans. **Holes:** 18. **Par:** 72/72.
Yards: 6,896/5,305. **Course rating:** 72.7/70.0. **Slope:** 132/118.
Opened: 1991. **Pace of Play rating:** 4:30. **Green fee:** $30/38.
Credit cards: MC, V. **Reduced fees:** Twilight, Juniors.
Caddies: No. **Golf carts:** Included in Green Fee.
Discount golf packages: Yes. **Season:** Year-round. **High:** April-July.
On-site lodging: No. **Rental clubs:** Yes.
Walking policy: Mandatory cart. **Range:** Yes (grass).
To obtain tee times: Call seven days in advance.
Subscriber comments: Open, straightaway, links style . . . Needs a
clubhouse, good course, good value . . . Too much water and out-of-
bounds every hole . . . Almost no pro shop to speak of . . . Plays long with
wind . . . Best course for public in the area . . . Deep bunkers, fast greens,
very fair from the blues, very harsh from the golds. Wind off the lake is
always a factor. Slicers need plenty of water balls . . . Lots of blind shots.
Not in good condition . . . Thinking player's course . . . Plenty of steep-
faced fairway bunkers. Good staff and practice area . . . Mounds, mounds,
everywhere . . . With money and attention this course may become an
outstanding layout.

★½ QUERBES PARK GOLF COURSE

PU—3500 Beverly Place, Shreveport (318)673-7773.
Holes: 18. **Par:** 71/71.
Yards: 6,207/5,360. **Course rating:** 69.0/70.0. **Slope:** 118/110.
Opened: 1992. **Pace of Play rating:** N/A. **Green fee:** $12.
Credit cards: MC, V. **Reduced fees:** Weekdays, Twilight, Seniors,
Juniors.
Caddies: No. **Golf carts:** $16 for 18 holes.
Discount golf packages: No. **Season:** Year-round. **High:** N/A.
On-site lodging: No. **Rental clubs:** Yes.
Walking policy: Unrestricted walking. **Range:** Yes (grass).
To obtain tee times: Call pro shop.
Subscriber comments: Tight old course . . . Poor condition, crowded
and slow . . . Good course for seniors, no water, no traps, very hard greens
. . . Chip-and-putt course . . . Old course with lots of walkers . . . Fun to
play . . . Nice easy pace for playing . . . Small pro shop, staff is helpful and
courteous.

★★★½ SANTA MARIA GOLF COURSE

PU—19301 Old Perkins Rd., Baton Rouge (504)752-9667.
Holes: 18. **Par:** 72/72.
Yards: 7,051/5,267. **Course rating:** 72.9/69.6. **Slope:** 124/120.
Opened: 1986. **Pace of Play rating:** 4:15. **Green fee:** $16/20.
Credit cards: MC, V. **Reduced fees:** Twilight, Seniors, Juniors.
Caddies: No. **Golf carts:** $8 for 18 holes.

Discount golf packages: No. **Season:** Year-round. **High:** April-Oct.
On-site lodging: No. **Rental clubs:** No.
Walking policy: Unrestricted walking. **Range:** Yes (grass).
To obtain tee times: Call up to seven days in advance.
Subscriber comments: Wonderful, challenging, beautiful . . . R.T. Jones
layout . . . Greens hard, not very receptive. Sand traps are dirt pits at best
. . . Could not find yardage markers . . . Some short par 4s are repetitive
. . . Well designed, large greens . . . Range good, needs new balls . . .
Warm and friendly staff . . . No. 15 is great . . . Good pace, good service
. . . Most underrated course in Louisiana . . . Recommend turkey sandwich
at concession stand . . . Some hills and trees . . . Nice clubhouse facility . . .
Multiple tees so you can pick your poison . . . Plenty of sharp teeth . . .
Love the trees, fairways, sand and greens, hate the bayou! . . . Forget your
wedges, must bump and run on rock hard fairways.

★★½ TORO HILLS LODGE

R—P.O. Box 460, Florien (318)586-4661.
72 miles northwest of Alexandria. **Holes:** 18. **Par:** 72/72.
Yards: 6,550/6,300. **Course rating:** N/A. **Slope:** 120/118.
Opened: N/A. **Pace of Play rating:** N/A. **Green fee:** N/A.
Credit cards: All major. **Reduced fees:** Weekdays.
Caddies: No. **Golf carts:** $18 for 18 holes.
Discount golf packages: Yes. **Season:** Year-round. **High:** April-Sept.
On-site lodging: Yes. **Rental clubs:** Yes.
Walking policy: N/A. **Range:** Yes (grass).
Subscriber comments: All trees . . . Toughest finishing holes in state
(nine and 18) . . . Course is very well taken care of, it's hilly and very
difficult to play, the course is located in an isolated area, the staff is
courteous and the facilities are great . . . Very scenic . . . Too many short
doglegs . . . Fast greens . . . A course for good players . . . Dining and
lodging need upgrading . . . Leave driver at home . . . Good quick pace,
good condition considering all the trees, hills and water, tough course . . .
You pay for practically every mistake.

★ WEBB MEMORIAL GOLF COURSE

PU—1352 Country Club Dr., Baton Rouge (504)383-4919.
Holes: 18. **Par:** 72/72.
Yards: 6,412/5,442. **Course rating:** 70.1/70.3. **Slope:** 120/N/A.
Opened: 1932. **Pace of Play rating:** 4:00. **Green fee:** $6.
Credit cards: MC, V. **Reduced fees:** Twilight, Juniors.
Caddies: No. **Golf carts:** $13 for 18 holes.
Discount golf packages: No. **Season:** Year-round. **High:** May-Aug.
On-site lodging: No. **Rental clubs:** Yes.
Walking policy: Unrestricted walking. **Range:** No.
To obtain tee times: Call up to three days in advance.
Subscriber comments: Fun design, crowded, slow pace, parts of fairway
without grass on sides, yardage not always well marked, tee boxes not well
kept up . . . Old, established public course, overplayed, fair shape,
inexpensive . . . Must improve everywhere . . . Some greens too small . . .
Good service, good carts . . . Cheap round of golf, perfect for practice . . .
Clubhouse facilities could be cleaner . . . Greens take too much abuse . . .
Worn out, plenty of play, but for six bucks, what do you expect?

MICHIGAN

★★½ A-GA-MING GOLF CLUB
PU—McLachlan Rd., Kewadin (616)264-5081, (800)678-0122.
22 miles northeast of Traverse City. **Holes:** 18. **Par:** 72/73.
Yards: 6,663/5,125. **Course rating:** 73.2/69.2. **Slope:** 133/124.
Opened: 1986. **Pace of Play rating:** 4:34. **Green fee:** $29.
Credit cards: All major. **Reduced fees:** Low season, Resort guests,
Twilight, Juniors.
Caddies: No. **Golf carts:** $12 for 18 holes.
Discount golf packages: Yes. **Season:** April-Oct. **High:** July-Sept.
On-site lodging: Yes. **Rental clubs:** Yes.
Walking policy: Walking at certain times. **Range:** Yes (grass).
To obtain tee times: Call in advance.
Subscriber comments: Lots of terrain, great views of the lake. A couple
of funny holes . . . Too tricked up . . . Back nine has breathtaking holes
. . . Great views of Torch Lake . . . Each hole is different . . . Better the
second time around . . . Torch Lake is a nice backdrop . . . Good greens
. . . Beautifully landscaped . . . Some strange holes. I'm not impressed . . .
Simply gorgeous . . . Excellent layout except for the 16th . . . Take clubs
and your camera . . . Views are unbelievable . . . Good start and finish, so-
so middle . . . Gimmicky.

ALPENA GOLF CLUB★
PU—1135 Golf Course Rd., Alpena (517)354-5052.
250 miles north of Detroit. **Holes:** 18. **Par:** 71/71.
Yards: 6,407/5,048. **Course rating:** 70.5/69.0. **Slope:** 120/113.
Opened: 1934. **Pace of Play rating:** N/A. **Green fee:** $17/22.
Credit cards: MC, V. **Reduced fees:** Resort guests, Seniors, Juniors.
Caddies: No. **Golf carts:** $17 for 18 holes.
Discount golf packages: Yes. **Season:** April-Oct. **High:** July-Aug.
On-site lodging: No. **Rental clubs:** Yes.
Walking policy: Unrestricted walking. **Range:** Yes (grass).
To obtain tee times: Call.

★★★½ ANTRIM DELLS GOLF CLUB
PU—Rt. No. 1, Box 108, Ellsworth (616)599-2679.
35 miles north of Traverse City. **Holes:** 18. **Par:** 72/72.
Yards: 6,606/5,493. **Course rating:** N/A. **Slope:** 125/121.
Opened: N/A. **Pace of Play rating:** N/A. **Green fee:** N/A.
Credit cards: MC, V. **Reduced fees:** Low season, Twilight.
Caddies: No. **Golf carts:** Included in Green Fee.
Discount golf packages: No. **Season:** April-Oct. **High:** July-Aug.
On-site lodging: No. **Rental clubs:** No.
Walking policy: N/A. **Range:** Yes (grass).
Subscriber comments: Hard-surfaced greens . . . Second nine a real treat
. . . Scenic, helpful, friendly staff . . . Three good opening holes, two best
finishing holes in Michigan . . . Challenging course . . . A visual delight
. . . A million pines . . . Design much better than average . . . Always have
fun on this course . . . Very pretty . . . Wonderful contrast between front
and back nines . . . Very walkable . . . Back nine more interesting.

★½ ARROWHEAD GOLF CLUB
PU—2797 Lapeer Rd., Auburn Hills (313)373-6860.
Call club for further information.
Subscriber comments: Too many players allowed at once . . . No sand,
no water . . . Convenient at best . . . Not an exciting course, but the
fairways were in great shape . . . No challenge . . . Holes too close together
. . . Affected by climatic extremes . . . Nothing spectacular.

★★ BALD MOUNTAIN GOLF COURSE
PU—3350 Kern Rd., Lake Orion (810)373-1110.
25 miles north of Detroit. **Holes:** 18. **Par:** 71/72.
Yards: 6,624/5,775. **Course rating:** 71.2/72.9. **Slope:** 120/120.
Opened: 1929. **Pace of Play rating:** 4:15. **Green fee:** $19/24.
Credit cards: All major. **Reduced fees:** Low season, Twilight.
Caddies: No. **Golf carts:** $20 for 18 holes.

Discount golf packages: No. **Season:** April-Nov. **High:** May-Sept.
On-site lodging: No. **Rental clubs:** No.
Walking policy: Unrestricted walking. **Range:** Yes (grass).
To obtain tee times: Call one day in advance for weekdays and seven days in advance for weekends and holidays.
Subscriber comments: Greens could use some work . . . Wilfred Reid a real treasure . . . Nothing outstanding, a nice relaxing atmosphere . . . Nice elevation . . . Nice. Slight challenge . . . Great terrain . . . Good solid course . . . Need to restore traps . . . Challenging but forgiving. A very open course.

★★½ BAY COUNTY GOLF COURSE

PU—584 Hampton Rd., Essexville (517)892-2161.
6 miles northeast of Bay City. **Holes:** N/A. **Par:** 72/74.
Yards: 6,557/5,706. **Course rating:** 71.3/72.4. **Slope:** 113/114.
Opened: 1966. **Pace of Play rating:** 4:00. **Green fee:** $14/15.
Credit cards: MC, V. **Reduced fees:** Weekdays, Seniors, Juniors.
Caddies: No. **Golf carts:** $18 for 18 holes.
Discount golf packages: No. **Season:** March-Dec. **High:** May-Aug.
On-site lodging: No. **Rental clubs:** Yes.
Walking policy: Unrestricted walking. **Range:** Yes (grass).
To obtain tee times: Tee times accepted for weekends and holidays. Call Tuesday from 7:30 a.m. to noon. Call or come in person after noon on Tuesday. Reservations taken for 18 holes and foursomes only.
Subscriber comments: Awesome views . . . Very flat, many parallel fairways . . . Flat, lifeless course . . . No easy holes . . . Well-kept for a county-supported course . . . Nice attitude by the staff . . . Can be cold and windy, especially in the spring. Gets winds right off the bay.

★★★ BAY VALLEY GOLF CLUB

R—2470 Old Bridge Rd., Bay City (517)686-5400, (800)292-5028.
5 miles south of Bay City. **Holes:** 18. **Par:** 71/71.
Yards: 6,610/5,151. **Course rating:** 71.3/68.5. **Slope:** 125/114.
Opened: 1973. **Pace of Play rating:** 4:00. **Green fee:** $46/54.
Credit cards: All major. **Reduced fees:** Weekdays, Low season.
Caddies: No. **Golf carts:** Included in Green Fee.
Discount golf packages: No. **Season:** April-Oct. **High:** June-Sept.
On-site lodging: Yes. **Rental clubs:** Yes.
Walking policy: Mandatory cart. **Range:** Yes (grass).
To obtain tee times: Call in advance.
Subscriber comments: What a course! . . . Generally right-to-left . . . A few great holes . . . Much water . . . Beautiful course with rolling hills . . . A step above. Facilities are getting old, run-down . . . Blind holes with water . . . Too much water . . . Good resort course, a little overpriced . . . Early Nicklaus/Muirhead course . . . Condition needs work . . . Water on 13 holes . . . Best layout in the area, but traps need work . . . Nice place for business and golf.

★★★½ BEDFORD VALLEY GOLF COURSE

PU—23161 Waubascon Rd., Battle Creek (616)965-3384.
Holes: 18. **Par:** 71/72.
Yards: 6,876/5,104. **Course rating:** 73.8/70.0. **Slope:** 135/119.
Opened: 1966. **Pace of Play rating:** 4:15. **Green fee:** $23/26.
Credit cards: MC, V. **Reduced fees:** Weekdays, Low season, Resort guests, Twilight, Juniors.
Caddies: No. **Golf carts:** $11 for 18 holes.
Discount golf packages: Yes. **Season:** April-Nov. **High:** May-Aug..
On-site lodging: No. **Rental clubs:** Yes.
Walking policy: Walking at certain times. **Range:** Yes (grass).
To obtain tee times: Call.
Subscriber comments: Old, established course . . . Exceptional public course . . . Traditional golf . . . Long par 3s with well-placed bunkers . . . Not much water but tough enough . . . Competitive . . . Lots of bunkers . . . Huge greens . . . Large greens . . . Beautiful, tough par 3s . . . Hard

course to find but worth looking for . . . No tricks, straight golf . . . The BIG course . . . Huge greens, huge bunkers, huge trees. A true championship course.

★★★★ BELVEDERE GOLF CLUB

SP—Ellsworth Rd., Charlevoix. (616)547-2611.
40 miles northeast of Traverse City. **Holes:** 18. **Par:** 72/74.
Yards: 6,715/5,629. **Course rating:** 72.1/72.9. **Slope:** 124/124.
Opened: 1927. **Pace of Play rating:** 4:00. **Green fee:** $30/55.
Credit cards: MC, V. **Reduced fees:** Weekdays, Low season, Resort guests, Twilight.
Caddies: Yes. **Golf carts:** $11 for 18 holes.
Discount golf packages: Yes. **Season:** April-Oct. **High:** July-Aug.
On-site lodging: No. **Rental clubs:** No.
Walking policy: Unrestricted walking. **Range:** Yes (grass).
To obtain tee times: Call.
Subscriber comments: Nice greens, great shaped fairways, beautiful . . . A northern Michigan treasure . . . Scottish tradition . . . The most underrated course in northwest Michigan . . . Nearly as good as Crystal Downs . . . A great old course . . . Always treated well . . . Good old-fashioned course . . . Small greens . . . Requires good tee shots.

★ BENT PINE GOLF CLUB

PU—2480 Duck Lake Rd., Whitehall (616)766-2045.
8 miles north of Muskegon. **Holes:** 18. **Par:** 71/72.
Yards: 6,007/5,429. **Course rating:** N/A. **Slope:** N/A.
Opened: 1970. **Pace of Play rating:** 4:00. **Green fee:** $8/13.
Credit cards: None. **Reduced fees:** Weekdays, Low season, Seniors, Juniors.

Caddies: No. **Golf carts:** $8 for 18 holes.
Discount golf packages: No. **Season:** March-Nov. **High:** May-Sept..
On-site lodging: No. **Rental clubs:** Yes.
Walking policy: Unrestricted walking. **Range:** No.
To obtain tee times: Call.
Subscriber comments: Ten pounds in a five-pound bag. Always have a fear of getting hit . . . Limited golf experience . . . A shooting gallery . . . You have to dodge other golf balls . . . Was an old airstrip . . . New changes a real improvement . . . Some trees, but mostly open.

★★★ BINDER PARK GOLF COURSE

PU—6723 B Drive S., Battle Creek (616)966-3459.
Holes: 18. **Par:** 72/75.

Yards: 6,328/4,965. **Course rating:** 69.9/68.4. **Slope:** 114/109.
Opened: 1962. **Pace of Play rating:** 4:20. **Green fee:** $12/13.
Credit cards: None. **Reduced fees:** Seniors, Juniors.
Caddies: No. **Golf carts:** $19 for 18 holes.
Discount golf packages: Yes. **Season:** April-Oct. **High:** June-Aug.
On-site lodging: No. **Rental clubs:** Yes.
Walking policy: Unrestricted walking. **Range:** No.
To obtain tee times: Call.
Subscriber comments: Some great golf holes . . . Scenic, playable, and challenging . . . Seasoned course, beautiful setting . . . Brutal when the wind blows . . . Superb green fees . . . Can be busy.

★½ BLOSSOM TRAILS GOLF COURSE

SP—1565 E. Britain Ave., Benton Harbor (616)925-4951.
90 miles east of Chicago. **Holes:** 18. **Par:** 70/70.
Yards: 5,980/4,957. **Course rating:** 68.3/N/A. **Slope:** 121/118.
Opened: 1959. **Pace of Play rating:** 3:30-4:00. **Green fee:** $16/18.
Credit cards: MC, V, DISC. **Reduced fees:** Weekdays, Low season.
Caddies: No. **Golf carts:** $9 for 18 holes.
Discount golf packages: No. **Season:** March-Nov. **High:** May-Aug.
On-site lodging: No. **Rental clubs:** Yes.
Walking policy: Unrestricted walking. **Range:** Yes (grass).

To obtain tee times: Call.

Subscriber comments: Short but interesting. A duffers' course . . . Set among apple trees on the back nine . . . Cheap to play . . . For the average golfer.

BOYNE HIGHLANDS RESORT

R—600 Highland Dr., Harbor Springs (616)526-3029x182, (800)462-6963. 6 miles north of Petoskey.
Credit cards: MC, V, AMEX.
Caddies: No. **Golf carts:** Included in Green Fee.
Discount golf packages: Yes. **Season:** May–Oct. **High:** June-Aug.
On-site lodging: Yes. **Rental clubs:** Yes.
Walking policy: Mandatory cart. **Range:** Yes (grass).
To obtain tee times: All anytime.

★★★★ DONALD ROSS MEMORIAL COURSE

Holes: 18. **Par:** 72/72.
Yards: 6,840/4,977. **Course rating:** 73.4/68.5. **Slope:** 132/119.
Opened: 1985. **Pace of Play rating:** 4:30. **Green fee:** $40/89.
Reduced fees: Low season, Resort guests.
Ranked 32nd in America's 75 Best Resort Courses by Golf Digest. Ranked 22nd in Michigan by Golf Digest.
Subscriber comments: Great holes, very different, new course feel . . . Replica of famous Donald Ross holes fun to play . . . Copies not very good . . . Best collection of short par 4s on the planet . . . Unique concept, tough on your rhythm . . . Marvelous! It ate us alive . . . Different holes from different courses give this course no continuity . . . Easy to love, especially with one of the amazing designers of all time . . . A beautiful, interesting layout . . . Staff very pleasant . . . Interesting. A good challenge . . . Great tribute to Donald Ross . . . Good service . . . Overrated . . . Condition marginal in the fall . . . Lots of fun . . . Possibly the best course in the state . . . A hard course for weekend golfers . . . No. 10 is a killer . . . Florida to Scotland to Michigan, it's all here.

★★★★ THE HEATHER COURSE

Holes: 18. **Par:** 72/72.
Yards: 7,210/5,245. **Course rating:** 74.0/67.8. **Slope:** 131/111.
Opened: 1968. **Pace of Play rating:** 4:00. **Green fee:** $46/98.
Reduced fees: Low season, Resort guests, Twilight.
Ranked 74th in America's 75 Best Resort Courses by Golf Digest. Ranked 13th in Michigan by Golf Digest.
Subscriber comments: Older Robert Trent Jones Sr. design . . . Expensive for Michigan . . . Restored to its former elegance . . . A classic . . . The staff and amenities make this worth the price . . . One of the best in the north . . . One of Trent Jones' best, not a weak hole among the 18 . . . Hitting greens in regulation is difficult . . . Worth playing again and again . . . Computerized golf carts, cool! . . . Great scenery . . . $10 more than Moor but the distance computer is really great . . . Solid, wonderful . . . The electronic display was very useful . . . On-board distance computers helpful with club selections . . . Cart computers helpful, but they slow down play . . . Makes you think about every shot.

★★★ THE MOOR COURSE

Holes: 18. **Par:** 72/72.
Yards: 7,179/5,459. **Course rating:** 74.0/70.0. **Slope:** 131/118.
Opened: 1972. **Pace of Play rating:** 4:00. **Green fee:** $33/69.
Reduced fees: Low season, Resort guests, Twilight.
Subscriber comments: Somewhat of a "muscle" course . . . Not in the greatest shape . . . Should be played . . . Tough holes, lots of water and sand . . . Good resort, neither great nor memorable . . . A great, peaceful ride in the woods . . . Beautiful course, especially with morning wildlife . . . Not too long, accuracy is a must. A very peaceful experience . . . The least difficult at Boyne . . . Almost as good as the Heather . . . Too tricked up with water . . . A better bargain than the Heather.

MICHIGAN

BOYNE MOUNTAIN RESORT
R—Deer Lake Rd., Boyne Falls (616)549-6029, (800)462-6963.
18 miles south of Petoskey.
Credit cards: All major. **Reduced fees:** Low season, Resort guests,
Twilight.
Caddies: No. **Golf carts:** Included in Green Fee.
Discount golf packages: Yes. **Season:** April-Oct. **High:** June-Aug.
On-site lodging: Yes. **Rental clubs:** Yes.
Walking policy: Mandatory cart. **Range:** Yes (grass).
To obtain tee times: Call 800 number for golf package reservations. Call
30 days in advance for weekends.

★★★½ ALPINE COURSE
Holes: 18. **Par:** 72/72.
Yards: 7,017/4,986. **Course rating:** 73.6/68.4. **Slope:** 129/114.
Pace of Play rating: 4:00. **Green fee:** $41/69.
Subscriber comments: Beautiful from start to finish . . . Play begins at
the top of a mountain . . . One-mile cart ride up Boyne Mountain to the
first tee . . . Holes are nicely varied, scenery is beautiful . . . A little bit of
heaven . . . Great layout, warmup for sister course . . . A must play . . .
Great views . . . The most scenic course I've ever played . . . Tee off at the
mountain top, fun all the way down . . . No gimmicks, old-style design
. . . Awesome scenery, a very "glad to meet you" staff . . . First-hole view
is outstanding . . . All holes play downhill . . . I expected some rolling
greens, seemed like every putt was flat . . . Greens were absolutely perfect
. . . One of the best in Michigan . . . A downhill, fun-filled experience.

★★★★ MONUMENT COURSE
Holes: 18. **Par:** 72/72.
Yards: 7,086/4,909. **Course rating:** 75.0/68.9. **Slope:** 139/122.
Pace of Play rating: 4:00. **Green fee:** $47/79.
Subscriber comments: Fabulous . . . Wonderful design . . . Outstanding
resort course . . . A great way to use the backside of a mountain . . . Great
first 12 holes, so-so last six . . . A memorable experience . . . Memorable
first tee shot . . . Has some tricked-up holes . . . Not as well-conditioned as
the Alpine, but overall a better test . . . Very exciting first few holes . . .
Enjoy the peacefulness. First hole an adventure . . . Some of the best golf in
northern Michigan . . . The 18th is a great test . . . Newer style . . . More
man-made architecture, sometimes too much.

★½ BRIAR DOWNS GOLF COURSE
PU—5441 E. M-115, Mesick (616)885-1220.
26 miles south of Traverse City. **Holes:** 18. **Par:** 71/71.
Yards: 5,759/4,481. **Course rating:** N/A. **Slope:** N/A.
Opened: 1989. **Pace of Play rating:** N/A. **Green fee:** $14/22.
Credit cards: MC, V. **Reduced fees:** Weekdays, Low season, Twilight.
Caddies: No. **Golf carts:** $8 for 18 holes.
Discount golf packages: No. **Season:** April-Oct. **High:** June-Aug.
On-site lodging: No. **Rental clubs:** Yes.
Walking policy: Unrestricted walking. **Range:** No.
To obtain tee times: Call one month in advance.
Subscriber comments: 90-degree dogleg, blind first hole . . . Nice
women's course . . . An English flavor . . . Best greens in the area . . .
High-handicap heaven . . . Some holes are full of gimmicks . . . Not much
of a course . . . An interesting little course.

★★ BRIAR HILL GOLF COURSE
PU—950 W. 40th St., Fremont (616)924-2070.
40 miles northwest of Grand Rapids. **Holes:** 18. **Par:** 72/71.
Yards: 6,134/4,624. **Course rating:** 67.5/65.8. **Slope:** 113/104.
Opened: 1928. **Pace of Play rating:** 3:37. **Green fee:** $15/16.
Credit cards: . **Reduced fees:** Weekdays, Low season, Resort guests,
Twilight, Seniors.
Caddies: No. **Golf carts:** N/A.
Discount golf packages: No. **Season:** March-Dec. **High:** June-Aug.
On-site lodging: No. **Rental clubs:** Yes.
Walking policy: Unrestricted walking. **Range:** Yes (grass).

To obtain tee times: Call. No restrictions.
Subscriber comments: Small greens, nothing fancy . . . Slow pace of play
. . . Only three real hard holes in the 18 . . . Good course.

★★½ BRIGADOON GOLF CLUB
PU—12559 Bagley Ave., Grant (616)834-8200, (800)839-8206.
30 miles north of Grand Rapids. **Holes:** 18. **Par:** 72/72.
Yards: 6,115/4,825. **Course rating:** 70.9/68.6. **Slope:** 135/124.
Opened: 1989. **Pace of Play rating:** N/A. **Green fee:** $11/21.
Credit cards: MC, V. **Reduced fees:** Weekdays, Low season, Seniors.
Caddies: No. **Golf carts:** $8 for 18 holes.
Discount golf packages: Yes. **Season:** April-Nov. **High:** May-Aug.
On-site lodging: No. **Rental clubs:** Yes.
Walking policy: Walking at certain times. **Range:** Yes (grass).
To obtain tee times: Call.
Additional 9 holes to open July 1995.
Subscriber comments: Target golf to the max . . . Too many blind shots
. . . Fantastic layout . . . Blind shots, but great . . . Novelty course . . . Par
5s are ridiculous, take your driver out of the game . . . It's not a golf course,
it's an experience . . . Very challenging, very different . . . Better known as
"bring-a-dozen", play it once for grins . . . Designed by a dentist, it's a real
pain . . . Appeals to the brave and the young . . . The most unusual course
I've every played . . . Too cutesy . . . Many unique holes . . . Blind wedge
shots turn me off . . . Homemade design . . . Blind shots to greens
surrounded by water . . . He should stick to dentistry . . . Major league
tricked-up course . . . Tremendous terrain . . . Many surprises.

★½ BURNING OAK COUNTRY CLUB
PU—4345 Redwood Dr., Higgins Lake (517)821-9821.
62 miles southeast of Traverse City. **Holes:** 18. **Par:** 72/72.
Yards: 6,240/5,256. **Course rating:** 69.7/70.0. **Slope:** 117/115.
Opened: 1962. **Pace of Play rating:** 4:00. **Green fee:** $17.
Credit cards: MC, V. **Reduced fees:** N/A.
Caddies: No. **Golf carts:** $9 for 18 holes.
Discount golf packages: No. **Season:** April-Oct. **High:** June-Aug.
On-site lodging: No. **Rental clubs:** Yes.
Walking policy: Unrestricted walking. **Range:** Yes (grass).
To obtain tee times: Call.
Subscriber comments: Duffers do well . . . Easier course . . . Too short
. . . They seem like nice people . . . Small greens . . . Not much trouble
. . . Well-kept.

★★ BURR OAK GOLF CLUB
PU—3491 N. Parma Rd., Parma (517)531-4741.
5 miles east of Jackson. **Holes:** 18. **Par:** 72/72.
Yards: 5,906/5,011. **Course rating:** 69.7/N/A. **Slope:** N/A.
Opened: 1965. **Pace of Play rating:** 4:00. **Green fee:** $10/13.
Credit cards: None. **Reduced fees:** Twilight, Seniors, Juniors.
Caddies: No. **Golf carts:** $8 for 18 holes.
Discount golf packages: Yes. **Season:** April-Oct. **High:** May-Aug.
On-site lodging: No. **Rental clubs:** Yes.
Walking policy: Unrestricted walking. **Range:** Yes (grass).
To obtain tee times: Call anytime.

BUTTERNUT BROOK GOLF COURSE★
PU—2200 Island Hwy., Charlotte (517)543-0570.
12 miles southwest of Lansing. **Holes:** 18. **Par:** 71/71.
Yards: 6,289/5,307. **Course rating:** 70.3/69.2. **Slope:** N/A.
Opened: 1970. **Pace of Play rating:** 4:30. **Green fee:** $10/13.
Credit cards: None. **Reduced fees:** Weekdays, Seniors.
Caddies: No. **Golf carts:** $18 for 18 holes.
Discount golf packages: No. **Season:** April-Oct. **High:** May-Aug.
On-site lodging: No. **Rental clubs:** Yes.
Walking policy: Unrestricted walking. **Range:** Yes (grass).
To obtain tee times: First come, first served.

★½ BYRON HILLS GOLF CLUB
PU—7330 Burlingame Rd., Byron Center (616)878-1522.
10 miles south of Grand Rapids. **Holes:** 18. **Par:** 72/76.
Yards: 6,045/5,645. **Course rating:** 69.5/N/A. **Slope:** N/A.
Opened: 1963. **Pace of Play rating:** N/A. **Green fee:** $16/17.
Credit cards: MC, V. **Reduced fees:** Weekdays, Low season, Seniors,
Juniors.
Caddies: No. **Golf carts:** $27 for 18 holes.
Discount golf packages: No. **Season:** March-Dec. **High:** May-Sept..
On-site lodging: No. **Rental clubs:** Yes.
Walking policy: Unrestricted walking. **Range:** No.
To obtain tee times: Call up to a month in advance for weekends only.

Subscriber comments: Kind of open, but in very good shape . . . Pitch-
and-putt course . . . Not much challenge . . . Simple, fairly competitive
layout . . . Awkward layout . . . Too flat and short . . . Typical Ma and Pa
public . . . Needs raised tee boxes and more hazards . . . Hackers' haven
. . . Not much trouble.

★★★ CANDLESTONE GOLF CLUB
R—8100 N. Storey, Belding (616)794-1580.
20 miles east of Grand Rapids. **Holes:** 18. **Par:** 72/74.
Yards: 6,692/5,547. **Course rating:** 72.8/73.1. **Slope:** 129/126.
Opened: 1975. **Pace of Play rating:** N/A. **Green fee:** $21/25.
Credit cards: All major. **Reduced fees:** Weekdays, Low season, Resort
guests, Twilight, Juniors.
Caddies: No. **Golf carts:** $11 for 18 holes.
Discount golf packages: Yes. **Season:** March-Oct. **High:** May-Sept.
On-site lodging: Yes. **Rental clubs:** Yes.
Walking policy: Unrestricted walking. **Range:** Yes (grass).
To obtain tee times: Call one week in advance.
Subscriber comments: Long and challenging . . . Interesting without
tricks . . . Average western Michigan golf course: up, down, around . . .
Holes very similar . . . Four of the toughest finishing holes in golf . . . Play
in early autumn and bring a camera . . . You must stay in the fairway . . .
Very nice people in the shop . . . No bad holes . . . Uncluttered . . .
Excellent par 3s . . . Nicely conditioned course . . . Not championship
caliber as advertised . . . A good test of golf . . . Long and wooded . . . A
very nice mix of holes . . . Easy to lose balls . . . Locker room needs help
. . . Great playability.

★★½ CAPTAIN'S CLUB AT WOODFIELD
PU—1 Golfside Dr., Grand Blanc (810)695-4653.
30 miles north of Detroit. **Holes:** 18. **Par:** 72/72.
Yards: 6,780/5,071. **Course rating:** 73.3/68.3. **Slope:** 133/121.
Opened: 1994. **Pace of Play rating:** 4:30. **Green fee:** $30/40.
Credit cards: MC, V. **Reduced fees:** Weekdays, Low season, Twilight,
Seniors, Juniors.
Caddies: No. **Golf carts:** Included in Green Fee.
Discount golf packages: Yes. **Season:** April-Oct. **High:** June-Aug.
On-site lodging: No. **Rental clubs:** Yes.
Walking policy: Unrestricted walking. **Range:** Yes (grass).
To obtain tee times: Call up to one month in advance.
Subscriber comments: No frills, expensive food and drink . . . Wetlands,
often too wet . . . New course . . . Many doglegs . . . Needs filling in . . .
Disappointing . . . Excellent greens . . . You need all the shots to score well
. . . Too much play allowed before it matured . . . Picturesque and wild
. . . Wonderful setting . . . Club selection is important . . . Design can't
overcome a mediocre piece of land . . . Could be a sleeper in southern
Michigan . . . Best course in Genesee County.

★★½ CARLETON GLEN GOLF CLUB
SP—13470 Grafton Rd., Carleton (313)654-6201.
19 miles southwest of Detroit. **Holes:** 18. **Par:** 71/71.
Yards: 6,496/5,602. **Course rating:** 70.5/73.0. **Slope:** 120/112.
Opened: 1961. **Pace of Play rating:** 4:30. **Green fee:** $20/22.

Credit cards: MC, V. **Reduced fees:** Low season, Seniors, Juniors.
Caddies: No. **Golf carts:** N/A.
Discount golf packages: No. **Season:** April-Nov. **High:** May-Sept.
On-site lodging: No. **Rental clubs:** No.
Walking policy: Unrestricted walking. **Range:** Yes (grass).
To obtain tee times: Call seven days in advance. Send money for earlier times.
Subscriber comments: Front too easy, back too hard. Minimal leagues, easy to get on . . . Beautiful, hard greens . . . Well designed, short par 4s . . . Well groomed . . . Be prepared for golf bag search (products bought off the golf course not allowed).

★★★½ CASCADES GOLF COURSE

PU—1992 Warren Ave., Jackson (517)788-4323.
37 miles east of Battle Creek. **Holes:** 18. **Par:** 72/73.
Yards: 6,614/5,282. **Course rating:** 71.8/70.5. **Slope:** 122/117.
Opened: 1929. **Pace of Play rating:** N/A. **Green fee:** $13/17.
Credit cards: None. **Reduced fees:** Weekdays, Low season, Twilight, Seniors, Juniors.
Caddies: No. **Golf carts:** N/A.
Discount golf packages: No. **Season:** March-Oct. **High:** July-Sept.
On-site lodging: No. **Rental clubs:** Yes.
Walking policy: Walking at certain times. **Range:** Yes (grass).
To obtain tee times: Call one week in advance.
Subscriber comments: Popular course, very busy . . . Very playable . . . Great public course . . . Best value for its quality of play in Michigan . . . Everytime I play it, I appreciate it more . . . Best muny in southern Michigan . . . Great course to just enjoy a round of golf . . . Rolling, hilly front nine . . . Long and scenic. The green on No. 17 will drive you nuts if you hit it deep . . . Very challenging . . . Fantastic value, the state's best secret . . . Lots of mature trees . . . Goose droppings a pain on the back . . . A little flat and repetitive . . . Cannot be beat . . . The best in Jackson . . . First two holes are par 5s . . . Spacious layout. Opening par 5s are killers . . . No better course in Michigan for the price . . . Always a summer stop . . . Cost is less than $1 per hole . . . Dave and Mike Hill cut their teeth here, still good.

★★½ CATTAILS GOLF CLUB

PU—57737 W. 9 Mile Rd., South Lyon (810)486-8777.
20 miles west of Detroit. **Holes:** 18. **Par:** 72/72.
Yards: 6,418/4,987. **Course rating:** 71.8/70.3. **Slope:** 132/117.
Opened: 1991. **Pace of Play rating:** 4:30. **Green fee:** $23/33.
Credit cards: MC, V. **Reduced fees:** Weekdays, Low season, Twilight, Seniors.
Caddies: No. **Golf carts:** $12 for 18 holes.
Discount golf packages: Yes. **Season:** April-Nov. **High:** June-Aug.
On-site lodging: No. **Rental clubs:** Yes.
Walking policy: Walking at certain times. **Range:** Yes (grass).
To obtain tee times: Call one week in advance.
Subscriber comments: Target style . . . Unforgiving . . . Not for the average hacker . . . Unreasonably hard . . . Go for it on No. 10 . . . Wetlands interfere with golf on some holes . . . Too much position golf . . . Cattails everywhere . . . More fun after you have played it once . . . Some forced holes . . . Think before you hit . . . No. 10 may be the toughest hole in Michigan . . . Too many blind, layup holes . . . No. 10 will get your attention . . . Holes would look nice on a calendar . . . No. 10 is a great hole.

★½ CEDAR GLEN GOLF CLUB

PU—36860 25 Mile Rd., New Baltimore (313)725-8156.
Call club for further information.
Subscriber comments: Short, short course, in decent condition . . . Back nine new, more interesting than front . . . Crowded, but I don't know why . . . Swampy in the spring, rock hard in summer . . . Plenty of trouble . . . Won't kill you. Getting better.

★★½ CENTENNIAL ACRES GOLF COURSE
PU—12485 Dow Rd., Sunfield (517)566-8055.
15 miles west of Lansing. **Holes:** 18. **Par:** 72/72.
Yards: 6,551/4,979. **Course rating:** 72.2/67.7. **Slope:** 118/111.
Opened: 1979. **Pace of Play rating:** 4:00. **Green fee:** $15/18.
Credit cards: MC, V, DISC. **Reduced fees:** Low season, Seniors, Juniors.
Caddies: No. **Golf carts:** $10 for 18 holes.
Discount golf packages: Yes. **Season:** April-Nov. **High:** June-Aug.
On-site lodging: No. **Rental clubs:** Yes.
Walking policy: Unrestricted walking. **Range:** No.
To obtain tee times: Call.
Subscriber comments: Well run . . . A pretty good course . . . A real
sleeper . . . Wide open front nine with huge greens, tight target golf on the
back nine . . . Best-kept secret in middle Michigan . . . Fun course . . .
Beautiful clubhouse . . . Newer nine has to grow up . . . Some water, not
much sand . . . Back nine enclosed by woods . . . Often wet, nice folks.

★★ CHASE HAMMOND GOLF COURSE
PU—2454 N. Putnam Rd., Muskegon (616)766-3035.
Call club for further information.
Subscriber comments: Very woody . . . Grounds upkeep below standard
. . . Short and straight . . . Beautiful walk in a pine forest . . . Overplayed
with leagues . . . Shoestring budget . . . Lined with trees . . . Putting
surfaces need work . . . Needs some renovation . . . Very pretty course,
could use more care.

★★ CHEBOYGAN GOLF & COUNTRY CLUB
SP—1431 Old Mackinaw Rd., Cheboygan (616)627-4264.
Holes: 18. **Par:** 70/71.
Yards: 6,003/4,653. **Course rating:** 67.4/67.7. **Slope:** 120/113.
Opened: 1922. **Pace of Play rating:** N/A. **Green fee:** $16/22.
Credit cards: MC, V. **Reduced fees:** Low season, Twilight, Seniors,
Juniors.
Caddies: No. **Golf carts:** $12 for 18 holes.
Discount golf packages: No. **Season:** April-Oct. **High:** June-Aug.
On-site lodging: No. **Rental clubs:** Yes.
Walking policy: Unrestricted walking. **Range:** Yes (grass).
To obtain tee times: Call 24 hours in advance.
Subscriber comments: Back nine is tight . . . Good value in an area of
fairly high-priced courses . . . Mix of average and tough holes . . . Odd
layout.

★★★ CLEARBROOK GOLF CLUB
SP—6494 Clearbrook Dr., Saugatuck (616)857-2000.
25 miles west of Grand Rapids. **Holes:** 18. **Par:** 72/74.
Yards: 6,453/5,153. **Course rating:** 72.8/70.0. **Slope:** 132/127.
Opened: 1920. **Pace of Play rating:** 4:00. **Green fee:** $19/30.
Credit cards: All major. **Reduced fees:** Low season.
Caddies: No. **Golf carts:** $10 for 18 holes.
Discount golf packages: No. **Season:** April-Oct. **High:** June-Aug.
On-site lodging: No. **Rental clubs:** Yes.
Walking policy: Unrestricted walking. **Range:** Yes (grass).
To obtain tee times: Tee times taken six days in advance.
Subscriber comments: Some good holes, some not very interesting . . .
Some blind shots. Attracts vacationers . . . Pleasant course, classic club-
house . . . Some tricky holes . . . Uncrowded. Excellent staff. Good dining
. . . Several redesigned holes . . . Back nine is a good test . . . Great greens.

★½ CRACKLEWOOD GOLF CLUB
PU—18215 24 Mile Macomb Township, Mt. Clemens (810) 781-0808.
Call club for further information.
Subscriber comments: Maturing nicely, no duplicate holes . . . Blue-
collar course, caters to retirees . . . Nice layout, rough condition . . . Open
six years and still no clubhouse yet . . . Needs polish.

★ CROOKED CREEK GOLF CLUB
PU—9387 Gratiot Rd., Saginaw (517)781-0050.
Call club for further information.
Subscriber comments: Lacks character . . . Open and fun . . . Not very demanding or interesting . . . Creek prone to flooding . . . Basic public course . . . Uninspiring. Cheap price for a practice course . . . Was not impressed . . . Forgiving course.

CROOKED TREE GOLF CLUB★
PU—600 Crooked Tree Dr., Petoskey (616)348-7000.
100 miles north of Grand Rapids. **Holes:** 18. **Par:** 71/71.
Yards: 6,584/4,713. **Course rating:** N/A. **Slope:** N/A.
Opened: 1995. **Pace of Play rating:** 4:00. **Green fee:** $35/60.
Credit cards: MC, V. **Reduced fees:** Weekdays, Low season, Twilight.
Caddies: No. **Golf carts:** Included in Green Fee.
Discount golf packages: No. **Season:** April-Nov. **High:** June-Aug.
On-site lodging: No. **Rental clubs:** Yes.
Walking policy: Walking at certain times. **Range:** Yes (grass).
To obtain tee times: Call. Must use a credit card.

★★½ CRYSTAL LAKE GOLF CLUB
PU—Hwy. 31, Beulah (616)882-4061.
Call club for further information.
Subscriber comments: Inconsistent greens . . . Beautiful course . . . Beautiful views . . . An overlooked northern Michigan gem . . . Making great steps to improve an already great course . . . Nice people in pro shop . . . Nice little course . . . Too pricey . . . Good views of Crystal Lake . . . Pleasantly surprised. Thought there would be more views of Crystal . . . Not a tough layout.

CRYSTAL MOUNTAIN RESORT
★★★ MOUNTAIN MEADOWS/MOUNTAIN RIDGE/MOUNTAIN CREEK
R—12500 Crystal Mountain Dr., Thompsonville (616)378-2000, (800)968-7686.
30 miles north of Traverse City. **Holes:** 27. **Par:** 72/71/71.
Yards: 6,689/6,372/6,215. **Course rating:** 72.1/70.5/70.0.
Slope: 127/129/126.
Opened: N/A. **Pace of Play rating:** 4:00. **Green fee:** $40.
Credit cards: All major. **Reduced fees:** Weekdays, Low season, Resort guests, Twilight.
Caddies: No. **Golf carts:** $12 for 18 holes.
Discount golf packages: Yes. **Season:** April-Oct. **High:** June-Aug.
On-site lodging: Yes. **Rental clubs:** Yes.
Walking policy: Walking at certain times. **Range:** Yes (grass).
To obtain tee times: Call 800 number.
Subscriber comments: Mountain Ridge only nine worth playing . . . Too easy . . . Very pretty course with demanding mountain shots . . . New nine makes this a better course . . . Nice (but not outstanding) northern Michigan resort course. Accommodations are excellent . . . Gnats have always been bad here . . . Breathtaking views . . . Mountain Ridge has spectacular views . . . All kinds of holes . . . Ridge is spectacular, a true Northwoods experience . . . Love the Ridge.

CURRIE MUNICIPAL GOLF COURSE
★½ EAST 18/WEST 9
PU—1006 Currie Pkwy., Midland (517)839-9600.
Holes: 27. **Par:** 72/36.
Yards: 6,368/5,292. **Course rating:** 70.2/71.2. **Slope:** 112/113.
Opened: 1954. **Pace of Play rating:** 4:00. **Green fee:** $13.
Credit cards: None. **Reduced fees:** Twilight, Seniors, Juniors.
Caddies: No. **Golf carts:** $10 for 18 holes.
Discount golf packages: No. **Season:** April-Oct. **High:** May-Sept.
On-site lodging: No. **Rental clubs:** Yes.

Walking policy: Unrestricted walking. **Range:** Yes (grass).
To obtain tee times: Call three days in advance.
Subscriber comments: If they ever stop reconstruction, this can be a good publinks . . . Great par 3s . . . Well-kept course, easy and tough holes . . . West course negelected badly but under improvement. East course crowded, very slow pace . . . Tough tabletop greens . . . You need a smooth stroke on the greens . . . Could be very good.

DEER RUN GOLF COURSE★
PU—Pineview Dr., Mancelona (616)585-6800, (800)851-4653.
18 miles southwest of Gaylord. **Holes:** 18. **Par:** 72/74.
Yards: 6,996/5,465. **Course rating:** 73.3/71.3. **Slope:** 130/123.
Opened: 1974. **Pace of Play rating:** 4:15. **Green fee:** $25/36.
Credit cards: MC, V, DISC. **Reduced fees:** Weekdays, Low season, Twilight, Juniors.
Caddies: No. **Golf carts:** Included in Green Fee.
Discount golf packages: Yes. **Season:** April-Oct. **High:** July-Aug.
On-site lodging: Yes. **Rental clubs:** Yes.
Walking policy: Unrestricted walking. **Range:** Yes (grass).
To obtain tee times: Call.

DEVIL'S RIDGE GOLF CLUB★
PU—3700 Metamora Rd., Oxford (810)969-0100.
11 miles north of Pontiac. **Holes:** 18. **Par:** 72/72.
Yards: 6,722/4,130. **Course rating:** N/A. **Slope:** N/A.
Opened: 1995. **Pace of Play rating:** 4:30. **Green fee:** $37/45.
Credit cards: All major. **Reduced fees:** Twilight.
Caddies: No. **Golf carts:** Included in Green Fee.
Discount golf packages: No. **Season:** April-Nov. **High:** April-Nov.
On-site lodging: No. **Rental clubs:** Yes.
Walking policy: Mandatory cart. **Range:** Yes (grass).
To obtain tee times: Call seven days in advance.

★★★½ DUNHAM HILLS GOLF AND COUNTRY CLUB
PU—13561 Dunham Rd., Hartland (810)887-9170.
23 miles west of Pontiac. **Holes:** 18. **Par:** 72/74.
Yards: 6,763/5,310. **Course rating:** 72.3/70.8. **Slope:** 128/121.
Opened: 1968. **Pace of Play rating:** 3:54. **Green fee:** $20/40.
Credit cards: MC, V. **Reduced fees:** Weekdays, Twilight, Seniors, Juniors.
Caddies: No. **Golf carts:** Included in Green Fee.
Discount golf packages: No. **Season:** March-Nov. **High:** May-Sept..
On-site lodging: No. **Rental clubs:** No.
Walking policy: Walking at certain times. **Range:** Yes (grass).
To obtain tee times: Call.
Subscriber comments: Fairly tough, greens usually slippery . . . Cramped . . . A few unusual holes . . . Holes too close together . . . Beautiful in the fall . . . Tough for most . . . If you score well here, you're a good player . . . Demanding layout . . . Hilly, tough, scenic . . . Location difficult and out of the way . . . wooded, water, some tight holes . . . Sidehill lies . . . Bring your "A" game and patience . . . Toughest public test of golf I've found in Michigan . . . Undulating greens . . . One of the best in lower Michigan . . . Needs improvement on turf care in hot months . . . No level lies . . . Country club greens . . . Really a tough monkey.

★★★★ DUNMAGLAS GOLF CLUB
SP—09031 Boyne City Rd., Charlevoix (616)547-1022.
50 miles north of Traverse City. **Holes:** 18. **Par:** 72/74.
Yards: 6,897/5,334. **Course rating:** 74.0/70.9. **Slope:** 142/127.
Opened: 1992. **Pace of Play rating:** 4:40. **Green fee:** $50/80.
Credit cards: MC, V, DISC. **Reduced fees:** Low season, Twilight.
Caddies: No. **Golf carts:** $10 for 18 holes.
Discount golf packages: No. **Season:** May-Oct. **High:** July-Aug.
On-site lodging: No. **Rental clubs:** Yes.
Walking policy: Unrestricted walking. **Range:** Yes (grass).

To obtain tee times: Call pro shop no more than two months in advance of desired time.

Ranked 6th in Michigan by Golf Digest.

Subscriber comments: Very difficult, very imaginative, gorgeous vistas and elevations . . . Too difficult . . . No clubhouse . . . Tight landing areas . . . Must play it once . . . The toughest course in Michigan . . . Target golf taken one step too far . . . Unbelievable scenery . . . Fantastic elevation changes . . . Toughest resort course in Michigan . . . Unforgettable first hole . . . Entry road is a goat path . . . Stunning views, natural setting. Saw three deer on No. 4 . . . Unfair and unforgiving . . . Errant shots are lost balls . . . Great variey . . . Very memorable. The drive into the course gets the heart pumping . . . Great views of Lakes Michigan and Charlevoix . . . Incredible first 11 holes, then opens up forest lined to heather lined . . . Maybe overpriced . . . Price is as steep as some of its hills.

★★★½ EAGLE GLEN GOLF COURSE
PU—1251 Club House Dr., Farwell (517)588-9357.
Holes: 18. **Par:** 72/72.
Yards: 6,602/5,119. **Course rating:** 71.1/69.2. **Slope:** 123/116.
Opened: 1992. **Pace of Play rating:** 4:30. **Green fee:** $21/28.
Credit cards: MC, V, DISC. **Reduced fees:** Weekdays, Low season, Resort guests, Seniors, Juniors.
Caddies: No. **Golf carts:** $9 for 18 holes.
Discount golf packages: Yes. **Season:** April-Oct. **High:** June-Oct.
On-site lodging: No. **Rental clubs:** Yes.
Walking policy: Walking at certain times. **Range:** Yes (grass).
To obtain tee times: Call anytime.
Subscriber comments: Good pace . . . Challenging rough . . . Great new course . . . Superb in every way. The best new course in the area . . . Different, but challenging . . . Some really tough holes . . . A jewel . . . Exceptional greens . . . Needs maturity . . . Too short, rough delays your game . . . Did a lot with available land, but pasture clover does not pass for heather . . . Too spread out.

★★★★ ELK RIDGE GOLF CLUB
PU—9400 Rouse Rd., Rte. 1, Box 28A, Atlanta (517)785-2275, (800)626-4355.
30 miles east of Gaylord. **Holes:** 18. **Par:** 72/72.
Yards: 7,058/5,261. **Course rating:** 75.0/73.1. **Slope:** 144/135.
Opened: 1991. **Pace of Play rating:** 4:58. **Green fee:** $45/60.
Credit cards: MC, V. **Reduced fees:** Weekdays, Low season, Twilight, Seniors, Juniors.
Caddies: No. **Golf carts:** Included in Green Fee.
Discount golf packages: Yes. **Season:** May-Oct. **High:** June-Aug.
On-site lodging: No. **Rental clubs:** Yes.
Walking policy: Mandatory cart. **Range:** Yes (grass).
To obtain tee times: Call proshop anytime. Guarantee with credit card.
Selected as runner-up for Best New Public Course of 1991 by Golf Digest.
Ranked 18th in Michigan by Golf Digest.
Subscriber comments: Beautiful northern Michigan property . . . Impossible par 5s . . . Much wildlife . . . Top-notch, but expensive . . . Beautiful, scenic course . . . All woods played as lateral hazards . . . Out of the way . . . Destined to be great . . . Very high on my list . . . Some of the nicest golf holes you'll ever play . . . I wish I lived in the upper Michigan area . . . Cool course . . . Golfing nirvana. Secluded golf all day . . . Great layout for a fade . . . Unusual 10th hole . . . A very pleasant surprise . . . Very clean carts . . . Watch for bull elk in the fall . . . Great layout with pines, marshes, water. A treat . . . Contrast of the course, wilderness is stunning . . . All the par 5s are double doglegs. Several great par 4s on the back . . . Each hole is a picture . . . Another northern Michigan beauty, but expensive as usual . . . Bring your straight game, very narrow . . . Pig-shaped bunker on the par-3 10th hole is unique . . . Location a drawback, but hike if you have to . . . No lodging close to the course . . . Too many doglegs; never got a chance to hit my driver.

★★½ ELLA SHARP PARK GOLF COURSE

PU—3225 4th St., Jackson (517)788-4066.

Call club for further information.

Subscriber comments: Nice public course . . . Fine layout, great price
. . . Additional plantings have added to the beauty . . . Real nice people . . .
Great for kids . . . Slightly flat . . . Ninth hole drainage very poor . . . Back
nine has too much standing water . . . Not too long but lots of trees . . .
Too many holes in too little space . . . Too many balls to choose from . . .
Bumpy greens . . . Friendly.

★★½ ELMBROOK GOLF COURSE

PU—420 Hammond Rd., Traverse City (616)946-9180.

1 miles north of Traverse City. **Holes:** 18. **Par:** 72/72.

Yards: 6,131/5,194. **Course rating:** 68.4/68.5. **Slope:** 114/112.

Opened: 1966. **Pace of Play rating:** 4:00. **Green fee:** $18/20.

Credit cards: MC, V. **Reduced fees:** Low season, Resort guests.

Caddies: No. **Golf carts:** $30 for 18 holes.

Discount golf packages: Yes. **Season:** April-Nov. **High:** June-Aug.

On-site lodging: No. **Rental clubs:** Yes.

Walking policy: Unrestricted walking. **Range:** Yes (grass).

To obtain tee times: Phone up to 24 hours or longer for out-of-town
visitors and golf outings.

Subscriber comments: Beautiful views of lake. A good course for the
average player . . . One trap designed like the state of Michigan . . . Well-
maintained, extremely scenic, very hilly but not overly challenging . . .
Traverse Bay can be seen from a couple of holes . . . Routine course . . .
Run-of-the-mill . . . Interesting . . . Nice country setting . . . Old favorite,
hanging in there.

★½ ENGLISH HILLS GOLF COURSE

PU—1200 Four Mile Rd., Grand Rapids (616)784-3420.

Call club for further information.

Subscriber comments: The front nine needs help . . . Basic golf . . . Not
one of the better ones in the Grand Rapids area . . . Made for short hitters
. . . Pace sometimes slow . . . Leave it for the leagues . . . Should be
categorized as a par-3 course . . . Cheap but plays like it.

★★★ FAULKWOOD SHORES GOLF CLUB

PU—300 S. Hughes Rd., Howell (517)546-4180.

20 miles west of Detroit. **Holes:** 18. **Par:** 72/72.

Yards: 6,828/5,341. **Course rating:** 74.3/71.8. **Slope:** 140/128.

Opened: 1967. **Pace of Play rating:** 4:30. **Green fee:** $22/35.

Credit cards: MC, V. **Reduced fees:** Weekdays, Low season, Twilight,
Seniors, Juniors.

Caddies: No. **Golf carts:** Included in Green Fee.

Discount golf packages: No. **Season:** April-Nov. **High:** June-Sept.

On-site lodging: No. **Rental clubs:** Yes.

Walking policy: Walking at certain times. **Range:** Yes (grass).

To obtain tee times: Call seven days in advance for weekdays and call
Monday for the upcoming weekend.

Subscriber comments: Greens very fast, two to three greens are too
sloped . . . You need to play it more than once . . . Some unseen water
hazards . . . Very hard the first time . . . Cut down trees on Nos. 1 and 18
. . . First hole is a throwaway . . . Sweetheart . . . Location is a minus . . .
Clubhouse should be in better shape . . . Good old lady . . . Need to be
straight . . . Everything you could hope for . . . Must be played very
strategically, excellent hazard placement . . . One of the better courses in the
area . . . Two severely banked greens . . . No. 18 a 443-yard par 4 over
greenside pond . . . No. 18 a tough hole.

FELLOWS CREEK GOLF CLUB
★★ EAST/SOUTH/WEST

PU—2936 Lotz Rd., Canton (313)728-1300.

20 miles west of Detroit. **Holes:** 27. **Par:** 72/72/72.

Yards: 6,489/6,430/6,399. **Course rating:** 71.0/70.9/70.9.
Slope: 118/118/118.
Opened: 1965. **Pace of Play rating:** N/A. **Green fee:** $19/22.
Credit cards: MC, V. **Reduced fees:** Weekdays, Low season, Twilight,
Seniors, Juniors.
Caddies: No. **Golf carts:** $11 for 18 holes.
Discount golf packages: No. **Season:** April-Dec. **High:** June-Aug.
On-site lodging: No. **Rental clubs:** No.
Walking policy: Unrestricted walking. **Range:** No.
To obtain tee times: Call during the week for a weekend time.
Subscriber comments: Three nines, no waiting, tight with very tough
sand . . . East and South better than the West . . . Fairways very good,
greens always spiked up, rough is long . . . Flat, few trees, very little water
and sand . . . Nice layout to experience . . . Service very good . . . Good
diversity . . . Good for large events.

★★ FENTON FARMS GOLF CLUB
PU—12312 Torrey Rd., Fenton (810)629-1212.
10 miles south of Flint. **Holes:** 18. **Par:** 72/72.
Yards: 6,509/5,424. **Course rating:** 69.0/69.6. **Slope:** 113/113.
Opened: 1940. **Pace of Play rating:** 4:00. **Green fee:** $18/24.
Credit cards: MC, V. **Reduced fees:** Weekdays, Low season, Twilight,
Seniors, Juniors.
Caddies: No. **Golf carts:** $12 for 18 holes.
Discount golf packages: No. **Season:** April-Nov. **High:** May-Sept.
On-site lodging: No. **Rental clubs:** No.
Walking policy: Unrestricted walking. **Range:** Yes (grass).
To obtain tee times: Call within seven days.
Subscriber comments: In excellent shape with some very interesting holes
. . . Not in the greatest condition . . . Making steady improvements . . .
Easy but fun . . . Relatively new management . . . Has come a long way
with new owners.

FERN HILL GOLF AND COUNTRY CLUB★
PU—17600 Clinton River Rd., Clinton Township (313)286-4700.
20 miles north of Detroit. **Holes:** 18. **Par:** 70/73.
Yards: 6,018/4,962. **Course rating:** 67.6/65.7. **Slope:** 115/108.
Opened: 1972. **Pace of Play rating:** 4:30. **Green fee:** $10/17.
Credit cards: MC, V. **Reduced fees:** Low season, Seniors.
Caddies: No. **Golf carts:** $15 for 18 holes.
Discount golf packages: Yes. **Season:** April-Nov. **High:** June-Sept.
On-site lodging: No. **Rental clubs:** No.
Walking policy: Unrestricted walking. **Range:** No.
To obtain tee times: Call pro shop.

★★★★ THE FORTRESS
R—950 Flint St., Box 304, Frankenmuth (517)652-9229.
15 miles north of Saginaw. **Holes:** 18. **Par:** 72/72.
Yards: 6,825/4,875. **Course rating:** 72.8/68.1. **Slope:** 132/121.
Opened: 1992. **Pace of Play rating:** 3:55. **Green fee:** $39/59.
Credit cards: All major. **Reduced fees:** Weekdays, Low season, Resort
guests, Twilight, Seniors, Juniors.
Caddies: No. **Golf carts:** Included in Green Fee.
Discount golf packages: Yes. **Season:** April-Oct. **High:** June-Sept.
On-site lodging: No. **Rental clubs:** Yes.
Walking policy: Walking at certain times. **Range:** Yes (grass).
To obtain tee times: Call, credit card used to guarantee tee time. 48-hour
cancellation policy.
Subscriber comments: This is the best. Gets better as it gets older . . .
You have to stay in the fairways . . . Outstanding, links feel is refreshing
. . . Wonderful testy course . . . They treat you like a king on a great
conditioned course . . . Incredible greens, wonderful conditions . . . Best
course in mid-Michigan, worth the money . . . A beautiful, challenging
course . . . Close to home but feels like a resort . . . Testy par 3s . . .

Roughs are rough . . . Lots of heather . . . Best manicured course I played this year . . . Diversity in the layout . . . Finishing five holes are first rate . . . Four beautiful finishing holes . . . Exceptional layout. Fairway distances are marked to front, middle and back of greens . . . Most courteous golf staff I have ever seen . . . Best yardage markers I have ever seen . . . Hilly course, lots of blind shots, moderately tight . . . Tough on windy days.

★★½ FIREFLY GOLF LINKS

PU—7795 S. Clare Ave., Clare (517)386-3510.
45 miles east of Saginaw. **Holes:** 18. **Par:** 72/72.
Yards: 5,658/4,470. **Course rating:** N/A. **Slope:** N/A.
Opened: 1932. **Pace of Play rating:** 4:00. **Green fee:** $18/20.
Credit cards: MC, V, DISC. **Reduced fees:** Weekdays, Low season, Seniors.
Caddies: No. **Golf carts:** $9 for 18 holes.
Discount golf packages: Yes. **Season:** April-Oct. **High:** June-Aug.
On-site lodging: No. **Rental clubs:** Yes.
Walking policy: Unrestricted walking. **Range:** No.
To obtain tee times: Call pro shop.
Subscriber comments: Tight, tough greens, excellent hospitality . . . Large, excellent greens . . . Good value at a friendly mom and pop course.

FOREST AKERS GOLF CLUB

PU—Mich. St. Univ. Harrison Rd., East Lansing (517)355-1635.
3 miles east of Lansing.
Credit cards: MC, V. **Reduced fees:** No.
Caddies: No. **Golf carts:** $24 for 18 holes.
Discount golf packages: No. **Season:** March-Oct. **High:** May-Sept.
On-site lodging: No. **Rental clubs:** Yes.
Walking policy: Unrestricted walking. **Range:** Yes (grass).
To obtain tee times: Call two days in advance.
EAST COURSE★
Holes: 18. **Par:** 71/73.
Yards: 6,510/5,380. **Course rating:** 70.4/70.4. **Slope:** 113/115.
Opened: 1972. **Pace of Play rating:** 4:30. **Green fee:** $18/20.
Subscriber comments: Best greens in Central Michigan . . . East is good for the average player . . . East Course is fine. Nothing to write home about . . . Well-maintained . . . Always in impeccable condition . . . Average East course . . . Open and rolling . . . Very little water . . . East Course, horrible fairways, no imagination in design . . . East is far easier . . . Good practice course.
WEST COURSE★
Holes: 18. **Par:** 72/72.
Yards: 7,003/5,251. **Course rating:** 74.4/70.0. **Slope:** 139/119.
Opened: 1958. **Pace of Play rating:** 4:30. **Green fee:** $30/34.
Subscriber comments: Redesigned West course is tops . . . An Arthur Hills redesign . . . Arthur Hills redesign turned an ordinary course into an outstanding one . . . West Course very demanding . . . West Course is a great college course . . . West Course, beautiful layout with great greens and lush fairways . . . West is a monster . . . Some inconsistency between old and new holes . . . Big time Big Ten. Not for faint of shaft . . . Absolutely wonderful since its renovation . . . West Course promises more than it delivers . . . Every tree native to Michigan is on the course.

★★ FOX CREEK GOLF COURSE

PU—36000 Seven Mile, Livonia (313)471-3400.
Call club for further information.
Subscriber comments: Not in good shape . . . Subpar, needs all-around attention . . . Nothing special . . . Front is tight and short, back longer and open, fairways are too hard . . . Frustrating . . . Great staff and accommodating to women walk-ons.

FOX HILLS COUNTRY CLUB

PU—8768 N. Territorial Rd., Plymouth (313)453-7272.

25 miles west of Detroit. **Credit cards:** All major.

Caddies: No. **On-site lodging:** No. **Rental clubs:** Yes.

Range: Yes.

To obtain tee times: Call seven days in advance for weekdays and 10 days in advance for weekends.

★★★½ GOLDEN FOX COURSE

Holes: 18. **Par:** 72/72.

Yards: 6,783/5,040. **Course rating:** 73.0/69.7. **Slope:** 136/122.

Opened: 1989. **Pace of Play rating:** 4:45. **Green fee:** $45/50.

Reduced fees: Weekdays, Low season, Twilight, Seniors.

Golf carts: Included in Green Fee.

Discount golf packages: Yes. **Season:** April-Nov. **High:** May-Sept.

Walking policy: Mandatory cart.

Subscriber comments: Fairly challenging . . . Arthur Hills designed, difficult premium public course . . . Terrific conditions . . . Tour caliber, almost too long . . . Food is excellent . . . One of three hidden Arthur Hills gems in our area . . . Demanding but reasonable . . . Long, narrow greens make it a challenge . . . Love the Scottish look with the long grasses. Hate to be forced to ride, though . . . Great track, but always wet . . . Outstanding . . . Playable . . . Some fun holes . . . Overrated . . . Easy, interesting . . . Difficult 18th . . . No. 5 is very strange: elephant mounds block the green from fairway . . . Greens do not hold well . . . Great greens but relatively flat; not as hilly as those on the other three nines . . . Interesting features, bring a drop wedge.

★★ HILLS/WOODLANDS/LAKES

Holes: 27. **Par:** 70/71/71.

Yards: 6,398/6,514/6,784. **Course rating:** 67.4/67.8/69.4.

Slope: 104/112/112.

Opened: 1921. **Pace of Play rating:** N/A. **Green fee:** $19/23.

Reduced fees: Weekdays, Low season, Twilight, Seniors, Juniors.

Golf carts: $23 for 18 holes.

Discount golf packages: Yes. **Season:** March-Dec. **High:** May-Sept.

Walking policy: Unrestricted walking.

Subscriber comments: Designed for players who hit the ball high . . . Interesting holes . . . All three nines are great for outings . . . Nice terrain . . . Well-staffed, friendly, well-organized . . . Some fairways too close together . . . Good variety in each hole . . . Gets lots of play . . . Rolling with trees and water . . . Condition not what it used to be . . . Woodlands is nicest nine: hills, trees and water galore . . . Excessive play has taken its toll. Beware of stones in the bunkers.

★★★ FOX RUN COUNTRY CLUB

PU—5825 W. Four Mile Rd., Grayling (517)348-4343.

40 miles east of Traverse City. **Holes:** 18. **Par:** 72/72.

Yards: 6,268/4,809. **Course rating:** 70.4/68.5. **Slope:** 126/117.

Opened: 1990. **Pace of Play rating:** 3:52. **Green fee:** $25.

Credit cards: MC, V. **Reduced fees:** Twilight.

Caddies: No. **Golf carts:** $15 for 18 holes.

Discount golf packages: No. **Season:** April-Oct. **High:** June-Sept.

On-site lodging: No. **Rental clubs:** Yes.

Walking policy: Walking at certain times. **Range:** Yes (grass).

Subscriber comments: Nice course in the boonies . . . Very enjoyable. Only a few plain holes detract . . . A lovely golf course . . . Excellent staff . . . Tricky greens, no gimmicks . . . Front nine flat and straightforward, back nine has more character . . . Some nondescript holes . . . Lush fairways and rough, enjoyed it . . . Interesting new course . . . No. 4 and No. 5 greens too severe.

GARLAND GOLF RESORT

R—HCR No. 1, Box 364M, Lewiston (517)786-2211, (800)968-0042.

30 miles east of Gaylord.

Credit cards: All major. **Reduced fees:** Weekdays, Low season, Resort guests, Twilight, Juniors.

Caddies: No. **Golf carts:** Included in Green Fee.
Discount golf packages: Yes. **Season:** April–Oct. **High:** June–Aug.
On–site lodging: Yes. **Rental clubs:** Yes.
Walking policy: Mandatory cart. **Range:** Yes (grass).
To obtain tee times: Call pro shop and ask for reservationist.
New 18-hole Fountains course to open August, 1995.

★★★½ MONARCH COURSE

Holes: 18. **Par:** 72/72.
Yards: 7,188/4,904. **Course rating:** 75.6/69.5. **Slope:** 140/123.
Opened: . **Pace of Play rating:** 4:30. **Green fee:** $72.
Subscriber comments: Great golf, great resort, great staff . . . A great
place to vacation . . . Most beautifully-kept complex of courses in northern
Michigan. Lodge rooms the most luxurious in Michigan, although the most
recent cabin construction detracts from the rest of the complex. Best lunch
room of any course in Michigan . . . 35 miles from nowhere . . . A
beautiful setting . . . Lots of deer . . . Must hit the greens . . . Best of the
three . . . The Augusta of northern Michigan . . . Every resort owner
should visit Garland to find out how customers should be treated . . .
Probably the best manicured greens in Michigan . . . Bring your ball
retriever: water, water everywhere . . . Great use of Michigan nature . . .
Brutally hard . . . Pricey but you get full value . . . Lots of water, layups
and yes, butterflies . . . Not a bad lie in the place . . . The wildlife is
fantastic, very picturesque.

★★★ REFLECTIONS COURSE

Holes: 18. **Par:** 72/72.
Yards: 6,434/4,778. **Course rating:** 70.4/66.9. **Slope:** 120/110.
Opened: 1990. **Pace of Play rating:** 4:30. **Green fee:** $65.
Subscriber comments: Love to play . . . Slow play . . . Great course in a
beautiful setting . . . Unique, secluded, and romantic . . . Not too difficult,
some trees in front of the green, perfectly conditioned . . . Bugs are
unbelievable . . . Garland is first-class in all aspects. Reflections cheapest of
the three . . . Great food and hospitality . . . Lots of par 3s and par 5s . . .
Tight, even for northern Michigan standards . . . As good as any private
course . . . Total beauty from the clubhouse to the grounds . . . Best golf
facility east of the Mississippi . . . Easiest of the three Garland courses . . .
Lots of wildlife, bring a camera.

★★★½ SWAMPFIRE COURSE

Holes: 18. **Par:** 72/72.
Yards: 6,854/4,791. **Course rating:** 73.9/68.4. **Slope:** 138/121.
Opened: N/A. **Pace of Play rating:** 4:30. **Green fee:** $72.
Subscriber comments: Clubhouse is stunning. Wildlife galore . . . Eats
my lunch . . . Each course different . . . Interesting golf variety . . . Too
many people, too many flies . . . Best of the three . . . A real test . . . More
woods and water . . . Absolutely tops in Michigan . . . Wildlife all over . . .
Very challenging . . . Very picturesque and playable . . . Uses water instead
of good architecture for its challenge . . . A beauty . . . You will have to
have your ball retriever regripped when you're done . . . Simply awesome
. . . What swamp? . . . A really attractive course, well-maintained but
costly . . . So much water you'll need to rent a wet suit . . . Swampfire is
the best of the three.

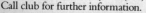

★★★ GAYLORD COUNTRY CLUB

SP—P.O. Box 207, Gaylord (616)546-3376.
Call club for further information.
Subscriber comments: Weak opening holes . . . Made for lefthanders . . .
The forgotten gem in Gaylord . . . In the heart of northern Michigan . . .
Some holes bad, others good . . . Best buy in the Gaylord area . . . First
three holes belie a great layout . . . Gets tight after No. 5 . . . Fun to play to
tune up for the Treetop courses . . . A rarity in northern Michigan: a course
that's playable, affordable and has four-hour rounds . . . Ho-hum start, but
it gets better . . . Fair; minimal gimmicks . . . Classic old-style layout . . .
Professional staff excellent . . . Bargain of the north.

★★★ GIANT OAKS GOLF COURSE

PU—1024 Valetta Dr., Temperance (313)847-6733.
Call club for further information.
Subscriber comments: Great challenges, exciting . . . Front nine has three
par 5s . . . Well-maintained, interesting and challenging . . . Condition
comes and goes . . . Four miles from the Ohio border.

GLACIER CLUB★

SP—8000 Glacier Club Dr., Washington (810)781-2288.
27 miles north of Detroit. **Holes:** 18. **Par:** 72/72.
Yards: 7,018/4,937. **Course rating:** 74.1/68.5. **Slope:** 134/116.
Opened: 1994. **Pace of Play rating:** N/A. **Green fee:** $30/50.
Credit cards: MC, V, AMEX. **Reduced fees:** Weekdays, Twilight,
Seniors, Juniors.
Caddies: No. **Golf carts:** Included in Green Fee.
Discount golf packages: No. **Season:** April-Dec. **High:** May-Sept.
On-site lodging: No. **Rental clubs:** Yes.
Walking policy: Mandatory cart. **Range:** Yes (grass).
To obtain tee times: Call seven days in advance.

★★ GLENEAGLE GOLF CLUB

PU—6150 14th Ave., Hudsonville (616)457-3680.
5 miles west of Grand Rapids. **Holes:** 18. **Par:** 71/72.
Yards: 6,125/4,971. **Course rating:** 69.4/68.8. **Slope:** 125/124.
Opened: 1960. **Pace of Play rating:** 4:00. **Green fee:** $16/18.
Credit cards: MC, V. **Reduced fees:** Low season, Seniors, Juniors.
Caddies: No. **Golf carts:** $18 for 18 holes.
Discount golf packages: No. **Season:** April-Nov. **High:** June-Aug.
On-site lodging: No. **Rental clubs:** Yes.
Walking policy: Unrestricted walking. **Range:** Yes (grass).
To obtain tee times: Call at least one-week in advance.
Formerly known as Fairway Golf Club.
Subscriber comments: Good views, good challenge . . . Some really
sharp holes . . . Some holes had me nervous, windows left and right . . .
Some interesting holes . . . Character is building in layout revisions . . .
Soft all around . . . Chopped-up layout designed to fit between the condos
. . . Nondescript. New holes are something of an improvement . . .
Getting better all the time.

★½ GLENHURST GOLF COURSE

PU—25345 W. 6 Mile Rd., Redford (313)592-8758.
18 miles west of Detroit. **Holes:** 18. **Par:** 70/72.
Yards: 5,508/4,978. **Course rating:** 65.5/70.6. **Slope:** 107/115.
Opened: 1932. **Pace of Play rating:** 4:30. **Green fee:** $9/19.
Credit cards: None. **Reduced fees:** Weekdays, Low season, Twilight,
Seniors, Juniors.
Caddies: No. **Golf carts:** $20 for 18 holes.
Discount golf packages: No. **Season:** March-Jan. **High:** June-Aug.
On-site lodging: No. **Rental clubs:** Yes.
Walking policy: Unrestricted walking. **Range:** No.
To obtain tee times: Tee times for weekends and holidays only.
Reservations taken one week in advance.
Subscriber comments: Fairly open, short, fun to play, great snack bar . . .
Old lady, easy . . . Typical muny . . . OK for practice . . . Service OK . . .
Very good greens the only redeeming value on an overplayed course . . .
Very friendly . . . Renovations in progress . . . Great chili dogs.

GRACEWIL COUNTRY CLUB

PU—2597 Four Mile Rd. N.W., Grand Rapids (616)784-2455.
Opened: 1929. **Green fee:** $14/17.
Credit cards: MC, V. **Reduced fees:** Weekdays, Low season, Twilight,
Seniors, Juniors.
Caddies: No. **Golf carts:** $18 for 18 holes.
Discount golf packages: No. **Season:** March-Nov. **High:** June-Aug.

On-site lodging: No. **Rental clubs:** Yes.
Walking policy: Unrestricted walking. **Range:** No.
To obtain tee times: Call up to ten days in advance. Tee times taken on weekends only until 4 p.m.

★ **EAST COURSE**
Holes: 18. **Par:** 72/72.
Yards: 6,180/5,025. **Course rating:** 69.9/71.3. **Slope:** N/A.
Pace of Play rating: 4:30.
Subscriber comments: Decent and cheap, open until the snow falls . . . Greens vary by hole . . . No bunkers . . . Pace can be slow . . . Boring walk, back and forth . . . In an old apple orchard . . . Hit it straight or you're in the apple trees.

★ **WEST COURSE**
Holes: 18. **Par:** 72/72.
Yards: 6,070/4,840. **Course rating:** 69.7/71.0. **Slope:** N/A.
Pace of Play rating: 4:00.
Subscriber comments: Not very challenging . . . It needs hazards . . . For seniors and league play . . . Gets lots of play . . . Not the greatest.

★★ **GRACEWIL PINES GOLF CLUB**
PU—5400 Trailer Park Dr., Jackson (517)764-4200.
20 miles north of Lansing. **Holes:** 18. **Par:** 72/72.
Yards: 6,170/4,405. **Course rating:** N/A. **Slope:** N/A.
Opened: 1984. **Pace of Play rating:** 4:30. **Green fee:** $10/13.
Credit cards: V. **Reduced fees:** Weekdays, Low season, Twilight, Seniors, Juniors.
Caddies: No. **Golf carts:** $18 for 18 holes.
Discount golf packages: Yes. **Season:** March-Nov. **High:** May-Aug.
On-site lodging: No. **Rental clubs:** Yes.
Walking policy: Unrestricted walking. **Range:** No.
To obtain tee times: Call pro shop.
Subscriber comments: Back nine is better . . . Short, tight front nine . . . Straight shooters will score well . . . Mosquitoes . . . Too much swamp . . . Lined with pine trees. Keeping the ball in play is the key . . . Tightest fairways I've ever seen . . . Very cheap . . . Great for the money . . . On the upswing, some fine holes . . . Short but challenging . . . Cut through the trees with rolling terrain . . . Needs maturity.

★★★½ **GRAND HAVEN GOLF CLUB**
SP—17000 Lincoln St., Grand Haven (616)842-4040.
28 miles east of Grand Rapids. **Holes:** 18. **Par:** 72/72.
Yards: 6,789/5,536. **Course rating:** 71.9/71.4. **Slope:** 124/119.
Opened: 1965. **Pace of Play rating:** 4:30. **Green fee:** $20/32.
Credit cards: MC, V. **Reduced fees:** Weekdays, Low season, Twilight.
Caddies: No. **Golf carts:** $10 for 18 holes.
Discount golf packages: No. **Season:** March-Nov. **High:** June-Aug.
On-site lodging: No. **Rental clubs:** Yes.
Walking policy: Unrestricted walking. **Range:** Yes (grass).
To obtain tee times: Weekday: as far in advance as customer would like to book a reservation. Weekend: one week in advance from date which customer would like to play.
Ranked in Third 25 of America's 75 Best Public Golf Courses by Golf Digest.
Subscriber comments: Very difficult but fun . . . Tough greens . . . Very narrow fairways, a must-play course . . . Easy to double-bogey plenty of holes if you're not careful . . . You'd better be accurate off the tee . . . "Corridor" golf but be patient, pain is only momentary . . . Greens need to be quicker . . . Nice layout in the woods . . . Overrated . . . Good combination of sand and pines, makes you play all the shots . . . Always among the state's best, a must-play on any Michigan trip . . . Beautiful setting . . . Only good players can enjoy . . . Still the best course in the area, old granddaddy . . . Too tight, too hilly, too expensive . . . Best kept secret in western Michigan . . . Keep it in the fairway or learn to hit out of the trees . . . Tightest course I play . . . If you get hit, it's because you're in

the woods trying to hit out . . . Worth the drive to play . . . Outstanding natural design . . . Holes well-separated by giant hardwoods . . . Only one fairway bunker . . . Could have been the Pinehurst of Michigan . . . Very similar to courses in northern Michigan with forests left and right.

★½ GRAND ISLAND GOLF RANCH

PU—6266 W. River Dr., Belmont (616)363-1262.
10 miles southwest of Grand Rapids. **Holes:** 18. **Par:** 72/73.
Yards: 6,266/5,522. **Course rating:** 71.9/71.4. **Slope:** 124/119.
Opened: 1965. **Pace of Play rating:** 4:30. **Green fee:** $16/17.
Credit cards: MC, V, DISC. **Reduced fees:** Low season, Seniors, Juniors.
Caddies: No. **Golf carts:** $16 for 18 holes.
Discount golf packages: Yes. **Season:** March-Dec. **High:** May-Sept.
On-site lodging: No. **Rental clubs:** Yes.
Walking policy: Unrestricted walking. **Range:** Yes (grass).
To obtain tee times: Call one week in advance.
Subscriber comments: Not cheap for a less-than-great course. You don't get what you pay for . . . Flat, back-and-forth golf, no challenge . . . Stays open longer than any other course . . . Wet in the spring . . . Very short . . . Typical muny . . . Greens in very poor shape.

GRAND RAPIDS GOLF CLUB
★½ WHITE/RED/BLUE

PU—4300 Leonard N.E., Grand Rapids (616)949-2820.
5 miles east of Grand Rapids. **Holes:** 27. **Par:** 72/70/72.
Yards: 6,127/5,887/6,194. **Course rating:** 70.3/68.5/69.8.
Slope: 116/116/115.
Opened: 1969. **Pace of Play rating:** N/A. **Green fee:** $17/19.
Credit cards: MC, V. **Reduced fees:** Weekdays, Low season, Seniors, Juniors.
Caddies: No. **Golf carts:** $20 for 18 holes.
Discount golf packages: No. **Season:** March-Nov. **High:** May-Aug.
On-site lodging: No. **Rental clubs:** Yes.
Walking policy: Unrestricted walking. **Range:** Yes (grass).
To obtain tee times: Call pro shop.
Subscriber comments: Nothing special . . . White and blue nines are very good . . . Greens don't last . . . Regular muny . . . Could have been one great 18 . . . Hilly in spots . . . Firm greens, small . . . Unimaginative . . . Starting to get rundown.

GRAND TRAVERSE RESORT

R—6300 U.S. 31 N., Acme (616)938-1620, (800)748-0303.
6 miles from Traverse City.
Credit cards: All major. **Reduced fees:** Weekdays, Low season, Resort guests, Twilight.
Caddies: No. **Golf carts:** Included in Green Fee.
Discount golf packages: Yes. **Season:** April-Oct. **High:** June-Aug.
On-site lodging: Yes. **Rental clubs:** Yes.
Walking policy: Mandatory cart. **Range:** Yes (grass).
To obtain tee times: Call one week in advance.
★★★½ SPRUCE RUN COURSE
Holes: 18. **Par:** 72/73.
Yards: 6,741/5,139. **Course rating:** 73.7/70.7. **Slope:** 137/131.
Opened: 1979. **Pace of Play rating:** 4:00. **Green fee:** $30/70.
Subscriber comments: The Bear is a bear, but Spruce Run is fun . . . As enjoyable as The Bear, maybe moreso . . . A solid compliment to The Bear . . . Average resort course . . . Wonderful resort . . . Nothing outstanding . . . Relaxing golf . . . Picture-postcard images of every hole . . . Short season . . . Beautiful condition, great fun . . . Good treatment of golfers if you stay at the resort . . . They cater to the customer . . . Better value than the Bear . . . A lot of nice holes . . . Very pretty and a fair challenge . . . Perfect greens . . . Best greens by far.

★★★★ THE BEAR
Holes: 18. **Par:** 72/72.
Yards: 7,065/5,281. **Course rating:** 75.8/72.0. **Slope:** 149/131.
Opened: 1985. **Pace of Play rating:** 4:20. **Green fee:** N/A.
Ranked 50th in America's 75 Best Resort Courses by Golf Digest.
Ranked 20th in Michigan by Golf Digest.
Subscriber comments: Wonderful greens, mega-different from the back tees . . . Not for a beginner . . . Not user-friendly . . . Out-of-this-world green fees . . . Some exceptional holes . . . Has everything, a must to play . . . Very challenging, but ugly . . . Too much and too hard . . . Difficult judging distances . . . Extraordinarily difficult . . . A course you play once . . . Unforgiving . . . Some great holes if you can thread a needle from 150 yards . . . Pricey, but you have to play it once . . . Typical Nicklaus target golf . . . Not for wimps! . . . Does not live up to its hype . . . It's a bear . . . Wonderful holes . . . Greens are very fast . . . Fun for anyone who has a sense of humor . . . Tough, don't take the wife . . . Golfers are kings and queens here . . . The course gives me goosebumps . . . Long tortuous journey . . . Eight-foot deep bunkers . . . Unforgiving greens . . . Should putt each one twice to get a good read . . . Fiendish and irresistable . . . Too tough for mere mortals . . . The few holes in the trees were remarkable . . . Nicklaus' toughest 18 . . . Terrible for tourists, too slow . . . Not very scenic . . . Leave your ego at home and bring extra balls . . . There is no let-up hole or shot . . . One of Jack's best jobs.

★★★ GRAND VIEW GOLF COURSE
PU—5464 S. 68th Ave., New Era (616)861-6616.
20 miles south of Muskegan. **Holes:** 18. **Par:** 71/71.
Yards: 6,258/4,737. **Course rating:** N/A. **Slope:** N/A.
Opened: 1993. **Pace of Play rating:** 4:30. **Green fee:** $15/16.
Credit cards: MC, V. **Reduced fees:** Weekdays, Seniors.
Caddies: No. **Golf carts:** $8 for 18 holes.
Discount golf packages: No. **Season:** April-Oct. **High:** June-Aug.
On-site lodging: No. **Rental clubs:** Yes.
Walking policy: Unrestricted walking. **Range:** Yes (grass).
To obtain tee times: Call ahead. Tee times recommended.
Subscriber comments: Can be very windy in the higher elevations of the course . . . Refreshing, proves that the little things don't cost much . . . Looks nice . . . Very forgiving fairways sloped towards center . . . Up-and-down front nine, rolling back nine, many uphill iron shots . . . Super treatment . . . Cut through an old cherry orchard, nice views . . . Absolutely beautiful . . . Excellent first-year course . . . Great bargain . . . Pleasant . . . Mom and Pop design . . . Everything mowed at one height.

(FRUGAL PICK)

★★★ GRANDVIEW GOLF CLUB
PU—3003 Hagni Rd., Kalkaska (616)258-3214.
Call club for further information.
Subscriber comments: New back nine . . . Ends with relief . . . Not much . . . Flat course, flat greens, flat golf . . . Very nice people, great scenery . . . Very beautiful during the autumn months with the leaves colored . . . Disappointing, not very interesting.

★★★ GREYSTONE GOLF CLUB
PU—67500 Mound Rd., Romeo (810)752-7030.
15 miles northeast of Troy. **Holes:** 18. **Par:** 72/71.
Yards: 6,861/4,816. **Course rating:** 73.3/67.5. **Slope:** 131/120.
Opened: 1992. **Pace of Play rating:** 4:00. **Green fee:** $43/48.
Credit cards: All major. **Reduced fees:** Low season, Twilight, Seniors, Juniors.
Caddies: No. **Golf carts:** Included in Green Fee.
Discount golf packages: No. **Season:** April-Nov. **High:** June-Aug.
On-site lodging: No. **Rental clubs:** Yes.
Walking policy: Mandatory cart. **Range:** Yes (grass).
To obtain tee times: Call for tee times seven days in advance. More than seven days a deposit is required.

Subscriber comments: Greens are lacking . . . Only three exceptional holes are 16, 17 and 18 . . . Very tough finishing holes, great clubhouse . . . Three of the best finishing holes anywhere . . . Last three holes are worth the price . . . 16th, 17th, 18th holes are a reality check . . . Best finishing holes in southeast Michigan . . . Love the mounding, except in front of the 15th green. Might as well build a brick wall . . . Last three holes are monsters . . . No place to hit the ball on the last three holes . . . Country club flavor, three unfair closing holes . . . Play is terribly slow . . . Great three-hole finish around water . . . Last three holes are thrillers around a quarry . . . Final three holes are fantastic . . . You're thinking about 16 through 18 all day . . . Did not like the design of the 17th and 18th holes . . . Try hitting the 16th green on a windy day.

GULL LAKE VIEW GOLF CLUB
PU—7417 N. 38th St., Augusta (616)731-4148.
15 miles southwest of Kalamazoo.
Opened: 1963. **Pace of Play rating:** 4:15. **Green fee:** $23/26.
Credit cards: MC, V. **Reduced fees:** Weekdays, Low season, Resort guests, Twilight, Juniors.
Caddies: No. **Golf carts:** $22 for 18 holes.
Discount golf packages: Yes. **Season:** April-Nov. **High:** May-Aug.
On-site lodging: Yes. **Rental clubs:** Yes.
Walking policy: Walking at certain times. **Range:** No.
To obtain tee times: Call pro shop.
★★★½ **EAST COURSE**
Holes: 18. **Par:** 70/70.
Yards: 6,002/4,918. **Course rating:** 69.4/68.5. **Slope:** 124/118.
Subscriber comments: Best golf for the money in the state . . . Picturesque, challenging . . . Short and tight, hills and small, bunkered greens. Not much use for your driver . . . Better than the West course . . . Short, tight, sporty and scenic . . . Lots of water, but well-placed . . . One of the prettiest courses in state . . . Affordable . . . Several novelty holes . . . Scenery is beautiful . . . Requires local knowledge . . . Prettiest par 3 around.

★★★ **WEST COURSE**
Holes: 18. **Par:** 71/72.
Yards: 6,300/5,218. **Course rating:** 70.6/69.0. **Slope:** 123/114.
Subscriber comments: Not as difficult as the East, but sporty . . . Excellent condition, play moved very well . . . Best golf package in the Midwest . . . Traditional . . . Woods and water, hilly . . . In great shape . . . Beautiful views make play more memorable . . . Nos. 10, 11, 12 are the three toughest holes in a row I've ever played . . . Back nine has some spongy fairways . . . Low land, no roll . . . As much variety as the East.

★★★½ **HAMPSHIRE COUNTRY CLUB**
SP—29592 Pokagon Hwy., Dowagiac (616)782-7476.
Holes: 18. **Par:** 72/75.
Yards: 7,030/6,185. **Course rating:** 72.6/73.0. **Slope:** 120/N/A.
Opened: 1962. **Pace of Play rating:** 4:30. **Green fee:** $15/17.
Credit cards: MC, V. **Reduced fees:** Weekdays, Twilight, Juniors.
Caddies: No. **Golf carts:** $18 for 18 holes.
Discount golf packages: Yes. **Season:** April-Nov. **High:** June-Aug.
On-site lodging: No. **Rental clubs:** Yes.
Walking policy: Unrestricted walking. **Range:** No.
To obtain tee times: One week in advance.
Subscriber comments: Excellent older course . . . Great test of ability . . . Long par 4s . . . New West course will only make the place better . . . Trees add real difinition . . . Few bunkers, fast greens . . . Just a great gem . . . A true challenge . . . Something for everyone . . . Will always want to play this one again . . . Average condition.

SUPER VALUE

HARTLAND GLEN GOLF AND COUNTRY CLUB
PU—12400 Highland Rd., Hartland (810)887-3777.
25 miles north of Ann Arbor.
Opened: 1972. **Pace of Play rating:** 4:15. **Green fee:** $12/20.

Credit cards: None. **Reduced fees:** Weekdays, Low season, Twilight, Seniors, Juniors.
Caddies: No. **Golf carts:** $10 for 18 holes.
Discount golf packages: No. **Season:** April-Oct. **High:** June-Aug.
On-site lodging: No. **Rental clubs:** Yes.
Walking policy: Unrestricted walking. **Range:** Yes (grass).
To obtain tee times: Call one week in advance.

★★ NORTH COURSE
Holes: 18. **Par:** 71/71.
Yards: 6,260/5,109. **Course rating:** 68.9/69.0. **Slope:** 113/113.
Subscriber comments: My "sneak in nine" course . . . Some clever holes, good price . . . Heavy play . . . Lack of design feature . . . Newest 18 not ready yet, but it will be great . . . Good layout for a pleasant course, not demanding.

SOUTH COURSE★
Holes: 18. **Par:** 71/71.
Yards: 6,175/4,661. **Course rating:** N/A. **Slope:** N/A.

★★★ HEATHER HIGHLANDS GOLF CLUB
PU—11450 E. Holly Rd., Holly (810)634-6800.
50 miles north of Detroit. **Holes:** 18. **Par:** 72/72.
Yards: 6,845/5,764. **Course rating:** 72.4/72.6. **Slope:** 121/120.
Opened: 1966. **Pace of Play rating:** 4:30. **Green fee:** $17/24.
Credit cards: MC, V. **Reduced fees:** Low season.

Caddies: No. **Golf carts:** $20 for 18 holes.
Discount golf packages: Yes. **Season:** April-Nov. **High:** May-Sept.
On-site lodging: No. **Rental clubs:** Yes.
Walking policy: Walking at certain times. **Range:** Yes (grass).
To obtain tee times: Call six days in advance.
Subscriber comments: Very playable public course . . . Large greens . . . Giant greens . . . Best for the average, economy-minded player . . . Good course, nice people, fair test, great for the buck . . . Good challenge, not boring . . . Difficult on a windy day . . . Well-balanced . . . One of the best courses for the money in the area . . . Good course, nothing spectacular . . . Use all of your clubs . . . Always in good shape . . . Underrated for the area, few traps.

HERITAGE GLEN GOLF CLUB★
PU—29795 Heritage Lane, Paw Paw (616)657-2552.
15 miles west of Kalamazoo. **Holes:** 18. **Par:** 72/72.
Yards: 6,598/4,946. **Course rating:** 70.1/68.4. **Slope:** N/A.
Opened: 1994. **Pace of Play rating:** 4:30. **Green fee:** $21/24.
Credit cards: MC, V. **Reduced fees:** No.
Caddies: No. **Golf carts:** $13 for 18 holes.
Discount golf packages: Yes. **Season:** April-Nov. **High:** May-Sept.
On-site lodging: No. **Rental clubs:** Yes.
Walking policy: Unrestricted walking. **Range:** Yes (grass).
To obtain tee times: Call anytime.

★★★ HIDDEN VALLEY RESORT AND CLUB
R—P.O. Box 556, Gaylord (517)732-4653.
60 miles northeast of Traverse City. **Holes:** 18. **Par:** 71/71.
Yards: 6,305/5,591. **Course rating:&** N/A. **Slope:** 121/113.
Opened: . **Pace of Play rating:** . **Green fee:** N/A.
Credit cards: All major. **Reduced fees:** Weekdays, Low season, Resort guests, Twilight.
Caddies: No. **Golf carts:** N/A.
Discount golf packages: Yes. **Season:** April-Oct. **High:** June-Aug.
On-site lodging: Yes. **Rental clubs:** No.
Walking policy: N/A. **Range:** Yes (grass).
Subscriber comments: Great greens, classic . . . Old course needs some work . . . Challenging course but not equal to others in area . . . Eye-catching beauty . . . Back nine a little tougher . . . Some interesting holes . . . Friendliest staff in Michigan . . . Not too imaginative, but has outstanding greens . . . Doesn't measure up to a Treetops course, but

neither does the price. Has some good looking holes . . . Husband-and-wife golf, enjoyable, quiet . . . You tee off on time . . . Greens near perfect, but layout is repetitive.

★★★ HIGH POINTE GOLF CLUB

PU—5555 Arnold Rd., Williamsburg (616)267-9900, (800)753-7888.
10 miles northeast of Traverse City. **Holes:** 18. **Par:** 71/72.
Yards: 6,849/5,101. **Course rating:** 72.9/69.6. **Slope:** 135/121.
Opened: 1989. **Pace of Play rating:** 4:15. **Green fee:** $15/30.
Credit cards: All major. **Reduced fees:** Weekdays, Low season, Resort guests, Twilight, Seniors, Juniors.
Caddies: No. **Golf carts:** $14 for 18 holes.
Discount golf packages: Yes. **Season:** April-Oct. **High:** June-Aug.
On-site lodging: No. **Rental clubs:** Yes.
Walking policy: Unrestricted walking. **Range:** Yes (grass).
To obtain tee times: Call. Credit cards may be required for advance tee times and groups.
Ranked in Third 25 of America's Best Public Golf Courses by Golf Digest.
Subscriber comments: Both nines provide different challenges . . . Good design, not always in good condition . . . Back nine much more interesting; almost two courses . . . Used 300 acres to build a 200-acre golf course . . . Not as good as touted . . . Funny grass to play on . . . Overpublicized . . . Can be very fast or very slow, pace of play depending on your tee time . . . Environmentally sensitive . . . Nice mix of conditions and setting from front to back . . . As challenging as The Bear at Grand Traverse Resort without the extravagant price tag . . . Front nine lures you into believing you can conquer the back nine. Wrong! . . . Pitch-and-run on links nine, target golf on wooded nine . . . Made an improvement . . . Challenging yet friendly holes offer options; mistakes aren't death sentences . . . Incredible . . . Nothing flashy . . . Front nine a Scottish course, back nine traditional American . . . Some small redesigning has improved an already superior track.

HIGHLAND GOLF CLUB★

SP—3011 U.S. 2-41, Escanaba (906)466-7457.
90 miles north of Green Bay, WI. **Holes:** 18. **Par:** 71/72.
Yards: 6,237/5,499. **Course rating:** 69.3/71.0. **Slope:** 117/115.
Opened: 1930. **Pace of Play rating:** N/A. **Green fee:** $16.
Credit cards: MC, V. **Reduced fees:** N/A.

Caddies: No. **Golf carts:** N/A.
Discount golf packages: No. **Season:** April-Oct. **High:** June-Aug.
On-site lodging: No. **Rental clubs:** Yes.
Walking policy: Unrestricted walking. **Range:** No.
To obtain tee times: Call three days in advance.

★½ HILLTOP GOLF COURSE

PU—47000 Powell Rd., Plymouth (313)453-9800.
Call club for further information.
Subscriber comments: Greens are the slickest I've ever played. Two are sloped so great that they are impossible . . . Short and hilly, small, quick greens . . . Supreme mental and physical challenge . . . Fairways and tee boxes are too close together . . . Toughest greens around this area. You can four-putt from four feet . . . Fair but not spectacular . . . Greens are very steep and undulating . . . I've seen the cosmetologist bikini wax the greens.

★★½ HUDSON MILLS METRO PARK GOLF COURSE

PU—4800 Dexter-Pickney Rd., Dexter (313)426-0466, (800)477-3191.
12 miles north of Ann Arbor. **Holes:** 18. **Par:** 71/71.
Yards: 6,560/5,411. **Course rating:** 70.6/70.2. **Slope:** 116/113.
Opened: 1991. **Pace of Play rating:** 4:30. **Green fee:** $17/19.
Credit cards: None. **Reduced fees:** Weekdays, Low season, Seniors, Juniors.
Caddies: No. **Golf carts:** $19 for 18 holes.
Discount golf packages: No. **Season:** March-Nov. **High:** May-Sept..
On-site lodging: No. **Rental clubs:** Yes.

Walking policy: Unrestricted walking. **Range:** No.
To obtain tee times: Call seven days in advance.
Subscriber comments: Back better than front . . . Short par 5s mean birdies . . . Very different nines, open and flat vs. tight with lots of trees . . . Two great par 5s on the back. Flat, relatively easy, low fees, walking allowed . . . Two par 5s on back nine are tree-lined and gorgeous . . . Well-constructed and maintained . . . A little tougher than most of the metro park courses.

★★★½ HURON BREEZE GOLF AND COUNTRY CLUB
PU—5200 Huron Breeze Dr., Au Gres (517)876-6868.
50 miles north of Saginaw. **Holes:** 18. **Par:** 72/72.
Yards: 6,806/5,075. **Course rating:** 73.1/69.4. **Slope:** 133/123.
Opened: 1991. **Pace of Play rating:** 4:09. **Green fee:** $14/24.
Credit cards: MC, V. **Reduced fees:** Weekdays, Low season, Twilight, Seniors, Juniors.
Caddies: No. **Golf carts:** $10 for 18 holes.
Discount golf packages: Yes. **Season:** April-Oct. **High:** June-Sept.
On-site lodging: No. **Rental clubs:** Yes.
Walking policy: Unrestricted walking. **Range:** Yes (grass).
To obtain tee times: Call in advance, no restrictions.
Subscriber comments: Mature, wooded setting . . . The equal of higher price resort courses . . . Nice course, people glad to see you . . . Excellent . . . Loved this course . . . The only thing I hated was that they time your play . . . Cut through Michigan pines . . . Short, but trees more than make up for it . . . All 18 holes have woods and/or water . . . Tight and tough . . . An absolute bargain . . . Hidden beauty . . . Well-designed . . . Abundant wildlife . . . Don't assume that you need driver off every tee.

★★★ HURON GOLF CLUB
R—1275 Huron St., Ypsilanti (313)487-2441.
15 miles west of Detroit. **Holes:** 18. **Par:** 72/72.
Yards: 6,750/5,185. **Course rating:** 73.6/69.7. **Slope:** 138/124.
Opened: 1989. **Pace of Play rating:** 4:30. **Green fee:** $35.
Credit cards: MC, V, AMEX. **Reduced fees:** Weekdays, Low season, Twilight, Seniors, Juniors.
Caddies: No. **Golf carts:** Included in Green Fee.
Discount golf packages: Yes. **Season:** March-Nov. **High:** June-Aug.
On-site lodging: Yes. **Rental clubs:** Yes.
Walking policy: Walking at certain times. **Range:** Yes (grass).
To obtain tee times: Call up to 14 days in advance.
Subscriber comments: Next to Ford Lake . . . Great back nine . . . Nice layout . . . Takes strategic tee shots . . . Toughest and best-kept course in southeast Michigan, loads of fun . . . Fifteen great holes, three poor ones. Still worth playing once a year . . . One of the best back nines in southeast Michigan. Greens sometimes spotty from overplay . . . Should be a better deal for students and alumni . . . Lots of water . . . Occasional slow play . . . Forces longer hitters to think . . . The view of the lake is very nice . . . Very picturesque . . . Gets heavy play.

★½ HURON HILLS GOLF COURSE
PU—3465 E Huron River Dr., Ann Arbor (313)971-6840.
Call club for further information.
Subscriber comments: Nice course, combo of tight and open holes . . . Very short, not much challenge . . . Tee shots a key on the back nine . . . Good course for beginners . . . Very flat . . . A good place to start kids golfing.

★★½ HURON MEADOWS GOLF COURSE
PU—8765 Hammel Rd., Brighton (810)685-1561.
Call club for further information.
Subscriber comments: Open metro park course, no trouble spots, easy to score on . . . Large greens, a short player's dream . . . One of the best maintained courses in the metro system . . . Trees and water and traps . . . Acceptable . . . Incorporates wildlife preserve. Sandhill cranes live on course.

★★★ INDIAN RIVER GOLF CLUB

SP—6460 Chippewa Beach Rd., Indian River (616)238-7011.
20 miles north of Gaylord. **Holes:** 18. **Par:** 72/72.
Yards: 6,718/5,277. **Course rating:** 72.4/71.3. **Slope:** 124/119.
Opened: 1921. **Pace of Play rating:** 4:15. **Green fee:** $20/26.
Credit cards: MC, V. **Reduced fees:** Weekdays, Low season, Twilight,
Juniors.
Caddies: No. **Golf carts:** $15 for 18 holes.
Discount golf packages: Yes. **Season:** May-Oct. **High:** July-Aug.
On-site lodging: No. **Rental clubs:** No.
Walking policy: Unrestricted walking. **Range:** No.
To obtain tee times: Call anytime.
Subscriber comments: A sleeper; old-style front nine, woodsy back, fun
. . . Good condition . . . Back nine is a lot better than front . . . Some nice
secluded holes . . . Stay out of the woods and you'll want to return.

★½ INDIAN RUN GOLF CLUB

PU—6359 E. RS Ave., Scotts (616)327-1327.
6 miles south of Kalamazoo. **Holes:** 18. **Par:** 72/72.
Yards: 6,808/5,028. **Course rating:** 72.1/68.8. **Slope:** 126/115.
Opened: 1966. **Pace of Play rating:** 4:00. **Green fee:** $17/20.
Credit cards: MC, V, DISC. **Reduced fees:** Weekdays, Low season,
Seniors, Juniors.
Caddies: No. **Golf carts:** $11 for 18 holes.
Discount golf packages: Yes. **Season:** April-Oct. **High:** May-Sept.
On-site lodging: No. **Rental clubs:** Yes.
Walking policy: Unrestricted walking. **Range:** Yes (grass).
To obtain tee times: Call.
Subscriber comments: Best suited for long hitters. The longest course in
the county . . . Tight holes . . . Maintenance could improve . . . Tied up
with leagues in the afternoon.

★★★ INDIAN SPRINGS METRO PARK GOLF COURSE

PU—5200 Indian Trail, White Lake (313)625-7870.
Call club for further information.
Subscriber comments: Metro park course, always in good shape . . .
Relaxing environment . . . Fairly long for a public course . . . Lush rough
can make it play even longer . . . No longer a secret . . . Several unfair
domed greens . . . Best of the metro park courses . . . One par 5 is 602
yards from the back . . . Rock-hard greens . . . Greens unpredictable . . .
Not memorable . . . Some exciting holes . . . No traps. You can walk.

★½ INDIAN TRAILS GOLF COURSE

PU—2776 Kalamazoo Ave S.E., Grand Rapids (616)245-2021.
Holes: 18. **Par:** 68/72.
Yards: 5,100/4,785. **Course rating:** 66.8/71.6. **Slope:** N/A.
Opened: 1921. **Pace of Play rating:** N/A. **Green fee:** $13.
Credit cards: None. **Reduced fees:** Weekdays, Low season, Seniors,
Juniors.
Caddies: No. **Golf carts:** N/A.
Discount golf packages: Yes. **Season:** April-Oct. **High:** June-July.
On-site lodging: No. **Rental clubs:** Yes.
Walking policy: Unrestricted walking. **Range:** No.
To obtain tee times: No tee times required.
Subscriber comments: Not a bad course for a quick 18 . . . Easy to get on
. . . Very short but acceptable . . . It's close and cheap . . . Needs length:
only one par 5.

★½ IRONWOOD GOLF CLUB

PU—3750 64th St. S.W., Byron Center (616)538-4000.
Call club for further information.
Subscriber comments: Some narrow, wooded fairways. An iron course
. . . In poor shape . . . Typical Ma and Pa public . . . Short, straight and
slow play . . . Good for beginners, women, lefthanders and bowlers.

IRONWOOD GOLF CLUB★
PU—6902 (M-59) Highland Rd, Howell (517)546-3211.

31 miles northwest of Lansing. **Holes:** 18. **Par:** 72/72.
Yards: 6,083/5,172. **Course rating:** 68.3/67.7. **Slope:** 116/117.
Opened: 1972. **Pace of Play rating:** 4:00. **Green fee:** $18/24.
Credit cards: MC, V. **Reduced fees:** Weekdays, Low season, Twilight, Seniors, Juniors.
Caddies: No. **Golf carts:** $20 for 18 holes.
Discount golf packages: No. **Season:** March-Nov. **High:** June-Sept.
On-site lodging: No. **Rental clubs:** Yes.
Walking policy: Unrestricted walking. **Range:** No.
To obtain tee times: Call.
Subscriber comments: Greens too small . . . Really shaping up . . . Friendly, helpful staff . . . Improving every year . . . A great job of redesigning . . . Gently rolling course. Both open and tree-lined holes.

★★★ KATKE GOLF COURSE
PU—1003 Perry St., Big Rapids (616)592-2213.
50 miles north of Gran Rapids. **Holes:** 18. **Par:** 72/72.
Yards: 6,729/5,344. **Course rating:** 72.5/70.8. **Slope:** 124/119.
Opened: 1974. **Pace of Play rating:** 4:00-4:30. **Green fee:** $18/20.
Credit cards: MC, V, DISC. **Reduced fees:** Weekdays, Low season, Resort guests, Seniors, Juniors.
Caddies: No. **Golf carts:** $10 for 18 holes.
Discount golf packages: Yes. **Season:** April-Nov. **High:** May-Sept.
On-site lodging: Yes. **Rental clubs:** Yes.
Walking policy: Unrestricted walking. **Range:** Yes (grass).
To obtain tee times: Call up to two weeks in advance.
Subscriber comments: Holes too close together, lots of places to get hit . . . Staff was exceptionally acoommodating . . . Ferris State University course, no flat lies, tough par 3s . . . Best value in Grand Rapids . . . Great golf layout for any experience level . . . Could be in better shape for the college . . . Nothing exceptional . . . Front so-so, back challenging . . . Large traps.

★★★ KENSINGTON METRO PARK GOLF CLUB
PU—2240 W. Buno Rd., Milford (313)685-9332.
Call club for further information.
Subscriber comments: Greens are always in good condition . . . Leaves tee times open for walk-ons . . . Old-fashioned but likeable course . . . Lots of wildlife: deer, swans, etc. . . . Get rid of the geese . . . In consistently great shape . . . A good challenge for us all . . . Watch out for deer . . . Best of the metro park system . . . Somewhere between special and ordinary . . . No sand but lots of trees . . . Another good muny on rolling terrain.

(FRUGAL PICK)

★★★½ L.E. KAUFMAN GOLF COURSE
PU—4829 Clyde Park S.W., Wyoming (616)538-5050.
Call club for further information.
Subscriber comments: Excellent greens, as good as any private course. Good test . . . Nicely kept secret . . . Best public course I have ever played . . . Excellent greenskeeping . . . Fast greens . . . Best public course in Michigan . . . Best public course in Grand Rapids . . . One of Michigan's best-kept secrets . . . Lots of doglegs, challenging . . . Best public course in western Michigan . . . Great price . . . Could be a country club . . . Best course, value in all of Michigan . . . Great variety of unique hole designs . . . Pinehurst in Michigan . . . Everything a course should be.

(SUPER VALUE)

★½ LAKE CORA HILLS GOLF COURSE
PU—Red Arrow Hwy., Paw Paw (616)657-4074.
Call club for further information.
Subscriber comments: Short course, but interesting . . . Better each season . . . Front nine quite hilly, difficult sidehill lies . . . Lacks top-notch maintenance . . . Back nine needs work . . . Blind, downhill par-3 first hole typifies a funky design.

★★★ LAKE DOSTER GOLF CLUB

SP—136 Country Club Blvd., Plainwell (616)685-5308.
40 miles north of Grand Rapids. **Holes:** 18. **Par:** 72/72.
Yards: 6,570/5,530. **Course rating:** 72.7/72.8. **Slope:** 134/128.
Opened: 1969. **Pace of Play rating:** 4:00. **Green fee:** $22/25.
Credit cards: MC, V, DISC. **Reduced fees:** No.
Caddies: No. **Golf carts:** $10 for 18 holes.
Discount golf packages: Yes. **Season:** April-Oct. **High:** June-Aug.
On-site lodging: No. **Rental clubs:** Yes.
Walking policy: Walking at certain times. **Range:** Yes (grass).
To obtain tee times: Call anytime.
Subscriber comments: Good test . . . Terrible sand in traps . . . Hilly
terrain tests your shotmaking ability . . . Pretty . . . Back nine more
interesting . . . Secluded, many strategic holes . . . Very scoreable par 5s
. . . Great par 3s, sneaky, tough . . . Not long but fun . . . No bad holes
. . . Third hole is ridiculous . . . You can spray the ball and still score . . .
Love the layout . . . Always disappointed by the greens . . . A blast to play!
Outstanding hilltop par 3 . . . .Great third hole, little killer par 3.

★★★ THE LAKE GOLF CLUB

R—1535 Opal Lake Rd., Gaylord (517)731-1406, (800)525-3719.
45 miles of Traverse City. **Holes:** 18. **Par:** 72/72.
Yards: 6,508/5,000. **Course rating:** N/A. **Slope:** 141/130.
Opened: N/A. **Pace of Play rating:** N/A. **Green fee:** N/A.
Credit cards: MC, V. **Reduced fees:** Weekdays, Low season, Resort
guests, Twilight.
Caddies: No. **Golf carts:** Included in Green Fee.
Discount golf packages: Yes. **Season:** April-Oct. **High:** June-Aug.
On-site lodging: Yes. **Rental clubs:** No.
Walking policy: N/A. **Range:** Yes (grass).
Formerly called Michaywe Hills Golf Club (Lake Course).
Subscriber comments: Has it all: water, sand, trees, elevation, marsh . . .
Keep it in the fairway . . . Golfer-friendly . . . Many picture postcard holes
. . . You must be able to place the ball . . . Some great holes with great
views . . . Reworking of the layout hasn't hurt it too much . . . Front nine
runs hot and cold, back is fabulous . . . Many water holes . . . Top 10
among the Gaylord courses. Bring your long irons . . . New clubhouse.

★★★½ LAKE MICHIGAN HILLS GOLF CLUB

PU—2520 Kerlikowske Rd., Benton Harbor (616)849-2722.
Call club for further information.
Subscriber comments: Very challenging . . . The best public course in
southwest Michigan . . . Like a country club . . . Tough layout, lots of
traps . . . Very playable, even in early spring . . . Always seems to play
with a lot of wind . . . Large greens that putt true . . . Large bunkers . . .
An enjoyable course to play . . . More Illinois players than Michigan ones
. . . Tough first hole.

★½ LAKELAND HILLS GOLF COURSE

PU—5119 Page Ave., Jackson (517)764-5292.
50 miles west of Detroit. **Holes:** 18. **Par:** 72/72.
Yards: 6,199/5,090. **Course rating:** 68.9/68.4. **Slope:** 110/109.
Opened: 1969. **Pace of Play rating:** 4:30. **Green fee:** $11/15.
Credit cards: MC, V. **Reduced fees:** Resort guests, Twilight, Seniors,
Juniors.
Caddies: No. **Golf carts:** $18 for 18 holes.
Discount golf packages: Yes. **Season:** March-Dec. **High:** April-Sept.
On-site lodging: No. **Rental clubs:** Yes.
Walking policy: Unrestricted walking. **Range:** No.
To obtain tee times: Call one week in advance.
Subscriber comments: Needs hazards . . . Too short, too many doglegs
. . . Flat and open . . . Birdies waiting . . . Little trouble . . . Not much
scenery . . . A good course if you don't plan on losing any golf balls.

LAKEVIEW HILLS COUNTRY CLUB & RESORT

R—6560 Peck Rd. (M-90), Lexington (810)359-8901.
20 miles north of Port Huron.
Credit cards: MC, V, AMEX. **Caddies:** No.
Discount golf packages: Yes. **Season:** April-Oct. **High:** July-Sept.
On-site lodging: Yes. **Rental clubs:** Yes. **Range:** Yes (grass).
To obtain tee times: Call.

★★½ **NORTH COURSE**
Holes: 18. **Par:** 72/74.
Yards: 6,852/4,995. **Course rating:** 73.5/71.8. **Slope:** 139/131.
Opened: 1990. **Pace of Play rating:** 4:00-4:30. **Green fee:** $37/44.
Reduced fees: Weekdays, Low season.
Golf carts: Included in Green Fee.
Walking policy: Mandatory cart.
Subscriber comments: Not for a beginner . . . Lots of potential . . .
Course needs help; too gimmicky . . . Improving with age . . . A couple of
unfair holes . . . Tough to find your ball.

★★½ **SOUTH COURSE**
Holes: 18. **Par:** 72/74.
Yards: 6,290/4,707. **Course rating:** 70.1/67.6. **Slope:** 119/116.
Opened: 1935. **Pace of Play rating:** 3:30-4:00. **Green fee:** $18/22.
Reduced fees: Weekdays, Low season, Twilight, Seniors, Juniors.
Golf carts: $11 for 18 holes.
Walking policy: Unrestricted walking.
Subscriber comments: The old nine is still great . . . Demands good shot
selection . . . Fast play . . . Hilly, a little easier than the North.

LAKEWOOD SHORES RESORT

R—7751 Cedar Lake Rd., Oscoda (517)739-2073, (800)882-2493.
80 miles north of Saginaw.
Credit cards: MC, V. **Reduced fees:** Weekdays, Low season, Resort
guests, Twilight.
Caddies: No. **Golf carts:** $11 for 18 holes.

Discount golf packages: Yes. **Season:** April-Oct. **High:** June-Sept.
On-site lodging: Yes. **Rental clubs:** Yes.
Walking policy: Unrestricted walking. **Range:** Yes (grass).
To obtain tee times: Call as far in advance as you wish.

★★★★½ **THE GAILES COURSE** *GREAT VALUE*
Holes: 18. **Par:** 72/73.
Yards: 6,954/5,246. **Course rating:** 74.6/72.0. **Slope:** 137/132.
Opened: 1992. **Pace of Play rating:** 4:30. **Green fee:** $30/50.
Selected as Best New Resort Course of 1993 by Golf Digest. Ranked 4th in
Michigan by Golf Digest.
Subscriber comments: Wonderful . . . Good for all abilities . . . Different
from most in Michigan . . . Completely different . . . Like being in
Scotland . . . Scottish heaven . . . Big, big greens . . . Bunkers are hot tubs
half full of sand . . . You'd better be in the fairway . . . Why go to
Scotland? Best resort course in Michigan . . . Manicuring is top-notch . . .
Plays different everytime . . . Fun, fun, fun . . . A real treat . . .
Magnificent resort course . . . Hidden bunkers . . . A million subtle rolls in
every fairway . . . Old Tom Morris would be at home . . . An unforget-
table experience . . . Seeing is believing, totally unique . . . Perfect from top
to bottom . . . Learn to run it up . . . Best course north of the 45th parallel
. . . I lived in the U.K. for five years, and this is a true links-type course.

★★★½ **THE RESORT COURSE**
Holes: 18. **Par:** 72/74.
Yards: 6,806/5,295. **Course rating:** 72.9/70.9. **Slope:** 120/115.
Opened: 1969. **Pace of Play rating:** 4:00. **Green fee:** $23/30.
Subscriber comments: Nicely kept . . . Beautiful fairways, greens and
scenery . . . Very pleasant staff . . . No parallel fairways . . . Best lunch
room in Michigan . . . Beautiful flowers . . . Ugly stepsister to the Gailes.
A good warm-up before the test of the Gailes . . . A traditional country
club layout with no surprises . . . Playable from any position.

★★★ LESLIE PARK GOLF CLUB
PU—2120 Traver Rd., Ann Arbor (313)994-1163.
Call club for further information.
Subscriber comments: Old, established course . . . A very good course but not always in good shape . . . Too hilly, greens too slick . . . Unfair tees on some of the holes . . . Gets too much play . . . Some greens are automatic three-putts . . . Absurd slopes . . . Several strange holes being rebuilt in '95 by Arthur Hills . . . The only course I play where I would never walk . . . Possibly the best community course in Michigan . . . Bring your "A" game and a hot putter.

★★½ LINCOLN GOLF COURSE
PU—4907 N. Whitehall, Muskegon (616)766-2226.
Call club for further information.
Subscriber comments: Recent changes may help . . . They try hard, but the layout is only adequate . . . Some dramatic elevation changes. Cherry tree-lined holes are beautiful in the spring, provide good eating after a wayward drive.

★★★ LINCOLN HILLS GOLF CLUB
PU—1527 N. Lakeshore Dr., Ludington (616)843-4666.
Call club for further information.
Subscriber comments: Two new holes . . . A neat little course on the big lake . . . Can be conquered by players of all abilities . . . Best scenery in the state . . . Getting better.

★★★ THE LINKS AT PINEWOOD
PU—8600 P.G.A. Dr., Walled Lake (810)669-9802.
30 miles north of Detroit. **Holes:** 18. **Par:** 70/70.
Yards: 6,572/5,559. **Course rating:** 72.0/72.3. **Slope:** 125/124.
Opened: 1985. **Pace of Play rating:** N/A. **Green fee:** $25/42.
Credit cards: MC, V, AMEX. **Reduced fees:** Weekdays, Low season, Twilight.
Caddies: No. **Golf carts:** Included in Green Fee.
Discount golf packages: No. **Season:** March-Dec. **High:** May-Sept.
On-site lodging: No. **Rental clubs:** Yes.
Walking policy: Walking at certain times. **Range:** No.
To obtain tee times: Call up to six days in advance.
Subscriber comments: Unusual pine tree-lined fairways . . . A wet course: on two holes, a good drive is almost a guaranteed plug . . . Beautiful array of pines . . . Good design . . . Great locker room . . . Gets tons of play and the greens show it: spike-mark city . . . Plays tight, no bunkers.

THE LINKS OF NOVI
★★★ EAST/SOUTH/WEST
PU—50395 Ten Mile Rd., Novi (810)380-9595.
15 miles west of Detroit. **Holes:** 27. **Par:** 69/70/71.
Yards: 5,795/5,899/6,358. **Course rating:** 67.9/68.3/71.2.
Slope: 118/119/127.
Opened: 1991. **Pace of Play rating:** N/A. **Green fee:** $29/34.
Credit cards: MC, V. **Reduced fees:** Twilight, Seniors, Juniors.
Caddies: No. **Golf carts:** $11 for 18 holes.
Discount golf packages: No. **Season:** April-Dec. **High:** June-Aug.
On-site lodging: No. **Rental clubs:** Yes.
Walking policy: Walking at certain times. **Range:** Yes (grass).
To obtain tee times: Call six days in advance for weekdays. Call Monday for the upcoming weekend.
Subscriber comments: Too tough for the general public . . . Insufficient topsoil over the rocks . . . Third nine borders on being an executive course . . . Challenging course . . . East course very tough, good mix of holes, well-laid out . . . Good reception . . . There are many interesting, but short, holes thru woods . . . Greens get so hard, sparks fly when the ball

lands . . . East and west nines very challenging . . . Shotmaking required
. . . Lots of variety . . . Variety in types of holes requires course
management. A little pricey for suburban courses . . . Not every hole has a
bail-out area.

★★★★ LITTLE TRAVERSE BAY GOLF CLUB

GREAT VALUE

PU—995 Hideaway Valley Dr., Harbor Springs (616)526-6200.
80 miles east of Traverse City. **Holes:** 18. **Par:** 72/72.
Yards: 6,865/5,061. **Course rating:** 72.9/69.2. **Slope:** 131/119.
Opened: 1991. **Pace of Play rating:** 4:30. **Green fee:** $55/75.
Credit cards: MC, V. **Reduced fees:** Weekdays, Low season, Juniors.
Caddies: No. **Golf carts:** Included in Green Fee.
Discount golf packages: No. **Season:** May-Oct. **High:** June-Sept.
On-site lodging: No. **Rental clubs:** Yes.
Walking policy: Mandatory cart. **Range:** Yes (grass).
To obtain tee times: Call pro shop. Credit card needed to reserve.
Cancellations can be made 48 hours prior to play.
Subscriber comments: Beautiful views from great elevations . . . Best
northern Michigan course for the average golfer. Outstanding . . . Severe
terrain . . . Clubhouse is in the style of Augusta National's . . . Most
spectacular views in Michigan . . . A must-play . . . Great design . . . 9th
and 18th holes should be ski slopes . . . Fantastic! . . . Couldn't score
because I paid too much attention to beautiful scenery . . . Impeccable
scenery . . . No holes abut or cross each other: it's like you're alone . . .
Huge greens . . . Every tee box a Kodak moment . . . Tons of fun . . .
Severe uphill finishing holes . . . No. 9 and No. 18 straight uphill . . . Feel
like you can drive 400 yards from most tees . . . Views of the bay are
unbelieveable . . . The most scenic course ever!

★★½ THE LOON GOLF CLUB

R—4400 Clubhouse Dr., Gaylord (517)732-4454.
55 miles northeast of Traverse City. **Holes:** 18. **Par:** 71/71.
Yards: 6,670/5,059. **Course rating:** 72.5/71.1. **Slope:** 128/121.
Opened: 1994. **Pace of Play rating:** 4:30. **Green fee:** $50.
Credit cards: MC, V. **Reduced fees:** Low season, Resort guests.
Caddies: No. **Golf carts:** Included in Green Fee.
Discount golf packages: Yes. **Season:** April-Sept. **High:** June-Sept.
On-site lodging: No. **Rental clubs:** Yes.
Walking policy: Mandatory cart. **Range:** No.
To obtain tee times: Call seven days in advance.
Subscriber comments: Very good shape for first year . . . Friendly, scenic
. . . Calls for control . . . Freeway noise detracts from the natural beauty
. . . Great finishing hole . . . Promising . . . A really new course . . . Some
good holes, some poor . . . Holes a little close together . . . Once it
matures, it will be one of the nicest in northern Michigan . . . A strategic
challenge . . . Good mix of holes.

THE MAJESTIC AT LAKE WALDEN
★★★★ FIRST/SECOND/THIRD

PU—9600 Crouse Rd., Hartland (810)632-5235, (800)762-3280.
45 miles west of Detroit. **Holes:** 27. **Par:** 72/72.
Yards: 7,035/6,757/6,612. **Course rating:** 73.8/72.0/71.4.
Slope: 132/132/132.
Opened: 1994. **Pace of Play rating:** N/A. **Green fee:** $50/55.
Credit cards: MC, V. **Reduced fees:** Weekdays, Resort guests, Twilight.
Caddies: No. **Golf carts:** Included in Green Fee.
Discount golf packages: No. **Season:** April-Nov. **High:** June-Aug.
On-site lodging: No. **Rental clubs:** Yes.
Walking policy: Mandatory cart. **Range:** Yes (grass).
To obtain tee times: Call up to one week in advance.
Subscriber comments: Great layout, greens super, can only get better . . .
Most interesting course I played all year, lots of variety . . . New, exciting,
fantastic, check this course out. The talk of southern Michigan . . . Only
two years old but seems to be more mature than that . . . A must round . . .

Beautiful scenery . . . Has all the ingredients . . . Golf doesn't get much nicer . . . Best course in southeast Michigan . . . Will probably win some awards . . . A Matthews gem . . . Many memorable and scenic holes . . . Makes you think . . . Best Matthews design in state . . . Finest golf course for the money in southern Michigan . . . The best new course in Michigan . . . Cannot be walked. Layed out over seven miles . . . Nine out, nine back . . . Layout is special though still a baby; has to grow . . . Terrific for a brand new course . . . A most excellent course . . . Distance between holes hurts . . . What a vista.

MAPLE LEAF GOLF COURSE
★★★ EAST/NORTH/WEST
PU—158 N. Mackinaw Rd., Linwood (517)697-3531.
10 miles north of Bay City. **Holes:** 27. **Par:** 71/71/70.
Yards: 5,762/5,997/5,697. **Course rating:** 67.6/68.3/66.4.
Slope: 116/114/109.
Opened: 1963. **Pace of Play rating:** N/A. **Green fee:** $15/16.
Credit cards: MC, V, DISC. **Reduced fees:** Weekdays, Low season, Seniors, Juniors.
Caddies: No. **Golf carts:** $16 for 18 holes.
Discount golf packages: No. **Season:** April-Nov. **High:** June-Aug.
On-site lodging: No. **Rental clubs:** Yes.
Walking policy: Unrestricted walking. **Range:** No.
To obtain tee times: Call two days in advance for tee times weekends and holidays.
Subscriber comments: North nine exciting, East interesting yet short . . . Family atmosphere . . . Water everywhere . . . Best dollar value in middle Michigan . . . West nine mediocre . . . Hitting driver straight is very important . . . Three completely different nines . . . Nice greens . . . Nice place to play your league . . . New North nine is the toughest. All three are worth playing . . . Nothing spectacular, but not bad.

★★ MARION OAKS GOLF CLUB
PU—2255 Pinckney Rd., Howell (517)548-0050.
Call club for further information.
Subscriber comments: Roughs are planted with wildflowers . . . Need to do something about the wildflower drop rule . . . Wildflowers everywhere . . . Wildflowers makes you feel like you're playing in a garden, not a golf course . . . Beautiful wildflowers everywhere, but they insist that you not retrieve your ball from them . . . Uses O.B. to prevent you from taking obvious shortcuts . . . Grow some grass, please! . . . Free drops from wildflower beds, I love it! . . . Three par 3s in each nine.

★★★ MARSH RIDGE RESORT
R—4815 Old 27 S., Gaylord (517)731-1563, (800)968-2633.
120 miles north of Saginaw. **Holes:** 18. **Par:** 71/71.
Yards: 6,100/5,088. **Course rating:** 69.7/65.7. **Slope:** 126/117.
Opened: 1992. **Pace of Play rating:** 4:30. **Green fee:** $35/54.
Credit cards: MC, V, AMEX. **Reduced fees:** Weekdays, Low season, Resort guests, Juniors.
Caddies: No. **Golf carts:** Included in Green Fee.
Discount golf packages: Yes. **Season:** April-Oct. **High:** June-Sept.
On-site lodging: Yes. **Rental clubs:** Yes.
Walking policy: Mandatory cart. **Range:** Yes (grass).
To obtain tee times: Call anytime in advance.
Subscriber comments: Beautiful layout over blueberry bogs . . . Too tight for most players . . . Lovely course, birch trees frame many fairways . . . Challenging par 3s . . . Elevation changes make many shots interesting . . . Best flat course there is . . . Leave your woods in the trunk, bring your rabbit's foot . . . Great preservation of wetlands . . . Narrow, long carries, but beautiful . . . Unique, must hit over marshes . . . Fun if you "go for it" . . . Toughest 6,100 yards you'll ever play . . . In a forest . . . Some unique holes, excellent practice area . . . Marsh everywhere . . . Wetlands are fine but the holes aren't.

★★½ MARYWOOD GOLF CLUB
PU—21310 N. Ave., Battle Creek (616)968-1168.
Holes: 18. **Par:** 72/72.
Yards: 6,729/5,342. **Course rating:** 73.0/71.6. **Slope:** 132/126.
Opened: 1926. **Pace of Play rating:** N/A. **Green fee:** $20/40.
Credit cards: All major. **Reduced fees:** Weekdays, Low season, Twilight.
Caddies: No. **Golf carts:** $12 for 18 holes.
Discount golf packages: Yes. **Season:** April-Nov. **High:** June-Sept.
On-site lodging: No. **Rental clubs:** Yes.
Walking policy: Walking at certain times. **Range:** Yes (grass).
To obtain tee times: Call anytime.
Subscriber comments: One of the prettiest courses in Michigan . . . An absolute gem . . . Still plays like a country club course . . . Condition seems to have dropped . . . One of a kind, like a paradise garden . . . Beautiful landscaping with bedding plants . . . No easy holes, really hilly, staff treats you well . . . Good mix of holes . . . First-class golf experience on and off the course . . . Too many flowers on tee boxes, but otherwise a fantastic course . . . PGA Tour quality, blue-collar wallet . . . Watch out for No. 14 . . . Fabulous layout.

★½ MASON HILLS GOLF COURSE
SP—2602 Tomlinson Rd., Mason (517)676-5366.
10 miles southeast of Lansing. **Holes:** 18. **Par:** 72/72.
Yards: 6,348/5,550. **Course rating:** N/A. **Slope:** N/A.
Opened: 1926. **Pace of Play rating:** N/A. **Green fee:** $7/15.
Credit cards: None. **Reduced fees:** Weekdays, Low season, Twilight, Seniors, Juniors.
Caddies: No. **Golf carts:** $18 for 18 holes.
Discount golf packages: Yes. **Season:** March-Oct. **High:** May-Aug.
On-site lodging: No. **Rental clubs:** Yes.
Walking policy: Unrestricted walking. **Range:** Yes (grass).
To obtain tee times: Call.

★★½ MATHESON GREENS GOLF COURSE
PU—Matheson Rd., Northport (616)386-5171, (800)443-6883.
25 miles north of Traverse City. **Holes:** 18. **Par:** 72/72.
Yards: 6,609/4,716. **Course rating:** 72.1/67.2. **Slope:** 132/116.
Opened: 1991. **Pace of Play rating:** 4:05. **Green fee:** $29/42.

Credit cards: All major. **Reduced fees:** Low season, Twilight, Juniors.
Caddies: No. **Golf carts:** Included in Green Fee.
Discount golf packages: Yes. **Season:** April-Oct. **High:** July-Aug.
On-site lodging: No. **Rental clubs:** Yes.
Walking policy: Walking at certain times. **Range:** Yes.
To obtain tee times: Call as far in advance as you wish.
Subscriber comments: Isolated . . . A good course at a nice price . . . In the spring, the whole course smells like cherry blossoms. Fall is spectacular . . . Michigan's hidden jewel. The wind makes the course a real challenge . . . Fast greens. Requires every shot in your bag . . . Staff very courteous . . . Great scenery . . . Superb use of terrain . . . Beautiful locale . . . Unfair first hole, blind shot off the tee.

MCGUIRE'S RESORT
★★½ SPRUCE COURSE
R—7880 Mackinaw Trail, Cadillac (616)775-9949, (800)632-7302.
Holes: 18. **Par:** 71/71.
Yards: 6,443/5,107. **Course rating:** 71.3/69.6. **Slope:** 124/118.
Opened: 1954. **Pace of Play rating:** 4:30. **Green fee:** $32/48.
Credit cards: All major. **Reduced fees:** Resort guests, Twilight.
Caddies: No. **Golf carts:** Included in Green Fee.
Discount golf packages: Yes. **Season:** April-Oct. **High:** May-Sept.
On-site lodging: Yes. **Rental clubs:** No.
Walking policy: Mandatory cart. **Range:** Yes (grass).
To obtain tee times: Call in advance.
Subscriber comments: Good dining . . . Nice shape . . . Pleasant, variable . . . Short, interesting layout . . . Nice looking nine in the pines.

Not an exceptional design . . . An OK course that is not too tough . . .
Norway course: short, good, fast nine holes . . . Comfortable . . . Good
staff, nothing special . . . Norway course: trees totally obscure some par-4
greens.

★★★½ THE MEADOWS GOLF CLUB
PU—4645 W. Campus Dr., Allendale (616)895-1000.
15 miles west of Grand Rapids. **Holes:** 18. **Par:** 71/72.
Yards: 7,034/4,777. **Course rating:** 74.5/67.4. **Slope:** 133/117.
Opened: 1994. **Pace of Play rating:** 4:30. **Green fee:** $18/33.
Credit cards: All major. **Reduced fees:** Weekdays, Low season, Twilight,
Juniors.
Caddies: No. **Golf carts:** $10 for 18 holes.
Discount golf packages: No. **Season:** April–Oct. **High:** June–Sept.
On-site lodging: No. **Rental clubs:** Yes.
Walking policy: Unrestricted walking. **Range:** Yes (grass).
To obtain tee times: Call up to ten days in advance. Multiple tee times
require credit card guarantee.
Subscriber comments: Different layout, needs some time. Placement
shots . . . Front nine tight with carries over wetlands, back nine is open.
Great practice center . . . A couple of holes are too close for comfort . . .
Sneaky hard, good conservation . . . Disappointing. Road noise distracting,
course crammed on too small an area . . . Not particularly scenic . . . Best
course in west Michigan, a winner . . . Strategically placed hazards . . .

Good from all tees, no bad holes . . . Impression improved later in season as
things filled in . . . Marsh or water on some holes, more a mental than a
physical hazard . . . Awesome new course . . . Lots of mounds, not many
trees . . . Requires a few times around to conquer.

MICHAYWE HILLS RESORT
★★★ PINES GOLF CLUB
R—1535 Opal Lake Rd., Gaylord (517)939-8911, (800)322-6636.
5 miles south of Traverse City. **Holes:** 18. **Par:** 72/73.
Yards: 6,835/5,901. **Course rating:** 73.6/74.4. **Slope:** 129/126.
Opened: 1972. **Pace of Play rating:** 4:30. **Green fee:** $40/42.
Credit cards: MC, V. **Reduced fees:** Weekdays, Low season, Resort
guests, Twilight, Juniors.
Caddies: No. **Golf carts:** $10 for 18 holes.
Discount golf packages: Yes. **Season:** April–Oct. **High:** June–Aug..
On-site lodging: Yes. **Rental clubs:** Yes.
Walking policy: Walking at certain times. **Range:** Yes (grass).
To obtain tee times: Call anytime. Credit card necessary to hold tee time.
Subscriber comments: One of the best Northern Michigan courses . . .
Wide, tree-lined fairways. Big, deep bunkers . . . Recommend highly . . .
Old-style course feeling . . . Pretty, not much character . . . Well-
bunkered, excellent bent grass greens . . . Relatively flat . . . Lacks
character; holes are all too similar . . . A bald eagle flew above our fairway;
what a sight!

MIDDLE CHANNEL GOLF & COUNTRY CLUB★
PU—2306 Golf Course Rd., Harsens Island (810)748-9922.
25 miles northeast of Mt. Clemens. **Holes:** 18. **Par:** 70.
Yards: 6,100. **Course rating:** N/A. **Slope:** N/A.
Opened: 1923. **Pace of Play rating:** 4:00–4:30. **Green fee:** $16/19.
Credit cards: MC, V. **Reduced fees:** Weekdays, Low season, Twilight,
Seniors, Junior
Caddies: No. **Golf carts:** $16 for 18 holes.
Discount golf packages: No. **Season:** April–Oct. **High:** June–Aug.
On-site lodging: No. **Rental clubs:** Yes.
Walking policy: Unrestricted walking. **Range:** No.
To obtain tee times: Call anytime.

★★★ MILHAM PARK MUNICIPAL GOLF COURSE

PU—4200 Lovers Lane, Kalamazoo (616)344-7639.
Holes: 18. **Par:** 73/72.
Yards: 6,578/5,582. **Course rating:** 71.3/71.8. **Slope:** 120/120.

Opened: 1931. **Pace of Play rating:** N/A. **Green fee:** $14.
Credit cards: None. **Reduced fees:** Seniors, Juniors.
Caddies: No. **Golf carts:** None.
Discount golf packages: No. **Season:** March-Dec. **High:** June-Aug.
On-site lodging: No. **Rental clubs:** Yes.
Walking policy: Unrestricted walking. **Range:** Yes (grass).
To obtain tee times: Call three days in advance for weekends and holidays only.
Subscriber comments: Keeps me off the more expensive courses . . . A true golf course, one of the best munys . . . Condition better than many country clubs . . . Best public course in Michigan . . . Great clubhouse . . . Always busy and slow . . . Best feature: no carts . . . I hope they never change: golf is for walking . . . Best public course in western Michigan . . . Great public course . . . Best merchandise in the area . . . Many very good holes. Friendly greens . . . Public courses don't get any better.

★★★½ MISTWOOD GOLF COURSE

PU—7568 Sweet Lake Rd., Lake Ann (616)275-5500.
18 miles southwest of Traverse City. **Holes:** 18. **Par:** 71/71.
Yards: 6,715/5,070. **Course rating:** 72.4/69.6. **Slope:** 130/120.

Opened: 1993. **Pace of Play rating:** N/A. **Green fee:** $29/32.
Credit cards: All major. **Reduced fees:** Weekdays, Low season, Twilight, Seniors, Juniors.
Caddies: No. **Golf carts:** $10 for 18 holes.
Discount golf packages: No. **Season:** April-Nov. **High:** June-Aug.
On-site lodging: No. **Rental clubs:** Yes.
Walking policy: Unrestricted walking. **Range:** Yes (grass).
To obtain tee times: Call anytime.
Subscriber comments: Great new course . . . Needs better yardage markings . . . Superb new course . . . Wide fairways, hard greens require bump-and-run approaches . . . Best new course for the money . . . Sneaky hard . . . An up-and-coming championship golf course . . . Fastest greens in the state . . . So much beautiful land in the area, why such a mediocre course? . . . Excellent bent grass fairways . . . Not memorable . . . Nice people running it . . . Absolutely beautiful. Very tight . . . Best new course in northern Michigan, a real gem . . . Another Matthews gem . . . Front had lots of character.

★★★ THE NATURAL AT BEAVER CREEK RESORT

R—5004 W. Otsego Lake Dr., Gaylord (517)732-1785.
50 miles northeast of Traverse City. **Holes:** 18. **Par:** 71/71.
Yards: 6,350/4,830. **Course rating:** 69.5/69.0. **Slope:** 129/117.
Opened: 1992. **Pace of Play rating:** 4:10. **Green fee:** $40/45.
Credit cards: MC, V. **Reduced fees:** Weekdays, Low season, Resort guests, Twilight.
Caddies: No. **Golf carts:** Included in Green Fee.
Discount golf packages: Yes. **Season:** May-Oct. **High:** June-Aug.
On-site lodging: Yes. **Rental clubs:** Yes.
Walking policy: Walking at certain times. **Range:** Yes (grass).
To obtain tee times: Call.
Subscriber comments: Tight, gimmicky par 3s. Friendly staff . . . Challenging for the right price . . . Very tough, a zillion trees . . . Slow pace because of trouble . . . Staff made us feel very welcome . . . Very interesting . . . Best value in northern Michigan . . . A real sleeper. One hole too short . . . Great name and logo doesn't measure up; yardage is padded . . . Long carries, wide fairways . . . An enjoyable experience . . . Keep it in play or you'll pay. Play the percentages . . . Nice, but some holes are unfair . . . Short and squeezed . . . Beautiful setting, course takes good advantage of it. Name is apt . . . Always backed up . . . Don't hook or slice here or you'll never find it.

★★ NORTHWOOD GOLF COURSE
PU—2888 Comstock Ave., Fremont (616)924-3380.
40 miles northwest of Grand Rapids. **Holes:** 18. **Par:** 71/71.
Yards: 6,313/5,600. **Course rating:** 69.7/66.1. **Slope:** 115/111.
Opened: 1968. **Pace of Play rating:** 4:00. **Green fee:** $16.
Credit cards: MC, V. **Reduced fees:** Seniors.
Caddies: No. **Golf carts:** N/A.
Discount golf packages: No. **Season:** April-Oct. **High:** July-Aug.
On-site lodging: No. **Rental clubs:** Yes.
Walking policy: Unrestricted walking. **Range:** Yes.
To obtain tee times: Call anytime.
Subscriber comments: Hilly, with small domed greens . . . Great country
course in an orchard . . . An enjoyable course . . . Greens are rounded like
top of a basketball, ball rolls off easily . . . Sporty, fun, shortish . . . Greens
could be better.

★★½ OAK LANE GOLF COURSE
PU—800 N. Main St., Webberville (517)521-3900.
20 miles east of Lansing. **Holes:** 18. **Par:** 70/71.
Yards: 5,714/5,115. **Course rating:** 67.3/69.1. **Slope:** 107/115.
Opened: 1967. **Pace of Play rating:** 4:00. **Green fee:** $14/17.
Credit cards: MC, V. **Reduced fees:** Twilight, Seniors, Juniors.
Caddies: No. **Golf carts:** $9 for 18 holes.
Discount golf packages: No. **Season:** April-Oct. **High:** June-Aug.
On-site lodging: No. **Rental clubs:** Yes.
Walking policy: Unrestricted walking. **Range:** No.
To obtain tee times: Call or come in up to two weeks in advance. Groups
of 20 or more need a deposit.
Subscriber comments: Nice little course, family owned and run . . .
Short, but pretty. Play it in the fall . . . Lots of hills . . . Lack of bunkers
and delineated fairways . . . Has had maintenance problem due to a flood
. . . Decent value.

★½ OAK RIDGE GOLF CLUB
PU—35035 26 Mile Rd., New Haven (810)749-5151.
20 miles northeast of Detroit. **Holes:** 18. **Par:** 72/72.
Yards: 6,811/5,637. **Course rating:** 71.0/72.6. **Slope:** 117/119.
Opened: 1966. **Pace of Play rating:** N/A. **Green fee:** $18/21.
Credit cards: MC, V. **Reduced fees:** Weekdays, Low season, Twilight,
Seniors, Juniors.
Caddies: No. **Golf carts:** $22 for 18 holes.
Discount golf packages: Yes. **Season:** April-Nov. **High:** April-Sept.
On-site lodging: No. **Rental clubs:** Yes.
Walking policy: Unrestricted walking. **Range:** Yes (grass).
To obtain tee times: Call two weeks in advance.
Subscriber comments: Nice clubhouse, slow play . . . Always crowded,
lots of waiting . . . Needs much better maintenance . . . Enjoyable course
. . . Scenic front nine, good food.

OAK RIDGE GOLF CLUB★
PU—513 W. Pontaluna Rd., Muskegon (616)798-4591.
Call club for further information.
Subscriber comments: Nice layout on the edge of Lake Michigan, open
but sporty . . . Course getting worse each year . . . Rarely in good shape
. . . Drainage and turf problems.

★★ OAKLAND HILLS GOLF CLUB
PU—11619 H Drive N., Battle Creek (616)965-0809.
Call club for further information.
Subscriber comments: Flawless greens . . . OK once in a while . . . Fast
greens that will hold anything you hit in there . . . Beautiful greens . . .
Interesting but mostly flat . . . Lush fairways.

★★½ OCEANA COUNTRY CLUB

PU—3333 W. Weaver Rd., Shelby (616)861-4211.
25 miles north of Muskegon. **Holes:** 18. **Par:** 73/71.
Yards: 6,172/5,403. **Course rating:** 70.0/71.8. **Slope:** 120/123.
Opened: 1962. **Pace of Play rating:** 4:00. **Green fee:** $17/18.
Credit cards: MC, V. **Reduced fees:** Low season, Juniors.
Caddies: No. **Golf carts:** $9 for 18 holes.
Discount golf packages: No. **Season:** April-Oct. **High:** June-Aug.
On-site lodging: No. **Rental clubs:** Yes.
Walking policy: Unrestricted walking. **Range:** Yes.
To obtain tee times: Call anytime.
Subscriber comments: Not very interesting, many back-and-forth holes
. . . Have seen it in better shape . . . Back and forth across a field,
monotonous . . . Hilly in sections . . . A short, demanding track . . . Front
has undulating greens and doglegs, back is long and straight.

★★½ OLD CHANNEL TRAIL GOLF CLUB

PU—Rt. 3, Old Channel Trail, Montague (616)894-5076.
20 miles north of Muskegon. **Holes:** 18. **Par:** 71/74.
Yards: 6,166/5,115. **Course rating:** 69.1/68.4. **Slope:** 113/112.
Opened: 1927. **Pace of Play rating:** . **Green fee:** $14/17.
Credit cards: MC, V. **Reduced fees:** Weekdays, Low season, Twilight,
Seniors.
Caddies: No. **Golf carts:** $16 for 18 holes.
Discount golf packages: Yes. **Season:** April-Oct. **High:** July-Aug.
On-site lodging: No. **Rental clubs:** Yes.
Walking policy: Walking at certain times. **Range:** Yes (grass).
To obtain tee times: Call.
Subscriber comments: Back nine very interesting . . . Back nine has grass
bunkers, a different touch . . . Old-fashioned back nine is beautiful . . .
Best-kept secret on the shores of Lake Michigan . . . 1927 old course;
newer, different nine . . . Just added another nine by Jerry Matthews . . .
Scottish style back nine . . . Two completely different nines . . . Not too
challenging . . . Lots of character . . . Front nine has too many flat fairways
too close together.

★★★★ THE ORCHARDS GOLF CLUB

PU—62900 Campground Rd., Washington (810)786-7200.
30 miles north of Detroit. **Holes:** 18. **Par:** 72/72.
Yards: 7,026/5,158. **Course rating:** 73.9/70.1. **Slope:** 133/122.
Opened: 1993. **Pace of Play rating:** 4:22. **Green fee:** $35/50.
Credit cards: MC, V, AMEX. **Reduced fees:** Low season, Twilight.
Caddies: No. **Golf carts:** Included in Green Fee.
Discount golf packages: No. **Season:** April-Oct. **High:** May-Sept.
On-site lodging: No. **Rental clubs:** Yes.
Walking policy: Unrestricted walking. **Range:** Yes (grass).
To obtain tee times: Call 30 days in advance.
Ranked 12th in Michigan by Golf Digest.
Subscriber comments: A new course with great potential . . . Each hole
is new and different . . . The best public course in Michigan . . . The best
value for a quality course that I have seen, staff is courteous, professional
and well-informed . . . Wonderfull all the way around . . . Treated better
than most private clubs . . . Wonderful Trent Jones Jr. layout, teriffic
clubhouse, excellent staff . . . 90-degree rule makes it a pain to play . . .
Where's the beef? Kind of barren land . . . Some holes tricked up. Holes are
either very easy or very difficult . . . Every hole is unique . . . One of the
best in Oakland County . . . Unbelievable . . . Use your head and score.
Like being in northern Michigan, but only 30 miles from Detroit . . . Hold
this course back . . . Nicest new course in southeast Michigan . . . Great
course with a feeling of being a club member . . . A Robert Trent Jones Jr.
masterpiece . . . Bring your sand wedge . . . Terrific . . . Lots of sand.
You'd better bring a camel.

★★ OXFORD HILLS GOLF CLUB

PU—300 E. Drahner Rd., Oxford (810)628-2518.
8 miles north of Pontiac. **Holes:** 18. **Par:** 72/72.
Yards: 6,522/5,312. **Course rating:** 71.4/70.5. **Slope:** 120/116.
Opened: 1964. **Pace of Play rating:** 4:30. **Green fee:** $17/21.
Credit cards: MC, V, AMEX. **Reduced fees:** Weekdays, Low season,
Seniors, Juniors.
Caddies: No. **Golf carts:** $10 for 18 holes.
Discount golf packages: No. **Season:** April-Nov. **High:** June-Aug.
On-site lodging: No. **Rental clubs:** Yes.
Walking policy: Unrestricted walking. **Range:** No.
To obtain tee times: Call in advance.
Subscriber comments: Good public course, great greens . . . Front nine is
nothing but the back nine takes some golf . . . Back nine: bring a cannon
. . . Front nine a short teaser for the back . . . Tee locations confusing for a
first-timer . . . You'll want to ride . . . Long hitters have fun . . . Back nine
is prettier.

PARTRIDGE CREEK GOLF COURSE

PU—43843 Romeo Plank Rd., Clinton Twp. (810)228-3030.
30 miles northwest of Mt. Clemens.
Opened: 1960. **Pace of Play rating:** 4:00. **Green fee:** $16/18.
Credit cards: MC, V. **Reduced fees:** Weekdays, Low season, Twilight,
Seniors, Juniors.
Caddies: No. **Golf carts:** $20 for 18 holes.
Discount golf packages: No. **Season:** Year-round. **High:** May-Aug.
On-site lodging: No. **Rental clubs:** Yes.
Walking policy: Unrestricted walking. **Range:** No.
To obtain tee times: Call for reservations for weekends only.
BLUE COURSE★
Holes: 18. **Par:** 72/72.
Yards: 6,616/5,121. **Course rating:** 70.5/68.5. **Slope:** 118/103.
GREEN COURSE★
Holes: 18. **Par:** 72/72.
Yards: 6,036/5,227. **Course rating:** 68.0/69.0. **Slope:** 103/105.

PAW PAW LAKE GOLF COURSE★

PU—4548 Forest Beach Rd., Watervliet (616)463-3831.
10 miles northwest of Benton Harbor. **Holes:** 18. **Par:** 70/73.
Yards: 5,457/5,064. **Course rating:** N/A. **Slope:** N/A.
Opened: 1928. **Pace of Play rating:** 4:00. **Green fee:** $16/19.
Credit cards: None. **Reduced fees:** Weekdays, Low season, Twilight.
Caddies: No. **Golf carts:** $10 for 18 holes.
Discount golf packages: No. **Season:** April-Nov. **High:** June-Aug.
On-site lodging: No. **Rental clubs:** Yes.
Walking policy: Unrestricted walking. **Range:** Yes (grass).
To obtain tee times: Call pro shop.
Subscriber comments:

★½ PEBBLE CREEK GOLF COURSE

PU—24095 Currie Rd., South Lyon (810)437-5411.
Call club for further information.
Subscriber comments: Nice course . . . Outlying country course in good
shape . . . 18 holes stuffed into an area big enough for only nine . . . Holes
too close to each other . . . Borderline maintenance.

PINE HILL GOLF CLUB
NARROWS COURSE★

PU—3459 U.S. 31 N., Brutus (616)529-6574.
12 miles south of Petoskey. **Holes:** 18. **Par:** 71/72.
Yards: 6,007/5,059. **Course rating:** 71.0/72.0. **Slope:** 113/113.
Opened: 1991. **Pace of Play rating:** 3:30-4:00. **Green fee:** $18/25.
Credit cards: MC, V. **Reduced fees:** Low season, Twilight, Seniors,
Juniors.
Caddies: No. **Golf carts:** $20 for 18 holes.

Discount golf packages: Yes. **Season:** April-Oct. **High:** June-Aug.
On-site lodging: No. **Rental clubs:** Yes.
Walking policy: Unrestricted walking. **Range:** Yes (grass).
To obtain tee times: Not required in advance.
Also has an 18-hole par-54 executive course.

★★★ PINE KNOB GOLF CLUB

PU—5580 Waldon Rd., Clarkston (810)625-4430.
9 miles north of Pontiac. **Holes:** 18. **Par:** 72/70.
Yards: 6,647/5,227. **Course rating:** 71.4/69.9. **Slope:** 123/120.
Opened: 1972. **Pace of Play rating:** 4:00. **Green fee:** $39/47.
Credit cards: All major. **Reduced fees:** No.
Caddies: No. **Golf carts:** Included in Green Fee.
Discount golf packages: No. **Season:** April-Oct. **High:** June-Sept.
On-site lodging: No. **Rental clubs:** Yes.
Walking policy: Mandatory cart. **Range:** Yes.
To obtain tee times: Call seven days in advance.
Subscriber comments: Must have a good tee ball . . . Mountaintop views
and mansion clubhouse make it a must play . . . Nice setting, expensive for
bluegrass fairways . . . Big greens . . . The view at No. 10 is outstanding
. . . A fun course, needs attention . . . Beautiful flowers, well kept . . .
No. 10 has the view of a lifetime . . . Very scenic 10th hole . . . A fine
course needing a few extras.

★ PINE LAKE GOLF COURSE

PU—1018 Haslett Rd., Haslett (517)339-8281.

10 miles east of Lansing. **Holes:** 18. **Par:** 71/71.
Yards: 6,155/4,677. **Course rating:** 69.1/66.3. **Slope:** 122/122.
Opened: 1954. **Pace of Play rating:** N/A. **Green fee:** $16/18.
Credit cards: None. **Reduced fees:** Weekdays, Low season, Twilight,
Seniors, Juniors.
Caddies: No. **Golf carts:** $11 for 18 holes.
Discount golf packages: Yes. **Season:** March-Dec. **High:** June-July.
On-site lodging: No. **Rental clubs:** No.
Walking policy: Unrestricted walking. **Range:** No.
To obtain tee times: Call pro shop.

★★★ PINE RIVER GOLF CLUB

PU—2244 Pine River Rd., Standish (517)846-6819.
30 miles north of Bay City. **Holes:** 18. **Par:** 71/74.
Yards: 6,250/5,156. **Course rating:** 70.8/70.7. **Slope:** 126/126.
Opened: 1966. **Pace of Play rating:** 4:00. **Green fee:** $16/20.
Credit cards: MC, V. **Reduced fees:** Weekdays, Seniors, Juniors.
Caddies: No. **Golf carts:** $10 for 18 holes.
Discount golf packages: No. **Season:** April-Oct. **High:** June-Aug.
On-site lodging: No. **Rental clubs:** No.
Walking policy: Unrestricted walking. **Range:** Yes (grass).
To obtain tee times: Call pro shop.
Subscriber comments: Good course for average seniors . . . Nice course,
nice people . . . Original nine a fair test, new nine a little short but tight . . .
Fantastic back nine . . . Going to be even better as it matures . . . Back nine
cut of the woods . . . They need to buy new power carts.

★★★ PINE TRACE GOLF CLUB

PU—3600 Pine Trace Blvd., Rochester Hills (810)852-7100.
30 miles north of Detroit. **Holes:** 18. **Par:** 72/72.
Yards: 6,610/4,974. **Course rating:** 72.8/69.9. **Slope:** 139/125.
Opened: 1989. **Pace of Play rating:** 4:20. **Green fee:** $40/48.
Credit cards: MC, V. **Reduced fees:** Low season, Seniors, Juniors.
Caddies: No. **Golf carts:** Included in Green Fee.
Discount golf packages: No. **Season:** March-Nov. **High:** May-Sept.
On-site lodging: No. **Rental clubs:** No.
Walking policy: Walking at certain times. **Range:** Yes.
To obtain tee times: Tee times can be reserved up to one week in
advance.

Subscriber comments: Beautiful design by Arthur Hills . . . A little too tough . . . Excellent course; too interested in play time . . . Clock on every hole to pace golfers . . . No. 18 can wreck your score . . . Receives too much play . . . Works hard on pace of play . . . Lighten up a little! . . . For a Detroit area course, the speed of play is excellent . . . New pace clocks a great idea. Other courses should follow their lead . . . Several side-to-side identical holes . . . Probably the best public course in the metro Detroit area . . . Clocks on every tee have kept pace of play up . . . Public courses do not get much better . . . Designed around wetlands . . . Sand traps need maintenance.

PINE VALLEY GOLF CLUB
★★½ RED/BLUE/GOLD
PU—16801 31 Mile Rd., Ray (810)752-9633.
12 miles north of Mt. Clemens. **Holes:** 27. **Par:** 72/71/71.
Yards: 6,259/6,021/6,138. **Course rating:** 69.5/68.3/69.0.
Slope: 118/114/110.
Opened: 1968. **Pace of Play rating:** 4:30. **Green fee:** $18/23.
Credit cards: MC, V. **Reduced fees:** Weekdays, Low season, Twilight, Seniors.
Caddies: No. **Golf carts:** $20 for 18 holes.
Discount golf packages: No. **Season:** March-Nov. **High:** May-Sept.
On-site lodging: No. **Rental clubs:** Yes.
Walking policy: Walking at certain times. **Range:** Yes (grass).
To obtain tee times: Call seven days in advance.
Subscriber comments: Well-maintained, good pace . . . Great fun to play . . . A morale maker . . . Good balance of difficult and not-so-difficult holes.

★★½ PINE VIEW GOLF CLUB
PU—5820 Stoney Creek Rd., Ypsilanti (313)481-0500, (800)214-5963.
15 miles west of Ypsilanti. **Holes:** 18. **Par:** 72/72.
Yards: 6,533/5,267. **Course rating:** 71.3/70.7. **Slope:** 124/119.
Opened: 1990. **Pace of Play rating:** 4:03. **Green fee:** $12/27.
Credit cards: MC, V. **Reduced fees:** Weekdays, Low season, Twilight, Seniors, Juniors.
Caddies: No. **Golf carts:** $11 for 18 holes.
Discount golf packages: Yes. **Season:** March-Dec. **High:** April-Sept.
On-site lodging: No. **Rental clubs:** Yes.
Walking policy: Unrestricted walking. **Range:** Yes (grass).
To obtain tee times: Call seven days in advance; for groups of 20 or more tee times can be made a year in advance.
Also has 9-hole par-30 executive course.
Subscriber comments: Good for people wild off tee. Pace of play was perfect . . . Back nine is outstanding. The regulars don't appreciate its beauty . . . Majestic pines . . . Beautifully scenic . . . Backwoodsy and narrow . . . Up north feel on the back nine . . . Friendly staff, facility improves each year.

★★★½ PINECROFT GOLF CLUB

PU—8260 Henry Rd., Beulah (616)882-9100.
Call club for further information.
Subscriber comments: A real hidden gem, inexpensive, great views and elevation changes . . . Fantastic views, well-maintained, a little short . . . Best way to describe Pinecroft is fun. Fantastic views of Crystal Lake . . . I do not want to play anywhere else . . . Deceiving to the eye to play . . . Feels like a northern Michigan course. Lots of pines . . . Just gorgeous . . . Too many hills to walk . . . Best views in northwest Michigan . . . Some greens sloped too severely . . . Smallest greens I've played.

★★★ PLEASANT HILLS GOLF CLUB
PU—4452 E. Millbrook Rd., Mt. Pleasant (517)772-0487.
50 miles west of Saginaw. **Holes:** 18. **Par:** 72/72.
Yards: 6,012/4,607. **Course rating:** 68.2/65.9. **Slope:** 110/107.
Opened: 1964. **Pace of Play rating:** 4:00. **Green fee:** $15/16.

Credit cards: None. **Reduced fees:** Weekdays, Low season, Twilight, Seniors, Juniors.
Caddies: No. **Golf carts:** $18 for 18 holes.
Discount golf packages: No. **Season:** March-Dec. **High:** June-Aug.
On-site lodging: No. **Rental clubs:** Yes.
Walking policy: Unrestricted walking. **Range:** No.
To obtain tee times: Call 24 hours in advance.
Subscriber comments: Very challenging. Always very scenic, a great place to play . . . Very little water or sand . . . Very good price.

★★★½ POHLCAT GOLF COURSE

R—6595 E. Airport Rd., Mt. Pleasant (517)773-4221, (800)292-8891.
60 miles north of Lansing. **Holes:** 18. **Par:** 72/72.
Yards: 6,810/5,140. **Course rating:** 74.2/70.8. **Slope:** 139/124.
Opened: 1991. **Pace of Play rating:** 4:30. **Green fee:** $39/59.
Credit cards: MC, V, AMEX. **Reduced fees:** Weekdays, Low season, Resort guests, Twilight, Seniors, Juniors.
Caddies: No. **Golf carts:** Included in Green Fee.
Discount golf packages: Yes. **Season:** April-Nov. **High:** July-Sept.
On-site lodging: Yes. **Rental clubs:** Yes.
Walking policy: Walking at certain times. **Range:** Yes (grass).
To obtain tee times: Call above 800 number after Feb 1 for anytime.
Subscriber comments: No. 10 one tough hole into an everpresent wind . . . No.18 a great finishing hole . . . Nice course for central Michigan . . . Don't miss the greens long . . . Four or five great holes; the rest are open and boring . . . Some picturesque spots . . . No. 17 is fun to play . . . Has a great future . . . Bent-grass fairways and greens . . . Interesting course . . . Great design; there's room to hit the ball . . . Very tight on interior holes . . . Greens perfect in the morning, too spiked-up in the afternoon . . . Shorter than you'd expect from Dan Pohl . . . User-friendly. Spacious . . . Large greens . . . Dan Pohl did a great job with the property he had to work with . . . Needs an improved clubhouse . . . Great stretch of finishing holes . . . Uninteresting except for the last four holes.

★½ PRAIRIEWOOD GOLF COURSE

PU—315 Prairiewood Dr., Otsego (616)694-6633.
14 miles north of Kalamazoo. **Holes:** 18. **Par:** 72/72.
Yards: 6,519/4,705. **Course rating:** 70.4/66.2. **Slope:** 114/106.
Opened: 1990. **Pace of Play rating:** 4:00. **Green fee:** $17.
Credit cards: MC, V. **Reduced fees:** Low season, Seniors, Juniors.
Caddies: No. **Golf carts:** $10 for 18 holes.
Discount golf packages: No. **Season:** April-Nov. **High:** June-Aug.
On-site lodging: No. **Rental clubs:** Yes.
Walking policy: Unrestricted walking. **Range:** Yes (grass).
To obtain tee times: Call.
Subscriber comments: Good character . . . Front nine too open, back nine too tight, design is ordinary, rough condition . . . Opened before it was ready . . . Will only get better . . . In the midst of pristine woods. Very pretty . . . Greens level to the ground . . . Some holes are interesting.

★★★ THE QUEST GOLF CLUB

PU—116 Questview Dr., Houghton Lake (517)422-4516.
115 miles north of Lansing. **Holes:** 18. **Par:** 72/72.
Yards: 6,773/5,027. **Course rating:** 72.0/73.0. **Slope:** 130/118.
Opened: 1994. **Pace of Play rating:** 4:30. **Green fee:** $48/58.
Credit cards: MC, V. **Reduced fees:** Weekdays, Low season.
Caddies: No. **Golf carts:** Included in Green Fee.
Discount golf packages: Yes. **Season:** April-Oct. **High:** May-Oct.
On-site lodging: No. **Rental clubs:** Yes.
Walking policy: Walking at certain times. **Range:** Yes (grass).
To obtain tee times: Call pro shop. Groups of nine or more are required to send a deposit or provide a credit card number.
Subscriber comments: Pace fast. Needs another year to mature . . . Fairways were great . . . Staff cares . . . Lots of variety . . . New course in

area . . . Playable, rolling, water, good design . . . Real scenic if you like K-mart parking lots . . . Brand new. It's going to be great . . . Has a beautiful par 3 with a K-mart in the background. Hello?

★★½ RACKHAM GOLF CLUB

PU—10100 W. Ten Mile Rd., Huntington Woods (810)543-4040.
15 miles north of Detroit. **Holes:** 18. **Par:** 71/72.
Yards: 6,555/5,413. **Course rating:** 71.1/70.7. **Slope:** 118/115.
Opened: 1924. **Pace of Play rating:** 3:45. **Green fee:** $18/22.
Credit cards: MC, V. **Reduced fees:** Weekdays, Low season, Twilight, Seniors, Juniors.
Caddies: No. **Golf carts:** $20 for 18 holes.
Discount golf packages: Yes. **Season:** Year-round. **High:** May-Sept.
On-site lodging: No. **Rental clubs:** Yes.
Walking policy: Unrestricted walking. **Range:** No.
To obtain tee times: Phone reservations accepted with a credit card guarantee.
Subscriber comments: Good city course . . . A Donald Ross original. First six holes redesigned, remainder still in their original state . . . Classic Donald Ross course in the middle of a city . . . Best condition ever . . . Plenty of sand, tough par 3s . . . Never a hold up . . . Making a real come-back . . . True man-sized par 3s and 4s on back . . . Great refurbished Ross . . . Rebounding classic . . . Helps if you can hit it a ton on long par 4s.

RAISIN RIVER COUNTRY CLUB

PU—1500 N. Dixie Hwy., Monroe (313)289-3700, (800)321-9564.
25 miles south of Detroit.
Credit cards: None.
Caddies: No. **Golf carts:** $9 for 18 holes.
Discount golf packages: Yes. **Season:** March-Nov. **High:** May-Sept.
On-site lodging: Yes. **Rental clubs:** Yes.
Walking policy: Unrestricted walking. **Range:** Yes (grass).
To obtain tee times: Call eight days in advance for weekend and holidays only. No tee times needed for weekday play.

★★½ EAST COURSE

Holes: 18. **Par:** 71/71.
Yards: 6,930/5,580. **Course rating:** 73.1/68.4. **Slope:** N/A.
Opened: 1974. **Pace of Play rating:** 4:15. **Green fee:** $17.
Reduced fees: Low season, Resort guests.
Subscriber comments: Tough and long with big greens . . . The more you play it, the blander it becomes . . . Boring, bring some beer . . . Huge greens make club selection interesting . . . A fun place to test your game . . . Huge flat greens on a flat course . . . The nicer of the two courses . . . Big greens, but always slow.

★★½ WEST COURSE

Holes: 18. **Par:** 70/74.
Yards: 6,255/5,880. **Course rating:** 68.5/N/A. **Slope:** N/A.
Opened: 1964. **Pace of Play rating:** N/A. **Green fee:** $15.
Reduced fees: Resort guests, Seniors, Juniors.
Subscriber comments: Long hitters can reach the par 5s . . . No trees . . . Front nine has four holes in one direction followed by five holes in the opposite . . . Two or three badly designed holes . . . Nice views, not too hard . . . Fairly easy except when windy . . . Good pace of play.

★★ RAISIN VALLEY GOLF CLUB

PU—4057 Comfort Rd., Tecumseh (517)423-2050.
35 miles north of Toledo, OH. **Holes:** 18. **Par:** 71/71.
Yards: 5,650/4,630. **Course rating:** 67.5/69.0. **Slope:** N/A.
Opened: 1969. **Pace of Play rating:** 4:30. **Green fee:** $10/18.
Credit cards: MC, V. **Reduced fees:** Weekdays, Low season, Seniors, Juniors.
Caddies: No. **Golf carts:** $18 for 18 holes.
Discount golf packages: No. **Season:** April-Nov. **High:** June-Aug.
On-site lodging: No. **Rental clubs:** No.
Walking policy: Unrestricted walking. **Range:** No.

To obtain tee times: Call one week in advance.
Subscriber comments: Chip-and-putt course, too easy, a few challenging holes . . . Much shorter than marked . . . Well kept public course . . . General upkeep is very good . . . Seldom overcrowded . . . Short, tricky, fun . . . Way too short, don't make a special trip to play here.

★★★ RATTLE RUN GOLF COURSE

PU—7163 St. Clair Hwy., China Township (810)329-2070.
23 miles north of Detroit. **Holes:** 18. **Par:** 72/75.
Yards: 6,891/5,085. **Course rating:** 75.1/70.4. **Slope:** 139/124.
Opened: 1977. **Pace of Play rating:** 4:30. **Green fee:** $29/39.
Credit cards: All major. **Reduced fees:** Low season, Twilight, Seniors, Juniors.
Caddies: No. **Golf carts:** Included in Green Fee.
Discount golf packages: Yes. **Season:** April-Nov. **High:** May-Sept.
On-site lodging: No. **Rental clubs:** Yes.
Walking policy: Walking at certain times. **Range:** Yes (grass).
To obtain tee times: Call up to two weeks in advance.
Ranked in Third 25 of America's 75 Best Public Golf Courses by Golf Digest.
Subscriber comments: Great holes, very poor condition . . . Not always in good condition but very challenging . . . A couple of holes are unfair . . . Probably the best track in southeast Michigan. New ownership is polishing this into a real diamond . . . Needs a new clubhouse badly . . . One of the toughest courses in the state . . . Bring your driver, you'll use it . . . Still has mosquitoes . . . Excellent service treats you like a king and a queen . . . Seems to be coming back . . . Tough but thrilling.

★★ REDDEMAN FARMS GOLF COURSE

PU—555 S. Dancer Rd., Chelsea (313)475-3020.
9 miles west of Ann Arbor. **Holes:** 18. **Par:** 72/72.
Yards: 6,513/5,813. **Course rating:** 71.4/73.4. **Slope:** 122/126.
Opened: 1991. **Pace of Play rating:** 4:00. **Green fee:** $21/25.
Credit cards: MC, V. **Reduced fees:** Weekdays, Low season, Twilight, Seniors, Junior
Caddies: No. **Golf carts:** $10 for 18 holes.
Discount golf packages: No. **Season:** April-Nov. **High:** June-Sept.
On-site lodging: No. **Rental clubs:** Yes.
Walking policy: Unrestricted walking. **Range:** Yes (grass).
To obtain tee times: Call anytime.
Subscriber comments: Has developed into an enjoyable course . . . Fun if dry, but easily gets really wet . . . Flat course . . . Straight and fun, long difficult carries over water . . . Memorable Nos. 9 and 18, both long par 4s over water . . . Relaxing . . . Lots of character . . . Undiscovered gem by most golfers, even in this area . . . Four years old, has character . . . Not too creative.

RICHMOND FOREST GOLF CLUB★

PU—33300 32 Mile Rd., Lenox (810)727-4742.
30 miles north of Detroit. **Holes:** 18. **Par:** 72/72.
Yards: 6,542/5,288. **Course rating:** N/A. **Slope:** N/A.
Opened: 1994. **Pace of Play rating:** 4:15. **Green fee:** $20/22.
Credit cards: MC, V. **Reduced fees:** Weekdays, Low season, Twilight, Seniors, Juniors.
Caddies: No. **Golf carts:** $10 for 18 holes.
Discount golf packages: No. **Season:** March-Nov. **High:** June-Aug.
On-site lodging: No. **Rental clubs:** Yes.
Walking policy: Unrestricted walking. **Range:** Yes (grass).
To obtain tee times: Call or come in up to seven days in advance.

RIVERVIEW HIGHLANDS GOLF CLUB
★★ RED/GOLD/BLUE

R—15015 Sibley Rd., Riverview (313)479-2266.
20 miles south of Detroit. **Holes:** 27. **Par:** 72/72/72.
Yards: 6,732/6,667/6,485. **Course rating:** 69.2/71.4/70.8.
Slope: 115/119/119.

Opened: 1973. **Pace of Play rating:** 4:18. **Green fee:** $18.
Credit cards: All major. **Reduced fees:** Weekdays, Low season, Twilight, Seniors, Juniors.
Caddies: No. **Golf carts:** $20 for 18 holes.
Discount golf packages: Yes. **Season:** March-Dec. **High:** May-Sept.
On-site lodging: No. **Rental clubs:** Yes.
Walking policy: Unrestricted walking. **Range:** No.
To obtain tee times: Call.
Subscriber comments: Each course is different. Blue has a lot of water . . . One par 5 is right next to a landfill . . . Good variety on flat land . . . Too many geese! . . . Cheap but wide open.

RIVERWOOD RESORT
★★½ WHITE/RED/BLUE
R—1313 E. Broomfield Rd., Mt. Pleasant (517)772-5726, (800)882-5211.
45 miles north of Lansing. **Holes:** 27. **Par:** 72/72/72.
Yards: 6,600/6,182/6,100. **Course rating:** 72.0/70.3/70.3.
Slope: 125/121/116.
Opened: 1932. **Pace of Play rating:** 4:10. **Green fee:** $17/21.
Credit cards: MC, V, DISC. **Reduced fees:** Low season, Resort guests, Twilight, Seniors
Caddies: No. **Golf carts:** $10 for 18 holes.
Discount golf packages: Yes. **Season:** March-Oct. **High:** June-Aug.
On-site lodging: Yes. **Rental clubs:** Yes.
Walking policy: Walking at certain times. **Range:** Yes (grass).
To obtain tee times: Call two months in advance.
Subscriber comments: Long, tight holes . . . Could use more grass seed . . . Not too challenging . . . Extremely slow pace . . . Just a fun 27 holes of golf at the right price . . . Several hard holes offset by some easier ones . . . Something for everyone. Food is supreme . . . Design is a little bland and dated . . . Needs to be upgraded.

★★★★ THE ROCK AT DRUMMOND ISLAND
R—26 Maxton Rd., Drummond Island (906)493-1006, (800)999-6343.
60 miles southeast of Sault Ste. Marie. **Holes:** 18. **Par:** 71/71.
Yards: 6,837/4,992. **Course rating:** 74.9/70.9. **Slope:** 142/130.
Opened: 1989. **Pace of Play rating:** 4:42. **Green fee:** $30/65.
Credit cards: All major. **Reduced fees:** Weekdays, Low season, Resort guests, Twilight, Juniors.
Caddies: No. **Golf carts:** Included in Green Fee.
Discount golf packages: Yes. **Season:** May-Oct. **High:** June-Aug.
On-site lodging: Yes. **Rental clubs:** Yes.
Walking policy: Mandatory cart. **Range:** Yes (grass).
To obtain tee times: Call pro shop between 9 a.m. and 5 p.m.
Subscriber comments: Fun to play . . . Beautiful . . . Terrific beauty, great conditions . . . A nice layout, hard to get to . . . Too far from civilization . . . Well designed . . . Lots of deer . . . Say bad things about The Rock. I want to keep it to myself . . . Very lightly played . . . Best "get away from it all" place to play . . . Too bad it's on an island . . . Just super as far as aesthetics go! . . . A visual experience with abundant wildlife . . . Wooded and tight, beautiful and secluded . . . Very few people made for a great round . . . Don't hit deer on your follow-through . . . Wild game, deer, bear and birds abound.

★★ ROGELL GOLF COURSE
PU—18601 Berg Rd., Detroit (313)935-5331.
Call club for further information.
Subscriber comments: Don't walk without a note from your cardiologist . . . Rouge River comes into play on two holes. Any hole can be tough . . . Best city course in Detroit . . . In good shape, greens are true, be careful of the trees . . . In sad shape, but interesting . . . Needs more care.

★★ ROGUE RIVER GOLF COURSE
PU—12994 Paine Ave., N.W., Sparta (616)887-7182.
Call club for further information.
Subscriber comments: The old guys love this course . . . Beautiful, challenging . . . Always in good shape . . . Apparent cash cow . . . Slow, slow, slow . . . Ego builder. Excellent greens, really an easy course.

★½ ROLLING HILLS GOLF CLUB
PU—3274 Davison Rd., Lapeer (810)664-2281.
20 miles east of Flint. **Holes:** 18. **Par:** 71/72.
Yards: 6,456/5,184. **Course rating:** 69.9/69.8. **Slope:** 113/112.
Opened: . **Pace of Play rating:** 4:00. **Green fee:** $15/17.
Credit cards: None. **Reduced fees:** Weekdays, Low season, Twilight, Seniors, Juniors.
Caddies: No. **Golf carts:** $22 for 18 holes.
Discount golf packages: No. **Season:** April-Oct. **High:** June-Aug.
On-site lodging: No. **Rental clubs:** Yes.
Walking policy: Unrestricted walking. **Range:** Yes (grass).
To obtain tee times: Call. Tee times not always required.
Subscriber comments: Old course in great shape . . . Swampy front . . . T-shirt or no shirt OK . . . Wide-open course . . . Nice variety of holes.

★½ ROLLING HILLS GOLF COURSE
PU—3100 Baldwin Dr., Hudsonville (616)669-9768.
Call club for further information.
Subscriber comments: Yardages not accurate . . . Nice, open course . . . Beautiful in the fall . . . Very hard to walk . . . Short, straight and slow play.

★★½ ROMEO GOLF & COUNTRY CLUB
PU—14600 - 32 Mile Rd., Washington (810)752-9673.
Call club for further information.
Subscriber comments: Best place in the state for seniors . . . One of the cheapest fees . . . New course; flat, but nice . . . Caters to seniors . . . Very playable.

★★★ ROUGE PARK GOLF CLUB
PU—11701 Burt Rd., Detroit (313)837-5900.
Call club for further information.
Subscriber comments: Par-4 10th crosses over the river twice, favors a draw. One of many dogleg lefts . . . Nice course . . . A great improvement to an old city course . . . Beautiful old design . . . Difficult. Take one ball as a sacrifice to the river bed . . . A treasured gem in the city of Detroit . . . Rouge River in play on many holes. Rewards good shots and penalizes severely poor shots . . . No. 2 very tough.

★★½ ROYAL SCOT GOLF COURSE
PU—4722 W. Grand River, Lansing (517)321-4653.
Holes: 18. **Par:** 71/71.
Yards: 6,606/4,685. **Course rating:** 71.7/66.8. **Slope:** 123/117.
Opened: 1962. **Pace of Play rating:** 4:00. **Green fee:** $15/21.
Credit cards: All major. **Reduced fees:** Weekdays, Low season, Resort guests, Twilight, Seniors, Juniors.
Caddies: No. **Golf carts:** $21 for 18 holes.
Discount golf packages: Yes. **Season:** Year-round. **High:** May-Aug.
On-site lodging: No. **Rental clubs:** Yes.
Walking policy: Unrestricted walking. **Range:** Yes (grass).
To obtain tee times: Call.
Subscriber comments: Course is fine, but they try to get too many groups on . . . Good layout, fast greens . . . Nice overall course improved by recent course construction . . . Gets lots of play . . . Quick greens and well-maintained fairways . . . No great holes, no weak ones.

★★★ SALEM HILLS GOLF CLUB
PU—8810 W. Six Mile Rd., Northville (810)437-2152.
25 miles northwest of Detroit. **Holes:** 18. **Par:** 72/76.
Yards: 6,966/5,874. **Course rating:** 72.9/73.4. **Slope:** 121/119.
Opened: 1961. **Pace of Play rating:** 3:50. **Green fee:** $19/38.
Credit cards: None. **Reduced fees:** Twilight, Seniors, Juniors.
Caddies: No. **Golf carts:** $11 for 18 holes.
Discount golf packages: No. **Season:** April-Nov. **High:** May-Sept.
On-site lodging: No. **Rental clubs:** Yes.
Walking policy: Walking at certain times. **Range:** Yes (grass).
To obtain tee times: Call one week in advance and guarantee with credit card.
Subscriber comments: Good local course . . . Plays like a private country club . . . Big greens . . . Long and fair . . . Best greens . . . Wasn't impressed . . . Overrated . . . Some great holes . . . Wide open on many holes, narrow on some . . . Tough par 4s . . . One of the best for public play . . . No. 18 green slopes into a pond! . . . Has always been overrated and undermaintained.

★½ SANDY RIDGE GOLF COURSE
PU—2750 W. Lauria Rd., Midland (517)631-6010.
100 miles north of Detroit. **Holes:** 18. **Par:** 72/72.
Yards: 6,385/5,304. **Course rating:** 70.4/70.2. **Slope:** 118/115.
Opened: 1966. **Pace of Play rating:** N/A. **Green fee:** $17.
Credit cards: MC, V, DISC. **Reduced fees:** Seniors, Juniors.
Caddies: No. **Golf carts:** $20 for 18 holes.
Discount golf packages: Yes. **Season:** April-Oct. **High:** June-Aug.
On-site lodging: No. **Rental clubs:** Yes.
Walking policy: Unrestricted walking. **Range:** Yes (grass).
To obtain tee times: Call up to three days in advance.
Subscriber comments: Pretty, open, front nine more interesting than the back . . . Conditions improving . . . Good course, good service, good pace . . . It has a bad location . . . Added trees will fill out in three to five years.

SASKATOON GOLF CLUB
PU—9038 92nd St., Alto (616)891-9229.
12 miles southeast of Grand Rapids.
Opened: 1970. **Green fee:** $16/18.
Credit cards: MC, V, DISC. **Reduced fees:** Seniors.
Caddies: No. **Golf carts:** $9 for 18 holes.
Discount golf packages: No. **Season:** March-Dec. **High:** May-July.
On-site lodging: No. **Rental clubs:** Yes.
Walking policy: Unrestricted walking. **Range:** Yes (grass).
To obtain tee times: Call two weeks prior to play for weekdays and one week in advance for weekends.

★★★ BLUE/WHITE
Holes: 18. **Par:** 73/73.
Yards: 6,750/6,125. **Course rating:** 70.7/71.7. **Slope:** 123/122.
Pace of Play rating: 4:20.
Subscriber comments: Superbly run . . . Best burgers in clubhouse . . . Total of four nines. Best muny course I have played . . . Tests your range of shots . . . Treated well in a busy period . . . Pines galore. Lush . . . Rough is too high . . . Best public course in Kent County . . . Requires straight shoots . . . Four nines of varying difficulty. Nice scenery. Greens don't hold well . . . A shotmaker's dream . . . Blue and White are the best nines on the west side of the state . . . Do they ever mow the fairways?

RED/GOLD★
Holes: 18. **Par:** 71/70.
Yards: 6,300/5,300. **Course rating:** 68.8/67.7. **Slope:** 117/114.
Pace of Play rating: 5:00.
Subscriber comments: Gold course is a Scottish links . . . Love the Gold Course . . . Gold Course is best of the nines.

SAULT STE. MARIE COUNTRY CLUB★

SP—1520 Riverside Dr., Sault Ste. Marie (906)632-7812.
Holes: 18. **Par:** 71/72.
Yards: 6,295/5,100. **Course rating:** 70.6/70.0. **Slope:** 125/119.
Opened: 1903. **Pace of Play rating:** 3:52. **Green fee:** $18/22.
Credit cards: MC, V. **Reduced fees:** Low season.
Caddies: No. **Golf carts:** $16 for 18 holes.
Discount golf packages: No. **Season:** April-Oct. **High:** June-Aug.
On-site lodging: No. **Rental clubs:** Yes.
Walking policy: Unrestricted walking. **Range:** Yes (grass).
To obtain tee times: Call up to three days in advance.

★★★ SCOTT LAKE COUNTRY CLUB

SP—911 Hayes Rd., Comstock Park (616)784-1355.
10 miles north of Grand Rapids. **Holes:** 18. **Par:** 72/72.
Yards: 6,333/4,794. **Course rating:** 70.8/67.6. **Slope:** 122/110.
Opened: 1962. **Pace of Play rating:** 3:49. **Green fee:** $16/20.
Credit cards: All major. **Reduced fees:** Weekdays, Low season, Seniors, Juniors.
Caddies: No. **Golf carts:** $9 for 18 holes.
Discount golf packages: No. **Season:** April-Nov. **High:** May-Sept.
On-site lodging: No. **Rental clubs:** Yes.
Walking policy: Unrestricted walking. **Range:** Yes (grass).
To obtain tee times: Call one week in advance.
Subscriber comments: Hilly course, forces good tee shots . . . Surprising, nice elevations . . . Very hilly and unique . . . Lots of ups and downs . . . Enjoyable . . . Lots of uphill, downhill and sidehill shots . . . Layout could be improved but is still an adequate test of golf . . . This is a public country club . . . Plays a little short . . . Four blind shots to be played.

SHANTY CREEK RESORT

R—One Shanty Creek Rd., Bellaire (616)533-8621, (800)678-4111.
35 miles northeast of Traverse City.
Credit cards: All major. **Reduced fees:** Resort guests, Twilight.
Caddies: No. **Golf carts:** Included in Green Fee.
Discount golf packages: Yes. **Season:** April-Oct. **High:** July-Aug.
On-site lodging: Yes. **Rental clubs:** Yes.
Walking policy: Walking at certain times. **Range:** Yes (grass).
To obtain tee times: Advance tee times suggested. Hotel Guests: Tee times may be made with hotel reservations. Non-guests: Tee time request for play on Monday through Thursday are accepted one month prior to play. Requests taken two weeks prior to play for Friday through Sunday.

★★★½ SCHUSS MOUNTAIN COURSE

Holes: 18. **Par:** 72/72.
Yards: 6,922/5,423. **Course rating:** 73.4/71.2. **Slope:** 127/126.
Opened: 1972. **Pace of Play rating:** 4:50. **Green fee:** $65.
Subscriber comments: Good layout, interesting holes . . . Great design on the back nine . . . A real challenge . . . Well-groomed . . . Probably the finest, most underrated course up north . . . Better than average . . . Best omelette I've ever had . . . Just fun to play . . . Great elevations with lots of trees . . . Nice scenery . . . Generous driving areas . . . You'll pay if you don't hit it straight . . . You can't go wrong playing the Schuss . . . Lots of doglegs, not too long . . . Drivers take aim . . . Two distinct nines: front full of trees, back is grassland hills.

★★½ SHANTY CREEK COURSE

Holes: 18. **Par:** 71/71.
Yards: 6,276/4,545. **Course rating:** 71.7/70.7. **Slope:** 120/116.
Opened: 1965. **Pace of Play rating:** 4:50. **Green fee:** $50.
Subscriber comments: Course has really improved in the last two years. Fast greens . . . Not much character . . . Easiest of the Shanty Creek courses . . . Very pretty . . . Heavily wooded and challenging . . . Good resort course . . . Great vistas . . . Uninspired open course, not in same league as other northern Michigan courses . . . Holes too close together . . . Should redesign the course again . . . A fair course without much flash.

★★★★½ **THE LEGEND COURSE**
Holes: 18. **Par:** 72/72.
Yards: 6,764/5,801. **Course rating:** 73.6/69.4. **Slope:** 137/121.
Opened: 1985. **Pace of Play rating:** 4:50. **Green fee:** $0/95.
Ranked 19th in America's 75 Best Resort Courses by Golf Digest. Ranked 25th in Michigan by Golf Digest.
Subscriber comments: Requires a previous round to understand and enjoy . . . Could be the prettiest course in state. A great test of golf . . . Awesome . . . Wait until you hone your game before you tackle the Legend . . . Next hole better than the last, 18 times . . . Only bad hole is the 2nd; it helps if you draw ball off tee . . . Probably the most breathtaking scenery of any Michigan course . . . Best course in Michigan, but expensive . . . Lots of up-and-down terrain . . . Beautiful routing . . . A champion course . . . Groomed to perfection . . . The scenery is great! I'll go back . . . Unbelievable elevation changes . . . This is a shrine to golf . . . What golf in heaven should be . . . Wish I could afford to play it more . . . Great layout . . . Northern Michigan golf at its best . . . A wonderful experience . . . Arnold Palmer course, awesome . . . Deserves Mr. Palmer's name . . . A Palmer masterpiece with beautiful vistas . . . A great northern Michigan landmark . . . Ignore hole No. 2 . . . Playable and pretty . . . The most memorable tee shots anywhere. You feel like you're the only one on the course.

SPRING VALLEY GOLF COURSE★
PU—7336 W. U.S. 10, Hersey (616)832-5041.
70 miles north of Grand Rapids. **Holes:** 18. **Par:** 72/74.
Yards: 6,439/5,273. **Course rating:** N/A. **Slope:** N/A.
Opened: 1962. **Pace of Play rating:** 3:00. **Green fee:** $14/16.
Credit cards: MC, V. **Reduced fees:** Weekdays, Low season, Seniors.
Caddies: No. **Golf carts:** $16 for 18 holes.
Discount golf packages: No. **Season:** April-Oct. **High:** June-Aug.
On-site lodging: No. **Rental clubs:** Yes.
Walking policy: Unrestricted walking. **Range:** Yes (grass).
To obtain tee times: Call pro shop.

★★★ **SPRINGFIELD OAKS GOLF COURSE**
PU—12450 Andersonville Rd., Davisburg (810)625-2540.
15 miles northwest of Pontiac. **Holes:** 18. **Par:** 71/71.
Yards: 6,235/5,372. **Course rating:** 69.4/70.3. **Slope:** 115/114.
Opened: 1970. **Pace of Play rating:** 4:00. **Green fee:** $12/18.
Credit cards: MC, V. **Reduced fees:** Weekdays, Low season, Twilight, Seniors, Juniors.
Caddies: No. **Golf carts:** $19 for 18 holes.
Discount golf packages: No. **Season:** March-Nov. **High:** June-Aug.
On-site lodging: No. **Rental clubs:** Yes.
Walking policy: Unrestricted walking. **Range:** No.
To obtain tee times: Weekdays: three days in advance. Weekends & Holidays: preceding Wednesday evening starting at 6:00 p.m. in person or 6:15 p.m. by phone.
Subscriber comments: Best value in Michigan . . . A gem, worth the ride, always a pleasure . . . Nice, little course . . . A remarkably enjoyable experience . . . Wonderful shape, best muny in southeast Michigan . . . Best-kept county course in the area . . . Exhilarating . . . Beautiful clubhouse . . . A great mix of holes.

★★★½ **STONEBRIDGE GOLF CLUB**
PU—5315 Stonebridge Drive S., Ann Arbor (313)429-8383.
30 miles west of Detroit. **Holes:** 18. **Par:** 72/72.
Yards: 6,932/5,075. **Course rating:** 74.2/71.0. **Slope:** 139/128.
Opened: 1991. **Pace of Play rating:** 4:15. **Green fee:** $30/40.
Credit cards: MC, V. **Reduced fees:** Low season, Twilight, Seniors, Juniors.
Caddies: No. **Golf carts:** $10 for 18 holes.
Discount golf packages: Yes. **Season:** March-Dec. **High:** June-Aug.
On-site lodging: No. **Rental clubs:** Yes.
Walking policy: Walking at certain times. **Range:** Yes (grass).

To obtain tee times: Maximum five days in advance.
Subscriber comments: Layout is great but maintenance has slipped . . .
Bah humbug . . . Championship caliber, best-kept secret in Michigan . . .
Best set of four par 3s in the area . . . Two or three hidden Arthur Hills
gems in our area . . . Driving range stinks; could develop into a very good
facility . . . Nice trail . . . In the path of an airport . . . Has variety: long and
open, short and tight, lots of hazards . . . Don't try to walk . . . Majority of
greens have elephants buried in them . . . I should play it again to determine
whether I played that bad or if the course is that difficult . . . No notable
features . . . A real pleasure . . . Long putts are tough . . . Well-maintained,
water, sand, mounds, woods: it's all there . . . Features a 471-yard par 4
into the prevailing wind.

★★★★ STONEHEDGE GOLF COURSE

PU—15503 E. M-89, Augusta (616)731-2300.
20 miles northeast of Kalamazoo. **Holes:** 18. **Par:** 72/72.
Yards: 6,656/5,191. **Course rating:** 72.4/70.3. **Slope:** 133/120.
Opened: 1988. **Pace of Play rating:** 4:20. **Green fee:** $23/26.
Credit cards: MC, V. **Reduced fees:** Weekdays, Low season, Resort
guests, Juniors.
Caddies: No. **Golf carts:** $11 for 18 holes.
Discount golf packages: Yes. **Season:** April-Nov. **High:** May-Aug.
On-site lodging: No. **Rental clubs:** Yes.

Walking policy: Walking at certain times. **Range:** Yes (grass).
To obtain tee times: Call pro shop.
Subscriber comments: Great resort course, requires control . . . Wooded
and pretty . . . A real gem. Very crowded on weekends . . . Terrific
finishing holes . . . Interesting design with a stone wall . . . Great accent,
great layout . . . Not many flat lies . . . Not long, but tight . . . Fair par 5s
. . . No water, but tight . . . Lots of elevation, bring a camera. A great test
. . . Maybe the most beautiful course in Michigan . . . No bad holes . . .
Great course despite no water hazards . . . Too many sidehill lies . . .
Stonehedge is the prettiest public golf course I have ever played . . . Many
hills and trees . . . Busy for a reason . . . A very worthwhile outing . . .
Fantastic scenery, the best public course in Michigan.

★★ STONY CREEK GOLF COURSE

PU—5140 Main Pkwy., Shelby Township (810)781-9166.
Call club for further information.
Subscriber comments: Quite ragged, greens too slow . . . Too bad they
don't take care of this course . . . When it's in good condition, it's a great
course . . . Good course for the metro park type . . . Fruit orchards all
around, many blind holes . . . Sand traps always wet and very heavy . . .
Slow play detracts.

SUGAR LOAF RESORT GOLF CLUB★

PU—4500 Sugar Loaf Mtn. Rd., Cedar (616)228-1880, (800)968-0576.
18 miles southeast of Traverse City. **Holes:** 18. **Par:** 72/74.
Yards: 6,813/5,134. **Course rating:** 73.3/70.5. **Slope:** 125/117.
Opened: 1965. **Pace of Play rating:** 4:50. **Green fee:** $39/45.
Credit cards: All major. **Reduced fees:** Weekdays, Twilight.
Caddies: No. **Golf carts:** Included in Green Fee.
Discount golf packages: Yes. **Season:** May-Oct. **High:** July-Aug.
On-site lodging: Yes. **Rental clubs:** Yes.
Walking policy: Walking at certain times. **Range:** Yes (grass).
To obtain tee times: Call pro shop.

SUGARBUSH GOLF CLUB★

PU—1 Sugarbush Dr., Davison (810)653-3326.
8 miles east of Flint. **Holes:** 18. **Par:** 72/72.
Yards: 7,285/5,667. **Course rating:** N/A. **Slope:** N/A.
Opened: 1995. **Pace of Play rating:** 4:00. **Green fee:** $48/52.
Credit cards: MC, V, AMEX. **Reduced fees:** Weekdays, Low season,
Twilight, Seniors, Juniors.
Caddies: No. **Golf carts:** Included in Green Fee.

Discount golf packages: Yes. Season: April-Nov. High: June-Aug.
On-site lodging: No. Rental clubs: Yes.
Walking policy: Unrestricted walking. Range: Yes (grass).
To obtain tee times: Call two weeks in advance.

★★ SWARTZ CREEK GOLF COURSE

PU—1902 Hammerberg Rd., Flint (313)766-7463.
Call club for further information.
Subscriber comments: Too close to the freeway, noisy . . . Tough to
read greens . . . Good mix of difficulty levels . . . Nothing spectacular . . .
A family course . . . Just a steady stream of good golf holes . . . Great
layout, zero upkeep.

SYCAMORE HILLS GOLF CLUB
★★★ NORTH/SOUTH/WEST

PU—48787 N. Ave., Mt. Clemens (810)598-9500.
20 miles north of Detroit. Holes: 27. Par: 72/72/72.
Yards: 6,255/6,305/6,250. Course rating: 70.3/70.7/70.2.
Slope: 123/130/132.
Opened: 1990. Pace of Play rating: 4:00. Green fee: $25/30.
Credit cards: MC, V. Reduced fees: Weekdays, Low season, Twilight,
Seniors, Juniors.
Caddies: No. Golf carts: $10 for 18 holes.
Discount golf packages: No. Season: March-Dec. High: May-Sept.
On-site lodging: No. Rental clubs: Yes.
Walking policy: Walking at certain times. Range: Yes (grass).
To obtain tee times: Call pro shop.
Subscriber comments: Some good holes, nice clubhouse, great pro shop
. . . Tough, tight . . . In satisfactory shape, but the course was unappealing
. . . Three separate nines, make the turn and wait . . . A short-hitter's
course.

★★★ TANGLEWOOD GOLF CLUB
NORTH/SOUTH/WEST

PU—53503 W. Ten Mile Rd., South Lyon (810)486-3355.
25 miles northwest of Detroit. Holes: 27. Par: 72/72/72.
Yards: 7,077/6,922/7,117. Course rating: 73.6/73.0/76.4.
Slope: 129/128/138.
Opened: 1991. Pace of Play rating: 4:15. Green fee: $30/35.
Credit cards: MC, V, AMEX. Reduced fees: Low season, Twilight,
Seniors, Juniors.
Caddies: No. Golf carts: $10 for 18 holes.
Discount golf packages: Yes. Season: March-Nov. High: May-Aug.
On-site lodging: Yes. Rental clubs: Yes.
Walking policy: Walking at certain times. Range: Yes (grass).
To obtain tee times: Call pro shop.
Subscriber comments: Hidden pond in the first fairway . . . Country club
atmosphere, great staff and food . . . Good design, can play slow . . . Front
nine is short and open with water, back nine much tougher, country club-
style clubhouse . . . They make a great Bloody Mary . . . Layout of the first
hole is awful.

★★★ TAYLOR MEADOWS GOLF CLUB

PU—25360 Ecorse Rd., Taylor (313)295-0506.
15 miles southwest of Detroit. Holes: 18. Par: 71/71.
Yards: 6,075/5,118. Course rating: 67.8/67.6. Slope: 114/111.
Opened: 1989. Pace of Play rating: 4:30-5:00. Green fee: $15/20.
Credit cards: MC, V. Reduced fees: Weekdays, Low season, Twilight,
Seniors, Juniors.
Caddies: No. Golf carts: $20 for 18 holes.
Discount golf packages: No. Season: March-Dec. High: May-Oct.
On-site lodging: No. Rental clubs: Yes.
Walking policy: Unrestricted walking. Range: Yes.
To obtain tee times: Call 2 days in advance, Thursday at noon for
weekends.

Subscriber comments: Short but fun. Taylor made something out of nothing . . . Easy scoring . . . A pleasant experience . . . The best fairways I played all year . . . Along noisy freeway . . . Short . . . Crowded day and night. Short and sweet, you'll feel like a pro . . . Arthur Hills course gets heavy play . . . Too short on too little land; not a compliment to Mr. Hills' ability . . . Will not hurt your ego.

★★★ THORNAPPLE CREEK GOLF CLUB
PU—6415 W. F Ave., Kalamazoo (616)344-0040.
5 miles north of Kalamazoo. **Holes:** 18. **Par:** 72/72.
Yards: 6,960/4,948. **Course rating:** 73.7/68.9. **Slope:** 137/121.
Opened: 1979. **Pace of Play rating:** 4:00-4:30. **Green fee:** $18/24.
Credit cards: MC, V, DISC. **Reduced fees:** Weekdays, Low season.
Caddies: No. **Golf carts:** $20 for 18 holes.
Discount golf packages: Yes. **Season:** April-Nov. **High:** June-Aug.
On-site lodging: No. **Rental clubs:** Yes.
Walking policy: Unrestricated walking. **Range:** Yes (grass).
To obtain tee times: Call in advance one week. Groups of 12 or larger can book any day or time but need to put down deposit.
Subscriber comments: Difficult hazards . . . Greens do not have a flat zone . . . Challenging, interesting . . . Fowl droppings everywhere . . . Three holes, greens not fair . . . Several challenging shots . . . Water and length . . . Greens are multi-tiered and tricky . . . Tough course . . . Hilly course . . . Back nine hilly and challenging, seldom crowded . . . A monster 13th hole . . . Pleasant place . . . Tough island-type green on 16. . . . Even if you like to walk, you'd better ride this one!

★★★★½ THOROUGHBRED GOLF CLUB
R—6886 Water Rd., Rothbury (616)893-4653.
20 miles north of Muskegon. **Holes:** 18. **Par:** 72/72.
Yards: 6,900/4,851. **Course rating:** 74.4/69.5. **Slope:** 147/126.
Opened: 1993. **Pace of Play rating:** N/A. **Green fee:** $45/59.
Credit cards: MC, V, DISC. **Reduced fees:** Low season, Resort guests, Twilight.
Caddies: No. **Golf carts:** Included in Green Fee.
Discount golf packages: Yes. **Season:** April-Nov. **High:** June-Sept.
On-site lodging: Yes. **Rental clubs:** Yes.
Walking policy: Unrestricted walking. **Range:** Yes (grass).
To obtain tee times: Tee times made for the entire year with a $59 deposit. Times can be made seven days in advance with no deposit.
Ranked 10th in Michigan by Golf Digest.
Subscriber comments: Exciting, challenging, beautiful . . . Best in western Michigan . . . Too many blind and surprise holes, maybe better next time . . . The average golfer will be humbled . . . Too hard for the wife . . . Super layout . . . Best course within 100 miles . . . Very scenic, don't miss it . . . Best-kept secret in Michigan . . . A scenic must . . . Arthur Hills' finest, expensive but worth every dollar . . . Some par 4s too tough . . . I call it the Rawhide . . . One great hole after another . . . An exciting layout, you have to play it more than once . . . 18th hole a little unfair off tee . . . Best unknown course in Michigan . . . No. 2, No. 18 are heroic holes . . . Little costly, but I'll definitely be back . . . Great scenery, sort of gimmicky . . . Very pretty golf course, but it needs a few years to grow . . . One of Michigan's most beautiful . . . Hilly lies . . . Every hole can be on a postcard. A class course . . . Another Hills' masterpiece . . . Spectacularly beautiful . . . Great wilderness course . . . Entire staff, including starters and rangers, was always helpful.

THUNDER BAY GOLF RESORT★
R—27800 M-32 East, Hillman (517)742-4875, (800)729-9375.
22 miles west of Alpena. **Holes:** 18. **Par:** 73/75.
Yards: 6,466/5,584. **Course rating:** 72.1/72.1. **Slope:** 129/124.
Opened: 1971. **Pace of Play rating:** 4:30. **Green fee:** $16/20.
Credit cards: All major. **Reduced fees:** Resort guests, Seniors, Juniors.
Caddies: No. **Golf carts:** $12 for 18 holes.

Discount golf packages: Yes. **Season:** April-Nov. **High:** June-Sept.
On-site lodging: Yes. **Rental clubs:** Yes.
Walking policy: Walking at certain times. **Range:** Yes (grass).
To obtain tee times: Call.

★★★½ TIMBER RIDGE GOLF COURSE

PU—16339 Park Lake Rd., East Lansing (517)339-8000, (800)874-3432.
5 miles east of Lansing. **Holes:** 18. **Par:** 72/72.
Yards: 6,497/5,048. **Course rating:** 72.7/70.4. **Slope:** 137/129.
Opened: 1989. **Pace of Play rating:** 4:30-5:00. **Green fee:** $40.
Credit cards: MC, V, DISC. **Reduced fees:** Weekdays, Low season,
Twilight, Seniors.
Caddies: No. **Golf carts:** $10 for 18 holes.
Discount golf packages: Yes. **Season:** March-Nov. **High:** May-Sept.
On-site lodging: No. **Rental clubs:** Yes.
Walking policy: Walking at certain times. **Range:** Yes (grass).
To obtain tee times: Call seven days prior for a foursome group; groups
of eight or more may book in advance.
Ranked in Third 25 of America's 75 Best Public Golf Courses by Golf
Digest.
Subscriber comments: Sister course to Elk Ridge. A little older and fairer
. . . Tight landing areas . . . Maintenance needs improvement . . . High
handicappers have walked off because of its toughness . . . Way too tight
. . . A nice test of shotmaking . . . Trees, trees, and more trees . . . Feels
like up north . . . Pro-type course with rolling hills, wildlife . . . You'd
better hit it straight! . . . No bail-out areas, trees immediately on sides of the
fairways with no rough to stop a rolling ball . . . Among the state's best in
scenery and amenities. However, most greens get too much shade and are
subpar . . . Wonderful layout and landscape . . . Fantastic course . . . What
exemplifies better Michigan courses: pines, hardwoods, water and hills . . .
Typical Matthews, almost too many holes are too tight . . . Lots of trees
makes it hard to grow grass . . . Has the design and look of a resort course
. . . Stay out of the woods . . . Pretty pricey for Lansing . . . When will
they clean up the woods? . . . Like playing a private course . . . One of
Matthews' best . . . Chronically bad greens . . . Punative course . . .
They're letting a great track go . . . I think they live on their past reputation
. . . Excellent rolling course through the woodlands . . . Demanding shot
placement . . . You can't reach No. 18 if the wind is in your face . . . Some
of the most challenging and breathtaking holes in the state.

TOMAC WOODS GOLF COURSE★

PU—14827 26½ Mile Rd., Albion (517)629-8241.
20 miles east of Battle Creek. **Holes:** 18. **Par:** 72/72.
Yards: 6,290/5,800. **Course rating:** 69.8/76.0. **Slope:** N/A.
Opened: 1964. **Pace of Play rating:** 4:00-4:30. **Green fee:** $10/12.
Credit cards: MC, V. **Reduced fees:** Weekdays, Low season, Twilight,
Seniors, Juniors.
Caddies: No. **Golf carts:** $8 for 18 holes.
Discount golf packages: No. **Season:** April-Oct. **High:** June-July.
On-site lodging: No. **Rental clubs:** Yes.
Walking policy: Unrestricted walking. **Range:** Yes (grass).
To obtain tee times: Call anytime.

TREETOPS SYLVAN RESORT

R—3962 Wilkinson Rd., Gaylord (517)732-6711, (800)444-6711.
50 miles northeast of Traverse City.
Credit cards: MC, V, AMEX. **Reduced fees:** Low season, Resort guests,
Twilight.
Caddies: No. **Golf carts:** Included in Green Fee.
Discount golf packages: Yes. **Season:** April-Oct. **High:** June-Sept.
On-site lodging: Yes. **Rental clubs:** No.
Walking policy: Mandatory cart. **Range:** Yes (grass).
To obtain tee times: Call.

★★★★ **ROBERT TRENT JONES MASTERPIECE COURSE**
Holes: 18. **Par:** 71/71.
Yards: 7,060/4,972. **Course rating:** 75.8/70.2. **Slope:** 146/124.
Opened: 1987. **Pace of Play rating:** 4:33. **Green fee:** $72.
Ranked 27th in America's 75 Best Resort Courses by Golf Digest. Ranked 17th in Michigan by Golf Digest.

Subscriber comments: Too severe. No landing areas or alternate way to hit greens . . . At Treetops, the first was worst . . . Play in the fall when the tree colors are great . . . Magnificent scenery, magnificent golf . . . Gracious hosts . . . Too hard for most golfers. Resort golf should be fun . . . Don't play from the back tees. Incredible par 3s . . . 18 beautiful holes . . . No. 16 is breathtaking . . . A must-play in October . . . Almost mountain golf . . . Worth it for the views of Pigeon River Valley . . . Playable if you use the right tees . . . A classic course . . . Every hole is memorable . . . Hole Nos. 2 through 5 too tough in the early going . . . Some holes punish good shots . . . Forget yardage markers on par 3s; go with your gut feeling . . . Easier than the Fazio course but a strong test . . . Great vistas . . . It will get your attention . . . Very demanding . . . You'll need all your shots . . . The Pinehurst of the north when it comes to service . . . Terrific views . . . Fantastic. This is where golf was meant to be played . . . No better view in Michigan than that on No. 6 . . . Couldn't walk it if you had a week . . . Try the par-3 course . . . The second-best course at the resort . . . A Trent Jones Sr. masterpiece: each hole is "easy to bogey, hard to par".

★★★★ **RICK SMITH SIGNATURE COURSE**
Holes: 18. **Par:** 70/70.
Yards: 6,653/4,604. **Course rating:** 72.7/66.8. **Slope:** 137/118.
Opened: 1993. **Pace of Play rating:** 4:33. **Green fee:** $68.
Ranked 23rd in Michigan by Golf Digest.
Subscriber comments: Great layout, generous landing areas . . . Outstanding views . . . I want to play it again! I was impressed . . . Huge greens . . . Many bunkers that frame the holes . . . More playable than the Fazio course . . . Big areas loaded with bunkers . . . Looks like a first attempt at design . . . Toughest greens I've ever putted. But I loved every minute . . . Still developing. Dramatic views . . . Every hole a challenge . . . Blink your eyes and you're on the Fazio course with $25 still in your pocket . . . First design effort, every bit as good as Fazio course . . . Beautiful course with all the elements . . . Best of the Treetops courses . . . A good imitation of the Fazio course . . . Spectacular, especially in autumn . . . We need more Smith courses . . . Ruthless greens . . . More open than the Jones or the Fazio. I'll remember hole No. 11, the "Sanctuary" . . . My top choice to play in Michigan . . . This is a great course . . . Great use of bunkers . . . Many holes and greens too difficult for the average player . . . Very limited landing areas off the tee . . . Most tee shots are downhill . . . Nearly every tee has a 25-mile view . . . You must also play the "Threetops" par-3 course . . . Best par-3 course, includes a 170-foot drop on the third hole called "Devils' Drop."

★★★★½ **TOM FAZIO PREMIER COURSE**
Holes: 18. **Par:** 72/72.
Yards: 6,832/5,039. **Course rating:** 73.2/70.1. **Slope:** 135/123.
Opened: 1992. **Pace of Play rating:** 4:33. **Green fee:** $80.
Ranked 5th in Michigan by Golf Digest.
Subscriber comments: An excellent resort course: interesting, difficult but playable . . . Outstanding . . . A Fazio gem. You don't feel like you have been beaten badly when you are done . . . Not as good as the RTJ . . . Dramatic . . . Thought this was the best in Gaylord until I played the Smith Course . . . Gorgeous course, imaginative holes, forgiving . . . One of Fazio's best . . . Beautiful par 3s . . . Wide fairways, tricky approach shots . . . Fairways are like carpet . . . Outstanding, one of the finest courses around. A place to visit again and again . . . Many memorable holes . . . A wonderful total golf experience . . . Golf's hottest designer scores big in Michigan . . . What a delight! . . . Architecture is very good . . . Easier than the other Treetops courses . . . What a view . . . Exceedingly difficult . . . One of the best if not the best in Michigan . . . Highlight of my summer golfing was a trip to Treetops . . . Beautiful, imaginative,

challenging . . . Two thumbs up . . . Stunning vistas . . . Unfairly tough uphill putts roll backward past the point of beginning. Can you believe the green on No. 7? . . . A joy to play and see . . . The best of all the northern Michigan courses.

★★★½ UNIVERSITY OF MICHIGAN GOLF COURSE

SP—500 E. Stadium Blvd., Ann Arbor (313)663-5005.
Holes: 18. **Par:** 71/75.
Yards: 6,687/5,331. **Course rating:** 72.5/71.0. **Slope:** 135/125.
Opened: 1931. **Pace of Play rating:** 4:30. **Green fee:** $40/50.
Credit cards: MC, V, AMEX. **Reduced fees:** N/A.
Caddies: No. **Golf carts:** $22 for 18 holes.
Discount golf packages: No. **Season:** April-Oct. **High:** May-Sept.
On-site lodging: No. **Rental clubs:** Yes.
Walking policy: Unrestricted walking. **Range:** Yes (grass).
Ranked 16th in Michigan by Golf Digest.
Subscriber comments: Arthur Hills did great job restoring to the original Mackenzie specs . . . Another Michigan treasure . . . Very tough to hold your game together for 18 holes here . . . Huge, immaculate greens . . . Always a great track . . . First-class . . . The best course in southeast Michigan . . . Wonderfully restored by Arthur Hills to all of its original

Alister Mackenzie splendor. A great value for University of Michigan students and employees . . . You must be a good putter . . . Bunkers frame the holes nicely. I loved the large trees that line the fairways . . . Great old fashioned track . . . It does not get any better than this . . . Condition was great, sand traps great . . . All putts break toward State Street.

★★★ VASSAR GOLF AND COUNTRY CLUB

SP—3509 Kirk Rd., Vassar (517)823-7221.
Call club for further information.
Subscriber comments: Very reasonable . . . Nicely located in Michigan's thumb. A down-home course . . . Beautiful course, well cared-for, constantly improving . . . Worth the trip to the boondocks, No. 10 a challenge . . . Don't let the looks fool you. Surprisingly fun.

★★★½ WALLINWOOD SPRINGS GOLF CLUB

SP—8152 Weatherwax, Jenison (616)457-9920.
15 miles west of Grand Rapids. **Holes:** 18. **Par:** 72/72.
Yards: 6,751/5,067. **Course rating:** 72.4/69.1. **Slope:** 128/115.
Opened: 1992. **Pace of Play rating:** N/A. **Green fee:** $24/27.
Credit cards: MC, V, DISC. **Reduced fees:** Weekdays.
Caddies: No. **Golf carts:** $11 for 18 holes.
Discount golf packages: Yes. **Season:** April-Nov. **High:** June-Aug.
On-site lodging: No. **Rental clubs:** Yes.
Walking policy: Walking at certain times. **Range:** No.
To obtain tee times: Call.
Subscriber comments: A sleeping giant with great variety, makes you think. Wet back nine . . . Excellent holes along Grand River . . . Two dramatically different nines. The back nine winds around the river . . . Great potential . . . Flood damage on three holes altered the course design . . . Back nine needs better drainage . . . Well-laid out . . . No. 11 is murder . . . Front nine plays short wih many moguls.

WARREN VALLEY GOLF COURSE

PU—26116 W. Warren, Dearborn Heights (313)561-1040.
10 miles west of Detroit.
Opened: 1927. **Pace of Play rating:** 4:30-5:00. **Green fee:** $15/19.
Credit cards: MC, V. **Reduced fees:** Weekdays, Low season, Twilight, Seniors, Juniors.
Caddies: Yes. **Golf carts:** $20 for 18 holes.
Discount golf packages: No. **Season:** March-Nov. **High:** May-Oct.
On-site lodging: No. **Rental clubs:** No.
Walking policy: Unrestricted walking. **Range:** No.
To obtain tee times: Call one week in advance.

★★ EAST COURSE

Holes: 18. **Par:** 72/72.
Yards: 6,189/5,328. **Course rating:** 69.1/70.0. **Slope:** 114/113.
Subscriber comments: Short, fun, pretty, affordable . . . Heavily played
. . . New clubhouse . . . A Donald Ross classic, being restored . . .
Wooded and tight, short but most par 4s take the driver away. Greens are
very small and fast . . . Good for outings . . . Very positive changes in the
past few years . . . Dramatic recent improvements . . . Had fallen on hard
times, but is now improving . . . Needs more traps.

★★ WEST COURSE

Holes: 18. **Par:** 71/71.
Yards: 6,066/5,150. **Course rating:** 68.5/69.2. **Slope:** 115/114.
Subscriber comments: Great old course, fun to play . . . Tricky on some
holes . . . Dramatic recent improvements to the Donald Ross design . . .
West is tougher than the East . . . Two decent courses a little too close
together.

WASHAKIE GOLF CLUB★

PU—3461 Burnside Rd., North Branch (810)688-3235.
30 miles northeast of Flint. **Holes:** 18. **Par:** 72/72.
Yards: 5,805/5,152. **Course rating:** N/A. **Slope:** N/A.
Opened: 1986. **Pace of Play rating:** 4:30. **Green fee:** $15/17.
Credit cards: None. **Reduced fees:** Seniors.
Caddies: No. **Golf carts:** $9 for 18 holes.
Discount golf packages: No. **Season:** April–Nov. **High:** May–Aug.
On-site lodging: Yes. **Rental clubs:** Yes.
Walking policy: Unrestricted walking. **Range:** No.
To obtain tee times: First come, first served.

WEST BRANCH COUNTRY CLUB★

SP—198 Fairview, West Branch (517)345-2501.
60 miles north of Saginaw. **Holes:** 18. **Par:** 72/73.
Yards: 6,402/5,436. **Course rating:** 70.5/71.4. **Slope:** 122/119.
Opened: 1930. **Pace of Play rating:** 4:00. **Green fee:** $22/28.
Credit cards: MC, V. **Reduced fees:** Low season, Twilight, Seniors.
Caddies: No. **Golf carts:** $12 for 18 holes.
Discount golf packages: Yes. **Season:** April–Oct. **High:** May–Sept..
On-site lodging: No. **Rental clubs:** Yes.
Walking policy: Unrestricted walking. **Range:** Yes (grass).
To obtain tee times: Call pro shop up to two weeks in advance.
Subscriber comments: Professionally run course is almost equal to
resorts, at a reasonable cost . . . Good greens, fun to play . . . Pace good
along with service . . . Usually in nice shape . . . Relaxing . . . A friendly
stop on your way to pricier courses . . . OK. Nothing spectacular.

★½ WEST OTTAWA COUNTRY CLUB

PU—6045 136th Ave., Holland (616)399-1678.
7 miles north of Holland. **Holes:** 18. **Par:** 70/67.
Yards: 6,250/5,700. **Course rating:** 68.5/66.0. **Slope:** N/A.
Opened: 1965. **Pace of Play rating:** 4:30. **Green fee:** $16/18.
Credit cards: MC, V. **Reduced fees:** Weekdays, Low season, Seniors,
Juniors.
Caddies: No. **Golf carts:** $19 for 18 holes.
Discount golf packages: No. **Season:** March–Nov. **High:** July–Aug.
On-site lodging: No. **Rental clubs:** Yes.
Walking policy: Unrestricted walking. **Range:** Yes (grass).
To obtain tee times: Call pro shop.
Also has additional 9 holes.
Subscriber comments: OK golf . . . Needs a facelift! Water the fairways
and add some bunkers . . . Very flat, not expensive . . . Good weekenders'
course . . . Unimaginative . . . Good-sized greens.

★½ WHIFFLE TREE HILL GOLF COURSE

PU—15700 Homer Rd., Concord (517)524-6655.
15 miles west of Jackson, Wy. **Holes:** 18. **Par:** 70/70.
Yards: 6,300/5,250. **Course rating:** N/A. **Slope:** N/A.
Opened: 1959. **Pace of Play rating:** 4:00. **Green fee:** $7/13.
Credit cards: MC, V. **Reduced fees:** Weekdays, Low season, Twilight,
Seniors, Junior
Caddies: No. **Golf carts:** $10 for 18 holes.
Discount golf packages: Yes. **Season:** April–Oct. **High:** May–Sept.
On-site lodging: No. **Rental clubs:** Yes.
Walking policy: Unrestricted walking. **Range:** Yes (grass).
To obtain tee times: Call pro shop.
Subscriber comments: Making good changes, being made better . . .
Nice course . . . Middle holes wide-open, little trouble . . . On the
upswing.

★★★ WHISPERING PINES GOLF CLUB

PU—2500 Whispering Pines Dr., Pinckney (313)878-0009.
Call club for further information.
Subscriber comments: Need to be a trick-shot artist with narrow greens,
90-degree shots . . . Holes past window-intensive homes . . . Northern flair
with a few too many blind shots . . . A shotmaker's course . . . You're
penalized at times for good tee shots . . . Nice course. Too bad they're
building homes on it . . . Far too tight and short, a couple par 4s must be
played with 6- or 7-irons off the tee . . . Southeastern Michigan course with
the flavor of upper Michigan . . . Beautiful terrain, a real test . . . Punishing
layout, scenic . . . Unfair fairways slope to roughs. I won't play there again
until they use chainsaws as a remedy . . . These pines don't whisper. Golf
balls make a lot of noise . . . Needs more grooming . . . Unique, eccentric
layout.

★★ WHISPERING WILLOWS GOLF COURSE

PU-20500 Newburg Rd., Livonia (313)476-4493.
Call club for further information.
Subscriber comments: Easy muny, fun to play . . . Greens in poor shape
. . . Accommodating to women walk-ons . . . Livonia's best course, but
needs better range . . . Watch for goose droppings in the fall . . . Slow play
much of the time.

★★ WHITE DEER COUNTRY CLUB

PU—1309 Bright Angel Dr., Prudenville (517)366-5812.
70 miles north of Saginaw. **Holes:** 18. **Par:** 72/72.
Yards: 6,311/5,290. **Course rating:** 68.8/69.9. **Slope:** 115/116.
Opened: 1965. **Pace of Play rating:** 3:35. **Green fee:** $16.
Credit cards: None. **Reduced fees:** Low season, Twilight.
Caddies: No. **Golf carts:** $8 for 18 holes.
Discount golf packages: Yes. **Season:** April–Oct. **High:** July–Aug.
On-site lodging: No. **Rental clubs:** Yes.
Walking policy: Unrestricted walking. **Range:** No.
To obtain tee times: Call pro shop.
Subscriber comments: A duffer's course . . . Typical public course, needs
a capital infusion . . . Some good greens . . . Needs constant watering . . .
Green fees are right . . . They have deer statues as 150 yard markers . . .
Very hospitable.

WHITE PINE NATIONAL GOLF CLUB★

PU—3450 N. Hubbard Lake Rd., Spruce (517)736-3279.
30 miles north of Alpena. **Holes:** 18. **Par:** 72/72.
Yards: 6,987/5,337. **Course rating:** N/A. **Slope:** N/A.
Opened: 1994. **Pace of Play rating:** 4:30. **Green fee:** $35/40.
Credit cards: MC, V. **Reduced fees:** Weekdays, Twilight, Juniors.
Caddies: No. **Golf carts:** Included in Green Fee.
Discount golf packages: Yes. **Season:** May–Nov. **High:** May–Sept.

On-site lodging: No. **Rental clubs:** Yes.
Walking policy: Walking at certain times. **Range:** Yes (grass).
To obtain tee times: Call pro shop.

WILDERNESS VALLEY GOLF CLUB

R—7519 Mancelona Rd., Gaylord (616)585-7090.
15 miles southwest of Gaylord.
Credit cards: All major. **Reduced fees:** Weekdays, Low season, Resort guests, Twilight, Seniors, Juniors. **Caddies:** No.
Discount golf packages: Yes. **Season:** April–Oct. **High:** July–Aug.
On-site lodging: Yes. **Rental clubs:** Yes.
Walking policy: Unrestricted walking. **Range:** Yes (grass).
To obtain tee times: Call pro shop.

★★★½ BLACK FOREST COURSE

Holes: 18. **Par:** 73/74.
Yards: 7,044/5,282. **Course rating:** 75.3/71.8. **Slope:** 145/131.
Opened: 1992. **Pace of Play rating:** 4:01. **Green fee:** $20/38.
Golf carts: $20 for 18 holes.
Ranked 21st in Michigan by Golf Digest
Subscriber comments: Tremendous layout. Straight-up golf, no tricks, small greens . . . In great shape in the fall . . . Dirty clubhouse . . . Remote facilities . . . Second-hardest course in state . . . An average course amidst the giants of the Gaylord area . . . Neat Tom Doak design . . . A shotmaker's course, no bail-out room around the greens . . . Hard to find, but worth it . . . Best combination of Gaylord resort courses . . . Yes, the forest there is black . . . Very strange greens, highly contoured . . . Appeared to have an irrigation system, but no evidence it was ever used . . . Marvelous use of elevation changes . . . Some silly holes . . . For a supposed gem, it is a fake . . . Best-kept secret of the north; never a wait on a tee box . . . Hard, long, fun . . . Some great holes . . . Black flies are a pest. Bring repellent . . . Bunkering is unparalleled. Doak's course is a classic . . . Course could be longer . . . Some greens a little too hilly . . . Takes advantage of its setting . . . You need hiking boots, not golf shoes . . . Greens are terrible, take the fun out of golf . . . This course is cool . . . Beauty and the Beast, a beautiful-but-brutal course . . . Needs its own clubhouse . . . Best wooded course, toughest greens around . . . Great sand, great scenery . . . Beautiful bunkering . . . Toughest three closing holes anywhere.

★★★ VALLEY COURSE

Holes: 18. **Par:** 71/71.
Yards: 6,485/4,889. **Course rating:** 70.6/67.8. **Slope:** 126/115.
Opened: 1971. **Pace of Play rating:** 3:47. **Green fee:** $15/23.
Golf carts: $15 for 18 holes.
Subscriber comments: Many different challenges due to terrain and layout . . . Short, open course, a poor sister to Black Forest . . . Mature, scenic, average . . . Too many short doglegs . . . A medium-length course . . . You can walk it easily . . . Beautiful surroundings, but not too much course . . . A good warm-up course . . . Short, fun, reasonable. Played it after the Black Forest, was like a nice warm-down . . . Much easier than the Black Forest . . . They want it to be a fun day.

WINDING CREEK GOLF COURSE★

PU—4514 Ottogan St., Holland (616)396-4516.
20 miles southwest of Grand Rapids. **Holes:** 18. **Par:** 72/72.
Yards: 6,665/5,027. **Course rating:** 71.9/69.0. **Slope:** 122/114.
Opened: 1968. **Pace of Play rating:** 4:30. **Green fee:** $18/19.
Credit cards: MC, V. **Reduced fees:** Weekdays, Low season, Twilight, Seniors, Juniors.
Caddies: No. **Golf carts:** $9 for 18 holes.
Discount golf packages: No. **Season:** April–Oct. **High:** May–Aug.
On-site lodging: No. **Rental clubs:** Yes.
Walking policy: Unrestricted walking. **Range:** Yes (grass).
To obtain tee times: Call or come in two days in advance.

WOLVERINE GOLF CLUB
★★ **RED/GOLD/BLUE/GREEN/WHITE**
PU—17201 25 Mile Rd., Mt. Clemens (313)781-5544.
Call club for further information.
Subscriber comments: Play is sometimes slow . . . Hook yourself up to this conveyor belt . . . Nice parking, nice facilities, courses not too tough but still challenging. Everything is packaged for convenience . . . User-friendly, moves well . . . Typical north Macomb County course: long, flat, and wide . . . No big deal . . . Like the Gold Course best . . . Features five nines.

WOODLAND HILLS GOLF CLUB★
PU—320 N. Gates Rd., Sandusky (810)648-2400, (800)648-2400.
65 miles west of Saginaw. **Holes:** 18. **Par:** 71/71.
Yards: 6,606/5,441. **Course rating:** 70.7/71.0. **Slope:** 121/117.
Opened: 1980. **Pace of Play rating:** 4:15. **Green fee:** $13/17.
Credit cards: MC, V. **Reduced fees:** Twilight, Seniors.
Caddies: No. **Golf carts:** $9 for 18 holes.
Discount golf packages: Yes. **Season:** April-Oct. **High:** May-Aug.
On-site lodging: No. **Rental clubs:** Yes.
Walking policy: Walking at certain times. **Range:** Yes (grass).
To obtain tee times: Call pro shop.

Notes

MINNESOTA

★ AFTON ALPS GOLF COURSE
PU—6600 Teller Ave. S., Hastings (612)436-1320.
Call club for further information.
Subscriber comments: Front nine is fairly flat . . . Back nine built on ski slopes . . . Great scenery . . . The course was in fair to good condition . . . Greens need work . . . Bring oxygen for back nine . . . Have to be mountain goat for back nine.

ALBANY GOLF COURSE★
PU—500 Church Ave., Albany (612)845-2505.
Call club for further information.
Subscriber comments: Very little trees . . . Good course for fall play . . . Very open course . . . . Good beginner's course . . . A real find in an unlikely location . . . Just plain golf.

★★★ ALBION RIDGES GOLF COURSE
PU—Wright County Rd. 105, Annadale (612)963-5500.
Call club for further information.
Subscriber comments: Open . . . Long and tough in wind . . . Good practice facilities . . . I played 42 courses in 1994, this was the best . . . Relatively new . . . Needs growth . . . Good layout . . . Interesting . . . Long and flat . . . Fine greens . . . Needs maturing.

★★★½ ALEXANDRIA GOLF CLUB
SP—Country Rd. No. 42, Alexandria (612)763-3605.
Call club for further information.
Subscriber comments: Home course of Tom Lehman . . . Just a nice place to play . . . Some greens shaped like states . . . Nice clubhouse . . . Great membership . . . Best outside of St. Paul . . . Kept in great shape . . . Staff is accommodating.

★★★½ BAKER NATIONAL GOLF COURSE
PU—2935 Parkview Dr., Medina (612)473-0800.
20 miles west of Minneapolis. **Holes:** 18. **Par:** 72/74.
Yards: 6,762/5,395. **Course rating:** 74.2/72.7. **Slope:** 133/129.
Opened: 1990. **Pace of Play rating:** 4:20. **Green fee:** $22.
Credit cards: MC, V, DISC. **Reduced fees:** Seniors, Juniors.
Caddies: No. **Golf carts:** $20 for 18 holes.
Discount golf packages: No. **Season:** April-Oct. **High:** June-Aug.
On-site lodging: No. **Rental clubs:** Yes.
Walking policy: Unrestricted walking. **Range:** Yes (grass).
To obtain tee times: Call three days in advance.
Subscriber comments: Tight fairways . . . Need good course management to score well . . . Hell of a test from the tips . . . U.S. Open rough around greens . . . . Beautiful . . . As good a public as I've seen . . . For a county park it's great . . . Always busy . . . Fast . . . Very tight . . . In the fairway or you can drop another . . . Many long par 4s . . . Challenging due to its length . . . One of the best in Twin Cities area . . . Practice area includes bunker . . . All holes are different . . . Maybe the best practice range in state . . . Great staff . . . Most holes hilly.

★★★ BALMORAL GOLF COURSE
PU—Rte. 3 Box 119, Battle Lake (218)864-5414.
Call club for further information.
Subscriber comments: Woods on every hole . . . Accuracy counts, distance no problem . . . Woodsy . . . Very scenic . . . Well groomed . . . Not overly tough . . . Tight fairways . . . Entertaining layout.

★★½ BELLWOOD OAKS GOLF COURSE
PU—13239 210th St., Hastings (612)437-4141.
25 miles south of St. Paul. **Holes:** 18. **Par:** 73/74.
Yards: 6,775/5,707. **Course rating:** 71.3/71.2. **Slope:** 115/115.
Opened: 1972. **Pace of Play rating:** 4:30. **Green fee:** $15/17.
Credit cards: None. **Reduced fees:** Seniors.

Caddies: No. **Golf carts:** $10 for 18 holes.
Discount golf packages: Yes. **Season:** April–Nov. **High:** May–Sept.
On-site lodging: No. **Rental clubs:** Yes.
Walking policy: Unrestricted walking. **Range:** Yes (grass).
To obtain tee times: Call five days in advance.
Subscriber comments: Well maintained and laid out . . . Great for all abilities . . . Friendly stafff . . . Challenging for the beginner . . . Makes medium handicappers feel good . . . Open but maturing . . . Easy to get on in short notice . . . Well taken care of . . . Challenging . . . Very enjoyable . . . Little trouble . . . Nice honest golf course . . . Not real difficult but many interesting holes.

★★★½ BEMIDJI TOWN AND COUNTRY CLUB
R—Birchmont Dr. N.E., Bemidji (218)751-9215.
220 miles north of Minneapolis/St. Paul. **Holes:** 18. **Par:** 72/72.
Yards: 6,535/5,058. **Course rating:** 71.8/69.1. **Slope:** 127/120.
Opened: 1920. **Pace of Play rating:** 4:00–4:30. **Green fee:** $16/26.
Credit cards: MC, V. **Reduced fees:** Low season, Resort guests, Twilight.
Caddies: No. **Golf carts:** $10 for 18 holes.
Discount golf packages: No. **Season:** April–Oct. **High:** June–Aug.
On-site lodging: No. **Rental clubs:** Yes.
Walking policy: Unrestricted walking. **Range:** Yes (grass).
To obtain tee times: Call one week in advance.
Subscriber comments: Long narrow fairways encased in trees . . . Great service . . . Beautifully hilly . . . Long but fair . . . Well kept . . . Easy to get on . . . Redesigned holes are well done . . . A joy to play . . . Hit it straight . . . Beautiful setting . . . Course is full of variations due to terrain and trees.

★½ BLUFF CREEK GOLF COURSE
PU—1025 Creekwood, Chaska (612)445-5685.
3 miles south of Minneapolis. **Holes:** 18. **Par:** 70/76.
Yards: 6,359/5,093. **Course rating:** 69.9/68.3. **Slope:** 115/109.
Opened: 1972. **Pace of Play rating:** 4:15. **Green fee:** $13/22.
Credit cards: None. **Reduced fees:** Weekdays, Low season, Twilight, Seniors, Juniors.
Caddies: No. **Golf carts:** $22 for 18 holes.
Discount golf packages: No. **Season:** April–Nov. **High:** June–Aug.
On-site lodging: No. **Rental clubs:** Yes.
Walking policy: Unrestricted walking. **Range:** Yes (grass).
To obtain tee times: For weekdays call seven days in advance. For Weekends and holidays call up to three days in advance.
Subscriber comments: Course has improved maintenance but is only acceptable . . . Target golf . . . Tight . . . Long with recent additions of trees . . . Very nice . . . Hilly . . . Can be walked . . . Short, tight course . . . Mature . . . Small greens . . . Very hilly with some blind shots . . . Suitable for average to above average players.

★★★ BRAEMAR GOLF COURSE
RED/WHITE/BLUE
PU—6364 John Harris Dr., Edina (612)941-2072.
81 miles northeast of Minneapolis. **Holes:** 27. **Par:** 71/71/72.
Yards: 6,739/6,377/6,692. **Course rating:** 71.8/71.6/73.0.
Slope: 124/129/134.
Opened: 1964. **Pace of Play rating:** 3:59. **Green fee:** $20.
Credit cards: None. **Reduced fees:** Low season, Juniors.
Caddies: Yes. **Golf carts:** $20 for 18 holes.
Discount golf packages: No. **Season:** April–Oct. **High:** May–Sept.
On-site lodging: No. **Rental clubs:** Yes.
Walking policy: Unrestricted walking. **Range:** Yes (grass).
To obtain tee times: First come, first served.
Subscriber comments: New nine is really fun . . . Greens are difficult . . . A well-manicured public track . . . Great greens . . . . Very busy . . .

Excellent for a five- to 19-handicapper . . . Staff was accommodating . . . Hard to get tee times unless residents of Edina . . . My home course for years . . . Continually improving the course . . . Well maintained . . . Residents have playing and cost privileges . . . Course is good test for golfers and is fair.

BREEZY POINT RESORT
R—HCR 2 Box 70 County Rd. 11, Breezy Point (218)562-7177, (800)950-4960.

20 miles north of Brainerd.
Credit cards: All major. **Reduced fees:** Weekdays, Low season, Twilight.
Caddies: No. **Golf carts:** $24 for 18 holes.
Discount golf packages: Yes. **Season:** April-Oct. **High:** June-Sept.
On-site lodging: Yes. **Rental clubs:** Yes.
Walking policy: Unrestricted walking. **Range:** Yes (grass).
To obtain tee times: Call 48 hours in advance on 800 number.

★★½ CHAMPIONSHIP COURSE
Holes: 18. **Par:** 72/76.
Yards: 6,601/5,718. **Course rating:** 71.8/75.4. **Slope:** 124/128.
Opened: 1981. **Pace of Play rating:** N/A. **Green fee:** $28/32. **Subscriber comments:** Some holes very easy . . . Some impossible . . . Beautiful layout . . . Nice fairways . . . Lined with trees . . . Staff friendly and helpful . . . Well worth the drive . . . . Fabulous trees and fairways . . . Beautiful scenery . . . Holes 15 through 17 are the best three consecutive holes.

★★ TRADITIONAL COURSE
(218)562-7166, (800)950-4961.
Holes: 18. **Par:** 68/N/A.
Yards: 5,192/N/A. **Course rating:** 62.9/N/A. **Slope:** 114/111.
Opened: 1930. **Pace of Play rating:** N/A. **Green fee:** $25/28.
Subscriber comments: Short holes . . . Goes back to '20s . . . Short but narrow . . . Leave driver home . . . Sharp doglegs . . . Carved out of a forest . . . Bring plenty of balls . . . Short . . . Good condition . . . Great for ladies, old men, beginners . . . Resort course for medium handicap players.

★★★ BROOKTREE MUNICIPAL GOLF COURSE
PU—1369 Cherry St., Owatonna (507)451-0730.
40 miles south of Minneapolis/St. Paul. **Holes:** 18. **Par:** 71/72.
Yards: 6,648/5,534. **Course rating:** 71.9/71.3. **Slope:** 121/121.
Opened: 1957. **Pace of Play rating:** 4:00. **Green fee:** $14/16.
Credit cards: None. **Reduced fees:** Weekdays.
Caddies: No. **Golf carts:** $17 for 18 holes.
Discount golf packages: No. **Season:** April-Oct. **High:** June-Aug.
On-site lodging: No. **Rental clubs:** Yes.
Walking policy: Unrestricted walking. **Range:** No.
To obtain tee times: Call three days in advance.
Subscriber comments: Upper nine long, open newer . . . Lower nine nice . . . Older trees . . . Very reasonable cost for course with lots of variety . . . Great condition . . . Courteous and helpful staff.

★★ BROOKVIEW GOLF COURSE
PU—200 Brookview Pkwy., Golden Valley (612)544-8446.
5 miles west of Minneapolis. **Holes:** 18. **Par:** 72/72.
Yards: 6,369/5,436. **Course rating:** 70.2/71.2. **Slope:** 122/121.
Opened: N/A. **Pace of Play rating:** 4:20. **Green fee:** $20.
Credit cards: MC, V. **Reduced fees:** Twilight, Seniors, Juniors.
Caddies: No. **Golf carts:** $20 for 18 holes.
Discount golf packages: No. **Season:** April-Oct. **High:** June-Sept.
On-site lodging: No. **Rental clubs:** Yes.
Walking policy: Unrestricted walking. **Range:** Yes (grass).
To obtain tee times: Call two days in advance. Patron card holders may call from three to seven days in advance.
Also has a 9-hole par-3 course.

Subscriber comments: Short course . . . Beautiful setting with grand oaks
. . . Mature parkland course . . . A little boring . . . Tighter than it looks
. . . Brookview was formerly a private club . . . Mature trees . . . Lots of
water . . . Long par 5s . . . Geese! . . . Nice course . . . Play early or bring a
chair . . . Get ready for six hours rounds.

★★★★ BUNKER HILLS GOLF COURSE
NORTH/EAST/WEST

PU—Highway 242 and Foley Blvd., Coon Rapids (612)755-4141.
15 miles south of Minneapolis. **Holes:** 27. **Par:** 72/72/72.
Yards: 6,799/6,938/6,901. **Course rating:** 72.7/73.1/73.4.
Slope: 130/135/133.
Opened: 1968. **Pace of Play rating:** 4:20. **Green fee:** $22/24.
Credit cards: None. **Reduced fees:** Seniors, Juniors.
Caddies: No. **Golf carts:** $24 for 18 holes.
Discount golf packages: No. **Season:** April-Nov. **High:** June-Aug.
On-site lodging: No. **Rental clubs:** Yes.
Walking policy: Unrestricted walking. **Range:** Yes (grass).
To obtain tee times: Call three days in advance after 2 p.m.
Also has a 9-hole executive course.
Subscriber comments: Good test of golf, you use every club . . . Long
and hard enough but won't kill high handicapper . . . North nine always
challenging . . . Tight fairways lined with tall pines on either side. Staff,
service, pace excellent . . . This course is a must . . . They don't get any
better than this . . . Worth playing all 27 holes . . . Excellent course . . .
Excellent staff . . . Hosts Senior PGA Tour's Burnet Senior Classic . . .
Was late for tee time and they still squeezed us in . . . Course plays long . . .
Subtle tricky greens . . . Outstanding! . . . Great shape with many rounds
played . . . Great course . . . Big greens, excellent test.

★★★ CANNON GOLF CLUB

SP—8606 295th St. E., Cannon Falls (507)263-3126.
25 miles south of Minneapolis. **Holes:** 18. **Par:** 71/71.
Yards: 6,200/5,011. **Course rating:** 67.4/68.9. **Slope:** 121/121.
Opened: N/A. **Pace of Play rating:** 4:00-4:30. **Green fee:** $18/22.
Credit cards: MC, V. **Reduced fees:** Weekdays, Seniors.
Caddies: No. **Golf carts:** $20 for 18 holes.
Discount golf packages: No. **Season:** April-Oct. **High:** April-Oct.
On-site lodging: No. **Rental clubs:** Yes.
Walking policy: Unrestricted walking. **Range:** Yes (grass).
To obtain tee times: Call pro shop.
Subscriber comments: Hidden value . . . Well manicured . . . Very short
. . . Back nine real tough . . . Pleasant staff . . . Cannon River makes for
interesting shot placement . . . Gorgeous views . . . Best greens . . . Lots of
water . . . Target golf . . . River makes it difficult . . . Nicely laid out . . .
Scenic course . . . Kept in good shape.

★★★ CEDAR RIVER COUNTRY CLUB

PU—Hwy. 56 W., Adams (507)582-3595.
16 miles northwest of Austin. **Holes:** 18. **Par:** 72/74.
Yards: 6,211/5,517. **Course rating:** 70.3/72.0. **Slope:** 124/124.
Opened: 1969. **Pace of Play rating:** 4:00. **Green fee:** $16.
Credit cards: None. **Reduced fees:** Low season.
Caddies: No. **Golf carts:** $18 for 18 holes.
Discount golf packages: Yes. **Season:** March-Nov. **High:** June-Aug.
On-site lodging: No. **Rental clubs:** Yes.
Walking policy: Unrestricaed walking. **Range:** Yes (grass).
To obtain tee times: Call pro shop.
Subscriber comments: Always fun for any type of player . . . Good shape
. . . Mix of new and old trees . . . Nice greens . . . Treated good . . .
Excellent condition all year . . . Surprisingly good for a rural course.

★★½ CHICAGO LAKES GOLF COURSE

PU—292nd St., Lindstrom (612)257-1484.
Call club for further information.
Subscriber comments: New back nine fun and challenging . . . Great bar
. . . Well-balanced course with good greens . . . Lots of water . . . Well-
maintained course . . . Pleasant staff . . . Challenging course from back
tees.

★½ CHOMONIX GOLF COURSE

PU—646 Sandpiper Dr., Lino Lakes (612)482-8484.
12 miles north of Minneapolis. **Holes:** 18. **Par:** 72/72.
Yards: 6,579/5,918. **Course rating:** 71.3/73.1. **Slope:** 120/121.
Opened: 1970. **Pace of Play rating:** N/A. **Green fee:** $14/16.
Credit cards: None. **Reduced fees:** Weekdays, Seniors, Juniors.
Caddies: No. **Golf carts:** $9 for 18 holes.
Discount golf packages: No. **Season:** April-Nov. **High:** June-Aug.
On-site lodging: No. **Rental clubs:** Yes.
Walking policy: Unrestricted walking. **Range:** Yes (grass).
To obtain tee times: Call four days in advance starting at 2 p.m.
Subscriber comments: Good family course . . . A little wet . . . A metro
course through woods and wetlands . . . Good for average golfer . . .
Pleasant . . . Can be questionable in rainy periods . . . Bring a lot of balls
. . . Many swamps, O.B.s and creeks . . . Must be straight . . . Nice staff.

★★ COLUMBIA GOLF COURSE

PU—3300 Central Ave., Minneapolis (612)789-2627.
Holes: 18. **Par:** 71/71.
Yards: 6,385/5,489. **Course rating:** 70.0/71.9. **Slope:** 121/123.
Opened: 1920. **Pace of Play rating:** 4:00. **Green fee:** $18.
Credit cards: MC, V. **Reduced fees:** Twilight, Seniors, Juniors.
Caddies: No. **Golf carts:** $20 for 18 holes.
Discount golf packages: No. **Season:** April-Nov. **High:** May-Aug.
On-site lodging: No. **Rental clubs:** Yes.
Walking policy: Unrestricted walking. **Range:** Yes (grass).
To obtain tee times: For weekends only. Come in person Tuesday 6 a.m.
or call Wednesday for $2 fee.
Subscriber comments: Nice course in downtown . . . Tough municipal
. . . Remodeling and drainage fixes makes it more playable . . . Very hilly
. . . Shorter than normal but fun . . . Good city course . . . All levels of
play . . . OK condition but heavily played . . . Hilly front nine . . . Some
long walks from green to tee . . . True roll on greens.

★½ COMO GOLF COURSE

PU—1431 N. Lexington Pkwy., St. Paul (612)488-9673.
Holes: 18. **Par:** 70/70.
Yards: 5,821/5,077. **Course rating:** 70.4/68.6. **Slope:** 125/121.
Opened: N/A. **Pace of Play rating:** 4:15. **Green fee:** $17.
Credit cards: MC, V. **Reduced fees:** Low season, Twilight, Seniors,
Juniors.
Caddies: No. **Golf carts:** $10 for 18 holes.
Discount golf packages: No. **Season:** April-Oct. **High:** June-Aug.
On-site lodging: No. **Rental clubs:** Yes.
Walking policy: Unrestricted walking. **Range:** No.
To obtain tee times: Call one day in advance for weekdays. For weekends
you must sign up in person the Thursday before. For holidays call the
Thursday before at 7 a.m.
Subscriber comments: Jammed together . . . Short but not too easy . . .
Water on closing holes offers bird watching for those who won't birdie . . .
Very tight, bring your hard hat . . . Holes 15 through 18 excellent and play
on them can be viewed from clubhouse . . . Lots of parallel fairways.

★★★½ CUYUNA COUNTRY CLUB

SP—P.O. Box 40, Deerwood (218)534-3489.
90 miles north of Minneapolis. **Holes:** 18. **Par:** 71/71.
Yards: 6,273/5,627. **Course rating:** 71.3/73.6. **Slope:** 129/135.
Opened: 1923. **Pace of Play rating:** N/A. **Green fee:** $24/26.
Credit cards: MC, V. **Reduced fees:** Weekdays, Low season, Resort guests, Twilight.
Caddies: Yes. **Golf carts:** $22 for 18 holes.
Discount golf packages: Yes. **Season:** April-Oct. **High:** July-Aug.
On-site lodging: No. **Rental clubs:** Yes.
Walking policy: Unrestricted walking. **Range:** Yes (grass).
To obtain tee times: Call or come in three days in advance.
Subscriber comments: Newer nine is very tight . . . Front nine is for average player . . . Back nine requires skill . . . Many hills . . . Lots of trees on the back . . . Challenges your accuracy . . . Staff eager to please . . . Very fun course . . . Some hills . . . Tight fairways cut through forest . . . Old established course with many more improvements.

★★½ DAHLGREEN GOLF CLUB

PU—6940 Dahlgreen Rd., Chaska (612)448-7463.
20 miles southwest of Minneapolis. **Holes:** 18. **Par:** 72/72.
Yards: 6,887/5,850. **Course rating:** 72.5/72.1. **Slope:** 124/120.
Opened: 1971. **Pace of Play rating:** N/A. **Green fee:** $24/24.
Credit cards: None. **Reduced fees:** Weekdays, Low season, Seniors, Juniors.
Caddies: No. **Golf carts:** $22 for 18 holes.
Discount golf packages: Yes. **Season:** March-Nov. **High:** June-Aug.
On-site lodging: No. **Rental clubs:** Yes.
Walking policy: Unrestrictd walking. **Range:** Yes (grass).
To obtain tee times: Call three days in advance.
Subscriber comments: Straight and long . . . Par 5s can cost you . . . Almost always windy . . . Water, hills, trees . . . A good all-around test of golf . . . Rural course in good shape . . . Wonderful country golf . . . Mature trees . . . Great greens . . . Staff good . . . Back and forth . . . Up and down.

★½ DAYTONA COUNTRY CLUB

PU—14740 Lawndale Lane, Dayton (612)427-6110.
20 miles northwest of Minneapolis. **Holes:** 18. **Par:** 72/73.
Yards: 6,363/5,468. **Course rating:** 69.7/70.7. **Slope:** 118/112.
Opened: 1964. **Pace of Play rating:** 4:00-5:00. **Green fee:** $16/19.
Credit cards: None. **Reduced fees:** Weekdays, Low season, Twilight, Seniors, Juniors.
Caddies: No. **Golf carts:** $21 for 18 holes.
Discount golf packages: No. **Season:** Year-round. **High:** April-Nov.
On-site lodging: No. **Rental clubs:** Yes.
Walking policy: Unrestricted walking. **Range:** Yes (grass).
To obtain tee times: Call or come in up to seven days in advance.
Subscriber comments: Long and open . . . Great for power . . . Stays open until first snow . . . Usually get a tee time even on holidays . . . Greens are elevated above fairways . . . Wide open . . . Little trouble . . . Public course of good quality . . . Staff is great.

★★ DEER RUN GOLF CLUB

PU—8661 Deer Run Dr., Victoria (612)443-2351.
20 miles southwest of Minneapolis. **Holes:** 18. **Par:** 71/71.
Yards: 6,265/5,541. **Course rating:** 70.5/72.1. **Slope:** 122/121.
Opened: 1989. **Pace of Play rating:** 4:00. **Green fee:** $21/25.
Credit cards: MC, V. **Reduced fees:** Twilight, Seniors, Juniors.
Caddies: No. **Golf carts:** $21/25 for 18 holes.
Discount golf packages: No. **Season:** March-Nov. **High:** June-Aug.
On-site lodging: No. **Rental clubs:** No.
Walking policy: Unrestricted walking. **Range:** Yes (grass).
To obtain tee times: Call three days in advance.

Subscriber comments: Tight front nine . . . Front nine more difficult than back nine . . . Relatively new course . . . Hilly and long but good challenge . . . Needs a few years to mature . . . As long as they continue to improve the course layout, someday it will be fine . . . Housing development course . . . Well kept . . . Challenging . . . OK, that's enough houses.

★★★ DETROIT COUNTRY CLUB
R—Rte. 5, Detroit Lakes (218)847-5790.
47 miles east of Fargo, ND. **Holes:** 18. **Par:** 71/72.
Yards: 5,941/5,508. **Course rating:** 69.5/71.8. **Slope:** 124/127.
Opened: 1917. **Pace of Play rating:** 4:00. **Green fee:** $22.
Credit cards: MC, V. **Reduced fees:** N/A.
Caddies: Yes. **Golf carts:** $20 for 18 holes.
Discount golf packages: No. **Season:** May-Oct. **High:** June-Aug.
On-site lodging: No. **Rental clubs:** Yes.
Walking policy: Unrestricted walking. **Range:** Yes (grass).
To obtain tee times: Call one week in advance.
Also has 18-hole executive Lakeview Course.
Subscriber comments: Very nice fairways . . . New greens and tees should help . . . Superb old course . . . Great layout . . . Wonderfully kept . . . . Hilly short course . . . Hard for a short course . . . Small greens fast . . . Staff excellent . . . Nice course . . . Tough during tournament . . . Nice little course you never get tired of playing.

★★½ EASTWOOD GOLF CLUB
PU—3505 Eastwood Rd. S.E., Rochester (507)281-6173.
Holes: 18. **Par:** 70/70.
Yards: 6,178/5,289. **Course rating:** 69.9/71.0. **Slope:** 120/121.
Opened: 1968. **Pace of Play rating:** N/A. **Green fee:** $17.
Credit cards: ,V. **Reduced fees:** N/A.
Caddies: No. **Golf carts:** $16 for 18 holes.
Discount golf packages: No. **Season:** April-Nov. **High:** May-Aug.
On-site lodging: No. **Rental clubs:** Yes.
Walking policy: Unrestricted walking. **Range:** Yes (grass).
To obtain tee times: Call two days in advance.
Subscriber comments: Small, fast greens . . . Nice course . . . Course conditioning is not consistent . . . Pro and staff outstanding especially with tournaments . . . Easy to get on . . . Long par 3s.

★★★★ EDINBURGH USA GOLF CLUB
PU—8700 Edinbrook Crossing, Brooklyn Park (612)424-7060.
12 miles north of Minneapolis. **Holes:** 18. **Par:** 72/72.
Yards: 6,701/5,255. **Course rating:** 73.0/71.4. **Slope:** 133/128.
Opened: 1987. **Pace of Play rating:** 4:20. **Green fee:** $31/31.
Credit cards: MC, V, AMEX. **Reduced fees:** Twilight, Seniors, Juniors.
Caddies: Yes. **Golf carts:** $24 for 18 holes.
Discount golf packages: No. **Season:** April-Oct. **High:** June-Aug.
On-site lodging: No. **Rental clubs:** Yes.
Walking policy: Unrestricted walking. **Range:** Yes (grass).
To obtain tee times: Call four days in advance of play at 2 p.m.
Ranked in Second 25 of America's 75 Best Public Golf Courses by Golf Digest. Ranked 14th in Minnesota by Golf Digest.
Subscriber comments: Country club-like atmosphere . . . Very difficult for 10 handicap and up . . . Play here . . . Sand/water placement is key . . . Best public course I've played . . . Sand and water everywhere . . . Almost too tough for high handicapper . . . Rough is murder . . . Target golf but fair layout . . . Excellent greens . . . If this course was in Illinois, Kemper Lakes might be out of business . . . Carts should be allowed off paths . . . Premium quality layout . . . Course is tight . . . Bring your straight driver

. . . Treated very well by staff . . . Fun . . . Need to hit good irons . . . Bring your whole bag and plenty of balls . . . Home of LPGA event . . . Top notch municipal . . . Twilight special is superb . . . The Sahara of Minnesota . . . Sugar sand is tough . . . Top course . . . Treatment by staff was excellent . . . Lady pros play here.

★★★ ELK RIVER COUNTRY CLUB

SP—20015 Elk Lake Rd., Elk River (612)441-4111.
Call club for further information.
Subscriber comments: Good for all abilities . . . Reasonable, tight and fun . . . Tough, small, elevated greens . . . Many dogleg fairways . . . Excellent variety of challenges . . . Hilly with some blind holes . . . A very nice course . . . Great greens . . . Not overly long yet enjoyable for all levels of players.

★★ ENGER PARK GOLF CLUB

PU—1801 W. Skyline Blvd., Duluth (218)723-3451.
Holes: 27. **Par:** 72/72/72.
Yards: 6,434/6,325/6,499. **Course rating:** 70.9/70.3/71.0.
Slope: 124/121/121.
Opened: 1927. **Pace of Play rating:** 4:30. **Green fee:** $18.
Credit cards: None. **Reduced fees:** Low season, Twilight, Seniors, Juniors.
Caddies: No. **Golf carts:** $18 for 18 holes.
Discount golf packages: No. **Season:** April-Nov. **High:** June-Aug.
On-site lodging: No. **Rental clubs:** Yes.
Walking policy: Unrestricted walking. **Range:** Yes (grass).
To obtain tee times: Call 72 hours in advance.
Also has 9-hole par-36 Back course.
Subscriber comments: Beautiful layout with panoramic views of Lake Superior . . . Good layout with water on several holes . . . New work has vastly improved layout . . . Front all hills . . . Be in good shape . . . Lots of hills . . . Lots of interesting holes . . . A course with character that's still healing from the scars of redesign.

FALCON RIDGE GOLF COURSE★

PU—33942 Falcon Ave., Stacy (612)462-5797.
Call club for further information.
Subscriber comments: Great place for beginners . . . Has string of wonderful holes on back nine . . . Wish it were closer . . . New course . . . Will improve in time.

★½ FOUNTAIN VALLEY GOLF CLUB

PU—2830 220th St. W., Farmington (612)463-2121.
30 miles south of Minneapolis. **Holes:** 18. **Par:** 72/72.
Yards: 6,540/5,980. **Course rating:** 70.9/72.8. **Slope:** 117/120.
Opened: 1977. **Pace of Play rating:** 4:00. **Green fee:** $17/20.
Credit cards: None. **Reduced fees:** Weekdays, Seniors.
Caddies: No. **Golf carts:** $18 for 18 holes.
Discount golf packages: No. **Season:** April-Oct. **High:** June-Aug.
On-site lodging: No. **Rental clubs:** Yes.
Walking policy: Unrestricted walking. **Range:** Yes (grass).
To obtain tee times: Call seven days in advance.
Subscriber comments: Cordial and super staff . . . Real wide open course . . . Good beginner's course . . . Spray hitter's course . . . Back nine starting to develop.

★★★ FOX HOLLOW GOLF CLUB

SP—4780 Palmgren Lane N.E., Rogers (612)428-4468.
30 miles west of Minneapolis. **Holes:** 18. **Par:** 72/72.
Yards: 6,726/5,161. **Course rating:** 72.7/70.8. **Slope:** 129/122.
Opened: 1989. **Pace of Play rating:** 4:20. **Green fee:** $20/22.
Credit cards: MC, V. **Reduced fees:** Weekdays, Low season, Seniors, Juniors.

Caddies: No. **Golf carts:** $22 for 18 holes.
Discount golf packages: No. **Season:** April–Nov. **High:** June–Aug.
On-site lodging: No. **Rental clubs:** Yes.
Walking policy: Unrestricted walking. **Range:** Yes (grass).
To obtain tee times: Call three days in advance at 7 a.m.
Subscriber comments: Big elevated greens . . . Lots of sand and water
. . . Very nice newer course . . . Will be great in four to five years . . .
Excellent Joel Goldstrand design . . . Good variety of holes . . . Very
challenging . . . Slow to come back from 1993 floods. A couple of quirky
holes . . . Great staff, pleasant, greet you by name . . . Very nice . . .
Beautiful island par 3 on river . . . Links style with several holes playing
over and along a river.

★★½ FRANCIS A. GROSS GOLF COURSE

PU—2201 St. Anthony Blvd., Minneapolis (612)789-2542.
Holes: 18. **Par:** 71/71.
Yards: 6,575/5,824. **Course rating:** 70.1/73.2. **Slope:** 120/121.
Opened: 1925. **Pace of Play rating:** 4:30. **Green fee:** $18.
Credit cards: , V. **Reduced fees:** Weekdays, Twilight, Seniors, Juniors.
Caddies: No. **Golf carts:** $21 for 18 holes.
Discount golf packages: Yes. **Season:** April–Nov. **High:** June–Aug.
On-site lodging: No. **Rental clubs:** Yes.
Walking policy: Unrestricted walking. **Range:** Yes (grass).
To obtain tee times: For weekends come in person on Tuesday or call on
Wednesday. For Monday through Friday come in person three days in
advance or all two days in advance.
Subscriber comments: Established course . . . Fair to golfers . . . Nice
clubhouse . . . A mature course that will keep you coming back . . . Flat
. . . Lots of trees . . . Flat greens . . . Sees lots of play . . . Near downtown
. . . Lots of trees . . . Grand old oaks . . . Has had National Publinx . . .
Fun.

★½ GOODRICH GOLF COURSE

PU—1820 N. Van Dyke, Maplewood (612)777-7355.
3 miles north of St. Paul. **Holes:** 18. **Par:** 70/72.
Yards: 6,015/5,728. **Course rating:** 67.8/71.8. **Slope:** 105/111.
Opened: 1959. **Pace of Play rating:** 4:00. **Green fee:** $18.
Credit cards: None. **Reduced fees:** Weekdays, Twilight, Seniors, Juniors.
Caddies: No. **Golf carts:** $20 for 18 holes.
Discount golf packages: No. **Season:** April–Nov. **High:** June–Aug.
On-site lodging: No. **Rental clubs:** Yes.
Walking policy: Unrestricted walking. **Range:** No.
To obtain tee times: Call four days in advance.
Subscriber comments: Senior course . . . Easy, flat . . . Good beginner
course . . . Postage stamp greens . . . Open fairways with some water and
more sand . . . Short, sporty . . . Good for beginners to average golfers . . .
Cash-only policy is stupid.

GRAND NATIONAL GOLF CLUB★

PU—300 Lady Luck Dr., Hinckley (612)384-7427.
60 miles north of Minneapolis/St.Paul. **Holes:** 18. **Par:** 72/72.
Yards: 6,894/5,100. **Course rating:** 72.0/68.7. **Slope:** 123/117.
Opened: 1995. **Pace of Play rating:** N/A. **Green fee:** $21/24.
Credit cards: MC, V. **Reduced fees:** No.
Caddies: No. **Golf carts:** $21 for 18 holes.
Discount golf packages: Yes. **Season:** April–Oct. **High:** June–Aug.
On-site lodging: Yes. **Rental clubs:** Yes.
Walking policy: Unrestricted walking. **Range:** Yes (grass).
To obtain tee times: Call seven days in advance.

★★★★½ GRAND VIEW LODGE
THE PINES - LAKES/WOODS/MARSH

R—S. 134 Nokomis, Nisswa (218)963-3146, (800)432-3788.
120 miles north of Minneapolis. **Holes:** 27. **Par:** 72/72/72.

Yards: 6,874/6,883/6,837. **Course rating:** 74.2/73.3/73.7.
Slope: 137/132/134.
Opened: 1990. **Pace of Play rating:** 4:15. **Green fee:** $39/46.
Credit cards: All major. **Reduced fees:** Weekdays, Low season, Resort guests, Twilight.
Caddies: No. **Golf carts:** $14 for 18 holes.
Discount golf packages: Yes. **Season:** April–Oct. **High:** June–Sept.
On-site lodging: Yes. **Rental clubs:** Yes.
Walking policy: Unrestricted walking. **Range:** Yes (grass).
To obtain tee times: June 15th through September 15th call 48 hours in advance with credit card. Lodge guests up to one year in advance with confirmed reservation. April 15th through June 15th and September 15th to end of season, up to one month in advance with credit card.
Ranked 6th in Minnesota by Golf Digest.
Subscriber comments: The best public course I've played . . . Well worth the money . . . The gem of the north . . . Top service . . . Top new clubhouse . . . One of the finest golf experiences you'll ever have . . . Everything Golf Digest said it was . . . A must if you're in the area . . . Keep the ball in play or you'll never find it . . . Wooded course that allows use of a driver . . . Many deer and even saw a bear one morning . . . Carved from forest but wide fairways . . . Can order food on ninth hole phone . . . A novel course everyone should play at least once . . . The best resort course in Minnesota.

★½ GREEN LEA GOLF COURSE
PU—101 Richway Dr., Albert Lea (507)373-1061.
90 miles south of Minneapolis. **Holes:** 18. **Par:** 73/77.
Yards: 6,157/5,764. **Course rating:** 68.1/71.8. **Slope:** 109/117.
Opened: 1947. **Pace of Play rating:** 3:30–4:00. **Green fee:** $15/17.
Credit cards: MC, V. **Reduced fees:** Weekdays, Low season, Twilight, Seniors, Juniors.
Caddies: No. **Golf carts:** $8 for 18 holes.
Discount golf packages: Yes. **Season:** April–Oct. **High:** June–Aug.
On-site lodging: No. **Rental clubs:** Yes.
Walking policy: Unrestricted walking. **Range:** No.
To obtain tee times: Call two days in advance for weekends and holidays.
Subscriber comments: An average public course . . . Narrow fairways . . . Lots of trees . . . Improving yearly . . . Not spectacular . . . Good for exercise . . . Very challenging . . . Trees are in play here.

★★★ HEADWATERS COUNTRY CLUB
SP—County Rd. 99, Park Rapids (218)732-4832.
112 miles north of St. Cloud. **Holes:** 18. **Par:** 72/72.
Yards: 6,455/5,362. **Course rating:** 70.9/71.0. **Slope:** 120/118.
Opened: 1969. **Pace of Play rating:** 4:15. **Green fee:** $18/20.
Credit cards: MC, V. **Reduced fees:** Low season, Twilight, Juniors.
Caddies: No. **Golf carts:** $20 for 18 holes.
Discount golf packages: No. **Season:** March–Nov. **High:** June–Aug.
On-site lodging: No. **Rental clubs:** Yes.
Walking policy: Unrestricted walking. **Range:** Yes (grass).
To obtain tee times: Local call two days in advance. Out of town, call anytime.
Subscriber comments: Trees and narrow fairways . . . Lot of water and sand on back nine . . . Good small town course . . . Great course, great staff . . . A real secret . . . Front nine tight, back nine very hilly. Wide open . . . Always windy . . . Good greens . . . Like two different courses . . . Front wooded . . . Back water.

★½ HIAWATHA GOLF COURSE
PU— 4553 Longfellow Ave. S., Minneapolis (612)724-7715.
Holes: 18. **Par:** 73/74.
Yards: 6,645/5,796. **Course rating:** 70.6/71.7. **Slope:** 114/123.
Opened: 1934. **Pace of Play rating:** 4:40. **Green fee:** $18.
Credit cards: ,V. **Reduced fees:** Weekdays, Low season, Twilight,

Seniors, Juniors.
Caddies: No. **Golf carts:** $20 for 18 holes.
Discount golf packages: Yes. **Season:** April-Nov. **High:** June-Aug.
On-site lodging: No. **Rental clubs:** Yes.
Walking policy: Unrestricted walking. **Range:** Yes (grass).
To obtain tee times: Come in person on Tuesday for the upcoming
weekend and by phone from Wednesday on. For weekend tee times a $2
starting fee is required.
Subscriber comments: Good layout . . . Sits on an old marsh . . .
Fairways wavy . . . A challenging course for average golfer . . . Plays long
. . . Small greens . . . Good test . . . Needs yardage markers . . . OK public
course, with a little more work could be very good.

★★½ **HIDDEN GREENS GOLF CLUB**
PU—12977 200th St. E., Hastings (612)437-3085.
24 miles southeast of Minneapolis. **Holes:** 18. **Par:** 72/72.
Yards: 5,954/5,599. **Course rating:** 68.8/72.2. **Slope:** 72.2/127.
Opened: 1986. **Pace of Play rating:** N/A. **Green fee:** $14/16.
Credit cards: None. **Reduced fees:** Weekdays, Seniors.
Caddies: No. **Golf carts:** $16 for 18 holes.
Discount golf packages: No. **Season:** April-Nov. **High:** July-Aug.
On-site lodging: No. **Rental clubs:** Yes.
Walking policy: Unrestricted walking. **Range:** Yes (grass).
To obtain tee times: Call after 9 a.m. on Tuesday.
Subscriber comments: Narrow fairways, most tree lined . . . Good staff
. . . Giant park . . . Lots of wildlife . . . Good condition . . . Something for
everyone . . . Hewn from hardwoods and evergreens . . . Must be straight
. . . No sand . . . Bring your chainsaw . . . Short but challenging, narrow
fairways . . . Tight . . . Lots of oak trees . . . Good family course . . . Very
tight . . . Lots of trees . . . Bring lots of balls.

★½ **HIGHLAND PARK GOLF COURSE**
PU—1403 Montreal Ave., St. Paul (612)699-5825.
Holes: 18. **Par:** 72/73.
Yards: 6,265/5,600. **Course rating:** 69.0/71.1. **Slope:** 111/N/A.
Opened: 1929. **Pace of Play rating:** 4:30. **Green fee:** $19.
Credit cards: MC, V. **Reduced fees:** Low season, Twilight, Seniors,
Juniors.
Caddies: No. **Golf carts:** $20 for 18 holes.
Discount golf packages: No. **Season:** April-Nov. **High:** May-Sept.
On-site lodging: No. **Rental clubs:** Yes.
Walking policy: . **Range:** Yes (grass).
To obtain tee times: For weekdays call 8 a.m. one day in advance. For
weekends come in Wednesday in person 6 a.m. to 7 a.m. or call on
Thursday after 7 a.m.
Subscriber comments: Good city course with mature trees . . . Great for
hackers or with the family . . . Open, predictable . . . Saw a slow foursome
thrown off the course, was gratified . . . Fair layout . . . Not a great
challenge . . . Easy par 5s.

★½ **HOLLYDALE GOLF COURSE**
PU—4710 Holly Lane N., Plymouth (612)559-9847.
Call club for further information.
Subscriber comments: Easy but fun . . . Low scores quite possible . . .
Was a better course before they allowed golf carts . . . Very roomy with
little trouble . . . Good for the ego . . . Pretty good grass . . . Ball sits up
. . . Popular with high handicappers . . . Only two traps . . . Rolling
terrain . . . Needs sand traps.

★★★ **INVERWOOD GOLF COURSE**
PU—1850 70th St. E., Inver Grove Heights (612)457-3667.
8 miles south of St. Paul. **Holes:** 18. **Par:** 72/72.
Yards: 6,724/5,175. **Course rating:** 72.5/70.3. **Slope:** 135/124.
Opened: 1991. **Pace of Play rating:** 4:02. **Green fee:** $22.

Credit cards: MC, V. **Reduced fees:** Juniors.
Caddies: No. **Golf carts:** $20 for 18 holes.
Discount golf packages: No. **Season:** April-Oct. **High:** May-Aug.
On-site lodging: No. **Rental clubs:** Yes.
Walking policy: Unrestricted walking. **Range:** Yes (grass).
To obtain tee times: Call or come in three days in advance.
Also has 9-hole course.
Subscriber comments: Good design and maturing . . . Hilly, water, greens big and fast . . . Reminds me of northern Michigan golf in metro area . . . Beautiful terrain . . . Will be outstanding . . . No forgiving holes . . . Out-of-bounds are everywhere . . . Varied terrain on back nine . . . Lots of challenging holes . . . Straight drives a must . . . Many blind shots . . . Come only with a single-digit handicap . . . Friendly staff . . . Bring balls . . . Excellent range.

★★★½ ISLAND VIEW COUNTRY CLUB

SP—P.O. Box 93, Waconia (612)442-5666.
Call club for further information.
Subscriber comments: Back nine short, par 4s stir a frenzy . . . Bring all your clubs . . . Nice old course in good shape . . . Shotgun starts speeds play . . . Semi-private but always accommodating . . . Great course . . . Great people . . . Great shape . . . Well worth the money . . . A Hazeltine for muny players . . . Feels like private course . . . Well groomed . . . Good pace . . . Private course atmosphere . . . Lots of trees . . . Average length . . . Fun to play . . . Tough course to walk . . . Well maintained . . . Nice staff.

★★★ IZATYS GOLF AND YACHT CLUB

R—Rte. 1 Izatys Rd., Onamia (612)532-4575, (800)533-1728.
90 miles north of Minneapolis. **Holes:** 18. **Par:** 72/72.
Yards: 6,481/4,939. **Course rating:** 72.1/69.7. **Slope:** 132/127.
Opened: N/A. **Pace of Play rating:** 4:30. **Green fee:** $30/50.
Credit cards: All major. **Reduced fees:** Weekdays, Resort guests, Twilight.
Caddies: No. **Golf carts:** $25 for 18 holes.
Discount golf packages: Yes. **Season:** April-Oct. **High:** June-Sept.
On-site lodging: Yes. **Rental clubs:** Yes.
Walking policy: Unrestricted walking. **Range:** Yes (grass).
To obtain tee times: Anytime for resort guests or members. Nonguests call four days in advance.
Subscriber comments: The more you play the better it gets . . . Extremely difficult from back tees . . . Good fast greens . . . Tight . . . Lots of trouble . . . Better hit it straight . . . Short . . . Some great holes . . . Staff is great . . . Bring balls . . . Course needs a few years to mature . . . Fun course . . . Back nine better than front nine . . . Frustrating unless you're a very experienced golfer . . . One of the best target courses . . . Demands good course management . . . Close tree line . . . Undulating greens . . . Deep bunkers.

★★★ KELLER GOLF COURSE

PU—2166 Maplewood Dr., St. Paul (612)484-3011.
Holes: 18. **Par:** 72/73.
Yards: 6,566/5,373. **Course rating:** 71.7/71.4. **Slope:** 127/124.
Opened: 1929. **Pace of Play rating:** 4:30. **Green fee:** $18.
Credit cards: None. **Reduced fees:** Low season, Twilight, Seniors, Juniors.
Caddies: No. **Golf carts:** $20 for 18 holes.
Discount golf packages: No. **Season:** March-Nov. **High:** May-Sept.
On-site lodging: No. **Rental clubs:** Yes.
Walking policy: Unrestricted walking. **Range:** Yes (grass).
To obtain tee times: Call four days in advance starting at 7 a.m.
Subscriber comments: Home of the old St. Paul Open . . . The greens were more challenging than I had anticipated . . . Old, great traditional classic . . . The putting surfaces are inconsistent . . . Traditional city

parkland course . . . Inspirational photos of St. Paul Open champs . . . .
Very old course . . . The staff is very professional . . . Site of '32 and '54
PGA championships . . . Need to keep their greens in better shape . . .
Course could be a "five" . . . Would be excellent if course conditions were
consistent.

★★★ LES BOLSTAD GOLF CLUB
PU—2275 W. Larpenteur Ave., St. Paul (612)627-4000.
Call club for further information.
Subscriber comments: Many sidehill lies . . . Very good risk/reward
holes . . . Short, tight, but fun old layout . . . Small but good greens . . .
Mature trees . . . Smallish greens . . . Old classic . . . Subtle but brilliant
design . . . Shotmaker's course . . . Huge oak trees . . . Mature trees and
tight fairways . . . A classic played all season . . . Owned and operated by
the University of Minnesota . . . Well groomed and kept course . . .
Returned to excellent condition in '94 . . . Very busy . . . Not too long . . .
Small, raised greens . . . Maintenance is getting better . . . Large driving
range . . . Challenging shots on approach . . . Great shape in fall . . . Great
value . . . Nice staff.

★½ LESTER PARK GOLF CLUB
FRONT/BACK/LAKE
PU—1860 Lester River Rd., Duluth (218)525-1400.
Holes: 27. **Par:** 72/72/72.
Yards: 6,371/6,606/6,599. **Course rating:** 70.8/71.7/71.7.
Slope: 118/126/125.
Opened: 1931. **Pace of Play rating:** N/A. **Green fee:** $18.
Credit cards: None. **Reduced fees:** Low season, Twilight, Seniors,
Juniors.
Caddies: No. **Golf carts:** $18 for 18 holes.
Discount golf packages: No. **Season:** April-Nov. **High:** June-July.
On-site lodging: No. **Rental clubs:** Yes.
Walking policy: Unrestricted walking. **Range:** Yes (grass).
To obtain tee times: Call 72 hours in advance.
Subscriber comments: Lake Superior view is outstanding . . . Best in fall
. . . All holes overlook Lake Superior . . . Best views in Duluth . . . Scenic
holes . . . Bring camera not clubs . . . The new Lake nine is most
challenging and scenic layout imaginable . . . Very hilly . . . Pretty views ..
Some greens are optical illusions . . . Everything breaks towards lake.

★★★½ THE LINKS AT NORTHFORK
PU—9333 153rd Ave., Ramsey (612)241-0506.
20 miles southwest of Minneapolis. **Holes:** 18. **Par:** 72/72.
Yards: 6,989/5,242. **Course rating:** 73.7/70.5. **Slope:** 127/117.
Opened: 1992. **Pace of Play rating:** N/A. **Green fee:** $27/29.
Credit cards: MC, V, AMEX. **Reduced fees:** Weekdays, Low season,
Twilight, Seniors, Juniors.
Caddies: No. **Golf carts:** $22 for 18 holes.
Discount golf packages: Yes. **Season:** April-Oct. **High:** June-Aug.
On-site lodging: No. **Rental clubs:** Yes.
Walking policy: Unrestricted walking. **Range:** Yes (grass).
To obtain tee times: Call three days in advance for an additional charge.
Subscriber comments: The links style gives one confidence but course
isn't easy . . . Scottish look . . . Lots of heather . . . Huge practice facility
. . . Usually windy . . . Nice condition . . . Would play this course for the
rest of my days! . . . Have to hit fairways . . . A joy to play . . . Varied
holes . . . Fun layout . . . Waste areas . . . True links . . . Won't see a tree
for 13 holes.

LITCHFIELD GOLF COURSE★
PU—W. Pleasure Dr., Litchfield (612)693-6059.
Call club for further information.
Subscriber comments: Plays fairly short . . . Tough in the wind . . . No driving range . . . Open, flat course . . . Nice course . . . Some tough holes . . . Pretty good shape . . . Nice, plain course.

★★★ LITTLE CROW COUNTRY CLUB

SP—Highway 23, Spicer (612)354-2296.
47 miles southwest of St. Cloud. **Holes:** 18. **Par:** 72/72.
Yards: 6,765/5,757. **Course rating:** 72.3/73.1. **Slope:** 123/125.
Opened: 1969. **Pace of Play rating:** N/A. **Green fee:** $15/20.
Credit cards: MC, V. **Reduced fees:** Weekdays, Low season.
Caddies: No. **Golf carts:** $9 for 18 holes.
Discount golf packages: No. **Season:** April-Nov. **High:** June-Aug.
On-site lodging: No. **Rental clubs:** Yes.
Walking policy: Unrestricted walking. **Range:** Yes (grass).
To obtain tee times: Call one day in advance.
Subscriber comments: Good course suited for average player . . . Favors the left to right player . . . Very challenging . . . Plush and well kept . . . Pleasure to play . . . Best-kept secret in Minnesota . . . Has it all . . . Good, fair test . . . Excellent country course . . . Good condition . . . Not busy.

★★½ LITTLE FALLS COUNTRY CLUB
PU—1 Edgewater Dr., Little Falls (612)632-3584.
25 miles north of St. Cloud. **Holes:** 18. **Par:** 72/72.
Yards: 6,051/5,713. **Course rating:** 69.0/72.0. **Slope:** 121/125.
Opened: 1982. **Pace of Play rating:** 4:00. **Green fee:** $17.
Credit cards: None. **Reduced fees:** Low season, Seniors, Juniors.
Caddies: No. **Golf carts:** $17 for 18 holes.
Discount golf packages: Yes. **Season:** April-Oct. **High:** June-Aug.
On-site lodging: No. **Rental clubs:** Yes.
Walking policy: Unrestricted walking. **Range:** Yes (grass).
To obtain tee times: Call up to one week in advance.
Subscriber comments: Great small town course . . . Very friendly to out-of-towners . . . Narrow fairways . . . Large oaks . . . Average player well treated . . . Not crowded . . . Course fun through trees . . . Takes some thinking . . . Look for cute black squirrels while playing.

MADDEN'S ON GULL LAKE
R—8001 Pine Beach Peninsula, Brainerd (218)829-7118.
120 miles north of Minneapolis.
Green fee: $26/27
Credit cards: MC, V. **Reduced fees:** Weekdays, Resort guests, Twilight.
Caddies: No. **Golf carts:** $25 for 18 holes.
Discount golf packages: Yes. **Season:** April-Oct. **High:** July-Aug.
On-site lodging: Yes. **Rental clubs:** Yes.
Walking policy: Unrestricted walking. **Range:** Yes(grass).
To obtain tee times: Resort guests may call 24 hours in advance with confirmation number. Public, call after 6 p.m. day before.
★★½ PINE BEACH EAST COURSE
Holes: 18. **Par:** 72/72.
Yards: 5,956/5,352. **Course rating:** 67.9/70.9. **Slope:** 119/116.
Opened: 1926. **Pace of Play rating:** 4:00.
Subscriber comments: Greens are fast but true . . . Fine greens . . . Short and easy but good for average resort guest . . . Only par 6 hole that I've played . . . A very fine resort course . . . Well managed and well kept . . . Features an interesting 600 plus yard hole . . . Perfect resort course . . . Improved every year . . . Fun to play.
★★½ PINE BEACH WEST COURSE
Holes: 18. **Par:** 67/67.
Yards: 5,049/4,662. **Course rating:** 64.0/66.7. **Slope:** 103/107.
Opened: 1950. **Pace of Play rating:** 3:30.

Subscriber comments: Nice resort course with trees and some hills . . . Heavy play . . . Shorter resort course . . . Fast sloping greens . . . Not very long but tight, scenic . . . Wooded . . . Short woodsy course . . . Leave your driver behind . . . Resort course . . . Short . . . Very tight and heavy woods.

MAJESTIC OAKS GOLF CLUB

PU—701 Bunker Lake Blvd., Ham Lake (612)755-2142.
20 miles north of Minneapolis.
Credit cards: MC, V, AMEX. **Reduced fees:** Weekdays, Low season, Twilight, Seniors, Juniors.
Caddies: No. **Golf carts:** $20 for 18 holes.
Discount golf packages: No. **Season:** April-Oct. **High:** June-Aug.
On-site lodging: No. **Rental clubs:** No.
Walking policy: N/A. **Range:** Yes (grass).

★★ GOLD COURSE

Holes: 18. **Par:** 72/72.
Yards: 6,396/4,848. **Course rating:** N/A. **Slope:** 122/118.
Opened: N/A. **Pace of Play rating:** N/A. **Green fee:** N/A.
Subscriber comments: Good course for all levels . . . Very long . . . Condition a problem . . . Caters to leagues and tourneys . . . Newer course, more open . . . Less challenging . . . Very difficult for average golfer.

★★★ PLATINUM COURSE

Holes: 18. **Par:** 72/72.
Yards: 7,013/5,268. **Course rating:** 73.9/71.1. **Slope:** 132/124.
Opened: 1972. **Pace of Play rating:** 4:30. **Green fee:** $16/22.
On-site lodging: Yes. **Rental clubs:** Yes.
Walking policy: Unrestricted walking. **Range:** Yes (grass).
To obtain tee times: Call four days in advance.
Also has 9-hole executive course.
Ranked in Third 25 of America's 75 Best Public Golf Courses by Golf Digest.
Subscriber comments: Holes you will remember . . . Condition is inconsistent . . . Difficult . . . Requires a tee ball and nice approaches . . . A lot of potential . . . Course never lets up . . . Long 7,000 plus . . . Need to work the ball . . . Course needs some more work . . . Fun and challenging holes . . . Fair conditions due to heavy play . . . Great old course with many trees . . . Need to hit straight . . . Not the course it used to be, but better this year than last four . . . Make sure you carry a sand wedge.

★★ MANITOU RIDGE GOLF COURSE

PU—3200 N. McKnight Rd., White Bear Lake (612)777-2987.
15 miles north of St. Paul. **Holes:** 18. **Par:** 71/71.
Yards: 6,422/5,556. **Course rating:** 70.5/71.5. **Slope:** 120/119.
Opened: N/A. **Pace of Play rating:** 4:15. **Green fee:** $17.
Credit cards: MC, V, DISC. **Reduced fees:** Seniors, Juniors.
Caddies: No. **Golf carts:** $19 for 18 holes.
Discount golf packages: No. **Season:** April-Oct. **High:** April-Oct.
On-site lodging: No. **Rental clubs:** Yes.
Walking policy: Unrestricted walking. **Range:** Yes (grass).
To obtain tee times: Call four days in advance.
Subscriber comments: Short and postage-stamp greens . . . Small elevated greens make a good short game a must . . . Tight, rolling . . . Lots of blind shots . . . New clubhouse . . . Some funky holes make it difficult . . . Sporty for average players . . . Shop helpful . . . Interesting holes and scenery . . . Hills . . . Long par 4s . . . Good testing holes . . . Good prices on equipment . . . Wide open course . . . Great staff in clubhouse.

★★★ MAPLE VALLEY GOLF AND COUNTRY CLUB

SP—8600 Maple Valley Rd. S.E., Rochester (507)285-9100.
Holes: 18. **Par:** 71/71.
Yards: 6,270/5,330. **Course rating:** 68.9/68.5. **Slope:** 108/108.
Opened: 1964. **Pace of Play rating:** N/A. **Green fee:** $16.

Credit cards: MC, V. **Reduced fees:** N/A.
Caddies: No. **Golf carts:** N/A.
Discount golf packages: No. **Season:** March-Nov. **High:** July-Aug.
On-site lodging: No. **Rental clubs:** Yes.
Walking policy: Unrestricted walking. **Range:** No.
To obtain tee times: Call five days in advance.
Subscriber comments: Great scenery . . . No bunkers . . . Very hilly . . .
Great valley holes . . . Will challenge anyone's game . . . Great golf course
to play in autumn . . . Mature course . . . A little hilly . . . Beautiful course
hidden in the trees and bluffs . . . Watch for bald eagles in bluffs.

★★★ MARSHALL GOLF CLUB

SP—800 Country Club Dr., Marshall (507)537-1622.
90 miles northeast of Souix Falls, SD. **Holes:** 18. **Par:** 72/72.
Yards: 6,565/5,136. **Course rating:** 71.6/69.5. **Slope:** 123/120.
Opened: N/A. **Pace of Play rating:** 4:00. **Green fee:** $22/28.
Credit cards: None. **Reduced fees:** No.
Caddies: No. **Golf carts:** $20 for 18 holes.
Discount golf packages: No. **Season:** April-Oct. **High:** May-Sept.
On-site lodging: No. **Rental clubs:** Yes.
Walking policy: Unrestricted walking. **Range:** Yes (grass).
To obtain tee times: Call one week in advance.
Subscriber comments: Interesting greens . . . Very well kept . . . Use
every shot . . . Great fun at tournament . . . Easy . . . Fun layout.

★★ MEADOWBROOK GOLF COURSE

PU—201 Meadowbrook Rd., Hopkins (612)929-2077.
3 miles west of Minneapolis. **Holes:** 18. **Par:** 72/72.
Yards: 6,593/5,610. **Course rating:** 69.9/71.1. **Slope:** 113/122.
Opened: 1926. **Pace of Play rating:** 4:30. **Green fee:** $17.
Credit cards: V. **Reduced fees:** Low season, Twilight, Seniors, Juniors.
Caddies: No. **Golf carts:** $20 for 18 holes.
Discount golf packages: No. **Season:** April-Nov. **High:** May-Aug.
On-site lodging: No. **Rental clubs:** Yes.
Walking policy: Unrestricted walking. **Range:** No.
To obtain tee times: For weekdays come in three days in advance. For
weekends come in person the Tuesday before.
Subscriber comments: A good public links course . . . Tough par fours
. . . Only one dogleg . . . Hilly! A good municipal but seems tired . . .
Conditions varied . . . Typical muny course, crowded most of the time . . .
Many elevated greens . . . Could use some updating . . . Fivesomes
allowed despite atrociously slow play . . . Best hot dog I've ever had.

MESABA COUNTRY CLUB★

SP—415 E. 51st St., Hibbing (218)263-4826.
70 miles northwest of Duluth. **Holes:** 18. **Par:** 72/74.
Yards: 6,792/5,747. **Course rating:** 71.7/73.0. **Slope:** 131/129.
Opened: 1923. **Pace of Play rating:** 4:05. **Green fee:** $22/27.
Credit cards: None. **Reduced fees:** Weekdays.
Caddies: No. **Golf carts:** $18 for 18 holes.
Discount golf packages: No. **Season:** April-Oct. **High:** June-Aug.
On-site lodging: No. **Rental clubs:** Yes.
Walking policy: Unrestricted walking. **Range:** Yes (grass).
To obtain tee times: Call pro shop.

★½ MILLE LACS GOLF RESORT

R—18314 Captive Lake Rd., Garrison (612)692-4325, (800)435-8720.
95 miles north of Minneapolis. **Holes:** 18. **Par:** 71/72.
Yards: 6,290/5,106. **Course rating:** 69.7/68.7. **Slope:** 119/113.
Opened: 1964. **Pace of Play rating:** 4:30. **Green fee:** $20/25.
Credit cards: MC, V. **Reduced fees:** Resort guests, Twilight, Seniors,
Juniors.
Caddies: No. **Golf carts:** $24 for 18 holes.
Discount golf packages: Yes. **Season:** April-Oct. **High:** June-Aug.

On-site lodging: Yes. **Rental clubs:** Yes.
Walking policy: Unrestricted walking. **Range:** Yes (grass).
To obtain tee times: Call pro shop.
Subscriber comments: Potential to be a good course . . . Need attention to detail . . . Fair condition . . . Extremely cordial . . . Back nine makes the course . . . Decent woodland course . . . Hilly course with large trees . . . Not overly tough course, but enjoyable . . . Front nine tight . . . Back open . . . Good shotmaking course . . . Some cute holes.

★★½ MINNEWASKA GOLF CLUB
PU—Golf Course Rd., Glenwood (612)634-3680.
120 miles east of Minneapolis. **Holes:** 18. **Par:** 72/73.
Yards: 6,457/5,398. **Course rating:** 70.7/71.7. **Slope:** 122/123.
Opened: 1923. **Pace of Play rating:** 4:00. **Green fee:** $15/20.
Credit cards: MC, V. **Reduced fees:** Weekdays, Low season, Resort guests, Juniors.
Caddies: No. **Golf carts:** $20 for 18 holes.
Discount golf packages: Yes. **Season:** April-Oct. **High:** June-Sept.
On-site lodging: No. **Rental clubs:** Yes.
Walking policy: Unrestricted walking. **Range:** Yes (grass).
To obtain tee times: Call pro shop.
Subscriber comments: New nine still a little rough . . . Extremely cordial . . . Great improvements in 1993-94 . . . Good public course . . . Western jewel . . . Great course to spend a day at . . . Great photos in clubhouse . . . Open course with a few tight holes . . . Not busy.

★★★½ MISSISSIPPI NATIONAL GOLF LINKS
LOWLANDS/MIDLANDS/HIGHLANDS
PU—409 Golf Links Dr., Red Wing (612)388-1874.
50 miles south of Minneapolis. **Holes:** 27. **Par:** 70/71/71.
Yards: 6,035/6,488/6,215. **Course rating:** 70.0/71.5/71.1.
Slope: 125/128/130.
Opened: 1987. **Pace of Play rating:** N/A. **Green fee:** $21/23.
Credit cards: MC, V. **Reduced fees:** Weekdays.
Caddies: No. **Golf carts:** $11 for 18 holes.
Discount golf packages: No. **Season:** April-Oct. **High:** June-Aug.
On-site lodging: No. **Rental clubs:** Yes.
Walking policy: Unrestricted walking. **Range:** Yes (grass).
To obtain tee times: Call up to seven days in advance.
Subscriber comments: Pretty course in the river valley . . . Scenic . . . Challenging greens are difficult to read . . . 27 holes and variety of tees presents a good challenge for all levels . . . Scenic beauty as good as any in Midwest . . . Better than most . . . Fun to play . . . Gorgeous in the autumn . . . Lowlands and Midlands nice . . . Everyone should play Highlands once . . . Nice clubhouse . . . Highlands scenic and tight . . . Other nines are good tests of golf . . . Not for beginners . . . Hilly course with marvelous views of Mississippi River . . . Try to play all three . . . Excellent test for above average golfers . . . Worth the drive from Twin Cities . . . Spend the day . . . Looking for diversity in Minnesota? Come here . . . What a view! . . . Has three different nines . . . One and two great . . . Three newest and very gimmicky . . . Exhillarating . . . Lots of wildlife . . . Great views . . . Good condition.

★★★ MONTICELLO COUNTRY CLUB
PU—1201 Golf Course Rd., Monticello (612)295-4653.
30 miles west of Minneapolis. **Holes:** 18. **Par:** 71/72.
Yards: 6,390/5,298. **Course rating:** 70.4/70.8. **Slope:** 118/119.
Opened: 1969. **Pace of Play rating:** N/A. **Green fee:** $16/22.
Credit cards: MC, V. **Reduced fees:** Weekdays, Low season, Seniors.
Caddies: No. **Golf carts:** $22 for 18 holes.
Discount golf packages: No. **Season:** April-Oct. **High:** June-Aug.
On-site lodging: No. **Rental clubs:** Yes.
Walking policy: Unrestricted walking. **Range:** Yes (grass).
To obtain tee times: Call five days in advance.

Subscriber comments: Hidden gem . . . Great shape . . . Lots of flower beds . . . Good staff . . . Nice large greens . . . Challenges average golfer . . . Like course . . . Fun and tough . . . Good variety . . . Good seniors course . . . Nice course for couples . . . Well conditioned . . . Pleasant staff . . . Comfortable pace . . . Fun course . . . Like two courses . . . Old nine and new nine . . . Nice layout for average golfer . . . Large flat greens . . . Interesting mix of holes . . . Odd contoured greens . . . Mix of links and parkland holes . . . Enjoyable course . . . Worth the 45-minute drive from Minneapolis area.

★★½ MOUNT FRONTENAC GOLF COURSE

PU—Hwy. 61, Frontenac (612)388-5826.
9 miles south of Red Wing. **Holes:** 18. **Par:** 70/70.
Yards: 6,050/4,832. **Course rating:** 69.2/67.7. **Slope:** 119/117.
Opened: 1985. **Pace of Play rating:** 4:00. **Green fee:** $14/17.
Credit cards: MC, V. **Reduced fees:** Weekdays, Twilight, Seniors.
Caddies: No. **Golf carts:** $18 for 18 holes.
Discount golf packages: Yes. **Season:** April-Oct. **High:** June-Aug.
On-site lodging: No. **Rental clubs:** Yes.
Walking policy: Unrestricted walking. **Range:** No.
To obtain tee times: Call ten days in advance.
Subscriber comments: Great views . . . Rolling hills on top of bluff over Mississippi . . . Nice staff . . . Sleeper course . . . Pretty holes atop river bluffs . . . Average course . . . Beautiful views . . . Constantly being improved . . . Unknown . . . Excellent greens will hold any shot . . . Course is built at a ski resort . . . Nice scenery.

★★★ NEW PRAGUE GOLF CLUB

PU—400 Lexington Ave. S., New Prague (612)758-3126.
40 miles southwest of Minneapolis. **Holes:** 18. **Par:** 72/72.
Yards: 6,335/5,032. **Course rating:** 69.5/68.3. **Slope:** 121/116.
Opened: 1929. **Pace of Play rating:** 4:00. **Green fee:** $22.
Credit cards: MC, V. **Reduced fees:** Low season, Seniors, Juniors.
Caddies: No. **Golf carts:** $22 for 18 holes.
Discount golf packages: Yes. **Season:** April-Oct. **High:** May-Aug.
On-site lodging: No. **Rental clubs:** No.
Walking policy: Unrestricted walking. **Range:** Yes (grass).
To obtain tee times: Call four days in advance.
Subscriber comments: Small town friendliness is the rule here . . . Nice public course . . . Older small-town course . . . Good shape . . . Nice . . . Fun . . . A wonderful course . . . Don't tell anyone about it . . . Course is hilly . . . Tee times are easy to get because of location . . . One of the best public courses I've been on . . . Front nine boring . . . Newer back nine OK . . . Fairways and greens well kept . . . Well-placed traps . . . Challenging approach shots.

★★★ NORTH LINKS GOLF COURSE

PU—Nicollet County Rd. 66, North Mankato (507)947-3355.
80 miles southwest of Minneapolis. **Holes:** 18. **Par:** 72/72.
Yards: 6,073/4,659. **Course rating:** 69.5/66.9. **Slope:** 117/114.
Opened: 1993. **Pace of Play rating:** 4:15. **Green fee:** $17/20.
Credit cards: MC, V. **Reduced fees:** Twilight, Seniors, Juniors.
Caddies: No. **Golf carts:** $15 for 18 holes.
Discount golf packages: No. **Season:** April-Nov. **High:** June-Aug.
On-site lodging: No. **Rental clubs:** Yes.
Walking policy: Unrestricted walking. **Range:** Yes (grass).
To obtain tee times: Call up to three days in advance.
Subscriber comments: New course . . . Will be good course in time . . . A bit short for the longer hitters . . . Good course for the average golfer . . . Need accuracy with short irons . . . Too many par 4s . . . Could be much better if longer . . . Short but fantastic condition . . . . Excellent clubhouse . . . Still new with lots of potential . . . Quick greens . . . Short overall length . . . No. 7 is fantastic.

★★★ NORTHERN HILLS GOLF COURSE
PU—4805 N.W. 41st Ave. N.W., Rochester (507)281-6170.
65 miles south of Minneapolis. **Holes:** 18. **Par:** 72/72.
Yards: 6,315/5,456. **Course rating:** 70.4/71.6. **Slope:** 123/123.
Opened: 1976. **Pace of Play rating:** 4:00. **Green fee:** $17.
Credit cards: MC, V. **Reduced fees:** N/A.
Caddies: No. **Golf carts:** $8 for 18 holes.
Discount golf packages: No. **Season:** April-Oct. **High:** May-Sept.
On-site lodging: No. **Rental clubs:** Yes.
Walking policy: Unrestricted walking. **Range:** Yes (grass).
To obtain tee times: Call two days in advance.
Subscriber comments: Challenging course, good condition . . . A good
variety of hole layouts . . . Hidden gem . . . Hit it straight . . . Very
friendly staff . . . Challenging but nice . . . My kind of golf . . . Good pro
shop.

★★★½ NORTHFIELD GOLF CLUB
SP—707 Prairie St., Northfield (507)645-4026.
25 miles south of Minneapolis. **Holes:** 18. **Par:** 69/71.
Yards: 5,856/5,103. **Course rating:** 68.7/70.4. **Slope:** 128/126.
Opened: 1926. **Pace of Play rating:** 4:00. **Green fee:** $25/35.
Credit cards: MC, V, AMEX. **Reduced fees:** N/A.
Caddies: Yes. **Golf carts:** $20 for 18 holes.
Discount golf packages: No. **Season:** April-Oct. **High:** April-Sept..
On-site lodging: No. **Rental clubs:** Yes.
Walking policy: Unrestricted walking. **Range:** No.
To obtain tee times: Call or come in two days in advance.
Subscriber comments: Beautiful par 69 . . . Very challenging . . . Unique
greens . . . Par 3s make the course . . . Beautiful finishing hole . . .
Beautifully manicured, fast greens . . . Short in length . . . Narrow
fairways . . . Fast greens . . . Must have good short game . . . Well kept
. . . Many flowers . . . Challenging . . . Good greens . . . Small clubhouse
. . . Difficult second shots on par 4s . . . A diamond in the rough . . . Very
good staff . . . Good food . . . Unique layout . . . Par 69 . . . With six par
3s . . . The feeling of a private club . . . Nice quiet secret in a neat little
historic town . . . Nice club and clubhouse . . . Friendly staff . . . Super
little course 45 minutes from Minneapolis.

★★★ OAK GLEN GOLF CLUB
PU—1599 McKusick Rd., Stillwater (612)439-6963.
20 miles east of St. Paul. **Holes:** 18. **Par:** 72/72.
Yards: 6,550/5,626. **Course rating:** 72.4/73.4. **Slope:** 131/130.
Opened: 1982. **Pace of Play rating:** 4:15. **Green fee:** $21/26.
Credit cards: MC, V. **Reduced fees:** Twilight.
Caddies: No. **Golf carts:** $10 for 18 holes.
Discount golf packages: No. **Season:** April-Nov. **High:** June-Aug.
On-site lodging: No. **Rental clubs:** Yes.
Walking policy: Unrestricted walking. **Range:** Yes (grass).
To obtain tee times: Call two days in advance.
Also has 9-hole short course.
Subscriber comments: Tight fairways . . . Beautiful homes on course . . .
Tight layout but excellent condition . . . Nice clubhouse . . . Lots of water
. . . Traditional course well trapped . . . Very challenging, suited for better
players . . . Good condition but young, course needs maturing . . . Better
players predominate . . . Good pro shop . . . Can be quite windy . . . Need
to be a shotmaker . . . Good use of water . . . Good greens . . . Thinking
man's golf course . . . Very tight but nice . . . Staff is polite.

OAK SUMMIT GOLF COURSE★
PU—2751 County Rd. 16 S.W., Rochester (507)252-1808.
Holes: 18. **Par:** 72/72.
Yards: 6,364/5,535. **Course rating:** 69.4/70.4. **Slope:** 113/115.
Opened: 1992. **Pace of Play rating:** 4:00-4:30. **Green fee:** $13/15.
Credit cards: MC, V. **Reduced fees:** Weekdays, Seniors.

Caddies: No. **Golf carts:** $16 for 18 holes.
Discount golf packages: No. **Season:** April-Nov. **High:** June-Aug.
On-site lodging: No. **Rental clubs:** Yes.
Walking policy: Unrestricted walking. **Range:** No.
To obtain tee times: Call up to three days in advance.

★★★ OAKS COUNTRY CLUB

SP—Country Club Rd., Hayfield (507)477-3233.
20 miles west of Rochester. **Holes:** 18. **Par:** 72/72.
Yards: 6,404/5,663. **Course rating:** 69.7/71.7. **Slope:** 114/118.
Opened: 1977. **Pace of Play rating:** N/A. **Green fee:** $16.
Credit cards: MC, V. **Reduced fees:** Low season.
Caddies: No. **Golf carts:** $9 for 18 holes.
Discount golf packages: Yes. **Season:** April-Oct. **High:** June-Aug.
On-site lodging: No. **Rental clubs:** Yes.
Walking policy: Unrestricted walking. **Range:** Yes (grass).
To obtain tee times: Nonmembers contact pro shop five days in advance.
Subscriber comments: Get on course anytime . . . Plays tough into
frequent northwest winds . . . Few hazards . . . Big greens . . . Easy
walking . . . Beautiful course . . . Pro shop staff excellent . . . Good small
town course.

ORTONVILLE MUNICIPAL GOLF COURSE★

PU—R.R. 1, Ortonville (612)839-3428.
Call club for further information.
Subscriber comments: Front nine outstanding . . . Back nine needs
maturing . . . Nice course . . . Fair for average player . . . Pretty country
course . . . Good maintenance with low budget.

★★★★ PEBBLE CREEK COUNTRY CLUB

PU—14000 Club House Lane, Becker (612)261-4653.
17 miles northwest of St. Cloud. **Holes:** 27. **Par:** 72/72/72.
Yards: 6,820/6,649/6,769. **Course rating:** 73.2/72.2/72.4.
Slope: 129/126/129.
Opened: 1987. **Pace of Play rating:** 4:30. **Green fee:** $19/23.
Credit cards: MC, V. **Reduced fees:** Seniors, Juniors.
Caddies: Yes. **Golf carts:** $10 for 18 holes.
Discount golf packages: No. **Season:** April-Nov. **High:** June-Sept.
On-site lodging: No. **Rental clubs:** Yes.
Walking policy: Unrestricted walking. **Range:** Yes (grass).
To obtain tee times: Call two days in advance.
Subscriber comments: Great scenery and nice value . . . Wonderful
public course . . . well maintained with many interesting holes . . . Just gets
better with time . . . Real nice course, water and tight . . . Very nice course
. . . Usually windy . . . Nice rural course . . . Relatively new . . .
Improved nicely . . . Definitely worth the drive from the Twin Cities . . .
Beautiful with something for every golfer . . . You don't have to spend a
day looking for golf balls . . . Long ride from Twin Cities . . . Over hill,
over dale. This course fun and exciting . . . Staff was friendly . . . Original
18 excellent . . . Very good diversity on the holes . . . They worked very
well with the existing terrain . . . Woods, water to come up with some real
challenges for all handicaps . . . Many fun holes . . . Too far from home
. . . I wish I could play more . . . Rolling . . . Some water holes . . .
Interesting . . . Great golf staff . . . Run like a private course for all players
. . . Excellent golf . . . Fun course . . . Well treated.

★★★ PEBBLE LAKE GOLF CLUB

PU—County 82 S., Fergus Falls (218)736-7404.
175 miles northwest of Minneapolis. **Holes:** 18. **Par:** 72/74.
Yards: 6,711/5,531. **Course rating:** 72.3/72.1. **Slope:** 128/126.
Opened: 1941. **Pace of Play rating:** 4:00. **Green fee:** $20.
Credit cards: MC, V. **Reduced fees:** Low season, Twilight, Seniors,
Juniors.
Caddies: No. **Golf carts:** $18 for 18 holes.

Discount golf packages: No. **Season:** April-Oct. **High:** June-Aug.
On-site lodging: No. **Rental clubs:** Yes.
Walking policy: Unrestricted walking. **Range:** Yes (grass).
To obtain tee times: Call up to one week in advance.
Subscriber comments: Challenging with many different shot choices . . .
Very tough, makes you think . . . Fun little course . . . Played in fall, nice
shape then . . . Hilly, beautiful . . . Older course . . . Mature trees . . .
Good shape . . . Straight ball will score.

★★★½ PERHAM LAKESIDE COUNTRY CLUB

PU—P.O. Box 313, Perham (218)346-6070.
20 miles southeast of Detroit Lakes. **Holes:** 18. **Par:** 72/72.
Yards: 6,575/5,312. **Course rating:** 72.5/71.1. **Slope:** 128/122.
Opened: 1938. **Pace of Play rating:** N/A. **Green fee:** $20.
Credit cards: MC, V. **Reduced fees:** Low season, Twilight.
Caddies: No. **Golf carts:** $19 for 18 holes.
Discount golf packages: No. **Season:** April-Nov. **High:** June-Aug.
On-site lodging: No. **Rental clubs:** Yes.
Walking policy: Unrestricted walking. **Range:** Yes (grass).
To obtain tee times: Call up to one week in advance.
Subscriber comments: Good course . . . Lots of trees . . . Tough but fair
. . . Not as easy as one would think . . . Beautiful with good combination
of water, sand, and choices . . . Nice rural course in resort area . . .
Relaxing family type . . . New nine is great.

★½ PEZHEKEE GOLF CLUB

R—2500 S. Lakeshore Dr., Glenwood (612)634-4501, (800)356-8654.
120 miles northwest of Minneapolis/St. Paul. **Holes:** 18. **Par:** 72/75.
Yards: 6,454/5,465. **Course rating:** 70.8/71.5. **Slope:** 119/122.
Opened: 1967. **Pace of Play rating:** 3:48. **Green fee:** $20/23.
Credit cards: MC, V. **Reduced fees:** Weekdays, Low season, Resort
guests, Twilight, Juniors.
Caddies: No. **Golf carts:** $10 for 18 holes.
Discount golf packages: Yes. **Season:** May-Oct. **High:** June-Sept.
On-site lodging: Yes. **Rental clubs:** Yes.
Walking policy: Unrestricted walking. **Range:** No.
To obtain tee times: Call in advance or walk on.
Subscriber comments: Has promise . . . Hilly, beautiful . . . New second
nine has character . . . Short but outstanding . . . Fun resort course . . .
Sporting and picturesque.

★★ PHALEN PARK GOLF COURSE

PU—1615 Phalen Dr., St.Paul (612)778-0413.
Holes: 18. **Par:** 70/71.
Yards: 6,101/5,439. **Course rating:** 68.7/70.7. **Slope:** 121/121.
Opened: 1920. **Pace of Play rating:** 4:00. **Green fee:** $19.
Credit cards: MC, V. **Reduced fees:** Twilight, Seniors, Juniors.
Caddies: No. **Golf carts:** $20 for 18 holes.
Discount golf packages: No. **Season:** March-Nov. **High:** June-Aug.
On-site lodging: No. **Rental clubs:** Yes.
Walking policy: Unrestricted walking. **Range:** Yes (grass).
To obtain tee times: Monday through Friday call one day in advance.
You can make tee time for Monday on Friday at 8 a.m. Nonresident can
call on Thursday at 6 a.m. for upcoming weekend.
Subscriber comments: Short, many doglegs . . . Fun but no pushover
. . . Very busy with smallish greens . . . Back nine more challenging . . .
Heavy play . . . Many retirees . . . Short course . . . Keep it straight and
you can really score . . . Friendly people and the best breakfast in town . . .
Old favorite . . . Learned golf here . . . Mature . . . Lots of oak trees . . .
Very busy . . . Fairly short . . . Course suffering from too much play.

★★ PHEASANT RUN GOLF CLUB

PU—10705 County Rd. 116, Rogers (612)428-8244.
20 miles northwest of Minneapolis. **Holes:** 18. **Par:** 71/72.
Yards: 6,400/5,200. **Course rating:** 69.9/68.7. **Slope:** 117/115.
Opened: 1988. **Pace of Play rating:** 4:15. **Green fee:** $14/20.
Credit cards: MC, V. **Reduced fees:** Weekdays, Low season, Twilight,
Seniors, Juniors.
Caddies: No. **Golf carts:** $20 for 18 holes.
Discount golf packages: No. **Season:** April–Nov. **High:** June–Sept.
On-site lodging: No. **Rental clubs:** Yes.
Walking policy: Unrestricted walking. **Range:** Yes (grass).
To obtain tee times: Call Tuesday for weekend times; Saturday for
weekdays.
Subscriber comments: Could use more sand . . . Open . . . Some hills
. . . Fairly easy . . . Need water on back nine . . . Newer . . . Wide open
. . . Nice rural course . . . Getting better every year . . . Needs another five
years maturity . . . Let it rip here, wide open course . . . Very friendly staff
that makes you feel at home . . . Confidence booster . . . Great staff . . .
Makes you feel they're glad you came . . . Course fun . . . Lots of straight
holes . . . Not much trouble . . . A well-kept confidence builder if you can
master the greens.

★★★½ PINE MEADOWS GOLF COURSE

PU—500 Golf Course Dr., Brainerd (218)829-5733, (800)368-2048.
120 miles northwest of Minneapolis/St. Paul. **Holes:** 18. **Par:** 72/74.
Yards: 6,200/5,538. **Course rating:** 70.7/72.7. **Slope:** 129/133.
Opened: N/A. **Pace of Play rating:** 4:00. **Green fee:** $23/26.
Credit cards: All major. **Reduced fees:** Weekdays, Low season, Resort
guests, Twilight, Seniors, Juniors.
Caddies: No. **Golf carts:** $11 for 18 holes.
Discount golf packages: Yes. **Season:** April–Oct. **High:** June–Aug.
On-site lodging: No. **Rental clubs:** Yes.
Walking policy: Unrestricted walking. **Range:** Yes (grass).
To obtain tee times: Call pro shop up to four days in advance.
Subscriber comments: Need good short game . . . Many improvements
last two years . . . Short but lots of trees and water . . . Lots of water . . .
This course will be sure to surprise . . . Watch out for the third hole from
the back tees . . . There is not a tougher par 4 around . . . Much improved
over last two years . . . Took a fairly easy course and made it a challenge
with pot bunkers, etc. . . . Very helpful, courteous staff . . . Must keep ball
in play.

★★★½ POKEGAMA GOLF CLUB

PU—3910 Golf Course Rd., Grand Rapids (218)326-3444.
4 miles west of Grand Rapids. **Holes:** 18. **Par:** 71/72.
Yards: 6,481/4,979. **Course rating:** 70.3/67.7. **Slope:** 121/116.
Opened: 1926. **Pace of Play rating:** 4:30. **Green fee:** $18/22.
Credit cards: MC, V. **Reduced fees:** Weekdays, Resort guests, Twilight,
Juniors.
Caddies: No. **Golf carts:** $18 for 18 holes.
Discount golf packages: No. **Season:** April–Oct. **High:** June–Aug.
On-site lodging: No. **Rental clubs:** Yes.
Walking policy: Unrestricted walking. **Range:** Yes (grass).
To obtain tee times: Call one week in advance.
Subscriber comments: One of the most beautiful and challenging I've
ever played . . . Very good small-town course . . . Good greens . . . Real
narrow but nice for price . . . Plush . . . As you can see, I love this course
. . . Nice country course . . . Fun layout . . . Good conditions . . . Tight
fairways . . . Small greens good shape . . . Nice views . . . Scenic layout
. . . Good for average golfer . . . Wide fairways . . . A fairly mature course
which is a fair test for average player.

PRAIRIE VIEW GOLF COURSE★
PU—Highway 266 N., Worthington (507)372-8670.
50 miles east of Sioux Falls. **Holes:** 18. **Par:** 71/71.
Yards: 6,366/5,103. **Course rating:** 69.9/68.3. **Slope:** 112/113.
Opened: 1983. **Pace of Play rating:** 4:00. **Green fee:** $13/16.
Credit cards: None. **Reduced fees:** Weekdays, Twilight.
Caddies: No. **Golf carts:** $8 for 18 holes.
Discount golf packages: No. **Season:** April–Oct. **High:** June–Aug.
On-site lodging: No. **Rental clubs:** Yes.
Walking policy: Unrestricted walking. **Range:** Yes (grass).
To obtain tee times: Call Thursday for weekend times.

PRINCETON GOLF CLUB★
SP—Golf Club Rd., Princeton (612)389-5109.
45 miles north of Minneapolis/St. Paul. **Holes:** 18. **Par:** 71/71.
Yards: 6,250/4,815. **Course rating:** 69.9/67.5. **Slope:** 117/112.
Opened: 1951. **Pace of Play rating:** 3:45. **Green fee:** $16/18.
Credit cards: MC, V, DISC. **Reduced fees:** Weekdays, Twilight,
Seniors, Juniors.
Caddies: No. **Golf carts:** $10 for 18 holes.
Discount golf packages: Yes. **Season:** April–Oct. **High:** June–Aug.
On-site lodging: No. **Rental clubs:** Yes.
Walking policy: Unrestricted walking. **Range:** Yes (grass).
To obtain tee times: Call five days in advance.

★★★½ PURPLE HAWK GOLF CLUB
SP—N. Hwy. 65, Cambridge (612)689-3800.
60 miles north of Minneapolis. **Holes:** 18. **Par:** 72/74.
Yards: 6,679/5,748. **Course rating:** 72.3/73.5. **Slope:** 132/131.
Opened: 1970. **Pace of Play rating:** 4:00. **Green fee:** $18/22.
Credit cards: MC, V, DISC. **Reduced fees:** Twilight, Seniors, Juniors.
Caddies: No. **Golf carts:** $22 for 18 holes.
Discount golf packages: No. **Season:** April–Oct. **High:** June–Aug.
On-site lodging: No. **Rental clubs:** Yes.
Walking policy: Unrestricted walking. **Range:** Yes (grass).
To obtain tee times: Call up to five days in advance.
Subscriber comments: Everything, I mean everything, is great . . .
Excellent course in rural area . . . Hidden gem . . . Would like to play more
often . . . A lot of new improvements . . . Beautiful . . . Good fairways
. . . Great greens . . . Keeps getting better and better . . . Best secret in
Twin Cities . . . Tough putting on very undulating greens . . . Small town
course always in great shape . . . Friendly staff . . . Greens always in great
shape . . . Mid-low handicapper . . . Staff was outstanding . . . Hour drive
from metro area . . . A sleeper . . . Long course . . . Hit all clubs . . . Fairly
open.

★★ RAMSEY GOLF CLUB
PU—R.R. No.1 Box 83, Austin (507)433-9098.
90 miles south of Minneapolis/St. Paul. **Holes:** 18. **Par:** 71/72.
Yards: 5,987/5,426. **Course rating:** 68.2/70.7. **Slope:** 120/117.
Opened: 1940. **Pace of Play rating:** 4:00. **Green fee:** $13/14.
Credit cards: None. **Reduced fees:** Low season.
Caddies: No. **Golf carts:** $16 for 18 holes.
Discount golf packages: Yes. **Season:** April–Nov. **High:** May–Sept.
On-site lodging: No. **Rental clubs:** Yes.
Walking policy: Unrestricted walking. **Range:** Yes (grass).
To obtain tee times: First come, first served. Cart reservations are
available.
Subscriber comments: Very short . . . Nice course . . . Great par 5s . . .
Good test of golf . . . Heavily used . . . Par 4s too short.

★½ RICH ACRES GOLF COURSE
PU—2201 E. 66th St., Richfield (612)861-9341.
10 miles of Minneapolis. **Holes:** 18. **Par:** 71/73.
Yards: 6,606/5,746. **Course rating:** 71.1/72.3. **Slope:** 116/119.
Opened: 1980. **Pace of Play rating:** 4:00-4:30. **Green fee:** $16/17.
Credit cards: MC, V. **Reduced fees:** Weekdays, Low season, Twilight,
Seniors, Juniors.
Caddies: No. **Golf carts:** $20 for 18 holes.
Discount golf packages: No. **Season:** April-Nov. **High:** April-Nov.
On-site lodging: No. **Rental clubs:** Yes.
Walking policy: Unrestricted walking. **Range:** Yes (grass).
To obtain tee times: Call (612)861-9345.
Subscriber comments: Flat . . . Close to Minneapolis/St. Paul airport . . .
Low jets add interest . . . Outstanding driving range . . . Easy course . . .
Easy to get on . . . Owned and operated by city of Richfield . . . Mature
course that is fairly open and not restricted . . . Well kept and managed . . .
Crowded on weekends . . . Always windy . . . Open course . . . Long . . .
Greens are its best defense.

★★ RICH SPRING GOLF COURSE
SP—17467 Fairway Circle, Cold Spring (612)685-8810.
20 miles southwest of St. Cloud. **Holes:** 18. **Par:** 72/72.
Yards: 6,542/5,347. **Course rating:** 69.7/70.0. **Slope:** 119/110.
Opened: 1962. **Pace of Play rating:** 4:00. **Green fee:** $15/17.
Credit cards: None. **Reduced fees:** Seniors.
Caddies: No. **Golf carts:** $10 for 18 holes.
Discount golf packages: No. **Season:** April-Oct. **High:** June-Aug.
On-site lodging: No. **Rental clubs:** Yes.
Walking policy: Unrestricted walking. **Range:** Yes (grass).
To obtain tee times: Call up to three days in advance.
Subscriber comments: Average track for average golfers . . . A spray
hitter's paradise . . . Very friendly staff . . . Uncrowded . . . Consistent
speed, but soft enough to hold the high approach shot . . . Just enjoy the
course . . . It's fun . . . Small town, but nice course . . . Excellent value.

RIDGEWOOD GOLF COURSE
PU—County Rd. 7, Longville (218)363-2444.
Call club for further information.
Subscriber comments: Front nine beautiful . . . Back nine still new . . .
Needs time . . . Newer course . . . Generally flat . . . Heavily wooded front
nine . . . Nice and tight . . . Some tricky holes . . . Second time better.

ROSE LAKE GOLF COURSE*
PU—R.R. No.2, Fairmont (507)235-5274.
Call club for further information.
Subscriber comments: Good condition . . . Nice variety of holes . . .
Good test for average golfer.

★★ RUM RIVER HILLS GOLF CLUB
PU—16659 St. Francis Blvd., Anoka (612)753-3339.
15 miles north of Minneapolis. **Holes:** 18. **Par:** 71/71.
Yards: 6,338/5,095. **Course rating:** 71.3/70.1. **Slope:** 122/119.
Opened: 1986. **Pace of Play rating:** 4:00. **Green fee:** $18/22.
Credit cards: MC, V. **Reduced fees:** Twilight, Seniors, Juniors.
Caddies: No. **Golf carts:** $22 for 18 holes.
Discount golf packages: Yes. **Season:** March-Nov. **High:** June-Aug.
On-site lodging: No. **Rental clubs:** Yes.
Walking policy: Unrestricted walking. **Range:** Yes (grass).
To obtain tee times: Call three days in advance.
Subscriber comments: Some very challenging holes . . . Nice course . . .

Ten to 12 years old . . . Need to be straight . . . Lots of water . . . Testy
. . . Water on the 14th hole . . . Opens early and stays open late . . . Tough
little course if you don't like water and fast greens . . . Play here . . .
Another fairly short, open course . . . Drove a couple of par 4s . . . Sneaky
good course . . . Hidden difficulty.

★★★ RUTTGER'S BAY LAKE LODGE
THE LAKES COURSE
R—Rte. 2, Deerwood (218)678-2885, (800)450-4545.
15 miles west of Brainerd. **Holes:** 18. **Par:** 72/72.
Yards: 6,750/5,100. **Course rating:** 72.5/69.3. **Slope:** 132/125.
Opened: 1992. **Pace of Play rating:** 4:00. **Green fee:** $24/40.
Credit cards: All major. **Reduced fees:** Low season, Resort guests,
Twilight.
Caddies: Yes. **Golf carts:** $14 for 18 holes.
Discount golf packages: Yes. **Season:** April-Oct. **High:** May-Sept.
On-site lodging: Yes. **Rental clubs:** Yes.
Walking policy: Unrestricaed walking. **Range:** Yes (grass).
To obtain tee times: Call 800 number anytime.
Subscriber comments: A mix and match from old course with new . . .
Some good holes and bad . . . Great course . . . Tough and beautiful . . .
Very challenging course for skilled players . . . When the new nine matures
this will really be a great course . . . More doglegs than a pound . . . Front
nine new but challenging . . . Back nine beautiful . . . Is better every year
. . . Very scenic . . . Lots of water and trees . . . Great 18th hole . . .
Another course that keeps improving . . . Very friendly staff.

ST. CHARLES GOLF CLUB★
SP—1920 Park Rd., St. Charles (507)932-5444.
20 miles east of Rochester. **Holes:** 18. **Par:** 71/71.
Yards: 6,347/5,877. **Course rating:** 69.3/72.6. **Slope:** 111/116.
Opened: 1991. **Pace of Play rating:** 4:00. **Green fee:** $16.
Credit cards: MC, V. **Reduced fees:** N/A.
Caddies: No. **Golf carts:** $17 for 18 holes.
Discount golf packages: No. **Season:** March-Nov. **High:** July-Aug.
On-site lodging: No. **Rental clubs:** Yes.
Walking policy: Unrestricted walking. **Range:** Yes (grass).
To obtain tee times: Tee times taken seven days in advance.

★★ SAWMILL GOLF CLUB
SP—11177 McKusick Rd., Stillwater (612)439-7862.
20 miles east of St. Paul. **Holes:** 18. **Par:** 70/71.
Yards: 6,300/5,300. **Course rating:** 70.2/69.5. **Slope:** 125/122.
Opened: 1983. **Pace of Play rating:** 4:00. **Green fee:** $18/20.
Credit cards: MC, V. **Reduced fees:** Low season, Twilight, Seniors,
Juniors.
Caddies: No. **Golf carts:** $10 for 18 holes.
Discount golf packages: No. **Season:** April-Nov. **High:** May-Sept.
On-site lodging: No. **Rental clubs:** Yes.
Walking policy: Unrestricted walking. **Range:** Yes (grass).
To obtain tee times: Call three days in advance.
Subscriber comments: Easy to get on . . . Great German food and drink
. . . Need compass to get from some greens to next tee . . . Balance of good
long and short holes . . . You must hit it straight . . . Keep in play as rough
is unplayable . . . Pretty course . . . Can play tough . . . Varied terrain . . .
Some areas wooded . . . Four practice greens . . . Three sand trap practice
areas . . . Only two or three houses in view of course . . . Gives impression
of being way out in the country . . . Give it a few more years . . . Big
numbers from the tips . . . On its way to outstanding if continues
improvements being made.

★★★ SOUTHERN HILLS GOLF CLUB

PU—18950 Chippendale Ave., Farmington (612)463-4653.
20 miles south of Minneapolis. **Holes:** 18. **Par:** 71/71.
Yards: 6,314/4,970. **Course rating:** 70.4/68.3. **Slope:** 123/116.
Opened: 1989. **Pace of Play rating:** 4:15. **Green fee:** $16/20.
Credit cards: MC, V. **Reduced fees:** Weekdays, Low season, Twilight,
Seniors, Juniors.
Caddies: No. **Golf carts:** $19 for 18 holes.
Discount golf packages: No. **Season:** April-Oct. **High:** June-Aug.
On-site lodging: No. **Rental clubs:** Yes.
Walking policy: Unrestricted walking. **Range:** Yes (grass).
To obtain tee times: Public may call one week in advance.
Subscriber comments: Open course with killer rough . . . Large greens
. . . Tough in wind . . . Some blind shots . . . Some tees and greens are too
close . . . Links course just planted 300 trees. Why? . . . Great for average
golfer . . . No. 5 is a bear . . . Great driving range . . . Good course to walk
. . . Beautiful course . . . Challenging but fair . . . Sneaky tough . . . Fine
course on unpromising terrain.

★★★½ STONEBROOKE GOLF CLUB

SP—2693 County Rd. 79, Shakopee (612)496-3171.
20 miles southwest of Minneapolis. **Holes:** 18. **Par:** 71/71.
Yards: 6,604/5,033. **Course rating:** 71.7/69.3. **Slope:** 133/118.
Opened: 1989. **Pace of Play rating:** 4:20. **Green fee:** $24/32.
Credit cards: MC, V. **Reduced fees:** N/A.
Caddies: No. **Golf carts:** $22 for 18 holes.
Discount golf packages: No. **Season:** April-Oct. **High:** June-July.
On-site lodging: No. **Rental clubs:** Yes.
Walking policy: Unrestricted walking. **Range:** Yes (grass).
To obtain tee times: Call three days in advance.
Subscriber comments: Short but nice . . . Challenging, lots of water . . .
You ride a ferry . . . 9th hole is a pretty hole . . . Boat ride on 8th is unique
. . . Short, target golf . . . A lot of water . . . Some long forced carries . . .
Good pro shop, bar, and staff . . . Nice layout and mix of holes . . . 16, 17,
18 a fun finish . . . A lot of doglegs . . . Good rangers . . . Short par 5s
make it fairly easy . . . Skipper always provides a cold one either way . . .
Pretty interesting layout but power lines a pain . . . Fun course . . . Large
undulating greens . . . Manicured nicely . . . Groomed all over . . . Plenty
of water . . . Strategic tee shots . . . Beautiful layout . . . Some great holes,
some just fair . . . As course matures it will be a great challenge.

★★★½ SUPERIOR NATIONAL AT LUTSEN GOLF COURSE

PU—P.O. Box 177, Lutsen (218)663-7195.
90 miles south of Duluth. **Holes:** 18. **Par:** 72/72.
Yards: 6,323/5,174. **Course rating:** 70.9/70.4. **Slope:** 130/123.
Opened: 1992. **Pace of Play rating:** 4:25. **Green fee:** $25/35.
Credit cards: MC, V. **Reduced fees:** Weekdays, Low season, Resort
guests, Twilight, Juniors.
Caddies: No. **Golf carts:** $25 for 18 holes.
Discount golf packages: Yes. **Season:** May-Oct. **High:** July-Sept.
On-site lodging: No. **Rental clubs:** Yes.
Walking policy: Unrestricted walking. **Range:** Yes (grass).
To obtain tee times: Call Wednesday for upcoming weekend. Must
guarantee with credit card.
Subscriber comments: Some great views . . . Be straight off tee . . . Very
lovely hills, water, trees . . . Worth the drive . . . Great view of Lake
Superior . . . A great getaway location . . . Beautiful, tight . . . Birch and
pine-lined holes . . . No. 17 is spectacular . . . Take a lot of balls and pack a
lunch . . . I saw one bear, five deer, and a timber wolf . . . Lost six balls . . .
A jewel in the north woods . . . Friendly staff . . . Bring your camera . . .
Well kept . . . Watch the weather . . . Can be windy and cool.

★★ THEODORE WIRTH GOLF COURSE

PU—1300 Theodore Wirth Pkwy., Minneapolis (612)522-4584.
Holes: 18. **Par:** 72/72.
Yards: 6,408/5,639. **Course rating:** 71.7/72.8. **Slope:** 129/123.
Opened: 1916. **Pace of Play rating:** 4:00-4:50. **Green fee:** $17.
Credit cards: None. **Reduced fees:** Weekdays, Low season, Twilight, Seniors, Juniors.
Caddies: No. **Golf carts:** $19 for 18 holes.
Discount golf packages: No. **Season:** April-Nov. **High:** June-Aug.
On-site lodging: No. **Rental clubs:** Yes.
Walking policy: Unrestricted walking. **Range:** No.
To obtain tee times: Call three days in advance.
Subscriber comments: Played revamped front nine. When mature will be excellent improvement . . . Small greens . . . Good casual play . . . Tough back nine . . . Contrasting nines . . . One hilly and one fairly flat . . . Congested on weekends . . . Tough city course in a spectacular wooded hill setting . . . Single can always play.

★★★ TIANNA COUNTRY CLUB

SP—PO Box 177, Walker (218)547-1712.
60 miles north of Brainerd. **Holes:** 18. **Par:** 72/74.
Yards: 6,550/5,681. **Course rating:** 70.7/73.5. **Slope:** 127/127.
Opened: 1925. **Pace of Play rating:** 4:00. **Green fee:** $20.
Credit cards: All major. **Reduced fees:** Twilight.
Caddies: No. **Golf carts:** $20 for 18 holes.
Discount golf packages: No. **Season:** May-Oct. **High:** June-Aug.
On-site lodging: No. **Rental clubs:** Yes.
Walking policy: Unrestricted walking. **Range:** Yes (grass).
To obtain tee times: Call pro shop.
Subscriber comments: Great views . . . 4½ hours from Minneapolis but worth the drive . . . Picturesque and hilly . . . Generous fairways . . . Very nice small town course . . . Always tee times available . . . Small greens . . . Hilly . . . Get fishing tips from staff . . . Excellent condition . . . Back nine flatter and not as interesting as front . . . Have to be familiar with course because of hidden green sites.

VALLEY GOLF ASSOCIATION★

SP—1800 21st St. N.W., East Grand Forks (218)773-1207.
5 miles northeast of Grand Forks, ND. **Holes:** 18. **Par:** 72/72.
Yards: 6,210/5,261. **Course rating:** 69.6/69.2. **Slope:** 118/112.
Opened: 1971. **Pace of Play rating:** 3:30. **Green fee:** $12/15.
Credit cards: MC, V. **Reduced fees:** Twilight, Seniors, Juniors.
Caddies: No. **Golf carts:** $15 for 18 holes.
Discount golf packages: No. **Season:** April-Oct. **High:** May-Aug.
On-site lodging: No. **Rental clubs:** Yes.
Walking policy: Unrestricted walking. **Range:** No.
To obtain tee times: First come, first served. Tee times for members only.

VIRGINIA GOLF COURSE★

PU—9th. St. N., Virginia (218)741-4366.
59 miles north of Duluth . **Holes:** 18. **Par:** 71/74.
Yards: 6,181/5,460. **Course rating:** 69.5/70.9. **Slope:** 118/129.
Opened: 1930. **Pace of Play rating:** 4:00-4:30. **Green fee:** $17.
Credit cards: None. **Reduced fees:** N/A.
Caddies: No. **Golf carts:** $19 for 18 holes.
Discount golf packages: No. **Season:** May-Oct. **High:** July-Aug.
On-site lodging: No. **Rental clubs:** Yes.
Walking policy: Unrestricted walking. **Range:** Yes (grass).
To obtain tee times: Call anytime.
Subscriber comments: Glad they've renovated . . . Front nine was closed but will be open in 1995.

MINNESOTA

★★★½ WEDGEWOOD GOLF CLUB
SP—9555 Wedgewood Dr., Woodbury (612)731-4779.
10 miles west of St. Paul. **Holes:** 18. **Par:** 72/72.
Yards: 6,717/5,267. **Course rating:** 72.3/70.1. **Slope:** 120/121.
Opened: 1985. **Pace of Play rating:** 4:15. **Green fee:** $25/30.
Credit cards: All major. **Reduced fees:** Weekdays, Twilight, Juniors.
Caddies: No. **Golf carts:** $13 for 18 holes.
Discount golf packages: No. **Season:** March-Nov. **High:** April-Sept.
On-site lodging: No. **Rental clubs:** Yes.
Walking policy: Unrestricted walking. **Range:** Yes (grass).
To obtain tee times: Credit card guarantee required with 24 hour
cancellation policy.
Subscriber comments: Best suited for long, low ball hitters . . . Wind is
always a factor . . . Fast play selectively enforced . . . Private course quality
. . . Good true test of skills . . . No gimmicks . . . Solid, challenging . . .
Three good finishing holes . . . Great Keep Pace program . . . Lightning
fast greens . . . Don't leave yourself above the hole. A must play from the
back tees . . . Good course with many O.B.s . . . Plays through housing
development.

WENDIGO GOLF COURSE★
PU—750 Golf Crest Dr., Grand Rapids (218)327-2211.
Holes: 18. **Par:** 72/72.
Yards: 6,756/5,151. **Course rating:** 72.0/70.0. **Slope:** 132/127.
Opened: 1995. **Pace of Play rating:** 4:00. **Green fee:** $20/22.
Credit cards: MC, V. **Reduced fees:** Twilight.
Caddies: No. **Golf carts:** $22 for 18 holes.
Discount golf packages: Yes. **Season:** April-Oct. **High:** June-Aug.
On-site lodging: No. **Rental clubs:** Yes.
Walking policy: Unrestricted walking. **Range:** Yes (grass).
To obtain tee times: Call three days in advance.

WHITEFISH GOLF CLUB★
SP—Rte. 1, Pequot Lakes (218)543-4900.
36 miles north of Brainerd. **Holes:** 18. **Par:** 72/72.
Yards: 6,407/5,682. **Course rating:** 70.4/72.6. **Slope:** 122/124.
Opened: 1966. **Pace of Play rating:** 4:30. **Green fee:** $22/29.
Credit cards: MC, V. **Reduced fees:** Weekdays, Low season, Resort
guests, Twilight.
Caddies: No. **Golf carts:** $22 for 18 holes.
Discount golf packages: No. **Season:** April-Oct. **High:** June-Aug.
On-site lodging: No. **Rental clubs:** Yes.
Walking policy: Unrestricted walking. **Range:** Yes (grass).
To obtain tee times: Call pro shop.

★★★½ WILDFLOWER AT FAIR HILLS
PU—R.R. 1, Detroit Lakes (218)439-3357, (800)323-2849.
45 miles east of Fargo, ND. **Holes:** 18. **Par:** 72/72.
Yards: 6,965/5,250. **Course rating:** 74.8/71.8. **Slope:** 136/124.
Opened: 1993. **Pace of Play rating:** 4:25. **Green fee:** $22/25.
Credit cards: All major. **Reduced fees:** Weekdays, Low season, Resort
guests, Twilight, Seniors, Juniors.
Caddies: No. **Golf carts:** $20 for 18 holes.
Discount golf packages: Yes. **Season:** May-first snow. **High:** June-Aug.
On-site lodging: Yes. **Rental clubs:** Yes.
Walking policy: Unrestricted walking. **Range:** Yes (grass).
To obtain tee times: Call one week in advance.
Subscriber comments: Challenging new course laid out in hilly county
should be good in a few years . . . Some unique holes . . . Long, fairly wide
open . . . New course needs maturing . . . Excellent driving range . . .
Long holes through prairie and woods . . . Fun to play.

GREAT VALUE

★★★★ **WILLINGER'S GOLF CLUB**
PU—6900 Canby Trail, Northfield (612)440-7000.
40 miles south of Minneapolis. **Holes:** 18. **Par:** 72/72.
Yards: 6,711/5,166. **Course rating:** 73.3/71.6. **Slope:** 140/130.
Opened: 1992. **Pace of Play rating:** 4:30. **Green fee:** $23/29.
Credit cards: MC, V. **Reduced fees:** Twilight, Seniors, Juniors.
Caddies: No. **Golf carts:** $22 for 18 holes.
Discount golf packages: No. **Season:** April-Oct. **High:** June-Aug.
On-site lodging: No. **Rental clubs:** Yes.
Walking policy: Unrestricted walking. **Range:** Yes (grass).
To obtain tee times: Call four days in advance for weekend times; seven
days in advance for weekday times.
Subscriber comments: Excellent for its age . . . Great use of its natural
surroundings . . . Very challenging with water and marsh on front nine . . .
Back nine is tree lined with some water . . . Shotmaker's course . . .
Excellent range and practice green for sand and chip shots . . . Super staff
. . . Very well maintained . . . Natural layout . . . Great par 3s . . . Great
improvement since '92 . . . A gem . . . A lot of surprises . . . Excellent
service . . . Great facilities . . . Target golf all the way . . . Suited for players
able to hit specific target with either woods or irons . . . This will be a
potential Tour site . . . Front Carolinas . . . Back Minnesota . . . Staff is
friendly . . . One of the ten courses I would play if I had a little time to live
. . . One of the best in the Twin Cities . . . Requires deft shot placement
. . . Need course knowledge to score . . . Play with someone experienced
there . . . Play three times, outstanding course and superb staff.

WILLMAR GOLF CLUB★
SP—1000 26th Ave. N.E., Willmar (612)235-1166.
80 miles west of Minneapolis. **Holes:** 18. **Par:** 72/73.
Yards: 9,317/5,271. **Course rating:** 70.8/70.9. **Slope:** 129/127.
Opened: 1930. **Pace of Play rating:** 4:00. **Green fee:** $20.
Credit cards: MC, V. **Reduced fees:** No.
Caddies: No. **Golf carts:** $20 for 18 holes.
Discount golf packages: Yes. **Season:** April-Oct. **High:** May-Aug.
On-site lodging: No. **Rental clubs:** Yes.
Walking policy: Unrestricted walking. **Range:** Yes (grass).
To obtain tee times: Call 24 hours in advance.

★★★ **WILLOW CREEK GOLF CLUB**
SP—1700 S.W. 48th St., Rochester (507)285-0305.
65 miles south of Minneapolis. **Holes:** 18. **Par:** 70/70.
Yards: 6,053/5,293. **Course rating:** 69.1/70.5. **Slope:** 117/121.
Opened: 1974. **Pace of Play rating:** 4:15. **Green fee:** $16.
Credit cards: MC, V. **Reduced fees:** No.
Caddies: No. **Golf carts:** $9 for 18 holes.
Discount golf packages: No. **Season:** March-Nov. **High:** June-Aug.
On-site lodging: No. **Rental clubs:** Yes.
Walking policy: Unrestricted walking. **Range:** Yes (grass).
To obtain tee times: Call seven days in advance.
Subscriber comments: Front nine flat . . . Back nine challenge . . .
Fantastic back nine . . . I plan on playing a lot more . . . Placement course
. . . Staff is nice . . . Mature course . . . Hills and flats, well mixed.

★ BELTON MUNICIPAL GOLF COURSE

PU—4200 Bong Ave., Belton (816)331-6777.
25 miles south of Kansas City. **Holes:** 18. **Par:** 72/73.
Yards: 6,855/5,500. **Course rating:** 73.1/71.0. **Slope:** 134/119.
Opened: 1965. **Pace of Play rating:** N/A. **Green fee:** $12/14.
Credit cards: None. **Reduced fees:** Seniors, Juniors.
Caddies: No. **Golf carts:** $21 for 18 holes.
Discount golf packages: No. **Season:** Year-round. **High:** May-Sept.
On-site lodging: No. **Rental clubs:** Yes.
Walking policy: Unrestricted walking. **Range:** Yes (grass).
To obtain tee times: Call Wednesday prior to weekend.
Subscriber comments: Good greens but course needs help in design . . .
Poorly conditioned and noisy . . . Old military course . . . Hard as a
runway in summer . . . Rough fairways, hard to walk, can get on anytime
. . . Staff good . . . Pace good . . . Play in spring or fall.

★★★½ BENT CREEK GOLF COURSE

SP—1 Bent Creek Dr., Jackson (314)243-6060.
100 miles south of St. Louis. **Holes:** 18. **Par:** 72/72.
Yards: 6,958/5,148. **Course rating:** 72.5/69.8. **Slope:** 136/112.
Opened: 1990. **Pace of Play rating:** 4:30. **Green fee:** 25/34.
Credit cards: MC, V, AMEX. **Reduced fees:** Weekdays, Low season,
Twilight, Seniors, Juniors.
Caddies: No. **Golf carts:** Included in Green Fee.
Discount golf packages: Yes. **Season:** Year-round. **High:** May-Sept.
On-site lodging: No. **Rental clubs:** Yes.
Walking policy: Walking at certain times. **Range:** Yes (grass).
To obtain tee times: Call seven days in advance.
Subscriber comments: Reasonable green fees, demanding greens that are
in excellent shape year round, courteous staff . . . Overbooked, pace was
very slow . . . You'll get to use all your clubs. Keep it straight or you'll also
use a lot of golf balls . . . Great holes, good condition, a "must play" . . .
Wonderful course and good staff with the exception that some of the
marshals need a course in courtesy . . . Tee shots, approach shots are well
laid out.

★★ BENT OAK GOLF CLUB

SP—1300 S.E. 30th, Oak Grove (816)690-3028.
20 miles east of Kansas City. **Holes:** 18. **Par:** 72/73.
Yards: 6,855/5,500. **Course rating:** 73.1/71.0. **Slope:** 134/119.
Opened: 1980. **Pace of Play rating:** 4:00. **Green fee:** $15/17.
Credit cards: MC, V. **Reduced fees:** Weekdays, Low season, Twilight,
Seniors, Juniors.
Caddies: No. **Golf carts:** $22 for 18 holes.
Discount golf packages: Yes. **Season:** Year-round. **High:** May-Sept.
On-site lodging: No. **Rental clubs:** Yes.
Walking policy: Unrestricted walking. **Range:** Yes (grass).
To obtain tee times: Call up to seven days in advance.
Subscriber comments: Nice staff, fairway watering has greatly improved
conditions . . . Some very good holes, overall a good place to play . . .
Good target golf without being too penal . . . Fast greens with more than
average contour . . . Greens usually in great shape. Condition of tee boxes
and fairways a problem.

★★ BILL AND PAYNE STEWART GOLF COURSE

PU—1825 E. Norton, Springfield (417)833-9962.
Holes: 18. **Par:** 70/72.
Yards: 6,043/5,693. **Course rating:** 68.4/71.3. **Slope:** 113/117.
Opened: 1947. **Pace of Play rating:** 4:00. **Green fee:** $10/11.
Credit cards: None. **Reduced fees:** Weekdays, Seniors, Juniors.
Caddies: No. **Golf carts:** $8 for 18 holes.
Discount golf packages: No. **Season:** Year-round. **High:** March-Oct.
On-site lodging: No. **Rental clubs:** Yes.
Walking policy: Unrestricted walking. **Range:** Yes (grass).

To obtain tee times: Call pro shop.
Also has 9-hole par-3 Oscar Blom Course.
Subscriber comments: Well-run public course, city owned, good tee times . . . Friendly staff, good conditions, easy layout, no water . . . Wide open, no rough, great confidence builder . . . Fun to play but slow on weekends because of crowds . . . Very slow play when I was there, 5½ hours.

★★ CARTHAGE MUNICIPAL GOLF COURSE

PU—2000 Oak St., Carthage (417)358-8724.
10 miles east of Joplin. **Holes:** 18. **Par:** 71/73.
Yards: 6,402/5,469. **Course rating:** 69.4/70.5. **Slope:** 124/115.
Opened: 1937. **Pace of Play rating:** 4:00. **Green fee:** 8/9.
Credit cards: None. **Reduced fees:** Weekdays, Juniors.
Caddies: No. **Golf carts:** $8 for 18 holes.
Discount golf packages: No. **Season:** Year-round. **High:** April-Aug.
On-site lodging: No. **Rental clubs:** Yes.
Walking policy: Unrestricted walking. **Range:** No.
To obtain tee times: Call or come in one week in advance.
Subscriber comments: Tight tree-lined fairways, small greens, for straight hitters . . . Plays long, no distance markers . . . People friendly and play usually fast . . . Dry thin grass cover in midsummer . . . Greens were hard to putt . . . Two different nines: one is old, wooded; the other, new and not wooded; in average condition.

CASSVILLE GOLF CLUB★

SP—Highway 112 S., Cassville (417)847-2399.
55 miles southwest of Springfield. **Holes:** 18. **Par:** 72/72.
Yards: 6,620/5,802. **Course rating:** 71.3/79.8. **Slope:** 118/117.
Opened: 1966. **Pace of Play rating:** 4:00. **Green fee:** $14/17.
Credit cards: None. **Reduced fees:** No.
Caddies: No. **Golf carts:** $N/A for 18 holes.
Discount golf packages: No. **Season:** Year-round. **High:** April-Oct.
On-site lodging: No. **Rental clubs:** Yes.
Walking policy: Unrestricted walking. **Range:** Yes (grass).
To obtain tee times: Call up to two weeks in advance.

★ CHAPEL WOODS GOLF COURSE

PU—800 Woods Chapel Rd., Lees Summit (816)795-8870
Call club for further information.
Subscriber comments: Course has some tough holes but condition is poor . . . Tends to be crowded . . . Very few fairway hazards, little sand . . . Poorly designed, but a tee time is always available . . . Very hard ground, no sprinklers on fairways . . . Fairly short, nice place to take children to learn to play . . . Needs bunkers and new clubhouse.

★★★ CHERRY HILLS GOLF CLUB

PU—16700 Manchester Rd., Grover (314)458-4113.
12 miles west of St. Louis. **Holes:** 18. **Par:** 71/72.
Yards: 6,450/5,491. **Course rating:** 71.1/72.6. **Slope:** 132/120.
Opened: 1964. **Pace of Play rating:** N/A. **Green fee:** $30/50.
Credit cards: MC, V. **Reduced fees:** Low season, Twilight, Seniors.
Caddies: No. **Golf carts:** Included in Green Fee.
Discount golf packages: No. **Season:** Year-round. **High:** May-Aug.
On-site lodging: No. **Rental clubs:** Yes.
Walking policy: Unrestricted walking. **Range:** Yes(grass).
To obtain tee times: Call up to seven days in advance. Weekend tee times require credit card to reserve.
Subscriber comments: Just plain straight holes, boring. Service good . . . Short course, staff not very helpful . . . Fairways in great shape, tee boxes OK, greens need a little work . . . Former private club . . . Overpriced for average golfer . . . Good course design, good clubhouse.

★½ CLAYCREST GOLF CLUB

SP—925 N. Lightburne, Liberty (816)781-6522.
15 miles north of Kansas City. **Holes:** 18. **Par:** 72/72.
Yards: 6,457/5,375. **Course rating:** 69.5/68.2. **Slope:** 115/109.
Opened: 1967. **Pace of Play rating:** 4:30. **Green fee:** $14/16.
Credit cards: MC, V. **Reduced fees:** Seniors.
Caddies: No. **Golf carts:** $24 for 18 holes.
Discount golf packages: No. **Season:** Year-round. **High:** April–Nov.
On-site lodging: No. **Rental clubs:** Yes.
Walking policy: Unrestricted walking. **Range:** Yes.
To obtain tee times: Call 7 a.m. Wednesday prior to weekend.
Subscriber comments: Needs watered fairways to be a good course . . .
All players treated A-1 . . . Greens good, fairway grass is thin, blind shots
. . . Slow play a problem . . . Interesting but too expensive . . . No beer
allowed.

★½ CRACKERNECK GOLF CLUB

PU—18800 E. 40 Hwy., Independence (816)795-7771.
Holes: 18. **Par:** 72/74.
Yards: 6,209/5,175. **Course rating:** 69.1/68.8. **Slope:** 114/108.
Opened: 1964. **Pace of Play rating:** N/A. **Green fee:** $13/15.
Credit cards: MC, V. **Reduced fees:** Weekdays, Low season, Twilight,
Seniors.
Caddies: No. **Golf carts:** $20 for 18 holes.
Discount golf packages: No. **Season:** Year-round. **High:** June–Aug.
On-site lodging: No. **Rental clubs:** Yes.
Walking policy: Unrestricted walking. **Range:** Yes.
To obtain tee times: First come, first served.
Subscriber comments: Poor layout, several tees too close to adjacent
fairways . . . Good walking course, long par 3s, poor maintenance . . .
Good service, well worth the money . . . Poorly managed, took 5½ hours
. . . Bad fairways, worse greens, lousy tee boxes . . . Good hot dogs.

★★★ CRYSTAL HIGHLANDS GOLF CLUB

PU—3030 U.S. Highway 61, Festus/Crystal City (314)931-3880.
30 miles south of St. Louis. **Holes:** 18. **Par:** 72/72.
Yards: 6,480/4,946. **Course rating:** 71.6/68.0. **Slope:** 135/109.
Opened: 1988. **Pace of Play rating:** 4:16. **Green fee:** $20/27.
Credit cards: MC, V. **Reduced fees:** Weekdays, Low season, Twilight,
Juniors.
Caddies: No. **Golf carts:** $10 for 18 holes.
Discount golf packages: No. **Season:** Year-round. **High:** April–Oct.
On-site lodging: No. **Rental clubs:** Yes.
Walking policy: Walking at certain times. **Range:** Yes (grass).
To obtain tee times: Call five days in advance.
Subscriber comments: Good course, have problem with greens in heat
. . . Lots of blind shots to greens . . . Service OK . . . Too crowded, some
good holes . . . Needs better cart paths . . . Rough cut too high . . . Snack
bar too slow on service, causes delays . . . A pleasure to play, clubhouse
overlooks course, great view . . . Too many tiered, gimmicky, funky
greens for serious golf . . . Beautifully manicured. Greens are very fast and
multilevel . . . Beautiful scenery of Ozark Valley, great condition in
spring/summer . . . Nice hilly track, best off back tees; some maintenance
problems; worth the trip; nice staff.

★½ DOGWOOD HILLS GOLF CLUB

R—State Rd. KK, Osage Beach (314)348-3153.
160 miles southwest of St. Louis. **Holes:** 18. **Par:** 71/71.
Yards: 6,105/4,604. **Course rating:** 68.9/65.6. **Slope:** 112/95.
Opened: 1963. **Pace of Play rating:** 4:00. **Green fee:** $36/42.
Credit cards: All major. **Reduced fees:** Weekdays, Low season, Resort
guests, Twilight, Seniors, Juniors.
Caddies: No. **Golf carts:** Included in Green Fee.
Discount golf packages: Yes. **Season:** March–Nov. **High:** Spring/Fall.

On-site lodging: Yes. **Rental clubs:** Yes.
Walking policy: Walking at certain times. **Range:** Yes (grass).
To obtain tee times: Call two weeks in advance.
Subscriber comments: Relatively easy layout . . . Good shape for high level of play . . . Well-maintained, good for tourist, treated well by staff . . . Course needs work. Greens burned out late summer . . . Resort course, good service, driving range, very good value . . . Wide open, small greens. Well-laced trees, has Bermuda fairways . . . Fairways too close together . . . Good package deals.

★★★½ EAGLE LAKE GOLF CLUB

SP—4215 Hunt Rd., Farmington (314)756-6660.
70 miles south of St. Louis. **Holes:** 18. **Par:** 72/72.
Yards: 7,093/5,648. **Course rating:** 73.9/N/A. **Slope:** 130/N/A.
Opened: 1993. **Pace of Play rating:** N/A. **Green fee:** $14/28.
Credit cards: All major. **Reduced fees:** Low season, Twilight, Seniors.
Caddies: No. **Golf carts:** $10 for 18 holes.
Discount golf packages: Yes. **Season:** Year-round. **High:** April-Oct.
On-site lodging: No. **Rental clubs:** Yes.
Walking policy: Walking at certain times. **Range:** Yes (grass).
To obtain tee times: Call seven days in advance.
Subscriber comments: Beautiful track, needs trees but has lush fairways and greens, fine clubhouse, good restaurant . . . Excellent, four-hour golf . . . Great condition, nice people, fun for all levels . . . Staff very accommodating . . . Long and interesting layout, great course for the money . . . Open course, well maintained . . . Going to be a great course; needs a couple of years to mature . . . Out of the way but enjoyable . . . Excellent amenities . . . Good weekend golf package.

(GREAT VALUE)

★★ EAGLE SPRINGS GOLF COURSE

PU—2575 Redman Rd., St. Louis (314)355-7277.
Holes: 18. **Par:** 72/72.
Yards: 6,679/5,533. **Course rating:** 71.4/72.3. **Slope:** 122/121.
Opened: 1989. **Pace of Play rating:** N/A. **Green fee:** $19/25.
Credit cards: MC, V. **Reduced fees:** Weekdays, Low season, Seniors, Juniors.
Caddies: No. **Golf carts:** $10 for 18 holes.
Discount golf packages: No. **Season:** Year-round. **High:** May-Sept.
On-site lodging: No. **Rental clubs:** Yes.
Walking policy: Unrestricted walking. **Range:** Yes (grass).
To obtain tee times: Call for weekends only.
Also has 9-hole par-3 course.
Subscriber comments: Nice course, good service . . . Nice layout, treated nicely at clubhouse . . . You can walk 18 in the morning in under four hours . . . Just a nice course to play, good service and treatment . . . Friendly staff and marshals . . . Sometimes slow but they make a good effort to improve pace . . . Poor rough, short, few bunkers, good greens, always crowded . . . Give it a few more years . . . This course suffers from layout and maintenance.

★★½ EXCELSIOR SPRINGS GOLF CLUB

PU—1201 E. Golf Hill Dr., Excelsior Springs (816)630-3731.
28 miles northeast of Kansas City. **Holes:** 18. **Par:** 72/72.
Yards: 6,650/5,450. **Course rating:** 69.5/67.9. **Slope:** 116/110.
Opened: 1915. **Pace of Play rating:** 4:30. **Green fee:** $14/16.
Credit cards: None. **Reduced fees:** Weekdays, Twilight.
Caddies: No. **Golf carts:** $9 for 18 holes.
Discount golf packages: No. **Season:** Feb-Dec. **High:** May-Sept.
On-site lodging: No. **Rental clubs:** No.
Walking policy: Unrestricted walking. **Range:** No.
To obtain tee times: Call on Monday prior to the weekend of play. Weekends and holiday tee times only.

Subscriber comments: Challenging, inexpensive, friendly . . . All services excellent . . . Country club allows walk-ons . . . One of oldest west of Mississippi River . . . Well maintained . . . Enjoyable if you like unfairly fast greens . . . Open course, little sand, new fairway watering system . . . Very long with fast greens.

★★ FAIRVIEW GOLF COURSE
PU—33rd and Pacific Sts., St. Joseph (816)364-9055.
Call club for further information.
Subscriber comments: Great course for the amount of play it gets . . . Too much slow play . . . Good staff, well kept . . . Old course, hills and large trees . . . City owned, maintenance average.

★½ FOREST PARK GOLF COURSE
PU—5591 Grand Dr., St. Louis (314)367-1337.
Call club for further information.
Subscriber comments: Great design, horrible shape . . . Never had sufficient maintenance . . . Overplayed, due to location and low rates for seniors on weekdays . . . Old city muny built in 1912 . . . Fun to play. Problem with picnickers . . . Too crowded and tee times aren't spaced out . . . Weeds in fairways . . . Great layout and price but needs better maintenance . . . Fun layout, five to six hour rounds, poor service (Don't think they ever heard of a marshal) . . . Slowest play ever.

★★ AL GUSTIN GOLF CLUB
PU—Stadium Blvd., Columbia (314)882-6016.
Call club for further information.
Subscriber comments: Not well maintained. Poor clubhouse . . . Very small greens are in great condition for amount of play, staff excellent . . . Target course . . . Needs work, fun, could drive 12 holes . . . Not a bad layout. Condition of fairway and rough poor . . . Slow on weekends . . . Very hilly, walking not recommended for weak of heart.

HAWK RIDGE GOLF CLUB★
PU—18 Hawk Ridge Dr., Lake St. Louis (314)516-2828.
40 miles west of St. Louis. **Holes:** 18. **Par:** 72/72.
Yards: 6,619/4,883. **Course rating:** 70.8/67.2. **Slope:** 127/105.
Opened: 1995. **Pace of Play rating:** 4:20. **Green fee:** $23/30.
Credit cards: MC, V. **Reduced fees:** Weekdays, Twilight, Juniors.
Caddies: No. **Golf carts:** $11 for 18 holes.
Discount golf packages: Yes. **Season:** Year-round. **High:** April-Oct.
On-site lodging: No. **Rental clubs:** Yes.
Walking policy: Walking at certain times. **Range:** Yes (grass).
To obtain tee times Call one week in advance.

★★½ HIDDEN VALLEY GOLF LINKS
PU—Rte. 1, Clever (417)743-2860.
18 miles southwest of Springfield. **Holes:** 18. **Par:** 73/75.
Yards: 6,611/5,288. **Course rating:** 71.9/N/A. **Slope:** 118/N/A.
Opened: 1975. **Pace of Play rating:** 4:00. **Green fee:** $10/13.
Credit cards: MC, V. **Reduced fees:** Seniors.
Caddies: No. **Golf carts:** $8 for 18 holes.
Discount golf packages: No. **Season:** Year-round. **High:** May-Sept.
On-site lodging: No. **Rental clubs:** Yes.
Walking policy: Unrestricted walking. **Range:** No.
To obtain tee times: Call Monday for upcoming weekend.
Subscriber comments: Secluded, excellent greens, great layout, water, sand, challenging . . . Tough to walk, killer in summer heat, gimmicky in places . . . Lots of water and forest land . . . Friendly owners . . . Wide open with lots of newly planted trees . . . Interesting course, longish but fair, can be slow . . . Beautiful river valley setting; challenging, wooded course.

★★ HODGE PARK GOLF COURSE
PU—7000 N.E. Barry Rd., Kansas City (816)781-4152.
Holes: 18. **Par:** 71/71.
Yards: 6,181/5,707. **Course rating:** N/A. **Slope:** 117/110.
Opened: N/A. **Pace of Play rating:** N/A. **Green fee:** $N/A.
Credit cards: V. **Reduced fees:** Twilight.
Caddies: No. **Golf carts:** $N/A for 18 holes.
Discount golf packages: No. **Season:** Year-round. **High:** April-Oct.
On-site lodging: No. **Rental clubs:** N/A.
Walking policy: N/A. **Range:** Yes.
Subscriber comments: Nice fairway hazards, nice greens . . . Takes too long per round, crowded tee times . . . Course not well marked . . . Heavily played, short course; a seniors' favorite, easy to walk.

★★★ HONEY CREEK GOLF CLUB
PU—R.R. 1, Aurora (417)678-3353.
28 miles southwest of Springfield. **Holes:** 18. **Par:** 71/79.
Yards: 6,732/5,972. **Course rating:** 71.9/N/A. **Slope:** 118/N/A.
Opened: 1932. **Pace of Play rating:** N/A. **Green fee:** $12/15.
Credit cards: MC, V, DISC. **Reduced fees:** No.
Caddies: No. **Golf carts:** $17 for 18 holes.
Discount golf packages: No. **Season:** Year-round. **High:** April-Oct.
On-site lodging: No. **Rental clubs:** Yes.
Walking policy: Unrestricted walking. **Range:** Yes (grass).
To obtain tee times: Call Wednesday for weekends.
Subscriber comments: Poorly designed, good greens, courtesy treatment . . . Outstanding service, poor carts . . . Best bent grass greens I've ever played . . . Front nine is very old, designed by Horton Smith. Course offers everything. Water, traps, creeks, tree lined narrow fairways . . . Great little resort, best value at Lake of Ozarks . . . Homemade brownies and deli sandwiches are legendary.

★½ HORTON SMITH GOLF COURSE
PU—2409 S. Scenic, Springfield (417)889-7510.
Holes: 18. **Par:** 70/71.
Yards: 6,317/5,199. **Course rating:** 69.5/68.5. **Slope:** 103/101.
Opened: 1962. **Pace of Play rating:** N/A. **Green fee:** $8/11.
Credit cards: MC, V. **Reduced fees:** Weekdays, Seniors, Juniors.
Caddies: No. **Golf carts:** $8 for 18 holes.
Discount golf packages: No. **Season:** Year-round. **High:** May-Sept.
On-site lodging: No. **Rental clubs:** Yes.
Walking policy: Unrestricted walking. **Range:** Yes (grass).
To obtain tee times: Call pro shop.
Subscriber comments: Improving each year, fine maintenance . . . Rough fairways, small greens, easy to walk, high handicappers' course . . . Fun to play but slow on weekends because of crowds . . . Renovated and rough but much improved.

★★★ INNSBROOK ESTATES GOLF CLUB
R—1 Innisbrook Estates Dr., Wright City (314)745-3000.
Call club for further information.
Subscriber comments: Great course, staff and course conditions very good . . . Costs more to play in p.m. than in a.m . . . .Great winter course . . . Some tough, beautiful holes . . . Watch for deer on fairways . . . Great golf, great people, great challenge, great price . . . Great varied layout . . . Condition impeccable . . . Nice course, can get crowded . . . Good lodging, dining, and conference facilities available . . . Food and beverages expensive.

★★½ KIRKSVILLE COUNTRY CLUB
SP—S. Highway 63, Kirksville (816)665-5335.
85 miles north of Columbia. **Holes:** 18. **Par:** 71/71.
Yards: 6,418/5,802. **Course rating:** 70.9/71.6. **Slope:** 118/114.
Opened: 1921. **Pace of Play rating:** 4:15. **Green fee:** $14/18.

Credit cards: MC, V, DISC. **Reduced fees:** No.
Caddies: No. **Golf carts:** $16 for 18 holes.
Discount golf packages: No. **Season:** March-Dec. **High:** June-Aug.
On-site lodging: No. **Rental clubs:** Yes.
Walking policy: Unrestricted walking. **Range:** Yes (grass).
To obtain tee times: Nonmembers first come, first served.
Subscriber comments: Wide open course, good condition in summer, watered fairways . . . Has some great holes . . . Good staff and fast rounds. Excellent condition . . . Long and short holes, greens above average . . . Nice rolling layout . . . Nice people.

★★★ LAKE VALLEY GOLF CLUB

PU—Lake Rd. 54-79, Camdenton (314)346-7218.
90 miles northeast of Springfield. **Holes:** 18. **Par:** 72/74.
Yards: 6,430/5,320. **Course rating:** 71.1/70.5. **Slope:** 121/118.
Opened: 1968. **Pace of Play rating:** 4:30. **Green fee:** $25/43.
Credit cards: MC, V. **Reduced fees:** Low season, Resort guests, Twilight, Juniors.
Caddies: No. **Golf carts:** $N/A for 18 holes.
Discount golf packages: Yes. **Season:** Year-round. **High:** April-Oct.
On-site lodging: No. **Rental clubs:** Yes.
Walking policy: Walking at certain times. **Range:** Yes (grass).
To obtain tee times: Call seven days in advance.
Subscriber comments: Good value, not crowded, well-kept . . . Very good staff, can be difficult to get a tee time in the busy months . . . Resort area course . . . Good value and nice layout . . . Second nine opened too early, fairways thin . . . Greens very good all year . . . Bermuda fairways are excellent . . . Very good condition . . . Great fairways and greens.

LOMA LINDA GOLF CLUB

PU—Rte. 5, Joplin (417)781-2620.
Call club for further information.
★★½ NORTH COURSE

Subscriber comments: Could be a great course, needs some TLC . . . Tough to walk, long and hilly . . . Service excellent . . . Not as well kept as it could be, but much fun . . . Great course with terrific package plans . . . Great place to stay.
★½ SOUTH COURSE

Subscriber comments: New course getting better with age, sparse amenities . . . Ball eater . . . New course, fairways rough, small greens . . . Fees too high for course . . . Hilly layout . . . Very interesting; good facilities.

★★★ LONGVIEW LAKE GOLF COURSE

PU—1100 View High Dr., Kansas City (816)761-9445.
Holes: 18. **Par:** 72/72.
Yards: 6,835/5,534. **Course rating:** 71.9/70.8. **Slope:** 121/113.
Opened: 1986. **Pace of Play rating:** 4:30. **Green fee:** $12/16.
Credit cards: MC, V. **Reduced fees:** Weekdays, Seniors, Juniors.
Caddies: No. **Golf carts:** $22 for 18 holes.
Discount golf packages: No. **Season:** Year-round. **High:** May-Aug.
On-site lodging: No. **Rental clubs:** Yes.
Walking policy: Unrestricted walking. **Range:** Yes (grass).
To obtain tee times: Call seven days in advance.
Also has 9-hole par-3 course.
Subscriber comments: Normally in good shape, hard to get tee times . . . Good layout with zoysia fairways; greens need work . . . Well maintained; nice clubhouse; fair prices . . . Attractive links-type layout OK for walking . . . Pleasant staff. Service good. Pace medium . . . Would be outstanding if greens were fixed . . . Lots of potential . . . Poor system for getting tee times . . . Pro shop and snack bar poor.

MARRIOTT'S TAN-TAR—A RESORT
★★★½ THE OAKS COURSE
R—State Rd. KK, Osage Beach (314)348-8521, (800)826-8272.
45 miles west of Jefferson City. **Holes:** 18. **Par:** 71/70.
Yards: 6,442/3,943. **Course rating:** 72.1/62.5. **Slope:** 143/103.
Opened: 1980. **Pace of Play rating:** 4:30. **Green fee:** $49/60.
Credit cards: All major. **Reduced fees:** Weekdays, Low season, Twilight.
Caddies: No. **Golf carts:** Included in Green Fee.
Discount golf packages: Yes. **Season:** Year-round. **High:** May-Oct.
On-site lodging: Yes. **Rental clubs:** Yes.
Walking policy: Mandatory cart. **Range:** Yes (grass).
To obtain tee times: Members and hotel guests call up to 30 days in
advance. Public call 14 days in advance.
Also has 9-hole par-35 Hidden Lakes Course.
Subscriber comments: Don't ever stray from cart path or the "police"
will get you . . . Hills, woods, hazards, course well-tended . . .
Overcrowded, six-hour rounds are common . . . Great shape in July, which
in Missouri is saying something . . . Treated like it was a private club . . .
Waterfall at 18th a perfect ending . . . Only flaw is too many layup holes
. . . Great staff, good food . . . Lovely.

★½ MINOR PARK GOLF CLUB
PU—11215 Holmes Rd., Kansas City (816)942-4033.
Call club for further information.
Subscriber comments: Beautiful scenery including beverage cart driver;
courteous staff with tee times always pretty much on time . . . Nice for
senior players to walk . . . Short, boring course, five-plus hours minimum
. . . Short, flat layout, good beginner's course, not much trouble . . . Well
taken care of . . . Often crowded.

MISSOURI BLUFFS GOLF CLUB★
PU—18 Research Park Circle, St. Charles (314)939-6494.
20 miles west of St. Louis. **Holes:** 18. **Par:** 71/71.
Yards: 7,047/5,197. **Course rating:** 74.4/69.2. **Slope:** 140/115.
Opened: 1994. **Pace of Play rating:** 4:00. **Green fee:** $75/100.
Credit cards: MC, V. **Reduced fees:** Twilight.
Caddies: No. **Golf carts:** Included in Green Fee.
Discount golf packages: No. **Season:** March-Nov. **High:** May-Oct.
On-site lodging: No. **Rental clubs:** Yes.
Walking policy: Unrestricted walking. **Range:** Yes (grass)
To obtain tee times: Call four days in advance.

★½ NEW MELLE LAKES GOLF CLUB
PU—404 Foristel Rd., New Melle (314)398-4653.
30 miles west of St. Louis. **Holes:** 18. **Par:** 71/71.
Yards: 6,348/4,905. **Course rating:** 69.8/68.6. **Slope:** 126/120.
Opened: 1993. **Pace of Play rating:** 4:30. **Green fee:** $28/38.
Credit cards: All major. **Reduced fees:** Twilight, Seniors, Juniors.
Caddies: No. **Golf carts:** Included in Green Fee.
Discount golf packages: No. **Season:** Year-round. **High:** April-Oct.
On-site lodging: No. **Rental clubs:** Yes.
Walking policy: Walking at certain times. **Range:** Yes(grass).
To obtain tee times: Call or come in seven days in advance.
Subscriber comments: Staff and course condition very good . . . Good
food . . . Owners seem committed to making it a nice course . . . Straight
hitters only, service and pace OK . . . Good layout, friendly . . . Too many
blind shots . . . Excellent facilities . . . Great sporty layout, tight fairways,
postage stamp greens.

★½ NORMANDIE PARK GOLF CLUB
PU—7605 St. Charles Rock Rd., St. Louis (314)862-4884.
Holes: 18. **Par:** 71/77.
Yards: 6,534/5,943. **Course rating:** 71.1/73.1. **Slope:** 120/133.

Opened: 1901. **Pace of Play rating:** 4:30. **Green fee:** $22/30.
Credit cards: MC, V. **Reduced fees:** Weekdays, Low season, Seniors, Juniors.
Caddies: No. **Golf carts:** $20 for 18 holes.
Discount golf packages: No. **Season:** Year-round. **High:** April-Oct.
On-site lodging: No. **Rental clubs:** Yes.
Walking policy: Unrestricted walking. **Range:** Yes (grass).
To obtain tee times: Call anytime.
Subscriber comments: Terrific layout but very poorly maintained . . .
Slow play, very congenial staff, needs renovation of clubhouse . . . Old
course in bad shape . . . Great layout, poor conditions all year, poorly
marshaled, slow pace . . . A great old course that has fallen on hard times
. . . Terrible course in summer, no water for fairways.

NORTH PORT NATIONAL GOLF CLUB
★★★½ **OSAGE COURSE**
R—Osage Hills Rd., Lake Ozark (314)365-1100.
175 miles southwest of St. Louis. **Holes:** 18. **Par:** 72/72.
Yards: 7,150/5,252. **Course rating:** 75.6/70.5. **Slope:** 145/122.
Opened: 1992. **Pace of Play rating:** 4:30. **Green fee:** $50/52.
Credit cards: MC, V, AMEX. **Reduced fees:** Weekdays, Low season,
Resort guests, Twilight, Seniors, Juniors.
Caddies: No. **Golf carts:** Included in Green Fee.
Discount golf packages: Yes. **Season:** Year-round. **High:** April-Oct.
On-site lodging: Yes. **Rental clubs:** Yes.
Walking policy: Mandatory cart. **Range:** Yes (grass).
To obtain tee times: Call up to two weeks in advance.
Subscriber comments: Great course, great condition, excellent value . . .
Design great, played late in season, maintenance not up to par . . . Low
key, friendly service . . . Very crowded . . . Scenery is fantastic on the front
nine . . . A little pricey . . . The course was in very good condition . . .
Service needs improving . . . A lot of hills, some real tough holes, great
condition . . . Tough Arnold Palmer course, found 25 balls . . . Great staff,
good food.

★ PADDOCK COUNTRY CLUB
PU—15 50 Country Club Lane, Florissant (314)741-4334.
15 miles north of St. Louis. **Holes:** 18. **Par:** 72/73.
Yards: 6,493/5,593. **Course rating:** 69.9/71.0. **Slope:** 120/114.
Opened: 1964. **Pace of Play rating:** 4:30. **Green fee:** $16/18.
Credit cards: MC, V. **Reduced fees:** Seniors, Juniors.
Caddies: No. **Golf carts:** $10 for 18 holes.
Discount golf packages: Yes. **Season:** March-Dec. **High:** April-Oct.
On-site lodging: No. **Rental clubs:** Yes.
Walking policy: Unrestricted walking. **Range:** Yes (grass).
To obtain tee times: Call seven days in advance.
Subscriber comments: Lacking in general maintenance, tee boxes need
work, landing areas and greens in good condition, rest of golf course is poor
. . . Don't see some greens until second shot . . . Tough course with lots of
sand . . . No problem with OB . . . Greens are always perfect, rough and
tee boxes need improvement.

PARADISE POINTE GOLF CLUB
PU—18212 Golf Course Rd., Smithville (816)532-4100.
25 miles north of Kansas City. **Green fee:** $15/20.
Credit cards: MC, V, AMEX. **Reduced fees:** Weekdays, Low season,
Seniors.
Caddies: No. **Golf carts:** $11 for 18 holes.
Discount golf packages: No. **Season:** Year-round. **High:** May-Oct.
On-site lodging: No. **Rental clubs:** Yes.
Walking policy: Unrestricted walking. **Range:** Yes (grass).
To obtain tee times: Weekend tee times required. Call Tuesday for
upcoming weekend.

MISSOURI

★★★ OUTLAW COURSE
Holes: 18. **Par:** 72/72.
Yards: 6,988/5,322. **Course rating:** 73.8/67.0. **Slope:** 138/118.
Opened: 1994. **Pace of Play rating:** N/A.
Subscriber comments: Course set up as a lakeside links style . . . Fun to play . . . Great course, great views, a truly outstanding course . . . Good design, pace real good, excellent staff . . . Conditions good all year, slow on weekends . . . Will be among the best when it matures . . . Next to a lake, pretty course, geese droppings are a real problem.

★★½ POSSE COURSE
Holes: 18. **Par:** 72/73.
Yards: 6,663/5,600. **Course rating:** 71.8/70.0. **Slope:** 125/115.
Opened: 1982. **Pace of Play rating:** N/A.
Subscriber comments: Resembles an oceanside course . . . Windy and difficult to play but enjoyable . . . Lots of sand . . . Good course for all levels of players; excellent value but crowded and slow play . . . Well marshaled . . . Staff is excellent, very polite and polished in their jobs . . . Overcrowded.

★ PARADISE VALLEY GOLF AND COUNTRY CLUB
PU—Old Hillsboro Rd., St. Louis County (314)225-5157.
19 miles west of St. Louis. **Holes:** 18. **Par:** 70/72.
Yards: 6,185/5,102. **Course rating:** 68.2/67.6. **Slope:** 112/101.
Opened: 1965. **Pace of Play rating:** N/A. **Green fee:** $30/34.
Credit cards: MC, V, AMEX. **Reduced fees:** Weekdays, Juniors.
Caddies: No. **Golf carts:** Included in Green Fee.
Discount golf packages: No. **Season:** Year-round. **High:** May-Sept.
On-site lodging: No. **Rental clubs:** Yes.
Walking policy: Walking at certain times. **Range:** Yes (grass).
To obtain tee times: Call pro shop.
Subscriber comments: Overcrowded, poor layout, very short, no challenge . . . Fairways and greens need attention . . . Excellent practice facility . . . Extremely short, listed yardage is greatly exaggerated . . . Took six hours to play 18 . . . Needs more marshaling to control goof-offs . . . Staff friendly.

FRANK E. PETERS MUNICIPAL GOLF COURSE★
PU—Rte. 3, Box 261-A, Nevada (417)448-2750.
100 miles south of Kansas City. **Holes:** 18. **Par:** 72/72.
Yards: 6,512/5,159. **Course rating:** 70.1/68.2. **Slope:** 109/110.
Opened: 1978. **Pace of Play rating:** N/A. **Green fee:** $8/10.
Credit cards: MC, V. **Reduced fees:** Weekdays, Twilight.
Caddies: No. **Golf carts:** $N/A for 18 holes.
Discount golf packages: No. **Season:** Year-round. **High:** April-Sept.
On-site lodging: No. **Rental clubs:** Yes.
Walking policy: Unrestricted walking. **Range:** Yes (grass).
To obtain tee times: First come, first served.

★★★ POINTE ROYALE GOLF CLUB
SP—1000 Pointe Royale Dr., Branson (417)334-4477.
Call club for further information.
Subscriber comments: Would not go to Branson just to play this course . . . Poorly designed . . . Great layout, good condition, nice course . . . Played here first week of April, practically had the course to ourselves . . . Wonderful layout for a short resort course . . . Difficult course, overpriced, rocky fairways . . . Maintenance needed . . . Staff very good.

★★★½ QUAIL CREEK GOLF CLUB
PU—6022 Wells Rd., St. Louis (314)487-1988.
Holes: 18. **Par:** 72/72.
Yards: 6,984/5,244. **Course rating:** N/A. **Slope:** 141/109.
Opened: N/A. **Pace of Play rating:** N/A. **Green fee:** $N/A.
Credit cards: MC, V, AMEX. **Reduced fees:** Weekdays, Low season, Twilight.

Caddies: No. **Golf carts:** $N/A for 18 holes.
Discount golf packages: No. **Season:** Year-round. **High:** April-Oct.
On-site lodging: No. **Rental clubs:** No.
Walking policy: N/A. **Range:** Yes.
Subscriber comments: Takes too long to play . . . Best of everything in golf . . . Marshals work well . . . Little too tight . . . A great public golf course in all respects, designed by Hale Irwin . . . A little pricey . . . Will not let you walk on weekends before 2 p.m. . . . Staff, service good; pace of play poor.

★½ RAINTREE GOLF CLUB
SP—5925 Plantation Dr., Hillsboro (314)797-4020.
45 miles south of St. Louis. **Holes:** 18. **Par:** 72/71.
Yards: 6,125/4,959. **Course rating:** 73.1/69.4. **Slope:** 121/119.
Opened: 1980. **Pace of Play rating:** 4:30. **Green fee:** $15/21.
Credit cards: MC, V. **Reduced fees:** Weekdays, Low season, Juniors.
Caddies: No. **Golf carts:** $10 for 18 holes.
Discount golf packages: No. **Season:** Year-round. **High:** May-Sept.
On-site lodging: No. **Rental clubs:** Yes.
Walking policy: Walking at certain times. **Range:** Yes (grass).
To obtain tee times: Call or come in four days to one week in advance.
Subscriber comments: Narrow, hilly fairways, woods all sides . . .
Seems like every shot is from a sidehill lie . . . Fast, sloping greens, courteous staff, blind par 3s . . . Course layout terrible, good shots shouldn't be penalized by poorly designed fairway . . . Need one leg shorter (or longer) than other . . . No fun . . . You've got to see to believe . . . Two blind par 3s . . . Service good, pace OK.

★½ RIVER OAKS GOLF CLUB
PU—14204 St. Andrews Rd., Grandview (816)966-8111.
Call club for further information.
Subscriber comments: Short course, long distance between green and next tee box . . . Never a problem with tee times . . . Staff friendly . . . Great layout but too much play . . . Tough to walk.

RIVERSIDE GOLF COURSE★
PU—1210 Larkin Williams, Fenton (314)343-6333.
10 miles southwest of St. Louis. **Holes:** 18. **Par:** 69/70.
Yards: 5,800/5,400. **Course rating:** 67.5/67.5. **Slope:** 99/99.
Opened: 1964. **Pace of Play rating:** 4:30. **Green fee:** $19/22.
Credit cards: MC, V. **Reduced fees:** Weekdays, Low season, Twilight, Seniors, Juniors.
Caddies: No. **Golf carts:** $20 for 18 holes.
Discount golf packages: No. **Season:** Year-round. **High:** April-Oct.
On-site lodging: No. **Rental clubs:** No.
Walking policy: Unrestricted walking. **Range:** No.
To obtain tee times: First come, first served.
Also has 9-hole par-3 course.

ROYAL MEADOWS GOLF COURSE
★ WEST/EAST COURSE
PU—10501 E. 47th, Kansas City (816)353-1323.
Holes: 18. **Par:** 73.
Yards: 5,994/5,176. **Course rating:** 68.3/68.0. **Slope:** 110/113.
Opened: 1930. **Pace of Play rating:** N/A. **Green fee:** $13/16.
Credit cards: MC, V. **Reduced fees:** Weekdays, Low season, Twilight, Seniors, Juniors.
Caddies: No. **Golf carts:** $N/A for 18 holes.
Discount golf packages: No. **Season:** Year-round. **High:** March-Oct.
On-site lodging: No. **Rental clubs:** Yes.
Walking policy: Unrestricted walking. **Range:** No.
To obtain tee times: Call five days in advance.
Also has 9-hole North Course.

Subscriber comments: Course needs attention, pace slow, service OK
. . . Overcrowded on weekends . . . Not enough time between tee times,
slow play . . . Hard as a rock, boring course, greens are either shaggy or
bald . . . Very reasonable, no sand traps . . . Staff OK, course acceptable,
value good.

★★ SCHIFFERDECKER GOLF COURSE

PU—506 Schifferdecker, Joplin (417)624-3533.
Holes: 18. **Par:** 71/72.
Yards: 6,123/5,251. **Course rating:** 68.7/69.7. **Slope:** 108/117.
Opened: 1920. **Pace of Play rating:** 4:00. **Green fee:** $7/8.
Credit cards: MC, V. **Reduced fees:** Twilight, Seniors, Juniors.
Caddies: No. **Golf carts:** $7 for 18 holes.
Discount golf packages: No. **Season:** Year-round. **High:** April-Sept.
On-site lodging: No. **Rental clubs:** Yes.
Walking policy: Unrestricted walking. **Range:** No.
To obtain tee times: Call on Thursday prior to weekend.
Subscriber comments: Well-maintained public course, few amenities . . .
Wide open, super greens . . . Short and open but still requires thought . . .
Usually in great shape . . . Best greens . . . Good treatment, pace OK . . .
Best kept course in Joplin but can be very slow due to inexperienced golfers
. . . Greens good for the amount of traffic. Parallel fairways can grind play
to standstill . . . Really inexpensive golf . . . Fun course, friendly staff.

★★★★ SHIRKEY GOLF CLUB

SP—409 Wollard Blvd., Richmond (816)776-9965.
38 miles northeast of Independence. **Holes:** 18. **Par:** 71/74.
Yards: 6,907/5,516. **Course rating:** 71.3/73.1. **Slope:** 136/129.
Opened: 1968. **Pace of Play rating:** 4:30. **Green fee:** $18/22.
Credit cards: None. **Reduced fees:** Weekdays, Seniors.
Caddies: No. **Golf carts:** $22 for 18 holes.
Discount golf packages: No. **Season:** Year-round. **High:** May-Oct.
On-site lodging: No. **Rental clubs:** Yes.
Walking policy: Walking at certain times. **Range:** Yes (grass).
To obtain tee times: Call seven days in advance for weekends.
Subscriber comments: Nice staff, good layout, good value, not crowded
. . . Best putting greens, watered fairways, championship caliber . . .
Hidden jewel, fast but true greens, old established course, big trees, super
value, worth trouble to find . . . All services excellent . . . A pleasure to
play, challenging but fair and well-kept . . . Fairways are a lush bluegrass
with bent grass greens always manicured to perfection . . . Clubhouse needs
remodeling.

★½ SOUTHVIEW GOLF CLUB

PU—16001 S. 71 Hwy., Belton (816)331-4042.
5 miles south of Kansas City. **Holes:** 18. **Par:** 72/73.
Yards: 6,594/5,805. **Course rating:** 70.6/73.0. **Slope:** 115/113.
Opened: 1955. **Pace of Play rating:** 4:00. **Green fee:** $13/15.
Credit cards: None. **Reduced fees:** Weekdays, Seniors, Juniors.
Caddies: No. **Golf carts:** $11 for 18 holes.
Discount golf packages: No. **Season:** Year-round. **High:** May-Aug.
On-site lodging: No. **Rental clubs:** Yes.
Walking policy: Unrestricted walking. **Range:** Yes (grass).
To obtain tee times: First come, first served.
Also has 9-hole par-3 course.
Subscriber comments: Heavily-used course, no tee times, first come, first
play . . . Good practice course . . . Staff friendly, good maintenance . . .
Easy to walk . . . Pace of play great . . . Fast greens . . . Has a couple of
neat holes around water, mostly flat . . . Good test, small greens.

SUN VALLEY GOLF COURSE★

PU—Rte. 2, Elsberry (314)898-2613, (800)737-4653.
55 miles north of St. Louis. **Holes:** 18. **Par:** 70/70.
Yards: 6,395/5,036. **Course rating:** 70.5/69.3. **Slope:** 134/109.

Opened: 1988. **Pace of Play rating:** N/A. **Green fee:** $16/22.
Credit cards: MC, V. **Reduced fees:** Weekdays, Low season, Seniors, Juniors.
Caddies: No. **Golf carts:** $8 for 18 holes.
Discount golf packages: No. **Season:** Year-round. **High:** June-Sept.
On-site lodging: No. **Rental clubs:** Yes.
Walking policy: Unrestricted walking. **Range:** Yes (grass).
To obtain tee times: Call or come in one week in advance.

★★★ SWOPE MEMORIAL GOLF COURSE
PU—6900 Swope Memorial Dr., Kansas City (816)523-9081.
Holes: 18. **Par:** 72/72.
Yards: 6,274/4,517. **Course rating:** 70.9/65.9. **Slope:** 128/107.
Opened: 1934. **Pace of Play rating:** N/A. **Green fee:** 13.
Credit cards: MC, V. **Reduced fees:** Twilight, Seniors, Juniors.
Caddies: No. **Golf carts:** $10 for 18 holes.
Discount golf packages: No. **Season:** Year-round. **High:** April-Oct.
On-site lodging: No. **Rental clubs:** Yes.
Walking policy: Unrestricted walking. **Range:** No.
To obtain tee times: Call one day in advance.
Subscriber comments: Tillinghast design, short but tough . . . Old, big trees, beautiful in late afternoon . . . Needs better upkeep . . . Hilly, bunkered, five-hour rounds, gets constant play . . . Need a cart, too many blind shots . . . Very poorly marshaled . . . Very accessible, thinkers' course, new fairways will improve rating . . . Classic course . . . Hilly, fast greens, tight . . . Changing fairways to zoysia, which will help.

★★★★ TAPAWINGO NATIONAL GOLF CLUB
PU—13253 W. Watson Rd., St. Louis (314)349-3100.
Holes: 18. **Par:** 72/72.
Yards: 7,151/5,566. **Course rating:** 75.1/72.2. **Slope:** 144/121.
Opened: 1994. **Pace of Play rating:** N/A. **Green fee:** $45/55.
Credit cards: MC, V, AMEX. **Reduced fees:** Weekdays, Twilight, Seniors, Juniors.
Caddies: No. **Golf carts:** Included in Green Fee.
Discount golf packages: No. **Season:** Year-round. **High:** April-Oct.
On-site lodging: No. **Rental clubs:** Yes.
Walking policy: Walking at certain times. **Range:** No.
To obtain tee times: Call up to seven days in advance. All tee times must be guaranteed with a credit card.
Subscriber comments: Great Gary Player course . . . Best new course in St. Louis . . . Spectacular vistas, but overdesigned . . . Good variety of holes, friendly staff, good pace, service limited . . . Currently most expensive course in area, but well-worth an occasional visit . . . Almost golfing heaven . . . Slow play, but love the design . . . Staff, service good, pace of play average . . . Five sets of tees.

THE LODGE OF FOUR SEASONS
R—State Rd. HH and Duckhead Rd., Lake Ozark (314)365-8544, (800)843-5253.
150 miles west of St. Louis. **Holes:** 18. **Par:** 72/72.
Yards: 6,416/4,627. **Course rating:** 71.4/71.0. **Slope:** 130/118.
Opened: 1991. **Pace of Play rating:** 4:15-4:30. **Green fee:** $49/59.
Credit cards: All major. **Reduced fees:** Weekdays, Low season, Twilight.
Caddies: No. **Golf carts:** Included in Green Fee.
Discount golf packages: Yes. **Season:** Year-round. **High:** May-Oct.
On-site lodging: Yes. **Rental clubs:** Yes.
Walking policy: Mandatory cart. **Range:** Yes (grass).
To obtain tee times: Call pro shop.
★★★½ SEASONS RIDGE COURSE
Subscriber comments: Terrific newer course, staff outstanding, great layout, tee to green great, must play . . . Very slow play, course could be kept in better shape . . . Great course, best in Ozarks . . . Poor bunker maintenance. Par 3s too short . . . Priced too high for services rendered . . .

Poor clubhouse . . . Great course for women . . . Breathtaking views, target golf course for better than average golfer . . . Temporary clubhouse . . . Course gets better every year . . . Scenic, lots of elevation changes.

★★★½ ROBERT TRENT JONES COURSE
Holes: 18. **Par:** 71/71.
Yards: 6,567/5,238. **Course rating:** 71.4/70.8. **Slope:** 136/124.
Opened: 1969. **Pace of Play rating:** 4:15–4:30. **Green fee:** $58/66.
Subscriber comments: Great course, great place to stay . . . Too tight and too hard to judge distance . . . Very slow play . . . Lake course, great. Staff great . . . Excellent course, great greens . . . Gorgeous, long distances between green and next tee, long carries over water, must have good short game . . . Old, private course atmosphere . . . An excellent course in an area rich with good courses . . . Service is what a resort course should be.

WHITMOOR COUNTRY CLUB
★★★ EAST COURSE
PU—1100 Whitmoor Dr., St. Charles (314)926-9622x2.
20 miles north of St. Louis. **Holes:** 18. **Par:** 71/71.
Yards: 6,646/4,658. **Course rating:** N/A. **Slope:** 132/110.
Opened: N/A. **Pace of Play rating:** N/A. **Green fee:** $N/A.
Credit cards: All major. **Reduced fees:** Low season, Twilight.
Caddies: No. **Golf carts:** $N/A for 18 holes.
Discount golf packages: No. **Season:** Year-round. **High:** April-Sept.
On-site lodging: No. **Rental clubs:** No.
Walking policy: N/A. **Range:** Yes (grass).
Subscriber comments: Fairways in very poor shape, tee boxes need work, greens good . . . Nice layout in excellent condition . . . Couple holes a bit squirrely . . . Beautiful clubhouse . . . Rolling hills, water, lots of trees, fast play . . . Good golf . . . Tight doglegs, thick, lush fairways . . . Great staff, good clubhouse, course in very good condition, prices a little high but worth the money.

★½ WINDBROOK COUNTRY CLUB
SP—10306 N.W. 45 Hwy., Parkville (816)741-9520.
10 miles northwest of Kansas City. **Holes:** 18. **Par:** 71/70.
Yards: 6,253/4,939. **Course rating:** 69.8/67.4. **Slope:** 119/112.
Opened: 1955. **Pace of Play rating:** 4:00–4:30. **Green fee:** $24/28.
Credit cards: None. **Reduced fees:** Seniors.
Caddies: No. **Golf carts:** Included in Green Fee.
Discount golf packages: No. **Season:** Year-round. **High:** May-Sept.
On-site lodging: No. **Rental clubs:** Yes.
Walking policy: Mandatory cart for nonmembers. **Range:** Yes (grass).
To obtain tee times: Call Friday for upcoming weekend and holidays. Members have preference for tee times.
Subscriber comments: Challenging layout, greens poor. Price OK. . . . Many blind shots because of hills . . . Good food . . . Hilly, punitive type course, unfair in many aspects, not maintained really well . . . Could be an excellent course, but condition rough.

Notes

MONTANA

★★½ BIG SKY SKI AND SUMMER RESORT
BIG SKY GOLF CLUB
PU—2160 Black Otter Rd., Meadow Village, Big Sky (406)995-4706.
45 miles north of Bozeman. **Holes:** 18. **Par:** 72/72.
Yards: 6,748/5,374. **Course rating:** 69.0/67.4. **Slope:** 111/104.
Opened: 1975. **Pace of Play rating:** 4:00. **Green fee:** $32.
Credit cards: All major. **Reduced fees:** Twilight, Juniors.
Caddies: No. **Golf carts:** $20 for 18 holes.
Discount golf packages: No. **Season:** May-Oct. **High:** June-Sept.
On-site lodging: No. **Rental clubs:** No.
Walking policy: Unrestricted walking. **Range:** Yes (grass).
To obtain tee times: Call seven days in advance.
Subscriber comments: Nice Palmer course, back nine especially fun and
scenic . . . Fun course, not long, improving every year . . . Pretty view of
the mountains . . . Fair greens.

★★½ BILL ROBERTS MUNICIPAL GOLF COURSE
PU—220 Cole Ave., Helena (406)442-2191.
Holes: 18. **Par:** 72/72.
Yards: 6,782/4,700. **Course rating:** 70.5/65.1. **Slope:** 117/101.
Opened: 1950. **Pace of Play rating:** 4:30. **Green fee:** $18.
Credit cards: None. **Reduced fees:** Seniors, Juniors.
Caddies: No. **Golf carts:** $20 for 18 holes.
Discount golf packages: Yes. **Season:** March-Nov. **High:** April-Sept.
On-site lodging: No. **Rental clubs:** Yes.
Walking policy: Unrestricted walking. **Range:** Yes (grass).
To obtain tee times: Call two days in advance.
Subscriber comments: Six holes on old nine redone with water, traps and
new greens . . . Great improvements! Shows what a public course can do
. . . Redone, nice layout . . . harder than it looks . . . New greens need time
to mature . . . One of best municipal courses in state.

★★★½ BUFFALO HILL GOLF COURSE
CHAMPIONSHIP COURSE
PU—1176 North Main St., Kalispell (406)756-4547.
200 miles east of Spokane. **Holes:** 18. **Par:** 72/74.
Yards: 6,525/5,258. **Course rating:** 71.4/70.3. **Slope:** 131/125.
Opened: 1933. **Pace of Play rating:** 4:20. **Green fee:** $25.
Credit cards: MC, V. **Reduced fees:** Twilight.
Caddies: No. **Golf carts:** $10 for 18 holes.
Discount golf packages: No. **Season:** April-Oct. **High:** May-Sept.
On-site lodging: No. **Rental clubs:** Yes.
Walking policy: Unrestricted walking. **Range:** Yes.
To obtain tee times: Call 48 hours in advance.
Also has 9-hole par-35 Cameron Course.
Subscriber comments: As good as a public course gets . . . Narrow
fairways, lots of doglegs . . . Beautiful, tough course, great for a getaway
weekend . . . Overcrowded . . . Hilly . . . Up and down with narrow
fairways . . . Front nine on top of a plateau gradually descending down into
a canyon for back nine. Back nine is like being in another world . . .
Treelined beauty that gets a lot of play . . . Tough, very tough, every club
in your bag . . . Buffalo Hill is not for a golfer who grips and rips. You
need to be accurate because of narrow fairways . . . Good variety of holes
. . . Great scenery . . . Good hike . . . Shotmaking test . . . Valley holes are
great . . . Very enjoyable golf experience.

EAGLE BEND GOLF CLUB
★★★½ RIDGE/LAKES COURSE
PU—279 Eagle Bend Dr., Bigfork (406)837-7302, (800)255-5641.
15 miles south of Kalispell. **Holes:** 18. **Par:** 72/72.
Yards: 6,639/5,382. **Course rating:** 71.4/70.0. **Slope:** 124/119.
Opened: 1984. **Pace of Play rating:** 4:30. **Green fee:** $45.
Credit cards: All major. **Reduced fees:** Twilight, Juniors.
Caddies: No. **Golf carts:** $12 for 18 holes.
Discount golf packages: Yes. **Season:** April-Oct. **High:** June-Aug.

On-site lodging: Yes. **Rental clubs:** Yes.
Walking policy: Unrestricted walking. **Range:** Yes (grass).
To obtain tee times: Call (800)392-9795 (Flathead Valley Central
Reservations) or club at 837-7300.
New nine for Ridge Course opened July 1, 1995.
Ridge and Lakes nines ranked in Second 25 of America's 75 Best Public Golf
Courses by Golf Digest. Ridge and Lake nines selected as runner-up for
Best New Public Course of 1989 by Golf Digest. Ridge and Lake nines
ranked 1st in Montana by Golf Digest.
Subscriber comments: God's country! . . . Very beautiful . . . Excellent
in all respects . . . Good chow, beautiful track . . . Beautifully laid out, lots
of water but fairly placed . . . Pretty course, easy to get on in the afternoons
. . . Long and winding course, lots of variety . . . Fairways cut out of pine
forest . . . This is heaven . . . Other than Augusta National, one of the most
picturesque courses I've ever played . . . Spectacular scenery, course well
designed . . . Exceptional conditions . . . Long ball hitter course, stay on
fairways!! Lots of water! . . . Very scenic, some big changes in elevation
. . . Old nine is great . . . Excellent practice facility . . . Really quick greens
. . . Very clean course. Great scenery . . . Great front nine . . . Beautifully
landscaped, long walks between holes . . . The best Montana has to offer.

★★ FAIRMONT HOT SPRINGS RESORT

R—1500 Fairmont Rd., Anaconda (406)797-3241, (800)332-3272.
20 miles west of Butte. **Holes:** 18. **Par:** 72/72.
Yards: 6,741/5,921. **Course rating:** 68.5/70.7. **Slope:** 107/109.
Opened: 1974. **Pace of Play rating:** 4:00. **Green fee:** $26.
Credit cards: All major. **Reduced fees:** Resort guests.
Caddies: No. **Golf carts:** $22 for 18 holes.
Discount golf packages: No. **Season:** March-Oct. **High:** June-Aug.
On-site lodging: Yes. **Rental clubs:** Yes.
Walking policy: Unrestricted walking. **Range:** Yes (grass).
To obtain tee times: Call pro shop.
Subscriber comments: Not much trouble but long . . . Great scenery,
good price, need better maintenance . . . Longest par 5 ever . . . 640-yard-
par 5 . . . Nice view of the mountains . . . Very uncrowded.

★★★ HAMILTON GOLF CLUB

PU—570 Country Club Lane, Hamilton (406)363-4251.
Call club for further information
Subscriber comments: Plays fast, wide open . . . Front older style, back
nine challenging, long and breathtaking . . . Like playing two different
courses, old nine and new nine . . . Back nine is tougher . . . Big hitter's
paradise . . . A real gem.

★½ LAKE HILLS GOLF COURSE

SP—1930 Clubhouse Way, Billings (406)252-9244.
Holes: 18. **Par:** 72/74.
Yards: 6,802/6,105. **Course rating:** 70.1/72.3. **Slope:** 112/109.
Opened: 1956. **Pace of Play rating:** 4:00-4:30. **Green fee:** $14.
Credit cards: MC, V. **Reduced fees:** Low season, Seniors, Juniors.
Caddies: No. **Golf carts:** $7 for 18 holes.
Discount golf packages: No. **Season:** Year-round. **High:** May-Sept.
On-site lodging: No. **Rental clubs:** Yes.
Walking policy: Unrestricted walking. **Range:** Yes (grass).
To obtain tee times: Call two days in advance. For weekend tee times call
Thursday a.m.
Subscriber comments: Pretty good course for an inexpensive price . . .
Would be an excellent course with some work on fairways, add some
bunkers . . . Crowded . . . Small children allowed on weekends . . . Well
kept considering the heavy traffic . . . Nice mix of holes . . . First to open,
last to close every year . . . Play in spring, too dry in summer . . . King of
rolling hills and medium-sized greens.

★★★ LARCHMONT GOLF COURSE
PU—3200 Old Fort Rd., Missoula (406)721-4416.
Holes: 18. **Par:** 72/72.
Yards: 7,114/5,936. **Course rating:** 72.7/72.9. **Slope:** 118/118.
Opened: 1982. **Pace of Play rating:** 4:00. **Green fee:** $16/18.
Credit cards: All major. **Reduced fees:** Weekdays, Seniors, Juniors.
Caddies: No. **Golf carts:** $20 for 18 holes.
Discount golf packages: No. **Season:** March-Oct. **High:** May-Aug.
On-site lodging: No. **Rental clubs:** Yes.
Walking policy: Unrestricted walking. **Range:** Yes (grass).
To obtain tee times: Call one day in advance.
Subscriber comments: Modern layout, easy to walk, big greens, good condition and service . . . Will be tougher when trees get bigger . . . Grip it and rip it course . . . Hidden ponds . . . New clubhouse . . . Long par 4s . . . Great staff and value . . . Flat course . . . Greenkeepers do an excellent job all year . . . No complaints . . . The setting is in the beautiful Missoula Valley . . . Has a great future.

★★★ MEADOW LAKE GOLF RESORT
R—490 St. Andrews Dr., Columbia Falls (406)892-2111, (800)321-4653.
12 miles north of Kalispell. **Holes:** 18. **Par:** 72/73.
Yards: 6,714/5,344. **Course rating:** 70.9/69.8. **Slope:** 124/121.
Opened: 1984. **Pace of Play rating:** 4:30-5:00. **Green fee:** $25/35.
Credit cards: All major. **Reduced fees:** Low season, Resort guests, Twilight.
Caddies: No. **Golf carts:** $11 for 18 holes.
Discount golf packages: Yes. **Season:** April-Nov. **High:** June-Sept.
On-site lodging: Yes. **Rental clubs:** Yes.
Walking policy: Mandatory cart. **Range:** Yes (grass).
To obtain tee times: Call pro shop. Credit card needed to guarantee.

Subscriber comments: My Montana favorite . . . Short, good layout, scenic . . . Hard because need to hit ball straight . . . Meadow Lake is fast becoming best golf course in Flathead Valley . . . Heavily wooded . . . Nice on-site accommodations . . . Lot of tricky shots . . . A good test of golf . . . Moderately demanding . . . Great scenery . . . Slow play at season's peak . . . Too many houses and condos . . . Number two course in Flathead.

★★★ MISSION MOUNTAIN COUNTRY CLUB
SP—640 Stagecoach Trail, Ronan (406)676-4653.
60 miles south of Missoula. **Holes:** 18. **Par:** 72/73.
Yards: 6,478/5,074. **Course rating:** 69.7/67.5. **Slope:** 114/108.
Opened: 1988. **Pace of Play rating:** 4:00. **Green fee:** No.
Credit cards: MC, V. **Reduced fees:** No.
Caddies: No. **Golf carts:** $20 for 18 holes.
Discount golf packages: No. **Season:** March-Oct. **High:** June-Aug.
On-site lodging: No. **Rental clubs:** Yes.
Walking policy: Unrestricted walking. **Range:** Yes (grass).
To obtain tee times: Call two days in advance.
Subscriber comments: Another one we would like to keep to ourselves . . . Relaxing atmosphere, excellent view . . . Beautiful sand, water, trees . . . Good shape . . . Scenery was breathtaking . . . Interesting holes . . . Best greens around . . . Great split fairway par 5 . . . Excellent greens . . . Newer course with wide open fairways . . . Staff personable . . . Outstanding scenery . . . Short but nice.

★★ PETER YEGEN JR. GOLF CLUB
PU—3400 Grand Ave., Billings (406)656-8099.
Holes: 18. **Par:** 71/71.
Yards: 6,617/4,994. **Course rating:** 69.7/67.0. **Slope:** 112/109.
Opened: 1993. **Pace of Play rating:** 4:30. **Green fee:** $15/16.
Credit cards: MC, V. **Reduced fees:** Weekdays.
Caddies: No. **Golf carts:** $15 for 18 holes.
Discount golf packages: Yes. **Season:** Year-round. **High:** April-Oct.
On-site lodging: No. **Rental clubs:** Yes.

Walking policy: Unrestricted walking. **Range:** Yes (grass).
To obtain tee times: Call three days in advance.
Subscriber comments: New course . . . Not many hazards . . . Has potential . . . Congenial staff . . . Course is very flat and wide open. In the middle of old corn field . . . Course greens are in very good condition . . . Needs some maturing and definition . . . Will be a good course with a few more trees.

★★★ POLSON COUNTRY CLUB

PU—111 Bayview Dr., Polson (406)883-2440.
60 miles north of Missoula. **Holes:** 18. **Par:** 72/72.
Yards: 6,756/5,215. **Course rating:** 70.9/68.4. **Slope:** 119/114.
Opened: 1936. **Pace of Play rating:** 4:00. **Green fee:** $20.
Credit cards: MC, V. **Reduced fees:** No.
Caddies: No. **Golf carts:** $10 for 18 holes.
Discount golf packages: Yes. **Season:** March-Nov. **High:** June-Aug.
On-site lodging: No. **Rental clubs:** Yes.
Walking policy: Unrestricted walking. **Range:** Yes (grass).
To obtain tee times: Call up to two days in advance.
Subscriber comments: Beautiful course on lake . . . Fun to play because of difference between front and back nines . . . Spectacular views . . . Excellent condition, friendly, helpful staff . . . Wide open front nine, no contest to narrow tree-lined back nine . . . Back nine is the old nine, hard driving, small greens, great challenge . . . Old nine holes excellent, new nine needs maturing . . . Course easy to walk . . . Elevation and trees are main hazards . . . Beautiful views of Flathead Lake, longer playing season.

★½ R.O. SPECK MUNICIPAL GOLF COURSE

PU—29th and River Dr. N., Great Falls (406)761-1078.
Holes: 18. **Par:** 72/73.
Yards: 6,830/5,817. **Course rating:** 69.6/71.4. **Slope:** 111/115.
Opened: N/A. **Pace of Play rating:** 3:55-4:00. **Green fee:** $16.
Credit cards: None. **Reduced fees:** Twilight, Juniors.
Caddies: No. **Golf carts:** $15 for 18 holes.
Discount golf packages: No. **Season:** March-Oct. **High:** April-Oct.
On-site lodging: No. **Rental clubs:** Yes.
Walking policy: Unrestricted walking. **Range:** Yes (grass).
To obtain tee times: Call two days in advance.
Subscriber comments: OK course, no trouble . . . Needs sand traps and water hazards . . . Slow play . . . Old course, lots of play . . . Easy access.

★★ RED LODGE MOUNTAIN GOLF COURSE

R—828 Upper Continental Dr., Red Lodge (406)446-3344.
60 miles southwest of Billings. **Holes:** 18. **Par:** 72/72.
Yards: 6,779/6,445. **Course rating:** 69.3/70.4. **Slope:** 115/115.
Opened: 1983. **Pace of Play rating:** N/A. **Green fee:** $20.
Credit cards: MC, V, DISC. **Reduced fees:** No.
Caddies: No. **Golf carts:** $16 for 18 holes.
Discount golf packages: No. **Season:** May-Oct. **High:** July-Aug.
On-site lodging: No. **Rental clubs:** Yes.
Walking policy: Unrestricted walking. **Range:** Yes (grass).
To obtain tee times: Call pro shop.
Subscriber comments: Good resort course . . . Working on many course improvements. Beautiful view of the Beartooth Mountains and ski runs . . . Pretty surroundings . . . Friendly staff, magnificent views . . . Numerous streams cutting across fairways . . . Play smart or the water will eat your golf balls . . . Short season . . . Nice variations on holes, needs better upkeep . . . Mountain views are great.

WHITEFISH LAKE GOLF CLUB
★★★½ **NORTH COURSE**

PU—Hwy. 93 N., Whitefish (406)862-5960.
130 miles north of Missoula. **Holes:** 18. **Par:** 72/72.
Yards: 6,556/5,556. **Course rating:** 69.8/70.1. **Slope:** 118/115.
Opened: 1936. **Pace of Play rating:** 4:20. **Green fee:** $28.
Credit cards: MC, V. **Reduced fees:** Resort guests, Twilight.
Caddies: No. **Golf carts:** $12 for 18 holes.
Discount golf packages: No. **Season:** April-Oct. **High:** June-Sept.
On-site lodging: No. **Rental clubs:** Yes.
Walking policy: Unrestricted walking. **Range:** Yes (grass).
To obtain tee times: Call two days in advance starting at 7 a.m.
Ranked 4th in Montana by Golf Digest.
Subscriber comments: This is a must if you come to Montana . . . Lot of
trees, play it straight . . . Club selection critical for tee shots on the par-4
holes . . . Great scenery . . . Good test but slow play always . . . Superb
golf . . . Big Mountain ski hill a great backdrop . . . Some very scenic
holes, well bunkered . . . Forgiving, but never dull, traditional layout
improved recently . . . Don't miss these two courses . . . Mature
landscaping . . . Best buy in valley . . . Beautiful forest course . . . Best
course in the Flathead Valley.

★★★½ **SOUTH COURSE**

PU—Highway 93 North, Whitefish (406)862-5960.
130 miles south of Missoula. **Holes:** 18. **Par:** 71/72.
Yards: 6,563/5,358. **Course rating:** 70.5/70.3. **Slope:** 122/120.
Opened: 1980. **Pace of Play rating:** 4:20. **Green fee:** $28/ 28.
Credit cards: MC, V. **Reduced fees:** Resort guests, Twilight.
Caddies: No. **Golf carts:** $12 for 18 holes.
Discount golf packages: Yes. **Season:** April-Oct. **High:** June-Sept.
On-site lodging: Yes. **Rental clubs:** Yes.
Walking policy: Unrestricted walking. **Range:** Yes(grass).
To obtain tee times: Call two days in advance starting at 7 a.m.
Subscriber comments: Best new course in the Pacific Northwest,
fantastic service . . . Incredible views, great restaurant . . . New nine very
interesting . . . Outstanding lakeside holes, great addition to existing holes
. . . Beautiful layout . . . Some housing too close to fairways . . .
Outstanding scenery and accommodations . . . Almost every hole could be
a signature hole . . . Most challenging course in Montana.

NEBRASKA

★★ APPLEWOOD GOLF COURSE

PU—6111 S. 99th St., Omaha (402)444-4656.
Holes: 18. **Par:** 72/76.
Yards: 6,916/6,014. **Course rating:** 72.4/74.6. **Slope:** 121/126.
Opened: 1971. **Pace of Play rating:** 4:00-4:30. **Green fee:** $12/13.
Credit cards: None. **Reduced fees:** Weekdays, Seniors, Juniors.
Caddies: No. **Golf carts:** $8 for 18 holes.
Discount golf packages: No. **Season:** Year-round. **High:** May-Sept.
On-site lodging: No. **Rental clubs:** No.
Walking policy: Unrestricted walking. **Range:** Yes (grass).
To obtain tee times: Call one week in advance.
Subscriber comments: Average public course . . . Very good course
design . . . Very reasonable . . . In good shape despite lots of play . . .
Many blind approaches, need pin placement guide . . . Gets lots of play!
Conditions deteriorate late in year . . . Lots of trees and rolling hills. Fun
course . . . Greens need work . . . Making some improvements.

★★ ASHLAND COUNTRY CLUB

SP—R2, Ashland (402)944-3388.
25 miles west of Omaha. **Holes:** 18. **Par:** 70/74.
Yards: 6,337/5,606. **Course rating:** 70.0/69.8. **Slope:** 112/112.
Opened: 1967. **Pace of Play rating:** 3:30-4:00. **Green fee:** $18/20.
Credit cards: None. **Reduced fees:** No.
Caddies: No. **Golf carts:** $18 for 18 holes.
Discount golf packages: No. **Season:** March-Oct. **High:** June-Sept.
On-site lodging: No. **Rental clubs:** Yes.
Walking policy: Unrestricted walking. **Range:** No.
To obtain tee times: Call seven days in advance.
Subscriber comments: Nice course for a small town . . . Flat with little
interest . . . Easy layout, few trees, hazards . . . Short but still has good
holes . . . Flat, easily walked. Two water holes, some trees . . . Good
greens . . . Basic layout good, maintained so-so . . . Used to be a great
course. Made it too easy.

★★½ BENSON PARK GOLF COURSE

PU—5333 N. 72nd St., Omaha (402)444-4626.
Holes: 18. **Par:** 72/78.
Yards: 6,814/6,085. **Course rating:** 72.1/73.4. **Slope:** 120/121.
Opened: 1964. **Pace of Play rating:** 4:00. **Green fee:** $12/13.
Credit cards: None. **Reduced fees:** Seniors, Juniors.
Caddies: No. **Golf carts:** $16 for 18 holes.
Discount golf packages: Yes. **Season:** March-Dec. **High:** May-Sept.
On-site lodging: No. **Rental clubs:** Yes.
Walking policy: Unrestricted walking. **Range:** No.
To obtain tee times: Call one week in advance.
Subscriber comments: Older course with a lot of big old trees . . .
Recently underwent renovation . . . Challenging municipal course . . .
Should continue to improve . . . Nice layout, not boring . . . Staff works
hard to keep course . . . Has private practice range next to it . . . Very long
for women . . . Best public course in Omaha.

COVINGTON LINKS GOLF COURSE★

PU—497 Golf Rd., South Sioux City (402)494-9841.
10 miles south of Sioux City, IA. **Holes:** 18. **Par:** 71/71.
Yards: 5,977/5,263. **Course rating:** N/A. **Slope:** N/A.
Opened: 1977. **Pace of Play rating:** 4:00. **Green fee:** $11/13.
Credit cards: MC, V. **Reduced fees:** No.
Caddies: No. **Golf carts:** $15 for 18 holes.
Discount golf packages: No. **Season:** March-Nov. **High:** June-Aug.
On-site lodging: No. **Rental clubs:** No.
Walking policy: Unrestricted walking. **Range:** No.
To obtain tee times: Weekend tee times only. Call Thursday prior to
weekend after 8 a.m.

Subscriber comments: Tight, great condition all year, don't need any woods . . . Took fine nine hole course, crammed in awkward back nine . . . Staff very friendly . . . Greens very nice.

★★★ GRAND ISLAND MUNICIPAL GOLF COURSE

PU—2800 Shady Bend Rd., Grand Island (308)385-5340.
90 miles east of Lincoln. **Holes:** 18. **Par:** 72/72.
Yards: 6,752/5,487. **Course rating:** 71.3/70.8. **Slope:** 118/112.
Opened: 1977. **Pace of Play rating:** 4:00. **Green fee:** $8/9.
Credit cards: None. **Reduced fees:** Seniors, Juniors.
Caddies: No. **Golf carts:** $15 for 18 holes.
Discount golf packages: No. **Season:** Year-round. **High:** April-Sept.
On-site lodging: No. **Rental clubs:** Yes.
Walking policy: Unrestricted walking. **Range:** Yes (grass).
To obtain tee times: Call one week in advance.

Subscriber comments: A great place to play, prices are amazingly low . . . Great greens . . . Huge greens . . . Good public course, good service & pace of play . . . Flat layout in good condition and very economical . . . Not many trees . . . Best value in U.S.A.

★★★★ HERITAGE HILLS GOLF COURSE

SP—6000 Clubhouse Dr., McCook (308)345-5032.
240 miles southwest of Lincoln. **Holes:** 18. **Par:** 72/72.
Yards: 6,715/5,475. **Course rating:** 72.7/71.1. **Slope:** 130/127.
Opened: 1981. **Pace of Play rating:** 4:00-4:30. **Green fee:** $20/30.
Credit cards: None. **Reduced fees:** Twilight, Juniors.
Caddies: No. **Golf carts:** $18 for 18 holes.
Discount golf packages: No. **Season:** Year-round. **High:** May-Sept.
On-site lodging: No. **Rental clubs:** Yes.
Walking policy: Unrestricted walking. **Range:** Yes (grass).
To obtain tee times: Call one week in advance.

Subscriber comments: Real gem in the middle of nowhere . . . Long drive worth it, through Nebraska known as great experience . . . The ultimate challenge for all levels of golfers . . . Best kept secret in golf . . . Many blind holes . . . Toughest course in Nebraska, too far from major cities . . . Much character, unusual . . . Very good greens, design is different but challenging . . . Best greens I've ever played . . . Not suitable for beginners . . . Best greens in the area . . . This is a great course, lots of fun, great value . . . Scenic and beautiful, best public course in Nebraska.

★ HIDDEN VALLEY GOLF COURSE
EAST COURSE

PU—10501 Pine Lake Rd., Lincoln (402)483-2532.
Holes: 18. **Par:** 71/75.
Yards: 6,080/5,411. **Course rating:** 68.3/71.6. **Slope:** 110/114.
Opened: 1962. **Pace of Play rating:** 3:30. **Green fee:** $11.
Credit cards: None. **Reduced fees:** Weekdays, Low season, Seniors, Juniors.
Caddies: No. **Golf carts:** $18 for 18 holes.
Discount golf packages: Yes. **Season:** March-Dec. **High:** June-Aug.
On-site lodging: No. **Rental clubs:** Yes.
Walking policy: Unrestricted walking. **Range:** Yes (grass).
To obtain tee times: Call one week in advance.
Also has 9-hole par-35 West Course.

Subscriber comments: Natural terrain, only fair condition . . . West nine wonderful . . . Treated well, staff OK . . . Needs a lot of work . . . Rocky . . . Don't expect too much . . . Tougher than it looks . . . Not in very good shape ever, but you can usually get on to play . . . Fun place to play.

★★★½ HIGHLANDS GOLF COURSE

PU—5501 N.W. 12th St., Lincoln (402)441-6081.
Holes: 18. **Par:** 72/72.
Yards: 7,021/5,280. **Course rating:** 72.5/69.4. **Slope:** 119/111.
Opened: 1993. **Pace of Play rating:** N/A. **Green fee:** $11/12.

Credit cards: MC, V. **Reduced fees:** Seniors, Juniors.
Caddies: No. **Golf carts:** $10 for 18 holes.
Discount golf packages: No. **Season:** Year-round. **High:** April-Oct.
On-site lodging: No. **Rental clubs:** Yes.
Walking policy: Unrestricted walking. **Range:** Yes.
To obtain tee times: Call one week in advance.
Subscriber comments: Newest course in Lincoln, you have to hit it straight . . . Calm day, it's a great place to play . . . Open, wind-blown, always tough . . . Many large fairway bunkers, huge greens . . . Need to know how to play in wind . . . Fantastic for a public course . . . A lot of sand . . . Wide open but long . . . Nos. 9 and 18 are difficult but fun . . . Must be a good putter . . . Great secret, this links-style course . . . Many mounds, bunkers . . . Outstanding young course . . . No wind, no problem . . . Many long walks between holes (worst feature) . . . Big greens, but never flat.

★★★ HIMARK GOLF COURSE

PU—9001 Pioneers Blvd., Lincoln (402)488-7888.
Holes: 18. **Par:** 72/70.
Yards: 6,700/4,900. **Course rating:** 71.3/67.1. **Slope:** 120/111.
Opened: 1993. **Pace of Play rating:** 4:00. **Green fee:** $14/16.
Credit cards: MC, V. **Reduced fees:** Weekdays, Low season, Twilight, Seniors, Juniors.
Caddies: No. **Golf carts:** $10 for 18 holes.
Discount golf packages: No. **Season:** March-Nov. **High:** June-Aug.
On-site lodging: No. **Rental clubs:** Yes.
Walking policy: Unrestricted walking. **Range:** Yes (grass).
To obtain tee times: Call five days in advance.
Subscriber comments: Country-club atmosphere for the public golfer . . . Half a dozen great holes . . . Fine bunch of people who run it . . . Best greens in city . . . New course being constantly improved . . . Excellent practice range . . . Course maintenance and attention to detail higher than others . . . Fairly new . . . It's a long walk . . . Wide open from tee, challenging approaches . . . Lincoln has the right idea, lots of courses, reasonable rates . . . Two years old, great conditioning.

★★★ HOLMES PARK GOLF COURSE

PU—3701 S. 70th St., Lincoln (402)441-8960.
Holes: 18. **Par:** 72/74.
Yards: 6,805/6,054. **Course rating:** 72.2/73.8. **Slope:** 120/126.
Opened: 1964. **Pace of Play rating:** 4:00. **Green fee:** $11/14.
Credit cards: MC, V. **Reduced fees:** Weekdays, Seniors, Juniors.
Caddies: No. **Golf carts:** $20 for 18 holes.
Discount golf packages: Yes. **Season:** March-Dec. **High:** July.
On-site lodging: No. **Rental clubs:** Yes.
Walking policy: Unrestricted walking. **Range:** Yes (grass).
To obtain tee times: Call one week in advance.
Subscriber comments: Old faithful in Lincoln . . . Excellent staff, actually have marshals on the course . . . Greens fast, but true putting . . . Good greens, good in wind, good use of contours and hills . . . Long-time Lincoln standard . . . Well cared for public course . . . Too many blind shots and similar holes . . . Well cared for public course . . . Starter works you in . . . Good basic midwestern course . . . A muny with character . . . Receives lots of play . . . Open course, bring your driver . . . Best muny greens in town . . . Best municipal course in Lincoln.

★★★½ INDIAN CREEK GOLF COURSE

PU—20100 W. Maple Rd., Elkhorn (402)289-0900.
5 miles east of Omaha. **Holes:** 18. **Par:** 72/72.
Yards: 7,236/5,149. **Course rating:** 75.5/68.9. **Slope:** 129/112.
Opened: 1992. **Pace of Play rating:** 4:00. **Green fee:** $18/22.
Credit cards: MC, V. **Reduced fees:** Seniors.
Caddies: No. **Golf carts:** $16 for 18 holes.
Discount golf packages: No. **Season:** March-Nov. **High:** June-July.

On-site lodging: No. **Rental clubs:** Yes.
Walking policy: Unrestricted walking. **Range:** Yes (grass).
To obtain tee times: Call seven days in advance.
Subscriber comments: Best track in the area . . . Adding new holes will hopefully speed up play, best of public Omaha . . . Variety of tees make it playable for all . . . Longest course from champion tees in Nebraska . . . Super condition . . . One of the best in eastern Nebraska . . . One of Nebraska's fine golf experiences . . . Long, long, long . . . Best track in the area . . . Great clubhouse . . . Building another nine holes . . . Great course for her . . . Long, interesting layout . . . Scenery, challenge, length and at fair price, love it!

★★ INDIANHEAD GOLF COURSE
PU—4100 Husker Hwy., Grand Island (308)381-4653.
Holes: 18. **Par:** 72/72.
Yards: 6,597/5,664. **Course rating:** 70.9/71.9. **Slope:** 122/117.
Opened: 1990. **Pace of Play rating:** 4:00 - 4:30. **Green fee:** $9/11.
Credit cards: MC, V. **Reduced fees:** Weekdays, Twilight, Seniors, Juniors.
Caddies: No. **Golf carts:** $9 for 18 holes.
Discount golf packages: Yes. **Season:** Year-round. **High:** May-Sept.
On-site lodging: No. **Rental clubs:** Yes.
Walking policy: Unrestricted walking. **Range:** Yes (grass).
To obtain tee times: Call seven days in advance.
Subscriber comments: Newer course . . . Front nine unimaginative . . . Bland but cheap . . . Back nine great value . . . Rather flat and unexciting in design . . . Well kept . . . People friendly . . . Nice course for beginner.

★★½ MAHONEY GOLF COURSE
PU—7900 Adams St., Lincoln (402)441-8969.
Holes: 18. **Par:** 70/72.
Yards: 6,300/5,607. **Course rating:** 72.3/70.3. **Slope:** 125/118.
Opened: 1975. **Pace of Play rating:** 4:30. **Green fee:** $11/14.
Credit cards: All major. **Reduced fees:** Seniors, Juniors.
Caddies: No. **Golf carts:** $10 for 18 holes.
Discount golf packages: No. **Season:** April-Nov. **High:** June-Aug.
On-site lodging: No. **Rental clubs:** Yes.
Walking policy: Unrestricted walking. **Range:** Yes (grass).
To obtain tee times: Call seven days in advance.
Subscriber comments: Good public course . . . Very busy but playable . . . No. 8 toughest hole in Lincoln . . . Undistinguished layout . . . Play in the winter, good . . . Open, lots of potential . . . Good shape year-around . . . Fun but difficult greens . . . A bit short . . . Too many parallel, similar holes . . . Will toughen up as trees grow.

★★★½ MEADOWLARK HILLS GOLF COURSE
SP—3300 30th Ave., Kearney (308)233-3265.
120 miles west of Lincoln. **Holes:** 18. **Par:** 71/72.
Yards: 6,485/4,967. **Course rating:** 70.4/68.2. **Slope:** 119/112.
Opened: 1994. **Pace of Play rating:** 4:28. **Green fee:** $7/18.
Credit cards: MC, V. **Reduced fees:** Low season, Twilight, Seniors, Juniors.
Caddies: No. **Golf carts:** $10 for 18 holes.
Discount golf packages: No. **Season:** Year-round. **High:** May-Aug.
On-site lodging: No. **Rental clubs:** Yes.
Walking policy: Unrestricted walking. **Range:** Yes (grass).
To obtain tee times: Call six days in advance.
Subscriber comments: Nice new course in Kearny . . . Best course of area, up and down rare in Platte Valley, watch yardage closely . . . Brand new, needs to mature, nice layout . . . Hilly, tight back nine . . . Deceptive, looks easy, is not . . . Excellent design, good variety of terrain . . . Best new course in Nebraska, watch this one.

★★ MIRACLE HILL GOLF AND TENNIS CENTER

PU—1401 N. 120th St., Omaha (402)498-0220.

Holes: 18. **Par:** 70/70.
Yards: 6,412/5,069. **Course rating:** 71.0/69.0. **Slope:** 129/117.
Opened: 1960. **Pace of Play rating:** 4:00. **Green fee:** $15/22.
Credit cards: MC, V. **Reduced fees:** Twilight, Seniors.
Caddies: No. **Golf carts:** $19 for 18 holes.
Discount golf packages: No. **Season:** Year-round. **High:** May-Aug.
On-site lodging: No. **Rental clubs:** Yes.
Walking policy: Unrestricted walking. **Range:** Yes (grass).
To obtain tee times: Call seven days in advance.
Subscriber comments: Straight-away golf holes . . . Lots of sand . . . All holes look the same . . . Drainage difficulty . . . Old course, plenty of room, large trees . . . Old public course, very crowded . . . Unimaginative . . . Flat greens . . . Greens need work . . . Forgiving . . . Easy walking . . . Relatively wide open . . . Very short but always well groomed.

★★★ PIONEERS GOLF COURSE

PU—3403 W. Van Dorn, Lincoln (402)441-8966.

2 miles west of Lincoln. **Holes:** 18. **Par:** 71/74.
Yards: 6,478/5,771. **Course rating:** 69.2/73.2. **Slope:** 110/114.
Opened: 1930. **Pace of Play rating:** 4:00. **Green fee:** $12.
Credit cards: MC, V. **Reduced fees:** Weekdays, Seniors, Juniors.
Caddies: No. **Golf carts:** $20 for 18 holes.
Discount golf packages: No. **Season:** Year-round. **High:** June-Aug.
On-site lodging: No. **Rental clubs:** Yes.
Walking policy: Unrestricted walking. **Range:** Yes (grass).
To obtain tee times: General public can call up to one week in advance.
Subscriber comments: Old course, new greens many large trees . . . Very interesting terrain . . . Mature, traditional course, no sand bunkers . . . Big greens that grow fast . . . Love the back nine . . . A good money value . . . Beautiful pines driving accuracy a must . . . Great course for the money and view . . . No bunkers but need to play from hillsides . . . A good solid public track . . . Best public course in Lincoln . . . Nebraska's best old course. Fits the natural setting of a pine forest on the plain. Very reasonable!

★★★ QUAIL RUN GOLF COURSE

PU—327 South 5th St., Columbus (402)564-1313.

80 miles southeast of Omaha. **Holes:** 18. **Par:** 72/72.
Yards: 7,024/5,147. **Course rating:** 75.1/70.7. **Slope:** 140/125.
Opened: 1991. **Pace of Play rating:** 4:14. **Green fee:** $12/15.
Credit cards: None. **Reduced fees:** Weekdays, Twilight, Seniors, Juniors.
Caddies: No. **Golf carts:** $16 for 18 holes.
Discount golf packages: No. **Season:** April-Oct. **High:** June-Aug.
On-site lodging: No. **Rental clubs:** Yes.
Walking policy: Unrestricted walking. **Range:** Yes (grass).
To obtain tee times: Call three days in advance for weekdays.
Subscriber comments: New muny, super track, huge trees . . . Greens fantastic . . . One of best layouts in Nebraska . . . Interesting riverside course . . . Problems with flooding on holes near river . . . Interesting links and wooded mix . . . Best kept secret in Nebraska . . . Fast greens . . . Top notch if the river doesn't rise.

★★★★ SHADOW RIDGE COUNTRY CLUB

SP—1501 S. 188th Plaza, Omaha (402)333-0500.

Holes: 18. **Par:** 72/72.
Yards: 7,013/5,176. **Course rating:** 74.6/69.8. **Slope:** 137/116.
Opened: 1994. **Pace of Play rating:** 4:06. **Green fee:** $35/45.
Credit cards: MC, V. **Reduced fees:** Twilight.
Caddies: No. **Golf carts:** $12 for 18 holes.
Discount golf packages: No. **Season:** March-Oct. **High:** May-Sept.
On-site lodging: No. **Rental clubs:** Yes.
Walking policy: Unrestricted walking. **Range:** Yes (grass).

To obtain tee times: Call seven days in advance.

Ranked 2nd in Nebraska by Golf Digest.

Subscriber comments: A beautiful new course, immaculately maintained . . . Just like the courses you see pros play on TV . . . A player's course, long par 4s play into prevailing winds . . . Wonderful fairways, fast greens . . . Area's best! . . . One of the best in Nebraska . . . Different holes . . . New course, can only get better . . . Best in Nebraska, by far an A + . . . Unmowed rough is death . . . Pricey for Omaha . . . Top notch like a resort course, worth the money . . . Greens superfast . . . Deluxe but too much for most amatuers . . . Get rid of trap in the sixth green . . . As their logo indicates this is golf the way it was meant to be, first class . . . Great condition . . . In a few years will be outstanding . . . Like the idea they have of putting the pin placements on the golf cart. Excellent bent-grass fairways . . . Fun course that challenges you, but not discourages.

SKYVIEW GOLF COURSE*

PU—R.R. 2, Alliance (308)762-1446.

45 miles northeast of Scottsbluff. **Holes:** 18. **Par:** 70/72.

Yards: 6,501/5,364. **Course rating:** 70.0/70.6. **Slope:** 112/115.

Opened: 1953. **Pace of Play rating:** 3:30 - 4:00. **Green fee:** $11/13.

Credit cards: None. **Reduced fees:** Juniors.

Caddies: No. **Golf carts:** $7 for 18 holes.

Discount golf packages: No. **Season:** March-Nov. **High:** June-Aug.

On-site lodging: No. **Rental clubs:** Yes.

Walking policy: Unrestricted walking. **Range:** Yes (grass).

To obtain tee times: First come, first served.

★★ THE KNOLLS GOLF COURSE

PU—11630 Sahler St., Omaha (402)493-1740.

Holes: 18. **Par:** 71/71.

Yards: 6,300/5,111. **Course rating:** 69.8/69.8. **Slope:** 123/N/A.

Opened: 1976. **Pace of Play rating:** 4:10. **Green fee:** $14/18.

Credit cards: MC, V, AMEX. **Reduced fees:** Twilight, Seniors, Juniors.

Caddies: No. **Golf carts:** $9 for 18 holes.

Discount golf packages: Yes. **Season:** Year-round. **High:** April-Oct.

On-site lodging: No. **Rental clubs:** Yes.

Walking policy: Unrestricted walking. **Range:** Yes.

To obtain tee times: Call or come in.

Subscriber comments: Started as nine, now 18, each nine different . . . Fairly wide open, short course . . . Typical public course, not hard . . . Has several nice holes . . . Tight and short . . . Back nine older than front . . . A tough one to walk the hills are killers . . . Long walk uphill on back nine . . . Heavy use . . . Typical course, okay place . . . Inexpensive golf . . . Tight front nine . . . Have to play different types of shots.

★★★ THE PINES COUNTRY CLUB

SP—7516 N. 286th St., Valley (402)359-4311.

30 miles west of Omaha. **Holes:** 18. **Par:** 72/72.

Yards: 6,650/5,370. **Course rating:** 69.9/ 70.2. **Slope:** 117/117.

Opened: 1979. **Pace of Play rating:** 4:30. **Green fee:** $15/22.

Credit cards: MC, V. **Reduced fees:** Weekdays, Seniors, Juniors.

Caddies: No. **Golf carts:** $9 for 18 holes.

Discount golf packages: No. **Season:** March-Oct. **High:** May-Aug.

On-site lodging: No. **Rental clubs:** Yes.

Walking policy: Unrestricted walking. **Range:** Yes (grass).

To obtain tee times: Call one week in advance for weekday play and Friday for upcoming weekend.

Subscriber comments: Best greens around . . . Great course to walk . . . Staff is second to none! . . . Almost always blustery . . . Uninspired layout . . . Flat course always wind . . . Challenges many skills . . . A hidden treasure.

★★★ TIBURON GOLF CLUB

SP—10302 S. 168th St., Omaha (402)895-2688.
Holes: 27. **Par:** 72/72/72.
Yards: 6,887/6,932/7,005. **Course rating:** 73.4/73.4/74.2.
Slope: 131/131/137.
Opened: 1989. **Pace of Play rating:** 4:15. **Green fee:** $18/23.
Credit cards: All major. **Reduced fees:** Weekdays, Seniors, Juniors.
Caddies: No. **Golf carts:** $10 for 18 holes.
Discount golf packages: No. **Season:** March-Nov. **High:** June-Sept.
On-site lodging: No. **Rental clubs:** Yes.
Walking policy: Unrestricted walking. **Range:** Yes (grass).
To obtain tee times: Call seven days in advance for weekdays ; weekend times taken five days in advance.
Subscriber comments: Lush greens and nice layout but needs more trees . . . One of the best in area . . . Newly added 3rd nine needs time to mature . . . Improved dramatically, new nine very challenging . . . Very big & fast greens, difficult when windy . . . Huge greens not many trees . . . can be best in Nebraska . . . 11-12-13 are three great holes . . . Few trees on a very exposed and windy sight . . . Lots of potential, wide open . . . Holes 5-14 best in Omaha . . . Still improving . . . Slow play is it's only downfall . . . With 27 holes its one of the best in Omaha.

★★ WILLOW LAKES GOLF CLUB

SP—Bldg. 9950 Offutt AFB, 25th St., Bellevue (402)292-1680.
Call club for further information.
Subscriber comments: Only Robert Trent Jones course in Nebraska . . . Military course must go public . . . Was once perfect . . . Used to really like it . . . Very small greens, water is a factor . . . Good course if kept up . . . Has gone downhill badly in last two years . . . Lots of water and bunkers.

★★★★ WOODLAND HILLS GOLF COURSE

PU—6000 Woodland Hills Dr., Eagle (402)475-4653.
12 miles east of Lincoln. **Holes:** 18. **Par:** 71/71.
Yards: 6,592/4,945. **Course rating:** 71.3/69.8. **Slope:** 125/121.
Opened: 1991. **Pace of Play rating:** 4:00. **Green fee:** $15/30.
Credit cards: MC, V, DISC. **Reduced fees:** Weekdays, Low season, Resort guests, Twilight, Seniors, Juniors.
Caddies: Yes. **Golf carts:** $10 for 18 holes.
Discount golf packages: Yes. **Season:** Year-round. **High:** July-Aug.
On-site lodging: No. **Rental clubs:** Yes.
Walking policy: Unrestricted walking. **Range:** Yes (grass).
To obtain tee times: Call up to 30 days in advance.
Ranked 5th in Nebraska by Golf Digest.
Subscriber comments: Very scenic, great design, best value in the area . . . Worth the small fee . . . Fabulous . . . Built on an old tree farm, beautiful . . . Bent grass, excellent layout . . . For the type of course you would almost expect to pay more in green fees . . . Awesome! Just needs a little length and it's perfect . . . Absolutely the finest in area, all bent, super, super . . . Keep it secret . . . One of the best anywhere . . . I hope new owners keep improving course shape . . . Back to back par 5s . . . Trees, trees, trees . . . A real jewel . . . Perhaps the most enjoyable course in Nebraska . . . Pines, ponds . . . Great golf. Great views. Great value . . . Hard to believe you're in Nebraska . . . Cleverly laid out . . . The pine trees make you think you're in North Carolina.

ANGEL PARK GOLF CLUB

PU—100 S. Rampart Blvd., Las Vegas (702)254-4653.
Opened: 1989. **Pace of Play rating:** N/A. **Green fee:** $50/90.
Credit cards: MC, V, AMEX. **Reduced fees:** Low season, Twilight, Juniors.
Caddies: No. **Golf carts:** Included in Green Fee.
Discount golf packages: No. **Season:** Year-round. **High:** Feb.–June/Sept.–Nov.
On-site lodging: No. **Rental clubs:** Yes.
Walking policy: Mandatory cart. **Range:** Yes (grass).
To obtain tee times: Call 30 days in advance.

★★★ MOUNTAIN COURSE

Holes: 18. **Par:** 71/72.
Yards: 6,722/5,164. **Course rating:** 72.4/69.9. **Slope:** 128/119.
Subscriber comments: New "sorta" desert course . . . Beautiful mountain and city views . . . Not as good as Palm . . . Tough when windy . . . Generally in good shape. Slow play . . . Good Palmer course . . . One of the best in Las Vegas area, nice to play target golf, driver not needed . . . Many long carries, greens like rocks . . . Course is challenging and in good condition . . . A fun course, forgiving . . . Wide open. Stood on first tee and could see 14 of the holes . . . Great driving range, polite staff . . . No homes around golf course.

★★★ PALM COURSE

Holes: 18. **Par:** 70/70.
Yards: 6,530/4,570. **Course rating:** 72.6/67.6. **Slope:** 130/110.
Subscriber comments: Fine course and well maintained, superb staff and clubhouse . . . Hit your ball in the high rough, you lose it . . . Tough when windy . . . Good layout, above average greens . . . Greens very hard and fast, surprising contours for desert course . . . Desert hills, different . . . Some changes to the layout added interest . . . Very hard course . . . Tough putting . . . Nice, tight, good experience but not special . . . A lot of danger spots . . . Loved the practice range, staff is very kind, felt like a king.

★½ BLACK MOUNTAIN GOLF AND COUNTRY CLUB

SP—500 E. Greenway Rd., Henderson (702)565-7933.
15 miles from Las Vegas. **Holes:** 18. **Par:** 72/72.
Yards: 6,541/5,478. **Course rating:** N/A. **Slope:** 123/125.
Opened: N/A. **Pace of Play rating:** N/A. **Green fee:** N/A.
Credit cards: MC, V. **Reduced fees:** Low season.
Caddies: No. **Golf carts:** N/A.
Discount golf packages: No. **Season:** Year-round. **High:** Jan.–May.
On-site lodging: No. **Rental clubs:** No.
Walking policy: N/A. **Range:** Yes (grass).
Subscriber comments: Another good test of golf for us older guys . . . Basic, no-thrills golf course . . . Average condition, nothing special . . . Has improved . . . Under-developed, overpriced, greens look like quilts . . . Bump and run to greens. Greens and fairways in poor condition . . . Old layout, needs help . . . Acceptable alternative to pricy Vegas courses.

★★ BOULDER CITY GOLF CLUB

PU—1 Clubhouse Dr., Boulder City (702)293-9236.
20 miles south of Las Vegas. **Holes:** 18. **Par:** 72/72.
Yards: 6,561/5,566. **Course rating:** 70.2/70.7. **Slope:** 110/113.
Opened: 1972. **Pace of Play rating:** 4:00. **Green fee:** $23.
Credit cards: MC, V. **Reduced fees:** Low season, Twilight.
Caddies: No. **Golf carts:** N/A.
Discount golf packages: Yes. **Season:** Year-round. **High:** Spring/Fall.
On-site lodging: No. **Rental clubs:** Yes.
Walking policy: Unrestricted walking. **Range:** Yes (grass).
To obtain tee times: Call seven days in advance weekdays and eight and nine days for weekends.
Subscriber comments: Fun little layout . . . Basic no-thrills golf. Residents usually play here to avoid tourists . . . Very forgiving course. Service was good . . . Front nine is ho-hum, but back nine rambles more than it is flat . . . Older parkland course, well maintained . . . Best buy in

Las Vegas . . . Very nice muny facility . . . Good course for sprayers . . . Not very punishing for an errant shot, you can recover . . . Greens very inconsistent . . . OK for quick round.

★★★ CALVADA VALLEY GOLF AND COUNTRY CLUB

SP—Red Butte & Mt. Charleston Rd., Pahrump (702)727-4653.
63 miles southwest of Las Vegas. **Holes:** 18. **Par:** 71/73.
Yards: 7,025/5,948. **Course rating:** 73.2/74.3. **Slope:** 124/123.
Opened: 1978. **Pace of Play rating:** 4:00-4:30. **Green fee:** $42.
Credit cards: MC, V. **Reduced fees:** Seniors, Juniors.
Caddies: No. **Golf carts:** Included in Green Fee.
Discount golf packages: Yes. **Season:** Year-round. **High:** Feb.-May/Sept.-Nov.
On-site lodging: No. **Rental clubs:** Yes.
Walking policy: Mandatory cart. **Range:** Yes (grass).
To obtain tee times: Call three days in advance starting at 7 a.m.
Subscriber comments: Down home folks in the clubhouse . . . Use of water overrated . . . Always in great shape, no sand bunkers . . . Don't let the lack of sand fool you, grass bunkers are not user-friendly . . . Not much imagination in design . . . Nice course, good condition . . . Tight with a lot of trees . . . Great condition, tough too.

★½ CRAIG RANCH GOLF COURSE

PU—628 W. Craig Rd., North Las Vegas (702)642-9700.
Holes: 18. **Par:** 70/70.
Yards: 6,001/5,221. **Course rating:** 66.8/67.4. **Slope:** 105/101.
Opened: 1962. **Pace of Play rating:** 4:00. **Green fee:** $13.
Credit cards: None. **Reduced fees:** No.
Caddies: No. **Golf carts:** N/A.
Discount golf packages: No. **Season:** Year-round. **High:** March-May/Oct.-Nov.
On-site lodging: No. **Rental clubs:** Yes.
Walking policy: Unrestricted walking. **Range:** Yes (grass).
To obtain tee times: Call up to seven days in advance.
Subscriber comments: Older course, but easy to get on . . . Decent for area . . . Many trees (hit it straight or you won't score), tight fairways, greens not soft enough to hold, most are sloped so ball rolls off, no traps, just trees . . . Narrow with lots of trees . . . OK-to-poor shape . . . Very nice people . . . Short course in pine trees, small greens, always in bad shape . . . Fairly tight course but short . . . Greens are horrible, like putting on shag carpet . . . Always busy, lots of duffers.

★★★½ DAYTON VALLEY COUNTRY CLUB

SP—51 Palmer Dr., Dayton (702)246-7888.
35 miles southeast of Reno. **Holes:** 18. **Par:** 72/72.
Yards: 7,218/5,161. **Course rating:** 72.9/68.4. **Slope:** 136/121.
Opened: 1991. **Pace of Play rating:** N/A. **Green fee:** $25/70.
Credit cards: MC, V. **Reduced fees:** Weekdays, Low season, Twilight, Juniors.
Caddies: No. **Golf carts:** Included in Green Fee.
Discount golf packages: No. **Season:** Year-round. **High:** May-Oct.
On-site lodging: No. **Rental clubs:** Yes.
Walking policy: Unrestricted walking. **Range:** Yes (grass).
To obtain tee times: Call two weeks in advance.
Ranked 5th in Nevada by Golf Digest.
Subscriber comments: Arnold Palmer designed . . . Wow! A class act, tough . . . Good course, artificial . . . Watch out for wind . . . Worth the drive from Reno . . . In the high desert, Arnold did a great job with plenty of sand and water. Target golf at its best, not an easy course . . . Great Palmer course with dramatic mountain surroundings . . . Fun course, nice challenge . . . Great last three holes on each nine. Best greens in Reno area . . . Windy, windy, windy! . . . Seven, eight and nine are a real challenge, good golf course . . . A real sleeper . . . Incredible fairways . . . Play early a.m., strong p.m. wind . . . Best condition in northern Nevada . . . Best-kept secret in the Tahoe area.

★★★½ DESERT INN GOLF CLUB
R—3145 Las Vegas Blvd. South, Las Vegas (702)733-4290, (800)634-6909.
Holes: 18. **Par:** 72/72.
Yards: 7,066/5,791. **Course rating:** 73.9/72.7. **Slope:** 124/121.
Opened: 1952. **Pace of Play rating:** 4:30-5:00. **Green fee:** $100/165.
Credit cards: All major. **Reduced fees:** Low season, Resort guests.
Caddies: No. **Golf carts:** Included in Green Fee.
Discount golf packages: No. **Season:** Year-round. **High:** Feb.-May.
On-site lodging: Yes. **Rental clubs:** Yes.
Walking policy: Mandatory cart. **Range:** Yes (grass).
To obtain tee times: Call.
Ranked 65th in America's 75 Best Resort Courses by Golf Digest. Ranked 6th in Nevada by Golf Digest.
Subscriber comments: If you want the most memorable Las Vegas golf this is it . . . Great urban course . . . Good shape . . . Anybody can have fun . . . Great layout and views of holes . . . Should have gone to a show . . . As good as any in the USA . . . Fine resort course, well maintained . . . An old master better than recent pretenders,

★ DESERT ROSE GOLF COURSE
PU—5483 Clubhouse Dr., Las Vegas (702)431-4653.
Holes: 18. **Par:** 71/71.
Yards: 6,511/5,458. **Course rating:** 70.7/69.6. **Slope:** 112/107.
Opened: 1962. **Pace of Play rating:** N/A. **Green fee:** $48.
Credit cards: MC, V. **Reduced fees:** Low season, Twilight, Seniors, Juniors.
Caddies: No. **Golf carts:** N/A.
Discount golf packages: No. **Season:** Year-round. **High:** Sept.-June.
On-site lodging: No. **Rental clubs:** Yes.
Walking policy: Unrestricted walking. **Range:** Yes (grass).
To obtain tee times: Call seven days in advance for weekdays and three days in advance for weekend play.
Subscriber comments: Layout good but condition of course suspect . . . This course is anything but a rose . . . Slow, flat and hard. What happened to grass seed? . . . Flat and predictable layout . . . Sloping fairways, some water, lined with houses . . . Rough shape . . . Ball washers with liquid needed . . . Poorly maintained . . . The ditch! . . . Don't use your good set of clubs.

EAGLE VALLEY GOLF CLUB
PU—3999 Centennial Park Dr., Carson City (702)887-2380.
30 miles south of Reno.
Pace of Play rating: 4:00.
Credit cards: None. **Reduced fees:** Twilight. **Caddies:** No.
Discount golf packages: No. **Season:** Year-round. **High:** May-Sept.
On-site lodging: No. **Rental clubs:** Yes.
To obtain tee times: Call Friday at 3 p.m. for the following Monday through Sunday.

★★★ EAST COURSE
Holes: 18. **Par:** 72/72.
Yards: 6,658/5,980. **Course rating:** 68.7/72.8. **Slope:** 117/123.
Opened: 1977. **Green fee:** $18.
Golf carts: $17 for 18 holes.
Walking policy: Walking at certain times. **Range:** Yes (grass).
Subscriber comments: Grip and rip it. Fun, flat course . . . Straight, wide open, boring . . . Flat but good, high desert condition . . . Fun course, open, easy to hit greens . . . Real easy course . . . Your basic flat easy muny that is fun to walk and play . . . Loved it! Challenge for anyone. Links setup is ideal for rolling sagebrush hills . . . Average design and experience . . . Long course, very windy . . . Open and a challenge . . . Excellent staff, best deal in Nevada . . . Terrific value if you're staying in Tahoe.

★★★ WEST COURSE
Holes: 18. **Par:** 72/72.
Yards: 6,851/5,293. **Course rating:** 73.5/68.8. **Slope:** 131/117.
Opened: 1987. **Green fee:** $33.
Golf carts: Included in Green Fee.

Walking policy: Mandatory cart. **Range:** Yes (grass).
Subscriber comments: More difficult than East Course . . . Good test from tips, very friendly staff . . . Some great holes, especially No. 3, tough . . . Excellent target golf facility . . . Target concept of golf, championship tees will challenge the best . . . 180 degrees from East Course. This is a rip and chip layout . . . Mountainside greens are getting too fast . . . When the wind blows it's impossible, otherwise straight forward . . . Great scenery, championship quality, always fun . . . A gorgeous setting . . . So, the wind doesn't bother you? Try this in the p.m. hours . . . Usually in good shape, very challenging.

★★★★½ **EDGEWOOD TAHOE GOLF COURSE**
R—U.S. Hwy. 50 and Lake Pky., Stateline (702)588-3566.
50 miles southwest of Reno. **Holes:** 18. **Par:** 72/72.
Yards: 7,491/5,749. **Course rating:** 75.1/71.5. **Slope:** 136/130.
Opened: 1968. **Pace of Play rating:** 4:00. **Green fee:** $125.
Credit cards: MC, V, AMEX. **Reduced fees:** No.
Caddies: Yes. **Golf carts:** Included in Green Fee.
Discount golf packages: No. **Season:** May-Oct. **High:** July-Sept.
On-site lodging: No. **Rental clubs:** Yes.
Walking policy: Unrestricted walking. **Range:** Yes (grass).
To obtain tee times: Call two weeks, to the day, in advance.
Ranked in First 25 of America's 75 Best Public Golf Courses by Golf Digest. Ranked 2nd in Nevada by Golf Digest.
Subscriber comments: Finest public course in the West . . . A real joy to play . . . Too bad Nevada golf has to be so expensive . . . Spectacular, what an enjoyment . . . Absolutely gorgeous, great views of lake . . . Quality golf in beautiful setting, must do it once . . . Overrated, some tough holes . . . Best in northern Nevada . . . Beautiful and scenic, is best in Lake Tahoe, well kept . . . Immaculate conditions . . . Cart rule silly . . . Best in Tahoe area . . . Back tees make it hardest course on the West Coast . . . Awesome scenery. Large fairways and greens . . . Great facility, good people . . . Like playing in a postcard . . . Better than Pebble, enough said! . . . High altitude golf at its finest, No. 16 is one of the best holes in the world . . . From the tips in breeze is a killer . . . Beautiful setting, lush . . . Fairly flat, wide fairways and lots of trees . . . A must play. Tahoe's beauty plus great golf.

★★½ **EMERALD RIVER GOLF COURSE**
PU—1155 W. Casino Dr., Laughlin (702)298-0061.
90 miles south of Las Vegas. **Holes:** 18. **Par:** 72/72.
Yards: 6,809/5,205. **Course rating:** 73.6/71.3. **Slope:** 144/129.
Opened: 1990. **Pace of Play rating:** N/A. **Green fee:** $29.
Credit cards: MC, V. **Reduced fees:** Weekdays, Low season, Resort guests, Twilight, Seniors, Juniors.
Caddies: No. **Golf carts:** Included in Green Fee.
Discount golf packages: Yes. **Season:** Year-round. **High:** Jan.-May/Oct.-Nov.
On-site lodging: No. **Rental clubs:** Yes.
Walking policy: Mandatory cart. **Range:** Yes (grass).
To obtain tee times: Call seven days in advance unless staying on a golf package, then it's 10 days in advance.
Subscriber comments: Toughest course around . . . Course condition was unacceptable . . . I enjoy target courses . . . Someday it might be great . . . Tough challenge . . . Nice layout along the river . . . This is the hardest golf course I have ever played . . . Golf course from hell, will help you appreciate your home course . . . Too many layup shots on par 4s . . . Fun and narrow . . . Barren and windy . . . Course has potential but needs better conditioning . . . Not a flat lie on the whole course . . . Lovely and long, you must have a mental game here . . . Great target course, a desert classic . . . Has some truly bizarre holes and greens . . . Gnats are terrible . . . Tough links along Colorado River . . . Desert heat and winds make for tough rounds. You gotta hit straight here . . . Better than the slots.

★★★★ THE GOLF CLUB AT GENOA LAKES

PU—1 Genoa Lakes Dr., Genoa (702)782-4653.
15 miles east of So. Lake Tahoe. **Holes:** 18. **Par:** 72/72.
Yards: 7,263/5,008. **Course rating:** 73.5/67.6. **Slope:** 134/117.
Opened: 1993. **Pace of Play rating:** 4:30. **Green fee:** $40/75.
Credit cards: MC, V, AMEX. **Reduced fees:** Weekdays, Low season.
Caddies: No. **Golf carts:** Included in Green Fee.
Discount golf packages: No. **Season:** Year-round. **High:** May-Sept.
On-site lodging: No. **Rental clubs:** Yes.
Walking policy: Unrestricted walking. **Range:** Yes (grass).
To obtain tee times: Call up to 30 days in advance.
Ranked 3rd in Nevada by Golf Digest.
Subscriber comments: Great new course, greens surprisingly good . . .
Could hold a PGA Tour event . . . Very enjoyable . . . Too many blind
shots for the first-time player . . . Second best-kept secret in Tahoe . . .
Don't play in the afternoon. Gale-force winds . . . Every club in your bag.
Overtime for your putter . . . Finally, another Edgewood on the south side
of the lake . . . Numerous tees, course may be too tough for average player,
too many forced carries . . . Great diversity of hole design, gorgeous
scenery . . . Very tough, expecially in usual afternoon winds . . . Great
creative design. Beautiful, a must . . . Open desert course but plays tough,
par 5 No. 9 is a great hole . . . A great memorable course. Look out if the
strong wind is blowing, water is everywhere . . . Tricky but nice . . . Still
new, no clubhouse . . . One of the best courses in the West.

INCLINE VILLAGE GOLF RESORT
★★★★ CHAMPIONSHIP COURSE

R—955 Fairway Blvd., Incline Village (702)832-1144.
30 miles southwest of Reno. **Holes:** 18. **Par:** 72/72.
Yards: 6,915/5,350. **Course rating:** 72.6/70.5. **Slope:** 129/126.
Opened: 1964. **Pace of Play rating:** 4:30. **Green fee:** $100.
Credit cards: MC, V. **Reduced fees:** Twilight.
Caddies: No. **Golf carts:** Included in Green Fee.
Discount golf packages: No. **Season:** May-Oct. **High:** June-Sept.
On-site lodging: No. **Rental clubs:** Yes.
Walking policy: Unrestricted walking. **Range:** Yes.
To obtain tee times: Call two weeks in advance.
Ranked in Third 25 of America's 75 Best Public Golf Courses by Golf
Digest. Ranked 9th in Nevada by Golf Digest.
Subscriber comments: Nothing but great golf . . . Best course at the lake
. . . Starting to feel like a muny . . . One of the most overrated in the West
. . . Beautiful course, good shape . . . Fine course, some spectacular holes
. . . Best course in Nevada, nice challenge . . . A two-putter wins all the
bets. Putts from hell . . . Has slipped lately in conditioning . . . Good solid
muny . . . Rank course not too far behind Edgewood . . . Beautiful views,
tough test in woods . . . Must be low handicap to play from back tees . . .
Challenging. Beautiful scenery. Nice fairways and greens . . . If vacationing
at Tahoe, it's a must play.

JACKPOT GOLF CLUB★

PU—P.O. Box 388, Jackpot (702)755-2260.
Call club for further information.
Subscriber comments: Only green spot for miles . . . Fun course . . .
Excellent condition year round . . . Well-kept.

★★★ LAKERIDGE GOLF COURSE

PU—1200 Razorback Rd., Reno (702)825-2200.
Holes: 18. **Par:** 71/71.
Yards: 6,703/5,159. **Course rating:** 70.8/68.5. **Slope:** 127/117.
Opened: 1969. **Pace of Play rating:** 4:14. **Green fee:** $36/58.
Credit cards: MC, V. **Reduced fees:** Low season, Twilight.
Caddies: No. **Golf carts:** Included in Green Fee.
Discount golf packages: No. **Season:** March-Dec. **High:** April-Oct.
On-site lodging: No. **Rental clubs:** Yes.
Walking policy: Walking at certain times. **Range:** Yes.

To obtain tee times: Call seven days in advance.
Subscriber comments: What can I say? Another Trent Jones gem . . .
Some fantastic holes; really liked signature hole . . . Conditioning not the
best . . . 15th island green spectacular . . . The island hole belongs in a
miniature golf course . . . No. 15 spectacular . . . Island green is beautiful
. . . Interesting 15th hole . . . Best guest service in Nevada . . . Drought has
hurt condition of the fairways; 15th hole is best in Reno . . . Front nine flat
and boring, back nine better . . . No. 15 the most dramatic par 3 I've ever
seen. Great course . . . No. 15 is a great hole, the rest is pretty ordinary . . .
Good solid golf course, many different looks. The island 15th worth it all
. . . Wide fairways, a lot of elevation change . . . Be a man, play the 15th
from back tees.

★★½ LAS VEGAS GOLF CLUB

PU—4300 West Washington, Las Vegas (702)646-3003.
Holes: 18. **Par:** 72/72.
Yards: 6,631/5,715. **Course rating:** 71.8/71.2. **Slope:** 117/113.
Opened: 1947. **Pace of Play rating:** 4:20. **Green fee:** $21.
Credit cards: None. **Reduced fees:** Twilight, Seniors, Juniors.
Caddies: No. **Golf carts:** N/A.
Discount golf packages: No. **Season:** Year-round. **High:** Year-round.
On-site lodging: No. **Rental clubs:** Yes.
Walking policy: Unrestricted walking. **Range:** Yes (grass).
To obtain tee times: Call up to seven days in advance.
Subscriber comments: Municipal with lots of trees . . . Good for all, staff
good, good pace . . . Slow play due to numbers, conditions vary greatly
. . . Well-kept . . . A place to swing your clubs . . . Hard to beat for a great
day . . . Sardine course, way too many people for one can.

★★★½ LAS VEGAS HILTON COUNTRY CLUB

R—1911 E. Desert Inn Rd., Las Vegas (702)796-0013, (800)884-1818.
Holes: 18. **Par:** 71/71.
Yards: 6,815/5,741. **Course rating:** 72.1/72.9. **Slope:** 130/127.
Opened: 1961. **Pace of Play rating:** 4:30-5:00. **Green fee:** $110/125.
Credit cards: MC, V, AMEX. **Reduced fees:** Weekdays, Low season,
Twilight, Juniors.
Caddies: No. **Golf carts:** Included in Green Fee.
Discount golf packages: No. **Season:** Year-round. **High:** Feb.-May.
On-site lodging: No. **Rental clubs:** Yes.
Walking policy: Mandatory cart. **Range:** Yes (grass).
To obtain tee times: Sixty day advance tee times with American Golf
Corporations Resort time office. Credit card required.
Formerly known as Sahara Country Club
Subscriber comments: Old, cultured course . . . Simple layout but very
challenging . . . Older course, but in great shape . . . Tight and tough . . .
Excellent course, computerized yardage, super greens . . . Mature ho-hum
course . . . Cut like a tour event, three distinct cuts on fairway . . . Still one
of best in Las Vegas . . . Mature course, very challenging from the tips,
could easily be walked but a cart is unfortunately required . . . Changed
name, same old course . . . Wonderful test with lots of history, recently
conditions have been rough . . . Excellent course, significant improvements
in last two years.

LAS VEGAS PAUITE RESORT★

PU—Snow Mtn. Rd., Las Vegas (702)658-1400.
Holes: 18. **Par:** 72/72.
Yards: 7,158/5,241. **Course rating:** 73.9/70.4. **Slope:** 125/117.
Opened: 1995. **Pace of Play rating:** 4:00. **Green fee:** $85.
Credit cards: MC, V, AMEX. **Reduced fees:** Twilight.
Caddies: No. **Golf carts:** Included in Green Fee.
Discount golf packages: No. **Season:** Year-round. **High:** May-Oct.
On-site lodging: No. **Rental clubs:** Yes.
Walking policy: Mandatory cart. **Range:** Yes (grass).
To obtain tee times: Call seven days in advance.

NEVADA

★★★½ THE LEGACY GOLF CLUB
PU—130 Par Excellence Dr., Henderson (702)897-2187.
10 miles southeast of Las Vegas. **Holes:** 18. **Par:** 72/72.
Yards: 7,233/5,340. **Course rating:** 74.9/71.0. **Slope:** 136/120.
Opened: 1989. **Pace of Play rating:** 4:00-4:30. **Green fee:** $95.
Credit cards: MC, V, AMEX. **Reduced fees:** Twilight.
Caddies: No. **Golf carts:** Included in Green Fee.
Discount golf packages: No. **Season:** Year-round. **High:** Sept.-June.
On-site lodging: No. **Rental clubs:** Yes.
Walking policy: Mandatory cart. **Range:** Yes (grass).
To obtain tee times: Tee times can be made with a credit card to
guarantee.
Ranked 8th in Nevada by Golf Digest.
Subscriber comments: Many different looks and shots. Great layout . . .
Nice course . . . Long, tough course. Conditions sometimes weak. Play
early in day to beat wind and heat . . . Fantastic course, very playable, no
hidden gimmicks or hazards . . . Classic tee boxes on the 10th. Awesome
track . . . Tees were prettiest I've ever seen . . . Absolute enjoyment from
tee to green . . . Very challenging course, slow play . . . Nice, excellent
greens. Don't hit it in the lava rock . . . Worth the cab ride from the strip.

★★★ NORTHGATE GOLF COURSE
R—1111 Clubhouse Dr., Reno (702)747-7577.
Holes: 18. **Par:** 72/72.
Yards: 6,966/5,521. **Course rating:** 72.3/70.2. **Slope:** 131/127.
Opened: 1988. **Pace of Play rating:** N/A. **Green fee:** $26/39.
Credit cards: MC, V. **Reduced fees:** Weekdays, Low season, Resort
guests, Twilight.
Caddies: No. **Golf carts:** Included in Green Fee.
Discount golf packages: No. **Season:** Year-round. **High:** June-Sept.
On-site lodging: No. **Rental clubs:** Yes.
Walking policy: Unrestricted walking. **Range:** Yes (grass).
To obtain tee times: Call seven days in advance.
Subscriber comments: Links layout stunning, requires thoughtful golf
. . . Course stays in good condition all season. Local knowledge helpful . . .
Too many blind shots, wind, moguls in hitting area, bad bounce . . . Very
hilly, like playing on the moon . . . Links style, lots of target shots . . .
Must play with someone that has played it often . . . Drought conditions
makes course poor, super elevated 15th hole, scenic . . . Blind shots galore.
Work, not fun . . . Great course if you are playing well . . . Best and fastest
greens in Reno . . . Survived drought by reducing watered areas . . .
Fabulous views of Reno . . . No straight putts . . . Fairways and greens
very undulating with severe uphill and downhill lies . . . If you like lots of
sand, little fairway grass, go to it.

OASIS RESORT HOTEL CASINO
R—(800)621-0187. 77 miles northeast of Las Vegas.
Credit cards: All major.
Caddies: No. **Golf carts:** Included in Green Fee.
Season: Year-round. **High:** Jan.-May/Oct.-Nov.
On-site lodging: Yes. **Rental clubs:** Yes. **Range:** Yes (grass).
To obtain tee times: Call up to 28 days in advance.
OASIS GOLF COURSE★
851 Oasis Blvd., Mesquite (702)346-7820.
Holes: 18. **Par:** 72/N/A.
Yards: 6,982/N/A. **Course rating:** N/A. **Slope:** N/A.
Opened: 1955. **Pace of Play rating:** N/A. **Green fee:** $125.
Reduced fees: No.
Discount golf packages: No. **Walking policy:** N/A.
★★★½ PALMS GOLF COURSE
2200 Hillside Dr., Mesquite (702)346-5232.
Holes: 18. **Par:** 72/72.
Yards: 7,008/6,284. **Course rating:** 74.9/70.4. **Slope:** 137/122.
Opened: 1989. **Pace of Play rating:** N/A. **Green fee:** $65/85.
Reduced fees: Weekdays, Low season, Resort guests, Twilight.
Discount golf packages: Yes. **Walking policy:** Mandatory cart.
Formerly known as Peppermill Palms Golf Club.

Subscriber comments: Great course in middle of nowhere . . . Watery front and scenic back . . . Lots of water . . . Each nine completely different . . . Back nine is spectacular . . . Back nine damn difficult, uphill and downhill . . . Don't try to walk back nine unless you're a goat! . . . Florida front, very mountainous back . . . Front side vs. back side, night vs. day . . . Best-kept fairways . . . Lush, green in desert; long, tough par 5s . . . Fun course, management very professional . . . Back nine makes it all worthwhile . . . No waiting, got right on. Beautiful, lush course . . . Back nine has some awesome cliff golf . . . Course is tired.

★★★½ PAINTED DESERT GOLF CLUB

PU—5555 Painted Mirage Way, Las Vegas (702)645-2568.
Holes: 18. **Par:** 72/72.
Yards: 6,840/5,711. **Course rating:** 73.7/72.7. **Slope:** 136/120.
Opened: 1987. **Pace of Play rating:** N/A. **Green fee:** $90.
Credit cards: MC, V, AMEX. **Reduced fees:** Low season, Twilight, Juniors.
Caddies: No. **Golf carts:** Included in Green Fee.
Discount golf packages: No. **Season:** Year-round. **High:** Sept.-June.
On-site lodging: No. **Rental clubs:** Yes.
Walking policy: Mandatory cart. **Range:** Yes (grass).
To obtain tee times: Call seven days in advance.
Subscriber comments: Very nice course which mixes the desert . . . Too many fairway homes . . . Long and narrow . . . Howling winds . . . Dirt devils everywhere . . . Away from strip . . . Has become way too expensive . . . Beautifully maintained, target golf, a long day awaits if you can't get off the tee . . . On "carts path only" holes, better yardage markers needed . . . Too narrow for a driver . . . Desert course, but nothing special . . . Always in great condition, you have to hit it straight . . . Very challenging, but too many houses around course . . . But becoming more difficult with houses going up . . . Fast but true greens, exceptionally well-manicured fairways; beautiful mountain scenery surrounds the course.

★★★ ROSEWOOD LAKES GOLF COURSE

PU—6800 Pembroke Dr., Reno (702)857-2892.
Holes: 18. **Par:** 72/72.
Yards: 6,693/5,082. **Course rating:** 71.1/68.2. **Slope:** 127/117.
Opened: 1991. **Pace of Play rating:** 4:30. **Green fee:** $12/24.
Credit cards: MC, V. **Reduced fees:** Low season, Twilight, Seniors, Juniors.
Caddies: No. **Golf carts:** $18 for 18 holes.
Discount golf packages: No. **Season:** Year-round. **High:** April-Nov.
On-site lodging: No. **Rental clubs:** Yes.
Walking policy: Unrestricted walking. **Range:** Yes (grass).
To obtain tee times: Call one week in advance for weekdays and Monday prior for weekends.
Subscriber comments: New course, wetlands make it scenic . . . Target golf, short but tight, leave driver in car . . . Summer mosquitoes . . . Lots of trouble . . . Short but very challenging . . . Picturesque wetlands . . . If you are errant, can be very penal . . . Some monotony in hole similarity, easy to walk . . . Geese and ducks have taken over course, droppings everywhere . . . Not a lot of trees, well maintained . . . Fun and challenging . . . Excellent layout, wetlands area, mosquitoes . . . Pace of play one of the best in area.

★★★½ RUBY VIEW GOLF COURSE

PU—2100 Ruby View Dr., Elko (702)738-6212.

SUPER VALUE

Holes: 18. **Par:** 72/72.
Yards: 6,928/5,958. **Course rating:** 70.5/72.5. **Slope:** 118/123.
Opened: 1967. **Pace of Play rating:** 4:00. **Green fee:** $18.
Credit cards: None. **Reduced fees:** Twilight.
Caddies: No. **Golf carts:** $16 for 18 holes.
Discount golf packages: No. **Season:** March-Nov. **High:** June-Aug.
On-site lodging: No. **Rental clubs:** Yes.
Walking policy: Unrestricted walking. **Range:** Yes (grass).
To obtain tee times: Call one week in advance.
Subscriber comments: Exceptionally well-conditioned public course with

great shot values and plenty of length and bunkers . . . Some good holes, fairly wide open, very good greens . . . Great staff, great place to play . . . Great par 4s . . . Not too difficult . . . Course in great shape even in drought . . . Greens very fast and lots of breaks, fairways forgiving and in great shape . . . Easy walking course. Very level and limited water hazards . . . Great layout and facility for a muny, not many like this one.

★ SIERRA SAGE GOLF COURSE
PU—6355 Silverlake Rd., Reno (702)972-1564.
Holes: 18. **Par:** 71/72.
Yards: 6,650/5,573. **Course rating:** 69.3/69.6. **Slope:** 120/113.
Opened: 1963. **Pace of Play rating:** 4:15. **Green fee:** $15/23.
Credit cards: None. **Reduced fees:** Weekdays, Low season, Twilight, Seniors, Juniors.
Caddies: No. **Golf carts:** N/A.
Discount golf packages: No. **Season:** Year-round. **High:** May-Oct.
On-site lodging: No. **Rental clubs:** Yes.
Walking policy: Unrestricted walking. **Range:** Yes (grass).
To obtain tee times: Call on Monday for upcoming weekend unless it's a holiday, then call Tuesday 7 a.m. Weekdays, call one week in advance.
Subscriber comments: Another easy walking course . . : Must keep ball in the fairways or you will be hitting out of sagebrush and rocks . . . Good for a public course, don't go off the fairway . . . Drought has hurt fairways . . . Needs a lot of help . . . It's golf . . . Staff OK, snail's pace . . . Overplayed muny course, fairways are poor . . . If in rough, practice hitting off 2x4's . . . Known locally as TPC: Terrible Playing Conditions.

SPRING CREEK GOLF COURSE★
PU—431 E. Spring Creek Pkwy., Elko (702)753-6331.
240 miles west of Salt Lake City. **Holes:** 18. **Par:** 71/71.
Yards: 6,258/5,658. **Course rating:** N/A. **Slope:** 125/119.
Call club for further information.

SUN CITY LAS VEGAS GOLF CLUB
(702)254-7010.
Opened: 1989. **Pace of Play rating:** N/A. **Green fee:** $35/95.
Credit cards: MC, V, AMEX. **Reduced fees:** Weekdays, Low season, Juniors.
Caddies: No. **Golf carts:** Included in Green Fee.
Discount golf packages: No. **Season:** Year-round. **High:** Oct.-May.
On-site lodging: No. **Rental clubs:** Yes.
Walking policy: Mandatory cart. **Range:** Yes (grass).
To obtain tee times: Call seven days in advance for weekends and three days in advance for weekdays after 2 p.m.
★★★½ HIGHLAND FALLS COURSE
SP—10201 Sun City Blvd., Las Vegas
Holes: 18. **Par:** 72/72.
Yards: 6,512/5,099. **Course rating:** 71.2/68.8. **Slope:** 126/110.
Subscriber comments: Top drawer . . . Finishing hole a must-see . . . Newer course, great future . . . Greg Nash, Billy Casper design . . . Nice retirement course . . . Breathtaking views . . . Super layout . . . Well maintained, challenging . . . Outstanding layout, especially from blue tees . . . Greens are still maturing . . . Scenic interest adds pleasure to a wide, well-maintained course . . . Panoramic views of Las Vegas.
★★★½ PALM VALLEY COURSE
SP—9201-B Del Webb Blvd, Las Vegas.
Holes: 18. **Par:** 72/72.
Yards: 6,849/5,502. **Course rating:** 72.3/71.5. **Slope:** 127/124.
Subscriber comments: Very good overall . . . Maturing very well, fine greens and traps . . . Greg Nash, Billy Casper design, a good balance . . . Good conditioning, staff good, not as breathtaking as sister course Highland Falls . . . Undulating bent grass greens . . . Good layout, similar to European courses with many moguls. Wide fairways, but when rough is allowed to grow one needs to be straight and narrow . . . Wide, green and rolling . . . Excellent condition, Sun City seniors hangout.

TOANA VISTA GOLF COURSE★
PU—2319 Pueblo Blvd., Wendover (702)664-4300.
Call club for further information.
Subscriber comments: Tight desert course in great shape, real challenge from back tees, water in play on several holes . . . Variety to course, blind shots, narrow, tough fairways . . . Tough, tough greens and tight fairways. Nice course . . . Can't believe there's a course this nice at the edge of hell.

★½ WASHOE COUNTY GOLF CLUB
PU—2601 South Arlington, Reno (702)828-6640.
Holes: 18. **Par:** 72/74.
Yards: 6,695/5,863. **Course rating:** 70.0/72.9. **Slope:** 119/122.
Opened: 1948. **Pace of Play rating:** 4:30. **Green fee:** $15/20.
Credit cards: None. **Reduced fees:** Low season, Twilight, Seniors, Juniors.
Caddies: No. **Golf carts:** N/A.
Discount golf packages: No. **Season:** Year-round. **High:** April-Oct.
On-site lodging: No. **Rental clubs:** Yes.
Walking policy: Unrestricted walking. **Range:** Yes.
To obtain tee times: Call one week in advance.
Subscriber comments: Good economy course . . . Lack of water, dry fairways . . . Very small, hard greens . . . Needs new sprinklers, straight and level tee boxes . . . Pro shop people were nice, but course condition wasn't . . . Nice county course, well kept . . . Yawn. Slow pace, unexciting. Fairways spotty . . . Nice old course, never in good shape . . . Is great in the summer.

★★½ WILD HORSE GOLF CLUB
R—1 Showboat Club Dr., Henderson (702)434-9009, (800)468-7918.
8 miles southeast of Las Vegas. **Holes:** 18. **Par:** 72/72.
Yards: 7,053/5,372. **Course rating:** 75.2/71.3. **Slope:** 135/125.
Opened: 1969. **Pace of Play rating:** N/A. **Green fee:** $65/85.
Credit cards: MC, V, AMEX. **Reduced fees:** Low season, Twilight, Juniors.
Caddies: No. **Golf carts:** Included in Green Fee.
Discount golf packages: No. **Season:** Year-round. **High:** Oct.-May.
On-site lodging: No. **Rental clubs:** Yes.
Walking policy: Mandatory cart. **Range:** Yes (grass).
To obtain tee times: Call (800)468-7918 for 60 days in advance. Golf shop will book seven days in advance.
Formerly known as Royal Kenfield Golf Club.
Subscriber comments: Fine rebuilt course, interesting layouts, each hole seems different . . . Nice course. Improving. Interesting, tight layout, a few tricked up holes . . . Nice layout . . . Toughest course in Las Vegas . . . Gets better every day, slow greens . . . Good layout, fun course . . . Well-bunkered like a Palm Springs course . . . Could be a good course if taken care of . . . Old Showboat course . . . If they ever get it in shape, tough . . . Always changing names.

★½ WILDCREEK GOLF COURSE
PU—3500 Sullivan Lane, Sparks (702)673-3100.
1 miles north of Reno. **Holes:** 18. **Par:** 72/72.
Yards: 6,932/5,472. **Course rating:** 73.0/70.5. **Slope:** 133/120.
Opened: 1978. **Pace of Play rating:** 4:35. **Green fee:** $28/48.
Credit cards: MC, V. **Reduced fees:** Low season, Twilight.
Caddies: No. **Golf carts:** Included in Green Fee.
Discount golf packages: Yes. **Season:** Feb.-Dec. **High:** April-Oct.
On-site lodging: No. **Rental clubs:** Yes.
Walking policy: Walking at certain times. **Range:** Yes (grass).
To obtain tee times: Call seven days in advance.
Subscriber comments: Good course when it has water . . . Will someday be a great course if a water source is found . . . Back nine is challenging . . . Must know where to hit it from tee . . . Water, good par 3s, par 5s short . . . It dried up . . . Good course when it has water . . . Rock-hard, cement greens . . . Hilly, fast greens, wide open . . . Enjoyable, great vistas, this is golf . . . 50% of course on steep hillside, greens are hard to read and putt . . . Best course in northern Nevada when they have water.

★★½ ANGEL FIRE COUNTRY CLUB

R—Drawer B, Angel Fire (505)377-3055.
150 miles from Albuquerque. **Holes:** 18. **Par:** 72/72.
Yards: 6,624/5,328. **Course rating:** N/A. **Slope:** 128/118.
Opened: N/A. **Pace of Play rating:** N/A. **Green fee:** N/A.
Credit cards: All major. **Reduced fees:** Low season, Resort guests.
Caddies: No. **Golf carts:** $20 for 18 holes.
Discount golf packages: Yes. **Season:** May-Oct. **High:** June-Sept.
On-site lodging: Yes. **Rental clubs:** No.
Walking policy: N/A. **Range:** Yes.
Subscriber comments: Great views, especially from one downhill par 3
. . . Scenic layout, some excellent holes, very long with elevation . . .
Mountain golf, short front, better back, C+ . . . A few great holes, a few
botched holes, high altitude, distance, friendly staff . . . A good resort
course with some fun holes . . . Beautiful layout of holes. Very scenic.
Maintenance poor . . . Saw a bear on No. 2 . . . Great back nine, beautiful
scenery, greens in bad shape.

★★½ ARROYO DEL OSO MUNICIPAL GOLF COURSE

PU—7001 Osuna Rd. N.E., Albuquerque (505)884-7505.
Holes: 18. **Par:** 72/73.
Yards: 6,892/5,998. **Course rating:** 72.3/72.3. **Slope:** 125/120.
Opened: 1966. **Pace of Play rating:** N/A. **Green fee:** $13.
Credit cards: MC, V, DISC. **Reduced fees:** Twilight, Seniors, Juniors.
Caddies: No. **Golf carts:** $10 for 18 holes.
Discount golf packages: No. **Season:** Year-round. **High:** April-Nov.
On-site lodging: No. **Rental clubs:** Yes.
Walking policy: Unrestricted walking. **Range:** Yes (grass).
To obtain tee times: First come, first served all days except Saturdays,
Sundays and holidays.
Also has 9-hole Dam Course
Subscriber comments: Tough course, great personnel but needs some
grass work . . . Plain Jane course, good condition, no imagination . . . Pace
of play somewhat slow, staff is excellent . . . Excellent municipal course,
crowded, challenging . . . Too many rounds detract . . . Best public course
in Albuquerque. Always well-maintained . . . Good use of hills and
arroyos, fun course, nice mountain scenery . . . Fun to play, but wouldn't
want it for a home course . . . Flat course, not very challenging.

★★★½ COCHITI LAKE GOLF COURSE

PU—5200 Cochiti Hwy., Cochiti Lake (505)465-2239.
35 miles southwest of Santa Fe. **Holes:** 18. **Par:** 72/72.
Yards: 6,451/5,292. **Course rating:** 71.2/70.6. **Slope:** 131/121.
Opened: 1981. **Pace of Play rating:** 4:00-4:30. **Green fee:** $18/20.
Credit cards: MC, V, DISC. **Reduced fees:** Weekdays.
Caddies: No. **Golf carts:** $10 for 18 holes.
Discount golf packages: No. **Season:** Year-round. **High:** March-Oct.
On-site lodging: No. **Rental clubs:** Yes.
Walking policy: Unrestricted walking. **Range:** Yes (grass).
To obtain tee times: Call up to seven days in advance.
Ranked in First 25 of America's 75 Best Public Golf Courses by Golf
Digest. Ranked 4th in New Mexico by Golf Digest.
Subscriber comments: Worth the extra miles to get there, tough . . .
Great course layout by R.T. Jones Jr. exceptional course, killer greens . . .
No. 1 in state . . . Excellent, looks like PGA West . . . Over 6,000 feet,
don't try to walk this one . . . Gorgeous course in very good condition . . .
What a find! . . . Great views. Can be difficult . . . Sometimes has poor
maintenance . . . Absolutely marvelous, all alone with nature, top public
course for sure . . . Lovely setting, good assortment of holes . . . Fantastic
vistas, golf course not in great condition . . . Course in great condition, a
hidden gem, lacks clubhouse.

GREAT VALUE

★½ DOS LAGOS GOLF CLUB

PU—232 Duffer Lane, Anthony (505)882-2830.
20 miles north of El Paso. **Holes:** 18. **Par:** 72/72.
Yards: 6,424/5,658. **Course rating:** 70.4/70.6. **Slope:** 120/111.

Opened: 1963. **Pace of Play rating:** 4:00. **Green fee:** $10/12.
Credit cards: None. **Reduced fees:** Twilight.
Caddies: No. **Golf carts:** $16 for 18 holes.
Discount golf packages: No. **Season:** Year-round. **High:** May-Aug.
On-site lodging: No. **Rental clubs:** Yes.
Walking policy: Unrestricted walking. **Range:** No.
To obtain tee times: Weekends and holidays call up to one week in
advance. Weekdays, call prior day.
Subscriber comments: A pleasure to play . . . Good for beginner, so-so
condition . . . I wouldn't go out of my way to play this course . . .
Relatively easy course to sharpen up your game. In beautiful scenery . . .
Easy, flat course. Lined with pecan trees, good fairways . . . Wide-open
course, poor upkeep . . . Flat and short, not very challenging.

★★★★ INN OF THE MOUNTAIN GODS GOLF CLUB

R—P.O. Box 269, Rte. 4, Mescalero (505)257-5141, (800)446-2963.
80 miles northeast of Las Cruces. **Holes:** 18. **Par:** 72/72.
Yards: 6,834/5,478. **Course rating:** 72.1/65.5. **Slope:** 132/116.
Opened: 1975. **Pace of Play rating:** 4:00. **Green fee:** $35/50.
Credit cards: All major. **Reduced fees:** No.
Caddies: No. **Golf carts:** $20 for 18 holes.
Discount golf packages: No. **Season:** March-Dec. **High:** May-Oct.
On-site lodging: Yes. **Rental clubs:** Yes.
Walking policy: Mandatory cart. **Range:** Yes (grass).
To obtain tee times: Resort guests may call anytime. Nonguests call two
weeks in advance.
Ranked 8th in New Mexico by Golf Digest.
Subscriber comments: If there's a golf course in Heaven, this is it . . .
Beautiful course, difficult to keep your mind on golf, tough greens . . .
Greens are like putting on ice . . . Beautiful and a true test of golf . . . No. 8
from back tees is a great par 3 . . . Postcard pretty, but the strategic
examination is strangely absent . . . Course was in reasonable shape; staff
could have been more cooperative . . . Great mountain course in southern
Rockies . . . Hard in wind, challenging . . . Unbelieveable views and great
golf holes from the tips. The name doesn't do it justice. Simply beautiful
and a great test of golf.

★★ LADERA GOLF COURSE

PU—3401 Ladera Dr. N.W., Albuquerque (505)836-4449.
Holes: 18. **Par:** 72/72.
Yards: 7,107/5,966. **Course rating:** 73.0/72.8. **Slope:** 123/116.
Opened: 1980. **Pace of Play rating:** 4:15. **Green fee:** $10/13.
Credit cards: MC, V, AMEX. **Reduced fees:** Weekdays, Low season,
Twilight, Seniors, Juniors.
Caddies: No. **Golf carts:** N/A.
Discount golf packages: Yes. **Season:** Year-round. **High:** April-Sept.
On-site lodging: No. **Rental clubs:** Yes.
Walking policy: Unrestricted walking. **Range:** Yes (grass).
To obtain tee times: Call or come in Wednesday before weekend or
holiday at 7 a.m.
Also has 9-hole executive course.
Subscriber comments: Well kept-up for a city course . . . Good grass and
fast greens . . . Good municipal course . . . Course could be very good . . .
Easiest course in area, fairways wide, little challenge . . . Nice course layout
. . . Layout is nothing special but greens in excellent condition . . . Some
very good holes, some very boring holes . . . Too heavily used, poor
maintenance . . . Wide fairways and huge greens. Good for your head. Nice
staff.

★★★½ THE LINKS AT SIERRA BLANCA

PU—105 Sierra Blanca Dr., Ruidoso (505)258-5330, (800)854-6571.
170 miles northwest of El Paso. **Holes:** 18. **Par:** 72/72.
Yards: 7,003/5,202. **Course rating:** 72.9/68.9. **Slope:** 136/111.
Opened: 1990. **Pace of Play rating:** 4:30-5:00. **Green fee:** $26/65.
Credit cards: MC, V, AMEX. **Reduced fees:** Weekdays, Low season,
Twilight, Seniors, Juniors.

Caddies: No. **Golf carts:** $11 for 18 holes.
Discount golf packages: No. **Season:** Year-round. **High:** June-Sept.
On-site lodging: No. **Rental clubs:** Yes.
Walking policy: Walking at certain times. **Range:** Yes (grass).
To obtain tee times: Call two weeks in advance.
Ranked 7th in New Mexico by Golf Digest.
Subscriber comments: Thinking man's course . . . . At more than 7000
feet elevation, your ball goes farther . . . Accuracy off tees essential.
Beautiful course in the mountains . . . The best I have ever played on,
wonderful view . . . Young course, but fun and getting better . . . Most
desirable course in the Southwest . . . I will definitely return . . . It's like
playing two courses, front and back nines totally different . . . Excellent
condition . . . Great links course . . . Tough if you're not familar with hilly
terrain . . . Very accomodating pro shop, enjoyable experience . . . Great
layout is challenging and beautiful.

★★ LOS ALAMOS GOLF CLUB
PU—4250 Diamond Dr., Los Alamos (505)662-8139.
35 miles north of Santa Fe. **Holes:** 18. **Par:** 71/74.
Yards: 6,440/5,499. **Course rating:** 69.7/69.8. **Slope:** 118/113.
Opened: 1947. **Pace of Play rating:** 4:18. **Green fee:** $14/18.
Credit cards: MC, V. **Reduced fees:** Weekdays.
Caddies: No. **Golf carts:** $8 for 18 holes.
Discount golf packages: Yes. **Season:** March-Nov. **High:** June-Sept.
On-site lodging: No. **Rental clubs:** Yes.
Walking policy: Unrestricted walking. **Range:** Yes.
To obtain tee times: Call the day prior for weekdays and Wednesday for
upcoming weekend and holidays.
Subscriber comments: Beautiful mountain course, friendly staff . . .
Course in good condition . . . Excellent greens, fun layout . . . Beautiful
scenery, challenging golf . . . Good experience for the off-the-beaten-track
traveler . . . Great views, difficult, usually well-maintained . . . Work on
the course should improve it . . . Had trouble in 1994 with burnt greens due
to a dry winter, then some winter-kill . . . Could be better maintained.

★★ LOS ALTOS GOLF COURSE
PU—9717 Copper N.E. St., Albuquerque (505)298-1897.
Holes: 18. **Par:** 71/74.
Yards: 6,459/5,895. **Course rating:** 69.9/71.9. **Slope:** 110/113.
Opened: 1960. **Pace of Play rating:** 4:00. **Green fee:** $13.
Credit cards: MC, V, DISC. **Reduced fees:** Low season, Twilight,
Seniors, Juniors.
Caddies: No. **Golf carts:** N/A.
Discount golf packages: No. **Season:** Year-round. **High:** May-Aug.
On-site lodging: No. **Rental clubs:** Yes.
Walking policy: Unrestricted walking. **Range:** Yes (grass).
To obtain tee times: Call Wednesday for upcoming weekend.
Subscriber comments: Easiest 18-hole course in Albuquerque . . . Flat
course, suited for beginners and retirees . . . Very good municipal course
. . . Good for beginners . . . Layout was great. Staff very helpful . . . Big
trees; wide, flat fairways, big greens . . . Good muny course, crowded . . .
Flat city . . . If you want to shoot in the 60s, here's the course . . .
Confidence builder.

★★★ NEW MEXICO STATE UNIVERSITY GOLF COURSE
PU—P.O. Box 30001, Dept. 3595, Las Cruces (505)646-3219.
45 miles north of El Paso, Tx. **Holes:** 18. **Par:** 72/74.
Yards: 7,040/5,858. **Course rating:** 74.1/70.7. **Slope:** 133/120.
Opened: 1962. **Pace of Play rating:** 4:20. **Green fee:** $17.
Credit cards: MC, V. **Reduced fees:** Weekdays, Twilight.
Caddies: No. **Golf carts:** $7 for 18 holes.
Discount golf packages: No. **Season:** Year-round. **High:** Spring/Fall.
On-site lodging: No. **Rental clubs:** Yes.
Walking policy: Unrestricted walking. **Range:** Yes (grass).
To obtain tee times: Call Friday for the following weekdays and call
Wednesday for the upcoming weekend.

Subscriber comments: Nos. 10, 11 and 12 excellent holes, force you to be straight . . . Greens could be better . . . Seems wide open, but placement required . . . Arroyos in the rough are tough . . . Usually in excellent condition, fun to play. Friendly staff . . . Long for the high handicapper. Wonderful desert course with a classic feel . . . Good course, good use of hills and water, very enjoyable . . . Excellent course . . . Challenging but fair, some college kids with attitudes.

★★★ NEW MEXICO TECH GOLF COURSE

PU—1 Canyon Rd., Socorro (505)835-5335.
75 miles south of Albuquerque. **Holes:** 18. **Par:** 72/73.
Yards: 6,688/5,887. **Course rating:** 71.2/72.8. **Slope:** 126/122.
Opened: 1953. **Pace of Play rating:** N/A. **Green fee:** $11/13.
Credit cards: MC, V, DISC. **Reduced fees:** Weekdays, Twilight, Juniors.
Caddies: No. **Golf carts:** N/A.
Discount golf packages: Yes. **Season:** Year-round. **High:** April-Oct.
On-site lodging: No. **Rental clubs:** Yes.
Walking policy: Unrestricted walking. **Range:** Yes (grass).
To obtain tee times: Call one week in advance.
Subscriber comments: Long, hard course . . . Wonderful, small greens . . . New sprinkler system will improve conditions . . . Some interesting holes, one green in the side of a mountain . . . Gem in the middle of nowhere . . . Nice layout, but greens are too small and hard . . . Needs additional and more accurate yardage markers . . . A hidden old jewel in the state of New Mexico, well maintained . . . Flower in the desert, nice layout . . . Postage-stamp greens.

★★½ OCOTILLO PARK GOLF COURSE

PU—N. Lovington Hwy., Hobbs (505)397-9297.
4 miles northeast of Hobbs. **Holes:** 18. **Par:** 72/72.
Yards: 6,716/5,245. **Course rating:** 70.5/69.0. **Slope:** 121/108.
Opened: 1955. **Pace of Play rating:** 4:00. **Green fee:** $6/8.
Credit cards: All major. **Reduced fees:** Weekdays, Twilight, Seniors, Juniors
Caddies: No. **Golf carts:** $8 for 18 holes.
Discount golf packages: Yes. **Season:** Year-round. **High:** April-Aug.
On-site lodging: No. **Rental clubs:** Yes.
Walking policy: Unrestricted walking. **Range:** Yes (grass).
To obtain tee times: Call Wednesday 8 a.m.
Subscriber comments: Outstanding greens. A challenge for low or high handicappers . . . This course stays in great shape year-round . . . Flat, not interesting . . . Average muny, tough in the wind . . . Excellent fairways and greens, some very challenging holes . . . Well-kept, friendly staff. Rewards accuracy. Not crowded.

★★½ PARADISE HILLS GOLF CLUB

PU—10035 Country Club Lane, Albuquerque (505)898-7001.
Holes: 18. **Par:** 72/74.
Yards: 6,801/6,090. **Course rating:** 71.7/73.5. **Slope:** 125/118.
Opened: 1963. **Pace of Play rating:** 3:55. **Green fee:** $18/26.
Credit cards: MC, V. **Reduced fees:** Low season, Twilight, Seniors.
Caddies: No. **Golf carts:** $7 for 18 holes.
Discount golf packages: Yes. **Season:** Year-round. **High:** April-Sept.
On-site lodging: Yes. **Rental clubs:** Yes.
Walking policy: Unrestricted walking. **Range:** Yes (grass).
To obtain tee times: Call seven days in advance for weekdays and four days in advance for weekends.
Subscriber comments: Greatly improved in last two years . . . Good layout, enjoyable, family golf course . . . Don't let the name fool you . . . Well-kept, small greens . . . Average . . . Extensive remodeling has really helped out this older country club course now open to the public. . . . Too tough for the average hacker . . . Suited to all handicaps, very good treatment by staff.

NEW MEXICO

★★★★★ **PINON HILLS GOLF COURSE**
PU—2101 Sunrise Pkwy., Farmington (505)326-6066.
Holes: 18. **Par:** 72/72.
Yards: 7,249/5,522. **Course rating:** 73.3/71.1. **Slope:** 130/126.
Opened: 1989. **Pace of Play rating:** 4:20. **Green fee:** $11/13.
Credit cards: MC, V. **Reduced fees:** Weekdays.
Caddies: No. **Golf carts:** $14 for 18 holes.
Discount golf packages: No. **Season:** Year-round. **High:** May-Oct.
On-site lodging: No. **Rental clubs:** Yes.
Walking policy: Unrestricted walking. **Range:** Yes (grass).
To obtain tee times: Call one week in advance.
Ranked 1st in New Mexico by Golf Digest.
Subscriber comments: Love the foxes . . . A family of red foxes followed us for five holes! . . . Hands down the best course I've ever played, superb, challenging but fair, it can humble and reward the scratch or high handicapper . . . Course is always in great condition, pace of play is okay, a real joy to play here . . . Best public course in USA . . . Best in New Mexico, incredible beauty . . . Muny with great layout, views are championship quality . . . It's 500 miles to play this course and it's worth every mile . . . Unbelievable course in remote location . . . Best public course in New Mexico. Layout, design, condition, all No.1 . . . Great golf course and well taken care of. Tough if not in fairways . . . Course very good for all levels of playing.

RIO MIMBRES COUNTRY CLUB★
SP—Rte. 2, Deming (505)546-9481.
100 miles west of El Paso. **Holes:** 18. **Par:** 72/72.
Yards: 3,701/5,454. **Course rating:** 72.0/69.0. **Slope:** 125/111.
Opened: 1950. **Pace of Play rating:** 4:00. **Green fee:** $13/14.
Credit cards: None. **Reduced fees:** Juniors.
Caddies: No. **Golf carts:** $7 for 18 holes.
Discount golf packages: Yes. **Season:** Year-round. **High:** June-Aug.
On-site lodging: No. **Rental clubs:** Yes.
Walking policy: Unrestricted walking. **Range:** Yes (grass).
To obtain tee times: Tee times for weekends only. Members have priority until Friday morning of that week.

★★ **RIO RANCHO GOLF AND COUNTRY CLUB**
SP—500 Country Club Dr. S.E., Rio Rancho (505)892-8440.
Call club for further information.
Subscriber comments: Great layout, poorly maintained . . . Course varies from poor to good . . . Course has been allowed to deteriorate . . . Narrow fairways . . . Course set up short and open . . . Course maintenance inconsistent. Can be difficult, eight holes with water . . . Nice layout, fun.

★★★½ **SANTA ANA GOLF COURSE**
TAMAYA/RIO GRANDE/CORONADO
PU—288 Prairie Star Rd., Bernalillo (505)867-9464.
15 miles north of Albuquerque. **Holes:** 27. **Par:** 71/72/71.
Yards: 7,108/7,007/7,117. **Course rating:** 72.7/72.7/72.4.
Slope: 122/123/121.
Opened: 1991. **Pace of Play rating:** 4:00. **Green fee:** $18/23.
Credit cards: MC, V, AMEX. **Reduced fees:** Weekdays, Low season, Twilight, Seniors, Juniors.
Caddies: No. **Golf carts:** $10 for 18 holes.
Discount golf packages: No. **Season:** Year-round. **High:** March-Oct.
On-site lodging: No. **Rental clubs:** Yes.
Walking policy: Unrestricted walking. **Range:** Yes (grass).
To obtain tee times: Call one week in advance for weekdays and three days in advance for weekends.
Formerly known as Valle Grande Golf Club.
Tamaya and Rio Grande 9s ranked 9th in New Mexico by Golf Digest.

Subscriber comments: Be prepared for wind gusts . . . Best-kept secret, links-type course, very playable . . . Solid but not exciting, beautiful vista of Rio Grande river . . . Great 27 holes played in any order . . . Will be really exciting with maturity . . . If you can't hit it straight, watch out for rattlesnakes . . . 27 holes pretty much all alike but good . . . Beautiful views of mountains, a must-play . . . Must be accurate, plays short . . . Open course and no trees . . . Host of many USGA qualifiers, great, fast greens.

★★★★ TAOS COUNTRY CLUB

SP—Hwy. 570 W., Rancho de Taos (505)758-7300.
58 miles north of Santa Fe. **Holes:** 18. **Par:** 72/72.
Yards: 7,302/5,310. **Course rating:** 73.6/69.0. **Slope:** 129/125.
Opened: 1992. **Pace of Play rating:** 4:20. **Green fee:** $22/25.
Credit cards: MC, V, AMEX. **Reduced fees:** Weekdays, Twilight.
Caddies: Yes. **Golf carts:** $20 for 18 holes.
Discount golf packages: Yes. **Season:** March-Nov. **High:** June-Sept.
On-site lodging: No. **Rental clubs:** Yes.
Walking policy: Unrestricted walking. **Range:** Yes (grass).
To obtain tee times: Call one week in advance.
Ranked 3rd in New Mexico by Golf Digest.
Subscriber comments: Incredible scenery, setting . . . Views great, course OK . . . Beautiful setting, great layout, tough new course . . . New course, excellent conditioning . . . Chronically windy . . . Beautiful links cut out of sagebrush . . . Excellent condition, only course I've found with caddies available to public . . . Beautiful views, actually spectacular with trees, mountain in background. More like a links course than a desert course, short course with lots of doglegs . . . Marvelous labor of love. Building, conditions like a country club, great shot values . . . Watch for the rattlers.

★★½ TIERRA DEL SOL GOLF COURSE

SP—1000 Golf Course Rd., Belen (505)865-5056.
34 miles south of Albuquerque. **Holes:** 18. **Par:** 72/72.
Yards: 6,703/5,512. **Course rating:** 71.0/71.2. **Slope:** 117/114.
Opened: 1971. **Pace of Play rating:** 4:00. **Green fee:** $15/19.
Credit cards: MC, V. **Reduced fees:** Weekdays, Twilight, Juniors.
Caddies: No. **Golf carts:** $9 for 18 holes.
Discount golf packages: No. **Season:** Year-round. **High:** April-Oct.
On-site lodging: No. **Rental clubs:** Yes.
Walking policy: Walking at certain times. **Range:** Yes (grass).
To obtain tee times: Call up to one week in advance.
Also has an executive course.
Subscriber comments: Could be a nice course, grounds need work . . . Hard greens, narrow fairways, and too many O.B. . . . Semiprivate, not a bad course, greens have hard surfaces, balls hard to keep on . . . Nicely manicured . . . Short but tricky, greens hard to putt . . . Funky golf course . . . Medium difficulty . . . Fun course, well-maintained with a friendly staff . . . Too many mosquitoes in the summer . . . Retirement community golf.

★★★★ UNIVERSITY OF NEW MEXICO GOLF COURSE CHAMPIONSHIP COURSE

PU—3601 University Blvd., S.E., Albuquerque (505)277-4546.
Holes: 18. **Par:** 72/73.
Yards: 7,248/6,031. **Course rating:** 74.7/75.1. **Slope:** 138/131.
Opened: 1966. **Pace of Play rating:** 4:00. **Green fee:** $18/40.
Credit cards: MC, V. **Reduced fees:** Weekdays, Twilight, Seniors, Juniors.
Caddies: No. **Golf carts:** $20 for 18 holes.
Discount golf packages: No. **Season:** Year-round. **High:** May-Sept.
On-site lodging: No. **Rental clubs:** Yes.
Walking policy: Unrestricted walking. **Range:** Yes (grass).

To obtain tee times: Call Thursday at 7:30 a.m. for Saturday through Friday tee time.

Ranked in Third 25 of America's 75 Best Public Golf Courses by Golf Digest. Ranked 5th in New Mexico by Golf Digest.

Subscriber comments: Monster! Beautiful condition, wonderful views . . . Challenging . . . The mosquitoes were brutal. Help! . . . Long, must stay in fairways, well-maintained . . . Beautifully conditioned, desert-type course . . . Excellent course. Very long, always in great shape, this course will test your skills at all levels . . . Best-maintained course in Albuquerque, lush fairways . . . A championship course for all golfers . . . Clubhouse staff needs customer relationship classes . . . Best course in New Mexico . . . Very demanding, courteous staff, impossible roughs . . . Outstanding course; very, very tough, excellent variety . . . Long, but a lot of fun.

Notes

★★★ BOIS DE SOUIX GOLF CLUB

PU—North 4th St. and 13th Ave., Wahpeton (701)642-3673.
45 miles south of Fargo. **Holes:** 18. **Par:** 72/72.
Yards: 6,675/5,500. **Course rating:** 71.3/71.4. **Slope:** 122/119.
Opened: 1924. **Pace of Play rating:** 4:00. **Green fee:** $16/18.
Credit cards: None. **Reduced fees:** Weekdays.
Caddies: No. **Golf carts:** $18 for 18 holes.
Discount golf packages: No. **Season:** April-Nov. **High:** April-Sept.
On-site lodging: No. **Rental clubs:** Yes.
Walking policy: Unrestricted walking. **Range:** Yes (grass).
To obtain tee times: Call seven days in advance.
Subscriber comments: A two-state challenge . . . Front nine in North
Dakota and back nine in Minnesota, front nine flat and wide open, back
nine fine test . . . Older back nine more interesting and difficult . . . Good
value, even for a small town . . . A must in North Dakota.

★★★½ EDGEWOOD GOLF COURSE

PU—3218 2nd St., N., Fargo (701)232-2824.
Holes: 18. **Par:** 71/71.
Yards: 6,369/5,176. **Course rating:** 68.4/68.9. **Slope:** 122/115.
Opened: 1915. **Pace of Play rating:** 4:00. **Green fee:** $14/16.
Credit cards: MC, V. **Reduced fees:** Twilight, Seniors, Juniors.
Caddies: No. **Golf carts:** $17 for 18 holes.
Discount golf packages: Yes. **Season:** April-Nov. **High:** July-Aug.
On-site lodging: No. **Rental clubs:** Yes.
Walking policy: Unrestricted walking. **Range:** Yes (grass).
To obtain tee times: Call three days in advance.
Ranked 5th in North Dakota by Golf Digest.
Subscriber comments: Best public golf course anywhere . . . Well-
groomed, bunkers edged, sand raked . . . Exceptional treatment, played in
four hours . . . Tight layout . . . Beautiful old trees cover course . . . A
gem of a public course . . . Good variety of holes, course conditions not
always ideal . . . Good solid golf course with tight landing and large greens
. . . Worth the trip to Fargo . . . Spring flood damage most years . . . A
"must play" if you're in the Dakotas . . . Short 4s are challenging . . . Best
course in North Dakota regardless of money.

★★½ HEART RIVER GOLF COURSE

PU—R.R. No. 4, Dickinson (701)225-9412.
90 miles west of Bismark. **Holes:** 18. **Par:** 72/71.
Yards: 6,652/5,583. **Course rating:** 70.8/71.0. **Slope:** 125/116.
Opened: 1983. **Pace of Play rating:** 4:30. **Green fee:** $12.
Credit cards: None. **Reduced fees:** Juniors.
Caddies: No. **Golf carts:** $15 for 18 holes.
Discount golf packages: No. **Season:** March-Oct. **High:** June-Aug.
On-site lodging: No. **Rental clubs:** Yes.
Walking policy: Unrestricted walking. **Range:** Yes (grass).
To obtain tee times: Call three days in advance.
Subscriber comments: A very good course, would surprise most . . .
Course relatively flat and open with some trees and creek to cross on several
holes . . . Difficult in the wind . . . Older back nine much better, front has
lots of growing up to do . . . Good course to get your scoring average done
if you can hit straight.

★½ LINCOLN PARK GOLF CLUB

PU—P.O. Box 248, Grand Forks (701)746-2788.
Call club for further information.
Subscriber comments: Wide fairways . . . Clubhouse facilities are meager
. . . Short, flat, slow greens . . . Small slow greens. Few traps . . . sees lots
of traffic . . . A golf course, that's all.

MANVEL GOLF COURSE★
PIONEER/SETTLER'S
PU—County Rd. No. 5, Manvel (701)696-8268.
10 miles northwest of Grand Forks. **Holes:** 9. **Par:** 72/72.
Yards: 6,357/5,146. **Course rating:** 70.6/69.1. **Slope:** 126/118.
Opened: 1993. **Pace of Play rating:** N/A. **Green fee:** $12.
Credit cards: None. **Reduced fees:** Juniors.
Caddies: No. **Golf carts:** $15 for 18 holes.
Discount golf packages: No. **Season:** April-Oct. **High:** April-June.
On-site lodging: No. **Rental clubs:** Yes.
Walking policy: Unrestricted walking. **Range:** No.
To obtain tee times: Call up to one week in advance.
Subscriber comments: Tough nine-hole course . . . Unique reversing
nine. Play one direction then the next day the course reverses . . .
Confusing layout . . . .New course can be played in opposite directions . . .
Ingenious challenging design.

★★★½ MINOT COUNTRY CLUB
SP—Highway 15 West, Minot (701)839-6169.
Holes: 18. **Par:** 72/72.
Yards: 6,667/6,217. **Course rating:** N/A. **Slope:** 124/121.
Opened: N/A. **Pace of Play rating:** N/A. **Green fee:** N/A.
Credit cards: MC, V. **Reduced fees:** Weekdays.
Caddies: No. **Golf carts:** N/A. for 18 holes.
Discount golf packages: No. **Season:** April-Nov. **High:** June-Aug.
On-site lodging: No. **Rental clubs:** No.
Walking policy: N/A. **Range:** Yes (grass).
Ranked 4th in North Dakota by Golf Digest.
Subscriber comments: Old beauty, makes you want to play . . . Fairways
generally lined with ponderosa pine, several water holes . . . One of best
courses in North Dakota . . . Not really long; premium on accuracy . . .
One on North Dakota's finest . . . .Gorgeous golf course, well groomed
. . . Short course but really well manicured, great hospitality . . . Beautiful
trees, you forget you're out on the great prairie . . . Incredible for North
Dakota, real pleasure to play.

★★★ PRAIRIE WEST GOLF COURSE
PU—2709 Long Spur Trail, Mandan (701)667-3222.
2 miles east of Bismarck. **Holes:** 18. **Par:** 72/72.
Yards: 6,681/5,452. **Course rating:** 71.6/70.1. **Slope:** 127/118.
Opened: 1992. **Pace of Play rating:** 4:30. **Green fee:** $14.
Credit cards: None. **Reduced fees:** Seniors, Juniors.
Caddies: No. **Golf carts:** $16 for 18 holes.
Discount golf packages: Yes. **Season:** April-Oct. **High:** July-Aug.
On-site lodging: No. **Rental clubs:** Yes.
Walking policy: Unrestricted walking. **Range:** Yes (grass).
To obtain tee times: Call one day in advance.
Subscriber comments: Up-and-coming course . . . Fairways, greens
and rough need filling in . . . No.11 tough off tee for slicer (trees tight on
left with pond to right full length) . . . Excellent treatment . . . New course
with work continuing . . . Some great holes . . . Prevailing north wind
makes the course play harder . . . Staff excellent . . . .New course with
excellent potential.

★★★½ RIVERWOOD GOLF CLUB
PU—725 Bismarck Dr, Bismarck (701)222-6462.
Holes: 18. **Par:** 72/72.
Yards: 6,941/5,196. **Course rating:** 70.0/ 68.6. **Slope:** 130/112.
Opened: 1969. **Pace of Play rating:** 4:15. **Green fee:** $15.
Credit cards: MC, V, DISC. **Reduced fees:** Seniors, Juniors.
Caddies: No. **Golf carts:** $16 for 18 holes.
Discount golf packages: No. **Season:** April-Oct. **High:** June-Sept.
On-site lodging: No. **Rental clubs:** Yes.

Walking policy: Unrestricted walking. **Range:** Yes (grass).
To obtain tee times: Call one day in advance.
Ranked 3rd in North Dakota by Golf Digest.
Subscriber comments: Fun, tight course . . . Heavily tree-lined, two ponds but not intimidating . . . Great course . . . Beautiful setting, cut through trees 40 feet tall . . . Shotmaking a must and tee shot critical to scoring . . . Crowded . . . Deer roaming fairways . . . Lots of fall leaves . . . Nice old layout! . . . Large cottonwood trees . . . Very tight through trees . . . Could be best track in North Dakota.

★★½ ROSE CREEK GOLF COURSE
PU—15000 Rose Creek Pkwy., Fargo (701)235-5100.
Holes: 18. **Par:** 72/72.
Yards: 6,616/5,062. **Course rating:** 71.4/68.8. **Slope:** 123/114.
Opened: 1993. **Pace of Play rating:** 4:00. **Green fee:** $14/16.
Credit cards: MC, V. **Reduced fees:** Twilight, Seniors, Juniors.
Caddies: No. **Golf carts:** $17 for 18 holes.
Discount golf packages: Yes. **Season:** April-Nov. **High:** May-Aug.
On-site lodging: No. **Rental clubs:** Yes.
Walking policy: Unrestricted walking. **Range:** Yes (grass).
To obtain tee times: Call seven days in advance.
Subscriber comments: Very nice new public course, made for walking . . . Very windy location . . . Finishing holes 15 to 18 are highlight . . . Demanding course . . . Interesting holes . . . Needs to mature . . . Really a beautiful place that will only get better.

★★★ SOURIS VALLEY GOLF CLUB
PU—2400 14th Ave. S.W., Minot (701)838-4112.
Holes: 18 **Par:** 72/ 72.
Yards: 6,815/5,474. **Course rating:** 72.5/71.2. **Slope:** 126/118.
Opened: 1968. **Pace of Play rating:** 4:00. **Green fee:** $13.
Credit cards: None. **Reduced fees:** Twilight, Seniors, Juniors.
Caddies: No. **Golf carts:** $15 for 18 holes.
Discount golf packages: No. **Season:** April-Sept. **High:** June-Aug.
On-site lodging: No. **Rental clubs:** Yes.
Walking policy: Unrestricted walking. **Range:** Yes (grass).
To obtain tee times: Call pro shop 24 hours in advance.
Subscriber comments: Most difficult in North Dakota . . . Long in the wind . . . Wonderful scenery . . . Enjoyable course that is very long . . . Nice test of game; variety of holes . . . A "must play" at this price . . . Tough in the wind . . . Lots of variety . . . Service and treatment excellent . . . River valley course, but open in spots . . . Lots of water for North Dakota . . . The best muny I've ever seen for $12.50.

★½ TOM O'LEARY GOLF COURSE
PU—1200 N. Washington St., Bismarck (701)222-6462.
Holes: 18. **Par:** 68/68.
Yards: 5,800/4,026. **Course rating:** 65.0/62.3. **Slope:** 110/97.
Opened: 1969. **Pace of Play rating:** 4:15. **Green fee:** $15.
Credit cards: MC, V, DISC. **Reduced fees:** Seniors, Juniors.
Caddies: No. **Golf carts:** $16 for 18 holes.
Discount golf packages: No. **Season:** April-Oct. **High:** June-Sept.
On-site lodging: No. **Rental clubs:** Yes.
Walking policy: Unrestricted walking. **Range:** Yes (grass).
To obtain tee times: Call one day in advance.
Subscriber comments: Fun layout with a very friendly atmosphere . . . Greens are like postage stamps . . . Challenge is on the front nine . . . Shorter course, rolling fairways, few trees.

★★½ ADAMS MUNICIPAL GOLF COURSE

PU—5801 E. Tuxedo Blvd., Bartlesville (918)337-5313.
45 miles north of Tulsa. **Holes:** 18. **Par:** 72/74.
Yards: 6,819/5,655. **Course rating:** 72.0/71.8. **Slope:** 119/117.
Opened: 1963. **Pace of Play rating:** 4:00. **Green fee:** $15.
Credit cards: None. **Reduced fees:** Weekdays, Twilight, Seniors, Juniors.
Caddies: No. **Golf carts:** $16 for 18 holes.
Discount golf packages: No. **Season:** Year-round. **High:** March-Oct.
On-site lodging: No. **Rental clubs:** Yes.
Walking policy: Unrestricted walking. **Range:** Yes (grass).
To obtain tee times: Come in person one week in advance for weekdays.
For weekend play call five days in advance.
Subscriber comments: Well-maintained, good balance of short and long
holes . . . Old, tree-lined course, courteous staff, good pace, well kept . . .
Lots of water . . . Course is continually being improved through additional
tree plantings . . . Tee boxes and fairways need attention . . . Great greens,
interesting layout.

★★ ARROWHEAD GOLF COURSE

PU—HC-67, Box 6, Canadian (918)339-2769.
20 miles south of McAlester. **Holes:** 18. **Par:** 72/75.
Yards: 6,741/5,342. **Course rating:** 71.4/NA. **Slope:** 119/NA.
Opened: 1965. **Pace of Play rating:** 4:00. **Green fee:** $9/11.
Credit cards: MC, V, DISC. **Reduced fees:** Weekdays, Low season,
Twilight, Seniors, Juniors.
Caddies: No. **Golf carts:** $8 for 18 holes.
Discount golf packages: Yes. **Season:** Year-round. **High:** April-Sept.
On-site lodging: Yes. **Rental clubs:** Yes.
Walking policy: Unrestricted walking. **Range:** Yes (grass).
To obtain tee times: Call one week in advance.
Subscriber comments: Course and accommodations need more care . . .
Beautiful scenery, deer and wild turkey can be seen . . . Narrow and tree
lined fairways, greens are seasonal . . . Decent staff . . . Sometimes slow
. . . State operated . . . Good lake vistas.

★★★½ BAILEY GOLF RANCH

PU—10105 Larkin Bailey Blvd., Owasso (918)272-9339.
8 miles north of Tulsa. **Holes:** 18. **Par:** 72/72.
Yards: 6,753/4,898. **Course rating:** 73.1/68.4. **Slope:** 132/115.
Opened: 1993. **Pace of Play rating:** 4:00. **Green fee:** $14/22.
Credit cards: MC, V, DISC. **Reduced fees:** Weekdays, Low season,
Twilight, Seniors, Juniors.
Caddies: No. **Golf carts:** $10 for 18 holes.
Discount golf packages: No. **Season:** Year-round. **High:** April-Oct.
On-site lodging: No. **Rental clubs:** Yes.
Walking policy: Walking at certain times. **Range:** Yes (grass).
To obtain tee times: Call pro shop three days in advance beginning at 11
a.m.
Subscriber comments: Great track, staff superb, 3½, 4 hours norm . . .
Course is two years old, and still no clubhouse . . . Pace good, better than
my country club . . . Fair test of golf; every golf hole unique and different,
challenge for all skill levels, great condition, tee, fairways, greens. Pace of
play good . . . Daily pin location sheets very helpful . . . Better than
average practice areas . . . Not too long, subtle greens, still maturing.

★★★½ BOILING SPRINGS GOLF CLUB

PU—R.R. 2, Woodward (405)256-1206.
83 miles west of Enid. **Holes:** 18. **Par:** 71/75.
Yards: 6,454/4,944. **Course rating:** 69.6/68.6. **Slope:** 117/117.
Opened: 1979. **Pace of Play rating:** N/A. **Green fee:** $8/13.
Credit cards: MC, V, DISC. **Reduced fees:** Weekdays, Seniors, Juniors.
Caddies: No. **Golf carts:** $15 for 18 holes.
Discount golf packages: No. **Season:** Year-round. **High:** April-Oct.
On-site lodging: No. **Rental clubs:** Yes.

SUPER VALUE

Walking policy: Unrestricted walking. **Range:** Yes (grass).
To obtain tee times: First come, first served.
Subscriber comments: For the money one of best anywhere, leave driver at home . . . Excellent greens, beautiful countryside . . . Great design, large elevation changes . . . If in a big town you would never get on . . . Sand dunes, hills, trees, doglegs and undulating greens, plays short but missed fairways are very costly . . . Serves cold beer . . . Good staff.

★★½ CEDAR CREEK GOLF COURSE
R—P.O. Box 10, Broken Bow (405)494-6456.
60 miles northeast of Paris, Tex. **Holes:** 18. **Par:** 72/72.
Yards: 6,724/5,762. **Course rating:** 72.1/N/A. **Slope:** 132/N/A.
Opened: 1975. **Pace of Play rating:** 4:00. **Green fee:** $8/11.
Credit cards: MC, V, DISC. **Reduced fees:** Weekdays, Low season, Resort guests, Twilight, Seniors, Juniors.
Caddies: No. **Golf carts:** $15 for 18 holes.
Discount golf packages: Yes. **Season:** Year-round. **High:** April-Oct.
On-site lodging: Yes. **Rental clubs:** Yes.
Walking policy: Unrestricted walking. **Range:** Yes (grass).
To obtain tee times: Call at least seven days in advance.
Subscriber comments: Very challenging and can be set up to play long
. . . Front nine very good, back new and needs time . . . Beautiful surroundings but a little rough . . . Old holes excellent, new fairways too hard . . . New holes need softer fairways.

CEDAR VALLEY GOLF CLUB
PU—210 Par Ave., Guthrie (405)282-4800.
30 miles north of Oklahoma City. **Green fee:** $10/11.
Credit cards: MC, V, AMEX. **Reduced fees:** Weekdays.
Caddies: No. **Golf carts:** $16 for 18 holes.
Discount golf packages: No. **Season:** Year-round. **High:** May-Aug.
On-site lodging: No. **Rental clubs:** Yes.
Walking policy: Unrestricted walking. **Range:** Yes (grass).
To obtain tee times: Call one day in advance for weekdays. Call seven days in advance for weekends.

★★★ AUGUSTA COURSE
Holes: 18. **Par:** 70/72.
Yards: 6,602/5,170. **Course rating:** 70.3/69.1. **Slope:** 108/117.
Opened: 1975. **Pace of Play rating:** 4:00.
Subscriber comments: Lots of water and cedar trees, friendliest personnel around . . . Very enjoyable to walk . . . Need a guide for yardages . . . Great challenge at low cost, pace acceptable . . . No sand bunkers on this course . . . Narrow course, can get crowded . . . Suited to all players. Always in good condition . . . Great family course, fairest female tees I've found.

★★ INTERNATIONAL COURSE
Holes: 18. **Par:** 70/72.
Yards: 6,520/4,955. **Course rating:** 71.1/68.4. **Slope:** 112/115.
Opened: 1975. **Pace of Play rating:** 4:00.
Subscriber comments: No sand; flat and wide open, few trees, links style course . . . Nice layout, not long wait, but too many swarms of bugs . . . Wide open, hard fairways, good greens . . . Staff always makes this a great place to play . . . Home of hard pan golf, need sprinklers in fairways.

CIMARRON NATIONAL GOLF CLUB
PU—500 Duffy's Way, Guthrie (405)282-7888.
20 miles north of Oklahoma City. **Green fee:** $12/16.
Credit cards: MC, V, AMEX. **Reduced fees:** Weekdays, Low season, Seniors.
Caddies: No. **Golf carts:** $18 for 18 holes.
Discount golf packages: No. **Season:** Year-round. **High:** May-Sept.
On-site lodging: No. **Rental clubs:** Yes.
Walking policy: Walking at certain times. **Range:** Yes (grass).

To obtain tee times: Call one day in advance for weekdays. Call one week in advance for weekends and holidays.

★★½ AQUA CANYON COURSE

Holes: 18. **Par:** 70/71.

Yards: 6,515/5,439. **Course rating:** 69.6/66.4. **Slope:** 114/110.

Opened: 1992. **Pace of Play rating:** 4:15.

Subscriber comments: This course is open, best suited for high handicapper, very fast greens. Duffy Martin and staff are great . . . Exciting short course, challenging water . . . No sand . . . Pretty place, enough water to irrigate Texas . . . Back nine fairways too close together . . . Service and pace good . . . Water on almost every hole.

★★★ CIMARRON COURSE

Holes: 18. **Par:** 70/70.

Yards: 6,653/5,559. **Course rating:** 68.1/66.1. **Slope:** 120/113.

Opened: 1992. **Pace of Play rating:** 4:15.

Subscriber comments: Very difficult. Requires several layup shots. Greens steeply sloped . . . Private quality at public prices, very satisfying . . . Many holes over water, not for high handicap . . . Greens and fairways excellent condition . . . Service excellent, pace somewhat slow . . . Magnificent clubhouse and a staff that features hospitality . . . Short but well maintained . . . Landing areas often slope to water . . . Worth playing . . . U.S. Open-type greens . . . Need to play a couple of times for club selections.

★★★½ COFFEE CREEK GOLF COURSE

PU—4000 N. Kelly, Edmond (405)340-4653.

15 miles north of Oklahoma City. **Holes:** 18. **Par:** 70/70.

Yards: 6,700/5,200. **Course rating:** 71.5/70.5. **Slope:** 129/122.

Opened: 1991. **Pace of Play rating:** 4:20. **Green fee:** $16/20.

Credit cards: All major. **Reduced fees:** Weekdays, Twilight, Seniors, Juniors.

Caddies: No. **Golf carts:** $9 for 18 holes.

Discount golf packages: No. **Season:** Year-round. **High:** May-Sept.

On-site lodging: No. **Rental clubs:** Yes.

Walking policy: Unrestricted walking. **Range:** Yes (grass).

To obtain tee times: Call seven days in advance.

Subscriber comments: Tee boxes too far from greens . . . Tight, lot of trees on most holes . . . Uncrowded, tough course. Makes you want to return again and again . . . Excellent course, tee times hard to get . . . Exceptionally nice all around, staff, carts, greens . . . Well maintained year round . . . Good course, crowded most of the time.

EARLYWINE PARK GOLF COURSE

PU—11500 S. Portland, Oklahoma City (405)691-1727.

Green fee: $12.

Credit cards: MC, V, AMEX. **Reduced fees:** Weekdays, Low season, Twilight, Seniors, Juniors.

Caddies: No. **Golf carts:** $16 for 18 holes.

Discount golf packages: No. **Season:** Year-round. **High:** March-Nov.

On-site lodging: No. **Rental clubs:** Yes.

Walking policy: Unrestricted walking. **Range:** Yes (grass).

To obtain tee times: Call one day in advance for weekdays and for weekends call the previous weekend.

NORTH COURSE★

Holes: 18. **Par:** 72/72.

Yards: 6,721/4,843. **Course rating:** 71.9/70.4. **Slope:** 126/122.

Opened: 1993. **Pace of Play rating:** 3:30-4:30.

★★★ SOUTH COURSE

Holes: 18. **Par:** 71/71.

Yards: 6,728/5,388. **Course rating:** 69.5/71.6. **Slope:** 107/117.

Opened: 1976. **Pace of Play rating:** 3:30-4:30.

Subscriber comments: South 18 holes are good, North 18 holes just opened, excellent layout, going to be a good one . . . Friendly staff . . .

Need marshals badly . . . Tough but fair, hilly and challenging, don't walk unless you're in good shape . . . Easy to get tee time on South Course, difficult to get tee time on North . . . More daily maintenance needed . . . South Course extremely hard fairways in summer . . . North Course great.

ELK CITY GOLF AND COUNTRY CLUB★
SP—108 Lakeridge Rd., Elk City (405)225-3556.
105 miles west of Oklahoma City. **Holes:** 18. **Par:** 71/71.
Yards: 6,208/4,678. **Course rating:** 89.9/65.9. **Slope:** 106/98.
Opened: 1954. **Pace of Play rating:** 4:30. **Green fee:** $11/13.
Credit cards: None. **Reduced fees:** Weekdays, Twilight.
Caddies: No. **Golf carts:** $17 for 18 holes.
Discount golf packages: No. **Season:** Year-round. **High:** May-Oct.
On-site lodging: No. **Rental clubs:** Yes.
Walking policy: Unrestricted walking. **Range:** Yes (grass).
To obtain tee times: Call pro shop.

★★★ FALCONHEAD RANCH AND COUNTRY CLUB
SP—605 Falconhead Dr., Burneyville (405)276-9284.
25 miles north of Ardmore. **Holes:** 18. **Par:** 72/71.
Yards: 6,400/5,280. **Course rating:** 69.9/70.3. **Slope:** 118/120.
Opened: 1960. **Pace of Play rating:** 4:00. **Green fee:** $15/20.
Credit cards: All major. **Reduced fees:** Seniors.
Caddies: No. **Golf carts:** $15 for 18 holes.
Discount golf packages: Yes. **Season:** Year-round. **High:** April-Oct.
On-site lodging: Yes. **Rental clubs:** Yes.
Walking policy: Mandatory cart. **Range:** Yes (grass).
To obtain tee times: Call one day in advance.
Subscriber comments: Good layout, uncrowded . . . Good greens . . . Fun to play, accommodations fair . . . Good mixture of holes, some tight, some wide open . . . Excellent condition. Outstanding value . . . Local pro and staff courteous and professional.

★★½ FIRE LAKE GOLF COURSE
PU—1901 S. Gordon Cooper, Shawnee (405)275-4471.
30 miles east of Oklahoma City. **Holes:** 18. **Par:** 70/71.
Yards: 6,335/4,992. **Course rating:** 69.6/N/A. **Slope:** 121/N/A.
Opened: 1983. **Pace of Play rating:** N/A. **Green fee:** $6/11.
Credit cards: MC, V, DISC. **Reduced fees:** Weekdays, Twilight, Seniors, Juniors.
Caddies: No. **Golf carts:** $16 for 18 holes.
Discount golf packages: No. **Season:** Year-round. **High:** May-July.
On-site lodging: No. **Rental clubs:** Yes.
Walking policy: Unrestricted walking. **Range:** Yes (grass).
To obtain tee times: Call one week in advance.
Subscriber comments: Lots of water. Walkable. Not crowded . . . Greens need to be redone, good price . . . Needs to improve staff . . . Super greens. Golf carts need upgrade . . . Very well groomed . . . Variety of holes. Good par 3s. Good restaurant.

★★★★ FOREST RIDGE GOLF CLUB
PU—7501 E. Kenosha, Broken Arrow (918)357-2282.
12 miles southeast of Tulsa. **Holes:** 18. **Par:** 72/72.
Yards: 7,069/5,341. **Course rating:** 74.0/70.5. **Slope:** 134/112.
Opened: 1989. **Pace of Play rating:** 4:15. **Green fee:** $30/60.
Credit cards: All major. **Reduced fees:** Weekdays, Low season, Twilight.
Caddies: No. **Golf carts:** Included in Green Fee.
Discount golf packages: No. **Season:** Year-round. **High:** March-Oct.
On-site lodging: No. **Rental clubs:** Yes.
Walking policy: Unrestricted walking. **Range:** Yes (grass).
To obtain tee times: Call four days in advance.
Subscriber comments: Has it all! Period. Could play everyday . . . Great layout, very challenging . . . Best public challenge in Tulsa . . . Not very

walkable. Excellent large greens . . . Expensive but worth the price. Great condition . . . Tough course, lots of dense growth contributes to lost balls . . . Never crowded weekdays. Excellent layout. Feel like you are alone in paradise . . . Pace of play is kept fast, four hours.

★★ FORT COBB STATE PARK GOLF COURSE
PU—P.O. Box 497, Fort Cobb, (405)643-2398.
Call club for further information.
Subscriber comments: Greens terribly rough . . . Front side builds confidence, back brings you back to reality, lots of geese and other wildlife, good scenery . . . Very difficult, tight, lots of water, thick rough . . . Fairways need work . . . Staff very down home. No waiting.

★★ FOUNTAINHEAD STATE PARK GOLF COURSE
PU—HC60 Box 1350, Checotah (918)689-3209.
60 miles north of Tulsa. **Holes:** 18. **Par:** 72/72.
Yards: 6,919/4,864. **Course rating:** 71.3/67.3. **Slope:** 116/98.
Opened: 1964. **Pace of Play rating:** 4:00. **Green fee:** $9/11.
Credit cards: MC, V, DISC. **Reduced fees:** Twilight, Seniors, Juniors.
Caddies: No. **Golf carts:** $15 for 18 holes.
Discount golf packages: No. **Season:** Year-round. **High:** March-Oct.
On-site lodging: No. **Rental clubs:** Yes.
Walking policy: Unrestricted walking. **Range:** Yes (grass).
To obtain tee times: Call seven days in advance.
Subscriber comments: Lots of uphill and downhill lies, be in good shape if you want to walk . . . Good state-run public layout in fair shape . . . Pace of play really good . . . Well kept, best time to play spring and fall . . . Have excellent package deal.

THE GOLF CLUB AT CIMARRON TRAILS★
PU—1400 Lovers Lane, Perkins (405)547-5701–.
70 miles southwest of Oklahoma City. **Holes:** 18. **Par:** 72/72.
Yards: 6,959/5,128. **Course rating:** 74.0/65.8. **Slope:** 124/106.
Opened: 1994. **Pace of Play rating:** 4:00. **Green fee:** $12/25.
Credit cards: MC, V. **Reduced fees:** Twilight.
Caddies: No. **Golf carts:** $9 for 18 holes.
Discount golf packages: Yes. **Season:** Year-round. **High:** March-Oct.
On-site lodging: No. **Rental clubs:** Yes.
Walking policy: Walking at certain times. **Range:** Yes(grass).
To obtain tee times: Call seven days in advance.

★★★ HERITAGE HILLS GOLF COURSE
PU—3140 Tee Dr., Claremore (918)341-0055.
30 miles north of Tulsa. **Holes:** 18. **Par:** 71/72.
Yards: 6,760/5,324. **Course rating:** 72.6/71.0. **Slope:** 120/N/A.
Opened: 1977. **Pace of Play rating:** 4:00. **Green fee:** $14.
Credit cards: None. **Reduced fees:** Weekdays, Twilight, Seniors, Juniors.
Caddies: No. **Golf carts:** $8 for 18 holes.
Discount golf packages: Yes. **Season:** Year-round. **High:** April-Sept.
On-site lodging: No. **Rental clubs:** Yes.
Walking policy: Unrestricted walking. **Range:** Yes (grass).
To obtain tee times: For weekday tee time call one day in advance or come in two days in advance. For weekends and holidays call Wednesday prior at 7 a.m. by phone or in person.
Subscriber comments: Excellent layout, great value, friendly staff, not crowded on weekdays . . . Best low green fee course in northeast Oklahoma . . . Tee times hard to get if not a local . . . I never met a golf course I did not like. See Will Rogers museum nearby . . . Good course to walk . . . Constantly improving. New sprinklers. Concrete cart paths . . . Always good greens, good pace of play.

★★★ JOHN CONRAD REGIONAL GOLF COURSE

PU—711 S. Douglas Blvd., Midwest City (405)732-2209.
1 mile east of Oklahoma City. **Holes:** 18. **Par:** 72/74.
Yards: 6,854/5,511. **Course rating:** 72.0/70.8. **Slope:** 115/119.
Opened: 1971. **Pace of Play rating:** 4:30. **Green fee:** $12.
Credit cards: None. **Reduced fees:** Twilight, Seniors, Juniors.
Caddies: No. **Golf carts:** $17 for 18 holes.
Discount golf packages: Yes. **Season:** Year-round. **High:** April-Oct.
On-site lodging: No. **Rental clubs:** Yes.
Walking policy: Unrestricted walking. **Range:** Yes (grass).
To obtain tee times: Call 24 hours in advance.
Subscriber comments: Always in great condition, good staff, nice
clubhouse . . . Played every day . . . Staff needs to improve . . . Lot of
noise from aircraft traffic . . . Good layout, usually very slow play . . . Full
of retired Air Force personnel. Quick, efficient, courteous . . . Well
maintained. Greens a problem in August . . . Effective marshaling . . .
Interesting, narrow fairways, lots of trees.

★★★★½ KARSTEN CREEK GOLF COURSE

SP—Rte. 5, P.O. Box 159, Stillwater (405)743-1658.
55 miles northeast of Oklahoma City. **Holes:** 18. **Par:** 72/72.
Yards: 7,095/4,906. **Course rating:** 74.8/70.1. **Slope:** 142/127.
Opened: 1994. **Pace of Play rating:** 4:00. **Green fee:** $125.
Credit cards: MC, V, AMEX. **Reduced fees:** No.
Caddies: Yes. **Golf carts:** Included in Green Fee.
Discount golf packages: No. **Season:** Year-round. **High:** April-Sept.
On-site lodging: No. **Rental clubs:** No.
Walking policy: Unrestricted walking. **Range:** Yes (grass).
To obtain tee times: Call two days in advance.
Selected Best New Public Course of 1994 by Golf Digest. Ranked 3rd in
Oklahoma by Golf Digest.
Subscriber comments: Fast greens, perfect use of existing land . . . Very
difficult, beautiful layout and grounds . . . Too expensive . . . Best course
in Oklahoma . . . Karsten Creek is absolutely the finest golf course in a 500-
mile radius. PGA quality, excellent service, you never know that there is
anyone else on the course . . . Superb, great staff, beautiful scenery, brisk
pace, a must play . . . Definitely upscale . . . With five sets of tees on some
holes anybody can play . . . Magnificent Tom Fazio design . . . Very good
condition for new course.

★★★ KICKINGBIRD GOLF COURSE

PU—1600 E. Danforth Rd., Edmond (405)341-5350.
10 miles north of Oklahoma City. **Holes:** 18. **Par:** 71/72.
Yards: 6,816/4,801. **Course rating:** 71.4/68.5. **Slope:** 127/117.
Opened: 1972. **Pace of Play rating:** 4:00-4:30. **Green fee:** $12.
Credit cards: None. **Reduced fees:** Twilight, Seniors, Juniors.
Caddies: No. **Golf carts:** $8 for 18 holes.
Discount golf packages: No. **Season:** Year-round. **High:** May-Sept.
On-site lodging: No. **Rental clubs:** Yes.
Walking policy: Unrestricted walking. **Range:** Yes (grass).
To obtain tee times: Call one day in advance for weekdays and one week
in advance for weekends.
Subscriber comments: Course in excellent condition, tough greens . . .
Way too crowded, 3½ hours for nine holes . . . Good layout, lots of trees
and squirrels . . . Great condition in summer. Friendly staff and good layout
. . . Marshals hurry play . . . Excellent course, priced right . . . Good
elevation change in a flat state . . . Tough course. Still allows some
fivesomes . . . Too easy.

★★ LAFORTUNE PARK GOLF CLUB

PU—5501 S. Yale Ave., Tulsa (918)596-8627.
Holes: 18. **Par:** 72/73.
Yards: 6,970/5,780. **Course rating:** 72.8/72.9. **Slope:** 123/117.
Opened: 1960. **Pace of Play rating:** N/A. **Green fee:** $9/15.

Credit cards: None. **Reduced fees:** Twilight, Seniors, Juniors.
Caddies: No. **Golf carts:** $9 for 18 holes.
Discount golf packages: No. **Season:** Year-round. **High:** March–Aug.
On-site lodging: No. **Rental clubs:** Yes.
Walking policy: Unrestricted walking. **Range:** Yes (grass).
To obtain tee times: Call Xeta Reservation up to one week in advance.
Call pro shop for same day reservation.
Also has 18-hole par-3 course.
Subscriber comments: Busy golf course, not well maintained . . .
Crowded every day, worn out tee boxes . . . Good staff, excellent practice
facility . . . Good course, needs marshals . . . Tank tops and thongs . . .
Hard to get tee time . . . Great practice facilities . . . Long par 72 can be
walked, also a par 3 lighted course . . . Good city location.

LAKE HEFNER GOLF CLUB
PU—4491 S. Lake Hefner Dr., Oklahoma City (405)843-1565.
Green fee: $10/11.
Credit cards: None. **Reduced fees:** Twilight, Seniors, Juniors.
Caddies: No. **Golf carts:** $15 for 18 holes.
Discount golf packages: No. **Season:** Year-round. **High:** March–Sept.
On-site lodging: No. **Rental clubs:** Yes.
Walking policy: Unrestricted walking. **Range:** Yes(grass).
To obtain tee times: Call one day in advance for weekends and one week
in advance for weekends and holidays.
Also has new 3-hole par-9 Academy Course.
★★★ NORTH COURSE
Holes: 18. **Par:** 72/72.
Yards: 6,970/5,169. **Course rating:** 74.2/69.6. **Slope:** 128/117.
Opened: 1994. **Pace of Play rating:** 4:00.
Subscriber comments: Lots of merchandise. Open with water, great
condition . . . Pace is slow, but golf is delightful, clubhouse is excellent . . .
Nice to see public course upgraded. Wind off lake tough . . . Cart trails
only, can walk . . . Five hours to play 18 . . . Plays slow, lots of beginners
. . . Staff very accommodating and pace wonderful.
★★ SOUTH COURSE
Holes: 18. **Par:** 70/73.
Yards: 6,305/5,393. **Course rating:** 68.9/71.2. **Slope:** 111/115.
Opened: 1950. **Pace of Play rating:** 4:00.
Subscriber comments: Flat, short, good shape. Same staff and clubhouse
as North . . . Course OK, pace of play very slow, too crowded . . .
Practice facilities are well laid out, staff is always helpful . . . Tee times
bunched up to maximize profit. Five hours to play 18 . . . Needs better
maintenance of fairways.

★½ LAKE MURRAY GOLF COURSE
PU—3310 S. Lake Murray Dr., Ardmore (405)223-6613.
Call club for further information.
Subscriber comments: Good variety of holes . . . New design, nice holes
but poor grass conditions during peak months . . . Tall trees, tight,
uphill/downhill shots, good condition . . . Staff OK, pace slow, overplayed
greens, very busy . . . Biggest problem is that it is owned by the state of
Oklahoma.

★★ LAKE TEXOMA GOLF RESORT
R—P.O. Box 279, Kingston (405)564-3333.
110 miles south of Oklahoma City. **Holes:** 18. **Par:** 71/74.
Yards: 6,145/5,145. **Course rating:** 67.8/68.7. **Slope:** 112/108.
Opened: 1971. **Pace of Play rating:** 4:30. **Green fee:** $10/12.
Credit cards: MC, V, DISC. **Reduced fees:** Weekdays, Low season,
Resort guests, Twilight, Seniors, Juniors.
Caddies: No. **Golf carts:** $15 for 18 holes.
Discount golf packages: Yes. **Season:** Year-round. **High:** April–Oct.
On-site lodging: Yes. **Rental clubs:** Yes.
Walking policy: Unrestricted walking. **Range:** Yes (grass).

To obtain tee times: Call on Wednesday at noon for upcoming weekend and holidays only.
Subscriber comments: Short course, hit straight, score well . . .
Clubhouse amenities fair, staff courteous, traffic moderate, greens condition very good . . . Right beside airport and lodge . . . Cheap golf . . .
Recommend Tuesday or Wednesday to golf here.

★★½ LAKESIDE MEMORIAL GOLF CLUB
PU—Rte. 2, Box 685, Stillwater (405)372-3399.
Call club for further information.
Subscriber comments: Too much competition with Karsten Creek to keep this course full of life . . . Weekdays it's a pleasure, not too challenging . . . Great golf, low cost, very friendly people, greens get rough in summer . . . Service good, play slow . . . Many approach shots require manuevering around, over or under trees from fairway . . . A workout if walked.

★★★ LAKEVIEW GOLF COURSE
PU—3905 N. Commerce, Ardmore (405)223-4260.
88 miles south of Oklahoma City. **Holes:** 18. **Par:** 71/72.
Yards: 6,881/5,032. **Course rating:** 71.2/67.5. **Slope:** 114/113.
Opened: 1971. **Pace of Play rating:** 4:00. **Green fee:** $9/11.
Credit cards: None. **Reduced fees:** Weekdays, Twilight, Seniors, Juniors.
Caddies: No. **Golf carts:** $17 for 18 holes.
Discount golf packages: No. **Season:** Year-round. **High:** April-Sept.
On-site lodging: No. **Rental clubs:** Yes.
Walking policy: Unrestricted walking. **Range:** Yes(grass).
To obtain tee times: Call Wednesday for upcoming weekend.
Subscriber comments: Clubhouse adequate, carts good, traffic very heavy, staff on course to speed play in courteous manner . . . Good maintenance, greens slick . . . Very well maintained, very scenic . . . A nice course, an excellent price . . . Some greens have severe breaks.

★★★ LEW WENTZ MEMORIAL GOLF COURSE
PU—L.A. Cann Dr., Ponca City (405)767-0433.
80 miles northwest of Tulsa. **Holes:** 18. **Par:** 71/70.
Yards: 6,400/5,450. **Course rating:** 70.0/71.8. **Slope:** 125/123.
Opened: 1940. **Pace of Play rating:** 4:00. **Green fee:** $10/12.
Credit cards: None. **Reduced fees:** Weekdays, Seniors, Juniors.
Caddies: No. **Golf carts:** $16 for 18 holes.
Discount golf packages: No. **Season:** Year-round. **High:** April-Oct.
On-site lodging: No. **Rental clubs:** Yes.
Walking policy: Unrestricted walking. **Range:** No.
To obtain tee times: Call two days in advance.
Subscriber comments: Very friendly staff, limited facilities . . . Nice holes along lake edge . . . Fairways need more coverage . . . . Water problems. Excellent greens, good value . . . Wentz is a fun course, a lot of hills, sand and water.

LINCOLN PARK GOLF COURSE
PU—4001 N.E. Grand Blvd., Oklahoma City (405)424-1421.
Green fee: $6/11.
Credit cards: None. **Reduced fees:** Weekdays, Twilight, Seniors, Juniors.
Caddies: No. **Golf carts:** $N/A for 18 holes.
Discount golf packages: No. **Season:** Year-round. **High:** April-Sept.
On-site lodging: No. **Rental clubs:** Yes.
Walking policy: Unrestricted walking. **Range:** Yes (grass).
To obtain tee times: Call or come in one week in advance for weekends and call or come in one day in advance for weekdays.
★★ EAST COURSE
Holes: 18. **Par:** 70/71.
Yards: 6,508/5,467. **Course rating:** 70.0/66.2. **Slope:** 120/112.
Opened: 1960. **Pace of Play rating:** 4:00.
Subscriber comments: Short, slow play, fair condition, good clubhouse

. . . The two Lincoln Park courses are two of the best maintained, city-run courses around . . . Slow play, lots of hacks. Golf carts from hell . . . Fairly easy but interesting . . . Lots of hills for an Oklahoma golf course.

★★½ WEST COURSE

Holes: 18. **Par:** 70/71.
Yards: 6,508/5,587. **Course rating:** 70.7/68.4. **Slope:** 121/115.
Opened: 1922. **Pace of Play rating:** 4:00.
Subscriber comments: Long, more camouflage than East . . . Greens are ragged and beat-up . . . Old hackers course . . . Course isn't always very well maintained but can be enjoyed . . . Large greens, fairways wide with a lot of trees . . . Pro shop people very helpful for walk-ons and tee times . . . Old Arthur Jackson course. Great buy . . . Too crowded, do not walk . . . Long! Fairly open, grip it and rip it.

MOHAWK PARK GOLF CLUB

PU—5223 E. 41st St. N., Tulsa (918)425-6871.
Green fee: $8/15.
Credit cards: None. **Reduced fees:** Twilight, Seniors, Juniors.
Caddies: No. **Golf carts:** $17 for 18 holes.
Discount golf packages: No. **Season:** Year-round. **High:** June-July.
On-site lodging: No. **Rental clubs:** Yes.
Walking policy: Unrestricted walking. **Range:** Yes.
To obtain tee times: You can call seven days in advance if you are a member of Tee Time Service Computer.

★★½ WOODBINE COURSE

Holes: 18. **Par:** 72/76.
Yards: 6,898/6,202. **Course rating:** 71.0/73.9. **Slope:** 115/127.
Opened: 1927. **Pace of Play rating:** 4:15.
Subscriber comments: Old course needs some course changes, greens poor . . . Too crowded . . . Friendly staff, T-shirt and cutoffs, round was five hours . . . Regulars do not know or care about ball marks . . . Could be very good.

★½ PECAN VALLEY COURSE

Holes: 18. **Par:** 70/70.
Yards: 6,499/5,130. **Course rating:** 71.6/69.6. **Slope:** 124/119.
Opened: 1957. **Pace of Play rating:** 4:15.
Credit cards: None. **Reduced fees:** Twilight, Seniors, Juniors.
Caddies: No. **Golf carts:** $17 for 18 holes.
Discount golf packages: No. **Season:** Year-round. **High:** June-July.
On-site lodging: No. **Rental clubs:** Yes.
Walking policy: Unrestricted walking. **Range:** No.
To obtain tee times: Call seven days in advance. Must be a member of Tee Time Service Computer.
Subscriber comments: Just remodeled, needs it again . . . City course, needs work, fairways poor shape . . . Staff good for getting you on . . . The playing regulars don't value divot repair . . . Very flat course, lots of trees, not good in fall leaves . . . Play can be slow due to novices.

PAGE BELCHER GOLF COURSE

PU—6666 S. Union Ave., Tulsa (918)446-1529
Green fee: $13/15.
Credit cards: None. **Reduced fees:** Weekdays, Twilight, Seniors, Juniors.
Caddies: No. **Golf carts:** $9 for 18 holes.
Discount golf packages: No. **Season:** Year-round. **High:** April-Oct.
On-site lodging: No. **Rental clubs:** Yes.
Walking policy: Unrestricted walking. **Range:** Yes (grass).
To obtain tee times: Call (918)582-6000.

★★★ OLD PAGE COURSE

Holes: 18. **Par:** 71/71.
Yards: 6,826/5,532. **Course rating:** 72.0/71.5. **Slope:** 121/118.
Opened: 1977. **Pace of Play rating:** 4:30.
Subscriber comments: Super municipal layout . . . Good zoysia fairways, open, huge greens . . . Slow play . . . Very good course, well maintained . . . Good course, needs marshals that will speed up play . . . Staff great.

Service great. Play is fine, just hard to get on . . . Great course, good facilities . . . Long, pretty wide open, five-hour round normal.

★★★½ STONE CREEK COURSE

Holes: 18. **Par:** 71/71.

Yards: 6,539/5,144. **Course rating:** 72.3/69.9. **Slope:** 126/127.

Opened: 1987. **Pace of Play rating:** 4:30.

Subscriber comments: Excellent shape, excellent layout, good test for all abilities . . . Great design . . . Water in play most holes, good staff, slow pace, slow greens all year . . . Hard to walk, too far from green to next tee . . . Greens are slightly thin in summer . . . Pro shop is run great . . . Tricky greens, lots of trouble . . . Difficult to get tee time. Crowded, but well kept . . . Five-hour round normal.

★★ QUARTZ MOUNTAIN GOLF COURSE

R—Rte. 1, Box 35, Lone Wolf (405)563-2520.

70 miles northwest of Lawton. **Holes:** 18. **Par:** 71/71.

Yards: 6,595/5,706. **Course rating:** N/A. **Slope:** N/A.

Opened: N/A. **Pace of Play rating:** 4:00. **Green fee:** $8/11.

Credit cards: MC, V, DISC. **Reduced fees:** Resort guests, Twilight, Seniors, Juniors.

Caddies: No. **Golf carts:** $15 for 18 holes.

Discount golf packages: Yes. **Season:** Year-round. **High:** May-Aug.

On-site lodging: Yes. **Rental clubs:** Yes.

Walking policy: Unrestricted walking. **Range:** Yes (grass).

To obtain tee times: Call after 10 a.m. Wednesday for following weekend or holiday.

Subscriber comments: There are no amenities. Course is challenging, but poorly designed . . . Back nine is new, should improve . . . Better maintenance of course needed, good potential if in good shape . . . Good course, short, nice, helpful staff.

★★ SAND SPRINGS MUNICIPAL GOLF COURSE

PU—1801 N. McKinley, Sand Springs (918)245-7551.

8 miles northwest of Tulsa. **Holes:** 18. **Par:** 71/70.

Yards: 6,113/4,692. **Course rating:** 68.9/68.4. **Slope:** 115/118.

Opened: 1956. **Pace of Play rating:** 3:45. **Green fee:** $7/13.

Credit cards: MC, V. **Reduced fees:** Weekdays, Low season, Twilight, Seniors, Juniors.

Caddies: No. **Golf carts:** $8 for 18 holes.

Discount golf packages: Yes. **Season:** Year-round. **High:** April-Oct.

On-site lodging: No. **Rental clubs:** Yes.

Walking policy: Unrestricted walking. **Range:** No.

To obtain tee times: Call pro shop.

Subscriber comments: Too hilly to walk . . . Mountain goat course . . . Short, fun to play once a year . . . Big, fun, elevation changes. One par 3, 156 yards out and 180 feet down . . . Service and staff excellent. Play is slow at times but OK . . . Picture perfect, short course, love hidden greens . . . Holes have personality, needs better defined fairways . . . Several blind approaches.

SAPULPA MUNICIPAL GOLF COURSE★

PU—Off Highway 66, Sapulpa (918)224-0237.

12 miles west of Tulsa. **Holes:** 18. **Par:** 70/0.

Yards: 6,523/N/A. **Course rating:** 71.3/N/A. **Slope:** 123/N/A.

Opened: 1995. **Pace of Play rating:** 4:00 **Green fee:** $12/14.

Credit cards: None. **Reduced fees:** Twilight, Seniors, Juniors.

Caddies: No. **Golf carts:** $16 for 18 holes.

Discount golf packages: No. **Season:** Year-round. **High:** June-Aug.

On-site lodging: No. **Rental clubs:** Yes.

Walking policy: Unrestricted walking. **Range:** No.

To obtain tee times: Call two days in advance.

★½ SEQUOYAH STATE PARK GOLF CLUB

R—Rte. 1, Box 201, Hulbert (918)772-2297.

45 miles east of Tulsa. **Holes:** 18. **Par:** 70/73.

Yards: 5,860/5,555. **Course rating:** 66.7/69.9. **Slope:** 109/113.

Opened: 1954. **Pace of Play rating:** 4:00. **Green fee:** $8/11.

Credit cards: MC, V, DISC. **Reduced fees:** Weekdays, Low season, Resort guests, Twilight, Seniors, Juniors.

Caddies: No. **Golf carts:** $16 for 18 holes.

Discount golf packages: Yes. **Season:** Year-round. **High:** June-Aug.

On-site lodging: Yes. **Rental clubs:** Yes.

Walking policy: Unrestricted walking. **Range:** Yes (grass).

To obtain tee times: Call seven days in advance for weekends and holidays.

Subscriber comments: Short, hills and trees, poor staff, slow pace, very rocky . . . Greens and fairways in poor shape most of the year . . . Beautiful layout, state should spend some money on this . . . Excellent course, priced right.

SHANGRI-LA GOLF RESORT

R—R.R. No. 3, Afton (918)257-4204, (800)331-4060.

70 miles northeast of Tulsa. **Green fee:** $50/70.

Credit cards: All major. **Reduced fees:** Weekdays, Low season, Resort guests.

Caddies: No. **Golf carts:** Included in Green Fee.

Discount golf packages: Yes. **Season:** Year-round. **High:** April-Oct.

On-site lodging: Yes. **Rental clubs:** Yes.

Walking policy: Walking at certain times. **Range:** Yes (grass).

To obtain tee times: Call two weeks in advance.

★★★½ BLUE COURSE

Holes: 18. **Par:** 72/73.

Yards: 7,012/5,892. **Course rating:** 74.0/74.8. **Slope:** 132/126.

Opened: 1970. **Pace of Play rating:** 4:30.

Subscriber comments: Challenging resort course with nice amenities . . . Beautiful course . . . Best golf getaway in Oklahoma . . . Great fairways and greens . . . Good staff, good pace, good condition summer . . . Bruce Lietzke likes it, so do I . . . .Quite forested and hilly, great facilities . . . Oklahoma's best resort . . . Good pace and treated well . . . Very good course for vacationers, fast play, little trouble . . . Beautiful setting with Grand Lake on three sides, great condition.

★★★ GOLD COURSE

Holes: 18. **Par:** 70/71.

Yards: 5,932/4,517. **Course rating:** 66.8/66.8. **Slope:** 123/112.

Opened: 1970. **Pace of Play rating:** 4:30.

Subscriber comments: Good weekend outing . . . Seven par 3s, six par 4s and five par 5s, easier than Blue Course . . . Golf staff was great, beautiful greens . . . Bring your sand wedge and know how to use it . . . Hosts the Mickey Mantle Classic each October . . . Relatively short. Fun for high handicapper . . . Combined with Blue, it's a good outing.

★★★ SILVERHORN GOLF CLUB

SP—11411 N. Kelley Ave., Oklahoma City (405)752-1181.

Holes: 18. **Par:** 71/71.

Yards: 6,800/4,943. **Course rating:** 73.4/71.0. **Slope:** 128/113.

Opened: 1991. **Pace of Play rating:** 4:00. **Green fee:** $24/28.

Credit cards: All major. **Reduced fees:** Weekdays, Low season, Twilight, Seniors, Juniors.

Caddies: No. **Golf carts:** $9 for 18 holes.

Discount golf packages: No. **Season:** Year-round. **High:** April-Sept.

On-site lodging: No. **Rental clubs:** Yes.

Walking policy: Unrestricted walking **Range:** Yes (grass).

To obtain tee times: Call five days in advance.

Subscriber comments: Beautiful course and layout, challenging, long . . . New, great layout, lots of hazards, good play, well manicured, recommended for low handicap players . . . Club-like atmosphere, great greens . . . Members need to take better care of traps and greens . . . Great pro shop and service, slow on weekends . . . Beautiful clubhouse . . . Big, undulating fast greens, good condition, fast pace of play . . . If you like doglegs, you will love this course.

★★½ SOUTH LAKES GOLF COURSE
PU—9253 S. Elwood, Jenks (918)746-3760.
3 miles southwest of Tulsa. **Holes:** 18. **Par:** 71/71.
Yards: 6,340/5,242. **Course rating:** 68.6/70.4. **Slope:** 113/116.
Opened: 1989. **Pace of Play rating:** 4:00. **Green fee:** $15.
Credit cards: None. **Reduced fees:** Twilight, Seniors, Juniors.
Caddies: No. **Golf carts:** $17 for 18 holes.
Discount golf packages: No. **Season:** Year-round. **High:** April-Sept.
On-site lodging: No. **Rental clubs:** Yes.
Walking policy: Unrestricted walking. **Range:** Yes(grass).
To obtain tee times: Call pro shop.
Subscriber comments: Great to walk, 4½ hours . . . Short course, good for seniors . . . Good staff, fair pace, very good condition all year . . . Staff and service rushed. Play very slow . . . Noisy, in flight path to airport . . . Executive course deluxe . . . Good use of mounding . . . Course layout is crowded into too small a space.

★★ SPUNKY CREEK COUNTRY CLUB
SP—1890 Country Club Dr., Catoosa (918)266-2207.
3 miles east of Tulsa. **Holes:** 18. **Par:** 72/73.
Yards: 6,639/5,748. **Course rating:** 71.5/72.9. **Slope:** 124/127.
Opened: 1921. **Pace of Play rating:** 4:00. **Green fee:** $14/16.
Credit cards: MC, V. **Reduced fees:** Weekdays, Low season, Twilight, Seniors, Juniors.
Caddies: No. **Golf carts:** $9 for 18 holes.
Discount golf packages: No. **Season:** Year-round. **High:** March-Oct.
On-site lodging: No. **Rental clubs:** Yes.
Walking policy: Unrestricted walking. **Range:** No.
To obtain tee times: Call two days in advance beginning at 7 a.m.
Subscriber comments: Still recovering from tornado two years ago that destroyed most trees . . . New facilities A-plus . . . Great course and facilities outstanding, course lost some personality with tornado.

★★★ SUNSET HILLS GOLF COURSE
PU—Sunset Lane, Guymon (405)338-7404.
120 miles north of Amarillo, Tex. **Holes:** 18. **Par:** 71/74.
Yards: 6,732/5,780. **Course rating:** 67.5/68.0. **Slope:** 108/112.
Opened: 1932. **Pace of Play rating:** 4:30. **Green fee:** $9/11.
Credit cards: None. **Reduced fees:** Twilight.
Caddies: No. **Golf carts:** $16 for 18 holes.

Discount golf packages: No. **Season:** Year-round. **High:** June-Aug.
On-site lodging: No. **Rental clubs:** Yes.
Walking policy: Unrestricted walking. **Range:** Yes.
To obtain tee times: First come, first served.
Subscriber comments: Good grass and greens, well maintained, good lunches . . . Nice course for Oklahoma anhandle . . . Good condition in middle of summer . . . Wide open with lots of hills, wind and undulating greens.

★★½ TROSPER PARK GOLF COURSE
PU—2301 S.E. 29th, Oklahoma City (405)677-8874.
Holes: 18. **Par:** 72/72.
Yards: 6,928/6,450. **Course rating:** N/A. **Slope:** 118/116.
Opened: N/A. **Pace of Play rating:** N/A. **Green fee:** $N/A.
Credit cards: N/A. **Reduced fees:** Twilight.
Caddies: No. **Golf carts:** $N/A for 18 holes.
Discount golf packages: No. **Season:** Year-round. **High:** March-Sept.
On-site lodging: No. **Rental clubs:** No.
Walking policy: N/A. **Range:** Yes (grass).

Subscriber comments: Well worth cost, heavily used . . . Great shape, difficult mid- length, great clubhouse and staff . . . Maintenance not up to par, too much hardpan . . . Enjoyable, well paced play. Never crowded . . . Former stepchild to Lincoln Park, now it is better than Lincoln . . . Excellent greens, wide open, short rough.

★★ UNIVERSITY OF OKLAHOMA GOLF COURSE
PU—1 Par Dr., Norman (405)325-6716.
20 miles south of Oklahoma City. **Holes:** 18. **Par:** 72/74.
Yards: 6,941/5,394. **Course rating:** 72.9/70.7. **Slope:** 123/116.
Opened: 1951. **Pace of Play rating:** N/A. **Green fee:** $11.
Credit cards: None. **Reduced fees:** Twilight, Seniors, Juniors.
Caddies: No. **Golf carts:** $7 for 18 holes.
Discount golf packages: No. **Season:** Year-round. **High:** April-Oct.
On-site lodging: No. **Rental clubs:** Yes.
Walking policy: Unrestricted walking. **Range:** Yes (grass).
To obtain tee times: Call Wednesday at 7 a.m. for upcoming weekend. Open play weekdays.
Subscriber comments: Greens were excellent, fairways need sprinkler system . . . Nice course, improving . . . Clubhouse is small . . . With irrigation and just a little work becomes four or five in rating . . . Need to spend some football income on their golf course . . . University should be ashamed of the condition of this great course . . . If this course had a water system, it could be best in Oklahoma .

★★½ WESTWOOD PARK GOLF COURSE
PU—2400 Westport Dr., Norman (405)321-0433.
17 miles south of Oklahoma City. **Holes:** 18. **Par:** 70/74.
Yards: 6,015/5,525. **Course rating:** 67.7/71.0. **Slope:** 108/120.
Opened: 1967. **Pace of Play rating:** 3:30. **Green fee:** $4/11.
Credit cards: None. **Reduced fees:** Weekdays, Twilight, Seniors.
Caddies: No. **Golf carts:** $8 for 18 holes.
Discount golf packages: No. **Season:** Year-round. **High:** April-Sept.
On-site lodging: No. **Rental clubs:** Yes.
Walking policy: Unrestricted walking. **Range:** Yes (grass).
To obtain tee times: Weekend tee times only. Call as early as Saturday for following weekend.
Subscriber comments: Well maintained, very popular, good fairways and greens. Not too difficult, easy to walk . . . Staff fair at best . . . Flat and dry . . . Slow play. No water . . . Stay off while school's out, course full of kids that play slow.

WHITE HAWK GOLF CLUB★
SP—14515 S. York Ave., Bixby (918)366-4653.
10 miles north of Tulsa. **Holes:** 18. **Par:** 72/72.
Yards: 6,982/5,148. **Course rating:** 74.1/N/A. **Slope:** 134/N/A.
Opened: 1994. **Pace of Play rating:** 4:15. **Green fee:** $22/27.
Credit cards: MC, V, AMEX. **Reduced fees:** Weekdays, Low season, Twilight, Seniors, Juniors.
Caddies: No. **Golf carts:** $10 for 18 holes.
Discount golf packages: Yes. **Season:** Year-round. **High:** May-Oct.
On-site lodging: No. **Rental clubs:** Yes.
Walking policy: Unrestricted walking. **Range:** Yes (grass).
To obtain tee times: Nonmembers call two weeks in advance. First come, first served.
Subscriber comments: Good grass and greens.

★★★ AWBREY GLEN GOLF CLUB
SP—2500 N.W. Awbrey Glen Dr., Bend (503)388-8526.
Holes: 18. **Par:** 72/72.
Yards: 7,007/5,459. **Course rating:** 73.7/69.6. **Slope:** 135/119.
Opened: 1993. **Pace of Play rating:** 4:00. **Green fee:** $45/50.
Credit cards: MC, V. **Reduced fees:** Low season, Juniors.
Caddies: No. **Golf carts:** $11 for 18 holes.
Discount golf packages: Yes. **Season:** March–Oct. **High:** May–Sept.
On-site lodging: No. **Rental clubs:** Yes.
Walking policy: Walking at certain times. **Range:** Yes (grass).
To obtain tee times: Call three days in advance.
Subscriber comments: Terrific practice facility . . . Best in central
Oregon, everything finest, class staff . . . Beautiful new course, not for high
handicapper . . . Open, little trees . . . Hills, hills, hills, cart, cart, cart . . .
Needs seasoning, not a walking course . . . Beautiful, scenic . . . New
tricky . . . Wow! What a view . . . One of my favorite courses, good
golfers will love it . . . Great diversity of interesting and challenging holes
. . . You remember each hole.

BLACK BUTTE RANCH
R—Hwy. 20, Black Butte (503)595-6689, (800)399-2322.
25 miles northeast of Bend. **Green fee:** $36/45.
Credit cards: All major. **Reduced fees:** Low season.
Caddies: No. **Golf carts:** $28 for 18 holes.
Discount golf packages: No. **Season:** March–Nov. **High:** June–Sept.
On-site lodging: Yes. **Rental clubs:** Yes.
Walking policy: Unrestricted walking. **Range:** Yes (grass).
To obtain tee times: Call one day in advance for weekdays. Guests
staying at the ranch call the Monday prior to upcoming weekend beginning
at 8:30 a.m. All others may call the Thursday prior to weekend.

★★★½ BIG MEADOW COURSE
Holes: 18. **Par:** 72/72.
Yards: 6,870/5,716. **Course rating:** 72.0/70.5. **Slope:** 127/115.
Opened: 1971. **Pace of Play rating:** 4:10.
Subscriber comments: Spectacular views . . . Beautiful meandering
layout . . . Great beauty . . . Great fairways . . . Fast greens . . . Good
variety among holes . . . My favorite, No. 2 only to Sandpines . . . Best in
the state, everything first class . . . Room for error . . . Better test from the
blues for good players . . . For these courses you better have your driver
ready and your putter tuned in . . . The better of the new Black Butte
courses . . . Personal favorite . . . Best place if you had to die on a golf
course . . . More open than sister course . . . Typical central Oregon golf,
lots of trees.

★★★ GLAZE MEADOW COURSE
Holes: 18. **Par:** 72/72.
Yards: 6,560/5,616. **Course rating:** 71.5/72.1. **Slope:** 128/120.
Opened: 1982. **Pace of Play rating:** 4:10.
Subscriber comments: Beautiful course . . . High in mountain, more
interesting than Big Meadow, higher altitude means longer drives . . . Very
narrow . . . Beautiful but tight . . . Beautiful course, plays long, winding
through pines . . . Scenery adds to enjoyment . . . Great if you draw the
ball . . . Need to play it twice . . . Love this challenge, beautiful condition
. . . Scenic front nine. Tough back side . . . Best setting in Oregon, peaceful
. . . Tight but demanding, great mountain views . . . When considering
everything, one of the best . . . Harder than Big Meadow, not as scenic, but
still beautiful.

★★ BROADMOOR GOLF COURSE
PU—3509 N.E. Columbia Blvd., Portland (503)281-1337.
4 miles northeast of Portland. **Holes:** 18. **Par:** 72/74.
Yards: 6,498/5,384. **Course rating:** 70.3/69.9. **Slope:** 118/110.
Opened: 1931. **Pace of Play rating:** 4:30-5:00. **Green fee:** $18/20.
Credit cards: MC, V. **Reduced fees:** Weekdays, Low season.
Caddies: No. **Golf carts:** $10 for 18 holes.
Discount golf packages: No. **Season:** Year-round. **High:** May–Sept.

On-site lodging: No. **Rental clubs:** Yes.
Walking policy: Unrestricted walking. **Range:** Yes (grass).
To obtain tee times: Call pro shop one week in advance.
Subscriber comments: Easy to walk . . . Wet course . . . Older course, not as good shape as could be but for price a good deal . . . Fun course, lots of birdie holes . . . Courteous staff . . . Course is too soft anytime of year . . . Too close to airport . . . Old city course . . . Treelined, straightaway course . . . Not too busy, but fun, great if you like planes.

★★ CEDAR LINKS GOLF COURSE
PU—3155 Cedar Links Dr., Medford (503)773-4373.
Holes: 18. **Par:** 70/71.
Yards: 6,142/5,145. **Course rating:** 68.9/68.7. **Slope:** 114/112.

Opened: 1972. **Pace of Play rating:** 4:30. **Green fee:** $20.
Credit cards: MC, V. **Reduced fees:** No.
Caddies: No. **Golf carts:** $18 for 18 holes.
Discount golf packages: No. **Season:** Year-round. **High:** May-Sept.
On-site lodging: No. **Rental clubs:** Yes.
Walking policy: Unrestricted walking. **Range:** Yes.
To obtain tee times: Call pro shop seven days in advance.
Subscriber comments: Course under new management, quality improving . . . Fair challenge, friendly staff . . . Nicest course in the area, in good condition . . . The pears on the back nine are delicious in the fall . . . Nice for an old course.

★★ COLWOOD NATIONAL GOLF CLUB
PU—7313 N.E. Columbia Blvd., Portland (503)254-5515.
Holes: 18. **Par:** 72/77.
Yards: 6,400/5,800. **Course rating:** 70.2/71.5. **Slope:** 113/111.
Opened: 1930. **Pace of Play rating:** 4:00. **Green fee:** $16/18.
Credit cards: None. **Reduced fees:** Juniors.
Caddies: No. **Golf carts:** $28 for 18 holes.
Discount golf packages: No. **Season:** Year-round. **High:** April-Oct.
On-site lodging: No. **Rental clubs:** Yes.
Walking policy: Unrestricted walking. **Range:** No.
To obtain tee times: Call seven days in advance.
Subscriber comments: Wonderful, Average-Joe public course . . . Do not have to be a power hitter to play on this course . . . Not long but tight . . . Easy to get on without tee times . . . Nice old clubhouse . . . Like going through a well-trained drive-through restaurant . . . Minutes from the car to the tee.

EAGLE CREST RESORT
R—1522 Cline Falls Rd., Redmond (503)923-4653.
7 miles east of Redmond. **Green fee:** $37.
Credit cards: All major. **Reduced fees:** Low season, Resort guests, Juniors.
Caddies: No. **Golf carts:** $25 for 18 holes.
Discount golf packages: Yes. **Season:** Year-round. **High:** April-Oct.
On-site lodging: Yes. **Rental clubs:** Yes.
Walking policy: Walking at certain times. **Range:** Yes (grass).
To obtain tee times: Public may call two weeks in advance but must guarantee with a credit card. Owners, one month in advance; tournaments six months in advance with credit card guarantee.
★★★ RESORT COURSE
Holes: 18. **Par:** 72/72.
Yards: 6,673/5,395. **Course rating:** 71.5/69.8. **Slope:** 123/109.
Opened: 1986. **Pace of Play rating:** 4:30.
Subscriber comments: The friendliest staff around, also promote junior golf . . . Staff excellent, service good, course very good . . . Beautiful scenery . . . Resort course, very pretty but not very easy. Accuracy a plus . . . Signature hole is a drive into a canyon . . . A few goofy holes . . . Harder than it appears, green speed can be awesome . . . Challenging but user-friendly . . . Very sporty.

★★★½ RIDGE COURSE
(503)923-5002.
Holes: 18. **Par:** 72/72.
Yards: 6,477/4,773. **Course rating:** 70.8/N/A. **Slope:** 123/N/A.
Opened: 1993. **Pace of Play rating:** 4:30.
Subscriber comments: Scenic time-share resort . . . Short but sweet . . .
Slick greens . . . Good value for a resort course . . . Short but a challenge,
has character . . . Each hole interesting . . . Wildlife . . . Many fairway
mounds that tend to keep ball in fairway . . . Nice staff . . . No homes,
cars, dogs, etc., just golf . . . Wind can add spice . . . Helpful staff . . .
Memorable . . . Well designed. Good variety. Fun track . . . Nice new
course, beautiful surroundings . . . No houses yet . . . First experience with
desert golf . . . Windy, wide landing areas.

★★★ EASTMORELAND GOLF COURSE
PU—2425 S.E. Bybee Blvd., Portland (503)775-2900.
Holes: 18. **Par:** 72/74.
Yards: 6,529/5,646. **Course rating:** 71.7/71.4. **Slope:** 123/117.
Opened: 1921. **Pace of Play rating:** 4:30. **Green fee:** $15/17.
Credit cards: None. **Reduced fees:** Seniors, Juniors.
Caddies: No. **Golf carts:** $22 for 18 holes.
Discount golf packages: No. **Season:** Year-round. **High:** June-Sept.
On-site lodging: No. **Rental clubs:** Yes.
Walking policy: Unrestricted walking. **Range:** Yes.
To obtain tee times: Call six days in advance.
Ranked in First 25 of America's 75 Best Public Golf Courses by Golf
Digest.
Subscriber comments: Beautiful old design, narrow tree-lined fairways,
inventive holes . . . Good conditions for such heavy play . . . One of the
better city courses . . . Good test with a great variety of holes, very good
value . . . Best public course in the state, built around lake on back nine . . .
A classic but needs attention . . . Back nine watery and challenging . . .
Great in spring when rhodies are in bloom . . . Best snack bar food and
coldest beer . . . Crowded, old style muny . . . Beautiful parklike setting
. . . Tough, good challenge, even low handicappers struggle.

★★★ EMERALD VALLEY GOLF CLUB
SP—83301 Dale Kuni Rd., Creswell (503)895-2174.
10 miles south of Eugene. **Holes:** 18. **Par:** 72/73.
Yards: 6,873/5,371. **Course rating:** 73.6/74.7. **Slope:** 130/129.
Opened: 1964. **Pace of Play rating:** 4:15. **Green fee:** $22/25.
Credit cards: MC, V, AMEX. **Reduced fees:** Weekdays, Twilight,
Seniors, Juniors.
Caddies: No. **Golf carts:** $18 for 18 holes.
Discount golf packages: No. **Season:** Year-round. **High:** June-Sept.
On-site lodging: No. **Rental clubs:** Yes.
Walking policy: Unrestricted walking. **Range:** Yes (grass).
To obtain tee times: Call up to one week in advance.
Subscriber comments: Interesting course, beautiful setting . . . Old, well
established. Country club atmosphere . . . Nice walkable course . . . Would
be outstanding if maintained better . . . Nice layout, good value . . . Price
comparable to most in area.

★★★ FOREST HILLS GOLF COURSE
SP—36260 S.W. Tongue Lane, Cornelius (503)357-3347.
25 miles southwest of Portland. **Holes:** 18. **Par:** 72/74.
Yards: 6,173/5,673. **Course rating:** 69.7/71.7. **Slope:** 122/114.
Opened: 1927. **Pace of Play rating:** 4:00. **Green fee:** $22.
Credit cards: MC, V. **Reduced fees:** Juniors.
Caddies: No. **Golf carts:** $20 for 18 holes.
Discount golf packages: No. **Season:** Year-round. **High:** May-Sept.
On-site lodging: No. **Rental clubs:** Yes.
Walking policy: Unrestricted walking. **Range:** Yes (grass).
To obtain tee times: Call pro shop seven days in advance. Saturday,
Sunday and holidays no nine hole play or twosomes before 1 p.m.

Subscriber comments: Good 18 hole public course, improvements being made . . . A good everyday golf course . . . Good public course . . . My favorite course in the area, great staff . . . A real surprise . . . My own favorite . . . Fun to play . . . Charming old course . . . Lovely countryside setting.

★½ GEARHART GOLF LINKS

PU—N. Marion St., Gearhart (503)738-3538.
90 miles northwest of Portland. **Holes:** 18. **Par:** 72/74.
Yards: 6,089/5,882. **Course rating:** 68.7/72.7. **Slope:** 114/123.
Opened: 1892. **Pace of Play rating:** 4:00. **Green fee:** $20.
Credit cards: MC, V. **Reduced fees:** No.
Caddies: No. **Golf carts:** $20 for 18 holes.
Discount golf packages: No. **Season:** Year-round. **High:** April-Oct.
On-site lodging: Yes. **Rental clubs:** Yes.
Walking policy: Unrestricted walking. **Range:** No.
To obtain tee times: Call anytime.
Subscriber comments: Good course in the spring . . . Good old course with poor maintenance . . . Seaside course, gets lots of play . . . Touted as the oldest course in Oregon . . . No clubhouse, busy public course . . . Friendly people . . . Courteous staff . . . Played late summer, fairways burned up.

GLENDOVEER GOLF COURSE

PU—14015 N.E. Glisan, Portland (503)253-7507.
Green fee: $15/17.
Credit cards: None. **Reduced fees:** Seniors, Juniors.
Caddies: No. **Golf carts:** $22 for 18 holes.
Discount golf packages: No. **Season:** Year-round. **High:** May-Sept.
On-site lodging: No. **Rental clubs:** Yes.
Walking policy: Unrestricted walking. **Range:** Yes.
To obtain tee times: Call tee time number (292-8570) six days in advance.
★★ EAST COURSE
Holes: 18. **Par:** 73/75.
Yards: 6,296/5,142. **Course rating:** 69.3/73.5. **Slope:** 119/120.
Opened: 1926. **Pace of Play rating:** 4:00.
Subscriber comments: Up and down course . . . Very popular, conditions not always good . . . Wide open, go for it . . . 36 holes on this one, could be better maintained . . . Short but fun . . . Greens need work, ongoing repair of bunkers . . . Hills, good for excercise . . . Has potential not realized . . . Easy to walk.
★½ WEST COURSE
Holes: 18. **Par:** 71/75.
Yards: 5,922/5,117. **Course rating:** 67.5/70.8. **Slope:** 111/110.
Opened: 1926. **Pace of Play rating:** 4:00.
Subscriber comments: Crowded . . . Easy to walk on, cheap fees . . . Flat course . . . Short, tree-lined . . . Great old course, needs better conditioning.

★★★ GRANTS PASS COUNTRY CLUB

SP—230 Espey Road, Grants Pass (503)476-0849.
Call club for further information.
Subscriber comments: A delight to play, front nine is level with narrow tree-lined fairways . . . A super public course, hardest in Portland from tips . . . Fun course . . . Front nine flat, back nine hilly . . . Pretty tough, be careful to choose driver on the right holes.

★★ HARBOR LINKS GOLF COURSE

PU—601 Harbor Isles Blvd., Klamath Falls (503)882-0609.
Holes: 18. **Par:** 72/72.
Yards: 6,272/5,709. **Course rating:** 69.3/71.2. **Slope:** 117/119.
Opened: 1986. **Pace of Play rating:** 4:00. **Green fee:** $23/25.
Credit cards: MC, V. **Reduced fees:** Weekdays, Low season, Twilight, Seniors, Juniors.
Caddies: No. **Golf carts:** $20 for 18 holes.

Discount golf packages: No. **Season:** Year-round. **High:** June-Sept.
On-site lodging: No. **Rental clubs:** Yes.
Walking policy: Unrestricted walking. **Range:** Yes.
To obtain tee times: Call anytime one week in advance.
Subscriber comments: Staff and setting are excellent . . . Easy to walk
. . . Course is challenging with many water hazards.

HERON LAKES GOLF COURSE
PU—3500 N. Victory Blvd., Portland (503)289-1818.
Green fee: $14/25.
Credit cards: None. **Reduced fees:** Weekdays, Seniors, Juniors.
Caddies: No. **Golf carts:** $22 for 18 holes.
Discount golf packages: No. **Season:** Year-round. **High:** March-Oct.
On-site lodging: No. **Rental clubs:** Yes.
Walking policy: Unrestricted walking. **Range:** Yes (grass).
To obtain tee times: Call Tee Time Inc. at (503)292-8570.

★★★½ GREAT BLUE COURSE
Holes: 18. **Par:** 72/72.
Yards: 6,916/5,285. **Course rating:** 73.6/69.8. **Slope:** 132/120.
Opened: 1971. **Pace of Play rating:** 4:50.
Ranked in Third 25 of America's 75 Best Public Golf Courses by Golf
Digest.
Subscriber comments: One of the best courses in Oregon, tough course
from back tees . . . Good public course . . . Bring your "A" game . . .
Excellent Trent Jones Jr. course . . . Tough when the wind blows . . . Very
busy . . . Bring water balls . . . Requires all the shots . . . A great design,
not in very good shape during peak season . . . Solid course . . .
Challenging, fun, risk/reward, back nine can eat you up . . . Lots of birds
(real birds) eagles, hawks, even blue heron . . . Front nine easier than
difficult back.

★★★ GREENBACK COURSE
Holes: 18. **Par:** 72/72.
Yards: 6,595/5,224. **Course rating:** 71.4/69.4. **Slope:** 124/113.
Opened: 1970. **Pace of Play rating:** 4:50.
Subscriber comments: Fun to play with my wife . . . Great layout, a little
too crowded . . . Majestic, challenging municipal course . . . Shows heavy
use . . . Few tees, lots of water, no houses, joggers, many birds . . . Very
good shape in spring . . . Lots of golf . . . Easy after playing Great Blue . . .
Not as challenging as Great Blue, but solid.

★★★ INDIAN CREEK GOLF CLUB
PU—3605 Brookside Dr., Hood River (503)386-7770.
Call club for further information.
Subscriber comments: Great scenery . . . Short course, long walk
between holes . . . Public course, fast greens, very windy, some tricky holes
. . . Mt. Hood and Mt. Adams beautiful . . . Fun course. Don't usually
ride, glad I did . . . Puts real meaning to "it's up and down" . . . Beautiful
scenery.

★½ JUNIPER GOLF CLUB
SP—139 S.E. Sisters Ave., Redmond (503)548-3121, (800)600-3121.
125 miles southeast of Portland. **Holes:** 18. **Par:** 72/72.
Yards: 6,525/5,598. **Course rating:** 71.3/70.9. **Slope:** 124/115.
Opened: 1953. **Pace of Play rating:** 4:00. **Green fee:** $20/25.
Credit cards: MC, V. **Reduced fees:** Weekdays, Low season, Juniors.
Caddies: No. **Golf carts:** $20 for 18 holes.
Discount golf packages: No. **Season:** Year-round. **High:** May-Oct.
On-site lodging: No. **Rental clubs:** Yes.
Walking policy: Unrestricted walking. **Range:** Yes (grass).
To obtain tee times: Call one month in advance.
Subscriber comments: Lots of water, wonderful people . . . Course has
physically improved . . . Maintenance not always there . . . Must know the
course in order to score . . . Not bad for price, several tight driving holes,
greens inconsistent . . . Nice view of Cascades.

★★ KAH-NEE-TA RESORT GOLF CLUB

R—P.O. Box K, Warm Springs (503)553-1112, (800)831-0100.
115 miles east of Portland. **Holes:** 18. **Par:** 72/73.
Yards: 6,352/5,195. **Course rating:** 73.1/70.0. **Slope:** 123/116.
Opened: 1972. **Pace of Play rating:** 4:30. **Green fee:** $18/28.
Credit cards: All major. **Reduced fees:** Low season, Seniors, Juniors
Caddies: No. **Golf carts:** $24 for 18 holes.
Discount golf packages: Yes. **Season:** Year-round. **High:** March–Oct.
On-site lodging: Yes. **Rental clubs:** Yes.
Walking policy: Unrestricted walking. **Range:** Yes (grass).
To obtain tee times: Call for times up to two weeks in advance.
Subscriber comments: Not very good shape . . . Open front nine, tight
back nine . . . Peaceful course . . . Strange layout . . . .Well maintained
beautiful course, well worth the drive . . . Good course, great housing . . .
Very nice, never crowded.

THE KNOLLS GOLF CLUB★

PU—1919 Recreation Lane, Sutherlin (503)459-4422.
50 miles south of Eugene. **Holes:** 18. **Par:** 72/73.
Yards: 6,346/5,427. **Course rating:** 70.3/71.5. **Slope:** 121/122.
Opened: 1970. **Pace of Play rating:** 3:50. **Green fee:** $18.
Credit cards: MC, V. **Reduced fees:** Twilight.
Caddies: No. **Golf carts:** $18 for 18 holes.
Discount golf packages: No. **Season:** Year-round. **High:** June–Aug.
On-site lodging: No. **Rental clubs:** Yes.
Walking policy: Unrestricted walking. **Range:** Yes (grass).
To obtain tee times: Call one week in advance.

LAKESIDE GOLF CLUB★

SP—3245 Club House Dr., Lincoln City (503)994-8442.
50 miles west of Salem. **Holes:** 18. **Par:** 66/71.
Yards: 5,007/4,318. **Course rating:** 64.9/66.2. **Slope:** 109/104.
Opened: N/A. **Pace of Play rating:** 4:00. **Green fee:** $24/31.
Credit cards: MC, V. **Reduced fees:** Twilight, Seniors, Juniors.
Caddies: No. **Golf carts:** $25 for 18 holes.
Discount golf packages: No. **Season:** Year-round. **High:** Aug.–Sept.
On-site lodging: No. **Rental clubs:** Yes.
Walking policy: Unrestricted walking. **Range:** Yes (grass).
To obtain tee times: Call pro shop.

LANGDON FARMS GOLF CLUB★

PU—24377 N.E. Airport Rd., Aurora (503)678-4653.
15 miles north of Portland. **Holes:** 18. **Par:** 71/71.
Yards: 6,930/5,249. **Course rating:** 73.3/69.4. **Slope:** 125/114.
Opened: 1995. **Pace of Play rating:** 4:15. **Green fee:** $45/50.
Credit cards: All major. **Reduced fees:** Twilight, Seniors.
Caddies: No. **Golf carts:** $10 for 18 holes.
Discount golf packages: Yes. **Season:** Year-round. **High:** April–Oct.
On-site lodging: No. **Rental clubs:** Yes.
Walking policy: Unrestricted walking. **Range:** Yes (grass).
To obtain tee times: Call 30 to 60 days in advance.

★★★ MEADOW LAKES GOLF COURSE

PU—300 Meadow Lakes Dr., Prineville (503)447-7113, (800)577-2797.
38 miles northeast of Bend. **Holes:** 180. **Par:** 72/72.
Yards: 6,731/5,155. **Course rating:** 73.1/69.0. **Slope:** 131/121.
Opened: 1993. **Pace of Play rating:** 4:15. **Green fee:** $25.
Credit cards: MC, V. **Reduced fees:** Low season.
Caddies: No. **Golf carts:** $11 for 18 holes.
Discount golf packages: Yes. **Season:** Year-round. **High:** June–Sept.
On-site lodging: No. **Rental clubs:** Yes.
Walking policy: Unrestricted walking. **Range:** Yes (grass).
To obtain tee times: Call up to one year in advance guaranteed with credit
card, otherwise six days without credit card.

FRUGAL PICK

Subscriber comments: Unique . . . Uses effluent water . . . Great young
golf course . . . Water on nearly every hole, need a lot of balls . . .
Friendliest staff I have ever seen anywhere . . . Restaurant grand . . . Proves
what can be done if you want to really try . . . Great golf . . . Flat with
much water. Puts premium on control.

★½ MERIWETHER NATIONAL GOLF CLUB

PU—5200 S.W. Rood Bridge Rd., Hillsboro (503)648-4143.
25 miles west of Portland. **Holes:** 27. **Par:** 72/72/72.
Yards: 6,719/6,779/6,752. **Course rating:** 71.3/71.2/71.3.

Slope: 121/117/115.
Opened: 1960. **Pace of Play rating:** 4:30. **Green fee:** $16/18.
Credit cards: MC, V. **Reduced fees:** Juniors.
Caddies: No. **Golf carts:** Included in Green Fee.
Discount golf packages: No. **Season:** Year-round. **High:** April-Oct.
On-site lodging: No. **Rental clubs:** Yes.
Walking policy: Walking at certain times. **Range:** Yes (grass).
To obtain tee times: Call seven days in advance.
Subscriber comments: Easy walking but carts mandatory on Saturday
. . . Beautiful new clubhouse, course needs better maintenance . . . A fun
course to play. Gets a little marshy . . . Do yourself a favor, play the back
nine twice and skip the front . . . Should have skipped new clubhouse, put
$$into course . . . Nice layout.

★½ MOUNTAIN VIEW GOLF CLUB

PU—27195 S.E. Kelso Rd., Boring (503)663-4869.
20 miles east of Portland. **Holes:** 180. **Par:** 71/73.
Yards: 6,056/5,294. **Course rating:** 69.2/69.2. **Slope:** 122/111.
Opened: 1963. **Pace of Play rating:** 4:25. **Green fee:** $18/20.
Credit cards: MC, V. **Reduced fees:** Weekdays, Seniors, Juniors.
Caddies: No. **Golf carts:** $20 for 18 holes.
Discount golf packages: No. **Season:** Year-round. **High:** April-Oct.
On-site lodging: No. **Rental clubs:** Yes.
Walking policy: Unrestricted walking. **Range:** Yes (grass).
To obtain tee times: Call pro shop.
Subscriber comments: Great location, beautiful . . . Front nine almost
boring, back nine has some character . . . Great scenery . . . Poor
maintenance . . . Overpriced, needs upgrading . . . No. 12 is a 200-foot
vertical drop par 3. You gotta see this.

★½ OAK KNOLL GOLF COURSE

PU—6335 Hwy. 22, Independence (503)378-0344.
6 miles west of Salem. **Holes:** 18. **Par:** 72/72.
Yards: 6,208/5,239. **Course rating:** 68.6/69.2. **Slope:** 113/113.
Opened: 1926. **Pace of Play rating:** 4:00. **Green fee:** $15/20.
Credit cards: MC, V. **Reduced fees:** Low season, Seniors, Juniors.
Caddies: No. **Golf carts:** $20 for 18 holes.
Discount golf packages: Yes. **Season:** Year-round. **High:** June-Oct.
On-site lodging: No. **Rental clubs:** Yes.
Walking policy: Unrestricted walking. **Range:** Yes (grass).
To obtain tee times: Call pro shop.
Subscriber comments: Great walker's course . . . Good service . . .
Poorly maintained . . . Unimaginative design.

★★½ OCEAN DUNES GOLF LINKS

PU—3345 Munsel Lake Rd., Florence (503)997-3232, (800)468-4833.
60 miles west of Eugene. **Holes:** 18. **Par:** 70/72.
Yards: 5,670/4,868. **Course rating:** 68.5/69.5. **Slope:** 124/124.
Opened: 1963. **Pace of Play rating:** 4:30. **Green fee:** $25.
Credit cards: MC, V, DISC. **Reduced fees:** Twilight, Seniors, Juniors.
Caddies: No. **Golf carts:** $10 for 18 holes.
Discount golf packages: No. **Season:** Year-round. **High:** April-Nov.
On-site lodging: No. **Rental clubs:** Yes.
Walking policy: Unrestricted walking. **Range:** Yes (grass).

To obtain tee times: Call pro shop.
Subscriber comments: Very narrow, windy, sand dunes, dry and firm, great staff and layout . . . Take a lot of balls and a dune buggy . . . Must stay in fairway . . . Tough course . . . Nice course . . . Extremely narrow but interesting short course.

★ PROGRESS DOWNS GOLF COURSE
PU—8200 S.W. Scholls Ferry Rd., Beaverton (503)646-5166.
4 miles west of Portland. **Holes:** 18. **Par:** 71/73.
Yards: 6,426/5,626. **Course rating:** 69.8/71.7. **Slope:** 112/115.
Opened: 1966. **Pace of Play rating:** 4:20. **Green fee:** $15/17.
Credit cards: None. **Reduced fees:** Weekdays, Seniors, Juniors.
Caddies: No. **Golf carts:** $10 for 18 holes.
Discount golf packages: No. **Season:** Year-round. **High:** April-Oct.
On-site lodging: No. **Rental clubs:** Yes.
Walking policy: Unrestricted walking. **Range:** Yes.
To obtain tee times: In person seven days in advance or phone in six days in advance.
Subscriber comments: Would be a very good track if city would maintain it adequately . . . Most played course in Oregon . . . Great pro shop staff . . . Best driving range . . . Overplayed, needs improvement . . . Very busy, generally well maintained.

★★★★½ PUMPKIN RIDGE GOLF CLUB
GHOST CREEK COURSE
PU—12930 Old Pumpkin Ridge Rd., Cornelius (503)647-9977.
20 miles west of Portland. **Holes:** 18. **Par:** 71/71.
Yards: 6,839/5,326. **Course rating:** 73.8/71.0. **Slope:** 140/121.
Opened: 1992. **Pace of Play rating:** 4:20. **Green fee:** $60/75.
Credit cards: All major. **Reduced fees:** Weekdays, Low season, Twilight.
Caddies: Yes. **Golf carts:** $20 for 18 holes.
Discount golf packages: No. **Season:** Year-round. **High:** April-Oct.
On-site lodging: No. **Rental clubs:** Yes.
Walking policy: Unrestricted walking. **Range:** Yes (grass).
To obtain tee times: Eight days with frequent player card; six days in person; seven days by phone.
Selected as Best New Public Course of 1992 by Golf Digest. Ranked 3rd in Oregon by Golf Digest.
Subscriber comments: Gotta play this one, fairways like carpet with a 3-inch pad . . . Tough but fair . . . One of the best in the West . . . Terrific everything . . . First class all the way . . . In winter course was still in great shape . . . More fun than its private partner . . . Country club atmosphere . . . Each hole delights, great value at summer twilight rates . . . Cupp outdid himself . . . A public country club . . . One of the best courses in the Northwest . . . Carts stay on paths. Better to walk . . . Worthy of all the praise . . . The ultimate golf experience . . . Provides difficulty without intimidation . . . U.S. Amateur next year. Good choice . . . A one day country club experience . . . Excellent course.

★★★ QUAIL VALLEY GOLF COURSE
PU—12565 N.W. Aerts Rd., Banks (503)324-4444.
20 miles west of Portland. **Holes:** 18. **Par:** 72/72.
Yards: 6,603/5,519. **Course rating:** 71.6/71.5. **Slope:** 122/117.
Opened: 1994. **Pace of Play rating:** 4:15. **Green fee:** $25.
Credit cards: MC, V, AMEX. **Reduced fees:** No.
Caddies: No. **Golf carts:** $22 for 18 holes.
Discount golf packages: No. **Season:** Year-round. **High:** June-Sept.
On-site lodging: No. **Rental clubs:** Yes.
Walking policy: Unrestricted walking. **Range:** Yes (grass).
To obtain tee times: Call seven days in advance.
Subscriber comments: Has good potential . . . New links-style course, great fun, friendly staff . . . Give it time to grow . . . Doug Hixson's shop a class act . . . New course, immature, very open and playable . . . Excellent

condition for new course, many challenging holes . . . Flail at Quail, can mis-hit shots and still par . . . New course, short but water and rough make good challenge . . . Amen Corner is fun!

★★½ THE RESORT AT THE MOUNTAIN
R—68010 E. Fairway Ave., Welches (503)622-3151, (800)669-4653.
45 miles southeast of Portland. **Holes:** 27. **Par:** 72/70/70.
Yards: 6,443/5,776/6,032. **Course rating:** 70.0/68.0/68.0.
Slope: 119/116/116.
Opened: 1928. **Pace of Play rating:** 4:00-4:30. **Green fee:** $20/33.
Credit cards: All major. **Reduced fees:** Weekdays, Low season, Resort guests, Twilight, Juniors.
Caddies: No. **Golf carts:** $25 for 18 holes.
Discount golf packages: Yes. **Season:** Year-round. **High:** May-Oct.
On-site lodging: Yes. **Rental clubs:** Yes.
Walking policy: Unrestricted walking. **Range:** No.
To obtain tee times: General public two weeks in advance; hotel guests may reserve tee times at time of reservation.
Subscriber comments: Fantastic place to play, too bad the season is so short . . . Short and sporty . . . Sets down in a valley, good condition, polite and business-like shop . . . Great for the office outing . . . Great wildlife, fairly well maintained.

★★★ RIVER'S EDGE GOLF COURSE
PU—200 N.W. Mt. Washington Dr., Bend (503)389-2828.
Holes: 18. **Par:** 72/73.
Yards: 6,647/5,380. **Course rating:** 72.2/71.8. **Slope:** 139/135.
Opened: 1988. **Pace of Play rating:** 4:00. **Green fee:** $29.
Credit cards: MC, V. **Reduced fees:** Low season, Resort guests, Twilight, -Juniors.
Caddies: No. **Golf carts:** $13 for 18 holes.
Discount golf packages: Yes. **Season:** Year-round. **High:** May-Sept.
On-site lodging: Yes. **Rental clubs:** Yes.
Walking policy: Unrestricted walking. **Range:** Yes (grass).
To obtain tee times: Call pro shop. Credit card will hold reservation more than one week.
Subscriber comments: Steep grades on holes . . . Not for the weak . . . Difficult, gorgeous course, waterfalls, ultra views, cheap . . . Narrow fairways, severe elevation changes . . . Lots of fun and trouble, short front, long back . . . Tough and narrow . . . Hard course to walk, good view of city of Bend . . . Great golf and scenery.

★★½ RIVERIDGE GOLF COURSE
PU—3800 N. Delta, Eugene (503)345-9160.
Holes: 18. **Par:** 71/71.
Yards: 6,256/5,146. **Course rating:** 68.6/67.7. **Slope:** 116/112.
Opened: 1990. **Pace of Play rating:** 4:00. **Green fee:** $19/21.
Credit cards: MC, V. **Reduced fees:** Low season, Twilight, Seniors, Juniors.
Caddies: No. **Golf carts:** $20 for 18 holes.
Discount golf packages: Yes. **Season:** Year-round. **High:** May-Sept.
On-site lodging: No. **Rental clubs:** Yes.
Walking policy: Unrestricted walking. **Range:** Yes (grass).
To obtain tee times: Call seven days in advance.
Subscriber comments: Good year-round course . . . Still young, small trees . . . Growing slowly and logically, becoming one of the fine golf attractions in the Willamette Valley . . . Pace is great, two hours on the dot for nine . . . For price, few better . . . Best course in Eugene . . . Good, easy course for beginners, little trouble. Friendly staff.

★★ ROSE CITY MUNICIPAL GOLF CLUB
PU—2200 N.E. 71st, Portland (503)253-4744.
Holes: 18. **Par:** 72/72.
Yards: 6,455/5,619. **Slope:** 118/117.

Call course for further information.

Subscriber comments: Good basic course . . . The sleeper of Portland munys . . . Good city course, good old layout, great value . . . Needs work on course upkeep . . . Stately fir trees . . . Nice public course, easy to get tee time . . . Best place if you just want to play with your father . . . True city course, long and overplayed, been there forever.

★★★ SALEM GOLF CLUB

PU—2025 Golf Course Rd., Salem (503)363-6652.
Holes: 18. **Par:** 72/72.
Yards: 6,200/5,163. **Course rating:** 69.6/70.0. **Slope:** 118/N/A.
Opened: 1928. **Pace of Play rating:** 4:00. **Green fee:** $28.
Credit cards: MC, V. **Reduced fees:** Low season, Juniors.
Caddies: Yes. **Golf carts:** $20 for 18 holes.
Discount golf packages: No. **Season:** Year-round. **High:** July-Sept.
On-site lodging: No. **Rental clubs:** Yes.
Walking policy: Unrestricted walking. **Range:** Yes (grass).
To obtain tee times: Call two days in advance for weekdays or on Monday for the upcoming weekend.
Subscriber comments: Beautiful parkland course, always fun to play . . . Great older course, tree-lined fairways . . . Narrow fairways, nice clubhouse . . . Great course for the money . . . Short, but tight . . . Stately old course, easy to get in trouble . . . Great public course, needs some work now . . . Classy old course.

★★★ SALISHAN GOLF LINKS

R—Hwy. 101, Gleneden Beach (503)764-3632, (800)452-2300.
58 miles east of Salem. **Holes:** 18. **Par:** 72/72.
Yards: 6,439/5,693. **Course rating:** 72.1/73.6. **Slope:** 128/127.
Opened: 1965. **Pace of Play rating:** 4:00. **Green fee:** $25/36.
Credit cards: All major. **Reduced fees:** Juniors.
Caddies: No. **Golf carts:** $26 for 18 holes.
Discount golf packages: Yes. **Season:** Year-round. **High:** June-Oct.
On-site lodging: Yes. **Rental clubs:** Yes.
Walking policy: Unrestricted walking. **Range:** Yes.
To obtain tee times: Call two weeks in advance.
Ranked 73rd in America's 75 Best Resort Courses by Golf Digest.
Subscriber comments: Difficult seaside course, great dining room . . . Course maintenance has slipped a little . . . Is presently being overhauled. In two years, will be like new . . . Super setting . . . Good ocean course, wind and weather change conditions drastically . . . Great ocean course, worth stopping by . . . Very nice staff, great views of ocean . . . Magical place, great golf and accommodations, staff very friendly . . . Bring a lot of golf balls and a windbreaker! . . . One of the prettiest beach courses . . . Don't miss when in area.

★★★★½ SANDPINES GOLF RESORT

PU—1201 35th St., Florence (503)997-1940, (800)917-4653.
60 miles west of Eugene. **Holes:** 18. **Par:** 72/72.
Yards: 6,954/5,346. **Course rating:** 74.0/65.8. **Slope:** 129/111.
Opened: 1993. **Pace of Play rating:** 4:30. **Green fee:** $25/50.
Credit cards: MC, V. **Reduced fees:** Twilight.
Caddies: Yes. **Golf carts:** $26 for 18 holes.
Discount golf packages: Yes. **Season:** Year-round. **High:** June-Oct.
On-site lodging: No. **Rental clubs:** Yes.
Walking policy: Unrestricted walking. **Range:** Yes (grass).
To obtain tee times: Call two weeks in advance or sign up for golf package (800)422-5091.
Selected as Best New Public Course of 1993 by Golf Digest. Ranked 5th in Oregon by Golf Digest.
Subscriber comments: Windy, but great fun, Nos. 16, 17, and 18 best final three in state, beautiful course . . . Staff a ten . . . Contrasting nines, beautiful layout, super condition . . . Better than Pinehurst No. 2 . . . Played in off-season, low rates . . . Beautiful coastal course, plays long,

wind gives problems . . . When the wind begins midday, kiss your handicap goodbye . . . Best of the West . . . If Pebble Beach is better, it's not by much . . . Put the Rees Jones name on it and people will come . . . Pumpkin Ridge at the coast . . . What a golf course should be . . . Should be Top 100 in America easy . . . Rated No. 1 by Golf Digest. We thought so, too . . . Twilight rates good . . . Built on Oregon sand dunes . . . Interesting contrast with weather and ocean . . . You're like a kid in the candy store, because it doesn't get much play and you might have the course almost to yourself . . . Starts off sleepy and then the ocean winds pick up. Great test of golf . . . Pray that the wind doesn't blow.

★★½ SANTIAM GOLF CLUB

PU—8724 Golf Club Rd. S.E., Aumsville (503)769-3485.
15 miles east of Salem. **Holes:** 18. **Par:** 72/72.
Yards: 6,392/5,469. **Course rating:** 70.4/72.2. **Slope:** 115/122.
Opened: 1958. **Pace of Play rating:** 4:00. **Green fee:** $20.
Credit cards: None. **Reduced fees:** Seniors, Juniors.
Caddies: No. **Golf carts:** $20 for 18 holes.
Discount golf packages: No. **Season:** Year-round. **High:** July-Sept.
On-site lodging: No. **Rental clubs:** Yes.
Walking policy: Unrestricted walking. **Range:** Yes.
To obtain tee times: Call one week in advance for Friday through Monday.
Subscriber comments: Well kept, walk the course . . . Good winter course . . . Pretty flat, but watch out for water . . . Small town but not small-town course . . . Nice public course, easy to score well.

SHADOW BUTTE GOLF CLUB★

PU—Hwy. 201, Ontario (503)889-9022.
60 miles east of Boise, ID. **Holes:** 18. **Par:** 72/74.
Yards: 6,800/6,200. **Course rating:** 69.8/71.2. **Slope:** 111/111.
Opened: 1968. **Pace of Play rating:** 5:00. **Green fee:** $11.
Credit cards: MC, V. **Reduced fees:** Weekdays, Seniors, Juniors.
Caddies: No. **Golf carts:** $15 for 18 holes.
Discount golf packages: No. **Season:** March-Nov. **High:** May-July.
On-site lodging: No. **Rental clubs:** Yes.
Walking policy: Unrestricted walking. **Range:** Yes (grass).
To obtain tee times: Not needed.

SUNRIVER LODGE AND RESORT

R—P.O. Box 4818, Sunriver (503)593-1221.
20 miles south of Bend. **Credit cards:** All major. **Reduced fees:** No.
Caddies: No. **Golf carts:** Included in Green Fee.
Discount golf packages: No. **Season:** April-Oct. **High:** April-Oct.
On-site lodging: Yes. **Rental clubs:** Yes.
Walking policy: Unrestricted walking. **Range:** Yes (grass).
To obtain tee times: Lodge guests may make tee times at time of reservation. Public call 30 days with credit card.

CROSSWATER COURSE★

Holes: 18. **Par:** 72/72.
Yards: 7,693/5,389. **Course rating:** 74.0/69.8. **Slope:** 146/125.
Opened: 1995. **Pace of Play rating:** N/A. **Green fee:** $95.

★★★★ NORTH WOODLANDS COURSE

Holes: 18. **Par:** 72/72.
Yards: 6,880/5,446. **Course rating:** 73.0/70.3. **Slope:** 131/118.
Opened: 1981. **Pace of Play rating:** 4:30. **Green fee:** $39/59.
Reduced fees: Low season, Resort guests, Twilight, Juniors.
Golf carts: $25 for 18 holes.
Discount golf packages: Yes. **Season:** April-Oct. **High:** June-Aug.
Ranked 20th in America's 75 Best Resort Courses by Golf Digest. Ranked 7th in Oregon by Golf Digest. Site of Golf Digest Schools.
Subscriber comments: Beautiful layout and tough course, great staff . . . Spectacular course in an area that's becoming a golf mecca . . . Be sure to have tee time . . . Will occasionally run mid-week specials during slow

season . . . Take the kids, there's a lot to do! . . . Great sunsets . . . Favorite course after Sandpines . . . Solid golf . . . Classic Trent Jones Jr., all holes interesting . . . Condition not up to design . . . Good fall values available . . . Good test . . . Great views of Mt. Bachelor . . . Wonderful experience, over too soon . . . One of best in the West, I'm going to retire here.

★★★ SOUTH MEADOWS COURSE
Holes: 18. **Par:** 72/72.
Yards: 6,960/5,847. **Course rating:** 72.9/71.7. **Slope:** 130/116.
Opened: 1968. **Pace of Play rating:** 4:30. **Green fee:** $29/49.
Reduced fees: Low season, Resort guests, Twilight, Juniors.
Discount golf packages: Yes. **Season:** April-Oct. **High:** June-Aug.

Site of Golf Digest Schools.
Subscriber comments: Better golf and better price than the more famous North Course . . . Decent little brother to the North, tough par 3s . . . They allow kids to play . . . Oregon's best resort, by far . . . Recent upgrading. Equal to most resort courses . . . Save your money, play North Course . . . Doesn't compare with the North Course . . . Wide open with beautiful views . . . Good fall value . . . Easiest of three Sunriver courses . . . A good tough resort course . . . Better driving course than North . . . Overshadowed by Sunriver North, but a good course.

★★★★ TOKATEE GOLF CLUB
PU—54947 McKenzie Hwy., Blue River (503)822-3220, (800)452-6376.
47 miles east of Eugene. **Holes:** 18. **Par:** 72/72.
Yards: 6,842/5,651. **Course rating:** 72.0/71.2. **Slope:** 126/115.
Opened: 1966. **Pace of Play rating:** 4:00. **Green fee:** $28.
Credit cards: None. **Reduced fees:** Juniors.
Caddies: No. **Golf carts:** $11 for 18 holes.
Discount golf packages: No. **Season:** Feb-Nov. **High:** June-Sept.
On-site lodging: No. **Rental clubs:** Yes.
Walking policy: Unrestricted walking. **Range:** Yes (grass).
To obtain tee times: Call in advance.
Ranked in First 25 of America's 75 Best Public Golf Courses by Golf Digest. Ranked 8th in Oregon by Golf Digest.
Subscriber comments: Beautiful drive from Eugene . . . A real secret in the Cascade foothills, great locale . . . For a golfer this is Shangri-La . . . Ideal for golf nuts . . . Best value for quality, isolated, timbered course . . . Great track, great scenery, staff treats you like royalty . . . Incredible top of mountain course . . . Excellent course in good condition . . . God's golf course . . . The sleeper in Oregon . . . Beautiful place to spend a day . . . Another wow! . . . Well-run public course . . . Great value . . . Simply wonderful . . . Out of the way but worth it . . . Golf heaven . . . A religious experience . . . Like playing in Switzerland . . . A very good Ted Robinson course . . . A jewel in the mountains.

GREAT VALUE

★★★ TRYSTING TREE GOLF CLUB
PU—34028 Electric Rd., Corvallis (503)752-3332.
34 miles southwest of Salem. **Holes:** 18. **Par:** 72/72.
Yards: 7,014/5,516. **Course rating:** 73.9/71.3. **Slope:** 129/118.
Opened: 1988. **Pace of Play rating:** 4:00. **Green fee:** $23.
Credit cards: None. **Reduced fees:** Juniors.
Caddies: Yes. **Golf carts:** $11 for 18 holes.
Discount golf packages: No. **Season:** Year-round. **High:** May-Oct.
On-site lodging: No. **Rental clubs:** Yes.
Walking policy: Unrestricted walking. **Range:** Yes (grass).
To obtain tee times: Call seven days in advance.
Subscriber comments: Oregon State's home course . . . Good test at fair price . . . Links-style course features fast, terraced greens . . . Get a tee time, very few walk ons . . . Wide open, slug away, exhuberant and brawny, tough finishing holes . . . One of the best public courses in Oregon . . . I travel 45 minutes to play . . . Front nine pretty forgiving, back nine can grab you . . . When rough is high, plays six-eight strokes tougher.

UMATILLA GOLF COURSE★
PU—705 Willamette, Umatilla (503)922-3006.
54 miles southwest of Walla Walla. WA. **Holes:** 18. **Par:** 70/72.
Yards: 6,000/5,700. **Course rating:** 68.9/74.0. **Slope:** 119/113.
Opened: 1968. **Pace of Play rating:** 3:30. **Green fee:** $10/16.
Credit cards: MC, V, DISC. **Reduced fees:** Low season, Juniors.
Caddies: No. **Golf carts:** $24 for 18 holes.
Discount golf packages: Yes. **Season:** Year-round. **High:** March-Oct.
On-site lodging: Yes. **Rental clubs:** Yes.
Walking policy: Unrestricted walking. **Range:** Yes (grass).
To obtain tee times: Show up or call within half an hour.

★★★½ WIDGI CREEK GOLF CLUB
SP—P.O. Box 1207, Bend (503)382-4449.
Call club for further information.
Formerly known as Seventh Mountain Golf Village.
Subscriber comments: Beautiful setting, pretty hard, good par 3s . . .
Will be better in a couple of years . . . Good playable design . . . Some very
tight holes, well maintained . . . Narrow, but fair . . . Tight layout . . .
Tight, sporty, good test . . . As with all courses in Bend, just very good.

Notes

★★★ FOX RUN GOLF COURSE
PU—600 W. 27th St., Yankton (605)665-8456.
60 miles southwest of Sioux Falls. **Holes:** 18. **Par:** 72/72.
Yards: 6,696/5,209. **Course rating:** 70.8/68.6. **Slope:** 122/115.
Opened: 1993. **Pace of Play rating:** 4:00. **Green fee:** $13/15.
Credit cards: MC, V. **Reduced fees:** Weekdays.
Caddies: No. **Golf carts:** $8 for 18 holes.
Discount golf packages: No. **Season:** March-Oct. **High:** May-Aug.
On-site lodging: No. **Rental clubs:** Yes.
Walking policy: Unrestricted walking. **Range:** Yes (grass).
To obtain tee times: Call pro shop one week in advance.
Subscriber comments: Good public course . . . Super shape for a new
course, pace fast and nice staff . . . I had fun on this layout, especially on
approach shots to Nos. 9 and 18 over water.

★★½ ELMWOOD GOLF COURSE
PU—2604 W. Russell, Sioux Falls (605)367-7092.
Holes: 18. **Par:** 72/72.
Yards: 6,850/5,750. **Course rating:** 72.1/72.0. **Slope:** 129/125.
Opened: 1923. **Pace of Play rating:** 4:00. **Green fee:** $11/13.
Credit cards: MC, V, DISC. **Reduced fees:** No.
Caddies: No. **Golf carts:** $9 for 18 holes.
Discount golf packages: No. **Season:** April-Oct. **High:** May-Aug.
On-site lodging: No. **Rental clubs:** Yes.
Walking policy: Unrestricted walking. **Range:** Yes (grass).
To obtain tee times: In person seven days in advance or call six days in
advance.
Also has 9-hole East Course.
Subscriber comments: Crowded . . . Good layout . . . Noise from
airport . . . Nice for municipal course . . . Staff very good . . . Mature
course.

★★★★ HILLCREST GOLF AND COUNTRY CLUB
SP—2206 Mulberry, Yankton (605)665-4621.
51 miles northwest of Sioux City, IA. **Holes:** 18. **Par:** 72/73.
Yards: 6,874/5,726. **Course rating:** 72.2/72.2. **Slope:** 130/126.
Opened: 1953. **Pace of Play rating:** 3:30-4:00. **Green fee:** $25/29.
Credit cards: MC, V. **Reduced fees:** Weekdays.
Caddies: No. **Golf carts:** $9 for 18 holes.
Discount golf packages: No. **Season:** April-Nov. **High:** June-Aug.
On-site lodging: No. **Rental clubs:** Yes.
Walking policy: Unrestricted walking. **Range:** Yes (grass).
To obtain tee times: Call one week in advance.
Subscriber comments: Good conditions, good staff . . . Still one of the
best in South Dakota . . . Played in under 3½ hours.

★★½ HILLSVIEW GOLF CLUB
PU—4201 SD Hwy. 34, Pierre (605)224-6191.
180 miles east of Rapid City. **Holes:** 18. **Par:** 72/73.
Yards: 6,828/5,470. **Course rating:** 71.4/73.9. **Slope:** 122/119.
Opened: 1965. **Pace of Play rating:** 4:00. **Green fee:** $15.
Credit cards: MC. **Reduced fees:** Juniors.
Caddies: No. **Golf carts:** $8 for 18 holes.
Discount golf packages: No. **Season:** April-Oct. **High:** June-Aug.
On-site lodging: No. **Rental clubs:** Yes.
Walking policy: Unrestricted walking. **Range:** Yes (grass).
To obtain tee times: Call pro shop.
Subscriber comments: Wide open course, favors long hitter, good
condition . . . Good municipal course . . . Big greens.

★★½ LAKEVIEW GOLF COURSE
PU—3300 N. Ohlman, Mitchell (605)996-1424.
60 miles east of Sioux Falls. **Holes:** 18. **Par:** 72/73.
Yards: 6,670/5,808. **Course rating:** 71.3/72.6. **Slope:** 124/125.

Opened: 1928. **Pace of Play rating:** 3:30–3:45. **Green fee:** $13.
Credit cards: V. **Reduced fees:** Juniors.
Caddies: No. **Golf carts:** $15 for 18 holes.
Discount golf packages: No. **Season:** April–Oct. **High:** June–Aug.
On-site lodging: No. **Rental clubs:** Yes.
Walking policy: Unrestricted walking. **Range:** Yes (grass).
To obtain tee times: Call pro shop or stop by and play within 20 minutes.
Staff can work groups into play in a reasonable time.
Subscriber comments: One of best conditioned munys in South Dakota,
excellent test . . . Wide open. Fairly easy . . . It's like playing two courses.
Old nine has trees, new nine is open with lots of water.

★★★½ MEADOWBROOK GOLF COURSE

PU—3625 Jackson Blvd., Rapid City (605)394-4191.

Holes: 18. **Par:** 72/72.
Yards: 7,054/5,603. **Course rating:** 73.0/71.1. **Slope:** 138/130.
Opened: 1976. **Pace of Play rating:** N/A. **Green fee:** $9/17.
Credit cards: None. **Reduced fees:** Low season, Twilight, Seniors,
Juniors.
Caddies: No. **Golf carts:** $18 for 18 holes.
Discount golf packages: No. **Season:** Year-round. **High:** April–Oct.
On-site lodging: No. **Rental clubs:** Yes.
Walking policy: Unrestricted walking. **Range:** Yes (grass).
To obtain tee times: Call 24 hours in advance or by advance booking
which is an additional $4 per player.
Ranked in Second 25 of America's 75 Best Public Golf Courses by Golf
Digest. Ranked 2nd in South Dakota by Golf Digest.
Subscriber comments: Great golf course . . . Nice, flat layout with
stream meandering throughout, pleasant place to play and enough challenge
. . . Heavy traffic . . . Typical public course problems . . . Good staff, good
test for anyone, good condition, fast play . . . Signs on tees keeps play
moving.

(GREAT VALUE)

★★★★ MOCCASIN CREEK COUNTRY CLUB

SP—4807 40th Ave. N.E., Aberdeen (605)226-0989.
180 miles south of Fargo. **Holes:** 18. **Par:** 72/73.
Yards: 7,125/5,416. **Course rating:** 72.5/69.4. **Slope:** 138/127.
Opened: 1971. **Pace of Play rating:** 4:00. **Green fee:** $25.
Credit cards: None. **Reduced fees:** No.
Caddies: No. **Golf carts:** $18 for 18 holes.
Discount golf packages: No. **Season:** April–Nov. **High:** June–Aug.
On-site lodging: No. **Rental clubs:** Yes.
Walking policy: Unrestricted walking. **Range:** Yes (grass).
To obtain tee times: Call 48 hours in advance.
Subscriber comments: Service great, great course, long but has multiple
tees, super . . . Tall, mature trees throughout but adequate landing areas
. . . Best for long hitters . . . Great condition . . . Major improvements
over last few years . . . Beautiful greens, fair but challenging course.

PRAIRIE GREEN GOLF COURSE*

PU—600 E. 69th St., Sioux Falls (605)339-6076.
Holes: 18. **Par:** 72/72.
Yards: 7,179/5,250. **Course rating:** 74.2/70.2. **Slope:** 134/122.
Opened: 1995. **Pace of Play rating:** N/A. **Green fee:** $18/22.
Credit cards: MC, V, DISC. **Reduced fees:** Weekdays, Twilight.
Caddies: No. **Golf carts:** $9 for 18 holes.
Discount golf packages: No. **Season:** April–Oct. **High:** May–Sept.
On-site lodging: No. **Rental clubs:** Yes.
Walking policy: Unrestricted walking. **Range:** Yes (grass).
To obtain tee times: Come in person seven days in advance or call six
days in advance.

SOUTH DAKOTA

★★★★ SOUTHERN HILLS GOLF COURSE

PU—236 S. 3rd St., Hot Springs (605)745-6400.
Call club for further information.
Subscriber comments: Finest course in region, short and tight, very fast greens . . . Nicest nine hole course around, extremely hilly and tree-lined makes driving important, nicest staff in area . . . Best kept course in state . . . I wish there were 18 holes like the first nine.

★★★½ TWO RIVERS GOLF CLUB

PU—150 S. Oak Tree Lane, Dakota Dunes (605)232-3241.
6 miles north of Sioux City, IA **Holes:** 18. **Par:** 72/73.
Yards: 6,181/5,603. **Course rating:** 69.0/71.0. **Slope:** 120/112.
Opened: 1921. **Pace of Play rating:** 3:45–4:00. **Green fee:** $13/16.
Credit cards: All major. **Reduced fees:** Low season.
Caddies: No. **Golf carts:** $9 for 18 holes.
Discount golf packages: No. **Season:** April–Oct. **High:** June–Sept.
On-site lodging: No. **Rental clubs:** Yes.
Walking policy: Unrestricted walking. **Range:** Yes (grass).
To obtain tee times: Call seven days in advance.
Subscriber comments: Short older course with trees . . . Attentive staff treats everyone like a private country club . . . Superior value . . . Perfect conditioning . . . Great atmosphere.

★★½ WATERTOWN MUNICIPAL GOLF COURSE

PU—315 S. Lake Dr., Watertown (605)886-3618.
Holes: 18. **Par:** 72/78.
Yards: 5,220/5,858. **Course rating:** 67.4/71.3. **Slope:** 106/114.
Opened: N/A. **Pace of Play rating:** 4:30. **Green fee:** $12/14.
Credit cards: None. **Reduced fees:** Twilight.
Caddies: No. **Golf carts:** $17 for 18 holes.
Discount golf packages: No. **Season:** April–Oct. **High:** May–Sept.
On-site lodging: No. **Rental clubs:** Yes.
Walking policy: Unrestricted walking. **Range:** Yes (grass)
To obtain tee times: Call seven days in advance for weekends.
Subscriber comments: Staff was very pleasant, played all seasaon . . . Small greens, need to stay on fairways for best scores.

★★★★ WILLOW RUN GOLF COURSE

PU—E. Hwy. 38/42, Sioux Falls (605)335-5900.
Holes: 18. **Par:** 71/71.
Yards: 6,505/4,855. **Course rating:** 71.1/68.7. **Slope:** 127/119.
Opened: 1988. **Pace of Play rating:** 4:15. **Green fee:** $14/17.
Credit cards: MC, V. **Reduced fees:** Weekdays, Twilight, Seniors, Juniors.
Caddies: No. **Golf carts:** $9 for 18 holes.
Discount golf packages: Yes. **Season:** March–Nov. **High:** May–Oct.
On-site lodging: No. **Rental clubs:** Yes.
Walking policy: Unrestricted walking. **Range:** Yes (grass).
To obtain tee times: Call seven days in advance.
Subscriber comments: Super course . . . Very challenging, every hole is different . . . Need to select right club on every tee box, can't just grab driver and step up . . . Favorite course in Sioux Falls, it's improved last two years . . . We play early each day, course is dewy but in great shape all year round . . . Good target course . . . Excellent public course . . . One of my favorites in South Dakota . . . Requires all the shots, must work the ball . . . Some very memorable holes.

★½ ALICE MUNICIPAL GOLF COURSE

PU—Texas Blvd., Alice (512)664–7033.
40 miles west of Corpus Christi. **Holes:** 18. **Par:** 71/72.
Yards: 5,991/4,853. **Course rating:** 67.8/65.6. **Slope:** 100/N/A.
Opened: N/A. **Pace of Play rating:** N/A. **Green fee:** $6/7.
Credit cards: MC, V. **Reduced fees:** Twilight, Seniors.
Caddies: No. **Golf carts:** $14 for 18 holes.
Discount golf packages: No. **Season:** Year-round. **High:** April-Aug.
On-site lodging: No. **Rental clubs:** No.
Walking policy: Unrestricted walking. **Range:** No.
To obtain tee times: Call Wednesday for upcoming weekend.
Subscriber comments: Flat, no sand, very good greens, some tricky holes
. . . Small, open fairways . . . Lots of traffic . . . Poor clubhouse . . . Staff
good . . . Fairways very dry . . . Very friendly atmosphere.

★★★ ANDREWS COUNTY GOLF COURSE

PU—920 Golf Course Rd., Andrews (915)524–1462.
36 miles north of Odessa. **Holes:** 18. **Par:** 70/72.
Yards: 6,300/5,331. **Course rating:** 68.9/69.7. **Slope:** 116/110.
Opened: N/A. **Pace of Play rating:** 3:30. **Green fee:** $10/15.
Credit cards: MC, V. **Reduced fees:** No.
Caddies: No. **Golf carts:** $17 for 18 holes.
Discount golf packages: No. **Season:** Year-round. **High:** May-July.
On-site lodging: No. **Rental clubs:** No.
Walking policy: Unrestricted walking. **Range:** Yes (grass).
To obtain tee times: Call pro shop.

Subscriber comments: Excellent course for the size of town . . .
Clubhouse only fair . . . Course well conditioned . . . Great layout, some
blind shots, but otherwise a fair course . . . Previously private facility . . .
Very flat, tree-lined course . . . A secret . . . Straight player rewarded. Wild
player is history . . . One of the best courses in west Texas.

★½ ASCARATE PARK GOLF COURSE

PU—6900 Delta Dr., El Paso (915)772-7381.
Holes: 18. **Par:** 71/72.
Yards: 6,505/5,650. **Course rating:** 69.4/66.2. **Slope:** 114/107.
Opened: 1958. **Pace of Play rating:** 4:30. **Green fee:** $5/10.
Credit cards: None. **Reduced fees:** Weekdays, Twilight, Seniors, Juniors.
Caddies: No. **Golf carts:** $16 for 18 holes.
Discount golf packages: No. **Season:** Year-round. **High:** Year-round.
On-site lodging: No. **Rental clubs:** Yes.
Walking policy: Unrestricted walking. **Range:** Yes (grass).
To obtain tee times: Call one week in advance for weekends only.
Also has 9-hole course.
Subscriber comments: Spacious . . . Course always in poor shape, greens
bumpy, every year county is going to improve it but doesn't . . . The
course in general is in dire need of a complete sprinkler system . . . No
trees, no shade, once out of the fairways, lots of trouble, all natural desert,
enough water to keep you honest . . . The staff is excellent, but the course
conditions are not very good.

BARTON CREEK RESORT AND COUNTRY CLUB

R—8212 Barton Club Dr., Austin (512)329-4608, (800)336-6158.
Credit cards: MC, V, AMEX. **Reduced fees:** Weekdays.
Caddies: No. **Golf carts:** $12 for 18 holes.
Discount golf packages: Yes. **Season:** Year-round. **High:** Spring/Fall.
On-site lodging: Yes. **Rental clubs:** Yes.
Walking policy: Unrestricted walking. **Range:** Yes (grass).
To obtain tee times: Must be an overnight resort guest, member or
conference guest to obtain a tee time.

★★★½ CRENSHAW AND COORE COURSE

Holes: 18. **Par:** 71/71.
Yards: 6,678/4,843. **Course rating:** 71.0/67.2. **Slope:** 124/110.
Opened: 1991. **Pace of Play rating:** 4:15. **Green fee:** $80/90.

Subscriber comments: Tree-studded layout, ground-ball shots required to side-sloped greens; pretty . . . Huge greens; beautiful Hill Country; deer everywhere . . . Greens very challenging . . . Huge greens . . . Fastest greens in Texas . . . Not as pretty as Fazio, Bermuda greens fast as lightning . . . Staff and service very good . . . One of the three best in Austin . . . Huge greens, must be good putter . . . A great resort . . . Fazio more interesting course . . . Bring your best putting stroke . . . Not fond of all the blind shots . . . Old course style . . . Middle of summer, course was hot, empty . . . Extra large greens, short overall . . . Greens not defined from fairway . . . A combination of Hawaii, Augusta and Scotland in one.

★★★★½ **FAZIO COURSE**
(512)329–4001.
Holes: 18. **Par:** 72/72.
Yards: 6,956/5,207. **Course rating:** 74.0/69.4. **Slope:** 135/120.
Opened: 1986. **Pace of Play rating:** 4:15. **Green fee:** $115.
Ranked 94th in America's 100 Greatest Golf Courses by Golf Digest. Ranked 21st in America's 75 Best Resort Courses by Golf Digest. Ranked 2nd in Texas by Golf Digest.
Subscriber comments: Best golf experience in texas . . . Difficult to get on, first class . . . Beautiful, good shape, poor driving range . . . Ambiance is outstanding . . . Fantastic layout . . . Very interesting test for shotmaking . . . It doesn't get any better than this in Texas . . . Prettiest golf course in Texas . . . Every hole is a masterpiece . . . Beautiful waterfalls . . . Dramatic, but not easy . . . Miles from green to next tee . . . Harder to get on than Crenshaw/Coore . . . Gorgeous . . . Accommodations great . . . Play it at any cost, one of the world's most beautiful . . . The more you play it, the more you'll want to play it again . . . Outstanding . . . Compare it to Pebble Beach without the ocean . . . Wow! . . . The most fun course to play in Texas.

★★★★ **PALMER—LAKESIDE COURSE**
R—1800 Clubhouse Hill Dr., Spicewood (210)693–4589, (800)888–2257.
25 miles west of Austin. **Holes:** 18. **Par:** 71/71.
Yards: 6,657/5,067. **Course rating:** 71.0/74.0. **Slope:** 124/135.
Opened: 1986. **Pace of Play rating:** 3:15. **Green fee:** $80/90.
Subscriber comments: Hidden treasure . . . Not a blade of grass out of place . . . Beautiful Hill Country views, worth the money . . . Great course, underplayed . . . Staff and service very good . . . Great bent greens . . . Not for walkers . . . Beautiful vistas, uncrowded and excellent condition . . . Great par 3s . . . Best of the three . . . Three-wood course . . . Not in same league as Crenshaw or Fazio . . . After the Fazio course, nothing compares . . . Friendly . . . Excellent variety of holes . . . Some holes have too much carry over tough hazard for women players . . . Long drive from resort, but worth it.

★½ **BATTLE LAKE GOLF COURSE**
PU—Rte. 1, Mart (817)876–2837.
15 miles southeast of Waco. **Holes:** 18. **Par:** 72/74.
Yards: 6,608/5,254. **Course rating:** 70.7/69.3. **Slope:** 116/112.
Opened: N/A. **Pace of Play rating:** 4:00. **Green fee:** $5/10.
Credit cards: MC, V, DISC. **Reduced fees:** Weekdays, Low season, Twilight, Seniors, Juniors.
Caddies: No. **Golf carts:** $8 for 18 holes.
Discount golf packages: No. **Season:** Year-round. **High:** March–Oct.
On-site lodging: No. **Rental clubs:** Yes.
Walking policy: Unrestricted walking. **Range:** Yes.
To obtain tee times: Call one week in advance for weekends and holidays.
Subscriber comments: Simple but tough . . . Rural-type course, good value but nothing fancy . . . Hard to find . . . A well laid out course, good staff, rates make it a desirable course for the area . . . Always has good Bermuda greens . . . Constantly being upgraded.

★★★ BAY FOREST GOLF COURSE

PU—201 Bay Forest Dr., LaPorte (713)471-4653.
20 miles southeast of Houston. **Holes:** 18. **Par:** 72/72.
Yards: 6,756/5,094. **Course rating:** 72.4/69.0. **Slope:** 126/113.
Opened: 1988. **Pace of Play rating:** 4:30. **Green fee:** $11/17.
Credit cards: MC, V. **Reduced fees:** Twilight, Seniors.
Caddies: No. **Golf carts:** $9 for 18 holes.
Discount golf packages: No. **Season:** Year-round. **High:** April-Oct.
On-site lodging: No. **Rental clubs:** Yes.
Walking policy: Unrestricted walking. **Range:** Yes (grass).
To obtain tee times: Call Monday for following seven days.
Subscriber comments: Short course, but trouble can be found easily;
water, trees . . . Plenty of water . . . Very good muny . . . Congenial pro/
staff . . . Must guard against hitting into a number of well placed water
hazards. Mosquitoes have home course advantage during summer . . .
Could improve maintenance . . . One of the best kept secrets in the
Houston area . . . Water on almost every hole . . . Bring plenty of balls . . .
Another good test, but just not special . . . The greens are kept very short
and hard, making the ball stick very difficult . . . Best golf value in Houston
area.

(FRUGAL PICK)

★★ BAYOU DIN GOLF CLUB
FRONT/BACK/NEW

PU—2722 Route 2, Beaumont (409)796-1327.
Holes: 27. **Par:** 71/71/72.
Yards: 6,285/6,495/7,020. **Course rating:** 68.5/70.6/72.1. **Slope:**
108/118/116.
Opened: 1959. **Pace of Play rating:** 4:00. **Green fee:** $8/15.
Credit cards: MC, V. **Reduced fees:** Weekdays, Seniors, Juniors.
Caddies: No. **Golf carts:** $7 for 18 holes.
Discount golf packages: No. **Season:** Year-round. **High:** March-Aug.
On-site lodging: No. **Rental clubs:** Yes.
Walking policy: Unrestricted walking. **Range:** Yes (grass).
To obtain tee times: Call pro shop.
Subscriber comments: Good place to sharpen game . . . New nine is the
best in town . . . Short holes, small greens, heads up, fairways run into each
other . . . New nine very nice, could water fairways more . . . New nine
much better than original 18 . . . Course is flat, holds water after it rains . . .
Good service, pace.

★★½ BAYOU GOLF CLUB

PU—2800 Ted Dudley Dr., Texas City (409)643-5850.
15 miles northwest of Galveston. **Holes:** 18. **Par:** 72/73.
Yards: 6,665/5,448. **Course rating:** 71.0/73.0. **Slope:** 114/118.
Opened: 1974. **Pace of Play rating:** 3:40. **Green fee:** $9/13.
Credit cards: None. **Reduced fees:** Twilight, Seniors.
Caddies: No. **Golf carts:** $16 for 18 holes.
Discount golf packages: No. **Season:** Year-round. **High:** N/A.
On-site lodging: No. **Rental clubs:** Yes.
Walking policy: Unrestricted walking. **Range:** Yes (grass).
To obtain tee times: Residents call Wednesday for upcoming weekend;
nonresidents call Thursday. Open play weekdays.
Subscriber comments: Spartan layout . . . Could use some more trees
. . . Low ball course, a lot of wind . . . Lack of trees makes course
unattractive . . . Usually very windy . . . Greens are very good . . . Wind is
a constant threat . . . Coastal course . . . Not very imaginative . . . Course
should improve due to new automated sprinklers.

BEAR CREEK GOLF WORLD

PU—16001 Clay Rd., Houston (713)855-4720.
Green fee: $17/49.
Credit cards: MC, V, AMEX. **Reduced fees:** Weekdays, Low season,
Twilight, Seniors, Juniors.
Caddies: No. **Golf carts:** $11 for 18 holes.

Discount golf packages: No. **Season:** Year-round. **High:** April-Oct.
On-site lodging: No. **Rental clubs:** Yes.
Walking policy: Walking at certain times. **Range:** Yes (grass).
To obtain tee times: Call seven days in advance.

★★ CHALLENGER COURSE

Holes: 18. **Par:** 66/66.
Yards: 5,295/4,432. **Course rating:** 64.2/64.7. **Slope:** 103/103.
Opened: 1968. **Pace of Play rating:** 4:00.
Subscriber comments: Not a bad executive-type course . . . Crowded weekends, great for mid-week . . . Short but challenging, friendly starters . . . Good complex, good staff, good value if walking . . . Not much of a challenge . . . Lots of par 3s . . . Lots of water . . . Eight par 3s . . . Par 66, great place to work on iron play, lot of bunkers . . . Good to practice iron play on . . . Wide open fairways, big greens, pace of play slow.

★★★ MASTERS COURSE

Holes: 18. **Par:** 72/72.
Yards: 7,131/5,544. **Course rating:** 74.1/72.1. **Slope:** 133/125.
Opened: 1972. **Pace of Play rating:** 4:30.
Ranked in Second 25 of America's 75 Best Public Golf Courses by Golf Digest.
Subscriber comments: Has everything, length, sand, and water . . . Nine and 18 very difficult . . . Good layout, not playable after heavy rains . . . Difficult from the whites because of out-of-bounds, heavily tree-lined . . . Best for control player . . . Staff very courteous . . . Take your A game . . . Good track when it's not flooded . . . Play is painfully slow . . . Post flood clean up exceptional . . . Staff helpful . . . Almost too hard . . . Challenging course . . . Excellent fairways, very good lies everywhere . . . A great finishing hole . . . The best of Bear Creek.

★★ PRESIDENTS COURSE

Holes: 18. **Par:** 72/72.
Yards: 6,562/5,728. **Course rating:** 69.1/70.6. **Slope:** 110/111.
Opened: 1968. **Pace of Play rating:** 4:00.
Subscriber comments: Great beginner's course . . . Greens are too slow, tees torn up . . . Course gets heavy play, pace good, too much hard-pan . . . Needs more bunkers . . . Good course to work on swing . . . Play a little slow . . . No challenge. Needs sand traps, out-of-bounds . . . No trouble . . . Vanilla golf . . . No trees . . . Ordinary at best.

★½ BLACKHAWK GOLF CLUB

PU—225 Kelly Lane, Pflugerville (512)251-9000.
15 miles northeast of Austin. **Holes:** 18. **Par:** 72/72.
Yards: 7,103/5,538. **Course rating:** 73.5/71.1. **Slope:** 123/121.
Opened: 1991. **Pace of Play rating:** 4:00. **Green fee:** $13/22.
Credit cards: MC, V, AMEX. **Reduced fees:** Weekdays, Low season, Twilight, Seniors, Juniors.
Caddies: No. **Golf carts:** $9 for 18 holes.
Discount golf packages: No. **Season:** Year-round. **High:** April-Sept.
On-site lodging: No. **Rental clubs:** Yes.
Walking policy: Walking at certain times. **Range:** Yes (grass).
To obtain tee times: Call up to five days in advance.
Subscriber comments: Hurrah! Bent greens are gone! . . . Flat open course, very few trees . . . New Bermuda greens are terrific, staff among the best . . . Tough course when wind blows. Ninth is meanest par 4 in Austin with or without wind . . . Nothing to get excited about . . . Not many trees . . . Courteous staff with good service . . . Won't allow walking weekends before 1 p.m. . . . Fairways best in area.

★★ BLUEBONNET COUNTRY CLUB

PU—Box 3471, Navasota (409)894-2207.
Call club for further information.
Subscriber comments: Course is secluded, so very peaceful . . . Good layout, fun to play, needs cart paths to improve fairway . . . Good layout, semi-poor condition . . . Poor maintenance . . . Always trampled . . . Nice landscape . . . A bit far out in the country . . . Friendly staff, great practice

facility, interesting low profile layout, speedy play . . . More fun to play second time . . . Quiet and not very crowded . . . Greens are large and hard to read . . . Lots of water, trees, must hit straight . . . Very poor turf, sand traps, poorly kept . . . Service was excellent . . . Could be one of the best in Texas.

★★½ BLUEBONNET HILL GOLF CLUB
PU—9100 Decker Lane, Austin (512)272-4228.
Holes: 18. **Par:** 72/72.
Yards: 6,503/5,241. **Course rating:** 70.0/68.2. **Slope:** 113/107.
Opened: 1991. **Pace of Play rating:** 4:15. **Green fee:** $9/18.
Credit cards: MC, V. **Reduced fees:** Weekdays, Twilight, Seniors, Juniors.
Caddies: No. **Golf carts:** $16 for 18 holes.
Discount golf packages: Yes. **Season:** Year-round. **High:** March-Aug.
On-site lodging: No. **Rental clubs:** Yes.
Walking policy: Unrestricted walking. **Range:** Yes (grass).
To obtain tee times: Call five days in advance for weekdays; call on Thursday at 7:30 a.m. for upcoming weekend.
Subscriber comments: Good job with poor piece of land, friendly staff . . . Marshal keeps pace of play four hours or less . . . Now maturing into good course . . . Open, fair condition . . . Not an easy course to walk . . . High volume . . . Great weekday rate for seniors . . . Major attraction is enforcement of speedy play . . . Too many shirtless hackers . . . Fairways are too close together . . . Racetrack pace . . . Steadily improving course . . . Lots of elevation change . . . Treated like a member . . . Open with terrain changes . . . Windswept every time I've played . . . Best course in area to walk up and get on.

★½ BRACKENRIDGE PARK MUNICIPAL GOLF COURSE
PU—2315 Ave. B, San Antonio (210)226-5612.
Holes: 18. **Par:** 72/72.
Yards: 6,185/5,216. **Course rating:** 67.0/69.2. **Slope:** 122/112.
Opened: 1922. **Pace of Play rating:** 4:15. **Green fee:** $11/16.
Credit cards: MC, V. **Reduced fees:** Weekdays, Low season, Twilight, Seniors, Juniors.
Caddies: No. **Golf carts:** $15 for 18 holes.
Discount golf packages: Yes. **Season:** Year-round. **High:** March-Nov.
On-site lodging: No. **Rental clubs:** Yes.
Walking policy: Unrestricted walking. **Range:** No.
To obtain tee times: Call pro shop.
Subscriber comments: Short, tight, historic golf course. Straight hitters can really score here . . . Flat course, lots of senior walkers . . . Trip down memory lane . . . A delight . . . Once sporty . . . Very poorly maintained, grounds and club . . . Too short, needs better upkeep . . . Lots of trees . . . A once grand course of Texas . . . 30 years ago it was a good test but not today . . . No wonder so many PGA records have been set here . . . Lots of history and trees . . . Good setting in inner city . . . Little rough around the edges; lots of character.

★★½ BRIARWOOD GOLF CLUB
SP—4511 Briarwood Dr., Tyler (903)593-7741.
84 miles east of Dallas. **Holes:** 18. **Par:** 71/71.
Yards: 6,512/4,735. **Course rating:** 70.6/66.1. **Slope:** 118/111.
Opened: 1955. **Pace of Play rating:** 4:00. **Green fee:** $15/22.
Credit cards: None. **Reduced fees:** Low season.
Caddies: No. **Golf carts:** $9 for 18 holes.
Discount golf packages: No. **Season:** Year-round. **High:** May-June.
On-site lodging: No. **Rental clubs:** Yes.
Walking policy: Unrestricted walking. **Range:** Yes (grass).

To obtain tee times: Call pro shop.
Subscriber comments: Friendly, informal golf course . . . Good course from back tees, somewhat short from front tees . . . Staff and service very good . . . "Bikini-wax" greens . . . Slow play . . . Front nine hilly, back nine flat.

★★ BROCK PARK GOLF COURSE

PU—8201 John Ralston Rd., Houston (713)458-1350.
Call club for further information.
Subscriber comments: Hilly terrain, good soft greens . . . Kind of run down . . . Needs better care of fairways . . . A little care would help, premier layout, terrible maintenance . . . Crowded, cart paths poor . . . Long wait to tee off . . . Not kept up, it's a shame . . . Could be one of Houston's best . . . Challenging from blue tees . . . 14th hole 225-yard par 3 hardest golf hole in Houston.

★½ BROWNSVILLE COUNTRY CLUB

PU—1800 W. San Marcelo, Brownsville (210)541-2582.
Call club for further information.
Subscriber comments: Sporty course . . . Too much traffic, poor condition . . . Not much vegetation . . . Summer, green, very dry . . . Rundown . . . Greens are fast and small, very tight fairways . . . Staff is great.

★½ BRYAN GOLF COURSE

PU—206 W. Villa Maria, Bryan (409)823-0126.
84 miles northwest of Houston. **Holes:** 18. **Par:** 70/70.
Yards: 6,280/4,576. **Course rating:** 69.7/65.5. **Slope:** 110/103.
Opened: 1925. **Pace of Play rating:** 4:00. **Green fee:** $10/13.
Credit cards: MC, V. **Reduced fees:** Weekdays, Low season, Twilight, Seniors, Juniors.
Caddies: No. **Golf carts:** $9 for 18 holes.
Discount golf packages: No. **Season:** Year-round. **High:** April-Aug.
On-site lodging: No. **Rental clubs:** Yes.
Walking policy: Unrestricted walking. **Range:** No.
To obtain tee times: Call pro shop.
Subscriber comments: Typical muny . . . If the fairways were as good as the greens it would be great . . . Course badly conditioned, pace of play slow . . . Pace OK, depending on student traffic . . . Great staff and atmosphere . . . Lots of hazards . . . The only place I have ever lost a ball in the fairway. Do they ever pick up leaves?

★★★★ BUFFALO CREEK GOLF CLUB

PU—624 Country Club Dr., Rockwall (214)771-4003.
15 miles east of Dallas. **Holes:** 18. **Par:** 71/71.
Yards: 7,018/5,209. **Course rating:** 73.8/67.0. **Slope:** 133/113.
Opened: 1992. **Pace of Play rating:** 4:15. **Green fee:** $30/60.
Credit cards: MC, V, AMEX. **Reduced fees:** Low season, Twilight, Seniors, Juniors.
Caddies: No. **Golf carts:** Included in Green Fee.
Discount golf packages: No. **Season:** Year-round. **High:** March-June.
On-site lodging: No. **Rental clubs:** Yes.
Walking policy: Walking at certain times. **Range:** Yes (grass).
To obtain tee times: Call four days in advance.
Subscriber comments: Wonderful design . . . Great course, Weiskopf/Morrish design . . . Great design, constantly outstanding conditions . . . Needs better food facilities . . . Best bent grass greens in area . . . Good people, slow play, crowded . . . Great staff, great driving range . . . Top three in DFW area . . . Pick the right tees . . . Very accommodating to walker . . . Best kept secret in Texas, fine test of ability . . . Very playable for the grip it and rip it . . . Tough layout, but very enjoyable from

the proper tees, good service . . . Great par 5s . . . Great getaway for small-town boy . . . Great course but too expensive . . . Uses rolling terrain uncommon in Dallas area . . . Public but run like a country club . . . A little pricey, although a great course . . . One of the finest public courses in north Texas.

★★★ CAPE ROYALE GOLF COURSE
PU—Lake Livingston, Coldspring (409)653-2388.
Call club for further information.
Subscriber comments: Beautiful lake layout . . . Greens will ruin your putting, fastest I've ever been on . . . Very different look for southeast Texas golf . . . Rolling scenic beauty . . . Trickiest greens ever putted on . . . Short hilly layout good value . . . Not heavily played . . . Plenty of blind shots . . . A pleasant experience . . . Some great elevated views of Lake Livingston . . . Most hilly course in Houston area, few hazards . . . Short and cutesy . . . Real surprise . . . Not a flat lie on the course . . . Off beaten path . . . Tees need to be rebuilt . . . Service was impeccable.

CASA BLANCA GOLF COURSE★
PU—3900 Casa Blanca, Laredo (210)791-7262.
Holes: 18. **Par:** 72/72.
Yards: 6,390/5,631. **Course rating:** 71.0/68.9. **Slope:** 115/115.
Opened: 1922. **Pace of Play rating:** 4:30. **Green fee:** $8/10.
Credit cards: All major. **Reduced fees:** Weekdays, Seniors, Juniors.
Caddies: No. **Golf carts:** $14 for 18 holes.
Discount golf packages: Yes. **Season:** Year-round. **High:** Feb-Oct.
On-site lodging: No. **Rental clubs:** Yes.
Walking policy: Unrestricted walking. **Range:** Yes (grass).
To obtain tee times: Call on Wednesday for upcoming weekend.

★★★½ CEDAR CREEK GOLF COURSE
PU—8250 Vista Colina, San Antonio (210)695-5050.

Holes: 18. **Par:** 72/72.
Yards: 7,103/5,535. **Course rating:** 73.4/70.8. **Slope:** 132/113.
Opened: 1989. **Pace of Play rating:** 4:30. **Green fee:** $10/40.
Credit cards: All major. **Reduced fees:** Weekdays, Low season, Twilight, Seniors, Juniors.
Caddies: No. **Golf carts:** $8 for 18 holes.
Discount golf packages: No. **Season:** Year-round. **High:** Year-round.
On-site lodging: No. **Rental clubs:** Yes.
Walking policy: Unrestricted walking. **Range:** Yes (grass).
To obtain tee times: Call pro shop.
Subscriber comments: Excellent Hill Country course . . . Beautiful vistas, sprawling holes with numerous challenges . . . Great value, good views, needs better conditions . . . A monster from the back tees . . . Staff friendly, slow play, let fivesomes play . . . No place for carts off path on front nine, hillsides make it very hard to get from cart to ball lying on fairways in the valleys . . . Tough to get tee time . . . Best municipal in Texas . . . Physically demanding . . . Slow play due to difficult terrain . . . Lots of slopes . . . Better than a lot of private courses . . . Pace of play terrible, 5½-hour rounds . . . Poor circulation patterns . . . Great setting . . . Severely sloped three-club greens. Great value . . . A picture perfect setting . . . Bring your long shots . . . Long holes, plenty of traps, lots of hills, tight fairways . . . Exceptional views . . . One of Texas' best-kept secrets . . . If you don't mind slow golf, best value in Texas . . . Fairways always seem to be wet, even in late afternoon . . . Built in ravines. Very hot, no breeze in summer . . . Makes me wish I lived in San Antonio . . . Best of San Antonio munys.

★★ CEDAR CREST GOLF COURSE
PU—1800 Southerland, Dallas (214)670-7615.
Holes: 18. **Par:** 71/75.
Yards: 6,550/5,594. **Course rating:** 71.0/76.0. **Slope:** 121/116.
Opened: 1923. **Pace of Play rating:** 4:00. **Green fee:** $11/14.

Credit cards: All major. **Reduced fees:** Twilight, Seniors, Juniors.
Caddies: Yes. **Golf carts:** $18 for 18 holes.
Discount golf packages: No. **Season:** Year-round. **High:** April–Sept.
On-site lodging: No. **Rental clubs:** Yes.
Walking policy: Unrestricted walking. **Range:** Yes (grass).
To obtain tee times: Call two days in advance.
Subscriber comments: Tillinghast layout . . . Old course, small greens
. . . Good friendly staff, great value . . . Nice layout, but needs work on
fairways . . . Back nine as tough as you want . . . Hardpan . . . School kids
cutting through course very irksome . . . Impossible to imagine this place
hosted a major (1927 PGA), downhill ever since . . . Not the greatest . . .
Tough opening hole and par 3s . . . Old traditional layout, excellent
condition . . . Hagen played here . . . Former grand old dame now an old
maid.

THE CEDARS ON BERGSTROM★
PU—Bldg. 3711, Old Bergstrom AFB, Austin (512)385-4653.
10 miles southeast of Austin. **Holes:** 18. **Par:** 71/72.
Yards: 6,501/5,377. **Course rating:** 69.5/70.5. **Slope:** 115/116.
Opened: 1954. **Pace of Play rating:** 4:00. **Green fee:** $10/13.
Credit cards: MC, V, AMEX. **Reduced fees:** Weekdays, Twilight,
Seniors, Juniors.
Caddies: No. **Golf carts:** $8 for 18 holes.
Discount golf packages: No. **Season:** Year-round. **High:** May–Oct.
On-site lodging: No. **Rental clubs:** Yes.
Walking policy: Unrestricted walking. **Range:** Yes (grass).
To obtain tee times: Call up to one week in advance.

★★½ CHAMBERS COUNTY GOLF COURSE
PU—1 Pinchback Dr., Anahuac (409)267-8235.
15 miles east of Baytown. **Holes:** 18. **Par:** 72/73.
Yards: 6,909/5,014. **Course rating:** 71.5/67.5. **Slope:** 116/106.
Opened: 1975. **Pace of Play rating:** 4:20. **Green fee:** $9/11.
Credit cards: MC, V, Pulse. **Reduced fees:** Weekdays, Twilight.
Caddies: No. **Golf carts:** $7 for 18 holes.
Discount golf packages: No. **Season:** Year-round. **High:** Summer.
On-site lodging: No. **Rental clubs:** Yes.
Walking policy: Unrestricted walking. **Range:** Yes (grass).
To obtain tee times: Call pro shop Thursday 7 a.m.
Subscriber comments: Staff very easy to get along with . . . Nice layout,
good staff, good condition . . . Short holes and big greens . . . Level mostly
. . . Little water, manageable trees . . . Excellent piney woods course . . .
Very economical, well worth the money . . . Lots of trees . . . A diamond
in the rough . . . No need to be long, must be straight . . . Can play 18
holes on the weekend in 4½ hours . . . Nice layout, needs more bunkers.

(FRUGAL PICK)

CHASE OAKS GOLF CLUB★
BLACK JACK COURSE
PU—7201 Chase Oaks Blvd., Plano (214)517-7777.
14 miles north of Dallas. **Holes:** 18. **Par:** 72/72.
Yards: 6,762/5,105. **Course rating:** 74.4/70.0. **Slope:** 139/128.
Opened: 1986. **Pace of Play rating:** 4:30. **Green fee:** $34/44.
Credit cards: All major. **Reduced fees:** Weekdays, Low season, Twilight,
Seniors, Juniors.
Caddies: No. **Golf carts:** $11 for 18 holes.
Discount golf packages: No. **Season:** Year-round. **High:** April–Nov.
On-site lodging: No. **Rental clubs:** Yes.
Walking policy: Walking at certain times. **Range:** Yes (grass).
To obtain tee times: Call three days in advance at 8 a.m.
Also has 9-hole course.

★★½ CHESTER W. DITTO GOLF CLUB

PU—801 Brown Blvd., Arlington (817)275-5941.
20 miles west of Dallas. **Holes:** 18. **Par:** 72/72.
Yards: 6,727/5,555. **Course rating:** 70.8/71.2. **Slope:** 117/116.
Opened: 1982. **Pace of Play rating:** 4:30. **Green fee:** $10/12.
Credit cards: MC, V, DISC. **Reduced fees:** Weekdays, Twilight,
Seniors, Juniors.
Caddies: No. **Golf carts:** $8 for 18 holes.
Discount golf packages: No. **Season:** Year-round. **High:** April-Sept.
On-site lodging: No. **Rental clubs:** Yes.
Walking policy: Unrestricted walking. **Range:** Yes (grass)
To obtain tee times: Call Tuesday at 6 a.m. for Wednesday through the
next Tuesday.
Subscriber comments: Decent shape for a city course . . . Hard ground,
lots of roll, poor grass . . . Layout has great potential, needs better care . . .
Tough but fair, a round could last 4½ to 6 hours . . . Back nine seemed like
different course from the front . . . Easy front and hard back . . . Driving
range, pitching area, easy to walk . . . Deceptively difficult . . . Best value
in Arlington . . . Greens a little rough, plays fast and challenging, service is
good . . . First eight holes lull one to sleep, then watch out . . . Improved
tremendously over the past two years.

★★★ CIELO VISTA GOLF COURSE

PU—1510 Hawkins, El Paso (915)591-4927.
Holes: 18. **Par:** 71/71.
Yards: 6,411/5,421. **Course rating:** 69.4/69.4. **Slope:** 122/113.
Opened: 1977. **Pace of Play rating:** 4:00-4:30. **Green fee:** $12/15.
Credit cards: MC, V. **Reduced fees:** Weekdays, Twilight.
Caddies: No. **Golf carts:** $8 for 18 holes.
Discount golf packages: Yes. **Season:** Year-round. **High:** April-Oct.
On-site lodging: No. **Rental clubs:** Yes.
Walking policy: Unrestricted walking. **Range:** Yes(grass).
To obtain tee times: Call Tuesday at 7 a.m. for upcoming weekend.
Subscriber comments: Nice looking course . . . The pace is usually slow
due to the crowds. The staff is OK . . . Great condition for the desert area
. . . Short, flat, easy, big greens, few bunkers . . . Good course for seniors
. . . Great greens . . . Exceptionally slow play, no course marshals . . . Easy
to walk . . . Nice practice facility, but no practice bunkers.

★★★½ CIRCLE C GOLF CLUB

PU—11511 FM 1826, Austin (512)288-4297.
Holes: 18. **Par:** 72/72.
Yards: 6,859/5,236. **Course rating:** 72.7/69.9. **Slope:** 122/120.
Opened: 1992. **Pace of Play rating:** 4:15. **Green fee:** $29/47.
Credit cards: MC, V, AMEX. **Reduced fees:** Weekdays, Low season,
Twilight, Juniors.
Caddies: No. **Golf carts:** Included in Green Fee.
Discount golf packages: Yes. **Season:** Year-round. **High:** Spring/Fall
On-site lodging: No. **Rental clubs:** Yes.
Walking policy: Walking at certain times. **Range:** Yes(grass).
To obtain tee times: Call three days in advance. Earlier tee times for
groups of 12 or more.
Subscriber comments: A secret gem . . . First tee half mile from pro
shop, walking is tough . . . Very fine layout . . . Staff excellent . . . Must
be a mile from clubhouse to first tee . . . Not for crooked hitters, fairway or
no way . . . Harmonious with Hill Country setting . . . Still developing
. . . Laid out over ample areas. Feeling of wide open spaces. Feels like a
resort course . . . Fairway bunkers aplenty . . . Like the straightforward
look of holes . . . Lots of risk, reward . . . Lack of water in summer created
toasty fairways . . . Best public course in Austin.

★★ CLEAR LAKE GOLF CLUB
PU—1202 Reseda Dr., Houston (713)488-0252.
Call club for further information.
Subscriber comments: Tricky, but not hard to score . . . Flat, wet, cart trails very poor, but improving . . . Fantastic greens, service good, pace slow . . . Turn on the sprinklers . . . Some holes are too similar . . . Crossing a main thoroughfare twice is not my idea of fun . . . Wide fairways, not much trouble . . . Nice, nothing exciting . . . Rather plain and flat . . . Boring subdivision course.

★★★★ THE CLIFFS GOLF CLUB
R—Star Rte. Box 19, Graford (817)779-3926, (800)621-8534.
75 miles northwest of Fort Worth. **Holes:** 18. **Par:** 71/71.
Yards: 6,808/4,888. **Course rating:** 73.8/69.5. **Slope:** 139/121.
Opened: 1988. **Pace of Play rating:** 4:30. **Green fee:** $45.
Credit cards: All major. **Reduced fees:** Weekdays, Twilight, Juniors.
Caddies: No. **Golf carts:** $13 for 18 holes.
Discount golf packages: Yes. **Season:** Year-round. **High:** April-Sept.
On-site lodging: Yes. **Rental clubs:** Yes.
Walking policy: Mandatory cart. **Range:** Yes (grass).
To obtain tee times: Call one week in advance.
Subscriber comments: What a scenic and tough course . . . Hidden jewel, tough course . . . A full day trip from Dallas . . . Beautiful piece of property, new owners have got it back in great shape . . . New clubhouse . . . Many blind shots . . . Bring plenty of balls, monster from the tips . . . Take your camera and lots of balls . . . Unusual and difficult layout . . . Spectacular scenery . . . Great views, snake country . . . Very hard to find if you don't know how to get there . . . A must play! . . . Fantastic scenery . . . Beautiful course has cliffs overlooking lake . . . Watch for rattlers in summer . . . Moguls, moguls, moguls . . . Dramatic course, superb greens, visually stunning . . . Use a lot of irons off tees . . . Very interesting, next to lake . . . Most beautiful layout in Texas . . . Ridiculously difficult . . . Impossibly hard, but incredibly scenic.

★★★ COLUMBIA LAKES GOLF CLUB
R—188 Freeman Blvd., West Columbia (409)345-5455, (800)231-1030.
50 miles southeast of Houston. **Holes:** 18. **Par:** 72/72.
Yards: 6,967/5,280. **Course rating:** 75.7/71.7. **Slope:** 131/122.
Opened: 1972. **Pace of Play rating:** N/A. **Green fee:** $40/55.
Credit cards: All major. **Reduced fees:** Weekdays, Low season, Resort guests.
Caddies: No. **Golf carts:** Included in Green Fee.
Discount golf packages: Yes. **Season:** Year-round. **High:** April-June.
On-site lodging: Yes. **Rental clubs:** Yes.
Walking policy: Unrestricted walking. **Range:** Yes (grass).
To obtain tee times: Guest of a member, resort guests, or reciprocal guests outside of a 100 mile radius of Columbia Lakes may call for tee times.
Subscriber comments: Good out-of-the-way weekend place . . . Tight driving course . . . Well kept, speed of play good, staff good, great facility/ lodging . . . Too many houses, but nice course . . . Beautiful Spanish moss covered trees . . . Good resort close to Houston . . . It reeks with class from the moment you drive in . . . Wide fairways, small greens, fast and lots of break . . . Outstanding clubhouse . . . Some great golf holes. Precision drives required . . . Outstanding greens . . . Great practice facility.

★★½ COMANCHE TRAIL GOLF CLUB
PU—4200 S. Grand, Amarillo (806)378-4281.
Holes: 18. **Par:** 72/72.
Yards: 7,180/5,524. **Course rating:** 72.9/70.0. **Slope:** 117/108.
Opened: 1990. **Pace of Play rating:** 4:00. **Green fee:** $8/10.
Credit cards: None. **Reduced fees:** Seniors, Juniors.
Caddies: No. **Golf carts:** $16 for 18 holes.
Discount golf packages: No. **Season:** Year-round. **High:** March-Sept.
On-site lodging: No. **Rental clubs:** Yes.

Walking policy: Unrestricted walking. **Range:** Yes (grass).
To obtain tee times: Call Thursday mornings 7 a.m. for upcoming
weekend; one day in advance for any other day.
Subscriber comments: Fine municipal course, made out of flat land . . .
Greens need a little work, course always wet . . . Can't they dry it out? . . .
Young course with good layout, great staff, good pro shop . . . Rough too
high and yardage marks hard to find . . . No sand, but good challenge . . .
No trees, lots of water . . . Perfect fit for Texas Panhandle winds . . . Open
enough, even sprayed shots can be playable . . . Best suited for a calm day.

★★ CONNALLY GOLF COURSE
PU—7900 Concord Rd., Waco (817)799-6561.
Holes: 18. **Par:** 72/73.
Yards: 6,975/5,950. **Course rating:** 72.5/73.8. **Slope:** 116/120.
Opened: 1959. **Pace of Play rating:** 4:00. **Green fee:** $8/10.
Credit cards: MC, V. **Reduced fees:** Twilight, Seniors, Juniors.
Caddies: No. **Golf carts:** $9 for 18 holes.
Discount golf packages: No. **Season:** Year-round. **High:** April-Sept.
On-site lodging: No. **Rental clubs:** Yes.
Walking policy: Unrestricted walking. **Range:** Yes (grass).
To obtain tee times: Call seven days in advance for weekends and
holidays only.
Subscriber comments: Old established course . . . Wide open, flat, some
hazards with no warning (hidden water) . . . Old style layout, very
marginal maintenance, friendly staff . . . Small greens . . . Fast play . . .
Some good tight driving . . . Little sand; Bermuda greens, small and hard,
especially in heat . . . Very acceptable.

★★½ COTTONWOOD CREEK GOLF COURSE
PU—5200 Bagby Dr., Waco (817)752-2474.
Holes: 18. **Par:** 72/72.
Yards: 7,123/5,724. **Course rating:** 73.3/71.9. **Slope:** 129/120.
Opened: 1983. **Pace of Play rating:** 4:30. **Green fee:** $9/12.
Credit cards: MC, V. **Reduced fees:** Weekdays, Low season, Seniors,
Juniors.
Caddies: No. **Golf carts:** $8 for 18 holes.
Discount golf packages: No. **Season:** Year-round. **High:** March-Oct.
On-site lodging: No. **Rental clubs:** Yes.
Walking policy: Unrestricted walking. **Range:** Yes (grass).
To obtain tee times: Call three to five days in advance.
Subscriber comments: Not bad for a public course . . . Something for all
. . . Large waste bunkers, huge greens . . . Play slow on weekends . . . Par
3s are great . . . Challenge to a newcomer . . . Has great senior program
. . . Staff always pleasant, marshals do good job to keep play moving . . .
Sand and hills make course fun and challenging . . . Bent grass greens and
rough suffer in summer . . . Best daily fee in Waco.

★★ COUNTRY VIEW GOLF CLUB
PU—240 W. Beltline Rd., Lancaster (214)227-0995.
13 miles south of Dallas. **Holes:** 18. **Par:** 71/71.
Yards: 6,609/5,048. **Course rating:** 71.0/68.2. **Slope:** 120/114.
Opened: 1989. **Pace of Play rating:** 4:00. **Green fee:** $12/17.
Credit cards: MC, V, DISC. **Reduced fees:** Low season, Twilight,
Seniors, Juniors.
Caddies: No. **Golf carts:** $20 for 18 holes.
Discount golf packages: No. **Season:** Year-round. **High:** April-Oct.
On-site lodging: No. **Rental clubs:** Yes.
Walking policy: Unrestricted walking. **Range:** Yes (grass).
To obtain tee times: Call three days prior to play.
Subscriber comments: Built in flood plain . . . Staff helpful, good 19th
hole . . . Elevated greens . . . Tough to walk due to raised tees and greens
. . . No. 17 is a killer . . . No. 17 a really tough par 4 . . . Elevated greens

are a challenge . . . Too far from greens to tee boxes to walk . . . Elevated greens on nine holes . . . Friendly personnel . . . Course is suited for a good player because of its elevated greens, sand traps, and creeks . . . Course is on the comeback.

CROSS TIMBERS GOLF COURSE★

PU—1181 S. Stewart, Azle (817)444-4940.
14 miles north of Fort Worth. **Holes:** 18. **Par:** 72/72
Yards: 6,734/5,051. **Course rating:** 71.5/N/A. **Slope:** 128/N/A.
Opened: 1995. **Pace of Play rating:** 4:30. **Green fee:** $18/22.
Credit cards: MC, V, AMEX. **Reduced fees:** Weekdays, Twilight,
Seniors, Juniors.
Caddies: No. **Golf carts** $10 for 18 holes.
Discount golf packages: No. **Season:** Year-round. **High:** March–Oct.
On-site lodging: No. **Rental clubs:** Yes.
Walking policy: Unrestricted walking. **Range:** Yes (grass).
To obtain tee times: Call three days prior to play.

★ CRYSTAL FALLS GOLF COURSE

PU—3400 Crystal Falls Pkwy., Leander (512)259-5855.
14 miles north of Austin. **Holes:** 18. **Par:** 72/72.
Yards: 6,654/5,194. **Course rating:** 72.3/70.0. **Slope:** 126/123.
Opened: 1990. **Pace of Play rating:** 4:00. **Green fee:** $18/25.
Credit cards: MC, V. **Reduced fees:** Weekdays, Low season, Twilight,
Seniors, Juniors.
Caddies: No. **Golf carts:** $8 for 18 holes.
Discount golf packages: Yes. **Season:** Year-round. **High:** April–Oct.
On-site lodging: No. **Rental clubs:** Yes.
Walking policy: Unrestricted walking. **Range:** Yes (grass).
To obtain tee times: Call three days in advance.
Subscriber comments: Unique course . . . Very unfair course . . . greens had dead spots . . . Could be fun course with work . . . Fairways hard and severely pitched, hit a shot down the middle and it ends up in a hazard . . . Too many blind shots . . . Needs watering system, hard as a pool table all year . . . Driving range is better . . . No level landing areas, lose balls in middle of fairway . . . Strategy is key, friendly staff . . . Love the high tee box on No. 2 and No. 11 . . . Great location . . . Rocks, rocks, rocks . . . Blind par 3s . . . You'd better be able to work ball against sloping.

CYPRESSWOOD GOLF CLUB

PU—21602 Cypresswood Dr., Spring (713)821-6300.
25 miles south of Houston. **Green fee:** $26/47.
Credit cards: MC, V, AMEX. **Reduced fees:** Weekdays, Twilight,
Seniors, Juniors.
Caddies: No. **Golf carts:** $17 for 18 holes.
Discount golf packages: No. **Season:** Year-round. **High:** March–Oct.
On-site lodging: No. **Rental clubs:** Yes.
Walking policy: Unrestricted walking. **Range:** Yes (grass).
To obtain tee times: Call automated system three days in advance.
★★★½ CREEK COURSE
Holes: 18. **Par:** 72/72.
Yards: 6,937/5,549. **Course rating:** 72.0/69.1. **Slope:** 124/113.
Opened: 1988. **Pace of Play rating:** 4:00.
Subscriber comments: Beautiful natural setting . . . Heavily wooded, damaged by recent floods . . . Beautiful layout, expensive but worth it . . . Good design, tees to suit all, too crowded at times . . . Quality course in good condition . . . Fairways always in great shape . . . In great shape right after major flood . . . Excellent golf course, good people, good pace . . . Good test . . . Meanders through large trees, with rolling fairways . . . Creek better than Cypress . . . Watch for water moccasins . . . Nice pair of courses . . . Demanding course, well trapped . . . All players, very nice, normal pace . . . Best public access course in Houston.

★★★½ CYPRESS COURSE
Holes: 18. **Par:** 72/72.
Yards: 6,906/5,599. **Course rating:** 71.8/67.6. **Slope:** 123/111.
Opened: 1987. **Pace of Play rating:** 4:00.
Subscriber comments: A super test of golf for a publicly played course
. . . Great layout, gets too much play, bad greens . . . The trees add to the
beauty . . . Really enjoyed this course, natural flows with the terrain . . .
Well maintained, polite and courteous staff . . . Practice facilities are
excellent . . . Not for hooker . . . Designed for shotmaking . . . Ample
room for long drives on par 5s, tricky par 3s, greens large, three-club depths
. . . Difficult to get a tee time . . . Many blind shots . . . Excellent value for
seniors . . . Generous landings . . . No problems with excessive back up
. . . Must use course management to score.

★★★ DEL LAGO RESORT
R—500 La Costa, Montgomery (409)582-6100x3300.
50 miles north of Houston. **Holes:** 18. **Par:** 71/71.
Yards: 6,907/6,467. **Course rating:** N/A. **Slope:** 122/113.
Opened: N/A. **Pace of Play rating:** N/A. **Green fee:** N/A.
Credit cards: All major. **Reduced fees:** Weekdays, Resort guests,
Twilight.
Caddies: No. **Golf carts:** N/A.
Discount golf packages: Yes. **Season:** Year-round. **High:** May-Oct.
On-site lodging: Yes. **Rental clubs:** No.
Walking policy: N/A. **Range:** Yes (grass).
Subscriber comments: All around good course, lots of trees . . . Long
drive from Houston . . . Hilly, narrow fairways, fast pace, friendly staff
. . . Not a difficult course, good service, some pretty holes . . . Greens are
very spotty . . . Well kept resort course . . . Beautiful clubhouse . . . Heavy
traffic . . . Good mix of hard and easy holes . . . A nice change from
Houston flat courses . . . Beautiful and fun on the lake . . . Nice amenities
and resort . . . Fairly simple, worth playing.

★★★ DELAWARE SPRINGS GOLF COURSE
PU—Hwy. 281 S., Burnet (512)756-8951.
50 miles northwest of Austin. **Holes:** 18. **Par:** 72/71.
Yards: 6,819/5,770. **Course rating:** 72.0/66.5. **Slope:** 121/107.
Opened: 1992. **Pace of Play rating:** 4:15. **Green fee:** $20.
Credit cards: All major. **Reduced fees:** Twilight, Seniors, Juniors.
Caddies: No. **Golf carts:** $9 for 18 holes.
Discount golf packages: No. **Season:** Year-round. **High:** March-Sept.
On-site lodging: No. **Rental clubs:** Yes.
Walking policy: Walking at certain times. **Range:** Yes (grass).
To obtain tee times: Call on Thursday for following weekend; call one
week in advance for holidays.

Subscriber comments: Unique Texas Hill Country course. Very
enjoyable to play . . . Fast pace, excellent golf at right price . . . Quiet, laid
back . . . Nothing fancy, but good test . . . People very friendly . . . Big
greens, can walk . . . Once played 36 and never saw another golfer . . . A
pleasant surprise . . . Super friendly staff and pro, outstanding fairways and
greens year round, well manicured, slow play never a problem . . .
Country jewel, worth the drive . . . Only negative is high rough with
rattlesnakes . . . Last holes are great, wonderful minimalism in the Hill
Country, boon to town . . . Each hole has character . . . A hidden treasure
. . . Ball hog, but pretty . . . Outstanding food . . . A little ragged . . .
Unwalkable . . . Scrub oak atmosphere . . . Would love to play here every
day . . . Need to cut back rough and brush . . . Never been treated better.

★★½ DEVINE GOLF COURSE
PU—116 Malone Dr., Devine (210)665-9943.
Call club for further information.
Subscriber comments: Fun course and friendly people . . . Always in
great shape . . . Most cooperative and helpful staff anywhere . . . A good
tough small town course.

ECHO CREEK COUNTRY CLUB★
SP—FM 317, Murchison (903)852-7094.
22 miles southwest of Tyler. **Holes:** 18. **Par:** 71/73.
Yards: 6,200/5,000. **Course rating:** 69.2/69.2. **Slope:** 120/118.
Opened: 1989. **Pace of Play rating:** 4:00. **Green fee:** $10/16.
Credit cards: None. **Reduced fees:** Resort guests, Seniors.
Caddies: No. **Golf carts:** $17 for 18 holes.
Discount golf packages: No. **Season:** Year-round. **High:** March-Aug.
On-site lodging: No. **Rental clubs:** Yes.
Walking policy: Unrestricted walking. **Range:** Yes (grass).
To obtain tee times: Call pro shop.

★★★ FAIRWAY FARM GOLF COURSE
PU—Highway 21E, San Augustine (409)275-5458.
Call club for further information.
Subscriber comments: Very good track in deep East Texas, No. 16
demands your three best shots . . . Tough, long course, needs to be
brought back into shape after being closed for two years . . . Interesting
course with interesting history, very peaceful . . . Lots of pine trees . . .
With tight, pine tree-lined fairway, course plays long, island green . . .
Excellent service, needs a lot of work . . . Must be longest course on earth.

★★★★ THE FALLS COUNTRY CLUB
SP—1001 N. Falls Dr., New Ulm (409)992-3128.
60 miles west of Houston. **Holes:** 18. **Par:** 72/73.
Yards: 6,757/5,326. **Course rating:** 72.3/70.0. **Slope:** 133/123.
Opened: 1985. **Pace of Play rating:** 4:10. **Green fee:** $42/52.
Credit cards: MC, V, AMEX. **Reduced fees:** Weekdays, Resort guests.
Caddies: No. **Golf carts:** Included in Green Fee.
Discount golf packages: No. **Season:** Year-round. **High:** April-July.
On-site lodging: Yes. **Rental clubs:** Yes.
Walking policy: Walking at certain times. **Range:** Yes (grass).
To obtain tee times: Call three days in advance.
Subscriber comments: Tight with trees, water, bunkers, and slick bent
greens . . . Great layout, fun to putt on bent grass . . . Super layout . . .
Pace of play excellent . . . Staff was great . . . If you don't mind drive, not
much play . . . Gorgeous in cool fall weather . . . Inconvenient location but
a wonderful course . . . Bent-grass greens a plus for Houston area . . .
Much scenery and wildlife . . . Bring your own food . . . You really have
to want to get there . . . Design among Texas' best . . . No one can figure
out how to make this gem shine . . . Lightning fast, crowned greens . . .
Crystal clear water . . . Beautiful terrain . . . Country atmosphere, outstanding layout . . . Bent greens can't take Texas summers, play in spring
and fall . . . A bit of a drive, but a good experience . . . Best greens in
Texas.

FIREWHEEL GOLF PARK
PU—600 W. Blackburn Rd., Garland (214)205-2795.
10 miles north of Dallas.
Green fee: $16/24.
Credit cards: MC, V, AMEX. **Reduced fees:** Twilight, Seniors.
Caddies: No. **Golf carts:** $9 for 18 holes.
Discount golf packages: No. **Season:** Year-round. **High:** April-Sept.
On-site lodging: No. **Rental clubs:** Yes.
Walking policy: Unrestricted walking. **Range:** Yes (grass).
To obtain tee times: Call Thursday at 8 a.m. for Friday through
Thursday.
★★★ LAKES COURSE
Holes: 18. **Par:** 71/71.
Yards: 6,625/5,215. **Course rating:** 72.0/69.1. **Slope:** 126/110.
Opened: 1987. **Pace of Play rating:** 4:00.
Subscriber comments: Great shotmakers' course . . . Tight front nine
with lots of water . . . Excellent service staff . . . Every hole seems to be
played into the wind . . . Tough par 5s . . . Doesn't drain well . . . Good

clubhouse and tournament facility . . . Tough getting tee time . . . Slow rounds, hard to keep in great shape, too crowded . . . Tight and versatile . . . Needs traps . . . My woods hardly left my bag . . . Water into play on 11 holes . . . No drinking water . . . Greens need to improve . . . Best public course without being expensive.

★★★ OLD COURSE

Holes: 18. **Par:** 72/72.
Yards: 7,054/5,692. **Course rating:** 74.1/71.7. **Slope:** 129/117.
Opened: 1983. **Pace of Play rating:** 4:00.
Subscriber comments: Old course has it all . . . Same price as Lakes but lacks in conditioning . . . I don't see what everyone raves about . . . Greens are rough due to lack of winds, tough in heat . . . Don't be fooled by the openness of this course . . . Deceptively long . . . Good clubhouse, scenic . . . Longer than Lakes course . . . Nice traditional design, good par 5s . . . Lots of walking . . . Doglegs right and left . . . Better course than Lakes . . . Lots of character . . . Hard to get tee times if not a resident . . . More traditional holes than Lakes . . . Greens in poor condition in summer.

★★★ FLYING L RANCH GOLF COURSE

R—P.O. Box 1959, Bandera (210)460-3001, (800)646-5407.
40 miles northwest of San Antonio. **Holes:** 18. **Par:** 72/72.
Yards: 6,635/5,442. **Course rating:** 71.0/69.9. **Slope:** 123/109.
Opened: 1975. **Pace of Play rating:** 4:30. **Green fee:** $20/27.
Credit cards: All major. **Reduced fees:** Weekdays, Low season, Resort guests, Twilight, Seniors, Juniors.
Caddies: No. **Golf carts:** $9 for 18 holes.
Discount golf packages: Yes. **Season:** Year-round. **High:** April-Sept.
On-site lodging: Yes. **Rental clubs:** Yes.
Walking policy: Unrestricted walking. **Range:** Yes (grass).
To obtain tee times: Call in advance.
Subscriber comments: Scenic Hill Country course . . . Nice course . . . Staff really cooperative, many improvements in last two years . . . Greens good . . . Can walk . . . Some holes subject to flooding . . . Fun, but not memorable, poor man's country club . . . Overpriced but beautiful . . . Tricky holes (hit fairway and still have tree trouble) . . . Beautiful new clubhouse with great service . . . Tee times stacked too close . . . Some very scenic hilltop holes . . . Great little course for the money.

★★★½ FOREST CREEK GOLF CLUB

PU—99 Twin Ridge Pkwy., Round Rock (512)388-2874.
10 miles south of Austin. **Holes:** 18. **Par:** 72/72.
Yards: 7,084/5,601. **Course rating:** 72.8/71.9. **Slope:** 130/124.
Opened: 1989. **Pace of Play rating:** 4:30. **Green fee:** $30/45.
Credit cards: All major. **Reduced fees:** Twilight, Seniors, Juniors.
Caddies: No. **Golf carts:** Included in Green Fee.
Discount golf packages: No. **Season:** Year-round. **High:** June-July.
On-site lodging: No. **Rental clubs:** Yes.
Walking policy: Walking at certain times. **Range:** Yes (grass).
To obtain tee times: Call seven days in advance.
Subscriber comments: Outstanding public course . . . Keep it a secret from the tourists . . . Stay away from the electric fences . . . Course is in great shape . . . Pleasant, excellent pace, very good course year round . . . Big greens, nice staff . . . Hard to figure yardage, plays harder than it looks . . . Slow play often a problem, even during the week . . . Staff cooperative, but sometimes overwhelmed with play . . . Tree-lined fairways . . . Beautiful layout. Challenging. Two- tiered greens . . . Country club golf at municipal price . . . One of the best public courses in Austin area . . . Too expensive . . . Always in good shape and playable . . . One of the nicest designs in Austin, but losing character to housing development . . . Narrow, wooded, uneven lies in fairway . . . Tricky par 3s . . . Tight, blind shots must play several times to know where to hit . . . Most challenging course in central Texas.

★½ FORT BROWN MUNICIPAL GOLF COURSE
PU—300 River Levy, Brownsville (210)541-0394.
Call club for further information.
Subscriber comments: Self-esteem builder . . . On the lower end of the scale . . . Short course, very hard, dry fairways, good greens . . . Staff above average. Few obstacles, wide open . . . Not particularly challenging . . . Pace of play very fast.

FOUR SEASONS RESORT AND CLUB
R—4150 N. MacArthur Blvd, Irving (214)717-2530, (800)332-3442.
10 miles northwest of Dallas. **Green fee:** $68/116.
Credit cards: MC, V, AMEX, Diners Club. **Reduced fees:** Low season, Resort guests, Twilight.
Caddies: No. **Golf carts:** Included in Green Fee.
Discount golf packages: Yes. **Season:** Year-round. **High:** Feb.–Oct.
On-site lodging: Yes. **Rental clubs:** Yes.
Walking policy: Mandatory cart. **Range:** Yes (grass).
To obtain tee times: Hotel guests may call up to 45 days in advance.
★★★½ TPC COURSE
Holes: 18. **Par:** 70/70.
Yards: 6,899/5,340. **Course rating:** 73.5/70.6. **Slope:** 135/116.
Opened: 1986. **Pace of Play rating:** 4:30.
Subscriber comments: What a surprise . . . Well maintained, short from white tees . . . Need a good short game . . . Must be good iron player . . . Expensive, staff and facilities top notch . . . Very interesting greens, a bit pricey . . . 5½ hours to play . . . Impressive clubhouse . . . Weird driving course, trees in center of fairway . . . Depends on wind for difficulty . . . No tricks, pretty plain . . . Want to impress a customer? . . . Beautiful hotel . . . Excellent course . . . Best TPC in Texas.
COTTONWOOD VALLEY COURSE★
Holes: 18. **Par:** 71/72.
Yards: 6,862/5,320. **Course rating:** 73.4/70.6. **Slope:** 133/116.
Opened: 1983. **Pace of Play rating:** 4:00.

★ FOX CREEK GOLF COURSE
PU—Rte. 3, Hempstead (409)826-2131.
40 miles northwest of Houston. **Holes:** 18. **Par:** 70/70.
Yards: 5,750/4,680. **Course rating:** N/A. **Slope:** N/A.
Opened: N/A. **Pace of Play rating:** N/A. **Green fee:** N/A.
Credit cards: MC, V. **Reduced fees:** Weekdays, Twilight.
Caddies: No. **Golf carts:** N/A for 18 holes.
Discount golf packages: No. **Season:** Year-round. **High:** March–Sept.
On-site lodging: No. **Rental clubs:** No.
Walking policy: N/A. **Range:** Yes (grass).
Subscriber comments: A small out-of-the-way course, fun with challenge . . . Three good holes . . . Good course for duffers. Flat as a pancake and reasonably priced . . . Treatment good, slow play . . . Routine maintenance lacking . . . Always fun, when your game needs an ego boost.

★½ GABE LOZANO SR. GOLF CENTER
PU—4401 Old Brownsville Rd., Corpus Christi (512)883-3696.
Call club for further information.
Subscriber comments: Very good, just too much wind . . . Greens see lots of traffic, learn to play the wind . . . Lousy drainage after rain . . . Always windy, best staff ever for public course . . . As with all Corpus Christi area munys, poorly maintained . . . Let fivesomes go. Expect 4–5 hour round . . . Many bare spots in fairway . . . Very good greens, well maintained . . . Better of the two munys in Corpus.

★½ GAINESVILLE MUNICIPAL GOLF CLUB
PU—200 S. Rusk, Gainesville (817)665-2161.
Call club for further information.
Subscriber comments: Very cheap, good greens, fast play . . . Course was in good shape in winter . . . Easy access . . . Fairways very nice, greens were pretty nice . . . Getting better every year.

★★★ GALVESTON ISLAND MUNICIPAL GOLF COURSE
PU—1700 Sydnor Lane, Galveston (409)744-2366.
50 miles south of Houston. **Holes:** 18. **Par:** 72/73.
Yards: 6,969/5,407. **Course rating:** 73.0/71.4. **Slope:** 131/121.
Opened: 1989. **Pace of Play rating:** 4:30. **Green fee:** $13/21.
Credit cards: MC, V, AMEX. **Reduced fees:** Weekdays, Resort guests, Twilight, Seniors, Juniors.
Caddies: No. **Golf carts:** $10 for 18 holes.
Discount golf packages: Yes. **Season:** Year-round. **High:** April-Oct.
On-site lodging: No. **Rental clubs:** Yes.
Walking policy: Unrestricted walking. **Range:** Yes (grass).
To obtain tee times: Times taken Wednesday morning 8 a.m. and four days before holiday.
Subscriber comments: Very open windy environment . . . A bit windy, a real test of golf, nice folks . . . Water, water everywhere . . . Few trees . . . Too much perimeter water . . . Very challenging . . . Tests your game in strong Gulf winds . . . Water on almost every hole . . . Needs maintenance . . . Good facilities . . . Too many blind shots . . . Plain Jane fairways and greens . . . Lots of trouble . . . Windy, windy, windy . . . Wind is a killer . . . Long and challenging to any player, a lot of water, great greens . . . Surprisingly good for coastal course.

GARDEN VALLEY GOLF RESORT
R—22049 FM 1995, Lindale (903)882-6107, (800)443-8577.
80 miles east of Dallas. **Credit cards:** MC, V, AMEX. **Reduced fees:** Weekdays, Low season, Twilight, Seniors.
Caddies: No. **Golf carts:** $12 for 18 holes.
Discount golf packages: Yes. **Season:** Year-round. **High:** April-Oct.
On-site lodging: Yes. **Rental clubs:** Yes.
Walking policy: Mandatory cart. **Range:** Yes (grass).
To obtain tee times: Call 800 direct line to golf shop. If local call pro shop number.

★★★½ DOGWOOD COURSE
Holes: 18. **Par:** 72/72.
Yards: 6,754/5,532. **Course rating:** 72.4/72.5. **Slope:** 132/130.
Opened: 1992. **Pace of Play rating:** 4:00. **Green fee:** $40.
Subscriber comments: Beautiful course in the middle of nowhere . . . Excellent golf. Beautiful color in spring . . . Dogwood aptly named . . . Fantastic tree lined golf course . . . Beautifully maintained . . . Reminiscent of Pinehurst . . . The best, most beautiful course I've ever played . . . Shot placement important . . . As close to Augusta as I will probably get . . . Fantastic clubhouse . . . A visual delight, fun to play . . . Modern type course, good condition all year, pine trees . . . Good service . . . Wonderful place to visit . . . Beautiful azaleas, dogwood, and pine trees . . . Beautiful course routed through pines, rolling hills, and lakes . . . Heaven in Texas . . . Let's keep this course a secret. Fabulous deep woods scenery . . . Best course in East Texas.

★★★ HUMMINGBIRD COURSE
Holes: 18. **Par:** 71/71.
Yards: 6,446/5,131. **Course rating:** 71.0/69.0. **Slope:** N/A.
Opened: N/A. **Pace of Play rating:** 4:00. **Green fee:** $19.
Subscriber comments: Older of the two . . . Maintenance of course is superb, nice pro shop and clubhouse . . . Excellent condition, pleasant staff, quick pace . . . Beautiful scenery, great finishing hole . . . Sister to Dogwood, just not as good . . . Staff very nice, excellent pace of play . . .

fun to play . . . Trees in middle of fairways . . . Not as well maintained due to new course . . . Slow play most of time . . . Kind of an East Texas Augusta National . . . Prettiest place to play in spring . . . Not too long or difficult . . . Good in all aspects.

★★ GLENBROOK GOLF COURSE

PU—8205 N. Bayou Dr., Houston (713)649-8089.
15 miles south of Houston. **Holes:** 18. **Par:** 71/71.
Yards: 6,427/5,258. **Course rating:** 70.7/70.7. **Slope:** 120/117.
Opened: N/A. **Pace of Play rating:** 4:50. **Green fee:** $11/14.
Credit cards: MC, V. **Reduced fees:** Weekdays, Low season, Twilight, Seniors, Juniors.
Caddies: No. **Golf carts:** $9 for 18 holes.
Discount golf packages: Yes. **Season:** Year-round. **High:** April-Oct.
On-site lodging: No. **Rental clubs:** Yes.
Walking policy: Unrestricted walking. **Range:** No.
To obtain tee times: Call or stop by anytime after Thursday at 7 a.m.
Subscriber comments: Houston's version of the Grand Canyon . . . Overplayed . . . Very short, but can be penal . . . Too tight, lots of "fores" . . . Not always wood off the tee . . . Concrete-lined bayou crosses several fairways requiring 170-175 yard carry . . . How many times did I cross that bayou? . . . Holes back and forth over river get tiresome . . . No character . . . Concrete bayous ruin course . . . Nothing special . . . Tee times stacked too close . . . A good course ruined by flood control.

★★★ THE GOLF CLUB AT CINCO RANCH

PU—23030 Cinco Ranch Blvd., Katy (713)395-4653.
20 miles west of Houston. **Holes:** 18. **Par:** 72/72.
Yards: 7,044/5,263. **Course rating:** 73.7/70.3. **Slope:** 132/118.
Opened: 1994. **Pace of Play rating:** 4:15. **Green fee:** $35/50.
Credit cards: All major. **Reduced fees:** Weekdays, Twilight, Seniors, Juniors.
Caddies: No. **Golf carts:** Included in Green Fee.
Discount golf packages: No. **Season:** Year-round. **High:** April-June.
On-site lodging: No. **Rental clubs:** Yes.
Walking policy: Mandatory cart. **Range:** Yes (grass).
To obtain tee times: Call three days in advance for public; five days for residents.
Subscriber comments: Two thumbs up! . . . This will be a very good course in 25 years if the trees grow . . . New course, needs to mature, service good . . . Lots of trouble . . . Excellent throughout, great staff . . . Greens outstanding and fairways fair . . . Well-designed, wind really increases toughness . . . Too many holes alike . . . Wind, wind, wind . . . Big multitiered greens . . . Two killer 4s . . . Not a great course, but OK . . . Best new course in Houston area.

★★½ GRAND PRAIRIE MUNICIPAL GOLF COURSE
BLUE/RED/WHITE

PU—3202 S.E. 14th St., Grand Prairie (214)263-0661.
5 miles south of Dallas. **Holes:** 27. **Par:** 72/71/71.
Yards: 6,500/6,309/6,219. **Course rating:** 71.0/69.5/69.5. **Slope:** 118/112/94.
Opened: 1964. **Pace of Play rating:** 4:00. **Green fee:** $14/16.
Credit cards: None. **Reduced fees:** Twilight, Seniors, Juniors.
Caddies: No. **Golf carts:** $19 for 18 holes.
Discount golf packages: No. **Season:** Year-round. **High:** May-Sept.
On-site lodging: No. **Rental clubs:** Yes.
Walking policy: Unrestricted walking. **Range:** Yes (grass).
To obtain tee times: 7 a.m. in person or 8 a.m. by phone on Thursdays for weekends and holidays only.
Subscriber comments: Good muny course has some personality . . . The course is great if you like water hazards, no sand traps; the staff is great, always friendly and helpful . . . An unusual way of using 27 holes . . .

Tough par 3s . . . Best putting greens around in mid summer . . . Many players don't wear shirts . . . Easy to walk . . . Tough water holes, long par 3s from back, nicely shaped greens . . . Overlooks lake . . . Excellent food at snack bar . . . Best muny course in Dallas/Ft. Worth.

★★½ GRAPEVINE GOLF COURSE

PU—3800 Fairway Dr., Grapevine (817)481-0421.
15 miles west of Dallas. **Holes:** 18. **Par:** 72/72.
Yards: 6,953/5,786. **Course rating:** 72.0/72.5. **Slope:** 113/113.
Opened: 1979. **Pace of Play rating:** 4:20. **Green fee:** $13.
Credit cards: MC, V, AMEX. **Reduced fees:** Twilight, Seniors, Juniors.
Caddies: No. **Golf carts:** $17 for 18 holes.
Discount golf packages: No. **Season:** Year-round. **High:** April-Sept.
On-site lodging: No. **Rental clubs:** Yes.
Walking policy: Unrestricted walking. **Range:** Yes (grass).
To obtain tee times: Call three days in advance, 7 a.m. in person or 1 p.m. by phone.
Subscriber comments: Long, heavily wooded, huge greens, bring every shot . . . Play is too slow . . . Hard to get a tee time . . . Little ragged in spots, great white sand bunkers . . . Undulating greens, must hit irons to correct spots on green . . . Very scenic, good range, some hills in Dallas . . . A lot harder than it looks on paper . . . Interesting . . . Needs better maintenance . . . Difficult to get a tee time but worth the effort . . . Good looking course but bad green problems . . . Deserves much more credit than it gets.

GRAYSON COUNTY COLLEGE GOLF COURSE★

PU—7109 Dinn, Denison (903)786-9719.
70 miles north of Dallas. **Holes:** 18. **Par:** 72/72.
Yards: 6,452/4,876. **Course rating:** 70.0/N/A. **Slope:** 114/N/A.
Opened: 1961. **Pace of Play rating:** 4:00. **Green fee:** $8/12.
Credit cards: MC, V. **Reduced fees:** Weekdays, Twilight.
Caddies: No. **Golf carts:** $16 for 18 holes.
Discount golf packages: No. **Season:** Year-round. **High:** May-June.
On-site lodging: No. **Rental clubs:** Yes.
Walking policy: Unrestricted walking. **Range:** Yes (grass).
To obtain tee times: Call 7 a.m. Thursday for upcoming weekend.

★★★½ GREATWOOD GOLF CLUB

PU—6767 Greatwood Pkwy., Sugar Land (713)343-9999.
20 miles southwest of Houston. **Holes:** 18. **Par:** 72/72.
Yards: 6,836/5,220. **Course rating:** 72.6/70.0. **Slope:** 130/125.
Opened: 1990. **Pace of Play rating:** 4:20. **Green fee:** $44/58.
Credit cards: All major. **Reduced fees:** Twilight.
Caddies: No. **Golf carts:** Included in Green Fee.
Discount golf packages: No. **Season:** Year-round. **High:** March-Oct.
On-site lodging: No. **Rental clubs:** Yes.
Walking policy: Mandatory cart. **Range:** Yes (grass).
To obtain tee times: Call three days in advance of the day you wish to play, starting at 8 a.m.
Subscriber comments: Very good for a development course . . . Lots of water makes this a challenge . . . Target golf at its best . . . Difficult first time, can't see the trouble . . . Would play it every day . . . Beautiful river bottom course, hot hot summer . . . Crowded but fairly quick five hour round . . . Stays soggy after rains . . . Best deal in Houston area . . . Country club atmosphere and conditions . . . Exceptionally well marshaled . . . One of the best places to play in Houston . . . Soon to become Texas masterpiece . . . Outstanding maintenance reflected in $50 green fee . . . Fairways and scenery are terrific . . . Course, pro shop people, all good . . .

Cart is needed due to length between holes . . . Course plays long with lots of water and beautiful sand . . . Excellent yardage markers . . . Lot of hidden pins and doglegs . . . Two par 5s are quirky . . . Best golf course in Houston area.

★½ GREEN MEADOWS GOLF CLUB

PU—I-10, Katy (713)391-3670.
Call club for further information.
Subscriber comments: Short but comfortable . . . Tight course, easy access, good practice course . . . Too close, no sand . . . Busy course but good, narrow fairways . . . No amenities . . . Not a lot of traffic, no bunkers but lots of water and trees . . . Side by side fairways . . . Watch out for mosquitoes . . . Staff very accommodating to walk-on players . . . Well cared for, people are great.

★★ GROVER C. KEATON GOLF COURSE

PU—2323 Jim Miller Rd., Dallas (214)670-8784.
Holes: 18. **Par:** 72/72.
Yards: 6,511/5,054. **Course rating:** 70.6/68.1. **Slope:** 113/113.
Opened: 1978. **Pace of Play rating:** 4:30. **Green fee:** $11/14.
Credit cards: MC, V, AMEX. **Reduced fees:** Weekdays, Low season, Twilight, Seniors, Juniors.
Caddies: No. **Golf carts:** $17 for 18 holes.
Discount golf packages: No. **Season:** Year-round. **High:** March-Aug.
On-site lodging: No. **Rental clubs:** Yes.
Walking policy: Unrestricted walking. **Range:** Yes (grass).
To obtain tee times: Call two days in advance.
Subscriber comments: A typical municipal course . . . Decent muny, good value, small clubhouse . . . Tight fairways, plenty of water, good playability . . . Good inner-city course, friendly people . . . Poorly maintained . . . Too short, a lot of 310-yard par 4s . . . Floods easily . . . Relaxed pace . . . Good service . . . Tightest Dallas municipal . . . Needs better greens . . . Pecan trees . . . Underrated Dallas municipal.

★½ GUS WORTHAM PARK GOLF COURSE

PU—7000 Capitol, Houston (713)921-3227.
Holes: 18. **Par:** 72/74.
Yards: 6,400/6,000. **Course rating:** 69.5/74.2. **Slope:** 113/118.
Opened: N/A. **Pace of Play rating:** 4:00. **Green fee:** $10/14.
Credit cards: MC, V, AMEX. **Reduced fees:** Weekdays, Twilight, Seniors, Juniors.
Caddies: No. **Golf carts:** $18 for 18 holes.
Discount golf packages: No. **Season:** Year-round. **High:** April-May.
On-site lodging: No. **Rental clubs:** Yes.
Walking policy: Unrestricted walking. **Range:** Yes (grass).
To obtain tee times: Call one day in advance.
Subscriber comments: Course is well designed but needs maintenance . . . Many recent improvements . . . Lots of wood and water . . . No sprinkler system, as a result the course can dry out and the grass dies . . . Overused and needs more and better fairway grass, but good value . . . Old style . . . Takes 5½ to 6 hours on weekends, very short par 3s and 4s, never seen both greens and fairways in good condition . . . Watch your clubs . . . Fun to play if you can keep ball sellers away from you.

★½ HENRY HOMBERG MUNICIPAL GOLF COURSE

PU—5940 Babe Zaharias Dr., Beaumont (409)842-3220.
25 miles east of Houston. **Holes:** 18. **Par:** 72/73.
Yards: 6,786/5,660. **Course rating:** 71.2/70.0. **Slope:** 116/116.
Opened: 1930. **Pace of Play rating:** 4:00 **Green fee:** $8.
Credit cards: MC, V, AMEX. **Reduced fees:** Weekdays, Twilight, Seniors, Juniors.
Caddies: No. **Golf carts:** $8 for 18 holes.
Discount golf packages: No. **Season:** Year-round. **High:** March-June.
On-site lodging: No. **Rental clubs:** Yes.

Walking policy: Unrestricted walking. **Range:** Yes (grass).
To obtain tee times: Call two days in advance for weekends or holidays at 9 a.m.
Subscriber comments: Average muny with lots of rounds . . . Staff is very courteous, well trained . . . Pace of play varies from good to very good, marshals are effective yet courteous . . . Small greens . . . Senior citizen special rates . . . Usually in good condition for the amount of play . . . Flat, tree-lined. Some interesting holes . . . A PGA tour site it is not.

★½ HERMANN PARK GOLF COURSE
PU—6201 Golf Course Dr., Houston (713)526-0077.
Holes: 18. **Par:** 71/72.
Yards: 5,966/5,369. **Course rating:** 68.1/64.5. **Slope:** 103/97.
Opened: 1922. **Pace of Play rating:** 4:00. **Green fee:** $10/15.
Credit cards: MC, V, AMEX. **Reduced fees:** Twilight, Seniors, Juniors.
Caddies: No. **Golf carts:** $16 for 18 holes.
Discount golf packages: No. **Season:** Year-round. **High:** April-Sept.
On-site lodging: No. **Rental clubs:** Yes.
Walking policy: Walking at certain times. **Range:** Yes (grass).
To obtain tee times:&F
First come, first served.
Subscriber comments: Old course with some history . . . Short course . . . Some fairways overlap . . . Not many hazards, good beginner's course, very slow . . . Biggest worry is the wind . . . Good location, in town . . . Tee times always 30 minutes behind schedule . . . Short; some fun holes . . . Limited staff . . . High density park, too close to park areas . . . Hard to find your next tee box . . . Greens are great in the fall.

★★★ HIDDEN HILLS PUBLIC GOLF COURSE
PU—N. Hwy. 70, Pampa (806)669-5866.
56 miles northeast of Amarillo. **Holes:** 18. **Par:** 71/71.
Yards: 6,463/5,196. **Course rating:** 69.4/68.0. **Slope:** 122/116.
Opened: 1990. **Pace of Play rating:** 3:30. **Green fee:** $6/11.
Credit cards: MC, V. **Reduced fees:** Weekdays, Twilight, Seniors, Juniors.
Caddies: No. **Golf carts:** $16 for 18 holes.
Discount golf packages: No. **Season:** Year-round. **High:** May-Sept.
On-site lodging: No. **Rental clubs:** Yes.
Walking policy: Unrestricted walking. **Range:** Yes (grass).
To obtain tee times: Call for tee times on Saturday, Sunday, and holidays.
Subscriber comments: Interesting, fun course in canyon . . . Hilly, hard to walk, windy always . . . Excellent fairways, greens good, good test of sidehill lies . . . Hilly and not easy walking, well maintained and friendly staff . . . Challenging course that would be really good with more water on it . . . Not a flat spot on it . . . Nice course considering land they had to work with . . . Great golf in the middle of nowhere, nice staff, fair pro shop.

★★★★ HILL COUNTRY GOLF CLUB
R—9800 Hyatt Resort Dr., San Antonio (210)520-4040.
15 miles west of San Antonio. **Holes:** 18. **Par:** 72/72.
Yards: 6,913/4,781. **Course rating:** 73.9/67.8. **Slope:** 136/114.
Opened: 1993. **Pace of Play rating:** 4:50. **Green fee:** $60/90.
Credit cards: All major. **Reduced fees:** Weekdays, Low season, Twilight, Juniors.
Caddies: No. **Golf carts:** Included in Green Fee.
Discount golf packages: Yes. **Season:** Year-round. **High:** March-Sept.
On-site lodging: Yes. **Rental clubs:** Yes.
Walking policy: Unrestricted walking. **Range:** Yes (grass).
To obtain tee times: Hotel guests call pro shop 30 days prior to arrival; all others call seven days in advance.
Subscriber comments: A Hills design in beautiful Hill Country . . . Beautiful layout . . . First class operation all the way; great attention to details . . . Well marshaled . . . Scenic beauty, very playable despite trees

galore . . . Nice surprise . . . Long but not too tough . . . Greens are excellent . . . Take what it gives . . . Slick greens . . . An outstanding new course . . . Play in April when the wildflowers bloom . . . A real sleeper . . . Arthur Hills layout has good variety of holes . . . Good vacation resort . . . Great par 3s. Long par 4s . . . Great atmosphere . . . Great hotel . . . Providing recommended strategy for each hole is a great idea . . . One of the best in Texas.

★½ HOGAN PARK GOLF COURSE
PU—3600 N. Fairground Rd., Midland (915)685-7360.
300 miles east of Fort Worth. **Holes:** 27. **Par:** 70/71/71.
Yards: 6,615/6,730/6,705. **Course rating:** 68.5/69.3/68.9. **Slope:** 110/112/111.
Opened: 1959. **Pace of Play rating:** 4:30. **Green fee:** $9/13.
Credit cards: MC, V. **Reduced fees:** Weekdays, Low season, Twilight, Seniors, Juniors.
Caddies: No. **Golf carts:** $15 for 18 holes.
Discount golf packages: No. **Season:** Year-round. **High:** June–Nov.
On-site lodging: No. **Rental clubs:** Yes.
Walking policy: Unrestricted walking. **Range:** Yes (grass).
To obtain tee times: Call pro shop.
Subscriber comments: Very good fairways, passable greens, slow play on weekends . . . Very heavy play wears course very thin . . . Only a few good holes . . . Staff is courteous and helpful . . . The mesquite needs to be cut back on some holes . . . Extremely rough . . . Little sand, water . . . All-day green fees.

HORSESHOE BAY RESORT
R—Bay West Blvd., Horseshoe Bay (210)598-6561.
52 miles west of Austin. **Green fee:** $60/85.
Credit cards: All major. **Reduced fees:** Weekdays, Low season, Resort guests, Juniors.
Caddies: No. **Golf carts:** $10 for 18 holes.
Discount golf packages: Yes. **Season:** Year-round. **High:** March–Nov.
On-site lodging: Yes. **Rental clubs:** Yes.
Walking policy: Mandatory cart. **Range:** Yes (grass).
To obtain tee times: Call seven days in advance.

★★★★ APPLEROCK COURSE
Holes: 18. **Par:** 72/72.
Yards: 6,999/5,509. **Course rating:** 73.9/71.6. **Slope:** 134/117.
Opened: 1986. **Pace of Play rating:** 4:15.
Selected Best New Resort Course of 1986 by Golf Digest.
Subscriber comments: Robert Trent Jones at his best, challenging without overkill . . . Best view in Texas . . . Picturesque Hill Country . . . Unbelievably beautiful . . . Staff and service very good . . . Just about as good as it gets . . . Immaculately kept . . . Long tough holes . . . A-1 condition . . . Best layout in Texas, very scenic . . . Great clubhouse . . . Take along plenty of balls, if out of play don't look (snakes) . . . What's not to like about an uncrowded, great course? . . . Hill Country heaven . . . Lots of sand and water. Wish they'd let you walk . . . Wonderful holes and views . . . Friendly, rustic beauty, lots of relief, tough greens . . . Significant elevation changes . . . Great cooperation between Robert Trent Jones and Mother Nature.

★★★★½ RAM ROCK COURSE
Holes: 18. **Par:** 71/71.
Yards: 6,946/5,306. **Course rating:** 73.9/71.4. **Slope:** 137/121.
Opened: 1981. **Pace of Play rating:** 5:00.
Ranked 40th in America's 75 Best Resort Courses by Golf Digest. Ranked 6th in Texas by Golf Digest.
Subscriber comments: Beguiling beauty that will break your heart . . . A hidden jewel, this one's great . . . Summer takes toll on greens . . . One incredibly tough hole after another . . . Excellent facility, great place to play, very pretty . . . Unforgettable experience, deer in fairways . . . Outstanding in every way . . . Too expensive . . . Tough test, long and lots

of trouble, local knowledge big help . . . Best layout in Texas . . . Too tough for the average resort guest . . . Nice accommodations . . . Beautiful but treacherous . . . Tough with large elevation changes. Slick bent- grass greens . . . Death by golf, but incredible views . . . Top of the line . . . Sand everywhere, makes you glad you're finished . . . Meanest in state, big greens, big views . . . Great staff, service, and pace of play . . . World class . . . Magnificent! . . . The best. No comparison . . . Ate my lunch . . . Toughest in Texas from back tees.

★★★★ SLICK ROCK COURSE
Holes: 18. **Par:** 72/72.
Yards: 6,834/5,832. **Course rating:** 72.6/70.2. **Slope:** 125/115.
Opened: 1972. **Pace of Play rating:** 4:15.
Subscriber comments: Most scenic . . . Could play it everyday and find tees as I get older to keep it fun . . . Excellent facility, great place to play, very pretty . . . Guaranteed to three-putt at least a few times . . . Typical resort course except for waterfall holes . . . Memorable . . . A good Trent Jones standard . . . Very challenging but very playable . . . Great 14th hole waterfall . . . Spectacular landscaping, gets a lot of play . . . The perfect resort course.

HYATT BEAR CREEK GOLF AND RACQUET CLUB
PU—3500 Bear Creek Court, DFW Airport (214)615-6800.
Green fee: $48/60.
Credit cards: All major. **Reduced fees:** Weekdays, Low season, Twilight, Seniors, Juniors.
Caddies: No. **Golf carts:** $12 for 18 holes.
Discount golf packages: Yes. **Season:** Year-round. **High:** April-Nov.
On-site lodging: No. **Rental clubs:** Yes.
Walking policy: Unrestricted walking. **Range:** Yes (grass).
To obtain tee times: Call five days in advance.

★★★½ EAST COURSE
Holes: 18. **Par:** 72/72.
Yards: 6,670/5,620. **Course rating:** 72.5/72.4. **Slope:** 127/124.
Opened: 1981. **Pace of Play rating:** 4:30.
Subscriber comments: Great convenience to DFW Airport . . . No carts on fairway, slow golf . . . Better of two courses . . . Greens too bumpy, need to be rolled . . . Excellent condition year-round . . . Great staff, dedicated, the best . . . Good character . . . Solid design . . . Lots of sand and water . . . Doesn't look like Texas . . . Too many irons off tee boxes, not a power hitter's course . . . Good food and beverage . . . DFW jets are distracting . . . Best corporate golf outing selection in Texas . . . Not as pleasing to the eye as West . . . Too much air traffic . . . Playing here a super pleasure . . . Can't use driver . . . Best bent-grass greens, hot climate . . . I like the big planes overhead . . . If low flying aircraft are your bag, you'll like it.

★★★½ WEST COURSE
Holes: 18. **Par:** 72/72.
Yards: 6,675/5,570. **Course rating:** 72.7/72.5. **Slope:** 130/122.
Opened: 1981. **Pace of Play rating:** 4:30.
Subscriber comments: Another fantastic course . . . One of the best in the Metroplex . . . Better than East course . . . Lots of trees for North Texas . . . Tougher than East, be prepared for low flying jets . . . One of hillier courses in Dallas area . . . Very good championship course, carts on paths only, slow . . . Solid design, well maintained . . . Lots of traps, trees, trouble, must hit straight . . . Great circuit for airplane lover . . . Great golf accompanied by long waits . . . Loud . . . Fastest greens in Dallas . . . All year long course is superb . . . More personality than East . . . Very enjoyable course in West Dallas . . . One of the best in Dallas.

INDIAN CREEK GOLF CLUB
PU—1650 W. Frankford, Carrollton (214)492-3620, (800)369-4137.
10 miles north of Dallas. **Green fee:** $23.
Credit cards: MC, V, DISC. **Reduced fees:** Weekdays, Twilight,

Seniors, Juniors.
Caddies: No. **Golf carts:** $8 for 18 holes.
Discount golf packages: No. **Season:** Year-round. **High:** March–Oct.
On-site lodging: No. **Rental clubs:** Yes.
Walking policy: Unrestricted walking. **Range:** Yes (grass).
To obtain tee times: Call three days in advance.

★★★ CREEKS COURSE
Holes: 18. **Par:** 72/72.
Yards: 7,218/4,967. **Course rating:** 74.7/68.2. **Slope:** 136/114.
Opened: 1984. **Pace of Play rating:** 4:30.
Subscriber comments: Challenging course with good fairways and
trouble . . . Best value in Metroplex . . . Better layout than Lakes . . . If
you like water, you'll love this course . . . Very large greens, very good
short game a must . . . Several quirky par 4 driving holes . . . Hard greens,
too crowded . . . First class municipal . . . Not lush . . . Hit ball between
mesquite trees that all look the same . . . Not a friendly driver course . . .
Lots of water . . . Too hard to get tee times . . . Good shape for as much
play as it gets . . . Attracts tank top and sneaker crowd . . . Has more scenic
layout but Lakes' Course. Bermuda greens are much better . . . Be on your
game . . . One of the best deals in the Dallas area.

★★★ LAKES COURSE
Holes: 18. **Par:** 72/72.
Yards: 7,060/5,367. **Course rating:** 72.9/69.9. **Slope:** 135/114.
Opened: 1987. **Pace of Play rating:** 4:30.
Subscriber comments: Standard for public play in DFW area . . . Other
local pros come here to play, best bent greens in Metroplex . . . Good
finishing holes . . . Great greens, impossible to get tee times . . . Well
managed, marshaled and manicured . . . Mucho water, long, tough, scenic,
slow . . . Very affordable . . . They don't call it the "Lakes" for nothing
. . . 90 degree rule for carts . . . Water on most holes . . . Bent grass greens
like glass . . . Not for the hydrophobic . . . Floods too much, poor drainage
all year . . . Tight driving, plenty of trees, no straight holes . . . Wider
fairways than Creek course . . . Need to water course better during hot
summer months . . . One of the nicest municipal courses in area.

★★★ IRON HORSE GOLF CLUB
PU—6200 Skylark Circle, North Richland Hills (817)485-6666.
20 miles southwest of Fort Worth. **Holes:** 18. **Par:** 70/70.
Yards: 6,580/5,083. **Course rating:** 71.8/69.6. **Slope:** 130/119.
Opened: 1990. **Pace of Play rating:** 4:15. **Green fee:** $22/30.
Credit cards: MC, V, AMEX. **Reduced fees:** Weekdays, Twilight,
Seniors, Juniors.
Caddies: No. **Golf carts:** $10 for 18 holes.
Discount golf packages: No. **Season:** Year-round. **High:** April–Aug.
On-site lodging: No. **Rental clubs:** Yes.
Walking policy: Unrestricted walking. **Range:** Yes (grass).
To obtain tee times: Call three days in advance.
Subscriber comments: Dick Phelps did well . . . Not a walking course,
about half a mile from 18th green to clubhouse . . . Shot selection crucial
. . . Tough, tight layout . . . Staff and service very good . . . A confined
layout . . . Greens seem to always need work . . . Play is often very slow
. . . Nice refreshment stops . . . Put your drive in the right place to score
. . . Some great holes . . . Difficult to get on . . . Wonderful from practice
tee to grill room . . . Good design, well maintained, enjoyable to play . . .
No. 3 hardest hole in world . . . Great shotmaking course . . . Too many
lay ups . . . Very slow play on weekends . . . Good looking course . . .
Great secret, should be packed all the time.

★★★ J.F. SAMMONS PARK GOLF COURSE
PU—2220 W. Ave. D, Temple (817)778-8282.
50 miles north of Austin. **Holes:** 18. **Par:** 70/70.
Yards: 6,100/4,450. **Course rating:** 69.8/65.8. **Slope:** 129/110.
Opened: 1987. **Pace of Play rating:** 4:15. **Green fee:** $6/13.

Credit cards: MC, V. **Reduced fees:** Weekdays, Low season, Twilight, Seniors, Juniors.
Caddies: No. **Golf carts:** $9 for 18 holes.
Discount golf packages: No. **Season:** Year-round. **High:** March-Aug.
On-site lodging: No. **Rental clubs:** Yes.
Walking policy: Unrestricted walking. **Range:** Yes (grass).
To obtain tee times: Call seven days in advance. Deposit required for goups of 16 or more.
Subscriber comments: Short municipal . . . Good fairways, well kept . . . Lots of water, comes into play 14 holes . . . Island green par 4 . . . Better be good with irons, lots of water (understatement) . . . Easy if you hit straight. Wet if you don't . . . Great facilities, staff is very friendly . . . Barely crowded. You better not be afraid of water . . . Affordable for average income people.

★★ JERSEY MEADOW GOLF COURSE
RED/WHITE/BLUE
PU—8502 Rio Grande, Houston (713)896-0900.
Holes: 27. **Par:** 72/72/72.
Yards: 6,583/6,383/6,400. **Course rating:** 70.5/70.4/68.9. **Slope:** 120/118/118.
Opened: 1956. **Pace of Play rating:** 4:05. **Green fee:** $27/36.
Credit cards: MC, V, AMEX. **Reduced fees:** Weekdays, Low season, Twilight, Seniors, Juniors.
Caddies: No. **Golf carts:** Included in Green Fee.
Discount golf packages: No. **Season:** Year-round. **High:** April-Oct.
On-site lodging: No. **Rental clubs:** Yes.
Walking policy: Walking at certain times. **Range:** Yes (grass).
To obtain tee times: Call Wednesday a.m. for weekend tee times. Call one week in advance for weekdays.
Subscriber comments: Mature 18 . . . Lots of traps in front of greens . . . Holes bunched too close together . . . Too much play, service OK . . . Lots of tight fairways . . . Fairly good layout, not much of anything else . . . Excellent value . . . Easy to get on . . . 27-hole design lets you mix it up . . . Newest nine too short . . . Newest nine best of the holes.

★★½ JIMMY CLAY GOLF COURSE
PU—5400 Jimmy Clay Dr., Austin (512)444-0999.
Holes: 18. **Par:** 72/72.
Yards: 6,857/5,036. **Course rating:** 72.4/68.5. **Slope:** 124/110.
Opened: 1974. **Pace of Play rating:** N/A. **Green fee:** $11/13.
Credit cards: None. **Reduced fees:** Weekdays, Twilight, Seniors, Juniors.
Caddies: No. **Golf carts:** $8 for 18 holes.
Discount golf packages: No. **Season:** Year-round. **High:** Aug.
On-site lodging: No. **Rental clubs:** Yes.
Walking policy: Unrestricted walking. **Range:** Yes (grass).
To obtain tee times: Call one day in advance except Friday make tee time for both Saturday and Sunday.
Subscriber comments: Budget municipal by Joe Finger that has aged well . . . Next to impossible to get tee times . . . Good except for greens, need to rework . . . Too much play. Usually 4½ to 5 hour ordeal . . . Greens are either great or terrible . . . Hectic for municipal . . . Staff most cooperative, always busy . . . Two of the toughest par 4s in area . . . . Trees, trees, trees . . . Some great holes . . . Nice old course with huge oak trees . . . Texas Hill Country challenge without all the blind shots . . . Too many fivesomes . . . Long knocker's dream . . . Plenty of room . . . . Carts are from the Hogan era . . . Austin's longest municipal. Good greens and wide fairways.

TEXAS

★★★ JOHN PITMAN MUNICIPAL GOLF COURSE
PU—S. Main St., Hereford (806)363-7139.
Call club for further information.
Subscriber comments: Good course for a small town . . . Small greens
. . . Hard par 3s . . . Best course in Amarillo area; distinct nines . . . Best
secret in Texas Panhandle . . . Worth driving to, neat layout, well kept, nice
people.

★½ KILLEEN MUNICIPAL GOLF COURSE
PU—406 Roy Reynolds Drive, Killeen (817)699-6034.
50 miles north of Austin. **Holes:** 18. **Par:** 72/72.
Yards: 6,700/5,109. **Course rating:** 69.5/68.3. **Slope:** 107/109.
Opened: 1969. **Pace of Play rating:** 4:00. **Green fee:** $8/9.
Credit cards: MC, V. **Reduced fees:** Twilight, Seniors, Juniors.
Caddies: No. **Golf carts:** $14 for 18 holes.
Discount golf packages: No. **Season:** Year-round. **High:** March-Oct.
On-site lodging: No. **Rental clubs:** Yes.
Walking policy: Unrestricted walking. **Range:** Yes (grass).
To obtain tee times: Call Wednesday for upcoming weekend.
Subscriber comments: Very good course for small town. Good length,
good greens . . . Hard greens, service and staff fair . . . Lots of play year-
round, conditions good year round, play can be slow on weekends, 4½ to 5
hours for foursome . . . First nine a real challenge, rest on the back side . . .
No. 9 is as beautiful a hole as any in or around Austin . . . Taking necessary
steps to get better.

★★½ KINGWOOD COVE GOLF CLUB
PU—805 Hamblen Rd., Kingwood (713)358-1155.
20 miles north of Houston. **Holes:** 18. **Par:** 71/71.
Yards: 6,722/5,601. **Course rating:** 71.9/73.2. **Slope:** 118/114.
Opened: N/A. **Pace of Play rating:** 4:15. **Green fee:** $24/34.
Credit cards: All major. **Reduced fees:** Weekdays, Low season, Twilight,
Seniors, Juniors.
Caddies: No. **Golf carts:** $12 for 18 holes.
Discount golf packages: Yes. **Season:** Year-round. **High:** Spring/Fall.
On-site lodging: No. **Rental clubs:** Yes.
Walking policy: Unrestricted walking. **Range:** Yes (grass).
To obtain tee times: Call seven days in advance.
Subscriber comments: Good subdivision course . . . Needs better
maintenance, but interesting holes . . . Lots of trees, hilly, blind shots . . .
Excellent facilities . . . Interesting . . . Needs fertilizer and maintenance . . .
Gorgeous course all around . . . Flood ravaged in 1994 . . . Always
crowded . . . Clubhouse nice . . . Fairly open course in pine trees, some
sand and water . . . Better be straight . . . Friendly service . . . Scenic but
needs better conditioning.

★★ L.B. HOUSTON PARK GOLF COURSE
PU—11223 Luna Rd., Dallas (214)670-6322.
Call club for further information.
Subscriber comments: Friendly, helpful people . . . Gets heavy play, very
few memorable holes . . . Only problem is third and fourth holes are next
to rifle range . . . Carved out of North Dallas mesquite patch . . . Layout
good, but a problem in wet weather . . . Fairways hard as a rock in
summer, greens fair, not well maintained . . . Located in flood plain, not
much fun when it rains . . . Lots of traffic . . . Poor maintenance, few ball
washers, slow play . . . Sand on both sides of every tee shot . . .
Uninspiring course . . . Wear a flack jacket.

★★ L.E. RAMEY GOLF COURSE
PU—FM 3320, Kingsville (512)592-1101.
Call club for further information.
Subscriber comments: Good mix on layout, good fairways, fair greens
. . . Sneaky, tight, typical South Texas windy course . . . Fun course,
cordial staff . . . Great improvement in last two years . . . Friendly staff . . .
Keeps you on your toes, thinking man's course.

LA CANTERA GOLF CLUB★
R—16401 La Cantera Pkwy., San Antonio (210)558-4653, (800)446-5387.
Holes: 18. **Par:** 72/72.
Yards: 6,892/4,953. **Course rating:** N/A. **Slope:** N/A.
Opened: 1994. **Pace of Play rating:** N/A. **Green fee:** $65/80.
Credit cards: All major. **Reduced fees:** Weekdays.
Caddies: Yes. **Golf carts:** Included in Green Fee.
Discount golf packages: No. **Season:** Year-round. **High:** March-Oct.
On-site lodging: No. **Rental clubs:** Yes.
Walking policy: Unrestricted walking. **Range:** Yes (grass).
To obtain tee times: Call up to six days in advance. Seven–14 days in
advance with additional $10 per person charge.
Subscriber comments: Great new course . . . Flat out gorgeous! . . .
Looks great from road . . . Could be the best in San Antonio.

★★★ LADY BIRD JOHNSON MUNICIPAL GOLF COURSE
PU—Hwy. 16 S., Fredericksburg (210)997-4010, (800)950-8147.
70 miles north of San Antonio. **Holes:** 18. **Par:** 72/72.
Yards: 6,432/5,092. **Course rating:** 70.3/68.0. **Slope:** 125/112.
Opened: 1969. **Pace of Play rating:** 4:00. **Green fee:** $10/15.
Credit cards: None. **Reduced fees:** Weekdays.
Caddies: No. **Golf carts:** $8 for 18 holes.
Discount golf packages: No. **Season:** Year-round. **High:** March-Nov.
On-site lodging: No. **Rental clubs:** Yes.
Walking policy: Unrestricted walking. **Range:** Yes (grass).
To obtain tee times: Call pro shop.
Subscriber comments: Little-known gem . . . Nice course with lots of
large live oaks, well maintained, can walk . . . Beautiful setting . . .
Personnel very helpful . . . Beautiful rolling course . . . Friendly. Good
pace . . . Fairly crowded . . . Great practice facilities . . . Newest nine holes
contrast and compliment old nine . . . Great fun to play . . . Very
interesting course. Not long but tricky.

(FRUGAL PICK)

★½ LAKE ARLINGTON GOLF COURSE
PU—1516 Green Oaks Blvd. W., Arlington (817)451-6101.
25 miles west of Dallas. **Holes:** 18. **Par:** 71/71.
Yards: 6,637/5,485. **Course rating:** 70.7/71.0. **Slope:** 117/114.
Opened: 1963. **Pace of Play rating:** 4:15. **Green fee:** $10/12.
Credit cards: MC, V, DISC. **Reduced fees:** Twilight, Seniors, Juniors.
Caddies: No. **Golf carts:** $8 for 18 holes.
Discount golf packages: No. **Season:** Year-round. **High:** April-Aug.
On-site lodging: No. **Rental clubs:** Yes.
Walking policy: Unrestricted walking. **Range:** No.
To obtain tee times: Call on Tuesday starting 6 a.m. for Wednesday
through next Tuesday.
Subscriber comments: Typical flat municipal course . . . No imagination
. . . Usually crowded . . . Extremely poor conditions in spring . . .
Fairways and greens not very healthy, always construction going on . . .
No sand . . . No driving range . . . Poor greens, scruffy fairways . . . 70%
wide open . . . Shortage of parking . . . Back nine has good elevation
differences.

★★½ LAKE HOUSTON GOLF CLUB

PU—27350 Afton Way, Huffman (713)324-1841.
20 miles northeast of Houston. **Holes:** 18. **Par:** 72/74.
Yards: 6,850/5,759. **Course rating:** 72.6/73.3. **Slope:** 128/131.
Opened: 1971. **Pace of Play rating:** 4:30. **Green fee:** $20/30.
Credit cards: MC, V, AMEX. **Reduced fees:** Weekdays, Twilight,
Seniors, Juniors.
Caddies: No. **Golf carts:** Included in Green Fee.
Discount golf packages: No. **Season:** Year-round. **High:** Spring/Fall.
On-site lodging: No. **Rental clubs:** Yes.
Walking policy: Walking at certain times. **Range:** Yes (grass).
To obtain tee times: Call up to two weeks in advance.
Subscriber comments: Tucked nicely away in pines . . . Great layout,
doesn't get much play, needs some work . . . Great but call it Mosquito
Junction . . . Big greens and fast, beautiful scenery . . . Trees, sand, water,
and long from all tees . . . Pretty . . . Good service . . . Front wooded; back
more open . . . Fast greens and large mosquitoes . . . Long back nine can
wear you out . . . Lots of storm damage but coming back.

LAKE WHITNEY COUNTRY CLUB★

SP—Route 1, Whitney (817)694-2313.
55 miles south of Dallas. **Holes:** 18. **Par:** 70/71.
Yards: 6,296/5,020. **Course rating:** 67.6/69.8. **Slope:** N/A.
Opened: 1968. **Pace of Play rating:** 4:30. **Green fee:** $14.
Credit cards: None. **Reduced fees:** Weekdays, Low season, Twilight,
Seniors, Juniors.
Caddies: No. **Golf carts:** N/A.
Discount golf packages: Yes. **Season:** Year-round. **High:** March-Nov.
On-site lodging: Yes. **Rental clubs:** Yes.
Walking policy: Unrestricted walking. **Range:** Yes.
To obtain tee times: Call pro shop.

LAKEWAY RESORT

R—602 Lakeway Dr., Austin (512)261-7573.
Green fee: N/A.
Credit cards: MC, V, AMEX. **Reduced fees:** Weekdays.
Caddies: No. **Golf carts:** N/A.
Discount golf packages: Yes. **Season:** Year-round. **High:** Spring/Fall.
On-site lodging: Yes. **Rental clubs:** No.
Walking policy: N/A. **Range:** Yes (grass).

★★★ LIVE OAK COURSE

Holes: 18. **Par:** 72/72.
Yards: 6,643/5,472. **Course rating:** N/A. **Slope:** 121/122.
Opened: N/A. **Pace of Play rating:** N/A.
Subscriber comments: Good challenge, good service, no hold up . . .
Fine older course, good condition . . . Well kept resort course . . . Staff was
excellent . . . No sandtraps . . . Quite charming . . . Middle of summer
take a cooler . . . Lots of blind shots . . . Easy walking, course needs sand
and tree grooming . . . Small, hard to read greens . . . Weak for a resort
course . . . Both courses are very well kept and views are great.

★★★ YAUPON COURSE

Holes: 18. **Par:** 72/72.
Yards: 6,565/5,032. **Course rating:** N/A. **Slope:** 123/119.
Opened: N/A. **Pace of Play rating:** N/A.
Subscriber comments: Scenic lake course . . . Several blind holes (over
hills) . . . Relaxed pace, beautiful scenery . . . Great staff . . . Beautiful
views from course . . . Hill Country indeed . . . Hard to walk . . . Very
exciting to play . . . Tricky but not impossible . . . A lot of different shots
. . . Great shape; challenging course; good value.

★½ LANDA PARK MUNICIPAL GOLF COURSE

PU—350 Landa Park Dr., New Braunfels (210)608-2174.
Call club for further information
Subscriber comments: In pleasant setting . . . Greens especially smooth

and true . . . Very good course, anyone can play it, staff and service very good . . . Small greens . . . Lots of traffic . . . Great condition, short, good for seniors . . . Course needs fairway watering . . . Some tees are too close to last green . . . Short and no character . . . Confidence builder, if you can't score well here, take up tennis.

★½ LEON VALLEY GOLF COURSE
PU—709 E. 24th Ave., Belton (817)939-5271.
6 miles northeast of Temple. **Holes:** 18. **Par:** 72/73.
Yards: 6,610/5,412. **Course rating:** 67.8/66.7. **Slope:** N/A.
Opened: 1962. **Pace of Play rating:** 4:00. **Green fee:** $9/11.
Credit cards: None. **Reduced fees:** Seniors, Juniors.
Caddies: No. **Golf carts:** $9 for 18 holes.
Discount golf packages: No. **Season:** Year-round. **High:** June-Aug.
On-site lodging: No. **Rental clubs:** Yes.
Walking policy: Unrestricted walking. **Range:** No.
To obtain tee times: Call on Thursday for Saturday and Sunday only.
Subscriber comments: Straight back and forth and side by side . . . Tee boxes were hard to find . . . Fairways are long and straight . . . Not that inspiring. Out of the way and not crowded . . . Greens always good, fairways burn up in summer . . . Very long, especially par 3s.

★★½ THE LINKS AT TENNWOOD
PU—Magnolia Rd., Hockley (713)757-5465, (800)865-4657.
30 miles northwest of Houston. **Holes:** 18. **Par:** 72/73.
Yards: 6,880/5,238. **Course rating:** 70.8/68.3. **Slope:** 120/109.
Opened: 1985. **Pace of Play rating:** N/A. **Green fee:** $10/25.
Credit cards: MC, V, AMEX. **Reduced fees:** Weekdays, Twilight, Seniors, Juniors.
Caddies: No. **Golf carts:** $9 for 18 holes.
Discount golf packages: Yes. **Season:** Year-round. **High:** Spring/Fall.
On-site lodging: No. **Rental clubs:** Yes.
Walking policy: Walking at certain times. **Range:** Yes (grass).
To obtain tee times: Call one day in advance for weekdays and Thursday at 9 a.m. for upcoming weekend.
Subscriber comments: One of the most peaceful golfing experiences I've had . . . Speed of play good, staff and service OK . . . Links nine and a wooded nine . . . Two very different nines . . . Trees make tight layout . . . Wooded nine. Open nine . . . For a new course, good shape. Will get better with seasoning . . . Pretty easy course with wide fairways . . . Flat, unimaginative greens . . . Back nine three times as difficult as front . . . Out in the country.

★★½ LIONS MUNICIPAL GOLF COURSE
PU—2901 Enfield Rd., Austin (512)477-6963.
Holes: 18. **Par:** 71/71.
Yards: 6,001/4,931. **Course rating:** N/A. **Slope:** 118/N/A.
Opened: N/A. **Pace of Play rating:** N/A. **Green fee:** N/A.
Credit cards: N/A. **Reduced fees:** Twilight.
Caddies: No. **Golf carts:** N/A.
Discount golf packages: No. **Season:** Year-round. **High:** June-Aug.
On-site lodging: No. **Rental clubs:** No.
Walking policy: N/A. **Range:** Yes.
Subscriber comments: Wonderful old Austin course, near downtown . . . Scenic, historic, challenging . . . Old tried and true muny . . . Needs work to keep it up . . . A landmark . . . Well kept for a high capacity course . . . Very slow play during summer . . . Great to walk, some of the most scenic holes ever . . . Very crowded and slow play . . . Could be magnificent with money . . . Fairways too close to major roads . . . Most fairways could use some fill dirt and thicker grass . . . Quaint muny with one of Hogan's favorite holes . . . Bunkers not a factor . . . Very slow play, lots pull carts, students . . . Playing "Hogan's Hole" is a treat.

★★★½ MARRIOTT'S GOLF CLUB AT FOSSIL CREEK

PU—3401 Clubgate Dr., Fort Worth (817)847-1900.
Holes: 18. **Par:** 72/72.
Yards: 6,865/5,066. **Course rating:** 73.6/68.5. **Slope:** 131/111.
Opened: 1987. **Pace of Play rating:** 4:30. **Green fee:** $46/60.
Credit cards: MC, V, AMEX. **Reduced fees:** Weekdays, Twilight.
Caddies: No. **Golf carts:** Included in Green Fee.
Discount golf packages: No. **Season:** Year-round. **High:** March-June/Sept.
On-site lodging: No. **Rental clubs:** Yes.
Walking policy: Mandatory cart. **Range:** Yes (grass).
To obtain tee times: Call five days in advance.
Subscriber comments: Interesting course, variety of holes . . . Course generally in great shape; good staff . . . Excellent greens . . . Outstanding condition . . . Good value, good pace, people are friendly . . . Plays differently than other locals . . . Too long and too tough for senior circuit . . . Good layout, good condition . . . Great scenery with greens on top of rock ledges . . . A real beauty . . . Good food and beverages . . . Variety and scenic . . . Nicest public access course in Southwest . . . Outstanding amenities . . . Run like a country club . . . Best public golf course in Metroplex, must try hot homemade cookies at turn . . . Good pro shop . . . Fine golf experience . . . Great job, Arnie . . . Cart path only. Could see no reason for it . . . Several impact holes . . . Geared more toward resort . . . Everything needed for a great golf day . . . Landscaping and greens in great shape . . . Great Palmer course, successful gambles rewarded, spread my ashes on No. 12.

★★ MAXWELL GOLF CLUB

PU—1002 S. 32nd St., Abilene (915)692-2737.
160 miles west of Dallas. **Holes:** 18. **Par:** 71/71.
Yards: 6,125/5,031. **Course rating:** 68.1/66.5. **Slope:** 111/105.
Opened:1930. **Pace of Play rating:** 3:30. **Green fee:** $11/15.
Credit cards: MC, V. **Reduced fees:** Twilight, Seniors, Juniors.
Caddies: No. **Golf carts:** $24 for 18 holes.
Discount golf packages: No. **Season:** Year-round. **High:** July-Aug.
On-site lodging: No. **Rental clubs:** Yes.
Walking policy: Unrestricted walking. **Range:** Yes (grass).
To obtain tee times: Call one week in advance.
Subscriber comments: Good municipal layout . . . Very high traffic, great condition . . . The guys in the golf shop really bend over backwards . . . Bent greens are fast . . . Plain course, reasonably priced.

★★ MEADOWBROOK GOLF COURSE

PU—1815 Jenson Rd., Fort Worth (817)457-4616.
Call club for further information.
Subscriber comments: Another good municipal course in Metroplex . . . Not bad, very hilly . . . Good layout, could be better taken care of . . . Great hidden greens and tight fairways . . . Short, tight, hilly . . . Many elevated approach shots . . . Nice staff . . . Some good holes, some "junk" holes . . . Good mix of easy and hard holes . . . Mostly open. Three tough holes, especially No. 5 . . . good course to practice fairway shots . . . The history of the course is the best part.

MEADOWBROOK MUNICIPAL GOLF COURSE

PU—601 Municipal Dr., Lubbock (806)765-6679.
Green fee: $10/13.
Credit cards: MC, V, DISC. **Reduced fees:** Weekdays, Twilight, Seniors, Juniors.
Caddies: No. **Golf carts:** $9 for 18 holes.
Discount golf packages: No. **Season:** Year-round. **High:** June-Oct.
On-site lodging: No. **Rental clubs:** Yes.
Walking policy: Unrestricted walking. **Range:** Yes (grass).
To obtain tee times: Call five days in advance.

★ MEADOWBROOK COURSE
Holes: 18. **Par:** 71/72.
Yards: 6,450/5,686. **Course rating:** 71.6/74.3. **Slope:** 118/N/A.
Opened: 1934. **Pace of Play rating:** 4:15.
Subscriber comments: Municipal course now under private management
. . . Best local course because it's not all flat . . . Good layout, awful
condition . . . The layout is excellent since it is in the canyon . . . Needs
maintenance . . . Could be so much . . . New management recently,
promised good things ahead.

★ SQUIRREL HOLLOW COURSE
Holes: 18. **Par:** 70/70.
Yards: 6,200/5,055. **Course rating:** 69.0/70.5. **Slope:** 113/N/A.
Opened: 1934. **Pace of Play rating:** 4:15.
Subscriber comments: The Squirrel is quite a challenge . . . Some
fairways lack definition . . . New management . . . Good layout, awful
condition . . . Play early part of year. Hot and dry in summer . . . Fairways
have more rocks than the rough . . . Expect improvements.

★★ MEMORIAL PARK GOLF COURSE
PU—1001 Memorial Loop Park E., Houston (713)862-4033.
Holes: 18. **Par:** 72/72.
Yards: 7,380/6,140. **Course rating:** N/A. **Slope:** N/A.
Opened: N/A. **Pace of Play rating:** N/A. **Green fee:** N/A.
Credit cards: N/A. **Reduced fees:** Weekdays, Twilight.
Caddies: No. **Golf carts:** N/A.
Discount golf packages: No. **Season:** Year-round. **High:** April-Aug.
On-site lodging: No. **Rental clubs:** No.
Walking policy: N/A. **Range:** N/A.
Subscriber comments: Remarkable, long, fine public layout . . .
Complete renovations underway, due to reopen fall of '95 . . . Being
revamped . . . Once was THE course . . . Being restored to original
splendor, will be one of best municipals in U.S . . . .Closed for one year for
rebuilding . . . Heavy play will increase when reopened.

★½ MESQUITE GOLF COURSE
PU—825 N. Hwy. 67, Mesquite (214)270-7457.
15 miles east of Dallas. **Holes:** 18. **Par:** 71/72.
Yards: 6,280/5,028. **Course rating:** 69.1/70.2. **Slope:** 116/113.
Opened: 1963. **Pace of Play rating:** 4:00. **Green fee:** $5/16.
Credit cards: MC, V. **Reduced fees:** Weekdays, Low season, Twilight,
Seniors, Juniors.
Caddies: No. **Golf carts:** N/A.
Discount golf packages: No. **Season:** Year-round. **High:** March-Oct.
On-site lodging: No. **Rental clubs:** Yes.
Walking policy: Unrestricted walking. **Range:** Yes (grass).
To obtain tee times: Call Thursday for Saturday, Sunday and holidays.
Weekdays call two days in advance.
Subscriber comments: Fun place to play, nice layout . . . Poor greens,
generally poorly maintained . . . Staff seems overworked . . . Fairways and
greens not in really good shape . . . No regard for pace of play, muddy in
wet weather . . . Very few memorable golf holes.

★★★½ MILL CREEK GOLF AND COUNTRY CLUB
R—Old Mill Rd., Salado (817)947-5698, (800)736-3441.
50 miles north of Austin. **Holes:** 18. **Par:** 71/73.
Yards: 6,486/5,250. **Course rating:** 72.1/69.6. **Slope:** 128/114.
Opened: 1981. **Pace of Play rating:** 4:00. **Green fee:** $35/45.
Credit cards: MC, V. **Reduced fees:** Weekdays, Resort guests.
Caddies: No. **Golf carts:** $12 for 18 holes.
Discount golf packages: Yes. **Season:** Year-round. **High:** March-Oct.
On-site lodging: Yes. **Rental clubs:** Yes.
Walking policy: Mandatory cart. **Range:** Yes (grass).
To obtain tee times: Call two days in advance.
Subscriber comments: Isolated and enjoyable . . . Beautiful course, fun,

condition was great . . . Very interesting course, creek comes in and out of play . . . Beautiful settings . . . Good pro shop . . . Well maintained, good staff . . . Nice Hill Country layout, Bermuda greens . . . Very challenging in the wind . . . Very pretty, scenic, well kept secret . . . Best golf package in Texas . . . Nice staff . . . Great setting, fun area to visit . . . Challenging with sand and water everywhere . . . Town is wonderful . . . Great atmosphere . . . Great accommodations . . . A fun course, can make the 18-handicapper look like a hero . . . One would never tire of playing this course.

★★★ MISSION DEL LAGO GOLF COURSE
PU—1250 Mission Grande, San Antonio (210)627-2522
Holes: 18. **Par:** 72/72.
Yards: 7,004/5,301. **Course rating:** 72.6/69.2. **Slope:** 127/113.
Opened: 1989. **Pace of Play rating:** 4:30. **Green fee:** $14/16.
Credit cards: All major. **Reduced fees:** Weekdays, Low season, Resort guests, Twilight, Seniors, Juniors.
Caddies: No. **Golf carts:** $16 for 18 holes.
Discount golf packages: Yes. **Season:** Year-round. **High:** March-July/Oct-Dec.
On-site lodging: No. **Rental clubs:** Yes.
Walking policy: Unrestricted walking. **Range:** Yes (grass).
To obtain tee times: Call seven days in advance.
Subscriber comments: A beautiful municipal that's not too packed . . . Outstanding city course, good condition, treated well by staff . . . Fivesomes play, too slow . . . Greens are sometimes very poor . . . Potentially a very good design . . . Challenging course in mundane setting . . . Course in good shape all year, pace good, lots of play . . . Deep bunkers and plenty of 'em . . . Wide fairway . . . Wide open. Usually easy to walk on . . . San Antonio's best muny . . . Very long, lots of water . . . Real flat, real windy . . . Beautiful during sunset . . . Humongous greens . . . A pleasant surprise.

★½ MORRIS WILLIAMS GOLF CLUB
PU—4305 Manor Rd, Austin (512)926-1298.
Holes: 18. **Par:** 72/72.
Yards: 6,636/5,273. **Course rating:** 71.5/70.4. **Slope:** 121/117.
Opened: 1964. **Pace of Play rating:** 4:12. **Green fee:** $11/13.
Credit cards: None. **Reduced fees:** Weekdays, Twilight, Seniors, Juniors.
Caddies: No. **Golf carts:** $8 for 18 holes.
Discount golf packages: Yes. **Season:** Year-round. **High:** March-Nov.
On-site lodging: No. **Rental clubs:** Yes.
Walking policy: Unrestricted walking. **Range:** Yes (grass).
To obtain tee times: Call one day in advance for weekdays and Friday a.m. for weekends and holidays.
Subscriber comments: Austin's toughest municipal . . . Flat course, very close to airport . . . Some holes need help . . . Good layout but too much play . . . Try putting with a jet 100 feet over your head . . . Golf carts in poor condition . . . Small greens test your short game . . . Need more water and grass on fairways and a marshal to keep play moving . . . A lot of up and down. Not much imagination . . . Jet noise can get to you . . . On airport glide path . . . The planes that land at the airport are spectacular from a couple of holes.

★★½ NOCONA HILLS GOLF COURSE
R—179 Country Club Drive, Nocona (817)825-3444.
Call club for further information.

FRUGAL PICK

Subscriber comments: Very pretty for northern Texas . . . Allows walking, but no one would want to. Tough to walk . . . Middle of nowhere, staff excellent . . . Fairway needs working on . . . Short and tight, could use a little better maintenance . . . Some of the best people in Texas.

★★★½ OLD ORCHARD GOLF CLUB
STABLES/BARN/RANGE
PU—13134 FM 1464, Richmond (713)277-3300.
15 miles southwest of Houston. **Holes:** 27. **Par:** 72/72/72.
Yards: 6,888/6,927/6,687. **Course rating:** 73.5/73.6/71.7. **Slope:** 130/127/124.
Opened: 1990. **Pace of Play rating:** 4:30. **Green fee:** $25/50.
Credit cards: MC, V, AMEX, Pulse Pay. **Reduced fees:** Twilight, Seniors, Juniors.
Caddies: No. **Golf carts:** Included in Green Fee.
Discount golf packages: No. **Season:** Year-round. **High:** Spring/Fall.
On-site lodging: No. **Rental clubs:** Yes.
Walking policy: Unrestricted walking. **Range:** Yes (grass).
To obtain tee times: Call or come in up to six days in advance.
Subscriber comments: Two of three nines tight and tree lined . . . Big problem with leaves in fall . . . Excellent condition, fine staff . . . Stables/Barn combination wonderful . . . Tight fairways surrounded by huge pecan trees, slow play during peak times . . . Fun, not overplayed . . . Fabulous 27 holes, but the barbecue at the turn, wow! . . . Clubhouse friendly . . . Good facilities . . . Forget Range nine, other two much better . . . Wooded with some sand and water . . . Winding through pecan orchard . . . Fast greens in mid-summer. Impressive . . . Range is average. Barn/Stables is outstanding . . . Prettiest and best public course in the area.

★½ OLMOS BASIN GOLF CLUB
PU—7022 N. McCullough, San Antonio (210)826-4041.
Call club for further information.
Subscriber comments: Long par 3s, generally good greens . . . A few decent holes . . . Heavy play, not always in shape . . . Flat, easy walker . . . Very crowded, poorly maintained, greens need lot of work . . . Fairways are like concrete . . . Not bad, not good.

★½ OSO BEACH MUNICIPAL GOLF COURSE
PU—5601 S. Alameda, Corpus Christi (512)991-5351.
Holes: 18. **Par:** 70/70.
Yards: 6,223/4,994. **Course rating:** 69.9/68.8. **Slope:** 119/118.
Opened: 1938. **Pace of Play rating:** 4:00. **Green fee:** $9/11.
Credit cards: MC, V. **Reduced fees:** Twilight, Seniors, Juniors.
Caddies: No. **Golf carts:** $7 for 18 holes.
Discount golf packages: No. **Season:** Year-round. **High:** Jan.-April.
On-site lodging: No. **Rental clubs:** Yes.
Walking policy: Walking at certain times. **Range:** No.
To obtain tee times: Call Wednesday for Saturday and Sunday.
Subscriber comments: Good layout, very small greens, usually windy . . . Staff is friendly and helpful, pace of play slow on weekends . . . Greens erratically kept . . . Mosquitoes everywhere, uneven layout . . . Poor condition year round . . . Some long rounds (five hours), lots of water, poor sand traps . . . Open course with some damage on fairways . . . Don't fear the water.

★★★★½ PAINTED DUNES DESERT GOLF COURSE
PU—12000 McCombs, El Paso (915)821-2122.
Holes: 18. **Par:** 72/72.
Yards: 6,925/5,717. **Course rating:** 74.0/74.5. **Slope:** 137/123.
Opened: 1991. **Pace of Play rating:** 4:15. **Green fee:** $9/16.
Credit cards: MC, V, AMEX. **Reduced fees:** Twilight, Seniors, Juniors.
Caddies: No. **Golf carts:** $9 for 18 holes.
Discount golf packages: No. **Season:** Year-round. **High:** April-May/Sept.
On-site lodging: No. **Rental clubs:** Yes.
Walking policy: Unrestricted walking. **Range:** Yes (grass).
To obtain tee times: Call up seven days in advance for weekdays and call Monday starting at 7 a.m. for upcoming weekend.
Subscriber comments: Fantastic course, not much water, lots of bunkers

. . . Well-designed course . . . Bring plenty of golf balls if you can't hit them straight . . . Well laid out desert course . . . Desert dirt and hills and water . . . Pleasant pros . . . Nice facilities, nice staff . . . Punishing roughs, play a little slow on weekends . . . This is best course in El Paso . . . Great golf year round . . . Beautiful fairways, but if you're not in it you are in the desert . . . None better at same price . . . Wow! What a course . . . I don't think there are many private clubs that are better . . . What an experience, country club golf on a beer salary . . . El Paso needs more courses like this one . . . A bit too "deserty" . . . Will make you concentrate off the box . . . Best in West Texas.

★★½ PALO DURO CREEK COUNTRY CLUB

SP—50 Country Club Dr., Canyon (806)655-1106.
Call club for further information.
Subscriber comments: Good layout . . . Needs permanent restrooms and water facilities . . . Poor maintenance, lots of water on back nine . . . Needs more watering in fairways . . . Staff friendly. Back nine a real challenge.

★½ PASADENA MUNICIPAL GOLF COURSE

PU—1000 Duffer, Houston (713)481-0834.
Holes: 18. **Par:** 72/72.
Yards: 6,750/4,910. **Course rating:** 72.2/67.9. **Slope:** 118/108.
Opened: 1978. **Pace of Play rating:** 4:00. **Green fee:** $6/10.
Credit cards: MC, V. **Reduced fees:** Weekdays, Twilight, Seniors, Juniors.
Caddies: No. **Golf carts:** $8 for 18 holes.
Discount golf packages: No. **Season:** Year-round. **High:** March-Aug.
On-site lodging: No. **Rental clubs:** Yes.
Walking policy: Unrestricted walking. **Range:** Yes (grass).
To obtain tee times: Call 7:30 a.m. Wednesday for weekend/holiday tee times.
Subscriber comments: Hard to walk, good bargain . . . Convoluted layout from green to next tee box . . . Extreme walks from some greens to tees (600 yards or more) . . . Always in good shape, lots of water, helpful staff . . . Not marked well . . . Airbase noise distracting . . . Fairways need to be built up for better drainage . . . Weirdest layout of holes I've seen. Ride a cart . . . Long and windy, a lot of water, service and pace very good.

PEACH TREE GOLF CLUB

SP—6212 CR 152 W., Bullard (903)894-7079.
9 miles south of Tyler. **Green fee:** $14/25.
Credit cards: MC, V, DISC. **Reduced fees:** Weekdays, Twilight, Seniors.
Caddies: No. **Golf carts:** $9 for 18 holes.
Discount golf packages: No. **Season:** Year-round. **High:** April-Sept.
On-site lodging: No. **Rental clubs:** Yes.
Walking policy: Unrestricted walking. **Range:** Yes (grass).
To obtain tee times: Call six days in advance.

★★★½ OAKHURST COURSE
Holes: 18. **Par:** 72/72.
Yards: 6,813/5,086. **Course rating:** 72.1/68.4. **Slope:** 126/113.
Opened: 1993. **Pace of Play rating:** 4:00.
Subscriber comments: Outstanding course . . . Beautiful new course . . . Will be great in a couple of years . . . Staff and service very good . . . Huge greens, up and coming course, exciting . . . Hard No. 16 . . . Some greens unrealistic . . . Good for iron play, short course . . . Top notch layout with laid-back country atmosphere . . . Nice but hard greens, lots of water . . . Has a lot of possibilities.

★½ PEACH TREE COURSE
Holes: 18. **Par:** 70/71.
Yards: 5,556/4,467. **Course rating:** 65.7/65.5. **Slope:** 109/113.
Opened: 1986. **Pace of Play rating:** 3:45. **Green fee:** $10/14.
Credit cards: MC, V, DISC. **Reduced fees:** Weekdays, Twilight, Seniors, Juniors.

Subscriber comments: First attempt at golf course development for Peach Tree . . . Definitely not manicured . . . Easy, no need for long irons, many eagle holes . . . Tees and greens need work . . . Service good, set your own pace . . . Play when you need a boost to your game . . . Popular with seniors.

★★★½ PECAN VALLEY GOLF CLUB

PU—4700 Pecan Valley Dr., San Antonio (210)333-9018, (800)336-3418.
Holes: 18. **Par:** 71/72.
Yards: 7,071/5,621. **Course rating:** 73.9/71.3. **Slope:** 136/113.
Opened: 1963. **Pace of Play rating:** 4:20. **Green fee:** $30/55.
Credit cards: MC, V, AMEX. **Reduced fees:** Weekdays, Low season, Twilight, Seniors, Juniors.
Caddies: No. **Golf carts:** Included in Green Fee.
Discount golf packages: No. **Season:** Year-round. **High:** Spring/Fall.
On-site lodging: No. **Rental clubs:** Yes.
Walking policy: Mandatory cart. **Range:** Yes (grass).
To obtain tee times: Call two weeks in advance with credit card or one month in advance through hotel.
Ranked in Second 25 of America's 75 Best Public Golf Courses by Golf Digest.

Subscriber comments: Press Maxwell design, mature trees make it more challenging than '68 PGA conditions . . . Still a good course but living in the past . . . Not in as good of shape as others . . . All players treated A-1; winter, course in super shape . . . Best suited for long driver, greens putt true and fast . . . Fine old course . . . History contributes to fun . . . Old minimalism, big trees, great tradition . . . Requires good course management to score well . . . Long, tight course lined with gorgeous oak and pecan trees. If your putter isn't working the greens here will eat your lunch . . . Overgrown and in need of tree trimmers . . . Still one of top courses in the country . . . Course excellent, clubhouse shabby . . . Doglegs and elevation variance fun . . . San Antonio's Colonial . . . Best old course in city . . . Very friendly staff . . . No gimmicks, just good golf . . . I tried the putt at 18 that Arnold Palmer missed in '68; I missed too.

PECAN VALLEY GOLF COURSE

PU—6400 Pecan Dr., Fort Worth (817)249-1845.
Holes: 18. **Par:** 72/72.
Yards: 6,577/5,275. **Course rating:** 71.4/69.7. **Slope:** 128/115.
Opened: N/A. **Pace of Play rating:** 4:30. **Green fee:** $11/13.
Credit cards: All major. **Reduced fees:** Weekdays, Low season, Twilight, Seniors, Juniors.
Caddies: No. **Golf carts:** $16 for 18 holes.
Discount golf packages: Yes. **Season:** Year-round. **High:** April-Nov.
On-site lodging: No. **Rental clubs:** Yes.
Walking policy: Unrestricted walking. **Range:** Yes (grass).
To obtain tee times: Call Monday at noon for that week.

★★ HILLS COURSE

Subscriber comments: Nice municipal . . . Wide open, three good holes . . . Decent course, plays long, greens always in bad shape . . . Thin on fairway grass, good for crowded public course . . . Staff was excellent . . . Always able to get on. Friendly . . . Good course in summer, average in winter . . . Landscaping not as good as River course.

★★½ RIVER COURSE

Holes: 18. **Par:** 71/72.
Yards: 6,562/5,419. **Course rating:** 71.3/69.6. **Slope:** 124/109.
Opened: N/A. **Pace of Play rating:** 4:30.
Subscriber comments: Course is old and trees are established, long and pretty tough driving holes . . . Crowded, long waits, play slow, good

greens . . . Fun to play . . . Great layout, challenging, easy to walk . . . Course with character . . . Well maintained, beautifully wooded, surprisingly fast, courteously staffed . . . Better than Hills . . . One of the best courses in Fort Worth area . . . Easiest decent course in Metroplex to obtain a weekend tee time.

PHEASANT TRAILS GOLF COURSE★
PU—Hwy. 119, Dumas (806)935-7375.
45 miles north of Amarillo. **Holes:** 18. **Par:** 71/71.
Yards: 6,481/5,292. **Course rating:** 69.5/70.5. **Slope:** 111/117.
Opened: 1945. **Pace of Play rating:** 4:12. **Green fee:** $8/10.
Credit cards: MC, V. **Reduced fees:** Twilight, Juniors.
Caddies: No. **Golf carts:** $17 for 18 holes.
Discount golf packages: No. **Season:** Year-round. **High:** March-Nov.
On-site lodging: No. **Rental clubs:** Yes.
Walking policy: Unrestricted walking. **Range:** Yes (grass).
To obtain tee times: Call Friday for weekend.

★★ PHILLIPS COUNTRY CLUB
PU—Sterling Rd., Borger (806)274-6812.
Call club for further information.
Subscriber comments: Nicely matured course, nice staff, could improve pro shop . . . Excellent greens . . . Native grass fairways . . . Short, results in many birdies . . . The course has improved since last year, fairways are much better.

PINE RIDGE GOLF COURSE★
PU—Pine Mill Rd., Paris (903)785-8076.
56 miles east of Sherman. **Holes:** 18. **Par:** 72/72.
Yards: 5,855/4,462. **Course rating:** N/A. **Slope:** N/A.
Opened: 1987. **Pace of Play rating:** 4:00. **Green fee:** $7/9.
Credit cards: MC, V, DISC. **Reduced fees:** Weekdays.
Caddies: No. **Golf carts:** $15 for 18 holes.
Discount golf packages: No. **Season:** Year-round. **High:** April-Oct.
On-site lodging: No. **Rental clubs:** Yes.
Walking policy: Unrestricted walking. **Range:** Yes (grass).
To obtain tee times: Call for weekends.

PINNACLE COUNTRY CLUB★
SP—200 Pinnacle Club Dr., Mabank (903)451-9797.
60 miles southeast of Dallas. **Holes:** 18. **Par:** 71/71.
Yards: 6,641/5,222. **Course rating:** 72.9/70.8. **Slope:** 135/129.
Opened: 1988. **Pace of Play rating:** 4:00. **Green fee:** $16/24.
Credit cards: MC, V, AMEX. **Reduced fees:** Weekdays, Twilight, Seniors.
Caddies: No. **Golf carts:** $8 for 18 holes.
Discount golf packages: Yes. **Season:** Year-round. **High:** March-Aug.
On-site lodging: No. **Rental clubs:** Yes.
Walking policy: Walking at certain times. **Range:** Yes (grass).
To obtain tee times: Call three days in advance.

★★ PLANO MUNICIPAL GOLF COURSE
PU—4501 E. 14th St., Plano (214)423-5444.
Call club for further information
Subscriber comments: Open fairways, but still challenging enough to improve one's game . . . Tough final holes eat people up . . . Good during hot, dry summer, marshland when wet . . . Made some great recent improvements . . . Ruined by redesigning of No. 14 and No. 17 . . . Heavy year round play, poor drainage . . . Some creative holes . . . Summertime "Bakeouts" . . . Fairly easy driver, wedge . . . 16 through 18 a real challenge . . . Good staff and service.

★★ PLANTATION RESORT GOLF CLUB
PU—4701 Plantation Lane, Frisco (214)335-4653.
20 miles north of Dallas. **Holes:** 18. **Par:** 72/72.
Yards: 6,382/5,945. **Course rating:** N/A. **Slope:** 122/117.
Opened: N/A. **Pace of Play rating:** N/A. **Green fee:** $/A.
Credit cards: MC, V, AMEX. **Reduced fees:** Weekdays, Twilight.
Caddies: No. **Golf carts:** Included in Green Fee.
Discount golf packages: Yes. **Season:** Year-round. **High:** Year-round.
On-site lodging: No. **Rental clubs:** No.
Walking policy: N/A. **Range:** Yes (grass).
Subscriber comments: Shot placement course . . . Wind always blows
. . . Lots of water, good greens, lots of layup holes . . . Little challenge . . .
Wonderful course for the Sunday hacker . . . Play is much too slow on
weekends . . . Leave driver at home . . . Keeping ball in fairway a
premium, good clubhouse . . . Too many tee shots require irons, too many
mounded greens with water in front and back . . . Six-minute tee times, too
many houses along fairways, felt like golfing in someone's backyard . . .
Routed through housing canyons . . . Water everywhere . . . Subdivision
course . . . No walking . . . More scenery in the parking lot . . . Too many
straight holes . . . Short holes but lots of water . . . Very easy, sociable
course, good staff.

★★★★ THE QUARRY GOLF CLUB
PU—444 E. Basse Rd., San Antonio (210)824-4500.
Holes: 18. **Par:** 71/71.
Yards: 6,740/4,897. **Course rating:** 71.0/67.0. **Slope:** 122/110.
Opened: 1993. **Pace of Play rating:** 4:15. **Green fee:** $55/65.
Credit cards: All major. **Reduced fees:** Twilight.
Caddies: Yes. **Golf carts:** Included in Green Fee.
Discount golf packages: No. **Season:** Year-round. **High:** March-Nov.
On-site lodging: No. **Rental clubs:** Yes.
Walking policy: Unrestricted walking. **Range:** Yes (grass).
To obtain tee times: Call seven days in advance with credit card.
Ranked 4th in Texas by Golf Digest.
Subscriber comments: Everything I'd heard; a must to play . . . Fantastic
staff, very playable, outstanding condition . . . Tricked up . . . Back nine
outstanding . . . Out of price range for many, but worth playing at least
once . . . Lovely dining room . . . All around great . . . Very interesting,
but price makes it one-timer . . . Interesting concept, rock quarry, caddie
very helpful . . . Remarkable . . . Awesome tee shots in quarry holes . . .
Back nine takes guts . . . Outstanding, loved it, best ever . . . Boring front
nine compared to back . . . Unique holes on back . . . Breathtaking scenery
. . . Worth every dollar . . . Tough. Tough. Tough . . . Unbelievably
good for a new course . . . Back nine is one of most unique layouts ever
. . . Spectacular course in Quarry nine . . . Super new course . . . The back
nine make you forget the front completely . . . Service great, it seems like a
resort course . . . One of the most interesting courses in the country . . .
Worth a little more . . . Best public course in Texas.

★★★½ THE RANCH COUNTRY CLUB
SP—5901 Glen Oaks Dr., McKinney (214)529-5990.
15 miles north of Dallas. **Holes:** 18. **Par:** 72/72.
Yards: 7,087/5,053. **Course rating:** 73.8/69.4. **Slope:** 130/117.
Opened: 1988. **Pace of Play rating:** 4:00. **Green fee:** $30/50.
Credit cards: MC, V. **Reduced fees:** Weekdays, Low season, Resort
guests, Twilight.
Caddies: No. **Golf carts:** $12 for 18 holes.
Discount golf packages: Yes. **Season:** Year-round. **High:** May-Sept.
On-site lodging: Yes. **Rental clubs:** Yes.
Walking policy: Unrestricted walking. **Range:** Yes (grass).
To obtain tee times: Call three days in advance starting at noon.
Subscriber comments: Fine Arthur Hills design always in good shape . . .
Outstanding design, great condition . . . Nice pro-shop, poor service in
restaurant . . . Good facilities . . . Links type course, well maintained year-

round . . . Beautiful par 3s . . . Neat course, good staff, lots of blind shots
. . . Large beautiful greens and bunkers . . . Challenging Arthur Hills
design. Great amenities . . . Very interesting layout . . . Well maintained,
challenging . . . Great people in pro shop. Restaurant is a great place to eat
. . . Tough, exciting layout . . . Probably best kept secret in Texas.

RANCHO VIEJO RESORT AND COUNTRY CLUB

R—No. 1 Rancho Viejo Dr., Rancho Viejo (210)350-4000.
3 miles north of Brownsville. **Green fee:** $35/40.
Credit cards: MC, V, AMEX. **Reduced fees:** Resort guests.
Caddies: No. **Golf carts:** $12 for 18 holes.
Discount golf packages: Yes. **Season:** Year-round. **High:** Oct-May.
On-site lodging: Yes. **Rental clubs:** Yes.
Walking policy: Walking at certain times. **Range:** Yes (grass).
To obtain tee times: Resort guests 30 days in advance.

★★½ EL ANGEL COURSE

Holes: 18. **Par:** 70/70.
Yards: 6,518/4,776. **Course rating:** 71.5/67.6. **Slope:** 120/113.
Opened: 1971. **Pace of Play rating:** 3:30.
Subscriber comments: Tough in windy conditions . . . Planted many
trees in past year . . . Staff very good . . . Overbooked mostly . . . Could
be great resort course, but maintenance has gone downhill . . . Nice service,
old clientele . . . For South Texas, these are decent resort-type courses.

★★½ EL DIABLO COURSE

Holes: 18. **Par:** 70/71.
Yards: 6,847/5,197. **Course rating:** 73.7/70.7. **Slope:** 129/122.
Opened: 1971. **Pace of Play rating:** 3:30.
Subscriber comments: Course lives up to its name . . . Good service and
accommodations . . . Longer, tighter than El Angel . . . Good course,
excellent staff, good pace . . . Best course in lower valley . . . Sand traps
need work . . . Flat and hard, not much character, too cramped . . .
Challenging, well maintained course . . . If you play only one, make it El
Diablo.

★★★ RATLIFF RANCH GOLF LINKS

PU—7500 N. Grandview, Odessa (915)368-4653.
Holes: 18. **Par:** 72/72.
Yards: 6,800/4,900. **Course rating:** 73.0/68.9. **Slope:** 122/110.
Opened: 1988. **Pace of Play rating:** 4:00. **Green fee:** $10/15.
Credit cards: MC, V, DISC. **Reduced fees:** Weekdays, Twilight,
Seniors, Juniors.
Caddies: No. **Golf carts:** $8 for 18 holes.
Discount golf packages: No. **Season:** Year-round. **High:** March-Sept.
On-site lodging: No. **Rental clubs:** Yes.
Walking policy: Unrestricted walking. **Range:** Yes (grass).
To obtain tee times: Call Wednesday for upcoming weekend or holiday.
Subscriber comments: Good links course . . . Lots of scrub, balls out of
fairway, say bye . . . Plenty of sand and water . . . Good food. Nice staff
. . . Layout is fantastic, greens very undulating, also well trapped . . . On
some holes the fairways and rough lack sufficient turf . . . No trees . . .
Good greens, with new water system. Watch this for the future.

★★★½ RAYBURN COUNTRY CLUB AND RESORT
BLUE/GOLD/GREEN

R—1000 Wingate Blvd., Sam Rayburn (409)698-2958, (800)882-1442.
82 miles north of Beaumont. **Holes:** 27. **Par:** 72/72/72.
Yards: 6,731/6,719/6,728. **Course rating:** 71.3/72.5/72.2. **Slope:**
116/129/124.
Opened: 1967. **Pace of Play rating:** 4:00. **Green fee:** $28/35.
Credit cards: All major. **Reduced fees:** Weekdays, Low season, Twilight,
Juniors.
Caddies: No. **Golf carts:** $20 for 18 holes.
Discount golf packages: Yes. **Season:** Year-round. **High:** Spring/Fall.
On-site lodging: Yes. **Rental clubs:** Yes.

Walking policy: Walking at certain times. **Range:** Yes (grass).
To obtain tee times: Call pro shop.
Subscriber comments: Three distinctly different nines, Gold and Green best . . . Course always in great condition, best resort in Southeast Texas . . . All levels of difficulty, fast pace, superb staff . . . Very challenging, many blind shots . . . Grass in rough impossible for average player . . . High grass around greens is ridiculous . . . Food in restaurant is excellent . . . Blue and Gold challenging, Green is shotmaker's course . . . Too bad it's so far from civilization . . . Fairways up and down . . . Old type course, good area, pine trees . . . Rolling, woodsy, three good designers . . . Best kept secret in Texas. I hope it doesn't change.

★★★ RIO COLORADO GOLF COURSE

PU—FM 2668 and Riverside Pk., Bay City (409)244-2955.
80 miles south of Houston. **Holes:** 18. **Par:** 72/72.
Yards: 6,824/5,020. **Course rating:** 73.1/69.1. **Slope:** 127/116.
Opened: 1993. **Pace of Play rating:** 4:00. **Green fee:** $16/21.
Credit cards: MC, V, AMEX. **Reduced fees:** Low season, Twilight, Seniors, Juniors.
Caddies: No. **Golf carts:** $9 for 18 holes.
Discount golf packages: Yes. **Season:** Year-round. **High:** April-Oct.
On-site lodging: No. **Rental clubs:** Yes.
Walking policy: Unrestricted walking. **Range:** Yes (grass).
To obtain tee times: Call two days in advance at 8 a.m. for weekend and holidays.
Subscriber comments: What a find! . . . Best public course on midcoastal plain . . . Excellent municipal golf, nine holes links-style, nine holes wooded . . . Watch out during heavy rain, place floods terribly . . . New layout imitates a links-type with four holes in woods, fun place . . . Front nine, sneaky, tough; back nine, pretty . . . Good hamburgers . . . Front and back nines totally different . . . Staff is very helpful.

(FRUGAL PICK)

★★½ RIVER BEND GOLF CLUB

R—Rte. 8, Brownsville (210)548-0192.
Holes: 18. **Par:** 72/72.
Yards: 6,828/5,836. **Course rating:** 71.9/67.5. **Slope:** 113/104.
Opened: 1985. **Pace of Play rating:** 3:50. **Green fee:** $15.
Credit cards: MC, V. **Reduced fees:** No.
Caddies: No. **Golf carts:** $8 for 18 holes.
Discount golf packages: Yes. **Season:** Year-round. **High:** Nov.-March.
On-site lodging: Yes. **Rental clubs:** Yes.
Walking policy: Walking at certain times. **Range:** Yes (grass).
To obtain tee times: For weekends, call Wednesday 8 a.m. For weekdays, start calling Monday 8 a.m.
Subscriber comments: Very nice setting along Rio Grande, several water holes . . . One of top courses in Rio Grande Valley . . . Greens usually overwatered . . . Beautiful fairways and greens . . . Fairways marginal, greens OK . . . Tough par 3s . . . Very few amenities . . . Too many long-into-the wind holes . . . Long, open, and lots of sand on front nine. Trees on back nine . . . Unique layout . . . River location adds to atmosphere . . . Delightful surprise . . . Long course to walk.

★★ RIVER CREEK PARK GOLF COURSE

PU—FM 1177, Burkburnett (817)855-3361.
10 miles north of Wichita Falls. **Holes:** 18. **Par:** 71/73.
Yards: 6,800/5,100. **Course rating:** 69.0/69.1. **Slope:** 104/104.
Opened: N/A. **Pace of Play rating:** 4:00. **Green fee:** $7/8.
Credit cards: MC, V. **Reduced fees:** Twilight, Seniors, Juniors.
Caddies: No. **Golf carts:** $10 for 18 holes.
Discount golf packages: No. **Season:** Year-round. **High:** May-July.
On-site lodging: No. **Rental clubs:** Yes.
Walking policy: Unrestricted walking. **Range:** Yes (grass).
To obtain tee times: Call up to one week in advance.
Subscriber comments: Great greens, but poor fairways, no bunkers . . .

Staff is helpful and polite . . . Wide open course, permits fast play, not real challenging . . . Not a lot of trouble . . . So-so course, nice bent grass greens . . . Very cheap. Very wide open. Very windy. Very dry. Don't light a match.

★★★½ RIVER PLACE GOLF CLUB

SP—4207 River Place Blvd., Austin (512)346-6784.
Holes: 18. **Par:** 71/71.
Yards: 6,611/4,878. **Course rating:** 72.0/65.5. **Slope:** 128/113.
Opened: 1984. **Pace of Play rating:** 4:30. **Green fee:** $40/50.
Credit cards: MC, V, AMEX. **Reduced fees:** Twilight, Seniors, Juniors.
Caddies: No. **Golf carts:** Included in Green Fee.
Discount golf packages: No. **Season:** Year-round. **High:** March–Oct.
On-site lodging: No. **Rental clubs:** Yes.
Walking policy: Mandatory cart. **Range:** Yes (grass).
To obtain tee times: Call seven days in advance for weekdays; call Wednesday for upcoming weekend.
Subscriber comments: Tom Kite design, many elevation changes . . . Absolutely beautiful, not too long, a real pleasure to play . . . Beautiful view, narrow fairways . . . Beautiful condition, good value, great service . . . Brutally hot in summer . . . Hilly target golf at its best . . . Difficult, but terrific Hill Country views . . . Excellent staff, course is maintained well . . . You will enjoy scenic views . . . Tough putting . . . Cart-path-only rule for carts makes playing an endurance test . . . Every hole is a postcard, bring extra balls . . . Lots of blind shots . . . Great course if playing well, a really long day if you're not . . . Hazards galore . . . Carts in awful shape . . . What a track . . . Difficult but playable . . . Flatlanders, better have a bag of balls . . . Miss the fairway, you're dead! . . . Private club atmosphere and amenities . . . Excellent clubhouse and snack bar . . . Uneven fairway lies . . . Every hole seems to have a canyon, ravine, or gully . . . Beautiful but tough, especially when windy . . . No level ground, even on tees . . . Loved the elevation changes from tee to green . . . Hole for hole, prettiest course in Texas.

★★½ RIVERCHASE GOLF CLUB

PU—700 Riverchase Dr., Coppell (214)462-8281.
5 miles northwest of Dallas. **Holes:** 18. **Par:** 71/71.
Yards: 6,593/6,041. **Course rating:** N/A. **Slope:** 124/114.
Opened: N/A. **Pace of Play rating:** N/A. **Green fee:** N/A.
Credit cards: MC, V, AMEX. **Reduced fees:** Weekdays, Low season, Twilight.
Caddies: No. **Golf carts:** N/A.
Discount golf packages: No. **Season:** Year-round. **High:** April–Oct.
On-site lodging: No. **Rental clubs:** No.
Walking policy: N/A. **Range:** Yes.
Subscriber comments: Hilly, deceptively hard, windy . . . Floods during rains . . . Best municipal greens one could expect . . . Lots of water on almost every hole . . . Some houses are too close to the fairways . . . Good conditions, open layout off tee . . . Has a few holes that were crammed in . . . Excellent staff and facilities . . . No imagination, not scenic . . . Windy all the time . . . Speeding up play would make it better . . . Par 5s reachable, wide open on most drives . . . Easy to get on . . . Little character, except for 10th hole . . . Like the bent greens. Some interesting holes . . . Too much water and close out-of-bounds . . . No trees to speak of . . . Lots of sand . . . Make every effort to get you a tee time. Food and beverage service very good.

★★ RIVERSIDE GOLF CLUB

PU—2600 N. Randolph, San Angelo (915)653-6130.
Call club for further information.
Subscriber comments: Typical West Texas course, well maintained . . .

The staff really tries to make you feel at home . . . Packed all the time . . . Tight fairways. Small greens. Very nice course. Not a lot of hazards. Limited staff and service . . . Be prepared to stay awhile . . . Best game in town.

★★★ RIVERSIDE GOLF CLUB

PU—3000 Riverside Pkwy., Grand Prairie (817)640-7800.
20 miles west of Dallas. **Holes:** 18. **Par:** 72/72.
Yards: 7,025/5,175. **Course rating:** 74.4/69.5. **Slope:** 132/113.
Opened: 1984. **Pace of Play rating:** 4:30. **Green fee:** $40/55.
Credit cards: MC, V, AMEX. **Reduced fees:** Weekdays, Twilight, Seniors, Juniors.
Caddies: No. **Golf carts:** Included in Green Fee.
Discount golf packages: No. **Season:** Year-round. **High:** March–Oct.
On-site lodging: No. **Rental clubs:** Yes.
Walking policy: Walking at certain times. **Range:** Yes (grass).
To obtain tee times: Call three days in advance. Credit card required to hold weekend reservation. Times are available farther out with prepayment of full amount.
Subscriber comments: Not bad for a flood plain; when dry it is a good deal . . . Good value, nice range, water holes are difficult, with island green on No. 18 . . . Lots of golfers and traffic, need a cart . . . Best outings, accommodating people . . . Bent grass greens and overseeding make it a good choice in off season . . . Can wave hello to the pilots on approach to DFW . . . Challenging course . . . Need escalators to greens . . . Too many balls to the water monsters . . . Good combination of water and sand . . . Creative course . . . Fantastic greens . . . Good test but gets flooded . . . Last hole difficult into wind . . . Several really neat holes . . . Keep this one above water and they will come.

★★½ RIVERSIDE GOLF COURSE
BLUE/RED/WHITE

PU—302 McWright Rd., Victoria (512)573-4521.
Call club for further information.
Subscriber comments: Just a nice all-around course . . . This course was made for the long hitter . . . Blue nine best . . . Very mature course. Large trees. No range . . . Course varies sporadically from good to very poor . . . Well kept for public course.

★★ RIVERSIDE GOLF COURSE

PU—1020 Grove Blvd., Austin (512)389-1070.
Holes: 18. **Par:** 71/71.
Yards: 6,562/5,334. **Course rating:** 70.3/69.6. **Slope:** 122/112.
Opened: 1948. **Pace of Play rating:** 4:00. **Green fee:** $12/16.
Credit cards: MC, V, AMEX. **Reduced fees:** Weekdays, Twilight, Seniors, Juniors.
Caddies: No. **Golf carts:** $10 for 18 holes.
Discount golf packages: No. **Season:** Year-round. **High:** May–Aug.
On-site lodging: No. **Rental clubs:** Yes.
Walking policy: Unrestricted walking. **Range:** No.
To obtain tee times: Call three days in advance.
Subscriber comments: Original Austin Country Club, excellent for visitors . . . Where Crenshaw and Kite learned to play . . . Good staff, course in good condition . . . Original holes, a good layout, course on rebound . . . Poor marshaling, always a wait on weekends . . . Original design whittled down to accommodate a college . . . Part of the layout (first nine) is good . . . Classic Perry Maxwell design . . . Fairways were beat . . . Maintenance is a problem, no range . . . Original Austin Country Club holes are outstanding . . . Course needs a sprinkler system . . . Too heavily used . . . Great old oaks . . . Easily walked . . . Still maintains some of the magic of Harvey Penick . . . Trying to squeeze out the last blood of this course . . . Not what it used to be according to oldtimers . . . Back to back par 3s, then you go back to back par 5s . . . Some holes rerouted . . . needs to be restored to the glory that it once had.

★★½ RIVERSIDE MUNICIPAL GOLF COURSE

PU—203 McDonald, San Antonio (210)533-8371.
Holes: 18. **Par:** 72/72.
Yards: 6,729/5,730. **Course rating:** 72.0/72.0. **Slope:** 128/121.
Opened: 1929. **Pace of Play rating:** 4:30. **Green fee:** $6/16.
Credit cards: All major. **Reduced fees:** Weekdays, Low season, Resort guests, Twilight, Seniors, Juniors.
Caddies: No. **Golf carts:** $15 for 18 holes.
Discount golf packages: Yes. **Season:** Year-round. **High:** April-Sept.
On-site lodging: No. **Rental clubs:** Yes.
Walking policy: Unrestricted walking. **Range:** No.
To obtain tee times: May call up to a week in advance.
Also 9-hole par-3 course.
Subscriber comments: Tight, tough, old-style needing better maintenance . . . Staff friendly . . . Easy course if you stay out of trees . . . greens better than average . . . Great weekday play . . . Fairways need attention . . . Many big trees . . . Best par 5s in town.

ROCKWOOD GOLF COURSE
★½ RED/WHITE COURSE

PU—1851 Jacksboro Hwy., Fort Worth (817)624-1771.
Holes: 18. **Par:** 71.
Yards: 6,340/5,556. **Course rating:** 72.0/N.A. **Slope:** 115/N.A.
Opened: 1940. **Pace of Play rating:** 4:15. **Green fee:** $12/14.
Credit cards: MC, V, AMEX. **Reduced fees:** Weekdays, Twilight, Seniors, Juniors.
Caddies: No. **Golf carts:** $17 for 18 holes.
Discount golf packages: No. **Season:** Year-round. **High:** March-Oct.
On-site lodging: No. **Rental clubs:** Yes.
Walking policy: Unrestricted walking. **Range:** Yes (grass).
To obtain tee times: Call seven days in advance.
Subscriber comments: A four-hour course most of the time . . . Long, straight par 4s . . . Used to be one of best munys in town . . . Nothing noteworthy . . . Easy walking . . . Red and White OK but Blue needs work . . . Staff always pleasant, good pace.
BLUE COURSE★
Holes: 9 (played twice). **Par:** 72/76.
Yards: 7,200/5,928. **Course rating:** 69/N.A. **Slope:** 112/N.A.

★★ ROLLING HILL GOLF CLUB

R—P.O. Box 1242, Hilltop Lakes (409)855-2100.
38 miles northeast of Bryan-College Station. **Holes:** 18. **Par:** 72/73.
Yards: 6,330/5,635. **Course rating:** 70.1/71.5. **Slope:** 111/117.
Opened: 1958. **Pace of Play rating:** 4:00. **Green fee:** $14/17.
Credit cards: MC, V, AMEX. **Reduced fees:** No.
Caddies: No. **Golf carts:** $16 for 18 holes.
Discount golf packages: No. **Season:** Year-round. **High:** May-Aug.
On-site lodging: Yes. **Rental clubs:** Yes.
Walking policy: Unrestricted walking. **Range:** Yes grass).
To obtain tee times: Call pro shop.
Subscriber comments: Long-iron course . . . Fine Hill Country golf. Very courteous staff . . . Could use better maintenance for a resort course . . . Greens are excellent, never crowded.

ROSS ROGERS GOLF CLUB

PU—722 N.W. 24th St., Amarillo (806)378-3086.
Green fee: $8/9.
Credit cards: MC, V, DISC. **Reduced fees:** Weekdays, Seniors, Juniors.
Caddies: No. **Golf carts:** $16 for 18 holes.
Discount golf packages: No. **Season:** Year-round. **High:** May-Oct.
On-site lodging: No. **Rental clubs:** Yes.
Walking policy: Unrestricted walking. **Range:** Yes (grass).
To obtain tee times: Call or come in.

★★½ EAST COURSE
Holes: 18. **Par:** 72/72
Yards: 6,858/5,575. **Course rating:** 70.8/69.5. **Slope:** 112/111.
Opened: 1938. **Pace of Play rating:** 4:00
Subscriber comments: Pretty good municipal . . . Course overall good; greens, tees, fairways need to be mowed more frequently . . . Course was shaggy . . . Good staff and pace of play, too busy in summer . . . West easy, East tough . . . Could use some natural grasses to perk up some of the prairie and rock roughs . . . Staff works you in very quickly if you do not have a tee time . . . No sand . . . Well watered all year . . . Easy to walk . . . More challenging than West Course . . . West old style, easy; East modern, tough . . . Wide open, you won't lose too many balls here . . . Not shabby for West Texas municipal.

WEST COURSE★
Holes: 18. **Par:** 72/72.
Yards: 6,602/5,392. **Course rating:** 69.2/68.2. **Slope:** 110/108.
Opened: 1938. **Pace of Play rating:** 4:00.

ROY KIZER GOLF COURSE★
PU—5400 Jimmy Clay Dr., Austin (512)444-0999.
Holes: 18. **Par:** 71/71.
Yards: 6,749/5,018. **Course rating:** N/A. **Slope:** N/A .
Opened: 1994. **Pace of Play rating:** N/A. **Green fee:** $16/21.
Credit cards: All major. **Reduced fees:** Weekdays, Twilight, Seniors, Juniors.
Caddies: No. **Golf carts:** $8 for 18 holes.
Discount golf packages: No. **Season:** Year-round. **High:** Aug.
On-site lodging: No. **Rental clubs:** Yes.
Walking policy: Unrestricted walking. **Range:** Yes (grass).
To obtain tee times: Call Tuesday for Friday, Saturday and Sunday. Weekdays, call three days in advance.

★½ RUNAWAY BAY GOLF CLUB
SP—400 Half Moon Way, Bridgeport (817)575-2228.
45 miles northwest of Fort Worth. **Holes:** 18. **Par:** 71/71.
Yards: 6,650/5,197. **Course rating:** 70.9/68.2. **Slope:** 116/108.
Opened: 1968. **Pace of Play rating:** 3.50. **Green fee:** $15/20.
Credit cards: MC, V, DISC. **Reduced fees:** Resort guests, Twilight, Juniors.
Caddies: No. **Golf carts:** $9 for 18 holes.
Discount golf packages: Yes. **Season:** Year-round. **High:** April-June/Oct.
On-site lodging: No. **Rental clubs:** Yes.
Walking policy: Walking at certain times. **Range:** Yes (grass).
To obtain tee times: Call pro shop up to seven days in advance.
Subscriber comments: Always can get a tee time, long drive from Metroplex . . . Could be a very good course with better care . . . Tee boxes hard and had not been watered . . . Some holes require accuracy . . . Plain Jane . . . Beautiful views, awful condition . . . Short . . . Nice staff.

★★★½ SAN SABA MUNICIPAL GOLF COURSE
PU—Golf Course Rd., San Saba (915)372-3212.
90 miles north of Austin. **Holes:** 18. **Par:** 72/72.
Yards: 6,904/5,246. **Course rating:** 72.5/69.0. **Slope:** 119/113.
Opened: 1972. **Pace of Play rating:** 4:00. **Green fee:** $9/13.
Credit cards: MC, V, AMEX. **Reduced fees:** No.
Caddies: No. **Golf carts:** $8 for 18 holes.
Discount golf packages: No. **Season:** Year-round. **High:** March–Oct.
On-site lodging: No. **Rental clubs:** Yes.
Walking policy: Unrestricted walking. **Range:** Yes (grass).
To obtain tee times: First come, first served.
Subscriber comments: One of the best kept secrets in Texas . . . Fun course. Good closing hole . . . Original nine really tough . . . Slow on weekends . . . Great place, great people . . . Back nine outstanding, front

GREAT VALUE

nine fair . . . Great back nine in huge trees . . . Fairways and greens good in summer . . . Best golf course in central Texas for the price . . . Staff treatment and service very good . . . Great mix of old and new . . . Need larger clubhouse . . . Big city fellows, eat your heart out.

★½ SCOTT SCHREINER MUNICIPAL GOLF COURSE

PU—1 Country Club Dr., Kerrville (210)257-4982.
60 miles northwest of San Antonio. **Holes:** 18. **Par:** 72/72.
Yards: 6,504/5,258. **Course rating:** 70.0/69.2. **Slope:** 118/117.
Opened: 1921. **Pace of Play rating:** 4:00 **Green fee:** $8/11.
Credit cards: None. **Reduced fees:** No.
Caddies: No. **Golf carts:** $8 for 18 holes.
Discount golf packages: No. **Season:** Year-round. **High:** April-Oct.
On-site lodging: No. **Rental clubs:** Yes.
Walking policy: Unrestricted walking. **Range:** Yes (grass).
To obtain tee times: Call three days in advance.
Subscriber comments: Old municipal course needs improvements . . .
Very tempting, hills, trees, water, traps, fun . . . Rental clubs are pitiful . . .
Short course with pleasurable elevation changes . . . Fast pace of play if you walk . . . Hard fairways . . . Easy for walk-ons. Staff very amiable.

SEVEN OAKS RESORT AND COUNTRY CLUB★

SP—1300 Circle Dr., Mission (210)581-6267.
7 miles west of McAllen. **Holes:** 18. **Par:** 70/70.
Yards: 6,089/4,867. **Course rating:** 69.2/66.8. **Slope:** 108/98.
Opened: 1983. **Pace of Play rating:** 4:15. **Green fee:** $14.
Credit cards: MC, V. **Reduced fees:** Juniors.
Caddies: No. **Golf carts:** $9 for 18 holes.
Discount golf packages: No. **Season:** Year-round. **High:** Nov.-March.
On-site lodging: No. **Rental clubs:** Yes.
Walking policy: Unrestricted walking. **Range:** Yes (grass).
To obtain tee times: Call 24 hours in advance.

★½ SHADOW HILLS GOLF COURSE

PU—6002 3rd Street, Lubbock (806)793-9700.
Call club for further information.
Subscriber comments: Plain West Texas course . . . Good greens, poor drainage . . . Better every time I play it . . . Heavily-watered, flat, 2,500 trees planted . . . Needs conditioning but fun to play, plenty of wind . . .
Neat, clean, friendly, affordable . . . Service is good . . . Soft greens . . .
Dull and too easy; sadly, the best municipal in Lubbock.

★½ SHARPSTOWN MUNICIPAL GOLF COURSE

PU—8200 Bellaire Blvd., Houston (713)988-2099.
Call club for further information.
Subscriber comments: Hacker's hangout. "Fore!" most common sound
. . . Longish. Kind of dull . . . Slow play . . . Needs more bunkers, fairly open fairways . . . Almost no sand or water . . . Too many ditches . . . Go early and play quicker . . . Decent course, if you like spending your day with 500 hackers.

★★★ SHARY MUNICIPAL GOLF COURSE

PU—2201 Mayberry, Mission (210)580-8770.
6 miles west of McAllen. **Holes:** 27. **Par:** 71/70/73.
Yards: 6,025/5,883/6,528. **Course rating:** 68.9/68.9/68.9. **Slope:** 105/105/105.
Opened: 1929. **Pace of Play rating:** 4:30. **Green fee:** $9/10.
Credit cards: None. **Reduced fees:** Juniors.
Caddies: No. **Golf carts:** $8 for 18 holes.
Discount golf packages: No. **Season:** Year-round. **High:** Jan.-March.
On-site lodging: No. **Rental clubs:** Yes.
Walking policy: Unrestricted walking. **Range:** Yes (grass).
To obtain tee times: Call one day in advance.

Subscriber comments: Short but nice . . . Narrow but challenging, very friendly . . . Tee boxes and green too close to each other . . . New nine holes, greatly improved course . . . Best course in South Texas . . . Good staff but limited. Can get very crowded . . . Very difficult to get tee times during winter months.

SHERRILL PARK GOLF COURSE
PU—2001 E. Lookout Dr., Richardson (214)234-1416.
10 miles south of Dallas. **Green fee:** $14/17.
Credit cards: None. **Reduced fees:** Weekdays, Low season, Twilight, Seniors, Juniors.
Caddies: No. **Golf carts:** $8 for 18 holes.
Discount golf packages: Yes. **Season:** Year-round. **High:** May-Nov.
On-site lodging: No. **Rental clubs:** Yes.
Walking policy: Unrestricted walking. **Range:** Yes (grass).
★★½ **COURSE NO. 1**
Holes: 18. **Par:** 72/72.
Yards: 6,800/5,455. **Course rating:** 72.6/72.0. **Slope:** 126/118.
Opened: 1971. **Pace of Play rating:** 4:00.
To obtain tee times: Weekend times taken on Friday by phone. Weekdays, first come, first served.
Subscriber comments: Nice traditional design . . . Good golf for the traffic it gets . . . Great staff . . . Tight, water, trees, not for beginners . . . Play slow . . . Great customer service . . . Not well maintained, greens bad, usually weedy . . . Lots of traffic . . . Greens worn . . . Much better than No. 2 course . . . Needs better maintenance and better traps . . . Marshals did good job . . . Crowded, but play moves along smartly . . . Big trees . . . Longer of two courses . . . Not bad on the pocket.
★½ **COURSE NO. 2**
Holes: 18. **Par:** 70/70.
Yards: 6,083/5,476. **Course rating:** 66.0/68.0. **Slope:** 113/113.
Opened: 1971. **Pace of Play rating:** 4:00.
To obtain tee times: Weekdays, call one week in advance. Weekends, call the Friday before.
Subscriber comments: Short, snappy par 70 on an old landfill . . . Greens are improved, but have to train golfers how to repair ball marks . . . Bent grass greens abused by players and not maintained . . . Big trees . . . Courteous staff . . . Eight years ago this was the best municipal course in the area . . . Short and tight with billions of new trees. Killer in 20 years . . . Not enough grass, overplayed . . . Good pace, four hours . . . Not one of better municipals in area, can do better . . . Great starter course.

★★ SLEEPY HOLLOW GOLF AND COUNTRY CLUB RIVER COURSE
SP—4747 South Loop 12, Dallas (214)371-3433.
Call club for further information.
Subscriber comments: Some good holes on this one . . . Fairways need work . . . Trees, long, long par 4s . . . A lot of water, narrow course . . . Finishing holes very demanding with levee and river on left.

★★★½ SOUTHWYCK GOLF CLUB
PU—2901 Clubhouse Dr., Pearland (713)436-9999.
10 miles south of Houston. **Holes:** 18. **Par:** 72/72.
Yards: 7,015/5,211. **Course rating:** 72.9/68.9. **Slope:** 123/112.
Opened: 1988. **Pace of Play rating:** 4:30. **Green fee:** $25/45.
Credit cards: MC, V, AMEX. **Reduced fees:** Weekdays, Low season, Twilight, Seniors, Juniors.
Caddies: No. **Golf carts:** Included in Green Fee.
Discount golf packages: Yes. **Season:** Year-round. **High:** Spring/Fall.
On-site lodging: No. **Rental clubs:** Yes.
Walking policy: Walking at certain times. **Range:** Yes (grass).
To obtain tee times: Call (713)777-1100.
Subscriber comments: Scotland comes to Texas . . . A true test of links golf . . . Can't help but feel you're in Scotland . . . Almost always windy

. . . Best golf value on the prairie . . . Too tough for me when it's windy . . . Unique links layout . . . Impossible to walk with 100 to 300 yards green to tee . . . Not very pretty, lots of water and deep rough . . . Links style is fun for a change . . . Always in great shape . . . No trees . . . Requires good placement shots . . . Best links course in Texas . . . It seems the wind is always blowing . . . Could use some trees . . . bring a knockdown shot . . . Home of University of Houston golf team . . . Impossible to play in wind . . . Awesome design, but greens are seasonal . . . Every hole is a new challenge . . . The staff here is excellent . . . Good service . . . Super par 3s . . . Facilities all first class.

★★★★ SQUAW VALLEY GOLF COURSE
PU—HCR 51-45B Hwy. 67, Glen Rose (817)897-7956, (800)831-8259. 60 miles southwest of Fort Worth. **Holes:** 18. **Par:** 72/72. **Yards:** 7,062/5,014. **Course rating:** 73.6/N/A. **Slope:** 130/N/A. **Opened:** 1992. **Pace of Play rating:** 4:15. **Green fee:** $19/23. **Credit cards:** MC, V, DISC. **Reduced fees:** Weekdays, Twilight, Seniors.
Caddies: No. **Golf carts:** $33 for 18 holes.
Discount golf packages: No. **Season:** Year-round. **High:** April–Oct.
On-site lodging: No. **Rental clubs:** Yes.
Walking policy: Walking at certain times. **Range:** Yes (grass).
To obtain tee times: Call or come in five days in advance. Tee times for weekends only.
Subscriber comments: A very pleasant surprise . . . Great new course, excellent greens, well kept . . . Rural location, links–type front nine, more character in back . . . Worth the drive . . . Long but fair, great shape for new course . . . Well maintained course. Front nine hilly . . . Great challenge, bogey hell, out in the boonies . . . Completely different front and back nines . . . Nice place . . . One I could play weekly . . . Off the beaten path but worth the ride . . . Lot of fun to play . . . Layout is great . . . Cut out of beautiful landscape; terrifically fun . . . Everyone should play this course . . . A "hidden gem" . . . Wonderful clubhouse . . . Marshals keep pace moving . . . Secluded, tucked away and quiet . . . Open front nine with mounds. Back nine has character . . . Better than many private courses in the area . . . Best course near DFW.

★★ STEPHEN F. AUSTIN STATE PARK GOLF COURSE
PU—Box 227, San Felipe (409)885-2811.
Call club for further information.
Subscriber comments: Not a tough course. Just a fun day . . . Pecan trees abundant . . . Nice variety to layout, subject to flooding . . . Good pace . . . Beautiful scenery and many deer . . . Short course near river, fun for RVers . . . Tough little course on the Brazos River . . . Greens tiny and hard, fairways like rock most of year . . . Beautiful scenic course but horribly rundown . . . Can't remember too much, other than lots of trees.

★★ STEVENS PARK GOLF COURSE
PU—1005 N. Montclair, Dallas (214)670-7506.
Holes: 18. **Par:** 71/71.
Yards: 6,005/5,000. **Course rating:** 65.0/68.0. **Slope:** 98/118.
Opened: 1922. **Pace of Play rating:** 4:10. **Green fee:** $6/14.
Credit cards: MC, V. **Reduced fees:** Weekdays, Low season, Twilight, Seniors, Juniors.
Caddies: No. **Golf carts:** $18 for 18 holes.
Discount golf packages: Yes. **Season:** Year-round. **High:** Spring/Fall.
On-site lodging: No. **Rental clubs:** Yes.
Walking policy: Unrestricted walking. **Range:** No.
To obtain tee times: Call two days in advance for weekdays; weekend times available Thursday 6 a.m. in person or noon by phone.
Subscriber comments: Short but very playable, great old style, small greens . . . Makes you think . . . Great old mature muny, good value . . . Couple of gimmicky holes . . . In old residential area . . . Service and pace

excellent . . . Greens never seem to be in good shape . . . Narrow fairways, tough elevation changes . . . Courteous and accommodating staff . . . Short, lots of trouble, good condition for municipal . . . Repair of washed-out creek banks has helped.

★★★½ SUGARTREE GOLF CLUB

SP—Hwy. 1189, Dennis (817)441-8643.
35 miles west of Fort Worth. **Holes:** 18. **Par:** 71/71.
Yards: 6,775/5,254. **Course rating:** 72.8/71.0. **Slope:** 138/125.
Opened: 1987. **Pace of Play rating:** 4:00. **Green fee:** $15/27.
Credit cards: All major. **Reduced fees:** Weekdays, Low season, Twilight, Seniors, Juniors.
Caddies: No. **Golf carts:** $9 for 18 holes.
Discount golf packages: No. **Season:** Year-round. **High:** March-Oct.
On-site lodging: No. **Rental clubs:** Yes.
Walking policy: Unrestricted walking. **Range:** Yes (grass).
To obtain tee times: Maximum of seven days in advance.
Subscriber comments: Nature that didn't let golf get in the way; wonderfully tight . . . Excellent course located in a quiet country setting on the Brazos River . . . Tree lined . . . Excellent layout, good greens, hard to get to . . . Quick rounds, tight but fun, great condition off season . . . 'Watch out for snakes . . . Greens burned in August but by September in great shape . . . Best kept secret in North Texas . . . Extremely tight . . . Great for a quiet peaceful round of golf, nice bent grass greens . . . May see deer standing in fairway . . . Fine course if you can find it . . . Excellent service . . . Need to play a few times to know how to play its blind shots . . . Little known treasure . . . Nice scenery, nice people, maybe too many blind shots . . . Gets better the more it's played . . . Great test in a picturesque setting . . . First-class, shotmaker's delight . . . Truly outstanding course and value in middle of nowhere.

SWEETWATER COUNTRY CLUB★

SP—1900 Country Club Lane, Sweetwater (915)235-8093.
45 miles east of Abilene. **Holes:** 18. **Par:** 71/72.
Yards: 6,362/5,316. **Course rating:** 70.0/N/A. **Slope:** 118/N/A.
Opened: 1957. **Pace of Play rating:** 3:30. **Green fee:** $15/20.
Credit cards: None. **Reduced fees:** No.
Caddies: No. **Golf carts:** $13 for 18 holes.
Discount golf packages: No. **Season:** Year-round. **High:** April-Aug.
On-site lodging: No. **Rental clubs:** Yes.
Walking policy: Unrestricted walking. **Range:** Yes (grass).
To obtain tee times: Call pro shop.

★★★ TANGLEWOOD RESORT

R—Hwy. 120 N., Pottsboro (903)786-4140, (800)833-6569.
68 miles north of Dallas. **Holes:** 18. **Par:** 72/72.
Yards: 6,993/4,925. **Course rating:** 73.7/67.5. **Slope:** 128/104.
Opened: 1971. **Pace of Play rating:** 4:00. **Green fee:** $27/33.
Credit cards: All major. **Reduced fees:** Twilight.
Caddies: No. **Golf carts:** $12 for 18 holes.
Discount golf packages: Yes. **Season:** Year-round. **High:** Spring/Fall.
On-site lodging: Yes. **Rental clubs:** Yes.
Walking policy: Walking at certain times. **Range:** Yes (grass).
To obtain tee times: Call golf shop up to four weeks in advance.
Subscriber comments: Course has really improved over the years . . . Course in good shape, must stay at resort to play . . . Good weekend golf outing . . . Clubhouse and supervision very good . . . Best shape ever . . . Wide open and long, excellent fairways and greens . . . Expensive, bad location for a good course . . . Course tough from back tees, some blind shots . . . Unknown gem, tough course, terrific greens . . . I'd play this course all the time if it was closer to Dallas.

★★★½ TAPATIO SPRINGS RESORT AND CONFERENCE CENTER
R—West Johns Rd., Boerne (210)537-4197, (800)999-3299.
25 miles north of San Antonio. **Holes:** 18. **Par:** 72/72.
Yards: 6,472/5,179. **Course rating:** 70.9/69.5. **Slope:** 122/118.
Opened: 1980. **Pace of Play rating:** 4:20. **Green fee:** $65/75.
Credit cards: All major. **Reduced fees:** Resort guests, Juniors.
Caddies: No. **Golf carts:** Included in Green Fee.
Discount golf packages: Yes. **Season:** Year-round. **High:** Spring/Fall.
On-site lodging: Yes. **Rental clubs:** Yes.
Walking policy: Mandatory cart. **Range:** Yes (grass).
To obtain tee times: Call seven days in advance, resort guest 30 days in advance with hotel confirmation.
Also 9-hole executive course.
Subscriber comments: Gorgeous course out in the middle of Hill Country . . . Great accommodations, great layout . . . Very pretty, scenic, lots of wild game . . . First class in every way . . . Lots of sand, water, trees, and deer, with fun executive nine . . . Nice weekend retreat . . . Lots of variety and visual challenges . . . Although we took carts and course was dry, had to stay on cart trails . . . Too many blind holes . . . Wild deer, goats, turkey . . . Greens are rock hard . . . Great fun on every hole! . . . Spacing of players could be better . . . Friendly staff and nice hotel . . . They need to water more often . . . The executive nine is a blast, take three clubs and enjoy . . . Good ambiance . . . Scenic valley . . . Relatively short. Back nine has character . . . Excellent place for a meeting . . . Needs better marshaling to control players.

TENISON PARK GOLF COURSE
PU—3501 Samuell, Dallas (214)670-1402.
Green fee: $6/14.
Credit cards: MC, V, AMEX. **Reduced fees:** Weekdays, Low season, Twilight, Seniors, Juniors.
Caddies: No. **Golf carts:** $17 for 18 holes.
Discount golf packages: Yes. **Season:** Year-round. **High:** April-Oct.
On-site lodging: No. **Rental clubs:** Yes.
Walking policy: Unrestricted walking. **Range:** No.
To obtain tee times: For weekend times come in person on Thursday at 6 a.m. or phone in at noon.
★★ EAST COURSE
Holes: 18. **Par:** 72/75.
Yards: 6,802/5,444. **Course rating:** 72.0/70.2. **Slope:** 123/113.
Opened: 1927. **Pace of Play rating:** 4:30.
Subscriber comments: Great old course with a lot of trees . . . One of Dallas' best public courses . . . Challenging, trees, river and other water come into play . . . Memories of Titanic Thompson and Lee Trevino . . . Short, open fun, most golfers would enjoy, staff OK, service good, play slow, course dry in summer . . . Condition slowly going downhill . . . Poor facilities . . . Nice new clubhouse . . . Fallen leaves are problem in autumn . . . Lots of hardpan . . . Staff was great, they treated us like we were either owners of the course or PGA Tour players . . . Creek runs throughout course, easy to walk, No. 17 a nightmare par 5 . . . Sand traps would make this one tough, very tough . . . No wonder Trevino is such a good shotmaker.
★★½ WEST COURSE
Holes: 18. **Par:** 72/75.
Yards: 6,902/5,747. **Course rating:** 72.0/72.2. **Slope:** 121/118.
Opened: 1927. **Pace of Play rating:** 4:30.
Subscriber comments: Better of two courses . . . Great long-shot course . . . Tough, demanding . . . Lots of water to cross, nice fairways . . . Lots of history . . . Greens hard to putt, nice fairways . . . Heavy traffic . . . Must know where to miss and hit it straight . . . It is suited for the average

player but challenging enough for good players . . . Hilly back nine, difficult to walk . . . West very muddy when wet . . . No sand, great old trees come into play . . . Hilly tree-lined fairways make back nine toughest municipal stretch . . . America was built quicker than the new clubhouse!

★½ TEXAS A&M UNIVERSITY GOLF COURSE
PU—Bizzell St., College Station (409)845-1723.
100 miles northwest of Houston. **Holes:** 18. **Par:** 70/73.
Yards: 6,513/5,238. **Course rating:** 71.0/68.3. **Slope:** 122/109.
Opened: 1951. **Pace of Play rating:** N/A. **Green fee:** $8/16.
Credit cards: All major. **Reduced fees:** Weekdays, Twilight.
Caddies: No. **Golf carts:** $8 for 18 holes.
Discount golf packages: No. **Season:** Year-round. **High:** April-Oct.
On-site lodging: No. **Rental clubs:** Yes.
Walking policy: Unrestricted walking. **Range:** No.
To obtain tee times: Only one week in advance available on Friday, Saturday, Sunday.
Subscriber comments: Compact course, a lot of fun to play. Be very accurate . . . Not very challenging . . . Good college course for limited funds . . . Gets long in tooth in deep summer . . . Pace of play is slow, slow, slow . . . On campus . . . Could be in better physical condition . . . Extremely affordable and easy to get on.

★★★½ TIMARRON GOLF AND COUNTRY CLUB
PU—14000 Byron Nelson Pkwy., South Lake (817)481-7529.
20 miles east of Fort Worth. **Holes:** 18. **Par:** 72/72.
Yards: 7,100/5,330. **Course rating:** 74.2/71.3. **Slope:** 137/120.
Opened: 1994. **Pace of Play rating:** 4:30. **Green fee:** $45/60.
Credit cards: MC, V, AMEX. **Reduced fees:** Weekdays.
Caddies: No. **Golf carts:** Included in Green Fee.
Discount golf packages: No. **Season:** Year-round. **High:** March-April.
On-site lodging: No. **Rental clubs:** Yes.
Walking policy: Mandatory cart. **Range:** Yes (grass).
To obtain tee times: Call three days in advance.
Subscriber comments: Awesome course . . . Great design . . . Friendly staff, outstanding layout . . . Will be top 10 course . . . Brand new course . . . None better in Dallas area . . . Greens were thin . . . Has great potential . . . Great condition, no walking, always cart path only . . . Byron Nelson design, great layout, greens need to mature . . . It was a bad year for bent grass.

★★½ TONY BUTLER GOLF COURSE
PU—2640 S. M St., Harlingen (210)430-6685.
26 miles north of Brownsville. **Holes:** 18 **Par:** 71/71.
Yards: 6,320/5,123. **Course rating:** 69.1/69.1. **Slope:** 113/112.
Opened: 1904. **Pace of Play rating:** 4:30. **Green fee:** $10.
Credit cards: MC, V. **Reduced fees:** Juniors.
Caddies: No. **Golf carts:** $9 for 18 holes.
Discount golf packages: No. **Season:** Year-round. **High:** Oct-March.
On-site lodging: No. **Rental clubs:** Yes.
Walking policy: Unrestricted walking. **Range:** Yes (grass).
To obtain tee times: Call one day in advance starting at 6:30 a.m. Tee times required every day during Oct./March.
Subscriber comments: A real pleasure to play . . . All players treated A-1 . . . Nice scenery and landscape . . . Has character . . . Good starters under heavy traffic, best we found in area . . . Lots of winter tourists, slow pace . . . Greens very fast, fairly wide . . . Limited staff and service, can get very crowded . . . Biggest gripe is that they allow fivesomes at all times . . . Watering system saturates course every morning, creating permanent areas of casual water . . . Good course conditions, greens are in excellent condition.

★★★½ **TOUR 18**
PU—3102 FM 1960 E., Humble (713)540-1818.
14 miles northeast of Houston. **Holes:** 18. **Par:** 72/72.
Yards: 6,807/5,583. **Course rating:** 72.2/66.6. **Slope:** 126/113.
Opened: 1992. **Pace of Play rating:** 5:00. **Green fee:** $55/75.
Credit cards: All major. **Reduced fees:** Twilight, Juniors.
Caddies: Yes. **Golf carts:** Included in Green Fee.
Discount golf packages: Yes. **Season:** Year-round. **High:** April-May.
On-site lodging: No. **Rental clubs:** Yes.
Walking policy: Mandatory cart. **Range:** Yes (grass).
To obtain tee times: Call seven days in advance begining at 7:15 a.m.
Subscriber comments: Eighteen knock-off holes from famous courses
. . . A unique experience . . . Excellent service . . . Everybody should play
it once, but that's all . . . Very expensive . . . Tee times one month in
advance . . . 18 great holes . . . Every hole a beauty and challenge . . .
Enjoyable day playing the world's best . . . Don't feel you are playing a real
golf course . . . Unique layout . . . Great layout, less traffic would help give
the course a rest . . . Greens way below par . . . Not nearly as gimmicky as
I thought it would be . . . It's just fun to look at . . . Nice copies of famous
holes . . . Greens in terrible shape, bring lots of balls, must have chosen
only holes loaded with water . . . Amen Corner is tough . . . Country club
atmosphere . . . Amen Corner was outstanding . . . Excellent service . . .
Would be fantastic if the greens were better . . . Nice novelty, but course
and play are too "touristy" . . . Big landing areas . . . Staff, pro shop and
practice area outstanding . . . Novel, great one-time course . . . All hype.
Complete letdown . . . Marshals were informative . . . Must ride and stay
on path (90-degree rule) . . . Amen Corner a blast . . . Replica holes were
fun . . . A curious novelty . . . Can't decide if I loved it or despised it.

TURTLE HILL GOLF COURSE★
PU—Rte. 373 N., Muenster (817)759-4896.
15 miles west of Gainsville. **Holes:** 18. **Par:** 72/72.
Yards: 6,824/5,150. **Course rating:** 72.2/69.5. **Slope:** 123/116.
Opened: 1993. **Pace of Play rating:** 4:00. **Green fee:** $12/16.
Credit cards: MC, V. **Reduced fees:** Weekdays, Twilight, Juniors.
Caddies: No. **Golf carts:** $15 for 18 holes.
Discount golf packages: Yes. **Season:** Year-round. **High:** April-Sept.
On-site lodging: No. **Rental clubs:** Yes.
Walking policy: Unrestricted walking. **Range:** Yes (grass).
To obtain tee times: Call one week in advance.
Subscriber comments: Not a bad country course. Nice people . . . Staff
good, pace medium to fast . . . Fun layout . . . A potential to be great when
it matures.

TWIN CREEKS GOLF CLUB★
PU—501 Twin Creeks Dr., Allen (214)390-8888.
30 miles north of Dallas. **Holes:** 18. **Par:** 72/72.
Yards: 6,924/4,790. **Course rating:** N/A. **Slope:** N/A.
Opened: 1995. **Pace of Play rating:** 4:30. **Green fee:** $38/48.
Credit cards: MC, V, AMEX. **Reduced fees:** Weekdays, Twilight,
Juniors.
Caddies: No. **Golf carts:** Included in Green Fee.
Discount golf packages: No. **Season:** Year-round. **High:** April-Oct.
On-site lodging: No. **Rental clubs:** Yes.
Walking policy: Unrestricted walking. **Range:** Yes (grass).
To obtain tee times: Call five days in advance.

★½ **TWIN WELLS GOLF COURSE**
PU—2000 E. Shady Grove Rd., Irving (214)438-4340.
5 miles west of Dallas. **Holes:** 18. **Par:** 72/72.
Yards: 6,636/6,239. **Course rating:** N/A. **Slope:** 117/113.
Opened: N/A. **Pace of Play rating:** N/A. **Green fee:** N/A.
Credit cards: MC, V. **Reduced fees:** Weekdays, Low season, Twilight.
Caddies: No. **Golf carts:** N/A.

Discount golf packages: Yes. **Season:** Year-round. **High:** March-Dec.
On-site lodging: No. **Rental clubs:** No.
Walking policy: N/A. **Range:** Yes.
Subscriber comments: Another confidence builder . . . Long hitters love this course, wide open fairways . . . Wasn't impressed . . . Long holes into the wind, short holes with the wind . . . Elevated greens . . . Limited enjoyment . . . Quick tee times . . . Many similar holes . . . Bottomland . . . No frills . . . Pace very slow . . . Some shotmaking par 4s . . . Too flat . . . Needs some sand traps in key spots to make the course more challenging.

UNDERWOOD GOLF COURSE
SP—3200 Coe Ave., El Paso (915)562-1273.
Green fee: $7/14.
Credit cards: MC, V. **Reduced fees:** Weekdays, Twilight.
Caddies: No. **Golf carts:** $9 for 18 holes.
Discount golf packages: No. **Season:** Year-round. **High:** April-Nov.
On-site lodging: No. **Rental clubs:** Yes.
Walking policy: Unrestricted walking. **Range:** Yes (grass).
To obtain tee times: Call for weekday tee times only. Lottery system for weekends.
★½ **SUNSET COURSE**
Holes: 18. **Par:** 72/72.
Yards: 6,629/5,531. **Course rating:** 70.1/70.4. **Slope:** 116/109.
Opened: 1945. **Pace of Play rating:** 4:00.
Subscriber comments: Very short, lots of par 3s . . . Needs more cart paths badly, has been neglected because of new course being built . . . Not very challenging . . . Waiting for new course to open . . . No hazards, OK service, pace OK . . . Very high traffic and not enough water to keep it green . . . Just added new desert course . . . Perfect practice range with bunkers . . . Staff is friendly and competent . . . A few good holes . . . Give old course a chance to breathe; newly installed water system should help.

★★½ VALLEY INN AND COUNTRY CLUB
PU—FM Rd. 802 and Central Blvd., Brownsville (210)546-5331.
Call club for further information.
Subscriber comments: Popular course . . . Bare spots on fairways, facilities worn out . . . Greens like shag carpet, some fairways terrible . . . Good restaurant . . . A few very good holes . . . Course needs work . . . Extremely nice and hospitable . . . Helpful staff, and uncrowded.

★★★½ WATERWOOD NATIONAL RESORT AND COUNTRY CLUB
R—One Waterwood, Huntsville (409)891-5050, (800)441-5211.
75 miles north of Houston. **Holes:** 18. **Par:** 71/73.
Yards: 6,872/5,029. **Course rating:** 73.7/68.0. **Slope:** 142/117.
Opened: 1975. **Pace of Play rating:** 4:30. **Green fee:** $28/40.
Credit cards: All major. **Reduced fees:** Low season, Twilight, Seniors.
Caddies: No. **Golf carts:** $10 for 18 holes.
Discount golf packages: Yes. **Season:** Year-round. **High:** April-June.
On-site lodging: Yes. **Rental clubs:** Yes.
Walking policy: Unrestricted walking. **Range:** Yes (grass).
To obtain tee times: Call 48 hours in advance.
Ranked 9th in Texas by Golf Digest.
Subscriber comments: This one's tough . . . True championship golf at public course rates . . . Pete Dye course . . . No. 14 unbelievable par 3 . . . The beast, can be tamed. Could leave crying . . . Gorgeous lakeside views . . . A little too challenging for higher handicappers . . . Being made easier for resort players . . . Toughest course in Texas . . . Too many railroad ties . . . Big challenge . . . Very picturesque . . . Beautiful scenery on Lake Livingston . . . Large elevation changes . . . Terrific pro shop and starter . . . Many 450-plus-yards par 4s and forced carries . . . Was the best until

mid-80's; on comeback trail . . . One tough par 3 . . . Few outstanding holes but tough, long and tight . . . Course has it all, challenging for all skill levels, very good condition . . . Water and woods . . . Can play in 3½ hours.

★★½ WEDGEWOOD GOLF CLUB
PU—5454 Hwy. 105 W., Conroe (409)441-4653.
50 miles north of Houston. **Holes:** 18. **Par:** 72/72.
Yards: 6,817/5,071. **Course rating:** 73.7/69.6. **Slope:** 134/128.
Opened: 1988. **Pace of Play rating:** 4:30. **Green fee:** $18/38.
Credit cards: MC, V, AMEX. **Reduced fees:** Weekdays, Twilight, Seniors, Juniors.
Caddies: No. **Golf carts:** $10 for 18 holes.
Discount golf packages: No. **Season:** Year-round. **High:** Spring/Fall.
On-site lodging: No. **Rental clubs:** Yes.
Walking policy: Unrestricted walking. **Range:** Yes (grass).
To obtain tee times: Call one week in advance for weekdays and call Wednesday for upcoming weekend.
Subscriber comments: What a change from flat Houston-area courses . . . Fairways so narrow you never get to "rip it" . . . Tough course, lot of blind shots . . . Roller coaster golf. Gee, wonder if I'll get a level lie today? Bring your machete . . . Good staff, slow pace . . . Too hot for summer play . . . Tougher than a possum's tail . . . Tough, tough, very unforgiving . . . Course dictates what club you have to use, very few options . . . Very hilly course with lots of water hazards and sand traps. Very tough course due to hilly fairways. Staff very friendly . . . Could be a good course with a little work . . . Narrow fairways, big greens, and fast . . . Too many doglegs . . . Must keep it straight . . . Don't expect to score as well as you do on most Houston area courses . . . Maximum target golf, don't bring your driver . . . One of best shotmaking courses . . . Will bring you down to earth . . . Tight, tight . . . Love to see what pros would do . . . Very hard and unfair . . . A challenge of the first order; every hole must be well played.

★★ WEEKS PARK MUNICIPAL GOLF
PU—Lake Park Dr., Wichita Falls (817)767-6107.
Call club for further information.
Subscriber comments: Like a lot of flat municipals in Texas . . . Needs some work, crowded on weekends . . . Fairways on inward nine need improvement, only one bunker . . . Good greens, staff is great, variety of hole types, long and short . . . Good food . . . The best in Wichita Falls.

★★ WESTERN OAKS COUNTRY CLUB
SP—1600 Western Oaks Dr., Waco (817)772-8100.
Holes: 18. **Par:** 70/70.
Yards: 6,400/5,040. **Course rating:** 70.7/68.7. **Slope:** 122/120.
Opened: 1969. **Pace of Play rating:** 3:40. **Green fee:** $10/13.
Credit cards: MC, V. **Reduced fees:** Weekdays, Low season, Resort guests, Twilight, Juniors.
Caddies: No. **Golf carts:** $9 for 18 holes.
Discount golf packages: Yes. **Season:** Year-round. **High:** April-Nov.
On-site lodging: No. **Rental clubs:** Yes.
Walking policy: Unrestricted walking. **Range:** Yes (grass).
To obtain tee times: Call up to seven days in advance. Call up to 60 days in advance for multiple groups.
Subscriber comments: Varied types of holes and shots . . . Cart path all the way (90-degree rule), good Bermuda greens . . . Narrow and demanding . . . Doglegs and hills . . . Course plays short, not crowded . . . Poor layout, many greens in path of oncoming tee shots . . . Could be a really nice course if they weren't always closing part of it for repairs.

★★★ WHITE BLUFF GOLF CLUB

SP—Golf Drive 1, Whitney (817)694-3656.
40 miles northwest of Waco. **Holes:** 18. **Par:** 72/72.
Yards: 6,845/5,292. **Course rating:** 73.3/72.4. **Slope:** 132/128.
Opened: 1992. **Pace of Play rating:** 4:05. **Green fee:** $45/79.
Credit cards: All major. **Reduced fees:** Twilight.
Caddies: No. **Golf carts:** Included in Green Fee.
Discount golf packages: No. **Season:** Year-round. **High:** April-Oct.
On-site lodging: Yes. **Rental clubs:** Yes.
Walking policy: Unrestricted walking. **Range:** Yes (grass).
To obtain tee times: Call one week in advance.
Subscriber comments: Kind of far away . . . Back nine very exciting and
scenic . . . Picturesque par 3 overlooking cliffs . . . Well kept secret at Lake
Whitney . . . Nice staff, great shape, quiet . . . Great greens and fairways
. . . Easy to get around . . . A destination course . . . Open, resort-style
front nine. Tight, hilly back nine . . . Back nine unfair to women players
. . . Can tell it's a Bruce Lietzke design, lots of left to right holes.

★★½ WILLOW SPRINGS GOLF CLUB

PU—202 Coliseum Rd., San Antonio (210)226-6721.
Call club for further information.
Subscriber comments: Good old municipal . . . Course too crowded,
upkeep not excellent, staff OK . . . Look out for No. 2 . . . No frills nor
much maintenance . . . Generally forgiving . . . Trees and creeks . . .
Fivesomes, slow play . . . Put this baby in top notch condition and speed up
play, WOW!

★★ WOODLAND HILLS GOLF COURSE

PU—319 Woodland Hills Dr., Nacogdoches (409)564-2762.
120 miles northeast of Houston. **Holes:** 18. **Par:** 72/72.
Yards: 6,672/6,218. **Course rating:** N/A. **Slope:** 123/114.
Opened: N/A. **Pace of Play rating:** N/A. **Green fee:** N/A.
Credit cards: MC, V. **Reduced fees:** Weekdays, Twilight.
Caddies: No. **Golf carts:** N/A.
Discount golf packages: No. **Season:** Year-round. **High:** April-Aug.
On-site lodging: No. **Rental clubs:** No.
Walking policy: N/A. **Range:** Yes (grass).
Subscriber comments: Hilly with lots of bends . . . Staff and service very
good . . . Tree-lined fairways . . . Has improved a great deal since last year
. . . Beautiful setting with wide fairways in piney woods.

THE WOODLANDS RESORT AND COUNTRY CLUB

R—2301 N. Millbend Dr., The Woodlands (713)367-1100.
25 miles north of Houston. **Credit cards:** All major. **Reduced fees:**
Weekdays, Low season, Twilight.
Caddies: No. **Golf carts:** N/A.
Discount golf packages: Yes. **Season:** Year-round. **High:** Spring/Fall.
On-site lodging: Yes. **Rental clubs:** N/A.
Walking policy: N/A. **Range:** Yes (grass).
★★★★ NORTH COURSE
Holes: 18. **Par:** 72/72.
Yards: 6,881/6,339. **Course rating:** N/A. **Slope:** 126/122.
Opened: N/A. **Pace of Play rating:** 4:30. **Green fee:** N/A.
Subscriber comments: Well designed, challenges and fun on each hole
. . . Best course in north Houston . . . If I see another OB stake I'm gonna
blow it up . . . Need every kind of shot, especially fairway bunker shot . . .
Well conditioned, great staff . . . Very good accommodations, lots of sand
. . . Full-blown resort . . . Particularly good condition in the winter . . .
Always in great condition . . . Sand and bunker capital of golfdom . . . Pace
good and treated A-1 . . . Great restaurant . . . Some unnecessary trick
holes . . . Great weekend resort package . . . More interesting than TPC
. . . Bunkers the size of Rhode Island . . . Just as good as the TPC course
and less expensive.

TEXAS

★★★★ TPC AT THE WOODLANDS
Holes: 18. **Par:** 72/72.
Yards: 7,045/5,302. **Course rating:** 73.6/70.3. **Slope:** 135/120.
Opened: 1985. **Pace of Play rating:** 4:30. **Green fee:** $60/90.
Ranked 13th in Texas by Golf Digest.
Subscriber comments: A real class act. Love all the Woodlands courses
. . . Challenging, lots of trouble . . . One of von Hagge/Devlin's best . . .
Great condition but overrated, some holes seem contrived . . . One of the
best TPC courses . . . Better have a big drive . . . Good friendly staff, try to
accommodate . . . This course is immaculate, accurate drives required . . .
Plush fairways . . . Bring your nerves, a lot of water in play . . . Top of the
line resort-type course, one bad shot equals a double bogey . . . Site of Shell
Houston Open . . . Excellent facilities and staff . . . Always in great shape
. . . Railroad ties and traps . . . Very commercial, no charm . . . Murderous
rough, lots of humidity . . . Super design, never tire of playing . . . A grind
on every shot . . . Sheer pleasure . . . Pleasure to play a TPC . . . Typical
TPC course target golf . . . Add gallery noise and you feel like you are on
tour . . . Typical TPC, playable and unspectacular . . . Golf does not get
any better than this!

★½ WORLD HOUSTON GOLF CLUB
PU—4000 Greens Rd., Houston (713)449-8384.
Holes: 18. **Par:** 72/72.
Yards: 6,642/5,204. **Course rating:** 71.2/71.4. **Slope:** 117/N/A.
Opened: N/A. **Pace of Play rating:** N/A. **Green fee:** $20.
Credit cards: MC, V, AMEX. **Reduced fees:** Low season.
Caddies: No. **Golf carts:** Included in Green Fee.
Discount golf packages: Yes. **Season:** Year-round. **High:** March-Oct.
On-site lodging: No. **Rental clubs:** Yes.
Walking policy: Unrestricted walking. **Range:** Yes (grass).
To obtain tee times: Call pro shop.
Subscriber comments: Open and rather easy . . . Cheap place to play,
easy course, not very exciting . . . Bring your earplugs, near the airport . . .
Bring your hardhat, not a bad course, just built on too small a piece of land
. . . Tee boxes hit into narrow fairways that are too close to adjoining
fairways . . . Can be a shooting gallery . . . Water will bite you . . . Greens
are good, easy walking.

★½ Z BOAZ GOLF COURSE
PU—3240 Lackland Rd., Fort Worth (817)738-6287.
Holes: 18. **Par:** 70/70.
Yards: 6,033/4,782. **Course rating:** 69.6/68.0. **Slope:** 124/107.
Opened: 1937. **Pace of Play rating:** N/A. **Green fee:** $11/13.
Credit cards: MC, V. **Reduced fees:** Weekdays, Twilight, Seniors,
Juniors.
Caddies: No. **Golf carts:** $8 for 18 holes.
Discount golf packages: No. **Season:** Year-round. **High:** N/A.
On-site lodging: No. **Rental clubs:** Yes.
Walking policy: Unrestricted walking. **Range:** No.
To obtain tee times: Call Mondays after noon for the following week.
Subscriber comments: Dan Jenkins put it on the map . . . Great "Goat
Hills Open" . . . A municipal golf icon, home of annual Dan Jenkins
Partnership . . . Good par 3s . . . Can drive three of the par 4s . . . Short,
easy fun . . . Very short with elevated tees . . . Famous . . . Good people,
pleasant . . . Right in the middle of Fort Worth . . . I felt like John Daly
driving the par 4s . . . Possible eagles.

★★★½ BIRCH CREEK GOLF CLUB
PU—600 E. Center St., Smithfield (801)563-6825.
Call club for further information.
Subscriber comments: Fun to play . . . May be best kept secret in Utah
. . . A hidden treasure. When you pay green fees, you feel like you are
stealing . . . A walking workout . . . Out of the way and worth it.

★★★ BONNEVILLE GOLF COURSE
PU—954 Connor St., Salt Lake City (801)583-9513.
Holes: 18. **Par:** 72/74.
Yards: 6,824/5,860. **Course rating:** 71.0/71.6. **Slope:** 120/119.
Opened: 1929. **Pace of Play rating:** 4:45. **Green fee:** $15/17.
Credit cards: MC, V. **Reduced fees:** Seniors, Juniors.
Caddies: No. **Golf carts:** $8 for 18 holes.
Discount golf packages: No. **Season:** March-Nov. **High:** April-Sept.
On-site lodging: No. **Rental clubs:** Yes.
Walking policy: Unrestricted walking. **Range:** Yes (grass).
To obtain tee times: Call central computer system seven days in advance
(972-7888) or pro shop 30 days prior to day of play.
Subscriber comments: Easy walking . . . Quick greens, everything
breaks towards the city . . . Old course, well designed. Close to town . . .
Best muny in Salt Lake, No. 9 very memorable and tough . . . Always
crowded . . . Probably most popular course in state. Sometimes plays slow
. . . Poorman's country club . . . Good condition for the amount of play it
receives . . . Has everything good golf requires.

★★★½ BOUNTIFUL CITY GOLF COURSE
PU—2430 S. Bountiful Blvd., Bountiful (801)298-6040.
5 miles north of Salt Lake City. **Holes:** 18. **Par:** 71/72.
Yards: 6,630/5,012. **Course rating:** 70.1/68.6. **Slope:** 117/115.
Opened: 1975. **Pace of Play rating:** 4:20. **Green fee:** $15.
Credit cards: MC, V. **Reduced fees:** Seniors, Juniors.
Caddies: No. **Golf carts:** $15 for 18 holes.
Discount golf packages: Yes. **Season:** March-Nov. **High:** May-Aug.
On-site lodging: No. **Rental clubs:** Yes.
Walking policy: Unrestricted walking. **Range:** No.
To obtain tee times: Call one day in advance for weekdays. Call
Thursday prior to weekends and holidays.
Subscriber comments: Beautiful view. Good test of golf . . . Hilly, scenic
. . . A great course for couples to play . . . Beautiful city course . . . Great
value . . . Tight course, lots of brush . . . Beautiful view of Salt Lake valley
. . . Lots of elevation changes . . . Good greens . . . Must bring camera . . .
Beautiful wooded course, Great staff, fast pace of play . . . Well maintained.

★★★ DAVIS PARK GOLF COURSE
PU—1074 E. Nicholls Rd., Fruit Heights (801)546-4154.
17 miles north of Salt Lake City. **Holes:** 18. **Par:** 71/71.
Yards: 6,481/5,295. **Course rating:** 69.3/68.7. **Slope:** 117/114.
Opened: 1964. **Pace of Play rating:** 4:30. **Green fee:** $15.
Credit cards: None. **Reduced fees:** Seniors, Juniors.
Caddies: No. **Golf carts:** $8 for 18 holes.
Discount golf packages: No. **Season:** March-Nov. **High:** May-Aug.
On-site lodging: No. **Rental clubs:** Yes.
Walking policy: Unrestricted walking. **Range:** Yes (grass).
To obtain tee times: Call one day in advance for weekdays and Thursday
for upcoming weekend.
Subscriber comments: Short but well kept . . . Playable . . . Super muny
. . . Good tune-up and confidence builder . . . Mature layout . . . Busy.
Reservations recommended . . . Fun course . . . Local favorite. Some
elevated tees and greens.

★★★ EAGLE MOUNTAIN GOLF COURSE

PU—960 E. 700 S., Brigham City (801)723-3212.
55 miles north of Salt Lake City. **Holes:** 18. **Par:** 71/71.
Yards: 6,769/4,767. **Course rating:** 71.4/65.4. **Slope:** 119/101.
Opened: 1989. **Pace of Play rating:** 4:00-4:30. **Green fee:** $15.
Credit cards: None. **Reduced fees:** No.
Caddies: No. **Golf carts:** $8 for 18 holes.
Discount golf packages: No. **Season:** March-Nov. **High:** April-Sept.
On-site lodging: No. **Rental clubs:** Yes.
Walking policy: Unrestricted walking. **Range:** Yes (grass).
To obtain tee times: Call one day in advance for weekdays and two days
in advance for weekends and holidays.
Subscriber comments: Great view. A little windy . . . Wide open, good
condition . . . Scenic . . . Plays tough from the back . . . Fun, tight course.
Great course for small city . . . Mountainside course.

★★★ EAGLEWOOD GOLF COURSE

PU—1110 E. Eaglewood Dr., North Salt Lake City (801)299-0088.
Holes: 18. **Par:** 71/71.
Yards: 6,800/5,200. **Course rating:** 71.1/68.8. **Slope:** 121/112.
Opened: 1994. **Pace of Play rating:** 4:30. **Green fee:** $16/17.
Credit cards: MC, V. **Reduced fees:** Weekdays, Low season, Juniors.
Caddies: No. **Golf carts:** $9 for 18 holes.
Discount golf packages: Yes. **Season:** March-Nov. **High:** June-July.
On-site lodging: No. **Rental clubs:** Yes.
Walking policy: Unrestricted walking. **Range:** Yes (grass).
To obtain tee times: Call two days in advance.
Subscriber comments: Spectacular view of Great Salt Lake . . . Steep
terrain . . . Hard to walk . . . Great test of golf, use all clubs, hilly . . .
Services and staff are great . . . Needs to mature . . . Brand new and
promising course . . . Nice clubhouse.

★★ EAST BAY GOLF COURSE

PU—1860 S. East Bay Blvd., Provo (801)379-6612.
Holes: 18. **Par:** 71/72.
Yards: 6,932/5,125. **Course rating:** 67.6/66.6. **Slope:** 116/106.
Opened: 1986. **Pace of Play rating:** 4:00. **Green fee:** $10/16.
Credit cards: None. **Reduced fees:** No.
Caddies: No. **Golf carts:** $16 for 18 holes.
Discount golf packages: No. **Season:** March-Nov. **High:** May-Sept.
On-site lodging: No. **Rental clubs:** Yes.
Walking policy: Unrestricted walking. **Range:** Yes (grass).
To obtain tee times: Call one day in advance. May call Thursday for
weekend reservations.
Also has 9-hole executive course.
Subscriber comments: Flat, water comes into play on almost every hole,
well trapped . . . Accommodating staff . . . Layout has potential . . .
Tough from tips.

★★★ GLADSTAN GOLF CLUB

PU—One Gladstan Dr., Payson (801)465-2549, (800)634-3009.
20 miles south of Provo. **Holes:** 18. **Par:** 71/71.
Yards: 6,509/4,782. **Course rating:** 70.7/67.4. **Slope:** 121/111.
Opened: 1988. **Pace of Play rating:** 4:15. **Green fee:** $15.
Credit cards: MC, V. **Reduced fees:** Seniors, Juniors.
Caddies: No. **Golf carts:** $15 for 18 holes.
Discount golf packages: Yes. **Season:** March-Nov. **High:** May-Aug.
On-site lodging: No. **Rental clubs:** Yes.
Walking policy: Unrestricted walking. **Range:** Yes (grass).
To obtain tee times: Call Monday for the following week.
Subscriber comments: High mountain course . . . Really different nine-
hole layouts. Great clubhouse and cordial staff . . . Must be a straight hitter,
elevation changes . . . Beautiful mountain course . . . Great views . . . Fun
canyon holes.

★★ GLENDALE GOLF COURSE
PU—1560 W. 2100 S., Salt Lake City (801)974-2403
Holes: 18. **Par:** 72/73.
Yards: 7,000/5,930. **Course rating:** 70.9/72.5. **Slope:** 117/120.
Opened: 1973. **Pace of Play rating:** 4:00. **Green fee:** $14/15.
Credit cards: MC, V. **Reduced fees:** Weekdays, Seniors, Juniors.
Caddies: No. **Golf carts:** $8 for 18 holes.
Discount golf packages: No. **Season:** March-Nov. **High:** May-Aug.
On-site lodging: No. **Rental clubs:** Yes.
Walking policy: Unrestricted walking. **Range:** Yes (grass).
To obtain tee times: Call computer system one week in advance or pro shop one day in advance.
Subscriber comments: Long and flat . . . Good range . . . City course . . . Some water, but mostly wide open . . . Easy course to score on . . . Crowded at peak season . . . Friendliest staff, best greens in metro area, great practice facility.

★★ GLENMOOR GOLF AND COUNTRY CLUB
PU—9800 S. 4800 W., South Jordan (801)280-1742.
12 miles south of Salt Lake City. **Holes:** 18. **Par:** 72/72.
Yards: 6,900/5,800. **Course rating:** 70.9/72.0. **Slope:** 117/118.
Opened: 1965. **Pace of Play rating:** 4:30. **Green fee:** $15/16.
Credit cards: None. **Reduced fees:** Weekdays, Seniors.
Caddies: No. **Golf carts:** $16 for 18 holes.
Discount golf packages: No. **Season:** Year-round. **High:** June-July.
On-site lodging: No. **Rental clubs:** Yes.
Walking policy: Unrestricted walking. **Range:** Yes (grass).
To obtain tee times: Call seven days in advance.
Subscriber comments: Nice place to play, varied layout . . . Windy, hilly . . . Fair shape . . . Wind makes it a different course each time . . . Good greens . . . Friendly staff.

★★★½ GREEN SPRING GOLF COURSE
PU—588 N. Green Spring Dr., Washington (801)673-7888.
2 miles north of St. George. **Holes:** 18. **Par:** 71/71.
Yards: 6,717/5,042. **Course rating:** 72.6/69.8. **Slope:** 131/119.
Opened: 1989. **Pace of Play rating:** 5:00. **Green fee:** $18/27.
Credit cards: MC, V. **Reduced fees:** Weekdays, Low season, Twilight, Juniors.
Caddies: No. **Golf carts:** $10 for 18 holes.
Discount golf packages: Yes. **Season:** Year-round. **High:** Oct.-May.
On-site lodging: No. **Rental clubs:** Yes.
Walking policy: Unrestricted walking. **Range:** Yes (grass).
To obtain tee times: Call Monday at 7 a.m. for the following Monday through Sunday.
Ranked 6th in Utah by Golf Digest.
Subscriber comments: Amazing canyon holes . . . Incredible views from most tees . . . Desert to jungle, great variety . . . Outstanding views, snow capped mountains, red cliffs . . . Very tough from back tees . . . The greenest grass I have ever seen . . . Toughest course in Utah. Conditioning back on track . . . Worth the trip from Las Vegas.

★★★★ HOBBLE CREEK GOLF CLUB
PU—E. Hobble Creek Canyon Rd, Springville (801)489-6297.
15 miles north of Provo. **Holes:** 18. **Par:** 71/73.
Yards: 6,315/5,435. **Course rating:** 69.4/69.5. **Slope:** 120/117.
Opened: 1966. **Pace of Play rating:** 4:25. **Green fee:** $15.
Credit cards: None. **Reduced fees:** Seniors, Juniors.
Caddies: No. **Golf carts:** $16 for 18 holes.
Discount golf packages: No. **Season:** March-Nov. **High:** July-Sept.
On-site lodging: No. **Rental clubs:** Yes.
Walking policy: Unrestricted walking. **Range:** Yes (grass).

To obtain tee times: Call Monday for Tuesday through the following Monday.

Subscriber comments: Best course in Utah . . . Every hole different . . . One pretty course! Can't beat this in Utah . . . Gives a lot of different shots . . . Good test of game . . . Beautiful mountain setting . . . In a canyon, beautiful, quiet . . . Best all around . . . Fall colors are beautiful . . . Best deal in Utah.

★★★ HOMESTEAD GOLF CLUB

R—700 N. Homestead Dr., Midway (801)654-5588, (800)327-7220.
30 miles east of Salt Lake City. **Holes:** 18. **Par:** 72/72.
Yards: 6,967/5,131. **Course rating:** 72.8/68.8. **Slope:** 135/118.
Opened: 1990. **Pace of Play rating:** 4:30. **Green fee:** $15/30.
Credit cards: All major. **Reduced fees:** Weekdays, Low season, Resort guests, Twilight, Seniors.
Caddies: No. **Golf carts:** $10 for 18 holes.
Discount golf packages: Yes. **Season:** April-Oct. **High:** June-Sept.
On-site lodging: Yes. **Rental clubs:** Yes.
Walking policy: Unrestricted walking. **Range:** Yes (grass).
To obtain tee times: Hotel guests call 14 days in advance, others call one week in advance.
Ranked 7th in Utah by Golf Digest.
Subscriber comments: Nice resort, high mountain course, stay the weekend . . . Fun course for all players . . . Good service, excellent food . . . Frequent bargain days . . . Farm-type setting . . . New course starting to mature . . . Terrific pro shop . . . Some great holes.

★★★½ LOGAN RIVER GOLF COURSE

PU—550 W. 1000 S., Logan (801)750-0123.
80 miles north of Salt Lake City. **Holes:** 18. **Par:** 71/71.
Yards: 6,502/5,048. **Course rating:** 70.5/78.9. **Slope:** 124/117.
Opened: 1993. **Pace of Play rating:** 4:07. **Green fee:** $15.
Credit cards: MC, V. **Reduced fees:** Seniors, Juniors.
Caddies: No. **Golf carts:** $9 for 18 holes.
Discount golf packages: No. **Season:** March-Oct. **High:** June-Sept.
On-site lodging: No. **Rental clubs:** Yes.
Walking policy: Unrestricted walking. **Range:** Yes (grass).
To obtain tee times: Call one week in advance.
Subscriber comments: Beautiful course, a lot of water . . . New, very good layout, scenic . . . Shotmaker's paradise . . . Very challenging, some narrow fairways . . . Every hole curves through reeds and river . . . Keep the ball straight.

★½ MEADOW BROOK GOLF COURSE

PU—4197 S. 1300 W., Taylorsville (801)266-0971.
4 miles south of Salt Lake City. **Holes:** 18. **Par:** 72/72.
Yards: 6,800/5,605. **Course rating:** 70.0/67.9. **Slope:** 110/104.
Opened: 1953. **Pace of Play rating:** 4:30. **Green fee:** $15/16.
Credit cards: None. **Reduced fees:** Weekdays, Seniors, Juniors.
Caddies: Yes. **Golf carts:** $17 for 18 holes.
Discount golf packages: No. **Season:** March-Dec. **High:** May-Oct.
On-site lodging: No. **Rental clubs:** Yes.
Walking policy: Unrestricted walking. **Range:** Yes (grass).
To obtain tee times: Call pro shop.
Subscriber comments: Old and flat . . . Popular local course . . . Good staff . . . Old-style course, small elevated greens . . . An old standby.

★★★½ MOAB GOLF CLUB

PU—2705 S.E. Bench Rd., Moab (801)259-6488.
220 miles southeast of Salt Lake City. **Holes:** 18. **Par:** 72/72.
Yards: 6,819/4,725. **Course rating:** 72.2/69.6. **Slope:** 125/110.
Opened: 1960. **Pace of Play rating:** 4:30. **Green fee:** $15.
Credit cards: MC, V. **Reduced fees:** Juniors.
Caddies: No. **Golf carts:** $8 for 18 holes.
Discount golf packages: Yes. **Season:** Year-round. **High:** Spring/Fall.

On-site lodging: No. **Rental clubs:** Yes.
Walking policy: Unrestricted walking. **Range:** Yes (grass).
To obtain tee times: Call 30 days in advance with credit card.
Subscriber comments: An oasis in the desert, best deal in Utah . . . A personal favorite . . . Beautiful redrock background, good condition, great staff, great value . . . I'll drive six hours for one round. It's fun . . . Accuracy a must . . . Take a camera . . . Nice mixture of the new nine holes with the old nine.

★★½ MOUNT OGDEN GOLF COURSE
PU—1787 Constitution Way, Ogden (801)629-8700.
Holes: 18. **Par:** 71/72.
Yards: 6,300/4,980. **Course rating:** 70.5/69.5. **Slope:** 121/111.
Opened: 1985. **Pace of Play rating:** 4:30. **Green fee:** $15.
Credit cards: None. **Reduced fees:** No.
Caddies: No. **Golf carts:** $8 for 18 holes.
Discount golf packages: No. **Season:** March-Nov. **High:** April-Oct.
On-site lodging: No. **Rental clubs:** Yes.
Walking policy: Unrestricted walking. **Range:** Yes (grass).
To obtain tee times: Call on Wednesday for weekend tee times. Weekdays, call one day in advance.
Subscriber comments: Very challenging course, must hit the fairways . . . Hilly . . . Toughest test of golf in Utah . . . Super shape, steep walking . . . Hit it straight . . . Toughest course I've ever played . . . Take a lot of balls . . . Outstanding scenery, narrow fairways, rough is oak brush.

MOUNTAIN DELL GOLF CLUB
PU—3287 Cummings Rd., Salt Lake City (801)582-3812.
Green fee: $18.
Credit cards: MC, V. **Reduced fees:** Weekdays, Twilight, Seniors, Juniors.
Caddies: No. **Golf carts:** $8 for 18 holes.
Discount golf packages: No. **Season:** April-Nov. **High:** June-Aug.
On-site lodging: No. **Rental clubs:** Yes.
Walking policy: Unrestricted walking. **Range:** Yes (grass).
To obtain tee times: Automated tee time system (801)972-7888.
★★★ CANYON COURSE
Holes: 18. **Par:** 72/73.
Yards: 6,787/5,447. **Course rating:** 71.3/71.1. **Slope:** 126/112.
Opened: 1962. **Pace of Play rating:** 5:00. **Subscriber comments:** Hard walk . . . Another mountain gem . . . Accuracy required . . . Blend of traditional and target golf . . . Great summer course . . . Wonderful staff . . . Play golf with the deer and elk . . . Steep hills . . . Great views.
★★★ LAKE COURSE
Holes: 18. **Par:** 71/71.
Yards: 6,709/5,066. **Course rating:** 72.2/67.6. **Slope:** 129/109.
Opened: 1962. **Pace of Play rating:** 5:00.
Subscriber comments: Lots of trouble . . . Beautiful holes, mountain views, valley views . . . Tough starting holes and super vistas . . . One of the most challenging courses in Utah . . . Local knowledge helps . . . Beautiful canyon course . . . Wide open.

★½ MOUNTAIN VIEW GOLF CLUB
PU—2400 W. 8660 S., West Jordan (801)255-9211.
Call club for further information.
Subscriber comments: Let-the-shaft-out course. You can usually recover . . . Playable . . . Flat, wide fairways, big greens, good shape, enjoyable . . . Good for beginners, open and forgiving, nice staff, easy tee times.

★★ MURRAY PARKWAY GOLF CLUB
PU—6345 S. Murray Pkwy. Blvd., Murray (801)262-4653.
8 miles south of Salt Lake City. **Holes:** 18. **Par:** 72/72.
Yards: 6,800/5,800. **Course rating:** 71.3/71.0. **Slope:** 120/118.
Opened: 1986. **Pace of Play rating:** 4:30. **Green fee:** $17.
Credit cards: MC, V. **Reduced fees:** Juniors.

Caddies: No. **Golf carts:** $8 for 18 holes.
Discount golf packages: No. **Season:** March-Nov. **High:** June-Aug.
On-site lodging: No. **Rental clubs:** Yes.
Walking policy: Unrestricted walking. **Range:** Yes.
To obtain tee times: Call Monday for Tuesday and Wednesday tee times; call Wednesday for Thursday and Friday and call Thursday for Saturday, Sunday and Monday.
Subscriber comments: Nice pro shop, driving range . . . Very busy, needs more trees, nice course . . . Not much variety . . . Wind is the challenge.

★★★½ PARK CITY GOLF COURSE
PU—Lower Park Ave., Park City (801)649-8701.
25 miles east of Salt Lake City. **Holes:** 18. **Par:** 72/72.
Yards: 6,754/5,600. **Course rating:** 71.7/71.4. **Slope:** 127/123.
Opened: 1963. **Pace of Play rating:** 4:30. **Green fee:** $20/25.
Credit cards: MC, V. **Reduced fees:** Low season.
Caddies: No. **Golf carts:** $10 for 18 holes.
Discount golf packages: No. **Season:** April-Oct. **High:** May-Sept.
On-site lodging: No. **Rental clubs:** Yes.
Walking policy: Unrestricted walking. **Range:** Yes (grass).
To obtain tee times: Call seven days in advance. Two or more tee times require a credit card.
Subscriber comments: Good, mature . . . Seems more like a resort course than muny . . . Beautiful layout, excellent maintenance . . . One of the best secrets in the state . . . Vacation layout between condos . . . Beautiful mountain setting, streams. One of my favorites . . . Picturesque . . . Course is always in good shape . . . Holes all different . . . Busy . . . Ideal course.

★★★★ PARK MEADOWS GOLF CLUB
PU—2000 Meadows Dr., Park City (801)649-2460.
30 miles west of Salt Lake City. **Holes:** 18. **Par:** 72/73.
Yards: 7,400/5,816. **Course rating:** 74.4/72.2. **Slope:** 129/125.
Opened: 1983. **Pace of Play rating:** 4:30. **Green fee:** $35/59.
Credit cards: MC, V, AMEX. **Reduced fees:** Low season, Twilight, Seniors.
Caddies: No. **Golf carts:** Included in Green Fee.
Discount golf packages: Yes. **Season:** April-Oct. **High:** June-Aug.
On-site lodging: No. **Rental clubs:** Yes.
Walking policy: Mandatory cart. **Range:** Yes (grass).
To obtain tee times: Call seven days in advance.
Ranked 8th in Utah by Golf Digest.
Subscriber comments: The best of the best . . . Beautiful but very long with hazards . . . Looks easy, plays hard, long par 4s . . . A great Nicklaus course . . . Well groomed . . . Requires long irons and sand wedge . . . Best in state, tough but fair, nice clubhouse . . . Free range balls . . . Altitude is helpful but wind is unforgiving.

RIVERBEND GOLF COURSE★
PU—12800 S. 1040 W., Riverton. (801)253-3673.
15 miles south of Salt Lake City. **Holes:** 18. **Par:** 72/72.
Yards: 6,876/5,081. **Course rating:** 69.9/68.7. **Slope:** 118/111.
Opened: 1994. **Pace of Play rating:** 4:00. **Green fee:** $16/18.
Credit cards: MC, V. **Reduced fees:** Seniors, Juniors.
Caddies: No. **Golf carts:** $9 for 18 holes.
Discount golf packages: No. **Season:** Year-round. **High:** April-Oct.
On-site lodging: No. **Rental clubs:** Yes.
Walking policy: Unrestricted walking. **Range:** Yes (grass).
To obtain tee times: Call Thursday for upcoming weekend.

★★ ROSE PARK GOLF CLUB
PU—1386 N. Redwood Rd., Salt Lake City (801)596-5030.
Holes: 18. **Par:** 72/ 75.
Yards: 6,696/5,816. **Course rating:** 69.6/70.8. **Slope:** 109/112.

Opened: N/A. **Pace of Play rating:** 4:30. **Green fee:** $15/16.
Credit cards: MC, V. **Reduced fees:** Seniors, Juniors.
Caddies: No. **Golf carts:** $16 for 18 holes.
Discount golf packages: Yes. **Season:** Feb.-Dec. **High:** May-Sept.
On-site lodging: No. **Rental clubs:** Yes.
Walking policy: Unrestricted walking. **Range:** Yes (grass).
To obtain tee times: Call seven days in advance.
Subscriber comments: Great for walking . . . Old established downtown Salt Lake course . . . Fun, short course, bring your wife or kids . . . Good greens . . . Great place to work on your game . . . City course . . . Beautifully maintained . . . Relaxing track.

SCHNEITER'S BLUFF AT WEST POINT★
PU—300 N. 3500 W., West Point (801)773-0731.
20 miles north of Salt Lake City. **Holes:** 18. **Par:** 72/72.
Yards: 6,833/5,419. **Course rating:** N/A. **Slope:** N/A.
Opened: 1995. **Pace of Play rating:** 4:00. **Green fee:** $15.
Credit cards: MC, V. **Reduced fees:** Seniors, Juniors.
Caddies: No. **Golf carts:** $16 for 18 holes.
Discount golf packages: Yes. **Season:** March-Nov. **High:** June-Sept.
On-site lodging: No. **Rental clubs:** Yes.
Walking policy: Unrestricted walking. **Range:** Yes (grass).
To obtain tee times: Call Thursday for upcoming weekend. Call one day in advance for weekday.

★★½ SCHNEITER'S RIVERSIDE GOLF COURSE
PU—5460 S. Weber Dr., Ogden (801)399-4636.
Holes: 18. **Par:** 71/71.
Yards: 6,177/5,217. **Course rating:** 68.4/68.5. **Slope:** 114/113.
Opened: 1961. **Pace of Play rating:** 4:00. **Green fee:** $15.
Credit cards: MC, V. **Reduced fees:** Seniors, Juniors.
Caddies: No. **Golf carts:** $16 for 18 holes.
Discount golf packages: No. **Season:** March-Nov. **High:** May-Aug.
On-site lodging: No. **Rental clubs:** Yes.
Walking policy: Walking at certain times. **Range:** Yes grass).
To obtain tee times: Call Thursday for upcoming weekend. Weekdays, call one day in advance.
Subscriber comments: Always busy . . . Nice course, some tough holes, green all year . . . Can walk 18 fairly easily . . . Short but demanding . . . Crowded . . . Pleasant setting . . . Friendly staff is very accommodating.

★★ SHERWOOD HILLS RESORT GOLF COURSE
R—Highway 89-91, Sardine Canyon (801)245-6055.
6 miles south of Logan. **Holes:** 9. **Par:** 36/37.
Yards: 3,315/2,830. **Course rating:** N/A. **Slope:** N/A.
Opened: 1973. **Pace of Play rating:** N/A. **Green fee:** $17.
Credit cards: MC, V. **Reduced fees:** Weekdays, Resort guests, Seniors.
Caddies: No. **Golf carts:** $18 for 18 holes.
Discount golf packages: Yes. **Season:** April-Nov. **High:** June-Aug.
On-site lodging: Yes. **Rental clubs:** Yes.
Walking policy: Unrestricted walking. **Range:** Yes (grass).
To obtain tee times: Call anytime in advance.
Subscriber comments: Nine-hole course with beautiful mountain scenery . . . Challenging.

★★ SOUTHGATE GOLF CLUB
PU—1975 S. Tonaquint Dr., St. George (801)628-0000.
110 miles northest of Las Vegas. **Holes:** 18. **Par:** 70/70.
Yards: 6,400/4,463. **Course rating:** 70.2/66.8. **Slope:** 120/112.
Opened: 1984. **Pace of Play rating:** 4:30. **Green fee:** $29.
Credit cards: MC, V. **Reduced fees:** Low season, Twilight, Juniors.
Caddies: No. **Golf carts:** $19 for 18 holes.
Discount golf packages: No. **Season:** Year-round. **High:** Oct-April.

On-site lodging: No. **Rental clubs:** Yes.
Walking policy: Unrestricted walking. **Range:** Yes (grass).
To obtain tee times: Call two weeks in advance.

★★★ SPANISH OAKS GOLF CLUB

PU—2300 Powerhouse Rd., Spanish Fork (801)798-9816.
7 miles north of Provo. **Holes:** 18. **Par:** 72/73.
Yards: 6,358/5,319. **Course rating:** 68.7/68.9. **Slope:** 116/113.
Opened: 1983. **Pace of Play rating:** N/A. **Green fee:** $15.
Credit cards: All major. **Reduced fees:** Twilight, Seniors, Juniors.
Caddies: No. **Golf carts:** $15 for 18 holes.
Discount golf packages: No. **Season:** March-Oct. **High:** May-Sept.
On-site lodging: No. **Rental clubs:** Yes.
Walking policy: Unrestricted walking. **Range:** Yes (grass)
To obtain tee times: Call one week in advance.
Subscriber comments: Relaxed, fun, not particularly difficult . . . Back
nine mountain course . . . Two different nines . . . Foothill course without
a lot of brush . . . Windy mornings.

★★ ST. GEORGE GOLF CLUB

PU—2190 S. 1400 E., St. George (801)634-5854.
110 miles northeast of Las Vegas. **Holes:** 18. **Par:** 73/73.
Yards: 7,211/5,216. **Course rating:** 73.1/68.9. **Slope:** 126/114.
Opened: 1975. **Pace of Play rating:** 4:00. **Green fee:** $29.
Credit cards: None. **Reduced fees:** No.
Caddies: No. **Golf carts:** Included in Green Fee.
Discount golf packages: No. **Season:** Year-round. **High:** Oct-May.
On-site lodging: No. **Rental clubs:** Yes.
Walking policy: Unrestricted walking. **Range:** No.
To obtain tee times: Call one week in advance.
Subscriber comments: Variety of holes . . . Wide open but long, good
greens . . . Course is a real sleeper . . . Lot of improvements over the years
. . . Friendly personnel.

★★ STANSBURY PARK GOLF CLUB

PU—One Country Club Dr., Tooele (801)328-1483.
25 miles east of Salt Lake City. **Holes:** 18. **Par:** 72/72.
Yards: 6,831/5,722. **Course rating:** 71.6/71.5. **Slope:** 125/121.
Opened: 1972. **Pace of Play rating:** 4:30. **Green fee:** $13/15.
Credit cards: None. **Reduced fees:** Weekdays, Low season.
Caddies: No. **Golf carts:** $7 for 18 holes.
Discount golf packages: No. **Season:** Feb.-Nov. **High:** June-Aug.
On-site lodging: No. **Rental clubs:** Yes.
Walking policy: Unrestricted walking. **Range:** Yes.
To obtain tee times: Call Thursday for weekends. For weekdays, call
Saturday and Sunday.
Subscriber comments: Nice layout, poorly maintained . . . Fun to play
. . . Easy walk . . . Good links style course. Water will test your game . . .
Best value in Utah, pay for 18 and can play all day; water on 16 of 18 holes.

★★★★ SUNBROOK GOLF CLUB

PU—2240 Sunbrook Dr., St. George (801)634-5866.
120 miles northeast of Las Vegas. **Holes:** 18. **Par:** 72/72.
Yards: 6,800/5,286. **Course rating:** 73.0/71.1. **Slope:** 129/121.
Opened: 1990. **Pace of Play rating:** N/A. **Green fee:** $18/29.
Credit cards: MC, V. **Reduced fees:** Low season.
Caddies: No. **Golf carts:** $10 for 18 holes.
Discount golf packages: No. **Season:** Year-round. **High:** Jan.-
May/Oct.-Nov.
On-site lodging: No. **Rental clubs:** Yes.
Walking policy: Unrestricted walking. **Range:** Yes (grass).
To obtain tee times: Call Monday for the following week.
Ranked 1st in Utah by Golf Digest.
Subscriber comments: Finest all-around course in Utah . . . Mountain

course, as beautiful as any anywhere . . . The best in golf . . . Four sets of tees . . . Tough but great design. Great winter golf . . . A must place to play . . . Best staff/club in state . . . Fantastic Ted Robinson layout . . . You really get your money's worth here . . . Lots of personality.

★★★ TRI-CITY GOLF COURSE
PU—1400 N. 200 E., American Fork (801)756-3594.
30 miles south of Salt Lake City. **Holes:** 18. **Par:** 72/75.
Yards: 7,077/6,304. **Course rating:** 73.0/75.0. **Slope:** 125/127.
Opened: 1972. **Pace of Play rating:** 4:15. **Green fee:** $13.
Credit cards: None. **Reduced fees:** Seniors,Juniors.
Caddies: No. **Golf carts:** $14 for 18 holes.
Discount golf packages: No. **Season:** March-Oct. **High:** May-Aug.
On-site lodging: No. **Rental clubs:** Yes.
Walking policy: Unrestricted walking. **Range:** Yes (grass).
To obtain tee times: Call up to ten days in advance.
Subscriber comments: Tough course, excellent shape, walkable . . . Old trees . . . Uncrowded, good value . . . Fun course, needs local knowledge . . . Tough and long but in good shape, shoot a good score and you've played very well . . . Good staff . . . Beautiful wooded course, well maintained, must be straight.

★★★★ VALLEY VIEW GOLF COURSE
PU—2501 E. Gentile, Layton (801)546-1630.
15 miles north of Salt Lake City. **Holes:** 18. **Par:** 72/74.
Yards: 6,652/5,755. **Course rating:** 71.2/72.3. **Slope:** 119/120.
Opened: 1974. **Pace of Play rating:** 4:30. **Green fee:** $15.
Credit cards: MC, V, AMEX. **Reduced fees:** Seniors, Juniors.
Caddies: No. **Golf carts:** $8 for 18 holes.
Discount golf packages: No. **Season:** March-Nov. **High:** May-Sept.
On-site lodging: No. **Rental clubs:** Yes.
Walking policy: Unrestricted walking. **Range:** Yes (grass).
To obtain tee times: Call Thursday 7 a.m. for Friday, Saturday, Sunday and Monday holidays. Call one day in advance for weekdays.
Subscriber comments: Tough course but can be tamed . . . Excellent staff . . . Best muny in Utah . . . Will rival any country club . . . A true test . . . Good service . . . Lots of elevation changes, tough from back tees. Last three holes very tough, uphill and long . . . Play if in Ogden area . . . Busy . . . Reservations recommended . . . Slick greens in good shape . . . Great view.

★★★★ WASATCH STATE PARK GOLF CLUB CANYON/LAKE/MOUNTAIN
PU—P.O. Box 10, Midway (801)654-0532.
Call club for further information.
Subscriber comments: A must play when fall colors turn . . . Spend a day and play all 27 . . . Very busy but great beauty . . . Nice variety between the three nines . . . Unbelievable scenery . . . Play it in September, you won't go home.

★★ WEST BOUNTIFUL CITY GOLF COURSE
PU—1201 N. 1100 W., West Bountiful (801)295-1019.
10 miles north of Salt Lake City. **Holes:** 18. **Par:** 71/72.
Yards: 6,030/4,895. **Course rating:** 67.2/66.5. **Slope:** 113/115.
Opened: 1966. **Pace of Play rating:** 4:20. **Green fee:** $15.
Credit cards: None. **Reduced fees:** Seniors, Juniors.
Caddies: No. **Golf carts:** $8 for 18 holes.
Discount golf packages: No. **Season:** March-Oct. **High:** June-Aug.
On-site lodging: No. **Rental clubs:** Yes.
Walking policy: Unrestricted walking. **Range:** Yes (grass).
To obtain tee times: Call Monday for Tuesday-Friday. Call Thursday for Saturday, Sunday and Monday.
Subscriber comments: Country golf . . . Nice course, great for practice rounds . . . Flat, easy course to learn on . . . Lots of diverse shots, great price.

★★★ WEST RIDGE GOLF COURSE
PU—5055 S. West Ridge Blvd., West Valley City (801)966-4653.
10 miles west of Salt Lake City. **Holes:** 18. **Par:** 71/71.
Yards: 6,734/5,027. **Course rating:** 72.2/68.1. **Slope:** 125/118.
Opened: 1991. **Pace of Play rating:** 4:30-5:00. **Green fee:** $15/17.
Credit cards: All major. **Reduced fees:** Weekdays, Seniors, Juniors.
Caddies: No. **Golf carts:** $8 for 18 holes.
Discount golf packages: Yes. **Season:** March-Nov. **High:** April-Aug.
On-site lodging: No. **Rental clubs:** Yes.
Walking policy: Unrestricted walking. **Range:** Yes (grass).
To obtain tee times: Call Monday at 7 a.m. for Tuesday/Wednesday. Call
Wednesday at 7 a.m. for Thursday/Friday. Call Thursday at 7 a.m. for
Friday-Monday tee times.
Subscriber comments: Can be challenging in wind . . . Courteous staff
. . . Fun golf . . . Never busy . . . Narrow fairways . . . New course, good
potential . . . Long, well groomed, best of local courses.

★★★½ WINGPOINTE GOLF COURSE
PU—3602 W., 100 N., Salt Lake City (801)575-2345.
Holes: 18. **Par:** 72/72.
Yards: 7,101/5,228. **Course rating:** 73.3/72.0. **Slope:** 131/125.
Opened: 1990. **Pace of Play rating:** 4:30. **Green fee:** $16/18.
Credit cards: MC, V. **Reduced fees:** Weekdays, Low season, Seniors,
Juniors.
Caddies: No. **Golf carts:** $16 for 18 holes.
Discount golf packages: No. **Season:** Year-round. **High:** May-Oct.
On-site lodging: No. **Rental clubs:** Yes.
Walking policy: Walking at certain times. **Range:** Yes (grass).
To obtain tee times: Call (801)972-7888 up to seven days in advance.
Ranked 9th in Utah by Golf Digest.
Subscriber comments: Arthur Hills' best value . . . Great use of poor
land, right by airport, traveler's dream . . . Windy, difficult links course
. . . Walk or ride . . . Best driving range in state . . . My favorite SLC
course . . . Best public course in the state, the St. Andrews of Utah . . .
Noisy, by airport . . . Tough from tips . . . Utah's best.

★★★½ WOLF CREEK RESORT GOLF COURSE
R—3900 N. Wolf Creek Dr., Eden (801)745-3365.
14 miles north of Ogden. **Holes:** 18. **Par:** 72/72.
Yards: 6,845/5,332. **Course rating:** N/A. **Slope:** 134/127.
Opened: N/A. **Pace of Play rating:** N/A. **Green fee:** N/A.
Credit cards: MC, V, AMEX. **Reduced fees:** Weekdays, Low season,
Resort guests, Twilight.
Caddies: No. **Golf carts:** N/A.
Discount golf packages: Yes. **Season:** March-Nov. **High:** May-Sept.
On-site lodging: Yes. **Rental clubs:** N/A.
Walking policy: N/A. **Range:** No.
Subscriber comments: Scenery is outstanding . . . Great setting . . .
Another mountain resort course, good staff . . . Two nines are extremely
different . . . Separates the men from the boys yet fun for ladies . . .
Difficult greens . . . Unbeatable mountain peak and valley views . . . Stay
in the condos, play again tomorrow . . . Has potential to be one of the best
in Utah.

★★½ ALDERBROOK GOLF AND YACHT CLUB

R—300 Country Club Dr. E., Union (360)898-2560.

35 miles northwest of Olympia. **Holes:** 18. **Par:** 72/73.

Yards: 6,326/5,500. **Course rating:** 70.9/72.2. **Slope:** 122/125.

Opened: 1966. **Pace of Play rating:** 4:30. **Green fee:** $27/33.

Credit cards: MC, V. **Reduced fees:** Weekdays, Low season, Resort guests, Seniors.

Caddies: No. **Golf carts:** $13 for 18 holes.

Discount golf packages: Yes. **Season:** Year-round. **High:** April-Oct.

On-site lodging: Yes. **Rental clubs:** Yes.

Walking policy: Unrestricted walking. **Range:** Yes (grass).

To obtain tee times: Call Monday prior to weekend or holiday.

Subscriber comments: Demanding front nine, relax and enjoy scenery on the back . . . Plays long with some difficult par fives, one with double dog-leg . . . Scenic tight fairways . . . Good course for nearly everyone . . . Pro shop staff tops in customer service . . . One of the best-kept secrets in NW . . . Could improve maintenance . . . Beautiful setting on Hood Canal.

★★★★ APPLE TREE GOLF COURSE

PU—8804 Occidental Ave., Yakima (509)966-5877.

140 miles southeast of Seattle. **Holes:** 18. **Par:** 72/72.

Yards: 6,892/5,428. **Course rating:** 73.3/72.0. **Slope:** 129/124.

Opened: 1992. **Pace of Play rating:** 4:50. **Green fee:** $25/45.

Credit cards: MC, V. **Reduced fees:** Weekdays, Low season, Twilight, Seniors, Junior

Caddies: No. **Golf carts:** $12 for 18 holes.

Discount golf packages: No. **Season:** Year-round. **High:** March-Oct.

On-site lodging: No. **Rental clubs:** Yes.

Walking policy: Unrestricted walking. **Range:** Yes (grass).

To obtain tee times: Call up to one month in advance when calling from outside the Yakima area; call one week in advance in the Yakima area. Groups of 16 or more may book six months to one year in advance.

Subscriber comments: We were treated like royalty . . . Very well laid out, great signature hole, apple-shaped 17th . . . Best small-town clubhouse anywhere! . . . Take your camera . . . Traditional-style course with modern twists . . . Five sets of tees . . . Very fair course . . . Good breakfast . . . Through apple orchards to island green, exciting! . . . Love Nos. 9, 17 and 18 . . . Good course to play when traveling.

★★ AUBURN GOLF COURSE

29630 Green River Rd., Auburn (206)833-2350.

Call club for further information.

Subscriber comments: Best value in dry weather . . . Family of bobcats frequently seen on sixth tee . . . Doing much work to improve . . . Best city course in King County . . . Easy, flat greens, you better score here . . . Staff is great . . . Best public course in the sound area . . . Great pro! . . . Pleasant course . . . Good old track . . . Front nine flat, back nine hilly . . . New drainage system . . . Good recent upgrades.

★★★ AVALON GOLF CLUB

NORTH/WEST/SOUTH

PU—1717 Kelleher Rd., Burlington (206)757-1900, (800)624-0202.

55 miles north of Seattle. **Holes:** 27. **Par:** 72/72/72.

Yards: 6,597/6,576/6,771. **Course rating:** 72.5/72.3/73.3.

Slope: 127/129/129.

Opened: 1991. **Pace of Play rating:** 3:00. **Green fee:** $22/37.

Credit cards: MC, V. **Reduced fees:** Weekdays, Low season, Twilight, Seniors, Juniors.

Caddies: Yes. **Golf carts:** $22 for 18 holes.

Discount golf packages: Yes. **Season:** Year-round. **High:** May-Sept.

On-site lodging: No. **Rental clubs:** Yes.

Walking policy: Unrestricted walking. **Range:** Yes (grass).

To obtain tee times: Phone up to five days in advance.

Subscriber comments: Course is constantly being improved . . . Always an inviting place to play . . . Tight, tough layout . . . Three distinct nines . . . $20 twilight that begins seven hours before sunset . . . Beautiful walk . . . Caddies available, great . . . Super deals for fall and winter play . . . Super staff, let me try out a new set of clubs on the range . . . Stunning view of Skagit Valley . . . Other specials for birthday and Mother's Day . . . Better hit the ball straight to play here.

★½ BATTLE CREEK GOLF COURSE

PU—6006 Meridian Ave. N., Marysville (206)659-7931.
30 miles north of Seattle. **Holes:** 18. **Par:** 73/73.
Yards: 6,575/5,391. **Course rating:** 71.4/70.9. **Slope:** 125/124.
Opened: 1990. **Pace of Play rating:** 4:30. **Green fee:** $18/23.
Credit cards: MC, V. **Reduced fees:** Weekdays, Low season, Seniors, Juniors.
Caddies: No. **Golf carts:** $21 for 18 holes.
Discount golf packages: Yes. **Season:** Year-round. **High:** May-Aug.
On-site lodging: No. **Rental clubs:** Yes.
Walking policy: Unrestricted walking. **Range:** Yes (grass).
To obtain tee times: Reservations can be made seven days in advance.
Subscriber comments: Staff is very friendly . . . Great property, could be a great course . . . Greens still inconsistant . . . Nice views of Puget Sound from many holes . . . Improved course conditions as compared to 1993 . . . Getting a little better . . . Interesting layout, very hilly . . . Extensive wetland protection . . . Great potential.

★★ BROOKDALE GOLF COURSE

PU—1802 Brookdale Rd. E., Tacoma (206)537-4400, (800)281-2428.
Holes: 18. **Par:** 71/74.
Yards: 6,425/5,847. **Course rating:** 69.6/72.2. **Slope:** 112/123.
Opened: 1931. **Pace of Play rating:** 3:31. **Green fee:** $18.
Credit cards: MC, V. **Reduced fees:** Low season, Twilight, Seniors, Juniors.
Caddies: No. **Golf carts:** $18 for 18 holes.
Discount golf packages: Yes. **Season:** Year-round. **High:** April-Oct.
On-site lodging: No. **Rental clubs:** Yes.
Walking policy: Unrestricted walking. **Range:** Yes.
To obtain tee times: Call or stop by pro shop one week in advance.
Subscriber comments: The staff goes out of its way to make you feel so good . . . A very forgiving course, with wide fairways and large greens, fun to play . . . Great breakfast by a friendly crew . . . Great mobile snack cart! . . . Straightforward, not fancy, especially good in winter . . . No practice range, but has an interesting warm-up facility.

★★★½ CANYON LAKES GOLF COURSE

PU—3700 Canyon Lakes Dr., Kennewick (509)582-3736.
210 miles southeast of Seattle. **Holes:** 18. **Par:** 72/72.
Yards: 6,973/5,565. **Course rating:** 73.7/71.1. **Slope:** 135/132.
Opened: 1981. **Pace of Play rating:** 4:00-4:30. **Green fee:** $18/20.
Credit cards: MC, V. **Reduced fees:** Juniors.
Caddies: No. **Golf carts:** $24 for 18 holes.
Discount golf packages: Yes. **Season:** Year-round. **High:** March-Nov.
On-site lodging: No. **Rental clubs:** Yes.
Walking policy: Unrestricted walking. **Range:** Yes (grass).
To obtain tee times: Call one week in advance.
Subscriber comments: This course can handle all the shots in your bag . . . Water, sand, all holes different . . . Great test, tournament ready . . . Extremely challenging, especially when it's windy . . . Staff and marshal helpful . . . Huge, fast greens . . . For the money, best value in Washington State! . . . Beautiful setting . . . Nice driving range and putting greens.

★★★ CAPITOL CITY GOLF CLUB
PU—5225 Yelm Hwy. S.E., Olympia (206)491-5111, (800)994-2582.
Holes: 18. **Par:** 72/72.
Yards: 6,536/5,510. **Course rating:** 70.9/71.7. **Slope:** 123/122.
Opened: 1961. **Pace of Play rating:** 4:15. **Green fee:** $17/ 22.
Credit cards: MC, V. **Reduced fees:** Weekdays, Low season, Twilight, Seniors, Juniors.
Caddies: No. **Golf carts:** $13 for 18 holes.
Discount golf packages: No. **Season:** Year-round. **High:** June-Aug.
On-site lodging: No. **Rental clubs:** Yes.
Walking policy: Unrestricted walking. **Range:** Yes (grass).
To obtain tee times: Call seven days ahead.
Subscriber comments: Beautiful view of Mount Rainier . . . Best winter course in the Northwest . . . A year-round course. Staff and service good. Drains well in wet weather . . . Flat, tree-lined fairways with homes on both sides . . . Fun course . . . Easy to walk . . . Tight fairways through housing development.

★½ CEDARCREST GOLF CLUB
PU—6810 84th St. N.E., Marysville (206)659-3566.
35 miles north of Seattle. **Holes:** 18. **Par:** 70/72.
Yards: 5,390/5,086. **Course rating:** 65.4/67.8. **Slope:** 110/110.
Opened: 1927. **Pace of Play rating:** 4:00. **Green fee:** $14.
Credit cards: None. **Reduced fees:** No
Caddies: No. **Golf carts:** $16 for 18 holes.
Discount golf packages: No. **Season:** Year-round. **High:** June-Aug.
On-site lodging: No. **Rental clubs:** Yes.
Walking policy: Unrestricted walking. **Range:** No.
To obtain tee times: Call seven days in advance.
Subscriber comments: Can't beat fees . . . Nicest pro around . . . Continually working to improve course . . . Fairly short course with some drivable par 4s, also some tight driving holes . . . Walkable at any age . . . Nice local course, very friendly staff!

★★ CEDARS GOLF CLUB
PU—15001 N.E. 181st St., Brush Prairie (206)687-4233.
20 miles north of Portland, OR. **Holes:** 18. **Par:** 72/72.
Yards: 6,423/5,216. **Course rating:** 71.2/71.1. **Slope:** 129/117.
Opened: 1975. **Pace of Play rating:** 4:30-5:00. **Green fee:** $16/18.
Credit cards: None. **Reduced fees:** Juniors.
Caddies: No. **Golf carts:** $20 for 18 holes.
Discount golf packages: No. **Season:** Year-round. **High:** May-Oct.
On-site lodging: No. **Rental clubs:** Yes.
Walking policy: Walking at certain times. **Range:** Yes (grass).
To obtain tee times: Call up to seven days in advance.
Subscriber comments: Excellent use of the natural terrain, beautiful water hazards . . . Tough but wet . . . Fantastic layout . . . Needs some TLC . . . Nice wooded setting.

★★½ CHEWELAH GOLF AND COUNTRY CLUB
SP—2537 Sand Canyon Rd., Chewelah (509)935-6807.
60 miles north of Spokane. **Holes:** 18. **Par:** 72/74.
Yards: 6,511/5,672. **Course rating:** 70.9/72.2. **Slope:** 125/124.
Opened: 1976. **Pace of Play rating:** 4:30. **Green fee:** $8/15.
Credit cards: None. **Reduced fees:** Seniors, Juniors.
Caddies: No. **Golf carts:** $20 for 18 holes.
Discount golf packages: No. **Season:** April-Oct. **High:** May-Sept.
On-site lodging: No. **Rental clubs:** Yes.
Walking policy: Unrestricted walking. **Range:** Yes.
To obtain tee times: Call one month in advance.
Subscriber comments: Heavily wooded and narrow, a real shotmaker's course . . . Control a must . . . One of my all-time favorites . . . Friendly, efficient staff and a scenic hilltop setting . . . Worthwhile stop . . . Fun to play, easy walking.

★★★½ CLASSIC COUNTRY CLUB

PU—4908 208th St. E., Spanaway (206)847-4440, (800)924-9557.
60 miles south of Seattle. **Holes:** 18. **Par:** 72/72.
Yards: 6,793/5,580. **Course rating:** 73.6/73.3. **Slope:** 133/128.
Opened: 1991. **Pace of Play rating:** 4:30. **Green fee:** $20/45.
Credit cards: MC, V, AMEX, JCB. **Reduced fees:** Weekdays, Low
season, Twilight, Seniors, Juniors.
Caddies: No. **Golf carts:** $23 for 18 holes.
Discount golf packages: Yes. **Season:** Year-round. **High:** May-Oct.
On-site lodging: No. **Rental clubs:** Yes.
Walking policy: Unrestricted walking. **Range:** Yes (grass).
To obtain tee times: In person or by phone up to seven days in advance.
Ranked 6th in Washington by Golf Digest.
Subscriber comments: Great pin placements . . . Great views of Mount
Rainier . . . Fine condition on a public track . . . Good walking course . . .
Tough but fair greens quick and true . . . No weak holes . . . Service good
. . . Long, narrow, challenging course. Friendly, helpful staff . . . Lots of
sand, but fun to play . . . Need to hit straight . . . Best greens in the state
winter or summer . . . Best greens in Washington . . . Best course Tacoma
area.

★★½ DESERT AIRE GOLF COURSE

SP—505 Club House Way W., Desert Aire (509)932-4439.
60 miles east of Yakima. **Holes:** 18. **Par:** 72/73.
Yards: 6,501/5,786. **Course rating:** 70.5/72.6. **Slope:** 115/120.
Opened: 1975. **Pace of Play rating:** 4:00-4:30. **Green fee:** $16/18.
Credit cards: MC, V. **Reduced fees:** No.
Caddies: No. **Golf carts:** $15 for 18 holes.
Discount golf packages: Yes. **Season:** Year-round. **High:** June-Oct.
On-site lodging: Yes. **Rental clubs:** Yes.
Walking policy: Unrestricted walking. **Range:** Yes (grass).
To obtain tee times: Call one week in advance.
Subscriber comments: Playable all year round except when it snows . . .
Short but fun course with plenty of challenge . . . Open in winter when
most Northwest courses are not . . . New nine surprisingly nice . . .
Course condition much improved over last few years.

★★★★ DESERT CANYON GOLF RESORT

R—114 Brays Rd., Orondo (509)784-1111, (509)258-4173.
25 miles south of Wenatchee. **Holes:** 18. **Par:** 72/72.
Yards: 7,293/4,899. **Course rating:** 74.0/67.5. **Slope:** 127/104.
Opened: 1993. **Pace of Play rating:** 5:00. **Green fee:** $35/59.
Credit cards: MC, V. **Reduced fees:** Weekdays, Low season, Twilight,
Juniors.
Caddies: No. **Golf carts:** Included in Green Fee.
Discount golf packages: Yes. **Season:** March-Nov. **High:** July-Aug.
On-site lodging: No. **Rental clubs:** Yes.
Walking policy: Mandatory cart. **Range:** Yes (grass).
To obtain tee times: Call seven days in advance.
Ranked 2nd in Washington by Golf Digest.
Subscriber comments: Fairways like playing on carpet . . . Awesome
views . . . Nearby is an 18-hole putting course . . . Five sets of tees . . .
Need to play course more than once . . . Desert golf in the northwest . . .
Target golf if you like that . . . Great views of the Columbia River . . .
Bring your camera. Great twilight rates . . . Extremely difficult with wind
from tips.

★★★ DOWNRIVER GOLF CLUB

PU—N. 3225 Columbia Circle, Spokane (509)327-5269.
Holes: 18. **Par:** 71/ 73.
Yards: 6,130/5,.592. **Course rating:** 68.8/70.9. **Slope:** 115/114.
Opened: 1927. **Pace of Play rating:** 4:00-4:30. **Green fee:** $18.
Credit cards: MC, V. **Reduced fees:** No.
Caddies: No. **Golf carts:** $22 for 18 holes.

Discount golf packages: No. **Season:** Feb-Nov. **High:** May-Sept.
On-site lodging: No. **Rental clubs:** Yes.
Walking policy: Unrestricted walking. **Range:** Yes.
To obtain tee times: Call anytime.
Subscriber comments: Wooded but forgiving . . . Historic city course
aging nicely . . . Easy walk . . . Best public course in area . . . An old-time
favorite, visitors are treated very well . . . Heavy play, but good condition
. . . Beautiful muny.

★★★ DUNGENESS GOLF AND COUNTRY CLUB

SP—1965 Woodcock Rd., Sequim (206)683-6344, (800)447-6826.
105 miles west of Tacoma. **Holes:** 18. **Par:** 72/72.
Yards: 6,372/5,344. **Course rating:** 70.4/70.1. **Slope:** 121/119.
Opened: 1964. **Pace of Play rating:** 4:30. **Green fee:** $15/25.
Credit cards: MC, V. **Reduced fees:** Weekdays, Twilight, Juniors.
Caddies: No. **Golf carts.** $20 for 18 holes.
Discount golf packages: Yes. **Season:** Year-round. **High:** April-Oct.
On-site lodging: No. **Rental clubs:** Yes.
Walking policy: Unrestricted walking. **Range:** Yes (grass).
To obtain tee times: Call anytime.
Subscriber comments: Gets lots of play, worth the wait to get on . . .
Best food of any clubhouse restaurant in Northwest . . . Will bite you if the
wind blows, great finishing hole . . . Beautiful course on Olympic
Peninsula . . . Varying wind conditions make it a real test.

EAGLEMONT GOLF CLUB★

SP—4127 Eaglemont Dr., Mt. Vernon (206)424-0800.
23 miles south of Bellingham. **Holes:** 18. **Par:** 72/72.
Yards: 7,006/5,307. **Course rating:** 73.4/70.7. **Slope:** 134/124.
Opened: 1994. **Pace of Play rating:** 4:30. **Green fee:** $45/60.
Credit cards: MC, V, AMEX. **Reduced fees:** Weekdays, Low season,
Twilight.
Caddies: No. **Golf carts.** Included in Green Fee.
Discount golf packages: No. **Season:** Year-round. **High:** June-Aug.
On-site lodging: No. **Rental clubs:** Yes.
Walking policy: Mandatory cart. **Range:** Yes (grass).
To obtain tee times: Call seven days in advance.

★★ ECHO FALLS COUNTRY CLUB

SP—20414 121st Ave. S.E., Snohomish (206)668-3030, (800)377-2420.
10 miles east of Bellevue. **Holes:** 18. **Par:** 70/71.
Yards: 6,123/4,357. **Course rating:** 68.9/64.6. **Slope:** 126/115.
Opened: 1992. **Pace of Play rating:** 4:30. **Green fee:** $23/40.
Credit cards: MC, V. **Reduced fees:** Weekdays, Low season, Resort
guests, Twilight, Seniors, Juniors.
Caddies: No. **Golf carts:** $10 for 18 holes.
Discount golf packages: Yes. **Season:** Year-round. **High:** April-Sept.
On-site lodging: No. **Rental clubs:** Yes.
Walking policy: Unrestricted walking. **Range:** Yes.
To obtain tee times: Call five days in advance.
Subscriber comments: Great finishing holes Nos.17 and 18 (par 3 with
island green) . . . Getting better, state-of-the art facilities . . . Huge power
lines through some holes . . . Too short . . . Super club building . . . Short
but narrow and hilly . . . 18 will try your nerves . . . Fun layout,
improving.

★★ESMERALDA GOLF COURSE

PU—3933 E. Courtland, Spokane (509)487-6291.
Holes: 18. **Par:** 70/72.
Yards: 6,249/5,594. **Course rating:** 69.2/70.8. **Slope:** 114/117.
Opened: 1956. **Pace of Play rating:** 4:00. **Green fee:** $14/18.
Credit cards: MC, V. **Reduced fees:** Twilight, Seniors.
Caddies: No. **Golf carts:** $20 for 18 holes.
Discount golf packages: No. **Season:** Feb.-Nov. **High:** May-Aug.
On-site lodging: No. **Rental clubs:** Yes.

Walking policy: Unrestricted walking. **Range:** Yes (grass).
To obtain tee times: Call one day in advance for weekdays or one week in advance for weekends.
Subscriber comments: Very good city course . . . Needs some TLC . . . Wide fairways, flat large fast greens, good for everyone . . . Great folks . . . Busy . . . Spokane's best city course . . . Nice walking course . . . No longer "Easy Essie" as growing trees add difficulty.

★½ FOSTER GOLF LINKS

PU—13500 Interuban Ave. S., Tukwila (206)242-4221.
6 miles south of Seattle. **Holes:** 18. **Par:** 69/70.
Yards: 4,930/4,695. **Course rating:** 62.3/65.1. **Slope:** 94/98.
Opened: 1925. **Pace of Play rating:** 4:00. **Green fee:** $15.
Credit cards: MC, V. **Reduced fees:** Twilight, Seniors, Juniors.
Caddies: No. **Golf carts:** $18 for 18 holes.
Discount golf packages: No. **Season:** Year-round. **High:** N/A.
On-site lodging: No. **Rental clubs:** Yes.
Walking policy: Unrestricted walking. **Range:** No.
To obtain tee times: Call seven days in advance.
Subscriber comments: Needed improvements and have been started . . . Easy to walk, friendly staff . . . Decent greens, little challenge, a place to stroll and swing . . . Mats on some tees . . . Old course, needs updating . . . They should build more courses like this rather than 7,000 yards.

★★½ GALLERY GOLF COURSE

PU—3065 N. Cowpens Rd., Whidbey Island, Oak Harbor (206)257-6585.
Call club for further information.
Subscriber comments: Two different nines, tough course, great condition . . . Great scenery (mountains/Puget Sound) . . . Fun layout . . . Small greens.

GLENEAGLES GOLF COURSE★

PU—7619 Country Club Dr., Arlington. (206)435-6713.
42 miles north of Seattle. **Holes:** 18. **Par:** 70/70.
Yards: 6,002/4,937. **Course rating:** N/A. **Slope:** N/A.
Opened: 1995. **Pace of Play rating:** 4:00. **Green fee:** $20/25.
Credit cards: MC, V, AMEX. **Reduced fees:** Twilight, Seniors, Juniors.
Caddies: No. **Golf carts:** $10 for 18 holes.
Discount golf packages: No. **Season:** Year-round. **High:** April-Sept.
On-site lodging: No. **Rental clubs:** Yes.
Walking policy: Unrestricted walking. **Range:** Yes (grass).
To obtain tee times: Call seven days in advance.

★★★½ GOLD MOUNTAIN GOLF COURSE

PU—7263 W. Belfair Valley Rd., Bremerton (206)674-2363, (800)249-2363.
25 miles west of Seattle. **Holes:** 18. **Par:** 72/75.
Yards: 6,749/5,428. **Course rating:** 71.8/70.6. **Slope:** 120/116.
Opened: 1969. **Pace of Play rating:** 4:00-4:30. **Green fee:** $18/22.
Credit cards: MC, V. **Reduced fees:** Twilight, Seniors, Juniors.
Caddies: No. **Golf carts:** N/A.
Discount golf packages: No. **Season:** Year-round. **High:** April-Oct.
On-site lodging: No. **Rental clubs:** Yes.
Walking policy: Unrestricted walking. **Range:** Yes (grass).
To obtain tee times: Call one week in advance at 11 a.m.
Subscriber comments: A true gem, No.1 hole best starting hole around . . . Staff and service great, well-stocked pro shop . . . Busy . . . Country club golf . . . Great, but don't let others know . . . Good practice area . . . Western Washington's best public course! A must . . . Best surprise of the year . . . Should be a best value . . . Hilly, wide open, beautiful setting . . . Fast, true greens . . . Fun course to play year round . . . Pride of ownership shows through . . . Drains and dries very quickly.

SUPER VALUE

WASHINGTON

★★★½ HANGMAN VALLEY GOLF COURSE
PU—E. 2210 Hangman Valley Rd., Spokane (509)448-1212.
Holes: 18. **Par:** 72/71.
Yards: 6,904/5,699. **Course rating:** 71.9/71.8. **Slope:** 126/125.
Opened: 1969. **Pace of Play rating:** 4:15. **Green fee:** $13/18.
Credit cards: None. **Reduced fees:** Seniors, Juniors.
Caddies: No. **Golf carts:** $20 for 18 holes.
Discount golf packages: No. **Season:** March-Oct. **High:** May-Sept.
On-site lodging: No. **Rental clubs:** Yes.
Walking policy: Unrestricted walking. **Range:** Yes.
To obtain tee times: Call Tuesday at 7 a.m. for Wednesday through
following Tuesday.
Subscriber comments: Long course, fast greens . . . Polite crew . . .
Accuracy a necessity . . . Recently upgraded, this course will test any level
of golfer . . . Local favorite . . . Long course . . . Good three-shot par 5s
. . . One of Spokane's most difficult courses . . . 18 different holes . . .
Beautiful clubhouse . . . Water driving range.

★★★ HARBOUR POINTE GOLF CLUB
PU—11817 Harbour Pointe Blvd., Mukilteo (206)355-6060, (800)233-3128.
15 miles north of Seattle. **Holes:** 18. **Par:** 72/72.
Yards: 6,862/4,842. **Course rating:** 72.8/68.8. **Slope:** 135/117.
Opened: 1990. **Pace of Play rating:** 4:30. **Green fee:** $25/45.
Credit cards: MC, V. **Reduced fees:** Weekdays, Low season, Twilight,
Seniors, Juniors.
Caddies: No. **Golf carts:** $13 for 18 holes.
Discount golf packages: No. **Season:** Year-round. **High:** May-Oct.
On-site lodging: No. **Rental clubs:** Yes.
Walking policy: Unrestricted walking. **Range:** Yes (grass).
To obtain tee times: Call seven days in advance.
Selected as Best New Public Course of 1991 by Golf Digest.
Subscriber comments: Great views, hilly play . . . Greens need help . . .
Not walker friendly . . . Great layout . . . View of Puget Sound . . . Two
distinct nines . . . Front nine water, back woods . . . Very busy . . .
Beautiful layout and scenery . . . Demanding . . . Too many houses . . .
No clubhouse . . . Potential to be outstanding.

★★ HIGH CEDARS GOLF CLUB
PU—14604 149th St. Court E., Orting (360)893-3171.
14 miles southeast of Tacoma. **Holes:** 18. **Par:** 71/72.
Yards: 6,303/5,651. **Course rating:** 70.2/75.6. **Slope:** 116/126.
Opened: 1971. **Pace of Play rating:** 4:15. **Green fee:** $22/27.
Credit cards: MC, V. **Reduced fees:** Weekdays, Twilight, Seniors,
Juniors.
Caddies: No. **Golf carts:** $22 for 18 holes.
Discount golf packages: Yes. **Season:** Year-round. **High:** April-Nov.
On-site lodging: No. **Rental clubs:** Yes.
Walking policy: Unrestricted walking. **Range:** Yes.
To obtain tee times: Call one week in advance.
Also has 9-hole executive course.
Subscriber comments: Nice course set in old nursery . . . Mount Rainier
looks reachable on most holes . . . Nice, friendly locally-owned course, also
has par-3 course . . . Dry and playable . . . Watch for bald eagles.

HOMESTEAD GOLF AND COUNTRY CLUB★
SP—115 E. Homestead Blvd., Lynden (206)345-1196.
15 miles north of Bellingham. **Holes:** 18. **Par:** 72/72.
Yards: 6,927/5,570. **Course rating:** 73.2/72.0. **Slope:** 129/124.
Opened: 1995. **Pace of Play rating:** 4:30. **Green fee:** $28/36.
Credit cards: MC, V. **Reduced fees:** Weekdays, Low season, Twilight,
Seniors, Juniors.
Caddies: No. **Golf carts:** $10 for 18 holes.

Discount golf packages: No. **Season:** Year-round. **High:** April–Oct.
On-site lodging: No. **Rental clubs:** Yes.
Walking policy: Unrestricted walking. **Range:** Yes (grass).
To obtain tee times: Call seven days in advance.

★★½ HORSESHOE LAKE GOLF CLUB
PU—15932 Sidney Rd., Port Orchard (206)857-3326.
Call club for further information.
Subscriber comments: Dogleg heaven . . . Only a few years old and
getting better . . . Very hilly back nine, mandatory cart . . . Good shape for
relatively new course, short and very tight.

HOT SPRINGS GOLF COURSE★
PU—One St. Martin Rd., Carson (509)427-5150, (800)755-5661.
45 miles east of Portland, OR. **Holes:** 18. **Par:** 73/73.
Yards: 6,559/5,365. **Course rating:** 72.1/68.9. **Slope:** 125/116.
Opened: 1991. **Pace of Play rating:** 4:30. **Green fee:** $10/16.
Credit cards: MC, V. **Reduced fees:** Low season, Seniors.
Caddies: No. **Golf carts:** $16 for 18 holes.
Discount golf packages: Yes. **Season:** Year-round. **High:** May–Sept.
On-site lodging: No. **Rental clubs:** Yes.
Walking policy: Unrestricted walking. **Range:** Yes (grass).
To obtain tee times: Call pro shop.

★★★½ INDIAN CANYON GOLF COURSE
PU—W. 4304 W. Dr., Spokane (509)747-5353.
Holes: 18. **Par:** 72/72.
Yards: 6,255/5,943. **Course rating:** 70.7/65.9. **Slope:** 126/115.
Opened: 1935. **Pace of Play rating:** N/A. **Green fee:** $22.
Credit cards: None. **Reduced fees:** Twilight, Juniors.
Caddies: No. **Golf carts:** $22 for 18 holes.
Discount golf packages: No. **Season:** March–Oct. **High:** May–Sept.
On-site lodging: Yes. **Rental clubs:** Yes.
Walking policy: Unrestricted walking. **Range:** Yes (grass).
To obtain tee times: Call as far in advance as needed.
Ranked in First 25 of America's 75 Best Public Golf Courses by Golf
Digest. Ranked 7th in Washington by Golf Digest.
Subscriber comments: The best muny in this area, requires all the shots
. . . A course you could play forever . . . Test of long ball . . . Shotmaker's
delight from lies of all angles . . . Splendid tradition . . . Deserves Top 100
ranking . . . Eastern Washington's best public links . . . . The history of the
clubhouse is worth the visit . . . Top public golf course as good as any
country club but at a fraction of the cost . . . Well-maintained older gem
. . . Still revered as a hilly test of accuracy and strategy . . . Every shot
counts, requires good course management . . . Beautiful views . . . Favorite
course ever . . . An existing definition of what the game is all about . . .
Great hamburger . . . Best deal in Washington state.

★½ JEFFERSON PARK GOLF COURSE
PU—4101 Beacon Ave., Seattle (206)762-4513.
Holes: 18. **Par:** 70/70.
Yards: 6,019/5,449. **Course rating:** N/A. **Slope:** 115/112.
Opened: N/A. **Pace of Play rating:** N/A. **Green fee:** N/A.
Credit cards: MC, V. **Reduced fees:** Twilight.
Caddies: No. **Golf carts:** N/A.
Discount golf packages: No. **Season:** Year-round. **High:** March–Oct.
On-site lodging: No. **Rental clubs:** No.
Walking policy: . **Range:** Yes.
Subscriber comments: Old muny course, needs work . . . Back nine is
hilly and fun to play . . . Fred Couples' home course . . . Very busy and
tough to get tee time . . . Simple layout . . . Short and narrow, easy to walk
. . . Heavy traffic.

★★★★ **KAYAK POINT GOLF COURSE**
PU—15711 Marine Dr., Stanwood (360)652-9676, (800)562-3094.
45 miles south of Seattle. **Holes:** 18. **Par:** 72/72.
Yards: 6,719/5,346. **Course rating:** 72.7/72.8. **Slope:** 133/129.
Opened: 1977. **Pace of Play rating:** 4:30-4:37 **Green fee:** $20/30.
Credit cards: MC, V. **Reduced fees:** Weekdays, Seniors, Juniors.
Caddies: No. **Golf carts:** $25 for 18 holes.
Discount golf packages: No. **Season:** Year-round. **High:** May-Sept.
On-site lodging: No. **Rental clubs:** Yes.
Walking policy: Unrestricted walking. **Range:** Yes (grass).
To obtain tee times: Call one week in advance for weekdays. Weekend
tee times are given on Monday morning. Advanced reservations for both
weekdays and weekends with prepayment of green fees.
Ranked in Second 25 of America's 75 Best Public Golf Courses by Golf
Digest.
Subscriber comments: Best muny ever played . . . A real test . . . Pick
correct tees, you'll have a great time . . . Fantastic views . . . A real find . . .
Lots of trees, hilly, narrow and challenging . . . Best public course in
Washington . . . Good food, clubhouse, and conditions year round . . .
Too bad a few houses are being built around it . . . Rate this one
comparable to Spyglass without the ocean . . . A gem . . . Better value if a
county resident.

★ **KENWANDA GOLF COURSE**
PU—14030 Kenwanda Dr., Snohomish (206)668-1166.
15 miles east of Everett. **Holes:** 18. **Par:** 69/72.
Yards: 5,336/5,336. **Course rating:** 65.3/70.4. **Slope:** 119/126.
Opened: 1962. **Pace of Play rating:** 4:00. **Green fee:** $17.
Credit cards: MC, V. **Reduced fees:** No.
Caddies: No. **Golf carts:** N/A.
Discount golf packages: Yes. **Season:** Year-round. **High:** June-Aug.
On-site lodging: No. **Rental clubs:** Yes.
Walking policy: Unrestricted walking. **Range:** No.
To obtain tee times: Call up to seven days in advance.
Subscriber comments: Good practice course . . . Loved it. Got my hole
in one on 16th, great hole . . . A course you can play all year round . . .
Greens inconsistent . . . Easy course . . . Staff courteous.

★★½ **LAKE CHELAN GOLF COURSE**
PU—1501 Golf Course Dr., Chelan (509)682-5421.
45 miles north of Wenatchee. **Holes:** 18. **Par:** 72/72.
Yards: 6,440/5,501. **Course rating:** 70.3/70.9. **Slope:** 119/113.
Opened: 1971. **Pace of Play rating:** 4:00. **Green fee:** $24.
Credit cards: MC, V. **Reduced fees:** No.
Caddies: No. **Golf carts:** $20 for 18 holes.
Discount golf packages: Yes. **Season:** March-Nov. **High:** June-Aug.
On-site lodging: No. **Rental clubs:** Yes.
Walking policy: Unrestricted walking. **Range:** Yes (grass).
To obtain tee times: Call up to seven days in advance.
Subscriber comments: Good lunch . . . Spectacular views . . . Small
elevated greens makes accuracy a must . . . Friendly staff . . . Can be windy
. . . Nice pro shop.

★★★ **LAKE PADDEN GOLF COURSE**
PU—4882 Samish Way, Bellingham (206)738-7400.
Holes: 18. **Par:** 72/72.
Yards: 6,675/5,496. **Course rating:** 71.3/71.9. **Slope:** 122/126.
Opened: 1970. **Pace of Play rating:** 4:30. **Green fee:** $15/23.
Credit cards: MC, V. **Reduced fees:** Seniors, Juniors.
Caddies: No. **Golf carts:** $20 for 18 holes.
Discount golf packages: No. **Season:** Year-round. **High:** May-Sept.
On-site lodging: No. **Rental clubs:** Yes.
Walking policy: Unrestricted walking. **Range:** Yes (grass).

To obtain tee times: Call seven days in advance.
Subscriber comments: Outstanding value . . . Friendly people . . . Best place in town to buy golf equipment . . . The "sleeper" of Washington . . . Very busy . . . Hilly layout. Cut out of the forest . . . Best public golf course in state . . . Excellent staff and scenery . . . Best municipal around!

★★★ LAKE SPANAWAY GOLF COURSE
PU—15602 Pacific Ave., Tacoma (206)531-3660.
Holes: 18. **Par:** 72/74.
Yards: 6,810/5,935. **Course rating:** 71.8/73.4. **Slope:** 121/123.
Opened: 1968. **Pace of Play rating:** 4:10. **Green fee:** $12/18.
Credit cards: MC, V. **Reduced fees:** Weekdays, Seniors, Juniors.
Caddies: No. **Golf carts:** $9 for 18 holes.
Discount golf packages: No. **Season:** Year-round. **High:** May-Oct.
On-site lodging: No. **Rental clubs:** Yes.
Walking policy: Unrestricted walking. **Range:** Yes (grass).
To obtain tee times: Call five days in advance.
Subscriber comments: Easy to walk . . . Tough par 4s . . . One of the best muny courses in Puget Sound . . . Tough course; if I lived closer I'd play every weekend . . . Good course for the amount of play it gets . . . Play year round . . . Long and challenging . . . One of best public tests of golf in Northwest! . . . Magnificent fir trees line fairways.

★½ LAKE WILDERNESS GOLF COURSE
PU—25400 Witte Rd. S.E., Maple Valley (206)432-9405.
30 miles south of Seattle. **Holes:** 18. **Par:** 70/70.
Yards: 5,218/4,544. **Course rating:** 66.1/66.6. **Slope:** 118/117.
Opened: N/A. **Pace of Play rating:** N/A. **Green fee:** $10/20.
Credit cards: MC, V. **Reduced fees:** Weekdays, Low season, Twilight, Seniors, Juniors
Caddies: No. **Golf carts:** $20 for 18 holes.
Discount golf packages: Yes. **Season:** Year-round. **High:** June-Aug.
On-site lodging: No. **Rental clubs:** Yes.
Walking policy: Unrestricted walking. **Range:** No.
To obtain tee times: Call or come in two weeks in advance.
Subscriber comments: Greens close to homes! . . . Staff good, narrow, lots of target holes . . . Has made improvements . . . "All day" green fee.

★★★ LEAVENWORTH GOLF CLUB
SP—9101 Icicle Rd., Leavenworth (509)548-7267.
110 miles east of Seattle. **Holes:** 18. **Par:** 71/71.
Yards: 5,711/5,343. **Course rating:** 67.0/69.6. **Slope:** 116/119.
Opened: 1927. **Pace of Play rating:** 4:15. **Green fee:** $18.
Credit cards: MC, V. **Reduced fees:** No.
Caddies: No. **Golf carts:** $20 for 18 holes.
Discount golf packages: No. **Season:** April-Nov. **High:** April-Oct.
On-site lodging: No. **Rental clubs:** Yes.
Walking policy: Unrestricted walking. **Range:** No.
To obtain tee times: Call Thursday for weekend and call one day in advance for weekdays.
Subscriber comments: Short and tight. Nice people . . . Most peaceful, relaxing golf course in Northwest . . . Beautiful mountain, river views . . . Seasonal course on the east side of Cascades . . . Views and surroundings make the golf secondary . . . Short course but lots of fun.

★½ LEGION MEMORIAL GOLF COURSE
PU—144 W. Marine View Dr., Everett (206)259-4653.
Call club for further information.
Subscriber comments: Wide open, great for the weekend warrior . . . Getting better, drainage improving . . . Nice "city fun course" . . . Plays well all year . . . Easy, walkable.

★★ LIBERTY LAKE GOLF CLUB

PU—E. 24403 Sprague, Liberty Lake (509)255-6233.
20 miles west of Spokane. **Holes:** 18. **Par:** 70/74.
Yards: 6,398/5,886. **Course rating:** 69.8/75.7. **Slope:** 121/134.
Opened: 1959. **Pace of Play rating:** 3:30-4:30. **Green fee:** $14/18.
Credit cards: None. **Reduced fees:** Seniors, Juniors.
Caddies: No. **Golf carts:** $20 for 18 holes.
Discount golf packages: No. **Season:** Year-round. **High:** June-Sept.
On-site lodging: No. **Rental clubs:** Yes.
Walking policy: Unrestricted walking. **Range:** Yes (grass).
To obtain tee times: Call Tuesday for following week.
Subscriber comments: Country course, nice to play . . . Pretty flat, long
holes, but can score pretty well . . . Only closed when snow covered . . .
Good staff and a nice complement to neighboring Meadowwood . . . Busy
muny, can walk . . . Nice pro . . . Basic public course.

★★ LIPOMA FIRS GOLF COURSE
GREEN/GOLD/BLUE

PU—18615 110th Ave. E., Puyallup (206)841-4396, (800)649-4396.
10 miles southeast of Tacoma. **Holes:** 27. **Par:** 72/72/72.
Yards: 6,722/6,805/6,687. **Course rating:** 72.2/72.1/72.0.
Slope: 122/122/122.
Opened: 1989. **Pace of Play rating:** 4:30. **Green fee:** $16/21.
Credit cards: None. **Reduced fees:** Weekdays, Low season, Twilight,
Seniors, Juniors.
Caddies: No. **Golf carts:** $18 for 18 holes.
Discount golf packages: No. **Season:** Year-round. **High:** April-Oct.
On-site lodging: No. **Rental clubs:** Yes.
Walking policy: Unrestricted walking. **Range:** Yes (grass).
To obtain tee times: Call seven days in advance.
Subscriber comments: Beautiful view Mount. Rainier . . . Rocky . . . 27
holes now, Green nine is a great walk . . . Built for winter drainage, this
means rocks . . . With age this 27-holer will be a great one . . . Very rocky
off fairways . . . Need more topsoil.

★★ MADRONA LINKS GOLF COURSE

PU—3604 22nd Ave. N.W., Gig Harbor (206)851-5193.
2 miles northwest of Tacoma. **Holes:** 18. **Par:** 71/73.
Yards: 5,602/4,737. **Course rating:** 65.5/68.1. **Slope:** 110/115.
Opened: 1978. **Pace of Play rating:** 4:30. **Green fee:** $18/19.
Credit cards: MC, V. **Reduced fees:** Twilight, Seniors, Juniors.
Caddies: No. **Golf carts:** $19 for 18 holes.
Discount golf packages: No. **Season:** Year-round. **High:** March-Oct.
On-site lodging: No. **Rental clubs:** Yes.
Walking policy: Unrestricted walking. **Range:** Yes (grass).
To obtain tee times: Call or come in seven days in advance.
Subscriber comments: Good restaurant and friendly staff . . . Confidence
builder . . . Keep it in the fairway, or deal with the madrona trees . . .
Walkable . . . A fun, moderately hilly short course . . . Very short, drivable
greens. Can score with good short game, average long game.

★½ MAPLEWOOD GOLF CLUB

PU—4000 Maple Valley Hwy., Renton (206)255-3194.
15 miles southeast of Seattle. **Holes:** 18. **Par:** 71/72.
Yards: 5,620/5,082. **Course rating:** 66.9/68.0. **Slope:** 111/113.
Opened: 1928. **Pace of Play rating:** 4:30. **Green fee:** $11/16.
Credit cards: None. **Reduced fees:** Seniors, Juniors.
Caddies: No. **Golf carts:** $18 for 18 holes.
Discount golf packages: No. **Season:** Year-round. **High:** March-Nov.
On-site lodging: No. **Rental clubs:** Yes.
Walking policy: Unrestricted walking. **Range:** Yes.
To obtain tee times: Call one week in advance for weekdays and Monday
for upcoming weekend.

Subscriber comments: Undergoing significant improvements now . . .
Play all year . . . Short course . . . Front nine old and tight, new nine
wonderful to play . . . Course and clubhouse being reworked, definitely
getting better.

★★★★ MCCORMICK WOODS GOLF COURSE

PU—5155 McCormick Woods Dr. S.W., Port Orchard (206)895-0130.
20 miles northwest of Tacoma. **Holes:** 18. **Par:** 72/72.
Yards: 7,040/5,299. **Course rating:** 74.1/71.1. **Slope:** 135/122.
Opened: 1988. **Pace of Play rating:** 4:30. **Green fee:** $20/45.
Credit cards: MC, V, DISC. **Reduced fees:** Weekdays, Low season,
Twilight, Seniors.
Caddies: No. **Golf carts:** $20 for 18 holes.
Discount golf packages: Yes. **Season:** Year-round. **High:** June–Sept.
On-site lodging: No. **Rental clubs:** Yes.
Walking policy: Unrestricted walking. **Range:** Yes (grass).
To obtain tee times: Call 30 days in advance if out of state; homeowners
call seven days in advance; general public call five days in advance beginning
at 9 a.m. Weekends and holidays require a credit card to reserve.
Ranked in Second 25 of America's 75 Best Public Golf Courses by Golf
Digest. Ranked 10th in Washington by Golf Digest.
Subscriber comments: My favorite course in Washington . . . New
clubhouse next year . . . Play after 2 p.m. during the summer for best value
. . . Great folks . . . Great course through the pines . . . Best public course
in state . . . Play year round . . . Makes me want to move to Port Orchard
. . . This course just keeps getting better . . . Great layout. Tough . . . I
love this course . . . Northwest golf at its very best . . . 18 separate holes,
wild flowers, wetlands, deer . . . They don't call it "woods" for nothing
. . . Each hole requires different mental approach.

★★½ MEADOW PARK GOLF COURSE

PU—7108 Lakewood Dr. W., Tacoma (206)473-3033.
Holes: 18. **Par:** 71/73.
Yards: 6,093/5,262. **Course rating:** 69.0/70.3. **Slope:** 114/118.
Opened: 1917. **Pace of Play rating:** 4:30. **Green fee:** $17/19.
Credit cards: MC, V. **Reduced fees:** Weekdays, Seniors, Juniors.
Caddies: No. **Golf carts:** $18 for 18 holes.
Discount golf packages: No. **Season:** Year-round. **High:** May–Sept.
On-site lodging: No. **Rental clubs:** Yes.
Walking policy: Unrestricted walking. **Range:** Yes.
To obtain tee times: Call one week in advance.
Subscriber comments: New layout much better . . . Nicely redesigned
municipal course . . . Lynn Rautio top notch pro . . . New club house and
some holes . . . Friendly management.

★★★★ MEADOWWOOD GOLF COURSE

PU—East 24501 Valley Way, Liberty Lake (509)255-9539.
12 miles east of Spokane. **Holes:** 18. **Par:** 72/72.
Yards: 6,846/5,880. **Course rating:** 72.4/74.1. **Slope:** 126/127.
Opened: 1988. **Pace of Play rating:** 4:30-5:00. **Green fee:** $18.
Credit cards: None. **Reduced fees:** Seniors, Juniors.
Caddies: No. **Golf carts:** $20 for 18 holes.
Discount golf packages: No. **Season:** March-Nov. **High:** May-Aug.
On-site lodging: No. **Rental clubs:** Yes.
Walking policy: Walking at certain times. **Range:** Yes.
To obtain tee times: Call 10 days in advance for nonresidents.
Subscriber comments: Excellent condition, rates with Indian Canyon as
best muny . . . Best in Northwest . . . Fine groundskeeping all year . . .
Nos. 16,17,18 are great finishing holes . . . Walkable . . . Nothing but
green grass everywhere . . . The more you play this course, the more you'll
like it . . . 16th is toughest par 5 in the state. Great value . . . Good blend of
water and open layout . . . Don't tell anyone about this one, too good to be
true.

GREAT VALUE

MERIWOOD GOLF COURSE★

PU—9051 46th Ave. N.E., Lacey. (206)412-0495.
10 miles south of Olympia. **Holes:** 18. **Par:** 72/72.
Yards: 7,170/5,600. **Course rating:** 74.6/72.8. **Slope:** 128/123.
Opened: 1995. **Pace of Play rating:** 4:30. **Green fee:** $32/35.
Credit cards: MC, V. **Reduced fees:** Weekdays, Low season, Twilight,
Seniors, Juniors.
Caddies: No. **Golf carts:** Included in Green Fee.
Discount golf packages: Yes. **Season:** Year-round. **High:** April-Sept.
On-site lodging: No. **Rental clubs:** Yes.
Walking policy: Mandatory cart. **Range:** Yes (grass).
To obtain tee times: Call 30 days in advance.

★★½ MINT VALLEY GOLF CLUB

FRUGAL PICK

PU—4002 Pennsylvania St., Longview (206)577-3395.
Call club for further information.
Subscriber comments: Gorgeous, short, placement course . . . Nice
design . . . Good staff . . . Same architects as Kayak Point . . . Wet areas in
winter . . . Challenging course, off the beaten path, exceptional value.

★★½ MOUNT ADAMS COUNTRY CLUB

SP—1250 Rockyford, Toppenish (509)865-4440.
Call club for further information.
Subscriber comments: Owl in tree to greet you . . . Flat, long, but a great
value . . . Flat, small fast greens, great staff . . . Heavily-played and loved
by the locals . . . Best greens in eastern Washington . . . Honest golf.

★★ MOUNT SI GOLF COURSE

PU—9010 Meadowbrook - Northbend Rd. S.E., Snoqualmie (206)881-
1541.
27 miles southeast of Seattle. **Holes:** 18. **Par:** 72/72.
Yards: 6,304/5,439. **Course rating:** N/A. **Slope:** N/A.
Opened: 1927. **Pace of Play rating:** 4:15. **Green fee:** $25/ 25.
Credit cards: None. **Reduced fees:** Low season, Seniors, Juniors.
Caddies: No. **Golf carts:** $22 for 18 holes.
Discount golf packages: No. **Season:** Year-round. **High:** April-Sept.
On-site lodging: No. **Rental clubs:** Yes.
Walking policy: Unrestricted walking. **Range:** Yes(grass).
To obtain tee times: Call anytime.
Subscriber comments: Scenic course, can play most of the year . . . New
layout should improve golf rating . . . Very short and tight . . . Fun course
in mountain setting . . . Good cheeseburgers . . . Right at the base of
mountain. Beautiful . . . Added new greens and tees, nice improvement.

★½ NEWAUKUM VALLEY GOLF COURSE

PU—153 Newaukum Golf Dr., Chehalis (206)748-0461.
85 miles east of Seattle. **Holes:** 18. **Par:** 72/72.
Yards: 6,512/5,628. **Course rating:** 70.7/71.4. **Slope:** 126/126.
Opened: 1979. **Pace of Play rating:** 4:30. **Green fee:** $10/18.
Credit cards: MC, V. **Reduced fees:** Weekdays, Low season, Twilight,
Seniors, Juniors.
Caddies: No. **Golf carts:** $16 for 18 holes.
Discount golf packages: Yes. **Season:** Year-round. **High:** May-Sept.
On-site lodging: No. **Rental clubs:** Yes.
Walking policy: Unrestricted walking. **Range:** No.
To obtain tee times: Call anytime.
Additional 9 holes to open June 1995.
Subscriber comments: Easy walk, not difficult . . . Front nine wide open.
Back nine tighter holes . . . New nine in progress, could use better care.

★★½ NORTH SHORE GOLF AND COUNTRY CLUB

PU—4101 N. Shore Blvd. N.E., Tacoma (206)927-1375, (800)447-1375.
Holes: 18. **Par:** 71/73.
Yards: 6,305/5,442. **Course rating:** 69.9/70.7. **Slope:** 120/119.
Opened: 1961. **Pace of Play rating:** 4:00. **Green fee:** $20/28.

Credit cards: MC, V, AMEX. **Reduced fees:** Weekdays, Low season, Twilight, Juniors.
Caddies: No. **Golf carts:** $20 for 18 holes.
Discount golf packages: No. **Season:** Year-round. **High:** May-Sept.
On-site lodging: No. **Rental clubs:** Yes.
Walking policy: Unrestricted walking. **Range:** Yes (grass).
To obtain tee times: Call seven days in advance.
Subscriber comments: Great range/practice area . . . Too many apartments . . . Good course, nice greens . . . Nice variety of holes . . . Usually crowded but managed well . . . Best pro shop in Northwest.

★★ OCEAN SHORES GOLF COURSE
R—500 Canal Dr. N.E., Ocean Shores (206)289-3357.
130 miles southwest of Seattle. **Holes:** 18. **Par:** 71/72.
Yards: 6,252/5,173. **Course rating:** 70.2/69.6. **Slope:** 115/115.
Opened: 1965. **Pace of Play rating:** 4:00. **Green fee:** $15/23.
Credit cards: MC, V. **Reduced fees:** Low season, Seniors, Juniors.
Caddies: No. **Golf carts:** $22 for 18 holes.
Discount golf packages: Yes. **Season:** Year-round. **High:** May-Sept.
On-site lodging: No. **Rental clubs:** Yes.
Walking policy: Unrestricted walking. **Range:** No.
To obtain tee times: Call up to one year in advance. But advised to call at least one week in advance.
Subscriber comments: Windy seaside course that's easy to walk, small greens . . . Needs work . . . Friendly staff . . . Front nine links style, back nine upland forest.

★★★★ PORT LUDLOW GOLF COURSE
TIDE/TIMBER/TRAIL
R—751 Highland Dr., Port Ludlow (206)437-0272, (800)732-1239.
20 miles northwest of Seattle. **Holes:** 27. **Par:** 72/72/72.
Yards: 6,746/6,683/6,787. **Course rating:** 73.6/73.1/72.7.
Slope: 138/138/131.
Opened: 1975. **Pace of Play rating:** 4:30. **Green fee:** $25/55.
Credit cards: MC, V, AMEX. **Reduced fees:** Weekdays, Low season, Resort guests, Twilight.
Cadd·s: No. **Golf carts:** $13 for 18 holes.
Discount golf packages: Yes. **Season:** Year-round. **High:** May-Sept.
On-site lodging: Yes. **Rental clubs:** Yes.
Walking policy: Unrestricted walking. **Range:** Yes (grass).
To obtain tee times: Resort guests may make tee times upon room confirmation. Public call one week in advance unless guaranteed with credit card.
Tide and Timber nines ranked 46th in America's 75 Best Resort Courses by Golf Digest. Tide and Timber nines ranked 9th in Washington by Golf Digest.
Subscriber comments: A course you must play when in area . . . Perhaps the best resort complex for golf in Washington State . . . Take your camera and a straight driver . . . Unbelievable, like a magical mystery tour . . . In mountains overlooking Puget Sound . . . Awesome course, new nine is as difficult as Kiawah and PGA West Stadium . . . Old course is the best . . . Staff very accommodating.

★★ QUAIL RIDGE GOLF COURSE
PU—3600 Swallows Nest Dr., Clarkston (509)758-8501.
100 miles south of Spokane. **Holes:** 18. **Par:** 71/71.
Yards: 5,861/4,720. **Course rating:** 68.1/66.2. **Slope:** 114/107.
Opened: 1966. **Pace of Play rating:** 4:15. **Green fee:** $13.
Credit cards: MC, V, DISC. **Reduced fees:** Juniors.
Caddies: No. **Golf carts:** $20 for 18 holes.
Discount golf packages: No. **Season:** Year-round. **High:** April-Sept.
On-site lodging: No. **Rental clubs:** Yes.
Walking policy: Unrestricted walking. **Range:** Yes.
To obtain tee times: Call one week in advance.
Subscriber comments: Friendly staff.

★★ RIVERBEND GOLF COMPLEX

PU—2019 W. Meeker St., Kent (206)854-3673.
18 miles south of Seattle. **Holes:** 18. **Par:** 72/72.
Yards: 6,603/5,485. **Course rating:** 71.8/70.4. **Slope:** 125/124.
Opened: 1989. **Pace of Play rating:** 4:15. **Green fee:** $17/23.
Credit cards: MC, V. **Reduced fees:** Weekdays, Low season, Seniors,
Juniors.
Caddies: No. **Golf carts:** $20 for 18 holes.
Discount golf packages: Yes. **Season:** Year-round. **High:** April-Sept.
On-site lodging: Yes. **Rental clubs:** Yes.
Walking policy: Unrestricted walking. **Range:** Yes (grass).
To obtain tee times: Call pro shop.
Also has a 9-hole par-3 course.
Subscriber comments: Too popular for own good . . . Good muny, flat
but tough, good layout, easy to walk . . . The way a muny course should
be run . . . Even better course when trees mature . . . Flat course on river
bank . . . Played on an inclement day, great staff bought us lunch.

★★★½ RIVERSIDE COUNTRY CLUB

PU—1451 N.W. Airport Rd., Chehalis (206)748-8182, (800)242-9486.
27 miles south of Olympia. **Holes:** 18. **Par:** 71/72.
Yards: 6,155/5,456. **Course rating:** 68.3/71.0. **Slope:** 117/121.
Opened: 1945 **Pace of Play rating:** 4:00. **Green fee:** $12/20.
Credit cards: MC, V. **Reduced fees:** Low season, Juniors.
Caddies: No. **Golf carts:** $20 for 18 holes.
Discount golf packages: No. **Season:** Year-round. **High:** April-Sept.
On-site lodging: No. **Rental clubs:** No.
Walking policy: Unrestricted walking. **Range:** Yes (grass).
To obtain tee times: Call pro shop.
Subscriber comments: Nice short course, great for family golf . . . Great
fourth hole . . . A good walking course, can play in under four hours . . .
Best-kept secret in western Washington . . . Great surprise . . . Best-kept
course around, short but tricky with narrow fairways . . . This is a jewel,
convenient driving range, good folks, small town.

★★★★ SEMIAHMOO GOLF AND COUNTRY CLUB

R—8720 Semiahmoo Pkwy., Blaine (206)371-7005, (800)770-7992.
40 miles south of Vancouver BC. **Holes:** 18. **Par:** 72/72.
Yards: 7,005/5,288. **Course rating:** 74.5/71.6. **Slope:** 130/126.
Opened: 1986. **Pace of Play rating:** 4:15. **Green fee:** $20/66.
Credit cards: MC, V, AMEX. **Reduced fees:** Weekdays, Low season,
Resort guests, Twilight.
Caddies: Yes. **Golf carts:** $14 for 18 holes.
Discount golf packages: Yes. **Season:** Year-round. **High:** July-Sept.
On-site lodging: Yes. **Rental clubs:** Yes.
Walking policy: Unrestricted walking. **Range:** Yes (grass).
To obtain tee times: Call 72 hours in advance Monday-Friday; 24 hours in
advance for Saturday and 48 hours in advance for Sunday play. Guests at the
hotel call 90 days in advance through hotel.
Ranked 18th in America's 75 Best Resort Courses by Golf Digest. Selected
Best New Resort Course of 1987 by Golf Digest. Ranked 4th in
Washington by Golf Digest.
Subscriber comments: Beautiful clubhouse . . . One of Palmer's best . . .
Best course in Washington State bar none . . . A great vacation spot . . .
Great challenge a lot like target golf in the desert . . . Could be the best
course north of San Francisco . . . Aging very well, superb design, excellent
contour to greens . . . Great course, no complaints . . . Beautiful pro shop,
bar and grill.

★★★★ SHUKSAN GOLF CLUB

PU—1500 E. Axton Rd., Bellingham (206)398-8888.
Holes: 18. **Par:** 72/72.
Yards: 6,706/5,253. **Course rating:** 70.3/68.5. **Slope:** 128/118.
Opened: 1994. **Pace of Play rating:** 4:15. **Green fee:** $32/38.

Credit cards: MC, V. **Reduced fees:** Weekdays, Low season, Twilight, Seniors, Juniors.
Caddies: No. **Golf carts:** Included in Green Fee.
Discount golf packages: No. **Season:** Year-round. **High:** April–Oct.
On-site lodging: No. **Rental clubs:** Yes.
Walking policy: Unrestricted walking. **Range:** Yes (grass).
To obtain tee times: Call seven days in advance.
Subscriber comments: Best new course in Northwest . . . My new favorite course . . . Great course, great views, great staff, great experience . . . Elevated tees . . . Service from staff outstanding . . . New kid on the block . . . Can walk but course is long and distance from green to tee is often long . . . What golf should be . . . I wished I lived closer so I could play it more . . . Tough walk.

★ SIMILK BEACH GOLF COURSE

PU—1250 Christiansen Rd., Anacortes (206)293-3444.
31 miles south of Bellingham. **Holes:** 18. **Par:** 72/76.
Yards: 6,205/5,934. **Course rating:** 68.9/73.3. **Slope:** 111/121.
Opened: 1955. **Pace of Play rating:** 4:15. **Green fee:** $17/19.
Credit cards: MC, V. **Reduced fees:** Weekdays, Low season, Juniors.
Caddies: No. **Golf carts:** $20 for 18 holes.
Discount golf packages: No. **Season:** Year-round. **High:** March–Sept.
On-site lodging: No. **Rental clubs:** Yes.
Walking policy: Unrestricted walking. **Range:** Yes (grass).
To obtain tee times: Call anytime in advance.
Subscriber comments: Staff always friendly . . . Good walking, can usually walk on . . . Old course being spruced up . . . Wide- open course, fun to play.

★★½ BRIDGE OF THE GODS GOLF COURSE

R—1131 Skamania Lodge Way, Stevenson (509)427-2541.
50 miles east of Portland. **Holes:** 18. **Par:** 70/69.
Yards: 5,776/4,362. **Course rating:** 68.9/65.2. **Slope:** 127/115.
Opened: 1993. **Pace of Play rating:** N/A. **Green fee:** $18/32.
Credit cards: All major. **Reduced fees:** Low season, Twilight.
Caddies: No. **Golf carts:** $27 for 18 holes.
Discount golf packages: Yes. **Season:** Year-round. **High:** June–Oct.
On-site lodging: Yes. **Rental clubs:** Yes.
Walking policy: Unrestricted walking. **Range:** Yes (grass).
To obtain tee times: Lodge guests upon confirmation of reservations. Others, up to two weeks in advance.
Subscriber comments: Excellent meal and wine . . . Great resort accommodations . . . Short but tough . . . Leave your driver home, beautiful tree-lined fairways, a real joy . . . Very narrow, no room for error.

★★★ SNOHOMISH GOLF COURSE

PU—7806 147th Ave. S.E., Snohomish (206)568-2676.
20 miles northeast of Seattle. **Holes:** 18. **Par:** 72/74.
Yards: 6,858/5,980. **Course rating:** 72.7/74.1. **Slope:** 126/129.
Opened: 1967. **Pace of Play rating:** 4:30. **Green fee:** $20.
Credit cards: None. **Reduced fees:** Twilight, Seniors, Juniors.
Caddies: No. **Golf carts:** $23 for 18 holes.
Discount golf packages: Yes. **Season:** Year-round. **High:** May-Sept.
On-site lodging: No. **Rental clubs:** Yes.
Walking policy: Unrestricted walking. **Range:** Yes (grass).
To obtain tee times: Call one week in advance.
Subscriber comments: Good junior program . . . One of the best public courses in the Puget Sound area . . . Hit it straight . . . Not a pushover . . . Outstanding public course . . . Cut out of woods and hills . . . Heavily used course that sometimes takes a beating . . . Long, old but good . . . Classic Northwest course, lots of trees, smallish greens . . . Nice staff.

★★★ SUDDEN VALLEY GOLF AND COUNTRY CLUB

SP—2145 Lake Whatcom Blvd., Bellingham (360)734-6435, (800)734-6903.
Holes: 18. **Par:** 72/72.
Yards: 6,553/5,627. **Course rating:** 72.4/72.5. **Slope:** 129/131.
Opened: 1970. **Pace of Play rating:** 4:20. **Green fee:** $25/34.
Credit cards: MC, V. **Reduced fees:** Weekdays, Low season, Twilight, Juniors.
Caddies: No. **Golf carts:** $23 for 18 holes.
Discount golf packages: No. **Season:** Year-round. **High:** July-Sept.
On-site lodging: Yes. **Rental clubs:** Yes.
Walking policy: Unrestricted walking. **Range:** Yes (grass).
To obtain tee times: Call up to seven days in advance. Tournaments may book up to one year in advance.
Subscriber comments: Nine holes hilly, nine holes flat . . . Service excellent . . . Picturesque . . . No. 5 is great hole . . . Good summer course . . . Beautiful, scenic, in mountains . . . Exceptional views . . . Could be drained better.

★★★ SUN WILLOWS GOLF CLUB

PU—2035 N. 20th St., Pasco (509)545-3440.
Call club for further information.
Subscriber comments: Best golf value in area. Greens are exceptional . . . Continues to improve, excellent greenskeeper . . . Municipal, well maintained . . . Fun for everyone; good conditioning . . . Open course . . . Better conditions this year . . . Lots of greenside bunkers.

★½ SUNDANCE GOLF COURSE

PU—W. 7003 Kendick Rd., Nine Mile Falls (509)466-4040.
Call club for further information.
Subscriber comments: Narrow tree-lined fairways, small, fast greens, short and flat . . . Short, not very difficult . . . Can walk.

★★½ SUNLAND GOLF AND COUNTRY CLUB

SP—109 Hilltop Dr., Sequim (206)683-8365.
100 miles east of Seattle. **Holes:** 18. **Par:** 72/73.
Yards: 6,319/5,557. **Course rating:** 70.4/71.5. **Slope:** 120/120.
Opened: 1971. **Pace of Play rating:** 4:00. **Green fee:** $28/33.
Credit cards: MC, V. **Reduced fees:** Juniors.
Caddies: No. **Golf carts:** $22 for 18 holes.
Discount golf packages: No. **Season:** Year-round. **High:** April-Sept.
On-site lodging: No. **Rental clubs:** Yes.
Walking policy: Unrestricted walking. **Range:** Yes (grass).
To obtain tee times: Call seven days in advance.
Subscriber comments: Fun course, great walking course . . . Tight front nine, open back nine, almost like two different courses . . . Houses too close to fairways . . . Need straight shots.

★½ SUNTIDES GOLF COURSE

PU—231 Pence Rd., Yakima (509)966-9065.
Holes: 18. **Par:** 70/71.
Yards: 6,232/5,509. **Course rating:** 67.8/70.6. **Slope:** 120/122.
Opened: 1963. **Pace of Play rating:** 4:00-4:20. **Green fee:** $17.
Credit cards: MC, V. **Reduced fees:** Juniors.
Caddies: No. **Golf carts:** $20 for 18 holes.
Discount golf packages: No. **Season:** Feb.-Nov. **High:** May-June.
On-site lodging: No. **Rental clubs:** Yes.
Walking policy: Unrestricted walking. **Range:** Yes.
To obtain tee times: Call Tuesday for Friday tee times, Wednesday for Saturday/Sunday tee times. Monday thru Thursday are first come, first served.
Subscriber comments: Good for quick golf pick me up . . . Well maintained . . . Condition varies . . . Flat course, no trouble . . . Narrow fairways, some good holes . . . Easy to play, good scores.

★ **TALL CHIEF GOLF COURSE**
PU—1313 Snoqualmie River Rd. S.E., Fall City (206)222-5911.
21 miles southeast of Seattle. **Holes:** 18. **Par:** 70/71.
Yards: 5,422/4,867. **Course rating:** 66.0/66.5. **Slope:** 119/117.
Opened: 1965. **Pace of Play rating:** 4:00. **Green fee:** $20/23.
Credit cards: MC, V, AMEX. **Reduced fees:** Weekdays, Low season,
Twilight, Seniors, Juniors.
Caddies: No. **Golf carts:** $20 for 18 holes.
Discount golf packages: Yes. **Season:** Year-round. **High:** June-Sept.
On-site lodging: No. **Rental clubs:** Yes.
Walking policy: Unrestricted walking. **Range:** No.
To obtain tee times: Call six days in advance.
Subscriber comments: Scenic . . . Short layout . . . Back nine is steep . . .
Always available for a tee time . . . Areas of poor drainage . . . Back nine all
sidehill lies.

★★★ **THE CREEK AT QUALCHAN GOLF COURSE**
PU—301 E. Meadowlane Rd., Spokane (509)448-9317.
Holes: 18. **Par:** 72/72.
Yards: 6,577/5,533. **Course rating:** 71.1/72.3. **Slope:** 124/126.
Opened: 1993. **Pace of Play rating:** 4:15. **Green fee:** $17/22.
Credit cards: MC, V. **Reduced fees:** Juniors.
Caddies: No. **Golf carts:** $22 for 18 holes.
Discount golf packages: Yes. **Season:** March-Oct. **High:** May-Sept.
On-site lodging: No. **Rental clubs:** Yes.
Walking policy: Unrestricted walking. **Range:** Yes (grass).
To obtain tee times: Call anytime, must guarantee with credit card.
Subscriber comments: Tough from the blacks . . . Tee shots are key . . .
Needs to mature . . . Best new course in Spokane . . . Exacts penalties for
bad shots . . . Tight, target course . . . New course with some great holes
. . . Good staff . . . Great for a muny . . . Fun course, a couple weak holes
. . . Tough unless you are long and straight.

★★½ **THREE RIVERS GOLF COURSE**
PU—2222 S. River Rd., Kelso (206)423-4653.
40 miles north of Portland. **Holes:** 18. **Par:** 72/72.
Yards: 6,846/5,455. **Course rating:** 72.1/68.5. **Slope:** 127/120.
Opened: 1983. **Pace of Play rating:** 4:00. **Green fee:** $10/16.
Credit cards: MC, V. **Reduced fees:** Low season, Twilight, Seniors,
Juniors.
Caddies: No. **Golf carts:** $20 for 18 holes.
Discount golf packages: No. **Season:** Year-round. **High:** May-Sept.
On-site lodging: No. **Rental clubs:** Yes.
Walking policy: Unrestricted walking. **Range:** Yes (grass).
To obtain tee times: Tee times can be made by phone or in person in the
pro shop up to one week in advance.
Subscriber comments: Easy course to play . . . Great dry winter course
. . . Built on dredgings from the Cowlitz River after Mount Saint Helens
erupted . . . Nice muny, flat walker course . . . Best in Washington year
round . . . Great winter course, built on volcanic ash, drains instantly.

★★½ **TRI-CITY COUNTRY CLUB**
SP—314 N. Underwood, Kennewick (509)783-6014.
120 miles south of Spokane. **Holes:** 18. **Par:** 65/65.
Yards: 4,700/4,400. **Course rating:** 62.5/65.2. **Slope:** 112/115.
Opened: 1938. **Pace of Play rating:** 3:45. **Green fee:** $15/20.
Credit cards: None. **Reduced fees:** Juniors.
Caddies: No. **Golf carts:** $20 for 18 holes.
Discount golf packages: No. **Season:** Year-round. **High:** May-Sept.
On-site lodging: No. **Rental clubs:** Yes.
Walking policy: Unrestricted walking. **Range:** No.
To obtain tee times: Tee times can be made by calling the pro shop.
Nonmembers call two days in advance.
Subscriber comments: Short, tough course, polite staff, accuracy a

requisite,. . . No amenities . . . Deceptively tight course . . . Excellent greenskeeper . . . Good for iron practice.

TRI-MOUNTAIN GOLF COURSE★
PU—1701 N.W. 299th St., Ridgefield. (206)887-3004.
15 miles south of Vancouver. **Holes:** 18. **Par:** 72/72.
Yards: 6,580/5,284. **Course rating:** 74.3/77.0. **Slope:** 127/133.
Opened: 1994. **Pace of Play rating:** 4:00. **Green fee:** $25/29.
Credit cards: MC, V. **Reduced fees:** Twilight, Seniors, Juniors.
Caddies: No. **Golf carts:** $20 for 18 holes.
Discount golf packages: Yes. **Season:** Year-round. **High:** April-Oct.
On-site lodging: No. **Rental clubs:** Yes.
Walking policy: Unrestricted walking. **Range:** No (grass).
To obtain tee times: Call seven days in advance.

★★½ TUMWATER VALLEY GOLF CLUB
PU—4611 Tumwater Valley Dr., Tumwater (206)943-9500.
60 miles south of Seattle. **Holes:** 18. **Par:** 72/72.
Yards: 7,154/5,504. **Course rating:** 73.1/70.4. **Slope:** 120/114.
Opened: 1970. **Pace of Play rating:** N/A. **Green fee:** $17/24.
Credit cards: MC, V. **Reduced fees:** Weekdays, Low season, Twilight, Seniors, Juniors.
Caddies: No. **Golf carts:** $20 for 18 holes.
Discount golf packages: No. **Season:** Year-round. **High:** May-Oct.
On-site lodging: No. **Rental clubs:** Yes.
Walking policy: Unrestricted walking. **Range:** Yes (grass).
To obtain tee times: Call up to eight days in advance.
Subscriber comments: Soggy when wet . . . Great driving course . . . Good practice area . . . Wet in winter . . . A great course during summer and fall . . . Large greens . . . Open, varied, reasonable, wide . . . Wide-open flat course plays long, longer when wet . . . Good quality public course . . . Hit the driver, hardly any trouble.

★ TYEE VALLEY GOLF COURSE
PU—2401 S. 192nd, Seattle (206)878-3540.
Call club for further information.
Subscriber comments: Sporty course, next to busy airport . . . Bring ear plugs . . . Very friendly staff . . . Challenging holes on each nine, easy walking course . . . Variety of holes, flat and hilly.

★★½ VETERANS MEMORIAL GOLF COURSE
PU—201 E. Rees, Walla Walla (509)527-4507.
Holes: 18. **Par:** 72/72.
Yards: 6,311/5,732. **Course rating:** N/A. **Slope:** 114/121.
Opened: N/A. **Pace of Play rating:** N/A. **Green fee:** N/A.
Credit cards: N/A. **Reduced fees:** N/A.
Caddies: No. **Golf carts:** N/A.
Discount golf packages: No. **Season:** Year-round. **High:** April-Sept.
On-site lodging: No. **Rental clubs:** No.
Walking policy: N/A. **Range:** Yes (grass).
Subscriber comments: One of area's nicest, mature, well kept . . . Nice public course in serene setting . . . Big old trees . . . Good value . . . Friendly, heavy traffic in peak season sometimes slows play.

★★½ WANDERMERE GOLF COURSE
PU—N. 13700 Division St., Spokane (509)466-8023.
Holes: 18. **Par:** 70/73.
Yards: 6,095/5,760. **Course rating:** 68.6/72.2. **Slope:** 119/126.
Opened: 1929. **Pace of Play rating:** 4:00-4:30. **Green fee:** $14/15.
Credit cards: MC, V. **Reduced fees:** Seniors, Juniors.
Caddies: No. **Golf carts:** $22 for 18 holes.
Discount golf packages: No. **Season:** March-Nov. **High:** June-Sept.
On-site lodging: No. **Rental clubs:** Yes.

Walking policy: Unrestricted walking. **Range:** Yes (grass).
To obtain tee times: One day ahead on weekdays; one week ahead on weekends. Start making times at 6:30 a.m.
Subscriber comments: Wide flat fairways, large fast greens, some water, good for everyone . . . Recent and ongoing improvements add spice . . . Gets lots of play . . . North Spokane's best . . . Tees and greens too close together.

★★ WEST SEATTLE GOLF COURSE
PU—4470 35th Ave. S.W., Seattle (206)935-5187.
Holes: 18. **Par:** 72/72.
Yards: 6,600/5,700. **Course rating:** 70.9/72.6. **Slope:** 119/123.
Opened: 1939. **Pace of Play rating:** 4:30. **Green fee:** $15.
Credit cards: None. **Reduced fees:** Twilight, Seniors, Juniors.
Caddies: No. **Golf carts:** $18 for 18 holes.
Discount golf packages: No. **Season:** Year-round. **High:** May-Sept.
On-site lodging: No. **Rental clubs:** Yes.
Walking policy: Unrestricted walking. **Range:** No.
To obtain tee times: Call up to seven days in advance.
Subscriber comments: Best city course for money . . . Hilly with lots of difficult lies . . . Great view on No. 12 . . . Heavy use, good bread-and-butter practice course . . . Most accessible of public courses . . . Good staff and service . . . Strict tee times . . . Undergoing improvement . . . Drainage a problem.

WILLOWS RUN GOLF CLUB★
PU—10402 Willows Rd. N.E., Redmond. (206)883-1200.
7 miles south of Bellevue. **Holes:** 18. **Par:** 72/72.
Yards: 6,806/5,633. **Course rating:** 71.6/71.4. **Slope:** 119/121.
Opened: 1994. **Pace of Play rating:** 4:30. **Green fee:** $29/39.
Credit cards: MC, V. **Reduced fees:** Twilight, Seniors, Juniors.
Caddies: No. **Golf carts:** $10 for 18 holes.
Discount golf packages: No. **Season:** Year-round. **High:** March-Oct.
On-site lodging: No. **Rental clubs:** Yes.
Walking policy: Unrestricted walking. **Range:** No (grass).
To obtain tee times: Call seven days in advance.

Notes

★★★½ ABBEY SPRINGS GOLF COURSE
R—Country Club Dr., Fontana on Geneva Lake (414)275-6111.
50 miles southeast of Milwaukee. **Holes:** 18. **Par:** 72/72.
Yards: 6,466/5,439. **Course rating:** 71.4/72.4. **Slope:** 133/129.
Opened: 1971. **Pace of Play rating:** 4:30. **Green fee:** $60.
Credit cards: All major. **Reduced fees:** Low season, Juniors.
Caddies: No. **Golf carts:** Included in Green Fee.
Discount golf packages: Yes. **Season:** April-Nov. **High:** June-Sept.
On-site lodging: No. **Rental clubs:** Yes.
Walking policy: Walking at certain times. **Range:** Yes (grass).
To obtain tee times: Call up to one month in advance.
Subscriber comments: Walk only if you are marathon fit . . . Wonderful
layout . . . Be straight and long . . . Very scenic, overlooking Lake Geneva
. . . Outstanding landscaping and vistas . . . One of the most scenic courses
in a very scenic state . . . Fastest greens around. Very tight fairways. A bit
too hilly.

★★ ALPINE RESORT GOLF COURSE
RED/WHITE/BLUE
R—P.O. Box 200, Egg Harbor (414)868-3232.
Call club for further information.
Subscriber comments: Outstanding cliff holes, some very short par 4s
. . . Ninth hole on Blue nine is breathtaking . . . The staff is short handed,
works hard . . . A view you'll never forget . . . Too tight, too many people
. . . Pretty course somewhat touristy . . . Relatively new third nine has
some imagination . . . Shows its age; some gimmicks, such as tram to
elevated tee . . . Cliff nine is worth playing, rest is kind of dry.

★★★ ANTIGO BASS LAKE COUNTRY CLUB
SP—P.O. Box 268, Antigo (715)623-6196.
Call club for further information.
Subscriber comments: Beautiful setting . . . Woods, hills, lakes, nice
course . . . Lay it up here or you're in the woods . . . A short, well-
conditioned course with challenges . . . Great food, better drinks . . . Horse
flies a real problem . . . Harder than you'd think . . . Treated very well . . .
Rolling fairways.

★★ BARABOO COUNTRY CLUB
SP—1010 Lake St., Baraboo (608)356-8195, (800)657-4981.
35 miles north of Madison. **Holes:** 18. **Par:** 72/72.
Yards: 6,570/5,681. **Course rating:** 71.3/72.5. **Slope:** 124/124.
Opened: 1962. **Pace of Play rating:** 4:30. **Green fee:** $17/26.
Credit cards: MC, V. **Reduced fees:** Weekdays, Low season, Twilight.
Caddies: No. **Golf carts:** $24 for 18 holes.
Discount golf packages: Yes. **Season:** April-Oct. **High:** June-Aug.
On-site lodging: No. **Rental clubs:** Yes.
Walking policy: Unrestricted walking. **Range:** Yes (grass).
To obtain tee times: Call or come in one week in advance.
Subscriber comments: Playable . . . Small track, some blind holes . . .
Very hilly, be in shape to walk . . . Uneven design . . . Nice people, good
greens . . . Old Indian grounds . . . Some patchy fairways . . . Finishing
holes blind and no fun.

BLACKWOLF RUN GOLF CLUB
R—1111 W. Riverside Dr., Kohler (414)457-4446, (800)344-2838.
55 miles north of Milwaukee.
Credit cards: All major. **Reduced fees:** Low season, Twilight.
Caddies: No. **Golf carts:** $15 for 18 holes.
Discount golf packages: No. **Season:** April-Oct. **High:** June-Sept.
On-site lodging: Yes. **Rental clubs:** Yes.
Walking policy: Unrestricted walking. **Range:** Yes (grass).
To obtain tee times: Call two weeks in advance. Guests may make tee
times at time of confirmed hotel reservation.

★★★★½ **MEADOW VALLEYS COURSE**

Holes: 18. **Par:** 72/72.
Yards: 7,142/5,065. **Course rating:** 74.7/69.5. **Slope:** 143/125.
Opened: 1988. **Pace of Play rating:** 5:03. **Green fee:** $71.
Ranked 5th in Wisconsin by Golf Digest.
Subscriber comments: Still in a class by itself . . . Better value than River Course . . . Huge greens . . . If wind is blowing at the turn, buy a dozen! Back nine finest in the country . . . Just as difficult as River Course . . . Sandtraps 150 yds long . . . Picture perfect golf holes . . . Service outstanding . . . Must play at least once a year . . . Great finishing hole with salmon . . . Each nine has different feeling . . . I have seen heaven, and it is named Blackwolf Run . . . Incredibly beautiful, subtle, devilish . . . The finest! . . . Staff treats everyone like a king . . . Fairer than River Course . . . Conditions are always impeccable.

★★★★★ **RIVER COURSE**

Holes: 18. **Par:** 72/72.
Yards: 6,991/5,115. **Course rating:** 74.9/70.7. **Slope:** 151/128.
Opened: 1988. **Pace of Play rating:** 5:09. **Green fee:** $100.
Ranked 62nd in America's 100 Greatest Golf Courses by Golf Digest. Selected as Best New Public Course of 1988 by Golf Digest. Ranked 1st in Wisconsin by Golf Digest.
Subscriber comments: What golf is all about. Best course in Wisconsin . . . Service is excellent . . . Grueling, beloved, a jewel . . . Easy to forget the outside world . . . Premier course . . . Pete Dye's best! Par 3s brutal from the blues or the blacks . . . Either course snow-covered would play better than most . . . None are the caliber of this one . . . Bring your camera and enjoy . . . Scenery is second to none . . . The Pebble Beach of Wisconsin . . . It will invigorate and exhaust you . . . Most challenging, most scenic, most variety of hazards, obstacles, best service . . . U.S. Open-caliber course . . . Don't try to cut the doglegs: you can't . . . Beyond incredible. The ultimate Midwest golf experience . . . Big bucks, tall grass, scenic views . . . Not to be missed . . . A challenge for anyone . . . On a par with Spyglass, Pinehurst No. 2 . . . Tee times a scarce commodity . . . Toughest in the state . . . Killer course . . . If you can play only once in Cheeseland, play this . . . It's a bear . . . Ruthless, stunning, painful . . . Expensive per hole, inexpensive per stroke . . . Leave your ego at home . . . The River is everywhere . . . Tougher than any other course from the black tees . . . Nonstop Dye punishment . . . Worth the price just to walk it.

BRIDGEWOOD GOLF COURSE★
PU—1040 Bridgewood Dr., Neenah (414)722-9819.
Holes: 18. **Par:** 71/71.
Yards: 6,015/5,907. **Course rating:** N/A. **Slope:** N/A.
Opened: 1949. **Pace of Play rating:** 4:00. **Green fee:** $12/14.
Credit cards: None. **Reduced fees:** Seniors, Juniors.
Caddies: No. **Golf carts:** $10 for 18 holes.
Discount golf packages: No. **Season:** April-Nov. **High:** May-Aug.
On-site lodging: No. **Rental clubs:** Yes.
Walking policy: Unrestricted walking. **Range:** No.
Subscriber comments: If you like a foundry as a backdrop, it's for you . . . OK as a beginner course.

BRIGHTON DALE GOLF CLUB
PU—830-248th Ave., Kansasville (414)878-1440.
21 miles southwest of Racine.
Pace of Play rating: 4:30. **Green fee:** $18/20.
Credit cards: None. **Reduced fees:** Weekdays.
Caddies: No. **Golf carts:** No,$18 for 18 holes.
Discount golf packages: No. **Season:** April-Nov. **High:** May-Sept.
On-site lodging: No. **Rental clubs:** Yes.
Walking policy: Unrestricted walking. **Range:** Yes.
Also has a nine-hole course.

★★★ WHITE BIRCH COURSE
Holes: 18. **Par:** 72/72.
Yards: 6,977/6,206. **Course rating:** 73.3/73.2. **Slope:** 130/126.
Opened: 1992.
Subscriber comments: Very scenic . . . 45-hole complex outstanding value . . . Too many long par 3s . . . Nice layout mixing old holes with new . . . Still kind of young . . . Some of the newer par 5s are unfair . . . Will develop into a fine course . . . Very well laid out. Very challenging . . . Picturesque, best value in the Midwest . . . Not enough distance info . . . Has everything, woods, water, character. Needs to age a little.

★★★ BLUE SPRUCE
Holes: 18. **Par:** 72/72.
Yards: 6,687/5,988. **Course rating:** 72.0/72.1. **Slope:** 129/125.
Opened: 1971.
Subscriber comments: Better of the two courses . . . Tough, tight layout . . . Good 19th hole . . . Ample challenge . . . Best public course for the money in southeast Wisconsin . . . Nice straightforward course . . . A pleasure to play, relaxing . . . New expanded course . . . Isolated, backwoodsy . . . Under-appreciated . . . Outstanding county park. Will go back and play again and again.

★★★★ BROWN COUNTY GOLF COURSE
PU—897 Riverdale Dr., Oneida (414)497-1731.
7 miles west of Green Bay. **Holes:** 18. **Par:** 72/73.
Yards: 6,729/5,801. **Course rating:** 72.1/72.7. **Slope:** 133/127.
Opened: 1957. **Pace of Play rating:** 5:00. **Green fee:** $21.
Credit cards: None. **Reduced fees:** Seniors, Juniors.
Caddies: No. **Golf carts:** $10 for 18 holes.
Discount golf packages: No. **Season:** April-Oct. **High:** June-Aug.
On-site lodging: No. **Rental clubs:** Yes.
Walking policy: Unrestricted walking. **Range:** Yes (grass).
To obtain tee times: Call one day in advance for weekdays. Call Monday at 6 p.m. for upcoming weekend and holidays.
Ranked in Second 25 of America's 75 Best Public Golf Courses by Golf Digest.
Subscriber comments: Excellent for a municipal course . . . Easy to get on during Packer home games. Same designer as Mascoutin and Chaska; this is the best of the three . . . Fantastic condition for a public course . . . Ninth hole is the toughest I have ever played . . . It feels tight now . . . For the price it's a steal . . . One of the finest public courses anywhere . . . Wished I had a chainsaw in my bag . . . Good elevation changes . . . Some holes good, some terrible . . . Immaculate county course. Fast greens . . . Conditions and layout many private clubs would envy . . . Best-kept secret in Wisconsin . . . Keep it on the fairway and you're okay. Woods? You're gone.

★★★★ BROWN DEER GOLF COURSE
PU—7835 N. Green Bay Rd., Milwaukee (414)352-8080.
Holes: 18. **Par:** 71/71.
Yards: 6,763/5,965. **Course rating:** N/A. **Slope:** 130/131.
Call club for further information.
Subscriber comments: Great old course . . . New Andy North holes look out of place . . . Traditional . . . Host to GMO in '94, mature trees, needs another year or two to grow in fairways . . . Should be great in '95. Pros didn't shoot 600 under! . . . Classic . . . Best value in midwest . . . Bent-grass fairways . . . Will be tougher when young trees grow up . . . Overrated due to the GMO, actually easier to play since improvements . . . Best muny in the state . . . It's good enough for the Tour and it was super for me . . . Best course in Milwaukee . . . Aesthetically satisfying . . . Great fun for a public course . . . Brown Deer is back . . . Now top notched . . . Unbelievable rough . . . Very reasonable cost . . . North work made a great layout better . . . Renovations have produced a public country club . . . Granddad of Milwaukee municipal courses . . . Solid old tree-lined course . . . Expected a pro course. Just a real good public course.

★★ BROWNS LAKE GOLF COURSE

PU—3110 S. Browns Lake Dr., Burlington (414)763-6065.
25 miles northeast of Milwaukee. **Holes:** 18. **Par:** 72/75.
Yards: 6,449/6,206. **Course rating:** 70.2/75.8. **Slope:** 122/132.
Opened: 1923. **Pace of Play rating:** 4:00. **Green fee:** $18/19.
Credit cards: None. **Reduced fees:** Seniors, Juniors.
Caddies: No. **Golf carts:** $12 for 18 holes.
Discount golf packages: No. **Season:** March-Oct. **High:** June-Sept.
On-site lodging: No. **Rental clubs:** Yes.
Walking policy: Unrestricted walking. **Range:** Yes (grass).
To obtain tee times: Call one week in advance for a $4 charge.
Subscriber comments: Something for all golfers. Enjoy being able to
walk on almost anytime! . . . Three par 5s on the front, back nine more
secluded and scenic . . . First four holes all a shooting gallery . . . Sporty
. . . Beautiful scenery . . . Cross Fox River twice.

★★½ CAMELOT COUNTRY CLUB

SP—W192 Highway 67, Lomira (414)269-4949.
Call club for further information.
Subscriber comments: Fun, scenic, saddleback greens could use a few flat
spots . . . Short but interesting . . . I love the elevated tee on the par 3s . . .
Par 3s could be downhill ski slopes . . . A lot of hills and trees but also some
wide open holes . . . Staff is great, ditto for the food . . . Rolling fairways.
Hard walking . . . . Very tough greens, need to avoid the high side of the
hole . . . Short and funky; small, mounded greens.

CASTLE ROCK GOLF COURSE★

PU—W. 6285 Welch Prairie Rd., New Lisbon (608)847-4658,
(800)851-4853.
2 miles north of Wisconsin Dells. **Holes:** 18. **Par:** 72/71.
Yards: 6,160/5,318. **Course rating:** 70.1/70.6. **Slope:** 126/122.
Opened: 1991. **Pace of Play rating:** N/A. **Green fee:** $18/21.
Credit cards: MC, V, DISC. **Reduced fees:** Weekdays, Twilight,
Seniors, Juniors.
Caddies: No. **Golf carts:** $20 for 18 holes.
Discount golf packages: Yes. **Season:** April-Oct. **High:** June-Aug.
On-site lodging: No. **Rental clubs:** Yes.
Walking policy: Unrestricted walking. **Range:** Yes (grass).
To obtain tee times: Call.

★★½ CHASKA GOLF COURSE

PU—Hwy. 10 and 45, Appleton (414)757-5757.
90 miles north of Milwaukee. **Holes:** 18. **Par:** 72/72.
Yards: 6,854/5,847. **Course rating:** 72.5/73.1. **Slope:** 128/126.
Opened: 1975. **Pace of Play rating:** 4:00. **Green fee:** $15/17.
Credit cards: MC, V. **Reduced fees:** Twilight, Seniors, Juniors.
Caddies: No. **Golf carts:** $20 for 18 holes.

Discount golf packages: No. **Season:** April-Nov. **High:** May-Aug.
On-site lodging: No. **Rental clubs:** Yes.
Walking policy: Unrestricted walking. **Range:** Yes (grass).
To obtain tee times: Call five days in advance.
Subscriber comments: Nicely wooded back nine . . . Save this gem . . .
Wish the trees would grow . . . Front side open . . . Nearby highway
detracts from course . . . Lots of sand, little water . . . Well designed . . .
Good golf, good price, nothing special . . . For the price, the best there is
. . . Inconsistent greens . . . Too much sand.

★★ CHERRY HILLS GOLF COURSE

R—5905 Dunn Rd., Sturgeon Bay (414)743-3240, (800)545-2307.
40 miles northeast of Green Bay. **Holes:** 18. **Par:** 72/72.
Yards: 6,163/5,432. **Course rating:** 69.2/71.0. **Slope:** 121/122.
Opened: 1977. **Pace of Play rating:** 4:00. **Green fee:** $16/25.
Credit cards: All major. **Reduced fees:** Weekdays, Low season, Twilight,
Seniors, Juniors.
Caddies: No. **Golf carts:** $11 for 18 holes.

Discount golf packages: Yes. **Season:** April-Oct. **High:** June-Aug.
On-site lodging: Yes. **Rental clubs:** Yes.
Walking policy: Unrestricted walking. **Range:** Yes (grass).
To obtain tee times: Call. No restrictions.
Subscriber comments: Pretty course . . . Has undergone a substantial
upgrade . . . Another young course I'd like to play again in 10 years . . .
Lots of hills . . . Very playable . . . Small greens . . . Too much slope on
greens . . . Small, convex greens . . . Hilly lies abound.

★½ CHRISTMAS MOUNTAIN VILLAGE GOLF CLUB

R—S. 944 Christmas Mountain Rd., Wisconsin Dells (608)254-3971.
40 miles northwest of Madison. **Holes:** 18. **Par:** 71/71.
Yards: 6,589/5,479. **Course rating:** 72.1/72.1. **Slope:** 129/126.
Opened: 1970. **Pace of Play rating:** 4:30. **Green fee:** $36.
Credit cards: All major. **Reduced fees:** Low season, Seniors.
Caddies: No. **Golf carts:** Included in Green Fee.
Discount golf packages: Yes. **Season:** March-Nov. **High:** May-Sept.
On-site lodging: Yes. **Rental clubs:** Yes.
Walking policy: Walking at certain times. **Range:** Yes (grass).
To obtain tee times: Call up to 14 days in advance or book a golf package
anytime.
Subscriber comments: Easy to play . . . A handful of challenging holes
. . . Wanted to like more . . . Below par but worth playing once a year . . .
Heavily played . . . Excellent views from tees, need to think before each
shot . . . Not in great shape . . . Awkward layout, pace was slow . . . A
wide range of holes . . . The greens were as slow as the people.

CLIFTON HOLLOW GOLF CLUB★

PU—12166 W. 820th. Ave., River Falls (715)425-9781, (800)487-8879.
30 miles east of St. Paul. **Holes:** 18. **Par:** 71/72.
Yards: 6,381/5,117. **Course rating:** 69.6/68.6. **Slope:** 118/114.
Opened: 1973. **Pace of Play rating:** N/A. **Green fee:** $16/20.
Credit cards: MC, V. **Reduced fees:** Weekdays, Seniors, Juniors.
Caddies: No. **Golf carts:** $21 for 18 holes.
Discount golf packages: No. **Season:** April-Nov. **High:** June-Aug.
On-site lodging: No. **Rental clubs:** Yes.
Walking policy: Unrestricted walking. **Range:** Yes (grass).
To obtain tee times: Call one week in advance.

★★★ COUNTRY CLUB OF WISCONSIN

PU—2241 Highway W., Grafton (414)375-2444.
20 miles south of Milwaukee. **Holes:** 18. **Par:** 72/72.
Yards: 7,108/5,499. **Course rating:** 74.7/67.4. **Slope:** 137/119.
Opened: 1994. **Pace of Play rating:** 4:30. **Green fee:** $20/49.
Credit cards: MC, V. **Reduced fees:** Weekdays, Twilight, Seniors,
Juniors.
Caddies: No. **Golf carts:** $12 for 18 holes.
Discount golf packages: No. **Season:** April-Nov. **High:** May-Sept.
On-site lodging: No. **Rental clubs:** Yes.
Walking policy: Unrestricted walking. **Range:** Yes (grass).
To obtain tee times: Call seven days in advance.
Subscriber comments: Had a very good first year . . . Developers need
remember it is the course, not the clubhouse, we come for . . . Is very
rough, has potential . . . New rough far too penal, some holes seem
squeezed together . . . Country club quality . . . Outstanding . . . Opened
too soon . . . Needs time to mature . . . Not marked well . . . Swampy
terrain is problematic . . . Interesting blind shots . . . Too many blind shots.

★ COUNTRYSIDE GOLF CLUB

PU—W. 726 Weiler Rd., Kaukauna (414)766-2219.
15 miles south of Green Bay. **Holes:** 18. **Par:** 71/73.
Yards: 6,140/5,947. **Course rating:** 68.9/73.2. **Slope:** 114/122.
Opened: 1964. **Pace of Play rating:** 4:00. **Green fee:** $13/15.
Credit cards: MC, V. **Reduced fees:** Weekdays, Low season, Seniors,
Juniors.

Caddies: No. **Golf carts:** N/A.
Discount golf packages: Yes. **Season:** April-Oct. **High:** June-Aug.
On-site lodging: No. **Rental clubs:** Yes.
Walking policy: Unrestricted walking. **Range:** Yes (grass).
To obtain tee times: Call in advance.
Subscriber comments: Average golf course . . . No $ put into the course
. . . Nice beginner course.

CRYSTAL SPRINGS GOLF CLUB★

PU—N. 8055 French Rd., Seymour (414)833-6348, (800)686-2984.
17 miles west of Green Bay. **Holes:** 18. **Par:** 72/73.
Yards: 6,596/5,497. **Course rating:** 70.7/74.5. **Slope:** 120/124.
Opened: 1967. **Pace of Play rating:** 4:30. **Green fee:** $15/17.
Credit cards: None. **Reduced fees:** Twilight, Seniors, Juniors.
Caddies: No. **Golf carts:** $20 for 18 holes.
Discount golf packages: No. **Season:** April-Nov. **High:** June-Aug.
On-site lodging: No. **Rental clubs:** Yes.
Walking policy: Walking at certain times. **Range:** Yes (grass).
To obtain tee times: Call pro shop.

★★ CURRIE PARK GOLF COURSE

PU—3535 N. Mayfair Rd., Milwaukee (414)453-7030.
Call club for further information.
Subscriber comments: Relaxing course . . . Real easy. Lots of play, OK
for an early-morning nine . . . Short and simple . . . Milwaukee's best-kept
secret . . . No big challenge, but fun . . . Back nine is next to the freeway
. . . Strange layout, but playable.

★★★ DEERTRAK GOLF COURSE

PU—W. 930 Hwy O, Oconomowoc (414)474-4444.
Call club for further information.
Subscriber comments: Nice setting . . . Good morale booster . . . Short
front nine; decent back nine . . . Greens were good . . . Too short . . . A
good course with lack of players . . . Short but testy . . . Good mix of tight
and open, fairways aren't in the greatest shape . . . Five water holes. Pretty
course with a waterfall.

★★½ DEVIL'S HEAD RESORT AND CONVENTION CENTER

R—S. 6330 Bluff Rd., Merrimac (608)493-2251, (800)472-6670.
35 miles north of Madison. **Holes:** 18. **Par:** 73/73.
Yards: 6,725/5,141. **Course rating:** 71.6/64.4. **Slope:** 127/113.
Opened: 1973. **Pace of Play rating:** 4:00. **Green fee:** $26/30.
Credit cards: MC, V. **Reduced fees:** Low season, Twilight.
Caddies: No. **Golf carts:** Included in Green Fee.
Discount golf packages: Yes. **Season:** April-Oct. **High:** June-Aug.
On-site lodging: Yes. **Rental clubs:** Yes.
Walking policy: Walking at certain times. **Range:** Yes.
To obtain tee times: Nonguests call two weeks in advance for weekday
and 24 hours in advance for weekend tee time.
Subscriber comments: Appears to be underplayed . . . Did not do the
land justice with the course design . . . Scenic . . . A good resort course,
many tough holes . . . Nice course, but nothing to go with it . . . Hills,
woods, etc. . . . A real challenge with large greens . . . Greens always need
cutting . . . Lacks conditioning.

★★½ DOOR CREEK GOLF CLUB

PU—4321 Vilas, Cottage Grove (608)839-5656.
Call club for further information.
Subscriber comments: Great shape for a relatively new course . . . A
hidden gem, still relatively unknown . . . Some interesting holes . . .
Friendliest staff in Wisconsin . . . Not long but plenty of water . . . Greens
on the shaggy side . . . Good, basic course.

★★★ DRETZKA PARK GOLF COURSE

PU—12020 W. Bradley Rd., Milwaukee (414)354-7300.
Holes: 18. **Par:** 72/72.
Yards: 6,832/5,680. **Course rating:** 70.8/74.6. **Slope:** 124/123.
Opened: 1967. **Pace of Play rating:** 4:35. **Green fee:** $13/17.
Credit cards: MC, V. **Reduced fees:** Twilight, Seniors, Juniors.
Caddies: No. **Golf carts:** $10 for 18 holes.
Discount golf packages: No. **Season:** March-Nov. **High:** May-Sept.
On-site lodging: No. **Rental clubs:** Yes.
Walking policy: Unrestricted walking. **Range:** Yes (grass).
To obtain tee times: Call.
Subscriber comments: Not too much trouble, just hit it long . . . A long track built into the natural lay of the land . . . Interesting . . . Tough course because of length . . . GMO should be here . . . Much tougher than most county courses . . . Best of the county courses . . . Rock-hard fairways . . . Sculptured fairways are ridiculous . . . U.S. Open-type rough all year . . . Usually good conditions . . . Could be great if the eighth hole were redesigned . . . More challenging than Brown Deer . . . No wind, it's easy . . . Change in elevation make this an interesting course . . . One of the best county courses in Wisconsin . . . Could be another Brown Deer at half price . . . More than worth any wait . . . Only a few sand traps, but a little creek meanders all over.

★★★ EAGLE RIVER GOLF COURSE

PU—527 McKinley Blvd., Eagle River (715)479-8111.
70 miles north of Wausau. **Holes:** 18. **Par:** 71/72.
Yards: 6,103/5,167. **Course rating:** 69.3/67.8. **Slope:** 121/119.
Opened: 1923. **Pace of Play rating:** 4:10. **Green fee:** $17/25.
Credit cards: MC, V. **Reduced fees:** Low season, Resort guests, Twilight, Seniors, Juniors.
Caddies: No. **Golf carts:** $11 for 18 holes.
Discount golf packages: Yes. **Season:** May-Oct. **High:** July-Aug.
On-site lodging: No. **Rental clubs:** Yes.
Walking policy: . **Range:** Yes (grass).
To obtain tee times: Call seven days in advance for three to four players and two days in advance for one to two players.
Subscriber comments: Fun northern course, getting better each year . . . Favorite despite the mosquitos . . . Cut out of the woods . . . Beautiful in the fall . . . More tough holes than easy ones . . . Through the woods we go . . . A lot of pin placements on humps . . . Augusta National of Wisconsin. Very pretty course.

★★½ EVANSVILLE COUNTRY CLUB

PU—Cemetery Rd., Evansville (608)882-6524.
30 miles south of Madison. **Holes:** 18. **Par:** 72/72.
Yards: 6,559/5,366. **Course rating:** 71.0/70.3. **Slope:** 127/122.
Opened: 1964. **Pace of Play rating:** 4:04. **Green fee:** $17/19.
Credit cards: MC, V. **Reduced fees:** Low season, Juniors.
Caddies: No. **Golf carts:** $20 for 18 holes.
Discount golf packages: No. **Season:** April-Oct. **High:** June-Aug.
On-site lodging: No. **Rental clubs:** Yes.
Walking policy: Unrestricted walking. **Range:** Yes (grass).
To obtain tee times: Call up to one week in advance.
Subscriber comments: Has recently expanded to 18 holes. Some of the new holes need time . . . Hilly terrain . . . Original nine is beautiful . . . Newly opened nine holes are subtly challenging . . . New nine will be excellent . . . Honest, traditional layout.

EVERGREEN GOLF CLUB
★★★ NORTH/EAST/SOUTH

PU—Hwys. No.12 and 67N., Elkhorn (414)723-5722, (800)868-8618.
40 miles southwest of Milwaukee. **Holes:** 27. **Par:** 72/72/72.
Yards: 6,431/6,501/6,280. **Course rating:** 71.7/71.7/70.8.
Slope: 128/127/125.

Opened: 1973. **Pace of Play rating:** 4:20. **Green fee:** $23/28.
Credit cards: MC, V, DISC. **Reduced fees:** Weekdays, Low season, Twilight, Juniors.
Caddies: No. **Golf carts:** $12 for 18 holes.
Discount golf packages: Yes. **Season:** March-Dec. **High:** May-Sept.
On-site lodging: No. **Rental clubs:** Yes.
Walking policy: Walking at certain times. **Range:** Yes (grass).
To obtain tee times: Tee times required. Make reservations in advance. 48 hour cancellation required.
Subscriber comments: A delightful 27 holes. Excellent services . . . Very good staff. Just added a new nine . . . Some unique holes . . . Sporty . . . Rough is brutal . . . Too much in-course O.B. . . . Country club conditions . . . Heavy play equals poor greens . . . For the cash, it's great fun . . . Some excellent holes . . . Deceptively tight . . . Contoured greens are an extra challenge . . . Interesting in spite of homes . . . Lots of sand . . . Everything neat as a pin. Very pretty.

FAR VU GOLF COURSE★

PU—4985 State Road 175, Oshkosh (414)231-2631.
Holes: 18. **Par:** 71/73.
Yards: 6,191/5,555. **Course rating:** 69.3/71.1. **Slope:** N/A.
Opened: 1964. **Pace of Play rating:** 4:00. **Green fee:** $13.
Credit cards: None. **Reduced fees:** Seniors, Juniors.
Caddies: No. **Golf carts:** $17 for 18 holes.
Discount golf packages: No. **Season:** April-Oct. **High:** June-Aug.
On-site lodging: No. **Rental clubs:** Yes.
Walking policy: Unrestricted walking. **Range:** No.
To obtain tee times: Call one week in advance.

FOREST RIDGES GOLF COURSE★

R—HC 73, Box 715, Cable. (715)794-2561
80 miles southeast of Duluth. **Holes:** 18. **Par:** 71/71.
Yards: 6,270/4,442. **Course rating:** N/A. **Slope:** N/A.
Opened: 1995. **Pace of Play rating:** 4:00. **Green fee:** $45.
Credit cards: All major. **Reduced fees:** Low season, Resort guests, Twilight.
Caddies: No. **Golf carts:** Included in Green Fee.
Discount golf packages: Yes. **Season:** May-Oct. **High:** June-Sept.
On-site lodging: Yes. **Rental clubs:** Yes.
Walking policy: Mandatory cart. **Range:** Yes (grass).
To obtain tee times: Call seven days in advance.

FOX HILLS RESORT

R—250 W. Chruch St., Mishicot (414)755-2831, (800)950-7615.
30 miles southeast of Green Bay.
Green fee: $12/28.
Credit cards: All major. **Reduced fees:** Weekdays, Low season, Twilight, Seniors.
Caddies: No. **Golf carts:** $12 for 18 holes.
Discount golf packages: Yes. **Season:** April-Nov. **High:** June-Aug.
On-site lodging: Yes. **Rental clubs:** Yes.
Walking policy: Unrestricted walking. **Range:** Yes (grass).
To obtain tee times: Call, no requirements.
★½ **CLASSIC COURSE-FRONT/BACK/BLUE**
Holes: 27. **Par:** 72/71/0.
Yards: 6,374/6,410/N/A. **Course rating:** 70.5/70.0/N/A.
Slope: 123/122/N/A.
Opened: 1961. **Pace of Play rating:** 4:30.
Subscriber comments: My kids might enjoy it . . . Fairway quality is inconsistent . . . All types of conditions . . . Accommodations below most; updated clubhouse . . . Much in-course O.B. . . . Short, fair greens, easy scoring . . . Woods and clover.

★★½ FOX HILLS NATIONAL GOLF CLUB
Holes: 18. **Par:** 72/72.
Yards: 7,017/5,366. **Course rating:** 73.8/71.0. **Slope:** 136/124.
Opened: 1988. **Pace of Play rating:** 4:30.
Subscriber comments: Dunes style, a bear when the wind is really blowing . . . Side-by-side par 4s with mounds between . . . Clay base: fake moguls! . . . Links style . . . A bit out of place in Wisconsin . . . Very poor imitation of Scottish golf . . . Waste areas are gravel pits . . . No restrooms anywhere . . . Requires some shotmaking and imagination . . . No trees, lots of water. You either love it or hate it. I love it . . . Flat and boring, no trees; tight par 3s.

GENEVA NATIONAL GOLF CLUB
R—1221 Geneva National Ave. S., Lake Geneva (414)245-7000.
45 miles southwest of Milwaukee.
Opened: 1991. **Pace of Play rating:** 4:12. **Green fee:** $75/85.
Credit cards: MC, V, AMEX. **Reduced fees:** Low season, Resort guests.
Caddies: No. **Golf carts:** Included in Green Fee.
Discount golf packages: Yes. **Season:** March-Oct. **High:** May-Sept.
On-site lodging: Yes. **Rental clubs:** Yes.
Walking policy: Mandatory cart. **Range:** Yes (grass).
To obtain tee times: Call two weeks in advance.

★★★★ PALMER COURSE
Holes: 18. **Par:** 72/72.
Yards: 7,171/4,904. **Course rating:** 74.8/68.7. **Slope:** 140/122.
Subscriber comments: No. 17 is Pebble Beach-like . . . Not a weak hole on the course. Good finishing hole . . . You don't need a Cadillac to play . . . Cut out of the woods . . . Bent-grass conditions are good . . . Beautiful, lots of trouble . . . Beautiful scenes . . . First-class operation . . . A true test of golf . . . Bring a good putter . . . Targets too small for long irons . . . Need to know the course to play well . . . Will get better with age . . . 12 exciting golf holes . . . Rolling fairways, tight greens, not for everybody . . . Three of the finest finishing holes in the state.

★★★★ TREVINO COURSE
Holes: 18. **Par:** 72/72.
Yards: 7,120/5,193. **Course rating:** 74.5/70.1. **Slope:** 137/124.
Ranked 8th in Wisconsin by Golf Digest.
Subscriber comments: Fader's dream . . . A better track to play than the Palmer . . . High quality courses and customer treatment . . . One nice par 5 through the woods; the other holes I've already forgotten . . . A lot of different looks . . . Great layout . . . The better of the two . . . Too expensive for the golf experience that one gets . . . A lot of character, like a country club open to the public . . . Very fair . . . One of the best . . . Excellent variety of holes.

THE GOLF COURSES OF LAWSONIA
R—W2615 S. Valley View Dr., Green Lake (414)294-3320, (800)529-4453.
35 miles southwest of Oshkosh.
Pace of Play rating: 4:30. **Green fee:** $33/48.
Credit cards: All major. **Reduced fees:** Low season, Resort guests, Twilight.
Caddies: No. **Golf carts:** Included in Green Fee.
Discount golf packages: Yes. **Season:** April-Nov. **High:** June-Sept.
On-site lodging: Yes. **Rental clubs:** Yes.
Walking policy: Walking at certain times. **Range:** Yes (grass).
To obtain tee times: Call anytime in advance up to eight months.

★★★★ LINKS COURSE
Holes: 18. **Par:** 72/71.
Yards: 6,764/5,078. **Course rating:** 72.8/68.9. **Slope:** 130/114.
Opened: 1930.
Ranked in Third 25 of America's 75 Best Public Golf Courses by Golf Digest. Ranked 10th in Wisconsin by Golf Digest.
Subscriber comments: Very tough bunkers . . . A classic . . . Great old course with three-puttable greens . . . Exceptional place . . . Difficult greens . . . Probably couldn't afford the beer they don't serve anyway . . .

Absolutely unique and frustrating . . . Elevated greens are fascinating . . . Don't tell anyone, it might get busier . . . Many fairway bunkers, fun to play . . . Bunkers are nasty . . . Bunkers, bunkers and larger bunkers . . . Uncut clover in rough worse than U.S. Open rough . . . Challenging, historic, unique . . . Every hole memorable . . . If you like links, you'll like this course . . . Proves that you don't need trees . . . No one outside of central Wisconsin has heard of Lawsonia . . . Two different courses, both outstanding . . . Woodlands, be straight. Links, play low ball . . . A challenging course from another era . . . Wisconsin's best links course . . . Wisconsin's British Open course . . . Killer long.

★★★★ THE WOODLANDS

Holes: 18. **Par:** 72/72.
Yards: 6,618/5,106. **Course rating:** 71.5/69.1. **Slope:** 129/120.
Opened: 1982.
Subscriber comments: A great track cut through heavy woods . . . Beauty only matched by Blackwolf Run . . . Some great, tough holes, but greens are only OK . . . Beautiful lake, interesting grounds . . . Great addition to the Links Course . . . Better than the Links Course . . . Woods, wildlife. Great layout . . . Great views, bring your best game to play here . . . Beautiful views of Green Lake . . . Has one hole of every kind . . . Hills, woods, and elevated greens . . . Toughest 18 holes of golf I played in Wisconsin, but also the most beautiful . . . Third and fourth holes are fantastic . . . You always see deer . . . Cut out of virgin timber . . . Deer, hawks, eagles in view . . . For the money, the best course in Wisconsin . . . Completely different from the Links . . . Too tight for me . . . Many well-designed holes.

GRAND GENEVA RESORT AND SPA

R—7036 Grand Way at Hwys. 50 and 12, Lake Geneva (414)248-2556, (800)558-3417.
40 miles southwest of Milwaukee.
Pace of Play rating: 4:30-5:00. **Green fee:** $75/85.
Credit cards: All major. **Reduced fees:** Low season, Twilight.
Caddies: No. **Golf carts:** Included in Green Fee.
Discount golf packages: Yes. **Season:** April-Nov. **High:** May-Sept.
On-site lodging: Yes. **Rental clubs:** Yes.
Walking policy: Mandatory cart. **Range:** Yes (grass).
To obtain tee times: Call tee time number and ask for golf tee times. Times are taken 30 days in advance with a hotel confirmation number for our guests or two weeks in advance on a major credit card for nonresort guests.

★★★ THE BRIAR PATCH COURSE

Holes: 18. **Par:** 71/71.
Yards: 6,478/4,950. **Course rating:** 71.7/65.0. **Slope:** 133/117.
Opened: 1970.
Ranked 9th in Wisconsin by Golf Digest.
Subscriber comments: A little costly, but average for the Lake Geneva area . . . Best it's ever been . . . Pete Dye course, short and lots of fun . . . Fast greens . . . Difficult . . . Tight . . . A little bit of Scotland . . . Some spectacular holes . . . Condition not as good as the Brute . . . You better hit it straight . . . Too much stuff going on . . . Interesting . . . Two or three questionable holes.

★★★★ THE BRUTE COURSE

Holes: 18. **Par:** 72/74.
Yards: 6,997/5,408. **Course rating:** 73.4/67.5. **Slope:** 135/122.
Opened: 1968.
Subscriber comments: Has gone downhill . . . Super-fast greens. The name describes the course . . . Sprawling, challenging course. Up, down, around, flat, has it all . . . Elevated tees on almost every hole, huge greens . . . Lots of water, a great golf course . . . Way too long! Immense greens . . . Large sand traps . . . Fairway woods a must . . . Both courses are a good challenge . . . A bit overwhelming at times . . . Fun from beginning to end . . . Humongous greens . . . Every hole is a challenge.

★★ GRANT PARK GOLF COURSE

PU—100 Hawthorne Ave., South Milwaukee (414)762-4646.
12 miles south of Milwaukee. **Holes:** 18. **Par:** 67/71.
Yards: 5,174/5,147. **Course rating:** 64.1/68.4. **Slope:** 110/103.
Opened: 1920. **Pace of Play rating:** 4:30. **Green fee:** $8/16.
Credit cards: None. **Reduced fees:** Weekdays, Low season, Twilight,
Seniors, Juniors.
Caddies: No. **Golf carts:** $20 for 18 holes.
Discount golf packages: No. **Season:** Year-round. **High:** June-Aug.
On-site lodging: No. **Rental clubs:** Yes.
Walking policy: Unrestricted walking. **Range:** Yes.
To obtain tee times: Same day at the course or use the automated system
up to one week in advance.
Must be a member of system. Walk-ons accepted.
Subscriber comments: Great course for irons only . . . Clubhouse
converted from an old home . . . If the course was longer it would be great
. . . Not in great shape, but very pretty . . . Victorian clubhouse. Great
hamburgers . . . Challenges you to place the ball . . . One of the oldest
courses in Milwaukee.

★★ GREENFIELD PARK GOLF COURSE

PU—2028 S. 124th. St., West Allis (414)342-8878.
Call club for further information.
Subscriber comments: Medium course . . . Play too slow for a course
this size . . . Basic, no-frills course . . . No hazards . . . Very busy . . .
Tends to be slow but worth the wait.

★★½ HARTFORD GOLF CLUB

SP—7072 Lee Rd., Hartford (414)673-2710.
30 miles northwest of Milwaukee. **Holes:** 18. **Par:** 72/74.
Yards: 6,406/5,850. **Course rating:** 69.7/72.9. **Slope:** 114/119.
Opened: 1933. **Pace of Play rating:** 4:00. **Green fee:** $21/24.
Credit cards: MC, V. **Reduced fees:** Twilight.
Caddies: Yes. **Golf carts:** $11 for 18 holes.
Discount golf packages: No. **Season:** April-Dec. **High:** May-Sept.
On-site lodging: No. **Rental clubs:** Yes.
Walking policy: Unrestricted walking. **Range:** Yes (grass).
To obtain tee times: Call seven days in advance.
Subscriber comments: Greens fast and consistent . . . Not overbearing.
Two cuts of rough . . . Fairway bunkers, walkable . . . Finish in under four
hours or adios! Much improved in recent years . . . Small-town, fun,
homey . . . Always the same but never first-class . . . Easy to get on . . .
Allows spraying . . . Longest course in Wisconsin for women . . . Only
two water holes, but is well-trapped.

★★½ HAWTHORNE HILLS GOLF CLUB

PU—4720 Hwy. 1, Saukville (414)692-2151.
25 miles north of Milwaukee. **Holes:** 18. **Par:** 72/72.
Yards: 6,595/5,307. **Course rating:** 70.5/69.1. **Slope:** 118/114.
Opened: 1965. **Pace of Play rating:** 4:30. **Green fee:** $12/19.
Credit cards: MC, V. **Reduced fees:** Seniors, Juniors.
Caddies: No. **Golf carts:** $20 for 18 holes.
Discount golf packages: No. **Season:** April-Oct. **High:** April-Oct.
On-site lodging: No. **Rental clubs:** Yes.
Walking policy: Unrestricted walking. **Range:** No.
To obtain tee times: Residents up to one week in advance; non-residents
up to three days prior.
Subscriber comments: Large greens . . . Nice scenery . . . Hilly, little
rough . . . Average course . . . Good condition and greens . . . Good
variety of holes . . . Good putter has an advantage on very sloped greens
. . . New tee boxes . . . There is room to stray.

★★★ HAYWARD GOLF AND TENNIS CENTER

PU—RR No.10, Wittwer St., Hayward (715)634-2760.
Call club for further information.
Subscriber comments: In the heart of muskie country . . . Best suited for players with a long ball . . . Surprising, enjoyable . . . great greens . . . Par 3s are a little too easy . . . Northwoods golf at a fair price . . . Have to keep it in play.

★½ HIGH CLIFF GOLF COURSE

PU—W. 5075 Golf Course Rd., Menasha (414)734-1162.
Call club for further information.
Subscriber comments: Course improvements make it tough to play . . . Has three or four awesome holes in the woods . . . Unimaginative, not enough sand or water . . . Good views of lake and harbor . . . Great views from the tees . . . Great scenery on back nine . . . Nice fairways, poor rough.

★★½ HILLMOOR GOLF CLUB

SP—Hwy. 50 E., Box 186, Lake Geneva (414)248-4570.
50 miles north of Chicago. **Holes:** 18. **Par:** 72/72.
Yards: 6,350/5,360. **Course rating:** 71.0/65.3. **Slope:** 123/113.
Opened: 1924. **Pace of Play rating:** 3:30-4:00. **Green fee:** $22/32.
Credit cards: MC, V. **Reduced fees:** Weekdays, Low season, Twilight, Juniors.
Caddies: No. **Golf carts:** $13 for 18 holes.
Discount golf packages: Yes. **Season:** March-Dec. **High:** May-Oct.
On-site lodging: Yes. **Rental clubs:** Yes.
Walking policy: Walking at certain times. **Range:** Yes (grass).
To obtain tee times: Call in advance.
Subscriber comments: Wide open, needs trees . . . Overlapping holes, congested . . . Neat layout . . . A couple of nice holes, but mostly pretty bland . . . Nice old-style golf . . . Very nice people . . . Holes seven through 13 in low ground area and very wet.

HON-E-KOR COUNTRY CLUB
★★ BLUE/RED/WHITE

SP—1141 Riverview Dr., Box 439, Kewaskum (414)626-2520.
5 miles north of West Bend. **Holes:** 27. **Par:** 70/70/70.
Yards: 5,959/6,033/5,958. **Course rating:** 71/71. **Slope:** 123/117.
Opened: 1962. **Pace of Play rating:** 4:30. **Green fee:** $20/25.
Credit cards: MC, V. **Reduced fees:** Weekdays, Low season, Seniors, Juniors.
Caddies: No. **Golf carts:** $12 for 18 holes.
Discount golf packages: No. **Season:** April-Nov. **High:** May-Sept.
On-site lodging: No. **Rental clubs:** Yes.
Walking policy: Unrestricted walking. **Range:** Yes (grass).
To obtain tee times: Call two days in advance.
Subscriber comments: White nine is challenging, but the rest needs work . . . Easy course . . . No imagination here . . . 27 holes, very tight, short course . . . A place to play, not much else . . . Decent shape, good mix of easy and tough holes.

★★½ IDLEWILD GOLF COURSE

PU—4146 Golf Valley Dr., Sturgeon Bay (414)743-3334.
40 miles northeast of Green Bay. **Holes:** 18. **Par:** 72/76.
Yards: 6,889/5,886. **Course rating:** 72.7/73.4. **Slope:** 130/128.
Opened: 1978. **Pace of Play rating:** 4:30. **Green fee:** $20.
Credit cards: MC, V. **Reduced fees:** Twilight, Seniors, Juniors.
Caddies: No. **Golf carts:** $12 for 18 holes.
Discount golf packages: No. **Season:** April-Oct. **High:** June-Sept.
On-site lodging: No. **Rental clubs:** Yes.
Walking policy: Unrestricted walking. **Range:** Yes (grass).
To obtain tee times: Phone or in person up to 14 days in advance.
Formerly called Lost Creek Golf Course.

Subscriber comments: Water on many holes, but all of it is fair . . . Nice balance, good but tough greens . . . Numerous improvements . . . Best-kept secret in the resort area.

★★★ IVES GROVE GOLF LINKS

PU—14101 Washington Ave., Sturtevant (414)878-3714.
6 miles west of Racine. **Holes:** 18. **Par:** 72/72.
Yards: 6,915/5,410. **Course rating:** 72.5/70.7. **Slope:** 129/123.
Opened: 1971. **Pace of Play rating:** 4:30. **Green fee:** $18/19.
Credit cards: None. **Reduced fees:** Seniors, Juniors.
Caddies: No. **Golf carts:** $23 for 18 holes.
Discount golf packages: No. **Season:** March-Nov. **High:** May-Sept.
On-site lodging: No. **Rental clubs:** No.
Walking policy: Unrestricted walking. **Range:** Yes (grass).
To obtain tee times: Call one week in advance.
Subscriber comments: A good municipal . . . Too many back-and-forth holes . . . Large greens . . . Always in nice shape . . . Limited trees . . . Always very windy . . . Attractive . . . New nine holes will help it improve . . . Did someone forget to plant some trees? . . . Good county greens . . . Course shaped like a big wheel . . . Windiest course in Wisconsin . . . Sand left, sand right . . . Many holes look alike.

★★★ JOHNSON PARK GOLF COURSE

PU—6200 Northwestern Ave., Racine (414)637-2840.
20 miles south of Milwaukee. **Holes:** 18. **Par:** 72/74.
Yards: 6,683/5,732. **Course rating:** 70.8/73.0. **Slope:** 117/120.
Opened: 1939. **Pace of Play rating:** 4:27. **Green fee:** $10/18.
Credit cards: None. **Reduced fees:** Weekdays, Low season, Seniors, Juniors.
Caddies: No. **Golf carts:** $9 for 18 holes.
Discount golf packages: No. **Season:** April-Nov. **High:** June-Aug.
On-site lodging: No. **Rental clubs:** Yes.
Walking policy: Unrestricted walking. **Range:** Yes (grass).

To obtain tee times: One week in advance, in person in golf shop. Call-ins available 6 p.m. night before or same day.
Subscriber comments: They have improved the fairways over the years . . . Classic layout . . . Greens could be better, some unfair pin placements . . . Fun golf . . . Clubhouse poorly kept up . . . Need work on traps.

KETTLE HILLS GOLF COURSE

PU—3375 State Hwy. 167 W., Richfield (414)255-2200.
20 miles northwest of Milwaukee.
Green fee: $20/24.
Credit cards: MC, V. **Reduced fees:** Low season, Twilight, Seniors, Juniors.
Caddies: No. **Golf carts:** $11 for 18 holes.
Discount golf packages: No. **Season:** April-Nov. **High:** May-Sept.
On-site lodging: No. **Rental clubs:** Yes.
Walking policy: Unrestricted walking. **Range:** Yes (grass).
To obtain tee times: Call up to nine days in advance.
★★★ PONDS/WOODS
Holes: 18. **Par:** 72/72.
Yards: 6,787/5,171. **Course rating:** 72.5/69.6. **Slope:** 128/123.
Opened: 1987. **Pace of Play rating:** 4:30
Subscriber comments: Should have hired an architect. Had the terrain, could ski downhill on a few greens! . . . Often better to play out of the rough . . . Very challenging and different nines . . . Real effort to upgrade here, Nos. 17 and 18 are nasty . . . Pretty course . . . Interesting course . . . Cut the fairways and this becomes a good course . . . Original 18 is scenic and challenging . . . Many good golf holes with rewards for risk-taking . . . 17th and 18th holes the two most interesting in Wisconsin . . . Last two holes are killers . . . 17th and 18th greens are unfair . . . Some unique holes . . . Two-inch long grass for fairways, c'mon . . . Original course offers a unique blend of tight fairways shots, hidden water hazards, blind lay-up shots . . . This is one course where you need to study the golf card map.

VALLEY COURSE*
Holes: 18. **Par:** 72/72.
Yards: 6,455/5,088. **Course rating:** 70.9/69.2. **Slope:** 122/116.
Opened: 1990. **Pace of Play rating:** N/A.
Subscriber comments: Latest nine not bad . . . Now 36 hilly holes . . .
Now nine has many hidden hazards to the newcomer.

★★★ KETTLE MORAINE GOLF CLUB
SP—4299 Highway 67, Dousman (414)965-6200.
Call club for further information.
Subscriber comments: Sporty, above average . . . Avoid after heavy rain
. . . Go before leaves fall . . . A couple holes along creek are boggy . . .
Most holes keep you thinking . . . Most greens quite small . . . Lots of
interesting holes . . . Environmental success . . . Nice variety of short and
long holes.

★★½ KRUEGER MUNICIPAL GOLF CLUB
PU—1611 Hackett St., Beloit (608)362-6503.
Call club for further information.
Subscriber comments: Took forever to get around . . . Well-maintained
muny . . . Good and improving . . . New sand traps . . . Par 3s make
course . . . Too many holes run in the same direction.

★★★★ LAKE ARROWHEAD GOLF COURSE
PU—1195 Apache Lane, Nekoosa (715)325-2929.

13 miles south of Wisconsin Rapids. **Holes:** 18. **Par:** 72/72.
Yards: 6,624/5,213. **Course rating:** 72.3/70.2. **Slope:** 135/125.
Opened: 1983. **Pace of Play rating:** 4:30. **Green fee:** $27/38.
Credit cards: MC, V. **Reduced fees:** Low season, Twilight.
Caddies: No. **Golf carts:** $11 for 18 holes.
Discount golf packages: Yes. **Season:** April-Oct. **High:** May-Sept.
On-site lodging: Yes. **Rental clubs:** No.
Walking policy: Unrestricted walking. **Range:** Yes (grass).
To obtain tee times: Call one month in advance. Groups of 16 or more
may call more than one month in advance.
Subscriber comments: Lush fairways make you feel like you're at a major
tournament . . . One of Wisconsin's best . . . As good as Blackwolf, but at
⅓ of the price . . . Don't stray into pine trees . . . Best-kept secret in
Wisconsin . . . Tall pines, lots of sand . . . If it were two hours closer to
Milwaukee you wouldn't be able to get a tee time . . . Next to Blackwolf
Run, the best . . . A hidden gem! Don't tell anyone . . . The best value I've
ever seen . . . Very fine condition, lots of beauty, top-notch staff . . .
Terrific holes . . . Beauty amidst the scrub pines . . . More sand than the
Sahara . . . Bunkers are huge . . . Augusta National without the flowers
. . . Velvet greens . . . A solid, great course . . . Best course in Wisconsin
for the money . . . Fast greens with big slopes . . . One of the top public
courses in state . . . Good layout, but not truly memorable . . . Superb
layout . . . 18 great holes . . . Well laid out . . . A shotmaker's course . . . A
gem in the woods, you have to see it . . . Strategic course, pines and sand
give it a Southern feel . . . Pinehurst in Wisconsin.

★½ LAKE BREEZE GOLF CLUB
PU—6333 Highway 110, Winneconne (414)582-7585, (800)330-9189.
10 miles northwest of Oshkosh. **Holes:** 18. **Par:** 72/72.
Yards: 6,896/5,748. **Course rating:** 72.2/71.9. **Slope:** 120/117.
Opened: 1991. **Pace of Play rating:** 4:15. **Green fee:** $13/16.
Credit cards: MC, V. **Reduced fees:** Low season, Twilight, Seniors,
Juniors.
Caddies: No. **Golf carts:** $9 for 18 holes.
Discount golf packages: Yes. **Season:** April-Oct. **High:** June-Aug.
On-site lodging: No. **Rental clubs:** Yes.
Walking policy: Unrestricted walking. **Range:** Yes (grass).
To obtain tee times: Call 24 hours in advance.
Subscriber comments: Fun back nine . . . Expect extra putts here . . .
Front nine long and tight, back nine short and open . . . Two good holes
. . . Needs years to mature.

★★ LAKE LAWN LODGE GOLF COURSE
R—Highway 50 East, Delavan (414)728-7950, (800)338-5253.
45 miles south of Milwaukee. **Holes:** 18. **Par:** 70/70.
Yards: 6,418/5,215. **Course rating:** 69.2/64.1. **Slope:** 120/107.
Opened: N/A. **Pace of Play rating:** 4:30. **Green fee:** $48/56.
Credit cards: All major. **Reduced fees:** Weekdays, Low season, Resort guests, Twilight, Seniors, Juniors.
Caddies: No. **Golf carts:** Included in Green Fee.
Discount golf packages: Yes. **Season:** April-Oct. **High:** June-Aug.
On-site lodging: Yes. **Rental clubs:** Yes.
Walking policy: Walking at certain times. **Range:** Yes (grass).
To obtain tee times: Guests of the resort may call two weeks in advance. Public may call two days in advance. Golf Package one year in advance.
Subscriber comments: Only three or four good holes . . . Take bug spray . . . Redone several years ago into championship caliber . . . Good resort course . . . Fast, hard greens . . . Mature with big trees.

LAKE PARK GOLF COURSE
★★ RED/WHITE/BLUE
PU—N. 112 W. 17300 Mequon Rd., Germantown (414)255-4200.
15 miles north of Milwaukee. **Holes:** 27. **Par:** 72/72/72.
Yards: 6,979/6,781/6,642. **Course rating:** 73.4/72.7/71.9.
Slope: 131/126/126.
Opened: 1974. **Pace of Play rating:** 4:30. **Green fee:** $9/23.
Credit cards: MC, V. **Reduced fees:** Weekdays, Low season, Twilight, Seniors.
Caddies: No. **Golf carts:** $11 for 18 holes.
Discount golf packages: No. **Season:** April-Oct. **High:** May-Sept.
On-site lodging: No. **Rental clubs:** No.
Walking policy: Unrestricted walking. **Range:** No.
To obtain tee times: Call pro shop.
Subscriber comments: Too much water . . . Greens could be kept up . . . Added a new nine last year . . . Good variety . . . Way too many goose droppings . . . Average public course for metro Milwaukee . . . Overcrowded . . . Some poor greens . . . Covered with goose dung . . . Large greens, little sand, short doglegs force you to lay up . . . More water than Lake Michigan . . . Water on most holes.

★★ LAKE SHORE GOLF COURSE
PU—2175 Punhoqua St., Oshkosh (414)235-6200.
85 miles north of Milwaukee. **Holes:** 18. **Par:** 70/71.
Yards: 6,030/5,162. **Course rating:** 68.2/69.4. **Slope:** 120/119.
Opened: 1920. **Pace of Play rating:** 3:50. **Green fee:** $11.
Credit cards: MC, V. **Reduced fees:** Seniors, Juniors.
Caddies: No. **Golf carts:** $0 for 18 holes.
Discount golf packages: No. **Season:** April-Nov. **High:** June-Aug.
On-site lodging: No. **Rental clubs:** Yes.
Walking policy: Unrestricted walking. **Range:** Yes (grass).
To obtain tee times: Call one week in advance for weekends and holidays.
Subscriber comments: Overplayed muny . . . Nice little course . . . Gets lots of play . . . Too many short par 4s and long par 3s that look alike . . . Cheap, short, simple . . . Love to play it . . . Small greens, very good price.

LAKE WINDSOR GOLF CLUB
★½ RED/WHITE/BLUE
PU—4628 Golf Rd., Windsor (608)255-6100.
5 miles north of Madison. **Holes:** 27. **Par:** 72/71/71.
Yards: 6,228/5,983/6,157. **Course rating:** 69.2/68.0/68.5.
Slope: 118/115/118.
Opened: 1963. **Pace of Play rating:** 4:30. **Green fee:** $10/20.
Credit cards: MC, V. **Reduced fees:** Weekdays, Low season, Twilight, Seniors, Juniors.
Caddies: No. **Golf carts:** $9 for 18 holes.
Discount golf packages: No. **Season:** March-Nov. **High:** June-Aug.
On-site lodging: No. **Rental clubs:** Yes.

Walking policy: Unrestricted walking. **Range:** No.
To obtain tee times: Call one week in advance.
Subscriber comments: Nothing special . . . Usually very wet . . . No great holes, not much trouble . . . Plenty of creeks come into play . . . Between the interstate highway and airport: too much noise . . . A tasty course . . . Trying to get better . . . Fairways always seem muddy . . . An outings course. Be prepared for a five-hour round.

★★½ MADELINE ISLAND GOLF CLUB

SP—P.O. Box 83, LaPointe (715)747-3212.
Call club for further information.
Subscriber comments: Double greens due to limited space. Fun, must take a ferry to the island . . . Unique Robert Trent Jones Sr. layout worth experiencing . . . Take the early morning ferry and have the course to yourself . . . Beautiful views of Lake Superior . . . Tough and fair, great scenery and atmosphere.

★★ MAPLE GROVE COUNTRY CLUB

SP—W. 4142 CTH B, West Salem (608)786-0340.
10 miles west of LaCrosse. **Holes:** 18. **Par:** 71/71.
Yards: 6,485/5,578. **Course rating:** 70.1/70.9. **Slope:** 122/121.
Opened: 1929. **Pace of Play rating:** 4:20 **Green fee:** $17/19.
Credit cards: MC, V. **Reduced fees:** Weekdays, Low season, Seniors.
Caddies: No. **Golf carts:** $20 for 18 holes.
Discount golf packages: Yes. **Season:** April-Nov. **High:** June-Aug.
On-site lodging: No. **Rental clubs:** Yes.
Walking policy: Unrestricted walking. **Range:** Yes (grass).
To obtain tee times: Call seven days in advance. Groups of 30-plus call anytime.
Subscriber comments: Scenic, good diversity of holes . . . Poor care . . . Multiple types of greens, varied topography . . . Has potential . . . Mature trees, huge new clubhouse.

★★★ MAPLECREST COUNTRY CLUB

SP—9401 18th St., Kenosha (414)859-2887.
20 miles south of Milwaukee. **Holes:** 18. **Par:** 70/70.
Yards: 6,396/5,056. **Course rating:** 70.9/71.0. **Slope:** 121/124.
Opened: 1929. **Pace of Play rating:** 4:30. **Green fee:** $14/19.
Credit cards: None. **Reduced fees:** Low season, Twilight, Seniors.
Caddies: No. **Golf carts:** N/A.
Discount golf packages: No. **Season:** March-Nov. **High:** May-Sept.
On-site lodging: No. **Rental clubs:** Yes.
Walking policy: Unrestricted walking. **Range:** Yes (grass).
To obtain tee times: Call one week in advance.
Subscriber comments: Long, narrow fairways, fast greens, plenty of sand . . . Deceptively difficult . . . Killer greens. Not very widely known . . . Best greens of any public course . . . Too many trees. Enjoyed greatly . . . No. 5 is a 613-yard par 5 . . . A lot of traps.

★★★½ MASCOUTIN GOLF CLUB

PU—Rte. 2 County Trunk A, Berlin (414)361-2360.
20 miles west of Oshkosh. **Holes:** 18. **Par:** 72/73.
Yards: 6,821/5,133. **Course rating:** 72.2/68.9. **Slope:** 123/114.
Opened: 1975. **Pace of Play rating:** 4:00. **Green fee:** $20/35.
Credit cards: MC, V. **Reduced fees:** Weekdays, Low season, Twilight, Seniors, Juniors.
Caddies: No. **Golf carts:** $12 for 18 holes.
Discount golf packages: Yes. **Season:** April-Oct. **High:** May-Sept.
On-site lodging: No. **Rental clubs:** Yes.
Walking policy: Unrestricted walking. **Range:** Yes (grass).
To obtain tee times: Call anytime.
Subscriber comments: Have to be the most challenging greens in the state . . . Nice, fun course, not too hard . . . Good variety . . . Wish it had some water on the front nine . . . Good combination of length, water, sand, hills . . . Fantastic scenery . . . Fastest greens in Wisconsin . . . Probably best greens in eastern Wisconsin . . . Fine layout, great people . . . A classic layout . . . A real challenge . . . Well maintained!

★★ MAXWELTON BRAES GOLF RESORT

R—7200 Hwy. 57, Baileys Harbor (414)839-2321.
Call club for further information.
Subscriber comments: Very nice, but very short . . . No water, no rough, wide fairways . . . Has wonderful possibilities . . . Lack of care, investment and upkeep obvious.

★★ MAYVILLE GOLF CLUB

PU—325 S. German St., Mayville (414)387-2999.
25 miles south of Fond du Lac. **Holes:** 18. **Par:** 71/72.
Yards: 6,173/5,235. **Course rating:** 68.9/69.1. **Slope:** 113/112.
Opened: 1931. **Pace of Play rating:** 3:45. **Green fee:** $11/18.
Credit cards: MC, V. **Reduced fees:** Weekdays, Low season, Twilight, Seniors, Juniors.
Caddies: No. **Golf carts:** $9 for 18 holes.
Discount golf packages: No. **Season:** April-Oct. **High:** June-Aug.
On-site lodging: No. **Rental clubs:** Yes.
Walking policy: Unrestricted walking. **Range:** No.
To obtain tee times: Call one week in advance.
Subscriber comments: Wide-open fairways, easy, relaxing . . . Interesting course, playable. Clubhouse burned down . . . New nine opened a year too early.

MERRILL GOLF CLUB★

PU—1604 O'Day St., Merrill (715)536-2529.
20 miles north of Wausau. **Holes:** 18. **Par:** 71/71.
Yards: 6,348/5,392. **Course rating:** 70.2/70.0. **Slope:** 120/111.
Opened: 1932. **Pace of Play rating:** 4:00. **Green fee:** $10/18.
Credit cards: All major. **Reduced fees:** Weekdays, Twilight, Seniors, Juniors.
Caddies: No. **Golf carts:** $18 for 18 holes.
Discount golf packages: No. **Season:** April-Oct. **High:** June-Aug.
On-site lodging: No. **Rental clubs:** Yes.
Walking policy: Unrestricted walking. **Range:** No.
To obtain tee times: Call seven days in advance.

★★ MID-VALLEE GOLF COURSE

PU—Highway 41, De Pere (414)532-6674.
Call club for further information.
Subscriber comments: Requires greenside touch. Unique par 3s . . . Back nine is long, some holes mediocre . . . Improves each year . . . Great looking course.

★★★ MILL RUN GOLF COURSE

PU—3905 Kane Rd., Eau Claire (715)834-1766, (800)260-3000.
65 miles east of Minneapolis/St. Paul. **Holes:** 18. **Par:** 70/71.
Yards: 6,065/4,744. **Course rating:** 68.7/66.6. **Slope:** 116/109.
Opened: 1981. **Pace of Play rating:** 4:00. **Green fee:** $16/18.
Credit cards: MC, V. **Reduced fees:** Seniors, Juniors.
Caddies: No. **Golf carts:** $19 for 18 holes.
Discount golf packages: Yes. **Season:** April-Oct. **High:** April-Oct.
On-site lodging: No. **Rental clubs:** Yes.
Walking policy: Unrestricted walking. **Range:** Yes (grass).
To obtain tee times: Call anytime.

★★ MUSKEGO LAKES COUNTRY CLUB

SP—S. 100 W. 14020 Loomis Rd., Muskego (414)425-6500.
13 miles southwest of Milwaukee. **Holes:** 18. **Par:** 71/72.
Yards: 6,498/5,493. **Course rating:** 71.5/71.7. **Slope:** 126/123.
Opened: 1969. **Pace of Play rating:** 4:00-4:30. **Green fee:** $16/25.
Credit cards: MC, V. **Reduced fees:** Weekdays, Low season, Seniors, Juniors.
Caddies: No. **Golf carts:** $11 for 18 holes.
Discount golf packages: No. **Season:** April-Nov. **High:** May-Sept.
On-site lodging: No. **Rental clubs:** Yes.

Walking policy: Unrestricted walking. **Range:** Yes (grass).
To obtain tee times: Call up to four days in advance, foursomes required on weekends before 1 p.m.
Subscriber comments: Too many bare spots . . . Water, water, water . . . 10th hole is one of the best in the state . . . Greens are very well-guarded . . . Mature course, not overbearing . . . Lots of O.B. . . . Fairways need work . . . Shape not always good, but playable . . . Short but watery.

★½ MYSTERY HILLS GOLF CLUB

PU—1800 Nobleman Court, Green Bay (414)336-6077.
Call club for further information.
Subscriber comments: Wear a helmet . . . Stays open until snow flies . . . Hundreds of trees added to the course . . . Lacks sand bunkers . . . Tricky greens . . . Most holes are fair, not cutesy . . . Want to golf in December? This is your course . . . Conditions unpredictable . . . You'd better know how to putt.

★★★½ NAGA-WAUKEE GOLF COURSE

PU—1897 Maple Ave., Pewaukee (414)367-2153.
20 miles west of Milwaukee. **Holes:** 18. **Par:** 72/72.
Yards: 6,780/5,796. **Course rating:** 71.8/72.6. **Slope:** 125/125.
Opened: 1966. **Pace of Play rating:** 3:47. **Green fee:** $17/26.
Credit cards: MC, V. **Reduced fees:** Weekdays, Low season, Twilight, Seniors, Juniors.
Caddies: No. **Golf carts:** $11 for 18 holes.
Discount golf packages: No. **Season:** April-Dec. **High:** May-Sept.
On-site lodging: No. **Rental clubs:** Yes.
Walking policy: Unrestricted walking. **Range:** Yes (grass).
To obtain tee times: Call four days in advance.
Subscriber comments: Couldn't ask for a better municipal. Beautiful terrain . . . Tough roughs, narrow fairways . . . Best kept county secret in golf . . . Mature, hilly course . . . Exceptional value, exceptional scenery . . . Condition a lilttle shaggy . . . Hills, water, woods . . . What a course with a view . . . You'd better like hills! . . . Great county course, lots of elevation, super value, a "must play" . . . Championship quality, period . . . Back nine tight and scenic . . . Most beautiful public course in southeast Wisconsin . . . Some of the prettiest holes in Wisconsin . . . 14th and 16th overlook Pewaukee Lake . . . The Brown Deer of Waukesha County . . . One of southeast Wisconsin's best . . . A riding cart helps on those last three holes.

(GREAT VALUE)

NEMADJI GOLF COURSE

PU—5 N. 58th St. E., Superior (715)394-9022.
Green fee: $12/18.
Credit cards: MC, V. **Reduced fees:** Low season, Twilight, Juniors.
Caddies: Yes. **Golf carts:** $18 for 18 holes.
Discount golf packages: No. **Season:** April-Oct. **High:** June-Aug.
On-site lodging: No. **Rental clubs:** Yes.
Walking policy: Unrestricted walking. **Range:** Yes (grass).
To obtain tee times: Call three weeks in advance.

★★★★ EAST/WEST

Holes: 18. **Par:** 72/72.
Yards: 6,701/5,252. **Course rating:** 72.7/70.7. **Slope:** 133/124.
Opened: 1981. **Pace of Play rating:** 4:00.
Subscriber comments: For players with a long ball . . . Well laid-out . . . Lots of trouble but fair . . . Straight hitter's paradise . . . A championship course. Water, sand, excellent . . . Golf staff is great . . . Greens crew has done an outstanding job.

(SUPER VALUE)

★★½ NORTH/SOUTH

Holes: 18. **Par:** 71/71.
Yards: 6,362/4,983. **Course rating:** 69.7/67.8. **Slope:** 120/114.
Opened: 1932. **Pace of Play rating:** 4:00.
Subscriber comments: Front nine best . . . Good greens all year . . . Mature layout . . . Dress warmly, even in the summer . . . Fast greens and tight fairways.

★½ NEW BERLIN HILLS GOLF COURSE

PU—13175 W. Graham St., New Berlin (414)797-2443.
Call club for further information.
Subscriber comments: Much water . . . Back nine more interesting . . .
Made some improvements . . . Golf on concrete . . . Fairways should be
reseeded.

★★★★ NEW RICHMOND GOLF CLUB

SP—1226 180th Ave., New Richmond (715)246-6724.
20 miles northeast of St. Paul, MN. **Holes:** 18. **Par:** 72/73.
Yards: 6,716/5,547. **Course rating:** 72.5/71.7. **Slope:** 136/129.
Opened: 1923. **Pace of Play rating:** 4:30. **Green fee:** $22/26.
Credit cards: N/A. **Reduced fees:** Weekdays, Low season, Seniors,
Juniors.
Caddies: No. **Golf carts:** $11 for 18 holes.
Discount golf packages: No. **Season:** April-Oct. **High:** June-Aug.
On-site lodging: No. **Rental clubs:** Yes.
Walking policy: Unrestricted walking. **Range:** Yes (grass).
To obtain tee times: Call two days in advance.
Subscriber comments: Best-kept secret in the Midwest . . . The best,
least-known course in Wisconsin . . . Must drive the ball straight . . .
Tough, could hold a state open . . . Very accommodating staff.

★★★ NORTHBROOK COUNTRY CLUB

PU—407 NorthBrook Dr., Luxemburg (414)845-2383.
Call club for further information.
Subscriber comments: Some of the best greens I'll ever putt on . . .
Slopes much too severe . . . Greens tough . . . Great Northbrook burgers
. . . Trees and course well grown in . . . Will play again . . . Short, tight,
country club fairways . . . Simple design but in great condition . . . No. 10
worth the trip . . . Some extraordinary holes. Very deceptive greens.

★★★★ NORTHWOOD GOLF COURSE

PU—6301 Hwy. 8 W., Rhinelander (715)282-6565.
50 miles north of Wausau. **Holes:** 18. **Par:** 72/72.
Yards: 6,719/5,338. **Course rating:** 72.8/71.0. **Slope:** 135/127.
Opened: 1989. **Pace of Play rating:** 4:28. **Green fee:** $23.
Credit cards: MC, V. **Reduced fees:** Juniors.
Caddies: No. **Golf carts:** $22 for 18 holes.
Discount golf packages: Yes. **Season:** April-Oct. **High:** June-Sept.
On-site lodging: No. **Rental clubs:** Yes.
Walking policy: Unrestricted walking. **Range:** Yes (grass).
To obtain tee times: Call up to 14 days in advance.
Subscriber comments: Challenging layout, fun experience . . . Can you
hit your long irons long and straight? A real test . . . Narrow, tree-lined,
leave your driver in car! . . . Back tees, forget it . . . No rough, just woods,
rocks and water . . . Take your compass . . . Best in Northwoods,
especially for fishermen! . . . The narrowest fairways in the state . . .
Awesome scenic holes . . . Too much trouble. I can't keep hitting the ball
that straight for 18 holes . . . Carved out of the forest . . . Staff very friendly
and accommodating . . . A real jewel cut in the forest . . . Great physical
layout . . . Treacherous . . . Best course in northern Wisconsin . . . A
couple of island greens.

★★★ OAKWOOD PARK GOLF COURSE

PU—3600 W. Oak Ridge Rd., Franklin (414)281-6700.
8 miles south of Milwaukee. **Holes:** 18. **Par:** 72/72.
Yards: 6,972/6,179. **Course rating:** 71.4/74.4. **Slope:** 118/123.
Opened: 1971. **Pace of Play rating:** 4:06. **Green fee:** $14/18.
Credit cards: MC, V. **Reduced fees:** Weekdays, Seniors, Juniors.
Caddies: No. **Golf carts:** $20 for 18 holes.
Discount golf packages: No. **Season:** April-Oct. **High:** June-Aug.
On-site lodging: No. **Rental clubs:** Yes.
Walking policy: Walking at certain times. **Range:** Yes (grass).

To obtain tee times: Call Hotline (414)643-4653 anytime.
Subscriber comments: One of the longest courses in Wisconsin. Great greens . . . Favors power players . . . Long, long and more long . . . Best greens in the county . . . Has really matured in last five years . . . Solid public course . . . Wide open and long . . . You need every shot in the bag . . . A golfer's delight . . . Nos. 3 and 9 greens are real challenges . . . Always slow and crowded.

★★½ ODANA HILLS GOLF COURSE
PU—4635 Odana Rd., Madison (608)266-4078.
Call club for further information.
Subscriber comments: Good public course considering all the traffic . . . Busiest course in town . . . Greens inconsistent . . . Nothing special. Fairly easy . . . Very low cost . . . Greens can get beaten up . . . Known in Madison as "Slow-dana" . . . Best city course in Madison.

★★★★ OLD HICKORY GOLF CLUB
SP—Hwy. 33 E., Beaver Dam (414)887-7577.
30 miles north of Madison. **Holes:** 18. **Par:** 72/73.
Yards: 6,688/5,644. **Course rating:** 72.5/72.8. **Slope:** 129/127.
Opened: 1920. **Pace of Play rating:** 4:00-4:15. **Green fee:** $40/50.
Credit cards: MC, V. **Reduced fees:** Low season.
Caddies: No. **Golf carts:** Included in Green Fee.
Discount golf packages: No. **Season:** April-Oct. **High:** June-Aug.
On-site lodging: No. **Rental clubs:** Yes.
Walking policy: Walking at certain times. **Range:** Yes (grass).
To obtain tee times: Call one week in advance.
Subscriber comments: Traditional course; plays tough because of hard, elevated greens . . . Top-of-the-line staff . . . Mature trees cause trouble. Fun course, a challenge . . . Great greens . . . A hidden gem . . . Friendly, small town atmosphere . . . Beautiful clubhouse . . . Interesting layout . . . Many classic holes . . . Beautiful countryside . . . Tight and woody . . . I would never tire of playing here . . . They don't call it Old Hickory for nothing . . . Lots of bluebirds . . . Fast greens, many sidehill lies . . . Heavily wooded . . . Very, very fast greens . . . Great track.

★★ OLYMPIA RESORT GOLF CLUB
R—1350 Royale Mile Rd., Oconomowoc (414)567-2577.
30 miles west of Milwaukee. **Holes:** 18. **Par:** 72/71.
Yards: 6,458/5,735. **Course rating:** 70.5/72.4. **Slope:** 118/119.
Opened: 1971. **Pace of Play rating:** 4:30 **Green fee:** $23/27.
Credit cards: All major. **Reduced fees:** Low season, Twilight, Seniors, Juniors.
Caddies: No. **Golf carts:** $11 for 18 holes.
Discount golf packages: Yes. **Season:** April-Nov. **High:** June-Sept.
On-site lodging: Yes. **Rental clubs:** Yes.
Walking policy: Walking at certain times. **Range:** Yes (grass).
To obtain tee times: Call pro shop.
Subscriber comments: Facilities not too good . . . Flat and open, not much challenge . . . Don't waste time on the front side. Play the back twice . . . Interesting . . . Will get better . . . Tough par 3s . . . Has been greatly improved.

★½ PAGANICA GOLF COURSE
PU—3850 Silverlake, Oconomowoc (414)567-0171.
29 miles east of Milwaukee. **Holes:** 18. **Par:** 72/74.
Yards: 6,698/6,021. **Course rating:** 70.2/73.0. **Slope:** 108/102.
Opened: 1965. **Pace of Play rating:** 4:30. **Green fee:** $21/24.
Credit cards: None. **Reduced fees:** Low season.
Caddies: No. **Golf carts:** $10 for 18 holes.
Discount golf packages: No. **Season:** March-Dec. **High:** June-Aug.
On-site lodging: No. **Rental clubs:** Yes.
Walking policy: Unrestricted walking. **Range:** Yes (grass).
To obtain tee times: Call one week in advance.

Subscriber comments: Postage-stamp greens . . . Narrow, parallel fairways; you and everyone else are always in the wrong fairway . . . Not in good shape . . . Lots of water, no sand . . . Opens early each year . . . Avoid in springtime as there is always standing water.

★★★ PENINSULA STATE PARK GOLF COURSE

PU—Highway 42, Fish Creek (414)854-5791.
Call club for further information.
Subscriber comments: Not easy. Tough putting . . . Dazzling scenes . . . Beautifully scenic views overlooking Lake Michigan . . . A treat to play anytime, but very slow and crowded . . . Fascinating terrain . . . Lovely in the fall . . . Tight par-3 17th . . . Very hilly, rent a cart . . . A little tough to walk . . . Greens need work . . . Has a downhill par 3 only 69 yards long . . . Downhill par 3s are spectacular . . . Great views and hot dogs . . . A Chicago hang-out.

★★★ PETRIFYING SPRINGS GOLF COURSE

PU—4909 7th St., Kenosha (414)552-9052.
Holes: 18. **Par:** 71/72.
Yards: 5,979/5,588. **Course rating:** 67.8/70.9. **Slope:** 119/122.
Opened: 1936. **Pace of Play rating:** 4:10. **Green fee:** $18/20.
Credit cards: MC, V. **Reduced fees:** N/A.
Caddies: No. **Golf carts:** $18 for 18 holes.
Discount golf packages: No. **Season:** April-Oct. **High:** July.
On-site lodging: No. **Rental clubs:** Yes.
Walking policy: Unrestricted walking. **Range:** No.
To obtain tee times: Call 12 days in advance for a fee of $4.
Subscriber comments: Scenic front nine . . . Scenic back nine . . . Lots of back and forth holes . . . Short but interesting . . . Greens are slanted, Nos. 16, 17 and 18 are great but hard finishing holes . . . Glacier-sculpted beauty . . . Sporty, short older course.

★★★ PLEASANT VIEW COUNTRY CLUB

SP—4279 Pleasant View Dr., Middleton (608)831-6666.
Call club for further information.
Subscriber comments: Thick roughs. Rolling hills . . . Many hidden greens . . . Recent improvements have been great . . . Hilly, interesting, not too difficult . . . Pleasant view of Wisconsin capitol building several miles away . . . Great setting . . . Crowded and very average . . . Best conditioned public course in area . . . Greens are A-1, smooth, fast . . . Tough course to play with hills and in the wind . . . A good, honest test of golf.

★★½ PORTAGE COUNTRY CLUB

SP—E. Hwy. No. 31, Portage (608)742-5121.
Call club for further information.
Subscriber comments: Short but lots of different holes . . . Must start enforcing rule that nobody hits until the bell is rung on blind shots . . . Very short. Hole along the lake is the best on the course . . . Very narrow course. Too many tricked-up holes . . . Very scenic No. 3 hole, a tough par 3 along Swan Lake . . . Back nine is long . . . Very funny layout . . . Nice mix of holes . . . Bring your iron game . . . Needs work on traps.

★★★ QUIT-QUI-OC GOLF CLUB

PU—500 Quit-Qui-Oc Lane, Elkhart Lake (414)876-2833.
50 miles north of Milwaukee. **Holes:** 18. **Par:** 70/71.
Yards: 6,178/5,134. **Course rating:** 69.6/64.9. **Slope:** 119/109.
Opened: 1925. **Pace of Play rating:** 4:10. **Green fee:** $15/22.
Credit cards: MC, V. **Reduced fees:** Weekdays, Low season, Twilight, Seniors, Juniors.
Caddies: No. **Golf carts:** $10 for 18 holes.
Discount golf packages: No. **Season:** April-Nov. **High:** May-Sept.
On-site lodging: No. **Rental clubs:** Yes.
Walking policy: Unrestricted walking. **Range:** Yes (grass).
To obtain tee times: Call four days in advance.

Subscriber comments: A tough test but fun . . . No. 15 signature hole, superb! . . . A few challenging greens . . . Rolling . . . Wow. What a beauty . . . Not long but requires good shotmaking . . . Could be wonderful . . . Nice diversity in hole length . . . As many as three signature holes . . . Six par 3s . . . Elevated small greens. Lots of woods . . . Cute layout; fun, fast play, easy, good condition . . . Beautiful setting, panoramic views, an old course with traditional feeling . . . Just average.

★★★ RAINBOW SPRINGS GOLF CLUB
SP—S103 W. 33599 Hwy. 99, Mukwonago (414)363-4550, (800)465-3631.
30 miles southwest of Milwaukee. **Holes:** 18. **Par:** 72/72.
Yards: 6,914/5,135. **Course rating:** 73.4/69.8. **Slope:** 132/120.
Opened: 1964. **Pace of Play rating:** 4:15. **Green fee:** $32/38.
Credit cards: MC, V. **Reduced fees:** Weekdays, Low season, Twilight, Seniors, Juniors.
Caddies: No. **Golf carts:** Included in Green Fee.
Discount golf packages: Yes. **Season:** April-Nov. **High:** June-Sept.
On-site lodging: No. **Rental clubs:** Yes.
Walking policy: Walking at certain times. **Range:** No.
To obtain tee times: Call up to 14 days in advance. Credit card is required. Cancellation no less than 48 hours prior to tee time.
Also has 18 hole executive course.
Subscriber comments: No sand, but the water makes up for it . . . This one will keep you thinking . . . Lots of hidden danger . . . Abandoned resort on the course is spooky . . . Tough country course with no sand . . . Lost class when shortened . . . Woods and a river winding around a nice layout . . . Hazards should be more clearly defined . . . Water on 15 of 18 holes . . . Brought me to my knees . . . Either you love it or you hate it, unique . . . Much improved playing conditions . . . Toughest course in Wisconsin without a sand trap . . . Too much water . . . Very expensive for a mediocre course . . . Unique layout . . . Enjoyable challenge . . . No. 12 unfairly hard.

★★★ REEDSBURG COUNTRY CLUB
SP—Hwy. 33, Reedsburg (608)524-6000.
14 miles south of Wisconsin Dells. **Holes:** 18. **Par:** 72/73.
Yards: 6,300/5,324. **Course rating:** 70.5/70.3. **Slope:** 129/124.
Opened: 1924. **Pace of Play rating:** 4:00-4:30. **Green fee:** $30.
Credit cards: MC, V. **Reduced fees:** Twilight.
Caddies: Yes. **Golf carts:** $12 for 18 holes.
Discount golf packages: No. **Season:** March-Nov. **High:** June-Aug.
On-site lodging: No. **Rental clubs:** Yes.
Walking policy: Unrestricted walking. **Range:** Yes (grass).
To obtain tee times: Call up to 30 days in advance.
Subscriber comments: Average in every respect . . . Short but interesting holes . . . Some great holes, some weak, good diversity . . . Fun to play, but not a classic . . . Super greens . . . A hidden jewel, shhh! . . . A short, very challenging course . . . Back nine younger, needs to age a little . . . Putting heaven, slick and true.

★★½ REID GOLF COURSE
PU—1100 E. Fremont, Appleton (414)832-5926.
Call club for further information.

FRUGAL PICK

Subscriber comments: Average municipal . . . Don't hook it; clubhouse in play on No. 18 . . . Unique municipal course in the middle of town, interesting design . . . Every cosmetic change has been for the worse . . . Fairways need work . . . Best finishing holes I have played. Very good people operating course . . . Water, lots of trees.

★★ THE RIDGES GOLF CLUB
SP—2311 Griffith Ave., Wisconsin Rapids (715)424-1111.
100 miles south of Madison. **Holes:** 18. **Par:** 72/72.
Yards: 6,289/5,018. **Course rating:** 71.3/69.9. **Slope:** 129/122.
Opened: 1963. **Pace of Play rating:** 4:00-4:15. **Green fee:** $16/20.

Credit cards: MC, V. **Reduced fees:** Low season, Twilight.
Caddies: No. **Golf carts:** $18 for 18 holes.
Discount golf packages: Yes. **Season:** April-Oct. **High:** June-Aug.
On-site lodging: No. **Rental clubs:** Yes.
Walking policy: Unrestricted walking. **Range:** Yes (grass).
To obtain tee times: Call anytime.
Subscriber comments: Front nine greener than the back. Some very sharp doglegs on the back nine . . . Beautifully wooded back nine, other nine is flat and plain . . . Back nine has spectacular scenery . . . Easy front nine, too tight and hard on the back.

RIVER FALLS GOLF CLUB★

SP—1011 E. Division St., River Falls (715)425-0032, (800)688-1511.
35 miles east of St. Paul, MN. **Holes:** 18. **Par:** 72/72.
Yards: 6,471/5,166. **Course rating:** 71.0/69.5. **Slope:** 123/116.
Opened: 1929. **Pace of Play rating:** 4:15. **Green fee:** $17/25.
Credit cards: MC, V. **Reduced fees:** Weekdays, Twilight, Seniors, Juniors.
Caddies: No. **Golf carts:** $20 for 18 holes.
Discount golf packages: No. **Season:** April-Oct. **High:** May-Sept.
On-site lodging: No. **Rental clubs:** Yes.
Walking policy: Unrestricted walking. **Range:** Yes.
To obtain tee times: Call three days in advance.

★★½ RIVERMOOR COUNTRY CLUB

SP—30802 Waterford Dr., Waterford (414)534-2500.
20 miles southwest of Milwaukee. **Holes:** 18. **Par:** 70/72.
Yards: 6,256/5,839. **Course rating:** 68.7/72.7. **Slope:** 121/125.
Opened: 1929. **Pace of Play rating:** 4:15. **Green fee:** $20/25.
Credit cards: MC, V, DISC. **Reduced fees:** Low season, Twilight, Seniors.
Caddies: No. **Golf carts:** $11 for 18 holes.
Discount golf packages: No. **Season:** March-Nov. **High:** June-Aug.
On-site lodging: No. **Rental clubs:** Yes.
Walking policy: Unrestricted walking. **Range:** No.
To obtain tee times: Call one week in advance.
Subscriber comments: Tight park course. Small but good greens . . . Trees will penalize errant shots . . . Short, tight, scenic . . . Trees tough . . . All the par 4s look alike . . . A tight, mature course . . . Unexciting . . . Nice, short, groomed course . . . Very narrow.

★★★½ RIVERSIDE GOLF COURSE

PU—2100 Golf Course Rd., Janesville (608)757-3080.
35 miles south of Maidson. **Holes:** 18. **Par:** 72/72.
Yards: 6,508/5,147. **Course rating:** 70.7/68.9. **Slope:** 123/116.
Opened: 1924. **Pace of Play rating:** 4:30. **Green fee:** $19/22.
Credit cards: MC, V. **Reduced fees:** Weekdays, Seniors, Juniors.
Caddies: No. **Golf carts:** $11 for 18 holes.
Discount golf packages: No. **Season:** April-Nov. **High:** June-Aug.
On-site lodging: No. **Rental clubs:** Yes.
Walking policy: Unrestricted walking. **Range:** Yes (grass).
To obtain tee times: Call Monday for upcoming weekend.
Subscriber comments: Interesting course, but small greens . . . One of the better munys in this area . . . No. 10 is unique . . . Scenery is outstanding, with mature oak trees lining each of the fairways . . . Sets the standard for municipal courses . . . Long par 4s . . . Old, well-groomed, well-managed and fun to play . . . Most fun course in Wisconsin.

(GREAT VALUE)

★★★ ROCK RIVER HILLS GOLF COURSE

PU—Main Street Rd., Horicon (414)485-4990.
Call club for further information.
Subscriber comments: Cheap hidden jewel, good scenery by the marsh . . . Need more sand in their bunkers . . . Too short, too flat, good for kids . . . Good back nine, water in play on several holes . . . Good, out-of-the-way public course . . . Some pin placements unfair . . . Nice course, very nice staff . . . Great pin placements.

WISCONSIN

★½ ROYAL SCOT COUNTRY CLUB
SP—4831 Church Rd., New Franken (414)866-2731.
Call club for further information.
Subscriber comments: Demands a variety of shots . . . Play the front nine twice, if possible . . . Very poor fairways, like playing in a swampy bog . . . Wisconsin version of target golf . . . Water on the back, woods on the front . . . More bland holes than good ones.

★½ SCENIC VIEW COUNTRY CLUB
PU—4415 Club Dr., Slinger (414)644-5661.
20 miles northwest of Milwaukee. **Holes:** 18. **Par:** 72/71.
Yards: 6,296/5,358. **Course rating:** 68.6/70.1. **Slope:** 115/115.
Opened: 1961. **Pace of Play rating:** 4:00. **Green fee:** $16/19.
Credit cards: MC, V. **Reduced fees:** Weekdays, Low season, Seniors.
Caddies: No. **Golf carts:** $22 for 18 holes.
Discount golf packages: No. **Season:** March-Nov. **High:** June-Aug.
On-site lodging: No. **Rental clubs:** Yes.
Walking policy: Unrestricted walking. **Range:** Yes (grass).
To obtain tee times: Call up to seven days in advance.
Subscriber comments: Hacker's paradise, wear a hard hat. Nos. 1 and 10 elevated. Seems like there's nine holes in one area. Fore! . . . Fairways too close to each other . . . Making great new changes . . . New greens . . . You have to look for trouble . . . Too easy and too slow.

★★★★ SENTRYWORLD GOLF COURSE
PU—601 N. Michigan Ave., Stevens Point (715)345-1600.
90 miles north of Madison. **Holes:** 18. **Par:** 72/72.
Yards: 7,055/5,197. **Course rating:** 74.5/71.6. **Slope:** 144/130.
Opened: 1981. **Pace of Play rating:** 4:30-5:00. **Green fee:** $45/55.
Credit cards: MC, V, AMEX. **Reduced fees:** Low season, Twilight, Juniors.
Caddies: No. **Golf carts:** Included in Green Fee.
Discount golf packages: Yes. **Season:** April-Oct. **High:** June-Aug.
On-site lodging: No. **Rental clubs:** Yes.
Walking policy: Unrestricted walking. **Range:** Yes (grass).
To obtain tee times: Call pro shop.
Ranked in First 25 of America's 75 Best Public Golf Courses by Golf Digest. Selected Best New Public Course of 1983 by Golf Digest. Ranked 4th in Wisconsin by Golf Digest.
Subscriber comments: Nice course . . . Bring your A-1 sand game . . . Unfair if you don't know the course . . . Great flowers, better than the course . . . Excellent . . . Outstanding par 3s . . . Still great, condition is slipping . . . Staff is great . . . Very nice, but not the excitement it should have . . . Interesting Robert Trent Jones Jr. layout . . . A real test of your skills . . . It's scenery is outstanding with mature oak trees . . . Incredible . . . Bent-grass fairways, private-club conditions for the public . . . Flowers are overrated . . . Visually attractive . . . Probably worth leaving behind a couple sleeves . . . "Flower hole" No. 16 is probably one of the prettiest holes you'll find anywhere . . . Too many flowers . . . A championship golf course . . . Has no flow . . . Too much sand . . . Photo-op at the 16th . . . There's a green somewhere in that garden . . . Design encourages risk, but at a price . . . One of the state's very best.

★★½ SHAWANO LAKE GOLF CLUB
PU—W5714 Lake Dr., Shawano (715)524-4890.
25 miles west of Green Bay. **Holes:** 18. **Par:** 71/75.
Yards: 6,211/5,516. **Course rating:** 72.9/70.4. **Slope:** 128/128.
Opened: 1922. **Pace of Play rating:** 4:15. **Green fee:** $12/16.
Credit cards: MC, V. **Reduced fees:** Weekdays, Low season, Resort guests, Twilight, Seniors, Juniors.
Caddies: No. **Golf carts:** $9 for 18 holes.
Discount golf packages: Yes. **Season:** April-Nov. **High:** June-Sept.
On-site lodging: No. **Rental clubs:** Yes.
Walking policy: Unrestricted walking. **Range:** Yes (grass).

To obtain tee times: Call up to two weeks in advance.
Subscriber comments: Now being worked upon . . . Excellent 70-year-old routing . . . Put the driver away, opt for a 3-wood or iron . . . Placement over distance on some holes a must, too many trees just off the fairways . . . Unique holes. Five blind shots . . . Small greens a real challenge.

★★★ SKYLINE GOLF CLUB
PU—11th & Golf Rd., Black River Falls (715)284-2613.
100 miles north of Madison. **Holes:** 18. **Par:** 72/72.
Yards: 6,371/5,122. **Course rating:** 70.6/69.4. **Slope:** 123/112.
Opened: 1956. **Pace of Play rating:** 4:00-4:30. **Green fee:** $10/20.
Credit cards: MC, V. **Reduced fees:** Low season, Resort guests.
Caddies: No. **Golf carts:** $19 for 18 holes.
Discount golf packages: No. **Season:** April-Nov. **High:** May-Aug.
On-site lodging: No. **Rental clubs:** Yes.
Walking policy: Unrestricted walking. **Range:** Yes (grass).
To obtain tee times: Call pro shop.
Subscriber comments: A trophy! Variety of terrain, good shape, very nice staff . . . A good idea gone bad, needs lots of work . . . Hilly . . . Lots of character.

★½ SONGBIRD HILLS GOLF COURSE
PU—W259-N8700 Hwy. J, Hartland (414)246-7050.
15 miles west of Milwaukee. **Holes:** 18. **Par:** 70/70.
Yards: 5,541/5,066. **Course rating:** 66.2/64.0. **Slope:** 110/105.
Opened: 1992. **Pace of Play rating:** N/A. **Green fee:** $18/23.
Credit cards: None. **Reduced fees:** Weekdays, Low season, Twilight, Seniors, Juniors.
Caddies: No. **Golf carts:** $10 for 18 holes.
Discount golf packages: No. **Season:** April-Nov. **High:** June-Aug.
On-site lodging: No. **Rental clubs:** Yes.
Walking policy: Unrestricted walking. **Range:** No.
To obtain tee times: Call pro shop.
Subscriber comments: Not for anyone serious about golf . . . Mostly open fairways . . . Brand new, still has growing pains . . . Two or three poorly designed blind holes . . . New, tight, very interesting layout . . . Very short but surprisingly tough . . . Three good holes, confusing layout.

★★★½ SPARTA MUNICIPAL GOLF CLUB
PU—1210 E Montgomery St., Sparta (608)269-3022.
Call club for further information.
Subscriber comments: Wide fairways, very playable . . . Condition tops for our area . . . A "must play" in western Wisconsin . . . Very friendly place . . . Greens a little slow.

GREAT VALUE

★★★ SPOONER GOLF CLUB
SP—County Trunk H N., Spooner (715)635-3580.
60 miles south of Duluth. **Holes:** 18. **Par:** 71/72.
Yards: 6,407/5,084. **Course rating:** 70.1/68.7. **Slope:** 125/120.
Opened: 1930. **Pace of Play rating:** 4:15. **Green fee:** $18/20.
Credit cards: None. **Reduced fees:** Weekdays, Twilight.
Caddies: No. **Golf carts:** $10 for 18 holes.
Discount golf packages: No. **Season:** April-Oct. **High:** June-Aug.
On-site lodging: No. **Rental clubs:** Yes.
Walking policy: Unrestricted walking. **Range:** Yes (grass).
To obtain tee times: Call one month in advance starting on the 25th of the preceeding month.
Subscriber comments: For players with a long ball . . . Rolling fairways . . . Nicest course in the state north of Wisconsin Rapids . . . Fast greens . . . Lacks a little something in every category . . . Always good condition . . . Modified Tom Vardon design . . . Nice layout, tough No. 18. A hidden treasure in the north . . . One nine strong, the other one weak.

WISCONSIN

★★★ SPRING VALLEY COUNTRY CLUB
PU—23913 Wilmot Rd., Salem (414)862-2626.
9 miles west of Kenosha. **Holes:** 18. **Par:** 70/0.
Yards: 6,450/5,950. **Course rating:** 69.8/69.5. **Slope:** 123/114.
Opened: 1924. **Pace of Play rating:** 4:00. **Green fee:** $18.
Credit cards: None. **Reduced fees:** Weekdays, Low season, Twilight,
Seniors.
Caddies: No. **Golf carts:** $10 for 18 holes.
Discount golf packages: No. **Season:** Year-round. **High:** April-Nov.
On-site lodging: No. **Rental clubs:** No.
Walking policy: Unrestricted walking. **Range:** Yes (grass).
To obtain tee times:
Call anytime.
Subscriber comments: Friendly neighborhood course . . . Laid back
atmosphere . . . Old-fashioned golf course; small greens, no bunkers . . .
Easy except for two holes.

THE SPRINGS GOLF CLUB RESORT
FRONT/BACK/NORTH★
R—400 Springs Dr., Spring Green (608)588-7707.
35 miles west of Madison. **Holes:** 27. **Par:** 72/72/72.
Yards: 6,554/6,534/6,544. **Course rating:** 71.5/71.9/71.6.
Slope: 132/134/130.
Opened: 1969. **Pace of Play rating:** N/A. **Green fee:** $58.
Credit cards: MC, V, DISC. **Reduced fees:** Low season, Twilight.
Caddies: No. **Golf carts:** Included in Green Fee.
Discount golf packages: Yes. **Season:** Year-round. **High:** April-Oct.
On-site lodging: Yes. **Rental clubs:** Yes.
Walking policy: Walking at certain times. **Range:** Yes (grass).
To obtain tee times: General public call six days in advance. Hotel guests
and members are allowed seven days in advance.

★½ SQUIRES COUNTRY CLUB
PU—4970 Country Club Rd., Port Washington (414)285-3402.
25 miles north of Milwaukee. **Holes:** 18. **Par:** 70/70.
Yards: 5,800/5,067. **Course rating:** 67.3/68.2. **Slope:** 112/112.
Opened: 1927. **Pace of Play rating:** 4:00. **Green fee:** $21.
Credit cards: MC, V, DISC. **Reduced fees:** Weekdays, Twilight,
Seniors.
Caddies: No. **Golf carts:** $11 for 18 holes.
Discount golf packages: No. **Season:** April-Oct. **High:** May-Oct.
On-site lodging: No. **Rental clubs:** Yes.
Walking policy: Unrestricted walking. **Range:** Yes (grass).
To obtain tee times: Call one week in advance.
Subscriber comments: Not a very picturesque course, could be kept up
better . . . Mature, overlooks Lake Michigan . . . Fifth hole is a winner . . .
The grill at No. 10 tee is a great idea . . . Two unfairly sloped greens . . .
Need substantial work . . . Too short with greens too slow.

★★★½ TRAPPERS TURN GOLF CLUB
PU—652 Trappers Turn Dr., Wisconsin Dells (608)253-7000, (800)221-
8876.
50 miles north of Madison. **Holes:** 18. **Par:** 72/72.
Yards: 6,550/5,013. **Course rating:** 71.7/69.3. **Slope:** 129/119.
Opened: 1991. **Pace of Play rating:** 4:00. **Green fee:** $32/52.
Credit cards: MC, V, DISC. **Reduced fees:** Weekdays, Low season,
Resort guests, Twilight.
Caddies: No. **Golf carts:** Included in Green Fee.
Discount golf packages: Yes. **Season:** April-Oct. **High:** July-Aug.
On-site lodging: No. **Rental clubs:** Yes.
Walking policy: Walking at certain times. **Range:** No.
To obtain tee times: Call up to 30 days in advance.
Subscriber comments: Fabulous Andy North and Roger Packard design
. . . Excellent golf, aethetics; no practice tees . . . North, Packard looks
great here . . . Fun and challenging . . . Great setting, stay away . . . Best

course in the area . . . A couple of tough greens . . . Mix of links, woodland holes. Very courteous staff . . . This is a sleeper . . . Too many moguls . . . Best front nine in Wisconsin . . . Interesting holes, but greens small . . . Really felt they wanted me there . . . Few level lies, scenic . . . Some holes are great . . . Terrific course with some tricky holes . . . Some frankly unfair holes.

★★ TROUT LAKE GOLF AND COUNTRY CLUB

PU—3800 Hwy. 51 N., Arbor Vitae (715)385-2189.
80 miles north of Wausau. **Holes:** 18. **Par:** 72/71.
Yards: 6,175/5,263. **Course rating:** 69.9/70.3. **Slope:** 124/122.
Opened: 1926. **Pace of Play rating:** 4:15. **Green fee:** $18/26.
Credit cards: MC, V. **Reduced fees:** Low season, Twilight.
Caddies: No. **Golf carts:** $11 for 18 holes.
Discount golf packages: No. **Season:** April-Oct. **High:** June-Sept.
On-site lodging: No. **Rental clubs:** Yes.
Walking policy: Unrestricted walking. **Range:** No.
To obtain tee times: Call two weeks in advance.
Subscriber comments: Sleepy Northwoods course . . . Ninth hole distant from the clubhouse . . . Has personality . . . I love it, but I recognize it isn't great . . . Some challenging holes, open front nine, back gets tighter . . . Wildwoodsy . . . Excellent greens.

★★★★ TURTLEBACK GOLF AND COUNTRY CLUB

PU—W. Allen Rd., Rice Lake (715)234-7641.
80 miles south of Duluth. **Holes:** 18. **Par:** 71/72.
Yards: 6,132/5,328. **Course rating:** 68.6/69.6. **Slope:** 116/115.
Opened: N/A. **Pace of Play rating:** N/A. **Green fee:** $17/18.
Credit cards: MC, V. **Reduced fees:** Weekdays.
Caddies: No. **Golf carts:** $9 for 18 holes.
Discount golf packages: No. **Season:** April-Oct. **High:** June-Aug.
On-site lodging: No. **Rental clubs:** Yes.
Walking policy: Unrestricted walking. **Range:** Yes (grass).
To obtain tee times: Call up to two weeks in advance.
Subscriber comments: Beautiful, challenging but playable . . . In excellent shape. Food is great . . . First nine is new . . . Staff is great, interesting layout . . . If walking 18 you might want to start on the hilly back side . . . Some tough holes . . . New nine very nice, old nine has too many blind pins.

(GREAT VALUE)

★★½ TUSCUMBIA GOLF CLUB

SP—Illinois Ave., Green Lake (414)294-3240, (800)294-3381.
65 miles north of Milwaukee. **Holes:** 18. **Par:** 71/71.
Yards: 6,301/5,619. **Course rating:** 70.1/73.2. **Slope:** 122/123.
Opened: 1896. **Pace of Play rating:** 4:15. **Green fee:** $24/36.
Credit cards: MC, V, DISC. **Reduced fees:** Low season, Twilight, Seniors, Juniors.
Caddies: No. **Golf carts:** $24 for 18 holes.
Discount golf packages: Yes. **Season:** April-Oct. **High:** June-Sept.
On-site lodging: No. **Rental clubs:** Yes.
Walking policy: Unrestricted walking. **Range:** Yes (grass).
To obtain tee times: Call pro shop.
Subscriber comments: Oldest course in Wisconsin . . . Large landing areas . . . Enjoy seeing an older course design . . . Small greens . . . Not bad for an old track . . . Narrow, old, enjoyable . . . A real old course . . . Hard greens . . . Not very difficult . . . Needs new infusion . . . Fairways are too narrow . . . Not bad, but lots of bugs.

TWIN LAKES COUNTRY CLUB★

SP—1230 Legion Dr., Twin Lakes (414)877-2500.
50 miles south of Milwaukee. **Holes:** 18. **Par:** 70/71.
Yards: 5,930/4,946. **Course rating:** 67.2/67.3. **Slope:** 115/113.
Opened: 1910. **Pace of Play rating:** 4:00. **Green fee:** $14/19.
Credit cards: None. **Reduced fees:** Weekdays, Twilight, Seniors.

Caddies: No. **Golf carts:** $10 for 18 holes.
Discount golf packages: No. **Season:** March–Nov. **High:** June–Aug.
On-site lodging: No. **Rental clubs:** Yes.
Walking policy: Unrestricted walking. **Range:** Yes (grass).
To obtain tee times: Call one week in advance.

★ TWIN OAKS COUNTRY CLUB
PU—4871 County Hwy. R, Denmark (414)863-2716.
5 miles south of Green Bay. **Holes:** 18. **Par:** 72/72.
Yards: 6,468/5,214. **Course rating:** 69.6/68.3. **Slope:** 116/103.
Opened: 1968. **Pace of Play rating:** 4:15. **Green fee:** $14/16.
Credit cards: None. **Reduced fees:** Weekdays, Low season, Seniors, Juniors.
Caddies: No. **Golf carts:** $9 for 18 holes.
Discount golf packages: No. **Season:** March–Nov. **High:** June–Aug.
On-site lodging: No. **Rental clubs:** Yes.
Walking policy: Unrestricted walking. **Range:** Yes (grass).
To obtain tee times: Call up to seven days in advance.
Subscriber comments: Play during Packer games and have the course to yourself . . . Too many beginners . . . Some holes lack definition . . . Fairly wide open . . . Slicer's nightmare . . . Back nine too undistinguished . . . Not exciting. Hit the ball and follow . . . Little variety.

★★★★ UNIVERSITY RIDGE GOLF COURSE
PU—7120 City Trunk Rd., Verona (608)845-7700, (800)897-4343.
8 miles southwest of Madison. **Holes:** 18. **Par:** 72/72.
Yards: 6,825/5,005. **Course rating:** 73.2/68.9. **Slope:** 142/121.
Opened: 1991. **Pace of Play rating:** 4:30 **Green fee:** $29/41.
Credit cards: MC, V, AMEX. **Reduced fees:** Low season, Twilight, Juniors.
Caddies: No. **Golf carts:** $13 for 18 holes.
Discount golf packages: No. **Season:** April–Oct. **High:** May–Sept.
On-site lodging: No. **Rental clubs:** Yes.
Walking policy: Walking at certain times. **Range:** Yes (grass).
To obtain tee times: Call up to five days in advance starting at 7 p.m. Tee times for outings are taken anytime in advance with groups of 12 or more. Ranked 3rd in Wisconsin by Golf Digest.
Subscriber comments: Very difficult but playable . . . Very scenic . . . Could be the best in Wisconsin . . . Rough is so thick and long you cannot recover if in it . . . Too frustrating to play with those roughs . . . Prices are a little steep . . . Great track . . . Outstanding . . . Good mix of style . . . Good for bombers and finesse players . . . Wonderful design . . . If you buy a large bucket of balls, plan on being there a long time . . . Some great golf holes . . . Wish I lived closer . . . Too much hype, overplayed . . . Fantastic. Woods, water, doglegs, narrow and wide holes . . . You won't find a better value for your dollar anywhere . . . Best golf experience in the state . . . .Not walkable . . . Beautiful rolling hills, front and back completely different woods and open . . . Diversity between nines makes it very interesting . . . Resort atmosphere. Not one weak hole . . . University of Wisconsin owned . . . Beautiful greens . . . Everything about this place is super . . . The class act of Madison . . . Still spectacular on a dreary day . . . It does Wisconsin proud. Go Badgers! . . . Each nine different. Like playing two courses . . . Memorable experience . . . Breathtaking beauty and superb layout . . . Doesn't anyone replace divots anymore?

★★★½ VOYAGER VILLAGE COUNTRY CLUB
SP—28851 Killkare Rd., Danbury (715)259-3911.
Call club for further information.
Subscriber comments: For players with a long ball . . . Very nice layout for all . . . Watch out for incoming planes . . . All in all, real plush . . . More of a target course . . . Out in the middle of nowhere.

★★ WESTERN LAKES GOLF CLUB

PU—W287 N1963, Pewaukee (414)691-1181.
Call club for further information.
Subscriber comments: Average . . . Fairly long, some water . . . A cow pasture. (I'm from Wisconsin and I know.) . . . Nothing outstanding . . . Sinkhole . . . In poor shape . . . Very sporty.

★★½ WESTHAVEN GOLF CLUB

PU—1400 Westhaven St., Oshkosh (414)233-4640.
Call club for further information.
Subscriber comments: Bowl-shaped greens . . . Greens unfair . . . Not the greatest greens . . . Front nine very short, back nine good . . . Heavy play . . . Easy to score on.

★★½ WHITNALL PARK GOLF COURSE

PU—5879 S. 92nd St., Hales Corners (414)425-7931.
15 miles southwest of Milwaukee. **Holes:** 18. **Par:** 71/74.
Yards: 6,216/5,778. **Course rating:** 69.9/72.1. **Slope:** 117/119.
Opened: 1932. **Pace of Play rating:** 4:10. **Green fee:** $20.
Credit cards: MC, V. **Reduced fees:** Low season, Twilight, Seniors, Juniors.
Caddies: No. **Golf carts:** $10 for 18 holes.
Discount golf packages: No. **Season:** April-Nov. **High:** June-Sept.
On-site lodging: No. **Rental clubs:** Yes.
Walking policy: Unrestricted walking. **Range:** No.
To obtain tee times: Call same day.
Subscriber comments: Nice county course. Not difficult, just nice . . . If you can't play well here, take up jogging . . . Older layout, scenic setting . . . Not always in good shape . . . Each hole is completely different . . . Old public course, wooded and tight; greens could be better . . . Very little sand.

★½ WILLOW RUN GOLF CLUB

SP—N12 W26506 Golf Rd., Pewaukee (414)544-8585.
15 miles west of Milwaukee. **Holes:** 18. **Par:** 71/71.
Yards: 6,521/5,233. **Course rating:** 70.0/69.1. **Slope:** 115/112.
Opened: 1960. **Pace of Play rating:** 5:00. **Green fee:** $22.
Credit cards: MC, V, DISC. **Reduced fees:** Weekdays, Twilight, Seniors, Juniors.
Caddies: No. **Golf carts:** $24 for 18 holes.
Discount golf packages: Yes. **Season:** March-Dec. **High:** June-Sept.
On-site lodging: Yes. **Rental clubs:** Yes.
Walking policy: Unrestricted walking. **Range:** Yes (grass).
To obtain tee times: Call up to seven days in advance.
Subscriber comments: Too low and long for my tastes . . . Greens are inconsistent . . . Plain, little challenge . . . Excellent par 3s . . . Improving . . . Back nine needs to mature . . . Last six holes too short and easy.

★½ WISCONSIN RIVER COUNTRY CLUB

SP—705 West River Dr., Stevens Point (715)344-9152.
Call club for further information.
Subscriber comments: Getting better . . . Greens were hard and fast . . . Not too tough . . . Flood waters hurt the course . . . Has challenging holes, needs conditioning . . . Many wet spots . . . Unimaginative, average scenery, recent improvements help a little.

YAHARA HILLS GOLF COURSE
PU—6701 East Broadway, Madison (608)838-3126.
Opened: 1967. **Pace of Play rating:** 4:15. **Green fee:** $14/18.
Credit cards: MC, V. **Reduced fees:** Low season, Seniors, Juniors.
Caddies: No. **Golf carts:** $20 for 18 holes.
Discount golf packages: No. **Season:** April-Nov. **High:** April-Aug.
On-site lodging: No. **Rental clubs:** Yes.
Walking policy: Unrestricted walking. **Range:** Yes (grass).
To obtain tee times: One week in advance.

★★½ **EAST COURSE**
Holes: 18. **Par:** 72/72.
Yards: 7,200/6,115. **Course rating:** 71.9/73.4. **Slope:** 116/118.
Subscriber comments: Busy, long with wide fairways . . . Two side-by-side 18s are well-designed, groomed, and a pleasure to play . . . Nothing special . . . Both courses a little repetitive . . . You can forget which one you're on . . . A bit dull . . . Just tee it up and rip it, long but wide open . . . Huge greens . . . Greens in very good shape for a public course . . . Nothing exceptional . . . Another basic municipal . . . Plays a stroke or two harder than the West . . . Course gets played a lot and you can tell.

★★½ **WEST COURSE**
Holes: 18. **Par:** 72/73.
Yards: 7,000/5,705. **Course rating:** 71.6/71.4. **Slope:** 118/116.
Subscriber comments: Nothing special . . . Interesting holes . . . Good municipal course with good prices . . . Some fairways were poor all summer . . . A bit dull, greens too large . . . Both play harder than they first appear because of long rough . . . Holes all look alike . . . Good 36 hole facility . . . Basic golf . . . They both look alike . . . They have par 3s right next to each other that play the same . . . Good place to learn to chip . . . Big fairway and big greens, lots of room . . . Big bunkers.

Notes

★ AIRPORT GOLF COURSE

PU—4801 Central, Cheyenne (307)637-6418.
Holes: 18. **Par:** 70/70.
Yards: 6,121/5,661. **Course rating:** N/A. **Slope:** 99/113.
Opened: N/A. **Pace of Play rating:** N/A. **Green fee:** N/A.
Credit cards: MC, V. **Reduced fees:** Twilight.
Caddies: No. **Golf carts:** N/A.
Discount golf packages: No. **Season:** Year-round. **High:** May-Oct.
On-site lodging: No. **Rental clubs:** No.
Walking policy: N/A. **Range:** Yes (grass).
Subscriber comments: Front nine much better than back . . . Nice place
to take the family.

★★★½ BELL NOB GOLF CLUB

PU—4600 Overdale Dr., Gillette (307)686-7069.
140 miles west of Rapid City, SD **Holes:** 18. **Par:** 72/72.
Yards: 7,024/5,555. **Course rating:** 70.8/70.6. **Slope:** 119/116.
Opened: 1981. **Pace of Play rating:** 4:00. **Green fee:** $15.
Credit cards: MC, V. **Reduced fees:** No.
Caddies: No. **Golf carts:** $9 for 18 holes.
Discount golf packages: No. **Season:** April-Oct. **High:** May-July.
On-site lodging: No. **Rental clubs:** Yes.
Walking policy: Unrestricted walking. **Range:** Yes (grass).
To obtain tee times: Call anytime one week in advance.
Subscriber comments: Antelope on the course make for interesting
hazards . . . Wide open, hilly . . . Well maintained, can't beat the price.

★★★½ BUFFALO GOLF CLUB

PU—P.O. Box 759, Buffalo (307)684-5266.
110 miles north of Casper. **Holes:** 18. **Par:** 71/72.
Yards: 6,684/5,512. **Course rating:** 70.9/69.8. **Slope:** 116/115.
Opened: 1928. **Pace of Play rating:** 3:20. **Green fee:** $18.
Credit cards: MC, V. **Reduced fees:** No.
Caddies: No. **Golf carts:** N/A.
Discount golf packages: No. **Season:** March-Nov. **High:** May-Sept.
On-site lodging: No. **Rental clubs:** Yes.
Walking policy: Unrestricted walking. **Range:** Yes (grass).
To obtain tee times: Call anytime.
Subscriber comments: Beautiful course at the base of the Rockies . . .
Well maintained, short, hilly course . . . Poirot and family run a great shop,
easy access . . . Base of Big Horn Mountains . . . Should become a
destination resort . . . Beautiful scenery.

★★½ CASPER MUNICIPAL GOLF COURSE

PU—2120 Allendale, Casper (307)234-2405.
Holes: 18. **Par:** 70/72.
Yards: 6,234/5,472. **Course rating:** 67.9/69.2. **Slope:** 112/112.
Opened: 1929. **Pace of Play rating:** 4:00. **Green fee:** $10/12.
Credit cards: None. **Reduced fees:** Weekdays.
Caddies: No. **Golf carts:** $7 for 18 holes.
Discount golf packages: No. **Season:** March-Oct. **High:** May-Aug.
On-site lodging: No. **Rental clubs:** Yes.
Walking policy: Unrestricted walking. **Range:** Yes (grass).
To obtain tee times: Call one day in advance beginning at 7 a.m.
Subscriber comments: Small greens, big wind . . . You can't beat the
green fees . . . Suited for all levels . . . Good condition.

★★½ DOUGLAS COMMUNITY CLUB

PU—64 Golf Course Rd., Douglas (307)358-5099.
50 miles east of Casper. **Holes:** 18. **Par:** 71/72.
Yards: 6,253/5,323. **Course rating:** 68.4/68.5. **Slope:** 107/103.
Opened: 1974. **Pace of Play rating:** 4:00. **Green fee:** $12/15.
Credit cards: None. **Reduced fees:** Weekdays.
Caddies: No. **Golf carts:** $8 for 18 holes.
Discount golf packages: No. **Season:** April-Oct. **High:** June-Aug.
On-site lodging: No. **Rental clubs:** Yes.

Walking policy: Unrestricted walking. **Range:** Yes (grass).
To obtain tee times: Call pro shop.
Subscriber comments: Fun course . . . Nothing special but price is right . . . Good stretch stop between Denver and Billings, Montana.

★★FRANCIS E. WARREN AFB GOLF COURSE

PU—7103 Randall Ave., F.E. Warren AFB (307)775-3556.
1 mile north of Cheyenne. **Holes:** 18. **Par:** 71/75.
Yards: 6,585/5,186. **Course rating:** 68.2/67.0. **Slope:** 105/102.
Opened: 1949. **Pace of Play rating:** 4:00. **Green fee:** $9/16.
Credit cards: MC, V. **Reduced fees:** Twilight.
Caddies: No. **Golf carts:** $14 for 18 holes.
Discount golf packages: Yes. **Season:** Year-round. **High:** April-Oct.
On-site lodging: Yes. **Rental clubs:** Yes.
Walking policy: Unrestricted walking. **Range:** Yes (grass).
To obtain tee times: Call two days in advance.
Subscriber comments: The scenery was outstanding with wildlife (antelope, deer, etc.) roaming the course undisturbed.

★★ GLENN "RED" JACOBY GOLF CLUB

PU—30th and Willett, Laramie (307)745-3111.
120 miles north of Denver, CO. **Holes:** 18. **Par:** 70/72.
Yards: 6,540/5,395. **Course rating:** 67.3/68.1. **Slope:** 108/109.
Opened: 1932. **Pace of Play rating:** 3:30-4:00. **Green fee:** $14.
Credit cards: MC, V. **Reduced fees:** Juniors.
Caddies: No. **Golf carts:** $15 for 18 holes.
Discount golf packages: No. **Season:** April-Oct. **High:** June-Aug.
On-site lodging: No. **Rental clubs:** Yes.
Walking policy: Unrestricted walking. **Range:** Yes (grass).
To obtain tee times: Call Tuesdays for upcoming weekend.
Subscriber comments: Very friendly staff, course pretty easy . . . An amateur's delight . . . Small greens . . . Wide fairways . . . Well-run shop.

★★½ GREEN HILLS MUNICIPAL GOLF COURSE

PU—1455 Airport Rd., Worland (307)347-8972.
180 miles north of Billings, MT. **Holes:** 18. **Par:** 72/73.
Yards: 6,444/5,104. **Course rating:** 69.3/68.0. **Slope:** 113/113.
Opened: 1954. **Pace of Play rating:** 3:30-4:00. **Green fee:** $16/18.
Credit cards: None. **Reduced fees:** Juniors.
Caddies: No. **Golf carts:** $16 for 18 holes.
Discount golf packages: No. **Season:** April-Oct. **High:** June-Aug.
On-site lodging: No. **Rental clubs:** Yes.
Walking policy: Unrestricted walking. **Range:** Yes (grass).
To obtain tee times: Call anytime.
Subscriber comments: Fun, easy . . . Two distinct nines, old big trees on front, wide open back.

★★★★ JACKSON HOLE GOLF AND TENNIS CLUB

R—5000 Spring Gulch Rd., Jackson (307)733-3111.
Holes: 18. **Par:** 72/73.
Yards: 7,168/6,036. **Course rating:** 72.3/73.2. **Slope:** 133/125.
Opened: 1967. **Pace of Play rating:** 4:15. **Green fee:** $40/73.
Credit cards: MC, V, AMEX. **Reduced fees:** Low season, Twilight.
Caddies: No. **Golf carts:** Included in Green Fee.
Discount golf packages: No. **Season:** April-Oct. **High:** June-Aug.
On-site lodging: No. **Rental clubs:** Yes.
Walking policy: Walking at certain times. **Range:** Yes (grass).
To obtain tee times: Call anytime with credit card.
Ranked in First 25 of America's 75 Best Public Golf Courses by Golf Digest. Ranked 10th in America's 75 Best Resort Courses by Golf Digest. Ranked 1st in Wyoming by Golf Digest.
Subscriber comments: Great view of the Tetons . . . R.T. Jones

masterpiece, golf at its finest, my favorite . . . Scenery is so great you don't care what you shoot . . . Fancy shop . . . Excellent golf, breathtaking views . . . A few great holes, but not enough for the price.

★★½ KENDRICK GOLF COURSE
PU—Big Goose Rd., Sheridan (307)674-8148.
125 miles southeast of Billings, MT. **Holes:** 18. **Par:** 72/73.
Yards: 6,800/5,549. **Course rating:** 71.3/70.8. **Slope:** 116/113.
Opened: 1940. **Pace of Play rating:** 4:15. **Green fee:** $15.
Credit cards: None. **Reduced fees:** Juniors.
Caddies: No. **Golf carts:** N/A.
Discount golf packages: No. **Season:** April-Oct. **High:** May-July.
On-site lodging: No. **Rental clubs:** Yes.
Walking policy: Unrestricted walking. **Range:** Yes (grass).
To obtain tee times: Call one week in advance.
Ranked 5th in Wyoming by Golf Digest.
Subscriber comments: Nice course with lots of hills . . . New greens on front nine . . . Great views . . . Easy access.

★★★ OLIVE GLENN GOLF AND COUNTRY CLUB
SP—802 Meadow Lane, Cody (307)587-5551.
102 miles south of Billings, Mont. **Holes:** 18. **Par:** 72/72.
Yards: 6,880/5,654. **Course rating:** 71.6/71.2. **Slope:** 124/120.
Opened: 1970. **Pace of Play rating:** 4:00. **Green fee:** $21.
Credit cards: MC, V. **Reduced fees:** Juniors.
Caddies: No. **Golf carts:** $10 for 18 holes.
Discount golf packages: Yes. **Season:** April-Oct. **High:** June-Aug.
On-site lodging: No. **Rental clubs:** Yes.
Walking policy: Unrestricted walking. **Range:** Yes (grass).
To obtain tee times: Call up to seven days in advance.
Ranked 4th in Wyoming by Golf Digest.
Subscriber comments: Excellent condition, long course, great views, very good value . . . Windy, tough par 4s . . . Nice public course . . . Priced high for Cody, but a very nice course.

★★★½ RIVERTON COUNTRY CLUB
SP—4275 Country Club Dr., Riverton (307)856-4779.
117 miles west of Casper. **Holes:** 18. **Par:** 72/72.
Yards: 7,064/5,549. **Course rating:** 72.2/71.0. **Slope:** 128/119.
Opened: 1970. **Pace of Play rating:** N/A. **Green fee:** $20/30.
Credit cards: MC, V. **Reduced fees:** No.
Caddies: No. **Golf carts:** $10 for 18 holes.
Discount golf packages: No. **Season:** March-Oct. **High:** June-Aug.
On-site lodging: No. **Rental clubs:** Yes.
Walking policy: Unrestricted walking. **Range:** Yes (grass).
To obtain tee times: Call up to seven days in advance.
Subscriber comments: Tough course, has potential . . . Fun to play . . . Good all around course, caters to locals.

(GREAT VALUE)

★★★★ TETON PINES RESORT AND COUNTRY CLUB
R—3450 Clubhouse Dr., Jackson (307)733-1733, (800)238-2223.
Holes: 18. **Par:** 72/72.
Yards: 7,412/5,486. **Course rating:** 74.2/70.8. **Slope:** 137/117.
Opened: 1987. **Pace of Play rating:** 4:00-4:15. **Green fee:** $70/95.
Credit cards: MC, V, AMEX, Diners Club. **Reduced fees:** Low season, Resort guests, Juniors.
Caddies: Yes. **Golf carts:** Included in Green Fee.
Discount golf packages: Yes. **Season:** May-Oct. **High:** June-Sept.
On-site lodging: Yes. **Rental clubs:** Yes.
Walking policy: Mandatory cart. **Range:** Yes (grass).
To obtain tee times: Call anytime during the year.
Ranked 49th in America's 75 Best Resort Courses by Golf Digest. Ranked 2nd in Wyoming by Golf Digest.

Subscriber comments: Great golf course, good staff . . . Best in all categories . . . Leave your driver at home but bring your wallet . . . Excellent test, par 3s are a highlight, excellent views . . . Beautiful course and the Tetons!

WHITE MOUNTAIN GOLF COURSE
PU—1501 Clubhouse Dr., Rock Springs (307)382-5030.
Holes: 18. **Par:** 72/73.
Yards: 7,000/5,666. **Course rating:** 72.4/73.1. **Slope:** 118/115.
Opened: 1979. **Pace of Play rating:** 4:30–5:00. **Green fee:** $15.
Credit cards: None. **Reduced fees:** Juniors.
Caddies: No. **Golf carts:** $15 for 18 holes.
Discount golf packages: No. **Season:** April–Nov. **High:** June–Sept.
On-site lodging: No. **Rental clubs:** Yes.
Walking policy: Unrestricted walking. **Range:** Yes (grass).
To obtain tee times: Call one week in advance.
Subscriber comments: Good risk and reward course . . . Good dining room . . . Excellent practice areas . . . If the wind is blowing, go bowling . . . Quiet, uncrowded, very friendly.

Notes

CANADA

ALBERTA

★★★½ BANFF SPRINGS GOLF COURSE
RUNDLE/SULPHER/TUNNEL
R—One Golf Course Rd., Banff (403)762-6833.
70 miles west of Calgary. **Holes:** 27. **Par:** 36/35/36.
Yards: 3,174/3,452/3,269. **Course rating:** N/A. **Slope:** N/A.
Opened: 1928. **Pace of Play rating:** 4:15. **Green fee:** $58/78.
Credit cards: All major. **Reduced fees:** Low season.
Caddies: No. **Golf carts:** Included in Green Fee.
Discount golf packages: Yes. **Season:** May-Oct. **High:** May-Sept.
On-site lodging: Yes. **Rental clubs:** Yes.
Walking policy: Walking at certain times. **Range:** Yes.
To obtain tee times: Call or fax with a credit card to guarantee tee time.
Subscriber comments: Original 18 excellent, new nine so-so . . . Classic
course, excellent fairways for mountain course . . . A "must" . . .
Something for every type of player . . . Always let the elk play through . . .
Gotta play it once, great setting . . . Spectacular scenery and good test of
golf . . . Hotel overlooking course is unbelievable. Banff will be a lifetime
of memories . . . Still one of the world's outstanding golf courses . . . Great
mountain golf . . . Original 18 was fabulous . . . Great old design, beautiful
views.

★★★ BARRHEAD GOLF COURSE
PU—P.O. Box 4090, Barrhead (403)674-3053.

60 miles northwest of Edmonton. **Holes:** 18. **Par:** 72/72.
Yards: 6,600/5,351. **Course rating:** 72.0/70.0. **Slope:** 127/129.
Opened: 1991. **Pace of Play rating:** 4:30. **Green fee:** $15/23.
Credit cards: MC, V. **Reduced fees:** Low season, Twilight.
Caddies: No. **Golf carts:** N/A.
Discount golf packages: Yes. **Season:** April-Oct. **High:** N/A.
On-site lodging: No. **Rental clubs:** Yes.
Walking policy: Unrestricted walking. **Range:** Yes(grass).
To obtain tee times: Call seven days in advance.
Subscriber comments: Friendly atmosphere . . . A hidden gem 70
minutes from Edmonton . . . A beautiful rustic course in a remote area . . .
Wooded course. Challenging for high or low handicapper.

★★ BROADMOOR PUBLIC GOLF COURSE
PU—2100 Oak St., Sherwood Park (403)467-7373.
Call club for further information.
Subscriber comments: Good public course. Pace is better because of new
nine . . . Typical flat municipal course in Alberta . . . Reconstructed back
nine great . . . Tight course and small greens demand accuracy.

CANMORE GOLF AND CURLING CLUB★
SP—2000 8th Ave., Canmore (403)678-4784.
55 miles west of Calgary. **Holes:** 18. **Par:** 71/71.
Yards: 6,309/5,258. **Course rating:** 69.1/70.3. **Slope:** 122/125.
Opened: 1961. **Pace of Play rating:** 4:30. **Green fee:** $34.
Credit cards: MC, V, AMEX. **Reduced fees:** Low season, Resort guests,
Juniors.
Caddies: No. **Golf carts:** $12 for 18 holes.
Discount golf packages: No. **Season:** April-Oct. **High:** June-Aug.
On-site lodging: No. **Rental clubs:** Yes.
Walking policy: Unrestricted walking. **Range:** Yes.
To obtain tee times: Hotel and golf packages available up to 60 days in
advance. Others call three days in advance.

★★★½ COLONIALE GOLF AND COUNTRY CLUB
SP—10 Country Club Dr., Beaumont (403)929-4653.
2 miles south of Edmonton. **Holes:** 18. **Par:** 72/72.
Yards: 7,020/5,344. **Course rating:** 73.8/72.1. **Slope:** 145/126.
Opened: 1993. **Pace of Play rating:** 4:19. **Green fee:** $27/35.
Credit cards: MC, V. **Reduced fees:** Weekdays, Low season, Twilight,
Seniors, Juniors.

Caddies: No. **Golf carts:** $22 for 18 holes.
Discount golf packages: Yes. **Season:** April–Oct. **High:** May–Sept.
On-site lodging: No. **Rental clubs:** Yes.
Walking policy: Unrestricted walking. **Range:** Yes (grass).
To obtain tee times: Call 48 hours in advance. Unlimited advance
guaranteed booking by credit card only. 24-hour cancellation policy.
Subscriber comments: Best in north Alberta . . . Very good test of golf,
links-type course . . . Another outstanding new layout, something for
every level . . . Best kept course in Edmonton area . . . Tough but excellent
. . . Needs time to mature . . . Extremely enjoyable layout . . . Great
course for aggressive players.

★½ CONNAUGHT GOLF CLUB
PU—2802 13th Ave. S.E., Medicine Hat (403)526-0737.
Call club for further information.
Subscriber comments: Excellent fairways. Small greens . . . Not real
difficult, forgiving.

★★★ COTTONWOOD GOLF AND COUNTRY CLUB
SP—Site 2, R.R. No. 1, De Winton (403)938-7200.
10 miles southeast of Calgary. **Holes:** 18. **Par:** 72/72.
Yards: 6,747/5,054. **Course rating:** 71.5/67.5. **Slope:** 129/N/A.
Opened: 1990. **Pace of Play rating:** 4:00. **Green fee:** $40.
Credit cards: MC, V, AMEX. **Reduced fees:** Twilight, Juniors.
Caddies: No. **Golf carts:** $24 for 18 holes.
Discount golf packages: No. **Season:** April–Oct. **High:** June-July.
On-site lodging: No. **Rental clubs:** Yes.
Walking policy: Unrestricted walking. **Range:** Yes (grass).
To obtain tee times: Call 3½ days in advance starting at noon.
Subscriber comments: Playable for all levels of golfers . . . Use all your
clubs . . . Nice design, easy walking, good service . . . Nicely maintained,
fun, can't get in much trouble . . . Excellent condition and very playable.

COUNTRYSIDE GOLF COURSE★
PU—51466 Range Rd. 232, Sherwood Park (403)467-9254.
14 miles southeast of Edmonton. **Holes:** 18. **Par:** 72.
Yards: 5,890. **Course rating:** 68.5. **Slope:** 113.
Opened: 1986. **Pace of Play rating:** 4:30. **Green fee:** $16/20.
Credit cards: MC, V. **Reduced fees:** Weekdays, Seniors.
Caddies: No. **Golf carts:** $22 for 18 holes.
Discount golf packages: Yes. **Season:** April–Oct. **High:** N/A.
On-site lodging: No. **Rental clubs:** Yes.
Walking policy: Unrestricted walking. **Range:** Yes.
To obtain tee times: Call for weekends only.

★★★★ D'ARCY RANCH GOLF CLUB
PU—Hwy. 29 and Milligan Dr., Okotoks (403)938-4455, (800)803-8810.
18 miles south of Calgary. **Holes:** 18. **Par:** 72/73.
Yards: 6,919/5,529. **Course rating:** 72.3/71.3. **Slope:** 126/122.
Opened: 1991. **Pace of Play rating:** 4:00-4:30. **Green fee:** $38.
Credit cards: MC, V, AMEX. **Reduced fees:** Twilight.
Caddies: No. **Golf carts:** $24 for 18 holes.
Discount golf packages: No. **Season:** April–Oct. **High:** May-Sept.
On-site lodging: No. **Rental clubs:** Yes.
Walking policy: Unrestricted walking. **Range:** Yes(grass).
To obtain tee times: Outside of province call one week in advance, local
call two days in advance. Call Thursday 7 a.m. for weekends and holidays.
Subscriber comments: Great facilites. Tough track . . . Treat you like a
member of a private club . . . Scottish style, beautiful course, windy . . .
Very hilly . . . First class pro shop . . . Good use of natural surrounding . . .
Pleasant, friendly staff, great views all over course . . . Difficult, each hole a
new experience.

★★★ THE DUNES GOLF AND WINTER CLUB
PU—R.R. No.1, Site 4, Box 1, Grande Prairie (403)538-4333.
Holes: 18. **Par:** 71/72.
Yards: 6,373/5,274. **Course rating:** 70.5/70.0. **Slope:** 116/122.
Opened: 1992. **Pace of Play rating:** 4:15. **Green fee:** $20/25.
Credit cards: MC, V, AMEX. **Reduced fees:** Low season, Seniors.
Caddies: Yes. **Golf carts:** N/A.
Discount golf packages: Yes. **Season:** March-Oct. **High:** April-Sept.
On-site lodging: No. **Rental clubs:** Yes.
Walking policy: Unrestricted walking. **Range:** Yes(grass).
To obtain tee times: Call one day in advance for weekdays. Call Friday for weekend and holidays. Reserve tee times two weeks in advance with credit card.
Subscriber comments: Best course in northern Alberta . . . Can play from 5:30 a.m. to 11:45 p.m. at end of June . . . Great course . . . Very friendly staff. Good golf.

★½ EAGLE ROCK GOLF COURSE
PU—RO 1, R.R. 1, South Edmonton (403)464-4653.
Call club for further information.
Subscriber comments: Great practice facility . . . Will be much better with age.

★★★½ GOOSE HUMMOCK GOLF CLUB
R—P.O. Box 1221, Gibbons (403)921-2444.
20 miles north of Edmonton. **Holes:** 18. **Par:** 71/71.
Yards: 6,604/5,408. **Course rating:** 74.0/71.5. **Slope:** 141/121.
Opened: 1989. **Pace of Play rating:** 4:30-5:00. **Green fee:** $22/25.
Credit cards: MC, V, AMEX. **Reduced fees:** Twilight, Seniors, Juniors.
Caddies: No. **Golf carts:** $22 for 18 holes.
Discount golf packages: No. **Season:** April-Oct. **High:** June-Aug.
On-site lodging: No. **Rental clubs:** Yes.
Walking policy: Unrestricted walking. **Range:** Yes (grass).
To obtain tee times: Call two weeks in advance with credit card. May book 48 hours in advance.
Subscriber comments: Very imaginative . . . Super use of property . . . Water on 15 of 18 holes . . . Not everyone's cup of tea . . . Can't wait to try again . . . Makes you think about your shot . . . A complete adventure in golf.

★★★ HENDERSON LAKE GOLF CLUB
PU—P.O. Box 1094, South Parkside Dr., Lethbridge (403)329-6767.
120 miles south of Calgary. **Holes:** 18. **Par:** 70/75.
Yards: 6,512/5,976. **Course rating:** 70.5/73.1. **Slope:** 120/123.
Opened: 1917. **Pace of Play rating:** 4:00. **Green fee:** $25.
Credit cards: MC, V. **Reduced fees:** Low season, Twilight, Juniors.
Caddies: No. **Golf carts:** $22 for 18 holes.
Discount golf packages: Yes. **Season:** April-Oct. **High:** May-Aug.
On-site lodging: No. **Rental clubs:** Yes.
Walking policy: Unrestricted walking. **Range:** No.
To obtain tee times: Call two days in advance.
Subscriber comments: Super pro shop, friendly staff . . . Great old track, small greens.

★★★½ HERITAGE POINTE GOLF AND COUNTRY CLUB
POINTE/DESERT/HERITAGE
R—R.R. No.1, Heritage Pointe Dr., De Winton (403)256-2002.
6 miles south of Calgary. **Holes:** 27. **Par:** 72/72/72.
Yards: 6,936/6,904/7,044. **Course rating:** 73.0/73.0/74.0.
Slope: 131/137/128.
Opened: 1992. **Pace of Play rating:** 4:30. **Green fee:** $43/48.
Credit cards: MC, V, AMEX. **Reduced fees:** Twilight, Seniors, Juniors.
Caddies: No. **Golf carts:** $12 for 18 holes.
Discount golf packages: Yes. **Season:** April-Oct. **High:** June-Aug.
On-site lodging: No. **Rental clubs:** Yes.

Walking policy: Walking at certain times. **Range:** Yes (grass).
To obtain tee times: Call one week in advance with credit cart.
Subscriber comments: Staff very friendly . . . Three great nines . . . Best clubhouse . . . Target golf course, favors good iron players . . . 27 challenging holes . . . First class for a public course, can play very tough . . . Tough walk, lots of variety.

HINTON GOLF CLUB★
PU—Hwy. 16 W., Hinton (403)865-2904.
175 miles east of Edmonton. **Holes:** 18. **Par:** 72/72.
Yards: 6,729/5,700. **Course rating:** 72.0/70.0. **Slope:** 125/N/A.
Opened: 1964. **Pace of Play rating:** N/A. **Green fee:** $23/25.
Credit cards: MC, V. **Reduced fees:** Weekdays, Twilight, Juniors.
Caddies: No. **Golf carts:** $22 for 18 holes.
Discount golf packages: Yes. **Season:** April-Oct. **High:** May-Aug.
On-site lodging: No. **Rental clubs:** Yes.
Walking policy: Unrestricted walking. **Range:** Yes (grass).
To obtain tee times: Call anytime.
Subscriber comments: New nine needs a few years to mature.

★★ INDIAN LAKES GOLF CLUB
PU—Site 2, R.R. No. 1, Winterburn (403)470-4653.
Call club for further information.
Subscriber comments: Good layout . . . Not spectacular but honest . . . Course could have lots of potential . . . Nice variety of scenic golf holes.

★★★ IRONHEAD GOLF AND COUNTRY CLUB
SP—P.O. Box 69, Wabamun (403)892-4653.
Call club for further information.
Subscriber comments: Good layout . . . Fun to play . . . Good test, use whole bag . . . Well-kept secret, outstanding value . . . Run by local Indian tribe.

★★★½ JASPER PARK LODGE GOLF COURSE
R—Box 40, Jasper (403)852-6089.
210 miles west of Edmonton. **Holes:** 18. **Par:** 71/75.
Yards: 6,598/6,037. **Course rating:** 70.5/73.5. **Slope:** 121/N/A.
Opened: 1925. **Pace of Play rating:** 4:30-5:00. **Green fee:** $36/50.
Credit cards: All major. **Reduced fees:** Low season, Twilight.
Caddies: No. **Golf carts:** $15 for 18 holes.
Discount golf packages: Yes. **Season:** April-Oct. **High:** June-Sept.
On-site lodging: Yes. **Rental clubs:** Yes.
Walking policy: Unrestricted walking. **Range:** Yes (grass).
To obtain tee times: Call anytime.
Subscriber comments: Beautiful golf course . . . Gorgeous setting . . . Great old course . . . You'll pay the price here, but these courses are worth every penny . . . The best course in the Rocky Mountains . . . Best scenery in the world . . . Old and stately course . . . Great view plus course . . . Course is potentially fabulous . . . Reconstructed bunkers near completion, returning to original Stanley Thompson form.

KANANASKIS COUNTRY GOLF CLUB
R—P.O. Box 1710, Kananaskis Village (403)591-7070.
50 miles southwest of Calgary. **Green fee:** $38.
Credit cards: MC, V, AMEX. **Reduced fees:** Twilight, Seniors, Juniors.
Caddies: No. **Golf carts:** $13 for 18 holes.
Discount golf packages: No. **Season:** May-Oct. **High:** June-Sept.
On-site lodging: Yes. **Rental clubs:** Yes.
Walking policy: Unrestricted walking. **Range:** Yes (grass).
To obtain tee times: Call up to 60 days in advance with credit card.
★★★★½ MT. KIDD COURSE
Holes: 18. **Par:** 72/72.
Yards: 7,083/5,539. **Course rating:** 72.8/71.5. **Slope:** 134/N/A.
Opened: 1983. **Pace of Play rating:** 4:30.
Subscriber comments: A must play when in Canadian Rockies, breathtaking views . . . Golf and value . . . About 30 minutes from Banff. All worth the trip. Mountain rangers you only see in books and scenery you'll never forget . . . Fantastic service . . . Best resort value in North

America . . . Crystal clear mountain streams . . . Well designed R.T. Jones
. . . Well run by well trained staff . . . Best of the Rockies! An absolute
must . . . Two jewels in the Rocky Mountains . . . Five-star service, great
price . . . Not recommended for first time or beginner golfer.

★★★★ MT. LORETTE COURSE

Holes: 18. **Par:** 72/72.
Yards: 7,102/5,429. **Course rating:** 74.1/72.0. **Slope:** 137/N/A.
Opened: 1983. **Pace of Play rating:** 4:30.
Subscriber comments: A touch easier than sister Kidd . . . Very walkable
. . . Treat you royally . . . Keeps play moving through reward systems,
must keep carts on paths . . . R.T. Jones gem in Rockies . . . Great course
but I prefer Mt. Kidd.

(SUPER VALUE)

★★★ LAKESIDE GREENS GOLF AND COUNTRY CLUB

SP—555 Lakeside Greens Dr., Chestermere (403)569-9111.
Call club for further information.
Subscriber comments: Good greens . . . Sleeper, five minutes outside
Calgary . . . Very good value, new course, will be excellent.

★★★ LAND-O-LAKES GOLF CLUB

SP—102 Fairway Dr., Coaldale (403)345-2582.
6 miles east of Lethbridge. **Holes:** 18. **Par:** 71/72.
Yards: 6,459/5,634. **Course rating:** 72.0/73.0. **Slope:** 119/126.
Opened: 1907. **Pace of Play rating:** 4:15. **Green fee:** $20/25.
Credit cards: MC, V. **Reduced fees:** Weekdays, Juniors.
Caddies: No. **Golf carts:** $20 for 18 holes.
Discount golf packages: Yes. **Season:** April-Oct. **High:** N/A.
On-site lodging: No. **Rental clubs:** Yes.
Walking policy: Unrestricted walking. **Range:** Yes (grass).
To obtain tee times: Call two days in advance.
Subscriber comments: Good staff . . . Good layout.

★★★ THE LINKS AT SPRUCE GROVE

PU—Calahoo Rd., Spruce Grove (403)962-4653.
10 miles east of Edmonton. **Holes:** 18. **Par:** 72/72.
Yards: 6,767/5,748. **Course rating:** 71.0/72.0. **Slope:** 125/N/A.
Opened: 1983. **Pace of Play rating:** 4:30. **Green fee:** $23/25.
Credit cards: MC, V. **Reduced fees:** Low season, Twilight, Seniors,
Juniors.
Caddies: No. **Golf carts:** $11 for 18 holes.
Discount golf packages: No. **Season:** April-Oct. **High:** June-Aug.
On-site lodging: No. **Rental clubs:** Yes.
Walking policy: Unrestricted walking. **Range:** Yes (grass).
To obtain tee times: Call 48 hours in advance.
Subscriber comments: Excellent staff, best public for the price in area . . .
Not for the faint of heart . . . Good layout, great condition, fun clubhouse
. . . Great staff.

★½ MCCALL LAKE GOLF COURSE

PU—2108 23rd Ave., S.W., Calgary (403)974-1805.
Call club for further information.
Subscriber comments: Best city-owned course . . . Windy, next to
airport.

★★★ MEDICINE HAT GOLF AND COUNTRY CLUB

SP—P.O. Box 232, Medicine Hat (403)527-8086.
180 miles west of Calgary. **Holes:** 18. **Par:** 72/72.
Yards: 6,612/5,606. **Course rating:** 72.5/72.5. **Slope:** 131/123.
Opened: 1933. **Pace of Play rating:** 4:30. **Green fee:** $14/27.
Credit cards: All major. **Reduced fees:** Low season, Twilight.
Caddies: No. **Golf carts:** $24 for 18 holes.
Discount golf packages: No. **Season:** April-Oct. **High:** N/A.
On-site lodging: No. **Rental clubs:** Yes.
Walking policy: Unrestricted walking. **Range:** Yes.
To obtain tee times: Call two days in advance.
Subscriber comments: Staff good, good shape . . . Fairly open course
. . . Short but well treed.

★★ OLDS GOLF CLUB

PU—R.R. No.1, Site 2, Box 13, Olds (403)556-8008.
Call club for further information.
Subscriber comments: Nice small town community course . . . Good municipal course, flat and windy.

★★★★ PARADISE CANYON GOLF AND COUNTRY CLUB

SP—185 Canyon Blvd., Lethbridge (403)381-7500.
120 miles south of Calgary. **Holes:** 18. **Par:** 71/71.
Yards: 6,810/5,282. **Course rating:** 73.1/70.6. **Slope:** 132/127.
Opened: 1992. **Pace of Play rating:** 4:30. **Green fee:** $30.
Credit cards: MC, V, AMEX. **Reduced fees:** Twilight.
Caddies: No. **Golf carts:** $24 for 18 holes.
Discount golf packages: No. **Season:** April-Nov. **High:** May-Aug.
On-site lodging: No. **Rental clubs:** Yes.
Walking policy: Unrestricted walking. **Range:** Yes (grass).
To obtain tee times: Call three days in advance.
Subscriber comments: One of my best rounds of golf with borrowed clubs and running shoes . . . Entertaining layout, combination of desert and valley holes . . . Rewards are big for good shots, misses kill you . . . Fantastic value with all-day green fee . . . Always windy but that's part of the fun . . . Oasis in the desert . . . Beautiful cliffs in a beautiful canyon . . . Spectacular par 3 cut out of canyon wall.

(GREAT VALUE)

PHEASANTBACK GOLF AND COUNTRY CLUB★

PU—P.O. Box 1621, Stettler (403)742-4653.
70 miles east of Red Deer. **Holes:** 18. **Par:** 71/71.
Yards: 6,104/4,631. **Course rating:** N/A. **Slope:** N/A.
Opened: 1995. **Pace of Play rating:** 4:00. **Green fee:** $20.
Credit cards: MC, V. **Reduced fees:** Low season, Resort guests, Twilight, Seniors, Juniors.
Caddies: No. **Golf carts:** $10 for 18 holes.
Discount golf packages: Yes. **Season:** April-Oct. **High:** May-June.
On-site lodging: No. **Rental clubs:** Yes.
Walking policy: Unrestricted walking. **Range:** Yes (grass).
To obtain tee times: Call one week in advance.

PICTURE BUTTE GOLF AND WINTER CLUB★

SP—P.O. Box 359, Picture Butte (403)732-4157.
20 miles north of Lethbridge. **Holes:** 18. **Par:** 72/73.
Yards: 6,390/5,127. **Course rating:** 70.5/71.5. **Slope:** N/A.
Opened: 1963. **Pace of Play rating:** 4:00. **Green fee:** $19/23.
Credit cards: MC, V. **Reduced fees:** Low season, Twilight, Seniors, Juniors.
Caddies: No. **Golf carts:** $23 for 18 holes.
Discount golf packages: No. **Season:** March-Oct. **High:** May-Sept.
On-site lodging: No. **Rental clubs:** Yes.
Walking policy: Unrestricted walking. **Range:** Yes (grass).
To obtain tee times: Call two days in advance.

★★★ PONOKA COMMUNITY GOLF COURSE

PU—P.O. Box 4145, Ponoka (403)783-4626.
Call club for further information.
Subscriber comments: Here's where you're made to feel at home . . . One of the best-kept secrets in central Alberta . . . Hidden gem . . . Very well kept, mature course.

(FRUGAL PICK)

★★½ THE RANCH GOLF AND COUNTRY CLUB

SP—52516 Range Rd. 262, Spruce Grove (403)470-4700.
3 miles west of Edmonton. **Holes:** 18. **Par:** 71/71.
Yards: 6,526/5,082. **Course rating:** 70.4/70.7. **Slope:** 129/124.
Opened: 1989. **Pace of Play rating:** 4:30. **Green fee:** $24/29.
Credit cards: MC, V, AMEX. **Reduced fees:** Weekdays, Low season, Twilight, Seniors, Juniors.
Caddies: No. **Golf carts:** $12 for 18 holes.
Discount golf packages: No. **Season:** April-Oct. **High:** May-Aug.
On-site lodging: No. **Rental clubs:** Yes.

Walking policy: Unrestricted walking. **Range:** Yes.
To obtain tee times: Call 48 hours in advance.
Subscriber comments: Some design problems but many interesting holes
. . . Improved drastically . . . Klondike Days Golf Classic played here . . .
Good course with lots of variety, suits all players.

★★★½ REDWOOD MEADOWS GOLF AND COUNTRY CLUB

SP—Box 1 Site 7 R.R. No.1, Calgary (403)949-3663.
Holes: 18. **Par:** 72/73.
Yards: 7,000/6,108. **Course rating:** 72.7/74.0. **Slope:** 129/134.
Opened: 1976. **Pace of Play rating:** 4:30. **Green fee:** $35.
Credit cards: MC, V, AMEX. **Reduced fees:** Juniors.
Caddies: No. **Golf carts:** $24 for 18 holes.
Discount golf packages: No. **Season:** April-Oct. **High:** May-Sept.
On-site lodging: No. **Rental clubs:** Yes.
Walking policy: Unrestricted walking. **Range:** Yes (grass).
To obtain tee times: Call three days in advance for weekdays only.
Subscriber comments: Staff ultra-courteous. No. 15 ranks with best par
3s in western. Canada . . . Mint condition . . . Similar feel to Kananaskis
courses . . . Best fairways in Alberta . . . Limited public play.

★★½ RIVER BEND GOLF COURSE

PU—P.O. Box 157, Red Deer (403)343-8311.
79 miles south of Edmonton. **Holes:** 18. **Par:** 72/72.
Yards: 6,451/5,551. **Course rating:** 71.5/70.5. **Slope:** N/A.
Opened: 1986. **Pace of Play rating:** 4:30. **Green fee:** $23.
Credit cards: MC, V. **Reduced fees:** Weekdays, Twilight.
Caddies: No. **Golf carts:** $22 for 18 holes.
Discount golf packages: No. **Season:** April-Oct. **High:** June-Aug.
On-site lodging: No. **Rental clubs:** Yes.
Walking policy: Unrestricted walking. **Range:** Yes (grass).
To obtain tee times: Call two days in advance.
Subscriber comments: Beautiful water holes . . . Very heavily used . . .
Easy to walk, suitable for all, polite, friendly staff . . . Good food at great
prices . . . Built in bend of river.

★★½ RIVERSIDE GOLF COURSE

PU—8630 Rowland Rd., Edmonton (403)496-8702.
Holes: 18. **Par:** 71/75.
Yards: 6,306/5,984. **Course rating:** 71.0/74.0. **Slope:** 114/N/A.
Opened: 1951. **Pace of Play rating:** N/A. **Green fee:** $20/23.
Credit cards: MC, V. **Reduced fees:** Low season.
Caddies: No. **Golf carts:** $20 for 18 holes.
Discount golf packages: No. **Season:** April-Oct. **High:** May-Aug.
On-site lodging: No. **Rental clubs:** Yes.
Walking policy: Unrestricted walking. **Range:** No.
To obtain tee times: Call two days in advance.
Subscriber comments: Good public course with nice location along river
in center of city . . . The very best public course in Edmonton . . . Always
well taken care of . . . Seems straight forward but at least one hole will get
you.

★½ SHAGANAPPI POINT GOLF COURSE

PU—P.O. Box 2100, Station M, Calgary (403)974-1810.
Call club for further information.
Subscriber comments: Easy to walk on, 3½-hour rounds common . . .
For weekend golfer . . . Municipal course . . . Very busy.

★½ SHAW-NEE SLOPES GOLF COURSE

SP—820 146 Ave. S.W., Calgary (403)256-1444.
Holes: 18. **Par:** 72/73.
Yards: 6,478/5,691. **Course rating:** 70.5/71.9. **Slope:** 124/126.
Opened: 1965. **Pace of Play rating:** 4:15. **Green fee:** $27/32.
Credit cards: MC, V. **Reduced fees:** Weekdays, Twilight, Seniors.
Caddies: No. **Golf carts:** $24 for 18 holes.
Discount golf packages: No. **Season:** April-Nov. **High:** June-Aug.
On-site lodging: No. **Rental clubs:** Yes.

Walking policy: Unrestricted walking. **Range:** Yes.
To obtain tee times: Call up to four days in advance.
Subscriber comments: An easy, fun day can be had here . . . "Sorry about the window" . . . Lots of homes . . . A good outing, enjoyable . . . Good for all caliber of players.

SHERWOOD PARK GOLF COURSE★
PU—52321 Range Rd. 233, Sherwood Park (403)467-5060.
5 miles southeast of Edmonton. **Holes:** 18. **Par:** 72/70.
Yards: 6,045/5,859. **Course rating:** 67.3/69.0. **Slope:** 112/N/A.
Opened: 1960. **Pace of Play rating:** 4:30. **Green fee:** $18/22.
Credit cards: MC, V. **Reduced fees:** Weekdays, Low season.
Caddies: No. **Golf carts:** $12 for 18 holes.
Discount golf packages: No. **Season:** April-Oct. **High:** May-Sept.
On-site lodging: No. **Rental clubs:** Yes.
Walking policy: Unrestricted walking. **Range:** Yes (grass).
To obtain tee times: Call Wednesday for weekend tee time. Call two days in advance for weekdays.

SPRUCE MEADOWS GOLF AND COUNTRY CLUB★
PU—P.O. Box 548, Sexsmith (403)568-4653.
12 miles north of Grand Prairie. **Holes:** 18. **Par:** 71/72.
Yards: 6,527/5,909. **Course rating:** 73.0/73.0. **Slope:** 117/N/A.
Opened: 1982. **Pace of Play rating:** N/A. **Green fee:** $16/20.
Credit cards: MC, V. **Reduced fees:** Weekdays, Low season, Resort guests.
Caddies: No. **Golf carts:** $19 for 18 holes.
Discount golf packages: Yes. **Season:** April-Oct. **High:** N/A.
On-site lodging: No. **Rental clubs:** Yes.
Walking policy: Unrestricted walking. **Range:** Yes (grass).
To obtain tee times: Call anytime.

★½ VICTORIA GOLF COURSE
PU—12130 River Rd., Edmonton (403)496-4710.
Call club for furthr information.
Subscriber comments: Busiest course in Canada . . . Nice tradition to it . . . Oldest muny course in Canada . . . In very good shape for a very busy public course . . . Nice practice facilities.

★★½ WINTERGREEN GOLF AND COUNTRY CLUB

SP—P.O. Bag No. 2, Bragg Creek (403)949-3333.
29 miles west of Calgary. **Holes:** 18. **Par:** 71/71.
Yards: 6,624/5,152. **Course rating:** 72.0/69.9. **Slope:** N/A/125.
Opened: 1991. **Pace of Play rating:** 4:00. **Green fee:** $32/35.
Credit cards: MC, V. **Reduced fees:** Weekdays, Low season, Twilight, Seniors, Juniors.
Caddies: No. **Golf carts:** $11 for 18 holes.
Discount golf packages: No. **Season:** April-Oct. **High:** June-Sept.
On-site lodging: No. **Rental clubs:** Yes.
Walking policy: Unrestricted walking. **Range:** Yes (grass).
To obtain tee times: Call four days in advance.
Subscriber comments: Tougher than you think . . . Needs a few years for fairways to grow . . . Drainage problems . . . Good potential . . . Interesting holes . . . Be straight and true, potential to be great, especially when dry.

★★★★ WOLF CREEK GOLF RESORT
WEST/EAST/SOUTH
R—R.R. No. 3 Site 10, Ponoka (403)783-6050.
70 miles south of Edmonton. **Holes:** 27. **Par:** 70/70/70.
Yards: 6,516/6,818/6,730. **Course rating:** 74.0/75.0/74.0. **Slope:** N/A.
Opened: 1984. **Pace of Play rating:** 4:30. **Green fee:** $32.
Credit cards: MC, V, AMEX. **Reduced fees:** Seniors, Juniors.
Caddies: Yes. **Golf carts:** $24 for 18 holes.
Discount golf packages: No. **Season:** April-Oct. **High:** June-Sept.
On-site lodging: No. **Rental clubs:** Yes.

Walking policy: Unrestricted walking. **Range:** Yes (grass).
To obtain tee times: Call anytime with credit card.
Subscriber comments: Pay your health care cuz the Wolf will bite you
. . . Great links course, home of Alberta Open . . . Bring all your clubs,
you'll need them . . . Toughest layout in Alberta . . . Memorable in all
respects . . . All three nines are fun, interesting and challenging . . . Nice
course with rustic look . . . When the wind blows the Wolf howls! . . .
Very different place, you gotta play once . . . Treated superbly by staff.

BRITISH COLUMBIA

★★½ ARBUTUS RIDGE GOLF AND COUNTRY CLUB
SP—3515 Telegraph Rd., Cobble Hill (604)743-5000.
18 miles north of Victoria. **Holes:** 18. **Par:** 72/72.
Yards: 6,478/5,241. **Course rating:** 72.3/70.2. **Slope:** 134/122.
Opened: 1988. **Pace of Play rating:** 4:30. **Green fee:** $22/30.
Credit cards: MC, V, AMEX. **Reduced fees:** Low season, Twilight,
Juniors.
Caddies: No. **Golf carts:** $25 for 18 holes.
Discount golf packages: Yes. **Season:** Year-round. **High:** May-Sept.
On-site lodging: No. **Rental clubs:** Yes.
Walking policy: Unrestricted walking. **Range:** Yes.
To obtain tee times: Call four days in advance.
Subscriber comments: Scenery, wildlife, clubhouse, would play again
. . . Houses too close to course . . . Hilly, tight course, long walks between
holes . . . Spectacular scenery.

★★ BELMONT GOLF COURSE
SP—22555 Telegraph Trail, Langley (604)888-9898.
20 miles east of Vancouver. **Holes:** 18. **Par:** 70/70.
Yards: 6,416/4,951. **Course rating:** 70.5/68.1. **Slope:** 122/114.
Opened: 1993. **Pace of Play rating:** 4:00-4:30. **Green fee:** $25/36.
Credit cards: MC, V. **Reduced fees:** Weekdays, Low season, Twilight,
Seniors, Juniors.
Caddies: No. **Golf carts:** $24 for 18 holes.
Discount golf packages: No. **Season:** Year-round. **High:** July-Aug.
On-site lodging: No. **Rental clubs:** Yes.
Walking policy: Unrestricted walking. **Range:** No.
To obtain tee times: Call three days in advance at 9 a.m.
Subscriber comments: Too many par 3s (six) . . . New course, will
improve when trees mature . . . Very playable new course . . . Bent grass,
nice to play . . . Fun golf course.

★★★★ BIG SKY GOLF AND COUNTRY CLUB
R—Airport Rd., Pemberton (604)894-6106, (800)668-7900.
85 miles north of Vancouver. **Holes:** 18. **Par:** 72/72.
Yards: 7,001/5,208. **Course rating:** 73.5/N/A. **Slope:** 133/N/A.
Opened: 1994. **Pace of Play rating:** 4:15. **Green fee:** $70/80.
Credit cards: MC, V, AMEX. **Reduced fees:** Weekdays, Low season,
Twilight, Juniors.
Caddies: Yes. **Golf carts:** $10 for 18 holes.
Discount golf packages: Yes. **Season:** April-Oct. **High:** June-Sept.
On-site lodging: No. **Rental clubs:** Yes.
Walking policy: Unrestricted walking. **Range:** Yes (grass).
To obtain tee times: Call.
Subscriber comments: Tough to get to but worth the trip . . . Great
practice facility, beautiful location . . . Great scenery and setting.

★★★½ CASTLEGAR GOLF CLUB
PU—P.O. Box 3430, Castlegar (604)365-5006, (800)666-0324.
180 miles north of Spokane, WA. **Holes:** 18. **Par:** 72/76.
Yards: 6,677/6,178. **Course rating:** 72.6/75.9. **Slope:** 127/133.
Opened: 1966. **Pace of Play rating:** 4:00-4:30. **Green fee:** $24/27.
Credit cards: MC, V. **Reduced fees:** Twilight.
Caddies: No. **Golf carts:** $25 for 18 holes.
Discount golf packages: Yes. **Season:** April-Oct. **High:** July-Sept.
On-site lodging: No. **Rental clubs:** Yes.

GREAT VALUE

Walking policy: Unrestricted walking. **Range:** Yes.
To obtain tee times: Outside 60 miles may call anytime within reason.
Subscriber comments: Beautiful mountain course. Excellent pro shop staff . . . One of the best in area . . . Homey attitude . . . Bear resting on 11th fairway! . . . A jewel, you'll want to play this course again and again . . . A must stop . . . Excellent established condition.

★★★★½ CHATEAU WHISTLER GOLF CLUB

R—4612 Blackcomb Way, Whistler (604)938-2095.
75 miles north of Vancouver. **Holes:** 18. **Par:** 72/72.
Yards: 6,635/5,157. **Course rating:** 73.0/70.0. **Slope:** 142/124.
Opened: 1993. **Pace of Play rating:** N/A. **Green fee:** $70/105.
Credit cards: MC, V, AMEX. **Reduced fees:** Weekdays, Low season, Twilight.
Caddies: No. **Golf carts:** Included in Green Fee.
Discount golf packages: Yes. **Season:** May-Oct. **High:** June-Sept.
On-site lodging: Yes. **Rental clubs:** Yes.
Walking policy: Mandatory cart. **Range:** No.
To obtain tee times: Call seven days a week. Resort guests may book within same calendar year.
Subscriber comments: A must on any golf trip, what beauty . . . Breathtaking scenery, superb layout, maybe best in western Canada . . . Worthy of Tour event . . . A must course with good staff . . . Absolutely gorgeous scenery up the mountain and down again . . . This one is a jewel . . . Great resort course in great resort area.

★★★ CHRISTINA LAKE GOLF CLUB

SP—339 2nd Ave., Christina Lake (604)447-9313.
12 miles west of Grand Forks. **Holes:** 18. **Par:** 72/73.
Yards: 6,615/5,725. **Course rating:** 71.5/71.3. **Slope:** 125/123.
Opened: 1963. **Pace of Play rating:** 4:00. **Green fee:** $24/30.
Credit cards: MC, V. **Reduced fees:** Twilight, Juniors.
Caddies: No. **Golf carts:** N/A.
Discount golf packages: Yes. **Season:** April-Oct. **High:** July-Sept.
On-site lodging: No. **Rental clubs:** Yes.
Walking policy: Unrestricted walking. **Range:** Yes (grass).
To obtain tee times: Out of town may book tee times in advance.
Subscriber comments: Great combination . . . Mums the word . . . Great holiday area as well . . . Huge trees . . . Good quality course with great value . . . Hidden little jewel. A joy for all level golfers . . . Country-style golf course, away from city . . . Nice walk, long, established course.

★★★½ CORDOVA BAY GOLF COURSE

PU—5333 Cordova Bay R., Victoria (604)658-4075.
Holes: 18. **Par:** 72/72.
Yards: 6,642/5,269. **Course rating:** 71.9/72.3. **Slope:** 128/129.
Opened: 1991. **Pace of Play rating:** 4:30. **Green fee:** $38/42.
Credit cards: MC, V, AMEX. **Reduced fees:** Weekdays, Low season, Twilight, Juniors.
Caddies: No. **Golf carts:** $23 for 18 holes.
Discount golf packages: No. **Season:** Year-round. **High:** May-Sept.
On-site lodging: No. **Rental clubs:** Yes.
Walking policy: Unrestricted walking. **Range:** Yes.
To obtain tee times: Call up to one year in advance with credit card.
Subscriber comments: Deer and eagles in view . . . The best public course in Victoria . . . Challenging yet forgiving . . . Good walking course . . . Drainage is excellent . . . Canadian Tour course . . . No tough hills so walking is great.

★★★★ CROWN ISLE GOLF CLUB

SP—Clubhouse Rd., Courtenay (604)338-6811, (800)668-3244.
100 miles northwest of Vancouver. **Holes:** 18. **Par:** 72/72.
Yards: 7,024/5,169. **Course rating:** 74.2/N/A. **Slope:** 133/N/A.
Opened: 1993. **Pace of Play rating:** 4:00. **Green fee:** $25/35.
Credit cards: MC, V. **Reduced fees:** Low season, Twilight, Juniors.
Caddies: No. **Golf carts:** $25 for 18 holes.
Discount golf packages: Yes. **Season:** Year-round. **High:** April-Oct.

On-site lodging: No. **Rental clubs:** Yes.
Walking policy: Unrestricted walking. **Range:** Yes (grass).
To obtain tee times: Call pro shop.
Subscriber comments: Lots of O.B. because of housing development . . .
Palm Springs' best has come to British Columbia . . . Good walking. Use
every club in bag . . . Country club quality, layout and conditioning . . .
Helpful staff . . . Best practice facilities I ever used in North America . . .
Gem on Vancouver Island.

★★½ DUNCAN LAKES GOLF AND COUNTRY CLUB
PU—Hwy. 18, Duncan (604)746-6789.
35 miles north of Victoria. **Holes:** 18. **Par:** 72/72.
Yards: 6,698/5,483. **Course rating:** 73.1/67.8. **Slope:** 130/117.
Opened: 1992. **Pace of Play rating:** N/A. **Green fee:** $15/28.
Credit cards: MC, V. **Reduced fees:** Weekdays, Low season, Resort
guests, Twilight, Juniors.
Caddies: No. **Golf carts:** $22 for 18 holes.
Discount golf packages: No. **Season:** Year-round. **High:** June-Aug.
On-site lodging: No. **Rental clubs:** Yes.
Walking policy: Unrestricted walking. **Range:** Yes (grass).
To obtain tee times: Call up to seven days in advance.
Subscriber comments: Course has excellent potential . . . Still maturing
. . . A fair nine- holer redesigned to a great 18 . . . Best cold beer around.

★★★ EAGLE POINT GOLF AND COUNTRY CLUB
PU—8888 Barnhartvale Rd., Kamloops (604)573-2453.
225 miles north of Vancouver. **Holes:** 18. **Par:** 72/72.
Yards: 6,762/5,315. **Course rating:** 73.4/70.6. **Slope:** 137/126.
Opened: 1991. **Pace of Play rating:** 4:00-4:30. **Green fee:** $35/38.
Credit cards: MC, V, AMEX, Interact Direct Payment. **Reduced fees:**
Weekdays, Low season, Resort guests, Twilight, Seniors, Juniors.
Caddies: No. **Golf carts:** $26 for 18 holes.
Discount golf packages: Yes. **Season:** March-Oct. **High:** April-Sept.
On-site lodging: No. **Rental clubs:** Yes.
Walking policy: Unrestricted walking. **Range:** Yes (grass).
To obtain tee times: Call pro shop.
Subscriber comments: On a par with any in the Northwest . . . Through
natural ponderosa pine forest . . . User-friendly course . . . Key to this
course is hitting landing areas . . . A fun course in the hills . . . Uses whole
bag . . . Carolina golf in B.C. interior . . . Hilly.

★½ EAGLECREST GOLF CLUB
SP—2035 Island Hwy. W., Qualicum Beach (604)752-6311, (800)567-1320.
25 miles north of Nanaimo. **Holes:** 18. **Par:** 71/71.
Yards: 6,350/5,430. **Course rating:** 70.6/71.0. **Slope:** 122/123.
Opened: 1971. **Pace of Play rating:** 4:15. **Green fee:** $20/30.
Credit cards: MC, V. **Reduced fees:** Low season, Resort guests,
Twilight, Juniors.
Caddies: No. **Golf carts:** $25 for 18 holes.
Discount golf packages: Yes. **Season:** Year-round. **High:** May-Oct.
On-site lodging: No. **Rental clubs:** Yes.
Walking policy: Unrestricted walking. **Range:** Yes.
To obtain tee times: Call anytime or book through hotel. Credit card
may be needed to guarantee time.
Subscriber comments: Courteous staff. Narrow fairways . . . Housing
encroaches on course . . . Long walk between holes . . . All shots explored.

★★½ FAIRMONT HOT SPRINGS RESORT
MOUNTAINSIDE COURSE
R—P.O. Box 10, Fairmont Hot Springs (604)345-6514, (800)663-4979.
200 miles west of Calgary. **Holes:** 18. **Par:** 72/72.
Yards: 6,505/5,554. **Course rating:** 71.1/72.5. **Slope:** 127/125.
Opened: 1963. **Pace of Play rating:** 4:30. **Green fee:** $35/38.
Credit cards: All major. **Reduced fees:** Weekdays, Low season, Resort
guests, Twilight, Juniors.
Caddies: No. **Golf carts:** $22 for 18 holes.
Discount golf packages: Yes. **Season:** March-Oct. **High:** May-Sept.

On-site lodging: Yes. **Rental clubs:** Yes.
Walking policy: Unrestricted walking. **Range:** No.
To obtain tee times: Call pro shop.
Subscriber comments: The toughest track in Alberta . . . Great scenery, well laid out. I would return . . . Beautiful setting . . . Hillside golf course, scenic, older course . . . Treated like kings by staff.

★★★½ FAIRVIEW MOUNTAIN GOLF CLUB

(GREAT VALUE)

SP—Old Golf Course Rd., Oliver (604)498-3521.
70 miles south of Kelowna. **Holes:** 18. **Par:** 72/73.
Yards: 6,557/5,382. **Course rating:** 71.3/71.0. **Slope:** 123/131.
Opened: 1991. **Pace of Play rating:** 4:15. **Green fee:** $25/33.
Credit cards: MC, V, AMEX. **Reduced fees:** Low season, Twilight, Juniors.
Caddies: No. **Golf carts:** $13 for 18 holes.
Discount golf packages: Yes. **Season:** March-Oct. **High:** June-Sept.
On-site lodging: No. **Rental clubs:** Yes.
Walking policy: Unrestricted walking. **Range:** Yes.
To obtain tee times: Call five days in advance.
Subscriber comments: British Columbia's hidden secret . . . Mountain golf at its best, staff excellent . . . Pro shop very friendly . . . Best-kept secret in Western Canada, spectacular holes . . . Excellent test of golf . . . Best value of any course we have played . . . Hilly layout, fast pace, no waits.

★★★ FAIRWINDS GOLF AND COUNTRY CLUB

R—3730 Fairwinds Dr., Nanoose Bay (604)468-7666.
Call club for further information.
Subscriber comments: Great clubhouse . . . Hilly, seaside course . . . Fun place . . . Staff is easygoing . . . Just seeing the eagles makes playing here worthwhile. Good resort course . . . Very nice layout . . . Golf, swim, fish in same day.

★½ FORT LANGLEY GOLF COURSE

SP—9782 McKinnon Crescent, Fort Langley (604)888-5911.
14 miles northwest of Langley. **Holes:** 18. **Par:** 70/75.
Yards: 6,428/5,681. **Course rating:** 70.0/71.5. **Slope:** 115/126.
Opened: 1968. **Pace of Play rating:** 4:30. **Green fee:** $29/34.
Credit cards: MC, V. **Reduced fees:** Weekdays, Low season, Twilight, Seniors, Juniors.
Caddies: No. **Golf carts:** $25 for 18 holes.
Discount golf packages: No. **Season:** Year-round. **High:** May-Sept.
On-site lodging: No. **Rental clubs:** Yes.
Walking policy: Unrestricted walking. **Range:** Yes.
To obtain tee times: Call one week in advance for weekdays. Call Thursday from 7 a.m. for weekends.
Subscriber comments: Good layout on low, rolling land . . . Has potential . . . Reasonable course, good price . . . Well established, nice surroundings.

★½ FRASERVIEW GOLF COURSE

PU—7800 Vivian St., Vancouver (604)280-8633.
Holes: 18. **Par:** 71/74.
Yards: 6,346/6,058. **Course rating:** 69.8/72.0. **Slope:** 118/121.
Opened: 1960. **Pace of Play rating:** 4:00-4:30. **Green fee:** $30.
Credit cards: MC, V. **Reduced fees:** Twilight, Seniors, Juniors.
Caddies: No. **Golf carts:** $24 for 18 holes.
Discount golf packages: No. **Season:** Year-round. **High:** April-Oct.
On-site lodging: No. **Rental clubs:** Yes.
Walking policy: Unrestricted walking. **Range:** Yes.
To obtain tee times: Call two days in advance at noon for weekdays. Call Thursdays at noon for weekends.
Subscriber comments: Don't feed coyotes . . . Busiest course in Canada . . . Traditional tree-lined course . . . Redesign scheduled for 1997 . . . Right in the city . . . Good test on municipal course.

★★ FURRY CREEK GOLF AND COUNTRY CLUB

R—Hwy. 99, P.O. Box 1000, Lions Bay (604)922-9461.

27 miles north of Vancouver. **Holes:** 18. **Par:** 72/70.
Yards: 6,184/4,525. **Course rating:** 72.1/N/A. **Slope:** 136/N/A.
Opened: 1993. **Pace of Play rating:** 4:30–5:00. **Green fee:** $60/80.
Credit cards: MC, V, AMEX, Diners, JCB. **Reduced fees:** Weekdays,
Low season, Resort guests, Twilight, Seniors, Juniors.
Caddies: No. **Golf carts:** Included in Green Fee.
Discount golf packages: Yes. **Season:** March–Nov. **High:** July–Sept.
On-site lodging: No. **Rental clubs:** Yes.
Walking policy: Mandatory cart. **Range:** Yes.
To obtain tee times: Call ten days in advance.
Subscriber comments: Best golf value and challenge in the Pacific
Northwest . . . Target golf . . . Spectacular ocean views . . . Built on the
side of a mountain . . . Mountain course, novelty holes . . . Not a typical
design.

★★★★ GALLAGHER'S CANYON GOLF AND COUNTRY CLUB
CANYON COURSE

SP—4320 Gallagher's Dr. W., Kelowna (604)861-4240.

250 miles north of Vancouver. **Holes:** 18. **Par:** 72/73.
Yards: 6,890/5,505. **Course rating:** 73.5/73.8. **Slope:** 136/131.
Opened: 1980. **Pace of Play rating:** 4:30. **Green fee:** $44.
Credit cards: MC, V. **Reduced fees:** Twilight, Juniors.
Caddies: No. **Golf carts:** $25 for 18 holes.
Discount golf packages: Yes. **Season:** April–Oct. **High:** May–Sept.
On-site lodging: No. **Rental clubs:** Yes.
Walking policy: Unrestricted walking. **Range:** Yes (grass).
To obtain tee times: Call as far in advance as you like within same
calendar year.
Also has 9-hole par-32 course.
Subscriber comments: Good layout . . . Hosted Canadian Amateur in
1988 . . . Best course in Kelowna . . . Always play when I'm in area, must
play . . . One of B.C.'s best . . . Great layout for all levels . . . Fun, fun,
fun all day . . . Hilly . . . Many elevated tee boxes . . . My favorite in the
area.

★★★½ GOLDEN GOLF AND COUNTRY CLUB

SP—P.O. Box 1615, Golden (604)344-2700.
Call club for further information.
Subscriber comments: 11th hole is outstanding . . . Best value in the west
. . . Friendly people . . . Best-kept secret in B.C. . . . A must to play . . .
New back nine by Les Furber is great . . . A new gem in the Okanagan . . .
Watch out for bears . . . Can be walked, snack shop great.

★★★½ HARVEST GOLF CLUB

R—2725 KLO Rd., Kelowna (604)862-3103, (800)257-8577.

200 miles northeast of Vancouver. **Holes:** 18. **Par:** 72/72.
Yards: 7,104/5,454. **Course rating:** 73.0/61.1. **Slope:** 126/N/A.
Opened: 1994. **Pace of Play rating:** 4:15. **Green fee:** $45/55.
Credit cards: MC, V, AMEX. **Reduced fees:** Low season, Resort guests,
Twilight, Juniors.
Caddies: No. **Golf carts:** $55 for 18 holes.
Discount golf packages: Yes. **Season:** March–Oct. **High:** May–Sept.
On-site lodging: No. **Rental clubs:** Yes.
Walking policy: Unrestricted walking. **Range:** Yes (grass).
To obtain tee times: Call from November 1 for entire following season.
Subscriber comments: The best in B.C., in the middle of apple orchard
. . . Most pleasant staff I have ever met. Lemonade coolers on course . . .
Great practice facility . . . Nice layout, no trouble . . . Immaculately
groomed, vacuumed fairways . . . Great service.

★★★★ KELOWNA SPRINGS GOLF CLUB

R—480 Penno Rd., Kelowna (604)765-8511.

Call club for further information.

Subscriber comments: Good facilities . . . Manager made us very welcomed . . . Fun to play . . . Short but great conditioning . . . Nice, flat course, many hazards but wide enough to steer clear.

★★★½ KOKANEE SPRINGS GOLF RESORT

R—Box 96, Crawford Bay (604)227-9362, (800)979-7999.

120 miles north of Spokane, WA. **Holes:** 18. **Par:** 71/74.

Yards: 6,537/5,747. **Course rating:** 72.8/74.6. **Slope:** 143/138.

Opened: 1967. **Pace of Play rating:** 5:00. **Green fee:** $39.

Credit cards: MC, V, AMEX. **Reduced fees:** Resort guests, Twilight, Juniors.

Caddies: No. **Golf carts:** N/A.

Discount golf packages: Yes. **Season:** April-Oct. **High:** July-Sept.

On-site lodging: Yes. **Rental clubs:** Yes.

Walking policy: Unrestricted walking. **Range:** Yes (grass).

To obtain tee times: Call 800 number.

Subscriber comments: Best course I played . . . Some of most scenic holes in Northwest . . . View is out of this world . . . Wish it could be kept a secret . . . Golf at its best . . . A "10" all the way . . . Play in July and pick cherries from the cherry trees . . . Heaven in a cove . . . Beautiful place to spend a quiet week . . . Could use better traps . . . Outstanding golf holes . . . Awesome.

THE LONE WOLF GOLF CLUB★

PU—P.O. Box 300, Taylor (604)789 -3711.

12 miles from Fort St. John. **Holes:** 18. **Par:** 72/73.

Yards: 6,817/5,968. **Course rating:** 72.5/68.5. **Slope:** N/A.

Opened: 1995. **Pace of Play rating:** 4:00. **Green fee:** $18/22.

Credit cards: MC, V, AMEX, Debit Card. **Reduced fees:** Weekdays, Low season.

Caddies: No. **Golf carts:** $20 for 18 holes.

Discount golf packages: Yes. **Season:** April-Oct. **High:** June-Aug.

On-site lodging: No. **Rental clubs:** Yes.

Walking policy: Unrestricted walking. **Range:** Yes (grass).

To obtain tee times: Call one day in advance.

Formerly known as Taylor Golf and Country Club.

★★½ MAYFAIR LAKES GOLF AND COUNTRY CLUB

SP—5460 N. 7 Rd., Richmond (604)276-0505.

7 miles south of Vancouver. **Holes:** 18. **Par:** 71/72.

Yards: 6,641/5,277. **Course rating:** 73.0/71.0. **Slope:** 123/123.

Opened: 1989. **Pace of Play rating:** 4:30. **Green fee:** $40/45.

Credit cards: MC, V, AMEX. **Reduced fees:** Weekdays, Low season, Twilight, Seniors, Juniors.

Caddies: No. **Golf carts:** $28 for 18 holes.

Discount golf packages: No. **Season:** Year-round. **High:** April-Oct.

On-site lodging: No. **Rental clubs:** Yes.

Walking policy: Unrestricted walking. **Range:** Yes (grass).

To obtain tee times: Call two days in advance at 9 a.m. for weekdays and on Friday 9 a.m. for weekends.

Subscriber comments: A different course when wind blows . . . Bring your best game . . . Four sets of tees . . . Site of Canadian Tour's Pacific Open . . . Tight . . . Flat course with lots of lakes . . . 14 water holes . . . Links style, plays longer than yardage . . . Greens OK and getting better.

MEADOW GARDENS GOLF CLUB★

SP—19675 Meadow Garden Way, Pitt Meadows (604)465-5474.

12 miles east of Vancouver. **Holes:** 18. **Par:** 72/72.

Yards: 7,041/5,519. **Course rating:** 74.7/72.8. **Slope:** 134/130.

Opened: 1994. **Pace of Play rating:** 4:30. **Green fee:** $45/55.

Credit cards: MC, V, AMEX. **Reduced fees:** Twilight, Seniors, Juniors.

Caddies: No. **Golf carts:** $30 for 18 holes.

Discount golf packages: No. **Season:** Year-round. **High:** April-Oct.

On-site lodging: No. **Rental clubs:** Yes.

Walking policy: Unrestricted walking. **Range:** Yes (grass).
To obtain tee times: Call seven days in advance.

★★★½ MORNINGSTAR GOLF CLUB
SP—525 Lowry's Rd., Parksville (604)248-8161.
Call club for further information.
Subscriber comments: Great Les Furber layout . . . Conditioning could improve. Great otherwise . . . Long . . . Lots of wildlife . . . Pretty course . . . Long walks from green to next tee . . . Use all the clubs . . . Host to two CPGA events . . . Lots of variety.

NORTHVIEW GOLF AND COUNTRY CLUB
PU—6857 168th St., Surrey (604)576-4653.
18 miles southeast of Vancouver. **Green fee:** $40/45.
Credit cards: MC, V, AMEX. **Reduced fees:** Weekdays, Low season, Twilight, Seniors, Juniors.
Caddies: No. **Golf carts:** $13.40 for 18 holes.
Discount golf packages: No. **Season:** Year-round. **High:** April-Sept.
On-site lodging: No. **Rental clubs:** Yes.
Walking policy: Unrestricted walking. **Range:** Yes (grass).
To obtain tee times: Call three days in advance at 9 a.m.
CANAL COURSE★
Holes: 18. **Par:** 72/72.
Yards: 7,191/5,394. **Course rating:** N/A. **Slope:** N/A.
Opened: 1995. **Pace of Play rating:** 4:30-5:00.
★★★★ **RIDGE COURSE**
Holes: 18. **Par:** 72/72.
Yards: 6,900/5,131. **Course rating:** 73.4/N/A. **Slope:** 139/N/A.
Opened: 1994. **Pace of Play rating:** 4:30-5:00.
Subscriber comments: Palmer course is very good from word go . . . One word describes, "class" . . . Eyestopper clubhouse, biggest practice green . . . Excellent service . . . Tough opening holes . . . Second 18 opened . . . Very narrow in places . . . Wildflowers . . . Outstanding 18th hole . . . Best new course in the area . . . What a great layout for all players.

★★★½ OLYMPIC VIEW GOLF CLUB
PU—643 Latoria Rd., Victoria (604)474-3671.
Holes: 18. **Par:** 72/71.
Yards: 6,513/5,220. **Course rating:** 73.1/70.5. **Slope:** 142/124.
Opened: 1990. **Pace of Play rating:** 4:15. **Green fee:** $32/48.
Credit cards: MC, V, AMEX. **Reduced fees:** Weekdays, Low season, Twilight, Juniors.
Caddies: No. **Golf carts:** $25 for 18 holes.
Discount golf packages: Yes. **Season:** Year-round. **High:** April-Oct.
On-site lodging: No. **Rental clubs:** Yes.
Walking policy: Unrestricted walking. **Range:** Yes.
To obtain tee times: Call three days in advance or reserve up to three months in advance with credit card.
Subscriber comments: Worth the trip to the island . . . Fantastic waterfalls . . . Beautiful location . . . Real target golf . . . Super service and facilities . . . Some very tight holes, used lots of irons . . . Difficult, great course . . . Fabulous views . . . Beautiful clubhouse . . . VIP treatment from all staff.

★★ OSOYOOS GOLF AND COUNTRY CLUB
PARK/DESERT/MEADOWS
SP—12300 46th Ave., Osoyoos (604)495-7003.
81 miles south of Kelowna. **Holes:** 27. **Par:** 72/72/72.
Yards: 6,223/6,318/6,323. **Course rating:** 69.6/70.6/72.6.
Slope: 120/116/127.
Opened: 1971. **Pace of Play rating:** 4:15. **Green fee:** $18/25.
Credit cards: MC, V. **Reduced fees:** Low season, Twilight.
Caddies: No. **Golf carts:** $25 for 18 holes.
Discount golf packages: Yes. **Season:** March-Dec. **High:** July-Aug.
On-site lodging: No. **Rental clubs:** Yes.
Walking policy: Unrestricted walking. **Range:** Yes.

To obtain tee times: Call pro shop.
Subscriber comments: First course to open in year . . . New third nine enhances good layout . . . Let it rip, desert holes pretty . . . Staff good . . . Not too tough for vacationers . . . 27 picturesque holes . . . Some reconstruction and new housing development, great potential.

★★★½ PEACE PORTAL GOLF COURSE
SP—16900 4th Ave., South Surrey (604)538-4818.
30 miles south of Vancouver. **Holes:** 18. **Par:** 72/73.
Yards: 6,363/5,621. **Course rating:** 70.7/73.5. **Slope:** 127/133.
Opened: 1928. **Pace of Play rating:** 4:15. **Green fee:** $38/40.
Credit cards: MC, V, AMEX, Interac Debit Card. **Reduced fees:** Low season, Twilight.
Caddies: No. **Golf carts:** $26 for 18 holes.
Discount golf packages: No. **Season:** Year-round. **High:** April-Sept.
On-site lodging: No. **Rental clubs:** Yes.
Walking policy: Unrestricted walking. **Range:** Yes (grass).
To obtain tee times: Call 48 hours in advance at 8 a.m. For weekends, call Thursday at 8 a.m.
Subscriber comments: Great staff . . . Top-notch public layout, deceptively tough, Nos. 5 and 12 are classics . . . Best value for public course . . . PGA could play here . . . Accuracy a must, ravines a challenge . . . One of the best public courses and the only one that plays in Washington state and Canada . . . Beautiful, a must . . . Use credit card for best exchange rate . . . Great variety of holes . . . Mature, treed layout, gem . . . Must think your way around course, use all clubs.

★★ PENTICTON GOLF AND COUNTRY CLUB
SP—Eckhardt Ave. W., Penticton (604)492-8727.
27 miles south of Kelowna. **Holes:** 18. **Par:** 70/71.
Yards: 6,131/5,664. **Course rating:** 71.1/74.2. **Slope:** 133/137.
Opened: 1920. **Pace of Play rating:** 4:00. **Green fee:** $32.
Credit cards: MC, V. **Reduced fees:** Low season, Resort guests, Twilight, Juniors.
Caddies: No. **Golf carts:** $24 for 18 holes.
Discount golf packages: Yes. **Season:** Feb.-Nov. **High:** April-Oct.
On-site lodging: No. **Rental clubs:** Yes.
Walking policy: Unrestricted walking. **Range:** No.
To obtain tee times: Call 24 hours in advance.
Subscriber comments: Target golf . . . Enjoyable, easy to walk . . . Water in play, discretion a must, don't get greedy . . . Old, mature, fun, great, good condition . . . Tough, short course.

★★½ PITT MEADOWS GOLF CLUB
SP—P.O. Box 29, 13615 Harris Rd., Pitt Meadows (604)465-4711.
Call club for further information.
Subscriber comments: Suitable for all players.

★★★★ PREDATOR RIDGE GOLF RESORT
R—360 Commonage Rd., Vernon (604)542-3436.
36 miles north of Kelowna. **Holes:** 18. **Par:** 73/73.
Yards: 7,156/5,475. **Course rating:** 76.0/72.9. **Slope:** 131/131.
Opened: 1991. **Pace of Play rating:** 4:30. **Green fee:** $35/45.
Credit cards: MC, V, AMEX. **Reduced fees:** Low season, Resort guests, Twilight, Juniors.
Caddies: Yes. **Golf carts:** $27 for 18 holes.
Discount golf packages: Yes. **Season:** April-Oct. **High:** June-Sept.
On-site lodging: No. **Rental clubs:** Yes.
Walking policy: Unrestricted walking. **Range:** Yes (grass).
To obtain tee times: Call up to one year in advance with credit card.
Subscriber comments: Unique target golf track, fun to play . . . Outstanding scenery . . . Good mountain course combined with desert holes . . . For scenery and hospitality as good as Arizona resorts . . . PGA-class course . . . Gorgeous clubhouse . . . Two nines contrast, links to trees . . . One of the best in B.C. . . . This course dares you to hit landing areas that are surrounded by water and sand . . . The pinnacle of target golf. Reduced rates are a steal. Free valet parking a classy touch . . . Plays long and is a long walk.

★★★★ **RIVERSHORE GOLF CLUB**
SP—Comp 1 Site 13 R.R. No. 2, Kamloops (604)573-4622.
Holes: 18. **Par:** 72/72.
Yards: 7,007/5,445. **Course rating:** 74.7/71.3. **Slope:** 134/122.
Opened: 1982. **Pace of Play rating:** 4:00-4:30. **Green fee:** $32/42.
Credit cards: MC, V. **Reduced fees:** Low season, Resort guests,
Twilight, Juniors.
Caddies: No. **Golf carts:** $13 for 18 holes.
Discount golf packages: Yes. **Season:** March-Oct. **High:** April-Sept.
On-site lodging: Yes. **Rental clubs:** Yes.
Walking policy: Unrestricted walking. **Range:** Yes (grass).
To obtain tee times: Call pro shop.
Subscriber comments: Watch out for feathered friends . . . Country club
atmosphere . . . Good length for the big whacker . . . Good facilities to
practice . . . Great R.T. Jones track . . . He should be proud . . .
Outstanding grooming . . . Nice flow to holes.

★★★ **RIVERSIDE GOLF RESORT AT FAIRMONT**
R—5099 Riverview Dr., Fairmont Hot Springs (604)345-6346.
180 miles east of Calgary. **Holes:** 18. **Par:** 71/71.
Yards: 6,507/5,349. **Course rating:** 71.0/71.3. **Slope:** 131/126.
Opened: 1988. **Pace of Play rating:** 4:30. **Green fee:** $39.
Credit cards: MC, V, AMEX. **Reduced fees:** Resort guests, Twilight,
Juniors.
Caddies: Yes. **Golf carts:** $25 for 18 holes.
Discount golf packages: Yes. **Season:** March-Oct. **High:** May-Aug.
On-site lodging: No. **Rental clubs:** Yes.
Walking policy: Unrestricted walking. **Range:** Yes (grass).
To obtain tee times: Call in advance, credit card required.
Subscriber comments: Good use of terrain . . . Good walkable course
. . . Mountain course you don't have to be a mountain goat to walk. Views
match great weather . . . Use the caddies, they're great . . . Course keeps
getting better every year . . . Wonderful resort course with friendly helpful
staff . . . Potential for top rating . . . Columbia River winds through course
. . . Tempting short cuts . . . Several river shots.

ROSSLAND TRAIL COUNTRY CLUB
★★★ **BIRCHBANK COURSE**
SP—P.O. Box 221, Trail (604)693-2255.
100 miles north of Spokane, WA. **Holes:** 18. **Par:** 71/72.
Yards: 6,413/5,712. **Course rating:** 69.7/72.8. **Slope:** 122/129.
Opened: 1963. **Pace of Play rating:** 4:00-4:15. **Green fee:** $28.
Credit cards: MC, V, AMEX. **Reduced fees:** Twilight, Juniors.
Caddies: No. **Golf carts:** $25 for 18 holes.
Discount golf packages: Yes. **Season:** March-Oct. **High:** June-Aug.
On-site lodging: No. **Rental clubs:** Yes.
Walking policy: Unrestricted walking. **Range:** Yes (grass).
To obtain tee times: Call pro shop or book through hotel.
Also has 9-hole par-36 Rossland Course.
Subscriber comments: Nice walking, good shape . . . Almost always
four-hour rounds . . . Pretty view . . . Great value . . . Pro shop great staff.

★★ **SHADOW RIDGE GOLF CLUB**
PU—3770 Bulman, P.O. Box 2284R, Kelowna (604)765-4414.
Call club for further information.
Subscriber comments: The old stand by . . . Nice recreational layout . . .
Tight, short course, good value . . . Pleasant golfing.

★½ **SHANNON LAKE GOLF COURSE**
PU—2649 Shannon Lake Rd., Westbank (604)768-4577.
5 miles north of Kelowna. **Holes:** 18. **Par:** 72/72.
Yards: 6,151/5,075. **Course rating:** 69.9/70.1. **Slope:** 122/126.
Opened: 1985. **Pace of Play rating:** 4:20. **Green fee:** $20/30.
Credit cards: MC, V. **Reduced fees:** Low season, Resort guests,
Twilight, Juniors.
Caddies: No. **Golf carts:** $24 for 18 holes.
Discount golf packages: Yes. **Season:** March-Nov. **High:** June-Aug.
On-site lodging: No. **Rental clubs:** Yes.

Walking policy: Unrestricted walking. **Range:** Yes (grass).
To obtain tee times: Call pro shop or fax.
Subscriber comments: Excellent food . . . Quite short but demanding.

★★½ SPALLUMCHEEN GOLF AND COUNTRY CLUB

SP—P.O. Box 218, Vernon (604)545-5811.
Call club for further information.
Subscriber comments: Accuracy more than length, fast greens . . .
Friendliest people one can meet . . . Good shape . . . Playable.

★★★★ THE SPRINGS AT RADIUM GOLF COURSE

PU—Stanley St. and Columbia Ave., Radium Hot Springs (604)347-6444,
(800)667-6446.
90 miles northeast of Banff, Alberta. **Holes:** 18. **Par:** 72/72.
Yards: 6,801/5,163. **Course rating:** 74.0/70.8. **Slope:** 143/126.
Opened: 1988. **Pace of Play rating:** 4:00-4:30. **Green fee:** $40/45.
Credit cards: MC, V. **Reduced fees:** Weekdays, Twilight, Juniors.
Caddies: No. **Golf carts:** $25 for 18 holes.
Discount golf packages: No. **Season:** March-Oct. **High:** June-Sept.
On-site lodging: No. **Rental clubs:** Yes.
Walking policy: Unrestricted walking. **Range:** Yes (grass).
To obtain tee times: Call from January 9th on for the upcoming year with
a credit card.
Subscriber comments: My favorite golf course in B.C., a pleasure to play
. . . The second-best course in Rocky Mountains . . . Exceptional practice
area prepares you for a greater course which follows . . . Beautiful layout,
great variety of holes, use every club, great service . . . I spend a week here
every year . . . Terrific layout over Columbia Valley . . . Hills, canyons,
water . . . Perfect! . . . Best with cart, tough walk . . . Well run . . . Great
par 3s . . . Best in valley.

★★ SQUAMISH VALLEY GOLF AND COUNTRY CLUB

SP—2458 Mamquam Rd., Squamish (604)898-9691.
50 miles north of Vancouver. **Holes:** 18. **Par:** 72/72.
Yards: 6,411/5,580. **Course rating:** 71.4/71.3. **Slope:** 125/119.
Opened: 1971. **Pace of Play rating:** 4:00. **Green fee:** $16/32.
Credit cards: MC, V. **Reduced fees:** Low season, Twilight, Seniors,
Juniors.
Caddies: No. **Golf carts:** $14 for 18 holes.
Discount golf packages: No. **Season:** March-Nov. **High:** May-Sept.
On-site lodging: No. **Rental clubs:** Yes.
Walking policy: Unrestricted walking. **Range:** No.
To obtain tee times: Call up to seven days in advance.
Subscriber comments: In glacial valley . . . Good golf, value and staff . . .
Beautiful scenery . . . Solid basic golf . . . Scenic mountains behind and
river, nice layout.

★★★½ STOREY CREEK GOLF CLUB

SP—McGimasey Rd., Campbell River (604)923-3673.
90 miles north of Nanaimo. **Holes:** 18. **Par:** 72/72.
Yards: 6,695/5,428. **Course rating:** 73.1/72.4. **Slope:** 141/136.
Opened: 1989. **Pace of Play rating:** 4:00. **Green fee:** $23/32.
Credit cards: MC, V. **Reduced fees:** Low season, Resort guests,
Twilight, Juniors.
Caddies: No. **Golf carts:** $22 for 18 holes.
Discount golf packages: Yes. **Season:** Year-round. **High:** April-Oct.
On-site lodging: No. **Rental clubs:** Yes.
Walking policy: Unrestricted walking. **Range:** Yes (grass).
To obtain tee times: Call two days in advance.
Subscriber comments: The best course on Vancouver Island . . . Wildlife
abound: deer, elk, bear, eagles plus spawning salmon in the creek . . .
Thoroughly enjoyable golf experience . . . Bring your "A" game . . .
Solitude . . . Fabulous nature park . . . What a treat, a great walk in the
forest, and fishing too . . . Jewel in the forest . . . Requires good golf skills.

★½ SUMMERLAND GOLF AND COUNTRY CLUB

SP—2405 Mountain Ave., Summerland (604)494-9554.
36 miles south of Kelowna. **Holes:** 18. **Par:** 72/72.
Yards: 6,535/5,655. **Course rating:** 70.7/73.4. **Slope:** 121/128.

Opened: 1980. **Pace of Play rating:** 4:00–4:30. **Green fee:** $28.
Credit cards: MC, V. **Reduced fees:** Low season, Resort guests,
Twilight, Juniors.
Caddies: No. **Golf carts:** $25 for 18 holes.
Discount golf packages: Yes. **Season:** March-Oct. **High:** June-Sept.
On-site lodging: No. **Rental clubs:** Yes.
Walking policy: Unrestricted walking. **Range:** Yes.
To obtain tee times: Call for weekdays. For tee times prior to 11 a.m. on
weekends, call the day before. For times after 11 a.m. call four days in
advance.
Subscriber comments: The old Dr. Jekyll and Mr. Hyde layout . . . Flat
nine, hilly nine. A course all levels can enjoy . . . Great staff . . . Improving
over time with work on course.

★★ SUNSET RANCH GOLF AND COUNTRY CLUB
SP—4001 Anderson Rd., Kelowna (604)765-7671.
Call club for further information.
Subscriber comments: Tight layout but a good mix of holes . . . Some
very challenging holes . . . Must keep ball in play on tight fairways through
pine forest . . . Interesting.

SWAN-E-SET BAY RESORT AND COUNTRY CLUB
★★★ THE RESORT COURSE
PU—16651 Rennie Rd., Pitt Meadows (604)465-3888.
27 miles east of Vancouver. **Holes:** 18. **Par:** 72/72.
Yards: 7,000/5,632. **Course rating:** 73.8/71.5. **Slope:** 130/120.
Opened: 1993. **Pace of Play rating:** 4:10. **Green fee:** $45/55.
Credit cards: MC, V, AMEX. **Reduced fees:** Juniors.
Caddies: No. **Golf carts:** $25 for 18 holes.
Discount golf packages: No. **Season:** Year-round. **High:** April-Oct.
On-site lodging: No. **Rental clubs:** Yes.
Walking policy: Unrestricted walking. **Range:** Yes (grass).
To obtain tee times: Call three days in advance.
Subscriber comments: Varied layout, good condition . . . What a setting,
what a clubhouse, great course, great service! . . . Gets my vote for best
new course in Canada . . . Lee Trevino design is fun and playable . . .
Classy clubhouse . . . A good new course . . . Two courses, one public,
one private . . . Clubhouse is like Taj Majal . . . Nice resort course.

★★★★ TRICKLE CREEK GOLF RESORT
R—P.O. Box 190, Kimberley (604)427-3389.
200 miles southwest of Calgary. **Holes:** 18. **Par:** 72/72.
Yards: 6,896/5,080. **Course rating:** 74.8/71.1. **Slope:** 143/131.
Opened: 1993. **Pace of Play rating:** 4:25. **Green fee:** $37.
Credit cards: MC, V. **Reduced fees:** Weekdays, Twilight.
Caddies: No. **Golf carts:** $24 for 18 holes.
Discount golf packages: Yes. **Season:** May-Oct. **High:** May-Sept.
On-site lodging: No. **Rental clubs:** Yes.
Walking policy: Unrestricted walking. **Range:** Yes (grass).
To obtain tee times: Call anytime starting January 1st for the upcoming
year.
Subscriber comments: Great new course. Real Rocky Mountain golf . . .
The best of everything . . . One of the top courses in Canada . . . Second-
best value in the West . . . For a new course it doesn't get any better . . .
Third-best course in western Canada . . . Position golf . . . Better the more
you play.

(GREAT VALUE)

★★½ UNIVERSITY GOLF CLUB
PU—5185 University Blvd., Vancouver (604)224-1818.
Holes: 18. **Par:** 72/72.
Yards: 6,584/5,653. **Course rating:** 71.5/71.9. **Slope:** 122/122.
Opened: 1929. **Pace of Play rating:** 4:15-4:30. **Green fee:** $28/41.
Credit cards: MC, V, AMEX. **Reduced fees:** Low season, Twilight.
Caddies: No. **Golf carts:** $32 for 18 holes.
Discount golf packages: No. **Season:** Year-round. **High:** April-Oct.
On-site lodging: No. **Rental clubs:** Yes.
Walking policy: Unrestricted walking. **Range:** Yes (grass).
To obtain tee times: Call seven days in advance with credit card.
Subscriber comments: Best head pro in B.C. . . . . A great public course in

the heart of Vancouver . . . Good shape considering the amount of rounds played . . . A good old track. A nice walk in the park . . . Right downtown . . . Old style design, good for walking, many varieties of trees.

★★ VERNON GOLF AND COUNTRY CLUB
SP—800 Kalamalka Lake Rd., Vernon (604)542-9126.
20 miles north of Kelowana. **Holes:** 18. **Par:** 72/74.
Yards: 6,460/5,771. **Course rating:** 70.0/73.1. **Slope:** 120/128.
Opened: 1913. **Pace of Play rating:** 4:00. **Green fee:** $17/32.
Credit cards: MC, V. **Reduced fees:** Low season, Twilight.
Caddies: No. **Golf carts:** $25 for 18 holes.
Discount golf packages: Yes. **Season:** March-Oct. **High:** May-Aug.
On-site lodging: No. **Rental clubs:** Yes.
Walking policy: Unrestricted walking. **Range:** Yes.
To obtain tee times: Call Thursday after 2 p.m. for Saturday, Sunday and Monday. Call Sunday after 2 p.m. for weekdays.
Subscriber comments: Interesting layout . . . Excellent dining room.

WESTWOOD PLATEAU GOLF AND COUNTRY CLUB★
PU—3251 Plateau Blvd., Coquitlam (604)941-4236.
12 miles east of Vancouver. **Holes:** 18. **Par:** 72/72.
Yards: 6,770/5,014. **Course rating:** N/A. **Slope:** N/A.
Opened: 1995. **Pace of Play rating:** N/A. **Green fee:** N/A.
Credit cards: MC, V, AMEX, Diners Club. **Reduced fees:** No.
Caddies: No. **Golf carts:** N/A.
Discount golf packages: No. **Season:** March-Oct. **High:** May-Sept.
On-site lodging: No. **Rental clubs:** Yes.
Walking policy: Walking at certain times. **Range:** Yes (grass).
Also has 9-hole par-31 course.

★★★ WHISTLER GOLF CLUB
R—4010 Whistler Way, Whistler (604)932-3280, (800)944-7853.
100 miles north of Vancouver. **Holes:** 18. **Par:** 72/72.
Yards: 6,400/5,434. **Course rating:** 71.3/70.5. **Slope:** 128/120.
Opened: 1982. **Pace of Play rating:** 4:00. **Green fee:** $50/70.
Credit cards: MC, V, AMEX. **Reduced fees:** Low season, Twilight.
Caddies: No. **Golf carts:** $25 for 18 holes.
Discount golf packages: Yes. **Season:** May-Oct. **High:** June-Sept.
On-site lodging: Yes. **Rental clubs:** Yes.
Walking policy: Unrestricted walking. **Range:** Yes (grass).
To obtain tee times: Call within 30 days of play. Hotel guests may call anytime.
Subscriber comments: Back catches you unaware, easy to shoot 36-45 . . . Shotmaker's course . . . Staff meets you at parking lot and are extremely helpful . . . Mountain peaks everywhere . . . Palmer course requires thought on tee . . . Great views among the ski hills . . . Great excursion . . . Surrounded by snow-covered mountains, spectacular beauty, good layout, a "must play" even for a high price.

MANITOBA

★★★½ CLEAR LAKE GOLF COURSE
PU—Box 328, Onanole (204)848-4653.
150 miles northwest of Winnipeg. **Holes:** 18. **Par:** 72/72.
Yards: 6,070/6,070. **Course rating:** 69.3/72.7. **Slope:** 120/130.
Opened: 1933. **Pace of Play rating:** . **Green fee:** $22/24.
Credit cards: MC, V. **Reduced fees:** Low season, Twilight, Juniors.
Caddies: No. **Golf carts:** $12 for 18 holes.
Discount golf packages: No. **Season:** May-Oct. **High:** June-Aug.
On-site lodging: No. **Rental clubs:** Yes.
Walking policy: Unrestricted walking. **Range:** No.
To obtain tee times: Call two days to one week in advance.
Subscriber comments: Maybe the most enjoyable round I've ever played . . . Best in Manitoba . . . Rolling fairways make interesting lies . . . What a way to get away from it all.

★★★½ FALCON BEACH GOLF COURSE
PU—Falcon Beach P.O., Falcon Lake (204)349-2554.
85 miles east of Winnipeg. **Holes:** 18. **Par:** 72/72.
Yards: 6,937/5,917. **Course rating:** 72.6/72.0. **Slope:** 121/115.

Opened: 1958. **Pace of Play rating:** 4:00-4:30. **Green fee:** $18/20.
Credit cards: MC, V. **Reduced fees:** Weekdays, Twilight, Seniors, Juniors.
Caddies: No. **Golf carts:** $9 for 18 holes.
Discount golf packages: Yes. **Season:** April-Oct. **High:** July-Aug.
On-site lodging: Yes. **Rental clubs:** Yes.
Walking policy: Unrestricted walking. **Range:** Yes (grass).
To obtain tee times: Call two days in advance. Write if more than two days in advance, reservation fee of $1 per person required.
Subscriber comments: Lovely park setting in cottage country . . . Best course in the province . . . Scenic course through forest . . . An aesthetically beautiful course with huge evergreens most every hole . . . Wide variety of golfers . . . Nice layout.

★★★½ HECLA GOLF COURSE
R—P.O. Box 1000, Riverton (204)475-2354.
110 miles from Winnipeg. **Holes:** 18. **Par:** 72/72.
Yards: 6,678/5,535. **Course rating:** N/A. **Slope:** N/A.
Opened: N/A. **Pace of Play rating:** N/A. **Green fee:** N/A.
Credit cards: All major. **Reduced fees:** Twilight.
Caddies: No. **Golf carts:** N/A.
Discount golf packages: Yes. **Season:** May-Oct. **High:** June-Aug.
On-site lodging: Yes. **Rental clubs:** No.
Walking policy: N/A. **Range:** Yes (grass).
Subscriber comments: One of the four best golf courses in Manitoba . . . Tough drive in, especially the last stretch of gravel, but worth it! . . . Scenic . . . Beautiful views . . . Not overly difficult, nicely cared for, a good resort course . . . Wild, rugged beauty.

★½ JOHN BLUMBERG GOLF COURSE
PU—4540 Portage Ave., Headingley (204)986-3490.
1 mile west of Winnipeg. **Holes:** 18. **Par:** 71/71.
Yards: 6,343/5,844. **Course rating:** 70.2/68.0. **Slope:** 116/111.
Opened: 1969. **Pace of Play rating:** N/A. **Green fee:** $16.
Credit cards: MC, V, AMEX. **Reduced fees:** Twilight, Seniors, Juniors.
Caddies: No. **Golf carts:** $10 for 18 holes.
Discount golf packages: No. **Season:** April-Nov. **High:** May-Sept.
On-site lodging: No. **Rental clubs:** Yes.
Walking policy: Unrestricted walking. **Range:** Yes (grass).
To obtain tee times: Call one day in advance.
Also 9-hole, par-34 course.
Subscriber comments: Open, public course, staff cordial . . . Heavy traffic, nice along river . . . Easily best local muny, little effort would greatly improve course . . . Wide open course, easy to get on anytime.

★★½ LARTERS ST. ANDREWS GOLF AND COUNTRY CLUB
SP—30 River Rd., St. Andrews (204)334-2107.
5 miles from Winnipeg. **Holes:** 18. **Par:** 71/71.
Yards: 6,526/5,374. **Course rating:** 71.0/69.7. **Slope:** 122/113.
Opened: 1990. **Pace of Play rating:** 4:15. **Green fee:** $27.
Credit cards: MC, V, AMEX. **Reduced fees:** Weekdays, Low season, Twilight, Juniors.
Caddies: No. **Golf carts:** $24 for 18 holes.
Discount golf packages: Yes. **Season:** April-Oct. **High:** May-Sept.
On-site lodging: No. **Rental clubs:** Yes.
Walking policy: Unrestricted walking. **Range:** Yes (grass).
To obtain tee times: Nonmembers call one day in advance.
Subscriber comments: Gets better every time I play it . . . Holes along river are tough. . . . Newer course that has come a long way and will improve even more . . . Continuously upgrading, improving each year . . . Beautiful facilities . . . Nice clubhouse.

★★★★ THE LINKS AT QUARRY OAKS
PU—Box 3629, Hwy. 311 E., Steinbach (204)326-4653.
35 miles southeast of Winnipeg. **Holes:** 18. **Par:** 72/72.
Yards: 7,009/5,422. **Course rating:** 73.0/70.0. **Slope:** 133/121.
Opened: 1992. **Pace of Play rating:** 4:30. **Green fee:** $35/38.
Credit cards: MC, V, AMEX. **Reduced fees:** Weekdays, Low season, Twilight, Seniors, Juniors.

Caddies: No. **Golf carts:** $13 for 18 holes.
Discount golf packages: Yes. **Season:** April-Oct. **High:** July-Aug.
On-site lodging: No. **Rental clubs:** Yes.
Walking policy: Unrestricted walking. **Range:** Yes (grass).
To obtain tee times: Call two weeks in advance with credit card.
Subscriber comments: Best course in Manitoba . . . Excellent staff . . .
Clubhouse is excellent . . . Not for faint hearts . . . The treatment you
receive when you arrive is the best . . . Memorable layout combined with
challenge . . . Links style built around and through an old rock quarry . . .
Private club service . . . Two very different nines . . . Back nine in quarry
. . . Les Furber designed . . . Benchmark course . . . Good use of reclaimed
land.

★★½ SELKIRK GOLF AND COUNTRY CLUB
PU—P.O. Box 15, Selkirk (204)482-5911.
Call club for further information.
Subscriber comments: Friendly and courteous staff.

★★½ STEINBACH FLY-IN GOLF COURSE
R—P.O. Box 3716, Steinbach (204)326-6813.
Call club for further information.
Subscriber comments: Nice course for the average guy who can't hit
every shot exactly where he wants to . . . Two very different nines . . .
Good course . . . Hit from grass on range.

★★½ TEULON GOLF AND COUNTRY CLUB
PU—Hwy. 7 N., Teulon (204)886-4653.
30 miles north of Winnipeg. **Holes:** 18. **Par:** 72/71.
Yards: 6,426/5,256. **Course rating:** 71.0/69.0. **Slope:** 115/111.
Opened: 1961. **Pace of Play rating:** 4:30. **Green fee:** $11/22.
Credit cards: MC, V. **Reduced fees:** Weekdays, Low season, Twilight,
Seniors, Junior
Caddies: No. **Golf carts:** $20 for 18 holes.

Discount golf packages: Yes. **Season:** April-Oct. **High:** June-Aug.
On-site lodging: No. **Rental clubs:** Yes.
Walking policy: Unrestricted walking. **Range:** Yes (grass).
To obtain tee times: Call two days in advance. Walk-ons not a problem
during non-peak times.
Subscriber comments: This course is improving every year . . . Happy
atmosphere . . . Excellent staff . . . Best value in province.

SASKATCHEWAN

★★★ COOKE MUNICIPAL GOLF COURSE
PU—900 22nd St. E., Prince Albert (306)763-2502.
93 miles northeast of Saskatoon. **Holes:** 18. **Par:** 71/72.
Yards: 6,319/5,719. **Course rating:** 69.4/72.6. **Slope:** 118/124.
Opened: 1935. **Pace of Play rating:** 4:20. **Green fee:** $18.
Credit cards: MC, V, AMEX. **Reduced fees:** Low season, Twilight,
Seniors, Juniors.
Caddies: No. **Golf carts:** $20 for 18 holes.
Discount golf packages: Yes. **Season:** April-Oct. **High:** June-Aug.
On-site lodging: No. **Rental clubs:** Yes.
Walking policy: Unrestricted walking. **Range:** Yes (grass).
To obtain tee times: Call one day in advance at 8 a.m. Call Friday a.m.
for Saturday and Sunday.
Subscriber comments: Every hole offers a different challenge . . . The
new changes really make Cooke a tough challenge . . . A classic . . . Better
since improvements . . . Treelined, scenic.

(FRUGAL PICK seal)

★★½ ELMWOOD GOLF CLUB
PU—P.O. Box 13, Swift Current (306)773-2722.
Call club for further information.
Subscriber comments: Good variety with water and blind tee shots . . .
Real gem on the prairies . . . Accommodating staff . . . Worth stopping
. . . You had better know how to play in wind . . . Very fun place for a
small-town course.

★★½ ESTEVAN WOODLAWN GOLF CLUB
PU—P.O. Box 203, Estevan (306)634-2017.
134 miles southeast of Moose Jaw. **Holes:** 18. **Par:** 71/72.
Yards: 6,320/5,409. **Course rating:** 70.0/73.0. **Slope:** 123/118.
Opened: N/A. **Pace of Play rating:** 4:00. **Green fee:** $20.
Credit cards: MC, V. **Reduced fees:** Juniors.
Caddies: No. **Golf carts:** $20 for 18 holes.
Discount golf packages: No. **Season:** May-Oct. **High:** June-Aug.
On-site lodging: No. **Rental clubs:** Yes.
Walking policy: Unrestricted walking. **Range:** Yes (grass).
To obtain tee times: Call 24 hours in advance.
Subscriber comments: Back nine, look out! . . . Good course, potential is
there . . . Staff helpful . . . Wide-open front.

★★½ NORTH BATTLEFORD GOLF AND COUNTRY CLUB
PU—P.O. Box 372, North Battleford (306)937-5659.
Call club for further information.
Subscriber comments: Staff makes players feel welcome . . . Good test of
golf skills . . . Challenge, challenge, challenge . . . Super club for a small
city.

★★★½ WASKESIU GOLF COURSE
PU—P.O. Box 234, Waskesiu (306)663-5302.
50 miles north of Prince Albert. **Holes:** 18. **Par:** 70/71.
Yards: 6,051/5,710. **Course rating:** 67.5/71.0. **Slope:** 111/111.
Opened: 1936. **Pace of Play rating:** 4:00-4:30. **Green fee:** $18/22.
Credit cards: MC, V, AMEX. **Reduced fees:** Low season, Twilight,
Juniors.
Caddies: No. **Golf carts:** $22 for 18 holes.
Discount golf packages: No. **Season:** May-Sept. **High:** July-Aug.
On-site lodging: No. **Rental clubs:** Yes.
Walking policy: Unrestricted walking. **Range:** Yes.
To obtain tee times: Call one day in advance at 9 a.m. or come in when
pro shop opens.
Subscriber comments: Take time to learn some of the course history . . .
Best value in Saskatchewan . . . A jewel set in the forest . . . Park course
. . . Classic course in a tremendous setting . . . Stanley Thompson design
. . . Walkable, wildlife . . . Beautiful, fun to play from novice to pro.

THE WILLOWS GOLF AND COUNTRY CLUB
PU—382 Cartwright Rd., Saskatoon (306)956-1100.
Green fee: $23/25.
Credit cards: MC, V, AMEX. **Reduced fees:** Weekdays, Twilight,
Seniors, Juniors.
Caddies: No. **Golf carts:** $11 for 18 holes.
Discount golf packages: No. **Season:** April-Oct. **High:** May-Aug.
On-site lodging: No. **Rental clubs:** Yes.
Walking policy: Unrestricted walking. **Range:** Yes (grass).
To obtain tee times: Call or come in three days in advance. Unlimited
advance when held with a credit card number.
★★½ LAKES/ISLAND
Holes: 18. **Par:** 71/71.
Yards: 6,839/5,137. **Course rating:** 72.5/70.0. **Slope:** 125/N/A.
Opened: 1991. **Pace of Play rating:** 4:00.
Subscriber comments: Much water (hence the names) . . . Many holes
have a similar layout. Island green par-3 17th is a beauty . . . Excellent
clubhouse and pro shop . . . Staff treats you like a member . . . Nicest
clubhouse in Canada . . . Lakes favorite of two courses . . . Good tracks,
worth your time . . . Great island par 3 on Island Course.
★★ XENA/BRIDGES
Holes: 18. **Par:** 72/72.
Yards: 7,070/5,564. **Course rating:** 73.1/72.0. **Slope:** 130/N/A.
Opened: 1991. **Pace of Play rating:** 4:00.
Subscriber comments: Public golf at muny price . . . Easily walkable . . .
Wide open . . . New course needs time.

MEXICO

Baja Norte

BAJA COUNTRY CLUB★
SP—Ensenada (011)52-61-730303.
8 miles south of Ensenada. **Holes:** 18. **Par:** 72/72.
Yards: 6,834/5,203. **Course rating:** 73.1/69.5. **Slope:** 137/117.
Opened: 1991. **Pace of Play rating:** N/A. **Green fee:** $28/34.
Credit cards: MC, V. **Reduced fees:** Weekdays.
Caddies: No. **Golf carts:** Included in Green Fee.
Discount golf packages: Yes. **Season:** Year-round. **High:** N/A.
On-site lodging: No. **Rental clubs:** Yes.
Walking policy: Mandatory cart. **Range:** Yes.
To obtain tee times: Call anytime.

BAJAMAR GOLF COURSE★
R—KM 77.5 Carrectora Esenica Tijuana, Ensenada, (800)225-2418.
20 miles south of Ensenada. **Holes:** 18. **Par:** 71/71.
Yards: 6,968/4,696. **Course rating:** 74.9/66.6. **Slope:** 143/113.
Opened: 1975. **Pace of Play rating:** 4:00. **Green fee:** $45/55.
Credit cards: MC, V. **Reduced fees:** Weekdays, Resort guests, Twilight,
Seniors.
Caddies: No. **Golf carts:** Included in Green Fee.
Discount golf packages: Yes. **Season:** Year-round. **High:** May-Sept.
On-site lodging: Yes. **Rental clubs:** Yes.
Walking policy: Mandatory cart. **Range:** Yes (grass).
To obtain tee times: Call direct to pro shop. Pro shop number is 011-52-
615-50161; fax number is 011-52-615-50150.

REAL DEL MAR GOLF CLUB★
R—19½ KM Ensenada, Toll Rd., Tijuana.
Holes: 18. **Par:** 72/72.
Yards: 6,403/5,033. **Course rating:** 70.5/68.5. **Slope:** 131/119.
Opened: 1993. **Pace of Play rating:** 4:00. **Green fee:** $43/49.
Credit cards: MC, V, AMEX. **Reduced fees:** Weekdays, Low season,
Resort guests, Twilight, Juniors.
Caddies: Yes. **Golf carts:** Included in Green Fee.
Discount golf packages: No. **Season:** Year-round. **High:** June-Sept.
On-site lodging: Yes. **Rental clubs:** Yes.
Walking policy: Walking at certain times. **Range:** Yes (grass).
To obtain tee times: Call seven days in advance.

TIJUANA COUNTRY CLUB★
SP—Blvd. Agua Caliente No. 11311, Col. Avia, Tijuana. (011)52-66-
817855.
20 miles south of San Diego. **Holes:** 18. **Par:** 72/72.
Yards: 6,869/5,517. **Course rating:** 73.0/72.0. **Slope:** 129/127.
Opened: 1942. **Pace of Play rating:** N/A. **Green fee:** $22/27.
Credit cards: MC, V. **Reduced fees:** Twilight, Seniors, Juniors.
Caddies: Yes. **Golf carts:** $20 for 18 holes.
Discount golf packages: Yes. **Season:** Year-round. **High:** N/A.
On-site lodging: No. **Rental clubs:** Yes.
Walking policy: Unrestricted walking. **Range:** Yes (grass).
To obtain tee times: Call pro shop up to 30 days in advance.

Baja Sur

CABO SAN LUCAS COUNTRY CLUB★
SP—Cabo San Lucas, (011)52-11-434653, (800)854-2314.
Holes: 18. **Par:** N/A.
Yards: N/A. **Course rating:** N/A. **Slope:** N/A.
Opened: 1994. **Pace of Play rating:** N/A . **Green fee:** $55/83.
Credit cards: MC, V, AMEX, Banamex Mexican CC. **Reduced fees:**
Low season.
Caddies: No. **Golf carts mandatory?** Yes, included in Green Fee.

Discount golf packages: Yes. **Season:** Year-round. **High:** Nov.-May.
On-site lodging: No. **Rental clubs:** Yes.
Walking policy: Mandatory cart. **Range:** Yes (grass).
To obtain tee times: Call pro shop.

THE OCEAN COURSE AT CABO DEL SOL★
PU—KM-75, Los Cabos, (011)-52-11-433149, (800)637-2226.
4 miles northeast of Cabo San Lucas. **Holes:** 18. **Par:** 72/72.
Yards: 7,037/4,696. **Course rating:** N/A. **Slope:** N/A.
Opened: 1994. **Pace of Play rating:** 4:15. **Green fee:** $99/132.
Credit cards: MC, V, AMEX. **Reduced fees:** Low season, Resort guests,
Juniors.
Caddies: No. **Golf carts mandatory?** Yes, included in Green Fee.
Discount golf packages: Yes. **Season:** Year-round. **High:** Oct.-June.
On-site lodging: Yes. **Rental clubs:** Yes.
Walking policy: Walking at certain times. **Range:** Yes (grass).
To obtain tee times: Call 800 number for prepaid advance tee times.
Local, call no more than one week in advance.

PALMILLA GOLF CLUB
MOUNTAIN/ARROYO/OCEAN★
SP—Carretera Transpeninsular KM 27, San Jose del Cabo (011)52-11-
420583, (800)386-2465.
Holes: 27. **Par:** 72/72/72.
Yards: 7,114/6,849/6,939. **Course rating:** 74.9/73.4/74.3.
Slope: 139/136/144.
Opened: 1992. **Pace of Play rating:** 4:30. **Green fee:** $55/105.
Credit cards: MC, V, AMEX. **Reduced fees:** Low season, Resort guests.
Caddies: No. **Golf carts:** Included in Green Fee.
Discount golf packages: Yes. **Season:** Year-round. **High:** Oct.-May.
On-site lodging: Yes. **Rental clubs:** Yes.
Walking policy: Mandatory cart. **Range:** Yes.
To obtain tee times: Call ahead.

Colima

LAS HADAS RESORT
LA MANTARRAYA CLUB LAS HADAS★
R—Manzanillo. (011)52-33-340000.
Holes: 18. **Par:** 71/71.
Yards: 6,492/5,535. **Course rating:** 73.7/69.1. **Slope:** 132/126.
Opened: 1974. **Pace of Play rating:** N/A. **Green fee:** $56.
Credit cards: MC, V, AMEX. **Reduced fees:** No.
Caddies: Yes. **Golf carts:** $44 for 18 holes.
Discount golf packages: Yes. **Season:** Year-round. **High:** Year-round.
On-site lodging: Yes. **Rental clubs:** Yes.
Walking policy: Unrestricted walking. **Range:** Yes (grass).

Guerrero

ACAPULCO PRINCESS CLUB DE GOLF★
R—A.P. 1351, Acapulco. (011)52-74-691000.
Holes: 18. **Par:** 72/72.
Yards: 6,355/5,400. **Course rating:** 69.4/69.6. **Slope:** 117/115.
Opened: 1971. **Pace of Play rating:** . **Green fee:** $60/80.
Credit cards: MC, V, AMEX, Diners. **Reduced fees:** Resort guests,
Twilight.
Caddies: No. **Golf carts:** Included in Green Fee.
Discount golf packages: No. **Season:** Year-round. **High:** Nov.-April.
On-site lodging: Yes. **Rental clubs:** Yes.
Walking policy: Mandatory cart. **Range:** Yes (grass).
To obtain tee times: Guests of hotel may call up to two days in advance.
Nonguests call one day in advance.
Subscriber comments: A little short, otherwise excellent.

IXTAPA GOLF COURSE★

PU—Blvd. Ixtapa S/N, Ixtapa. (011)91-75-331063.
Holes: 18. **Par:** 72/72.
Yards: 6,868/5,801. **Course rating:** 70.0/N/A. **Slope:** N/A.
Opened: 1975. **Pace of Play rating:** N/A. **Green fee:** $50.
Credit cards: MC, V, AMEX. **Reduced fees:** Twilight.
Caddies: Yes. **Golf carts:** N/A.
Discount golf packages: No. **Season:** Year-round. **High:** Nov.-April.
On-site lodging: No. **Rental clubs:** Yes.
Walking policy: Carts or caddies are required. **Range:** Yes (grass).
To obtain tee times: First come, first served.

MARINA IXTAPA CLUB DE GOLF★

R—Calle De La Darsena s/n, Lote 8, Ixtapa, Zihuatanejo.
Holes: 18. **Par:** 72/72.
Yards: 6,800/5,197. **Course rating:** N/A. **Slope:** N/A.
Opened: 1994. **Pace of Play rating:** 4:20. **Green fee:** $45/55.
Credit cards: MC, V, AMEX. **Reduced fees:** Low season, Twilight.
Caddies: Yes. **Golf carts:** Included in Green Fee.
Discount golf packages: Yes. **Season:** Year-round. **High:** Dec.-April.
On-site lodging: No. **Rental clubs:** Yes.
Walking policy: Mandatory cart. **Range:** Yes (grass).
To obtain tee times: Call pro shop.
Subscriber comments: New course, good pro and staff.

PIERRE MARQUEZ GOLF CLUB★

R—Acapulco.
Contact club for further information.
Subscriber comments: Good test . . . Adequate condition . . . Good pace
and service.

Jalisco

MARINA VALLARTA CLUB DE GOLF★

SP—Puerto Vallarta.
Contact club for further information.
Subscriber comments: Fun track for area, friendly caddies . . . Good
pace.

Morelos

COUNTRY CLUB COCOYOC★

R—Circuito Dll Hombre S/N, Cocoyoc. (011)52-73-561139.
65 miles south of Mexico City. **Holes:** 18. **Par:** 72/72.
Yards: 6,287/5,250. **Course rating:** 69.7/68.1. **Slope:** 127/116.
Opened: 1977. **Pace of Play rating:** N/A. **Green fee:** $90.
Credit cards: MC, V. **Reduced fees:** Weekdays, Resort guests.
Caddies: Yes. **Golf carts:** N/A.
Discount golf packages: Yes. **Season:** Year-round.
On-site lodging: Yes. **Rental clubs:** Yes.
Walking policy: Unrestricted walking. **Range:** Yes (grass).

Oaxaca

TANGOLUNDA GOLF COURSE★

SP—Huatulco. (011)91-95-810059.
Call club for further information.

EL CID GOLF AND COUNTRY CLUB★
R—Mazatlan. (011)-52-69-133333.
Holes: 18. **Par:** 72/72.
Yards: 6,729/5,752. **Course rating:** 73.2/72.0. **Slope:** 132/127.
Opened: 1973. **Pace of Play rating:** N/A. **Green fee:** N/A.
Credit cards: MC, V, AMEX. **Reduced fees:** Resort guests.
Caddies: Yes. **Golf carts:** N/A.
Discount golf packages: No. **Season:** Year-round. **High:** Feb.–March.
On-site lodging: No. **Rental clubs:** Yes.
Walking policy: Walking at certain times. **Range:** Yes (grass).
To obtain tee times: Call pro shop.

Notes

America's 100 Greatest Golf Courses

As ranked by GOLF DIGEST (1995)

Includes private (not covered in this book)
as well as public and resort courses.

1. **Pine Valley Golf Club,** Pine Valley, N.J.
2. **Augusta National Golf Club,** Augusta, Ga.
3. **Pebble Beach Golf Links,** Pebble Beach, Calif.
4. **Cypress Point Club,** Pebble Beach, Calif.
5. **Merion Golf Club,** Ardmore, Pa.
6. **Shinnecock Hills Golf Club,** Southampton, N.Y.
7. **Oakmont Country Club,** Oakmont, Pa.
8. **Winged Foot Golf Club (West),** Mamaroneck, N.Y.
9. **Pinehurst Country Club (No. 2),** Pinehurst, N.C.
10. **The Country Club (Open),** Brookline, Mass.
11. **The Olympic Club (Lake),** San Francisco, Calif.
12. **Oakland Hills Country Club (South),** Bloomfield Hills, Mich.
13. **Crystal Downs Country Club,** Frankfort, Mich.
14. **Medinah Country Club (No. 3),** Medinah, Ill.
15. **Seminole Golf Club,** North Palm Beach, Fla.
16. **Muirfield Village Golf Club,** Dublin, Ohio
17. **Shadow Creek Golf Club,** North Las Vegas, Nev.
18. **Chicago Golf Club,** Wheaton, Ill.
19. **National Golf Links,** Southampton, N.Y.
20. **Oak Hill Country Club (East),** Rochester, N.Y.
21. **Prairie Dunes Country Club,** Hutchinson, Kan.
22. **Quaker Ridge Golf Club,** Scarsdale, N.Y.
23. **San Francisco Golf Club,** San Francisco, Calif.
24. **Baltusrol Golf Club (Lower),** Springfield, N.J.
25. **Southern Hills Country Club,** Tulsa, Okla.
26. **Peachtree Golf Club,** Atlanta, Ga.
27. **Winged Foot Golf Club (East),** Mamaroneck, N.Y.
28. **The Golf Club,** New Albany, Ohio
29. **Riviera Country Club,** Pacific Palisades, Calif.
30. **Garden City Golf Club,** Garden City, N.Y.
31. **Cherry Hills Country Club,** Englewood, Colo.
32. **Wade Hampton Golf Club,** Cashiers, N.C.
33. **Los Angeles Country Club (North),** Los Angeles, Calif.
34. **Spyglass Hill Golf CSE. ,** Pebble Beach, Calif.
35. **Inverness Club,** Toledo, Ohio
36. **Scioto Country Club,** Columbus, Ohio
37. **The Honors Course,** Chattanooga, Tenn.
38. **Maidstone Club,** East Hampton, N.Y.
39. **Cascades Golf Club,** Hot Springs, Va.
40. **TPC at Sawgrass (Stadium),** Ponte Vedra Beach, Fla.
41. **Colonial Country Club,** Fort Worth
42. **Baltimore Country Club (East),** Timonium, Md.
43. **Plainfield Country Club,** Plainfield, N.J.
44. **Forest Highlands Golf Club,** Flagstaff, Ariz.
45. **Laurel Valley Golf Club,** Ligonier, Pa.
46. **Long Cove Club,** Hilton Head Island, S.C.
47. **Wannamoisett Country Club,** Rumford, R.I.
48. **Castle Pines Golf Club,** Castle Rock, Colo.
49. **Butler National Golf Club,** Oak Brook, Ill.
50. **Hazeltine National Golf Club,** Chaska, Minn.
51. **Valhalla Golf Club,** Louisville, Ky.
52. **Salem Country Club,** Peabody, Mass.
53. **Bellerive Country Club,** St. Louis
54. **Interlachen Country Club,** Edina, Minn.
55. **Black Diamond (Quarry),** Lecanto, Fla.

56. **Canterbury Golf Club,** Shaker Heights, Ohio
57. **Harbour Town Golf Links,** Hilton Head Island, S. C.
58. **Kittansett Club,** Marion, Mass.
59. **Cog Hill Golf and Country Club (No. 4),** Lemont, Ill.
60. **Somerset Hills Country Club,** Bernardsville, N. J.
61. **Shoal Creek,** Shoal Creek, Ala.
62. **Blackwolf Run Golf Club (River),** Kohler, Wis.
63. **Olympia Fields Country Club (North),** Olympia Fields, Ill.
64. **Jupiter Hills Club (Hills),** Tequesta, Fla.
65. **Point O'Woods Golf and Country Club,** Benton Harbor,
    Mich.
66. **Crooked Stick Golf Club,** Carmel, Ind.
67. **Desert Forest Golf Club,** Carefree, Ariz.
68. **Congressional Country Club (Blue),** Bethesda, Md.
69. **Oak Tree Golf Club,** Edmond, Okla.
70. **Mauna Kea Golf CSE. ,** Kohala Coast, Hawaii
71. **Haig Point Club (Calibogue),** Daufuskie Island, S. C.
72. **The Prince Golf and Country Club,** Princeville, Kauai, Hawaii
73. **NCR Country Club (South),** Kettering, Ohio
74. **Eugene Country Club,** Eugene, Ore.
75. **Sycamore Hills Golf Club,** Fort Wayne, Ind.
76. **Stanwich Club,** Greenwich, Conn.
77. **Aronimink Golf Club,** Newtown Square, Pa.
78. **Country Club of North Carolina,** (Dogwood) Pinehurst, N. C.
79. **Valley Club of Montecito,** Santa Barbara, Calif.
80. **Troon Golf and Country Club,** Scottsdale, Ariz.
81. **Greenville Country Club (Chanticleer),** Greenville,
    South Carolina
82. **Shadow Glen Golf Club,** Olathe, Kan.
83. **Saucon Valley Country Club (Grace),** Bethlehem, Pa.
84. **Camargo Club,** Indian Hill, Ohio
85. **Milwaukee Country Club,** Milwaukee, Wis.
86. **Pine Tree Golf Club,** Boynton Beach, Fla.
87. **Sahalee Country Club (South/North),** Redmond, Wash.
88. **Old Waverly Golf Club,** West Point, Miss.
89. **Bay Hill Club,** Orlando, Fla.
90. **Troon North Golf Club,** Scottsdale, Ariz.
91. **Wild Dunes (Links),** Isle of Palms, S. C.
92. **Wilmington Country Club (South),** Greenville, Del.
93. **Old Warson Country Club,** Ladue, Mo.
94. **Barton Creek Country Club (Fazio),** Austin, Tex.
95. **Sherwood Country Club,** Thousand Oaks, Calif.
96. **Atlanta Country Club,** Marietta, Ga.
97. **Ridgewood Country Club (East/West),** Paramus, N. J.
98. **Desert Highlands Golf Club,** Scottsdale, Ariz.
99. **Pasatiempo Golf Club,** Santa Cruz, Calif.
100. **Desert Mountain (Renegade),** Scottsdale, Ariz.

America's 75 Best Resort Courses

As ranked by GOLF DIGEST (1992)

FIRST 25

Pebble Beach, Pebble Beach, Calif.
Pinehurst (No. 2), Pinehurst, N.C.
The Ocean Course, Kiawah Island, S.C.
Kapalua (Plantation), Kapalua, Maui, Hawaii
Prince Golf & Country Club, Princeville, Kauai, Hawaii
Spyglass Hill, Pebble Beach, Calif.

TPC at Sawgrass (Stadium), Ponte Vedra, Fla.
Mauna Kea, Kohala Coast, Hawaii
Harbour Town, Hilton Head Island, S.C.
Jackson Hole, Jackson Hole, Wyo.
Coeur d'Alene Resort, Coeur d'Alene, Idaho
The Homestead (Cascades), Hot Springs, Va.
Wild Dunes (Links), Isle of Palms, S.C.
Stonehenge, Fairfield Glade, Tenn.
Kauai Lagoons (Kiele), Lihue, Kauai, Hawaii
PGA West (Stadium), La Quinta, Calif.
Bay Hill (Challenger/Champion), Orlando, Fla.
Semiahmoo, Blaine, Wash.
Shanty Creek (Legend), Bellaire, Mich.
Sunriver (North), Sunriver, Ore.
Barton Creek (Fazio), Austin, Tex.
Innisbrook (Copperhead), Tarpon Springs, Fla.
Pinehurst (No. 7), Pinehurst, N.C.
Spanish Bay, Pebble Beach, Calif.
The Kings' Course, Waikoloa, Hawaii

SECOND 25

Samoset, Rockport, Me.
Treetops Sylvan (Jones), Gaylord, Mich.
Ventana Canyon (Mountain), Tucson
The Broadmoor (East), Colorado Springs, Colo.
Golden Horseshoe (Gold), Williamsburg, Va.
Kapalua (Village), Kapalua, Maui, Hawaii
Donald Ross Memorial, Harbor Springs, Mich.
The Greenbrier (Greenbrier), White Sulphur Springs, W. Va.
Stoney Creek, Wintergreen, Va.
PGA West (Nicklaus Resort), La Quinta, Calif.
Kapalua (Bay), Kapalua, Maui, Hawaii
Tamarron, Durango, Colo.
Eagle Ridge (South), Galena, Ill.
Eagle Ridge (North), Galena, Ill.
Horseshoe Bay (Ram Rock), Horseshoe Bay, Tex.
Keystone Ranch, Keystone, Colo.
Doral (Blue), Miami
Marriott's Bay Point (Lagoon Legend), Panama City Beach, Fla.
Turtle Point, Kiawah Island, S.C.
The Concord (Monster), Kiamesha Lake, N.Y.
Port Ludlow, Port Ludlow, Wash.
The New Course at Grand Cypress, Orlando, Fla.
Princeville Makai (Ocean/Lakes), Princeville, Kauai, Hawaii
Teton Pines, Jackson, Wyo.
Grand Traverse (Bear), Acme, Mich.

THIRD 25

Long Point, Amelia Island, Fla.
The Boulders (North), Carefree, Ariz.
Singletree, Edwards, Colo.
Osprey Point, Kiawah Island, S.C.
Grand Cypress (North/South), Orlando, Fla.
Callaway Gardens (Mountain View), Pine Mountain, Ga.
Palm Beach Polo (Dunes), West Palm Beach, Fla.
The Broadmoor (West), Colorado Springs, Colo.
La Paloma (Ridge/Canyon), Tucson
Sun Valley, Sun Valley, Idaho
Walt Disney World (Palm), Lake Buena Vista, Fla.
Sea Island (Plantation/Seaside), St. Simons Island, Ga.
Sugarloaf, Carrabassett Valley, Me.

Radisson Elkhorn Sun Valley, Sun Valley, Idaho
Desert Inn, Las Vegas
Wailea (Blue), Wailea, Maui, Hawaii
Ko Olina, Ewa Beach, Oahu, Hawaii
La Quinta Hotel (Citrus), La Quinta, Calif.
New Seabury (Blue), New Seabury, Mass.
Grenelefe (West), Haines City, Fla.
Innisbrook (Island), Tarpon Springs, Fla.
PGA National (Champion), Palm Beach Gardens, Fla.
Salishan, Gleneden Beach, Ore.
Boyne Highlands (Heather), Harbor Springs, Mich.
La Quinta Hotel (Dunes), La Quinta, Calif.

America's 75
Best Public Golf Courses
As ranked by GOLF DIGEST (1990)

Listed alphabetically.

FIRST 25

Bull Creek (Wh./Bl.), Midland, Ga.
Cantigny (Premier), Wheaton, Ill.
The Captains, Brewster, Mass.
Cochiti Lake, Cochiti Lake, N.M.
Cog Hill (No. 4), Lemont, Ill.
Eastmoreland, Portland, Ore.
Edgewood Tahoe, Stateline, Nev.
Forest Preserve National, Oak Forest, Ill.
Hog Neck (Ch.), Easton, Md.
Hominy Hill, Colts Neck, N.J.
Hyland Hills (Gld.), Westminster, Colo.
Indian Canyon, Spokane, Wash.
Jackson Hole, Jackson Hole, Wyo.
Kemper Lakes, Hawthorn Woods, Ill.
Otter Creek, Columbus, Ind.
Pasatiempo, Santa Cruz, Calif.
Pine Meadow, Mundelein, Ill.
Richter Park, Danbury, Conn.
Riverdale (Dunes), Brighton, Colo.
Sandpiper, Goleta, Calif.
Sentryworld, Stevens Point, Wis.
Spook Rock, Ramapo, N.Y.
Tanglewood Park (Championship), Clemmons, N.C.
Tokatee, Blue River, Ore.
Wailua, Kauai, Hawaii

SECOND 25

Bear Creek (Masters), Houston, Tex.
Bethpage (Black), Farmingdale, N.Y.
Brown County, Oneida, Wis.
Colony West (Ch.), Tamarac, Fla.
Desert Dunes, Palm Springs, Calif.
Eagle Bend, Bigfork, Mont.
Eastwood, Fort Myers, Fla.
Edinburgh USA, Brooklyn Park, Minn.
Heather Glen (Nos. 1/2), Little River, S.C.

Heritage, Pawleys Island, S.C.
Howell Park, Farmingdale, N.J.
Hunter's Creek, Orlando, Fla.
Kayak Point, Stanwood, Wash.
Key Biscayne, Key Biscayne, Fla.
Lagoon Park, Montgomery, Ala.
Marsh Harbour, Calabash, N.C.
McCormick Woods, Port Orchard, Wash.
Meadowbrook, Rapid City, S.D.
Montauk Downs, Montauk, N.Y.
Oyster Bay, Sunset Beach, N.C.
Pecan Valley, San Antonio, Tex.
The Pit, Pinehurst, N.C.
Torrey Pines (So.), La Jolla, Calif.
TPC of Scottsdale (Stadium), Scottsdale, Ariz.
West Palm Beach, West Palm Beach, Fla.

THIRD 25

Alvamar, Lawrence, Kan.
Ancil Hoffman, Carmichael, Calif.
Arrowhead, Littleton, Colo.
Blue Ash, Blue Ash, Ohio
Eagle Creek (Ch.), Indianapolis
Fall Creek Falls, Pikeville, Tenn.
Golden Ocala, Ocala, Fla.
Grand Haven, Grand Haven, Mich.
Heron Lakes (White/Blue), Portland, Ore.
High Pointe, Williamsburg, Mich.
Hulman Links, Terre Haute, Ind.
Incline Village, Incline Village, Nev.
Golf Club of Indiana, Zionsville, Ind.
Jones Creek, Evans, Ga.
Lawsonia Links (West/East), Green Lake, Wis.
Lick Creek, Pekin, Ill.
Majestic Oaks, Ham Lake, Minn.
Moreno Valley Ranch (Mountain/Lake), Moreno Valley, Calif.
Oak Hollow, High Point, N.C.
Pole Creek, Winter Park, Colo.
Rattle Run, St. Clair, Mich.
Stone Mountain (Stonemont/Woodmont), Stone Mountain, Ga.
Timber Ridge, East Lansing, Mich.
Torrey Pines (No.), La Jolla, Calif.
University of New Mexico (South), Albuquerque, N.M.

Geographical Directory by Town/City

A

Abaco
Treasure Cay Golf Club *535*
Aberdeen, N.C.
Legacy Golf Links *317*
Aberdeen, S.Dak.
Moccasin Creek Country Club *962*
Abilene, Texas
Maxwell Golf Club *993*
Absecon, N.J.
Marriott's Seaview Resort *246*
Acapulco, Guerrero
Acapulco Princess Club de Golf *1106*
Pierre Marquez Golf Club *1107*
Acme, Mich.
Grand Traverse Resort *821*
Acton, Ontario
Blue Springs Golf Club *547*
Acworth, Ga.
The Boulders Course at Lake Acworth *117*
Cenntennial Golf Club *119*
Adams, Minn.
Cedar River Country Club *863*
Addison, Ill.
Oak Meadows Golf Club *756*
Afton, N.Y.
Afton Golf Club *255*
Afton, Okla.
Shangri-La Golf Resort *945*
Aiea (Oahu), Hawaii
Pearl Country Club *717*
Aiken, S.C.
Cedar Creek Golf Club *445*
Midland Valley Golf Club *462*
Akron, N.Y.
Dande Farms Country Club *266*
Rothland Golf Course *287*
Akron, Ohio
J.E. Good Park Golf Club *362*
Turkeyfoot Lake Golf Links *386*
Valley View Golf Club *387*
Alachua, Fla.
Heritage Links Country Club at Turkey Creek *75*
Alameda, Calif.
Chuck Corica Golf Complex *615*
Albany, Minn.
Albany Golf Course *860*
Albany, N.Y.
The New Course at Albany *283*
Albert Lea, Minn.
Green Lea Golf Course *869*
Albion, Mich.
Tomac Woods Golf Course *853*
Albuquerque, N.Mex.
Arroyo del Oso Municipal Golf Course *925*
Ladera Golf Course *926*
Los Altos Golf Course *927*
Paradise Hills Golf Club *928*
University of New Mexico Golf Course *930*
Aledo, Ill.
Hawthorne Ridge Golf Club *745*
Alexandria, Minn.
Alexandria Golf Club *860*
Alexandria, Ohio
St. Albans Golf Club *381*
Algonquin, Ill.
Golf Club of Illinois *744*
Alhambra, Calif.
Alhambra Municipal Golf Course *605*
Alice, Texas
Alice Municipal Golf Course *964*
Allen, Texas
Twin Creeks Golf Club *1013*
Allendale, Mich.
The Meadows Golf Club *705*
Allentown, Pa.
Allentown Municipal Golf Course *391*
Alliance, Nebr.
Skyview Golf Course *913*
Alliance, Ohio
Tannenhauf Golf Club *384*
Allison Park, Pa.
North Park Golf Course *419*
Alloway, N.J.
Holly Hills Golf Club *244*
Alpena, Mich.
Alpena Golf Club *802*
Alpharetta, Ga.
The Champions Club of Atlanta *119*
Riverpines Golf Club *132*
White Columns Golf Club *138*
Alpine, Ala.
Alpine Bay Golf and Country Club *18*
Alto, Mich.
Saskatoon Golf Club *847*
Alton, Ill.
Spencer T. Olin Community Golf Course *766*
Alton, Ontario
Osprey Valley Heathlands Golf Course *557*
Altoona, Pa.
Park Hills Country Club *420*
Sinking Valley Country Club *427*
Amana, IA
Amana Colonies Golf Course *775*
Amarillo, Texas
Comanche Trail Golf Club *973*
Ross Rogers Golf Club *1005*
Ambler, Pa.
Horsham Valley Golf Club *410*

Bangor Municipal Golf Course *180*

Banks, Oreg.
Quail Valley Golf Course *955*

Banning, Calif.
Sun Lakes Country Club *679*

Bar Harbor, Maine
Kebo Valley Golf Course *182*

Baraboo, Wis.
Baraboo Country Club *1048*

Barberton, Ohio
Barberton Brookside Country Club *342*

Barboursville, W.Va.
Esquire Country Club *526*

Bardstown, Ky.
Maywood Golf Course *174*
My Old Kentucky Home State Park Golf Club *174*

Barre, Vt.
Country Club of Barre *497*

Barrhead, Alberta
Barrhead Golf Course *1082*

Barrie, Ontario
Horseshoe Valley Resort *553*

Barrington, Ill.
Thunderbird Country Club *769*

Bartlesville, Okla.
Adams Municipal Golf Course *935*

Bartlett, Ill.
Bartlett Hills Golf Course *732*
Villa Olivia Country Club *770*

Bartlett, Tenn.
Quail Ridge Golf Course *492*

Bastian, Va.
Wolf Creek Golf & Country Club *525*

Basye, Va.
Bryce Resort Golf Course *506*

Batavia, Ill.
Settler's Hill Golf Course *765*

Batavia, N.Y.
Batavia Country Club *256*
Terry Hills Golf Course *294*

Bath, Pa.
White Tail Golf Club *435*

Bathurst, New Brunswick
Gowan Brae Golf & Country Club *543*

Baton Rouge, La.
Howell Park Golf Course *799*
Santa Maria Golf Course *800*
Webb Memorial Golf Course *801*

Battle Creek, Mich.
Bedford Valley Golf Course *803*
Binder Park Golf Course *804*
Marywood Golf Club *834*
Oakland Hills Golf Club *837*

Battle Lake, Minn.
Balmoral Golf Course *860*

Bay City, Mich.
Bay Valley Golf Club *803*

Bay City, Texas
Rio Colorado Golf Course *1002*

Bayou La Batre, Ala.

Bay Oaks Golf Club *18*

Bayside, N.Y.
Clearview Golf Club *264*

Bayville, N.J.
Cedar Creek Golf Course *238*

Bear Mountain, N.Y.
Rockland Lake State Park Golf Club *286*

Beaufort, S.C.
Callawassie Island Club *444*
Cat Island Golf Club *445*
Country Club of Beaufort *448*

Beaumont, Alberta
Coloniale Golf and Country Club *1082*

Beaumont, Calif.
Oak Valley Golf Club *651*

Beaumont, Texas
Bayou Din Golf Club *966*
Henry Homberg Municipal Golf Course *983*

Beaver Dam, Wis.
Old Hickory Golf Club *1067*

Beaver Falls, Pa.
Black Hawk Golf Corporation *392*
Fox Run Golf Course *404*

Beaver, W.Va.
Grandview Country Club *527*

Beaverton, Oreg.
Progress Downs Golf Course *955*

Becker, Minn.
Pebble Creek Country Club *879*

Bedford, Ind.
Otis Park Golf Club *154*

Bedford, Ohio
Shawnee Hills Golf Course *379*

Bedford, Pa.
Bedford Springs Golf Course *392*

Beecher, Ill.
Shady Lawn Golf Course *765*

Belding, Mich.
Candlestone Golf Club *808*

Belen, N.Mex.
Tierra del Sol Golf Course *930*

Belfast, N.Y.
Six-S Golf Course *290*

Bellaire, Mich.
Shanty Creek Resort *848*

Belle Vernon, Pa.
Cedarbrook Golf Course *396*

Belleair, Fla.
Belleview Mido Country Club *53*

Bellefontaine, Ohio
Bellefontaine Country Club *343*
Cherokee Hills Golf Course *348*

Belleville, Ill.
The Orchards Golf Club *758*

Belleville, N.J.
Hendricks Field Golf Course *244*

Belleville, Ontario
Bay of Quinte Country Club *547*

Bellevue, Nebr.
Willow Lakes Golf Club *914*

Bellingham, Mass.
Maplegate Country Club *209*

New England Country Club *209*
Bellingham, Wash.
Lake Padden Golf Course *1036*
Shuksan Golf Club *1042*
Sudden Valley Golf and Country Club *1044*
Belmont, Mich.
Grand Island Golf Ranch *821*
Beloit, Wis.
Krueger Municipal Golf Club *1061*
Belpre, Ohio
Oxbow Golf and Country Club *370*
Belton, Mo.
Belton Municipal Golf Course *889*
Southview Golf Club *900*
Belton, Texas
Leon Valley Golf Course *992*
Belvidere, N.J.
Apple Mountain Golf Club *236*
Bemidji, Minn.
Bemidji Town and Country Club *861*
Bend, Oreg.
Awbrey Glen Golf Club *948*
River's Edge Golf Course *956*
Widgi Creek Golf Club *960*
Bennington, Vt.
Mt. Anthony Golf & Tennis Center *500*
Bensenville, Ill.
White Pines Golf Club *772*
Benton, Ark.
Longhills Golf Club *601*
Benton Harbor, Mich.
Blossom Trails Golf Course *804*
Lake Michigan Hills Golf Club *829*
Benton, Ill.
Rend Lake Golf Course *763*
Benton, Pa.
Mill Race Golf Course *415*
Berkeley, Calif.
Tilden Park Golf Course *682*
Berkeley Springs, W.Va.
Cacapon State Park Resort *526*
Berlin, Md.
The Bay Club *187*
The Beach Club Golf Links *187*
Berlin, Md.
Eagle's Landing Golf Club *189*
Ocean City Golf and Yacht Club *194*
River Run Golf Club *196*
Berlin, Wis.
Mascoutin Golf Club *1063*
Bermuda Dunes, Calif.
Sun City Palm Springs Golf Club *678*
Bernalillo, N.Mex.
Santa Ana Golf Course *929*
Bernardston, Mass.
Crumpin-Fox Club *204*
Bessemer, Ala.

Bent Brook Golf Course *19*
Frank House Municipal Golf Club *21*
Bethel Island, Calif.
The Island Club *634*
Bethel, Maine
Bethel Inn and Country Club *180*
Bethlehem, N.H.
Bethlehem Country Club *226*
Maplewood Country Club *230*
Bethlehem, Pa.
Bethlehem Municipal Golf Club *392*
Green Pond Country Club *406*
Bettendorf, Iowa
Palmer Hills Municipal Golf Course *782*
Beulah, Mich.
Crystal Lake Golf Club *811*
Pinecroft Golf Club *841*
Beverly Hills, Fla.
Twisted Oaks Golf Club *111*
Big Canoe, Ga.
Sconti Golf Club *134*
Big Rapids, Mich.
Katke Golf Course Karsten Golf Course at ASU *828*
Big Sky, Mont.
Big Sky Golf Club *903*
Bigfork, Mont.
Eagle Bend Golf Club *903*
Billings, Mont.
Lake Hills Golf Course *904*
Peter Yegen Jr. Golf Club *905*
Biloxi, Miss.
Broadwater Resort *219*
Edgewater Bay Golf Course *220*
Southwind Country Club *223*
Sunkist Country Club *223*
Binghamton, N.Y.
Ely Park Muni Golf Course *270*
Birmingham, Ala.
Don A. Hawkins Golf Course *21*
Eagle Point Golf Club *21*
Oxmoor Valley Golf Club *30*
Bishop, Ga.
Lane Creek Golf Club *127*
Bismarck, Ark.
DeGray State Park Golf Course *600*
Bismarck, N.Dak.
Tom O'Leary Golf Course *934*
Bixby, Okla.
White Hawk Golf Club *947*
Black Butte, Oreg.
Black Butte Ranch *948*
Black Mountain, N.C.
Black Mountain Golf Course *301*
Black River Falls, Wis.
Skyline Golf Club *1072*
Blackfoot, Idaho
Blackfoot Municipal Golf Course *724*
Blackshear, Ga.
Lakeview Golf Club *127*
Blackwood, N.J.

ckory Ridge Golf Center *746*

Carbondale, Pa.
Skyline Golf Course *427*
Carefree, Ariz.
The Boulders Club *571*
Carleton, Mich.
Carleton Glen Golf Club *808*
Carlisle, Ontario
Carlisle Golf and Country Club *549*
Carlisle, Pa.
Cumberland Golf Club *399*
Mayapple Golf Links *414*
Carlsbad, Calif.
Aviara Golf Club *607*
La Costa Resort and Spa *636*
Carmel, Calif.
Carmel Valley Ranch Golf Club *613*
Rancho Canada Golf Club *661*
Carmel, Ind.
Brookshire Golf Club *141*
Carmichael, Calif.
Ancil Hoffman Golf Course *606*
Carpentersville, Ill.
Bonnie Dundee Golf Club *733*
Carrabassett Valley, Maine
Sugarloaf Golf Club *185*
Carroll, Ohio
Pine Hill Golf Club *371*
Carrollton, Ohio
Carroll Meadows Golf Course *347*
Carrollton, Texas
Indian Creek Golf Club *986*
Carson City, Nev.
Eagle Valley Golf Club *917*
Carson, Wash.
Hot Springs Golf Course *1035*
Carter Lake, Iowa
Shoreline Golf Course *783*
Cartersville, Ga.
Royal Oaks Golf Club *133*
Carterville, Ill.
Crab Orchard Golf Club *738*
Carthage, Mo.
Carthage Municipal Golf Course *890*
Cary, Ill.
Chalet Hills Golf Club *736*
Cary, N.C.
Lochmere Golf Club *319*
Casa Grande, Ariz.
Casa Grande Municipal Golf Course *572*
Dave White Municipal Golf Course *574*
Francisco Grande Resort and Golf Club *578*
Cashiers, N.C.
High Hampton Inn and Country Club *314*
Casper, Wyo.
Casper Municipal Golf Course *1078*
Cassville, Mo.
Cassville Golf Club *890*

Cassville, W.Va.
Meadow Ponds Golf Course *530*
Castle Rock, Colo.
Plum Creek Golf and Country Club *700*
Castlegar, British Columbia
Castlegar Golf Club *1090*
Castro Valley, Calif.
Willow Park Golf Club *687*
Caswell Beach, N.C.
Oak Island Golf and Country Club *324*
Cathedral City, Calif.
Desert Princess Country Club and Resort *620*
Lawrence Welk's Desert Oasis Country Club *639*
Catoosa, Okla.
Spunky Creek Country Club *946*
Cave Creek, Ariz.
Rancho Manana Golf Course *589*
Tatum Ranch Golf Club *594*
Cave Springs, Ark.
The Creeks Public Links *600*
Cavendish, P.E.I.
Green Gables Golf Course *562*
Cedar Falls, Iowa
Pheasant Ridge Municipal Golf Course *782*
Cedar, Mich.
Sugar Loaf Resort Golf Club *850*
Cedar Rapids, Iowa
Ellis Park Municipal Golf Course *778*
St. Andrews Golf Club *783*
Celina, Ohio
Northmoor Golf Club *369*
Center Square, Pa.
Center Square Golf Club *396*
Center Valley, Pa.
Center Valley Club *396*
Centerburg, Ohio
The Golf Club at Yankee Trace *384*
Table Rock Golf Club *383*
Wyandot Golf Course *390*
Central Valley, N.Y.
Central Valley Golf Club *263*
Centralia, Ill.
Greenview Country Club *745*
Centreville, Ill.
Grand Marais Golf Course *744*
Chambersburg, Pa.
Majestic Ridge Golf Club *413*
Champion, Pa.
Seven Springs Mountain Resort Golf Course *426*
Chandler, Ariz.
Ocotillo Golf Club *584*
San Marcos Golf & Country Club *590*
Channahon, Ill.
Heritage Bluffs Golf Club *745*
Chapel Hill, N.C.
Finley Golf Club *311*
Chapel Hill, Tenn.

Henry Horton State Park Golf
  Course *487*
Chapin, S.C.
Timberlake Plantation Golf Club
  475
Chaptico, Md.
Wicomico Shores Municipal Golf
  Course *199*
Chardon, Ohio
Chardon Lakes Golf Club *348*
Pleasant Hill Golf Course *372*
Charles Town, W.Va.
Locust Hill Golf Course *530*
Sleepy Hollow Golf & Country
  Club *531*
Charleston, S.C.
Charleston Municipal Golf Course
  446
Shadowmoss Plantation Golf Club
  473
Charlevoix, Mich.
Belvedere Golf Club *804*
Dunmaglas Golf Club *812*
Charlotte, Mich.
Butternut Brook Golf Course *807*
Charlotte, N.C.
Charlotte Golf Links *305*
Highland Creek Golf Club *314*
Pawtucket Golf Club *325*
Charlottesville, Va.
Birdwood Golf Course *504*
Meadowcreek Golf Course *516*
Chaska, Minn.
Bluff Creek Golf Course *861*
Dahlgreen Golf Club *865*
Chatham, Ontario
Indian Creek Golf and Country
  Club *554*
Chattanooga, Tenn.
Brainerd Golf Course *482*
Brown Acres Golf Course *482*
Moccasin Bend Golf Club *490*
The Quarry Golf Club *492*
Chautauqua, N.Y.
Chautauqua Golf Club *263*
Cheboygan, Mich.
Cheboygan Golf & Country Club
  810
Checotah, Okla.
Fountainhead State Park Golf
  Course *939*
Chehalis, Wash.
Newaukum Valley Golf Course
  1040
Riverside Country Club *1042*
Chelan, Wash.
Lake Chelan Golf Course *1036*
Chelsea, Mich.
Reddeman Farms Golf Course
  844
Chenango Forks, N.Y.
Chenango Valley Golf Cours *263*
Cheraw, S.C.
Cheraw State Park Golf Club *446*
Cherokee Village, Ark.
Cherokee Village *599*

Cherry Valley, Ill.
Elliott Golf Course *740*
Chester, S.C.
Chester Golf Club *447*
Chester, Va.
River's Bend Golf & Country
  Club *520*
Chesterfield, Va.
Birkdale Golf & Country Club
  505
Chesterland, Ohio
Fowler's Mill Golf Club *354*
Orchard Hills Golf and Country
  Club *370*
Chestermere, Alberta
Lakeside Greens Golf and Country
  Club *1086*
Chewelah, Wash.
Chewelah Golf and Country Club
  1030
Cheyenne, Wyo.
Airport Golf Course *1078*
Chico, Calif.
Bidwell Park Golf Course *609*
Canyon Oaks Golf Club *612*
Chicopee, Mass.
Chicopee Golf Club *203*
Chillicothe, Ohio
Jaycee Golf Course *363*
Running Fox Golf Course *377*
China Lake, Calif.
China Lake Golf Club *615*
China Township, Mich.
Rattle Run Golf Course *844*
Chino, Calif.
El Prado Golf Course *623*
Chino Hills, Calif.
Los Serranos Lakes Golf and
  Country Club *642*
**Christina Lake, British
  Columbia**
Christina Lake Golf Club *1091*
Chuckey, Tenn.
Graysburg Hills Golf Course *486*
Chula Vista, Calif.
EastLake Country Club *622*
Cicero, Ind.
Bear Slide Golf Club *140*
Cincinnati, Ohio
Avon Field Golf Course *342*
Blue Ash Golf Course *344*
California Golf Course *347*
Glenview Golf Course *355*
Neumann Golf Course *369*
Reeves Golf Course *375*
Sharon Woods Golf Course *379*
The Vineyard Golf Course *385*
Winton Woods Golf Club *389*
Citronelle, Ala.
Citronelle Municipal Golf Course
  20
City of Industry, Calif.
Industry Hills Sheraton Resort and
  Conference Cent *633*
Clare, Mich.
Firefly Golf Links *816*

Claremore, Okla.
Heritage Hills Golf Course *939*
Clarion, Pa.
Mayfield Golf Club *414*
Clarkston, Mich.
Pine Knob Golf Club *840*
Clarkston, Wash.
Quail Ridge Golf Course *1041*
Clarksville, Ind.
Wooded View Golf Club *165*
Clarksville, Tenn.
Eastland Green Golf Course *484*
Swan Lake Country Club *494*
Clayton, Calif.
Oakhurst Country Club *651*
Clayton, N.C.
The Neuse Golf Club *323*
Clemmons, N.C.
Tanglewood Park Golf Course *336*
Clendenin, W.Va.
Sandy Brae Golf Course *531*
Clermont, Fla.
Clerbrook Resort *58*
Palisades Golf Club *89*
Cleveland, Ohio
Highland Park Golf Club *360*
Clever, Mo.
Hidden Valley Golf Links *893*
Clifton, Va.
Twin Lakes Golf Course *524*
Clinton, Ind.
Geneva Hills Golf Course *147*
Clinton, Iowa
Valley Oaks Golf Club *784*
Clinton, N.J.
Beaver Brook Country Club *236*
Clinton Township, Mich.
Fern Hill Golf and Country Club *815*
Clinton Twp., Mich.
Partridge Creek Golf Course *839*
Clyde, Ohio
Green Hills Golf Club *356*
Sleepy Hollow Golf Course *380*
Clymer, N.Y.
Peek'N Peak Resort *284*
Coaldale, Alberta
Land-O-Lakes Golf Club *1086*
Cobble Hill, British Columbia
Arbutus Ridge Golf and Country Club *1090*
Cochiti Lake, N.Mex.
Cochiti Lake Golf Course *925*
Cocoa Beach, Fla.
Cocoa Beach Golf Course *58*
Cocoyoc, Morelos
Country Club Cocoyoc *1107*
Cody, Wyo.
Olive Glenn Golf and Country Club *1080*
Coeur d'Alene, Idaho
Coeur d'Alene Resort Golf Course *725*
Cohutta, Ga.
Nob North Golf Course *129*

Cold Spring, Minn.
Rich Spring Golf Course *883*
Coldspring, Texas
Cape Royale Golf Course *970*
Colfax, N.C.
Sandy Ridge Golf Course *332*
College Park, Md.
University of Maryland Golf Course *198*
College Station, Texas
Texas A&M University Golf Course *1012*
Collingwood, Ontario
Monterra Golf Course *556*
Colorado Springs, Colo.
Broadmoor Golf Club *690*
Patty Jewett Golf Club *149*
Pine Creek Golf Club *700*
Valley Hi Golf Course *706*
Colts Neck, N.J.
Hominy Hill Golf Course *244*
Columbia Falls, Mont.
Meadow Lake Golf Resort *905*
Columbia, Ill.
Columbia Golf Club *738*
Columbia, Mo.
Al Gustin Golf Club *893*
Columbia, S.C.
LinRick Golf Course *461*
Northwoods Golf Club *463*
Oak Hills Golf Club *463*
Columbia Station, Ohio
Dorlon Park Golf Course *351*
Emerald Woods *352*
Columbia Township, Ohio
Hickory Nut Golf Club *359*
Columbiana, Ohio
Copeland Hills Golf Course *349*
Columbus, Ga.
Bull Creek Golf Course *118*
Maple Ridge Golf Club *128*
Columbus–Galloway, Ohio
Thorn Apple Country Club *385*
Columbus, Ind.
Otter Creek Golf Club *154*
Columbus, Nebr.
Quail Run Golf Course *912*
Columbus, Ohio
Airport Golf Course *341*
Champions Golf Course *347*
Minerva Lake Golf Club *368*
Raymond Memorial Golf Club *374*
Comstock Park, Mich.
Scott Lake Country Club *848*
Concho, Ariz.
Concho Valley Country Club *573*
Concord, Calif.
Diablo Creek Golf Course *620*
Concord, Mich.
Whiffle Tree Hill Golf Course *857*
Concord, N.H.
Beaver Meadow Golf Club *226*
Concord Country Club *228*
Concord, Ohio
Quail Hollow Resort *373*

Conklin, N.Y.
Conklin Players Club *265*
Conneaut Lake, Pa.
Park Golf Course *420*
Conover, N.C.
Rock Barn Club of Golf *332*
Conroe, Texas
Wedgewood Golf Club *1015*
Conway, S.C.
Burning Ridge Golf Club *443*
Wild Wing Plantation *478*
The Witch *479*
Conyers, Ga.
Highland Golf Club *124*
Cookeville, Tenn.
Ironwood Golf Course *488*
Coon Rapids, Minn.
Bunker Hills Golf Course *863*
Coopersburg, Pa.
Locust Valley Golf Club *412*
Wedgewood Golf Club *434*
Cooperstown, N.Y.
Leatherstocking Golf Course *278*
Copetown, Ontario
Flamborough Hills Golf Club *552*
Coppell, Texas
Riverchase Golf Club *1003*
Copper Mountain, Colo.
Copper Creek Golf Club *692*
Coquitlam, British Columbia
Westwood Plateau Golf and
  Country Club *1101*
Coral Gables, Fla.
The Biltmore Golf Course *53*
Coral Springs, Fla.
Continental Golf Club at Coral
  Springs *59*
Corapolis, Pa.
Bon Air Golf Club *393*
Cordele, Ga.
Georgia Veterans State Park Golf
  Course *123*
Cornelius, Oreg.
Forest Hills Golf Course *950*
Pumpkin Ridge Golf Club *955*
Corner Brook, Newfoundland
Blomidon Golf & Country Club
  544
Cornwall, Ontario
Summerheights Golf Links *561*
Corona, Calif.
Green River Golf Course *628*
Mountain View Country Club *650*
Coronado, Calif.
Coronado Golf Course *617*
Corpus Christi, Texas
Gabe Lozano Sr. Golf Center *979*
Oso Beach Municipal Golf Course
  996
Corry, Pa.
North Hills Golf Club *419*
Cortland, N.Y.
Elm Tree Golf Course *270*
Cortland, Ohio
Tamer Win Golf and Country
  Club *383*

Corvallis, Oreg.
Trysting Tree Golf Club *959*
Costa Mesa, Calif.
Costa Mesa Country Club *617*
Cottage Grove, Wis.
Door Creek Golf Club *1053*
Council Bluffs, Iowa
Dodge Park Golf Complex *777*
Courtenay, British Columbia
Crown Isle Golf Club *1091*
Coventry, Conn.
Twin Hills Country Club *45*
Covington, Ga.
The Oaks Golf Course *130*
Coyote, Calif.
Riverside Golf Club *666*
Crab Orchard, Tenn.
Briarwood Golf Course *482*
Craig, Colo.
Yampa Valley Golf Club *707*
Cranbury, N.J.
Cranbury Golf Club *239*
Cranston, R.I.
Cranston Country Club *437*
Craryville, N.Y.
Copake Country Club *265*
**Crawford Bay, British
  Columbia**
Kokanee Springs Golf Resort
  1095
Cream Ridge, N.J.
Cream Ridge Golf Club *239*
Gambler Ridge Golf Club *242*
Crested Butte, Colo.
Skyland Mountain Golf Resort
  703
Creston, Ohio
Hawks Nest Golf Club *357*
Crestview, Fla.
Foxwood Country Club *70*
Shoal River Country Club *105*
Creswell, Oreg.
Emerald Valley Golf Club *950*
Crete, Ill.
Balmoral Woods Country Club
  731
Cross Junction, Va.
Summit Golf Club *523*
Crossville, Tenn.
Deer Creek Golf Club *484*
Thunderhollow Golf Club *495*
Crown Point, Ind.
Oak Knoll Golf Course *154*
Pheasant Valley Golf Club *156*
Summertree Golf Club *161*
Crownsville, Md.
Eisenhower Golf Course *189*
Crystal River, Fla.
Plantation Inn and Golf Resort *94*
Cumberland, Maine
Val Halla Golf Course *186*

D

Dacula, Ga.
Hamilton Mill Golf Club *123*

Hidden Lakes Golf Course 790

Derwood, Md.
Needwood Golf Course 193

Des Moines, Iowa
A.H. Blank Golf Course 775
Grandview Golf Course 779
Waveland Golf Course 785

Desert Aire, Wash.
Desert Aire Golf Course 1031

Desert Hot Springs, Calif.
Desert Dunes Golf Club 619
Mission Lakes Country Club 646

Destin, Fla.
Emerald Bay Golf Course 66
Indian Bayou Golf and Country
    Club 77
Sandestin Resort 101
Seascape Resort 103

Detroit Lakes, Minn.
Detroit Country Club 866
Wildflower at Fair Hills 887

Detroit, Mich.
Rogell Golf Course 845
Rouge Park Golf Club 846

Devine, Texas
Devine Golf Course 976

Dewey, Ariz.
Prescott Country Club 588

Dexter, Mich.
Hudson Mills Metro Park Golf
    Course 825

DFW Airport, Texas
Hyatt Bear Creek Golf and
    Raquet Club 986

Diamond Bar, Calif.
Diamond Bar Golf Club 621

Diamond City, Ark.
Diamond Hills Golf Course 600

Diamondhead, Miss.
Diamondhead Country Club 219

Dickinson, N.Dak.
Heart River Golf Course 932

Digby, Nova Scotia
The Pines Resort Hotel Golf
    Course 546

Dodge City, Kans.
Mariah Hills Golf Course 791

Donegal, Pa.
Donegal Highlands Golf Club 400

Dorado, P.R.
Hyatt Dorado Beach Resort 539
Hyatt Regency Cerromar Beach
    540

Dorchester, Ontario
Pine Knot Golf and Country Club
    558

Dorval, Quebec
Dorval Golf Club 564

Dothan, Ala.
Highland Oaks Golf Club 25
Olympia Spa Golf Resort 29

Douglas, Ga.
Beaver Kreek Golf Club 116

Douglas, Wyo.
Douglas Community Club 1078

Douglassville, Pa.

Arrowhead Golf Course 391
Blackwood Golf Course 392

Douglaston, N.Y.
Douglaston Golf Club 267

Dousman, Wis.
Kettle Moraine Golf Club 1061

Dowagiac, Mich.
Hampshire Country Club 823

Downey, Calif.
Rio Hondo Golf Club 665

Downington, Pa.
Downington Country Club 400

Doylestown, Ohio
Chippewa Golf Club 349

Draper, Va.
Draper Valley Golf Club 508

Dresher, Pa.
Twining Valley Golf Club 432

Drummond Island, Mich.
The Rock at Drummond Island
    845

Drums, Pa.
Edgewood in the Pines Golf
    Course 401

Duanesburg, N.Y.
Sycamore Greens Golf Cours 293

Dubois, Pa.
Treasure Lake Golf Club 432

Dubuque, Iowa
Bunker Hill Golf Course 777

Duluth, Ga.
St. Marlo Country Club 133

Duluth, Minn.
Enger Park Golf Club 867
Lester Park Golf Club 872

Dumas, Texas
Pheasant Trails Golf Course 999

Duncan, British Columbia
Duncan Lakes Golf and Country
    Club 1092

Duncan, S.C.
River Falls Plantation 470

Dundee, Ill.
Randall Oaks Golf Club 762

Dunedin, Fla.
Dunedin Country Club 65

Dunkirk, Md.
Twin Shields Golf Club 198

Dunrobin, Ontario
Eagle Creek Golf Club 551

Durango, Colo.
Dalton Ranch Golf Club 692
Hillcrest Golf Club 696

Durham, N.C.
Duke University Golf Club 308

Dyersburg, Tenn.
Dyersburg Municipal Golf Course
    484

E

E. Sandwich, Mass.
Round Hill Country Club 213
Eagle, Idaho
Eagle Hills Golf Course 725
Eagle, Nebr.

Woodland Hills Golf
Course *914*
Eagle River, Wis.
Eagle River Golf Course *1054*
East Amherst, N.Y.
Glen Oak Golf Course *272*
East Brunswick, N.J.
Tamarack Golf Course *252*
East Dennis, Mass.
Dennis Pines Golf Course *205*
East Dubuque, Ill.
Lacoma Golf Course *750*
East Grand Forks, Minn.
Valley Golf Association *886*
East Hartford, Conn.
East Hartford Golf Course *36*
East Lansing, Mich.
Forest Akers Golf Course *816*
Timber Ridge Golf Course *853*
East Meadow, N.Y.
Eisenhower Park Golf *269*
East Moline, Ill.
Golfmohr Golf Club *744*
East Syracuse, N.Y.
Arrowhead Golf Course *256*
Eastman, Ga.
Pine Bluff Golf and Country
Club *131*
Easton, Md.
Hog Neck Golf Course *191*
Eatonton, Ga.
Reynold's Plantation *131*
Eatontown, N.J.
Old Orchard Country Club *248*
Eau Claire, Wis.
Mill Run Golf Course *1064*
Eckton, Fla.
St. Johns County Golf Club *100*
Eden, Utah
Wolf Creek Resort
Golf Course *1027*
Edgefield, S.C.
Pine Ridge Country Club *468*
Edina, Minn.
Braemar Golf Course *861*
Edinboro, Pa.
Culbertson Hills Golf Resort *399*
Edisto Island, S.C.
Edisto Beach Golf Club *451*
Edmond, Okla.
Coffee Creek Golf Course *937*
Kickingbird Golf Course *940*
Edmonton, Alberta
Riverside Golf Course *1088*
Victoria Golf Course *1089*
Edwards, Colo.
The Club at Cordillera *704*
Sonnenalp Golf Club *703*
Edwardsville, Ill.
Fox Creek Golf Club *741*
Egg Harbor, Wis.
Alpine Resort Golf Course *1048*
El Cajon, Calif.
Rancho San Diego Golf Club *662*
Singing Hills Country Club *675*
El Mirage, Ariz.

Pueblo El Mirage Country Club
588
El Paso, Texas
Ascarate Park Golf Course *964*
Cielo Vista Golf Course *972*
Painted Dunes Desert Golf Course
996
Underwood Golf Course *1014*
Elburn, Ill.
Hughes Creek Golf Club *747*
Elgin, Ill.
Spartan Meadows Golf Club *766*
Elizabeth, Pa.
Butler's Golf Course *394*
Seven Springs Country Club *426*
Elizabethton, Tenn.
Elizabethton Municipal Golf Club
485
Elizabethtown, Ky.
Pine Valley Country Club &
Resort *175*
Elk City, Okla.
Elk City Golf and Country Club
938
Elk Grove Village, Ill.
Fox Run Golf Links *741*
Elk River, Minn.
Elk River Country Club *867*
Elkhart Lake, Wis.
Quit-Qui-Oc Golf Club *1068*
Elkhorn, Nebr.
Indian Creek Golf Course *910*
Elkhorn, Wis.
Evergreen Golf Club *1054*
Elko, Nev.
Ruby View Golf Course *922*
Spring Creek Golf Course *923*
Elkton, Md.
Brantwood Golf Club *188*
Ellabell, Ga.
Black Creek Golf Club *117*
Ellenville, N.Y.
Nevele Country Club *283*
Ellicott City, Md.
Turf Valley Hotel and Country
Club *197*
Ellicottville, N.Y.
Holiday Valley Resort *275*
Ellsworth, Mich.
Antrim Dells Golf Club *802*
Elma, N.Y.
Elma Meadows Golf Club *270*
Elmer, N.J.
Centerton Golf Club *239*
Elmira, N.Y.
Mark Twain Golf Club *280*
Elmore, Ohio
Sugar Creek Golf Course *381*
Eloy, Ariz.
Eloy-Tohono Municipal Golf
Course *576*
Elsberry, Mo.
Sun Valley Golf Course *900*
Elverta, Calif.
Cherry Island Golf Course *615*
Elyria, Ohio

Pala Mesa Resort *654*
Fancy Gap, Va.
Skyland Lakes Golf Course *521*
Fargo, N.Dak.
Edgewood Golf Course *932*
Rose Creek Golf Course *934*
Farmingdale, Maine
Kennebec Heights Golf Club *182*
Farmingdale, N.J.
Howell Park Golf Course *245*
Spring Meadow Golf Course *252*
Farmingdale, N.Y.
Bethpage State Park Golf Courses
258
Farmington, Conn.
Tunxis Plantation Country Club
45
Farmington, Minn.
Fountain Valley Golf Club *867*
Southern Hills Golf Club *885*
Farmington, Mo.
Eagle Lake Golf Club *892*
Farmington, N.Mex.
Pinon Hills Golf Course *929*
Farmington, Pa.
Nemacolin Woodlands Resort *418*
Farwell, Mich.
Eagle Glen Golf Course *813*
Fayetteville, Ga.
River's Edge Golf Course *132*
Whitewater Creek Country Club
138
Fayetteville, N.C.
Gates Four Country Club *312*
Fayetteville, N.Y.
Green Lakes State Park Golf Club
273
Fayetteville, Pa.
Penn National Golf Club *420*
Feeding Hills, Mass.
Oak Ridge Golf Club *210*
Fenton, Mich.
Fenton Farms Golf Club *815*
Fenton, Mo.
Riverside Golf Course *899*
Fenwick, Ontario
Peninsula Lakes Golf Club *558*
Fergus Falls, Minn.
Pebble Lake Golf Club *879*
Fernandina Beach, Fla.
Fernandina Beach Municipal Golf
Course *68*
Festus/Crystal City, Mo.
Crystal Highlands Golf Club *891*
Fillmore, Calif.
Elkins Ranch Golf Club *624*
Findlay, Ill.
Eagle Creek Resort Golf Course
739
Findlay, Ohio
Hillcrest Golf Club *360*
Fish Creek, Wis.
Peninsula State Park Golf Course
1068
Fishers, Ind.
Ironwood Golf Club *151*

Flagstaff, Ariz.
Elden Hills Golf Club *575*
Flanders, N.J.
Flanders Valley Golf Course *241*
Fleetwood, Pa.
Rich Maiden Golf Course *424*
Fletcher, N.C.
French Broad Golf Center *312*
Flint, Mich.
Swartz Creek Golf Course *851*
Florence, Ala.
McFarland Park Golf Course *29*
Florence, Ky.
Boone Links *167*
Florence, Oreg.
Ocean Dunes Golf Links *954*
Sandpines Golf Resort *957*
Florence, S.C.
Oakdale Country Club *464*
Florien, La.
Toro Hills Lodge *801*
Florissant, Mo.
Paddock Country Club *897*
Flowery Branch, Ga.
Royal Lakes Golf and Country
Club *133*
Floyd Knobs, Ind.
Valley View Golf Club *163*
Flushing, N.Y.
Kissena Park Golf Course *277*
Foley, Ala.
Glenlakes Country Club *22*
Fontana on Geneva Lake, Wis.
Abbey Springs Golf Course *1048*
Ford City, Pa.
Lenape Heights Golf Course *411*
Forest, Va.
Ivy Hill Golf Club *513*
Forestville, N.Y.
Tri County Country Club *296*
Forsyth, Ga.
Forsyth Country Club *122*
Fort Cobb, Okla.
Fort Cobb State Park Golf Course
939
Fort Collins, Colo.
Collindale Golf Club *692*
Ptarmigan Country Club *701*
Southridge Golf Club *703*
Fort Dodge, Iowa
Lakeside Municipal Golf Course
781
Fort Fairfield, Maine
Aroostook Valley Country Club
180
Fort Langley, British Columbia
Fort Langley Golf Course *1093*
Fort Lauderdale, Fla.
Rolling Hills Hotel and Golf
Resort *99*
Fort Madison, Iowa
Sheaffer Golf Course *783*
Fort Mill, S.C.
Fort Mill Golf Club *451*
Regent Park Golf Club *470*
Fort Morgan, Colo.

Pezhekee Golf Club *880*
Golden, British Columbia
Golden Golf and Country Club
1094
Golden, Colo.
Applewood Golf Course *688*
Golden Valley, Minn.
Brookview Golf Course *862*
Goldsboro, N.C.
Lane Tree Golf Course *317*
Goleta, Calif.
Sandpiper Golf Course *670*
Gonic, N.H.
Rochester Country Club *233*
Goodyear, Ariz.
Eagle's Nest Country Club at
Pebble Creek *575*
Estrella Mountain Golf Course
577
Palm Valley Golf Club *585*
Goose Creek, S.C.
Crowfield Golf & Country Club
449
Gordonsville, Va.
Shenandoah Crossing Resort and
Country Club *520*
Gorham, Maine
Gorham Golf Club *182*
Gormley, Ontario
Fire Fighters Gormley Green Golf
Club *551*
Fire Fighters Rolling Hills Golf
Club *552*
Goshen, Ind.
Black Squirrel Golf Club *140*
Graeagle, Calif.
Graeagle Meadows Golf
Course *628*
Graford, Texas
The Cliffs Golf Club *973*
Grafton, Ohio
Pine Brook Golf Course *371*
Grafton, W.Va.
Tygart Lake Country Club *532*
Grafton, Wis.
Country Club of Wisconsin *1052*
Graham, N.C.
Quarry Hills Country Club *330*
Gramling, S.C.
Village Green Golf Club *476*
Granby, Mass.
Westover Golf Course *217*
Grand Blanc, Mich.
Captain's Club at Woodfield *808*
Grand Forks, N.Dak.
Lincoln Park Golf Club *932*
Grand Haven, Mich.
Grand Haven Golf Club *820*
Grand Island, N.Y.
Beaver Island State Park Golf
Course *257*
River Oaks Golf Club *286*
Grand Island, Nebr.
Grand Island Municipal Golf
Course *909*
Indianhead Golf Course *911*

Grand Lake, Colo.
Grand Lake Golf Course *695*
Grand Prairie, Texas
Grand Prairie Municipal Golf
Course *981*
Riverside Golf Club *1004*
Grand Rapids, Mich.
English Hills Golf Course *814*
Gracewil Country Club *819*
Grand Rapids Golf Club *821*
Indian Trails Golf Course *827*
Grand Rapids, Minn.
Pokegama Golf Club *881*
Wendigo Golf Course *887*
Grande Prairie, Alberta
The Dunes Golf and Winter Club
1084
Grandview, Mo.
River Oaks Golf Club *899*
Granger, Ind.
Juday Creek Golf Course *151*
Granger, Iowa
Jester Park Golf Course *780*
Granite City, Ill.
Legacy Golf Club *751*
Grant, Mich.
Brigadoon Golf Club *807*
Grantham, N.H.
Eastman Golf Links *228*
Grants Pass, Oreg.
Grants Pass Country Club *951*
Grantville, Pa.
Manada Golf Club *413*
Granville, Ohio
Granville Golf Club *356*
Raccoon International Golf Club
374
Grapevine, Texas
Grapevine Golf Course *982*
Grass Valley, Calif.
Alta Sierra Golf and Country
Club *605*
Grayling, Mich.
Fox Run Country Club *817*
Graysville, Ala.
Mountain View Golf Club *29*
Great Falls, Mont.
R.O. Speck Municipal Golf
Course *906*
Great River, N.Y.
Timber Point Golf Course *295*
Greeley, Colo.
Highland Hills Golf Courses *695*
Green Bay, Wis.
Mystery Hills Golf Club *1065*
Green Lake, Wis.
The Golf Courses of Lawsonia
1056
Tuscumbia Golf Club *1074*
Green Lane, Pa.
Macoby Run Golf Course *413*
Green Valley, Ariz.
Canoa Hills Golf Course *572*
Haven Golf Club *580*
San Ignacio Golf Club *590*
Greencastle, Pa.

Hanover, N.H.
Hanover Country Club *229*
Hanover, Pa.
South Hills Golf Club *428*
Harbor Springs, Mich.
Boyne Highlands Resort *805*
Little Traverse Bay Golf Club *832*
Harborcreek, Pa.
Downing Golf Course *400*
Hardy, Va.
Chestnut Creek Golf Club *507*
Harlingen, Texas
Tony Butler Golf Course *1012*
Harmony, Pa.
Deep Valley Golf Course *407*
Harmony, R.I.
Melody Hill Golf Course *438*
Harpster, Ohio
Hickory Grove Golf Course *358*
Harrisburg, Pa.
Sportsmans Golf Club *428*
Harrison, Ohio
Miami Whitewater Forest Golf
  Course *367*
Harrisonburg, Va.
Lakeview Golf Course *515*
Massanutten Golf Club *516*
Harrisville, R.I.
Country View Golf Club *437*
Harrodsburg, Ky.
Bright Leaf Golf Resort *168*
Harsens Island, Mich.
Middle Channel Golf & Country
  Club *835*
Hartford City, Ind.
Laurel Lakes Golf Course *152*
Hartford, Conn.
Goodwin Park Golf Course *37*
Keney Golf Course *38*
Hartford, Wis.
Hartford Golf Club *1058*
Hartland, Mich.
Dunham Hills Golf and Country
  Club *812*
Hartland Glen Golf and Country
  Club *823*
The Majestic at Lake Walden *832*
Hartland, Wis.
Songbird Hills Golf Course *1072*
Harvard, Ill.
Plum Tree National Golf Club
  760
Harvard, Mass.
Shaker Hills Golf Club *214*
Harwich, Mass.
Cranberry Valley Golf Course *203*
Haslett, Mich.
Pine Lake Golf Course *840*
Hastings, Minn.
Afton Alps Golf Course *860*
Bellwood Oaks Golf Course *860*
Hidden Greens Golf Club *870*
Hatchville, Mass.
Cape Cod Country Club *202*
Hattiesburg, Miss.
Timberton Golf Club *224*

USM's Van Hook Golf Course *224*
Hauppauge, N.Y.
Hauppauge Country Club *274*
Marriott's Golf Club at Wind
  Watch *281*
Haverhill, Mass.
Crystal Springs Golf Club *204*
Hawley, Pa.
Country Club at Woodloch
  Springs *399*
Hayden Lake, Idaho
Avondale Golf Club *724*
Hayesville, N.C.
Chatuge Shores Golf Course *305*
Hayfield, Minn.
Oaks Country Club *879*
Hayward, Calif.
Skywest Golf Club *675*
Hayward, Wis.
Hayward Golf and Tennis Center
  1059
Headingley, Manitoba
John Blumberg Golf Course *1102*
Heber Springs, Ark.
The Red Apple Inn and Country
  Club *603*
Hebron, Conn.
Blackledge Country Club *34*
Tallwood Country Club *44*
Hedgesville, W.Va.
The Woods Resort *533*
Helen, Ga.
Innsbruck Resort and Golf Club
  125
Helena, Mont.
Bill Roberts Municipal Golf
  Course *903*
Hellertown, Pa.
Woodland Hills Country Club
  436
Hemet, Calif.
Seven Hills Golf Course *672*
Hempstead, Texas
Fox Creek Golf Course *979*
Henderson, Nev.
Black Mountain Golf and Country
  Club *915*
The Legacy Golf Club *921*
Wild Horse Golf Club *924*
Hendersonville, Tenn.
Country Hills Golf Course *483*
Hereford, Texas
John Pitman Municipal Golf
  Course *989*
Hermitage, Pa.
Tam O'Shanter Pa. *430*
Hernando, Fla.
Citrus Hills Golf and Country
  Club *57*
Herndon, Va.
Herndon Centennial Golf Club
  511
Hersey, Mich.
Spring Valley Golf Course *849*
Hershey, Pa.
Hershey Country Club *408*

Hershey Parkview Golf Course 409

Hertford, N.C.
The Sound Golf Links 337

Hesperia, Calif.
Hesperia Golf and Country Club 631

Hesston, Kans.
Hesston Municipal Golf Park 789

Hibbing, Minn.
Mesaba Country Club 875

Hidden Valley, Pa.
Golf Club at Hidden Valley 409

Higgins Lake, Mich.
Burning Oak Country Club 807

High Point, N.C.
Blair Park Golf Club 301
Oak Hollow Golf Course 323

Highland, Ind.
Wicker Memorial Park Golf Course 165

Highland Park, Ill.
Highland Park Country Club 746
Sunset Valley Golf Club 768

Hillman, Mich.
Thunder Bay Golf Resort 852

Hillsboro, Mo.
Raintree Golf Course 899

Hillsboro, Ohio
Rocky Fork Golf and Tennis Center 377

Hillsboro, Oreg.
Meriwether National Golf Club 954

Hilltop Lakes, Texas
Rolling Hill Golf Club 1005

Hilton Head Island, S.C.
Country Club of Hilton Head 449
Harbour Town Golf Links 453
Hilton Head National Golf Club 455
Indigo Run Golf Club 456
Oyster Reef Golf Club 465
Palmetto Dunes Resort 465
Palmetto Hall Plantation 466
Port Royal Golf Club 469
Sea Pines Sports and Conference Center 473
Shipyard Golf Club 474

Hinckley, Minn.
Grand National Golf Club 868

Hinckley, Ohio
Hinckley Hills Golf Course 360
Ironwood Golf Course 362
Pine Hills Golf Club 371
Skyland Golf Club 380

Hingham, Mass.
South Shore Country Club 214

Hinton, Alberta
Hinton Golf Club 1085

Hixson, Tenn.
Creek's Bend Golf Club 483

Hobart, Ind.
Cressmoor Country Club 143

Hobbs, N.Mex.
Ocotillo Park Golf Course 928

Hobe Sound, Fla.
Lost Lake Golf Club 82

Hockley, Texas
The Links at Tennwood 992

Hoffman Estates, Ill.
Highland Woods Golf Course 747
Hilldale Golf Club 747
Poplar Creek Country Club 760

Holland, Mich.
West Ottawa Country Club 856
Winding Creek Golf Course 858

Hollis, N.H.
The Overlook Country Club 231

Hollister, Calif.
Ridgemark Golf and Country Club 664

Holly, Mich.
Heather Highlands Golf Club 824

Holly Springs, Miss.
Kirkwood National Golf Club 220

Holly Springs, N.C.
Devil's Ridge Golf Club 308

Hollywood, S.C.
Links at Stono Ferry 460

Homestead, Fla.
Redland Golf and Country Club 96

Honolulu (Oahu), Hawaii
Ala Wai Golf Course 708
Hawaii Kai Golf Course 709

Hood River, Oreg.
Indian Creek Golf Club 952

Hope Mills, N.C.
Cypress Lakes Golf Course 307

Hopewell Junction, N.Y.
Beekman Golf Club 257

Hopewell, Va.
Jordan Point Golf Club 513

Hopkins, Minn.
Meadowbrook Golf Course 875

Hopkinsville, Ky.
Western Hills Golf Course 179

Hopkinton, Mass.
Saddle Hill Country Club 213

Horicon, Wis.
Rock River Hills Golf Course 1070

Hornby, Ontario
Hornby Tower Golf Club 553

Horseheads, N.Y.
Soaring Eagles Golf Club 291

Horseshoe Bay, Texas
Horseshoe Bay Resort 985

Hot Springs, Ark.
Hot Springs Country Club 601

Hot Springs, S.Dak.
Southern Hills Golf Course 963

Hot Springs, Va.
The Homestead Resort 512

Houghton Lake, Mich.
The Quest Golf Club 842

Houston, Texas
Bear Creek Golf World 966
Brock Park Golf Course
Broadwater Resort 969
Clear Lake Golf Club 973

Ixtapa Golf Course *1107*
Marina Ixtapa Club de Golf *1107*

J

Jackpot, Nev.
Jackpot Golf Club *919*
Jackson, Mich.
Cascades Golf Course *809*
Ella Sharp Park Golf Course *814*
Gracewil Pines Golf Club *820*
Lakeland Hills Golf Course *829*
Sonny Guy Municipal Golf
Course *223*
Jackson, Mo.
Bent Creek Golf Course *889*
Jackson Springs, N.C.
Foxfire Resort and Country
Club *311*
Jackson, Wyo.
Jackson Hole Golf and Tennis
Club *1079*
Teton Pines Resort and Country
Club *1080*
Jacksonville, Fla.
Baymeadows Golf Club *52*
Champions Club at Julington
Creek *57*
Cimarrone Golf and Country
Club *57*
The Course at Westland *60*
Golf Club of Jacksonville *72*
Hyde Park Golf Club *76*
Jacksonville Beach Golf Club *79*
Mill Cove Golf Club *87*
Windsor Parke Golf Club *114*
Jacksonville, Ill.
The Links Golf Course *753*
Jaffrey, N.H.
Shattuck Golf Course *233*
James City County, Va.
The Colonial Golf Course *507*
Jamestown, N.C.
Jamestown Park Golf Club *316*
Jamul, Calif.
Steele Canyon Golf Club *678*
Janesville, Wis.
Riverside Golf Course *1070*
Jasper, Alberta
Jasper Park Lodge Golf Course
1085
Jasper, Ind.
Jasper Municipal Golf Course *151*
Sultan's Run Golf Course *161*
Jefferson, N.C.
Jefferson Landing Club *316*
Jefferson, N.H.
Waumbek Golf Club *235*
Jeffersonton, Va.
South Wales Golf Course *522*
Jeffersontown, Ky.
Charlie Vettiner Golf Course *168*
Jekyll Island, Ga.
Jekyll Island Golf Resort *125*
Jenison, Mich.
Wallinwood Springs Golf Club *855*

Jenks, Okla.
South Lakes Golf Course *946*
Jericho, Vt.
West Bolton Golf Club *502*
Jeromesville, Ohio
Mohican Hills Golf Club *368*
Johns Island, S.C.
Oak Point Golf Course *464*
Johnsonville, S.C.
The Wellman Club *796*
Johnstown, N.Y.
Alban Hills Country Club *255*
Johnstown, Pa.
North Fork Golf and Tennis
Club *418*
Joliet, Ill.
Inwood Golf Course *748*
Wedgewood Golf Course *771*
Woodruff Golf Course *774*
Jonesboro, Ga.
The Links Golf Club *128*
Jonesborough, Tenn.
The Crossings Golf Club *483*
Jonestown, Pa.
Monroe Valley Golf Club *416*
Jonesville, Va.
Cedar Hill Country Club *507*
Joplin, Mo.
Loma Linda Golf Club *895*
Schifferdecker Golf Course *900*
Julian, N.C.
Walnut Wood Golf Course *338*
Jupiter, Fla.
Indian Creek Golf Club *77*

K

Kahuku (Oahu), HI
Turtle Bay Hilton Golf and
Tennis Resort *719*
Kailua-Kona, Hawaii
Kona Surf Resort and Country
Club *713*
Makalei Hawaii Country Club *714*
Kalamazoo, Mich.
Milham Park Municipal Golf
Club *836*
Thornapple Creek Golf Club *852*
Kalispell, Mont.
Buffalo Hill Golf Course *903*
Kamloops, British Columbia
Eagle Point Golf and Country
Club *1092*
Rivershore Golf Club *1098*
Kamuela, Hawaii
Hapuna Golf Course *709*
Mauna Kea Beach Golf
Course *715*
Waikoloa Beach Resort *721*
Waimea Country Club *722*
Kananaskis Village, Alberta
Kananaskis Country Golf
Club *1085*
Kanata, Ontario
Kanata Lakes Golf and Country
Club *554*

Lakewood, Calif.
Lakewood Country Club *639*
Lakewood, Colo.
Fox Hollow at Lakewood Golf
    Course *694*
Lakewood, Ill.
Lakewood Golf Club *751*
Lakewood, N.J.
Lakewood Country Club *246*
Woodlake Golf and Country Club
    254
Lanai City (Lanai), Hawaii
The Challenge at Manele *708*
The Experience at Koele *708*
Lancaster, Ohio
Estate Golf Club *353*
Lancaster, Pa.
Overlook Golf Course *420*
Lancaster, Texas
Country View Golf Club *974*
Langhorne, Pa.
Middletown Country Club *415*
Langley, British Columbia
Belmont Golf Course *1090*
Lansdale, Pa.
Pine Crest Golf Club *422*
Lansdowne, Va.
Lansdowne Golf Course *515*
Lansing, Mich.
Royal Scot Golf Course *846*
Lapeer, Mich.
Rolling Hills Golf Club *846*
LaPointe, Wis.
Madeline Island Golf Club *1063*
LaPorte, Texas
Bay Forest Golf Course *966*
Laramie, Wyo.
Glenn "Red" Jacoby Golf Club
    1079
Laredo, Texas
Casa Blanca Golf Course *970*
Largo, Fla.
Bardmoor North Golf Club *52*
Las Croabas, P.R.
The Golf Club at El Conquistador
    539
Las Cruces, N.Mex.
New Mexico State University
    Golf Course *927*
Las Vegas, Nev.
Angel Park Golf Club *915*
Desert Inn Golf Club *917*
Desert Rose Golf Course *917*
Las Vegas Golf Club *920*
Las Vegas Hilton Country Club
    920
Las Vegas Paiute Resort *920*
Painted Desert Golf Club *922*
Sun City Las Vegas Golf Club *923*
LaSalle, Ill.
Oak Ridge Golf Club *756*
Laughlin, Nev.
Emerald River Golf Course *918*
Laurel Fork, Va.
Olde Mill Golf Course *518*
Laurel, Md.

Patuxent Greens Country Club
    194
Lauringburg, N.C.
The Lodge Golf Course *337*
Lavalette, W.Va.
Lavelette Golf Club *529*
Sugarwood Golf and Country
    Club *532*
Laveen, Ariz.
PohlCat Mountain View Golf
    Club *587*
Lawrence, Kans.
Alvamar Golf Club *787*
Lawrenceburg, Ky.
Bob-O-Link Golf Course *167*
Layton, Utah
Valley View Golf Course *1026*
Laytonsville, Md.
Laytonsville Golf Course *192*
Le Roy, N.Y.
Le Roy Country Club *278*
Leander, Texas
Crystal Falls Golf Course *975*
Leavenworth, Wash.
Leavenworth Golf Club *1037*
Lebanon, Ind.
Cool Lake Golf Club *143*
Golf Club of Indiana *147*
Lebanon, Ohio
Shaker Run Golf Course *378*
Lebanon, Pa.
Royal Oaks Golf Course *425*
Lebanon, Tenn.
Hunters Point Golf Club *488*
Leesburg, Va.
Goose Creek Golf Club *509*
Leesburg Westpark Hotel Golf
    Club *516*
Leesport, Pa.
Willow Hollow Golf Course *436*
Lehigh, Fla.
Admiral Lehigh Golf and Resort
    50
Lemont, Ill.
Cog Hill Golf Club *737*
Gleneagles Golf Club *743*
Ruffled Feathers Golf Club *763*
Lemoore, Calif.
Lemoore Golf Course *640*
Lenox, Mich.
Richmond Forest Golf Club *844*
Leonardtown, Md.
Breton Bay Golf & Country Club
    188
Less Summit, Mo.
Chapel Woods Golf Course *890*
Lethbridge, Alberta
Henderson Lake Golf Club *1084*
Paradise Canyon Golf and
    Country Club *1087*
Lewisburg, Pa.
Bucknell Golf Club *394*
Lewisburg, W.Va.
Greenbrier Valley Country Club
    528
Lewisburg Elks Country Club *529*

Camelot Country Club *1051*
Lompoc, Calif.
La Purisima Golf Course *636*
London, Ky.
Crooked Creek Golf Club *169*
London, Ontario
Fanshawe Golf Club *551*
Forest City National Golf Club *552*
River Road Golf Course *559*
Thames Valley Golf Course *561*
Lone Wolf, Okla.
Quartz Mountain Golf Course *944*
Long Beach, Calif.
El Dorado Park Golf Club *623*
Recreation Park Golf Course *663*
Skylinks Golf Club *675*
Long Grove, Ill.
Kemper Lakes Golf Course *749*
Long Grove, Iowa
Glynns Creek Golf Course *779*
Longboat Key, Fla.
Longboat Key Club *82*
Longmont, Colo.
Lake Valley Golf Club *698*
Twin Peaks Golf Course *705*
Longs, S.C.
Buck Creek Golf Plantation *443*
Colonial Charters Golf Club *448*
The Long Bay Club *461*
Longview, Wash.
Mint Valley Golf Club *1040*
Longville, Minn.
Ridgewood Golf Course *883*
Longwood, Fla.
Sabal Point Country Club *100*
Wekiva Golf Club *113*
Lore City, Ohio
Salt Fork State Park Golf Course *378*
Lorton, Va.
Pohick Bay Regional Golf Course *519*
Los Alamitos, Calif.
Cypress Golf Club *618*
Los Alamos, N.Mex.
Los Alamos Golf Club *927*
Los Angeles, Calif.
Chester Washington Golf Course *615*
Griffith Park *629*
Rancho Park Golf Course *662*
Los Cabos, Baja Sur
The Ocean Course at Cabo del Sol *1106*
Louisville, Colo.
Coal Creek Golf Course *691*
Louisville, Ky.
Iroquois Golf Course *171*
Quail Chase Golf Club *176*
Seneca Golf Course *176*
Shawnee Golf Course *177*
Loveland, Colo.
Loveland Golf Club *698*
Mariana Butte Golf Course *699*

Loveland, Ohio
Eagles Nest Golf Course *352*
Hickory Woods Golf Course *359*
Lowellville, Ohio
Bedford Trails Golf Course *342*
Countryside Golf Course *350*
Lubbock, Texas
Meadowbrook Municipal Golf Course *993*
Shadow Hills Golf Course *1007*
Lucas, Ky.
Barren River State Park Golf Course *167*
Ludington, Mich.
Lincoln Hills Golf Club *831*
Lumber Bridge, N.C.
Scothurst Country Club *332*
Luray, Va.
Caverns Country Club *506*
Lutherville, Md.
Pine Ridge Golf Course *194*
Lutsen, Minn.
Superior National at Lutsen Golf Course *885*
Lutz, Fla.
Tournament Players Club of Tampa Bay *110*
Luxemburg, Wis.
Northbrook Country Club *1066*
Lydia, S.C.
Fox Creek Golf Club *452*
Lynden, Wash.
Homestead Golf and Country Club *1034*
Lynn, Mass.
Gannon Municipal Golf Cour *206*
Lynnfield, Mass.
Sagamore Springs Golf Club *213*
Lyons, N.Y.
Wayne Hills Country Club *297*

M

Mabank, Texas
Pinnacle Country Club *999*
Macon, Ga.
Barrington Hall Golf Club *116*
Madera, Calif.
Madera Municipal Golf Course *643*
Madison, Ohio
Powderhorn Golf Course *373*
Madison, Wis.
Odana Hills Golf Course *1067*
Yahara Hills Golf Course *1077*
Maggie Valley, N.C.
Maggie Valley Resort Golf Club *319*
Magnolia, N.C.
Magnolia Country Club *320*
Mahanoy City, Pa.
Mountain Valley Golf Cours *417*
Mahomet, Ill.
Lake of the Woods Golf Club *750*
Mahopac, N.Y.
Putnam Country Club *285*

Mahwah, N.J.
Darlington Golf Course 240
Malibu, Calif.
Malibu Country Club 643
Malone, N.Y.
Malone Golf Club 280
Manahawkin, N.J.
Ocean Acres Country Club 247
Manakin Sabot, Va.
Sycamore Creek Golf Course 523
Mancelona, Mich.
Deer Run Golf Course 812
Manchester, N.H.
Derryfield Country Club 228
Manchester Village, Vt.
Gleneagles Golf Course 498
Mandan, N.Dak.
Prairie West Golf Course 933
Manhattan, Kans.
Stagg Hill Golf Club 793
Manorville, N.Y.
Pine Hills Country Club 285
Rock Hill Country Club 286
Swan Lake Golf Club 293
Mansfield, Ohio
Twin Lakes Golf Course 387
Wooldridge Golf and Swim Club
   373
Mansfield, Pa.
Corey Creek Golf Club 398
Mansonville, Quebec
Owl's Head 566
Manvel, N.Dak.
Manvel Golf Course 933
Manzanillo, Colima
La Mantarraya Club Las Hadas
   1126
Maple Valley, Wash.
Lake Wilderness Golf Course 1037
Maplewood, Minn.
Goodrich Golf Course 868
Marengo, Ill.
Marengo Ridge Golf Club 753
Margaretville, N.Y.
Hanah Country Club 274
Margate, Fla.
Oriole Golf and Tennis Club of
   Margate 89
Marietta, Ga.
City Club Marietta 120
Marion, Ind.
Hart Golf Course 149
Shady Hills Golf Course 160
Walnut Creek Golf Course 164
Marion, Iowa
Squaw Creek Golf Course 784
Marion, Va.
Holston Hills Golf Club 512
Markham, Ontario
Angus Glen Golf Club 547
Markham Green Golf and
   Country Club 556
Mars, Pa.
Venango Trail Golf Course 434
Marshall, Minn.
Marshall Golf Club 875

Marshall's Creek, Pa.
Mountain Manor Inn and Golf
   Club 417
Marshfield, Mass.
Green Harbor Golf Club 207
Marstons Mills, Mass.
Olde Barnstable Fairgrounds Golf
   Course 211
Mart, Texas
Battle Lake Golf Course 965
Martinsburg, W.Va.
Stonebridge Golf Club 532
Marysville, Calif.
Plumas Lake Golf and Country
   Club 659
Marysville, Ohio
Darby Creek Golf Course 350
Flagstone Golf Club 354
Marysville, Wash.
Battle Creek Golf Course 1029
Cedarcrest Golf Club 1030
Maryville, Tenn.
Lambert Acres Golf Club 489
Mashpee, Mass.
Quashnet Valley Country Club
   212
Mason, Mich.
Mason Hills Golf Course 834
Mason, Ohio
Crooked Tree Golf Club 350
The Golf Center at Kings Island
   384
Kingswood Golf Course 363
Western Row Golf Course 388
Mason, W.Va.
Riverside Golf Club 531
Massena, N.Y.
Massena Country Club 281
Mather, Calif.
Mather Golf Course 644
Maunaloa (Molokai), Hawaii
Kaluakoi Golf Course 710
Mayesville, S.C.
Pineland Plantation Golf Club 468
Mayville, Wis.
Mayville Golf Club 1064
McAfee, N.J.
Great Gorge Country Club 243
McCall, Idaho
McCall Municipal Golf Course
   726
McCook, Nebr.
Heritage Hills Golf Course 909
McCormick, S.C.
Hickory Knob Golf Club 454
McDonough, Ga.
Georgia National Golf Club 122
McHenry, Md.
The Golf Club at Wisp 191
McKee City, N.J.
Mays Landing Country Club 246
McKenzie, Tenn.
Carroll Lake Golf Club 483
McKinleyville, Calif.
Beau Pre Golf Club 608
McKinney, Texas

The Ranch Country Club 1000
McMurray, Pa.
Rolling Green Golf Club 425
McPherson, Kans.
Turkey Creek Golf Course 795
McRae, Ga.
Wallace Adams Golf Course 138
Mechanicsburg, Ohio
Indian Springs Golf Club 361
Mechanicsburg, Pa.
Silver Springs Golf Course 427
Medford, N.J.
Golden Pheasant Golf Club 242
Medford, Oreg.
Cedar Links Golf Course 949
Media, Pa.
Paxon Hollow Country Club 420
Medicine Hat, Alberta
Connaught Golf Club 1083
Medicine Hat Golf and Country
  Club 1086
Medina, Minn.
Baker National Golf Course 860
Medina, Ohio
Bunker Hill Golf Course 346
Pleasant Valley Country Club 373
Ridge Top Golf Course 376
Melbourne, Fla.
Baytree National Golf Links 52
Memphis, Tenn.
Audubon Park Golf Course 481
Davy Crockett Golf Course 484
Fox Meadows Golf Course 486
Pine Hill Golf Course 492
Stonebridge Golf Course 493
T.O. Fuller Golf Course 494
Menasha, Wis.
High Cliff Golf Course 1059
Menifee, Calif.
Menifee Lakes Country Club 645
Mercer, Pa.
Mercer Public Golf Course 415
Meredith, N.H.
Waukewan Golf Club 234
Meriden, Conn.
Hunter Golf Club 38
Merrill, Wis.
Merrill Golf Club 1064
Merrillville, Ind.
Broadmoor Country Club 141
Turkey Creek Country Club 163
Merrimac, Wis.
Devil's Head Resort and
  Convention Center 1053
Merritt Island, Fla.
Savannahs at Sykes Creek Golf
  Club 103
Mesa, Ariz.
Arizona Golf Resort 570
Dobson Ranch Golf Club 574
Las Sendas Golf Club 581
Painted Mountain Golf Club 585
Red Mountain Ranch Country
  Club 589
Superstition Springs Golf Club
  594

Mescalero, N.Mex.
Inn of the Mountain Gods Golf
  Club 926
Mesick, Mich.
Briar Downs Golf Course 806
Mesquite, Nev.
Oasis Resort Hotel Casino 921
Mesquite, Texas
Mesquite Golf Course 994
Methuen, Mass.
Merrimack Golf Club 209
Miami Beach, Fla.
Bayshore Golf Course 52
Normandy Shores Golf Course 88
Miami, Fla.
Doral Golf Resort and Spa 64
Doral Park Golf and Country
  Club 65
Fontainebleau Golf Course 68
Golf Club of Miami 72
Melreese Golf Course 86
Palmetto Golf Course 92
Miami Lakes, Fla.
Don Shula's Golf Club 64
Miami Shores, Fla.
Miami Shores Country Club 86
Miamisburg, Ohio
Pipestone Golf Club 372
River Bend Golf Course 376
Michigan City, Ind.
Michigan City Municipal Course
  154
Middle Island, N.Y.
Middle Island Country Club 282
Spring Lake Golf Club 292
Middleburg, Fla.
Ravines Golf and Country Club
  96
Middlebury, Vt.
Ralph Myhre Country Club 500
Middlefield, Conn.
Lyman Orchards Golf Club 39
Middlefield, Ohio
Grandview Golf Club Grandview
  Golf Club 356
Middleton, Wis.
Pleasant View Country Club 1068
Middletown, Ind.
Tri County Golf Club 163
Valley View Golf Course 164
Middletown, N.Y.
Town of Wallkill Golf Club 296
Middletown, Ohio
Green Crest Golf Course 356
Pleasant Hill Golf Club 372
Weatherwax Golf Course 387
Middletown, Pa.
Sunset Golf Course 430
Midland, Mich.
Currie Municipal Golf Course
  811
Sandy Ridge Golf Course 847
Midland, Ontario
Brooklea Golf and Country Club
  548
Midland, Texas

Hogan Park Golf Course 985
Midway, Pa.
Quicksilver Golf Club 424
Midway, Utah
Homestead Golf Club 1021
Wasatch State Park Golf Club 1026
Midwest City, Okla.
John Conrad Regional Golf Course 940
Milford, Kans.
Rolling Meadows Golf Course 792
Milford, Mich.
Kensington Metro Park Golf Club 828
Mililani (Oahu), Hawaii
Mililani Golf Club 716
Millersburg, Ind.
Timber Ridge Golf Club 162
Millington, Tenn.
Big Creek Golf Club 481
Orgill Park Golf Course 491
Milpitas, Calif.
Spring Valley Golf Club 677
Summit Pointe Golf Club 678
Milton, Fla.
The Moors Golf Club 87
Tanglewood Golf and Country Club 108
Milton, N.J.
Bowling Green Golf Club 237
Milton, Pa.
Turbot Hills Golf Course 432
Milwaukee, Wis.
Brown Deer Golf Course 1050
Currie Park Golf Course 1053
Dretzka Park Golf Course 1054
Mineral Wells, W.Va.
Woodridge Plantation GC 533
Minerva, Ohio
Great Trail Golf Course 356
Minneapolis, Minn.
Columbia Golf Course 864
Francis A. Gross Golf Course 868
Hiawatha Golf Course 869
Theodore Wirth Golf Course 886
Minot, N.Dak.
Minot Country Club 933
Souris Valley Golf Club 934
Mishicot, Wis.
Fox Hills Resort 1055
Mission, Texas
Seven Oaks Resort and Country Club 1007
Shary Municipal Golf Course 1007
Missoula, Mont.
Larchmont Golf Course 905
Mitchell, Ind.
The Links Golf Course 153
Mitchell, S.Dak.
Lakeview Golf Course 961
Mitchellville, Md.
Enterprise Golf Course 190
Moab, Utah

Moab Golf Club 1021
Mobile, Ala.
Azalea City Golf Club 18
The Linksman Golf Club 27
Modesto, Calif.
Creekside Golf Course 617
Dryden Park Golf Course 622
Moncks Corner, S.C.
Berkeley Country Club 442
Monmouth, Ill.
Gibson Woods Golf Club 742
Monroe, Conn.
Whitney Farms Golf Course 46
Monroe, La.
Chennault Park Golf Course 798
Monroe, Mich.
Raisin River Country Club 843
Monroe, N.C.
Monroe Country Club 321
Mont Tremblant, Quebec
Gray Rocks Golf Club 565
Montague, Mich.
Old Channel Trail Golf Club 838
Montague, N.J.
High Point Country Club 244
Montauk, N.Y.
Montauk Downs State Park 282
Montebello, Calif.
Montebello Golf Club 647
Montebello, Quebec
Le Chateau Montebello 565
Montego Bay, Jamaica
Half Moon Golf Club 537
Wyndham Rose Hall Resort 538
Monterey, Calif.
Laguna Seca Golf Club 637
Old Del Monte Golf Course 653
Montgomery, Ala.
Lagoon Park Golf Course 26
Montgomery, N.Y.
Stony Ford Golf Club 292
Montgomery, Pa.
White Deer Park and Golf Course 435
Montgomery, Texas
Del Lago Resort 976
Monticello, Minn.
Monticello Country Club 876
Monticello, N.Y.
Kutsher's Country Club 277
Montpelier, Va.
Hollows Golf Course 511
Montreal, Quebec
Montreal Municipal Golf Course 566
Moodus, Conn.
Banner Resort and Country Club 34
Moorefield, W.Va.
Valley View Golf Course 533
Moorestown, N.J.
Willow Brook Country Club 253
Mooresville, N.C.
Mallard Head Country Club 320
Mooresville Golf Course 321
Mooretown, Ontario

St. Clair Parkway Golf Course *560*
Morehead City, N.C.
Brandywine Bay Golf and
  Country Club *302*
Morehead City Country Club *321*
Morehead, Ky.
Eagle Trace Golf Course *170*
Morell, P.E.I.
The Links at Crowbush Cove *563*
Moreno Valley, Calif.
Moreno Valley Ranch Golf Club
  647
Morganton, N.C.
Quaker Meadows Golf Club *330*
Morgantown, W.Va.
Lakeview Resort &Conference
  Center *529*
Morris, Ill.
Nettle Creek Golf Club *755*
Morrisburg, Ontario
Upper Canada Golf Course *561*
Morro Bay, Calif.
Morro Bay Golf Course *648*
Morton Grove, Ill.
Chick Evans Golf Course *736*
Mosca, Colo.
Great Sand Dunes Country Club
  695
Moscow, Idaho
University of Idaho Golf Course
  729
Mount Dora, Fla.
Country Club of Mount Dora *60*
Mount Pocono, Pa.
Mount Airy Lodge Golf Course
  416
Mount Vernon, Wash.
Eaglemont Golf Club *1032*
Mountain City, Tenn.
Roan Valley Golf Estates *493*
Mountain Home, Ark.
Twin Lakes Golf Club *603*
Mountain View, Calif.
Shoreline Golf Links *673*
Mouton, Ala.
Deer Run Golf Course *21*
Mt. Clare, W.Va.
Bel Meadow Country Club *526*
Mt. Clemens, Mich.
Cracklewood Golf Club *810*
Sycamore Hills Golf Club *851*
Wolverine Golf *859*
Mt. Juliet, Tenn.
Windtree Golf Course *496*
Mt. Laurel, N.J.
Ramblewood Country Club *250*
Mt. Pleasant, Mich.
Pleasant Hills Golf Club *841*
PohlCat Golf Course *842*
Riverwood Resort *845*
Mt. Pleasant, Pa.
Mulberry Hill Golf Club *418*
Mt. Pleasant, S.C.
Charleston National Country
  Club *446*
The Dunes West Golf Club *450*

Patriots Point Links *467*
Mt. Prospect, Ill.
Old Orchard Country Club *757*
Mt. Sterling, Ohio
Deer Creek State Park Golf
  Course *350*
Mt. Vernon, Ohio
Hiawatha Golf Course *358*
Irish Hills Golf Course *362*
Muenster, Texas
Turtle Hill Golf Course *1013*
Mukilteo, Wash.
Harbour Pointe Golf Club *1034*
Mukwonago, Wis.
Rainbow Springs Golf Club *1069*
Mullens, W.Va.
Twin Falls State Park Golf Course
  532
Muncie, Ind.
Maplewood Golf Club *153*
Mundelein, Ill.
Pine Meadow Golf Club *759*
Steeple Chase Golf Club *767*
Village Green Country Club *770*
Murchison, Texas
Echo Creek Country Club *977*
Murfreesboro, Tenn.
Indian Hills Golf Club *488*
Murphy, N.C.
Cherokee Hills Golf and Country
  Club *305*
Murray, Ky.
Frances E. Miller Golf Course *170*
Murray, Utah
Murray Parkway Golf Club *1022*
Murrells Inlet, S.C.
Blackmoor Golf Club *442*
Murrieta, Calif.
The SCGA Members' Club at
  Rancho California *667*
Murrysville, Pa.
Meadowink Golf Club *414*
Murrysville Golf Club *418*
Muscatine, Iowa
Muscatine Municipal Golf Course
  781
Muscle Shoals, Ala.
Cypress Lakes Golf and Country
  Club Cypress Knoll Golf Club
  21
Muskego, Wis.
Muskego Lakes Country Club
  1064
Muskegon, Mich.
Chase Hammond Golf Course
  810
Lincoln Golf Course *831*
Oak Ridge Golf Club *837*
Myrtle Beach, S.C.
Arcadian Shores Golf Club *441*
Arrowhead Country Club *441*
Heron Point Golf Club *454*
Island Green Golf Club *456*
Myrtle Beach National Golf Club
  462
Myrtlewood Golf Club *463*

New Palestine, Ind.
The Links Golf Club 153
New Philadelphia, Ohio
Green Valley Golf Club 357
New Port Richey, Fla.
Fox Hollow Golf Club 69
Magnolia Valley Country Club 83
Seven Springs Golf and Country
Club 104
New Prague, Minn.
New Prague Golf Club 877
New Richmond, Wis.
New Richmond Golf Club 1066
New Seabury, Mass.
New Seabury Country Club 209
New Smyrna Beach, Fla.
Sugar Mill Country Club 107
New Ulm, Texas
The Falls Country Club 977
New Vienna, Ohio
Snow Hill Country Club 381
Newark, Ohio
Licking Springs Trout and Golf
Club 364
Newbury, Ohio
Punderson State Park Golf Course
373
Newland, N.C.
Mountain Glen Golf Club 322
Newmarket, Ontario
Silver Lakes Golf and Country
Club 560
Newnan, Ga.
Orchard Hills Golf Club 130
Newport Coast, Calif.
Pelican Hill Golf Club 657
Newport, N.H.
John H. Cain Golf Club 230
Newport News, Va.
Kiln Creek Golf & Country Club
513
Newport News Golf Club at Deer
Run 517
Newport, Vt.
Newport Country Club 500
Newton, Iowa
Westwood Golf Club 785
Niagara Falls, N.Y.
Hyde Park Golf Course 275
Niagara Falls, Ontario
Beechwood Golf and Country
Club 547
Whirlpool Golf Course 562
Willo-Dell Golf Club 562
Niceville, Fla.
Bluewater Bay Resort 54
Nicholasville, Ky.
Connemara Golf Links 169
Nine Mile Falls, Wash.
Sundance Golf Course 1044
Nipoma, Calif.
Black Lake Golf Club 609
Nisswa, Minn.
Grand View Lodge 868
Nobelton, Ontario
Nobleton Lakes Golf Club 556

Noblesville, Ind.
Fox Prairie Golf Club 146
**Pebble Brook Golf and Country
Club 155**
Nocona, Texas
Nocona Hills Golf Course 995
Nokomis, Fla.
Calusa Lakes Golf Course 56
Norfolk, Va.
Lake Wright Golf Course 514
Ocean View Golf Course 517
Normal, Ill.
Illinois State University Golf
Course 747
Ironwood Golf Course 749
Norman, Okla.
University of Oklahoma Golf
Course 947
Westwood Park Golf Course 947
**North Battleford,
Saskatchewan**
North Battleford Golf and
Country Club 1104
North Bend, Ohio
Shawnee Lookout Golf Club 379
North Branch, Mich.
Washakie Golf Club 856
North Conway, N.H.
North Conway Country Club 231
North East, Pa.
Green Meadows Golf Course 406
North Fort Myers, Fla.
Lochmoor Country Club 82
North Gower, Ontario
Manderley on the Green 555
North Hampton, N.H.
Sagamore-Hampton Golf Club
233
North Kingstown, R.I.
North Kingstown Municipal Golf
Course 439
North Las Vegas, Nev.
Craig Ranch Golf Course 916
North Lawrence, Ohio
The Elms Country Club 352
North Little Rock, Ark.
Burns Park Golf Course 599
Quapaw Golf Links 602
North Madison, Ohio
Erie Shores Golf Course 353
North Mankato, Minn.
North Links Golf Course 877
North Myrtle Beach, S.C.
Azalea Sands Golf Club 441
Beachwood Golf Club 442
Eagle Nest Golf Club 450
Robbers Roost Golf Course 471
North Palm Beach, Fla.
North Palm Beach Country Club
88
North Salt Lake City, Utah
Eaglewood Golf Course 1019
North Sutton, N.H.
The Country Club of New
Hampshire 228
North Tonawanda, N.Y.

Shadow Ridge Country Club *912*
Tiburon Golf Club *914*
Onamia, Minn.
Izaty's Golf and Yacht Club *871*
Onanole, Manitoba
Clear Lake Golf Course *1101*
Oneida, Wis.
Brown County Golf Course *1050*
Onset, Mass.
Bay Pointe Country Club *200*
Ontario, Oreg.
Shadow Butte Golf Club *958*
Opelika, Ala.
Grand National Golf Club *22*
Orange, Conn.
Grassy Hill Country Club *37*
Orange Hills Country Club *40*
Orange Park, Fla.
Eagle Harbor Golf Club *65*
Orangeburg, S.C.
Hillcrest Golf Club *455*
Orangeville, Ontario
Hockley Valley Resort *553*
Oregon, Ohio
Maumee Bay State Park Golf
   Course *366*
Orilla, Ontario
Hawk Ridge Golf Club *553*
Oriskany Falls, N.Y.
Barker Brook Golf Course *256*
Orland Park, Ill.
Silver Lake Country Club *766*
Orlando, Fla.
Arnold Palmer's Bay Hill Club and
   Lodge *570*
Eastwood Golf Club *66*
Grand Cypress Golf Club *73*
Hunter's Creek Golf Course *76*
International Golf Club *78*
Marriott's Orlando World Center
   85
MetroWest Country Club *86*
Rosemont Golf and Country
   Club *99*
Orleans, Vt.
Orleans Country Club *500*
Ormond Beach, Fla.
Halifax Plantation Golf Club *75*
River Bend Golf Club *97*
Riviera Country Club *98*
Tomoka Oaks Golf and Country
   Club *109*
Orondo, Wash.
Desert Canyon Golf Resort *1031*
Orono, Maine
Penobscot Valley Country Club
   183
Oroville, Calif.
Table Mountain Golf Course *680*
Orting, Wash.
High Cedars Golf Club *1034*
Ortonville, Minn.
Ortonville Municipal Golf Course
   879
Osage Beach, Mo.
Dogwood Hills Golf Club *891*

Marriott's Tan-Tar-A Resort *896*
Oscoda, Mich.
Lakewood Shores Resort *830*
Oshkosh, Wis.
Far Vu Golf Course *1055*
Lake Shore Golf Course *1062*
Oshkosh, Wis.
Westhaven Golf Club *1076*
Oskaloosa, Iowa
Edmundson Golf Course *777*
Osoyoos, British Columbia
Osoyoos Golf and Country Club
   1096
Ostrander, Ohio
Mill Creek Golf Club *367*
Oswego, Ill.
Fox Bend Golf Course *741*
Otsego, Mich.
Prairiewood Golf Course *842*
Ottawa, Ohio
Country Acres Golf Club *349*
Ottumwa, Iowa
Ottumwa Municipal Golf Course
   782
Overland Park, Kans.
Deer Creek Golf Club *788*
Overland Park Golf Club *791*
St. Andrew's Golf Course *793*
Oviedo, Fla.
Ekana Golf Club *66*
Owasco, N.Y.
Dutch Hollow Country Club *268*
Owasso, Okla.
Bailey Golf Ranch *935*
Owatonna, Minn.
Brooktree Municipal Golf Course
   862
Owens Cross Roads, Ala.
Hampton Cove Golf Club *24*
Oxford, Ind.
Oak Grove Country Club *154*
Oxford, Mich.
Devil's Ridge Golf Club *812*
Oxford Hills Golf Club *839*
Oxford, Miss.
Grand Oaks Resort *220*
Ole Miss Golf Club *222*
Oxford, N.Y.
Blue Stone Golf Course *259*
Oxford, Ohio
Hueston Woods State Park Golf
   Resort *361*
Oxford, Pa.
Wyncote Golf Club *436*
Oxnard, Calif.
River Ridge Golf Club *665*
Ozawkie, Kans.
Village Greens Golf Course *795*

P

Pacific Grove, Calif.
Pacific Grove Municipal Golf
   Links *654*
Pacifica, Calif.
Sharp Park Golf Course *673*

Pacoima, Calif.
Hansen Dam Golf Course 631
Paducah, Ky.
Paxton Park Golf Club 175
Pagosa Springs, Colo.
Fairfield Pagosa Golf Club 693
Pahrump, Nev.
Calvada Valley Golf and Country
    Club 916
Painesville, Ohio
Fairway Pines Golf Course 353
Pakenham, Ontario
Pakenham Highlands Golf Club
    557
Palatine, Ill.
Palatine Hills Golf Course 758
Palm Beach, Fla.
The Breakers Club 55
Palm Beach Gardens, Fla.
Palm Beach Gardens Municipal
    Golf Course 90
PGA National Golf Club 93
Palm Coast, Fla.
Matanzas Woods Golf Club 85
Palm Harbor Golf Club 91
Pine Lakes Country Club 93
Palm Desert, Calif.
Desert Falls Country Club 620
Marriott's Desert Springs Resort
    and Spa 643
Palm Desert Resort Country
    Club 655
Palm Harbor, Fla.
Innisbrook Hilton Resort 78
Lansbrook Golf Club 80
Tarpon Woods Golf and Country
    Club 108
Palm Springs, Calif.
Canyon South Golf Course 612
Mesquite Golf and Country Club
    645
Tahquitz Creek Palm Springs Golf
    Resort 681
Palmer, Alaska
Palmer Golf Course 569
Palmetto, Fla.
Imperial Lakes Golf Club 77
Palmyra, Va.
Lake Monticello Golf Club 514
Palos Heights, Ill.
Westgate Valley Country Club 772
Palos Park, Ill.
Palos Country Club 759
Palos Verdes Estates, Calif.
Palos Verdes Golf Club 655
Pampa, Texas
Hidden Hills Public Golf Course
    984
Panama City Beach, Fla.
Hombre Golf Club 76
Marriott's Bay Point Resort 84
Signal Hill Golf and Country
    Club 105
Panora, Iowa
Lake Panorama National Golf
    Course 780

Parachute, Colo.
Battlement Mesa Golf Club 689
Paradise Valley, Ariz.
Stonecreek, The Golf Club 593
Paramus, N.J.
Paramus Golf Club 248
Paris, Ontario
The Oaks of St. George Golf Club
    557
Paris, Texas
Pine Ridge Golf Course 999
Park City, Ky.
Park Mammoth Golf Club 175
Park City, Utah
Park City Golf Course 1023
Park Meadows Golf Club 1023
Park Rapids, Minn.
Headwaters Country Club 869
Parker, Ariz.
Emerald Canyon Golf Course 576
Parkersburg, W.Va.
South Hills Golf Club 532
Parksville, British Columbia
Morningstar Golf Club 1096
Parkville, Mo.
Windbrook Country Club 902
Parma, Mich.
Burr Oak Golf Club 807
Parsippany, N.J.
Knoll Country Club 245
Pasadena, Calif.
Brookside Golf Club 610
Pasco, Wash.
Sun Willows Golf Club 1044
Paso Robles, Calif.
Hunter Ranch Golf Course 632
Pass Christian, Miss.
Pass Christian Isles Golf Club 222
Pataskala, Ohio
Willow Run Golf Course 389
Paw Paw, Mich.
Heritage Glen Golf Club 824
Lake Cora Hills Golf Course 828
Pawcatuck, Conn.
Elmridge Golf Course 37
Pawley's Island, S.C.
Caledonia Golf and Fish Club 444
Heritage Club 454
Litchfield Country Club 461
Pawley's Plantation Golf Club 467
The River Club 470
Sea Gull Golf Club 473
Willbrook Plantation Golf Club
    479
Payette, Idaho
Scotch Pines Golf Course 728
Payson, Ariz.
Payson Golf Course 586
Payson, Utah
Gladstan Golf Club 1019
Pearce, Ariz.
Shadow Mountain Golf Club 591
Pearl River, N.Y.
Blue Hill Golf Club 259
Pearland, Texas
Southwyck Golf Club 1008

Rutland, Vt.
Rutland Country Club *501*
Rutledge, Ga.
Hard Labor Creek State Park Golf
Course *124*

S

S. Williamstown, Mass.
Waubeeka Golf Links *217*
Saco, Maine
Biddeford Saco Golf Club *181*
Sacramento, Calif.
Bartley W. Cavanaugh Golf Course
608
Bing Maloney Golf Course *609*
Haggin Oaks Golf Course *630*
Safford, Ariz.
Mt. Graham Municipal Golf
Course *584*
Saginaw, Mich.
Crooked Creek Golf Club *811*
Salado, Texas
Mill Creek Golf and Country
Club *994*
Salem, N.H.
Campbell's Scottish Highlands
Golf Course *227*
Salem, Ohio
Salem Hills Golf and Country
Club *377*
Salem, Oreg.
Salem Golf Club *957*
Salem, Va.
Hanging Rock Golf Club *510*
Salem, Wis.
Spring Valley Country Club *1073*
Salina, Kans.
Salina Municipal Golf Club *793*
Salinas, Calif.
Salinas Fairways Golf Course *667*
Salisbury, Md.
Nutters Crossing Golf Club *193*
Salt Lake City, Utah
Bonneville Golf Course *1018*
Glendale Golf Course *1020*
Mountain Dell Golf Club *1022*
Rose Park Golf Club *1023*
Wingpointe Golf Course *1027*
Saltillo, Miss.
Natchez Trace Golf Club *221*
Saluda, S.C.
Persimmon Hill Golf Club *467*
Sam Rayburn, Texas
Rayburn Country Club and
Resort *1001*
San Angelo, Texas
Riverside Golf Club *1003*
San Antonio, Texas
Brackenridge Park Municipal Golf
Course *968*
Cedar Creek Golf Course *970*
Hill Country Golf Club *984*
La Cantera Golf Club *990*
Mission Del Lago *995*
Olmos Basin Golf Club *996*

Pecan Valley Golf Club *998*
The Quarry Golf Club *1000*
Riverside Municipal Golf Course
1005
Willow Springs Golf Club *1016*
San Augustine, Texas
Fairway Farm Golf Course *977*
San Bernardino, Calif.
San Bernardino Golf Club *667*
Shandin Hills Golf Club *673*
San Clemente, Calif.
San Clemente Municipal Golf
Club *667*
San Diego, Calif.
Balboa Park Golf Club *608*
Carmel Highland Doubletree Golf
and Tennis Resort *612*
Carmel Mountain Ranch Country
Club *613*
Rancho Bernardo Inn and
Country Club *660*
San Dimas, Calif.
San Dimas Canyon Golf Club *668*
San Felipe, Texas
Stephen F. Austin State Park Golf
Course *1009*
San Francisco, Calif.
Harding Park Golf Club *631*
Lincoln Park Golf Course *640*
San Geronimo, Calif.
San Geronimo Golf Club *668*
San Jacinto, Calif.
Soboba Springs Country Club
676
San Jose, Calif.
San Jose Municipal Golf
Course *668*
Santa Teresa Golf Club *671*
San Jose del Cabo, Baja Sur
Palmilla Golf Club *1106*
San Juan Capistrano, Calif.
San Juan Hills Country Club *669*
San Leandro, Calif.
Tony Lema Golf Club *683*
San Marcos, Calif.
Twin Oaks Golf Course *684*
San Mateo, Calif.
City of San Mateo Golf Course
616
San Rafael, Calif.
Peacock Gap Golf and Country
Club *656*
San Ramon, Calif.
Canyon Lakes Country Club *611*
San Ramon Royal Vista Golf Club
669
San Saba, Texas
San Saba Municipal Golf Course
1006
Sand Springs, Okla.
Sand Springs Municipal Golf
Course *944*
Sandpoint, Idaho
Hidden Lakes Golf Resort *726*
Sandusky, Mich.
Woodland Hills Golf Club *859*

Selkirk, Manitoba
Selkirk Golf and Country Club
1103
Sellersburg, Ind.
Covered Bridge Golf Club 143
Hidden Creek Golf Club 149
Selma, Calif.
Selma Valley Golf Course 672
Semmes, Ala.
Magnolia Grove Golf Club 28
Sequim, Wash.
Dungeness Golf and Country
Club 1032
Sunland Golf and Country Club
1044
Seven Devils, N.C.
Hawksnest Golf and Ski Resort
314
Sewell, N.J.
Ron Jaworski's Eagles' Nest
Country Club 251
Sexsmith, Alberta
Spruce Meadows Golf and
Country Club 1089
Seymour, Wis.
Crystal Springs Golf Club 1053
Shakopee, Minn.
Stonebrooke Golf Club 885
Shalimar, Fla.
Shalimar Pointe Golf and Country
Club 105
Shallotte, N.C.
Brierwood Golf Club 302
Sharon Center, Ohio
Western Reserve Golf and
Country Club 388
Sharon, Ontario
Pheasant Run Golf Club 558
Shawano, Wis.
Shawano Lake Golf Club 1071
Shawnee, Kans.
Tomahawk Hills Golf Club 794
Shawnee, Okla.
Fire Lake Golf Course 938
Shawnee-on-Delaware, Pa.
Shawnee Inn and Golf Resort 426
Shediac, New Brunswick
Pine Needles Golf & Country
Club 543
Shelburne, Vt.
Kwiniaska Golf Club 499
Shelby, Mich.
Oceana Country Club 838
Shelby, N.C.
Pine Grove Golf Club 326
River Bend Golf Club 331
Shelby Township, Mich.
Stony Creek Golf Course 850
Shelbyville, Ky.
Weissinger Hills Golf Course 178
Shenandoah, Iowa
American Legion Country Club
775
Sheridan, Wyo.
Kendrick Golf Course 1080
Sherwood Park, Alberta

Broadmoor Public Golf Course
1082
Countryside Golf Course 1083
Sherwood Park Golf Course 1089
Shoemakersville, Pa.
Perry Golf Course 421
Short Hills, N.J.
East Orange Golf Course 240
Shortsville, N.Y.
Winged Pheasant Golf Links 299
Shreveport, La.
Huntington Park Golf Course 799
Querbes Park Golf Course 800
Sicklerville, N.J.
Freeway Golf Course 242
Sidney, Ohio
Shelby Oaks Golf Club 379
Sierra Vista, Ariz.
Pueblo Del Sol Golf Course 588
Siloam Springs, Ark.
Dawn Hill Golf Club 600
Silverthorne, Colo.
Eagles Nest Golf Club 693
Simi Valley, Calif.
Simi Hills Golf Club 675
Sinking Spring, Pa.
Manor Golf Club 413
Sioux City, Iowa
Green Valley Golf Course 780
Sioux Falls, S.Dak.
Elmwood Golf Course 961
Prairie Green Golf Course 962
Willow Run Golf Course 963
Sky Valley, Ga.
Sky Valley Golf Club 135
Skytop, Pa.
Skytop Lodge Golf Club 427
Slidell, La.
Oak Harbor Golf Club 800
Slinger, Wis.
Scenic View Country Club 1071
Smithfield, Utah
Birch Creek Golf Club 1018
Smithtown, N.Y.
Smithtown Landing Golf Club
291
Smithville, Mo.
Paradise Pointe Golf Club 897
Smyrna, Del.
Ron Jaworski's Garrisons Lake
Golf Club 47
Sneads Ferry, N.C.
North Shore Country Club 323
Snoqualmie, Wash.
Mount Si Golf Course 1040
Snohomish, Wash.
Echo Falls Country Club 1032
Kenwanda Golf Course 1036
Snohomish Golf Course 1043
Snow Camp, N.C.
Sourwood Golf Course 335
Snow Hill, Md.
Nassawango Country Club 193
Snowmass Village, Colo.
The Snowmass Club Golf Course
705

Snowshoe, W.Va.
Hawthorne Valley Golf Course
528
Socorro, N.Mex.
New Mexico Tech Golf Course
928
Solvang, Calif.
The Alisal Ranch Golf Course
605
River Course at The Alisal 665
Somers, Conn.
Cedar Knob Golf Club 35
Somers Point, N.J.
Greate Bay Resort & Country
Club 243
Somerset, Ky.
Eagle's Nest Country Club 170
Somerset, N.J.
Quail Brook Golf Course 249
Spooky Brook Golf Course 251
Sonoma, Calif.
Sonoma Golf Club 676
Sonora, Calif.
Mountain Springs Golf Club 650
South Alburg, Vt.
Alburg Country Club 497
South Bend, Ind.
Blackthorn Golf Club 140
Elbel Park Golf Course 144
Erskine Park Golf Club 144
South Boston, Va.
Green's Folly Golf Course 510
South Edmonton, Alberta
Eagle Rock Golf Course 1084
South Fallsburg, N.Y.
Tarry Brae Golf Club 293
South Jordon, Utah
Glenmoor Golf and Country
Club 1020
South Lake Tahoe, Calif.
Lake Tahoe Golf Course 638
South Lyon, Mich.
Cattails Golf Club 809
Pebble Creek Golf Course 839
Tanglewood Golf Club 851
South Madison, Ohio
Thunder Hill Golf Club 385
South Milwaukee, Wis.
Grant Park Golf Course 1058
South Portland, Maine
Sable Oaks Golf Club 184
South Rustico, P.E.I.
Rustico Resort Golf & Country
Club 563
South Sioux City, Nebr.
Covington Links Golf Course 908
**South Surrey, British
Columbia**
Peace Portal Golf Course 1097
South Yarmouth, Mass.
Bass River Golf Course 200
Southampton, Bermuda
Port Royal Golf Course 534
Southampton, Ontario
Chippewa Golf and Country Club
549

Southern Pines, N.C.
The Club at Longleaf 306
Hyland Hills Golf Club 315
Mid Pines Golf Club 320
Pine Needles Golf Club 326
Southern Pines Golf Club 335
Talamore Resort 336
Southington, Conn.
Pine Valley Country Club 41
Southington Country Club 43
Southington, Ohio
Forest Oaks Golf Course 354
Southlake, Texas
Timarron Golf and Country Club
1012
Southport, N.C.
The Gauntlet at St. James
Plantation 313
Spanaway, Wash.
Classic Country Club 1031
Spanish Fork, Utah
Spanish Oaks Golf Club 1025
Sparks, Nev.
Wildcreek Golf Course 924
Sparta, Mich.
Rogue River Golf Course 846
Sparta, Wis.
Sparta Municipal Golf Club 1072
Spencer, Iowa
Spencer Golf and Country Club
784
Spencerport, N.Y.
Braemar Country Club 260
Salmon Creek Country Club 288
Spicer, Minn.
Little Crow Country Club 873
Spicewood, Texas
Barton Creek Resort and Country
Club 964
Spirit Lake, Iowa
Okoboji View Golf Course 781
Spokane, Wash.
The Creek at Qualchan Golf
Course 1045
Downriver Golf Club 1031
Esmeralda Golf Course 1032
Hangman Valley Golf Course 1034
Indian Canyon Golf Course 1035
Wandermere Golf Course 1046
Spooner, Wis.
Spooner Golf Club 1072
Spring Green, Wis.
The Springs Golf Club Resort
1073
Spring Hill, Fla.
Oak Hills Golf Club 88
Seven Hills Golfers Club 104
Spring Hill Golf Club 106
Spring, Texas
Cypresswood Golf Club 975
Springboro, Ohio
Heatherwoode Golf Club 357
Springfield, Ill.
Bunn Golf Course 734
Lincoln Greens Golf Course 752
The Rail Golf Club 762

Ste. Adele, Quebec
Le Golf Chantecler 565
Steamboat Springs, Colo.
Sheraton Steamboat Golf Club
702
Steinbach, Manitoba
The Links at Quarry Oaks 1102
Steinbach Fly-In Golf Course
1103
Sterling, Va.
Algonkian Regional Park Golf
Course 504
Stettler, Alberta
Pheasantback Golf and Country
Club 1087
Stevens, Pa.
Foxchase Golf Club 404
Stevens Point, Wis.
SentryWorld Golf Course 1071
Wisconsin River Country Club
1076
Stevenson, Wash.
Bridge of the Gods Golf Course
1043
Stewartstown, Pa.
Pleasant Valley Golf Club 423
Stillwater, Minn.
Oak Glen Golf Club 878
Sawmill Golf Club 884
Stillwater, Okla.
Karsten Creek Golf Course 940
Lakeside Memorial Golf Club 942
Stockbridge, Ga.
Southerness Golf Club 136
Stockton, Calif.
Swenson Park Golf Club 680
Van Buskirk Park Golf Course 685
Stone Mountain, Ga.
Stone Mountain Park Golf Course
136
Stoney Creek, N.C.
Stoney Creek Golf Club 336
Stouffville, Ontario
Maples of Ballantrae Lodge and
Golf Club 556
Stow, Mass.
Stow Acres Country Club 214
Stow, Ohio
Fox Den Golf Club 354
Stowe, Vt.
Stowe Golf Course 501
Stoystown, Pa.
Oakbrook Golf Course 419
Stratton Mountain, Vt.
Stratton Mountain CC 501
Stroudsburg, Pa.
Glen Brook Country Club 405
Stuart, Fla.
The Champions Club at
Summerfield 57
Martin County Golf and Country
Club 85
Stuart, Va.
Gorden Trent Golf Course 510
Sturgeon Bay, Wis.
Cherry Hills Golf Course 1051

Idlewild Golf Course 1059
Sturtevant, Wis.
Ives Grove Golf Links 1060
Suffern, N.Y.
Spook Rock Golf Course 291
Suffolk, Va.
Sleepy Hole Golf Course 521
Suffolk Golf Course 523
Sugar Hill, Ga.
Sugar Hill Golf Club 137
Sugar Land, Texas
Greatwood Golf Club 982
Sugarcreek, Ohio
Sugarcreek Golf Course 382
Sugarloaf, Pa.
Sugarloaf Golf Club 430
**Summerland, British
Columbia**
Summerland Golf and Country
Club 1099
Summerside, P.E.I.
Summerside Golf Club 564
Summerton, S.C.
Foxboro Golf Club 452
Summerville, S.C.
George Miler Golf Course 453
Kings Grant Country Club 458
Legend Oak's Plantation Golf
Club 459
Pine Forest Country Club 467
Sumter, S.C.
Lakewood Links 459
Pocalla Springs Country Club 469
Sun City West, Ariz.
Hillcrest Golf Club 580
Sun Valley, Idaho
Elkhorn Country Club 725
Sun Valley Resort Golf Course 728
Sunbury, Ohio
Bent Tree Golf Club 343
Sunfield, Mich.
Centennial Acres Golf Course 810
Sunnyvale, Calif.
Sunnyvale Municipal Golf Course
679
Sunol, Calif.
Sunol Valley Golf Course 679
Sunrise, Fla.
Sunrise Country Club 108
Sunriver, Oreg.
Sunriver Lodge and Resort 958
Sunset Beach, N.C.
Lion's Paw Golf Links 318
Oyster Bay Golf Links 325
Pearl Golf Links 325
Sandpiper Bay Golf and Country
Club 332
Sea Trail Plantation 333
Superior, Wis.
Nemadji Golf Course 1065
Supply, N.C.
Lockwood Golf Links 319
Surfside Beach, S.C.
Deer Track Golf Resort 449
Indigo Creek Golf Club 456
Surprise, Ariz.

Coyote Lakes Golf Club *573*
Happy Trails Golf Resort *580*
Surrey, British Columbia
Northview Golf & Country Club
  1096
Sutherlin, Oreg.
The Knolls Golf Club *953*
Sutter, Calif.
Southridge Golf Club *677*
Suwanee, Ga.
Olde Atlanta Golf Club *130*
Swansboro, N.C.
Silver Creek Golf Club *334*
Swansea, Mass.
Swansea Country Club *215*
Swanton, Ohio
Valleywood Golf Club *387*
Swedesboro, N.J.
Beckett Golf Club *237*
Sweetwater, Texas
Sweetwater Country Club *1010*
Swift Current, Saskatchewan
Elmwood Golf Club *1103*
Sydney, Nova Scotia
Lingan Country Club *546*
Syracuse, Ind.
Maxwelton Golf Club *153*
South Shore Golf Club *161*
Syracuse, N.Y.
Drumlins West Golf Club *267*

T

Tacoma, Wash.
Brookdale Golf Course *1029*
Lake Spanaway Golf Course *1037*
Meadow Park Golf Course *1039*
North Shore Golf and Country
  Club *1040*
Talladega, Ala.
Timber Ridge Golf Club *32*
Tallahassee, Fla.
Hilaman Park Municipal Golf
  Course *75*
Killearn Country Club and Inn *79*
Seminole Golf Club *104*
Tamarac, Fla.
Colony West Country Club *59*
Tamiment, Pa.
Tamiment Resort & Conference
  Center GC *431*
Tampa, Fla.
Babe Zaharias Golf Course *51*
Northdale Golf Club *88*
Rocky Point Golf Course *98*
Rogers Park Golf Course *98*
University of South Florida Golf
  Course *111*
Westchase Golf Club *114*
Tavares, Fla.
Deer Island Golfers Club *62*
Taylor, British Columbia
The Lone Wolf Golf Club *1095*
Taylor, Mich.
Taylor Meadows Golf Club *851*
Taylor, Pa.

Pine Hills Golf Course *422*
Taylorsville, Ill.
Lake Shore Golf Club *751*
Taylorsville, Ky.
Tanglewood Golf Course *177*
Taylorsville, N.C.
Brushy Mountain Golf Club *303*
Taylorsville, Utah
Meadow Brook Golf Course *1021*
Teaneck, N.J.
Overpeck Golf Course *248*
Tecumseh, Mich.
Raisin Valley Golf Club *843*
Tehachapi, Calif.
Horse Thief Country Club *631*
Temecula, Calif.
Redhawk Golf Club *663*
Temecula Creek Inn *681*
Tempe, Ariz.
Karsten Golf Course at ASU *880*
Ken McDonald Golf Club *581*
Temperance, Mich.
Giant Oaks Golf Course *819*
Temple, Texas
J.F. Sammons Park Golf Course
  987
Terre Haute, Ind.
Hulman Links Golf Course *150*
Rea Park Golf Course *157*
Terrebonne, Quebec
Golf Le Mirage *564*
Teulon, Manitoba
Teulon Golf and Country Club
  1103
Tewksbury, Mass.
Trull Brook Golf Course *216*
Texarkana, Ark.
South Haven Golf Club *603*
Texas City, Texas
Bayou Golf Club *966*
Thendara, N.Y.
Thendara Golf Club *294*
Thiells, N.Y.
Philip J. Rotella Golf Course *285*
Thompson, Conn.
Raceway Golf Club *41*
Thompsonville, Mich.
Crystal Mountain Resort *811*
Thomson, Ga.
Belle Meade Country Club *116*
Thornton, Colo.
Thorncreek Golf Club *705*
Thousand Oaks, Calif.
Los Robles Golf Club *641*
Thurmont, Md.
Maple Run Golf Club *192*
Tigerville, S.C.
The Gauntlet Golf at Laurel Valley
  452
Tijuana, Baja Norte
Real Del Mar Golf Club *1105*
Tijuana Country Club *1105*
Tinley Park, Ill.
Odyssey Golf Course *756*
Tipp City, Ohio
Hidden Lake Golf Course *359*

Lake Breeze Golf Club *1061*
Winnetka, Ill.
Winnetka Golf Course *773*
Winslow, N.J.
Pinelands Golf Club *249*
Winston-Salem, N.C.
Hillcrest Golf Club *315*
Reynolds Park Golf Club *331*
Winter Park, Colo.
Pole Creek Golf Club *700*
Winterburn, Alberta
Indian Lakes Golf Club *1085*
Wintergreen, Va.
Wintergreen Resort *524*
Wisconsin Dells, Wis.
Christmas Mountain Village Golf
Club *1052*
Trappers Turn Golf Club *1073*
Wisconsin Rapids, Wis.
The Ridges Golf Club *1069*
Wolfville, Nova Scotia
Ken-Wo Country Club *545*
Wood River, Ill.
Belk Park Golf Club *732*
Woodbury, Minn.
Wedgewood Golf Club *887*
Woodbury, N.J.
Westwood Golf Club *253*
Woodbury, N.Y.
Oyster Bay Town Golf Course *284*
Woodland Park, Colo.
Woodland Park Fujiki Golf and
Country Club *707*
The Woodlands, Texas
The Woodlands Resort and
Country Club *1016*
Woodlawn, Md.
Diamond Ridge Golf Course *189*
Woodridge, Ill.
Seven Bridges Golf Club *765*
Village Greens of Woodridge *771*
Woodstock, Ga.
Eagle Watch Golf Club *121*
Towne Lake Hills Golf Club *137*
Woodstock, N.H.
Jack O'Lantern Resort *229*
Woodstock, Vt.
Woodstock Country Club *503*
Woodville, Ohio
Hidden Hills Golf Club *359*
Woodward, Okla.
Boiling Springs Golf Club *935*
Worland, Wyo.
Green Hills Municipal Golf
Course *1079*

Worthington, Minn.
Prairie View Golf Course *882*
Wright City, Mo.
Innsbrook Estates Golf Club *894*
Wrightstown, N.J.
Hanover Country Club *243*
Wrightsville, Pa.
Cool Creek Country Club *398*
Wyoming, Mich.
L.E. Kaufman Golf Club *828*

Y

Yakima, Wash.
Apple Tree Golf Course *1028*
Suntides Golf Course *1044*
Yankton, S.Dak.
Fox Run Golf Course *961*
Hillcrest Golf and Country Club
961
Yonkers, N.Y.
Dunwoodie Golf Club *267*
Sprain Lake Golf Club *292*
York, Pa.
Briarwood Golf Club *968*
Grandview Golf Club *406*
Heritage Hills Golf Resort *408*
Honey Run Golf and Country
Club *410*
York, S.C.
Spring Lake Country Club *474*
Yorktown Heights, N.Y.
Mohansic Golf Club *282*
Youngsville, La.
Les Vieux Chenes Golf Club *799*
Ypsilanti, Mich.
Huron Golf Club *826*
Pine View Golf Club *841*
Yucca Valley, Calif.
Blue Skies Country Club *609*
Yuma, Ariz.
Desert Hills Golf Course *574*
Zanesville, Ohio
Eagle Sticks Golf Course *351*
Jaycee Public Golf Course *363*
Zellwood, Fla.
Zellwood Station Country Club
115
Zephyrhills, Fla.
The Links of Lake Bernadette *82*
Silver Oaks Golf and Country
Club *105*
Zoar, Ohio
Zoar Village Golf Club *390*

Alphabetical Directory by Course

A

A.H. Blank Golf Course 775
A-Ga-Ming Golf Club 802
Abbey Springs Golf Course 1048
Abercrombie Golf Club 544
Acapulco Princess Club de Golf 1106
Adams Municipal Golf Course 935
Adirondack Golf & Country Club 255
Admiral Lehigh Golf and Resort 50
Adobe Creek Golf Club 605
Adobe Creek National Golf Course 688
Afton Alps Golf Course 860
Afton Golf Club 255
Ahwatukee Country Club 570
Airport Golf Course (Cheyenne, Wyo.) 1078
Airport Golf Course (Columbus, Ohio) 341
Al Gustin Golf Club 893
Ala Wai Golf Course 708
Alban Hills Country Club 255
Albany Golf Course 860
Albion Ridges Golf Course 860
Alburg Country Club 497
Aldeen Golf Club 730
Alderbrook Golf and Yacht Club 1028
Alexandria Golf Club 860
Algonkian Regional Park Golf Course 504
The Algonquin Resort 543
Alhambra Municipal Golf Course 605
Alice Municipal Golf Course 964
The Alisal Ranch Golf Course 605
Allentown Municipal Golf Course 391
Alling Memorial Golf Course 34
Alpena Golf Club 802
Alpine Bay Golf and Country Club 18
Alpine Resort Golf Course 1048
Alta Sierra Golf and Country Club 605
Alvamar Golf Club 787
Amana Colonies Golf Course 775
Amelia Island Plantation 50
American Legion Country Club 775
Amherst Audubon Golf Course 255
Amherst Country Club 226
Amherst Golf Club 544

Amsterdam Municipal Golf Course 255
Anaheim Hills Golf Course 606
Anchorage Golf Course 568
Ancil Hoffman Golf Course 606
Andrews County Golf Course 964
Angel Fire Country Club 925
Angel Park Golf Club 915
Angus Glen Golf Club 547
Annbriar Golf Course 730
Antelope Hills Golf Course 570
Antigo Bass Lake Country Club 1048
Antioch Golf Club 730
Antrim Dells Golf Club 802
Apollo Beach Golf and Sea Club 50
Apple Mountain Golf Club 236
Apple Tree Golf Course 1028
Apple Valley Golf Club 341
Appletree Golf Course 688
Applewood Golf Course (Golden, Colo.) 688
Applewood Golf Course (Omaha, Nebr.) 908
Aptos Seascape Golf Course 606
Arboretum Golf Club 730
Arbutus Ridge Golf and Country Club 1090
Arcadian Shores Golf Club 441
Arizona Biltmore Country Club 571
Arizona Golf Resort 570
Arnold Palmer's Bay Hill Club and Lodge 50
Arnold's Golf Club 391
Aroostook Valley Country Club 180
Arrowhead Golf Club (Auburn Hills, Mich.) 802
Arrowhead Golf Club (Littleton, Colo.) 688
Arrowhead Golf Club (Myrtle Beach, S.C.) 441
Arrowhead Golf Club (Wheaton, Ill.) 731
Arrowhead Golf Course (Canadian, Okla.) 935
Arrowhead Golf Course (Davie, Fla.) 51
Arrowhead Golf Course (Douglassville, Pa.) 391
Arrowhead Golf Course (East Syracuse, N.Y.) 256
Arrowhead Ranch Country Club 571
Arroyo del Oso Municipal Golf Course 925
Arthur Pack Desert Golf Club 571
Ascarate Park Golf Course 964
Ash Brook Golf Course 236

C

Golf Club of Illinois 744
Golf Club of Indiana 147
Golf Club of Jacksonville 72
Golf Club of Miami 72
Golf Club of West Virginia 527
The Golf Courses at Kenton County 178
The Golf Courses of Lawsonia 1056
Golf Hammock Country Club 73
Golf Le Mirage 564
Golf Resort at Indian Wells 627
Golfmohr Golf Club 744
Goodrich Golf Course 868
Goodwin Park Golf Course 37
Goose Creek Golf Club 509
Goose Hummock Golf Club 1084
Goose Pond Colony Golf Course 22
Gorden Trent Golf Course 510
Gorham Golf Club 182
Goshen Plantation Country Club 123
Gowan Brae Golf & Country Club 543
Gracewil Country Club 819
Gracewil Pines Golf Club 820
Graeagle Meadows Golf Course 628
Grand Cypress Resort 73
Grand Geneva Resort and Spa 1057
Grand Haven Golf Club 820
Grand Island Golf Ranch 821
Grand Island Municipal Golf Course 909
Grand Lake Golf Course 695
Grand Marais Golf Course 744
Grand National Golf Club (Hinckley, Minn.) 868
Grand National Golf Club (Opelika, Ala.) 22
Grand Oak Golf Club 147
Grand Oaks Resort 220
Grand Palms Golf and Country Club Resort 73
Grand Prairie Municipal Golf Course 981
Grand Rapids Golf Club 821
Grand Traverse Resort 821
Grand View Golf Course 822
Grand View Lodge 868
Grandote Golf and Country Club 695
Grandview Country Club 527
Grandview Golf Club (Middlefield, Ohio) 356
Grandview Golf Club (New Era, Mich.) 822
Grandview Golf Club (York, Pa.) 406
Grandview Golf Course (Des Moines, Iowa) 779
Grant Park Golf Course 1058
Grants Pass Country Club 951
Granville Golf Club 356

Grapevine Golf Course 982
Grassy Hill Country Club 37
Gray Rocks Golf Club 565
Grayhawk Golf Club 579
Graysburg Hills Golf Course 486
Grayson County College Golf Course 982
Great Gorge Country Club 243
Great Sand Dunes Country Club 695
Great Smokies Resort Golf Club 313
Great Trail Golf Course 356
Greate Bay Resort and Country Club 243
Greatwood Golf Club 982
Green Acres Golf Club (Kokomo, Ind.) 148
Green Acres Golf Club (Titusville, Pa.) 406
Green Crest Golf Course 356
Green Gables Golf Course 562
Green Harbor Golf Club 207
Green Hills Golf Club 356
Green Hills Municipal Golf Course 1079
Green Knoll Golf Course 243
Green Lakes State Park Golf Club 273
Green Lea Golf Course 869
Green Meadow Golf Club 229
Green Meadows Golf Club 983
Green Meadows Golf Course (North East, Pa.) 406
Green Meadows Golf Course (Volant, Pa.) 406
Green Pond Country Club 406
Green River Golf Course 628
Green Spring Golf Course 1020
Green Tree Golf Club 629
Green Valley Country Club 438
Green Valley Golf Club 357
Green Valley Golf Course 780
Green's Folly Golf Course 510
The Greenbrier 527
Greenbrier Valley Country Club 528
Greencastle Greens Golf Club 407
Greenfield Country Club 148
Greenfield Park Golf Course 1058
Greenhills Country Club 528
The Greens of Fredericksburg 510
Greenview Country Club 745
Grenelefe Golf and Tennis Resort 74
Greystone Golf Club 822
Griffith Park 629
Grossinger Resort 273
The Grove Park Inn Resort 314
Grover C. Keaton Golf Course 983
Grover Cleveland Golf Course 273
Gulf Shores Golf Club 23
Gulf State Park Golf Course 24
Gull Lake View Golf Club 823

Club 1095
Mayfield Golf Club 414
Mays Landing Country Club 246
Mayville Golf Club 1064
Maywood Golf Course 174
McCabe Field Golf Course 490
McCall Lake Golf Course 1086
McCall Municipal Golf Course 726
McCann Memorial Golf Club 281
McCormick Ranch Golf Club 584
McCormick Woods Golf Course 1039
McFarland Park Golf Course 29
McGuire's Resort 834
Meadow Brook Golf Course 1021
Meadow Gardens Golf Club 1095
Meadow Hills Golf Course 699
Meadow Lake Country Club 644
Meadow Lake Golf Resort 905
Meadow Lakes Golf Course 953
Meadow Park Golf Course 1039
Meadow Ponds Golf Course 530
Meadowbrook Golf Club 86
Meadowbrook Golf Course (Fort Worth, Tex.) 993
Meadowbrook Golf Course (Hopkins, Minn.) 875
Meadowbrook Golf Course (Rapid City, S.Dak.) 962
Meadowbrook Municipal Golf Course 993
Meadowcreek Golf Course 516
Meadowink Golf Club 414
Meadowlark Hills Golf Course 911
Meadows Farms Golf Course 516
Meadows Golf Club 247
The Meadows Golf Club 705
The Meadows Golf Club of Blue Island 754
Meadowwood Golf Course 1039
Medicine Hat Golf and Country Club 1086
Melody Hill Golf Course 438
Melreese Golf Course 86
Memorial Park Golf Course 994
Menifee Lakes Country Club 645
Mercer Oaks Golf Club 247
Mercer Public Golf Course 415
Meriwether National Golf Club 954
Meriwood Golf Course 1040
Merrill Golf Club 1064
Merrimack Golf Club 209
Mesaba Country Club 875
Mesquite Golf and Country Club 645
Mesquite Golf Course 994
Metropolitan Golf Club 128
MetroWest Country Club 86
Miami Shores Country Club 86
Miami Shores Golf Course 367
Miami Whitewater Forest Golf

Course 367
Michaywe Hills Resort 835
Michigan City Municipal Golf Course 154
Micke Grove Golf Links 645
Mid Pines Golf Club 320
Mid-Vallee Golf Course 1064
Middle Channel Golf & Country Club 835
Middle Island Country Club 282
Middletown Country Club 415
Midland Valley Golf Club 462
Midlane Country Club 754
Mile Square Golf Club 646
Milham Park Municipal Golf Club 836
Mililani Golf Club 716
Mill Cove Golf Club 87
Mill Creek Golf and Country Club 994
Mill Creek Golf Club 367
Mill Creek Park Golf Course 368
Mill Quarter Plantation Golf Course 517
Mill Race Golf Course 415
Mill River Golf Course 563
Mill Run Golf and Country Club 556
Mill Run Golf Course 1064
Millbrook Golf Course 39
Mille Lacs Golf Resort 875
Minerva Lake Golf Club 368
Mingo Springs Golf Course 182
Minnewaska Golf Club 876
Minor Park Golf Club 896
Minot Country Club 933
Mint Valley Golf Club 1040
Miracle Hill Golf and Tennis Center 912
Miry Run Country Club 247
Mission Del Lago Golf Course 995
Mission Hills North Golf Course 646
Mission Inn Golf and Tennis Resort 87
Mission Lakes Country Club 646
Mission Mountain Country Club 905
Mississippi National Golf Club 221
Mississippi National Golf Links 876
Mississippi State University Golf Course 221
Missouri Bluffs Golf Club 896
Mistwood Golf Course 836
Moab Golf Club 1021
Moccasin Bend Golf Club 490
Moccasin Creek Country Club 962
Moccasin Run Golf Course 415
Mohansic Golf Club 282
Mohawk Park Golf Club 943
Mohawk Trails Golf Course 416
Mohican Hills Golf Club 368

Monarch Beach Golf Links *647*
Moncton Golf Club *543*
Monroe Country Club *321*
Monroe Valley Golf Club *416*
Montague Golf Club *499*
Montauk Downs State Park Golf Course *282*
Montaup Country Club *438*
Montebello Golf Club *647*
Monterra Golf Course *556*
Montgomery Bell State Park Golf Course *490*
Monticello Country Club *876*
Montreal Municipal Golf Course *566*
Mooresville Golf Course *321*
The Moors Golf Club *87*
Moose Run Golf Course *568*
Morehead City Country Club *321*
Moreno Valley Ranch Golf Club *647*
Morningstar Golf Club *1096*
Morris Williams Golf Club *995*
Morro Bay Golf Course *648*
Mosholu Golf Course and Driving Range *283*
Mount Adams Country Club *1040*
Mount Airy Lodge Golf Course *416*
Mt. Anthony Golf & Tennis Center *500*
Mount Frontenac Golf Course *877*
Mt. Graham Municipal Golf Course *584*
Mount Mitchell Golf Club *321*
Mount Odin Park Golf Club *416*
Mount Ogden Golf Course *1022*
Mount Pleasant Golf Club *192*
Mount Si Golf Course *1040*
Mount Snow Golf Club *499*
Mount Washington Golf Course *231*
Mt. Woodson Country Club *648*
Mountain Aire Golf Club *322*
Mountain Dell Golf Club *1022*
Mountain Glen Golf Club *322*
Mountain Laurel Golf Club *417*
Mountain Manor Inn and Golf Club *417*
Mountain Meadows Golf Club *649*
Mountain Ranch Golf Club *602*
Mountain Shadows Golf Course *649*
Mountain Springs Golf Club *650*
Mountain Valley Golf Course *417*
Mountain View Country Club *650*
Mountain View Golf Club (Boring, Oreg.) *954*
Mountain View Golf Club (Grayville, Ala.) *29*
Mountain View Golf Club (West Jordan, Utah) *1022*

Mountain View Golf Course (West Trenton, N.J.) *247*
Mulberry Hill Golf Club *418*
Mullet Bay Golf Club *541*
Murray Parkway Golf Club *1022*
Murrysville Golf Club *418*
Muscatine Municipal Golf Course *781*
Muskego Lakes Country Club *1064*
My Old Kentucky Home State Park Golf Club *174*
Myrtle Beach National Golf Club *462*
Myrtle West Golf Club *462*
Myrtlewood Golf Club *463*
Mystery Hills Golf Club *1065*
Mystery Valley Golf Course *128*

N

Naga-Waukee Golf Course *1065*
Nags Head Golf Links *322*
Napa Municipal Golf Club *650*
Naperbrook Golf Course *754*
Naples Beach Hotel and Golf Club *88*
Nashboro Village Golf Course *491*
Nassawango Country Club *193*
Natanis Golf Club *183*
Natchez Trace Golf Club *221*
The Natural *836*
Needles Municipal Golf Course *650*
Needwood Golf Course *193*
Nemacolin Woodlands Resort *418*
Nemadji Golf Course *1065*
Nettle Creek Golf Club *755*
Neumann Golf Course *369*
The Neuse Golf Club *323*
Nevel Meade Golf Course *175*
Nevele Country Club *283*
New Berlin Hills Golf Course *1066*
The New Course at Albany *283*
New England Country Club *209*
New Melle Lakes Golf Club *896*
New Mexico State University Golf Course *927*
New Mexico Tech Golf Course *928*
New Prague Golf Club *877*
New Richmond Golf Club *1066*
New Seabury Country Club *209*
Newaukum Valley Golf Course *1040*
Newman Golf Course *755*
Newport Country Club *500*
Newport News Golf Club at Deer Run *517*
Niagara County Golf Course *283*
Nob North Golf Course *129*
Nobleton Lakes Golf Club *556*
Nocona Hills Golf Course *995*
Nordic Hills Resort *755*
Normandie Park Golf Club *896*

Salem Golf Club 957
Salem Hills Golf and Country Club 377
Salem Hills Golf Club 847
Salina Municipal Golf Club 793
Salinas Fairways Golf Course 667
Salishan Golf Links 957
Salmon Creek Country Club 288
Salt Creek Golf Club 159
Salt Fork State Park Golf Course 378
Saluda Valley Country Club 472
Samoset Resort Golf Club 185
San Bernardino Golf Club 667
San Clemente Municipal Golf Club 667
San Dimas Canyon Golf Club 668
San Geronimo Golf Club 668
San Ignacio Golf Club 590
San Jose Municipal Golf Course 668
San Juan Hills Country Club 669
San Luis Rey Downs Country Club 669
San Marcos Golf & Country Club 590
San Ramon Royal Vista Golf Club 669
San Saba Municipal Golf Course 1006
San Vicente Golf Club 670
Sand Creek Golf Club 728
Sand Springs Municipal Golf Course 944
Sandals Golf and Country Club 537
Sandalwood Golf Course 718
Sandestin Golf Course 101
Sandpines Golf Resort 957
Sandpiper Bay Golf and Country Club 332
Sandpiper Golf and Country Club 101
Sandpiper Golf Course 670
Sandridge Golf Club 102
Sandy Brae Golf Course 531
Sandy Burr Country Club 214
Sandy Hollow Golf Course 764
Sandy Lane Golf Club 536
Sandy Pines Golf Course 159
Sandy Ridge Golf Course (Colfax, N.C.) 332
Sandy Ridge Golf Course (Midland, Mich.) 847
Santa Ana Golf Course 929
Santa Anita Golf Course 670
Santa Barbara Golf Club 671
Santa Clara Golf and Tennis Club 671
Santa Maria Golf Course 800
Santa Rita Golf Club 590
Santa Rosa Golf and Beach Club 102
Santa Teresa Golf Club 671
Santee National Golf Club 472
Santiam Golf Club 958

Sapulpa Municipal Golf Course 944
Sarah Shank Golf Course 159
Sarasota Golf Club 102
Saratoga Spa Golf Course 288
Saskatoon Golf Club 847
Sault Ste. Marie Country Club 848
Savannahs at Sykes Creek Golf Club 103
Sawmill Creek Golf and Racquet Club 378
Sawmill Golf Club 884
Saxon Golf Course 426
Saxon Woods Golf Course 288
Scarlet Oaks Country Club 531
Scenic Hills Country Club 103
Scenic View Country Club 1071
The SCGA Members' Club at Rancho California 667
Schalamar Creek Golf and Country Club 103
Schaumburg Golf Club 764
Schenectady Golf Course 288
Scherwood Golf Course 160
Schifferdecker Golf Course 900
Schneiter's Bluff at West Point 1024
Schneiter's Riverside Golf Course 1024
Sconti Golf Club 134
Scotch Pines Golf Course 728
Scothurst Country Club 332
Scott Lake Country Club 848
Scott Schreiner Municipal Golf Course 1007
Scottsdale Country Club 591
Scranton Municipal Golf Course 426
Sea Gull Golf Club 473
Sea Island Golf Club 134
Sea Palms Resort 135
Sea Pines Sports and Conference Center 473
The Sea Ranch Golf Links 672
Sea Scape Golf Course 333
Sea Trail Plantation and Golf Links 333
Seamountain Golf Course 719
Seascape Resort 103
Sebastian Municipal Golf Course 103
Sedona Golf Resort 591
Segalla Country Club 289
Selkirk Golf & Country Club 1103
Selma Valley Golf Course 672
Semiahmoo Golf and Country Club 1042
Seminole Golf Club 104
Seneca Golf Course 176
SentryWorld Golf Course 1071
Sepulveda Golf Course 672
Sequoyah State Park Golf Club 945
Settler's Hill Golf Course 765

Notes

Notes

Notes

Notes

Notes

Notes

Notes

Notes